A   Volume 1

The World Book Encyclopedia

WORLD

The World Book Encyclopedia

For information on other World Book publications, visit our website at **www.worldbook.com** or call **1-800-WORLDBK (967-5325).** For information about sales to schools and libraries, call **1-800-975-3250 (United States); 1-800-837-5365 (Canada).**

World Book, Inc.
180 North LaSalle Street
Suite 900
Chicago, Illinois 60601
USA

Library of Congress Cataloging-in-Publication Data

Title: The World Book Encyclopedia
Description: Chicago, IL: World Book Inc., [2022] | Includes index.
Identifiers: LCCN 2021041068 | ISBN 9780716601227 (set)
Subjects: LCSH: Encyclopedias and dictionaries.
Classification: LCC AE5 .W55 2022 | DDC 031--dc23
LC record available at https://lccn.loc.gov/2021041068

Printed in the United States of America by LSC Communications, Willard, Ohio
1st printing November 2021

About the SPINESCAPE®

Dinosaurs roamed Earth for about 160 million years. Even though these animals died out millions of years ago, they have fascinated people ever since they were first described in the early 1800's. And scientists continue to discover new species and learn more about these fantastic creatures and the world in which they lived.

Featured on *The World Book Encyclopedia* 2022 Spinescape® is a *Giganotosaurus,* one of the largest meat-eating dinosaurs that ever lived. Its saw-edged, daggerlike teeth could easily slice flesh. It weighed approximately 8 tons (7.3 metric tons), measured about 45 feet (14 meters) in length, and stood about 15 feet (4.6 meters) tall at the hips.

The **Dinosaur** article in the 2022 edition of *The World Book Encyclopedia* has been fully revised to reflect the most recent findings in the field of paleontology. Highlights include an in-depth look into the life cycle of a dinosaur and detailed descriptions of many important dinosaur groups. The article features realistic illustrations of dinosaurs in their natural habitats as well as a detailed family-tree graphic depicting dinosaur origins and relationships over time.

Staff

Preface

The World Book Encyclopedia, a publication of World Book, Inc., was first published in 1917 as an 8-volume set. The encyclopedia has been expanded many times through the years and now has 22 volumes. Throughout its publishing history, *World Book* has sought new and better ways to serve its readers. For a brief summary of *World Book*'s development, see the article **Encyclopedia** (History).

Aims and objectives

The *World Book* editorial staff presents information from the vast reservoir of knowledge in the most accessible and usable form. Editors craft *World Book* articles especially to meet the reference and study needs of students in elementary school, junior high school, and high school. *World Book* can be used as a review and reinforcement tool by college students and also serves as a general family reference tool. Librarians, teachers, and the general public likewise turn to *World Book* to satisfy their everyday reference needs.

Authority

Central to *World Book*'s editorial process are its contributors and consultants. These outstanding scholars and specialists include experts in such major academic fields as biological sciences, humanities, physical sciences, regional studies, social sciences, and sports. They provide guidance in the planning and ongoing evaluation of *World Book* content.

World Book reflects the combined expertise of more than 4,500 such individuals. The name of the contributor or reviewer appears at the end of *World Book* articles. *World Book* contributors and consultants are listed in the front of the "A" volume. In addition, some *World Book* entries are critically reviewed by authoritative organizations. The publishers of *World Book* also employ artists, cartographers, content creators, editors, graphic designers, indexers, researchers, and technological-support personnel.

Selection of contents

Ongoing evaluation and research help the editors make decisions on the encyclopedia's contents. Editors and content creators stay abreast of developments in a variety of topic areas, as well as trends in user research. They also make decisions about *World Book*'s content based on contributor expertise and feedback from sales personnel about the needs of teachers and librarians. In addition, analyses of curriculum guides and of national and state standards provide information on current and new and emerging school topics.

Presentation of information

World Book is organized so that readers may quickly find the information they are seeking. This is achieved through a single alphabetical arrangement of articles and entry cross-references, a carefully designed page and article format, and a comprehensive, single-volume index.

World Book uses a modified unit-letter arrangement of volumes. All entries that begin with the letter "A" are found in Volume A, all entries that begin with the letter "B" are found in volume B, and so on throughout most of the set. In some cases, entries that start with two or more consecutive letters of the alphabet are combined in one volume. In two instances, a single volume is not large enough to accommodate all the articles that start with the same letter, and the entries are divided between two volumes.

Most reference questions are answered by referring to Volumes 1 through 21, where the reader finds either an article or a cross-reference to such an article. If there is no article or cross-reference, the reader can turn to Volume 22, the Research Guide/Index. In this way, *World Book* provides the reader with both an extensive system of alphabetically arranged articles and cross-references, and a comprehensive, in-depth index.

All topics are arranged alphabetically, using the word-by-word system. For example, **Arab League** precedes **Arabian Desert,** and **New Mexico** appears before **Newark.** For more information on *World Book*'s alphabetical system, see page VIII of this volume. Thousands of cross-references form part of this alphabetical arrangement. They guide the reader to a subject or to some information that may be a part of another article, or that may appear as an alternative title. *See* and *See also* cross-references are included within many articles. A list of *Related articles* at the end of many *World Book* articles guides the reader to additional pertinent information in the encyclopedia.

World Book's page format is designed for maximum usefulness. Page numbers and guide words at the top of a page provide rapid access to subjects. Within articles, topics and subtopics stand out in boldface center headings and boldface side headings.

World Book's fourfold plan for major articles brings together four basic elements: (1) an outline, (2) a complete story, (3) visual aids, and (4) related articles.

1. An outline gives readers an overall view of the article and shows the interrelationship of its components.

2. The complete story gives readers a solid foundation of information about a subject.

3. A wide variety of visual aids clarifies meaning and reinforces learning. Photographs, drawings, paintings, maps, diagrams, charts, and graphs make information come alive.

4. A list of related *World Book* articles encourages readers to broaden their study of a subject.

Some articles also include lists of books for further reading on the subject.

Readability

World Book editors present information in a clear, direct style that meets the most exacting standards of readability. Curriculum analysis and testing of text samples according to established measurement systems help the editors design articles to be understandable at the age levels where they are most commonly used. Vocabulary is geared to the proper age group. For example, the **Mouse** article was written especially for younger children, and **Cell** was aimed at advanced readers. Many long articles are designed to present simpler concepts and reading levels at the beginning. These articles build toward more sophisticated concepts and reading levels toward the end. The **Leaf** article is an excellent example of this simple-to-more-complex approach.

In developing an article, the editor checks its vocabulary against a list of about 44,000 words created especially for *World Book* by its readability consultants.

World Book editors use words that can be understood at the grade level of the article, but they use technical terms where needed. Such words are defined immediately in the article, thus ensuring understanding and helping vocabulary development. In the **Moon** article, for example, the section on *The movements of the moon* uses the words *elliptical, perigee, apogee, synodic month,* and *sidereal month.* These words are printed in italics, and their meanings are given in parentheses or defined within the context of the sentence in which they appear. Similar techniques are used throughout the set to define difficult words and clarify meanings.

Illustrations and maps

Illustrations are combined with text in *World Book* to achieve the most effective communication of information. An illustration is placed close to the portion of subject matter that it is designed to clarify, supplement, or complement. *World Book* has more than 20,000 illustrations, including maps, most of them in color. Many *World Book* illustrations were created exclusively for the encyclopedia by specially commissioned illustrators and photographers. For example, the color photographs in the **Mineral** article were obtained by a specially assigned photographer working with museum experts. Specialists in depicting nature subjects have illustrated such articles as **Animal, Bird, Flower, Insect, Spider,** and **Tree.**

World Book's treatment of the fine arts is exemplified by the **Painting** article. This 64-page article features reproductions of about 100 paintings from the world's leading museums and private collections. In addition, numerous biographies of artists are illustrated with color reproductions of their work.

In illustrating historical articles, *World Book* uses period art where appropriate. For example, the article **United States, History of the,** includes more than 20 pieces of art, some by such well-known artists as Currier and Ives and Benjamin West. Illustrated time lines in such articles as **Classical music** and **Medicine** help place people and events in historical perspective.

World Book has about 2,000 maps, all of them in color. The publisher has conducted research that analyzes type size and placement, color, symbolization, captioning, scale, and other elements involved in map design. Design principles based on such research are incorporated in *World Book* maps. Examples of maps that use these principles are the thematic maps in articles on the states, provinces, major countries, and continents. These maps convey basic information on such topics as climate, economy, population distribution, and historical development. The maps on climate, economy, and population distribution are based on the latest available data, including official government and United Nations sources.

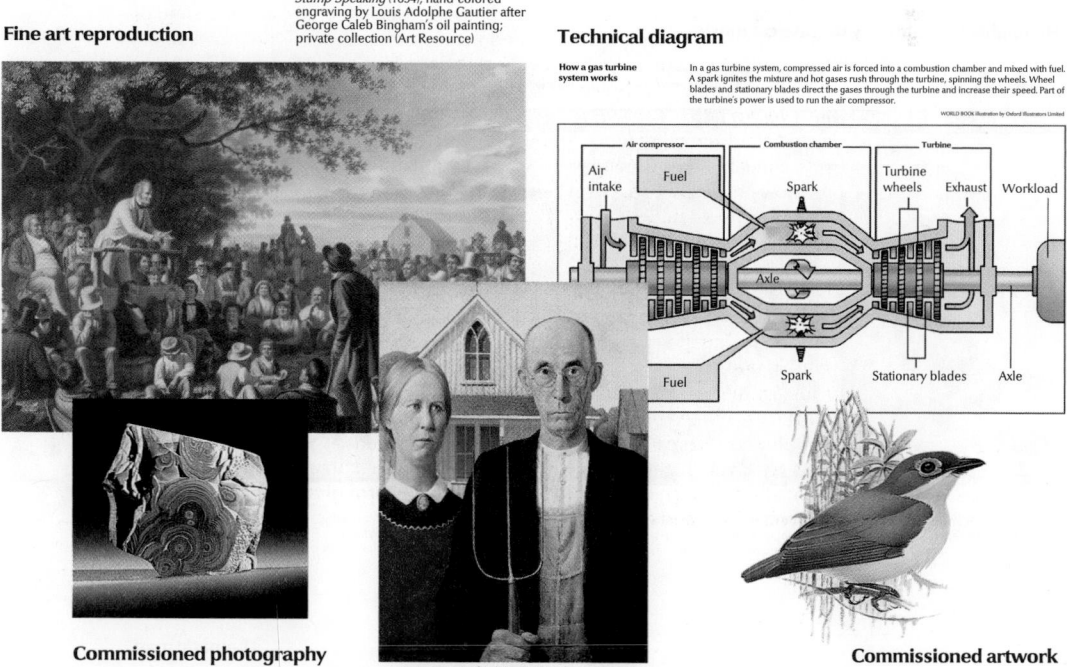

Fine art reproduction

Stump Speaking (1854), hand-colored engraving by Louis Adolphe Gautier after George Caleb Bingham's oil painting; private collection (Art Resource)

Technical diagram

How a gas turbine system works

In a gas turbine system, compressed air is forced into a combustion chamber and mixed with fuel. A spark ignites the mixture and hot gases rush through the turbine, spinning the wheels. Wheel blades and stationary blades direct the gases through the turbine and increase their speed. Part of the turbine's power is used to run the air compressor.

WORLD BOOK illustration by Oxford Illustrators Limited

Commissioned photography

American Gothic (1930) oil on beaverboard by Grant Wood, The Art Institute of Chicago; © All Rights Reserved by the Art Institute of Chicago and VAGA, New York, NY, 1930.934

Commissioned artwork

Research aids

Many research aids have been built into *World Book*. These aids facilitate the search for information within *World Book* and assist the reader in finding information beyond the encyclopedia. These research aids appear both in the alphabetical volumes and in Volume 22, the Research Guide/Index.

Listings of *Related articles* at the end of many *World Book* articles lead the reader to additional, related information on the subject. For example, after reading the section *The Era of Expansion (1831-1870)* in the **American literature** article, a reader might want to learn more about Emily Dickinson, Walt Whitman, and other poets of the period. The *Related articles* section at the end of the **American literature** article includes an alphabetical listing of articles on the writers of this period.

The *Additional resources* heading that follows hundreds of articles in *World Book* leads the user to further reading on the subject. These lists of books have been carefully selected to represent current, balanced scholarship. In some instances, the books have been grouped on two levels, with Level I books being simpler than Level II books.

An instructional section called *A Student Guide to Better Writing, Speaking, and Research Skills* in Volume 22 gives students practical, easy-to-understand guidance in carrying out everyday school assignments. It includes writing tips and advice on preparing different types of written reports; advice on preparing and delivering an oral report; and detailed information on using the library and tapping other reference sources.

Illustrated timeline

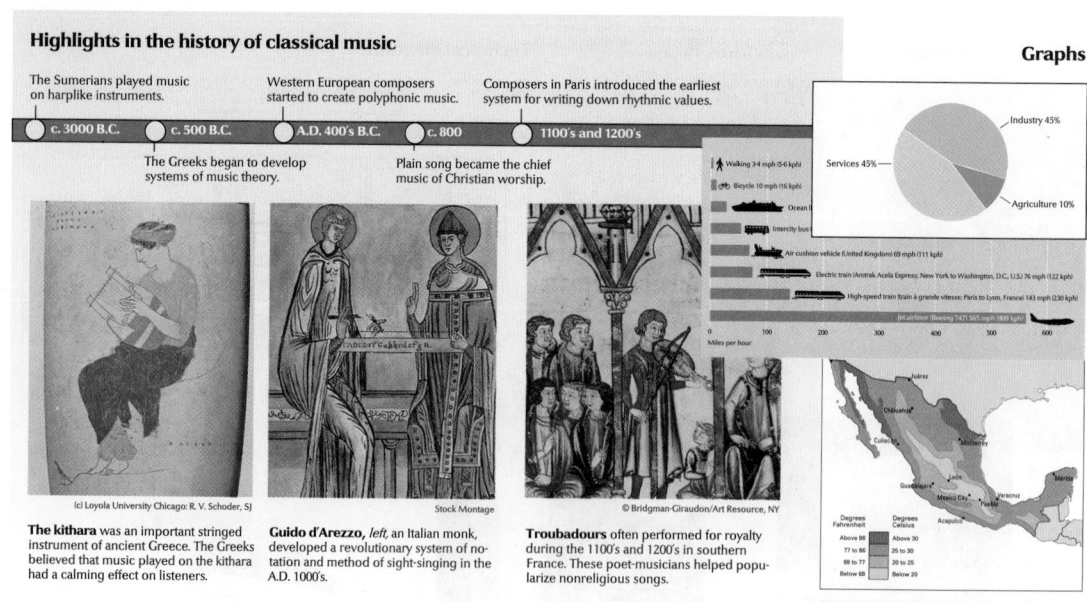

Highlights in the history of classical music

Graphs

The Sumerians played music on harplike instruments.

Western European composers started to create polyphonic music.

Composers in Paris introduced the earliest system for writing down rhythmic values.

c. 3000 B.C. | c. 500 B.C. | A.D. 400's B.C. | c. 800 | 1100's and 1200's

The Greeks began to develop systems of music theory.

Plain song became the chief music of Christian worship.

Industry 45%
Services 45%
Agriculture 10%

(c) Loyola University Chicago: R. V. Schoder, SJ

Stock Montage

© Bridgman-Giraudon/Art Resource, NY

The kithara was an important stringed instrument of ancient Greece. The Greeks believed that music played on the kithara had a calming effect on listeners.

Guido d'Arezzo, *left,* an Italian monk, developed a revolutionary system of notation and method of sight-singing in the A.D. 1000's.

Troubadours often performed for royalty during the 1100's and 1200's in southern France. These poet-musicians helped popularize nonreligious songs.

In summer, Mexico's climate is warm in the central regions of the country, and hot along the coasts. July temperatures in Mexico City range from 53 to 73 °F (12 to 23 °C).

Thematic map

Revision program

An encyclopedia must be up to date if it is to serve the best interests of its users. A revised edition of *World Book* is published each year. Each edition reflects up-to-date information and the latest changes in educational viewpoints. Every subject area is under continuing surveillance. The annual revision program is never confined to a single area or to certain volumes. Hundreds of articles are added or updated each year.

To keep *World Book* owners abreast of world events, *The World Book Year Book*, an annual supplement, is published; the supplement reviews the events of the previous year. It reports major news developments, chronologically listed, to update *World Book*. It also publishes a selection of new or revised articles from the current edition of *World Book*.

Physical format

The high goals of *World Book*'s editorial processes also characterize its manufacturing processes. *World Book* is printed on modern web offset presses. *World Book*'s presses allow the use of color throughout the set. The paper used in *World Book* is especially manufactured to achieve the best results from color printing.

The text type used in *World Book*—World Book Modern—was created exclusively for *World Book* by Hermann Zapf, an internationally renowned type designer. His specifications for the text type have been incorporated into a page format that facilitates readability and the search for information.

World Book's attractive and practical binding materials were selected for their durability, dirt resistance, and high scuff resistance.

Tests at every stage of production during the printing and binding processes are conducted at the press facilities.

Electronic versions

The content of *The World Book Encyclopedia* and selected other World Book general reference publications is available online on a subscription basis.

For more information, please
    call:
        1-800-967-5325
    write to:
        World Book, Inc.
        180 North LaSalle Street
        Suite 900
        Chicago, Illinois 60601
        USA
    visit World Book's website at:
        www.worldbook.com

The editors

How to use *World Book*

Assigned a written or oral report? Turn to *A Student Guide to Better Writing, Speaking, and Research Skills* in Volume 22 for advice on how to go about it.

World Book is a tool for learning—a general encyclopedia that tells about people, places, things, events, and ideas. It provides accurate information that is easy to find and easy to understand.

You may come to the encyclopedia for the answer to a particular question, such as "How high is a badminton net?" or "What is the population of Haiti?" Or you may seek general information for a school assignment. Parents and young people, when they plan together for the future, often come to *World Book* to find out about the possibilities in various careers. And, of course, many people like simply to explore *World Book*, letting one topic lead them to another. Browsing or skimming through the encyclopedia is an enjoyable way to pick up interesting information on many subjects.

All articles, generally called *entries* in *World Book*, are arranged alphabetically, volume by volume and subject by subject. Included in this alphabetical arrangement are also thousands of *entry cross-references*. Cross-references are explained in detail later in this section.

All entries that begin with the letter "A" are found in Volume A, everything that starts with "B" is in Volume B, and so on throughout most of the set. In some cases, entries that start with two or more consecutive letters of the alphabet are combined in one volume. Or, a single volume may not be large enough to hold all the articles that start with the same letter. In such cases, entries starting with the same letter are divided between two volumes. For example, *World Book* articles that begin with the letter "C" are contained in two volumes—C to Ch and Ci to Cz.

In most instances, *World Book*'s alphabetical arrangement of articles and cross-references will enable you to find the information you are seeking. However, if you do not find the information, turn to Volume 22, the Research Guide/Index. Its approximately 170,000 index entries provide access to the wealth of information in *World Book*.

Volume 22 also includes an instructional section titled *A Student Guide to Better Writing, Speaking, and Research Skills*. This feature has been designed to help students assigned a written or oral report.

For information on using the index, see Volume 22, the Research Guide/Index.

The word-by-word arrangement

In the *word-by-word* alphabetical system used in *World Book*, commas and then spaces precede letters of the alphabet. For example: **Marsh; Marsh, Ngaio; Marsh hen; Marshall, George Catlett.** In word-by-word order, the **New York** article appears ahead of the **Newark** article.

Exceptions to word-by-word order are made in certain cases in which a word or name may or may not contain spaces. A preposition (such as *De* or *Von*) or an article (such as *El* or *La*) is alphabetized with the word it precedes as though the space between the two words did not exist. For example: **Delacroix, Eugène; De la Roche, Mazo; Delaware; De la Warr, Lord; Delft.** Hyphenated prefixes (such as *anti-*, *pre-*, and *un-*) are alphabetized in a similar manner. For example: **Antidote; Anti-Federalists; Antifreeze.** This exception allows similar words to appear together even though they are punctuated differently.

An additional exception applies to personal names used with roman numerals, as with monarchs or popes. This kind of name appears ahead of the same name when it is separated from another word by a comma or space. For example: **Mary; Mary I; Mary II; Mary, Queen of Scots; Mary Magdalene.**

Guide words

At the top of most pages is a *guide word*. The purpose of the guide word is to help you locate quickly the entry you are seeking. On a left-hand page, the guide word (or words) may be the title of the first entry that appears in the first column of that page. Or, the guide word may be the title of an article that is continued from a preceding page, if the continuation takes up the whole first column. On a right-hand page, the guide word is the title of the last article on that page.

Let us say your question is: "What are the different branches of law?" First, select the *key word*—the most important word—in the question: "Law." In most cases, this word will be the same as the entry in *World Book*. So, look for **Law** in Volume L. Start leafing through Volume L, noting the guide words on the tops of the pages.

Leaf forward until you see guide words that begin with "La," for example **Language**. If you come upon such guide words as **Lawn** or **Laxative**, you know you must go back to find the **Law** article in its alphabetical place. Finding an entry in *World Book* is very much like finding a word in a dictionary.

Entry cross-references

Thousands of *cross-references* are important aids to finding information in *World Book*. There are several types of cross-references. The principal type is the *entry cross-reference*. Entry cross-references appear in heavy type—the same as article titles—and are included in *World Book*'s alphabetical arrangement.

Some entry cross-references provide you with the titles of topics that can be found in the set under other names. For example, in Volume P you will find the entry **PET. See Positron emission tomography**. That entry directs you to the place where *World Book* provides the most specific information on this topic.

Other entry cross-references tell you in what section of an article to find information. If you want to know about the corolla of a flower's petals, you look up the topic *Petal* in its proper alphabetical place in Volume P. You will find the entry cross-reference: **Petal. See Flower** (The corolla). Then you would turn to the **Flower** article and look for the section titled *The corolla*.

---

130   **Law** ▪

Law is the set of enforced rules under which people are governed. Law is one of the most basic social institutions—and one of the most necessary. No society could exist if all people did just as they pleased, without regard for the rights of others. Nor could a society exist if its members did not recognize that they also have certain obligations toward one another. The law thus establishes the rules that define a person's rights and obligations. The law also sets penalties for people who violate

cases are called *lawsuits* or *civil suits*.

Private law can be divided into six major branches according to the kinds of legal rights and obligations involved. These branches are (1) contract and commercial law, (2) tort law, (3) property law, (4) inheritance law, (5) family law, and (6) corporation law. The dividing line between the various branches is not always clear, however. For example, many cases of property law also involve contract law.

PET. See Positron emission tomography.

Pétain, *PAY TAN*, **Henri Philippe,** *ahn REE fee LEEP* (1856-1951), became a national hero of France because of his military leadership in World War I. Yet he was tried and imprisoned for treason in his old age because of his collaboration with the Germans in World War II.

Military hero. Pétain was born on April 24, 1856, at Cauchy-la-Tour. He was educated at the French military academy of Saint Cyr and served as an army officer. In 1916, during World War I, he commanded the French forces in the heroic defense of Verdun (see **Verdun, Battles of**). Here he spoke his famous words "They shall not pass." In April 1917, Pétain was made chief of staff. He served as commander in chief on the Western Front from May 1917 to March 1918. Pétain was made a Marshal of France in 1918.

Political career. Pétain served briefly as minister of war in 1934. His critics accused him of secret hostility to the French Republic and also of sympathy for the dictatorial government of Francisco Franco in Spain. He served as ambassador to Spain in 1939 and 1940. Pétain was called home to be vice premier of France in the

Henri Philippe Pétain

desperate World War II days of May 1940, when France was unable to stop the German invasion. On June 16, 1940, at the age of 84, Pétain became premier. Against the objections of some of his colleagues, he arranged the armistice with Germany.

Collaborator. Pétain became "chief of state" in the French government when its capital moved to Vichy. He accepted collaboration with the Germans as an inescapable necessity. But he also saw it as an opportunity to reshape France along authoritarian lines. His government undertook measures against Jews, paid heavy financial tribute to the Germans, and sent many French workers to Germany. Pétain's chief supporters included veterans who had served under him in World War I.

The Germans overran all of France in 1942. But Pétain, though essentially powerless, insisted on maintaining a false appearance of French sovereignty. After the Allied troops landed in France in June 1944, the Germans took him to Baden, where he remained until after the war. In 1945, Pétain was returned to France. He was tried for treason and was convicted. Pétain died in prison on July 23, 1951, at the age of 95.   *John F. Sweets*

Petal. See Flower (The corolla).

Peter I (1844-1921), became Serbia's first constitutional monarch in 1903, following the assassination of King Alexander Obrenovic. As monarch, Peter's aggressive policies led to the expansion of Serbian territory through the Balkan Wars of 1912 and 1913. In 1914, Peter, who was in poor health, gave control of the government to his son Alexander, who served as *regent* (temporary ruler). During World War I (1914-1918), a combined invasion by Austria-Hungary, Bulgaria, and Germany forced Peter and the Serbian army to retreat into exile on the Greek island of Corfu. In 1918, at the

conclusion of the war, the Kingdom of the Serbs, Croats, and Slovenes (later renamed Yugoslavia) was formed. Peter became its first king.

Peter Karadjordjevic was born in Belgrade on July 11, 1844. His name is also spelled Petar. He spent most of his early life in exile in France and Switzerland. He died on Aug. 16, 1921. His son Alexander I succeeded him as king.   *Thomas A. Emmert*

Peter I, the Great (1672-1725), was one of the most famous rulers in history. A member of the Romanov *dynasty* (family of rulers), he ruled first as *czar* (king) of Russia and later became Russia's first emperor. Peter transformed Russia from an isolated and backward country into a great European power.

Early life. Peter was born on June 9, 1672, in Moscow. His father was Czar Alexis. Alexis died in 1676 and was succeeded as czar by his oldest son, Fedor. Fedor died in 1682. Peter then came to the throne at the age of 10, along with his weak-minded half brother Ivan V. However, Peter's half sister Sophia actually ruled Russia until 1689. Peter's followers forced Sophia to retire that year, and Peter eventually became the sole ruler of Russia.

Peter had been interested in military matters as a youth. He also had enjoyed spending time with foreign military officers who lived in Moscow, and he learned much about European civilization from them. In 1695, a number of these officers helped Peter lead a force against the Ottoman Empire. Peter conquered the Ottoman port of Azov on the Black Sea in 1696.

In 1697 and 1698, Peter toured Western Europe with a group of Russian delegates to seek allies for Russia against the Ottoman Empire. He traveled for about 17 months, mostly in England and the Netherlands. Peter also recruited Western experts to bring modern techniques of engineering, architecture, art, and science to Russia. At the time, Russia lagged far behind other European nations in those areas.

A revolt of his royal guards forced Peter to return to Russia in 1698. Peter crushed the revolt. This victory

© Prisma Archivo/Alamy Images

▪ **Peter the Great** was a powerful ruler who succeeded in bringing Western European culture and customs to Russia.

Cross-references within the text

In addition to the entry cross-references, *World Book* provides many cross-references within the text of articles and at the end of articles. These "see" and "see also" cross-references direct you to particular maps, charts, pictures, or articles and sections of articles for additional information on material that you have just read. Good examples of this kind of cross-reference are "see **Artificial intelligence**" found in the **Bionics** article and the "See also" cross-reference at the end of the **Ben Bella, Ahmed** article.

Article headings

We have told you about finding articles in *World Book*. Now, look at some of the aids that help you find information quickly *within* most of the articles. Turn to the **Tree** article. You will notice this long article is divided into sections, each with its own *head* or *heading*—words in large type that tell you what information will be found in the section—for example:

How a tree grows

Every section has been divided into *subsections*, each with a *subhead* or *subheading* in heavy type that pinpoints particular kinds of information. For example, under the heading *How a tree grows,* you will find these subheads: **How seeds sprout into trees; How leaves make plant food; How trees grow taller; How trunks and branches grow thicker;** and **How trees reproduce.** All of these heads and subheads lead you to the particular kinds of information you might be seeking if you did not wish to read the entire **Tree** article.

Note also that the color diagrams in the article have special headings that serve a similar purpose, for example: **How a tree reveals its history.** Many medium-length and short articles in *World Book* are also divided into sections that have heads and subheads, but of course some articles are so short that they do not require separate sections.

Captions

The illustrations in *World Book* all have *captions*—special text which usually starts with heavy type that quickly identifies the subject. Captions give information that clarifies or adds to the information given in the article. A caption will be found close to an illustration.

■ **Swimming** 1043

ect, you can throw a life preserver, a board, or any other object that will float and support the swimmer.

■ Swimming kicks and strokes

Swimmers move their legs, feet, arms, and hands in certain ways to propel themselves through the water easily and quickly. The movements of the legs and feet are called *kicks.* These movements combined with movements of the arms and hands are called *strokes.*

---

418 Tree ■

■ *How a tree grows*

Most trees begin life as a seed. The young tree that develops from this seed is called a *seedling.* After a tree reaches a height of 6 feet (1.8 meters) or more and its trunk becomes 1 to 2 inches (2.5 to 5 centimeters) thick, it is called a *sapling.* Many trees reach a height of more than 100 feet (30 meters). Some old trees have trunks more than 10 feet (3 meters) in diameter.

Trees need great amounts of water. A large apple tree in full leaf may absorb 95 gallons (360 liters) from the soil daily. Most of the water goes to the leaves. On a sunny summer day, some trees move water up through their trunks at the rate of 3 feet (91 centimeters) per minute. A tree's wood is about half water.

■ **How seeds sprout into trees.** A seed contains parts that develop into the trunk and roots of a tree. It also has one or more cotyledons and a supply of plant food. After a seed has left the parent tree, it rests for a while on the ground. Water, air, and sunshine help the seed *germinate* (begin to grow). The part of the seed that develops into the trunk points upward toward the sunlight. As the seed absorbs water, the root part swells and bursts through the seed's shell. As the root grows, it pushes down into the soil. The food stored in the seed nourishes the tree. As the root begins to soak up water from the soil, the trunk begins to develop leaves.

■ **How leaves make plant food.** As a leaf develops, it gets sap from the roots. It also absorbs carbon dioxide from the air. The leaf uses the energy of sunlight to change the sap and carbon dioxide into sugar, a process called *photosynthesis.* The sugar provides food for the trunk, branches, and roots. During photosynthesis, the leaves also produce oxygen and release it into the atmosphere. See Leaf (How a leaf makes food). ■

■ **How trees grow taller.** Trees grow taller only at the tips of their trunk and branches. Each year, the tips of the trunk and of each branch develop a *bud.* The bud

contains a tiny, leafy green stem called a *shoot.* The bud is wrapped in a protective covering of *bud scales.* After a period of rest, the buds swell and open. The shoots that were inside the buds begin to grow and so make the trunk and branches taller. Another type of bud grows on the sides of the trunk and branches. These buds contain a shoot that develops into a leaf-bearing *twig* after the bud opens. As a twig grows larger, it becomes another branch of the tree. Some tree buds develop into flowers. Still others develop into twigs that bear both leaves and flowers. In warm climates, trees produce buds frequently during the year or continue to grow without forming buds. In colder climates, trees produce buds only in the summer. These buds rest during the winter and open after warm weather arrives in spring.

Trees without branches—cycads, most palms, and tree ferns—grow somewhat differently. For example, a young palm tree does not grow taller for a number of years. Its short trunk thickens and produces more and larger leaves each year. After the trunk and crown reach adult size, the tree begins to grow taller. The trunk stays about the same thickness for the rest of the tree's life.

■ **How trunks and branches grow thicker.** The trunk and branches of a broadleaf or needleleaf tree grow thicker as long as the tree lives. The cambium tissue just underneath the inner bark causes this thickening. It uses the sugar produced by the leaves to make new plant tissue. On its outside, the cambium makes new phloem, or inner bark, and on its inside, new xylem, or wood.

Wood consists largely of *cellulose,* a tough substance made from sugar. The xylem has two kinds of wood—*sapwood* and *heartwood.* The wood nearest the cambium is the sapwood. It is living wood and contains the tiny pipelines that carry sap. In tropical climates, the sapwood thickens all year. In cooler climates, a new layer of

---

■ **How a tree reveals its history**

Most trees in temperate regions grow a layer of wood each year. After such a layer has been cut down, the layers can be seen as rings in the trunk. These *annual rings* reveal the tree's life story. The pine log in this drawing has 72 annual rings, showing that the tree lived for 72 years.

■ **Narrow center rings** indicate that other trees shaded the young tree, depriving it of moisture and sunlight.

■ **Wider rings** on the log's lower side after the 30th year show that the tree was slightly bent in this direction. The tree then began to grow more wood on this side than on the other to keep from falling. Most rings after the 38th year are wider than the center rings. This indicates that many surrounding trees had been removed, giving the tree more moisture and sunlight. Differences in the width of rings after the 38th ring were caused mainly by varying amounts of rainfall from year to year.

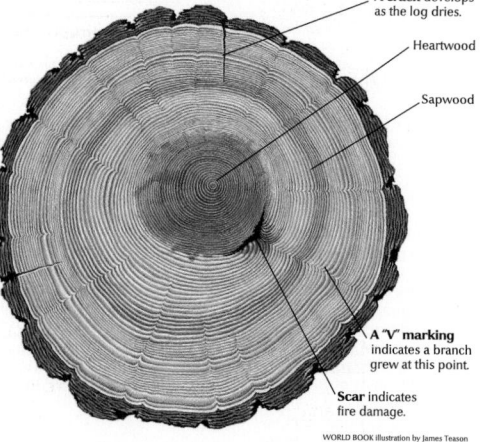

A crack develops as the log dries.

Heartwood

Sapwood

A "V" marking indicates a branch grew at this point.

Scar indicates fire damage.

WORLD BOOK illustration by James Teason

Other research aids

On this page, a number of special research aids found in *World Book* are shown. If you make good use of them, they will facilitate your search for information. Browse through the set and you will find these special features in many articles. They have been developed to help you get the most out of *World Book.*

Facts in brief

Capital: London
Official language: English.
Area: 50,301 mi² (130,279 km²). *Greatest distances*—north-south, about 360 mi (579 km); east-west, about 270 mi (435 km). *Coastline*—about 1,150 mi (1,851 km).
Elevation: *Highest*—Scafell Pike, 3,210 ft (978 m) above sea level. *Lowest*—Great Holme Fen, near the River Ouse in Cambridgeshire, 9 ft (2.7 m) below sea level.

Facts in brief tables are found in state, province, country, continent, and many other articles. They provide information at a glance.

Horse terms

Bronco, or **Bronc,** is an untamed Western horse.
Colt, technically, is a male horse 4 years old or less. However, the word colt is often used for any young horse.
Crossbred means bred from a sire of one breed and a dam of another.
Dam is the mother of a foal.
Filly is a female horse 4 years old or less.

Tables of terms present information that defines certain words or phrases used in discussing specialized or highly technical topics.

Important dates in Kennedy's life

1917	(May 29) Born in Brookline, Massachusetts.
1940	Graduated from Harvard University.
1941-1945	Served in the U.S. Navy during World War II.
1946	Elected to the U.S. House of Representatives.
1952	Elected to the U.S. Senate.
1953	(Sept. 12) Married Jacqueline Lee Bouvier.

Tables of important dates are included in many articles. They provide quick reference to outstanding events in the history of a topic.

Additional resources

Level I
Fletcher, Patricia. *Why Do People Have Chins? And Other Curious Human Adaptations.* Gareth Stevens, 2018.
Midthun, Joseph. *Building Blocks of Science.* World Bk., 2014. This multivolume series includes titles on systems of the human body.
Randolph, Joanne, ed. *The Amazing Human Body.* 6 vols. Enslow, 2018.

Level II
Houston, Rob, ed. *How the Body Works.* DK Pub., 2016.
Macaulay, David. *The Way We Work.* Houghton, 2008.
Roberts, Alice M., ed. *The Complete Human Body.* 2nd ed. DK Pub., 2016.
Shubin, Neil. *Your Inner Fish: A Journey into the 3.5-Billion-Year History of the Human Body.* Pantheon, 2008.

Additional resources at the end of articles lead to further reading. Sometimes, books are grouped on two levels, with Level I books being simpler than Level II books.

Related articles. See Literature for children and its list of *Related articles.* See also the following:

Colonial literature (1608-1764)

Bay Psalm Book	Mather, Cotton
Bradford, William (1590-1657)	Mather, Richard
Bradstreet, Anne Dudley	Poor Richard's Almanac
Byrd, William, II	Smith, John
Edwards, Jonathan	Taylor, Edward
Franklin, Benjamin	Wigglesworth, Michael
Great Awakening	

The revolutionary period (1765-1787)

Crèvecoeur, Michel-Guillaume Jean de	Paine, Thomas
	Warren, Mercy Otis

Related articles listings at the end of many articles direct the reader to additional, related information in *World Book.*

Key to pronunciation

The World Book Encyclopedia provides pronunciation for many unusual or unfamiliar words, either with the article title or where the word appears in the text. In the pronunciation, the words are divided into syllables and respelled according to the way each syllable sounds. The syllables appear in *italic* letters. For example, here is an article title along with the respelled pronunciation for it:

Antibiotic, *AN tee by AHT ihk*

The syllable that bears the greatest emphasis when the word is spoken appears in capital letters *(AHT).* If the word is long enough to have a syllable that receives secondary emphasis, that syllable appears in small capitals *(AN).* More than one pronunciation appears for words that have several accepted pronunciations in English, for words that have distinctive pronunciations in other languages, and for names that have distinctive local pronunciations (such as **Arkansas River,** *AHR kuhn saw* or *ahr KANS zuhs).*

World Book uses a number of diacritical marks and special characters to indicate the correct spellings for many words and names in languages other than English. These marks have various meanings, according to the languages in which they are used. An acute accent mark (´) over an *e* in a French word indicates that the *é* is pronounced *ay.* An acute accent mark over an *e* in a Spanish word indicates that the syllable containing the *é* bears the main emphasis in the word. The accented characters may look difficult, and some of them represent sounds that are hard for English-speaking people to make. But the respelled pronunciation normally makes the sounds clear, as in **Dvořák,** *DVAWR zhahk,* or **Łódź,** *looj* or *lahdz.*

The pronunciation key at the right shows how common word sounds are indicated by diacritical marks, and by respelling in *The World Book Encyclopedia.* The key also shows examples of the *schwa,* or unaccented vowel sound. The schwa is represented by ə.

Letter or mark	As In	Respelling		Example
a	h*a*t, m*a*p	a	**Alphabet**	*AL fuh beht*
ā	*a*ge, f*a*ce	ay	**Asia**	*AY zhuh*
ã	c*a*re, *air*	ai	**Bareback**	*BAIR bak*
ä	f*a*ther, f*ar*	ah	**Armistice**	*AHR muh stihs*
ch	*ch*ild, mu*ch*	ch	**China**	*CHY nuh*
e	l*e*t, b*e*st	eh	**Essay**	*EHS ay*
ē	*e*qual, s*ee*, ma*ch*ine, cit*y*	ee	**Leaf** **Marine**	*leef* *muh REEN*
ėr	t*er*m, l*ear*n, s*ir*, w*or*k	ur	**Pearl**	*purl*
i	*i*t, p*i*n, h*y*mn	ih	**System**	*SIHS tuhm*
ī	*i*ce, f*i*ve, *i*con	y	**Ohio**	*oh HY oh*
		eye	**Iris**	*EYE rihs*
k	*c*oat, loo*k*	k	**Corn**	*kawrn*
o	h*o*t, r*o*ck	ah	**Ottawa**	*AHT uh wuh*
		or o	**Hospice**	*HOS pihs*
ō	*o*pen, g*o*, gr*o*w, tabl*eau*	oh	**Rainbow** **Château**	*RAYN boh* *shah TOH*
ô	*o*rder, *a*ll	aw	**Orchid** **Mall**	*AWR kihd* *mawl*
oi	*oi*l, v*oi*ce	oy	**Coinage**	*KOY nihj*
ou	h*ou*se, *ou*t	ow	**Fountain**	*FOWN tuhn*
s	*s*ay, ni*c*e	s	**Spice**	*spys*
sh	*sh*e, aboli*ti*on	sh	**Motion**	*MOH shuhn*
u	c*u*p, b*u*tter, fl*oo*d	uh	**Study** **Blood**	*STUHD ee* *bluhd*
ù	f*u*ll, p*u*t, w*oo*d	u	**Fulbright** **Wool**	*FUL bryt* *wul*
ü	r*u*le, m*o*ve, f*oo*d, m*u*sic	oo	**Zulu**	*ZOO loo*
		yoo	**Muses**	*MYOOZ ehz*
zh	plea*s*ure	zh	**Asia**	*AY zhuh*
ə	*a*bout, ameb*a*	uh	**Burma**	*BUR muh*
	tak*e*n, purpl*e*	uh	**Fiddle**	*FIHD uhl*
	penc*i*l	uh	**Citizen**	*SIHT uh zuhn*
	lem*o*n	uh	**Lion**	*LY uhn*
	circ*u*s	uh	**Cyprus**	*SY pruhs*
	lab*y*rinth	uh	**Physique**	*fuh ZEEK*
	curt*ai*n	uh	**Mountain**	*MOWN tuhn*
	Egypt*ia*n	uh	**Georgia**	*JAWR juh*
	sec*tio*n	uh	**Legion**	*LEE juhn*
	fabul*ou*s	uh	**Anonymous**	*uh NAHN uh muhs*

Contributors and Consultants

A person whose name appears at the end of an article in *The World Book Encyclopedia* either wrote it originally or reviewed it later for accuracy and currency. The content of *The World Book Encyclopedia* reflects assistance and advice contributed, over the course of its publication history, by experts in such areas as cartography and readability.

A

Aaron, Henry J., Ph.D. Sr. Fellow, Brookings Inst.

Abadinsky, Howard, Ph.D. Professor, Criminal Justice & Legal Studies, St. John's Univ.

Abbate, Carolyn, Ph.D. Christopher H. Browne Dist. Prof. of Music, Univ. of Pennsylvania.

Abbott, Carl, Ph.D. Prof. of Urban Studies and Planning, Portland State Univ.

Abbott, Kathryn A., Ph.D. Assoc. Prof. of History, Western Kentucky Univ.

Abeloff, Martin D., M.D. Former Prof. and Dir., Johns Hopkins Oncology Ctr.

Abels, Richard P., Ph.D. Prof. of History, U.S.; Tills-V Naval Academy, Annapolis.

Abrams, Suzanne R., Ph.D. Principal Research Officer, Plant Biotechnology Inst., Natl. Research Council of Canada.

Abramson, Charles I., Ph.D. Prof. of Psychology, Oklahoma State Univ.

Abu Jaber, Kamel S., Ph.D. Prof. Emer. of Political Science, Jordan Univ.

AbuKhalil, As'ad, Ph.D. Prof. of Politics, California State Univ., Stanislaus.

Aby, Anne J., M.A. Former Prof., Minnesota West Community and Technical Coll.; editor, *The North Star State: A Minnesota History Reader.*

Acheson, Donald T., Ph.D. Consultant; former Staff Scientist, Natl. Weather Service.

Acheson, T. W., Ph.D. Former Prof. of History, Univ. of New Brunswick.

Ackroyd-Kelly, Ian H., Ph.D. Prof. of Geography, East Stroudsburg Univ.

Adam, Mohammed M., M.J. Journalist/Municipal Reporter, *Ottawa* (ON) *Citizen.*

Adams, Clark E., Ph.D. Prof. of Wildlife and Fisheries Sciences, Texas A&M Univ.

Adams, Jack, B.S. Regional Dir. for Canada of the Natl. Horseshoe Pitchers Assoc. of America.

Adams, Nicholas, Ph.D. Prof. of Art, Vassar Coll.

Adams, Robert L. A., Ph.D. Former Assoc. Prof. of Geography, Univ. of New Hampshire.

Adams, Russ, B.S. Owner, BarCode-1.com.

Adams, William D., M.Sc. Content Creator, World Book, Inc.

Adamson, Douglas H., Ph.D. Assoc. Prof., Univ of Connecticut.

Adamson, Jeremy, Ph.D. Dir. for Collections and Services, Library of Congress.

Adewumi, Michael A., Ph.D. Prof. of Petroleum and Natural Gas Engineering, Penn. State Univ.

Adler, Thomas P., Ph.D. Prof. Emer. of English, Purdue Univ.

Agnew, John, Ph.D. Prof., Dept. of Geography, Univ. of California, Los Angeles.

Agranoff, Robert, Ph.D. Prof. Emer. of Public and Environmental Affairs, Indiana Univ.

Ahearne, Michael, Ph.D. Assoc. Prof. of Marketing and Exec. Dir. of the Sales Excellence Inst., Univ. of Houston.

Ahlgrim, Kevin C., Ph.D. Assoc. Prof., Dept. of Finance, Insurance, and Law, Illinois State Univ.

Ahlquist, Jon E., Ph.D. Assoc. Prof., Dept. of Meteorology, Florida State Univ.

Ahlschwede, William T., Ph.D. Swine Production Consultant, Genetic Advisory Service, Univ. of Tennessee, Martin.

Ahrens, Richard A., Ph.D. Prof. Emer., Grad. Program in Nutrition, Univ. of Maryland.

Aiken, Charles S., Ph.D. Prof. Emer. of Geography, Univ. of Tennessee, Knoxville.

Aikin, Arthur C., Ph.D. Sr. Scientist Emer., National Aeronautics and Space Administration/Goddard Space Flight Center.

Ajayi, J. F. Ade, LL.D. Former Professor of History, University of Ibadan.

Akerman, James, Ph.D. Dir., Herman Dunlap Smith Ctr. for the History of Cartography, Newberry Library.

Aksan, Virginia H., Ph.D. Chair, Department of History, McMaster University.

Alahi, Peter, M.D. Professor of Clinical Psychiatry, Univ. of Illinois College of Medicine, Peoria.

Albert, James S., Ph.D Professor, Department of Biology, University of Louisiana, Lafayette.

Albrecht, Randy, Ph.D. Postdoctoral Fellow, Mount Sinai School of Medicine.

Albright, Jonathan, Ph.D. Assistant Professor, School of Communications, Elon University.

Albro, Ward S., Ph.D. Prof. Emer. of History, Texas A&M Univ., Kingsville.

Alcock, James E., Ph.D. Prof. of Psychology, York Univ.

Alcorn, Peter W., M.S. Botanist, Wild Things, Inc.

Aldeman, Matthew R., Ph.D. Assistant Professor of Technology, Illinois State University.

Alex-Assensoh, Yvette M., Ph.D. Vice President for Equity and Inclusion, University of Oregon.

Alexander, Duane F., M.D. Dir., Natl. Inst. of Child Health and Human Dev., Natl. Inst. of Health.

Alfaro, Luis D., Ph.D. Consulting Engineer, Ingenieros Geotécnicos, S.A. (Panama)

Ali, Asra, M.D. Dermatologist, Texas Dermatology Specialists.

Allard, Scott W., Ph.D. Assoc. Prof., Univ. of Chicago, School of Social Service.

Allen, Anita L., J.D. Prof. of Law and Philosophy, Univ. of Pennsylvania.

Allen, Delmas J., Ph.D. Former Pres. for Academic Affairs, North Georgia Coll.

Allen, Garland E., Ph.D. Prof. of Biology, Washington Univ., St. Louis.

Allen, John L., Ph.D. Prof. Emer. of Geography, Univ. of Wyoming and Univ. of Connecticut.

Allen, Michael I., Ph.D. Assoc. Prof. of Classics, Univ. of Chicago.

Allen, Richard, Ph.D. Former Minister Responsible for Intl. Trade, Government of Ontario.

Allen, Roger, D.Phil. Emeritus Prof. of Arabic, Univ. of Pennsylvania.

Allen, William Hand, M.S. Pres., Allen & Shariff Corp.

Allen, William Sheridan, Ph.D. Prof. Emer. of History, State Univ. of New York, Buffalo.

Alley, Phillip W., Ph.D. Prof. Emer. of Physics, State Univ. of New York, Geneseo.

Allin, Craig W., Ph.D. Professor of Political Science, Cornell Coll.

Allinson, Gary D., Ph.D. Former Ellen Boyard Weedon Prof. of Modern Japanese History, Univ. of Virginia.

Allison, David G., Ph.D. Sr. Lecturer, Univ. of Manchester.

Allison, Mary Ann, Ph.D. Assoc. Prof. of Journalism, Media Studies, and Public Relations, School of Communication, Hofstra Univ.

Allison, Robert J., Ph.D. Chair and Prof., History Dept., Suffolk Univ.

Allmand, C. T., D.Phil. Prof. Emer. of History, Univ. of Liverpool.

Allocca, Michaelangelo F., M.A. Basic Program Lecturer/Instructor, Univ. of Chicago, Graham School of Continuing Educ.

Alman, Bob, Owner and Managing Editor, *Croquet World Online Magazine.*

Almond, Gabriel A., Ph.D. Coauthor, *The Struggle for Democracy in Germany.*

Alsop, Fred J., III, Ph.D. Prof., Dept. of Biological Science, East Tennessee State Univ.

Alten, Stanley R., Ph.D. Prof. Emer., Newhouse School of Public Communications, Syracuse Univ.; author, *Audio in Media.*

Altrock, Uwe, Dr.-Ing. Prof. for Urban Regeneration and Planning, Univ. of Kassel.

Aman, Mohammed M., Ph.D. Prof., School of Information Studies, Univ. of Wisconsin.

Ambler, Susan H., Ph.D. Assoc. Prof. of Sociology, Maryville Coll.

Ambrose, Stephen E., Ph.D. Author of a three-volume study of Richard M. Nixon and numerous books on World War II.

Ameriks, Karl, Ph.D. Prof. of Philosophy, Univ. of Notre Dame.

Ammirati, Joe F., Ph.D. Prof. of Biology, Univ. of Washington.

Ammons, Patty Former Features Editor, (Augusta, ME) *Kennebec Journal.*

Amrine, Frederick, Ph.D. Assoc. Prof. of German, Univ. of Michigan.

Andaya, Leonard Y., Ph.D. Prof. of History, Univ. of Hawaii, Honolulu.

Anderson, Albert G., Ph.D. Research Assoc., E. I. du Pont de Nemours & Company, Inc.

Anderson, Barrie, M.D. Prof. of Obstetrics and Gynecology; Dir., Fellowship in Gynecologic Oncology, Univ. of Iowa Hospitals and Clinics.

Anderson, Bertin W., Ph.D. Pres., Revegetation and Wildlife Management Ctr.

Anderson, Celia Catlett, Ph.D. Prof. Emer. of English, Eastern Connecticut State Univ.

Anderson, Dan R., Ph.D. Prof. of Business, Univ. of Wisconsin.

Anderson, David L., Ph.D. Prof. of History, California State Univ., Monterey Bay.

Anderson, Fred W., Ph.D. Prof. of History, Univ. of Colorado, Boulder.

Anderson, John F., Ph.D. Dir., Connecticut Agricultural Experiment Station.

Anderson, John G., Ph.D. Prof., Univ. of Nevada.

Anderson, Michael A., Ph.D. Associate Professor, Dept. of Classics, San Francisco State Univ.

Anderson, Stannie Former Writing Coach, *Topeka* (KS) *Capital-Journal.*

Andreasen, Nancy C., M.D., Ph.D. Chair of Psychiatry, Univ. of Iowa Hospitals and Clinics.

Andrews, Frank C., Ph.D. Prof. Emer. of Chemistry, Univ. of California, Santa Cruz.

Andrews, Melodie, Ph.D. Assoc. Prof. of History, Minnesota State Univ., Mankato.

Andrews, William L., Ph.D. E. Maynard Adams Prof. of English, Univ. of North Carolina.

Angel, J. Roger P., D.Phil. Regents Prof., Prof. of Astronomy and Optical Sciences, Univ. of Arizona.

Angell, Carole S., M.Ed. Teacher, Fairfax County Public Schools.

Anner, Mark, Ph.D. Assoc. Prof. of Labor and Employment Relations and Political Science; Director, Ctr. for Global Workers' Rights, Penn. State Univ.

Ansari, Ali M., Ph.D. Prof. of Iranian Hist. and Dir. of the Inst. of Iranian Studies, Univ. of St. Andrews.

Antonello, Alessandro, Ph.D. Research Fellow, Robert D. Clark Honors College, Univ. of Oregon.

Antonini, Gustavo A., Ph.D. Former Prof. of Latin American Studies and Geography, Univ. of Florida.

Aponte-Parés, Luis, Ph.D. Assoc. Prof., Coll. of Public and Community Service, Univ. of Mass.

Appelman, Evan H., Ph.D. Former Sr. Chemist, Argonne Natl. Laboratory.

Applegate, David M., B.A. Freelance writer.

Appleman, Jean, J.D. Attorney and legal author.

Appleton, Jon H., M.A. Prof. of Music, Dartmouth Coll.

Apseloff, Marilyn Fain, M.A. Prof. Emer. of English, Kent State Univ.

Arbic, Brian K., Ph.D. Assoc. Prof., Dept. of Earth and Environmental Sciences, Univ. of Michigan.

Archambault, Jo Allyn, Ph.D. Dir., American Indian Program in the Natl. Museum of Natural History, Smithsonian Inst.

Ard, Josh, Ph.D., J.D. Adjunct Professor, Michigan State University College of Law.

Argall, Brenna D., Ph.D. Assistant Professor of Rehabilitation Robotics, Northwestern University.

Argote-Freyre, Frank, Ph.D. Asst. Prof., Kean Univ.

Argrow, Brian M., Ph.D. Prof., Dept. of Aerospace Engineering Sciences, Univ. of Colorado.

Ariew, Roger, Ph.D. Prof. and Chair, Dept. of

Philosophy, University of South Florida.

Armbruster, David C., Ph.D. Pres., Armbruster Assoc. Inc., Chemical Consultants and Specialty Products.

Armstrong, Charles K., Ph.D. Professor of Korean Studies, Dept. of History, Columbia University.

Armstrong, Joseph E., Ph.D. Prof. of Botany, Illinois State Univ.

Arndt, Roger E. A., Ph.D. Prof. of Hydromechanics, St. Anthony Falls Laboratory.

Arno, Janet N., M.D. Medical Dir., Bell Flower Clinic; Assoc. Prof. of Clinical Medicine, Indiana Univ. School of Medicine.

Arnold, Eric A., Jr., Ph.D. Former Assoc. Prof. of History, Univ. of Denver.

Arnold, James D., Ph.D. Former Prof. of Agriculture, Texas A&M Univ., Kingsville.

Arreola, Daniel D., Ph.D. Prof., School of Geographical Sciences and Urban Planning, Arizona State Univ.

Arshadi, Nasser, Ph.D. Prof. of Finance, Univ. of Missouri.

Art, Robert J., Ph.D. Herter Prof. of Intl. Relations, Brandeis Univ.

Asay, Kay H., Ph.D. Former Research Geneticist, Agriculture Research Service, U.S. Dept. of Agriculture.

Ash, Stephen V., Ph.D. Professor Emeritus of History, University of Tennessee.

Ashe, Arthur J., III, Ph.D. Prof. Emer. of Chemistry, Univ. of Michigan.

Ashley, Susan A., Ph.D. William R. Hochman Prof. of History, Colorado Coll.

Ashton, Dore, M.A. Prof. of Art History, Cooper Union.

Ashton, Peter S., Ph.D. Charles Bullard Professor of Forestry, Emeritus, Harvard University.

Askin, Ronald G., Ph.D. Professor and Director, School of Computing, Informatics, and Decision Systems Engineering, Arizona State University.

Assensoh, A. B., Ph.D. Dir. of Grad. Studies and Admissions, African American and African Diaspora Studies, Indiana Univ., Bloomington.

Atkinson, Ronald R., Ph.D. Assoc. Prof. Emeritus of African History, Univ. of South Carolina.

Audesirk, Gerald J., Ph.D. Prof. Emer., Univ. of Colorado, Denver.

Augee, Michael L., Ph.D. Member, Nature Conservation Council of NSW, Karst Management Advisory Committee.

Austin, Daniel F., Ph.D. Book Review Editor, *Economic Botany.*

Austin, Max E., Ph.D. Prof. Emer. of Horticulture, Univ. of Georgia.

Autry, William O., B.A. Consultant, Anthropological Research Assoc., South Bend.

Avallone, Linnea M., Ph.D. Prof., Lab. for Atmospheric and Space Physics, Univ. of Colorado.

Avella, Steven M., M.Div., Ph.D. Professor of History, Marquette University.

Averett, John E., Ph.D. Prof. and Chair, Dept. of Biology, Georgia Southern Univ.

Avery, Mary Ellen, M.D. Dist. Prof. of Pediatrics Emer., Harvard Medical School.

Awbery, Gwenllian, Ph.D. Former Coordinating Lecturer for Welsh, Centre for Lifelong Learning, Cardiff University.

Axelrod, Steven Gould, Ph.D. Prof. of English, Univ. of California, Riverside.

Axen, Gary J., Ph.D. Assoc. Prof. of Earth and Environmental Science, New Mexico Inst. for Mining and Technology.

Axtell, James, Ph.D. Kenan Prof. of Humanities, Coll. of William and Mary.

Ayers, Catherine R., Ph.D. Asst. Prof., Dept. of Psychiatry, Univ. of California, San Diego.

B

Babayan, Kathryn, Ph.D. Asst. Prof. of Iranian History and Culture, Univ. of Michigan, Ann Arbor.

Bach, Andrew J., Ph. D. Assoc. Prof., Huxley Coll. of Environmental Studies, Western Wash. Univ.

Bachrach, Bernard S., Ph.D. Prof. of Medieval History, Univ. of Minnesota, Twin Cities Campus.

Bachrach, David S., Ph.D. Professor of Medieval History, University of New Hampshire.

Badyaev, Alexander V., Ph.D. Prof., Dept. of Ecology & Evolutionary Biology, Univ. of Arizona.

Baeder, Paul S., B.S. Instructor, Major Appliance and Refrigeration Technol., Renton Technol. Coll.

Baerwald, Thomas J., Ph.D. Program Dir., Div. of Social and Econ. Science, Natl. Science Found.

Bagley, Will, B.A. Independent historian; columnist, *The Salt Lake* (UT) *Tribune.*

Bagshaw, David A., M.B.A. General Manager, W. H. Bagshaw Company, Inc.

Bahrke, Michael S., Ph.D. Acquisitions Editor, Human Kinetics.

Bailey, Don, Ph.D. Dist. Fellow, Early Childhood Dev., RTI Intl., Triangle Park, North Carolina.

Bailey, Donald A., Ph.D. Prof. of History, Univ. of Winnipeg.

Bailey, George S., Ph.D. Former Professor, Department of Environmental and Molecular Toxicology, Oregon State University.

Bailey, Robert C., Ph.D. Prof. of Epidemiology, School of Public Health, Univ. of Illinois, Chicago.

Bailey, Ted E., M.S. Owner, flight-toys.com.

Bailey, William L. Pres., Auto-Foto.

Bain, Carol, M.A. Former Archivist, Folklore Archives, Indiana Univ., Bloomington.

Baker, Alton F., III, B.A. Editor and Publisher, *The* (Eugene, OR) *Register-Guard.*

Baker, Carrie N., Ph.D. Prof. and Dir., Program for the Study of Women and Gender, Smith Coll.

Baker, Chris, Ph.D. Independent researcher.

Baker, John F., M.A. Former Editorial Dir., *Publishers Weekly.*

Baker, Vaughan B., Ph.D. Prof. Emer. of History and Geography, Univ. of Southwestern Louisiana.

Balcer, Jack Martin, Ph.D. Former Prof. of Ancient History, Ohio State Univ.

Baldrige, Letitia, B.A. Former Pres., Letitia Baldrige Enterprises, Inc.

Balgooyen, Thomas G., Ph.D. Professor Emeritus of Biological Sciences, San Jose State Univ.

Balistreri, William F., M.D. Dir., Pediatric Liver Care Ctr., Cincinnati Children's Hospital; and Prof., Univ. of Cincinnati Coll. of Medicine.

Ball, David W., Ph.D. Prof. of Chemistry, Cleveland State Univ.

Ball, Deborah Loewenberg, Ph.D. Prof. of Mathematics Educ., Univ. of Michigan.

Ball, Samuel, Ph.D. Emer. Prof., CEO, Board of Studies, Victoria, Australia.

Ballinger, Pamela, Ph.D. Assoc. Prof. of Anthropology, Bowdoin Coll.

Balmer, Randall, Ph.D. Prof. of American Religious History, Barnard Coll., Columbia Univ.

Balonek, Thomas J., Ph.D. Professor of Physics and Astronomy, Colgate University.

Balph, Martha Hatch, Ph.D. Former Research Assoc. Prof., Fisheries and Wildlife, Utah State Univ.

Bamber, Greg J., Ph.D. Professor and Co-Director, Australian Consortium for Research in Employment and Work, Monash University.

Bamforth, Charlie, Ph.D., D.Sc. Chair and Prof., Dept. of Food Science and Technology, Univ. of California, Davis.

Banerdt, W. Bruce, Ph.D. Principal Investigator, InSight Mission to Mars, Jet Propulsion Laboratory, California Institute of Technology.

Banko, Paul C., Ph.D. Project Leader, USGS Pacific Island Ecosystems Research Ctr.

Bannatyne, Lesley P., B.A. Author, *A Halloween How-To: Costumes, Parties, Decorations and Destinations.*

Bannon, C. J., Ph.D. Assoc. Prof., Dept. of Classical Studies, Indiana Univ.

Baranski, Michael J., Ph.D. Professor Emeritus of Biology, Catawba College.

Baratta, Joseph Preston, Ph.D. Cofounder and Co-Dir., Ctr. for Global Community and World Law.

Barbash, Jack, M.A. Author, *The Elements of Industrial Relations.*

Barbe, Serge, B.A. Community Records Archivist, City of Ottawa Archives.

,**Barber, Katrine,** Ph.D. Assoc. Prof. of History, Portland State University.

Barber, Valerie A., Ph.D. Asst. Research Prof. and Forestry Specialist, Univ. of Alaska, Fairbanks.

Barbezat, Daniel, Ph.D. Prof. of Economics, Amherst Coll.

Barbosa, Francisco J., Ph.D. Asst. Prof. of History, Univ. of Colorado, Boulder.

Barbour, Barton H., Ph.D. Associate Prof. of History, Boise State Univ.

Barbour, Michael G., Ph.D. Prof. Emer. of Plant Ecology, Univ. of California, Davis.

Bard, Allen J., Ph.D. Prof. of Chemistry, Univ. of Texas, Austin.

Barden, John A., Ph.D. Prof. Emer. of Horticulture, Virginia Polytechnic Institute and State Univ.

Bardolph, Richard, Ph.D. Former Prof. of History, Univ. of North Carolina, Greensboro.

Bareegt, René W., Ph.D. Assoc. Dean, Faculty of Arts and Science, Univ. of Lethbridge.

Barefoot, Aldos C., Jr., D.F. Former Prof. of Wood and Paper Sci., North Carolina State Univ.

Barenbaum, Nicole B., Ph.D. Prof. of Psychology, Univ. of the South.

Barfuss, Steven L., M.S. Research Asst. Prof., Utah Water Research Laboratory, Utah State Univ.

Barkan, Elliott Robert, Ph.D. Prof. Emer. of History, California State Univ., San Bernardino.

Barker, Brett R., Ph.D. Asst. Prof. of History, Univ. of Wisconsin, Marathon County.

Barker, Fiona, Ph.D. Lecturer, Victoria Univ. of Wellington.

Barker, Rodney, Ph.D. Emer. Prof. of Government, London School of Economics and Polit. Sci.

Barlow, Nadine G., Ph.D. Asst. Prof., Dept. of Physics and Astronomy, Northern Arizona Univ.

Barman, Jean, Ed.D. Prof. Emer., History of Education, Univ. of British Columbia.

Barnbaum, Cecilia, Ph.D. Prof. of Physics and Astronomy, Valdosta State Univ.

Barnes, Andrew, Ph.D. Assoc. Prof. of Political Science, Kent State Univ.

Barnes, L. Diane, Ph.D. Assoc. Prof. of History, Youngstown State Univ.

Barnes, Gary, Ph.D. Prof. of Meteorology, Univ. of Hawaii, Honolulu.

Barnes, Robert D., Ph.D. Former Prof. of Biology, Gettysburg Coll.

Barnes, Timothy David, D.Phil. Former Prof. of Classics, Univ. of Toronto.

Barnett, Jeffrey C., Ph.D. Dean, Coll. of Educ., Univ. of Wisconsin, Whitewater.

Barnett, Roger, Ph.D. Prof. Emer. of Geography, Univ. of the Pacific.

Barnhardt, Robert A., Ed.D. Dean Emer. and Prof., Coll. of Textiles, North Carolina State Univ.

Baron, John H., Ph.D. Prof. of Musicology, Tulane Univ.

Barone, Michael, LL.B. Political analyst; coauthor, *The Almanac of American Politics.*

Barr, William, M.S. Emer. Prof. of Geography, Univ. of Saskatchewan.

Barrett, Alan D. T., Ph.D. Assoc. Dir., Sealy Ctr. for Vaccine Dev., Univ. of Texas Medical Branch.

Barrett, Anthony A., Ph.D. Professor Emeritus of Classics, Univ. of British Columbia.

Barrett, Eugene J., Ph.D. Prof. of Medicine, Univ. of Virginia.

Barrett, Gerald V., Ph.D. Former Prof. and Head, Dept. of Psychology, Univ. of Akron.

Barrett, John Q., J.D. Prof. of Law, St. John's Univ.

Barrett, Lisa Feldman, Ph.D. Prof. of Psychology, Boston Coll.

Barrett, Nora A., M.D. Fellow in Pulmonary Medicine, Brigham and Women's Hospital.

Barron, Andrew R., Ph.D. Prof., Dept. of Chemistry, Rice Univ.

Barron, Neil, M.L.S. Former librarian and freelance editor.

Barrow, Bruce B., Ph.D. Consultant in telecommunications; Chair, Metric Practice Committee, Inst. of Electrical and Electronics Engineers.

Barrows, Robert G., Ph.D. Assoc. Prof. of History, Indiana Univ., Indianapolis.

Barry, Roger D., Ph.D. Former Prof. and Head, Dept. of Chemistry, Northern Michigan Univ.

Barth, Daniel S., Ph.D. Prof. of Neuroscience, Dept. of Psychology, Univ. of Colorado, Boulder.

Barth, James R., Ph.D. Lowder Eminent Professor of Finance, Auburn University, and Senior Finance Fellow, Milken Institute.

Bartlett, Charles, B.A. Former Pres., Jefferson Foundation; winner of Pulitzer Prize for Natl. Reporting, 1956.

Bartlett, Richard A., Ph.D. Former Professor of

History, Florida State University.

Bartley, W. W., III, Ph.D. Former Sr. Research Fellow, Hoover Inst. on War, Revolution, and Peace, Stanford Univ.

Bartone, Chris G., Ph.D. Prof., School of Electrical Engineering and Computer Science, Ohio Univ.

Basil, Jennifer, Ph.D. Assoc. Prof., Dept. of Biology, Brooklyn Coll., City Univ. of New York.

Basinger, James F., Ph.D. Prof. of Geological Sciences, Univ. of Saskatchewan.

Baskin, Jerry M., Ph.D. Prof. of Biological Sciences, Univ. of Kentucky.

Basofin, Peter, M.L.S. Dir. of Editorial Research, *The Sacramento* (CA) *Bee.*

Basri, Gibor, Ph.D. Prof. of Astronomy, Univ. of California.

Bass, Hyman, Ph.D. Prof. of Mathematics and Mathematics Educ., Univ. of Michigan.

Bassett, Sharon, Ph.D. Emer. Prof. of English, California State Univ., Los Angeles.

Bassett, Thomas J., Ph.D. Prof. of Geography, Univ. of Illinois, Urbana-Champaign.

Bassiouni, M. Cherif, LL.D. Former Research Prof. of Law and former Pres. of the Intl. Human Rights Law Institute, DePaul College of Law.

Basso, Keith H., Ph.D. Former Prof. of Anthropology, Univ. of New Mexico.

Bates, Robert H., Ph.D. Eaton Prof. of the Science of Government and Faculty Fellow of the Ctr. for Intl. Dev., Harvard Univ.

Batra, Subhash K., Ph.D. Dir. Emer., Nonwovens Cooperative Research Ctr., Coll. of Textiles, North Carolina State Univ.

Battenburg, John D., Ph.D. Prof. of English, California Polytechnic State Univ.

Battestin, Martin C., Ph.D. Former William R. Kenan, Jr., Prof. of English, Univ. of Virginia.

Bauer, Brian S., Ph.D. Professor, Department of Anthropology, University of Illinois at Chicago.

Bauer, Marc, M.A. Head Wrestling Coach, Univ. of Nebraska at Kearney.

Bauer, Raymond T., Ph.D. Prof. of Biology, Univ. of Louisiana, Lafayette.

Baughn, W. H., Ph.D. Author, *International Bankers Handbook.*

Bauman, Thomas A., Ph.D. Prof., Bienen School of Music, Northwestern Univ.

Baumgartner, William A., M.D. Cardiac Surgeon-in-Charge, Johns Hopkins Hospital.

Baxevanis, John J., Ph.D. Prof. Emer. of Geography, East Stroudsburg Univ.

Baybutt, Richard C., Ph.D. Assoc. Prof., Dept. of Human Nutrition, Kansas State Univ.

Bayer, Barbara M., Ph.D. Assoc. Prof. of Pharmacology, Georgetown Univ.

Bays, Brad A., Ph.D. Assoc. Prof. of Geography, Oklahoma State Univ.

Beall, Jo, Ph.D. Prof. of Dev. Studies and Dir., Dev. Studies Inst., London School of Economics.

Beam, James C. "Jim", M.A. Columnist, *Lake Charles* (LA) *American Press.*

Bean, Mark C. Pres., Match Division, D. D. Bean & Sons Company.

Bean, Pat Former City Editor, (Ogden, UT) *Standard-Examiner.*

Bearman, Alan, Ph.D. Asst. Prof. of History, Washburn Univ.

Beart, Robert W., Jr., M.D. Chairman, Dept. of Colorectal Surgery, Univ. of Southern California.

Beasley, Maurine H., Ph.D. Prof. Emer. of Journalism, Univ. of Maryland.

Beaulieu, Michel S., Ph.D. Professor of History, Lakehead University.

Beaulieu, Robert J., B.S. Asst. Prof. of Textile Dev. and Marketing, Fashion Inst. of Technology.

Beaulieu, Norman C., Ph.D. Dept. of Electrical and Computer Engineering, Univ. of Alberta.

Bebb, Phillip N., Ph.D. Former Prof. of History, Ohio Univ.

Beck, Alan M., Sc.D. Prof. of Animal Ecology and Dir., Ctr. for the Human-Animal Bond, School of Veterinary Medicine, Purdue Univ.

Beck, Boyde, M.A. Curator of History, Prince Edward Island Museum and Heritage Foundation.

Beck, Hermann, Ph.D. Prof., Dept. of History, Univ. of Miami.

Beck, John H., M.M. Prof. Emer. of Percussion, Eastman School of Music; Timpanist, Rochester Philharmonic Orchestra.

Beck, Laurence H., M.D. Chairman, Dept. of Internal Medicine, Cleveland Clinic Florida, Weston.

Beck, Robert F., Ph.D. Prof. of Naval Architecture and Marine Engineering, Univ. of Michigan.

Becker, Anne E., M.D., Ph.D. Assoc. Prof. of Medical Anthropology and Asst. Prof. of Psychiatry, Harvard Medical School.

Becker, Brenda, B.S. Biological Science Technician, National Marine Fisheries Service.

Becker, Christian M., M.D. Resident, Dept. of Obstetrics and Gynecology, Free Univ., Berlin.

Becker, Robert A., Ph.D. Prof. Emer. of History, Louisiana State Univ.

Becker, William H., Ph.D. Prof. of History, George Washington Univ.

Beckett, Ian F. W., Ph.D. Professor of Military History, University of Kent.

Beckles, Hilary, Ph.D. Pro-Vice-Chancellor, Principal, Univ. of the West Indies, Cave Hill, Barbados.

Beckman, Gary, Ph.D. Prof. of Hittite and Mesopotamian Studies, Univ. of Michigan.

Bednarek, Janet R., Ph.D. Prof. of History, Univ. of Dayton.

Beebe, Ralph K., Ph.D. Prof. Emer. of History, George Fox Univ.

Beehler, Bruce M., Ph.D. Vice Pres. for Pacific Island Programs, Melanesia Ctr. for Biology Conservation Intl.

Beeley, Christopher A., Ph.D. Walter H. Gray Assoc. Prof. of Anglican Studies and Patristics, Yale Divinity School.

Beem, John K., Ph.D. Prof. Emer. of Mathematics, Univ. of Missouri, Columbia.

Beemyn, Genny, Ph.D. Director, University of Massachusetts Stonewall Center.

Beermann, Donald H., Ph.D. Prof. Emer., Dept. of Animal Science, Univ. of Nebraska, Lincoln.

Behler, Deborah A., B.A. Former Editor in Chief, *Wildlife Conservation* magazine.

Behrman, Cynthia F., Ph.D. Prof. Emer. of History, Wittenberg Univ.

Behrooz, Maziar, Ph.D. Assoc. Prof. of History, San Francisco State Univ.

Beidelman, T. O., D.Phil. Prof. of Anthropology, New York Univ.

Beiswenger, Ronald E., Ph.D. Prof. Emer. of Geography, Univ. of Wyoming.

Beiswenger, Vivian M., B.S. Dir. of Dance Sport, Pennsylvania Performing Arts Academy.

Bekker, Matthew F., Ph.D. Associate Professor, Department of Geography, Brigham Young Univ.

Bélanger, Éric, Ph.D. Professor, Department of Political Science, McGill University.

Bélanger, Patrice C., Ph.D. Dir., Quality Assurance, Merck Frosst Canada, Inc.

Belbruno, Edward, Ph.D. Visiting Research Collaborator, Astrophysical Sciences, Princeton Univ.

Belk, Keith E., Ph.D. Prof., Dept. of Animal Science, Colorado State Univ.

Bell, Stephen, Ph.D. Assoc. Prof. of Geography and History, Univ. of California, Los Angeles.

Bellegarde-Smith, Patrick, Ph.D. Prof. Emeritus of Africology, Univ. of Wisconsin, Milwaukee.

Beller, Steven, Ph.D. Independent scholar.

Belmont, Patrick, Ph.D. Asst. Prof., Utah State Univ.

Belt, Mike, B.S. Staff Writer, *Kansas City* (KS) *Kansan.*

Bender, Gerald J., Ph.D. Assoc. Prof. Emeritus of International Relations, Univ. of Southern Calif.

Bender, Ronald, B.A. Former City Editor, *Rapid City* (SD) *Journal.*

Benford, Gregory, Ph.D. Prof. Emeritus, Dept. of Physics and Astronomy, Univ. of Calif., Irvine.

Ben-Harosh, Jesse Service Manager, Lakewood Stereo and TV Repair.

Benjamin, Gerald, Ph.D. Director, The Benjamin Center, State University of New York, New Paltz.

Benkov, KeMith J., M.D. Pediatric Gastroenterologist, Mount Sinai School of Medicine.

Bennett, Albert F., Ph.D. Professor Emeritus, Department of Ecology and Evolutionary Biology, University of California, Irvine.

Bennett, Andrew, Ph.D. Prof. of Government, Georgetown Univ.

Bennett, J. Michael, Ed.D. Prof. Emer. of Rhetoric, Univ. of Minnesota, Twin Cities Campus.

Bensinger, Gad J., Ph.D. Former Prof. of Criminal Justice, Loyola Univ., Chicago.

Benson, Barbara E., Ph.D. Former Exec. Dir., Historical Society of Delaware.

Benson, Keith R., Ph.D. Prof. of Medical History and Ethics, Univ. of Washington.

Bentler, Ruth A., Ph.D. Prof., Dept. of Speech Pathology and Audiology, Univ. of Iowa.

Bentley, James, D.Phil. Author, *Schweitzer: The Enigma.*

Bentley, Jerry H., Ph.D. Former Professor of History, University of Hawaii.

Bercuson, David J., Ph.D. Professor of History, University of Calgary.

Berdahl, Robert M., Ph.D. Pres., Assoc. of American Universities; Former Prof. of Public Policy and History, Univ. of Calif., Berkeley.

Berenbaum, Michael, Ph.D. Dir., Sigi Ziering Inst., Univ. of Judaism.

Berenson, Edward, Ph.D. Prof. and Dir., Inst. of French Studies, New York Univ.

Berentsen, William H., Ph.D. Prof., Dept. of Geography, Univ. of Connecticut.

Berg, Darrell Matthews, Ph.D. Honorary Assoc. Prof. of Music, Blewitt Hall, Wash. Univ., St. Louis.

Berger, Melvin, M.A. Author, *The Story of Folk Music.*

Berger, Rainer, Ph.D. Former Prof. of Anthropology, Geography, and Geophysics, Univ. of Calif., Los Angeles.

Berger, Richard E., M.D. Prof. of Urology, Univ. of Washington.

Berghahn, Klaus J., D.Phil. Emer. Dir., Ctr. for German and European Studies, Univ. of Wisconsin, Madison.

Bergstresser, Paul R., M.D. Prof. and Chairman, Dept. of Dermatology, Univ. of Texas Southwestern Medical Ctr.

Berkey, Braden R., Psy.D. Pres., Prairie Psychological Services.

Berkhofer, Robert F., Jr., Ph.D. Prof. Emer. of History, Univ. of Calif., Santa Cruz.

Berkowitz, Gerald M., Ph.D. Former Prof. of English, Northern Illinois Univ.

Berkowitz, Luci, Ph.D. Prof. Emer. of Classics, Univ. of Calif., Irvine.

Berlin, Michael J., M.S.J. Assoc. Prof. Emer. of Journalism, Boston Univ.

Berlinsky, David, Ph.D. Prof., Dept. of Biological Sciences, Univ. of New Hampshire.

Berman, David R., Ph.D. Prof. Emer. of Political Science, Arizona State Univ.

Berman, Russell A., Ph.D. Walter A. Haas Prof. in the Humanities, Stanford Univ.

Bernat, James L., M.D. Prof. of Medicine (Neurology), Dartmouth Medical School.

Bernault, Florence, Ph.D. Prof. of African History, Univ. of Wisconsin, Madison.

Bernheimer, Martin, M.A. Music critic.

Bernstein, I. Melvin, Ph.D. Former Provost and Sr. Vice Pres. for Academic Affairs, Brandeis Univ.

Berrey, Ellen, Ph.D. Assistant Professor of Sociology, University of Toronto, Mississauga.

Berst, Charles A., Ph.D. Prof. Emer. of English, Univ. of Calif., Los Angeles.

Berta, Annalisa, Ph.D. Professor of Biology, San Diego State University.

Bertacco, Valeria, Ph.D. Assoc. Prof., Univ. of Michigan.

Bertoldi, Gilbert L., M.S. Sr. Research Hydrologist Emer., U.S. Geological Survey.

Besch, Henry R., Jr., Ph.D. Former Prof. and Chair, Dept. of Pharmacology and Toxicology; Prof. of Medicine, Indiana Univ. School of Medicine.

Bevin, A. Griswold, M.D. Former Prof. of Plastic Surgery, Univ. of North Carolina Sch. of Medicine.

Bewley, Joel J., B.A. Former Reporter, *Times of Trenton* (NJ); Adjunct Prof., Rider Univ.

Beyerstein, Barry L., Ph.D. Former Prof., Dept. of Psychology, Simon Fraser Univ.

Bianchina, Paul General contractor, Spectrum Builders, Inc.; author.

Bidlack, Richard H., Ph.D. Assoc. Prof. of History and Chairman of the Russian Studies Program, Washington and Lee Univ.

Bierman, Paul R., Ph.D. Prof. of Geology and Natural Resources, Univ. of Vermont.

Bigelow, Bruce, Ph.D. Professor of Geography,

Butler University.

Biggar, Jeanne C., Ph.D. Former Assoc. Prof. of Sociology, Univ. of Virginia.

Bilik, Dorothy S., Ph.D. Former Assoc. Prof., Germanic and Slavic Lang., Univ. of Maryland.

Billy, Rich Manager-Editor, *The* (Flin Flon, MB) *Reminder.*

Bilocerkowycz, Jaroslaw, Ph.D. Assoc. Prof. of Political Science, Univ. of Dayton.

Bilstein, Roger E., Ph.D. Prof. Emer. of History, Univ. of Houston, Clear Lake.

Bindschadler, Robert, Ph.D. Glaciologist, NASA (Emer.) and Goddard Earth Sciences and Technology Ctr., Univ. of Maryland, Baltimore County.

Birdsall, Stephen S., Ph.D. Prof. of Geography, Univ. of North Carolina, Chapel Hill.

Birkner, Michael J., Ph.D. Prof. of History, Gettysburg Coll.

Bish, David L., Ph.D. Haydn Murray Chair of Applied Clay Mineralogy, Indiana Univ., Bloomington.

Bishop, Finley C., Ph.D. Former Assoc. Prof. of Geology, Northwestern Univ.

Bix, Amy Sue, Ph.D. Assoc. Prof. of History, Iowa State Univ.

Blachman, Morris J., Ph.D. Asst. Dean of Continuing Medical Educ. and Faculty Dev., Univ. of South Carolina School of Medicine.

Black, Donald W., M.D. Prof. of Psychiatry, Univ. of Iowa, Roy J. and Lucille A. Carver Coll. of Medicine.

Blackhawk, Ned, Ph.D. Assoc. Prof. of History and American Indian Studies, Univ. of Wisconsin.

Blacklow, Neil R., M.D. Prof. Emer., Dept. of Medicine, Univ. of Mass. Medical School.

Blackwell, James H. Former Exec. Secretary, American Saddle Horse Breeders Assoc.

Blaufarb, Rafe, Ph.D. Prof. of History, Florida State Univ.

Blecha, Michael E., B.A. Former Opinion Page Editor, *Green Bay* (WI) *Press-Gazette.*

Blewitt, Richard F., M.B.A. Former Chief Executive Officer - Washington, Rowan & Blewitt, Inc.

Bliss, Lawrence C., Ph.D. Emer. Prof. of Botany, Univ. of Washington.

Bliss, Michael, Ph.D. Univ. Prof. Emer., Univ. of Toronto.

Bliss, Neil W., Ph.D. Consultant; Former Chief Geologist, Alcan Intl.

Blomberg, S. Brock, Ph.D. Robin and Peter Barker Prof. of Econ., Claremont McKenna Coll.

Bloom, Ken Author, *American Song: The Complete Musical Theatre Companion.*

Bloy, Marjorie, Ph.D. Former Lecturer in History, Rotherham Coll. of Arts and Technology, England.

Blue, Todd I., M.A. Pres., The Blue Review, Inc.; Former Pres./Instructor, Construction and Civil Technology, Blue Skye Inst.

Bluestein, Howard B., Ph.D. Prof. of Meteorology, School of Meteorology, Univ. of Oklahoma.

Blumberg, Jeffrey B., Ph.D. Prof. of Nutrition, School of Nutrition Science and Policy, Tufts Univ.

Blumhofer, Edith L., Ph.D. Dir., Inst. for the Study of American Evangelicals, Wheaton Coll.

Boal, Jean Geary, Ph.D. Prof., Dept. of Biology, Millersville Univ.

Bodman, Andrew R., Ph.D. Provost and Vice Pres. of Academic Affairs, Calif. State Univ., San Bernardino.

Boehm, Robert F., Ph.D. Professor of Mechanical Engineering, University of Utah.

Boehme, Sarah E., M.A. Managing Dir., Stark Museum of Art.

Bogus, John D., M.S.E. Dept. Head, Office of Naval Intelligence.

Bohannan, Paul, D.Phil. Former Prof. of Anthropology, Univ. of Southern Calif.

Bohren, Craig F., Ph.D. Prof. Emer. of Meteorology, Pennsylvania State Univ.

Bolen, Eric G., Ph.D. Prof. Emer. of Biology, Univ. of North Carolina, Wilmington.

Bolick, Margaret R., Ph.D. Curator of Botany and Assoc. Prof. of Biological Sciences, Univ. of Nebraska.

Bolin, David A., B.A. Teacher, Clark County School District, Las Vegas, Nevada.

Bollinger, Paul P., Jr., B.S. Deputy Asst. Secretary of the Army.

Bonato, Maud, Ph.D. Professor of Animal Sci-

ence, University of Stellenbosch.

Bond, David P. G., Ph.D. Research Fellow, School of Environmental Sciences, Univ. of Hull.

Bondar, Roberta L., Ph.D. Chancellor of Trent Univ.; former astronaut.

Bonello, Frank J., Ph.D. Assoc. Prof. of Economics, Univ. of Notre Dame.

Bonevac, Daniel, Ph.D. Prof. of Philosophy, Univ. of Texas, Austin.

Bonfante, Larissa, Ph.D. Prof. of Classics, New York Univ.

Bonner, Phillip L., Ph.D. Prof. of History, Univ. of the Witwatersrand.

Bonney, Richard E., Jr., M.P.S. Dir., Educ. and Citizen-Science Programs, Cornell Laboratory of Ornithology.

Bonn-Miller, Marcel O., Ph.D. Asst. Prof., Perelman School of Medicine, Univ. of Pennsylvania.

Booth, John A., Ph.D. Regents Prof. of Political Science, Univ. of North Texas.

Bordman, Gerald, Ph.D. Author, *American Musical Theatre: A Chronicle* and the *Oxford Companion to American Theatre.*

Borish, Steven M., Ph.D. Asst. Prof. of Anthropology, Swarthmore Coll.

Boritt, Gabor S., Ph.D. Fluhrer Prof. of Civil War Studies and Dir., Civil War Inst., Gettysburg Coll.

Borklund, Elmer W., Ph.D. Emer. Prof. of English, Pennsylvania State Univ.

Borkowski, Raymond P., Ph.D. Prof. of Chemistry, King's College, Wilkes-Barre, Pennsylvania.

Born, Brad S., Ph.D. Vice Pres. for Academic Affairs; Assoc. Prof. of English, Bethel Coll.

Born, George H., Ph.D. Dir., Colorado Ctr. for Astrodynamics, Univ. of Colorado, Boulder.

Borrowman, Merle L., Ed.D. Former Prof. of Education, Univ. of Calif., Berkeley.

Bos, Nick, Ph.D. Postdoctoral Researcher, Department of Biology, University of Copenhagen.

Bosland, Paul W., Ph.D. Prof. and Dir., Chile Pepper Inst., New Mexico State Univ.

Bostian, Charles W., Ph.D. Prof. Emer., Bradley Dept. of Electrical and Computer Engineering, Virginia Polytechnic Institute and State Univ.

Bosworth, Mary, Ph.D. Univ. Lecturer, Univ. of Oxford.

Bothwell, Robert, Ph.D. Prof. of History, Univ. of Toronto.

Bouchard, Constance B., Ph.D. Dist. Prof. of History, Univ. of Akron.

Boucher, Rod C. Educ. Services Manager, *The* (Hobart, Tasmania, Australia) *Mercury.*

Boulard, Garry, Freelance writer and author.

Boullata, Joseph I., Pharm.D. Assoc. Prof. of Pharmacy and Therapeutics, Univ. of Pennsylvania School of Nursing.

Boulton, Roger, Ph.D. Prof. of Enology, Univ. of Calif., Davis.

Bourguignon, Erika, Ph.D. Prof. Emer. of Anthropology, Ohio State Univ.

Bourke, Joanna, Ph.D. Prof. of History, School of History, Classics, and Archaeology, Birkbeck Coll.

Boutin, Stan, Ph.D. Prof., Dept. of Biological Sciences, Univ. of Alberta.

Bowden, Henry Warner, Ph.D. Prof. of Religion, Rutgers, the State Univ. of New Jersey.

Bowden, Mark E., B.A. Exec. Editor, *The Cedar Rapids* (IA) *Gazette.*

Bowen, D. Q., Ph.D. Professor, Department of Earth Sciences, Cardiff University.

Bowen, William A., Ph.D. Prof. Emer. of Geography, Calif. State Univ., Northridge.

Bowers, Douglas E., Ph.D. Chief Historian, U.S. Dept. of Agriculture.

Bowers, Jane Ann Raymond, Ph.D. Prof. Emer. of Foods and Nutrition, Kansas State Univ.

Bowles, Edgar B., Jr., M.S. Dir., Fluids Engineering Dept., Mechanical and Materials Engineering Division, Southwest Research Inst.

Bowman, Kenneth A., Ph.D. Sr. Technical Specialist, Alcoa Laboratories.

Bowman, Larry W., Ph.D. Prof. Emer. of Political Science, Univ. of Connecticut.

Bowyer, Jim L., Ph.D. Former Dir., Forest Products Management Dev. Inst., Univ. of Minnesota, Twin Cities Campus.

Boyarsky, Bill, B.A. Former *Los Angeles Times* journalist and author of *Ronald Reagan: His Life*

and Rise to the Presidency.

Boyce, David, Ph.D. Prof. Emer. of Transportation and Regional Science, Univ. of Ill., Chicago.

Boyd-Ball, Alison J., Ph.D. Research Assoc., Child and Family Ctr., Univ. of Oregon; Sapsik'walá Project Dir., College of Education, Univ. of Oregon.

Boyd, Belvel J., M.A. Former Deputy Editorial Page Editor, (Minneapolis, MN) *Star Tribune.*

Boyd, Bill Columnist, *The Macon* (GA) *Telegraph.*

Boyd, David R., M.D., C.M. Consultant on Emergency Medical Services.

Boyer, John W., Ph.D. Martin A. Ryerson Dist. Service Prof. of History, Univ. of Chicago.

Boyer, LeRoy T., Ph.D. Prof. Emer. of Civil Engineering, Univ. of Illinois, Urbana-Champaign.

Boyer, Tina, Ph.D. Assistant Professor, Department of Russian and German, Wake Forest Univ.

Boyko, Christopher B., Ph.D. Asst. Prof. of Biology, Dowling Coll.

Boylan, Dan, Ph.D. Prof. of History, University of Hawaii, West Oahu.

Bradford, James C., Ph.D. Prof. of History, Texas A&M Univ.

Bradley, Bruce Author, *Hugh Glass.*

Bradnock, Robert W., Ph.D. Sr. Lecturer, Dept. of Geography, King's Coll., London.

Bradsher, Henry S., B.J. Author, foreign affairs analyst.

Brail, Shauna, Ph.D. Associate Professor, Institute for Management and Innovation, University of Toronto, Mississauga.

Brana-Shute, Gary, Ph.D. Former Sr. Consultant, U.S. State Dept.

Branch, William D., Ph.D. Prof. of Agronomy, Univ. of Georgia.

Brand, Larry R., M.S.M.E. Principal Technology Manager, Building Systems Research, Gas Research Inst.

Brand, Osa E., Ph.D. Former Dir. of Educ. Affairs, Assoc. of American Geographers.

Brand, Paul, D.Phil. Emeritus Fellow, All Souls College, University of Oxford.

Brandão, José António, Ph.D. Assoc. Prof. of History, Western Michigan Univ.

Brands, H. W., Ph.D. Dickson Allen Anderson Centennial Prof. of History, Univ. of Texas at Austin.

Brasser, T., Drs. Former Staff Ethnologist, Natl. Museum of Man.

Braswell, G. S., Ph.D. Assoc. Prof., Dept. of Psychology, Illinois State Univ.

Brauer, Kinley J., Ph.D. Former Prof. of History, Univ. of Minnesota, Twin Cities Campus.

Braverman, Alan C., M.D. Prof. of Medicine, Cardiovascular Division, Dept. of Medicine, School of Medicine, Washington Univ., St. Louis

Brazas, Julia Borst, Ed.D. Curriculum Specialist, Educ. and Public Outreach, Chicago Public Schools-Univ. of Chicago Internet Project, Dept. of Astronomy and Astrophysics, Univ. of Chicago.

Brearley, Joan McDonald Writer, lecturer, editor, consultant, and American Kennel Club judge.

Brecher, Kenneth, Ph.D. Prof. of Astronomy and Physics, Boston Univ.

Breckenridge, Roy M., Ph.D. Dir. and State Geologist, Idaho Geological Survey, Univ. of Idaho.

Breen, Jon L., M.S. Former Professor of English, Rio Hondo College.

Breen, T. H., Ph.D. William Smith Mason Prof., Northwestern Univ.

Brehm, Lawrence P., Ph.D. Staff Physicist, Intl. Business Machines Corp.

Bremer, William W., Ph.D. Former Prof. of History, Lawrence Univ.

Bremner, Robert H., Ph.D. Former Prof. of History, Ohio State Univ.

Brendel, Dale, B.J. Exec. Editor/General Manager, *The* (Independence, MO) *Examiner.*

Brennan, Shawn, B.A. Sr. Editor, World Book, Inc.

Brennan, Troyen, M.D. Exec. Vice Pres., Chief Medical Officer, CVS Caremark; former Prof., Dept. of Health Policy and Management, Harvard School of Public Health.

Brent, Harold Patrick, Ph.D. Prof. of English, Baruch Coll., City Univ. of New York.

Bretos, Miguel A., Ph.D. Sr. Scholar, Natl. Portrait Gallery, Smithsonian Inst.

Brett, Judith, Ph.D. Professor and Head of

School of Social Science, La Trobe University.

Brewer, Bruce A., Ph.D. General Manager, Cheetah Conservation Fund.

Brewer, Kelly, B.A. Former Editor and Pres., *The Albuquerque* (NM) *Tribune.*

Bridges, David H., Ph.D. Assoc. Prof. of Aerospace Engineering, Mississippi State Univ.

Bridges, Julian C., Ph.D. Prof. Emer., Dept. of Sociology, Hardin-Simmons Univ.

Bridges, Roger D., Ph.D. Exec. Dir. Emer., Rutherford B. Hayes Pres. Ctr.

Brierley, John S., Ph.D. Prof. of Geography, Univ. of Manitoba.

Brieske, Thomas J., Ph.D. Former Prof., Mathematics and Computer Science, Georgia State Univ

Briggs, Tony, B.A. Managing Editor/Online Services, *Daytona Beach* (FL) *News-Journal.*

Bright, George W., Ph.D. Prof. Emer. of Mathematics Educ., Univ. of North Carolina.

Brimeyer, Jack, B.S. Managing Editor, *Peoria* (IL) *Journal Star.*

Brinkman, John A., Ph.D. Prof. Emer. of Mesopotamic History, Oriental Inst., Univ. of Chicago.

Briscoe, David L., Ph.D. Professor of Sociology, University of Arkansas at Little Rock.

Bristow, Edward, Ph.D. Prof. of History, Fordham Univ.

Britcher, Colin P., Ph.D. Prof. of Aerospace Engineering, Old Dominion Univ.

Brito, André F., Ph.D. Assoc. Prof., Dept. of Biological Sciences, Univ. of New Hampshire.

Brittain, James E., Ph.D. Prof. Emer., School of History, Technology, and Society, Georgia Inst. of Technology.

Brittin, Helen C., Ph.D. Prof. of Food and Nutrition, Coll. of Human Sciences, Texas Tech Univ.

Brockmann, H. Jane, Ph.D. Prof., Dept. of Biology, Univ. of Florida.

Broder, David S., M.A. Former Political Correspondent, *Washington Post;* winner of Pulitzer Prize for Commentary, 1973.

Broderick, Carlfred B., Ph.D. Former Prof. of Sociology, Univ. of Southern Calif.

Brodman, James W., Ph.D. Prof. of History, Univ. of Central Arkansas.

Brodsky, Arthur R., M.S.J. Communications Dir., Public Knowledge, Washington, D.C.

Brody, David, Ph.D. Prof. Emer. of History, Univ. of Calif., Davis.

Bromke, Adam, Ph.D. Prof. Emer. of Political Science, McMaster Univ.; author, *Poland, The Protracted Crisis.*

Bromley, Ray, Ph.D. Prof., Geography and Planning, Univ. at Albany, State Univ. of New York.

Bronner, Simon J., Ph.D. Dist. Prof. of American Studies and Folklore, Penn. State Univ., Harrisburg.

Brookhiser, Richard Sr. Editor, *Natl. Review;* author of *Alexander Hamilton, American.*

Brooks, John L., II, B.S. Sr. Special Agent, U.S. Fish and Wildlife Service.

Brooks, Nathan M., Ph.D. Assoc. Prof. of History, New Mexico State Univ.

Brooks, Tim, M.A. Freelance writer, commentator, and development consultant for the sport of cricket.

Broome, Richard, Ph.D. Assoc. Prof. of History, La Trobe Univ.

Brosman, Catharine Savage, Ph.D. Gore Professor of French, Emeritus, Tulane University.

Broun, Elizabeth, Ph.D. Dir., Natl. Museum of American Art.

Brouwer, Mark, B.A. Copywriter, *Thomson Reuters.*

Brower, Kenneth S., B.S.E. Pres., Spectrum Assoc. Inc.

Brown, Alison K., Ph.D. CEO/Pres., NAVSYS Corp., Colorado Springs.

Brown, Calvin R., Jr., M.D. Assoc. Prof. of Medicine and Orthopaedic Surgery, Rush-Presbyterian-St. Luke's Medical Ctr., Chicago.

Brown, Kris, Ph.D. Research Fellow, Inst. of Irish Studies, Queen's Univ., Belfast.

Brown, Michael B., M.A. Doctoral Candidate, Life Sciences Center, Dartmouth College.

Brown, Michael S., M.D. Prof., Dept. of Molecular Genetics, Univ. of Texas Southwestern Medical Ctr.

Brown, Richard D., Ph.D. Board of Trustees Distinguished Professor of History Emeritus; Director, Humanities Institute, Univ. of Connecticut.

Brown, Richard D., Ph.D. Chair, Biology Dept., Brunswick Community Coll.

Brown, Robert Craig, Ph.D. Emer. Prof. of History, Univ. of Toronto.

Brown, Stephen W., Ph.D. Dean, Coll. of Business, Humanities, and Sciences, West Virginia Univ. Inst. of Technology.

Brown, Susan L., Ph.D. Prof. of Sociology; Co-Dir., Natl. Ctr. for Family and Marriage Research, Bowling Green State Univ.

Brown, Thomas G., Ph.D. Assoc. Prof., The Inst. of Optics, Univ. of Rochester.

Browne, Mark J., Ph.D. Prof., Univ. of Wisconsin, Madison.

Broyde, Michael J., J.D. Prof. of Law and Academic Dir., Law and Religion Program, Emory Univ. School of Law.

Brubaker, John H., III, B.A. Editor of the Editorial Page and Columnist, *Lancaster* (PA) *New Era.*

Brubaker, Linda B., Ph.D. Prof. Emer. of Forest Resources, Univ. of Washington.

Bruce, Robert B., Ph.D. Assoc. Prof. of History, Sam Houston State Univ.

Bruce, Timothy J., Ph.D. Prof. and Assoc. Chair, Dept. of Psychiatry and Behavioral Medicine, University of Illinois College of Medicine, Peoria.

Brudvig, Jon L., Ph.D. Prof. of History and Dir., Theodore Roosevelt Honors Program, Dickinson State Univ.

Brugh, Max, D.V.M., Ph.D. Former Research Veterinarian, U.S. Dept. of Agriculture.

Brumfiel, Elizabeth M., Ph.D. Prof. of Anthropology, Weinberg Coll. of Arts and Sciences, Northwestern Univ.

Brumm, Thomas J., Ph.D. Asst. Prof. of Agriculture and Biosystems Engineering, Iowa State Univ.

Brunelle, Gayle K., Ph.D. Professor of History, California State University, Fullerton.

Bruning, Donald F., Ph.D. Chair, Curator, Dept. of Ornithology, Wildlife Conservation Society.

Brunk, Samuel, Ph.D. Prof. of History, Univ. of Texas, El Paso.

Brusca, Richard C., Ph.D. Dir. of Science, Arizona-Sonora Desert Museum.

Bryan, Harvey, Ph.D. Prof. of Architecture, Arizona State Univ.

Bryant, Jonathan M., Ph.D. Assoc. Prof. of History, Georgia Southern Univ.

Bryen, Diane Nelson, Ph.D. Former Prof., Coll. of Educ.; former Exec. Dir., Inst. on Disabilities, Temple Univ.

Buchenau, Jürgen, Ph.D. Prof. of History and Dir. of Latin American Studies, Univ. of North Carolina at Charlotte.

Bucholz, Robert, D.Phil. Prof. of History, Loyola Univ.

Bucki, James, M.B.A. Assistant Professor, Genesee Community College.

Buckley, Thomas H., Ph.D. Prof., American History; Assoc. Dean, Grad. School, Univ. of Tulsa.

Buckner, Phillip, Ph.D. Former Prof. of History, Univ. of New Brunswick.

Buenker, John D., Ph.D. Emer. Prof. of History, Univ. of Wisconsin, Parkside; editor, *The Historical Dictionary of the Progressive Era.*

Buethe, Chris, Ed.D. Prof. of Educ. Emer., Indiana State Univ., Terre Haute.

Buffalohead, Priscilla Giddings, M.S. Lecturer, Cultural Anthropology and Women's Studies, Augsburg College.

Buffalohead, W. Roger, M.A. Dean, Inst. of American Indian Arts, New Mexico.

Bugajski, Janusz, M.Phil. Dir., New European Democracies Project and Sr. Fellow in the Europe Program at the Ctr. for Strategic and Intl. Studies, Washington, D.C.

Bugeja, Michael J., Ph.D. Dir., School of Journalism and Communication, Iowa State Univ.

Bukowski, Douglas, Ph.D. Author, *Big Bill Thompson, Chicago, and the Politics of Image.*

Bulik, Cynthia M., Ph.D. Dir., UNC Eating Disorders Program, Univ. of North Carolina, Chapel Hill.

Bullion, John L., Ph.D. Professor of History, University of Missouri, Columbia.

Bumgardner, Jake, B.A. Author; Former Editor in Area Studies, World Book, Inc.

Bump, Jerome, Ph.D. Professor of English, University of Texas, Austin.

Bumsted, J. M., Ph.D. Prof. of History, St. John's Coll., Univ. of Manitoba.

Bunten, Alexis Celeste, Ph.D. Senior Researcher, FrameWorks Institute.

Burd, Larry, Ph.D. Dir., North Dakota Fetal Alcohol Syndrome Ctr., Univ. of North Dakota.

Burda, Angela N., Ph.D. Assoc. Prof., Dept. of Communication Sciences and Disorders, Univ. of Northern Iowa.

Burdick, Glenn A., Ph.D. Dist. Prof. and Dean Emer., Coll. of Engineering, Univ. of South Florida.

Burg, B. R., Ph.D. Prof. of History, Arizona State Univ.

Burger, William C., Ph.D. Curator Emer. of Botany, Field Museum of Natural History.

Burgess, Paul L., Ph.D. Prof. Emer. of Economics, Arizona State Univ.

Burghardt, Gordon M., Ph.D. Prof., Dept. of Psychology and Dept. of Ecology and Evolutionary Biology, Univ. of Tennessee.

Burich, Raymond L., Ph.D. Assoc. Prof. Emer., School of Biological Sciences, Univ. of Missouri, Kansas City.

Burke, Ronald, Ph.D. Former Prof. of Philosophy and Religion, Univ. of Nebraska.

Burke, William T., J.S.D. Prof. of Law Emer., Univ. of Washington.

Burkemper, Nicole M., M.D. Asst. Prof. of Dermatology and Pathology, St. Louis Univ.

Burkholder, JoAnn M., Ph.D. Prof., Dept. of Botany, North Carolina State Univ.

Burks, R. V., Ph.D. Author, *Dynamics of Communism in Eastern Europe.*

Burnett, Adam W., Ph.D. William R. Kenan Jr. Prof. of Geography, Colgate Univ.

Burnett, David, Ph.D. Independent consultant and writer.

Burns, Robin B., Ph.D. Former Prof. of History, Bishop's Univ.

Burns, Sarah, Ph.D. Ruth N. Halls Prof., Dept. of History of Art, Indiana Univ., Bloomington.

Burrell, David B., Ph.D. Prof. Emer. of Philosophy and Theology, Univ. of Notre Dame.

Burrill Korshet, Melinda J., Ph.D. Prof. Emer., Dept. of Animal and Veterinary Sciences, Calif. State Polytechnic Univ.

Burrowes, Robert D., Ph.D. Former Adjunct Prof. of Political Science, Univ. of Washington.

Burton, David H., Ph.D. Editor, *Collected Works of William Howard Taft,* and author of several books on Taft.

Burton, John W., Ph.D. Prof. of Anthropology; Dir. of Africana Studies, Connecticut Coll.

Burton, Nelson, Jr., Announcer, ABC Sports.

Burtt, Edward H., Jr., Ph.D. Prof. of Zoology, Ohio Wesleyan Univ.

Bury, Charles Former Editor in Chief, *The Sherbrooke* (QC) *Record.*

Busch, A. J., Ph.D. Prof. of History and Dept. Chairman, Fort Hays State Univ.

Busch, August A., III Former Chairman of the Board, Anheuser-Busch Companies, Inc.

Busch, Marianna A., Ph.D. Prof. of Chemistry and Co-Dir., Ctr. for Analytical Spectroscopy, Dept. of Chemistry and Biochemistry, Baylor Univ.

Busch-Vishniac, Ilene J., Ph.D. Provost and Vice Pres. and Prof. of Mechanical Engineering, McMaster Univ., Hamilton, Ontario.

Bush, Sargent, Ph.D. Former John Bascom Prof. of English, Univ. of Wisconsin, Madison.

Bushbaum, Michael J., J.D. Associate Law Librarian for Access Services, Valparaiso Univ. School of Law.

Bushnell, Cheryl D., M.D., M.H.S. Assoc. Prof. of Neurology, Dir. of WFUBMC stroke center, Wake Forest Univ. Health Sciences.

Butler, Christopher J., Asst. Prof. of Biology, Univ. of Central Oklahoma.

Butler, John C., Ph.D. Former Professor of Geosciences, University of Houston.

Butterfield, David A., Ph.D. Sr. Research Scientist, Univ. of Washington.

Butts, Thomas, Ph.D. Professor of Mathematics Education, University of Texas, Dallas.

Butzer, Karl W., D.Sc. Dickson Centennial Prof. of Liberal Arts, Univ. of Texas, Austin.

Byrd, Jason H., Ph.D. Associate Director, Maples

Center for Forensic Medicine, Univ. of Florida.

Byrd, Ryland P., Jr., M.D.   Prof. of Medicine, James H. Quillen Coll. of Medicine.

Byrne, Joseph P., Ph.D.   Prof. of Honors, Belmont Univ.

Byrnes, Giselle M., Ph.D.   Pro Vice-Chancellor, Faculty of Law, Education, Business and Arts, Charles Darwin Univ.

C

Cadigan, Sean, Ph.D.   Prof. of History, Memorial Univ. of Newfoundland.

Cady, Edwin H., Litt.D.   Former Prof. of English, Duke Univ.

Cafruny, Alan W., Ph.D.   Henry Platt Bristol Prof. of Intl. Affairs, Hamilton Coll.

Caldarelli, David D., M.D.   Prof. and Chairman, Dept. of Otolaryngology, Rush-Presbyterian-St. Luke's Medical Ctr., Chicago.

Caldwell, Dan, Ph.D.   Prof. of Political Science, Pepperdine Univ.

Caldwell, Janalee P., Ph.D.   Professor Emeritus, Department of Biology, University of Oklahoma.

Caldwell, Robert J., B.S.   Former Editorial Page Editor, *The* (Portland) *Oregonian.*

Cale, Jen Shunatona, B.S.   Pawnee author.

Calhoun, Charles W., Ph.D.   Prof. of History, Dept. of History, East Carolina Univ.

Calhoun, Ralph V., Ph.D.   Sr. Vice Pres., Sverdrup Technology, Inc.

Calinger, Ronald S., Ph.D.   Professor Emeritus, Dept. of History, Catholic Univ. of America.

Callahan, Sean, B.A.   Former Public Relations Dir., U.S. Intl. Speedskating Assoc.

Callahan, William R.   Former Managing Editor, *The* (St. John's, NF) *Evening Telegram.*

Callan, Terrance D., Ph.D.   Former Professor of Biblical Studies, Athenaeum of Ohio.

Callejo Pérez, David M., Ed.D.   Carl A. Gerstacker Endowed Chair in Education, Saginaw Valley State Univ.

Callender, Craig Adam, Ph.D.   Prof. of Philosophy, Univ. of Calif., San Diego.

Calvert, John C. M., Ph.D.   Professor of History, Creighton University.

Cameron, Ewen A., Ph.D.   Professor of Scottish History and Palaeography, Univ. of Edinburgh.

Camilleri, Joseph, Ph.D.   Managing Director, Alexandria Agenda; Professor Emeritus of International Relations, La Trobe University.

Cammett, Melani, Ph.D.   Professor of Government, Harvard University.

Camp, Roderic A., Ph.D.   McKenna Prof. of the Pacific Rim, Claremont McKenna Coll.

Campbell, David J., Ph.D.   Prof. of Geography and African Studies, Michigan State Univ.

Campbell, I. C., Ph.D.   Sr. Lecturer in History, Univ. of Canterbury.

Campbell, James N., M.D.   Prof. of Neurosurgery, Johns Hopkins Univ.

Campbell, Tracy, Ph.D.   Prof. of History, Univ. of Kentucky.

Cancalon, Elaine D., Ph.D.   Former Prof. of French, Florida State Univ.

Cane, Mark A., Ph.D.   G. Unger Vetlesen Prof. of Earth and Climate Sciences, Columbia Univ.

Canemaker, John, M.F.A.   Film animator; winner, 2006 Academy Award for best animated short subject; author, *Treasures of Disney Animation Art.*

Canfield, Paul C., Ph.D.   Prof. of Physics, Iowa State Univ.

Cannistraro, Philip V., Ph.D.   Prof. of History, Drexel Univ.

Cannon, Brian Q., Ph.D.   Professor of History, Brigham Young University.

Cantrell, Gregg, Ph.D.   Prof. of History, Texas Christian Univ.

Cao, Tian Yu, Ph.D.   Professor of Philosophy, Boston University.

Capelli, Gregory M.,   Former Professor of Aquatic Biology, College of William and Mary.

Caplan, Arthur, Ph.D.   Prof. of Bioethics, New York University School of Medicine.

Cardona, George, Ph.D.   Professor of Linguistics, University of Pennsylvania.

Carey, James W., Ph.D.   Former CBS Prof. of Intl. Journalism, Grad. School of Journalism, Columbia Univ.

Carey, Lisa A., M.D.   Assoc. Prof. of Medicine; Medical Dir., Breast Ctr., Univ. of North Carolina.

Carico, James E., Ph.D.   Prof. Emer., Biology and Environmental Science Programs, Lynchburg Coll.

Carlos, Ann M., Ph.D.   Prof. of Economics, Univ. of Colorado, Boulder.

Carlson, Ann D., D.L.S.   English and Fine Arts Librarian, Oak Park and River Forest High School.

Carlson, John, Ph.D.   Prof., Dept. of Agriculture, Western Illinois Univ.

Carlson, W. Bernard, Ph.D.   Prof., Technology, Culture, and Communication, Univ. of Virginia.

Carlson, William H., Ph.D.   Prof. Emer. of Horticulture, Michigan State Univ.

Carlton, Charles, Ph.D.   Prof. Emer. of History, North Carolina State Univ.

Carlton, James T., Ph.D.   Dir., Maritime Studies Program, Williams Coll., Mystic Seaport.

Carman, Greg P., Ph.D.   Prof., Mechanical and Aerospace Engineering, Univ. of Calif., LA.

Carpenter, Kenneth, Ph.D.   Paleontologist, Denver Museum of Natural History.

Carpenter, Thomas P., Ph.D.   Dir., Natl. Ctr. for Improving Student Learning and Achievement in Mathematics and Science, Univ. of Wisconsin, Madison.

Carr, Anne E., Ph.D.   Prof. Emer. of Theology, Univ. of Chicago Divinity School.

Carr, Dale C., M.A.   Chief Music Librarian, Public Library, Groningen, Netherlands.

Carr, Stephen H., Ph.D.   Assoc. Dean of Engineering, Northwestern Univ.

Carrasco, David, Ph.D.   Neil L. Rudenstine Prof. of Latin America, Harvard Divinity School.

Carraway, Kermit L., Ph.D.   Prof., Dept. of Cell Biology, Univ. of Miami School of Medicine.

Carrigan, Mellonee, B.A.   Former Editor, World Book, Inc.

Carriker, Robert C., Ph.D.   Prof. of History, Gonzaga Univ.

Carroll, Bob, B.A.   Former Exec. Dir., Pro Football Researchers Assoc.

Carroll, Chris, Ph.D.   Assistant Professor, Civil Engineering, University of Louisiana, Lafayette.

Carroll, John L., M.D.   Prof., Pediatrics and Physiology; Dir., Pediatric Pulmonary Division, Arkansas Children's Hospital.

Carroll, Joseph, Ph.D.   Asst. Prof., Medical Coll. of Wisconsin, The Eye Inst.

Carroll, Peter N., Ph.D.   Author, *It Seemed Like Nothing Happened: America in the 1970s.*

Carson, Clayborne, Ph.D.   Prof. of History and Dir., Martin Luther King, Jr., Papers Project, Stanford Univ.

Carson, Culley C., M.D.   Rhodes Dist. Prof. and Chief of Urology, Univ. of North Carolina.

Carson, Robert B., Ph.D.   Prof. Emer. of Econ. and Business, State University of New York, Oneonta.

Carter, Dan T., Ph.D.   Educ. Foundation Prof. of History, Univ. of South Carolina.

Carter, David, Ph.D.   Prof. of Australian Lit. and Cultural Studies, Univ. of Queensland.

Carter, David C., Ph.D.   Assoc. Prof. of History, Auburn Univ.

Carter, Lisle Carleton, Jr., LL.B.   Former attorney at law.

Carter, William E., Ph.D.   Former Research Geodesist, Natl. Oceanic and Atmospheric Admin.

Cartwright, Donald G., Ph.D.   Prof. Emer. of Geography, Univ. of Western Ontario.

Casa, Douglas J., Ph.D.   Associate Professor of Kinesiology, University of Connecticut.

Case, Karl E., Ph.D.   Katherine Coman and A. Barton Hepburn Prof. of Economics, Wellesley Coll.

Case, William B., Ph.D.   Prof. of Physics, Grinnell College.

Cashdan, Elizabeth, Ph.D.   Prof. and Chair of Anthropology, Univ. of Utah.

Cashman, Katharine V., Ph.D.   Prof. Dept. of Geological Sciences, Univ. of Oregon.

Caskey, C. Thomas, M.D.   Dir. and CEO, Brown Foundation Inst. of Molecular Medicine for the Prevention of Human Diseases, Univ. of Texas.

Cassanelli, Lee V., Ph.D.   Assoc. Prof. of History, Univ. of Pennsylvania.

Cassara, Catherine, Ph.D.   Assoc. Prof., Dept. of Journalism, School of Communication Studies, Bowling Green State Univ.

Cassidy, David C., Ph.D.   Prof. of Natural Science, Hofstra Univ.

Cast, David, Ph.D.   Prof. of History of Art, Bryn Mawr Coll.

Castaneda, Terri A., Ph.D.   Assoc. Prof.; Museum Dir., Anthropology Museum, Dept. of Anthropology, Calif. State Univ., Sacramento.

Castellanos, F. Xavier, M.D.   Dir., Inst. for Pediatric Neuroscience, New York Univ. School of Medicine.

Casto, James E., M.A.   Sr. Public Information Specialist, Robert C. Byrd Inst. for Advanced Flexible Manufacturing.

Catanese, Anthony James, Ph.D.   Pres. and Prof., Florida Atlantic Univ.

Cateforis, David, Ph.D.   Prof. of Art History, Univ. of Kansas.

Cathey, James E., Ph.D.   Prof. Emer. of German & Scandinavian Studies, Univ. of Massachusetts, Amherst; coauthor, *Old Icelandic.*

Catto, Norm, Ph.D.   Prof. of Geography, Memorial Univ.

Causey, Virginia E., Ph.D.   Assoc. Prof., Dept. of History, Columbus State Univ.

Cauvin, Jean-Pierre, Ph.D.   Prof. of French, Univ. of Texas.

Cave, Steve, B.A.   Skateboarding Guide, *About. com.*

Cayton, Andrew, Ph.D.   Dist. Prof. of History, Miami Univ.

Cazorla-Sánchez, Antonio, Ph.D.   Assoc. Prof. of History, Trent Univ.

Cech, John, Ph.D.   Dir., Ctr. for the Study of Children's Lit. and Media, Univ. of Florida.

Ceci, Lynn, Ph.D.   Former Assoc. Prof., Anthropology, Queen's Coll., City Univ. of New York.

Cereghino, Régis, Ph.D.   Prof., Université de Toulouse, France.

Cerulo, Karen A., Ph.D.   Prof. of Sociology, Rutgers, the State Univ. of New Jersey.

Chalmers, David, Ph.D.   Dist. Service Prof. Emer. of History, Univ. of Florida.

Chalupnik, James D., Ph.D.   Prof. Emer., Dept. of Mechanical Engineering, Univ. of Washington.

Chamberlain, David S., Ph.D.   Former Prof. of English, Univ. of Iowa.

Chamblee, Theresa S., M.S.   Principal Scientist, Flavor Research and Dev., The Coca-Cola Company.

Champlin, Charles, A.B.   Freelance writer.

Chan, Julia Y., Ph.D.   Prof. of Chemistry, Louisiana State Univ.

Chandler, David P., Ph.D.   Prof. Emer. of History, Monash Univ.; Adjunct Prof. of Asian Studies, Georgetown Univ.; author, *A History of Cambodia.*

Chang, Parris H., Ph.D.   Former Dir., Ctr. for East Asian Studies, Pennsylvania State Univ.

Channell, David F., Ph.D.   Prof. of Historical Studies, Univ. of Texas, Dallas.

Chapman, Graham P., Ph.D.   Former Professor of Geography, Lancaster University, and former Fellow, Centre for Advanced Study, Oslo.

Chapple, Christopher Key, Ph.D.   Prof. of Theological Studies, Loyola Marymount Univ.

Charbonneau, Hubert, Ph.D.   Prof. Emer. of Demography, Univ. of Montreal.

Charles, Robert W., Ph.D.   Former Group Leader, Univ. of Calif., Los Alamos Natl. Laboratory.

Charlesworth, J. H., Ph.D.   Prof. of New Testament Lang. and Lit; Dir., Dead Sea Scrolls Project, Princeton Theological Seminary.

Charlton, Jane C., Ph.D.   Prof. of Astronomy and Astrophysics, Pennsylvania State Univ.

Chase, Philander D., Ph.D.   Former Editor in Chief, *The Papers of George Washington* Project.

Chatfield, Charles, Ph.D.   Emer. Prof. of History, Wittenberg Univ.

Chatterjee, Sankar, Ph.D.   Paul Whitefield Horn Professor of Geosciences and Curator of Paleontology, Texas Tech University.

Chatziioanou, Alypios, Ph.D.   Prof., Civil and Environmental Engineering, Calif. Polytechnic State Univ.

Chege, Michael, Ph.D.   Director, Center for African Studies, University of Florida.

Chen, Qingyan, Ph.D.   Prof. of Mechanical Engineering, Purdue Univ.

Chen, Tung-Ling Li, Ph.D.   Principal and Chinese Lang. Teacher, Chicago North Chinese School.

Cherchi, Paolo, Ph.D. Former Prof. of Italian Lit., Univ. of Chicago.

Cherkauer, Douglas S., Ph.D. Prof. of Geosciences, Univ. of Wisconsin, Milwaukee.

Cherny, Robert W., Ph.D. Prof. of History, San Francisco State Univ.

Chertow, Marian, Ph.D. Professor, Yale School of Forestry & Environmental Studies.

Cheshewalla, Cherokee Interim Dir., Wah Zha Zhi Cultural Ctr.

Chesick, John P., Ph.D. Former Prof. of Chemistry, Haverford Coll.

Chikeka, Charles O., Ph.D. Assoc. Prof. of History, Morgan State Univ.

Child, Jois C., Ph.D. Former Asst. Prof. of Geography, Eastern Washington Univ.

Childress, Dudley S., Ph.D. Dir. Emer., Prosthetics Research Laboratory and Rehabilitation Engineering Research Program, Feinberg School of Medicine, Northwestern Univ.

Childs, William R., Ph.D. Prof. of History, Ohio State Univ.

Chirikjian, Gregory S., Ph.D. Prof., Dept. of Mechanical Engineering, Johns Hopkins Univ.

Chism, Grady W., Ph.D. Prof. Emer. of Food Science and Technology, Ohio State Univ.

Christ, Carol Tecla, Ph.D. Pres., Smith Coll.

Christensen, Norman L., Jr., Ph.D. Prof. of Ecology, Nicholas School of the Environment and Earth Sciences, Duke Univ.

Christensen, Tom, Ph.D. Prof. of Physics, Univ. of Colorado at Colorado Springs.

Christiansen, John B., Ph.D. Prof. of Sociology, Gallaudet Univ.

Christianson, Eric Howard, Ph.D. Assoc. Prof. of History, Univ. of Kentucky.

Chudler, Eric H., Ph.D. Research Assoc. Prof., Dept. of Bioengineering, Univ. of Washington.

Church, Andrew, Ph.D. Prof. of Geography, School of the Environment, Univ. of Brighton.

Churchill, James E. Former freelance writer.

Cicale, Annie, M.F.A. Professional calligrapher.

Ciochon, Russell L., Ph.D. Prof. of Anthropology, Univ. of Iowa.

Clancy, Lou Former Managing Editor, *The Toronto Star.*

Clapp, John M., Ph.D. Prof., Dir. Ctr. for Real Estate and Urban Econ. Studies, Univ. of Connecticut.

Clapp, Stephen, M.Sc. Dean Emer. and Violin Faculty Member, Juilliard School.

Clark, Alan F., Ph.D. Div. Chief, Magnetic Technol. Division, Natl. Inst. of Standards and Technol.

Clark, C. B., Ph.D. Former Prof. of American Indian Studies, Calif. State Univ.

Clark, Charles W., Ph.D. Prof., Dept. of History, Univ. of West Georgia.

Clark, Clifford E., Jr., Ph.D. Prof. of History; Hulings Prof. of American Studies, Carleton Coll.

Clark, Edward W., Ph.D. Former Prof. of English, Winthrop Univ.

Clark, J. C. D., Ph.D. Prof., Hall Ctr. for the Humanities, Univ. of Kansas.

Clark, J. Derrell, D.Sc. Former Prof. of Medical Microbiology, Univ. of Georgia.

Clark, James M., Ph.D. Prof., Dept. of Biology, George Washington Univ.

Clark, Larry V., Ph.D. Asst. Prof., Indiana Univ.

Clark, Michael P., B.A. Editorial Page Editor, *The* (Jacksonville) *Florida Times-Union.*

Clark, Nancy L., Ph.D. Dean, Honors Coll., Louisiana State Univ.

Clark, Perry, Ph.D. Professor of Dairy Science, University of Wisconsin, River Falls.

Clark, Robert E., Ph.D. Former Asst. Prof. of Geography, Univ. of Northern Iowa.

Clark, Robert Sadler, B.A. Pres., United States Surfing Committee.

Clark, Scott, B.A. Pres., Elgin Bonsai Study Group; Member, Board of Dirs., Bonsai Clubs Intl.; Pres., Owner, Bonsai Interunion.

Clark, Terry Nichols, Ph.D. Prof. of Sociology, Univ. of Chicago.

Clark, W. Dennis, Ph.D. Former Assoc. Prof. of Botany, Arizona State Univ.

Clark, William W., Ph.D. Prof. of Art, Queens Coll. and Grad. Ctr., City Univ. of New York.

Clarke, Simon James, Ph.D. Postdoctoral Researcher, Natl. Wine and Grape Industry Centre, Charles Sturt Univ.

Claus, Michael J., Ph.D. Asst. Prof., Chemistry Dept., Adrian Coll.

Clauson, Barbara L., M.S. Former Adjunct Curator, Univ. of Kansas Natural History Museum.

Clavin, Matthew, Ph.D. Assoc. Prof. of History, Univ. of Houston.

Clawson, David L., Ph.D. Prof. Emer., Dept. of Geography, Univ. of New Orleans.

Clay, Keith, Ph.D. Prof. of Biology, Indiana Univ.

Clayton, Daniel, Ph.D. Assoc. Prof. of History and Dir., the Regis Univ. Ctr. for the Study of War Experience, Regis Univ.

Clayton, Lawrence A., Ph.D. Prof. of History Emer., Univ. of Alabama.

Clayton, Paula J., M.D. Former Chairman, Department of Psychiatry, University of Minnesota, Twin Cities Campus.

Cleeton, David L., Ph.D. Prof. and Assoc. Provost, Economics Dept., Oberlin Coll.

Clemens, Diane Shaver, Ph.D. Prof. of History, Univ. of Calif., Berkeley.

Clemens, Paul G. E., Ph.D. Prof. of History, Rutgers, the State Univ. of New Jersey.

Clements, Kendrick A., Ph.D. Prof. Emer. of History, Univ. of South Carolina.

Clendenning, John, Ph.D. Former Prof. of English, Calif. State Univ., Northridge.

Cliffe, Rebecca, Ph.D. Founder and Executive Director, Sloth Conservation Foundation.

Clifton, Robert G., B.S. Former Managing Dir., American Brush Manufacturers Assoc.

Cline, Erin M., Ph.D. Asst. Prof., Dept. of Theology, Georgetown Univ.

Cliver, Dean O., Ph.D. Prof. Emer., Food Safety, School of Vet. Medicine, Univ. of Calif., Davis.

Clonts, Howard A., Jr., Ph.D. Dir., Environmental Inst. and Water Resources Research Inst., Auburn Univ.

Cloos, Mark, Ph.D. Prof. of Geological Sciences, Univ. of Texas, Austin.

Clothey, Fred W., Ph.D. Prof. Emer., Dept. of Religious Studies, Univ. of Pittsburgh.

Clout, Hugh D., Ph.D. Prof. of Geography, Univ. Coll. London.

Clum, James A., Ph.D. Prof., Dept. of Materials Science and Engineering, Univ. of Wisconsin, Madison.

Coakley, Timothy N., M.A. Copy Editor, *The* (Schenectady, NY) *Daily Gazette.*

Coale, Samuel Chase, Ph.D. Prof. of English, Wheaton Coll.

Coates, Colin M., Ph.D. Canada Research Chair in Canadian Cultural Landscapes, Glendon Coll., York Univ.

Coates, Julia M., Ph.D. Asst. Prof., Native American Studies, Univ. of Calif., Davis.

Coates, Ken S., Ph.D. Canada Research Chair in Regional Innovation, Johnson-Shoyama Graduate School of Public Policy, Univ. of Saskatchewan.

Cobb, William E., Ph.D. Prof. Emer. of Economics, West Virginia Grad. Coll.

Coble, Harold D., Ph.D. Former Prof. of Crop Science, North Carolina State Univ.

Cockroft, Irene, Dip. History. Author, *Books of the Month.*

Coclanis, Peter A., Ph.D. Albert Ray Newsome Dist. Prof., Dept. of History, and Dir., Global Research Inst., Univ. of North Carolina, Chapel Hill.

Coddington, Jonathan A., Ph.D. Curator of Arachnids and Myriapods, Natl. Museum of Natural History, Smithsonian Inst.

Coffman, John Edwin, Ph.D. Former Assoc. Prof. of Geography, Univ. of Houston.

Cohen, Daniel, B.J. Writer.

Cohen, Gary B., Ph.D. Prof. of History, Univ. of Minnesota, Twin Cities Campus.

Cohen, Jacob, M.A. Prof. and Chairman, Dept. of American Studies, Brandeis Univ.

Cohen, Jeremy, Ph.D. Associate Vice President and Sr. Associate Dean for Undergraduate Education, Pennsylvania State University.

Cohen, Philip N., Ph.D. Professor, Department of Sociology, University of Maryland.

Cohen, Ralph L., Ph.D. Prof. of Mathematics, Stanford Univ.

Cohen, S. Marc, Ph.D. Professor Emeritus of Philosophy, University of Washington.

Cohen, Sarah Blacher, Ph.D. Former Prof. Emer. of English, State Univ. of New York, Albany.

Cohen, Steve, B.A. Boot Ed., *Ski Press* magazine.

Cohen, Stuart E., M.Arch. Architect; Prof. Emer. of Architecture, Univ. of Illinois, Chicago.

Cohn, Martin A., M.D. Dir., Sleep Disorders Ctr. of Southwest Florida, Naples.

Cohn, Sherman L., LL.M. Prof. of Law, Georgetown Univ.

Cole, Christine W., Ph.D. Prof. of Materials Science and Engineering and Dir., Clemson Apparel Research, Clemson Univ.

Cole, David E., Ph.D. Chairman Emer., Ctr. for Automotive Research, Altarum Inst.

Cole, Francis T., Ph.D. Former Physicist, Fermi Natl. Accelerator Laboratory.

Cole, Hugh M., Ph.D. Author, *The Ardennes Campaign.*

Cole, Madison B., Jr., Ph.D. Former Chief, Electron Microscopy Laboratory, Hines Veterans Admin. Hospital.

Coleman, Dorothy S., B.A. Author, *Lenci Dolls;* coauthor, *The Collector's Encyclopedia of Dolls.*

Coleman, Evelyn Jane, M.A. Coauthor, *The Collector's Encyclopedia of Dolls.*

Coleman, J. M., Ph.D. Boyd Prof. Emer., Coastal Studies Inst., Louisiana State Univ.

Coles, William E., Jr., Ph.D. Former Prof. of English, Univ. of Pittsburgh.

Colgan, Charles T., J.D. Former Exec. Vice Pres., Natl. Steeplechase Assoc.

Collier, Billie J., Ph.D. Prof. and Dean, Florida State Univ.

Collins, Arlene R., Ph.D. Assoc. Prof. of Microbiology, State Univ. of New York, Buffalo, School of Biomedical Sciences.

Collins, K. K., Ph.D. Assoc. Prof. of English and Dist. Teacher, Southern Illinois Univ., Carbondale.

Collins, Nigel Writer, ESPN.com.

Collins, Theresa M., Ph.D. Assoc. Editor, Thomas A. Edison Papers Project, Rutgers, the State Univ. of New Jersey.

Colman, Penny, M.A.T. Dist. Lecturer, Queens Coll., City Univ. of New York.

Colten, Craig E., Ph.D. Professor, Dept. of Geography and Anthropology, Louisiana State Univ.

Coltoff, Philip, M.S.W. Special Adviser, former CEO and Exec. Dir., Children's Aid Society.

Colvin, Howard A., Ph.D. Project Manager, New Solutions Polymer and Catalyst Research, Goodyear Tire & Rubber Company.

Combs, Jerald A., Ph.D. Prof. Emer. of History, San Francisco State Univ.

Commins, Stephen K., Ph.D. Lecturer in Urban Planning, UCLA School of Public Affairs.

Concepcion, Anne-Marie, M.A. President, Seneca Design and Consulting.

Conger, Clement Ellis, D.H.L. Former Chairman, Fine Arts Committee, U.S. Dept. of State.

Conlan, Thomas D., Ph.D. Professor of East Asian Studies and History, Princeton University.

Conn, Phyllis, Ph.D. Assistant Professor of History, St. John's University.

Connelly, Thomas L., Ph.D. Former Prof. of History, Univ. of South Carolina.

Conniff, Michael L., Ph.D. Prof. of History, San Jose State Univ.

Connor, Lawrence J., Ph.D. Owner and Dir., Beekeeping Educ. Service, Wicwas Press.

Connors, Peter G., Ph.D. Principal Museum Scientist, Bodega Marine Lab., Univ. of Calif., Davis.

Conover, Mary E., Ph.D. Assoc. Prof. of Industrial and Engineering Technology, Murray State Univ.

Conrad, Barnaby, III, B.A. Contributing Editor, *Horizon.*

Consroe, Paul, Ph.D. Prof. Emer., Dept. of Pharmacology and Toxicology, Univ. of Arizona.

Constant, Kristen P., Ph.D. Prof. and Chair, Materials Science and Engineering, Iowa State Univ.

Conway, John R., III, Ph.D. Prof. of Biology, Univ. of Scranton.

Cook, Chris, D.Phil. Dir., Modern Archives Unit, London School of Economics.

Cook, Eddie Publisher, Editor in Chief, and Managing Dir., *Jazz Journal Limited.*

Cook, Leon F., M.S.W. Assistant to the President

for Diversity, Augsburg College.

Cook, Noble David, Ph.D. Prof. of Latin American History, Florida Intl. Univ.

Cook, Robert B., Ph.D. Prof. and Head, Dept. of Geology, Auburn Univ.

Cook, Robert Francis, Ph.D. Former Prof. of French, Univ. of Virginia.

Cook, Theodore F., Jr., Ph.D. Prof. of History, William Paterson Univ.

Cooke, Roger, Ph.D. Prof. Emer. of Mathematics, Univ. of Vermont.

Cooksey, D. Kay, Ph.D. Prof., Packaging Science Dept., Clemson Univ.

Cooley, Marianne, Ph.D. Assoc. Prof. Emer. of English, Univ. of Houston.

Coomes, Oliver T., Professor of Geography, McGill University.

Cooper, Barry, Ph.D. Prof. of Political Science, Univ. of Calgary.

Cooper, Belinda, J.D. Sr. Fellow, World Policy Inst.

Cooper, Christine Elizabeth, Ph.D. Sr. Lecturer, Dept. of Environment and Agriculture, Curtin Univ.

Cooper, Leon N., Ph.D. Prof. of Science, Dir., Inst. for Brain and Neural Systems, and Brain Science Program, Brown Univ.; winner of Nobel Prize in Physics, 1972.

Cope, Doris K., M.D. Prof. and Vice Chairman of Pain Medicine, Dept. of Anesthesiology, Univ. of Pittsburgh Medical Ctr. Pain Medicine Program.

Copeland, James M., M.A. Exec. Secretary, Natl. Forensic League.

Coppa, Frank J., Ph.D. Prof. of History and Dir. of Doctor of Arts Program in Modern World History, St. John's Univ.

Coran, Arnold Gerald, M.D. Head, Pediatric Surgery, Univ. of Michigan Medical School; Surgeon in Chief, C. S. Mott Children's Hospital.

Corbett, Amanda H., Pharm.D. Clinical Asst. Prof., Eshelman School of Pharmacy, Univ. of North Carolina.

Corbett, J. D., Ph.D. Former Dist. Prof. of Chemistry, Iowa State Univ.

Corbitt, Mary Kay, Ed.D. Assoc. Prof. Emer., Mathematics, Valdosta State Univ.; author, *Plane Geometry.*

Cord, Robert L., Ph.D. Matthews Dist. Univ. Prof. and Prof. of Political Science, Northeastern Univ.

Cordell, Dennis D., Ph.D. Former Prof. of History, Southern Methodist Univ., and Adjunct Prof. of Demography, Université de Montréal.

Cordes, Joseph J., Ph.D. Prof. of Economics, George Washington Univ.

Coren, Stanley, Ph.D. Prof. Emer., Psychology Dept., Univ. of British Columbia

Corey, Jason, Ph.D. Assoc. Prof. and Chair, Dept. of Performing Arts Technology, Univ. of Michigan.

Corradini, Michael L, Ph.D. Wisconsin Dist. Prof., Dept. of Engineering Physics, Univ. of Wisconsin, Madison.

Corwin, Nancy A., Ph.D. Former Asst. Prof. of Art History, Kansas City Art Inst.

Cosgrove, John H., Ph.D. Former Manager, Avtex Fibers, Inc.

Cosman, Pamela C., Ph.D. Prof. of Electrical and Computer Engineering, Univ. of Calif., San Diego.

Costa, Daniel P., Ph.D. Prof. of Ecology and Evolutionary Biology, Univ. of Calif., Santa Cruz.

Costello, Bonnie, Ph.D. Prof. of English, Boston Univ.

Cotilla-Sanchez, J. Eduardo, Ph.D. Assistant Professor, Oregon State Univ.

Couclelis, Helen, Ph.D. Prof., Dept. of Geography, Univ. of Calif., Santa Barbara.

Coulter, C. Brewster, Ph.D. Former Prof. of History, Univ. of Puget Sound.

Courtenay, William J., Ph.D. Prof. Emer. of Medieval History, Univ. of Wisconsin, Madison.

Coutts, Robert, M.A. Manager, Heritage Presentation, Western and Northern Services Ctr. of Parks Canada.

Covell, Charles V., Jr., Ph.D. Prof. Emer. of Biology, Univ. of Louisville.

Cox, Kevin R., Ph.D. Dist. Univ. Prof. of Geography, Ohio State Univ.

Coxford, Arthur F., Jr., Ph.D. Former Prof. of Mathematics Educ., Univ. of Michigan.

Coy, Patrick G., Ph.D. Prof. of Political Science, Kent State Univ.

Coyne, Jerry A., Ph.D. Prof. of Ecology and Evolution, Univ. of Chicago.

Cracraft, James, Ph.D. Prof. Emer. of History and Univ. Scholar, Univ. of Illinois, Chicago.

Cragan, Janet D., M.D. Pediatrician and medical epidemiologist in Atlanta, GA.

Craig, William J., Ph.D. Assoc. Dir., Ctr. for Urban and Regional Affairs, Univ. of Minnesota, Twin Cities Campus.

Craker, Lyle E., Ph.D. Prof. and Head of Plant and Soil Sciences, Univ. of Massachusetts, Amherst.

Cramer, Christopher S., Ph.D. Professor of Horticulture, New Mexico State University.

Crandall, Suzanne, B.S. Tour Specialist, Rockford Area Convention and Visitors Bureau.

Crane, Peter, Ph.D. Prof. of Geophysical Sciences, Univ. of Chicago.

Crane, Sir Peter, Ph.D. John and Marion Sullivan Univ. Prof., Univ. of Chicago, and Fellow of the Royal Society.

Crane, Robert I., Ph.D. Former Ford-Maxwell Prof. of South Asian History, Syracuse Univ.

Crawford, Heide A., Ph.D. Lecturer in German, The University of Georgia.

Crawford, Joseph P., B.A. Independent writer, editor, and political consultant.

Crawford, Maria Luisa, Ph.D. Prof. of Geology, Bryn Mawr Coll.

Crawford, Michael H., M.D. Chief of Clinical Cardiology, Univ. of Calif. San Francisco Medical Ctr.

Crawford, Michael J., Ph.D. Head, Early History Branch, Naval Historical Ctr.

Crawford, Nicholas C., Ph.D. Dist. Univ. Prof., Dept. of Geography and Geology, Western Kentucky Univ.

Crawford-Brown, Douglas John, Ph.D. Adjunct Prof. of Environmental Sciences and Engineering, Univ. of North Carolina, Chapel Hill.

Cray, Ed, B.A. Prof., School of Journalism, Univ. of Southern Calif.

Creech, James, Ph.D. Prof. of French and Italian, Miami Univ.

Creevey, Lucy E., Ph.D. Prof. Emer. of Political Science, Univ. of Connecticut; author, *Muslim Brotherhoods and Politics in Senegal.*

Crew, Michael A., Ph.D. Prof., Dept. of Finance and Economics, School of Business, Rutgers, the State Univ. of New Jersey.

Crimmins, Timothy J., Ph.D. Prof. of History, Georgia State Univ.

Crispens, Charles G., Jr., Ph.D. Former Prof. of Biology, Univ. of Alabama, Birmingham.

Croan, Melvin, Ph.D. Prof. Emer. of Political Science, Univ. of Wisconsin, Madison.

Croat, Thomas B., Ph.D. P. A. Schulze Curator of Botany, Missouri Botanical Garden.

Croft, W. Bruce, Ph.D. Dist. Univ. Prof., Computer Science, Univ. of Massachusetts.

Crompton, Paul, B.A. Dir., Paul H. Crompton, Ltd.

Crone, Anna Lisa, Ph.D. Former Prof. of Slavic Langs. and Lits., Univ. of Chicago.

Cronin, Bruce, Ph.D. Dir., Masters Program in Intl. Relations, City Coll. of New York.

Cronin, R. E. Former Editor in Chief, West Australian Newspapers, Ltd.

Cronin, Thomas E., Ph.D. Former Pres., Whitman Coll.

Cronk, Brian, Ph.D. Prof. of Psychology, Missouri Western State Univ.

Crossley, William A., Ph.D. Professor, School of Aeronautics and Astronautics, Purdue Univ.

Crouch, Harold, Ph.D. Sr. Fellow, Political and Social Change, Australian Natl. Univ.

Crouch, Tom D., Ph.D. Sr. Curator, Dept. of Aeronautics, Natl. Air and Space Museum, Smithsonian Inst.

Crovello, Theodore J., Ph.D. Prof. Emer. of Biology and former Dean, Grad. Studies and Research, Calif. State Univ., Los Angeles.

Crowe, Michael J., Ph.D. Rev. John J. Cavanaugh Prof. Emer. of History and Philosophy of Science, Univ. of Notre Dame.

Cruz, Jesus, Ph.D. Prof., Dept. of History, Univ. of Delaware.

Crystal, Eric, Ph.D. Former Lecturer, Group in Asian Studies, Univ. of Calif., Berkeley.

Cubbins, Octavia N., M.Ed. Dir. of Educ., Mariners Museum.

Cullen, Charles T., Ph.D. Former Pres. and Librarian, Newberry Library.

Cullis, Christopher, Ph.D. Professor, Department of Biology, Case Western Reserve University.

Cummings, Charles W., M.D. Prof. and Chairman, Dept. of Otolaryngology-Head and Neck Surgery, Johns Hopkins Univ. Medical Ctr.

Cummings, S. C., Ph.D. Prof. Emer. of Chemistry, Wright State Univ.

Cunningham, Frank R., Ph.D. Prof. Emer. of English, Univ. of South Dakota.

Cuno, Kenneth M., Ph.D. Assoc. Prof. of History, Univ. of Illinois, Urbana-Champaign.

Cupp, E. W., Ph.D. Prof. Emer. of Entomology, Auburn Univ.

Cupp, Melanie Johns, Pharm.D. Clinical Asst. Prof., West Virginia Univ. School of Pharmacy.

Curran, Claude W., Ph.D. Prof. Emer. of Geography, Southern Oregon Univ.

Curran, Ronald T., Ph.D. Assoc. Prof. Emer. of English, Univ. of Pittsburgh.

Current, Richard N., L.H.D. Former Prof. of History, Univ. of North Carolina, Greensboro.

Currie, Sean E., Ph.D. candidate and Graduate Instructor, University of South Florida.

Curtin, Michael, Ph.D. Mellichamp Prof. of Global Media Studies, Univ. of Calif., Santa Barbara.

Curtis, James C., Ph.D. Former Prof. of History, Univ. of Delaware.

Cushing, Katherine Kao, Ph.D. Associate Professor, Department of Environmental Studies, San Jose State University.

Cutler Egbert, Susan, Ph.D. Asst. Prof. of Social Work, Utah State Univ.

Cypher, Brian, Ph.D. Assoc. Dir. and Research Ecologist, Endangered Species Recovery Program, California State University, Stanislaus.

Cyr, Arthur I., Ph.D. Dist. Prof., Political Economy and World Business; Dir., Intl. Political Economy Program, Carthage Coll.

D

Daehn, Glenn S., Ph.D. Prof., Dept. of Materials Science and Engineering, Ohio State Univ.

Daeschler, Ted, Ph.D. Assoc. Curator of Vertebrate Zoology, Academy of Natural Sciences.

Dagg, Anne Innis, Ph.D. Senior Academic Advisor, Independent Studies, Univ. of Waterloo.

Dagnelie, Gislin, Ph.D. Assoc. Prof. of Ophthalmology, Johns Hopkins Univ. School of Medicine.

Dahlinger, Fred, Jr., B.S. Former Dir. of Historic Resources and Facilities, Circus World Museum.

Dalrymple, G. Brent, Ph.D. Dean Emeritus, College of Oceanic & Atmospheric Sciences, Oregon State University.

Dalton, C. David, Ph.D. Prof. of History, Coll. of the Ozarks.

Daly, Mary, D.Phil. Coll. Principal, Univ. Coll. Dublin.

Dalzell, Robert F., Jr., Ph.D. Professor of History, Williams College.

Dalziel, Ian W. D., Ph.D. Sr. Research Scientist, Assoc. Dir., Univ. of Texas Inst. for Geophysics; Prof. of Geological Sciences, Univ. of Texas, Austin.

D'Amato, Anthony, Ph.D. Leighton Prof. of Law, Northwestern Univ. Law School.

DaMatta, Roberto, Ph.D. Prof. Emer. of Anthropology, Univ. of Notre Dame.

D'Ambrosio, Beatriz S., Ph.D. Prof. of Mathematics and Statistics, Miami Univ.

Daniell, Jere, Ph.D. Former Prof. of History, Dartmouth Coll.

Daniels, George H., Ph.D. Former Chair, Dept. of History, Univ. of South Alabama.

Daniels, Peter T., M.A. Coeditor, *The World's Writing Systems.*

Daniere, Amrita G., Ph.D. Assoc. Prof., Dept. of Geography, Univ. of Toronto.

Danker, George J., B.A. Vice Pres. and Chief Technol. Officer, Akro Fireguard Products, Inc.

Dann, Wanda, Ph.D. Assoc. Teaching Prof., Computer Science, Carnegie Mellon Univ.

D'Arcy, William G., Ph.D. Former Sr. Curator, Missouri Botanical Garden.

Darden, Robert F., M.A. Professor of Journalism, Public Relations and New Media, Baylor Univ.

Darian-Smith, Kate, Ph.D. Prof. of Australian Studies and History, Univ. of Melbourne.

Darvick, Herman, M.S. Chief Cataloguer and Authenticator, Gallery of History; author, *Collecting Autographs.*

Daryaee, Touraj, Ph.D. Prof. of History, Univ. of Calif., Irvine.

Das, Mihir K., Ph.D., M.E. Prof. Emer. of Mechanical and Aerospace Engineering, Calif. State Univ.

Dattwyler, Raymond J., M.D. Prof. of Medicine and Microbiology/Immunology and Chief of Allergy, Immunology and Rheumatology, New York Medical Coll.

Daub, Edward E., Ph.D. Former Prof. Emer. of Engineering, Univ. of Wisconsin, Madison.

Dauben, Joseph W., Ph.D. Dist. Prof. of History and the History of Science, City Univ. of New York.

Dauphin, Roma, M.A. Dean of Faculty of Arts and Prof. of Economics, Univ. of Sherbrooke.

Davenport, Fionn, M.A. Author, Historian.

Davenport, Ronald R., LLM. Chairman, Sheridan Broadcasting Corp.

Davey, Kent, Ph.D. Research Scientist, Ctr. for Electromechanics, Univ. of Texas.

Davidson, Fiona M., Ph.D. Assoc. Prof., Dept. of Geosciences, Univ. of Arkansas.

Davidson, Roger H., Ph.D. Prof. of Government and Politics Emer., Univ. of Maryland, Coll. Park.

Davidson, William V., Ph.D. Former Chair, Dept. of Geography-Anthropology, Louisiana State Univ.

Davidson-Arnott, Robin G. D., Ph.D. Prof. Emer. of Geography, Univ. of Guelph.

Davies, Brian, M.A. Teacher and Lecturer of Polit. and Communic. Studies, Univ. of Liverpool.

Davies, Fred T., Jr., Ph.D. Prof. of Horticultural Sciences and Molecular and Environmental Plant Sciences, Texas A&M Univ.

Davis, Allen F., Ph.D. Prof. of Hist., Temple Univ.

Davis, Audrey B., Ph.D. Former Curator of Medical Sciences, Natl. Museum of American History, Smithsonian Inst.

Davis, Carl L., Ph.D. Prof. Emer. of History, Stephen F. Austin State Univ.

Davis, Carolyne Kahle, Ph.D. Former Intl. Health Care Adviser, Ernst & Young.

Davis, Clark, Ph.D. Former Assoc. Prof. of History, Calif. State Univ., Fullerton.

Davis, David Brion, Litt.D. Former Sterling Professor of American History, Yale University.

Davis, Dick, Ph.D. Professor of Persian and Chair, Department of Near Eastern Languages and Cultures, Ohio State University.

Davis, Gregory W., PhD. P.E., Prof., Dept. of Mechnical Engineering, Kettering Univ.

Davis, Jack L., Ph.D. Prof. of Greek Archaeology, Univ. of Cincinnati.

Davis, James N., M.D. Former Prof. and Chairman of Neurology, State Univ. of New York, Stony Brook.

Davis, John A., D.Phil. Emiliana Pasca Noether Chair in Italian History, Univ. of Connecticut.

Davis, Joseph A., B.S. Former Editor, Concept Omega Corp.

Davis, Lee, Ph.D. Former Asst. Prof. of Anthropology, Univ. of Nebraska, Lincoln.

Davis, Paul E., B.S. Former Manager, Tin Research Inst., Inc., Palo Alto, CA.

Davis, Raymond E., Ph.D. Prof. Emer. of Chemistry, Univ. of Texas, Austin.

Davis, Richard L., Ph.D. Prof. of History and East Asian Studies, Brown Univ.

Davis, Richard S., Ph.D. Head, Mass Section, Intl. Bureau of Weights and Measures.

Davis, Richard W., Ph.D. Prof. Emer. of History, Washington Univ., St. Louis.

Davis, Rochelle, Ph.D. Assoc. Prof., Center for Contemporary Arab Studies, Georgetown Univ.

Davis, Stephen M., Ph.D. Pres., Davis Global Advisors, Inc.

Davis, Tamra S., Ph.D. Asst. Prof., Dept. of Marketing, Illinois State Univ.

Davison, Brian D., Ph.D. Assoc. Prof., Computer Science and Engineering, Lehigh Univ.

Dawson, David A., B.A. Managing Editor, *Herald and Review,* Decatur, IL.

Dawson, Todd E., Ph.D. Prof. of Biology, Univ. of Calif., Berkeley.

Day, Janet, M.A. Deputy Managing Editor, *The Denver Post.*

Dean, Dennis R., Ph.D. Former Prof. of English

and Humanities, Univ. of Wisconsin, Parkside.

Dean, James A., B.A. Sr. Copy Editor, *Battle Creek* (MI) *Enquirer.*

Dean, Richard H., M.D. Pres., Wake Forest Univ. Health Sciences, and Dir., Wake Forest Univ. Baptist Medical Ctr.

Dean, Walter E., Jr., Ph.D. Scientist Emer., U.S. Geological Survey.

DeAngelis, Martin, B.A. Columnist, *The Press of Atlantic City* (NJ).

Dearborn, Lynne M., Ph.D. Asst. Prof., School of Architecture, Univ. of Illinois at Urbana-Champaign.

Decalo, Samuel, Ph.D. Managing Editor, Florida Academic Press.

Decker, Hannah S., Ph.D. Prof. of History, Univ. of Houston.

Deeb, Marius, Ph.D. Prof. of Middle East Studies, School of Advanced Intl. Studies, Johns Hopkins Univ.

Deer, Ada E., M.A. Former Asst. Secretary for Indian Affairs, Dept. of the Interior.

Deese, David A., Ph.D. Professor of Political Science, Boston College.

DeFrank, Thomas M., M.A. Washington Bureau Chief, *NY Daily News.*

DeFriend, Kimberly, Ph.D. Technical Staff Member, Los Alamos Natl. Laboratory.

De Hertogh, August A., Ph.D. Prof. Emer. of Horticultural Science, North Carolina State Univ.

Deitzer, Gerald F., Ph.D. Assoc. Prof. Emer. of Horticulture, Univ. of Maryland.

De Jong, James A., Th.D. Pres. Emer., Calvin Theological Seminary.

De Jong, Mayke, Ph.D. Prof. of Medieval History, Univ. of Utrecht.

DeLancey, Mark W., Ph.D. Prof. Emer. of Government and Intl. Studies, Univ. of South Carolina.

Dela Cruz, Charles S., M.D., Ph.D. Assistant Professor of Medicine, Yale School of Medicine.

DeLaria, Giacomo A., M.D. Head of Cardiac Surgery, Scripps Clinic and Research Foundation.

De La Rosa, Jeff, B.A. Manager, New Content. World Book, Inc.

de la Torre, Carlos, Ph.D. Director and Prof., Center for Latin American Studies, Univ. of Florida.

DeLay, Dorothy, L.H.D. Former Starling Prof. of Violin, Juilliard School and Univ. of Cincinnati.

Deliyannis, Deborah Mauskopf, Ph.D. Assoc. Prof., Dept. of History, Indiana Univ., Bloomington.

del Mar, David Peterson, Ph.D. Associate Professor, Department of History, Portland State Univ.

Delpar, Helen, Ph.D. Prof. Emer. of History, Univ. of Alabama.

DeMallie, Raymond J., Ph.D. Prof. of Anthropology and Dir. of the American Indian Studies Research Inst., Indiana Univ.

Demars, Stanford E., Ph.D. Emeritus Professor and Director of Geography, Rhode Island College.

DeMasse, Richard J. Former Regional Manager, Coats American.

de Meneses, Filipe Ribeiro, Ph.D. Prof. of History, National University of Ireland, Maynooth.

Demers, Raymond, M.D. Prof. of Family Medicine, Wayne State Univ.

Dempewolff, Richard F., B.S. Former Science Writer and Editor, *Science Digest.*

Dempsey, Kristi H., B.S. Editor, *Scottsdale* (AZ) *Tribune.*

DeNardo, Dale F., Ph.D. Univ. Veterinarian and Asst. Prof., Arizona State Univ.

De Nault, Kenneth J., Ph.D. Assoc. Prof. of Geology, Univ. of Northern Iowa.

Denkin, Nathan M., Ph.D. Consulting Member of Technical Staff, Lucent Technologies, Inc.

Denlinger, David L., Ph.D. Dist. Univ. Prof., Ohio State Univ.

Dennhardt, Andrew J., M.S. Graduate Research Assistant, Department of Fisheries and Wildlife, Michigan State University.

Dennis, Anthony W. Sr. Journalist, *The Sydney* (Australia) *Morning Herald.*

Denton, Melinda F., Ph.D. Former Curator of the Herbarium, Univ. of Washington.

D'Entremont, Jeremy Author, *The Lighthouses of Massachusetts, The Lighthouses of Rhode Island.*

Depcik, Christopher, Ph.D. Asst. Prof., Univ. of Kansas.

Deresiewicz, William, Ph.D. Dance critic.

Derman, Gordon H., M.D. Asst. Prof. of Plastic Surgery and Hand Surgery, Rush Medical Coll., Rush-Presbyterian-St. Luke's Medical Ctr.

Dernburg, Thomas F., Ph.D. Former Prof. of Economics, American Univ.

Derocher, Andrew E., Ph.D. Prof., Dept. of Biological Sciences, Univ. of Alberta.

Desanker, Paul V., Ph.D. Assoc. Prof., Dept. of Geography, Pennsylvania State Univ.

Desbarats, Catherine, Ph.D. Assoc. Prof. of History, McGill Univ.

Désilets, Andrée, Ph.D. Prof. Emer. of History, Univ. of Sherbrooke.

De Simone, Daniel V., J.D. Consultant; former Exec. Dir., Amer. Assn. of Engineering Societies.

Destler, I. M., Ph.D. Dir., Intl. Security and Economic Policy Specialization, Univ. of Maryland.

Dethloff, Henry C., Ph.D. Former Prof. of History, Texas A&M Univ.

Dettman, Matthew A., M.S. James D. Scott Prof. of Civil Engineering, Western Kentucky Univ.

De Turk, William, M.Mus. Director, Carillon Services, Bok Tower Gardens.

DeVault, Ileen A., Ph.D. Prof. of Labor Relations, Law, and History, Cornell Univ.

De Villiers, Marq, B.A. Author.

Devine, Theresa, M.F.A. Assistant Professor, Arizona State University.

Devlin, Iseult, B.A. Freelance writer; author, *Winter Sports: A Ragged Mountain Press Woman's Guide.*

Devlin, J. Paul, Ph.D. Prof. Emer. of Chemistry, Oklahoma State Univ.

De Vos, Paula S., Ph.D. Associate Professor, Department of History, San Diego State University.

De Vries, Jan, Ph.D. Prof. of History and Economics, Univ. of Calif., Berkeley.

DeVries, Marvin F., Ph.D. Prof. Emer., Mechanical Engin. Dept., Univ. of Wisconsin, Madison.

Dewald, William G., Ph.D. Former Dir. of Research, Federal Reserve Bank of St. Louis.

DeWit, Andrew, Ph.D. Prof., Dept. of Economic Policy Studies, Coll. of Economics, Rikkyo Univ.

Dewulf, Jeroen, Ph.D. Dir., Dutch Studies Program, Dept. of German, Univ. of Calif., Berkeley.

De Wit, Cary W., Ph.D. Assoc. Prof. of Geography, Univ. of Alaska, Fairbanks.

Diamond, Jay, M.A. Prof. of Marketing, Retailing, and Fashion, Nassau Community Coll.

Diamond, Norma, Ph.D. Prof. Emer. of Anthropology, Univ. of Michigan.

Dick, Christopher W., Ph.D. Asst. Prof. of Ecology and Evolutionary Biology, Univ. of Michigan.

Dickinson, John A., Ph.D. Former Professor and Chair of History, Université de Montréal.

Dickson, James S., Ph.D. Prof. of Animal Science, Iowa State Univ.

Dickson, W. Patrick, Ph.D. Prof. of Educ. Psychology and Educ. Technol., Michigan State Univ.

Diehl, Paul B., Ph.D. Emer. Assoc. Prof., Dept. of English, Univ. of Iowa.

Diehl, Stephen J., M.S. Prof. of Photography, Coll. of Imaging Arts and Sciences, Rochester Inst. of Technology.

Dienes, Leslie, Ph.D. Prof. of Geography, Univ. of Kansas.

Dieter, Steven, C.D., B.A., B.Ed. Associate Air Force Historian, Royal Canadian Air Force.

Dietrich, Michael R., Ph.D. Prof., Dept. of Biological Sciences, Dartmouth Coll.

Dietz, John L., Ph.D. Prof. Emer. of Geography, Univ. of Northern Colorado.

Dillard, Dudley, Ph.D. Former Prof. of Economics, Univ. of Maryland, Coll. Park.

Dillman, Lisa, B.A. Reporter, the *Los Angeles Times.*

Dillon, Alexander, Ph.D. Visiting Prof., Faculty of Humanities, Ukrainian Catholic Univ.

Dilly, Barbara J., Ph.D. Asst. Prof. of Sociology and Anthropology, Creighton Univ.

DiMichele, William A., Ph.D. Curator of Fossil Plants, Dept. of Paleobiology, Natl. Museum of Natural History, Smithsonian Inst.

Dine, Michael, Ph.D. Professor of Physics, University of California, Santa Cruz.

Dinsmore, James J., Ph.D. Former Prof. of Animal Ecology, Iowa State Univ.

Dinwiddie, Stephen H., M.D. Professor of Psychiatry, Northwestern University.

Diosady, Levente L., Ph.D. Prof. of Food Engineering and Applied Chemistry, Univ. of Toronto.

DiPaolo, Carolyn M., B.A. Managing Editor, *The* (Fort Wayne, IN) *News-Sentinel.*

Dippie, Brian W., Ph.D. Prof. Emer. of History, Univ. of Victoria.

Dirks, Richard A., Ph.D. Assoc. Dir., Joint Office for Science Support, Natl. Ctr. for Atmospheric Research.

Dirlik, Arif, Ph.D. Former Prof. of History, Duke Univ.

Dirr, Michael A., Ph.D. Prof. of Horticulture, Univ. of Georgia.

Diver, Stephen G., M.S. Technical Specialist, Appropriate Technology Transfer for Rural Areas.

Dmochowski, Roger R., M.D. Prof., Dept. of Urology, Vanderbilt Univ. Medical Ctr., Nashville.

Dmowski, W. Paul, M.D., Ph.D. Pres. Oak Brook Fertility Ctr. and Endometriosis Inst.

Doan, James E., Ph.D. Prof. of Humanities, Nova Southeastern Univ.

Doan-Crider, Diana, Ph.D. Director, Animo Partnership in Natural Resources.

Dobelle, William H., Ph.D. Former Chairman, Dobelle Inst.

Dobler, Scott A., M.A. Instructor, Geography and GIS, Western Kentucky Univ.

Dobris, Joel C., LL.B. Prof. of Law Emer., School of Law, Univ. of Calif., Davis.

Dobyns, Henry F., Ph.D. Author, *The Pima-Maricopa.*

Docherty, David C., Ph.D. Dean of Arts, Wilfrid Laurier Univ.

Dodelson, Scott, Ph.D. Professor of Physics, Carnegie Mellon University.

Dodge, Richard E., Ph.D. Dean and Prof., Nova Southeastern Univ. Oceanographic Ctr.

Dodson, Peter, Ph.D. Prof. of Earth and Environmental Science, Univ. of Pennsylvania.

Dodson-Robinson, Sally, Ph.D. Asst. Prof., Dept. of Astronomy, The Univ. of Texas at Austin.

Doerr, Paul W., Ph.D. Assoc. Prof., Dept. of History, Acadia Univ.

Doherty, Carroll J., M.A. Staff Writer, *Congressional Quarterly.*

Doherty, Donna K., B.A. Editor, *Tennis.*

Dolan, James M., Ph.D. Dir. of Collections, Zoological Society of San Diego.

Dolbear, Geoffrey E., Ph.D. Pres., G. E. Dolbear and Assoc.

Domer, Dennis, Ph.D. Prof. of Architecture, Coll. of Architecture, Univ. of Kentucky.

Domingo, Vernon, Ph.D. Prof. of Geography, Bridgewater State College.

Domjan, Laszlo K., B.J. Night News Editor, *St. Louis* (MO) *Post Dispatch.*

Domski, Mary, Ph.D. Asst. Prof., Dept. of Philosophy, Univ. of New Mexico.

Donahue, Matthew, Ph.D. Lecturer, Department of Popular Culture, Bowling Green State University.

Donald, David Herbert, Ph.D. Former Prof. of History, Harvard Univ.; winner of Pulitzer Prize for Biography or Autobiography, 1961 and 1988.

Donaldson, Gary A., Ph.D. Prof. of History, Xavier Univ. of Louisiana.

Donnelly, John Patrick, Ph.D. Prof. Emer. of History, Marquette Univ.

Donoghue, Michael E., Ph.D. Assoc. Prof. of History, Marquette Univ.

Donovan, Dianne, M.A. Independent Media Consultant and Editor, Zanvyl Krieger School of Arts and Sciences, Johns Hopkins Univ.

Donovan, James, Ph.D. Asst. Prof., Dept. of Mining Engineering, Univ. of Utah.

Donovan, Jane, B.A. Coauthor, *Historical Dictionary of Washington, D.C.*

Dooley, John F., M.S., M.E.E. William and Marilyn Ingersoll Prof. of Computer Sci., Knox College.

Doolittle, William E., Ph.D. Erich W. Zimmermann Regents Prof., Dept. of Geography, Univ. of Texas, Austin.

Dorman, Gary Jay, Ph.D. Former Sr. Vice Pres., National Economic Research Associates, Inc.

Dormon, James H., Ph.D. Prof. Emer., History and American Studies, Univ. of Southwestern Louisiana.

Dornbos, Stephen Q., Ph.D. Assoc. Prof., Dept. of Geosciences, Univ. of Wisconsin, Milwaukee.

Dossani, Rafiq, Ph.D. Sr. Research Scholar, Shorenstein Asia-Pacific Research Ctr., Stanford Univ.

Doty, R. G., Ph.D. Former Curator, National Numismatic Collection, Smithsonian Institution.

Dougan, Michael B., Ph.D. Emer. Prof. of History, Arkansas State Univ.

Doughty, Robert A., Ph.D. Former Head, Dept. of History, U.S. Military Academy, West Point.

Douglas, Patricia Casey, Ph.D. Assoc. Prof., Loyola Marymount Univ.

Doumato, Eleanor Abdella, Ph.D. Former Visiting Fellow, Watson Institute for International and Public Affairs, Brown University.

Dowd, Gregory Evans, Ph.D. Prof. of Hist. and American Culture, Univ. of Michigan, Ann Arbor.

Downhower, Jerry F., Ph.D. Professor of Zoology, Ohio State University.

Dowse, Robert E., Ph.D. Professor Emeritus of Politics, University of Western Australia.

Doyle, Daryl J., Ph.D. Prof. of Chemistry, Kettering Univ.

Doyle, Jeffrey Scott, B.S. Firearms Examiner, Kentucky State Police.

Doyle, William, Ph.D. Emer. Prof. of History, Univ. of Bristol.

Drake, Frank D., Ph.D. Prof. Emer., Astronomy and Astrophysics, Univ. of Calif., Santa Cruz.

Drescher, Seymour, Ph.D. Univ. Prof. of History, Univ. of Pittsburgh.

Driever, Steven L., Ph.D. Prof. of Geography and Chair of the Dept. of Geosciences, Univ. of Missouri, Kansas City.

Drotman, D. Peter, M.D., M.P.H. Sr. Medical Officer, Natl. Ctr. for Infectious Diseases, Ctrs. for Disease Control and Prevention.

Druesedow, Jean L., A.M. Dir., Kent State Univ. Museum.

Druker, Brian J., M.D. Prof. of Medicine, Oregon Health and Science Univ.

Drury, George H., M.A. Writer, *Rail Travel Guidebooks.*

Dry, Peter, Ph.D. Assoc. Prof., Dept. of Wine and Horticulture, Univ. of Adelaide.

Dubois, André, Ph.D. Former Research Prof. of Medicine, Uniformed Services Univ. of the Health Sciences.

Dudley, Theodore R., Ph.D. Former Lead Scientist and Research Botanist, U.S. Natl. Arboretum.

Duffey, Bernard, Ph.D. Former Prof. of English, Duke University.

Dugas, Daniel P., Ph.D. Asst. Prof. of Geography, New Mexico State Univ.

Duis, Perry R., Ph.D. Prof. Emer. of History, Univ. of Illinois, Chicago.

Dumaine, Deborah Pres., Better Communications; author, *Write to the Top.*

Dumas, Ernest C., B.J. Political columnist, *Arkansas Times.*

Dumenil, Lynn, Ph.D. Prof. of History, Occidental Coll.

Dungy, Kathryn R., Ph.D. Asst. Prof. of History, New Coll. of Florida.

Dunleavy, Janet Egleson, Ph.D. Prof. Emer. of English and Comparative Lit., Univ. of Wisconsin, Milwaukee.

Dunn, Casey, Ph.D. Asst. Prof. of Biology, Dept. of Ecology and Evolutionary Biology, Brown Univ.

Dunn, Richard J., Ph.D. Prof. Emer. of English, Univ. of Washington.

Dunn, Sarah E., M.A. Doctoral student in clinical psychology, Georgia State Univ. and Emory Univ.

Dunsworth, Holly M., Ph.D. Asst. Prof. of Anthropology, Univ. of Rhode Island.

Duram, Leslie, Ph.D. Prof. of Geography and Environmental Resources, Southern Illinois Univ., Carbondale.

Durant, Jack D., Ph.D. Former Prof. of English, North Carolina State Univ.

Durbin, Lynn, Ph.D. Sr. Editor/Researcher, World Book, Inc.

Durocher, Claudette, B.A. Former Editorial Page Editor, *The* (Nashua, NH) *Telegraph.*

DuRoss, Michael, B.A. Former Physical Sciences Editor, World Book, Inc.

Dutch, Steven I., Ph.D. Prof. of Earth Science, Dept. of Natural and Applied Sciences, Univ. of Wisconsin, Green Bay.

Dutcher, Janice Phillips, M.D. Prof. of Medicine, Assoc. Dir. for Clinical Affairs, Our Lady of Mercy Medical Ctr., Comprehensive Cancer Ctr.

Dwyer, Johanna T., D.Sc. Prof. of Medicine and Community Health, Tufts Univ. Schools of Medicine and Nutrition.

Dykstra, Daniel J., S.J.D. Former Prof. of Law, Univ. of Calif., Davis.

E

Earle, Claudette, Dip.Mass.Com. Editor, Guyana Natl. Newspapers.

Earle, Rosalie, B.S. Managing Editor, *The Charleston* (WV) *Gazette.*

Easby, Rebecca Jeffrey, Ph.D. Associate Professor of Art History, Trinity Washington University.

Eastman, Joel Webb, Ph.D. Former Prof. of History, Univ. of Southern Maine.

Eaton, George W., Ph.D. Prof. Emer., Univ. of British Columbia.

Eaton, William J., M.S.J. Former Curator, the Humphrey Program at the Univ. of Maryland; winner of Pulitzer Prize for Natl. Reporting, 1970.

Eaves, Peter J., O.N.C. Chem. Technical Dir., WRS Film and Video Laboratory.

Ebersole, Lynn A., Ph.D. Former Assoc. Prof., Dept. of Biological Sciences, Northern Kentucky Univ.

Ebert, Roger, B.S. Former film critic, *Chicago Sun-Times;* winner of Pulitzer Prize for Criticism, 1975.

Echtle, Edward L., Jr., M.A. Treasurer, Bigelow House Museum.

Eck, Paul, Ph.D. Former Prof. of Horticulture, Rutgers, the State Univ. of New Jersey.

Ecke, Paul, III, M.S., M.B.A. Chief Exec. Officer, Paul Ecke Ranch.

Eckert, Carter J., Ph.D. Prof., Dept. of East Asian Lang. and Civilizations, Harvard Univ.

Eckman, James R., M.D. Prof. of Hematology-Oncology and Medicine at Emory Univ. School of Medicine and Dir. of the Georgia Sickle Cell Ctr. at Grady Health System.

Eckstein, Arthur M., Ph.D. Prof. of History, Univ. of Maryland.

Economides, Michael J., Ph.D. Former Prof., Dept. of Chemical Engineering, Univ. of Houston.

Eden, Guinevere, Ph.D. Assoc. Prof. of Pediatrics, Georgetown Univ.

Eddy, William P., B.S. Feature Sections Editor, *Lincoln* (NE) *Journal Star.*

Edelman, Jerome P. Shorthand Production Manager and Platewriter, McGraw-Hill Book Co.

Edgerton, Samuel Y., Jr., Ph.D. Professor Emeritus of Art History, Williams College.

Edie, Carlene J., Ph.D. Prof. of Political Science, Univ. of Massachusetts.

Edmonds, Richard Louis, Ph.D. Associate Member, Ctr. for East Asian Studies, Univ. of Chicago.

Edmunds, R. David, Ph.D. Watson Prof. of American History, Univ. of Texas, Dallas.

Edwards, Andrew, Ph.D. Lecturer, School of History, Welsh History, and Archaeology, Univ. of Wales, Bangor.

Edwards, M. U., Ph.D. Pres. Emer., St. Olaf Coll.

Edwards, Paul N., Ph.D. Assoc. Prof., School of Information, Univ. of Michigan, Ann Arbor.

Edwards, R. Lawrence, Ph.D. Dist. McKnight Univ. Prof., Dept. of Geology & Geophysics, Univ. of Minnesota.

Edwards, R. Wayne, Ed.D. Dir. of Athletics, Towson Univ.

Edwards, Richard A., Ph.D. Former Assoc. Prof. of Theology, Marquette Univ.

Egan, Clifford L., Ph.D. Former Prof. of History, Univ. of Houston.

Egerton, Douglas R., Ph.D. Prof. of History, Le Moyne Coll.

Ehinger, John, M.A. Former Editorial Page Editor, *The Huntsville* (AL) *Times.*

Ehrick, Christine, Ph.D. Associate Professor, Department of History, University of Northern Iowa.

Eichhorn, Donald H., D.Ed. Former Superintendent, Lewisburg (PA) Area Schools.

Eidt, Robert C., Ph.D. Former Professor of Geography and Director, State Soils Laboratory, University of Wisconsin, Madison.

Eifrig, David E., M.D.   Former Professor of Ophthalmology, University of North Carolina.

Eilers, H. Peter, Ph.D.   Prof., Dept. of Earth Science, Willamette Univ.

Eils, Larry M., M.P.H.   Former Sr. Dir., Technical Services, Natl. Automatic Merchandising Assoc.

Einhorn, Robin L., Ph.D.   Prof. of History, Univ. of Calif., Berkeley.

Einstein, Herbert H., Dipl. Ing. ETH   Prof. of Civil Engineering, Massachusetts Inst. of Technology.

Ekirch, Arthur A., Jr., Ph.D.   Former Prof. of History, State Univ. of New York, Albany.

Ela, Patrick H., M.B.A.   Former Chair, Board of Trustees, Craft and Folk Art Museum, Los Angeles.

Elbl, Martin Malcolm, Ph.D.   Managing Editor, *Portuguese Studies Review;* independent scholar.

Elbourne, Elizabeth, Ph.D.   Assoc. Prof. of History, McGill Univ.

Elbow, Gary S., Ph.D.   Assoc. Dean of the Honors Coll. and Prof. of Geography, Texas Tech Univ.

Elder, E. Rozanne, Ph.D.   Professor Emeritus, Department of History, Western Michigan Univ.

Eldredge, Charles C., Ph.D.   Hall Dist. Prof. of American Art, Univ. of Kansas.

Elfenbein, Jessica I., Ph.D.   Assoc. Prof. of History and Community Studies, Univ. of Baltimore.

Elhardt, Matt, B.S.   Marketing Dir., Longview Fibre Company.

Eliashberg, Jehoshua, D.B.A.   Prof. of Marketing, Wharton School, Univ. of Pennsylvania.

Ellenbogen, Rudolph, M.S.   Former Curator of Rare Books, Columbia Univ.

Ellerbach, Susan, B.S.   Managing Editor, *Tulsa* (OK) *World.*

Elliot, James L., Ph.D.   Former Prof. of Physics and of Earth, Atmospheric, and Planetary Sciences, Massachusetts Inst. of Technology.

Elliott, Charles N., M.A.   Instructor of History, Southeastern Louisiana Univ.

Elliott, Robert, Ph.D.   Prof. of Counselling in the Counselling Unit, Univ. of Strathclyde, Glasgow, Scotland.

Ellis, Bill, Ph.D.   Prof. Emer., American Studies, Pennsylvania State Univ., Hazleton.

Ellis, Elizabeth Garrity, Ph.D.   Former Asst. Prof. of Art History, Southern Methodist Univ.

Ellis, Hayne, IV, B.A.   Former Dir. of Communications, Colorado Avalanche.

Ellis, Mark A.   Sr. Reporter, *The Columbus* (OH) *Dispatch.*

Ellis, Richard E., Ph.D.   Former Prof. of History, State Univ. of New York, Buffalo.

Ellison, William L., Jr., M.A.   Former Deputy Managing Editor, *The* (Louisville, KY) *Courier-Journal.*

Ellison, Sara Fisher, Ph.D.   Senior Lecturer, Dept. of Economics, Mass. Institute of Technology.

Elman, Yaakov, Ph.D.   Associate Professor of Jewish Studies, Yeshiva University.

Ellwood, Robert S., Jr., Ph.D.   Former Prof. of Religion, Univ. of Southern Calif.

Elmore, Barbara, B.A.   Freelance writer/editor.

Elmstrom, Gary W., Ph.D.   Former Plant Breeder, Sunseeds.

Elrod, Linda Henry, J.D.   Dist. Prof. of Law, Washburn Univ. School of Law.

Emanel, Kerry A., Ph.D.   Prof. of Atmospheric Science, Mass. Inst. of Technology.

Embry, Patrick S. "Pat"   Editorial Director, Magellan Press.

Emery, Michael, Ph.D.   Former Prof. of Journalism, Calif. State Univ., Northridge.

Eminov, Ali, Ph.D.   Prof. Emer. of Anthropology, Wayne State Coll.

Emling, Shelley, B.A.   Author, *The Fossil Hunter: Dinosaurs, Evolution, and the Woman Whose Discoveries Changed the World.*

Emmert, Thomas A., Ph.D.   Former Professor of History, Gustavus Adolphus College.

Emy, Hugh V., Ph.D.   Former Prof. of Politics, Monash Univ.

Enderle, John D., Ph.D.   Dir. and Prof. of Biomedical Engineering, Univ. of Connecticut, Storrs.

Engel, David, Ph.D.   Greenberg Prof. of Holocaust Studies, New York Univ.

Engel, Toby R., M.D.   Cardiologist, Cooper Univ. Cardiology.

Engels, Donald, Ph.D.   Former Asst. Prof. of History, Wellesley Coll.

Englehart, Neil A., Ph.D.   Assoc. Prof. of Political Science, Bowling Green State Univ.

English, John, Ph.D.   Dist. Prof. Emer. of History, Univ. of Waterloo.

English, Peter C., Ph.D.   Assoc. Prof. of Pediatrics and of History, Duke Univ.

Engst, Elaine D., M.A.   Archivist, Cornell Univ.

Enlow, Harold L.   Woodcarver and author, *Patterns for Wood Carving.*

Epps, Helen H., Ph.D.   Prof. of Textiles, Merchandising, and Interiors, Univ. of Georgia.

Epstein, Cynthia Fuchs, Ph.D.   Dist. Prof. of Sociology, Grad. Ctr., City Univ. of New York.

Epstein, William H., Ph.D.   Prof. of English, Univ. of Arizona.

Erhardt, Andreas, Ph.D.   Lecturer, Univ. of Basel.

Erickson, H. T., Ph.D.   Prof. of Horticulture, Purdue Univ.

Erickson, Stephen A., Ph.D.   E. Wilson Lyon Prof. of Humanities and Chairman, Philosophy Dept., Pomona Coll.

Ernst, Carl W., Ph.D.   William R. Kenan, Jr., Dist. Prof., Dept. of Religious Studies, The Univ. of North Carolina, Chapel Hill.

Errington, Wayne, Ph.D.   Lecturer in Politics, School of History and Politics, Univ. of Adelaide.

Eschman, Donald F., Ph.D.   Prof. Emer. of Geology, Univ. of Michigan.

Eschmeyer, William N., Ph.D.   Sr. Curator, Dept. of Ichthyology, Calif. Academy of Sciences.

Esenwein, George R., Ph.D.   Assoc. Prof. of History, Univ. of Florida.

Esler, William C., B.A.   Former Editor in Chief, *Graphic Arts Monthly.*

Esposito, Matthew D., Ph.D.   Assoc. Prof. of History, Drake Univ.

Essex, Randy, B.A.   Former Assistant Managing Editor, *Des Moines* (IA) *Register.*

Esslinger, Gary L., B.S.   Treasurer/Manager, Elephant Butte Irrigation District.

Esters, Onikia N., Ph.D., R.D.   Postdoctoral Research Assoc., Purdue Univ.

Etcheson, Nicole, Ph.D.   Alexander M. Bracken Prof. of History, Ball State Univ.

Euraque, Dario A., Ph.D.   Prof. of History and Intl. Studies, Trinity Coll.

Evans, Andrea E., Ph.D.   Director, Carruthers Ctr. for Inner City Studies, Northeastern Illinois Univ.

Evans, Larry, B.A.   Five-time U.S. chess champion; author, *Chess: Beginner to Expert.*

Evans, Simon M., Ph.D.   Former Assoc. Prof. of Geography, Memorial Univ. of Newfoundland.

Eve, Raymond A., Ph.D.   Prof. Emer. of Sociology, Univ. of Texas, Arlington.

Everard, J. A., Ph.D.   Senior Research Associate, Acta of the Plantagenets Project, Faculty of History, University of Cambridge.

Everson, Jeff M., Ph.D.   Editor in Chief, *Planet Muscle Magazine.*

Evert, Chris   Tennis champion.

Eves, Howard W., Ph.D.   Former Dist. Visiting Prof. of Mathematics, Univ. of Central Florida.

Ewen, Charles R., Ph.D.   Prof. of Anthropology, East Carolina Univ.

Exline, Christopher H., Ph.D.   Former Professor and Chairman, Department of Geography, University of Nevada, Reno.

Eybel, Carl E., M.D.   Sr. Attending Asst. Prof., Rush-Presbyterian-St. Luke's Medical Ctr.

Eyman, Alice Page, M.A.   Former Dir. and Prof., Univ. of Delaware Laboratory Preschool, Coll. of Human Resources, Univ. of Delaware.

Eyster, Linda S., Ph.D.   Teacher, Milton Academy.

F

Faber, Betty Lane, Ph.D.   Former Staff Scientist, Liberty Science Ctr.

Faber, Sandra M., Ph.D.   Prof. of Astronomy, Lick Observatory, Univ. of Calif., Santa Cruz.

Fabian, Carol, M.D.   Prof. of Medicine, Division of Clinical Oncology, and Breast Program Dir., Kansas Univ. Cancer Ctr.

Fagan, Brian M., Ph.D.   Prof. Emer. of Anthropology, Univ. of Calif., Santa Barbara.

Fagan, Julie M., Ph.D.   Prof. of Animal Science, Rutgers, the State Univ. of New Jersey.

Fagin, Stephen, B.A.   Asst. Sunday Editor, The Day Publishing Company.

Fain, Stephen M., Ed.D.   Faculty Fellow in the Honors Coll., Florida Intl. Univ.

Fair, Laura, Ph.D.   Prof. of History, Univ. of Oregon.

Fairchild, Mark D., Ph.D.   Prof., Munsell Color Science Laboratory, Rochester Inst. of Technology.

Fairfield, John D., Ph.D.   Prof., Dept. of History, Xavier Univ., Cincinnati, Ohio.

Falk, Nancy E. Auer, Ph.D.   Prof. Emer. of Comparative Religion and Women's Studies, Western Michigan Univ.

Falkner, Kelly K., Ph.D.   Prof., Oregon State Univ.

Falta, Ronald W., Ph.D.   Prof. of Earth Sciences, Clemson Univ.

Fandy, Mamoun H., Ph.D.   Pres. of Fandy Associates, Washington, D.C.

Fantham, Elaine, Ph.D.   Former Professor of Latin, Department of Classics, Princeton University.

Farley, Fred, B.A.   Unlimited Hydroplane Historian, American Power Boat Assoc.

Farmer, Ken, B.A.   Section Chief, Leadership & Fire Risk Reduction, Natl. Fire Academy.

Farnham, Dale E., Ph.D.   Technology Dev. Manager, Monsanto.

Farr, D. M. L., D.Phil.   Prof. Emer. of History, Carleton Univ.

Faucher-King, Florence, Ph.D.   Assoc. Prof. of European Studies, Vanderbilt Univ.

Faulk, Odie B., Ph.D.   Former Prof. of History, Northeastern State Univ.

Fawcett, John, M.A.   Asst. Archivist for Pres. Libraries, Natl. Archives and Records Admin.

Fay, Matthew M., M.S.   Process Engineer, General Motors Corp.

Feather, Leonard   Author, *The Encyclopedia of Jazz.*

Feder, Robert, B.S.   Former Television and Radio Columnist, *Chicago Sun-Times.*

Feduccia, Alan, Ph.D.   S. K. Heninger Dist. Prof. Emer., Dept. of Biology, Univ. of North Carolina, Chapel Hill.

Fee, Elizabeth, Ph.D.   Chief, History of Medicine Division, Natl. Library of Medicine.

Fee, Margery, Ph.D.   Professor of English, University of British Columbia.

Fehl, Pamela J., B.A.   Dir., Graphic Artists Guild of New York.

Fehrs, Don, Ph.D.   Former Sr. Investment Officer, Cornell Univ.

Feigl, Dorothy M., Ph.D.   Vice Pres., Dean of Faculty, Prof. of Chemistry, St. Mary's Coll.

Feinberg, Gerald, Ph.D.   Former Prof. of Physics, Columbia Univ.

Feinberg, Jack, Ph.D.Phys.   Prof., Physics Dept., Univ. of Southern Calif.

Feldheim, Kevin A., Ph.D.   Manager, Pritzker Lab. for Molecular Systematics and Evolution, The Field Museum, Chicago.

Feldman, Gary J., Ph.D.   Frank B. Baird, Jr., Prof. of Science, Harvard Univ.

Feldman, Richard M., M.D.   Chairman, Dept. of Emergency Medicine, Advocate Illinois Masonic Medical Ctr.

Felkenes, George T., Dr.Crim.   Prof. Emer. of Political Science, Claremont Grad. Univ.

Felson, Nancy, Ph.D.   Prof. Emer. of Classics, Univ. of Georgia.

Fenton, M. B., Ph.D.   Prof. Emer., Dept. of Biology, Univ. of Western Ontario.

Fenwick, Lynda Beck, J.D.   Attorney and author of *Should the Children Pray?*

Ferdman, Ronald, M.D., M.Ed.   Asst. Prof., Dept. of Pediatrics, Keck School of Medicine, Univ. of Southern Calif.

Feretic, Eileen, B.A.   Former Editor in Chief, *Beyond Computing* magazine.

Ferguson, John C., Ph.D.   Former Prof. of Biology and Marine Science, Eckerd Coll.

Ferguson, R. Brian, Ph.D.   Professor of Sociology and Anthropology, Rutgers, the State University of New Jersey, Newark.

Fernandez, James W., Ph.D.   Prof. Emer. of Anthropology, Univ. of Chicago.

Fernandez, Michael, Ph.D.   Exec. Dir., Pew Initiative on Food and Biotechnology.

Ferrara, Ronald J., Ed.D.   Dir. of Aerospace Grad.

Programs, Middle Tennessee State Univ.

Ferrell, Keith Former freelance science writer; former Editor, *OMNI* magazine.

Ferrell, Ray E., Jr., Ph.D. Prof. of Geology, Louisiana State Univ.

Ferrell, Robert H., Ph.D. Former Distinguished Professor of History, Indiana Univ., Bloomington.

Ferrie, Gina M., M.A. Research Manager, Population Biologist, Disney's Animal Kingdom.

Ferrill, Arther, Ph.D. Prof. Emer. of History, Univ. of Washington.

Fetter, Bruce S., Ph.D. Prof. Emer. of History, Univ. of Wisconsin, Milwaukee.

Field, Bruce F., Ph.D. Acting Assoc. Dir., EEEL, Natl. Inst. of Standards and Technology.

Field, Christopher B., Ph.D. Dir., Dept. of Global Ecology, Carnegie Inst.

Field, Judith, Ph.D. Research Fellow/Lecturer in Archaeology, University of Sydney.

Fields, Clark L., Ph.D. Prof. of Chemistry, Univ. of Northern Colorado.

Fierman, William, Ph.D. Prof. Emer., Dept. of Central Eurasian Studies, Indiana Univ.

Filipi, Zoran, Ph.D. Timken Endowed Chair in Vehicle System Design, Department of Automotive Engineering, Clemson University.

Filler, Louis, Ph.D. Former historian, lexicographer, and editor.

Finch, Jerry, B.S. President, Habitat for Horses.

Finckenauer, James O., Ph.D. Prof. Emer. and Professorial Fellow, School of Criminal Justice, Rutgers, the State Univ. of New Jersey.

Findlay, Raymond D., Ph.D. Prof. Emer., Electrical and Computer Engineering, Power Research Laboratory, McMaster Univ.

Findlen, Paula, Ph.D. Prof. of History, Stanford Univ.

Findling, John E., Ph.D. Professor Emeritus of History, Indiana University Southeast.

Fine, Michael, Ph.D. Prof. of Biology, Virginia Commonwealth Univ.

Fingard, Judith, Ph.D. Former Prof. of History, Dalhousie Univ.

Fink, Peter E., M.Div. Prof. Emer. of Liturgical Theology, Weston Jesuit School of Theology; Assoc. Pastor, St. Francis Xavier Parish, New York City.

Finke, Wayne H., Ph.D. Prof. of Modern Lang., Baruch Coll.

Finkin, Matthew W., LL.M. Prof. of Law, Univ. of Illinois Coll. of Law.

Finkler, Michael S., Ph.D. Assoc. Prof. of Biology, Indiana Univ., Kokomo.

Finn, Bernard S., Ph.D. Curator, Natl. Museum of American History.

Finn, John W., M.D. Exec. Medical Dir., Hospice of Michigan.

Finn, Lee Samuel, Ph.D. Dir., Ctr. for Gravitational Wave Physics, and Prof. of Physics, Astronomy and Astrophysics, Pennsylvania State Univ.

Finnegan, Gregory Allan, Ph.D. Assoc. Librarian for Public Services and Head of Reference in the Tozzer Library, Harvard Univ.

Finney, Ben, Ph.D. Prof. Emer. of Anthropology, Univ. of Hawaii.

Firmage, Edwin B., S.J.D. Samuel D. Thurman Prof. Emer. of Law, Univ. of Utah Coll. of Law.

Firpo, Meri T., Ph.D. Asst. Prof., Stem Cell Inst., Dept. of Medicine, Endocrinology Division, Univ. of Minnesota.

Fischer, John E., Ph.D. Prof. of Materials Science, Univ. of Pennsylvania.

Fishback, Price V., Ph.D. Frank and Clara Kramer Prof. of Economics, Univ. of Arizona.

Fisher, Bart, B.S. Former Associate Director of Marketing and Communications, Central Connecticut State University.

Fisher, Deena K., Ed.D. Dean, Woodward Campus, and Assoc. Prof. of American History, Northwestern Oklahoma State Univ.

Fisher, James F., Ph.D. Prof. Emer. of Asian Studies and Anthropology, Carleton Coll.

Fisher, Louis, Ph.D. Scholar in Residence, the Constitution Project.

Fisher, Michael H., Ph.D. Robert S. Danforth Prof. of History, Oberlin Coll.

Fisher, Terri D., Ph.D. Prof. of Psychology, Ohio State Univ., Mansfield.

Fiss, Owen M., LL.B. Sterling Prof. Emer. of Law

and Professorial Lecturer in Law, Yale Law School.

Fitz, Earl E., Ph.D. Prof. of Portuguese, Spanish, and Comparative Lit., Vanderbilt Univ.

Fitzgerald, Alan, B.A. Communications consultant, Alan Fitzgerald & Assoc.

Fitzgerald, Ed Author, *The Ballplayer.*

Fitzgerald, F. Patrick, M.A.T. Former Prof. of Geography and History, Univ. of Alaska Southeast.

Fitzgerald, Oscar P., Ph.D. Adjunct Professor, Smithsonian/George Mason University M.A. Program in Decorative Arts.

Fitzpatrick, John W., Ph.D. Dir., Cornell Laboratory of Ornithology, Cornell Univ.

Fixico, Donald L., Ph.D. Dist. Foundation Prof. of History, Arizona State Univ.

Flecknell, Paul, Ph.D. Prof. of Laboratory Animal Science, Newcastle Univ.

Fleischner, Jeannette E., Ed.D. Former Prof. of Special Educ., Teachers Coll., Columbia Univ.

Fleishman, Avrom, Ph.D. Prof. of English, Johns Hopkins Univ.

Fleming, Henry P., Ph.D. Research Leader, Prof. Emer., Dept. of Food Science, U.S. Dept. of Agriculture.

Flick, George J., Jr., Ph.D. Univ. Dist. Prof., Food Science and Technology, Virginia Polytechnic Inst. and State Univ.

Flint, Harrison L., Ph.D. Prof. Emer. of Horticulture, Purdue Univ.

Flores, Dan L., Ph.D. Hammond Prof. of Western History, Univ. of Montana.

Florian, Kenneth (Kenny), B.S. Mixed martial artist and CEO/owner, Florian Martial Arts Ctr.

Flowers, Benjamin, Ph.D. Associate Professor, School of Architecture, Georgia Tech.

Floyd, Juliet, Ph.D. Prof. of Philosophy, Boston Univ.

Flynn, Michael, Ph.D. Prof. of Linguistics, Carleton Coll.

Flynn, Thomas P. Vice Pres. of Communications, (Rochester, NY) *Democrat and Chronicle.*

Fogarty, Gerald P., S.T.M. Prof. of Religious Studies and History, Univ. of Virginia.

Fogel, Daniel Mark, Ph.D. Pres., Univ. of Vermont, Burlington.

Foley, William E., Ph.D. Prof. Emer. of History, Central Missouri State Univ.

Fontaine, Carole R., Ph.D. Distinguished Taylor Professor of Biblical Theology and History, Andover Newton Theological School.

Fontana, Lynn A., Ph.D. Chief Academic Officer, Sylvan Learning.

Foody, James J., M.D. Assoc. Chairman of Clinical Affairs, Northwestern Univ.

Forbes, John Vernon Recording engineer, Frogg Mountain Recording Studio.

Forcey, Charles B., Ph.D. Former Prof. of History, Binghamton Univ.

Forcey, Linda R., Ph.D. Assoc. Prof., School of General Studies, State Univ. of New York, Binghamton.

Ford, John K. B., Ph.D. Head, Cetacean Research Program, Conservation Biology, Fisheries and Oceans Canada.

Forester, Don C., Ph.D. Professor of Biology, Towson University.

Forgeng, Jeffrey L., Ph.D. Adjunct Professor of History, Worcester Polytechnic Institute.

Forman, James D., LL.B. Attorney and author.

Forrest, Stephen R., Ph.D. Vice Pres. for Research and Prof. of Electrical Engineering and Computer Science, Physics, and Materials Science and Engineering, Univ. of Michigan.

Forrester, Sibelan E. S., Ph.D. Professor of Russian, Swarthmore College.

Forry, Nicole D., Ph.D. Research Scientist, Child Trends.

Forslund, Catherine, Ph.D. Isabel Ross Abbott Prof. of Hist. and Women's Studies, Rockford Univ.

Forsman, Eric, Ph.D. Research Wildlife Biologist, U.S. Forest Service.

Foss, Clive, Ph.D. Professor, Department of History, Georgetown University.

Foster, David E., Ph.D. Prof., Engine Research Ctr., Univ. of Wisconsin, Madison.

Foster, John Elgin, Ph.D. Former Prof. of History, Univ. of Alberta.

Foster, Stephen C., Ph.D. Professor of Art Histo-

ry, University of Iowa.

Fournier, Eric J., Ph.D. Prof. and Chair, Geography Dept., Samford Univ.

Fowler, Catherine S., Ph.D. Prof. Emer. of Anthropology, Univ. of Nevada, Reno.

Fowler, Don D., Ph.D. Prof. Emer. of Historic Preservation and Anthropology, Univ. of Nevada, Reno.

Fowler, Loretta, Ph.D. Prof. of Anthropology, Indiana Univ., Bloomington.

Fowler, William Morgan, Jr., Ph.D. Dist. Prof. of History, Northeastern Univ.

Fox, Eleanor M., LL.B. Prof. of Law, New York Univ. School of Law.

Fox, James Alan, Ph.D. The Lipman Family Prof. of Criminal Justice and Prof. of Law, Policy and Society, Northeastern Univ.

Fox, Marye Anne, Ph.D. Chancellor, Univ. of Calif., San Diego.

Fox, Stephen, Ph.D. Historian.

Frahm, Eckart, Ph.D. Prof. of Assyriology, Yale Univ.

Frances, Allen, M.D. Prof. of Psychiatry, Duke Univ. Medical School.

Francko, David A., Ph.D. Prof. and Chairman, Dept. of Botany, Miami Univ.

Frank, Elizabeth S., M.A. Former Curator of Large Mammals, Milwaukee County Zoo.

Frankfurter, David, M.D. Prof. of Obstetrics and Gynecology, The George Wash. Univ. Medical Ctr.

Franklin, James L., M.D. Assoc. Prof. of Internal Medicine and Gastroenterology, Rush-Presbyterian-St. Luke's Medical Ctr.

Franklin, William L., Ph.D. Mammalian Wildlife Ecologist, Iowa State Univ.

Franz, George W., Ph.D. Dir. Emer. of Academic Affairs, Pennsylvania State Univ., Delaware County Campus.

Fraser, Graham, M.A. Commissioner of Official Lang. of Canada.

Fraser, James E., Ph.D. Lecturer in Early Scottish History and Culture, Univ. of Edinburgh.

Fraser, Steven, Ph.D. Writer-Historian.

Fratkin, Elliot, Ph.D. Prof. of Anthropology, Smith Coll.

Fraze, Kathleen M., B.S. Asst. Managing Editor/ Features, *Akron (OH) Beacon Journal.*

Frazier, Gregory, M.A. Exec. Dir., AudioVision Inc.

Freas, Samuel James, Ed.D. Former Pres., Intl. Swimming Hall of Fame.

Frederic, Paul B., Ph.D. Former Prof. of Geography, Univ. of Maine, Farmington.

Frederick, Claire, M.D. Dist. Consulting Faculty, Grad. Coll. of Psychology and Humanistic Studies, Saybrook Univ.

Frederick, Jeff, Ph.D. Assoc. Prof. of History, Univ. of North Carolina, Pembroke.

Fredrickson, Leigh H., Ph.D. Former Rucker Prof. of Fisheries and Wildlife and former Dir., Gaylord Memorial Lab., Univ. of Missouri, Columbia.

Freedman, Lew, M.L.A. Freelance writer.

Freehling, William W., Ph.D. Singletary Prof. of the Humanities, Univ. of Kentucky.

Freeman, John G., M.A. Assoc. Prof. of Journalism, Univ. of Florida.

Freund, William Mark, Ph.D. Prof. Emer. of Economic History, Univ. of KwaZulu-Natal.

Frey, Linda S., Ph.D. Prof. of European History, Univ. of Montana.

Frey, Marsha L., Ph.D. Prof. of History, Kansas State Univ.

Frieden, Rob, J.D. Pioneers Chair and Prof. of Telecommunications and Law, Penn State Univ.

Friedman, Ann, Ph.D. Manager of Grants and Foundations, Nelson-Atkins Museum of Art, Kansas City, Missouri.

Frisch, Priscilla, Ph.D. Senior Scientist, Dept. of Astronomy and Astrophysics, Univ. of Chicago.

Fritz, Harry W., Ph.D. Prof. of History, Univ. of Montana.

Frodin, Joanna H., Ph.D. Vice Pres., Federal Reserve Bank of Philadelphia.

From, Milton, Ph.D. Assoc. Prof. of Physics, Western Washington Univ.

Fry, Edward S., Ph.D. Prof. of Physics, Texas A&M Univ.

Frye, B. E., Ph.D. Provost and Vice Pres. for Academic Affairs, Emory Univ.

Fugelsang, K. C., M.A. Former Professor of Enology, California State Univ., Fresno; coauthor, *Wine Microbiology* and *Wine Analysis and Production.*

Fuhrmann, Joseph T., Ph.D. Prof. of History, Murray State Univ.

Fujita, T. Theodore, Sc.D. Former Prof. of Meteorology, Univ. of Chicago.

Fulghum, Julia E., Ph.D. Vice Pres. for Research and Prof. of Chemical and Nuclear Engineering, Univ. of New Mexico.

Fulton, E. Kaye, B.A. Sr. Writer, *Maclean's* magazine.

Fumich, Frank F., M.D. Orthopaedic Spine Surgeon, Orthopaedic Inst. of Ohio.

Funkhouser, John G., Ph.D. Former Chemist, Michigan State Univ.

Fuson, Karen Connors, Ph.D. Prof. of Educ., Northwestern Univ.

G

Gab, Orville E., M.S. Asst. Prof., Dept. of Geography, South Dakota State Univ.

Gabel, Christopher R., Ph.D. Historian, U.S. Army Command and General Staff Coll.

Gable, John A., Ph.D. Former Exec. Dir., Theodore Roosevelt Assoc.

Gadwood, Robert C., Ph.D. Chief Exec. Officer, Kalexsyn, Inc.

Gager, Wyvolyn, B.A. Former Editor in Chief, *Gleaner Publications,* Kingston, Jamaica.

Gagliano, Joseph A., Ph.D. Former Professor of Latin American History, Loyola Univ. of Chicago.

Gagnon, Joe Talk show host, Talk Radio 1600 WAAM.

Gaines, Brian John, Ph.D. Assoc. Prof., Dept. of Political Science and Inst. of Government and Public Affairs, Univ. of Illinois, Urbana-Champaign.

Gaiser, Adam R., Ph.D. Professor of Religion, Florida State University.

Gait, Robert I., Ph.D. Curator Emer. of Mineralogy, Royal Ontario Museum, Toronto.

Gallagher, Charles M., B.S. Former Managing Editor, Reading Eagle Company.

Gallagher, Joan S., Ph.D. Research Assoc., Pathology/Immunology, Univ. of Cincinnati.

Gallagher, Rachel, B.A. Author, *Games in the Street.*

Gallawa, John C. Owner, Microtech; author, *The Complete Microwave Oven Service Handbook.*

Gallis, Paul E., Ph.D. Section Head, Europe and Eurasia Foreign Affairs, Defense, and Trade Division, Congressional Research Service.

Galloway, J. H., Ph.D. Prof. of Geography, Univ. of Toronto.

Gamble, Douglas W., Ph.D. Assoc. Prof. of Geography, Univ. of North Carolina, Wilmington.

Games, Ivan A., M.S. Doctoral Student/Researcher, Univ. of Wisconsin, Madison.

Gandy, Joan W., B.A. Former Managing Editor, *The Natchez* (MS) *Democrat.*

Gandy, Sam, M.D., Ph.D. Prof. of Neurology and Psychiatry, Mount Sinai Medical Ctr., New York City.

Gangel, Kenneth O., Ph.D. Former Academic Dean, Dallas Theological Seminary.

Gantz, Nelson M., M.D. Chairman, Dept. of Medicine and Chief, Division of Infectious Diseases, Pinnacle Health Hospitals.

Garavito, R. Michael, Ph.D. Prof. of Biochemistry, Michigan State Univ.

Garbarino, Merwyn S., Ph.D. Former Professor of Anthropology, Univ. of Illinois, Chicago.

Garber, Eugene K., Ph.D. Former Prof. of English, State Univ. of New York, Albany.

García-Guevara, Aldo V., Ph.D. Asst. Prof. of History and Political Science, Worcester State Coll.

García, Homer D. C., Ph.D. Former Pres., Henry Cogswell Coll.

Garcia, Jesus, Ed.D. Prof. of Social Studies Educ., Dept. of Curriculum and Instruction, Univ. of Nevada, Las Vegas.

García-Sastre, Adolfo, Ph.D. Professor of Microbiology, Mount Sinai School of Medicine.

Gardin, Julius M., M.D. Chief, Division of Cardiology, St. John Hospital & Medical Ctr.

Garfield, Robert, Ph.D. Assoc. Prof. of History, DePaul Univ.

Garibaldi, Louis E. Aquarium Consultant and former Dir. of the New York Aquarium.

Garman, Mary Van Vleck, Ph.D. Professor of Religion, Earlham College.

Garmon, Lucille B., Ph.D. Prof. Emer. of Chemistry, State Univ. of West Georgia.

Garnes, Sara, Ph.D. Prof. Emer. of English, Ohio State Univ.

Garnett, Sherman W., Ph.D. Dean, James Madison Coll., Michigan State Univ.

Garnick, Marc B., M.D. Gorman Brothers Professor of Medicine, Harvard Medical School; Physician, Beth Israel Deaconess Medical Center.

Garretson, Peter P., Ph.D. Assoc. Prof. of History, Florida State Univ.

Garrison, David L., Ph.D. Researcher, Inst. of Marine Sciences, Univ. of Calif., Santa Cruz.

Garrison, Dee, Ph.D. Former Prof. of History and Women's Studies, Rutgers, the State Univ. of New Jersey.

Garrow, David J., Ph.D. Author, *Bearing the Cross: Martin Luther King, Jr., and the Southern Christian Leadership Conference;* winner, Pulitzer Prize for Biography or Autobiography, 1987.

Gass, Susan M., Ph.D. Univ. Dist. Prof., Linguistics and Lang., and Dir., English Lang. Ctr., Michigan State Univ.

Gates, William C., Jr., M.A. Former Curator and Historian, Ohio Historical Society.

Gauthreaux, Sidney A., Jr., Ph.D. Prof. of Zoology, Clemson Univ.

Gavrilovich, Peter Deputy Nation/World Editor, *Detroit Free Press;* author, *The Detroit Almanac: 300 Years of Life in the Motor City.*

Gebissa, Ezekiel, Ph.D. Assoc. Prof. of History, Kettering Univ.

Geerken, John H., Ph.D. Prof. Emer. of History, Scripps Coll.

Geherin, David, Ph.D. Prof. Emer. of English, Eastern Michigan Univ.

Geiger, Gordon H., Ph.D. Consultant, T. P. McNulty & Assoc.

Geist, Valerius, Ph.D. Prof. Emer. of Environmental Sciences, Univ. of Calgary.

Gelles, Richard J., Ph.D. Former Joanne and Raymond Welsh Chair of Child Welfare and Family Violence, School of Social Policy & Practice, University of Pennsylvania.

Gellman, Andrew J., Ph.D. Prof. and Head of Chemical Engineering, Carnegie Mellon Univ.

Genovese, E. N., Ph.D. Prof. Emer., Classics and Humanities, San Diego State Univ.

Genovese, Michael A., Ph.D. Loyola Chair of Leadership, Loyola Marymount Univ.

Genoways, Hugh H., Ph.D. Prof. Emer., Univ. of Nebraska State Museum, Univ. of Nebraska, Lincoln.

Gentry, Alwyn H., Ph.D. Former Sr. Curator, Missouri Botanical Garden.

George, David B., B.S. Dir., Technology, Kennecott Utah Copper Corp.

Gerace, Paul L., Ph.D. Former Technical Specialist and Project Manager, Xerox Corp.

Gerard, Valrie A., Ph.D. Assoc. Prof. of Marine Sciences, State Univ. of New York, Stony Brook.

Gerber, Jane S., Ph.D. Prof. of History, Grad. Ctr., City Univ. of New York.

Gerbie, Melvin V., M.D. Prof. Emer., Clinical Obstetrics and Gynecology, Feinberg School of Medicine, Northwestern Univ.

Gerdes, Dick, Ph.D. Prof. of Latin-American Lit., Univ. of New Mexico.

Gereau, Roy E., M.S. Curatorial Asst., Missouri Botanical Garden.

Gergen, Kenneth J., Ph.D. Prof. of Psychology, Swarthmore Coll.

Gerking, Shelby, Ph.D. Galloway Prof. of Econ., Univ. of Central Florida, Coll. of Business Admin.

Gervais, Sarah J., M.S. Prof. of Psychology, Univ. of Nebraska, Lincoln.

Gervers, Michael, Ph.D. Prof. of History and Art History, Univ. of Toronto, Scarborough.

Getson, Heather-Anne, B.A. Curator of Collections, Fisheries Museum of the Atlantic.

Gettleman, Marvin E., Ph.D. Prof. of History, Polytechnic Inst. of New York.

Ghilarducci, Teresa, Ph.D. Prof. of Economics, Univ. of Notre Dame.

Giacumakis, George, Jr., Ph.D. Prof. of History

and Dir. of Calif. State Univ., Fullerton, Mission Viejo Campus.

Giannelli, Paul C., LL.M. Weatherhead Prof. of Law, Case Western Reserve Univ.

Giannetti, Louis, Ph.D. Author, *Understanding Movies.*

Gibbard, Bruce G., Ph.D. Sr. Physicist and Dir., RHIC and US ATLAS Computing Facilities, Brookhaven Natl. Laboratory.

Gibbons, Don C., Ph.D. Emer. Prof. of Sociology and Urban Studies, Portland State Univ.

Gibbons, J. Whitfield, Ph.D. Former Prof. of Ecology, Univ. of Georgia; former Sr. Research Ecologist, Savannah River Ecology Lab., Univ. of Georgia.

Gibbs, Gary G., Ph.D. Prof. of History, Roanoke Coll.

Giblin, James L., Ph.D. Prof. of History, Univ. of Iowa.

Gibson, Arrell Morgan, Ph.D. Former George Lynn Cross Research Prof., Univ. of Oklahoma.

Gibson, Lay James Prof. of Geography and Regional Dev. and Dir., Economic Dev. Research Program, Univ. of Arizona.

Gibson, Robert Ryder, B.A. Exec. Dir., Sorensen Inst. for Political Leadership, Univ. of Virginia.

Giddins, Gary, B.A. Former Columnist, Staff Writer, *Village Voice.*

Gies, David Thatcher, Ph.D. Commonwealth Professor of Spanish, University of Virginia.

Gilbert, Marc Jason, Ph.D. Prof. of History, North Georgia Coll. and State Univ.

Gilbert, Robert E., Ph.D. Prof. of Political Science, Northeastern Univ.

Gilbert, Roger, Ph.D. Prof. of English, Cornell Univ.

Gilderhus, Mark T., Ph.D. Prof. of History, Lyndon Baines Johnson Chair, Texas Christian Univ.

Gill, Anton, M.A. Historian, journalist, and author, *The Devil's Mariner.*

Gill, Thomas J., III, M.D. Menten Prof. of Experimental Pathology Emer., Univ. of Pittsburgh.

Gillenwater, Mack H., Ph.D. Prof. of Geography, Marshall Univ.

Gillespie, Thomas D., Ph.D., P.E. Research Prof. Emer., Univ. of Michigan, Ann Arbor.

Gillette, Robert, B.S. Former Staff Writer, Washington Bureau, *Los Angeles Times.*

Gilligan, Amy K. Editorial Writer, (Dubuque, IA) *Telegraph Herald.*

Gillingham, John, B.A., B.Phil. Prof. Emer. of History, London School of Economics and Polit. Sci.

Gillis, Chester, Ph.D. Prof. of Theology, Georgetown Univ.

Gillmor, Desmond A., Ph.D. Emer. Assoc. Prof. and Fellow, Trinity Coll., Univ. of Dublin.

Gilman, Alan David, M.D. Asst. Prof. of Medicine, Rush-Presbyterian-St. Luke's Medical Ctr.

Gilman, Rhoda M., M.A. Research Assoc., Minnesota Historical Society.

Gilmore, Jesse L., Ph.D. Former Prof. of History, Portland State Univ.

Ginter, T. N., Ph.D. Beam Delivery Physicist, Natl. Superconducting Cyclotron Laboratory.

Giometti, Carol S., Ph.D. Sr. Biochemist, Argonne Natl. Laboratory.

Girard, Philip, Ph.D. Prof., Dalhousie Law School.

Girguis, Peter R., Ph.D. Asst. Prof., Harvard Univ.

Gitelman, Zvi, Ph.D. Prof. of Political Science and Judaic Studies, Univ. of Michigan.

Gitlow, Howard Seth, Ph.D. Exec. Dir., Inst. for the Study of Quality, Univ. of Miami.

Gittleman, Arthur, Ph.D. Prof. of Mathematics and Computer Science, Calif. State Univ., Long Beach.

Givens, Beth, M.A. Dir. and Founder, Privacy Rights Clearinghouse.

Givens, David B., Ph.D. Director, Center for Nonverbal Studies.

Givens, Terryl L., Ph.D. Prof. of Lit. and Religion, Univ. of Richmond.

Glantz, Stanton A., Ph.D. Prof. of Medicine, Univ. of Calif., San Francisco.

Glaser, Dee Anna, M.D. Prof. and Vice Chairman, Dept. of Dermatology, St. Louis Univ.

Glaser, Donald A., D.Sc. Former Prof. of Physics and Neurobiology, Univ. of Calif., Berkeley; Winner of Nobel Prize in Physics, 1960.

Glazier, Stephen D., Ph.D. Professor of Anthropology, University of Nebraska.

Glendon, Mary Ann, M.Comp.L. Prof. Emer. of Law, Harvard Law School.

Glenn, Justin M., Ph.D. Former Prof. of Classics, Florida State Univ.

Glenn, Stanley L., Ph.D. Emer. Prof. of Dramatic Art, Univ. of Calif., Santa Barbara.

Glickman, Harvey, Prof. Emer. of Political Science, Haverford Coll.

Glover, Sandra J., Ph.D. Prof. Emer. of Biology, Appalachian State Univ.

Goates, Scott, B.A. Health Economics Researcher, School of Economic Sciences, Wash. State Univ.

Gocek, F. Muge, Ph.D. Assoc. Prof., Dept. of Sociology and the Program in Women's Studies, Univ. of Michigan.

Goda, Norman J. W., Ph.D. Assoc. Prof. of History, Ohio Univ.

Goddard, Peter A., D.Phil. Assoc. Prof., Dept. of History, Univ. of Guelph.

Goddard, Tara B., M.S. Ph.D. candidate, Graduate Student Researcher, Portland State University.

Godson, Roy, Ph.D. Prof. Emer. of Government, Georgetown Univ.

Godwin, Joscelyn, F.R.C.O. Prof. of Music, Colgate Univ.

Goering, Joseph, Ph.D. Prof. of History, Univ. of Toronto.

Goertzen, Valerie Woodring, Ph.D. Assoc. Prof. of Music History, Coll. of Music and Fine Arts, Loyola Univ. New Orleans.

Goetz, Alexander F. H., Ph.D. Emer. Prof. of Geological Sciences and Emer. Dir., Ctr. for the Study of Earth from Space, Univ. of Colorado.

Goetz, Thomas H., Ph.D. Prof. of French, State Univ. of New York Coll., Fredonia.

Goetzmann, William H., Ph.D. Former Prof. of History and American Studies, Univ. of Texas, Austin.

Goff, John S., J.D. Prof. Emer. of History, Phoenix Coll.

Goist, Park Dixon, Ph.D. Prof. Emer. of Theater Arts, Case Western Reserve Univ.

Goizueta, Roberto S., Ph.D. Prof. of Theology, Loyola Univ. of Chicago.

Gold, Alison Leslie, B.A. Coauthor, *Anne Frank Remembered.*

Gold, Mark S., M.D. Prof., Dept. of Psychiatry, Univ. of Florida Coll. of Medicine.

Goldberg, Alfred, Ph.D. Editor, *A History of the U.S. Air Force 1907-1957.*

Goldberg, Morton F., M.D. Prof. of Ophthalmology, Johns Hopkins School of Medicine.

Goldman, Eric F., LL.D. Former Rollins Prof. of History, Princeton Univ.

Goldman, Sheldon, Ph.D. Prof. of Political Science, University of Massachusetts, Amherst.

Goldman, Stuart D., Ph.D. Scholar in Residence, Natl. Council on Eurasian and East European Research (NCEEER).

Goldsmith, Timothy H., Ph.D. Prof. Emer. of Biology, Yale Univ.

Goldstein, Erik, Ph.D. Prof. of Intl. Relations, Boston Univ.

Goldstein, Jerome C., M.D. Exec. Vice Pres. Emer., American Academy of Otolaryngology-Head and Neck Surgery.

Goldstein, Joseph L., M.D. Prof. and Chairman, Dept. of Molecular Genetics, Univ. of Texas Southwestern Medical Ctr.

Goldstein, Malcolm, Ph.D. Prof. Emer. of English, Queens Coll., City Univ. of New York.

Golembiewski, Robert T., Ph.D. Research Prof. of Public Admin. and Management, Univ. of Georgia.

Goliber, Sue Helder, Ph.D. Prof. of History and Dist. Prof. of Teacher Dev., Mount St. Mary's Coll.

Golub, Leon, Ph.D. Sr. Astrophysicist, Harvard-Smithsonian Ctr. for Astrophysics.

Gondola, Ch. Didier, Ph.,D. Assoc. Prof. of History, Indiana Univ.

Gontrum, Peter, Ph.D. Prof. Emer. of German, Univ. of Oregon.

González, Echo Elise, B.A. Former Content Creator, World Book, Inc.

Good, Alice B. Former Dir., Arizona Dept. of Library and Archives.

Goode, Stephen, Ph.D. Sr. Writer, *Insight.*

Goodman, Alyssa A., Ph.D. Prof. of Astronomy, Harvard-Smithsonian Ctr. for Astrophysics.

Goodwin, Paul B., Jr., Ph.D. Prof. Emer., Coll. of Liberal Arts and Sciences, Univ. of Connecticut.

Gordon, Alan, Ph.D. Professor, History Department, University of Guelph.

Gordon, John W., Ph.D. Former Prof., Dept. of History, The Citadel.

Gordon, Leslie B., M.D., Ph.D. Asst. Prof. of Pediatrics Research, Brown Univ., and Medical Dir., The Progeria Research Foundation.

Gordon, Linda, Ph.D. Florence Kelley Prof. Emer. of History, Univ. of Wisconsin, Madison.

Gordon, Rich, B.A. Assoc. Prof. of Journalism, Medill School of Journalism, Northwestern Univ.

Gosner, Kevin, Ph.D. Assoc. Prof. of History, Univ. of Arizona.

Gottfried, Michael, Ph.D. Assoc. Prof., Dept. of Geological Sciences, Michigan State Univ.

Gottschalk, Stephen, Ph.D. Author, *The Emergence of Christian Science in American Religious Life.*

Goudie, Andrew S., Ph.D., D.Sc. Prof. of Geography, Oxford Univ.

Gough, Aidan R., LL.M. Former Prof. of Law, Santa Clara Univ.

Gough, Barry M., D.Lit. Prof. Emer. of History, Wilfrid Laurier Univ.

Gould, James L., Ph.D. Prof. of Ecology and Evolutionary Biology, Princeton Univ.

Gould, Lewis L., Ph.D. Prof. Emer. of History, Univ. of Texas, Austin.

Gouttierre, Thomas E., M.A. Dean Emer., Intl. Studies and Programs, Univ. of Nebraska, Omaha.

Gover, Kevin, J.D. Dir., Natl. Museum of the American Indian.

Govig, Valerie, B.A. Dir., KiteLines Bookstore, LLC.

Grabar, Oleg, Ph.D. Former Aga Khan Prof. of Islamic Art, Emer., Harvard Univ.

Grabiner, Judith V., Ph.D. Prof., Mathematics and Science, Technol., and Society, Pitzer College.

Graff, Harvey J., Ph.D. Prof., Dept. of History, Univ. of Texas, San Antonio.

Gragg, Larry, Ph.D. Prof. of History, Univ. of Missouri, Rolla.

Graham, Annette, Ph.D. Assoc. Prof., Coordinator of Food, Nutrition, and Hospitality, Ohio Univ.

Graham, Colin C., Ph.D. Pres., Compact Group, Bowen Island, British Columbia.

Graham, Larry L., Ph.D. Prof. Emer., Paper Science and Engin., Univ. of Wisconsin, Stevens Point.

Graham, Robert O., M.D. Ophthalmologist.

Graham-Campbell, James A., Ph.D. Prof. Emer. of Medieval Archaeology, Univ. Coll. London.

Granatstein, J. L., Ph.D. Professor Emeritus of History, York University.

Grant, Jonathan, Ph.D. Prof., Dept. of History, Florida State Univ.

Grant, Taran, Ph.D. Prof. of Vertebrate Systematics, Pontifical Catholic Univ. of Rio Grande do Sul.

Graves, Donald E., M.A. Managing Director, Ensign Heritage Group.

Gray, Patrick T. R., Th.D. Assoc. Prof. of Humanities, York Univ.

Graybill, John R., M.D. Prof. of Medicine, Univ. of Texas Health Science Ctr., San Antonio.

Grayson, George W., J.D. Class of 1938 Prof. of Government, Coll. of William and Mary.

Greaves, Richard L., Ph.D. Former Prof. and Chairman, Dept. of History, Florida State Univ.

Green, Charles P., B.A. Past Executive Director, Museum of Cartoon Art.

Green, David, Ph.D. Prof. Emer. of Medicine (Hematology/Oncology), Feinberg School of Medicine, Northwestern Univ.

Green, Jonathan, Ph.D. Prof. of Biology, Roosevelt Univ.

Green, Michael D., Ph.D. Prof. of American Studies and History, Univ. of North Carolina, Chapel Hill.

Green, Michael S., Ph.D. Prof. of History, Coll. of Southern Nevada.

Green, Paul J., Ph.D. Astrophysicist, Smithsonian Astrophysical Observatory.

Greenberg, Douglas, Ph.D. Vice Pres., American Council of Learned Societies.

Greenberger, Allen J., Ph.D. Professor Emeritus

of History, Pitzer College.

Greenblatt, Alan, M.A. Reporter, *Congressional Quarterly,* Washington, D.C.

Greenblatt, Stephen, Ph.D. Prof. of English, Univ. of Calif., Berkeley.

Greene, Charlotte H., Ph.D. Prof. of Physiology, Philadelphia Coll. of Osteopathic Medicine.

Greene, Jerome A., M.A. Former Historian, Natl. Park Service.

Greenfield, David W., Ph.D. Research Assoc., Dept. of Ichthyology, Calif. Academy of Sciences.

Greenfield, Eloise Author, *Paul Robeson.*

Greenfield, Richard P. H., Ph.D. Prof. and Chair, Dept. of History, Queen's Univ.

Greenspoon, Leonard J., Ph.D. Klutznick Chair in Jewish Civilization, Prof. of Theology and of Classical and Near Eastern Studies, Creighton Univ.

Greenwald, Carol S., Ph.D. Pres., Potomac Investment Company, Inc.

Greenwell, Francis M. Former Chief Taxidermist, Smithsonian Inst.

Gregory, Leonard W., B.A. Managing Editor, *Pueblo* (CO) *Chieftain.*

Gregory, Richard V., Ph.D. Prof. of Chemistry and Biochemistry, Old Dominion Univ.

Greiner, Alyson L., Ph.D. Assoc. Prof. of Geography, Oklahoma State Univ.

Grendler, Paul F., Ph.D. Prof. Emer. of History, Univ. of Toronto.

Greskovic, Robert, M.F.A. Freelance writer, *The Wall Street Journal.*

Gribben, Alan, Ph.D. Dept. Head and Dist. Research Prof., Dept. of English, Auburn Univ. Montgomery.

Grier, James W., Ph.D. Prof. Emer. of Zoology, Dept. of Biological Sci., North Dakota State Univ.

Griess, Thomas E., Ph.D. Former Prof., U.S. Military Academy, West Point; Brigadier Gen., U.S. Army, retired.

Grieve, Michael D., B.A. Managing Editor, (Thunder Bay, ON) *Times-News/Chronicle-Journal.*

Griffin, Robert B., Ph.D. Prof. Emer. of French and Comparative Lit., Univ. of Calif.

Griffis, Patrick D., M.S.E.E. Dir., Worldwide TV Standards and Strategy, Microsoft Corp.

Griffith, Clark, Ph.D. Prof. Emer. of English, Univ. of Oregon.

Griffiths, Ralph A., D.Litt. Prof. of Medieval History, Univ. of Wales, Swansea.

Griffiths, Richard E., Ph.D. Prof. of Physics, Carnegie Mellon Univ.

Griffy, Thomas A., Ph.D. Prof. Emer. of Physics, Univ. of Texas, Austin.

Grim, Pamela, M.D. Asst. Prof., Univ. of Chicago.

Grima, A. P. Lino, Ph.D. Assoc. Dir., Inst. for Environmental Studies, Univ. of Toronto.

Grimsley, Judy L. Information Resources Manager, *The Orlando* (FL) *Sentinel.*

Grodecki, Thomas S., M.A. Former Historian/Analyst, U.S. Army Ctr. of Military History.

Gronke, Paul, Ph.D. Assoc. Prof. of Political Science, Reed Coll.

Gross, Laurence F., Ph.D. Assoc. Prof., Dept. of Regional Economic and Social Dev., Univ. of Mass., Lowell.

Grossholtz, Jean, Ph.D. Prof. Emer. of Political Science, Mount Holyoke Coll.

Grossman, Gene M., Ph.D. Prof. of Intl. Economics, Princeton Univ.

Groth, Alexander J., Ph.D. Emer. Prof. of Political Science, Univ. of Calif., Davis.

Groth, Edward, III, Ph.D. Sr. Scientist, Consumers Union of United States, Inc.

Gruber, Helmut, Ph.D. Former Charles S. Baylis Prof. of History, Polytechnic Inst. of New York.

Gruenbacher, Don M., Ph.D. Associate Professor, Electrical and Computer Engineering, Kansas State University.

Gruenberg, Alan M., M.D. Prof. of Psychiatry and Human Behavior, Jefferson Medical Coll.

Grumet, Robert S., Ph.D. Anthropologist, New Hope, Pennsylvania.

Gubser, Peter, D.Phil. Pres., American Near East Refugee Aid.

Guelzo, Allen C., Ph.D. Henry R. Luce Prof. of Civil War Era Studies, Gettysburg Coll.

Guengerich, Thomas, B.A. General Manager, *Spencer County* (IN) *Journal-Democrat.*

Guentert, Kenneth, M.A. Editorial Director, Resource Publications, Inc.

Guiley, Rosemary Ellen, B.A. Author, *The Encyclopedia of Witches and Witchcraft.*

Gulley, Rosemarie C., M.A. Former Dir., Community Relations, WLS-TV, Chicago.

Gundersen, Joan R., Ph.D. Prof. Emer. of History, Calif. State Univ., San Marcos.

Gunter, Elsa L., Ph.D. Research Professor, Department of Computer Science, University of Illinois, Urbana-Champaign.

Gunzburger, Cecilia, M.A. Faculty Member, Decorative Arts and Design History Program, Smithsonian Inst. and George Washington Univ.

Gurel, Lois M., Ph.D. Former Assoc. Prof. of Clothing and Textiles, Virginia Polytechnic Inst. and State Univ.

Gurney, George, Ph.D. Deputy Chief Curator, Natl. Museum of American Art.

Gurshtein, Alexander A., D.Sc. Vice Pres. for the Commission on History of Astronomy, Intl. Astronomical Union.

Gurval, Robert, Ph.D. Prof. of Classics, Univ. of Calif., Los Angeles.

Gustafson, Bret, Ph.D. Asst. Prof. of Anthropology, Washington Univ., St. Louis.

Gustafson, Melanie S., Ph.D. Assoc. Prof. of History, Univ. of Vermont.

Gustin, Lawrence R., B.A. Manager, News Relations, Buick Motor Division; editor, *Picture History of Flint.*

Gutek, Gerald L., Ph.D. Former Prof. of Educ. and History, Loyola Univ. of Chicago.

Guthman, Julie, Ph.D. Assoc. Prof. of Community Studies, Univ. of Calif., Santa Cruz.

Gutierrez, Joseph A., Jr., M.A. Sr. Dir. for Museum Operations and Educ., Jamestown-Yorktown Foundation.

Gutnik, Martin J., M.S. Educator, Shorewood Public Schools, Wisconsin.

Guyot, James F., Ph.D. Prof. of Political Science and Public Admin., City Univ. of New York.

H

Haberman, David L., Ph.D. Prof. of Religious Studies, Indiana Univ.

Hachey, Thomas E., Ph.D. Exec. Dir., Ctr. for Irish Programs, Boston Coll.

Hackett, Perry B., Jr., Ph.D. Chief Science Officer, Discovery Genomics, Inc.

Hadler, Jeffrey, Ph.D. Associate Professor, Department of South and Southeast Asian Studies, University of California, Berkeley.

Hadow, Harlo H., Ph.D. Prof. of Biology, Coe Coll.

Haefeli, Evan, Ph.D. Associate Professor of History, Texas A&M University.

Haenlein, Joy L., M.S.J. Independent Writing and Editing Professional.

Hafner, James A., Ph.D. Prof., Geosciences, Morrill Science Ctr., Univ. of Mass.

Hagan, Kenneth J., Ph.D. Prof. Emer. of History, U.S. Naval Academy, Annapolis.

Hagedorn, John M., Ph.D. Assoc. Prof. of Criminal Justice, Univ. of Illinois, Chicago.

Hageman, Jon B., Ph.D. Assoc. Prof., Dept. of Anthropology, Northeastern Illinois Univ.

Hagen, Charles, M.F.A. Critic, *The New York Times.*

Hahn, H. George, Ph.D. Prof. of English, Towson Univ.

Hahn, Richard L., Ph.D. Sr. Chemist and Leader of Solar Neutrino Group, Chemistry Dept., Brookhaven Natl. Laboratory.

Hahn, Walther L., Ph.D. Prof. Emer. of German, Univ. of Oregon.

Haider-Markel, Donald P., Ph.D. Prof., Dept. of Political Science, Univ. of Kansas.

Haigler, Candace, Ph.D. Prof. of Crop Science and Plant Biology, North Carolina State Univ.

Haj, Samira, Ph.D. Prof. of History, Coll. of Staten Island Grad. Ctr., City Univ. of New York.

Halbert, Debora, Ph.D. Associate Prof. of Political Science, Univ. of Hawaii.

Halder, Rebat M., M.D. Prof., Chairman, Dept. of Dermatology, Howard Univ. Coll. of Medicine.

Halikowski Smith, Stefan, Ph.D. Lecturer in History, Univ. of Wales, Swansea.

Hall, Greg, Ph.D. Associate Professor of History,

Western Illinois University.

Hall-Milhouse, Virginia, Ph.D. Assoc. Prof., Dept. of Human Relations, Univ. of Oklahoma.

Haller, Gary L., Ph.D. Prof. of Chemical Engineering, Yale Univ.

Hallett, Judith P., Ph.D. Professor Emerita, Dept. of Classics, University of Maryland, College Park.

Hallett, Richard W., Ph.D. Prof. of Linguistics, Northeastern Illinois Univ.

Hallin, Gustav W., M.D. Former Asst. Prof. of Medicine, Univ. of New Mexico.

Hallion, Richard P., Ph.D. Air Force Historian, Bolling Air Force Base, Washington, D.C.

Hallman, Joseph M., Ph.D. Prof. Emer. of Theology, Univ. of St. Thomas.

Halman, Hugh Talat, Ph.D. Asst. Prof. of Religion, Central Michigan Univ.

Halper, Donna L., Ph.D. Author, *Icons of Talk: The Media Mouths That Changed America.*

Halpern, Bruce P., Ph.D. Prof. of Psychology and Prof. of Neurobiology and Behavior, Cornell Univ.

Halstead, Lois Kazmier, Ph.D., R.N. Vice-Provost and Vice Pres., Univ. Affairs, Rush Univ.

Halverson, Guy, M.A. Former New York Correspondent, *The Christian Science Monitor.*

Hamalainen, Pekka Kalevi, Ph.D. Prof. Emer. of History, Chair of the Western European Area Studies Program, Univ. of Wisconsin, Madison.

Hamby, Alonzo L., Ph.D. Prof. of Hist., Ohio Univ.

Hamel, Chouki El, Ph.D. Assoc. Prof. of History, Arizona State Univ.

Hames, Willis, Ph.D. Prof., Dept. of Geology and Geography, Auburn Univ.

Hamilton, Charles V., Ph.D. Former Wallace S. Sayre Prof. of Political Science, Columbia Univ.; author, *The Black Experience in American Politics.*

Hamilton, John, Ph.D. Assoc. Prof. of Classics, Coll. of the Holy Cross.

Hamilton, Phillip, Ph.D. Assoc. Prof. of History, Christopher Newport Univ.

Hamlin, Christine, Ph.D. Dissertator, Dept. of Anthropology, Univ. of Wisconsin, Milwaukee.

Hamre, Melvin L., Ph.D. Former Prof. of Animal Science, Univ. of Minnesota, Twin Cities Campus.

Han, MeiLan K., M.D. Asst. Prof. of Internal Medicine, Univ. of Michigan Health Ctr., Ann Arbor.

Hanauer, Stephen B., M.D. Prof. of Medicine, University of Chicago.

Hancock, Joseph G., Ph.D. Prof. Emer. of Plant Pathology, Univ. of Calif., Berkeley.

Hancock, M. Donald, Ph.D. Prof. of Political Science, Vanderbilt Univ.

Handelman, Howard, Ph.D. Prof. Emer. of Political Science, Univ. of Wisconsin, Milwaukee.

Handler, Arden S., Ph.D. Prof., Community Health Sciences, School of Public Health, Univ. of Illinois, Chicago.

Hanes, Jeffrey E., Ph.D. Assoc. Prof. of History, Univ. of Oregon.

Hankins, James, Ph.D. Prof. of History, Harvard Univ.

Hanks, Reuel, Ph.D. Prof. of Geography, Oklahoma State Univ.

Hanley, Anne G., Ph.D. Assoc. Prof. of History, Northern Illinois Univ.

Hanlon, David, Ph.D. Prof. of History, Univ. of Hawaii, Honolulu.

Hanna, Jack, B.A. Dir. Emer., Columbus Zoo and Aquarium.

Hannigan, James E., B.A.E. Former Sr. Staff Engineer, Eagle Technical Services, Inc.

Hansen, Ellen R., Ph.D. Assoc. Prof. of Geography, Dept. of Social Sciences, Emporia State Univ.

Hansen, James R., Ph.D. Alumni Prof./Historian for Natl. Aeronautics and Space Admin., Auburn Univ.

Hansen, Katherine, Ph.D. Prof. Emer. of Geography, Montana State Univ.

Hansen, William F., Ph.D. Prof. Emer. of Classical Studies and Folklore, Indiana Univ.

Hansma, Paul, Ph.D. Prof. of Physics, Univ. of Calif., Santa Barbara.

Hanson, Jarice, Ph.D. Prof., Dept. of Communication, Univ. of Mass., Amherst.

Hanson, Stephen E., Ph.D. Professor of Political Science, University of Washington.

Hapeman, Cathleen J., Ph.D. Research Chemist, Agriculture Research Service, U.S. Department of

Agriculture.

Harb, Imad K., Ph.D. Director of Research and Analysis, Arab Center Washington DC.

Hardcastle, David P., Ph.D. Writer and historian.

Harden, Lydia Dixon, B.S. Former Managing Editor, *Music City News.*

Hardin, Marie, Ph.D. Asst. Prof. of Communications, Pennsylvania State Univ.

Hardin-Jones, Mary, Ph.D. Prof., Craniofacial Disorders and Child Phonology, Univ. of Wyoming.

Harding, Cary O., M.D. Assoc. Prof. of Molecular and Medical Genetics, Oregon Health & Science Univ.

Hardy, Grant, Ph.D. Prof. of History and Religious Studies, Univ. of North Carolina, Asheville.

Hargis, B. M., Ph.D. Prof. and Dir., Poultry Health Research Lab., Ctr. of Excellence for Poultry Science, Univ. of Arkansas, Fayetteville.

Harik, Elsa Marston, M.S. Writer.

Harik, Iliya, Ph.D. Former Prof. of Political Science, Indiana Univ.

Harman, W. Dean, Ph.D. Prof. of Chemistry, Univ. of Virginia.

Harmon, Daniel P., Ph.D. Prof. Emer. of Classics, Univ. of Washington.

Harmon, Pat Former Curator-Historian, Coll. Football Hall of Fame.

Harmon, William, Ph.D. Prof. of Humanities, Univ. of North Carolina.

Harper, Craig, B.S.J. Former News Editor, *News/North,* Yellow Knife, NT.

Harper, Kimball T., Ph.D. Scholar in Residence, Plant Systematics and Natural Resource Management, Utah Valley State Coll.

Harran, Marilyn J., Ph.D. Prof. of History and Religious Studies, Stern Prof. of Holocaust Educ., Chapman Univ.

Harries, Keith D., Ph.D. Contributing author, *The Geography of Oklahoma.*

Harrington, John A., Jr., Ph.D. Prof., Dept. of Geography, Kansas State Univ.

Harris, Alan A., M.D. Hospital Epidemiologist, Prof., Asst. Chairman of Internal Medicine, Rush-Presbyterian-St. Luke's Medical Ctr., Chicago.

Harris, Anthony D., M.D. Assoc. Prof., Epidemiology and Preventive Medicine, Univ. of Maryland.

Harris, Jessica B., Ph.D. Prof., Dept. of English, Queens Coll., City Univ. of New York.

Harris, Michael H., Ph.D. Prof. Emer. of Library Science, Univ. of Kentucky.

Harris, Michael W., B.A. Assistant Editor, *Houseboat* magazine.

Harris, Neil, Ph.D. Prof. Emer. of History, Univ. of Chicago.

Harrison, Frederick W., Ph.D. Prof. Emer. of Biology, Western Carolina Univ.

Harrison, Gregory B., B.A.J. Vice Pres., Communications, American Motorcyclist Assoc.

Harrison, Timothy P., Ph.D. Prof. of Near Eastern Archaeology, Univ. of Toronto.

Harrod, William M., M.S. Sr. Editor, World Book, Inc.

Harrysson, Ola L. A., Ph.D. Assoc. Professor, Department of Industrial and Systems Engineering, North Carolina State University.

Harss, Marina, M.A. Freelance journalist specializing in dance.

Hart, Lynn W., Ph.D. Physicist, Principal Staff, Johns Hopkins Univ. Applied Physics Laboratory.

Hart, Paul, Ph.D. Assoc. Prof., Dept. of History, Texas State. Univ., San Marcos.

Hartl, Daniel L., Ph.D. Higgins Prof. of Biology, Harvard Univ.

Hartlein, Richard A., M.S.M.E. Program Manager, Underground Systems, Natl. Electric Energy Testing Research and Applications Ctr., Georgia Inst. of Technology.

Hartman, Ann, D.S.W. Dean Emer., Smith Coll. School for Social Work.

Hartman, J. P., Ph.D. Former Prof. of Engineering, Univ. of Central Florida, Orlando.

Hartman, Marvis E., Ph.D. Dir., Automotive Technologies Europe, PPG Industries.

Hartman, Mary S., Ph.D. Dir., Inst. for Women's Leadership, Rutgers, the State Univ. of New Jersey; author, *Victorian Murderesses.*

Hartwick, Brian, Ph.D. Assoc. Prof. of Biological Sciences, Simon Fraser Univ.

Harvey, Neil F., Ph.D.   Assoc. Prof., Dept. of Government, New Mexico State Univ.

Harvey, Maurice, B.A.   Air Commodore, Royal Air Force, retired; author, *Gibraltar.*

Harvey, Robert R., M.L.A.   Prof. Emer. of Landscape Architecture, Iowa State Univ.

Harvey, Thomas, Ph.D.   Prof., Dept. of Geography, Portland State Univ.

Hasan, Zoya, Ph.D.   Prof., Centre for Political Studies, School of Social Sciences, Jawaharlal Nehru Univ.

Haselkorn, Robert, Ph.D.   F. L. Pritzker Dist. Service Prof. of Molecular Genetics and Cell Biology, Univ. of Chicago.

Haskett, James P., Former Managing Editor, *Lethbridge* (AB) *Herald.*

Hassler, Kevin, B.A.   Assoc. Editor, *Enid* (OK) *News & Eagle.*

Hastings, Harold M., Ph.D.   Chair and Prof., Dept. of Physics and Astronomy, Hofstra Univ.

Hatch, Ronald B., Ph.D.   Associate Professor Emeritus of English, Univ. of British Columbia.

Hattendorf, John B., D. Phil.   Ernest J. King Prof. of Maritime History and Chairman, Maritime History Dept., Naval War Coll.

Hatzenbuehler, Ronald L., Ph.D.   Prof. of History, Idaho State Univ.

Haugland, H. Kristina, M.A.   Assoc. Curator, Costume and Textiles, Philadelphia Museum of Art.

Hauser, Richard J., Ph.D.   Prof. of Theology, Creighton Univ.

Haveman, Robert H., Ph.D.   Prof. Emer. of Economics, Univ. of Wisconsin, Madison.

Havens, Murray Clark, Ph.D.   Prof. Emer. of Political Science, Texas Tech Univ.

Haverdink, William H., M.S.E.M.   Staff Research Engineer, General Motors Research Laboratories.

Haverstock, Nathan A., A.B.   Affiliate Scholar, Oberlin Coll.

Hawks, John, Ph.D.   Professor, Department of Anthropology, University of Wisconsin, Madison.

Hay, John, Ph.D.   Assistant Professor of English, University of Nevada, Las Vegas.

Haycox, Stephen, Ph.D.   Prof. of History, Univ. of Alaska, Anchorage.

Hayes, Denis, J.D.   Pres. and CEO, Bullitt Foundation.

Hayes, Mary Eshbaugh, B.A.   Contributing Editor and Columnist, *The Aspen* (CO) *Times.*

Haymer, David S., Ph.D.   Professor, Department of Cell and Molecular Biology, Univ. of Hawaii.

Haynes, Allyson W., J.D.   Assoc. Prof. of Law, Charleston School of Law.

Haynes, Sam W., Ph.D.   Assoc. Prof. of History, Univ. of Texas, Arlington.

Hayward, Jane, Ph.D.   Former Curator, Cloisters, Metropolitan Museum of Art, New York City.

Hayward, Jason P., Ph.D.   Assoc. Prof., Dept. of Nuclear Engineering, The Univ. of Tennessee.

Hazel, Fred, B.A.   Editor Emer. and Columnist, New Brunswick Publishing, St. John.

Heard, Andrew D., Ph.D.   Professor, Department of Political Science, Simon Fraser University.

Hearn, M. F., Ph.D.   Prof. of Fine Arts and Dir. of Architectural Studies, Univ. of Pittsburgh.

Heath, James Edward, Ph.D.   Prof. Emer. of Physiology and Biophysics, Univ. of Illinois.

Heckel, Waldemar, Ph.D.   Prof. of Greek and Roman Studies, Univ. of Calgary.

Heckman, Timothy M., Ph.D.   Prof. of Physics and Astronomy, Johns Hopkins Univ.

Hedquist, Valerie Lind, Ph.D.   Professor of Art, University of Montana.

Hedrick, Philip W., Ph.D.   Ullman Prof. of Biology, Arizona State Univ.

Heelis, Roderick A., Ph.D.   Professor and Director, Hanson Center for Space Sciences.

Hehr, John G., Ph.D.   Prof. of Geography, Univ. of Arkansas, Fayetteville.

Heidenreich, Conrad E., Ph.D.   Prof. Emer. of Geography, York Univ.

Heidt, Gary A., Ph.D.   Prof. and Chair, Dept. of Biology, Univ. of Arkansas, Little Rock.

Heilbrun, Margaret, M.L.S., M.A.   Former Vice Pres., Library Services, New-York Historical Society.

Heinrich, Bernd, Ph.D.   Prof. Emer. of Biology, Univ. of Vermont.

Heister, Stephen, Ph.D.   Prof. of Aeronautics and Astronautics, Purdue Univ.

Heithaus, Michael R., Ph.D.   Dir., School of Environment and Society, Florida Intl. Univ.

Heitmann, John A., Ph.D.   Prof. of History, Univ. of Dayton.

Helfrick, Albert, Ph.D.   Prof., Aeronautical Science Dept., Embry-Riddle Aeronautical Univ.

Hellen, J. A., D.Phil.   Sr. Lecturer, Dept. of Geography, Univ. of Newcastle upon Tyne.

Hellickson, Martin L., Ph.D.   Prof. Emer., Dept. of Biological and Ecological Engineering, Oregon State Univ.

Hellinger, Daniel C., Ph.D.   Prof. of Political Science, Webster Univ.

Helm, Rebecca R., B.S.   Grad. Student, Brown Univ.

Helmer, William J., M.A.   Sr. Editor, *Playboy.*

Helms, Christine Moss, D.Phil.   Author, *Cohesion of Saudi Arabia: Evolution of Political Identity* and *Iraq: Eastern Flank of the Arab World.*

Helms, Joseph M., M.D.   Founding Pres., American Academy of Medical Acupuncture, and Pres., Helms Medical Inst.

Helms, Ronald N., Ph.D.   Prof. of Architectural Engineering, North Carolina Agricultural and Technical State Univ.; lighting consultant; expert witness.

Helper, Mark A., Ph.D.   Dist. Sr. Lecturer, Univ. of Texas, Austin.

Hemingway, Sam   News Columnist, *Burlington* (VT) *Free Press*

Hemley, Robin., M.F.A.   Director of Writing Programme, Prof. of Humanities, Yale-NUS College.

Henderson, David E., Ph.D.   Prof. of Chemistry, Trinity Coll.

Henderson, Karla A., Ph.D.   Professor Emeritus, Department of Parks, Recreation & Tourism Management, North Carolina State University.

Hendricks, Lewis T., Ph.D.   Former Prof. and Extension Specialist, Forest Products, Univ. of Minnesota, Twin Cities Campus.

Hendrickson, Chris, Ph.D.   Prof. of Civil and Environmental Engineering, Carnegie Mellon Univ.

Hendrix, Amanda R., Ph.D.   Research Scientist, Jet Propulsion Lab., Calif. Inst. of Technology.

Hoving, Henk-Jan, Ph.D.   Postdoctoral Fellow, Monterey Bay Aquarium Research Institute.

Henneman, John Bell, Ph.D.   Former History Bibliographer, Princeton Univ.

Hennessey, William J., Ph.D.   Dir., Chrysler Museum of Art.

Henning, Basil D., Ph.D.   Coauthor, *Crises in English History, 1066-1945.*

Henning, C. Randall, Ph.D.   Research Associate, Institute for International Economics.

Henry, Edward O., Ph.D.   Prof. Emer. of Anthropology, San Diego State Univ.

Henry, Richard W., Ph.D.   Prof. Emer. of Physics, Bucknell Univ.

Hentoff, Nat, B.A.   Former Columnist, *Washington Post* and *Village Voice.*

Hepner, George F., Ph.D.   Prof. of Geography, Univ. of Utah.

Hermalyn, Gary D., Ed.D.   Exec. Dir., Bronx County Historical Society; Editor of the Bicentennial of the United States Constitution Series.

Herman, Daniel, Ph.D.   Professor, Department of History, Central Washington University.

Hermann, William J., Jr., M.D.   Dir., Clinical Laboratories, Memorial Hospital-Memorial City.

Herndon, Christopher M., Pharm.D.   Asst. Prof., Southern Illinois Univ. Edwardsville School of Pharmacy.

Hernon, Joseph Martin, Jr., Ph.D.   Former Prof. of History, Univ. of Mass., Amherst.

Herr, Edwin L., Ed.D.   Dist. Prof. Emer. of Educ. and Assoc. Dean Emer., Pennsylvania State Univ.

Herrero-Olaizola, Alejandro, Ph.D.   Arthur F. Thurnau Professor of Spanish, Univ. of Michigan.

Herring, George C., Ph.D.   Prof. of History, Univ. of Kentucky.

Herron, Ron, A.B.J.   Opinion Editor, (Frankfort, KY) *State Journal.*

Hersey, G. L., Ph.D.   Former Prof. of the History of Art, Yale Univ.

Hershberg, Theodore, Ph.D.   Dir., Ctr. for Greater Philadelphia; Prof. of Public Policy and History, Univ. of Pennsylvania.

Hertsgaard, Doris F., Ph.D.   Director of Research, D H Research.

Herzstein, R. E., Ph.D.   Carolina Dist. Prof. of History, Univ. of South Carolina.

Hess, Andrew C., Ph.D.   Prof. of Diplomacy, Fletcher School of Law and Diplomacy, Tufts Univ.

Hess, David F., Ph.D.   Prof. Emer. of Geology, Western Illinois Univ.

Hesse, Mark B., M.A.   Treasurer, Rocky Mountain Field Inst.

Hester, Thomas R., Ph.D.   Prof. Emer. of Anthropology, Univ. of Texas, Austin.

Heupel, Michelle R., Ph.D.   Principal Research Fellow, School of Earth and Environmental Sciences, James Cook Univ., Australia.

Heymsfield, Andrew, Ph.D.   Sr. Scientist and Section Head, Natl. Ctr. for Atmospheric Research.

Heyl, Jeremy S., Ph.D.   Assoc. Prof. of Physics and Astronomy, Univ. of British Columbia.

Hickey, Donald R., Ph.D.   Prof. of History, Wayne State Coll.

Hickey, Eric W., Ph.D.   Criminologist, Walden University.

Hicks, Joyce E., M.A.   Director, Writing Center, Valparaiso Univ.

Higgins, Lynn A., Ph.D.   Prof. of French and Comparative Lit., Dartmouth Coll.

Hildebrand, Kurtis R., B.A.   Columnist, *Nevada Appeal.*

Hildebrandt, Jack, Ph.D.   Prof. of Physiology, Biophysics and Medicine, Univ. of Washington.

Hildesley, C. Hugh   Exec. Vice Pres., Sotheby's.

Hill, David T., Ph.D.   Prof. of Southeast Asian Studies, School of Social Sciences and Humanities, Murdoch Univ.

Hill, Fiona, Ph.D.   Sr. Fellow, Foreign Policy Studies Program, Brookings Inst.

Hill, James A., M.D.   Prof. of Clinical Orthopedic Surgery, Northwestern Univ. Medical School.

Hill, James E., Ph.D.   Chief, Building Environment Division, Natl. Inst. of Standards and Technology.

Hillard, Darla   Educ. Dir., Snow Leopard Conservancy.

Hillary, Sir Edmund P., LL.D.   First climber to reach the summit of Mount Everest; author, *High Adventure.*

Hilt, Richard L., Ph.D.   Prof. of Physics, Colorado Coll.

Hindman, Sandra L., Ph.D.   Prof. Emer. of Art History, Northwestern Univ.

Hinduja, Sameer, Ph.D.   Assoc. Prof. of Criminology and Criminal Justice, Florida Atlantic Univ.

Hing, Margaret Ng Thow, J.D.   Patent Manager, La Jolla Institute for Allergy and Immunology.

Hinman, Alan R., M.P.H.   Director, National Center for Prevention Services, Centers for Disease Control and Prevention.

Hirsch, Edward, Ph.D.   Prof. of English, Univ. of Houston.

Hirsch, Rick, B.S.   Managing Editor, *The Miami* (FL) *Herald.*

Hirsch, Robert, M.F.A.   Exec. Dir., Light Research.

Hirschhorn, Joel S., Ph.D.   Pres., Hirschhorn and Assoc.

Hirshman, Carol A., M.D.   Prof. of Anesthesiology and Pharmacology and Vice Chair for Research, Columbia Univ. Coll. of Physicians and Surgeons.

Hirsley, Michael,   Former boxing writer, *Chicago Tribune;* Member, Boxing Writers Assoc. of America.

Hiskey, Jonathan T., Ph.D.   Assoc. Prof. of Political Science, Vanderbilt Univ.

Hitchcock, Bert, Ph.D.   Former Hargis Prof. of American Lit., Auburn Univ.

Hitchman, Matthew H., Ph.D.   Professor, Department of Atmospheric and Oceanic Sciences, University of Wisconsin, Madison.

Hixon, Mark A., Ph.D.   Prof., Dept. of Zoology, Oregon State Univ.

Hobbs, Ray D., B.A.   Former Deputy Managing Editor, (Little Rock) *Arkansas Democrat-Gazette.*

Hobbs, Richard R., M.S.A.   Physics Teacher, Anne Arundel City (MD) Schools; author, *Marine Navigation.*

Hobson, Burton H., B.A.   EDP Manager, Sterling Publishing Company.

Hochfelder, David, Ph.D.   Asst. Prof., Dept. of History, State Univ. of New York at Albany.

Hocutt, Charles H., Ph.D. Ichthyologist, Ctr. for Environmental and Estuarine Studies, Univ. of Maryland.

Hodges, Paul D., Ph.D. Sessional Lecturer, Birkbeck Coll., Univ. of London.

Hodgetts, Richard M., Ph.D. Former Prof., Florida Intl. Univ.

Hodgkin, Georgia E., Ed.D. Prof., Nutrition and Dietetics, Loma Linda Univ.

Hodierne, Robert, B.A. Assoc. Prof. of Journalism, Univ. of Richmond.

Hoerr, David M., M.S. Lecturer, Engineering Mechanics, Univ. of Wisconsin, Madison.

Hoffman, Cyrus M., Ph.D. Adjunct Prof. of Physics, Los Alamos Natl. Laboratory.

Hoffman, M. Peter, Ph.D. Prof. of Animal Science, Iowa State Univ.

Hoffmann, Peter, Ph.D. Fellow of the Royal Society of Canada; Prof. of History, McGill Univ.

Hoffmann, Richard J., Ph.D. Assoc. Vice Pres., Academic Affairs & Research, Univ. of Nebraska.

Hoffmeister, Werner, Ph.D. Prof. of German and Comparative Lit., Dartmouth Coll.

Hogan, David Gerard, D.A. Prof. of History, Heidelberg Univ.

Hogan, Edward Patrick, Sr., Ph.D. Former Assoc. Vice Pres. for Academic Affairs and Chief Information Technology Officer, South Dakota State Univ.; State Geographer for South Dakota.

Hogg, R., Ph.D. Prof. Emer. of Mineral Processing and Geo-Environmental Eng., Penn. State Univ.

Holden, Heather, Ph.D. Asst. Prof., Dept. of Geography, Natl. Univ. of Singapore.

Holland, James C., Ph.D. Prof. Emer. of History, Shepherd Coll.

Hollander, Inez, Ph.D. Lecturer on Dutch Studies, Univ. of Calif., Berkeley.

Höllerer, Tobias, Ph.D. Professor, Computer Science Dept., University of California, Santa Barbara.

Hollingsworth, D. Keith, Ph.D. Prof., Dept. of Mechanical and Aerospace Engineering, Univ. of Alabama, Huntsville.

Hollister, C. Warren Former Prof. of History, Univ. of Calif., Santa Barbara.

Holloway, C. M. Journalist.

Holmes, Kim R., Ph.D. Asst. Secretary, Bureau of Intl. Organization Affairs, U.S. Dept. of State.

Holscher, Louis M., Ph.D. Prof., Mexican American Studies, San Jose State Univ.

Holt, Michael F., Ph.D. Prof. of History, Univ. of Virginia.

Holtzman, Neil A., M.D., M.P.H. Emer. Prof. of Pediatrics, Johns Hopkins Univ.

Holzer, Harold, B.A. Co-Chair, U.S. Lincoln Bicentennial Commission, Metropolitan Museum of Art.

Honig, Donald Novelist and baseball historian.

Honychurch, Lennox, D.Phil. Staff Tutor, Univ. of the West Indies, School of Continuing Studies; Curator, The Dominica Museum, Roseau.

Hood, Leroy, Ph.D. Pres., Inst. for Systems Biology, Seattle.

Hoogland, John L., Ph.D. Prof. of Biology, Univ. of Maryland.

Hoop, Jinger Gail, M.D., M.F.A. Former Asst. Prof., Asst. Dir., Empirical Ethics Group, Dept. of Psychiatry and Behavioral Medicine, Medical Coll. of Wisconsin.

Hooper-Bui, Linda M., Ph.D. Assoc. Prof., Dept. of Entomology, Louisiana State Univ.

Hooper, Dan, Ph.D. Assoc. Scientist, Theoretical Astrophysics Group, Fermi Natl. Accelerator Lab.

Hooper, Monica Webb, Ph.D. Assoc. Prof., Dept. of Psychology, Univ. of Miami.

Hopkins, Benjamin D., Ph.D. Assoc. Prof. of History and Intl. Affairs, The George Washington Univ.

Hopkins, Richard J., Ph.D. Former Assoc. Prof. of History, Ohio State Univ.

Hopper, Jennifer, Ph.D. Assistant Prof. of Political Science, Southern Connecticut State University.

Hordon, Robert M., Ph.D. Prof. Emer. of Geography, Rutgers, the State Univ. of New Jersey.

Horita, Robert E., Ph.D. Prof. Emer. of Physics, Univ. of Victoria.

Horle, Craig W., Ph.D. Chief editor, *Lawmaking and Legislators in Pennsylvania: A Biographical Dictionary.*

Horn, André, D.Phil. Assoc. Prof., Dept. of Geography, Geoinformatics and Meteorology, Univ. of Pretoria.

Horn, James, Ph.D. Vice Pres. of Research, Colonial Williamsburg Foundation.

Hornsby, Alton, Jr., Ph.D. Fuller E. Callaway Prof. of History, Morehouse Coll.

Horowitz, Leonard M., Ph.D. Prof. Emer. of Psychology, Stanford Univ.

Horsman, Reginald, Ph.D. Dist. Prof. Emer. of History, Univ. of Wisconsin, Milwaukee.

Horswill, Catharine, M.S. Ph.D. student, British Antarctic Survey.

Horwath, William R., Ph.D. Prof., Dept. of Land, Air and Water Resources, Univ. of Calif., Davis.

Horwitz, Barbara A., Ph.D. Prof. and Vice Provost, Academic Personnel, Univ. of Calif., Davis.

Hose, Louise D., Ph.D. Environmental Studies Program Dir., Westminster Coll.

Hoskote, Ranjit, M.A. Art Critic and Asst. Editor, *The Times of India.*

Hothersall, David, Ph.D. Prof. Emer. of Psychology, Ohio State Univ., Columbus.

Houghton, David D., Ph.D. Prof. Emer. of Atmospheric and Oceanic Sciences, Univ. of Wisconsin, Madison.

Houghton, Desmond Asst. Editor and Columnist, *The* (Brisbane, Australia) *Courier-Mail.*

Houston, Steve Customer Service Representative, White's Electronics, Inc.

Hovi, Michael A., B.S., L.M.T., N.C.T.M.B. Program Dir./Core Instructor, The Soma Inst.

Howard, Don, Ph.D. Prof., Dept. of Philosophy, Univ. of Notre Dame.

Howe, Daniel Walker, Ph.D. Rhodes Prof. Emer. of American History, Oxford Univ.

Howe, Russell Warren, License-ès-lettres. Former writer.

Howell, David L., Ph.D. Assoc. Prof. of East Asian Studies, Princeton Univ.

Howell, Roger, Jr., D.Phil. Former Prof. of History, Bowdoin Coll.

Howse, Robert, B.A. Editor in Chief, *The Halifax* (NS) *Chronicle-Herald.*

Hoyt, Reginald A., Sr. Vice Pres., Conservation and Science, Philadelphia Zoo.

Hoyt, Robert D., Ph.D. Prof. of Biology, Western Kentucky Univ.

Hoyt, Robert S., Ph.D. Author, *Europe in the Middle Ages.*

Hubbell, John T., Ph.D. Dir. Emer., Kent State Univ. Press.

Huddleston, Ellis W., Ph.D. Prof. Emer. of Entomology, New Mexico State Univ.

Hudecki, Michael S., D.Sc. Exec. Officer, Biological Sciences, State Univ. of New York, Buffalo.

Hudson, Charles, Ph.D. Prof. Emer. of Anthropology, Univ. of Georgia.

Hudson, John C., B.Sc. Former Regional Manager, Land Transportation, Public Works Canada.

Hudson, Michael C., Ph.D. Professor of International Relations and Arab Studies, Center for Contemporary Arab Studies, Georgetown University.

Huegele, Vinson B., M.S. Education Chairman, National Association of Rocketry.

Huey, Raymond B., Ph.D. Prof. of Zoology, and Chair, Dept. of Biology, Univ. of Washington.

Hufbauer, Gary, Ph.D. Reginald Jones Sr. Fellow, Inst. for Intl. Economics.

Hufbauer, Karl, Ph.D. Prof. Emer. of History, Univ. of Calif., Irvine.

Huff, Jerome J., Jr., B.A. Managing Editor, (Fort Smith, AR) *Southwest Times Record.*

Huff-Lonergan, Elisabeth, Ph.D. Prof., Dept. of Animal Science, Iowa State Univ.

Huffines, Marion Lois, Ph.D. Assoc. Vice Pres., Academic Affairs, Bucknell Univ.

Huffman, Carl A., Ph.D. Prof. of Classics, DePauw Univ.

Hughes, George R., M.S. Former Vegetable Crops Specialist and Specialist-in-Charge, Dept. of Horticulture Science, North Carolina State Univ.

Hughes, Robert M. Exec. Producer, Carr-Hughes Productions.

Hughes, Steven C., Ph.D. Prof. of History, Loyola Coll., Maryland.

Hughes, Terence, Ph.D. Dir., Centre for Coral Reef Biodiversity, School of Marine Biology, James Cook Univ.

Hummer, Robert A., Ph.D. Prof. and Chairperson, Dept. of Sociology, Univ. of Texas at Austin.

Humphreys, Ashlee, Ph.D. Asst. Prof., Medill School of Journalism, Northwestern Univ.

Hundy, Guy F., Ph.D. Technical consultant; former President, Institute of Refrigeration.

Hunkins, Francis P., Ph.D. Prof. Emer. of Educ., Curriculum, Social Studies, Univ. of Washington.

Hunner, Jon, Ph.D. Prof., Dept. of History, New Mexico State Univ.

Hunt, George L., Jr., Ph.D. Research Prof., Aquatic & Fishery Sciences, Univ. of Washington.

Hunt, Lester H., Ph.D. Prof. of Philosophy, Univ. of Wisconsin, Madison.

Hunt, Melody J., Ph.D. Sr. Environmental Scientist, Coastal Ecosystems Division, South Florida Water Management District.

Hunt, William R., Ph.D. J.D. Author, *Arctic Passage* and *To Stand at the Pole.*

Hunter, Albert, Ph.D. Prof. of Sociology, Northwestern Univ.

Hunter, Kathy Pres. and Founder, Intl. Rett Syndrome Assoc.

Hunter, O. Frank, M.S. Prof. Emer., Clemson Univ. School of Textiles, Fiber and Polymer Science.

Hunter, Rob Coauthor, *The Book of Knots.*

Hunter, William D. G. Emer. Prof. of Economics, McMaster Univ.

Hurst, Michael Emer. Fellow in Modern History and Politics, St. John's Coll., Oxford Univ.

Hurt, R. Douglas, Ph.D. Prof. of History, Purdue Univ.

Hurtado, W. Jean, M.A. Editor, HarperCollins Publishers.

Huse, Nancy Lyman, Ph.D. Prof. of English, Augustana Coll.

Huseboe, Arthur R., D.H.L. Exec. Dir., Ctr. for Western Studies, Augustana Coll.

Hussin, Nordin, Ph.D. Assoc. Prof., Dept. of History, Universiti Kebangsaan Malaysia.

Hustrulid, William, Ph.D. Prof. Emer., Mining Engineering Univ. of Utah.

Hutchinson, Dennis J., LL.M. William Rainey Harper Professor and Senior Lecturer in Law, University of Chicago.

Hutchison, Jane Campbell, Ph.D. Prof. of Art History, Univ. of Wisconsin, Madison.

Hutjens, Michael F., Ph.D. Prof. of Animal Sciences and Extension Dairy Specialist, Univ. of Illinois, Urbana-Champaign.

Hutson, James H., Ph.D. Chief, Manuscript Division, Library of Congress.

Hutyra, Lucy R., Ph.D. Asst. Prof., Dept. of Geography and Environment, Boston Univ.

Hvenegaard, Glen T., Ph.D. Prof. of Geography and Environmental Studies, Univ. of Alberta.

Hyatt, James A., Ph.D. Prof., Environmental Earth Science, Eastern Connecticut State Univ.

Hyland, Douglas K. S., Ph.D. Dir., San Antonio Museum of Art.

I

Ibbotson, Roger G., Ph.D. Prof. in the Practice of Finance, Yale School of Management.

Ifkovic, John W., Ph.D. Prof. of History, Westfield State Coll.

Ihde, Don, Ph.D. Prof. of Philosophy, State Univ. of New York, Stony Brook.

Ihler, Garret M., M.D. Prof. Emer. of Medical Biochemistry and Medical Genetics, Texas A&M Coll. of Medicine.

Ikeda, Tom, M.B.A. Exec. Dir., Densho: Japanese American Legacy Project.

Ikram, Salima, Ph.D. Professor of Egyptology, American University in Cairo.

Ilyin, Mary Alexander, B.S.M.E. Mechanical Engineer, Pacific Gas and Electric Company.

Imbelli, Robert P., Ph.D. Assoc. Prof. Emer. of Theology, Boston Coll.

Ingalls, Robert P., Ph.D. Prof. of History, Univ. of South Florida.

Ingersoll, Andrew P., Ph.D. Prof. of Planetary Science, Calif. Inst. of Technology.

Ingham, John N., Ph.D. Professor Emeritus of History, University of Toronto.

Inglesby, Thomas V., M.D. Director, Center for Health Security, Johns Hopkins Bloomberg School of Public Health.

Ingrao, Charles W., Ph.D. Professor Emeritus of History, Purdue University.

Inrig, Stephen, Ph.D. Asst. Prof., Dept. of Clinical Sciences, The Univ. of Texas Southwestern Medical Center.

Ingwersen, Niels, Cand. Mag. Prof. Emer. of Scandinavian Studies, Univ. of Wisconsin, Madison.

Insler, Stanley, Ph.D. Prof. Emer. of Sanskrit and Comparative Philology, Yale Univ.

Ioffe, Grigory, Ph.D. Prof. of Geography, Radford Univ.

Ireland, Patrick, Ph.D. Prof. of Polit. Sci. and Chair, Dept. of Social Sci., Illinois Inst. of Technol.

Irish, Jerry A., Ph.D. Prof. of Religious Studies, Pomona Coll.

Irland, Lloyd C., Ph.D. Pres., The Irland Group; former Budworm Program Coordinator, Maine Forest Service.

Isquith, Irwin Richard, Ph.D. Exec. Dir. for Global Partnerships and Prof. of Biology, Fairleigh Dickinson Univ.

Ito, Philip J., Ph.D. Prof. Emer. of Horticulture and Consultant on Tropical Fruits and Nuts, Univ. of Hawaii.

Ivers, Gregg, Ph.D. Prof., Dept. of Government, American Univ.

Ivinski, Pamela A., M.A. Art Historian, Grad. Ctr., City Univ. of New York.

Iwamoto, Tomio, Ph.D. Curator of Ichthyology, Calif. Academy of Sciences.

Izen, Judith, M.J.L.S. Doll and Toy Historian, Judith Izen Associates.

J

Jablonski, Daniel G., Ph.D. Research Physicist, Johns Hopkins Univ.

Jackson, Dennis R., M.A. Professional climbing guide and outdoor educator.

Jackson, Randall W., Ph.D. Prof. of Geology and Geography and Dir., Regional Research Inst., West Virginia Univ.

Jackson, Robert B., Ph.D. Prof. of Environmental Sciences, Duke Univ.

Jackson, Rodney, Ph.D. Founder-Dir., Snow Leopard Conservancy.

Jackson, W. Turrentine, Ph.D. Prof. of History, Emer., Univ. of Calif., Davis.

Jacob, Charles E., Ph.D. Prof. Emer. of Political Science, Rutgers, the State Univ. of New Jersey.

Jacob, Margaret C., Ph.D. Prof. of History, Univ. of Calif., Los Angeles.

Jacobs, Douglass F., Ph.D. Assoc. Prof., Dept. of Forestry and Natural Resources, Purdue Univ.

Jacobs, William Jay, Ed.D. Author; former Coordinator, History and the Social Sciences, Darien (CT) Public Schools.

Jacobsen, Krista S., Ph.D. Assoc., Covington & Burling LLP.

Jacobson, James E., M.A. Former Contributing Editor, *The Birmingham* (AL) *News.*

Jaeger, C. Stephen, Ph.D. Prof. Emer. of German and Comparative Lit., Univ. of Washington.

Jaenen, Cornelius J., LL.D. Prof. Emer. of History, Univ. of Ottawa.

Jaffe, Stephen, A.M. Prof. of Music, Duke Univ.

Jahncke, Michael L., Ph.D. Dir., Virginia Seafood Agricultural Research and Extension Ctr.

Jain, Anil K., Ph.D. Univ. Dist. Prof., Dept. of Computer Science and Engineering, Mich. State Univ.

Jalal, Ayesha, Ph.D. Mary Richardson Prof. of History, Tufts Univ.

Jalongo, Mary Renck, Ph.D. Professor of Education, Indiana University of Pennsylvania.

Jakosky, Bruce, Ph.D. Prof., Laboratory for Atmospheric and Space Physics, Univ. of Colorado.

James, D. Clayton, Ph.D. Former Prof. of History, Mississippi State Univ., Mississippi State; author, *The Years of MacArthur* and *A Time for Giants.*

Jamieson, Kay Franzen, Ph.D. Food consultant.

Janda, Kenneth, Ph.D. Prof. Emer. of Political Science, Northwestern Univ.

Janick, Jules, Ph.D. Prof. of Horticulture and Landscape Architecture, Purdue Univ.

Janke, Julie World champion logroller.

Jansen, Marius B., Ph.D. Former Prof. of History and East Asian Studies, Princeton Univ.

Jared, Alva H., Ed.D. Prof. Emer. and Chairman, Dept. of Industrial Studies, Univ. of Wisconsin, Platteville.

Jarvis, Donald K., Ph.D. Prof. Emer. of Russian, Brigham Young Univ.

Jarvis, Robert L., Ph.D. Prof. Emer. of Wildlife Ecology, Oregon State Univ.

Jarvis, William E., M.L.S. Knowledge Manager, Library Faculty, Washington State Univ. Libraries.

Jasek, Jacqueline, B.S. Former Editor, World Book, Inc.

Jaynes, Richard A., Ph.D. Horticulturalist and consultant, Broken Arrow Nursery.

Jeans, D. N., Ph.D. Assoc. Prof. of Geography, Univ. of Sydney.

Jednoralski, J. Neil, B.S. Water Resources Civil Engineer, Kirkham Michael and Assoc., Inc.

Jeffreys, David G., Ph.D. Senior Lecturer in Egyptian Archaeology, University College London Institute of Archaeology.

Jenkins, Jeffery A., Ph.D. Assoc. Prof., Dept. of Politics, Univ. of Virginia.

Jenkins, Phil, B.A. Managing Editor, *The* (Fredericksburg, VA) *Free Lance-Star.*

Jenkins, Reese V., Ph.D. Prof. Emer. of History, Rutgers, the State Univ. of New Jersey.

Jennings, Kathryn Pierson, M.L.S. Asst. Librarian, Hudson (WI) Public Library.

Jenniskens, Peter, Ph.D. Meteor Astronomer, SETI Inst.

Jensen, B., Ph.D. Former Assoc. Prof. of Physics, Univ. of Lowell.

Jespersen, James, M.S. Former Physicist, National Institute of Standards and Technology.

Jesseph, Douglas M., Ph.D. Prof. of Philosophy, Univ. of South Florida.

Jhutti-Johal, Jagbir Kaur, Ph.D. Lecturer in Sikh Studies, Univ. of Birmingham.

Jiménez García, Marilisa, Ph.D. Assistant Professor of English, Lehigh University.

Ji-Yeon Yuh, Ph.D. Assoc. Prof., Dept. of History, Northwestern Univ., Evanston.

Joel, Cliffe D., Ph.D. Prof. Emer. of Chemistry, Lawrence Univ.

Joes, Anthony James, Ph.D. Prof. of Political Science, St. Joseph's Univ.

Johannes, Michelle D., Ph.D. Research Physicist, U.S. Naval Research Laboratory.

Johanos, Thea, M.S. Research Wildlife Biologist, Pacific Islands Fisheries Science Center.

Johansen, Harley, Ph.D. Former Professor of Geography, University of Idaho.

Johnson, Alan Kim, Ph.D. F. Wendell Miller Dist. Prof. of Psychology and Pharmacology, Univ. of Iowa.

Johnson, Bob, M.L.S. Reference Librarian, Calif. Room, San Jose Public Library.

Johnson, Bobby H., Ph.D. Regents Prof. Emer. of History, Stephen F. Austin State Univ.

Johnson, Bonnie J. Former Technical Committee member, Intl. Federation of Trampoline and Tumbling.

Johnson, Brian C., B.A. Former Life Sciences Editor, World Book, Inc.

Johnson, Dale A., Th.D. Prof. Emer. of Church History, Vanderbilt Univ.

Johnson, Donald D., Ph.D. Former Prof. of History, Univ. of Hawaii.

Johnson, Doris McNeely, M.S. Assoc. Prof. of Psychology, Univ. of the District of Columbia.

Johnson, Douglas A., Ph.D. Plant Physiologist, Agriculture Research Service Forage and Range Research Lab., U.S. Dept. of Agriculture, Logan, Utah.

Johnson, Douglas L., Ph.D. Prof. of Geography, Grad. School of Geography, Clark Univ.; Editor, *The Geographical Review.*

Johnson, Eugene M., Jr., Ph.D. Prof. of Neurology, Molecular Biology, and Pharmacology, School of Medicine, Washington Univ., St. Louis.

Johnson, George B., Ph.D. Prof. Emer. of Biology, Washington Univ., St. Louis.

Johnson, James P., B.S. Captain, Instructor, Delta Air Lines; Consulting Meteorologist, James Johnson Associates.

Johnson, Jarrett R., Ph.D. Asst. Prof., Department of Biology, Western Kentucky University.

Johnson, Juliet, Ph.D. Associate Professor of Po-

litical Science, McGill University.

Johnson, Kristin, M.L.I.S. Librarian, Cataloging, Salt Lake Community Coll.; editor, *"Unfortunate Emigrants": Narratives of the Donner Party.*

Johnson, Maren Anderson, Ph.D. Assistant Professor of Nordic Studies, Luther College.

Johnson, Michael C., Ph.D. Research Scientist, Utah State Univ. Research Foundation.

Johnson, Ronald C., Ph.D. Prof. Emer. of Chemistry, Emory Univ.

Johnson, Sara Raup, Ph.D. Assoc. Prof. of Modern and Classical Lang., Univ. of Connecticut.

Johnson, Susan R., M.D. Prof. of Obstetrics and Gynecology; Prof. of Epidemiology, Univ. of Iowa.

Johnson, Thomas H., Ph.D. Prof. Emer. of Anthropology, Univ. of Wisconsin, Stevens Point.

Johnston, A. J. B., Ph.D. Historian and writer specializing in Atlantic Canada.

Johnston, J. H., III Former Exec. Editor, *The Leavenworth* (KS) *Times.*

Johnston, Laura, B.J. Former Exec. Editor, *North Platte* (NE) *Telegraph.*

Johnston, N. Paul, Ph.D. Prof. of Animal Science, Brigham Young Univ.

Johnston, Paul F., Ph.D. Curator, National Museum of American History.

Johnston, Richard F., Ph.D. Private consultant.

Johnston, Susan A., Ph.D. Professorial Lecturer in Anthropology, George Washington Univ.

Johnston, Taylor J., Ph.D. Prof., Dept. of Crop and Soil Sciences, Michigan State Univ.

Jok, Jok Madut, Ph.D. Assoc. Prof. of History, Loyola Marymount Univ.

Jokisch, Brad D., Ph.D. Assoc. Prof. of Geography, Ohio Univ.

Jolliffe, Lee B., Ph.D. Assoc. Prof., School of Journalism and Mass Communication, Drake Univ.

Jones, Catherine Children's author and private music educator.

Jones, Charles O., Ph.D. Prof. Emer. of Political Science, Univ. of Wisconsin, Madison.

Jones, Clyde, Ph.D. Prof. Emer. of Biological Sciences, Texas Tech Univ.

Jones, H. R., M.A. Prof. of Geography, Univ. of Dundee.

Jones, Ian Historian and author of *Ned Kelly: A Short Life.*

Jones, James W., Ph.D. Prof. and Chairman, Dept. of Surgery, Univ. of Missouri, Columbia.

Jones, Peter d'A., Ph.D. Former Prof. of History, Univ. of Illinois, Chicago.

Jones, Philip Dwight, Ph.D. Assoc. Prof. of History, Bradley Univ.

Jones, Ronald L., Ph.D. Prof. of Biology, Eastern Kentucky Univ.

Jones, Sidney, Ph.D. Scholar specializing in African American literature.

Jones, Stephen, Ph.D. Dir./Prof., Washington State Univ. Northwestern Washington Research and Extension Ctr.

Jones, Steve, Ph.D. Prof. of Communication, Univ. of Illinois, Chicago.

Jones, Susan C., Ph.D. Assoc. Prof. of Entomology, Ohio State Univ.

Jordan, David P., Ph.D. Prof. of History, Univ. of Illinois, Chicago.

Jordan, Terry G., Ph.D. Former Walter Prescott Webb Professor of Geography, Univ. of Texas.

Jordan, V. Craig, Ph.D., D.Sc. Scientific Dir. and Vice Chairman, Oncology, Lombardi Comprehensive Cancer Ctr., Georgetown Univ.

Joseph, Toni Grayson, M.P.A. Dir. of Laboratory Management, U.S. Dept. of Energy.

Judd, Denis, Ph.D. Prof. Emer. of History, Univ. of North London.

Judd, Richard W., Ph.D. Prof. of History, Univ. of Maine, Orono.

Judd, Walter S., Ph.D. Professor of Botany, University of Florida.

Juergensmeyer, Mark, Ph.D. Prof. of Sociology and Religious Studies, Univ. of Calif., Santa Barbara.

Juley, Michael, B.A. Racine County/Suburban Dev. Editor, *Milwaukee Journal Sentinel.*

K

Kaba, Lansiné, Ph.D. Prof. of History and African-American Studies, Univ. of Illinois, Chicago.

Kadia, Miriam Kingsberg, Ph.D. Assoc. Professor, Dept. of History, Univ. of Colorado, Boulder.

Kadlec, Daniel, B.A. Columnist, *Time* magazine.

Kado, Clarence I., Ph.D. Prof., Head Davis Crown Gall Group, Univ. of Calif., Davis.

Kagan, Donald, Ph.D. Former Sterling Professor of Classics and History, Yale University.

Kahn, Jeffrey P., Ph.D. Dir., Ctr. for Bioethics, Univ. of Minnesota.

Kahn, Wilma J., D.A. Instructor of English, Western Michigan Univ.

Kaiser, Peter K., Dipl. Ing. CEO and Pres., Mining Innovation, Rehabilitation, and Applied Research Corp., Laurentian Univ.

Kalberg, Stephen, Ph.D. Assoc. Prof. of Sociology, Boston Univ.

Kaler, James B., Ph.D. Prof. Emer. of Astronomy, Univ. of Illinois.

Kalish, Richard A. Former Clinical Prof. of Psychiatry, Univ. of New Mexico.

Kamp, Ulrich, Ph.D. Assoc. Prof. of Geography, Univ. of Montana.

Kane, William J., Ph.D. Prof. Emer. of Orthopaedic Surgery, Northwestern Univ.

Kapcia, Antoni, Ph.D. Prof. of Latin American History, Univ. of Nottingham.

Kaplan, Edgar Former Editor and Publisher, *The Bridge World.*

Kaplan, Edward K., Ph.D. Prof. of French and Comparative Lit., Brandeis Univ.

Kaplan, Lawrence, M.D. Prof. of Internal Medicine, Temple Univ. School of Medicine.

Karamanski, Theodore J., Ph.D. Grad. Dir. of Public History, Loyola Univ. Chicago.

Karan, P. P., Ph.D. Dist. Prof. of Geography, Univ. of Kentucky.

Karcheski, Walter J., Jr., M.Ed. Chief Curator of Arms and Armor, Frazier Historical Arms Museum.

Karlin, Eric F., Ph.D. Certified Sr. Ecologist, Ecological Society of America.

Karol, Paul J., Ph.D. Prof. of Chemistry, Carnegie Mellon Univ.

Karr, Paul, Ph.D. Prof. of Chemistry, Wayne State Coll.

Karskens, Grace, Ph.D. Assoc. Prof. and Convenor of Australian Studies Program, School of History and Philosophy, Univ. of New South Wales.

Kaslow, Nadine J., Ph.D. Prof. and Chief Psychologist, Emory Univ. School of Medicine.

Kasonde, Alexander Raymond Makasa, Ph.D. Research Scholar (Linguistics), Emory Univ.

Kastenbaum, Robert J. Prof. Emer. of Communication, Arizona State Univ.

Kates, Michael A., B.S.J. Sports editor.

Katz, Debora M., Ph.D. Prof. of Physics, U.S. Naval Academy, Annapolis.

Katz, Victor J., Ph.D. Prof. Emer. of Mathematics, Univ. of the District of Columbia.

Katzenberg, Dena S. Consultant Curator, Baltimore Museum of Art.

Katzner, Todd, Ph.D. Research Assistant Professor, Division of Forestry and Natural Resources, West Virginia University.

Kaufman, Burton I., Ph.D. Adjunct Prof. of History, Univ. of Utah.

Kaufman, Stuart J., Ph.D. Prof., Political Science and Intl. Relations, Univ. of Delaware.

Kaufmann, Arleen B., M.A. Freelance naturalist and photographer; Biological Scientist, State of Florida Dept. of Agriculture.

Kaufmann, John H., Ph.D. Prof. of Zoology, Univ. of Florida.

Kay, Jason, B.J. Editor in Chief, *The Hockey News.*

Kaye, Neil S., M.D. Asst. Clinical Prof. of Family Medicine, Jefferson Medical Coll.

Kazerounian, Kazem, Ph.D. Prof. of Mechanical Engineering, Univ. of Connecticut.

Kear, Benjamin P., Ph.D. Assistant Professor, Department of Earth Sciences, Uppsala University.

Kearley, F. Furman, Ph.D. Former Editor, *Gospel Advocate.*

Kearney, Janis F., B.A. Founding Publisher, Writing Our World Publishing, LLC.

Kearns, Robin A., Ph.D. Assoc. Prof., School of Geography and Environmental Science, Univ. of Auckland.

Keating, Michael, Ph.D. Asst. Prof. of Catholic Studies, Univ. of St. Thomas.

Keating, Richard C., Ph.D. Botanist, Missouri Botanical Garden.

Kechichian, Joseph A., Ph.D. Chief Exec. Officer, Kechichian and Assoc., LLC.

Kedward, H. R., M.Phil. Prof. Emer. of French History, Univ. of Sussex.

Keefe, John Webster, M.A. Former Curator of Decorative Arts, New Orleans Museum of Art.

Keelan, Brian W., Ph.D. Research Scientist, Eastman Kodak Company.

Keeling, David J., Ph.D. University Distinguished Professor of Geography, Western Kentucky Univ.

Keen, Charlotte E., Ph.D. Prof. Emer., Atlantic Geoscience Centre, Bedford Inst.

Keenan, Julian Paul, Ph.D. Dir., Cognitive Neuroimaging Laboratory, Montclair State Univ.

Kegerreis, Christopher, Ph.D. Lecturer, Dept. of History, University of California, Santa Barbara.

Kehoe, Alice B., Ph.D. Former Prof. of Anthropology, Marquette Univ.

Keil, David J., Ph.D. Prof. of Biology, Calif. Polytechnic State Univ.

Keinath, Thomas M., Ph.D. Dean Emer., Coll. of Engineering and Science, Clemson Univ.

Keith, Jennie, Ph.D. Prof. Emer. of Anthropology, Swarthmore Coll.

Keith-Lucas, Alan, Ph.D. Former Prof. of Social Work, Univ. of North Carolina, Chapel Hill.

Keller, D. Steven, Ph.D. Assoc. Prof., Paper & Chemical Engineering, Miami Univ.

Kelley, Ed, B.A. Editor, *The Daily* (Oklahoma City, OK) *Oklahoman.*

Kelley, Patricia H., Ph.D. Prof., Dept. of Geography & Geology, Univ. of North Carolina, Wilmington.

Kelly, Andrea, M.D. Attending Physician, Children's Hospital of Philadelphia; Asst. Prof., Univ. of Pennsylvania School of Medicine.

Kelly, James P., B.A. Editorial Page Editor, *The Honolulu* (HI) *Advertiser.*

Kelly, Joseph F., Ph.D. Professor, Dept. of Theology and Religious Studies, John Carroll University.

Kelly, Marcella J., Ph.D. Assoc. Prof., Dept. of Fisheries and Wildlife Sciences, Virginia Tech.

Kelso, Frank M., Ph.D. Faculty, Dept. of Mechanical Engineering, Univ. of Minnesota, Twin Cities Campus.

Kelting, M. Whitney, Ph.D. Asst. Prof. of Philosophy & Religion, Northeastern Univ.

Kemmick, Edward A. Community Affairs Reporter, *The Billings* (MT) *Gazette.*

Kenagy, G. J., Ph.D. Prof. of Zoology, Univ. of Washington.

Kenkel, Don, Ph.D. Prof., Dept. of Policy Analysis and Management, Cornell Univ.

Kennedy, Ann R., D.Sc. Richard Chamberlain Prof. of Research Oncology, Univ. of Pennsylvania School of Medicine.

Kennedy, Brian, M.A. Copy Editor, *Outback* magazine.

Kennedy, Christina Beal, Ph.D. Prof. Emer., Dept. of Geography, Planning and Recreation, Northern Arizona Univ.

Kennedy, Gavin, Ph.D. Managing Dir., Negotiate Ltd.

Kennedy, George, Ph.D. Prof. Emer. of Journalism, Univ. of Missouri, Columbia.

Kennedy, James E., Ph.D. Technical Staff Member, Los Alamos Natl. Laboratory.

Kennedy, Robert A., Ph.D. Pres., Univ. of Maine.

Kenoyer, Jonathan Mark, Ph.D. Prof. of Anthropology, Univ. of Wisconsin, Madison.

Kent, Neil, D.Phil. Professor, Russian Academy of Art; Associate, Scott Polar Research Institute, University of Cambridge.

Kerchner, Geoffrey A., M.D., Ph.D. Asst. Prof. of Neurology and Neurological Sciences, Stanford Univ.

Kerr, Donald R., Jr., Ph.D. Former Basic Skills Coordinator, Dept. of Mathematics, Indiana Univ.

Kerr, Ian J., Ph.D. Former Professor of History, University of Manitoba.

Kershaw, G. Peter, Ph.D. Assoc. Prof., Dept. of Earth and Atmospheric Sciences, Univ. of Alberta.

Kertzer, David I., Ph.D. Provost and Paul Dupee Univ. Prof. of Social Science, Brown Univ.

Kessel, John L., B.A. Dir. of Educ., Disabled, Grassroots, and Beach Volleyball, USA Volleyball.

Kessell, John L., Ph.D. Prof. Emer. of History, Univ. of New Mexico; Editor, *The Vargas Project.*

Kesselman, Mark, Ph.D. Prof. Emer. of Government, Columbia Univ.

Kester, Dana R., Ph.D. Former Prof. of Oceanography, Grad. School of Oceanography, Univ. of Rhode Island.

Kesterson, David B., Ph.D. Former Prof. of English and Provost and Vice Pres. for Academic Affairs, Univ. of North Texas.

Keszler, Douglas A., Ph.D. Dist. Prof. of Chemistry, Oregon State Univ.

Ketchum, Bostwick H., Sc.D. Former Sr. Scientist, Woods Hole Oceanographic Inst.

Kettering, Alison McNeil, Ph.D. William R. Kenan, Jr., Prof. of Art History, Carleton Coll.

Kettl, Donald F., Ph.D. Prof. of Political Science and Public Affairs, Univ. of Wisconsin, Madison.

Kevles, Daniel J., Ph.D. Prof. Emer. of Humanities, Calif. Inst. of Technology.

Keyder, Caglar, Ph.D. Prof. of Sociology, Binghamton Univ., State Univ. of New York.

Keyes, Charles, Ph.D. Prof. Emer. of Anthropology and Intl. Studies, Univ. of Washington.

Keyes, Jane, M.A. Author and editor.

Keyes, P. Landis, Ph.D. Prof. of Physiology, Univ. of Michigan.

Khalidi, Rashid I., D.Phil. Edward Said Prof. of Modern Arab Studies, Columbia Univ.

Kicza, John E., Ph.D. Former Prof. of History, Washington State Univ.

Kidder, Stanley Q., Ph.D. Sr. Research Scientist, Cooperative Inst. for Research in the Atmosphere, Colorado State Univ.

Kidwell, Clara Sue, Ph.D. Dir., Native American Studies, Univ. of Oklahoma.

Kidwell, Peggy Aldrich, Ph.D. Museum Specialist, Smithsonian Inst.

Kienzler, Michael F., M.A. Metro Editor, (Springfield, IL) *State Journal-Register.*

Kieren, Thomas E., Ph.D. Prof. Emer. of Educ., Univ. of Alberta.

Kierszenbaum, Felipe, Ph.D. Former Prof. of Microbiology, Michigan State Univ.

Kiger, Joseph C., Ph.D. Author, *Operating Principles of the Larger Foundations.*

Kilzer, Nicholas V., M.S. Associate Manager, Sciences, World Book, Inc.

Kimble, Mary, Ph.D. Assoc. Prof. of Biology, Northeastern Illinois Univ.

King, Dwight Y., Ph.D. Prof. of Political Science, Northern Illinois Univ.

King, Jerry W., Ph.D. Former Prof., Dept. of Chemical Engineering, Univ. of Arkansas.

King, John N., Ph.D. Prof. Emer. of English, Ohio State Univ.

King, Madeline, B.A. Content Creator, World Book, Inc.

King, Micki, M.A. Gold medal winner in diving, 1972 Olympic Games.

King, Pauline N., Ph.D. Assoc. Prof. of History, Univ. of Hawaii.

King, Wilma, Ph.D. Dist. Prof. of History, Univ. of Missouri, Columbia.

Kinkade, Richard P., Ph.D. Prof. of Spanish and Portuguese, Univ. of Arizona.

Kinkel, Doreen H. D., Ph.D. Prof. of Animal Science, Texas A&M Univ., Kingsville.

Kinney, Jeremy R., Ph.D. Curator, Smithsonian Natl. Air and Space Museum.

Kinzer, Bruce L., Ph.D. Professor of History, Kenyon College.

Kionka, Edward J., LLM. Prof. Emer. of Law, School of Law, Southern Illinois Univ.

Kirby, F. E., Ph.D. Prof. Emer. of Music, Lake Forest Coll.

Kirschenbaum, Howard, Ed.D. Author, educator, and consultant; Adjunct faculty, State University of New York, Brockport.

Kispert, Robert J., Ph.D. Former Assoc. Prof. of English, Univ. of Illinois, Chicago.

Kiste, Robert C., Ph.D. Emer. Dir. and Prof., Univ. of Hawaii Ctr. for Pacific Islands Studies.

Kitching, Brian Managing Partner, Kitching, Ruscoe Public Relations.

Kizirian, David, Ph.D. Curatorial Associate, American Museum of Natural History.

Klein, Donald W., Ph.D. Prof. Emer. of Political

Science, Tufts Univ.; Research Assoc., Fairbank Ctr. for East Asian Research, Harvard Univ.

Klein, Marcus, Ph.D. Prof. Emeritus of Modern American Lit., State Univ. of New York, Buffalo.

Klein, Milton M., Ph.D. Editor, *The Empire State: A History of New York.*

Klein, Richard G., Ph.D. Prof. of Anthropology, Stanford Univ.

Klein, Ronald, M.D. Prof. of Ophthalmology, Univ. of Wisconsin, Madison.

Klein, Samuel, M.D. Dir., Ctr. for Human Nutrition, School of Medicine, Wash. Univ., St. Louis.

Kleindorfer, Paul R., Ph.D. Anheuser-Busch Prof. of Management Science, Wharton School, Univ. of Pennsylvania.

Klement, Frank L., Ph.D. Prof. Emer. of History, Marquette Univ.

Klemm, David E., Ph.D. Prof. of Religion, Univ. of Iowa.

Klemm, Peri M., Ph.D. Assoc. Prof. of African, Oceanic, and Native American Art History, Calif. State Univ., Northridge.

Kline, Ronald R., Ph.D. Prof. in the History and Ethics of Professional Engineering, Cornell Univ.

Klocke, Robert A., M.D. Prof. of Medicine and Physiology, State Univ. of New York, Buffalo.

Klotzko, Arlene Judith, J.D. Writer in Residence, Science Museum, London.

Kluger, Matthew J., Ph.D. Prof., Health Admin. and Policy, George Mason Univ., Coll. of Health and Human Services.

Klymyshyn, Alexandra M. Ulana, Ph.D. Dir., Multicultural Programming, Central Michigan Univ.

Knapp, Gregory, Ph.D. Assoc. Prof. and Chair, Dept. of Geography, Univ. of Texas, Austin.

Knapp, Mark L., Ph.D. Jesse H. Jones Centennial Prof. Emer. in Communication and Dist. Teaching Prof., Univ. of Texas, Austin.

Knechtges, David R., Ph.D. Prof. Emer. of Chinese, Dept. of Asian Langs. and Lit., Univ. of Wash.

Kneebone, Sterling Features Editor, *The* (Fredericton, NB) *Daily Gleaner.*

Kneeshaw, Stephen, Ph.D. Prof. of History, Coll. of the Ozarks.

Knight, Charles A., Ph.D. Sr. Scientist, Natl. Ctr. for Atmospheric Research.

Knipe, C. Lynn, Ph.D. Assoc. Prof., Dept. of Food Science and Technology, Ohio State Univ.

Knoop, Michael, MLIS News Research Editor, *San Antonio Express-News.*

Knopf, Fritz L., Ph.D. Former Sr. Scientist, U.S. Geological Survey.

Kobasa, Paul A., M.S.L.S. Former Editor in Chief, World Book, Inc.

Kodesh, Neil, Ph.D. Asst. Prof. of History, Univ. of Wisconsin, Madison.

Koehler, Michael F., B.S. Pres. and CEO, Teradata Corp.

Koenker, Diane P., Ph.D. Prof. of History, Univ. of Illinois, Urbana-Champaign.

Koestner, Richard, Ph.D. Prof. of Psychology, McGill Univ.

Kolata, Alan L., Ph.D. Neukom Family Prof. of Anthropology, Univ. of Chicago.

Kolaz, David J., M.S. Chief, Bureau of Air, Illinois Environmental Protection Agency.

Koontz, Fred, Ph.D. Vice Pres. of Field Conservation, Woodland Park Zoo.

Kooyman, Gerald, Ph.D. Prof. of Biology, Emer., Scripps Inst. of Oceanography, Univ. of Calif., San Diego.

Korgel, Brian A., Ph.D. Edward S. Hyman Endowed Chair in Engineering and T. Brockett Hudson Professor of Chemical Engineering, University of Texas, Austin.

Kornbluh, Peter, M.A. Senior Analyst, Natl. Security Archive.

Kornblum, Aaron T., M.L.S. Archivist and Historical Collections Curator, Western Jewish History Ctr., Magnes Museum.

Kosel, Peter Bohdan, Ph.D. Dir., Gallium Arsenide Devices and Integrated Circuits Laboratory, Univ. of Cincinnati.

Koshan, Terry, M.A. Sports reporter, the *Toronto Sun*/Postmedia.

Kosinski, Leszek A., Ph.D. Secretary General Emer., Intl. Social Science Council, UNESCO.

Kosslyn, S. M., Ph.D. John Lindsay Professor of Psychology, Harvard University.

Kosta, Barbara, Ph.D. Professor and Head of German Studies, University of Arizona.

Koszczuk, Jackie, B.S. Natl. Congressional Correspondent, Knight Ridder Newspapers.

Kotek, Richard, Ph.D. Associate Professor, College of Textiles, North Carolina State University.

Kottak, Conrad Phillip, Ph.D. Prof. of Anthropology, Univ. of Michigan, Ann Arbor.

Kotynski, Tom, B.A. Former Assoc. Editor, *Great Falls* (MT) *Tribune.*

Koumoulides, John A., Ph.D. Prof. Emer. of History, Ball State Univ.

Kovacik, Charles F., Ph.D. Dist. Prof. Emer., Dept. of Geography, Univ. of South Carolina.

Kovacs, Zoltan, B.A. Opinion Editor, *The West Australian.*

Kovscek, A. R., Ph.D. Assoc. Prof., Dept. of Petroleum Engineering, Stanford Univ.

Kozloski, Lillian D., B.S. Former Museum Specialist, Natl. Air and Space Museum.

Krahmer, John, LL.M. Prof. of Law, Texas Tech Univ. School of Law.

Krajcik, Dawn M., B.A. Sr. Editor, World Book, Inc.

Kramer, Victor A., Ph.D. Prof. Emer. of English, Georgia State Univ.

Kranzberg, Melvin, L.H.D. Former Callaway Prof. of the History of Technol., Georgia Inst. of Technol.

Kraus, Pansy D., F.G.A. Gem consultant.

Krefman, Ronald A., O.D. Optometrist.

Kremer, Gary R., Ph.D. Prof. of History, William Woods Univ.

Kremkau, Frederick W., Ph.D. Prof. and Dir., Ctr. for Medical Ultrasound, Wake Forest Univ. School of Medicine.

Krentz, Peter, Ph.D. W. R. Grey Prof. of History, Davidson Coll.

Kress, Jack M., D.Crim. Exec. Dir., Advisory Committee on Organ Transplantation, U.S. Dept. of Health and Human Services.

Krier, James E., J.D. Earl Warren DeLano Prof. of Law, Univ. of Michigan Law School.

Krisciunas, Kevin, Ph.D. Lecturer, Dept. of Physics, Texas A&M Univ.

Kroeber, Donald W., Ph.D. Former Dean, Coll. of Business and Economics, Radford Univ.

Kroeger, Edwin Bane, Ph.D. Asst. Prof., Dept. of Mining and Mineral Resources Engineering, Southern Illinois Univ.

Kroeker, Scott, M.A. JCC Project Officer, Pacific Islands Dev. Program, East-West Ctr.

Kroenig, Matthew, Ph.D. Asst. Prof., Dept. of Government, Georgetown Univ.

Krolik, Jeffrey L., Ph.D. Prof. of Electrical and Computer Engineering, Duke Univ.

Kropf, Nancy P., Ph.D. Prof. and Doctoral Program Dir., School of Social Work, Univ. of Georgia.

Krosby, H. Peter, Ph.D. Prof. of History, State Univ. of New York, Albany.

Krugman, Karen, Owner, Lineages, Inc.

Krupczak, John J., Jr., Ph.D. Prof., Dept. of Physics, Hope Coll.

Krysko, Kenneth L., Ph.D. Research Scientist, Florida Museum of Natural Hist., Univ. of Florida.

Kuhn, George W. S., J.D. Research Fellow, Logistics Management inst.; former U.S. Army officer.

Kujawa-Holbrook, Sheryl A., Ph.D. Prof. of Practical Theology and Religious Educ., Claremont School of Theology.

Kulczycki, John J., Ph.D. Prof. Emer. of History, Univ. of Illinois, Chicago.

Kumbier, William A., Ph.D. Assoc. Prof. of English, Missouri Southern State Coll.

Kuntz, Kirby A., Ph.D. Project Manager, Hensel Phelps Construction Co.

Kupperman, Karen Ordahl, Ph.D. Prof. of History, Univ. of Connecticut.

Kurta, Allen, Ph.D. Professor of Biology, Eastern Michigan University.

Kurth, William S., Ph.D. Research Scientist, Dept. of Physics and Astronomy, Univ. of Iowa.

Kushma, David, M.S. Opinion Pages Editor, *The* (Toledo, OH) *Blade.*

Kusimba, Chapurukha, Ph.D. Prof. of Anthropology, American Univ.

Kutler, Stanley I., Ph.D. Prof. Emer. of American Inst., Univ. of Wisconsin, Madison.

Kuzen, Robin H., M.A. Senior Accountant and Financial Analyst, Miller Ctr. of Public Affairs, Univ. of Virginia.

Kyanka, George H., Ph.D. Prof. of Wood Products Engineering, State Univ. of New York.

Kyle, Richard, Ph.D. Prof. of History and Religion, Tabor Coll.

Kyvig, David E., Ph.D. Prof. of History, Univ. of Akron.

L

Labuza, Theodore P., Ph.D. Prof. of Food Science, Univ. of Minnesota, Twin Cities Campus.

Lack, Sylvia A., B.S. Dir., Chronic Pain Program; Staff Physician, Gaylord Hospital.

LaCourt, Jody, M.L.S. Sr. Teaching Specialist, Univ. of Minnesota Program of Mortuary Science.

Laderman, Scott, Ph.D. Professor of History, University of Minnesota, Duluth.

Laflen, John M., Ph.D. Dir., Natl. Soil Erosion Research Laboratory, U.S. Dept. of Agriculture.

LaFleur-Giambrone, Amanda, M.A. Coordinator of Cajun Studies, Louisiana State Univ.

LaFranco, Frank P., M.D. Vitreoretinal Surgeon, Retina Services Ltd.

Lahti, David C., Ph.D. Assistant Prof. of Biology, Queens College, The City University of New York.

Laidre, Kristin L., Ph.D. Oceanographer IV and Asst. Prof., Fisheries, Polar Science Ctr., Applied Physics Lab., Univ. of Washington.

Lal, Anil, M.A. Independent scholar; former Instructor of English, Truman Coll.

Lal, Brij V., Ph.D. Prof., School of Culture, History & Lang., Australian Natl. Univ., Canberra.

Lal, Vinay, Ph.D. Assoc. Prof. of History, Univ. of Calif., Los Angeles.

Laline, Brian J. Editor, *Staten Island* (New York, NY) *Advance.*

Lamar, Howard R., Ph.D. Prof. Emer. of History, Yale Univ.; author, *The Far Southwest, 1846-1912.*

Lamb, David R., Ph.D. Prof. Emer. of Exercise Physiology and Preventive Medicine, Ohio State Univ.

Lamb, Joseph F., Ph.D. Assoc. Dean of the Coll. of Fine Arts and Assoc. Prof. of Art at Ohio Univ.

Lamba, Savi, M.S.Ch.E. Vice Pres. and Technical Dir., James Finlay and Company (U.S.), Inc.

Lambert, B.A. Tandem & AFF Instructor, Skydive Orange. Former Managing Editor, *Parachutist Magazine.*

Lambert, John, D.Phil. Assoc. Prof., Dept. of History, Univ. of South Africa.

Lambert, Michael C., Ph.D. Assoc. Prof. of African Studies, Univ. of North Carolina.

Lambert, Peter, Ph.D. Professor of Latin American Studies, University of Bath.

Lambert, Wayne, Ph.D. Assoc. Prof. of Geology, West Texas A&M Univ.

Lamm, Darrell R., Ph.D. Chief Scientist, Electro-Optical Systems Lab., Georgia Tech Research Inst.

Lancaster, Nicholas, Ph.D. Research Prof. of Earth and Ecosystem Sciences, Desert Research Inst.

Lancaster, Roger A., M.S. General Manager, U.S. Dept. of Agriculture Employee Services and Recreation Assoc.

Lance, H. Darrell, Ph.D. Prof. Emer., Old Testament Interpretation, Colgate Rochester/Bexley/Crozer Theological Seminary.

Lance, Tony, B.S. Asst. Editor, *Tennis* magazine.

Land, Michael H., M.D. Asst. Prof. of Pediatrics, Duke Univ. School of Medicine.

Landen, Robert Geran, Ph.D. Former Dir., Ctr. for Programs in the Humanities, Virginia Polytechnic Inst. and State Univ.

Lander, Jesse M., Ph.D. Assoc. Prof. of English, Univ. of Notre Dame.

Landers, Jack M., Ed.D. Prof. Emer. of Industrial Technology, Central Missouri State Univ.

Landry, David T., Ph.D. Assoc. Prof. of Theology, Univ. of St. Thomas.

Lane, James B., Ph.D. Prof. Emer. of History, Indiana Univ. Northwest.

Lang, Jack Former Executive Secretary, Baseball Writers Association of America.

Lang, Kate, Ph.D. Assoc. Prof. of History, Univ. of Wisconsin, Eau Claire.

Lang, Robert J., Ph.D. Origami artist.

Langdon, Robert Former Visiting Fellow, Pacific and Asian History, Australian Natl. Univ.

Langerman, Michael A., Ph.D. Prof. of Mechanical Engineering, South Dakota School of Mines and Technology.

Langley, Susan K., Ph.D. Former Asst. Prof. of Geology and Geography, Georgia Southern Univ.

Lanphier, Bill Freelance writer and photographer.

Lansing, Richard H., Ph.D. Prof. of Italian and Comparative Lit., Brandeis Univ.

Lapidus, Leah Blumberg, Ph.D. Prof. Emer. of Psychology, Columbia Univ. Grad. School of Arts and Sciences.

LaPorte, Robert, Jr., Ph.D. Prof. of Public Admin. and Political Science, Pennsylvania State Univ.; author, *Power and Privilege: A Study of Influence and Decision Making in Pakistan.*

Lapp, Douglas M., Ed.D. Former Dir., Natl. Science Resources Ctr., Natl. Academy of Sciences/Smithsonian Inst.

Lara, Dulcinea M., Ph.D. Asst. Prof. of History, New Mexico State Univ.

Large, Daniel, M.Sc. Research Dir., Africa Asia Ctr., Univ. of London.

Larsen, Fenton E., Ph.D. Prof. Emer. of Horticulture, Washington State Univ.

Larsen, Kristine M., Ph.D. Prof. of Physics and Astronomy, Central Connecticut State Univ.

Larsen, Lawrence H., Ph.D. Coauthor, *The Gate City; A History of Omaha.*

Larsen, Michael D., Ph.D. Assoc. Prof. of Statistics, George Washington Univ.

Larson, André P., Ph.D. Prof. of Music and Dir., America's Shrine to Music Museum, Univ. of South Dakota.

Larson, Michael F., D.O. Clinical Instructor, Harvard Univ. Medical School.

Larter, David B., B.A. Naval Warfare Reporter, *Defense News.*

Lasch, Christopher, Ph.D. Former Prof. of History, Univ. of Rochester.

Lau, Tin-Man, M.A. Prof., Dept. of Industrial Design, Auburn Univ.

Laudan, Rachel, Ph.D. Prof. of General Science, Univ. of Hawaii, Honolulu.

Laugharne, Peter J., Ph.D. Sr. Lecturer, Dept. of Law, Governance and Intl. Relations, London Metropolitan Univ.

Laur, Timothy M., M.A. Lieutenant Colonel, retired, U.S. Air Force; consultant; lecturer.

Laurance, William F., Ph.D. James Cook Dist. Research Prof., James Cook Univ.

La Vere, David L., Ph.D. Prof. of History, Univ. of North Carolina, Wilmington.

Lawley, Mark A., Ph.D. Assoc. Prof., School of Industrial Engineering, Purdue Univ.

Lawrance, Benjamin N., Ph.D. Asst. Prof., Dept. of History, Univ. of Calif., Davis.

Lawrence, Keith, M.S. Sr. Writer, *Owensboro (KY) Messenger-Inquirer.*

Lawson, Wendy, Ph.D. Professor of Geography and Pro-Vice Chancellor of Science, University of Canterbury, Christchurch.

Lazarte, Jaime E., Ph.D. Lecturer-Researcher, Harvard Univ. School of Medicine, Ctr. for Blood Research.

Lea, David A. M., Ph.D. Former Exec. Dir., North Australia Research Unit.

Le Bon, Joel, Ph.D. Clinical Prof. of Marketing and Dir. of Exec. Educ. of the Sales Excellence Inst., Univ. of Houston.

Lecher, Alanna L., Ph.D. Assistant Professor of Scientific Literacy, Lynn University.

LeClair, James A., Ph.D. Assoc. Prof., Dept. of Geography, Nipissing Univ.

Ledbetter, Mary Lee S., Ph.D. Professor of Biology, College of the Holy Cross.

Ledeen, Lydia Hailparn, Ph.D. Prof. and Chair of Music Dept., Drew Univ.

Ledes, Allison Eckardt, B.A. Former Editor, *Antiques.*

Ledgerwood, Judy L., Ph.D. Assoc. Prof. and Chair, Dept. of Anthropology, Northern Illinois Univ., DeKalb.

LeDuc, Lawrence, Ph.D. Professor Emeritus, Dept. of Political Science, Univ. of Toronto.

LeDuff, Garry R., M.A.C.E. Exec. Dir., Assoc. of Independent Schools of South Australia (AISSA).

Lee, Chong-Sik, Ph.D. Prof. of Political Science, Univ. of Pennsylvania.

Lee, Cindy T., M.A. Research Analyst, Milken Institute.

Lee, Kwang-sun, M.D. Prof. of Pediatrics and Obstetrics/Gynecology, Univ. of Chicago.

Lee, Lloyd L., Ph.D. Associate Professor of Native American Studies, University of New Mexico.

Lee, Raphael C., M.D., Sc.D. Prof. of Surgery, Medicine, Anatomy, and Organismal Biology, Univ. of Chicago.

Lee, Russell, M.S. Aeronautics Curator, Smithsonian Natl. Air and Space Museum.

Lee, Warren F., Ph.D. Prof. Emer. of Agricultural, Environmental and Dev. Econ., Ohio State Univ.

Lefebvre, R. Craig, Ph.D. Vice Pres. and Chief Technical Officer, Intervention Services, Prospect Assoc.

Lefkowitz, Mary R., Ph.D. Andrew W. Mellon Prof. Emer. of Humanities, Dept. of Classical Studies, Wellesley Coll.

Le Gall, Michel, Ph.D. Assoc. Prof. of Middle Eastern History, St. Olaf Coll.

Legon, Ronald P., Ph.D. Former Provost and Prof. of History, Univ. of Baltimore.

Lehrer, Adrienne, Ph.D. Prof. of Linguistics, Univ. of Arizona.

Leiren, Terje I., Ph.D. Sverre Arestad Endowed Prof. in Norwegian Studies and Chair, Dept. of Scandinavian Studies, Univ. of Washington.

Lekakh, Simon, Ph.D. Research Assoc. Prof. of Metallurgical Engineering, Missouri Univ. of Science and Technology.

Lemanske, Robert F., Jr., M.D. Prof. of Pediatrics and Medicine, Univ. of Wisconsin Medical School.

Lemarchand, René, Ph.D. Regional consultant on Governance, U.S. Agency for Intl. Dev.

Lemberg, Dave, Ph.D. Assoc. Prof. of Geography, Western Michigan Univ.

Lemmon, Big Dave, B.A. Asst. Dir. of Public Relations, Miami Jai-Alai.

LeMone, Margaret A., Ph.D. Sr. Scientist, Natl. Ctr. for Atmospheric Research.

Lemons, J. Stanley, Ph.D. Prof. Emer. of History, Rhode Island Coll.

Lencki, Robert W., Ph.D. Assoc. Prof., Dept. of Food Science, Univ. of Guelph.

Lengle, James I., Ph.D. Prof. of Government, Georgetown Univ.

Lenkowsky, Leslie, Ph.D. Prof. of Public Affairs and Philanthropic Studies, Indiana Univ.

Leonard, Joseph W., III, M.S. Former Mining Engineering Foundation Prof., Univ. of Kentucky.

Leonard, Scott A., Ph.D. Prof. of English, Youngstown State Univ.

Leonard, Thomas C., Ph.D. Prof., Grad. School of Journalism, Univ. of Calif., Berkeley.

Lepore, Jill, Ph.D. Prof. of History, Harvard Univ.

Lerman, Robert I., Ph.D. Dir., Human Resources Policy Ctr., The Urban Inst.; Prof. of Economics, American Univ.

Lersten, Nels R., Ph.D. Prof. Emer. of Botany, Iowa State Univ.

Lesko, Leonard H., Ph.D. Prof. Emer., Egyptology, Brown Univ.

Lesser, Michael, Ph.D. Research Scientist, Univ. of Arizona.

Lester, Larry, B.S. Former Research Dir., Negro Leagues Baseball Museum.

Lev, Arlene, LCSW-R Lecturer, School of Social Welfare, State University of New York at Albany.

Levanon, Yosef, Ph.D. Adjunct Assoc. Prof. of Jewish History, Spertus Inst. of Jewish Studies.

Levere, Trevor H., D.Phil. Prof. Emer. of the History of Science, Univ. of Toronto.

Leveton, Deborah, M.A. Curator, Salisbury House Foundation, Des Moines, Iowa.

Leviatan, Uriel, Ph.D. Prof., Dept. of Sociology, Univ. of Haifa.

Levier, Francis, Ed.D. Consultant, Levier & Assoc.

Levine, Alan S., Ph.D. Dr. Alan Levine & Assoc., Biomedical Research Funding Consultants.

Levine, Gordon L., Ph.D. Former Dir., Intl. Educ. Office, Univ. of Minnesota, Duluth.

Levine, Michael P., Ph.D. Prof. of Philosophy, Univ. of Western Australia.

Levine, Robert M., Ph.D. Former Prof. and Dir. of Latin American Studies, Dept. of History, Univ. of Miami.

Levings, Darryl W., M.A. Asst. Managing Editor for Natl. News, *The Kansas City (MO) Star.*

Levinson, Paul, Ph.D. Prof. of Communication and Media Studies, Fordham Univ.

Levinson, Sanford, J.D. Prof. of Law and Government, Univ. of Texas Law School, Austin.

Levitzky, Michael G., Ph.D. Prof. of Physiology, Louisiana State Univ. Health Sciences Ctr.

Levy, B. Barry, Ph.D. Dean, Faculty of Religious Studies, McGill Univ.

Levy, David H., M.A. Observer, Jarnac Lab.

Lewis, Adrian R., Ph.D. Prof., Dept. of History, Univ. of Kansas.

Lewis, Anthony J., Ph.D. Prof. Emer. of Geography and Anthropology, Louisiana State Univ.

Lewis, B. M., M.Sc. Sr. Research Assoc., Natl. Astronomy and Ionosphere Ctr. (Arecibo).

Lewis, Cathleen S., M.A. Asst. Curator, Natl. Air and Space Museum, Smithsonian Inst.

Lewis, Daniel K., Ph.D. Assoc. Prof., History Dept., Calif. Polytechnic State Univ., Pomona.

Lewis, David L., Ph.D. Prof. of Business History, Univ. of Michigan.

Lewis, Finlay Washington Correspondent, Copley News Service.

Lewis, G. Malcolm, M.Sc. Consultant, G. Malcolm Lewis and S. Margaret Lewis History of Cartography Research.

Lewis, John P., Ph.D. Former Prof. of Economics and Intl. Policy, Princeton Univ.

Lewis, Jon, Ph.D. Prof. of English, Oregon State Univ.

Lewis, Laurence A., Ph.D. Prof. Emer. of Geography, Clark Univ.

Lewis, Mark J., Ph.D. Prof., Dept. of Aerospace Engineering, Univ. of Maryland, Coll. Park.

Lewis, Nancy Davis, Ph.D. Dir., Research Program, East-West Ctr.

Lewis, Thomas R., Ph.D. Assoc. Prof.-in-Residence, Geography Dept., Univ. of Connecticut.

Lewis, Tom Director of Communications, U.S. Track & Field and Cross Country Coaches Assoc.

Lewis, W. Joe, Ph.D. Research Entomologist, Agricultural Research Service, U.S. Dept. of Agriculture.

Ley, Klaus, M.D. Head, Division of Inflammation Biology, La Jolla Inst. for Allergy & Immunology.

Li, Cheng, Ph.D. Prof. of Govt., Hamilton Coll.; Fellow, Woodrow Wilson Intl. Ctr. for Scholars.

Li, Tong, Ph.D. Research Economist, Milken Inst.

Liao, Thomas T., Ed.D. Prof. and Chairman, Dept. of Technology and Society, State Univ. of New York, Stony Brook.

Libbrecht, Ken G., Ph.D. Prof. of Physics, Calif. Inst. of Technology.

Lichtor, J. Lance, M.D. Prof., Dept. of Anesthesia & Pediatrics, Univ. of Mass. Medical School.

Lieber, Charles S., M.D. Former Prof. of Medicine and Pathology, Mount Sinai School of Medicine, City Univ. of New York.

Lieberman, Jethro K., J.D. Vice Pres., Academic Publishing, and Prof. of Law, New York Law School.

Liebman, Dave, B.S. Composer; Founder and Artistic Dir., International Assoc. of Schools of Jazz.

Liebow, Charles, Ph.D. Prof., Dept. of Oral Surgery, School of Dental Medicine, State Univ. of New York, Buffalo.

Lilien, Gary L., Ph.D. Prof., Coll. of Business, Pennsylvania State Univ., Univ. Park.

Lillard, Paula P., M.Ed. Cofounder, Forest Bluff Montessori School.

Lin, C.-Y. Cynthia, Ph.D. Asst. Prof., Dept. of Agriculture and Resource Econ., Univ. of Calif., Davis.

Lincoln, Louise, M.A. Curator of African, Oceanic, and New World Cultures, Minneapolis Inst. of Arts.

Lindahl, Carl, Ph.D. Prof. of English, Univ. of Houston.

Lindgren, James, J.D. Prof. of Law, Northwestern Univ. School of Law.

Lindgren, Raymond E., Ph.D. Former Prof. Emer. of History, Calif. State Univ., Long Beach.

Lindheimer, Marshall D., M.D. Professor of Medicine, Obstetrics and Gynecology, and Clinical Pharmacology, Univ. of Chicago.

Lindow, John, Ph.D. Prof., Dept. of Scandinavian, Univ. of Calif., Berkeley.

Lindstrom, Lamont, Ph.D. Prof. of Anthropology, Univ. of Tulsa.

Lindstrom, Marilyn M., Ph.D. Planetary Scientist, Natl. Aeronautics and Space Admin., Johnson Space Ctr.

Lindstrom, Naomi, Ph.D. Prof. of Spanish and Portuguese, Univ. of Texas, Austin.

Lineback, Neal G., Ph.D. Prof. Emer., Dept. of Geography and Planning, Appalachian State Univ.; Editor, *Atlas of Alabama.*

Linhardt, Robert J., Ph.D. Prof. of Chemistry and Chemical Biology, Biology, and Chemical and Biological Engineering, Rensselaer Polytechnic Inst.

Linker, H. Michael, Ph.D. Prof. Emer., Dept. of Crop Science, North Carolina State Univ.

Linsley, Judith Walker, M.A. Educ. Coordinator, McFaddin-Ward House Museum.

Lipkin, W. Ian, M.D. Prof. of Epidemiology, Columbia Univ.

Lipking, Lawrence, Ph.D. Prof. Emer., Dept. of English, Northwestern Univ.

Lippy, Charles H., Ph.D. Leroy A. Martin Dist. Prof. of Religious Studies, Univ. of Tennessee, Chattanooga.

Lipscomb, Diana L., Ph.D. Prof. of Biology and Robert Weintraub Chair, George Wash. Univ.

Liptay, Albert, Ph.D. Dir., Research and Dev., Stoller Enterprises Inc.

Litchfield, R. Burr, Ph.D. Prof. Emer. of History, Brown Univ.

Litman, Diane J., Ph.D. Prof. of Computer Science, Univ. of Pittsburgh.

Little, Lawrence S., Ph.D. Assoc. Prof. of History, Villanova Univ.

Little, Richard Stark, Ph.D. Pres., Appalachian Geographic Information Systems.

Little, Trevor J., Ph.D. Head, Dept. of Textile and Apparel Technology and Management, Coll. of Textiles, North Carolina State Univ.

Little Soldier, Lee M., Ed.D. Prof. Emer. of Education, Texas Tech Univ.

Littleton, C. Scott, Ph.D. Former Prof. of Anthropology, Occidental Coll.; author, *The New Comparative Mythology* and *From Scythia to Camelot.*

Litz, Richard E., Ph.D. Prof., Univ. of Florida Tropical Research and Educ. Ctr.

Liu, Hau, M.D. Assoc. Chief of Endocrinology, Stanford Univ.

Liu, Kam-biu, Ph.D. Prof. of Oceanography and Coastal Sciences, Louisiana State Univ.

Liu, Philip L.-F., Sc.D. Prof. of Environmental Engineering, Cornell Univ.

Living, Patricia Communications Coordinator, Health and Social Services, Government of Yukon.

Lizzadro, John S. Exec. Dir., Lizzadro Museum of Lapidary Art.

Ljungquist, Kent, Ph.D. Prof., Dept. of Humanities & Arts, Worcester Polytechnic Inst.

Lloyd, Howell C., Ph.D. Former Prof. of Geography, Miami Univ.

Lloyd, James E., Ph.D. Former Prof. of Entomology and Nematology, Univ. of Florida.

Lo, Chor-Pang, Ph.D. Prof. of Geography, Univ. of Georgia.

Lobeck, Ânne, Ph.D. Prof. of English and Linguistics, Western Washington Univ.

Locascio, S. J., Ph.D. Prof. Emer. of Horticultural Sciences, Univ. of Florida.

Lochner, James C., Ph.D. Sr. Scientist, NASA/Goddard Space Flight Center.

Lockshin, Michael D., F.A.C.P. Dir., Barbara Volcker Ctr. for Women and Rheumatic Disease, and Co-Dir., Mary Kirkland Ctr. for Lupus Research, Hospital for Special Surgery.

Lofaro, Michael A., Ph.D. Prof. of American Lit. and American Studies, Univ. of Tennessee.

Loft, Abram, Ph.D. Prof. Emer. of Chamber Music, Eastman School of Music.

Loftus, Elizabeth F., Ph.D. Distinguished Professor, Department of Psychology and Social Behavior, University of California, Irvine.

Logan, B. Ikubolajeh, Ph.D. Prof. of Geography, Pennsylvania State Univ.

Logan, Bob, B.S. Former sportswriter, (Arlington Heights, IL) *Daily Herald.*

Loizides, Neophytos, Ph.D. Lecturer in Intl. Politics and Ethnic Conflict, Queen's Univ., Belfast.

Loizou, John Brendan Journalist, *The Southeast Asian Times.*

Lombardi, Michael A., B.S. Metrology Engineer, Natl. Inst. of Standards and Technology.

Lombardo, Robert M., Ph.D. Assoc. Prof., Dept. of Criminal Justice, Loyola University Chicago.

Londre, Felicia Hardison, Ph.D. Curators' Prof. of Theatre, Univ. of Missouri, Kansas City.

Long, Alexis B., Ph.D. Assoc. Research Prof. of Atmospheric Sciences, Desert Research Inst.

Long, Charles A., Ph.D. Prof. Emer. of Biology, Curator of Mammals, Univ. of Wisconsin, Stevens Point.

Long, Stephen K., M.L.S., M.A. Technical Services and Systems Librarian, and Music Librarian, Capital Univ.

Longman, Timothy, Ph.D. Assoc. Prof. of Political Science and Africana Studies, Vassar Coll.

Longyear, R. M., Ph.D. Former Prof. of Music, Univ. of Kentucky.

Looft, W. Gene, B.S. Pres., Aerospace Division, Rexnord Corp.

Lookingbill, Brad D., Ph.D. Professor of History, Columbia College of Missouri.

López-Portillo, José-Juan, B.A. Queen Mary Univ. of London.

Lorenz, John R., B.B. Transportation Analyst, New Century Freight Traffic Assoc.

Louie, Henry M., Ph.D. Asst. Prof., Dept. of Electrical and Computer Engineering, Seattle Univ.

Lourdou, Dorothy, M.L.S. Librarian III, New York Public Library.

Love, Jeffrey J., Ph.D. Geomagnetism Group Leader, United States Geological Survey.

Lovejoy, Donald W., Ph.D. Assoc. Prof. and Coordinator, Dept. of Earth Science and Oceanography, Palm Beach Atlantic Univ.

Lovejoy, Thomas E., Ph.D. Pres., Heinz Ctr. for Science, Economics and the Environment.

Lovell, Daniel J., M.D. Prof. of Pediatrics, Cincinnati Childrens Hospital.

Lovell, David J., Ph.D. Asst. Prof., Dept. of Civil Engineering, Univ. of Maryland, Coll. Park.

Loving, Jerome, Ph.D. Prof. of English, Texas A&M Univ.

Lovoll, Odd S., Ph.D. Prof. Emer. of History, St. Olaf Coll.

Low, Frank J., Ph.D. Former Regents Research Prof., Univ. of Arizona.

Low, John N., J.D., M.A. Visiting Lecturer, North Central Coll.

Loy, J. Brent, Ph.D. Prof. of Plant Biology, Univ. of New Hampshire.

Lubin, Nancy, Ph.D. Pres., JNA Assoc., Inc.

Lucey, John, Ph.D. Assoc. Prof., Dept. of Food Science, Univ. of Wisconsin, Madison.

Luckenbach, Mark, Ph.D. Prof. of Marine Science, Coll. of William and Mary.

Ludwickson, John, M.A. Curator of Anthropology, Nebraska State Historical Society.

Luecke, Greg R., Ph.D. Assoc. Prof. of Mechanical Engineering, Iowa State Univ.

Luhrmann, Tanya Marie, Ph.D. Prof. of Anthropology, Stanford Univ.

Lukas, J. Anthony Author and journalist.

Luker, Victoria, Ph.D. Research Fellow, Research School of Pacific and Asian Studies, Australian Natl. Univ.

Lukes-Lukaszewski, Edward A., Ph.D. Prof. of History, Hillsborough Coll.

Lum, P. Andrea, F.R.C.P.C. Abdominal Radiologist, Ottawa Civic Hospital, Ontario.

Lunenfeld, Marvin, Ph.D. Distinguished Teaching Professor Emeritus of History, Fredonia College, State University of New York.

Lunine, Jonathan I., Ph.D. Prof. of Physical Sciences, Cornell Univ.

Lussier, Frances M., Ph.D. Sr. Analyst, Congressional Budget Office.

Lutas, Elizabeth Mary, M.D. Attending Physician, Depts. of Community Medicine and Medicine, St. Vincent's Hospital.

Luteyn, James L., Ph.D. Senior Curator of Botany and Mary Flagler Curator of Botany, New York Botanical Garden.

Lutz, Thomas E., Ph.D. Former Professor of Astronomy, Washington State University.

Ly, Uy-Loi, Ph.D. Assoc. Prof., Dept. of Aeronau-

tics and Astronautics, Univ. of Washington.

Lyles, L. Ward, Ph.D. Asst. Prof., School of Architecture, Design & Planning, Univ. of Kansas.

Lynch, John H., M.D. Chairman of Urology, Prof., Dept. of Urology, Georgetown Univ. Medical Ctr.

Lynfield, Yelva Liptzin, M.D. Clinical Prof. of Dermatology, State Univ. of New York Health Sciences Ctr. at Brooklyn and Chairman of Dermatology Dept., Brookdale Univ. Medical Ctr.

Lyon, Bryce, Ph.D. Former Professor of History, Brown Univ.

Lyons, Charles R., Ph.D. Former Margery Bailey Prof. of English and Dramatic Lit., Stanford Univ.

Lyons, Leslie A., Ph.D. Assoc. Prof. of Genetics, Dept. of Population Health & Reproduction, Sch. of Veterinary Medicine, Univ. of California, Davis.

M

Ma, Kesen, Ph.D. Assoc. Prof., Univ. of Waterloo.

Maas, John L., Ph.D. Former Research Plant Pathologist, U.S. Dept. of Agriculture.

Mac Donald, Laura M., Author, *Curse of the Narrows.*

MacAndrews, Colin, Ph.D. Fellow, Dept. of Economics, Australian Natl. Univ.

MacDonald, Kevin C., Ph.D. Sr. Lecturer, Inst. of Archaeology, Univ. Coll. London.

MacDougall, Robert, Ph.D. Asst. Prof. of History, Univ. of Western Ontario.

Macinko, George, Ph.D. Prof. of Geography, Central Washington Univ.

Macintyre, Clement, Ph.D. Head, Dept. of Politics, Univ. of Adelaide.

Mack, Taylor E., Ph.D. Asst. Prof. of Geography, Louisiana Tech Univ.

Mackay, Bret P., Ph.D. Asst. Prof., Dept. of Economics, Brigham Young Univ.

Mackay, Christopher S., Ph.D. Prof., Dept. of History and Classics, Univ. of Alberta.

Mackey, Philip English, Ph.D. Consultant; author, *The Giver's Guide: Making Your Charity Dollars Count.*

Mackey, Robert R., Ph.D. Former Asst. Prof. of History, U.S. Military Academy, West Point.

MacKillop, James, Ph.D. Prof. of English, Onondaga Community Coll.; Reviewer of Theater and Films, *Syracuse* (NY) *New Times.*

Mackzum, Mary F., M.S.L.S. Head Librarian, *The* (Toledo, OH) *Blade.*

MacLeod, D. Peter, Ph.D. Asst. Prof. of History, Univ. of Ottawa.

Macleod, David I., Ph.D. Prof. of History, Central Michigan Univ.

Macleod, Roderick C., Ph.D. Prof. Emer. of History, Univ. of Alberta; author, *The Mounties.*

Macpherson, Anne S., Ph.D. Assoc. Prof. of History, The Coll. at Brockport, SUNY.

MacRitchie, Finlay, Ph.D. Prof., Dept. of Grain Science, Kansas State Univ.

Macsai, Marian S., M.D. Chief, Division of Ophthalmology, Evanston Northwestern Healthcare.

Maddalena, Ronald J., Ph.D. Astronomer, Natl. Radio Astronomy Observatory.

Madden, Thomas F., Ph.D. Prof. of History, St. Louis Univ.

Madelung, Wilferd, Ph.D. Prof. Emer. of Arabic, Oxford Univ.

Maehl, William H., Ph.D. Former Prof. of Modern History, Auburn Univ.

Magid, Shaul, Ph.D. Prof. of Jewish Studies, Indiana University.

Magrath, C. Peter, Ph.D. Pres. and Prof. of Polit. Sci., University of Minnesota, Twin Cities Campus.

Mahaney, William C., Ph.D. Prof. of Geography, York Univ.

Maher, Michael W., S.J., Ph.D. Assoc. Prof. of History and Dir., Catholic Studies, Gonzaga Univ.

Maier, Pauline, Ph.D. Former William R. Kenan, Jr., Prof. of History, Mass. Institute of Technology.

Makward, Edris, Ph.D. Vice Chancellor, Univ. of the Gambia, West Africa.

Malefakis, Edward, Ph.D. Professor Emeritus of History, Columbia University.

Malik, Iftikhar H., Ph.D. Professor of History, Bath Spa University.

Mamiya, Lawrence H., Ph.D. Prof. of Religion and Africana Studies, Vassar Coll.

Mampilly, Zachariah C., Ph.D. Assistant Professor of Political Science, Vassar College.

Maney, Patrick J., Ph.D. Prof. of History, Boston Coll.

Mangan, Frank, Ph.D. Extension Assoc. Prof. of Plant, Soil & Insect Sciences, Univ. of Mass.

Mango, Karin N., M.L.S. Writer; librarian; author, *Armor—Yesterday and Today.*

Mann, Alan E., Ph.D. Professor Emeritus of Anthropology, Princeton University.

Mann, Gurinder Singh, Ph.D. Prof. of Sikh Studies, Univ. of Calif., Santa Barbara.

Mann, S. Lee, M.F.A. Assoc. Prof. of Design, Univ. of Kansas.

Manning, Kenneth R., Ph.D. Thomas Meloy Prof. of Rhetoric and of the History of Science, Mass. Inst. of Technology.

Maor, Eli, Ph.D. Adjunct Prof. of Mathematics, Loyola Univ. Chicago.

Marble, Vern L., Ph.D. Extension Agronomist Emer., Univ. of Calif., Davis.

March, Robert H., Ph.D. Former Professor of Physics and Integrated Liberal Studies, University of Wisconsin, Madison.

Marcus, Abraham, Ph.D. Associate Professor Emeritus, Dept. of History, Univ. of Texas, Austin.

Marcus, Jane, Ph.D. Dist. Prof. of English, City Univ. of New York Grad. School and City Coll.

Marcus, Philip S., Ph.D. Prof. of Mathematics, Eureka Coll.

Marcus, Robert, M.D. Former Prof. of Medicine, Stanford Univ., and Dir., Aging Study Unit, VA Medical Ctr., Palo Alto, Calif.

Marfisi, Carol A., M.A. Staff person and course instructor, Inst. on Disabilities, Temple Univ.

Margheritis, Ana, Ph.D. Reader in International Relations, University of Southampton.

Mariani, John F., Ph.D. Freelance entertainment writer.

Marini, Richard, Ph.D. Prof. of Horticulture, Virginia Tech.

Markle, William H., M.D. Family Practice Program Dir., Univ. of Pittsburgh Medical Ctr., McKeesport Hospital.

Marks, Bonita L., Ph.D. Assoc. Prof. and Dir., Exercise Science Teaching Lab, Univ. of North Carolina, Chapel Hill.

Marland, Alex, Ph.D. Professor of Political Science, Memorial University of Newfoundland.

Marples, David R., Ph.D. Prof., Dept. of History and Classics, Univ. of Alberta.

Marquard, Katie Former Exec. Dir., United States Speedskating.

Marquardt, Thomas L., B.A. Editor and Publisher, Capital Gazette Communications.

Marquis, Greg, Ph.D. Prof. of History and Politics, Univ. of New Brunswick, St. John.

Marrin, Albert, Ph.D. Chairman, Dept. of History, Yeshiva Coll.

Marsh, Kevin R., Ph.D. Assoc. Prof. of History, Idaho State Univ.

Marshall, Andrew J., Ph.D. Asst. Prof., Dept. of Anthropology, Univ. of Calif., Davis.

Marshall, Brian D. Managing Editor, *Brandon (MB) Sun.*

Marshall, Donald G., Ph.D. Former Fletcher Jones Chair of Great Books, Pepperdine Univ.

Marshek, Kurt M., Ph.D. Harry L. Kent Prof. of Mechanical Engineering, Univ. of Texas.

Marszalek, John F., Ph.D. William L. Giles Dist. Prof. Emer. of History, Mississippi State Univ.

Martin, Dale Robert, M.A. Assoc. Prof. Emer. of Geography, Truman State Univ.

Martin, George C., Ph.D. Prof. Emer. of Pomology, Univ. of Calif., Davis.

Martin, George E., Ph.D. Prof. Emer., Mathematics and Statistics, State Univ. of New York, Albany.

Martin, James, B.A. Editor in Chief, *Tennis Magazine.*

Martin, James Kirby, Ph.D. Dist. Univ. Prof. of History, Univ. of Houston.

Martin, Jennifer L., Ph.D. Asst. Research Prof., Univ. of Calif., Los Angeles, Dept. of Medicine.

Martin, Paul W., Ph.D. Assistant Professor, Department of English, and Director, Canadian Studies Program, University of Vermont.

Martin, Philip L., Ph.D. Prof., Dept. of Agricultural & Resource Economics, Univ. of Calif., Davis.

Martin, Pierre, Ph.D. Professor of Political Sci-

ence, Université de Montréal.

Martin, Richard, M.Phil. Former Curator, Costume Inst., Metropolitan Museum of Art.

Martin, Richard A., Ph.D. Staff Member, Los Alamos Natl. Laboratory.

Martin, Richard C., Ph.D. Prof. of Religion, Emory Univ.

Martin, Steve W., Ph.D. Prof. of Materials Science and Engineering, Iowa State Univ.

Martin, Susan Taylor, B.A. Sr. Foreign Correspondent, *St. Petersburg* (FL) *Times.*

Martin, William H., Ph.D. Former Dir., Division of Natural Areas, Eastern Kentucky Univ.

Martinson, Candace, Ph.D. Former Asst. Curator of Entomology, Collection of Insects and Spiders, Ohio State Univ.

Martner, Brooks E., M.S. Former Research Meteorologist, Natl. Oceanic and Atmospheric Admin.

Marvin, Betty, M.A. Historic Preservation Planner, City of Oakland, Calif.

Marx, Robert F., B.A. Marine Archaeologist, Phoenician Explorations.

Masayesva-Jeanne, LaVerne, Ph.D. Assoc. Prof. of Anthropology, Univ. of Nevada, Reno.

Mason, Charles Exec. Editor, *Sail* magazine.

Mason, Sherri A., Ph.D. Professor of Chemistry, State University of New York, Fredonia.

Masotti, Louis H., Ph.D. Prof. Emer. of Management and Urban Dev., Univ. of Calif., Irvine.

Mass, Jeffrey P., Ph.D. Former Prof. of History, Stanford Univ.

Massey, J., Ph.D. Curator Emer., Herbarium, Univ. of North Carolina.

Mast, Roderic B. Vice Pres., Conservation Intl.

Mastny, Vojtech, Ph.D. Sr. Research Scholar, Woodrow Wilson Intl. Ctr. for Scholars; author, *Russia's Road to the Cold War.*

Mastrandrea, Michael D., Ph.D. Director, Near Zero climate change policy think tank; and Sr. Research Associate, Carnegie Institution for Science.

Matalon, Reuben, Ph.D. Former Prof. and Dir. Chief of Genetics, Miami Children's Hospital-Research Inst.

Mateo, Mario, Ph.D. Prof. of Astronomy, Univ. of Michigan, Ann Arbor.

Mather, A. S., Ph.D. Former Prof. of Geography, Univ. of Aberdeen.

Mather, Keith G., B.A. Author and expert on Africa and the Middle East.

Matheson, Katy, M.A. Coeditor, *Dance as a Theatre Art.*

Mathews, Thomas G., Ph.D. Secretary-General, Assoc. of Caribbean Universities.

Matloff, Maurice, Ph.D. Former Adjunct Prof. of History, Georgetown Univ.; former Chief Historian, U.S. Dept. of the Army.

Matolak, David W., Ph.D. Prof., School of Electrical Engineering and Computer Science, Ohio Univ.

Matta, Kristin Dir. of Natl. Governing Bodies Business Dev., U.S. Olympic Committee; former Dir. of Dev., U.S. Figure Skating Assoc.

Matthee, Rudi, Ph.D. Prof. of History, Univ. of Delaware.

Matthews, Anne L., Ph.D. Assoc. Prof. of Genetics and Dir., Genetic Counselling Training Program, Case Western Reserve Univ.

Matthews, Leslie S., M.D. Chief of Orthopaedic Surgery, Union Memorial Hospital, Baltimore.

Matthews, Peter Hans, Ph.D. Prof. of Econ. and Dir., Intl. Politics and Econ., Middlebury Coll.

Matthews, Robert W., Ph.D. Prof. Emer. of Entomology, Univ. of Georgia.

Maugh, Thomas H., II, Ph.D. Medical writer.

Mauseth, James D., Ph.D. Prof., Dept. of Integrative Biology, Univ. of Texas, Austin.

Mauskopf, Seymour Harold, Ph.D. Prof. of History, Duke Univ.

Maxwell, Clarence V. H., Ph.D. Asst. Prof., Dept. of History, Millersville Univ.

Maxwell, Jeanine M., B.S. Research Engineer, UMR Coatings Inst.

May, Jill P., M.S.L.S. Prof. of Children's Lit., Purdue Univ.

Maycock, Paul F., Ph.D. Professor Emeritus of Botany, Erindale College, University of Toronto.

Mayer, Jeremy D., Ph.D. Asst. Prof., School of Public Policy, George Mason Univ.

Mayer, Robert N., Ph.D. Professor, Department

of Family and Consumer Studies, Univ. of Utah.

Mays, Larry W., Ph.D. Professor, School of Sustainable Engineering and the Built Environment, Arizona State University.

Mazzone, Theodore, M.D. Chief, Section of Endocrinology, Diabetes and Metabolism, Univ. of Illinois at Chicago.

McAlister, Elizabeth, Ph.D. Assoc. Prof. of Religion, Wesleyan Univ.

McArthur, David S., Ph.D. Prof. Emer. of Geography, San Diego State Univ.

McCall, Benjamin J., Ph.D. Asst. Prof. of Chemistry and Astronomy, Univ. of Illinois, Urbana-Champaign.

McCall, Christina, B.A. Author, *Grits: An Intimate Portrait of the Liberal Party* and *Trudeau and Our Times.*

McCammon Feldman, Beth, Ph.D. Former owner, Lively Run Goat Dairy.

McCardell, John, Ph.D. Prof. of History and Pres. Emer., Middlebury Coll.

McCarthy, Justin, Ph.D. Prof. of History, Univ. of Louisville.

McCarthy, Kathryn L., Ph.D. Professor, Dept. of Food Science and Technol., Univ. of Calif., Davis.

McCarthy, Linda, B.S. President and cofounder, History is a Hoot, Inc.

McCarty, William H., Ph.D. Extension Prof. Emer., Mississippi State Univ.

McCausland, Ian Retired Editor, *The Mercury/ The Sunday Tasmanian.*

McClintock, Jeffrey E., Ph.D. Sr. Astrophysicist, Smithsonian Astrophysical Observatory.

McComb, David, Ph.D. Prof. of History, Colorado State Univ.

McCormick, Mark E., Dir. of Communications, Kansas Leadership Ctr.

McCosker, John E., Ph.D. Sr. Scientist and Chair of Aquatic Biology, Calif. Academy of Sciences.

McCoy, Donald R., Ph.D. Univ. Dist. Prof. of History, Univ. of Kansas.

McCoy, Jennifer L., Ph.D. Prof. of Political Science, Georgia State Univ.

McCracken, J. C., M.B.A. Former Production Dir., *The* (Parsippany, NJ) *Daily Record.*

McCusker, Jane, M.D. Prof., Dept. of Clinical Epidemiology and Community Studies, St. Mary's Hospital Ctr.

McDade, Barbara E., Ph.D. Assoc. Prof., Dept. of Geography, Univ. of Florida.

McDaniel, Ben T., Ph.D. Prof. of Animal Science, North Carolina State Univ.

McDermott, Vincent, Ph.D. Prof. of Music, Lewis and Clark Coll.

McDonald, Charles J., M.D. Prof. and Head, Division of Dermatology, Brown Univ. and Roger Williams General Hospital.

McDonald, Robert A. J., Ph.D. Assoc. Prof. of History, Univ. of British Columbia.

McDowall, Duncan, Ph.D. Prof., Dept. of History, Carleton Univ.

McEachran, John D., Ph.D. Prof. of Wildlife and Fisheries Sciences, Texas A&M Univ.

McFadden, Lucy-Ann, Ph.D. Assoc. Research Prof. of Astronomy, Univ. of Maryland.

McFall, Sara, D. Phil. Sr. Investigating Officer, Parliamentary and Health Service Ombudsman.

McFerrin, John B., Ph.D. Former Prof. of Finance, Univ. of Florida.

McGhee, Robert, Ph.D. Curator of Arctic Archaeology, Canadian Museum of Civilization.

McGiffert, Michael, Ph.D. Editor Emer. of *The William and Mary Quarterly,* and Prof. Emer. of History, Coll. of William and Mary.

McGill, Lawrence D., Ph.D. Technical Vice Pres., Animal Reference Pathology.

McGinley, P. A., B.Comm. Managing Dir., Europa Publications Ltd.

McGinnis, Christine, B.A. Editor, Special Editions, Arkansas Valley Publishing.

McGinnis, Terri, D.V.M. Veterinarian; author, *The Well Dog Book.*

McGirr, Lisa Maria, Ph.D. Prof. of History, Harvard Univ.

McGlathery, James M., Ph.D. Prof. of German and Head, Dept. of Germanic Langs. and Lits., Univ. of Illinois, Urbana-Champaign.

McGovern, James, B.S. Freelance writer.

McGovern, William M., LL.B. Professor Emeritus of Law, University of California, Los Angeles.

McGowan, Alan, B.E. Pres., Gene Media Forum, S. I. Newhouse School of Public Communications, Syracuse Univ.

McGowan, Kevin J., Ph.D. Editor, Cornell Laboratory of Ornithology, Cornell Univ.

McGowan, Mary Kate, Ph.D. Assoc. Prof. of Philosophy, Wellesley College.

McGrath, Roger D., Ph.D. Prof. of History, Univ. of Calif., Los Angeles.

McGrath, William J., Ph.D. Prof. Emer. of History, Univ. of Rochester.

McGuinn, Patrick, Ph.D. Professor of Political Science and Education, Drew University.

McInally, Mike, B.A. Former Editor, *Missoulian.*

McIntosh, Cecilia A., Ph.D. Prof., Dept. of Biology, East Tennessee State Univ.

McIntosh, Christopher, D.Phil. Author, *Astrology.*

McIntyre, Peggy Exec. Secretary and Editorial Asst., *The* (Charleston, SC) *Post and Courier.*

McKale, Donald M., Ph.D. Class of '41 Memorial Professor of Humanities, Dept. of History, Clemson Univ.

McKay, Kenneth B., M.Ed. Author, *Puppetry in Canada: An Art to Enchant.*

McKee, Ann C., M.D. Prof. of Neurology and Pathology, Boston Univ. School of Medicine.

McKeen, William, Ph.D. Acting Chair and Visiting Prof. of Journalism, Dept. of Journalism, Boston Univ.

McKeever, Merri-Lou General Manager, Eastman Kodak Company.

McKerns, Joseph P., Ph.D. Former Assoc. Prof. of Journalism, Ohio State Univ.

McKinley, Mary B., Ph.D. Professor Emeritus of French, University of Virginia.

McKinnon, William B., Ph.D. Prof. of Earth and Planetary Sciences, Washington Univ., St. Louis.

McKnight, Tom L., Ph.D. Prof. of Geography, Univ. of Calif., Los Angeles.

McLaughlin, John F., M.D. Prof. Emer., Dept. of Pediatrics, Univ. of Washington.

McLaughlin, P. A., Ph.D. Former Research Scientist, Shannon Point Marine Ctr., Western Washington Univ.

McLean, Margaret R., Ph.D. Dir., Biotechnology and Healthcare Ethics, Markkula Ctr. for Applied Ethics, Santa Clara Univ.

McLear, Patrick E., Ph.D. Professor Emeritus of History, Missouri Western State College.

McLeay, Elizabeth, Ph.D. Adjunct Professor of Political Science, Victoria University of Wellington.

McLeese, Don, M.A. Assoc. Prof., School of Journalism, Univ. of Iowa.

McLendon, George, Ph.D. Howard R. Hughes Provost and Prof. of Chemistry, Rice Univ.

McLure, Charles E., Jr., Ph.D. Sr. Fellow, Hoover Inst. on War, Revolution, and Peace, Stanford Univ.

McMahon, James D., Jr., M.A. Director, Milton Hershey School Heritage Center and Department of School History.

McManus, Ruth, Ph.D. Associate Professor in Geography, Dublin City University.

McNeese, Tim, M.A. Assoc. Prof. of History, York College.

McNulty, Michael L., Ph.D. Professor Emeritus of Geography, University of Iowa.

McPherson, H. J., Ph.D. Former Prof. of Geography, Univ. of Alberta.

McPherson, James M., Ph.D. Prof. Emer., Dept. of History, Princeton Univ.; author, *Battle Cry of Freedom: The Civil War Era;* winner of Pulitzer Prize for History, 1989.

McWilliams, Margaret, Ph.D. Author, *Food Fundamentals.*

Meade, Janet A., Ph.D. Assoc. Prof. of Accountancy and Taxation, Univ. of Houston.

Meade, Marion, M.S. Author, *Eleanor of Aquitaine.*

Meade, Teresa A., Ph.D. Professor of History, Union College, Schenectady.

Means, D. Bruce, Ph.D. Pres. and Exec. Dir., Coastal Plains Inst. and Land Conservancy; Adjunct Prof., Dept. of Biological Science, Florida State Univ.

Meeks, Brian Winston, Ph.D. Prof., Department of Government, Univ. of the West Indies, Mona.

Meeks, Harold A., Ph.D. Professor Emeritus of Geography, University of Vermont.

Meier, Heinz K., Ph.D. Former Prof. of History, Old Dominion Univ.

Meilach, Dona Z., M.A. Contributing Editor, *Presentations Magazine* and *Computer Pictures;* author of art, craft, and graphics books.

Meir, A. J., Ph.D. Prof., Dept. of Mathematics, Auburn Univ.

Meister, F. A., M.A. Pres. and CEO, Distilled Spirits Council of the United States, Inc.

Meixsel, Richard B., Ph.D. Associate Prof. of History, James Madison Univ.

Melder, Keith E., Ph.D. Former Curator of Political History, Natl. Museum of American History.

Meldrum, Jeff, Ph.D. Assoc. Prof. of Anatomy and Anthropology, Idaho State Univ.

Melford, Sara Steck, Ph.D. Assoc. Prof. Emer. of Chemistry, DePaul Univ.

Mellard, James M., Ph.D. Former Prof. of English, Northern Illinois Univ.

Mendelson, Joseph R., III, Ph.D. Director of Research, Zoo Atlanta.

Menden, Harvey A., Ph.D. Dir., Training and Organizational Dev., Adecco.

Mendilow, Jonathan, Ph.D. Prof. of Political Science, Rider Univ.

Menning, Carol Bresnahan, Ph.D. Prof. of History, Univ. of Toledo.

Merchant, Carolyn, Ph.D. Prof. of Conservation and Resource Studies, Univ. of Calif., Berkeley.

Merenstein, Gerald B., M.D. Former Prof. of Pediatrics and Sr. Assoc. Dean of Educ., Univ. of Colorado School of Medicine.

Merkel, Brian, Ph.D. Associate Professor of Human Biology, Univ. of Wisconsin, Green Bay.

Merkl, Peter H., Ph.D. Prof. Emer. of Political Science, Univ. of Calif., Santa Barbara.

Merriam, Alan P., Ph.D. Former Prof. of Anthropology, Indiana Univ., Bloomington.

Merrill, Chris, Ph.D. Prof., Technology Educ., Illinois State Univ.

Merritt, James Douglas, Ph.D. Former Prof. of English, Brooklyn Coll., City Univ. of New York.

Mertz, Barbara, Ph.D. Author, *Temples, Tombs and Hieroglyphs* and *Red Land, Black Land: Daily Life in Ancient Egypt.*

Metzler, John D., Ph.D. Asst. Prof. of African Studies and Educ., Michigan State Univ.

Meulenberg, Norman F., M.B.A. Marketing Manager, Mettler-Toledo, Inc.

Mews, Siegfried, Ph.D. Prof. Emer. of German, Univ. of North Carolina, Chapel Hill.

Meyendorff, Paul, Ph.D. Alexander Schmemann Prof. of Liturgical Theology, St. Vladimir's Orthodox Theological Seminary.

Meyer, B., Ph.D. Consultant; former Prof. of Chemistry, Univ. of Washington.

Meyer, Gary C., Ph.D. Prof. Emer. of Geography and Natural Resources, Univ. of Wisconsin, Stevens Point.

Meyer, John R., Ph.D. Prof., North Carolina State Univ.

Meyer-Arendt, Klaus J., Ph.D. Prof. and Chair, Dept. of Environmental Studies, Univ. of West Florida.

Meyers, Carol L., Ph.D. Professor of Religion, Duke University.

Meyers, Eric M., Ph.D. Prof. of Religion, Duke Univ.

Meyers, Jason, M.A. Curator, Museum of Funeral Customs.

Meyerson, Joel D., Ph.D. Chief, Histories Division, U.S. Army Ctr. of Military History.

Mezey, Susan Gluck, Ph.D. Prof. of Political Science, Loyola Univ.

Michaelides, Efstathios E., Ph.D. Prof., Dept. of Mechanical Engineering, Univ. of Texas at San Antonio.

Michielli, Zachariah, M.Arch. Ph.D. candidate, Yale School of Architecture.

Michopoulos, John G., Ph.D. Sr. Research Scientist, United States Naval Research Laboratory.

Mieczkowski, Yanek, Ph.D. Visiting Assistant Prof. of History, Univ. of Central Florida; author, *Gerald Ford and the Challenges of the 1970s.*

Mignot, Emmanuel, M.D.; Ph.D. Prof. of Psychology and Behavioral Sciences, Stanford Univ.

Mikalson, Jon D., Ph.D. Prof. of Classics and Dir. of Undergraduate Studies, Univ. of Virginia.

Miksic, John N., Ph.D. Professor, Department of Southeast Asian Studies, Natl. Univ. of Singapore.

Milanesio, Natalia, Ph.D. Associate Professor of History, University of Houston.

Milbert, Neil, B.A. Former Staff Reporter, *Chicago Tribune.*

Mildner, Gerard C. S., Ph.D. Assoc. Prof., School of Urban Studies and Planning, Portland State Univ.

Millar, F. G. B., D.Litt. Camden Prof. Emer. of Ancient History, Oxford Univ.

Millbrooke, Anne, Ph.D. Former Manager, Archive and Historical Resource Ctr., United Technologies Corp.

Miller, Arthur I., Ph.D. Prof. Emer. of History, Philosophy, and Communication of Science, Univ. Coll. London.

Miller, Bruce Granville, Ph.D. Prof., Dept. of Anthropology and Sociology, Univ. of British Columbia.

Miller, Carman, Ph.D. Prof. Emer. of History, McGill Univ.

Miller, Dean, B.A. Former Managing Editor, *The* (Idaho Falls, ID) *Post Register.*

Miller, E. Willard, Ph.D. Former Prof. of Geography and Assoc. Dean for Resident Instruction, Coll. of Earth and Mineral Sciences, Penn. State Univ.

Miller, J. Maxwell, Ph.D. Director, Graduate Studies in Religion, Emory University.

Miller, J. R., Ph.D. Canada Research Chair and Prof. of History, Univ. of Saskatchewan.

Miller, James E., M.S. Former Prof. of Meteorology, Polytechnic Univ. of New York.

Miller, James S., Ph.D. Dean and Vice Pres. for Science, New York Botanical Garden.

Miller, Jane K., Ph.D. Former Prof., Lone Mountain Coll.

Miller, Laura J., M.D. Dir., Women's Mental Health Program, Univ. of Illinois, Chicago.

Miller, Lee D., Ph.D. Curator, Allyn Museum of Entomology/Florida Museum of Natural History.

Miller, Leonard Scott, Ph.D. Chairman and Prof., Dept. of Aerospace Engineering, Wichita State Univ.

Miller, Raymond J., Jr., Ph.D. Dir., Intl. Program in Agriculture and Natural Resources, Univ. of Maryland, Coll. Park.

Miller, Timothy T., M.D. Clinical Asst. Prof. of Obstetrics and Gynecology, Univ. of Illinois Coll. of Medicine, Chicago.

Miller, William C., B.S.Ed. Marketing Manager, Clauss Cutlery Company.

Miller-Sanchez, Sandra Elizabeth, M.A. Lecturer, McGill University.

Millett, Allan R., Ph.D. Maj. Gen. Raymond E. Mason, Jr., Prof. Emer. of Military History, Mershon Ctr., Ohio State University.

Mills, Barbara J., Ph.D. Prof. of Anthropology, Univ. of Arizona.

Mills, Daniel Quinn, Ph.D. Prof. Emer. of Business Admin., Harvard Univ.

Mills, John R., Ph.D. Prof. of Accounting, Univ. of Nevada, Reno.

Millward, Hugh, Ph.D. Professor Emeritus of Geography, St. Mary's University.

Minch, Edwin W., Ph.D. Environmental Specialist, Arizona Dept. of Agriculture.

Miner, Todd, M.S. Instructor of Meteorology, Pennsylvania State Univ.

Minkler, Julie-Tsivakou, M.A. Senior Lecturer, Iowa State Univ.

Minor, Vernon Hyde, Ph.D. Prof. Emer. of Art History and Humanities, Univ. of Colorado.

Mintz, Steven, Ph.D. John and Rebecca Moores Prof. of History and Dir., American Cultures Program, Univ. of Houston.

Minutaglio, Bill, M.S. Author, *First Son: George W. Bush and the Bush Family Dynasty.*

Misa, Thomas J., Ph.D. Director, Charles Babbage Institute, University of Minnesota.

Misfeldt, Willard E., Ph.D. Former Professor of Art, Bowling Green State University.

Miskokomon, Roberta, M.L.S. First Nations Library Coordinator, Southern Ontario Library Service, London.

Mitchell, Adrian, Ph.D. Head, School of English, Art History, Film and Media, Univ. of Sydney.

Mitchell, Charlie, J.D. Executive Editor, *The*

Vicksburg (MS) *Post.*

Mitchell, Kelly L., Ph.D.   Prof., Fanshawe College.

Mitchell, Otis C., Ph.D.   Prof. of History, Univ. of Cincinnati.

Mitchener, Kris James, Ph.D.   Assoc. Prof. of Economics, Santa Clara Univ.

Mittermeier, Russell A., Ph.D.   Pres., Conservation Intl.

Mockaitis, Thomas R., Ph.D.   Professor of History, DePaul University.

Moczek, Armin, Ph.D.   Assoc. Prof. of Biology, Indiana Univ.

Modell, Harold I., Ph.D.   Dir., Natl. Resource for Computers in Life Science Educ.

Moe, Doug, B.A.   Journalist/Author, *The* (Madison, WI) *Capital Times.*

Moffroid, Mary T., Ph.D.   Prof. of Physical Therapy, Univ. of Vermont.

Mohamed, Fabian, Ph.D.   Prof., Faculty of Chemistry, Biochemistry, and Pharmacy, Natl. Univ. of San Luis, Argentina.

Mohanty, Manoj K., Ph.D.   Professor of Mining and Mineral Resources Engineering, Southern Illinois University, Carbondale.

Mokwa, Robert L., Ph.D.   Assoc. Prof., Dept. of Civil Engineering, Montana State Univ.

Molé, Paul A., Ph.D.   Former Prof. of Physical Educ., Univ. of Calif., Davis.

Molineux, Will, B.A.   Former Editorial Page Editor, (Newport News, VA) *Daily Press.*

Monath, Thomas P., M.D.   Vice Pres., Research and Medical Affairs, OraVax, Inc.

Moncton, David E., Ph.D.   Dir., MIT Nuclear Reactor Lab., Mass. Inst. of Technology.

Monet, Jacques, Ph.D.   Dir., Canadian Inst. of Jesuit Studies.

Money, K. E., N.D.C.   Sr. Scientist, Defence and Civil Inst. of Environmental Medicine.

Monk, Patricia, Ph.D.   Former Prof. of English, Dalhousie Univ.

Monnier, John D., Ph.D.   Assoc. Prof. of Astronomy, Univ. of Michigan.

Monteón, Michael, Ph.D.   Prof. of History, Univ. of Calif., San Diego.

Monto, Arnold S., M.D.   Prof. of Epidemiology, School of Public Health, Univ. of Michigan.

Moody, Joycelyn K., Ph.D.   Sue E. Denman Dist. Chair in American Lit., Dept. of English, Univ. of Texas at San Antonio.

Moody, Ken, Ph.D.   Chemist, Lawrence Livermore Natl. Laboratory.

Moody, Patricia A., Ph.D.   Assoc. Prof. of English, Syracuse Univ.

Moore, Clement Henry, Ph.D.   Prof. of Government, Univ. of Texas, Austin.

Moore, Duncan T., Ph.D.   Prof. of Optical Engineering, Univ. of Rochester.

Moore, Gerry, Ph.D.   Dir., Dept. of Science, Brooklyn Botanic Garden.

Moore, Janice, Ph.D.   Prof. of Biology, Colorado State Univ.

Moore, Paul H., Ph.D.   Research Leader, Agricultural Research Service, U.S. Dept. of Agriculture, Pacific Basin Agricultural Research Ctr.

Moore, Raymond K., Ph.D.   Prof. of Civil Engineering, Univ. of Kansas.

Moore, Stephen T., M.D.   Assoc. Prof. of History, Central Washington Univ.

Moorhouse, James   Dir. of Youth Natl. Teams, U.S. Soccer.

Moran, Joseph M., Ph.D.   Prof. Emer., Dept. of Earth Science, Univ. of Wisconsin, Green Bay; Assoc. Dir., Educ. Program, American Meteorological Society.

Moran, Robbin C., Ph.D.   Curator, New York Botanical Garden.

Moran-Taylor, Michelle, Ph.D.   Asst. Adjunct Prof. of Geography, Univ. of Denver.

Morcom, Nicole F., Ph.D.   Postdoctoral Fellow/Lecturer, Geography and Environmental Studies, Univ. of Adelaide.

Moreno, Cesáreo, M.F.A.   Visual Arts Dir., Mexican Fine Arts Ctr. Museum, Chicago.

Morgan, Anthony W., Ph.D.   Prof., Dept. of Educ. Leadership and Policy, Univ. of Utah.

Morgan, H. Wayne, Ph.D.   George Lynn Cross Research Prof. Emer. of History, Univ. of Oklahoma.

Morgan, T. Clifton, Ph.D.   Albert Thomas Profes-

sor of Political Science, Rice University.

Morrill, Bruce T., Ph.D.   Assoc. Prof. of Theology, Boston Coll.

Morrill, John S., DLiH; FBA   Prof. of British and Irish History, Selwyn Coll., Univ. of Cambridge.

Morring, Frank, Jr., A.B.   Sr. Space Technology Editor, *Aviation Week & Space Technology.*

Morris, M. Michelle, Ph.D.   Associate Professor of History, University of Missouri, Columbia.

Morris, Mark, Ph.D.   Prof. of Physics and Astronomy, Univ. of Calif., Los Angeles.

Morrissett, Irving   Emer. Prof. of Economics, Univ. of Colorado.

Morse, Edward E., M.D.   Former Prof. of Laboratory Medicine, Univ. of Connecticut.

Morstein-Marx, Robert, Ph.D.   Prof. of Classics, Univ. of Calif., Santa Barbara.

Morton, Desmond, Ph.D.   Dir. Emer., McGill Inst. for the Study of Canada.

Morton, Graeme, Ph.D.   Prof., Dept. of History, Univ. of Guelph.

Moser, Katrina A., Ph.D.   Assoc. Prof. of Geography, Univ. of Western Ontario.

Moses, Michele S., Ph.D.   Assoc. Prof. of Education Policy and Philosophy, Univ. of Colorado at Boulder.

Moss, Cynthia, B.A.   Dir., Amboseli Elephant Research Project.

Moss, Mark H., M.D.   Fellow in Allergy and Immunology, Univ. of Wisconsin Hospital & Clinics.

Mottram, Murray   Former Sr. Journalist, *The Age* (Melbourne, Australia).

Mould, Jeremy, Ph.D.   Dir., Mount Stromlo and Siding Spring Observatories, Natl. Australia Univ.

Moulton, Alice, B.Ed.   Former Teacher-Librarian, Winnipeg School Division #1.

Moulton, Edward C., Ph.D.   Sr. Scholar of History, Univ. of Manitoba.

Moulton, Gary E., Ph.D.   Thomas C. Sorensen Prof. Emer. of History, Univ. of Nebraska, Lincoln.

Mounfield, Peter R., Ph.D.   Former Sr. Lecturer in Geography, Univ. of Leicester.

Moyer, Ann E., Ph.D.   Assoc. Prof. of History, Univ. of Pennsylvania.

Mozdzen, Edward C., Ph.D.   Project Manager, Fuels Refinery and Oilfield, The Lubrizol Corp.

Muchie, Mammo, D.Phil.   Visiting Prof., Aalborg Univ., Denmark.

Muckleston, Keith W., Ph.D.   Prof. Emer. of Geography, Oregon State Univ.

Mueckler, Michael, Ph.D.   Prof. of Cell Biology and Medicine, Washington Univ., St. Louis.

Mueller, Robert C., J.D.   Litigation attorney, Rubin, Hay & Gould, P.C.

Mugnai, Robert   Vice Pres. and Publisher, *Salon News,* Fairchild Publications.

Mulder, John M., Ph.D.   Former Pres., Louisville Presbyterian Theological Seminary.

Mulholland, M. Robert, Jr., Th.D.   Vice Pres. and Chief Academic Officer, Asbury Theological Seminary.

Mullen, Kieran, Ph.D.   Associate Professor of Physics, University of Oklahoma.

Mullen, Patricia Ann, M.A.   President, Tigon American, Inc.

Muller, Edward K., Ph.D.   Prof. of History, Univ. of Pittsburgh.

Muller, Peter O., Ph.D.   Prof., Dept. of Geography, Univ. of Miami.

Mullin, James V., M.L.S.I.S., M.Ed.   Pres., Irish Famine Curriculum Committee.

Munski, Douglas C., Ph.D.   Prof. of Geography, Univ. of North Dakota; Chairperson, North Dakota Geographic Alliance.

Munson, Edwin S., M.D.   Former Diplomate of the American Board of Anesthesiology.

Murphy, Bruce Allen, Ph.D.   Fred Morgan Kirby Prof. of Civil Rights, Lafayette Coll.

Murray, Talbot, Ph.D.   Dir., T&T Pacific Ltd.

Muscari, Joseph A., Ph.D.   Program Manager, Lockheed Martin Corp.

Muscatine, L., Ph.D.   Prof. Emer. of Biology, Univ. of Calif., Los Angeles.

Musiek, Frank E., Ph.D.   Dir. of Audiology, Dartmouth Medical School.

Musto, David F., M.D.   Former Prof. of Child Psychiatry and History of Medicine, Yale Univ.

Mutu, Margaret, Ph.D.   Head, Dept. of Maori Studies, Univ. of Auckland.

Myers, Garth A., Ph.D.   Assoc. Prof. of Geography, Univ. of Kansas.

Myers, Robert J., M.A.   Author, *Celebrations, The Complete Book of American Holidays.*

Myhre, Larry, B.A.   Editor, *Sioux City* (IA) *Journal.*

Myles, Edward L., Ph.D.   Prof. Emer. of Geography, Calif. State Univ., Chico.

Myrsiades, Kostas, Ph.D.   Professor Emeritus, English Department, West Chester Univ.

N

Nabokov, Peter, Ph.D.   Professor, Culture and Performance, University of California, Los Angeles.

Nadeau, Roger, Ph.D.   Head, Dept. of Geography, Univ. of Sherbrooke.

Nadelson, Theodore, M.D.   Former Clinical Prof. of Psychiatry, Boston Univ. School of Medicine.

Nadler, Henry L., M.D.   Prof. Emer. of Pediatrics, Univ. of Illinois, Chicago.

Nadler, Steven, Ph.D.   Prof. of Philosophy, Univ. of Wisconsin, Madison.

Nagel, Roy K.   Former Editor, *The Prince George* (BC) *Citizen.*

Nagel, Sidney R., Ph.D.   Prof. of Physics, Univ. of Chicago.

Nagle, D. Brendan, Ph.D.   Prof. Emer. of History, Univ. of Southern Calif.

Najita, Tetsuo, Ph.D.   Prof. Emer. of History and East Asian Lang. and Civilizations, Univ. of Chicago.

Napier, Rita G., Ph.D.   Assoc. Prof. of History, Univ. of Kansas.

Nash, Bonnie, M.A.   Former Editor and Publisher, *Trap & Field* magazine.

Nash, Stanley L., Ph.D.   Prof. Emer. of Hebrew Lit., Hebrew Union Coll.–Jewish Inst. of Religion.

Nash, Suzanne, Ph.D.   Prof. Emer. of French, Princeton Univ.

Naske, Claus-M., Ph.D.   Coauthor, *Alaska: A History of the 49th State.*

Nassar, Jamal R., Ph.D.   Dean, Coll. of Social and Behavioral Sciences, Calif. State Univ., San Bernardino.

Natanson, Lisa J., Ph.D.   Research Fish Biologist, National Oceanic and Atmospheric Administration.

Nathan, Ronald G., Ph.D.   Former Prof. of Family Practice and Psychiatry, Albany Medical Coll.

Nathanson, Stephen, Ph.D.   Prof. of Philosophy, Northeastern Univ.

Natoli, Marie D., Ph.D.   Prof. of Political Science, Emmanuel Coll., Boston.

Navarrete Cálix, Daniela, M.A.   Chargé of Historical Ctrs. Unit, Honduran Inst. of Anthropology and History.

Navarro, Maria, Ph.D.   Assoc. Prof., College of Agricultural and Environmental Sciences, Univ. of Georgia.

Nazareth, Peter, B.A.   Prof. of English and African-American World Studies, Univ. of Iowa.

N'Diaye, Boubacar, Ph.D.   Associate Professor of African Studies, The College of Wooster.

Neal, Dan   Former Editor, *Casper* (WY) *Star-Tribune.*

Needles, Howard L., Ph.D.   Prof. Emer. of Textile and Materials Science, Univ. of Calif., Davis.

Neely, Mark E., Jr., Ph.D.   McCabe Greer Prof. of Civil War History, Pennsylvania State Univ.

Neely, Sharlotte, Ph.D.   Prof. of Anthropology, Northern Kentucky Univ.

Neiberg, Michael S., Ph.D.   Professor of History, U.S. Army War College.

Neil, Randy L., B.S.   Founder and Pres., Intl. Cheerleading Assoc., Inc.

Nelsen, David A., Jr., M.D.   Assoc. Prof., Family and Community Medicine, Univ. of Arkansas for Medical Sciences.

Nelson, Hank, Ph.D.   Prof. of Pacific and Asian History, Australian Natl. Univ.

Nelson, Mark D., M.F.A.   Former Assistant Professor of Music, Wabash College.

Nelson, Paul David, Ph.D.   Professor of History, Berea College.

Nelson, Roy Paul, M.S.   Prof. of Journalism, Univ. of Oregon; author, *The Cartoonist.*

Nelson, Tom, D.Phil.   Departmental Lecturer, Oriental Inst., Oxford Univ.

Nemerson, David, Ph.D.   Independent environmental consultant.

Neto, Francelina A., Ph.D. Prof., Dept. of Civil Engineering, Calif. State Polytechnic Univ., Pomona.

Neumann, Jeanne M., Ph.D. Prof. and Chair, Classics Dept., Davidson Coll.

Neumann, Robert G., Ph.D. Former Sr. Adviser, Ctr. for Strategic and Intl. Studies, Wash., D.C.

Neusner, Jacob, Ph.D. Dist. Service Prof. Emer. of the History and Theology of Judaism; Sr. Fellow, Institute of Advanced Theology, Bard College.

Neville, Cynthia J., Ph.D. Prof. of History, Dalhousie Univ.

Newman, Oscar, B.Arch. Pres. and Exec. Dir., Inst. for Community Design Analysis, Inc.

Nguyen Thi Dieu, Ph.D. Assoc. Prof. of History, Temple Univ.

Nice, Alex T., Ph.D. Former Visiting Assoc. Prof. of Classics, Classical Studies Program, Willamette Univ.

Nicely, Kenneth A., Ph.D. Prof. of Biology, Western Kentucky Univ.

Nicklas, Brian Museum Specialist, Archives Div., Natl. Air and Space Museum, Smithsonian Inst.

Nicodemus, Charles E., Jr., B.S. Former Government Reporter, *Chicago Sun-Times.*

Nielsen, Peter Editor in Chief, *SAIL* magazine.

Nieman, James M., M.D. Orthopaedic Surgeon, Orthopaedic Inst. of Ohio.

Niemeyer, Carl, Ph.D. Former Prof. of English, Union College.

Niesen, James R. Exec. Dir., Binding Industries of America.

Nightingale, Dave, B.S. Former freelance writer, *Inside Sports* and *Sport Magazine.*

Niiler, Pearn, Ph.D. Former Prof. of Oceanography, Scripps Inst. of Oceanography.

Niles, David M., Ph.D. Former Curator of Birds, Delaware Museum of Natural History.

Niles, Susan A., Ph.D. Professor Emeritus of Anthropology, Lafayette College.

Nilsson, Greta, A.A. Wildlife Consultant, Animal Welfare Inst.

Nisetich, Frank, Ph.D. Prof. of Classics, Univ. of Mass.

Nitzke, Susan, R.D., Ph.D. Former Prof., Nutritional Sciences, Univ. of Wisconsin, Madison.

Nix, J. Rayford, Ph.D. Former Nuclear Theory Staff Member, Los Alamos Natl. Laboratory.

Nixon, Donald M. Ph.D. Prof. of Agricultural Economics, Texas A&M Univ., Kingsville.

Noble, Thomas F. X., Ph.D. Former Professor of History, University of Notre Dame.

Nochimson, Martha, Ph.D. Author of *No End to Her: Soap Opera and the Female Subject.*

Nock, Steven L., Ph.D. Former Professor of Sociology, University of Virginia.

Nolan, Robert P., Ph.D. Associate Professor, Center for Applied Studies of the Environment, City University of New York.

Noll, Mark A., Ph.D. Professor of History, University of Notre Dame.

Nolon, John R., J.D. Law Prof., Pace Univ. School of Law.

Noone, Timothy B., Ph.D. Prof., School of Philosophy, Catholic Univ. of America.

Nordstrom, Byron J., Ph.D. Prof. Emer. of History and Scandinavian Studies, Gustavus Adolphus Coll.

Norell, Mark A., Ph.D. Curator, Paleontology Division, American Museum of Natural History.

Noren, David G., J.D. Attorney at law; former Acting Asst. Prof. of Law, New York Univ. School of Law.

Norfleet, Donald S., B.A. Business Editor, News Tribune Company, Inc., Publications.

Normile, Dwight, M.Ed. Editor, *International Gymnast.*

Norse, Elliott A., Ph.D. Chief Scientist, Marine Conservation Institute.

Northrop, Gretajo, Ph.D. Assoc. Prof. of Medicine and of Obstetrics and Gynecology and Assoc. Attending Physician, Rush-Presbyterian-St. Luke's Medical Center, Chicago.

Norwood, F. A., Ph.D. Former Professor of History of Christianity, Garrett-Evangelical Theological Seminary.

Noss, Reed F., Ph.D. Professor, Department of Biology, University of Central Florida.

Novick, Julius, D.F.A. Prof. Emer. of Drama Studies, Purchase Coll., State Univ. of New York.

Novick, Sheldon M. Scholar in Residence, Vermont Law School; author, *Law of Environmental Protection.*

Novotny, Donald W., Ph.D. Prof. Emer., Dept. of Electrical and Computer Engineering, Univ. of Wisconsin, Madison.

Nowell, April, Ph.D. Assoc. Prof. of Anthropology, Univ. of Victoria.

Nugent, Peter, Ph.D. Staff Scientist, Lawrence Berkeley Natl. Laboratory.

Nunan, Richard, Ph.D. Prof. of Philosophy and Chair, Dept. of Philosophy and Religious Studies, Coll. of Charleston.

Nunn, Kenneth B., J.D. Prof. of Law, Fredric G. Levin Coll. of Law, Univ. of Florida.

Nuttall, Mark, Ph.D. Prof. of Anthropology, Univ. of Alberta.

Nweeia, Martin T., D.M.D. Instructor, Advanced Dental Rotation, Harvard School of Dental Medicine; Research Assoc., Marine Mammal Program, Smithsonian Inst.

Nye, M. J., Ph.D. Horning Prof. of Humanities and Prof. of History, Oregon State Univ.

O

Oakes, David D., M.D. Prof. of Surgery, Stanford Univ. School of Medicine.

Oberg, James, M.S. Spaceflight engineer; author, *UFOs and Outer Space Mysteries.*

Oberright, John E., B.M.E. Advanced Missions Study Manager, Natl. Aeronautics and Space Admin./Goddard Space Flight Ctr.

O'Brian, Thomas R., Ph.D. Chief, Time and Frequency Div., Natl. Inst. of Standards and Technol.

O'Brien, David M., Ph.D. Prof. of Politics, Univ. of Virginia.

Ockert, Karl Brewmaster, BridgePort Brewing Company.

O'Connell, Anne C., M.S. Consultant Paediatric Dental Surgeon, Dublin Dental Univ. Hospital and The Natl. Children's Hospital, Tallaght, Ireland.

O'Connell, Marvin R., Ph.D. Prof. Emer. of History, Univ. of Notre Dame.

O'Dell, C. R., Ph.D. Dist. Research Prof. of Physics and Astronomy, Vanderbilt Univ.

Odell, Daniel K., Ph.D. Sr. Research Biologist, Hubbs-SeaWorld Research Inst.

Odom, Selma Landen, Ph.D. Prof. Emerita, Dept. of Dance, York Univ.

O'Donnell, John L., Jr., B.S. Former Dir. of Facilities, Dept. of Intercollegiate Athletics, Univ. of Illinois, Urbana-Champaign.

Oetinger, David F., Ph.D. Professor of Biology, Kentucky Wesleyan College.

Ogden, Michael R., Ph.D. Prof. of Communication, Central Washington Univ.

Ogden, Shepherd Author, *Step by Step Organic Flower Gardening* and *Step by Step Organic Vegetable Gardening.*

Oguchi, Takashi, Ph.D. Prof., Ctr. for Spatial Information Science, Univ. of Tokyo.

Oh, Bonnie Bongwan Cho, Ph.D. Dist. Prof. of Korean Studies Emer., Georgetown Univ.

Oh, John K. C., Ph.D. Former Banigan Prof. of Politics Emer., Catholic Univ. of America.

Ohnuki-Tierney, Emiko, Ph.D. William F. Vilas Research Prof. of Anthropology, Univ. of Wisconsin, Madison.

O'Keefe, F. Robin, Ph.D. Assoc. Prof., Dept. of Biology, Marshall Univ.

Okrant, Mark J., Ed.D. Prof. of Tourism Management and Dir. of the Inst. for New Hampshire Studies, Plymouth State Univ.

Olds, Shelley E., M.A. Science Education Specialist, UNAVCO.

O'Leary, Brendan, Ph.D. Lauder Prof. of Political Science and Dir. of the Penn Program in Ethnic Conflict, Univ. of Pennsylvania.

Olien, Roger M., Ph.D. Prof. of History, Univ. of Texas, Odessa.

Olinto, Angela V., Ph.D. Prof. and Chair, Dept. of Astronomy and Astrophysics, Univ. of Chicago.

Oliver, Dale Owner, Spintastics Skill Toys, Inc.; Founder, American Yo-Yo Assoc.

Olliff, Martin T., Ph.D. Assoc. Prof. of History and Dir., Archives of Wiregrass History and Culture, Troy Univ., Dothan.

Olsen, Gary J., Ph.D. Assoc. Prof. of Microbiology, Univ. of Illinois, Urbana-Champaign.

Olsen, Nora, Ph.D. Extension Potato Specialist, Univ. of Idaho.

Olshansky, S. Jay, Ph.D. Prof. of Epidemiology, Univ. of Illinois, Chicago.

Olson, Donald W., Ph.D. Prof., Dept. of Physics, Southwest Texas State Univ.

Olson, James S., Ph.D. Dist. Prof. of History, Sam Houston State Univ.

Olson, Judy M., Ph.D. Prof. Emer. of Geography, Michigan State Univ.

Olson, Mary K., Ph.D. Assoc. Prof. of Economics, Tulane Univ.

Olson, Maynard V., Ph.D. Prof. of Medicine and Genome Sciences, Univ. of Wash. Genome Ctr.

Olson, Richard G., Ph.D. Prof. of History, Dept. of Humanities and Social Sciences, Harvey Mudd Coll.

O'Neill, Michael P., Ph.D. Former Asst. Prof. of Geography, Virginia Polytechnic Inst. and State Univ.

Onwudiwe, Ebere, Ph.D. Exec. Dir., Ctr. for Intl. Studies, Central State Univ.

Opgrande, J. Donald, M.D. Chairman, Division of Orthopedic Surgery, Univ. of North Dakota School of Medicine.

Ophardt, Charles E., Ph.D. Prof. Emer. of Chemistry, Elmhurst Coll.

Oppel, Richard A., B.A. Former Editor, *Austin (TX) American-Statesman.*

Oppenheim, Lois Hecht, Ph.D. Prof. of Political Science, American Jewish Univ.

Oppenheimer, Bruce I., Ph.D. Prof. of Political Science, Vanderbilt Univ.

Oppenheimer, John R., Ph.D. Assoc. Prof., Biology; Dir., Environmental Science Masters Program, City Univ. of New York, Coll. of Staten Island.

Orel, Harold, Ph.D. Univ. Prof. Emer., Univ. of Kansas.

Orenstein, Eugene V., Ph.D. Assoc. Prof. of Jewish Studies, McGill Univ.

Oreskes, Michael Senior Managing Editor, *The Associated Press.*

Orgel, Stephen, Ph.D. Jackson Eli Reynolds Prof. of Humanities, Stanford Univ.

Orlin, Louis L., Ph.D. Prof. Emer. of Ancient Near Eastern History and Lit., Univ. of Michigan.

O'Rourke, Thomas D., Ph.D. Thomas R. Briggs Prof. of Engineering, School of Civil and Environmental Engineering, Cornell Univ.

Orozco, Cynthia E., Ph.D. Chair, History and Humanities Department, Eastern New Mexico University, Ruidoso.

Orr, Delilah, M.Ed. Professor, Department of English, Fort Lewis College.

Osler, Margaret J., Ph.D. Former Prof. of History and Adjunct Prof. of Philosophy, Univ. of Calgary.

Osman, M. O. M., Dr.Sc.Techn. Prof. Emer. of Engineering, Concordia Univ.

Oster, Harry, Ph.D. Former Prof. of English, Univ. of Iowa.

Ostler, Jeffrey, Ph.D. Prof. of History, Univ. of Oregon.

Ostrower, Gary B., Ph.D. Prof. of History, Alfred Univ.

O'Toole, Thomas, Ph.D. Prof. of Anthropology, St. Cloud State Univ.

Ouellet, Fernand, Ph.D. Prof. of History, York Univ., Canada.

Ouellette, Robert J., Ph.D. Prof. Emer. of Chemistry, Ohio State Univ.

Owen, Valerie, Ph.D. Assoc. Prof., Natl.-Louis Univ.

Owens, Robert A., Ph.D. Research Chemist, Molecular Plant Pathology Laboratory, Beltsville Agricultural Research Ctr., U.S. Dept. of Agriculture.

Owensby, Brian P., Ph.D. Prof. of History, Univ. of Virginia.

Ownby, Ted, Ph.D. Prof. of History and Southern Studies, Univ. of Mississippi.

Owusu-Ansah, David, Ph.D. Prof. of History, James Madison Univ.

Oxendine, Linda E., Ph.D. Professor and Chair, American Indian Studies, University of North Carolina, Pembroke.

Oxley, Jimmie, Ph.D. Professor of Chemistry, University of Rhode Island.

Oyler, David D. Copy Editor, *The* (Wilmington, DE) *News Journal.*

Ozment, Steven, Ph.D. McLean Professor of Ancient and Modern History, Emeritus, Harvard Univ.

P

Paaswell, Robert E., Ph.D. Dir., Univ. Transportation Research Ctr., and Dist. Prof. of Civil Engineering, City Coll. of New York.

Packer, Alex J., Ph.D. President Emeritus, FCD Educational Services.

Pagen, Dennis, B.S. Chairman, Competition Committee, Intl. Hang Gliding and Paragliding Commission.

Palfrey, Thomas R., III, Ph.D. Prof. of Economics and Political Science, Calif. Inst. of Technology.

Pallen Mark J., M.D., Ph.D. Prof. of Microbial Genomics, Univ. of Birmingham.

Palmer, Colin A., Ph.D. Dir., Scholars-in-Residence Program, Schomburg Ctr. for Research in Black Culture.

Palmer, Ruth, Ph.D. Assoc. Prof. of Classics and World Religions, Ohio Univ.

Pandya, Rajul E., Ph.D. Asst. Prof. of Atmospheric Science, West Chester Univ.

Panek, Mark, Ph.D. Assoc. Prof. of Humanities, Univ. of Hawaii, Hilo.

Pankhurst, Tim Chief Exec., Newspaper Publishers' Association of New Zealand.

Pannabecker, Rachel K., Ph.D. Dir., Kauffman Museum.

Panozzo, Michael E., B.A. Editor, *Billiards Digest.*

Pantozzi, Jill, B.A. Popular-culture journalist; Owner and Editor in Chief, TheNerdyBird.com.

Pantuso, Peter J. Pres. and CEO, American Bus Assoc.

Papalambros, Panos Y., Ph.D. Prof., Dept. of Mechanical Engineering, Univ. of Michigan.

Papenfuse, Edward C., Ph.D. Sr. Facility Assoc., Gradual Liberal Arts Program and Division of Undergraduate Studies, Johns Hopkins Univ.

Parascenzo, Marino A., B.A. Golf Writer, *Pittsburgh* (PA) *Post-Gazette.*

Parashonts, Travis N., B.A. Administrator, Dept. of Family Support, State of Utah.

Parangi, Sareh, M.D. Asst. Prof. of Surgery, Harvard Medical School.

Parish, M. E., Ph.D. Prof. and Chair, Dept. of Nutrition and Food Science, Univ. of Maryland.

Park, Eugene Y., Ph.D. Korea Foundation Associate Professor of History, University of Pennsylvania.

Parker, John, Ph.D. Former Curator, James Ford Bell Library, Univ. of Minnesota, Twin Cities Campus.

Parker, Laurence, Ph.D. Prof., Dept. of Educ. Policy Studies, Univ. of Illinois, Urbana-Champaign.

Parker, Sue Morrow, Ed.D. Assistant Professor Emeritus, Department of Clothing, Textiles and Design, University of Alabama.

Parker, Thomas J., B.E.E.T. Sr. Research Technologist II, Natl. Electric Energy Testing Research and Applications Ctr., Georgia Inst. of Technol.

Parkhurst, Carmen R., Ph.D. Prof. Emer., Dept. of Poultry Science, North Carolina State Univ.

Parkinson, Robert L., B.S. Former Research Ctr. Dir., Circus World Museum.

Parmentier, Eric, Ph.D. Research worker, Laboratory of Functional and Evolutionary Morphology, Univ. of Liège, Belgium.

Parmet, Robert D., Ph.D. Prof. of History, York Coll., City Univ. of New York.

Parrish, David J., Ph.D. Prof. Emer., Dept. of Crop & Soil Environmental Sciences, Virginia Tech.

Parrott, David, D.Phil. Fellow and Lecturer in History, New Coll., Oxford Univ.

Parrott, Marissa L., Ph.D. Reproductive Biologist, Zoos Victoria.

Parsons, Cóilín, Ph.D. Associate Professor of English, Georgetown University.

Parsons, Timothy H., Ph.D. Prof. of African and Afro-American Studies, Wash. Univ., St. Louis.

Partner, Nancy F., Ph.D. Prof. of History, McGill Univ.

Pasachoff, Jay M., Ph.D. Field Memorial Prof. of Astronomy and Dir., Hopkins Observatory of Williams Coll.

Pasachoff, Naomi, Ph.D. Research Associate, Williams College.

Passow, A. Harry, Ed.D. Former Prof. of Educ., Teachers Coll., Columbia Univ.

Patchin, Justin W., Ph.D. Assoc. Prof. of Criminal Justice, Univ. of Wisconsin, Eau Claire.

Patel, Medha S., B.A. Former Asst. in Dir.'s Office, Natl. Museum of American Art, Smithsonian Inst.

Patiño-Echeverri, Dalia, Ph.D. Gendell Asst. Prof. of Energy Systems and Public Policy, Duke Univ.

Patten, Steve, Ph.D. Assoc. Prof. of Political Science, Univ. of Alberta.

Patterson, James T., Ph.D. Prof. Emer. of History, Brown Univ.

Patterson, Victoria D., Ph.D. Educator, Redwood Region Consortium for Professional Dev., Mendocino Coll.

Patton, James L., Ph.D. Prof. Emer. and Curator of Mammals, Dept. of Integrative Biology, Museum of Vertebrate Zoology, Univ. of Calif., Berkeley.

Paul, Iain C., Ph.D. Prof. Emer. of Chemistry, Univ. of Illinois, Urbana-Champaign.

Paulins, V. Ann, Ph.D. Prof., School of Human and Consumer Sciences, Ohio Univ.

Paulson, Boyd C., Jr., Ph.D. Former Charles H. Leavell Prof. of Civil Engineering, Stanford Univ.

Paulson, Dennis, Ph.D. Dir. Emer., Museum of Natural History, Univ. of Puget Sound.

Pausch, Randy, Ph.D. Former Prof. of Computer Science, Carnegie Mellon Univ.

Pavelec, S. Mike, Ph.D. Associate Professor of Strategic Studies, School of Advanced Air and Space Studies, Air University, Maxwell Air Force Base, Montgomery, Alabama.

Pavonetti, Linda M., Ed.D. Prof. and Chair, Dept. of Reading and Language Arts, Oakland Univ.

Payne, Craig M., M.S. Instructor, Weapons and Systems Engineering, U.S. Naval Acad., Annapolis.

Payne, Robert B., Ph.D. Curator of Birds and Prof. of Biology, Univ. of Michigan.

Payne, Stanley G., Ph.D. Prof. Emer. of History, Univ. of Wisconsin, Madison; author, *A History of Spain and Portugal.*

Payton, Adina, Ph.D. Research Scientist, University of California, Santa Cruz.

Peace, Walter, Ph.D. Professor Emeritus, School of Geography and Earth Sciences, McMaster Univ.

Peach, Ceri, Ph.D. Prof. of Social Geography, School of Geography, Oxford Univ.

Peacock, James L., Ph.D. Prof. of Anthropology, Univ. of North Carolina.

Pearcy, Thomas L., Ph.D. Prof. of History, Slippery Rock Univ.

Pearson, Stuart, Ph.D. Conjoint Lecturer, School of Environmental and Life Sci., Univ. of Newcastle.

Peck, Chris Editor, *The Commercial Appeal,* Memphis

Peck, Malcolm C., Ph.D. Sr. Program Officer, Meridian Intl. Ctr., Programming Division; former Arabian Peninsula Affairs Analyst, Bureau of Intelligence and Research, U.S. Dept. of State.

Pecoraro, Vincent L., Ph.D. Prof. of Chemistry and Sr. Research Scientist, Biophysics Research Division, Univ. of Michigan, Ann Arbor.

Pelissero, John P., Ph.D. Prof. of Political Science, Loyola Univ. Chicago.

Pellegrini, Anthony D., Ph.D. Prof., Dept. of Educ. Psychology, Univ. of Minnesota, Twin Cities Campus.

Pellegrino, Charles, Ph.D. Paleontologist and archaeologist.

Pelletier, Kenneth R., M.D. Dir., Stanford Corporate Health Program, Stanford Univ. School of Medicine.

Pelley, Patricia M., Ph.D. Assoc. Prof. of History, Texas Tech Univ.

Pellis, Neal R., Ph.D. Dir., Division of Space Life Sciences, Universities Space Research Association.

Pelrine, Michael J., Mgr., *Delaware State News.*

Pemberton, William E., Ph.D. Prof. Emer. of History, Univ. of Wisconsin, La Crosse.

Pender, Michael R., M.S. Exec. Dir., World's Fair Collector's Society, Inc.

Pendleton, Wade C., Ph.D. Prof. Emer. of Anthropology, San Diego State Univ.

Penet, Laurent, Ph.D. Research Scholar, Dept. of Biological Sciences, Univ. of Pittsburgh.

Penn, Richard D., M.D. Prof. of Neurosurgery, Rush-Presbyterian-St. Luke's Medical Ctr.

Pennington, Kenneth, Ph.D. Kelly-Quinn Professor of Ecclesiastical and Legal History, Columbus School of Law, School of Religious Studies, Catholic University of America.

Pennycook, Stephen J., Ph.D. Corporate Fellow, Oak Ridge Natl. Laboratory.

Penslar, Derek J., Ph.D. Prof. of History, Univ. of Toronto.

Pepion, Donald D., Ed.D. Coll. Assoc. Prof. of Native American Studies, New Mexico State Univ.

Percy, Alan, M.D. Prof. of Pediatric Neurology, Univ. of Alabama at Birmingham School of Medicine.

Peregrin, M. Isabelle, B.S. Assoc. Editor, *The* (Hot Springs, AR) *Sentinel-Record.*

Perez, Daniel R., Ph.D. Assoc. Prof., Dept. of Veterinary Medicine, Univ. of Maryland, Coll. Park.

Pérez, Louis A., Jr., Ph.D. Prof. of History, Univ. of North Carolina, Chapel Hill.

Perini, Lynda, B.A. Marketing Mgr., Sony Corp.

Perkins, Barbara M., Ph.D. Adjunct Prof., Univ. of Toledo; Assoc. Editor, *Narrative.*

Perkins, Edwin J., Ph.D. Prof. Emer. of History, Univ. of Southern Calif.

Perkins, Kenneth J., Ph.D. Distinguished Professor Emeritus of History, Univ. of South Carolina.

Perman, Michael, Ph.D. Research Prof. in the Humanities, Univ. of Illinois, Chicago.

Pervin, Lawrence A., Ph.D. Prof. Emer. of Psychology, Rutgers, the State Univ. of New Jersey.

Pesely, George E., Ph.D. Prof. of History, Austin Peay State Univ.

Pesic, Peter, Ph.D. Tutor, St. John's Coll.; author, *Seeing Double: Shared Identities in Physics, Philosophy, and Literature.*

Petersen, Kurt E., Ph.D. Former Pres., Cepheid.

Peterson, Blake E., Ph.D. Prof., Dept. of Mathematics Educ., Brigham Young Univ.

Peterson, David L., Ph.D. Research Biologist, U.S. Forest Service.

Peterson, Deane, Ph.D. Assoc. Prof. Emer. of Astronomy, Stony Brook Univ.

Peterson, John W., B.S. Wildlife Biologist, Fish and Wildlife Service, U.S. Dept. of the Interior.

Peterson, Rolf O., Ph.D. Research Professor, Michigan Technological University.

Petrick, Gabriella M., Ph.D. Prof. of Food and Nutrition, Coll. of Human Sci., Texas Tech Univ.

Petrie, Joanne, J.D. Sr. Attorney, U.S. Dept. of Transportation.

Pettigrew, Thomas F., Ph.D. Research Prof. of Social Psychology, Univ. of Calif., Santa Cruz.

Petulla, Joseph M., Ph.D. Former Prof. of Environmental Management, Univ. of San Francisco.

Pfaff, Daniel W., Ph.D. Prof. Emer. of Journalism, Pennsylvania State Univ.

Pfeifer, Ellen Former Music Critic and Arts Writer, *The Boston Globe.*

Pham, J. Peter, Ph.D. Director, Michael S. Ansari Africa Center.

Phelps, Michael E., Ph.D. Prof. and Chair, Dept. of Molecular and Medical Pharmacology, Univ. of Calif., Los Angeles, School of Medicine.

Phelps, Robert, Ph.D. Assoc. Prof. of History, Calif. State Univ., East Bay.

Philips, F. Carter, Ph.D. Assoc. Prof. Emer. of Classics, Vanderbilt Univ.

Phillips, Anne K., Ph.D. Professor, English Department, Kansas State University.

Phillips, Bill Security consultant.

Phillips, Carla Rahn, Ph.D. Prof. of History, Univ. of Minnesota, Twin Cities Campus.

Phillips, Charles F., Jr., Ph.D. Robert G. Brown Prof. Emer. of Economics, Wash. and Lee Univ.

Phillips, David P., Ph.D. Assoc. Prof. of Interdisciplinary Humanities, Women's, Gender and Sexuality Studies, and Creativity, Innovation and Entrepreneurship., Wake Forest University.

Phillips, Gene D., Ph.D. Prof. of English, Loyola Univ. of Chicago.

Phillips, Lisa, Ph.D. Asst. Prof. of History, Indiana State Univ.

Phillips, William D., Jr., Ph.D. Prof. of History, Univ. of Minnesota, Twin Cities Campus.

Phongpaichit, Pasuk, Ph.D. Prof., Faculty of Economics, Chulalongkorn Univ.

Piatt, Mickie A., J.D. Associate Professor of Law; Executive Director, Program in Intellectual Proper-

Contributors and consultants

ty Law, Chicago-Kent College of Law.

Picard, Kristen, M.S. Instructor, Biomanufacturing Education and Training Center, Worcester Polytechnic Institute.

Picard, Louis A., Ph.D. Prof., Intl. Dev., Grad. School of Public and Intl. Affairs, Univ. of Pittsburgh.

Picciano, Mary Frances, Ph.D. Former Sr. Nutrition Research Scientist, Office of Dietary Supplements, Natl. Inst. of Health.

Pichler, Wayne K., B.S. Former Manager, Cartography, World Book, Inc.

Picus, Lawrence O., Ph.D. Prof. of Educ., Univ. of Southern Calif.

Picus, Mark, Ed.D. Training Specialist, The Univ. of Texas MD Anderson Cancer Ctr.

Piehl, Mel, Ph.D. Professor of Humanities and History, Christ College, Valparaiso University.

Pietsch, Theodore W., Ph.D. Prof., School of Aquatic and Fishery Sciences and Curator of Fishes, Burke Museum of Natural History and Culture, Univ. of Washington.

Pienta, Amy Mehraban, Ph.D. Inter-univ. Consortium for Political and Social Research, Univ. of Michigan.

Pierce, Thomas J., Ph.D. Prof. of Economics, California State Univ., San Bernardino.

Pike, Sarah M., Ph.D. Prof., Religious Studies, Calif. State Univ., Chico.

Pikula, Joan Brock, B.A. Former Associate Editor, *Dance Magazine.*

Pinder, D. A., Ph.D. Prof. Emer. of Economic Geography, Univ. of Plymouth.

Pineo, Ronn, Ph.D. Professor and Chair, Department of History, Towson University.

Pinkava, Donald J., Ph.D. Prof. Emer. of Botany, Arizona State Univ.

Pinyuh, George, M.A. Former Area Extension Agent, Washington State Univ.

Piper, Linda J., Ph.D. Assoc. Prof. of History, Univ. of Georgia.

Pisetsky, David S., M.D., Ph.D. Prof. of Medicine and Immunology, Duke Univ. Medical Ctr.

Pitblado, Bonnie L., Ph.D. Asst. Prof. of Anthropology, Utah State Univ.

Pittas-Herschbach, Mary, Ph.D. Affiliate Senior Lecturer, Department of Classics, University of Maryland, College Park.

Pitts, William Karl, Ph.D. Sr. Research Scientist II, Pacific Northwest Natl. Laboratory.

Plante, Michael, Ph.D. Jessie J. Poesch Prof. of Art History, Newcomb Art Dept., Tulane Univ.

Plaut, Andrew S., M.D. Staff Physician, Tufts Medical Ctr.

Pletcher, James, Ph.D. Assoc. Prof. of Political Science, Denison Univ.

Plotkin, Allen, Ph.D. Prof. of Aerospace Engineering, San Diego State Univ.

Plyler, Brett C., M.D. Psychiatrist, Northwestern Memorial Hosp. and Chicago Psychiatry Associates.

Poag, James F., Ph.D. Prof. Emer. of German, Washington Univ., St. Louis.

Pocius, Gerald L., Ph.D. Univ. Research Prof., Memorial Univ. of Newfoundland.

Poertner, Andrew, B.A. Managing Editor, *Roswell* (NM) *Daily Record.*

Pohlmann, Ken C., M.S.E.E. Prof. Emer., Music Engineering Technology, Univ. of Miami.

Pointer, Richard W., Ph.D. Prof. of History, Westmont Coll.

Polachek, Dora E., Ph.D. Visiting Assoc. Prof., Dept. of Romance Langs. and Lits., Binghamton Univ.

Polachek, Solomon W., Ph.D. Dist. Prof. of Economics, State Univ. of New York, Binghamton.

Polasky, Janet L., Ph.D. Professor of History, University of New Hampshire.

Polenberg, Richard, Ph.D. Goldwin Smith Prof. of American History, Cornell Univ., and author of *The World of Benjamin Cardozo.*

Polis, John E., B.A. Former Dir. of Communications, U.S. Soccer Federation.

Polito, Vito S., Ph.D. Prof. of Plant Sciences, Univ. of Calif., Davis.

Politoske, Daniel T., Ph.D. Prof. Emer. of Music History, Univ. of Kansas.

Polk, Noel, Ph.D. Professor Emeritus of English,

University of Southern Mississippi.

Pollard, James E., Ph.D. Assoc. Prof. of Plant Biology and Biology Program Coordinator, Univ. of New Hampshire.

Polmar, Norman, B.A. Author, *Ships and Aircraft of the U.S. Fleet* and *Guide to the Soviet Navy.*

Poluhowich, John J., Ph.D. Prof., Life, Earth, and Environmental Sciences, West Texas A&M Univ.

Polyné, Millery, Ph.D. Asst. Prof., Gallatin School for Individualized Study, New York Univ.

Pommer, David, B.A. City Hall Bureau Reporter, *The Calgary* (AB) *Herald.*

Pomory, Christopher, Ph.D. Associate Professor of Biology, University of West Florida.

Ponganis, Paul, Ph.D. Research Physiologist, Scripps Inst. of Oceanography, Univ. of Calif., San Diego.

Pope, Harrison G., Jr., M.D., M.P.H. Prof. of Psychiatry, Harvard Medical School.

Pope, Peter E., Ph.D. Prof. of Anthropology, Archaeology Unit, Memorial Univ.

Popoff, Wilfred Exec. Editorial Consultants, Saskatoon, SK.

Popova, Maria, Ph.D. Associate Professor, Department of Political Science, McGill University.

Popp, Michael, Ph.D. Prof., Dept. of Agricultural Economics and Agribusiness, Univ. of Arkansas.

Porch, Douglas, Ph.D. Dist. Prof., Dept. of National Security Affairs, Naval Postgraduate School.

Porciatti, Lara, B.A. Student, Univ. of Siena.

Porco, Carolyn, Ph.D. Prof., Cassini Imaging Central Laboratory for Operations, Southwest Research Inst.

Porter, Jonathan, Ph.D. Prof. of History, Univ. of New Mexico, Albuquerque.

Porter, Kimberly K., Ph.D. Prof. of History, Univ. of North Dakota.

Porter-Szűcs, Brian, Ph.D. Assoc. Prof. of History, Univ. of Michigan, Ann Arbor.

Portney, David, B.S. Manager of Media Relations and E-commerce, American Volleyball Coaches Association.

Porton, Gary G., Ph.D. Prof. Emer. of Religion, Univ. of Illinois, Urbana-Champaign.

Post, Robert C., Ph.D. Former Editor in Chief, *Technology and Culture.*

Poston, John W., Sr., Ph.D. Prof., Dept. of Nuclear Engineering, Texas A&M Univ.

Pottage, John C., Jr., M.D. Sr. Vice Pres., Chief Scientific and Medical Officer, ViiV Healthcare.

Potts, Daniel, Ph.D. Prof. of Archaeology, Univ. of Sydney.

Poulson, Barry W., Ph.D. Former Prof. of Economics, Univ. of Colorado, Boulder.

Poulson, Thad Editor, *Daily Sitka* (AK) *Sentinel.*

Poulson, Thomas L., Ph.D. Prof. of Biological Sciences, Univ. of Illinois, Chicago.

Pourshariati, Parvaneh, Ph.D. Assoc. Prof., Near Eastern Lang. and Cultures, Ohio State Univ.

Povey, Karen D., M.Ed. Assoc. Curator of Conservation and Educ., Point Defiance Zoo & Aquarium.

Powell, Evan, B.A. Dir. of Engineering, Southeastern Products, Inc.

Powell, Roger A., Ph.D. Assoc. Prof. of Zoology and Forestry, North Carolina State Univ.

Power, Harry W., Ph.D. Prof. Emer. of Behavioral Ecology, Rutgers, the State Univ. of New Jersey.

Powers, Lenita, B.A. Reporter, Reno Newspapers, Inc.

Powers, Richard Gid, Ph.D. Prof. of History, Coll. of Staten Island, City Univ. of New York.

Powless, Robert E., Ph.D. Former Professor and Department Head, American Indian Studies, University of Minnesota, Duluth.

Prah, Kwesi Kwaa, Ph.D. Dir. of the Centre for Advanced Studies of African Society.

Pranger, Robert J., Ph.D. Managing Editor, *Mediterranean Quarterly;* Adjunct Prof., American Univ.

Pratt, Robert A., Ph.D. Prof. of History, Univ. of Georgia.

Presley, Cora Ann, Ph.D. Assoc. Prof., African American Studies, Georgia State Univ.

Pressman, David, J.D. Patent lawyer and author.

Preston, Katherine K., Ph.D. Prof. of Music, Coll. of William and Mary.

Preston, Tim, M.A. Publishing Director, Puzzler Media Ltd.

Prezant, Robert S., Ph.D. Dean, Coll. of Science and Mathematics, Montclair State Univ.

Price, Hugh C., Ph.D. Prof. Emer., Dept. of Horticulture, Cornell Univ., Geneva.

Price, Richard, Ph.D. Prof. of American Studies, Anthropology, and History, Coll. of William and Mary.

Price, Steven D., LL.B. Author, *The Whole Horse Catalog.*

Priddle, George B., Ph.D. Former Assoc. Prof. of Environment and Resource Studies, Univ. of Waterloo, Ontario.

Prigo, Robert B., Ph.D. Prof. Emer. of Physics, Middlebury Coll.

Primack, Joel R., Ph.D. Prof. of Physics, Univ. of Calif., Santa Cruz.

Pritchett, Edward C., B.S. Former Chief, Geotechnical Branch, Headquarters, U.S. Army Corps of Engineers.

Prober, Charles G., M.D. Prof. of Pediatrics, Microbiology, and Immunology, Stanford Univ. School of Medicine.

Probst, Steven R., J.D., M.L.I.S. Educational Services Librarian, Valparaiso Univ. School of Law.

Prockter, Louise M., Ph.D. Sr. Professional Staff Scientist, Applied Physics Laboratory, Johns Hopkins Univ.

Procter, James E., B.A. Night Editor, *The* (Gary, IN) *Post-Tribune.*

Provenzo, Eugene F., Jr., Ph.D. Professor, Department of Teaching and Learning, School of Education, University of Miami.

Prum, Richard O., Ph.D. William Robertson Coe Prof. of Ornithology, Dept. of Ecology and Evolutionary Biology, Yale Univ.

Prusiner, Stanley B., M.D. Dir., Inst. for Neurodegenerative Diseases, Univ. of Calif., San Francisco; winner of Nobel Prize in physiology or medicine, 1997.

Pultz, John, Ph.D. Assoc. Prof., Kress Foundation Dept. of Art History, The Univ. of Kansas.

Putnam, Daniel H., Ph.D. Extension Specialist, Dept. of Plant Sciences, Univ. of Calif., Davis.

Putzel, James, D.Phil. Prof., Dept. of Intl. Development and Dir., Crisis States Research Centre, London School of Economics and Political Science.

Pyle, Kenneth B., Ph.D. Prof. of History and Asian Studies, Henry M. Jackson School of Intl. Studies, Univ. of Washington.

Q

Quere, Ralph W., Ph.D. Prof. Emer. of History and Theology, Wartburg Theological Seminary.

Quesal, Robert W., Ph.D. Prof. of Communication Sciences and Disorders, Western Illinois Univ.

Quimby, William R., B.S. Former Dir. of Publications, Safari Club Intl.

Quinn-Judge, Sophie, Ph.D. Assoc. Dir., Ctr. for Vietnamese Philosophy, Culture and Society, Temple Univ.

Quintiere, James G., Ph.D. Prof. of Fire Protection Engineering, Univ. of Maryland.

Quirarte, Jacinto, Ph.D. Dir., Research Ctr. for the Visual Arts, Univ. of Texas, San Antonio.

R

Raat, W. Dirk, Ph.D. Prof. Emer. of History, State Univ. of New York, Fredonia.

Rabiger, Michael, B.A. Former Chair, Film/Video Dept., Columbia Coll., Chicago.

Rabiner, Donald, Ph.D. Former Assoc. Prof. of Art History, Arizona State Univ.

Raboteau, Albert J., Ph.D. Henry W. Putnam Prof. of Religion, Princeton University.

Racaniello, Vincent R., Ph.D. Prof. of Microbiology, Columbia Univ. Coll. of Physicians and Surgeons.

Rack, Frank R., Ph.D. Assoc. Prof., Dept. of Geosciences, Univ. of Nebraska, Lincoln.

Rader, Patricia W., M.L.S. Asst. Catalog Librarian, Dance Collection, New York Public Library.

Radunsky, Michael B., Ph.D. Product Manager, New Focus.

Raedeke, Kenneth J., Ph.D. Research Assoc. Prof., Wildlife Sciences Program, Coll. of Forest Resources, Univ. of Washington.

Rahman, M. Omar, M.D., D.Sc. Associate Professor of Demography and Epidemiology, Harvard School of Public Health.

Raitt, Jill, Ph.D.   Prof. Emer., Dept. of Religious Studies, Univ. of Missouri, Columbia.

Raitz, Karl B., Ph.D.   Prof. of Geography, Univ. of Kentucky.

Raju, Tonse N. K., M.D., D.C.H.   Medical Officer, Eunice Kennedy Shriver Natl. Inst. of Child Health and Human Dev., Natl. Inst. of Health.

Rakov, Vladimir A., Ph.D.   Prof., Dept. of Electrical and Computer Engineering, Univ. of Florida.

Rakove, Jack N., Ph.D.   Coe Prof. of History and American Studies, Stanford Univ.

Raleigh, Donald J., Ph.D.   Jay Richard Judson Dist. Prof. of History, Univ. of North Carolina, Chapel Hill.

Ramanathan, Veerabhadran, Ph.D.   Alderson Prof. of Ocean Sciences, Univ. of Calif., San Diego.

Rambelli, Fabio, Ph.D.   Prof. of Religious Studies & East Asian Lang., Univ. of Calif., Santa Barbara.

Ramesh, Lalita, Ph.D.   Research Assoc., Milken Inst.

Ramet, Sabrina P., Ph.D.   Prof., Dept. of Sociology and Political Science, Norwegian Univ. of Science and Technology, Trondheim, Norway.

Ramey, Steven W., Ph.D.   Assoc. Prof. of Religious Studies, Univ. of Alabama.

Ramsay, O. Bertrand, Ph.D.   Prof. Emer. of Chemistry, Eastern Michigan Univ.

Ramsey, Matthew, Ph.D.   Assoc. Prof. of History, Vanderbilt Univ.

Rangarajan, Anusuya, Ph.D.   Assoc. Prof. of Horticulture, Cornell Univ.

Rankin, Joanna M., Ph.D.   Prof. of Physics, Univ. of Vermont.

Rapaport, Herman, Ph.D.   Prof. of English, Wake Forest Univ.

Rashkin, Esther, Ph.D.   Prof. of French and Comparative Lit., Univ. of Utah.

Rauber, Robert M., Ph.D.   Prof. of Atmospheric Sciences, Univ. of Illinois.

Raven, Peter H., Ph.D.   Pres. Emer., Missouri Botanical Garden; Prof. Emer. of Botany, Wash. Univ.

Rawls, James J., Ph.D.   Instructor of History, Diablo Valley Coll.

Ray, Brian D., Ph.D.   Pres., Natl. Home Educ. Research Inst.

Rebeck, Ken, Ph.D.   Assoc. Prof. of Economics, St. Cloud State Univ.

Rector, Lee, B.A.   Former Ed., *Music City News.*

Reddy, William M., Ph.D.   Laprade Prof. of History and Prof. of Cultural Anthropology, Duke Univ.

Reed, Brian V., Ph.D.   Assoc. Prof. of Rehabilitation and Movement Science, Univ. of Vermont.

Reed, David M., B.A.   Owner, Know the Net Consulting.

Reed, Gretchen, B.Ed.   Educ. Dir., Intl. Women's Air and Space Museum.

Reed, James S., Ph.D.   Former Prof. of Ceramic Engineering, New York State Coll. of Ceramics, Alfred Univ.

Reed, Sylvia L., M.A.   Grad. Assoc., Dept. of Linguistics, Univ. of Arizona.

Reed, William F., B.A.   Former columnist, *Lexington* (KY) *Herald-Leader.*

Reefe, Thomas Q., Ph.D.   Pres., Q Solutions.

Rees, Peter W., Ph.D.   Assoc. Prof. of Geography, Univ. of Delaware.

Reetz, Brian, B.A.   Sports Writer, *Lincoln* (NE) *Journal Star.*

Reeves, Thomas C., Ph.D.   Prof. Emer. of History, Univ. of Wisconsin, Parkside.

Regehr, T. D., Ph.D.   Professor Emeritus of History, University of Saskatchewan.

Rehkugler, Gerald E., Ph.D.   Prof. Emer. of Agricultural and Biological Engineering, Cornell Univ.

Reich, Bernard, Ph.D.   Prof., Political Science and Intl. Affairs, George Washington Univ.

Reich, Kenneth, M.A.   Former Reporter, *Los Angeles Times.*

Reich, Steven A., Ph.D.   Professor of History, James Madison University.

Reid, Donald J., Ph.D.   Prof., Dept. of Agricultural Sciences, Texas A&M Univ., Commerce.

Reid, W. W., M.A.   Former Editor, *All Hands* magazine, Navy Internal Relations Activity.

Reid, William J., Ph.D.   Coauthor, *Massachusetts.*

Reider, Bruce, M.D.   Prof. Emer., Dept. of Surgery, Univ. of Chicago.

Reider, Richard G., Ph.D.   Prof. Emer. of Geography, Univ. of Wyoming.

Reilingh, Maarten, Ph.D.   Freelance writer and editor.

Reilly, John G.   Assoc. Prof. of Culinary Arts, Culinary Inst. of America.

Reilly, Nolan J., Ph.D.   Prof. of History, Univ. of Winnipeg.

Reilly, Timothy F., Ph.D.   Assoc. Prof. of Historical Geography, Univ. of Louisiana at Lafayette.

Reimer, Michael J., Ph.D.   Assoc. Prof. of History, American Univ. in Cairo.

Reiners, Stephen, Ph.D.   Assoc. Prof. of Horticultural Sciences, Cornell Univ.

Reiners, William A., Ph.D.   Prof. of Botany, Univ. of Wyoming.

Reinersman, Melanie, M.A.   Editor, website and web magazine of the National Career Development Association.

Reinhartz, Dennis, Ph.D.   Prof. Emer. of History, Univ. of Texas, Arlington.

Reiss, David L., M.D.   Head of Endocrinology, Kaiser Permanente, Orange County, Calif.

Reiss, Edmund, Ph.D.   Author, *Arthurian Legend and Literature.*

Reiter, Russel J., Ph.D.   Prof. of Neuroendocrinology, Univ. of Texas Health Science Ctr.

Reitz, Bruce A., M.D.   Prof. Emer., Stanford Univ. School of Medicine, Cardiothoracic Surgery Clinic.

Rense, William C., Ph.D.   Former Prof. of Geography, Shippensburg Univ. of Pennsylvania.

Rentzepis, Peter M., Ph.D.   Pres. Chair and Prof. of Chemistry, Univ. of Calif., Irvine.

Restak, Richard, M.D.   Clinical Prof. of Neurology, George Washington Univ. Medical School.

Reyes, Carlos, B.S.   Founder, RCadvisor.com.

Reyes, Socorro L., Ph.D.   Assoc. Prof. of Political Science, De la Salle Univ.

Reynolds, Barbara A., M.S.   Pres., Reynolds News Service.

Reynolds, Frank E., Ph.D.   Prof. Emer. of Hist. of Religions and Buddhist Studies, Univ. of Chicago.

Reynolds, Terry S., Ph.D.   Former Prof. of History, Michigan Technological Univ.

Rezac, Edward J.   EVA (Extra-Vehicular Activity) Engineer, Lockheed Martin Corp.

Reznicek, Anton A., Ph.D.   Curator, Vascular Plants, Univ. of Michigan Herbarium.

Rhoades, Everett R., M.D.   Former Vice Chairman, Kiowa Tribe of Oklahoma.

Rhoades, Rex H.   Exec. Editor, (Lewiston, ME) *Sun Journal.*

Rhoades, Robert E., Ph.D.   Prof. of Anthropology, Univ. of Georgia.

Ribera, Feliciano M., Ph.D.   Former Prof. of History and Mexican American Studies, San Jose State Univ.

Rice, Janice M., M.L.S.   Outreach Coordinator, Coll. Library, General Library System, Univ. of Wisconsin, Madison.

Rice, Mark, Ph.D.   Assistant Professor of History, Baruch College, City University of New York.

Rice, Phillip L., Ph.D.   Prof. of Psychology, Moorhead State Univ.

Rich, George W., Ph.D.   Former Prof. of Anthropology, Calif. State Univ., Sacramento.

Richards, Joan L., Ph.D.   Prof. of History, Brown Univ.

Richards, Nancy E., M.A.   Chief Researcher, Cliveden.

Richards-Wilson, Stephani, Ed.D., Ph.D.   Visiting Prof. of Global Studies and Social Entrepreneurship, George Williams College of Aurora Univ.

Richards, William J., Ph.D.   Senior Scientist, Southeast Fisheries Center.

Richardson, D. H. S., D.Phil.   Former Dean of Science, St. Mary's Univ., Halifax, Nova Scotia.

Richardson, Deborah South, Ph.D.   Prof., Dept. of Psychology, Augusta State Univ.

Richardson, Elmo R., Ph.D.   Public Historian, Historians' Services of the Northwest

Richardson, James T., Ph.D.   Prof. of Sociology and Judicial Studies, Univ. of Nevada, Reno.

Richardson, Philip L., Ph.D.   Scientist Emer., Woods Hole Oceanographic Inst.

Richardson, S. Thomas, M.S.L.I.S.   Former Librarian/Researcher/Editor, World Book, Inc.

Richardson, Seth F. C., Ph.D.   Asst. Prof. of Ancient Near Eastern History, Oriental Inst., Univ. of Chicago.

Richmond, Martha E., Ph.D.   Prof. and Chair, Dept. of Chemistry and Biochemistry, Suffolk Univ.

Richter, Daniel K., Ph.D.   Prof. of History, Univ. of Pennsylvania.

Richter, David H., Ph.D.   Prof. of English, Queens Coll., City Univ. of New York.

Rickard, Lee J., Ph.D.   Research Astronomer, Naval Research Laboratory.

Rickspoone, Howard A., B.S.   Former Pres., American Contract, Inc.

Ricou, Laurie R., Ph.D.   Prof. Emer. of English, Univ. of British Columbia.

Rider, Jeff, Ph.D.   Prof. of French and Medieval Studies, Wesleyan Univ.

Ridker, Paul M., M.D.   Prof. of Medicine, Harvard Medical School.

Ridley, Mark, D.Phil.   Research Assoc., Oxford Univ. Dept. of Zoology.

Ridolfi, Mark, M.A.   Editor, Editorial Page, (Davenport, IA) *Quad-City Times.*

Rieck, James Nelson, Ph.D.   Former Sr. Research Scientist, Bayer Corp.

Rietz, Henry W. Morisada, Ph.D.   Assoc. Prof. of Religious Studies, Grinnell Coll.

Rigg, Jonathan, Ph.D.   Professor of Geography, University of Durham.

Riggs, Paula DeGraffenreid, M.D.   Assoc. Prof., Psychiatry, Univ. of Colorado School of Medicine.

Riley, Brendan, Ph.D.   Assoc. Prof. of English, Columbia Coll., Chicago.

Riley, Donald R., Ph.D.   Professor of Decision Information Technologies, Univ. of Maryland.

Riley, James D., Ph.D.   Former Assoc. Prof. of History, Catholic Univ. of America.

Riley, Jonathan, D.Phil.   Prof., Murphy Inst. of Political Economy, Tulane Univ.

Riley-Smith, Jonathan, Ph.D.   Former Prof. of Ecclesiastical History, Univ. of Cambridge.

Ring, Richard R., Ph.D.   Collection Dev. Librarian, Univ. of Kansas.

Ringler, Richard N., Ph.D.   Prof. Emer. of Scandinavian Studies, Univ. of Wisconsin, Madison.

Rink, Oliver A., Ph.D.   Prof. of History, Calif. State Univ., Bakersfield.

Rinke, Carlotta M., M.D.   Physician, Alexian Brothers Medical Center, Elk Grove Village, IL.

Risso, Patricia, Ph.D.   Prof. of History, Univ. of New Mexico.

Ristine, Karen Clark, B.S.   Minister, Mission Hills United Methodist Church, San Diego, CA.

Ritchie, Robert C., Ph.D.   Dir. of Research, Huntington Library, Art Gallery, and Botanical Gardens.

Ritchie, Susan, Ph.D.   Visiting Prof. of History, Star King School for the Ministry; Minister, North Unitarian Universalist Congregation.

Ritner, Robert K., Ph.D.   Prof. of Egyptology, Oriental Inst., Univ. of Chicago.

Ritter, Jay R., Ph.D.   Cordell Prof. of Finance, Univ. of Florida.

Ritter, Michael E., Ph.D.   Prof., Dept. of Geography and Geology, Univ. of Wisconsin, Stevens Point.

Rivers, Jeff, B.A.   Former writer and editor for *The Hartford* (CT) *Courant.*

Roan, Vernon P., Ph.D.   Former Prof. of Mechanical Engineering, Univ. of Florida.

Roark, Carol, M.L.S.   Manager, Dallas Public Library.

Robb, Edith, B.A.   Asst. Managing Editor, (Moncton, NB) *Times & Transcript.*

Robbins, Keith, D.Litt.   Emeritus Vice-Chancellor, Univ. of Wales, Lampeter; former Prof. of Modern History, Univ. of Glasgow.

Roberts, Jennifer Tolbert, Ph.D.   Prof. of Foreign Langs. and Lits., City Coll. of New York.

Roberts, Phil, Ph.D.   Associate Professor of History, University of Wyoming.

Roberts, W. Thomas, Jr., Ph.D.   Sr. Member, Technical Staff, Jet Propulsion Lab., Pasadena.

Roberts, William C., Ph.D.   Assoc. Prof. and Chair, Dept. of Anthropology and Sociology, St. Mary's Coll. of Maryland.

Robertson, Don, Ph.D. Former Deputy Manager, Marine Research, MAF Fisheries, New Zealand.

Robertson, John F., Ph.D. Prof. of History, Central Michigan Univ.

Robertson, Kenneth R., Ph.D. Plant Systematist Emeritus, Illinois Natural History Survey.

Robertson, Robert, Ph.D. Honorary Curator of Malacology, Academy of Natural Sciences of Philadelphia.

Robinowitz, Joe, B.S. Former Editor in Chief, *TV Guide*.

Robinson, David J., Ph.D. Dellplain Prof. of Latin American Geography, Syracuse Univ.

Robinson, David Mason, Ph.D. Former Assoc. Dir. for Scientific Programs, Division of Heart and Vascular Diseases, Natl. Inst. of Health.

Robinson, Geoffrey, Ph.D. Prof. of History, Univ. of Calif., Los Angeles.

Robinson, Glenn E., Ph.D. Assoc. Prof., Dept. of Defense Analysis, Naval Postgraduate School.

Robinson, June K., M.D. Prof. of Dermatology, Northwestern Univ.

Robinson, Michael F., Ph.D. Assoc. Prof. of History, Hillyer Coll., Univ. of Hartford.

Robinson, Neal, Ph.D. Former Prof. of Islamic Studies, Univ. of Wales.

Robinson, William W., A.B. Former Contributing Editor, *Cruising World Magazine*.

Robison, Henry W., Ph.D. Prof. of Biology, Southern Arkansas Univ.

Robock, Alan, Ph.D. Prof. of Environmental Sciences, Rutgers, the State University of New Jersey.

Rochfort, Heather Balogh, M.Ed. Freelance writer specializing in the outdoor recreation industry.

Rochon, Meredith, M.D. Physician, fetal and maternal medicine, Lehigh Valley Health Network, Allentown, PA.

Rock, Peter A., Ph.D. Former Dean, Division of Mathematical and Physical Sciences and Prof. of Chemistry, Univ. of Calif., Davis.

Rocke, Alan J., Ph.D. Prof. of History, Case Western Reserve Univ.

Rodabaugh, James H., Ph.D. Former Prof. of History, Miami Univ.

Rodd, Laurel Rasplica, Ph.D. Professor Emerita of Japanese, University of Colorado, Boulder.

Roddick, Daniel McCulloch, Ph.D. Writer, teacher and consultant.

Rodell, Roland L., Ph.D. Assoc. Prof. of Anthropology, Univ. of Wisconsin, Rock County.

Rodier, Patricia M., Ph.D. Prof. of Obstetrics/Gynecology and Dir., Collaborative Program of Excellence in Autism, Univ. of Rochester Medical Ctr.

Rodowskas, Christopher A., Jr., Ph.D. Prof. and Asst. Dean, Nova Southeastern Univ.

Rodway, George, Ph.D. Adjunct Asst. Prof., Internal Medicine, Univ. of Utah School of Medicine.

Roessel, Ruth W. Former Principal, Pinon Public School; former Dir., Navajo and Indian Studies Dept., Navajo Community Coll.

Roessler, David M., Ph.D. Web Designer/Developer, RWebMaker.com.

Rogers, George C., Jr., Ph.D. Former Chairman, Dept. of History, Univ. of South Carolina.

Rogers, Jefferson S., Ph.D. Prof. of Geography, The Univ. of Tennessee at Martin.

Rogers, Quinton R., Ph.D. Prof. of Physiological Chemistry, Univ. of Calif., Davis.

Rogers, Tracey, Ph.D. Assoc. Prof., School of Biology, Earth and Environmental Sciences, Univ. of New South Wales.

Rogerson, Robert J., Ph.D. Vice Pres. Academic, Univ. Canada West.

Rohli, Robert V., Ph.D. Professor, Dept. of Geography and Anthropology, Louisiana State Univ.

Rohrbough, Malcolm J., Ph.D. Professor Emeritus of History, University of Iowa.

Roisman, Joseph, Ph.D. Classics Dept., Colby Coll.

Rojas, Cristina, Ph.D. Prof. of International Affairs, Carleton Univ.

Rolfe, Stanley T., Ph.D. Albert P. Learned Professor of Civil and Environmental Engineering, University of Kansas.

Rollinson, Paul A., Ph.D. Prof., Dept. of Geography, Geology, and Planning, Missouri State Univ.

Romano, Frank J., M.A. Prof. Emer., School of

Print Media, Rochester Inst. of Technology.

Romanowicz, Barbara, Ph.D. Professor of Geophysics, University of California, Berkeley; Director, Berkeley Seismological Laboratory.

Romer, Grant B., M.F.A. Chief Conservator and Curator, Intl. Museum of Photography.

Romero, Christie, Former Dir., Ctr. for Jewelry Studies, Santiago Canyon Coll.

Romrell, Lynn J., Ph.D. Prof. of Biomedical Sciences and Assoc. Dean for Curriculum Dev. and Evaluation, Florida State Univ. Coll. of Medicine.

Roodman, G. David, Ph.D. Prof. of Medicine, Division of Hematology/Oncology, Univ. of Pittsburgh School of Medicine.

Roper, L. H., Ph.D. Professor of History, State University of New York, New Paltz.

Ropp, Steve C., Ph.D. Prof. Emer. of Political Science, Univ. of Wyoming.

Rorex, Robert A., Ph.D. Assoc. Prof. of Art and Art History, Univ. of Iowa.

Rosario, Ruben A., B.A. Columnist, *St. Paul* (MN) *Pioneer Press*.

Rose, C. Brian, Ph.D. James B. Pritchard Professor of Archaeology, University of Pennsylvania.

Rose, Deborah Bird, Ph.D. Former Adjunct Professor in Environmental Humanities, University of New South Wales.

Rose, Emily Jane, Ph.D. Science Educ. Consultant, Science Through Experiments Program.

Rose, Richard, D.Phil. Dir., Centre for the Study of Public Policy, Univ. of Strathclyde.

Rosen, Carol J., Ph.D. Prof. of Geography, Univ. of Wisconsin, Whitewater.

Rosenstone, Robert A., Ph.D. Prof. of History, Calif. Inst. of Technology.

Rosenthal, Joel T., Ph.D. Prof. Emer. of History, State Univ. of New York, Stony Brook.

Rosentreter, Roger L., Ph.D. Editor, *Michigan History* magazine and Visiting Assoc. Prof. of History, Michigan State Univ.

Ross, David A., Ph.D. Scientist Emer., Dept. of Geology and Geophysics, Woods Hole Oceanographic Inst.

Ross, Stewart L., Ph.D. Prof. of Music and former Dir. of Bands, Mankato State Univ.

Rossabi, Morris, Ph.D. Prof. of History, City Univ. of New York.

Rosseker, A. D. Exec. Dir., Saskatchewan Trucking Association.

Rotberg, Robert I., D.Phil. President Emeritus, World Peace Foundation.

Roth, Leland M., Ph.D. Marion D. Ross Distinguished Professor of Architectural History, Emeritus, Univ. of Oregon.

Rothman, Hal K., Ph.D. Former Prof. of History, Univ. of Nevada, Las Vegas.

Rourke, Ralph Martin, B.S. Former Dir., Hall of Fame for Great Americans, Bronx Community Coll.

Rouse, Greg, Ph.D. Professor, Scripps Institution of Oceanography, Univ. of California, San Diego.

Rowan, Andrew N., D.Phil. Sr. Vice Pres. and Chief of Staff, Research, Educ. and Intl. Issues, Humane Society of the United States.

Rowan, Carl T., M.A. Former Syndicated Columnist, *Chicago Sun-Times*.

Rowe, John A., Ph.D. Assoc. Prof. Emer. of History, Northwestern Univ.

Rowland, Scott K., Ph.D. Specialist, Dept. of Geology and Geophysics, Univ. of Hawaii, Manoa.

Rowley, William D., Ph.D. Griffen Prof., Dept. of History, Univ. of Nevada.

Roy, Neil J., Ph.D. Visiting Asst. Prof., Univ. of Notre Dame.

Royle, Stephen A., Ph.D. Prof. of Geography, Queen's Univ., Belfast.

Rozell, Mark J., Ph.D. Professor of Public Policy, George Mason University.

Rozenblit, Marsha, Ph.D. Prof. of History, Univ. of Maryland, Coll. Park.

Roznowsky, Wayne J. Former Managing Editor, *Prince Albert* (SK) *Daily Herald*.

Rubel, David, B.A. Pres., Agincourt Press.

Rubens, Jeff, M.A. Coeditor, *The Bridge World*.

Rubenstein, Allan E., M.D. Clinical Professor, Departments of Pediatrics and Neurology, NYU Langone Medical Center.

Rubenstein, Irwin, Ph.D. Prof. Emer. of Plant Biology, Univ. of Minnesota, Twin Cities Campus.

Rubin, Barnett R., Ph.D. Dir. of Studies, Ctr. on Intl. Cooperation, New York Univ.

Rubin, David T., M.D. Assoc. Prof. of Medicine, Univ. of Chicago Medical Ctr.

Rubin, Kenneth H., Ph.D. Prof. of Geology, Univ. of Hawaii.

Rubin, Ronald N., M.D. Prof. of Internal Medicine, Temple Univ. School of Medicine.

Rubinstein, Donald H., Ph.D. Prof. of Anthropology and Public Health, Micronesian Area Research Ctr., Univ. of Guam.

Ruck, Robert, Ph.D. Sr. Lecturer of History, Univ. of Pittsburgh.

Rudd, J. William, M.A. Dean Emer., Coll. of Architecture and Planning, Univ. of Tennessee, Knoxville.

Rudisill, Richard, Ph.D. Former Curator of Photographic History, Museum of New Mexico.

Rudnytsky, Peter L., Ph.D. Former Asst. Prof., English and Comparative Lit., Columbia Univ.

Rudolph, Frederick B., Ph.D. Former Professor of Biochemistry and Cell Biology, Rice Univ.

Rudwick, Elliott, Ph.D. Former Prof. of Sociology and History, Ctr. for Urban Regionalism, Kent State Univ.

Rugeley, Terry, Ph.D. Prof. of Mexican and Latin American History, Univ. of Oklahoma.

Ruhl, J. Mark, Ph.D. Prof. of Political Science, Dickinson Coll.

Rulon, Philip Reed, Ed.D. Prof. Emer. of History, Northern Arizona Univ.

Rumbaugh, Duane M., Ph.D. Dir. Emer., Lang. Research Ctr., Georgia State Univ.

Rumford, Beatrix T., M.A. Former Vice Pres., Special Projects, Colonial Williamsburg Foundation.

Rundel, Philip W., Ph.D. Dist. Prof., Dept. of Ecology and Evolutionary Biology, Univ. of Calif., L.A.

Rung, Margaret C., Ph.D. Assoc. Prof. of History and Dir., Ctr. for New Deal Studies, Roosevelt Univ.

Rupp, Jennifer A., M.D. Former Physician, Dept. of Infectious Diseases, Univ. of New Mexico.

Rupp, Richard E., Ph.D. Assoc. Prof. of Political Science, Purdue Univ.

Rushton, Alan R., Ph.D. Dept. of Pediatrics, Hunterdon Medical Ctr.

Ruskin, William R., B.S. Local Industry Program Coordinator, Colorado Springs Econ. Dev. Corp.

Russ, Jonathan S., Ph.D. Assoc. Prof., Dept. of History, Univ. of Delaware.

Russell, Christopher T., Ph.D. Prof. of Geophysics and Space Physics, Inst. of Geophysics and Planetary Physics, Univ. of Calif., Los Angeles.

Russell, Lynn M., Ph.D. Prof., Scripps Inst. of Oceanography, Univ. of Calif., San Diego.

Russell, Lynette, Ph.D. ARC Kathleen Fitzpatrick Laureate Fellow 2020-2025, Monash University.

Russell, Mona L., Ph.D. Asst. Prof., Dept. of History, East Carolina Univ.

Russell, Peter H., LL.D. Prof. Emer. of Political Science, Univ. of Toronto.

Rutger, J. Neil, Ph.D. Former Dir. and Supervisory Research Geneticist, Dale Bumpers Natl. Rice Research Ctr.

Rutledge, Albert J., M.L.A. Former Prof. of Landscape Architecture, Iowa State Univ.

Ryan, Julie J. C. H., D.Sc. Assoc. Prof. of Engineering Management and Systems Engineering, George Washington Univ.

Ryll, Thomas Hardy Former Reporter, *The* (Vancouver, WA) *Columbian*.

S

Saab, A. P., Ph.D. Prof. Emer. of History, Univ. of North Carolina, Greensboro.

Sabatino, Dominick, M.D. Dir., Pediatric Hematology/Oncology, Nassau Univ. Medical Ctr.

Sack, James J., Ph.D. Prof. of History, Univ. of Illinois, Chicago.

Sadosky, Leonard J., Ph.D. Independent scholar and freelance writer.

Saff, Grant, Ph.D. Assoc. Prof., Dept. of Global Studies and Geography, Hofstra Univ.

Saffell, David C., Ph.D. Professor Emeritus of Political Science, Ohio Northern University.

Saffman, Mark, Ph.D. Professor, Department of Physics, Univ. of Wisconsin, Madison.

Sagás, Ernesto, Ph.D. Associate Professor of

Ethnic Studies, Colorado State University.

St John, Ronald Bruce, Ph.D. Independent Middle East scholar and author.

St. John, Ronald K., M.D., M.P.H. Sr. Consultant, HIV/AIDS, Dept. of Health, Canada, and Assoc. Prof., Dept. of Medicine, Univ. of Ottawa Medical School.

St-Pierre, Georges Mixed martial artist, GSP Holdings, LP.

Sakagawa, Gary T., Ph.D. Former Chief, Pelagic Fisheries Resources Division, Southwest Fisheries Science Ctr.

Sakalas, Ray V., M.S. Dir., Vocational Rehabilitation, Rehabilitation Inst. of Chicago.

Sakalowsky, Peter P., Jr., Ph.D. Prof. of Geography, Southern Connecticut State Univ.

Sakmyster, Thomas, Ph.D. Prof. Emer. of History, Univ. of Cincinnati.

Saku, James C., Ph.D. Prof., Dept. of Geography, Frostburg State Univ.

Salisbury, David S., Ph.D. Assoc. Prof. of Geography and the Environment, University of Richmond.

Salter, C. L., Ph.D. Prof. and Chair Emer., Dept. of Geography, Univ. of Missouri, Columbia.

Saltzman, Arthur M., Ph.D. Former Prof. of English, Missouri Southern State Coll.

Saltzman, Martin D., Ph.D. Prof. of Natural Science, Providence Coll.

Salvador, Ricardo J., Ph.D. Assoc. Prof. of Agronomy, Iowa State Univ.

Salvatore, Nick, Ph.D. Prof., School of Industrial and Labor Relations, Cornell Univ.

Samhan, Helen Hatab, M.A. Treasurer, Arab American Institute Foundation.

Sammons, Jeffrey L., Ph.D. Leavenworth Prof. Emer. of German, Yale Univ.

Samuels, Gina Miranda, Ph.D. Assoc. Prof., School of Social Service Admin., Univ. of Chicago.

Samuels, Louis, M.D. Surgical Dir., Heart Failure and Transplant Program, Lankenau Hospital.

Sandbrook, Dominic, Ph.D. Author, *Eugene McCarthy and the Rise and Fall of Postwar American Liberalism.*

Sanders, I. J. Author, *English Baronies.*

Sanders, Joe Sutliff, Ph.D. Asst. Prof. of English, Calif. State Univ., San Bernardino.

Sanders, Keith P., Ph.D. Prof. Emer., School of Journalism, Univ. of Missouri.

Sanders, R. M. Managing Editor, *Lubbock* (TX) *Avalanche-Journal.*

Sandhu, Sarwan S., Ph.D. Prof. of Chemical Engineering, Univ. of Dayton.

Sanjana, Neville E., Ph.D. Core Faculty Member, New York Genome Center; Asst. Prof. of Biology, Neuroscience, and Physiology, New York Univ.

Sansone, Mike, B.S. Associate Sports Editor, the *Chicago Tribune.*

Santer, Richard A., Ph.D. Former Prof. of Geography, Ferris State Univ.

Santi, Peter A., Ph.D. Prof., Dept. of Otolaryngology, Univ. of Minnesota.

Santino, Jack, Ph.D. Prof. of Popular Culture, Bowling Green State Univ.

Sardar, Riffat, Ph.D. Project Officer, UNICEF.

Sarmiento, Fausto O., Ph.D. Assoc. Prof. of Mountain Science, Dept. of Geography, The Univ. of Georgia.

Sassoon, Vidal Author, *Cutting Hair the Vidal Sassoon Way.*

Sauers, Richard A., Ph.D. Military historian.

Saul, William E., P.E. Prof. Emer., Civil and Environmental Engineering, Michigan State Univ.

Saunders, Christopher, D.Phil. Prof. Emer. Dept. of Historical Studies, Univ. of Cape Town.

Saunders, Mike R., Ph.D. Asst. Prof. of Hardwood Silviculture, Purdue Univ.

Saunders, Richard, Jr., Ph.D. Prof. and Alumni Master Teacher, Dept. of History, Clemson Univ.

Sauro, Clare, M.A. Curator, Historic Costume Collection, Westphal College of Media Arts & Design, Drexel University.

Savage, Martha Kane, Ph.D. Sr. Lecturer, Inst. of Geophysics, Victoria Univ., Wellington.

Savage, Sean J., Ph.D. Professor of Political Science, St. Mary's College.

Savage, William W., Jr., Ph.D. Professor of History, University of Oklahoma.

Savaiano, Dennis A., Ph.D. Professor, Foods and Nutrition, Purdue University.

Sawisch, Leonard P., Ph.D. Former Pres., Little People of America Foundation; Co-founder, Dwarf Athletic Assoc. of America.

Sayre, Henry M., Ph.D. Dist. Prof. of Art History, Oregon State Univ.

Saywell, John T., Ph.D. Former Professor, Department of History, York University.

Scales, Jason A., M.S. Asst. Prof. of Agriculture Educ. and Mechanization, Central Missouri State Univ.

Scarborough, John, Ph.D. Prof., Hist. of Pharmacy and Medicine and Classics, Univ. of Wisconsin.

Scargill, D. Ian, D.Phil. Univ. Lecturer of Geography, Univ. of Oxford.

Scarre, Chris, Ph.D. Professor of Archaeology, Durham University.

Scavone, Daniel C., Ph.D. Prof. Emer. of History, Univ. of Southern Indiana.

Schachter, Ruth, M.S. Communications Coordinator, Footwear Industries of America.

Schaefer, Ernst J., M.D. Prof. of Medicine and Nutrition, Tufts Univ.

Schaetzl, Randall, Ph.D. Prof. of Geography, Michigan State Univ.

Schaffner, John A., M.D. Assoc. Prof., Dir. of Clinical Gastroenterology, Rush-Presbyterian-St. Luke's Medical Ctr.

Schagrin, Morton L., Ph.D. Prof. of Philosophy, State Univ. of New York, Fredonia.

Schaich, K. M., Sc.D. Prof. of Food and Lipid Chemistry, Rutgers, the State Univ. of New Jersey.

Schaller, George B., Ph.D. Vice Pres. for Science and Exploration, Wildlife Conservation Society, New York.

Schatz, Michael F., Ph.D. Assoc. Prof. of Physics, Georgia Inst. of Technology.

Schebera, Richard L., Ph.D. Former Assoc. Prof. of Religion, St. Louis Univ.

Schechter, Michael G., Ph.D. Prof. Emer. of International Relations, James Madison Coll., Michigan State Univ.

Schein, Jerome D., Ph.D. Author, *Speaking the Language of Sign.*

Scheina, Robert L., Ph.D. Prof. of History, Industrial Coll. of the Armed Forces.

Schiffman, Lawrence H., Ph.D. Edelman Prof. of Hebrew and Judaic Studies, New York Univ.

Schirmer, Bruce David, M.D. Prof. of Surgery, Univ. of Virginia School of Medicine.

Schlereth, Eric R., Ph.D. Asst. Prof. of History, Univ. of Texas, Dallas.

Schlesinger, Richard C., Ph.D. Research Forester, Forest Service, U.S. Dept. of Agriculture.

Schlessinger, David, Ph.D. Sr. Investigator and Chief, Human Genetics Unit; Chief, Laboratory of Genetics, Natl. Inst. on Aging, Natl. Inst. of Health.

Schlitter, Duane A., Ph.D. Curator of Mammals and Birds, Texas Cooperative Wildlife Collection, Dept. of Wildlife and Fisheries Sciences, Texas A&M Univ.

Schlosser, C. Adam, Ph.D. Researcher, Dept. of Earth, Atmospheric, and Planetary Sciences, Mass. Inst. of Technology.

Schmalz, Mathew N., Ph.D. Assoc. Prof. of Religious Studies, The Coll. of the Holy Cross.

Schmeltzer, John C., M.A. Financial Writer, *Chicago Tribune.*

Schmid-Schoenbein, Geert W., Ph.D. Prof. of Bioengineering, Univ. of Calif., San Diego.

Schmidlin, Thomas W., Ph.D. Prof. of Geography, Kent State Univ.

Schmidt, Jennifer V., Ph.D. Director of Science and Research, Shark Research Institute.

Schmittberger, R. Wayne, J.D. Editor in Chief, *Games* magazine.

Schneck, Stephen, Ph.D. Chair and Assoc. Prof., Dept. of Politics, Catholic Univ. of America.

Schneider, Edward L., M.D. Dean, Andrus Gerontology Ctr., Univ. of Southern Calif.

Schneider, Glenn, Ph.D. Astronomer, Steward Observatory, University of Arizona.

Schneider, Stephen H., Ph.D. Professor of Biological Sciences, Stanford University.

Schneir, Miriam Writer; editor, *Feminism: The Essential Historical Writings.*

Schober, Juliane, Ph.D. Professor, Religious Studies, Arizona State University.

Schoenbrun, David Lee, Ph.D. Asst. Prof. of History, Northwestern University.

Schoenherr, Steven E., Ph.D. Professor Emeritus of History, University of San Diego.

Schoenhals, Michael, Ph.D. Assoc. Prof., Dept. of East Asian Lang., Lund Univ.

Schonchin, Lynn J., Sr., B.S. Consultant; Educator, Klamath County School District.

Schonfeld, Paul M., Ph.D. Prof. of Civil and Environmental Engineering, Univ. of Maryland.

Schott, Jeffrey J. Senior Fellow, Peterson Institute for International Economics.

Schramm, David N., Ph.D. Former Louis Block Prof. of Physical Sciences, Univ. of Chicago.

Schroll, R. Craig, B.A.S. Pres., FIRECON.

Schuchat, Anne, M.D. Chief, Respiratory Diseases, Ctrs. for Disease Control and Prevention.

Schuelein, Marianne, M.D. Asst. Prof. of Pediatrics and Neurology, Georgetown Univ.

Schulman, Bruce J., Ph.D. Prof. of History, Boston Univ.

Schulman, Ivan A., Ph.D. Prof. of Spanish, Florida Intl. Univ.

Schultenover, David G., Ph.D. Prof. of Historical Theology, Marquette Univ.

Schultz, Donald O., M.P.A. Prof. of Criminal Justice, Broward Community Coll.

Schuman, Gerald E., Ph.D. Soil Scientist, Rangeland Resources Research, High Plains Grasslands Research Station.

Schumer, Peter, Ph.D. Prof. of Mathematics and Natural Philosophy, Middlebury Coll.

Schutt, Amy C., Ph.D. Lecturer of History, State Univ. of New York, Cortland.

Schuyler, David, Ph.D. Prof. of American Studies, Franklin and Marshall Coll.

Schwan, Adrian L., Ph.D. Prof., Dept. of Chemistry, Univ. of Guelph.

Schwartz, Adina, J.D. Assoc. Prof., Dept. of Law, Police Science and Criminal Justice Admin., John Jay Coll. of Criminal Justice, and Grad. Ctr., City Univ. of New York.

Schwartz, David G., Ph.D. Dir., Ctr. for Gaming Research, Univ. of Nevada, Las Vegas.

Schwartz, Stephen I., B.A. Editor, *The Nonproliferation Review;* Adjunct Prof., Monterey Inst. of Intl. Studies.

Schwarz, Carolyn, Ph.D. Visiting Asst. Prof., Dept. of Sociology and Anthropology, Goucher College.

Scollon, John D. Exec. Dir., Columbia Marionette Theatre.

Scott, Deborah Emont, M.A. Director/CEO, Taft Museum of Art.

Scott, J. W., Ph.D. Prof. of Horticultural Science, Univ. of Florida.

Scott, Jeffrey G., Ph.D. Prof., Dept. of Entomology, Cornell Univ.

Scoville, James G., Ph.D. Prof. Emer. of Industrial Relations, Univ. of Minnesota, Twin Cities Campus.

Scrivener, Leslie, M.S.J. Faith and Ethics Reporter, *Toronto Star.*

Scruggs, Otey M., Ph.D. Former Professor of History, Syracuse University.

Seaborne, Adrian A., Ph.D. Former Prof. of Geography, Univ. of Regina.

Searing, James F., Ph.D. Former Prof., Dept. of History, Univ. of Illinois, Chicago.

Searl, Gary H., M.S. Adjunct Asst. Prof. of Geography, Univ. of Oregon.

Sears, Stuart D., Ph.D. Writer/translator, Middle East Communications.

Sebranek, Joseph G., Ph.D. Univ. Prof. of Animal Science, and Food Science and Human Nutrition, Iowa State Univ.

Seed, Patricia, Ph.D. Prof. of History, Univ. of Calif., Irvine.

Seely, Bruce E., Ph.D. Dean, College of Sciences and Arts, Michigan Technological University.

Sefton, James E., Ph.D. Prof. of History, Calif. State Univ., Northridge.

Segovia-Bain, Rossana, M.S. Asst. Clinical Prof., Univ. of Calif., San Francisco, School of Nursing.

Seidel, George E., Jr., Professor of Biomedical Sciences, Colorado State University.

Seidel, Michael, Ph.D. Professor Emeritus of English and Comparative Literature, Columbia Univ.

Seigler, David S., Ph.D. Prof. Emer. of Plant Biology, Univ. of Illinois, Urbana-Champaign.

Seiler, Tamara Palmer, Ph.D. Professor and Division Head for Culture, Faculty of Communication and Culture, Univ. of Calgary.

Selamet, A., Ph.D. Prof., Dept. of Mechanical Engineering, Ohio State Univ.

Selgin, George, Ph.D. Professor of Economics, Terry Coll. of Business, Univ. of Georgia.

Sellar, Christian, Ph.D. Asst. Prof., Dept. of Public Policy Leadership, Univ. of Mississippi.

Sellers, John Irvin, B.A. Dir. of New Media, *The Mobile* (AL) *Press.*

Selman, Kelly, Ph.D. Assoc. Prof. Emer. of Anatomy and Cell Biology, Univ. of Florida Coll. of Medicine.

Seltzer, Vicki, M.D. Former Chairman, Obstetrics and Gynecology, Long Island Jewish Medical Ctr. and North Shore Univ. Hospital.

Selvi, Arthur M., D.Pol.Sc. Former Prof. of Modern Lang., Central Connecticut State Univ.

Semler, Charles E., Ph.D. Pres., Semler Materials Services.

Semple, John C., Ph.D. Prof. Emer. and Adjunct Prof., Dept. of Biology, Univ. of Waterloo.

Senghas, Ann, Ph.D. Asst. Prof. of Psychology, Barnard Coll.

Senften, Rick, B.A. Special Projects Editor, *The* (Canton, OH) *Repository.*

Senn, Frank C., Ph.D. Former Pastor, Immanuel Lutheran Church, Evanston, IL.

Senyard, June, Ph.D. Sr. Lecturer, Dept. of History, Univ. of Melbourne.

Serrano, Elena L., Ph.D. Asst. Prof., Dept. of Human Nutrition, Foods, and Exercise, Virginia Polytechnic Inst. and State Univ.

Serrano, Roberto, Ph.D. Prof. of Economics, Brown Univ.

Servheen, Christopher, Ph.D. Grizzly Bear Recovery Coordinator, U.S. Fish and Wildlife Service.

Setta, Susan M., Ph.D. Assoc. Prof. of Philosophy and Religion, Northeastern Univ.

Sewell, James P., Ph.D. Prof. Emer. of Politics, Brock Univ. and External Assoc., Centre for Intl. and Strategic Studies, York Univ.

Shackelford, James F., Ph.D. Prof., Dept. of Chemical Engineering and Materials Science, Univ. of Calif., Davis.

Shafer, Byron E., Ph.D. Andrew W. Mellon Prof. of American Government, Oxford Univ.

Shahady, Edward J., M.D. Medical Director, Diabetes Master Clinician Program, Diabetes Master Clinician Inc.

Shallat, Todd, Ph.D. Prof. of History, Boise State Univ.

Shamey, Renzo, Ph.D. Asst. Prof., Textile Engineering, Chemistry and Science Dept., Coll. of Textiles, North Carolina State Univ.

Shands, Kathryn N., M.D. Child psychiatrist; former Asst. to the Dir., Ctrs. for Disease Control.

Shangold, Mona M., M.D. Dir., Ctr. for Women's Health and Sports Gynecology.

Shannon, Daniel W., Ph.D. Dean, Graham School of General Studies, Univ. of Chicago.

Shannon, David A., Ph.D. Former Prof. of History, Univ. of Virginia.

Shapiro, Arthur M., Ph.D. Prof., Ctr. for Population Biology, Univ. of Calif.

Sharp, Andrew, Ph.D. Prof. Emer. of Political Studies, Univ. of Auckland.

Sharpe, James Anthony, D.Phil. Sr. Lecturer in History, Univ. of York.

Shastri, Amita, Ph.D. Prof. and Chair, Dept. of Political Science, San Francisco State Univ.

Shaw, Brian J., M.Sc. Honorary Research Fellow, School of Earth and Environment, Univ. of Western Australia.

Shaw, C. Frank, III, Ph.D. Prof. Emer. of Chemistry, Univ. of Wisconsin, Milwaukee.

Shaw, Robin M., M.D. Asst. Prof. of Medicine/Cardiology, Univ. of Calif., San Francisco.

Shearer, Ned A., Ph.D. Prof. Emer. of Communication Arts and Sciences, Western Illinois Univ.

Shedlin, Michele G., Ph.D. Principal Investigator and Associate Director, International and Immigrant Health Research, Institute for AIDS Research, National Development and Research Institute.

Sheehan, Colleen A., Ph.D. Professor and Direc-

tor, Matthew J. Ryan Center for the Study of Free Institutions and the Public Good.

Sheehan, James J., Ph.D. Professor Emeritus, Department of History, Stanford University.

Sheets, Debra J., Ph.D. Asst. Prof., Dept. of Health Sciences, Calif. State Univ., Northridge.

Sheets, Payson, Ph.D. Prof., Dept. of Anthropology, Univ. of Colorado.

Sheidley, Nathaniel, Ph.D. Historian and Director of Public History, The Bostonian Society, Old State House Museum.

Sheldon, Kathleen, Ph.D. Research Scholar, UCLA Ctr. for the Study of Women.

Shelmerdine, Cynthia W., Ph.D. Prof. Emer., Dept. of Classics, Univ. of Texas, Austin.

Shelton, Dinah L., J.D. Prof. Emer. of International Law, The George Washington Univ. Law School.

Shen, Xiaoping, Ph.D. Prof. of Geography, Central Connecticut State Univ.

Shenkman, Kenneth J., B.J. Sr. Editor, World Book, Inc.

Shepherd, Jeffrey P., Ph.D. Visiting Prof. of Native American/Western History, Univ. of Texas, El Paso.

Sheppard, Scott S., Ph.D. Astronomer, Carnegie Inst. of Washington.

Sheridan, Thomas E., Ph.D. Author, *Arizona: A History.*

Sherman, Carol L., Ph.D. Prof. of French, Dept. of Romance Lang., Univ. of North Carolina, Chapel Hill.

Sherman, Ed, B.A. Freelance golf writer; former Golf Writer, *Chicago Tribune.*

Sherman, Paul W., Ph.D. Prof. Emer. of Animal Behavior, Cornell Univ.

Shetlar, David J., Ph.D. Prof. of Landscape Entomology, Ohio State Univ.

Shi, Mingzheng, Ph.D. Regional Dir., Council on Intl. Educ. Exchange.

Shields, Dianne, Ph.D. Former Educ. Specialist, Evanston Hospital.

Shiff, Richard, Ph.D. Effie Marie Cain Regents Chair in Art, Univ. of Texas, Austin.

Shifflett, Crandall, Ph.D. Prof. of History, Virginia Polytechnic Inst. and State Univ.

Shikuma, Nicholas J., Ph.D. Assistant Professor, Dept. of Biology, San Diego State University.

Shilstone, Frederick W., Ph.D. Former Prof. of English, Clemson Univ.

Shimizu, Kay, Ph.D. Assistant Professor, Columbia University.

Shinnick, Thomas M., Ph.D. Chief, Tuberculosis/Mycobacteriology Branch, Ctrs. for Disease Control and Prevention.

Shriver, Duward F., Ph.D. Prof. Emer., Dept. of Chemistry, Northwestern Univ.

Shisler, Joanna L., Ph.D. Asst. Prof. of Microbiology, Univ. of Illinois.

Shopkow, Leah, Ph.D. Assoc. Prof., Dept. of History, Indiana Univ.

Shor, Molly H., Ph.D. Asst. Prof., Dept. of Electrical and Computer Engineering, Oregon State Univ.

Shorrock, William I., Ph.D. Former Vice Provost for Academic Affairs and Faculty Relations, Cleveland State Univ.

Short, John Rennie, Ph.D. Prof., Dept. of Public Policy, Univ. of Maryland, Baltimore County.

Shortridge, James R., Ph.D. Prof. of Geography, Univ. of Kansas.

Shortz, Will, J.D. Crossword Editor, *The New York Times.*

Shostak, Seth, Ph.D. Sr. Astronomer, SETI Inst.

Showalter, Gerald R., Ph.D. Former Assoc. Prof. of Geography, Ball State Univ.

Shriver, Duward F., Ph.D. Morrison Prof. of Chemistry, Northwestern Univ.

Shuchat, Alan, Ph.D. Prof. of Mathematics, Wellesley Coll.

Shumway, J. Matthew, Ph.D. Prof. and Chair of Geography, Brigham Young Univ.

Shurtleff, William, M.A. Pres., Soyfoods Ctr.

Siavelis, Peter M., Ph.D. Professor of Political Science, Wake Forest University.

Sicilia, David B., Ph.D. Associate Professor of History, University of Maryland.

Siddiquee, Baker A., Ph.D. Assoc. Prof. of Economics, Univ. of Illinois, Springfield.

Sidey, Hugh S., B.S. Author, *Hugh Sidey's*

Portraits of the Presidents.

Sidlo, Steven L., M.A. Managing Editor, *Dayton* (OH) *Daily News.*

Sieber, Harry, Ph.D. Professor of Spanish, Johns Hopkins University.

Siedentop, Daryl, P.E.D. Dir., P-12 Project, Ohio State Univ.

Sieger, Charles F., M.S.L.S. Dir., Lyndhurst Free Public Library.

Silver, David F., M.A. Pres., Intl. Photographic Historical Organization.

Silverman, Alan K., M.D.

Silvers, Anita, Ph.D. Prof. and Chair, Dept. of Philosophy, San Francisco State Univ.

Silverstein, Helena, Ph.D. Assoc. Prof. of Government and Law, Lafayette Coll.

Silverstein, Melvin J., M.D. Prof. of Surgery and Henrietta C. Lee Chair in Breast Cancer Research, Keck School of Medicine, and Dir., Harold E. and Henrietta C. Lee Breast Ctr., USC/Norris Comprehensive Cancer Ctr. and Hospital.

Silverstein, Michael, Ph.D. Charles F. Grey Dist. Service Prof. of Anthropology, Linguistics, and Psychology, Univ. of Chicago.

Simberloff, Daniel, Ph.D. Nancy Gore Hunger Prof. of Environmental Studies, Univ. of Tennessee, Knoxville.

Simco, Bill A., Ph.D. Prof. of Biology, Univ. of Memphis.

Simmons, William B., Jr., Ph.D. Univ. Research Prof., Dept. of Geology and Geophysics, Univ. of New Orleans.

Simms, Steven R., Ph.D. Prof. of Anthropology, Utah State Univ.

Simon, James E., Ph.D. Professor, Department of Plant Biology and Plant Pathology, Rutgers, the State University of New Jersey.

Simon, Steven L., Ph.D. Staff Scientist, Division of Cancer Epidemiology & Genetics, Natl. Cancer Inst.

Simone, Joseph V., M.D. Physician in Chief, Memorial Sloan-Kettering Cancer Ctr.

Simpson, Brooks D., Ph.D. Prof. of History, Arizona State Univ.

Sims, Phillip L., Ph.D. Research Leader and Range Scientist, Agricultural Research Service, U.S. Dept. of Agriculture.

Sims, Randi L., Ph.D. Prof., Huizenga School of Business & Entrepreneurship, Nova Southeastern Univ.

Sims, Robert C., Ph.D. Prof. Emer. of History, Boise State Univ.

Simson, Robin Peter, M.Sc. Former Principal, Redbank Plains High School.

Sine, Richard L., B.A. Pres., Envision; former Editorial Dir., Scott Publishing Company.

Singer, Franz J. Master Barber.

Singer, Marcus G., Ph.D. Emer. Prof. of Philosophy, Univ. of Wisconsin, Madison.

Singh, Rana P. B., Ph.D. Prof. of Cultural Geography, Banaras Hindu Univ.

Singh, Vijay P., Ph.D. Prof., Dept. of Civil and Environmental Engineering, Louisiana State Univ.

Sinha, Aseema, Ph.D. Asst. Prof., Dept. of Political Science, Univ. of Wisconsin, Madison.

Sinha, Surya Prakash, J.S.D. Former Prof. of Law, Pace Univ. School of Law.

Sinnigen, William G., Ph.D. Former Prof. of History, City Univ. of New York Hunter Coll.

Sivin, N., Ph.D. Prof. Emer. of Chinese Culture and of the Hist. of Science, Univ. of Pennsylvania.

Skeen, C. Edward, Ph.D. Emer. Prof. of History, Univ. of Memphis.

Skelley, George C., Ph.D. Prof. Emer. of Animal Science, Clemson Univ.

Skidmore, Bill, B.A. Former City Editor, *Helena* (MT) *Independent Record.*

Sklar, Kathryn Kish, Ph.D. Dist. Prof., State Univ. of New York, Binghamton.

Sklar, Robert, Ph.D. Former Prof. of Cinema Studies, New York Univ.

Skorupa, Joseph, B.A. Boating/Outdoors Editor, *Popular Mechanics.*

Skroch, Walter A., Ph.D. Former Prof. of Horticultural Science, North Carolina State Univ.

Slackman, Joel, M.S. Exec. Dir., Legislative and Regulatory Policy, Blue Cross Blue Shield Assoc.

Sladek, N. E., Ph.D. Professor of Pharmacology,

University of Minnesota, Twin Cities Campus.

Slater, Keith, F.T.I. Former Adjunct Professor, School of Engineering, University of Guelph.

Slatta, Richard W., Ph.D. Professor of History, North Carolina State University.

Slavin, Arthur J., Ph.D. Justus Bier Dist. Prof. Emer. of Humanities, Univ. of Louisville.

Slemrod, Joel, Ph.D. Prof. of Business Economics and Public Policy and Dir. of the Office of Tax Policy Research, Univ. of Michigan Business School.

Slider, Robin, B.S. Educator, Ypsilanti Community Schools, Ypsilanti, Michigan.

Sloan, Alice S., R.Ph. Pharmacy Consultant, HealthGuard of Lancaster, Inc.

Sloan, Douglas, Ph.D. Author of *Faith and Knowledge* and *Insight-Imagination.*

Sloan, Richard W., M.D. Chairman and Residency Program Dir., Dept. of Family Practice, York Hospital.

Sludikoff, Stanley R., B.Arch. Editor and Publisher, *Poker Player Newspaper.*

Small, Melvin, Ph.D. Dist. Prof. of History, Wayne State Univ.

Small, Stephen, Ph.D. Assoc. Prof. of African American Studies, Univ. of Calif., Berkeley.

Smelser, Marshall, Ph.D. Former Prof. of History, Univ. of Notre Dame.

Smelser, Neil J., Ph.D. Prof. Emer. of Sociology, Univ. of Calif., Berkeley.

Smidchens, Guntis, Ph.D. Sr. Lecturer, Dept. of Scandinavian Studies, Univ. of Washington.

Smidt, Warner K., Ph.D. Prof., Dept. of Industrial Studies, Univ. of Wisconsin, Platteville.

Smiley, J. H., Ph.D. Former Extension Prof. of Agronomy, Univ. of Kentucky.

Smit, Peter-Ben, Th.D. Prof. of Old Catholicism, Utrecht Univ.

Smith, A. Mark, Ph.D. Prof. of History, Univ. of Missouri, Columbia.

Smith, C. Wayne, Ph.D. Prof. of Cotton Breeding, Texas A&M Univ.

Smith, Carolyn J., Ph.D. Prof. of Chemistry, Delaware County Community Coll.

Smith, Dale C., Ph.D. Prof. of Military Medicine and History, Dir. of Military and Medical History, Uniformed Services Univ. of the Health Sciences.

Smith, David Glenn, Ph.D. Prof. of Anthropology, Univ. of Calif., Davis.

Smith, David R., M.L.S. Consultant and former Chief Archivist, Walt Disney Company.

Smith, David V., Ph.D. Former Prof. and Chair, Dept. of Anatomy and Neurobiology, Univ. of Tennessee Health Science Ctr.

Smith, Deborah K., Ph.D. Sr. Scientist, Woods Hole Oceanographic Inst.

Smith, Duane A., Ph.D. Former Professor of History and Southwest Studies, Fort Lewis College; author, *The Trail of Gold and Silver.*

Smith, George P., II, LLM. Prof. of Law, Catholic Univ. of America.

Smith, Glenn, Ph.D. Prof., Chair, Leadership and Educ. Policy Studies, Northern Illinois Univ.

Smith, Harding E., Ph.D. Prof. of Physics, Ctr. for Astrophysics and Space Sciences, Univ. of Calif., San Diego.

Smith, John E., LL.D. Former Professor of Philosophy, Yale University.

Smith, John M., Ph.D. Former Prof. of Mathematics, George Mason Univ.

Smith, Jonathan Z., Ph.D. Former Robert O. Anderson Distinguished Service Professor of the Humanities, University of Chicago.

Smith, Lahra, Ph.D. Asst. Prof. of African Studies, Georgetown Univ.

Smith, Lytton E., B.A. Former Chief Librarian, *Seattle Post-Intelligencer.*

Smith, Mary Frances, Ph.D. Asst. Prof., Dept. of History, Ohio Univ.

Smith, Matthew, Ph.D. Professor of History, The University of the West Indies, Mona.

Smith, Merritt Roe, Ph.D. Cutten Prof. of the History of Technology, Mass. Inst. of Technology.

Smith, Michael Author specializing in the history of polar exploration.

Smith, Pamela H., Ph.D. Prof. of History, Columbia Univ.

Smith, Philip Chadwick Foster, B.A. Former maritime historian.

Smith, Robert Freeman, Ph.D. Former Univ. Prof. of History, Univ. of Toledo.

Smith, Robert Powell, M.A. Prof. of Military Science, U.S. Army.

Smith, Robert William, Ph.D. Former Professor of Philosophy/Religion Studies, Maricopa Community Colleges.

Smith, Sam, M.A. Columnist, *Chicago Tribune.*

Smith, Suzanne J., M.D. Dir. of Breast Imaging, Columbia-Presbyterian Medical Ctr.

Smith, W. Calvin, Ph.D. Prof. of History, Univ. of South Carolina, Aiken.

Smith, W. David, Ph.D. Philip Morris Prof. of Crop Science, North Carolina State Univ.

Smith, Whitney, Ph.D. Former Director, Flag Research Center.

Smock, Raymond W., Ph.D. Coeditor, *Booker T. Washington Papers.*

Smolensky, Michael H., Ph.D. Prof. of Environmental Sciences, School of Public Health, Univ. of Texas Health Science Ctr., Houston.

Snaddon, Andrew, B.A. Former Publisher, *Medicine Hat* (AB) *News.*

Snipes, David S., Ph.D. Former Professor of Geology, Clemson University.

Snoble, Joseph J., Ph.D. Prof. Emer. of Physics/ Science Educ., Central Missouri State Univ.

Snodgrass, Michael, Ph.D. Assoc. Prof. of History, Indiana Univ.-Purdue Univ. Indianapolis

Snouffer, Chet A., B.S. Board of Dirs., U.S. Boomerang Assoc.

Snow, Dean, Ph.D. Professor Emeritus of Anthropology, Pennsylvania State University.

Snyder, Gregory K., Ph.D. Prof. of Biology, Univ. of Colorado.

Snyder, John W., Ph.D. Emer. Prof. of History, Kent State Univ.

Soast, Allen, B.A. Former Senior Editor, *Engineering News-Record.*

Sobel, Robert, Ph.D. Former Lawrence Stessin Prof. of Business History, Hofstra Univ.

Sobieszek, Robert A., M.Phil. Former Curator, Los Angeles County Museum of Art.

Sobré, Judith Berg, Ph.D. Prof. of Art History, Univ. of Texas, San Antonio.

Sochen, June, Ph.D. Prof. Emer. of History, Northeastern Illinois Univ.; author, *Herstory: A Record of the American Woman's Past.*

Sokal, Michael M., Ph.D. Prof. of History, Worcester Polytechnic Inst.

Sokolsky, Mark, Ph.D. Freelance writer and editor.

Soll, Ivan, Ph.D. Professor Emeritus of Philosophy, University of Wisconsin, Madison.

Solomon, Keith J., Ph.D. Asst. Vice Chancellor, Northern Territory Univ.

Solomon, Sean C., Ph.D. Dir., Dept. of Terrestrial Magnetism, Carnegie Inst. of Washington.

Somlo, Stefan, M.D. C. N. H. Long Prof. of Internal Medicine, Yale Univ. School of Medicine.

Sorrentino, Frank M., Ph.D. Prof. of Political Science, St. Francis Coll.

Southgate, W. M., Ph.D. Former Prof. of History, Denison Univ.

Sparks, Donald L., Ph.D. Prof. of Intl. Economics, The Citadel.

Spears, Ian S., Ph.D. Assoc. Prof. of Political Science, Univ. of Guelph.

Spencer, C. Bruce, B.A. Pres., Pipe Collectors International.

Sperandeo, Andy, M.A. Exec. Editor, *Model Railroader.*

Sperling, Elliot, Ph.D. Prof. of Tibetan Studies, Indiana Univ., Bloomington.

Spicer, Dag, Sr. Curator, Computer History Museum.

Spilman Vogt, Alexis K., Ph.D. Associate Professor of Optics, Monroe Community College.

Spindel, Donna J., Ph.D. Dean, Graduate College, and Prof., Dept. of History, Marshall Univ.

Spitler, G. Hollis, Ph.D. Agricultural Technician, Northwestern Washington Research and Extension Ctr., Washington State Univ.

Spitulnik, Debra, Ph.D. Asst. Prof., Dept. of Anthropology, Emory Univ.

Spitzer, Leo, Ph.D. Prof. Emer. of History, Dartmouth Coll.; author, *The Creoles of Sierra Leone.*

Splittstoesser, W. E., Ph.D. Professor of Plant Physiology in Horticulture, University of Illinois, Urbana-Champaign.

Spoehr, Luther, Ph.D. Lecturer, Educ. Dept., Brown Univ.

Sprugel, Douglas G., Ph.D. Prof. of Forest Ecology, Coll. of Forest Resources, Univ. of Washington.

Sprules, W. Gary, Ph.D. Professor Emeritus of Biology, University of Toronto, Mississauga.

Spudis, Paul D., Ph.D. Staff Scientist, Lunar and Planetary Inst., Houston.

Spurgeon, Thomas, B.S. Former Publisher/Editor, *The Comics Reporter.*

Spychalski, John C., D.B.A. Prof. of Business Logistics, Pennsylvania State Univ.

Squire, Kurt, Ph.D. Assoc. Prof. of Educ. Communications and Technology, Univ. of Wisconsin, Madison.

Stacks, Don W., Ph.D. Dir., Program in Advertising and Public Relations, School of Communication, Univ. of Miami.

Stadel, Christoph, Ph.D. Prof. Emer. of Geography and Geology, Univ. of Salzburg.

Staley, Richard, Ph.D. Asst. Prof. of History of Science, Univ. of Wisconsin, Madison.

Stallings, E. Fran, Ph.D. Former Dir., Southwest Florida Office, Florida Wildlife Federation.

Standen, S. Dale, Ph.D. Prof. of History, Trent Univ.

Stanford, Craig B., Ph.D. Prof. of Anthropology and Biological Sciences, Univ. of Southern Calif.

Stanley, Matthew, Ph.D. Professor, Gallatin School of Individualized Study, New York Univ.

Standiford, Les, Ph.D. Director, Creative Writing Program, Florida International University.

Stanley, Steven M., Ph.D. Prof. of Geobiology, Univ. of Hawaii.

Starrfield, Sumner, Ph.D. Regents Prof. of Physics and Astronomy, Arizona State Univ.

Stasik, Andrew J., Jr., M.F.A. Pres., Andrew Stasik Fine Arts; founder, *Print Review.*

Stavrou, Theofanis G., Ph.D. Prof. of Modern Russian and Near Eastern History, Univ. of Minnesota, Twin Cities Campus.

Stearns, Peter N., Ph.D. Heinz Prof. of History and Dean, Coll. of Humanities and Social Sciences, Carnegie-Mellon Univ.

Stecker, Ann Page, M.A. Prof. of Humanities, Colby-Sawyer Coll.

Stedman, Lew, B.S. Library Asst./Theremin Player, Newport Beach Public Library.

Steele, Russell W., M.D. Prof. and Vice Chairman of Pediatrics, Children's Hosp., New Orleans.

Steele, Valerie, Ph.D. Dir., Museum at the Fashion Inst. of Technology.

Steffen, Jerome O., Ph.D. Instructor of History, Univ. of Georgia; author, *Comparative Frontiers: A Proposal for Studying the American West.*

Steffes, Paul G., Ph.D. Prof. and Assoc. Chair for Research, School of Electrical and Computer Engineering, Georgia Inst. of Technology.

Steinberg, David J., Ph.D. Former Pres., Long Island Univ.

Steinberg, Laurence, Ph.D. Dist. Univ. Prof. and Laura H. Carnell Prof. of Psychology, Temple Univ.

Steinhardt, Paul Joseph, Ph.D. Prof. of Physics, Princeton Univ.

Steinhauer, Nathalie, Ph.D. student, Department of Entomology, University of Maryland.

Steinkamp, Myrna P., Ph.D. Former Research Assoc., Beet Sugar Dev. Foundation, USDA Crops Research Laboratory, Colorado State Univ.

Stekert, Ellen J., Ph.D. Prof. Emer. of English, American Studies, and Folklore, Univ. of Minnesota, Twin Cities Campus.

Stephan, Karl D., Ph.D. Professor, Ingram School of Engineering, Texas State Univ., San Marcos.

Stern, David, Ph.D. Assoc. Prof. of Asian and Middle Eastern Studies, Univ. of Pennsylvania.

Stern, Louis W., Ph.D. John D. Gray Dist. Prof. Emer. of Marketing, Kellogg School of Management, Northwestern Univ.

Stern, Robert M., Ph.D. Prof. Emer. of Economics and Public Policy, Univ. of Michigan.

Stern, Robert S., M.D. Prof. of Dermatology, Harvard Medical School; Chairman of Dermatology, Beth Israel Deaconess Medical Center.

Stern, S. Alan, Ph.D. Director, Department of

Space Studies, Southwest Research Institute.

Sternberg, Robert J., Ph.D. IBM Prof. of Psychology and Educ., Yale Univ.

Stevens, Charles F., M.D., Ph.D. Howard Hughes Medical Inst. Investigator, Salk Inst.

Stevens, Martin, Ph.D. Research Fellow, Dept. of Zoology, Univ. of Cambridge.

Stevens, Michael B., M.D. Assoc. Dir., Family Practice Residency Program, San Jose Medical Ctr., and Clinical Assoc. Prof. of Family and Community Medicine, Stanford Univ. School of Medicine.

Stevenson, David, Ph.D. Prof. of Intl. History, London School of Economics and Political Science.

Steverlynck, Astrid, D.Phil. Freelance writer.

Stewart, A. T. Q., Ph.D. Former Reader in Irish History, Queen's Univ., Belfast.

Stewart, David K., Ph.D. Prof. and Head, Dept. of Political Science, Univ. of Calgary.

Stewart, Garrett, Ph.D. Prof. of English, Univ. of Iowa.

Stewart, Kendra B., Ph.D. Assoc. Prof., Dept. of Government, Eastern Kentucky Univ.

Stewart, Robert K., Ph.D. Prof. of Journalism, Ohio Univ.

Stewart, Roderick J., B.A. Former Fellow, Bethune Coll., York Univ., Toronto.

Stiff-Roberts, Adrienne D., Ph.D. Assoc. Prof. of Electrical and Computer Engineering, Duke Univ.

Stinger, Charles L., Ph.D. Prof. of History, State Univ. of New York, Buffalo.

Stinson, Donald L., Ph.D. Consulting engineer.

Stipanuk, Martha H., Ph.D. Prof., Division of Nutritional Sciences, Cornell Univ.

Stivender, Donald L., M.S.E. Former owner, Stivender Engineering Associates.

Stock, Joann, Ph.D. Prof. of Geology and Geophysics, Calif. Inst. of Technology.

Stoker, H. Stephen, Ph.D. Prof. of Chemistry, Weber State Univ.

Stokes, Carol E., M.A.T. Command Historian, U.S. Army Signal Corps.

Stokesbury, James L., Ph.D. Author, *Navy and Empire* and *A Short History of Air Power.*

Stokstad, Marilyn, Ph.D. Judith Harris Murphy Dist. Prof. Emer. of Art History, Univ. of Kansas.

Stolar, Mark, M.D. Assoc. Prof. of Medicine, Northwestern Univ.

Stone, Andrew, B.A. Dip. Journalism. Sr. Journalist, *New Zealand Herald.*

Stone, David L., Ph.D. Asst. Prof. of Classics, Florida State Univ.

Stone, Joanne, M.D. Assoc. Prof., Mount Sinai School of Medicine, Mount Sinai Medical Ctr.

Stone, M. David, B.A. Freelance writer; Contributing Editor, *PC Magazine.*

Stone, Martha B., Ph.D. Prof., Dept. of Food Science and Human Nutrition, Colorado State Univ.

Stone, Neil J., M.D. Prof. of Clinical Medicine, Northwestern Univ. School of Medicine.

Stone-Ferrier, Linda, Ph.D. Prof. and Chair, Dept. of Art History, Univ. of Kansas.

Storbeck, Glenn, B.A. Special Collections Librarian, Tacoma Public Library.

Stout, Joseph A., Jr., Ph.D. Prof. Emer. of History, Oklahoma State Univ.

Stow, George B., Ph.D. Prof. of History, LaSalle Univ.

Stowasser, Barbara R. F., Ph.D. Prof. of Arabic, Ctr. for Contemporary Arab Studies, Georgetown Univ.

Stowers, Carlton Freelance journalist; author, *Dallas Cowboys: The First Twenty-Five Years.*

Stowers, Stanley K., Ph.D. Prof. of Religious Studies, Brown Univ.

Stoy, Walt Alan, Ph.D. Prof. and Dir., Emergency Medicine Program, Univ. of Pittsburgh.

Strahl, Stuart D., Ph.D. Former Coordinator, Tropical South America Program, WCI–New York Zoological Society.

Straus, E. G., Ph.D. Former Prof. of Mathematics, Univ. of Calif., Los Angeles.

Straus, Scott, Ph.D. Professor, Department of Political Science, University of Wisconsin, Madison.

Strauss, Arnold W., M.D. Prof.; Dir., Division of Pediatric Cardiology, Washington Univ.

Strauss, Jonathan, Ph.D. Assoc. Prof. and Chair, Dept. of French and Italian, Miami Univ.

Strauss, Michael A., Ph.D. Professor of Astrophysical Sciences, Princeton University.

Stricklin, George P., Ph.D. Prof. and Chief, Division of Dermatology, Vanderbilt Univ. Medical Ctr.

Striedter, Georg F., Ph.D. Professor, Dept. of Neurobiology & Behavior, Univ. of Calif., Irvine.

Stringer, Gary A., Ph.D. Prof. of English, Univ. of Southern Mississippi.

Strohm, Paul, Ph.D. Prof. Emer. of Humanities, Columbia Univ.

Strout, Jeffrey, B.A. Former Editor, *Bangor* (ME) *Daily News.*

Stuart, Paul H., Ph.D. Prof. of Social Work, Univ. of Alabama.

Stuart-Fox, Martin, Ph.D. Head, Dept. of History, Univ. of Queensland.

Stuckey, Kenneth A., M.L.S. Research Librarian, Perkins School for the Blind.

Stucky, Galen D., Ph.D. Prof. of Chemistry and of Materials, Univ. of Calif., Santa Barbara.

Studlar, Susan Moyle, Ph.D. Adjunct Assoc. Prof. of Biology, West Virginia Univ., Morgantown.

Stuewer, Roger H., Ph.D. Prof. of the History of Science and Technology, Univ. of Minnesota, Twin Cities Campus.

Stults, Taylor, Ph.D. Prof. of History, Muskingum Coll.

Su, Linli, B.S. Grad. Asst., Liquid Crystal Inst., Kent State Univ.

Subtelny, Orest, Ph.D. Prof. of History and Political Science, York Univ.

Suchlicki, Jaime, Ph.D. Prof., Grad. School of Intl. Studies, Univ. of Miami.

Sues, Hans-Dieter, Ph.D. Assoc. Dir. for Research and Collections, Natl. Museum of Natural History, Smithsonian Inst.

Sugar, Bert Randolph, J.D. Publisher-Editor, *Boxing Illustrated.*

Sulikowski, James, Ph.D. Associate Professor, University of New England.

Sullivan, Beth A., Ph.D. Associate Professor, Department of Molecular Genetics and Microbiology, Duke University School of Medicine.

Sullivan, Charles L., M.S. Archivist, Mississippi Gulf Coast Community Coll.

Sullivan, Charles M., M.C.P. Exec. Dir., Cambridge Historical Commission.

Sullivan, Christine, B.A. Former Sr. Ed., World Book, Inc.

Sullivan, Daniel R., Ph.D. Manager, Product Dev., Keebler Company.

Sullivan, Denis J., Ph.D. Prof. and Chair, Dept. of Political Science, Northeastern Univ.

Sullivan, Donald B., Ph.D. Former Chief, Time and Frequency Division, Natl. Inst. of Standards and Technology.

Sullivan, Margaret M., M.S.J. Editor and Vice Pres., *The Buffalo* (NY) *News.*

Sullivan, Michael E., Ph.D. Former Assoc. Prof. of Geography, Ball State Univ.

Sullivan, Michael P., Ph.D. Former Prof. of Political Science, Univ. of Arizona.

Sullivan, Peggy, Ph.D. Former Exec. Dir., American Library Assoc.

Sullivan, Rosemary, Ph.D. Professor Emeritus of English, University of Toronto.

Sullivan, Teresa A., Ph.D. President Emerita, University of Virginia.

Sulok, Nancy J., B.A. Columnist, *The South Bend* (IN) *Tribune.*

Summerhill, William R., Ph.D. Professor, Dept. of History, Univ. of California, Los Angeles.

Summers, David, Ph.D. Wm. R. Kenan, Jr., Prof. of the History of Art, Univ. of Virginia.

Summers, Hollis, D.Litt. Former Dist. Prof. of English, Ohio Univ.

Summers, Mark Wahlgren, Ph.D. Prof. of History, Univ. of Kentucky.

Summers, Michael E., Ph.D. Prof. of Planetary Science and Astronomy, George Mason University.

Summons, Roger E., Ph.D. Prof. of Geobiology, Mass. Inst. of Technology.

Sunley, Emil M., Ph.D. Asst. Dir. of Fiscal Affairs, Intl. Monetary Fund.

Superina, Mariella, Dr.med.vet., Ph.D. Research Scientist, Cuyo Institute of Experimental Medicine and Biology, Technological Scientific Center, National Scientific and Technical Research Council,

Mendoza, Argentina.

Surratt, Jerry L., Ph.D. Adjunct Prof. of History, Wingate Univ.

Susman, Randall L., Ph.D. Prof. of Anatomical Sciences, School of Medicine, Stony Brook Univ.

Sutcliffe, Anthony, F.R.H.S. Former Special Professor in the Dept. of History, Univ. of Nottingham.

Sutherland, D. A., Ph.D. Adjunct Prof. of History, Dalhousie Univ.

Sutherland, Donald, Ph.D. Prof. of History, Univ. of Maryland.

Sutton, Eva, M.F.A. Professor of Photography, Rhode Island School of Design.

Sviedrys, Romualdas, Ph.D. Assoc. Prof. of History of Science, Polytechnic Univ.

Svinth, Joseph, M.A. Editor, Electronic Journals of Martial Arts and Sciences.

Swade, Doron D., Ph.D. Guest Curator, Computer History Museum and Visiting Prof. of Computer Science, Portsmouth Univ.

Swain, Carol M., Ph.D. Prof. of Law and Prof. of Political Science, Vanderbilt Univ. Law School.

Swain, Joseph P., Ph.D. Assoc. Prof. of Music, Colgate Univ.

Swaisgood, Ronald, Ph.D. Dir., Applied Animal Ecology, San Diego Zoo Inst. for Conservation Research.

Swami, Praveen, B.A. Chief of Bureau, New Delhi, *Frontline* magazine.

Swan, Patricia B., Ph.D. Prof. Emer., Iowa State Univ.

Swank, Duane, Ph.D. Assoc. Prof. of Political Science, Marquette Univ.

Swayd, Samy, Ph.D. Visiting Prof. of Religious Studies, San Diego State Univ.

Swedlund, Alan, Ph.D. Prof. Emer. of Anthropology, Univ. of Mass., Amherst.

Sweet, David C., Ph.D. Pres., Youngstown State Univ.

Sweet, R. F. G., Ph.D. Prof. Emer. of Near Eastern Studies, Univ. of Toronto.

Sweetman, Jack, Ph.D. Former Naval and Military Historian, U.S. Naval Academy, Annapolis.

Sweets, John F., Ph.D. Prof. of History, Univ. of Kansas.

Sweitzer, James S., Ph.D. Pres. and Principal, Science Communications Consultants.

Swerdlow, David L., M.D. Medical Epidemiologist, Ctrs. for Disease Control and Prevention.

Swezey, Marilyn Pfeifer, M.A. Art historian.

Swinton, Elizabeth deS., Ph.D. Former Curator of Asian Art, Worcester Art Museum.

Sydnor, Charles W., Jr., Ph.D. Pres. and Chief Exec. Officer, Central Virginia Educ. Telecommunications Company, Inc.

Symonds, Deborah A., Ph.D. Prof., Dept. of History, Drake Univ.

Szporluk, Roman, Ph.D. M. S. Hrushevsky Prof. of Ukrainian History, Harvard Univ.

T

Tabuteau, Emily Zack, Ph.D. Assoc. Prof. of History, Michigan State Univ.

Taeuber, Karl, Ph.D. Prof. Emer. of Sociology, Univ. of Wisconsin, Madison.

Tager, Jack, Ph.D. Coauthor, *Massachusetts: A Concise History.*

Tait, Diane M., Ph.D. Postdoctoral Fellow, Medical Coll. of Wisconsin, The Eye Inst.

Taj, Afroz, Ph.D. Assoc. Prof., Dept. of Foreign Langs. and Literatures, North Carolina State Univ.

Takaha, Michael, B.S. Asst. Track Coach, Univ. of Houston.

Takim, Liyakat, Ph.D. Sharjah Chair in Global Islam, McMaster Univ.

Talbert, Richard J. A., Ph.D. Prof. of History and Classics, Univ. of North Carolina, Chapel Hill.

Talbott, Basil B., Jr., B.A. Washington Correspondent, *Chicago Sun-Times.*

Tanabe, Michael J., Ph.D. Prof. of Plant Science, Univ. of Hawaii, Hilo.

Tankersley, Kenneth Barnett, Ph.D. Asst. Prof. of Anthropology, Univ. of Cincinnati.

Tankersley, Richard, Ph.D. Prof., Dept. of Biological Sciences, Florida Inst. of Technology.

Tanner, Adrian, Ph.D. Professor, Department of Anthropology, Memorial University.

Tanner, Raymond L., Ph.D. Prof. Emer. of Radiology, Univ. of Tenn. Ctr. for the Health Sciences.

Tanzi, Vito, Ph.D. Dir., Fiscal Affairs Dept., Intl. Monetary Fund.

Tao, Eugene, M.A. Editor, (Hilo) *Hawaii Tribune-Herald.*

Tardif, Claude, M.B.A. Former Director, International Maple Syrup Institute.

Tarter, Brent, M.A. Course Leader, Osher Lifelong Learning Institute, School of Professional and Continuing Studies, University of Richmond.

Tarter, Jill C., Ph.D. Former Dir., SETI Research, SETI Inst.

Tatum, Henry K., B.A. Assoc. Editor, Editorial Page, *Dallas Morning News.*

Taubman, Paul, Ph.D. Prof. of Economics, University of Pennsylvania.

Taylor, Andrew C., III, B.S. Former Metro Editor, *Richmond* (VA) *Times-Dispatch.*

Taylor, C. Richard, Ph.D. Former Charles P. Lyman Prof. of Biology, Harvard Univ.

Taylor, Harriet V., Ph.D. Assoc. Prof. of Chemistry, Miami Univ.

Taylor, Heber, B.A. Editor, *The Galveston County* (TX) *Daily News.*

Taylor, Kathleen C., Ph.D. Former Chair, Board of Dirs. of the Centre for Automotive Materials and Manufacturing, General Motors of Canada.

Taylor, Leighton R., Jr., Ph.D. Research Assoc., Calif. Academy of Sciences.

Taylor, Michael J. H. Author and editor of books on aircraft.

Taylor, Michael P., Ph.D. Research Associate, Department of Earth Sciences, University of Bristol.

Taylor, R. Craig, Ph.D. Prof. of Chemistry, Oakland Univ.

Taylor, Robert H., Ph.D. Prof. of Politics, School of Oriental and African Studies, Univ. of London.

Taylor, Robert W., Ph.D. Professor of Criminology and Public Affairs, University of Texas, Dallas.

Teaiwa, Katerina Martina, Ph.D. Pacific Studies Convener, Australian Natl. Univ.

Tebben, Joseph R., Ph.D. Prof. of Greek and Latin, Ohio State Univ.

Teeter, Emily, Ph.D. Research Assoc., Oriental Inst., Univ. of Chicago.

Tefft, Stanton K., Ph.D. Prof. of Anthropology, Wake Forest Univ.

Temperley, Howard, Ph.D. Prof. of History, Univ. of East Anglia.

Temperley, Judith K., Ph.D. Chief, Weapons Analysis Branch, U.S. Army Research Laboratory.

Temple, Frederick T., Ph.D. Chief, Resident Mission in Turkey, World Bank.

Templeton, Alan R., Ph.D. Charles Rebstock Prof. of Biology and Prof. of Genetics and Biomedical Engineering, Washington Univ., St. Louis.

terHorst, J. F., B.A. Author, *Gerald Ford and the Future of the Presidency.*

Terrasse, Jean, Ph.D. Prof. of French Lang. and Lit., McGill Univ.

TeSelle, Eugene, Ph.D. Prof. of Church History and Theology, Divinity School, Vanderbilt Univ.

Tétreault, Mary Ann, Ph.D. Una Chapman Cox Dist. Prof. of Intl. Affairs, Dept. of Political Science, Trinity Univ.

Thayamballi, A., Ph.D. Sr. Technology Consultant, Chevron Shipping Company.

Thelen, David P., Ph.D. Prof. of History, Indiana Univ., Bloomington.

Thiel, Elizabeth, B.A. Day Metro Editor, *The* (Norfolk, VA) *Virginian-Pilot.*

Thomas, Bert J., Ph.D. Prof. and Head of Caribbean Studies, Brooklyn Coll., The City Univ. of New York.

Thomas, Ebony Elizabeth, Ph.D. Assistant Prof., Graduate School of Education, Univ. of Michigan.

Thomas, Samuel J., Ph.D. Prof. of History, Michigan State Univ.

Thomas, Steve, B.A. Economy Editor, *Savannah* (GA) *Morning News.*

Thomas, William G., III, Ph.D. Prof. of History, Univ. of Nebraska, Lincoln.

Thompsell, Angela D., Ph.D. Asst. Prof. of Hist., The College at Brockport, State Univ. of New York.

Thompson, Brian S., Ph.D. Prof. of Mechanical Engineering, Michigan State Univ.

Thompson, Carol L., M.A. Former Editor, *Cur-*

rent History magazine.

Thompson, David W., Ph.D. Professor Emeritus of Chemistry, College of William and Mary.

Thompson, Dennis L., Ph.D. Prof. of Political Science, Brigham Young Univ.

Thompson, Jerry, D.A. Regents Prof. of History, Texas A&M Intl. Univ.

Thompson, Larry C., Ph.D. Professor Emeritus of Inorganic Chemistry, Univ. of Minnesota, Duluth.

Thompson, Paul M., Ph.D. Assoc. Prof. of Neurology, Univ. of Calif., LA, School of Medicine.

Thompson, W. Scott, D.Phil. Adjunct Prof., Georgetown Univ. and Fletcher School of Law and Diplomacy, Tufts Univ.; editor, *The Third World.*

Thompson, Wayne, Ph.D. Historian, Ctr. for Air Force History, Headquarters, U.S. Air Force.

Thomson, Keith Stewart, Ph.D. Pres., Academy of Natural Sciences.

Thornton, John I., D.Crim. Emer. Prof. of Forensic Science, Univ. of Calif., Berkeley.

Thornton, Lee, Ph.D. Former Richard Eaton Prof. of Journalism, Univ. of Maryland, College Park.

Thursby, Gene R., Ph.D. Assoc. Prof. of Religion, Univ. of Florida.

Tidwell, William D., Ph.D. Prof. Emer. of Botany, Brigham Young Univ.

Tierney, Kevin, LLM. Prof. of Law, Hastings Coll. of the Law, Univ. of Calif., San Francisco.

Tiffney, Bruce H., Ph.D. Prof. of Geological Sciences, Univ. of Calif., Santa Barbara.

Tignor, Robert L., Ph.D. Prof. Emer. of History, Princeton Univ.

Tilbrook, Kym Group Manager Editorial, *The* (Adelaide, South Australia) *Advertiser and Sunday Mail.*

Tiller, Veronica E. Velarde, Ph.D. Pres., Tiller Research, Inc.

Tillman, Barrett, B.S. Secretary, American Fighter Aces Assoc.

Timm, Robert M., Ph.D. Curator of Mammals and Assoc. Prof. of Ecology and Evolutionary Biology, Museum of Natural History, Univ. of Kansas.

Timms, Howard, M.A. British author and journalist.

Tirro, Frank, Ph.D. Emeritus Professor of Music, Yale University.

Tismaneanu, Vladimir, Ph.D. Prof. of Government and Politics, Univ. of Maryland.

Titman, Rodger D., Ph.D. Prof. of Wildlife Biology, Macdonald Campus of McGill Univ.

Todd, James K., M.D. Prof. of Pediatrics, Microbiology and Preventive Medicine, Univ. of Colorado School of Medicine.

Todd, Malcolm, D.Litt. Former Professor of Archaeology, University of Exeter.

Tollefson, Derrik R., Ph.D. Research Assoc. Prof., Univ. of Utah Coll. of Social Work.

Tong, Phillip S., Ph.D. Prof., Dairy Products Technology Ctr., Calif. Polytechnic State Univ.

Tonos, Michael, B.A. Former Exec. Editor, *The* (Biloxi, MS) *Sun Herald.*

Toppin, Edgar Allan, Ph.D. Former Prof. of History, Virginia State Univ.

Torielli, Rose M., M.B.A. Researcher, Pennsylvania State University.

Tortike, W. Simon, Ph.D. Former Assoc. Prof. of Petroleum Engineering, Univ. of Alberta.

Tortora, Phyllis, Ph.D. Prof. Emer., Home Economics, Queens Coll., City Univ. of New York.

Tosney, Kathryn, Ph.D. Prof. and Chair, Dept. of Biology, The Univ. of Miami.

Townsend, Camilla, Ph.D. Assoc. Prof. of History, Rutgers, the State Univ. of New Jersey.

Trachtenberg, Barry, Ph.D. Asst. Prof. of European Jewish Studies, Univ. at Albany, State Univ. of New York.

Trachtenberg, Marc, Ph.D. Prof., Dept. of Political Science, Univ. of Calif., Los Angeles.

Trathan, Philip Neil, Ph.D. Head of Conservation Biology, British Antarctic Survey.

Travisono, Anthony P., B.A. Former Exec. Dir., American Correctional Assoc.

Trede, Larry D., Ph.D. Emer. Prof., Dept. of Agricultural Educ. and Studies, Iowa State Univ.

Trefil, James, Ph.D. Clarence J. Robinson Prof. of Physics, George Mason Univ.

Trevett, Jeremy, D.Phil. Associate Professor of History, York University.

Tripathi, Brenda, Ph.D. Prof. of Pathology and Adjunct Prof. of Ophthalmology, Univ. of South Carolina School of Medicine.

Tripathi, Ramesh C., F.R.C.Path. Former Prof. and Chairman, Dept. of Ophthalmology, Univ. of South Carolina School of Medicine.

Trotter, William R., B.A. Freelance writer; author, *A Frozen Hell: The Russo-Finnish Winter War of 1939-1940.*

Troy, Nancy J., Ph.D. Professor and Chair, Dept. of Art and Art History, Stanford University.

Troyan, Brett, Ph.D. Assoc. Professor, History Dept., State University of New York, Cortland.

Truemper, David G., S.T.D. Former Prof. and Chair of Theology, Valparaiso Univ.

Trujillo, Chadwick A., Ph.D. Science Fellow, Gemini Northern Observatory.

Trussell, James, Ph.D. Prof. of Economics and Public Affairs and Dir., Office of Population Research, Princeton Univ.

Tsai, Shih-shan Henry, Ph.D. Prof. Emer. of History and Dir. of Asian Studies, Univ. of Arkansas.

Tsang, Steve, D.Phil. Fellow and Reader in Politics, St. Anthony's Coll., Oxford Univ.

Tu, Anthony T., Ph.D. Prof. Emer. of Biochemistry and Molecular Biology, Colorado State Univ.

Tucholski, Edward J., Ph.D. Commander, U.S. Navy; Permanent Military Professor, U.S. Naval Academy.

Tuck, James A., Ph.D. Prof. Emer. of Archaeology, Memorial Univ. of Newfoundland.

Tucker, Barbara M., Ph.D. Prof. of History and Dir., Ctr. for Connecticut Studies, Eastern Connecticut State Univ.

Tunks, Thomas W., Ph.D. Assoc. Provost, Southern Methodist Univ.

Tunnell, Ted, Ph.D. Prof. of History, Virginia Commonwealth Univ.

Turits, Richard, Ph.D. Associate Professor of History, Africana Studies, and Latin American Studies, College of William and Mary.

Turley, William S., Ph.D. Prof., Dept. of Political Science, Southern Illinois Univ., Carbondale.

Turner, Howard, Ph.D. Prof., Dept. of Civil Engineering, Calif. State Polytechnic Univ., Pomona.

Turner, R. Carroll, M.B.A. Technical Assoc., Carpet and Rug Inst.

Turner, Robert L., M.P.A. Deputy Editor, Editorial page, *Boston Globe.*

Turner, Walter W. Vice Pres. and Manager, Marketing and Dev., Industrial Pitch, Koppers Industries, Inc.

Turner, Wendy C., Ph.D. Postdoctoral Researcher, Univ. of Calif., Berkeley.

Turque, Bill, B.A. Washington Correspondent, *Newsweek;* author, *Inventing Al Gore.*

Tushnet, Mark, J.D. Carmack Waterhouse Prof. of Constitutional Law, Georgetown Univ. Law Ctr.

Tye-Murray, Nancy, Ph.D. Research Prof., Dept. of Otolaryngology, School of Medicine, Washington Univ., St. Louis.

Tyler, Seth, Ph.D. Prof., Dept. of Biological Sciences, Univ. of Maine, Orono.

U

Ubelaker, Douglas H., Ph.D. Curator of Physical Anthropology, Smithsonian Institution.

Udelson, Joseph H., Ph.D. Prof. of History, Tennessee State Univ.

Uhalde, Kevin, Ph.D. Assoc. Prof., Dept. of History, Ohio Univ.

Uhler, Sharron G., B.Phil. Archivist, Colorado Springs Pioneers Museum.

Ujiie, Hitoshi, M.F.A. Assoc. Prof. of Textile Printing, Philadelphia Univ.

Ullrich, Arthur H., Jr. Fellow, Academy of Underwater Arts and Sciences; Member, Board of Advisers, Natl. Assoc. of Underwater Instructors.

Ultee, Maarten, Ph.D. Prof. Emer. of History, Univ. of Alabama.

Uman, Martin A., Ph.D. Prof. of Electrical and Computer Engineering, Univ. of Florida.

Unger, Richard W., Ph.D. Prof. of History, Univ. of British Columbia.

Urla, Jacqueline, Ph.D. Associate Professor of Anthropology, Univ. of Massachusetts, Amherst.

Urquhart, Gerald R., Ph.D. Assistant Professor of Biology, Michigan State University.

Urwin, Gregory J. W., Ph.D. Professor of History,

Temple University.

Usselman, Melvyn C., Ph.D. Prof. of Chemistry, Univ. of Western Ontario.

Utts, Jessica, Ph.D. Prof., Department of Statistics, Univ. of Calif., Davis.

V

Valbuena, Jose A. Fernandez, Ph.D. Lecturer in Anthropology, Baylor Univ.

Valgemae, Mardi, Ph.D. Prof. of English, City Univ. of New York Herbert H. Lehman Coll.

VanBlaricom, Glenn, Ph.D. Prof., School of Aquatic and Fishery Sciences, Univ. of Washington.

Vance, Charles C. Former Dir. of Public Relations, Natl. Safety Council.

Vancko, Robert M., Ph.D. Prof. Emer. of Mathematics, Ohio Univ.

Van De Mieroop, Marc, Ph.D. Professor of Ancient Near Eastern History, Columbia University.

Van den Berghe, Pierre L., Ph.D. Prof. Emer. of Sociology, Univ. of Washington.

van den Hout, Theo, Ph.D. Prof. of Hittite and Anatolian Languages, Univ. of Chicago.

VanderMeer, Philip R., Ph.D. Assoc. Prof. of History, Arizona State Univ.

Vander Zanden, James W., Ph.D. Former Prof. of Sociology, Ohio State Univ.

Vandiver, J. Kim, Ph.D. Dean for Undergraduate Research, Mass. Inst. of Technology.

vanEngelsdorp, Dennis, Ph.D. Assistant Professor, Dept. of Entomology, University of Maryland.

Vanlandingham, Karen M., Ph.D. Asst. Prof. of Geology and Astronomy, West Chester Univ.

Van Riper, Charles, III, Ph.D. Prof. of Wildlife and Fisheries Sciences, Univ. of Arizona, Tucson.

Van Riper, Sandra, M.S. Science writer.

Van Tine, Warren, Ph.D. Prof. Emer. of History, Ohio State Univ.

Van Vleet, Edward S., Ph.D. Prof. of Chemical Oceanography, Univ. of South Florida.

Vardy, Steven Bela, Ph.D. Prof. of History, Duquesne Univ.

Vatai, Frank L., Ph.D. Prof. of History, Calif. State Univ., Northridge.

Vaughn, Andrew G., Ph.D. Exec. Dir., American Schools of Oriental Research.

Vavreck, Lynn, Ph.D. Assoc. Prof. of Political Science, Univ. of Calif., Los Angeles.

Vealey, Randy B., B.A. Opinion Page Editor, *The* (Morgantown, WV) *Dominion Post.*

Vega, Robert D., M.L.I.S. Reference Services Librarian, Valparaiso Univ.

Vehrencamp, Sandra L., Ph.D. Prof. Emer. of Neurobiology and Behavior, Cornell Lab. of Ornithology.

Veillette, Robert D., B.G.S. Managing Editor, *The Waterbury* (CT) *Republican-American.*

Veit, Helen Zoe, Ph.D. Assistant Professor, Department of History, Michigan State University.

Velasco, Alejandro, Ph.D. Asst. Prof., Gallatin School of Individualized Study, New York Univ.

Venit, Marjorie S., Ph.D. Prof. of Art History and Archaeology, Univ. of Maryland.

Verderber, Nadine L., Ph.D. Former Prof. of Mathematics, Southern Illinois Univ., Edwardsville.

Veremakis, Dean S., M.A. Former Pres., Orders and Medals Society of America.

Vergano, Peter J., Sc.D. Prof. Emer. of Packaging Science, Clemson Univ.

Verity, John W. Dept. Editor, *Business Week.*

Ver Steeg, Clarence L., Ph.D. Former Prof. of History, Northwestern Univ.

Verts, William T., Ph.D. Asst. Prof., Dept. of Computer Science, Univ. of Mass., Amherst.

Veršič, Ronald J., Ph.D. Pres., Ronald T. Dodge Company.

Vescio, Theresa K., Ph.D. Assoc. Prof. of Psychology, Pennsylvania State Univ.

Vick, Brian, Ph.D. Assoc. Prof., Dept. of History, Emory Univ.

Vickery, John B., Ph.D. Former Professor of English, University of California, Riverside.

Videon, Fred F., Ph.D. Professor Emeritus, Department of Civil Engineering and Engineering Mechanics, Montana State University.

Vietor, Richard H. K., Ph.D. Professor of Business Administration and Sr. Assoc. Dean, Harvard

Univ. Grad. School of Business Administration.

Villard, Erik B., Ph.D. Historian, United States Army Ctr. of Military History.

Vincenti, Virginia B., Ph.D. Prof., Dept. of Family and Consumer Sciences, Univ. of Wyoming.

Vinetz, Joseph M., M.D. Prof. of Medicine, Univ. of Calif., San Diego.

Vink, Markus P. M., Ph.D. Assoc. Prof., Dept. of History, State Univ. of New York, Fredonia.

Vinquist, Mary, Ph.D. Author, *Performance Practice: A Bibliography.*

Vinzant, Carol Editor, AnimalTourism.com.

Vitt, Dale H., Ph.D. Prof. of Biological Sciences, Univ. of Alberta.

Vitt, Laurie J., Ph.D. Prof. of Zoology, Univ. of Oklahoma.

Vizenor, Gerald, B.A. Dist. Prof. of American Studies, Univ. of New Mexico.

Vogel, Morris J., Ph.D. President, Lower East Side Tenement Museum, New York City.

Vogele, William B., Ph.D. Professor of Political Science, Pine Manor College.

Vogt, Jay D., B.A. Dir. and State Historic Preservation Officer, South Dakota State Historical Society.

Voigt, Robert C., Ph.D. Professor, Pennsylvania State University.

Vontz, Thomas S., Ph.D. Assoc. Prof. and Dir., Ctr. for Social Studies Education, Kansas State Univ.

Voorhies, Michael R., Ph.D. Prof. Emer., Vertebrate Paleontology, Univ. of Nebraska State Museum.

Voyles, J. Bruce, B.A. Publisher and author, Chattanooga, TN.

W

Wacker, Peter O., Ph.D. Prof. Emer. of Geography, Rutgers, the State Univ. of New Jersey.

Waddell, Eileen, M.A. Asst. Managing Editor, *The* (Columbia, SC) *State.*

Wagner, David H., Ph.D. Sr. Scientist, Northwest Botanical Inst.

Wagner, John E., Jr., M.D. Prof. of Pediatrics and Director of the Division of Hematology-Oncology and Blood and Marrow Transplantation, Univ. of Minnesota, Twin Cities Campus.

Wagner-Martin, Linda, Ph.D. Hanes Prof. of English, Univ. of North Carolina, Chapel Hill.

Waiser, Bill, Ph.D. Historian and author; Distinguished Professor Emer., Univ. of Saskatchewan.

Waite, Scott W., Ph.D. Vice President of Technology, MPR Services, Inc.

Wakeman, Frederic, Jr., Ph.D. Former Haas Prof. of Asian Studies, Univ. of Calif., Berkeley.

Walch, Timothy, Ph.D. Dir., Herbert Hoover Pres. Library.

Walcott, Charles, Ph.D. Prof. Emer., Dept. of Neurobiology and Behavior, Cornell Univ.

Walczak, Claire, Ph.D. Prof. of Biochemistry & Molecular Biology, Indiana Univ.

Waldinger, Roger, Ph.D. Distinguished Professor of Sociology, Univ. of California, Los Angeles.

Waldstreicher, David, Ph.D. Prof. of History, Temple Univ.

Wales, Patience, B.A. Chief Ed., *Sail* magazine.

Wales, Robert W., Ph.D. Prof. of Geography, Univ. of Southern Mississippi.

Walk, Deborah W., M.L.S. Assistant Director of Legacy and Circus, The John & Mable Ringling Museum of Art, Florida State University.

Walker, Corey D. B., Ph.D. Assoc. Prof. and Chair, Dept. of Africana Studies, Brown Univ.

Walker, Deward E., Jr., Ph.D. Prof. of Anthropology, Univ. of Colorado.

Walker, James C. G., Ph.D. Prof. Emer. of Atmospheric Science, Univ. of Michigan.

Walker, Jearl, Ph.D. Prof. of Physics, Cleveland State Univ.

Walker, Jerry T., Ph.D. Former Prof., Coll. of Agricultural and Environmental Sciences, Univ. of Georgia, Georgia Station.

Wallechinsky, David Exec. Committee Member, International Society of Olympic Historians.

Waller, Bruce F., M.D. Cardiologist, Nasser Smith Pinkerton Cardiology, St. Vincent Hospital, Indianapolis.

Waller, John F., M.D. Chief, Foot Service, Mount Sinai Hospital.

Wallerstein, Immanuel, Ph.D. Former Distin-

guished Professor of Sociology, Binghamton University, State University of New York.

Walsberg, Glenn E., Ph.D. Prof. of Biology, Arizona State Univ.

Walsh, John C., Ph.D. Asst. Prof. of History, Carleton Univ.

Walsh, J. Michael, Ph.D. Pres., Walsh Group, Public Accountants.

Walsh, M. Eileen, Ph.D. Assoc. Prof., Coll. of Nursing, Univ. of Toledo.

Walter, Hartmut S., Ph.D. Professor Emeritus, Dept. of Geography, Univ. of Calif., Los Angeles.

Walters, James C., Ph.D. Prof. of Geology, Univ. of Northern Iowa.

Walters, William D., Jr., Ph.D. Prof. Emer. of Geography, Illinois State Univ.

Walton, Clyde C., M.A. Former Dir. of Libraries, Univ. of Colorado, Boulder.

Walton, Craig, Ph.D. Former Prof. of Philosophy, Univ. of Nevada, Las Vegas.

Walton, Hanes, Jr. Prof., Dept. of Political Science, Univ. of Michigan.

Walvoord, Barbara E., Ph.D. Fellow Emer., Inst. of Educ. Initiatives, Univ. of Notre Dame.

Walz, Arthur H., Jr., M.S. Sr. Water Resources Engineer, Gannett Fleming.

Wang, Chien Yi, Ph.D. Research Horticulturist, Produce Quality and Safety Laboratory, U.S. Dept. of Agriculture.

Wanner, Anja, Ph.D. Prof., Dept. of English, Univ. of Wisconsin.

Ward, Roger, Ph.D. Chief Curator and Curator of European Art, Norton Museum of Art.

Ward, Steven, Ph.D. Research Geophysicist, Inst. of Geophysics and Planetary Physics, Univ. of Calif., Santa Cruz.

Ward, William A., Ph.D. Former Visiting Prof. of Egyptology, Brown Univ.

Wardowski, Wilfred F., Ph.D. Coauthor, *Florida Citrus Diagnostic Guide.*

Ware, Donna M. Eggers, Ph.D. Emer. Research Assoc. Prof. of Biology, Coll. of William and Mary.

Wareham, Rachel E. Former Editor, *International Old Lacers.*

Waring, Geo. H., Ph.D. Prof. of Ethology, Southern Illinois Univ.

Warkentin, Germaine, Ph.D. Prof. Emer., Dept. of English, Univ. of Toronto.

Warner, Ralph P., M.Ed. Former Pres., RAM Radio Controlled Models, Inc.

Warren, Ann Alexander, M.A. Instructor, Kansas State Univ.

Warren, Cliff, M.A. Pres., Raytek, Inc.; former Managing Dir., AGA Infrared Systems.

Warrington, Molly, Ph.D. Sr. Lecturer, Dept. of Geography, Univ. of Cambridge.

Washington, Margaret, Ph.D. Prof., Dept. of History, Cornell Univ.

Waterford, Jack Editor-at-large, *The Canberra* (Australia) *Times.*

Waterland, Larry R., Ph.D. Operations Manager, Energy Systems, Arthur D. Little, Inc.

Watermeier, Daniel J., Ph.D. Prof. Emer. of Theatre, Film, and Dance, Univ. of Toledo.

Waters, Janet, B.S. Baking and Pastry Arts Program Coordinator, Lake Wash. Technical Coll.

Watson, David Lowes, Ph.D. Prof. Emer. of Theology and Congregational Life and Mission, Wesley Theological Seminary, Washington, D.C.

Watson, Harry L., Ph.D. Prof. of History, Dir. of the UNC Ctr. for the Study of the American South, Univ. of North Carolina, Chapel Hill.

Watson, John L., Ph.D. Former Dean, School of Engineering and Mines, Univ. of North Dakota.

Watt, Ian, M.A. Former Prof. of English, Stanford Univ.

Wawro, Geoffrey, Ph.D. Prof. of Military History, Univ. of North Texas.

Wayman, Michael L., Ph.D. Professor Emeritus, Department of Chemical & Materials Engineering, University of Alberta, Edmonton.

Wearing, J. P., Ph.D. Professor Emeritus of English, University of Arizona.

Weart, Spencer R., Ph.D. Former Dir., Ctr. for History of Physics, American Inst. of Physics.

Weatherford, Doris Independent scholar/author.

Weaver, David C., Ph.D. Former Prof. and Chair,

Dept. of Geography, Univ. of Alabama.

Weaver, Karol K., Ph.D. Assoc. Prof., Dept. of History, Susquehanna Univ.

Weaver, Robert F., Ph.D. Prof. Emer., Dept. of Molecular Biosciences, Univ. of Kansas.

Webb, Charles H., D.M. Dean Emer., School of Music, Indiana Univ.

Webb, Leland F., Ph.D. Prof. Emer., Dept. of Mathematics, Calif. State Univ., Bakersfield.

Webby, Elizabeth, Ph.D. Emeritus Professor of Australian Literature, University of Sydney.

Weber, Darrell J., Ph.D. Former Prof. of Botany, Brigham Young Univ.

Weber, Herb, Ph.D. Prof. Emer., Work Physiology Laboratory, East Stroudsburg Univ.

Weber, Joan, B.A. Consumer Affairs Manager, Wm. Wrigley, Jr., Company.

Webster, Frederick E., Jr., Ph.D. Charles Henry Jones Third Century Prof. of Management, Tuck School of Business, Dartmouth Coll.

Weeks, Kent R., Ph.D. Prof. Emer. of Egyptology, American Univ. in Cairo.

Wegner, Mary-Ann Pouls, Ph.D. Asst. Prof. of Egyptian Archaeology, Univ. of Toronto.

Wehner, Todd, Ph.D. Prof., Dept. of Horticultural Sciences, North Carolina State Univ., Raleigh.

Weigl, Peter D., Ph.D. Prof. of Biology, Wake Forest Univ.

Weil, Andrew, M.D. Assoc. Dir., Division of Social Perspectives in Medicine, Univ. of Arizona.

Wein, Ross W., Ph.D. Prof. Emer., Dept. of Renewable Resources, Univ. of Alberta.

Weiner, William J., M.D. Prof., Dept. of Neurology, Univ. of Maryland School of Medicine.

Weinhaus, Anthony J., Ph.D. Asst. Prof., Dept. of Integrative Biology and Physiology, Univ. of Minnesota.

Weintraub, Michael N., Ph.D. Asst. Prof., Dept. of Environmental Sciences, Univ. of Toledo.

Weir, Lorraine, Ph.D. Prof. of English and Comparative Lit., Univ. of British Columbia.

Weir, Robert M., Ph.D. Prof. Emer. of History, Univ. of South Carolina.

Weisberg, Martin, M.D. Physician, Obstetrics and Gynecology, Elkins Park, PA; former Clinical Assoc. Prof. of Obstetrics and Gynecology, Thomas Jefferson Univ.

Weishampel, David B., Ph.D. Prof., Johns Hopkins Univ. School of Medicine; coauthor, *The Evolution and Extinction of the Dinosaurs.*

Weishar, Peter, B.A. Dean, College of Visual Arts, Theatre & Dance, Florida State Univ.

Weiss, Nancy J., Ph.D. Prof. of History, Princeton Univ.

Weller, Milton W., Ph.D. Former Prof. and Kleberg Chair in Wildlife Ecology, Texas A&M Univ.

Wellford, Charles F., Ph.D. Prof. Emer. of Criminology and Criminal Justice, Univ. of Maryland.

Wells, Amy E., Ph.D. Asst. Prof. of Educ. Admin., Univ. of New Orleans.

Wells, Paul F., M.A. Dir. Emer., Ctr. for Popular Music, Middle Tennessee State Univ.

Welsch, Frank, D.V.M. Principal, Orbitox, Intl. Toxicology Consultants.

Weismantel, Mary, Ph.D. Prof., Dept. of Anthropology, Northwestern Univ.

Welsh, Helga, Ph.D. Prof. of Political Science, Wake Forest Univ.

Welty, Gus, B.A. Sr. Editor, *Railway Age.*

Wendel, Earl F., M.D. Assoc. Prof. of Urology, Northwestern Univ. Medical School.

Wendland, Wayne M., Ph.D. Prof. of Geography, Univ. of Illinois, Urbana-Champaign.

Wendt, Carl J., Ph.D. Assoc. Prof., Dept. of Anthropology, Calif. State Univ., Fullerton.

Wenig, Barry L., M.D. Chief, Division of Otolaryngology-Head and Neck Surgery, and Prof., Northwestern Univ. Medical School.

Wertlieb, Donald, Ph.D. Prof., Eliot-Pearson Dept. of Child Dev., Tufts Univ.

Wespestad, Vidar G., Ph.D. Chief Scientist, Pacific Whiting Conservation Cooperative.

Wessel, Frank J., Ph.D. Project Scientist, Dept. of Physics and Astronomy, Univ. of Calif., Irvine.

Wester, Lyndon, Ph.D. Professor of Geography, University of Hawaii.

Weston, Michele, B.A. Editor, American Power Boat Assoc.

Wetz, Max, B.S. Former City Editor, *Black Hills* (SD) *Pioneer.*

Weyant, Robert G., Ph.D. Prof. of General Studies, Univ. of Calgary.

Wharton, Annabel Jane, Ph.D. Prof. of Art History, Duke Univ.

Wheaton, Bruce R., Ph.D. Dir., Inventory of Sources for History of Twentieth-Century Physics.

Wheeler, Douglas L., Ph.D. Prof. Emer. of History, Univ. of New Hampshire, Durham; author, *Republican Portugal.*

Wheeler, James O., Ph.D. Merle Prunty, Jr., Prof. Emer. of Geography, Univ. of Georgia.

Wheeler, Maria S., B.A. Ph.D. candidate, Duquesne University.

Wheelwright, Julie, M.A. Dir., Creative Writing (Non-Fiction) M.A., City Univ., London.

Whitacre, J. F., Ph.D. Prof., Depts. of Materials Science and Engineering, and Engineering and Public Policy, Carnegie Mellon Univ.

Whitaker, Jim Columnist and Staff Writer, *Cynic Magazine Online.*

White, Charles S. J., Ph.D. Prof. Emer. of Philosophy and Religion, American Univ.

White, D. E., Ph.D. Assoc. Prof., Dept. of English, Emory Univ.

White, Geoffrey M., Ph.D. Prof., Dept. of Anthropology, Univ. of Hawaii, Honolulu.

White, George W., Ph.D. Head, Dept. of Geography, South Dakota State Univ.

White, John H., Jr., B.A. Curator Emer., Natl. Museum of American History.

White, John Kenneth, Ph.D. Prof. of Politics, Catholic Univ. of America.

White, Linda R., B.A. Former Asst. Production Dir., Portland Newspapers.

White, Raymond E., Ph.D. Prof. Emer., Dept. of Astronomy, Univ. of Arizona.

White, Richard D., Jr., Ph.D. Prof., Public Admin. Inst., Louisiana State Univ.

White, S. Elizabeth, M.A.Ed. Former Sr. Assoc., American Red Cross.

Whitehead, Nancy Dickerson, B.S. Author, *Among Those Present.*

Whitehorn, Alan, Ph.D. Prof. Emer., Dept. of Political Science, Royal Military College of Canada.

Whitmire, Kenton H., Ph.D. Prof. of Chemistry, Rice Univ.

Whitney, Nicholas M., Ph.D. Postdoctoral Scientist, Mote Marine Laboratory.

Whittaker, John C., Ph.D. Prof. of Anthropology, Grinnell Coll.

Whitworth, Jeff, Ph.D. Extension Specialist, Entomology, Kansas State Univ.

Whorton, M. Donald, M.D., M.P.H. Former Vice Pres., Epidemiologist, WorkCare, Inc.

Wichlinski, Lawrence J., Ph.D. Assoc. Prof. of Psychology, Carleton Coll.

Wicklund, Douglas M., M.A. Sr. Curator, Natl. Firearms Museum.

Wielebnowski, Nadja, Ph.D. Vice Pres. of Conservation Science, Chicago Zoological Society.

Wienecke, Barbara, Ph.D. Sea Bird Ecologist, Dept. of Sustainability, Environment, Water, Population and Communities, Australian Government.

Wiens, John A., Ph.D. Prof. of Biology, Univ. of New Mexico.

Wiese, Dorene P., Ed.D. Pres. and Prof., Leadership and Policy Studies, Native American Educ. Services Coll.

Wigge, Larry Hockey Editor/Chief Statistician, *The Sporting News.*

Wignall, P. B., Ph.D. Prof. of Palaeoenvironments, School of Earth and Environment, Univ. of Leeds.

Wilczek, Frank, Ph.D. Herman Feshbach Prof. of Physics, Mass. Inst. of Technology; winner of Nobel Prize in physics, 2004.

Wild, M. Trevor, Ph.D. Sr. Lecturer, Dept. of Geography, Univ. of Hull.

Wilentz, Sean, Ph.D. Prof. of History, Princeton Univ.

Wiles, Richard C., Ph.D. Charles Ranlett Flint Prof. Emer. of Economics, Bard Coll.

Wiley, James, Ph.D. Prof. of Global Studies and Geography, Hofstra Univ.

Wiley, Tonya R., B.S. Program Specialist II, Texas Parks and Wildlife Dept., Dickinson Marine Lab.

Wilkie, Richard W., Ph.D. Professor Emeritus of

Geosciences, Univ. of Massachusetts, Amherst.

Wilkins, Frederick C., Ph.D. Prof. and Chairman, Dept. of English, Suffolk Univ.

Wilkinson, Richard H., Ph.D. Prof. and Dir., Univ. of Arizona Egyptian Expedition.

Wilkinson, Sylvia, M.A. Journalist and author of books on automobile racing.

Willett, Debra A., B.A. Assoc. Dir., Long Island Studies, Hofstra Univ.

Williams, Andreá N., Ph.D. Assoc. Prof. of English, Ohio State Univ.

Williams, Bob, B.A.J. Contributing Editor, *PennEnergy.*

Williams, Edward V., Ph.D. Prof. of Music, Pennsylvania State Univ.

Williams, Irving G., Ph.D. Author, *The American Vice-Presidency: New Look.*

Williams, James G., Ph.D. Prof. Emer. of Information Sciences, Univ. of Pittsburgh.

Williams, Jerre S., J.D. Former Judge, United States Court of Appeals for the Fifth Circuit.

Williams, Jerry R., Ph.D. Prof. Emer. of Geography, Calif. State Univ., Chico.

Williams, John R., Ph.D. Associate Member, Center for East Asian Studies, Univ. of Chicago.

Williams, Larry E., Ph.D. Prof. of Viticulture and Enology, Univ. of Calif., Davis.

Williams, Nudie Eugene, Ph.D. Former Assoc. Prof. of History, Univ. of Arkansas, Fayetteville.

Williams, Patrick Ryan, Ph.D. Assoc. Curator, Archaeological Science, The Field Museum.

Williams, Peter W., Ph.D. Distinguished Prof. Emer. of Comparative Religion and American Studies, Miami Univ.

Williams, Robert E., Ph.D. Assoc. Prof. of Political Science, Pepperdine Univ.

Willis, Eliza J., Ph.D. Prof. of Political Science, Grinnell Coll.

Willmarth, Philip R., B.A. Former Exec. Editor and Business Manager, *The Linking Ring.*

Willmott, Cory, Ph.D. Assoc. Prof., Dept. of Anthropology, Southern Illinois Univ., Edwardsville.

Wills, John E., Jr., Ph.D. Prof. Emer. of History, Univ. of Southern Calif.

Wills, Jon, M.L.S. Former Librarian/Editorial Researcher, World Book, Inc.

Wilmeth, Don B., Ph.D. Co-editor, *Cambridge Guide to American Theatre.*

Wilson, Carroll, M.A. Managing Editor, *Temple* (TX) *Daily Telegram.*

Wilson, Dru, B.A. Feature Writer, *The* (Colorado Springs, CO) *Gazette.*

Wilson, James A., Jr., Ph.D. Assoc. Prof. of History, Prairie View A&M University.

Wilson, Janelle L., Ph.D. Assoc. Prof. of Sociology, Univ. of Minnesota, Duluth.

Wilson, John F., Ph.D. Collord Prof. of Religion, Princeton Univ.

Wilson, John S. Former freelance music critic.

Wilson, Margaret D., Ph.D. Former Prof. of Philosophy, Princeton Univ.

Wilson, Randy, M.A. Editor, (Flagstaff) *Arizona Daily Sun.*

Wilson, Samuel M., Ph.D. Prof. of Anthropology, Univ. of Texas, Austin.

Wilson, Terry P., Ph.D. Prof. Emer. of Ethnic Studies, Univ. of Calif., Berkeley.

Wilson, Theodore A., Ph.D. Prof. of History, Univ. of Kansas.

Wilson, W. Herbert, Jr., Ph.D. Leslie Brainerd Arey Prof. of Biosciences, Colby Coll.

Wilwerding, Terry, D.D.S. Prof., Dept. of Prosthodontics, Creighton Univ. School of Dentistry.

Winberry, John J., Ph.D. Former Prof. of Geography, Univ. of South Carolina.

Winchester, Juti A., Ph.D. Asst. Prof. of History, Fort Hays State Univ.

Winders, Bill, Ph.D. Associate Professor, Georgia Institute of Technology.

Windeyer, Kendal Former Transport Editor, *The* (Montreal) *Gazette.*

Windham, Lane, Ph.D. Postdoctoral Scholar, School of Labor & Employment Relations, Pennsylvania State University.

Winfield, Barry Editor-at-Large, *Car and Driver* magazine.

Wing, John F., M.B.A. Senior Vice President,

Booz Allen & Hamilton.

Winokur, James L., LL.B. Prof. of Law, Univ. of Denver; Special Counsel, Holme Roberts & Owen.

Winsboro, Irvin D. S., Ph.D. Prof. of History, African American Studies, and Southwest Florida Studies, Florida Gulf Coast Univ.

Winslow, David J., Ph.D. Folklorist and museum consultant.

Winston, Judith E., Ph.D. Curator of Marine Biology, Virginia Museum of Natural History.

Winter, Ruth, M.S. Author, *A Consumer's Dictionary of Cosmetic Ingredients.*

Winters, Jeffrey A., Ph.D. Assoc. Prof. and Honors Program Dir., Dept. of Political Science, Northwestern Univ.

Wise, Stephen R., Ph.D. Dir., Parris Island Marine Corps Museum.

Wise, Thomas N., M.D. Prof. of Psychiatry, Georgetown Univ. School of Medicine.

Wise, Wayne, M.A. Comics scholar and freelance journalist.

Wishart, David, Ph.D. Prof. of Geography, Univ. of Nebraska.

Wit, Lawrence C., Ph.D. Prof., Dept. of Biological Sciences, Auburn Univ.

Witham, Glenn, B.S. Exec. Editor, *Cornell Hotel Quarterly.*

Withuhn, William L., M.B.A. Curator Emer., Natl. Museum of American History, Smithsonian Inst.

Witvliet, John D., Ph.D. Dir./Prof., Calvin Inst. of Christian Worship.

Wohlstetter, Priscilla, Ph.D. Dir., Ctr. on Educ. Governance, Rossier School of Educ., Univ. of Southern Calif.

Wojcicki, Stanley G., Ph.D. Prof. Emer. of Physics, Stanford Univ.

Wolchik, Sharon L., Ph.D. Prof. of Political Science and Intl. Affairs, George Washington Univ.

Wolf, Aaron T., Ph.D. Prof. of Geography, Oregon State Univ.

Wolf, Kirsten, Ph.D. Prof. of Scandinavian Studies, Univ. of Wisconsin, Madison.

Wolf, Larry L., Ph.D. Prof. Emer. of Biology, Syracuse Univ.

Wolf, Richard M., Ph.D. Prof. Emer. of Psychology and Educ., Columbia Univ.

Wolf, Susan M., J.D. Faegre and Benson Prof. of Law and Prof. of Medicine, Univ. of Minnesota.

Wolf, Virginia L., Ph.D. Prof. of English, Univ. of Wisconsin, Stout.

Wolfe, Willard, Ph.D. Former Social Sciences Bibliographer, State Univ. of New York, Binghamton.

Wolff, David A., Ph.D. Assoc. Prof. of History, Black Hills State Univ.

Wolff, Margaret A., B.A. Author, *Finger Painting.*

Wolfgang, Marvin E., Ph.D. Former Prof. of Criminology and Law, Univ. of Pennsylvania.

Wolfson, Amy B., M.A. Dept. of African American Studies, Univ. of Calif., Berkeley.

Wolfson, Richard, Ph.D. Prof. of Physics, Middlebury Coll.

Wolk, Donald J., Ph.D. Clinical psychologist; former Prof. of Psychology, Univ. of Bridgeport.

Woll, Peter, Ph.D. Prof. of Politics, Brandeis Univ.

Wolman, Howard B., Ph.D. Prof. of Classics, Brooklyn Coll., City Univ. of New York.

Woloch, Isser, Ph.D. Prof. Emer. of History, Columbia Univ.

Woloch, Nancy, Ph.D. Author, *Women and the American Experience.*

Wolters, Timothy S., Ph.D. Asst. Prof. of History, Utah State Univ.

Wood, Peter W., Ph.D. Pres., Natl. Assoc. of Scholars, Northwestern Coll., St. Paul, Minnesota.

Woodard, Fredrick, Ph.D. Former Assoc. Prof., African-American World Studies, Univ. of Iowa.

Woodley, David T., M.D. Prof., Univ. of Southern Calif., Div. of Dermatology, LAC + USC Medical Ctr.

Woodside, Jeffrey R., M.B.A. Former Prof. of Urology and Exec. Dir., Univ. of Tennessee Medical Ctr., Univ. of Tennessee, Memphis.

Woodward, Susan L., Ph.D. Prof. Emerita of Geography, Radford Univ.

Woodworth, Steven E., Ph.D. Prof. of History, Texas Christian Univ.

Wooster, Robert, Ph.D. Professor of History, Texas A&M University, Corpus Christi.

Workman, Mark E., Ph.D. Prof. of English and Folklore and Sr. Honors Fellow, Honors Program, Academic Affairs Division, Univ. of North Florida.

Worley, Barbara A., Ph.D. Instructor of Anthropology, Univ. of Mass., Boston.

Worsey, Paul, Ph.D. Prof. of Mining Engineering; Director, Explosives Education, Missouri Univ. of Science and Technology.

Wortel, John P., M.S. Assoc. Clinical Prof. of General and Oral Pathology, Loyola Univ. School of Dentistry.

Worthy, Graham A. J., Ph.D. Prof. of Marine Mammalogy, Univ. of Central Florida.

Wright, Donald, Ph.D. Asst. Prof. of History, Brock Univ.

Wright, Glenn C., Ph.D. Assoc. Prof., Yuma Agriculture Ctr., Univ. of Arizona.

Wright, Grant, B.A. Former Publisher, *Thompson* (MB) *Citizen.*

Wright, Paul W., M.D. Prof. of Family Practice, Univ. of Texas Health Ctr., Tyler.

Wright, Robert E., Ph.D. Nef Family Chair of Political Economy, Augustana Coll.

Wrighton, Mark S., Ph.D. Chancellor, Washington Univ., St. Louis.

Wuhl, Charles Michael, M.D. Clinical Asst. Prof. of Psychiatry, New York Univ.

Wunn, J. Scott, M.A. Exec. Dir., Natl. Forensic League.

Wuntch, Philip, B.A. Former Film Critic, *Dallas Morning News.*

Würsig, Bernd, Ph.D. Prof. of Marine Biology, Texas A&M Univ., Galveston.

Wych, Robert D., Ph.D. Sr. Research Scientist, Pioneer Hi-Bred Intl., Inc.

Wynn, Graeme, Ph.D. Prof. of Geography, Univ. of British Columbia.

Wyse, Roger E., Ph.D. Dean and Dir., Coll. of Agricultural and Life Sciences, Univ. of Wisconsin, Madison.

X

Xiang, Lanxin, Ph.D. Professor, Graduate Institute of International Studies.

Xiong, Victor Cunrui, Ph.D. Prof. of History, Western Michigan Univ.

Y

Yaffe, Michael P., Ph.D. Prof. of Biology, Univ. of Calif., San Diego.

Yago, Glenn, Ph.D. Director, Capital Studies, Milken Institute.

Yap, Foong Ha, Ph.D. Asst. Prof., Dept. of Linguistics and Modern Lang., Chinese Univ. of Hong Kong.

Yasso, Warren E., Ph.D. Former professor of Natural Sciences, Teachers Coll., Columbia Univ.

Yates, Dave, Pres., F. W. Behler, Inc.

Yatskievych, George, Ph.D. Curator of Missouri Plants, Missouri Botanical Garden.

Yelle, Roger V., Ph.D. Prof. of Planetary Science, Univ. of Arizona.

Yeninas, Barbara, M.A. Exec. Dir., Containerization and Intermodal Inst.

Yeomans, Donald K., Ph.D. Sr. Research Scientist, Jet Propulsion Laboratory.

Yesalis, C. E., M.P.H., Sc.D. Professor Emeritus of Health Policy and Administration, and Kinesiology, Pennsylvania State University.

Yezzi, David, M.F.A. Exec. Ed., *The New Criterion.*

Yoffee, Norman, Ph.D. Prof. Emer. of Near Eastern Studies, Univ. of Michigan.

Yoo Kyung Sung, Ph.D. Assistant Professor, Department of Language, Literacy, and Sociocultural Studies, University of New Mexico.

Young, Hugh D., Ph.D. Prof. of Physics, Carnegie-Mellon Univ.

Young, M. Crawford, Ph.D. Prof. Emer. of Political Science, Univ. of Wisconsin, Madison.

Young, Vincent B., M.D., Ph.D. Professor, Department of Microbiology & Immunology, University of Michigan.

Youngman, Joan, J.D. Sr. Fellow, Lincoln Inst. of Land Policy.

Yu, Victor L., M.D. Prof. of Medicine, Univ. of Pittsburgh.

Z

Zabik, Mary E., Ph.D. Univ. Dist. Prof. of Food Science and Human Nutrition and Assoc. Dean for Academic Affairs, Michigan State Univ.

Zablocki, Benjamin, Ph.D. Prof. of Sociology, Rutgers, the State Univ. of New Jersey.

Zaffiro, James J. Ph.D. Prof. of Political Science, Central Coll.

Zafran, Eric M., Ph.D. Curator, Dept. of European Paintings and Sculpture, Wadsworth Atheneum.

Zagare, Frank C., Ph.D. Prof., Dept. of Political Science, State Univ. of New York, Buffalo.

Zalom, Frank G., Ph.D. Prof. of Entomology, Univ. of Calif., Davis.

Zanca, Russell, Ph.D. Prof. of Anthropology, Northeastern Illinois Univ.

Zangari, Amanda M., Ph.D. Postdoctoral Researcher, Southwest Research Institute.

Zapotoczny, Walter S., Jr., M.A. Author, Historian, Speaker.

Zebley, Eric, B.A. Sr. Communications Manager, Crayola LLC.

Zee, Yuan Chung, Ph.D. Prof. of Veterinary Microbiology and Immunology, Univ. of Calif. School of Veterinary Medicine, Davis.

Zeff, Dan, M.S.J. Former Sr. Editor in Humanities and Sports, World Book, Inc.; theater critic.

Zehnder, Kirk Lee, B.A. Vice Pres., Intl. Marketing and Logistics, Mercado Latino, Inc.

Zeitlin, Irving M., Ph.D. Prof. of Sociology, Univ. of Toronto.

Zeleza, Paul Tiyambe, Ph.D. Prof. of African American Studies, Univ. of Illinois at Chicago.

Zenilman, Jonathan M., M.D. Prof. of Medicine, Johns Hopkins Univ. School of Medicine.

Zerega, Nyree J. C., Ph.D. Dir., Grad. Program in Plant Biology and Conservation, Northwestern Univ. and the Chicago Botanic Garden.

Zetter, Bruce R., Ph.D. Prof. of Cell Biology and Surgery, Harvard Medical School.

Zettl, J. Robert, M.P.A.; DABFE Pres., Forensic Consultant, Inc.

Zettler, Richard L., Ph.D. Assoc. Prof. of Near Eastern Lang. and Civilizations, Univ. of Penn.

Zhong, Bu, Ph.D. Asst. Prof. of Journalism, Penn. State Univ.

Ziegler, Gregory R., Ph.D. Prof. of Food Science, Penn. State Univ.

Ziegler, Philip G., Th.D. Senior Lecturer in Systematic Theology, School of Divinity, History and Philosophy, Univ. of Aberdeen.

Zietlow, Rebecca E., J.D. Professor of Law, University of Toledo College of Law.

Zilinskas, Raymond A., Ph.D. Sr. Scientist, James Martin Ctr. for Nonproliferation Studies, Middlebury Institute of International Studies at Monterey.

Zils, John J., M.S. Senior Structural Consultant, Skidmore, Owings, & Merrill.

Zimmer, David E., Ph.D. Technology Transfer Coordinator, Agricultural Research Service, U.S. Dept. of Agriculture.

Zimring, Franklin E., J.D. Prof. of Law and Dir., Criminal Justice Research Program, Earl Warren Legal Inst., Univ. of Calif., Berkeley.

Zobel, Donald B., Ph.D. Prof. of Botany, Oregon State Univ.

Zobell, Charles, B.A. Managing Editor, *Las Vegas* (NV) *Review-Journal.*

Zolberg, Aristide R., Ph.D. Former Professor of Political Science, New School University.

Zook, Melinda S., Ph.D. Professor of History, Purdue University.

Zophy, Jonathan W., Ph.D. Prof. of History, Univ. of Houston, Clear Lake.

Zuber, Maria T., Ph.D. E. A. Griswold Prof. of Geophysics, Mass. Inst. of Technology.

Zuhur, Sherifa, Ph.D. Faculty Assoc., Ctr. for Near Eastern Studies, Univ. of Calif., Los Angeles.

ZumBrunnen, Craig, Ph.D. Prof. of Geography, Univ. of Washington.

Zurick, David, Ph.D. Professor Emeritus, Department of Geosciences, Eastern Kentucky University.

Zwicker, Steven N., Ph.D. Prof. of English, Washington Univ., St. Louis.

Aa

A is the first letter of the alphabet used for the modern English language. It is also used in a number of other languages, including French, German, and Spanish.

The letter *A* is the first of the English vowel letters (see **Vowel**). The letter can be pronounced in different ways. The sound of long *A* can be heard in the word *fate* and the sound of short *A* in *cat.*

Scholars believe the letter *A* evolved from an Egyptian *hieroglyph* (pictorial symbol) that represented an ox head. Hieroglyphs were adapted to be used for a Semitic language by around 1500 B.C. The alphabet for this Semitic language—the earliest known alphabet—is called Proto-Sinaitic. By 1100 B.C., an alphabet for another Semitic language, Phoenician, had evolved from Proto-Sinaitic. See **Semitic languages.**

The Phoenician letter that can be traced to the Egyptian ox-head hieroglyph is the first letter of the Phoenician alphabet, *alp.* The Phoenicians used the letter to represent the beginning sound of *alp,* which was their word for *ox.* Language scholars call the *alp* sound a *glottal stop.* This sound is heard in the middle of the phrase "Uh-oh," but it is not used in actual English words. This sound was not used by the ancient Greeks either. When the Greeks adapted the Phoenician alphabet around 800 B.C., they changed *alp* to *alpha* and used the letter for the *ah* sound at the beginning of the word *alpha.* The letter kept that sound when it was adopted by the Etruscans starting about 700 B.C. and by the Romans by around 650 B.C.   Peter T. Daniels

See also **Alphabet.**

WORLD BOOK map and illustrations

Development of the letter *A*

Seafarers and traders aided the transmission of letters along the coast of the Mediterranean Sea.

Faster ways of writing letters developed during Roman times. Curved, connected lines were faster to write than imitations of the *inscriptional* (carved) Roman letters. The inscriptional forms of the letters developed into capital letters. The curved forms developed into small letters. The form of most small letters, including *a,* was set by around A.D. 800.

A.D. 300   1500   Today

The Latin alphabet was adopted from the Etruscan alphabet by the Romans around 650 B.C. The letter *A* in the *inscriptional* (carved) form of Latin letters was much more linear.

The Etruscan alphabet was adopted from the Greek about 700 B.C. The Etruscan letter that evolved from *alpha* was slightly more rounded.

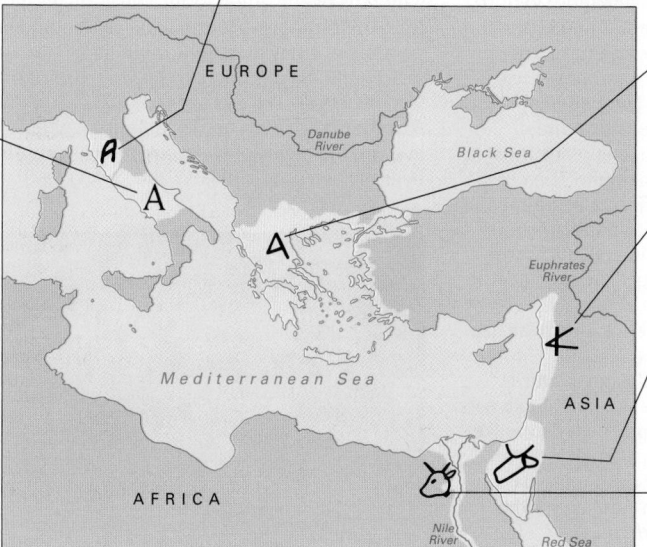

The Greek alphabet evolved from the Phoenician by around 800 B.C. The Phoenician letter *alp* was rotated to form the Greek letter *alpha.*

The Phoenician alphabet had evolved from the Proto-Sinaitic by around 1100 B.C. The Phoenician letter *alp* was a simpler version of an ox head.

A Proto-Sinaitic alphabet for a Semitic language evolved from Egyptian hieroglyphs by around 1500 B.C. The Proto-Sinaitic letter that came from the ox head hieroglyph resembled the Egyptian symbol.

The Egyptians, about 3000 B.C., drew a hieroglyph representing an ox head.

A.A. See Alcoholics Anonymous.

Aachen, *AH kuhn* (pop. 236,420), is the westernmost city in Germany. It sits near the junction of the borders of Belgium and the Netherlands. The city is also known by its French name, Aix-la-Chapelle *(EHKS lah shah PEHL),* after the Palatine Chapel in Aachen Cathedral. For the location of Aachen, see **Germany** (political map).

Roman soldiers established a settlement on the site of Aachen shortly after the birth of Christ. The city grew up around the Roman baths and eventually became the capital of the Frankish empire of Charlemagne. The magnificent Aachen Cathedral was begun by Charlemagne during the 700's and contains his tomb. More than 30 German kings were crowned there. The Gothic Rathaus, or city hall, dates from 1330 and houses a number of art treasures. Each year, thousands of people visit the city's resort, Bad Aachen *(BAHD AH kuhn),* where hot mineral springs are believed to cure some ailments. Aachen produces machinery, metal products, and textiles. The city is famous for its *printen* (spicy gingerbread) and has a number of museums, theaters, and universities.

A devastating fire in 1656 caused much of the city to be rebuilt. The Congress of Aix-la-Chapelle in 1818 helped to preserve the peace following the Napoleonic Wars. During World War II (1939-1945), Aachen was the first German city to be taken by the Allies. Much of the city was destroyed during the fighting, but the Rathaus and the cathedral survived. The German architect Ludwig Mies van der Rohe was born in Aachen.

Peter H. Merkl

See also **Aix-la-Chapelle, Congress of; Charlemagne.**

Aalto, *AHL taw,* **Alvar,** *AHL vahr* (1898-1976), was a Finnish architect, town planner, and furniture designer. He gained fame for buildings that imaginatively combine modern design principles with traditional materials, especially wood. Aalto often used flowing, wavy forms that marked a strong departure from the strict geometric lines favored by other modern architects.

Aalto designed his first two major works in the 1920's: a tuberculosis sanitarium in Paimio, Finland, near Turku, and a municipal library in Viipuri, Finland (now Vyborg, in Russia). He designed birchwood tables and chairs for these projects that made him famous as a furniture designer. His other buildings include a number of civic, university, and apartment buildings. The Hall of Residence (1947-1949), at the Massachusetts Institute of Technology, with its curved facade, is one of his most famous buildings in North America. The Aalto Theater, an opera house he designed in Essen, Germany, opened in 1988, after his death. Aalto's projects as a town planner include a town center in Seinäjoki, Finland. It features several small wedge-shaped buildings, largely made of wood.

Aalto was born on Feb. 3, 1898, in Kuortane, near Vaasa. He died on May 11, 1976.   Nicholas Adams

See also **Furniture** (Scandinavian design [picture]).

Aardvark, *AHRD vahrk,* is an African mammal that eats ants and termites. It has an arched body with a tubelike snout, large ears, and a long tail. The animal hunts for food at night and sleeps in a burrow during the day. In the 1600's, Dutch settlers in southern Africa gave the aardvark its name, which means *earth pig.*

Aardvarks grow 4 ½ to 6 ½ feet (1.4 to 2 meters) long and weigh 110 to 155 pounds (50 to 70 kilograms). Their

Norman Myers, Bruce Coleman Ltd.

The aardvark rips open the nests of ants and termites with its claws. Then it catches the insects with its long, sticky tongue.

coarse hair ranges from pinkish to grayish. The animals lack front teeth. But peglike molars on the sides of their mouths grow continuously. Unlike teeth of many mammals, aardvarks' molars have no enamel coating. Instead, a hard tissue called *cementum* covers the teeth. Aardvarks have four sharp, spoon-shaped claws on their front feet and five on their hind feet. If attacked, they roll on their backs and use their claws for defense. People, large cats, hyenas, and wild dogs hunt aardvarks.

An aardvark digs burrows faster than most other animals. It can make a deep hole in only a few minutes. Permanent burrows may extend to 43 feet (13 meters) in length. The aardvark does not have good eyesight, but it uses its excellent senses of smell and hearing to find prey. When an aardvark searches for food, its snout stays close to the ground and its ears point forward. The animal uses its claws to rip open ant or termite nests, and it licks up the insects with its long, sticky tongue. The tongue is about 12 inches (30 centimeters) long.

Females give birth to one baby at the start of the rainy season. Young aardvarks start digging burrows at about 6 months of age. After about a year, males move away from their mothers. Young females also become independent but stay near their mothers.   Duane A. Schlitter

Scientific classification. The aardvark's scientific name is *Orycteropus afer.*

Aardwolf, *AHRD wulf,* is an unusual type of hyena that lives on the plains of southern and eastern Africa. Most hyenas have powerful jaws and strong teeth, but the

© Tom McHugh, Photo Researchers

The aardwolf is tawny-colored with black stripes, black feet, and a black-tipped bushy tail. It is not a wolf but a hyena.

aardwolf's teeth are small, weak, and cone-shaped. It feeds chiefly on termites, which it laps up with its broad, sticky tongue. The aardwolf is unlike other hyenas because it has five toes on its front feet, and four toes on its hind feet. Other kinds of hyenas have four toes on each foot. It is also smaller than other hyenas, standing 20 inches (51 centimeters) high at the shoulder.

Aardwolves live alone, in pairs, or in family groups with two to four young. Along its back the aardwolf has a mane, which it can raise to make itself look larger.

The name *aardwolf,* which is Afrikaans for *earth wolf,* was given to the animal because it lives in a burrow. Aardwolves come out only at night. Anne Innis Dagg

Scientific classification. The aardwolf is *Proteles cristatus.*

Aaron, *AIR uhn,* in the Bible, was the brother of Moses and Miriam. In earlier Biblical traditions, he was seen as a prophet and as Moses's helper. In later traditions, he was viewed as the first high priest of Israel. Aaron may have originally played a role independent from Moses in the Israelites' deliverance from slavery in Egypt. Like Moses, Aaron was denied entrance into Canaan and died on Mount Hor in Edom.

The priestly traditions in the Bible give Aaron an expanded role in Israelite religious life and consider him founder of the Aaronite priesthood. This priesthood became important in Jerusalem after the Israelite return from exile in 538 B.C. Carole R. Fontaine

See also **Birthstone; High priest; Moses.**

Aaron, *AIR uhn,* **Hank** (1934-2021), was one of the best hitters in baseball history. For more than 30 years, he held the major league career record for regular-season home runs, with 755. He hit his 715th homer, which broke Babe Ruth's record of 714, on April 8, 1974. Aaron's record was broken in 2007 by Barry Bonds.

Aaron played for the Milwaukee (later Atlanta) Braves of the National League (NL) from 1954 through 1974. He was traded to the Milwaukee Brewers of the American League (AL) following the 1974 season, and he retired after the 1976 season. Aaron played right field most of his career but also played left field, center field, and first base.

Aaron led the National League in home runs in 1957, 1963, 1966, and 1967. He won the league batting title twice. He holds the major league career record for runs batted in— 2,297. Aaron led the NL in

Atlanta Braves

Hank Aaron

runs batted in four times. He received the 1976 Spingarn Medal, and he was elected to the National Baseball Hall of Fame in 1982 (see **Spingarn Medal**). In 2002, he received the Presidential Medal of Freedom. Henry Louis Aaron was born on Feb. 5, 1934, in Mobile, Alabama. He died on Jan. 22, 2021. Dave Nightingale

See also **Baseball** (picture).

AARP, *ahrp* or *ay ay ahr pee,* is one of the world's largest private nonprofit membership organizations. Its members must be 50 years old or older.

AARP's main purpose is to address the needs of older people in the United States. It does this by providing them with education and services and by representing their interests before government agencies and other public bodies. AARP also works to improve the lives of older people by promoting their independence and dignity and by encouraging them to pursue personal goals. The organization's magazine, *AARP The Magazine,* is the largest circulation magazine in the United States.

Ethel Percy Andrus, a retired educator, founded the American Association of Retired Persons in 1958. It changed its name to AARP in 1998. Its headquarters are in Washington, D.C. For more information, see its website at http://www.aarp.org. Critically reviewed by AARP

See also **Retirement.**

Abacá, *AH buh KAH,* is a plant grown in Borneo, the Philippines, and Sumatra for its fiber. Abacá grows about 20 feet (6 meters) high. Large, oblong leaves grow from the plant's trunk. The bases of the leaves form a *sheath* (covering) around the trunk that contains the valuable fiber. Abacá fiber is sold under the name *manila,* after the capital of the Philippines. See also **Philippines** (picture: Manila hemp). Christine W. Cole

Scientific classification. The abacá plant is *Musa textilis.*

Abacus, *AB uh kuhs,* is an ancient device used in China and other countries to perform arithmetic problems. It can be used to add, subtract, multiply, and divide, and to calculate square roots and cube roots. The abacus consists of a frame containing columns of beads. The beads, which represent numbers, are strung on wires or narrow wooden rods attached to the frame.

The abacus was used by the ancient Greeks and Romans. The Chinese abacus is called *suanpan,* which means *counting,* or *reckoning, board.* A typical Chinese abacus has columns of beads. The first column on the right is the ones column. The second column is the tens column. The third column is the hundreds column, and so on. In addition, the columns are divided by a crossbar. Each column has two beads above the crossbar and five below it. Each upper bead represents five units— that is, five ones, five tens, and so on. Each lower bead represents one unit. The number 153, for example, is represented by moving 3 lower beads in the ones column up to the crossbar, 1 upper bead in the tens column down to the crossbar, and 1 lower bead in the hundreds column up to the crossbar.

The Japanese abacus, called the *soroban,* used rods with just one bead above the partition and four beads below it. The electronic calculator made both types of abacus obsolete. Eli Maor

Abadan, *AH bah DAHN* (pop. 250,555), is a refining center for Iran's oil industry. It lies on Abadan Island, on the Shatt al Arab River in southwestern Iran (see **Iran** [map]). Pipelines link Abadan with Iranian oil fields. The city's petroleum refinery, completed in 1913, ranks among the largest in the world. It was badly damaged by Iraqi forces in 1980, during a war between Iran and Iraq. The Anglo-Persian Oil Company, a British firm, began the development of Abadan in the early 1900's. Michel Le Gall

Abalone, *AB uh LOH nee,* is an ocean snail found in most mild and tropical seas. It is sometimes called an *ear shell* or *ormer.* It lives along the coasts of Australia, Japan, New Zealand, South Africa, Europe, and western North America. It clings to submerged rocks with its flat, muscular foot. It feeds on plants it scrapes off the rocks with a filelike tongue. Abalone steak, the snail's muscular foot, is a popular seafood dish around the world. Some kinds of abalone are endangered, and many countries regulate the harvesting of abalone. The colorful interior of the abalone's shell, which may be from 1 to 12 inches (2.5 to 30 centimeters) long, is used in making costume jewelry. See also **Mother-of-pearl.**   Robert Robertson

Scientific classification. Abalones make up the genus *Haliotis.*

Abandonment is a legal term that has two chief meanings. In the field of property law, abandonment occurs when a person intentionally gives up all rights to something he or she owns. For example, if a person purposely throws away a ring, it has been abandoned. In family law, abandonment refers to the desertion of a husband, wife, or child without intention to support the person. Most states of the United States make it a crime for a parent to abandon a child. A father or mother who does this may lose the right to raise the child.

Abandonment, also called *desertion,* has traditionally been grounds for divorce in the United States (see **Desertion**). But in the last half of the 1900's, all U.S. states legalized *no-fault divorce,* which requires only that one of the partners testify that the marriage has failed. As a result of no-fault divorce, few U.S. residents seek divorce on the ground of abandonment.   Mary Ann Glendon

Abbado, Claudio (1933-2014), was an internationally known Italian symphony orchestra and opera conductor. Abbado served as music director of several major orchestras and opera companies in Europe.

Abbado was born on June 26, 1933, in Milan, Italy. He studied piano with his father, and at the Milan Conservatory. He then studied conducting at the Vienna Academy of Music. He won two prestigious international conducting competitions in 1958 and 1963. Abbado quickly became one of the leading conductors of his generation.

In 1968, Abbado became principal conductor of the La Scala opera in Milan. He served as the institution's music director from 1971 to 1986. He won praise for raising the artistic standards of the La Scala orchestra both in opera and in concert performances. Abbado was principal conductor for the London Symphony Orchestra from 1979 to 1988. He was also music director for the Vienna State Opera from 1986 to 1991.

Abbado served as artistic director and principal conductor of the Berlin Philharmonic Orchestra from 1989 to 2002. Over the years, Abbado established several new orchestras and music festivals, including the Lucerne Festival Orchestra in Switzerland in 2003. He was especially interested in training young musicians. Abbado died on Jan. 20, 2014.   John H. Baron

Abbas I, *ab BAHS* (1571-1629), was the *shah* (king) of the Safavid dynasty in Southwest Asia from 1587 until his death in 1629. Under Abbas, the Safavids reached the height of their power, ruling all or parts of present-day Iran, Iraq, Azerbaijan, Turkmenistan, and Afghanistan.

Abbas brought peace and stability to an empire that had been weakened by internal conflict since the 1570's. Before Abbas's reign, the Safavids relied on Turkic warriors called Qizilbash (Red Heads) for military and administrative support. But Qizilbash tribes constantly fought with one another for power. As shah, Abbas reduced Qizilbash influence by creating an army of Georgian, Armenian, and Circassian slaves who were loyal only to him. He also seized land that had been under Qizilbash control. Under Abbas, the Safavids regained territory that had been lost to the Ottoman Empire in the west and to the Uzbek and Mughal empires in the east.

Abbas relocated the Safavid capital to the Persian city of Isfahan in 1598. He turned Isfahan into a splendid capital with a magnificent public square and beautiful mosques, palaces, and gardens.

Abbas was born on Jan. 27, 1571, in Herat, a city in what is now Afghanistan. He died on Jan. 19, 1629, in Ashraf (now Behshahr).   Kathryn Babayan

See also **Isfahan; Safavid dynasty.**

Abbas, *ah BAHS,* **Mahmoud,** *mah MOOD* (1935-), also known as Abu Mazen, is head of the Palestine Liberation Organization (PLO) and president of the Palestinian Authority (PA). His first name is also spelled Mahmud. The PLO is a political body that represents the Palestinian people. Its goal is to establish an independent Palestinian state in the West Bank and Gaza Strip, territories captured by Israel in 1967. Israel, the Gaza Strip, and the West Bank make up the historic region of Palestine. The PA is the government that has limited control over parts of the West Bank and Gaza Strip.

Abbas is chairman of the PLO Executive Committee, the highest PLO post. He became chairman in 2004, after the death of Yasir Arafat, who had been chairman since 1969. In 2005, Abbas was elected president of the PA.

Abbas was born in Zefat in what is now northern Israel. After the state of Israel was created in 1948, Abbas sought refuge in Syria with his family. In the 1950's, he joined the Palestinian independence movement and helped found Fatah, a guerrilla group that is now part of the PLO. In 1958, he earned a bachelor's degree in law from the University of Damascus in Syria. In 1982, he earned a doctor's degree in history from the Institute of Oriental Studies in Moscow. In 1995, Abbas returned to live in Palestine. He became secretary-general of the PLO Executive Committee in 1996. In 2003, he briefly served as prime minister of the PA.   Jamal R. Nassar

Abbot is the religious superior of a monastery of an early Christian religious order, such as the Benedictines and Cistercians. The term comes from the Aramaic word *abba,* which means *father.* Young Egyptian monks first used the title in the early 300's. They would seek an older monk or a hermit of the desert, whom they called *abba,* to teach them. In the 500's, the Benedictines established the title for the monk who had authority over other monks and monastic property.   David G. Schultenover

Abbott was the name of two sisters who were American social-work pioneers. They were born in Grand Island, Nebraska—Edith on Sept. 26, 1876, and Grace on Nov. 17, 1878.

Edith Abbott (1876-1957) taught at the Chicago School of Civics and Philanthropy and was dean of the University of Chicago's School of Social Service Administration from 1924 to 1942. She fought for better treatment of the poor and criticized politics in welfare programs. Abbott helped awaken the government to its responsibility for welfare. She died on July 28, 1957.

Grace Abbott (1878-1939) was chief of the United States Children's Bureau from 1921 to 1934 and fought for the rights of women and children worldwide. She was on the Committee on Economic Security, which developed the Social Security Act. She died on June 19, 1939.   Alan Keith-Lucas

Sir John Joseph Caldwell Abbott

Prime minister of Canada
1891-1892

Macdonald	Abbott	Thompson
1878-1891	1891-1892	1892-1894

The Public Archives of Canada, Ottawa

Abbott, Sir John Joseph Caldwell (1821-1893), served as prime minister of Canada from June 1891 to November 1892. He succeeded Sir John A. Macdonald, who died in office. Abbott inherited many problems from Macdonald's administration that he could not solve. They included a severe nationwide depression and major conflicts between English- and French-speaking Canadians. Abbott became prime minister at the age of 70 and resigned after a brief and frustrating administration because of poor health.

Abbott was a distinguished lawyer, a position that drew him into politics. Before he became prime minister, he had served in the legislature of the Province of Canada and, later, in the Parliament of the Dominion of Canada. He also had been dean of the law school of McGill College (now McGill University) in Montreal.

Abbott claimed he disliked politics. He said he held political office because he believed public service was his duty. Shortly before taking office as prime minister, Abbott wrote a friend, "I hate notoriety, public meetings, public speeches, caucuses, and everything that I know of what is apparently the necessary incident of politics—except doing public work to the best of my ability."

Abbott had a wide range of interests. He owned a salmon stream where he often fished, and he grew many varieties of rare orchids. He also loved animals and helped establish the Canadian Society for the Prevention of Cruelty to Animals.

Early life. John Abbott was born on March 12, 1821, in St. Andrews, near Montreal, Lower Canada (in present-day Quebec province). His father, Joseph Abbott, was an Anglican missionary who had moved there from England in 1818. Soon after arriving in Canada, he married Harriet Bradford, a Canadian minister's daughter.

The Abbott family moved to Grenville, Lower Canada, in 1830, but John spent much time with an uncle in St. Andrews. He learned about astronomy and mathematics from a retired sea captain there and attended school in the nearby village of Carillon.

Abbott left home at age 17 and began a business career, which he followed most of the time through the mid-1840's. He conducted his activities, which included selling cloth, packing apples, and buying grain, in Montreal, then Canada's leading commercial center. He interrupted these activities to study law at McGill College.

Abbott received a law degree in 1847 and began to practice in Montreal that year. He specialized in corporation law and soon became known as an authority in this field. In 1849, he married Mary Bethune, whose father was the principal of McGill College. Abbott served as dean of the law school at McGill from 1855 to 1880.

Early political career. Abbott was elected to the Assembly of the Province of Canada in 1857 and served until 1867. He entered politics as a Liberal but gradually shifted toward the Conservative Party. In the early 1860's, a coalition of Conservative and Reform politicians favored the unification under one government of all the British colonies in North America. In 1865, Abbott joined this coalition in support of confederation. The Dominion of Canada was established in 1867. It consisted of New Brunswick, Nova Scotia, Ontario, and Quebec provinces. That same year, Abbott was elected to the Dominion's first House of Commons, where he served until 1874.

Abbott continued his thriving law practice while serving as a legislator. During the early 1870's, he became involved in negotiations for the construction of a Canadian transcontinental railroad. Two financial groups were competing for the construction contract. Sir Hugh Allan, a Montreal shipping line owner and a client of Abbott, headed one group. Abbott tried to unite the two groups into one company, but he was unsuccessful. Allan's group eventually received the construction contract.

The Pacific Scandal. In 1873, a clerk in Abbott's office stole some papers that revealed large campaign contributions by Allan to the Conservatives in the 1872 general election. The papers included a telegram in which Prime Minister John A. Macdonald, the Conservative leader, had demanded of Allan: "Send me another ten thousand. Do not fail me." Liberal members of Parliament acquired the papers and revealed their contents. Macdonald admitted to receiving the money, but he denied that the contributions had influenced his decision to give the contract to Allan. The government appointed a royal commission to investigate the case, which became known as the Pacific Scandal.

The scandal finally forced Macdonald to resign as prime minister in November 1873 and led to the formation of a Liberal government headed by Alexander Mackenzie. Abbott lost his seat in the House in the 1874 election. Historians disagree about the extent of Abbott's involvement in the scandal. Most believe he was innocent of personal misconduct but was probably aware of some of the dealings between Macdonald and Allan.

The railroad project was abandoned after the Pacific Scandal, and Mackenzie failed to reorganize it. The Conservatives took control of Parliament in 1878, and Macdonald became prime minister. He revived the railroad plans. In 1880, Abbott became the lawyer of the Canadian Pacific Railway, based in Montreal. He wrote the charter for the railroad, which was completed in 1885.

Return to Parliament. Abbott was reelected to the Canadian House of Commons in 1880 and served until 1887. He was then appointed to Macdonald's Cabinet and to the Canadian Senate, where he served as government leader. In 1887, Abbott was also elected mayor of Montreal, a position he held until 1889. In 1891, Macdonald wanted to increase Abbott's duties in the Cabinet. But Abbott refused because he did not feel capable of handling more speeches and public meetings.

Prime minister. Macdonald died in June 1891. The Conservatives wanted either Sir John S. D. Thompson, the Minister of Justice, or Sir Charles Tupper, the Canadian high commissioner in the United Kingdom, to be the party leader. Both Thompson and Tupper refused the position, however, and the Conservatives chose Abbott. They believed he would appeal to both English- and French-speaking members of the troubled party. Abbott, who preferred Thompson for the leadership, reluctantly took over as party leader and prime minister. He relied on Thompson to handle many of the responsibilities in the House of Commons and in the Cabinet.

Even before Abbott took office, a scandal in the public works department had shaken the Conservative government. Some employees in that department were found guilty of awarding railroad contracts to companies in exchange for money. An investigation was conducted, and the department head, Sir Hector-Louis Langevin, was found to have been negligent. Abbott asked for his res-

ignation, and Langevin submitted it in September 1891.

A dispute about schools in the province of Manitoba caused additional problems within Abbott's party. In 1890, Manitoba's government passed a law that abolished tax support for Roman Catholic and French-language schools. It then set up a single nonreligious, English-language school system. Manitoba's Roman Catholic and French-speaking population argued that abolishing tax support violated an earlier law passed in 1870. The English-speaking wing of the national Conservative Party largely approved of the 1890 law. But the Catholic and French-speaking wing of the party was outraged. In 1891, Canada's Supreme Court declared the 1890 law unconstitutional. But in 1892, the British Privy Council, then the highest court of appeal, reversed the ruling. Tension between English- and French-speaking Canadians rose. But Abbott, with Thompson's help, prevented a political crisis by keeping the dispute in court.

An economic depression that had begun in the 1870's worsened during Abbott's term. His health began to fail, and he was able to handle fewer responsibilities. Queen Victoria of the United Kingdom knighted Abbott in May 1892. He went to London in October for medical advice but resigned from office in November. Thompson succeeded Abbott as leader of the Conservative Party and as prime minister. Abbott later returned to Montreal, where he died on Oct. 30, 1893.   Duncan McDowall

See also **Prime minister of Canada.**

Abbott, Robert Sengstacke (1868-1940), was an African American journalist. He founded the *Chicago Defender,* which became one of the nation's largest and most influential African American newspapers.

Under Abbott's leadership, the *Defender* encouraged Southern blacks to move to the industrial states of the North. Beginning in the 1910's, and continuing after World War I (1914-1918), hundreds of thousands of African Americans moved to the North in search of better job opportunities. Abbott's editorials demanded full equality for African Americans.

Abbott was born on Nov. 28, 1868, on St. Simon's Island, Georgia. His parents had been slaves. He learned printing at his stepfather's newspaper, the *Woodville (Georgia) Times,* and at Hampton Institute in Virginia. Abbott put himself through Kent Law School (now Chicago-Kent College of Law) by working as a printer. He graduated in 1899 and became a lawyer. But he decided he could better serve blacks by publishing a newspaper. He founded the *Chicago Defender,* a weekly, in 1905. He died in Chicago on Feb. 29, 1940. In 1956, under John H. H. Sengstacke, Abbott's nephew and successor, the *Defender* became a daily. Sengstacke built the largest chain of African American newspapers in the United States around the *Defender.*   Robert K. Stewart

Abbott, Tony (1957-   ), was prime minister of Australia from 2013 to 2015. He led the Liberal Party and a coalition of the Liberal and National parties. The Liberal Party is generally conservative on social issues. It favors *free enterprise,* a system that allows people to carry out most economic activities free from government control.

Anthony John Abbott was born in London on Nov. 4, 1957. His parents were Australian, and the family moved to Australia when Tony was a boy. After graduating from the University of Sydney, Abbott received a Rhodes Scholarship and studied at the University of Oxford in

England. He graduated from Oxford with a master's degree in politics and philosophy. Abbott returned to Australia in 1984 and later began a career as a journalist.

Abbott began working for the Liberal Party in 1990. He was first elected to Australia's Parliament in 1994. He replaced Malcolm Turnbull as leader of the Liberal Party on Dec. 1, 2009. In 2013, Abbott's coalition defeated Kevin Rudd's Australian Labor Party in a general election. Abbott then became prime minister. Abbott was criticized by members of his own party for not sufficiently strengthening Australia's economy. In September 2015, Turnbull ousted Abbott as leader of the Liberal Party and became prime minister. Abbott lost his seat in Parliament in a 2019 federal election.   Wayne Errington

Abbreviation is a shortened form of a word or a phrase. Some abbreviations include only initial letters of a word, as when *Feb.* stands for *February.* Other abbreviations use first and last letters, as when *VT* stands for *Vermont.* Key letters in a word or phrase may also be used, as when *LOL* stands for *laughing out loud.*

Abbreviations save space. They are used in tables, in technical and scientific material, and in indexes, footnotes, and bibliographies. They are also used instead of long official names, as in *AFL-CIO* (American Federation of Labor and Congress of Industrial Organizations). Abbreviations called *acronyms* are words made up of the first letters or syllables of other words, such as *UNESCO* (United Nations Educational, Scientific and Cultural Organization). Such abbreviations are often written without periods. Symbols that are not made up of letters of the alphabet are not abbreviations, but they serve the same purpose abbreviations do (see **Symbol**).

Abbreviations have been found on the earliest known tombs, monuments, and coins. When manuscripts were written by hand, abbreviations were used to save time and space. Many Latin abbreviations are still used.

Many *World Book* articles contain abbreviations in lists, tables, picture credits, and captions. Abbreviations are also used to a limited extent in the text of articles. This article includes a table of abbreviations commonly used in published works. Other categories of abbreviations can be found in the following *World Book* articles:

Canadian provinces. Abbreviations are given in the Canada article in the table *The provinces and territories of Canada.*

College degrees. Some common abbreviations can be found in the article **Degree, College.**

New Deal agencies. Abbreviations for many New Deal agencies are in a table in the article **New Deal.**

Proofreading. Abbreviations and marks used by proofreaders are in a table in the article **Proofreading.**

States. Abbreviations for the states can be found in a table with the article **United States.**

United Nations. Abbreviations for United Nations agencies and committees are given in the table *The United Nations system* with the article **United Nations.**

Weights and measures. Abbreviations are in tables with the article **Weights and measures.**   Sara Garnes

ABC is a major broadcasting network in the United States. ABC stands for American Broadcasting Company. ABC is owned by the Walt Disney Company.

ABC was created as a result of a Federal Communications Commission (FCC) radio network monopoly investigation that took place from 1938 to 1941. The FCC ordered the NBC network to sell one of its two chains of affiliates. In 1943, NBC sold its Blue Network to the American Broadcasting System, Inc. In 1945, the American Broadcasting System was renamed the American Broadcasting Company.

ABC's first television broadcast was in 1948. In 1953, ABC merged with United Paramount Theatres Inc. Successful TV programs during ABC's early years included "Disneyland," "American Bandstand," and "Cheyenne." Popular ABC shows of the 1960's included "Marcus Welby, M.D.," "Batman," "That Girl," "Bewitched," "The Brady Bunch," and "The Mod Squad." ABC also pioneered modern sports programming with "Wide World of Sports" (1961-1997) and brought sports to prime time with "Monday Night Football" in 1970. Other popular ABC programs of the 1970's included "Baretta," "Happy Days," "Charlie's Angels," "The Six Million Dollar Man," "The Love Boat," and the miniseries *Roots.* Successful

Common abbreviations

A.A.—Alcoholics Anonymous; Associate in Arts
AC—alternating current
A.D.—*anno Domini* (in the year of our Lord)
ad lib—*ad libitum* (as one pleases)
AFL-CIO—American Federation of Labor and Congress of Industrial Organizations
AIDS—acquired immunodeficiency syndrome
a.k.a.—also known as
ALA—American Library Association
AM—amplitude modulation
a.m., A.M.—*ante meridiem* (before noon)
assn.—association
assoc.—associate; association
asst.—assistant
ATM—automated teller machine
atty.—attorney

ave.—avenue
AWOL—absent without leave
b.—born
B.C.—before Christ
biog.—biography
bldg.—building
blvd.—boulevard
Btu—British thermal unit
c.—*circa* (about); *centum* (century); copy; copyright
cal, cal.—calorie (heat)
Cal, Cal.—calorie (nutrition)
CD—compact disc; certificate of deposit
CD-ROM—compact disc read-only memory
CDT—Central Daylight Time
cent.—century
CEO—chief executive officer
ch., chap.—chapter
CO—commanding officer
c/o—in care of
Cong.—Congress
cont.—continued

corp.—corporation
CPA—certified public accountant
CST—Central Standard Time
CT—computed tomography
D—Democrat
d.—died
D.A.—district attorney
db, dB—decibel
D.C.—District of Columbia
DC—direct current
DDT—dichloro-diphenyl-trichloroethane
dec.—deceased
Dem.—Democrat
DNA—deoxyribonucleic acid
DOA—dead on arrival
DST—daylight saving time
DUI—driving under the influence
DVR—digital video recorder
ECG—electrocardiogram
ed.—edition; editor; edited

e.g.—*exempli gratia* (for example)
eq.—equal; equation
ERA—Equal Rights Amendment; earned run average
ESP—extrasensory perception
esp.—especially
EST—Eastern Standard Time
E.T.A.—estimated time of arrival
et al.—*et alibi* (and elsewhere); *et alii* (and others)
etc.—*et cetera* (and so forth)
ff.—folios (page numbers); following (pages)
fig.—figure
FM—frequency modulation
GDP—gross domestic product
GED—General Educational Development
GI—government (or general) issue; gastrointestinal
gig, GB—gigabyte

Common abbreviations (continued)

GNP—gross national product
Gov.—Governor
h.—hour
HIV—human immunodeficiency virus
HMO—health maintenance organization
HMS—His (or Her) Majesty's Ship
Hon.—Honorable
H.P., h.p.—horsepower
HQ—headquarters
hr.—hour
Hz—hertz
ibid.—ibidem (in the same place)
ICBM—intercontinental ballistic missile
ICU—intensive care unit
id.—idem (the same)
i.e.—id est (that is)
ill.—illustrated
inc.—incorporated; including
I.O.U.—I owe you
IQ—intelligence quotient
IRA—Irish Republican Army; individual retirement account
J—joule
Jr.—Junior
k.—carat; knot
kHz—kilohertz
lat.—latitude
LLC—limited liability company
log.—logarithm
lon., long.—longitude
Ltd.—Limited
m.—minute; mile; meter
max.—maximum
meg, MB—megabyte
mfd.—manufactured
mfg.—manufacturing

mfr.—manufacturer
MHz—megahertz
M.I.A.—missing in action
misc.—miscellaneous
M.P.—Member of Parliament
MP—Military Police
mph—miles per hour
MRI—magnetic resonance imaging
MST—Mountain Standard Time
Mt.—Mount
n.—noun; note (footnote)
natl.—national
NCAA—National Collegiate Athletic Association
NCO—noncommissioned officer
no.—numero (number)
non seq.—non sequitur (it does not follow)
N.P.—notary public
N/S, N.S.F.—not sufficient fund
OK, O.K.—correct; all right
op. cit.—opere citato (in the work cited)
OPEC—Organization of the Petroleum Exporting Countries
p.—page; part
PAC—political action committee
Parl.—Parliament
pat.—patent; patented
PC—personal computer
PCB—polychlorinated biphenyl
PIN—personal identification number
pl.—plural; place; plate
PLC—public limited company

p.m., P.M.—post meridiem (after noon)
P.O.—post office
pop.—population
POW—prisoner of war
ppd.—prepaid
pref.—preface
pro tem.—pro tempore (for the time being)
prov.—province
P.S.—post scriptum (postscript)
pseud.—pseudonym
PST—Pacific Standard Time
quot.—quotation
q.v.—quod vide (which see)
R.—rex (king); regina (queen); Republican; River
RAF—Royal Air Force
RAM—random-access memory
R.C.—Red Cross; Roman Catholic
R.D.—rural delivery
rd.—road
ref.—refer; reference
reg.—region; regulation
Rep.—Republic; Republican; Representative
Rev.—Reverend
R.I.P.—requiescat in pace (rest in peace)
R.N.—Royal Navy; registered nurse
RNA—ribonucleic acid
ROM—read-only memory
rpm—revolutions per minute
R.R.—railroad; rural route
R.S.V.P.—Répondez, s'il vous plaît (Answer, if you please)
Rt. Rev.—Right Reverend
RV—recreational vehicle
R.V.—Revised Version (Bible)

s—second
sci.—science; scientific
sec.—second
secy.—secretary
Sen.—Senator
sig.—signature
sing.—singular
sp.—spelling; species
sq.—square
Sr.—Senior
S.S.—steamship
St.—Saint; strait; street
STD—sexually transmitted disease
Ste.—Sainte
Supt.—Superintendent
syn.—synonym
tech.—technical; technology
temp.—temperature
theol.—theological; theology
TNT—trinitrotoluene
tp., twp.—township
treas.—treasurer
UFO—unidentified flying object
UHF—ultrahigh frequency
univ.—university
URL—uniform resource locator
v.—verb
V—volt
v., vid.—vide (see)
v., vs.—versus (against)
VAT—value-added tax
vet.—veteran, veterinarian
VHF—very high frequency
VIP—very important person
vol.—volume
v.p.—vice president
W—Watt
wt.—weight
Xmas—Christmas
zool.—zoology

ABC shows of the 1980's and 1990's included "America's Funniest Home Videos," "NYPD Blue," and "Roseanne."

ABC was sold in 1986 to Capital Cities Communications. It was then sold in 1995 to the Walt Disney Company. Successful shows under Disney ownership include "Lost," "Desperate Housewives," "Dancing with the Stars," and "Who Wants to Be a Millionaire?" In 2013, with the Spanish-language TV network Univision, ABC News launched Fusion, an English-language cable TV network targeted toward Hispanic Americans.   Michael Curtin

See also **Walt Disney Company.**

Abdomen is a large body cavity between the *thorax* (chest) and the pelvic cavity. A strong wall of muscle, called the *diaphragm,* separates the abdomen from the thorax. But no structure separates the abdomen from the pelvic cavity. The abdominal organs include the stomach, liver, pancreas, intestines, kidneys, adrenal glands, and spleen. A thin membrane known as the *peritoneum* lines the entire abdominal cavity and covers most of the abdominal organs. Two large blood vessels, the *aorta* and *vena cava,* run along the spine and pass through the diaphragm and into the thorax.

The front wall of the abdomen consists of layers of sheetlike muscles attached to the ribs above and the

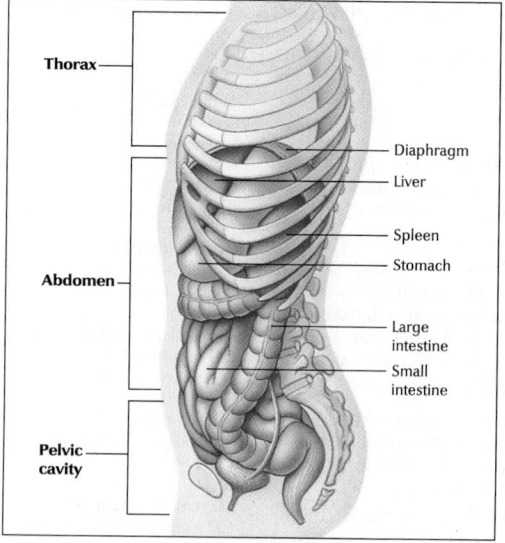

WORLD BOOK illustration by Robert Demarest

The abdomen is a large body cavity that lies between the *thorax* (chest) and the pelvic cavity.

pelvic bones below. These muscles hold in the abdominal organs and assist in bending and rotating the body trunk. Other muscles and the backbone form the abdomen's rear wall. The abdomen is the part of the body behind the thorax of insects, crustaceans, and certain other kinds of animals without backbones.   Laurence H. Beck

Related articles in *World Book* include:

Appendix	Human body	Intestine	Pelvis
Coelom	(Anatomy of	Kidney	Solar plexus
Diaphragm	the human	Liver	Spleen
	body)	Pancreas	Stomach

Abduction. See Kidnapping.

Abduh, *AHB doo,* **Muhammad,** *moo HAM uhd* (1849-1905), an Egyptian theologian, led a movement in the late 1800's to modernize Islamic thinking. He tried to bring Islamic law, education, and theology in line with the findings of science and the conditions of the modern world. His ideas have had a lasting effect on Islam.

Abduh was born in the Nile Delta area of Egypt. In 1877, he graduated from al-Azhar University in Cairo. As a young man, Abduh was a follower of Iranian philosopher and politician Jamāl al-Din al-Afghānī, who called for the unity of all Muslims worldwide. For many years, Abduh favored resistance to European power in Egypt. But he later supported limited cooperation with Egypt's British rulers to achieve educational and social change. In 1899, Abduh became *grand mufti* (chief legal expert) of Egypt. He died on July 11, 1905.   Neal Robinson

Abdul-Jabbar, *AHB dool juh BAHR,* **Kareem,** *kuh REEM* (1947-   ), became one of the greatest centers in basketball history. Standing 7 feet 2 inches (218 centimeters) tall, he combined his height advantage with quick, graceful movements, fine shooting, and excellent teamwork. He was especially known for a sweeping hook shot that became known as the "sky hook."

Abdul-Jabbar played in the National Basketball Association (NBA) from 1969 until his retirement at the end of the 1988-1989 season. During his professional career, he scored a record 38,387 regular-season points. He played in 1,560 regular season games over 20 seasons. Abdul-Jabbar led the NBA in scoring in the 1970-1971 and 1971-1972 seasons. He was named the league's Most Valuable Player six times. During his college career, Abdul-Jabbar led UCLA to national championships in 1967, 1968, and 1969. After graduation, he joined the Milwaukee Bucks of the NBA. In 1975, he was traded to the Los Angeles Lakers, finishing his career with that team.

Abdul-Jabbar was born Ferdinand Lewis Alcindor, Jr., in New York City on

Focus on Sports

Kareem Abdul-Jabbar scored more points than any other player in the history of the National Basketball Association.

April 16, 1947. He took the name Kareem Abdul-Jabbar when he became a Muslim in 1971. He made it his legal name that year.

Abdul-Jabbar has written or co-written a number of books, including the autobiographies *Giant Steps* (1987); *Kareem* (1990); *Coach Wooden and Me* (2017); and *Becoming Kareem* (with Raymond Obstfeld, 2017). His other books include *Black Profiles in Courage* (2000), which contains portraits of notable black men and women; *Brothers in Arms* (2004), an account of the first all-black armored unit to fight in World War II (1939-1945); and *On the Shoulders of Giants* (2007), a personal account of African American history in the early 1900's. Abdul-Jabbar wrote two children's books with Obstfeld—*What Color Is My World?* (2012) and *Sasquatch in the Paint* (2013). He also has written a series of detective novels with Anna Waterhouse. The series begins with *Mycroft Holmes* (2015) and features the older brother of Sherlock Holmes. With Obstfeld, Abdul-Jabbar wrote the graphic novel *Mycroft Holmes and the Apocalypse Handbook* (2017, illustrated by John Cassara).   Bob Logan

See also **Basketball** (picture).

Abdullah, *ab DUHL uh* or *ab dool LAH* (1924?-2015), served as king and prime minister of Saudi Arabia from 2005 to 2015. He previously had assumed the position of commander of the Saudi National Guard in 1962. He came to power after the death of his half brother King Fahd, who had ruled Saudi Arabia since 1982. In the mid-1990's, Fahd suffered a stroke, and his health began to decline. Abdullah became increasingly responsible for governing the country. In 2000, Abdullah assumed the title of *regent* (one who governs in place of the king).

Abdullah supported moderate reforms within Saudi Arabia. He also became a spokesman for the Arab world and played a leadership role in trying to peacefully settle the Israeli-Palestinian conflict.

Abdullah ibn Abd al-Aziz Al Saud was born in Riyadh. He was educated at the royal court, but he lived part of his youth with Bedouin tribes in the deserts of Saudi Arabia. He died on Jan. 23, 2015.   Joseph A. Kechichian

Abdullah II, *ab DUHL uh* or *ab dool LAH* (1962-   ), became king of Jordan in 1999, following the death of his father, Hussein. He is the oldest son of Hussein and his second wife, Princess Muna al-Hussein. Before taking the throne, Abdullah was a career military officer.

Abdullah ibn al-Hussein was born on Jan. 30, 1962, in Amman, the capital of Jordan. He attended high school in the United States. In the 1980's, he studied international relations at Oxford University in the United Kingdom and Georgetown University in the United States. He also had military training at schools in both countries.

In 1981, Abdullah joined the Jordanian army as a second lieutenant. He was promoted to colonel in 1993 and became commander of Jordan's special forces in 1994. While in the military, Abdullah represented his father on diplomatic missions to the Middle East, Europe, and the United States.   Peter Gubser

Abel, *AY buhl,* in the Bible, was a shepherd and the second son of Adam and Eve (Genesis 4). He offered some of the first born of his flocks as a sacrifice to the Lord. His sacrifice was accepted. But when his older brother, Cain, a farmer, offered "fruit of the ground," his sacrifice was refused. Cain grew angry and killed Abel. See also **Adam and Eve; Cain.**   Carole R. Fontaine

Abelard, *AB uh LAHRD,* **Peter** (1079-1142), was a leading philosopher and theologian of the Middle Ages, a period in Europe from about the A.D. 400's through the 1400's. But Abelard is probably best known for his love affair with Héloïse, a gifted young Frenchwoman.

Abelard was born near Nantes, France. His father, a nobleman, planned a military career for him, but Abelard became a scholar. From 1113 to 1118, he taught theology in Paris. There, he founded a school that, along with two others, developed into the University of Paris.

In 1113, Abelard became the tutor of Héloïse, the niece of an official of the Cathedral of Notre Dame. Abelard and the young woman became lovers, and she became pregnant. Soon after the birth of their baby in 1118, the couple secretly married. Fulbert, Héloïse's uncle, learned of the marriage and was outraged. In anger, Fulbert hired several men who broke into Abelard's house and castrated him. After the attack, Abelard and Héloïse separated. Abelard became a monk, and Héloïse joined an order of nuns. Their tragic love affair became famous from the many letters they exchanged.

Abelard's major contributions to medieval thought were in the areas of logic and theology. He urged the use of logic to understand and defend Christianity. Abelard compiled a book called *Sic et Non (Yes and No,* about 1120). It consisted of conflicting views of theological authorities on various religious problems and principles. The work became an influential textbook in the medieval philosophical system called Scholasticism (see **Scholasticism**). Abelard also wrote a book on ethics and *The Story of My Misfortunes* (about 1130), a revealing autobiography. He died April 21, 1142.   Timothy B. Noone

Aberdeen, *AB uhr DEEN* (pop. 222,793), is the third largest city in Scotland. Only Glasgow and Edinburgh have more people. Aberdeen lies on the east coast of northern Scotland, along the North Sea and between the Rivers Dee and Don (see **Scotland** [political map]). Aberdeen is called the *Granite City* due to its many gleaming, gray granite buildings. It has long been the main port and distribution center for northern Scotland. In Scottish Gaelic, Aberdeen is called *Obar Dheathain.*

Aberdeen dates from the 1100's. The Aberdeen Harbour Board, established in 1136, is the oldest recorded business in the United Kingdom. Much of the modern city dates from the late 1700's and the 1800's, when Aberdeen became a center for the agricultural, fishing, granite, and textile industries. Granite quarrying ended in 1971, but petroleum fields in the North Sea brought new growth and prosperity to Aberdeen.   A. S. Mather

Aberdeen and Temair, *AB ur DEEN, tuh MAIR,* **Marquess of** (1847-1934), a British politician, was governor general of Canada from 1893 to 1898. In 1896, he set an example for future governors general when he refused to approve last-minute political appointments recommended by outgoing Prime Minister Sir Charles Tupper.

Aberdeen was born John Campbell Hamilton-Gordon on Aug. 3, 1847, in Edinburgh, Scotland. He became the seventh Earl of Aberdeen in 1870. Lord Aberdeen attended St. Andrews University and Oxford University. He began his political career as a Conservative but later joined the Liberal Party. Aberdeen was the chief British administrator in Ireland in 1886 and from 1905 to 1915. He became a marquess in 1916. Aberdeen and his wife wrote a book about their life called *We Twa* (1925). He

died on March 7, 1934.   Jacques Monet

Abernathy, Ralph David (1926-1990), was an American civil rights leader. He served as president of the Southern Christian Leadership Conference (SCLC) from 1968 to 1977. He succeeded Martin Luther King, Jr., who was murdered in 1968. In 1955 and 1956, Abernathy helped King lead a bus boycott in Montgomery, Alabama, to protest racial discrimination. He and King helped organize the SCLC in 1957. Abernathy became the SCLC's vice president at large in 1965. In 1968, he led the "Poor People's March" on Washington, D.C., which dramatized problems faced by poor people.

© Alamy Images
Ralph David Abernathy

Abernathy was born on March 11, 1926, in Linden, Alabama. He earned a B.S. degree at Alabama State College and an M.S. degree at Atlanta University. He became a Baptist minister in 1948. Abernathy ran unsuccessfully for a Georgia congressional seat in 1977. His autobiography, *And the Walls Came Tumbling Down,* was published in 1989. Abernathy died on April 17, 1990.   Robert A. Pratt

Aberration, in optics, is the failure of a lens or mirror to produce an image that is sharply focused and has the same proportions as the object being viewed. There are three main kinds of aberration: (1) *point aberration,* (2) *distortion,* and (3) *chromatic aberration.*

Point aberration produces a fuzzy image by failing to focus light to a point. The three primary types of point aberration are (1) *spherical aberration,* (2) *astigmatism,* and (3) *coma.*

Spherical aberration occurs in a lens in which one or both sides are curved like a portion of the surface of a sphere. A spherical surface is easy and inexpensive to produce. As a result, a typical lens in a camera, a pair of binoculars, or a small telescope is a piece of glass with spherical surfaces. This kind of lens focuses light well enough for those applications.

To understand spherical aberration, imagine that parallel rays of light strike a lens as shown in the illustration on the facing page. If there were no aberration, all the rays would come to a focus at a point on the other side of the lens. But because of aberration, rays that pass through different parts of the lens come to a focus at different points. All the points are along the *optical axis,* an imaginary line through the center of the lens. Rays that pass through the lens near its center come to a focus at a point relatively far from the lens. Rays passing through the lens near its edge come to a relatively close focus. An inward-curving spherical mirror produces spherical aberration in a similar way. Aberrations are not necessarily a result of manufacturing errors. For example, even a lens with perfectly spherical sides could not focus all parallel rays that pass through it to a single point.

In astigmatism, light comes to a focus as a line rather than as a point. In coma, the light focuses in the shape of a cone. Astigmatism and coma make the image blurry at its edge but not at its center.

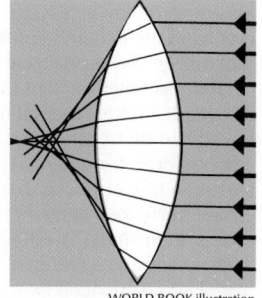

Spherical aberration occurs in a lens because light rays that pass through the lens at different distances from its center come to a focus at different distances from its edge.

WORLD BOOK illustration

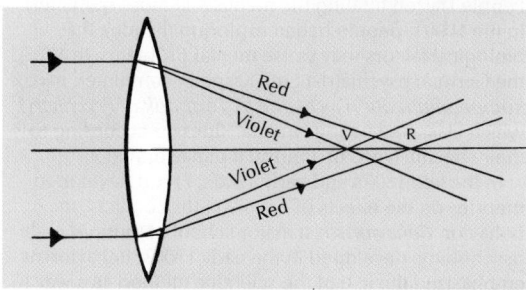

WORLD BOOK illustration

Chromatic aberration occurs because a lens focuses different colors of light at different points—violet light at the nearest point, red at the farthest, and the other colors at points in between.

Distortion results when a lens or mirror focuses light at an incorrect distance from the optical axis. The image appears either stretched or compressed near the edges.

Chromatic aberration occurs in lenses but not in mirrors. It occurs because a lens focuses light rays of different colors at different distances. The distance to the focal point of a light ray depends on the *wavelength*. Wavelength is the distance between successive crests of a wave. Each color has its own wavelength. From longest to shortest wavelength, the colors of visible light include red, orange, yellow, green, blue, and violet.

In *longitudinal chromatic aberration,* a lens focuses the different colors at different points on the optical axis. Violet light comes to a focus that is closest to the lens. Then comes the focal point for blue light, then the point for green, and so forth. In *lateral chromatic aberration,* focal points are also offset above and below the optical axis—red the least, violet the most. W. Thomas Roberts, Jr.

See also **Lens; Mirror; Parabola; Telescope.**

Abidjan, *AB ih JAHN* (pop. 3,788,400), is the largest city in the African nation of Côte d'Ivoire (also known as Ivory Coast). Abidjan is one of the busiest seaports in western Africa. It lies along a lagoon that is connected by a canal to the Gulf of Guinea, an arm of the Atlantic Ocean. For location, see **Côte d'Ivoire** (map).

Abidjan is an important center of import and export activities in western Africa. It is also a chief industrial and commercial center. The city is known for its culture and music industry. Abidjan is divided into neighborhood administrative areas called *communes.* The city has many high-rise office and apartment buildings and single-family houses. But it also has areas of overcrowded slums, especially on the city's outskirts.

The French took control of Côte d'Ivoire in the late 1800's and began to develop Abidjan in the early 1900's.

In 1934, Abidjan became the capital. Abidjan grew rapidly after 1950, when the canal linking the lagoon with the ocean was completed. Côte d'Ivoire gained independence in 1960. In 1983, Yamoussoukro replaced Abidjan as the capital. However, most government business continued to take place in Abidjan. Boubacar N'Diaye

Abilene, *AB uh LEEN* (pop. 6,844), a city in east-central Kansas, is a railroad shipping center for crops raised in the east-central part of the state. For Abilene's location, see **Kansas** (political map). Abilene is the seat of Dickinson County.

From 1867 to 1872, cowhands drove longhorn cattle over the Chisholm Trail to Abilene, where the stock was loaded and shipped to Eastern markets. Probably the top year was 1871, when 5,000 cowhands and 700,000 head of cattle came to Abilene from Texas. Wild Bill Hickok became famous as a "two-gun marshal" of Abilene.

President Dwight D. Eisenhower grew up in Abilene. The city is the site of the Dwight D. Eisenhower Presidential Library, Museum, and Boyhood Home. This complex also includes the Place of Meditation, where Eisenhower is buried. The city has a council-manager form of government. James R. Shortridge

See also **Westward movement in America** (Cattle frontiers).

Abkhazia, *ahb KAH zee uh,* is a region at the western end of the Caucasus Mountains bordering the Black Sea. For location, see **Georgia** (map). Abkhazia is officially part of Georgia. However, it declared its independence in 1992 and operates under its own government.

Abkhazia's population was about 540,000 in 1990, but many of its people fled the fighting that broke out in the early 1990's following its declaration of independence. The native language of Abkhazia is Abkhaz, which belongs to the Caucasian language family. A majority of people in Abkhazia are Eastern Orthodox Christians. Most of the remaining people are Muslims.

In the A.D. 780's, Abkhazian ruler Leon II conquered what is now western Georgia and made it an independent kingdom. In 1008, Bagrat III, king of Abkhazia, united the rest of Georgia with his kingdom. Abkhazia fell to the Ottomans in the late 1500's and to the Russians in the early 1800's. In the 1860's and 1870's, Russia smashed a rebellion in Abkhazia and exiled about half its people to the Ottoman Empire.

Abkhazia fought against Georgia during the civil war in Russia (1918-1921). After the war, Abkhazia became part of Georgia in the Soviet Union. When the Soviet Union broke apart in 1991, Georgia became independent. Abkhazia declared its independence from Georgia in 1992, and Georgian troops invaded. In 1993, Abkhazian forces, with aid from Russia, drove the Georgian troops out of Abkhazia. Peacekeeping forces have since helped maintain a cease-fire, but talks to resolve the conflict have made little progress. In 2016, Russia and Abkhazia created a joint military force. The United States and Georgia do not recognize the joint force as legitimate or legal under international law. Stuart J. Kaufman

Abnormal psychology, also called *psychopathology,* is the scientific study of psychological or mental disorders. These disorders affect the way people think, speak, feel, and behave. The term *abnormal* can refer to something strange or rare. But standards of behavior differ among societies and change as social conditions and customs change. This article uses *abnormal* to refer to a pattern of thoughts, feelings, and behavior that is thought to have a biological or psychological cause and that leads to significant distress, disability, or danger to oneself or others. Psychologists do not consider behavior that is simply different to be a mental disorder.

Studies in abnormal psychology are conducted by professionals in clinical psychology, psychiatry, and social work. Investigators collect data on peoples' thoughts, feelings, and actions through observation, interviews, questionnaires, and psychological tests. Some studies, called *idiographic studies,* focus on only one person. Other studies, called *nomothetic studies,* involve a group or groups of people.

Researchers often examine environmental or biological differences between people with a mental disorder and a *control group* of similar people without the disorder. Environmental factors that may affect behavior include past experiences or family interactions. Biological factors may include variations in brain chemicals called *neurotransmitters,* hormones, or nutrition. Research in abnormal psychology helps mental health professionals understand how mental problems may develop and how they may be treated.

Theories of abnormal psychology guide how scientists think about, study, and treat psychological problems. These theories describe the characteristics of mental disorders, suggest possible causes, and propose methods of treating them. The major theories guiding abnormal psychology today are the (1) biological, (2) cognitive behavioral, and (3) psychodynamic.

Biological theories focus on the role that bodily structures and functions play in producing behavior, thoughts, and feelings. Biological theorists also investigate the role that heredity and genes play in the development of mental disorders. Studies may look at how medical conditions, such as disease or injury, or drugs and other substances affect the way people think, feel, and behave. Treatments developed from biological theories typically involve using medication, and sometimes surgery, to relieve distressing or disabling symptoms.

Cognitive-behavioral theories focus on environmental influences on behavior. Known principles of learning, such as *modeling* (imitation), *operant conditioning* (learning through rewards and punishments), and *classical conditioning* (learning by association) came historically from what are now called cognitive-behavioral theories. Cognitive-behavioral studies may look at how rewards or punishments in the past or present influence how people act, think, or feel. Cognitive-behavioral treatments try to help troubled people change the way they think and act in situations. They may encourage an individual to try new ways of thinking or behaving that help them, for example, overcome a fear or experience more pleasure and less sadness.

Psychodynamic theories focus on how human behavior and relationships are shaped by conscious and unconscious influences. They highlight the role of unresolved conflicts in early life and how they may be influencing the way people behave, feel, and think. These theories developed from the work of Sigmund Freud, an Austrian physician. Freud theorized that *intrapsychic conflicts* (conflicts within the individual) between basic biological urges and societal standards lead to abnormal behavior. Psychodynamic therapies focus on resolving the patient's conflicted feelings from the past that may be influencing current problems.

History. Since ancient times, people have tried to understand and treat mental disorders. Many societies believed that demons caused abnormal behavior. People who suffered from mental problems were often feared and seen as dangerous. Many disturbed individuals were imprisoned in miserable conditions, sometimes in chains, in institutions called *insane asylums.*

During the late 1700's, old ideas about abnormal behavior were replaced by more personal explanations. People started treating the mentally ill more humanely. In the 1800's, people began exploring the idea that biological factors may cause mental problems. In 1883, the German psychiatrist Emil Kräpelin completed his *Kompendium der psychiatrie (A Textbook of Psychiatry),* which classified various mental illnesses according to their specific types of abnormal behaviors.

In the late 1800's and early 1900's, Freud developed theories on the effects of unconscious conflicts on behavior. *Behaviorism,* a major school of thought in psychology, developed in the early 1900's. Behaviorists emphasized the use of the scientific method as a way to understand the role that learning and the environment play in the development of behavior. The emergence of cognitive psychology in the late 1900's led to studies aimed at understanding how a person's unique view of the environment determines his or her emotional and behavioral response to it. Today, psychologists focus on how biological, psychological, and social factors may interact to shape the development of normal and abnormal thoughts, feelings, and behavior.   Timothy J. Bruce

See also **Mental illness** and its list of *Related articles.*

Abolition movement was the organized effort to end slavery in the Americas. The movement was centered in the United Kingdom and the United States, but antislavery efforts occurred in other countries as well.

Abolitionist activity began during the colonial period, when Quakers in Pennsylvania condemned slavery on moral grounds. In the late 1700's, prominent leaders of the American revolutionary movement, including Thomas Jefferson, Patrick Henry, and Thomas Paine, spoke out against slavery. British abolitionists included William Wilberforce, Thomas Clarkson, and the formerly enslaved African Olaudah Equiano. In 1807, British abolitionists persuaded Parliament to pass a bill outlawing the Atlantic slave trade. In 1833, another bill abolished slavery throughout the British Empire.

In the United States, abolitionists heeded the call of free Black people for the immediate and universal ending of slavery. Many abolitionists came from New England. They included the newspaper editor William Lloyd Garrison and the renowned orator Wendell Phillips. Others, such as the merchant brothers Arthur and Lewis Tappan and the reformer Theodore Weld, came from Middle Atlantic or Midwestern states. A number of abolitionists came from prominent slaveholding families in the South, including Moncure Daniel Conway and the sisters Sarah and Angelina Grimké. Women made significant contributions to the movement as writers, speakers, organizers, and fund-raisers.

In 1831, Garrison began publication of his influential antislavery newspaper, *The Liberator.* The American

Anti-Slavery Society, founded in 1833, supported Garrison's crusade. The abolitionist movement gradually spread throughout the Northern States despite bitter and violent opposition by Southern slaveholders and Northerners who favored slavery. Abolitionists faced incredible dangers. In 1835, a mob dragged Garrison through the streets of Boston with a noose around his neck. Two years later, antiabolitionists in Alton, Illinois, murdered Elijah P. Lovejoy, a well-known antislavery newspaper editor.

The abolitionist movement entered a new phase in 1840, when some of its leaders entered politics and founded the Liberty Party. James G. Birney, a former slaveholder, ran as the party's candidate for president in 1840 and 1844. In 1848, abolitionists became an important element in the Free Soil Party. After 1854, most abolitionists supported the Republican Party. A small group of enthusiasts formed the Radical Abolition Party in 1855.

Even after abolitionists entered politics, they remained more interested in their cause than in political offices. They combined political protest with direct action. Their homes often became stations on the *underground railroad,* a system that helped slaves fleeing to the free states or to Canada.

In 1859, John Brown led a small group of radical abolitionists in a military invasion of Harpers Ferry, Virginia, the site of a federal arsenal. Brown modeled his plan on a successful slave revolt in the French West Indies, a group of Caribbean islands under French control. Brown's raid sought to end slavery by sparking a massive slave rebellion. Though his mission failed, it led to heightened tensions between the North and South.

After the American Civil War began in 1861, abolitionists rallied to the Union cause. The abolitionists rejoiced when President Abraham Lincoln issued the Emancipation Proclamation on Jan. 1, 1863, declaring the slaves free in numerous parts of the South. In 1865, the 13th Amendment to the Constitution of the United States abolished slavery throughout the republic. By the end of the 1800's, slavery had disappeared from the Western Hemisphere completely.   Matthew Clavin

Related articles in *World Book* include:

Abominable Snowman. See Yeti.

Aboriginal peoples of Australia, *AB uh RIHJ uh nuhl,* are the first people who lived in Australia and their descendants. Today, Australia has about 700,000 Aboriginal people—about 3 percent of the country's population. They include peoples of mainland Australia, Tasmania, and some other nearby islands. The descendants of early Australians who lived on islands off the northern tip of Queensland, however, make up a separate collection of cultural groups known as the Torres Strait Islander peoples. To refer together to the Aboriginal and Torres Strait Islander peoples, Australians use the terms *Indigenous peoples of Australia, First Australians,* or *First Nations peoples.* The word *indigenous* means *native.*

Australians use the term Aboriginal peoples (with an *s*) to emphasize the diversity of culture and language among the several hundred Aboriginal groups, or *peoples,* from different parts of the Australian continent. The terms Aboriginal persons or Aboriginal people (without an *s*) are often used when discussing Aboriginal people as individuals rather than the groups.

According to Aboriginal traditions, Aboriginal people have always lived in Australia. The ancestors of today's Aboriginal peoples likely have lived in Australia for more than 65,000 years. Scientists who analyze population characteristics and trends estimate that from 500,000 to 1 million people lived throughout the continent when European colonists first reached Australia in 1788. These inhabitants belonged to about 600 groups (sometimes termed *tribes).* The groups spoke hundreds of distinct languages and dialects.

The arrival of European colonizers, described by Aboriginal peoples as an invasion, devastated Aboriginal communities. Diseases previously unknown in Australia, violent conflict with settlers, *dispossession* (the taking of lands), and the loss of traditional foods and resources wiped out whole families, lineages, and clans.

Many white colonizers did not value the Aboriginal cultures and made little effort to understand them. They assumed that the Aboriginal peoples would either die out or *assimilate* (be absorbed) and live like Europeans. Aboriginal peoples were often treated unfairly and did not have the rights of other Australians.

Since the mid-1900's, Aboriginal people have won greater recognition of their rights as citizens and to land. Today, many people also realize that the Aboriginal cultures were complex, sophisticated, and well-adapted to the environments in which the first Australians lived.

The earliest Australians. *Archaeologists* (scientists who study the cultural remains left behind by past civilizations) estimate that Australia's Aboriginal people came by boat from Southeast Asia. By about 40,000 years ago, Aboriginal people lived in most parts of Australia, from the tropical rain forests to the central desert.

Aboriginal life. Over time, Aboriginal peoples developed food gathering methods, fishing techniques, clothing, and shelters suited to each area. They had social systems and beliefs that varied across the continent.

Those Aboriginal peoples who were nomadic hunter-gatherers traveled according to the seasons to locate food, water, and other resources by hunting animals and gathering plants. Eventually, some groups in southern Australia began to live in semi-permanent villages.

Men hunted large land and sea animals, such as emu, kangaroo, and sea turtles. Women hunted small animals and gathered plants. People developed ways to influence their environment to increase their food sources. Many Aboriginal groups burned certain sections of their lands at certain times to encourage the growth of useful plants or to create grasslands that would attract animals to hunt. This is called *firestick farming*. Some people may have scattered grains to grow in certain places. Some built traps and holding ponds for fish and eels.

Aboriginal people lived in family groups. They wore ornaments and waistbands but little other clothing. In colder areas, they made cloaks of kangaroo and possum fur. They made tools of stone and wood. The tools included boomerangs, digging sticks, grindstones, knives, and spears. Aboriginal peoples had their own music, songs, and stories. Religious beliefs varied across the groups. According to some Aboriginal beliefs, people had a spiritual relationship to the land through *ancestral beings* who created the world long ago during a period called the *Dreaming,* or *Dreamtime*. These ancestral beings never died but merged with the natural world.

Territorial rights were based on descent, birth, and ceremonial ties to a region. The land was divided into areas known today as *countries,* each inhabited by a group of related families called a *clan*. A clan cared for its country, and the country provided food and water. The idea of country (often spelled with a capital *C*) is still important to Aboriginal peoples. Clans were part of larger groups, today called tribes and nations, that were distinguished by their dialects. No formal governments existed. Leadership depended on age and knowledge.

The arrival of British colonizers in 1788 brought new diseases and conflicts, which together devastated the Aboriginal population. Europeans did not understand the Aboriginal ways of land management. They assumed the land was *terra nullius,* a Latin term meaning *land belonging to no one*, and free for settlement. For Aboriginal peoples, removal from their lands meant loss of their food sources and ways of life.

In the late 1800's and early 1900's, government legislation strictly controlled how Aboriginal peoples lived. From about 1870 to 1970, many Aboriginal and Torres Strait Islander children were separated from their families and placed in institutions, missions, and foster homes. The removals were part of a policy to control Indigenous people and force them to adopt Western culture. The children are called the *Stolen Generations*.

Recognition of rights. Since the mid-1900's, protests and political efforts by Aboriginal peoples have won greater recognition of their rights as citizens. In 1976, the government passed the Aboriginal Land Rights (Northern Territory) Act, which allowed Aboriginal groups in the Northern Territory to reclaim their traditional lands. The 1992 decision by the High Court of Australia in *Mabo v. Queensland* declared the theory of *terra nullius* was illegal. It recognized that a form of land possession termed *native title* had existed when Europeans colonized Australia, and still existed where Aboriginal and Torres Strait Islander peoples continued to occupy their land. A 1997 government report condemned the earlier child removal policies as acts of *genocide* (extermination of an entire people).

Australia's Aboriginal peoples have made great gains in the areas of civil and land rights and in overcoming discrimination. Aboriginal languages, art, religion, ritual, and other aspects of their traditional life have gained increasing acceptance and support within Australia and abroad. Despite these gains, the Aboriginal peoples still face prejudice and difficulties. It still is often hard for individuals to get a good education, a job, or housing.

Since the early 1990's, there has been an official process of settling disagreements between Aboriginal and non-Aboriginal groups and bringing them together in friendship. This process, called *reconciliation,* was formalized by an act of Parliament. In 2008, the government of Australia formally apologized for the child removal policy and other past wrongs and policies that inflicted grief, suffering, and loss among Aboriginal and Torres Strait Islander peoples.   Lynette Russell

Related articles in *World Book* include:

Australia	Races, Human (Climatic
Boomerang	adaptations)
Bora ground	Stolen Generations
Dreamtime	Tasmania

© David Gray, Reuters/Alamy Images

Australia's annual National Reconciliation Week encourages equality, justice, and mutual understanding among Indigenous and non-Indigenous Australians. Here, Aboriginal people participate in a *corroboree,* an Aboriginal celebration at which people exchange songs and rituals, as a part of the week's activities.

Abortion is the ending of a pregnancy before birth. Early in a pregnancy, the fertilized egg that grows and develops is called an *embryo*. After three months of development, it is usually called a *fetus*. An abortion causes the embryo or fetus to die. In a *spontaneous abortion,* also called a *miscarriage,* the fetus passes from the woman's body. Spontaneous abortions may result from such natural causes as an abnormality in the embryo, a hormonal imbalance, a long-term disease, or some other disorder in the woman. In an *induced abortion,* the fetus is purposely removed from the woman's body. This article deals with induced abortion.

Abortion methods. Physicians perform abortions in several ways. During the first trimester of pregnancy, the most common method is *suction curettage,* also known as *vacuum aspiration*. This method involves removing the fetus by suction, then scraping the woman's uterus with surgical instruments called *curettes*.

Abortion can also be caused in the first trimester by a drug called *mifepristone* or *RU-486*. The drug blocks the action of the hormone *progesterone* in the woman's body. Normally, this hormone prepares the woman's uterus to receive and nourish the embryo.

In the second trimester, many doctors use a method called *dilation and evacuation,* or simply *D and E.* In this way, the fetus is taken apart in the uterus and removed. Another method involves adding a salt solution to the *amniotic fluid,* the liquid that surrounds the fetus. The fetus then dies and passes from the woman's body. An abortion also may be performed by adding hormonelike drugs called *prostaglandins* to the amniotic fluid. The drugs cause muscle contractions that expel the fetus.

Induced abortion has been a topic of dispute for hundreds of years. People disagree on two basic questions. One question is whether the law should permit a woman to have an abortion and, if so, under what circumstances. The other is whether the law should protect the unborn. Those who wish to legally limit or forbid abortion describe their position as "right-to-life" or "pro-life." Those who believe a woman should have the right to an abortion refer to themselves as "pro-choice."

Arguments against abortion are generally based on the belief that an abortion is the unjustified killing of an unborn child. Most people who oppose abortion believe that human life begins as soon as a sperm fertilizes an egg. Some believe that human embryos and fetuses should have legal rights and that abortion is actually a form of murder. Many pro-life people believe that legalization of abortion increases the number of irresponsible pregnancies and leads to a disrespect for human life.

The Roman Catholic Church is probably the leading opponent of abortion. Conservative branches of other religions also disapprove of abortion.

Arguments for abortion. Many people would allow abortion under certain circumstances. Some approve of abortion if a woman's life or health is endangered by her pregnancy. Others find abortion permissible if medical tests predict that the child will be born with a serious mental or physical defect. Some people would permit abortion when a pregnancy has resulted from rape or incest. Others believe that a woman should have an unrestricted right to an abortion, especially before the fetus becomes *viable*—that is, capable of living outside the mother's body. Most fetuses become viable after the sixth month of the pregnancy.

People who favor an unrestricted right to abortion during early pregnancy often separate human life from *personhood.* They argue that personhood includes an ability to experience self-consciousness and to be accepted as a member of a community. These people believe fetuses are not persons and thus should not be granted the rights given to persons. Such pro-choice thinkers consider birth the beginning of personhood.

Another pro-choice argument is that legal abortion eliminates many of the illegal abortions performed by unskilled individuals under unsanitary conditions. These abortions cause many women permanent injury or result in their deaths. Also, some argue that women should not have to give birth to unwanted children because the world's population is growing rapidly and natural resources are becoming scarce.

Abortion history. Abortion has been practiced and debated since ancient times. The ancient Hebrews permitted it in cases where the mother's life was at risk.

The early Christian church generally opposed abortion. For hundreds of years, however, the church debated whether abortion might be justifiable before *anima-* tion. Church scholars defined animation as the point at which the fetus received a soul. According to church teachings, animation occurred between 40 and 80 days after *conception* (fertilization). From about the 1300's to the 1800's, abortion before animation became generally accepted in Europe if the pregnancy endangered the life of the mother. If an abortion before animation took place for a less serious reason, many church scholars considered it to be wrong, but not homicide.

In 1869, Pope Pius IX condemned abortion from the moment of conception, but some Catholic church scholars continued to teach that abortions performed to save the mother were morally acceptable. In 1895, the Roman Catholic Church declared that abortion is never justifiable. Today, the Catholic church condemns all forms of *direct abortion—that is, the intentional ending of pregnancy. Current Catholic teaching permits* indirect abortion, *in which the fetus is lost as a side effect of medical treatment designed to save the mother's life.*

Abortion in the United States is a subject of public debate. Opinion polls show that most people think abortion should be legal. These people might disapprove of abortion or disagree with some of the reasons that women seek abortions, but they would permit a legal choice. Some believe only the states—and not the federal government—should regulate or outlaw abortion.

Before the mid-1800's, abortion was not a crime under U.S. common law if it took place before *quickening.* Quickening is the time when the mother first feels the fetus moving. State laws prohibiting abortion began to appear in the 1820's. By 1900, every state except Kentucky had made abortion a serious crime. But some courts refused to impose penalties for early abortion.

By the 1960's, pro-choice organizations in the United States had begun working to change state abortion laws. By the early 1970's, 14 states had laws permitting abortion if the woman's health was in danger or if the woman was a victim of incest or rape.

In 1973, the Supreme Court of the United States delivered a historic decision on abortion in the case of *Roe v. Wade.* The court ruled that states could not forbid a woman to have an abortion during the first *trimester* (three months) of pregnancy. The court also ruled that, during the second trimester, states may regulate abortion only to protect women's health. Once the fetus becomes viable in the third trimester, states may regulate abortion to protect the interests of both women and the unborn. The *Roe v. Wade* decision stated that the U.S. Constitution implies the right of privacy and allows a woman to decide for herself if she will have an abortion.

The 1973 decision also defined when a fetus becomes viable. It stated, "Viability is usually placed at about seven months (28 weeks) but may occur earlier, even at 24 weeks." The court said that states may forbid abortion of a viable fetus except when the abortion is necessary to protect the mother's life or health.

Since the *Roe v. Wade* decision, many groups have organized to oppose abortion and the legislation and court decisions that permit it. These groups include the National Right to Life Committee, the Christian Coalition, and Operation Rescue. Most pro-life groups strongly oppose illegal acts. But some individuals have vandalized, bombed, or set fire to abortion clinics. Others have attacked and killed doctors and other clinic employees.

Pro-choice groups also have expanded their efforts. They contact lawmakers, hold demonstrations, and attack restrictive abortion laws in court. Pro-choice organizations include NARAL Pro-Choice America, Planned Parenthood Federation of America, and the National Organization for Women.

Since 1973, some Supreme Court rulings have limited the influence of *Roe v. Wade.* One such case was *Webster v. Reproductive Health Services* (1989). The Supreme Court ruled that states may require doctors to test a fetus's viability before performing an abortion on a woman pregnant for 20 weeks or more. The court also ruled that states may outlaw abortions in public hospitals and prohibit public employees from assisting in abortions.

Following the *Roe v. Wade* decision, the federal government and many state governments began to pay for abortions for poor women under the Medicaid program. Many opponents of abortion objected to this use of government funds. In 1977, the Supreme Court ruled that the government was not obligated to finance abortions considered unnecessary to preserve the mother's physical or emotional health. In 1980, the court said the government had no obligation to pay for even most medically necessary abortions. This ruling upheld a federal law called the Hyde Amendment.

In 1990, the Supreme Court decided that states may require minors to obtain parental or court consent before having an abortion. In *Planned Parenthood of Eastern Pennsylvania v. Casey* (1992), both sides of the dispute asked the Supreme Court to review the ruling in *Roe v. Wade.* The justices upheld the ruling by a vote of 5 to 4. The court also ruled that states may require women seeking an abortion to first receive counseling by a doctor about fetal development and abortion risks. The court also decided that states may require women to wait 24 hours between the counseling and the abortion.

The case of *National Organization for Women v. Scheidler* (1994) was a legal response to incidents at abortion clinics. The Supreme Court decided that protesters who block access to clinics can be prosecuted under federal racketeering laws. In 1994, Congress passed the Freedom of Access to Clinic Entrances Act, which protects abortion clinics and their staff members from violence and blockades.

In *Stenberg v. Carhart* (2000), the Supreme Court ruled that a Nebraska law banning what pro-life activists call *partial-birth abortions* was unconstitutional. The procedure, which doctors call *intact dilation and extraction,* involves aborting a fetus after it has been partially removed from a woman's body. The court stated that the Nebraska law placed an "undue burden" on a woman's right to choose an abortion and did not allow the procedure even to protect a woman's health. In 2003, however, Congress passed a similar law banning the procedure. Pro-choice organizations quickly challenged the law in court, and several federal court rulings blocked full enforcement of the ban.

In September 2000, the U.S. Food and Drug Administration approved the sale of the abortion drug mifepristone, marketed by the name Mifeprex. The decision allows women to buy pills through physicians to end pregnancies. Supporters of the drug claimed it would enable women to end their pregnancies earlier, more safely, and with greater privacy than before. The drug had been available in Europe for more than 10 years.

In other countries, abortion laws differ. Lawmakers in some countries have considered abortion an effective tool for limiting family size and combating poverty. In China, for example, abortions are legal and common because the government allows only a limited number of children per family. Chinese women may have an abortion at any time during their pregnancy. In Russia, abortion is allowed up to the 29th week of pregnancy. Japan restricts abortions to the first 24 weeks of pregnancy.

In the United Kingdom, an abortion may be performed up to the 24th week of pregnancy. However, it must be shown that continuing the pregnancy would endanger the physical or mental health of the woman or her children. Canadian law permits abortion at any time during pregnancy and for any reason. But most physicians avoid performing abortions during the later stages and do not offer abortion as a method of birth control. A few countries, including El Salvador, Malta, and Nicaragua, ban abortion in all cases.   David M. O'Brien

See also **Miscarriage; National Right to Life Committee; Planned Parenthood Federation of America; Roe v. Wade.**

Additional resources

Gold, Susan D. *Roe v. Wade: A Women's Choice.* Benchmark Bks., 2005.
Hull, N. E. H., and others, eds. *The Abortion Rights Controversy in America: A Legal Reader.* Univ. of N. C. Pr., 2004.

Abraham was the founder of Judaism and the ancestor of both the Arabs and the Jews. The Arabs trace their ancestry to Abraham's oldest son, Ishmael. The Jews consider Abraham their ancestor through another son, Isaac. Abraham, Isaac, and Isaac's son Jacob are called the *patriarchs* (founding fathers) of the Jews.

Many scholars believe that Abraham lived between about 1800 and 1500 B.C. The story of his life is told in Genesis, the first book of the Bible. During his early life, Abraham was called Abram. He was born in the city of Ur, in ancient Mesopotamia (now mostly Iraq). The people of Ur, like most people then, worshiped many gods. But Abram believed in one God. Abram left Ur and traveled west with his wife, Sarah; his nephew Lot; and other members of his household. At God's command, he went to a land called Canaan. Canaan consisted roughly of an area that extended from east of the Jordan River to the Mediterranean Sea. God told Abram that the land would belong to Abram and his descendants.

Abram settled in Canaan, where God made a *covenant* (special agreement) with him. The covenant promised that Abram would have many descendants and that Canaan would be their "everlasting possession" if they remained faithful to God (Genesis 17:4-8). To symbolize his pledge, God changed Abram's name to Abraham, which means *father of many nations.* God commanded him and all males in his family to be circumcised as a symbol of this covenant (see **Circumcision**).

God repeatedly promised Abraham many children. But he and Sarah remained childless. Following a custom of the time, Sarah gave her maid Hagar to Abraham to bear him a child. Hagar bore Abraham a son, Ishmael.

When Abraham and Sarah were very old, God promised them a son within a year. God also told Abraham that he intended to destroy the cities of Sodom and Gomorrah because nearly all the people were wicked.

Abraham pleaded with God to spare the cities for the sake of the righteous but could not persuade him to do so. But God saved Lot, who lived in Sodom. The next year, Abraham and Sarah had a son, Isaac.

God later gave Abraham his greatest test of faith and obedience. He commanded him to sacrifice Isaac. Abraham took his son to a mountaintop, laid him on an altar, and prepared to kill him. But at the last minute, God stopped Abraham and provided a ram for the sacrifice.

The Bible says Abraham died at an advanced age. According to tradition, he was buried in the Cave of Machpelah in Hebron, in what is now the West Bank region of Southwest Asia.　　　Eric M. Meyers

See also **Isaac; Ishmael; Jews** (Beginnings); **Judaism** (The covenant with God); **Lot.**

Abscess, *AB sehs,* is a collection of pus within an infected part of the body. Pus contains bacteria, blood plasma, and debris from dead cells. It also contains white blood cells, which the body uses to combat infection. An abscess often appears as a red and swollen lump, which may open and drain. Abscesses may occur in any tissue that becomes infected by bacteria.

When abscesses form, blood vessels *dilate* (expand) and fluid from the blood collects in the injured tissue. Serum and white blood cells help destroy the invading bacteria and their poisons. Abscesses swell because the blood vessels expand and the amount of blood in the infected area increases. An abscess is painful because the pus presses on the nerve endings.

Small superficial abscesses, such as pimples, need no special treatment. Boils, carbuncles, or internal abscesses are treated with antibiotics, such as penicillin, and surgical incision if necessary (see **Antibiotic**). An abscess at the root of a tooth should be treated by a dentist. No abscess, regardless of size, should be squeezed, because bacteria can enter the bloodstream and produce infection elsewhere.　　　David T. Woodley

See also **Boil; Teeth** (Diseases and defects of the teeth).

Absolute zero is the temperature at which atoms and molecules have the least amount of heat possible. The atoms and molecules that make up matter are in constant motion relative to each other. What we think of as heat is actually a measure of the energy of this motion. If all the heat in a substance were removed, its molecular and atomic motion would virtually stop. The substance's temperature would be considered to be absolute zero. On the three most widely used temperature scales, absolute zero is −273.15 °C, −459.67 °F, or 0 Kelvin.

According to a widely accepted law of *thermodynamics*—the study of various kinds of energy, including heat—it is impossible for a substance to actually reach absolute zero. Even so, scientists have come extremely close. In 2003, researchers at the Massachusetts Institute of Technology (MIT) reached 0.00000000045 K—one-half of one-billionth of a Celsius degree above absolute zero.

Scientists have discovered that many materials have unusual properties near absolute zero. Some materials develop *superconductivity,* the ability to conduct electric current without resistance. Such materials include many metals, metallic compounds, and ceramics. Superconducting magnets of such materials are used to make *magnetic resonance imaging* (MRI) machines and powerful particle colliders. MRI is a medical technique used by doctors to reveal internal body parts without surgery.

Near absolute zero, liquid helium develops *superfluidity.* Superfluidity is the ability to flow without friction. Other materials can become *Bose-Einstein condensates.* A Bose-Einstein condensate is a cluster of atoms that behaves somewhat like a single atom. Both superfluid helium and Bose-Einstein condensates have been used to study various principles of physics, including gravity, light, and the properties of molecules. Achieving low temperatures and studying their effect on materials is called *cryogenics.*　　　Jerry W. King

Absolutism, *AB suh loo TIHZ uhm,* is a form of government in which one or more persons rule with power unlimited by law. It includes *absolute monarchies* and *dictatorships.*

The power of absolute monarchs is unlimited and inherited, and is based on the *divine right of kings*—the belief that monarchs receive their power directly from God. The monarch may do what he or she wishes. In practice, however, judges, governors, and other officials within an absolute monarchy also carried out government functions according to laws, customs, or simply their own judgment. Absolute monarchs ruled ancient China, Egypt, and Rome. Absolute rulers called *czars* governed Russia until the early 1900's.

Most dictatorships are run by a ruler or rulers who seized power by force. In some dictatorships, the government is satisfied to keep the people from revolting while the rulers obtain advantages for themselves. Other dictatorships try to maintain almost complete control over people so as to make great changes in society. Adolf Hitler of Germany and Joseph Stalin of the Soviet Union headed such governments.　　　Thomas S. Vontz

Related articles in *World Book* include:

Authoritarianism	Divine right of	Monarchy
Despotism	kings	Totalitarianism
Dictatorship	Fascism	Tyranny

Absorption and adsorption, *ab SAWRP shuhn, ad SAWRP shuhn,* are processes by which substances take in matter or energy, or both. In *absorption,* the matter or energy taken in becomes distributed throughout the absorbing material. *Adsorption* is the gathering of matter only. The matter collects on the surface of the adsorbing material. It does not enter the interior.

Absorption. There are many familiar examples of absorption. Heavy drapes absorb sound energy. The sound waves make the fibers in the drapes vibrate and rub together. Friction turns the sound energy into heat

Water drops soak entirely through sponge.
Absorption

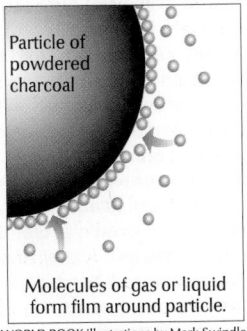
Molecules of gas or liquid form film around particle.
Adsorption

WORLD BOOK illustrations by Mark Swindle

so the sound cannot be reflected as an echo (see **Insulation** [Insulation against sound]). Colored objects and filters selectively absorb light energy. White light is composed of all colors of light. When white light strikes a colored object, some colors of light energy are absorbed. The absorbed light energy *excites* electrons in the atoms of the colored object—that is, it raises them to higher energy levels. The object will transmit or reflect the colors that have not been absorbed. Dry earth absorbs water by a process called *capillarity* (see **Capillarity**). The water in a lake absorbs oxygen by dissolving it.

Adsorption. Usually only solid material can act as an adsorbent. The adsorbed matter can be the molecules of a liquid or a gas, or tiny particles of a solid. Adsorption is often highly selective, making it useful for separating or purifying liquids and gases. A charcoal filter adsorbs molecules on the surface of each charcoal particle. Silica gel adsorbs water molecules from moist air and holds them on the surface of each grain. Adsorption releases heat called *heat of adsorption.*

The interaction of adsorbed molecules with the adsorbing surface may be weak or strong. Molecules are weakly held when physical attraction holds them to the adsorbing surface (see **Molecule** [Molecules and matter]). This process is called *physiosorption.* When adsorbed molecules are united chemically with the surface, they are strongly held. This process is called *chemisorption.* In chemisorption, the adsorbed molecules form a single layer. In physiosorption, they may form layers several molecules deep.   Robert B. Prigo

See also **Plant** (Movement of water).

Abstract art is a style of art that discards identifiable subject matter. The style originated in the early 1900's. It is sometimes called *nonobjective art* or *nonfigurative art.*

Abstract art broke with a long tradition in Western culture that considered art a kind of refined illustration. Works of art were often admired because of the importance given to the story or theme they represented. This view began to change in the early 1900's. At that time, painters allowed the means of imagemaking—brushstrokes, color, and shapes—to overshadow or distort the subject matter. They discovered that the formal characteristics of painting were interesting in their own right.

The first abstract art was produced by painters identified with such movements as Fauvism, Expressionism, Cubism, and Futurism. Their paintings were called "abstract," though subject matter could still be recognized in their work.

After about 1910, some artists eliminated all subject matter in favor of pure forms. Two distinct and opposite theoretical defenses of totally abstract art emerged. The Spiritualists worked from the belief that the elements of art could stir the soul and spirit directly. For these artists, references to the material world hindered their ability to convey emotional messages directly and powerfully. Leading Spiritualists were Wassily Kandinsky and Kasimir Malevich of Russia and Piet Mondrian of the Netherlands. Kandinsky was a founder of a German art movement known as Der Blaue Reiter (The Blue Rider). Malevich was a leader of a Russian movement called Suprematism. Mondrian was a member of a Dutch art movement known as Neoplasticism or Die Stijl.

The other major theory of abstract art was grounded on Materialism. It appeared first in the work of the Con-

structivist artists in Russia about 1915. Their art essentially dealt with textures, shapes, colors, and patterns, and rejected storytelling, poetry, or emotional experiences. To portray objectively the new age and its scientific basis, artists stressed geometric forms; flat, unmodulated colors; and an impersonal approach to their art. Leading Russian Constructivists included Vladimir Tatlin, El Lissitsky, Naum Gabo, and Alexander Rodchenko.

The term *abstract art* was originally confusing because it could mean art with altered but still recognizable content, or totally nonfigurative or nonobjective art. However, by the end of World War II in 1945, the term was used primarily as a synonym for art completely without recognizable subject matter. Total abstraction was given wide publicity through the work of the Abstract Expressionist, or New York School, artists such as Jackson Pollock, Willem de Kooning, Arshile Gorky, Franz Kline, and Robert Motherwell.   David Cateforis

Related articles in *World Book* include:
Abstract Expressionism
Cubism
Expressionism
Fauves
Futurism
Malevich, Kasimir

Painting (The 1900's in Europe;
The 1900's in North
America)
Sculpture (Modern
international sculpture)

Abstract Expressionism was a movement in American painting that flourished from the mid-1940's to the mid-1950's. The Abstract Expressionists developed a revolutionary approach to the nature and purpose of painting. They influenced artists in many countries.

The Abstract Expressionists rejected many of the customs and rules of earlier art. They did not paint traditional pictures that told a story or created the appearance of reality. Instead, the Abstract Expressionists emphasized

West Brant (1960), an oil painting on canvas by Franz Kline;
collection of Mr. and Mrs. Graham Gund (Art Resource)

Abstract Expressionist paintings include *West Brant,* a powerful black-and-white work by Franz Kline.

color, the physical qualities of paint, and the enveloping character of extremely large paintings.

The Abstract Expressionist movement was more a philosophical attitude than a style. For example, certain Abstract Expressionist works feature many shapes and thick paint, while others are simple and thinly painted. Some painters deliberately left portions of the canvas unpainted to provide a contrast with the painted areas. But all the diverse personalities in this movement shared the belief that both the figurative and abstract traditions of modern art could be used freely to express their feelings and their attitude toward life. They maintained that no matter how abstract their paintings appeared, there was always an underlying serious subject.

One of the important Abstract Expressionists was Jackson Pollock. He placed his canvas on the floor and dripped and splattered the paint from above. This technique led some critics to call Pollock and certain other members of the movement *action painters.* Other leading Abstract Expressionists included Willem de Kooning, Helen Frankenthaler, Adolph Gottlieb, Philip Guston, Franz Kline, Joan Mitchell, Robert Motherwell, Barnett Newman, Mark Rothko, Clyfford Still, and Bradley Walker Tomlin.   Dore Ashton

Each artist discussed in this article has a biography in *World Book.* See also **Painting** (Abstract Expressionism).

Abū Bakr. See Muslims (The early caliphs).

Abu Dhabi, *AH boo DAH bee* (pop. 1,267,000), also spelled *Abu Zaby,* is the capital of the United Arab Emirates (UAE), a confederation of seven Arab states. Abu Dhabi is also the capital of the emirate of Abu Dhabi, which is the largest of the seven states. The city is governed by the al-Nahyan family, which belongs to a large group of related Arab families called the Bani Yas. Members of another branch of the Bani Yas rule Dubai (also spelled *Dubayy),* the largest city in the UAE.

Abu Dhabi was founded about 1761. It soon became a pearl-fishing port. It lies on an island in the southeastern Persian Gulf and is linked to the mainland by two bridges. The city has developed rapidly since oil production from land-based and offshore fields began in the early 1960's. A national development program has helped the city improve its harbor and construct buildings, roads, parks, and an airport.   Imad Harb

See also **United Arab Emirates.**

Abu Simbel, *AH boo SIHM buhl,* **Temples of,** are two ancient Egyptian temples that were carved in a mountainside beside the Nile River in southern Egypt. The pharaoh Ramses II built the temples in the 1200's B.C. The Great Temple extended 200 feet (60 meters) into the mountainside. Four seated figures of Ramses II, each 67 feet (20 meters) high, guarded the entrance. Four figures of Ramses II and two of his wife, Queen Nefertari, stood at the entrance to the other temple.

The temples' original location is now covered by Lake Nasser, which was formed by the Aswan High Dam. In the mid-1960's, the temples were cut into huge blocks and moved to higher ground. About 50 nations contributed funds to this project.   Richard H. Wilkinson

See also **Egypt, Ancient** (map); **Ramses II.**

Abuja, *ah BOOH jah* (pop. 3,564,126), is the capital of Nigeria. The city lies in a hilly region in the central part of the country. For location, see **Nigeria** (political map).

Abuja is part of the Abuja Federal Capital Territory,

which has an area of about 3,100 square miles (8,000 square kilometers). The city itself covers about 100 square miles (260 square kilometers).

Abuja's major buildings include the National Mosque and the administrative headquarters of the Economic Community of West African States. Many modern roads connect Abuja with surrounding cities and towns. The city has a light-rail system and an international airport. Rock formations lying in or near the city include Aso and Zuma rocks. The Nigerian president's official residence stands near Aso Rock and is itself nicknamed Aso Rock.

Nigeria created the capital territory in 1976 mainly because Lagos, the former capital, was overcrowded and lacked room for expansion. Construction of the new city of Abuja has occurred since the 1980's. Abuja officially became the new capital in 1991. By the late 1990's, all of Nigeria's government ministries had moved their headquarters from Lagos to Abuja.   Ebere Onwudiwe

See also **Nigeria** (picture).

Abyssinia. See Ethiopia.

Abzug, *AB zuhg,* **Bella Savitzky** (1920-1998), a Democrat from New York, served in the United States House of Representatives from 1971 to 1977. She gained fame for her support of women's rights. In addition, Abzug supported legislation that promoted federal job programs, public transportation, and the individual's right to privacy. She served on the House Government Operations Committee.

Abzug was born on July 24, 1920, in New York City. She earned a law degree from Columbia University. In 1961, she helped establish Women Strike for Peace, a group that worked for nuclear disarmament. In 1971, Abzug helped found the National Women's Political Caucus, which aids women running for office. She died on March 31, 1998.   Guy Halverson

AC. See Electric current.

Acacia, *uh KAY shuh,* is the name given to a variety of trees and shrubs known for their sharp spines. But the many acacias that grow in Australia do not grow spines. In addition to Australia, acacias grow in parts of Africa, Asia, and the Americas. There are hundreds of *species* (kinds) of acacia. The flowers of most acacias are yellow or white and grow in round or long clusters. Many species of acacia have compound leaves consisting of

The catclaw acacia grows in the southwestern United States. The plant has yellow flowers. Its seeds grow in pods.

numerous leaflets. In some species, the leaves grow from wide, flat leafstalks. Other species lack true leaves and have only the leafstalks. Certain species, including the catclaw acacia of the southwestern United States and the bullhorn acacia of Mexico, have sharp spines. The bullhorn acacia has large, paired hornlike spines that are partly hollow and often inhabited by ferocious ants. These ants attack any other animal that invades the tree. Some acacias produce a gum called *gum arabic* that is used in making foods, drugs, and other products. The bark of various acacias produces *tannin,* a substance used to make leather. In arid regions, acacia leaves and fruits provide food for livestock and other animals. Several kinds of acacia have become endangered, mostly due to habitat destruction.   J. Massey

Scientific classification. Acacias belong to the pea family, Fabaceae or Leguminosae. The catclaw acacia is *Acacia greggii.* The bullhorn acacia is *A. cornigera.*

See also **Catechu; Mimosa.**

Academic freedom is a term that refers primarily to certain rights claimed by professors at universities and colleges. It also refers to rights claimed by students at those institutions and by the institutions themselves.

For professors, academic freedom means the right to teach, to conduct research, and to write without fear of dismissal, so long as the researcher or teacher has followed the academic discipline's standards for seeking the truth. For students, it means the right to challenge a professor's views without being penalized for being outspoken. For the institutions, it means the right to determine what is taught and what research is conducted on the campus, free of control from outside the university. For teachers, academic freedom has also included the freedom to engage in political speech and activities.

Academic freedom grew out of freedom of thought and expression, a basic right of any free society. Scholars insist on having the freedom to present the truth as they find it, even if it conflicts with popular belief, as long as they adhere to scholarly standards of care. Without such freedom, scholars cannot perform their vital role of seeking and spreading new knowledge. Scholars believe that creative research is impossible if its findings must be withheld or distorted to agree with established views. This spirit of free inquiry and teaching helps give universities and colleges their unique character.

The chief importance of academic freedom is that society benefits from the knowledge discovered by scholars. Yet, the history of academic freedom is largely the history of the many attacks on it.

Beginnings. The idea of academic freedom developed with the rise of universities in Europe during the 1100's and 1200's. The universities were self-governing, *ecclesiastical* (church) bodies, and many of these universities became famous and powerful. But even the most powerful could be subject to church control. The church persecuted many scholars whose ideas and teaching contradicted religious beliefs. One such scholar was the Italian astronomer and physicist Galileo, who had been a member of the faculty of the University of Padua. The church silenced him in 1633 for arguing that Earth moved around the sun. But over time, the rise of commerce and the need for knowledge sustained the idea of the university as a place where knowledge can freely be tested, sought, and taught.

By the early 1800's, the concept of academic freedom had been established in Germany, along with the idea of the university as a research institution. Professors could teach whatever they desired and could undertake any research. Students could study whatever they wanted, subject only to their taking a final examination. Such ideas influenced the growth of American universities.

In the United States, academic freedom has faced a variety of threats. In colonial times, religious intolerance presented the biggest danger to academic freedom. Universities dismissed many teachers whose religious beliefs conflicted with the established views. During the late 1800's, economic and political power became the major source of threats to academic freedom in the United States. Many private universities had wealthy benefactors as trustees, and most state universities had politically appointed trustees. Some trustees felt that the teaching in their universities should agree with their own economic and political views. As a result, a number of professors lost their jobs for teaching certain economic or political concepts. However, most university trustees respected academic freedom.

The 1900's. After World War II ended in 1945, academic freedom in the United States came under attack by many people who feared possible Communist infiltration of universities. An investigation by the Un-American Activities Committee of the U.S. House of Representatives found a few Communists on the faculty of a small number of universities. As a result, many people feared that most universities were full of Communists. A number of professors were unjustly accused of supporting Communism and lost their jobs.

In the 1960's, academic freedom faced new challenges—from the campus itself. Many students opposed the U.S. role in the Vietnam War (1957-1975)—and all forms of war as well. They resented having military research conducted on campus. They thought that funds spent for military purposes should go instead to help minority groups gain equality and to eliminate poverty and pollution. Some students also questioned the relationship of some of their courses to current problems.

The 2000's. In the early 2000's, a new challenge emerged from outside the universities. Organized groups mounted an effort for the states to enact a "Student Bill of Rights," limiting what professors can say in the classroom. Professors and college and university presidents strongly opposed these proposals as infringing, not protecting, academic freedom. No state has yet enacted the proposed law limiting the freedom to teach.

Matthew W. Finkin

Academy is the general name for a group of people or an organization that promotes art, literature, science, or some other field of knowledge. Some high schools are also called academies. See also **American Academy of Arts and Sciences; Education** (The 1700's); **French Academy; National Academies.**

Academy Award. See Motion picture (table: Academy Award winners).

Academy of Motion Picture Arts and Sciences is an honorary nonprofit organization. The academy was founded in 1927. Its members include leaders in every phase of filmmaking. Its purposes are to advance the arts and sciences of motion pictures; to foster cooperation in the industry for cultural, educational, and technological progress; and to recognize outstanding film achievements through the presentation of annual awards called Oscars. See also **Motion picture** (table).

Critically reviewed by the Academy of Motion Picture Arts and Sciences

Acadia, *uh KAY dee uh,* was a region and French colony in what is now mostly eastern Canada. It was part of New France, the French colonial empire in North America. Acadia included what are now the provinces of Nova Scotia, New Brunswick, and Prince Edward Island. Also in Acadia were parts of what are now the province of Quebec and the state of Maine. Acadia is best known as the setting for the romantic poem *Evangeline* (1847) by Henry Wadsworth Longfellow, an American poet.

The French explorer Pierre du Gua, Sieur de Monts, founded the original settlement in Acadia in 1604. Acadia remained a French settlement until the early 1700's, when it became involved in the struggle for control of North America between France and England.

During Queen Anne's War (1702-1713), Port-Royal, the seat of the Acadian government, surrendered to the British. The Treaty of Utrecht, which ended the war, gave Acadia to Britain. But a dispute arose when France only *ceded* (surrendered) what is now mainland Nova Scotia. The other parts of Acadia tried to remain neutral.

In 1755, during the French and Indian War (1754-1763), British officials tried to force the Acadians to swear allegiance to the British king. But the Acadians refused to do so. Between 1755 and 1763, about 10,000 men, women,

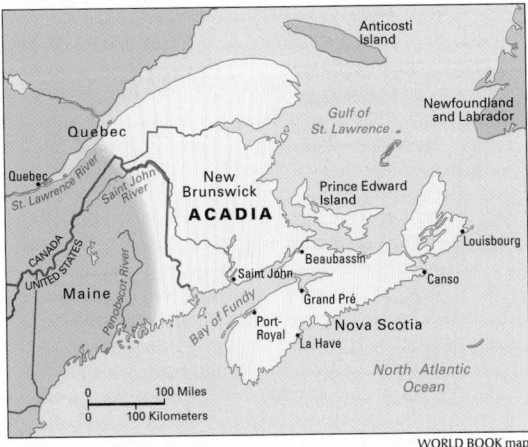

Location of Acadia

WORLD BOOK map

and children were forced to move to colonies farther south. After much hardship, most of these people in time returned to Acadia and settled in southeastern New Brunswick. More than 350,000 of their descendants still live there. About 4,000 Acadians went to Louisiana, a former French colony. Descendants of these Acadians are called Cajuns. Many of them still speak a French dialect. Since the early 1900's, many Cajuns have moved from Louisiana to eastern Texas to work in the petroleum industry and other businesses there.   John A. Dickinson

See also **Cajuns; Du Gua, Pierre, Sieur de Monts; French and Indian wars; Grand Pré; Nova Scotia** (The struggle in Acadia).

Acadia National Park, *uh KAY dee uh,* was the first national park established in the United States east of the

Mississippi River. It lies in Maine on Mount Desert Island, Isle au Haut, and the Schoodic Peninsula. The community of Bar Harbor lies next to the park. For the park's area, see **National Park System** (table: National parks).

Acadia National Park contains Cadillac Mountain (1,530 feet, or 466 meters), the highest granite mountain on the eastern coast. Forests and lakes make the park an excellent wildlife sanctuary. Acadia National Park was established on land donated by residents of the island in 1916.   Critically reviewed by the National Park Service

Acanthus, *uh KAN thuhs,* is a group of shrubs or herbs found chiefly in Asia, Africa, and southern Europe. They spread from underground stems and sometimes become pests. The flowers vary in color from white to purple and develop on rigid spikes. The large leaves have many narrow, pointed lobes. Acanthus plants prefer rich soil and some shade and can live with little water. A common acanthus *species* (kind) of the southwestern United States is the desert honeysuckle. In architecture, acanthus refers to a leafy decoration that was popular in Greek and Roman times. The design at the top of the Corinthian column is an example of acanthus. See **Column.**   Melinda F. Denton

Scientific classification. Acanthus plants belong to the acanthus family, Acanthaceae. The desert honeysuckle is *Anisacanthus thurberi.*

Acapulco, *ah kah POOL koh* (pop. 658,609), is a Mexican port and resort city. It is officially named Acapulco de Juárez *(day HWAH rehz).* Acapulco lies on a large, deep-water bay on the Pacific coast in the state of Guerrero (see **Mexico** [political map]). Acapulco's beautiful scenery, warm climate, active night life, and water activities attract both Mexican and foreign visitors. Many cruise ships stop there.

People may have lived in the Acapulco region since about 3000 B.C., and possibly earlier. Some of the earliest known ceramics from Mesoamerica (Mexico and Central America) were discovered there.

Spaniards founded Acapulco in 1550. Acapulco served as the chief Pacific port for trade between Spanish colonies in Mexico and the Philippines for more than 200 years. In 1616, the Spaniards built Fort San Diego to defend the port from pirates. Clashes occurred at Acapulco during Mexico's independence war (1810-1821); the Revolution of Ayutla (1854), an attempt to over-

Miguel Angel Alvarez Bernardo (licensed under CC BY-SA 2.0)

Scenic Acapulco lies on Mexico's Pacific coast. The warm, sunny climate and beautiful beaches of this popular resort city attract thousands of visitors yearly.

throw dictator Antonio López de Santa Anna; and the French occupation of Mexico in the 1860's.

Acapulco became a prime resort destination for Hollywood actors and other wealthy travelers in the mid-1900's. The city's population grew rapidly during that time. Continued population growth and a dramatic increase in tourism led to serious pollution, especially in the bay. As a result of pollution and competition from other resorts, the city became less popular. In the late 1900's, the federal, state, and local governments began a major effort to clean up the city. This effort and the completion of a highway from Acapulco to Mexico City have helped revive tourism.   Paul Hart

Acceleration. See Falling bodies, Law of; Motion (Describing motion); Velocity (Acceleration).

Accelerator, Particle. See Particle accelerator.

Accent, *AK sehnt,* in language, is an emphasis placed on a syllable in a word and is often called *stress.* Dictionaries usually indicate an accented syllable by the mark, ', placed after the syllable. A secondary accent can be indicated by two marks, ", or by one light accent mark. Accented syllables can also be shown by capital letters or italics. Where pronunciations are given in *The World Book Encyclopedia,* capital letters are used for the syllable with the primary accent and small capital letters for the secondary accent. See **Key to pronunciation** at the beginning of the A volume.

The tendency in English is to shift the accent toward the beginning of the word. The accent in the word *re VOKE* shifts toward the beginning in the form *ir REV ocable.* This tendency often causes a change in the language. The accent in the word *BAL con y* was once placed on the second syllable *(bal CON y).*

Words spelled in the same way are sometimes accented on different syllables. This usually means they have different meanings or different usages. The verb of a pair of identical words may have the accent on the second syllable, although the noun or adjective has it on the first. For example, *ab SENT* is the verb, while *AB sent* is the adjective. Accent is important in sentences as well as in words.   Marianne Cooley

See also **Meter** (in poetry); **Music** (Rhythm).

Accommodation, in physiology. See **Eye** (Focusing).

Accordion is any of a family of portable reed instruments with bellows suspended in front of the player by shoulder straps. The player stretches and compresses the bellows by hand. These movements force air past metal reeds, making them vibrate and produce sounds. The right hand plays buttons or keys arranged in the order of the scale, like piano keys. The left hand presses buttons that produce single tones and chords. In many countries, accordions are used in folk and popular music. Cyrillys Damian invented an accordion in Vienna in 1829. But the principle had been known for centuries in China.   Valerie Woodring Goertzen

Accounting is a system of gathering, summarizing, and communicating financial information for a business firm, government, or other organization. Accounting, also called *accountancy,* enables decision makers to interpret financial information and use the results in planning for the future. Business people often call accounting the "language of business" because they use accounting data in communicating about a firm's activities. Information provided by accountants helps managers

and other executives understand the results of business transactions and evaluate the financial status of their organization. With this knowledge, managers can make informed decisions about such matters as production, marketing, and financing. Charities, churches, colleges, government agencies, and other nonprofit organizations also use accounting to keep track of their finances.

Accounting is closely related to *bookkeeping,* which deals mainly with recording and analyzing financial information. Accountants carry out these activities but also design and install information systems, perform audits, interpret financial statements, and prepare tax returns.

Financial reports

In the United States and many other countries, publicly owned businesses are required by law to issue financial reports. These reports are used by investors; officials of banks, government agencies, and labor unions; and others interested in a firm or its industry. Accountants prepare the reports, which provide summaries of the financial condition of a company. Firms within a country use similar accounting procedures so that their financial reports can be compared. These procedures are called *generally accepted accounting principles.* The Financial Accounting Standards Board (FASB), an organization of professional accountants, establishes generally

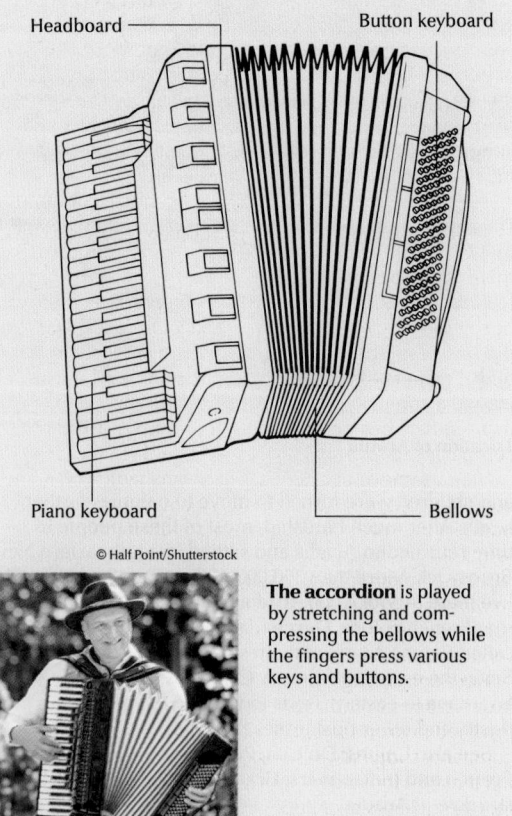

Headboard

Button keyboard

Piano keyboard

Bellows

© Half Point/Shutterstock

The accordion is played by stretching and compressing the bellows while the fingers press various keys and buttons.

accepted accounting principles for the United States.

The most important financial reports include *balance sheets, income statements,* and *statements of cash flows.* A balance sheet shows a company's assets, liabilities, and net worth. An income statement is a report of a firm's revenue and expenses during a certain period. The bottom line of an income statement shows whether the company had a net profit or a net loss for that period. A statement of cash flows shows the amounts of money flowing into a company and out of it as a result of its operating, investing, and financing activities.

Organizations that do not seek a profit need many of the same kinds of financial reports. For example, private schools must keep track of their tuition income and their expenses. A government agency may wish to compare the cost of a program with the benefits.

Fields of accounting

Accountants may be classified by the type of organization for which they work. For example, *business accountants* are employed by all types of companies. A small firm may have one general accountant who handles all financial records. But a large corporation may have many accountants for the various duties involved.

Organizations or individuals may hire professional *public accountants* for occasional tasks or special accounting services. In the United States, most public accountants have passed a state examination and obtained a license to practice as a *certified public accountant* (CPA). Such accountants are called *chartered accountants* in Canada, the United Kingdom, and some other countries. Many CPA's in the United States work for one of the four large public accounting firms that dominate the nation's accounting industry. These four firms, which provide a wide variety of services, are Deloitte Touche Tohmatsu; EY (formerly known as Ernst & Young); KPMG International; and PricewaterhouseCoopers.

Most accountants specialize in a field of accounting. The major fields include financial accounting, management accounting, tax accounting, auditing, and management consulting services.

Financial accounting involves the preparation of a business's financial statements, mainly for users outside the business. These reports are used by owners and potential owners of a business and by people who have loaned a company money. Some government agencies that regulate business and the stock market require companies to submit financial statements to them.

Management accounting helps managers plan and control a company's operations. Accountants prepare budgets to express management's goals in financial terms. After a budget has been adopted, *performance reports* compare actual results with the budget. *Cost accountants* help management keep track of how much it costs a company to make the product, or provide the service, it sells.

Tax accounting consists of preparing tax returns for organizations or individuals and determining the taxes involved in proposed business transactions. Tax accountants suggest ways to save money on taxes. They must have a thorough knowledge of the tax laws that affect their clients or employers. They also must know the details of court rulings in a wide variety of tax cases.

Auditing involves the examination of an organiza-

tion's financial statements and records. Auditors from outside the organization ensure that the organization's financial statements present information fairly and that they follow generally accepted accounting principles. People use such statements in deciding which companies to invest in and lend money to.

Internal auditors are employees of an organization who make sure that the organization follows the accounting procedures management wants. They also strive to increase efficiency and reduce waste.

Management consulting services consist of a variety of activities that many accountants perform. These services include the design and installation of computerized financial information systems, assistance in setting up employee pension plans, and the planning of an individual's personal finances.

The history of accounting

Accounting dates back to the earliest known civilizations of the Middle East and Central America. As these civilizations advanced, skilled people called *scribes* performed many of the accounting functions. They put business transactions in writing and assured compliance with commercial agreements. As commerce developed and economic systems became more complex, the need for accounting grew. Explanations of many bookkeeping techniques appeared in 1494 in *Summa de Arithmetica, Geometria, Proportioni et Proportionalita,* a mathematics book written by the Italian monk Luca Pacioli.

The later development of accounting largely paralleled the evolution of big business in industrialized countries. As commercial and industrial activity accelerated, the need for detailed and accurate financial information became increasingly important.

Following the stock market crash of 1929, the U.S. Congress passed legislation to address problems in financial reporting and in the regulation of *securities* (stocks and bonds). The Securities Exchange Act of 1934 established the Securities and Exchange Commission (SEC), a federal agency that administers and enforces securities laws.

In the early 2000's, a series of corporate failures related to faulty or dishonest accounting practices occurred. In November 2001, Enron Corporation, a U.S.-based energy company, revealed that it had overstated its earnings by several hundred million dollars. In June 2002, WorldCom Inc., a U.S.-based communications company, announced that it had improperly concealed billions of dollars of expenses. Both Enron and WorldCom filed for bankruptcy soon after their announcements. The failures led to criminal investigations and charges of fraudulent accounting practices. Many of the charges focused on Arthur Andersen, an accounting firm that worked with both Enron and WorldCom.

In July 2002, Congress passed the Sarbanes-Oxley Act, in response to the accounting scandals. The act's numerous provisions included the establishment of a new oversight board to monitor the accounting industry. The act also prohibited auditing firms from engaging in certain nonauditing services for corporate clients. In addition, it required executives of public corporations to certify the accuracy of financial information given to shareholders.   Patricia Casey Douglas

See also **Bookkeeping; Spreadsheet.**

Accra, *uh KRAH* or *AK ruh* (pop. 964,879; met. area pop. 1,420,065), is the capital and largest city of Ghana. It lies on the northern coast of the Gulf of Guinea. For the location of Accra, see **Ghana** (map). Accra's transportation facilities include a railroad and an international airport. The city's industries include the production of tile and brick and the processing of diamonds and lumber. The University of Ghana is in Legon, a residential area north of the city.

Accra was established by the Ga people by the mid-1600's. It was a center of the African slave trade from the 1500's to the mid-1800's. European nations competing for slaves built several forts in Accra. In 1923, a railroad linking Accra and the interior added to the city's economic importance.   Samuel Decalo

Acculturation. See Culture (Contact with other cultures).

Ace is a pilot who shot down at least five enemy aircraft during a war. By military custom, most air forces award a *victory* or a *kill* only when a pilot causes an enemy aircraft to crash or destroys it in flight. In addition, most air forces require confirmation by an eyewitness or by videotape or film of the incident. Because of human error and differences in counting practices, the actual number of aircraft a pilot has shot down can be higher or lower than a force's official tally of victories.

The custom of qualifying aces originated during World War I (1914-1918). A minimum of five victories became widely used as the standard for becoming an ace.

The leading aces of World War I became national heroes. The top ace of the war was Baron Manfred von Richthofen of Germany, who was known as the *Red Baron* or *Red Knight.* Richthofen shot down 80 enemy aircraft before he was killed in action in 1918. Aces from other countries included Captain René Fonck of France, with 75 kills; and Major Edward Mannock of the United Kingdom, with 61. Canadian Major Billy Bishop claimed 72 kills, but some historians have questioned that number. The top American ace, Captain Eddie Rickenbacker, had 26 kills.

During World War II (1939-1945), Major Erich Hartmann of Germany was the top ace, with 352 victories. In addition, thousands of other German aviators qualified as aces by U.S. standards, many with 100 victories or more. Warrant Officer Hiroyoshi Nishizawa of Japan destroyed or damaged 87 Allied planes. Major Richard I. Bong of the U.S. Army Air Force became the leading American ace, shooting down 40 Japanese planes. Six other Americans also equaled or surpassed Rickenbacker's record. The Soviet Union's top ace, Major Ivan Kozhedub, claimed 62 victories from 1942 to 1945.

During the Korean War (1950-1953), U.S. Air Force Captain James Jabara became the first jet-to-jet combat ace, destroying 15 enemy jets. During the Vietnam War (1957-1975), two American pilots became aces.
  Barrett Tillman

See also **Air Force, United States** (History); **Bishop, Billy; Richthofen, Baron Manfred von; Rickenbacker, Eddie.**

Acerola, *AS uh ROH luh,* is the fruit of a bushy tree that grows 10 to 15 feet (3.0 to 4.6 meters) tall. It is native to the West Indies and parts of Mexico, Central America, and northern South America. The tree has deep roots and grows well even in poor soil, if there is enough rain.

WORLD BOOK illustration by Kate Lloyd-Jones, Linden Artists Ltd.
Acerola is the nutritious fruit of a bushy tree that is also called the acerola. The ripened fruit resembles a deep red cherry.

The acerola is also called the *Puerto Rican, West Indian,* or *Barbados cherry.* The fruits are about the size of cherries. When ripe, acerolas have a deep red color and soft flesh. Most have a tart flavor.

The acerola ranks as the richest known natural source of vitamin C (ascorbic acid). The vitamin C content varies in different varieties and under different environmental conditions. Green fruits contain more vitamin C than ripe fruits. The edible part of the acerola has about 1 to 4 percent ascorbic acid. In other kinds of fruits, even 0.06 percent ascorbic acid is high. Jelly and juices made from acerolas retain the fruit's high vitamin C content.

The acerola was eaten by Indians long before the Europeans came to the Western Hemisphere. During the late 1940's, commercial canners began to use the acerola in fruit juice mixes. Today, the fruit is an important crop in Puerto Rico.   Philip J. Ito

Scientific classification. The acerola belongs to the malpighia family, Malpighiaceae. The scientific name is *Malpighia emarginata.* In the past, it was often classified as *M. glabra* or *M. puncifolia.*

Acetaminophen, *uh SEET uh MIHN uh fuhn,* is a commonly used drug that relieves pain and reduces fever. Many people take acetaminophen instead of aspirin because they are allergic to aspirin, have stomach ailments, or use *anticoagulants* (substances that prevent or slow blood clotting). Acetaminophen, unlike aspirin, does not irritate the stomach or interfere with blood clotting. However, acetaminophen cannot reduce inflammation nearly as well as aspirin. Therefore, it is not as useful in treating inflammatory conditions, such as arthritis or rheumatic fever.

Acetaminophen can be purchased without a prescription under many trade names, including Tylenol. Doctors advise people to be extremely careful not to take more than the recommended dose. The drug can cause liver damage that may, in some cases, progress to liver failure and death.

Acetaminophen was first used in medicine in 1893. However, it gained widespread use only after 1949, when scientists discovered that another popular drug, *phenacetin,* is converted to acetaminophen in the body. Acetaminophen proved to be as effective as phenacetin but less toxic.   Eugene M. Johnson, Jr.

Acetate, *AS uh tayt,* is a manufactured fiber produced from wood. It is delicate and resembles silk in feel and appearance. Acetate is used primarily in textiles, especially draperies, linings for clothing, and formal wear.

In a common method of acetate production, called *acetylation,* pulped wood is mixed with acetic acid, acetic anhydride, and sulfuric acid. The mixture is added to water, and white flakes of *cellulose acetate* form. The flakes are dried and dissolved in acetone. The resulting solution, pure or with dyes added, is then forced through a *spinneret* (plate with tiny holes), forming a continuous filament. Acetate filaments can be spun into threads and yarns of different thicknesses and textures.

Acetate's naturally shiny finish can be dulled by adding titanium dioxide to the solution before forcing it through the spinneret. Acetate melts when exposed to temperatures of 350 °F (177 °C) or higher, so acetate fabrics must be ironed at low settings.   Richard V. Gregory

Acetic acid, *uh SEE tihk,* is an important organic acid and industrial chemical. It gives vinegar its sour taste. Vinegar used in the home contains about 5 percent of the acid (see **Vinegar**). Pure acetic acid is called *glacial acetic acid* because it solidifies at 62 °F (17 °C), the temperature of a cool room. When diluted with water, it is known simply as acetic acid.

Georg Stahl, a German chemist, first isolated glacial acetic acid from vinegar in 1700. Commercially, the acid is usually produced by such chemical processes as the oxidation of acetaldehyde with air in the presence of catalysts. Acetaldehyde is itself formed from the oxidation of ethylene obtained from petroleum.

One of the chief uses of acetic acid is as an intermediate for making other chemicals. Manufacturers convert it into acetic anhydride and acetate esters. Acetic anhydride is used to make acetate fibers and cellulose acetate, a plastic. Ethyl acetate is an important ester used as a solvent for varnishes and in nail polish remover. As a reagent, acetic acid is used to make synthetic materials, rubber, and aspirin and other pharmaceuticals.

Acetic acid is a colorless liquid with a sharp, irritating odor. It is a caustic substance, and concentrated forms of it can cause severe burns. The chemical formula of acetic acid is CH_3COOH.   W. Dean Harman

Acetone, *AS uh tohn,* is an important industrial chemical. Its chief use is in making other compounds. Industry prepares acetone commercially from isopropyl alcohol, using brass or copper catalysts. Acetone can also be obtained from corn and other starchy products by fermenting them with a special bacteria and then distilling them.

Acetone also forms in the body of a diabetic person. Its presence in urine is one symptom of the disease.

Acetone dissolves many substances, including gums, oils, resins, fats, and cellulose. Industry uses acetone in paints, varnish removers, nail polish and nail polish removers, and some polishes and lacquers. It is a clear, colorless, flammable liquid with a fruity odor. It mixes easily with water. Its chemical formula is CH_3COCH_3, and it boils at 133.2 °F (56.2 °C).   Suzanne R. Abrams

See also **Acetylene.**

Acetylene, *uh SEHT uh leen,* also called *ethyne,* is a colorless, flammable gas used for welding and for preparing other chemical compounds. Its chemical formula is C_2H_2. Acetylene is poisonous if inhaled. It also forms explosive mixtures with air. Edmund Davy, an English chemist, first produced acetylene in 1836. The gas was forgotten until 1860, when the French chemist Marcellin Berthelot discovered a way to synthesize the gas from carbon and hydrogen, using an electric arc.

Acetylene mixed with oxygen produces a flame that reaches a temperature of about 6000 °F (3316 °C). This flame, called the *oxyacetylene flame,* is used to weld and cut metals. In welding, the edges of the metal are melted by the flame and then fused together (see **Welding**). In cutting, the metal to be cut is heated but not melted by the oxyacetylene flame. Then a fine stream of oxygen is sprayed onto the metal. The oxygen burns through the metal, leaving a clean-cut edge. Acetylene also serves as a raw material in the preparation of certain chemical compounds used to manufacture plastics. In addition, acetylene is used in the manufacture of vitamins.

Acetylene may be produced commercially by creating a chemical reaction between calcium carbide and water. It is also made in industry by decomposing methane at high temperatures. Acetylene is stored in cylinders under high pressure. If not properly handled, the compressed gas can break down chemically and explode. To prevent explosions, acetylene is dissolved in acetone in special cylinders.   Suzanne R. Abrams

See also **Acetone; Calcium carbide; Hydrocarbon.**

Acetylsalicylic acid. See **Aspirin.**

Achaeans, *uh KEE uhnz,* were people of ancient Greece. According to the Greek poet Homer, they once lived in the Peloponnesus (Greece's southern peninsula) and on the islands of Crete, Rhodes, Cephalonia, and Ithaca. The term *Achaeans* appears in Homer's epic poem the *Iliad* to identify the Greeks who fought in the Trojan War. Achaeans are also mentioned in Hittite documents from the 1300's and 1200's B.C., found in what is now Turkey. Some Achaeans may have taken part in sea raids on Egypt in the early 1100's B.C. Later in the 1100's B.C., Dorian invaders swept across Greece and drove the Achaeans to a region in the northern Peloponnesus. This region later became known as Achaea. In the 300's B.C., 12 Achaean cities formed a confederation that was known as the Achaean League. The league played an important part in Greek politics, opposing first the Macedonians and then the Romans. The Romans conquered Greece and broke up the league in 146 B.C.   Jack L. Davis

See also **Aeolians; Dorians; Iliad.**

Achebe, *ah CHAY bay,* **Chinua,** *CHIHN oo ah* (1930-2013), was a leading Nigerian author best known for novels that explore the psychological and social impact of Western colonialism on traditional African societies. Achebe, who wrote in English, also dealt with African life after Africans gained their independence from colonial powers in the mid-1900's. Critics have praised the simplicity of his language, his use of proverbs and folklore, his irony, and his objectivity in presenting complex issues. In 2007, Achebe received the Man Booker International Prize, now the International Booker Prize, for lifetime achievement in fiction published in English.

Achebe gained international recognition with his first novel, *Things Fall Apart* (1958). The work portrays the influence of colonial European missionaries and government on a west African tribe in the late 1800's. Achebe continued this theme in the novel *Arrow of God* (1964). He dealt with late colonial and postcolonial life in Africa in the novels *No Longer at Ease* (1960), *A Man of the People* (1966), and *Anthills of the Savannah* (1987).

Achebe also wrote the short-story collections *The Sacrificial Egg* (1962) and *Girls at War* (1973). He wrote a number of children's books, including *Chike and the River* (1966), *How the Leopard Got His Claws* (1972) as co-author, and *The Flute* and *The Drum* (both 1977). His poetry appears in *Beware, Soul-Brother* (1971), *Christmas in Biafra* (1973), and *Collected Poems* (2004). Many of his essays were published in *Morning Yet on Creation Day* (1975), *The Trouble with Nigeria* (1983), *Hopes and Impediments* (1988), and *The Education of a British-Protected Child* (2009). He also wrote a memoir, *There Was a Country: A Personal History of Biafra* (2012).

Albert Chinualumogu Achebe was born on Nov. 16, 1930, in Ogidi, Nigeria, which was then a British colony. He attended University College in Ibadan from 1948 to 1953. Achebe worked in broadcasting in Nigeria from 1954 to 1966 and was professor of English at the University of Nigeria from 1976 to 1981. In 1990, he was paralyzed from the waist down in an auto accident in Nigeria. He was Professor of Languages and Literature at Bard College in the United States from 1993 until he moved to Brown University in 2009. Achebe died on March 21, 2013.   Peter Nazareth

Acheron. See Hades.

Acheson, *ACH ih suhn,* **Dean Gooderham** (1893-1971), was United States secretary of state under President Harry S. Truman from 1949 to 1953. Earlier, he had served as undersecretary to three secretaries of state—Cordell Hull, James F. Byrnes, and George C. Marshall.

In the Acheson-Lilienthal Report of 1946, Acheson urged international control of nuclear power. He negotiated the treaty that led to the North Atlantic Treaty Organization (NATO) in 1949. He began carrying out the Marshall Plan in 1948. This plan aided the economic recovery of Europe after World War II (see **Marshall Plan**). Acheson began much of the Truman Doctrine to protect Greece and Turkey from Soviet imperialism (see **Truman, Harry S.** [The Truman Doctrine]).

Senator Joseph McCarthy and other people accused Acheson of "coddling" Communists in the State Department. His critics also blamed him for encouraging the Communist invasion of South Korea in 1950 and for the Communist victory in China in 1949. Most historians have rejected these charges against Acheson.

Acheson wrote many books, including *Present at the Creation: My Years in the State Department* (1969), which won the 1970 Pulitzer Prize for history. He was born on April 11, 1893, in Middletown, Connecticut. He died on Oct. 12, 1971.   William E. Pemberton

Achilles, *uh KIHL eez,* in Greek mythology, was the best Greek warrior in the Trojan War. In the 10th year of that war, the Greeks defeated the city of Troy.

The events in Achilles's life are legends but may have some historical basis. Achilles was the son of Peleus, the king of Phthia in Thessaly, and Thetis, an immortal sea nymph. Soon after Achilles was born, Thetis dipped him in the River Styx, whose water would make him invulnerable, like a god. However, the immortalizing water did not touch the heel by which Thetis held him.

When the Trojan War began, Agamemnon, the commander of the Greek forces, sent soldiers to recruit Achilles into the Greek army. Thetis feared her son, who was nearing manhood, would be killed in battle. She sent him, disguised in women's clothing, to live with King Lycomedes on the island of Skíros. But Odysseus (Ulysses in Latin), who was a cunning Greek general, saw through the disguise, and Achilles joined the army.

In the last year of the war, Achilles quarreled with Agamemnon, who took away Briseis, a young woman Achilles had captured as a prize of war. In anger, Achilles refused to fight any longer and, without him, the Greek forces began to lose. Achilles allowed Patroclus, his best friend, to join the battle wearing his armor. Patroclus was slain by Hector, the greatest Trojan warrior. Enraged, Achilles returned to the battlefield, slaughtering everyone in his path. He eventually killed Hector, aided by the goddess Athena. According to some stories, Hector's brother Paris shot an arrow into Achilles's heel, and Achilles died from the wound.   Nancy Felson

See also **Trojan War; Iliad; Hector; Priam.**

Achilles tendon, *uh KIHL eez,* is the tendon at the back of the ankle. It attaches the muscles of the calf to the heel bone and is one of the strongest tendons in the body. The name *Achilles tendon* comes from the legend of Achilles, a Greek hero killed by an arrow in the heel.

The Achilles tendon may rupture as the result of a powerful upward movement of the foot or a blow to the calf when the calf muscles are contracted. This injury most commonly occurs in people over the age of 30 who compete in sports that involve running. Complete rupture frequently is accompanied by a snap, severe pain, and the inability to push off or stand on the toes. As soon as possible, ice should be applied to the back of the ankle, and the leg should be raised and immobilized. Surgery may be necessary to sew the tendon together. The person should stay off the injured leg for up to two months before beginning a program of gradual stretching and strengthening exercises. Full recovery may take a year or more.   John R. Conway III

See also **Ankle** (illustration); **Tendon** (illustration).

Acid is any of a group of chemical compounds with certain similar properties. Solutions of acids have a sour taste and produce a prickling or burning sensation if they come into contact with the skin. They dissolve many metals and turn blue litmus paper red. Chemical compounds called *bases* or *alkalis* neutralize acids.

Many acids occur naturally and some are essential for life. For example, *hydrochloric acid* (HCl) is produced in the stomach of most people and helps digestion. Acids are also used widely in industry, and they are a part of a large number of foods and beverages. But many acids are poisonous, and strong acids can cause severe burns. Chemists use several definitions to describe the behavior of acids. When water is the solvent, an acid is often defined as a compound that dissolves to produce *hydrogen ions* (H+) in solution. A hydrogen atom consists of one proton, which has a positive electric charge, and one electron, which has a negative charge. A hydrogen ion is the proton that remains when the atom loses its electron. In solution, the proton is closely associated with solvent molecules, forming *hydronium ions* (H_3O+).

An acid may also be defined as a substance that serves as a *proton donor*—that is, it readily gives up a proton to another substance. However, acids are most broadly defined as compounds that are *electron pair acceptors*. This definition describes all acids, including those that have no hydrogen that they can release and that cannot serve as proton donors. The acid accepts a pair of electrons from another atom or molecule. In such cases, the acid and the electron pair donor form a new molecule in which they share the electrons.

The strength of an acid depends on the degree to which the acid *dissociates* (breaks up) in solution to form hydrogen ions. For example, in water solution, every molecule of hydrogen chloride (HCl) releases a hydrogen ion to form hydrochloric acid. Hydrochloric acid is therefore considered a strong acid. *Acetic acid* (CH_3COOH), which is found in vinegar, forms only a few hydrogen ions in solution. It is a weak acid.

Inorganic acids, in general, do not contain carbon atoms. Many inorganic acids are strong acids. They are used in the production of other chemicals, explosives, fertilizers, metals, paints, plastics, and synthetic fibers, and in the refining of petroleum. *Sulfuric acid* (H_2SO_4), a strong inorganic acid, is commonly used as the fluid in automobile batteries. Other important inorganic acids are hydrochloric acid and *nitric acid* (HNO_3).

Organic acids contain carbon atoms. They are used in beverages, cosmetics, detergents, foods, drugs, plastics, and soaps. Common organic acids include *citric acid* ($C_6H_8O_7$), which is found in citrus fruits; *ascorbic acid* ($C_6H_8O_6$), or vitamin C; and *acetylsalicylic acid* ($C_9H_8O_4$), or aspirin. *Amino acids,* which contain nitrogen, are also organic acids. Amino acids are the building blocks of proteins, and some of them are necessary for human life.   Marianna A. Busch

Related articles in *World Book* include:

Acids

Acetic acid	Lactic acid	Salicylic acid
Amino acid	Nitric acid	Stearic acid
Citric acid	Oxalic acid	Sulfuric acid
Formic acid	Phosphoric acid	Tannic acid
Hydrochloric acid	Prussic acid	Tartaric acid
Hypochlorous acid		

Other related articles

Acid rain	Base	pH
Anhydride	Litmus	Salt, Chemical

Acid rain is precipitation that has become acidic. It is caused by pollution in the air. The term also includes acidic sleet and snow. Acid rain harms thousands of lakes, rivers, and streams worldwide. It kills fish and other wildlife. It also damages buildings, bridges, and statues. In high concentrations, it can harm forests and soil.

Acid rain forms when water vapor in the air reacts with certain chemical compounds. For example, sulfur dioxide and nitrogen oxide react to form sulfuric and nitric acid. Such compounds come largely from the burning of *fossil fuels*—that is, fuels made from once-living material, such as coal, gasoline, and oil. Most automobiles, factories, and power plants burn such fuels for energy. Regions affected by acid rain include large parts of eastern North America, northern and central Europe, and parts of Asia. Tall smokestacks in urban areas have enabled winds to spread more pollutants—and more acid rain—farther away into rural areas.

Scientists and engineers have developed ways to reduce the acidity of rain. For example, several kinds of devices remove sulfur and nitrogen compounds from fuels or industrial emissions before they reach the atmosphere. Adding lime to lakes and rivers and their drainage areas temporarily neutralizes their acidity. But the neutralization may have harmful side effects.

In 1990, the United States Congress amended the Clean Air Act of 1970 to reduce acid rain in the United States and Canada. The amendments tightened emissions standards. They also required fuels that burn more cleanly. In 1999, the World Health Organization published air quality guidelines designed to reduce acid rain and other environmental problems.

Marian Chertow

See also **Air pollution.**

Acid reflux is a common medical condition in which acid from the stomach flows back into the esophagus. It is also called *gastroesophageal reflux.* Symptoms include heartburn, chest pain, gas, and vomiting. Prolonged acid reflux can cause inflammation of the esophagus. In a few cases, such inflammation can in turn lead to ulcerations, scarring, and even cancer of the esophagus. When acid reflux damages the esophagus, the condition is called *gastroesophageal reflux disease* (GERD).

Acid reflux is caused by weakness in the *lower esophageal sphincter*—the ring of muscles separating the stomach and the esophagus. This weakness allows stomach acid to leak back into the esophagus. Excessive body weight and dietary factors that increase the amount of stomach acid can also cause acid reflux. Dietary factors include alcohol, caffeine, chocolate, nicotine, and some antibiotics and other drugs.

Acid reflux is usually a temporary condition with symptoms that are easily treated. Making some lifestyle changes, such as maintaining normal body weight, eating a low-fat diet, and avoiding certain foods and drugs, can improve the condition. Antacids and medications that stop acid production in the stomach may also be useful. However, individuals should consult a physician if the symptoms of acid reflux persist.   Keith J. Benkov

See also **Esophagus; Heartburn.**

ACLU. See American Civil Liberties Union.

Acne is a skin disorder that occurs most commonly among teenagers. It consists of various kinds of blemishes, mainly on the face, upper chest, and back. A few blemishes are normal, but severe acne may result in permanent scarring. Some teenagers find severe acne so distressing that they develop emotional problems.

In most cases, acne appears during early adolescence—at about the age of 13, when a child starts to develop physically into an adult. Chemical substances called *hormones* control this development. One kind of hormone stimulates the oil glands in the skin. These glands, which are called *sebaceous glands,* grow larger and produce more oil. Each sebaceous gland empties into a *hair follicle,* a cylinderlike structure that surrounds a hair. Normally, the oil empties out of the follicle through a pore that opens onto the surface of the skin.

Sometimes, the pores become plugged and oil accumulates under the plugs. A plugged pore forms a blemish called a *blackhead* or *whitehead.* The black color of a blackhead comes from a normal skin pigment that darkens when exposed to air. A whitehead develops if a pore is so clogged that no air can enter.

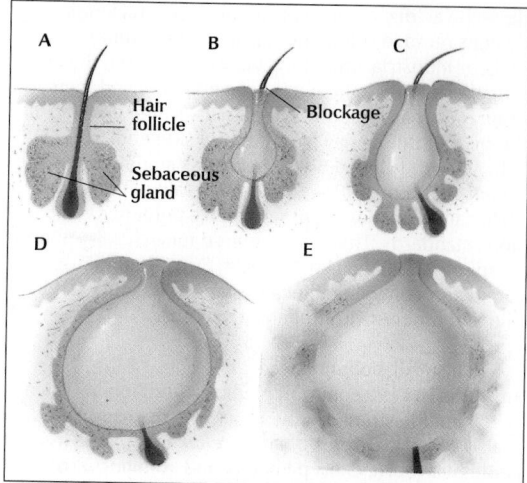

The development of an acne pimple is illustrated here. Figure A shows a normal hair follicle and sebaceous gland. In figure B, a blockage prevents the flow of oil out of the hair follicle. Bacteria breed in the backed-up oil. In figures C and D, the follicle swells with pus. The walls of the follicle eventually burst, and the pus drains away, as shown in figure E.

Small, pus-filled bumps called *pimples,* or tender red lumps called *cysts,* may also develop. In pimples and cysts, a type of bacteria called *Propionibacterium acnes* breeds in the follicles, sebaceous glands, and backed-up oil, producing inflammation that causes the redness and pus. Cysts may leave permanent scars, but pimples usually do not scar unless squeezed or picked.

A poor diet, worry, and various bad habits are often blamed for acne, but they have little to do with the disorder. A balanced diet, enough sleep and exercise, and regular washing are good for the complexion and general health but cannot prevent or cure acne. Mild acne can be treated with nonprescription lotions that contain benzoyl peroxide or other medications. Heavy makeup makes acne worse and should not be used.

Severe acne should be treated by a physician. An antibiotic called *tetracycline* may be prescribed. This drug blocks the growth and reproduction of *Propionibacterium acnes* bacteria. Medications containing vitamin A acid may be applied to the skin to help prevent new blemishes. Other treatment used by doctors includes removing blackheads, freezing the skin with dry ice or liquid nitrogen to make it peel, and using a sun lamp. A drug called *isotretinoin* may be used to treat severe acne. But this drug, which has the trade name Accutane, can cause birth defects. It should not be used by women who are pregnant or who may become pregnant while undergoing treatment.   David T. Woodley

See also **Abscess; Pimple.**

Aconcagua, *AH kahn KAH gwah,* is an eroded volcano that has long been dormant. It is the highest mountain in the Western Hemisphere and the highest peak outside of Asia. Aconcagua is part of the Andes mountain range in South America. It stands 22,841 feet (6,962 meters) high in western Argentina, near the border of Chile. Long ago, Aconcagua was probably more than 1,000 feet (300 meters) taller than it is today. However, the up-

per portion of the volcano has crumbled away, and few traces of its crater remain.   David J. Keeling

See also **Andes Mountains; Argentina** (terrain map); **Mountain** (diagram: Major mountains).

Aconite, *AK uh nyt,* is a group of flowering plants that thrive in cool, northern regions. They are *perennials,* which means they can live for more than two years. There are hundreds of aconite *species* (kinds). Most of them grow in Asia. Aconite flowers bloom in spring and summer and vary in color from purple-blue to yellow and white.

Aconites may grow from 1 to 6 feet (30 to 180 centimeters) high. The upper parts of their flowers resemble hoods or helmets. The roots, seeds, and leaves of some aconites are poisonous. A species of aconite called the common monkshood produces a drug also called *aconite.* This drug is used in traditional Asian medicine. The drug aconite contains a powerful poison, *aconitine,* that can be deadly.   Jerry M. Baskin

Scientific classification. Aconites make up the genus *Aconitum.* The common monkshood is *Aconitum napellus.*

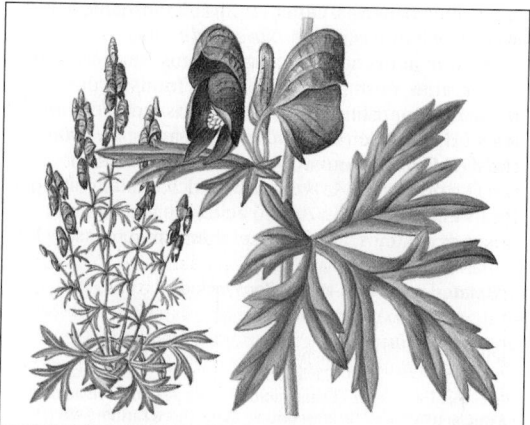

The common monkshood is an aconite that has purplish flowers. The plant produces a poisonous drug also called *aconite.*

Acorn is the nut produced by various kinds of oak trees. Acorns are sometimes used to feed hogs. Many wild birds and mammals, including quail, deer, and squirrels, eat acorns. Many kinds of acorns are bitter. American Indians crushed and soaked acorns in water to remove the bitterness. See also **Oak.**   Richard A. Jaynes

Acoustics, *uh KOO stihks,* is the branch of physics dealing with sound. Acoustics includes the study of how sound is produced, transmitted, detected, measured, and used. It is also concerned with the effect of sound on living things. Sound includes all mechanical vibrations that travel as waves through solid, liquid, or gas.

Sound waves are often described in terms of their *frequency,* the number of vibrations in a given time. Frequency is often measured in units called hertz. One hertz equals one vibration per second. The higher the frequency of a sound wave, the higher the sound's pitch. The *acoustic spectrum* (range of all possible frequencies) can be broken up into three regions: (1) audible sound; (2) infrasound; and (3) ultrasound. The audible part of the spectrum refers to sounds human beings can hear. Infrasound includes sounds too low in pitch to be heard by people (below about 20 hertz). Ultrasound contains sounds too high to be heard (above 20,000 hertz).

Human ears are sophisticated sound receivers. They can distinguish a sound's pitch, loudness, and direction. Sound waves make part of the ear vibrate. The vibration is converted to a nerve signal, which is sent to the brain.

Acousticians (scientists who specialize in acoustics) use microphones to measure sound in air. *Hydrophones* measure sound underwater. *Accelerometers* and *geophones* detect vibrations. They are often used in engineering design and geological studies. Laser beams can be reflected off an object to detect vibration without touching it. All of these devices produce electrical signals that can be studied with acoustic test equipment, such as *oscilloscopes* and *frequency analyzers.*

Because sound is a wave, it behaves much like light. When sound strikes an object, it can be *diffracted* (spread out), *dissipated* (absorbed), reflected, or *refracted* (bent). *Polarization* describes the direction of the vibrations, in relation to the wave's direction of travel. *Reverberation* is heard when a sound is received after reflection from many surfaces. The *Doppler effect* is a shift in the pitch of sound as its source moves toward or away from a receiver. It can be heard when a train or a vehicle with a siren passes by. *Interference* is the reinforcing or canceling effect between two or more sound waves traveling through the same space. Over time, interference between two tones similar in frequency can produce variations in volume called *beats. Resonance* is the vibration of an object at its natural frequency upon being struck by a sound wave of the same frequency.

There are many branches of acoustics. *Architectural acoustics* deals with making rooms and buildings quiet and providing good conditions for listening to speech and music. *Environmental acoustics* involves the control of *noise pollution* (unwanted sound). *Underwater acoustics* studies sound waves in water. It involves detecting objects underwater using *sonar,* a device similar to radar that relies on sound waves rather than radio waves. *Physiological acoustics* is the study of how people hear sounds. *Psychological acoustics* studies the way people interpret sounds. *Speech communication* studies the way people produce, transmit, and hear speech. *Musical acoustics* deals with the way instruments and voices produce sounds. *Medical acoustics* involves imaging and treating disease with sound. *Bioacoustics* studies the sounds emitted by animals and the effect of sound on animals.   Edward J. Tucholski

See also **Sound** and its list of *Related articles.*

Acquired immunodeficiency syndrome. See **AIDS.**

Acre is a unit of land area in the inch-pound system of measurement. One acre equals 160 square rods or 43,560 square feet (4046.856 square meters). An acre that is square in shape measures about 208.7 feet (63.6 meters) on each side. There are 640 acres in a square mile. In the metric system, one measure of land area is the *hectare,* which equals 10,000 square meters, or 2.471 acres.   Richard S. Davis

Acrobatics. See **Diving; Gymnastics.**

Acronym. See **Abbreviation.**

Acropolis, *uh KRAHP uh lihs,* was the religious and military center of a city-state in ancient Greece. A city-

© S. Borisov, Shutterstock

An *acropolis* (hill) served as the religious and military center of an ancient Greek city-state. The Acropolis in Athens includes the Parthenon, *upper right,* and ruins of other ancient temples.

state consisted of a city and the surrounding villages and farmland. The Greeks usually fortified a hill, called an acropolis, within or near the city for defense. The acropolis was often the first place to be inhabited. At the height of the Mycenaean era (1400 to 1200 B.C.), most local kings had their palace on a hill. The palace also served as a military fort and a refuge for the townspeople in emergencies. The most important temples were also on the hill, including the local shrines of the gods.

The most famous acropolis was in Athens. The Athenian Acropolis was originally the site of the armory and royal palace. The Persians demolished many buildings on the Acropolis during an invasion in 480 B.C. The Athenians then built a magnificent new group of temples. From 447 to 432 B.C., the Athenians built the Parthenon, dedicated to the virgin goddess Athena, the patron of the city (see **Parthenon**). The Erechtheum, built to honor the legendary founders of the city, was constructed from 421 to about 406 B.C. The Temple of Athena Nike, built about 425 B.C., honored Athena as the goddess of victory. Two theaters and several minor sanctuaries also occupied the slopes of the hilltop. On sacred holidays, a procession made its way up the slopes of the Acropolis and passed through the Propylaea, a large roofed gateway, to various temples.   William J. Hennessey

For pictures of the Acropolis in Athens, see **Athens; Greece.**

Acrylic, *uh KRIHL ihk,* is a kind of synthetic product made primarily from petroleum. Acrylics are manufactured as fibers or plastics or as substances called *resins* (see **Resin**). Common acrylics include Acrilan, Lucite, Orlon, and Plexiglas.

Acrylic fibers are woven or knitted into durable fabrics of various textures. These fabrics dry fast and resist fading, wrinkling, shrinkage, and mildew. They have a feel similar to that of wool and are used to make blankets, carpets, sweaters, and many other products.

Acrylic plastics are tough materials that resist weathering, sharp blows, and corrosion. Acrylic plastics are often used as substitutes for glass in such products as aircraft windows, television screens, automobile tail lights, and lighting fixtures. They are less breakable than glass but are more easily scratched. Liquid acrylic resins are used to make paints and waxes. Acrylic paints dry quickly and provide strong protection against the weather. High-gloss acrylic waxes are spread as protective coatings on floors and automobiles.

Acrylic adhesives and sealants are made from soft, elastic acrylic resins. They can bond to almost any sort of material. They are used in such products as prepasted wallpaper and tapes and in *cyanoacrylate* (super glue). Acrylic sealants are used to seal cracks and joints in buildings.   Scott W. Waite

ACT. See Australian Capital Territory.

Act of ... Laws that begin *Act of* or *Act for* appear under their key words, as in **Union, Act of.**

Acting. See Motion picture (Assembling the cast; Holding rehearsals); **Television; Theater** (The performers).

Actinide, also called an *actinoid,* is any of the 15 chemical elements that follow the element radium in the periodic table. In order of atomic number, the actinides are actinium (atomic number 89), thorium (90), protactinium (91), uranium (92), neptunium (93), plutonium (94), americium (95), curium (96), berkelium (97), californium (98), einsteinium (99), fermium (100), mendelevium (101), nobelium (102), and lawrencium (103). Scientists sometimes do not include actinium among the actinides.

Most periodic tables show the actinides and a series called the *lanthanides* separate from the rest of the elements in two long rows. If the rows were shown in place, the table would be too wide for easy display.

Actinide atoms have an increasing number of electrons in a region called the *5f subshell.* In general, each actinide has one more electron in the 5f subshell than the previous actinide. But several actinides do not follow this pattern, leading to unique electron arrangements.

In forming compounds, most actinides tend to lose three electrons, gaining a 3+ charge. However, some actinides are known to take on charges as high as 7+.

Only two actinide elements, thorium and uranium, are present on Earth in significant quantities. The other elements exist only in minute quantities or are made exclusively by human beings. All of the actinide elements are radioactive, limiting their use.

Uranium and plutonium are used to produce power in nuclear power plants and atomic bombs. Uranium is also used to make dense, armor-penetrating artillery shells. Americium is widely used as part of the electrical circuit by which smoke detectors operate.   David W. Ball

Related articles. Each of the actinide elements has a separate article in *World Book.*

Actinium, *ak TIHN ee uhm,* a chemical element, is an extremely rare, silvery-white, radioactive metal that glows in the dark. A radioactive element *decays* (breaks down) by sending out particles from its nucleus. In this process, it changes into another element. Natural actinium is itself a product of radioactivity. It is created by the decay of an *isotope* of uranium known as *uranium 235.* An element's isotopes have the same number of protons but different numbers of neutrons in their nucleus.

Actinium also can be artificially prepared from radium treated with neutrons in a nuclear reactor. Actinium is a difficult element to study because it can be produced only in extremely small quantities and because it decays into products that give off radiation.

Actinium's chemical symbol is Ac. Its *atomic number* (number of protons) is 89. Its most stable isotope has an atomic mass number (total number of protons and neutrons) of 227. That isotope has a *half-life* of 21.77 years—that is, due to radioactive decay, only half the atoms in a sample of actinium 227 would still be atoms of that isotope after 21.77 years. Actinium melts at 817 °C and boils at 2470 °C. Most simple actinium compounds, such as the oxides, hydrides, and halides, contain the positively charged actinium ion, Ac^{3+}. André Debierne, a French scientist, discovered actinium in 1899.   S. C. Cummings

Actinomycosis, *AK tuh nuh my KOH sihs,* is a rare, infectious disease that affects human beings. It is characterized by the formation of painful abscesses in the mouth, lungs, or digestive organs. These abscesses grow larger as the disease progresses, often over a period of months. In severe cases, the abscesses may bore through bone and muscle to the skin, where they break open and leak large amounts of pus. Actinomycosis can destroy a person's jaw or lungs. It can also block the passage of food through the digestive system. It occurs in cattle and other animals as a disease called *lumpy jaw.* This name refers to the large abscesses that grow on the head and neck of the infected animal.

Actinomycosis is caused by any of several members of a group of bacteria called *actinomyces.* These bacteria are *anaerobes*—that is, they cannot survive in the presence of large amounts of oxygen. Actinomyces normally live harmlessly in the small spaces between the teeth and gums. They cause infection only when they can multiply freely in places where oxygen cannot reach them. The three most common sites of infection are decayed teeth, the lungs, and the intestines. Doctors use penicillin to treat actinomycosis.   John R. Graybill

Actium, *AK tee uhm* or *AK shee uhm,* **Battle of,** was a primarily naval battle that settled the struggle for control of the Roman world between co-rulers Mark Antony and Octavian. Antony ruled Rome's eastern territories, and Octavian ruled its western ones. The battle took place on Sept. 2, 31 B.C., off the coast of northwestern Greece near present-day Preveza.

The battle centered around the Straits of Actium, which controlled access to the Gulf of Ambracia. The fleet and army of Antony and his ally Queen Cleopatra of Egypt were trapped near the straits by Octavian's fleet under the command of Marcus Agrippa. Antony's forces were suffering from desertion, disease, and hunger. Antony decided to try to break free of Octavian's forces by sea rather than by land. He prepared about 170 warships with 20,000 marines and 2,000 archers on board. Octavian prepared about twice this number of ships, although his ships were smaller. His ships' nimbleness may have convinced Cleopatra prematurely, after a couple hours of fighting, that Antony would lose. Cleopatra fled with her 60 ships and was joined by Antony. The battle continued indecisively into the night until Antony's fleet surrendered. His army surrendered several days later.   Richard J. A. Talbert

See also **Agrippa, Marcus; Antony, Mark.**

Acton, *AK tuhn,* **Lord** (1834-1902), was one of the most respected historians of the 1800's. Many of his works focused on the history of freedom. Acton also planned the massive *Cambridge Modern History* (1902-1912). His statement "Power tends to corrupt, and absolute power corrupts absolutely" has become a famous proverb.

Acton was a prominent liberal Roman Catholic. At Vatican Council I (1869-1870), he worked with bishops who opposed the church's adoption of the doctrine of *papal infallibility.* This doctrine states that the pope can commit no errors when he speaks as head of the church to define solemnly, in matters of faith and morals, what is to be accepted by all Roman Catholics.

John Emerich Edward Dalberg Acton was born on Jan. 10, 1834, in Naples, Italy. As a child, he moved with his family to the United Kingdom. In 1869, he became a baron. He was a professor of modern history at Cambridge University from 1895 until his death on June 19, 1902.

James C. Holland

Actor and actress. See the lists of biographies in the *Related articles* of **Motion picture** and **Theater.**

Acts of the Apostles is the fifth book of the New Testament. It continues the story that begins in the Gospel of Luke. Luke and Acts were written by the same author. They are volumes one and two of a single work that scholars refer to as Luke-Acts. According to Christian tradition, Saint Luke, a companion of Saint Paul, wrote Acts. Many scholars doubt that this is true. Most scholars believe that Luke and Acts were written between A.D. 85 and 95.

Acts tells of the beginning and expansion of the Christian church. Because the Christian church began within Judaism, the inclusion of Gentiles (non-Jews) was controversial. Acts justifies the mission to the Gentiles as the fulfillment of the Jewish scriptures. Acts also defends the church against charges that it was a threat to the Roman Empire. Acts provides an account of Paul joining the church and of his three missionary journeys in what is now Turkey and Greece.   Henry W. Morisada Rietz

See also **Bible** (The Acts of the Apostles); **Luke, Saint.**

Acuff, Roy (1903-1992), was an American country music singer and fiddler. Acuff and his band, the Smoky Mountain Boys, helped make Tennessee mountain music internationally known. Such recordings as "The Great Speckled Bird" and "Wabash Cannonball" (both 1936) became country music classics.

Roy Claxton Acuff was born on Sept. 15, 1903, in Maynardville, Tennessee. He joined a traveling show in 1932. Acuff became a radio entertainer and began recording in 1936. In 1938, he joined the "Grand Ole Opry" radio show in Nashville and became one of its longest-running performers. Acuff was elected to the Country Music Hall of Fame in 1962. He died on Nov. 23, 1992.

Lee Rector

Acupuncture, *AK yuh puhngk chuhr,* is an ancient Chinese method of inserting needles into the body to relieve pain and treat disease. According to Chinese philosophy, acupuncture influences a life force that flows along 12 paired and 2 unpaired *meridians.* The meridians are channels of energy that run the length of the body. Specialists called *acupuncturists* insert needles at points along these meridians or at painful points on the body. This practice is said to restore balance between two principal forces of nature called *yin* and *yang.* Acupuncturists believe disease and pain occur as a result of imbalance between these forces.

Insertion of the needles produces a pinching feeling. This feeling quickly disappears. It may be replaced by occasional tingling or a sense of numbness, heaviness, or soreness while the needles are in place.

Acupuncture is used alone or with Western medicine

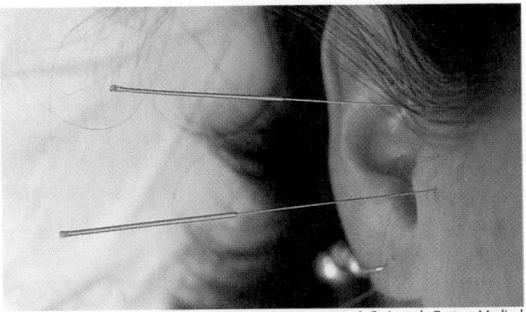

L. Steinmark, Custom Medical

Acupuncture relieves pain by the insertion of needles. This photo shows needles inserted near a person's ear.

or Chinese herbal preparations. It is most often used to relieve pain resulting from chronic illness and severe injury. Some common afflictions acupuncturists treat include headaches, sinusitis, chronic respiratory infections, digestive disturbances, and drug dependencies. Since the late 1950's, doctors in China have used acupuncture to relieve pain during major surgery. The patient is conscious and seems to feel little or no pain.

Scientists have determined that acupuncture triggers signals in the nervous system. These signals adjust the activities of the body's internal organs. They also change pain signals sent to the brain. Researchers have shown that acupuncture increases the brain's production of natural painkillers called *endorphins* (see **Endorphin**). But much of acupuncture's influence is not understood.

Acupuncture is practiced widely in Asia and Europe. It is gaining popularity and respect in the United States. Its practitioners include many medical doctors.

Joseph M. Helms

A.D. is the abbreviation for *anno Domini,* which is Latin for *in the year of our Lord.* In 532, the monk Dionysius Exiguus introduced a system of dating events, beginning with the year he believed Jesus Christ was born. In this system, the year of Christ's birth was A.D. 1, and the year before that was 1 B.C. (before Christ). Modern scholars believe Christ was actually born no later than 1 B.C. But people still determine dates using the original system.

Writers generally use *A.D.* and *B.C.* only to avoid confusion. When a writer mentions a year without using either abbreviation, readers should assume that the year was, or is, an "A.D." year.

Because there is no "year zero" in the dating system, it takes two steps to calculate an interval between a date in a "B.C." year and the same date in an "A.D." year. First, add the numbers representing the years. Then subtract 1. Thus, the interval between the end of 1 B.C. and the end of A.D. 1 was 1 year. The interval between the end of 2000 B.C. and the end of A.D. 2000 was 3,999 years.

An alternative system uses the same numbering method as that of Dionysius Exiguus but does not refer specifically to Christ. In the alternative system, *C.E.,* which stands for *common era,* replaces A.D.; and *B.C.E. (before the common era)* replaces B.C.   Michael Dine

See also **B.C.**

Ad Dawhah. See Doha.

Adam was the family name of two brothers—Robert Adam (1728-1792) and James Adam (1732-1794)—who were famous Scottish architects. Robert Adam settled in

A Robert Adam design for Kedleston Hall in Derbyshire is a masterpiece of English Neoclassical architecture. The state drawing room, *shown here,* was completed in the 1760's. It blends ceiling and wall decorations with paintings and furniture.

A. Haslam, Royal Oak Foundation

London in 1758 and formed a partnership with his brother. Their interest in ancient Roman architecture formed the basis for the light and delicate Neoclassical character of their work. The brothers are especially noted for their residential buildings, furniture, and interior design.

Robert Adam's best-known buildings include Syon House (1762-1769) and Osterley Park House (1763-1780), both in London. The brothers collaborated on the Adelphi (1772), a large row of residential and commercial buildings in London. Robert's book *Ruins of the Palace of the Emperor Diocletian at Spalato in Dalmatia* (1764) was a significant archaeological publication of the time.

Robert Adam was born in Kirkcaldy, Scotland, on July 3, 1728. He died in London on March 3, 1792. James Adam was born in Edinburgh on July 21, 1732. He died in London on Oct. 20, 1794.   J. William Rudd

See also **Architecture** (Neoclassical architecture; picture); **Furniture** (English neoclassical furniture; picture); **Museum** (picture: Museums).

Adam and Eve, according to the Bible, were the first man and woman created by God. The account of Adam and Eve is told in Genesis 2-3. According to Genesis, God created two human beings, later called Adam and Eve, and placed them in the Garden of Eden (see **Eden**). Adam and Eve lived in Eden, tending the garden of God. They were permitted to eat from any tree in the garden except from the tree of knowledge of good and evil. But a serpent persuaded Eve to eat fruit from this tree. Eve gave some to Adam, who also ate the fruit. Thus, they became mortal and God exiled them from Eden. Outside the garden, Adam had to work hard to make a living, and Eve also had to work and to bear many children.

The story of Adam and Eve begins a long Biblical narrative of human history. Their position at the beginning of the Bible makes them seem historical. But many Biblical scholars consider them as models who reveal the essential qualities of human existence. Their names are normally not proper names in Biblical Hebrew. They are general terms for *humanity* and *living being*.

According to one interpretation, the account of Adam and Eve focuses especially on those characteristics that define human nature as opposed to the nature of God and that of animals. Adam and Eve were made in God's image, and they gained wisdom, or knowledge of good and evil, which made them like God. But like animals, they had to die. Some people also believe the account emphasizes universal human fellowship by showing all humans as descendants of one couple.   Carol L. Meyers

See also **Abel; Cain; Genesis.**

Adams, Abigail Smith (1744-1818), was the wife of John Adams, the second president of the United States. She also was the mother of John Quincy Adams, the sixth president. Abigail Adams is known for many letters containing her opinions of the society of her time.

Abigail Smith was born in Weymouth, Massachusetts. She and Adams were married in 1764. They had four children besides John Quincy Adams. She managed the family farm in Braintree (now Quincy), Massachusetts, while Adams served in the Continental Congress and as a diplomat in Europe during the 1770's and 1780's.

Abigail Adams supported women's rights and provided her daughter, Abigail, with a broad education. Writing to Adams in Philadelphia in 1776, she urged him to "remember the ladies" in the new nation's laws. She also opposed slavery. During the American Revolution (1775-1783), Abigail Adams's letters to her husband contained valuable information about British troops and ships in the Boston area. In 1800, the Adamses became the first couple to live in the White House.   Kathryn Kish Sklar

See also **Adams, John** (Adams's family; picture).

Adams, Ansel (1902-1984), was an American photographer known for his dramatic photographs of the West. He took large pictures of landscapes that include mountains, forests, and rivers. Adams's interest in preserving wilderness areas also led him to become active in the conservation movement. Adams was a leading supporter of *straight photography,* a style featuring detailed, focused photos that portray subjects simply and directly. In 1932, he and six other photographers formed a group that promoted this style of photography.

In 1940, Adams helped found the Department of Photography at the Museum of Modern Art in New York City. In 1946, he established a photography department at the California School of Fine Arts (now the San Fran-

Ansel Adams

Nature's majestic beauty is portrayed in Ansel Adams's photo *Mt. Williamson, Sierra Nevada, from Manzanar, California 1944.*

cisco Art Institute). This department was the first of its kind at a United States college. He also wrote books on photography. Adams was born in San Francisco on Feb. 20, 1902, and died on April 22, 1984. Charles Hagen

Adams, Brooks (1848-1927), was an American historian and a critic of capitalism. He believed that commercial civilizations rise and fall in predictable cycles. First, people draw together in large population centers and engage in commercial activities. Then, as their desire for wealth grows, greed replaces spiritual and creative values. Finally, the society crumbles. In *The Law of Civilization and Decay* (1895), Adams noted that as new population centers emerged, centers of world trade shifted. They moved from Constantinople (now Istanbul, Turkey) to Venice, Italy, and then to London. Adams predicted in *America's Economic Supremacy* (1900) that Russia and the United States would become the leading world powers by 1950. He was born on June 24, 1848, in Quincy, Massachusetts, and died on Feb. 13, 1927. He was the son of U.S. diplomat Charles Francis Adams, brother of historian Henry Brooks Adams, and a grandson of President John Quincy Adams. Joseph Martin Hernon, Jr.

Adams, Charles Francis (1807-1886), was one of the most successful diplomats in United States history. He gained this reputation through his work as U.S. minister to the United Kingdom between 1861 and 1868. He helped keep the United Kingdom and France from recognizing the independence of the Confederacy during the American Civil War (1861-1865).

Adams was born on Aug. 18, 1807, in Boston. His father, John Quincy Adams, later became president of the United States. Charles spent his boyhood in Russia and the United Kingdom, where his father was U.S. minister. Charles graduated from Harvard University in 1825.

In the mid-1830's, Charles Adams became involved in the controversy over slavery in the United States. He served in the Massachusetts legislature from 1841 to 1845 and helped persuade fellow House members to take an open stand against slavery. He also edited the *Boston Daily Whig,* an antislavery party journal. Gradually, Adams became leader of the Conscience Whigs, an antislavery group. The group supported the Free Soil Party in 1848, which nominated Martin Van Buren for president and Adams for vice president. Zachary Taylor, the Whig candidate for president, won the election.

Adams devoted most of the 1850's to editing the 10-volume *Works of John Adams.* He was elected to the U.S. House of Representatives from Massachusetts in 1858 and 1860. In 1861, President Abraham Lincoln appointed Adams minister to the United Kingdom. There he had to face strong sympathy for the Southern States in the Civil War. As minister, Adam struggled to prevent British recognition of Confederate independence and urged British officials not to equip Confederate ships. In 1871, President Ulysses S. Grant chose Adams to represent the United States in the settlement of claims involving the Confederate cruiser *Alabama* (see **Alabama** [ship]). Adams died on Nov. 21, 1886. Elliott Robert Barkan

Adams, Gerry (1948-), was president of Sinn Féin *(shihn fayn),* an Irish nationalist political party, from 1983 to 2018. Sinn Féin is the political wing of the Irish Republican Army (IRA). The IRA is a group that has long sought to unite the country of Ireland with Northern Ireland, which is part of the United Kingdom.

For many years, Adams defended the IRA's use of violence to achieve its goals for Northern Ireland. However, he also sought a peaceful settlement to the conflict. Adams participated in talks that led to a 1998 agreement committing all sides to resolve their differences by peaceful means. On March 26, 2007, Adams met with Ian Paisley, president of the Democratic Unionist Party, which has supported Northern Ireland's continued union with the United Kingdom. The two leaders agreed to establish a power-sharing government in Northern Ireland. The government began in May 2007. See **Northern Ireland** (The Good Friday Agreement).

Gerard Adams was born on Oct. 6, 1948, in Belfast, Northern Ireland. In 1964, he joined Sinn Féin. He became involved in the movement to improve social and economic conditions for Roman Catholics in Northern Ireland. Authorities imprisoned him during much of the 1970's because of his suspected IRA role. In prison, Adams encouraged Irish nationalism in Northern Ireland. He has written several books, including *A Farther Shore: Ireland's Long Road to Peace* (2003). Kris Brown

See also **Irish Republican Army; Sinn Féin.**

Adams, Henry (1838-1918), was an American historian. His autobiography, *The Education of Henry Adams,* won a Pulitzer Prize in 1919. In this book, Adams painted a vivid picture of the increasing sense of disconnectedness, terrifying diversity, and rapid change that many people began to feel in Western society in the 1800's.

Adams's greatest contribution to American history was the nine-volume *History of the United States* (1889-1891). In it, he made extensive use of historical documents to establish sure facts with little personal comment. He thus helped found the "scientific method" of history-writing that developed in the late 1800's. His *Mont-Saint-Michel and Chartres* (1913) established him as one of the best American writers of medieval history.

Henry Brooks Adams was born in Boston on Feb. 16, 1838, the son of American diplomat Charles Francis Adams, the grandson of U.S. President John Quincy Adams, and the great-grandson of President John Adams. Henry graduated from Harvard University in 1858 and taught history there from 1870 to 1877. He edited the *North American Review* from 1870 to 1876. He also wrote two novels—*Democracy* (1880) and *Esther* (1884). He died on March 27, 1918. Daniel Mark Fogel

John Adams (signature)

**2nd president of
the United States 1797-1801**

Washington
1st president
1789-1797
No political
party

J. Adams
2nd president
1797-1801
Federalist

Jefferson
3rd president
1801-1809
Democratic-
Republican

**Thomas
Jefferson**
Vice president
1797-1801

Oil painting on canvas (1793) by John Trumbull; Fogg Art Museum, Harvard University

Adams, John (1735-1826), guided the young United States through some of its most serious troubles. He served under George Washington as the nation's first vice president and followed him as the second president. The United States government moved from Philadelphia to Washington, D.C., during Adams's administration, and he became the first president to live in the White House. Adams was the first chief executive whose son also served as president.

Adams played a leading role in the adoption of the Declaration of Independence, and was a signer of the historic document. He had spoken out boldly for separation from Great Britain (now called the United Kingdom) at a time when most colonial leaders still hoped to settle their differences with the British. As president, Adams fought a split in his own party over his determination to avoid war with France. He kept the peace, but in the process he lost a second term as president. He was succeeded by Thomas Jefferson.

In appearance, Adams was short and stout, with a ruddy complexion. He seldom achieved popularity during his long political career. Those close to him loved him, but his bluntness, impatience, and vanity made more enemies than friends. On most great decisions of his public career, history has proved him right and his opponents wrong. But his clumsiness in human relations often caused him to be misunderstood. Few people knew about another part of Adams's personality. His diary and personal letters show his pleasant, affectionate, and often playful nature.

During Adams's term, the United States took its first steps toward industrialization. The first woolen mills began operating in Massachusetts, and Congress established the Department of the Navy and the Marine Corps. Americans enjoyed such songs as "The Wearing of the Green" and "The Blue Bells of Scotland." People read and admired *The Life and Memorable Actions of George Washington* by Mason Locke Weems. On the frontier, Johnny Appleseed began wandering through Ohio and Indiana, planting apple seeds and teaching the Bible.

Early life

Childhood. John Adams was born in Braintree (now Quincy), Massachusetts, on Oct. 30, 1735. (The date was October 19 by the calendar then in use.) His father, also named John Adams, was a farmer, a deacon of the First Parish of Braintree, and a militia officer. His mother, Susanna Boylston Adams, came from a leading family of Brookline and Boston merchants and physicians.

The Adams farm lay at the foot of Penn's Hill. The National Park Service preserves as a memorial the house in which John Adams was born. The house stands close to the place where his great-great-grandfather, Henry Adams, settled before 1640. Henry Adams had sailed from Somerset, England, along with thousands of other Puritans, to escape the religious persecution found in his homeland.

Young John helped with the chores on the farm. He studied hard in the village school, but did not particularly enjoy books.

Education. Adams graduated from Harvard College in 1755, ranking 14th in a class of 24. In those days, a student's rank indicated social position, not scholarship, and Adams was one of the best scholars in his class.

After teaching school for a short time, Adams studied law in the office of James Putnam in Worcester, Massachusetts. Adams began to practice law in Braintree in 1758. He became a leading attorney of the Massachusetts colony.

Adams's family. In 1764, Adams married Abigail Smith (Nov. 22, 1744-Oct. 28, 1818), the daughter of a

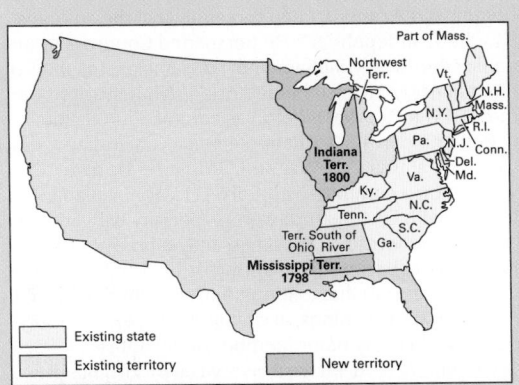

The world of President John Adams

The rebirth of the United States Navy was symbolized by the launching of the frigate *United States* in 1797. Two other ships launched that year, the *Constitution* and the *Constellation*, made up the core of the nation's first naval force since the American Revolution. Congress established a separate Department of the Navy in 1798.

The United States Marine Corps was established by Congress in 1798 as a separate military service. The nation's first marine corps had been dissolved after the American Revolution.

The first organized strike in the United States took place in 1799. A group of Philadelphia shoemakers refused to work for nine days, until their demands for higher wages were met.

Napoleon became First Consul of France in 1799 and began to rule as a dictator.

The Library of Congress was established in 1800. Congress appropriated $5,000 to buy books and to furnish a room in the Capitol to house the library.

The federal government moved to Washington, D.C., from Philadelphia in June 1800. Congress convened in the new capital city for the first time in November of that year.

France secretly reacquired Louisiana from Spain in 1800. The United States did not learn of the transaction until the following year.

Two new territories were organized during Adams's presidency—the Mississippi Territory in 1798 and the Indiana Territory in 1800. No new states entered the Union.

minister in Weymouth, Massachusetts. (Her birth date was November 11 by the calendar then in use.)

Like most women of her time, Abigail Adams had received little formal schooling. But she read widely, and became one of the best-informed women of the day. She wrote delightful letters to Adams during his absences from home. Mrs. Adams was a lively observer of people and events, and her letters provide colorful pictures of colonial life.

The Adamses' eldest child, Abigail, became the wife of Colonel William Stephens Smith, the secretary to the United States legation in London. The Adamses' eldest son, John Quincy, became the sixth president of the United States the year before his father died. The third child, Susanna, died in infancy. The fourth child, Charles, died while his father was president. Thomas, the youngest child, became a lawyer and a judge.

Political and public career

In New England. Adams took a leading part in opposing British colonial policies in America. The year 1765, when the British Parliament passed the Stamp Act, was a turning point in his life. This law taxed newspapers, legal papers, and other items. It hit Adams hard as a lawyer. He wrote: "This tax was set on foot for my ruin as well as that of Americans in general."

Adams wrote resolutions against the tax that were adopted by the Braintree town meeting. More than 40 other Massachusetts towns adopted these resolutions. The Boston town meeting appointed Adams to a committee to present a petition against the tax to the British

John Adams's birthplace stands in Quincy (then Braintree), Massachusetts. Farmland surrounded the house when Adams was born. The house is now preserved as a national historic site.

Important dates in Adams's life

1735 (Oct. 30) Born in Braintree (now Quincy), Massachusetts.
1764 (Oct. 25) Married Abigail Smith.
1774 Chosen a delegate to the First Continental Congress.
1777 Elected commissioner to France to negotiate a treaty of alliance.
1780-1782 Obtained recognition of American independence from the Netherlands.
1782-1783 Served on the commission that negotiated peace with Great Britain.
1785 Appointed minister to Great Britain.
1789 Elected vice president of the United States.
1792 Reelected vice president.
1796 Elected president of the United States.
1826 (July 4) Died in Quincy.

Oil painting on canvas (1785) by Mather Brown; New York
State Historical Association, Cooperstown, N.Y.

Abigail Smith Adams was an intelligent, well-read woman, and a keen observer of colonial life. She and her husband carried on a lively correspondence when he was away from home.

governor. Adams argued that the tax was illegal because the people had not consented to it. This amounted to saying that Parliament could not tax the colonies at all. Britain repealed the Stamp Act in 1766. See **Stamp Act**.

Adams rejoiced at every expression of popular opposition to the British. But the treatment of British soldiers who had taken part in the Boston Massacre distressed him (see **Boston Massacre**). His sense of justice led him to defend Captain Thomas Preston and the British soldiers charged with manslaughter. He felt that the soldiers should be freed, because the mob had provoked them to fire. Adams feared that his viewpoint would cost him popularity. Instead, his prestige rose. In 1770, the people of Boston chose him as one of their representatives in the colonial legislature. There, with the help of his cousin, Samuel Adams, he led the fight against British colonial policies.

The British tax on tea enraged Adams and most of his fellow colonists. When a band of patriots dumped large quantities of tea into Boston Harbor on Dec. 16, 1773, Adams called this act "the most magnificent movement of all." See **Boston Tea Party**.

National politics. In 1774, in response to the Tea Party, the British government passed several laws that became known as the Intolerable Acts (see **Intolerable Acts**). Under these laws, the British shut down the port of Boston and suspended the Massachusetts government. Massachusetts called for representatives from each colony to meet in Philadelphia. Adams was one of the four Massachusetts delegates at this meeting, later called the First Continental Congress. He and a few other men wanted to seek independence from Britain, but he knew it was too early to propose such drastic action.

Adams's influence had grown by the time the Second Continental Congress met in 1775. By this time, war had begun, and Adams argued forcefully that the colonies should be independent. He persuaded Congress to organize the 16,000 militiamen of New England as the Continental Army. He also helped bring about the appointment of George Washington as commander in chief.

Beginning in 1776, Adams served as chairman of the Continental Board of War and Ordnance. He also worked on a committee appointed to draft a plan for treaties with European powers, especially with France. Adams later wrote: "I was incessantly employed through the whole fall, winter, and spring of 1775 and 1776, in Congress during their sittings, and on committees in the mornings and evenings, and unquestionably did more business than any other member of the house."

On June 7, 1776, Richard Henry Lee of Virginia presented a resolution to Congress declaring that "these United Colonies are, and of right ought to be, free and independent States." Adams seconded the resolution. Congress chose him to be a member of the committee to prepare a declaration of independence. Adams urged Thomas Jefferson to draft the document. Adams defended the Declaration in the stormy debate that followed in Congress.

Diplomat. Early in 1778, Congress sent Adams to Paris to help Benjamin Franklin and Arthur Lee strengthen American ties with France and other European nations. Adams arrived in Paris to find that treaties had already been signed with France. He noted that friction had developed among the American ministers, and wrote to Congress proposing that one person take charge of affairs in France. Congress chose Franklin, and Adams sailed home in 1779.

Upon his return to Massachusetts, the people of Braintree elected Adams to the convention that framed a state constitution. Adams wrote almost all the constitution, which had a detailed bill of rights. The document also included a *separation of powers* that divided the government into three branches—the governor, the legislature, and the courts. In such a system, each branch can use its powers to *check and balance* (exercise control over) the other two. It would be a "government of laws, and not of men," Adams wrote. Many other states, and later the United States, adopted features of the Massachusetts Constitution of 1780. It is the oldest still-functioning written constitution in the world.

During the Massachusetts constitutional convention, Congress appointed Adams to negotiate treaties of peace and trade with Great Britain. He sailed for Paris, and arrived in February 1780. But the British were not prepared to negotiate. Adams then went to the Netherlands to seek diplomatic and commercial support for the American war effort. After two years of hard work, he obtained recognition of the United States as a *sovereign* (independent) power. He also obtained a loan of about $1,400,000 for the United States. Adams's mission to the Netherlands ranks among his greatest diplomatic achievements.

In the fall of 1782, Adams joined John Jay and Benjamin Franklin in Paris to meet British and French representatives and arrange a peace treaty. Adams and Jay distrusted the French foreign minister, Count de Vergennes. They feared he would sacrifice American interests to gain advantages for France and its ally, Spain. As a result, the Americans departed from their instructions and negotiated with the British without informing Vergennes of each step taken. Franklin smoothed over affairs with France after the British and Americans had agreed on peace terms.

British and American commissioners signed a preliminary peace treaty on Nov. 30, 1782. The document was signed again in Paris on Sept. 3, 1783, as the final peace treaty. Adams made sure that the United States kept fishing rights in North Atlantic waters. He also arranged provisions recommending *amnesty* (a general pardon) for Americans who had remained loyal to the British. During the next two years, Adams negotiated another Dutch loan and served in Paris on a commission to negotiate trade treaties with many European governments. He was proud when the French called him "the Washington of negotiations."

In 1785, Congress named Adams the first U.S. minister to Great Britain. He hoped to negotiate treaties that would encourage trade with Britain. But the British treated Adams coolly, and they made it clear that they would not relax their harsh trade policies. Adams eventually asked to be recalled, and returned home in 1788 after almost 10 years abroad.

Vice president. Adams had been home only a few months when he was elected vice president. At that time, every elector voted for two men for the presidency. The man who ran second became vice president. Each of the 69 electors voted for George Washington, and 34 gave their second vote to Adams.

Adams later wrote that the vice presidency was "the most insignificant office that ever the invention of man contrived or his imagination conceived." Washington relied on others for policy advice, and Adams was left to a vice president's duties—presiding over Senate debates in which he could not participate. Adams proposed giving the president what he thought was a more suitable title—"His High Mightiness, the President of the United States and Defender of their Liberties"—which earned

him ridicule and raised suspicions that Adams favored a monarchy.

The French Revolution, which lasted from 1789 to 1799, divided Americans. Many saw the French pursuit of liberty, equality, and fraternity as an extension of the American Revolution. Others feared the overthrow of established order and the *anarchy* (lawlessness) that might result. In reaction to the events in France, Adams wrote a series of newspaper articles called *Discourses on Davila.* Many readers thought these articles indicated that he had become much more conservative in his political views. Old friends, such as Thomas Jefferson, felt he had become too fond of kingly rule and too distrustful of popular government.

Washington and Adams were reelected to second terms as president and vice president, returning to office in 1793. Two political groups began to form in response to the French Revolution and to Washington's policies. Adams and Alexander Hamilton led a group that favored a strong federal government. This group, known as the Federalists, supported Washington's policies. James Madison and Thomas Jefferson led the Democratic-Republicans (called Republicans at the time, though later to become the Democratic Party) in fighting for strong states' rights. Jefferson resigned as secretary of state in 1793 because he disapproved of the growing dominance of Hamilton in the Cabinet.

By the time Washington refused in 1796 to seek a third term, the two parties had become well defined. The Federalists supported Adams for the presidency, and the Democratic-Republicans nominated Jefferson. Adams received only three more votes than Jefferson did, and the two rivals thus became president and vice president.

Adams's administration (1797-1801)

The Federalist split. During Adams's four years as president, the government faced many problems at home. Relations with European nations were also unsettled. To make his task more difficult, Adams could not

A View of the American Frigate, Constellation, Capturing the French National Frigate, L'Insurgente, engraving by an unknown artist (1800); New York Historical Society, New York City

Naval battles between U.S. and French ships occurred in spite of President Adams's efforts to keep the United States neutral during the European wars of the late 1700's.

John Adams was the first president to live in the White House. He and Mrs. Adams moved into the mansion in 1800, before it was completed, and suffered many inconveniences. The illustration above shows the original design for the White House by architect James Hoban.

count on the support of his party or his Cabinet. Disagreement over foreign policy split the Federalist Party into two groups. Adams led the more moderate of these groups. The other was led by Alexander Hamilton, who had left the Cabinet and returned to private life before Adams became president.

Difficulties with France. The French Revolution caused most of the problems that faced Adams. President Washington had insisted that neutrality was the best policy in case of a war in Europe. But, in the wars following the French Revolution, European warships attacked American ships. France and Great Britain claimed the right to seize American vessels. The United States was forced to protect itself, and the government launched several new warships, including the *Constitution* ("Old Ironsides").

The United States also became involved in the European wars on philosophical grounds. Jefferson believed that the French Revolution was a people's movement, like the American Revolution. His party sympathized with the French people, and wanted to aid them. But Hamilton led many Federalists in demanding a war against France. Adams was determined to keep the Unit-

ed States neutral, and deplored the policy of Hamilton and his followers. The split in the Federalist Party became irreparable.

One of Adams's first acts as president was to call a special session of Congress to consider ways of keeping peace. He sent ministers to France to work out a treaty. Three French diplomats offered to negotiate a pact if the United States would bribe Charles Maurice de Talleyrand-Périgord, the French foreign minister. This episode became known as the XYZ Affair, because the French diplomats were referred to by these initials instead of their names (see **XYZ Affair**). The Americans ended the negotiations late in 1797.

The XYZ Affair caused great anger in the United States. People rallied to the cry of "Millions for defense, but not one cent for tribute!" Congress began preparing for war with France. It established the Department of the Navy, ordered the construction of more warships, and summoned George Washington to command the Army. Neither nation declared war, but American and French ships fought many battles.

The Alien and Sedition Acts. The Federalists faced bitter criticism because of their opposition to France. Most of the criticism came from American citizens, but some of the critics were French. In 1798, the Federalists passed laws designed to limit this criticism. Two Alien Acts gave the president authority to banish or imprison foreigners. The Sedition Act made it a crime to criticize the government, the president, or Congress. Adams never used the Alien Acts, but a number of journalists who supported Jefferson were arrested for violation of the Sedition Act. See **Alien and Sedition Acts**.

These laws caused a storm of disapproval. Many people claimed they violated the guarantees of freedom of

Vice president and Cabinet

Vice president	*Thomas Jefferson
Secretary of state	*Timothy Pickering
	*John Marshall (1800)
Secretary of the treasury	Oliver Wolcott, Jr.
	Samuel Dexter (1801)
Secretary of war	*James McHenry
	Samuel Dexter (1800)
Attorney general	Charles Lee
Secretary of the Navy	*Benjamin Stoddert

*Has a separate biography in *World Book*.

speech and of the press. Jefferson wrote the resolutions adopted by the Kentucky legislature declaring the Alien and Sedition Acts unconstitutional (see **Kentucky and Virginia Resolutions**). Historians agree that the acts were unwise.

Adams and peace. Adams was still determined to keep peace. He again asked Talleyrand for a treaty. This time, Talleyrand was eager to negotiate, because he feared that the United States might join forces with Great Britain. Without consulting Congress, Adams sent a second commission to France. This act was the boldest of his career as president, and it lost him support in his own party. But he believed that avoiding war was the most important achievement of his administration.

Election of 1800. Hamilton strongly criticized Adams for not fighting France. This argument influenced many Federalist voters. The Democratic-Republicans denounced Adams for the Alien and Sedition Acts, and for hostility toward France. The Democratic-Republican presidential candidates, Thomas Jefferson and Aaron Burr, received 73 electoral votes each. Adams received 65 electoral votes. Because Jefferson and Burr had tied, the House of Representatives chose the president. It selected Jefferson.

Late in 1800, the government had moved from Philadelphia to the new capital in Washington, D.C. Adams made appointments to government offices until his last day in office. One of his most important appointments was that of John Marshall as chief justice of the United States (see **Marshall, John**).

Life in the White House. President Adams moved into the White House just a few months before the end of his administration. In one of his first letters from the White House, John wrote to Abigail, "I pray Heaven to bestow the best of Blessings on this House and all that shall hereafter inhabit it. May none but honest and wise men ever rule under this roof."

Quotations from John Adams
The following quotations come from some of John Adams's speeches and writings.

Liberty cannot be preserved without a general knowledge among the people ... but besides this, they have a right ... to that most dreaded and envied kind of knowledge, I mean of the characters and conduct of their rulers.
A Dissertation on the Canon and Feudal Law, 1765

Facts are stubborn things; and whatever may be our wishes, our inclinations, or the dictates of our passions, they cannot alter the state of facts and evidence.
Argument in defense of the British soldiers in the Boston Massacre trials, December 1770

As the happiness of the people is the sole end of government, so the consent of the people is the only foundation of it.
Proclamation, 1774

Education makes a greater difference between man and man than nature has between man and brute.
Letter to Abigail Adams, Oct. 29, 1775

When annual elections end, there slavery begins.
Thoughts on Government, 1776

The fundamental article of my political creed is that despotism, or unlimited sovereignty, or absolute power, is the same in a majority of a popular assembly, an aristocratic council, an oligarchical junto, and a single emperor.
Letter to Thomas Jefferson, Nov. 13, 1815

The unfinished Executive Mansion stood in isolated splendor amid a dismal, swampy landscape. Abigail Adams wrote to her sister: "As I expected to find it a new country, with houses scattered over a space of 10 miles, and trees and stumps in plenty with a castle of a house— so I found it." Only half a dozen rooms of the mansion were finished. Mrs. Adams had to dry the laundry in the East Room, because no drying yard had been provided.

The unfinished condition of the White House made it hard to carry on official social functions. But the Adamses worked to overcome their difficulties. As the first residents of the White House, they felt they should set a social tone appropriate to the home of the president. Mrs. Adams admired the courtly entertainments of Martha Washington and tried to follow her example.

Later years

John Adams was nearly 66 years old when he left the White House. His defeat, and the death of his son Charles, grieved him so much that he refused to stay in Washington for Jefferson's inauguration. He hurried off for his home in Quincy on the morning of March 4, 1801. Adams devoted himself to farming and to studying history, philosophy, and religion.

After Jefferson left office, he and Adams renewed their friendship. These two great Americans from North and South had met in Congress in 1775. Their friendship cooled steadily after about 1790, because they differed on the meaning of the French Revolution. But they forgot their political quarrels after retiring from public life.

By a remarkable coincidence, both men died on July 4, 1826. Adams died less than four months before his 91st birthday. His last words were: "Thomas Jefferson still survives." Adams was buried in Quincy, Massachusetts.   Robert J. Allison

Related articles in *World Book* include:

Outline

Additional resources

Adams, John. *John Adams: Revolutionary Writings, 1755-1775.* Ed. by Gordon Wood. Lib. of Am., 2011.
Ellis, Joseph J. *First Family: Abigail and John.* Knopf, 2010.
Gelles, Edith B. *Abigail and John: Portrait of a Marriage.* Morrow, 2009.
Wan, Rosana Y. *The Culinary Lives of John and Abigail Adams: A Cookbook.* Schiffer, 2014.

John Quincy Adams

**6th president of
the United States 1825-1829**

Monroe
5th president
1817-1825
Democratic-
Republican

J. Q. Adams
6th president
1825-1829
Democratic-
Republican/
National
Republican

Jackson
7th president
1829-1837
Democrat

**John C.
Calhoun**
Vice president
1825-1829

Oil painting on canvas (1824) by Thomas Sully; National Gallery of Art, Washington, D.C., Andrew W. Mellon Collection

Adams, John Quincy (1767-1848), was the first son of a president of the United States who also became president. The second father and son to be elected were George Herbert Walker Bush and George Walker Bush. Like his father, John Adams, John Quincy Adams failed to win a second term. But soon afterward, he was elected to the U.S. House of Representatives. This pleased him more, he said, than his election as president.

Before entering the presidency, Adams held several important diplomatic posts. He took part in the negotiations that ended the War of 1812. As secretary of state, he helped develop the Monroe Doctrine. Quarrels within his party hampered Adams as president, and he made little progress with his ambitious legislative program. His years in the White House were perhaps the unhappiest period of Adams's life.

Adams was short and stout, and his shrill voice often broke when he became excited. Yet he spoke so well he was nicknamed "Old Man Eloquent." He was affectionate with close friends, but more reserved toward others. He once referred to himself as "an unsocial savage."

During Adams's administration, Noah Webster brought out his two-volume *American Dictionary of the English Language* (1828), and James Fenimore Cooper wrote his famous novel *The Last of the Mohicans* (1826). The American labor movement began in Philadelphia.

Early life

Childhood. John Quincy Adams was born on July 11, 1767, in the family home in Braintree (now Quincy), Massachusetts. He was the second child and eldest son of the second president of the United States. During the 1770's, his father was away much of the time serving in the Continental Congresses. John Quincy had to help his mother manage a large farm. In February 1778, Con-

gress sent his father to France. John Quincy, although not yet 11, pleaded to go along on the dangerous voyage. His father proudly wrote in his diary: "Mr. Johnny's behavior gave me a satisfaction I cannot express. Fully sensible of our danger, he was constantly endeavoring to bear it with a manly patience, very attentive to me, and his thoughts constantly running in a serious vein."

Education. Adams attended schools in Paris, Amsterdam, and Leiden as his father moved from one diplomatic post to another. At 14, he went to St. Petersburg as private secretary to Francis Dana, the first American minister to Russia. The boy rejoined his father in 1783 and served as his private secretary. His father became minister to Britain (later also called the United Kingdom) in 1785, and the boy returned home and entered Harvard College. He said later: "By remaining much longer in Europe I saw the danger of an alienation from my own country." His previous studies enabled him to join the junior class at Harvard. He graduated in 1787.

Lawyer and writer. Adams read law for three years and began his own practice in 1790. But he had few clients and soon turned to political journalism.

Important dates in Adams's life

1767 (July 11) Born in Braintree (now Quincy), Massachusetts.
1794 Became minister to the Netherlands.
1797 (July 26) Married Louisa Catherine Johnson.
1803 Elected to the United States Senate.
1809 Appointed minister to Russia.
1814-1815 Helped negotiate peace with the United Kingdom.
1815 Became minister to the United Kingdom.
1817 Appointed secretary of state.
1825 Elected president of the United States.
1830 Elected to the U.S. House of Representatives.
1848 (Feb. 23) Died in Washington, D.C.

The Erie Canal, completed in 1825, linked Lake Erie with the Hudson River. It enabled freight to be shipped between the Atlantic Ocean and the Great Lakes.

The world of President John Quincy Adams

The first women's labor union was organized in 1825. The union was formed by women working in the garment industry in New York City.

Czar Nicholas I of Russia crushed the Decembrist uprising, a revolt of discontented nobles, in 1825. As a result of wars fought during the late 1820's, Russia expanded its borders to include important territory on the Black Sea.

July 4, 1826, marked the 50th anniversary of the adoption of the Declaration of Independence. In a remarkable coincidence, the deaths of two of the nation's Founding Fathers, Thomas Jefferson and John Adams, occurred that same day.

The Last of the Mohicans, one of James Fenimore Cooper's most popular works, was published in 1826.

The first overland expedition from Utah to California was led by the trader and explorer Jedediah Smith in 1826. Smith crossed Indian territories, the Mojave Desert, and the High Sierra in search of trade routes to California and the Northwest.

The Creek Indians signed treaties in 1826 and 1827 that transferred land in western Georgia to the U.S. government.

Artist and naturalist John James Audubon published the first part of his masterpiece, *Birds of America,* in 1827. The work, eventually completed in 1838, consisted of 435 life-sized, color engravings of Audubon's water colors.

Noah Webster published *An American Dictionary of the English Language* in 1828. The two-volume work included about 12,000 words and 40,000 definitions that had never appeared in any other dictionary.

View on the Erie Canal, a water color (1832) by John William Hill; Stokes Collection, New York Public Library

In 1791, Thomas Paine published the first part of *Rights of Man.* Adams considered Paine's ideas too radical and replied with 11 articles that he signed with the name "Publicola." A second series, signed "Marcellus," defended President George Washington's policy of neutrality. A third series, signed "Columbus," attacked French minister Edmond Genêt, who wanted America to join France in a war against Britain.

Political and public career

Diplomat. In 1794, Washington appointed Adams minister to the Netherlands. The French invaded the country three days after Adams arrived and overthrew the Dutch Republic. On a special assignment in London, Adams met his future wife, Louisa Catherine Johnson (Feb. 12, 1775-May 15, 1852), the daughter of a merchant who became the American consul general to London.

In 1796, Washington appointed Adams minister to Portugal. Just before he left for Lisbon, his father was elected president. Both men felt it would be undesirable for the son to hold such a post during his father's administration. But Washington urged that the younger Adams stay on, calling him "the most valuable public character now abroad." President Adams followed this recommendation and named his son minister to Prussia.

Adams's family. John Quincy married Louisa Johnson in 1797, just before leaving for Berlin. He served there more than four years. Adams and his wife had four children. Their only daughter, Louisa Catherine, died in infancy. George Washington Adams, the eldest son, died in 1829, at the close of his father's presidency. John, who was named for his grandfather, died five years later. The Adamses' youngest son, Charles Francis, served as minister to the United Kingdom during the American Civil War (1861-1865).

U.S. senator. Thomas Jefferson became president in 1801. John Quincy Adams soon returned home, and he was elected to the Massachusetts Senate in 1802. Adams soon displayed the independence that marked his entire career. Fisher Ames, the Federalist leader in Massachusetts, described him as "too unmanageable."

In 1803, the Federalists chose Adams to fill a vacant seat in the United States Senate. Although a Federalist, he often voted with the Democratic-Republicans. He broke with his party completely in 1807, when Congress passed the Embargo Act. The Federalists in New England wanted to trade with the British, but Adams supported the embargo, believing that it benefited the nation as a whole.

Doris S. Oberg, Quincy Historical Society

John Quincy Adams's birthplace stands in Quincy, Massachusetts. His father, John Adams, was born in a nearly identical house next door. The two buildings are now historic sites.

Oil painting on canvas (1821) by Gilbert Stuart; © White House Historical Association (National Geographic Society)

Louisa Johnson Adams was born in London, the daughter of an American diplomat. She first came to the United States in 1801, four years after she married John Quincy Adams.

Federalist leaders in Massachusetts felt that Adams had betrayed them. They elected another man to his Senate seat several months before the 1808 elections. Adams resigned immediately and prepared for a career as professor of rhetoric and oratory at Harvard.

Again a diplomat. Adams intended to stay out of public life permanently. But in 1809, President James Madison persuaded him to accept an appointment as minister to Russia. From mid-1814 to early 1815, Adams served as one of the American commissioners who negotiated the Treaty of Ghent with the British, ending the War of 1812. The negotiations gained respect for the United States, as well as for Adams as a diplomat.

Madison next appointed Adams as minister to the United Kingdom, a post once held by his father. While in London, Adams began discussions that led to improved relations along the U.S.-Canadian border. The United Kingdom and the United States agreed to stop using forts and warships in the Great Lakes region, leaving the frontiers of the two countries unguarded and open.

Secretary of state. In 1817, President James Monroe called Adams home to serve as secretary of state. Adams made an agreement with the United Kingdom for joint occupation of the Oregon region. He negotiated a treaty that quieted Spanish claims to territory in the northwest and also acquired Florida. But his most important achievement as secretary of state was to help develop the Monroe Doctrine.

Austria, Prussia, and Russia had formed the Holy Alliance in 1815, after the fall of Napoleon. During and after the Napoleonic Wars, the countries of Central and South America had revolted against Spanish rule. When King Ferdinand VII regained the Spanish throne in 1823, many people feared that the Holy Alliance might help Spain reconquer its former colonies. British Foreign Minister George Canning asked the United States to join in a declaration against any such move. However, Adams insisted that the United States should make its

own policy. He declared that America must not "come in as a cockboat (small rowboat) in the wake of the British man-of-war."

Adams made the first declaration of this policy in July 1823. He told the Russian minister that "the American continents are no longer subjects for any new European colonial establishments." President Monroe followed Adams's advice, and the Monroe Doctrine became a part of U.S. foreign policy. See **Monroe Doctrine**.

Election of 1824. Many Americans believed that Adams should follow Monroe as president. Both Madison and Monroe became president after serving as secretary of state. Adams felt he also should be elected but did little to attract votes. Three Democratic-Republicans opposed him: Henry Clay, William H. Crawford, and Andrew Jackson. John C. Calhoun was the running mate for both Adams and Jackson and was elected vice president. Crawford, the secretary of the treasury, had appeared to be the leading candidate, but he suffered a stroke during the campaign. Jackson received 99 electoral votes; Adams, 84; Crawford, 41; and Clay, 37. None had a majority, so the House of Representatives had to choose one of the first three men. Clay, the speaker of the House, then threw his support to Adams, who was elected in February 1825.

Adams's administration (1825-1829)

Democratic-Republican Party split. Even before the House elected Adams, followers of Jackson accused Adams of promising Clay a Cabinet post in return for his support. When Adams named Clay secretary of state, Jackson's powerful supporters charged that the two men had made a "corrupt bargain." This split the Democratic-Republican Party, and Adams's group became known as the National Republicans. Jackson's group fought Adams for the next four years.

Rebuff by Congress. Adams delivered his inaugural address in the Senate chamber of the unfinished Capitol. In this address, and in his first message to Congress, he recommended an ambitious program of national improvements. This program included the construction of highways, canals, weather stations, and a national university. He argued that if Congress did not use the powers of government for the benefit of all the people, it "would be treachery to the most sacred of trusts." But the majority in Congress disagreed. Adams's hopes for a partnership of government and science were not to be realized until after his lifetime.

The "tariff of abominations." By 1828, manufacturing had replaced farming as the chief activity in most New England states. These states favored high tariffs on imported goods. But high tariffs would make farmers in the South pay more for imported products. Southern leaders wanted a low tariff or free trade.

Jackson's supporters in Congress wrote a tariff bill that put high duties on manufactured goods. They hoped to make the duties so high that even New Englanders would oppose the bill. To everyone's surprise, enough New Englanders voted for the bill to pass it. The "tariff of abominations," as it became known, aroused bitter anger in the South.

Life in the White House. Adams threw all his energies into the presidency from the day he took office. Each day, he conferred with a steady procession of con-

Vice president and Cabinet

Vice president . . . .* John C. Calhoun	
Secretary of state . . . .* Henry Clay	
Secretary of the treasury . . . . . . .Richard Rush	
Secretary of war . . . . James Barbour	
	Peter B. Porter (1828)
Attorney general . . . . .William Wirt	
Secretary of the Navy . . . . .Samuel L. Southard	

*Has a separate biography in *World Book.*

Quotations from John Quincy Adams

The following quotations come from some of John Quincy Adams's speeches and writings.

... may our country be always successful, but whether successful or otherwise, always right.
Letter to John Adams, Aug. 1, 1816

Internal improvements was at once my conscience and my treasure.
Letter to Henry Clay, Sept. 30, 1842

... above all, let us never forget, in the most fervent heat of our party conflicts, that there is a cause, embracing and transcending all others— ... the cause of our country.
Lecture given at Providence, Rhode Island, Nov. 25, 1842

gressmen and department heads in his upstairs study in the White House. The president wrote in his diary: "I can scarcely conceive a more harassing, wearying, teasing condition of existence." He felt a lack of exercise, in spite of daily walks. In warm weather, Adams liked to swim in the Potomac River.

Mrs. Adams suffered ill health during her husband's term as president, but she overcame her sickness to serve as White House hostess. She was responsible for a brilliant series of parties during the visit of the Marquis de Lafayette in 1825.

Election of 1828. Adams had never been popular, chiefly because of his aloof manner. He had not even tried to defend himself against the attacks of Jackson and his followers, feeling it was below the dignity of the president to engage in political debate. At the same time, Jackson gained great popularity. In the election of 1828, Jackson won a popular vote proportionately larger than any other presidential candidate received during the rest of the 1800's. He and his running mate, Vice President Calhoun, won 178 electoral votes. Adams and Secretary of the Treasury Richard Rush had 83.

Back to Congress

Election to the House. Adams then retired to the family home in Quincy. But the people of Quincy asked him to run for Congress in 1830. He defeated two other candidates by large majorities and wrote in his diary: "My election as president of the United States was not half so gratifying." He took his seat in the House of Representatives in 1831 and served for 17 years.

Adams served at times as chairman of the House Foreign Affairs Committee and of the Committee on Manufactures. But he remained independent of party politics. He fought President Jackson's opposition to the second Bank of the United States. He also opposed Jackson's policy of recognizing the independence of Texas. But Adams supported Jackson's foreign policy and stern resistance to nullification (see Nullification).

The Gag Rules. Adams's greatest public role may have occurred during debates about slavery. Abolitionists sent many petitions to Congress urging that slavery be abolished in the District of Columbia and in new territories. These petitions took much of the lawmakers' time. In 1836, the House adopted the first of a series of resolutions called the Gag Rules to keep the petitions from being read on the floor. Adams believed these rules violated the constitutional rights of free speech and petition. He was strongly criticized in the House for opposing the Gag Rules, but he finally succeeded in having them abolished in 1844.

Adams became the first congressman to assert the right of the government to free slaves during time of war. President Abraham Lincoln based the Emancipation Proclamation on Adams's arguments.

The Amistad Rebellion. In 1841, Adams again publicly showed his opposition to slavery when he defended the Amistad rebels before the Supreme Court of the United States. The rebels were black Africans who had been captured and enslaved by whites. In 1839, they attacked their captors while on a ship called *La Amistad* in the Caribbean Sea. They killed two whites and took control of the vessel. They were later arrested in the United States for the killings and mutiny. Their case ended up in the Supreme Court. There, Adams strongly defended the rebels, arguing that every person has the right to freedom. The rebels were found not guilty. For more details, see **Amistad Rebellion.**

Death. On Feb. 21, 1848, he suffered a stroke at his House desk. Too ill to be moved from the building, he was carried to the speaker's room. He died there two days later. Adams was buried in the churchyard of the First Unitarian Church in Quincy, Massachusetts. His wife died on May 15, 1852, and was buried at his side. Their remains were later moved to the church crypt.

Robert J. Allison

Related articles in *World Book* include:

Outline

I. Early life
  A. Childhood
  B. Education
  C. Lawyer and writer

II. Political and public career
  A. Diplomat
  B. Adams's family
  C. U.S. senator
  D. Again a diplomat
  E. Secretary of state
  F. Election of 1824

III. Adams's administration (1825-1829)
  A. Democratic-Republican Party split
  B. Rebuff by Congress
  C. The "tariff of abominations"
  D. Life in the White House
  E. Election of 1828

IV. Back to Congress
  A. Election to the House
  B. The Gag Rules
  C. The Amistad Rebellion
  D. Death

Additional resources

Lewis, James E., Jr. *John Quincy Adams.* S R Bks., 2001.

Nagel, Paul C. *John Quincy Adams.* 1997. Reprint. Harvard Univ. Pr., 1999.
Parsons, Lynn H. *John Quincy Adams.* Madison Hse., 1998.
Remini, Robert V. *John Quincy Adams.* Times Bks., 2002.
Walker, Jane C. *John Quincy Adams.* Enslow, 2000. Younger readers.

Adams, Samuel (1722-1803), was an American patriot and politician who stirred opposition to British rule in the American Colonies. However, Adams attempted to make people work for their rights peacefully through committees and other meetings. He was willing to justify violent opposition to Britain only if all else failed. Adams was a signer of the Declaration of Independence.

Adams was born on Sept. 27, 1722, in Boston. He was the cousin of John Adams, who became the second president of the United States. Samuel graduated from Harvard College in 1740, received an M.A. degree from the college in 1743, and then entered private business. However, Adams failed in that career and by 1764 was deeply in debt.

The patriot. Adams became increasingly involved in politics. He belonged to several patriotic clubs and was a prominent figure in Boston town meetings. Adams opposed several laws passed by the British Parliament to raise revenue in the American Colonies. Those laws included the Sugar Act of 1764, the Stamp Act of 1765, and the Townshend Acts of 1767 (see **Stamp Act**). Adams served in the Massachusetts legislature from 1765 to 1774. As its clerk, he corresponded widely with other colonial leaders.

Parliament repealed the Stamp Act in 1766. In 1770, it canceled all the *duties* (import taxes) in the Townshend Acts except the tax on imported tea. Adams, however, believed American freedom was still in danger. In 1768, the British had sent soldiers to Boston. Adams thought the use of soldiers against civilians was a sign of tyranny. He served as a spokesman for the town of Boston after British troops killed several colonists in the Boston Massacre on March 5, 1770, and succeeded in getting the British troops sent elsewhere. In 1772, the Boston town meeting, spurred by Adams, set up a *committee of correspondence.* This committee published a declaration of colonial rights, which Adams had written, and sent it to other towns.

In 1773, Adams led Boston's resistance to the Tea Act, which gave a British company a monopoly on all tea exported to the colonies. The resistance reached its high point on the evening of Dec. 16, 1773, when a group of Bostonians dumped a cargo of British tea into the harbor (see **Boston Tea Party**).

The British Parliament responded in 1774 by passing the so-called Intolerable Acts. Those laws included measures that closed the port of Boston, restricted town meetings, and made it easier for Britain to use troops against American civilians (see **Intolerable Acts**). Adams then urged all the

Portrait by John Singleton Copley
Museum of Fine Arts, Boston

Samuel Adams

American Colonies to boycott trade with Britain. Representatives of 12 colonies soon assembled in the First Continental Congress in 1774 (see **Continental Congress**). The Massachusetts legislature sent Adams and four others to represent it at the congress. In 1775, Adams began serving in the Second Continental Congress, where he pleaded for independence and a *confederation* (union) of the colonies. He narrowly escaped arrest by the British in Lexington while he was on his way to Philadelphia. Congress approved the Declaration of Independence in 1776.

In office. Adams served in the Continental Congress until 1781, when he returned to Boston. He at first opposed the newly written Constitution of the United States. In the end, however, he supported its *ratification* (approval) in Massachusetts. Adams served as governor of Massachusetts from 1793 to 1797. A statue of Adams represents the state in the U.S. Capitol.   Pauline Maier

See also **Revere, Paul.**

Additional resources

Fradin, Dennis B. *Samuel Adams.* Clarion, 1998.
Irvin, Benjamin H. *Samuel Adams.* Oxford, 2002.

Adams, Samuel Hopkins (1871-1958), was an American journalist and author. Early in his career, Adams wrote newspaper and magazine articles that exposed dishonesty in business and government. His articles collected in *The Great American Fraud* (1906) dealt with patent medicine frauds and contributed to the passage of the first federal food and drug act in 1906.

About 1910, Adams began concentrating on fiction and wrote novels and short stories for both children and adults. Adams often used people and events from American history in his fiction. His most appealing historical works describe life along the Erie Canal in New York during the 1800's. His children's novel *Chingo Smith of the Erie Canal* (1958) is an example. Adams based his political novel *Revelry* (1926) on events in the administration of President Warren G. Harding. Adams also wrote several biographies and a number of mystery stories about an amateur detective called Average Jones. Adams's *Grandfather Stories* (1955) is a collection of essays. Adams was born on Jan. 26, 1871, in Dunkirk, New York.

Bert Hitchcock

Adams, Scott (1957-   ), an American cartoonist, created the comic strip "Dilbert." Dilbert is an engineer who struggles daily with the often ridiculous policies of corporate management. Other characters include fellow employees Alice and Wally; Catbert, a cat who is the human resources director; and Dogbert and Ratbert, a dog and a rat who serve as consultants. Adams bases many of his cartoons on stories that readers send him about actual experiences at their jobs.

Adams was born on June 8, 1957, in Windham, New York. He earned a graduate degree in business administration and held numerous jobs in technology and finance. "Dilbert" was first *syndicated*—that is, distributed to a large number of newspapers—in 1989. Several collections of Dilbert cartoons became best-selling books, including *The Dilbert Principle* (1996) and *Dogbert's Top Secret Management Handbook* (1996).   Pamela J. Fehl

Adams, Sherman (1899-1986), served as chief of staff to United States President Dwight D. Eisenhower from 1953 to 1958. He resigned after Democratic and Republican leaders criticized him for taking gifts from a Boston industrialist whose business affairs were under government investigation. Adams served as a Republican representative in Congress from 1945 to 1947, and as governor of New Hampshire from 1949 to 1953. He was born on Jan. 8, 1899, in East Dover, Vermont. He died on Oct. 27, 1986.   Yanek Mieczkowski

Adam's apple. See Larynx.

Adamson, Joy (1910-1980), was a wildlife conservationist and author who won wide recognition for her observations on animal behavior in Africa. She is best known for her books *Born Free* (1960), *Living Free* (1961), and *Forever Free* (1962), in which she describes the life of the lioness Elsa. Elsa was raised in the Adamson household. She was then trained to survive in the wild by Adamson and her husband, George Adamson, a wildlife conservationist and game warden. The movie *Born Free* (1966), based on Joy Adamson's books, helped spread her message of concern for wildlife.

Joy-Friederike Victoria Gessner was born on Jan. 20, 1910, in Troppau, Silesia (now Opava, the Czech Republic). She went to Kenya at the age of 27, where she married George Adamson and lived for the rest of her life. The couple acquired Elsa after George had shot a lioness, Elsa's mother, in self-defense. The Adamsons took Elsa and the lioness's two other orphaned cubs into their home. The couple trained Elsa to develop her natural hunting skills so that she could survive on her own. After her release into the wild, Elsa found a mate and raised three cubs.

The Adamsons were among the first conservationists to train a captive animal to establish its wild nature. They also worked to control *poaching,* the illegal killing of animals to obtain animal skins or the ivory of elephant tusks. Joy Adamson died of stab wounds inflicted on Jan. 3, 1980, by a former employee. George Adamson, who worked for Kenya's wildlife department, was fatally shot by poachers on Aug. 20, 1989.   G. J. Kenagy

Adaptation is a characteristic of an organism that makes it better able to survive and reproduce in its environment. For example, the long neck of a giraffe is an adaptation. It enables the giraffe to eat leaves high above the reach of many other animals.

Adaptations develop and spread through a process called *natural selection.* Natural selection occurs because every trait, such as size or color, shows some variation. Some individuals have variations that make them more likely to survive and reproduce in an environment. Other individuals do not compete as successfully for food, water, mates, and other necessities. The variations may result in whole or in part from *genetic* (hereditary)

© Shutterstock

An adaptation of color enables the butterflyfish to escape predators. The fish's markings make its tail look like a head. Confused predators do not know which end to attack.

differences among individuals. Genes that produce a helpful variation make the individual more likely to survive and reproduce. Such genes are thus more likely to be passed on to offspring. These genes tend to increase in frequency over generations, developing and spreading adaptations. See **Natural selection.**

Some organisms are adapted to living in many different environments. For example, people live in all kinds of climates. Thus, human beings are *generalized*—that is, the human body has adaptations that enable people to live in widely different environments. But other organisms are more *specialized.* Polar bears, for example, can live only in the cold climate around the Arctic Ocean.

Living things often die when they cannot adapt to a changing environment. For example, many animals became extinct around the end of the most recent ice age, about 11,500 years ago. As the climate became warmer, such animals as mammoths and saber-toothed cats struggled to adapt and eventually died out.

The word *adaptation* also refers to the ability of individuals to adjust to varying conditions in their environment. If a person moves to the mountains, his or her body adapts to the lower oxygen levels at high altitudes by making more oxygen-carrying red blood cells. A dog

DILBERT reprinted by permission of United Feature Syndicate, Inc.

A Scott Adams comic strip satirizes bureaucracy and mismanagement in business through the experiences of an engineer named Dilbert. The comic strip often pokes fun at the impact of computers in corporate activities.

adapts to warm weather by shedding its hair. Adaptations that occur over a relatively short time in an individual, particularly as a result of changes in climate, are often called *acclimatizations*.   Alan R. Templeton

See also **Animal** (The bodies of animals); **Environment; Evolution; Evolutionary psychology; Life** (Adaptation); **Plant** (The evolution of plants); **Races, Human** (Climatic adaptations).

Addams, Charles (1912-1988), an American cartoonist, became famous for the morbid humor of his drawings. He enjoyed turning ordinary situations into ghoulish comedy. His cartoons featured ghosts, monsters, haunted houses, and cemeteries. Addams was best known for creating the comically grotesque characters called the Addams family. The family inspired a popular television series (1964-1966), motion pictures, and a musical comedy.

Charles Samuel Addams was born on Jan. 7, 1912, in Westfield, New Jersey. He showed a fascination with the morbid at an early age, frequently visiting the cemetery. His neighborhood had a number of Victorian houses like the spooky mansion he drew for the Addams family.

Addams achieved his greatest popularity as a cartoonist with *The New Yorker* magazine. He began publishing in *The New Yorker* in the 1930's and became one of the magazine's most celebrated cartoonists. Collections of Addams's cartoons have been published in several books. Addams died on Sept. 29, 1988.   Pamela J. Fehl

See also **Cartoon** (picture: A gag cartoon).

Addams, Jane (1860-1935), was an American social worker, woman suffrage leader, and peace activist. She was a founder of Hull House, a Chicago settlement house that provided services for people in need (see **Hull House; Settlement house**). Addams shared the 1931 Nobel Peace Prize with the American educator Nicholas Murray Butler. She received the award for her work with the Women's International League for Peace and Freedom.

Addams was born on Sept. 6, 1860, in Cedarville, Illinois. She graduated from Rockford Female Seminary in 1881 and received a bachelor's degree the next year after it became Rockford College. She attended the Woman's Medical College of Pennsylvania from 1881 to 1882. In 1888, Addams visited Toynbee Hall, a settlement house in London, after she became interested in humanitarian work. Upon returning to the United States, she and Ellen Gates Starr, a fellow social reformer, founded Hull House in 1889. Hull House offered a variety of programs—including day nurseries and language classes—that assisted immigrants and the poor.

Addams believed strongly in the need for research into the causes of poverty and crime, in the importance of trained social workers, and in the need to press for social reforms. Among the reforms for which she was largely responsible were the first eight-hour law for working women, the first state

University of Illinois at Chicago Library, Jane Addams Memorial Collection

Jane Addams

child-labor law, housing reform, and the first juvenile court. In 1909, she became the first woman president of the National Conference of Charities and Corrections (later called the National Conference on Social Welfare).

Addams actively supported the peace and woman suffrage movements. She served as a vice president of the National American Woman Suffrage Association from 1911 to 1914. She helped found and served as chair of the Woman's Peace Party, which evolved into the Women's International League for Peace and Freedom (WILPF) in 1919. She served as the international president of the WILPF from 1915 to 1929.

Addams wrote and spoke on a variety of social issues, including child labor, public health, unemployment relief, and social insurance. Her books include *Democracy and Social Ethics* (1902), *The Spirit of Youth and the City Streets* (1909), *Twenty Years at Hull-House* (1910), *A New Conscience and an Ancient Evil* (1912), *Women at The Hague* (1915), and *Peace and Bread in Time of War* (1922). Addams died on May 21, 1935.   Melanie S. Gustafson

See also **Nobel Prizes** (picture).

Addax, *AD aks,* is an antelope that lives in the deserts of northern Africa. The addax resembles its close relative, the oryx.

The addax is well suited for desert life. It can withstand hot temperatures, go without water for long periods, and eat coarse desert plants. The animal stands about 3 ½ feet (107 centimeters) high at the shoulder. Its

© Gail Rubin, Photo Researchers

The addax is an antelope with spirally twisting horns. During the summer, it can have nearly white coloring, as shown here. Addaxes live in North African deserts in herds of 5 to 30 animals.

body and neck are grayish-brown in the winter and sandy to almost white in summer. A patch of chestnut-colored hair lies on the forehead. The spirally twisting horns grow about 4 feet (1.2 meters) long. The addax usually runs in herds of from 5 to 30 animals. It is in great danger of extinction due mostly to overhunting.
William L. Franklin

Scientific classification. The addax's scientific name is *Addax nasomaculatus.*

See also **Antelope** (Kinds of antelope).

Adder is a name given to several *species* (kinds) of snakes in various parts of the world. Most of these snakes are *venomous* (poisonous) and deadly to humans. The European viper is frequently called *adder* in the United Kingdom. It is the only venomous snake

WORLD BOOK illustration by Richard Lewington, The Garden Studio, London

An adder commonly known as the *European viper, shown here,* is the only poisonous snake that is found in the United Kingdom.

there. The puff adder of Africa is a large, deadly snake with distinct markings. It has a thick body and long fangs. The death adder is a dangerous snake of Australia. The hognose snakes of the United States are commonly called "puff adders." They get this name from their behavior of hissing and flattening the front part of their bodies when disturbed. Although hognose snakes are considered harmless, their venom can cause harmful reactions in some people.   Kenneth L. Krysko

Scientific classification. The scientific name of the European viper is *Vipera berus.* The puff adder is *Bitis arietans.* The death adder is *Acanthophis antarcticus.* Hognose snakes belong to the genus *Heterodon.*

See also **Snake** (pictures: The North American hognose snake).

Adder's-tongue. See Dogtooth violet.

Addiction. See Drug abuse.

Addis Ababa, *AD ihs AB uh buh* (pop. 3,400,000), is the capital and largest city of Ethiopia. It is a leading city of Africa and the headquarters of important regional organizations. Addis Ababa lies in central Ethiopia. For location, see **Ethiopia** (map).

Addis Ababa lies on the southern slopes of the Entoto

Four by Five

Addis Ababa, the capital of Ethiopia, lies in the central part of the country on the southern slopes of the Entoto Mountains. It is Ethiopia's largest city and a major commercial center.

Mountains. Deep ravines cut through the city. Many eucalyptus trees grow in and near Addis Ababa.

Ethiopia's national government occupies the palace of a former emperor, Menelik II, in Addis Ababa. The Jubilee Palace, the residence of former Emperor Haile Selassie I, is in the city. The African Union (AU) and the United Nations Economic Commission for Africa have their headquarters in Addis Ababa. The National Theater, Addis Ababa University, and several museums are also in the city.

Homes of wealthy and poor people stand next to each other throughout Addis Ababa. The city's housing ranges from high-rise apartment buildings and European-style homes to traditional African mud houses.

Addis Ababa is an important commercial center and has one of the largest open-air markets in Africa. This market is called the Mercato. The city's products include cement, sugar, textiles, and tobacco. Addis Ababa has an international airport, and a railroad links the capital with Djibouti, a city on the Gulf of Aden. A rapidly growing population and other factors have made unemployment a problem in Addis Ababa.

Addis Ababa was founded in 1887 by Menelik II, who was then king of Shawa Province. Menelik made Addis Ababa the capital of the province. He took the throne as emperor of Ethiopia in 1889, and Addis Ababa became the nation's capital.

Until 1974, much of Addis Ababa's land was owned by the emperor's family, members of the nobility, and the Ethiopian Orthodox Church. That year, a revolution headed by Ethiopian military leaders overthrew Emperor Haile Selassie I. Most of the city's land then came under government control.   Kenneth J. Perkins

See also **Ethiopia** (picture: Addis Ababa).

Addison, Joseph (1672-1719), was an English author and politician. He is best known for his collaboration with Sir Richard Steele in writing and publishing *The Spectator,* a series of 555 popular essays published in 1711 and 1712. The authors intended these essays to improve manners and morals, raise the cultural level of the middle-class reader, and popularize serious ideas in science and philosophy. Most of the essays deal with social behavior, love and marriage, and literature. Addison wrote with charm and polish, and Steele with liveliness and feeling. See **Steele, Sir Richard.**

The Spectator became popular because it expressed in a natural but sophisticated manner the ideals admired by its readers. The essays also gave middle-class readers a pleasant sense of self-improvement in manners and taste. To add to the interest of the essays, Addison and Steele introduced a set of representative English characters. The most famous of these characters was the simple but delightful country squire, Sir Roger de Coverley.

Addison also contributed to *The Tatler* (1709-1711), a periodical started by Steele. Addison's verse tragedy, *Cato* (1713), ran for a month on the London stage and was admired for its patriotic sentiments.

Addison was born in Milston in Wiltshire on May 1, 1672. While attending Oxford University from 1687 to 1699, he earned a reputation as a classical scholar. He was rather reserved, but his personal charm and wit won him powerful friends in London. He entered politics after achieving sensational success with a patriotic poem, "The Campaign" (1704), describing the English victory in the Battle of Blenheim. He served in Parliament from 1708 until his death and also held several government appointments. In 1717, Addison was appointed secretary of state. Illness forced him to resign in 1718.

Gary A. Stringer

Addison, Thomas (1793-1860), was a British doctor famous for his description of Addison's disease (see **Addison's disease**). Addison reported this condition, in which bronzed skin is found together with diseased adrenal glands, in a research paper in 1855. He also described Addison's anemia, known today as *pernicious anemia* (see **Anemia**).

During his lifetime, Addison's reputation rested largely on his outstanding ability as a doctor and teacher. His painstaking examinations of patients and his uncanny diagnoses became a legend.

Addison was born near Newcastle, England. He obtained his medical degree at the University of Edinburgh in 1815 and started his practice in London. In 1824, Addison was appointed assistant physician at Guy's Hospital in London. He began teaching and conducting clinical medical studies there, and his work eventually made Addison a leading figure in British medicine.

Dale C. Smith

Addison's disease is a disorder that gradually destroys the adrenal glands, causing them to produce insufficient amounts of certain hormones. The body has two adrenal glands, one located on top of each kidney. The most common cause of Addison's disease is an *autoimmune disorder* in which the body's immune system attacks and destroys the adrenal glands. Other causes of Addison's disease include cancer, infectious diseases such as tuberculosis, and such fungal diseases as histoplasmosis. Addison's disease is named after the British doctor Thomas Addison, who first described the disorder in 1855.

Addison's disease develops gradually, and patients are unable to say exactly when their symptoms began. Almost all patients experience weakness and fatigue, and most suffer weight loss. Many patients experience nausea, vomiting, and diarrhea. The disease also is characterized by abnormal skin *pigmentation* (coloration). In most patients, the skin becomes darker than normal. Abnormal pigmentation may be especially evident in areas of the body exposed to light.

Doctors treat Addison's disease by prescribing drugs to replace the missing hormones. One of the most widely used drugs is hydrocortisone. The majority of patients who receive treatment can live full, active lives.

David L. Reiss

Addition is a way of putting together two or more things to find out how many there are all together. Only *like things* can be added. This is, you cannot add apples and pencils together.

Suppose you have a set of 5 apples and a set of 3 apples on a table:

Now put the sets together in a new set of 8 apples.

You *add* when you put together two or more sets to find out how many there are all together.

Learning to add

To find out how many things you have added to make a new set, you can *count* them or *think* them together.

Addition by counting. Ralph has 3 red marbles and 4 blue marbles. He puts them together in one set.

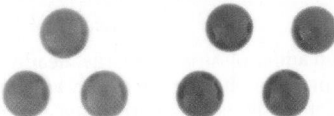

How many marbles are there in the first set? Count them. There are 3 marbles. How many marbles are there in the second set? Count them. There are 4 marbles. Now, put the marbles together and count them in the third set. There are 7 marbles. We call this *counting together*. You counted to find how many 3 marbles and 4 marbles are together. You discovered that 3 and 4 are 7.

Suppose you have drawn 3 circles. Now draw 4 more circles next to the first 3.

You know that there were already 3 circles. So you can think "3" and point to each of the 4 new circles, and count "4, 5, 6, 7." This is called *counting on*. You can find out how many 3 and 4 are together by thinking "3" for the first set, and counting on until you have counted the 4 circles in the second set. Counting on serves as a quicker way of adding things than counting them together.

Addition by thinking. Suppose there are 4 girls at the blackboard and 5 girls at the reading table. You find how many girls there are all together by thinking. For example, you could think: "I already know that 4 and 4 are 8, so 4 and 5 will be 1 more. That means that 4 and 5 are 9." Or, you could think: "4 girls and 5 girls are 9 girls." We call this *thinking together*. Thinking together is a quicker way of adding than counting together or counting on.

Addition terms

Addend. In 4 + 9 = 13, the numbers which are added, 4 and 9, are both addends.
Addition fact is a basic statement in addition. For example, 2 + 3 = 5 and 8 + 7 = 15 are addition facts.
Carry in addition means to transfer a number from one place in the sum to the next. A 10 in the 1's place must be carried to the 10's place.
Sum. In 4 + 9 = 13, the total, 13, is the sum.

Regrouping. Suppose you want to put together two sets in a new set and the new set will be more than 10. For example, Nancy wanted to know how many 9 and 6 are. To find out, she drew a *number line:*

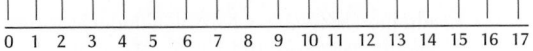

Then, she drew lines to show 9 and 6 as shown below:

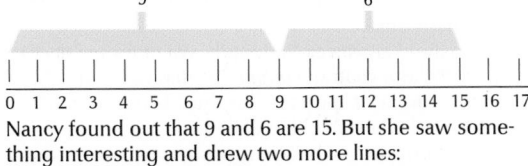

Nancy found out that 9 and 6 are 15. But she saw something interesting and drew two more lines:

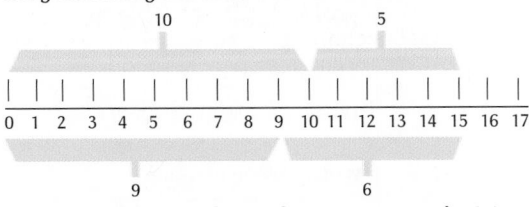

Nancy found that 9 and 6 are the same as 10 and 5. It is easier for beginners to add 10 and 5 than it is to add 9 and 6. We call changing the sets 9 and 6 to the sets 5 and 10 *regrouping.* Here are some examples:

8 and 4 are 12   **(10 and 2)**
7 and 8 are 15   **(10 and 5)**
9 and 4 are 13   **(10 and 3)**

Writing addition. You should write down your addition problems, so you have a record of your counting or thinking.

You can make a record with pictures:

Or you can make a record with numbers and words:
2 and 4 are 6

But it is easiest and best to make a record with numbers and signs:

$$2 + 4 = 6 \quad \text{or} \quad \begin{array}{r} 2 \\ 4 \\ \hline 6 \end{array}$$

In the first example, the plus sign (+) tells you to add. You can read 2 + 4 as "two and four." The equals sign (=) means that the sets on one side of the sign are *equal* to the set on the other side of the sign. You can read 2 + 4 = 6 as "two and four are six." The second example shows how you write an addition problem when you want to work out the answer on paper. The two or more groups you want to put together, or add, are called *addends.* The new group is called the *sum.*

$$\begin{array}{r} 2 \\ 4 \\ \hline 6 \end{array} \begin{array}{l} \Longleftarrow Addend \\ \Longleftarrow Addend \\ \Longleftarrow Sum \end{array}$$

Addition facts. By putting together sets, you have discovered that 5 + 3 = 8, 3 + 4 = 7, and 9 + 6 = 15. We call these *addition facts.* Each addition fact is made up of two addends and a sum. You can discover all the addition facts by putting together sets of things. Some beginners practice with sets of pennies or bottle caps.

The 81 addition facts

1	1	1	1	1	1	1	1	1
1	2	3	4	5	6	7	8	9
2	3	4	5	6	7	8	9	10
2	2	2	2	2	2	2	2	2
1	2	3	4	5	6	7	8	9
3	4	5	6	7	8	9	10	11
3	3	3	3	3	3	3	3	3
1	2	3	4	5	6	7	8	9
4	5	6	7	8	9	10	11	12
4	4	4	4	4	4	4	4	4
1	2	3	4	5	6	7	8	9
5	6	7	8	9	10	11	12	13
5	5	5	5	5	5	5	5	5
1	2	3	4	5	6	7	8	9
6	7	8	9	10	11	12	13	14
6	6	6	6	6	6	6	6	6
1	2	3	4	5	6	7	8	9
7	8	9	10	11	12	13	14	15
7	7	7	7	7	7	7	7	7
1	2	3	4	5	6	7	8	9
8	9	10	11	12	13	14	15	16
8	8	8	8	8	8	8	8	8
1	2	3	4	5	6	7	8	9
9	10	11	12	13	14	15	16	17
9	9	9	9	9	9	9	9	9
1	2	3	4	5	6	7	8	9
10	11	12	13	14	15	16	17	18

It is best to learn the addition facts so you can use them quickly and easily. You will be able to use them in your daily life. You will also need them to add larger numbers and solve problems.

Learning these addition facts looks like work at first. But there are several ways to make learning the facts easier. For instance, if you look at all the facts in which a number and 1 are added, you will see that learning them is something like ordinary counting. Also, many of the pairs of addends are just the *reverse* of each other. For example, 4 + 5 adds up to the same thing as 5 + 4. We call a fact like 3 + 3 = 6 a *double.* Knowing doubles is useful. If you know that 4 + 4 = 8, then 4 + 3 is 1 less than 8, and 4 + 5 is 1 more than 8. You should be able to think of other ways to help you learn the addition facts.

Adding larger numbers

You use the addition facts and the idea of place value to add larger numbers.

Adding 10's. Last week, Tom earned 2 dimes, or 20¢. This week, Tom earned 3 dimes, or 30¢. How much has

Tom earned all together? You can find the answer by counting.

   1   2   3   4   5

You find that Tom earned 5 dimes, or 50¢. You can find the answer by adding.

2 dimes	20¢
3 dimes	30¢
5 dimes	50¢

If you know that 2 + 3 = 5, you know that 2 dimes and 3 dimes are 5 dimes. A dime is 10¢, so you can see that 20¢ + 30¢ = 50¢.

Here is another example:

4	**4 tens**	40
2	**2 tens**	20
6	**6 tens**	60

You can see that 4 + 2 = 6, 4 tens + 2 tens = 6 tens, and 40 + 20 = 60. The 6 in the 60 shows six 10's because it is in the 10's place. *You add 10's the same way you add 1's. But you must write the sum in the 10's place.* And you must remember to write a zero in the 1's place to show that the sum is 10's, not 1's.

Here is a third example:

8	**8 tens**	80
9	**9 tens**	90
17	**17 tens**	170

Here the sum of the 10's is seventeen 10's. Seventeen 10's is the same as ten 10's and seven 10's. But ten 10's is 100. So you must write the sum in the 10's and 100's places, and write in a zero to show that the answer is one 100, seven 10's, and no 1's.

Adding 10's and 1's. Suppose there are 23 boys and 24 girls in a school play. To find out how many children there are all together, you must add 23 and 24

2 tens and 3 ones	23
2 tens and 4 ones	24
4 tens and 7 ones	

We call the numbers 23 and 24 *two-place numbers.* When you add two-place numbers, you add the 1's first. In this example, three 1's and four 1's are 3 + 4 = 7. You write the sum of the 1's in the 1's place of the answer:

$$\begin{array}{r} 23 \\ 24 \\ \hline 7 \end{array}$$

Next, you add the 10's. Two 10's and two 10's are added as 2 + 2 = 4. The 4 stands for four 10's. You write the sum of the 10's in the 10's place of the answer:

$$\begin{array}{r} 23 \\ 24 \\ \hline 47 \end{array}$$

So there are 47 children in the school play.

Here is another example:

$$\begin{array}{r} 72 \\ 43 \\ \hline 115 \end{array}$$

First, you add the 1's: 2 + 3 = 5. Next, you find that seven 10's and four 10's are eleven 10's. Eleven 10's are the same as ten 10's and one 10, or one 100 and one 10. So you must write the sum of the 10's in the 10's and 100's places in the answer.

When there are several addends, we often speak of the 1's, 10's, and 100's as *columns.* When you add columns, you must learn to *think* the additions. At first it may help to keep some kind of record.

22 31 45 98	1's	**Think:** 2 + 1 = 3. 3 + 5 = 8. **Write:** 8 in the 1's place.
	10's	**Think:** 2 tens + 3 tens = 5 tens. 5 tens + 4 tens = 9 tens. **Write:** 9 in the 10's place.

With practice, adding two-place numbers and long columns will be easy.

How to carry. When you add two-place numbers, the sum of the 1's column is often 10 or more. To add such numbers, you must learn to *carry.*

Here is an example of carrying:

45 27 2	1's	**Think:** Five 1's and seven 1's are twelve 1's: 5 + 7 = 12. Twelve is one 10 and 2 ones. **Write:** 2 in the 1's place.
	Carry	From the 1's column, there is a 10 to be added to the 10's column. Write a 1 for the one 10 at the top of the column. This is what *carrying* means.
1 45 27 72	10's	**Think:** One 10 + four 10's + two 10's = seven 10's. 1 + 4 + 2 = 7 **Write:** 7 in the 10's place.

You add longer columns the same way.

$$\begin{array}{r} 24 \\ 52 \\ 17 \end{array}$$

First, add the 1's column: 4 + 2 = 6, and 6 + 7 = 13. Thirteen is one 10 and three 1's. Write the 3 in the 1's place of the answer. Carry the one 10 to the 10's column by writing a 1 at the top of the 10's column.

$$\begin{array}{r} 1 \\ 24 \\ 52 \\ 17 \\ \hline 3 \end{array}$$

Now add the 10's column: 1 + 2 = 3, 3 + 5 = 8, and 8 + 1 = 9. This 9 means nine 10's. Write the 9 in the 10's place.

```
   1
  24
  52
  17
  93
```

Adding three-place and four-place numbers is no more difficult than the examples you have just done. You must always remember to keep the columns straight, and to add 1's, 10's, 100's, and so on, in order. Here is an example:

```
 371
 403
 139
```

First, add the 1's column: 1 + 3 + 9 = 13. Write 3 for three 1's in the 1's place of the answer. Carry the 10 by writing 1 for one 10 at the top of the 10's column.

```
   1
 371
 403
 139
   3
```

Next, add the 10's column: 1 + 7 + 0 + 3 = 11. This is *not* eleven 1's. It is eleven 10's. Eleven 10's is one 100 and one 10. So write 1 for the one 10 in the 10's place of the answer. Carry the 100 by writing 1 for one 100 at the top of the 100's column.

```
  11
 371
 403
 139
  13
```

Now add the 100's column: 1 + 3 + 4 + 1 = 9. This 9 is nine 100's. Write 9 in the 100's place of the answer.

```
  11
 371
 403
 139
 913
```

The sum is 913. You use the same method of carrying for 1,000's and larger numbers.

Here is an example in which the number you carry is more than one 10:

```
 37
 29
 18
```

First, add the 1's column: 7 + 9 + 8 = 24. Twenty-four is two 10's and four 1's. Write the 4 in the 1's place in the answer. Carry the two 10's to the 10's column by writing a 2 at the top of the 10's column.

```
  2
 37
 29
 18
  4
```

Now add the 10's column: 2 + 3 + 2 + 1 = 8. This 8 means eight 10's. Write the 8 in the 10's place of the answer.

```
  2
 37
 29
 18
 84
```

The sum is 84. The numbers you carry may often be 20's or 30's or 40's, and so on.

Checking addition

Good workers always check their addition to see if they have made any mistakes. There are several ways to check addition.

Adding up. You have learned to add a column of figures by starting at the top and adding down. After you have written the sum, you can check your answer by *adding up*. That is, starting at the bottom of the column and adding up to the top. Here is an example:

```
21
34
42
97
```

	Check		
1's	2 + 4 = 6.	6 + 1 = 7
10's	4 + 3 = 7.	7 + 2 = 9

If you get the same answer adding up as you did adding down, your answer is probably right.

Subtraction can be used to check problems with only two addends (see **Subtraction**). Here is an example:

```
  422
+ 736
 1158
```

To check the addition, subtract one of the addends from the sum. For example, subtract 736 from 1,158. The subtraction should leave 422 if the addition is correct:

```
 1158
- 736
  422
```

Estimating is a good way of checking addition, but it will not catch small mistakes. If you estimate before you work a problem, you will have an idea of your answer in advance. You should get into the habit of always estimating your answer first. Here is an example:

```
 32
 46
 71
149
```

Estimating
(Think)
32 is about 30.
45 is about 50.
30 and 50 are 80.
71 is about 70.
80 and 70 are 150.
The answer should be about 150.

There are other methods of checking used in arithmetic. Some of them can be used for addition.

Addition rules to remember

1. Remember what addition means. You can find the answers to addition problems by counting. But it is quicker and easier to *think* the answers.

2. Learning the 81 addition facts will help you think the answers to addition problems.

3. You can put the addends in any order without changing the sum of the equation. For example, 3 + 2 + 7 = 12, 2 + 7 + 3 = 12, and 7 + 3 + 2 = 12.

4. You can add only quantities of the same kind. That is, you must add 1's to 1's and 10's to 10's, and be careful not to mix them up.

Fun with addition

Two winks. Make a pack of 20 cards on which the numbers from 1 to 10 have been written. Make two cards for each number. Divide the pack of cards into two piles, and put one pile facedown in front of each player. The first player turns a card and holds it up for both players to see. The second player does the same thing from the other pile of cards. The player who first sees that the sum of the numbers on the two cards is 10 or more calls out "Two winks!" Then, that player takes

the two cards. If the two cards do not equal 10 or more, the players put them back in the piles. The game continues, with two new players turning the cards. When all of the cards have been turned, the player with the most cards wins.

Tick-tack-toe puzzle. Each player draws a tick-tack-toe figure on a piece of paper.

Then, each tries to fill in the spaces with the numbers from 1 to 9, so that if three numbers are added across, up and down, or diagonally the sums will be 15. The player must use each number from 1 to 9. The first player with the correct answer wins.   Nadine L. Verderber

Related articles in *World Book* include:

Abacus	Fraction
Algebra (Addition)	Mathematics
Arithmetic	Multiplication
Decimal system	Subtraction
Division	

Outline

I. **Learning to add**
    A. Addition by counting   D. Writing addition
    B. Addition by thinking   E. Addition facts
    C. Regrouping

II. **Adding larger numbers**
    A. Adding 10's   C. How to carry
    B. Adding 10's and 1's

III. **Checking addition**
    A. Adding up   B. Subtraction   C. Estimating

IV. **Addition rules to remember**

V. **Fun with addition**

Practice addition examples

In each of the first six problems, what number should be used to replace the N?

1. 5 + 2 = 7	2. 8 + 6 = 14	3. 5 + 9 = 14	4. 3 + 6 = N	5. 7 + 9 = N	6. 8 + N = 13
2 + N = 7	N + 8 = 14	9 + 5 = N	6 + 3 = N	9 + N = 16	5 + 8 = N

7. 4
  2
	10. 34
	   2
		13. 35
		   6
			16. 20¢
			  80¢
				19. 10
				  70
					22. 74¢
					  65¢
						25. 14
						  64
							28. 37¢
							  56¢

8. 14
  2
	11. 5
	  6
		14. 45
		   6
			17. 60¢
			  70¢
				20. 37¢
				  42¢
					23. 65
					  23
						26. 65¢
						  18¢
							29. 98
							  69

9. 24
  2
	12. 25
	  6
		15. 40¢
		  30¢
			18. 50
			  90
				21. 56¢
				  33¢
					24. 43
					  52
						27. 29¢
						  48¢
							30. 75
							  58

31. 3¢ 9¢ 4¢ 6¢	32. 6¢ 8¢ 6¢ 3¢	33. 6 5 4 7	34. 7 8 4 6	35. $2.49 1.29 36. $7.65 1.82	37. $3.95 4.89 38. 525 482	39. 618 489 40. 311 299	41. 30 78 62 50	42. 43 20 80 7	43. 402 187 260 517	44. 5627 1872 9000 4351	45. 7269 143 2425 82

Answers to the practice examples

1. 5	6. 5, 13	11. 11	16. $1.00	21. 89¢	26. 83¢	31. 22¢	36. $9.47	41. 220
2. 6	7. 6	12. 31	17. $1.30	22. $1.39	27. 77¢	32. 23¢	37. $8.84	42. 150
3. 14	8. 16	13. 41	18. 140	23. 88	28. 93¢	33. 22	38. 1,007	43. 1,366
4. 9, 9	9. 26	14. 51	19. 80	24. 95	29. 167	34. 25	39. 1,107	44. 20,850
5. 16, 7	10. 36	15. 70¢	20. 79¢	25. 78	30. 133	35. $3.78	40. 610	45. 9,919

Address, Forms of, are courteous, formal ways to introduce, speak to, write to, or send e-mail to other people. In most cases, you can address another person as "Mr. Green" or "Ms. Green" or by using that person's title before his or her last name. In business correspondence, use "Miss" or "Mrs." only when you know that the recipient prefers such a form of address. Government officials, members of royalty, religious dignitaries, and members of certain professions merit special forms of address. This article gives some of the most commonly used forms of address for people in such positions.

"Yours truly" is a common closing for letters, though there are many others. Certain situations require a more formal closing such as "Respectfully yours."

In the examples listed here, the first indentation under each entry provides the formal way to introduce or refer to the person in each position. The second indentation gives the proper salutation to use for communicating with the person in writing or by e-mail. An acceptable closing is also included for positions in which "yours truly" is considered insufficiently formal.

Officials of the United States

President
    The President
    Dear Mr. *or* Madam President:
Closing: Respectfully,
Vice president
    The Vice President
    Dear Mr. *or* Madam Vice President:
Cabinet member (except attorney general)
    The Honorable John *or* Mary Green, Secretary of (State *or* Transportation, for example)
    Dear Mr. *or* Madam Secretary: *or* Dear Secretary Green:
(Deputy secretaries, assistant secretaries, and undersecretaries are addressed by their specific title, but the salutation is "Dear Mr. *or* Ms. Green".)
Assistant to the president
    The Honorable John *or* Mary Green *or* Assistant to the President Green
    Dear Mr. *or* Ms. Green:
Attorney general
    The Attorney General
    Dear Mr. *or* Madam Attorney General:
Chief justice of the United States
    The Chief Justice of the United States
    Dear Mr. *or* Madam Chief Justice:
Associate justice of the Supreme Court
    Justice Green
    Dear Mr. *or* Madam Justice: *or* Dear Justice Green:
United States senator
    The Honorable John *or* Mary Green
    Dear Senator: *or* Dear Senator Green:
United States representative
    The Honorable John *or* Mary Green
    Dear Mr. *or* Ms. Green: *or* Dear Representative Green: *or* Dear Congressman *or* Congresswoman Green:
Speaker of the House of Representatives
    The Honorable John *or* Mary Green
    Dear Mr. *or* Madam Speaker:
Member of an agency, bureau, or commission
    The Honorable John *or* Mary Green
    Dear Mr. *or* Madam Chairman: *or* Dear Mr. *or* Ms. Green:
(For a commissioner, the salutation is generally "Dear Commissioner Green".)
Ambassador
    The Honorable John *or* Mary Green, Ambassador of the United States of America
    Sir *or* Madam: *or* Dear Mr. *or* Madam Ambassador:

Closing: Very truly yours,
(Although it is permissible to refer to a United States ambassador as "American Ambassador," it is best not to do so because other Western Hemisphere ambassadors also consider themselves Americans. Ministers, chargés d'affaires, consuls, and secretaries all use their full title in place of "Ambassador" but are addressed as "Dear Mr. *or* Ms. Green".)
Governor of a state
    The Honorable John *or* Mary Green
    Dear Sir *or* Madam: *or* Dear Governor Green:
State senator
    The Honorable John *or* Mary Green
    Dear Sir *or* Madam: *or* Dear Senator Green:
State representative
    The Honorable John *or* Mary Green
    Dear Sir *or* Madam: *or* Dear Representative Green:
Mayor or city manager
    The Honorable John *or* Mary Green
    Dear Sir *or* Madam: *or* Dear Mayor Green:
(City managers do not use "Honorable" except at ceremonies. They are addressed as "Mr. John Green" *or* "Ms. Mary Green" and "Dear Mr. Green" *or* "Dear Ms. Green".)

Officials of the Commonwealth of Nations

King or queen
    His *or* Her Majesty
    Your Majesty: *or* Madam:
Closing: Respectfully, *or* Respectfully yours,
Prince or princess
    His Royal Highness, the Prince John *or* Her Royal Highness, the Princess Mary
    Your Royal Highness:
Closing: Respectfully, *or* Respectfully yours,
Knight or dame
    Sir John Green *or* Dame Mary Green
    Dear Sir John Green *or* Dear Dame Mary Green:
(A knight's or dame's name is followed by initials that designate the order of knighthood. For example, *KCB* or *DCB* stand for *Knight Commander of the Bath* or *Dame Commander of the Bath;* and *KG* or *DG* stand for *Knight of the Garter* or *Dame of the Garter.*)
Prime minister
    The Right Honourable John *or* Mary Green, Prime Minister of (Canada or the United Kingdom, for example)
    Dear Sir *or* Madam: *or* Dear Prime Minister:
Closing: Respectfully yours, *or* Very truly yours,
Member of the House of Lords of the United Kingdom
    The Right Honourable the (Duke *or* Earl *or* Viscount, for example) Green
    My Lord:
Member of the House of Commons
    John *or* Mary Green, M.P.
    Dear Sir *or* Madam:
Governor general
    His *or* Her Excellency the Right Honourable John *or* Mary Green, Governor General of (Canada, for example)
    Dear Sir *or* Madam: *or* Sir *or* Madam:
Premier or prime minister of a province
    The Honourable John *or* Mary Green, Prime Minister of (Ontario, for example)
    Dear Sir *or* Madam: *or* Sir *or* Madam:
Senator
    The Honourable John *or* Mary Green
    Dear Sir *or* Madam:
Minister of a department
    John *or* Mary Green, Minister of (Transport, for example)
    Dear Sir *or* Madam:
Judge
    The Honourable Mr. Justice John Green *or* The Honourable Ms. Justice Mary Green
    Dear Justice Green:
(A High Court judge is addressed as "Your Lordship" or "My Lord" only when the court is in session. An English or Australian

justice of the peace on the bench is addressed in court as "Your Worship." In Canada, judges for county and district courts are addressed as "His or Her Honour Judge Green.")

Mayor
His Worship Mayor John Green or
Her Worship Mayor Mary Green
Dear Sir or Madam: or Dear Sir or Madam Mayor:

President
The Right Honourable John or Mary Green, President of the Republic
Dear Sir or Madam: or Dear Sir or Madam President:

Foreign officials in the United States

Ambassador to the United States
His or Her Excellency John or Mary Green,
Ambassador of (Australia, for example)
Dear Mr. or Madam Green: or Dear Mr. or
Madam Ambassador:

Secretary-general of the United Nations
His or Her Excellency John or Mary Green,
Secretary-General of the United Nations
Sir or Madam: or Dear Mr. or Madam Secretary-General:
(Ambassadors and representatives to the United Nations use the form "Representative of Brazil to the United Nations.")

Representative to the United Nations
You may use the forms of address for Ambassador as a general guide for addressing United Nations representatives. However, each member nation awards its own titles to its individual representatives to the United Nations. Whenever possible, the representatives should be addressed by the titles conferred by their country.

Members of the clergy

Roman Catholic archbishop or bishop
Your excellency or Archbishop Green
Your excellency or Bishop Green
Archbishop or Bishop of (Chicago, for example)
Dear Archbishop or Bishop Green:
(Episcopal bishops often use "The Right Reverend." Greek Orthodox bishops often use "The Very Reverend.")

Roman Catholic cardinal
His Eminence John Cardinal Green
Your Eminence: or My Dear Cardinal Green:

Roman Catholic priest
The Reverend Father John Green
Dear Father Green: or Reverend Father:

Roman Catholic nun
Sister Mary Xavier, T.O.S.F.
Dear Sister Xavier:

Church of England archbishop
The Most Reverend John Green, the Lord Archbishop of (Canterbury, for example)
Your Grace: or My Dear Archbishop:

Church of England bishop
The Right Reverend John or Mary Green
Dear Bishop or Dear Bishop Green:

Church of England priest
The Reverend John or Mary Green
Dear John or Mary Green: or Dear Mr. or Ms. Green: or Dear Father Green:

Church of England canon
The Reverend Canon John Green
Dear Canon Green:

Protestant minister
The Reverend John or Mary Green
Dear Reverend Green:
(If a minister has a doctor's degree from a university, it is often used in the salutation in place of "Reverend,"as "Dear Doctor Green:".)

Rabbi
Rabbi Jacob or Miriam Green
Dear Rabbi Green:

Other forms

President or chancellor of a university or college
President or Chancellor John Green or President or Chancellor Mary Green
Dear President or Chancellor Green:

Professor
Professor John or Mary Green
Dear Professor Green:
(Full professors, associate professors, and assistant professors can be addressed as "Professor." Lecturers, instructors, and fellows are addressed as "Mr." or "Ms.")

Lawyer
John R. Green, Esq.
Dear Mr. Green:
(Attorneys, especially in the United States, usually address each other by "Esq." This abbreviation stands for "esquire."In the United Kingdom, Queen's Counsel add the initials Q.C. after the name.)

Doctor of medicine or dentistry
Medicine: Dr. John or Mary Green, or John or Mary Green, M.D.
Dentistry: Dr. John or Mary Green, or John or Mary Green, D.D.S.
(In the United States, all medical doctors and dentists are addressed as "Dr." In the United Kingdom, surgeons and specialists are more often addressed as "Mr." Dentists are rarely addressed as "Dr."

Doctor of veterinary medicine:
Dr. John or Mary Green, or John or Mary Green, D.V.M.
Dear Dr. Green:

Doctor of an academic discipline
Dr. John or Mary Green, or John or Mary Green, Ph.D. or Ed.D.
Dear Dr. Green:
(People outside the medical and health professions who hold a doctorate may choose whether or not to be addressed as "Dr.")

Military officer
Captain John or Mary Green, U.S. Coast Guard
Dear Captain Green:
(All people who hold rank that has subgrades, such as vice admiral, second lieutenant, or master sergeant, are addressed by their rank without qualification—as, for example, "Dear Admiral:", "Dear Lieutenant," or "Dear Sergeant:".)

Widow
Mrs. John Green
Dear Mrs. Green:
(If a widow or a divorced woman signs her own name to a letter "Mrs. Betty Green," then the person writing to this woman should use the same form of address.)　Deborah Dumaine

See also **Letter writing.**

Ade, ayd, **George** (1866-1944), was an American humorist, playwright, and journalist. He won fame for his comic stories written in the everyday speech and popular slang of the rural Midwest, especially his home state of Indiana. Ade's best-known work is *Fables in Slang* (1899), a collection of stories modeled on *Aesop's Fables.* The work consists of humorous tales of country life and of country people living in the city. It also makes fun of show-offs and bigots.

Ade was also a noted comic playwright and author of musical comedies. His most successful works for the musical stage were *The Sultan of Sulu* (1902) and *The Sho-Gun* (1904). His most significant plays were two comedies of small-town life in the United States, *The County Chairman* (1903) and *The College Widow* (1904). Although Ade's theater works are rarely staged today, they provide a significant record of American life in the early 1900's.

Ade was born on Feb. 9, 1866, in Kentland, Indiana. In the 1890's, he worked as a reporter for the Chicago *Record.* Many of his stories originally appeared in a column he wrote for the newspaper. Ade died on March 16, 1944. Samuel Chase Coale

Adelaide, *AD uh* LAYD (pop. 1,165,632; met. area pop. 1,295,714), is the capital of the state of South Australia, as well as the state's largest city, its economic center, and its chief port. The city lies on a plain on Australia's southern coast and extends inland from Gulf St. Vincent, an inlet off the Indian Ocean. For the location of Adelaide, see **Australia** (political map). The city was named for Queen Adelaide, whose husband, William IV, ruled the United Kingdom from 1830 to 1837.

The Torrens River flows through Adelaide. The city's central business district is on both banks of the river, 6 miles (10 kilometers) inland from Gulf St. Vincent. A belt of beautiful parkland surrounds the central business district. Adelaide's residential, commercial, and industrial areas spread north and south along the plain. The Mount Lofty Ranges rise east of the city.

Manufacturing is a major economic activity in the Adelaide area. Products include machinery, motor vehicles, electrical goods, and processed foods. The city also has a significant defense industry. Adelaide hosts an international Festival of Arts every two years.

Adelaide was first settled by Europeans in 1836. Colonel William Light, the first surveyor general of South Australia, completed a city plan for Adelaide in 1837. The city quickly became an important center for nearby agricultural and mining activities. Many new industries were established in Adelaide after World War II ended in 1945. The city's population has grown greatly since then and now accounts for about 70 percent of South Australia's population. Garry R. LeDuff

See also **South Australia** (picture).

Adélie penguin, *uh* DAY *lee,* is a medium-sized penguin. It stands about 18 inches (46 centimeters) tall and weighs 8 ½ to 12 pounds (4 to 5.5 kilograms). It lives in Antarctica and the surrounding Southern Ocean.

An adult Adélie penguin has a black face. The head, back, and tail are also black. The underparts are white. The Adélie penguin has a white ring around the eyes. The beak appears short because nearly half of it is covered in feathers.

The Adélie penguin lives in colonies on the coast of

© Shutterstock

The Adélie penguin is a medium-sized penguin of Antarctica and the Southern Ocean. Adélie penguins gather in rocky areas to form large nesting colonies.

Antarctica or nearby islands. It requires a rocky area free from ice. The colonies may be quite large. The largest colony at Cape Adare, in the Ross Sea, can have more than 300,000 breeding pairs. In winter, the penguins move north into the pack ice that surrounds Antarctica.

The Adélie penguin eats mainly shrimplike animals called krill and other *crustaceans*—a type of animal with a shell and jointed legs. It also feeds on small fish and some squid. Most of the prey is caught at depths of less than 130 feet (40 meters). The penguin is capable of diving to 575 feet (175 meters).

At sea, the Adélie penguin is hunted by leopard seals and killer whales. Birds called skuas prey on eggs and chicks at the colonies.

The Adélie penguin builds nests from pebbles. The female lays two eggs. Both parents take turns incubating the eggs, for a total of up to about 39 days. Chicks leave the colony when they are about 50 days old. The Adélie penguin lives for 10 to 20 years. It starts to breed when it is 5 to 6 years old. Barbara Wienecke

Scientific classification. The scientific name of the Adélie penguin is *Pygoscelis adeliae.*

Aden, *AHD uhn* or *AYD uhn* (pop. 800,000), is the second largest city of Yemen. Only Sanaa has more people. Aden lies on a small peninsula that extends into the Gulf of Aden (see **Yemen** [map]). Aden has served as an important port and trading center since ancient times.

Aden has both broad streets lined by modern buildings and winding, narrow streets bordered by old, thick-walled Arab buildings. The city serves as the trading center for its region and as a refueling place for ships. It has a large oil refinery. Manufactured products include cooking oil and textiles.

Aden became an important Roman trading center during ancient times. In 1839, British forces took over the city. In 1967, Yemen (Aden) became an independent nation with Aden as its capital. In 1990, Yemen (Aden) and Yemen (Sanaa) merged and became the country of Yemen, with Sanaa as the capital.

In 2013, fighting between Islamic extremists, southern rebels, and government forces erupted in parts of Yemen. In 2015, the violence escalated and spread to Aden, damaging large parts of the city. Many people died in the fighting and many more fled the city.

Robert Geran Landen

Adena Indians. See Mound builders.

Adenauer, *AH duh* NOW *uhr,* **Konrad** (1876-1967), served as chancellor of the West German Republic from its formation in 1949 until he retired in 1963. Under his leadership, West Germany gained its sovereignty, made an extraordinary economic recovery, built its military power, and played a major role in Western European affairs. Adenauer's accomplishments were all the more remarkable because he was 73 years old when he started his 14 years as chancellor.

Adenauer helped bring Germany into the North Atlantic Treaty Organization (NATO), the Council of

Wide World

Konrad Adenauer

Europe, the European Coal and Steel Community, and the European Economic Community. Adenauer allied his country with the Western powers. He acknowledged Germany's responsibility for the crimes committed against Jews during World War II (1939-1945), and Germany paid war reparations to the Jewish state of Israel. Adenauer and French President Charles de Gaulle signed a Franco-German Treaty of Cooperation in 1963. The treaty was seen as a symbol of reconciliation between France and Germany, which had traditionally been enemies.

As chancellor, Adenauer exercised strong rule. He treated his ministers as subordinates rather than as his colleagues. During his later years as chancellor, Adenauer's actions were criticized both by his own Christian Democratic Union Party members and by his opponents.

Adenauer was born on Jan. 5, 1876, in Cologne, Germany. He studied at the universities of Freiburg, Munich, and Bonn, and became a lawyer. He served as mayor of Cologne from 1917 to 1933. During World War II, the Nazis imprisoned him several times.

The Allies made Adenauer mayor of Cologne when they occupied Germany after World War II. However, the British dismissed him, and Adenauer entered national politics in 1947 as the leader of the Christian Democratic Party. He played an important role in drafting the West German Constitution, which went into force in 1949. That year, Adenauer won his first election as chancellor. After Adenauer retired in 1963, his vice chancellor, Ludwig Erhard, was elected chancellor. Adenauer died on April 19, 1967.   Otis C. Mitchell

Adenoids. See Tonsil.

ADHD. See Attention deficit disorder.

Adhesion, *ad HEE zhuhn,* is the property of two unlike substances that causes them to stick together. Adhesion occurs because of the attraction between all molecules and atoms.

Adhesive strength varies, depending on the characteristics of the substances coming together. The adhesion between the surfaces of two solid substances tends to be low, even if they seem perfectly flat and clean. The surfaces are actually rough when viewed through a microscope, and touch each other at relatively few places. But if one of the substances is part or all liquid, contact between the surfaces is much greater.

The strongest adhesives are applied as thin layers of liquids. In many cases, these liquids are solutions of *polymers,* large molecules formed by the chemical linking of many smaller molecules into a long chain. As these solutions set, their molecules become immovable. The adhesion can be so good that a strong force will cause the substance, but not the adhesive bond, to break.   Robert B. Prigo

See also **Cohesion.**

Adhesion, *ad HEE zhuhn,* in the body, is a term for bands of scar tissue that sometimes bind together internal organs that are normally separate. The tough, fibrous tissue usually grows as a result of inflammation or a surgical operation. Adhesions are frequently painful and may interfere with the normal work of the internal organs. Diseases of the heart or lungs may result in painful adhesions between those organs and the surrounding parts of the body. After abdominal operations, adhesions sometimes cause parts of the intestine to grow to-

gether or to the lining of the abdomen. If the adhesions interfere with digestion, additional surgical operations may be necessary. See also **Tissue.**   David T. Woodley

Adhesive is a substance that bonds surfaces together. Adhesives include such materials as cement, epoxy, paste, polyurethane, white glue, and cyanoacrylate (super glue). Adhesives are used in homes, offices, and schools. They also play an important role in the manufacture of many products, including aircraft, automobiles, books, furniture, and toys. In addition, they are used in the construction of buildings and roads. Many people use adhesives to make simple household repairs.

Since ancient times, people have made adhesives from such natural materials as beeswax, egg yolks, tree sap, and proteins from animal hides, hooves, and blood. Today, most adhesives are made from plastics and other synthetic materials.

Adhesives vary in the way they are applied and in the manner in which they form a bond. Adhesives made from the synthetic materials *polyethylene* and *polyvinyl acetate,* called *hot melt adhesives,* are heated to a liquid state before being applied. The bond forms as the adhesive cools and hardens. Epoxy adhesives are usually sold as two substances in separate tubes. The two substances must be mixed before being applied to the surfaces to be joined. The molecules of epoxy adhesives *cross-link* (interconnect) to form a *thermoset material,* which cannot be deformed by heat or pressure. Cyanoacrylate reacts with water on the joined surfaces to create a strong, but brittle, adhesive bond.   Daryl J. Doyle

See also **Adhesion; Glue; Gum.**

Adirondack Mountains, *AD uh RAHN dak,* are a group of mountains that covers about 12,000 square miles (31,000 square kilometers) in northeastern New York. Millions of tourists, hikers, and sports enthusiasts are drawn every year to the Adirondacks for their beautiful scenery, wildlife, and recreational opportunities.

More than 40 of the Adirondack Mountains rise above 4,000 feet (1,220 meters). Mount Marcy, at 5,344 feet (1,629 meters), is the highest point in New York. There are over 2,300 lakes and ponds in the region. Lake George and Lake Placid are the region's most famous resort areas. Lake Champlain lies in a broad lowland to the east of the mountains (see **Lake Champlain**).

The mountains were formed when powerful geological forces lifted Earth's crust more than a billion years ago. Glaciers later created most of the area's lakes. The Adirondack Park has 6 million acres (2.4 million hectares) of public and private lands. The 2 ½ million acres (1 million hectares) of public land makes up the largest wilderness preserve in the eastern United States. The word *Adirondack* comes from the Iroquois Indian word for *bark eater.* The Iroquois may have used the term to describe the neighboring Algonquin Indians.

Ray Bromley

See also **Lake Placid; New York** (picture).

Adjective is a part of speech that describes, qualifies, or places limits on a noun or pronoun. Adjectives are said to *modify* nouns or pronouns.

As a part of speech, adjectives are single words. However, clauses and phrases may serve roughly the same function. For example, in *the angry woman* and *the woman angered by his crude behavior,* the phrase *angered by his crude behavior* modifies the noun woman, just as the word *angry* does. Relative clauses generally function as adjectives. For example, in "The man *whose sister is arriving from France,*" the relative clause *whose sister is arriving from France* modifies *the man.* These clauses and phrases that serve as adjectives are called *adjectival* clauses and phrases.

A speaker or writer uses adjectives to add detail, to make distinctions, and to be precise about what they are saying. For example, various adjectives can make the noun *tulip* more and more specific. *A red tulip* adds a quality. *A big, beautiful, red tulip* adds even more detail. Sometimes the effects are more dramatic. *An alleged murderer* is not necessarily a murderer. *A false prophet* is not a prophet at all.

The position of adjectives. Adjectives can occupy three different positions in a sentence. An adjective can come before a noun, as in *wild animal.* Or an adjective can follow a noun, as in the title *Captains Courageous.* When adjectives are themselves modified by a prepositional phrase, the adjective and prepositional phrase follow the noun *(The wet shirt* versus *The shirt wet with perspiration).*

Adjectives can also follow a *linking verb.* Linking verbs include the verb *to be* and such verbs as *seem, become, feel,* or *taste.* In the sentence *The furniture is durable,* the adjective *durable* follows the linking verb *is* and modifies the noun *furniture.*

Adjectives that follow a linking verb are called *predicate adjectives.* Adjectives that follow nouns and repeat the meaning of the noun in different words are called *adjective appositives.* For example, *The boring lecture, long and dull, lasted until 9 p.m.*

Comparison of adjectives. Adjectives show differences in amount or degree by the addition of *function words* or by changes in form. The function words *less* and *least* show decreasing amounts or degrees. The function words *more* and *most* show increasing amounts or degrees. Adjectives have three degrees of comparison, called the *positive,* the *comparative,* and the *superlative.* Some adjectives, usually those of one or two syllables, add *-er* to form the comparative and *-est* to form the superlative, as shown in the following examples:

Positive	Comparative	Superlative
dry	drier	driest
free	freer	freest
happy	happier	happiest
high	higher	highest
rich	richer	richest
slow	slower	slowest
warm	warmer	warmest

The comparative and superlatives here show increasing amounts or degrees. Adjectives of more than two syllables use function words, as shown in the next examples:

Positive	Comparative	Superlative
accurate	more accurate	most accurate
accurate	less accurate	least accurate
beautiful	more beautiful	most beautiful
beautiful	less beautiful	least beautiful
interesting	more interesting	most interesting
interesting	less interesting	least interesting

Many adjectives, including *handsome, happy, lovely,* and *proud,* may be compared by either method—for ex-

ample, *happy, happier, happiest;* or *happy, more happy, most happy.*

A special group of adjectives show comparison by *irregular* forms. That is, their changes in form follow no set rules. Here are some examples:

Positive	Comparative	Superlative
bad	worse	worst
far	farther, further	farthest, furthest
good	better	best
little	littler, less, lesser	littlest, least
many, much	more	most

Although many adjectives show three degrees of comparison, such adjectives as *chief, main,* and *foremost* exist in only one degree and cannot be compared at all. There is a difference of opinion about whether adjectives such as *round, perfect,* and *unique* can be compared. Many persons consider them absolute adjectives that cannot show degree, except in phrases such as *almost round, more nearly perfect,* and *almost completely unique.* However, such comparisons as *more round, more perfect,* and *most unique* have become increasingly common in informal usage.

Classifying adjectives. Adjectives are classified into several types according to their meaning and function.

Descriptive adjectives specify the kind, nature, or condition of the words they modify, as in *When we saw the fierce dog, we grew* cautious.

Proper adjectives come from a proper name and are written with a capital letter. Some examples of proper adjectives are: *American flag, Roman numerals,* and *Shakespearean sonnets.*

Interrogative adjectives ask a question, as in *Which car do you mean?* or *What difference does it make?*

Determiners are adjectives that place limits on a noun rather than add description. Several groups of words serve as determiners. They include the articles *a, an,* and *the;* the *demonstrative* adjectives *that, this, these,* and *those;* and the *indefinite* adjectives *all, each, no, some, other,* and *much;* and such numbers as *one box* and *second place.* Some scholars consider determiners to be a separate part of speech.

Usage. The careful use of adjectives can clarify meaning, but too many adjectives in a sentence may confuse a reader or listener. One carefully chosen adjective often can express more information than two or three vague ones.

Sometimes a person may have difficulty in deciding whether to use an adjective or an adverb after certain verbs. If the sentence requires a word to modify the verb, the choice should be an adverb—for example, *Helen sings well,* not *Helen sings good.* If the sentence requires a word following a linking verb to modify the subject, the choice should be an adjective—for example, *I feel bad,* not *I feel badly.* In the sentence *He looked calmly at the judge,* the word *calmly* is an adverb that modifies *looked.* It describes the manner in which the person acted. In the sentence *He looked calm,* the word *calm* is a predicate adjective that modifies *he.* It describes the condition of the subject.

Errors in agreement can be created when such words as *kind, sort,* and *type* are used with the demonstrative adjectives *this* or *that.* In such cases, both the adjective and the noun should be either singular or plural. For example, *I like this kind of motion picture* or *I like these kinds of motion pictures,* but not *I like these kind of motion pictures.*   Susan M. Gass

See also **Adverb; Apposition; Article; Comparison; Parts of speech.**

Adjutant, *AJ uh tuhnt,* is a large bird in the stork family. Adjutants are found in India and Southeast Asia. There are two *species* (kinds) of adjutants. The *greater adjutant* stands about 5 feet (1.5 meters) high, and the *lesser adjutant* measures up to 4 feet (1.2 meters) tall. Both birds have a white body, and the back and wings are dark gray. The greater adjutant has a long bag of skin that hangs under its bare neck. The bird can puff out this skin and fill it with air. Adjutants have become endangered due to habitat destruction and overhunting. Laws protect them in several countries.   Eric G. Bolen

Scientific classification. The greater adjutant's scientific name is *Leptoptilos dubius.* The lesser adjutant is *L. javanicus.*

See also **Marabou; Stork.**

E. R. Degginger

The adjutant is the largest member of the stork family. It has a long beak and a white body with a gray back and wings.

Adler, Alfred (1870-1937), an Austrian psychiatrist, developed important theories concerning the motivation of human behavior. According to Adler, the major force of all human activity is a striving from a feeling of inferiority toward perfection. Adler at first referred to this force as an *aggressive drive.* He later called the force a *striving for superiority.* Adler termed his school of thought *individual psychology.* Today, it is often referred to as *Adlerian psychology.*

Adler taught that everyone experiences feelings of inferiority and each person strives to overcome such feelings according to a unique set of goals. Every individual, he said, also has a unique way of attempting to achieve the goals. Adler used the term *style of life* for the person's goals and methods of pursuing them. He claimed that the style of life becomes established by the age of 4 or 5. He also believed that an individual's self-image and opinion of the world reflect the person's style of life.

Adler emphasized the importance of social forces in determining behavior. He believed everyone is born with a trait called *social interest,* which enables a person to relate to other people and to place the good of society above their own interests. Many of Adler's ideas have become part of the theory and practice of psychiatry.

Adler was born on Feb. 7, 1870, near Vienna, Austria.

He received his M.D. degree from the University of Vienna in 1895. Adler was an eye specialist and a neurologist before becoming a psychiatrist. From 1902 to 1911, he worked with the famous Austrian neurologist and psychoanalyst Sigmund Freud. From 1921 to 1934, Adler established child guidance clinics in Vienna. He trained teachers, worked with parents, and supervised teachers' clinical activities with disturbed children. Adler moved to New York City in 1934. He died on May 28, 1937.
Hannah S. Decker

Adler, Dankmar (1844-1900), was an American architect noted primarily for his association with architect Louis H. Sullivan. The two formed the partnership of Adler & Sullivan in 1883. Together they designed such important structures as the Auditorium Building (1889) in Chicago and the Wainwright Building (1891) in St. Louis. These buildings helped define the influential Chicago School of architecture. The firm's other notable Chicago structures include the Chicago Joint Board Building (1884), the Garrick Theater in the Schiller Building (1892), the Transportation Building (1893) at the World's Columbian Exposition, and the Stock Exchange Building (1894).

In spite of Adler's training as an architect, his responsibilities within the firm seem to have been limited to structure, ventilation, and acoustics, in which he was an expert. Adler was also an excellent business manager. The partnership was dissolved in 1895 following the construction of the Guaranty Building (1895) in Buffalo, New York.

Adler was born on July 3, 1844, near Eisenach, Germany, and immigrated with his family to the United States in 1854. He moved to Chicago in 1861 and served as an engineer in the Union Army during the American Civil War (1861-1865). Adler returned to Chicago in 1866. He died on April 16, 1900.   Nicholas Adams

See also **Sullivan, Louis Henri; Architecture** (Early modern architecture in America).

Administrator is a person who takes charge of the property of a person who has died. Probate courts appoint administrators to handle the property of a person who leaves no will, or who leaves a will but names no executor. An *executor* is a person who is named in a will to handle property (see **Executor**). The administrator's duty is to collect the assets of the dead person's estate, pay claims against the estate, and then distribute the balance to the person's heirs and next of kin—or to the *legatees* (beneficiaries) of the will if there is one.

Courts usually name a qualified close relative of the deceased to serve as administrator. In many large cities, officials called *public administrators* manage the estates of dead people who have no relatives. When citizens of another country die while in the United States without leaving a will, their country's consul is usually named to administer the estate.   William M. McGovern

See also **Probate; Will** (document); **Heir.**

Admiral is the highest rank in the navies of many countries. Most admirals command fleets or specially organized naval units called *task forces* or *task groups.*

There are four basic grades of admiral in the United States Navy. They are—from the lowest to the highest—rear admiral, vice admiral, admiral, and fleet admiral. A rear admiral wears the insignia of two stars and generally commands a task group. A vice admiral wears three stars and commands a task force. An admiral, with four stars, commands a fleet. The rank of fleet admiral carries five stars. It was created in 1944 and was held by four Americans in World War II—William F. Halsey, Ernest J. King, William D. Leahy, and Chester W. Nimitz.

The word *admiral* comes from the Arabic term *amir-albahr,* which means "commander of the sea." The title of admiral was introduced into Europe during the Crusades (A.D. 1096-1500's). In the United States, captains were the highest-ranking Navy officers until 1862, when the rank of rear admiral was adopted. David G. Farragut became the first person to hold this rank. He also became the Navy's first vice admiral in 1864 and its first admiral in 1866. In 1899, Congress created the honorary rank of Admiral of the Navy for George Dewey, a hero of the Spanish-American War.   Ann Alexander Warren

See also **Rank, Military.**

Admiralty, *AD muhr uhl tee,* is a department of a nation's government that directs naval affairs. For example, the Admiralty Board in the United Kingdom controls the Royal Navy. Beginning in the 1300's, the lord high admiral commanded the Royal Navy. In 1708, the Board of Admiralty (now Admiralty Board) assumed control of naval affairs. Its powers are about the same as those of the Department of the Navy in the United States and of the Royal Canadian Navy. The term *admiralty law* applies to a body of laws relating to ships and shipping. It covers wrecks, collisions, and cargo damage. In the United States, district courts hear these cases. See also **Maritime law.**   Ann Alexander Warren

Admiralty Islands, *AD muhr uhl tee,* a group of islands in the South Pacific Ocean, are part of the nation of Papua New Guinea. Also known as the Manus Islands, they cover 800 square miles (2,072 square kilometers). The group includes one large island (Manus); several small, hilly volcanic islands; and about 100 low reef islands (see **New Guinea** [map]). About 60,500 people live on the islands. They rely on income from crops, fishing, and *remittances* (money sent) from family living abroad. Lorengau, the principal town, is on Manus Island.

Hunters and gatherers first settled the islands approximately 40,000 years ago. Archaeologists have found several sites in the islands from the seafaring and farming Lapita culture, which arose 3,500 years ago. The first Europeans to reach the islands were probably the Dutch navigators Willem Schouten and Jacob Le Maire. In 1616, they found the islands inhabited by Melanesians. Germany claimed the group in 1884. Australians captured the islands in World War I (1914-1918), and Japan occupied them in 1942, during World War II (1939-1945). In 1944, American and Australian troops recaptured the islands.   Victoria Luker

See also **Bismarck Archipelago; Pacific Islands.**

Admiralty law. See Maritime law.

Adobe, *uh DOH bee,* is the Spanish name for sun-dried bricks, or for a house built with such bricks. A less common type of adobe is made with dampened earth pressed down in building forms similar to those used for poured concrete walks.

People have used adobe to build houses and other structures in desert regions for thousands of years. The ancient Egyptians and Babylonians used adobe.

To make adobe, workers mix sandy clay or *loam* (a mixture of sand, clay, and silt) with water and a small quantity of straw, grass, or similar material. The straw holds the mixture together, giving the bricks greater stability. The mixture is placed in wooden forms that shape it into bricks. Workers remove the forms when the bricks are dry. Then they bake the bricks in the heat of the sun for several days or weeks.

Adobe houses are common in Mexico and the southwestern part of the United States. Traditional adobe houses are covered with mud. Modern adobe houses are covered with a plasterlike material called *stucco.* Adobe houses are cooler than uninsulated homes made of wood or stone, but adobe is not suitable for use in cold or damp regions. The bricks will crumble if they are exposed to rain or to periods of freezing temperatures followed by thaws.   Jack M. Landers

© M. Gebicki, Lonely Planet Images/Getty Images

Manus Island, *shown here,* is the largest of the Admiralty Islands. It is covered by a dense tropical forest.

© Bill Florence, Shutterstock

Adobe structures are made of sun-dried bricks. Since ancient times, people living in desert regions have built adobe houses. Adobe consists mostly of clay, which stays cool in extreme heat.

© Lawrence Migdale

WORLD BOOK photo by Steven Spicer (Jones Metropolitan High School
of Business and Commerce, a Chicago Public High School)

During adolescence, relationships with *peers* (people of one's own age) take on great importance.
Teen-agers spend much time with their peers in such activities as eating together or chatting after
school. The students shown above right attend a high school with a strict dress code.

Adolescent

Adolescent refers to a person who is experiencing the
period of development between childhood and adulthood. This period is often called *adolescence.* Many experts in human development believe adolescence begins at about the age of 10. They recognize adolescence
as a period of growth with many distinctive features.
These features involve changes in the individual's body,
thinking abilities, psychological concerns, and place in
society.

Human beings, like all mammals, go through a series
of physical and biological changes, called *puberty,* that
prepares them for sexual reproduction. As a biological
phenomenon, therefore, adolescence has always existed
as a period in human development. However, adolescence as a separate psychological and social stage is a
concept that was developed in industrialized nations
during the mid-1800's.

The "invention" of adolescence

Before the 1800's, adults did not make important distinctions among children of different ages. However,
new patterns of work and family life came with industrialization in the 1800's. Individuals from age 12 to 16 were
greatly affected by these changes. As work shifted away
from farming and became less tied to the family, young
people needed a new kind of preparation for adulthood.
Children in working-class families often took jobs in
mines, factories, and mills. Others were apprenticed to
craftworkers to learn a trade. Adolescents in middle-
class families were expected to attend school, where
they were grouped with others of the same age. At

*Laurence Steinberg, the contributor of this article, is Professor
of Psychology at Temple University and co-author of* You and
Your Adolescent: A Parent's Guide for Ages 10 to 20.

school, they could be better educated for a rapidly
changing workplace.

By the early 1900's, adolescence in some societies and
some social and economic classes had become a
lengthy period of preparation for adulthood. During this
time, young people remained grouped with people
their own age, often referred to as their *peers,* and were
economically dependent on adults. This role is still what
is expected of adolescents in most societies today.

How society regards adolescence has a tremendous
impact on the psychological and social development of
individuals. Before the 1800's, the lives of adolescents
did not revolve around socializing with their friends.
There was no such thing as a "teen culture." Young people seldom felt compelled to take a certain action, adopt
certain values, or otherwise conform to be accepted by
the group. Today, social pressure from people their
own age, known as *peer pressure,* is a major influence
on many adolescents.

Before adolescence became defined as a distinct developmental stage, most young people did not struggle
to develop a clear sense of self or to sort out what they
would become in the future. Most young people had
few real choices open to them. Today, psychological experts use the term *identity crisis* to refer to the psychological distress many adolescents feel as they seek a
sense of purpose and an acceptable role in the world.
Peer pressure, popular culture, and identity crises may
seem to make up the core of adolescence, but they are
actually consequences of how adolescence is defined
today.

Physical development

Puberty is the most obvious sign that an individual has
entered adolescence. Technically, puberty refers to the
period during which the individual becomes capable of
sexual reproduction. More broadly, however, puberty is
used as a collective term for all the physical

changes that occur in a growing girl or boy as the individual passes from childhood to adulthood.

The physical changes of adolescence are triggered by *hormones* (chemical substances in the body) that act on specific organs and tissues. In boys, a major change is increased production of the hormone *testosterone,* while girls experience increased production of the hormones called *estrogens.* In both sexes, a rise in growth hormone produces a growth spurt. During this spurt, which lasts two or more years, an individual commonly grows 2 to 4 inches (5 to 10 centimeters) taller per year.

Sexual development. Many of the most dramatic changes of puberty involve sexual development. Internally, adolescents become capable of sexual reproduction. Externally, as secondary sexual characteristics appear, girls and boys begin to look more like mature women and men. The term *secondary sexual characteristics* refers to a variety of physical traits, such as body shape, voice, and facial hair.

Not everyone goes through puberty at the same time or rate. In Western industrialized societies today, the adolescent growth spurt occurs, on average, between the ages of 12 and 14 in boys, and 10 and 12 in girls. But some young people start puberty when they are 8 or 9, and others not until they are in their mid-teens. Generally, girls begin puberty about two years earlier than boys. The duration of puberty also varies greatly, from $1\frac{1}{2}$ to 6 years in girls and from 2 to 5 years in boys.

Adolescent "awkwardness." Because different parts of the body grow at different rates during puberty, many adolescents temporarily look and feel awkward. For many years, psychologists believed that puberty was stressful for young people. According to one theory, changes in hormones made young adolescents moody, irritable, and depressed. We now know that most emotional disturbances in adolescence result from changes in the teen-ager's roles and relationships. Adolescents can minimize difficulties associated with adjusting to puberty by knowing what changes to expect and having healthy attitudes toward them.

The timing of puberty may affect an adolescent's social and emotional development in important ways. Because early-maturing boys and girls appear older physically, people often treat them as if they were more mature psychologically than they are. Early maturers will more likely engage in risky behavior during early adolescence, such as experimentation with drugs, sex, or delinquency. Many psychologists believe these risky actions result from the influence of older teen-agers, who befriend early maturers more often than they befriend younger-looking adolescents.

Because of the emphasis many boys place on athletics, early-maturing boys may have temporary advantages over their peers. As a result, during the first years of adolescence, early-maturing boys tend to be more popular, have higher self-esteem, and have more self-confidence than average- or late-maturing boys.

In contrast, the effects of early maturation on girls are more mixed. Early-maturing girls tend to be more popular with their peers. But they are also more likely to feel awkward and self-conscious, perhaps because they are uncomfortable with the attention, both welcome and unwelcome, their new appearance draws.

Over time, puberty has begun at younger and young-

National Archives/Photo Researchers

An adolescent of the past worked long hours in a factory, *shown here.* Before the 1800's, adolescence was not regarded as a separate psychological and social stage of development.

er ages. Part of the trend is due to improvements in nutrition and health care. The trend appears to be leveling off, however.

Intellectual development

Compared with children, adolescents begin to think in ways more like adults. Their thinking becomes more advanced, more efficient, and generally more effective. These improvements appear in five chief ways.

(1) An adolescent's thinking is less bound to concrete events than that of a child. Children's thinking focuses on things and events that they can observe directly in the present. Adolescents can better compare what they observe with what they can imagine.

(2) During adolescence, individuals become better able to think about abstract things. Adolescents have an increased interest in relationships, politics, religion, and morality. These topics involve such abstract concepts as loyalty, faith, and fairness.

(3) Adolescents think more often about the process of thinking itself. As a result, they can develop better ways to remember things and to monitor their own thinking.

(4) Adolescents have the ability to think about things in several ways at the same time. Adolescents can give much more complicated answers than children to such questions as "What caused the American Civil War?" Adolescents have more sophisticated, complicated relationships with others because they can better understand other people's feelings. They also understand that social situations can have different interpretations, depending on one's point of view.

(5) Children tend to see things in absolute terms. Adolescents often see things as relative. They are more likely to question statements and less likely to accept "facts" as unquestionably true. This change can be frustrating to parents, who may feel that their adolescent children question everything just for the sake of argument. However, such questioning is normal and helps teen-agers develop individuality and personal convictions.

One by-product of these changing aspects of intellectual development is the tendency for adolescents to become self-conscious and self-absorbed. This tendency is sometimes called *adolescent egocentrism*. Intense self-consciousness sometimes leads teen-agers mistakenly to believe that others are constantly watching and evaluating them. A related problem is an adolescent's incorrect belief that his or her problems are unique. For example, a teen-ager who has just broken up with a girlfriend or boyfriend may say that nobody else could possibly understand what he or she is feeling, even though such breaking up is a common experience.

Psychological development

Identity and self-esteem. As individuals mature, they come to see themselves in more sophisticated, complicated ways. Adolescents can provide complex, abstract psychological descriptions of themselves. As a result, they become more interested in understanding their own personalities and why they behave the way they do. Teen-agers' feelings about themselves may fluctuate, especially during early adolescence. However, self-esteem increases over the course of middle and late adolescence, as individuals gain more confidence.

Some adolescents go through periods when they genuinely wonder what their "real" personality is. Adolescents who have gone through a prolonged identity crisis may feel a stronger sense of identity as a result of taking the time to examine who they are and where they are headed.

Independence and responsibility. During adolescence, individuals gradually move from the dependency of childhood to the independence of adulthood. Older adolescents generally do not rush to their parents whenever they are upset, worried, or need assistance. They solve many problems on their own. In addition, most adolescents have a great deal of emotional energy wrapped up in relationships outside the family. They may feel just as attached to their friends as to their parents. By late adolescence, children see their parents, and interact with them, as people—not just as a mother and father. Unlike younger children, adolescents do not typically see their parents as all-knowing or all-powerful.

Being independent also means being able to make one's own decisions and behave responsibly. In general, decision-making abilities improve over the course of the adolescent years, with gains in being able to handle responsibility continuing into the late years of high school.

During childhood, boys and girls are dependent upon and relate closely to their parents rather than their peers. During early adolescence, conformity to parents begins to decline, while peer pressure and conformity to peers increase. Peer pressure is particularly strong during junior high school and the early years of high school.

Adolescents yield more often to peer pressure when it involves day-to-day social matters, such as styles of dress, tastes in music, and choices among leisure activities. But teen-agers are mainly influenced by their parents and teachers when it comes to long-range questions concerning educational or occupational plans, or decisions involving values, religious beliefs, or ethics.

Becoming independent involves learning how to cope with peer pressure. During middle adolescence,

individuals begin to act the way they think is right, rather than trying to impress their friends or please their parents.

Social development

Relationships with peers change in four important ways during the teen-age years: (1) There is a sharp increase in the amount of time adolescents spend with their peers compared to the time they spend with adults or their families. (2) Peer groups function much more often without adult supervision than they do during childhood. (3) In most societies, there is much more contact with peers of the opposite sex. (4) Adolescents tend to move in much larger peer groups than they did in childhood. Crowds tend to dominate the social world of the school.

The increased importance of peers during early adolescence coincides with changes in an individual's need for intimacy. As adolescents begin to share secrets with their friends, a new sense of loyalty and commitment grows between them. An adolescent's discovery that he or she thinks and feels the same way as someone else becomes an important basis of friendship and helps in the development of a sense of identity.

Dating and sex. In industrialized societies, most young people begin dating sometime during early to mid-adolescence. Dating can mean a variety of activities, from gatherings that bring males and females together, to group dates, in which a group of boys and girls go out jointly. There can be casual dating in couples or serious involvement with a boyfriend or girlfriend.

Most adolescents' first experience with sex does not involve another person. Many boys and girls report having sexual fantasies about someone they know or wish they knew. It is also fairly common for adolescents to *masturbate* (handle or rub their sex organs).

By the time many adolescents have reached high school, they have had some experience with intimate sexual contact, such as kissing, caressing, or sexual intercourse. During the 1970's and 1980's, more adolescents became sexually active than in the past and they became sexually active at an earlier age. By the late 1990's and the 2000's, however, surveys indicated that the trend toward becoming sexually active at an early age was leveling off. Many individuals and religious groups consider sexual activity outside of marriage to be morally wrong. They also urge adolescents to avoid sexual activity for health reasons.

Family relationships change most about the time of puberty. Conflict can increase between parents and adolescents, and closeness between them diminishes somewhat. Changing adolescent views on family rules and regulations may contribute to increased disagreement between young people and their parents.

Although young people may distance themselves from their parents as they enter adolescence, this period is not normally a time of family stress. Most conflicts take the form of minor arguments over day-to-day issues. In many families, the decline in closeness between parents and children in early adolescence results from the adolescent's increased desire for privacy. In addition, teen-agers and parents may express affection for each other less often. Generally, this distancing is temporary, and family relationships become closer and less conflict-ridden during middle and late adolescence.

Certain constants remain in family life. Among the most important is an adolescent's need for parents who are both nurturing and demanding. This combination of warmth and strictness is associated with healthy psychological development. Children raised by loving parents who maintain clear and constant personal and social standards are more likely to have good feelings about themselves than children brought up by harsh or lax parents. Adolescents raised with both warmth and firmness are more likely to excel in school, to have close and satisfying relationships with others, and to avoid trouble with drugs and delinquency.

Special problems and challenges

Adjusting to school life. A young person's move from elementary school to middle school or junior high school can be difficult. In elementary school, the child had a single homeroom teacher who knew him or her personally. In middle school or junior high, the child usually has a different teacher for each subject. In elementary school, children are rewarded for trying hard. In middle or junior high school, grades are based more on performance than on effort. In elementary school, children work under close supervision all day. In middle school or junior high, young people must learn to work more independently.

For such reasons, many students are temporarily disoriented during the transition between schools. Their self-esteem falters, and their grades may drop off slightly. Their interest in school activities declines. They may feel anonymous, isolated, and vulnerable. Parents can help by talking to the child before school begins about the differences he or she will experience.

Alcohol and drug abuse. Many adolescents in industrialized countries experiment with alcohol, tobacco, and marijuana. Adolescents may experiment with such substances because of a desire to fit in with their friends. Many adolescents see smoking, drinking, and using drugs as a key to popularity. Other reasons adolescents experiment with drugs and alcohol include boredom, and a desire to feel grown-up—that is, they see drugs as a way to prove they are adults and no longer under adult control.

Young people who abuse drugs and alcohol are more likely to experience problems at school, to suffer from psychological distress and depression, to have unsafe sex, and to become involved in dangerous activities. Alcohol and drugs often contribute to automobile accidents, the leading cause of death among American teenagers. Adolescent substance abusers also expose themselves to long-term health risks that result from drug addiction or dependency.

Pregnancy. Some young women become pregnant before the end of adolescence. Adults can help adolescents prevent unwanted pregnancies. For example, parents and teachers can provide sex education to instruct young people in how to deal with their sexual feelings before they become sexually active. Adults also can make adolescents feel more comfortable about discussing sexual matters so that young people will examine their own behavior seriously and thoughtfully.

Establishing a sexual identity. Normal developmental tasks of adolescence include learning to think of one-

© Bob Higbee, Berg & Associates

Dating normally begins during adolescence. Learning to enjoy a new kind of closeness with another person is a normal developmental task of this period of life, as well as learning to think of oneself as a sexual being and to deal with sexual feelings.

self as a sexual being, to deal with sexual feelings, and to enjoy a new kind of closeness with another person. Part of this involves developing a sexual identity. Sexual identity includes *sexual orientation*—that is, whether a person is sexually attracted to the opposite sex or the same sex. People who are primarily attracted to members of their own sex are called *homosexual, gay,* or, if they are women, *lesbian*. People who are attracted to the opposite sex are called *heterosexual* or *straight*. No one factor determines sexual orientation.

At some time, almost all young adolescents worry that they might be homosexual. At the age when children enter puberty, they still spend most of their time with members of the same sex. As a result, many adolescents begin to experience sexual feelings before they have much contact with the opposite sex. This does not mean that all of these young adolescents have homosexual desires. Their sexual development is just ahead of their social development.

Unfavorable attitudes toward homosexuality may cause significant psychological distress for adolescents who experience gay and lesbian feelings, especially if they encounter hostility from those around them. The psychological tasks of adolescence, such as developing a sense of identity, present great challenges for all teenagers. These challenges may be intensified for those adolescents attracted to members of the same sex. They may have to resolve these issues without the social support available to their heterosexual peers.

Eating disorders. Some adolescents, especially females, become so concerned about weight control that they take drastic and dangerous measures to remain

© Billy E. Barnes, Photo Edit

Conflicts between adolescents and their parents can arise because adolescents are more likely than children to question what they are told and more likely to disagree with family rules.

thin. Some overeat and then force themselves to vomit to avoid gaining weight. This pattern is associated with an eating disorder called *bulimia*. Young women with a disorder called *anorexia nervosa* actually starve themselves to keep their weight down. Adolescents with eating disorders have an extremely disturbed body image. They see themselves as overweight when they are actually underweight. Bulimia and anorexia nervosa are rare before the age of 10. It was once believed that eating disorders were more common in North America and Western Europe than in other parts of the world, and were more common among the prosperous and well educated. However, research studies have found these disorders to be common among all social and economic levels, and in many countries throughout the world.

Although the incidence of anorexia and bulimia is small, many adolescents, especially females, remain unhappy with their body shape or weight. Many girls whose weight is normal by medical and health standards believe they are overweight. A majority of adolescent girls report that they would like to be thinner. Most believe that being thinner would make them happier, more successful, and more popular.

Delinquency. Violations of the law are far more common among adolescents and young adults than in any other age group. Violent crimes and crimes against property peak during high school.

Violent crime is a serious concern to youths as well as to adults. Adolescents are the age group most likely to become victims of such crimes as theft, robbery, rape, and assault. However, adolescents may also commit such violent crimes. Delinquents who repeatedly commit serious crimes typically come from disrupted or badly functioning families, and they frequently abuse alcohol or drugs. Hostile, neglectful, or unfit parents may mistreat children and fail to instill in them proper standards of behavior or the psychological foundations of self-control.

Risk taking. Many adolescent health problems result from behaviors that can be prevented. These behaviors include substance abuse, reckless driving, unprotected sex, and violence. One particular concern is sexually transmitted diseases, such as AIDS, among teen-agers. Some people mistakenly consider AIDS a homosexual disease, but the virus can be transmitted from male to female or female to male. The virus is also transmitted through needles and syringes that are used in taking drugs. It may even be spread by tattooing or body piercing if the instruments were previously used on an infected person.

Suicide. The suicide rate among teen-agers has risen dramatically since the mid-1900's. Four factors in particular place an adolescent at risk for a suicide attempt: (1) suffering from low self-esteem or an emotional problem, such as depression; (2) being under stress, especially in school or because of a romantic relationship; (3) experiencing family disruption or family conflict; and (4) having a history of suicide in the family or a friend who has committed suicide.

Any threat of suicide demands immediate professional attention. Anyone who suspects an adolescent is considering suicide should immediately call a suicide hot line or the emergency room of a local hospital.

Planning for the future

Career planning is part of the identity development process during adolescence. Occupational plans develop in stages. Prior to adolescence, children express career interests that are often little more than fantasies and have little bearing on the plans they eventually make. In adolescence, individuals begin to develop self-concepts and ideas about work that will guide them in their educational and occupational decisions. Although adolescents may not settle on a particular career at this point, they do begin to narrow their choices according to their interests, values, and abilities.

One problem all young people face in making career plans is obtaining accurate information about the labor market and the best ways of pursuing positions in various fields. One goal of career education is to help adolescents make more informed choices about their careers and to free them from misinformation that inhibits their choices. For a discussion of how to choose and plan a career, see the **Careers** article.

Education is essential today for any person who wants a well-paying job with a promising future. Young people need at least a high school education to compete in the job market. Those young people who want to go into a craft or trade usually need a two-year course of college study.

Most of the better jobs go to individuals with at least some college education. However, getting a job is not the only reason for going to college. College plays a critical role in a young person's psychological development. College not only provides occupational advantages but also affects where individuals will live, whom they will marry, who their lifelong friends will be, and, most important, who they become.   Laurence Steinberg

Related articles in *World Book* include:

Acne	Bulimia
Anorexia nervosa	Child
Boys Town	Developmental psychology

Outline

I. The "invention" of adolescence
II. Physical development
  A. Sexual development
  B. Adolescent "awkwardness"
  C. The timing of puberty
III. Intellectual development
IV. Psychological development
  A. Identity and self-esteem
  B. Independence and responsibility
V. Social development
  A. Relationships with peers
  B. Dating and sex
  C. Family relationships
VI. Special problems and challenges
  A. Adjusting to school life
  B. Alcohol and drug abuse
  C. Pregnancy
  D. Establishing a sexual identity
  E. Eating disorders
  F. Delinquency
  G. Risk taking
  H. Suicide
VII. Planning for the future
  A. Career planning
  B. Education

Questions

What is *peer pressure?*
How does puberty affect an adolescent's social and emotional
  development?
What challenges does an adolescent face in moving into a mid-
  dle or junior high school?
Why is education important for an adolescent?
When did the term *adolescent* first emerge?
What are the chief reasons why some adolescents experiment
  with alcohol, drugs, and tobacco?
What are the two most important adolescent eating disorders?

Additional resources

Adams, Gerald R., and Berzonsky, M. D. *Blackwell Handbook of
  Adolescence.* Wiley, 2003.
Arnett, Jeffrey J., ed. *International Encyclopedia of Adolescence.*
  2 vols. Routledge, 2007.
Bashe, Philip. *Caring for Your Teenager.* Ed. by Donald E. Grey-
  danus. Bantam, 2003.
Burningham, Sarah O. *How to Raise Your Parents: A Teen Girl's
  Survival Guide.* Chronicle, 2008.
Faber, Adele, and Mazlish, Elaine. *How to Talk So Teens Will Lis-
  ten and Listen So Teens Will Talk.* HarperCollins, 2005.
Johnson, Patrick B., and Malow-Iroff, M. S. *Adolescents and Risk.*
  Praeger, 2008.
Middleman, Amy B., and Pfeifer, K. G. *American Medical Associ-
  ation Boy's Guide to Becoming a Teen.* Jossey-Bass, 2006.
  *American Medical Association Girl's Guide to Becoming a
  Teen.* 2006.
Phillips, Sherre F. *The Teen Brain.* Chelsea Hse., 2007.
Shannon, Joyce B., ed. *Adolescent Health Sourcebook.* 2nd ed.
  Omnigraphics, 2007.
Webber, Diane. *The Skin You're In: Staying Healthy Inside and
  Out.* Watts, 2008.

Adolphus, Gustavus. See Gustavus Adolphus.
Adonis, *uh DAHN ihs,* was a handsome youth in Greek

Marble sculpture (mid-1600's) by Dionisio Mazzuoli;
Hermitage museum, St. Petersburg (Bridgeman Art Library)

Adonis was a handsome young man in Greek mythology. According to one myth, he was killed by a boar he was hunting.

mythology. Adonis's beauty attracted Aphrodite, the
goddess of love. According to one myth, Aphrodite
warned him of the dangers of hunting. But Adonis did
not heed her advice and was killed by a boar, or by Hephaestus, Aphrodite's jealous husband, disguised as a
boar. A flower called the *anemone* sprang either from
Adonis's blood or from Aphrodite's tears at his death.

According to another myth, Aphrodite placed the infant Adonis in a chest and gave it to Persephone, the
queen of the underworld, for safekeeping. Persephone
became enchanted with the youth and wanted to keep
him. To settle the quarrel between the goddesses, Zeus,
king of the gods, ruled that Adonis would spend part of
the year with Aphrodite and part of the year with Persephone. When Adonis stayed with Aphrodite on earth,
plants and crops flourished. During his time in the underworld, vegetation died. The Greeks used this myth to
explain why the seasons changed. They honored Adonis
in ceremonies and by cultivating plants that grew and
died quickly.   Nancy Felson

Adonis, *uh DAHN ihs,* is the name of a group of plants
that grow wild in Europe and Asia. Adonis plants are
sometimes cultivated in gardens in North America.
Some types of Adonis plants may grow 1 foot (30 centimeters) high. The *autumn Adonis,* also called
pheasant's-eye, has flowers with bright red petals.

WORLD BOOK illustration by Christabel King

The autumn Adonis has bright red flowers. It grows wild in Europe and Asia but is sometimes cultivated in gardens.

The *spring Adonis* has flowers with gold petals.

Kenneth A. Nicely

Scientific classification. Adonis plants are members of the crowfoot family, Ranunculaceae. The scientific name for the autumn Adonis is *Adonis annua.* The spring Adonis is *A. vernalis.*

Adoption is a legal process by which people take as their own son or daughter a person not born to them. Most *adoptees* (adopted people) are adopted when they are children. Adoptees are entitled to the same privileges as children born to a parent or parents, including the right to inherit property. This article chiefly discusses the adoption of children.

Many adoptions occur partly out of a need to find permanent, loving families for children whose birth parents cannot raise them. Many adults adopt children because they are, for medical reasons, unable to become birth parents. Other people choose to become adoptive parents in addition to, or instead of, being birth parents. Research shows that most adoptions work out well and that most adopted children develop normally.

The adoption process is similar in the United States and Canada. In the United States, licensed agencies arrange most adoptions by nonrelatives. These agencies are either privately funded or public and tax-supported. In Canada, provincial agencies handle most adoptions by nonrelatives. Agency adoptions involve three steps: (1) the legal separation of a child from the birth parents, (2) the transfer of custody to a qualified adoption agency, and (3) the transfer of parental rights and responsibilities to the adoptive parents.

When a couple apply to an adoption agency, the agency assigns them a caseworker. The caseworker obtains information about the couple's health and emotional maturity and answers their questions about the physical and emotional development of the child they want to adopt. The caseworker also makes sure the couple have a stable relationship and can afford to support the child. This process often is called the *home study.*

Single people are increasingly becoming adoptive parents. Sometimes agencies place children who have special needs with single individuals when two-parent homes cannot be found. Children with special needs include disabled, emotionally disturbed, or older children; ethnic minorities; and brothers and sisters who need to be adopted together. Most special needs children in the United States for whom adoptive parents have not been found live in *foster care* (see **Foster care**).

Some people adopt a child without the services of an agency. In many of these cases, physicians and lawyers put birth parents in touch with couples or individuals wishing to adopt. These adoptions are called *private,* or *independent,* adoptions. Many private adoptions do not involve a thorough home study. Private adoptions are illegal in some states.

In most states and provinces, adoptions do not become legal until children have lived in the home of their adoptive parents for 6 to 12 months. A lawyer then prepares a formal request for adoption. The adoptive parents submit the request to the proper court. If the court approves the request, the adoption becomes legal.

International adoptions. Most adoptive parents adopt children who were born in the country in which the adoptive parents live. Since the 1960's, however, the number of people waiting to adopt children has risen while the number of available children has declined. Therefore, some people adopt children from other countries. In the early 2000's, the largest numbers of international adoptees in the United States arrived from China, Guatemala, and Russia.

The United Nations has established guidelines concerning the rights of international adoptees. These guidelines recommend using authorized adoption agencies that can provide the same protection that children receive in national adoptions. According to the guidelines, the child should have an official name, nationality, and legal representative at every stage of the adoption process. In 1993, the Hague Convention on Intercountry Adoption outlined rules to protect children and their birth families from illegal adoption processes. The rules also served to prevent the abduction or the selling of children. But not all countries follow these standards.

Transracial adoptions. A transracial adoption occurs when a couple or a person adopts someone of another race or ethnic heritage. Many international adoptions are transracial adoptions. Transracial adoptions make up a small percentage of all adoptions. In the past, transracial adoptions were used as a method of cultural and racial *assimilation* (blending into a new culture).

Increasingly, agencies encourage people interested in transracial adoption to undergo special training and to participate in support groups. Some organizations provide culture camps for transracial adoptees and their families. Some adult adoptees have developed organizations to support other adoptees who are growing up in international or transracial adoptive families.

Black market adoptions. The scarcity of adoptable infants has led, in some cases, to the buying and selling of babies. Such transactions, known as black market adoptions, are against the law.

Rights of adoptive parents and adoptees. Most states and provinces keep adoption records secret once a child is adopted. The state or province issues a new birth certificate showing only the names of the adoptive parents. However, many adopted people want to know more about their backgrounds. Some organizations concerned about the rights of adopted people have proposed that nonidentifying information about the child be given to the adoptive parents. Such information does not reveal the identity of the birth parents but might include their medical and ethnic histories. This practice has been especially important for international adoptees. In a small number of states, adopted adults have a legal right to see their original birth certificates.

Adoptees and birth parents may decide that they want to contact one another. Some states and provinces maintain registries to aid these people. However, adopted children may not register until they reach adulthood. In addition, both the adopted person and the birth parents must register before contact may be established.

Some adoptive parents and birth parents now agree to *open adoptions*. In an open adoption, the birth parent or parents meet the adoptive parents and participate in the adoption process. There are many ways open adoptions are arranged. Some private agencies allow birth parents to choose the couple or individual who will raise their child. Some birth parents give up their basic parental rights but keep the right to remain in contact with the child. The birth parents might have the right to know where the child lives and to keep informed about the child's well-being. Other birth parents only request the exchange of pictures as the child grows up.

History. People have been adopting children for thousands of years. In ancient times, a childless person often adopted an individual to provide a legal heir. Adoptions were common among the ancient Assyrians, Babylonians, Greeks, and Romans. One of the first written law codes, the Babylonian Code of Hammurabi (1700's B.C.), includes a lengthy section about adoption. In the United States, the first adoption law was passed in Massachusetts in 1851.   Gina Miranda Samuels

Adrenal gland, *uh DREE nuhl,* is a small, pyramid-shaped organ that secretes many important hormones. The body has two adrenal glands, one on top of each kidney. The adrenals, also called *suprarenals,* measure about 2 inches (5 centimeters) each in diameter. Each adrenal gland consists of a *medulla* (inner core) and a *cortex* (outer shell).

The adrenal medulla is controlled by the nervous system. Nerve signals stimulate the medulla to secrete *epinephrine* (also called *adrenalin)* and norepinephrine (also called *noradrenalin)* into the blood. These hormones help the body adjust to sudden stress. For example, they increase the rate and strength of the heartbeat, raise the blood pressure, and speed up the body's energy-producing processes.

The adrenal cortex secretes many hormones, some of which are essential to life. These hormones, called *corticosteroids,* belong to three main groups—(1) glucocorticoids, (2) mineralocorticoids, and (3) sex hormones.

Glucocorticoids regulate the use of digested foods and help the body adapt to stress. The most important glucocorticoid is *cortisol,* also called *hydrocortisone.* The secretion of the glucocorticoids is controlled by *adrenocorticotropic hormone* (ACTH). ACTH is produced by the *pituitary gland,* a small organ near the base of the brain. Physicians use cortisol, and synthetic compounds that resemble it, to control inflammation.

Mineralocorticoids regulate the excretion of sodium and potassium by the kidneys. *Aldosterone* is the most important mineralocorticoid. *Renin,* a hormone secreted

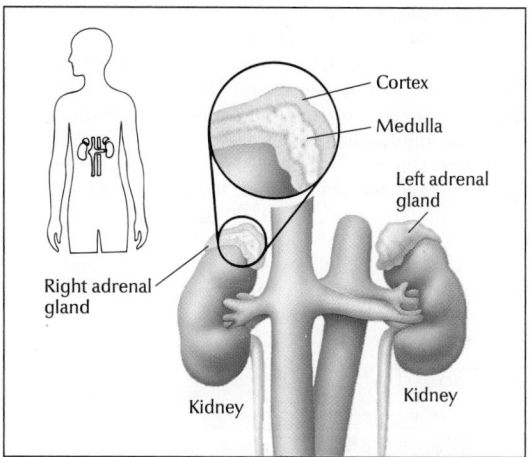

WORLD BOOK illustration by Leonard Morgan

The adrenal glands are important hormone-producing organs that lie atop the kidneys. As shown in the circle, each gland consists of two parts, an outer *cortex* and an inner *medulla.*

by the kidneys, controls the production of aldosterone. Overproduction of aldosterone causes high blood pressure in some people.

The adrenal glands produce only small amounts of sex hormones, chiefly the male sex hormones called *androgens.* The adrenal androgens help regulate the development of pubic hair and other early sexual characteristics in both males and females during the period just prior to puberty.   Charlotte H. Greene

Related articles in *World Book* include:

Addison's disease	Hormone (Human hormones)
Cortisone	Hypertension
Epinephrine	Steroid
Gland (Endocrine glands)	

Adrenalin. See Epinephrine.

Adrian, Roman emperor. See Hadrian.

Adrian IV (about 1110-1159) was the only English pope. He was elected pope in 1154. The city of Rome was in revolt against the papacy at the time of his election. Adrian placed Rome under an *interdict*—that is, a ban depriving Romans of certain religious privileges and rites. With the cooperation of the Holy Roman Emperor Frederick I, Adrian regained control of the city. Adrian made great claims for papal authority, and his policies led to a split between the empire and the papacy after his death.

At the imperial Diet of Besançon in 1157, Adrian sent a letter to Frederick in which he claimed that he had bestowed the empire on Frederick as a fief of the papacy. The letter caused a great uproar because it implied that the emperor was subordinate to the pope. Adrian explained that the translation of an ambiguous word led to the misunderstanding, and that he had only meant that the emperor had received "gifts" from the pope. The exchange destroyed the relationship between the pope and the emperor. The next year, at the Diet of Roncaglia, Frederick declared imperial authority over all of northern Italy. Adrian threatened to excommunicate Frederick if he did not withdraw his claims. But the pope died on Sept. 1, 1159, soon after the confrontation.

Adrian was born near St. Albans. His given and family name was Nicholas Breakspear.   Kenneth Pennington

Adrianople. See Edirne.

Adriatic Sea, *AY dree AT ihk,* is an extension of the Mediterranean Sea. It lies east of Italy and separates Italy from Croatia, Montenegro, and Albania. The Strait of Otranto joins the Adriatic to the Ionian Sea, another arm of the Mediterranean.

The Adriatic Sea is about 480 miles (772 kilometers) long. It has an average width of 100 miles (160 kilometers) and an area of about 60,000 square miles (160,000 square kilometers).

The Po and Adige rivers empty into the Adriatic. The Dalmatian coast, in Croatia, and the Albanian coast are

Adriatic Sea

WORLD BOOK map

rocky and dotted with islands. The Italian coast is low and flat.

Both the Italian and Croatian coasts are popular tourist regions. They are noted for their scenery and mild climate. Major port and resort cities on the Adriatic include Trieste, Venice, Ancona, Pescara, and Bari in Italy; and Rijeka, Split, and Dubrovnik in Croatia. Ferry services connect Italian ports on the western coast of the Adriatic Sea with ports on the eastern coast.

Industry and other factors have polluted many areas of the Adriatic. Navigation in the Adriatic is hazardous in winter because of sudden storms. The sea was named for the city of Adria in Italy, once an important Roman port.   Howell C. Lloyd

Adsorption. See Absorption and adsorption.

Adult education is a broad term that covers a variety of types of learning by adult students. Students are usually considered adults if they have completed high school or are at least 18 years of age.

Educators use many different terms when referring to adult education. Often, the term used depends on the location or sponsor of the learning activities. For example, universities and colleges tend to use *continuing*

studies or *continuing education.* A community-based nonprofit organization, such as a YMCA, might call its adult education offerings *lifelong learning.* In a workplace, the terms *training* or *professional development* might be used.

Adult education is found in most countries of the world. In the United States, for example, a large percentage of adults participate in some type of formal educational activity. Many adult students participate in work-related courses or training. Some adult learners study English as a Second Language (ESL). Others take General Educational Development (GED) preparation classes, which lead to a high school equivalency diploma. Some adult learners are enrolled in college or university degree or certificate programs. Others are involved in vocational or technical training programs.

Adult education can enable people to improve their quality of life. It is also a way of helping people to feel more included in society and of supporting their participation in a strong civic community. Adult education is often a means of economic development for states, regions, and nations as well.

Types of adult education. Adult education can be grouped into categories depending upon the type of instruction as well as the setting where learning takes place.

Formal adult education consists of classes taught by an instructor in an educational setting. Such settings include community colleges, universities, museums, and libraries. Formal institutions frequently award a student who has completed a course of study with a degree or certificate.

Corporate "universities" also employ instructors in an educational setting. Such universities teach management and business skills for a specific corporation. In addition, some corporate university programs offer courses that grant college credits. The Boeing and Walt Disney companies and the McDonald's Corporation are just a few of the many businesses that have a corporate university.

Nonformal adult education uses an instructor but does not take place in a school or other formal educational setting. Nonformal adult education classes are

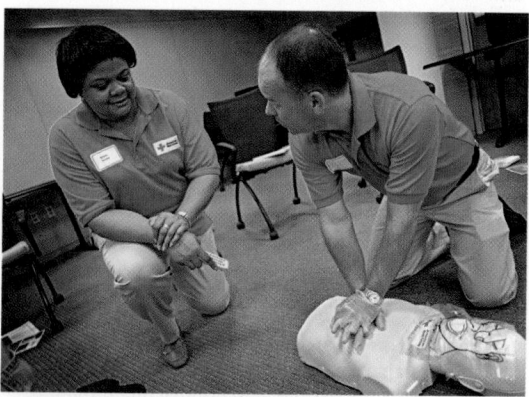

© Daniel Cima, American Red Cross

An adult learner at a first aid class receives instruction in cardiopulmonary resuscitation (CPR). Each year, many millions of adults take classes to acquire special skills.

usually focused on a particular problem, issue, or activity. They typically run for a short period. The setting for such classes is often a community-based organization. Examples of nonformal adult education include scuba-diving instruction at a YMCA; home-improvement instruction at a building center; or emergency medical training, such as training in cardiopulmonary resuscitation (CPR) at a Red Cross office.

Informal adult education, additionally known as *self-directed adult education,* is most often started and managed by the learners themselves without the aid of an instructor. Informal learners want to gain new knowledge or skills to address an issue, a problem, or an interest that they themselves have identified. For instance, a person could build a birdhouse by following the directions in a book.

Distance learning. Since the 1990's, all types of adult education have expanded their range with distance learning. Distance learning, also called *distance education,* is a process in which students learn by using resources that are far away from them, even in another city or country. The students gain access to the resources, including instructors, by using available communications systems. During the late 1800's and early 1900's, for example, a form of distance learning called *correspondence study* used the mail. In the mid-1900's, distance classes were taught on radio, and in the late 1900's, they were taught on television.

Internet-based online education became the most common means of teaching at a distance in the 2000's. Programs of study using podcasts, e-book readers, applications for smartphones and tablet computers, and conventional computers all work to allow students to learn in nearly any setting. The availability of these technologies has significantly changed adult education. It is possible now to knit together adult students from many parts of the world into a single learning environment.

History of adult education in the United States. Adult education has its roots in colonial America. Apprenticeships in the various trades were used prior to the founding of the United States. These apprenticeships represent an early system of vocational training. Formal organizations of adult learners emerged in colonial times as well. For example, the American inventor and statesman Benjamin Franklin established an organization called the Junto in 1727. The Junto created opportunities for working men, businessmen, and professionals to debate politics, business affairs, philosophy, and moral behavior.

In the mid-1800's, the Industrial Revolution changed the pattern of adult education. The Industrial Revolution was a period during which technology advanced rapidly. The development of industrialization caused businesses to need a more skilled and educated work force. Workers also saw education as a way to increase their chance of employment. From these needs emerged the *mechanics' institutes,* schools formed for the education of manual workers. Mechanics' institutes allowed members of various trades to learn from one another. The institutes often included lectures on applied science, a library, a laboratory, and museum.

From the 1820's until after the American Civil War (1861-1865), organizations called *lyceums* sponsored lectures, concerts, and other adult education programs.

© Salah Malkawi, Getty Images

Adult women learn how to read at a literacy center in Amman, Jordan. Classes in such skills as reading allow adults to significantly improve the quality of their lives.

Lyceums provided adults with a place for discussing and understanding the political and educational issues of the time. Teachers' institutes also came about in the 1800's as a place to hear lectures and discussions on topics of importance to educators. Institutes for teachers most often took place in the summer at some appealing location, such as the mountains or seaside.

Farmers' clubs and farmers' institutes were started and grew in the period following the creation of land-grant universities. These universities began with the passage of the Morrill Act of 1862, which granted every state a piece of land to be sold. The income from the sale was used to create and maintain colleges. These new American universities focused on teaching agriculture and the mechanical arts. Such schools took the university to the farmer with workshops, lectures, and correspondence study.

In the late 1800's, a system of education aimed at adult learners called the *Chautauqua movement* was established. The movement began as a church camp for Sunday school teachers. It evolved into a nationwide, year-round program of lectures and readings. The movement provided education that brought adults into contact with current thought on scientific and social issues. It provided a way for people to participate in discussions on such issues. Chautauqua argued that education for adults was both a right and a duty. Chautauqua leaders believed that adults were able to learn and that education should be extended beyond formal schooling. The Chautauqua movement believed in the idea that learning should be lifelong.

University extension programs developed in the late 1800's. These programs were used to reach students who lived far from a university or who could not attend full time. The Chautauqua movement had a strong influence on the establishment of university extension programs. Many Chautauqua leaders went on to work in higher education and brought the values of the movement to the colleges and universities they joined. Most notable among the Chautauqua leadership in higher education was William Rainey Harper, the founding president of the University of Chicago. Harper founded an extension division at that university in 1892.

The establishment of American adult education in the 1800's supported many changes in the following decades. It allowed adult education to help meet many of the social and economic needs of the country. Adult education in the 1920's, for example, was a means of educating teachers who did not have bachelor's degrees. In the 1930's, during the worldwide economic slump known as the Great Depression, adult education sponsored by the Civilian Conservation Corps (CCC) aimed at improving job prospects for its members. Adult education was a part of the continuing education of U.S. armed forces after World War II (1939-1945). It was also an important tool in President Lyndon B. Johnson's War on Poverty in the 1960's.

Adult education continues to play an important role in the country's history into the 2000's as a means of economic development and enriching the lives of an increasingly older population.   Daniel W. Shannon

Related articles in *World Book* include:
Chautauqua
Correspondence school
Distance learning
Library (Services for adults)
Lyceum
Vocational education

Additional resources

Aspin, David N. *International Handbook of Lifelong Learning.* 2 vols. Kluwer Academic, 2001.
Vella, Jane K. *Taking Learning to Task: Creative Strategies for Teaching Adults.* Jossey-Bass, 2000.
Wilson, Arthur L., and Hayes, E. R., eds. *Handbook of Adult and Continuing Education.* 2nd ed. Jossey-Bass, 2000.

Advent, *AD vehnt,* is the season that marks the beginning of the Christian church year. For most Christians, it starts on the Sunday nearest St. Andrew's Day (November 30) and continues until Christmas Eve (December 24). The term comes from the Latin word *adventus,* which means *coming* or *arrival.* The season is thus one of preparation for the celebration of the feast of the Nativity of Jesus Christ on Christmas Day. See **Christmas** (Developing Christmas traditions; Europe).

Beginning in the 500's, the Advent season was marked by a spirit of penitence, and it lasted as long as six weeks. Under the influence of the church in Rome, the season was gradually reduced to four weeks. The season in modern times has taken on a spirit of somber yet joyful preparation for the Advent of Christ, both in his birth in Bethlehem and on Judgment Day. During Advent, many members of the clergy wear vestments of royal purple or royal blue.   David G. Truemper

Adventists, *AD vehn tihsts,* are members of religious groups that stress the doctrine of the Second Coming. That is, they believe that Jesus Christ may return to the earth at any moment.

Such questions as when, where, and how Jesus would return have excited the curiosity of Christians. Interest was particularly high during the early 1800's. William Miller, a Baptist minister in Low Hampton, New York, was one of many students of the Bible who tried to find the answers. For years, Miller studied the prophecies recorded in the Old Testament Book of Daniel and the New Testament Book of Revelation. After many cal-

culations, he announced in 1831 that the Second Advent would occur in 1843 or 1844. Thousands of people believed him, and some sold their possessions. His followers, called Millerites, waited for the coming of Christ and the end of the world.

When the world did not end in 1844, many of Miller's followers were bitterly disappointed. They abandoned his movement to form new ones. The largest one—the Seventh-day Adventist Church—emerged about the time of the American Civil War (1861-1865). This group also stressed the doctrine of the Second Coming. But it avoided Miller's inclination to predict the specific time of Jesus's return.

The Seventh-day Adventists believe the body is the temple of the Holy Spirit. They abstain from anything that might affect bodily health, including tobacco, alcohol, tea, and coffee. The Adventists conduct an extensive missionary program because they believe the Second Coming cannot take place until all nations have heard the Gospel.   Charles H. Lippy

See also **Seventh-day Adventists.**

Adverb is a part of speech that adds meaning to a verb, to an adjective, to another adverb, or to an entire sentence. Adverbs are single words *(quickly).* Groups of words that act as an adverb are known as *adverbials.* These groups of words can take the form of adverbial phrases *(in the morning)* or adverbial clauses *(if the meeting continues).*

A speaker or writer uses adverbs or adverbials to add details that describe *how, when, where,* or *why* a thing happened. For example, *My brother crawled* becomes more specific when adverbs and adverbials are added: *After the accident, my brother crawled painfully from the car.* Adverbs and adverbials modify the verb *crawled. After the accident* is an adverbial phrase that tells *when.* The adverb *painfully* describes *how,* and the adverbial phrase *from the car* shows *where.*

Classifying adverbs and adverbials

Adverbs can be distinguished by their use as simple adverbs, sentence modifiers, conjunctive adverbs, or intensifiers.

Simple adverbs are single words. Most of them end in *-ly,* as in *certainly* and *deeply.* Some simple adverbs do not have an *-ly* ending. They include *above, ahead, down, too,* and *well.*

A few simple adverbs may be used either as adverbs or as adjectives. They include *better, early, fast, much, more,* and *late.* These words function as an adjective when they modify a noun *(a late breakfast)* and as an adverb when they modify a verb *(they arrived late).* Another group of adverbs has two accepted forms: *close, closely; cheap, cheaply; slow, slowly; even, evenly; deep, deeply; tight, tightly; loud, loudly.* The *-ly* form is preferred in formal usage.

Not all words that end in *-ly* are adverbs. For example, *lovely* and *jolly* are adjectives.

Sentence modifiers are adverbs and adverbials that modify the whole action of a sentence or clause rather than a single word in it. They often appear at the beginning of a sentence. For example:

Frankly, *I don't want to hear about it.*
As I recall, *nobody asked any questions.*
Fortunately, *we could reach him before he left town.*

Conjunctive adverbs serve a double purpose. Although these adverbs can modify other words or phrases, they frequently act as sentence modifiers. However, conjunctive adverbs additionally serve as *structure words*—words that connect one part of a sentence to another.

> *You have made a few payments;* however, *we must ask you to send checks regularly.*

The adverb *however* connects the two clauses as a conjunction. It also modifies the final clause. Other words commonly used as conjunctive adverbs include *therefore, still, otherwise, also, moreover, nevertheless,* and *yet.* Phrases that are frequently used as conjunctive adverbs include *for example, that is, on the other hand,* and *in conclusion.*

Intensifiers do not alter the meaning of the words they modify, but they add emphasis to those words. For example, when intensifiers are added—as in *very* proud, *extremely* quiet, *quite* concerned, and *too* loud—additional force is given to the verb they modify.

Position of adverbs

An adverb can occupy a number of positions in a sentence:

> Slowly *she walked off the stage.*
> *She walked* slowly *off the stage.*
> *She walked off the stage* slowly.

In these three sentences, the position of the adverb *slowly* changes the emphasis, but not the overall meaning, of the sentence. In some instances, however, the placement of certain adverbs can change both the emphasis and the meaning of a sentence. The following three sentences show how meaning can be changed by altering the placement of the adverb *only:*

> Only *my brother asked to see the gift.*
> *My brother* only *asked to see the gift.*
> *My brother asked to see* only *the gift.*

Other adverbs whose placement can affect the emphasis and meaning of a sentence include *almost, ever, hardly, just, merely, nearly, normally, quite, scarcely,* and *somewhat.*

Usage

Adverb-adjective confusion. Through usage, certain words have been established as only adverbs and others as only adjectives. Confusion between some of these adjectives and adverbs is common because they are similar in form. For example, *sure* is an adjective meaning firm or secure; *surely* is an adverb meaning certainly. Consider the use of adverbs in the following three sentences:

> *He was* surely *(not* sure) *afraid of his mother.*
> *It was a* really *(not* real) *good game.*
> *He did* very *well (not* good) *on his first test.*

People often find the following adverbs and adjectives to be confusing:

Adjectives	Adverbs
good (kind, agreeable, satisfactory)	well (in a satisfactory or desirable way)
real (authentic, genuine)	really (actually)
sure (firm, secure)	surely (certainly)
some (in an indefinite amount)	somewhat (to a certain extent)

Confusing adverbs and adjectives is common after linking verbs (some form of the verb *to be* or verbs like *feel, seem, hear,* or *smell).* A linking verb should be followed by an adjective modifying the subject, not an adverb. But the adverb form may be used to modify the verb. For example:

> *He felt* bad *(not* badly) *because he had played so* poorly *(not* poor).

The adjective *bad,* modifying *he,* appears after *felt.* But *poorly,* the adverb, is used to modify *played.*

The use of the adjective *most* in place of the adverb *almost* appears frequently in informal usage. However, the less formal substitution should be avoided in formal writing.

> *Almost all the elephants died,* not *Most all the elephants died.*

Unnecessary adverbs can clutter and confuse a sentence. Often, a single specific verb can replace an adverb and sharpen expression. *Hurried* is preferable to *moved quickly,* and *grasped* is better than *took eagerly.* Such adverbs as *hardly, barely,* and *scarcely* carry a negative meaning. Using the adverb *not* with these words is unnecessary and confusing:

> *The family had scarcely enough to eat,* not *The family did not have scarcely enough to eat.*
> *I can hardly remember the incident,* not *I cannot hardly remember the incident.*

Unnecessary adverbs also may merely repeat and confuse the meaning of the words that they modify. For example:

> *The old man reverted (not* reverted back) *to the days of his childhood.*
> *He advanced (not* advanced forward) *to his position in the line.*
> *This (not* this here) *book has more pictures than that (not* that there) *one.*

Adverbs that split an infinitive. An infinitive is the base part of a verb, such as *go* or *see.* It is often used with the word *to,* as in *to go* or *to see. Splitting an infinitive* means placing one or more words between *to* and the verb form, as in *to quickly go* or *to readily see.*

Splitting an infinitive with an adverb is a matter of style rather than correct grammar. It can sometimes result in an awkward expression. This is especially true when the infinitive is separated from its verb by more than one word. For example:

> *We want to slowly and carefully reorganize the workflow of this organization.*
> *He promised to faithfully and cheerfully work with his teacher.*

In the first example, *slowly and carefully* splits the infinitive *to reorganize.* Reordering the sentence to read *to reorganize slowly and carefully* improves clarity. In the second example, the placement of the words *faithfully and cheerfully* splits the infinitive *to work.* The sentence would be easier to understand if the adverbs did not split the infinitive: For example:

> *He promised to work faithfully and cheerfully with his teacher.*

In other cases, however, splitting the infinitive may be the only way to get the special emphasis and meaning a writer wants. For example:

> *I prefer to actually see a play, not just read it.*

Placing *actually* in any other position would alter the meaning of the sentence.   Anja Wanner

See also **Adjective.**

Advertising messages promote a wide variety of products, services, and ideas in nearly all the world's countries. The streets of the Ginza district of Tokyo, *shown here,* are lined with brightly colored signs and displays that advertise specific brands of automobiles, beverages, and other goods.

Advertising

Advertising is a message designed to promote a product, a service, or an idea. In everyday life, people come into contact with many kinds of advertising. Printed advertisements make up a large part of newspapers and magazines. Poster ads appear in many buses, subways, and trains. Neon signs along downtown streets flash advertisements. Billboards dot the roadsides. Commercials interrupt TV and radio programs. Advertisements appear on many sites on the internet.

The purpose of most advertising is to sell products or services. Manufacturers advertise to try to persuade people to buy their products. Large business firms also use advertising to create a favorable "image" of their company. Local businesses use it to gain new customers and increase sales. Advertising thus plays a key role in the competition among businesses for the consumer's dollar. In many businesses, the volume of sales depends largely on the amount of advertising done.

Advertising is also used by individuals, political parties and candidates, social organizations, special-interest groups, and the government. Many people advertise to sell used cars, homes, or other property. Political parties and candidates use advertising to try to win votes. Social organizations and special-interest groups often advertise to promote a cause or to influence the way people think or act. For example, the American Cancer Society sponsors ads designed to educate people about cancer risks and to raise money for cancer research. The United States government uses advertising chiefly to recruit volunteers for the armed forces.

Advertising is a multibillion-dollar industry. About $250 billion is spent on advertising in the United States each year. About $400 billion is spent on advertising in other countries.

Advertising is common in almost all countries. In many countries, however, advertising is more restricted than it is in the United States. In most of the countries of western Europe, for example, governments limit the amount of advertising that appears on television. In addition, these governments make greater use of advertising for social, political, and educational purposes.

Ways of advertising

Advertising reaches people through various forms of mass communication. These *media* include newspapers, magazines, television, the internet, and radio. Advertisers buy *space* in newspapers and magazines and on websites to publish their ads. They buy *time* on television and radio to broadcast their commercials. National advertisers, such as automobile makers and fast-food

© Reed Kaestner, Corbis

Television is the chief medium used by national advertisers. Companies use TV commercials to reach large numbers of consumers who view programs, movies, and sports events on TV.

AP/Wide World

Store displays called *point-of-purchase displays* advertise products within a store. These displays often involve colorful signs, banners, and the careful arrangement of items for sale.

AP/Wide World

Outdoor advertising is effective in communicating brief messages to large numbers of people. Some companies place advertisements on airships called *blimps,* which then fly over highly populated areas and popular events.

restaurants, use the media to reach consumers throughout large parts of the country or all of it. Local advertisers, such as department stores and supermarkets, use the media to reach consumers within a city or town.

The chief advertising media in the United States are (1) television, (2) newspapers, (3) the Internet, (4) direct mail, (5) magazines, (6) radio, and (7) outdoor signs.

Television is the chief medium used by national advertisers. Much television advertising is for car companies, financial and insurance companies, food companies, restaurants, retail stores, telecommunications companies, and companies that sell medicines.

A main advantage of television to advertisers is that it brings sight, sound, and action directly to consumers in their homes. Advertisers can explain and demonstrate their products to viewers who are enjoying a TV pro-

gram. In addition, network television reaches a vast, nationwide audience at a low cost per viewer. For example, a 30-second commercial on a TV network may cost $1 million. But if 50 million viewers watch the commercial, the advertiser pays only 2 cents for each person who sees the ad.

The majority of TV commercials consist of short *spot announcements,* most of which last 30 seconds. The commercials are usually run in groups of three to six.

Advertisers can buy *spot time* from local TV stations or *network time* from one of the national TV networks. Sometimes an advertiser will choose to run ads on a cable channel to reach a specific audience. In addition, advertisers can either sponsor an entire TV program or buy *scatter packages.* In scatter packages, the commercials are aired at various times for several weeks. Most advertisers buy scatter packages. But special entertainment programs, sports events, and certain motion pictures are often sponsored by one advertiser. In this way, the advertiser hopes to gain added recognition by being identified with the program.

Newspapers, on the average, devote more than half of their space to advertising. Local businesses and individuals place most of this advertising. National advertisers sometimes use newspapers to inform consumers of the names and locations of local stores where the advertiser's products are available. National advertisers also use newspapers when they want to concentrate their sales efforts in particular regions of the country.

Newspapers offer advertisers several advantages over other media. Many newspaper readers specifically check the ads for information about products or services. Daily newspapers also offer the advantage of timeliness. An advertiser can prepare and publish an advertisement within a day. Newspaper ads can thus quickly reflect a sudden demand for certain merchandise. For example, a department store can advertise snow shovels in a newspaper the day after the city has its first snowfall of the season.

The Internet. Advertising on the Internet includes small signs on web pages, called *text ads,* and larger signs, called *banner ads.* Other forms of Internet advertising include listings in online directories and e-mails sent to lists of potential customers. Many companies also maintain websites to promote their products and services.

The cost to advertise on the Internet can vary greatly. Banner advertising is generally sold in one of two types. The first type is called *cost per million* (CPM), and the cost depends on the number of visitors to the website. The second type is called *cost per click* (CPC), and the cost depends on how many people click through to the advertiser's website. One benefit of Internet advertising is that advertisers can access minute-by-minute information about consumer response to advertising. This allows them to know what advertising is effective and what elements of the advertising should be changed.

One form of Internet advertising is called social-media marketing. This kind of advertising uses existing networks of friends or communities of Internet users to spread a promotional message about a product or service. This form of advertising can be especially effective, because people tend to pay more attention to, and show more trust in, messages that come from someone they know.

Direct mail includes leaflets, brochures, catalogs, and other printed advertisements that are delivered by a postal service. Mail-order firms, which sell largely through the mail, are the primary users of direct-mail advertising.

The effectiveness of advertising by direct mail depends mainly on the quality of the *mailing list.* Some lists consist of all the addresses in a city and are simply sent to "Occupant." Other mailing lists consist of individual names with addresses. Some firms specialize in preparing lists of people according to their occupation, age, income, interests, or other characteristics. For example, a firm might assemble a list of 20,000 new mothers or 10,000 lawyers. These lists are sold to advertisers. Some advertisers assemble their own mailing lists.

Direct-mail advertising costs more per person reached than do other ways of advertising. However, advertisers who obtain special mailing lists know they are reaching good prospects. In addition, advertisers can choose from many different sizes and forms of advertisements. Some products or services are too complicated to be explained in any other medium.

Radio. Local advertisers place most of the advertising on radio stations. The rest is placed by national advertisers, who buy time either from individual stations in various cities and towns or from one of the radio networks.

One advantage of advertising on radio is that people can listen to programs while doing other things. Another advantage is that radio audiences, in general, are more highly selected by the type of programming than are television audiences. For example, stations that feature country music attract different kinds of listeners than do those that play rock. By selecting the station, advertisers can reach the people most likely to buy their products.

Radio commercials include direct sales announcements, dramatized stories, and songs. Most commercials last 30 or 60 seconds. In general, radio stations have more commercial time per hour than television stations. Thus, a major drawback of radio is that listeners often hear so many commercials that it is difficult for any one ad to make an impression.

Magazines. Most magazines have a nationwide circulation and so are used chiefly by national advertisers. Magazines have a number of advantages over newspapers as an advertising medium. They are usually read in a leisurely manner and are often kept for weeks or months before being discarded. In many cases, several members of a family read each copy of a magazine. Another advantage of magazines is that they offer better printing and color reproduction than newspapers do.

AP/Wide World

Direct-mail advertising involves the mailing of leaflets, catalogs, brochures, and other printed materials. This man is gathering envelopes stuffed with ads to be sent to potential customers.

© TH Foto from Alamy.com

Newspapers and magazines devote large amounts of their space to advertising. The wide variety of publications allows advertisers to target readers of a certain age or location, or with specific areas of interest.

Advertisers can thus show off their products to greater advantage in magazines.

Advertisers can choose from a wide variety of magazines. Some magazines, such as newsmagazines, appeal to a mass audience. Others are designed for specific groups of people, such as teenagers or amateur photographers. Certain companies advertise in *trade publications,* which are devoted to particular businesses, industries, or professions. For example, farm magazines are used by advertisers who sell agricultural equipment and supplies. Drug firms advertise in medical journals to reach doctors and druggists.

Outdoor signs. Most advertising on outdoor signs is for local businesses. One of the main advantages of outdoor signs is that people pass by the signs repeatedly. In addition, large, colorful signs easily attract attention. However, the ads on outdoor signs must be short and simple because most passers-by see a sign for only a few seconds.

The main kinds of outdoor signs are (1) posters, (2) painted bulletins, and (3) electronic billboards. Posters, commonly called *billboards,* are the most widely used form of outdoor advertising. They consist of printed sheets of paper that are pasted on large billboards. The billboards are owned by local companies and are rented by the month to advertisers. Painted bulletins are signs painted on buildings or billboards. Electronic billboards are large illuminated displays. Many feature changing messages and moving pictures. Electronic billboards are the most expensive kind of outdoor sign.

Other ways of advertising include the use of (1) transit signs, (2) displays, (3) product placement, (4) novelties, and (5) sponsorship.

Transit signs are small posters placed in or on local trains, subways, buses, and taxicabs. Posters placed inside vehicles can carry a longer message than outside ads because riders have more time to read it.

Displays. Window displays are designed to draw customers into a store. Point-of-purchase displays are arrangements of signs, banners, and other items within a store. These displays highlight certain products and are designed to encourage *impulse buying*—that is, buying without previous thought or planning. Many stores have a promotion department, whose duties include preparing displays. Other stores hire display firms. Many manufacturers supply display materials to retailers that sell their products.

Product placement involves the promotion of products within such media as a television show, a movie, or a book. Typically, a company will pay to have its products incorporated into the script or manuscript, or the product is used as a prop.

Novelties are inexpensive items that many advertisers give away. Such items include calendars, pens, and key rings that carry an advertiser's name and message. Peo-

WORLD BOOK photo by Jeff Guerrant

Novelty items that carry an advertiser's name and message are often given away to potential customers. Such items include calendars, matchbooks, mugs, pens, and T-shirts.

Transit signs may be placed on or inside buses, subway cars, taxis, and trains to help spread a company's message. This city bus in San Francisco, California, is advertising an aquarium in nearby Monterey.

ple are reminded of the advertiser as long as they use the item.

Sponsorship involves a company giving money to support an event or award. For example, the Booker Prizes, major British literary awards, have a single sponsor. Such big events as the Olympics often have multiple sponsors. Sponsorship is useful for shaping a company's image over a long period.

Advertising techniques

Advertising is designed to inform, influence, or persuade people. To be effective, an advertisement must first attract attention and gain a person's interest. It may then provide reasons for buying a product and for believing the advertiser's claims.

Advertisers use a variety of techniques to create effective advertisements. They start with a basic *appeal,* which is the main selling point, or theme, of an advertisement. Advertisers then use certain specific techniques. The most commonly used techniques include (1) attention-getting headlines, (2) slogans, (3) testimonials, (4) product characters, (5) comparison of products, and (6) repetition.

Basic appeals. Advertisers rely on many kinds of appeals to persuade people to buy. In general, appeals can be classified as *informational* or *transformational.* Advertisements that use an informational approach describe the *demonstrable* characteristics of a product. Such ads tell what the product is, how it works, or how it is made. Advertisements that use a transformational appeal stress the ways in which a product will provide personal satisfaction. Such an ad might suggest that the product will satisfy the consumer's need for love, security, or prestige.

Advertisers often use sexual themes that appeal to a person's desire to be attractive. For example, an advertisement for after-shave lotion might suggest that the product will cause a man to be found more attractive.

To persuade the largest possible number of people, many advertisements combine different types of appeals. Appeals may also be aimed at a large general audience or targeted at a limited group of people, such as business executives or young married couples.

Attention-getting headlines are an important feature of printed advertisements. A successful headline leads a person into reading the rest of the ad. Some headlines attract attention by promising the reader a personal benefit, such as a savings in money or an improvement in physical appearance. Other headlines are cleverly worded to arouse a person's curiosity. Still other headlines carry news, such as an announcement of a new product. Headlines also attract attention by directly addressing a specific group. For example, a headline might read: "For the Working Mom." The opening lines in a radio or TV commercial serve the same purpose as headlines in printed ads.

Slogans are short phrases that are used over and over. Good slogans are easy to remember. The majority of slogans are designed to help create a favorable image of a company and its products. Most such slogans do not relate to particular features of a product. Companies also use slogans in advertising inexpensive products, such as chewing gum or soft drinks.

Testimonials are advertisements in which a person endorses a product. The person may be someone who looks like an average user of the product. Advertisers also pay movie and TV stars, popular athletes, and other celebrities to endorse products. A celebrity helps attract attention to an advertisement. Under United States government regulations, endorsers must use the advertised product if they claim they do so.

Product characters are fictional people and cartoon animals or characters that are used in advertisements over a long period. Many advertisers use product characters to deliver sales messages for a whole line of products. The characters become highly familiar to people and so provide lasting identification with a company's products. Product characters are often used in advertising aimed at children because such characters delight many young people.

Comparison of products is used most frequently to sell products that compete heavily with other brands. Advertisers compare their product with similar brands and point out the advantages of using their brand. A competitor's product may be named, or it may be referred to as "Brand X" or "the leading brand."

Repetition is one of the most basic techniques advertisers use to get their message across. Advertisers may broadcast their commercials several times a day for weeks on TV or radio. Or they may publish their ads frequently in printed media. Repetition can help build or reinforce a company's reputation. Advertisers also believe that the more often people see or hear an advertisement, the more likely they are to accept the message and want the product. However, if a message is repeated too often, people can begin to ignore or dislike it.

Creating advertisements

Most business firms hire advertising agencies to create their advertisements and place them in the various media. In most cases, individual advertisements form part of an *advertising campaign*. A campaign is an organized sales effort that may run for several months and that usually involves more than one medium.

In planning an advertising campaign, the agency must first determine the objective of the campaign. The objective may be to prove a product's superiority over competing brands, to change the image of the company, or to achieve some other goal. The agency must additionally determine the *target market*—that is, the people who are likely users of a product and at whom the advertising will be aimed. Finally, the agency has to estimate how much money and time will be needed to carry out the campaign.

Large advertising agencies generally assign a team of people from the various departments of the agency to handle all the advertising for a specific advertiser, or *client*. The typical agency includes a research department, creative department, media department, and production department. An *account manager,* or *account executive,* has overall responsibility for planning and directing a client's advertising. The following discussion describes in broad terms the way an agency creates advertisements. The main steps in the process include (1) research, (2) media selection, (3) creative work, and (4) production.

Research. Information gathered from consumers provides the basis for many advertising decisions. It helps an agency determine the kinds of people at whom to aim advertisements, the types of appeals to use, and in which media to place the ads. The chief kinds of research include (1) market research, (2) motivation research, and (3) media research.

Market research seeks information about consumers and their buying habits. The information is obtained from a sample of consumers by means of surveys. The information includes the age, sex, income, and occupation of potential consumers. Researchers may also learn how consumers rate various brands of a product, in-

cluding the advertiser's brand. Such information helps advertisers decide on the best way to present the features of their products.

Motivation research tries to find out why people buy certain products. Motivation researchers gather such information in personal interviews, during which they use techniques developed by psychologists and sociologists. By discovering the motives for people's buying behavior, advertisers hope to find the most effective appeal to use in their advertisements. For example, advertisers may learn that many people buy certain kinds of automobiles chiefly to impress their friends. The motivations of consumers are complex, and the study of motivations is therefore more difficult than most other types of research.

Media research. Various research firms measure the size and makeup of radio and TV audiences at different times of the day. The Audit Bureau of Circulations—an organization of advertisers, advertising agencies, and publishers—measures the circulations of publications. Advertisers use information on audience size and makeup in selecting media in which to place ads.

Media selection. The members of an agency's media department compare the various media in terms of audience size and makeup. They decide which particular magazines, newspapers, and radio and television stations or networks to use to reach the target market. They then prepare a media plan that will give an effective combination of *reach* and *frequency* within the limita-

An emotional appeal is used in many advertisements to attract attention so that people will learn about the product. This advertisement appeals to parents' love and concern for their children and then gives reasons for buying the product.

Testimonials include advertisements in which a celebrity endorses a product or service. In amusing television commercials, actress Sofia Vergara, *shown here,* urges viewers to sample a Diet Pepsi.

PepsiCo

tions of the budget. Reach is the number of people who will see or hear the advertisement. Frequency is the number of times that they will see or hear it. The media planners may decide to reach a large number of people a few times or to reach fewer people more often.

The recommendations of the media department must be approved by the client. The media planners then buy time and space from the media and schedule the advertisements for specific dates.

Creative work. An agency's creative department develops the central theme of an advertising campaign. The department then designs individual advertisements. The theme, and the ideas for carrying it out, must be approved by the account manager and the client.

For printed advertisements, a copywriter prepares the *copy* (written words) and an artist prepares a *layout* of the advertisement. A layout shows the placement of the copy and illustrations. The illustrations may consist of artwork or photographs or both. The copy, illustrations, and layout may be revised several times. The finished artwork may be prepared by an artist in the agency or by a *free-lance* (independent) artist. Photographs are taken by professional photographers who are hired by the agency or chosen from a *stock photography* catalog, which has images that are offered for sale.

For radio commercials, a copywriter prepares the script, which may consist simply of a sales message to be read by a radio announcer. Some scripts are skits that feature dialogue and perhaps sound effects or background music. Original music or songs are written by composers commissioned by the agency.

For television commercials, a copywriter creates the script and an artist designs a *storyboard,* which is a series of drawings of the planned action. The storyboard is combined with the script and includes directions for filming the commercial.

Production. The production of printed advertisements, radio commercials, and TV commercials is

arranged by the production department of an advertising agency. The production department deals with *advertising service and supply houses,* which include graphic arts firms and producers of radio and TV commercials. In each case, the client has to approve the final advertisements before they are printed or broadcast.

For printed advertisements, the production department works with graphic arts firms, which set the copy in type and prepare the film or other material for printing the type and illustrations. This material is then sent to the publications in which the ads will appear. Newspaper advertisements are sometimes produced by the newspaper printers themselves.

For radio commercials, the production department may simply deliver the script to the radio station where it will be read by an announcer. If the script has dialogue, the commercial must be prerecorded, and so the agency hires a radio producer. The producer selects performers to read the commercial and sets up rehearsals. If necessary, a musical director and an orchestra are also hired. The commercial is then recorded on tape in a studio and delivered for broadcasting.

The agency also uses a producer for television commercials. If the commercial is to be filmed or videotaped, the producer may work with a director. These two individuals select performers and arrange rehearsals. After the commercial is shot in the studio or on location, the production department combines it with the sound track and edits it. After the producer has approved the finished commercial, the commercial is sent to the TV stations or network where it will be aired.

Some TV commercials consist of *stop-motion* films or animated cartoons. Stop motion is a method of photographing objects in different positions so that, when the film is run, they appear to move. For example, bottles may seem to dance across a table.

Animated cartoons produced in the traditional way require many individual drawings that must be filmed in sequence. Modern computer-generated animation and special effects are much easier to produce. For example, an electronic device called a *scanner* can convert the colors and shades of illustrations or photos into *digital* (numerical) code, then feed this code to a computer. An animator can then use the computer to manipulate the illustrations.

If the commercial is a live announcement, the producer makes sure the script, product, and furniture or other objects are supplied to the station. The producer also supervises the rehearsals. Today, live announcements are rare.

The advertising industry

Advertising is a global industry. Most advertising agencies are owned by one of four large international companies: WPP Group, based in London; Publicis Groupe, based in Paris; and Interpublic Group of Companies and Omnicom Group, both based in New York City.

Advertising agencies. The United States has thousands of advertising agencies. These agencies range in size from one-person organizations to huge agencies with several thousand employees and with offices in several U.S. and foreign cities.

An advertising agency's chief service is to create and place advertising for clients. Some agencies also provide information and advice on selling plans, packaging designs, and other marketing operations.

Advertising agencies receive income in three main ways: (1) from commissions paid by the media, (2) from service charges paid by clients for materials and work purchased from graphic arts firms and other companies, and (3) from fees paid by clients. The standard commission is 15 percent of the cost of the space or time that an agency buys for a client. The agency charges the client the total cost of the space or time and deducts 15 percent before paying the media.

Advertising departments. Most large business companies have an advertising department. In some companies, the department prepares all the company's advertising and so functions as an *in-house agency.* Among those firms that employ an advertising agency, the company's advertising department works closely with the agency. The department might also prepare such materials as point-of-purchase displays and direct-mail brochures, which are not usually considered part of an agency's duties.

Some companies that manufacture a large number of products have *brand managers.* A brand manager supervises the advertising and promotion of one or a few products.

Newspapers, magazines, and radio and television stations and networks also have advertising departments. These departments collect and publish information designed to persuade advertisers to use their particular media vehicle. They supply advertisers and advertising agencies with reports on the vehicle's circulation, listening audience, or viewing audience. They may also provide production assistance.

Advertising associations work to promote the industry and to raise the standards of advertising. The leading advertising organizations in the United States include the Association of National Advertisers, the American Advertising Federation, and the Association of National Advertisers.

Two other important advertising organizations are the Advertising Council and the National Advertising Review Board. The Advertising Council prepares public service ads, such as those that promote highway safety and energy conservation. The National Advertising Review Board fosters self-regulation of the advertising industry. It evaluates complaints about *deceptive* (false or misleading) advertisements. If the council judges an advertisement to be deceptive, it asks the advertiser to discontinue the ad.

Most countries have one to several advertising associations. The Institute of Communication Agencies works to improve advertising standards in Canada. In the United Kingdom, the Advertising Association represents the British advertising industry. In Australia, associations include the Advertising Federation of Australia and the Australian Association of National Advertisers.

Regulation of advertising. Both the U.S. government and the state governments have laws designed to protect consumers from deceptive advertising. They also have laws that prohibit certain kinds of advertising. For example, a federal law bans cigarette advertising on radio and television. However, the Supreme Court of the United States has ruled that advertising and the advertising industry have some protection under the First Amendment to the Constitution of the United States. Thus, regulations concerning advertising must be no more restrictive than necessary to accomplish the goals of state and federal governments.

Federal laws against deceptive advertising are enforced chiefly by the Federal Trade Commission (FTC). The FTC monitors all advertising and may ask advertisers for proof of their claims. If the FTC decides that an advertisement is false or misleading, it may order an advertiser to withdraw the ad. The FTC may further require an advertiser to run "corrective" advertising to inform the public that former advertisements were deceptive. However, the FTC rarely requires this. Advertisers may be fined for violating an FTC order. Some advertisers are also subject to regulation by the Federal Communications Commission (FCC), the Food and Drug Administration (FDA), the Securities and Exchange Commission (SEC), and certain other federal agencies.

Advertising in other countries. Many of the largest advertisers in the United States also spend significant amounts of money to advertise in other countries. These companies may use local agencies or branch offices of U.S.-based agencies to create ad campaigns. Many large U.S. agencies have acquired foreign-based local agencies or developed a network of international offices to handle the advertising of multinational corporations.

In Western Europe, government had regulated broadcasting tightly until the 1980's. The state owned the broadcast industry, each country had only one or two television channels, and the amount of advertising time was severely restricted. In the 1980's, more channels were added by the state and private companies, and advertising restrictions were loosened. In addition, satellites began to beam TV signals to rooftop antennas on individual homes. Most such signals reach consumers in more than one country. Because of increased access to consumers, the trend among major European advertis-

AP/Wide World

International ad campaigns can spread an advertiser's message to people throughout the world. This billboard for a U.S.-based computer company appeared in Yangon, Myanmar.

ers has been to develop a single ad campaign for several countries.

Regulations on advertising differ in other parts of the world. In Australia, for example, most ads must be produced locally. China charges higher ad rates for foreign advertisers than for local companies or joint ventures.

Agencies throughout the world support the International Advertising Association, which has headquarters in New York City. This organization works for truth in advertising, the protection of commercial speech, and improvements in the quality of media research.

Effects of advertising

Advertising greatly influences many aspects of life in the United States. This section deals with some of its economic, social, and political effects.

Economic effects. Advertising plays a major role in the distribution of goods from manufacturers to consumers. It provides an effective way for sellers to inform buyers about products. Advertising thus helps manufacturers sell their products and benefits consumers by providing them with shopping information.

Advertising also helps the economy grow by stimulating demand for new products. Manufacturers spend much money to develop new products. Through advertising, they can speed up the process of creating a market for a product and so recover their costs more quickly. Fewer new products would be developed if manufacturers could not use advertising to help sell the products.

Some economists believe that a large amount of the money spent on advertising is wasted. They argue that much advertising simply leads consumers to switch from one brand of a product to another brand. Brand-switching may increase the profits of a particular firm but has no positive effect on the overall economy.

Advertisers include the expense of advertising in the sales price of a product. In some cases, advertising raises the price of a product. In other cases, advertising helps lower prices by creating the *mass demand* that supports mass production. Successful advertising makes many people want a product. By mass producing a product and developing a large volume of sales, the manufacturer can charge less per unit.

Social effects. Perhaps the most important social contribution of advertising is that it supports the mass communication media. Advertising pays all the costs of commercial television and radio. It provides viewers with free entertainment and news programs, though viewers are often irritated by commercial interruptions. Advertising also pays much of the costs of newspapers and magazines. Without advertising, readers would have to pay a higher price for newspapers and magazines, and many of the publications would go out of business.

Because the mass media depend on advertising to stay in business, many people question whether advertisers control the media. Generally, media do not allow advertisers to influence their programming or editorial content. However, many broadcasters and publishers do not hesitate to run favorable information about their advertisers, and they sometimes refuse to run unfavorable information. Critics of commercial television maintain that dependence on advertising lowers the quality of TV programming. In order to sell advertising time at high prices, TV stations try to attract the largest possible audience. Critics argue that the stations therefore broadcast too many general entertainment programs and not enough informational and cultural programs.

Many critics also charge that advertising persuades people to buy products they do not need or want through the use of psychological techniques. Advertisers reply that they do not have the means to make people buy unwanted products. They argue that adults freely choose what to buy or what not to buy. Most experts agree, however, that advertising is particularly persuasive to young children, who do not have the ability or experience to judge advertising critically. For this reason, the Federal Trade Commission and the Federal Communications Commission have strict regulations governing advertising aimed at children.

Political effects. Little attention was paid to political advertising until 1952, when Dwight D. Eisenhower successfully ran for the U.S. presidency. Advertising executives, rather than politicians, directed Eisenhower's presidential campaign. Much of Eisenhower's campaign consisted of a flood of spot announcements on television stations.

Since 1952, advertising executives have played an increasingly important role in political campaigns. In addition, TV spot announcements have become a major feature of campaigns for public offices at the national and state levels. The chief criticism of political advertising concerns the use of such spot announcements, which

Political advertising has played an important role in election campaigns since the mid-1900's. President Dwight D. Eisenhower, shown here with his wife, Mamie, used television to reach out to voters during the 1950's.

may concentrate on creating an image of a candidate and tend to oversimplify the issues. Critics object to candidates being "sold" through advertising methods like those used to sell products. Another complaint is that candidates with the most money to spend on advertising have an unfair advantage over their opponents. Because of this complaint, Congress passed a law in 1974 that limits the amount of money candidates may spend in presidential campaigns.

History

Most historians believe that outdoor signs above shop doors were the first form of advertising. As early as 3000 B.C., the Mesopotamians, who lived in what is now Iraq, used such signs to advertise their stores. The ancient Greeks and Romans also hung signs outside their shops. Few people could read, and so merchants used symbols carved in stone, clay, or wood for the signs. For example, a bush indicated a wine shop, and a boot advertised a shoemaker's shop.

In ancient Egypt, merchants hired *criers* to walk through the streets and announce the arrivals of ships and their cargo. By the A.D. 900's, town criers, who called out the news, were common in European countries. They also were hired by merchants to direct customers to shops and to tell them about goods and prices in the marketplace.

The impact of printing. About 1440, Johannes Gutenberg of Germany invented movable type in Europe. His invention led to the first forms of mass advertising—printed posters, handbills, and newspaper ads. William Caxton, who introduced printing into England, produced the first printed advertisement in English in 1472. It was a poster announcing the sale of a book and was tacked on church doors.

The first newspaper regularly printed in England, a weekly newssheet, appeared in 1622. In the years that followed, more English newspapers were started, and advertising soon became a standard feature of newspapers.

The first newspaper advertisement in the American Colonies appeared in *The Boston News-Letter* in 1704.

Many of the early magazines in the United States either refused to print advertisements or carried only certain kinds of ads. But in the mid-1800's, more and more magazines began to accept advertising, and magazine advertising grew quickly. Some magazines were started chiefly to earn advertising money.

Many early ads in both the United States and England paid little heed to the truth. Advertisers made wildly exaggerated claims. Ads for nonprescription drugs, for example, boasted cures for all kinds of ailments.

The development of advertising agencies. The first advertising agencies acted as *brokers*—that is, they bought space at a discount from newspapers and resold it to advertisers. The ads were prepared by the advertisers themselves or by hired writers.

Volney B. Palmer started the first U.S. advertising agency in Philadelphia in 1841. Palmer worked as an agent for newspaper publishers. He received 25 percent commission on the space that he sold to advertisers.

In 1875, N. W. Ayer & Son, another Philadelphia advertising agency, began to emphasize agency services to advertisers. In time, the firm hired writers and artists and carried out complete advertising campaigns for clients. N. W. Ayer & Son thus became the first "modern" advertising agency. By 1900, most agencies in the United States were writing copy for advertisers. By the 1920's, they had assumed responsibility for complete advertising campaigns.

The rise of radio and television provided advertisers with new, powerful media. Commercial radio stations began operating in the United States in the 1920's. Radio soon became a major medium for national advertisers. It enabled them to reach the large, captive audiences that tuned in to popular programs. Many of the radio shows were produced by advertising agencies. The popularity of radio soared for about 20 years, until television began to boom after World War II (1939-1945). Radio then lost much of the business of national advertisers, though it continued to be an important medium for local advertisers.

The rise of coast-to-coast TV broadcasts in the 1950's

221

TRUAX & COMPANY

ELECTRIC BELTS.

Try it and be Convinced.

DISCOUNT, ONE-THIRD.

THIS BELT CURES

PARALYSIS,	LUMBAGO,	MALARIA,
NEURALGIA,	DYSPEPSIA.	LAME BACK,
RHEUMATISM,	FEVER AND AGUE,	LIVER COMPLAINT,
SPINAL IRRITATION.	SEMINAL WEAKNESS,	KIDNEY DISEASES,
NERVOUS EXHAUSTION.	FEMALE COMPLAINTS,	GENERAL DEBILITY.

FAC-SIMILE OF LABEL.

COMMON SENSE ELECTRIC BELT,

THE BELT FOR THE MILLION.

Warranted Equal to any of the High Priced Belts and Sold at a REASONABLE Price.

Manufactured by the

Common Sense Electric Belt Co.

Pat. Sept. 20, 1881.   CHICAGO, ILL.

Price, according to quality, $3.00, $4.00 and $5.00 each.

Sent by mail on receipt of price.   Address your orders to our agents,

CHAS. TRUAX & CO.

Historical Pictures Service

Exaggerated claims were made in many ads in the 1800's for medicines and such "medical aids" as electric belts, *shown here.*

provided national advertisers with access to mass audiences far larger than the listeners reached by radio. By 1955, advertisers were spending over $1 billion a year on television.

Recent developments. Advertising expenditures in the United States have increased tremendously since

World War II. In 1950, about $7.4 billion was spent on advertising worldwide. Advertising expenditures are now about $600 billion a year.

The growth of advertising since the 1950's has been accompanied by criticism of advertising practices. Much of the criticism has focused on the use of psychological techniques in advertising. Advertising has also been criticized for its stereotypical portrayal of women, elderly people, and racial minorities. As a consequence, many advertisers have broadened the variety of roles played by members of these groups in ads. In addition, some advertisers have used people with physical disabilities in commercials for products and services not related to the disabilities.

Since the 1980's, many new advertising media have appeared. For example, advertisements are now seen in motion-picture theaters and on DVD's prior to the featured movie. They appear in high school classroom news programming. Supermarket shoppers may be exposed to in-store radio and grocery carts with miniature billboards or video screens advertising products.

Advertising on the Internet began in the early 1990's. Companies developed a variety of new techniques for advertising on the Internet. In addition to using e-mail, banner ads, and social media, companies used "viral" campaigns designed to be communicated from person to person. Advertisers referred to the excitement about a product or service that these ads created as *buzz.* Companies also began to use part of their advertising budget to pay Internet search engines to list their company website at the side of a page showing a search response for a certain keyword. To contact potential customers directly, advertisers bought lists of e-mail addresses to send direct messages through e-mail. When this e-mail was unwanted, excessive, or annoying, however, customers called it *spam.*

In the 1990's, advertisers also began to spend more money on promotional campaigns. Promotions involving coupons, rebates, premiums, or sweepstakes

1929

1983

1994

Coca-Cola Company

Advertising over many years has helped establish the widespread popularity of Coca-Cola. Distinctive slogans and an emphasis on youth, enjoyment, and success have long characterized Coke ads. The company regularly updates its ads to appeal to more consumers.

awards may provide a short-term boost in sales. But some industry experts believe the increase in sales comes at the expense of the long-term image of the brand or product.

Careers

The field of advertising offers a wide variety of job opportunities for people with creative, analytic, business, or technical skills. The industry needs writers, artists, researchers, media buyers, salespeople, production managers, and account executives. Jobs can be found with advertisers, advertising agencies, the advertising media, or advertising service and supply houses.

The majority of jobs in advertising require a college education or special training. A number of colleges and universities offer major programs in the field of advertising. People with education in the liberal arts, journalism, behavioral sciences, business, or commercial art may also find employment in the advertising industry.

The websites of the American Advertising Federation (http://www.aaf.org) and the American Association of Advertising Agencies (http://www.aaaa.org) have information about careers in advertising.   Ashlee Humphreys

Related articles in *World Book* include:
Commercial art
Computer graphics (In advertising)
Consumer protection (The right to information)
Internet (Advertising)
Magazine
Mail-order business
Market research
Marketing
Modeling
Motion picture (Distribution)
Motivation research
Newspaper
Packaging
Poster
Propaganda (Businesses)
Public opinion poll
Public relations
Radio
Sales
Television

Outline

I. Ways of advertising
  A. Television
  B. Newspapers
  C. Internet advertising
  D. Direct mail
  E. Radio
  F. Magazines
  G. Outdoor signs
  H. Other ways of advertising
II. Advertising techniques
  A. Basic appeals
  B. Attention-getting headlines
  C. Slogans
  D. Testimonials
  E. Product characters
  F. Comparison of products
  G. Repetition
III. Creating advertisements
  A. Research   C. Creative work
  B. Media selection   D. Production
IV. The advertising industry
  A. Advertising agencies
  B. Advertising departments
  C. Advertising associations
  D. Regulation of advertising

  E. Advertising in other countries
V. Effects of advertising
  A. Economic effects
  B. Social effects
  C. Political effects
VI. History
VII. Careers

AEC. See Atomic Energy Commission.

Aëdes aegypti. See Finlay, Carlos J.; Yellow fever.

A.E.F. is the abbreviation for the American Expeditionary Forces sent to Europe during World War I (1914-1918). The A.E.F. was the first United States army ever sent to Europe. General John J. Pershing trained and led the A.E.F. from a small group of regulars in 1917 to a force of 2 million men by the end of the war.

American troops reached the Western Front in France in October 1917 and quickly suffered their first killed and wounded. The first major action involving the A.E.F. occurred on April 20, 1918, near Saint-Mihiel in Lorraine. By mid-summer, American troops were committed in larger and larger numbers, stopping a German attack at Château-Thierry and launching their own attacks at Belleau Wood and Cantigny. By July 4, the A.E.F. was 1 million strong, and 250,000 more were arriving every month. On September 12, the A.E.F. led a victorious offensive at Saint-Mihiel. Exactly two weeks later, the A.E.F. launched the massive Meuse-Argonne Offensive, the U.S. Army's largest battle up to that time. The A.E.F. continued to fight until the war's end on November 11.

The soldiers, marines, sailors, airmen, and others of the A.E.F.—collectively known as the "Doughboys"—reached Europe in time to rally the Allies and provide sufficient strength and advantage to assure victory. The A.E.F. succeeded at a price, however, suffering 53,402 killed in action and another 63,114 dead of other causes—nearly half from influenza. Another 204,002 were wounded in action.   Jake Bumgardner

See **American Legion; Harlem Hellfighters; Pershing, John Joseph; World War I** (The United States enters the war).

Aegean civilization, *ih JEE uhn,* consisted of four cultures that flourished on the islands and shores of the Aegean Sea between about 3000 and 1100 B.C. These cultures are called the Cycladic, Minoan, Mycenaean, and western Anatolian cultures. The Cycladic culture developed on a group of islands called the Cyclades. The Minoan culture arose on the island of Crete, and the Mycenaean culture flourished on the mainland of Greece. The city of Troy, in the northwestern part of ancient Anatolia (now part of Turkey), was a center of western Anatolian culture.

The Aegean civilization arose after the people of the area discovered how to make bronze. During this period, called the Aegean Bronze Age, the people became highly skilled in architecture, painting, and various crafts. They built richly decorated palaces and used systems of writing. The Aegean Bronze Age ranks as one of the greatest artistic and cultural ages in history.

The Aegean civilization collapsed around 1100 B.C. The craftwork skills, the systems of writing, and the building knowledge were lost, and most trade ended. The region was relatively isolated from other parts of the Mediterranean world during the next 300 years.

The Aegean people left no written history. However,

© Shutterstock

The Aegean people were highly skilled architects, artists, and craftworkers. The Minoans on the island of Crete produced such works as the painting shown here. The painting is in the ruins of the Palace of Minos at Knossos.

Spread of Greek culture
worldbook.com/gc-14

their descendants told stories about gods, great kings and heroes, and bloody wars. Some of these stories may have been based on actual people and events. The tales formed the basis for the epics the *Iliad* and the *Odyssey,* attributed to the Greek poet Homer. The Aegean people also kept some records written on clay tablets. These records were written in characters that were deciphered as an early form of Greek in A.D. 1953.

Archaeologists have uncovered most of the information known about the Aegean civilization. In the 1870's, the German archaeologist Heinrich Schliemann began research on the civilization. He believed that many stories in classical Greek literature were based on real events, and he searched for the sites of legendary cities. In 1870, using legends as a guide, Schliemann conducted the first major excavation on the site of Troy. In 1876, he launched the study of the Mycenaean culture. Schliemann discovered royal graves in Mycenae on the Greek mainland.

In the late 1800's, James T. Bent, a British scholar, and Christos Tsountas, a Greek archaeologist, explored the Cycladic culture. In 1900, Arthur Evans, another British scholar, began excavating the Palace of Minos in Knossos on the island of Crete. His research provided much of the present-day knowledge of Minoan culture.

The Cycladic culture flourished on a number of Aegean islands, including Milos, Naxos, Siros, and Thira. Many Cycladic people made their living by fishing. Others worked as sailors and traders. Still others were farmers, many of whom grew grapes for use in producing wine. Cycladic craftworkers made distinctively designed pottery and stone figurines. After 1900 B.C., the Cycladic culture declined and adopted many features of the Minoan and Mycenaean cultures.

The Minoan culture, which arose on Crete, was named for Minos, the legendary king of the island. According to tradition, Minos ruled the Aegean Sea and kept the Minotaur, a monster that was half man and half bull. See **Minos; Minotaur.**

The Minoans were skilled artists and architects and active traders. They built the Palace of Minos in Knossos,

as well as palaces in Zakros, Mallia, Galatas, and Phaistos. The Minoans traded throughout the Aegean region and in Egypt. Other Aegean people copied Minoan designs in pottery and other craftwork. The Minoans developed a decimal system and used a writing system in which complex symbols represented syllables of words. The Mycenaeans on the mainland of Greece later adapted the Minoan writing system to their language.

After about 1450 B.C., fire destroyed nearly all of Crete's towns and palaces. Although it was damaged, the palace in Knossos survived and Mycenaeans gained control of it. The Mycenaeans finally abandoned the palace in the early 1300's B.C. Minoan culture began to decline after the palace was lost. The culture disappeared about 1100 B.C.

WORLD BOOK map

Aegean civilization flourished on the islands and shores of the Aegean Sea between 3000 and 1100 B.C. Four cultures—the Cycladic, Minoan, Mycenaean, and Anatolian—developed there.

The Mycenaean culture, also called the Helladic culture, centered on Mycenae, a powerful city on the mainland of Greece. By about 2000 B.C., a group of people had moved to the Peloponnesus, the southern peninsula of Greece, and had established Mycenae. Archaeologists do not know where these people came from. The people introduced new styles of pottery to the area and built houses that had a large central room. Scholars believe the Mycenaeans may have spoken a dialect that later developed into the Greek language.

By the 1500's B.C., the Mycenaeans had grown rich and powerful, and they greatly influenced Aegean culture. For this reason, archaeologists call the late Bronze Age in Greece the Mycenaean period. The Mycenaeans used Minoan architecture as a model for their palaces. During the 1300's B.C., they built palaces in Mycenae and in such places as Athens, Pylos, Thebes, and Tiryns. The palace in Mycenae was surrounded by massive walls with a huge gateway called the Lion Gate.

By about 1200 B.C., the Mycenaean civilization had collapsed, and its main centers had been destroyed. Scholars do not know whether the civilization fell because of internal disorder or under attack from invaders. According to one traditional account, the Mycenaeans were invaded by the Dorians, a people from northwestern Greece. But many experts now believe the Dorians did not actually exist.

Anatolian culture. The city of Troy was one center of western Anatolian culture. The people of Troy are known as Trojans. Archaeologists have uncovered the remains of nine cities on the site of Troy. Each successive city was built on the ruins of the one before it. Archaeologists believe the seventh city was the legendary Troy described in the *Iliad* and the *Odyssey*. This city was built in the mid-1200's B.C. It was set afire and destroyed around 1200 B.C., possibly by invaders from the mainland of Greece.　Jack L. Davis

Related articles in *World Book* include:

Architecture (Minoan architecture; Mycenaean architecture; picture: Greek architecture)
Crete
Evans, Sir Arthur John
Greece, Ancient (History)
Knossos
Labyrinth
Mycenae
Painting (Aegean painting)
Sculpture (Aegean; pictures: Cycladic monumental figure; Woman praying)
Ship (Minoan and Mycenaean ships)
Trojan War
Troy
Ventris, Michael George Francis

Aegean Sea, *ih JEE uhn,* is a gulf or arm of the Mediterranean Sea. It lies between Greece on the west and north, Turkey on the east, and the island of Crete to the south. The Aegean covers about 69,000 square miles (179,000 square kilometers). It is approximately 400 miles (640 kilometers) long and more than 200 miles (320 kilometers) wide at its widest point. The Dardanelles, a strait on the northeast shore, links the Aegean to the Sea of Marmara.

Around a thousand islands, known as the Grecian Archipelago, lie throughout the clear blue waters of the Aegean Sea. Some have fertile plains, and others are rocky and barren volcanic islands. Some islands have large deposits of pure white marble or black obsidian. Wheat, wine, olive oil, and figs are all produced on the Aegean islands. Fishing and tourism are the two biggest industries.

The Aegean islands and shores are famous in Greek history and legend, having given birth to the Minoan and Mycenean civilizations. Three major island groups—the Cyclades, the Dodecanese, and the Sporades—contain such historically important islands as Delos, Samos, and Rhodes.　John J. Baxevanis

See also **Aegean civilization; Dardanelles; Lesbos; Rhodes.**

Aegis, *EE jihs,* in Greek and Roman mythology, was the name of the shield or breastplate made for the Greek god Zeus (Jupiter in Roman mythology) by Hephaestus (Vulcan). Zeus created thunder with it. Athena (Minerva), Zeus's daughter, carried it as a sign of authority when she went on missions for her father. In its center was the head of Medusa, which had the power of turning men to stone. See also **Athena; Medusa.**

Mary R. Lefkowitz

Aeneas, *ih NEE uhs,* was a Trojan hero in Greek and Roman mythology. The Romans believed he was an ancestor of Romulus and Remus, the mythical founders of Rome. The Roman poet Virgil celebrated the adventures of Aeneas in the *Aeneid,* Rome's national epic.

Aeneas was the son of the Trojan prince Anchises and the Greek goddess Aphrodite (called Venus by the Romans). When Troy fell, Aeneas fled with his father and his son Ascanius from the burning city (see **Trojan War**). On nearby Mount Ida, Aeneas gathered the few other Trojan survivors and sailed away to found a new home. They stopped at various places and had many adventures. In the city of Carthage in Africa, Aeneas met Queen Dido. She fell in love with him and committed suicide when a sense of duty to his destined role as a founder of a new home for the Trojans compelled him to leave her.

Aeneas finally arrived in Italy. He visited the lower world, where he learned about Rome's future glory. Ae-

Aegean Sea

WORLD BOOK map

neas then traveled to the Italian region of Latium, where he became friends with King Latinus. The king offered his daughter Lavinia in marriage. Aeneas married Lavinia and founded the city of Lavinium.

Aeneas later disappeared from this world during a battle with a neighboring people called the Etruscans. Some versions of the myth say he was taken to heaven and became the god Jupiter Indiges.   Daniel P. Harmon

See also **Aeneid; Dido; Virgil.**

Aeneid, *ih NEE ihd,* the national epic of ancient Rome, is one of the world's greatest poems of heroic adventure. It was written by the Roman poet Virgil between 30 and 19 B.C. This period was one of national pride for the Romans. The emperor Augustus had just united the people of the Italian peninsula to defeat Rome's enemies in the eastern provinces. Virgil chose the myth of the Trojan hero Aeneas to express ancient Rome's moral and religious values and to honor Augustus, who was believed to be Aeneas's descendant.

The *Aeneid* contains 12 books. The first 6 books imitate the Greek epic the *Odyssey.* They describe Aeneas's adventures at sea following the capture of Troy by the Greeks during the Trojan War.

As the *Aeneid* begins, a storm shipwrecks Aeneas and his Trojan followers near Carthage in North Africa. There, Aeneas falls in love with the queen, Dido. But the gods order him to leave for Italy. In despair, Dido commits suicide. After Aeneas finally reaches Italy, he goes down to the underworld and learns about his future descendants, the Romans.

Virgil bases the last six books of the *Aeneid* on the Greek epic the *Iliad.* They begin as Aeneas arrives near the future site of Rome. There, the local king, Latinus, offers him land for his people and marriage to his daughter, Lavinia. Turnus, Lavinia's jealous suitor, attacks the Trojans and kills the young soldier Pallas, whom Aeneas has promised to protect. Aeneas later fights Turnus and

Venus, Mother of Aeneas, Presenting Him with Arms Forged by Vulcan (1635), an oil painting on canvas by Nicolas Poussin; Art Gallery of Ontario, Toronto, gift of the Reuben Wells Leonard estate, 1948

The Trojan hero Aeneas receives weapons and armor from his mother, the goddess Aphrodite (Venus). According to tradition, Aeneas survived Troy's defeat by the Greeks and founded a colony in Italy. The ancient Romans traced their origin to Aeneas.

kills him in punishment for the death of Pallas.

Aeneas's obedience to the gods costs him his personal happiness and the lives of those he loves. Yet he retains his sense of duty and commitment to creating a new nation in an unknown land.   Elaine Fantham

See also **Aeneas; Dido; Sibyl; Troy; Virgil.**

Aeolian harp, *ee OH lee uhn,* is an unusual ancient musical instrument. It consists of a wooden box with from 8 to 15 strings of various thickness stretched along the top. The strings are raised slightly by low bridges near each end of the box. The instrument produces soft, exotic sounds when the wind blows on the strings, causing them to vibrate. The Aeolian harp is named for Aeolus, the ancient Greek god of the winds.   Abram Loft

Aeolians, *ee OH lee uhnz,* were a group of ancient Greeks who once lived in a large part of east-central Greece. Around 1000 B.C., other Greeks known as Dorians may have invaded Aeolian territory, and many Aeolians moved to the nearby islands of Lesbos and Tenedos and to the western coast of Asia Minor (present-day Turkey). The coastal district where they settled was known as *Aeolis.* Some of the Aeolians probably organized themselves into a loose confederacy. The island of Lesbos became a minor trading center and the home of some renowned poets, the most famous of whom included Alcaeus and Sappho.   Jack L. Davis

See also **Achaeans; Dorians; Greece, Ancient** (History); **Ionians; Sappho.**

Aeolus, *EE uh luhs,* was the keeper of the winds in Greek mythology. Aeolus lived on a floating island, which scholars believe was one of the Aeolian Islands near Sicily. These islands were named for him. Aeolus kept the winds confined in a cave on the island and released them whenever he wished.

Aeolus plays an important part in two great epic poems, the *Odyssey* and the *Aeneid.* In the *Odyssey,* Aeolus gives the Greek hero Odysseus (Ulysses in Latin) a leather bag containing the winds that could prevent Odysseus from sailing home. Odysseus's sailors open the bag because they mistakenly believe that it contains treasure. The winds escape from the open bag and blow Odysseus's ship off its course. At the start of the *Aeneid,* the goddess Juno, an enemy of the Trojan hero Aeneas, persuades Aeolus to release winds that cause a storm. The storm then scatters Aeneas's fleet.   Nancy Felson

Aerated water. See Mineral water.

Aerial. See Antenna.

Aerial photography. See Archaeology (Locating sites; picture: Aerial photography); **Photogrammetry.**

Aerial surveying. See Photogrammetry; Surveying.

Aerobatics. See Airplane (Special-purpose planes; picture: Aerobatic planes).

Aerobics, *air OH bihks,* is a system of exercises designed to promote the supply and use of oxygen in the body. These exercises include bicycling, dancing, jogging, rowing, skating, swimming, and fast walking. Many people participate in aerobics programs to increase their endurance and energy and to achieve and maintain their proper weight. Regular aerobic exercise may also help lessen the risk of heart disease.

A regular, vigorous program of aerobic exercises helps the body process large amounts of oxygen efficiently. The presence of oxygen in the muscle cells is necessary for the formation of a compound called *adenosine triphosphate* (ATP). The breakdown of ATP produces the energy for all muscular activity. During vigorous activity, more oxygen is inhaled and passes from the lungs into the blood. More oxygen-rich blood is delivered to the muscles, creating more ATP. This increased amount of ATP produces more energy for the body. If the circulatory system cannot supply enough oxygen to the muscles or if the muscles cannot use oxygen efficiently, the body produces a smaller amount of ATP. This results in early fatigue.

For maximum effectiveness, individuals should perform aerobic exercises continuously for 15 minutes to an hour 3 to 5 times a week. Men and women over the age of 35 should get a medical examination before beginning an aerobics program.   Herb Weber

See also **Jogging; Physical fitness; Running.**

Aerodynamics, AIR *oh dy NAM ihks,* is the study of forces that act on an object as it moves through air or another fluid. Aerodynamic forces act on airplanes and all other objects that fly through the air. These forces also act on automobiles and other objects that move partly through the air and partly along a solid surface. In addition, aerodynamic forces act on ships, which move partly through the air and partly through water. Such forces even act on buildings due to the wind that blows around them. Scientists, engineers, and architects study aerodynamics to learn to design vehicles and structures.

Principles of aerodynamics

There are two basic aerodynamic forces—*lift* and *drag.* Both result from a transfer of force from a fluid to the surface of a solid object. The force from the fluid creates a *pressure* and a *shear stress* on the surface.

Pressure is force per unit area, with the force applied perpendicular to the surface. Pressure can be measured in *pounds per square inch* in the system of units customarily used in the United States. The pounds are a measure of the force, and the square inch is the unit of surface area. In the metric system, a common unit of pressure is the *kilopascal.* One kilopascal equals a force of 0.1 newton on an area of 1 square centimeter. One pound per square inch equals about 6.9 kilopascals.

Shear stress is also force per unit area, but this force is applied along the surface. Shear stress occurs in a fluid due to the fluid's *viscosity,* its internal friction that resists motion. Friction occurs in a fluid whenever one layer of the fluid slides over another layer. Because of friction, the layers resist sliding.

The *total aerodynamic force* transferred from the fluid to the surface is a result of the pressure and the shear stress acting over the entire surface. Lift and drag are *components* (parts) of the total aerodynamic force. Lift is the component that is perpendicular to the direction of motion of the object. In the case of an airplane that is flying horizontally, the lift is applied in the upward direction. Drag is the component that pushes in the direction opposite that of the object's motion. Thus, drag opposes the motion of the object.

Lift keeps an airplane in the air by balancing the weight of the plane. This aerodynamic force is created along a wing by the motion of the wing through the air.

Lift can be analyzed in terms of the motion of an *airfoil* (cross section of a wing) through the air. The motion creates lift by producing a difference in air pressure. The air

How lift occurs

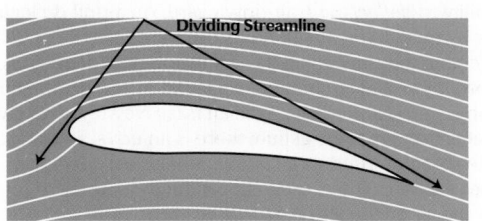

WORLD BOOK diagram by Jonathan Simpson

Lift can occur when the airflows along the top and bottom surfaces of an airplane wing are *unsymmetrical* (unbalanced). The air approaching the wing's rounded edge splits smoothly along a line called a *dividing streamline* and merges smoothly at the sharp edge.

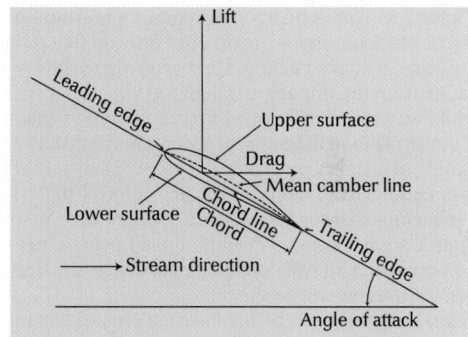

WORLD BOOK diagram by Jonathan Simpson

Factors that create lift in an airplane include (1) the *angle of attack* that each wing makes with the airstream and (2) the shape of the *mean camber line* that represents the average curvature of the wing's upper and lower surfaces. At the leading edge of the wing, the mean camber line curves upward from the straight *chord line* connecting the leading and trailing edges.

pressure on the lower surface of the airfoil becomes greater than the air pressure on the upper surface.

The pressure difference is a result of a difference in the speed of the air flowing along the two surfaces. According to a principle discovered by Daniel Bernoulli, a Swiss mathematician, the pressure of a fluid increases as the speed of the fluid decreases. The air pressure on the lower surface of the airfoil is greater because the air flows more slowly along that surface.

Lift can occur when the airflows along the top and bottom surfaces are *unsymmetrical* (unbalanced). Unsymmetrical flow is a result of one or both of the following factors: (1) the *camber* (curved shape) of the airfoil and (2) the *angle of attack* (the angle at which the airflow meets the airfoil). A typical airfoil has a rounded *leading* (front) edge and a sharp *trailing* (rear) edge. As the air approaches the leading edge, it splits to go around the airfoil. The air that travels along the top accelerates as it goes around the highly curved leading edge. As a result, the speed of the air on the upper surface is greater.

Also, the airflows along the top and bottom of the airfoil merge smoothly as they leave the trailing edge. This condition is called the *Kutta condition*—named for its discoverer, Martin W. Kutta, a German mathematician.

Another explanation for lift is related to an airfoil's ability to *deflect* (turn) air downward. An airfoil deflects air by guiding the air along its cambered surface and by meeting the air at an angle. Deflection produces lift according to a law of motion explained in 1687 by the English scientist and mathematician Isaac Newton. This law states that, for every action, there is an equal and opposite reaction. Thus, as an airfoil deflects air downward, the reaction to the deflection produces an upward force by the air on the airfoil.

The amount of lift created by the airflow along a wing depends mainly on the wing's angle of attack, speed, and camber. The area of the wing and the density of the air also affect the amount of lift.

Angle of attack is the angle that a wing makes with the air flowing past it. A pilot can change this angle by changing the plane's position in space. Increasing the angle of attack increases the lift—but only up to a point. If the angle of attack becomes too large, the airflow will separate from the upper surface of the wing. As a result, lift will decrease sharply, producing a condition called *stall*. An airplane at the point of stalling may crash unless the angle of attack is quickly reduced. Airplanes fly at angles of about 3 to 15 degrees. An airplane will stall if the angle becomes larger than 15 or 20 degrees.

Speed. A wing's speed through the air helps determine how much lift will occur. The faster the airplane is flying, the greater will be the lift.

Wing area. An increase in wing area creates extra lift by increasing the total forces due to air pressure and shear stress. If the air pressure and the shear stress are held constant, the amount of force depends only on the area: The greater the area, the greater the force.

Air density. Air that is relatively dense creates more lift than does relatively thin air. This happens because, according to Bernoulli's principle, pressure increases with density.

Creating extra lift. During take-offs and landings, pilots want to fly as slowly as possible. Special parts called *high-lift devices* enable a plane to fly at minimum speeds. These devices are extensions that fit smoothly against the wing while the airplane is cruising. The pilot can lower them when they are needed. The extension at the leading edge of the wing is called a *slat*. The extension at the trailing edge is a *flap*. When lowered, these extensions increase the wing camber and area, furnishing extra lift.

Drag is a force that resists the forward motion of a solid object in a fluid. The object's shape affects the amount of drag. Objects shaped to produce little drag are called *streamlined* or *aerodynamically clean.*

Two types of drag—*friction drag* and *form drag*—act on all moving objects. A third type, *induced drag,* affects only objects with lift. Still another kind of drag, *wave drag,* results when an object moves faster than the speed of sound. Wave drag also occurs when a ship generates waves on the surface of the water. This section discusses friction drag, form drag, and induced drag. For a discussion of wave drag, see the section *Shock waves* later in this article.

Friction drag is a component of the drag due to shear stress. Friction has its strongest effect in the *boundary layer,* a thin layer of fluid next to the surface.

The amount of friction drag depends upon whether the fluid flow is *laminar* or *turbulent.* In laminar flow, the fluid molecules move in orderly paths essentially along the direction of the surface. Turbulent flow occurs at higher speeds. In turbulent flow, the fluid's speed and direction of flow vary randomly from an average value. This variation increases the shear stress. As a result, friction drag is much higher when flow is turbulent than it is when flow is laminar.

Airflow is usually laminar near a wing's leading edge, and it becomes turbulent farther along the surface. Airplane designers try to delay the change from laminar flow to turbulent flow. One way to do this is to make the surface as smooth as possible.

Form drag is a component of the drag due to pressure. The amount of form drag on an object depends on the object's form, or shape. If the object is not streamlined, the drag force is mostly form drag. If the object is streamlined, the drag force is mostly friction drag.

In form drag, the flowing fluid separates from the object. The pressure next to the rear surface of the object therefore decreases. This decrease makes the pressure on the front surface larger than that on the rear surface. The net result is a force that pushes against the front of the object. This force is the form drag. Designers can reduce form drag by streamlining the object.

Induced drag is a result of a phenomenon that is also responsible for lift. Airflow will lift an airplane wing if the air pressure on the wing's lower surface is greater than that on the upper surface. However, this difference in pressure also makes air flow at the tip of the wing. The air at the tip moves from the lower surface to the upper surface. This flow creates *vortices,* swirling streams of air that flow away from the tip and continue behind the wing.

The creation of wing-tip vortices uses energy that could otherwise be spent to provide lift and propel the aircraft. In addition, the vortices threaten the safety of airplanes flying close behind. Aircraft designers lessen induced drag by giving airplanes long, narrow wings.

Lift and drag in a sailboat. The principles of aerodynamics also apply to objects that move through air but

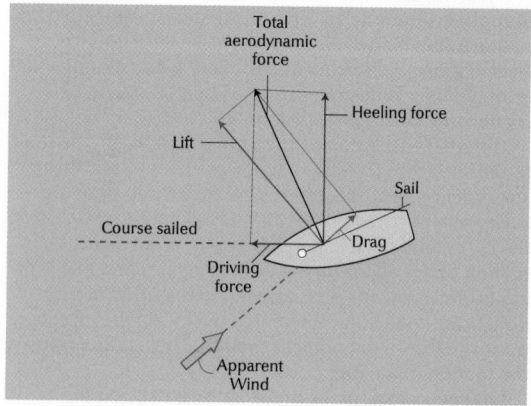

WORLD BOOK diagram by Jonathan Simpson

A boat sails into the wind. When the wind blows past the sail, it creates a total aerodynamic force that can be represented by a *driving force,* which propels the boat, and a *heeling force.* This diagram also shows lift and drag forces for comparison with the corresponding forces on an airplane wing.

do not fly. One can use these principles to explain, for example, how a sailboat sails into the wind.

When the wind puffs the sail out, the sail resembles a cambered airplane wing. The *apparent wind*—the wind measured by an observer on the boat—thus generates a total aerodynamic force that corresponds to the force on a wing. This force can be *resolved into* (represented by) two components relative to the apparent wind: (1) lift, which tends to push the sail in a direction perpendicular to the apparent wind; and (2) drag, which resists the movement of the boat directly against the wind.

The total aerodynamic force can also be resolved into another pair of components: (1) a *driving force* in the sailing direction, and (2) a *heeling force,* which is perpendicular to the driving force. The driving force propels the boat. As the boat moves, the water exerts an aerodynamic force on its hull and *keel.* The keel is the main timber that extends the entire length of the bottom of the boat.

The boat will sail at constant speed when the aerodynamic force generated on the sail is both equal to and opposite the corresponding aerodynamic force that the water exerts on the hull and keel. This condition also has the effect of canceling the heeling force.

Supersonic aerodynamics

Effects of supersonic aerodynamics occur when the airplane flies at speeds greater than the speed of sound. *Supersonic* means *faster than the speed of sound.* Two of the major effects of supersonic aerodynamics are *shock waves* and *sonic booms.* Both are created by pressure disturbances that a moving airplane produces in the air.

These disturbances result from the flow of air around the plane. The disturbances travel away from the plane just as ripples in a pond spread from the spot where a stone falls into the water. Pressure disturbances travel at the speed of sound—about 760 miles per hour (mph), or

about 1,225 kilometers per hour (kph), at sea level.

Sound itself is a pressure disturbance, and so some of the disturbances produced by the airplane can be heard. If the plane is flying at less than the speed of sound, the sound of the plane travels ahead of the plane. Thus, people on the ground can hear the plane coming toward them. However, the sound of a plane flying faster than the speed of sound cannot be heard on the ground until the aircraft has passed.

Engineers and pilots use special numbers called *Mach numbers* to describe the speed of planes flying near or above the speed of sound. A Mach number is found by dividing the speed of an airplane by the speed of sound at the plane's altitude. For example, the Mach number of a plane flying at 1,520 mph at sea level would be 2. Modern airliners cruise at an altitude of about 35,000 feet (9,000 meters) and a speed of about Mach 0.80 to Mach 0.85.

Flight that is slightly faster or slower than Mach 1 is known as *transonic* flight. Flight that is significantly slower than Mach 1 is *subsonic.* Flight that is significantly faster than Mach 1 is *supersonic,* and flight at or faster than about Mach 5 is *hypersonic.* Mach numbers are named for the Austrian physicist and psychologist Ernst Mach.

Shock waves are pressure disturbances produced by the flight of an airplane at supersonic speed. Because disturbances cannot move ahead of the plane, they build up into shock waves. The waves then attach themselves to the front and rear of the plane. An airplane flying at slightly less than the speed of sound can also produce shock waves. These waves occur because the airflow next to some surfaces of the plane is actually supersonic.

Shock waves create wave drag, thereby increasing the total amount of drag on the plane. A plane designed for transonic and supersonic flight therefore has features that help reduce wave drag. For example, its nose is

NASA/Ames Research Center

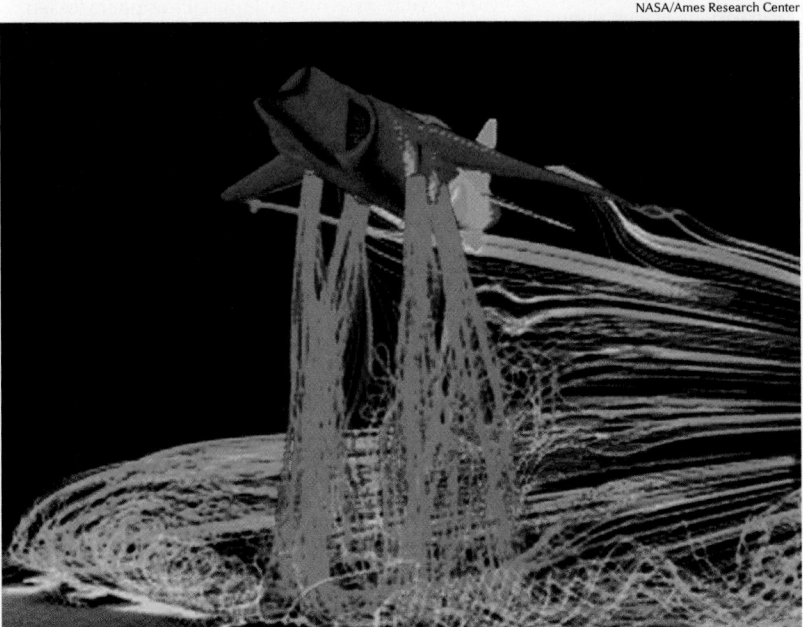

Stringlike lines represent airflow in this illustration drawn by a supercomputer. Engineers typically use such *computer simulations* to evaluate proposed designs for an airplane. The engineers then select a design and build a physical model for testing.

How a sonic boom is created

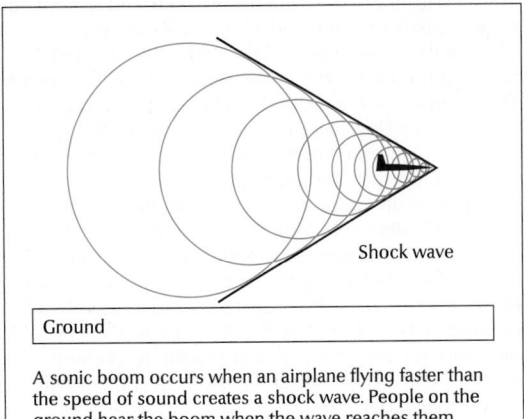

Shock wave

Ground

A sonic boom occurs when an airplane flying faster than the speed of sound creates a shock wave. People on the ground hear the boom when the wave reaches them.

WORLD BOOK diagram

sharply pointed, and its wings have sharp, thin edges that can knife through the air. The wings may also be angled back from the body of the plane.

Sonic boom. After a supersonic airplane flies overhead, people on the ground may hear a sharp "bang." This sound, called a *sonic boom,* is caused by shock waves from the plane. A plane flying at a supersonic speed sends out at least two shock waves—one from its front and the other from its rear. But the two waves may reach the ground so close together that people hear only one boom. A sonic boom may be strong enough to break windows or damage buildings.

Applying aerodynamic principles

To design an airplane, engineers need to determine how the airflow will interact with the surfaces of the plane. They need to know in detail how strong the air pressure and shear stress will be at various places along the body, the wings, and other parts of the airplane. To gather the information they need, the engineers must study more than the layers of air next to the surfaces. They must investigate the entire *flow field,* the large region of space in which the airflow and the plane will interact. To study flow fields, aircraft design engineers almost always use a combination of two techniques— *wind-tunnel testing* and *computational fluid dynamics.*

Wind-tunnel testing. A wind tunnel is a ground-based facility in which a stream of air is blown at an object at uniform speed. Some wind tunnels are so huge that they can be used to test full-sized experimental airplanes. But most wind tunnels are relatively small facilities that are used to test scaled-down models.

Engineers can obtain much valuable information from wind-tunnel testing. However, the models are expensive to build. Furthermore, as the design evolves, the engineers often must test a large number of different airplane shapes.

Computational fluid dynamics employs *supercomputers,* the fastest and largest computers. In this technique, a supercomputer solves equations describing physical laws that govern what happens at a large number of points in a flow field. The equations contain a

huge number of factors that are related to one another in complex ways. Some factors pertain to features of the airplane, such as the sizes and shapes of various parts of the plane. Other factors have to do with flying conditions, including aircraft speed, wind speed, angle of attack, and air density.

The engineers first enter the equations into the supercomputer. Next, they enter the numerical values that apply to the plane they are designing and to the flying conditions. The computer then calculates the corresponding pressures, shear stresses, and other results. These calculations *simulate* (represent) how the airplane would interact with the air. In many cases, the computer creates a motion picture that shows a few moments of flight. The engineers evaluate the results and change the design as necessary.   Allen Plotkin

Related articles in *World Book* include:

Air	Helicopter	Shock wave
Airplane	Jet propulsion	Sonic boom
Bernoulli's principle	Propeller	Streamlining
Glider	Rocket	Wind tunnel

Aerogel, *AIR uh jehl,* is an artificial, dry solid known for its exceptionally low density. Like a sponge, an aerogel contains many tiny holes or pores. In the case of an aerogel, these pores are much smaller—measuring *nanometers* (billionths of a meter) in size—and are filled with air. Aerogels typically consist of from 95 percent to more than 99 percent air. Aerogels appear ghostly and translucent and thus have been nicknamed "frozen smoke" or "solid smoke."

The name *aerogel* comes from the way these solids are produced. First, a gel is made by combining a liquid with a substance such as silica, carbon, or metal oxides. This substance forms clusters of long molecule chains surrounded and supported by the liquid. Under high pressure and temperature, the liquid is removed and replaced with air. The molecules left behind retain their clustered structure, creating a finished aerogel.

JPL/NASA

An aerogel is an extremely light solid. Tiny holes fill aerogels, much like the holes in a sponge, only smaller. Aerogels have been nicknamed "frozen smoke" for their ghostly appearance.

Because of their high air content and complex molecular structure, aerogels make extremely effective *thermal insulators,* substances that block the flow of heat. Scientists are working to produce cheap aerogels for use in such products as refrigerators and winter jackets. Aerogels have other unique properties that make them desirable for use in catalysts, filters, optics, sensors, and other applications.

The American chemical engineer Steven Kistler wrote the first scientific paper on aerogels, published in 1931. Since then, scientists have continued to study and improve aerogels. In 2004, the United States probe Stardust used an aerogel collector to capture space dust and particles given off by a comet.   Kimberly DeFriend

Aeronautics. See Aviation.

Aeronautics and Space Administration, National. See National Aeronautics and Space Administration.

Aeroplane. See Airplane.

Aerosol, *AIR uh sahl,* is a mixture of extremely small particles in gas. The particles may consist of liquid droplets or bits of solid material *suspended* (distributed) throughout the gas. Aerosol particles vary in size, from about 10 *nanometers* to 100 micrometers (.004 inch) in diameter. One nanometer equals one billionth of a meter, or $\frac{1}{25,400,000}$ inch. Smaller particles, like those that make up smoke, can remain suspended for days or weeks. Larger particles, such as rain, may stay suspended for only minutes. Aerosols in the air can affect health, visibility, and climate. Clouds and fog are aerosols that occur naturally. Cans of deodorant and devices called *inhalers* for treating asthma produce aerosols when used.

Fine particles and vapor constantly enter Earth's atmosphere, producing *atmospheric aerosols.* Natural particles, such as pollen, volcanic ash, and dust, stimulate the formation of clouds. Human activities release additional dust, soil, smoke, other particles, and vapors into the air. These particles and vapors form additional atmospheric aerosols that contribute to air pollution.

Light scattered by atmospheric aerosols produces the sky's red glow at sunset. Particles also reflect some solar radiation back into space, slightly lowering Earth's surface temperature. In heavily polluted areas, sunlight reacts with atmospheric aerosols to produce smog. Heavy concentrations of smog reduce visibility and affect human health by damaging lung tissue.

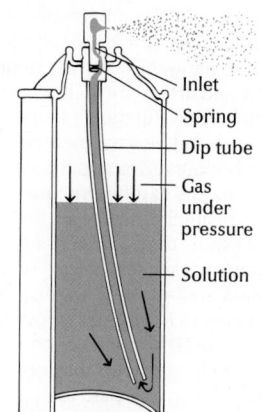

An aerosol container sprays out such products as deodorizers and paints in the form of a fine mist. The product is mixed with a liquefied gas, called a *propellant,* and is held in the container under pressure. When the cap of the container is pushed down, the inlet opens and the solution moves through the dip tube. As the solution reaches the opening in the cap, the propellant vaporizes and the particles shoot into the air.

Inlet
Spring
Dip tube
Gas under pressure
Solution

WORLD BOOK diagram

Manufacturers package aerosol products in containers called *aerosol cans.* Within such cans, the product remains dissolved in a *propellant,* usually a liquefied gas. The contents of the can are sealed under pressure. Opening a release valve ejects the pressurized solution. The released propellant vaporizes while the product suspended in it condenses to form an aerosol. Inhalers convert medicine into aerosols that can be breathed into the lungs. These *pharmaceutical aerosols* are used to treat asthma and other respiratory problems. Some products in pressurized cans, such as whipped cream, are not aerosols because they are gases suspended in a liquid rather than solids or liquids suspended in gas.

Lynn M. Russell

See also Air (Particles in the air); Chlorofluorocarbon.

Aerospace industry. See Aviation.

Aerospace medicine is the field of medical science concerned with the effects of flight on human health. It deals with *aviation medicine,* the care of airplane crews and passengers; and *space medicine,* the care of astronauts. Doctors and scientists in this field try to increase the job performance and safety, as well as the health, of people who fly.

Aviation medicine. There are many common stresses of air travel. They include motion sickness, noise, vibration, changes in oxygen levels, and rapid changes in speed and atmospheric pressure.

An important stress in fighter aircraft is a rapid upward acceleration. This movement can cause blood to be *pooled,* or concentrated, in the lower parts of the body. The flow of blood to the heart may then be insufficient for the heart to maintain adequate circulation to the brain, causing unconsciousness. As a result, fighter pilots must wear special trousers called *G suits* that squeeze blood out of the legs and back to the heart.

Doctors who specialize in aviation medicine are called flight surgeons. Flight surgeons help to design equipment and develop crew selection and training programs. Other areas of aviation medicine include investigating accidents, training crews for survival after crashing, and transporting sick or injured people by air.

Space medicine. During space travel, *weightlessness* (freedom from the pull of gravity) can cause several disorders. These include motion sickness, *disorientation* (loss of a sense of direction), and a shift of blood and other fluids from the feet and legs to the chest and head. Weightlessness also can cause the loss of bone and muscle tissue in the feet and legs. This condition probably occurs because the bones and muscles no longer need to work against the pull of gravity. Researchers are seeking a combination of exercises, drugs, and special diets that will reduce bone and muscle loss.

Another hazard of space flight is radiation from the sun and other objects in space. Being exposed to radiation increases a person's chances of developing leukemia and other cancers. Astronauts exposed to more than a certain amount of radiation would be grounded. Today's spacecraft have too little protection against radiation for long-duration flights into *deep space* (space beyond Earth and the moon).

Some scientists have suggested that the most serious problem for astronauts on long missions could be psychological. Space travelers have found that after 30 days of being confined together in a small space on a flight scheduled to last many months, they develop an intense dislike for each other and a strong desire to go home.

K. E. Money

See also **Anoxia; Bends; G** (symbol); **Space exploration.**

Aeschylus, *EHS kuh luhs* (525-456 B.C.) was the earliest writer of Greek tragedy whose plays exist in complete form. He wrote over 80 plays, of which 7 survive. These seven plays reveal a deeply patriotic and religious artist who brought Greek tragedy to maturity. Before Aeschylus, tragedies had a single actor who could only respond to the questions or suggestions of the chorus. He increased the number of actors to two, which created dialogue that permitted interaction between characters.

Aeschylus's plots are simple. Most of them center on a conflict between an individual's will and the divine powers that rule the world. Aeschylus wrote tragedy in the grand manner, with a richness of language and complexity of thought that only the English playwright William Shakespeare has rivaled. Aeschylus's greatest work is the *Oresteia* (458 B.C.), which consists of three plays forming one drama. They are *Agamemnon, Choephori (The Libation Bearers),* and *The Eumenides (The Furies).* In these plays, Aeschylus turned the violence after the return of King Agamemnon from Troy into a drama about the reconciliation of human suffering with divine power. Aeschylus's other surviving plays are *The Persians* (472), *Seven Against Thebes* (467), *The Suppliants* (463?), and *Prometheus Bound,* which was probably written late in Aeschylus's life. Aeschylus was born into a prominent family in Eleusis, near Athens.   Luci Berkowitz

See also **Drama** (Greek drama).

Aesculapius. See Asclepius.

Aesop's fables, *EE sahps,* are a collection of stories attributed to a Greek slave named Aesop, who died about 565 B.C. Like all fables, each of these tales teaches a moral and offers useful advice. Most of the characters in Aesop's fables are animals that talk and act like humans. They show the failings and virtues of human nature in a simple, humorous way. Each fable ends with a proverb that sums up the fable's moral and advice.

The best-known of Aesop's fables is probably "The Tortoise and the Hare." It tells of a race between a slow tortoise and a swift hare. Halfway through the race, the hare is so far ahead and so sure of victory that he takes a nap. The tortoise plods along steadily and eventually passes the hare, who awakens and sees the tortoise crossing the finish line. The proverb "Slow and steady wins the race" sums up the moral of this story, teaching that persistence can be more important than speed.

Another favorite fable, "The Ant and the Grasshopper," illustrates the value of hard work and preparation for the future. In this fable, the grasshopper frolics all summer, while the ant stores food. When winter comes, the ant has plenty to eat, but the grasshopper starves.

Aesop's fables have provided popular expressions. For example, an enemy who pretends to be a friend is sometimes called "a wolf in sheep's clothing." This comes from the fable in which a wolf disguises himself in a sheepskin. The wolf then moves among a herd of sheep and kills them for food. But the shepherd also mistakes the wolf for a sheep and kills him for supper.

No one knows how many of the stories attributed to Aesop were actually composed by him. Some of the fables originated from more ancient sources, and Aesop may have been responsible only for retelling them and making them popular.

For many years, Aesop's fables were handed down orally from generation to generation. About 300 B.C., an Athenian politician named Demetrius of Phaleron gathered about 200 of them into a collection called *Assemblies of Aesopic Tales.* This collection was translated into Latin about 300 years later by Phaedrus, a freed Greek slave. About A.D. 230, the Greek writer Valerius Babrius combined Aesop's fables with some from India and translated all of them into Greek verse. Since then, other writers have retold the fables and expanded their meaning, but the tales have never lost their original charm and simplicity.   Cynthia W. Shelmerdine

See also **Allegory; Fable; La Fontaine, Jean de.**

Aesthetics, *ehs THEHT ihks,* also spelled *esthetics,* is the study of theories that apply to the arts in a broad and fundamental way. People think about aesthetics when they ask why some things are beautiful and some are not, or whether there are basic rules for creating or interpreting good paintings, poems, and music.

Aestheticians study the arts in general. They compare arts from different cultures and from different periods of history, in order to organize our knowledge of them systematically. For many years, the study of beauty was regarded as the central problem of aesthetics. Now the subject has broadened to include many other aspects of art. Aestheticians try to understand how art is related to what people feel, to what they learn, and to the cultures in which they live. To gain this understanding, they collect, organize, and interpret information about the arts and aesthetic experience. They try to find whether there are standards of art criticism. This helps people appreciate different kinds of art and judge them intelligently.

In addition to studying theories about works of art, aestheticians want to understand artists and audiences. They can understand art better if they have learned how artists imagine, create, and perform, and what makes artists' activities different from the work of nonartists. They also try to understand what happens to people's feelings when they experience art. Aestheticians study how art affects people's moods, beliefs, and values.

Aesthetics is the youngest branch of philosophy to be given its own name, which was first used in the late 1700's. But philosophers from the ancient Greeks to the present day have discussed the philosophy of art. Almost all of them have talked about whether art is good for people and for society. Some point out that art can have dangers as well as benefits, and a few argue that art and artists are so disruptive that they threaten the social order. But most philosophers believe art is good because it allows us to express our emotions, teaches us about ourselves and the world, or communicates the traditions of different times and cultures.

Aestheticians use art history to understand the art of previous times. They use the psychology of art to learn how our senses interact with our imagination and understanding when we experience art. Art criticism serves as a guide to enjoy each individual work of art. The social sciences, such as anthropology and sociology, help aestheticians understand how creating and appreciating art relate to other human activities. The social sciences also indicate how art varies in relation to physical, social, and cultural environments.   Anita Silvers

See also **Art and the arts; Philosophy** (Aesthetics).

Affenpinscher, *AH fuhn PIHN shuhr,* is a small, shaggy, black dog. It weighs about 8 pounds (3.6 kilograms) and stands only 10 inches (25 centimeters) high. It has bushy eyebrows that hang down over its eyes. Tufts of hair stick out all over its face, and it has a mustache. The name *affenpinscher* comes from the German words meaning *monkey terrier.* The affenpinscher is bold, quick on its feet, and playful. See also **Dog** (picture: Toy dogs).   Critically reviewed by the American Kennel Club

Affirmative action is a type of policy or program that attempts to increase the participation of certain groups within a society. In the United States, for example, such groups include African Americans, Latinos, Native Americans, women, and people with disabilities. The purpose of affirmative action is to ensure that such groups have a fair chance to be employed at jobs and to be admitted to colleges and universities. Governments, employers, and educational institutions use affirmative action policies and programs to increase the number of people from *marginalized* (excluded) groups in an organization and to better ensure their success.

There are different ways to apply affirmative action, and different programs have different goals. For example, a military organization could send recruiters to underfunded schools with mostly Black or Latino students, because such schools often have limited resources to inform students about a military career. Or a technology company could create a mentoring program for its women engineers. Relatively few women are engineers, and the male-dominated environment at many technology firms can be unsupportive of women employees. Or a university might consider an applicant's racial identity when deciding whom to admit, to create a diverse student body and thus improve the learning environment.

Affirmative action exists because people of color, minority groups, and women have faced discrimination, often by a majority group made up of white people and men. Historically, members of these marginalized groups have not been hired for the top jobs or admitted to elite universities, although they might be qualified. In the United States, racial and gender discrimination have been illegal since the 1960's. But past discrimination still has an impact today, and people of color and women still face many unfair barriers. For example, when universities decide whom to admit, they often consider factors that are racially biased, although the racial bias may not be obvious. A university might favor students whose parents or grandparents attended that school, but many universities did not admit people of color in the past. Affirmative action aims to counteract such barriers.

Affirmative action policies, especially those that consider race in college admissions, have proven controversial. Supporters of affirmative action give different reasons for using it. Some want to remedy discrimination. Others wish to educate people from disadvantaged communities who later might work as doctors, lawyers, or other professionals in such communities. Many people reason that affirmative action creates more diverse institutions that are better at educating all students, providing national security, and conducting business. They argue that affirmative action results in a broader variety of viewpoints in colleges, greater trust and understanding between military ranks, and a wider variety of products and services for companies to sell. For supporters, affirmative action is a useful, if flawed, tool for creating greater opportunity in a society where discrimination still exists.

Those who oppose affirmative action argue that making decisions based on race or gender violates a person's right to be treated as an individual, rather than part of a group. For opponents, affirmative action is unfair, especially to white people and men. Opponents of affirmative action have filed many lawsuits to try to end the practice. The U.S. Supreme Court, the country's highest court, has decided many such cases.

Affirmative action in the United States began during the 1960's. The first programs chiefly favored African Americans. In 1965, President Lyndon B. Johnson signed Executive Order 11246. It established affirmative action requirements for the federal government and for companies with government contracts. Since then, the U.S. government and larger government contractors have been required to use affirmative action.

American universities and colleges adopted affirmative action voluntarily. In the 1960's, the leaders of some elite, predominantly white, universities created the first policies that considered race in recruitment and admissions. They were inspired by the civil rights movement in the Southern States, and also pressured by student activists. Many state and local governments, businesses, and schools have created their own affirmative action policies and programs. Affirmative action law generally has become stricter over the years, placing more limits on how organizations can apply affirmative action policies. Some U.S. states have banned affirmative action in hiring and college admissions.

Other countries also have affirmative action policies and programs that favor racial minorities, women, and other groups, such as people with disabilities and members of lower *castes* (inherited social classes). Such countries include Brazil, Canada, India, Rwanda, and South Africa. In many countries with affirmative action programs, the national constitution gives the government responsibility for promoting equality, and affirmative action is considered "positive discrimination." In contrast, the Constitution of the United States does not give the government such responsibility. Nor does U.S. law support positive discrimination. Rather, it largely forbids discrimination based on race, sex, and other legally "protected" characteristics, such as age, national origin, and religion. This legal environment has made it easier for opponents of affirmative action to challenge such policies in U.S. courts of law.   Ellen Berrey

See also **African Americans** (Economic and social progress; Education; Affirmative action); **Bakke case; Civil rights** (Major changes in the field of civil rights).

Afghan hound, *AF guhn,* is a dog known for its speed and agility. It has been used for hunting gazelles and hares in Afghanistan for hundreds of years. It has long ears, large feet, and a heavy coat of long, silky hair. It can be any of many colors. It is about 27 inches (69 centimeters) tall at the shoulder and weighs about 50 to 60 pounds (23 to 27 kilograms). It moves with its head and tail held high. No one knows just where or when the Afghan hound originated. See also **Dog** (picture: Hounds).   Critically reviewed by the Afghan Hound Club of America

AP/Wide World

Kabul, Afghanistan's capital and largest city, has both traditional and modern buildings. Traditional mud-brick dwellings, such as those on the hillside, are found throughout Afghanistan. Some modern buildings rise in downtown Kabul.

Afghanistan

Afghanistan, a nation in southwest Asia, has towering mountains, scorching deserts, fertile valleys, and rolling plains. Afghanistan is completely surrounded by six other countries and has no seacoast. It is bordered by Turkmenistan, Uzbekistan, and Tajikistan on the north, China on the far northeast, Pakistan on the east and south, and Iran on the west.

Afghanistan is one of the world's least developed countries. Decades of war have devastated the country. Many Afghan workers farm small plots of land. Since the beginning of the 2000's, there has been a large migration of people to the cities, especially to Kabul, the country's capital and largest city.

Almost all the people of Afghanistan are Muslims. The population of Afghanistan consists of numerous ethnic groups. Many of the ethnic groups have distinct languages and cultures.

Afghanistan has a long and complicated history. It has been invaded and conquered by numerous peoples and powers, including Persians, Greeks, and Mongols. From 1979 to 1989, the Soviet Union occupied Afghanistan. Nevertheless, the country also has a rich history of trade and peaceful interactions with its neighbors.

In the 1990's, a conservative Islamic group called the Taliban came to power. The Taliban allowed international terrorist organizations to run training camps in Afghanistan. After terrorist attacks against the United States in 2001, the United States and anti-Taliban forces within Afghanistan drove the Taliban from power. Afghans, with assistance from the United States, the United Nations, and other international agencies then worked to establish a new democratic government for the country. However, the Taliban regrouped. As U.S. and other international forces withdrew in 2021, Taliban forces seized control of Afghanistan once again.

Government

According to Afghanistan's 2004 Constitution, a president is head of state. The president and two vice presidents are elected by the people to five-year terms. The legislature consists of the *Wolesi Jirga* (House of the People) and the *Meshrano Jirga* (House of the Elders). The 250 members of the Wolesi Jirga are elected by the people to five-year terms. The Meshrano Jirga has 102 members. One-third of these members are chosen by

Facts in brief

Capital: Kabul.
Official languages: Pashto (also called Pakhto) and Dari.
Official name: *Da Afghanistan Enteqali Islami Daulat* (in Pashto) or *Daulat e Entaqali Islami Afghanistan* (in Dari), both meaning Islamic Republic of Afghanistan.
Area: 251,827 mi² (652,230 km²). *Greatest distances*—east-west, 820 mi (1,320 km); north-south, 630 mi (1,012 km).
Elevation: *Highest*—Nowshak, 24,557 ft (7,485 m) above sea level. *Lowest*—In Sistan Basin, 1,640 ft (500 m) above sea level.
Population: *Estimated 2022 population*—40,803,000; population density, 162 per mi² (63 per km²); distribution, 74 percent rural, 26 percent urban. *2012 official government estimate*—25,500,100.
Chief products: *Agriculture*—beef and dairy cattle, fruits, goats, Karakul skins, nuts, rice, vegetables, wheat. *Manufacturing*—carpets, cement, leather goods, processed foods. *Mining*—coal, lapis lazuli, natural gas.
National anthem: "Milli Surood" ("National Anthem").
Money: *Basic unit*—afghani.

Noreen S. Ahmed-Ullah © *Chicago Tribune*

A *jirga* (council) is a traditional Afghan community meeting. This jirga near Khowst, in eastern Afghanistan, met to choose delegates to send to a national *loya jirga* (grand council) in Kabul.

Afghanistan's 34 provincial councils, one-third by district councils, and one-third by the president. Afghanistan's highest court is the Supreme Court. Its nine members each serve a single 10-year term. Men and women were guaranteed equal rights under the 2004 Constitution. However, after the Taliban seized control in 2021, they installed an interim government. They named a prime minister and cabinet to run the country.

Afghan communities often hold smaller *jirgas* (councils) to decide matters of local importance. Local jirgas may include all of a single community's adult men or the leaders from several neighboring communities.

People

Ancestry. Most Afghans are a blend of early peoples who came to the country as invaders or settlers. These groups included Aryans, Persians, Arabs, Mongolians, Turkish-speaking people from central Asia, and people from the Xinjiang region of western China.

Ethnic groups and languages. Afghanistan has about 20 ethnic groups, many of which have their own language, culture, and traditions. Some ethnic groups consist of smaller communities known as *qawms* (pronounced *komz*), which can be translated as *tribe, nation,* or *family*. There can be as much difference between qawms within the same ethnic group as between different ethnic groups.

The largest ethnic groups are the Pashtuns (or Pakhtuns) and the Tajiks. The Pashtuns and Tajiks make up about 70 percent of the population. Historically, most Pashtuns lived in the south and east, and Tajiks lived in the north and east of the country. But the violence of the late 1900's and early 2000's has led to significant migration within Afghanistan. Other important ethnic groups

include the Aimak, Baloch, Hazara, Qizilbash, Turkmen, and Uzbek.

Afghanistan has two official languages—Pashto (or Pakhto) and Dari, which is also known as Afghan Persian. There are a number of local languages spoken by different ethnic groups and communities as well. Many Afghans speak more than one language.

Way of life. Afghanistan's rural people live in homes made of sun-dried mud bricks. City dwellers live in modern homes and apartment buildings. A small number of nomadic and seminomadic people live in tents made of goat hair. Nomads are people who move from place to place with their herds of sheep or goats.

Traditional Afghan clothing includes a *posteen*, a heavy winter coat made of sheepskin, quilted fabric, or felt. Some men wear a turban and others wear a woolen cap called a *pakool*. Such headwear can indicate a person's ethnic identity or place of origin. Afghanistan is a socially conservative country, and women's modesty in dress is expected and enforced in public. Women are expected to cover their heads. Some women, mainly Pashtuns, wear a garment called a *burqa* that covers the body from head to toe.

Afghans usually serve flat loaves of whole-grain, sourdough bread at meals. They also enjoy vegetables, yogurt, chicken, beef, mutton, and rice. Popular desserts include nuts and fruits. Tea is the favorite drink.

Women have traditionally played a secondary role in

© Gil C, Shutterstock   © Gil C, Shutterstock

Symbols of Afghanistan. Afghanistan's flag and coat of arms were adopted in 2004. The flag has black, red, and green vertical stripes, and the coat of arms in the center. The coat of arms features a *mosque* (Islamic house of worship) with flags on each side, surrounded by a wreath of wheat bound by a ribbon.

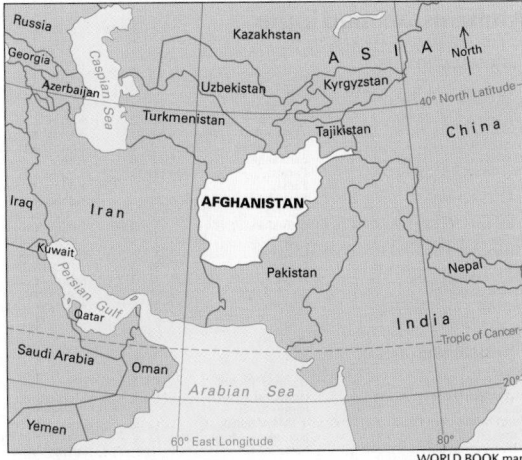

WORLD BOOK map

Afghanistan is a landlocked country in southwestern Asia. It is surrounded by six other countries.

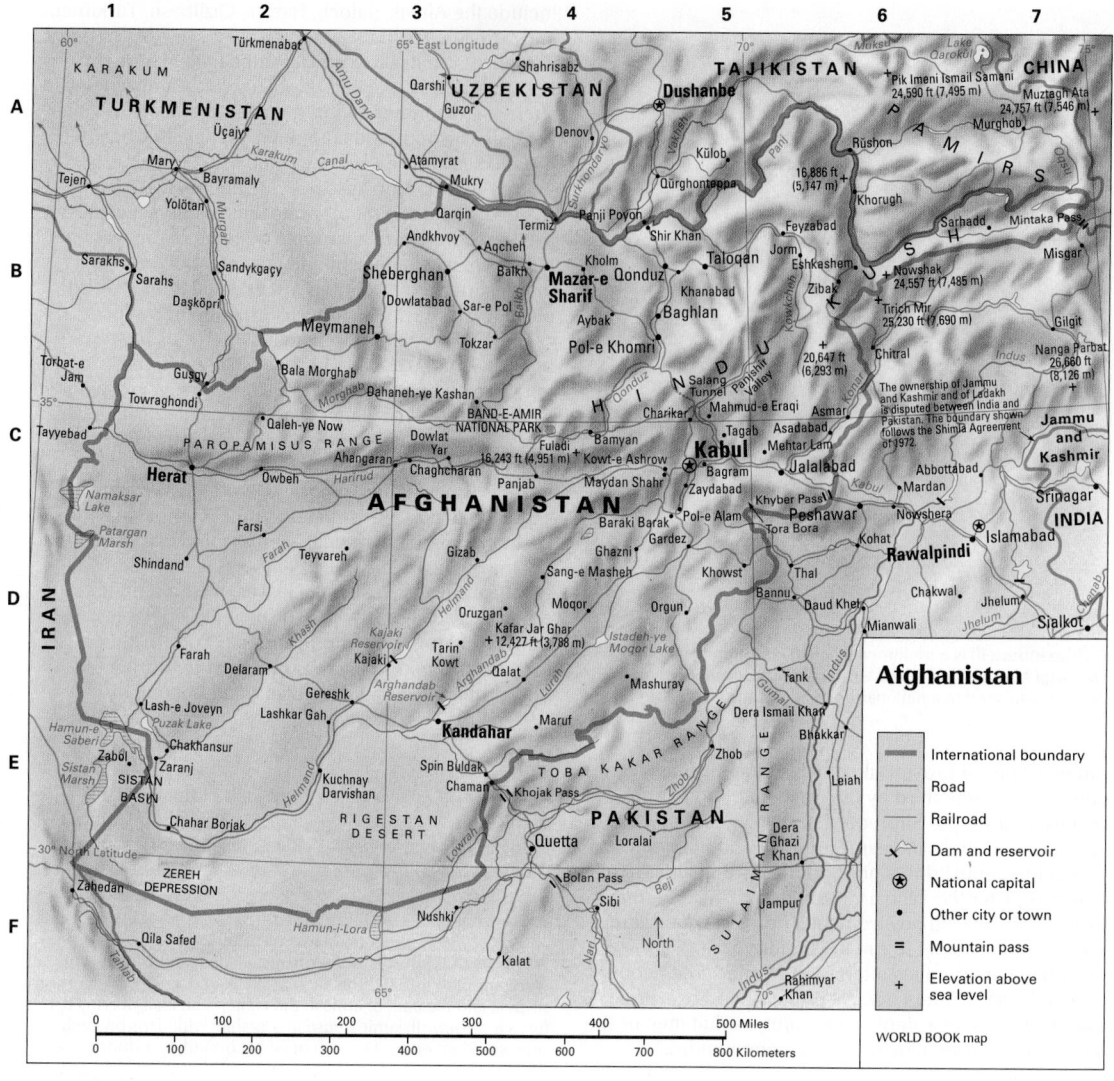

Afghanistan map index

Cities and towns

Physical features

*Does not appear on map; key shows general location.
Source: 2012 official estimates.

Islam greatly influences family and community relationships and almost all other aspects of Afghan life. This beautiful blue *mosque* (Islamic house of worship) is in Mazar-e Sharif.

© F. Jack Jackson, Alamy Images

Afghan society. Their opportunities for education and careers have been limited, especially in rural areas. Afghan society is *patriarchal* (controlled by men). For example, some Afghan communities require women to be accompanied by a male relative in public. Some families practice *purdah,* which involves segregating men and women in the home except in cases of close relatives.

During the 1900's, several Afghan governments gave women more legal rights. In 1964, for example, a new constitution granted Afghan women equal status with men, and the social and economic position of some women improved. In practice, however, few women fully enjoyed these rights.

In the 1990's and early 2000's, the Taliban greatly limited the freedom of women. The Taliban required all women to cover themselves completely when in public. They also prohibited women from working outside their homes. Women who violated Taliban laws were punished severely.

After the Taliban fell in 2001, many Afghan women hoped to reclaim their rights. Several women played significant roles in the national councils that created a transitional government and adopted a new constitution for the country. The 2004 Constitution reserved several seats for women in the National Assembly.

Religion. Nearly all Afghans are Muslims. Most are Sunni Muslims, though some are Shi`ites. The latter include Ismailis, a small religious minority found mainly in Badakhshan in the far northeast. Sufism, the mystical tradition of Islam, has long been important in Afghanistan. Other religious communities, such as Sikhs, are mainly found in Kabul and other large cities.

Education. About 60 percent of Afghanistan's people 15 years of age or older cannot read and write. The country lacks sufficient schools and teachers, largely be-

AP/Wide World

The blue *burqa* (or *chadri)* is a full-length hooded garment worn by most Pashtun women in Afghanistan. Some Afghan women drape a shawl over their heads.

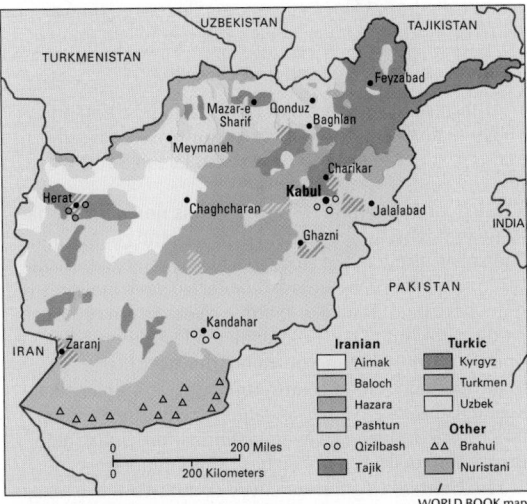

WORLD BOOK map

Afghanistan's major ethnic groups inhabit various parts of the country. The map key arranges the ethnic groups by their language types. For example, the language spoken by the Pashtuns is an Iranian language, but that spoken by Uzbeks is Turkic. Stripes indicate areas shared by more than one ethnic group.

© SuperStock

Goat herders lead their herd over an arid mountain path. Afghanistan's economy depends heavily on agriculture. Many of the country's farmers practice sheep and goat herding.

cause of the upheaval caused by decades of war. Muslim religious schools known as *madrasahs* have in many places met this need. Afghanistan has a few universities, including Kabul University and Nangarhar University in Jalalabad.

The arts. Folklore, songs, and dances play an important part in Afghan life. They enable the people to pass their values and traditions on from one generation to the next. The *attan* (also spelled *atan)* is an energetic folk dance. Pashtuns dance the attan at weddings and other community celebrations. Afghanistan also has a long tradition of poetry, both religious and *secular* (nonreligious). Poetry competitions continue to be a central source of entertainment and are sometimes broadcast on national radio.

Recreation. Afghans enjoy sports and games, such as soccer and cricket. Men of the northern plains play a game called *buzkashi.* In the game, dozens of horsemen try to grab a headless calf and carry it across a goal.

The land and climate

Afghanistan is made up of three main land regions. These regions are, from north to south: (1) the Northern Plains, (2) the Central Highlands, and (3) the Southwestern Lowlands.

The Northern Plains stretch across northern Afghanistan and consist of mountain plateaus and rolling hills. The soil is fertile in the Northern Plains but can be cultivated only where water is available. Large irrigation systems have been built along some rivers in the region, including the Amu Darya. Nomadic and seminomadic people raise sheep and goats on the vast grasslands.

Temperatures in the Northern Plains of Afghanistan average about 38 °F (3 °C) in January and approximately 90 °F (32 °C) in July. The average annual precipitation in the region totals about 7 inches (18 centimeters).

The Central Highlands cover about two-thirds of Afghanistan. They consist of the Hindu Kush mountain range and its branches. Snow-capped peaks rise about 25,000 feet (7,620 meters) along the Pakistani border in the northeast. The range gradually descends to a rolling plain in the southwest. Kabul lies in a valley in these

mountains, surrounded by ridges of the Hindu Kush.

The Central Highlands have an average temperature of about 25 °F (–4 °C) in January and about 75 °F (24 °C) in July. The region receives about 15 inches (38 centimeters) of precipitation yearly.

The Southwestern Lowlands lie in southern and southwestern Afghanistan and consist mainly of desert or semidesert land. The region is crossed by the Helmand River, which flows from the Hindu Kush to the Sistan Basin on the Iranian border. The basin has several slightly salty lakes and marshes. Barley, corn, fruits, and wheat are grown in the Helmand Valley, which is the site of important irrigation works.

Temperatures in the lowlands of Afghanistan average about 35 °F (2 °C) in January and about 85 °F (29 °C) in July. The average annual precipitation ranges from 2 to 9 inches (5 to 23 centimeters).

Economy

Historically, Afghanistan's economy has benefited from the country's location along the Silk Road and other ancient trade routes. The Italian trader Marco Polo's journals from the 1200's detail his journey through the country. As these routes died out, Afghanistan's economy suffered. Afghanistan has long benefited from foreign money through trade, plunder, or international aid. The country's internal resources have proven insufficient to support government expenditure. Throughout the 1900's, Afghan governments attempted to develop the country's economy and to improve educational opportunities. But decades of war and internal struggles at the end of the 1900's reversed most of these advances.

Agriculture. Although little of Afghanistan's land is suitable for farming, many Afghan workers earn at least part of their living from agriculture. Wheat is Afghanistan's chief crop. Other crops include barley, corn, cotton, fruits, nuts, rice, and vegetables. Agricultural production has been limited since the 1980's, with war limiting access to machinery, fertilizer, and water.

In the 1980's, Afghanistan became one of the world's leading producers of opium, which is used to make the illegal drug heroin. Wartime conditions led many Afghan farmers, especially in the south and northeast, to raise opium poppies rather than grow food crops. In 2000, the Taliban began enforcing a strict ban on poppy farming, but the practice resumed after the Taliban were driven from power in 2001. Despite the efforts of the Afghan government and its allies, Afghanistan produces the vast majority of the world's opium.

Afghanistan raises beef and dairy cattle, chickens, goats, and sheep. The skins of Karakul sheep, a fat-tailed sheep known for its silky pelt, are especially valuable.

Mining. Afghanistan is rich in minerals. However, because of the country's rugged terrain, frequent conflicts, and poor infrastructure, most of the deposits are largely undeveloped. In the 1960's, large deposits of natural gas were discovered in northern Afghanistan. Since then, the production of natural gas has become an important part of the nation's economy. Afghanistan also produces some coal and salt. Some of the world's finest *lapis lazuli,* a valuable azure-blue stone, and other gemstones are mined in Afghanistan.

Manufacturing. Afghanistan has little industry because of war damage and a scarcity of raw materials.

Skilled craftworkers in their homes or small shops make carpets, leather goods, and other handicraft items. A few mills produce textiles, and small factories turn out such products as cement and processed foods.

International trade. Illegal opium accounts for much of Afghanistan's exports. Afghanistan's leading legal exports include animal skins, carpets, cotton, and fruits and nuts. The country's leading imports include food, machinery, petroleum products, and textiles. Afghanistan's main trading partners include China, India, Iran, and Pakistan. *Remittances* (sums of money sent) from Afghans working overseas are extremely important to the Afghan economy.

Transportation and communication. Many of Afghanistan's roads are unpaved. Decades of war have heavily damaged the paved roads, making many of them unusable. The country has limited rail service. Kabul has an international airport.

Afghanistan's most famous transportation route is the Khyber Pass, which crosses the border between Afghanistan and Pakistan. The pass cuts through the Safid Kuh mountains, which are part of the Hindu Kush range. Conquerors, such as Alexander the Great of Macedonia, used the pass to invade South Asia. The Khyber Pass has been an important trade route for centuries. See **Khyber Pass.**

Several newspapers are published in Afghanistan. Radio and television stations operate under both private and public ownership. Cell phone usage increased rapidly in the early 2000's. Few people use the Internet.

History

Prehistoric hunting people lived in what is now Afghanistan as early as 100,000 years ago. After many thousands of years, the people learned how to farm and to herd animals. Agricultural villages then developed. By about 4000 to 2000 B.C., a number of these villages had grown into small cities.

Early invasions. About 1500 B.C., the Aryans, a central Asian people, invaded the region. Scholars believe they killed many of the area's inhabitants and intermarried with others. In the mid-500's B.C., Persians invaded northern Afghanistan, a region then called Bactria. The Persians ruled Bactria until about 330 B.C., when Greeks and Macedonians led by Alexander the Great conquered the region and much of the rest of Afghanistan.

About 246 B.C., the Bactrians revolted. They eventually conquered much of Afghanistan and formed a kingdom that lasted about 150 years. They were conquered by the Kushans of central Asia. Sasanians from Persia invaded in the A.D. 200's, and White Huns from central Asia defeated the Kushans and Sasanians in the 400's.

The coming of Islam. Arab Muslim armies swept into parts of what is now Afghanistan during the late 600's. Three Muslim dynasties—the Tahirid, the Samanid, and the Saffarid—controlled much of the region during the 800's and 900's. Under these dynasties, most local inhabitants converted to Islam.

Turkic-speaking peoples from eastern Persia and central Asia ruled Afghanistan from about 900 to 1200. The most famous of these were the Ghaznavids, who, under Mahmud of Ghazni, conquered much of northern India. Afghanistan was conquered by Mongols led by Genghis Khan in the 1200's and led by Timur, also called Tamer-

lane, in the 1300's. Safavids from Persia and Mughals from India struggled for control of Afghanistan from the mid-1500's to the early 1700's.

United Afghanistan. In 1747, Ahmad Khan Abdalli came to power. He took the title *shah* (king) and adopted the name *Durrani* (Pearl of the Age). Ahmad Shah Durrani united the many Pashtun tribes, establishing the Durrani Empire. This marked the beginning of modern Afghanistan, though it included territory stretching far beyond the country's current borders.

Ahmad Shah established his capital at Kandahar. His son and successor, Timur Shah, moved the capital from Kandahar to Kabul in 1775. Timur Shah and his successors struggled to keep the Afghans united and lost control of most of the territory beyond the current borders of Afghanistan.

In 1819, civil war broke out among rival groups that wanted to rule the country. The war lasted until 1826, when Dost Muhammad Khan gained control. He took the title of *amir* (prince). Dost Muhammad's descendants ruled the country for the next 150 years.

The Anglo-Afghan wars. During the 1800's, the United Kingdom and Russia competed for control of Afghanistan. The United Kingdom wanted to protect its empire in India, which was threatened by Russia's expansion in Afghanistan. In 1839, British Indian troops invaded Afghanistan to stop Russia's perceived influence in the region. The invasion set off the First Anglo-Afghan War, which lasted until the British withdrew in 1842.

In 1878, the United Kingdom invaded the country again, starting the Second Anglo-Afghan War. The British found it difficult to establish control of Afghanistan. They recognized Abdur Rahman Khan as amir in 1880, though his authority was limited to the country's internal affairs. In return, Abdur Rahman accepted British India's control of Afghanistan's foreign relations. Abdur Rahman Khan, often called the "Iron Amir," strengthened the national government and reduced the power of tribal leaders. After he died in 1901, his policies were continued by his son Habibullah Khan.

Independence. Early in 1919, Habibullah Khan was assassinated. One of his sons, Amanullah Khan, then became amir and attacked British troops in India, beginning the Third Anglo-Afghan War. The United Kingdom had just finished fighting in World War I (1914-1918). After a brief conflict, it decided to end its involvement in Afghanistan. In August 1919, Afghanistan became fully independent.

Amanullah began many reforms, challenging long-held traditions and customs. The nation's first constitution was adopted in 1923, and Amanullah changed his title from amir to shah in 1926. But tribal and religious leaders resisted the reform movement and forced Amanullah Shah to give up the throne in 1929.

Late in 1929, Muhammad Nadir Shah became king. In 1931, Afghanistan adopted a new constitution, under which Nadir Shah planned a program of gradual reform. But he was assassinated in 1933, before many of the reforms were begun. Muhammad Zahir Shah, Nadir Shah's son, then became king.

The mid-1900's. Afghanistan avoided involvement in World War II (1939-1945). By the early 1950's, Afghanistan had developed good relations with the United States and many Western European nations. But the

Afghans feared the intentions of the Soviet Union, their country's powerful Communist neighbor. In 1953, Muhammad Daoud Khan, the king's cousin and brother-in-law, took control of the government and made himself prime minister. Under Daoud, Afghanistan took no side in the Cold War, a period of hostility between Communist and non-Communist nations. It received aid from both the United States and the Soviet Union.

Border disputes with Pakistan and other problems led to pressures that forced Daoud to resign in 1963. In 1964, under the leadership of Zahir Shah and Western-educated scholars and thinkers, Afghanistan adopted a constitution that provided for a democratic government for the first time. But many problems arose. Zahir Shah and the legislature could not agree on the role of political parties within the reform program. Parliament often deadlocked on key issues. As a result, the new democratic system failed to bring about the progress that the framers of the Constitution had hoped for.

In 1973, Daoud overthrew Zahir Shah. He established the Republic of Afghanistan and assumed the offices of president and prime minister.

The Soviet invasion. In 1978, the People's Democratic Party of Afghanistan (PDPA), the country's Communist party, overthrew Daoud, who was killed in the uprising. The PDPA established a Communist government. Many in Afghanistan opposed the new government. They believed its policies conflicted with the teachings of Islam. They also resented Soviet influence on the government. A rebellion against the government soon broke out.

The Soviet Union became concerned that the rebels, who called themselves *mujahideen* (holy warriors), might defeat the Afghan government forces. On Dec. 25, 1979, the Soviet Union invaded Afghanistan. Over the next decade, the Soviet Union sent more than 100,000 troops to join the fight against the rebels. The Soviets had better equipment than their opponents. But the rebels were supplied by countries opposed to the Soviet Union, including the United States and Saudi Arabia. The mujahideen used guerrilla tactics to overcome the Soviet advantage.

In 1988 and 1989, the Soviet Union withdrew its troops from Afghanistan. But fighting between the mujahideen and government forces continued until 1992, when the rebels overthrew the government.

Afghanistan under the Taliban. Continued fighting among mujahideen groups prevented the establishment of a stable government. In the mid-1990's, a conservative Islamic organization called the Taliban rose to power.

Pashtun religious students who had fled to Pakistan during the Soviet invasion started the Taliban movement. The Taliban were supported by Pakistan's military and by militant Arab Islamic groups. By the late 1990's, the Taliban controlled nearly all of Afghanistan. They established a Council of Ministers to rule the country.

The Taliban imposed their strict interpretation of Islam on the people. They banned television and most other modern forms of entertainment, and they established rules for dress and grooming. All women were forced to cover themselves completely when in public, and men were required to grow beards. The Taliban also prohibited girls from attending school and forbade women from working outside the home.

The Taliban destroyed many artifacts of the country's heritage that they claimed were un-Islamic. They demolished two ancient statues of Buddha carved into a mountainside near Bamyan, a city northwest of Kabul. The Taliban also destroyed many works of art in the country's museums.

Recent developments. In 2001, members of a terrorist organization called al-Qa`ida attacked the World Trade Center in New York City and the Pentagon Building near Washington, D.C. (see **September 11 terrorist attacks**). The United States accused the Taliban of harboring and assisting al-Qa`ida, which had been founded in the late 1980's by Saudi-born millionaire Osama bin Laden to resist the Soviet occupation of Afghanistan. The United States demanded that the Taliban arrest bin Laden and other Qa`ida leaders and shut down their training camps. The Taliban refused to do so, and the United States and its allies launched a military campaign against the Taliban.

The campaign included air strikes in support of the Northern Alliance and other Afghan rebel groups who opposed the Taliban. This support enabled the rebels to drive the Taliban from power in late 2001. An international peacekeeping force known as the International Security and Assistance Force arrived in Kabul in late 2001 and early 2002. In the following years, the force extended its duties from Kabul throughout Afghanistan. However, in the absence of a strong central government, warlords and rebel groups continued to compete for territory and power. Taliban and Qa`ida forces also continued to battle U.S., Afghan, and allied troops.

Meanwhile, the United Nations brought representatives of Afghanistan's leading groups together in Bonn, Germany, to discuss the formation of a new national government. In June 2002, a *loya jirga* (grand council) met in Kabul, established a two-year transitional government, and chose Hamid Karzai, a prominent member of the Popalzai tribe, as the country's transitional president.

In December 2003 and January 2004, another loya jirga met in Kabul and adopted a new constitution. In October 2004, a presidential election was held under the new Constitution, and Karzai was elected president. Parliamentary and provincial elections were held in 2005.

Karzai was reelected in 2009. From 2011 to 2013, national peacekeeping and security duties were transferred to Afghan forces. International troops shifted into a supporting role. But Taliban and Qa`ida forces continued to fight international troops across the country.

A disputed presidential election in 2014 resulted in a deadlock between the two leading candidates, former surgeon Abdullah Abdullah and former Finance Minister Ashraf Ghani. Each accused the other of fraud. After negotiations, a power-sharing agreement made Ghani, who had received the most votes, president. Abdullah assumed the new office of chief executive.

In 2014, the United States and the North Atlantic Treaty Organization (NATO) formally ended their combat missions in Afghanistan. However, thousands of their forces remained in the country to train and advise Afghan troops. The Taliban soon renewed its insurgency.

A disputed election in 2019 was settled in 2020. Ghani remained president. Abdullah became chairman of a High Commission for National Reconciliation, with primary responsibility for negotiations with the Taliban.

In 2020, the United States negotiated an agreement

with the Taliban. The Taliban agreed not to allow terrorist groups to operate from bases in Afghanistan, and the United States agreed to withdraw its troops. The Taliban resisted negotiating with the Afghan government, but talks slowly began in September.

As U.S. and other allied forces withdrew, however, the Taliban and other militant groups increased their violence against the Afghan government. In 2021, the Taliban seized more territory, and the Afghan military collapsed. On August 15, Taliban forces took control of the capital, Kabul, and gained control of the country. The United States and its allies evacuated about 123,000 Afghani civilians. In September, the Taliban's leaders named an interim government.   Benjamin D. Hopkins

Related articles in *World Book* include:

Outline

I. Government
II. People
    A. Ancestry   E. Religion
    B. Ethnic groups   F. Education
        and languages   G. The arts
    C. Way of life   H. Recreation
    D. Women
III. The land and climate
    A. The Northern Plains
    B. The Central Highlands
    C. The Southwestern Lowlands
IV. Economy
    A. Agriculture   D. International trade
    B. Mining   E. Transportation and
    C. Manufacturing   communication
V. History

Afghanistan War, a long and destructive international conflict, began in 2001. It started in response to the September 11 terrorist attacks on the United States. The U.S. government linked those attacks to an Islamic extremist group called al-Qa'ida (also spelled *al-Qaeda*). The Taliban, a militant Islamic group that controlled Afghanistan, had hosted al-Qa'ida since 1996.

Following the September 11 attacks, the United States demanded that the Taliban arrest Qa'ida leaders. When the Taliban refused to do so, the United States and its allies launched a military campaign. With assistance from U.S. and other allied forces, Afghan anti-Taliban groups began taking control of major cities and towns. On Dec. 9, 2001, Afghan forces took Kandahar, bringing Taliban rule in Afghanistan to an end.

In late 2001, the United Nations (UN) sponsored a meeting of delegates from Afghanistan's main ethnic and regional groups. The delegates chose Hamid Karzai, a member of the Popalzai tribe of the Pashtun ethnic group, to head a temporary government. The UN also established the International Security Assistance Force to lead foreign forces providing security for the new government. Eventually, about 50 countries sent troops to Afghanistan.

In November 2004, Karzai was elected president. Still, despite steps toward democracy, the Afghanistan War dragged on. Fighters loyal to the Taliban and al-Qa'ida launched attacks on U.S. and allied forces from bases in Pakistan. The insurgents staged ambushes, carried out suicide bomb attacks, and used other guerrilla tactics.

Allied forces established outposts throughout much of Afghanistan. They worked to convince Afghan civilians not to support the insurgents. Troops provided security for villages and performed such humanitarian tasks as digging wells, building schools and roads, and providing medical care.

Pakistan became an important U.S. ally. The United States and its allies used the Pakistani port of Karachi as a transportation hub. Trucks carried supplies from Karachi into northwestern Pakistan and across the border into Afghanistan. The war strained Pakistan's relationship with the United States. The U.S. military used unpiloted aircraft called *drones* to launch attacks on targets they believed to be Taliban and Qa'ida strongholds in Pakistan. Many Pakistanis opposed the drone strikes.

Some international affairs experts accused Pakistan's leaders of harboring top Qa'ida figures, including the organization's head, Osama bin Laden. Pakistan denied the allegations. However, American intelligence tracked bin Laden to Abbottabad, a Pakistani city northeast of Islamabad. A U.S. special forces team killed bin Laden there on May 2, 2011 (May 1 in the United States).

From 2011 to 2013, international troops transferred peacekeeping and security duties to Afghan forces. In 2014, the U.S. and the North Atlantic Treaty Organization (NATO) formally ended their combat missions in Afghanistan. But thousands of their forces remained in advisory and support roles. More than 3,500 coalition soldiers, mostly Americans, died in the conflict in Afghanistan.

The Taliban regrouped, and fighting among Afghans continued. In 2020, the United States concluded a treaty with the Taliban. The Taliban agreed not to allow such terrorist organizations as al-Qa'ida and the Islamic State (ISIS) to operate in Afghanistan. The U.S. agreed to withdraw its troops. But as the U.S. and other allies withdrew, the Taliban and other militant groups increased their violence against the Afghan government.

In 2021, the United States announced it would withdraw its troops by August 31. It promised to continue to provide Afghan government troops with *reconnaisance* (data on enemy activity) from bases outside the country. The Taliban seized more territory, and hundreds of thousands of Afghans fled. The Afghan government's forces collapsed that summer. On August 15, Taliban troops took Kabul and gained control of the country.

The United States then sent forces to secure the Kabul airport during the evacuation of U.S. and NATO personnel and of Afghan allies and their families. Flights continued despite a suicide bomb attack on August 26 by the miltant group ISIS-K (Islamic State Khorasan—a branch of ISIS). The attack killed about 170 people waiting to enter the airport, as well as 13 U.S. troops. The last U.S. forces withdrew on August 30.   Robert Hodierne

Related articles in *World Book* include:

© Betty Press, Panos Pictures

Africa is a continent of striking contrasts. About two-fifths of African people live in cities, such as Lagos, Nigeria, *above*. The newer sections of many cities have hotels, tall office and apartment buildings, and large stores. The remaining three-fifths of Africans live in rural areas, chiefly villages.

Africa

Africa is the second largest continent in area and in population. Only Asia covers a larger area and has more people. Africa covers approximately 11,688,000 square miles (30,272,000 square kilometers), about a fifth of the world's land area, and has a population of more than 1.4 billion, about one-sixth of the world's people.

The African continent is an immense plateau, broken by a few mountain ranges and bordered in some areas by a narrow coastal plain. It is a land of striking contrasts and great natural wonders. In the tropical rain forests of western and central Africa, the towering treetops form a thick green canopy. The world's largest desert, the Sahara, stretches across northern Africa. It covers an area almost as large as the United States. Africa also has the world's longest river—the Nile. It flows more than 4,000 miles (6,400 kilometers) through northeastern Africa. Grasslands make up about a third of the continent. Elephants, giraffes, lions, zebras, and many other animals live in the vast grasslands in eastern and southern Africa.

Africa is divided into 54 independent countries and several other political units. The largest country, Algeria,

The contributors of this article are Paul Desanker, Associate Professor of Geography at Pennsylvania State University; Peri Klemm, Associate Professor of Art History at California State University at Northridge; Kenneth J. Perkins, Professor Emeritus of History at the University of South Carolina; Kwesi Kwaa Prah, Director of the Centre for Advanced Studies of African Society in Cape Town, South Africa; and Paul Tiyambe Zeleza, Professor of African American Studies at the University of Illinois at Chicago.

© Nigel Pavitt from John Warburton-Lee

Africa is famous for its wildlife. Millions of tourists come to see huge herds of wildebeest, *shown here,* and other animals at Kenya's Maasai Mara National Park and other wildlife preserves.

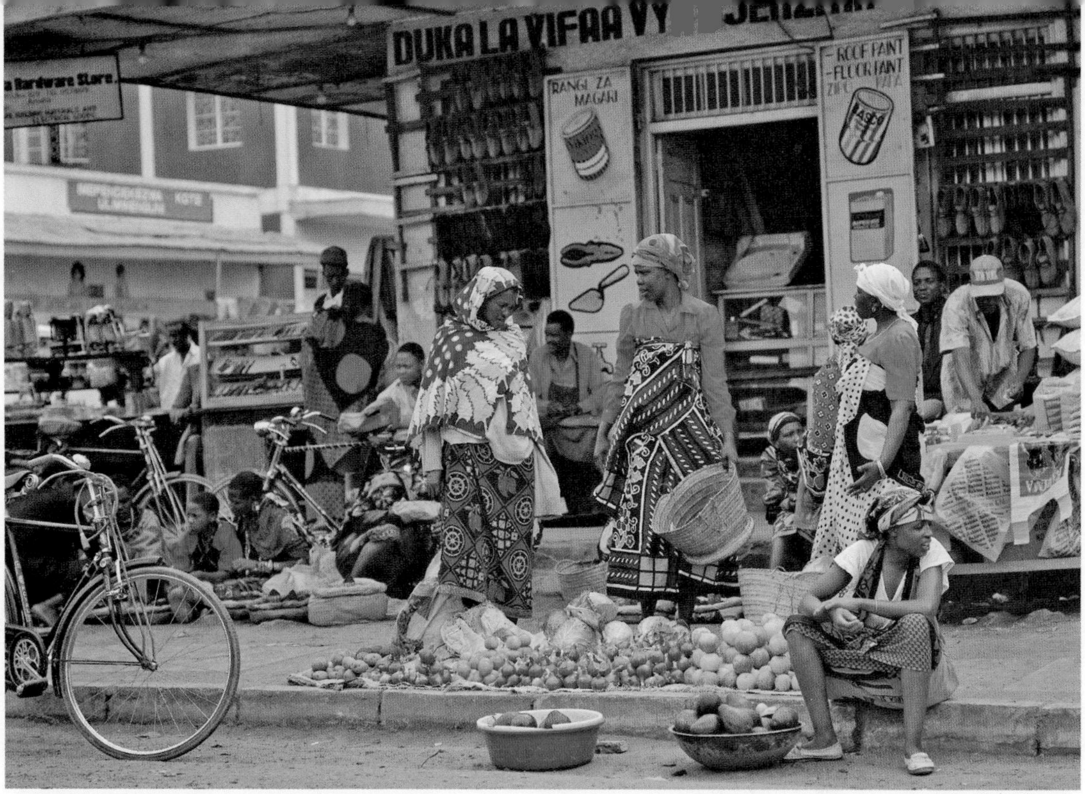

© Horst Klemm, Masterfile

A busy street in Arusha, Tanzania, is typical of most African towns. Shops, restaurants, and small roadside vendors line the main streets in towns throughout Africa south of the Sahara.

has an area of 919,595 square miles (2,381,741 square kilometers). The smallest, Seychelles, has a land area of only 176 square miles (455 square kilometers). The most heavily populated African nation, Nigeria, has about 220 million people. However, about 30 percent of all African countries have fewer than 5 million people each. About 1.2 billion people—about 85 percent of Africa's total population—live south of the Sahara in the vast region called *sub-Saharan Africa.*

There are several hundred ethnic groups throughout Africa, each with its own language or dialect and way of life. The large number and various sizes of ethnic groups has made it difficult for some African countries to develop into unified, modern nations. In some African countries, national boundaries cut across traditional ethnic homelands. As a result, people may feel closer ties to neighbors in another country than to other ethnic groups within their own country. Ethnic and religious

Facts in brief

Area: 11,688,000 mi^2 (30,272,000 km^2). *Greatest distances*—north-south, 5,000 mi (8,047 km); east-west, 4,700 mi (7,564 km). *Coastline*—22,921 mi (36,888 km).

Population: *Estimated 2022 population*—1,400,822,000; density, 120 per mi^2 (46 per km^2).

Elevation: *Highest*—Kilimanjaro in Tanzania, 19,340 ft (5,895 m) above sea level. *Lowest*—Lake Assal in Djibouti, 509 ft (155 m) below sea level.

Physical features: *Chief mountain ranges*—Ahaggar, Atlas, Drakensberg, Ruwenzori, Tibesti. *Chief rivers*—Congo, Limpopo, Niger, Nile, Orange, Zambezi. *Chief lakes*—Albert, Chad, Nyasa, Tanganyika, Turkana, Victoria. *Largest deserts*—Kalahari, Namib, Sahara.

Number of independent countries: 54.

© Gloria H. Chomica, Masterfile

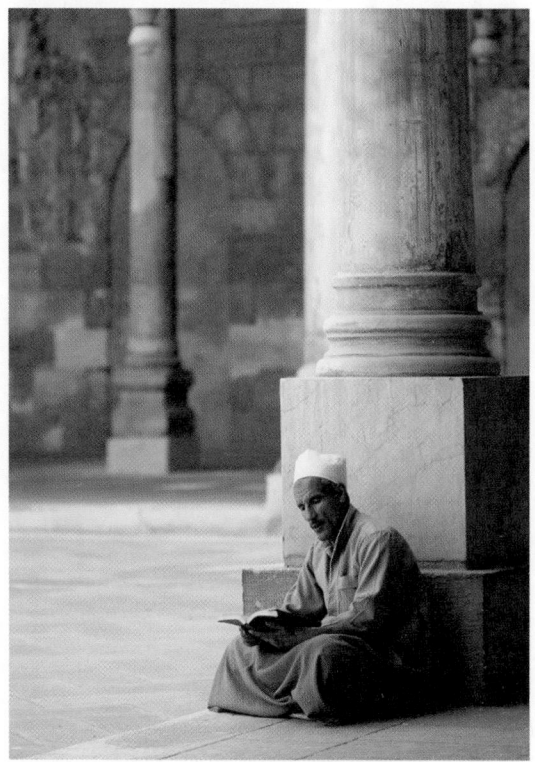

Arab culture and Islam have been important influences in northern Africa for centuries. Here, a man studies the Qur'ān in Cairo, Egypt, where the population is mainly Arab and Muslim.

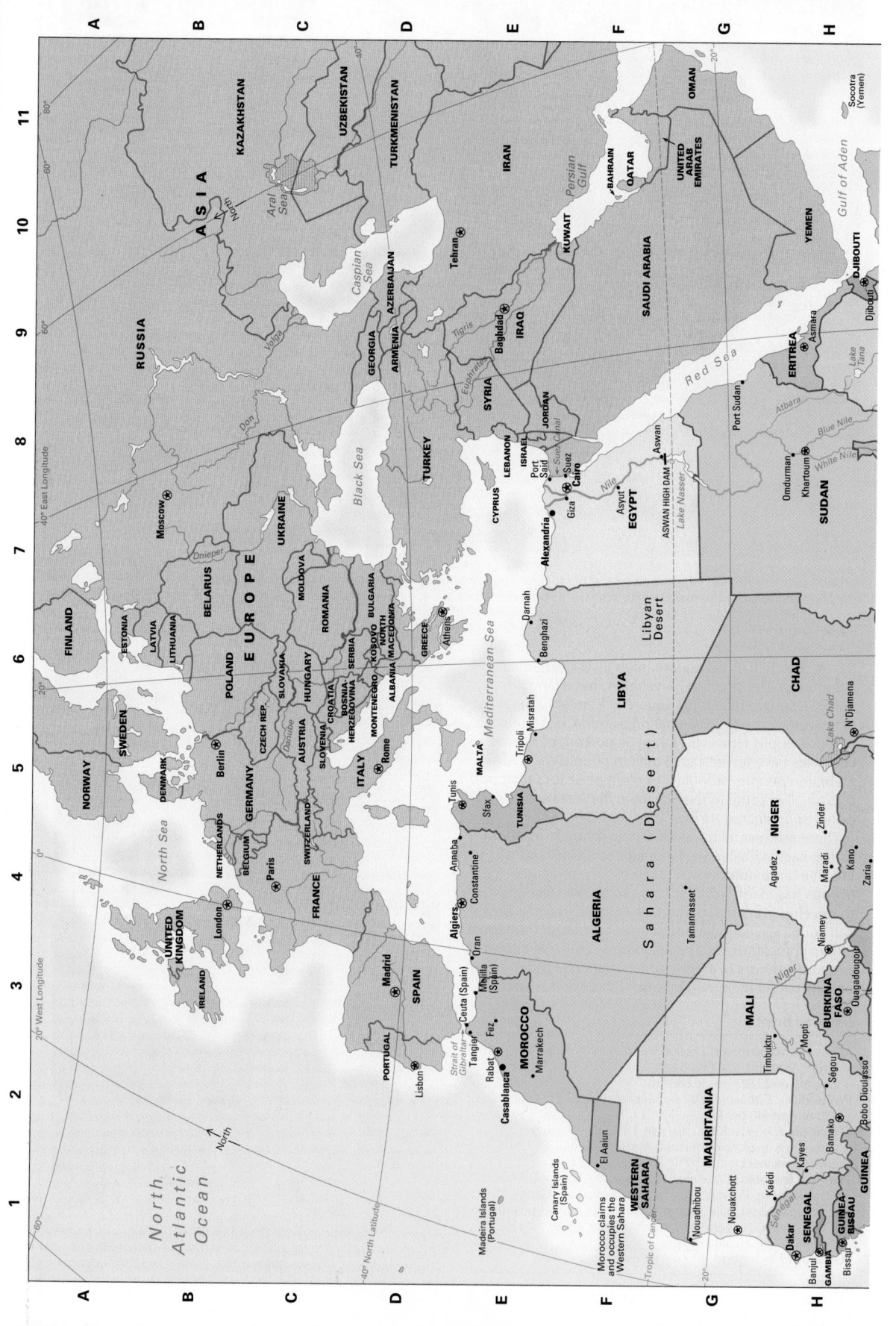

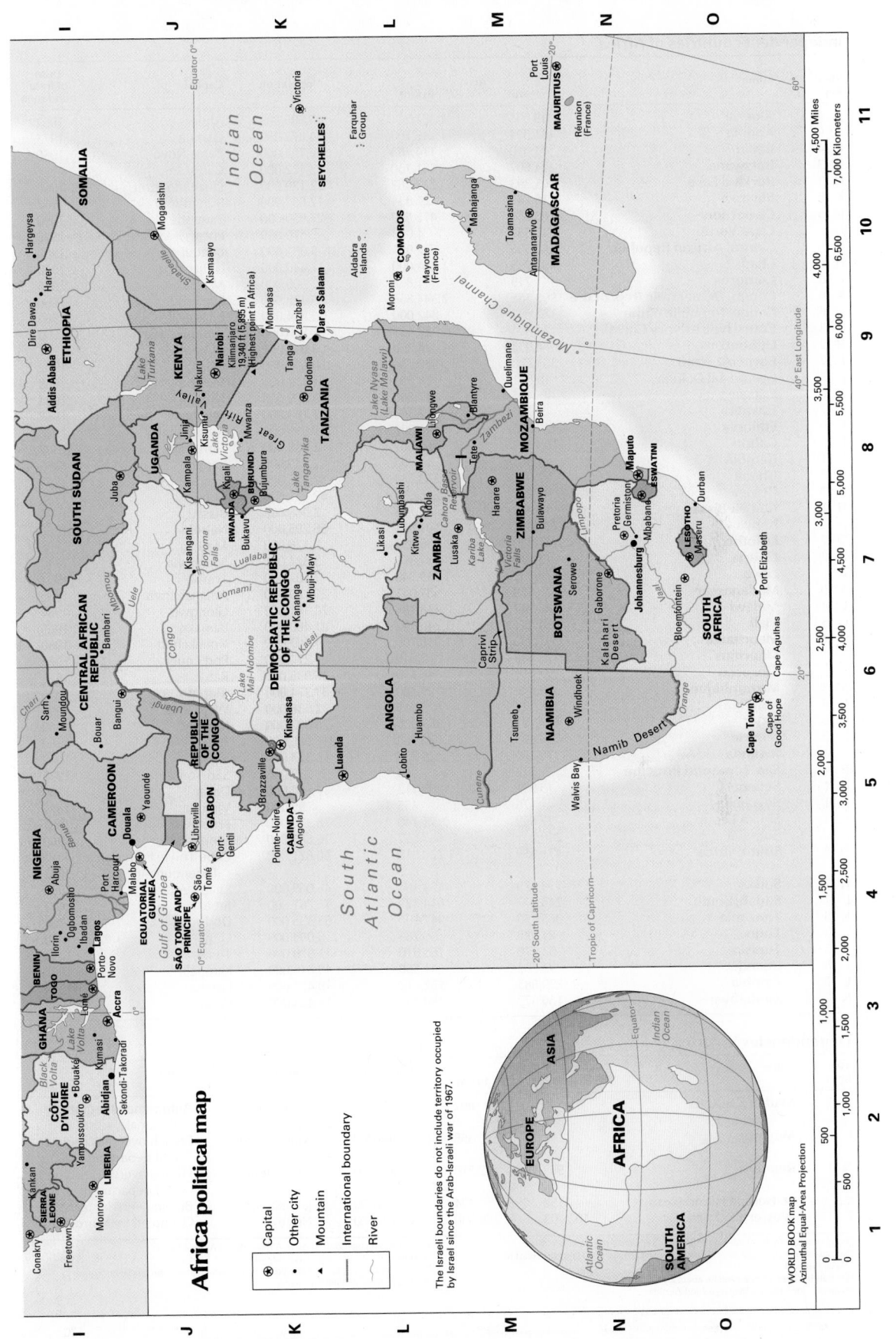

Africa political map

Capital ⊛
Other city •
Mountain ▲
International boundary ——
River 〰

The Israeli boundaries do not include territory occupied by Israel since the Arab-Israeli war of 1967.

WORLD BOOK map
Azimuthal Equal-Area Projection

Independent countries of Africa*

Map key	Name	Area In mi²	Area In km²	Population	Capital	Date of independence
F 4	Algeria	919,595	2,381,741	45,605,000	Algiers	1962
L 6	Angola	481,354	1,246,700	34,872,000	Luanda	1975
I 4	Benin	44,310	114,763	12,794,000	Porto-Novo	1960
N 7	Botswana	224,607	581,730	2,422,000	Gaborone	1966
H 3	Burkina Faso	105,393	272,967	22,120,000	Ouagadougou	1960
K 8	Burundi	10,747	27,834	12,652,000	Bujumbura	1962
I 5	Cameroon	183,650	475,650	27,950,000	Yaoundé	1960
†	Cape Verde	1,557	4,033	570,000	Praia	1975
I 6	Central African Republic	240,535	622,984	5,031,000	Bangui	1960
H 6	Chad	495,755	1,284,000	17,440,000	N'Djamena	1960
L 10	Comoros	719	1,862	909,000	Moroni	1975
K 6	Congo, Democratic Rep. of the	905,355	2,344,858	95,422,000	Kinshasa	1960
J 6	Congo, Republic of the	132,047	342,000	5,804,000	Brazzaville	1960
I 3	Côte d'Ivoire (Ivory Coast)	124,504	322,463	27,820,000	Yamoussoukro	1960
H 9	Djibouti	8,958	23,200	1,019,000	Djibouti	1977
F 7	Egypt (African)	363,220	940,736	104,691,000	Cairo	1922
J 5	Equatorial Guinea	10,831	28,051	1,471,000	Malabo	1968
H 8	Eritrea	45,406	117,600	3,630,000	Asmara	1993
N 7	Eswatini	6,704	17,363	1,183,000	Mbabane	1968
I 9	Ethiopia	426,373	1,104,300	119,699,000	Addis Ababa	‡
J 5	Gabon	103,347	267,667	2,238,000	Libreville	1960
H 1	Gambia	4,361	11,295	2,539,000	Banjul	1965
I 3	Ghana	92,098	238,533	32,326,000	Accra	1957
H 2	Guinea	94,926	245,857	12,551,000	Conakry	1958
H 1	Guinea-Bissau	13,948	36,125	2,068,000	Bissau	1974
J 9	Kenya	228,561	591,971	56,295,000	Nairobi	1963
O 7	Lesotho	11,720	30,355	2,176,000	Maseru	1966
I 2	Liberia	43,000	111,369	5,324,000	Monrovia	1847
F 6	Libya	679,362	1,759,540	7,107,000	Tripoli	1951
M10	Madagascar	226,658	587,041	29,189,000	Antananarivo	1960
L 8	Malawi	45,747	118,484	20,161,000	Lilongwe	1964
G 3	Mali	478,841	1,240,192	21,480,000	Bamako	1960
G 2	Mauritania	397,956	1,030,700	4,407,000	Nouakchott	1960
N 11	Mauritius	788	2,040	1,271,000	Port Louis	1968
E 2	Morocco	172,414	446,550	36,935,000	Rabat	1956
M 8	Mozambique	308,642	799,380	31,774,000	Maputo	1975
N 6	Namibia	318,772	825,615	2,636,000	Windhoek	1990
H 5	Niger	489,191	1,267,000	26,092,000	Niamey	1960
I 5	Nigeria	356,669	923,768	216,956,000	Abuja	1960
J 8	Rwanda	10,169	26,338	13,333,000	Kigali	1962
J 4	São Tomé and Príncipe	372	964	218,000	São Tomé	1975
H 1	Senegal	75,951	196,712	17,644,000	Dakar	1960
K 11	Seychelles	176	455	99,000	Victoria	1976
I 1	Sierra Leone	27,699	71,740	8,320,000	Freetown	1961
I 10	Somalia	246,201	637,657	16,805,000	Mogadishu	1960
O 7	South Africa	471,359	1,220,813	60,621,000	Cape Town; Pretoria; Bloemfontein	1931
H 7	Sudan	718,723	1,861,484	46,069,000	Khartoum	1956
I 7	Sudan, South	248,777	644,329	11,761,000	Juba	2011
K 8	Tanzania	365,756	947,303	63,335,000	Dodoma	1964§
I 3	Togo	21,925	56,785	8,088,000	Lomé	1960
E 5	Tunisia	63,170	163,610	11,970,000	Tunis	1956
J 8	Uganda	93,263	241,550	48,848,000	Kampala	1962
L 7	Zambia	290,585	752,612	19,477,000	Lusaka	1964
N 7	Zimbabwe	150,872	390,757	15,424,000	Harare	1980

Dependencies in Africa*

Map key	Name	Area In mi²	Area In km²	Population	Capital	Status
E 1	Madeira Islands	310	802	255,000	Funchal	Autonomous region of Portugal
L 10	Mayotte	142	368	260,000	Mamoudzou	French overseas region and department
N 11	Réunion	969	2,510	908,000	Saint-Denis	French overseas region and department
#	St. Helena Island Group	152	394	8,000	Jamestown	British overseas territory
F 1	Western Sahara	102,703	266,000	650,000	None	Occupied by Morocco**

*Every country and dependency in Africa has a separate article in *World Book*.
†Not shown on map. In the Atlantic Ocean, about 400 miles (640 kilometers) west of Dakar, Senegal.
‡Ethiopia has been independent for about 2,000 years.
§Date of union between Tanganyika and Zanzibar.

#Not shown on map. Southwest of Africa in South Atlantic Ocean.
**Claimed by Morocco and by the Polisario Front.
Populations are current estimates based on the latest figures from official government, United Nations, and other sources.

differences have led to civil wars in several countries.

Africa has great mineral wealth, including huge deposits of copper, diamonds, gold, and petroleum. It also has valuable forests. In addition, many African rivers and waterfalls could be used to produce hydroelectric power. Africa produces most of the world's cassava, cocoa beans, and yams. But Africa has the least developed economy of any continent except Antarctica.

Agriculture is the leading economic activity in Africa, but most farmers use outdated tools and methods to farm thin, poor soil. About two-thirds of all Africans live in rural areas, where they make a living growing crops or raising livestock. Since the mid-1900's, however, millions of rural Africans have flocked to cities and have adopted a more urban lifestyle. The development of manufacturing has been handicapped by a lack of money to build factories, a shortage of skilled workers, and competition from industries on other continents. Many African countries depend on only one or two farm or mineral products for more than half their export earnings. In case of crop failures or drops in world market prices, a country's economy suffers. The majority of African nations rely to some extent on aid from countries outside the continent.

One of the world's first great civilizations—ancient

Egypt—arose along the banks of the Nile River more than 5,000 years ago. Later, other powerful and culturally advanced kingdoms and empires developed in Africa. Even so, for many years Westerners referred to Africa as the "Dark Continent." They used this name because they knew little about Africa's interior geography, and they mistakenly believed that the people of the interior had not developed any important cultures.

During the late 1400's and 1500's, Europeans began to establish trading posts in Africa. Gold, ivory, and enslaved people became the continent's most valuable exports. By the late 1800's, European nations competed fiercely for control of Africa's resources. By the early 1900's, they had carved almost all of Africa into colonial empires. The European colonizers used their colonies as a source of wealth, exporting natural resources while most of the colonized people lived in poor conditions. Colonial rulers often cared little about local customs and ethnic boundaries.

Many Africans resisted colonial rule from the beginning. But the demands for independence did not become a powerful mass movement until the mid-1900's. Between 1950 and 1980, 47 African colonies gained independence. But years of colonial rule had left Africa poorly prepared in some ways to face the modern

Where the people of Africa live

Africa ranks second in population—after Asia—among the world's continents. This map shows where the people of Africa live and the location of its largest cities. Heavily populated areas are shown in darker colors.

Major urban centers

● More than 5 million inhabitants

• 2 million to 5 million inhabitants

○ Less than 2 million inhabitants

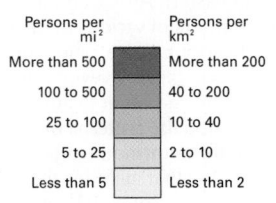

Persons per mi²		Persons per km²
More than 500		More than 200
100 to 500		40 to 200
25 to 100		10 to 40
5 to 25		2 to 10
Less than 5		Less than 2

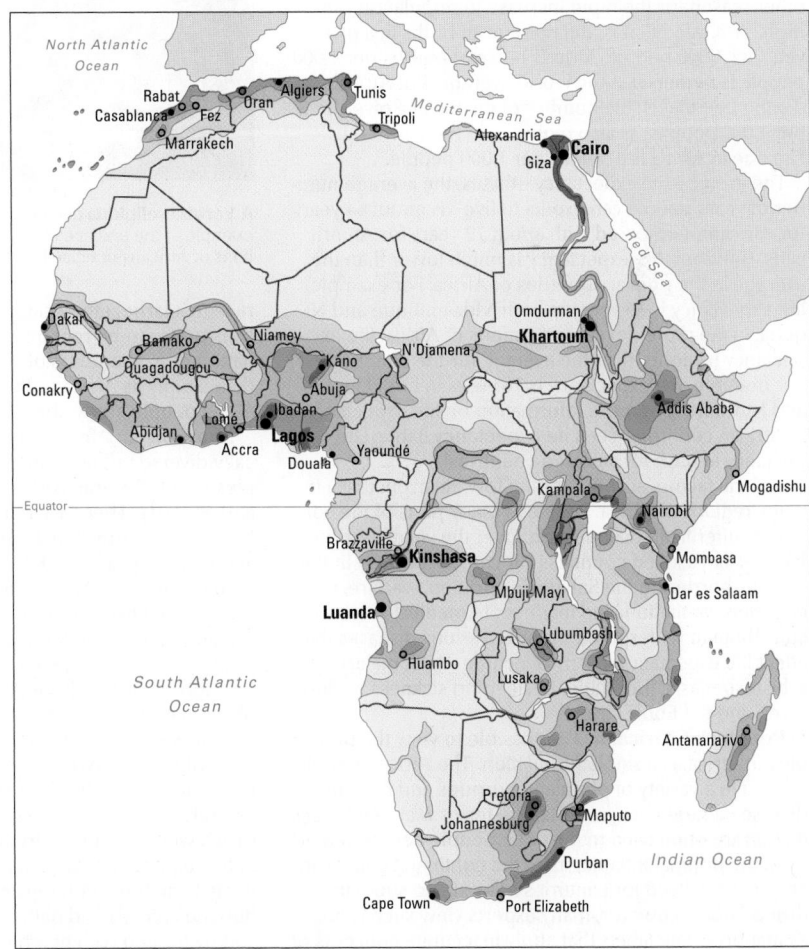

WORLD BOOK map

world. Leaders in many of the new nations managed their national economies poorly and struggled with the ethnic differences and other social challenges facing them. Military officers overthrew the governments of many nations. In a few countries, military dictatorships emerged. In most other countries, a single political party became the ruling power.

Today, ethnic rivalries and territorial disputes among nations continue to threaten the stability of Africa. Such problems as overpopulation, poverty, famine, corruption, and disease remain challenges for African leaders.

People

Population. Africa's population is distributed unevenly. Large areas of the Sahara and other deserts have no people at all. Some dry grasslands and tropical forests are also thinly populated. On the other hand, certain areas are greatly overcrowded. The Nile River Valley in Egypt is one of the most heavily populated regions on Earth. It has an average of about 3,500 people per square mile (1,352 per square kilometer). Other heavily populated areas include sections of the Mediterranean coast; parts of Nigeria and the west coast; the lakes region of eastern Africa; and the southeast coast.

Africa's population is increasing rapidly, partly because of improvements in medical care for children. Another reason for the rapid increase in population is a high birth rate—that is, the number of births in a given year per 1,000 people. Africa's rate of 34 births per 1,000 people is higher than the world average. But Africa's death rate—that is, the number of deaths in a given year per 1,000 people—is also higher than the world rate. The rate in Africa is 8 deaths per 1,000 people.

The average life expectancy—that is, the average number of years people can expect to live—is about 64 years for Africans, compared with about 79 years for Americans. However, life expectancy is much lower than the average in the poorer countries of Africa. For example, life expectancy is 55 years in both Mozambique and Nigeria. In the more developed nations of Africa, life expectancy is higher than the average for the continent. For example, life expectancy is 76 years in both Libya and Morocco. For more information on life expectancy in African countries, see **Life expectancy** (table: Life expectancy at birth for selected countries).

Several factors account for the low life expectancy in many regions of Africa. People in many parts of the continent suffer from malnutrition. Over the years, terrible famines have killed countless Africans, especially in the regions bordering the Sahara. In addition, warfare, poverty, poor sanitation, and inadequate medical services contribute to widespread disease. Serious diseases that affect life expectancy in Africa include AIDS, malaria, schistosomiasis, tuberculosis, sleeping sickness, yellow fever, and the Ebola virus.

Peoples of Africa. It is impossible to view the peoples of Africa as a single population. The African people belong to a variety of population groups and have many diverse cultural backgrounds. The terms *Black* and *Black African* are often used to describe people descended from the original inhabitants of the continent, whose ancestors have lived for centuries in west and sub-Saharan Africa. Today, however, many experts view such terms as inappropriate labels that apply inaccurate concepts of

© Sarah Errington Porlock, Eye Ubiquitous & Hutchinson

A Yoruba religious ceremony in Nigeria, *shown here,* is an example of the practice of an African traditional religion. Millions of Africans practice local traditional religions.

race to a large, ethnically diverse population. Most Africans prefer to be recognized as citizens of a particular nation or as members of a particular ethnic group rather than simply as Africans. In the north, for example, most of the people are Arabs.

Sub-Saharan Africans include the oldest, most genetically diverse human populations in the world. The peoples of sub-Saharan Africa have rich and varied cultures and ancestry. There are hundreds of ethnic groups. Some of the largest include the Igbo and Yoruba of west and central Africa, the Kikuyu of eastern Africa, and the Zulu of southern Africa. The members of various ethnic groups are linked by a shared history, culture, language, religion, artistic tradition, and way of life. However, migration, intermarriage, colonization, and other factors throughout history have complicated the patterns of physical and cultural diversity in this enormous region.

Pygmies are an African population that includes the Aka, Mbuti, Efe, Twa, and other ethnic groups who inhabit the tropical forests of the Congo River Basin in central Africa. The term *Pygmy* comes from an ancient Greek word and refers to the characteristic short stature of these people. Today, many people consider this name insulting. Traditionally, these people have lived by hunting animals and gathering plant foods in the forest and by trading with nearby agricultural groups.

The Khoikhoi and San are among the most ancient cultures in the world. The San and various Khoikhoi groups once lived throughout much of the southern and eastern parts of Africa. The two groups speak related languages characterized by clicking sounds. Today, the only remaining Khoikhoi populations are the Nama people who live in Namibia and a smaller population in Botswana and South Africa. The San live mainly in the Kalahari Desert of Botswana and Namibia and also in parts of South Africa and Angola.

Most of Africa's millions of Arabs live in Egypt, in northern Sudan, and along the Mediterranean coast. The first Arabs settled in northern Africa in the 600's.

Berbers have lived in the northwestern part of Africa since prehistoric times. The term *Berber* comes from a Greek word meaning *foreigner* or *non-Greek speaker.* Today, most Berbers and many experts prefer the term Amazigh instead of Berber (or the plural, Imazighen). The language they speak is called Tamazight. The Berbers live throughout much of northern Africa and the Sahara, mainly in Algeria, Libya, Morocco, Mauritania, Western Sahara, Mali, and Niger.

Europeans began to settle in Africa during the 1600's. Most of the continent's people of European ancestry are of British, Dutch, or French descent. The majority live along the Mediterranean coast, in the Republic of South Africa, in Zimbabwe, and in parts of east Africa.

Many people of Asian ancestry live in southern and eastern Africa. Most of them are descendants of people who came to Africa from India during the 1800's. Large numbers of people of Asian ancestry also live in Madagascar, an island country southeast of the African mainland. Their ancestors began to migrate to Madagascar from Indonesia about 2,000 years ago.

Languages. Most African ethnic groups have their own language or dialect. In some cases, members of different groups speak the same language. The peoples of Africa speak more than 1,000 languages. As a result, communication among Africans is difficult at times. But certain languages, such as Arabic, Swahili (also called Kiswahili), and Hausa, are widely spoken. In addition to their own language, millions of Africans speak one or more other languages, which they use when traveling or conducting business and government affairs. The languages spoken in Africa can be classified into six broad families: (1) Niger-Congo, (2) Nilo-Saharan, (3) Khoisan, (4) Afro-Asian, (5) Indo-European, and (6) Austronesian. The first three families, known as *indigenous African languages,* originated in Africa and are limited to the continent.

Niger-Congo languages make up the largest of the African language families and are spoken throughout sub-Saharan Africa. This family includes about 300 Bantu languages spoken in central, eastern, and southern Africa. The term *Bantu* refers to both the languages and the groups of people who speak them. Swahili is the most widely spoken Bantu language. Other important Bantu languages are Ganda (Luganda), Kikuyu (Kikikuyu or Gigikuyu), Kongo (Kikongo), Rundi (Kirundi), Sesotho, and Zulu (isiZulu). The Niger-Congo family also includes many non-Bantu languages spoken mainly in western and central Africa. These languages include Akan; Igbo, or Ibo; and Yoruba.

Nilo-Saharan languages are used by people who live in parts of Chad, Kenya, Mali, Niger, Sudan, Tanzania, and Uganda. Major languages in this family include Bari, Dinka, Kalenjin, Kanuri, and Maasai.

Khoisan languages are sometimes called *click languages* because many words are expressed with unusual click sounds. These languages are unrelated to any other African language. The San and Khoikhoi of southwestern Africa speak Khoisan languages. Two small ethnic groups in Tanzania, the Hadza and Sandawe, also speak these languages.

Afro-Asian languages are spoken throughout the northern half of Africa. The Afro-Asian language family includes Arabic and Berber (also called Tamazight), the two major languages of northernmost Africa. More Africans speak Arabic than any other single language. Other Afro-Asian languages include Amharic, Afaan Oromo, Hausa, and Somali.

Indo-European languages. A large number of educated Africans speak English, French, or Portuguese in addition to their local language. The use of these European languages remains as a reflection of colonial rule in many African nations. English, French, or Portuguese serves as the official language in many countries and helps unify the people. European languages are also important for communication in international business and government affairs. Two Indo-European languages—Afrikaans and English—are widely spoken in southern Africa. The Afrikaans language developed from the speech of early Dutch settlers in southern Africa. Many of the people of Asian descent who live in southern and eastern Africa speak various Indian languages. Most of them also know English.

Austronesian languages. The people of Madagascar—the Malagasy—speak Malagasy, a language of the Austronesian family. Their ancestors arrived in Madagas-

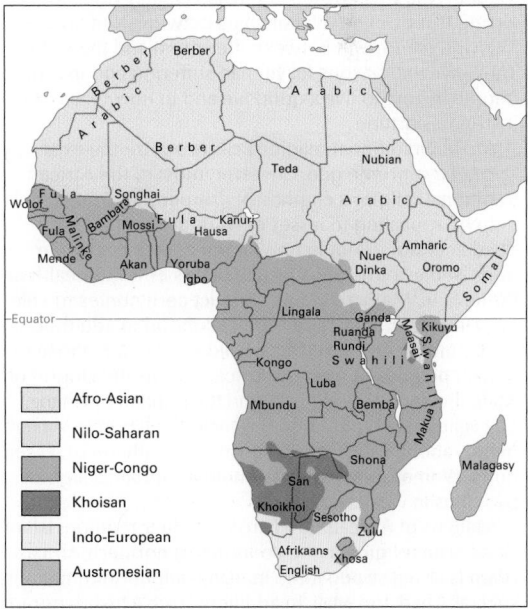

WORLD BOOK map

The major languages spoken in Africa are shown by labels on this map. The colors on the map indicate the language families to which the languages belong.

© Afrique Photo

Islam is one of the leading religions in Africa. Most people in the north practice Islam. But the religion is also practiced by many other Africans, such as these Nigerians praying to Allah.

car from southeast Asia around 2,000 years ago. This language family is not found among the ethnic groups of mainland Africa.

Religions. Millions of Africans practice local traditional religions. There are hundreds of African traditional religions because each ethnic group has its own set of beliefs and practices. In general, however, local religions have many features in common. They explain how the universe was created and teach what is right and wrong. They define relationships between human beings and nature and between the young and the old. They give the reasons for human suffering and instruct people in how to live a good life and in how to avoid or lessen misfortune.

African traditional religions all recognize the existence of a supreme god. However, most of the African traditional religions emphasize that people should seek help by appealing to lesser gods or to the spirits of dead ancestors. People pray or offer sacrifices to the gods or the spirits to gain such things as good health or fertile land. Many religions conduct ceremonies to celebrate a person's passage from childhood to adulthood.

The more complex African religions include those of certain peoples of western Africa, such as the Dogon of Mali, the Yoruba of Nigeria, and the Ashanti of Ghana. The religions of these peoples include elaborate sets of beliefs about a supreme being and a pantheon of lesser gods. Women as well as men hold important religious positions in western Africa.

Millions of Africans are Muslims. Their religion, Islam, is the state religion in the countries of northern Africa. Islam is also a strong force in many neighboring nations, such as Chad and Mali. In addition, large Muslim populations have great influence in such countries as Djibouti, Somalia, Sudan, Nigeria, and Tanzania.

Millions of other Africans are Christians. Most of them

© Afrique Photo

The Ethiopian Orthodox Church is a major Christian church in Ethiopia. In this picture, Abune Paulos, leader of the Ethiopian Orthodox Church, reads from the Bible.

The Nile River Valley in Egypt is one of the most densely populated regions on Earth. Today, Egyptian farmers work irrigated fields using age-old methods in the shadow of the pyramids, the remains of one of the world's oldest civilizations.

belong to the Roman Catholic Church or to various Protestant churches. The Ethiopian Orthodox Church is the largest church of Ethiopia. In Egypt, a few million people belong to the Coptic Orthodox Church. A growing number of Africans belong to *syncretic* African churches. These churches combine Christian or Islamic beliefs with traditional African practices.

Ways of life in northern Africa

The six countries of northern Africa—Mauritania, Morocco, Algeria, Tunisia, Libya, and Egypt—have much in common. A large majority of the people speak the same language, Arabic; practice the same religion, Islam; and share the same history. Northern Africa lies along the Mediterranean Sea, and the region has long been in close contact with Europe and the Middle East. The Middle East has been the most important influence on the culture and history of northern Africa since the arrival of the Arab people in the 600's. Today, northern Africa is an important part of the Arab world.

In addition to the Arab Muslim majority, northern Africa has minority groups that differ in language or religion. For example, the Berbers or Imazighen share the Islamic religion, but many maintain their own culture and language. Sub-Saharan Africans form another important minority group. Many of them speak Arabic and practice Islam. An important religious minority group in Egypt is the Copts. They are Christians who speak Arabic and follow many Arab ways of life.

The following discussion deals chiefly with the ways of life among the Arab Muslim majority in northern Africa, but even within this group there are important differences. For more information, see the separate articles on the countries that make up the region.

Rural life. About half the people in northern Africa live in rural areas. Most of them raise livestock or grow crops on small plots of land. They do much of the work by hand or with the help of animals. In some areas, farmers work on larger farms where machinery and modern agricultural practices are used. Governments or wealthy individuals own many of these large farms. Many rural people lack sufficient land to support their families and must work as laborers or move to the cities or to foreign countries to find jobs. Small groups of nomads called Bedouins tend camels, goats, and sheep. Today, less than 10 percent of north Africans live as nomads.

In many rural parts of northern Africa, the people live in flat-roofed houses with thick adobe walls that help keep out the region's intense heat. In highland areas, houses are more often made of stucco or stone. Most rural homes are simply furnished and lack many modern conveniences. Private generators supply power in many communities, and cellular telephones have enabled rural people to maintain contact with others.

City life. Cairo, the capital of Egypt, is the largest city in northern Africa. About 9 ½ million people live in the city. Other cities of northern Africa with more than a million people are Alexandria, Giza, and Shubra al Khaymah in Egypt; Algiers, Algeria; Casablanca, Morocco; and Tripoli, Libya.

The architecture of most cities in the north reflects a

A rural village in Morocco has houses with flat roofs and thick adobe walls. Many houses in northern Africa have thick walls to help keep out the region's intense heat.

A city square in Algiers, Algeria, is lined with small shops and residences. The large building in the background with the two towers is a *mosque* (Islamic house of worship).

© Shutterstock

combination of European and Islamic styles. Many *mosques* (Islamic houses of worship) and *suqs* (outdoor markets) are typical features of the large cities. Older neighborhoods often lie within the remnants of city walls, some of them centuries old. In these quarters, houses and shops are crowded along narrow, winding streets. Broad boulevards, parks, and modern apartment and office buildings occupy newer sections.

Most city dwellers in northern Africa have a higher standard of living than rural people. The cities offer better medical facilities and schools, and most city workers earn more than rural people. Factories and such services as banks, insurance companies, and government offices are concentrated in urban centers. Hospitals and clinics are also more common in the cities.

The attractions of urban life have led many rural people to move to the cities. Many move in with relatives, but others can afford to live only in slums. Such neighborhoods consist of substandard dwellings, have inadequate sanitary facilities, and lack many public services.

Marriage and family. At one time, Islamic traditions regulated marriage practices and family life throughout northern Africa. These traditions included *polygyny*—the right of a man to have more than one wife. They also required a bride's family to give a *dowry* of household goods or money to the bridegroom. In addition, parents usually selected a husband or wife for each of their children. Today, polygyny remains legal in every northern country except Tunisia. Dowries are less common, but many people still consider at least a token dowry as essential. Arranged marriages have also decreased, though parents exert more influence on their children's choice of a spouse than do parents in Western cultures.

A typical rural household in much of northern Africa consists not only of parents and children but also of grandparents, aunts, uncles, and cousins. These *extended families* provide security, financial help, and social life. In the cities, the *nuclear family,* which consists only of parents and their children, is more common. But even in urban areas, grandparents and other relatives often share the household with the nuclear family.

The traditional role of women in northern Africa has been to remain at home to care for their families. Many

© Thinkstock

Freshly baked bread is delivered daily to shops and restaurants throughout North Africa. Here, a bicyclist balances a load of bread amid busy Cairo traffic.

© Woodfin Camp, Inc.

Mint tea is a favorite ending to a meal among the people of northern Africa. The people also drink coffee, soft drinks, fruit juice, and other beverages.

in traditional clothing. The men wear long, loose robes and usually cover their heads with a turban or skullcap. In mountainous regions, where winter weather can be severe, a heavy, hooded woolen cloak called a *burnoose* provides additional warmth. The women wear long, simple dresses, sometimes with baggy trousers underneath. In public, rural women add a cloak or shawl, cover their heads, and often follow the Islamic tradition of covering the face with a veil.

Many city dwellers dress in clothing like that worn by Europeans and Americans, but more traditional forms of apparel have become increasingly popular, especially among women. Women who customarily dress in European or American fashions often wear a head covering in conformity with Muslim principles.

Education. Traditionally, only religious scholars received more than an elementary school education in northern Africa. During the colonial period, European settlers established schools, but the schools served only their own children and those of a handful of important local leaders. Today, about four-fifths of the people can read and write. The *literacy rate* (percentage of people who can read and write) is much lower in rural areas than in the cities and much lower among women than among men.

The nations of northern Africa are working to improve education, especially in rural areas. However, the population is growing faster than new schools can be built, and the costs of education are constantly increasing. Many areas have a shortage of qualified teachers, and many students must leave school to work and help support their families. Rural children often have to travel great distances to attend school. More students, however, are going on to high school and college. A few universities in northern Africa are among the most modern in the Arab world.

older women and those who live in rural regions still follow this tradition. But a growing number of younger women have taken advantage of education and career opportunities and now work outside the home.

Food and drink. Flat breads and other grain products are the basic foods in northern Africa. *Couscous,* coarse grains of wheat steamed and served with a spicy stew, is a common dish in much of the region. Vegetables, often served in soups, are an important part of regional diet, as are fresh fruits. People in coastal regions often eat fish and other seafoods. Refrigerated trucks now make it possible to ship seafood to the interior, where fish consumption has increased greatly. Meat is too expensive to be part of the daily diet of most people, but chicken, goat, or lamb are enjoyed occasionally.

Tea, mint tea, and coffee are preferred hot beverages. Soft drinks and citrus and other juices are locally produced in each country, as are a wide variety of canned and processed foods.

Clothing. Many people in rural northern Africa dress

Ways of life in sub-Saharan Africa

In general, sub-Saharan Africans follow their traditional ways and observe the customs of their ancestors. Most Africans live in rural areas and make a living by farming the land.

Mineral wealth has brought greater economic development to parts of southern Africa than to any other

© Giacomo Pirozzi, Panos Pictures

Educational opportunities in northern Africa have improved, especially in rural areas. These students in Algeria study local newspapers in a media-studies class. Many students go on to college.

© Eye Ubiquitous & Hutchinson

Cattle herding is a proud tradition south of the Sahara for such groups as the Dinka, Fulani, Maasai, and Turkana. Cattle symbolize wealth for these people. Most groups use dairy products from the cattle but seldom eat meat. The people move with their herds to seasonal pastures.

section of the continent. But much of the wealth from mineral production is held by people of European ancestry, who form a politically and economically powerful minority in parts of southern Africa.

This section mainly describes the ways of life among Africans living south of the Sahara. For additional information, see the separate country articles.

Rural life. About 60 percent of all Africans south of the Sahara live in rural areas, chiefly in villages. Villages vary considerably in size and population. Whatever its size, each village is a closely knit community of families usually belonging to the same ethnic group and often related through either birth or marriage.

Among some ethnic groups, kings and chiefs command great respect, though they may have limited political power. In most cases, the position of king or chief is inherited and serves as a means to link villages of the same ethnic group. Among other ethnic groups, village elders may handle matters of local concern.

Many villages are simply a cluster of houses, surrounded by farmland. Larger settlements may have a schoolhouse, a few shops, and perhaps such facilities as a medical dispensary or a courthouse. Most villages also have a central square. The people gather in the central square for visiting, entertainment, and ceremonies.

Rural housing varies from village to village, depending on climate, lifestyle, and tradition. Many Africans live in houses built of sun-dried mud with roofs of straw, grass, or leaves. As villagers become wealthy, they may construct houses of concrete blocks with sheet-metal roofs. Almost all villages have dwellings of this type. In parts of western Africa, some houses are covered with clay and decorated with sculptured designs. The houses of African Muslims may be built around a large courtyard so that the women can go about their tasks without being seen by people outside the family. This custom follows the traditions of Islam.

In many villages, the way of life has changed little

© John Henshall, Alamy Images

An outdoor market attracts shoppers in Basse Santa Su, a town in eastern Gambia. Many people gather at markets to hear news and socialize.

over the years. Most of the people farm the land and raise some livestock. Modern industrial methods of agriculture are used in parts of South Africa, Kenya, and Zimbabwe and in some countries of western Africa, such as Côte d'Ivoire. But the majority of farmers of sub-Saharan Africa use simple hand tools to work the land.

The soil is thin and poor in much of Africa. The people have thus traditionally practiced an agricultural technique called *shifting cultivation*. A farm community clears the land of trees and bushes and plants crops for several years, until the land wears out. The community then moves to a new location. The abandoned land eventually returns to grass or forest and can be farmed again. Shifting cultivation is still common in certain areas. But in heavily populated regions, resettlement is not possible. As a result, the farmers continue to work land that becomes poorer and poorer.

Most farm families grow food crops for their own use. In the grasslands of eastern and southern Africa, food crops include peanuts and such grains as corn, millet, and sorghum. In wetter areas, food crops include bananas, cassava, plantains, rice, and yams.

Farmers also grow various *cash crops,* including coffee; cacao, or cocoa beans; cotton; coconuts; and fruits. The farmers sell their cash crops for money to buy manufactured goods, especially canned food, clothing, kerosene, lamps, and batteries. The farmers may also use the money from their cash crops to pay taxes as well as medical expenses and school fees.

In addition to growing crops, almost all farmers raise chickens. Many keep goats and sheep. Farmers may also sell livestock or food crops for needed money.

A typical farm family has several widely scattered plots outside the village. Each plot is planted with a different crop. Families may also rent land or farm on land that is owned by village elders and chiefs. Some farmers also work part-time on large estates or plantations that produce cash crops. Both men and women work long hours at farming to make a living.

Rural women also spend much time doing such chores as collecting firewood, grinding grain, and obtaining water. In many villages, however, the introduc-

© Ron Giling, Peter Arnold Inc.

A woman harvests cacao pods by hand at a company-owned plantation in Ghana. The main ingredient in chocolate, cacao is one of Africa's largest export crops.

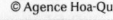
© Agence Hoa-Qui

A modern store in Dakar, Senegal, contrasts sharply with the traditional open-air markets of Africa. Traditional ways of life are changing as more and more rural Africans move to urban areas.

Soccer is popular throughout Africa. Soccer games draw large crowds in cities throughout the continent, and many countries have professional teams and established leagues. This African Champions League game is being played in Tunisia.

© Fethi Belaid, AFP/Getty Images

tion of such simple machines as water pumps and small hand- or machine-driven flour mills has given women more time to do other things. In most villages, everyone takes part in such major tasks as clearing new land and building new houses. The people work together on such tasks, while sharing food and drink and socializing.

Some African farmers—for example, those who live along the Nile River—irrigate their crops. But most farmers depend on seasonal rains. Work and other activities therefore follow a seasonal schedule. During the rainy season, farm families work long, hard days planting and tending their crops. Food may be in short supply at that time of year. During the dry season, after the crops have been harvested, food is more plentiful. The people also have more leisure time. They spend the extra hours repairing tools and houses, visiting with friends and relatives, and trading their crops for other goods. In western Africa, women have traditionally controlled trade activities. Some women have become wealthy as a result of their trading skill. In other areas of Africa, trade matters are handled either by men or women.

Community ceremonies, which are often held in the village square, are an important part of rural African life. They mark such occasions as the first rains of the growing season, the planting of crops, and harvesttime. Entire communities, as well as people from neighboring villages, may gather for ceremonies related to births, marriages, funerals, the curing of the sick, and the passage of children into adulthood. These community gatherings strengthen family ties and religious beliefs.

In many parts of rural Africa, young men leave their villages and work at least a few years as migrant laborers. They travel to cities and towns in hope of earning enough money to get married, to open a small business, or to go to school. In parts of central and southern Africa, many men work temporarily as miners. The women left behind in the villages must do much of the farm work themselves.

Nomadic herding is a way of life for people in parts of Africa, particularly in dry areas near the Sahara and in the highland regions of eastern Africa. Such nomadic

peoples as the Dinka, Fulani, Maasai, Toubou, Tuareg, and Turkana follow well-established routes to find grazing land for their herds of cattle, sheep, goats, or, in some cases, camels. Among some groups, including the Dinka, Maasai, and Nuer, cattle herding is an ancient and proud tradition. For these people, cattle are a measure of a person's wealth and social position as well as a major source of food and other necessities.

The nomadic herders depend mainly on their livestock for food. They also trade meat and milk for grain from neighboring farming groups. The men and boys tend the herds, and the women care for the household. Some nomadic groups, such as the Maasai of eastern Africa, build huge corrals for their livestock. Within the corrals, the people construct igloo-shaped houses of brush, mud, and dried manure. Other nomads live in tents made of animal skins.

City life. City dwellers make up only about 40 percent of sub-Saharan Africa's population. But the percentage is much higher in some countries, such as Angola, Djibouti, Gabon, Liberia, the Republic of the Congo, and South Africa. Throughout Africa, more and more rural people are moving to cities to seek work. Lagos, the chief commercial center of Nigeria, is the largest city in sub-Saharan Africa—and the largest city in Africa. About 12 ½ million people live there. Other cities in sub-Saharan Africa with populations of more than a million include Addis Ababa, Ethiopia; Cape Town, South Africa; Dar es Salaam, Tanzania; Johannesburg, South Africa; Kinshasa, Democratic Republic of the Congo; and Nairobi, Kenya.

In most cities of sub-Saharan Africa, the architecture reflects both traditional and modern styles. The newer sections of many cities have parks, hotels, tall office and apartment buildings, and large stores. Many older neighborhoods have houses and shops crowded along narrow streets. Open-air markets, where people buy food, clothing, and a variety of other goods, are common in many cities.

Like city people in northern Africa, most city dwellers in sub-Saharan Africa have a higher standard of living than rural people. The cities provide better schools and medical facilities than the countryside. For people with skills, the cities may offer well-paying job opportunities in government, business, industry, and other fields.

City lifestyles vary widely. Some people are wealthy and live in luxury apartments or large, modern houses. Most people, however, live in unplanned neighborhoods of small, one-story houses. Many houses are built of wood or concrete blocks with corrugated iron roofs.

Like cities in the north, most cities of sub-Saharan Africa face serious problems. The sharp increase in city populations has made it difficult for governments to provide enough housing and efficient public transportation. The water supply, sewerage, and electrical systems are overloaded. Many cities also have a large number of unemployed workers.

Marriage and family. Strong feelings of loyalty and cooperation bind African families together. Such feelings are shared among all family members, not only parents and children but also grandparents, aunts, uncles, and cousins. The family helps its members with business concerns, employment, legal matters, and other affairs. The family also cares for members who are sick or elderly. Most Africans still seek the advice and approval of their relatives before making any important decision.

According to traditional African beliefs, marriage is more than an agreement between a man and a woman to live together. Marriage is also a way to acquire more relatives, both by gaining in-laws and by having children. In general, the families of the bride and groom must consent to a marriage before it may take place. Among most African peoples, a man or his father or uncles must provide a gift of money, livestock, or other valuables to a woman's family before the man may marry her. This gift is called the *bride price* or *bridewealth*. Africans do not regard the bride price as a payment for the bride but as a way to show her importance and the value they place upon the new ties with her relatives.

Most African ethnic groups permit *polygyny* (marriage to more than one woman). Many men follow this custom and so have more than one wife. The husband is expected to divide his attention and possessions equally among his various families. Each wife expects to have her own house, livestock, and other goods. Feminists, both inside and outside of Africa, and foreign missionaries have tried to end the brideprice and polygyny. But the traditions remain among most sub-Saharan ethnic groups.

Among some African peoples, related families form larger groups called *lineages*. Related lineages are organized into larger groupings called *clans*. All the members of a clan consider themselves to be descended from the same ancestor. Clans are usually represented by symbols called *totems*. Often, members of the same clan are not allowed to marry. Like the family, the clan offers protection, security, and a sense of belonging for its members.

For some sub-Saharan Africans, the strength of family ties has decreased as more and more rural people have moved to the cities. But even in the cities, relatives may live in the same neighborhood, and most city dwellers keep in close touch with relatives in the country.

Food and drink. South of the Sahara, most Africans in both the cities and the countryside eat one large meal daily, usually in the evening. They have only light snacks

© Robert Frerck

Community feasts like this one in Ghana celebrate such events as marriages and births. The gatherings help strengthen the common beliefs and kinship ties that unite African communities.

© Agence Hoa-Qui

Women in Mali grind grain into flour, *shown here*. Both sexes share the farm work in Africa, but certain chores are assigned to either men or women. Food preparation is the work of women.

© Caroline Penn, Panos Pictures

African families are bound by strong feelings of loyalty and co-operation. Extended families with many relatives may live together in a single household, as does this family in Ghana.

at other times of the day. The main meal is a time for socializing with relatives and neighbors. The men and boys generally eat separately from the women and girls. In many households, the people gather around a large bowl of food set on the ground and scoop up the food with their fingers or with pieces of bread.

A typical sub-Saharan African meal consists of a starchy food, such as rice, cassava, or corn cooked into a porridge, or yams. The food is served with a sauce containing vegetables or bits of meat. A common food in tropical areas is the plantain, a large, starchy kind of banana. Plantains may be fried, boiled, baked, or grilled. They may also be dried and ground into flour.

For many African families, meat and fish are expensive and sometimes unavailable. Family members and guests expect such foods on special occasions, however. The people eat chicken, goat, lamb, or beef. Fish are important in the diet of people who live along seacoasts, rivers, and lakes. Africans who keep cattle live largely on milk, cheese, and a thick sour-milk product that resembles yogurt.

Many Africans make beer from honey or from such grains as corn and millet. They also make wine from the sap of certain kinds of palm trees.

In some parts of Africa, the people suffer from malnutrition because of periodic food shortages or the lack of a balanced diet. Long droughts, particularly in regions

near the Sahara, sometimes lead to terrible famines, and thousands of people may die of starvation.

Clothing. Clothing styles vary according to climate and custom throughout sub-Saharan Africa. City dwellers often wear clothing similar to that of North Americans and Europeans. But other city people and most villagers prefer more traditional African clothing, which often features bright colors and bold patterns.

In western Africa and regions near the Sahara, many men wear a long flowing robe or baggy trousers and a loose shirt or tunic. A small cap or turban is also customary among many African men. Many African women take a length of cloth and wrap it around themselves into a dress. They may also wrap a cloth around the head in the style of a turban or scarf. Some Muslim women follow Islamic tradition and cover the face with a veil when they go out in public. Many rural men and women tie a piece of fabric around the waist or at the shoulder to form a cloak. Some African herders wear simple garments made of leather. Colorful necklaces, bracelets, anklets, and earrings are part of the everyday clothing of some Africans. Among the Ashanti of Ghana and certain other ethnic groups, kings and their courts dress in gorgeous robes on special occasions.

Education. Centuries ago, Muslim scholars established near the edges of the Sahara some of the first schools in Africa. These schools taught Islam, the Arabic language, and science. But for most Africans, education did not involve going to school. Parents taught their children what they needed to know to get along in society and to make a living. Some young people, especially in western Africa, served as apprentices in craft associations, where they were trained in such skills as metalworking, woodcarving, pottery making, or weaving.

Christian missionaries taught some sub-Saharan Africans how to read and write as early as the 1500's. But large advances in education did not begin until the 1900's, when the European colonial powers decided they needed more Africans to fill jobs in government and industry. The United Kingdom, France, and other colonial powers established schools in Africa.

Today, many sub-Saharan African governments strive to build schools and to extend education to as many

© Beryl Goldberg

Mission schools were founded in Africa by European missionaries during the colonial period. Such schools remain important because of shortages of public schools and qualified teachers.

College education is available in most African countries. Before the 1940's, most Africans had to go abroad to get a college education. Since then, most countries have built modern universities. However, few Africans can afford to go to college. These students attend the University of Cape Town in the Republic of South Africa.

people as possible. A greater number of Africans than ever are attending elementary school and going on to high school and college.

Despite the progress in education, serious problems remain. A large number of adults in sub-Saharan Africa cannot read and write. However, the literacy rate varies greatly from country to country. In Namibia, South Africa, and Zimbabwe, for example, the literacy rate is higher than 85 percent. But in such countries as Guinea, Mali, and Niger, the literacy rate is less than 40 percent.

In many places, especially rural areas, there is a shortage of schools, educational materials, and qualified teachers. A large number of children do not attend school at all, and many others leave after only a few years to help their families earn a living.

The arts

When one visits a museum to see African art, one often finds masks hanging on a wall or objects placed behind glass cases. Most African art, however, was initially made to be used, whether in a sacred or a secular context. Art in Africa serves an important role as a form of communication.

Ancient art. The oldest known African artworks are prehistoric engravings and paintings that have been found in southern Africa, in the Sahara, and in other areas on rocks and on the walls of caves and rock shelters. They are between 2,000 and 20,000 years old and usually feature hunting scenes with men and animals.

Some of the oldest African sculptures come from ancient Egypt. These include small female figures made of clay and the gigantic Great Sphinx constructed about 4,500 years ago.

The oldest human sculptures from sub-Saharan Africa are *terra-cotta* (baked clay) figures created by the Nok culture of present-day Nigeria between 500 B.C. and A.D. 200. The Nok sculptures are human and animal figures. Most stand no more than 1 foot (30 centimeters) high, but some are nearly life-sized. The Nok people were also among the earliest ironworkers in sub-Saharan Africa. The remains of their low, circular iron-smelting furnaces are found in sites in Nigeria and Benin.

During the 1100's through the 1400's, Yoruba craftworkers in west Africa created tools, weapons, and artworks of brass and iron. In the city of Ife, in what is now Nigeria, artists produced lifelike brass heads depicting royalty, who were regarded as gods. Sculptors in the kingdom of Benin, which flourished in western Africa from the early 1400's to the late 1800's, produced more stylized brass figures of royalty.

Fine arts. The human figure is central to many African art forms. Many figures and masks do not depict an exact likeness of a human face or body. Instead, they highlight certain features that may correspond to a particular concept of beauty or to a belief system. Ashanti carvers of Ghana, for example, favor a high, glossy forehead in the sculpting of female figures. The Mende of Sierra Leone believe that women should be reserved and not talkative. Mende masks generally depict females with a small mouth.

Throughout Africa, the human body itself often becomes a canvas on which to create art. For example, Oromo women in eastern Ethiopia use hairstyle, jewelry, and face paint to communicate their ethnic identity and family to others. Among the Nuba of Sudan, body paintings identify a man's age group or the clan to which he belongs. Among the Nuer of Sudan, patterns of scars cut into the face indicate courage and maturity in men.

Male artists traditionally work with hard materials, such as wood, stone, metals, and bone. Men also produce most ceremonial items, including masks, figures, and musical instruments. African women traditionally work with soft fibrous materials to create such useful objects as baskets, mats, beadwork, and clothing. Some art-making practices, including sewing, leatherwork, pottery, and weaving, are done by either men or women. Male weavers often use a horizontal loom for weaving cloth, while women use a vertical loom.

Materials used in African art often depend on what is available in the environment. African ethnic groups in desert or grassland areas create artworks using such

© Nigel Pavitt from John Warburton-Lee

A beaded necklace worn by a Maasai woman is typical of the decorative objects that many African peoples create using available materials, such as leather, fiber, shells, and beads.

Detail of statue (A.D. 1100-1400); Nigerian Museum, Lagos (© Agence Hoa-Qui)

A metal sculpture from Nigeria is an image of a priest-king of a Yoruba civilization once centered at Ife. The people used sculptures of former kings in ceremonies honoring the dead.

Carved wooden mask; Nelson A. Rockefeller Collection (© Lee Boltin)

A ceremonial mask worn at certain royal events reflects the artistry of the Songe of the Democratic Republic of the Congo.

available materials as stone, bone, clay, leather, and fiber. Woodcarving is most common in west and central Africa where hardwood forests are found. From these materials they make such everyday items as spoons, stools, and headrests.

In northern Africa, artists create beautiful works in a distinct style called *Islamic art.* The artists of northern Africa are also known for their superb textiles, metalwork, glassware, and other craftwork.

Colonialism had a profound effect on the arts of Africa. As European colonial powers introduced Christianity, many art practices associated with traditional African religions declined. Manufactured items replaced handmade objects, such as ceramic vessels, hand-dyed cloth, and woven fiber baskets. However, African artists soon began catering to a new market of middle-class ur-

© Peri Klemm

A beaded gourd is a typical example of African art made for useful purposes.

A wooden stool supported by an ancestor figure symbolizes Songe royal authority.

A wooden spoon like this one is used by the Dan of Liberia to portion rice at feasts.

Nelson A. Rockefeller Collection (© Lee Boltin)

The royal emblem of the Ashanti Empire was a lion made of gold, *shown here.*

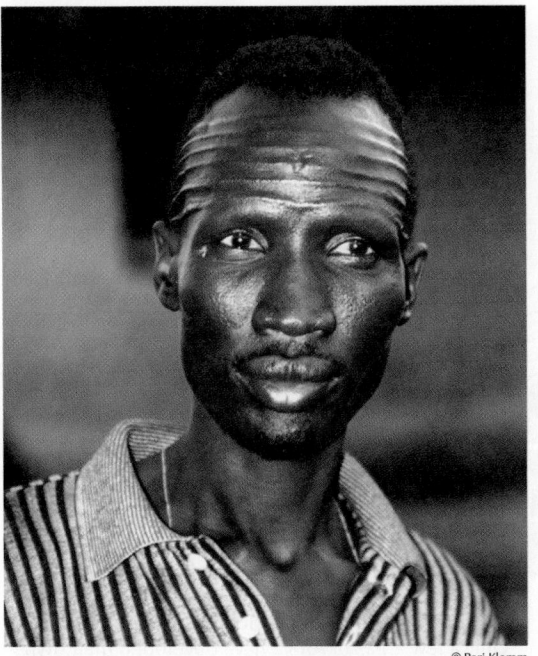

© Peri Klemm

African artists sometimes use the human body as a canvas on which to create art. The patterns of scars cut into the face of this Nuer man from Ethiopia indicate courage and maturity.

© Shutterstock

Rural housing varies according to climate, tradition, and available materials. Houses of the Ndebele of South Africa, *shown here*, are made of dried mud and are colorfully painted.

ban Africans and foreigners and developed new artistic practices.

Many African artists, either self-taught or educated in art academies or mission schools, began depicting their experiences with colonialism and independence. Many contemporary African artists are also heavily influenced by traditional African art forms.

Architecture. Women are the homebuilders in many societies throughout Africa. Among north African nomadic groups, such as the Tuareg, women construct temporary tentlike homes from animal skins supported by wooden posts. The Maasai of east Africa make distinctive loaf-shaped homes of mud, branches, and grass, plastered with cow manure. In southern Africa, Ndebele women build traditional homes and courtyards with a mud plaster. The Ndebele paint their buildings with geometric designs as well as symbols of modern technology, such as light bulbs and airplanes. Outstanding examples of Islamic architecture are seen in the many magnificent mosques throughout northern and western Africa.

Dance and music add to the expressiveness of many visual artworks in Africa. Dance and music often accompany the display of ceremonial art objects in public, such as at a funeral or the installation of a chief. In ceremonies and celebrations throughout Africa, dancers manipulate carved masks to the accompaniment of music. In royal festivals performed by the Kuba people of the Democratic Republic of the Congo, the beat of the drums is necessary to activate the spirit of the masks worn by dancers. Among the Yoruba, *talking drums* imitate the sounds of human speech and are used to relay messages from ancestors, who are embodied by masked dancers during a performance.

© Shutterstock

Architecture in northern Africa ranges from magnificent mosques to simple village houses. The mosque shown here was built in Al Qayrawan, Tunisia, in 1860. It is an excellent example of Islamic architecture.

Dance and music are important elements of ceremonies and celebrations that mark important events in everyday life, such as births, deaths, and harvesttime. The dancers shown here are Zulu people of South Africa.

© Hamilton Wright, Photo Researchers

Music also accompanies many daily events in life in Africa. Singing often sustains the rhythms of manual labor in fields and villages. Traditional African music includes choral singing, music performed for entertainment, and songs and dances for religious events. In Senegal and other parts of west Africa, a professional speaker called a *griot* plays music while reciting history and praising the sponsor of the performance in song.

African musicians use a variety of drums, string instruments, and wind instruments, including harps, horns, flutes, pipes, lyres, zithers, and xylophones. Today, the influence of African music can be heard in Western popular music and jazz, West Indian calypso, and Latin American dance music.

Literature. Africa has a rich tradition of oral literature passed from one generation to the next. This oral literature includes histories of ethnic and kinship groups, legends of heroes, animal fables, proverbs, riddles, and songs in praise of chiefs and kings. Oral literature plays an important role in religious ceremonies. It also serves to record the past, to teach morals and traditions to

young people, and to glorify political leaders.

Only a few areas of Africa have developed their own writing system. The ancient Egyptians developed a hieroglyphic writing system, where pictures represent ideas and sounds, nearly 5,000 years ago. Other African written literatures include *Ge`ez,* a religious script used in Ethiopia since the A.D. 300's. Muslim scholars in Africa have written works in Arabic since the mid-600's. They have written Swahili and Hausa works in Arabic script since the 1500's.

African writers began to produce literature in various sub-Saharan African languages in the 1800's. Most modern African literature is still written in English, French, or Portuguese, the languages of former colonial powers. The plays, novels, and poetry of modern African writers, such as Chinua Achebe and Chimamanda Adichie of Nigeria, Ama Ata Aidoo of Ghana, and Athol Fugard of South Africa, often deal with issues of modernity, colonialism, and postcolonial conditions in Africa.

The land

Africa is an enormous plateau, most of which is covered by deserts, forests, and grasslands.

Land regions. Africa can be divided into two major land regions: (1) Low Africa and (2) High Africa.

Low Africa consists of northern, western, and central Africa. Except for a few coastal plains and mountain ranges, most of the region lies from 500 to 2,000 feet (150 to 610 meters) above sea level. Low Africa can be subdivided into six smaller land regions. They are (1) the Coastal Lowlands, (2) the Northern Highlands, (3) the Saharan Plateau, (4) the Western Plateau, (5) the Nile Basin, and (6) the Congo Basin.

The Coastal Lowlands form a narrow border along most of northern Africa and the bulge of western Africa. The area has fertile farmland, forests, sandy beaches, deserts, and swamps.

The Northern Highlands are a mountainous region that stretches across parts of Algeria, Morocco, and Tunisia. The Atlas Mountains in this region have de-

© Owen Franken, Stock, Boston

Royal music of the Ashanti of Ghana, *shown here,* honors a new chief. Horns and trumpets are common musical instruments in Africa. They may be made of wood, ivory, or animal horns.

posits of phosphate rock, iron ore, and manganese.

The Saharan Plateau covers most of northern Africa. The Sahara, in turn, occupies most of the plateau. Isolated clusters of mountains rise from the plateau in places. Valuable deposits of petroleum and other minerals lie beneath the Sahara. The desert merges with a dry grassland called the Sahel at the southern boundary of the Saharan Plateau.

The Western Plateau lies south of the Saharan Plateau. It consists of forests and grasslands. The Niger and other rivers flow through the region.

The Nile Basin is a flat region that borders the Nile River and its tributaries in northeastern Africa. In addition to fertile farmland along the Nile, the region has deserts in the north and a huge swamp called the Sudd in the south.

The Congo Basin, in west-central Africa, includes the land drained by the Congo River and its tributaries. Tropical rain forests cover much of the Congo Basin.

High Africa consists of eastern and southern Africa. Most of the region is more than 3,000 feet (910 meters) above sea level. High Africa can be subdivided into five smaller land regions. They are (1) the Rift System, (2) the Eastern Highlands, (3) the Southern Plateau, (4) the Coastal Lowlands, and (5) Madagascar.

The Rift System extends from Eritrea to Mozambique. The region consists of the Great Rift Valley, which is a series of parallel cracks in the earth that form deep, steep-sided valleys. The three main lakes in this valley, Lake Victoria, Lake Tanganyika, and Lake Malawi, have many unique species of fish and add to the region's beauty. The region also has some of Africa's best farmland because of its rich volcanic soil.

The Eastern Highlands are grassy plains that provide grazing for livestock and many kinds of wild animals. The Rift System cuts through the Eastern Highlands.

The Southern Plateau covers most of southern Africa. Much of it is flat or rolling grassland used for crops and pasture. The region also has deserts, swamps, and forests. Rugged mountains and cliffs rim the plateau in the south and west. Deposits of diamonds and gold lie in the Southern Plateau.

The Coastal Lowlands border the high plateaus of eastern and southern Africa. The lowlands include productive farmland, sandy beaches, and swamplands.

Madagascar, the world's fourth largest island, lies about 240 miles (390 kilometers) southeast of the mainland in the Indian Ocean. The island can be divided into two chief land regions. The Coastal Lowlands form a narrow band along the east coast and broaden to a wide fertile plain on the west. The Central Highlands, which run almost the full length of the island, have some peaks over 9,000 feet (2,700 meters) above sea level.

Deserts, grasslands, and forests. Deserts cover about two-fifths of Africa. The Sahara, the world's largest desert, stretches across northern Africa from the Atlantic Ocean to the Red Sea. It covers about 3 ½ million square miles (9 million square kilometers). The Sahara is a region of bare rock, boulders, gravel, and sand dunes, broken only by a few oases and the fertile Nile Valley. The Namib Desert borders the Atlantic coast of southwestern Africa. The Kalahari Desert lies inland from the Namib.

Grasslands called *savannas* occupy more than two-

© Victor Englebert, Photo Researchers

Deserts cover about two-fifths of Africa. This oasis is in the Sahara, the world's largest desert. The Sahara stretches across northern Africa between the Atlantic Ocean and the Red Sea.

fifths of Africa. They form a broad curve that extends from the Atlantic coast just south of the Sahara, across eastern Africa, and back westward to the Atlantic south of the Congo Basin. Tall grasses, thorny bushes, and scattered trees grow in this area. Thicker woodlands cover areas with more rainfall. But closer to the deserts, there are fewer trees and shorter grasses.

Forests cover less than a fifth of Africa. Most of the forests are tropical rain forests. These forests, with many kinds of broadleaf evergreen trees, grow in the Congo

© Giacomo Pirozzi, Panos Pictures

Tropical rain forests cover parts of central and western Africa and Madagascar. The Mbuti people, *shown here,* live by hunting and gathering in the rain forest of the Congo Basin.

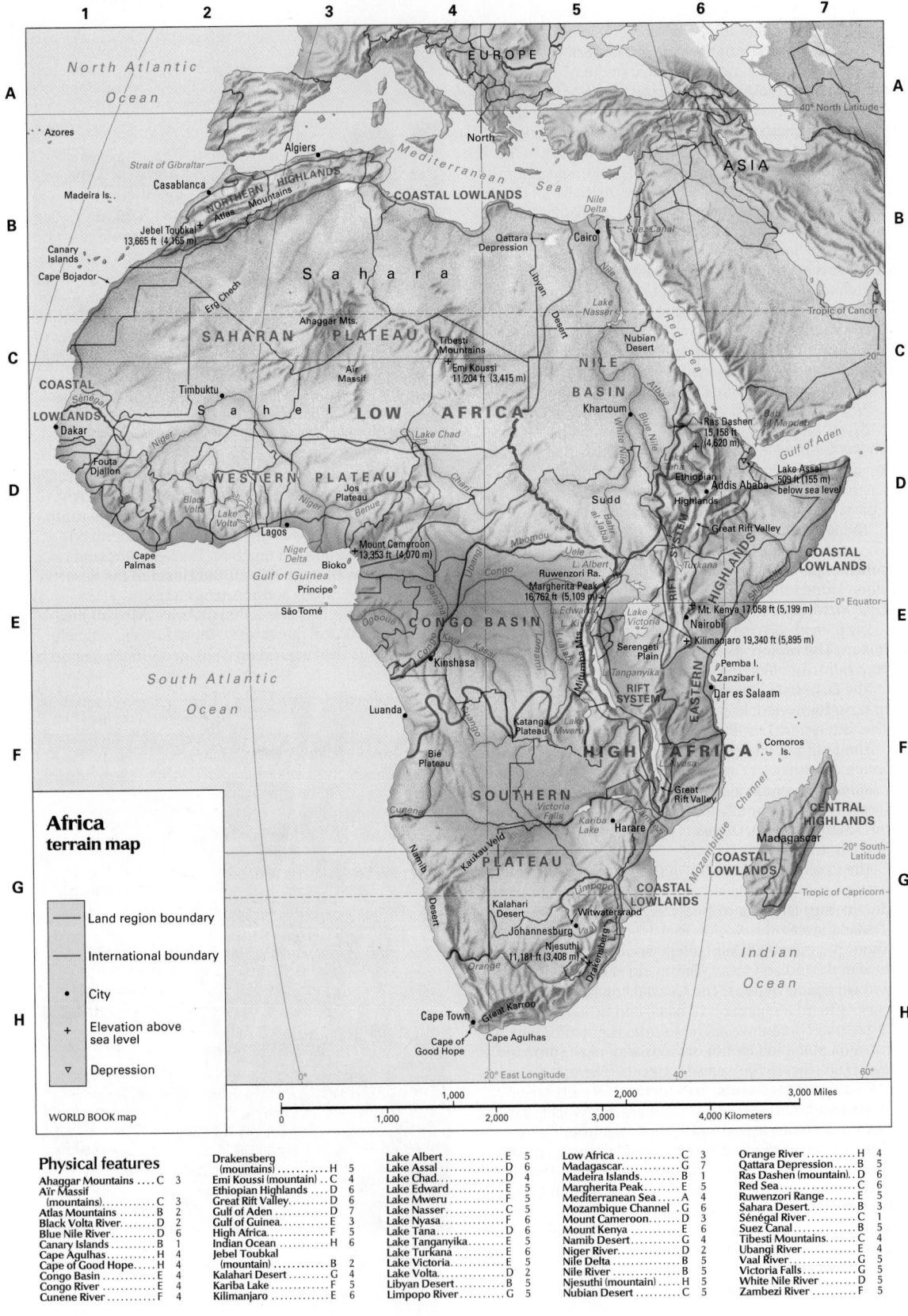

Africa
terrain map

Land region boundary

International boundary

• City

+ Elevation above sea level

▽ Depression

WORLD BOOK map

Physical features

Ahaggar Mountains .... C 3
Aïr Massif
  (mountains) .... C 3
Atlas Mountains .... B 2
Black Volta River ...... D 2
Blue Nile River .... D 6
Canary Islands .... B 1
Cape Agulhas .... H 4
Cape of Good Hope .... H 4
Congo Basin .... E 4
Congo River .... E 4
Cunene River .... F 4

Drakensberg
  (mountains) .... H 5
Emi Koussi (mountain) .. C 4
Ethiopian Highlands .... D 6
Great Rift Valley .... D 6
Gulf of Aden .... D 7
Gulf of Guinea .... E 3
High Africa .... F 5
Indian Ocean .... H 6
Jebel Toubkal
  (mountain) .... B 2
Kalahari Desert .... G 4
Kariba Lake .... F 5
Kilimanjaro .... E 6

Lake Albert .... E 5
Lake Assal .... D 6
Lake Chad .... D 4
Lake Edward .... E 5
Lake Mweru .... F 5
Lake Nasser .... C 5
Lake Nyasa .... F 6
Lake Tana .... D 6
Lake Tanganyika ..... E 5
Lake Turkana .... E 6
Lake Victoria .... E 5
Lake Volta .... D 2
Libyan Desert .... B 5
Limpopo River ...... G 5

Low Africa .... C 3
Madagascar .... G 7
Madeira Islands ...... B 1
Margherita Peak ..... E 5
Mediterranean Sea ... A 4
Mozambique Channel . G 6
Mount Cameroon .... D 3
Mount Kenya .... E 6
Namib Desert ...... G 4
Niger River .... D 2
Nile Delta .... B 5
Nile River .... B 5
Njesuthi (mountain) . H 5
Nubian Desert ..... C 5

Orange River .... H 4
Qattara Depression .... B 5
Ras Dashen (mountain) . D 6
Red Sea .... C 6
Ruwenzori Range ..... E 5
Sahara Desert .... B 3
Sénégal River .... C 1
Suez Canal .... B 5
Tibesti Mountains .... C 4
Ubangi River .... E 4
Vaal River .... G 5
Victoria Falls ...... G 5
White Nile River .... D 5
Zambezi River ...... F 5

© Norman Meyers, Bruce Coleman Collection

Africa's spectacular sights include Victoria Falls, *left*, and Kilimanjaro, *right*, a towering dormant volcano. Victoria Falls is on the Zambezi River, between Zambia and Zimbabwe. Kilimanjaro rises 19,340 feet (5,895 meters) in Tanzania. It is Africa's highest point.

Basin and in parts of western Africa and Madagascar. Other forests grow in the highlands of eastern Africa, the mountains of the northwest, and parts of the south.

Woodlands border the rain forests within the tropical region. Most of these woodlands contain patches of grassland. Dense pockets of tangled mangrove swamp, where the spreading roots of mangrove trees catch and hold soil, fringe some coastal areas. These swamps provide important breeding sites for fish, protect the coast from damaging waves, and clean the water by filtering sediment.

Rivers, waterfalls, and deltas. The Nile River, the world's longest river, flows 4,160 miles (6,695 kilometers) northward from east-central Africa to the Mediterranean Sea. Most of Africa's other major rivers, including the Congo and the Niger, empty into the Atlantic. Rivers that flow into the Indian Ocean include the Limpopo and the Zambezi. All of these rivers flow through several countries and serve as major sources of hydroelectric power. They also provide flood control and water for irrigation or industry. The rivers are also major centers of wildlife *biodiversity*—that is, a variety of plant and animal species—and important sources of fish.

Rapids and waterfalls make navigation difficult on many African rivers. Hydroelectric power projects have been built on a number of rivers. Scientists estimate that the Congo River has the potential to generate enough hydropower for all of Africa's energy needs. Several waterfalls, including spectacular Victoria Falls on the Zambezi, are popular tourist attractions.

Large deltas where the major rivers enter the ocean along the coasts of Africa are important sites for fishing and shrimp farming, as well as critical centers of biodiversity. Major river deltas include the Congo, Niger, Nile, and Zambezi deltas. The Niger Delta in Nigeria is also an important region for its oil deposits.

Lakes. Most of Africa's large lakes lie in the east, where chains of long, deep lakes have formed in the bottoms of the narrow valleys called *rift valleys.* One of these lakes, Tanganyika, is the longest freshwater lake in the world. It is 420 miles (680 kilometers) long and more than 4,700 feet (1,430 meters) deep. Other large rift lakes include Albert, Malawi, and Turkana. Africa's largest lake, Victoria, lies in a shallow basin between two chains of rift valleys. It covers 26,800 square miles (69,500 square kilometers) and is second in size only to Lake Superior in North America among the world's freshwater lakes. The rift valley lakes are centers of biodiversity and support many unique fish species.

Mountains. Volcanic activity created most of Africa's highest mountains. The two tallest peaks—19,340-foot (5,895-meter) Kilimanjaro and 17,058-foot (5,199-meter) Mount Kenya—were formed in this way. Although they rise near the equator in eastern Africa, both mountains have glaciers and are covered with snow much of the year. Volcanic activity also produced the Ethiopian Highlands; the isolated Tibesti Mountains in the Sahara; and Mount Cameroon, the highest peak in western Africa. Volcanic rock covers the Drakensberg, a mountainous region where the plateau of southeastern Africa drops sharply to the sea.

Two major nonvolcanic mountain ranges of Africa are the Ruwenzori Range and the Atlas Mountains. The Ruwenzori Range rises on the border of Uganda and the Democratic Republic of the Congo. The Atlas Mountains extend from Morocco to Tunisia and form Africa's longest mountain chain. The Atlas Mountains are part of the same mountain system as the European Alps.

Climate

Most of Africa has a warm or hot climate, but the humidity and amount of rainfall vary dramatically from area to area. The maps in this section illustrate Africa's climate patterns, the average January and July tempera-

Lake Turkana is one of the long, deep lakes common in east Africa. These lakes formed in the bottoms of narrow valleys called *rift valleys.* The Turkana people who live near the lake fish and raise livestock for a living.

© Nigel Pavitt from John Warburton-Lee

What Africa's climate is like

Much of Africa has a tropical or desert climate. This map and legend show what the climate is like throughout the continent.

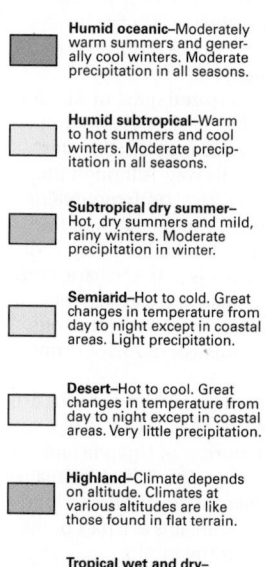

Humid oceanic–Moderately warm summers and generally cool winters. Moderate precipitation in all seasons.

Humid subtropical–Warm to hot summers and cool winters. Moderate precipitation in all seasons.

Subtropical dry summer–Hot, dry summers and mild, rainy winters. Moderate precipitation in winter.

Semiarid–Hot to cold. Great changes in temperature from day to night except in coastal areas. Light precipitation.

Desert–Hot to cool. Great changes in temperature from day to night except in coastal areas. Very little precipitation.

Highland–Climate depends on altitude. Climates at various altitudes are like those found in flat terrain.

Tropical wet and dry–Always hot, with alternate wet and dry seasons. Heavy precipitation in wet season.

Tropical wet–Always hot and wet. Heavy precipitation well distributed throughout year.

WORLD BOOK map

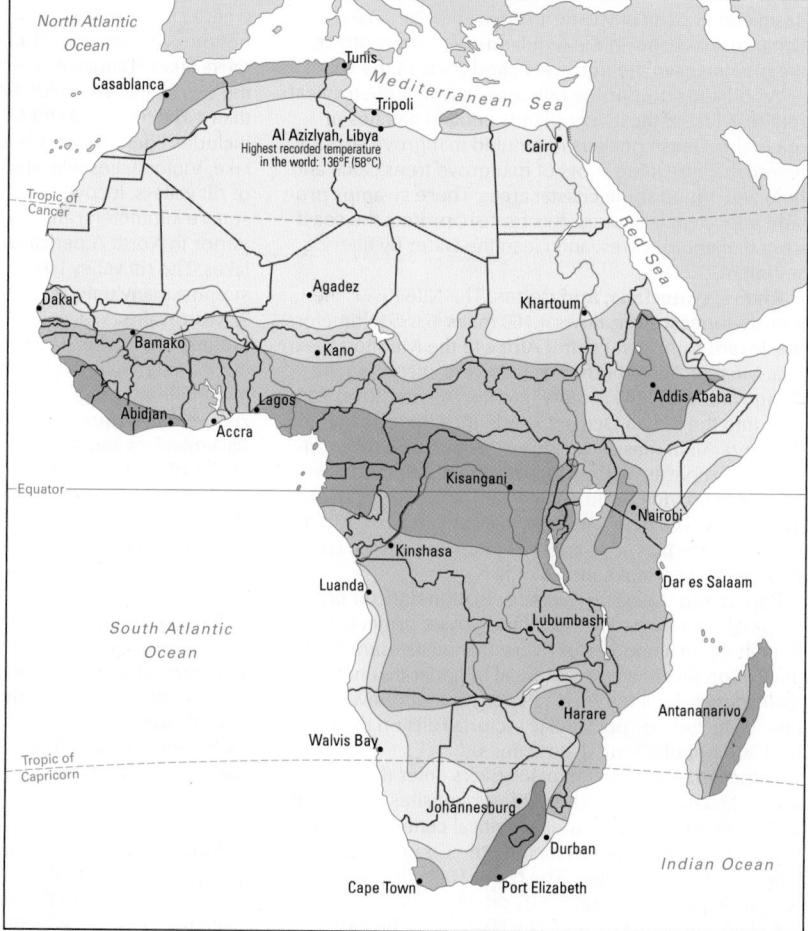

North Atlantic Ocean

Mediterranean Sea

Casablanca
Tunis
Tripoli
Cairo

Al Azizlyah, Libya
Highest recorded temperature
in the world: 136°F (58°C)

Tropic of Cancer

Red Sea

Dakar
Agadez
Khartoum

Bamako
Kano

Abidjan
Lagos
Accra
Addis Ababa

Equator

Kisangani
Nairobi

Kinshasa
Dar es Salaam

Luanda
Lubumbashi

South Atlantic Ocean

Harare
Antananarivo

Tropic of Capricorn

Walvis Bay

Johannesburg
Durban
Indian Ocean

Cape Town
Port Elizabeth

tures, and the average yearly *precipitation* (rain, melted snow, and other forms of moisture).

Africa has the largest tropical area of any continent in the world. The equator runs through the middle of Africa, and about 90 percent of the continent is located within the tropics. Temperatures are high the year around almost everywhere. The variations between summer and winter temperatures are slight. The difference between daytime and nighttime temperatures in most of the continent is greater than the difference in the average temperatures between the coldest and warmest months.

Africa's highest temperatures occur in the Sahara and in parts of Somalia. At I-n-Salah, Algeria, and along the north coast of Somalia, July temperatures soar to 115 °F (46 °C) or higher on most days. Nighttime temperatures, however, may drop sharply. In addition, the Sahara has the greatest seasonal range of temperatures in Africa. Temperatures during the winter in the Sahara average from 50 to 60 °F (10 to 16 °C). Near the equator, temperatures may average 75 °F (24 °C) or more the year around. However, temperatures of more than 100 °F (38 °C) are rare.

The coolest regions in Africa are the northwest, the eastern highlands, and parts of the south. In Johannesburg, South Africa, for example, the average temperature in January, the warmest month of the year, is 68 °F (20 °C). Frost and snowfall are common in the mountains of Africa.

Rainfall is distributed unevenly in Africa, and most areas receive either too much rain or too little. In parts of

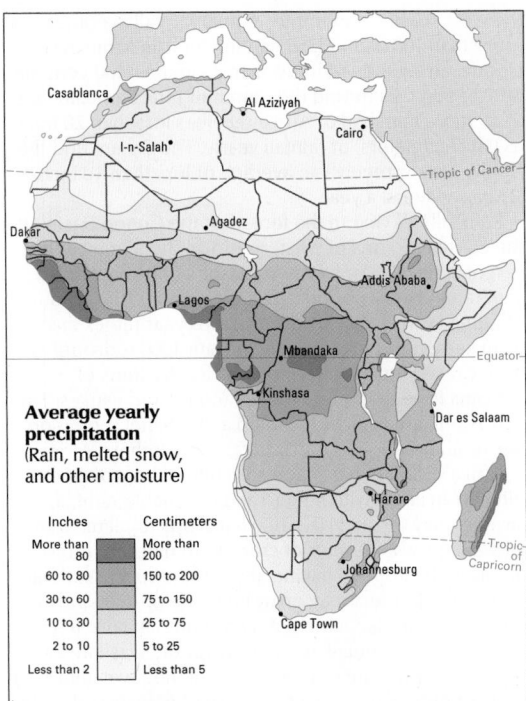

Rainfall is unevenly distributed in Africa. Equatorial regions receive 60 inches (150 centimeters) or more annually. The Sahara receives less than 2 inches (5 centimeters).

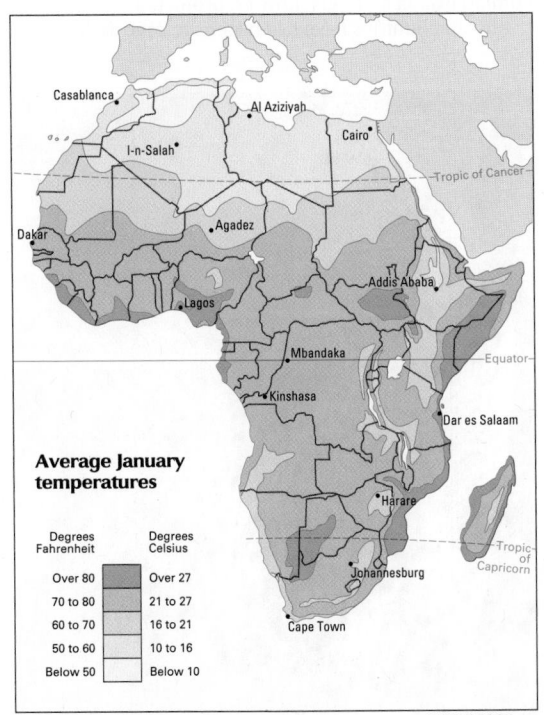

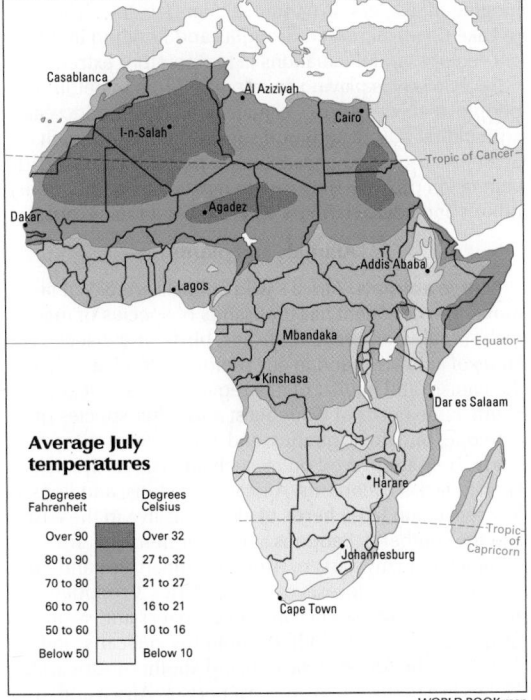

Temperatures are high all year throughout most of Africa. These maps show the average January and July temperatures across the continent. January is a winter month in the north and a summer month in the south. But in July, the north has summer, and the south has winter.

the west coast, for example, annual rainfall averages more than 100 inches (250 centimeters). In Monrovia, Liberia, an average of more than 40 inches (100 centimeters) of rain falls during the month of June alone. In contrast, more than half of Africa receives less than 20 inches (50 centimeters) of rainfall yearly. The Sahara and the Namib Desert receive an average of less than 10 inches (25 centimeters) a year.

Rain falls all year in the forests of the Congo Basin and the coastal regions of western Africa. But almost all the rest of Africa has one or two seasons of heavy rainfall separated by dry periods. In some regions, the amount of rainfall varies sharply from year to year rather than from season to season. Since the late 1960's, droughts have caused much suffering in Africa. Millions of Africans have died of starvation and related causes. The hardest-hit areas include Ethiopia, the Sahel region on the southern edge of the Sahara, and southern Africa.

Africa's climate has made agricultural improvement difficult. In areas with limited and unreliable rainfall, farmers may be uncertain of what crops to plant. Some farmers grow a number of crops with different moisture needs in the hope of having at least one successful harvest. Other farmers may grow only one or two kinds of crops and risk starvation if not enough rain falls. In areas with too much rainfall, heavy downpours wash away nourishing substances in the soil. The hot, wet climate in parts of Africa encourages the spread of insects that destroy livestock and cause diseases in people.

Many scientists suspect that global warming is responsible for an increasing occurrence of extremes in the weather and changes in seasonal patterns of rainfall in Africa. Signs of global warming in Africa include the melting of glaciers on Mount Kilimanjaro, the shrinking of Lake Chad, increased droughts and flooding in different regions, and fluctuations in temperature extremes.

Technology is playing an important role in helping people deal with Africa's climate in an effort to increase agricultural output and food supply on the continent. Scientists use weather satellites to monitor climate and vegetation growth. They can then predict weather conditions and advise farmers when to plant their crops.

Animals and plants

Native animals. Africa's wild animals are world famous. The continent has thousands of species of mammals, reptiles, amphibians, fishes, birds, and insects. The kinds of animals found in any region depend largely on the climate and habitat of that region. In the east and south, huge herds of wildebeest and other species of antelope, buffaloes, giraffes, and zebras roam the grasslands. They are preyed on by such animals as cheetahs, hyenas, jackals, leopards, African wild dogs, and lions. A few remaining large herds of elephants live in the east and the southeast. Baboons and other monkeys are common in many parts of Africa. Chimpanzees and gorillas dwell in the forests of central Africa. Crocodiles and hippopotamuses live in tropical rivers and swamps. Large water birds, including flamingos, pelicans, and storks, can be found in eastern and southern Africa. Ostriches live in the south and east parts of Africa and in the western Sahara. Many bird species migrate from Europe in winter to warmer regions of Africa.

Africa once had many more wild animals than it has

© George Holton, Photo Researchers

Gorillas are found only in the dense forests of Africa near the equator. Today, their survival is threatened by hunting and by the destruction of the forest environment in which they live.

today, and they were more widespread. Ancient paintings on rocks show that hippopotamuses and giraffes once lived in regions that are now deserts. Gradual changes in climate partly reduced the number and range of Africa's animals. But in many regions, people have overhunted the animals and destroyed much of their natural environment to make room for farms and cities. Intensive conservation efforts are necessary for many species. Some African animals, including the black rhinoceros, gorilla, and elephant, are in danger of becoming extinct and must now be protected.

African countries have taken steps to save their rich

© Peter Davey, Bruce Coleman Collection

Leopards are well adapted to Africa's savanna and bush environments. The big cat's coloration helps it blend in with tall grasses, bushes, and scattered trees while hunting prey.

wildlife heritage. Each country has established game reserves and national parks. Hunting is forbidden in these
areas, and modern methods of wildlife conservation are
practiced to protect the animals. Tourists come to view
wildlife in these protected areas and are an important
source of income to help in conservation efforts. In
some cases, hunters can go on regulated *safaris* (hunting expeditions). However, *poaching* (illegal hunting)
continues to be a problem.

Some rural Africans have opposed wildlife conservation efforts. In some areas, for example, wild animals
compete with farmers and herders for scarce land. Meat
from hunted wild animals, called *bush meat,* is important in the diet of some Africans. Some rare animals, including gorillas, elephants, and rhinoceroses, are
poached to sell certain body parts that are valued in
some countries for supposed healing powers or other
special qualities. International laws have been created to
end the illegal trade in endangered animals.

Native plants. Across Africa, the overall distribution

Animals of Africa   This map shows some of the mammals, birds, and reptiles of Africa. Wild animals were once much
more numerous and widespread there than today. Hunting and expanding settlement have greatly reduced the animal population and have put some species in danger of extinction.

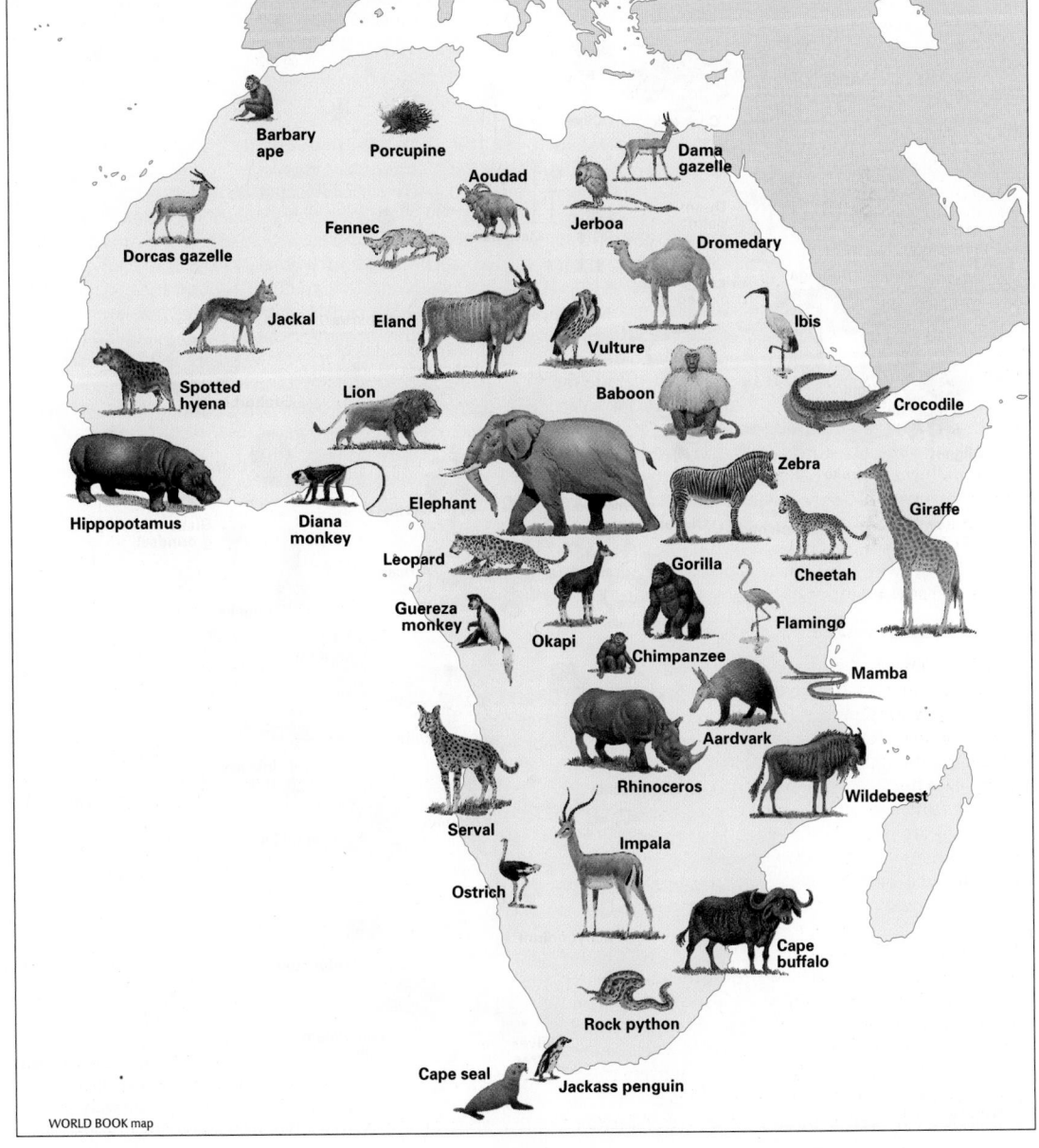

WORLD BOOK map

of plants is determined largely by temperature and rainfall. At local levels, plant variety is determined by many factors, including soil type, local climate, and habitat disturbances, such as wildfires. The spectacular rain forests of western and central Africa have hundreds of kinds of trees. They include oil palms; fruit trees; valuable timber trees, such as ebony, mahogany, and other hardwood trees; and softwood okoume trees, which are used to make furniture, plywood, and veneers. Mangrove trees stand on stiltlike roots in swampy areas along tropical

coasts. Olive and oak trees and such evergreen bushes as myrtle grow in the northwestern parts of Africa and at the southern tip of the continent.

Plants that withstand drought and fire cover the grasslands. In addition to various grasses, grassland plants include thick-trunked baobab trees, acacia trees, and thorny euphorbia bushes. Dry grasslands near the deserts, called *steppes,* have shorter grasses and fewer varieties of other plants. In the desert oases and *wadis* (dry valleys), there are date palms, doum palms,

Plants of Africa   Some of Africa's trees, shrubs, and other plants are pictured on this map. Much of Africa has a tropical climate. However, the land regions of the continent vary dramatically, ranging from deserts to tropical rain forests. As a result, Africa has a wide variety of plant life.

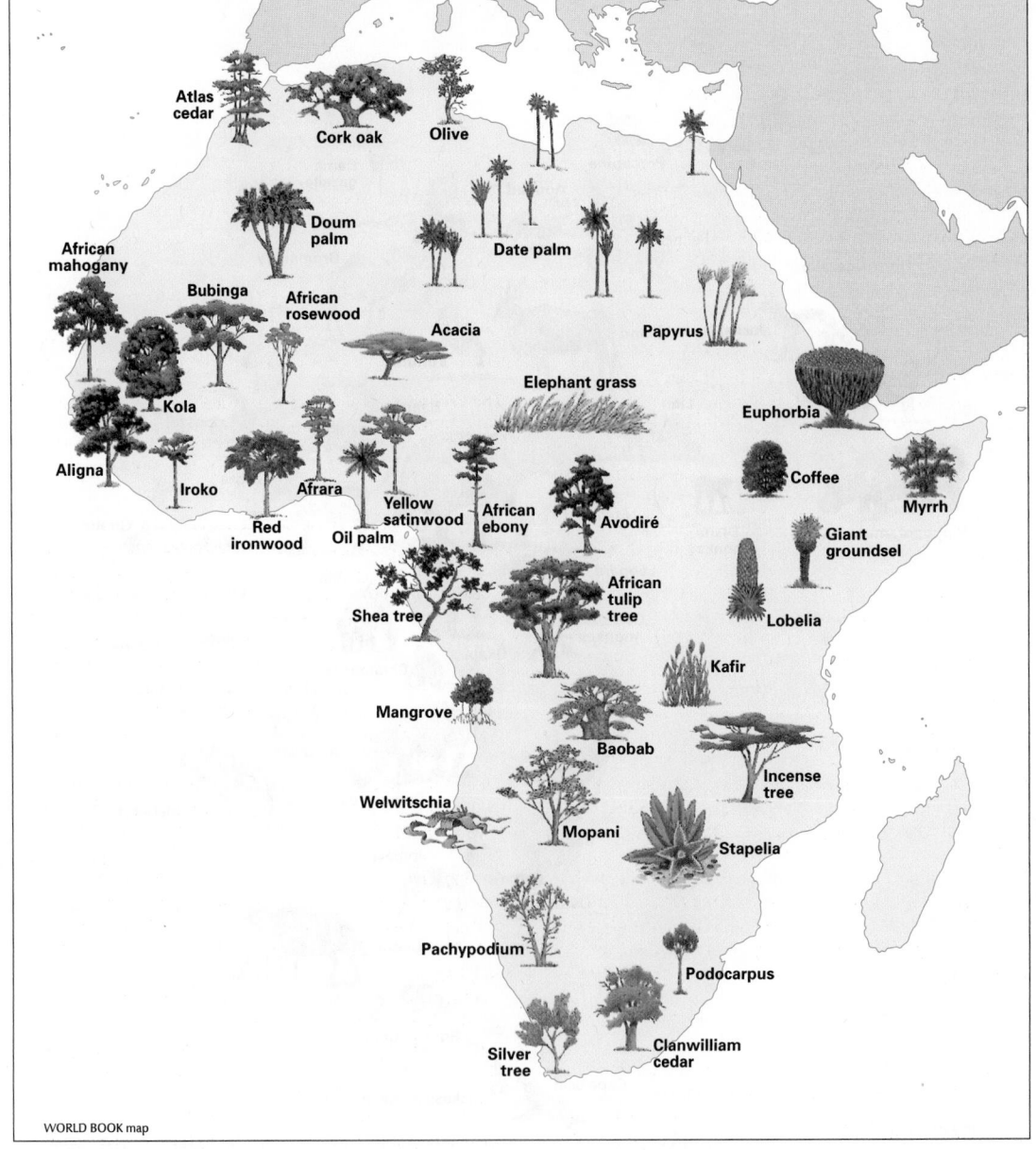

WORLD BOOK map

The baobab tree grows in grassland and bushland environments throughout Africa. The thick trunk helps protect the tree from drought and fires that occur in its dry environment.

© Shutterstock

tamarisks, and some kinds of acacias. Certain grasses and shrubs may appear briefly in the deserts after a rare rain.

In the mountainous highlands of Africa, bamboo thickets, podocarpus trees, tree ferns, and cedar trees grow on the lower slopes. On the upper slopes, meadows are covered with grasses, buttercups, and violets. Mosses and lichens grow near the mountaintops.

Land cleared for agriculture has destroyed portions of Africa's natural plant life. People use fire to clear land and to encourage grass growth for livestock. These fires suppress forest growth and maintain large areas as grasslands. Overgrazing by livestock has turned portions of the Sahel and other steppes into semidesert.

Introduced species. Some plants and animals that are common in Africa were introduced from other parts of the world by traders and colonists. These include some of Africa's most important food crops, including bananas, cassava, and corn, as well as such cash crops as cacao (cocoa) beans and tea. Eucalyptus trees, which originated in Australia, now grow in many parts of Africa and are widely used for firewood and construction. Pine trees, introduced from Mexico and other regions, are important for timber and paper. Camels, which provide food and other necessities in much of northern Africa, were domesticated in Asia.

Some introduced species have become pests. For example, eucalyptus trees use more water than native trees, reducing water available for other uses. Other species, called *invasive species,* have been introduced by accident and have spread quickly, destroying local habitats and species. For example, the water hyacinth was introduced from South America as a pond plant. However, it soon spread into rivers and lakes. The plant can cover entire lakes and rivers, choking out fish, limiting fishing, and making boating impossible. Nile perch were introduced into Lake Victoria to provide a new source of food fish for local people. However, this fish, which can grow to more than 200 pounds (91 kilograms), feeds on other fish. Since its introduction, the Nile perch has contributed to the loss of several fish species unique to Lake Victoria. Today, the fish are carefully monitored to prevent further destruction of native species.

Economy

African countries vary considerably in size, levels of economic development, rates of economic growth, economic development policies, and amounts of international trade. This variation is a result of unequal

© J. A. L. Cooke, Oxford Scientific Films

The Welwitschia plant grows only in the deserts of southwestern Africa. The plant bears a single pair of leaves. Older plants appear to have many leaves because hot winds, blowing sand, and age split the leaves into long, ribbonlike shreds.

distribution of natural resources, variation in political and economic systems, colonialism, and various other historical factors in countries across the continent.

Economic development in Africa can be measured by *gross domestic product* (GDP). GDP is the value of all goods and services produced in a country. In the late 2010's, the GDP for all of Africa was about one-eighth the GDP of the United States. Egypt, Nigeria, and South Africa have Africa's largest economies. Other countries with large economies include Algeria, Angola, Kenya, and Morocco.

African countries vary considerably in annual *per capita* (per person) GDP. The per capita GDP of a country is determined by dividing the total GDP of all people by the population. In the late 2010's, the average annual per capita GDP in Africa was about $2,000. At that time, more than 20 African countries each had an annual per capita GDP of less than $1,000. In comparison, the annual per capita GDP of the United States was about $60,000.

Agriculture. Production of agricultural crops and livestock employs more workers than any other economic activity in Africa. The countries with the largest areas of land under cultivation include Egypt, Ethiopia, Nigeria, South Africa, and Sudan.

African crop production is divided between *staple food crops* and *export crops*. Staple food crops produced in Africa include such grains as corn, millet, rice, sorghum, and wheat. Important root crops include cassava, potatoes, and yams. Other important staple crops include various *legumes* (peas, peanuts, and beans), fruits, and vegetables. Africa's leading export crops include *cacao* (cocoa), cashews, coffee, cotton, palm oil, sugar, and tobacco.

Most staple crops in Africa are produced for local consumption by farmers working on family-owned or family-rented farms. There are also large plantations owned by companies, wealthy individuals, or governments. These plantations are usually used for production of export crops, such as palm oil and cocoa.

Different crops are grown in various regions of Africa depending on the environmental conditions and historical preferences. Yams and cassava are more common in the wet tropical areas of western Africa, but corn is more common in the grasslands of eastern and southern Africa. Wheat is the major staple crop in northern Africa, where irrigation is also more commonly used. In the highlands of Ethiopia and other parts of eastern Africa, a plant called *khat* (also spelled *kat* or *qat*) has been an important crop for centuries. The leaves of this plant contain a stimulant and they produce a mild *euphoria*

(feeling of well-being) when chewed. Khat is grown for local use and export to the Arabian Peninsula, Europe, and North America.

In many African countries, food production has grown more slowly than the population. This situation leads to food shortages that must be offset by food imports. However, some countries lack the economic resources necessary to purchase food from abroad, and hunger or famine has sometimes resulted. In these countries, foreign food contributions and aid are essential. Periodic droughts also contribute to poor agricultural production and hunger in Africa.

In Africa, most fertile lands and resources, such as fertilizer, are used for production of cash crops grown for export rather than food crops. This is partly a continuation of colonial practices, when African farmers were forced to cultivate export crops demanded in Europe. However, the production of cash crops also reflects the policies of African governments. They use export crops to obtain foreign income to purchase imported goods and materials essential for economic development.

Livestock production is an important branch of the agricultural economy, mostly in the grassland regions. The main livestock raised in Africa include camels, cattle,

Agriculture and fishing in Africa

This map shows the major uses of land in Africa. It locates the chief agricultural products and shows the most important crops in large type. The map also shows the major fishing areas and kinds of fish caught.

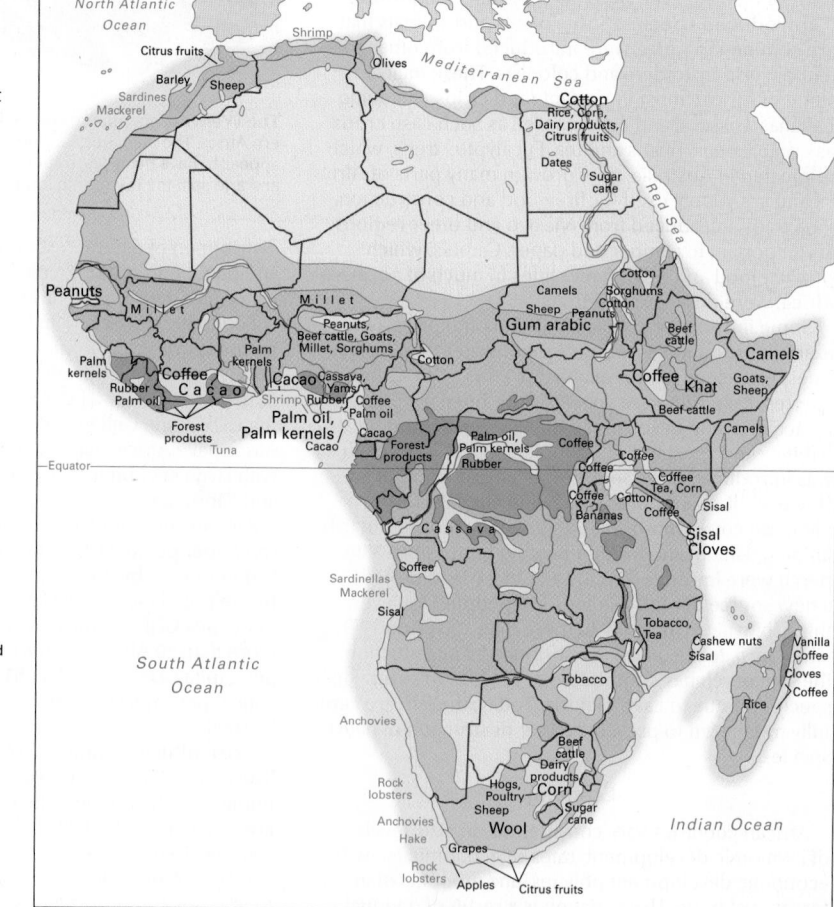

Africa has vast mineral resources, and many countries have a well-developed mining industry. This open-pit diamond mine in Botswana is among the largest in the world. The continent has large reserves of chromium, cobalt, gold, manganese, platinum, and uranium.

© Trygve Bolstad, Panos Pictures

chickens, goats, horses, pigs, and sheep. Some regions of Africa are not suitable for livestock due to infestation with tsetse flies. Tsetse flies transmit African sleeping sickness, a disease that is fatal for many species of domestic livestock.

Mining. Africa is richly endowed with mineral resources and has a large mining industry. The continent has among the world's largest reserves of chromium, cobalt, gold, manganese, phosphates, platinum, and uranium. Substantial quantities of other metals, including *bauxite* (aluminum ore), copper, nickel, and vanadium, are also found throughout Africa. Africa is also a major producer of oil and natural gas.

Africa's most developed mining industry is in the Republic of South Africa. Angola, Botswana, Zambia, and Zimbabwe also have large mining industries. South Africa is one of the world's largest gold producers, and Botswana is one of the world's leading producers of diamonds. The Democratic Republic of the Congo has a large copper industry, while Guinea and Morocco are Africa's leading producers of bauxite and phosphates. Algeria, Angola, Libya, and Nigeria are major petroleum-producing countries.

However, much of Africa has not benefited from its vast mineral resources. African countries have no control over prices of minerals on the global market, and many mining companies are foreign-owned. In addition, mining employs fewer workers than either agriculture or services, and is more expensive to operate.

In some instances, Africa's mineral wealth has contributed to environmental destruction and helped fuel political conflicts. Nigeria's large petroleum industry has contributed to pollution in the Niger River Delta. Money from illegal trade in diamonds helped finance a brutal civil war in Sierra Leone during the 1990's. Since the early 2000's, United Nations embargoes have tried to prevent trade in diamonds called *conflict diamonds* or *blood diamonds*, which are sold to fund the illegal operations of rebel, military, and terrorist groups.

Manufacturing. In much of Africa, the growth in the manufacturing industry occurred only after independence. By the 1960's, significant manufacturing industries had developed only in former colonies that had large European populations, such as Algeria, Kenya, Zimbabwe, and South Africa, or in countries that attained independence early, such as Egypt. Many African countries have since developed small manufacturing sectors mainly to produce consumer goods that they previously imported, such as beverages, processed foods, and textiles. Large-scale industrial manufacturing has proved

SABMiller

Small industries in many African countries produce mainly consumer goods that were previously imported, such as beverages, processed foods, and textiles. This brewery in Mozambique produces beverages for local and international markets.

more difficult and costly to implement. Currently, Africa produces only a small percentage of the total world manufacturing output.

Service industries in Africa include transactions conducted by the government, called the *public sector,* and by nongovernment businesses, the *private sector.* The private sector is further divided into *formal* and *informal* sectors based on their structure and size. Informal enterprises include small businesses that provide goods and services but are not accurately recorded in government figures or properly taxed as are businesses in the formal sector. The informal sector is large in many African countries.

Government spending plays a major role in all African economies. Education, health care, and other social services account for much of the expenditure of many governments.

Private service industries, including financial services, retail, and tourism, have grown in Africa since the mid-1900's. Retail services range from small roadside vendors to large stores and shopping malls.

Tourism is a leading source of income in many African nations, including Egypt, Gambia, Kenya, Mauritius, Morocco, Tanzania, and Uganda. To accommodate the tourists, these countries have constructed an extensive array of hotels and other facilities. Many foreign tourists come to visit the famous historic sites of Egypt or the game reserves of Botswana, Kenya, South Africa, Tanzania, and Uganda.

Transportation. The transportation system is poorly developed in many African countries. Many of Africa's roads are unpaved. The Democratic Republic of the Congo, Kenya, Nigeria, and South Africa have major railroad systems. Automobile ownership is limited to the middle and upper classes in most nations. The vast majority of Africans depend on public transportation, such as buses, minivans, and taxis. Many people rely on bicycles or walking. In some parts of Africa, camels and donkeys are still widely used to transport goods.

Major railroads are concentrated in only a few countries, chiefly Algeria, the Democratic Republic of the Congo, Egypt, South Africa, Sudan, and Tanzania. Africa's air transportation industry is well developed mainly in Algeria, Egypt, Ethiopia, Kenya, Morocco, and South Africa, though all African countries have large airports. The African coasts have few good natural harbors. But almost every coastal country has at least one harbor, and engineers are working to equip them with modern shipping facilities. Many harbors have been constructed along Africa's extensive rivers and lakes.

Mining and manufacturing in Africa

This map shows the location of Africa's chief mineral resources and manufacturing centers. Major mineral-producing areas are shown in large type, and lesser ones in small type. Manufacturing centers are in red.

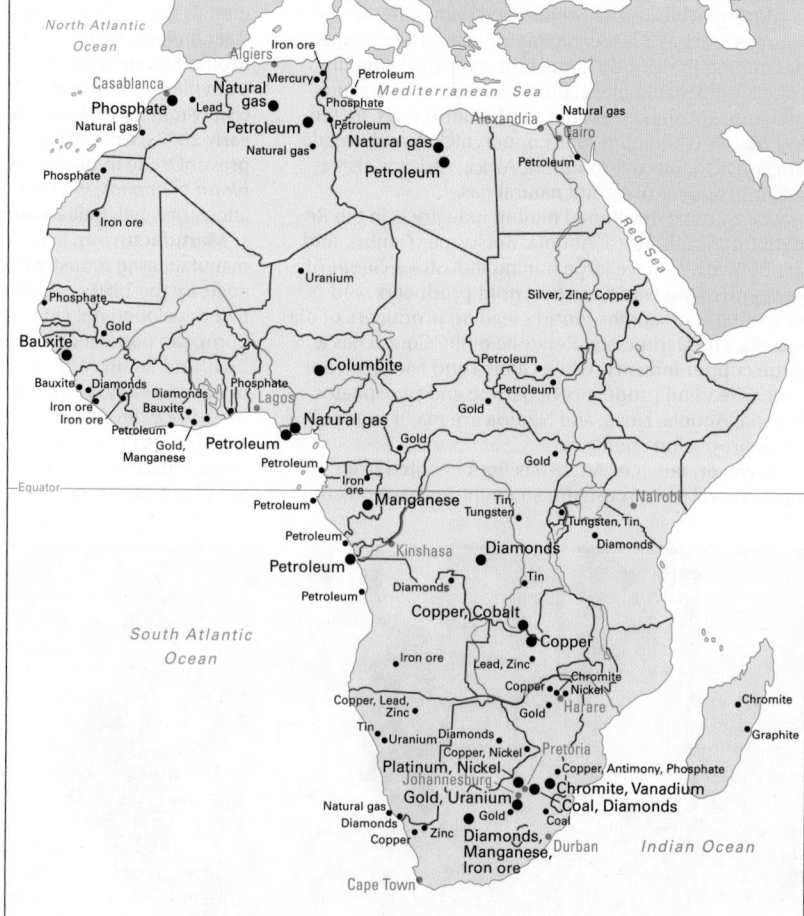

Communication. Africa's communication systems, despite some rapid expansion in the late 1900's and early 2000's, remain underdeveloped compared with non-African countries. The number of newspapers published in Africa has increased significantly since the 1990's. However, radio remains a popular form of mass communication. The number of public, private, and community radio stations has also grown dramatically since the 1990's. Television access is expanding on the continent. Motion-picture theaters are found only in cities, and few African countries have even small motion-picture industries.

Telephone service throughout Africa has improved greatly since the 1990's. Telephone ownership remains largely concentrated in major urban centers. However, cellular telephones are increasingly common in smaller towns and villages. Both cell phone and internet usage have increased rapidly since the early 2000's. However, Africa still lags behind other regions in the development of this technology. Computer and internet access and usage are concentrated in South Africa and urban areas of western and northern Africa.

International trade. Africa's leading merchandise exporters include Algeria, Angola, and South Africa. Petroleum ranks as Africa's major merchandise export. Other important exports include agricultural products, minerals, and manufactured products.

Africa's merchandise imports have also grown since the 1980's. Algeria, Egypt, Morocco, Nigeria, Somalia, and South Africa are among Africa's leading importing countries. Food imports are increasingly important as agricultural output has failed to keep up with population growth in many countries. Other key imports include fuel and manufactured goods.

Terms of trade refers to the relationship between the prices of imports and those of exports. Declining terms of trade occur when import prices rise faster than export prices. Rising terms of trade occur when export prices grow faster. Africa's terms of trade have tended to decline since the 1970's because Africa's exports consist of mainly agricultural products and minerals that are subject to frequent price fluctuations. Many African countries are also economically vulnerable because they depend on one or two major exports. As a result, African nations have been active in international efforts to control price changes and improve trade terms. For example, the African oil-producing countries belong to the Organization of the Petroleum Exporting Countries (OPEC), a group of nations that seeks to regulate the world market for oil.

Foreign aid, debt, and investment. Foreign aid to Africa includes grants, loans, and technical assistance in such areas as agriculture, education, and health care. The grants and loans come from a variety of international sources and are usually referred to as *official development assistance* (ODA). This aid is important for many African countries as they attempt to face their economic difficulties due in part to declining terms of trade.

Foreign aid has helped African countries to promote economic and social development. But it has also had some harmful effects. The loans have left many African countries with large debt and crippling interest payments. The bulk of Africa's debt is held by the larger countries, including Egypt and South Africa. But in

© Victor Englebert

Ashanti and Ewe weavers in Ghana are famous for producing colorful kente cloth. Garments and accessories of kente cloth manufactured in western Africa are exported worldwide.

smaller, poorer African countries, the debt load has the most severe impact. These countries must reduce investment in education, health care, and other economic development to repay debt.

In the 1980's and 1990's, international lending institutions, led by the World Bank and the International Monetary Fund, imposed strict conditions on African debtor nations. For example, they required borrowing countries to *devalue* (lower the value of) their currencies to promote exports and to reduce their budget deficits by cutting government funding of health care and education. Many experts believe that these strict conditions, called *structural adjustment programs* (SAP's), hurt a number of African economies. Today, lenders have relaxed the policy of SAP's, with the hope that African countries will return to economic growth.

History

Africa has been called the "cradle of humanity." Fossils discovered at sites in northern, eastern, and southern Africa provide the oldest evidence of humanlike creatures and people found anywhere in the world. From this evidence, most scientists have concluded that the earliest human beings lived about 2 million years ago in Africa. In time, human beings spread to other continents. For detailed information on the earliest human beings, see the article **Prehistoric people.**

This section discusses the broad outlines of African history. For the history of a particular country, see the *World Book* article on that country. See also the articles listed under "History" and "People" in the *Related articles* at the end of this article.

The development of agriculture. Africa played an important role in the development of agriculture in the world. Previously, people obtained food by hunting, fishing, and gathering wild plant foods. The transition from food gathering to agriculture in Africa was a long process that took place over many centuries. Archaeologists and historians have identified five major centers of development of African agriculture: the Nile Valley, Ethiopia, west Africa, central Africa, and east Africa.

In each of the regions of Africa, the domestication of native plants developed independently between about 7,000 and 2,000 years ago. In the Nile Valley, farmers domesticated sorghum. In Ethiopia, coffee, *noog* (an oil plant), *ensete* (a bananalike plant), millet, sorghum, and *teff* (a type of grain) were domesticated. In east Africa, farmers also grew varieties of sorghum and millet. In the savanna areas of west Africa, people cultivated varieties of African peanuts, African rice, cotton, millet, and sorghum. Crops that originated in the forest zones of central Africa include kola nuts, oil palm, and yams.

Some crops were introduced to Africa from other regions. Early farmers of western Asia probably introduced such domestic crops as barley and wheat to the Nile Valley by about 7,000 years ago. Bananas were introduced to Africa from Southeast Asia more than 2,000 years ago. By the late 1400's, agricultural exchanges between Africa and the Americas became important. Corn and cassava were introduced to Africa from the Americas and have since become important food crops.

In several regions of Africa, *pastoralism* (raising of livestock) began before farming. Domesticated cattle, sheep, and goats were raised by about 8,000 years ago in the northern Sahara region of Africa. At the time, the Sahara region was moist grassland and the center of thriving pastoral and farming communities. These communities migrated to the Nile Valley, the Mediterranean coast, and west African grasslands as the Sahara began to dry about 6,000 years ago. Pastoralism also developed before farming in east and southern Africa. Early Khoisan-speaking peoples of southern Africa were raising domestic cattle and sheep by about 2,500 years ago.

The development of agriculture had enormous consequences for Africa. Greater and more secure access to food contributed to population growth. The develop-

Reproduction of a rock painting (3500-3000 B.C.);
Musée de l'Homme, Paris © Erich Lessing, Magnum
Rock paintings on the walls of caves and rock shelters were made thousands of years ago by peoples who lived in Africa. This painting was found in the Tassili-n-Ajjer region of Algeria.

ment and spread of agriculture was made possible and accompanied by technological developments, including the production and use of metal tools. Agriculture also led to the establishment of permanent settlements.

Early civilizations. Africa's earliest civilizations emerged in the fertile plains of the Nile Valley, where thriving agricultural communities grew into small states. These states gradually developed into larger states, the most powerful of which emerged in what later became known as Egypt and Nubia.

Several small states had emerged in Egypt by about 4000 B.C. By 3500 B.C., two kingdoms called Upper Egypt and Lower Egypt were dominant. Menes, king of Upper Egypt, unified the kingdoms about 3100 B.C. Menes was given the title *pharaoh* and established the first *dynasty* (family of rulers) of ancient Egypt. Pharaohs from 30 dynasties ruled Egypt for the next 3,000 years.

Beginning around 1085 B.C., Egypt experienced a series of revolts, invasions, and foreign rule by Assyrians, Libyans, Nubians, and Persians lasting nearly 700 years. In 332 B.C., Alexander the Great of Macedonia conquered Egypt. Ptolemy, one of Alexander's generals, later took the title of king of Egypt and founded a dynasty that ruled until 30 B.C., when the Roman Empire conquered Egypt. Roman rule lasted in Egypt until A.D. 639.

The Kush civilization arose after 1000 B.C. in Nubia, south of Egypt. The Kush maintained close relations with Egypt. Kush culture, architecture, and writing both resembled and differed from Egyptian styles. Egypt ruled over Kush at times, but Kush conquered and ruled Egypt from about 750 to 660 B.C. Kush eventually declined due to environmental destruction, falling trade, and competition from neighbors. Around A.D. 350, Kush was invaded by Aksum, marking the end of this ancient civilization.

The kingdom of Aksum was in the Ethiopian highlands (now part of Ethiopia and Eritrea), a fertile region that was easy to defend from invasion. Aksum grew into a powerful kingdom by about A.D. 100, largely through control of trade on the Red Sea. The kingdom began to decline in the 600's due to environmental destruction and economic competition from Muslim traders.

The rise of Christianity. Egypt, Ethiopia, and Nubia were among the earliest centers of Christianity in Africa. Christianity was introduced to Egypt from western Asia sometime before A.D. 100. Over the next few hundred years, the religion spread throughout Egypt and other parts of north Africa. Historians believe Christianity was introduced in Ethiopia from Egypt in the 300's. Ezana, the king of Aksum, converted to Christianity around 333 and established it as the state religion. But Christianity did not spread to the rest of sub-Saharan Africa until the late 1400's, when missionaries introduced it from Europe.

North Africa produced many of early Christianity's most influential thinkers and writers. These include Saint Augustine and the early Christian philosopher Origen. Egyptian Christians, known as Copts, emphasized the practices of solitude and monasticism. Three popes in the early church were Africans. The last African pope was Saint Gelasius I, elected in 492.

Christianity in north Africa declined sharply following the rise of Islam and Arab conquests of the region in the 600's. In Egypt, the Coptic Church declined and survived only among a minority of the population. Arab invasions between 1050 and 1056 completed the conversion of northern Africa to Islam. Only in Ethiopia did Christianity survive as the official religion of the state and the majority of the population.

The rise of Islam. The development of Islam had a profound impact on African history. Islam emerged in Arabia during the early 600's, inspired by the teaching of the Prophet Muhammad. Within years of Muhammad's death, Arab followers began a rapid campaign of conquest and conversion. By the late 700's, Arab and Arabized Muslims had built an empire that stretched from Central Asia to northern Africa to Spain.

In northern Africa, Islam spread through Arab conquests and settlement. This spread was accompanied by the conversion of the Berbers, who also adopted many other elements of Arab culture. In west Africa, Islam was introduced in the 800's. The Berbers introduced Islam by way of trade routes that crossed the Sahara. The new religion appealed to sub-Saharan rulers. Islam spread throughout Ghana, Mali, and Songhai, and farther south.

In Sudan, Islam spread from Egypt along the Nile and through trade with Arab Muslims across the Red Sea. In Somalia, Eritrea, and Ethiopia, Muslim Arabs and Persians established coastal settlements from the 700's to the 900's. In eastern Africa, the spread of Islam was aided by Arab settlement in the region during the late 700's. Intermarriage between the Arab settlers and local Africans eventually led to east Africa's Swahili culture.

Islam strengthened Africa's contacts with the outside world. Africa became a key part of the Islamic empire stretching from Spain to Indonesia. The first Islamic universities were established in northern Africa beginning around 970. These universities taught religion, science, mathematics, philosophy, geography, medicine, and history. African scholars made important contributions to Islamic thought. Similarly, Islam transformed African cultural practices, ideas, and values. In addition, it promoted long-distance trade by providing a common culture and language throughout much of Africa.

The empires of west Africa emerged in the savanna zone below the Sahara beginning somewhat before A.D. 1000. Ghana, the first great empire to emerge, was founded by the Soninke people around A.D. 700. Soninke agricultural and iron-producing communities gradually expanded political control over neighboring regions and united them into a single empire. Ghana traded grain and iron with gold-producing states farther south. They then traded the gold with Arab merchants for other goods, developing enormous wealth. However, Ghana went into a period of decline from about 1000 due to attacks from external enemies, internal revolts, and climate change.

Mali, founded around 1000, rose as nearby Ghana declined. By the 1200's, Mali was the largest, wealthiest empire in all of Africa. The capital city of Niani was a major center of trade. Timbuktu, Mali's largest city, had a population of about 50,000 by the 1300's. Scholars from many parts of the Islamic world came to study at the university there. Mali began to decline in the 1400's, due to political conflicts and raids from outside enemies. The empire had disappeared by the early 1600's.

Songhai formed as part of the Mali empire. Songhai first rose to prominence during the 1300's as Mali declined. Songhai's capital was Gao, a major trading city on the banks of the Niger River. At Songhai's height in the 1500's, trade and learning flourished. Invasion from Morocco in 1591, however, greatly weakened the empire. By the early 1600's, Songhai and the other great empires of west Africa had all but disappeared.

States and kingdoms. The east African coast saw the rise of several *city-states*, independent states that consisted of a city and the surrounding area. The city-states arose from settlements that existed sometime after A.D. 100. The communities prospered for centuries through trade of materials from the African interior with merchants sailing from China, India, Indonesia, the Red Sea, and the Persian Gulf. East coast ports exported gold, copper, ivory, grain, iron, timber, and other products in exchange for such goods as cotton cloth, glass, porcelain, and silk. The people came to be known as *Swahili*, a word that comes from an Arabic word meaning *coast.*

By 1000, the Swahili city-states dominated trade along east Africa's coast. The largest cities included Manda, Mogadishu, Mombasa, Kilwa, and Zanzibar. The city-states were all independent, but rivalries sometimes led to conflicts and war. The Portuguese, attempting to gain control of the Indian Ocean trade, attacked Zanzibar in 1503 and destroyed Kilwa in 1505. These European invasions began the decline of the Swahili civilization.

Other states and kingdoms developed in southern Africa and central Africa. Great Zimbabwe was built

© David Wall, Alamy Images

Great Zimbabwe, the capital of an ancient African civilization, was built about A.D. 1100 in the plains of southern Africa. The city was an important center of trade in the region. The ruins of the spectacular walls and buildings of the capital remain today.

around the 1100's in the fertile plains of southern Africa. The region was rich in gold, iron, tin, copper, and granite. The granite was used to construct the spectacular walls and buildings of the capital and many smaller sites across the region. Great Zimbabwe declined toward the end of the 1400's due to environmental destruction, overpopulation, and a decline in trade.

The Kongo kingdom was one of a series of kingdoms that emerged in central Africa in the 1400's. It had a highly centralized government with its capital at Mbanza Kongo, in what is now the Democratic Republic of the Congo. Kongo was among the first African states in the region to have contact with European countries. During the 1400's, the Portuguese began to explore the west coast of Africa. They were interested in Africa's gold trade. Portugal established trading posts at São Jorge da Mina (now called Elmina, in modern-day Ghana) and in the Kongo kingdom. However, Portuguese merchants, seeking to monopolize trade, increasingly turned to trading in enslaved people instead of gold. The effects of the trade of enslaved people, internal conflicts, and wars with neighbors weakened the Kongo kingdom and led to its eventual collapse in the early 1700's.

The Atlantic slave trade. Soon after the Portuguese arrived in western Africa, they began to ship Africans to Europe as enslaved people, beginning what is known as the Atlantic slave trade. Africa had sent enslaved people to Asia and Europe long before the Portuguese arrived, but the Atlantic slave trade was vastly larger in scale than any slave trade that preceded it. Portugal, Britain, the Netherlands, the United States, and other countries all participated in this trade. Today, many scholars recognize it as the largest forced migration of people in history. They estimate that between 10 and 12 million people were sent as enslaved people to the Americas between the mid-1400's and mid-1800's.

African merchants and rulers were actively involved in the Atlantic slave trade. The trade in gold and enslaved people brought wealth and power to some African kingdoms. However, it was Europeans who came to purchase the enslaved people, transported them in ships to the Americas, and sold them to work on plantations and mines. Europe and the Americas were the greatest beneficiaries of the Atlantic slave trade.

The effects of the Atlantic slave trade on Africa were disastrous. Depopulation caused by raiding and warfare disrupted economic activities and development throughout much of Africa. The Atlantic slave trade also contributed to the growth of racist stereotypes against Africans, which were used to justify their enslavement

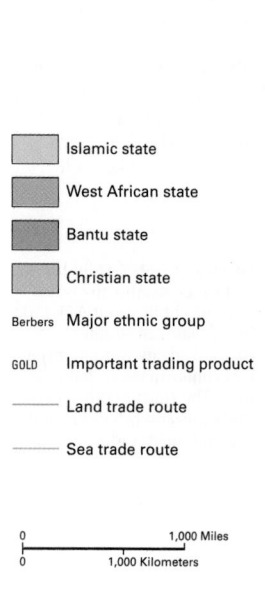

Africa in the 1400's

Africa had many highly organized states long before the European colonial period. This map shows the main states and trade routes of the 1400's.

Islamic state

West African state

Bantu state

Christian state

Berbers Major ethnic group

GOLD Important trading product

Land trade route

Sea trade route

0   1,000 Miles

0   1,000 Kilometers

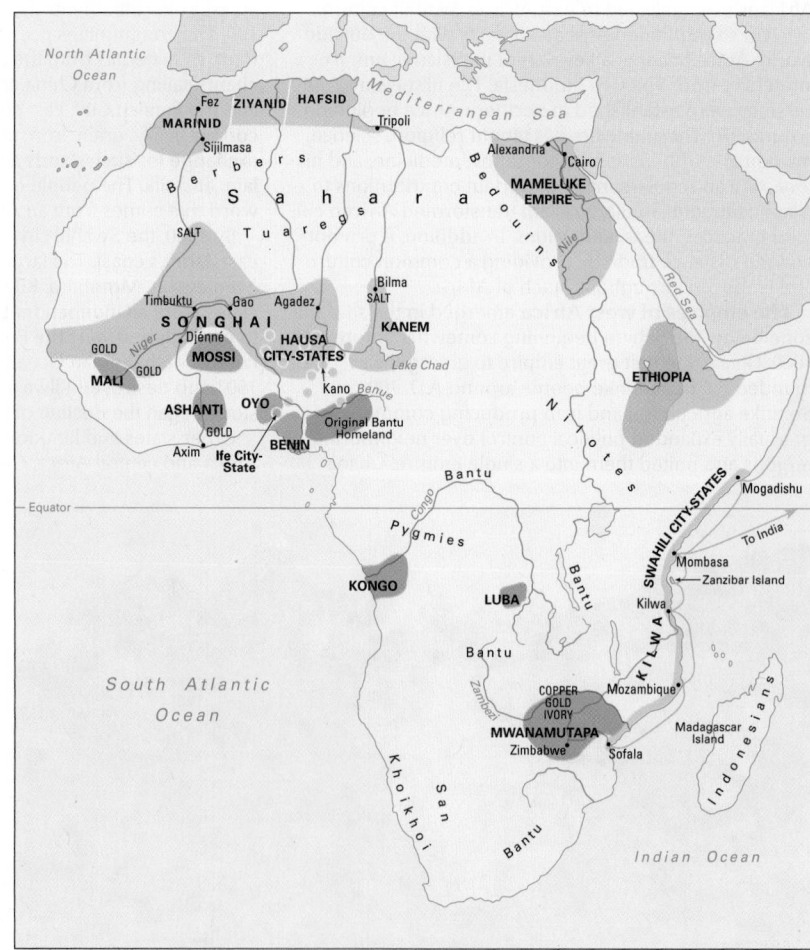

and eventual colonization by European powers.

African societies in the 1800's. The 1800's were a period of revolutionary changes across Africa. In west Africa, Islamic reformist movements led to the establishment of Islamic states. In southern Africa, political upheavals generated the rise of the Zulu empire. In north Africa, there was a drive toward modernization.

In west Africa, Muslim religious reformers accused local rulers of undermining or corrupting Islam. The reformers sought to purify and spread Islam and establish a new government based on Shari`a, the legal and moral code of Islam. In 1804, Muslim reformers declared *jihad* (holy war) that led to the establishment of the Sokoto caliphate, the largest state in west Africa at the time. The movement spawned other jihads that led to the creation of other Islamic states in west Africa.

Societies in southern Africa underwent revolutionary changes. A period of upheaval there between 1819 and 1838 is known to historians as the *Mfecane* (also called *Difaqane*). One center of conflict was Zululand, in what is now the South African province of KwaZulu-Natal. Competition for trade, grazing land, and water led to the emergence of several kingdoms in the region. Raids by European settlers and an increase in the trade of enslaved people and ivory heightened the struggle for re-

sources and forced local people to seek the protection of African military leaders ruling the kingdoms.

At the beginning of the 1800's, the Arab states of north Africa were struggling to rid themselves of foreign rule by the Ottoman Empire and to resist European intrusion. In Egypt, the government of Muhammad Ali began an ambitious program to modernize Egypt and to increase its wealth and power. This modernization program included political, military, economic, educational, and social reforms. However, heavy debt and internal disagreement over foreign involvement would eventually lead to the country's occupation by the British in 1882.

European colonization in Africa. European interest in Africa began growing in the 1400's as European nations acquired the military and technological capacities for overseas voyages and conquest. Merchant companies were the first Europeans to reach Africa, followed by explorers and missionaries. European intervention peaked in the late 1800's in colonial invasions by European governments.

Portugal led the European expansion into Africa, capturing Ceuta in Morocco (now a Spanish city at the Strait of Gibraltar) in 1415. Early in the 1500's, Portugal established trading posts along the east and west coasts. The Portuguese destroyed Kilwa in 1505 and seized other

European exploration of Africa

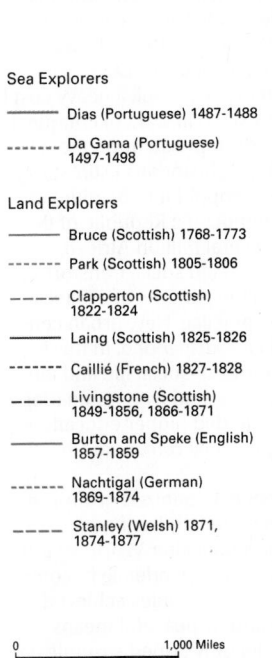

Sea Explorers

——— Dias (Portuguese) 1487-1488

------- Da Gama (Portuguese) 1497-1498

Land Explorers

——— Bruce (Scottish) 1768-1773

------- Park (Scottish) 1805-1806

— — — Clapperton (Scottish) 1822-1824

——— Laing (Scottish) 1825-1826

------- Caillié (French) 1827-1828

— — — Livingstone (Scottish) 1849-1856, 1866-1871

——— Burton and Speke (English) 1857-1859

------- Nachtigal (German) 1869-1874

— — — Stanley (Welsh) 1871, 1874-1877

0   1,000 Miles

0   1,000 Kilometers

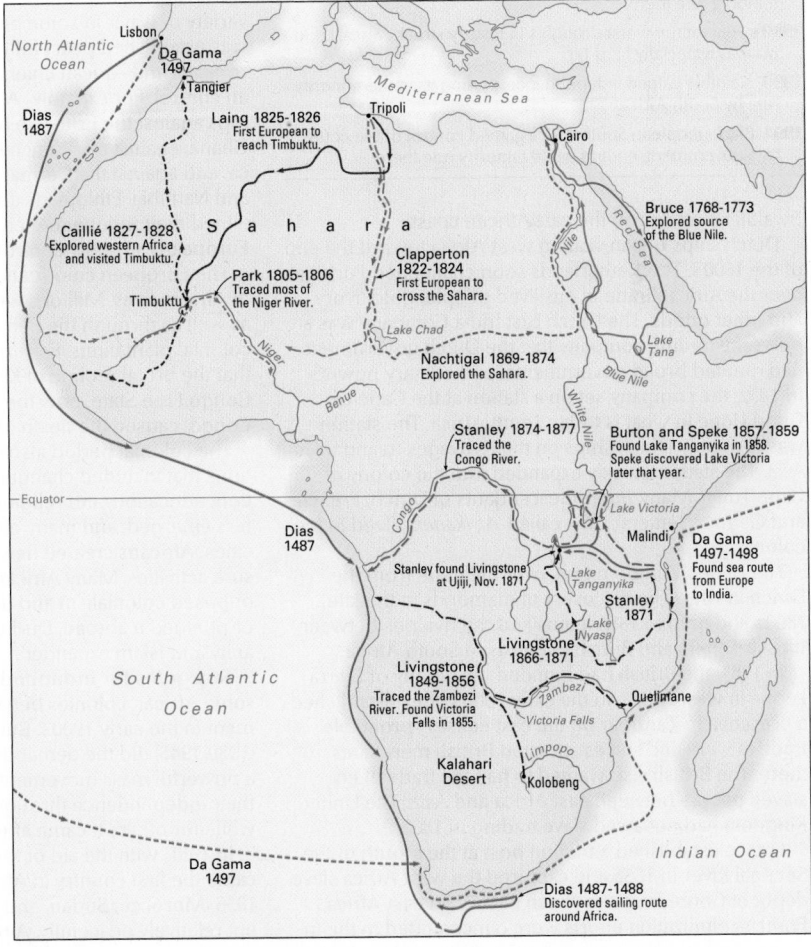

WORLD BOOK map

Important dates in Africa

c. 2,000,000 B.C. The earliest human beings may have lived in eastern Africa.

c. 5000 B.C. People in northern Africa practiced farming.

c. 4000 B.C. The Sahara began to turn into a desert.

c. 3100 B.C. Upper and Lower Egypt became one country.

30 B.C. The Roman Empire controlled northern Africa.

c. A.D. 1 Bantu-speaking peoples began southward migrations.

300's The Kingdom of Aksum became a Christian state.

500's The Nubian kingdoms were converted to Christianity.

639-710 Arab Muslims conquered northern Africa.

1000-1500 Large kingdoms were established in Africa south of the Sahara.

1400's The Portuguese began to explore Africa's west coast.

1652 The Dutch founded Cape Town.

Late 1700's Europeans began to explore the African interior.

1880's European governments began to claim parts of Africa.

1920's European colonial rule was firmly established in Africa.

1950's-1960's Most European colonies in Africa became independent.

1975 Portugal, the last European country with large African holdings, gave up its remaining colonies.

1979 Black Africans in Rhodesia (now known as Zimbabwe) gained control of the country's government, ending white-minority rule there.

1980's One of the worst droughts in history struck Africa. Ethiopia was especially hard-hit.

1990 Namibia gained independence, ending its white-minority rule by South Africa.

1994 Black people in South Africa gained control of the country's government, ending white-minority rule there.

Swahili city-states on the east African coast.

Dutch ships began visiting west Africa toward the end of the 1500's. The Netherlands soon challenged Portugal over the African trade in enslaved people, gold, ivory, and other goods. The Dutch East India Company was a powerful trading company that the Dutch government had granted broad governmental and military powers. In 1652, the company set up a station at the Cape of Good Hope in what is today South Africa. The station was to supply Dutch ships on their voyages to and from Asia. The station quickly expanded into the colony of Cape Town. Many *Boers* (descendants of Dutch, French, and German settlers), now called *Afrikaners*, lived in the colony.

The United Kingdom took over the Cape from the Dutch in 1814. The discovery of diamonds in the late 1860's and gold in 1886 intensified the rivalries between the Afrikaners and British colonists in South Africa.

In 1787, the British had founded the colony of Sierra Leone in west Africa. In the early 1800's, they established a presence in Zanzibar on the east coast. A profitable trade in ivory and spices attracted British merchants there. The British also wanted to halt the trade in enslaved people between east Africa and Asia. The United Kingdom had outlawed slave trading in 1807.

France established a trading post at the mouth of the Sénégal River in 1638 and captured the west Africa slave depot of Gorée from the Dutch in 1677. In east Africa, French colonization efforts were concentrated in the In-dian Ocean islands of Mauritius and Reunion. There, the French established plantations using enslaved laborers from east Africa. In 1830, the French colonized Algeria.

Colonial rule. As trade between Africa and Europe expanded, European merchants called upon their governments to establish political control in the regions where they were operating. By the 1880's, there were intense rivalries among the European nations as they staked claims to parts of Africa. This race to expand European colonial influence is often referred to by historians as the "scramble for Africa." In 1884, European powers convened the Berlin Conference to draw up rules among the nations establishing colonies and to prevent war over claims to African lands. No Africans were invited to attend the conference.

The Berlin Conference adopted a number of provisions. For example, it ruled that European nations had to actually occupy and administer African lands that they claimed. It also declared that a nation already holding colonies on the African coast would have first claim on the neighboring interior. The colonial borders that were established paid little attention to previous national, ethnic, and religious boundaries. By 1914, Belgium, France, Germany, Italy, Portugal, Spain, and the United Kingdom had divided almost all of Africa among themselves. Only Ethiopia and Liberia remained independent.

African societies responded to colonial conquest in a variety of ways. In some parts of Africa, colonial rule was established peacefully by treaties between the Europeans and African chiefs. But others resisted European control. For example, Africans staged violent uprisings against the British in Nigeria and what is now Ghana, against the French in western and northern Africa, and against the Germans in what are now Tanzania and Namibia. Ethiopians defeated Italian forces and retained their independence. By the mid-1920's, however, Europeans strongly controlled most of Africa.

The European colonization of Africa took a heavy cost in African lives. Millions were killed in wars of conquest as well as through the demands imposed upon them in colonial plantations. For example, historians estimate that the brutal regime of King Leopold II of Belgium in Congo Free State, now the Democratic Republic of the Congo, caused the death of several million Africans.

The colonial period also witnessed social transformations that included changes in the patterns of urbanization, education, and religious practice. New urban centers emerged, and many old cities expanded. In these cities, Africans created new forms of social life and leisure activities. Many Africans educated by missionaries opposed colonialism and demanded higher education or pursued it abroad. During colonial rule, both Christianity and Islam expanded.

Struggles for independence. Organized groups in some African colonies began to demand self-government in the early 1900's. But not until after World War II (1939-1945) did the demands for independence become a powerful mass movement. Some colonies achieved their independence through largely peaceful means, while for others it came after lengthy armed struggles.

In 1951, with the aid of the United Nations, Libya became the first country in Africa to gain independence. In 1956, Morocco, Sudan, and Tunisia became independent relatively peacefully. A bloody revolt against the

French in Algeria broke out in 1954. It lasted eight years and cost about 1 million Algerian lives before the country won independence in 1962.

In 1957, the Gold Coast became the first western African colony to gain independence. It won independence from the United Kingdom and took the name Ghana. In Kenya, a secret movement called Mau Mau began a revolt against British control in 1952. Although it failed, the revolt contributed to Kenya's eventual decolonization in 1963. By the mid-1960's, the United Kingdom, Belgium, and France had freed most of their colonies in east and west Africa. But in Guinea-Bissau, Africans waged war against the Portuguese until independence in 1974.

The most difficult wars of liberation were fought in southern Africa. Portugal fought costly wars in Angola and Mozambique before granting them freedom in 1975. In Rhodesia, Black people fought for years against white-minority rule. A government with a Black majority was finally elected in 1979. The next year, the United Kingdom recognized Rhodesia's independence, and the country was renamed Zimbabwe. South Africa's control over the territory of Namibia (called South West Africa until 1968) became an international issue during the mid-1900's. Most nations considered South Africa's control of Namibia illegal. In 1990, Namibia became an independent country. Finally, South Africa made the transition from *apartheid* (strict racial segregation) to a multiracial democracy under Black-majority rule in 1994. This transition marked the end of European colonialism in Africa.

Africa since independence. African countries were confronted with many challenges inherited from colonialism and brought by independence. Military officers overthrew civilian governments in many countries. In a few countries, military dictatorships emerged. Civil wars broke out in Chad, the Democratic Republic of the Congo (DRC), Nigeria, and other countries.

During the 1990's, struggles for democracy intensified across Africa. The majority of African countries are now democratic. However, the effectiveness of several African states in promoting good government and ending corruption remains a concern. In some areas, ethnic or religious loyalties often clash with national loyalties.

At independence, most African economies were small and underdeveloped. In the 1960's and 1970's, some Afri-

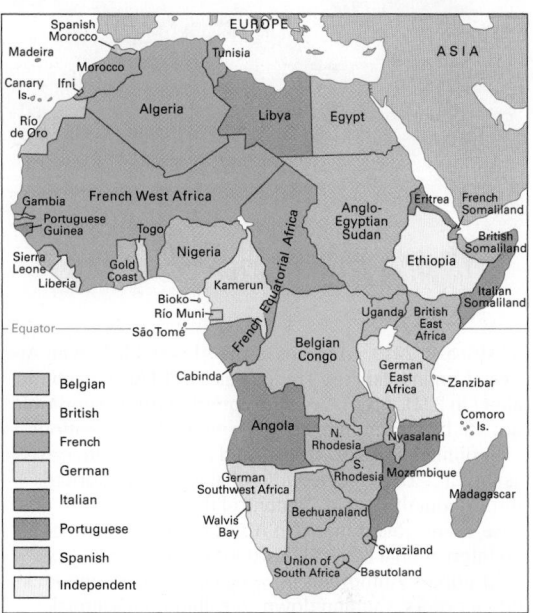

WORLD BOOK map

Africa in 1914 had only two independent countries—Ethiopia and Liberia. The rest of the continent was under colonial rule by European powers.

can countries opted for capitalism and free enterprise, while others pursued socialist strategies of state ownership. Most countries experienced economic growth. However, this changed in the late 1970's as prices for African goods, such as coffee and cocoa, fell in world markets. National debt rose in most nations.

Other challenges to African stability include disease and warfare. Since the 1970's, outbreaks of the Ebola virus have killed thousands of people. In the 1990's and early 2000's, the AIDS epidemic reached disastrous levels in parts of Africa. Internal conflicts and regional wars have devastated several countries in Africa since the 1990's. In 1994, Hutu militias massacred hundreds of thousands of Tutsi and moderate Hutu in Rwanda. Civil war in the DRC broke out in 1998 and involved several other countries. Even after the war ended in 2003, ethnic clashes continued. Since 1998, conflict in the DRC has claimed more than 5 million lives, mostly from disease and malnutrition.

Cooperation is the ideal behind the movement of *Pan-Africanism,* which promotes the unity of African countries. The 1990's saw the strengthening of regional economic blocs, including the Economic Community of West African States, the Southern African Development Community, and the Arab Maghreb Union. These organizations were formed to help Africa compete in the world economy.

The drive for regional and continental integration continued into the 2000's. The African Union (AU), an association of African states, was formed in 2002. It replaced the Organization of African Unity (OAU). The AU works to promote African economic and political cooperation. The AU has several administrative bodies, including a Pan-African Parliament and a Peace and Security Council, set up to promote good government, justice, and peace

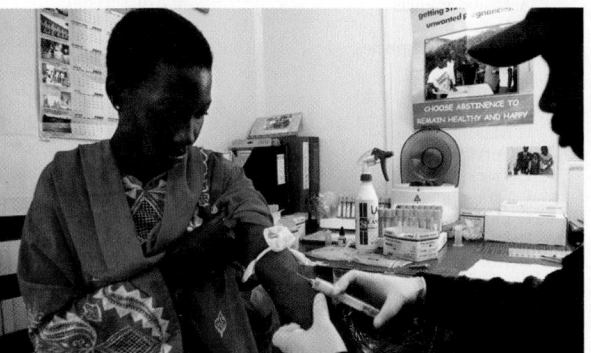

© Per-Anders Pettersson, Getty Images

A Ugandan woman is tested for HIV, the virus that causes AIDS, as part of a program to reduce HIV transmission. The AIDS epidemic reached disastrous levels in Africa by the early 2000's. But AIDS-related deaths dropped after 2010 with the introduction of antiretroviral therapy (ART).

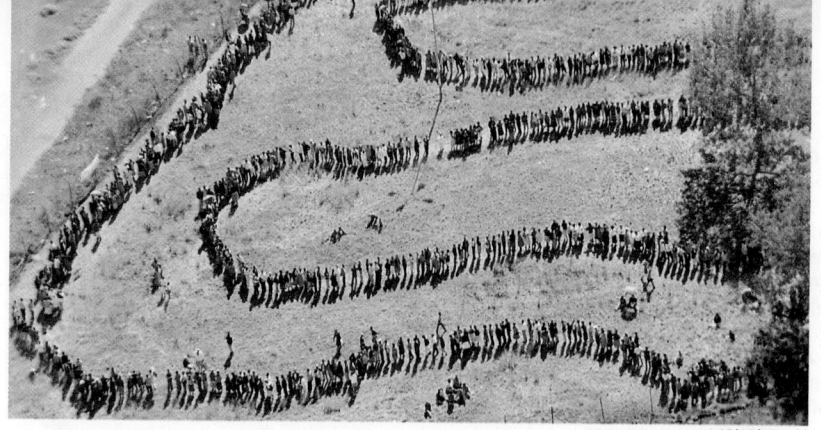

South Africa's first elections open to all races, held in 1994, drew long lines of voters to the polls. In the elections, Black Africans gained control of the government from the white minority. Previously, Black people, who make up a majority of the nation's population, could not vote.

in Africa. In 2019, countries of the AU established an African Continental Free Trade Area (AfCFTA). It went into effect in 2021. AfCFTA was designed to boost economic growth by making trade easier among African nations.

Beginning in 2020, Africa faced a public health crisis as the COVID-19 *pandemic* (global epidemic) spread throughout the world. To control the spread of the disease, many governments in Africa imposed restrictions on international travel and urged residents to stay in their homes. Authorities in some countries issued lockdown orders, shutting down so-called nonessential businesses. By mid-2020, many countries began to relax some restrictions as cases declined. Some African countries began a vaccination program in February 2021. However, a shortage of vaccines and the spread of new, more infectious variants of the virus caused sharp rises in cases and deaths in a number of countries by mid-2021.   Paul Desanker, Peri Klemm, Kenneth J. Perkins, Kwesi Kwaa Prah, and Paul Tiyambe Zeleza

Related articles in *World Book* include:

Countries and other political units

See the separate articles on African countries and other political units listed in the table with this article.

Biographies

Bruce, James	Dias, Bartolomeu	Shaka
Burton, Sir Richard F.	Park, Mungo	Stanley and Livingstone
	Rhodes, Cecil J.	

History

African Americans (The African background)	Egypt, Ancient	Mali Empire
	Exploration	Nok
African Union	French West Africa	Nubia
Aksum	Funj Sultanate	Numidia
Barbary States	Ghana Empire	Rwandan Genocide
Benin	Great Zimbabwe	Slavery
Berlin Conference	Guinea	Somaliland
Carthage	Ife	Songhai Empire
Colonialism	Islamic Empire	Timbuktu
Darfur	Kanem	Utica
Djénné	Kongo	World War II
	Kush	

People

Afrikaners	Copts	Igbo	Mandinka	Swahili
Arabs	Dinka	Khoikhoi	Moors	Tuareg
Ashanti	Fulani	Kikuyu	Nuer	Tutsi
Bantu	Ganda	Luba	Pygmies	Xhosa
Bemba	Hausa	Lunda	San	Yoruba
Berbers	Hutu	Maasai	Semites	Zulu

Physical features

See **Desert; Island; Lake; Mountain; River;** and **Waterfall.** See also:

Aswan High Dam	Cape of Good Hope
Great Rift Valley	Red Sea
Mediterranean Sea	Suez Canal
Olduvai Gorge	

Other related articles

Bank (Africa)	Sculpture (African sculpture)
Conservation (Africa)	Television (In Africa)
Flag	Third World
Music (African music)	United Nations (Working for
Races, Human	self-government)

Outline

I. People
  A. Population
  B. Peoples of Africa
  C. Languages
  D. Religions

II. Ways of life in northern Africa
  A. Rural life
  B. City life
  C. Marriage and family
  D. Food and drink
  E. Clothing
  F. Education

III. Ways of life in sub-Saharan Africa
  A. Rural life
  B. City life
  C. Marriage and family
  D. Food and drink
  E. Clothing
  F. Education

IV. The arts
  A. Ancient art
  B. Fine arts
  C. Architecture
  D. Dance and music
  E. Literature

V. The land
  A. Land regions
  B. Deserts, grasslands, and forests
  C. Rivers, waterfalls, and deltas
  D. Lakes
  E. Mountains

VI. Climate

VII. Animals and plants
  A. Native animals
  B. Native plants
  C. Introduced species

VIII. Economy
  A. Agriculture
  B. Mining
  C. Manufacturing
  D. Service industries
  E. Transportation
  F. Communication
  G. Interntational trade
  H. Foreign aid, debt, and investment

IX. History

African American literature is literature written by Black Americans of African descent. Its themes include the exploration of Black identity, the diversity of the Black experience, and the condemnation of racism. African American literature also celebrates the unique aspects of African American culture, from folklore to religion and music.

Early works. The earliest surviving works of African

American literature date from the mid-1700's. They were written by Africans who had been enslaved and brought to America. The oldest known example is "Bars Fight," a poem about a raid by Indigenous (native) people on a Massachusetts town. Lucy Terry, a 16-year-old enslaved woman living in New England, composed the poem in 1746. It was handed down orally before its publication in 1855. In the late 1700's, Phillis Wheatley, an enslaved woman who lived in Boston, became the first important Black poet. Her *Poems on Various Subjects, Religious and Moral*, published in London in 1773, is the first published book by an African American writer.

The 1800's. The oral tradition of fables, notably trickster tales, played a vital part in early African American culture. Trickster tales often involved a clever character outwitting a stronger adversary, as in the famous stories about the trickster Brer Rabbit. The stories were a significant form of entertainment for enslaved people and a way of indirectly discussing the institution of slavery.

Before the American Civil War (1861-1865), many Black writers were people who had escaped from slavery. Their texts described their experiences on plantations—including frequent beatings, harsh labor, and the separation of family members—in an attempt to persuade white readers that slavery was immoral and therefore should be abolished. Additionally, the texts showed the courage, humanity, and intelligence of people of African descent. The most important such autobiography of this period is the *Narrative of the Life of Frederick Douglass* (1845). Douglass became the leading spokesman for Black Americans in the 1800's. *Incidents in the Life of a Slave Girl* (1861), by Harriet Ann Jacobs, is rare among pre-Civil War autobiographical accounts because it focuses on the unique hardships suffered by enslaved Black women.

Twelve Years a Slave by Solomon Northup (1853) demonstrates how vulnerable all African Americans, enslaved or free, were at this time. Northup recounts being sold into slavery despite his status as a free man. Ellen and William Craft's *Running a Thousand Miles for Freedom; or, The Escape of William and Ellen Craft from Slavery* (1860) challenges the assumed boundaries between Blackness and whiteness. Ellen disguised herself as a white slave master and her husband, William, as her slave in order to escape to freedom.

Some lesser known texts, including *The Bondwoman's Narrative* (written about 1853-1860, first published in 2002), have been recently discovered and published. Historians believe the writer of this handwritten document was Hannah Bond, who used the pen name Hannah Crafts to hide her identity. Evidence suggests that she began writing it while still enslaved and finished after she escaped to freedom in about 1857.

Spiritual narratives that combined autobiography with religious or philosophical beliefs were also popular. *Meditations from the Pen of Mrs. Maria W. Stewart* (1832, expanded edition 1879) is one example. Maria Stewart was a free Black woman living in Massachusetts and a speaker on women's rights. A speech she gave in 1832 is the first known public speech on politics given by an American woman to an audience of both men and women. This period also saw the publication of the nation's first African American-owned newspaper, *Freedom's Journal* (1827 to 1829).

The first published African American fiction appeared in the mid-1800's. It included such novels about slavery as *Clotel, or The President's Daughter* (1853), by William Wells Brown, who had escaped from slavery himself; and *Our Nig* (1859), by Harriet E. Wilson, the first African American woman to publish a novel. Frances E. W. Harper's "The Two Offers" (1859) is the earliest published short story by an African American. Frank J. Webb's *The Garies and Their Friends* (1857) is a novel that describes the problems of a free family living in the North. *Blake* (1861-1862) by Martin Robison Delany tells about a free Black man who organizes a slave rebellion.

© Peter Newark American Pictures/ Bridgeman Art Library

Phillis Wheatley

After slavery was abolished in 1865, African American authors wrote in many literary forms to protest race discrimination. In the 1890's and early 1900's, Paul Laurence Dunbar was acclaimed for his romantic poems in Black dialect. However, some of his verses assert bitter social criticism. Charles Waddell Chesnutt portrayed formerly enslaved persons as intelligent and resourceful in his realistic short stories and novels. One of his better-known works is *The Conjure Woman* (1899). This collection of short stories draws in part on the trickster tradition. However, it also shows how impossible it was for African Americans to hold their families together under slavery.

Frances E. W. Harper and Pauline Hopkins were leading Black women writers. They challenged both racism and sexism in their novels and other works.

In the early 1900's, African American writers questioned how to produce art that told creative stories but also addressed issues of racial injustice after slavery. In Booker T. Washington's *Up From Slavery* (1901), he opposes efforts to protest racism. Instead, he champions a pacifist approach, in which skilled trade labor is key to resolving inequality.

This stance indirectly placed Washington in opposition to Douglass and to a number of contemporaries, including W. E. B. Du Bois. In 1910, Du Bois helped to establish *The Crisis*, which became one of the leading Black-owned magazines of the early 1900's. *The Crisis* addressed social and political issues concerning African Americans and became a platform for upcoming artists and writers. In his essay collection *The Souls of Black Folk* (1903), Du Bois showcases his background in sociology and his primary argument that intellectualism and the arts have pivotal roles in securing greater equality.

Du Bois became a leader among Black intellectuals who believed that Black artists should create for political purposes, with the goal of racial equality as their top priority. A second group, including the educator and writer Alain Locke, thought that artistic creativity should not be limited by pressure to create only positive images of Black life. This debate shaped many of the Black literary works of the 1900's.

The Harlem Renaissance. African American ethnic

pride and creativity flourished during the 1920's. The period's exceptional outpouring of Black literature came to be called the Harlem Renaissance because it began in Harlem, a district of New York City.

In the 1910's and 1920's, many African Americans moved to Harlem and other urban areas in the North. They hoped to find higher-paying industrial jobs and to escape the more violent and overt racism in the South. This mass exodus from the South came to be called the Great Migration.

Alain Locke theorized that African Americans were not only changing location, but also experiencing a drastic change in identity. He referred to this new identity as the New Negro. The New Negro became a popular term to describe the dramatic transformation from imitating old rural Southern stereotypes of Blackness to possessing a modern, urban identity grounded in racial pride and greater self-understanding.

Writers portrayed the idea of the New Negro in literature that reflected the social, cultural, and geographical variation of Black American experiences. Jean Toomer's *Cane* (1923) and Langston Hughes's *The Weary Blues* (1926) blend artistic *genres* (categories) by combining poetry, prose, and music to illustrate the struggles of working class Black people across the country. Toomer and Hughes drew stark contrasts between the tradition-bound South and the fast-paced, urban North. They envisioned the North as the ultimate place of refuge for African Americans.

Claude McKay's *Home to Harlem* (1928) shows how deeply embedded racism is in the nation's core institutions. McKay also revealed a much more complicated attitude towards the North, as a corrupt place but also as a means of escape for African Americans. Other important writers of the Harlem Renaissance include Sterling A. Brown, James Weldon Johnson, and Countee Cullen.

Women writers explored feminism and the journey that African American women endured to find their own artistic voice in such works as Jessie Redmon Fauset's *Plum Bun* (1928). Nella Larsen's novels *Quicksand* (1928) and *Passing* (1929) portray urban Black women's determination to achieve social and economic advancement at any cost. Zora Neale Hurston's *Their Eyes Were Watching God* (1937) continues the conversation about Black women's autonomy by suggesting that fulfillment does not exist in the traditional institution of marriage.

The mid-1900's and Naturalism. In the mid-1900's, much African American literature departed from the themes of the Harlem Renaissance by exposing the bleak conditions of Black life during and after the Great Depression of the 1930's. Writers also condemned discrimination against the poor of all races. As part of a literary movement called Naturalism, many writers created characters whose actions were fully determined by the characters' heredity or environment. They demonstrated the many ways that racism and sexism hindered African Americans' free will to pursue their dreams and passions.

Richard Wright's *Native Son* (1940) and Ralph Ellison's *Invisible Man* (1952) both describe Black men's quests for identity in a hostile country. James Baldwin explored related themes of identity and isolation in novels, essays, and dramas. His semiautobiographical novel *Go Tell It on the Mountain* (1953) follows a young Black man struggling to navigate the worlds of a repressive Black church and the city's temptations and oppression.

In 1950, Gwendolyn Brooks became the first African American to be awarded a Pulitzer Prize for poetry for her book *Annie Allen* (1949). Her novel *Maud Martha* (1953) details how exceptionally difficult adolescence can be for Black girls, who lack ways to express themselves or challenge their abilities. Like many black writers of the mid-1900's, Brooks examined the impact of race, alienation, and poverty on the African American's pursuit of the American dream. Lorraine Hansberry also explored these issues in *A Raisin in the Sun* (1959), the first play by an African American woman to be produced on Broadway.

Black pride and the arts. During the 1960's and 1970's, many African American writers gave up the hope of an integrated society and began to echo the call of the Black Pride Movement for a separate Black culture. The movement stressed the importance of Black nationalism and of independence from white mainstream media. For many writers, activism and art inspired each other. They saw art as a way to encourage racial pride and heighten social awareness and liberation in their Black audience.

Amiri Baraka (then known as LeRoi Jones) was a founder of the Black Arts Movement. His one-act play, *Dutchman* (1964), is a conversation between a well-to-do Black man and a white woman on a subway train. Despite the play's seeming simplicity, *Dutchman* explores the contradictions of Black-white race relations. It also portrays the identity crisis faced by Black men who strive for excellence, and as a result, are questioned about their loyalty to their racial identity.

The writers of the Black Arts Movement rejected traditional literary techniques and themes and developed their own forms of self-expression. Prominent authors included Ed Bullins, Etheridge Knight, Haki Madhubuti (born Don L. Lee), and Douglas Turner Ward.

Male voices dominated the movement, and many works presented masculinity as a solution to the generations-long degradation of African Americans. However, strong female voices also emerged, including Jayne Cortez, Nikki Giovanni, Carolyn Rodgers, Sonia Sanchez, and Ntozake Shange. Shange's choreopoem *for colored girls who have considered suicide/when the rainbow is enuff* (1975) is a series of monologues in which Black women recount stories of abuse and disillusionment. A choreopoem is a dramatic performance that includes music and dance as well as poetry or narrative. Shange and other women writers sought to build a sisterhood that reclaimed the Black female voice and honored the Black Arts Movement from a feminist perspective.

The artistic and political efforts of these authors of the mid-1900's formed the basis for courses in Black studies in many universities in the United States. *The Black Scholar* (founded in 1969) was the first schol-

Library of Congress

Richard Wright

arly journal to promote Black studies. *Negro Digest* became a major platform for up-and-coming Black writers of the movement. The magazine was published from 1942 to 1951 and from 1961 to 1970. It was published under the name *Black World* from 1970 to 1976.

The late 1900's. Much Black literature written in the late 1900's and early 2000's has been described as "post-soul" literature. The term was coined by Nelson George, a writer and editor of works on popular culture. It refers to writers born during or after the civil rights movement of the mid-1950's to late 1960's who were far enough removed from the movement to view it more critically.

Post-soul writers also criticized the Black Arts Movement era for oversimplifying racial issues. They explored such themes as the duality of being a Black American citizen and the irony of being both well versed on white culture and isolated from it. Toni Cade Bambara's *Salt Eaters* (1980), for example, depicts a disillusioned activist's failed suicide attempt and healing in order to re-imagine the path of post-civil rights African American activism.

Some authors sought to redefine Blackness to more fully recognize the diversity among Black people. They acknowledged that such factors as class, gender, political affiliation, regional location, and sexuality all influence the individual experiences of African Americans. In *Sister Outsider: Essays and Speeches* (1984), Audre Lorde famously challenges racism, sexism, and homophobia as interlocking systems of oppression for Black lesbians like herself. Lorde asserts that celebrating difference is the means for social progress. Percival Everett's satirical novel *Erasure* (2001) suggests that Black writers have had to perpetuate racial stereotypes in order to please literary critics.

The late 1900's saw a rise in publications from Black female writers, including Elizabeth Alexander, Maya Angelou, Lucille Clifton, Gayl Jones, Jamaica Kincaid, Paule Marshall, and Gloria Naylor. Alice Walker won the 1983 Pulitzer Prize for fiction for *The Color Purple* (1982), a novel about an isolated unwed mother forcibly separated from her children. Rita Dove was awarded the Pulitzer Prize for poetry in 1987 for *Thomas and Beulah* (1986). In 1988, Toni Morrison won the Pulitzer for her novel *Beloved* (1987). *Beloved* is about a formerly enslaved woman haunted by the ghost of her child, whom she killed during her attempt to escape from slavery. In 1993, Morrison became the first African American writer to be awarded the Nobel Prize in literature.

Other post-soul authors include Paul Beatty, Samuel R. Delany, Trey Ellis, Ernest J. Gaines, Danzy Senna, and Kevin Young. Yusef Komunyakaa won the 1994 Pulitzer prize in poetry for *Neon Vernacular* (1993).

The 2000's. African American voices and experiences have been central to American literature of the 2000's. August Wilson and Suzan-Lori Parks emerged as leading playwrights during the late 1900's and early 2000's. Before his death in 2005, Wilson completed a cycle of 10 major plays. The cycle traces the Black experience in the United States throughout the 1900's. Parks's plays explore such topics as slavery, racism, urban poverty, and the legacy of past discrimination. Wilson won Pulitzer Prizes for drama for *Fences* (1985) and *The Piano Lesson* (1987). Parks received the prize for *Topdog/Underdog* in 2001. Lynn Nottage became the first woman to receive

the Pulitzer Prize for drama twice, in 2009 for *Ruined* (2007) and in for 2017 for *Sweat* (2015).

Black poets in the early 2000's have combined various mediums and poetry forms, including the written word, the spoken word, and music. They tell compelling stories about the complexities of identity and African American experiences. *Don't Let Me Be Lonely: An American*

© Deborah Feingold, Getty Images
Toni Morrison

Lyric (2004) by the Jamaican-born poet Claudia Rankine incorporates poetry and photography to examine death, alienation, and the collective anxieties of Americans following the terrorist attacks of Sept. 11, 2001. Other prominent poets of this period include Robin Coste Lewis, Gregory Pardlo, Danez Smith, Tracy K. Smith, and Natasha Trethewey.

Black speculative fiction began to develop in African American literature in the late 1900's. Speculative fiction is literature, including science fiction and some fantasy, that intertwines aspects of the contemporary world with futuristic or supernatural elements. Historically, white male writers dominated speculative fiction, which emphasized adventure and the technical possibilities of the future. Octavia Butler's groundbreaking novel *Parable of the Sower* (1993) and its sequel, *Parable of the Talents* (1998), follow a young Black woman as she navigates through future social upheaval to establish her own religious commune as a refuge. The series illustrates the negative impacts of social and technological advances on communities of color. It also shows how the remnants of slavery can resurface in a seemingly advanced future.

Beginning in the late 1900's, many Black novelists began to produce works of myth, ritual, and magic realism to reflect on the legacies of slavery and racial prejudice. African spirituality and magic help young women fight oppression in such books as *Who Fears Death* (2010) by the Nigerian-born American author Nnedi Okorafor and *Children of Blood and Bone* (2018) by the African American author Tomi Adeyemi. Black speculative fiction departs from the focus on realism in much African American literature. Butler and her successors demonstrate how the otherworldliness of speculative fiction can speak to the alienation in the Black experience.

Another popular form of African American literature of the 2000's is historical fiction about African Americans who were silenced or completely erased from early recorded history. Alice Randall's *The Wind Done Gone* (2001) takes the focus away from the famed Scarlett O'Hara of the novel *Gone with the Wind* (1936) and redirects readers' attention to the lives of the enslaved Black characters of the book's Civil War setting. Colson Whitehead's *The Underground Railroad* (2016) illustrates the experiences and obstacles two fictional characters endure in seeking freedom through the underground railroad.   Sidney Jones

See also **African Americans** with its list of *Related articles,* including those on African American writers.

And the Migrants Kept Coming (1940-1941). Tempera on gesso composition board by Jacob Lawrence; The Museum of Modern Art, New York City (Digital Image © The Museum of Modern Art/Licensed by SCALA/Art Resource)

The history of African Americans is largely the story of their struggle for freedom and equality. This painting, titled *And the Migrants Kept Coming,* is from "The Migration Series" by the African American painter Jacob Lawrence. Lawrence painted the series of 60 panels in 1940 and 1941 when he was living in Harlem, a Black community in New York City. The paintings tell the story of African Americans who journeyed from rural areas in the southern United States to cities in the North between 1910 and 1930 in search of a better life. The movement was called the "Great Migration."

African Americans

African Americans are Americans mostly or partly of African descent. About 40 million African Americans live in the United States. They account for 13 percent of the nation's total population and, in number, trail only Hispanic Americans among minority groups. About half of all Black Americans live in the Southern States. Most of the rest live in large cities in other regions.

African Americans have used a number of terms to refer to themselves. The terms *Negro* (which means *black* in Spanish and Portuguese) and *colored* were commonly used until the mid-1960's. These terms referred to the dark brown skin color of many African Americans. Since then, most African Americans have chosen to express pride in their color or origin by using other terms. At various times, they have called themselves *blacks, Afro-Americans, black Americans,* or *African Americans.* Discussion of preferred names in African American communities continues today. For example, Black activists and scholars have argued for capitalization of the term *Black* and use of the term *Black Americans* (with an upper-case *B)* to recognize the shared culture, experiences, and identity of a people who have endured a centuries-long struggle for equality, recognition, and respect.

The majority of African Americans trace their origin to an area in western Africa that was controlled by three great and wealthy Black empires from about the A.D. 300's to the late 1500's. These empires—Ghana, Mali,

and Songhai—thrived on trade and developed efficient governments. During the early 1500's, European nations began a trade in which people from western Africa were enslaved and brought to European colonies in the Americas. For about the next 300 years, millions of enslaved Black Africans were shipped across the Atlantic Ocean to North and South America. About 500,000 of them were brought to what is now the United States.

The history of African Americans is largely the story of their struggle for freedom and equality. From the 1600's until the American Civil War (1861-1865), most Black Americans worked as slaves throughout the South. They did much to help Southern agriculture expand. At the same time, free Black Americans helped develop industry in the North. Even after 1865, when slavery was finally abolished in the United States, Black Americans suffered from widespread *segregation* (separation by race) and poverty. The determined efforts of Black people to achieve equality and justice led to the start of a strong civil rights movement in the United States in the 1950's.

The lives of African Americans have improved since the 1950's. Black Americans are making important contributions in all areas of American life. The election in 2008 of Barack Obama as the first African American president reflects the strides toward equality that have been made in the United States. However, many African Americans still suffer from segregation and poverty, discrimination in jobs and housing, and other problems.

This article describes the African background of Black Americans and traces their history since their arrival in North America. The section at the end of the article lists many related articles in *World Book*.

The African background

The cultural heritage. The ancestors of most Black Americans came from an area of Africa known as the western Sudan. This area was about as large as the United States, not including Hawaii and Alaska. It extended from the Atlantic Ocean in the west to Lake Chad in the east and from the Sahara in the north to the Gulf of Guinea in the south.

From about the A.D. 300's to 1591, three highly developed Black African empires, in turn, controlled all or most of the western Sudan. They were Ghana, Mali, and Songhai. Their economies were based on farming, on mining gold, and on trade with Arabs of northern Africa.

Ghana ruled much of the western Sudan from the 300's to the mid-1000's. The Ghanaians became the first people in western Africa to smelt iron ore. They made arrows, swords, and other weapons of iron, which helped them conquer nearby nations.

In 1235, the Malinke people of Mali began to develop the second great Black African empire of the western Sudan. By 1240, they controlled all Ghana. The Mali Empire's most famous ruler was Mansa Musa, who reigned from 1312 to about 1337. Mansa Musa encouraged the practice of Islam, the religion of the Muslims. Under his rule, Mali reached its height of wealth, political power, and cultural achievement.

Beginning in the 1400's, the Songhai Empire gained control of most of northwestern Africa south of the Sahara, including much of Mali. Under Askia Muhammad, who ruled Songhai from 1493 to 1528, the empire had a well-organized central government and excellent universities in such cities as Timbuktu and Djénné. Like Mansa Musa, Askia encouraged his people to practice the Islamic faith. Invaders from Morocco conquered Songhai in 1591.

Some ancestors of African Americans lived in smaller nations in the western Sudan. These nations included Ashanti, Benin, Dahomey, and Oyo. Their economies also depended on farming, trade, and gold mining. For more details on the major Black African empires, see **Ghana Empire; Mali Empire; Songhai Empire.**

Beginning of the slave trade. Africans had practiced slavery since ancient times. In most cases, people captured in warfare were enslaved and sold to Arab traders of northern Africa. Portugal and Spain became increasingly involved in the African slave trade during the early 1500's, after they had established colonies in the Americas. Portugal acquired Black Africans to work on sugar plantations that its colonists developed in Brazil. Spain used enslaved people on sugar plantations in the Caribbean. During the early 1600's, the Netherlands,

The North American slave trade

The map at the right shows the route ships used to carry enslaved people from western Africa to North America. On the map below, the red type indicates the groups from which most enslaved people were taken. The groups that captured the most Africans for European and American slave traders are shown in bold black type.

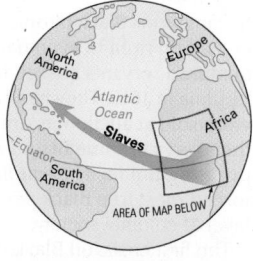

WORLD BOOK maps

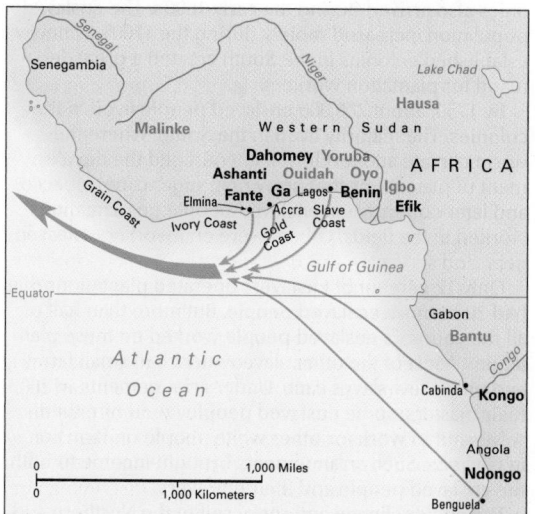

© INTERFOTO/Alamy Images

Africans marched captured enemies, *above,* to coastal slave markets. The cutaway drawing below shows the *tight packing* system used on ships taking enslaved people to North America.

Schomburg Collection, New York Public Library

Robert A. Pratt, the contributor of this article, is Professor of History at the University of Georgia.

France, and England also began to use enslaved Africans in their American colonies.

The Europeans obtained enslaved people from Africans who continued to sell their war captives or trade them for rum, cloth, and other items, especially guns. The Africans wanted the guns for use in warfare with neighboring peoples.

The slave trade took several triangular routes. Over one route, ships from Europe transported manufactured goods to the west coast of Africa. There, traders exchanged the goods for enslaved people. Next, the captives were carried across the Atlantic Ocean to the Caribbean Islands and sold for huge profits. This part of the route was called the Middle Passage because it was the middle leg of the journey from Africa to the New World. The traders used much of their earnings to buy coffee, sugar, and tobacco in the Caribbean. The ships then took these products to Europe.

On another triangular route, ships from the New England Colonies carried rum and other products to Africa, where they were exchanged for enslaved people. The ships then transported these people to the Caribbean to be sold. The slave traders used some of their profits to buy molasses and sugar, which they took back to New England and sold to rum producers.

The slave trade was conducted for profit. The captains of slave ships therefore tried to deliver as many healthy captives for as little cost as possible. Some captains used a system called *loose packing.* Under that system, captains transported fewer enslaved people than their ships could carry in the hope of reducing sickness and death among them. Other captains preferred *tight packing.* They believed that many of their captives would die on the voyages anyway and so carried as many enslaved people as their ships could hold.

The majority of the slave ship voyages across the Atlantic took several months. The enslaved people were chained below deck all day and all night except for brief periods of exercise. Their crowded conditions led to the chief horrors of the Middle Passage—filth, stench, disease, and death.

The Atlantic slave trade operated from the 1500's to the mid-1800's. Between 10 million and 12 million Africans were enslaved during this period. Of this total, what is now the United States received about 5 percent.

The years of slavery

Some scholars believe that the first Black Africans in America came with the expeditions led by Christopher Columbus, starting in 1492. Enslaved Black people traveled to North and South America with French, Portuguese, and Spanish explorers throughout the 1500's.

The best-known Black African to take part in the early explorations of North America was an enslaved man named Estevanico. In 1539, he crossed what are now Arizona and New Mexico on an expedition sent by Antonio de Mendoza, ruler of Spain's colony in America.

Colonial times. The first Black Africans in the American Colonies were brought in, like many lower-class white Europeans, as *indentured servants.* Most indentured servants had a contract to work without wages for a master for four to seven years, after which they became free. Black people brought in as slaves, however, had no right to eventual freedom. The first Black indentured servants arrived in Jamestown in the colony of Virginia in 1619. They had been captured in Africa and were sold at auction in Jamestown. After completing their service, some Black indentured servants bought property. But racial prejudice among white colonists forced most free Black people to remain in the lowest level of colonial society.

The first enslaved Black Africans in the American Colonies also arrived during the early 1600's. The enslaved population increased rapidly during the 1700's as newly established colonies in the South created a great demand for plantation workers.

By 1750, about 200,000 enslaved people lived in the colonies. The majority lived in the South, where the warm climate and fertile soil encouraged the development of plantations that grew rice, sugar cane, tobacco, and later cotton. Most enslaved people on plantations worked in the fields. Others were craftworkers, messengers, and servants.

Only 12 percent of enslavers operated plantations that had 20 or more enslaved people. But more than half of all the country's enslaved people worked on these plantations. Most of the other slaveowners had small farms and only a few slaves each. Under arrangements with their masters, some enslaved people could hire themselves out to work for other white people on farms or in city jobs. Such arrangements brought income to both the enslaved people and their enslavers.

The cooler climate and rocky soil of the Northern and

Notable African American "firsts"

1773 Phillis Wheatley, first important African American poet

1794 Absalom Jones founded first Episcopal Church for African Americans.

1816 Richard Allen founded the African Methodist Episcopal Church (A.M.E.), the first African American denomination in the United States.

1827 John Russwurm cofounded first U.S. newspaper owned and operated by African Americans.

1843 Sojourner Truth, first African American woman orator to speak out against slavery

1872 P. B. S. Pinchback, first African American to serve as governor of a U.S. state, Louisiana

1875 Blanche K. Bruce, first African American to serve a full term in the U.S. Senate

1875 James A. Healy, first African American bishop of the Roman Catholic Church

1890's Paul Laurence Dunbar, first African American to become nationally popular as a writer of both poetry and fiction

1895 W. E. B. Du Bois, first African American to receive a Ph.D. degree at Harvard University

1895 James Weldon Johnson founded first African American-oriented daily newspaper in the United States.

Late 1890's Charles Waddell Chesnutt, first major African American writer of fiction

Early 1900's Madam C. J. Walker, first African American woman to become a wealthy business owner

1907 Alain Locke, first African American to receive a Rhodes Scholarship to study at Oxford University

1908 Jack Johnson, first African American to win the world heavyweight boxing championship

1921 Bessie Coleman, first African American woman licensed as a pilot

1931 William Still, first African American composer to have a work performed by a major orchestra

1936 Mary McLeod Bethune, first African American woman to head a federal agency, the Division of Negro Affairs of the National Youth Administration

1940 Hattie McDaniel, first African American to win an Academy Award

1941 Gordon Parks, first African American photographer to work for major magazines

1942 Lena Horne, first African American performer signed to a long-term contract by a major Hollywood film studio, Metro-Goldwyn-Mayer

1947 Jackie Robinson, first African American to play modern major league baseball

1950 Gwendolyn Brooks, first African American to win a Pulitzer Prize

1950 Ralph Bunche, first African American to win the Nobel Peace Prize

1955 Marian Anderson, first African American soloist to sing with the Metropolitan Opera of New York City

1955 Arthur Mitchell, first African American to dance with a major classical ballet company, the New York City Ballet

1957 Althea Gibson, first African American tennis player to win at Wimbledon and U.S. Open

1959 Berry Gordy, Jr., first African American to own a record label that successfully promoted African American crossover artists

1959 Lorraine Hansberry, first African American playwright to achieve critical and popular success on Broadway

1960 Leontyne Price, first African American woman to sing a leading role with the LaScala opera company of Milan, Italy

1962 James Meredith, first African American to attend the University of Mississippi

1964 Sidney Poitier, first African American to win an Academy Award for a leading role

1964 Quincy Jones, first African American to hold an executive position with a major white-owned record company

1965 Bill Cosby, first African American actor to co-star in a prime-time TV dramatic series, "I Spy"

1966 Bill Russell, first African American head coach in major league professional sports

1966 Robert Weaver, first African American Cabinet member

1967 Edward W. Brooke, first African American elected to the Senate since the Reconstruction period

1967 Robert Henry Lawrence, Jr., first African American selected as an astronaut

1967 Thurgood Marshall, first African American justice on the Supreme Court of the United States

1967 Carl B. Stokes, first African American to be elected mayor of a major American city, Cleveland

1968 Arthur Ashe, first African American to win the U.S. men's national tennis singles championship

1969 Shirley Chisholm, first African American woman to serve in the U.S. Congress

1970 Charles Gordone, first African American playwright to win a Pulitzer Prize for drama

1973 Tom Bradley, first African American mayor of Los Angeles

1973 Barbara C. Jordan, first African American woman from a Southern state, Texas, to serve in the U.S. Congress

1973 Coleman A. Young, first African American mayor of Detroit

1975 Virginia Hamilton, first African American author to be awarded the Newbery Medal

1975 Daniel James, Jr., first African American U.S. four-star general

1975 Frank Robinson, first African American manager of a major league baseball team, the Cleveland Indians

1977 Patricia Roberts Harris, first African American woman to hold a U.S. Cabinet post, secretary of housing and urban development

1977 Andrew Young, Jr., first African American to serve as U.S. ambassador to the United Nations

1983 Guion S. Bluford, Jr., first African American astronaut to travel in space

1983 Harold Washington, first African American mayor of Chicago

1988 Eugene A. Marino, first African American to be named an archbishop of the Roman Catholic Church

1989 Ronald H. Brown, first African American to head a major U.S. political party, the Democratic Party

1990 David N. Dinkins, first African American mayor of New York City

1990 L. Douglas Wilder, first African American to be elected governor of a state, Virginia

1991 Sharon Pratt Kelly, first African American woman mayor of a major American city—Washington, D.C.

1992 Mae C. Jemison, first African American woman astronaut to travel in space

1992 Carol Moseley Braun, first African American woman elected to the U.S. Senate

1993 Joycelyn Elders, first African American to serve as U.S. surgeon general

1997 Tiger Woods, first golfer of African American heritage to win the Masters Tournament

1998 David Satcher, first African American man to serve as U.S. surgeon general

1999 J. C. Watts, Jr., first African American Republican to hold a leadership role in the House of Representatives—chairman of the House Republican Conference—since Reconstruction

2001 Colin L. Powell, first African American to serve as U.S. secretary of state

2002 Halle Berry, first African American to win an Oscar as best actress

2002 Suzan-Lori Parks, first African American female playwright to win a Pulitzer Prize for drama

2005 Condoleezza Rice, first African American woman to serve as U.S. secretary of state

2008 Barack Obama, first African American to be elected U.S. president

2008 Tyler Perry, first African American to own a major television and motion-picture studio, Tyler Perry Studios

2009 Michelle Obama, first African American first lady

2015 Misty Copeland, first African American woman to be named a principal dancer with the American Ballet Theater

2020 Kamala Harris, first African American (and first woman) to be elected vice president of the United States

Where African Americans live

This map shows the state-by-state distribution of African Americans in the United States, according to the 2010 census. The numbers on the map indicate the percentage of African Americans in the total population of each state.

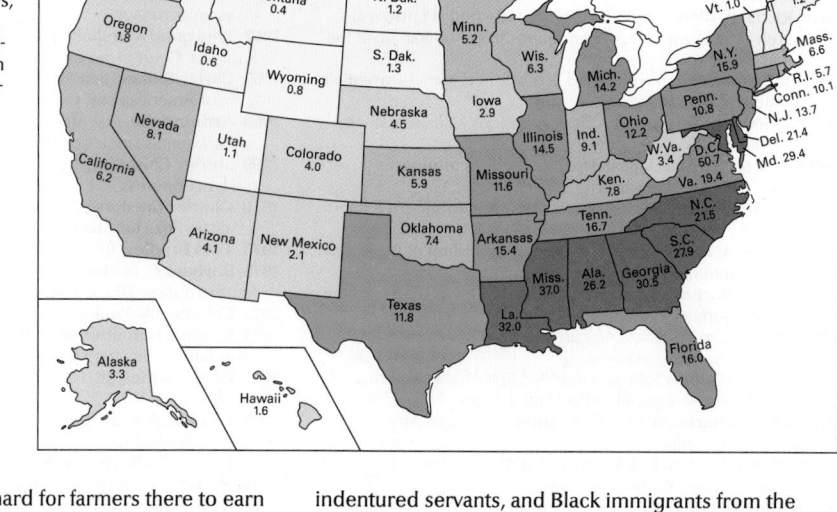

Percent of total population by state

▉	More than 20.0
▓	10.0 to 20.0
▒	5.0 to 10.0
░	1.5 to 5.0
□	Less than 1.5

WORLD BOOK map

Middle colonies made it hard for farmers there to earn large profits. Many enslaved people in those colonies worked as skilled and unskilled laborers in factories, homes, and shipyards and on fishing and trading ships.

During the mid-1600's, the colonies began to pass laws called *slave codes.* In general, these codes prohibited enslaved people from owning weapons, receiving an education, meeting one another or moving about without the permission of their enslavers, and testifying against white people in court. Enslaved people received harsher punishments for some crimes than white people. An enslaver usually received less punishment for killing a slave than for killing a free person. Enslaved people on small farms probably had more freedom than those on plantations, and slaves in urban areas had fewer restrictions than those in rural areas.

By 1770, there may have been 40,000 or more free Black people in the American Colonies. They included people who had escaped slavery, descendants of early indentured servants, and Black immigrants from the Caribbean. Many free Black people opposed British rule. One of the best-known African American patriots was Crispus Attucks, who died in the Boston Massacre of 1770 while mocking the presence of British soldiers.

During the American Revolution (1775-1783), most Black people probably favored the British. They believed that a British victory would offer them their earliest or best chance for freedom. But about 5,000 people of Black African descent fought on the side of the colonists. Most of them were freedmen or enslaved people from the Northern and Middle colonies. Black heroes of the war included Peter Salem and Salem Poor of Massachusetts, who distinguished themselves in the Battle of Bunker Hill in 1775.

The growth of slavery. By the early 1800's, more than 700,000 slaves lived in the South. They accounted for a third of the region's people. Enslaved people outnumbered white people in South Carolina and made up

© Thinkstock

Slave trading became increasingly profitable throughout the South from the time the first enslaved Africans arrived in the early 1600's. Buyers often paid more than $1,000 for a skilled, healthy person. Many enslaved people were sold at auctions.

Granger Collection

Crispus Attucks, *center,* was a leader of the patriot mob that was fired upon by British troops in the Boston Massacre of 1770. Attucks and many other free Black colonists who lived in the North opposed British rule in the American Colonies.

over half the population in both Maryland and Virginia.

Slavery began to develop even deeper roots in the South after Eli Whitney of Massachusetts invented his cotton gin in 1793. This machine removed the seeds from cotton as fast as 50 people working by hand. It probably contributed more to the growth of slavery than any other development. Whitney's gin enabled farmers to meet the rapidly rising demand for cotton. As a result, the Southern cotton industry expanded. The planters needed more and more workers to pick and bale the cotton, which led to large increases in the enslaved population. The thriving sugar cane plantations of Louisiana also used many enslaved people during the first half of the 1800's. By 1860, about 4 million slaves lived in the South.

Numerous enslaved people protested against their condition. They used such day-to-day forms of rebellion as destroying property, running away, pretending illness, and disobeying orders. Enslaved people received beatings or other physical punishment for refusing to work, attempting to run away, or participating in plots or rebellions against their enslavers. Some enslaved people were executed for rebelling.

Major protests by people who were enslaved included armed revolts and mutinies. The most famous of about 200 such revolts was led by Nat Turner, an enslaved preacher. The revolt broke out in 1831 in Southampton County in Virginia. The rebels killed about 60 white people before being captured. The best-known slave mutiny occurred in 1839 aboard *La Amistad,* off the coast of Cuba. A group of Africans, led by Joseph Cinque, brought the vessel to Long Island in New York. The Africans were given their freedom soon afterward.

Free Black people. The American Revolution helped lead to new attitudes about slavery, especially among white people in the North. The war inspired a spirit of liberty and an appreciation for the service of the Black soldiers. Partly for this reason, some Northern legislatures adopted laws during the late 1700's that provided for the immediate or gradual end of slavery. Another reason for such laws was simply that slaves had no essential role in the main economic activities of the North.

The census of 1790 revealed that the nation had about 59,000 free Black people, including about 27,000 in the North. By the early 1800's, most Northern states had taken steps to end slavery. Besides formerly enslaved people freed by law, free Black people included those who had been freed by their enslavers, who had bought their freedom, or who had been born of free parents.

After the American Revolution, numerous free Black people found jobs in tobacco plants, textile mills, and other factories. Some worked in shipyards, on ships, and later in railroad construction. Many became skilled in carpentry and other trades. Some became merchants and editors. The best-known editors were Samuel Cornish and John Russwurm, who helped start the first Black newspaper, *Freedom's Journal,* in 1827.

Most white people treated free Black Americans as inferiors. Many hotels, restaurants, theaters, and other public places barred them. Few states gave free Black people the right to vote. Their children had to attend separate schools. Some colleges and universities, such as Bowdoin in Maine, and Oberlin in Ohio, admitted Black students. But the limited number of admissions led to the opening of Black colleges, including Lincoln University in Pennsylvania in 1854 and Wilberforce University in Ohio in 1856.

In both the North and the South, churches either banned Black people or required them to sit apart from white people. As a result, some Black Americans set up their own churches. In 1816, Richard Allen, a Black Philadelphia minister, helped set up the African Methodist Episcopal Church, the first Black denomination in the country.

The rising number of free Black people alarmed many white people and led to further restrictions on their activities. In parts of New England, free Black Americans could not visit any town without a pass. They also needed permission to entertain enslaved people in their homes. In the South, free Black people could be enslaved if caught without proof that they were free. Fears that free Black people would lead slave revolts encouraged almost all states to pass laws severely limiting the right of free Black Americans to own weapons.

© Thinkstock

© North Wind Picture Archives/Alamy Images

The production of cotton increased rapidly in the South after Eli Whitney invented a faster way of cleaning cotton in 1793. Whitney's cotton gin, *left,* could clean as much cotton in a day as could 50 people working by hand and helped meet the growing demand for cotton. More workers were needed on plantations, *right,* which led to a huge growth in the enslaved population.

Increasing concern over the large number of free Black people led to the founding of the American Colonization Society in 1816. The society was sponsored by well-known supporters of slavery, including U.S. Representatives John C. Calhoun of South Carolina and Henry Clay of Kentucky. Their plan was to lessen "the race problem" by transporting free Black Americans on a voluntary basis to Africa. In 1822, the society established the Black American colony of Liberia on the continent's west coast. In 1847, Liberia became the first self-governing Black republic in Africa. However, most free Black people felt that the United States was their home. As a result, only about 12,000 of them had volunteered to settle in Liberia by 1850.

Despite their inferior position, a number of free Black people won widespread recognition during the late 1700's and early 1800's. For example, Phillis Wheatley gained fame for her poetry. Newport Gardner distinguished himself in music. Benjamin Banneker, a mathematician, published outstanding almanacs. Notable Black ministers included Absalom Jones in the North and George Liele and Andrew Bryan in the South. Paul Cuffe and James Forten gained wealth in business. Tom Molineaux became known for his boxing skills.

By 1860, the nation had about 490,000 free Black people. But most of them faced such severe discrimination that they were little better off than those who remained enslaved.

The antislavery movement. Many white Americans, particularly Northerners, felt that slavery was evil and violated the ideals of democracy. However, plantation owners and other supporters of slavery regarded it as natural to, and necessary for, the Southern way of life. They also argued that Southern culture introduced enslaved people to Christianity and helped them become "civilized." Most white Southerners held such beliefs by 1860, though less than 5 percent of them owned slaves and only about half the slaveowners had more than five enslaved people. In addition, Southern farmers insisted that they could not make money growing cotton without cheap slave labor.

The Southern States hoped to expand slavery as new states were admitted to the Union. However, the Northern States feared they would lose power in Congress permanently if more states that permitted slavery were admitted. The North and the South thereby became increasingly divided over the spread of slavery.

The slavery issue created heated debate in Congress after the Territory of Missouri applied for statehood in 1818. At the time, there were 11 slave states, in which slavery was allowed, and 11 free states, in which it was prohibited. Most Missourians supported slavery, but many Northern members of Congress did not want Missouri to become a slave state. In 1820, Congress reached a settlement known as the Missouri Compromise. This measure admitted Missouri as a slave state, but it also called for Maine to enter the Union as a free state. Congress thus preserved the balance between free and slave states at 12 each.

New, aggressive opponents of slavery began to spring up in the North during the 1830's. Their leaders included William Lloyd Garrison, Lucretia Mott, Lewis Tappan, and Theodore Dwight Weld. During the 1830's and 1840's, these white abolitionists were joined by many free Black people, including such formerly enslaved people as Frederick Douglass, Henry Highland Garnet, Sojourner Truth, and Harriet Tubman.

Abolitionist leaders attacked slavery in writings and public speeches. Garrison began to publish an antislavery newspaper, *The Liberator,* in 1831. Douglass, the most influential Black leader of the time, started an abolitionist newspaper called the *North Star* in 1847. Tubman and many other abolitionists helped Southern slaves escape to the free states and Canada. Tubman returned to the South 19 times and personally led about 300 enslaved people to freedom. She and others used a network of routes and housing to assist the escapees. This network became known as the *underground railroad.*

The deepening division over slavery. After 1848, Congress had to deal with the question of whether to permit slavery in the territories that the United States gained from Mexico as a result of the Mexican War (1846-1848). The territories covered what are now California, Nevada, Utah, and parts of four other states. Fol-

Frederick Douglass, *right,* was the most influential black leader in the United States during much of the 1800's. He started an abolitionist newspaper, the *North Star,* in 1847 and advised government leaders on the problems of free Blacks in the North.

Bloody conflicts broke out during the 1850's between supporters and opponents of a proposal to allow slavery in the Territory of Kansas. Because of shootings like this one, which occurred in 1858, the territory became known as "Bleeding Kansas."

lowing angry debates among the members of Congress, Senators Henry Clay of Kentucky and Daniel Webster of Massachusetts helped work out a series of measures that became known as the Compromise of 1850. The Compromise allowed slavery to continue but prohibited the slave trade in Washington, D.C. A key measure in the Compromise admitted California to the Union as a free state. Another agreement gave the residents in the other newly acquired areas the right to decide for themselves whether to allow slavery. The Compromise included a federal fugitive slave law designed to help enslavers get back enslaved people who had run away.

The Compromise of 1850 briefly ended the heated arguments in Congress over slavery. However, the abolitionist movement and the hostility between the North and the South continued. Harriet Beecher Stowe's antislavery novel *Uncle Tom's Cabin* (1851-1852) increased the tensions between Northerners and Southerners. In addition, attempts by Northerners to stop enforcement of the fugitive slave law further angered Southerners.

The quarrel over slavery flared again in Congress in 1854, when it passed the Kansas-Nebraska Act. This law created two federal territories, Kansas and Nebraska, and provided that the people of each territory could decide whether to permit slavery. Most Nebraskans opposed slavery. However, bloody conflicts broke out between supporters and opponents of slavery in Kansas. In 1856, for example, the militant abolitionist John Brown led a raid against supporters of slavery in a small settlement on Pottawatomie Creek in Kansas. Brown's group killed five men and focused the nation's attention on the conflict in the territory, which became known as "Bleeding Kansas." In the end, Kansas joined the Union as a free state in 1861.

Supporters of slavery won a major victory in 1857, when the Supreme Court of the United States issued its ruling in the case of *Dred Scott v. Sandford.* In the Dred Scott Decision, the court denied the claim of Scott, an enslaved man, that his residence in a free state and later a free territory for a time made him free. The court also declared that no Black person—free or enslaved—could be a U.S. citizen. In addition, it stated that Congress had

no power to ban the spread of slavery.

Tension in the South increased again in 1859, when John Brown led another abolitionist group in seizing the United States arsenal at Harpers Ferry in Virginia (now West Virginia). Federal troops quickly captured Brown, and he was executed later that year. But his raid helped convince many Southerners that the slavery issue would lead to fighting between the North and the South.

The end of slavery

Slavery became a major issue in the U.S. presidential election of 1860. Many Democrats in the North opposed the spread of slavery, but Democrats in the South favored it. Each group nominated its own candidate for president, thereby splitting their party. Most Republicans opposed the expansion of slavery. They chose Abraham Lincoln of Illinois as their presidential candidate. In November 1860, he was elected president.

The American Civil War (1861-1865). Southerners feared that Lincoln would limit or end slavery. On Dec. 20, 1860, South Carolina *seceded* (withdrew) from the Union. Early in 1861, six other Southern states seceded. The seceded states took the name Confederate States of America. On April 12, 1861, Confederate troops attacked Fort Sumter, a U.S. military base in South Carolina, and the American Civil War began. Four more slave states joined the Confederacy soon afterward. Four other slave states—Missouri, Kentucky, Maryland, and Delaware—remained loyal to the Union.

At the start of the Civil War, Lincoln's chief concern was to preserve the Union, not to end slavery. He therefore refused requests of African Americans to join the Union Army. He felt that their participation in the war could lead more slave states to secede. Lincoln also knew that many Northerners were hostile toward Black people and so might oppose the use of Black troops.

A number of developments gradually persuaded Lincoln to make the war a fight against slavery. For example, some Union military commanders, without the president's consent, had freed enslaved people in areas they had conquered. Furthermore, abolitionists and Black leaders urged that the war be fought to end slavery, and

Schomburg Collection, NYPL

Harriet Tubman, *left,* was a leader of the *underground railroad,* which helped slaves flee to freedom.

Library of Congress

The Emancipation Proclamation, issued on Jan. 1, 1863, freed the slaves in Confederate areas. Advancing Union troops told slaves they were free.

Chicago History Museum

Black troops made important contributions to the Union victory in the Civil War. Over 200,000 African Americans served in segregated Northern units, such as the 2nd U.S. Colored Artillery, *shown here.*

they demanded the use of Black troops. Most important-ly, the war was going badly for the Union. By fighting against slavery, Lincoln hoped to strengthen the war effort in the North and weaken it in the South.

In March 1862, Lincoln gave Congress a plan for the gradual freedom of enslaved people. The plan included payment for the enslavers. In April, Lincoln approved legislation that ended slavery in the District of Columbia and provided funds for any freed enslaved people who wished to move to Haiti or Liberia. In June, Lincoln signed a bill that ended slavery in all federal territories.

By July 1862, Lincoln was ready to accept African Americans in the Union Army. In September, he issued a preliminary order to *emancipate* (free) the slaves. It declared that all enslaved people in areas or states in re-bellion against the United States on Jan. 1, 1863, would be forever free. The order excluded areas still loyal to the Union, meaning that they might retain slaves. The or-der had no immediate effect in the Southern-controlled areas, but it meant that each Union victory brought the end of slavery closer. The final order was issued on Jan. 1, 1863, as the Emancipation Proclamation. African Americans referred to that day as the Day of Jubilee. Bells rang from the spires of most Northern Black churches to celebrate.

Over 200,000 African Americans fought on the side of the Union. They were discriminated against in pay, assignments, and rank. Nevertheless, many of them contributed greatly to the war effort. Robert Smalls of South Carolina, a harbor pilot, was one of the first Black heroes of the war. In 1862, he sailed a Confederate ship, the *Planter,* out of Charleston Harbor and turned it over to the Union. Smalls then joined the Union Navy. In 1863, Black regiments played an important role in the attack on Port Hudson, Louisiana. The fall of Port Hudson helped the Union gain control of the Mississippi River. Altogether, 23 Black soldiers won the Medal of Honor, the nation's highest military award, for heroism during the Civil War.

About 40,000 Black troops—nearly all of them Union troops—died during the war. In April 1865, the main Southern army surrendered. In December 1865, the

adoption of the 13th Amendment to the Constitution of the United States officially ended the institution of slav-ery throughout the nation.

The first years of freedom. The period of rebuilding that followed the Civil War became known as Recon-struction. A major concern during Reconstruction was the condition of the approximately 4 million *freedmen* (freed slaves). Most of them had no homes, were des-perately poor, and could not read and write.

To help the freedmen and homeless white people, Congress established the Bureau of Refugees, Freed-men, and Abandoned Lands. The agency, better known as the Freedmen's Bureau, operated from 1865 until 1872. It issued food and supplies to Black people; set up more than 100 hospitals; resettled more than 30,000 people; and founded over 4,300 schools. Some of the schools developed into outstanding Black institutions, such as Clark Atlanta University in Georgia, Fisk Univer-sity in Nashville, Hampton University in Virginia, and Howard University in Washington, D.C.

In spite of its achievements, the Freedmen's Bureau did not solve the economic problems of African Amer-icans. Most of them continued to live in poverty. They also suffered from racist threats and violence and from laws restricting their civil rights. All these problems cast a deep shadow over their new freedom.

Legal restrictions on Black civil rights arose in 1865 and 1866, when many Southern state governments passed laws that became known as the *black codes.* These laws were like the earlier slave codes. Some black codes prohibited Black people from owning land. Oth-ers set a nightly curfew for Black people. Some permit-ted states to jail Black Americans for being jobless.

The black codes shocked a powerful group of North-ern congressmen called Radical Republicans. These senators and representatives won congressional approv-al of the Civil Rights Act of 1866. The act gave African Americans the rights and privileges of full citizenship. The 14th Amendment to the Constitution, adopted in 1868, further guaranteed the citizenship of Black Amer-icans. However, most white Southerners resented the new status of Black people. The white people simply

Historical Pictures Service

Schools for Blacks were established by the Freed-men's Bureau during Reconstruction, the period of rebuilding after the Civil War. Some of the schools the bureau opened became outstanding Black colleges.

Historical Pictures Service

Ku Klux Klan members were white terrorists who tried to deny Blacks their rights after the Civil War.

Historical Pictures Service

African American voters helped the Republican Party win control of all the state governments in the South during the Reconstruction period.

could not accept the idea of formerly enslaved people voting and holding office. As a result, attempts by Southern Black citizens to vote, run for public office, or claim other civil rights were met by increasing violence from white people in the South. In 1865 and 1866, about 5,000 Southern Black people were murdered. Forty-six Black Americans were killed when their schools and churches were burned in Memphis in May 1866. In July of that year, 34 were killed during a race riot in New Orleans.

Some law enforcement officers encouraged or participated in assaults on Black people, but lawless groups carried out most attacks. One of the largest, the Ku Klux Klan, was organized in 1865 or 1866 in Pulaski, Tennessee. Bands of hooded Klansmen rode at night and beat and murdered many Black people and their white sympathizers. The Klan did much to deny Black Americans their civil and human rights throughout Reconstruction.

The federal government tried to maintain the rights of African Americans. In 1870 and 1871, Congress passed laws authorizing the use of federal troops to enforce the voting rights of Black citizens. These laws were known as the Enforcement Acts or the Ku Klux Klan Acts. In addition, President Ulysses S. Grant signed a proclamation demanding respect for the civil rights of all Americans.

Temporary gains. The policies of the Radical Republicans enabled African Americans to participate widely in the nation's political system for the first time. Congress provided for Black men to become voters in the South and called for constitutional conventions to be held in the defeated states. Many Black people attended the conventions held in 1867 and 1868. They helped rewrite Southern state constitutions and other basic laws to replace the black codes drawn up by white people in 1865 and 1866. In the legislatures elected under the new constitutions, however, Black lawmakers had a majority of seats only in the lower house in South Carolina. Most of the chief legislative and executive positions were held by Northern white Republicans who had moved to the South and by their white Southern allies. Angry white Southerners called the Northerners *carpetbaggers* to suggest that they could carry everything they owned when they came South in a *carpetbag,* or suitcase.

African Americans elected to important posts during Reconstruction included U.S. Senators Hiram R. Revels and Blanche K. Bruce of Mississippi and U.S. Representatives Joseph H. Rainey of South Carolina and Jefferson Long of Georgia. Others were Oscar J. Dunn, lieutenant governor of Louisiana; Richard Gleaves and Alonzo J. Ransier, lieutenant governors of South Carolina; P. B. S. Pinchback, acting governor of Louisiana; Francis L. Cardozo, secretary of state and state treasurer of South Carolina; and Jonathan Jasper Wright, an associate justice of the South Carolina Supreme Court. Most of them had college educations.

By the early 1870's, white Northerners had lost interest in the Reconstruction policies of the Radical Republicans. They grew tired of hearing about the continual conflict between Black and white people in the South. Most white Northerners wanted to put Reconstruction behind them and turn to other things. Federal troops sent to the South to protect Black citizens were gradually withdrawn. White Southerners who had stayed away from elections to protest Black participation started voting again. White Democrats then began to regain control of the state governments from the Black officials and their white Republican associates. In 1877, the last federal troops were withdrawn. By the end of that year, the Democrats held power in all the Southern state governments. For more details on the Reconstruction era, see **Reconstruction.**

The growth of discrimination

During the late 1800's, Black citizens in the South increasingly suffered from segregation, the loss of voting rights, and other forms of discrimination. Their condition reflected beliefs held by most white Southerners that white people were born superior to Black people with respect to intelligence, talents, and moral standards. In 1881, the Tennessee legislature passed a law that required railroad passengers to be separated by race. In 1890, Mississippi adopted several measures that in effect ended voting by Black citizens. These measures included the passing of reading and writing tests and the payment of a poll tax before a person could vote.

Library of Congress

George Washington Carver, *center,* won worldwide fame for agricultural research. He taught at Tuskegee (Alabama) Institute.

Historical Pictures Service

Booker T. Washington, principal of Tuskegee Institute, was the most influential African American leader of the early 1900's.

From *A Pictorial History of the Negro in America,* by Langston Hughes and Milton Meltzer

W. E. B. Du Bois, *second from right,* a sociologist and historian, helped lead the Black struggle for equality during the early 1900's. He directed the publications of the NAACP from 1909 until 1934.

Several U.S. Supreme Court decisions enabled Southern States to establish "legal" segregation. In 1883, for example, the court declared the Civil Rights Act of 1875 to be unconstitutional. That act had guaranteed Black people the right to be admitted to any public place.

The Civil Rights Act of 1866 and the 14th Amendment to the Constitution, ratified in 1868, had forbidden the states to deny equal rights to any person. But in 1896, the Supreme Court ruled in the case of *Plessy v. Ferguson* that a Louisiana law requiring the separation of Black and white railroad passengers was constitutional. The court argued that segregation in itself did not represent inequality and that separate public facilities could be provided for the races as long as the facilities were equal. This ruling, known as the "separate but equal doctrine," became the basis of Southern race relations. In practice, however, nearly all the separate schools, places of recreation, and other public facilities provided for Black people were far inferior to those provided for white people.

In spite of the increasing difficulties for African Americans, a number of them won distinction during the late 1800's. For example, Samuel Lowery started a school for Black students in Huntsville, Alabama, in 1875 and won prizes at international fairs for silk made at the school. In 1883, Jan E. Matzeliger invented a revolutionary shoe-lasting machine that shaped the upper part of a shoe and fastened it to the sole. In 1887, Joe Clark and other Black settlers founded Eatonville, Florida. It was the first African American settlement in the United States to be incorporated. Mary Church Terrell helped found the National Association of Colored Women in 1896 and advised government leaders on racial problems. Charles Waddell Chesnutt wrote *The Conjure Woman,* published in 1899. He became one of the first major African American novelists and short-story writers.

During the early 1900's, discrimination against Black Americans in the South became even more widespread. By 1907, every Southern state required racial segregation on trains and in churches, schools, hotels, restaurants, theaters, and other public places. The Southern States also adopted an election practice known as the *white primary.* The states banned Black citizens from voting in the Democratic Party's primary elections by calling them "private affairs." But the winners of the primary elections were certain of victory in the general elections because Republican and independent candidates got little support from white voters and rarely ran for office. By 1910, every Southern state had taken away or begun to take away the right of African Americans to vote.

The Ku Klux Klan used threats, beatings, and killings in its efforts to keep Black citizens from voting. More than 3,000 Black people had been lynched during the late 1800's. The Klan and similar groups lynched hundreds more throughout the South during the early 1900's.

African Americans had little opportunity to better themselves economically. Some laws prohibited them from teaching and from entering certain other businesses and professions. Large numbers of Black workers had to take low-paying jobs as farm hands or servants for white employers. Many other poor Black people became sharecroppers or tenant farmers. They rented a small plot of land and paid the rent with money earned from the crops. They had to struggle to survive, and many ran up huge debts to their white landlords or the town merchants.

The rise of new Black leaders. By the early 1900's, the educator Booker T. Washington had become the most influential African American leader. Washington, who had formerly been enslaved, had been principal of Tuskegee Institute (now Tuskegee University) in Alabama since 1881. He urged Black people to stop demanding political power and social equality and to concentrate on economic advancement. Washington especially encouraged Black people to practice thrift and respect hard work. He asked white people to help Black people gain an education and make a decent living. Washington believed his program would lead to progress for African Americans and keep peace between the races.

Many African Americans agreed with Washington's ideas. But many others strongly rejected them. The chief opposition came from W. E. B. Du Bois, a sociologist and historian at Atlanta University. Du Bois's reputation rested on such works as *The Suppression of the African Slave-Trade to the United States of America, 1638-1870*

© Everett Collection Alamy Images

Marcus Garvey founded the Universal Negro Improvement Association, which worked to create a new homeland in Africa for Black Americans. He wore a plumed hat for this parade in 1924.

Schomburg Collection, New York Public Library

Langston Hughes contributed to the Harlem Renaissance, an outpouring of Black literature in the early 1900's.

UPI/Bettmann Archive

Duke Ellington, playing the piano in this scene from the movie *Cabin in the Sky* (1943), became one of the greatest jazz musicians.

(1896) and *The Souls of Black Folk* (1903).

Du Bois argued that Washington's approach would not achieve economic security for African Americans. Instead, Du Bois felt Washington's acceptance of segregation and the rest of his program would strengthen the beliefs that Black people were inferior and could be treated unequally. As evidence for their position, Du Bois and his supporters pointed to the continuing lynching of Black people and to the passage of new segregation laws in the South. In 1905, Du Bois and other critics of Washington met in Niagara Falls, Canada, and organized a campaign to protest racial discrimination. Their campaign became known as the Niagara Movement.

Bitter hostility toward Black citizens erupted into several race riots during the early 1900's. Major riots broke out in Brownsville, Texas, and Atlanta, Georgia, in 1906 and in Springfield, Illinois, in 1908. The riots alarmed many white Northerners as well as many Black people. In 1909, a number of white Northerners joined some of the African Americans in the Niagara Movement to form the National Association for the Advancement of Colored People (NAACP). The NAACP vowed to fight for racial equality. The organization relied mainly on legal action, education, protests, and voter participation to pursue its goals.

The Black migration to the North. The efforts of new Black leaders and of the NAACP did little to end the discrimination, police brutality, and lynchings suffered by Black people in the South in the early 1900's. In addition, Southern farmers had great crop losses because of floods and insect pests. All these problems persuaded many Black Southerners to move to the North. This movement is sometimes called the "Great Migration."

During World War I (1914-1918), hundreds of thousands of Black Southerners migrated to the North to seek jobs in defense plants and other factories. The National Urban League, founded in New York City in 1910, helped the newcomers adjust to city life. About 400,000 African Americans served in the armed forces during World War I. They were put in all-Black military units.

Between 1910 and 1930, about 1 million Black people moved from the South to the North. Most of them quickly discovered that the North did not offer solutions to their problems. They lacked the skills and education needed for the jobs they sought. Many of them had to become laborers or servants and thus do the same kinds of work they had done in the South. Others could find no work at all. Numerous Black Americans were forced to live crowded together in cheap, unsanitary, run-down housing. Large all-Black slums developed in big cities throughout the North. The segregated housing promoted segregated schooling. Poverty, crime, and despair plagued the Black communities, which became known as *ghettos.*

After World War I, race relations grew increasingly tense in Northern cities. The hostility partly reflected the growing competition for jobs and housing between Black and white people. In addition, many Black veterans, after fighting for democracy, returned home with expectations of justice and equality. The mounting tension helped the Ku Klux Klan recruit thousands of members in the North. In the summer of 1918, 10 people were killed and 60 injured in racial violence in Chester and Philadelphia, Pennsylvania. A series of riots erupted in the summer of 1919. By the end of the year, 25 race riots had broken out across the country. At least 100 people died and many more were injured in the riots.

The Garvey movement offered new hope for many African Americans deeply disturbed by the race riots of 1918 and 1919 and the economic and social injustice they encountered. The movement had begun when Marcus Garvey founded the Universal Negro Improvement Association in Jamaica in 1914. In 1917, Garvey brought the movement to Harlem, a Black community in New York City. By the mid-1920's, he had established more than 700 branches of the association in 38 states.

Garvey tried to develop racial pride among America's Black citizens. But he doubted that their life in the United States would ever be much improved. Garvey urged the establishment of a new homeland in Africa for dissatisfied Black Americans. His plans collapsed, however, when he was sent to prison in 1925 after having been convicted of using the mails to commit fraud.

The Harlem Renaissance and other achievements. The Harlem Renaissance was an outpouring of African American literature chiefly in Harlem in the early

Marian Anderson sang at the Lincoln Memorial in 1939 after the DAR would not let her sing in Constitution Hall.

UPI/Bettmann Archive

During World War II, nearly 1 million African Americans served in the U.S. armed forces. Most were in such segregated units as the 92nd Division, *shown here.*

Signal Corps Photo

Jackie Robinson of the Brooklyn Dodgers became the first Black player in modern major league baseball in 1947. He helped break down racial barriers in professional sports.

UPI/Bettmann Archive

1900's, particularly in the 1920's. The writers drew their themes from the experiences of Black Americans in the Northern cities and the rural South. The best-known writers included Countee Cullen, Jessie Redmon Fauset, Langston Hughes, James Weldon Johnson, Nella Larsen, Claude McKay, and Jean Toomer.

African American musicians also gained fame during the early 1900's. A Black bandleader named W. C. Handy, who had composed "St. Louis Blues" in 1914, became known as the father of the blues. Jazz grew out of Black folk blues and ballads. The African American bandleaders Louis Armstrong and Duke Ellington became the country's leading jazz musicians.

Another noted African American of the early 1900's was the agricultural researcher George Washington Carver. Carver created hundreds of products from peanuts, sweet potatoes, and other plants and revolutionized Southern agriculture. Other famous African Americans of the time included labor leader A. Philip Randolph; journalist Ida Wells-Barnett; singer, actor, and political activist Paul Robeson; Hattie McDaniel, the first African American to win an Academy Award; dancer Bill Robinson; U.S. Representative Oscar DePriest of Illinois; Olympic track and field gold medalist Jesse Owens; and heavyweight boxing champions Jack Johnson and Joe Louis.

The Great Depression was a worldwide business slump in the 1930's. The Depression brought hard times for most Americans, but especially for Black people, who became the chief victims of job discrimination. They adopted the slogan "Last Hired and First Fired" to express their situation.

To help ease the poverty in the ghettos, African Americans organized cooperative groups. These groups included the Colored Merchants Association in New York City and "Jobs for Negroes" organizations in Chicago, Cleveland, New York City, and St. Louis. The groups bought food and other goods in large volume to get the lowest prices. They boycotted stores that had mostly Black customers but few, if any, Black workers.

Most African Americans felt that President Herbert Hoover, a Republican, had done little to try to end the Depression. In the elections of 1932, some Black voters deserted their traditional loyalty to the Republican Party. They no longer saw it as the party of Abraham Lincoln the emancipator but of Hoover and the Depression. In 1936, for the first time, most African Americans supported the Democratic Party candidate for president, Franklin D. Roosevelt, and helped him win reelection.

Roosevelt called his program the New Deal. It included measures of reform, relief, and recovery and benefited many Black Americans. A group of prominent Black citizens advised Roosevelt on the problems of African Americans. This group, called the Black Cabinet, included William H. Hastie and Mary McLeod Bethune. Hastie served as assistant solicitor in the Department of the Interior, as a U.S. district court judge in the Virgin Islands, and as a civilian aide to the secretary of war. Bethune, founder of what is now Bethune-Cookman University in Daytona Beach, Florida, directed the Black affairs division of a federal agency called the National Youth Administration. As a result of the New Deal, African Americans developed a strong loyalty to the Democratic Party.

African Americans deeply admired Roosevelt's wife, Eleanor, for her stand in an incident in 1939 involving the great concert singer Marian Anderson. The Daughters of the American Revolution (DAR), an organization of women directly descended from people who fought in the American Revolution (1775-1783), owned Constitution Hall in Washington, D.C. The DAR denied Anderson permission to perform there because she was Black. Eleanor Roosevelt then resigned from the DAR and helped arrange for Anderson to sing, instead, at the Lincoln Memorial on Easter Sunday. Over 75,000 people—both Black and white—attended the concert.

During the early 1940's, the NAACP stepped up its legal campaign against racial discrimination. The campaign achieved important victories, including several favorable rulings by the U.S. Supreme Court. In 1941, for example, the court ruled that separate facilities for white and Black railroad passengers must be significantly equal. In 1944, the court declared that the white primary, which excluded Black citizens from voting in the only meaningful elections in the South, was unconstitutional.

Besides taking legal action, African Americans used new tactics to attack segregation in public places. In

Carl Iwasaki, *Life* magazine, © Time Inc.

Linda Brown was the focus of a 1954 case in which the U.S. Supreme Court outlawed segregation in public schools.

AP/Wide World

Rosa Parks was arrested in 1955 when she refused to give up her seat on a bus in Montgomery, Alabama, to accommodate a white person.

Larry Obsitnik, *Arkansas Gazette*

United States troops enforced a federal court order to integrate Little Rock Central High School in Arkansas in 1957.

1943, for example, the Congress of Racial Equality (CORE) launched a *sit-in* at a Chicago restaurant. In this protest, Black demonstrators sat in places reserved for white people.

World War II (1939-1945) opened up new economic opportunities for African Americans. Like World War I, it expanded defense-related industries and encouraged many rural Black Southerners to seek jobs in Northern industrial cities. During the 1940's, about a million Black Southerners moved to the North. Discrimination again prevented many of them from getting work. In 1941, Black Americans led by A. Philip Randolph of the Brotherhood of Sleeping Car Porters threatened to march in Washington, D.C., to protest job discrimination. President Roosevelt then issued an executive order forbidding racial discrimination in defense industries.

Nearly 1 million African Americans served in the U.S. armed services during World War II, mostly in segregated units. In 1940, Benjamin O. Davis became the first Black brigadier general in the U.S. Army. His son, Benjamin O. Davis, Jr., later became the first Black lieutenant general in the Air Force. Desegregation of the armed forces began on a trial basis during the war. It became a permanent policy in 1948.

The civil rights movement

The beginning. After World War II, three major factors encouraged the beginning of a new movement for civil rights. First, many African Americans had served with honor in the war. Black leaders pointed to the records of these veterans to show the injustice of racial discrimination. Second, African Americans in the urban North had made economic gains, increased their education, and registered to vote. Third, the NAACP had attracted many new members and received increased financial support from both white and Black people. It also included a new group of bright young lawyers.

Rulings by the U.S. Supreme Court during the 1940's and 1950's brought major victories for African Americans. In several decisions between 1948 and 1951, the court ruled that separate higher education facilities for Black students must be equal to those for white students. Largely because of federal court rulings, laws

permitting racial discrimination in housing and recreation also began to be struck down. Many of these rulings came in cases brought by the NAACP.

The NAACP and the NAACP Legal Defense and Educational Fund won a historic victory in 1954. That year, the Supreme Court ruled in the case of *Brown v. Board of Education of Topeka* that segregation in the public schools was in itself unequal and thus unconstitutional. The suit had been filed because the school board had not allowed a Black student named Linda Brown to attend an all-white school near her home. The court's decision rejected the "separate but equal" ruling of 1896 and inspired African Americans to strike out against other discrimination, particularly in public places.

In 1955, Emmett Till, a Black teenager, was beaten and killed while visiting Money, Mississippi. Two white men were charged with the murder but were acquitted by an all-white jury. The men later admitted to the crime. Till's murder sparked widespread outrage and led to increased support for the civil rights movement.

Rosa Parks, a seamstress in Montgomery, Alabama, became a symbol of African Americans' bold new action to attain their civil rights. In 1955, she was arrested for disobeying a city law that required Black riders to give up their bus seats when white people wished to sit in their seats or in the same row. Montgomery's Black residents protested her arrest by refusing to ride the buses. Their protest began in late 1955 and lasted for over a year, ending when the U.S. Supreme Court declared segregated seating on the city's buses unconstitutional. The boycott was the first organized mass protest by Black Americans in Southern history. It also focused national attention on its leader, Martin Luther King, Jr., a Montgomery Baptist minister.

Many Southern communities acted slowly in desegregating their public schools. Governor Orval E. Faubus of Arkansas symbolized Southern resistance. In 1957, he defied a federal court order to integrate Little Rock Central High School. Faubus sent the Arkansas National Guard to prevent Black students from entering the school, but President Dwight D. Eisenhower used federal troops to enforce the court order.

The growing movement. In 1957, King and other

Pictorial Parade

Martin Luther King, Jr., spoke to over 250,000 civil rights demonstrators after a march in Washington, D.C., in 1963. His appeal for racial equality won wide support for the civil rights movement.

United Press Int.

Author James Baldwin became a leading critic of racial discrimination in the United States in the mid-1900's.

AP/Wide World

Black Muslim leaders of the 1950's and the 1960's included Malcolm X, *left,* and Elijah Muhammad, *right.*

Black Southern clergy formed the Southern Christian Leadership Conference (SCLC) to coordinate the work of civil rights groups. King urged African Americans to use peaceful means to achieve their goals. In 1960, a group of Black and white college students organized the Student Nonviolent Coordinating Committee (SNCC) to help in the civil rights movement. They joined with young people from the SCLC, CORE, and the NAACP in staging sit-ins, boycotts, marches, and *freedom rides* (bus rides to test the enforcement of desegregation in interstate transportation). During the early 1960's, the efforts of the civil rights groups ended discrimination in many public places, including hotels, restaurants, and theaters.

Numerous cities and towns remained unaffected by the civil rights movement. African American leaders therefore felt the United States needed a clear, strong federal policy that would erase the remaining discrimination in public places. To attract national attention to that need, King and such other leaders as A. Philip Randolph, Roy Wilkins of the NAACP, James L. Farmer of CORE, and Whitney M. Young, Jr., of the Urban League organized a march in Washington, D.C., in August 1963. About 250,000 people, including many white sympathizers, took part in the March on Washington.

A high point of the March on Washington was a stirring speech by King. He told the crowd that he had a dream that one day all Americans would enjoy equality and justice. Afterward, President John F. Kennedy proposed strong laws to protect the civil rights of all U.S. citizens. But many people, particularly white Southerners, opposed such legislation.

Kennedy was assassinated in November 1963, and Vice President Lyndon B. Johnson became president. Johnson persuaded Congress to pass Kennedy's proposed laws in the Civil Rights Act of 1964. This act prohibited racial discrimination in public places and called for equal opportunity in employment and education. King won the 1964 Nobel Peace Prize for leading nonviolent demonstrations for civil rights.

African American celebrities not directly involved with civil rights groups also contributed to the growing rights movement. Author James Baldwin criticized white Americans for their prejudice against Black people.

Other noted African Americans who promoted civil rights causes included boxer Muhammad Ali, singer Harry Belafonte, dancer Katherine Dunham, comedian Dick Gregory, gospel singer Mahalia Jackson, and artist Charles White.

Political gains. In the South, many elected officials and police officers refused to enforce court rulings and federal laws that gave Black citizens equality. In some cases, this opposition extended to the right to vote.

In 1965, a major dispute over voting rights broke out in Selma, Alabama. King had gone there in January to assist African Americans seeking the right to vote. He was joined by many Black and white people from throughout the country. In the next two months, at least three people were killed and hundreds were beaten as opposition to King's efforts increased. Authorities continued to deny Black Americans their voting rights. In late March, King began leading about 3,200 people, guarded by federal troops, from Selma to Montgomery. By the time the marchers reached the Montgomery State Capitol Building, the crowd had grown to 25,000. There, King demanded that African Americans be given the right to vote without unjust restrictions.

Largely as a result of the activities in Selma, Congress passed the Voting Rights Act of 1965. The act banned the use of a literacy test as a requirement to vote. The law also ordered the U.S. attorney general to begin court action that ended the use of a poll tax as a voting requirement. In places where voter registration had been unjustly denied, the Voting Rights Act provided for federal officials to supervise voter registration. The law also forbade major changes in voting laws without approval of the U.S. attorney general. The act gave the vote to hundreds of thousands of Southern Black citizens who had never voted. It thus led to a large increase in the number of Black elected officials.

African Americans began to take an increasingly important role in the national government during the mid-1900's. In 1950, U.S. diplomat Ralph J. Bunche became the first Black person to win the Nobel Peace Prize. In 1966, Robert C. Weaver became the first Black Cabinet member, as secretary of housing and urban development. In 1967, Thurgood Marshall became the first Black

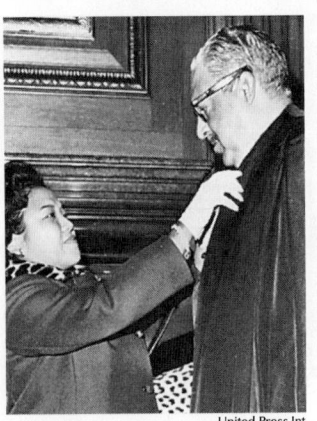

United Press Int.

Thurgood Marshall became the first Black associate justice of the Supreme Court of the United States in 1967.

© Corbis/Bettmann

Tom Bradley became the first African American mayor of Los Angeles in 1973. He was reelected in 1977, 1981, 1985, and 1989.

NASA

Guion S. Bluford, Jr., a U.S. astronaut, was the first African American to travel in space. He and four other astronauts traveled on the space shuttle Challenger in 1983.

justice on the Supreme Court. In 1969, Shirley Chisholm of New York became the first Black woman to serve in the U.S. House of Representatives.

Economic and social progress. In 1965, President Johnson declared that it was not enough simply to end *de jure* segregation—that is, separation of the races by law. It was also necessary to eliminate *de facto* segregation—that is, racial separation in fact and based largely on custom. Johnson called for programs of "affirmative action" that would offer Black people equal opportunity with white people in areas where discrimination had a long history and still existed. Many businesses and schools then began to adopt affirmative action programs. These programs, some of which were ordered by the federal government, gave hundreds of thousands of Black Americans new economic and educational opportunities.

Racial barriers fell in several professional sports and in the arts during the mid-1900's. In 1947, Jackie Robinson of the Brooklyn Dodgers became the first Black player in modern major league baseball. He had an outstanding career and became a national hero. Other Black sports heroes of the mid-1900's included Hank Aaron, Willie Mays, and Frank Robinson in baseball; Jim Brown and Gale Sayers in football; and Wilt Chamberlain, Oscar Robertson, and Bill Russell in basketball. In 1966, Russell became the first Black head coach in major league professional sports. He was named coach of the Boston Celtics of the National Basketball Association.

In the arts, Gwendolyn Brooks became the first African American to win a Pulitzer Prize. She received the award in 1950 for a collection of poems titled *Annie Allen*. In 1955, Marian Anderson became the first Black person to sing a leading role with the Metropolitan Opera in New York City. In 1958, Alvin Ailey formed one of the finest dance companies in the United States. In 1963, Sidney Poitier became the first African American to win the Academy Award for a leading role when he won the best actor award for *Lilies of the Field*.

Unrest in the cities. Since the start of the civil rights movement, various court decisions, laws, and protests had removed great legal injustices long suffered by African Americans. But many Black people continued to be discriminated against in jobs, law enforcement, and housing. They saw little change in the long-held racist attitudes of numerous white Americans.

During the 1960's, unrest among Black people living in urban ghettos exploded into a series of riots that shook the nation. The first riot occurred in Harlem in the summer of 1964. In August 1965, 34 people died and almost 900 were injured in an outburst in the Black ghetto of Watts in Los Angeles. During the next two summers, major riots erupted in cities across the nation.

The race riots puzzled many people because they came at a time when African Americans had made huge gains in the campaign for freedom. In 1967, President Johnson established a commission headed by Governor Otto Kerner of Illinois to study the causes of the outbreaks. In its 1968 report, the Kerner Commission put much of the blame on racial prejudice of white Americans. It said that the average Black American was still poorly housed, poorly clothed, underpaid, and undereducated. Black Americans, the report said, still often suffered from segregation, police abuse, and other forms of discrimination. The commission recommended programs to improve ghetto conditions and called for changes in the racial attitudes of white Americans.

Less than a month after the Kerner Commission report, race riots broke out in at least 100 Black communities across the nation. The rioting followed the assassination of Martin Luther King, Jr., on April 4 in Memphis. James Earl Ray, a white drifter, was convicted of the crime and sentenced to 99 years in prison. King's murder helped President Johnson persuade Congress to approve the Civil Rights Act of 1968. This law, also known in part as the Fair Housing Act of 1968, prohibited racial discrimination in the sale and rental of most housing.

Black militancy. During the height of the civil rights movement, some Black Americans claimed that it was almost impossible to change white racial attitudes. They saw the movement as meaningless and urged Black people to live apart from white people and, in some cases, to use violence to preserve their rights. Groups promoting these ideas included the Black Muslims, the Black Panthers, and members of the Black Power Movement.

© Ron Galella, WireImage/Getty Images

Oprah Winfrey hosted and produced a highly rated television talk show, which began national broadcasts in 1986.

J. L. Atlan, Sygma

Jesse Jackson ran for the Democratic presidential nomination in 1984 and 1988, drawing attention to minority issues.

© Ralf-Finn Hestoft, SABA

Carol Moseley Braun, *center,* of Illinois, became the first Black woman elected to the U.S. Senate when she won a seat in 1992.

The Black Muslims had been led since 1934 by Elijah Muhammad, who called white people "devils." He also criticized racial integration and urged formation of an all-Black nation within the United States. But the most eloquent spokesman for the Black Muslims during the 1950's and 1960's was Malcolm X. Malcolm wanted to unite Black people throughout the world. He was assassinated in 1965. Three Black men, at least two of whom were Black Muslims, were convicted of the murder.

The Black Panther Party was founded in 1966. Its two main founders, Huey P. Newton and Bobby Seale, had been inspired by Malcolm X. At first, the party favored violent revolution as the only way to end police actions that many Black people considered brutal and to provide opportunities for African Americans in jobs and other areas. The Panthers had many clashes with police and others. Later, the party became less militant and worked to achieve full employment for Black workers and other peaceful goals.

The Black Power Movement developed in 1966 after James H. Meredith, the first African American to attend the University of Mississippi, was shot on a march. The shooting and other racial violence made H. Rap Brown, Stokely Carmichael, and other members of the Student Nonviolent Coordinating Committee (SNCC) doubt the sincerity of white support for Black rights. Such doubts prompted SNCC to expel its white members.

Carmichael and other African Americans called for a campaign to achieve "Black Power." They urged Black people to gain political and economic control of their own communities and to reject the values of white people. The leaders stressed that "black is beautiful" and called on Black people to form their own standards. They suggested that Black Americans no longer refer to themselves as *Negroes* or *colored people* but as *blacks, African Americans,* or *Afro-Americans.*

Beyond the civil rights movement

Developments since 1970. African Americans have achieved great progress in education and politics since the 1970's. Many have also won great recognition in such fields as sports and the arts.

Education. From 1970 to the first decade of the 2000's,

college enrollment among African Americans rose from about half a million to about 2 million students. This gain resulted in part from affirmative action programs by predominantly white colleges and universities. By the first decade of the 2000's, about 20 percent of all Black Americans had received a bachelor's degree.

A Black studies movement emerged on college campuses throughout the nation during the 1970's and drew increasing attention to the heritage of African Americans. In addition, Black musical and theater groups and African American museums were established in almost every U.S. city with a large Black population.

In the 1980's and 1990's, courses of study based on an approach called Afrocentrism gained popularity. These courses aimed to teach the culture and history of Africans and African Americans. Educators soon developed a broader curriculum called *multicultural education,* designed to help students from all backgrounds appreciate diverse cultures and peoples. Most of the programs emphasized the past and presented accomplishments of African Americans and other groups. Educators think it is important to recognize the injustices that have sometimes been suffered by African Americans and other minority groups. Many educators also believe that such teaching builds the self-esteem of African American children and improves their success in school.

Another trend in education is the growing acceptance, among many educators, of African American English (AAE), a variation of English spoken by many Black Americans. AAE is also called Black English, *Ebonics (ee BAHN ihks),* African American Language, and African American Vernacular English. Educators have developed courses to teach the grammatical rules, pronunciation, and vocabulary of AAE. A knowledge of AAE can help teachers improve their instruction of African American students. Some schools also employ it as an aid in the teaching of standard English.

Affirmative action. Supreme Court decisions from the 1970's to the early 2000's sharply limited affirmative action programs. In 1978, the court ruled that racial quotas could not be used in admitting students to colleges and universities. In 1995, it ruled that federal programs requiring preferences based on race are unconstitutional

Jan Collsiöö, Pressens Bild

Toni Morrison received the Nobel Prize in literature in Stockholm, Sweden, in 1993. A novelist, she had won a Pulitzer Prize for her novel *Beloved* in 1988.

© Mike Blake, Reuters/Landov

Tiger Woods won the Masters Tournament for the first time in 1997. He was the first golfer of African American heritage to win the tournament.

© Trippett, Sipa Press

Colin Powell became the first Black chairman for the Joint Chiefs of Staff in 1989. In 2001, he became the first African American secretary of state.

unless preferences are designed to make up for specific instances of past discrimination. This meant that affirmative action could no longer be used to counteract racial discrimination by society as a whole. In 1989, the court had made a similar decision regarding state and local affirmative action programs.

The 1995 ruling was supported by Supreme Court Justice Clarence Thomas, an African American who replaced Thurgood Marshall on the court when Marshall retired in 1991. Thomas had long been an outspoken opponent of affirmative action. He based his opposition on the principle that the government may not treat individuals differently based on race. Many other Black Americans, however, continued to believe that broad affirmative action programs were needed to help minorities overcome past discrimination and eventually compete on an equal basis with white people. In 2003, the Supreme Court ruled that, within certain limits, colleges and universities could use race as a factor in selecting students for admission.

Politics. Many African American leaders stressed the use of political means to solve the problems of Black people. They urged more African Americans to vote and to run for public office. The Voting Rights Act of 1965 led to the removal of restrictions on voting in most places. As a result, African Americans helped elect a greater number of Black candidates to office. In 1973, for example, Tom Bradley was elected the first Black mayor of Los Angeles.

African Americans gained considerable influence in the administration of Jimmy Carter, who was president of the United States from 1977 to 1981. Under him, Andrew Young became the first Black U.S. ambassador to the United Nations (UN). Carter named Patricia Roberts Harris secretary of housing and urban development. She was the first Black woman to hold a Cabinet post.

In 1984 and 1988, Jesse L. Jackson, a Black civil rights leader and Baptist minister, waged strong campaigns to register new Black voters and win the Democratic presidential nomination. Jackson failed to win the nomination, but he became a hero to many African Americans.

In the 1990's, many African Americans focused on self-help programs to deal with crime, drug abuse,

poverty, and substandard education. For example, in 1995, hundreds of thousands of Black men marched in Washington, D.C., to declare their determination to improve conditions in Black communities. The event, called the Million Man March, was organized chiefly by Louis Farrakhan, leader of the Nation of Islam, a Black Muslim group.

Current challenges. Despite the considerable progress that African Americans have made since the civil rights movement began, many Black people continue to face economic struggles and other challenges. The Black middle class has expanded, but other African Americans live at the extremes of both wealth and poverty. Black entertainers and athletes have become enormously wealthy. But a significant number of Black Americans remain poor, isolated, and vulnerable to disease, drugs, crime, discrimination, and racism.

Housing and lending discrimination. Although housing discrimination occurs far less frequently than in the past, African Americans often live in the poorest communities with the least resources. Lenders often charge Black homeowners higher interest on mortgage loans than they charge white homeowners. Higher monthly payments sometimes mean severe economic strain for struggling Black families. During the economic downturns of the first decades of the 2000's, a large number of African Americans faced the risk of losing their homes to foreclosure. Many Black people became the victims of dishonest lending agencies that were more interested in selling houses than in the ability of their clients to pay for them.

Health issues. A large number of Black people have suffered from diseases associated with poverty, lack of education, and limited access to health care. For example, Black Americans have been much more likely than white Americans to contract HIV/AIDS. In the 2020's, Black Americans were about twice as likely as white Americans to die of the respiratory disease COVID-19.

Black Americans are also more likely to have diabetes than non-Hispanic white people are. In the first decade of the 2000's, more than 10 percent of all African Americans aged 20 years or older had the disease. In addition, Black American children and adults are three times

AP/Wide World

Denzel Washington and Halle Berry won Academy Awards in 2001. Berry was the first African American woman to win the Oscar for best actress.

© Luke Frazza, AFP/Getty Images

Condoleezza Rice became the first African American woman to serve as U.S. secretary of state. President George W. Bush appointed Rice in 2005.

© Dennis Brack, Bloomberg/Getty Images

Barack Obama became the first African American U.S. president in 2009. He won reelection as president in 2012.

A commemorative march crossed the Edmund Pettus Bridge in Selma, Alabama, in 2007. The marchers included Barack Obama, *in a white shirt, carrying his jacket;* Hillary Clinton, *wearing pale green;* her husband, Bill Clinton; and many civil rights activists. In 1965, civil rights leader Martin Luther King, Jr., led a five-day march from Selma to Montgomery, Alabama, to protest discrimination in voter registration.

more likely than white Americans to be hospitalized for asthma and to die from asthma. Substandard housing, resulting in increased exposure to certain indoor *allergens* (substances that cause allergies), contributes to an increased risk of asthma among some Black people.

Social struggles. Reductions in government spending have led to cutbacks in education and social programs, often hitting poor Black communities the hardest. In addition, changes in the U.S. economy, including the decline of manufacturing, have contributed to high unemployment rates among African Americans. A high dropout rate in schools leaves many young people unprepared for new types of well-paying jobs that require technical skills. Unemployment and poverty are often linked with criminal behavior, and in these situations, African American males are especially at risk. Black-on-Black violence—much of it gang-related—continues to plague poorer African American communities.

In 1980, about 145,000 African American men were in prison. Twenty-five years later, there were about four times that many. Many social scientists believed that a major cause of this increase in the imprisonment rate was a U.S. government policy known as the War on Drugs. The War on Drugs, begun in the 1970's, sought to reduce the illegal drug trade by imposing *manda-*

tory (required) prison sentences for drug possession. Some social scientists also saw racial bias in new laws imposing stiffer sentences for crack cocaine than for powder cocaine. Crack cocaine is a form of cocaine that is smoked, and it was more likely to be used by African Americans. Powder cocaine is usually snorted through the nose or injected, and it was more likely to be used by white people. In 2010, Congress passed a law that brought federal crack cocaine sentences in line with those for powder cocaine.

Race relations remain a sensitive issue in the United States. In 1992, riots broke out in Los Angeles and other U.S. cities. The riots erupted after a jury decided not to convict four white police officers of assaulting Rodney G. King, a Black motorist. No African Americans had served on the jury. The jury's decision shocked many people because a videotape of the officers beating King had been broadcast by TV stations throughout the country. Many African Americans felt the trial proved that the U.S. court system treated Black people unfairly. Fifty-three people died and over 4,000 were injured in the Los Angeles riots. Later that year, all four officers were indicted under federal laws for violating King's civil rights. Two of the officers were convicted in 1993.

Barack Obama's election to the presidency in 2008 was a historic milestone. His election stood as an example of the progress that came from the civil rights movement. Many Americans became hopeful that racism had diminished in the United States. Despite this progress, racial tensions still lingered.

Several incidents in 2014 highlighted tensions between police forces and African American communities in the United States. In July, Eric Garner, an African American man under arrest for a misdemeanor charge, died after a white police officer grabbed him across the neck in a choke hold. In the following months, police use of force led to the deaths of Black teenagers Michael Brown in Ferguson, Missouri, and LaQuan McDonald in Chicago; and of 12-year-old Tamir Rice in Cleveland, Ohio. People protested both the shootings and what many believed was a history of unfair treatment of Black people by white authorities. The protests at times involved damage to property, and national media broadcast images of protesters pitted against police clad in riot gear. The activist group Black Lives Matter,

Kamala Harris became in 2021 the first woman, and the first person of African descent, to serve as vice president of the United States. Harris served under President Joe Biden.

formed to campaign against racial injustice and police brutality, gained in prominence during the protests.

Other much-reported deaths resulting from police use of force included Freddie Gray of Baltimore, Maryland, in 2015; Alton Sterling of Baton Rouge, Louisiana, and Philando Castile of Falcon Heights, Minnesota, in 2016; and Breonna Taylor of Louisville, Kentucky, and George Floyd in Minneapolis, Minnesota, in 2020. Some of the killings were captured in videos that were then shared on social media. Following some of these incidents, police officers faced criminal charges, and police chiefs were fired or resigned. In addition, a number of officers were wounded or killed in retaliatory attacks.

The killings and the protests sparked a national dialogue about relations between police and minority groups, and about racial bias in criminal proceedings, employment, and social settings. Politicians regularly issued calls for reform and police retraining. Prominent athletes and entertainers promoted calls to end racial injustice. Increased media attention about such issues, however, led to a backlash among many conservative white Americans, including communities with strong ties to police. Commentators pointed to high rates of violent crime in poor Black communities and drew attention to images of looting that followed some protests. The challenges confronting African American communities, especially their poorest members, seemed likely to persist for years to come.

In 2021, former California Senator Kamala Harris became the first person of African American ancestry, and the first woman, to serve as U.S. vice president. Harris served under President Joe Biden, Obama's vice president from 2009 to 2017.

Robert A. Pratt

Related articles in *World Book* include:

Political figures

Bond, Julian
Bradley, Tom
Brooke, Edward William
Brown, Henry "Box"
Brown, Jesse
Brown, Linda
Brown, Ronald H.
Bruce, Blanche Kelso
Chisholm, Shirley
Dinkins, David N.
Espy, Mike
Harris, Kamala
Harris, Patricia R.
Hastie, William H.

Hatcher, Richard Gordon
Holder, Eric Himpton, Jr.
Jackson, Jesse L.
Jordan, Barbara C.
Kelly, Sharon P.
Lewis, John R.
Mfume, Kweisi
Moseley Braun, Carol
Obama, Barack
Pierce, Samuel Riley, Jr.
Pinchback, P. B. S.
Powell, Adam Clayton, Jr.

Powell, Colin L.
Price, Hugh Bernard
Revels, Hiram R.
Rice, Condoleezza
Smalls, Robert
Stokes, Carl B.
Sullivan, Louis W.
Washington, Harold
Watts, J. C., Jr.
Weaver, Robert C.
Wilder, L. Douglas
Young, Andrew Jackson, Jr.
Young, Coleman Alexander

Athletes and sports leaders

Aaron, Hank
Abdul-Jabbar, Kareem
Ali, Muhammad
Ashe, Arthur
Barkley, Charles
Baylor, Elgin
Biles, Simone
Brown, Jim
Bryant, Kobe
Campanella, Roy
Chamberlain, Wilt
Erving, Julius

Ewing, Patrick
Gibson, Althea
Gibson, Josh
Griffey, Ken, Jr.
Henderson, Rickey
Iverson, Allen
James, LeBron
Johnson, Jack
Johnson, Magic
Jordan, Michael
Joyner-Kersee, Jackie

Leonard, Sugar Ray
Lewis, Carl
Louis, Joe
Mays, Willie
Olajuwon, Hakeem
O'Neal, Shaquille
Owens, Jesse
Paige, Satchel
Payton, Walter
Rice, Jerry
Robertson, Oscar

Robinson, Frank
Robinson, Jackie
Robinson, Sugar Ray
Rose, Derrick
Rudolph, Wilma

Russell, Bill
Sanders, Deion
Simpson, O. J.
Tomlinson, LaDainian

Tyson, Mike
White, Bill
Williams, Serena
Williams, Venus
Woods, Tiger

Civil rights figures

Abernathy, Ralph David
Bridges, Ruby
Carmichael, Stokely
Du Bois, W. E. B.
Evers, Medgar
Evers-Williams, Myrlie
Farmer, James L.
Gregory, Dick
Hamer, Fannie Lou
Hooks, Benjamin Lawson
Jackson, Jesse L.
Jacob, John E.
Jordan, Vernon E.
King, Coretta Scott

King, Martin Luther, Jr.
Lewis, John Robert
Malcolm X
McKissick, Floyd Bixler
Meredith, James Howard
Parks, Rosa Louise
Randolph, A. Philip
Rustin, Bayard
Terrell, Mary C.
Wells-Barnett, Ida
White, Walter F.
Wilkins, Roy
Young, Whitney Moore, Jr.

Educators and scholars

Bethune, Mary McLeod
Cary, Mary Ann Shadd
Clark, Kenneth Bancroft
Franklin, John Hope
Frazier, Edward Franklin
Hope, John
Johnson, Charles Spurgeon

Locke, Alain LeRoy
Mays, Benjamin Elijah
Moton, Robert Russa
Nabrit, James Madison, Jr.
Quarles, Benjamin
Washington, Booker T.
Woodson, Carter Godwin

Jazz musicians and singers

Armstrong, Louis
Basie, Count
Bechet, Sidney
Blakey, Art
Coltrane, John
Davis, Miles
Ellington, Duke
Fitzgerald, Ella
Gillespie, Dizzy
Hampton, Lionel
Hancock, Herbie
Handy, W. C.
Hawkins, Coleman
Henderson, Fletcher
Hines, Earl

Holiday, Billie
Joplin, Scott
Lewis, John A.
Marsalis, Wynton
Mingus, Charles
Monk, Thelonious
Morton, Jelly Roll
Parker, Charlie
Rollins, Sonny
Shorter, Wayne
Smith, Bessie
Tatum, Art
Vaughan, Sarah
Waller, Fats
Young, Lester W.

Other singers and entertainers

Ailey, Alvin
Aldridge, Ira
Anderson, Marian
Baker, Josephine
Belafonte, Harry
Berry, Chuck
Berry, Halle
Brown, James
Burleigh, Harry T.
Carey, Mariah
Charles, Ray
Cole, Nat King
Cooke, Sam
Cosby, Bill
Dunham, Katherine

Franklin, Aretha
Gaye, Marvin
Gordy, Berry, Jr.
Handy, W. C.
Hayes, Roland
Horne, Lena
Jackson, Mahalia
Jackson, Michael
Johnson, Robert
Jones, James Earl
King, B. B.
Lee, Spike
Little Richard
Maynor, Dorothy
McDaniel, Hattie
Mitchell, Arthur

Murphy, Eddie
Poitier, Sidney
Price, Leontyne
Robeson, Paul
Robinson, Bill
Shakur, Tupac
Smith, Will
Turner, Tina
Washington, Denzel
Waters, Ethel
Waters, Muddy
West, Kanye
Williams, Bert
Winfrey, Oprah
Wonder, Stevie

Military figures

Attucks, Crispus
Christophe, Henri
Davis, Benjamin O., Jr.
Delany, Martin Robison
Dessalines, Jean-Jacques

James, Daniel, Jr.
Miller, Dorie
Salem, Peter
Toussaint Louverture

Scientists and inventors

Banneker, Benjamin
Carver, George Washington
Drew, Charles Richard
Julian, Percy Lavon

Latimer, Lewis Howard
Lawless, Theodore Kenneth
Matzeliger, Jan E.
McCoy, Elijah
Morgan, Garrett A.

Rillieux, Norbert
Tyson, Neil de-Grasse
Williams, Daniel Hale
Woods, Granville T.

Artists and writers

Angelou, Maya
Baldwin, James
Baraka, Amiri
Bearden, Romare
Bontemps, Arna W.
Bradford, Roark
Brooks, Gwendolyn
Chesnutt, Charles Waddell
Cleaver, Eldridge
Cullen, Countee
Dove, Rita
Dunbar, Paul L.

Ellison, Ralph
Giovanni, Nikki
Haley, Alex
Hamilton, Virginia
Hansberry, Lorraine
Harper, Frances E. W.
Himes, Chester
Hughes, Langston
Hurston, Zora N.
Johnson, James Weldon
Lawrence, Jacob
McKay, Claude

Morrison, Toni
Mosley, Walter
Myers, Walter Dean
Parks, Gordon
Parks, Suzan-Lori
Pippin, Horace
Tanner, Henry O.
Taylor, Mildred D.
Toomer, Jean
Walker, Alice
Wheatley, Phillis
Wilson, August
Wright, Richard

Antislavery leaders

Douglass, Frederick
Forten, James
Gabriel
Still, William

Truth, Sojourner
Tubman, Harriet
Turner, Nat
Vesey, Denmark
Walker, David

Religious leaders

Allen, Richard
Divine, Father
Farrakhan, Louis
Healy, James Augustine

Jones, Absalom
Marino, Eugene Antonio
Muhammad, Elijah

Other biographies

Abbott, Robert Sengstacke
Beckwourth, James
Bland, James A.
Bluford, Guion Stewart, Jr.
Bunche, Ralph Johnson
Coleman, Bessie
Cuffe, Paul
Du Sable, Jean Baptiste Point
Estevanico
Garvey, Marcus
Hall, Prince
Henson, Matthew Alexander
Jemison, Mae Carol
Johnson, John Harold

Lacks, Henrietta
Lafayette, James Armistead
Lawrence, Robert Henry, Jr.
Love, Nat
Marshall, Thurgood
Obama, Michelle Robinson
Pickett, Bill
Rowan, Carl T.
Russwurm, John B.
Still, William Grant
Sullivan, Leon H.
Thomas, Clarence
Walker, Madam C. J.

History

Abolition movement
Amistad Rebellion
Black codes
Black Seminole
Bloody Sunday
Brown v. Board of Education of Topeka
Buffalo Soldiers
Carpetbaggers
Civil Rights Act of 1964
Civil War, American (Black Americans and the war)
Dred Scott Decision
Emancipation Proclamation
Emmett Till case
Freedmen's Bureau
Freedom riders
Grandfather clause
Greensboro Four
Harlem Hellfighters

I Have a Dream
Jim Crow
Ku Klux Klan
Little Rock Nine
Lynching
March on Washington
Maroons
Middle Passage
Missouri Compromise
Montgomery bus boycott
Negro leagues
Niagara Movement
Proslavery movement
Reconstruction
Scalawags
Scottsboro case
Selma marches
Sit-in
16th Street Baptist Church bombing

Slavery
Tulsa race massacre of 1921
Tuskegee Airmen

Underground railroad
Voting Rights Act of 1965

Organizations

Association for the Study of African American Life and History
Black Caucus, Congressional
Black Panther Party
Congress of Racial Equality
Knights of Peter Claver
National Association for the Advancement of Colored People
National Medical Association
Southern Christian Leadership Conference
Student Nonviolent Coordinating Committee
United Negro College Fund
Urban League

Religion

African Methodist Episcopal Church
African Methodist Episcopal Zion Church
Black Muslims
Nation of Islam
National Baptist Convention, USA, Inc.
National Baptist Convention of America, Inc.

Other related articles

African American literature
American literature (The Harlem Renaissance; The African American experience; Works by minority writers)
Black History Month
Black Lives Matter
Blues
Civil rights
Cowboy (The early cowboys)
Dialect
Ethnic group
Family (Early American families)
Gospel music
Gullah
Hampton University
Harlem Renaissance
Henry, John
Hip-hop

Howard University
Jazz
Juneteenth
Kwanzaa
Martin Luther King, Jr., Day
Martin Luther King, Jr., National Historical Park
Minority group
Museum of African American History
Opera (Porgy and Bess)
Races, Human
Racial profiling
Racism
Rap music
Rhythm and blues
Segregation
Sickle cell anemia
Spingarn Medal
Spiritual
Stereotyping

African hunting dog is a wild dog known for its large, round ears and sparse, tricolored coat. This coat consists of irregular patches of black, brown, and white fur. The dog also has long legs, a deep chest, and powerful jaws and teeth. An adult African hunting dog weighs from 45 to 67 pounds (20 to 30 kilograms) and stands 24 to 30 inches (60 to 75 centimeters) tall at the shoulders.

African hunting dogs usually live in packs of about 10 to 40 animals. A dominant male and female, who form a breeding pair, lead each pack. The dominant female gives birth in a den to a litter of 6 to 16 pups. The pack assists in grooming, feeding, and protecting the litter.

African hunting dogs usually hunt gazelles and antelope, but they may also kill zebras and wildebeests. They hunt during the day in packs, often surrounding their victim and chasing it until it is exhausted.

African hunting dogs once roamed in large numbers throughout much of Africa. However, they are endangered today. Only a few thousand African hunting dogs remain, mostly on wildlife parks and reserves in the eastern and southern parts of Africa. Increasing human population, disease, competition from hyenas, and various other factors have greatly reduced the African

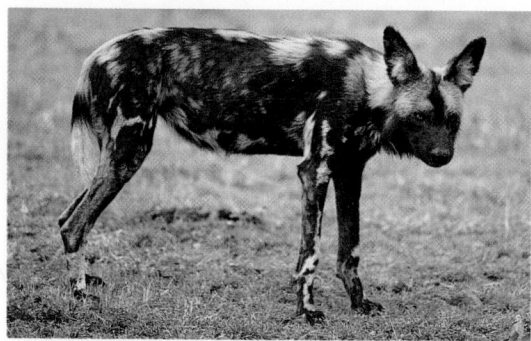

© Len Rue, Jr., Animals Animals
The African hunting dog is an endangered species.

hunting dog's population. Duane A. Schlitter

Scientific classification. The scientific name of the African hunting dog is *Lycaon pictus*.

African Methodist Episcopal Church (A.M.E.) is a Protestant denomination in the United States. It is one of the largest religious denominations in the country. The A.M.E. was founded by African American Methodists who withdrew in 1787 from St. George Methodist Episcopal Church in Philadelphia to protest segregation. Blacks then made up a large percentage of the Methodists in the United States. Two free Black men, Richard Allen and Absalom Jones, led the withdrawal. The church name was chosen to indicate it was formed by people of African descent. But the church has never had a policy of discrimination and has members of all races. See also **Allen, Richard.** Critically reviewed by the A.M.E. Church

African Methodist Episcopal Zion Church (A.M.E. Zion) is a Protestant religious denomination. It was formed in 1796 by a group of African Americans who withdrew from the John Street Methodist Episcopal Church in New York City. Many leaders of the movement in the 1800's to abolish slavery were members of the A.M.E. Zion Church, including Harriet Tubman, Sojourner Truth, and Frederick Douglass.

The General Conference, Board of Bishops, and a number of general officers or department heads administer the A.M.E. Zion. The General Conference meets every four years to set the business agenda and budget for the church. Bishops oversee the entire A.M.E. Zion as a board, and they individually lead separate *episcopal districts* (geographical divisions). General officers, each responsible to the Conference and a bishop, provide resources and services for A.M.E. Zion congregations. The church operates Livingstone College and Hood Theological Seminary in Salisbury, North Carolina, as well as two junior colleges, A.M.E. Zion University in Liberia, and Hood Speaks Theological Seminary in Nigeria.

Critically reviewed by the A.M.E. Zion Church

African National Congress (ANC) is a political party in South Africa. It played a major role in winning political and civil rights for the country's Black people, who make up about three-fourths of the population. Until 1994, South African law denied Black people the right to vote in national elections and to participate in the national government. Most ANC members are Black, but some members are white, Asian, or of mixed ancestry.

Black South Africans founded the ANC in 1912 to defend their political rights. In 1948, South Africa started a policy of rigid racial segregation called *apartheid*. Young ANC members, led by lawyer Nelson Mandela, began to resist the government, chiefly through civil disobedience. In 1960, the government outlawed the ANC. The ANC then began a policy of violent resistance. Many members, including Mandela, were imprisoned. Some were killed or exiled. Many nations opposed apartheid, and South Africa grew isolated in the world community.

In February 1990, South Africa legalized the ANC and released Mandela and other ANC leaders from prison. In May, the ANC and the government began talks aimed at giving nonwhite people the rights to vote and participate in government. In August, the ANC declared it would abandon the use of violence. In 1991, the government repealed the last of the apartheid laws.

In 1994, South Africa held its first national elections in which Black people were allowed to vote. The ANC won a majority of seats in the new National Assembly. The Assembly, in turn, elected Mandela president of South Africa. In elections held in 1999, the ANC again won a majority of seats in the Assembly, which then elected ANC leader Thabo Mbeki president of South Africa. Mandela had stepped down as head of the ANC in 1997 and had retired as South Africa's president in 1999.

The ANC again won a majority of Assembly seats in 2004, and the Assembly reelected Mbeki as president. In late 2007, Jacob Zuma defeated Mbeki in elections for the ANC presidency. The ANC won a majority of Assembly seats in elections in 2009, and Zuma became president of South Africa. The ANC and Zuma remained in power after elections in 2014, but Zuma resigned amid corruption allegations in 2018. Cyril Ramaphosa, the new head of the ANC, succeeded him as South African president. Ramaphosa remained in that office after the ANC won a parliamentary majority in 2019. Bruce Fetter

See also **Apartheid; Mandela, Nelson; Mbeki, Thabo; Xhosa.**

African Union, often called the AU, is an organization that works to achieve political, social, and economic cooperation among African governments and peoples. The membership of the organization consists of 54 independent countries and a government-in-exile. The AU replaced a previous group, the Organization of African Unity (OAU), in 2002. The structure of the AU is similar to that of the European Union (see **European Union**).

OAU leaders signed the Constitutive Act of the African Union in 2000. The act entered into force in 2001, and the African Union officially replaced the Organization of African Unity on July 9, 2002. The act outlines several objectives of the AU. These include working toward further political and economic integration of Africa; defending the independence of member states; promoting peace, cooperation, security, and stability in Africa; promoting democratic principles and human rights; raising the living standards of Africa's people; encouraging scientific and technological research; and working to eradicate diseases and promote good health. The act calls for participation of African peoples in AU activities. It also says the AU will reject unconstitutional changes of government in African countries.

The AU's supreme body is the Assembly of the Union, which consists of the member countries' heads of state and heads of government or their recognized representatives. It meets at least once a year. An Executive Coun-

Members of the African Union

Algeria	Libya
Angola	Madagascar
Benin	Malawi
Botswana	Mali
Burkina Faso	Mauritania
Burundi	Mauritius
Cameroon	Morocco
Cape Verde	Mozambique
Central African Republic	Namibia
Chad	Niger
Comoros	Nigeria
Congo, Democratic	Rwanda
Republic of the	Sahrawi Arab Democratic
Congo, Republic of the	Republic*
Côte d'Ivoire	São Tomé and Príncipe
Djibouti	Senegal
Egypt	Seychelles
Equatorial Guinea	Sierra Leone
Eritrea	Somalia
Eswatini	South Africa
Ethiopia	Sudan
Gabon	Sudan, South
Gambia	Tanzania
Ghana	Togo
Guinea	Tunisia
Guinea-Bissau	Uganda
Kenya	Zambia
Lesotho	Zimbabwe
Liberia	

*The Sahrawi Arab Democratic Republic is a government-in-exile formed by the Polisario Front, an organization seeking independence for the African territory of Western Sahara.

cil, made up of ministers of foreign affairs and other authorities representing the member states, makes administrative decisions on behalf of the Assembly. The AU also has a Peace and Security Council, which is modeled after the United Nations (UN) Security Council; a Pan-African Parliament; and an African Court on Human and Peoples' Rights. Other administrative bodies, including financial institutions, are being established. The headquarters of the AU are in Addis Ababa, Ethiopia. In 2019, the AU established an African Continental Free Trade Area (AfCFTA). It went into effect in 2021.   Mammo Muchie

African violet, also called *Saintpaulia,* is a tropical plant with beautiful flowers and heart-shaped, fuzzy leaves. It is not a true violet. A native of Africa, it is widely cultivated as a house plant. It thrives in moderate temperatures and soil rich in *humus* (decayed matter). The plant grows from 3 to 5 inches (8 to 13 centimeters) tall.

© Shutterstock

African violet flowers

The flowers grow to 1 inch (2.5 centimeters) wide, grow in clusters of three or more on slender stalks. They range in color from white to pink to violet. The name *Saintpaulia* comes from Baron Walter von Saint Paul-Illaire, a German nobleman who discovered the plant in 1892.   Thomas B. Croat

Scientific classification. The African violet's scientific name is *Saintpaulia ionantha.*

Afrikaners, *af ruh KAH nuhrz,* are people of Dutch, German, or French ancestry who live in South Africa. Most Afrikaners are of Dutch descent. The first Afrikaners were colonists sent to South Africa in 1652 by the Dutch East India Company, a trading firm. Many of the colonists became farmers. Afrikaners are also called Boers (pronounced *bawrz). Boer* is a Dutch term meaning *farmer.* Afrikaners speak the Afrikaans language, which is derived from Dutch.

The British occupied the colony the Afrikaners founded from 1795 until 1803. They seized the land again in 1806 and held it. In 1836, some Afrikaners left the colony to gain freedom from British rule. They moved northeast into lands that became known as Natal, the Orange Free State, and the Transvaal. On this "Great Trek," the Afrikaners faced grave dangers and hardships. Later, they lost to the British in the Anglo-Boer War of 1899-1902. Today, Afrikaners outnumber people of British descent in South Africa.   T. O. Beidelman

See also **Anglo-Boer Wars.**

Afro-Americans. See African Americans.

AFS Intercultural Programs is a nonprofit organization that promotes worldwide learning and living experiences for secondary school students, young adults, and families. It was formerly known as the American Field Service. AFS is active in more than 50 countries. Most AFS programs involve the international exchange of students 16 to 18 years old. The student lives with a family in another country for a summer or for a year and attends a local school. AFS also runs programs for young professionals in education, journalism, economics, banking, law, agriculture, and language.

The American Field Service was founded in 1914 as a volunteer ambulance corps during World War I (1914-1918). In 1947, it established the exchange program for students. In 1971, it expanded the program to include international exchanges that did not involve the United States as one of the partners. The organization adopted its present name in 1987. It has headquarters in New York City.   Lawrence O. Picus

Agamemnon, *AG uh MEHM nahn,* in Greek mythology, led the Greek army that conquered Troy in the Trojan War. Agamemnon was the king of Mycenae (or Argos). He married the princess Clytemnestra. Their children included Electra, Iphigenia, and Orestes.

Agamemnon assembled the Greek forces at Aulis before sailing for Troy. But the goddess Artemis refused to send favorable winds because Agamemnon had offended her. At Artemis's command, Agamemnon sacrificed his daughter Iphigenia so that the army could sail for Troy. One version tells that Iphigenia died in the sacrifice. Another tells that Artemis rescued her.

In the last year of the Trojan War, Agamemnon angered the god Apollo because he refused to return the captured maiden Chryseis to her father, a priest of Apollo. As punishment, Apollo sent a plague to afflict the Greek army. Agamemnon then returned Chryseis but, in exchange, he demanded the captive maiden Briseis from his rival, the warrior Achilles. The bitter quarrel that resulted between Achilles and Agamemnon became a major theme of the Greek epic the *Iliad.*

After Troy fell, Agamemnon returned to Mycenae with the Trojan princess Cassandra as his captive. Clytemnestra, aided by her lover, Aegisthus, killed

Agamemnon and Cassandra out of revenge for what she thought was the death of Iphigenia. Orestes killed his mother and Aegisthus to avenge the murder of Agamemnon.   F. Carter Philips

See also **Iliad; Iphigenia; Trojan War.**

Agana. See Hagåtña.

Agassi, *AG uh see,* **Andre** (1970-   ), ranks among the greatest players in the history of American men's tennis. Agassi became known for his powerful forehand and backhand strokes as well as for his ability to return an opponent's serve. Agassi retired as an active player in 2006 with 60 career tournament victories.

© Carmen Jaspersen, dpa/Landov
Andre Agassi

Agassi was the fifth man to win all four grand slam tennis tournaments during his career. He won Wimbledon in England in 1992; the United States Open in 1994 and 1999; the Australian Open in 1995, 2000, 2001, and 2003; and the French Open in 1999. He also won the gold medal in men's singles at the 1996 Summer Olympic Games. In 2001, he married the German tennis star Steffi Graf (see **Graf, Steffi**).

Andre Kirk Agassi was born on April 29, 1970, in Las Vegas. Agassi wrote *Open: An Autobiography* (2009).

Tony Lance

Agassiz, *AG uh see,* **Louis** (1807-1873), was a Swiss-born naturalist who studied many kinds of animals in Europe and America. He became noted for his work on both modern and fossil forms of fishes. He established a zoological laboratory on an island in Buzzards Bay off the coast of Massachusetts to study animals in their natural surroundings. Agassiz believed that animal species do not change, and he criticized the theory of evolution developed by the British naturalist Charles Darwin. As a geologist, Agassiz showed that glaciers once covered large areas of Earth.

Jean Louis Rodolphe Agassiz was born on May 28, 1807, in Motier-en-Vuly, Switzerland. He studied at the universities of Zurich, Heidelberg, and Munich. Agassiz came to the United States in 1846. In 1848, he became a professor of zoology and geology at Harvard University. He died on Dec. 14, 1873.

Carolyn Merchant

Agate, *AG iht,* is a banded form of *chalcedony,* a fine-grained, porous type of quartz. It commonly forms by precipitation in cavities of sedimentary and volcanic rocks (see **Sedimentary rock**). Most types of agates are dully colored. Their bands vary from white through gray to black. In some cases, the bands may be pale red, yellow, or blue. The colors result from the presence of such impurities as iron oxide and manganese oxide. Agates differ in the pattern of their bands. *Onyx* is a type of agate distinguished by parallel bands that lie in a plane. The bands of *eye agate* form circles that spread out from the center. *Moss agate* has delicate mosslike patterns.

Agate is used chiefly in making ornaments, such as pins and brooches. Most agate that is used for ornaments must be colored artificially. Agate's hardness and

ability to resist acids also make it valuable in the manufacture of mortars and pestles, tools used to crush and mix chemicals. Most agate comes from quarries in Brazil and Uruguay. Idar-Oberstein, in southwestern Germany, has been the main center for cutting and polishing agate for several hundred years.   Willis Hames

© Ted Kinsman, Photo Researchers
Bands of color in agate

See also **Chalcedony; Quartz; Sardonyx.**

Agate Fossil Beds National Monument is in northwestern Nebraska (see **Nebraska** [terrain map]). It has the fossil bones of extinct animals that lived about 20 million years ago. The fossils include those of two-horned rhinoceroses and of animals that had horselike heads, rhinoceroslike forelegs, bearlike hindlegs, and clawed feet. The monument was authorized in 1965. For its area, see **National Park System** (table: National monuments).   Critically reviewed by the National Park Service

Age of Reason. See Enlightenment.

Ageism, sometimes called *age discrimination,* is the unequal treatment of people because of their age. People may face ageism if they are believed to be too young or too old for a certain job, activity, or responsibility. Ageism can isolate people from mainstream society and severely limit their opportunities and social roles.

Some people hold oversimplified or false beliefs—called *stereotypes*—about people of certain age groups. Common stereotypes about older adults may label them as slow, incompetent, or depressed. Similarly, stereotypes about younger people may suggest that they are immature, inexperienced, or unreliable. People who hold such beliefs may practice age discrimination in employment, education, or other aspects of life.

Robert N. Butler, an American physician, introduced the term *ageism* in 1968. He compared ageism to other forms of discrimination, such as racism and sexism. Today, many governments seek to protect people against age discrimination. In the United States, for instance, the Age Discrimination in Employment Act of 1967 seeks to eliminate ageism in the workplace.   Debra J. Sheets

See also **Gray Panthers; Old age.**

Agency for International Development is an independent agency of the United States government that administers most of the nation's economic, technical, and humanitarian foreign aid programs. These programs are designed to improve the quality of life in developing countries in Africa, Asia, Latin America, and central and eastern Europe. The agency, which is commonly referred to as USAID or simply AID, helps these nations use their resources to become self-supporting.

USAID works to improve education, farm and industrial production, health care, nutrition, and population planning. It gives loans and grants to build hospitals, housing, and schools, and to set up small businesses. It also funds communications systems, small factories, power plants, and rural roads. USAID also provides famine and disaster relief, including food, medical aid, and temporary housing, to any needy nation.

Congress created the agency in 1961. From 1979 to 1999, it was part of the International Development Cooperation Agency.

Critically reviewed by the Agency for International Development

Agent is a person who represents someone else in legal, business, or other matters. The *principal* is the person who employs the agent. The agent's authority may be *express* or *implied.* Express authority involves doing exactly what the principal says to do. Implied authority involves doing anything that is a normal part of the agent's duties on behalf of the principal. For example, a corporation's president is an agent of the corporation. He or she has implied authority to perform the customary acts of a president, even without express authority.

If the principal allows an agent to appear as if he or she has more authority than the agent really has, the principal is bound by what the agent does. If the agent acts without authority, the principal is under no obligation unless the principal takes advantage of the act or approves it in some other way. If the principal does not approve the act, the agent may be liable for damages to the person the agent misled.

Edward J. Kionka

Agent Orange is the military code name for an *herbicide* (plant killer) used by the United States during the Vietnam War (1957-1975). In the 1960's and early 1970's, the U.S. armed forces sprayed Agent Orange over jungles and farms in South Vietnam and Laos. Agent Orange was used to *defoliate* (cause the leaves to fall off) trees and shrubs and to kill crop plants. The spraying revealed enemy hiding places and destroyed food crops.

Agent Orange consisted of mainly two plant-killing compounds: 2,4-D and 2,4,5-T. It also contained a type of compound called a *dioxin.* Some veterans of the war blamed Agent Orange for health problems. In 1990, the Centers for Disease Control (now the Centers for Disease Control and Prevention), a U.S. government agency, released a study which found no evidence that Agent Orange increased the risk of cancer among Vietnam veterans. That same year, a congressional committee declared the study flawed. In 1991, Congress passed a bill providing disability benefits for Vietnam veterans suffering from certain illnesses said to have been caused by exposure to Agent Orange. See **Dioxin.**

In 1993, the Institute of Medicine (now the National Academy of Medicine), an adviser to the U.S. government, released a study that linked exposure to Agent Orange to three kinds of cancer and two skin diseases. The study based its conclusions on civilians' exposure in their jobs or in job-related accidents. It recommended more studies before the effects of Agent Orange on veterans could be determined. Scott W. Waite

Aggression is a term psychologists use to refer to behavior intended to hurt others. Aggression may take a direct form, such as verbal abuse or a physical attack against people or their possessions. Indirect methods of aggression include spreading rumors and stealing.

People become aggressive for various reasons. Experiencing pain or danger can lead to aggression. In other cases, people behave aggressively to gain status, money, pleasure, or control over others.

Different approaches to understanding aggression emphasize different *determining factors* (causes). *Biological factors,* such as genes and hormones, and *person-*

ality characteristics, such as dominance or hostility, can lead to aggressive behavior. So can a person's *developmental history*—that is, how the person was raised. *Social factors,* including the presence of an audience and the sex, race, or other characteristics of the target, can also influence aggression.

Most theories of aggression recognize the relationship between emotions and aggression. People who experience frustration, anger, or fear may act aggressively. Some theories focus on *social learning,* the process by which individuals learn the behavior society expects of them. According to these theories, people may learn to be aggressive by witnessing aggressive behavior, such as family arguments and violent television programs. They may also learn aggression through *direct rewards* (getting what they want after acting aggressively). Social learning theories also emphasize the importance of *gender roles,* society's expectations about appropriate behavior for males and females.

Deborah South Richardson

See also **Bullying; Child** (Aggressive behavior); **Child abuse; Domestic violence; Personality** (Freud's psychoanalytic theory; Emotional reactions); **Psychology.**

Agincourt, *AZH ihn koor,* **Battle of,** took place between English and French armies near the village of Agincourt, in northern France, in 1415. The English had only about 6,000 troops. But its archers, firmly disciplined and backed by cavalry, routed a French army that probably consisted of about 20,000 to 30,000 troops. The battle marked the third great English victory in the Hundred Years' War. The English went on to conquer Normandy and to sign the favorable Treaty of Troyes in 1420. The English playwright William Shakespeare wrote about the battle in his history play *Henry V.* See also **Hundred Years' War; Shakespeare, William** (Shakespeare's plays *[Henry V]).*

C. T. Allmand

Aging is the process of growing old. As adults age, they become increasingly vulnerable to injury, illness, and death. Aging is a characteristic of almost all living things. The rate at which it occurs, however, varies within and across species. The biological changes associated with aging begin at the moment of *conception* (fertilization). In most human beings, the changes do not become visible until individuals reach 30 to 40 years of age. Age-related changes include graying or loss of hair, weakened muscles, wrinkled skin, and diminished sense of hearing and vision.

Why people age. Early scientists and philosophers viewed aging as a natural process that removed the elderly to make room for the young. This idea suggests that the natural lifespan of an organism is fixed and determined by genetic instructions that are present at birth. However, many scientists now believe that aging is the result of various natural biological processes rather than a predetermined genetic program. Most scientists think that aging and death occur at different rates and times among individuals because of a combination of genetic variation, differences in the way in which people live their lives, and the random nature of the biological processes that contribute to aging.

For most organisms, the timing of death is linked to the time in the life span when reproduction occurs. The timing of puberty and menopause is particularly important. After the reproductive period, the cells, tissues, and other components of the body have accumulated enough damage so that they can no longer function as well as before. This loss of function is expressed in the form of a wide range of diseases and disorders associated with aging.

How aging occurs. Scientists do not fully understand the precise biological changes in cells, tissues, and organs that contribute to aging. One important mechanism involved in aging is the damage that accumulates in cells from unstable molecules called *free radicals.* These molecules are produced from the natural biological processes as the body works to maintain a constant temperature and level of functioning.

The human body has many biological defense mechanisms designed to prevent or minimize free radical damage and repair the damage that does occur. Over time, however, the damage caused by free radicals accumulates and contributes to the many processes associated with aging. Scientists are looking for ways in which they can reduce or postpone the damage caused by free radicals and possibly delay the aging process.

Overcoming aging. Some of the effects of aging can be masked through the use of cosmetics, creams, lotions, and plastic surgery. Many people claim that vitamins, antioxidants, hormones, and various other substances have antiaging properties. Scientific research on these claims has yet to be completed, and most scientists doubt that they will work. However, scientific experiments have shown that it is possible to make some animals live longer by reducing their intake of food. Researchers are trying to understand how and why this method, called *caloric restriction,* works. Most scientists, however, believe that it is impossible to stop or reverse the process of aging.   S. Jay Olshansky

Related articles in *World Book* include:

Antioxidant	Old age
Life expectancy	Palliative care
Middle age	Progeria

Agnew, Spiro Theodore (1918-1996), became the only vice president of the United States to resign while under criminal investigation. In 1968 and 1972, Agnew won election as vice president under President Richard M. Nixon. Agnew resigned in 1973 after a federal grand jury began hearing charges that he had participated in graft as a Maryland officeholder.

Agnew was elected governor of Maryland in 1966. He was the first man of Greek descent to serve as governor of an American state, or as vice president. He became the second vice president to resign. In 1832, Vice President John C. Calhoun resigned after being chosen to fill a U.S. Senate seat from South Carolina.

Early life. Agnew was born on Nov. 9, 1918, in Towson, Maryland. His father, Theodore Spiro Agnew, had come to the United States in 1897. Theodore Agnew became a leader of the city's Greek community.

Office of the Vice President
Spiro T. Agnew

Agnew studied chemistry for three years at Johns Hopkins University and then transferred to the law school of the University of Baltimore. He served in the Army in Europe during World War II (1939-1945).

After the war, Agnew switched from the Democratic Party to the Republican Party. He married Elinor Isabel Judefind in 1942. They had three daughters and a son. Agnew received a law degree in 1947 and began practicing in Baltimore County.

Political career. Agnew entered politics in 1957, when he was appointed to the Baltimore County Board of Appeals. In 1962, he was elected county executive, the chief official of Baltimore County. In 1967, Agnew became the fifth Republican governor in Maryland history.

Agnew was little known outside Maryland when Nixon selected him to be his vice presidential running mate in 1968. Nixon—whose campaign stressed "law and order"—felt Agnew had taken a strong stand against the Baltimore riots that had erupted after the 1968 assassination of civil rights leader Martin Luther King, Jr.

In the 1968 election, Nixon and Agnew defeated the Democratic candidates, Vice President Hubert H. Humphrey and U.S. Senator Edmund S. Muskie. As vice president, Agnew soon became controversial. He accused newspapers and television networks of presenting news that was biased against the administration. He also harshly criticized student radicals and other dissenters. In 1972, Nixon and Agnew won a landslide victory over their Democratic opponents, George S. McGovern and Sargent Shriver.

In 1973, federal officials began to investigate charges that Agnew had accepted payments from contractors in return for helping them get state government work. The investigation covered the period Agnew had served as county executive, governor, and vice president.

Agnew denied any wrongdoing. But on October 10, he resigned as vice president under an agreement with the Department of Justice. Agnew pleaded *nolo contendere* (no contest) to a single charge—that he had cheated the government of $13,551 on his 1967 federal income taxes. The judge declared that the plea was "the full equivalent" of a guilty plea. Agnew was fined $10,000 and sentenced to three years probation.

House Minority Leader Gerald R. Ford succeeded Agnew as vice president in December 1973. In 1974, the Maryland Court of Appeals banned Agnew from practicing law in the state because of his *nolo contendere* plea. In 1981, another Maryland court ordered Agnew to pay the state for the illegal payments he had accepted, plus interest. In 1983, Agnew paid Maryland $268,482. Agnew wrote a memoir, *Go Quietly ... or Else* (1980). He died on Sept. 17, 1996.   Yanek Mieczkowski

See also **Ford, Gerald R.; Nixon, Richard M.; Vice president of the United States.**

Agnosticism, *ag NAHS tuh sihz uhm,* is the belief that ultimate questions, especially those about the existence of God, cannot be answered. The term comes from the Greek word *agnostos,* which means *not knowing.* It was first used by the British naturalist Thomas Henry Huxley in 1869. Agnosticism reflects the point of view that reason and scientific evidence should be the sole guides to finding truth. During the mid-1900's, the German American theologian Paul Tillich argued that a period of agnosticism—in the form of doubt—is a necessary stage before one can accept a meaningful faith. See **Atheism; Ingersoll, Robert Green.**   Mark Juergensmeyer

Agouti, *uh GOO tee,* is a rodent that lives in dense forests from southern Mexico to northern Argentina, and in the Caribbean region. Agoutis measure almost 2 feet (60 centimeters) long. They have small rounded ears, long legs, and either a short tail or no tail at all.

Most agoutis have brown, blackish-brown, or orange fur. The hair on the back is grayish. Agoutis run with a jumping motion, like deer.

Agoutis eat fruit, leaves, and roots. Most females bear their young in litters of two. The young have full coats of fur at birth, and their eyes are open. They can move about and take care of themselves soon after birth. However, they remain with their parents for as long as 20 weeks. Coatis, mountain lions, and jaguars prey on agoutis. In the tropics, people hunt agoutis for their meat. Agoutis make affectionate pets. Some kinds of agoutis have become endangered because the forests where they live have been destroyed.

© Shutterstock

Agouti

Charles A. Long

Scientific classification. Agoutis make up the genus *Dasyprocta.*

See also **Rodent.**

Agra, *AH gruh* (pop. 1,585,704; met. area pop. 1,746,467), is one of the largest cities in Uttar Pradesh, a state in northern India (see **India** [political map]). It is also one of the oldest cities on the Indian Peninsula. Agra is famous as the site of the Taj Mahal. In the 1600's, Emperor Shah Jahan ordered this magnificent marble tomb built as a memorial to his wife, Mumtaz-i-Mahal. Agra lies on the Yamuna River. The city centers around Agra Fort, which was built by the Mughal emperor Akbar about 1566. The northern part of the city has business and market districts. Modern factories lie north of the city along the river. Agra is an important trading center for cotton, grain, sugar, and tobacco. It is well known for the gold lace and delicate inlaid mosaics that its people make chiefly by hand.   P. P. Karan

See also **India** (picture: The art treasures of India); **Taj Mahal.**

Agribusiness, *AG ruh BIHZ nihs,* is the group of industries involved in the production, processing, and distribution of farm products. It includes grocery stores and food distributors as well as businesses that supply farmers with machinery, seeds, fertilizers and other chemicals, credit, and management information.

In most developed countries, agribusiness employs a sizable but shrinking proportion of workers. In the United States, where farmers represent less than 1 percent of the labor force, agribusiness employs about 1 out of every 6 workers. In less developed countries, it accounts for an even greater share of the labor force and the *gross domestic product* (GDP). GDP is the value of all the goods and services produced in a country during a year.

Providing a secure worldwide food supply ranks as a major challenge facing agribusiness. Companies are

also developing systems that track food products from the grower to the consumer to address food safety concerns and improve inventory management. Such tracking could be important in cases of food contamination and required recalls.   Michael Popp

Agricola, *uh GRIHK uh luh,* **Gnaeus Julius,** *NEE uhs* (A.D. 37?-93), was an able Roman general. He was given command in Britain by the emperor Domitian about A.D. 77 and ordered to complete the conquest of England. Seven years later, Agricola had conquered all of England and a part of Scotland. He also sent ships around the island of Great Britain to draw maps. Agricola then prepared to invade Ireland. But Domitian was displeased by the high cost of Agricola's operations. Agricola was relieved of his command and recalled to Rome. Agricola was born in what is now Frejus, France. He owes much of his fame to the writings of his son-in-law, the historian Tacitus.   Arther Ferrill

Agricultural Adjustment Administration (AAA). See **New Deal.**

Agricultural education is instruction about crop production, livestock management, soil and water conservation, and various other aspects of agriculture. Agricultural education includes instruction in food education, such as nutrition. Agricultural and food education improves the quality of life for all people by helping farmers increase production, conserve resources, and provide nutritious foods.

There are four major fields of agricultural education: (1) elementary agriculture, (2) vocational agriculture, (3) college agriculture, and (4) general-education agriculture. Elementary agriculture is taught in public schools and deals with such subjects as how plants and animals grow and how soil is farmed and conserved. Vocational agriculture trains people for jobs in such areas as production, marketing, and conservation. College agriculture involves training people to teach, conduct research, or provide information to advance agriculture and food science in other ways. General-education agriculture informs the public about food and agriculture.

In the United States

There are three chief sources of agricultural education in the United States. They are (1) high schools, (2) colleges and universities, and (3) youth organizations.

High schools. Most high school agriculture courses offer both classroom instruction and practical experience. For example, a student might raise a crop or an animal, work on a farm, or work for an agriculture business, such as a machinery dealer. Many schools offer adult education courses to help people improve their production, management, and computer skills.

Colleges and universities award bachelor's, master's, and doctor's degrees in agriculture. Many colleges and universities offer agricultural education via distance learning over the internet. Such classes are especially valuable for remote and rural populations.

Land-grant universities are state schools that receive federal aid under legislation that followed the Morrill Act of 1862. This act granted public lands to support agricultural or mechanical education. Land-grant universities have three chief functions: (1) teaching, (2) research, and (3) extension service.

Teaching. Colleges of agriculture prepare students

for careers in all aspects of the food and agriculture system. Some career choices include farming, food science, management, marketing, ranching, social services, teaching, and veterinary science.

Research. Each land-grant university has an agricultural experiment station equipped with laboratories and experimental farms. There, agricultural scientists work to develop better farming methods, solve the special problems of local farmers, and provide new technology.

Extension service. The Cooperative Extension System is a partnership of the federal, state, and county governments. This service distributes information gathered by the land-grant universities and the United States Department of Agriculture (USDA) to farmers, families, and young people. County extension agents, who work in most counties, train and support volunteer leaders. Agents and volunteers carry out extension programs through the internet, meetings, newsletters, radio, television, and visits.

Youth programs and organizations involved in agricultural education include 4-H and FFA (Future Farmers of America). Members of 4-H participate in projects dealing with conservation, food and agriculture, health and safety, and other subjects. The 4-H program in the United States is part of the National Institute of Food and Agriculture (NIFA), an agency of the USDA.

FFA is an integral part of the program of vocational agriculture in many high schools. Local chapters take field trips and conduct projects to develop leadership, citizenship, patriotism, and excellence in agriculture.

History. The rapid growth of agricultural education began during the late 1800's. In 1862, Congress created the Department of Agriculture to gather and distribute agricultural information. The Morrill Act, which provided for the land-grant schools, became law that same year. The Hatch Act of 1887 gave federal funds to establish agricultural experiment stations.

Government support for agricultural education increased during the 1900's. For example, the Smith-Lever Act of 1914 created what is now the Cooperative Extension System. The Smith-Hughes Act of 1917 and the George-Barden Act of 1946 financed high school instruction in farming. The Vocational Education Act of 1963 funded training in other fields of agriculture.

Agricultural science and education expanded after 1900 in response to a need for more technical knowledge and skill. This development led to the use of modern farming methods that required fewer farmworkers. Another result of this change was the creation of larger farms and ranches. This development increased the need for agricultural science and education. In the early 2000's, concern for the environment and the need for sustainable farming have driven agricultural research.

In other countries

Agricultural education in other countries resembles that in the United States. Canada has its own 4-H program. Agriculture and Agri-Food Canada, a government agency, distributes information on new farming methods and maintains experimental farms and research institutions throughout the country. In Australia, each state has several agricultural research stations and an extension service. The United Kingdom and New Zealand have programs of youth clubs called Young Farmers'

Clubs that resemble 4-H. In India, agricultural education is promoted by the Indian Council of Agricultural Research (ICAR).   Raymond J. Miller, Jr.

Related articles in *World Book* include:
Agricultural experiment station
FFA
4-H
Land-grant university

Agricultural experiment station is a research center that conducts scientific investigations to solve problems and suggest improvements in food and agriculture systems. Experiment station scientists work with farmers, ranchers, suppliers, processors, and others involved in food production and agriculture. Station scientists also work with natural resource and environmental organizations, rural communities, and consumers. Agricultural experiment stations have made outstanding contributions to the development of food and agriculture in the United States and Canada.

The United States has dozens of stations, including stations in the Virgin Islands and Puerto Rico. Each state has at least one main station at a state school called a *land-grant university.* Many states have branch stations to meet the needs of different climate and geographic zones in those states.

The United States stations are state institutions, but the federal and state governments cooperate in funding the research done at the stations. The states provide most of the government money. Additional income comes from competitive grants, contracts, and the sale of farm products.

Station scientists study biological, economic, and social problems of food, agriculture, and related industries in each state. They investigate such subjects as crop rotations, soil health, plant and livestock diseases, and environmentally friendly agriculture. They also work to develop and apply advanced technology to food and agriculture. The scientists work with specialists called *extension agents* or *county extension faculty,* who teach farmers about the latest local developments in agriculture. Most station scientists are faculty members of the land-grant universities.

The first state agricultural experiment station in the United States was organized in 1875 at Wesleyan University in Middletown, Connecticut. It was supported by private donations and state funds. Federal aid for experiment stations across the country began with the Hatch Act of 1887. The provisions of this act and later legislation providing increased funds were combined in the Hatch Act of 1955. The McIntire-Stennis Act of 1962 authorized forestry research at experiment stations. The federal government takes part in the experiment station program through the National Institute of Food and Agriculture of the U.S. Department of Agriculture. The department coordinates research activities among the state experiment stations.

In Canada, about 50 percent of the experiment stations are controlled by the Canadian government. The Central Experimental Farm in Ottawa is the headquarters of the federal system. Private industries, universities, and agricultural colleges control the rest of the stations. Each province has provincial stations.

Stephen Jones

See also **Land-grant university.**

© Yann Layma, Image Bank/Getty Images

Agriculture has reshaped many of Earth's natural features. Farmers in China, for example, have carved flat terraces into the slopes of hills and mountains. The terraces enable the farmers to grow rice in flooded sections, called *paddies*, without the water running down the slope.

Agriculture

Agriculture is the cultivation of plants and animals for human benefit. Agriculture provides us with almost all the food we eat. It also provides materials for clothing, industrial products, and fuel. Agriculture has reshaped much of Earth's natural environment, displacing or damaging many natural *ecosystems* (systems of living things along with their surroundings). But without agriculture, human civilization would not exist.

Agricultural products come from plants or from animals that eat plants. Such crops as corn, rice, and wheat provide food for billions of people. These crops also can provide food for livestock animals, which are raised for their meat, milk, or eggs. Some crops are grown to make fuel for automobiles. Others, such as cotton and linen, are used to make clothing and other materials.

Across the world, millions of farmers practice agriculture in a variety of ways. Some farmers use ancient methods to grow only enough food to feed their families. Other farmers use modern machines and chemicals. They raise large amounts of crops and animals and sell them at a profit. Some farms specialize in methods aimed at limiting the harmful impacts of agriculture.

Agriculture affects almost every part of human society. Everyone on Earth depends on agriculture's products to survive. In addition, many people work in the agricul-

ture industry as farmers, scientists, and businesspeople. Much economic activity involves trading agricultural products on the global market. Because growing and distributing food is so important, governments control and direct many aspects of the agriculture industry.

Agricultural activity has altered much of Earth's surface. People have destroyed forests, prairies, and other natural environments to make room for farmland. Such destruction displaces wild plants and animals, reducing the diversity of life in farmed regions. Modern technology enables farmers to harvest vast amounts of food. But the same technology can produce harmful pollution.

Before agriculture, people got their food by hunting wild animals and gathering wild plants. Small groups of such *hunter-gatherers* usually had to move around from place to place to find enough food. Human beings first started practicing agriculture about 10,000 years ago. Agriculture enabled people to grow their food in the same place year after year. Thus, people who practiced agriculture could establish villages where they could stay for their whole lives. These early farming communities gave rise to cities and, eventually, the world's great civilizations. Throughout history, the technological and social development of civilization has remained intertwined with the development of agriculture.

This article will discuss various agricultural products and the practices used to produce them. It will also discuss agriculture's impact on human society and on

Earth's environment. The final section will cover the history of agriculture. For more information on modern farming techniques, see **Farm and farming.** See **Food supply** for more information about how agriculture feeds the world's people. The **Gardening** and **Horticulture** articles cover gardening and the growing of plants on a smaller scale.

Agricultural products

Agricultural products come in a huge variety of shapes, sizes, flavors, and uses. They include eggs, flowers, grains, meat, milk, natural fibers, oils, vegetables, and wood. Manufacturers process agricultural products to create an even greater variety of goods, from candy bars to sweaters to fuel. For example, corn (also called *maize)* can become breakfast cereal, *fodder* (livestock feed) for chickens, sweetener for soft drinks, starch for binding books, and even fuel for automobiles.

All agricultural products share one thing in common—they depend on sunlight. Crops, like all plants, get energy directly from the sun. Livestock animals get energy by eating crops or other plants. Agriculture involves transforming the sun's energy into a form that human beings can use.

The most important form of energy that agriculture provides is food. Human beings require a wide range of *nutrients* (nourishing substances) to survive. The three most important are *carbohydrates* (mostly sugars and starches), proteins, and fats. Various agricultural products have different amounts of these nutrients.

Food from plants. Plants use a process called *photosynthesis* to capture the sun's energy. Photosynthesis takes place in special parts of a plant's leaves. These parts use the energy of sunlight to combine water with carbon dioxide from the air, making sugar. The sugar serves as food for the plant.

There are five main groups of plants raised as food crops. They are (1) cereal grains, (2) root crops, (3) pulses,

(4) sugar-bearing crops, and (5) other crops.

Cereal grains rank as the most important food crops. These plants are mostly grasses that are grown for their edible seeds. They include corn, rice, and wheat.

Many cereals are *staple crops.* A staple crop provides a large part of the world's nutrition and so is grown in huge quantities. People often eat some form of staple crops at every meal. For example, many American and European meals include wheat in the form of bread or pasta. Rice dishes make up much of Asian food. Cereals also serve as fodder for animals.

Root crops have large, nutritious underground roots. They include beets, carrots, potatoes, turnips, and such tropical plants as cassava and taro. Many root crops serve as staples in tropical areas. Root crops have large amounts of carbohydrates.

Pulses are a group of plants whose seeds are used for food, including beans and peas. Unlike most other plants, pulses contain high amounts of protein.

M. Stone, DPI

Miller Services

Food and other agricultural products come from plants and from animals that eat plants. Farmers grow wheat and other *cereal grains* for their edible seeds, *above.* Such *livestock* as sheep, *right,* provide milk and wool along with meat.

Leading groups of agricultural products

Product groups	Production		Leading countries
	in tons*	in metric tons*	
Cereal grains	3,283,766,000	2,978,982,000	
Corn	1,265,991,000	1,148,487,000	Argentina, Brazil, China, Ukraine, United States
Wheat	844,117,000	769,770,000	Canada, China, France, India, Russia, United States
Rice	832,767,000	755,474,000	Bangladesh, China, India, Indonesia, Vietnam
Sugar-bearing crops	2,345,507,000	2,127,808,000	
Sugar cane	2,148,747,000	1,949,310,000	Brazil, China, India, Mexico, Pakistan, Thailand
Sugar beets	196,760,000	178,498,000	France, Germany, Russia, Turkey, United States
Fruits and vegetables	2,219,636,000	2,013,620,000	
Tomatoes	199,261,000	180,766,000	China, Egypt, India, Iran, Turkey, United States
Bananas	128,730,000	116,782,000	Brazil, China, Ecuador, India, Indonesia, Philippines
Watermelons	110,689,000	100,415,000	Algeria, Brazil, China, India, Iran, Turkey
Oil-bearing crops†	1,213,983,000	1,101,307,000	
Palm oil	452,716,000	410,697,000	Colombia, Indonesia, Malaysia, Nigeria, Thailand
Soybeans	367,810,000	333,672,000	Argentina, Brazil, China, India, United States
Cottonseed	91,039,000	82,589,000	Brazil, China, India, Pakistan, United States
Milk (cow, buffalo, goat, and sheep)	973,654,000	883,284,000	Brazil, China, Germany, India, Pakistan, United States
Root crops	949,137,000	861,042,000	
Potatoes	408,336,000	370,437,000	China, India, Russia, Ukraine, United States
Cassava	334,627,000	303,569,000	Brazil, Democratic Republic of the Congo, Ghana, Indonesia, Nigeria, Thailand
Sweet potatoes	101,215,000	91,821,000	China, Malawi, Nigeria, Tanzania, Uganda
Meat	371,680,000	337,183,000	
Poultry	130,092,000	118,017,000	Brazil, China, India, Indonesia, Russia, United States
Pork	121,375,000	110,110,000	Brazil, China, Germany, Russia, Spain, United States
Beef	75,303,000	68,314,000	Argentina, Australia, Brazil, China, United States
Pulses	97,422,000	88,380,000	
Dry beans	31,860,000	28,903,000	Brazil, China, India, Myanmar, Tanzania
Chickpeas	15,704,000	14,246,000	India, Myanmar, Pakistan, Russia, Turkey
Eggs	97,295,000	88,264,000	Brazil, China, India, Indonesia, Mexico, United States

*The figures for products within a group may not add up to the group total. Only the leading products are listed.
†Used to make flour and meal as well as oil.
Source: FAOSTAT, Statistics Division, Food and Agriculture Organization of the UN (http://www.fao.org). Figures are for 2019. Data accessed in 2021.

Sugar-bearing crops—mainly sugar beets and sugar cane—are processed to make sugar. Sugar beets are root crops grown in cooler areas. Sugar cane is a tropical grass. Sugar processors can more easily extract sugar from sugar beets than from sugar cane.

Other food crops include fruits, nuts, vegetables, and such oil-bearing crops as canola and olives. Vegetables and fruits contain many nutrients and provide variety in diets. Farmers also grow such specialty crops as coffee and tea, as well as cacao beans for making chocolate.

Food from animals. People raise many livestock animals for their meat, eggs, or milk. Such animals include cattle, chickens, goats, hogs, sheep, and turkeys. Many animal products contain high amounts of protein.

All livestock eat plants to get the energy they need to grow and to produce eggs or milk. Some farmers raise their livestock on pastures, where the animals eat natural grasses. Many other farmers raise livestock animals in large pens called *feedlots*, where the animals eat fodder made from cereal grains.

Other food-producing animals important to agriculture include bees, fish, and shellfish. Beekeepers raise bees for their honey. Fishing crews take many fish and shellfish from open waters. However, in a type of farming known as *aquaculture,* farmers raise fish, shellfish, and aquatic plants in large underwater holding areas called *fish farms.*

Fuel and raw materials. Agriculture also plays a key role in producing fuel and nonfood materials for industry. Some products, such as cotton, come from plants raised for the sole purpose of producing that product.

Others, such as some biofuels, come from plants that also produce food.

Biofuels are fuels produced from agricultural crops. Such plants as corn, sugar cane, and switchgrass can be made into ethanol and biodiesel. These substances can be used in place of gasoline and diesel fuel.

Biofuels differ from such fuel sources as coal, petroleum, and natural gas. These other substances, called *fossil fuels,* consist of long-dead remains of living things compressed over millions of years. Fossil fuels provide much of the energy used to power modern society. But fossil fuels are a *nonrenewable resource*—that is, they exist in limited amounts, beyond which we cannot produce more. Biofuels, on the other hand, come from plants that can grow year after year.

Raw materials include natural fibers, timber, animal hides, and nonedible oils. Many of these materials are used to manufacture finished products. For example, cotton—a plant fiber—is used in many types of clothing, as well as such products as coffee filters. Silk from silkworms and wool from sheep also serve as important clothing fibers. Castor oil and linseed oil come from plants with high oil contents in their seeds. These oils are used to create paints, lubricants, medicines, and other products. Farmers also grow ornamental plants, including cut flowers and decorative trees.

Agricultural practices

Farmers have developed many methods of harvesting a vast number of crops. With the exception of the frigid polar regions, people practice some form of agriculture on almost all of Earth's land. Until the early 2000's, more people worked in agriculture than any other industry. Only the service industry employs more people today.

Agricultural practices vary widely based on climate, soil, and physical terrain. In mountainous areas, farmers often grow root crops on steplike terraces carved into slopes. In parts of Asia, farmers take advantage of heavy rains from *monsoons* (seasonal winds) to grow rice in flooded paddies. Farmers in dry regions often use irrigation to water their soil, bringing the water from distant rivers or other sources. Some grasslands with poor soils or too little water for growing food crops provide grazing for livestock animals instead.

Wealth, technology, and cultural history also influence how agriculture is practiced. In less developed parts of the world, farmers practice *subsistence agriculture* or *semisubsistence agriculture*. Such farmers grow food mostly for feeding their families, often using just the power of their own muscles and draft animals. In contrast, most farmers in developed countries practice *industrialized agriculture*. They use tractors, chemical fertilizers, and other modern technologies to help plant and harvest vast areas of land. In industrialized agriculture, the work of one farmer may feed dozens of families or more.

Subsistence agriculture has been the main form of agriculture for most of human history. Subsistence farmers *subsist*, or survive, almost entirely on what they can grow or raise. They have little food left over to sell and little money to buy other food. Semisubsistence farmers grow small amounts of extra food that they sell to others. Subsistence agriculture requires much human labor, leaving little time for other activities associated with modern civilization. Hundreds of millions of people in Africa, Asia, and Latin America practice subsistence or semisubsistence agriculture.

Subsistence farmers often practice *shifting cultivation*, which involves moving from one small plot of land to another. They use simple technology, such as plows attached to draft animals. They rarely have access to fertilizers other than natural fertilizers, such as manure. Another form of traditional agriculture is *pastoralism*, the raising of herds of grazing animals.

Shifting cultivation is an ancient method of farming. Farmers commonly practice it in tropical areas with poor soil. They clear a small area by cutting down trees and vegetation and burning them. The ashes help fertilize the soil. Because of these methods, shifting cultivation is sometimes called *slash-and-burn agriculture.*

The farmers typically grow crops in an area for one to three years. Eventually, the crops deplete the fertility of the soil. Then, farmers clear a new area and move the farm there. The first area may lie fallow for a number of years while its fertility recovers.

In shifting agriculture, farmers often plant crops by digging holes in the soil with sticks or simple tools and dropping the seeds in. The farmers typically grow a mixture of crops in the same field. This growing strategy is called *polyculture*. A traditional polyculture involves beans, corn, and squash. The sturdy corn stalks help support the beans. Together, the crops benefit the soil in ways they would not if planted separately.

Shifting cultivation can cause environmental problems, especially in areas with high populations. With more people to feed, farmers become pressured to slash and burn more land, damaging ecosystems. They also may leave the soil less time to recover.

Pastoralism involves the breeding and raising of such grazing animals as alpacas, camels, goats, sheep, and yaks. Most pastoralist peoples live in places that are too hot, cold, dry, or rocky to support food crops. The people live in small groups and move about constantly in search of water and pasture for their herds. A major region supporting millions of pastoralists stretches from northern Africa through the Arabian Desert into Mongolia and Tibet.

Some pastoralists trade milk, meat, and other animal products with nearby farmers. They may also graze their

Shifting cultivation, sometimes called *slash-and-burn agriculture,* is an ancient method of farming. It involves the periodic moving from one small farming area to another. Fire helps to clear new areas for planting, and the ashes fertilize the soil. Shifting agriculture is still practiced in some areas, as seen in this photo from Madagascar.

Agriculture by region

This graph compares various regions in terms of their percentage of the world's agricultural workers and percentage of world crop production. Over 90 percent of agricultural workers live in Asia and Africa. These regions include many developing areas, where farming requires large amounts of human labor. Europe, the United States, and Canada, on the other hand, together produce about 20 percent of the world's crops with only about 2 percent of the world's farmers.

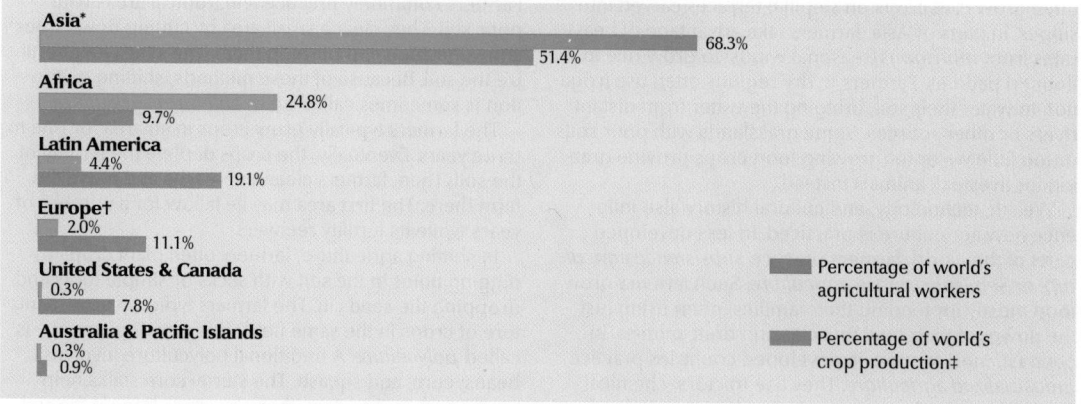

Asia*
68.3%
51.4%

Africa
24.8%
9.7%

Latin America
4.4%
19.1%

Europe†
2.0%
11.1%

United States & Canada
0.3%
7.8%

Australia & Pacific Islands
0.3%
0.9%

■ Percentage of world's agricultural workers

■ Percentage of world's crop production‡

*Including Asian part of Russia.   †Excluding Asian part of Russia.   ‡Crop production does not include forage crops.
Figures are for 2019 and may not add up to 100 percent due to rounding.
Source: FAOSTAT, Statistics Division, Food and Agriculture Organization of the UN (http://www.fao.org). Data accessed in 2021.

herds on unused farms. The animals help fertilize the soil with their manure.

Industrialized agriculture developed from technological advances made in the 1800's in Europe and America. It has since spread all over the world. In industrialized agriculture, machines perform much of the physical farm work, such as plowing and harvesting. Farmers use manufactured chemicals to fertilize the soil and keep pests away. Unlike subsistence farms, industrialized farms raise a surplus of crops. They sell these crops in national and global markets, often shipping them great distances.

Large corporations own and operate many industrialized farms. In addition to farming, such *agribusinesses* often control the processing, distribution, and marketing of farm products. Some agribusinesses employ *contract farmers,* also called *contract growers,* whom they pay to produce a certain amount.

As scientific and technological knowledge has increased, so has the efficiency of industrialized agriculture. In 1900, for example, a typical farmer in the United States could produce only enough food to feed several people. A modern farmer in the United States produces enough food to feed well over 100 people. Today, computers automate much industrialized farm work, such as irrigating soil, feeding livestock, and even operating tractors.

Industrialized farming techniques have made much of our modern civilization possible. However, their intensive use has also contributed to a number of environmental, ethical, and social concerns.

Growing plant crops. Unlike most subsistence farms, industrialized farms typically grow a single, uniform crop over large areas of land. Such a practice is called *monoculture.* Examples of monoculture include vast wheat and corn fields in North America, as well as large areas of oil palms in Southeast Asia. The uniformity of a monoculture enables farmers to efficiently grow and quickly harvest huge amounts of crops. For example, a single tractor or combine can run across a whole field, planting or harvesting all the crops at the same time.

The plants in a monoculture share *genetic* (inherited) similarities and so respond similarly to fertilizers, pesticides, and growing techniques. Many monocultures have special adaptations for the region in which they grow. On a farm with salty soil, for example, a farmer may plant a variety of tomato with a high salt tolerance. Farmers may also plant varieties that have resistance to certain diseases or pests, or that grow well with synthetic fertilizers. Such adaptations may be natural, developed through *breeding,* or introduced through *genetic engineering.* Breeding is the careful selection and pairing of plants or animals to bring about desired characteristics in their offspring. Genetic engineering is the direct manipulation of a living thing's *genes* (hereditary material) to change its inherited characteristics.

To protect crops from pests, industrialized farms often spray the plants with chemical pesticides. They also use chemical fertilizers to replenish soils and increase yields.

One major environmental and health concern in industrialized agriculture involves the widespread use of chemical pesticides. Pesticides are poisons, and large amounts of the chemicals can harm wildlife and human beings. In addition, diseases, weeds, and insects can often become resistant to a particular pesticide. If this happens, farmers must use more of a pesticide or researchers must develop a new pesticide.

Another major agricultural concern is the vulnerability of monocultures. In addition to sharing strengths, the plants in a monoculture have the same weaknesses. For this reason, a disease that harms a single plant will likely affect every plant in the field. Diseases and pests can become especially damaging to monocultures if a single crop variety is planted across a large region. For example, in 1970, a corn leaf blight fungus destroyed about 15 percent of the corn crop from Florida to Texas.

Raising livestock. In industrialized agriculture, farmers

increasingly raise animals in indoor pens or in crowded outdoor enclosures. *Feedlots* are outdoor pens that can hold thousands of cattle. Some cattle are born and raised on natural pastures and later moved to feedlots to gain weight before they are slaughtered.

Many modern farms resemble highly automated industrial factories. Such farms are often called *confined animal feeding operations* (CAFO's) or *factory farms.* They produce massive amounts of meat, dairy products, and eggs quickly and cheaply. Millions of hogs and chickens are raised in indoor factory farms.

Factory farms are designed for efficiency. The farmers give the animals high-energy feed, often made from cereal grain fodder. The animals are confined in dense groups. They gain weight rapidly before being slaughtered and sold as meat.

Reforming agricultural practices. One of the broadest criticisms of many industrialized techniques is that they are not *sustainable*—that is, they cannot be continued in the long-term because they cause irreparable damage to the environment, depletion of natural resources, and disruption of human communities. Monocultures, for example, have been attacked as unsustainable for their vulnerability to pests and diseases. Industrialized agriculture also relies heavily on fossil fuels, which are used to create synthetic fertilizers and pesticides and to transport farm products. Critics charge that such reliance on diminishing supplies of fossil fuels is not sustainable.

Much ethical criticism has centered on the use of factory farms to raise livestock. At such farms, the demands of efficiency tend to minimize concern for the welfare of animals. Many people consider the crowding, confinement, slaughtering techniques, and other elements of factory farming cruel and degrading to animals.

Another ethical and health concern in industrialized agriculture involves the widespread use of drugs to treat livestock. Diseases can spread easily among animals in crowded conditions. To prevent sickness, factory farms often give their animals regular doses of *antibiotics* (germ-fighting drugs). Cattle also typically receive vitamins and growth *hormones* (body chemicals) that boost their weight or cause them to produce more milk. Many people worry about the health effects of eating meat or drinking milk from animals exposed to large amounts of antibiotics and growth hormones. Many people also worry that the widespread use of antibiotics has led to more antibiotic resistance in disease-causing organisms.

Criticisms of industrialized agriculture have led to the development or proposal of practices considered to be more sustainable and kinder to livestock. They include organic agriculture and local food movements.

Organic agriculture is one response to many concerns about industrialized agriculture. Organic farms grow crops that are not genetically engineered using little or no pesticides, synthetic fertilizers, or other artificial chemicals. Organic meat, eggs, and dairy products come from animals raised on organically grown fodder or natural grasses. In addition, the animals must not receive antibiotics or growth hormones. Before a farmer can label and sell a food as *organic,* the farm and its products must pass a government certification process.

Organic farmers use natural processes and substances to fertilize their crops and to control pests and diseases. For example, organic farmers often apply *compost* (decaying plant and animal matter) to their crops instead of synthetic fertilizer.

Like industrialized farms, many organic farms are run by large agribusinesses. Many organic farms also grow crops in monocultures and transport them long distances to market.

Local food movements have increased in popularity since the late 1900's. Such movements assist consumers in the purchase of agricultural products from nearby farms. Supporters argue that local food movements allow farmers to develop a closer relationship with the people they feed. They also argue that buying local food helps reduce the use of fossil fuels used to transport products. In practice, however, local food production and distribution does not always use fuel as efficiently as large-scale, long-distance systems of agriculture.

In many cities, farmers' markets sell locally produced food and other products. Another form of local food distribution is called *community supported agriculture* (CSA). Members of a CSA organization directly pay a local farmer in advance for a certain amount of food. The members can then pick up fresh food from the farm

© Jacob Kearns, Shutterstock

Free-range chickens roam freely in an open pasture. Raising free-range animals serves as an alternative to raising them in cages or pens, a practice some people consider inhumane and unnecessary.

throughout the growing season. Some CSA members may work on the farm in exchange for food.

Agriculture and society

Agriculture is centrally important to human society. It provides materials for food and clothing—two of life's most basic necessities. Agriculture also plays a vital role in the global economy, and economic activity has a strong effect on agriculture. In addition, ensuring the safety of agricultural products is a major public health concern. For these and other reasons, governments throughout the world regulate and control many aspects of agriculture.

The global market shapes, and is shaped by, agricultural activity. Today, billions of people buy their food in supermarkets. A shopper in Europe or North America can buy bananas from Costa Rica, lamb from Australia, and a frozen dinner with ingredients from China. In late winter, the same shopper can buy fresh apples harvested and flown in from New Zealand—where it is late summer and apples are in season. The global market makes possible such a variety of food choices. Using modern communication and transportation, the market connects farmers, distributors, food processing companies, and consumers throughout the world.

Commodity trading. Many agricultural products are *commodities*—that is, raw, unprocessed goods that can easily be bought and sold in large amounts around the world. Commodities, or contracts to produce commodities, are bought and sold by investors at a commodity exchange. A global network of commodity exchanges enables food grown in one country to be bought and sold around the world.

The international trading of commodities affects farmers in a number of ways. It offers farmers a wide variety of overseas markets for selling their products. But it also exposes them to much more competition from farmers in other countries. Farmers in less developed countries may suffer because customers in such countries can often buy food from distant, industrialized farms more cheaply.

Changes in demand affect food prices and agricultural production. The greater the demand for an agricultural product, the more farmers can charge for it.

Modern demand for agricultural products has increased due to several factors. One factor is population growth—more people require more food. But the world's farms can produce only a limited supply of food, causing food to become more valuable—and expensive.

A second factor is the growth of wealth. As countries become more developed, their people generally want to consume more food—and in particular, more meat. A higher demand for meat increases not only the price of meat but also the price of cereal grains used as fodder. The resulting increase in staple grain prices can put particular pressure on poor people who rely on cereal grains as a central part of their diet.

A third factor increasing food prices is the development of biofuels. Some biofuels are made from important food crops, such as corn. An increase in fuel demand means that more crops may go to make biofuel for automobiles instead of providing food for people.

Government regulation. Governments around the world regulate the quality and safety of agricultural products that enter the market. Governments also use a number of methods to control agriculture's interaction with the economy.

Grades and labels of agricultural products exist to protect consumers from harm. In most cases, government agencies grade crops and animal products according to their quality. Only food with certain grades is considered fit for sale to people—though some food not suitable for human consumption can be sold for livestock and pets. Governments typically monitor crops for outbreaks of disease and coordinate responses to such outbreaks.

Governments also regulate the labeling of food products. Effective labeling ensures that consumers know the freshness, nutritional content, and ingredients of what they buy. Labels often include a *sell by* or *use by* date on the packaging. Such perishable foods as dairy, eggs, fish, and meat have especially strict labeling requirements. Governments regulate the *organic* label so that consumers know the food was raised according to specific standards. The European Union requires genetically modified food to have clear labels identifying it as such.

Economic controls are used by governments to ensure that the food supply remains stable, protecting people from shortages. The controls also serve to help farmers and agribusinesses make profits.

In general, the demand for a crop determines its price. Farmers tend to grow crops that they think will yield a high price at the markets. For example, a farmer might notice that corn sells for a high price, and so the farmer will plant fields with corn for next year's harvest. But if every farmer in the area did the same, they would produce a huge surplus of corn that nobody wanted. All the farmers would have to sell their corn at low prices and lose money.

Governments use several techniques to keep the supply of a crop from greatly exceeding the demand. A *price ceiling*—that is, a maximum price set for a crop—may discourage farmers from growing that crop. Governments also offer farmers *subsidies* (financial assistance) in exchange for not growing a certain kind of crop.

Price floors have the opposite effect, encouraging farmers to grow a crop by setting a minimum price above the market's price. Another way governments encourage agriculture production in their own countries is through tariffs and other trade barriers. A tariff is a tax on products imported from other countries. Because foreign products become more expensive with such taxes, more people will want to buy local products—which encourages domestic farmers to grow more. Less developed countries may also use subsidies and trade barriers to encourage more people to become farmers, creating sources of income and guarding against famine.

Agriculture and the environment

Agriculture has changed much of Earth's surface from its natural state. For at least 10,000 years, people have cut down forests to clear areas for farmland. They have dug canals and redirected water supplies to irrigate their farms. Even the crop plants and livestock animals have changed significantly from their wild ancestors through breeding. Since the 1980's, plants and animals have also been changed through genetic engineering.

The clearing of wilderness to make room for farmland

Genetically modified crops make up most of the crops grown in the United States and Canada. This photograph shows a worker inspecting genetically modified corn. Genetic engineering can help create more productive crops, but the use of such technology is controversial.

Food and farming
worldbook.com/ag-15

can damage topsoil and destroy fragile ecosystems. Planting monocultures and relying on only a few widespread crops threatens *biodiversity*, the variety of living things in the environment. Industrialized agriculture relies on large amounts of fossil fuels and synthetic chemicals, contributing to pollution. Today, agriculture has a greater impact on the environment than ever before.

Ecosystem destruction. The vast fields of modern farmland were once complex ecosystems, home to hundreds of *species* (kinds) of plants, animals, and other living things. Before agriculture, for example, forests covered much of Europe. The Great Plains of North America once supported vast prairies, which early explorers described as "seas of grass." Today, corn and wheat fields have replaced almost all the prairies.

In addition to destroying native ecosystems, agriculture can also damage topsoil. Soil is itself a kind of ecosystem, home to many kinds of worms, insects, and microorganisms. Topsoil can take hundreds of years to form. However, intensive farming can quickly drain topsoil of its nutrients and disrupt its ecosystem.

Farming can even strip topsoil altogether by contributing to erosion. Topsoil acts like a sponge, absorbing great amounts of moisture. If an area's topsoil erodes, the area can quickly dry out. In regions that are already dry, farming can contribute to the loss of fertile land known as *desertification*. Without healthy topsoil and native grasses, such areas lose their ability to hold any significant amount of water and become lifeless desert wastelands.

Threats to biodiversity. Prairies, forests, and even deserts support many different kinds of plants, fungi, insects, and large animals. But farmed areas tend to support relatively few living things. Monocultures, in particular, are created to support only a single kind of plant. As more wilderness areas have been converted into farmland, overall biodiversity has declined.

In addition to the diversity of species, modern agriculture also threatens genetic diversity within species. In natural ecosystems, different individuals of the same species often show much genetic variation. But in a monoculture, all the plants in the field have similar or even identical genetic makeup. This lack of diversity even threatens the crops themselves. If the genetic variety of a species becomes lost, farmers and scientists cannot breed new varieties to replace those that fail.

Pollution. Modern agriculture causes many kinds of pollution. Industrialized farms often spray crops with large amounts of pesticides. These chemical poisons can contaminate a region's soil and *ground water* (water beneath the surface). Pesticides can also kill harmless or beneficial insects and other organisms.

Ocean and lake ecosystems can be greatly harmed by fertilizers from crop fields and by livestock wastes. Fertilizers and animal wastes contain many nutrients that can help plants grow. But they also provide food for plantlike organisms called *algae*, which live in bodies of water. Rain often washes fertilizers and animal wastes from farms into rivers and streams that flow into the ocean and other bodies of water. There, the nutrients cause algae to rapidly multiply, creating *algal blooms* that use up all the oxygen in the water. Without oxygen, fish and other organisms in the water die.

Agriculture also heavily contributes to *global warming*—an observed increase in Earth's average surface temperature. Global warming is chiefly caused by *greenhouse gases,* which trap heat in Earth's atmosphere. Burning fossil fuels gives off greenhouse gases, and most modern farm machinery burns fossil fuels. Fossil fuels are also used to transport farm products around the world. Livestock animals produce large amounts of the greenhouse gas methane as they digest their food.

History

Before agriculture, human beings lived by hunting and gathering, also called *foraging.* People picked fruits, nuts, and seeds from their natural surroundings to eat. Many of these plants looked almost nothing like modern agricultural crops. Before people could farm, they first had to *domesticate* wild plants and animals—changing them into forms suitable for agriculture. People began to domesticate plants and animals for food around 9000 to 8500 B.C. Soon afterward, people began to farm.

As early farming communities developed agricultural technologies, they also expanded into new areas and traded with other peoples. As a result, new farming practices began to spread throughout the world. Eventually, certain farming communities developed into the first great civilizations.

Beginning in the late A.D. 1400's, Europeans sailed across the Atlantic Ocean to the Americas. They brought many native crops from the Americas—such as chocolate, potatoes, and tomatoes—back to Europe, Asia, and Africa. Europeans also introduced their own native crops and livestock onto American lands as they began settling and farming North and South America.

Industrialized agriculture emerged in Europe and the United States during the 1800's, greatly increasing agricultural productivity. In the mid-1900's, Western scientists helped spread the techniques and technologies of industrialized agriculture to less developed countries in Asia, Africa, and Central and South America. This expansion became known as the Green Revolution.

Today, the world's fast-growing population relies on highly productive industrialized farming to provide enough food. But many aspects of industrialized agriculture cannot be sustained indefinitely. Scientists and farmers are working to develop new methods to provide enough food for the world's people without depleting natural resources and destroying the environment.

Origins of agriculture. Like all living things, crop plants and livestock animals *evolve* (change over time) through a process called *natural selection*. In natural selection, certain organisms have traits that help them survive and reproduce more readily. These organisms produce more offspring, passing on those traits to a greater number of individuals. The traits thus survive and spread throughout a population. In effect, nature "selects" for traits that aid in survival and reproduction. See **Natural selection.**

In domestication, people also act as agents of selection. Hunter-gatherers learned to identify the tastiest and most nourishing varieties of wild plants. They selected the best individuals of such plants for their purposes and spread seeds from those individual plants more than the seeds of others. This practice ensured that more of the plants they considered best would survive and reproduce. Human selection transformed wild plants over a relatively short period into domesticated agricultural crops.

Human beings also changed livestock animals from their wild ancestors through domestication. In the past, people hunted wild animals for food. But a few species of wild animals had characteristics that made them suitable for domestication. For example, people could easily tame and herd some animals. Early farmers selected specific animals with such tameable characteristics, protected them from predators, and helped them reproduce. In this way, human selection transformed the animals into domesticated livestock.

Centers of domestication. Domestication did not occur as a single event or in a single place. Instead, people in a number of different regions independently domesticated various crops and livestock. Scientists often call such areas *centers of domestication.* From these loca-

tions, agriculture spread as people migrated to, or traded with, other lands.

The first domesticated crops probably emerged in an arc-shaped region of the Middle East called the Fertile Crescent. Beginning around 9000 to 8500 B.C., people in the Fertile Crescent domesticated barley, *lentils* (a type of seed vegetable), peas, and wheat from wild plants that were native to the region. Inhabitants of the Fertile Crescent also first domesticated goats and sheep, and were among the first to domesticate cattle and pigs. Soon afterward, many of these crops and livestock spread to northern Africa, Europe, and parts of Asia.

China was the second important center of domestication. People there first domesticated millet and rice by roughly 8000 B.C. Inhabitants of the area were also among the first to domesticate pigs and chickens.

Also around 8000 B.C.—on the other side of the world—people in the Andes region in South America domesticated squash. People there later domesticated such crops as lima beans, peanuts, and potatoes, along with such livestock as guinea pigs and llamas.

In Mesoamerica (Mexico and Central America), people independently domesticated squash around the same time as in South America. Mesoamericans later domesticated such crops as avocados, beans, and corn. Eventually, they also domesticated ducks and turkeys,

Where the world's crops and livestock are raised

Major crop-growing area

Major grazing area

Mostly nonagricultural

but their agriculture focused more on crops than it did on livestock.

Scientists believe another important center of domestication was the large island of New Guinea. People there may have been the first to domesticate yams and taro around 7000 B.C. They may also have been the first to domesticate bananas and sugar cane.

Scientists have identified a small number of additional centers of domestication, including areas in Africa and a region in what is now the eastern United States. These centers began domesticating plants and animals later than the other centers.

The transition to farming. In many ways, early agriculture required more time and labor than hunting and gathering. The earliest farmers had only simple tools to help them plant and raise crops. Their diets also relied on a few staple foods, often providing less nutrition than the more varied diets of hunter-gatherers. Crop failures could lead to widespread starvation. In addition, disease spread quickly through the crowded conditions in early farming communities. For these reasons, many scholars have wondered why early farmers would adopt agriculture as a way of life.

Scientists have developed several theories to explain this mystery. For example, many domesticated plants arose in marginal areas with poor soil or limited rainfall, or in places with changing climates. People in such areas may have intentionally domesticated plants to protect against famine. Farming would have been the only way they could get a reliable and adequate supply of food. Some scientists, on the other hand, think domestication may not have been entirely intentional. For example, hunter-gatherers may have unconsciously dispersed the seeds of their favorite food plants around their settlements. Over time, such plants would have evolved to thrive in the conditions around settlements, becoming domesticated.

In the prehistoric past, hunter-gatherers usually lived in small groups, constantly moving from place to place to obtain food. Once people began cultivating domestic crops and animals, they could settle in one place. A settled lifestyle enabled human populations to grow, leading to the first villages and towns. The conditions of settled life both made possible and required new forms of social, political, and economic interaction.

Once a community had settled and grown, hunting and gathering became impractical. Farming provided the only way to get enough food to feed large, concentrated populations.

Ancient civilizations. Over thousands of years, agricultural communities gradually developed into cities and, in some cases, *city-states*, kingdoms, and empires.

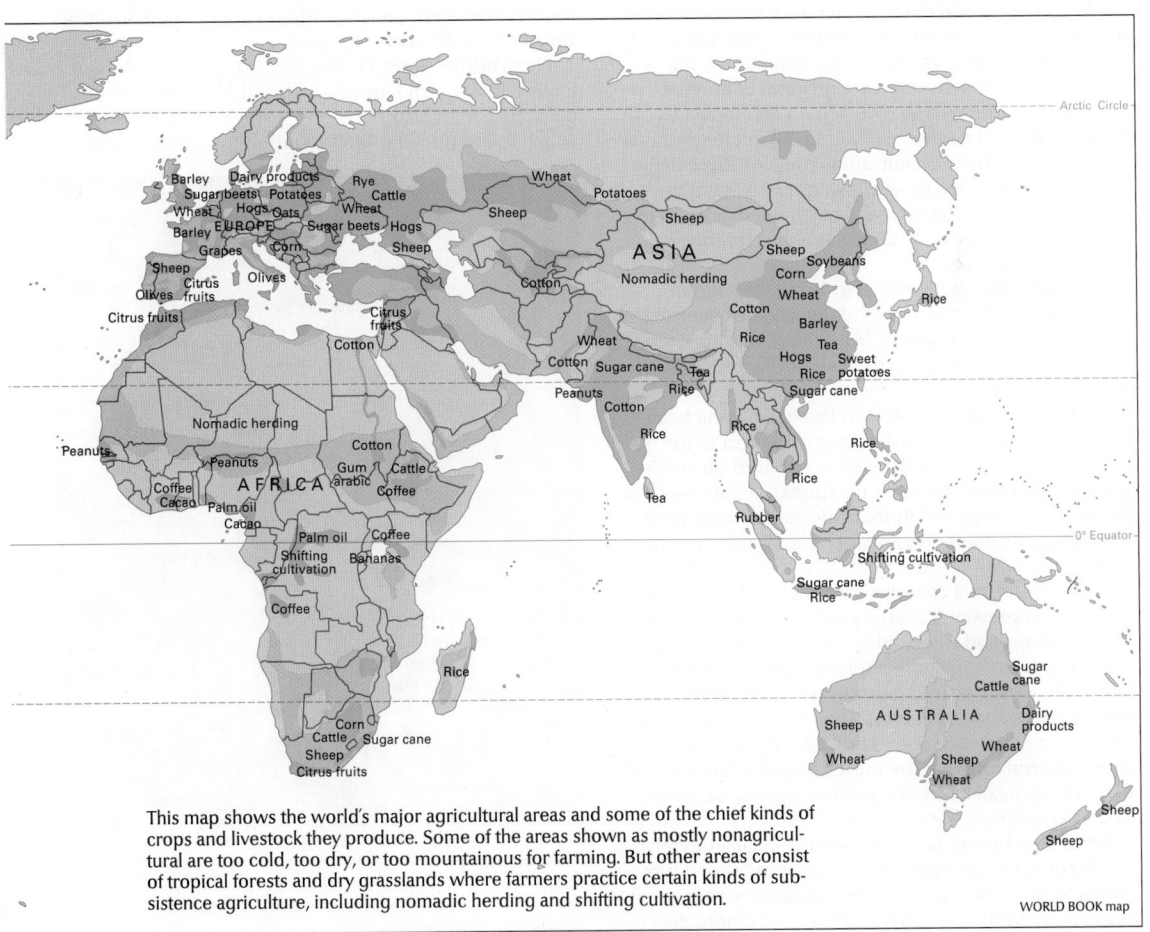

This map shows the world's major agricultural areas and some of the chief kinds of crops and livestock they produce. Some of the areas shown as mostly nonagricultural are too cold, too dry, or too mountainous for farming. But other areas consist of tropical forests and dry grasslands where farmers practice certain kinds of subsistence agriculture, including nomadic herding and shifting cultivation.

WORLD BOOK map

Detail of a clay seal (about 2900 B.C.) from Mesopotamia; the Louvre, Paris

Wheat was first cultivated in the Fertile Crescent, a region of the Middle East that includes parts of Iraq, Lebanon, and Syria.

Detail from a copy of a wall painting (about 1275 B.C.); Metropolitan Museum of Art, New York City, Egyptian Expedition Rogers Fund, 1930

Irrigation enabled the Egyptians to draw water from the Nile for their crops, which could flourish despite Egypt's dry climate.

A city-state is an independent state consisting of a city and its surrounding farmland and other territory. Several ancient civilizations made especially important contributions to the development of agriculture. They include the Sumerian and Egyptian civilizations, the Roman Empire, and the Han dynasty of China.

Mesopotamia and Egypt. Agriculture first arose in the Fertile Crescent, and this area also gave rise to the world's first great civilizations. One civilization, the Sumerians, lived between the Tigris and Euphrates rivers in what is now Iraq. This region is referred to as Mesopotamia. The other civilization, Egypt, formed just west of the Fertile Crescent, along the Nile River delta. Both civilizations dug canals linking the rivers to their farmland. These irrigation systems enabled farmers to grow crops all year, even though neither region received much rain.

The Sumerians and Egyptians also developed ox-drawn plows. These tools could quickly turn over large amounts of soil for planting. In addition, this advance saved farmers from having to push or drag the plows themselves.

Rome. By 272 B.C., the Roman Republic—which later became the Roman Empire—controlled most of the Italian Peninsula. Roman agriculture was based on farms spread throughout the lands the Romans controlled. As the Romans conquered more lands, they spread their agricultural technologies and techniques throughout much of Europe.

The Romans built complex irrigation systems featuring raised waterways called *aqueducts*, which brought water to farms and city residents from distant sources. Roman farmers who could afford to often left half their fields fallow each year to help restore nutrients to the soil for the next year's harvest. They also often alternated a field's crop between pulses and cereal grains, an example of *crop rotation*. The pulses helped restore the soil's nitrogen, an important nutrient quickly depleted by cereal grains.

China. The ancient Chinese, like the ancient Egyptians and Sumerians, developed irrigation systems and plows drawn by animals. During the Han dynasty, which ruled China from 206 B.C. to 220 A.D., Chinese farmers devel-

oped several technologies that helped them harness the power of flowing water. For example, they used water wheels to transport water from lower to higher elevations. The Chinese also invented a *trip hammer,* a mechanical hammer used to pound grain. The hammer, powered by water pressure, could quickly pound rice to separate the husk from the edible grain. People had previously done this work by hand.

The Middle Ages. During the A.D. 400's, the Roman Empire in western Europe collapsed. This collapse began a period of history known as the Middle Ages, which lasted until the 1400's. During the same period,

© Réunion des Musées Nationaux, Art Resource, NY

A manor was a type of estate that developed in western Europe during the Middle Ages, which began in the A.D. 400's. Farmers worked on the manor, which was controlled by a landlord, often a noble or church leader.

civilizations in the Middle East, China, and the Americas made a number of agricultural advances.

In western Europe, a new type of farming estate developed. Much of the land was divided into units sometimes known as *manors.* Each manor produced most of its own food and goods. The extensive long-distance agricultural trade that the Romans had developed decreased, and trade generally became more local.

A landlord, often a noble or church leader, controlled each manor. Tenants and laborers also lived on the manor and worked as farmers. The tenants and laborers supplied the lord with a certain amount of produce in exchange for the use of the land and protection from attackers. Some farmers, called *serfs,* were considered "bound to the soil," meaning that they were essentially part of the manor's property. Unlike slaves, serfs could not be sold, but they stayed on the land if a new lord acquired it. There were also some peasants who owned all or part of their land.

Some farmers replaced the Roman two-field system of crop rotation with three- or four-field systems. Instead of leaving half of their land fallow each year, such farmers left only a third or a fourth of it fallow, which could yield more food each year. They rotated such crops as wheat and barley on the remaining farmland.

In China and the Middle East, agriculture and farming technology continued to develop during the Middle Ages. In the 400's or possibly earlier, the Chinese developed a collar harness for hitching plows to horses. Horses could drag plows faster and for a longer period of time than oxen could. During China's Song dynasty (960-1279), farmers began using early-ripening rice. This rice could produce two or three harvests each year, which helped create and support a rapid growth in China's population.

By the mid-700's, Muslims controlled a vast empire in the Middle East. They put into use sophisticated crop rotation and improved irrigation. The long reach of the Islamic Empire during the Middle Ages created a more global system of trade and played a crucial role in the spread of several crops. Such foods as artichokes, lemons, oranges, and sugar were introduced to Europe through the Islamic Empire. People in the Islamic Empire also invented new ways of processing cotton, widely increasing that crop's importance.

In the Americas, several great civilizations had formed by the Middle Ages, supported by farming such products as beans, corn, and root crops. The Maya of Central America dug irrigation systems to water their crops. About 900, the Maya civilization began to decline, possibly in part because of crop failures and the exhaustion of natural resources.

The Aztec, a civilization of central Mexico, formed fertile islands for growing crops by scooping up and piling mud from lake bottoms. The Inca and other inhabitants of western South America used a method of freeze-drying potatoes for better storage.

European and American expansion. By the 1400's, a more interconnected system of trade was developing. Ships carrying agricultural products and other goods began sailing between Europe, Africa, India, and Southeast Asia. Merchants in European cities had access to goods produced as far away as China.

But this system of trade did not become truly global until 1492, when the Italian navigator Christopher Columbus sailed to North America. Before this time, agriculture in the Americas had developed completely independently from agriculture in the "Old World" of Europe, Africa, and Asia. Europeans had never seen such crops as cocoa, corn, peppers, potatoes, and tomatoes, which only grew in the Americas. Similarly, the Native Americans had never seen barley, cattle, sheep, wheat, and other plants and animals that had only existed in the Old World. The exchange of crops and livestock between these continents revolutionized agriculture in both places.

Colonial agriculture. By the 1600's, several European countries had established colonies throughout the Americas. The colonists established agricultural systems resembling those of their native countries. For example, Spanish colonists created large *haciendas* (farming estates) similar to those in southern Spain. They treated the Native Americans much like serfs. In the area that is now Canada, French colonists established estates controlled by nobles or merchants and rented out land to other settlers.

In the warm regions of the Americas, Europeans established large plantations that specialized in raising crops for export back to Europe. These crops included cocoa beans, coffee, cotton, sugar cane, and tobacco. At first, the colonists enslaved Native Americans to work on the plantations. Later, they began importing large numbers of black slaves from Africa.

In England's North American colonies, many early settlers cleared away forests to establish small subsistence or semisubsistence farms. Such farmers carried European agriculture farther and farther westward. But in the Southern Colonies, some wealthy farmers established huge plantations worked by slaves. The plantations typically grew export crops.

Europeans also established colonies in Asia during the 1600's and afterward. As in much of the Americas, agriculture in these colonies typically shifted to the production of export crops for the enrichment of the European countries. Plantation systems and tenant farming systems developed in some Asian colonies as a result of the shift, and many small farmers lost their land.

Technological advances. During the 1600's and 1700's, improvements in existing crop production and farm machinery helped make agriculture more efficient. One particularly important new device was the cotton gin, which was invented in 1793 by an American named Eli Whitney. The machine could remove the seeds from cotton fibers as fast as 50 people could by hand. The cotton gin thus made growing cotton much more profitable, and cotton soon replaced tobacco as the leading crop in the United States. As the cotton industry expanded, planters needed more and more workers to pick and bale the cotton. The demand for workers led to large increases in the population of African American slaves.

The industrialization of agriculture. In the late 1700's and early 1800's, technology advanced rapidly in Britain (now also known as the United Kingdom). This period, called the Industrial Revolution, radically changed European and American society. It also led to the emergence of industrialized agriculture, which transformed farming across the world.

A number of new developments led to agriculture's dramatic increase in productivity. They include: (1) the invention of powered machines; (2) the development of electric power; (3) the study of agricultural genetics; (4) the use of artificial fertilizer; and (5) the development of chemical pesticides.

Powered machines, driven by coal-fired steam, gasoline, or other fossil fuels, changed farming throughout the world. In the United States, for example, a number of railroad lines linked populated cities in the East to the vast, fertile Great Plains by the mid-1800's. This development enabled farmers to settle much of the Great Plains, replacing the prairies with farmland and shipping their agricultural products along railroad lines.

On the farms themselves, powered machines eliminated much of the need for manual labor. Before such machines, people either used draft animals—such as horses, mules, and oxen—to work their fields, or they worked with their own hands. Even such machines as Whitney's cotton gin had needed to be cranked or pulled by people or animals.

Early steam-powered tractors were used successfully

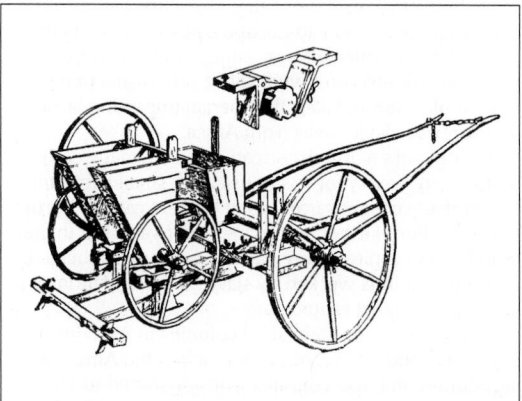

Detail of an engraving from *Horse-Hoeing Husbandry* (1731) by Jethro Tull; Historical Pictures Service

Technological advances during the 1700's gave rise to more complex farm machines, such as this horse-drawn seed drill.

Detail of an engraving (1869) in *Harper's Weekly* based on a drawing by William L. Sheppard (Library of Congress)

The cotton gin, invented by Eli Whitney of the United States in 1793, saved workers the labor of cleaning cotton by hand.

on some large farms. But despite their power, they were expensive and difficult to maintain. Their large size and awkward control made them impractical to use on many farms, especially smaller farms. In the late 1910's and early 1920's, lighter, gasoline-powered tractors became more popular. Many gasoline-powered tractors could pull and power a wide variety of farm equipment.

Although the machines needed fuel and maintenance, they quickly proved more effective than draft animals, which required food, shelter, and care even when not working. Fossil fuel-powered tractors soon became widespread on farms throughout the world.

Electric power became widespread on farms by the mid-1900's. In the United States, for example, the Rural Electrification Act of 1936 expanded electric service to rural areas. Before that time, only about 10 percent of American farmers had electric power. By the mid-1950's, electric power spread to more than 90 percent of American farmers. In Japan, Europe, and other developed countries, electric power also spread quickly from cities to farms.

Electric power enabled farmers to take advantage of a number of inventions that made their work easier and more productive. Such inventions included electric milking machines and egg incubators, as well as irrigation pumps and wells operated by electric power. Electric power also ran communication devices—such as telephones, radios, and televisions—that helped provide farmers with essential information about markets, weather, and growing conditions.

Agricultural genetics began with the work of an Austrian monk named Gregor Mendel. In the mid-1800's, Mendel determined that plants and animals inherit traits based on certain patterns. His work led to the science of genetics.

Before Mendel's studies, people bred animals without understanding the actual process behind inheritance. With a knowledge of genetics, scientists could breed new varieties of plants and animals even better suited for agricultural use. For example, in the early 1900's, botanists used genetics to successfully cross two varieties of corn, creating a new variety called a *hybrid.* The hybrid corn produced extremely high crop yields. By the 1960's, this hybrid variety made up 95 percent of all the corn planted in the United States.

Genetics also helped scientists and farmers refine *selective breeding.* Many livestock produced through selective breeding have traits that cause them to grow and fatten quickly, or to produce large amounts of eggs or milk. However, breeders must sometimes select certain genetic traits at the expense of others. For example, a tomato bred for a long shelf-life or a tough skin may lose traits responsible for its flavor.

Artificial fertilizers were developed with a new understanding of the chemical composition of the nutrients that plants need to grow. During the 1800's and early 1900's, scientists discovered that plants require three main nutrients from the soil: nitrogen, phosphorus, and potassium. Industrial processes can produce these chemicals directly using fossil fuels.

Before artificial fertilizers, farmers enriched their soil with such natural fertilizers as animal manure and decaying plant material. Using such natural fertilizers often resulted in a *closed nutrient cycle.* In a closed cycle, the

Detail of a photograph (about 1906) taken near Beloit, Wis.; State Historical Society of Wisconsin

Powered farm machines, such as this gasoline-powered tractor, helped lead to industrialized agriculture. Machines proved much more effective than draft animals for pulling farm equipment.

An ox-drawn plow
worldbook.com/ag-16

nutrients in the soil move into the plants, then into the livestock that eat the plants, and then back into the soil through the livestock's droppings. In a closed cycle, the nutrients do not leave the farmland, and the farmer need not add new nutrients.

The development and use of artificial fertilizers created *open nutrient cycles.* Farmers began buying artificial fertilizer produced in factories. They then harvested crops, often for sale in distant markets. Under this system, nutrients leave the farmland with each harvest, and farmers must add new nutrients back to the land in the form of fertilizers. But artificial fertilizers proved more efficient than natural fertilizers and so came into wide use.

Chemical pesticides include *herbicides* (weedkillers), *insecticides* (insect killers), *fungicides* (fungus killers), and other chemicals that kill agricultural pests and control livestock disease. Before such chemicals existed, farmers controlled weeds by pulling them up or hoeing them. They had little control over insects or diseases.

In 1939, a Swiss scientist named Paul Muller discovered the insect-killing properties of one of the most important chemical pesticides, DDT (dichloro-diphenyl-trichloroethane). DDT was widely used on farms and sprayed in areas with malaria-spreading mosquitos. But by the 1960's, scientists realized that DDT could poison other animal life, including human beings.

The Green Revolution. By the end of World War II (1939-1945), much of Europe and North America practiced industrialized agriculture and could efficiently produce huge amounts of crops and livestock. But the ideas and technologies of industrialized agriculture had not yet spread to less developed countries in Asia, Africa, and Central and South America. Farmers in such countries often could not produce enough food to feed their populations. The effort to improve such countries' food supplies with techniques from industrialized agriculture is known as the Green Revolution.

High-yield varieties (HYV's) of plants served as a cornerstone of the Green Revolution. They included varieties of corn, rice, and wheat that grew quickly and produced large grains. Scientists established a number of international agricultural research centers around the world. Each center focused on creating HYV crops for its region. Scientists bred HYV's using advanced genetic technology as well as plant varieties native to the growing area.

Plant breeders developed HYV's to grow well in the presence of artificial fertilizers and pesticides. In addition, HYV crops grew best in well-watered or irrigated regions. Thus, it was not enough to simply give farmers in less developed countries seeds for HYV crops. To fully benefit from the Green Revolution, farmers needed to acquire many of the other technologies of industrialized agriculture.

Effects of the Green Revolution. The Green Revolution had great success in raising food production in less developed countries. From 1960 to 1985, cereal grain production more than doubled in less developed countries. In the right conditions, an HYV rice called "miracle rice" could yield almost 10 times as much food as some traditional rice crops. The Green Revolution reduced the danger of famine in many less developed countries.

However, the Green Revolution also brought many of the problems associated with industrialized agriculture to less developed countries. The new crops depended on high levels of artificial fertilizers and pesticides, which damage the environment and often come from nonrenewable resources. In many places, industrialized monocultures replaced a wide variety of local crop plants.

The Green Revolution caused many social changes in traditional societies. In many cases, only wealthy farmers could afford the materials and technologies necessary to grow HYV's. Such wealthy farmers often outcompeted smaller farmers, driving them out of business and absorbing them into their work forces.

Recent developments. Earth has a limited amount of fertile land, but its population is constantly increasing. The development of industrialized agriculture and the Green Revolution have been essential in supporting the world's population. Using these methods, modern farmers have transformed much of Earth's surface into a highly productive source of food.

However, industrialized agriculture has contributed to environmental damage and global warming. Monocultures have reduced the genetic diversity of crop plants. Genetic engineering promises to develop more productive varieties of crops, but the practice is controversial. Eventually, the fossil fuels that power industrialized agriculture will run out. Farmers will need to develop and adopt new, sustainable agricultural methods to continue to feed the world population.

Genetic engineering. Almost all agricultural crops and animals have had their genes altered by domestication and selective breeding over the past 10,000 years. But modern scientists can alter an organism's genetic material directly, creating *genetically modified organisms* (GMO's).

The development and use of GMO's ranks as a major topic of controversy in agriculture. On one hand, genetic engineering enables scientists to even further increase the quality and productivity of crops and livestock. In some cases, scientists can even design GMO's with genetic resistance to pests and diseases, reducing the amount of pesticides needed to grow them.

But many people worry about the potential long-term consequences of releasing genetically modified crops into the environment. Critics have voiced concerns that GMO crops could accidentally crossbreed with other nearby plants—contaminating the environment with the engineered genes. Critics also worry that GMO crops could become herbicide-resistant "superweeds," or that they could help create such weeds by transferring their resistant properties to close plant relatives. In addition, in an environment full of GMO's, pests with resistance to the GMO crop's defenses will survive and reproduce more often.

A major controversy with genetically modified crops is whether they should be protected by patent. Agribusinesses spend large amounts of money developing new GMO's. They often seek to patent the genetically modified organism, preventing farmers from planting the seeds without paying the developer. Agribusinesses argue that without such patents, developing new crops would not be profitable enough to justify the investment. But opponents of such practices argue that patenting organisms may create problems. For example, it might hinder scientific research if corporations hold patents on organisms. Some people also argue that living things are part of nature, not anyone's invention, and so it would be wrong to patent organisms and put them under private control.

In most countries, genetically modified food must undergo a safety evaluation by the government before it can be sold. Some countries also have strict requirements for the labeling of such food. For example, Australia, New Zealand, and the countries of the European Union require genetically modified food to have clear labels, but Canada and the United States do not. In fact, many of the crops grown in Canada and the United States are GMO's.

Preserving genetic diversity. Over time, selective breeding and monoculture have drastically reduced the genetic diversity of many crop plants and animals. Some crops consist almost entirely of *clones* (genetic copies)

of one or a few individuals. Such crops may be extremely vulnerable to disease or environmental change. For this reason, scientists are working to preserve the genetic diversity of crop plants. Agricultural research centers and other organizations have established *gene banks.* Gene banks collect the genetic material of large numbers of crop varieties in case the material is needed to develop new varieties in the future. *Seed banks* have also been developed to preserve a variety of plant seeds.

Alternative sources of energy. The machines and vehicles used in industrialized farming require energy. Artificial fertilizers and other chemicals also require large amounts of energy to manufacture and distribute. Before the advent of biofuels, all of this energy came from diminishing supplies of fossil fuels. With biofuels, agriculture can create new sources of energy. But the process of deriving biofuel from crops often takes much energy itself. Biofuel crops can also replace food crops, reducing the availability of food.

Scientists hope to develop energy-efficient biofuels that do not crowd out the human food supply. Some biofuels can be produced from a by-product of food crops, such as the residue left over from turning sugar cane into sugar. Other biofuel crops, such as switchgrass, can thrive on land that is not suitable for food crops.

Adopting sustainable practices is another way to deal with diminishing fossil fuels and other environmental and social concerns. But such practices have their drawbacks. They tend to require more labor, which can make their products more expensive. They also generally produce lower yields than typical industrialized farms. Moreover, some experts question whether sustainable farming methods can supply enough food for a growing population.

Research centers, along with a number of governments and nonprofit groups, fund research into sustainable agriculture. Shifting from intensive industrialized techniques to sustainable techniques around the world would require many social, economic, and technological changes. But as natural resources run out, continuing industrialized practices may become impractical for our civilization, just as hunting and gathering became impractical for our ancestors.   Robert E. Rhoades

Related articles. See Farm and farming and its list of related articles. See also the *Agriculture* section of the state, province, country, and continent articles. Additional related articles in *World Book* include:

Biographies

Borlaug, Norman Ernest	McCormick, Cyrus Hall	Ruffin, Edmund Townshend, Viscount
Burbank, Luther	Mendel, Gregor Johann	
Carver, George Washington	Morton, Julius Sterling	Tull, Jethro
Deere, John		Wallace, Henry Agard
Lysenko, Trofim Denisovich	Pinckney, Eliza Lucas	Whitney, Eli

Kinds of farming

Aquaculture	Fur (Fur ranching)	Plantation
Collective farm	Gardening	Ranching
Dairying	Horticulture	Tenant farming
Dry farming	Hydroponics	Tree farming
Factory farming	Nursery	Truck farming
Floriculture		

Major crops

Alfalfa	Potato
Barley	Rice
Bean	Rye
Cassava	Sorghum
Coffee	Soybean
Corn	Sugar
Cotton	Sweet potato
Flax	Switchgrass
Fruit	Vegetable
Hemp	Wheat
Oats	

Chief kinds of livestock

Cattle	Hog	Rabbit
Chicken	Horse	Sheep
Duck	Poultry	Turkey
Goat		

Methods and problems

Cloud seeding	Herbicide
Conservation	Insecticide
Cropping system	Irrigation
Drainage	Land reform
Environmental pollution	Migrant labor
(Agriculture)	Pest control
Erosion	Weed
Fertilizer	Windbreak
Fungicide	

Education and research

Agricultural education	FFA
Agricultural experiment	4-H
station	Hybrid
Agronomy	Land-grant university
Breeding	Nutrition
Cooperative Extension System	

History of agriculture

Aztec (Agriculture)	Prehistoric people (The rise
Babylonia (Way of life)	of agriculture)
Colonial life in America	Rome, Ancient (Agriculture)
(Farming)	Serf
Egypt, Ancient (Agriculture)	Villein
Feudalism	Western frontier life in
Greece, Ancient (Farming)	America (Ranching;
Indian, American (Farming)	Farming)
Persia, Ancient (Economy)	Yeoman

Other related articles

Agribusiness	Insect (The importance
Animal (The importance	of insects)
of animals)	Livestock
Biofuel	Marketing
Crop	Plant (The importance
Food and Agriculture	of plants)
Organization	Soil
Food supply	Svalbard Global Seed Vault
Grain elevator	

Agriculture, Department of, is an executive department of the United States government. It works to maintain adequate supplies of farm products and to expand overseas markets for such products. The department helps to ensure reasonable incomes for farmers and reasonably priced farm products for consumers. It works to ensure the safety of the nation's food supply. The department also works to combat hunger in the United States and abroad and to improve the economy of rural America.

The secretary of agriculture, a member of the president's Cabinet, heads the department. The president appoints the secretary with the approval of the U.S. Senate.

The seal of the Department of Agriculture

Functions. The Department of Agriculture, also called the USDA, serves farmers and consumers in many ways. It works to safeguard the food supply by inspecting meat and poultry in slaughtering and processing plants. The USDA grades meat, poultry, and dairy products to indicate their quality. It establishes standards of quality for grain exported from the United States and administers a nationwide system of grain inspection. The department's regulatory programs help protect animals and plants from pests and diseases.

The department runs food assistance programs to fight hunger and to improve the diet of Americans. These programs include the Supplemental Nutrition Assistance Program (SNAP)—formerly the Food Stamp Program—which helps needy people purchase food; the National School Lunch Program; and a program to provide certain foods for pregnant women and for nursing mothers and their infants.

The USDA finances research in its own laboratories and in agricultural experiment stations at land-grant uni-

Secretaries of agriculture

Name	Took office	Under President
Norman J. Colman	1889	Cleveland
Jeremiah M. Rusk	1889	Harrison
*Julius S. Morton	1893	Cleveland
James Wilson	1897	McKinley,
		T. Roosevelt
	1909	Taft
David F. Houston	1913	Wilson
Edwin T. Meredith	1920	Wilson
Henry C. Wallace	1921	Harding,
		Coolidge
Howard M. Gore	1924	Coolidge
William M. Jardine	1925	Coolidge
Arthur M. Hyde	1929	Hoover
*Henry A. Wallace	1933	F. D. Roosevelt
Claude R. Wickard	1940	F. D. Roosevelt
Clinton P. Anderson	1945	Truman
Charles F. Brannan	1948	Truman
Ezra Taft Benson	1953	Eisenhower
Orville L. Freeman	1961	Kennedy,
		L. B. Johnson
Clifford M. Hardin	1969	Nixon
Earl L. Butz	1971	Nixon, Ford
John A. Knebel	1976	Ford
Robert S. Bergland	1977	Carter
John R. Block	1981	Reagan
Richard E. Lyng	1986	Reagan
Clayton K. Yeutter	1989	G. H. W. Bush
Edward R. Madigan	1991	G. H. W. Bush
*Mike Espy	1993	Clinton
Dan Glickman	1995	Clinton
Ann M. Veneman	2001	G. W. Bush
Mike Johanns	2005	G. W. Bush
Edward T. Schafer	2008	G. W. Bush
Tom Vilsack	2009	Obama
Sonny Perdue	2017	Trump
Tom Vilsack	2021	Biden

*Has a separate biography in *World Book.*

versities and other institutions. This research deals with such topics as plant and animal diseases, crop production, marketing of agricultural products, nutrition, pest control, and soil conservation. Together with state and county governments, the department sponsors a nationwide program of agricultural education.

The Department of Agriculture provides other services as well. It reports on crop production, crop prices, and farm operating costs. The department gathers world agricultural data and provides technical assistance to help developing nations improve food production. Its Forest Service manages national forests. In addition, the department provides financial aid and other assistance to communities, businesses, and utilities in rural areas. The department's website at https://www.usda.gov presents information on its activities.

History. Congress established the Department of Agriculture in 1862. In 1889, it became a Cabinet-level department headed by a secretary of agriculture.

From the start, the department devoted much of its attention to developing and distributing information that would help increase agricultural production. Later, as improved farming methods led to larger crop yields, the department increased its emphasis on marketing farm products and supporting prices. In the 1960's, the USDA began to give more attention to expanding the agricultural markets at home and abroad and to ensuring an adequate diet for all Americans.

Critically reviewed by the Department of Agriculture

Related articles in *World Book* include:

Agricultural experiment station	Food for Peace
Commodity Credit Corporation	Forest Service
	Rural Electrification Administration
Cooperative Extension System	Supplemental Nutrition
Farmers Home Administration	Assistance Program

Agrippa, *uh GRIHP uh,* **Marcus** (63-12 B.C.), was a Roman general who was the chief adviser and military leader of Augustus, Rome's first emperor. Agrippa was also a lifelong friend and loyal supporter of Augustus.

Agrippa rose to prominence during the civil wars that followed the assassination of the Roman leader Julius Caesar in 44 B.C. In these wars, Octavian, who later became the emperor Augustus, struggled against a number of enemies for control of Rome. Agrippa became Octavian's best commander, both on land and at sea. Agrippa's most important victory was the Battle of Actium, fought off the west coast of Greece in 31 B.C. There, he led a fleet that defeated the forces of Mark Antony, co-ruler of Rome with Octavian, and of Cleopatra, queen of Egypt. This victory cleared the way for Octavian to be named sole emperor of Rome, in 27 B.C.

Agrippa helped the new emperor in the reordering of Roman politics and society under one-person rule. When Augustus fell ill in 23 B.C., he gave Agrippa his seal ring. Augustus recovered, but the gift of the ring meant that Agrippa would have become emperor if Augustus had died. Agrippa married the emperor's daughter Julia in 21 B.C., another sign that he was the chosen successor. Agrippa held wide powers for the next 10 years, but he died in March of 12 B.C., before he could become emperor.   Arthur M. Eckstein

Agrippina the Younger, *AG ruh PY nuh* or *AG ruh PEE nuh* (A.D. 15-59), was one of the most powerful

women in ancient Rome, partly because of her family relationships with Rome's first five emperors. Her parents were Agrippina the Elder and the celebrated military commander Germanicus. On her mother's side, Agrippina the Younger was the great-granddaughter of the emperor Augustus. On her father's side, she was the great-niece and adoptive granddaughter of the emperor Tiberius. The emperor Caligula was Agrippina's brother. Agrippina greatly influenced two other Roman emperors—Claudius and Nero. Claudius was Agrippina's uncle and, later, her second husband. Nero was her son from her first marriage, to Gnaeus Domitius Ahenobarbus.

Caligula became emperor in A.D. 37. In A.D. 39, he banished Agrippina from Rome for her part in a plot against him. Agrippina returned from exile after her uncle Claudius became emperor in A.D. 41. She married Claudius in A.D. 49. The following year, she was honored by the founding of a Roman colony, Colonia Agrippinensis, at her birthplace in what is now Cologne, Germany. Agrippina persuaded Claudius to adopt Nero as his son and to name Nero as guardian of Britannicus, Claudius's son from an earlier marriage. Nero was only four years older than Britannicus.

Claudius died in A.D. 54, and Nero became emperor at the age of 17. Many Romans believed Agrippina had poisoned Claudius so that Nero could succeed to the throne. In the first year of Nero's reign, Agrippina held great political power. She received the honorary title of Augusta, the feminine form of Augustus, meaning *the revered.* She retired from the imperial court after Britannicus died, probably by poison at Nero's order, in A.D. 55. Nero had Agrippina murdered four years later, in A.D. 59. She wrote an autobiography that was quoted by ancient authors, but has not survived.   Judith P. Hallett

Agronomy, *uh GRAHN uh mee,* is a branch of agricultural science that deals with the study of crops and the soils in which they grow. Agronomists work to develop methods that will improve the use of the soil and increase the production of food and fiber crops. They conduct research in crop rotation, irrigation and drainage, plant breeding, molecular biology, soil classification, soil fertility, weed control, and other areas.

Plant breeding, a branch of agronomy, has increased crop yields and has improved the nutritional value of several crops, including corn, rice, soybeans, and wheat. It also has led to the development of new types of plants. For example, a hybrid grain called triticale was produced by crossbreeding rye and wheat. Triticale contains more usable protein than does either rye or wheat.

Agronomists study ways to make soils more productive. They classify soils and test them for substances vital for plant growth. In addition, agronomists develop methods to preserve the soil and to decrease the effects of erosion by wind and water. For example, a technique called reduced tillage may be used to prevent soil erosion and conserve rainfall. Researchers in agronomy also seek ways to use the soil more effectively in solving other problems. Such problems include the disposal of wastes; water pollution; and the unintended build-up in the soil of chemicals used to kill insects and weeds.

Most agronomists are researchers, consultants, or teachers. Many work for agricultural experiment stations, government agencies, industrial firms, universities, or international organizations.   Stephen Jones

See also **Agricultural experiment station; Cropping system; Soil.**

Aguascalientes, *ah gwahs kahl YEHN tays,* is a state in central Mexico. It has an area of 2,112 square miles (5,471 square kilometers). The name *Aguascalientes* comes from the Spanish words for *hot waters.* The area has numerous hot springs. At the time of the 2020 census, the population of Aguascalientes was 1,425,607. Most of the people live in or near the capital city, also called Aguascalientes.

The Sierra Madre Occidental mountain range rises in the western part of the state. The Mesa Central (Central Plateau) covers eastern and southern Aguascalientes. The state has a warm, dry climate. The economy depends on agriculture, manufacturing, and tourism.

Indigenous (native) Chichimec people lived in Aguascalientes before the Spanish conquered Mexico in the 1500's. Descendants of the Chichimec live in the state today. Aguascalientes became a territory of Mexico in 1835 and a state in 1857. Before 1835, it formed part of the state of Zacatecas.   Jurgen Buchenau

Aguilera, *ah gee LEH rah,* **Christina,** *krihs TEE nuh* (1980-   ), is a popular American singer. Aguilera has been successful recording pop songs in both Spanish and English. Her music has also included elements of jazz, blues, and rock. Aguilera is known for her powerful voice and a several-octave singing range.

Aguilera has won several Grammy Awards, beginning with being named Best New Artist in 2000. She also won Grammys for Best Female Pop Vocal Performance for "Beautiful" (2003) and "Ain't No Other Man" (2006). She won a Latin Grammy award for Best Female Pop Vocal Album, *Mi Reflejo* (2000).

Christina María Aguilera was born on Dec. 18, 1980, in the Staten Island borough of New York City. Her Hispanic heritage comes from her father, who was born in Ecuador. Aguilera began singing as a child, performing on national television when she was 8 years old. In the 1990's, she appeared on the Walt Disney TV variety series "The All New Mickey Mouse Club."

Aguilera recorded her first album, *Christina Aguilera,* in 1999, when she was 18. Her other hit songs include "Genie in a Bottle" (1999); "I Turn to You" (2000); a duet with Ricky Martin called "Nobody Wants to Be Lonely" (2001); and "Lady Marmalade" with Pink, Lil' Kim, and Mya (2001). Aguilera made her motion-picture debut in *Burlesque* (2010). She was a coach on the singing-competition television show "The Voice" from 2011 to 2013.

William McKeen

See also **Rock music** (picture: Modern rock stars).

Aguinaldo, *ah gee NAHL doh,* **Emilio,** *eh MEE lyoh* (1869-1964), was a leader in the fight for Philippine independence. In 1896 and 1897, he took part in an unsuccessful revolt against Spanish rule. In 1898, he led a Filipino army against Spain in the Spanish-American War. In June of that year, the Filipinos set up a revolutionary government and made Aguinaldo president. On June 12, he declared Philippine independence from Spain. In December 1898, Spain gave up the Philippines to the United States for $20 million. In January 1899, Aguinaldo established the Philippine Republic, and his troops began fighting U.S. forces in February. United States forces captured him in March 1901. In April, Aguinaldo took an oath of allegiance to the United States and retired. He

was born on March 23, 1869, near Cavite, Luzon. Aguinaldo died on Feb. 6, 1964. See also **Philippine-American War; Philippines** (History).   Socorro L. Reyes

Ahmadabad, *AH muhd ah BAHD* (pop. 5,577,940; met. area pop. 6,352,254), is the largest city in Gujarat, a state in western India. It lies on the Sabarmati River in India's cotton-growing region (see **India** [political map]).

The city is a manufacturing and trade center for the nation's cotton textile industry. Ahmadabad's chemical industry produces drugs, dyes, pesticides, and plastics. Chemical plants have caused widespread air pollution.

Ahmadabad was named after Ahmad Shah I, the sultan of Gujarat who founded the city in 1411. The overcrowded, older section of the city lies on the east bank of the Sabarmati. Ahmadabad has many historic monuments as well as busy shopping areas. Weaving mills and other factories stand near this section. The west bank of the river includes many upper-class neighborhoods and Gujarat University.   P. P. Karan

Ahmadinejad, *ah MAH dih nee ZHAHD,* **Mahmoud,** *mah MOOD* (1956-   ), was president of Iran from 2005 to 2013. Before his election, Ahmadinejad was mayor of Tehran. He was known for his conservative views and simple lifestyle.

Ahmadinejad was born in Garmsar, near Tehran, on Oct. 28, 1956. He belonged to a radical student group while he was a university student in Tehran. He has a Ph.D. degree in civil engineering from Iran University of Science and Technology, where he has also taught.

In the 1980's, during Iran's war with Iraq, Ahmadinejad served in the Revolutionary Guards. Since the 1980's, he has held a number of political posts, including adviser to the Ministry of Culture and Islamic Guidance and governor of the Ardabil province. The Tehran city council appointed him mayor in 2003. As mayor, he reversed many changes that moderate mayors before him had put into effect. In 2005, Ahmadinejad resigned to run for president. He defeated Hashemi Rafsanjani, a former president, in a runoff election. In 2009, Ahmadinejad was reelected president, defeating reformist candidate Mir Hussein Moussavi.   Ali M. Ansari

Ahura Mazda. See **Zoroastrianism.**

AID. See **Agency for International Development.**

Aid to Families with Dependent Children, often called AFDC, was a United States federal-state government program. It was created in 1935 to provide financial help to low-income families with children. Under AFDC, states determined benefit levels and administered the program. The federal government set many of the rules for determining who qualified for benefits, and it paid about half the costs of the program.

To qualify for AFDC, a family had to have one parent who was missing, dead, or unemployed. Divorced, separated, and never-married mothers headed most AFDC families. Many families received AFDC for less than one year. But by the mid-1990's, three-fourths of all people receiving AFDC had received it for five years or more.

In 1996, the federal government replaced AFDC with Temporary Assistance for Needy Families (TANF). TANF paid fixed grants to states, required that adult recipients work, and placed limits on the length of time recipients could obtain benefits. Under the new program, states received more authority to choose their own approach to assisting families.   Robert I. Lerman

© Herwig Prammer, Reuters

International cooperation in the fight against AIDS helps limit the spread of the disease. In this photograph, former U.S. president Bill Clinton addresses an international conference on AIDS.

AIDS

AIDS is the final, life-threatening stages of infection with the *human immunodeficiency virus* (HIV). HIV damages the immune system, the human body's most important defense against disease. *AIDS* stands for *a*cquired *i*mmuno*d*eficiency *s*yndrome or *a*cquired *i*mmune *d*eficiency *s*yndrome. A syndrome is a group of signs and symptoms that occur together as part of an illness.

People usually acquire HIV in one of three ways. They may become infected through (1) sexual intercourse, (2) direct exposure to infected blood, or (3) transmission from an infected mother to her baby. HIV is not transmitted through air, food, or water or by insects. No known cases of infection have occurred through the sharing of eating utensils, bathrooms, locker rooms, living space, or classrooms.

How HIV affects the body

Scientists have identified two different types of HIV. The first type identified was discovered by French researchers in 1983. It is now known as HIV-1. A second,

related virus, known as HIV-2, was isolated in 1985. Both viruses cause AIDS. But HIV-1 has spread throughout the world. It is the type most associated with the global problem of AIDS. HIV-2 occurs mainly in western Africa.

Once HIV enters the bloodstream, it infects certain white blood cells, called *T helper cells* and *macrophages.* These cells serve important functions in the immune system (see **Immune system** [Antigen-presenting cells; The cell-mediated immune response]). Together, these cells are often called *CD4 cells.* HIV attaches to proteins called *CD4 receptors* on the surface of the cells. Once attached, HIV enters the cell and inserts its own genes into the cell's reproductive system. These genes carry the genetic "instructions" for manufacturing more HIV. The infected cell thus acts as an HIV "factory," making thousands of copies of HIV. The HIV is then released to infect other CD4 cells throughout the body.

HIV kills the cells it infects. The immune system produces millions of CD4 cells every day. But HIV can destroy them as fast as they are produced. If left untreated, HIV infection thus disables the immune system. People then can become sick from other diseases and die.

Symptoms. People infected with HIV eventually develop symptoms that can also be caused by other disorders. These symptoms include fever, diarrhea, tiredness, night sweats, enlarged lymph glands, loss of appetite and weight, and yeast infections of the mouth and vagina. With HIV infection, however, the symptoms are more frequent. They are more severe and last longer.

HIV infection also commonly causes a "wasting syndrome." The syndrome results in weight loss, declining health, and in some cases, death. The virus can also infect the brain and nervous system, causing *dementia.* Dementia is a condition characterized by disorders of the senses, thinking, or memory. Infection of the brain may also cause problems with movement or coordination.

Opportunistic illness. HIV damages the immune system, leaving infected people vulnerable to other infections and conditions. Many of these illnesses do not usually bother people who are not infected with HIV. These illnesses are known as *opportunistic illnesses* because they take advantage of the opportunity presented by a damaged immune system. People with HIV infection may be diagnosed as having AIDS when they develop one or more opportunistic infections or one of several other severe illnesses. They may otherwise be diagnosed with AIDS when blood tests indicate that they have fewer than 200 CD4 cells per microliter (0.000001 liter) of blood.

A number of opportunistic illnesses typically affect AIDS patients. In North America and Europe, *Pneumocystis carinii* pneumonia (PCP) is most common. PCP is an infection of the lungs. It is a leading cause of death among AIDS patients. People with AIDS commonly develop yeast infections of the *esophagus* (the tube that carries food to the stomach). This infection can cause severe pain when swallowing, resulting in weight loss and *dehydration* (excessive loss of water from the body).

People with AIDS often develop a form of cancer called Kaposi's sarcoma. This cancer usually arises in the skin. It causes tumors that look like bruises. Kaposi's sarcoma is rare in healthy people and usually grows slowly. But in people with AIDS, the tumors grow quickly and spread. AIDS patients can also develop tuberculosis or an eye infection called cytomegalovirus retinitis.

It may take from 2 to 15 years after infection with HIV for a person to develop AIDS. For children born with HIV infection, the interval is usually much shorter. Doctors have discovered that 4 to 7 percent of HIV-infected people do not develop any symptoms or opportunistic infections over many years, even without treatment.

Stages of HIV infection

People infected with human immunodeficiency virus (HIV) go through three stages of infection. These stages are (1) acute retroviral syndrome and asymptomatic period, (2) symptomatic HIV infection, and (3) AIDS. The length of time any person stays in each stage varies greatly and depends on many factors, including medical treatment. HIV can be transmitted during all stages of infection, even when no symptoms occur.

Acute retroviral syndrome and asymptomatic period. Most people get a flulike or mononucleosis-like illness within 12 weeks after becoming infected with HIV. This illness, known as acute retroviral syndrome, usually goes away without treatment. From this point on, the infected person's blood tests positive for HIV antibodies even though symptoms usually do not develop for 2 to 15 years or more. During this early stage of infection, the patient maintains a near normal number of CD4 cells—that is, more than 500 CD4 cells per microliter of blood. CD4 cells are the white blood cells that are infected by HIV.

Symptomatic HIV infection. In this stage, a wide variety of mild or severe symptoms may appear. Common symptoms include tiredness, enlarged lymph glands, yeast infections, skin rashes, and dental disease. This stage of the infection may last from a few months to many years. During this time, the patient's CD4-cell count gradually declines, typically ranging from 500 to 200 CD4 cells per microliter of blood.

AIDS is characterized by severe damage to the immune system and such opportunistic infections as *Pneumocystis carinii* pneumonia and Kaposi's sarcoma. The progressive breakdown of the immune system eventually leads to death, usually within a few years. Most people with AIDS have fewer than 200 CD4 cells per microliter of blood, with most deaths occurring in patients with CD4-cell counts below 50.

Percentage of adults with HIV or AIDS

By 2018, an estimated 38 million people throughout the world had HIV or AIDS. The highest rates of infection were in central and southern Africa, where public health and education programs lacked resources to combat the epidemic.

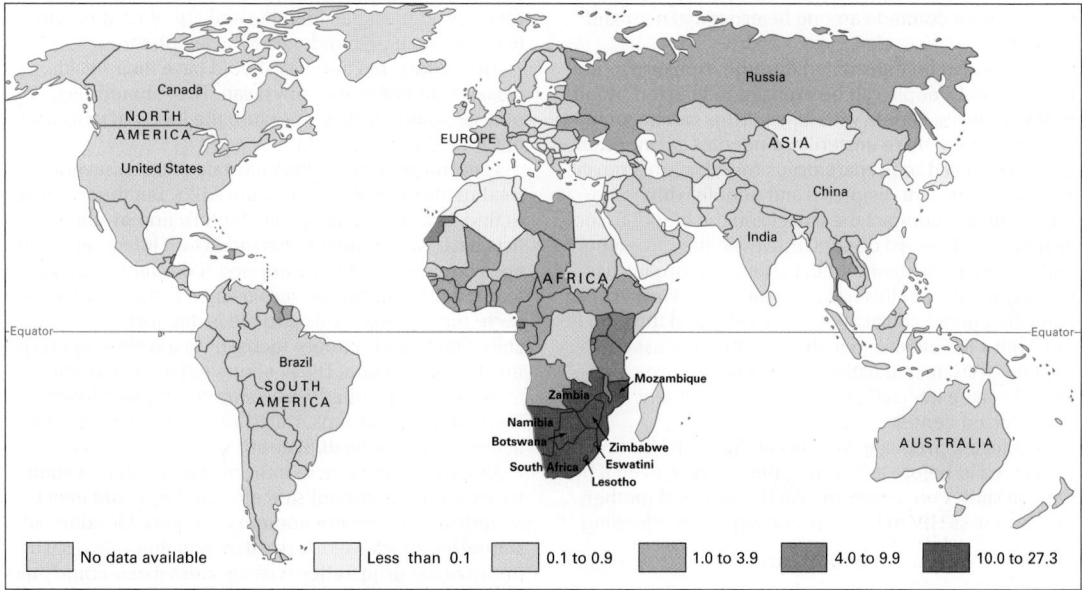

No data available	Less than 0.1	0.1 to 0.9	1.0 to 3.9	4.0 to 9.9	10.0 to 27.3

WORLD BOOK map; based on data from the Joint United Nations Programme on HIV/AIDS.

Estimated number of new HIV infections by year worldwide

The number of new HIV infections reported each year has risen dramatically since the early 1980's, especially among the poor. Education in HIV prevention has led to declines in infection rates in some areas. But most of the decline in this graph is attributed to more accurate infection-rate data.

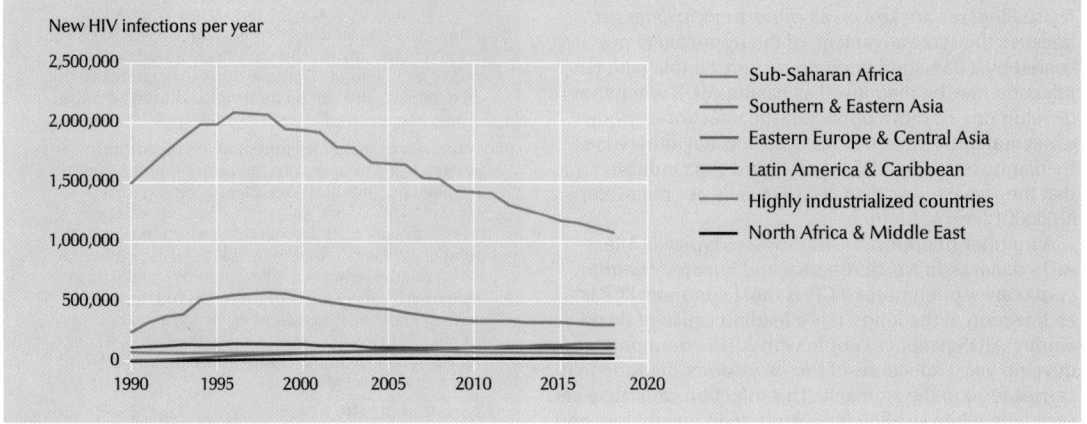

New HIV infections per year

- Sub-Saharan Africa
- Southern & Eastern Asia
- Eastern Europe & Central Asia
- Latin America & Caribbean
- Highly industrialized countries
- North Africa & Middle East

Source: Joint United Nations Programme on HIV/AIDS.

Medical professionals call such individuals *long-term nonprogressors.* A small percentage of people with HIV go 20 years without developing AIDS.

Medical treatment can delay the development of AIDS in several ways. It can inhibit the growth of HIV, preserve the immune system, and delay the onset of opportunistic infections. However, an infected person with or without symptoms can still transmit the virus to another person. Infection with HIV appears to be permanent in all who become infected.

How HIV is transmitted

The most common means of infection with HIV is sexual intercourse with an infected person. All forms of sexual intercourse can transmit HIV. In the United States, sexual transmission of HIV has occurred mainly among men who have sexual intercourse with men. But it is becoming more common among heterosexual men and women.

HIV can also be transmitted through exposure to infected blood. People can be exposed to infected blood in several ways. People who inject drugs can become exposed if they share unsterilized needles, syringes, or equipment used to prepare drugs for injection. Transfusion and transplant recipients and people with hemophilia can also contract the virus from the blood, tissues, or organs of infected donors. However, the screening and testing of donated blood, tissues, and organs has virtually eliminated this hazard. Health-care workers can come into direct contact with infected blood through injury with a needle or other sharp instrument used in treating HIV-infected patients. In a few instances, patients became infected after receiving treatment from an HIV-infected dentist or surgeon.

An infected pregnant woman can transmit HIV to her unborn child before and during the delivery, even if the woman shows no symptoms. An HIV-infected mother may also pass HIV to her baby through breast-feeding.

Medical care

Medical care for HIV and AIDS includes diagnosing

and treating the illness. It also includes preventing the spread of HIV infection.

Diagnosis. Tests for detecting evidence of HIV-1 in the blood became widely available in 1985. Tests for detecting HIV-2 in the blood became widely available in 1992. Both blood tests identify *antibodies* to the HIV virus. Antibodies are proteins produced by certain white blood cells in response to viruses or other invaders that enter the body. The presence of antibodies to HIV indicates infection with the virus. There is also an oral test for HIV-1 antibodies in mouth fluids.

Other tests directly measure the amount of HIV in the blood. These tests enable doctors to measure a patient's response to treatment. They also help to predict the patient's future health and estimated survival time. In 1996, the first home tests for HIV infection became available. People send in by mail a card holding a dried spot of their blood. Using an identification number, they can learn the results confidentially by telephone.

All HIV-infected patients should have their health closely monitored by a physician. They should receive periodic blood tests to measure the levels of virus and of CD4 cells in the blood.

Treatment. Researchers have developed several treatments for HIV infection and AIDS. But they have yet to find a cure. Ever since the identification of HIV, scientists have worked to understand how it infects and damages human cells. In one important discovery, scientists learned that HIV reproduces using an enzyme called *reverse transcriptase.* This enzyme is not normally found in cells. Scientists therefore focused on developing drugs that block its action. These efforts led to development of a class of drugs called *reverse transcriptase inhibitors.* The first of these drugs, called zidovudine or AZT, was licensed in the United States in 1987.

AZT and other reverse transcriptase inhibitors sometimes produce harmful side effects. These side effects include anemia severe enough to require blood transfusions. HIV also develops resistance to these drugs. To improve the drugs' effectiveness, doctors combine them and vary the order in which they are given.

In 1995 and 1996, the United States Food and Drug Administration (FDA) approved the first three of a class of drugs called *protease inhibitors* for treating HIV. These drugs block the action of *protease,* another HIV enzyme not found in healthy human cells. HIV uses protease at a later stage in its reproduction than it does reverse transcriptase. The first three protease inhibitors were indinavir, ritonavir, and saquinavir.

With the development of protease inhibitors, doctors began to combine them with other antiviral drugs. Studies showed that some antiviral drug combinations could decrease HIV in the blood to undetectable levels. At first, this kind of "drug cocktail" included several drugs taken at different times of the day for an indefinite period. But in 2006, the FDA approved the first single-dose combination pill. This combined therapy was originally called Highly Active Antiretroviral Therapy (HAART). Today, it is more commonly known as Antiretroviral Therapy (ART). ART helps people with HIV to live normal lives. It also reduces HIV in the blood to such low levels that transmission becomes extremely difficult. It therefore serves to both treat the disease and prevent its spread. In 2021, the FDA approved a new type of ART, given to patients by injection. The injection is an extended-release therapy, and thus is only needed once per month.

In the early 2000's, researchers developed *integrase inhibitors,* which block yet other stages in the reproduction of HIV. They also developed *fusion inhibitors* and *CCR5 antagonists*. These drugs work by blocking HIV from entering human cells.

As a result of the various types of drug developments, by the early 2020's, many doctors considered HIV to be a chronic, manageable condition. But HIV may still develop resistance to drugs. In addition, scientists have found that HIV persists inside CD4 cells. Even when the virus is managed, patients remain infected with HIV, and those who stop treatment will eventually develop AIDS.

Doctors also work with AIDS patients to prevent and treat opportunistic infections. PCP can be prevented with antibiotics. Physicians use chemotherapy and biological substances called *interferons* to treat Kaposi's sarcoma (see **Chemotherapy; Interferon**). They believe that any eventual cure for AIDS must not only stop the growth of the virus but also prevent opportunistic illnesses and restore normal immune function.

Prevention. To prevent HIV infection, a person must avoid sexual contact with anyone who is or might be infected with the virus. The most effective strategies are to refrain from all sexual intimacy or to restrict intimacy to one uninfected person. Health authorities recommend that a condom be used every time sexual intercourse occurs with a person who has HIV or whose infection status is unknown. Drug users should seek help to stop taking drugs. They should never share hypodermic needles, syringes, or other injection equipment.

Since 1985, health officials have used tests that detect the presence of HIV-1 to screen all donated blood and tissue products to ensure the safety of transfusions. Screening for HIV-2 began in 1992.

In 1994, researchers showed that AZT reduced the risk of transmission from an HIV-infected mother to her baby. Since then, other drugs have been developed. Today, physicians routinely administer a combination of three antiretroviral drugs to HIV-infected women during pregnancy and labor and to their newborn babies. Doctors advise HIV-infected women not to breast-feed.

In the late 1980's, researchers found evidence that male circumcision might help protect against the transmission of HIV (see **Circumcision**). By 2006, controlled trials in Africa indicated that male circumcision reduced the risk of HIV-1 transmission from females to males. Researchers did not find circumcision to have similar protective value for transmission from male to female or from male to male. In 2007, the World Health Organization recommended male circumcision as an effective intervention against HIV transmission.

Public health agencies have provided guidelines for preventing the transmission of HIV in health care settings. Physicians, dentists, and other health care workers wear gloves, masks, and other protective clothing during many examinations and procedures.

The search for a vaccine against HIV has proven difficult. HIV is a complicated virus that *mutates* (changes) rapidly, making traditional vaccines impossible to use. Nonetheless, researchers continue working to develop safe, effective, and economical vaccines against HIV infection. However, even if HIV transmission ended, AIDS cases would still occur because millions of people are already infected with the virus. As a result, scientists are also working to develop vaccines that would boost the immune systems of HIV-infected people.

Social issues

AIDS is a relatively new life-threatening disease. At first, it mainly affected young adults. In the public imagination, the disease soon became associated with risky sexual behavior and with drug abuse. For all these reasons, efforts to address AIDS or to prevent the spread of HIV have at times faced unique social challenges.

Education about AIDS, both in schools and in the community, has become the chief means of preventing infection. Some schools have established health clinics that distribute condoms to students. However, some people oppose even classroom discussion of condom use. They believe that such discussion implies acceptance of sexual intimacy outside of marriage.

Other important approaches to reducing transmission include preventing drug use and educating drug users about HIV. Some communities have launched sex education and *needle-exchange programs* among drug users. Needle-exchange programs provide sterilized needles for those who cannot or will not stop injecting drugs. But many people have criticized such programs for their implied acceptance of drug abuse.

In the United States, federal, state, and local governments have provided funds for AIDS education, treatment, and research. Public health clinics offer counseling and HIV-antibody testing to people who have symptoms or are at risk of infection. In addition, these clinics may privately and confidentially notify an infected person's sexual or needle-sharing partners of their risk. Once notified, such partners too can receive preventive counseling, testing, and medical services.

Public awareness. Many individuals and organizations have worked to increase public awareness of AIDS. The most active organizations include community-based groups and the American Red Cross. They hope that greater awareness will generate more compassion and support for people living with AIDS. They also hope to ensure adequate funding for HIV prevention, treatment, and research. One prominent project bringing attention to the crisis is the AIDS Memorial Quilt. Begun by the NAMES Project Foundation in 1987, the quilt consists of thousands of individually designed panels. The panels memorialize people who died of AIDS. The quilt has been displayed throughout the world.

Celebrities have also helped raise public consciousness of AIDS. Many well-known entertainers and athletes have participated in education and fund-raising efforts. The epidemic also has gained attention as a result of well-known people becoming infected with HIV or dying from AIDS. They include actor Rock Hudson, who died of AIDS in 1985, and tennis champion Arthur Ashe, who died in 1993. Basketball star Magic Johnson announced he was infected with HIV in 1991. Olympic diver Greg Louganis announced his infection in 1995.

Beginning in 1988, the United Nations has designated December 1 each year as World AIDS Day. On this day, public agencies and schools around the world sponsor education and prevention programs. Many people wear a red ribbon to show support for people with AIDS.

Discrimination. Poor understanding of HIV has at times stoked public fears, leading many people with the virus to suffer unjustly. Some of the infected have lost or been denied jobs or housing. Others have been denied medical care and health insurance. Many children with AIDS were initially barred from attending school or playing on sports teams. To prevent discrimination, people with HIV and AIDS are often included under laws protecting the rights of people with disabilities. The United States government and some states have also strengthened laws safeguarding the confidentiality of medical records relating to HIV infection and AIDS.

Preventing discrimination against people with HIV is not only just—it also protects public health. When people can live without fear of discrimination, they are more likely to seek counseling and treatment. In many cases, such measures lead to earlier diagnosis and a reduction in risky behavior.

Providing medical care for the hundreds of thousands of people with HIV and those with AIDS is expensive. Planning and paying for this care consumes considerable resources. Some of the burdens may be reduced through prevention efforts and by finding less expensive alternatives to hospital care. Such alternatives may include expanded home care services and *hospice* care. Hospices are places that care for people who are dying.

Antiviral drugs are effective in prolonging the lives of people with HIV. But the cost of the drugs exceeds what nearly any individual can pay. Patients in developing nations in particular often lack sufficient access to medical care and cannot afford these medications. Experts view this issue, as well as the public health impact of AIDS itself, as a major challenge to social and economic progress in developing nations. Even in developed nations, state funds for antiviral drugs can be limited.

AIDS around the world

AIDS occurs in every nation. In areas such as Africa south of the Sahara, Southeast Asia, and India, HIV transmission has occurred mostly among heterosexual men and women, particularly young adults and teens. Many developing nations carry enormous burdens of HIV infection. For example, the United Nations reports that in some parts of Africa, the infection rate may reach over 30 percent in some urban areas. The huge number of young adults dying of AIDS in Africa south of the Sahara has decreased overall life expectancy across the continent. A growing number of people have also become infected in countries with increasing drug use, such as Russia, China, and the nations of central Europe.

Since 1986, the international health community has worked to coordinate the global fight against HIV and AIDS. The World Health Organization's Global AIDS Programme formed the Joint United Nations Programme on HIV/AIDS (UNAIDS) in 1996. Since that time, UNAIDS has worked with other international partners to coordinate the global fight against HIV and AIDS.

History

Scientists do not know for certain exactly how, when, or where the AIDS virus evolved and first infected people. Researchers have shown that HIV-1 and HIV-2 are more closely related to viruses that infect monkeys and apes than to each other. They believe HIV evolved from viruses that originally infected monkeys and apes in Africa. The virus was somehow transmitted to people.

In 1999, U.S. researchers found evidence that HIV-1 most likely originated in chimpanzees in west Africa. Further genetic studies in 2006 supported this theory. The virus appears to have been transmitted to people who hunted, butchered, and consumed the chimpanzees for food. Later studies suggest HIV probably spread to humans between 1884 and 1924. Transportation routes created by colonial powers brought HIV-infected people to the growing cities of central Africa, facilitating the spread of the virus. HIV was transmitted between sexual partners and from mothers to babies.

Scientists believe HIV infection became widespread after major social changes in Africa during the 1960's and 1970's. Large numbers of people moved from rural areas to cities. This shift caused growth in crowding, unemployment, and prostitution, which in turn increased cases of sexually transmitted infections, including HIV. HIV may have been introduced into industrialized nations several times before it became widespread.

AIDS was first identified as a disease by physicians in California and New York City in 1981. Doctors recognized the condition as something new because all the patients were previously healthy, young gay men. They sought medical care because they were suffering from otherwise rare forms of cancer and pneumonia. In 1982, the disease was named AIDS. Scientists soon determined that AIDS occurred when the immune system became damaged. They also learned that the agent that caused the damage was spread through sexual contact, shared drug needles, and infected blood transfusions.

After researchers isolated HIV as the cause of AIDS in 1983 and 1984, they developed tests to detect HIV infection. Scientists have used these and other tests to analyze stored tissues from several people who died from the late 1950's through the 1970's. Scientists have concluded that some of these people died from AIDS.

Cases of HIV infection reported worldwide rose dramatically during the 1980's and 1990's. By 2010, experts estimated that about 33 million people were living with

HIV infection or AIDS throughout the world. More than 35 million people had died since the epidemic's beginning. But scientists have observed that the number of newly infected people has declined since the late 1990's, largely due to stabilizing rates of infection in Africa.

In the United States, about 50,000 people are infected with HIV each year. This rate has remained relatively steady since the late 1990's. In the early part of the epidemic, new infections occurred primarily among gay and bisexual men. In the late 1980's and 1990's, however, more women, children, and drug users became infected. Minority groups have suffered a disproportionately high rate of infection from the beginning of the epidemic. Today, African Americans make up the majority of new cases of HIV in the United States.

Some success has been achieved in controlling the spread of HIV. In the United States, for example, among gay and bisexual men, HIV has spread more slowly than it did in the early 1980's. These improvements result almost entirely from community-based education about AIDS prevention and the ensuing changes in sexual behavior. As a result of education, many gay and bisexual men report fewer sexual partners and increased use of condoms. HIV blood tests, which became available in 1985, caused a gradual decline in transfusion-related cases in the late 1980's. The rate of infection in other groups rose, however, during the 1980's and 1990's. These groups include heterosexual men and women and people who inject drugs.

During the mid-to-late 1990's, advances in HIV treatment slowed the progression of the infection into AIDS. This slowing has led to dramatic decreases in AIDS cases in the United States. In 2010, the United States released the first National HIV/AIDS Strategy (NHAS), to reduce the prevalence of HIV in the country. In 2021, the United States replaced the NHAS with the HIV National Strategic Plan (HIV Plan). The goal of the HIV Plan is to reduce nationwide HIV infections by 90 percent by 2030.

In 2012, the FDA approved the first combination of drugs to help prevent the transmission of HIV between people. Such medications are called *pre-exposure prophylaxis* (PrEP). In research studies, taking PrEP lowered a person's risk of contracting HIV by as much as 90 percent. But the high cost of PrEP drugs and the fact that they must be taken daily have limited their impact on infection rates. In 2021, the FDA approved a new treatment for HIV, given to patients by injection. The injection is a combination of the drugs cabotegravir and rilpivirine. Only one injection is needed per month. Doctors hope this new option will result in more patients getting treatment.   Stephen Inrig

Related articles in *World Book* include:

Adolescent (Risk taking)	Pneumonia
Antiviral drug	Retrovirus
Condom	Sexually transmitted disease
Disease (picture: Viruses)	Tuberculosis
Medicine (Unequal distribution of medical care)	

Aiken, *AY kuhn,* **Conrad Potter** (1889-1973), was an American poet, novelist, and critic. He was a sympathetic ally of Ezra Pound, T. S. Eliot, and others who used new methods in poetry. Aiken's verse, however, is relatively conservative and deeply personal, and especially influenced by the Austrian psychiatrist Sigmund Freud. Aiken's central poetic concern was the problem of achieving personal identity in an unstable world of change. The greatest strength of his poetry is its musicality, which often overwhelms the poem's ideas. His *Selected Poems* won the 1930 Pulitzer Prize for poetry.

Aiken was born in Savannah, Georgia, on Aug. 5, 1889, but grew up in New Bedford, Massachusetts. In addition to several novels and collections of stories and essays, he wrote *Ushant* (1952), an autobiographical fantasy. This work provides an eloquent account of the writer's development as an artist, despite personal setbacks and uncertainties. Aiken's *Collected Poems 1916-1970* was published in 1971. He died on Aug. 17, 1973.   Bonnie Costello

Aikido, *eye KEE doh,* is a popular martial art that originated in Japan. The word means *the way of spiritual harmony.* Aikido is a form of self-defense, but it is also a moral philosophy and sometimes a sport.

© Shutterstock

Aikido is a popular martial art that originated in Japan. Aikido is not based on physical strength. Practitioners use holds and throws to make opponents lose their balance, rather than attack opponents with kicks or hand blows.

Aikido traditionally is a method of fighting without weapons. It is not based on physical strength. Practitioners use holds and throws to make opponents lose their balance, rather than attack opponents with kicks or hand blows.

Aikido stresses the need for a healthy and relaxed body, with a mind and spirit free of bad habits. A central element in aikido is called *ki,* which followers believe is the internal energy everyone possesses but few know how to use. Aikido makes people aware of their ki and how to utilize it properly. Aikido followers are taught that their ki is a source of mental strength and power located just below the navel.

Aikido was founded about 1925 by Morihei Ueshiba, a Japanese teacher of martial arts. Ueshiba studied with Buddhist priests as a child and Shinto priests as an adult, and precepts of these religions are important in aikido. There are many systems of aikido. One system, called *Tomiki aikido,* is also known as *sport aikido.* In this system, tournaments are held in which players can test their skills against both armed and unarmed opponents.

See also **Martial arts.**

Aikman, *AYK muhn,* **Troy** (1966-   ), was a leading quarterback in the National Football League (NFL). Aikman played for the Dallas Cowboys from 1989 to 2000. He helped lead the team to victories in the Super Bowl in 1993, 1994, and 1996. He became known for his accurate passing and leadership skills on the field. Aikman retired in 2001 after Dallas released him. He became a television analyst for NFL games.

Aikman was born on Nov. 21, 1966, in West Covina, California. He played at the University of Oklahoma in 1984 and 1985 and then transferred to the University of California at Los Angeles (UCLA). After sitting out a year, he played for UCLA in 1987 and 1988, winning All-American honors his final year. Dallas selected him as the top choice in the 1989 draft. Aikman became the team's starting quarterback his rookie year. He was elected to the Pro Football Hall of Fame in 2006 and to the College Football Hall of Fame in 2008.   Neil Milbert

Ailanthus, *ay LAN thuhs,* is a hardy tree that thrives in cities and places where other trees fail to grow. It is also called the *tree of heaven.* Although native to the forests of China, the tree grows throughout much of the world.

An ailanthus has smooth brown-gray bark and small greenish flowers. Male flowers give off an unpleasant odor. During spring and summer, the tree produces *compound leaves* (leaves with more than one blade) that smell like peanut butter when broken. In autumn, ailanthuses develop attractive, reddish-brown, winged fruits.

Because the ailanthus can live in most soils and many climates, people often call it a "weed tree." It resists injury from insects, diseases, and pollution. Seedlings carried by the wind sprout almost anywhere they land. Many ailanthuses grow at roadsides and forest edges. They also flourish in vacant city lots and sidewalk cracks. The tree develops rapidly. From seed, it may grow 8 feet (2.4 meters) in one year. A mature ailanthus stands about 60 feet (18 meters) tall.   Norman L. Christensen, Jr.

Scientific classification. The scientific name of the ailanthus is *Ailanthus altissima.*

See also **Tree** (Broadleaf and needleleaf trees [picture]).

Ailey, *AY lee,* **Alvin** (1931-1989), was an American *choreographer* (creator of dances) and the director of the

© Hulton/Archive/Getty Images

Alvin Ailey, *center,* was an American choreographer and the director of the Alvin Ailey American Dance Theater. He composed many of his modern dances to black folk music and jazz.

Alvin Ailey American Dance Theater. Ailey's modern dances strongly reflected his Southern background. He composed many of them to black folk music and jazz. His works include *Revelations* (1960), *Mary Lou's Mass* (1971), and *Cry* (1971). He based *Survivors* (1986) on the antiapartheid movement in South Africa.

Ailey was born on Jan. 5, 1931, in Rogers, Texas. He studied and performed with the American choreographer Lester Horton. In 1958, Ailey formed his own dance company. In 1965, he retired from performing to focus on choreography. In addition to works created for his company, Ailey composed dances for ballet, television, and opera. In 1977, he received the Spingarn Medal for his achievement in modern dance (see **Spingarn Medal**). He died on Dec. 1, 1989. *Revelations,* an autobiography, was published six years later. Ailey received the Presidential Medal of Freedom, one of the country's highest civilian honors, in 2014, after his death.   Katy Matheson

AIM. See **American Indian Movement.**

Aimar, *eh MAHR,* **Pablo,** *PAHB loh* (1979-   ), is a former star soccer player from Argentina. Soccer is called *football* in many countries. A midfielder, Aimar gained international recognition for his exuberance and his creativity as a playmaker.

Pablo César Aimar was born on Nov. 3, 1979, in Rio Cuarto, Argentina. He began his career with River Plate in Argentina in 1996. In 1997, he helped lead Argentina to the World Youth Championship. He played with River Plate until 2001, when he joined Valencia CF in Spain. He helped lead Valencia to league championships in 2002 and 2004. Aimar also played in Valencia's Union of European Football Associations (UEFA) Cup and European Super Cup victories in 2004. From 2006 to 2008, Aimar played for Valencia's league rival Real Zaragoza. In 2008, he joined the Portuguese team Benfica. He helped lead the team to the 2010 Portuguese league championship. In 2013, he joined the Malaysian Super League team Johor Darul Takzim. Aimar returned briefly to River Plate in Argentina before retiring in 2015.   Neil Milbert

Ainu, *EYE noo,* are a group of people who may have been the first inhabitants of what is now Japan. There are about 15,000 Ainu. Most live on Hokkaido, Japan's northernmost main island. In the mid-1900's, many Ainu moved to Hokkaido from Sakhalin and the Kuril Islands. Sakhalin is a part of Russia. Russia claims and occupies all the Kurils, but Japan claims the southernmost ones.

Scientists are uncertain about the ancestry of the Ainu. Some anthropologists think the Ainu are related to European peoples. Other anthropologists believe they are related to Asian peoples or the Aboriginal people of Australia, Australia's original inhabitants. The Ainu language has not been clearly classified.

Through the centuries, many Ainu have intermarried with the Japanese and other neighboring peoples. The village was once the basic unit of Ainu society. Each village was headed by a leader and consisted of 5 to 30 one-room houses. Hunting, fishing, and gathering plants provided food for the community. The Ainu practiced a complicated set of religious ceremonies.

The Ainu have long been victims of discrimination. But they have started a movement to gain fair treatment in Japan. The Japanese government has begun a program of economic aid for the Ainu.   Emiko Ohnuki-Tierney

See also **Japan** (People [picture]).

Artstreet

Dave Woodward, Atoz Images

The air around us is invisible. But we can feel the air when it pushes against us as gusts of wind. Wind is simply moving air. We can also tell that air has weight. This weight enables hot-air balloons to rise above Earth because they are lighter than the surrounding air.

Air

Air is the mixture of gases that surrounds Earth. Air covers the land and sea and extends far above Earth's surface. We cannot see, smell, or taste air. But when the wind blows, it is the air you feel against your face. Wind is simply moving air. You can also see the effect of wind in drifting clouds, pounding waves, and trembling leaves. Moving air can turn windmills and blow large sailboats across the ocean. The word *air* is often used interchangeably with the word *atmosphere*. However, atmosphere refers to the air and all the elements in the air, such as clouds, dust, and smoke.

Everyone needs air to stay alive. People have lived more than a month without food and more than a week without water. But a person can live only a few minutes without air.

Air does much more than make it possible for us to breathe. Air shields Earth from most of the harmful radiation from the sun. At the same time, gases in the air absorb heat *emitted* (given off) by the ground that has been warmed by the sun. In this way, air helps keep Earth warm enough to support life. It shields our planet from meteors, most of which burn up in the atmosphere before striking the ground.

We also need air to hear. Sound must travel through the air or some other substance. Most of the sounds we hear travel through the air. Thus, the world would be silent if there were no air. Air has weight. This weight enables balloons filled with a light gas or heated air to rise high above Earth. They rise because they are lighter than the air around them. Air moving over the wings of airplanes, birds, and insects enables them to fly.

The quality of the air we breathe depends largely on the amount of *pollutants* (impurities) that people add to the atmosphere. Air pollution is a serious problem in most of the world's big cities. Motor vehicles and industrial processes produce most of the wastes that cause air pollution. But many other pollutants that affect air quality come from natural sources, such as volcanic ash, smoke from forest fires, pollen, and dust. Polluted air can harm the health of living things. It can also damage building materials and even affect the weather.

What is air?

Air consists of a mixture of gases that extends from Earth's surface to outer space. Earth's gravitational pull prevents the air from escaping out into space. The gases of the air move freely among one another. As sunlight passes through Earth's atmosphere, it strikes molecules of the gases. These molecules scatter the sunlight, which is a mixture of all colors, in every direction. The sky appears blue because the gas molecules scatter more blue light than any other color. See Sky.

Many small particles of dust are suspended among the gases of the air. The air also carries tiny water droplets and ice crystals in the form of clouds. Scientists do not consider dust, water droplets, and ice crystals to be part of the air. Scientists do consider these suspended substances to be a part of Earth's atmosphere.

Gases of the air. The principal gases of the air are nitrogen and oxygen. Other gases include argon, water vapor, carbon dioxide, methane, neon, helium, krypton, hydrogen, xenon, and ozone. The water vapor in the air is water in the form of an invisible gas. Nitrogen makes up about 78 percent of *dry air*—that is, air from which all water vapor has been removed. Oxygen accounts for about 21 percent of dry air. The remaining 1 percent

The gases of the air

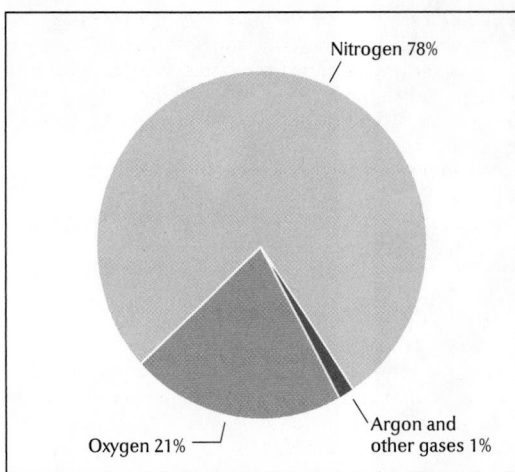

Nitrogen 78%

Oxygen 21%

Argon and other gases 1%

Air consists chiefly of nitrogen and oxygen. They make up about 99 percent of *dry air*—air from which all water vapor has been removed. Argon and other gases account for about 1 percent.

consists chiefly of argon, with only extremely small amounts of the other gases, often called *trace gases*. Except for water vapor, the gases in the atmosphere tend to be thoroughly mixed as high as an altitude of about 60 miles (100 kilometers).

Some gases of the atmosphere are particularly important. When we breathe, we take in oxygen from the air and give off carbon dioxide. Green plants take in carbon dioxide and give off oxygen in a food-making process called *photosynthesis* (see **Photosynthesis**). Most fuels must have oxygen to burn. Certain bacteria turn nitrogen that has passed into the soil from the atmosphere into chemicals that fertilize plants.

Water vapor and carbon dioxide are two of the primary gases in the air that help retain Earth's heat. They absorb *infrared radiation* (heat) emitted by the ground and oceans. In this way, the gases prevent some of the surface heat created by sunlight from escaping back into space. Ozone, a form of oxygen, absorbs many of the sun's harmful *ultraviolet rays,* an invisible form of light that has been linked to skin cancer.

Moisture in the air takes the form of water vapor and tiny particles of liquid water and ice. Water vapor enters the atmosphere when water evaporates from oceans, lakes, rivers, and soil. The leaves of plants also give off water in a process called *transpiration*. The total of evaporation and transpiration is called *evapotranspiration*.

The amount of vapor in the air depends on location. For example, air over oceans and in the tropics usually contains more vapor than air over the interior of continents or near the North and South poles. Furthermore, air near Earth's surface typically contains more vapor than air several miles or kilometers above the ground. The amount of water vapor in the air also depends on weather patterns and winds. For instance, air normally contains more vapor if it is blowing from an ocean.

Warm air can hold much more water vapor than cold air. Scientists express the ability of air to hold water vapor in terms of *relative humidity*—the air's vapor content

divided by its *vapor capacity*. Vapor capacity is often defined as the maximum amount of vapor the air could hold (see **Humidity**). According to this definition, air that is holding as much water vapor as possible has a relative humidity of 100 percent. Air just above water surfaces, such as the ocean, often has a relative humidity near 100 percent. Air over dry surfaces, such as deserts, usually has a low relative humidity.

However, air in clouds can actually have a relative humidity greater than 100 percent. If air is cooled enough, its vapor capacity decreases. The excess vapor can then change to tiny water droplets in a process called *condensation* or ice crystals in a process called *deposition*. The temperature at which water vapor begins to condense into tiny liquid droplets is called the *dew point*.

Air cools as it rises. Clouds form when masses of moist air rise and cool to below the dew point. The vapor in clouds condenses on tiny particles of matter called *cloud condensation nuclei*. These particles include sea salt, dust, soot, or such chemical compounds as ammonium sulfate or magnesium sulfate. Most ice crystals form in cold clouds as water vapor deposits onto tiny particles called *ice nuclei*.

Clouds consist of air filled with millions of water droplets, ice crystals, or both. Rain or snow develops after the growing droplets or crystals become heavy enough to fall out of the clouds. Fog is a cloud near Earth's surface.

Particles in the air. Air always contains many tiny solid particles called *aerosols*. Most aerosols measure only about $\frac{1}{250,000}$ inch (0.1 micrometer) in diameter. They are therefore invisible, except when crowded together in extremely large numbers.

Many aerosols enter the air from active volcanoes, automobile exhaust, forest and brush fires, and factory smoke. The wind carries particles of dust and sand up from the ground into the atmosphere. Other aerosols include pollen from plants, salt from the oceans, ashes of meteoroids, and tiny living things called *microbes*. In the presence of high humidity and sunlight, sulfur dioxide, a by-product of burning fossil fuels, turns into aerosols of sulfuric acid. In summer, a build-up of these aerosols may turn the sky a hazy shade of white.

Aerosols are always being added to the air. But they do not remain in the atmosphere forever. Rain and snow wash out many aerosols, so air is often fresher after it rains or snows. Other aerosols slowly fall to Earth.

Near Earth's surface, the number of aerosols in the air

How air pressure decreases with altitude

Altitude		Pressure	
In feet	In meters	In pounds per square inch	In kilopascals
50,000	15,000	1.8	12.1
40,000	12,000	2.8	19.4
30,000	9,000	4.5	30.8
20,000	6,000	6.8	47.2
10,000	3,000	10.2	70.1
Sea level	Sea level	14.7	101.3

varies greatly from place to place. The air over the oceans contains about 30 million aerosols per cubic foot (1 billion per cubic meter). However, the polluted air over a large city may contain about 3 billion aerosols per cubic foot (100 billion per cubic meter). Fewer aerosols float in the higher regions of the atmosphere. Thus, the air in mountainous regions is usually purer.

How air behaves

Weight and pressure. We do not usually notice the weight of air because air is much lighter than solids or liquids. At sea level, each cubic foot of air weighs only about 1 ⅕ ounces, a measurement equivalent to about 1.2 kilograms per cubic meter. But the weight of all the air around the world is more than 5,700 trillion tons (5,200 trillion metric tons). The gravitational pull of Earth maintains the atmosphere and prevents the air from escaping into outer space. The weight of the air pressing from the top of the atmosphere upon the layers of air below produces *air pressure,* also called *atmospheric pressure.* The air pressure at sea level averages 14.7 pounds per square inch (101.3 kilopascals). The air pressing down on your shoulders weighs about 1 ton (0.9 metric ton). You do not feel this weight because you are supported by equal air pressure on all sides.

An instrument called a *barometer* is used to measure air pressure. Air pressure is usually lower on stormy, wet days than on clear, dry days. Thus, a falling reading on a barometer often indicates that a storm is coming.

The upper atmosphere has less pressure than the air near Earth, simply because there is less air pressing down from above. When you ride up a tall building in a fast elevator, you can feel the air pressure changing. As you rise higher, the pressure of the air inside the elevator decreases, but the pressure inside your ears remains the same. This difference in pressure causes your eardrums to bulge outward slightly until some air finally forces its way out, causing your ears to "pop."

We use the pressing force of air in various ways. When we sip a soft drink through a straw, for example, we do not actually pull the liquid up through the straw. Instead, by sucking on the straw, we remove some of the air from inside it. As a result, the air pressure inside the straw becomes less than the pressure of the air on the liquid outside the straw. The greater pressure of the air outside then pushes the liquid up through the straw and into our mouths. Suction pumps and vacuum cleaners also work by means of air pressure.

Air movement. Air moves across the surface of Earth in the form of wind blowing from regions of high pressure to low pressure. These local areas of high and low pressure are primarily a result of the sun's uneven heating of Earth. Air above warm areas of Earth expands and becomes lighter. It then rises, creating an area of low pressure near the surface. Wind is produced when cooler, heavier air flows toward the low-pressure area, replacing the rising air. Wind often develops along an ocean shore during the day because land heats up more quickly than water does. The air over the shore is thus warmer than the air over the water. As the warm air over the shore rises, the cooler air from the sea moves inland and replaces it, producing a daytime sea breeze. At night, the air over the shore becomes cooler than the air over the water. Thus, the wind direction reverses, and a breeze blows out to sea as a land breeze.

The warm air above the equator is usually rising. Cooler air from north and south of the equator blows in steadily, replacing the rising air. This movement of air

Air pressure

The weight of the air pressing down all around us produces *air pressure.* The diagrams here show one common way we use the force of the air—to drink through a straw. Sucking on the straw creates a partial vacuum inside it. The greater air pressure outside then pushes the liquid in the glass up through the straw.

WORLD BOOK illustrations by Oxford Illustrators Limited

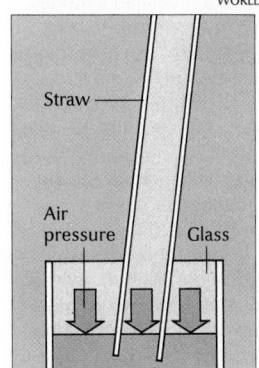

Equal air pressure

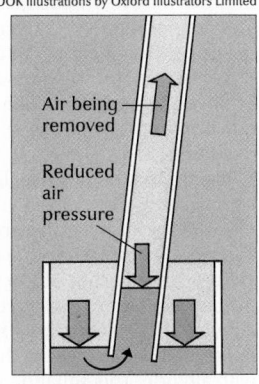

Unequal air pressure

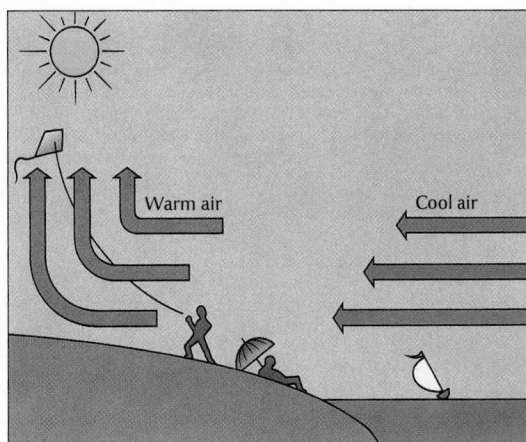

WORLD BOOK illustration by Oxford Illustrators Limited

Air movement. Wind results from differences in the temperature of the air. For example, on a sunny day, the air above an ocean shore is warmer than the air over the water. The warmer air over the shore expands, becomes lighter, and rises. The cooler air from the sea moves in, producing a sea breeze.

creates two vast belts of winds called the *trade winds.* The trade winds do not blow straight toward the equator because of Earth's rotation. The trade winds north of the equator are twisted to the right of their original direction, or toward the southwest. The trade winds south of the equator are shifted to their left, or toward the northwest. The alteration of wind flow due to Earth's rotation is called the *Coriolis force* or *Coriolis effect.* The Coriolis force also affects the flow pattern of two other great belts of winds that circle Earth, the *prevailing westerlies* and *polar easterlies.*

Bands of fast-moving winds occur about 6 to 9 miles (10 to 15 kilometers) above Earth. These bands are known as *jet streams.* Winds in the core of a jet stream may exceed 200 miles (320 kilometers) per hour. Systems of swirling winds, called *cyclones* and *anticyclones,* also form in the air. The winds of cyclones swirl inward toward a center of low pressure. Anticyclones whirl outward around a center of high pressure.

Air resistance. Air resists the motion of objects traveling through it. This resistance occurs because moving objects rub against the atoms and molecules of the gases that make up the air. A feather in the air floats slowly to the ground because of air resistance acting on its surface. Air resistance also slows a parachute jumper's fall.

During the early days of aviation, airplanes flew slowly partly because such parts as the wing braces and landing wheels rubbed against the air. Aviation engineers found that they could reduce air resistance and thus increase the speed of a plane by streamlining its shape. They removed outside wing supports and installed landing wheels that could be pulled up into the plane. They found that even smoothing down rivet heads helped reduce air resistance.

The faster objects move through the air, the more resistance they meet. For example, the faster you ride a bicycle, the stronger the air resistance against you will be. As you increase your speed, you can feel the air pushing harder against you. This air resistance generates heat, but you will actually feel cooler because the faster-moving air removes heat from your body more effectively. However, for objects traveling at great speeds, the heat generated by air resistance exceeds the cooling effect of the wind. Meteoroids speeding through the atmosphere encounter great air resistance and thus become hot enough to glow, producing streaks of light known as *meteors.* Most disintegrate before hitting the surface. Rockets traveling through Earth's atmosphere must be made of materials that can withstand the intense heat created by air resistance.

Air compression. Air can be pumped into cylinders or tanks until the air pressure is several hundred times greater than normal atmospheric pressure. Such air is called *compressed air.* When air is being compressed, the atoms and molecules of the air speed up. As their speed increases, the air gets warmer.

People use compressed air to inflate tires and air mattresses. Scuba divers breathe from tanks of compressed air strapped to their backs. Submarines carry cylinders of compressed air. A submarine dives as compartments called *ballast tanks* are flooded with water. It rises to the surface as the water is forced out of the ballast tanks by compressed air. Compressed air is also used to operate air brakes, certain insecticide and paint sprayers, and air hammers and other *pneumatic tools.*

Structure of the atmosphere

Scientists divide Earth's atmosphere into four layers according to differences in temperature. These layers, from the lowest to highest altitude, are (1) the troposphere, (2) the stratosphere, (3) the mesosphere, and (4) the thermosphere. The atmosphere becomes thinner with increasing height above Earth. This thinning occurs because the number of air molecules in a given amount of space decreases. The outer atmosphere gradually fades into space, where it meets the *solar wind*—that is, a continuous stream of charged particles from the sun.

The troposphere is the layer of the atmosphere closest to Earth—the layer in which we live. It contains more than 75 percent of Earth's air. Nearly all Earth's weather conditions—including most clouds, rain, and snow—occur in this layer. Scientists forecast weather by studying the behavior of the troposphere. Most of the aerosols and water vapor in the air are in the troposphere. Jet streams blow in the upper part of the troposphere.

The temperature of the troposphere decreases about 3.5 Fahrenheit degrees for every 1,000 feet (6.5 Celsius degrees for every 1,000 meters) of increase in altitude. The temperature stops decreasing at the *tropopause,* the upper boundary of the troposphere. The tropopause lies about 6 miles (10 kilometers) over the North and South poles and about 12 miles (19 kilometers) over the equator. At the tropopause, the air has become too thin to support life.

The troposphere is usually warmest near Earth's surface because the majority of sunlight that passes through the air heats the ground and seas. The ground and seas, in turn, warm the air directly above them.

Sometimes, especially at night and during the winter, the air near Earth's surface becomes cooler than the air above it. This cooling near the ground causes the temperature in a thin layer of the troposphere to increase with altitude. This situation is called a *temperature inversion* or *thermal inversion.* The worst outbreaks of air

Air resistance

Air resists the motion of objects traveling through it. This resistance slows a parachute jumper's fall, *shown here.* The jumper meets minimum air resistance and falls rapidly until the parachute is opened. The greater resistance acting on the surface of the parachute enables the jumper to float safely to the ground.

WORLD BOOK illustrations by Oxford Illustrators Limited

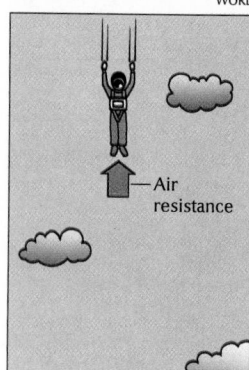

Minimum resistance   **Maximum resistance**

The layers of the atmosphere

Scientists divide Earth's atmosphere into four layers, according to differences in the temperature of the air. These layers are the *troposphere,* the *stratosphere,* the *mesosphere,* and the *thermosphere.* The outer atmosphere gradually fades into interplanetary space.

WORLD BOOK illustration by Oxford Illustrators Limited

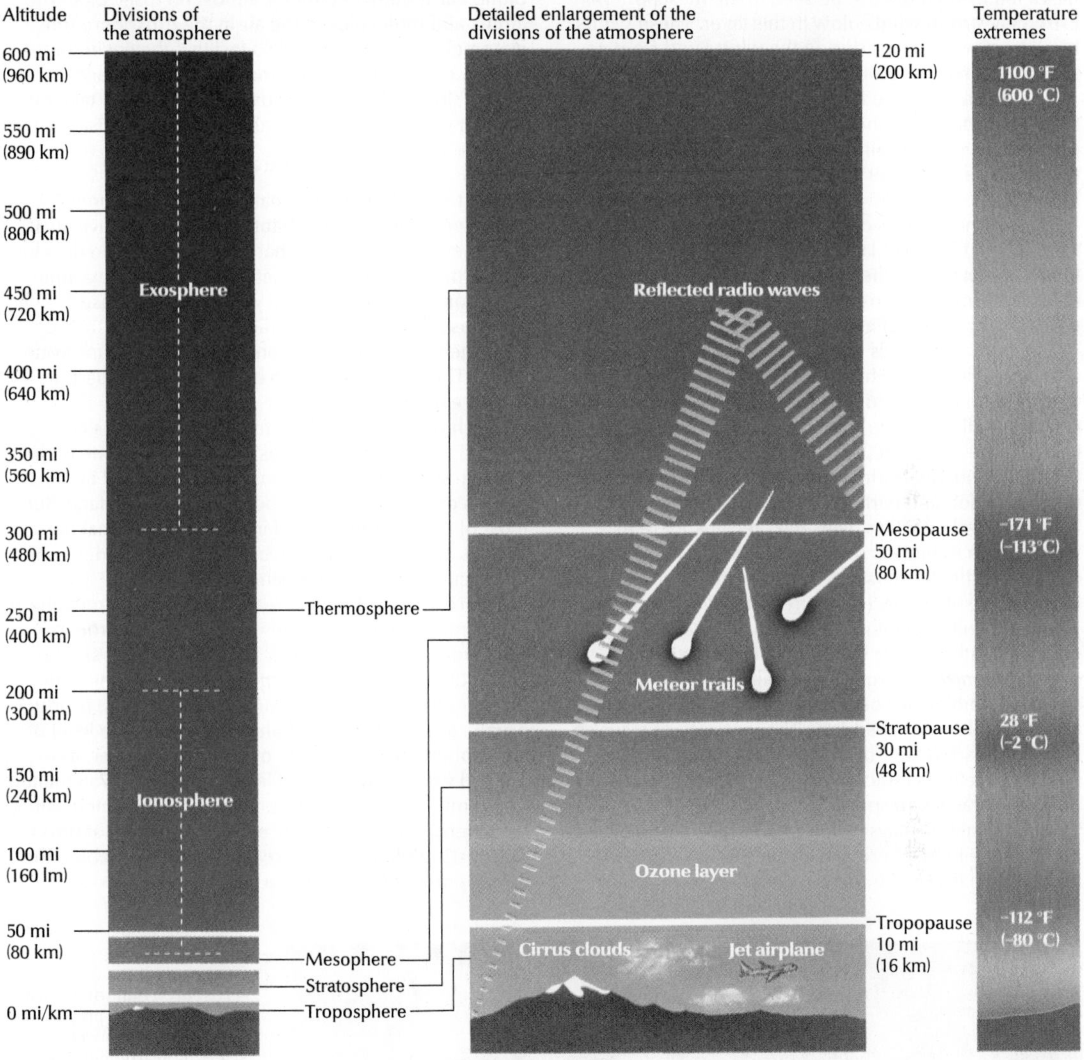

Altitude	Divisions of the atmosphere	Detailed enlargement of the divisions of the atmosphere	Temperature extremes
600 mi (960 km)		120 mi (200 km)	1100 °F (600 °C)
550 mi (890 km)			
500 mi (800 km)			
450 mi (720 km)	Exosphere	Reflected radio waves	
400 mi (640 km)			
350 mi (560 km)			
300 mi (480 km)		Mesopause 50 mi (80 km)	-171 °F (-113°C)
250 mi (400 km)	Thermosphere		
200 mi (300 km)		Meteor trails	
150 mi (240 km)	Ionosphere	Stratopause 30 mi (48 km)	28 °F (-2 °C)
100 mi (160 lm)		Ozone layer	
50 mi (80 km)	Mesophere	Tropopause 10 mi (16 km)	-112 °F (-80 °C)
	Stratosphere	Cirrus clouds Jet airplane	
0 mi/km	Troposphere		

pollution occur during temperature inversions. The warmer air overlying cold air traps pollutants and prevents them from rising and scattering. An inversion typically lasts until sunlight heats the air below or wind breaks up the overlying layer of warm air.

The coldest part of the troposphere is at the tropopause. Temperatures at the tropopause range from about -60 to -112 °F (-50 to -80 °C). The air is so cold that clouds can only exist as ice. The coldest part of the tropopause is over the equator. There, the temperature drops as low as -112 °F (-80 °C). The tropopause can be as much as 54 °F (30 °C) warmer over the poles than over the equator.

The stratosphere extends from the tropopause to about 30 miles (48 kilometers) above Earth's surface. Lit-

tle moisture enters the stratosphere, so clouds are rare. Often airline pilots on large jets prefer to fly in the stratosphere to stay above the weather disturbances in the troposphere. Temperatures are fairly steady in the lower stratosphere, typically hovering between -60 and -70 °F (-50 and -55 °C). Temperatures then increase with height in the rest of the stratosphere, reaching about 28 °F (-2 °C) at the top of the stratosphere, called the *stratopause.* The stratosphere contains most of the atmosphere's ozone. Ozone heats the air by absorbing the sun's ultraviolet rays. This ozone helps protect life on Earth from the harmful ultraviolet radiation of the sun.

The mesosphere extends from the stratopause to roughly 50 miles (80 kilometers) above Earth. The temperature of the mesosphere decreases with altitude. The lowest temperatures in Earth's atmosphere occur at the top of the mesosphere, called the *mesopause*. At the mesopause over the poles, the air temperature can drop below –200 °F (–130 °C) during the summer. Trails of hot gases left by meteors can be seen in the mesosphere. Extremely strong winds blow in this layer. These winds blow from west to east during the winter and from east to west during the summer.

The thermosphere begins at the mesopause and extends into space. It is the thickest layer of the atmosphere by height. The air in the thermosphere is extremely thin. More than 99.99 percent of the atmosphere lies below it.

The thermosphere's chemical composition differs from that of the lower layers of the atmosphere. In the lower regions of the thermosphere, many oxygen molecules are broken into oxygen atoms. The thermosphere's outer layer consists chiefly of hydrogen and helium.

The thermosphere is completely exposed to the sun's ultraviolet radiation, which heats the thin air there to extremely high temperatures. Ordinarily, the temperature climbs rapidly from the mesopause to about 1100 °F (600 °C) at 120 miles (200 kilometers) above Earth and then levels off. But during periods of peak solar activity, more radiation and particles strike the thermosphere. The increased radiation heats the thermosphere to a temperature as high as 4500 °F (2500 °C).

Much of the thermosphere, along with the upper part of the mesosphere, includes a region called the *ionosphere*. When radiation from the sun and from other sources in outer space strikes the air in the thermosphere, it *ionizes* (charges electrically) some of the atoms and molecules of the air. These charged atoms and molecules are called *ions*. The ionosphere plays an important part in long-distance radio communication because it reflects radio waves back to Earth that would otherwise travel into space.

Natural light displays called *auroras* also occur primarily in the ionosphere. The display in the Northern Hemisphere is called the *aurora borealis* or *northern lights*. The display in the Southern Hemisphere is called the *aurora australis* or *southern lights*.

The outer portion of the thermosphere, called the *exosphere*, has so little air that satellites and spacecraft orbiting Earth there encounter almost no resistance. The atoms and molecules of the air in the exosphere move extremely fast. Some travel so fast that they overcome the force of Earth's gravity and escape into space. Earth is thus slowly losing its atmosphere. But it will take billions of years before all the air around Earth disappears.

Origin of the atmosphere

Most scientists believe that Earth formed about 4 ½ billion years ago and probably did not then have an atmosphere. Slowly, gases that escaped from the developing Earth began to accumulate around it. For example, numerous volcanoes on the young Earth released such gases as ammonia, carbon dioxide, carbon monoxide, hydrogen, methane, nitrogen, sulfur dioxide, and water vapor. These volcanic gases made up a large part of Earth's earliest atmosphere.

Much of the water vapor from the volcanoes condensed, forming rivers, lakes, and oceans. Some of the other gases in the early atmosphere dissolved in the oceans or combined with rocks on Earth's surface. But most of the nitrogen stayed in the air. Additional gases, such as argon and xenon, were added by the decay of radioactive elements in Earth.

Before about 2.4 billion years ago, Earth's atmosphere held almost no oxygen. After 2.4 billion years ago, oxygen began to accumulate. Scientists think that single-celled organisms called *cyanobacteria* were the source of this initial oxygen. Like plants, cyanobacteria produce oxygen as a by-product of photosynthesis. The level of atmospheric oxygen varied over time. However, it remained well below current levels until about 750 million to 550 million years ago. Then oxygen began increasing to current levels, eventually even exceeding it at times. Scientists think that the increase in oxygen enabled the development of multicellular life.

A research balloon is inflated with helium in preparation for its launch, *shown here*. Scientific instruments aboard such balloons collect data about Earth's atmosphere.

Where space begins
worldbook.com/sp-14

Changes in the atmosphere

Human activity has caused small but important changes in the composition of the air. The amounts of many gases in the air, such as carbon dioxide, are increasing at significant rates. Carbon dioxide enters the atmosphere whenever coal, oil, or other fuels containing carbon are burned. Since the mid-1700's, the amount of carbon dioxide in the air has increased by about 40 percent, mainly because of the use of such fuels. Levels of methane and nitrous oxide have more than doubled.

Human activity has also added *chlorofluorocarbons* (CFC's) to the atmosphere. CFC's are synthetic substances used as refrigerants in air conditioners and refrigerators and as propellants in aerosol spray products. There were no CFC's in the atmosphere before 1930.

Earth's average surface temperature has risen sharply since the mid-1900's. Most scientists believe the *greenhouse effect* is responsible for most of this global warming. In the greenhouse effect, certain gases in the atmosphere trap heat from the sun, acting much like the glass roof and walls of a greenhouse. The chief greenhouse gases include methane and carbon dioxide. Modern industry has caused significant increases in greenhouse gases. Many scientists believe that CFC's also strengthen the greenhouse effect.

CFC's also weaken Earth's protective layer of ozone. When CFC's drift high in the atmosphere, they break apart and release chlorine atoms. The chlorine reacts with the ozone, converting it into ordinary oxygen molecules. This conversion enables an increased amount of harmful ultraviolet radiation to reach Earth's surface. By 2000, the United States and most other industrialized countries had ended production of CFC's.

The study of air

Since ancient times, people have known that air is important to life. During the 400's B.C., Empedocles, a Greek philosopher, suggested that four elements—air, earth, fire, and water—combined in various proportions to make up all objects in the universe. Many other Greek scholars accepted this theory. In the 300's B.C., the Greek philosopher Aristotle wrote *Meteorologica.* This book contained his thoughts on the earth sciences, including his theories about the nature of air and weather.

The early philosophers and scientists could not test their theories about the air because they had no instruments to measure the air's properties. Around 1600, scientists began to use a type of thermometer to study air. Evangelista Torricelli, an Italian mathematician and physicist, invented the mercury barometer in 1643. In the mid-1600's, the Irish chemist Robert Boyle used the barometer to formulate the relationship between the volume of air and its pressure.

In the 1700's, scientists began to study the gases that make up air. Oxygen was discovered by the Swedish chemist Carl Scheele in the early 1770's and independently by the English chemist Joseph Priestley in 1774. In 1777, Antoine Lavoisier, a French chemist, realized that oxygen in the air enables objects to burn. Daniel Rutherford, a Scottish physician, discovered nitrogen in 1772. In 1894, the Scottish chemist Sir William Ramsay and the English physicist Lord Rayleigh together isolated argon.

During the early 1900's, Norwegian researchers headed by the physicist Vilhelm Bjerknes discovered that the movement of enormous bodies of air, called *air masses,* helps determine weather conditions. The researchers used the term *front* to signify the location where two different air masses meet each other. They found that storms develop along fronts. Their model of weather systems improved the accuracy of weather forecasting.

Today, weather balloons, radars, satellites, and other devices monitor atmospheric conditions, air pollution levels, and changes in the composition of the air. Meteorologists can analyze the data to prepare detailed weather forecasts and to study Earth's climate.

In 1999, the National Aeronautics and Space Administration (NASA) launched Terra, the first of a series of satellites known as the Earth Observing System. Terra monitors clouds, water vapor, aerosol particles, and trace gases in the atmosphere linked to global climate change.　　Todd Miner

Related articles in *World Book.* For a discussion of the atmosphere of other planets, see the separate articles on the planets, such as **Venus** and **Mars.** See also:

Aerodynamics	Lavoisier, An-	Pressure	Torricelli,
Air pollution	toine L.	Priestley,	Evangelista
Air turbulence	Mesosphere	Joseph	Trade wind
Barometer	Nitrogen	Radiosonde	Troposphere
Climate	Oxygen	Stratosphere	Weather
Gas	Ozone	Thermosphere	Wind
Ionosphere	Ozone hole		

Air, Liquid. See Liquid air.

Air bag. See Airbag.

Air brake. See Brake (Air brakes).

Air cleaner, also called an *air purifier,* is a device that removes *contaminants* (impurities) from the air or other gases. Solid contaminants include dust, lint, pollen, and the tiny particles in smoke. Air cleaners also remove unwanted liquid and gaseous contaminants. By removing such contaminants, air cleaners can help prevent both indoor and outdoor air pollution.

Uses. Special types of air cleaners help eliminate pollen and dust in homes, bringing relief to those with hay fever and other allergies. Department stores may use air cleaners to keep merchandise clean and to reduce fire hazard by collecting lint or other burnable material that may be deposited in the ventilation system. Hospitals use air cleaners to prevent the spread of infection.

Without air cleaners, many industries could not operate efficiently. For example, food processing and electronic equipment manufacturing require relatively dust-free air. Air cleaners can lower expense by recirculating conditioned air from heating and air-conditioning systems. Air-cleaning systems also keep exhausted contaminants from reentering the factory. Sometimes industrial dust or odors must be removed to keep the air from harming people in the area nearby. Air cleaners also protect internal-combustion engines and other machinery from excessive wear.

Types of air cleaners. Air cleaners are often designed to remove certain types and amounts of contaminants. Some air-cleaning systems cost more to buy, operate, and maintain than others. Air cleaners are classified according to their principle of operation. The chief types of air cleaners are (1) filtration, (2) electrostatic precipitator, and (3) inertial.

Filtration air cleaners use a dry, uncoated filter made of such materials as wool felt, cotton batting, or cellulose fiber. The filters trap solid particles floating in the air. They come in both cleanable and throwaway types.

Dry filters can hold large amounts of lint. But accumulations can clog the filter pores, slowing the air flow through the filter and reducing effectiveness. The most familiar dry filters are those used in the air cleaners of automobiles and in the heating and cooling systems of homes.

Special dry filters, called HEPA (high efficiency particulate air) filters, can remove more than 99 percent of solid contaminants from the air. They contain such material as pleated cellulose-fiber paper, deep sand beds, a combination of fiberglass and wool, or a compressed fiberglass. The properties of such materials enable HEPA filters to remove from the air pollen, smoke, and tiny dust particles that air cleaners with other types of filters cannot catch.

Electrostatic precipitators are among the most efficient air cleaners in use today. Electrostatic precipitators are especially useful for removing particles of dust and smoke, but they also remove pollen and even bacteria from the air.

Some types of electrostatic precipitators are designed only for cleaning ventilating air in such places as homes, offices, hospitals, and stores. Other types of electrostatic precipitators are widely used in industry to clean air and gas.

An electrostatic precipitator consists of an *ionizer,* through which air passes; a *cell,* also called a *collector,* which removes the contaminant; and a *power pack,* which provides direct-current electric energy. A fan blows the contaminated air past a number of small, electrically charged wires in the ionizer. The particles receive an electric charge. The charged particles are said to be ionized. The ionized particles then pass to the cell, which consists of a series of metal plates. Some of the plates carry a positive charge, but others carry a negative charge. The ionized particles are attracted to the oppositely charged metal plates, because opposite charges attract each other, and like charges repel each other. The particles stick to the metal plates, which can then be cleaned.

Inertial air cleaners use the principle of centrifugal force (see **Centrifugal force**). They change the direction of the air flow so that dirt particles are thrown out of the air stream. Inertial air cleaners are primarily used in industry for the continuous removal of dust, granular material, and other contaminants.

Other types of air cleaners. Absorber cleaners use simple absorbing agents, such as water or alkali, to remove soluble gases in various industrial processes. The gases dissolve into the absorbing agent. *Adsorption* cleaners also remove gases, but the gas collects on the surface of the adsorbing material, instead of dissolving. Such materials include powdered charcoal and silica gel.

Combustion cleaners burn explosive industrial gases at a high temperature to ensure that the gases do not become dangerously concentrated in the air. Combustion cleaners also burn gases that have an unpleasant odor.

Some *scrubber* cleaners use water droplets in steam to wash the air. Scrubber cleaners also absorb gases or collect solid particles with wet filters or containers full of ceramic material.

Other air cleaners create ultraviolet radiation to kill harmful organisms and viruses in the air, or to transform harmful gases into harmless substances. Such cleaners must be used in combination with other filters to actually remove the contaminants.

Sarwan S. Sandhu

Related articles in *World Book* include:
Air conditioning (Cleaning the air)
Air pollution
Filter
Gasoline engine (The fuel system)
Ventilation

Air compressor is a device used to squeeze air into a smaller space, *compressing* it. When you squeeze a balloon, the air inside compresses, pushing back against your hand with force. Air compressors collect that force to power tools and other devices.

A common type of air compressor works on the same principle as a pump. A piston moves back and forth within a hollow cylinder, forcing air into a closed chamber. Pipes or hoses connected to the chamber channel the air to various devices.

Trains and heavy road vehicles have air compressors for powering their brakes (see **Brake** [Air brakes]). Air compressors also provide the air that runs *pneumatic* (air-powered) tools in manufacturing plants, construction sites, and home workshops (see **Pneumatic tool**). Such compressors may be driven by electric motors or by gasoline or diesel engines. *Rotary* (fan-type) compressors are used in gas turbines, jet engines, and other devices.   Evan Powell

See also **Pump** (Axial-flow pumps); **Turbine** (Gas turbines; diagram).

Air conditioning controls the temperature, moisture, cleanliness, and movement of indoor air. It cools the air when the weather is hot. It warms the air when the weather is cold. Comfort depends partly on humidity, and air conditioning removes moisture from the air or adds it as needed. Removing dirt and dust from air makes the air more healthful. By controlling air movement, air conditioning brings fresh air into a room and pushes out stale air. In all these ways, air conditioning provides air that makes people comfortable at work, at play, and while sleeping.

How we use air conditioning

For comfort. When the weather is hot, most people enjoy eating in cool, air-conditioned restaurants. They sleep better in air-conditioned bedrooms. Airplanes, trains, ships, buses, and automobiles that are air conditioned make traveling more pleasant.

Air conditioning helps keep homes clean by taking dirt from the air. It frequently relieves the discomfort that hay-fever victims experience, because it removes pollen from the air. Air-conditioned hospitals protect the health and improve the comfort of patients and hospital staffs.

During cold weather, air conditioning performs much the same services. It supplies clean, moist air that is warmed to the most comfortable temperatures for working and sleeping.

In business and industry, air conditioning improves the efficiency of workers. Employees stay more alert and become less tired in air-conditioned offices and factories. They make fewer mistakes and have fewer accidents. Air conditioning also protects workers against high temperatures and harmful dust, smoke, and fumes. In stores and shops, air conditioning keeps merchandise clean. It also increases sales, because people like to shop in comfort.

Several industries, such as the electronics industry, work with delicate parts and therefore require air-conditioned *clean rooms,* which are free of dust or germs. Companies in these industries make or assemble equipment in such rooms because the tiniest speck of dust could prevent the equipment from working properly.

Large computers become warm when in use and are sensitive to dust. A computer may break down unless air conditioning removes this heat and keeps the surrounding air clean.

Metals and other materials expand as the temperature rises, and contract as the temperature drops. For this reason, air conditioning is used to control the temperature in factories that manufacture tools or parts for instruments, watches, cameras, and other precision products. Changes in temperature would change the size of such products.

Many nonmetallic materials, including textiles, paper, and tobacco, absorb moisture from the air. Too much moisture may make these materials stretch out of shape. Too little moisture in the air makes these materials dry and brittle.

Almost all textile mills use air conditioning to control moisture so they can produce strong, uniform threads and fabrics. Some fibers, such as nylon and rayon, could not be made and woven into cloth without air conditioning. Even the sewing machines that mass-produce nylon stockings require proper temperature control. The nee-

dles of these machines are so small, and operate in such tiny spaces, that sudden temperature changes could cause them to jam and break.

Paper stretches in wet weather, and becomes brittle in dry weather. Air conditioning helps control moisture in printing plants so the paper will remain flexible and stay the same size. This makes possible high-speed printing of newspapers, magazines, and books throughout the year.

In bakeries, air conditioning controls the rising of bread dough. It also keeps flour from molding. Bread that is cooled in air-conditioned rooms has crack-free crusts.

In drug and chemical plants, air conditioning not only provides clean air but also removes germs from air. Air conditioning keeps moisture at the proper level so that powders, salts, and other chemical substances stay dry.

Air-conditioning systems in commercial buildings are being used increasingly for smoke control during fires. By controlling the airflow, the systems provide smoke-free areas for evacuation and fire-fighter access.

How air conditioners work

There are three main kinds of air-conditioning systems. *Summer air conditioning* cleans, cools, and removes moisture from air. *Winter air conditioning* cleans, heats, and adds moisture to air. *Year-round air conditioning* cleans and controls the temperature and moisture content of air throughout the year. All air-conditioning systems have some way of blowing, or circulating, the conditioned air through rooms.

Cleaning the air can be done in several ways. Some air conditioners force the air through *filters.* The filters usually consist of closely packed fiberglass wool or metal fibers that have been coated with a sticky oil or some other type of adhesive (see **Fiberglass**). As the air

How a window air conditioner works   A window air conditioner cools room air by means of a refrigerant. The liquid refrigerant absorbs heat from the air and becomes a vapor as it flows through the evaporator. A compressor pumps the vapor to the condenser, which discharges the heat and turns the vapor back to liquid.

WORLD BOOK diagram by Ramon Goas

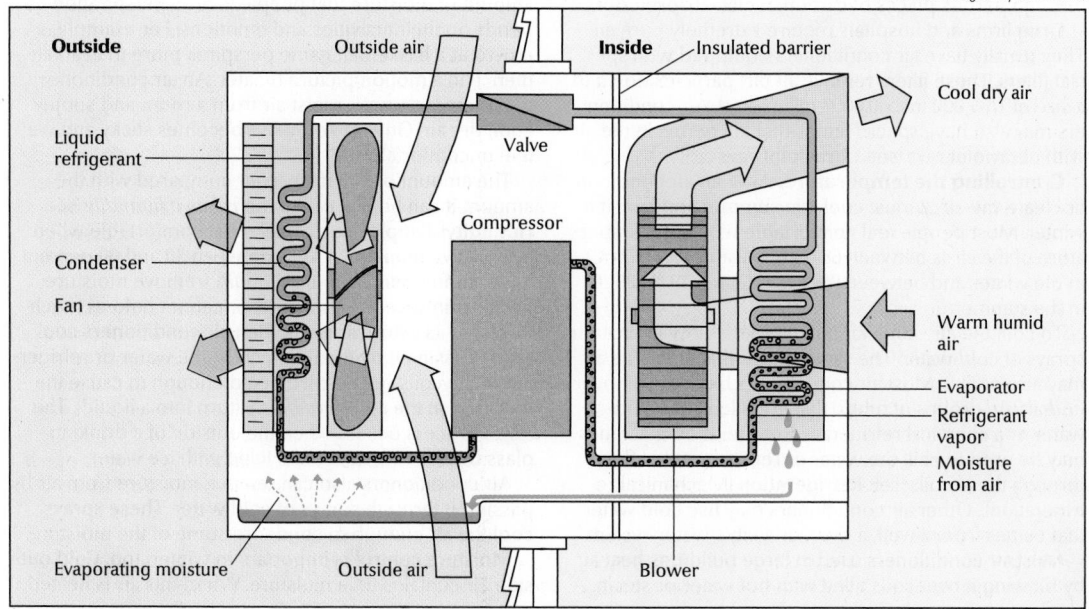

Outside — Outside air — Inside — Insulated barrier — Cool dry air — Liquid refrigerant — Valve — Compressor — Condenser — Fan — Warm humid air — Evaporator — Refrigerant vapor — Moisture from air — Evaporating moisture — Outside air — Blower

How home central air conditioning works

In a home central air conditioner, the refrigerant carries heat outside just as it does in a window unit. A system of *ducts* (pipes) and a blower on a furnace move the air cooled by the evaporator to all the rooms in the building. The compressor and condenser are in a separate unit outside.

WORLD BOOK diagram by Ramon Goas

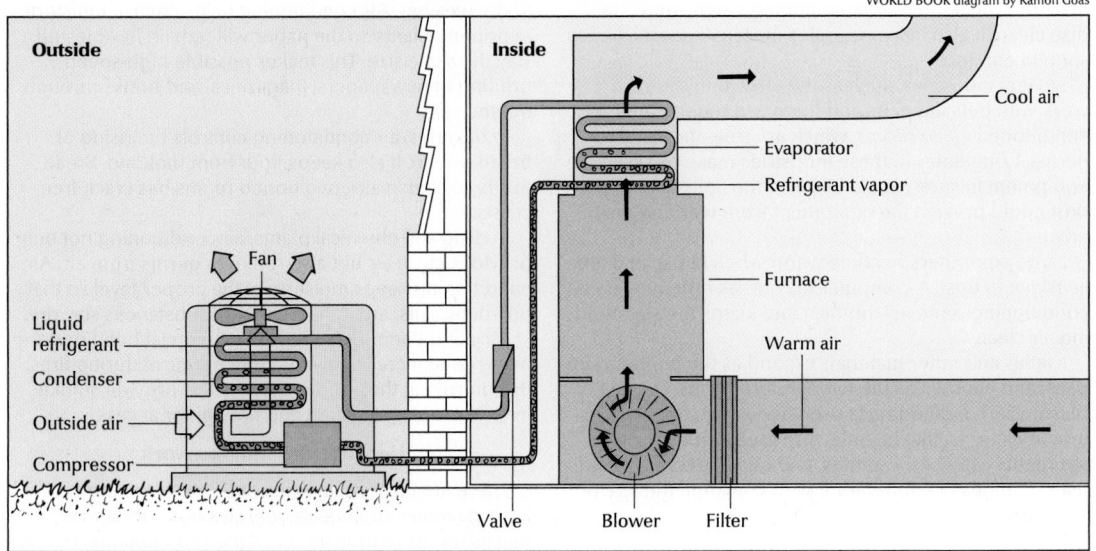

Outside

Inside

Cool air

Evaporator

Refrigerant vapor

Fan

Furnace

Liquid refrigerant

Warm air

Condenser

Outside air

Compressor

Valve   Blower   Filter

passes through, the dirt, dust, and soot in the air stick to the fibers. Air can also be cleaned by blowing it through sprays of water called *air washers*. A central air conditioner that uses this method has a row of nozzles that squirt a fine mist of water into the air. The water rinses out the dirt. Central air conditioners may also be equipped with *electrostatic filters,* or *electrostatic precipitators*. These devices put an electric charge on the particles of dirt in the air. Oppositely charged collector plates attract the charged particles out of the air (see **Air cleaner**). Some central air conditioners force the air through porous pieces of carbon, which absorb odors.

Drug firms and hospitals require extremely pure air. They usually have air conditioners equipped with special filters. These filters remove all dirt particles down to a size of 1/85,000 inch (0.0003 millimeter). Air conditioners may also have special lamps that kill germs in the air with ultraviolet rays (see **Ultraviolet rays**).

Controlling the temperature. After an air conditioner cleans the air, it must cool it in summer and heat it in winter. Most people feel comfortable when the temperature of the air is between 68 °F (20 °C) and 75 °F (24 °C) in the winter and between 73 °F (23 °C) and 79 °F (26 °C) in the summer.

To cool the air, some air conditioners blow it through sprays of cold water. The same sprays that clean the air may also cool it. Most air conditioners blow the air over *coils* (large groups of tubes) that are filled with cold water or a chemical refrigerant. Refrigeration machines may be used to chill the water or refrigerant that flows through these coils (see **Refrigeration** [Mechanical refrigeration]). Other air conditioners may use cold water that comes from a well, a river, or a city's water system.

Most air conditioners used in large buildings heat air by blowing it over coils filled with hot water or steam. A

boiler heated by a gas or oil burner produces the hot water or steam. In some air conditioners, electric heaters warm the air. These heaters have a screen of wires heated by electricity. The air is warmed as it passes through the screen.

Controlling the moisture. The evaporation of moisture from our skin helps cool our bodies. But in summer, air often becomes *humid* (moist). Humid air cannot pick up as much extra moisture as dry air can. We find it difficult to cool off in humid weather, because the air does not absorb the perspiration from our bodies. The amount of moisture that people lose as perspiration depends on their activities and emotions. For example, a crowd at a basketball game perspires more than an audience in a motion-picture theater. An air conditioner must remove warm, moist air from a room and supply cool, dry air. Otherwise, the air becomes sticky and we feel uncomfortable.

The amount of moisture in air compared with the amount it can hold is called the *relative humidity* (see **Humidity**). People usually feel most comfortable when the relative humidity is kept between 30 and 60 percent.

Air conditioners can *dehumidify* (remove moisture from) air in several ways. Cold air cannot hold as much moisture as warm air can. When air conditioners cool air by passing it over cooling coils, the water or refrigerant in the coils can be made cold enough to cause the moisture in the air to *condense* (turn into a liquid). The same process occurs when the outside of a drinking glass becomes moist as it is filled with ice water.

Air conditioners also can remove moisture from air by passing it through sprays of cold water. These sprays cool the air enough to condense some of the moisture.

Moisture control is important in winter, too. Cold outside air contains little moisture. When this air is heated, it becomes extremely dry. Such air dries the skin and may irritate the nose, throat, and lungs. To prevent these discomforts, air conditioners add moisture to the air in cold weather. They do this by passing air through sprays of water or over pans of heated water. The water evaporates into the air.

Circulating the air is important because most people feel uncomfortable in motionless air. The air in a room often becomes filled with moisture and odors. This air must be removed as conditioned air is blown in.

Fans blow conditioned air through the room. The air may be blown in directly or through *ducts* (pipes) that lead to various parts of a building. In large commercial buildings, other fans suck out used air. To eliminate smoke and odors, the fans *exhaust* some of the used air by blowing it out of the building. The remaining used air is returned to the air conditioner, where it is mixed with *ventilation air* drawn in from outside. This mixture of inside and outside air is then conditioned and returned to the cooled room. Eventually, an air conditioner replaces all the air in a room or building with ventilation air drawn in from outside. An air conditioner can circulate air through a room at a rate of about 15 to 40 cubic feet (0.4 to 1.1 cubic meters) per minute. The amount of air circulated through a room depends on the size and speed of the fan used in the air conditioner.

Kinds of air conditioners

Room air conditioners operate on electricity or gas, and are located partly in the room to be cooled. They are enclosed in a single cabinet. They blow the conditioned air directly into the room and do not have air ducts leading to and from them. The three chief types are (1) window air conditioners, (2) consoles, and (3) self-contained air conditioners.

Window air conditioners fit into the lower part of a window and can be moved from window to window. In the air-conditioning industry, these units are called *room air conditioners.*

Consoles are larger than window air conditioners and stand on the floor in the room. They must be near a window or a wall opening in order to obtain outside air.

Self-contained air conditioners are the largest room air conditioners. They may stand 7 feet (2 meters) tall, and can cool an entire large room, such as a restaurant.

Central air conditioners use electricity or gas. They can supply conditioned air to a number of rooms or to an entire building from one central source. Fans blow the conditioned air through air ducts from the air conditioner to the rooms.

Central conditioners have a number of advantages over other kinds. For example, all the equipment for air conditioning a large area is located in one place. This reduces the cost of cleaning and repairing. Central conditioners can also be *zoned.* That is, they can supply air of different temperatures to different parts of a building. A doctor with a crowded waiting room might want cooler air than a lawyer in a smaller office. Zoning makes it possible to serve both their needs.

Combination room and central air conditioners are used in large buildings. They combine the advantages of both types. One kind of combination system has a central conditioner to condition outside air. It circulates the conditioned air to a unit in each room. The room unit controls the temperature and moisture-content of the air.

Another type of combination system furnishes cold water or a refrigerant from a central refrigeration machine to a conditioner in every room. Each room conditioner has a fan, filter, and cooling coils to condition and circulate the air.

A third variety of combination system conditions a mixture of outside and inside air. This system supplies each room with cool, conditioned air through one duct, and warmed, conditioned air through another duct. A *mixing-box* unit in each room mixes the two air streams to provide the right temperature. Combination systems have the advantage of supplying conditioned air or a cooling fluid from a central source. This cuts the cost of maintaining them. At the same time, the individual room units allow the people in each room to adjust the temperature to suit their wishes.

Air conditioners for vehicles. In automobiles, the refrigeration unit is located under the hood near the engine. The engine drives the unit by means of a belt connected to the engine. Air ducts feed the conditioned air into the car.

Buses often have a separate motor to drive the refrigerating equipment. This equipment may be located either in the rear of the bus or under one side near the luggage compartment. The air conditioner is in the roof of the bus. It supplies cool, conditioned air to the seats through ducts running along the roof.

In a railroad passenger car, an electric motor or a gasoline engine drives a refrigeration unit located under the car. The air conditioner is mounted over the entrance at one end of the car. Fans in the conditioner blow the air through ducts to outlets that are located in the car.

Airplanes require special air-conditioning units. Much of the equipment is made of aluminum to save weight. The refrigeration and air-conditioning units for large airplanes are usually located in the wings. In smaller aircraft, these units may be in the body of the airplane. Air turbines drive the refrigeration equipment. Air ducts feed the conditioned air to different parts of the airplane.

On ships, the refrigeration equipment is installed in the engine room or in a mechanical equipment room. The air-conditioning units are located throughout the ship. Air-conditioning equipment for ships must be extra strong to withstand the rolling and pitching motion of the water. Special metals are used to resist corrosion by seawater.

Choosing a window air conditioner

Two facts should be kept in mind when selecting a window air conditioner. (1) The *capacity* (cooling power) of the air conditioner should be suitable for the room. (2) The electric power requirements for the air conditioner must match the electric system available for it.

Capacity of air conditioners. The size of a room and the number of people using it help determine the capacity of the air conditioner needed. So do the number, size, and direction of the windows in a room, the wattage of appliances and lights, and the amount of wall insulation.

An air conditioner that has a lower capacity than

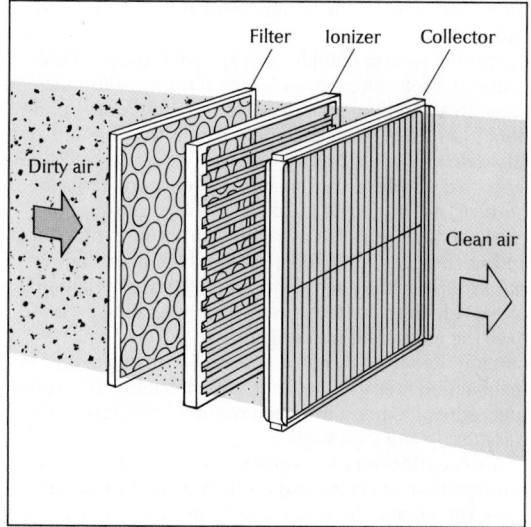

Filter   Ionizer   Collector

Dirty air

Clean air

WORLD BOOK diagram by Ramon Goas

An electrostatic filter, also called an *electrostatic precipitator,* removes particles of dust and smoke from the air. The ionizer gives the particles an electric charge. The oppositely charged collector then attracts and holds the particles.

needed will not keep a room cool. An oversized unit will control the temperature, but it may not reduce excess humidity. Such a unit will run only a short time before the temperature falls. It may not even run long enough to remove much moisture from the air.

Manufacturers rate the capacity of air conditioners in four ways: (1) British thermal units, (2) watts and kilowatts, (3) tons of refrigeration, and (4) horsepower.

British thermal units. One British thermal unit (Btu) equals the amount of heat needed to raise the temperature of 1 pound (0.45 kilogram) of water from 59 to 60 °F (15 to 15.56 °C). The *Btu per hour* rating is the basic measurement for air conditioning and should always be used to specify the capacity of an air conditioner. An air conditioner with a capacity of 12,000 Btu's per hour can remove enough heat from the air it is conditioning to raise 12,000 pounds (5,440 kilograms) of water one degree Fahrenheit each hour. The cooling capacities of room air conditioners range from 4,000 to 36,000 Btu's per hour.

Watts and kilowatts are the units used to measure air-conditioner capacity in the metric system. One watt equals 3.4 Btu's per hour.

Tons of refrigeration. One ton of refrigeration removes the amount of heat needed to melt 1 ton (0.9 metric ton) of ice at 32 °F (0 °C) in 24 hours. A one-ton air-conditioning unit can remove 288,000 Btu's of heat in 24 hours, or 12,000 Btu's per hour (3,510 watts). A two-ton air-conditioning unit can remove twice this amount, and so on.

Horsepower measures the power needed to run the refrigeration equipment that cools the air. One horsepower equals 745.7 watts.

Electric power requirements. Local electrical codes govern the kind of motor that can be connected to different kinds of electrical systems. Most air conditioners that have a capacity rating of up to 14,000 Btu's per hour

operate on 110-volt, single-phase current. Larger air conditioners need either 220-volt or 220-440-volt, three-phase current. See **Electric generator** (Kinds of AC generators).

Different air conditioners use various amounts of electric power to remove the same amount of heat. Engineers use a number, called the Energy Efficiency Ratio (EER), to measure how economically an air conditioner uses electric power. To find an air conditioner's EER, its Btu per hour rating is divided by the number of watts of electric power used by the unit. For example, an air conditioner that uses 600 watts to remove 5,000 Btu's per hour has an EER of 5,000 divided by 600, or 8.33. Most air conditioners have an EER of from 8 to 9. The higher the EER of a unit, the less electric power it uses—and the less it costs to operate.

History

The ancient Egyptians, Greeks, and Romans used wet mats to cool indoor air. They hung the mats over the doors to their tents and other dwellings. When wind blew through the mats, evaporation of the water cooled the air. The people of India later used this method to cool the royal palaces. About 1500, Leonardo da Vinci, the great Italian artist and scientist, built the first mechanical fan to provide ventilation. Water power turned the fan. In 1553, the English developed a rotary fan to ventilate mines.

Textile manufacturers made the first attempts at air conditioning. In 1719, a silk company in Derwent, England, installed a central system to heat and ventilate its mill. Early cloth makers in New England boiled water in huge pots near their looms to keep the air moist. Unfortunately, the heat injured the health of the workers and this method was discontinued.

About 1838, David B. Reid, an English scientist, provided the British House of Commons with a system to ventilate and humidify the air. In the mid-1800's, John Gorrie, an American, invented a cold-air machine to cool hospital rooms.

During the late 1800's, textile manufacturers in New England began using sprays of water to condition the air in their mills. In 1897, Joseph McCreery of Toledo, Ohio, received a patent for the type of spray now used in air conditioners.

By 1902, Alfred R. Wolff, a consulting engineer, had designed air-cooling systems for Carnegie Hall and several other buildings in New York City. That same year, Willis H. Carrier, a research engineer, designed the first scientific system to clean, circulate, and control the humidity of air.

In 1906, Stuart W. Cramer, a textile engineer from Charlotte, North Carolina, used the term *air conditioning* for the first time. Air conditioning became a recognized branch of engineering in 1911.

The Baltimore & Ohio Railroad installed the first air-conditioning system for trains in 1931. Air conditioning of apartments and homes also began during the 1930's. In 1939, Packard Motors introduced air-conditioning units for automobiles. The Greyhound Corporation installed the first bus air-conditioning systems in 1940. By the early 2010's, about 90 percent of all housing in the United States had some form of air conditioning. In addition, most of the new single-family homes that were built in the United States were equipped with central air conditioning.

Careers in air conditioning

Careers in air conditioning can be divided into five main fields: (1) designing, (2) manufacturing, (3) selling, (4) installing and servicing, and (5) teaching and research. College-educated engineers research and design air-conditioning systems. Skilled machinists, toolmakers, cabinetmakers, and similar craftworkers help manufacture air conditioners. Technical training, such as a degree in engineering, is often essential for positions in the selling and executive branches of air conditioning. Specially trained technicians, and operating and service engineers, install and maintain air conditioners.

James E. Hill

Related articles in *World Book* include:

Air	Heat pump	Refrigeration
Air cleaner	Heating	Solar energy
Air pollution	Humidifier	Thermostat
Heat	Humidity	Ventilation

Air-cooled engine. See Gasoline engine (Cooling).

Air cushion vehicle (ACV) is an *amphibious* (land and water) craft that travels on a layer of compressed air just above any kind of surface. The compressed air serves as an invisible cushion that eliminates almost all friction between the vehicle and the surface. ACV's, which are also known as *hovercraft,* can carry passengers, vehicles, and freight. Some ACV's can travel as fast as 80 miles (130 kilometers) per hour.

How an ACV works. An air cushion vehicle has one or more fans that suck air into the craft. The fans force the air underneath the vehicle, creating an air cushion between the ACV and the surface. ACV's are sometimes called *ground effect machines* because they use the surface to help trap the air.

A flexible rubberized skirt surrounds the lower edge of most ACV's. It fills with air forced in by the fans. The skirt enables the vehicle to travel over such rough obstacles as rocks and waves. Some ACV's have skirts only across the bow and stern. Rigid sidehulls run along the length of the craft. Such ACV's are called *surface effect ships* (SES's). They can be used only in water.

Gas turbines or lightweight diesel engines provide the power for the fans, and propellers drive the ACV forward. Most ACV's have small doors called *puff ports* and either rudders or propellers for steering. These

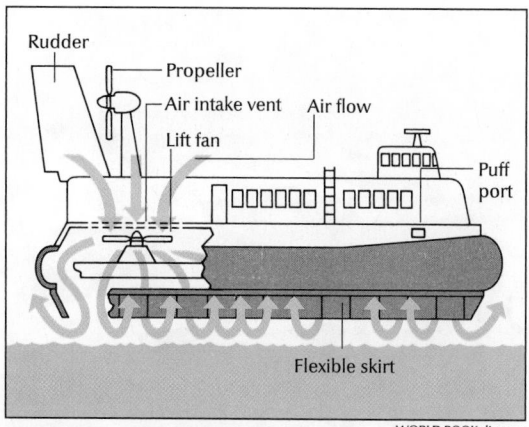

WORLD BOOK diagram

A "cushion" of air under pressure supports an air cushion vehicle. A powerful fan creates the cushion by blowing air beneath the vehicle's flexible skirt. A propeller drives the craft forward. The pilot steers the vehicle with an airplane-type rudder.

three devices enable the vehicle to travel backward, forward, or sideways, or to hover or turn.

History. ACV principles were recognized as early as the mid-1800's, but the technology did not exist for building a practical model. In the early 1900's, a limited number were built. The Austrian Navy demonstrated one in 1916. In the mid-1950's, Christopher Cockerell, an English inventor, improved the basic design. In the early 1960's, Japan, the Soviet Union, the United Kingdom, the United States, and other countries all tested ACV's.

In the late 1960's, the U.S. Navy and Army began to use ACV's in the Vietnam War for patrol duty and rescue missions. In 1968, the British began to use ACV's to carry passengers and cars across the English Channel. Development of *hoverbarges*—that is, ACV's that are pulled or pushed by another vehicle—began in the 1960's. In 1972, Canadian researchers discovered that ACV's could be used to break ice on waterways.

Today, manufacturers produce a number of models that vary in size, speed, and power. Modern ACV's accomplish many tasks. However, most ACV's are used for military missions. Russia and the United States are the world's largest users of the craft.

In the late 1950's, Jean Bertin, a French engineer, invented a special train called a *tracked air cushion vehicle* (TACV) or *air train.* This train ran only on land, and it required special tracks. It did not actually touch the tracks but used them as a guide. The train had a *linear electric motor,* which included electromagnets in the underside of the vehicle (see **Linear electric motor**). The tracked air cushion vehicle was powered by magnetic forces between the track and the electromagnets. It could also be powered by an auxiliary jet engine.

A vehicle called a *magnetic levitation train,* or *maglev train,* resembles the TACV. But a maglev train relies on a magnetic force between the vehicle and the guide rail—rather than on a cushion of compressed air—to hold the vehicle above the track.

Paul F. Johnston

Air embolism. See Diving, Underwater (Dangers of underwater diving).

Textron Marine Systems

An air cushion vehicle can travel on land or on water. This vehicle is a U.S. Navy Landing Craft, Air Cushion (LCAC). It can cross rough shores to land troops and equipment.

Fighter planes attack enemy aircraft and ground targets. In this photograph, three CF-18 Hornet fighters from the Canadian Air Force practice a maneuver. A Hornet fighter can carry missiles and other weapons at the tips of its wings and under its wings and main body.

Air force

Air force is the branch of a nation's armed forces responsible for military operations in the air. An air force consists of pilots and other personnel, aircraft, support equipment, and military bases. Some air forces also have guided missiles and spacecraft.

Most countries have some type of air force. More powerful nations have an independent air force equal in rank to the other branches of the nation's armed forces. These countries usually also have an air force unit in their army and navy. Many smaller, less powerful nations have an air unit as part of their army or navy.

Air forces differ greatly in size and fighting strength, depending on a nation's wealth, technology, and national defense needs. The large air forces of industrialized nations have modern bombers, fighters, transport planes, helicopters, and other aircraft. Most developing nations cannot afford the advanced technology required to build a modern air force. But some have assembled relatively strong air forces through loans and trade with industrialized nations. Many smaller developing nations have air forces that consist of older aircraft.

The United States and Russia have the most powerful and complex air forces. These forces include thousands

Timothy M. Laur, the contributor of this article, is a consultant and lecturer on military issues. He is a retired lieutenant colonel in the United States Air Force and author of An Encyclopedia of Modern Military Weapons.

of aircraft and long-range missiles, some with nuclear warheads. Other powerful nations, including China, France, and the United Kingdom, also have such missiles.

Until the development of airplanes and guided missiles in the 1900's, nations relied on armies and navies for military power. The operations of these forces, however, are limited by land and sea barriers. Today, armies and navies remain extremely important. But the main striking force of the most powerful nations consists of airplanes and guided missiles.

The role of air forces

A nation's air force may have several different roles depending on the country's security needs. Air forces within an army or navy support the operations of that branch. A navy's air force, for example, may operate attack and *reconnaissance* (observation) planes from aircraft carriers to obtain information about operations in enemy territory. A navy's air force may also patrol its country's coastline. An air force that serves as a separate military branch, however, usually has several roles related to establishing control of the air. These roles include (1) combat, (2) defense, and (3) transport.

Combat missions involve fighting directly against an enemy force. The two chief types of combat missions are *strategic* and *tactical.* In strategic missions, air forces operate over long distances, usually traveling from one continent to another. The most common strategic missions involve attacks with bombs and long-range missiles against specific targets in enemy cities and industrial areas. Strategic attacks are designed to destroy the enemy's ability and desire to fight.

Tactical missions are short- or medium-range operations carried out in cooperation with ground or sea forces in battle. Such missions include attacks on enemy ground forces and *counter air tactical missions.* In these missions, fighter planes may attack enemy aircraft to gain control of the air over a battle area. In *interdiction attacks,* aircraft strike transportation networks and other targets behind enemy lines. Such attacks prevent enemy forces and supplies from reaching the battlefield.

Defense missions protect a nation's territory from enemy attack. Advanced air forces use radar stations and satellites to detect surprise attacks by enemy bombers or missiles. In case of such an attack, an air force uses missiles and fighter planes to shoot down enemy bombers and missiles.

The threat of a counterattack can also serve as part of a nation's air defenses, especially among nations that have nuclear weapons. Nations may avoid launching a nuclear attack because of their fear of a counterattack.

Transport missions, also called *airlifts,* support a nation's combat operations by moving troops and equipment quickly by air. In a strategic airlift, aircraft transport troops and equipment over long distances. A tactical airlift provides air support to battlefield operations. For example, aircraft may drop paratroopers and supplies in a battle area or behind enemy lines. In peacetime, air forces may transport food and other supplies to areas struck by disaster.

Other missions include reconnaissance and air rescue. Reconnaissance missions gather military information using visual observation, or cameras, radar, and other sensing devices aboard aircraft and satellites. Air rescue missions use small airplanes or helicopters to rescue people trapped in dangerous areas.

The organization of air forces

The leader of an independent air force may be a chief of staff or air marshal and hold the rank of general. In the U.S. Air Force, however, the highest authority is the secretary of the Air Force, a civilian appointed by the president. Air forces of smaller countries often come under the command of the army or navy.

The *squadron* is the basic administrative unit of air forces. A squadron usually consists of aircraft of one type or model. Most fighter and attack squadrons have 18 to 24 assigned aircraft, which are usually grouped into smaller units of 2 to 4 planes called *flights.* Bomber squadrons typically have from 10 to 19 assigned aircraft. Two or more squadrons form units called *groups* or *wings.* In large air forces, these units may combine to form larger *divisions* or *commands.*

Aircraft and missiles

Aircraft are usually classified by their function. The main types of aircraft are (1) attack and fighter aircraft, (2) bombers, (3) transport aircraft, and (4) reconnaissance aircraft.

Attack and fighter aircraft are designed for speed and maneuverability in combat. They usually have a crew of one or two and carry missiles or bombs, depending on their mission. These aircraft attack enemy planes and ground targets or defend against air attacks.

Shaun Harris, Photo Press

Paratroopers drop from planes into battle areas or behind enemy lines, often surprising the enemy. *Above,* paratroopers from Britain's Royal Air Force train for an assault by air.

Bombers are usually large, medium-range or long-range planes that carry a combination of bombs and guided missiles for striking strategic targets. Only a few nations with powerful air forces have bombers. Bomber crews range in size from about four to six people.

Transport aircraft carry troops or cargo. The crew of a typical transport plane includes a pilot, copilot, navigator, flight engineer, and one or more *loadmasters* responsible for the cargo or passengers.

Reconnaissance aircraft carry cameras or electronic sensors to gather information about enemy forces. Reconnaissance aircraft include both airplanes specifically designed for reconnaissance and modified versions of other aircraft.

Other aircraft include trainers, tankers, and helicopters. Trainers are used to train pilots. Tankers refuel other aircraft in flight. Some helicopters transport troops and equipment over short distances. Others, called *helicopter gunships,* carry guns and missiles and are used in combat.

Missiles used by air forces may be launched from the ground or from aircraft. Ground-launched strategic missiles include intercontinental ballistic missiles (ICBM's) and intermediate-range ballistic missiles (IRBM's). ICBM's can deliver a nuclear warhead to a target up to 9,200 miles (15,000 kilometers) away. IRBM's can reach

Sovfoto

Russian-made MiG aircraft, such as this MiG-29K fighter from the Russian Air Force, are common in the world's air forces. India, Poland, and many other countries fly MiG's.

from about 1,700 to 3,400 miles (2,700 to 5,500 kilometers). In some nations, such as the United States, the air force is responsible for ICBM's. But in other nations, including China and Russia, these missiles fall under a separate command. Air forces defend against ballistic missile attacks with ground-launched antiballistic missiles (ABM's).

Air-launched missiles include both strategic and tactical missiles. Bombers carry air-launched strategic missiles, such as the cruise missile, that can hit targets hundreds of miles or kilometers away. Fighter and attack aircraft and helicopters fire tactical air-to-air missiles (AAM's) at enemy aircraft and air-to-surface missiles (ASM's) at ground targets.

Major air forces of the world

The power of an air force depends on the quality of its technology, training, and equipment. The world's most powerful air forces have advanced aircraft, well-trained crews, and efficient maintenance and supply systems. They include the air forces of the United States, China, Russia, India, France, North Korea, Germany, the United Kingdom, and Israel. Other important air forces include those of Italy, Turkey, and Ukraine. However, these forces are smaller and less technologically advanced.

The United States Air Force has about 2,800 combat aircraft, including about 1,300 fighter and attack aircraft and about 140 bombers on active duty. The Air National Guard also has about 580 fighter and attack aircraft, and the Air Force Reserve has about 125. The Air Force also operates several satellite and radar systems. It has about 320,000 active members, along with about 70,000 in the Air Force Reserve. An additional 105,000 people serve in Air National Guard units, which are administered by the states. The U.S. Air Force commands about 400 ICBM's but no IRBM's. Under a 1987 treaty, the United States and the Soviet Union agreed to eliminate their IRBM's.

The U.S. Army, Navy, Marine Corps, and Coast Guard all have their own air force units. The U.S. Navy has a large air arm with thousands of combat airplanes and hundreds of helicopters. The U.S. Army air unit includes thousands of helicopters.

The Chinese Air Force has about 2,400 combat planes. Many of its planes are based on Russian designs. About 400,000 people serve in the Air Force. China's Navy operates hundreds of additional combat aircraft. China also has about 100 ICBM's and IRBM's under a separate strategic force.

The Russian Air Force has about 1,200 active combat aircraft, primarily fighters. The Air Force has about 165,000 members. A separate strategic force controls about 330 ICBM's. Another force for space operations launches and operates military satellites. The Russian Navy's aviation branch has hundreds of additional combat airplanes and armed helicopters.

The Indian Air Force has about 810 combat aircraft. India's Air Force also controls a large arsenal of surface-to-air missiles. About 127,000 people serve in the Air Force. India's naval air force has additional combat airplanes and armed helicopters.

The French Air Force has about 290 combat aircraft, mostly fighter and attack planes. The force has about 41,000 members. A separate strategic air force operates about 20 bombers equipped with IRBM's. The French Navy has hundreds of additional combat airplanes and helicopters.

The North Korean Air Force has about 550 active combat planes. About 110,000 people serve in the Air Force.

The German air force, called the Luftwaffe, includes about 220 active attack and fighter aircraft, with additional combat airplanes and armed helicopters in the navy's air unit. About 28,000 people serve in the Luftwaffe.

The British air force, called the Royal Air Force (RAF), has about 250 active combat aircraft, mostly fighter and attack airplanes. It has about 33,000 members. The Royal Navy's air arm has hundreds of additional combat airplanes and helicopters.

The Israeli Air Force has about 350 active combat planes, and about 140 armed helicopters. The Air Force has about 34,000 members.

History

Early air forces. The first air force was established by France in 1794, during a war against several other Eu-

Skilled pilots are essential to an effective air force. Like all military pilots, this pilot from the Chinese Air Force must spend many hours training before he can fly sophisticated aircraft into dangerous combat areas.

Bettmann

The first air force was a French balloon corps, formed in 1794. Before airplanes were invented in 1903, warring nations used balloons to observe enemy troops and to drop bombs.

ropean nations. The air force flew large balloons filled with hot air or gas. The French used the balloons to observe movements of enemy troops.

The first air attack took place in 1849. Austria controlled much of Italy at that time, and the people of Venice revolted. The Austrians sent unmanned balloons carrying time bombs over the city. Some of the bombs exploded as planned. But the wind changed direction and blew several balloons back over the Austrian troops, where the rest of the bombs exploded.

During the American Civil War (1861-1865), both the Union and Confederate armies used balloons. The Union Army organized a balloon corps to direct artillery fire and observe Confederate troop movements. Almost every major army in the world soon established a balloon corps.

Balloons became much less important in warfare after Orville and Wilbur Wright made the world's first airplane flight in 1903. By 1909, France, Germany, Britain, Russia, and the United States had purchased planes for their armed forces. In 1912, Britain established the Royal Flying Corps as the air arm of the Royal Army and Navy. In 1918, the corps became the Royal Air Force, the first independent air force.

World War I began in 1914. In the war, the Allies, who included Britain, France, Russia, and the United States, fought the Central Powers, who included Germany and Austria-Hungary. At that time, most airplanes

flew at a maximum speed of about 75 miles (120 kilometers) per hour. They could reach an altitude of about 10,000 feet (3,000 meters). By 1918, when the war ended, the maximum speed of aircraft had reached about 120 miles (190 kilometers) per hour, and maximum altitude had more than doubled. Planes also had become much more maneuverable.

At the beginning of the war, the fighting nations used planes only for observing enemy ground movements. Aircraft soon began to exchange gunfire, but many could not shoot forward because the plane's propeller was in front. Bullets might shatter the spinning blades of the propeller. In 1915, a Dutch designer, Anthony Fokker, developed a machine gun for the Germans that fired only when the propeller blades were not blocking the muzzle. The Allies began to use a similar gun in 1917.

During the war, pilots fought air battles called *dogfights,* and fliers who shot down five or more enemy planes became known as *aces.* Toward the end of the war, battles between squadrons of airplanes replaced most combat between single pilots. Early in the war, pilots had dropped bombs by hand. Later, they used mechanical devices to release the bombs. By 1917, some planes could carry up to 3,000 pounds (1,400 kilograms) of bombs.

In September 1918, American officer Billy Mitchell directed the largest air assault of the war. He commanded about 1,500 Allied aircraft in a mission over St.-Mihiel in France, where the Germans had advanced. The Allied planes gained control of the air, dropped bombs behind the German lines, and attacked enemy ground forces. Two months later, the Allies won the war.

The growth of national air forces. Although many nations reduced their armed forces after World War I, the success of the airplane caused them to gradually develop their airpower. This policy often produced competition between a country's new air service and older army and navy. In the United States, for example, Billy Mitchell and other aviation leaders argued vigorously for greater emphasis on airpower. Mitchell became so bitter in his criticism of the U.S. defense program that he was court-martialed for defying his superior officers. In 1946, after events had confirmed many of Mitchell's predictions, he was awarded the Medal of Honor, the nation's highest military decoration. During the 1920's and early 1930's, France, Germany, Italy, and Sweden formed independent air forces.

World War II. Airpower played a vital role in deciding the outcome of World War II. In the war, Germany, Italy, Japan, and other Axis powers fought the Allies, who included Britain, Canada, China, the Soviet Union, and the United States.

The war began in 1939 when Germany invaded Poland. The Germans used a new method of warfare called *blitzkrieg* (lightning war). Germany's air force, the Luftwaffe, bombed Polish troops, destroyed airfields, and struck at key cities, highways, and railroads. On the ground, tanks and infantry overwhelmed the Polish forces. Between April and June 1940, Germany attacked and defeated Denmark, Norway, Luxembourg, the Netherlands, Belgium, and France.

The Germans planned to invade Britain next, but first they had to defeat the Royal Air Force. In July 1940, the

Luftwaffe started to bomb British ships and ports. German air raids on London began in September. The RAF was outnumbered, but it had better planes and pilots than the Luftwaffe. The British also had developed radar and a decoding device that enabled them to read coded German messages. Both developments were carefully guarded secrets that helped the RAF intercept Luftwaffe raids. By October, the RAF had shot down more than 1,700 attacking planes and had lost about 900 of its own. Germany postponed its plans to invade the United Kingdom, but air raids on British cities continued.

The United States entered the war on Dec. 8, 1941, the day after about 360 Japanese aircraft attacked the United States fleet at Pearl Harbor in Hawaii. The attack destroyed or damaged 21 ships and more than 300 planes, temporarily crippling the Pacific Fleet and Hawaii's air defense.

In mid-1942, American airpower halted Japanese advances in the Pacific in two important battles at sea. In the Battle of the Coral Sea, in May, each side attacked the other with planes launched from aircraft carriers. The opposing warships never got close enough to see or fire on an enemy ship. Japan lost more planes, but fewer ships, than the United States lost in the battle. Neither side won, but the battle prevented a Japanese assault on New Guinea. A month later, in the Battle of Midway, Japan lost 4 aircraft carriers and more than 200 planes. The United States lost 1 carrier and about 150 airplanes. The battle blunted Japan's naval strength for the rest of the war and ended the threat of a Japanese attack on Hawaii and the United States.

By mid-1942, Japan had captured large parts of China and had cut off the country's main supply routes. To help China continue fighting Japan, Allied forces flew supplies from India to China over the Himalaya, the world's tallest mountain range. This dangerous route was called the "Hump." During this airlift, which lasted almost three years, the Allies carried about 650,000 tons (590,000 metric tons) of supplies to China.

The Allies attacked Germany in 1943. The United Kingdom and the United States started a bombing offensive that lasted almost until the end of the war. The RAF bombed German cities at night, and American planes attacked enemy industries during the day. In 1944, the Luftwaffe began to use jet fighter planes. These planes could fly nearly 550 miles (885 kilometers) per hour, compared with about 400 miles (640 kilometers) per hour for propeller-driven fighters. Germany also developed the first guided missiles, the V-1 and V-2. In 1944 and 1945, the Germans fired more than 12,000 missiles at enemy cities. But these technological advances came too late to affect the outcome of the war. Germany surrendered in May 1945.

In August 1945, American B-29 bombers dropped atomic bombs on the Japanese cities of Hiroshima and Nagasaki. The bombers had flown from Tinian Island, 1,360 miles (2,189 kilometers) away. Japan surrendered in September, and the war ended.

The development of jet aircraft in the late 1930's and early 1940's greatly increased the range and speed of attacking planes. In 1939, a German Heinkel He 178 made the first successful jet-powered flight. By 1944, Germany had developed the Messerschmitt Me 262, the first jet to fly combat missions. The first American jet

plane, the Bell XP-59, flew in 1942 but was little used in World War II. After the war, several nations, including the United Kingdom, the Soviet Union, and the United States, rapidly developed jet-powered air forces. Soon each of these nations operated a fleet of jet fighters and long-range bombers. By the late 1950's, France and China also began developing jet-powered air forces.

Air forces in the nuclear age. The United States emerged as the most powerful nation at the end of World War II. It was the only nation with atomic weapons and the aircraft to use them. But the Soviet Union soon began to challenge the United States, competing for power and international influence in a struggle known as the Cold War. In 1949, the Soviet Union tested its first atomic bomb. Several other nations have developed nuclear weapons since then.

The Soviet Union successfully tested its first ICBM in 1957, several months before the first successful United States test. The Soviets also launched the first space satellite in 1957. The United States and the Soviet Union competed for supremacy in missiles and space. They also developed *antiballistic missiles* (ABM's) designed to destroy enemy missiles in flight. To provide warning of a missile attack, the two nations set up missile detection systems on the ground and in space.

By the late 1960's, the number of missiles and nuclear warheads had grown alarmingly large. In 1969, the United States and the Soviet Union began a series of conferences in an effort to limit each country's missile strength. After several more conferences in the 1970's and 1980's, they agreed to eliminate their IRBM's. See **Arms control.**

Many smaller nations established strong air forces during the 1980's by obtaining aircraft from the United States or the Soviet Union. These nations included Finland, Hungary, Kuwait, and Saudi Arabia.

The Soviet Union began withdrawing its forces from Eastern Europe in 1990. In 1991, the United States and the Soviet Union agreed to reduce their long-range missiles and bombers, including their ICBM forces, by about a third. They also ended a continuous alert for long-range bombers carrying nuclear weapons and took other steps to reduce the threat of a nuclear air attack. This alert had been in effect in the United States since 1957. In late 1991, the Soviet Union broke up. These developments reduced the threat of nuclear war and the need for huge armed forces. As a result, most major air forces made cuts in personnel and equipment during the 1990's.

Air forces in limited wars. Fear of a massive nuclear war has helped prevent nations with nuclear weapons from using them. In all wars since World War II, nations restricted the weapons they used, the targets they attacked, and the areas of battle to avoid a nuclear conflict. In such *limited wars,* air forces played an important role.

The Korean War (1950-1953) brought the first combat between jet aircraft. The United States and other members of the United Nations aided South Korea, and the Soviet Union and China assisted North Korea. United States military leaders limited attacks on military targets, but airplanes often fought each other. As many as 150 jet fighters took part in some air battles. Each side adopted the principle of *asylum,* which allowed aircraft to withdraw from the battle zone without being pursued. Neither side won complete victory in this war.

During the Vietnam War (1957-1975), the United States supported South Vietnam, and the Soviet Union and China backed North Vietnam and the Viet Cong rebels of South Vietnam. From 1965 to 1968, the U.S. Air Force and the air arm of the U.S. Navy conducted frequent bombing raids against North Vietnam and later attacked targets in South Vietnam, Cambodia, and Laos. The U.S. Air Force used helicopter gunships to locate and attack enemy forces in the jungles and mountains. United States helicopters also rescued downed aviators, transported the wounded, and carried supplies and troops. In 1969, the United States began withdrawing its troops from Vietnam. The United States removed the last of its troops and stopped its air attacks in 1973. Two years later, the war ended with a North Vietnamese and Viet Cong victory.

Wars in the Middle East. In 1967, the Israeli Air Force destroyed most of the air forces of Egypt, Jordan, and Syria in the Six-Day War. Egypt rebuilt its air force and, in 1973, staged a surprise attack with Syria against Israel. For a brief period, Egypt established control of the skies. Israel's airpower, however, regained control and helped drive back the attackers. An airlift of supplies from the United States also helped Israel win the war.

In the Persian Gulf War of 1991, airpower played a decisive role. In that war, a U.S.-led coalition drove Iraq out of Kuwait. Before the war began, the coalition moved huge amounts of equipment to the Persian Gulf region in one of the largest airlifts in history. Coalition air forces began the war in mid-January 1991 with massive bombing of targets in Iraq and Kuwait. The U.S. Air Force used precision-guided bombs and the F-117 "stealth" fighter-bomber. The design and surface materials of "stealth" aircraft make them difficult to detect with radar. The coalition quickly gained control of the air, destroying many Iraqi aircraft on the ground and forcing others to flee to Iran. When the coalition launched a ground attack in late February, the air war had so devastated the Iraqis that they surrendered within days.

In the Iraq War (2003-2011), a U.S.-led coalition sought to rid Iraq of banned weapons and to remove Iraqi dictator Saddam Hussein from power. The war started in March with intense bombing by coalition air forces of targets related to air defense, weapons systems, and the leadership of Iraq's ruling Baath Party. In April, after extensive air attacks against Iraqi ground troops, coalition ground forces captured Baghdad, Iraq's capital, ending Hussein's rule. Nearly every bomb dropped in the war was precision-guided by laser or satellite. The main combat phase of the war ended in May 2003. Coalition forces, facing strong opposition from Iraqi militants, remained in Iraq until late 2011.

Timothy M. Laur

Related articles in *World Book* include:

Wars

Afghanistan War	Vietnam War
Iraq War	World War I
Korean War	World War II
Persian Gulf War of 1991	

Weapons and equipment

Aircraft, Military	Balloon (Balloons	Guided missile
Airplane (Military	in war)	Helicopter
planes)	Bomb	Machine gun
Airship	Bomber	Nuclear weapon

Parachute	Unmanned aerial vehicle
Radar (In the military)	V/STOL
Rocket (Military use)	

Other related articles

Ace	Aircraft carrier	Luftwaffe
Aerospace	Amphibious	National Guard
medicine	warfare	Space exploration
Air Force, U.S.	Aviation	Test pilot
Airborne troops	Logistics	

Outline

I. **The role of air forces**
   A. Combat missions
   B. Defense missions
   C. Transport missions
   D. Other missions
II. **The organization of air forces**
III. **Aircraft and missiles**
   A. Aircraft
   B. Missiles
IV. **Major air forces of the world**
   A. The United States Air Force
   B. The Russian Air Force
   C. The Chinese Air Force
   D. The French Air Force
   E. The Indian Air Force
   F. The North Korean Air Force
   G. The German air force
   H. The British Air Force
   I. The Israeli Air Force
V. **History**

Questions

How do strategic missions differ from tactical missions?
What makes an air force powerful?
What type of aircraft is used to gather military information?
Which country had the first independent air force?
What is a *dogfight?* What is an *airlift?*
Which country has the largest air force?
What type of aircraft was the first to be used in war?
How do the air forces of industrialized nations and developing nations differ?

Additional resources

Boyne, Walter J., and Handleman, Philip, eds. *Brassey's Air Combat Reader: Historic Feats and Legends.* Brassey's, 1999.
March, Peter R. *Directory of Military Aircraft of the World.* Cassell, 2001.

Air Force, Department of the, is a military department within the Department of Defense of the United States government. It is located in Washington, D.C., and operates as Air Force headquarters. It provides support for national and international policy by organizing, training, and equipping the Air Force. Its major divisions include the secretariat and the air staff.

The *secretary of the Air Force,* a civilian, heads the department under the direction of the secretary of defense, and ranks equally with the secretaries of the Army and Navy. The principal civilian aides to the secretary of the Air Force include an undersecretary and three assistant secretaries.

The *chief of staff of the Air Force,* a general, is the secretary's chief military adviser. The chief of staff heads the air staff; supervises such members and units of the Air Force as are determined by the secretary; and is a member of the Joint Chiefs of Staff, a military group that advises the U.S. president. A vice chief of staff assists the chief of staff.

Congress set up the department as an executive agency within the National Military Establishment in 1947. Before then, the Department of War controlled military aviation. In 1949, the Department of the Air Force became a military agency.

Critically reviewed by the Department of Defense

See also **Air Force, United States; Defense, Department of.**

The U.S. Air Force Thunderbirds, a team of demonstration pilots, showcase the skill and talent of Air Force pilots at air shows, such as that shown in the photograph, in the United States and other countries. The Air Force's official symbol, *below right,* combines stylized wings with other emblems.

United States Air Force

Air Force, United States, is the branch of the United States armed forces responsible for most military operations in the air and in space. Air Force *reconnaissance* (information-gathering) satellites and aircraft constantly scan the earth for signs of hostile activity. The Air Force is ready to attack immediately with conventional or nuclear weapons. The Air Force also supports ground troops in battle and protects them from air attack. Air Force transport planes deliver troops and supplies.

Because the Air Force needs to use advanced technology, it has a large research and development organization, with laboratories and testing centers throughout the United States. In addition, thousands of civilian scientists and engineers at universities and in corporations conduct research for the Air Force. The Air Force has cooperated with the National Aeronautics and Space Administration (NASA) to send astronauts and satellites into space. The Air Force also tracks hurricanes, forecasts weather, and carries help to disaster victims.

The Air Force has about 320,000 men and women on active duty throughout the world. In addition, about 175,000 people serve in the Air Force Reserve or the Air National Guard. The Air Force also employs about 170,000 civilians. The Air Force has more than 5,000 active aircraft and about 400 *intercontinental ballistic missiles* (ICBM's), long-range missiles that can reach targets up to 9,200 miles (15,000 kilometers) away.

The Air Force's official colors are ultramarine blue and Air Force yellow. Its official song is the "United States Air Force Song" (1938), which begins, "Off we go into the wild blue yonder."

Congress created the Air Force in 1947 by reorganizing the Army Air Forces as a separate branch. The Army Air Forces developed from an Aeronautical Division that the Army Signal Corps set up in 1907.

Life in the Air Force

Men and women who serve in the United States Air Force give up some of the freedoms they protect for their country. They must go wherever they are sent, even on missions that may put their lives in great danger. The United States Air Force has about 85 major bases, many of which are overseas. Most Air Force members serve abroad at some time.

Recruit training. After enlisting, recruits receive eight and a half weeks of basic military training at Lack-

Grade insignias for officers

Air Force officers wear insignias made of metal or of thread or wire embroidery. Insignias decorate caps, shirt collars, or shoulders. Shoulder-board insignias are shown here.

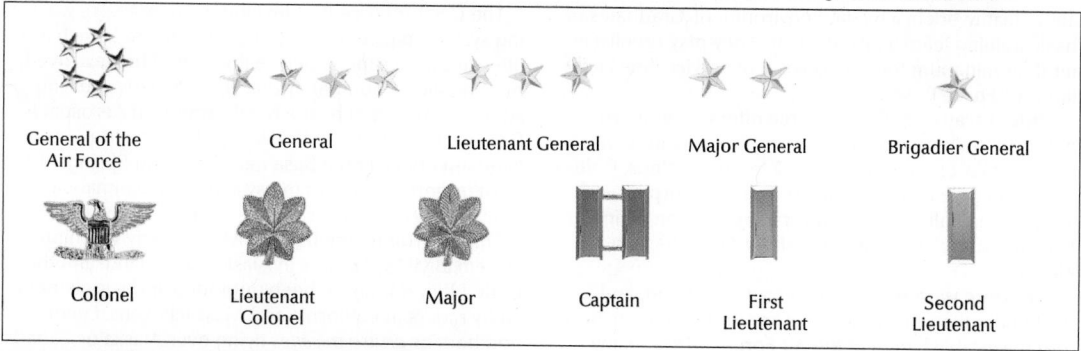

General of the Air Force

General

Lieutenant General

Major General

Brigadier General

Colonel

Lieutenant Colonel

Major

Captain

First Lieutenant

Second Lieutenant

U.S. Air Force

Dress uniforms for Air Force enlisted personnel are shown here. The uniforms for Air Force officers are similar, but officers' uniforms have grade insignias on the shoulder.

Grade insignias for enlisted men and women

The insignias of enlisted personnel, *shown here,* are worn on the sleeves of the uniform. Similar insignias are worn on the collar or shoulder of certain uniforms.

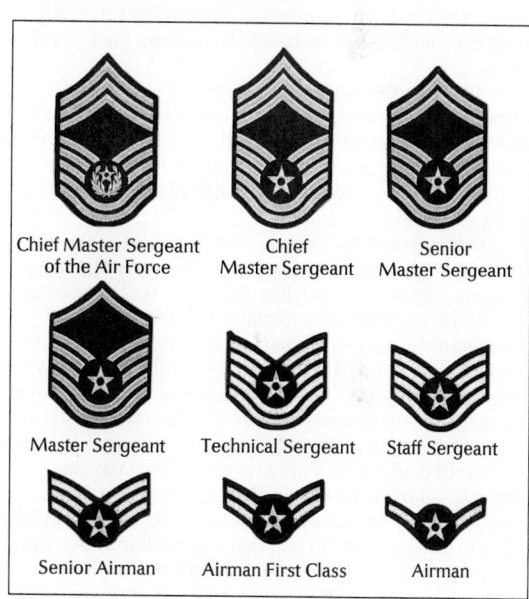

Chief Master Sergeant of the Air Force

Chief Master Sergeant

Senior Master Sergeant

Master Sergeant

Technical Sergeant

Staff Sergeant

Senior Airman

Airman First Class

Airman

Badges*

Air Force badges, *displayed here,* show the qualifications and area of specialization of personnel. Aircraft crews wear wing badges. Missile crews wear missile badges.

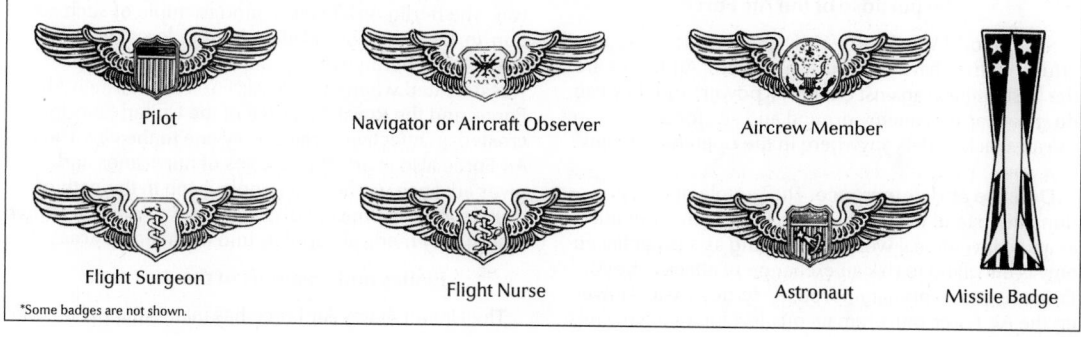

Pilot

Navigator or Aircraft Observer

Aircrew Member

Flight Surgeon

Flight Nurse

Astronaut

Missile Badge

*Some badges are not shown.

land Air Force Base near San Antonio. Through marching, exercise, and classroom studies, recruits learn about teamwork in a military environment. Graduates of basic training learn a job specialty. They may reenlist after their minimum four or six years of service. See **Lackland Air Force Base.**

Officer training. The Air Force offers several programs for training officers. The programs include those of the Air Force Academy near Colorado Springs, Colorado; Air Force Reserve Officers Training Corps (AFROTC) in colleges and universities; and the Officer Training School (OTS) at Maxwell Air Force Base in Alabama.

Air Force women are trained, administered, and paid under the same policies as are Air Force men. Before the establishment of the Air Force in 1947, many members of the Women's Army Corps (WAC) were assigned to the Army Air Forces.

During World War II (1939-1945), more than 40,000 "Air Wacs" served at air bases in the United States and in other parts of the world. Over 1,000 civilians served as Women Airforce Service Pilots, also known as WASP's, under the leadership of aviation pioneer Jacqueline Cochran (see **Cochran, Jacqueline**). The WASP's flew aircraft from factories to air bases throughout the United States.

In 1948, women became a permanent part of the armed forces. Women in the Air Force became known as WAF's. The Air Force dropped this term in the 1970's. The term *airman* is now used for all Air Force enlisted military personnel. About one-fourth of Air Force military personnel are women.

Careers in the Air Force provide opportunities for advanced education and promotion. Enlistment may prepare a person for a civilian job or an Air Force career. The Air Force offers jobs in many career fields. Applicants must be at least 17 years of age and not older than 34. They also must pass the Air Force's physical and written examinations. Air Force military personnel may retire after 20 years of service. But many personnel stay on active duty for 30 years and some even longer.

Members of the Air Force receive a base pay that is determined by their rank and length of service. They may receive extra money for special tasks, such as flying a plane or taking part in combat. The Air Force also pays for *quarters* (housing) or *subsistence* (food) when airmen are unable to live or eat on base. All Air Force personnel on active duty are eligible for 30 days' *leave* (vacation) a year. The Air Force provides free medical care to airmen and their families.

The purpose of the Air Force

Since World War I (1914-1918), the world's most powerful countries have built large air forces. Air forces are the best defense against enemy airpower, and they can do great harm to enemy ground and sea forces. Air forces can attack targets anywhere in the opening minutes of a war.

Defense and deterrence. The people of every nation understand the terrible destructive power of nuclear and conventional weapons. As long as a potential enemy is unwilling to risk an exchange of attacks, the Air Force serves its primary purpose—to deter war. However, the Air Force must remain on alert for an enemy missile or bomber attack and must be prepared to respond to such an attack.

The U.S. Air Force has developed an extensive warning system to give the United States time to launch its offensive air weapons before they could be destroyed by a missile or bomber attack. The U.S. early warning system is managed by the North American Aerospace Defense Command (NORAD), which has headquarters at Peterson Space Force Base near Colorado Springs. The most important parts of the system are reconnaissance satellites that orbit over various parts of the world.

On the ground, the Ballistic Missile Early Warning System (BMEWS) radars in Alaska, Greenland, and the United Kingdom have been upgraded and supplemented by radars in California and Massachusetts. Enemy bombers or *cruise missiles* flying over Alaska or Canada might be detected first by the North Warning System line of radars. Cruise missiles are jet-powered missiles that fly at low altitudes to avoid radar detection. A radar system in Maine can detect aircraft and cruise missiles approaching the east coast of the United States. See **North Warning System.**

The Air Force also carries radar aboard its Airborne Warning and Control System (AWACS) planes. In addition to performing its early warning function, an AWACS plane can fly to another part of the world and control U.S. air strikes. AWACS planes flew such missions during the Persian Gulf War of 1991 and the Iraq War (2003-2011).

Offense. The most important use of the Air Force during war is to attack the enemy. Air attack can hit unexpectedly, at long range, and with devastating power. Each flight a combat plane makes against the enemy is called a *sortie.* An attack by one or more planes is a *combat mission.* If 10 planes fly in a group, the group flies 1 combat mission, but 10 sorties.

Tactical air attacks are the direct help given to ground or sea units in battle. Tactical air units fight to control the air over a battle area by destroying planes in the air and on the ground. They attack enemy troops and supplies to *interdict* them—that is, keep them from reaching the battlefront. They provide *close support* for ground troops, attacking specific targets for them.

Strategic air attacks hit far behind the battle lines. Such attacks destroy the enemy's industries and war materials. They also ruin the enemy's transportation network so troops and supplies cannot be moved into battle. Strategic air attacks are designed to destroy the enemy's capability to make war or its will to fight.

Peacetime emergencies. Prompt action by the Air Force may at times relieve emergencies that are short of war. The Berlin Airlift was a good example of such action. In 1948, the Soviet Union tried to force the Allies out of West Berlin with a ground blockade. The plan was defeated when the U.S. Air Force, the French Air Force, and the Royal Air Force of the United Kingdom created an effective aerial supply line to the city. The U.S. Air Force also charts the courses of hurricanes and gives advance warning to people living in the path of such storms. In times of disaster, the Air Force has flown emergency medical supplies into the affected areas.

Planes and weapons of the Air Force

The United States Air Force has many kinds of aircraft.

A few are driven by propellers, but jet engines drive most Air Force planes today. Many planes carry only a pilot. Others have a crew of several members that may include a copilot, navigator, and flight engineer. Some aircraft are guided only by electronic devices.

Planes of the Air Force are designated by both letters and numbers. A letter in front of the numbers refers to the basic mission of the plane, and the numbers designate the model. Basic missions include *A,* attack; *B,* bomber; *C,* cargo transport; *F,* fighter; *H,* helicopter; *K,* tanker; *M,* multipurpose; *R,* reconnaissance; and *T,* trainer. For example, an F-15 is a fighter aircraft.

A letter following the numbers indicates a general modification of the design. The original design is designated *A,* but often this letter is not used. The first modification is designated *B;* the second, *C;* and so on. Thus, the fourth modification (the fifth general design) of the F-15 is the F-15E. Some designations have an additional letter indicating a special modification. This letter appears in front of what would otherwise be the first letter. For example, an AC-130 is a C-130 to which guns have been added to convert it to an attack aircraft.

Bombers drop explosives on enemy targets. These planes are equipped with radar and bombsights to find the target and direct bombs to it. The navigator guides the pilot over the target, then releases the bomb. Bombers also launch missiles. The B-52 is the oldest American bomber in service. The B-52's maximum range without refueling is more than 8,800 miles (14,000 kilometers), and its top speed is nearly 650 miles (1,050 kilometers) per hour. American bombers also include the B-1, which is smaller than a B-52 but carries a heavier bomb load. A third type of bomber, the B-2 "stealth" bomber, is a sleek plane designed to be nearly invisible to radar.

Fighters shoot down enemy aircraft and attack ground targets. They are smaller and generally faster than bombers. However, many fighters perform bombing missions. In fact, the leading precision bombers in the Iraq War were F-117 and F-15E fighters. The F-117 "stealth" fighters penetrated heavy air defenses without being hit. The two-seat F-15E lacks the "stealth" of the F-117, but it is faster and can reach a speed of *Mach 2.5.* Mach 2.5 is 2.5 times the speed of sound. Sound travels about 760 miles (1,220 kilometers) per hour at sea level. Equally fast is the single-seat F-15C, which has been the Air Force's best fighter for shooting down enemy aircraft. Lighter and slower than the two-engine F-15 is the single-engine F-16, which can be used in air-to-air combat or against ground targets. The Air Force's newest fighter, the F-35, combines stealth and speed.

Other aircraft include attack and reconnaissance planes, tankers, and transports. Attack planes, such as the A-10, are designed to provide low-flying air support for ground troops, particularly against armored targets. Reconnaissance planes observe and photograph enemy forces and installations. Tanker aircraft refuel other planes in flight.

Transport aircraft carry personnel and equipment and can evacuate wounded soldiers in battle. The C-5 Galaxy can carry tanks or helicopters. The C-5 and the smaller C-141 can fly long distances. The C-17 can carry a bigger load and land on a shorter runway than the C-141 can. The C-130 Hercules is used on shorter flights.

Remotely piloted aircraft called *drones* execute mili-

U.S. Air Force

A jet fighter shoots down enemy aircraft and attacks ground targets. This fighter, the single-seat F-15 Eagle, flies at more than twice the speed of sound.

tary missions without putting their pilots at risk. The MQ-1 Predator drone can perform reconnaissance or engage enemy ground targets. The *Q* denotes that it is a remotely piloted aircraft. A pilot flies the drone via satellite from a ground control station that can be thousands of miles away. The Predator's successor, the MQ-9 Reaper, is larger, faster, and can carry more weapons. Even with its improved speed, the Reaper only flies around 230 miles (370 kilometers) per hour. Therefore, such drones are transported to areas of conflict by cargo aircraft and are only used after fighters have established control of the air.

Missiles are a major weapon of the U.S. Air Force. They can be equipped with a conventional or nuclear warhead.

Surface-launched missiles are fired from the ground at enemy ground or air targets. The largest of these are intercontinental ballistic missiles (ICBM's), which can travel from one continent to another. The Minuteman

U.S. Air Force

A-10 Thunderbolt attack planes provide low-flying air support for ground troops, especially against armored targets. These single-seat planes are armed with guns and bombs.

Different types of U.S. Air Force planes carry out various missions. The KC-10 tanker refuels other planes in flight. The F-22 shoots down enemy aircraft and attacks ground targets. The B-2 "stealth" bomber is designed to avoid detection by radar. The AWACS airplane can use its radar dome to detect aircraft and missiles. The C-5A Galaxy transport carries tanks and other heavy equipment. The F-16 Fighting Falcon fighter, *right,* is armed with guided missiles.

U.S. Air Force

KC-10 tanker refueling a C-5A Galaxy transport

F-22 Photo Team from Lockheed Martin

F-22 jet fighter

U.S. Air Force

B-2 "stealth" bomber

Boeing Aerospace & Electronics

Airborne Warning and Control System (AWACS) aircraft

U.S. Air Force

C-5 Galaxy jet transport

F-16 Fighting Falcon jet fighters

ICBM can carry three nuclear warheads.

Air-launched missiles are carried by bombers and fighters. *Air-to-ground missiles* (AGM's) are fired at targets on the ground. The Maverick is an AGM guided by a television or *infrared* (heat) image of a target on the ground. Other AGM's include the *H*igh-speed *A*nti-*R*adiation *M*issile (HARM) and the Shrike, which destroy enemy radar by following the radar signal to its source. *Air interceptor missiles* (AIM's) are used against enemy planes. The *A*dvanced *M*edium-*R*ange *A*ir-to-*A*ir *M*issile (AMRAAM) and the Sparrow are AIM's guided by radar. Another AIM called the Sidewinder seeks the heat of the enemy aircraft's engine.

Organization of the Air Force

The Department of the Air Force operates under the secretary of the Air Force, a civilian directly responsible to the secretary of defense. The chief of staff, a four-star general, is the Air Force's top military officer. However, the chief of staff does not command the Air Force in wartime. When Air Force units go to war, they are part of joint commands that include all branches of the armed forces. The Air Force chief of staff and his or her subordinates are known formally as Headquarters United States Air Force and informally as the *air staff.*

The Air Force has a headquarters at the Pentagon Building near Washington, D.C., and nine major commands. These units can be roughly grouped into *combat commands* and *support commands.*

Combat commands provide forces that carry out the fighting assignments of the Air Force. A four-star general usually heads a major command. These major commands are divided into successively smaller units called *air forces, wings,* and *squadrons.* A squadron usually has 20 to 25 aircraft.

In peacetime, all combat-ready missiles, bombers, fighters, attack aircraft, and reconnaissance aircraft of the active Air Force belong to one of five commands. They are the Air Combat Command, headquartered at Langley Air Force Base, Virginia; Pacific Air Forces, headquartered at Joint Base Pearl Harbor-Hickam, Hawaii; United States Air Forces in Europe and Air Forces Africa, headquartered at Ramstein Air Base, Germany; Air Force Global Strike Command, headquartered at Barksdale Air Force Base, Louisiana; and Air Force Special Operations Command, headquartered at Hurlburt Field, Florida.

These Air Force combat commands make their forces available in wartime to joint commands. Joint commands include the Central Command for war in the Middle East and the Strategic Command for nuclear war. Air Combat Command was set up in 1992 by merging much of the Strategic Air Command with the Tactical Air Command. Air Combat Command controls most of the Air Force's fighters, bombers, and drones. Air Force Special Operations Command has helicopters and *gunships* (armed airplanes or helicopters). Air Force Global Strike Command has intercontinental ballistic missiles.

Support commands help the combat commands of all the services. Air Mobility Command transports troops and supplies and also extends the range of bombers and fighters by refueling them in the air. This command was formed in 1992 when its predecessor, Military Airlift Command, gained most of the air refueling aircraft that had belonged to the Strategic Air Command. The Air Force Materiel Command, formed in 1992, buys planes, missiles, and supplies. In 1993, the Air Training Command and the Air University joined to form the Air Education and Training Command. The Air Force Reserve Command became a major command in 1997. It provides aircraft, personnel, and support to the other major commands in time of war or national emergency.

The U.S. Space Force, a department of the Air Force, is the youngest branch of the United States armed forces. Founded in 2019, the Space Force operates military satellites and ground radar sites.

Components of the Air Force

The regular Air Force supplies the professional core of Air Force personnel. Its size is fixed by Congress. Regular Air Force personnel include regular officers who have graduated from an officer training program and regular airmen who enlist in the service.

Air Force reserves provide additional personnel and aircraft in emergencies. Even in times of peace, most junior Air Force officers on active duty are reservists, and reserve units perform important functions, such as air transport. The Ready Reserve consists of units and individuals trained and equipped to be called to duty in any emergency. The Standby Reserve includes personnel who can be called to duty in time of war. The Air National Guard is administered by the individual states, but can be called to duty by the president in emergencies.

Civil Air Patrol (CAP) is a civilian auxiliary of the Air Force. It trains young people in the science of aviation and conducts search and rescue missions.

History

United States military leaders sent up balloons to observe the enemy during the American Civil War (1861-1865) and the Spanish-American War (1898). But military officials did not begin to consider the airplane an important weapon until early in World War I.

Early years. On Dec. 17, 1903, two brothers, Wilbur and Orville Wright, flew the first successful engine-powered airplane to carry a pilot. In early 1905, the Wrights offered to sell planes to the U.S. government, but the government did not take them seriously at first. Finally, in 1907, President Theodore Roosevelt showed interest in the airplane. That year, an Aeronautical Division was established in the office of the chief signal officer of the U.S. Army to look into the new "air machines."

The Army bought its first airplane from the Wrights in 1909. In 1911, Congress appropriated the first funds for aviation—$125,000. But by 1914, when World War I erupted in Europe, the U.S. Army's air force owned only five planes. The airplane's military role had grown much faster in Europe. Germany had about 250 planes. France, Russia, and the United Kingdom each had over 100.

World War I pitted France, Russia, the United Kingdom, and other Allies against the Central Powers, including Germany and Austria-Hungary. Under the pressure of war, the European nations' air forces grew rapidly to several thousand airplanes. When the United States entered the war in April 1917, the Army had fewer than 300 training planes and no combat planes. Only American pilots who already had been flying in British and French units had significant combat experience. The Lafayette Escadrille, a French squadron which included some American pilots, already boasted several *aces,* aviators who had shot down at least five enemy aircraft.

Not all aircraft in the war were planes. Observation balloons were used for reconnaissance. Huge, *dirigible* (steerable) airships—most notably the German zeppelins—could drop bombs. See **Airship.**

At the start of the war, opposing armies used planes only to scout out enemy positions. Enemy pilots waved to each other when they passed in the sky. But soon they began to carry pistols and rifles and took potshots at each other. In 1915, a Dutch engineer, Anthony H. G. Fokker, perfected a machine gun that could fire between the revolving propeller blades. He transformed aerial warfare by making the airplane a true fighting machine. Now pilots sought enemy planes and tried to destroy them in airborne battles called *dogfights.*

Most of the airplanes used in World War I were small wood and canvas *biplanes* that had one wing above and one below the open cockpit. Plane design improved rapidly during the war. In 1914, most machines could fly only about 75 miles (120 kilometers) per hour. By 1918, planes were flying at 120 miles (190 kilometers) per hour.

As planes improved, pilots began to use them on bombing missions. At first, the pilot carried a sack of bombs in the cockpit and simply dropped them over the side. Later, mechanical devices released the bombs from under the fuselage. American pilots flew mostly French-built planes, such as Spads, Salmsons, and

Important dates in Air Force history

1907	The Army set up an Aeronautical Division in the Office of the Chief Signal Officer.
1909	The Army bought its first airplane from the Wright brothers.
1914	The Aviation Section of the Signal Corps took charge of aviation operation and training.
1917	The First Aero Squadron arrived in France during World War I.
1926	Congress established the U.S. Army Air Corps.
1940	President Franklin D. Roosevelt requested 50,000 planes for the Army and Navy.
1941	Congress set up the Army Air Forces.
1945	A B-29 dropped the first atomic bomb used in warfare, on Hiroshima, Japan.
1947	The United States Air Force was created as a separate service.
1947	Captain Charles E. Yeager piloted an X-1 rocket-powered aircraft through the sound barrier.
1948	The Berlin Airlift began.
1950	The U.S. Air Force was ordered into action in Korea. Dogfights between jet fighters occurred for the first time.
1957	The Air Force successfully fired its first intercontinental ballistic missile (ICBM).
1959	The U.S. Air Force Academy graduated its first class.
1962	Air Force U-2 reconnaissance aircraft took photographs indicating that Soviet ballistic missiles were being installed in Cuba.
1965	Air Force and Navy fighter planes bombed North Vietnam to begin Operation Rolling Thunder.
1968	The C-5 Galaxy jet transport, the world's largest aircraft at the time, made its first flight.
1971	Jeanne M. Holm became the first woman in the Air Force to be promoted to the rank of general.
1976	Women were admitted to the U.S. Air Force Academy for the first time.
1986	Air Force F-111's bombed the headquarters of Libya's leader Mu'ammar al-Qadhāfī.
1988	The Air Force unveiled its "stealth" bomber and fighter planes designed to be nearly invisible to radar.
1991	The Air Force helped drive Iraqi forces out of Kuwait during the Persian Gulf War of 1991.
1995	The Air Force helped end a war between Bosnian Serbs and government forces in the former Yugoslav republic of Bosnia-Herzegovina.
2003	The Air Force participated in the Iraq War, helping to end the rule of Iraqi dictator Saddam Hussein.

The first U.S. Army plane, *shown here,* was built by the Wright brothers in 1909. The aircraft, which cost $30,000, flew 42.5 miles (68.4 kilometers) per hour in a record flight that lasted 1 hour 12 minutes 40 seconds.

U.S. Air Force

Nieuports. The United States produced a version of the British de Havilland D.H.4, though most of these planes did not reach the front lines. The United States entered the war with almost no airpower, but Congress quickly appropriated $640 million for military aviation. Flying schools trained 8,688 flying cadets. Another 1,800 were trained in Europe. The 94th Pursuit Squadron entered combat in April 1918. American pilots destroyed about 750 enemy planes and 70 balloons. The leading American ace, Captain Eddie Rickenbacker, shot down 22 enemy planes and 4 balloons. The Allies won the war.

Between world wars. The most prominent American air combat leader of World War I was Brigadier General Billy Mitchell. In September 1918, Mitchell had commanded nearly 1,500 American, British, French, and Italian aircraft during the Battle of St.-Mihiel in France. The air assault had helped Allied ground forces win an easy victory at St.-Mihiel.

Mitchell's wartime experience convinced him that air units needed to be independent of ground units so that airpower could be concentrated where it was most needed. In July 1921, he demonstrated the power of the airplane by sinking a former German battleship with aerial bombs. Mitchell's criticism of the government's defense program was so outspoken that he was court-martialed for insubordination. He chose to resign from the Army rather than accept a five-year suspension. In 1946, after developments had confirmed many of Mitchell's ideas, he was awarded the Medal of Honor, the nation's highest military decoration.

The Air Service was renamed the Army Air Corps in 1926. In 1931, the first all-metal bomber was built. In 1935, the Army tested the first B-17, the Flying Fortress that would be important in World War II.

World War II was a huge war in which Germany, Italy, Japan, and other Axis powers fought the Allies, who included Canada, China, the Soviet Union, and the United Kingdom. The U.S. Army Air Forces (AAF) was formed in 1941. The United States entered the war in December of that year, after Japan attacked the U.S. naval base at Pearl Harbor, Hawaii. By the time of the attack, the United States had begun a program of building planes and training pilots.

General Henry H. "Hap" Arnold was the first commander of the AAF. Under Arnold, the AAF grew to its top strength during World War II of 2,411,000 members and 80,000 planes. Aircraft used by the AAF during World War II included the P-51 Mustang long-range fighter and such bombers as the B-17, the B-24 Liberator, the B-25, and the B-29.

During the war, the AAF dropped more than 2 million tons (1.8 million metric tons) of bombs and destroyed over 40,000 enemy planes. The most destructive raids were the firebombing of Tokyo in March 1945 and the atomic bombing of Hiroshima in August 1945. The Tokyo raid killed an estimated 80,000 to 125,000 people, and the bombing of Hiroshima killed an estimated 70,000 to 100,000 people. The fact that a single atomic bomb could destroy a large city made nuclear weapons a dominating factor in U.S. military planning.

The AAF lost about 23,000 planes, about half of them in combat. Others were lost in training or other non-combat operations. About 88,000 U.S. Army aviators died in the war, which ended in an Allied victory.

Separate Air Force. On Sept. 18, 1947, Congress created the United States Air Force as an equal partner with the Army and Navy. It also established the Department of the Air Force. Stuart Symington became the first secretary of the Air Force, and General Carl Spaatz became the first Air Force chief of staff.

The Berlin Airlift was the first big job of the new Air Force. After World War II, the Western Allies occupied western Germany, and the Soviet Union occupied the east. Berlin, in the east, was divided into Allied-occupied West Berlin and Soviet- occupied East Berlin. On June 26, 1948, Soviet troops blockaded all ground routes through the Soviet zone of occupation to West Berlin, stopping all food and supplies. The Air Force, with British and French units, supplied the city by air. Soon Allied planes were landing at Tempelhof airport every 3 ½ minutes. During the 462 days of "Operation Vittles," as U.S. pilots called it, Allied planes flew 277,000 flights carrying about 2,325,000 tons (2,109,000 metric tons) of supplies into West Berlin.

The Korean War (1950-1953) was a local war in Korea. The United States and other members of the United Nations aided South Korea, and the Soviet Union and China assisted North Korea. The war brought the first dogfights between jet fighters. In November 1950, Air Force F-86 fighters clashed with Soviet-made MiG fighters near the Chinese border along the Yalu River. Air Force pilots called this area "MiG Alley." They shot down 10 times as many jets as they lost there. When the Korean War ended, the Air Force had downed about 900 enemy planes and had lost 139 of its own planes in aerial combat. The Korean War ended without either side winning a complete victory.

The nuclear Air Force. After Korea, the Air Force found itself undergoing rapid change. It soon had thermonuclear hydrogen bombs thousands of times more powerful than the atomic bombs that ended World War II. Propeller aircraft rapidly became obsolete for most jobs. Newer planes, such as the B-52 bomber, had jet engines and carried nuclear weapons. Intercontinental ballistic missiles could be launched from the United States and the Soviet Union.

The Vietnam War (1957-1975) was a drawn-out conflict in Southeast Asia. In that war, the United States supported South Vietnam, and the Soviet Union and China backed North Vietnam and the Viet Cong rebels of South Vietnam. From 1961 to 1973, the United States dropped a much greater tonnage of conventional bombs in Southeast Asia than had been dropped by both sides in World War II. Most of this bombing took place in the jungles of South Vietnam by B-52's and fighter aircraft against Communist rebels and their North Vietnamese allies. The simultaneous bombing of North Vietnam was done mostly by F-105 and F-4 fighters. The Air Force also introduced laser-guided bombs, which rarely missed their targets. The war ended with a North Vietnamese and Viet Cong victory.

The Persian Gulf War of 1991. After Iraq occupied Kuwait in August 1990, the U.S. Air Force began its most extensive airlift. In six months, the Air Force transported more than 577,000 tons (523,000 metric tons) of supplies and 498,000 military passengers as far as 7,000 miles (11,000 kilometers) to points in the Middle East. After the war began in January 1991, the Air Force flew more than 37,000 combat sorties and lost only 14 aircraft. In their first extensive use, 42 F-117 "stealth" fighter-bombers dropped hundreds of laser-guided bombs without losing a plane. The air assault so devastated the Iraqis that they surrendered in February.

The Balkans. In Bosnia-Herzegovina, a war began in 1991 between Bosnian Serb rebels and the country's government, which was dominated by Bosniaks (sometimes called Bosnian Muslims). In 1995, the North Atlantic Treaty Organization (NATO) intervened in the war. As part of the NATO operation, the U.S. Air Force attacked Bosnian Serb forces to help provide relief to Bosnians under siege. Later that year, the groups involved in the war agreed to a peace treaty. In 1999, the Air Force took part in NATO air strikes against Serbia to end Serbian attacks on ethnic Albanians in its Kosovo province.

The war in Afghanistan. After the Sept. 11, 2001, terrorist attacks in the United States, U.S. forces waged war against the Taliban, the rulers of Afghanistan. The Taliban harbored and supported the terrorists of al-Qa'ida responsible for the attacks. The campaign included air strikes by the U.S. forces to support troops on the ground and Afghan rebel groups opposed to the Taliban. The rebels overthrew the Taliban in December, but the Taliban continued to violently resist the new government of Afghanistan for years. The U.S. Air Force continued operations in Afghanistan, often using drones to gather intelligence and launch missile attacks against Taliban forces.

The Iraq War (2003-2011) ended the rule of Iraqi dictator Saddam Hussein. Before the war began in March 2003, the Air Force airlifted troops and equipment to positions near Iraq, mostly in Kuwait. At the beginning of the war, the Air Force used precision-guided bombs to strike military targets and the leaders of Iraq's ruling Baath Party. In April, after extensive air attacks against Iraqi ground troops, U.S.-led forces captured Baghdad, Iraq's capital, ending Hussein's rule. The Air Force con-

tinued to strike Iraqi targets as militants in Iraq continued to fight U.S. forces and the new Iraqi government long after the end of Hussein's regime.   Wayne Thompson

Related articles in *World Book* include:

Biographies

Arnold, Henry H.	Mitchell, Billy
Chennault, Claire Lee	Rickenbacker, Eddie
Doolittle, James H.	Spaatz, Carl
James, Daniel, Jr.	Yeager, Chuck
LeMay, Curtis E.	

Air Force installations

Area 51	Scott Air Force Base
Edwards Air Force Base	United States Air Force
Lackland Air Force Base	Academy
Langley Air Force Base	Vandenberg Air Force Base
Offutt Air Force Base	

History

Ace	Pearl Harbor
Afghanistan War	Persian Gulf War of 1991
Cold War	Strategic Air Command
Iraq War	Vietnam War
Korean War	World War I
Midway Island	World War II

Organization

Air Force, Department of the
NORAD

Other related articles

Air Force One	General
Aircraft, Military	Guided missile
Cape Canaveral	Medals, decorations, and
Coast Guard, United States	orders
(Aircraft)	National Guard
Defense, Department of	RAND Corporation
Flag (picture: Flags of the	Rank, Military
armed forces)	Space exploration

Outline

I. **Life in the Air Force**
  A. Recruit training   C. Air Force women
  B. Officer training   D. Careers in the Air Force
II. **The purpose of the Air Force**
  A. Defense and deterrence
  B. Offense
  C. Peacetime emergencies
III. **Planes and weapons of the Air Force**
  A. Bombers   C. Other aircraft
  B. Fighters   D. Missiles
IV. **Organization of the Air Force**
  A. The Department of the Air Force
  B. Combat commands
  C. Support commands
  D. The U.S. Space Force
V. **Components of the Air Force**
  A. The regular Air Force   C. Civil Air Patrol (CAP)
  B. Air Force reserves
VI. **History**

Air Force Academy, United States. See United States Air Force Academy.

Air Force One is the aircraft that carries the president of the United States. The presidential fleet actually consists of two Boeing VC–25 airplanes, highly modified versions of the civilian Boeing 747-200B. The two planes are maintained and operated by the Presidential Airlift Group, part of the 89th Airlift Wing of the Air Mobility Command of the U.S. Air Force. The planes are based at Joint Base Andrews-Naval Air Facility Washington, in Maryland. When the president is aboard either plane, or on any other Air Force aircraft, that aircraft's radio call signal is "Air Force One."

The two aircraft of the presidential fleet have been designed to suit the president's requirements. Each contains a large room that can serve as a conference or dining room, quarters for the president and the first lady, and offices for senior staff members. Each plane also has extensive storage areas for food and equipment, two galleys, and work and rest areas for the presidential staff, reporters, and Air Force crews. Each plane can accommodate up to 76 passengers and 26 crew members. The aircraft are 231 feet 10 inches (70.7 meters) long, with wingspans of 195 feet 8 inches (59.6 meters). They can fly 7,800 miles (12,550 kilometers) without refueling.

The radio call sign "Air Force One" was first used by presidential aircraft in the 1950's. But the first aircraft to be popularly known as Air Force One was a Boeing VC–137C, a modified civilian 707-320B, which went into service for President John F. Kennedy in 1962. One of the current aircraft in the presidential fleet went into service in 1990, and the other in 1991.   Brian Nicklas

Air Line Pilots Association is the largest labor union of airline pilots in the world. It represents pilots at U.S. and Canadian airlines. The association seeks to improve pay, working conditions, seniority rights, pensions, and other benefits for airline pilots. It also works to establish standards for flight safety, aircraft performance, accident investigations, flight operations, and security.

The association was founded in 1931. Its full name is the Air Line Pilots Association, International. It is affiliated with the American Federation of Labor and Congress of Industrial Organizations (AFL-CIO). Headquarters are in Washington, D.C.

Critically reviewed by the Air Line Pilots Association, International

Air lock is a chamber with two airtight doors. It is used on submarines and spacecraft and in underwater construction. One door opens to the outside environment. The other door opens to a structure called a *pneumatic caisson.* The caisson contains compressed air. Caissons cannot be opened to the outer environment because air loss will occur. All movements to and from the caisson must take place through an air lock. The pressure in the air lock is regulated, depending on whether people or materials are entering or exiting the caisson. Separate

air locks are usually provided for people and materials.

To enter the caisson, a person first steps into the air lock. Compressed air holds the inner door of the air lock tightly shut. The outer door is then closed, and air with a pressure equal to that of the caisson is slowly introduced. When the pressures within the air lock and the caisson are equal, the inner door is opened and the person can enter the caisson. When exiting the caisson, a person moves into the air lock and the pressure in the lock is made to match the pressure outside. When they are equal, the outer door is opened and the person can leave. Lowering of the air pressure, or *decompression,* must be done slowly. If the pressure drops too rapidly, the person may develop a painful and dangerous condition called *bends.*

James Donovan

See also **Bends; Caisson.**
Air mail. See **Airmail.**
Air mass. See **Weather** (Air masses; map).
Air piracy. See **Hijacking.**
Air plant. See **Epiphyte.**
Air pollution occurs when wastes dirty the air. People produce most of the wastes that cause air pollution. Such wastes can be in the form of gases or *particulates* (particles of solid or liquid matter). These substances result chiefly from burning fuel to power motor vehicles and to heat buildings. Industrial processes and the burning of garbage also contribute to air pollution. Natural *pollutants* (impurities) include dust, pollen, soil particles, and naturally occurring gases.

The rapid growth of population and industry, and the increased use of automobiles and airplanes, have made air pollution a serious problem. The air we breathe has become so filled with pollutants that it can cause health problems. Polluted air also harms plants, animals, building materials, and fabrics. In addition, it causes damage by altering Earth's atmosphere.

Damage caused by air pollution costs billions of dol-

How an air lock works

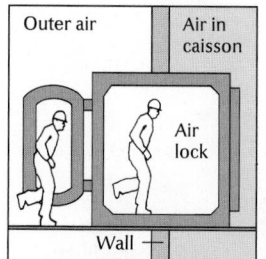
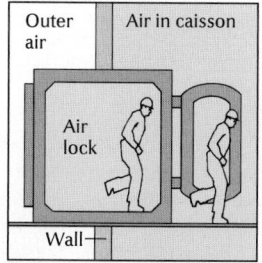

WORLD BOOK illustration by David Cunningham

Air locks enable people to enter caissons containing compressed air. When a person enters an air lock, *left,* its air pressure is the same as that outside. Air pressure in the air lock is slowly increased, *right,* to equal that inside the caisson. This action permits a person to enter the caisson without danger.

© Joe Sterling, Click/Chicago

Air pollution is a serious problem in many of the world's large cities. Heavy concentrations of air pollutants, often in the form of smog, settle over a city, creating a health hazard for its people.

lars each year. This includes money spent for health care and increased maintenance of buildings. Air pollution also causes irreversible damage to the environment.

Chief sources of air pollution

People depend on the atmosphere to dilute and remove pollutants as they are produced. But weather conditions called *thermal inversions* can trap pollutants over an area until they build up to dangerous levels. A thermal inversion occurs when a layer of warm air settles over a layer of cool air that lies near the ground. Impurities become trapped and cannot rise until rain or wind breaks up the layer of stationary warm air.

Forms of transportation, such as automobiles, airplanes, ships, and trains, are the leading source of air pollution in most industrial nations. The major pollutants produced by these sources are carbon monoxide, carbon dioxide, *hydrocarbons* (compounds of carbon and hydrogen), and *nitrogen oxides* (compounds of nitrogen and oxygen). Nitrogen oxides can react with hydrocarbons in the presence of sunlight to produce a form of oxygen called *ozone.* Ozone is the chief component of photochemical smog, which is a common form of air pollution (see **Smog**).

Fuel combustion for heating and cooling homes, of-

fice buildings, and factories contributes significantly to air pollution. Electric power plants that burn coal or oil also release pollutants into the atmosphere. The major pollutants from these sources are nitrogen oxides, sulfur oxides (compounds of sulfur and oxygen), particulates, and carbon dioxide.

Industrial processes produce a wide range of pollutants. Oil refineries discharge ammonia, hydrocarbons, organic acids, and sulfur oxides. Metal smelting plants give off large amounts of sulfur oxides and particulates containing lead and other metals. Plants that make aluminum expel fluoride dust. By 1996, most industrialized nations, including the United States, had ended production of *chlorofluorocarbons* (CFC's), compounds of chlorine, fluorine, and carbon. But normal operation of many older refrigerators and air conditioners produces CFC's.

Burning of solid wastes often creates a very visible form of air pollution—thick, black smoke. It also produces invisible pollution in the form of toxic chemicals called *dioxins.* Many cities and towns enforce bans on the burning of garbage, leaves, and other refuse.

Other sources of pollution include chemical sprays and organic chemicals used to start fires on charcoal grills. Forest fires and structural fires also contribute to air pollution. In rural areas and in developing countries,

Major air pollutants and their sources   Most air pollution results from human activity. These pie graphs represent the total emissions of each of the five major air pollutants in the United States in 2016. The legend identifies the sources of air pollution by color. Each graph shows how much each source contributed to that kind of air pollution. All natural sources of air pollution are included in "Miscellaneous," as well as other sources.

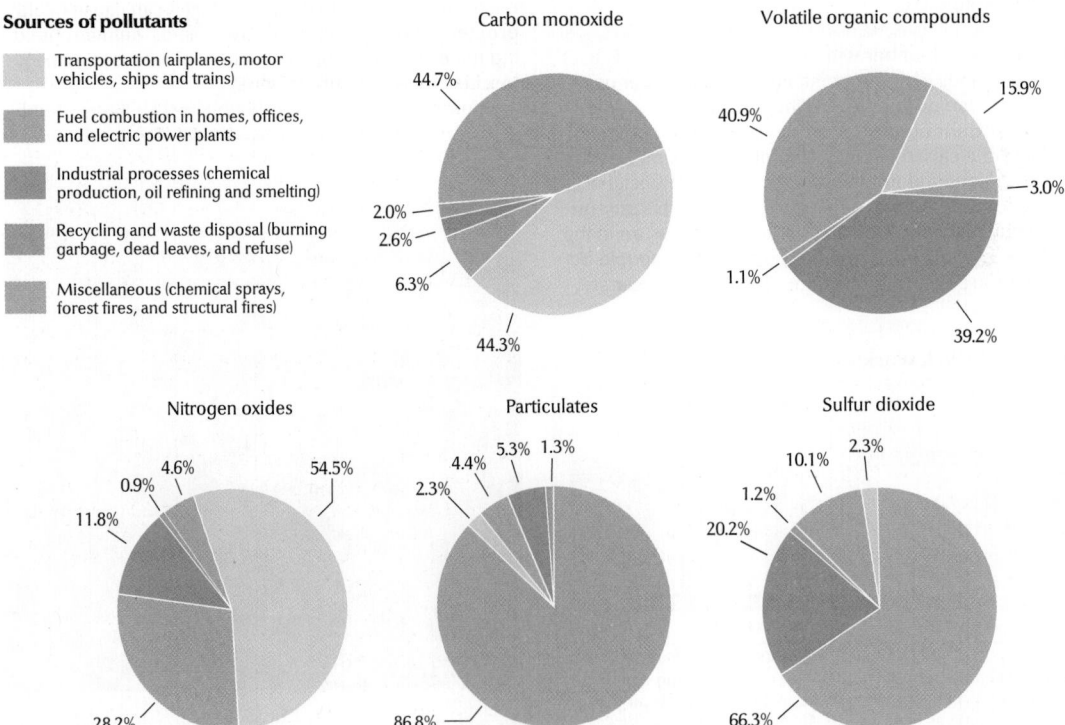

Sources of pollutants

- Transportation (airplanes, motor vehicles, ships and trains)
- Fuel combustion in homes, offices, and electric power plants
- Industrial processes (chemical production, oil refining and smelting)
- Recycling and waste disposal (burning garbage, dead leaves, and refuse)
- Miscellaneous (chemical sprays, forest fires, and structural fires)

Carbon monoxide
44.7%
2.0%
2.6%
6.3%
44.3%

Volatile organic compounds
15.9%
40.9%
3.0%
1.1%
39.2%

Nitrogen oxides
54.5%
4.6%
0.9%
11.8%
28.2%

Particulates
5.3% 1.3%
4.4%
2.3%
86.8%

Sulfur dioxide
2.3%
10.1%
1.2%
20.2%
66.3%

Figures are for 2019 and may not add up to 100 percent due to rounding. Source: U.S. Environmental Protection Agency.

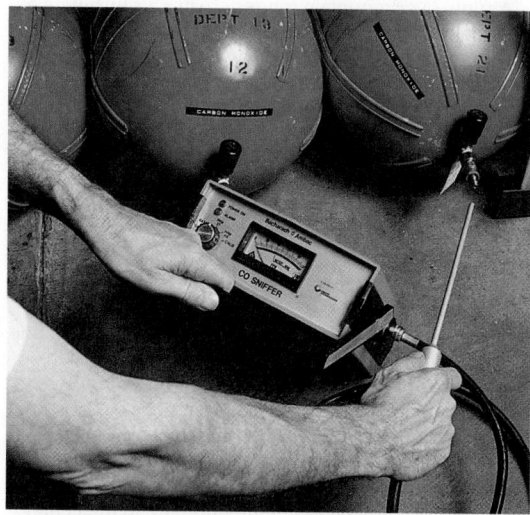

© Peter Vadnai, The Stock Market

A carbon monoxide detector is used in manufacturing facilities to test for leakage from tanks that store the gas. Carbon monoxide has many uses in industry, but it is a deadly poison.

the burning of forests and grasslands to clear areas for farming is a major source of air pollution.

Natural sources also contribute to air pollution. Volcanoes emit large amounts of sulfur oxides and particulates. Microbes in the digestive tracts of cattle and in rice fields break down plant materials and release an odorless gas called *methane,* a type of hydrocarbon.

Indoor air pollution occurs when energy-efficient houses and office buildings trap pollutants inside. As a result, some pollutants found outdoors are found indoors in even higher concentrations. Some plastic products, processed wood products, paints, and adhesives can give off hydrocarbons. Many cleaning products emit poisonous gases such as ammonia and chlorine. Soil and rocks release an odorless gas called *radon* into the atmosphere. The gas enters buildings through cracks in the foundation (see **Radon**).

Effects of air pollution

Health. When people breathe polluted air, the impurities can irritate their air passages and lungs. Particulates often stay in the lungs and can worsen such conditions as asthma and bronchitis. Radon can cause lung cancer if inhaled in large amounts. Certain chemical compounds can cause cancer and birth defects. Ozone reduces resistance to colds and pneumonia and can aggravate emphysema. Carbon monoxide interferes with the transfer of oxygen from the lungs to body tissues.

In London in 1952, about 4,000 people died of respiratory diseases during a "killer smog." More than 600 people died as a result of thermal inversions that occurred in New York City in 1953 and 1963. Today, such extreme events are rare in many countries because of government *emission standards,* which limit the amounts of pollutants that factories and other sources may release.

Agriculture. Air pollutants can stunt the growth of crops, harm livestock, and destroy crops. Such damage can prove costly to farmers. Forests also have been damaged by air pollution.

Atmosphere. Some pollutants can cause damage by altering Earth's atmosphere. For example, the amount of carbon dioxide in the atmosphere has been increasing since the early 1800's, chiefly as a result of the burning of coal, oil, and other carbon-containing fuels. Carbon dioxide allows sunlight to reach Earth and warm its surface, but it prevents some surface heat from escaping out of the atmosphere. This *greenhouse effect* can produce significant climatic changes, which will result in great environmental challenges. See **Greenhouse effect**.

CFC's break down the layer of ozone in Earth's upper atmosphere. This layer protects plants and animals from harmful ultraviolet rays (see **Ozone**).

Other effects. Most materials deteriorate faster when exposed to pollutants in the air. Concrete and stone are dissolved by air pollutants. Metals corrode faster than usual. Plastics, rubber, and fabrics are also damaged by air pollutants. Air pollution is closely related to other forms of pollution. Sulfur dioxide and nitrogen oxides can react with water droplets in the air to produce acid rain. Acid rain pollutes lakes and streams and, in high concentrations, can harm soil fertility (see **Acid rain**).

Control of air pollution

In the United States, all levels of government—federal, state, and local—have passed laws to control pollution. Congress passed the Air Quality Act in 1967. Under this act, the federal government sets goals called *air quality standards* for achieving cleaner air. The states must enforce air pollution controls to meet the goals. When states fail to enforce the regulations, the federal government can act against polluters by imposing fines.

The Clean Air Act of 1970, and its amendments, set strict standards for air quality and emissions. It requires fuel producers to develop cleaner-burning fuels. It also requires car manufacturers to equip new vehicles with pollution control devices called *catalytic converters.* In addition, the smokestacks of many electric power plants, incinerators, and factories must have *scrubbers* installed to remove pollutants before they can reach the air. New standards will remove most sulfur from fuels and reduce emissions of particulates. However, industry groups have repeatedly opposed stricter standards.

States may set stricter air standards than the federal government requires. Since 1970, California has set the strictest standards for motor-vehicle emissions. Several states require that a certain percentage of vehicles sold annually must be nonpolluting.

Efforts to control air pollution in the United States have been generally successful. Between 1970 and 1997, federal regulation resulted in a 98-percent reduction in lead emissions. During this same period, pollution by dust particles decreased by 75 percent. Pollution by sulfur dioxide decreased 35 percent. Both carbon monoxide and ozone emissions were reduced by more than 30 percent. Efforts to reduce nitrogen oxide pollution have met with the least success. Nitrogen oxide emissions decreased by only about 10 percent between 1970 and 1997. They increased for a number of years during this period before finally decreasing.

In other countries. The lack of controls on automobile emissions in Western Europe has contributed to extensive damage to forests there. Countries in Eastern Europe have lacked pollution controls altogether and, as a result, have suffered enormous environmental damage.

David E. Henderson

Related articles in *World Book* include:

Acid rain	Greenhouse effect
Automobile (Automobiles and	Incinerator
the environment)	Los Angeles (Recent
Catalytic converter	developments)
Coal (Coal as a fuel)	Ozone
Environmental pollution	Smog
Gasoline engine (Air pollution	Smoke
controls)	Soot
Global warming	

Air route. See Aviation (Aviation agencies).

Air sac. See Bird (The respiratory system); **Human body** (The air passages); **Lung** (Parts of the lungs).

Air traffic control center. See Airplane (Safety).

Air Transport Association of America (ATA) is an organization of scheduled airlines of the United States. ATA works to improve air safety, to help produce economical, efficient air service, and to coordinate the airlines' role in national defense. The organization was founded in 1936. The headquarters of ATA are in Washington, D.C.

Critically reviewed by the Air Transport Association of America

Air turbulence is a disturbance of the air that is often felt by the passengers and crew of aircraft. Air turbulence may produce only a slightly bumpy ride. But in some cases, luggage and even passengers have been tossed about the cabin.

A major source of air turbulence is *convective heating.* This phenomenon begins when the sun heats the ground. The ground, in turn, heats the air just above it. Because warm air is less dense than cool air, parcels of warm air rise in a *convection current.* Cooler air then moves downward and inward, filling the space beneath the rising air.

We can see an up-and-down movement of air parcels in puffy cumulus clouds. Air travelers who fly through even a small cumulus cloud usually experience some turbulence.

Much air turbulence is not readily visible and so is known as *clear-air turbulence.* Convective heating can create clear-air turbulence where there is not enough moisture to form clouds. In addition, clear-air turbulence occurs at extremely high altitudes, where clouds are rarely present.

An example of turbulence at high altitudes is a disturbance created by a *jet stream.* Jet streams are bands of fast-moving air that circle Earth at altitudes of about 30,000 to 45,000 feet (9,000 to 15,000 meters). Airflow in the core of the jet stream is usually smooth. However, near the outer edge of the stream, the high-speed air rubs against the surrounding low-speed air. This interaction leads to the creation of air turbulence pockets.

In the Northern Hemisphere, aircraft flying in an easterly direction frequently ride in a jet stream to reduce travel time. As an airplane crosses the stream's outer boundary, the occupants of the craft usually feel some turbulence.

Air turbulence is also associated with *weather fronts,* narrow zones between huge volumes of air that differ in temperature or humidity. These air masses move over Earth's surface much like blobs of molasses on an apple. Where air masses bump and rub against one another, pockets of air turbulence form.

Airflow over mountain ranges creates air turbulence at virtually all altitudes. Certain cloud formations sometimes indicate the presence of low-altitude disturbances. But clear-air turbulence also occurs over mountain ranges. The movement of an air mass over a range may create several disturbances at the same time. This turbulence can often be felt at altitudes as high as 60,000 feet (18,000 meters).   Brian M. Argrow

See also **Cloud; Weather** (Weather systems).

Airbag is a cloth bag that quickly fills with air during an automobile collision to cushion and protect the people inside. An airbag is most effective when used with lap and shoulder belts.

How airbags work. An airbag system consists of one or more cloth airbags, an inflator, and devices called *sensors.* The sensors can detect a sudden slowdown, which would occur in a frontal collision, or the jarring force of a side impact. Sensors for detecting frontal collisions are usually mounted at the front of the vehicle and in the passenger compartment. Those that detect side collisions are usually in the door and in the center pillar at the side of the vehicle. The sensors run on energy from the vehicle's battery or from a computerized control unit, a device that also monitors the system for malfunctions.

Airbags are designed to inflate in frontal or front-angle impacts in which the automobile strikes an immovable object at more than about 10 miles (16 kilometers) per hour or another car at about twice that speed. A side-impact airbag can be triggered by less impact.

After an impact, some airbag sensors send an electric current directly to an igniter system. Other sensors may send the current to a computerized control unit, which evaluates the situation before sending the current on to the igniter system. The electric current heats a *filament* (wire), which ignites a capsule. The capsule, in turn, ignites gas-generating pellets.

In most systems, the pellets are made of sodium azide, which produces nitrogen gas when it burns. The gas expands quickly and inflates the airbag, causing it to break through a plastic cover in the steering wheel, the dashboard, or a door panel. The whole process takes about 0.1 second from the moment a frontal impact is

General Motors

A cloth airbag helps protect the driver in a head-on collision. The bag inflates within a fraction of a second after a frontal or front-angle impact.

detected, and even less time in the event of a side impact. The airbag starts to deflate immediately, venting the harmless gas through holes in the back of the bag or through the fabric itself.

Safety concerns. Safety experts have raised concerns that airbags can injure children, pregnant women, and adults of below-average height by hitting them on the head or neck. Automobile manufacturers are developing systems that can adjust the position and inflation speed of an airbag based on the position and size of the person in the seat. The United States National Highway Traffic Safety Administration recommends placing all children 12 years old and younger in the back seat.

William H. Haverdink

Airborne troops are soldiers trained for assault by air. They may be dropped to the ground by parachute or transported to combat areas by airplanes. Airborne troops of the United States Army are volunteers. The chief center for training U.S. airborne troops is at Fort Bragg, North Carolina.

Volunteers must undergo a difficult three-week training course. In combat, airborne troops land behind enemy lines, blow up bridges, destroy communications, and cut off supplies and reinforcements. They often take the enemy by surprise and engage in fierce hand-to-hand fighting. Airborne troops carry heavy packs of equipment, including an automatic rifle, a machine gun, grenades, a medical kit, and radio equipment.

In World War II (1939-1945), the Allies and the Germans used airborne troops. The Germans first employed sky soldiers in the Netherlands in 1940 and in capturing the island of Crete in 1941. The Allies made the most effective use of paratroops. They formed a complete army of sky soldiers and coordinated parachute attacks with air, land, and naval operations. United States Army paratroopers spearheaded attacks in Sicily, Normandy, and the Netherlands. In the Philippines, airborne troops recaptured Corregidor from Japanese forces.

Airborne troops have taken part in all major military

Photri

Airborne troops drop by parachute from an airplane into a battle area or behind enemy lines.

operations since World War II. United States airborne troops are often called *paratroops, paratroopers,* and *sky soldiers.* S. Mike Pavelec

See also **Parachute.**

Airbrush is a tool used by photographers and commercial artists to apply color or shading to drawings, prints, and photographs. Photographers find it useful to bring out highlights and to supply backgrounds. The airbrush looks something like a pencil. It has a length of tubing at one end and a fine nozzle at the other. An electric pump or tank with a pressure gauge supplies a current of compressed air. The air enters the nozzle through the tubing and sends a stream of fine particles of liquid coloring matter out through the nozzle. The artist controls the air pressure by means of a valve to create different effects.

Kongsgaard Studio (WORLD BOOK photo by Steinkamp/Ballogg)

The airbrush blows out a mist of coloring matter that creates images with delicate tones and a smooth-looking surface.

The *spray gun* is a tool that works in the same way as an airbrush, but it takes less skill to operate. Painters use it to apply a coat of paint, varnish, shellac, and other finishing materials to all types of manufactured articles.

Andrew J. Stasik, Jr.

Aircraft. See Aircraft, Military; Airplane; Airship; Autogiro; Balloon; Glider; Guided missile; Helicopter; Rocket; V/STOL.

Aircraft, Military. Military aircraft are airplanes, helicopters, and other flying machines used for military purposes. Most military aircraft are operated by pilots. But *unmanned aerial vehicles* (UAV's)—often called *drones*— carry no crew and are guided by electronic devices.

Armed forces use military aircraft for a wide variety of tasks in both combat and peacetime. During a war, these aircraft attack enemy forces, protect and transport troops and supplies, defend territory, and carry out many other types of missions. Peacetime uses include rescue operations and scientific expeditions.

Military aircraft range from drones the size of small model airplanes to huge transport planes that carry tanks and trucks. Their speeds also vary greatly, reaching more than 2,000 miles per hour (mph), or 3,200 kilometers per hour (kph), for some jet planes. Some aircraft

U.S. Air Force

B-1B bomber

U.S. Air Force

KC-10 tanker

Master Sgt. Scott Reed, U.S. Air Force

MQ-1 Predator drone

Photri

Blackhawk UH-60 helicopter

Military aircraft, such as the United States aircraft shown here, are designed to perform various tasks. For example, bombers attack targets with bombs, missiles, rockets, and other weapons. Tankers refuel aircraft in flight. Unpiloted drones are flown by controllers on the ground to observe and attack enemy forces and bases. Transport helicopters are used to carry cargo.

are designed for specialized duties. For example, some military planes take off and land vertically, enabling them to operate from ships and rough terrain. Others can fly at extremely high altitudes to escape enemy missiles or at low altitudes to avoid detection by radar.

Types of military aircraft

Most military aircraft are *fixed-wing aircraft* (airplanes) or *rotary-wing aircraft* (helicopters). They are classified by their function. Those that can perform more than one type of mission are designated by their original or principal use. Military planes include (1) bombers, (2) fighters, (3) reconnaissance aircraft, (4) transports, (5) tankers, and (6) special-mission aircraft. Some of these classifications are also used for helicopters.

Bombers attack targets with bombs, missiles, rockets, and other weapons. The two main kinds of bombers are *strategic bombers* and *fighter-bombers.* Most strategic bombers are large, long-range airplanes that can attack targets deep inside enemy territory. They have two or more jet engines and a crew of two to six people.

One such strategic bomber, the American-made B-1B, can fly up to about 7,500 miles (12,000 kilometers) without refueling. Its top speed is *Mach 1.25,* which is 1 ¼ times the speed of sound. The American B-2 "stealth" bomber has special features that make it difficult to detect by radar. These features include surface materials that absorb radar energy and a winglike shape that deflects radar beams. See **Air Force, United States** (picture: B-2 "stealth" bomber).

Most fighter-bombers, also called *attack planes,* are small, short- to medium-range aircraft with one or two jet engines and a crew of one or two people. These planes are used primarily to attack ships and ground forces. One of the most advanced fighter-bombers is the American F-117 "stealth" fighter. Features much like those of the B-2 bomber make the F-117 difficult to detect by radar.

Fighters are used chiefly to intercept and attack other aircraft, but they also hit ground targets. These planes must be fast and easy to maneuver. Most fighters carry cannons, rockets, and missiles. Fighters have one or two jet engines and a crew of one or two people. Many have *swept-back wings,* which slant backward from the plane's body to the tip of the wing, or triangle-shaped *delta wings* to provide great speed. Two widely used fighters, the Russian MiG-29 and the French Mirage, can fly faster than Mach 2.

Reconnaissance aircraft are equipped with cameras or electronic sensing devices for collecting information about enemy forces. The TR-1, one of the few American reconnaissance aircraft, is used to locate enemy forces during wartime. The plane's sensing devices can detect signals from enemy radars, communications, and other electronic equipment.

Some reconnaissance aircraft photograph enemy forces and bases. However, artificial satellites that orbit the earth carry out most photographic reconnaissance today.

Transports carry military personnel and equipment. Almost any aircraft can be used as a transport, but some combat situations require specially designed planes. Most such specialized transports have oversized tires on their landing gear and high-lift devices on their wings that enable the planes to use runways that are short and unpaved.

The largest transport, the Russian Antonov An-124, can carry more than 330,000 pounds (150,000 kilograms). Some transports are equipped with guns to convert them to attack aircraft called *gunships.*

Tankers refuel other aircraft in flight. A tanker must be able to fly at the same speed and altitude as the planes it refuels. The planes approach the tanker from behind and below and pick up refueling tubes that trail from the tanker. Nearly all tankers are modified bombers, cargo aircraft, or commercial airliners. The U.S. Air Force uses the KC-135, a version of the Boeing 707 airliner, and the KC-10, a version of the McDonnell Douglas DC-10.

Special-mission aircraft include electronic support aircraft, trainers, and drones. Electronic support aircraft contain sensitive electronic instruments. Some of these aircraft are used to interfere with enemy radar and other electronic equipment. Others guard against air or ground attack and serve as command centers in a war.

The U.S. Air Force uses the Airborne Warning and Control System (AWACS) aircraft. A radar dome on top of these AWACS planes can detect and track aircraft and missiles. Trainers are used to train pilots and are designated by the stage of training in which they serve—primary, basic, or advanced. They range from planes with piston engines to jet aircraft that can be used for both training and combat.

Drones of various sizes are used for hazardous reconnaissance missions, for firing missiles at enemy targets, and as targets in combat practice. Some notable drones, such as the General Atomics MQ-1 Predator and MQ-9 Reaper, take off and land on runways. They are powered by turboprop jet engines and can circle slowly over targets for many hours. Smaller drones, such as the Aero-Vironment RQ-11 Raven, can be carried by troops into war zones and launched with a toss of the hand.

Helicopters play an important role in military operations because they can be used in a variety of missions. They have the ability to take off and land almost anywhere, and they can hover over one spot. Helicopters serve chiefly as attack aircraft, reconnaissance aircraft,

U.S. Air Force

The French Mirage 2000 is a fighter airplane designed mainly to intercept enemy planes. The missiles attached under its wings can be fired at enemy aircraft.

U.S. Air Force

The F-117 "stealth" American fighter is designed mainly to attack ground forces and ships. Flat surfaces on its fuselage deflect radar beams, making the plane difficult to detect.

The Boeing Company

The C-17 Globemaster III is a United States transport plane. It can carry about 205 troops or 160,000 pounds (72,500 kilograms) of cargo a distance of about 2,750 miles (4,450 kilometers).

and transports. Some attack helicopters are called *helicopter gunships.* A gunship, such as the American-made AH-64 Apache, can carry cannons and missiles to attack targets on the ground and in the air. Other helicopters are specially equipped for antisubmarine warfare. The American-made OH-58 Kiowa, the British Lynx, and other small helicopters are used for reconnaissance and light transport duty. The largest transport helicopters can pick up and carry planes, tanks, or trucks by using cables suspended from the helicopters.

History

The first military aircraft were balloons filled with gas or hot air. In 1794, the French Army sent up soldiers in balloons to observe enemy troop movements. During the 1800's, most major armies set up a balloon corps.

Heavier-than-air aircraft gained military importance after 1903, when the Wright brothers made the first successful plane flight. Early planes were made of cloth, wood, and wire and had a low-powered gasoline engine. Most of these aircraft were called *biplanes* because they had two main wings, one above and one be-

low the body of the plane. By 1914, biplanes could fly at an average of 75 mph (121 kph) and reach an altitude of about 10,000 feet (3,000 meters). Military use of the planes was limited largely to reconnaissance.

World War I (1914-1918) brought great changes in the design and performance of military aircraft. For example, the German Army used the engine-powered *airship,* a lighter-than-air aircraft, for reconnaissance and bombing missions. In addition, both sides recognized the possible advantages of using airplanes for attack as well as for reconnaissance. Engineers designed larger, more powerful planes that could carry bombs over long distances. The introduction of these bombers created a need for fighter aircraft to intercept them. As the war continued, fighters were armed with more effective weapons and became faster and easier to maneuver.

During the 1920's and 1930's, further improvements were made in military aircraft design. Biplanes were replaced by aluminum *monoplanes.* The monoplanes had one main wing, which extended outward from both sides of the body of the plane. Increasingly powerful engines and a streamlined design enabled monoplanes to

Early military aircraft

The first military aircraft were balloons used for reconnaissance. Heavier-than-air aircraft, developed during the early 1900's, played a major role in World War I (1914-1918). Some important early military aircraft are shown below. The dates indicate when the aircraft were first built.

WORLD BOOK illustrations by Tony Gibbons, Linden Artists Ltd.

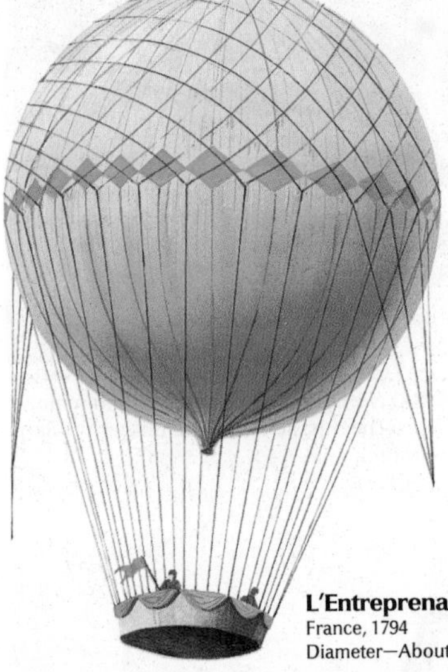

L'Entreprenant balloon
France, 1794
Diameter—About 27 ft 6 in (8 m)

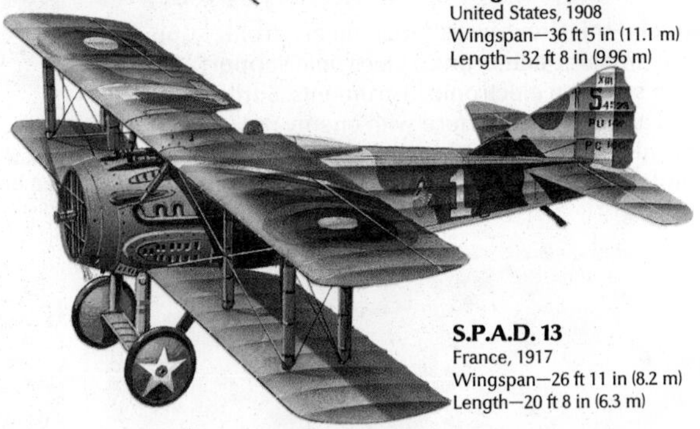

Wright A flyer
United States, 1908
Wingspan—36 ft 5 in (11.1 m)
Length—32 ft 8 in (9.96 m)

S.P.A.D. 13
France, 1917
Wingspan—26 ft 11 in (8.2 m)
Length—20 ft 8 in (6.3 m)

Fokker DR-1 triplane
Germany, 1917
Wingspan—23 ft 7 ½ in (7.2 m)
Length—18 ft 11 in (5.77 m)

Sopwith Camel
United Kingdom, 1917
Wingspan—28 ft (8.53 m)
Length—18 ft 9 in (5.72 m)

reach speeds of more than 300 mph (480 kph).

World War II (1939-1945) sped up the development of piston-engined aircraft and marked the first use of jet planes. One of the most advanced fighters was the British Spitfire, which could fly faster than 450 mph (724 kph) and higher than 40,000 feet (12,000 meters). Late in the war, Germany began to use the Messerschmitt Me 262, the first jet to fly in combat. This plane had a top speed of almost 550 mph (885 kph).

The jet age. Aircraft technology made further rapid progress in the 1950's, 1960's, and 1970's. For example, new types of wings and other structural improvements greatly increased the speed and maneuverability of jet planes. The United States and Soviet Union developed jet bombers that had the ability to fly nonstop from their own country to the other country in only a few hours.

At the same time, ground warfare was transformed by the widespread use of helicopters. Military helicopters were introduced on a large scale in the Korean War (1950-1953), chiefly for transporting supplies and wounded troops. In the late 1950's, the use of jet engines boosted the speed and lift capacity of helicopters.

During the Vietnam War (1957-1975), the United States Army, Navy, and Air Force used helicopters for attack, reconnaissance, and transport. Helicopters were also used to rescue pilots shot down in enemy territory.

Recent developments in military aircraft include improvements in design and materials. Surfaces that deflect radar beams and materials that absorb radar energy make "stealth" aircraft difficult to detect by radar. The *supercritical wing,* which is thinner and flatter than a standard wing, increases the speed and range of planes. Drones capable of shooting missiles at targets became increasingly common in warfare during the early 2000's.

S. Mike Pavelec

Related articles in *World Book* include:

Air force	Drone
Air Force, United States (Planes and weapons of the Air Force)	Guided missile
	Helicopter
	Navy, United States (Naval aviation)
Airplane (Types of airplanes; History)	Rocket
Army, United States (Army aviation)	Unmanned aerial vehicle
	V/STOL
Bomber	

Later military aircraft

Through the years, military aircraft have been improved to increase their speed and maneuverability. For example, the use of jet engines enabled planes to fly much faster than before. The Messerschmitt Me 262, built by Germany during World War II, was the first jet plane to fly in combat.

B-17G Flying Fortress bomber
United States, 1943
Wingspan—103 ft 9 in (31.62 m)
Length—74 ft 9 in (22.78 m)

A6M2 Zero fighter
Japan, 1939
Wingspan—39 ft 4 ½ in (12 m)
Length—29 ft 9 in (9.07 m)

Messerschmitt Me 262 fighter
Germany, 1944
Wingspan—41 ft (12.5 m)
Length—34 ft 9 ½ in (10.6 m)

P-51D Mustang fighter
United States, 1940
Wingspan—37 ft (11.28 m)
Length—32 ft 3 in (9.83 m)

F-14 Tomcat fighter
United States, 1970
Maximum wingspan—64 ft 1 ½ in (19.55 m)
Minimum wingspan—38 ft 2 in (11.63 m)
Length—62 ft (18.9 m)

MiG-21F fighter
Soviet Union, 1955
Wingspan—23 ft 5 ½ in (7.15 m)
Length—44 ft 2 in (13.46 m)

Avro Vulcan B.Mk.2 bomber
United Kingdom, 1952
Wingspan—111 ft (33.83 m)
Length—99 ft 11 in (30.45 m)

Aircraft carrier is a ship that is used as a mobile base for airplanes. With its aircraft striking force, the carrier is the most powerful surface warship. Carriers are often referred to as *flattops* because of their wide, flat decks. The only ships bigger than carriers are the largest oil tankers.

Aircraft carriers are equipped with only a minimum number of antiaircraft guns or defensive missiles. Carriers usually *steam* (travel) with other ships. Cruisers, destroyers, and submarines protect aircraft carriers from enemy missiles, planes, surface ships, and submarines. Such a fleet is referred to as a *carrier task force* or *battle group.*

Airplanes take off from, and land on, the *flight deck.* They are repaired and stored on the *hangar deck* just below it. Large elevators move the planes from one deck to the other. The *superstructure* of the ship, called the *island,* includes the command and navigation bridges, communications equipment, radar antennas, and smokestacks, unless the ship has nuclear power. The island rises on the flight deck's *starboard side* (right side facing forward). The rest of the deck is left clear for planes. A carrier also houses maintenance shops for the planes and living quarters and *mess* (cooking and eating areas) for the pilots, air crews, and ship's crew. It has storage space for bombs, ammunition, fuel, and food.

The United States Navy operates the world's largest carrier fleet, consisting of 11 major ships. The navies of Brazil, China, France, India, Russia, and the United Kingdom also have carriers that launch and land conventional aircraft. The U.S. Navy also operates 9 *amphibious assault ships,* which resemble small aircraft carriers. Helicopters and *V/STOL* (Vertical/Short Take-Off and Landing) aircraft operate from these ships. The navies of several countries, including Australia, Italy, Japan, South Korea, Spain, and Thailand include at least one of these small carriers.

Flight operations. Conventional airplanes are too heavy and require too great an air speed to take off from a carrier entirely under their own power. For this reason, they are launched by a catapult from the take-off areas (see **Catapult**). The carrier steams into the wind at high speed during take-offs. Wind speed plus the ship's speed helps lift the planes as they take off.

The carrier also heads into the wind when planes land. If a carrier steams at 25 *knots* (nautical miles per hour) into a wind blowing 25 knots, then the wind speed over the carrier's deck is 50 knots. A plane flying at 100 knots therefore has a relative landing speed of only 50 knots. *Arresting gear,* four steel cables stretched across the rear landing area of the deck, catch a tail hook lowered from the plane. The plane is brought to a stop over a distance of about 300 feet (91 meters).

Modern carriers for conventional aircraft have angled landing sections on their flight decks. The landing section, which takes up the rear two-thirds of the deck, angles toward the carrier's *port side* (left side facing forward) and extends over the water. A plane that makes a bad approach or misses the arresting wires with its tail hook may keep going and fly off the deck. Helicopters and certain other aircraft can take off and land vertically and so require no runway.

The United States carrier fleet. Aircraft carriers are the U.S. Navy's principal warships. They carry jet fighters and jet bombers. They also have radar, reconnaissance, and tanker planes, and antisubmarine aircraft. Each carrier usually carries six helicopters.

The Navy groups its carriers by *class.* The name of each class is that of the first ship built in the class. Most active carriers today are *Nimitz* class. These 10 nuclear-powered ships are the *Nimitz,* the *Dwight D. Eisenhower,* the *Carl Vinson,* the *Theodore Roosevelt,* the *Abraham Lincoln,* the *George Washington,* the *John C. Stennis,* the *Harry S. Truman,* the *Ronald Reagan,* and the *George H. W. Bush.*

Nimitz-class ships are among the world's largest warships measured in *displacement tonnage.* This measurement refers to the number of long tons or metric tons of water *displaced* (pushed aside) by a ship. Each *Nimitz*-class ship displaces 97,000 long tons (98,600 metric tons) when fully loaded. Each ship is 1,092 feet (333 meters) long, has a flight deck 252 feet (77 meters) wide, and can carry 85 aircraft and about 5,700 people.

The *Gerald R. Ford,* a nuclear-powered carrier with a

An aircraft carrier is a warship that serves as a mobile base for jet bombers, fighters, and other types of military planes. The nuclear-powered carrier *Carl Vinson, shown here,* is part of the *Nimitz* class of U.S. Navy carriers.

new design, was commissioned in 2017. It is the first of the *Ford* class of carriers built to replace older *Nimitz*-class ships. The *Gerald R. Ford* displaces about 100,000 long tons (102,000 metric tons).

The only aircraft the Navy's nine amphibious assault ships carry are V/STOL aircraft and helicopters. These ships are not nuclear-powered and are designed mainly for attacking targets on land. The Navy does not classify them as aircraft carriers, but they have capabilities similar to those of small carriers operated by other nations.

History. In 1910, British and American pilots began experimenting with take-offs and landings from ships. In 1917, the *Furious,* a British Royal Navy cruiser, was outfitted with a flight deck. The first ship to have a full, unobstructed flight deck was the Royal Navy's *Argus,* completed in 1918. The first aircraft carrier in the U.S. Navy was the *Langley,* a converted coal ship. It went into service in 1922. The *Ranger,* commissioned by the U.S. Navy in 1934, was the first ship built especially for aircraft.

During World War II (1939-1945), the warring nations built more than 150 aircraft carriers. They were the most important ships of the war. Planes launched from Japanese carriers attacked the U.S. naval base at Pearl Harbor, Hawaii, and the first U.S. air raid on Japan was made by bombers from the *Hornet.* British aircraft carriers escorted supply convoys in the Atlantic Ocean and the Mediterranean Sea, and also took part in fleet actions such as the sinking of the German battleship *Bismarck.*

After the war, many carriers were scrapped. By the 1960's, only the United States kept a large fleet of carriers. The *Forrestal,* commissioned in 1955, was the first U.S. carrier to have an angled flight deck and jet fighters. *Forrestal*-class ships carried more aircraft than previous carriers, and they were sometimes called *supercarriers.*

The *Kitty Hawk,* the first of several ships of the *Kitty Hawk* class of U.S. supercarriers, was commissioned in 1961. That same year, the U.S. Navy commissioned the *Enterprise,* the first nuclear-powered aircraft carrier in history. It was the only ship of its *Enterprise* class.

Norman Polmar

See also **Navy, United States; World War II** (The war in Asia and the Pacific; picture: The aircraft carrier).

Airedale terrier, *AIR DAYL,* is the name of a breed of large terriers. It weighs 50 to 60 pounds (23 to 27 kilograms) when full-grown. Its coat of wiry hair is black or grizzled on its back, and tan on the rest of its body.

The Airedale was named for the Aire Valley in northern England. The breed was developed in England about 1880. One of its ancestors was the otter hound. The Airedale is fearless, a good watchdog, and affectionate toward its owner. It also is a good swimmer.

Critically reviewed by the Airedale Terrier Club of America

See also **Dog** (picture: Terriers); **Terrier.**

Airline. See **Airport; Aviation.**

Airmail is mail sent by aircraft. It is the fastest way to send packages and many other types of mail to distant places. Airliners carry the mail between large cities. Some cities offer helicopter service between central and suburban post offices. Nearly all first-class mail going more than 200 miles (320 kilometers) travels by air.

Earle Ovington flew the first official airmail in the United States in 1911 between Garden City and Mineola, New York. The first continuous regular airmail service in the world started on May 15, 1918, with United States Army pilots flying between New York City, Philadelphia, and Washington, D.C.

On Aug. 12, 1918, the Post Office Department (now the United States Postal Service) began making contracts with private airlines to carry the mail. The first night airmail was flown from Omaha, Nebraska, to Chicago in 1921. Regular night airmail flights and regular transcontinental mail service began in 1924. The American Railway Express Company began shipping air express packages on airlines in 1927.

The cancellation of all airmail contracts in 1934 marked the beginning of airmail rate regulation. Rates were regulated by the Civil Aeronautics Administration (now part of the Federal Aviation Administration). The regulation of airmail rates and service ended on Dec. 31, 1984. In 1985, the U.S. Postal Service returned to contracting with passenger and freight airlines to transport mail. Critically reviewed by the United States Postal Service

See also **Airplane** (The golden age); **Aviation** (Aviation progress; picture).

WORLD BOOK illustration by Robert Keys

Parts of an aircraft carrier

Aircraft take off from and land on the *flight deck* of a carrier. This deck has catapults and arresting wires that assist planes. Elevators move aircraft to and from the *hangar deck,* where they are stored. The *island* houses communications and radar equipment.

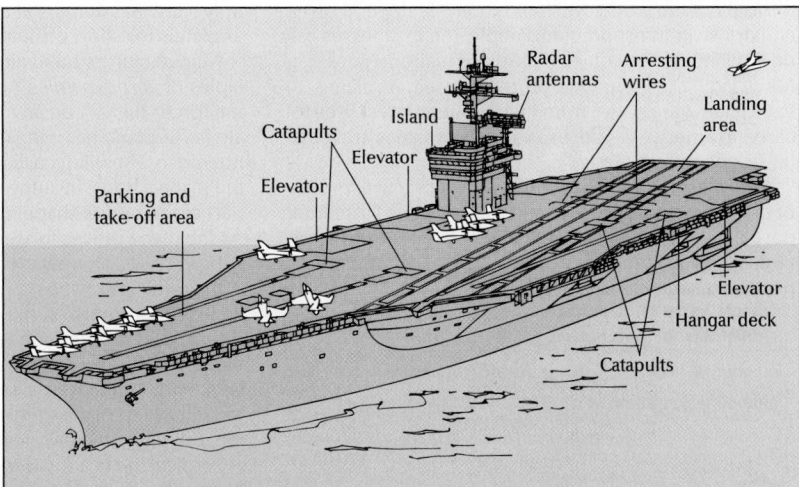

Radar antennas · Arresting wires · Landing area · Island · Catapults · Elevator · Parking and take-off area · Elevator · Elevator · Hangar deck · Catapults

The Boeing Company

A giant commercial airliner can fly hundreds of passengers long distances, bringing distant parts of the world within easy reach of one another. The Boeing 777-300, a large twin-engine passenger jet, can fly about a fourth of the way around the world without refueling.

Airplane

Airplane is a piloted, engine-driven machine that can fly through the sky, supported by the flow of air around its wings. Hundreds of thousands of airplanes are used throughout the world. Millions of people depend on aircraft for swift transportation. People and businesses rely on airplanes for the quick delivery of mail and packages. Many industries ship their products by air. Airplanes have many other uses, from helping fight forest fires to carrying emergency aid. In addition, airplanes are a major weapon of war.

Airplanes provide the world's fastest practical means of transporting passengers and freight. Most large transport planes routinely fly 500 to 600 miles per hour (mph), or 800 to 970 kilometers per hour (kph). The fastest airplanes are *supersonic,* which means they can fly faster

than sound travels. At sea level, sound has a speed of 760 mph (1,225 kph).

Airplanes range in size from training planes, which have only two seats, to jumbo jets, which can carry hundreds of passengers. In the United States, about 90 percent of all airplanes have one or two engines and carry only a few passengers at a time. Many people use such airplanes for short business or pleasure trips.

Manufacturers build airplanes according to the principles of *aerodynamics.* Aerodynamics is the study of the forces that act on an object as it moves through the air. An airplane has wings that are *fixed*—that is, they do not move. The wings usually extend from either side of the plane's body. In some cases, the wings are actually part of the body's shape. The wings are curved on top. As the plane moves forward, the flow of air around the wings creates an upward force called *lift.*

In addition to wings, a plane has one or more engines and various control surfaces. The engines must move the airplane fast enough to produce the lift needed for flight. The control surfaces are movable sections on the back edge of the wings and tail. The pilot adjusts them to control the plane's flight path. The activity of designing, building, and flying aircraft is called *aeronautics.*

An airplane is a *heavier-than-air* aircraft, meaning it is heavier than the air it displaces. Airplanes achieve flight

Timothy S. Wolters, the contributor of this article, is an Assistant Professor of History at Utah State University and former Ramsey Chair of Naval Aviation History at the National Air and Space Museum of the Smithsonian Institution. The drawings throughout this article, unless otherwise credited, were prepared for World Book by Tom Morgan.

© Chris Sorensen, The Stock Market

A powerful jet cargo plane can carry tons of goods nonstop for thousands of miles or kilometers. Privately operated package delivery services use planes such as the one above to deliver almost any kind of merchandise within a few days to customers throughout the world.

in a different way than do *airships,* such as blimps or dirigibles. These *lighter-than-air* aircraft rise and float because they are filled with a gas that is lighter than the surrounding air.

During the late 1700's, people made their first flights into the air using balloons. After the first balloon flights, inventors tried to develop a heavier-than-air flying machine. Some inventors experimented with *gliders* (engineless planes). They studied birds' wings and discovered that the wings are curved. By building gliders with curved wings instead of flat ones, they could make the vehicles fly hundreds of feet or meters. But heavier-than-air machines could not fly far until the invention of an engine light enough but powerful enough to keep a plane in flight. The first such engines were four-stroke gasoline engines, developed during the 1880's and initially used to power bicycles, boats, and carriages.

In 1903, the brothers Orville and Wilbur Wright—two American bicycle makers—made the first successful powered airplane flights in history near Kitty Hawk,

Henley & Savage, Uniphoto

Light planes make up most of the world's privately owned airplanes. Most light planes are propeller driven, have a single engine, and are small enough to land and take off at small airports.

Outline

I. Types of airplanes
  A. Commercial transport planes
  B. General aviation planes
  C. Military planes
  D. Seaplanes
  E. Special-purpose planes
II. The parts of an airplane
  A. The wing
  B. The fuselage
  C. The tail
  D. The landing gear
  E. The controls and instruments
  F. Propellers
III. Power for flight
  A. Reciprocating engines
  B. Jet engines
  C. Turboprop engines
  D. Rocket engines

IV. Principles of flight
  A. Gravity and lift   C. Changing altitude
  B. Drag and thrust   D. Changing direction
V. Flying an airplane
  A. Basic movements and controls
  B. Proper use of the controls
  C. Stalling
  D. Flying by instruments
  E. Measuring flying speed
  F. Learning to fly
VI. Air navigation
  A. Pilotage
  B. Dead reckoning
  C. Electronic navigation
  D. Inertial guidance
  E. Safety
VII. Building an airplane
  A. Design and testing   B. Mass production
VIII. History

North Carolina. After the Wright brothers' success, pilots and inventors worked continually to improve airplane design. By the late 1950's, passenger planes with jet engines had brought all countries within easy reach of one another.

This article provides an overview of airplanes and how they work. To learn about the aviation industry and careers in aviation, see the *World Book* article on **Aviation**.

Types of airplanes

There are many kinds of airplanes, and they vary greatly in size, speed, and function. Today's airplanes can be divided into five main groups: (1) commercial transport planes, (2) general aviation planes, (3) military planes, (4) seaplanes, and (5) special-purpose planes.

Commercial transport planes are large planes owned by airline companies. Most of these planes are *airliners*—planes that are designed to carry passengers and some cargo. Some commercial transports are designed to carry cargo only. The largest transport planes commonly used weigh about 400 tons (360 metric tons) when fully loaded.

Most large airliners can carry from 100 to 250 passengers. However, some can carry more. For example, the Airbus A380 has room for more than 550 passengers and carries more than 51,400 gallons (194,000 liters) of fuel. A typical interior layout includes 18 washrooms and multiple galleys.

Most airliners routinely fly 500 to 600 mph (800 to 970 kph). Supersonic transport planes have traveled at 1,350 mph (2,180 kph).

Most airliners are powered by jet engines, which enable the planes to travel long distances at high speeds without refueling. Most four-engine jets, such as the Boeing 747 or the Airbus A340, can fly at 600 mph (970 kph) nonstop for 6,000 miles (9,700 kilometers) or more—farther than the distance between New York City and Tokyo. Four-engine jet transports fly at an altitude of 30,000 to 45,000 feet (9,100 to 13,700 meters), and so they stay above most storms.

Many three-engine jets are designed for shorter flights than are four-engine jets. Three-engine jets can also use shorter runways. Some three-engine jetliners, such as the McDonnell Douglas DC-10, can carry as many passengers as most four-engine jets can carry.

Many twin-engine jetliners carry fewer passengers than three- or four-engine jets and are used for shorter trips to serve small and medium-sized cities. Other twin-engine jets fly long trips. The Boeing 777, for example, can carry more than 300 passengers over 7,200 miles (11,600 kilometers). Twin-engine, propeller-driven planes, such as the Beechcraft King Air, travel at less than 400 mph (640 kph) and make mostly short flights.

The Boeing Company

Cessna Aircraft Company

Passenger jets range in size from the enormous Boeing 747 jumbo jet, *above*, which could hold more than 400 people, to small business jets such as the Cessna Citation Bravo, *right*, which seats a maximum of 6 passengers. The 747 has ranked among the world's largest commercial airliners. Business executives use small jets such as the Citation Bravo to fly to out-of-town assignments or meetings.

General aviation planes are smaller than most commercial transports and can thus land and take off at smaller airfields. Most of these planes are *light planes,* which generally weigh less than 2,000 pounds (900 kilograms) when empty and have two to six seats.

Most light planes are single-engine, propeller-driven planes owned by individuals. Many people fly such planes for personal transportation and enjoyment. Light planes have hundreds of other uses. For example, they are used to inspect pipelines and power lines, to spot and fight forest fires, and to deliver emergency aid. Some light planes are used to haul light cargo, to take pictures from the air, and to teach student pilots to fly. Farmers use light planes to help them plant seeds, check soil erosion, and count livestock.

The largest general aviation planes have two engines. Air taxi services and commuter airlines use such planes to transport passengers—usually fewer than 20—be-

McDonnell Douglas Corporation

A three-engine jet transport, such as the DC-10, *above,* generally makes shorter flights than four-engine jets do. But some carry nearly as many passengers as jumbo jets carry.

U.S. Air Force

Four-engine jet transports are designed for long nonstop flights. Commercial airlines own and operate most of these planes. But some, such as the Lockheed C-5A Galaxy, *above,* are military transports. The Galaxy is one of the world's largest airplanes. It carries battle tanks and other military equipment.

Raytheon Aircraft

Propeller-driven light planes are used to carry passengers and lightweight or perishable goods. They also perform many other tasks, from scattering seeds to carrying emergency aid.

U.S. Air Force

Military planes carry out special duties for a nation's armed forces. Jet fighters, such as the U.S. Air Force's F-16, *left,* are used chiefly to intercept and attack enemy aircraft.

Aerobatic planes perform difficult maneuvers, such as flying in close formation. These military jets are flown by the Blue Angels, the U.S. Navy's famous aerobatic team.

David R. Frazier Photolibrary

tween small airports and the large airports that serve larger airliners.

Many businesses own single- or twin-engine airplanes. Such *business planes,* also called *corporate planes,* are used to fly employees to out-of-town assignments or meetings.

Extremely light aircraft are flown for recreation. In the United States, where they are called *ultralights,* these one-seat, single-engine aircraft weigh no more than 254 pounds (115 kilograms) and carry only 5 gallons (19 liters) of fuel or less. Ultralights are allowed to fly only below 10,000 feet (3,000 meters) and at a speed of 63 mph (101 kph) or less. In other countries, these light aircraft are commonly called *microlights* and usually have two seats. They may weigh up to 496 pounds (225 kilograms) and carry up to 15 gallons (57 liters) of fuel. They are allowed to fly only below 10,000 feet and at a speed of 40 mph (65 kph) or less.

Military planes carry out a variety of duties for a nation's armed forces. Some military planes are special models of transports or light planes that the armed forces have bought from aircraft manufacturers. For example, the United States armed forces use special models of the Boeing 707 as tankers for refueling other planes in the air. Many other kinds of military planes are custom-made. Most are *bombers,* which mainly attack ground targets, or *fighters,* which mainly attack other aircraft. *Fighter-bombers* can both fight and drop bombs. One of the most advanced fighter-bombers is the Lockheed F-117A "stealth" fighter, a sleek plane designed to be nearly invisible to radar.

Some military planes are designed for tasks other than attacks on an enemy. For example, the Lockheed C-5A Galaxy is an enormous transport plane that can carry two battle tanks weighing 50 tons (45 metric tons), or about 350 troops. Another Lockheed plane, the SR-71A, was one of the most advanced spy planes ever built. It carried cameras and instruments used to survey enemy forces and installations in the late 1900's. Today, survey tasks are often accomplished by pilotless aircraft called *unmanned aerial vehicles.* For more information on military planes, see **Air Force, United States** (Planes and weapons of the Air Force); **Aircraft, Military.**

Seaplanes can touch down and take off on water. There are three kinds of seaplanes: (1) floatplanes, (2) flying boats, and (3) amphibians. Floatplanes are equipped with big floats instead of wheels. Flying boats have a wa-

tertight body that floats in the water like the hull of a ship. Amphibians, which can land and take off on both land and water, are flying boats with retractable wheels attached to their floats or hull. The pilot raises the wheels when operating the plane on water and lowers the wheels on land.

Special-purpose planes. Many airplanes are built for particular jobs. For example, farmers use *agricultural spray planes* to spray their fields with liquid fertilizer or insecticide. These planes are built to fly slowly and to carry large tanks filled with chemicals. An amphibian plane made in Canada is designed for fighting forest fires. This plane can fly just above a lake and draw over 1,000 gallons (3,800 liters) of water into its tanks. The

Andy Sacks, Tony Stone Images

Agricultural spray planes, also known as crop dusters, are used to spray farm crops with liquid fertilizer or insecticide. These planes are built to carry large tanks of liquid chemicals.

Northrop Grumman Corporation

An amphibian plane can operate from land or water. An amphibian designed to fight forest fires, *above,* can draw lake water into tanks in its hull and spray the water on a fire from the air.

Vince Streano, The Stock Market

Ultralight planes, such as the one shown here, are flown for recreation. In the United States, ultralights weigh no more than 254 pounds (115 kilograms) and have one seat and one engine.

plane then flies to the fire and drops its load of water.

Special-purpose planes also include planes used for air races or for *aerobatics* (air acrobatics). These are light planes that can perform difficult maneuvers. Another large category of special-purpose planes consists of *home-built* airplanes, which are built from plans or manufactured in kits for assembly by the owner.

Aircraft called *V/STOL's* are designed to take off and land vertically or on a short runway. The term *V/STOL* stands for Vertical/Short Take-Off and Landing. V/STOL's have great military value because they can land on small airfields near battlefields and on ships smaller than aircraft carriers. See **V/STOL**.

The parts of an airplane

All airplanes, except for a few experimental planes, have the same basic parts. They are (1) the wing, (2) the *fuselage* (pronounced *FYOO zuh lahzh*)—that is, the body of the plane, (3) the tail, (4) the landing gear, and (5) the engine. All these parts—except the engine—make up a plane's *airframe.*

This section of the article discusses the basic parts of the airframe, as well as airplane controls and instruments and types of propellers. The airplane engine is described in the next section. For information about how the parts of an airplane work to move the plane through the air and how a pilot uses controls and instruments, see the section called *Principles of flight.*

The wing. People usually think of an airplane as having two wings, but modern planes actually have only one. This wing is a single, continuous structure that extends outward from each side of the fuselage. A wing has a nearly flat bottom and a curved top. This shape helps create the lift that raises an airplane off the ground and keeps it in the air.

Most airplane wings are metal. They have a skeleton of lengthwise *spars* and crosswise *ribs.* The skeleton has a thin covering, usually of an aluminum *alloy* (mixture of metals). Most planes have a *cantilever* wing, which is completely supported by its internal structure.

An airplane wing has a *root, tip, leading edge,* and *trailing edge.* The root is the part of the wing attached to the fuselage. The tip is the edge of the wing farthest from the fuselage. The leading edge is the curved front edge of the wing. The top of the wing thickens from the leading edge and then slopes back to the knifelike trailing edge. On most airplanes, the wing tips are slightly higher than the wing roots. Such wings are called *dihedral* wings. Many planes have a *low-wing* design—that is, the wing is joined to the lower part of the fuselage. In planes of *mid-wing* design, the wing is attached about halfway up the side of the fuselage. *High-wing* planes have the wing near the top.

In planes of *straight-wing* design, the wing's leading edge and the fuselage form a right angle. This design is common because it works over a broad range of speeds. Many high-speed airplanes, especially jets, have a *sweptwing.* Such a wing, also called a *swept-back wing,* slants backward from the root to the tip. A few planes have a wing that is *swept forward.* A *delta wing* is shaped like a triangle. The root may be almost as long as the fuselage, and the leading edge is deeply swept back for high-speed flight.

Most airplane wings have movable control surfaces that help balance the plane during flight. *Ailerons* are hinged sections along the trailing edge of the wing. They can be moved up or down to control the plane's *lateral stability* (balance from side to side). The ailerons are used to make the plane *bank* (tilt) to the right or to the left for a turn. When one aileron is raised, the other is lowered. On most planes, each aileron has a small

McDonnell Douglas Corporation

V/STOL's, or Vertical/Short Take-Off and Landing planes, can take off and land without runways or on short ones. These planes can land easily on ships and can also use small airfields in large cities or in rural areas.

The parts of an airplane This drawing shows the parts of a light plane, a Piper Cherokee. The basic parts are the wing, *fuselage* (body), tail, landing gear, and engine. Some other parts, such as the ribs and spars in the wing, are structural. Still other parts, including the ailerons, flaps, rudder, and stabilator, are used to control the plane. The drawing also shows the wing's root, tip, and leading and trailing edges.

WORLD BOOK illustration by Tom Morgan; courtesy of Piper Aircraft Corp.

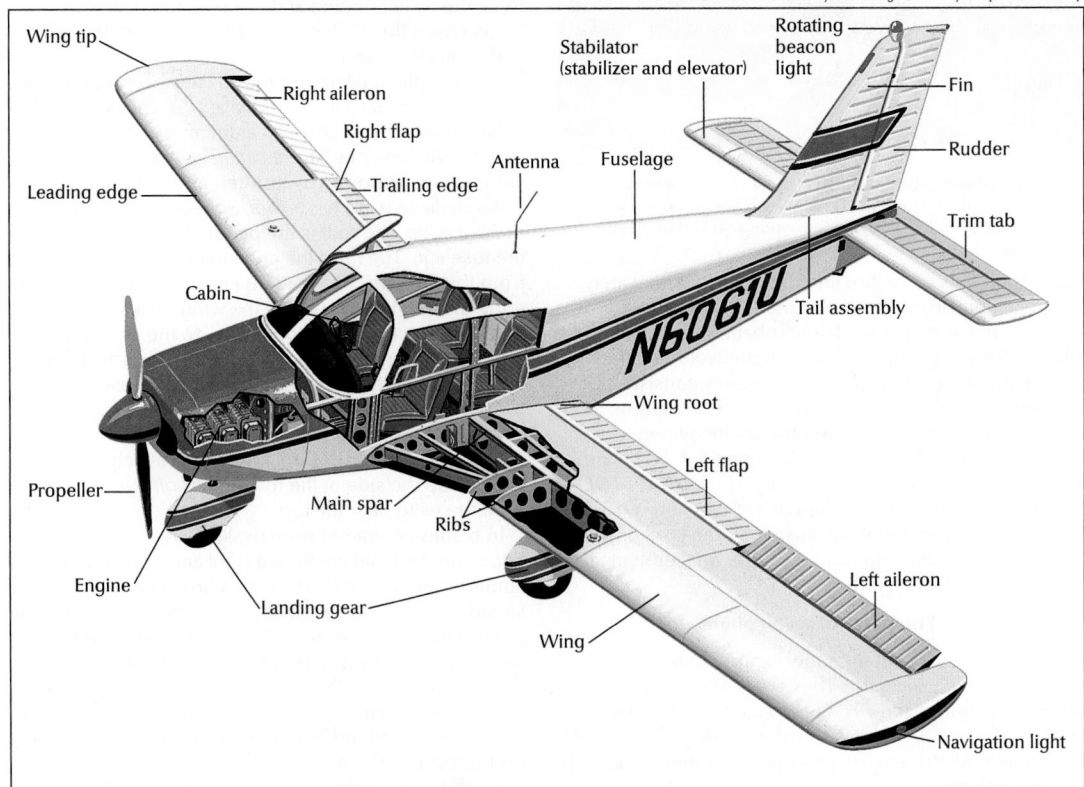

hinged section called a *trim tab*. A pilot uses the trim tabs to regulate the pressure that must be applied to other controls in keeping the plane in *trim* (balance) during flight. There are usually trim tabs on the movable parts of the tail as well as on the ailerons.

Many airplanes have *flaps*. Flaps are hinged sections along the trailing edge of the wing near the root. They are lowered to help increase the plane's lift during both take-off and landing.

Some planes have additional wing controls. A *spoiler* is a plate on the upper part of each side of the wing. A pilot can raise both spoilers to act as air brakes. If the pilot raises the spoiler on one side only, it makes the plane bank in that direction. Some planes have spoilers instead of ailerons. A *slat* is a hinged section on the leading edge of the wing. At low speeds, the slats slant forward and help to provide extra lift. A *slot* is an opening behind the leading edge near each wing tip. Slots also help produce more lift at low speeds.

Many airplanes have their engines on or in the wing. The engines are enclosed in metal casings called *nacelles (nuh SEHLZ)*. Most wings also have space inside for fuel tanks and landing gear. Various lights are also on the plane's wing. For example, each wing tip has a colored *navigation light*, also called a *position light*. The light on the plane's left wing tip is red, and the light on the right wing tip is green. By noting the position of

these two lights, a person can tell the direction in which a plane is traveling.

The fuselage of an airplane extends from the nose to the tail. Most airplane bodies have a tubelike shape and are covered with a lightweight aluminum skin. The name *fuselage* comes from the French word *fuselé*, which means *spindle-shaped*. The engine of most single-engine planes is in the front part of the fuselage. However, some multiengine jet planes have their engines at the rear of the fuselage.

The fuselage houses the controls, crew, passengers, and cargo. In the smallest airplanes, the fuselage contains a cockpit with room for only the pilot, or for the pilot and one passenger. In most planes that carry from two to six people, the pilot and passengers sit together in a single cabin. Most large planes have a cockpit for the crew and a cabin for the passengers and cargo. In major passenger airliners, such as the Airbus A340 and the Boeing 787, the cabin has separate *decks* (floors) for the passengers and cargo.

The tail, also called the *empennage (ehm PEHN ahj)*, is the rear part of a plane. It helps guide the plane and keep it balanced in flight, much as feathers do on an arrow. Most tails consist of a vertical *fin* and *rudder* and a horizontal *stabilizer* and *elevator*. The fin stands upright and does not move. It keeps the rear of the plane from swinging to the left or right. The rudder is hinged to the

Text continued on page 216.

Wing, tail, and landing gear designs

WORLD BOOK diagrams

Wings have various shapes, depending on the planes for which they are designed. *Straight wings* perform at both high and low speeds. *Sweptwings* (also called *swept-back wings), swept-forward wings,* and *delta wings* are used on high-speed jets.

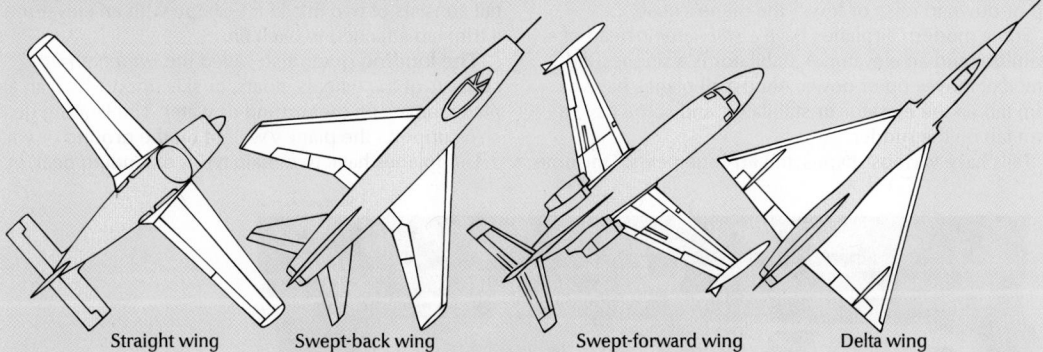

Straight wing   Swept-back wing   Swept-forward wing   Delta wing

Tails. The fin and rudder, which make up the vertical surfaces of the tail, may be at a right angle to the fuselage or swept back. Some planes have twin or triple fins. The stabilizer and elevator, the horizontal surfaces of the tail, are near the top of the vertical surfaces in a T-tail and attached to the fuselage in an anhedral tail. A V-tail has two fins in a V shape, each with an elevator and trim tab.

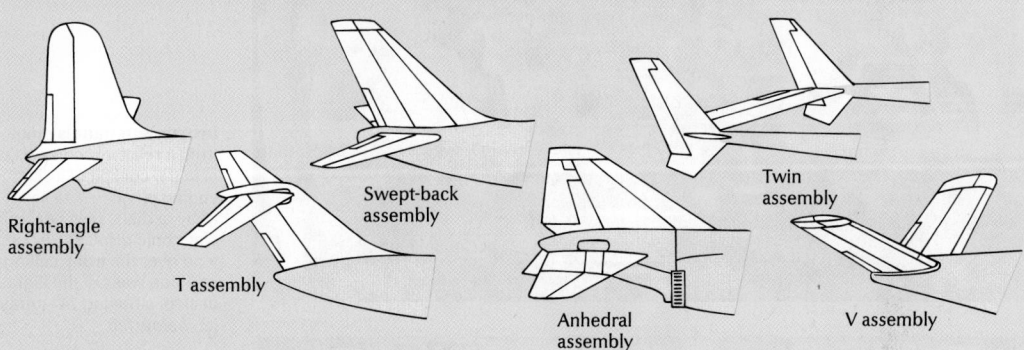

Right-angle
assembly

T assembly

Swept-back
assembly

Anhedral
assembly

Twin
assembly

V assembly

Landing gears. Some planes have a *tail-wheel landing gear*—1 wheel under the tail and 1 under each side of the fuselage or wing. Most planes have a *tricycle landing gear*—1 to 4 wheels under the nose and 2 to 20 under the midfuselage or 1 or 4 wheels under the nose and 1 to 10 under each side of the wing.

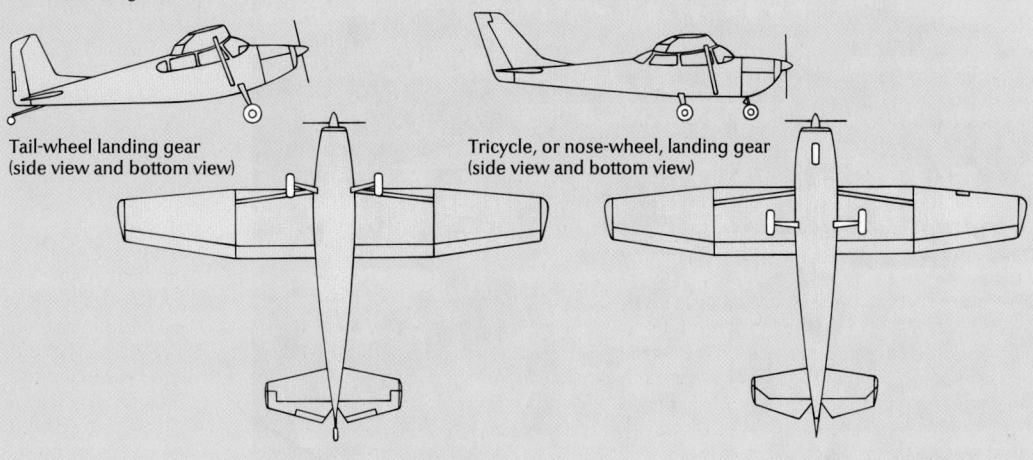

Tail-wheel landing gear
(side view and bottom view)

Tricycle, or nose-wheel, landing gear
(side view and bottom view)

rear edge of the fin and can be moved from side to side. It helps control the plane during a turn.

The stabilizer is like a small wing in the tail. It prevents the tail from bobbing up and down and so keeps the plane flying at a steady altitude. The elevator is hinged to the rear edge of the stabilizer. A pilot moves the elevator up or down to raise or lower the plane's nose.

Some modern airplanes have a *stabilator* instead of a stabilizer and an elevator. A stabilator is a single solid unit that moves up or down. Almost all planes have a trim tab on the elevator or stabilator, and some have a trim tab on the rudder.

Tails have various shapes and arrangements. On some planes, the fin and rudder stand upright at a right angle to the fuselage. On other planes, they slant back at a sharp angle. Most jet planes with engines at the rear of the fuselage have their horizontal stabilizer and elevator mounted across or near the top of a tall vertical fin and rudder. Some light airplanes have a V-tail. This type of tail consists of two fins in a V-shape with an elevator and a trim tab attached to each fin.

The landing gear, also called the *undercarriage,* consists of the wheels, floats, or skis upon which an airplane moves on the ground or water. The landing gear also supports the plane's weight on the ground or water.

Landplanes have two main types of landing gear. In

Raytheon Aircraft

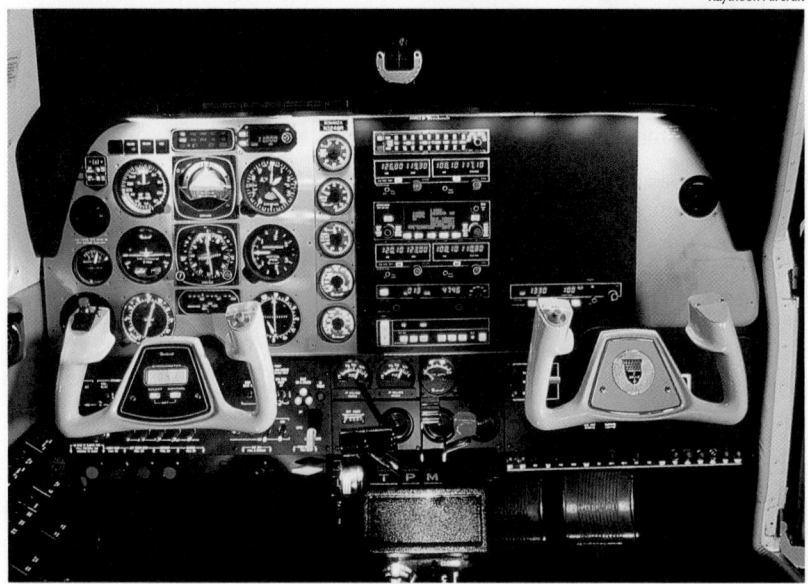

The Boeing Company

Instrument panels range from a relatively compact panel in the cockpit of a single-engine plane, *left,* to a vast array of dials, switches, and electronic displays that extend over the front, ceiling, and side walls of the flight deck of a Boeing 747 jumbo jet, *below left.*

some light planes, landing gear consists of a wheel under each side of the wing or front part of the fuselage
and a third wheel under the tail. Most airplanes, however, have a *tricycle landing gear.* On light planes, it consists of a wheel under the nose and two wheels under
the midfuselage or one under each side of the wing.
Many large airplanes have a tricycle landing gear made
up of (1) a *main gear* with from 1 to 10 wheels under
each side of the wing or from 2 to 20 wheels under the
midfuselage and (2) a *nose gear* with 2 or 4 wheels.

Landing gear may be fixed or retractable. Fixed landing gear remains extended in flight. The extended gear
increases air resistance and thus slows down the plane.
Retractable landing gear can be *retracted* (drawn back)
into either the wing or the fuselage after take-off. Most
high-speed planes use retractable landing gear.

The watertight body of a flying boat serves as both
landing gear and cabin. Floats are landing gear for floatplanes. Amphibians, which operate from land or water,
have retractable wheels in their floats or hull. Some
planes are equipped with skis for landing in snow.

The controls and instruments. Inside the cockpit,
the pilot has a variety of controls, instruments, and navigation aids. Most planes have a *yoke* (control wheel) that
operates the ailerons and elevator. A few special types
of planes, such as fighters and spray planes, have a control *stick* instead of a yoke. Two *rudder pedals* on the
floor control the rudder. Various engine instruments
display information on the fuel supply, oil pressure, and
other conditions affecting the engine. Flight instruments
show the plane's speed, altitude, and *attitude* (position in
relation to the horizon).

Some airplanes have an *automatic flight control system,* sometimes called an *automatic pilot* or *autopilot.*
This device is connected to the plane's controls and automatically keeps the plane on course.

Many airplanes have one or more flight recorders,
sometimes called *black boxes.* These devices record
flight data, such as speed and direction, or they record
conversations and other sounds in the cockpit. In case
of a crash or other incident, the flight recorders help investigators determine how the incident happened.

Propellers, also called *airscrews,* move turboprop
planes and planes with reciprocating engines through
the air. On most such planes, each propeller has its own
engine. However, a few planes have *coaxial propellers*—
two propellers turned by a single engine. On most
single-engine planes, the engine and a single propeller
are mounted at the front of the fuselage. Most propeller-
driven planes with more than one engine have their engines and propellers on the wing.

Small planes have a two- or three-bladed propeller.
Some planes have propellers with up to eight blades.
Many planes have *controllable-pitch propellers.* A pilot
can change the angle of the blades on these propellers
in flight. A particular blade angle is best suited to a particular speed or maneuver. With the blades at the proper angle, the plane operates most efficiently. On *fixed-
pitch propellers,* the angle of the blades cannot be
changed. *Constant-speed propellers* adjust their blade
angle automatically and so keep the plane's engine
speed steady during any maneuver.

The blades of *feathering propellers* can be turned to a
right angle so that their edges are parallel to the plane's

Airplane propellers

WORLD BOOK diagrams; courtesy of Hartzell Propeller, Inc.

Propeller designs vary according to the type of plane.
On most light planes, propellers have two or three
blades. On large planes, they have three to eight blades.

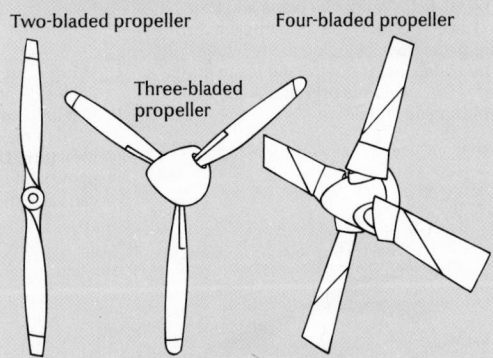

Two-bladed propeller   Four-bladed propeller

Three-bladed
propeller

A propeller blade resembles a plane wing. Like a wing,
it has a tip, root, leading edge, and trailing edge. The
blades are attached to an engine-driven shaft by a *hub.*

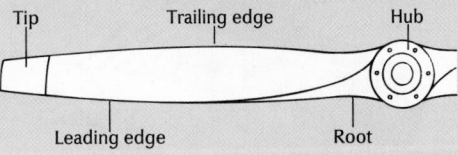

Tip   Trailing edge   Hub

Leading edge   Root

A feathering propeller has blades that can be turned
on edge if the engine fails. This action reduces air resistance and stops the propeller from spinning.

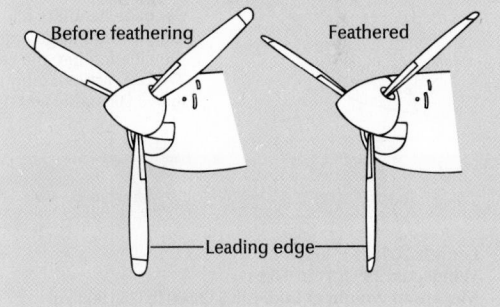

Before feathering   Feathered

Leading edge

flight path. If a plane's engine is disabled, a pilot angles
a feathering propeller to decrease air resistance. This action also keeps the wind from spinning the propeller
and so prevents possible damage to the engine.

Power for flight

An airplane's engine produces the power that moves
the plane fast enough to fly. Planes use four main types
of engines: (1) reciprocating engines, (2) jet engines, (3)
turboprop engines, and (4) rocket engines. Reciprocating engines are the heaviest and least powerful of these
engines, and rocket engines the most powerful. Most
small planes and many large ones have reciprocating

Text continued on page 220.

Parts of a passenger jet airplane

A large jet airliner can fly hundreds of passengers long distances. This drawing shows the features of a Boeing 777-200, one of the largest twin-engine jetliners.

WORLD BOOK illustrations by Kim Downing

Aileron

Flap

The tail

The tail helps guide the plane and keeps it balanced in flight. The *fin* keeps the rear of the plane from swinging to the left or right. The *rudder* helps control the plane during a turn. The *stabilizers* prevent the tail from bobbing up and down.

Fin

Wing control surfaces

Each side of a jetliner's wing has movable surfaces that help control the plane in flight. The *ailerons* are used to make the plane *bank* (tip) to the right or left for a turn. The *flaps* can be lowered to increase the plane's lift during both take-off and landing. The pilot can raise the *spoilers* to act as air brakes.

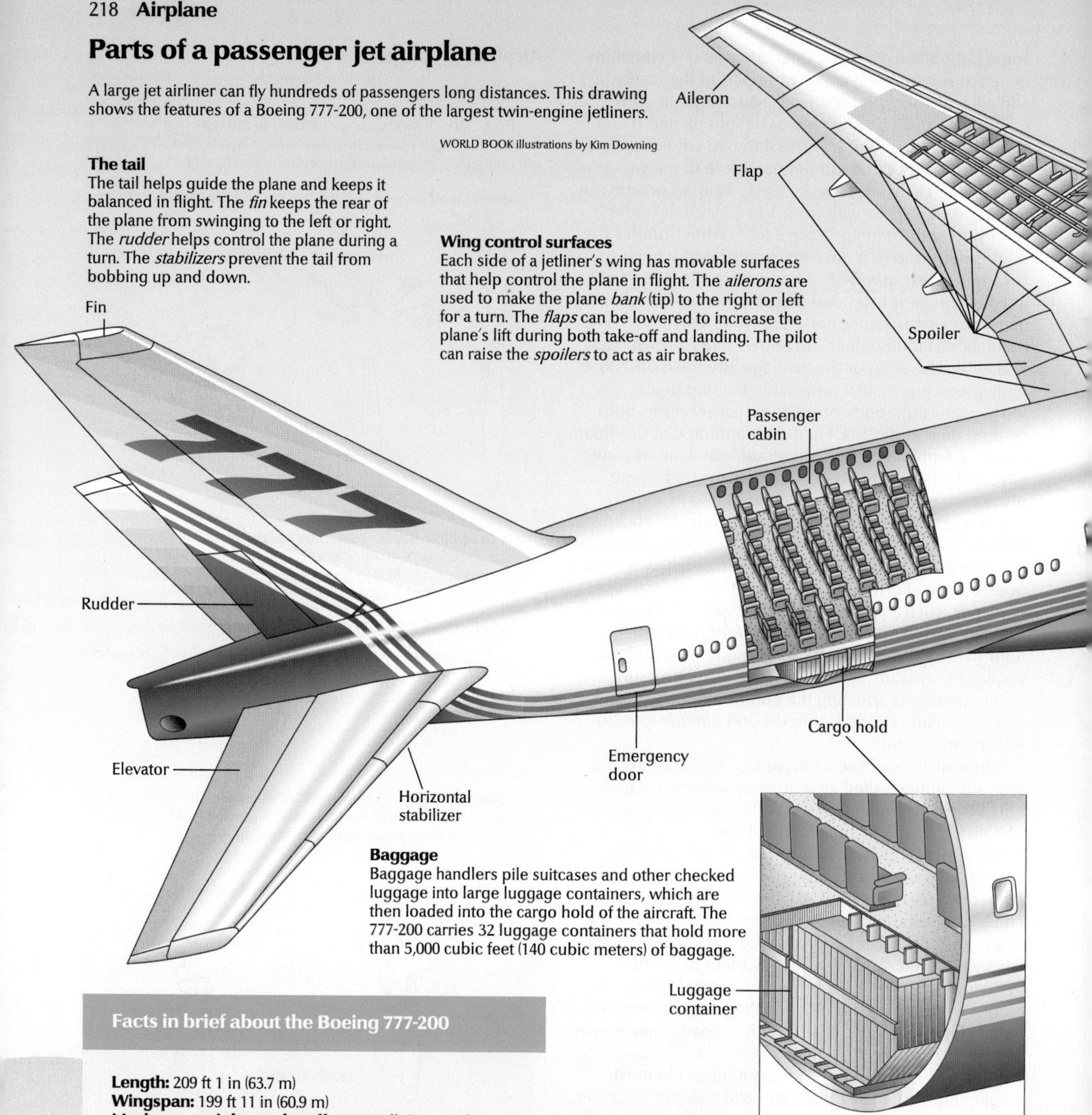

Spoiler

Passenger cabin

Rudder

Cargo hold

Elevator

Emergency door

Horizontal stabilizer

Baggage

Baggage handlers pile suitcases and other checked luggage into large luggage containers, which are then loaded into the cargo hold of the aircraft. The 777-200 carries 32 luggage containers that hold more than 5,000 cubic feet (140 cubic meters) of baggage.

Luggage container

Facts in brief about the Boeing 777-200

Length: 209 ft 1 in (63.7 m)
Wingspan: 199 ft 11 in (60.9 m)
Maximum weight at take-off: 632,500 lb (286,900 kg)
Range: 7,230 nautical mi (13,390 km)
Cruising speed: 550 mph (890 kph)

Flexible seating

Seating arrangements vary among airlines. A 777-200 may carry up to 440 passengers. But the maximum number varies depending on the seating plan. These diagrams show three common seating plans.

One class

The Boeing Company

418 passengers

Two classes

30 first class   345 economy class
375 passengers

Three classes

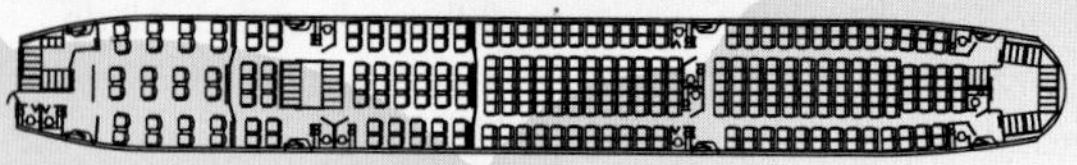

24 first class   54 business class   227 economy class
305 passengers

Fuel tanks
A jetliner's main fuel tanks are inside the right and left wing and in the center section of the plane. The 777-200's tanks hold 31,000 gallons (117,000 liters) of aviation fuel.

Engines
Most jetliners have *turbofan* engines, jet engines with a propellerlike fan at the front that draws in huge amounts of air. The 777-200 has two large turbofan engines that produce up to 84,000 pounds (374,000 newtons) of thrust each.

Engine

Flight deck
Instrument panels in the flight deck display information that helps the pilot and copilot keep the airplane on course and monitor the operation of the engines. The 777-200 has six large display screens that provide navigation information and engine data.

Flight deck

Nose landing gear

Landing gear
Most jetliners have *retractable* landing gear, which tucks away during flight. The 777-200's main landing gear is under the wing and not shown here. It has 12 wheels.

Galley

Engine

Spoiler

Meals in the air
Airline catering companies prepare and refrigerate hundreds of meals and load them onto the plane at the airport. At mealtime, flight attendants reheat the food in convection ovens in the galleys.

Other large jetliners

The twin-engine Boeing 777-200 is slightly larger than two other wide-bodied jets that serve similar markets, the four-engine Airbus A340-200 and three-engine McDonnell Douglas MD-11.

Boeing 777-200

Airbus A340-200

McDonnell Douglas MD-11

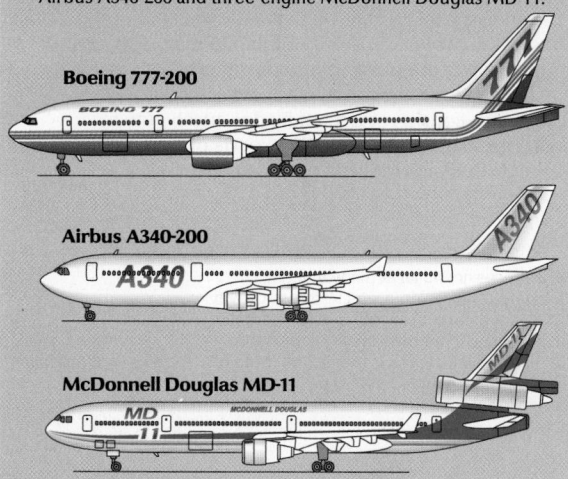

engines. Nearly all newer airliners and some private planes have jet engines. Turboprop aircraft have the power of jet aircraft but can operate at lower speeds. Rocket engines are used mainly for research.

Reciprocating engines, also called *piston engines,* are the most widely used type of airplane engine. Airplanes that use reciprocating engines also have one or more propellers. The engine turns the propeller, which moves the plane through the air.

A reciprocating engine in an airplane works much like one in an automobile. Both burn a mixture of gasoline and air inside cylinders. The burning mixture forms a fine spray, which explodes. The explosion drives pistons inside the cylinders up and down. This pumping motion rotates a crankshaft. In an airplane, the rotating crankshaft turns the propeller.

Reciprocating engines in airplanes differ from those in automobiles in some ways. In most airplane engines, for example, the cylinders are arranged in a circle or opposite each other. In automobile engines, they are arranged in a single line or a V-shape. In addition, most airplane engines are cooled by air, but most automobile cooling systems use a mixture of water and antifreeze.

The power of reciprocating engines is measured in units of horsepower or kilowatts. Most reciprocating engines made for airplanes range from 65 horsepower (50 kilowatts) for small single-engine planes to about 400 horsepower (300 kilowatts) for larger two-engine planes. The most powerful reciprocating engines ever used on an airplane were the 3,650-horsepower (2,722-kilowatt) engines of the huge B-36 bomber of the late 1940's. Large, high-speed airplanes no longer use such powerful reciprocating engines. These airplanes are powered by jet engines, which weigh less than reciprocating engines but produce much greater power. Reciprocating engines are still used for most light airplanes because they work better than jet engines at low speeds.

Jet engines enable large airplanes to travel long distances at high speeds. Airplanes use two main types of jet engines: (1) *turbojets* and (2) *turbofans* or *fanjets.*

The turbojet was the first successful jet engine and is still used on some airplanes. Like other jet engines, the turbojet takes air in through the front and burns it with fuel. This process forms a powerful jet exhaust. The exhaust moves backward through the engine at tremendous speed, which causes the engine to move forward at an equally high speed. Before the jet exhaust passes out the engine's tail pipe, it spins a device called a *turbine,* which consists of a set of blades attached to a shaft. The turbine runs the various parts of the engine. See **Jet propulsion** (How jet propulsion works).

Almost all new airliners have turbofan engines, which are an improvement on the turbojet. A turbofan works much like a turbojet, but it has a fan at the front that draws in huge amounts of air. Only part of the air is burned with the fuel to form the jet exhaust. The rest is added to the exhaust as it passes out the tail pipe. The resulting exhaust is much more powerful and much cooler than that of a turbojet. In addition, turbofans use less fuel than turbojets do, make much less noise, and operate better at low speeds.

Turboprop engines somewhat resemble jet engines but use a propeller—rather than the movement of air through the engine—to drive the plane forward. A turboprop engine uses the exhaust from a turbojet to turn a propeller. Turboprop planes combine the tremendous power of the jet engine with the propeller's ability to fly at low speed.

Rocket engines work much like jet engines, except that they do not need a supply of oxygen from outside the engine. A rocket engine operates best at high speeds. It also burns much fuel, and so it is expensive to operate. In addition, the possibility of explosion makes rocket engines too dangerous to power passenger airplanes. But a few jet and turboprop military planes use small rockets to help them take off quickly with heavy loads or on short runways. The rockets are attached to the plane's body or under its wing. This system is called Jet-Assisted Take-Off (JATO). Rocket engines have powered many supersonic test planes, such as the Bell X-1 and North American X-15. See **Rocket.**

Principles of flight

Four basic forces govern the flight of an airplane: (1) gravity, (2) lift, (3) drag, and (4) thrust. Gravity is the natural force that pulls a plane toward the ground. Lift is the force that pushes a plane upward against the force of gravity. It is created by the plane's wing as it moves through the air. Drag is the natural force of air that resists an airplane's forward movement. Thrust is the force that moves a plane forward. Thrust is created by a plane's propeller or by its jet engines.

Gravity and lift are opposing forces, as are drag and thrust. When a plane's lift equals the force of gravity and its thrust equals the drag, the plane is in level, cruising flight. When one or more of the four forces change, the plane begins to change its altitude, direction, or speed.

Gravity and lift. Gravity tends to keep an airplane on the ground or to pull it to Earth when in flight. The force of gravity on the ground equals the weight of the plane on the ground. For a plane to take off or to climb, its wing must create a lifting force greater than the down-

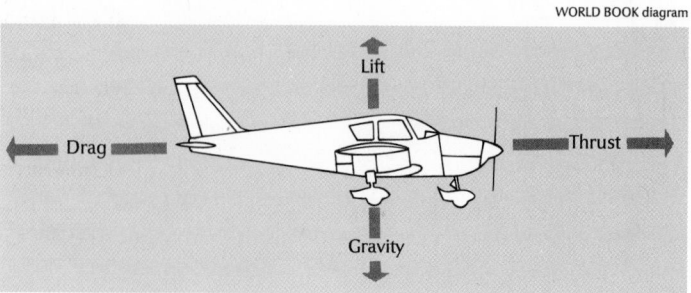

Four forces act on an airplane in flight: (1) gravity, (2) lift, (3) drag, and (4) thrust. Gravity is the natural force that pulls a plane toward the ground. Lift opposes gravity and pushes the plane upward. Drag is the natural force of air opposing a plane's forward movement. Thrust opposes drag and moves the plane forward.

Lift

Drag

Thrust

Gravity

ward force of gravity. For level flight, the wing must create a lifting force equal to the force of gravity.

Lift is created by the flow of air around the airplane's wing as the plane moves forward. Experts disagree on the best explanation of lift. According to one explanation, lift is produced by a difference in air pressure above and below the wing. As the wing moves through the air, air flows faster over its curved upper surface and slower along its bottom surface. The faster airflow reduces the air pressure above the wing. As a result, the air below the wing pushes more strongly than the air above the wing, producing lift.

Another explanation of lift is related to the wing's ability to *deflect* (turn) the airflow downward. The wing deflects the airflow by guiding air along its curved surface and by meeting the air at an angle. Deflection produces

How thrust is produced

Propellers produce thrust in gasoline-powered and turboprop airplanes. Jet engines produce thrust in jet planes.

WORLD BOOK diagrams

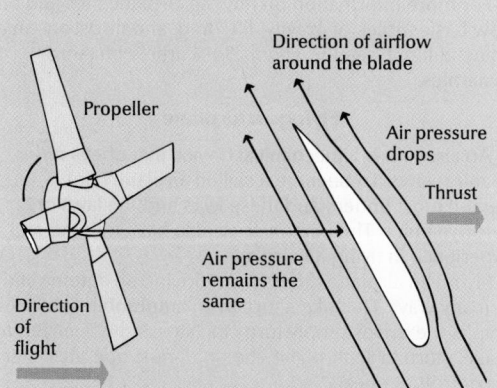

A spinning propeller produces thrust in much the same way as wings produce lift. According to one explanation, spinning decreases the air pressure on the curved front surface of the blades. The pressure on the back surface remains constant, pushing the blades forward. According to another theory, air pushes the blades forward as the blades push the air backward.

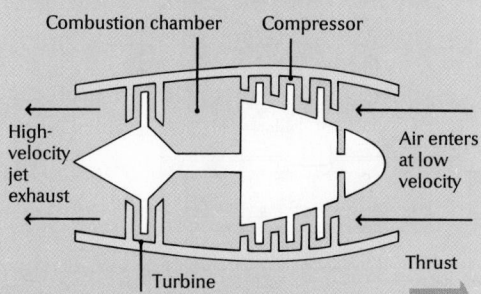

A jet engine takes in air at low *velocity* (speed). A *compressor* increases the pressure of the air. The compressed air is then burned with jet fuel in a *combustion chamber,* forming a high-velocity exhaust. The exhaust moves rapidly backward through the engine, which causes the engine to move forward. The exhaust also spins a *turbine,* which runs the engine parts.

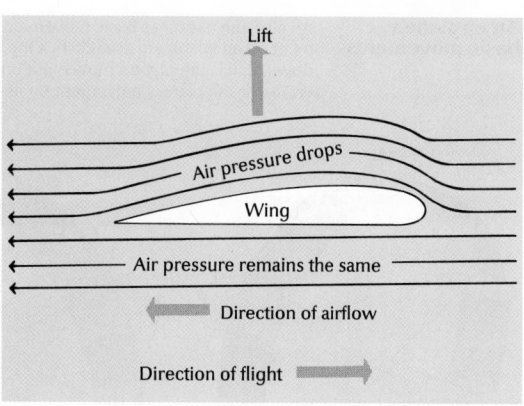

WORLD BOOK diagram

Lift is created by the flow of air around a plane's wing. According to one explanation of lift, the air pressure above the wing falls as air flows over the wing's curved upper surface. Thus, the air below the wing pushes more strongly than the air above the wing. Another explanation holds that as a wing *deflects* (turns) the airflow downward, the air pushes the wing upward.

lift according to the English scientist Isaac Newton's third law of motion. This law states that, for every action, there is an equal and opposite reaction. Thus, as a wing deflects air downward, the air pushes the wing upward.

The faster a wing moves, the more lift it creates. As an airplane accelerates down the runway before take-off, the amount of lift produced by its wing increases. When the lifting force becomes greater than the force of gravity, the plane takes off.

Drag and thrust. A wing can produce lift only if it is moving forward through the air. A plane needs thrust to create the required forward movement.

In a jet airplane, the rapid movement of gases through the jet engine produces thrust. Propellers produce thrust in turboprop planes and planes powered by reciprocating engines. Propeller blades produce thrust in much the same way that wings produce lift. As the propeller spins, the flow of air over the surface of the blades produces a force that pulls the airplane forward. The faster the jet engine works or the propeller spins, the greater the force of thrust.

To reduce drag, engineers design airplane bodies to be as streamlined as possible. They make them sleek and trim, and they design every part on the outside of the aircraft to slip through the air easily and smoothly.

Changing altitude. An airplane cruising in level flight has lift balanced against gravity and thrust balanced against drag. To descend, the pilot may decrease engine power. The propeller or engines slow down, reducing the plane's thrust. The reduction in thrust reduces lift, and the airplane begins to descend. At the same time, drag increases, further slowing the airplane and thus adding to the rate at which the plane descends.

For a sustained climb, the pilot increases the engine power, creating more thrust and moving the plane faster through the air. The faster speed increases lift, and the airplane begins to climb. However, climbing adds more drag, and so the plane needs still more lift. For additional lift, the pilot increases the airplane's *angle of attack*—that is, the angle at which the wing cuts through the air. The pilot uses the controls to make the aircraft's

An airplane's basic movements

An airplane has three basic movements: (1) *pitch,* (2) *roll,* and (3) *yaw.* The airplane makes each movement on an imaginary axis. Pitch is the plane's movement on its *lateral axis* as the nose moves up or down. Roll is the plane's movement on its *longitudinal axis* as one wing tip dips lower than the other. Yaw is the plane's movement on its *vertical axis* as the nose turns left or right.

WORLD BOOK diagrams

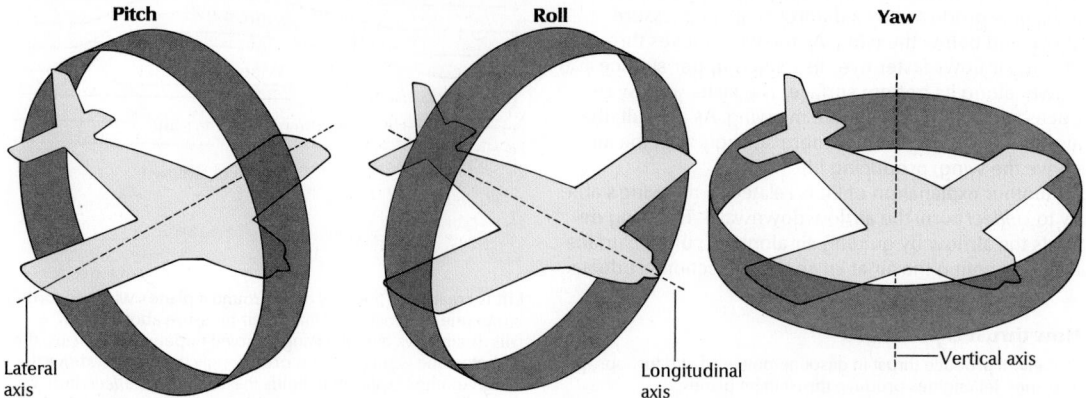

Pitch

Roll

Yaw

Lateral axis

Longitudinal axis

Vertical axis

nose point up slightly so that the wing is at an upward angle to the path of the plane's flight. Increasing the angle of attack alters the airflow around the wing, producing added lift.

Changing direction. A pilot turns a plane by *banking* (tilting) the wing left or right. Lift always occurs at a right angle to the surface of the wing. It is the lifting force of the wing, occurring at an angle to the horizon, that makes the airplane turn. The rudder is not used to turn the plane but only to balance the turn.

When a plane makes a turn, the amount of lift opposing the force of gravity is reduced. Unless the pilot brings lift and gravity back into balance, the plane begins to lose altitude. To produce greater lift, the pilot raises the nose slightly to increase the angle of attack. In making a steep turn, a pilot increases the angle of attack and the engine power at the same time to keep the plane from losing altitude.

For more information on how an airplane flies and on how basic forces of gravity, lift, drag, and thrust act on a plane in flight, see the *World Book* article on **Aerodynamics.**

Flying an airplane

An airplane is a mechanical device that obeys mechanical laws. To become a skilled airplane pilot, a person must understand these laws and the laws of aerodynamics. The person must also have training and experience in flying an airplane.

Flying an airplane differs from driving an automobile in many ways. To make a turn in an automobile, for example, the driver simply turns the steering wheel. But to make a turn in an airplane, the pilot must operate several controls at once.

Basic movements and controls. An airplane has three basic movements: (1) *pitch,* (2) *roll,* and (3) *yaw.*

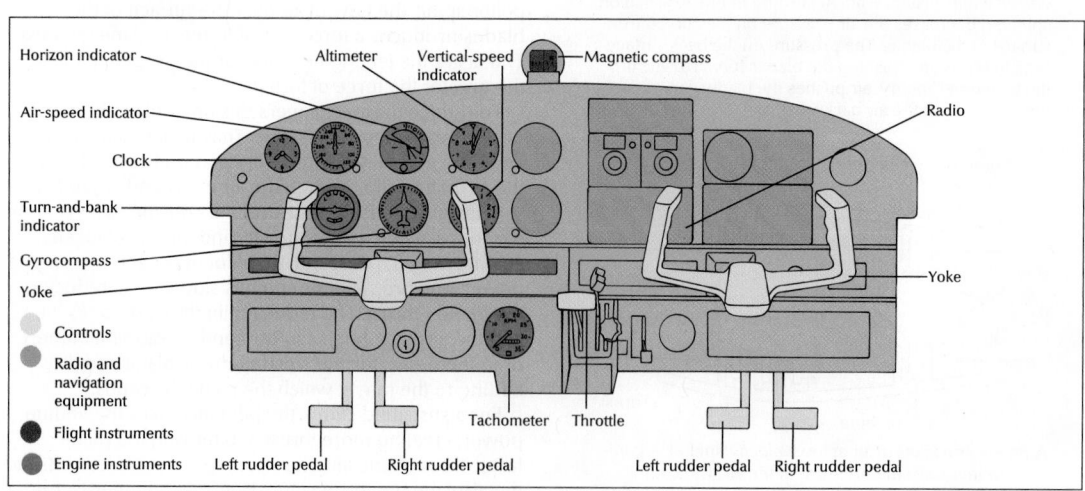

Horizon indicator

Altimeter

Vertical-speed indicator

Magnetic compass

Air-speed indicator

Radio

Clock

Turn-and-bank indicator

Gyrocompass

Yoke

Yoke

Controls

Radio and navigation equipment

Flight instruments

Engine instruments

Left rudder pedal

Right rudder pedal

Tachometer

Throttle

Left rudder pedal

Right rudder pedal

WORLD BOOK diagram; courtesy Piper Aircraft Corp.

Basic cockpit controls and instruments. Both the pilot's and copilot's yokes control the ailerons and elevator. Their pedals operate the rudder. The throttle controls engine power and speed. *Flight instruments,* such as the air-speed indicator and altimeter, help keep the plane on course. *Engine instruments,* such as the oil-pressure gauge and tachometer, measure engine operations.

Pitch is the motion of a plane as its nose moves up or down. A plane rolls when it banks—that is, when one wing tip dips lower than the other. Yaw is a plane's motion as the nose moves left or right. A pilot uses the controls to make these movements and to adjust for them.

An airplane has many controls, but four of them are basic. They are (1) the elevator, (2) the rudder, (3) the ailerons, and (4) the throttle. The elevator and rudder are parts of the tail assembly. The ailerons are on each side of the wing. A system of cables, rods, and pulleys leads from these outside flight controls to the pilot's controls in the cockpit. The pilot's yoke or stick controls the ailerons and elevator. The rudder pedals control the rudder. The pilot uses the throttle to control the engine speed and power.

The yoke and rudder pedals make the plane pitch, roll, or yaw. The yoke moves forward and backward and turns from side to side. Pushing the yoke forward or pulling it backward moves the elevator up or down and makes the plane pitch up or down. When the yoke is pushed forward, the elevator lowers and the nose drops. When the yoke is pulled back, the elevator moves up, forcing the nose up. Turning the yoke from side to side raises or lowers the ailerons and makes the plane roll. When the yoke is turned to the right, the right-wing aileron goes up and the left-wing aileron goes down. The plane then rolls to the right. Turning the yoke to the left makes the plane roll to the left. The pilot uses the rudder pedals to make the plane yaw. Pushing on the left pedal swings the rudder to the left, causing

Text continued on page 225.

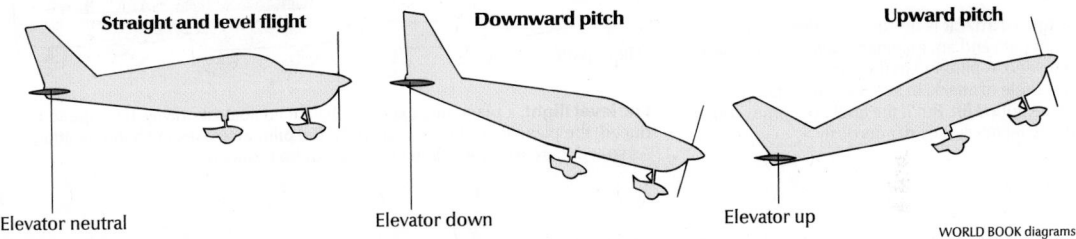

Straight and level flight   **Downward pitch**   **Upward pitch**

Elevator neutral   Elevator down   Elevator up

WORLD BOOK diagrams

To make a plane pitch, the pilot lowers or raises the elevator. The pilot lowers the elevator by pushing the yoke forward and raises it by pulling the yoke back.

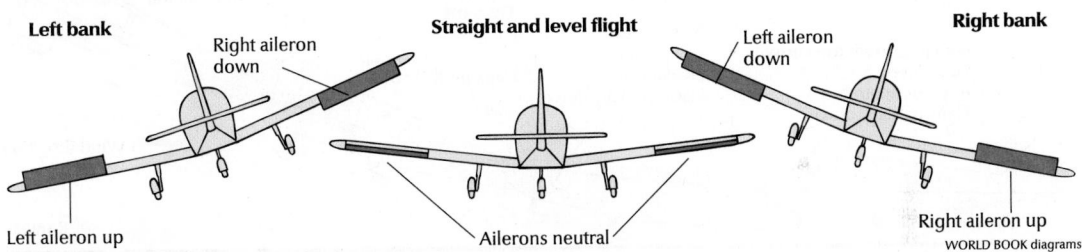

Left bank   **Straight and level flight**   **Right bank**

Right aileron down   Left aileron down

Left aileron up   Ailerons neutral   Right aileron up

WORLD BOOK diagrams

To make a plane roll, or *bank,* the pilot operates the ailerons. To make a left bank, for example, the pilot turns the yoke to the left, which raises the left aileron and lowers the right one.

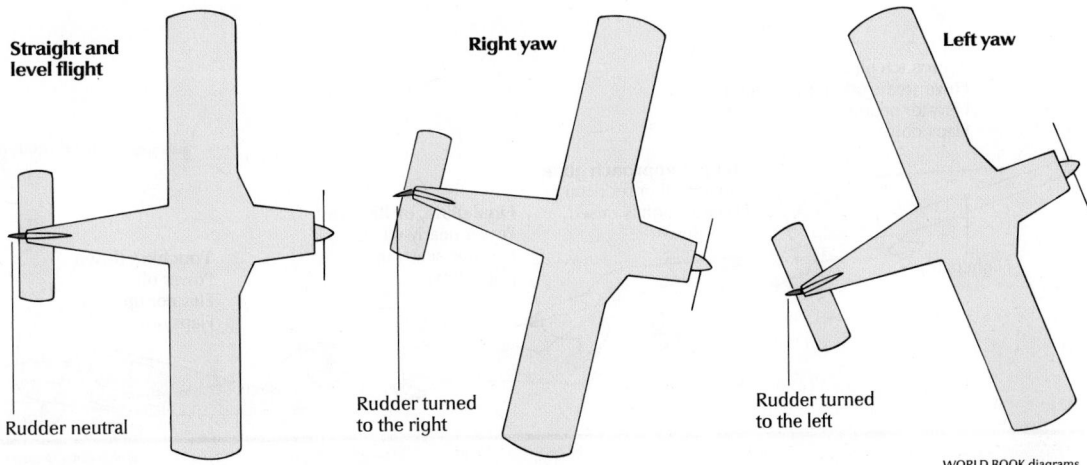

Straight and level flight   **Right yaw**   **Left yaw**

Rudder neutral   Rudder turned to the right   Rudder turned to the left

WORLD BOOK diagrams

To make a plane yaw, the pilot operates the two pedals that control the rudder. The pilot presses the right pedal to swing the rudder to the right and the left pedal to swing it to the left.

How a pilot uses angle of attack

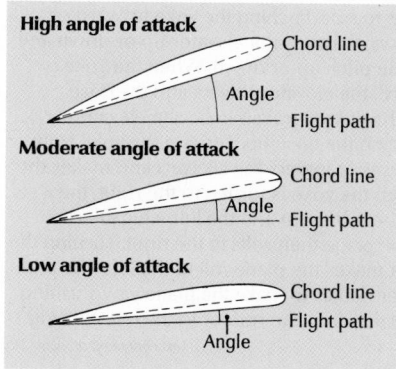

High angle of attack
Chord line
Angle
Flight path

Moderate angle of attack
Chord line
Angle
Flight path

Low angle of attack
Chord line
Flight path
Angle

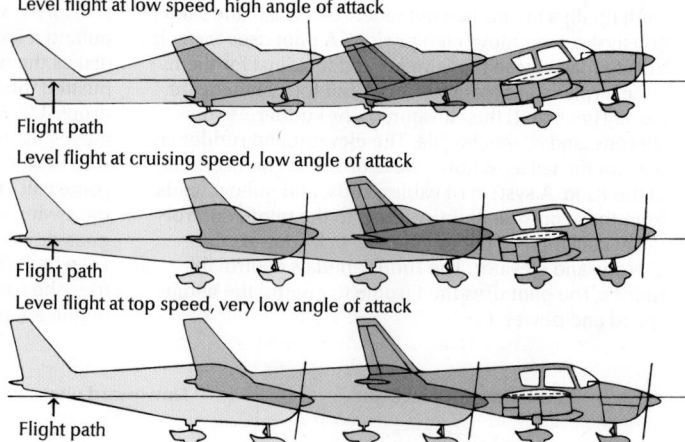

Level flight at low speed, high angle of attack
Flight path

Level flight at cruising speed, low angle of attack
Flight path

Level flight at top speed, very low angle of attack
Flight path

Angle of attack is the angle formed by a plane's flight path and an imaginary *chord line* through the wing. A pilot raises the elevator to increase the angle of attack. In so doing, the pilot gives the plane added lift. But if the angle becomes too great, lift decreases dangerously.

For level flight, a plane must keep lift balanced against gravity. If its speed is reduced, the plane loses lift. To regain lift, the pilot increases the angle of attack. As speed increases, the angle of attack can be reduced.

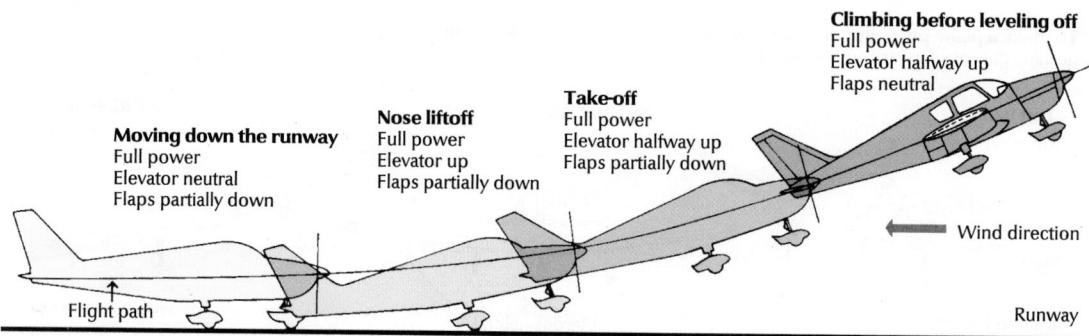

Climbing before leveling off
Full power
Elevator halfway up
Flaps neutral

Take-off
Full power
Elevator halfway up
Flaps partially down

Nose liftoff
Full power
Elevator up
Flaps partially down

Moving down the runway
Full power
Elevator neutral
Flaps partially down

Flight path

Wind direction

Runway

For take-off, a plane moves down the runway at high speed. The wind rushes around the wing, building up lift. To get more lift, the pilot raises the elevator, increasing the angle of attack. The pilot may also lower the flaps. When lift becomes greater than gravity, the plane takes off.

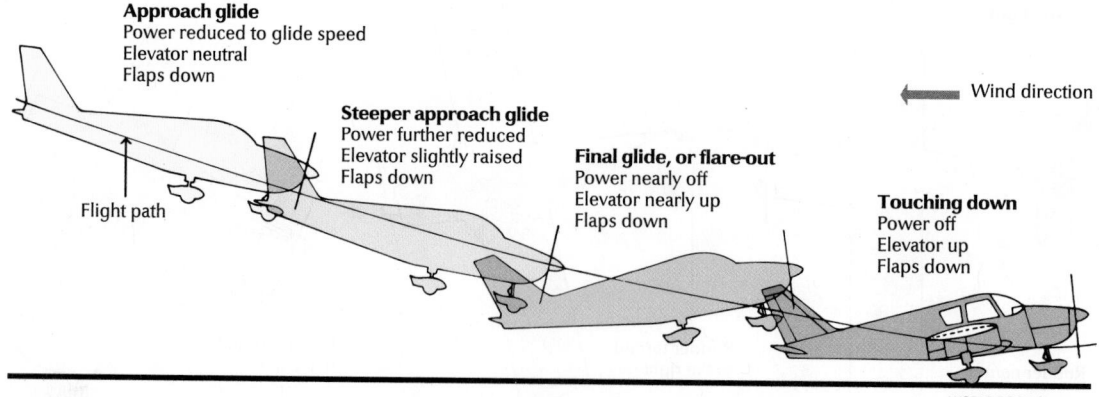

Approach glide
Power reduced to glide speed
Elevator neutral
Flaps down

Steeper approach glide
Power further reduced
Elevator slightly raised
Flaps down

Final glide, or flare-out
Power nearly off
Elevator nearly up
Flaps down

Touching down
Power off
Elevator up
Flaps down

Flight path

Wind direction

WORLD BOOK diagrams

For landing, a plane's speed must be reduced as much as possible, and so the pilot decreases the engine power. But reducing speed also reduces lift. The plane must recover enough lift to counteract gravity. To recover lift, the pilot increases the angle of attack and lowers the flaps.

the plane's nose to swing left also. Pushing on the right pedal swings the rudder and nose to the right.

The pilot also has cockpit controls for the trim tabs on the ailerons, elevator, and rudder. The trim tabs help keep a plane balanced in spite of changes in the plane's air speed or its center of gravity. A plane's center of gravity changes many times in flight. For example, the center of gravity changes as the fuel in the plane's tanks is used. To keep the plane from pitching up or down because its center of gravity is changing, the pilot would have to keep constant pressure on the yoke. But if the pilot adjusts the elevator trim tabs, they adjust the elevator to handle the change in the center of gravity and thus help keep the plane balanced.

Proper use of the controls. To make any maneuver, an airplane pilot never uses only one basic control. To make a left turn, for example, a pilot does not simply press down on the left rudder pedal. Using only this one control would send the airplane into a left *skid.* An airplane in a skid does not complete its turn. It returns to its original course of flight as soon as the pilot releases the rudder pedal.

To make a left turn in level flight, a pilot must (1) turn the yoke to the left to raise the left aileron and lower the right aileron for a left bank; (2) press down on the left rudder pedal to make the plane's nose swing to the left; and (3) pull back on the yoke to bring up the elevator and raise the nose, which increases the wing's angle of attack. In a steep turn, the pilot might also need to push the throttle forward to increase engine power. The pilot makes all these movements at the same time, but they soon become second nature for an experienced pilot.

For all other airplane maneuvers—from taking off to landing—a pilot must also keep all the forces of flight in balance, just as in making a turn. By using all the basic controls at once, a pilot balances lift against gravity and thrust against drag.

Stalling occurs when the wing's angle of attack becomes so great that the plane loses lift and begins to fall. If a pilot brings the plane's nose up so that the wing is at an angle of more than 15 to 20 degrees to the flight path, the air flowing over the wing will bubble wildly. As a result, the plane stalls. The pilot can bring the plane out of the stall by lowering the nose and letting gravity build up the speed needed for lift. The pilot can also increase engine power to regain flying speed.

Flying by instruments. A pilot can maneuver a plane without being able to see anything but the plane's instruments. This skill is necessary when flying in clouds, fog, or heavy rain. If a pilot cannot see the horizon or the ground below, it is difficult to know if the plane is on course, flying straight or turning, and losing or gaining altitude. Cockpit instruments provide this information. In addition, the instruments help pilots carry out various maneuvers without losing altitude or speed and help them land safely.

Measuring flying speed. A plane's speed is measured in several ways. The *indicated air speed* is the speed a pilot reads on an instrument called an *air-speed indicator.* But an air-speed indicator is affected by the changes in temperature and air pressure at different altitudes. As a result, a plane's indicated air speed differs from its *true air speed* and its *ground speed.* True air speed is the speed of the plane in relation to the air

How an airplane is turned   A pilot must use several controls to make a turn. This plane is beginning a right turn. The pilot has raised the right aileron to bank the wing to the right and has also turned the rudder to the right to steady the plane's nose. The lift on the left side of the wing has increased and is pulling the plane around the turn. But in turning, a plane loses lift. The pilot has therefore raised the elevator to increase the angle of attack. The pilot may also need to increase engine power for added thrust.

WORLD BOOK illustration by Tom Morgan; courtesy of Piper Aircraft Corp.

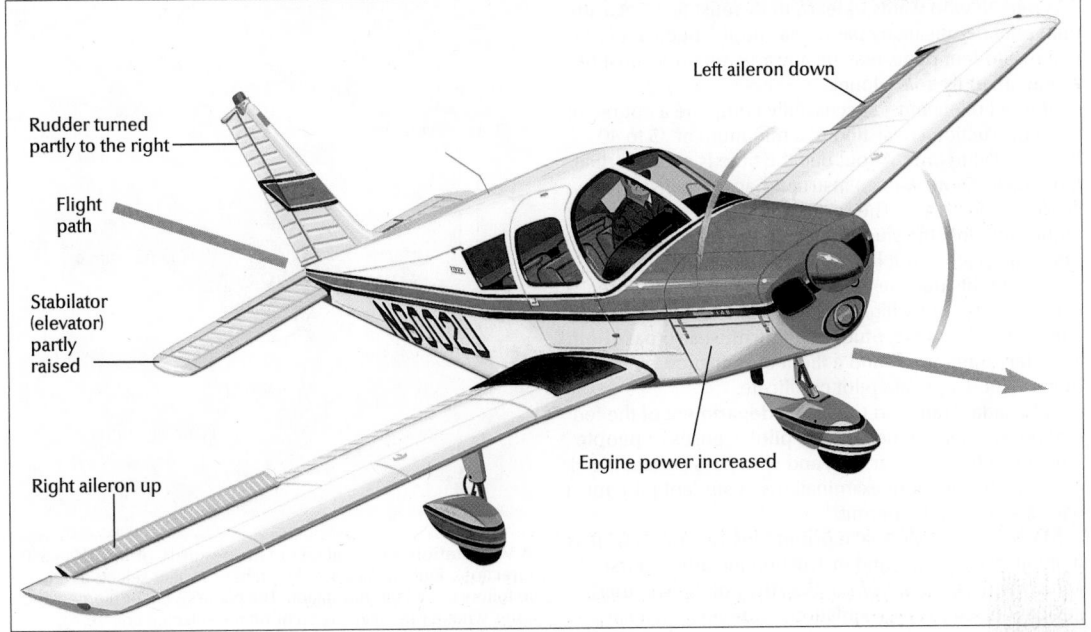

Left aileron down

Rudder turned partly to the right

Flight path

Stabilator (elevator) partly raised

Right aileron up

Engine power increased

through which it is moving. Ground speed is the speed of the plane in relation to the ground. A pilot can figure true air speed by checking the indicated air speed and the outside air temperature. Because the air is usually colder at higher altitudes, true air speed increases over indicated air speed about 2 percent for every 1,000 feet (300 meters) of altitude. For example, if a plane is flying at 10,000 feet and its air-speed indicator reads 100 mph, the plane's true air speed will probably be about 120 mph. A pilot can use true air speed to figure the ground speed if he or she knows the direction and speed of the wind. For example, if the true air speed is 120 mph and the plane is flying into a 30-mph headwind, the ground speed will be 90 mph.

A plane's *maximum speed,* also called *top speed,* is the fastest speed it can reach in level flight. Its *best rate of climb speed* is the speed at which it climbs the fastest. *Cruising speed* is the most suitable speed for long-distance flight. *Maneuvering speed* is the fastest speed at which an airplane can be flown in maneuvers or in *turbulence* (irregular air flow, often due to stormy weather) without endangering its structure.

Every plane also has a *yellow arc speed* and a *red line speed,* which are shown on the air-speed indicator. The area marked in yellow is a caution area. A pilot should not carry out sudden maneuvers or enter turbulence while flying at speeds in this range. The area marked in red indicates the fastest speed at which the plane can be flown under any conditions.

Every plane has a *stall speed*—the speed at which the wing loses lift. However, the indicated stall speed tells only the speed at which the airplane will stall in level flight. If the plane is turning, its stall speed will be higher than it is in level flight.

Learning to fly. The Federal Aviation Administration (FAA) issues private pilot certificates to qualified United States citizens who are at least 17 years old. A private pilot certificate authorizes a person to fly a plane carrying passengers without payment for his or her services.

A person who wants to learn to fly must first get a student pilot certificate by passing a simple medical examination. Student pilots may be any age, but they must be at least 16 to fly *solo* (alone).

Student pilots must successfully complete a course of flight instruction consisting of a minimum of 35 to 40 hours of flying time. About half the time is spent in dual flight instruction, with an instructor accompanying the student in the plane. The rest of the time is solo practice flight, with only the student pilot in the plane. Students must complete about half their solo hours in cross-country flights outside their local airport area. Before every cross-country flight, students check the weather and plot their course. Student pilots must also pass both a written examination and a flight examination before being issued a private pilot certificate.

In Canada, Transport Canada, a department of the federal government, issues private pilot licenses to people who are at least 17 years old and who pass certain physical, written, and flight examinations. A student pilot must have a student pilot permit.

Many student pilots take ground instruction as well as flight instruction. Ground instruction includes courses in aerodynamics, *meteorology* (the study of the weather), navigation, and flying regulations. Students must have good knowledge of all these subjects to pass their pilot examinations. However, students are not required to take formal instruction in these subjects and may, instead, use home-study materials.

Air navigation

Air navigation is the means by which pilots determine their plane's location in the air and direct its route of flight. Pilots use charts, compasses, radio systems, and computerized instruments to navigate accurately.

The three chief methods of air navigation are (1) pilotage, (2) dead reckoning, and (3) electronic navigation. Most pilots use a combination of all three methods. Some aircraft use *inertial guidance* as a navigational aid.

Pilotage, also called *piloting,* is the simplest and most common method of air navigation. Using this method, a pilot keeps on course by following a series of landmarks on the ground. Before take-off, the pilot plots his or her course on an *aeronautical chart,* a map that shows the location of various landmarks, such as bridges, highways, railroad tracks, rivers, and towns. An aeronautical chart also shows routes for aircraft, landing fields, and radio stations that broadcast air navigation signals. The U.S. Department of Commerce publishes such charts for all parts of the United States.

As the plane flies over each landmark on the plotted course, the pilot checks it off on the chart. If the plane does not pass over a landmark, the pilot must adjust the path of flight to resume its preplanned course.

Dead reckoning is a way of navigating when there are few or no visible landmarks. It demands more skill and experience than pilotage does. An aviator uses dead reckoning when flying over forests, deserts, large bodies of water, or heavy clouds. This method of navigation requires an aeronautical chart, an accurate clock, a compass, and a calculator for figuring time, speed, and distance. Working with the chart, the pilot plots a route in

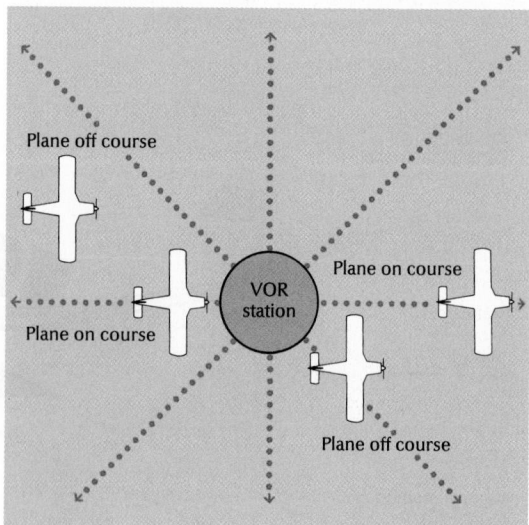

WORLD BOOK diagram

A VOR station sends out rays of radio signals, or *radials,* in 360 directions. Eight radials are shown here. A pilot selects a radial to follow to or from the station. The plane's VOR equipment indicates whether the plane is on or off the selected course.

advance. The pilot also figures how long it should take to reach the destination while flying at a constant speed. The pilot adjusts the course to allow for the wind.

In the air, the pilot watches the compass to keep the plane headed in the right direction. The plane should arrive at the destination when it has flown exactly the length of time planned. Dead reckoning is not always a successful method of navigation because changing winds may drive a plane slightly off course.

Electronic navigation involves the use of radio signals broadcast by satellites or by transmitters on the ground. Electronic devices on the airplane use the signals to determine the craft's position or direction of travel. Almost all pilots use electronic navigation.

Satellite navigation systems use radio signals broadcast by artificial satellites orbiting Earth. A receiver picks up signals from at least four satellites. It then calculates the plane's location based on the distances between each satellite and the receiver.

The most widely used satellite navigation system is the Global Positioning System (GPS). Pilots of small airplanes often use affordable handheld GPS receivers to aid them in piloting. Flying in poor visibility requires a more expensive and reliable GPS unit permanently installed in the craft.

Because satellite navigation does not rely on ground stations, it can be used anywhere on Earth. Ground-based systems, on the other hand, cannot be used over the oceans or wherever else ground stations are not available. A satellite network is also cheaper to maintain than a large network of ground-based stations. As satellite navigation becomes more accurate and reliable, it continues to replace ground-based systems.

Ground-based navigation systems still serve as an important aid to navigation in many areas. In the United States, for example, ground-based radio navigation stations guide aircraft en route and assist with navigation near airports. When pilots fly in or above the clouds, they use an IFR (*I*nstrument *F*light *R*ules) chart, a map of routes between radio navigation stations.

To navigate using ground-based stations, pilots first consult an aeronautical chart. The chart indicates which radio station to tune to in a particular area. The plane's navigation equipment picks up the appropriate signal. An indicator needle shows the pilot when the plane is flying on a direct course to or from the station. It also shows when the plane drifts off course. This system of navigation, which was designed for *civil* (nonmilitary) aircraft, is called VOR *(V*ery High Frequency *O*mnidirectional *R*ange). Most VOR stations also transmit signals for *DME (D*istance *M*easuring *E*quipment). DME tells the pilot how far the aircraft is from the VOR station. Military aircraft use a similar system called TACAN *(TAC*tical *A*ir *N*avigation). A combined civil and military system, called VORTAC, is used by both civil and military planes.

Inertial guidance does not rely on any information from outside the vehicle. Instead, devices on board the plane measure changes in the plane's speed and direction. The computer uses this information to calculate the position of the vehicle and to guide its flight.

Safety. Airplane pilots follow two sets of rules when flying. When the weather enables them to see clearly, pilots usually follow Visual Flight Rules (VFR). They observe Instrument Flight Rules (IFR) when they cannot see the ground or other aircraft in the sky. However, the U.S. government requires all jet airliners to operate under Instrument Flight Rules at all times.

Pilots have various navigation aids that help them take off, fly, and land safely. In the United States, one of the most important aids is a series of air route traffic control centers operated by the federal government. In the past, each center typically used radar to make sure all the planes in its vicinity were clear of other traffic. Today, centers use Automatic Dependent Surveillance-Broadcast (ADS-B). Airplanes carry special receivers and transmitters called *ADS-B In* and *ADS-B Out.* These devices use signals from Global Positioning System (GPS)

A wind tunnel enables aircraft designers and engineers to test how a plane will perform under various flying conditions. Air is forced through the tunnel at high speeds to study the effects of wind and air pressure on a scale model of the plane. This wind tunnel is operated by the United Kingdom's Defence Science and Technology Laboratory in Farnborough, near London.

The Boeing Company

Aircraft assembly takes place in some of the largest manufacturing plants in the world, such as this huge facility near Everett, Washington, where the Boeing 777 is manufactured.

satellites to safely communicate with air traffic controllers and other airplanes.

Most large and medium-sized airports also have air traffic control towers. In the towers, air traffic controllers also now use ADS-B to direct planes that are approaching and landing or taking off and departing. Most larger airports also have an Instrument Landing System (ILS) to guide pilots to the runway in bad weather. This system uses horizontal and vertical radio beams from the ground to operate an instrument in the cockpit of an airliner. By watching this instrument, pilots can tell their exact position in relation to the runway and so can make a safe landing.

Building an airplane

In the United States, the Federal Aviation Administration makes rules for the design and manufacture of airplanes. The agency sets standards that every airplane designer and manufacturer must meet. A manufacturer may not sell a plane until the aircraft receives certification from the FAA. The certification states that the plane meets FAA standards for "design, materials, workmanship, construction, and performance."

Some people build their own airplanes. The FAA sets different standards for home-built planes. Such a plane receives a certification that specifies (1) where and when it may fly and (2) how many passengers it may carry.

Design and testing. Designers and engineers begin to plan and test a new airplane long before it is ready

for mass production. Transports and other large planes require at least 8 to 10 years of planning. The design depends largely on how the plane is to be used. Transports must be able to carry heavy loads great distances, using as little fuel as possible. Light planes must be able to maneuver easily and to land on shorter runways. All planes must have a wing that gives great lift at low speed and little drag at high speed. The FAA requires that a wing be joined to the fuselage so firmly that it can produce lift four to six times the force of gravity on the plane. For example, if a plane weighs 2,000 pounds (910 kilograms), its wing must withstand a force of gravity of at least 8,000 pounds (3,600 kilograms).

Engineers carefully test the metal, plastics, wood, and other materials to be used in a plane. All the materials must be able to withstand tremendous air pressures and extreme weather conditions. Engineers may use a structure called a *wind tunnel* to test the effects of air flowing over the plane at various speeds and altitudes. Today, however, many airplane designs are tested using computers instead of wind tunnels. In addition to these tests, engineers build full-sized *mock-ups* (models) of aircraft from wood or metal—often complete in every detail—to test the arrangement of seats and equipment.

After years of planning and research, engineers build a *prototype* (full-sized test model) of the plane. They test it thoroughly on the ground, running the engines at high speed and taxiing the model on a runway as fast as it will go. Usually, engineers build several prototypes to

Flight of Daedalus and Fall of Icarus (1493), a woodcut
by an unknown German artist; the Science Museum, London

An ancient Greek story told how Daedalus and his son Icarus
flew with wings of feathers and wax. But Icarus flew too near the
sun. His wings melted, and he fell into the sea and drowned.

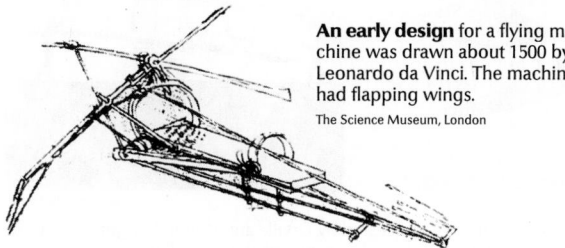

An early design for a flying machine was drawn about 1500 by
Leonardo da Vinci. The machine
had flapping wings.

The Science Museum, London

The first human flights were in balloons filled
with hot air. This balloon, built by the Montgolfier
brothers of France in 1783, carried two passengers about 5 miles (8 kilometers) across Paris.

discover how much wear the plane can take and to test
various systems. The engine and other parts on some
prototypes are tested until they fail. The manufacturer
then tests an experimental plane in flight. Following
these procedures, the FAA reviews every aspect of the
design, construction, and testing of the aircraft, including the flight testing. If the plane meets the FAA's strict
requirements, the agency gives the manufacturer a *type
certificate,* which allows the plane to be sold.

The Boeing 777, which entered service in 1995, was
completely planned with computers. Instead of making
paper drawings or building models, engineers used
computers to electronically design and test the entire
plane and ensure that the parts would fit together.

Mass production. Only a few companies manufacture airplanes. But thousands of factories supply the
parts needed to assemble the planes. Some suppliers
specialize in making such parts as fasteners, landing
gears, or instruments. Others build the larger parts of
the aircraft, including the wing, fuselage, and tail.

Airplane assembly is a complex process that takes
place in many stages. The smallest parts of an airplane
may be assembled by workers stationed along an *assembly line,* also called a *production line.* In the latter
stages of construction, airplanes are generally too large
to be moved down an assembly line. The planes remain
stationary in one part of the factory, with work crews
moving around to complete their assembly.

Each new plane receives a complete inspection, and a
test pilot flies it to make sure the engines and controls
are in perfect working order. After the plane passes

these final tests, it is ready for delivery to a customer.

History

For thousands of years, people dreamed of flying.
Some even tried to fly by tying feathers to their arms
and flapping them like wings. But most people believed
that flying was beyond the powers of ordinary human
beings. They told stories of godlike people who could
fly or who were carried through the air by winged animals. The ancient Greeks told a story about an inventor
named Daedalus and his son Icarus, both of whom flew
with wings made of feathers and wax. But Icarus flew
too close to the sun. The sun's heat melted his wings,
and he fell into the sea and drowned. See **Daedalus.**

Early experiments and ideas. About 400 B.C., a
Greek scholar named Archytas built a wooden pigeon
that moved through the air. No one knows how Archytas
made his pigeon fly. He may have attached the bird to a
revolving arm and used steam or compressed air to
move it in a circle. The people of China may have made
and flown kites as early as 1000 B.C. A kite is really a
form of glider. Later, large kites lifted people into the air.

In the 200's B.C., the Greek mathematician and
inventor Archimedes first described the principle of
buoyancy, which explains how objects float. For hundreds of years, people thought their bodies would float
or fly in the air, too, if they equipped themselves with
such devices as flowing cloaks or artificial wings. But all
of their attempts failed. About A.D. 1290, an English friar
named Roger Bacon wrote that air, like water, has something solid about it. Bacon had studied the ideas of

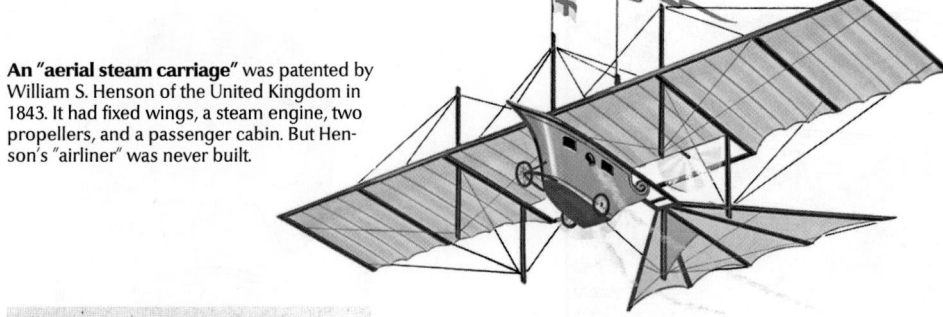

An "aerial steam carriage" was patented by William S. Henson of the United Kingdom in 1843. It had fixed wings, a steam engine, two propellers, and a passenger cabin. But Henson's "airliner" was never built.

Smithsonian Institution

The first glider flights in which a person actually piloted the glider were made in the early 1890's by Otto Lilienthal of Germany. But his gliders were difficult to control.

Improved gliders were built and tested by Orville and Wilbur Wright of the United States. Their first glider, *left*, was a large, two-wing kite built in 1899. After experiments with this and other gliders, the Wright brothers built a glider in 1902 that the pilot could control in the air, *right*.

Archimedes and concluded that if people could build the right kind of machine, the air would support it, as water supports a ship. About 1500, the Italian artist and inventor Leonardo da Vinci made drawings of *ornithopters,* flying machines with wings designed to flap like those of a bird. In 1680, Giovanni A. Borelli, an Italian mathematician, showed that people cannot fly by flapping wings. Borelli proved that people's muscles are too weak to flap the large surfaces that would be needed to support their weight in the air.

First human flights. In 1783, two Frenchmen—a doctor named Jean F. Pilâtre de Rozier and a nobleman, the Marquis d'Arlandes—made the first recorded free flight in an artificially created device. They floated for over 5 miles (8 kilometers) over Paris in a large linen and paper balloon. Two French papermakers—the brothers Jacques Étienne Montgolfier and Joseph Michel Montgolfier—had made the balloon, which was filled with hot air from burning wool and straw. The hot air made it rise. Less than two weeks later, the French chemist Jacques Alexandre Charles and his assistant Marie-Noel Robert became the first people to fly in a balloon filled with hydrogen, a gas lighter than air. Both of these efforts inspired other inventors.

Early balloons were hard to handle. But inventors continued their experiments and, during the mid-1800's, developed the airship. The airships had engines and propellers and so were easier to handle than free-floating balloons, whose course could not be controlled. See **Airship; Balloon.**

Meanwhile, other inventors had turned their attention to gliders, which are heavier-than-air aircraft without engines. In 1804, Sir George Cayley, a British inventor, built the first successful glider. It was a small craft that flew without a passenger. Cayley later built successful full-sized gliders. One of these carried his coachman across a small valley. Cayley also founded the science of aerodynamics and was probably the first person to describe a fixed-wing airplane powered by propellers.

From 1891 to 1896, Otto Lilienthal of Germany made the first successful flights in which a person actually piloted the glider. Before the end of the 1800's, other inventors, including Percy Pilcher of the United Kingdom and Octave Chanute of the United States, made similar flights. Some of these early gliders were so well built that they carried their pilots hundreds of feet or meters through the air. But gliders were often hard to control. They were also not designed to carry passengers or cargo and so were not a practical means of transportation.

Powered flight. In 1843, William S. Henson, a British inventor, patented plans for the first plane with an engine, propellers, and a fixed wing. But after building one unsuccessful model, he gave up the project. In 1848, his friend John Stringfellow built a small model plane using Henson's design. The model was successfully launched but could stay in the air only a short time. In 1890, Clé-

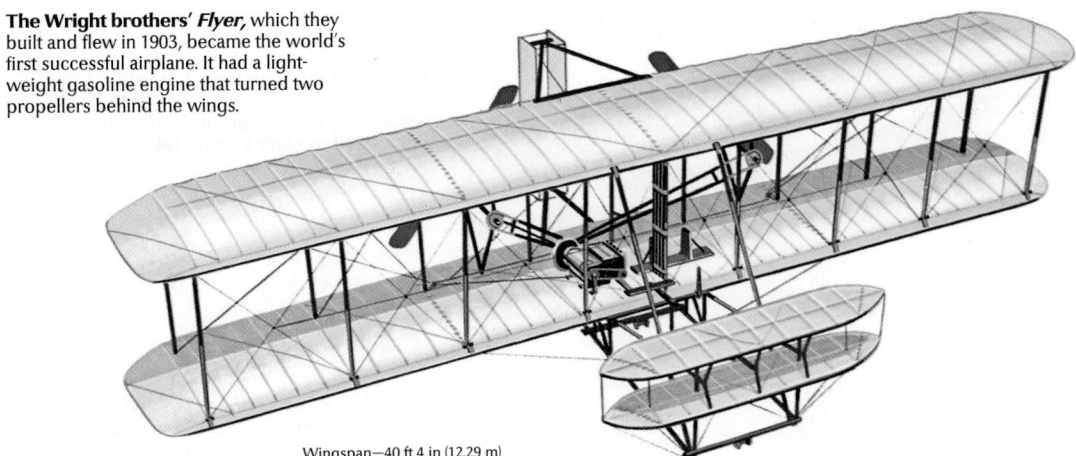

The Wright brothers' *Flyer,* which they built and flew in 1903, became the world's first successful airplane. It had a lightweight gasoline engine that turned two propellers behind the wings.

Wingspan—40 ft 4 in (12.29 m)
Length—21 ft 1 in (6.43 m)

ment Ader, a French engineer, took off in a steam-powered plane that he had built. But he could not control the plane or keep it in the air. About the same time, the inventor Hiram Maxim—an American who had become a British citizen—built a huge steam-powered flying machine. It had two wings, two engines, and two propellers. Maxim tested the plane in 1894. It lifted off the ground briefly but did not actually fly.

During the 1890's, Samuel P. Langley, an American scientist, built a steam-powered model airplane. Langley called his plane an *aerodrome.* In 1896, it flew over ½ mile (0.8 kilometer) in about 1 ½ minutes. Langley then built a full-sized aerodrome powered by a gasoline engine. A pilot attempted to fly the plane on Oct. 7 and on Dec. 8, 1903. Both times Langley's plane was launched

into the air from a houseboat on the Potomac River, and both times the airplane crashed into the water.

The Wright brothers. During the 1890's, Orville and Wilbur Wright became interested in flying while operating their bicycle-manufacturing shop in Dayton, Ohio. The brothers read every book about flying they could find. They started building gliders in 1899. The next year, they began making glider flights near Kitty Hawk, North Carolina, an area known for its steady winds and high sand dunes. After many experiments, the brothers worked out a system for controlling an aircraft in flight. In 1903, the Wright brothers built their first airplane, named the *Flyer.* It was a *biplane* (two-wing plane) with a 12-horsepower (9-kilowatt) gasoline engine that the brothers also built. The wings, which measured 40 feet 4

Text continued on page 233.

Important dates in airplane development

c. 1500 The Italian artist and inventor Leonardo da Vinci made drawings of flying machines with flapping wings.

1783 Two Frenchmen—Jean F. Pilâtre de Rozier and the Marquis d'Arlandes—made the first free lighter-than-air ascent. They made the ascent in a hot-air balloon.

1804 Sir George Cayley of the United Kingdom flew the first successful model glider.

1843 William S. Henson, a British inventor, patented plans for a steam-driven airplane that had many of the basic parts of a modern plane.

1848 John Stringfellow of the United Kingdom built a small model based on Henson's plane. It stayed in the air briefly.

1891-1896 Otto Lilienthal of Germany became the first person to successfully pilot gliders in flight.

1896 Samuel P. Langley of the United States flew a steam-powered model plane.

1903 Orville and Wilbur Wright of the United States made the first engine-powered, heavier-than-air flights, near Kitty Hawk, North Carolina. Their first flight went 120 feet (37 meters) and lasted only about 12 seconds.

1906 Trajan Vuia, a Romanian inventor, built the first full-sized monoplane, but it could not fly.

1909 Louis Blériot of France became the first person to fly across the English Channel.

1913 Igor I. Sikorsky, a Russian inventor, built and flew the first four-engine plane.

1915 The first flight of an all-metal, cantilever-wing plane, the Junkers J 1, took place in Germany.

1927 The Lockheed Vega, a single-engine transport, flew for the first time. It became one of the most popular transport planes of the 1920's and early 1930's.

1936 Douglas DC-3 transport planes entered airline service in the United States. They were the most widely used airliners in the mid-1900's.

1939 The first successful flight of a jet-engine airplane took place in Germany.

1947 Charles E. Yeager, a U.S. Air Force captain, made the first supersonic flight, in a Bell X-1 rocket plane.

1952 De Havilland Comets, the world's first large commercial jetliners, began service.

1953 The North American F-100 Super Sabre jet fighter became the first operational supersonic fighter.

1958 The Boeing 707 began the first U.S. jet transport service between the United States and Europe.

1968 Russian pilots test-flew the world's first supersonic transport plane, the Tu-144.

1970 The first jumbo jet, the Boeing 747, entered service.

1976-2003 The Concorde, built by the United Kingdom and France, provided supersonic transport service.

1983 The pilot of a Rockwell Sabreliner crossed the Atlantic Ocean guided only by satellite navigation.

1995 The Boeing 777 airliner, the world's largest twin-engine jet, began passenger service.

2011 The Boeing 787 Dreamliner, the first major airliner made mostly of lightweight composite materials, began service.

Wingspan—42 ft 6 in (13.89 m)
Length—30 ft (9.1 m)

The *June Bug* was designed by Glenn H. Curtiss. In July 1908, Curtiss used the plane to make the first official public airplane flight in the United States. But it was only a short, shaky flight.

Culver Pictures

Wingspan—25 ft 7 in (7.8 m)
Length—26 ft 3 in (8 m)

The Blériot XI, built and flown by Louis Blériot of France, in 1909 became the first plane to fly across the English Channel.

The Deperdussin racer, built in France in 1912, was one of the first planes with a *monocoque* (tubelike) body, reducing the need for body braces and so lightening the plane.

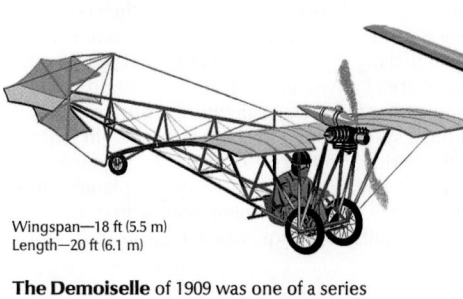

Wingspan—21 ft 10 in (6.65 m)
Length—20 ft (6.1 m)

Wingspan—18 ft (5.5 m)
Length—20 ft (6.1 m)

The Demoiselle of 1909 was one of a series of small lightweight planes built in France by Alberto Santos-Dumont, a Brazilian. The Demoiselles were among the first planes used for personal and pleasure flying.

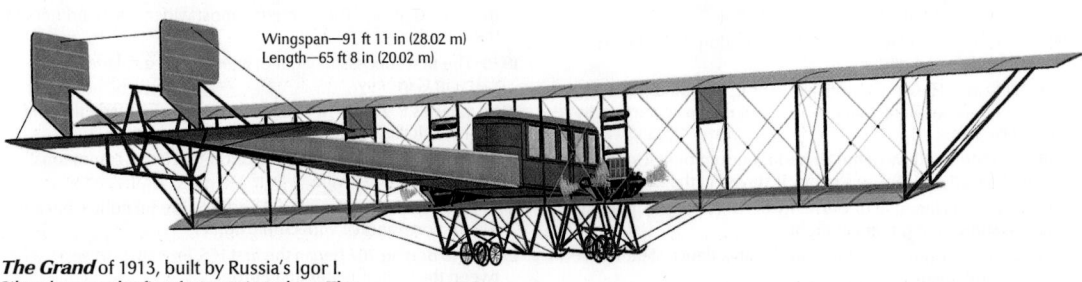

Wingspan—91 ft 11 in (28.02 m)
Length—65 ft 8 in (20.02 m)

The *Grand* of 1913, built by Russia's Igor I. Sikorsky, was the first four-engine plane. The engines were paired back to back.

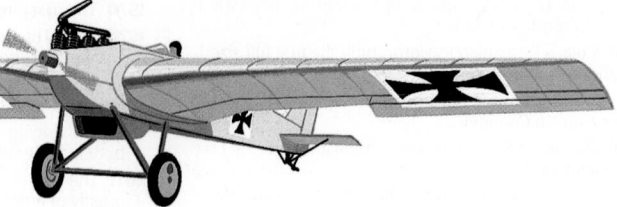

Wingspan—55 ft (16.8 m)
Length—29 ft 8 in (9.04 m)

The Junkers J 1, built in Germany in 1915, was the first plane with an all-metal body and a *cantilever* wing, which is supported by an internal framework instead of outside braces.

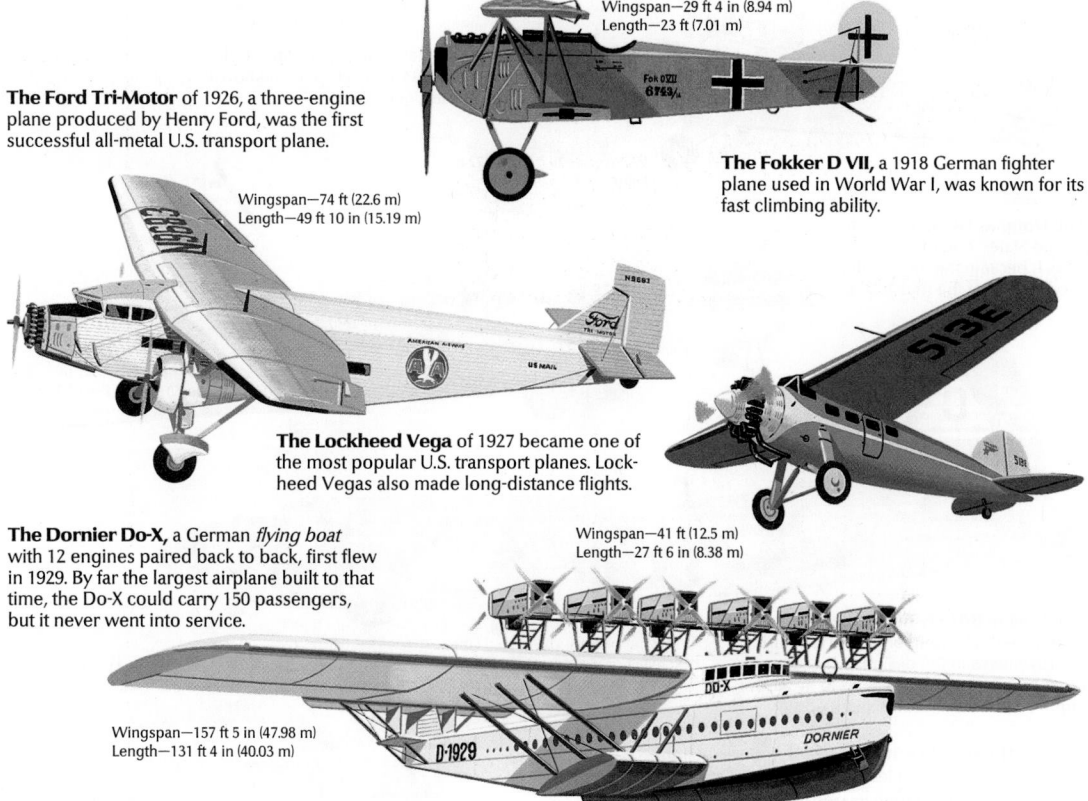

The Ford Tri-Motor of 1926, a three-engine plane produced by Henry Ford, was the first successful all-metal U.S. transport plane.

Wingspan—29 ft 4 in (8.94 m)
Length—23 ft (7.01 m)

The Fokker D VII, a 1918 German fighter plane used in World War I, was known for its fast climbing ability.

Wingspan—74 ft (22.6 m)
Length—49 ft 10 in (15.19 m)

The Lockheed Vega of 1927 became one of the most popular U.S. transport planes. Lockheed Vegas also made long-distance flights.

The Dornier Do-X, a German *flying boat* with 12 engines paired back to back, first flew in 1929. By far the largest airplane built to that time, the Do-X could carry 150 passengers, but it never went into service.

Wingspan—41 ft (12.5 m)
Length—27 ft 6 in (8.38 m)

Wingspan—157 ft 5 in (47.98 m)
Length—131 ft 4 in (40.03 m)

inches (12.29 meters) from tip to tip, were wooden frames covered with cotton cloth. The pilot lay in the middle of the lower wing. The engine, mounted to the pilot's right, turned two wooden propellers behind the wings. Instead of wheels, the plane had wooden runners. Most important of all, it had the successful control system that the brothers had developed for their gliders. A main feature of this system, called a *wing warp system,* was a device for twisting the wing tips to preserve balance in flight. The device consisted of a wire strung from each wing tip to a "cradle" that fitted around the pilot's hips. By moving their hips, the brothers could twist one wing tip or the other to maintain the plane's balance and control while in flight.

On Dec. 17, 1903, Orville Wright became the first person to successfully fly an engine-driven, heavier-than-air machine. The flight took place near Kitty Hawk. The brothers launched the plane from a 60-foot (18-meter) rail on a sand flat. The plane took off and flew 120 feet (37 meters) at about 30 mph (48 kph). The flight lasted only about 12 seconds. The Wright brothers made three more flights that day. Wilbur made the longest one—852 feet (260 meters) in 59 seconds.

Because the Wright brothers were secretive about their work, many people where skeptical of their achievement. But the men continued to improve their planes. By the end of 1905, they had built and flown the first plane that was fully maneuverable and could fly for more than a half hour at a time. But no important officials had seen the plane fly, and so the flights were not

officially recognized. In 1908, Wilbur made the first official public flights in France and amazed the world with the plane's flying ability.

Other pioneer planes and fliers. Alberto Santos-Dumont, a Brazilian who lived in France, became the third person to fly an airplane. In 1906, he made a few brief flights in a plane patterned after a box kite. He later built some of the first planes for personal and pleasure flying. Also in 1906, Trajan Vuia, a Romanian inventor living in France, constructed the first full-sized *monoplane* (single-wing plane). It had the propeller mounted in front of the wing rather than behind. Although the plane was unsuccessful, it influenced the design of later airplanes.

Glenn H. Curtiss, an American inventor, made the first important airplane flight in the United States after the Wright brothers. On July 4, 1908, he became the first American to make an official public flight of more than 1 kilometer (0.6 mile). He flew his biplane, the *June Bug,* 5,090 feet (1.55 kilometers) at 34 mph (55 kph). Henri Farman, an English flier living in France, had made a circular flight of 1 kilometer earlier in 1908. Then, on Oct. 30, 1908, Farman flew 16 ¾ miles (27.0 kilometers) directly across the French countryside in the first cross-country flight. The Wright brothers had made longer circular flights. Curtiss, Farman, and the Wright brothers all became successful airplane manufacturers. John A. D. McCurdy, a Canadian engineering student, made the first successful airplane flight in Canada. On Feb. 23, 1909, he flew his biplane—the *Silver Dart*—over ½ mile (0.8 kilometer) across Bras d'Or Lake in Nova Scotia.

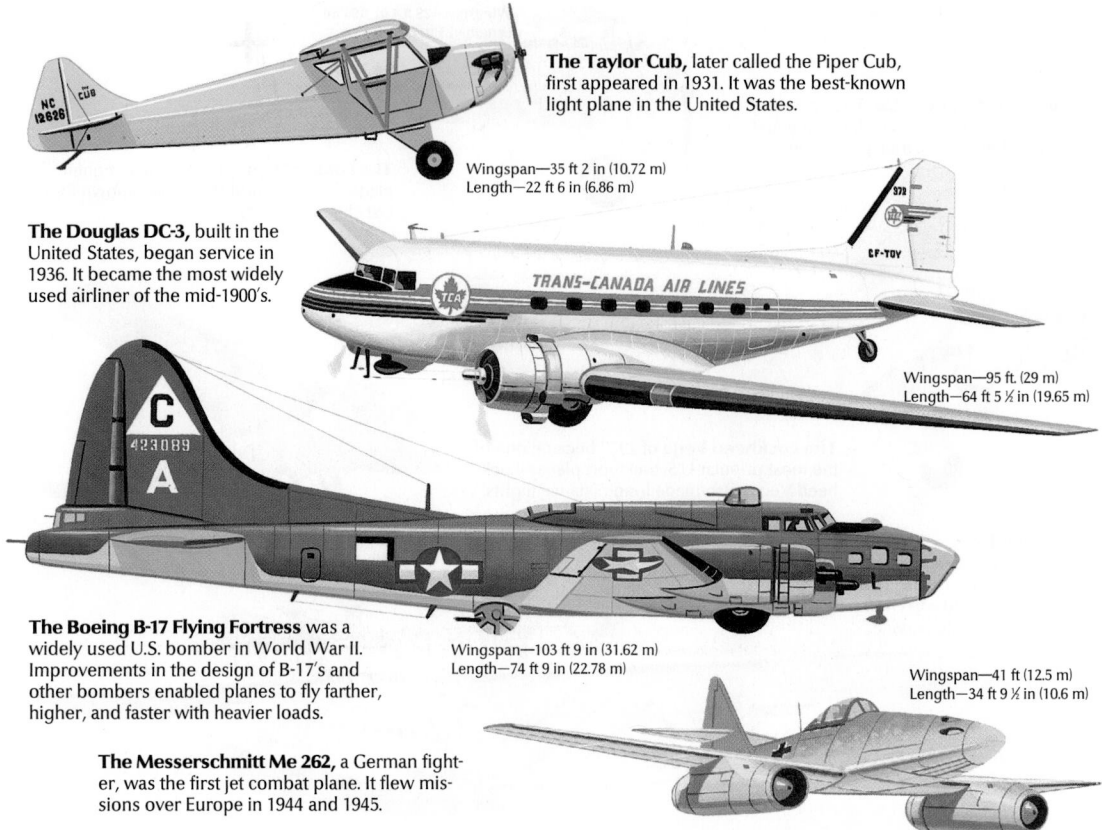

The Taylor Cub, later called the Piper Cub, first appeared in 1931. It was the best-known light plane in the United States.

Wingspan—35 ft 2 in (10.72 m)
Length—22 ft 6 in (6.86 m)

The Douglas DC-3, built in the United States, began service in 1936. It became the most widely used airliner of the mid-1900's.

Wingspan—95 ft. (29 m)
Length—64 ft 5 ½ in (19.65 m)

The Boeing B-17 Flying Fortress was a widely used U.S. bomber in World War II. Improvements in the design of B-17's and other bombers enabled planes to fly farther, higher, and faster with heavier loads.

Wingspan—103 ft 9 in (31.62 m)
Length—74 ft 9 in (22.78 m)

Wingspan—41 ft (12.5 m)
Length—34 ft 9 ½ in (10.6 m)

The Messerschmitt Me 262, a German fighter, was the first jet combat plane. It flew missions over Europe in 1944 and 1945.

Thomas E. Selfridge, a lieutenant in the U.S. Army Signal Corps and the first officer trained to fly, was the first person killed in a plane crash. The Army had decided to test the military value of the Wright brothers' airplane. On Sept. 17, 1908, Selfridge went up in a plane with Orville Wright. At an altitude of 75 feet (23 meters), one of the two propellers broke. The plane crashed, killing Selfridge and injuring Wright. But the Wrights were not discouraged. In 1909, they won an Army contract to build the world's first military plane.

A French inventor, Louis Blériot, made the first international airplane flight. In 1909, he flew his *Blériot XI* monoplane 23 ½ miles (37.8 kilometers) across the English Channel from France to England. The plane had a long, enclosed body, a tail for control at the rear, and a wheeled landing gear. Other successful monoplanes of the period included the *Antoinette* series designed by the French inventor Leon Levavasseur.

In 1911, Calbraith P. Rodgers made the first airplane flight across the United States—from Sheepshead Bay, New York, to Long Beach, California. During the 84-day journey, Rodgers landed—or crashed—his Wright airplane about 70 times. He had to replace almost every part of the plane before he reached Long Beach. His actual flying time was 3 days 10 hours 24 minutes.

In 1912, the Deperdussin Company of France built the Deperdussin monoplane racer, the first successful airplane of *monocoque* construction (pronounced *maw naw KAWK* or *MAHN uh kohk).* In this type of construction, the fuselage of the plane consisted of a structure

strong enough to bear the stresses of flight, reducing the need for external bracing. The monocoque design produced a streamlined aircraft that was lighter and created less drag. Meanwhile, two-engine planes had been developed. In 1913, a Russian inventor, Igor I. Sikorsky, flew his *Russky Vityaz* (Russian Knight), also called *The Grand,* the first four-engine plane. Most planes still had one engine.

The early fliers and their planes participated in many air races and air circuses. These tests of flying skill did much to improve airplane design and to make flying more popular. In 1913, a French pilot, Adolphe Pégoud, became noted for his skill at air acrobatics.

World War I (1914-1918) greatly advanced airplane development. Early in the war, both sides discovered the value of the airplane for locating enemy forces and military bases. Engineers designed more powerful engines to put swift fighter planes and heavy bombers into the skies. Germany, France, and Britain began to turn out thousands of these planes. *Dogfights* (air battles between fighters) became common. Seaplanes were used for taking pictures of enemy naval forces and for bombing enemy submarines. For the story of how airplanes were used in World War I, see **Air Force** (World War I); **World War I.**

At the beginning of the war, most planes could fly 60 to 70 mph (97 to 110 kph). By the war's end, many could go 130 mph (209 kph) or faster. Hugo Junkers, a German inventor and manufacturer, created one of the most influential airplane designs of the war. His plane, called

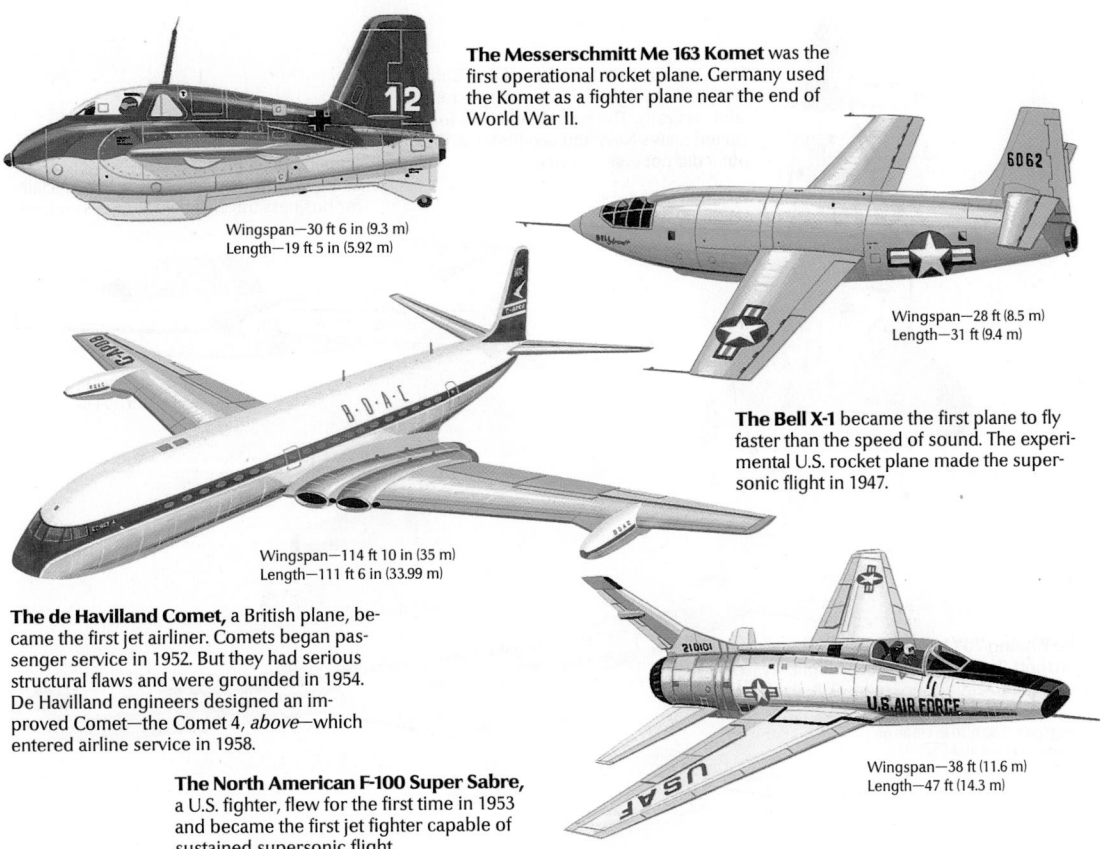

The Messerschmitt Me 163 Komet was the first operational rocket plane. Germany used the Komet as a fighter plane near the end of World War II.

Wingspan—30 ft 6 in (9.3 m)
Length—19 ft 5 in (5.92 m)

Wingspan—28 ft (8.5 m)
Length—31 ft (9.4 m)

The Bell X-1 became the first plane to fly faster than the speed of sound. The experimental U.S. rocket plane made the supersonic flight in 1947.

Wingspan—114 ft 10 in (35 m)
Length—111 ft 6 in (33.99 m)

The de Havilland Comet, a British plane, became the first jet airliner. Comets began passenger service in 1952. But they had serious structural flaws and were grounded in 1954. De Havilland engineers designed an improved Comet—the Comet 4, *above*—which entered airline service in 1958.

The North American F-100 Super Sabre, a U.S. fighter, flew for the first time in 1953 and became the first jet fighter capable of sustained supersonic flight.

Wingspan—38 ft (11.6 m)
Length—47 ft (14.3 m)

the Junkers J 1, made its first flight in 1915. The plane was the first to be made entirely of metal and the first to have a cantilever wing, which is completely supported by an internal framework. Earlier wings were supported by *struts* (braces) between the body and wings, which created drag and reduced the airplanes' speed.

The golden age in the development of the airplane occurred during the 1920's and 1930's. During this period, rapid advances were made in airplane design, and airlines began large-scale operations. It was also a time when daring pilots amazed the world with feats of flying skill and endurance.

In 1914, an American flier named Tony Jannus was the pilot of the world's first scheduled airline. Jannus used a small seaplane to carry passengers and freight across Tampa Bay between St. Petersburg and Tampa, Florida. The plane had room for one passenger, who paid $5 for the 22-mile (35-kilometer) flight. The airline had financial difficulties and lasted only a few months. In 1919, small airlines began to operate in Europe. They used rebuilt World War I bombers to carry passengers and mail on short flights between European cities. The cabins of some of the planes were elegantly decorated and furnished with comfortable armchairs. But the passengers could barely make themselves heard above the roar of the engines, and the cabins were unheated.

After World War I, the U.S. government offered thousands of surplus warplanes for sale at bargain prices. Although these planes were stronger than those built be-

fore the war, they still were not always safe. They were made mostly of wood and cloth and lacked satisfactory navigation equipment. But many former military pilots bought the planes and used them for an exciting and dangerous type of flying called *barnstorming*. Barnstormers toured the United States in the 1920's and put on daring air shows at county fairs and other events. The pilots flew the planes in wild acrobatics. Performers called *wing walkers* stepped from wing tip to wing tip in flight, or leaped from the wing of one flying plane to another. Many of the planes crashed, and a number of barnstormers were killed.

The United States Post Office, the forerunner of the U.S. Postal Service, also used modified military planes to fly mail between a few large cities. The Post Office began airmail service in 1918, operating its own planes. By 1927, the Post Office gave up operating its own planes and contracted with the airlines to carry airmail. Airmail greatly aided the growth of commercial aviation.

Meanwhile, engineers were working to design safer, more powerful transport planes. German engineers developed an all-metal, *trimotor* (three-engine) transport, the Junkers G 23. It flew for the first time in 1924 and was the first of a series of all-metal, trimotor planes made in Europe. The first such plane in the United States was developed from the ideas of William B. Stout, an aircraft manufacturer. Henry Ford, the automobile maker, bought Stout's company and began producing a trimotor plane in 1926. The Ford Tri-Motor could carry 10 pas-

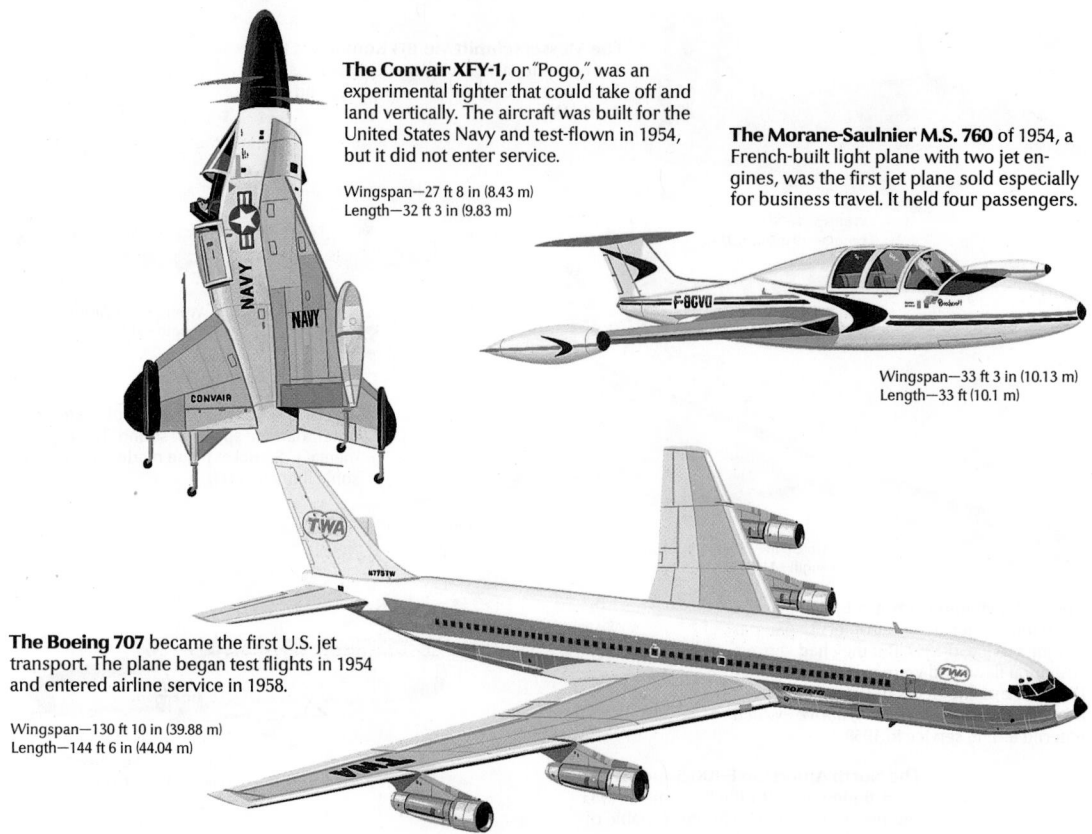

The Convair XFY-1, or "Pogo," was an experimental fighter that could take off and land vertically. The aircraft was built for the United States Navy and test-flown in 1954, but it did not enter service.

Wingspan—27 ft 8 in (8.43 m)
Length—32 ft 3 in (9.83 m)

The Morane-Saulnier M.S. 760 of 1954, a French-built light plane with two jet engines, was the first jet plane sold especially for business travel. It held four passengers.

Wingspan—33 ft 3 in (10.13 m)
Length—33 ft (10.1 m)

The Boeing 707 became the first U.S. jet transport. The plane began test flights in 1954 and entered airline service in 1958.

Wingspan—130 ft 10 in (39.88 m)
Length—144 ft 6 in (44.04 m)

sengers at 100 mph (160 kph) or more. In 1927, the Lockheed Company (now Lockheed Martin Corporation) produced the Vega, a single-engine transport that carried up to six passengers. It could fly 135 mph (217 kph) and travel 500 miles (800 kilometers) or farther without refu-

eling. The Ford Tri-Motor and the Lockheed Vega were among the most popular transport planes of the late 1920's and early 1930's.

Races helped encourage improvements in airplane design during the 1920's and 1930's. Important races in-

Notable airplane flights

1911 Calbraith P. Rodgers made the first flight across the United States. He flew from Sheepshead Bay, New York, to Long Beach, California, in a series of short flights that took 84 days.

1919 Two British fliers, John Alcock and Arthur Whitten Brown, made the first nonstop transatlantic flight. They flew 1,950 miles (3,138 kilometers) from St. John's, Newfoundland, to Clifden, Ireland.

1924 Two U.S. Army planes made the first round-the-world flight. They took nearly six months to complete the 26,345-mile (42,398-kilometer) journey.

1926 American explorers Richard E. Byrd and Floyd Bennett claimed the first airplane flight over the North Pole.

1927 Charles A. Lindbergh, a U.S. pilot, made the first solo nonstop transatlantic flight. He flew 3,610 miles (5,810 kilometers) from Garden City, New York, to Paris in 33 hours 31 minutes.

1928 Charles Kingsford Smith and his crew made the first flight across the Pacific—from Oakland, California, to Brisbane, Australia, with stops at Honolulu, Hawaii, and Suva, Fiji.

1929 Richard E. Byrd of the United States and his crew made the first flight over the South Pole.

1931 Two U.S. pilots, Clyde Pangborn and Hugh Herndon, made the first nonstop airplane flight across the Pacific. They flew from Tokyo to Wenatchee, Washington.

1932 Amelia Earhart of the United States became the first woman to fly across the Atlantic Ocean alone. She flew from Harbour Grace, Newfoundland, to a pasture near Londonderry,

Northern Ireland, in 15 hours 18 minutes.

1933 Wiley Post, a U.S. pilot, made the first solo round-the-world flight, traveling 15,596 miles (25,099 kilometers) in 7 days 18 hours 49 minutes.

1949 A U.S. Air Force crew made the first nonstop round-the-world flight, covering 23,452 miles (37,742 kilometers) in 3 days 22 hours 1 minute.

1992 French pilots Claude Delorme and Jean Boyé flew an Air France Concorde around the world in a record 32 hours 49 minutes 3 seconds.

2001 A solar-powered, propeller-driven airplane set an unofficial altitude record of 96,500 feet (155,302 meters). The craft, owned by NASA, was remotely piloted from the ground.

2004 NASA successfully tested a remotely-piloted scramjet-powered aircraft that reached Mach 7, or seven times the speed of sound.

2005 U.S. aviator Steve Fossett became the first person to make a nonstop solo flight around the world without refueling.

2006 Fossett made the longest nonstop flight in aviation history, traveling 26,389 miles (42,469 kilometers) in 3 days 4 hours 45 minutes.

2012 The Swiss pilot Bertrand Piccard flew from Spain to Morocco in a solar-powered airplane, the first intercontinental flight in such a craft.

2020 A British Airways plane made the fastest-ever flight from New York to London, in 4 hours 56 minutes.

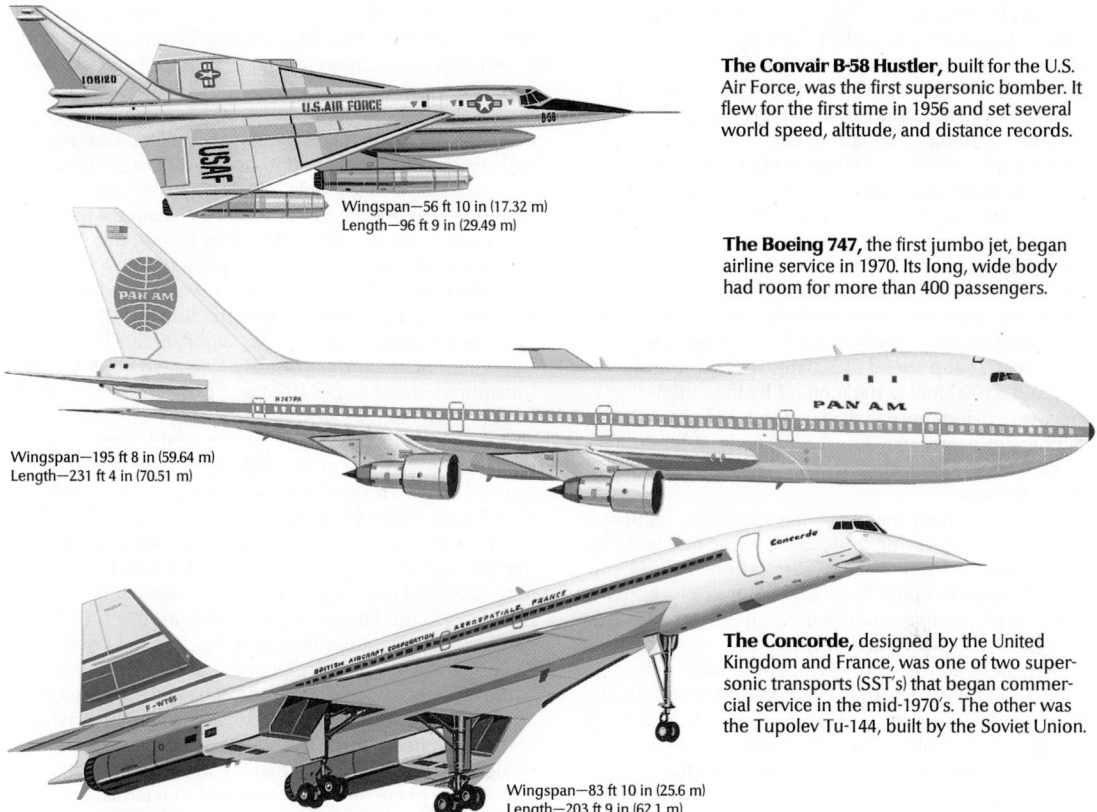

The Convair B-58 Hustler, built for the U.S. Air Force, was the first supersonic bomber. It flew for the first time in 1956 and set several world speed, altitude, and distance records.

Wingspan—56 ft 10 in (17.32 m)
Length—96 ft 9 in (29.49 m)

The Boeing 747, the first jumbo jet, began airline service in 1970. Its long, wide body had room for more than 400 passengers.

Wingspan—195 ft 8 in (59.64 m)
Length—231 ft 4 in (70.51 m)

The Concorde, designed by the United Kingdom and France, was one of two supersonic transports (SST's) that began commercial service in the mid-1970's. The other was the Tupolev Tu-144, built by the Soviet Union.

Wingspan—83 ft 10 in (25.6 m)
Length—203 ft 9 in (62.1 m)

cluded the Pulitzer Trophy races for small planes and the Schneider Trophy races for seaplanes. In 1920, the winner of the Schneider Trophy race flew at 107 mph (172 kph). The 1931 winner reached 340 mph (547 kph).

Fliers of the golden age. A number of American pilots made daring long-distance flights during the 1920's and early 1930's. Richard E. Byrd and Floyd Bennett are credited with flying the first plane to the North Pole, in May 1926. They flew a trimotor plane designed by the Dutch engineer Anthony Fokker. Fokker had built planes in Germany during World War I but moved his plant to the Netherlands after the war. In 1929, Byrd and Bernt Balchen made the first flight over the South Pole, in a Ford Tri-Motor. In 1927, Charles A. Lindbergh made the first solo nonstop flight across the Atlantic Ocean. His 3,610-mile (5,810-kilometer) flight—from Garden City, New York, to Paris—took 33 ½ hours. Lindbergh's plane, the *Spirit of St. Louis,* was a specially built Ryan monoplane with a Wright engine. It was a little larger than the Wright brothers' first airplane. It also had the most advanced aircraft instruments of the day, which helped Lindbergh find his way across the ocean without a radio.

In 1931, Hugh Herndon and Clyde Pangborn made the first nonstop flight across the Pacific. The next year, Amelia Earhart, flying an improved Lockheed Vega, became the first woman to cross the Atlantic solo and nonstop. In 1933, a former parachute jumper named Wiley Post flew a Vega in the first solo round-the-world flight.

Engineering improvements during the 1930's made it possible to build bigger planes that could fly faster,

farther, and higher—and carry heavier loads. Advances in aerodynamics helped engineers streamline planes so they could cut through the air with as little drag as possible. Engineers designed *controllable-pitch* propellers, with which pilots could set the propeller blade at the best angle for a particular air speed or altitude. Improved radio equipment enabled pilots to receive flight directions from the ground. Automatic flight control systems also came into use during the 1930's. These systems made possible more accurate navigation and enabled pilots to take rest breaks during long flights.

All the major advances in airplane design went into making the Douglas DC-3. This twin-engine transport made its first passenger flights in 1936. The DC-3 could carry 21 passengers and fly smoothly at 200 mph (320 kph). It soon became the most widely used airliner.

During the 1930's, many airline passengers traveled on *flying boats,* large, watertight seaplanes that could float in the water like the hull of a ship. Flying boats were used mainly for flights across oceans. One of the largest commercial flying boats was an enormous 12-engine plane built in Germany—the Dornier Do-X. It flew for the first time in 1929 but never became a popular airliner. One of the last and most famous flying boats was the Boeing 314 Clipper, which could carry up to 74 passengers. In 1939, 314's started the first regular passenger service across the Atlantic Ocean. But the development of more powerful landplanes—and of more airports with runways long enough to handle them—ended the day of the flying boats in most parts of the world.

As planes flew higher and higher, pilots and passengers had increased difficulty breathing in the thin air at high altitudes. So engineers designed *pressurized cabins,* in which the air inside is compressed at high altitudes to make breathing easier. Pressurized cabins became common in the late 1940's.

During World War II (1939-1945), the United Kingdom, Germany, Japan, the United States, and other countries turned out thousands of military planes. As in World War I, engineers made great advances in the design of bombers and fighters. Bombers developed during World War II could carry twice as heavy a load and travel nearly twice as far without refueling as prewar bombers could. Early in the war, fighter planes could reach a top speed of 300 mph (480 kph) and climb to about 30,000 feet (9,100 meters). By the end of the war, they were flying more than 400 mph (640 kph) and climbing to over 40,000 feet (12,000 meters). Jet fighters could fly even faster, though they were not used until late in the war.

In 1939, Germany made the first successful jet plane flight. The Messerschmitt Me 262 was the first jet to fly combat missions. It flew them over Europe in 1944 and 1945. This fighter could fly nearly 550 mph (885 kph). The Bell Aircraft Company (now a division of Textron Inc.) built the first U.S. jet plane in 1942.

German scientists had experimented with rocket planes as far back as 1928. Early in World War II, they developed the prototype Messerschmitt Me 163. This rocket-powered plane could fly at over 600 mph (970 kph). German engineers used it as a model for a fighter, the Me 163 Komet, which flew missions late in the war.

Transoceanic transports. Near the end of World War II, manufacturers began to develop nonstop transoceanic transports for commercial airlines. Four-engine transports developed during the war, such as the pressurized Douglas DC-4 and the Lockheed Constellation, were widely used for long-distance commercial passenger service after the war. But they had to stop for refueling on the longest ocean flights. Nonstop transoceanic flights required more powerful engines. By 1945, jet engines had the necessary power, but they used so much fuel that a jet could fly only a short distance without refueling. Instead of waiting for improved jet engines, the airlines built more powerful reciprocating engines. Two U.S. manufacturers created reciprocating engines of more than 3,000 horsepower (2,200 kilowatts) for the new transoceanic transports. These engines were used in the Douglas DC-7, the Lockheed Super Constellation, and the Boeing 377 Stratocruiser. Each plane could carry about 100 passengers nonstop between New York City and Paris at over 300 mph (480 kph).

The jet age. In the late 1940's, engineers worked to improve the crude jet engines built during World War II. The Soviet Union and the United States wanted jet engines to increase the power and speed of their bombers and fighters. By the time of the Korean War (1950-1953), both countries had highly effective jet planes. These planes included two famous fighters—the U.S. Air Force F-86 Sabre and the Soviet MiG-15.

In the United Kingdom, engineers produced the world's first large commercial jet airliner, the de Havilland Comet. Comets began passenger service in 1952. They flew at nearly 500 mph (800 kph) with little vibration or noise. The cabin was pressurized for safety and comfort. Then, in two separate accidents in January and April 1954, Comets tore apart in the air, killing all aboard. The fault proved to be in the plane's metal skin, which was too weak to withstand the stress of pressurization. The disasters led to the development of fuselage designs and structures more suited to pressurization in all airliners, including new Comets. Meanwhile, the United Kingdom had also produced the Vickers Viscount, a transport plane with propellers driven by jet engines. These turboprop planes began to carry passengers in 1953.

By the mid-1950's, U.S. engineers were also designing commercial jet airliners. In 1958, the Boeing 707, a four-engine jetliner, began passenger service between the United States and Europe. By 1960, two other U.S. jet transports—the Douglas DC-8 and the Convair 880—had begun passenger service. United States manufacturers also began to design a large jet that could carry several hundred passengers or 50 to 100 tons (45 to 90 metric tons) of cargo. The first of these giants, the Lockheed C-5A Galaxy military transport, began service in the U.S. Air Force in 1969. The world's first commercial jumbo jet, the Boeing 747, began service in 1970. It could carry more than 400 passengers. Newer versions of the Boeing 747 could travel longer distances, flying 14 hours or more without refueling. By 2017, the Boeing 747 was phased out in the United States, but it remained in the air fleet of a few countries. It has been replaced by the Boeing 787, also known as the Dreamliner, which entered service in 2011. The 787 is constructed with carbon-reinforced plastics that are lighter than metal, making the plane more fuel-efficient. The Dreamliner can hold 240 to 330 passengers.

Supersonic airplanes can fly faster than sound. At sea level, sound has a speed of about 760 mph (1,225 kph). But the speed of sound declines with altitude. At 50,000 feet (15,250 meters), for example, sound normally travels at about 660 mph (1,060 kph). No early jet plane was powerful enough or sturdy enough to fly faster than sound. A few approached this speed. When they did, shock waves tore them apart.

About 1943, U.S. engineers began work on rocket research planes for supersonic flight. These planes had to withstand the terrific air pressures at *Mach 1* (the speed of sound). In 1947, the Bell X-1 rocket plane, piloted by Chuck Yeager, a U.S. Air Force captain, made the first supersonic flight in history. In 1962, the North American X-15 rocket plane soared 314,750 feet (95,936 meters)—about 60 miles (96 kilometers) above Earth. Robert H. White, an Air Force major, piloted the plane. White thus became the first pilot to qualify as an astronaut by flying an airplane into space. In 1963, the X-15 raised the altitude record to 354,200 feet (107,960 meters)—about 67 miles (108 kilometers) above Earth. Later, it flew faster than Mach 6 (six times the speed of sound). Speeds of Mach 5 (five times the speed of sound) or higher are called *hypersonic.*

Meanwhile, engineers had developed jet engines capable of supersonic speeds. In 1953, the North American F-100 Super Sabre fighter became the first jet that could be operated at supersonic speeds in level flight. The first supersonic bomber was the U.S. Air Force's Convair B-58 Hustler. It flew for the first time in 1956.

At first, all the new supersonic jets were military

planes. Then in 1968, Soviet test pilots flew the world's first supersonic transport (SST), the Tupolev Tu-144. The United Kingdom and France cooperated to build an SST, the Concorde, which made its first test flight in 1969.

The Soviet Union began cargo service with the Tupolev Tu-144 in 1975 and started passenger service in 1977. But in 1983, the Soviet Union withdrew the plane from service because of technical and operational problems. The United Kingdom and France began passenger service with the Concorde in 1976. But all flights were suspended for more than a year beginning in 2000 after the crash of a Concorde in France following take-off. In 2003, the United Kingdom and France stopped all Concorde flights because they had become unprofitable. Traveling by supersonic airliner had been extremely expensive because the planes carried few passengers and used large amounts of fuel. In addition, the planes were extremely noisy, so some countries, including the United States, had restricted the Concorde to oceanic flights only.

Future developments. Engineers continue to search for ways to make airplanes faster, safer, quieter, and more efficient. One possible type of future airplane, called a *spaceplane* or *reusable launch vehicle* (RLV), would be powered by rocket engines. Spaceplanes could be launched into Earth's orbit and return to Earth and land on a runway. While in orbit, they would cruise at speeds of up to Mach 15 (15 times the speed of sound). Timothy S. Wolters

Related articles in *World Book* include:

Biographies

Alcock and Brown	Hughes, Howard R.
Blanchard, Jean-Pierre	Langley, Samuel P.
Blériot, Louis	Lindbergh, Charles A.
Boeing, William E.	Link, Edwin A.
Byrd, Richard E.	Mitchell, Billy
Coanda, Henri-Marie	Post, Wiley
Cochran, Jacqueline	Saint-Exupéry, Antoine de
Coleman, Bessie	Santos-Dumont, Alberto
Curtiss, Glenn H.	Sikorsky, Igor I.
De Seversky, Alexander P.	Wilkins, Sir Hubert
Doolittle, James H.	Wright brothers
Earhart, Amelia	Yeager, Chuck
Fokker, Anthony H. G.	

Parts of an airplane

Automatic flight control system	Magneto
	Propeller
Gasoline engine	Rocket
Gyroscope	Starter (Airplane starters)
Jet propulsion	

Other related articles

Aerodynamics
Aerospace medicine
Air force
Air Force, United States
Air Force One
Air turbulence
Aircraft, Military
Aircraft carrier
Airport
Airship
Autogiro
Aviation
Balloon
Contrail
Drone
Ducted propeller
Federal Aviation Administration
Glider
Global Positioning System
Helicopter
Hijacking
Inertial guidance
Jet propulsion
Jet stream
National Aeronautics and Space Administration
Navigation
Parachute
Radar
Streamlining
Test pilot
Unmanned aerial vehicle
V/STOL
Weather (Measuring the weather)
Wind shear

Outline

I. Types of airplanes
  A. Commercial transport planes
  B. General aviation planes
  C. Military planes
  D. Seaplanes
  E. Special-purpose planes

II. The parts of an airplane
  A. The wing
  B. The fuselage
  C. The tail
  D. The landing gear
  E. The controls and instruments
  F. Propellers

III. Power for flight
  A. Reciprocating engines
  B. Jet engines
  C. Turboprop engines
  D. Rocket engines

IV. Principles of flight
  A. Gravity and lift
  B. Drag and thrust
  C. Changing altitude
  D. Changing direction

V. Flying an airplane
  A. Basic movements and controls
  B. Proper use of the controls
  C. Stalling
  D. Flying by instruments
  E. Measuring flying speed
  F. Learning to fly

VI. Air navigation
  A. Pilotage
  B. Dead reckoning
  C. Electronic navigation
  D. Inertial guidance
  E. Safety

VII. Building an airplane
  A. Design and testing
  B. Mass production

VIII. History

Questions

What are *ailerons?* What are they used for?

Who made the first solo nonstop flight across the Atlantic Ocean?

What government agency sets standards for the design and manufacture of airplanes in the United States?

What four main types of engines are used to produce power for airplane flight?

In what ways did World War I and World War II contribute to airplane development?

What four forces act on a plane in flight?

What are an airplane's three basic movements?

What are the chief methods of air navigation?

Who was the first woman to make a solo flight across the Atlantic Ocean?

What is a V/STOL plane?

© John Boys

A control-line model airplane, *shown here,* has long wires attached to it. A person controls the flight of such a plane by holding onto the wires as the model whirls around.

Airplane, Model, is a miniature airplane. It may be a copy of a full-sized plane or have an original design. Building model airplanes is a popular hobby. There are flying and nonflying miniature aircraft of all types, including gliders and helicopters. Scale models can be of commercial and military planes. Scientists also use scale models of aircraft for testing before full-sized planes are built. They test the models in *wind tunnels,* where the airflow around the model is carefully controlled. See **Airplane** (Design and testing); **Wind tunnel.**

Models may be powered by twisted rubber bands, electric motors, gas or diesel engines, or compressed carbon dioxide. Most model planes take off under their own power, but some are hand-launched.

In the United States, the organization that regulates official model airplane contests is the Academy of Model Aeronautics (AMA). In Canada, it is the Model Aeronautics Association of Canada (MAAC). These groups certify flying records and sponsor contests in skills such as scale detail and accuracy of flight maneuvers.

Hobbyists generally build model airplanes from kits sold by hobby stores. Most kits of nonflying models consist of plastic parts that the modeler glues together. Balsa wood and foam rank as the most popular materials for flying models because they are light, strong, and easy to work with. Various kinds of synthetic materials may be used for parts of a model that require extra strength, such as the landing gear and engine mount. Hobbyists also build models from plans published in magazines. Advanced modelers sometimes design their own planes. Many planes are purchased assembled and ready to fly.

There are five main kinds of model airplanes. They are

© Jay Smith, Model Aviation Magazine

A free-flight model airplane, *shown here,* has no wires. A small engine powers this and many other flying model planes.

Radio control models,
left, are controlled by a transmitter that sends radio signals to a tiny receiver in the model. The receiver decodes the signals and passes the information to electric motors. The motors control the surfaces on the wings and tail assembly, allowing the model to maneuver. A radio control glider is shown here.

© Flyfoto/Alamy Images

(1) display, (2) indoor, (3) free-flight, (4) control-line, and (5) radio control.

Display models cannot fly. Hobbyists build them with the goal of duplicating the appearance of full-sized aircraft in every possible detail. Some display models have movable propellers, doors, and landing gear. Hobbyists take care in painting these models to make them look authentic. The models are judged at exhibitions on the basis of workmanship and accuracy of detail. Display models make attractive decorations in a home. Some modelers display their planes by hanging them from the ceiling by wires or exhibiting them in display cases.

Indoor models are flown only inside a building. They fly slowly, and some can stay aloft as long as 45 minutes. An indoor model is powered by twisted strands of rubber that turn the propeller as they unwind. These airplanes have a balsa frame covered by thin paper or a substance called *microfilm.* Microfilm is made by mixing lacquer and castor oil and floating the mixture on water to form a clear, thin film. The modeler removes the film with a wire loop and applies it to the plane's frame. Such models weigh ⅟₃₀ ounce (1 gram) or less. They are too fragile to be flown outdoors, where they might collapse at the slightest movement of air. Indoor gliders are typically made entirely of balsa.

Free-flight models may be powered by rubber strands or have a piston engine. Engine-powered free-flight models run on a mixture of methyl alcohol, nitromethane, and a lubricant. Diesel engines, using a mixture of kerosene, ether, and castor oil, are also used, and so are electric motors with rechargeable batteries. Such models built for competitive flying typically have wings from 3 to 6 feet (0.9 to 1.8 meters) long. After launching, a free-flight model climbs straight up for 5 to 15 seconds. A timing device then turns the engine off, and the plane goes into a slow glide for 3 to 5 minutes. Some engine-powered free-flight models that do not have a timing device can fly in a circular pattern for hours. Flying in rising air currents called *thermals* helps them remain airborne.

A free-flight glider may be hand-launched or it may be towed at the end of a cord and then released. Such gliders have remained airborne for many hours by flying in thermals.

Control-line models have piston or jet engines and fly at the end of wires. Most control-line models have two Dacron or steel wires that measure from 25 to 75 feet (8 to 23 meters) long. One end of each wire is attached to the model and moves the plane's *elevator,* a control surface on the tail assembly. The other end is fastened to a handle that the modeler uses to control the plane's altitude and flight path. When the hobbyist tilts the handle up, one wire raises the elevator, pointing the nose of the plane upward. Tilting the handle down causes the other wire to lower the elevator and point the plane's nose downward.

Some control-line models have only one line, which both raises and lowers the elevator. Others have a third line that controls the engine power and thus the speed of the plane. Jet-powered control-line models have flown nearly 250 miles (400 kilometers) per hour.

Radio control models are controlled by means of a transmitter that sends radio signals to the airplane. The model carries a tiny radio receiver that decodes the signals and passes the information to electric motor devices called *servos.* The servos move control surfaces on the wings and tail assembly, enabling the model to rise, sink, or turn. Servos can also control the speed of the plane's engine and even lift and lower the landing gear. Some radio control models are slow enough to be flown indoors. Radio control is also used to pilot model helicopters and racing and acrobatic model aircraft.

Some radio control gliders rank among the largest model airplanes. Their wings measure from 9 to 16 feet (3 to 4.9 meters) long. These long wings enable the plane to stay aloft for extended periods when steered into thermals.   Carlos Reyes

See also **Remote control.**

Airplane pilot. See Air Line Pilots Association; Airplane (Flying an airplane).

AP/Wide World

A major airport, such as Los Angeles International, *shown here,* may handle more than 200 take-offs and landings per hour at peak times. Thousands of passengers pass through the airport daily.

Airport

Airport is a place where airplanes and other aircraft take off and land, and load and unload passengers and cargo. Air travel has become the chief means of long-distance transportation, and modern aircraft provide the safest means of travel. Every day, the world's airports handle millions of passengers flying on thousands of commercial airplanes for business and leisure travel.

Airports are exciting places to see commercial airliners, general aviation aircraft, and sometimes even military aircraft. Overhead, planes approach or depart. On the ground, one plane after another takes off or lands. Automobiles, buses, taxis, and trains carry travelers to and from the passenger terminal. Thousands of people fill the terminal area. Most of them are passengers. Others are employees of the airport, airlines, or commercial establishments operating in the airport.

The largest airports resemble small cities. Many have hotels, restaurants, banks, post offices, and shops, as well as their own police force, fire departments, medical facilities, and utility plants and facilities. These services and facilities are important and useful for passengers and employees at an airport. In addition, some of them help produce the income necessary for the airport to operate successfully. During lengthy flight delays or emergencies, these services can become vital.

Airports differ from other transportation terminals, such as bus or train stations, in two important ways: (1) airports require more land, and (2) most airports are far from the centers of the cities they serve. An airport

needs much more land to accommodate the same number of passengers as a bus or train station. A medium-sized city airport needs from 700 to 3,000 acres (280 to 1,200 hectares). The largest airport in the world in area—King Fahd International Airport near Ad Dammam, Saudi Arabia—covers about 192,000 acres (78,000 hectares). The largest airport in the United States, Denver International Airport, has an area of approximately 34,000 acres (14,000 hectares).

National governments, state-sponsored bodies, local governments, and corporations own most of the world's large airports. Many small airports are privately owned.

In most countries, one or more federal agencies oversee airport certification, air safety, pilot qualifications, and the certification and inspection of aircraft. In the United States, for example, those agencies are the Transportation Security Administration (TSA) and the Federal Aviation Administration (FAA). In Australia, the agency is the Civil Aviation Safety Authority; in Canada, Transport Canada; in India, the Ministry of Civil Aviation; and in the United Kingdom, the Civil Aviation Authority. Nearly all countries, including Australia, Canada, India, South Africa, the United Kingdom, and the United States, belong to the International Civil Aviation Organization (ICAO) of the United Nations. The ICAO establishes standards for its members in such areas as airport safety, operations, and air traffic control.

The FAA is an agency of the U.S. Department of Transportation. In addition to licensing U.S. aircraft and pilots and certifying airports and airlines, the FAA regulates safety and sets design and operations standards for airports. The FAA also operates air navigational aids and controls air traffic. The TSA, an agency of the U.S. Department of Homeland Security, is responsible for airport and airline security in the United States.

Kinds of airports

Airports are classified in different ways in different countries. The FAA classifies most United States civilian airports as either *commercial service airports* or *general aviation airports*. Military airfields make up a third classification of airports.

Commercial service airports, also called *air carrier airports,* serve planes of commercial airlines. They may also serve such small aircraft as business, charter, or private planes. Nearly all major civilian airports are commercial service airports.

A commercial service airport may serve regional, national, or major airlines—or a combination of these types. *Regional airlines* generally fly short routes using smaller aircraft and connect small communities with one or two large airports. However, some regional jets fly routes of up to 1,000 miles (1,600 kilometers). *National airlines* fly from large airports as well as smaller ones, and they use both large and small jet aircraft. *Major airlines* are large air carriers that generate annual revenues of more than $1 billion in U.S. dollars. They generally provide both national and international flights.

Most airports that operate international flights have the word *international* in their names. International airports serve airlines of both their own country and other countries.

General aviation airports serve all types of aircraft except *scheduled airliners*—planes that operate over specified routes on a timetable. They serve business, charter, and private aircraft as well as scheduled air taxis, which carry passengers between towns and to and from commercial service airports. In addition, general aviation airports handle small aircraft used for aerial surveys, crop-dusting, and flight instruction. Airports that handle only specialized aircraft, such as helicopters or seaplanes, also fall into this category.

There are thousands of general aviation airports ranging from small grass or gravel strips to large, busy airports that handle huge corporate jets. The FAA classifies all general aviation airports—except those that serve only specialized aircraft—in four groups. The classifications are based on the size of the planes the airports can handle. *Basic utility airports* serve single-engine and some small twin-engine, propeller-driven planes. *General utility airports* can handle slightly heavier propeller aircraft. *Basic transport airports* can accommodate small jet airplanes. *General transport airports* handle all types of aircraft.

Special classifications of general aviation airports include *heliports* and *seaplane bases.* Heliports are areas where helicopters land and take off. A heliport may be on the ground, on the roof of a building, or on the deck of a ship. Seaplane bases are used by seaplanes and *amphibians.* Amphibians are aircraft that can land and take off on water or land. Seaplane bases may be on bays, lakes, or rivers. Most seaplane bases have onshore facilities to service the aircraft. The busiest seaplane base in

AP/Wide World
Airline personnel helping travelers at the check-in counter

© Karen Kent, The Stock Market
Workers loading food for passengers' meals

the world is in Anchorage, Alaska.

Military airfields are airports operated by the armed forces. Some military units, such as the U.S. Air National Guard, share facilities at commercial airports. Military airfields range in size from small fields for light planes to huge airports for heavy jet bombers.

Airport facilities

An airport's facilities depend on the size of the community it serves, the area of land it covers, and the type

© Thinkstock
Air traffic controllers directing aircraft movements

An overview of an airport

Airports provide facilities for aircraft and their crews, passengers, and cargo. The airport diagramed below is designed on the satellite plan. In this plan, departing passengers enter the main terminal, then go to separate terminals called *satellite terminals* to board their planes. The control tower is a navigation center from which air traffic controllers direct aircraft movements. The airport also has hangars in which aircraft are stored and repaired, runways where the planes take off and land, and cargo areas.

WORLD BOOK diagram by Russ Coombs, Steven Edsey and Sons

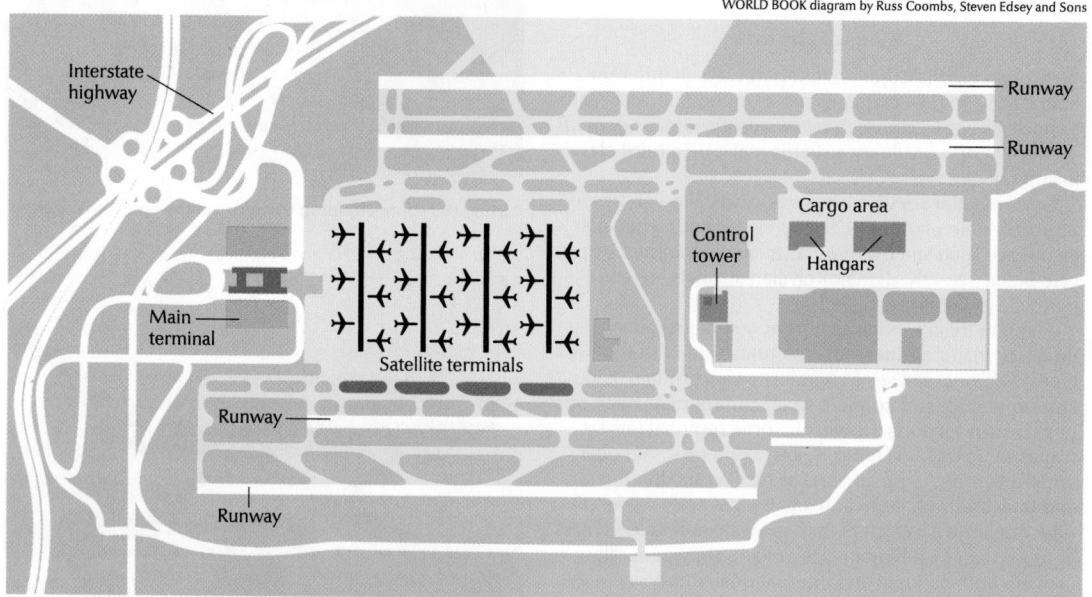

of air service it provides. This section deals chiefly with the numerous facilities provided by most large commercial service airports. The subsection *Planning and building an airport* later in this article discusses different types of designs for airport passenger terminals.

The passenger terminal. Passengers begin and end their flights at the passenger terminal. Airports may have one or more terminal buildings. At airline ticket counters, departing passengers purchase tickets, have their tickets checked, and receive boarding passes. They also can leave their baggage to be loaded into the airplane's cargo hold. Loudspeakers, flight monitors, and electronic message boards announce flight arrivals and departures. Boarding lounges provide seats for waiting travelers and airline crews.

Passengers board and leave aircraft from openings called *gates*. At most large airports, an enclosed walkway called a *boarding bridge*—or, under a common trade name, a *Jetway*—connects the terminal gate with the aircraft during boarding. Arriving passengers pick up their luggage at a baggage claim area in the passenger terminal.

Many of the activities in the passenger terminal take place behind the walls or under the floor. These activities include the transport of baggage and cargo from the ticket counter to the aircraft. In addition, airlines maintain offices in these areas.

Each airline has a *briefing room,* where pilots receive flight information. The briefing room includes a *dispatch office,* which handles communications with the airline's

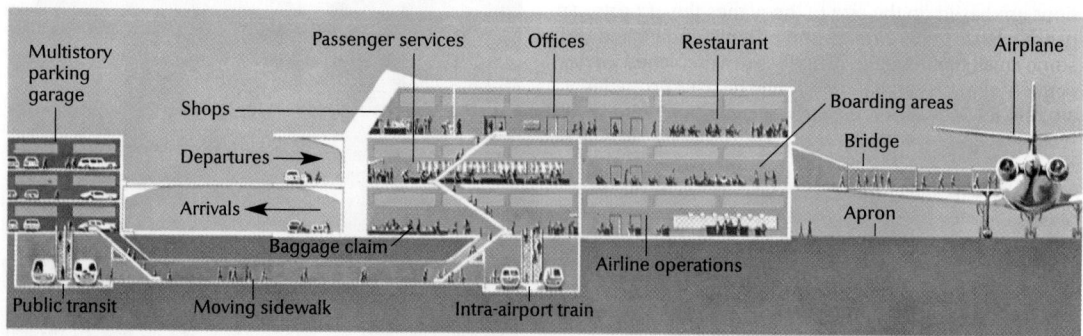

WORLD BOOK diagrams by Einbecker-Butler & Associates

The terminal area of many airports has three main levels that handle a variety of activities. An additional underground level may provide links with mass transportation and intra-airport trains.

operations center and with its airplanes, both on the ground and in flight. The airport manager and the management staff, who oversee the operation of the airport, also have offices at the airport.

Hangars are buildings in which aircraft are stored and repaired. Most airlines have their own hangars. Some hangars can hold several large jets at one time. Most airports locate hangars far enough from the terminal building to avoid interference with aircraft traffic on the ground.

The control tower is the air traffic nerve center. In the tower, air traffic controllers may use Automatic Dependent Surveillance-Broadcast (ADS-B), radar, signal lights, and other equipment. ADS-B, which replaces or supplements radar-based surveillance, is surveillance technology that uses signals from Global Positioning System (GPS) satellites to direct air traffic near the airport as well as aircraft on the ground. Control towers at the busiest airports may handle more than 200 landings and take-offs an hour during peak periods. Large, tinted windows enable controllers to see all the aircraft in motion at the airport. Some control towers are more than 400 feet (120 meters) tall.

Runways must be long enough and wide enough to handle the largest planes using the airport. They must be as level as possible. However, runways slope slightly from the center toward each side to provide good drainage. A government body usually sets minimum runway lengths for different types of aircraft. Many small airports use only strips of mowed grass called *landing strips.* Some of these strips are only 2,000 to 2,500 feet (610 to 760 meters) long. The runways of large airports are paved with concrete or asphalt. These runways may be as long as 13,000 to 14,000 feet (4,000 to 4,300 meters) to handle the biggest planes. Runways must have a *clear zone* at each end to give aircraft additional space to take off or land without endangering people or property on the ground.

Lines painted down the center and sides and across the ends of runways guide pilots in the air and on the ground. Numbers painted on each end of a runway tell pilots the compass direction in which the runway is laid out. For example, 18 and 36 indicate a north-south runway. The number 18 (an abbreviation for 180°) is painted on the north end of the runway, and the number 36 (360°) appears on the south end. Most airports design runways in at least two directions so planes can take off and land as nearly as possible into the wind.

At night and other periods of low visibility, white lights outline each runway. Green lights mark the beginning of a runway. Red and white approach lights shine in front of the area where a plane should touch down.

Loading aprons and taxiways. The aircraft parking area at the gates of the passenger terminal is called a *loading apron* or *tarmac.* Although the word *tarmac* originally referred to a paving material made of crushed rock and tar, the apron is actually made of concrete or asphalt because these materials better resist damage from heat and fuel leaks. While an airplane is on the apron, workers refuel it and load baggage, cargo, and meals for the passengers. The crew and passengers board airplanes on the loading apron. A small airport may service only 1 or 2 aircraft on the apron at one time. Large airports may service more than 100 planes at once.

Aircraft use lanes called *taxiways* to taxi from the apron to the runways and from the runways to the hangars. Many large airports have double taxiways so aircraft can move to and from the runways and hangars at the same time. At night, the taxiways are marked with blue lights. Red lights mark barriers or other dangers.

Ground transportation and parking. Large airports provide roadways alongside the terminal buildings where airport buses, hotel vans, private automobiles, limousines, and taxis can pick up and drop off passengers. Some airports are connected to the city center by light rail systems or subways.

All airports maintain parking facilities. Most large airports have multistory parking garages, which take less land than parking lots do to hold the same number of cars. Parking provides a major source of revenue for many airports.

Airport operations

The airport manager and the management staff direct the maintenance, operation, and safety of the entire airport. In some regions, they may be responsible for several airports. The management staff at a large airport is divided into several departments, such as administra-

World's 25 busiest airports

Airport	Passenger departures and arrivals*	Aircraft take-offs and landings
1. Hartsfield-Jackson Atlanta International	110,531,000	904,000
2. Beijing Capital International	100,014,000	594,000
3. Los Angeles International	88,068,000	691,000
4. Dubai International	86,397,000	373,000
5. Tokyo (Haneda) International	85,505,000	458,000
6. O'Hare International (Chicago)	84,649,000	920,000
7. Heathrow (London)	80,888,000	478,000
8. Pudong International (Shanghai)	76,153,000	512,000
9. Charles de Gaulle (Paris)	76,150,000	505,000
10. Dallas/Fort Worth International	75,067,000	720,000
11. Guangzhou Baiyun International	73,395,000	491,000
12. Schiphol (Amsterdam)	71,707,000	516,000
13. Hong Kong International	71,415,000	430,000
14. Incheon International	71,204,000	407,000
15. Frankfurt	70,556,000	514,000
16. Denver International	69,016,000	632,000
17. Indira Gandhi International (Delhi)	68,491,000	466,000
18. Singapore Changi	68,283,000	386,000
19. Suvarnabhumi International (Bangkok)	65,425,000	381,000
20. John F. Kennedy International (New York City)	62,551,000	456,000
21. Kuala Lumpur International	62,336,000	408,000
22. Madrid-Barajas	61,708,000	426,000
23. San Francisco International	57,419,000	458,000
24. Chengdu Shuangliu International	55,859,000	367,000
25. Soekarno-Hatta International (Jakarta)	54,497,000	391,000

*Includes only commercial airline traffic.   Figures are for 2019.
Source: Airports Council International (ACI) World, World Annual Traffic Reports.
https://store.aci.aero/product-category/economics-statistics/world-annual-traffic-reports-watr/

Airborne Express

WORLD BOOK photo

Cargo handling is a major airport activity. Many airlines have special cargo planes like the one above. Workers pack small cargo items in containers shaped to fit the airplane's interior. They load the cargo through the plane's wide door.

Refueling is one of the important activities carried out while a plane stands outside the terminal between flights.

tion, finance, operations, maintenance, planning, engineering, safety, security, and public affairs. The airport staff works to ensure that the airport operates safely and efficiently. Every day, the staff checks the safety of the airport's terminal, taxiways and runways, parking areas, and roadways.

An airport must operate like a business. Airports rent space to the airlines for offices, check-in counters, and baggage areas. In addition, airports give leases to restaurants, gift shops, hotels, and car rental agencies. The leases provide revenue to pay for the operation and development of the airport. In addition, the airport receives income from parking lots, telephones and advertisements in the terminal, and landing fees paid by the airlines. Most commercial service airports also get income from a *passenger facility charge,* a small fee as-sessed on each passenger's ticket.

Airline passenger services. Airline workers provide many services for passengers at commercial airports. Ticket counter employees sell tickets, check in passengers who already have tickets, and provide information about the times and gates for flight arrivals and departures. A passenger's ticket may be a printed ticket or an *e-ticket,* a ticket purchased over the telephone or the Internet and recorded electronically with the airline. Ticket counter agents use airline computer systems to quickly print boarding passes and baggage tags. Ticket kiosks at some airports enable passengers to check themselves in without the aid of a ticket agent.

Ticket counter workers also check in passengers' baggage. Baggage handlers and *ramp agents* (workers that service aircraft between flights) see that baggage is loaded on the correct flights. After a plane reaches its destination, handlers unload bags and transport them to the baggage claim area.

Other airline workers include an airline station manager, who oversees passenger services, and reservations agents, who keep records of flight reservations. The dispatch staff maintains contact with planes in the air and with other airports that the airline serves.

Cargo handling. Most airports use the term *cargo*

for mail and all other freight carried by aircraft except baggage. Much air cargo includes items that spoil rapidly, such as flowers, fruits, vegetables, seafood, and medical supplies, including organs for transplant. Other typical air cargo includes such products as electronic products and machinery parts. Both cargo aircraft and passenger aircraft carry cargo.

Large airports have several separate terminals for cargo processing. Cargo brought in from the surrounding area is often sorted at the airport for various flights. Postal workers sort any mail. Carts, towed by small vehicles called *tugs,* then carry the cargo to the apron, where workers load it into passenger or cargo aircraft.

Small aircraft services. Commercial service airports must provide many services for small planes that are not operated by commercial airlines. In the United States, these small planes account for about 10 percent of the traffic at most large commercial service airports and approximately 65 percent of the flights at small commercial service airports. A Fixed Base Operator provides these small aircraft with such services as fuel, hangars, mechanical maintenance, ground transportation, and food.

Air traffic control. In the control tower, the air traffic controllers guide aircraft as they land, take off, and taxi. The controllers see that traffic keeps moving smoothly, rapidly, and safely. They must have good eyesight, speak clearly over the radio, and think quickly. The controllers must also remain calm during periods of heavy air traffic. Their job becomes especially difficult when fog or other weather conditions reduce visibility. In such situations, the controllers must rely entirely on ADS-B technology, radar, or GPS satellite signals to locate and guide aircraft in flight.

Planes approach or depart on assigned routes called *traffic patterns.* Instruments in aircraft cockpits electronically display an airport's traffic patterns for pilots to follow. When necessary, a pilot can safely fly without instruments if the weather is clear enough to see other aircraft and the airport.

The control tower has several types of electronic all-weather landing equipment to help bring planes down

Airport terms

Cargo is all freight, except baggage, carried by an airplane.

Closed in means an airport is closed to air traffic because of bad weather.

Commercial service airport is an airport that serves planes of commercial airlines. Air carrier airports may also serve other types of aircraft, such as business, charter, or private planes.

Control tower is a glass-enclosed booth equipped with radar, radio, lights, and other navigation aids for directing aircraft movements on the ground and in the air. *Air traffic controllers* work in the tower or in buildings called *air route traffic control centers.*

Gate is the airport terminal entryway passengers use when boarding or leaving planes. Each airliner is assigned a *gate position* for loading or unloading passengers.

General aviation airport is an airport that does not serve scheduled airlines. General aviation airports serve mostly air taxis and business, charter, and private planes.

General aviation traffic is all air traffic except scheduled airline flights.

Heliport is an area where helicopters land and take off.

Instrument Landing System is an electronic aid used by most commercial airports. It sends radio signals to receivers on an airplane to help guide the pilot on the correct approach path to the airport.

Loading apron is the paved area around the terminal where aircraft are serviced, passengers board and leave planes, and baggage and cargo are loaded and unloaded.

Runway is a smooth, level strip of land on which aircraft take off and land. At a small airport, the runway may be only a strip of mowed grass called a landing strip. Large airports have many runways paved with concrete and asphalt.

Taxiway is a paved lane aircraft use to move between the apron, hangars, and runways. Aircraft follow a *taxi route* to reach a take-off point or parking area.

Terminal is the main airport building for passenger services. It also houses offices of airline employees and the airport management staff.

Other navigation aids include Airport Surveillance Radar (ASR) and the Global Positioning System. The ASR gives traffic controllers a view of all aircraft activity within about 60 miles (100 kilometers) of the airport. This information helps controllers prevent midair collisions by choosing the safest route for pilots to follow.

The GPS uses a network of navigation satellites to enable pilots anywhere on earth to determine their location. These satellites send out radio signals that are picked up by receivers on the aircraft. GPS equipment can compute an aircraft's position, speed, and time every second. The system bases the calculations on the distances between the satellites and the receiver. Many airports use a *wide-area augmentation system* (WAAS) that enhances GPS data to provide more accurate positioning information for approaches and landings. See **Global Positioning System.**

Airport security. Commercial service airports worldwide maintain a high level of security to prevent such dangerous activity as terrorist hijackings and bombings. TSA personnel search airplanes for hidden weapons and explosives. They also inspect passengers' baggage before it goes onto the plane. Passengers must pass through electronic scanners that detect guns, knives, and other metal objects.

The federal government has established security regulations for all air carrier airports in the United States. They include rules on inspection of planes, baggage, and passengers. The airports are required to have law enforcement personnel on the premises as part of their security programs. Federal legislation passed after terrorist attacks in the United States in September 2001 set deadlines for increased security measures at airports. They include screening all checked baggage for explosives. In addition, the new law transferred responsibility for the screening of passengers and baggage from personnel employed by private security firms to federal employees.

Other operations. Some airline and privately contracted employees work in the hangars. There, trained

safely. Most commercial airports have an electronic aid called an Instrument Landing System (ILS). The ILS sends radio signals to receivers on an airplane which show the pilot whether the plane is to the left, right, above, below, or directly on the correct approach path to the airport.

Making instrument landings

The *Instrument Landing System* (ILS) sends radio signals to receivers on a plane. A vertical *localizer beam* guides the plane to the runway. A *glide-slope beam* shows the angle on which the plane should descend. *Marker beacons* or special signals indicate the distance to the runway.

WORLD BOOK diagram by Einbecker-Butler & Associates

Outer marker beacon

Middle marker beacon

Localizer beam

Glide-slope transmitter and antenna

Localizer transmitter and antenna

Flight path

Glide-slope beam

End of runway

Runway

Touchdown

End of runway

½ mile (0.8 kilometer) to runway

Approach lights

5 miles (8 kilometers) to runway

Security checks at airports help prevent hijacking of planes. Passengers walk through a device that detects metal objects. Security personnel may also use a hand-held scanner, *shown here,* to be certain a passenger carries no concealed weapons.

An airline mechanic works to keep aircraft in safe flying condition. Mechanics perform routine checks and make needed repairs.

mechanics repair planes and other employees keep records of spare parts needed for urgent repairs. Many airline employees work in the apron area. Some direct aircraft into parking spaces. Mechanics check the engines and other equipment. Some employees clean the interior of airplanes between flights. After all the work has been completed, the captain of an aircraft notifies the dispatch office that the flight is ready to leave.

Airlines contract with commercial flight kitchens to prepare food for passengers on some flights. Dietitians plan the menus, chefs do the cooking, and food handlers transport the meals to waiting aircraft.

At most U.S. airports, FAA employees operate the control tower and maintain electronic equipment in the tower. The workers who do passenger and baggage inspection in U.S. airports are also federal employees. Other federal workers at airports include postal workers, customs and immigration officials, and security personnel.

Many large commercial service airports have a station for their national weather service. Airports and airlines typically use private weather services to check conditions in specific areas of interest. Such services provide airlines, pilots, and airport operators with world and national weather information.

Airport development

Planning and building an airport takes a long time because of the environmental and economic issues that must be considered. When a governmental body wishes to build an airport, it may take several years and many studies before construction can begin. The first step is to hire an airport planning firm to select the best site for the new airport. The planners evaluate each potential site for many factors, including environmental impact, distance to the city, homes and businesses that must be moved, and difficulty of building on the terrain. The governmental body then holds public hearings where elected officials and the public can express their opinions

about the site that has been chosen.

Following approval by the community and the federal government, funding for the airport must be arranged. Voters may be asked to approve a bond issue to help pay for the new facility. The governmental body then contracts with an architectural firm, an engineering firm, contractors and suppliers, and perhaps a project management firm to design and build the airport. The actual construction of a major airport usually takes three to five years.

Few cities build new airports. Instead, most cities expand or renovate their existing airports. Planners prepare a document called an *airport master plan.* The plan shows the airport's present facilities and describes how the airport should be developed to meet future needs. These plans generally show the location of new runways and terminal buildings so these areas can be protected for future development. The nation's government often funds such plans.

As cities allow homes and businesses to be built near an airport, they decrease the ability of the airport to grow in the future. Airports, airlines, the federal government, and local communities must all work together to ensure that airports operate safely and efficiently.

Terminal designs. Designs for airport passenger terminals use one of three types of plans. These plans are: (1) linear, (2) pier, and (3) satellite.

In a linear plan, arriving and departing passengers enter and exit the terminal at various points along the building's curb. Aircraft also park along the length of the building. This arrangement results in short walking distances for passengers. Linear plans work best for passengers beginning or ending their trips. Such plans are less efficient, however, for passengers or baggage transferring between flights.

A pier plan has a central terminal building with a pier or passageway called a *concourse* that extends onto the apron where the airplanes park. Although this type of plan may create longer walking distances, it allows

Types of airport passenger terminals

Common terminal designs include linear, pier, and satellite plans. In a *linear plan,* passengers arrive at points along the length of the building, and the planes park along the other side. A *pier plan* has a central terminal with piers that extend onto the apron where the aircraft park. In a *satellite plan,* people board and leave planes from separate satellite terminals.

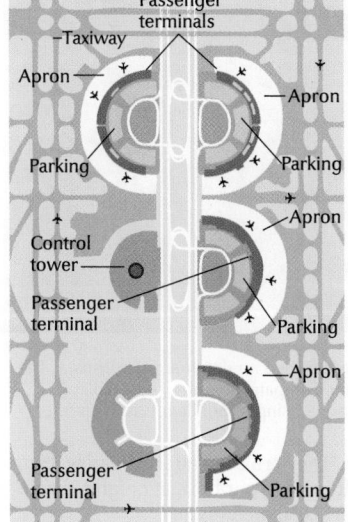

Linear plan

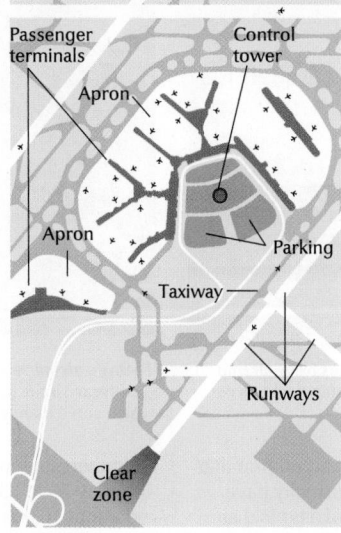

Pier plan

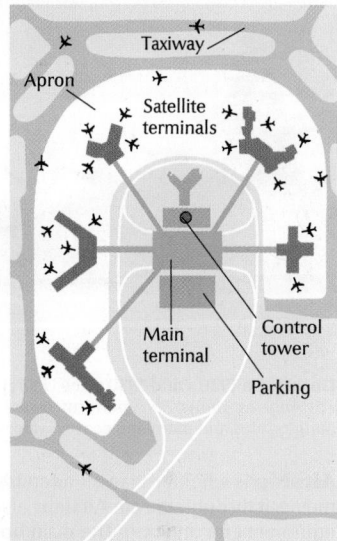

Satellite plan

WORLD BOOK diagrams by Russ Coombs, Steven Edsey and Sons

more aircraft to park near the building. It also centralizes such functions as baggage handling, ticketing, and check-in. Many modern pier terminals have moving sidewalks to help passengers who have to walk long distances.

In a satellite plan, passengers board aircraft from terminals called *satellite terminals.* Passengers travel from the main terminal to a satellite terminal by riding a shuttle or a driverless electric rail car called a *people mover.* Shuttles and people movers run at ground level, overhead, or underground from the main terminal. The satellite plan enables a greater number of aircraft to park at a terminal and shortens walking distances.

Airport noise. When airports were built years ago, they lay far from cities and people's homes. However, as cities have grown, more people have come to live near airports. As a result, aircraft noise has become an increasing problem. In the United States, federal noise laws have resulted in airlines phasing out old, noisy aircraft and purchasing quieter new planes, or replacing engine parts on existing aircraft. In addition, airports sometimes obtain federal funds to buy homes affected by noise or to pay for the soundproofing of schools, libraries, and homes. At many airports, pilots must follow specific approach and departure patterns to reduce the impact of noise on populated areas.

Paul P. Bollinger, Jr.

Related articles. See the *Transportation* section in the various city, country, state, and province articles. See also:

Airmail
Airplane
Aviation
Federal Aviation Administration
Radar

Outline

I. Kinds of airports
 A. Commercial service airports
 B. General aviation airports
 C. Military airfields
II. Airport facilities
 A. The passenger terminal
 B. Hangars
 C. The control tower
 D. Runways
 E. Loading aprons and taxiways
 F. Ground transportation and parking
III. Airport operations
 A. Airline passenger services
 B. Cargo handling
 C. Small aircraft services
 D. Air traffic control
 E. Airport security
 F. Other operations
IV. Airport development
 A. Planning and building an airport
 B. Terminal designs
 C. Airport noise

Questions

What security regulations do airports follow to prevent hijacking attempts?
What things are shown in an airport master plan?
What do the numbers on runways mean?
How do commercial service airports differ from general aviation airports?
What are some functions of federal employees at airports?
What is the job of the airport management staff?
What are some of the navigation aids used by air traffic controllers?
What are some major sources of revenue at commercial airports?
What are some of the responsibilities of the FAA?
What is the largest airport in the world? In the United States?

Culver

During the 1920's and 1930's, the United States Navy airship *Los Angeles, shown here,* performed such military tasks as escorting ships and patrolling coastal waters.

Goodyear

Today's airships are often used for commercial purposes. The Goodyear Tire & Rubber Company operates several blimps, which serve mainly as advertising or public relations craft.

Airship is a lighter-than-air aircraft with an engine that moves it through the air. Airships also normally have equipment for steering. The main body of a typical airship is a huge, cigar-shaped balloon filled with a lighter-than-air gas. The gas raises the craft and keeps it aloft.

An airship differs from a *free-floating balloon,* which is neither powered nor steered. Airships also differ from helicopters and airplanes, which are heavier than air. Helicopters and airplanes use their engines and blades or wings to lift them and keep them aloft.

Airships were introduced in the 1800's as the first flying machines capable of prolonged flight and of being steered. This feature led to the craft being called *dirigibles,* which comes from the Latin word *dirigere,* meaning *to direct.* In World War I (1914-1918), airships were used as bombers, for protecting ships against submarine attack, and for other duties. Before and after the war, they were used to carry passengers. Airship passenger services reached their height in the 1930's, but a series of disastrous crashes and the increasing popularity and long-range capability of the airplane brought airship passenger services to an end. Today, several countries have shown a renewed interest in airships for advertising, cargo operations, passenger transport, recreational flying, and surveillance.

Types of airships

There are three main types of airships: (1) nonrigid airships, (2) rigid airships, and (3) semirigid airships.

Nonrigid airships were the first airships and are the most popular type today. They have no major internal structures and no outer framework. Gas pressure causes the outer skin, called the *envelope,* to keep its shape. Modern envelopes are made of synthetic materials.

The smallest airships have been nonrigid craft. Some have measured less than 75 feet (23 meters) long. The largest nonrigid airships were the United States Navy's ZPG-3W airships. These craft were flown from 1958 to 1962 and were used for airborne early-warning duties. Each ZPG-3W measured about 403 feet (123 meters) long. Today's nonrigid airships average about 150 feet

(46 meters) in length. They cruise at approximately 35 to 40 miles (56 to 65 kilometers) per hour at heights reaching about 10,000 feet (3,050 meters).

The U.S. Navy's B-class nonrigid airships, built in 1917, gave rise to the term *blimp* for nonrigid craft. The term came from *B-nonrigid,* or *B-limp.*

Rigid airships, the largest airships, have a greater carrying capacity than nonrigid craft. But few are flown today. The main body of a rigid airship is called the *hull.* Most early rigid craft had a hull consisting of a wooden or metal framework that supported the outer skin. Today, composite materials can be used. The most famous rigid airships were called *zeppelins,* after Count Ferdinand von Zeppelin, a German airship pioneer.

Zeppelins were cigar-shaped and ranged from about 400 feet (120 meters) to over 800 feet (240 meters) long. Advanced models could reach speeds of about 80 miles (130 kilometers) per hour. Inside the hulls were several compartments, called *gas cells,* that held the lifting gas. Many hulls contained corridors along which cargo, crew quarters, and the fuel tanks were located.

Semirigid airships became fairly common in the early 1900's. They often resembled nonrigid ships, except that a support ran along most of the length of the envelope and helped maintain its shape and distribute loads. Semirigid airships were often larger than nonrigid craft. A few semirigid craft are being developed and flown today, but they are far less common than nonrigid craft.

How airships fly

Lift is the force that raises an airship off the ground and keeps it aloft. Airships generate lift because the gas they contain has a lower density than the air outside the craft. Airships hold enough of this lighter-than-air gas to overcome their own weight and rise from the ground.

Early airships contained hydrogen, the lightest of all gases. But hydrogen is highly flammable, which was an important factor in a number of airship disasters. As a result, helium replaced hydrogen for use in airships.

Thrust is the force that moves an airship through the air. Most airships use engines and propellers to obtain thrust. On large rigid airships of the early 1900's, the engines and propellers were in *gondolas* (cars) attached to the hull. Such craft had separate gondolas for the passengers and crew. On most nonrigid and semirigid airships, engines are mounted on a gondola that also holds the crew and passengers.

Control. Most airships have tail structures that include *fins, rudders,* and *elevators.* Fins are large, fixed surfaces. Typically, four fins are set equally distant from one another around the ship's *stern* (rear). The smaller, movable rudders and elevators are surfaces attached to the fins. A pilot moves the rudders to steer and the elevators to raise or lower the ship's nose.

For improved control, many early airships carried weight called *ballast,* usually water. If rain or other weather conditions made the craft heavier in flight, the pilot could release ballast to lighten the craft and thus maintain altitude. Some modern airships carry ballast.

Ballonets are air-filled bags or compartments inside the envelope of nonrigid and semirigid craft. Ballonets help maintain the shape of the envelope. If gas pressure in the envelope decreases, air is pumped into the ballonets so that the envelope will not sag. Ballonets can also be used to stiffen the envelope of a rigid airship.

Storage. Early airships were kept in huge hangars or sheds, but moving the craft in and out of these shelters sometimes proved disastrous. Engineers partly solved the problem when they developed the *mooring mast,* a high, stable tower to which an airship could be anchored without touching the ground. The bow of the airship was secured to the tower. Mooring masts allowed airships a limited amount of movement to help them survive high winds. To enter rigid craft, the crew and passengers passed up a staircase within the mast.

Low mooring masts were developed to secure nonrigid airships close to the ground. The crew and passengers can board these craft directly into the gondola. Some modern airships do not require masts at all.

History

The first airships evolved from balloons. Henri Giffard, a French engineer, built and piloted the first powered airship. As with many balloons, ropes covered the envelope and hung down to support an open gondola. But unlike the ball-shaped balloons, Giffard's airship was cigar-shaped, and the gondola supported a 3-horsepower (2.2-kilowatt) steam engine. A saillike rudder was carried in the gondola.

On Sept. 24, 1852, Giffard flew his craft about 17 miles (27 kilometers) from Paris to Trappes, near Versailles, at an average speed of 5 miles (8 kilometers) per hour. The small rudder and engine enabled him to alter his course, but the craft was not properly steerable.

In 1884, Charles Renard and Arthur Krebs, two French inventors, completed *La France.* This airship had a battery-powered electric motor that produced about 9 horsepower (7 kilowatts). It also had an efficient rudder and elevator. Renard and Krebs flew *La France* around a 5-mile (8-kilometer) circular course near Paris at speeds over 14 miles (23 kilometers) per hour. In 1901, the Brazilian-born inventor Alberto Santos-Dumont completed a controlled journey around the Eiffel Tower in

Kinds of airships   There are three main types of airships. A *nonrigid airship* has no framework supporting its gas-filled *envelope* (outer skin). In a *semirigid airship,* supports brace the craft's gas-filled bag. An extensive inner framework, usually of wood or metal, supports the gas bags of a *rigid airship.*

WORLD BOOK illustrations by Tony Gibbons, Linden Artists Ltd.

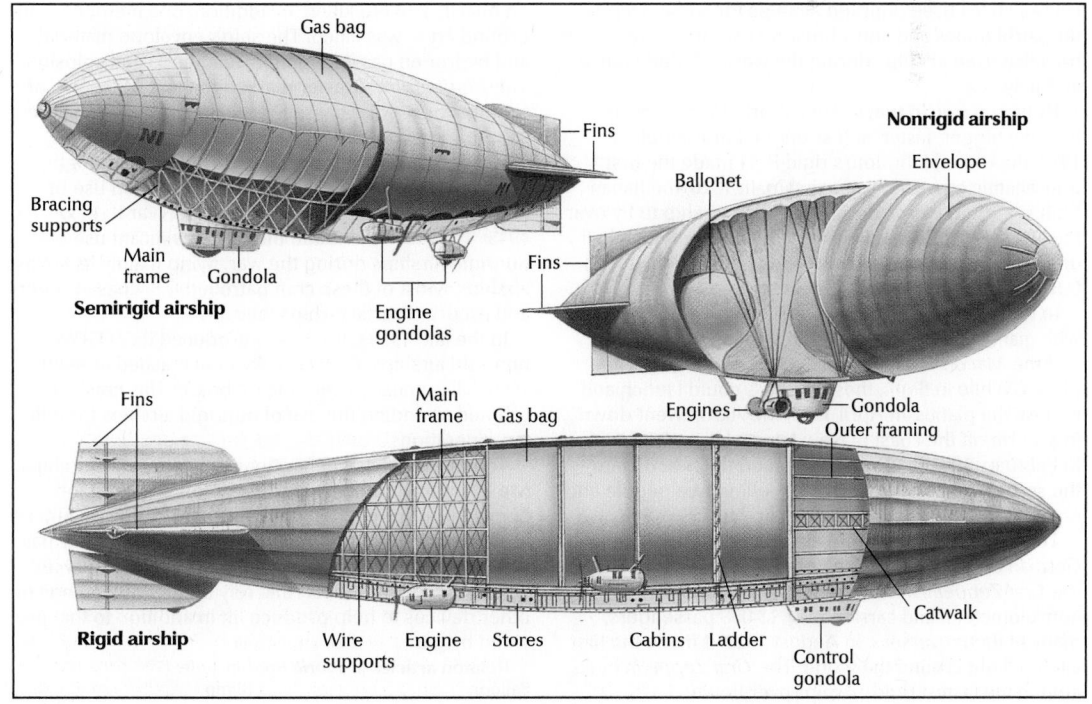

Gas bag

Fins

Nonrigid airship

Envelope

Ballonet

Bracing supports

Main frame   Gondola

Fins

Semirigid airship

Engine gondolas

Engines   Gondola
Outer framing

Fins

Main frame   Gas bag

Rigid airship   Wire supports   Engine   Stores   Cabins   Ladder   Control gondola   Catwalk

Paris. His adventures won him great popularity.

David Schwarz of Austria designed the first truly rigid airship. His craft flew on Nov. 3, 1897. But due to windy conditions, mechanical problems, and an inexperienced pilot, the craft crashed.

The zeppelins. In 1900, Count Ferdinand von Zeppelin flew his first airship, the LZ-1. It was 420 feet (128 meters) long and could reach a top speed of about 17 miles (27 kilometers) per hour. It made only three flights because it was underpowered and lacked proper control. Zeppelin completed the LZ-2 in 1905, and he launched the LZ-3 in 1906. The German Army later made the LZ-3 the first military zeppelin.

In 1909, Zeppelin helped establish the world's first commercial airline, known as DELAG. The *Deutschland,* DELAG's first airship, was over 485 feet (148 meters) long and had three 120-horsepower (90-kilowatt) engines. From 1910 to 1913, over 34,000 passengers flew by zeppelin airships on DELAG flights.

World War I. During World War I, Germany used zeppelins and other airships to patrol the North Sea and scout enemy craft and positions. Germany was also the only country to make major use of rigid airships for strategic bombing. But the frequent raids over England caused little damage. The largest user of rigid airships during the war was the German Naval Airship Division. It received about 70 zeppelin and Schütte-Lanz craft. Due to accidents, bad weather, and enemy fire, 53 of these airships were lost. The capabilities of zeppelins improved dramatically. For example, the L-59 once flew 4,200 miles (6,800 kilometers) nonstop. Its five engines could produce speeds of over 60 miles (95 kilometers) per hour.

The United Kingdom built and operated a large number of nonrigid airships during the war. British airships primarily protected ships from submarine attack. The United States used nonrigid airships for some overwater patrol duties and antisubmarine warfare. Other countries that used airships during the war included France and Italy.

Between world wars. After World War I, airships became bigger, faster, and stronger. For example, in 1919, the United Kingdom's rigid R-34 made the first transatlantic crossing by an airship. In 1926, the Italian-built semirigid *Norge* became the first airship to fly over the North Pole. The replacement of hydrogen with helium to prevent airship disasters began in the 1920's, on U.S. craft.

In the 1920's and 1930's, the U.S. Navy experimented with giant rigid airships. The *Akron,* launched in 1931, and the *Macon,* launched in 1933, carried fighter airplanes. While in flight, these airships could launch and receive the planes. In April 1933, the *Akron* went down in a storm off the coast of New Jersey, killing 73 people. In February 1935, bad weather forced the *Macon* into the sea off the coast of California, killing two people and ending U.S. construction of rigid airships.

The most successful rigid airship ever built was the German LZ-127 *Graf Zeppelin.* Between 1928 and 1937, the *Graf Zeppelin* flew more than 1 million miles (1.6 million kilometers) and carried over 13,000 passengers, many of them overseas. In August 1929, it made the first airship flight around the world. The *Graf Zeppelin* ranks among the fastest rigid airships ever flown.

News Syndicate Co., Inc.

The *Hindenburg* explosion marked the end of regular passenger service on airships. In 1937, this German airship, one of the largest ever built, burst into flames while approaching its dock in Lakehurst, New Jersey. The ship's envelope and hydrogen gas ignited, causing an explosion. Thirty-six people died in the disaster.

The *Hindenburg.* Construction and operation of rigid airships in Germany came to a swift end following the destruction of the *Hindenburg.* One of the largest airships ever built, the *Hindenburg* was about 804 feet (245 meters) long and 135 feet (41 meters) wide. It had a volume of 7,062,100 cubic feet (199,980 cubic meters) and cruised at 78 miles (126 kilometers) per hour. On May 6, 1937, while approaching its docking in Lakehurst, New Jersey, the *Hindenburg* exploded. Of the 97 people on board, 35 were killed. In addition, one member of the ground crew was killed. The ship's envelope material and hydrogen gas had ignited, leading to an explosion. The *Hindenburg* disaster marked the end of the use of airships for regular passenger services. In addition, development of rigid airships ended.

World War II to the present. The evolution of the airplane contributed greatly to the decreased use of the military nonrigid airship during World War II (1939-1945). The U.S. Navy made the only significant use of nonrigid airships during the war, flying mainly its K-class airships. Most of these craft patrolled U.S. coastal waters and escorted surface ships there.

In the late 1950's, the Navy introduced its ZPG-3W nonrigid airships. One ZPG-3W craft crashed at sea in 1960, killing nearly everyone on board. This crash contributed to ending the use of nonrigid airships for military operations.

Today, there has been a significant revival of airships. Most airship companies produce nonrigid craft for commercial and recreational purposes. Some manufacturers also design and build large rigid airships for passenger and heavy cargo operations. Other companies have created hybrid craft that rely on modified wings or other devices to help produce lift in addition to that provided by gas.   Michael J. H. Taylor

Related articles in *World Book* include:
Balloon   Blimp

Helium
Hindenburg
Hydrogen
Santos-Dumont, Alberto
Zeppelin, Ferdinand von

Aisne River, *ayn,* is a river in northeastern France. It rises in the forests of Argonne near Ste. Menehould. It flows north and then west before joining the Oise River near Compiègne. For location, see **France** (terrain map). The Aisne is about 180 miles (290 kilometers) long. Canals join the Aisne to the Seine and Meuse rivers. Three bitter battles of World War I (1914-1918) were fought in the valley of the Aisne.   Hugh D. Clout

Aitken, William M. See Beaverbrook, Lord.

Aix-la-Chapelle. See Aachen.

Aix-la-Chapelle, *EKHS lah shah PEHL* or *AYKS lah shah PEHL,* **Congress of,** met in Aachen (Aix-la-Chapelle), Germany, in 1818. It was the first summit meeting called to preserve the peace established by the Congress of Vienna in 1815.

In 1818, Europe was still struggling with problems that had grown out of the Napoleonic Wars. Even with Napoleon in exile, fear of France and of revolution persisted. The conservative monarchs Alexander I of Russia, Francis I of Austria, and Frederick William III of Prussia attended the congress. The United Kingdom was represented by the Duke of Wellington and Lord Castlereagh, Austria by Prince von Metternich, and France by the Duc de Richelieu. Richelieu convinced the congress that France would keep the peace, and the allies withdrew their occupying troops from France. The congress also discussed ways to end the slave trade, stop sea raids by the Barbary States, and persuade Spain's American colonies to accept Spanish rule.   Brian Vick

See also **Vienna, Congress of.**

Ajax the Greater, in Greek mythology, was one of the bravest Greek heroes who fought in the Trojan War. He is called Ajax the Greater to distinguish him from another Greek warrior, called Ajax the Lesser. After the Greek hero Achilles was killed in the war, his armor was unfairly awarded to Odysseus (Ulysses in Latin). Ajax went mad with despair at losing the prize and killed flocks of sheep and cattle that he believed were his enemies. When he regained his sanity, he committed suicide by falling on his sword. A flower is said to have sprung from his blood. Ajax was the son of King Telamon. *Ajax* is the Latin form of the Greek *Aias.*   F. Carter Philips

Ajax the Lesser, in Greek mythology, was a great Greek hero during the Trojan War. He is called Ajax the Lesser to distinguish him from another Greek hero of the Trojan War, called Ajax the Greater. Ajax had a sinful character. By raping the Trojan princess Cassandra in the temple of the goddess Athena, he brought divine wrath on the entire Greek force. Athena and the sea god Poseidon destroyed the ships of Ajax and other Greeks in a fierce storm in which Ajax died for his defiance of the gods. *Ajax* is the Latin form of the Greek *Aias.* Ajax was the son of King Oileus.   F. Carter Philips

Akbar, *AK bahr* (1542-1605), was the greatest ruler of the Mughal Empire of India. During his 49-year reign, from 1556 until his death on Oct. 27, 1605, he controlled most of north and central India and Afghanistan. He set up the governmental framework of the empire and organized new systems of coinage and taxation.

Akbar had a great interest in all religions and was known for his religious tolerance and his justice. Scholars, priests, and mystics of all religions debated before him. Despite resistance from orthodox Muslims, he won the support of many Hindus, including the Rajputs, who came from a tribal kingdom in northwestern India.

Akbar was born on Nov. 23, 1542, in Umarkot in what is now Pakistan. He was the grandson of Babur, the first Mughal emperor. Akbar became emperor at the age of 13 after the death of his father, Humayun.   Patricia Risso

See also **Babur; India** (The Mughal Empire).

Akhenaten, *ah kuh NAH tehn,* ruled ancient Egypt from about 1353 to 1336 B.C. Queen Nefertiti was his wife. Akhenaten was a religious reformer, devoted solely to the worship of Aten, a sun god. He abandoned the state religion of Amun and changed his name from Amenhotep, his father's name, to Akhenaten. He attacked the old religion, removed the name of Amun from monuments, and closed Amun's temples. Akhenaten built a new capital at Amarna and called it Akhetaten, meaning *horizon of Aten.* After his death, many later pharaohs tried to destroy Akhenaten's monuments. See also **Egypt, Ancient** (The New Kingdom); **Nefertiti.**

Art Resource
Akhenaten

Kent R. Weeks

Akihito, *ah kih HEE toh* (1933-   ), was emperor of Japan from 1989 to 2019. He became emperor upon the death of his father, Hirohito. *Heisei* was chosen as Akihito's reign name, and he is known as the Heisei Emperor.

Akihito was born on Dec. 23, 1933, in Tokyo. After World War II (1939-1945) ended, the life of Japan's imperial family changed. Akihito studied with an American tutor and toured the West. His marriage to a commoner, Michiko Shoda, in 1959

Simon Benainous, Gamma-Liaison
Akihito

was considered symbolic of Japan's new democracy. The couple had two sons and a daughter. Akihito *abdicated* (gave up the throne) on April 30, 2019. His elder son, Naruhito, became emperor on May 1.

Kenneth B. Pyle

See also **Hirohito; Naruhito.**

Akita is a breed of dog that originated in northern Japan. It was used to hunt bears and other large animals. Akitas were once owned by royalty in Japan, and the dogs are still revered in that country. Akitas are known for their loyalty. They are alert, responsive guard dogs.

Akitas are large and powerful, with heavy bones. Males stand from 26 to 28 inches (66 to 71 centimeters) tall at the shoulder. The short coat of the Akita may be

© Thinkstock

The Akita is a powerful dog that developed in Japan.

any color, or it may be a mixture of colors.

Critically reviewed by the Akita Club of America

Akiva ben Joseph, *ah KEE vah behn JOH zuhf* (A.D. 50?-135?), was a rabbi who profoundly influenced the development of Jewish law. His name is also spelled *Akiba.* He emphasized the importance for every Jew of studying the Torah, the first five books of the Bible. Akiva believed that each word and letter of the Bible was significant. He sought lessons from the spelling itself as well as from the wording of the text. He collected and explained legal traditions along with interpretations of the Bible. This work became the basis of the Mishnah, the fundamental code of Jewish law. Akiva was known for his modesty, optimism, concern for the poor, and love of Israel. He is the subject of many stories in Jewish literature.

Akiva was born in Judea in central Palestine. After the Roman rulers of Judea issued decrees forbidding the practice of Judaism, Akiva went to Rome on behalf of the Jewish community. However, the Romans did not relent. In 132, the Jews revolted under the leadership of the warrior Bar Kokhba. The Romans crushed the revolt in 135. They arrested Akiva and executed him for practicing his religion.   Lawrence H. Schiffman

Akkad. See Sargon of Akkad.

Akron (pop. 199,110; met. area pop. 703,200) is a city in northeastern Ohio. It lies on the Cuyahoga and Little Cuyahoga rivers. For the city's location, see **Ohio** (political map).

Akron was once the world's largest producer of tires, and it was known as the *Rubber Capital of the World.* Today, the city is a center for the research and development of rubber products. The Goodyear Tire & Rubber Company—one of the largest rubber companies in the United States—has its main office in Akron.

The city. Downtown Akron includes a federal courthouse and state government offices. A sports stadium is also located in the downtown area. A restaurant and entertainment district has developed around the stadium.

The former Goodyear Airdock, also called the Akron Airdock, is a well-known feature of the Akron skyline. Goodyear once built blimps in the building. It stands

more than 20 stories tall and covers 364,000 square feet (33,800 square meters) of floor space. It is one of the world's largest buildings without interior supports.

Akron's cultural attractions include the Akron Art Museum, which specializes in modern art, and the Akron Civic Theatre, built in 1929. Stan Hywet Hall, a mansion built by Goodyear founder F. A. Seiberling, is now used for cultural events. The Akron Symphony Orchestra performs at the Akron Civic Theatre and at E. J. Thomas Performing Arts Hall. Blossom Music Center, north of the city in Cuyahoga Falls, is the summer home of the Cleveland Orchestra and hosts other musical performances. Akron is host each year to the All-American Soap Box Derby (see **Soap Box Derby**).

The University of Akron is in downtown Akron. Kent State University is northeast of Akron in Kent. The Northeast Ohio Medical University is east of Akron in Rootstown.

Economy. Akron is a center for the research and development of rubber products. Service industries, such as health care and retail trade, are also important in Akron. The city has several hospitals and serves as a medical center for the region. It is also an important trucking center.

Akron-Canton Airport and Akron Fulton International Airport serve the city. Passenger trains and freight trains also serve Akron.

Government. Akron has a mayor-council form of government. The voters elect the mayor to a four-year term. They also elect 13 council members. Ten of the members, representing different sections of the city, serve for two years. Three of the members represent the entire city and serve for four years. Akron is the seat of Summit County.

History. Chippewa, Delaware, Erie, and other Native American groups lived in what is now the Akron area. In 1825, General Simon Perkins, a banker, developer, and land agent, and settler Paul Williams founded Akron on a ridge that rises 950 feet (290 meters) above sea level. The settlement's name was based on the Greek word *akros,* meaning *high point.* Akron became a thriving trade center after completion of the Ohio and Erie Canal in 1832 and the Pennsylvania and Ohio Canal in 1840. The canals opened the way for trade with cities in the eastern United States. Akron was incorporated in 1865.

During the 1800's, Akron was a center for the production of cereal, clay pipe, and farm equipment, but it was rubber that made the city famous. In 1870, Benjamin F. Goodrich, a New York doctor and rubber manufacturer, moved to Akron and established a rubber factory. Several other rubber companies later built factories in Akron, and the city grew rapidly. The development of the automobile industry in the early 1900's created a huge demand for rubber tires. Akron became the world's leading tire producer. The city's population soared, rising from about 70,000 in 1910 to nearly 210,000 in 1920. Military needs during World War II (1939-1945) led to an even greater demand for Akron's tires and other rubber products.

Rubber remained the city's main industry until about the 1970's. During the 1970's and 1980's, Akron, like other older cities of the North, lost many jobs and people to newer factories in the South and Southwest. In the late 1900's, the city worked to diversify its manufacturing base and to redevelop its downtown. Today, many small businesses occupy the buildings once dominated by the rubber industry.   Kathleen M. Fraze

Aksum, *AHK soom,* also spelled Axum, was a powerful ancient kingdom in East Africa. It occupied lands that are now Eritrea, northern Ethiopia, parts of Sudan and Djibouti, and at times parts of southwest Arabia. Aksum was the ancestor of Ethiopia. Aksum's capital, also called Aksum, stood on the site of what is now Aksum in Ethiopia. The kingdom became important about A.D. 50 and reached its greatest strength between the 300's and 600's.

Aksum grew rich and powerful in part because of Adulis, its port on the Red Sea. Adulis was a world trading center near what is now Massawa, Eritrea. Spices, ivory, ebony, animal skins, and tortoise shells were exported from Adulis in exchange for textiles, precious metal objects, wine, and olive oil. These imports came principally from Egypt and the Mediterranean area. Aksum's trade network also included Arabia and India and may have stretched as far as China.

At its peak, Aksum conquered other kingdoms along the Red Sea and the Blue Nile River. Aksumite kings built impressive fortresses, palaces, and granite monuments. During the 300's, King Ezana conquered the kingdom of Kush in what is now Sudan. Ezana also made Christianity the state religion of Aksum.

During the 600's, Muslim conquests in Arabia, Egypt, and along the Red Sea and east African coasts ended Aksum's role as a trading power. Islam, the religion of the Muslims, spread rapidly in Arabia and North Africa. As a result, the Christians of Aksum found themselves surrounded by Muslims and other non-Christians. From the 600's to about the 900's, the Aksumites fought the Muslims. Aksum lost power and territory. However, as-

The kingdom of Aksum about A.D. 400

Aksum, shown in yellow, occupied lands that are now Eritrea, northern Ethiopia, and parts of Sudan and Djibouti. By the middle of the A.D. 300's, Aksum had gained control of the land and sea routes from Africa to Europe and Asia. Present-day boundaries are shown as gray lines.

WORLD BOOK map

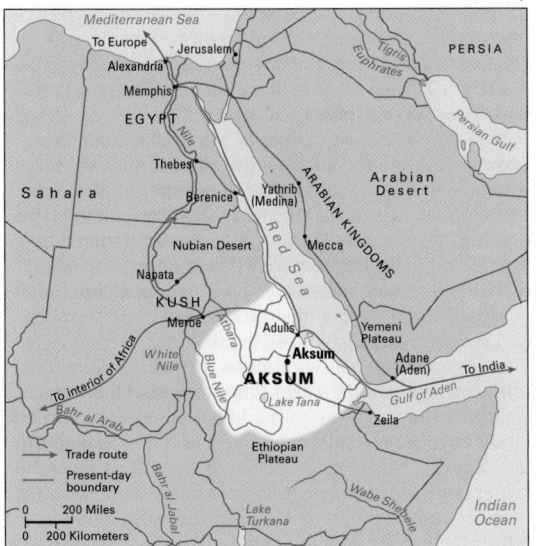

pects of Aksum's culture, particularly its Christian faith, survive today in Eritrea and Ethiopia. In addition, the ruins and monuments of Aksum's capital can still be seen in the present-day town of Aksum.   Kevin C. MacDonald

ALA. See **American Library Association.**

Alabama was the most famous of the 20 Confederate cruisers that attacked Union merchant ships and whalers during the American Civil War (1861-1865). Together with the *Florida, Shenandoah,* and 17 other cruisers, the *Alabama* destroyed 257 Union ships. The Confederate cruisers also forced more than 700 other Union ships to travel under foreign flags to avoid attack. The raiders had little effect on the outcome of the Civil War. But their actions disrupted trade and nearly destroyed the United States Merchant Marine.

The *Alabama* was built in England in 1862. Under the command of Confederate naval hero Raphael Semmes, it sank, burned, or captured 64 ships in the next two years. In June 1864, the USS *Kearsarge,* a Union warship commanded by Captain John A. Winslow, found the *Alabama* in the harbor of Cherbourg, France, where it had gone for repairs. On June 19, the *Alabama* engaged and fired on the *Kearsarge.* Within an hour, the *Kearsarge* sank the *Alabama.*

Combat of the Kearsarge and the Alabama (about 1865), an oil painting on canvas by Edouard Manet; the Philadelphia Museum of Art, the John G. Johnson Collection

The Confederate cruiser *Alabama* was sunk by the Union warship *Kearsarge* in a battle in the English Channel in 1864.

After the Civil War, the United States demanded that the British pay for damages inflicted on Northern shipping by the *Alabama* and other Confederate warships built in British ports. In 1872, under guidelines from the previous year's Treaty of Washington, the Geneva Tribunal of Arbitration decided that the United Kingdom had failed in its obligations of neutrality by aiding the Confederate Navy. The United Kingdom was obliged to pay the United States $15 ½ million for damages.

Gabor S. Boritt

See also **Washington, Treaty of.**

Noccalula Falls is a scenic waterfall in Gadsden, a city in northeastern Alabama. A 9-foot (2.7-meter) statue of Noccalula, a Native American princess of legend, was dedicated at the falls in 1969.

Public Domain

Alabama *The Heart of Dixie*

Alabama, one of the Southern States of the United States, is known as the *Heart of Dixie*. Alabama occupies a central place in the history of the South. The Constitution of the Confederacy was drawn up in Montgomery, the state capital, in 1861. The Alabama Capitol served as the first Confederate Capitol. There, Jefferson Davis took office as president of the Confederacy.

Today, Alabama has a vital part in the nation's future. Huntsville, called *Rocket City, U.S.A.,* is the site of the United States Army's Redstone Arsenal and the National Aeronautics and Space Administration's George C. Marshall Space Flight Center. Scientists at Huntsville developed many important rockets and space vehicles, including the Saturn V rocket system that carried the first astronauts to land on the moon.

Most parts of the South did not become widely industrialized until the 1900's. But heavy industry got a relatively early start in Alabama, mainly because of the

The contributors of this article are Eric J. Fournier, Professor and Chair of the Department of Geography at Samford University, and Martin T. Olliff, Associate Professor of History at Troy University.

state's rich mineral resources. Northern Alabama had all three main raw materials used in making steel—coal, iron ore, and limestone. Blast furnaces for making iron and steel began operating in Birmingham in the 1880's. After that, Birmingham grew rapidly. Today, it is Alabama's largest city and one of the state's important centers of service industries.

For many years, "King Cotton" ruled Alabama's farm economy. When the cotton crop was poor, or when it sold at low prices, Alabama farmers suffered. But serious crop failures during the early 1900's taught the farmers that they should plant a variety of crops. Then they would not lose all their money if the cotton crop failed. Alabama is still an important cotton producer. But much livestock and poultry and large crops of corn, peanuts, and soybeans are also raised in the state.

Forest-covered hills and ridges spread over much of northern Alabama. In places where the land has been cleared, bright red clay soils add splashes of color to the landscape. Many dams along rivers and creeks help prevent floods. Hydroelectric power stations at some of the larger dams produce electricity for homes and factories.

In the southern part of Alabama, the hills give way to thick pine forests, rolling grasslands, and low croplands.

Birmingham's City Hall stands near Linn Park in the city's downtown area. Birmingham is the largest city in Alabama.

© R. Krubner, Robertstock

Interesting facts about Alabama

WORLD BOOK illustrations by Kevin Chadwick

The first electric trolley streetcars in the United States began operating in Montgomery in 1866.

Little River, on Lookout Mountain in northeastern Alabama, is the only river in the United States that runs its entire course on the top of a mountain. It forms the Little River Canyon. Known as the "Grand Canyon of the South," it is the deepest gorge east of the Mississippi River.

First trolley streetcars

A monument to the boll weevil, erected in 1919, stands in the town of Enterprise. After the insect destroyed their cotton crops, Alabama farmers were forced to grow new and more diverse crops. As a result, the farmers became more prosperous. Enterprise then put up the monument "in profound appreciation of the boll weevil and what it has done as the herald of prosperity ... ."

George Washington Carver gained a reputation as one of the world's greatest agricultural scientists from the research he conducted at Alabama's Tuskegee Institute (now Tuskegee University). Among his discoveries were more than 300 new uses for peanuts and more than 100 new uses for sweet potatoes.

George Washington Carver

The black civil rights movement began at the Dexter Avenue Baptist Church in Montgomery in 1955. The church's minister, Martin Luther King, Jr., organized a nonviolent protest group to help carry out a boycott against the Montgomery bus system. This action came after a black passenger, Rosa Parks, was arrested for refusing to yield her seat to a white person.

The Mobile Delta area in the southern part of the state has numerous swamps and *bayous* (shallow channels filled with slow-moving water). At the southern tip of Alabama, sandy beaches border Mobile Bay and the Gulf of Mexico.

Mobile, at the mouth of the Mobile River, is a busy seaport. Oceangoing ships unload a wide variety of goods at the Alabama State Docks in Mobile Bay. The goods include minerals and other raw materials to be made into manufactured goods in Alabama factories. The ships carry away Alabama coal and a wide variety of the state's products, including iron and steel, petroleum products, pulp and other wood products, soybeans, and wheat.

The name *Alabama* comes from the name of an Indian tribe that once lived in the region. These Indians called themselves the *Alibamu,* meaning *I open* (or *I clear) the thicket.* One of Alabama's nicknames, the *Yellowhammer State,* began during the American Civil War (1861-1865). A company of Alabama troops paraded in uniforms trimmed with bits of bright yellow cloth. The soldiers reminded people of the birds called yellowhammers, which have yellow patches under their wings. After that, Alabama soldiers were known as *Yellowhammers.*

© GTD7/Shutterstock

The Port of Mobile, Alabama's only seaport, lies on Mobile Bay north of the Gulf of Mexico. Cargo passing through the port includes chemicals, coal, metal products, and petroleum products.

Alabama in brief

Symbols of Alabama

The state flag, adopted in 1895, bears a crimson cross on a white field. The state seal, first adopted in 1819, has a map of Alabama that shows the state's rivers and bordering states. The rivers served as important shipping routes when Alabama had few good roads. Today, the rivers remain vital to the state as sources of hydroelectric power.

State flag

State seal

Alabama (brown) ranks 29th in size among all the states and 5th in size among the Southern States (yellow).

Montgomery has housed the State Capitol since 1846. Earlier capitals were St. Stephens (1817-1819), Huntsville (1819-1820), Cahaba (1820-1826), and Tuscaloosa (1826-1846).

General information

Statehood: Dec. 14, 1819, the 22nd state.
State abbreviations: Ala. (traditional); AL (postal).
State motto: *Audemus Jura Nostra Defendere* (We Dare Defend Our Rights).
State song: "Alabama." Words by Julia S. Tutwiler; music by Edna Goeckel Gussen.

Land and climate

Area: 51,701 mi² (133,905 km²), including 1,057 mi² (2,738 km²) of inland water but excluding 518 mi² (1,342 km²) of coastal water.
Elevation: *Highest*—Cheaha Mountain, 2,407 ft (734 m) above sea level. *Lowest*—sea level along the Gulf of Mexico.
Coastline: 53 mi (85 km).
Record high temperature: 112 °F (44 °C) at Centreville on Sept. 5, 1925.
Record low temperature: –27 °F (–33 °C) at New Market on Jan. 30, 1966.
Average July temperature: 80 °F (27 °C).
Average January temperature: 46 °F (8 °C).
Average yearly precipitation: 56 in (142 cm).

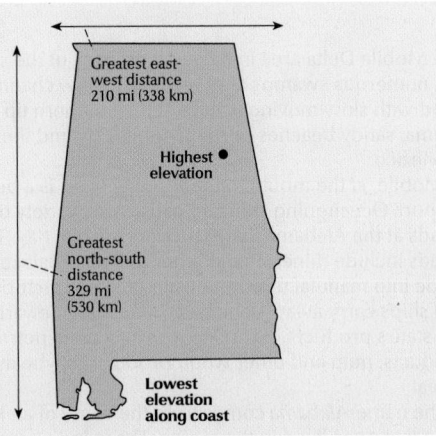

Greatest east-west distance 210 mi (338 km)

Highest elevation

Greatest north-south distance 329 mi (530 km)

Lowest elevation along coast

Important dates

French Canadians founded Fort Louis on the Mobile River. In 1711, the colony moved to Mobile.

The state's first blast furnace began operating in Birmingham.

| 1519 | 1702 | 1819 | 1880 |

Alonso Álvarez de Pineda sailed into Mobile Bay.

Alabama became the 22nd state on December 14.

State bird
Northern flicker (yellowhammer)

State flower
Common camellia

State tree
Longleaf pine

People

Population: 4,779,736
Rank among the states: 23rd
Density: 92 per mi² (36 per km²), U.S. average 85 per mi² (33 per km²)
Distribution: 59 percent urban, 41 percent rural
Largest cities in Alabama

Birmingham	212,237
Montgomery	205,764
Mobile	195,111
Huntsville	180,105
Tuscaloosa	90,468
Hoover	81,619

Source: 2010 census.

Population trend

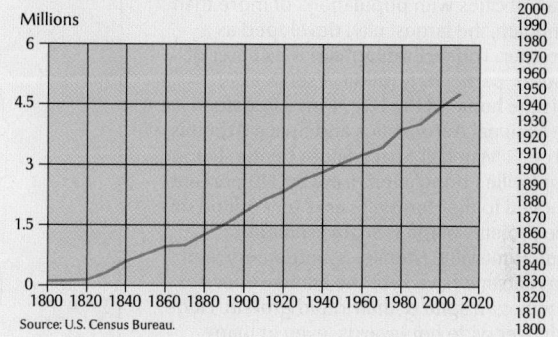

Millions

Source: U.S. Census Bureau.

Year	Population
2010	4,779,736
2000	4,447,100
1990	4,040,587
1980	3,893,888
1970	3,444,165
1960	3,266,740
1950	3,061,743
1940	2,832,961
1930	2,646,248
1920	2,348,174
1910	2,138,093
1900	1,828,697
1890	1,513,401
1880	1,262,505
1870	996,992
1860	964,201
1850	771,623
1840	590,756
1830	309,527
1820	127,901
1810	109,046
1800	101,250

Economy

Chief products

Agriculture: beef cattle, broilers, corn, cotton, eggs, greenhouse and nursery products, peanuts, soybeans.
Manufacturing: chemicals, food products, paper products, primary metal products, transportation equipment.
Mining: coal, lime, limestone, natural gas, petroleum, portland cement.

Gross domestic product

Value of goods and services produced in 2016: $203,355,000,000. *Services* include community, business, and personal services; finance; government; trade; and transportation and communication. *Industry* includes construction, manufacturing, mining, and utilities. *Agriculture* includes agriculture, fishing, and forestry.

Source: Bureau of Economic Analysis.

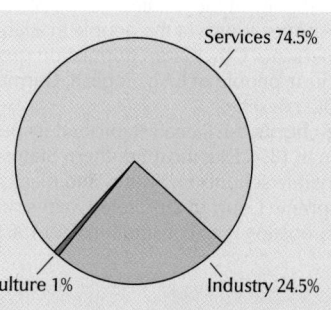

Services 74.5%
Agriculture 1%
Industry 24.5%

Government

State government
Governor: 4-year term
State senators: 35; 4-year terms
State representatives: 105; 4-year terms
Counties: 67

Federal government
United States senators: 2
United States representatives: 7
Electoral votes: 9

Sources of information

Alabama's official website at http://www.alabama.gov provides a gateway to much information on the state's government, history, and economy.

In addition, the website at http://www.alabama.travel provides information about tourism.

—The federal government created the Tennessee Valley Authority.

—Martin Luther King, Jr., led a march from Selma to Montgomery to protest discrimination in voter registration.

1933   **1960**   **1965**   **1985**

The George C. Marshall Space Flight Center was established in Huntsville.

Completion of the Tennessee-Tombigbee Waterway linked Alabama's port at Mobile with the Tennessee and Ohio rivers.

Population. The 2010 United States census reported that Alabama had 4,779,736 people. The state's population had increased 7 ½ percent over the 2000 census figure, 4,447,100. According to the 2010 census, Alabama ranks 23rd in population among the 50 states.

About 75 percent of the people of Alabama live in metropolitan areas. These areas are Anniston-Oxford-Jacksonville, Auburn-Opelika, Birmingham-Hoover, Daphne-Fairhope-Foley, Decatur, Dothan, Florence-Muscle Shoals, Gadsden, Huntsville, Mobile, Montgomery, and Tuscaloosa. The Columbus (Georgia) metropolitan area extends into Alabama. For the populations of these metropolitan areas, see the *Index* to the political map of Alabama. See **Metropolitan area.**

Alabama has 20 cities with populations of more than 25,000. Birmingham, the largest city, developed as a steelmaking center. Today, Birmingham is a center of service industries, particularly medical services.

Huntsville is the home of the U.S. Army's Redstone Arsenal and the National Aeronautics and Space Administration's George C. Marshall Space Flight Center. During the 1950's, Huntsville's population grew by 340 percent. Thousands moved to the Huntsville area to work on missile and space projects of the U.S. government.

Birmingham, Huntsville, Mobile, Montgomery, and other cities in Alabama have kept the attractiveness of small communities, in spite of their rapid growth. Huge oak trees arch over wide boulevards, even in many downtown areas. Stately old homes add to the charm and dignity of these cities.

About a fourth of the people in Alabama are African Americans. Other large population groups in the state include people of Irish, English, German, and American Indian descent.

Schools. Alabama established its public school system in 1854. Like most Southern States, Alabama had separate schools for whites and blacks. In 1954, the Supreme Court of the United States ruled that school segregation is unconstitutional. In 1963, Alabama began

Population density

Most of Alabama's most densely populated areas lie in the east and north. Much of the swampy Mobile River Delta area of southwestern Alabama is thinly populated.

Persons per mi²	Persons per km²
More than 100	More than 40
50 to 100	20 to 40
25 to 50	10 to 20
Less than 25	Less than 10

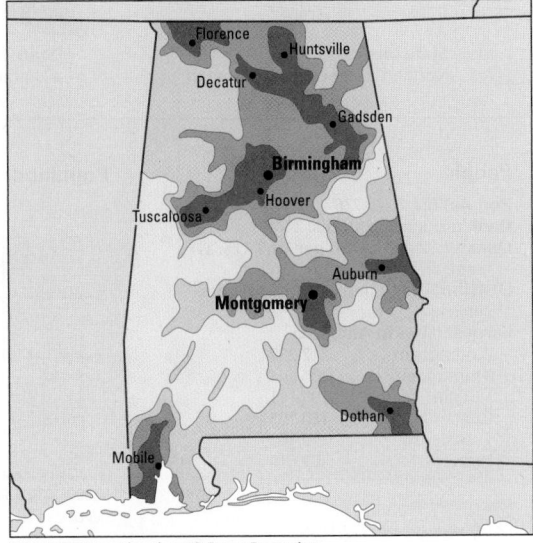

WORLD BOOK map; based on U.S. Census Bureau data.

to desegregate its public schools. By 1973, most of these schools had been integrated.

The superintendent of education heads Alabama's public school system. The superintendent is appointed by the State Board of Education. The nine-member Board of Education establishes policies for the public school system. The governor serves as president of the board. The other eight members are elected by the voters to four-year terms.

© Jeff Greenberg, Alamy Images

Alabama's Gulf Coast is the site of numerous resorts and vacation homes. This long, sandy peninsula extends into the Gulf of Mexico between Mobile and Perdido bays.

© Jeff Greenberg, Alamy Images

Auburn University has campuses at Auburn and Montgomery. Samford Hall, *shown here,* was one of the first buildings built on the Auburn campus. The campus was founded in 1856.

AP/Wide World

College football is a popular spectator sport throughout Alabama. The University of Alabama football team, *in red,* plays its home games in Tuscaloosa.

Universities and colleges

This table lists the nonprofit universities and colleges based in Alabama that grant bachelor's or advanced degrees and are accredited by the Southern Association of Colleges and Schools Commission on Colleges.

Name	Mailing address
Air University	Maxwell AFB
Alabama, University of	*
Alabama Agricultural and Mechanical University	Normal
Alabama State University	Montgomery
Amridge University	Montgomery
Athens State University	Athens
Auburn University	†
Birmingham-Southern College	Birmingham
Faulkner University	Montgomery
Huntingdon College	Montgomery
Jacksonville State University	Jacksonville
Judson College	Marion
Miles College	Fairfield
Mobile, University of	Mobile
Montevallo, University of	Montevallo
North Alabama, University of	Florence
Oakwood University	Huntsville
Samford University	Birmingham
South Alabama, University of	Mobile
Spring Hill College	Mobile
Stillman College	Tuscaloosa
Talladega College	Talladega
Troy University	Troy
Tuskegee University	Tuskegee
U.S. Sports Academy	Daphne
West Alabama, University of	Livingston

*For campuses, see Alabama, University of.
†For campuses, see Auburn University.

Alabama law requires children between the ages of 6 and 17 to attend school.

Libraries. Alabama's first large library, the Supreme Court Library in Montgomery, was created in 1828. In 1901, the state Legislature created the Department of Archives and History—the first state-supported archives in the United States. Today, the largest of Alabama's public libraries are in Birmingham, Huntsville, Mobile, and Montgomery. The Birmingham Public Library owns the Rucker Agee collection of rare maps, the Tutwiler collection on Southern history and literature, and a collection of civil rights documents. The University of Alabama's William Stanley Hoole Special Collections Library and the Auburn University libraries have materials on the history of the region.

Museums. The Anniston Museum of Natural History includes exhibits on the history of Earth and displays of birds in their natural surroundings. The McWane Science Center in Birmingham houses a wide variety of science exhibits and displays. The Tuskegee Institute National Historic Site at Tuskegee University features exhibits that illustrate contributions of African Americans to U.S. history. The University of Alabama's Moundville Archaeological Park exhibits a large collection of Native American items. The History Museum of Mobile has displays on the long history of the Mobile Bay area.

Alabama has notable art museums in Birmingham, Huntsville, Mobile, and Montgomery. Birmingham also is home to the Birmingham Civil Rights Institute and the Southern Museum of Flight. The U.S. Army Aviation Museum at Fort Rucker has one of the largest collections of military helicopters in the world.

Alabama Bureau of Tourism and Travel

The Tuskegee Institute National Historic Site at Tuskegee University has exhibits dealing with George Washington Carver and other famous African Americans.

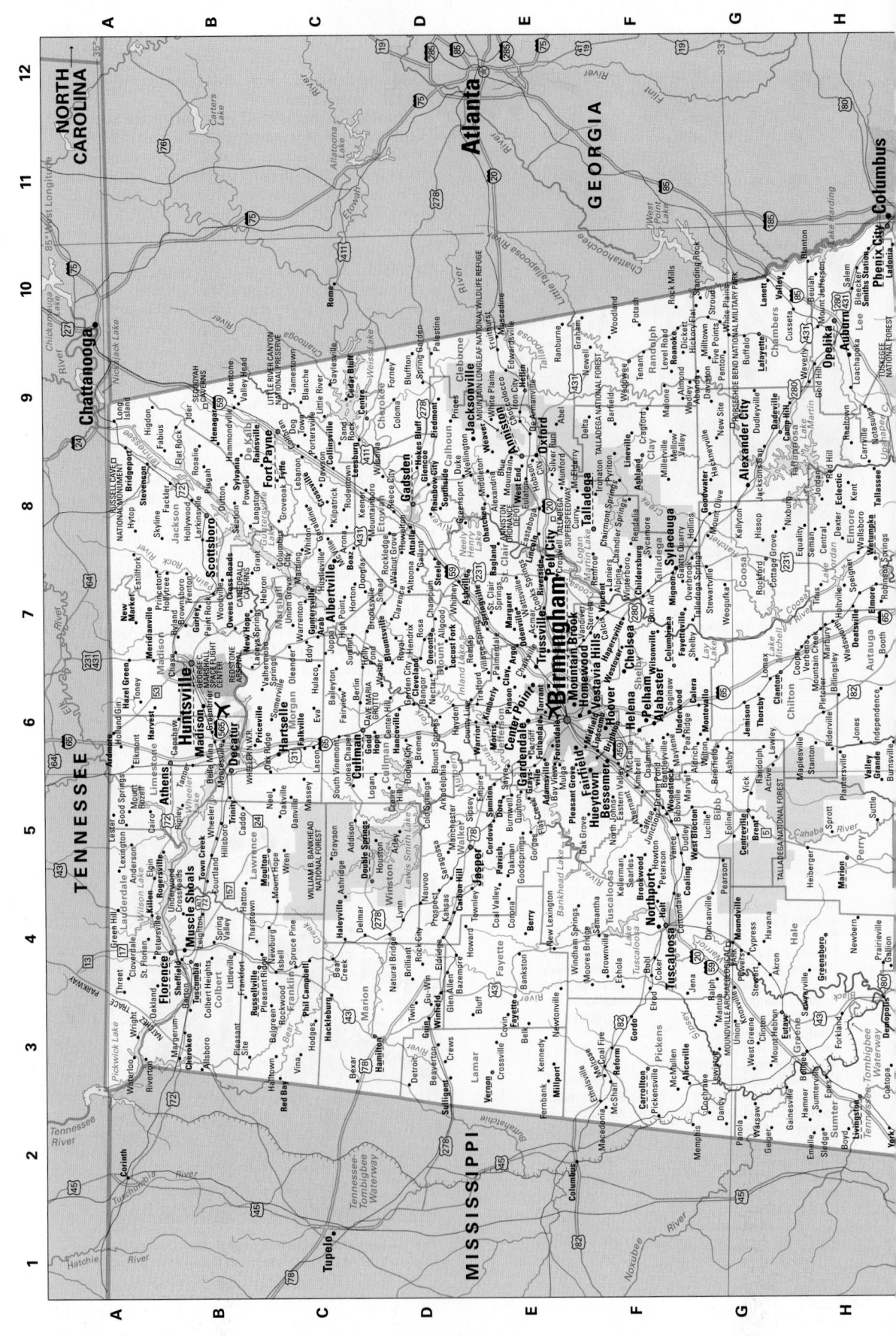

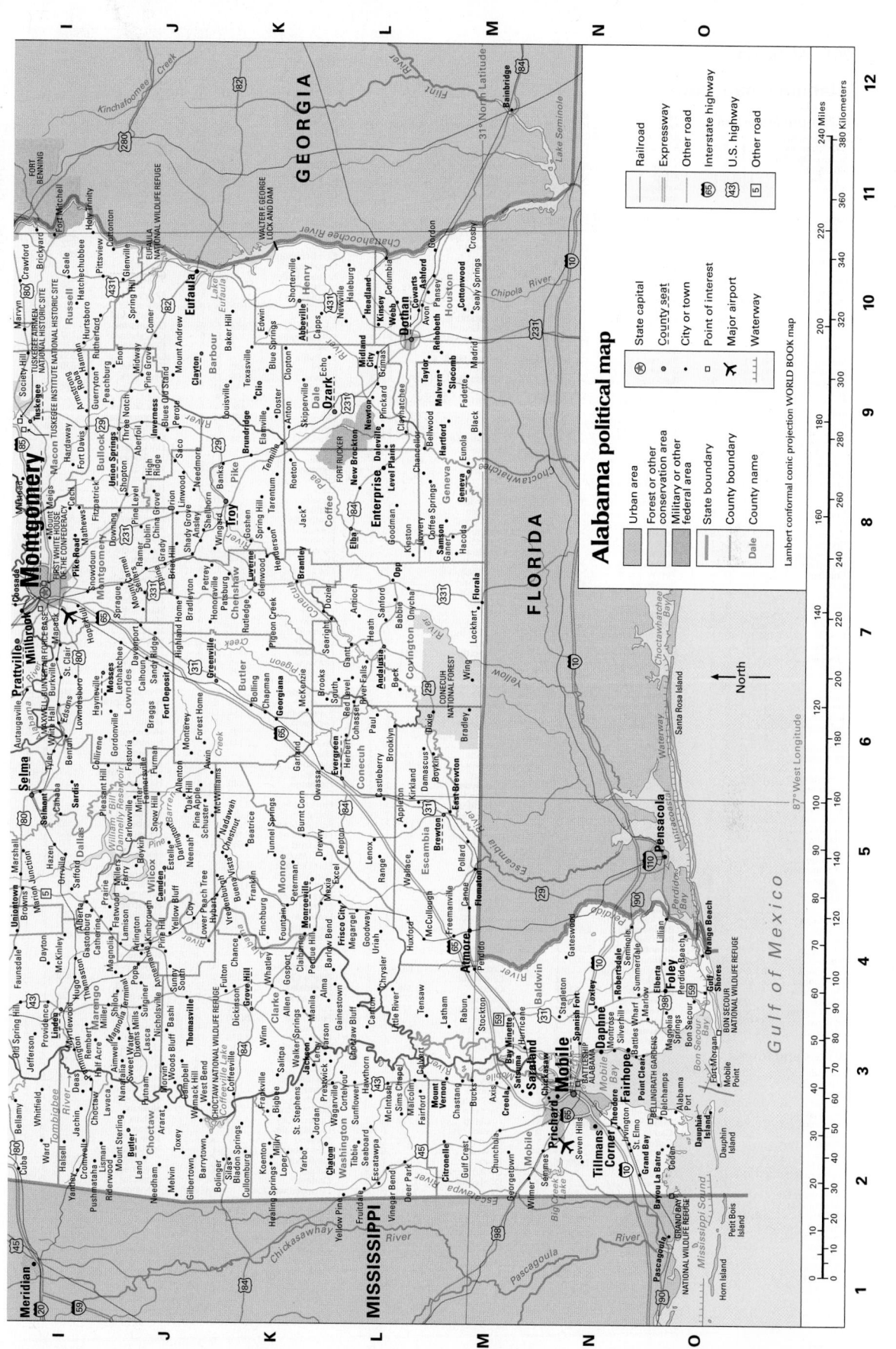

Alabama political map

| Urban area |
| Forest or other conservation area |
| Military or other federal area |

State boundary
County boundary

Dale — County name

⊛	State capital
•	County seat
•	City or town
□	Point of interest
✈	Major airport
⟝⟞	Waterway

	Railroad
	Expressway
	Other road
65	Interstate highway
43	U.S. highway
5	Other road

Lambert conformal conic projection WORLD BOOK map

North

0 20 40 60 80 100 120 140 160 180 200 220 240 Miles
0 20 40 60 80 100 120 140 160 180 200 220 240 260 280 300 320 340 360 380 Kilometers

GEORGIA

FLORIDA

MISSISSIPPI

Gulf of Mexico

Alabama map index

Metropolitan areas

Anniston-Oxford-Jacksonville 118,572
Auburn-Opelika 140,247
Birmingham-Hoover 1,128,047
Columbus (GA) 294,865 (241,918 in GA, 52,947 in AL)
Daphne-Fairhope-Foley 182,265
Decatur 153,829
Dothan 145,639
Florence-Muscle Shoals 147,137
Gadsden 104,430
Huntsville 417,593
Mobile 412,992
Montgomery 374,536
Tuscaloosa 230,162

Counties

Autauga 54,571 H 6
Baldwin 182,265 N 4
Barbour 27,457 J 9
Bibb 22,915 G 5
Blount 57,322 D 6
Bullock 10,914 I 9
Butler 20,947 K 6
Calhoun 118,572 D 8
Chambers 34,215 G 10
Cherokee 25,989 D 9
Chilton 43,643 H 6
Choctaw 13,859 J 2
Clarke 25,833 K 3
Clay 13,932 F 9
Cleburne 14,972 D 9
Coffee 49,948 L 8
Colbert 54,428 B 3
Conecuh 13,228 L 6
Coosa 11,539 G 7
Covington 37,765 L 7
Crenshaw 13,906 K 7
Cullman 80,406 D 6
Dale 50,251 K 9
Dallas 43,820 I 5
De Kalb 71,109 B 9
Elmore 79,303 H 8
Escambia 38,319 L 5
Etowah 104,430 D 8
Fayette 17,241 E 4
Franklin 31,704 B 3
Geneva 26,790 M 8
Greene 9,045 G 3
Hale 15,760 H 4
Henry 17,302 K 10
Houston 101,547 M 10
Jackson 53,227 B 8
Jefferson 658,466 E 6
Lamar 14,564 D 3
Lauderdale 92,709 A 4
Lawrence 34,339 B 5
Lee 140,247 H 10
Limestone 82,782 A 5
Lowndes 11,299 J 6
Macon 21,452 I 9
Madison 334,811 B 7
Marengo 21,027 I 4
Marion 30,776 C 3
Marshall 93,019 C 7
Mobile 412,992 M 2
Monroe 23,068 K 5
Montgomery 229,363 I 7
Morgan 119,490 C 6
Perry 10,591 H 4
Pickens 19,746 F 3
Pike 32,899 K 8
Randolph 22,913 F 9
Russell 52,947 I 10
St. Clair 83,593 E 7
Shelby 195,085 F 7
Sumter 13,763 H 2
Talladega 82,291 F 7
Tallapoosa 41,616 H 8
Tuscaloosa 194,656 F 4
Walker 67,023 E 5
Washington 17,581 L 2
Wilcox 11,670 J 5
Winston 24,484 D 4

Cities and towns

Abanda† 192 G 9
Abbeville° 2,688 K 10
Abel E 9
Acmar E 7
Adamsville 4,522 E 6
Addison 758 C 5
Akron 356 G 4
Alabama Port O 3
Alabaster 30,352 F 6
Alberta I 4
Albertville 21,160 C 8
Aldrich G 6
Alexander City 14,875 G 8
Alexandria† 3,917 E 8
Aliceville 2,486 G 3
Allen K 4
Allenton J 6
Allgood 622 D 7
Alpine F 7
Altoona 933 D 7
Andalusia° 9,015 L 7
Anderson 282 A 5
Anniston° 23,106 E 8
Arab 8,050 C 7
Ardmore 1,194 A 6
Argo 4,071 E 7
Ariton 764 K 9
Arley 357 D 5
Arlington J 4
Armstrong I 9
Ashby G 6
Ashford 2,148 L 10
Ashland° 2,037 F 8
Ashridge C 4
Ashville° 2,212 D 7
Athens° 21,897 B 6
Atmore 10,194 M 4
Attalla 6,048 D 8
Auburn 53,380 H 9
Autaugaville 870 I 6
Avon 543 L 10
Axis† 757 M 3
Babbie 603 L 7
Baileyton 610 C 6
Baker Hill 279 K 10
Bangor D 6
Banks 179 K 8
Bankston E 4
Barfield F 9
Barlow Bend L 4
Barton B 3
Bashi J 3
Battles Wharf N 3
Bay Minette° 8,044 M 4
Bay View E 6
Bayou La Batre 2,558 O 2
Bazemore D 4
Bear Creek 1,070 C 4
Beatrice 301 K 5
Beaverton 201 D 3
Belgreen† 129 C 3
Belk 215 E 3
Bellamy† 543 I 3
Belle Mina B 6
Bellwood L 9
Benton 49 I 6
Berry 1,148 E 4
Bessemer 27,456 F 6
Beulah H 10
Bexar C 3
Bibbville F 5
Billingsley 144 H 6
Birmingham° 212,237 E 6
Black 207 M 9
Bladon Springs K 2
Blanche C 9
Bleecker H 10
Blount Springs D 6
Blountsville 1,684 D 7
Blue Mountain E 8
Blue Ridge*† 1,341 H 8
Blue Springs 96 K 9
Boaz 9,551 C 8
Boligee 328 H 3
Bolinger K 2
Bolling K 6
Bon Air 116 F 7
Bon Secour O 4
Booth H 7
Boyd H 2
Boykin J 5
Boykin M 6
Bradley M 6
Bradleyton J 7
Braggs J 6
Brantley 809 K 7
Brantleyville† 884 F 6
Brent 4,947 G 5
Brewton° 5,408 M 5
Briar Hill J 8
Brickyard I 11
Bridgeport 2,418 A 9
Brierfield G 6
Brighton 2,945 F 6
Brilliant 900 D 4
Brooklyn L 6
Brooks L 6
Brookside* 1,363 E 6
Brookwood 1,828 F 5
Broomtown*† 182 C 9
Browns I 5
Brownsboro B 7
Brundidge 2,076 K 9
Bucks† 32 M 3
Buena Vista K 5
Buhl F 4
Burkville I 7
Burnsville H 6
Burnt Corn K 5
Burnwell E 5
Butler° 1,894 J 2
Caddo B 5
Caffee Junction F 5
Calcis F 7
Calera 11,620 G 6
Calhoun J 7
Calvert† 277 L 3
Camden° 2,020 J 5
Camp Hill 1,014 H 9
Canoe M 4
Capshaw B 6
Carbon Hill 2,021 D 4
Cardiff 55 E 6
Carlowville J 5
Carolina* 297 M 7
Carrollton° 1,019 F 3
Carrville H 8
Castleberry 583 L 6
Catherine† 22 I 4
Cecil I 8
Cedar Bluff 1,820 C 9
Center Hill D 6
Center Point† 16,921 E 6
Centre° 3,489 D 9
Centreville° 2,778 G 5
Chalkville E 6
Chance K 4
Chancellor L 8
Chandler Springs F 8
Chapman K 6
Chase B 7
Chastang M 3
Chatom° 1,288 L 2
Chelsea 10,183 F 6
Cherokee 1,048 B 3
Chickasaw 6,106 N 3
Childersburg 5,175 F 7
China Grove J 8
Choccolocco† 2,804 E 9
Choctaw I 3
Choctaw Bluff L 4
Chrysler L 4
Chunchula† 210 M 2
Citronelle 3,905 M 2
Claiborne K 4
Clanton° 8,619 G 6
Clarence D 7
Clay 9,708 E 6
Clayhatchee 589 L 9
Clayton° 3,008 J 9
Cleveland 1,303 D 7
Clinton G 3
Clio 1,399 K 9
Clopton K 10
Cloverdale A 4
Coal Fire F 3
Coal Valley E 5
Coaling 1,657 G 5
Coalmont F 6
Cobbtown, see West End [-Cobbtown]
Coffee Springs 228 L 8
Coffeeville 352 K 3
Cohasset L 6
Coker 979 F 4
Colbert Heights B 4
Cold Springs D 5
Collbran C 9
Collinsville 1,983 C 8
Collirene I 6
Colony* 268 C 6
Columbia 740 L 10
Columbiana° 4,197 F 7
Columbus City C 7
Comer J 10
Concord*† 1,837 F 6
Cooks Springs E 7
Cooper H 7
Coosada 1,224 I 7
Cordova 2,095 E 5
Corona E 4
Cortelyou L 3
Cottage Grove G 8
Cottondale F 4
Cottonton J 10
Cottonwood 1,289 M 10
County Line 258 D 6
Courtland 609 B 5
Covin E 3
Cowarts 1,871 L 10
Coy J 4
Cragford F 9
Craig I 6
Crane Hill D 5
Crawford I 10
Creola 1,926 M 3
Crews D 3
Cromwell I 2
Cropwell E 7
Crossville 1,862 C 8
Crossville E 3
Cuba 346 I 2
Cullman° 14,775 C 6
Cullomburg† 171 K 2
Curry F 8
Cusseta 123 H 10
Cypress G 4
Dadeville° 3,230 G 9
Daleville 5,295 L 9
Damascus L 6
Danville C 5
Daphne 21,570 N 3
Darlington J 5
Dauphin Island 1,238 O 3
Davenport J 7
Daviston 214 G 9
Dawson C 8
Dayton 52 I 4
De Armanville E 9
Deatsville 1,154 H 7
Decatur° 55,683 B 6
Deer Park† 188 L 2
Delmar C 4
Delta† 197 F 9
Demopolis 7,483 H 3
Detroit 237 D 3
Dickert G 9
Dickinson K 4
Dixie M 6
Dixons Mills J 4
Dodge City 593 D 6
Dora 2,025 E 5
Doster K 9
Dothan° 65,496 L 10
Double Springs° 1,083 D 5
Douglas 744 D 7
Dozier 329 K 7
Dublin J 8
Dudleyville G 9
Duke D 8
Duncanville G 4
Dutton 315 B 8
East Brewton 2,478 M 5
Eastaboga E 8
Eastern Valley F 6
Echo K 9
Echola F 4
Eclectic 1,001 H 8
Eddy C 7
Edgewater*† 883 E 6
Edwardsville 202 E 9
Edwin K 10
Elamville K 9
Elba° 3,940 L 8
Elberta 1,498 O 4
Eldridge 130 D 4
Elgin A 5
Elkmont 434 A 6
Elmore 1,262 H 7
Elrod F 4
Emelle 53 H 2
Empire E 6
Enon I 9
Enterprise 26,562 L 8
Eoline G 5
Epes 192 H 3
Equality H 8
Estillfork A 8
Ethelsville 81 F 3
Eufaula 13,137 J 10
Eulaton E 8
Eunola† 243 M 9
Eutaw° 2,934 G 3
Eva 519 C 6
Evergreen° 3,944 L 6
Excel 723 L 5
Fabius B 9
Fackler B 8
Fadette M 9
Fairfield 11,117 E 6
Fairfold† 186 L 3
Fairhope 15,326 N 3
Fairview 446 C 6
Falkville 1,279 C 6
Farmersville J 6
Faunsdale 98 I 4
Fayette° 4,619 E 3
Fayetteville† 1,284 G 7
Fernbank E 3
Fitzpatrick† 83 I 8
Five Points 141 G 10
Flat Creek E 5
Flat Rock B 9
Flatwood J 4
Flomaton 1,440 M 5
Florala 1,980 M 7
Florence° 39,319 B 4
Foley 14,618 O 4
Forest Home J 6
Forestdale† 10,162 E 6
Forkland 649 H 3
Fort Davis I 9
Fort Deposit 1,344 J 7
Fort Morgan O 3
Fort Payne° 14,012 C 9
Fort Rucker† 4,636 L 9
Fosters G 4
Fostoria J 6
Fountain K 4
Frankfort B 3
Franklin 149 K 5
Frankville K 3
Freemanville M 4
Frisco City 1,309 L 5
Fruitdale† 185 L 2
Fruithurst 284 E 9
Fulton 272 K 4
Fultondale 8,380 E 6
Furman J 6
Fyffe 1,018 C 8
Gadsden° 36,856 D 8
Gainesville 208 G 3
Gallant† 855 D 7
Gallion H 4
Ganer M 8
Gantt 222 L 7
Gantts Quarry G 7
Garden City 492 D 6
Gardendale 13,893 E 6
Garland K 6
Gastonburg I 4
Gaylesville 144 C 9
Geiger 170 G 2
Geneva° 4,452 M 8
Georgetown M 2
Georgiana 1,738 K 6
Geraldine 896 C 8
Gilbertown 215 J 2
Glen Allen 510 D 4
Glencoe 5,160 D 8
Glenville J 10
Glenwood 187 K 8
Goldville* 55 G 9
Good Hope 2,264 C 6
Good Springs A 5
Goodman L 8
Goodsprings E 5
Goodwater 1,475 G 8
Goodway L 4
Gordo 1,750 F 3
Gordon 332 L 10
Gordonville 326 I 6
Gorgas E 5
Goshen 266 K 8
Grady J 8
Graham† 211 F 10
Grand Bay† 3,672 N 2
Grant 896 B 7
Grayson C 5
Grayson Valley*† 5,736 E 6
Graysville 2,165 E 6
Green Hill A 4
Green Pond F 5
Greenbrier B 6
Greensboro° 2,497 H 4
Greenville° 8,135 J 7
Grimes 558 L 9
Grove Hill° 1,570 K 4
Groveoak C 8
Guin 2,376 D 3
Gulf Crest M 2
Gulf Shores 9,741 O 4
Guntersville° 8,197 C 7
Gurley 801 B 7
Gu-Win 176 D 3
Hackleburg 1,516 C 4
Hackneyville† 347 G 8
Hacoda M 8
Haleburg 103 L 10
Haleyville 4,173 C 4
Halltown C 3
Halsell I 2
Hamilton° 6,885 D 3
Hammondville 488 B 9
Hamner H 2
Hanceville 2,982 D 6
Hannon I 9
Hardaway I 8
Harpersville 1,637 F 7
Hartford 2,624 M 9
Hartselle 14,255 C 6
Harvest† 5,281 A 6
Hatchechubbee I 10
Hatton† 261 B 5
Havana G 4
Hayden 444 D 6
Hayneville° 932 I 7
Hazel Green† 3,630 A 7
Hazen I 5
Headland 4,510 L 10
Healing Springs K 2
Heath 254 L 7
Heflin° 3,480 E 9
Heiberger H 5
Helena 16,793 F 6
Henagar 2,344 B 9
Henderson K 8
Hickory Flat G 10
Higdon A 9
High Point C 7
Highland Home J 7
Highland Lake* 412 D 7
Hillsboro 552 B 5
Hissop† 658 G 8
Hobson City 771 E 8
Hodges 288 C 3
Hokes Bluff 4,286 D 8
Holland Gin A 6
Hollins† 545 G 8
Holly Pond 798 D 6
Hollytree B 7
Hollywood 1,000 B 8
Holt† 3,638 F 4
Holtville† 4,096 H 7
Holy Trinity I 11
Homewood 25,167 F 6
Honoraville J 7
Hoover 81,619 E 6
Hope Hull I 7
Horn Hill* 228 L 7
Horton C 7
Houston D 5
Howard D 4
Howton F 5
Hueytown 16,105 F 6
Huguley*† 2,540 G 10
Hulaco C 7
Huntsville° 180,105 B 7
Hurricane M 3
Hurtsboro 553 I 10
Huxford L 4
Hybart K 5
Hytop 354 A 8
Ider 723 B 9
Indian Springs Village* 2,363 F 6
Inverness J 9
Iron City E 9
Ironaton F 8
Irondale* 12,349 F 6
Irvington N 2
Isbell C 4
Jachin I 3
Jack K 8
Jackson 5,228 K 3
Jacksons Gap 828 G 9
Jacksonville 12,548 E 9

*Does not appear on map; key shows general location.
†Census designated place—unincorporated, but recognized as a significant settled community by the U.S. Census Bureau.
°County seat.
Places without population figures are unincorporated areas.
Source: 2010 census. Metropolitan area figures are based on the 2013 Office of Management and Budget reorganization of 2010 census data.

The beaches and hotels along Alabama's Gulf Coast are among the state's major attractions. Many vacationers visit the area each year. Many enjoy saltwater fishing in the Gulf of Mexico and freshwater fishing on inland lakes. Tourists also come to see Alabama's historic homes and beautiful gardens.

Alabama has many historic sites associated with the American Civil War (1861-1865) and the civil rights movement. Many cities have special tours that spotlight this heritage. Tourists can learn about these periods of history at such sites as the Alabama State Capitol in Montgomery, the National Voting Rights Museum and Institute in Selma, and the Birmingham Civil Rights Institute.

One of Alabama's outstanding annual events is the Mardi Gras celebration in Mobile. The festivities begin two weeks before Shrove Tuesday. They include colorful parades through the streets both during the day and in the evening.

Bellingrath Gardens in Mobile

Bellingrath Gardens

Places to visit

Following are brief descriptions of some of Alabama's many interesting places to visit:

Alabama Scenic River Trail, which begins on the Coosa River near the Alabama-Georgia border, extends more than 600 miles (970 kilometers) over several rivers and lakes to Mobile Bay. The route, accessible only by boat, is designated a National Recreational Trail by the National Park Service.

Ave Maria Grotto, in Cullman, features more than 125 miniature replicas of famous buildings and religious shrines constructed on a hillside. Joseph Zoettl, a Benedictine monk, constructed most of the buildings.

Barber Vintage Motorsports Museum, in Birmingham, has one of the largest collections of motorcycles in the United States. The museum exhibits hundreds of motorcycles and cars. A 2.38-mile (3.83-kilometer) track hosts motorcycle and car races.

Bellingrath Gardens and Home, near Mobile, is world famous for its displays of azaleas in the spring and chrysanthemums in the autumn. Flowers bloom in the gardens the year around. Many waterfowl populate the gardens.

Civil Rights Memorial Center, in Montgomery, honors the memory and achievements of those who lost their lives during the civil rights movement.

Dexter Avenue King Memorial Baptist Church, in Montgomery, was the site at which Martin Luther King, Jr., first preached his message of peace and brotherhood.

First White House of the Confederacy, in Montgomery, was the home of President and Mrs. Jefferson Davis during the first months of the Confederacy. The white frame house was built in 1835.

Ivy Green, in Tuscumbia, was the birthplace and home of Helen Keller. It was built in 1820 by Helen Keller's grandfather.

U.S. Space & Rocket Center, at Tranquility Base in Huntsville, houses a large collection of spacecraft, rockets, and hands-on astronaut training exhibits.

National forests, parks, and monuments. Alabama has four national forests: Talladega, William B. Bankhead, Conecuh, and Tuskegee. Talladega, the largest, has two divisions—one in central Alabama and the other in eastern Alabama.

Horseshoe Bend National Military Park, near Dadeville, marks the site where Andrew Jackson defeated the Creek Indians in 1814. Natchez Trace Parkway between Natchez, Mississippi, and Nashville, Tennessee, runs across northwestern Alabama. This parkway, which is administered by the National Park Service, follows a route that was used by pioneers to return north after floating goods down the Mississippi River on flatboats (see **Natchez Trace**).

At Russell Cave National Monument near Bridgeport, archaeologists have found tools and other items used by prehistoric people. These items show that people lived in the cave as early as 10,000 B.C., and that the cave was used as a shelter until about A.D. 1650.

State parks. Alabama has a number of state parks. The Alabama Historical Commission operates Fort Morgan on Mobile Bay. For more information, visit the official website of Alabama State Parks at http://www.alapark.com.

Alabama Bureau of Tourism and Travel

Jefferson Davis Home in Montgomery

Sequoyah Caverns

Rainbow Falls in Sequoyah Caverns at Valley Head

Debra Schulke, Black Star

United States Space and Rocket Center in Huntsville

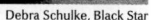

AP/Wide World

Commemoration of the 1965 Selma-to-Montgomery voting rights march

Land regions. Most of southern Alabama lies less than 500 feet (150 meters) above sea level. The surface of the state rises gradually toward the northeast. Alabama has six main land regions: (1) the East Gulf Coastal Plain, (2) the Black Belt, (3) the Piedmont, (4) the Appalachian Ridge and Valley Region, (5) the Cumberland Plateau, and (6) the Interior Low Plateau.

The East Gulf Coastal Plain is Alabama's largest land region. It covers the entire southern two-thirds of the state, except for a narrow strip of land called the Black Belt. In western Alabama, the plain extends north almost to Tennessee.

The plain has several sections. The low, swampy land of the *Mobile River Delta* makes up the southwestern section. The southeastern part is called the *Wiregrass* area. It is named for a tough grass that once grew there in pine forests. Today, the Wiregrass area is an important farming region. The northern part of the plain is often called the *Central Pine Belt* because many pine forests cover its low, rolling hills. In the western part of this section, the soils are gravelly and sandy, and are not good for growing crops.

The Black Belt is a narrow strip of rolling prairie wedged between the northern and southern parts of the East Gulf Coastal Plain. The Black Belt was named for the sticky black clay soils of its rolling uplands. Early in Alabama's history, farmers developed large plantations in this region. Boll weevils came to the Black Belt in 1915, and damaged the cotton crop. Some farmers then changed from growing cotton to raising livestock. Fish-farming operations in the region began to raise catfish in the 1960's. The industry expanded greatly after 1980.

The Piedmont, in east-central Alabama, is an area of low hills and ridges separated by sandy valleys. The clay soils of these hills and ridges have been badly eroded. Most of the land is forested. Cheaha Mountain, the highest point in Alabama, rises 2,407 feet (734 meters) on the northwestern edge of the Piedmont.

Deposits of coal, iron ore, limestone, and marble, together with electric power from projects on the Coosa and Tallapoosa rivers, make the Piedmont an important manufacturing area.

The Appalachian Ridge and Valley Region is an area of sandstone ridges and fertile limestone valleys. It lies northwest of the Piedmont. The region has coal, iron ore, and limestone—the three basic minerals used in making iron and steel. For this reason, Birmingham and other large cities in the region developed as centers of iron and steel production.

The Cumberland Plateau, also known as the *Appalachian Plateau,* lies northwest of the Appalachian Ridge and Valley Region. The surface varies from flat to gently rolling land. It reaches a height of about 1,800 feet (549 meters) above sea level in the northeast. The land slopes to about 500 feet (150 meters) where it meets the East Gulf Coastal Plain in the southwest. Farmers could not grow large crops in the plateau's sandy soils until the 1880's, when commercial fertilizers came into common use. Today, farmers raise hogs and poultry there, and grow cotton, hay, potatoes, and vegetables.

The Interior Low Plateau lies in the northwestern part of the state. Much of the land is in the valley of the Tennessee River. Farmers in the region grow corn, cotton, and hay. Water transportation and hydroelectric power support manufacturing in the region. Decatur and "The Shoals," the area of Muscle Shoals, Florence, Sheffield, and Tuscumbia, are industrial centers.

Coastline. Alabama's general coastline extends for 53 miles (85 kilometers) along the Gulf of Mexico. The tidal shoreline, which includes small bays and inlets, is 607 miles (977 kilometers) long. Mobile Bay, at the mouth of the Mobile River, is the chief feature of the Alabama coastline. It is an important harbor area. Mississippi Sound borders the coast west of Mobile Bay. Perdido Bay is at the border between Alabama and Florida. The long, sandy peninsula between Mobile and Perdido bays is known as the *Gulf Coast.* Dauphin Island, Alabama's largest coastal island, lies at the entrance to Mobile Bay. An overseas highway connects the island with the mainland.

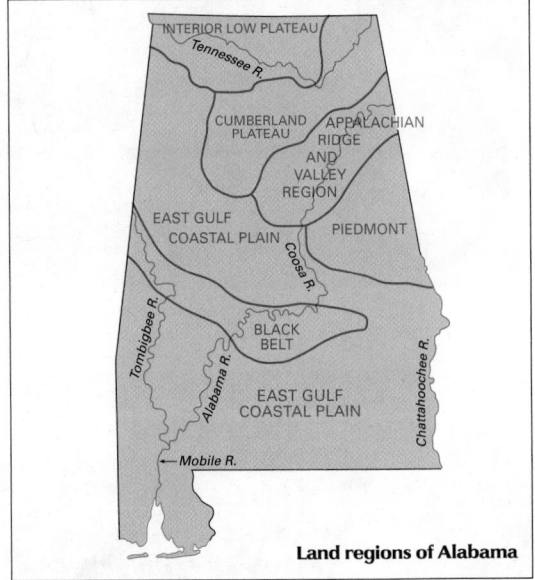

Land regions of Alabama

WORLD BOOK map

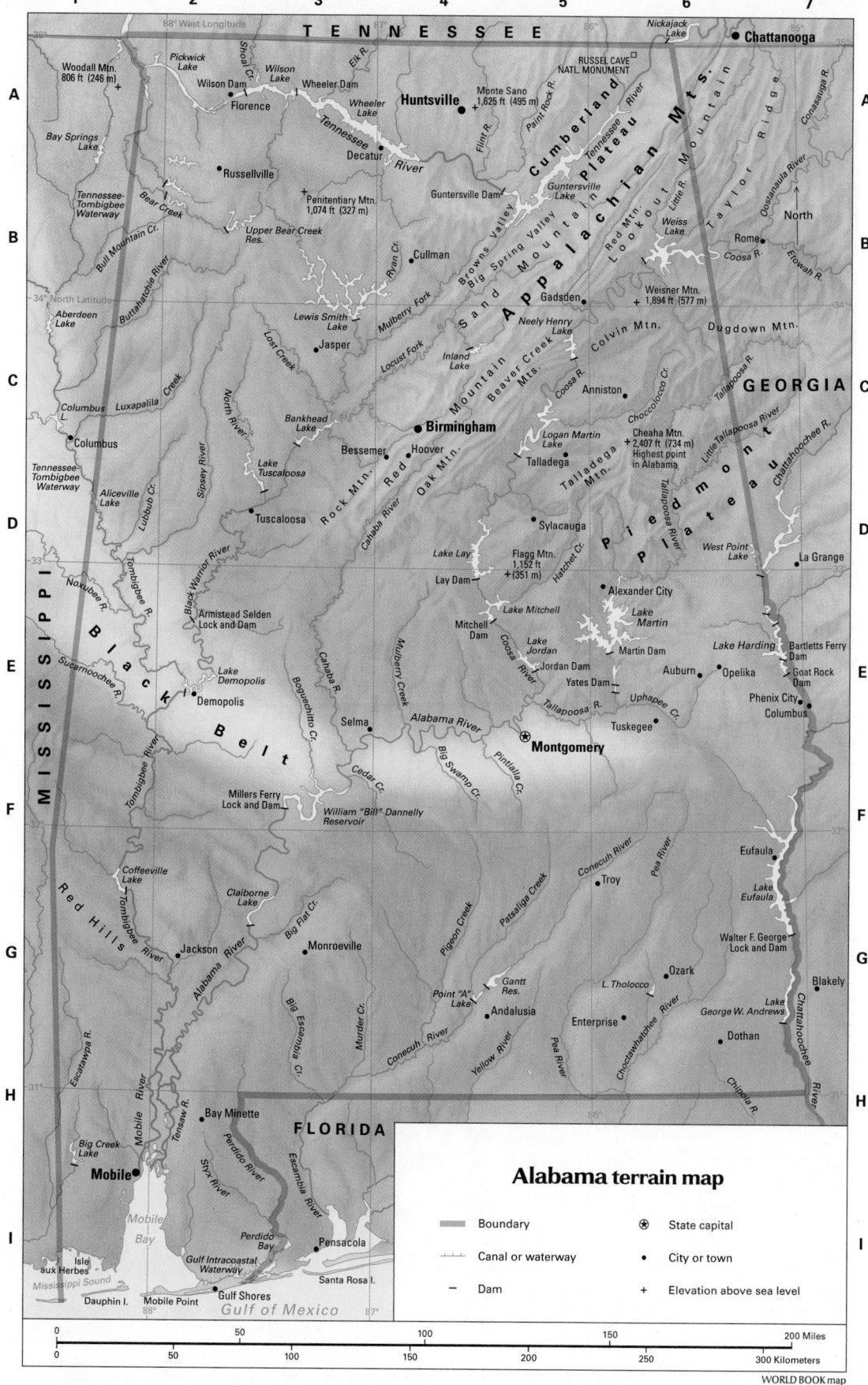

Alabama terrain map

Legend:
- ▬▬ Boundary
- ⊛ State capital
- ┴┴ Canal or waterway
- • City or town
- — Dam
- + Elevation above sea level

WORLD BOOK map

Dauphin Island lies at the entrance to Mobile Bay. It is Alabama's largest coastal island. This picture shows a boardwalk along a salt marsh at the Dauphin Island Sea Lab.

Rivers and lakes. Navigable rivers flow through almost every part of Alabama. The Mobile River and its tributaries flow south to the Gulf of Mexico. They form the most important river system in the state. The Alabama and the Tombigbee, Alabama's longest rivers, meet about 45 miles (72 kilometers) north of Mobile and form the Mobile River. The Alabama River begins where the Coosa and Tallapoosa rivers meet, just north of Montgomery. The Tombigbee starts in Mississippi and flows southeast into Alabama. Its main tributary in Alabama is the Black Warrior.

The Chattahoochee River forms much of the border between Alabama and Georgia. The Tennessee River is the most important river in northern Alabama. It flows west across almost the entire width of the state.

Alabama has no large natural lakes, but dams on rivers have created many artificial lakes. The largest of these, Guntersville Lake, covers 110 square miles (285 square kilometers). It is formed by Guntersville Dam on the Tennessee River. Other large artificially created

Average monthly weather

	Mobile						Birmingham				
	Temperatures °F		Temperatures °C		Days of rain or snow		Temperatures °F		Temperatures °C		Days of rain or snow
	High	Low	High	Low			High	Low	High	Low	
Jan.	60	40	16	4	10	Jan.	54	34	12	1	10
Feb.	63	44	17	7	9	Feb.	58	37	14	3	10
Mar.	70	50	21	10	9	Mar.	67	44	19	7	10
Apr.	76	57	24	14	7	Apr.	74	51	23	11	9
May	83	65	28	18	8	May	82	60	28	16	9
June	88	71	31	21	11	June	88	68	31	20	9
July	90	74	32	23	15	July	91	71	33	22	12
Aug.	91	74	33	23	13	Aug.	91	71	33	22	9
Sept.	87	70	31	21	9	Sept.	85	64	29	18	7
Oct.	79	59	26	14	6	Oct.	75	53	24	12	6
Nov.	70	50	21	10	7	Nov.	65	44	18	7	8
Dec.	62	43	17	6	9	Dec.	56	36	13	2	10

Average January temperatures

In winter, winds from the Gulf of Mexico bring mild air to southern Alabama. Winters are a little colder in the north.

Degrees Fahrenheit	Degrees Celsius
Above 48	Above 9
44 to 48	7 to 9
42 to 44	6 to 7
Below 42	Below 6

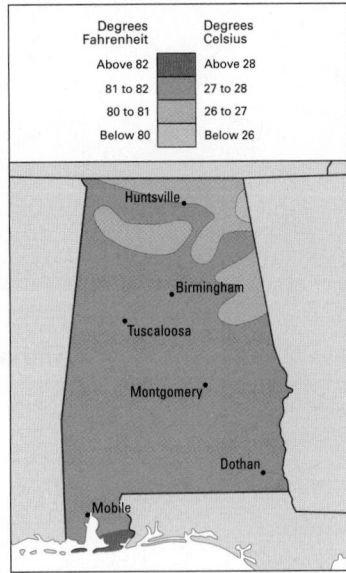

Average July temperatures

Summers in Alabama are long, hot, and humid. Higher elevations make the northeast slightly cooler.

Degrees Fahrenheit	Degrees Celsius
Above 82	Above 28
81 to 82	27 to 28
80 to 81	26 to 27
Below 80	Below 26

Average yearly precipitation

Alabama receives much rainfall, especially near the Gulf coast. Snowfall is light in the north and rare in the south.

WORLD BOOK maps

Inches	Centimeters
More than 60	More than 152
56 to 60	142 to 152
Less than 56	Less than 142

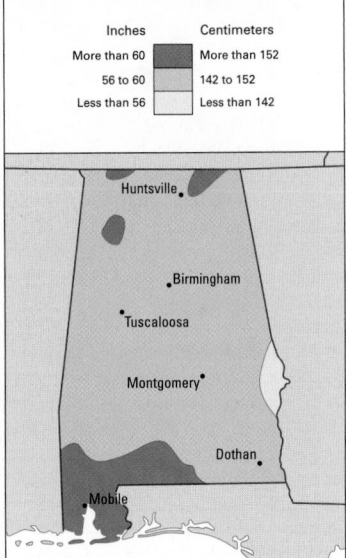

lakes, in order of size, include Wheeler on the Tennessee River, Martin on the Tallapoosa River, and Weiss on the Coosa River.

Plant and animal life. Forests cover about two-thirds of Alabama. Pine forests are the most common type of forest. Besides pines, other trees in the state include cedars, cypresses, hemlocks, and oaks.

In the spring, blooming shrubs and trees cover the Alabama countryside. The state is famous for its azaleas. It also has flowering dogwood, mountain laurel, and rhododendrons. Alabama's wildflowers include asters, Dutchman's-breeches, goldenrods, orchids, pinks, and southern camasses.

Bobcats, deer, minks, opossums, rabbits, raccoons, red and gray foxes, skunks, squirrels, and wild turkeys live in many parts of Alabama. Beaver colonies thrive in the swamps and lowlands. Some alligators can be found in the state's southern swamps and bayous (see **Bayou**). These areas also provide winter shelter for ducks,

geese, and other water birds that fly north in the spring. Freshwater fish in Alabama streams include bass, bream, buffalo fish, catfish, crappies, garfish, and shad. Drumfish, flounder, mackerel, mullet, red snapper, and tarpon are common in the Gulf of Mexico along Alabama's coast. Shellfish found in the Gulf include crabs, oysters, and shrimps.

Climate. Alabama has a mild climate. January temperatures average about 50 °F (10 °C) in the southern part of the state and about 41 °F (5 °C) in the north. July temperatures average about 81 °F (27 °C) throughout the state. Alabama's lowest temperature, –27 °F (–33 °C), occurred at New Market on Jan. 30, 1966. The state's highest temperature, 112 °F (44 °C), happened at Centreville on Sept. 5, 1925.

Alabama's annual precipitation averages from about 66 inches (168 centimeters) on the coast to 54 inches (137 centimeters) in the north. Snow falls in the north but is rare on the coast.

Economy

Through the years, Alabama's economy has been closely linked with major trends in the nation's history. In the early 1800's, plantation owners using slave labor made cotton the state's leading product. In the decades following the Civil War, northern Alabama became a center for the iron and steel industries. In the mid-1900's, the state became a leader in developing the rockets and satellites that brought the country into the space age.

Service industries, from health care to retail trade, form the leading part of Alabama's economy today. Manufacturing, mining, and farming also contribute to Alabama's economic output. Chemicals, motor vehicles, paper, and processed foods rank among the state's leading manufactures. Alabama is an important producer of coal, natural gas, and petroleum. Poultry products are the leading source of farm income in the state.

Natural resources of Alabama include thick pine forests, areas of fertile soil, valuable mineral deposits, and deep rivers.

Soil. Alabama's Black Belt is known for its black clay soils. Parts of the East Gulf Coastal Plain have sandy soils. Red soils cover most other parts of the state. In many areas, gray or yellow topsoil once covered these red soils. Erosion carried away much of the fertile topsoil after farmers cut down trees and plowed the land. Today, many Alabama farmers help save fertile soils by contour plowing, terracing, and other conservation methods.

Minerals. Valuable deposits of coal and limestone lie fairly close together in the Birmingham area. Alabama's most important coal beds lie in the north-central part of the state. Major deposits of limestone are also found in northern Alabama.

Alabama has important oil and natural gas fields in the west-central and southwestern parts of the state. Other mined products found in Alabama include bauxite, cement, clay, dolomite, gemstones, marble, salt, sand and gravel, and sandstone.

Service industries, as a group, contribute the greatest part of Alabama's employment and *gross domestic product*—the total value of all goods and services produced in the state in a year. Most of the service

industries are concentrated in the state's metropolitan areas.

Birmingham is Alabama's leading financial center. One of the South's largest banking companies, Regions Financial Corporation, has its headquarters in Birmingham. The city also ranks as Alabama's leading health care center. Many shipping companies are based in Mobile, which has one of the busiest ports in the United States.

Montgomery, the state capital, is the center of state government activities. Government services also include the operation of military establishments. Major military bases in the state include Fort Rucker, northwest of Dothan, and Maxwell Air Force Base, near Montgomery. The Huntsville area is home to the George C. Marshall Space Flight Center and the Redstone Arsenal.

Many hotels, restaurants, and retail trade establishments operate in the Birmingham, Huntsville, Mobile, and Montgomery areas. These businesses benefit especially from the spending of the millions of tourists who visit the state each year.

Manufacturing. Transportation equipment is one of Alabama's leading manufacturing industries. Cars and trucks are produced in Lincoln, Montgomery, and Vance. Space and military equipment are manufactured in the Huntsville area, and aircraft are manufactured in the Mobile area.

Chemicals, food products, paper products, primary metals, and wood products are also important. Alabama's most important chemical products are used by industry. The chief chemical production centers in the state include Decatur and Mobile. Meat packing is the state's most important food processing activity. Most meat products are made in northern and southwestern Alabama. The state's other food products include animal feed, baked goods, and dairy products. Mills in many parts of the state produce paper and wood products, especially in the northeastern and southeastern portions of the state. Primary metals manufacturing is centered mainly on the steel industry, which is concentrated in Birmingham.

Alabama economy

General economy

Gross domestic product (GDP)* (2017) $211,197,000,000
   Rank among U.S. states   27th
Unemployment rate (2018)   4.0% (U.S. avg: 3.9%)

*Gross domestic product is the total value of goods and services produced in a year.
Sources: U.S. Bureau of Economic Analysis and U.S. Bureau of Labor Statistics.

Agriculture

Cash receipts $5,490,773,000
   Rank among U.S. states   26th
Distribution   80% livestock, 20% crops
Farms   40,600
Farm acres (hectares)   8,600,000 (3,480,000)
   Rank among U.S. states   31st
Farmland   26% of Alabama

Leading products

1. Broilers   (ranks 3rd in U.S.)
2. Cattle and calves
3. Chicken eggs
4. Cotton
5. Peanuts   (ranks 3rd in U.S.)
Other products: corn, dairy products, greenhouse and nursery products, hay, hogs, peaches, pecans, soybeans, tomatoes, watermelon, wheat.

Manufacturing

Value added by manufacture* $46,264,355,000
   Rank among U.S. states   20th

Leading products

1. Transportation equipment
2. Chemicals
3. Primary metals products
4. Food and beverage products
5. Paper products
Other products: fabricated metal products, machinery, plastics and rubber products, wood products.

*Value added by manufacture is the increase in value of raw materials as they become finished products.

Mining

Nonfuel mineral production (2015) $1,370,000,000
   Rank among U.S. states   18th
Coal (tons*)   12,861,000
   Rank among U.S. states   14th
Crude oil (barrels†)   6,827,000
   Rank among U.S. states   17th
Natural gas (cubic feet‡)   150,084,000,000
   Rank among U.S. states   16th

*One ton equals 0.9072 metric ton.
†One barrel equals 42 gallons (159 liters).
‡One cubic foot equals 0.0283 cubic meter.

Leading products

1. Coal
2. Natural gas
3. Limestone
4. Petroleum
5. Lime   (ranks 1st in U.S.)
Other products: cement, clays, granite, salt, sand and gravel.

Figures are for 2017, except for the manufacturing figures, which are for 2016.
Sources: U.S. Census Bureau, U.S. Department of Agriculture, U.S. Energy Information Administration.

continued on page 273

Production and workers by economic activities

Economic activities	Percent of GDP produced	Employed workers	
		Number of people	Percent of total
Community, business, & personal services	20	818,100	31
Finance, insurance, & real estate	18	235,000	9
Government	17	401,400	15
Manufacturing	17	271,200	10
Trade, restaurants, & hotels	16	558,700	21
Transportation & communication	5	106,000	4
Construction	4	141,700	5
Utilities	3	15,000	1
Agriculture, forestry, & fishing	1	62,300	2
Mining	1	11,500	*
Total†	100	2,620,900	100

*Less than one-half of one percent.
†Figures do not add up to 100 percent, due to rounding.
Figures are for 2016; employment figures include full- and part-time workers.
Source: *World Book* estimates based on data from U.S. Bureau of Economic Analysis.

Economy of Alabama

This map shows the economic uses of land in Alabama and where the state's leading farm, mineral, and forest products are produced. Major manufacturing centers are shown in red.

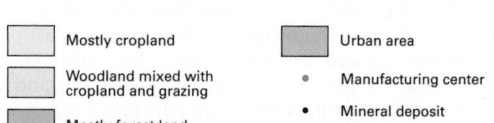

▢	Mostly cropland	▨	Urban area
▢	Woodland mixed with cropland and grazing	◦	Manufacturing center
▨	Mostly forest land	•	Mineral deposit

WORLD BOOK map

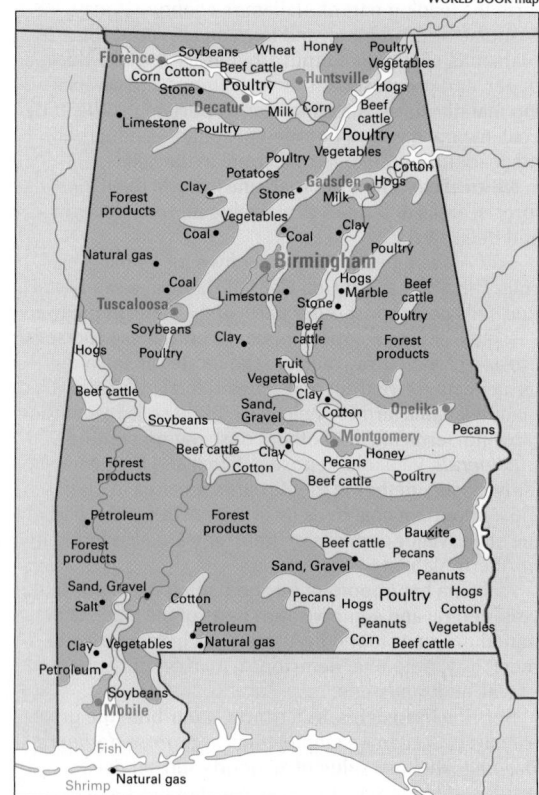

Fishing

Commercial catch	$50,797,000
Rank among U.S. states	15th

Leading catches

1. Shrimp (ranks 3rd in U.S.)
2. Crabs
3. Snapper (ranks 5th in U.S.)
4. Mackerel (ranks 5th in U.S.)

Other catches: finfish, ladyfish, mullet, oysters, sharks.

Electric power

Natural gas	37.9%
Nuclear	30.5%
Coal	22.5%
Hydroelectric	6.6%
Wood and wood waste	2.4%
Other	0.1%

Fishing figures are for 2016 and the electric power figures are for 2017.
Sources: U.S. Energy Information Administration, U.S. National Marine Fisheries Service.

Agriculture. Farms cover about one-fourth of Alabama's total land area. Livestock products account for about four-fifths of Alabama's farm income. Alabama ranks among the leading states in the production of *broilers* (young, tender chickens). Broilers are the most valuable farm product in the state. They provide more than half of the state's farm income. Counties in the northern part of the state produce the most broilers.

Beef cattle are another valuable farm product in Alabama. Cattle graze on grasslands throughout the state. Eggs and milk are also leading livestock products. Many hogs are raised in the northeast part of the state.

Until the early 1900's, cotton production employed many farmworkers and provided almost all of Alabama's agricultural wealth. Today, cotton is still one of Alabama's leading field crops, and the state is an important cotton producer. Mechanical pickers harvest much of the cotton crop.

Greenhouse and nursery products are an important source of farm income. Peanuts, which are grown in the southern portion of the state, are also important. Other field crops include corn, hay, soybeans, and wheat.

Peaches and watermelons are Alabama's leading fruit products. The state's leading vegetable crops include cucumbers, potatoes, sweet potatoes, sweet corn, and tomatoes. Many of the potatoes and sweet potatoes are produced in Baldwin, Cullman, and DeKalb counties. Pecans are another valuable farm product, produced mainly in the southern part of the state.

© Mira/Alamy Images

Alabama's steel industry has been centered in Birmingham since the late 1800's. In this picture, steelworkers inspect a length of tubular steel.

Mining. Alabama's most valuable mined products include coal, limestone, natural gas, petroleum, and portland cement. Jefferson, Tuscaloosa, and Walker counties in north-central Alabama produce most of the state's coal. The coal is a *bituminous* (soft) variety that is taken from both underground and surface mines. Large limestone quarries lie near Birmingham and Huntsville. Natural gas and petroleum are obtained mainly from wells in the west-central and southwestern part of the state. The production of methane gas from coal is a major activity in west-central Alabama. The state ranks as an important producer of portland cement. Other mined products include clays, lime, marble, salt, and sand and gravel.

Fishing industry. The Gulf of Mexico provides most of Alabama's fish catch. Shrimp are the most valuable product of Alabama's saltwater fishing industry. Blue crabs, mackerel, mullet, oysters, and red snapper are also leading products. Alabama's Black Belt region is the center of the state's fish-farming industry. Catfish, raised in artificial ponds on farms, are an important food crop.

Electric power and utilities. Plants that burn coal, natural-gas-burning plants, and nuclear plants are the leading sources of electric power in Alabama. Hydroelectric plants supply most of the remaining power. The Tennessee Valley Authority, a government corporation, operates hydroelectric and nuclear plants in northern Alabama.

Transportation. Alabama has an extensive system of roads and highways. The state also has thousands of miles of rail lines. Major rail lines provide freight service in Alabama. Most of Alabama's air traffic goes in and out of airports at Birmingham, Huntsville, and Mobile.

About 1,270 miles (2,040 kilometers) of navigable waterways cross the state. They include a small section of the Gulf Intracoastal Waterway between Brownsville, Texas, and Carrabelle, Florida. The Black Warrior-Tombigbee-Mobile river system is Alabama's longest navigable waterway. The Tennessee River connects northern Alabama with the Mississippi River system. The Tennessee-Tombigbee Waterway was completed in 1985. This waterway helps link the port at Mobile with inland ports on the Tennessee and Ohio rivers. Alabama has built dock facilities at Decatur, Eufaula, Huntsville, Phenix City, and other towns along waterways.

Mobile, on Mobile Bay, is Alabama's only seaport. The Alabama State Docks at Mobile are among the finest port facilities in the United States.

Communication. *The Mobile Register,* founded in 1813, is Alabama's oldest newspaper. Today, *The Birmingham News* has the largest circulation. Other leading papers include *The Huntsville Times,* the *Press-Register* of Mobile, and the *Montgomery Advertiser.*

Constitution of Alabama was adopted in 1901. The state had five earlier constitutions, adopted in 1819, 1861, 1865, 1868, and 1875. An amendment may be proposed either by the Alabama Legislature or by a constitutional convention. An amendment proposed by the Legislature must be approved by three-fifths of the members in each house. Then it must get the approval of a majority of the electors voting on the issue. Alabama's Constitution has been amended several hundred times, more than any other state constitution.

A majority of the members of each house of the legislature and a majority of the voters must approve calling a constitutional convention. An amendment proposed by the convention must be approved by a majority of the people voting on the issue in an election.

Executive. The governor of Alabama is elected to a four-year term. This official can serve more than one term. However, the governor is not allowed to serve three terms in a row. Alabama's other top executive officials include the lieutenant governor, secretary of state, attorney general, auditor, treasurer, and commissioner of agriculture and industries. Each of these officials is elected to a four-year term.

Legislature consists of a Senate of 35 members and a 105-member House of Representatives. Each of Alabama's 35 senatorial districts elects one senator. Each of the state's 105 representative districts elects one member to the House of Representatives. Senators and representatives serve four-year terms.

The Legislature holds regular sessions each year. Sessions may not last longer than 105 days, and the Legislature may not meet as a whole on more than 30 of these days. Sessions begin in March during the first year of the legislative term, in February during the second and third years, and in January during the fourth year.

Courts. The highest court in Alabama is the state Supreme Court. It has a chief justice and eight associate justices, and they are all elected to six-year terms. The Court of Criminal Appeals has five judges, and the Court of Civil Appeals has five judges. These judges also are all elected to six-year terms. Lower courts in Alabama include a circuit court, district court, probate court, and municipal courts.

Local government. Alabama has 67 counties. Each is governed by a board of commissioners. The boards are

AP/Wide World

The Alabama House of Representatives meets in the State House in Montgomery. The Senate meets in the same building.

The governors of Alabama

	Party	Term		Party	Term
William Wyatt Bibb	*Dem.-Rep.	1819-1820	Joseph Forney Johnston	Democratic	1896-1900
Thomas Bibb	Dem.-Rep.	1820-1821	William James Samford	Democratic	1900-1901
Israel Pickens	Dem.-Rep.	1821-1825	William Dorsey Jelks	Democratic	1901-1907
John Murphy	Dem.-Rep.	1825-1829	Braxton Bragg Comer	Democratic	1907-1911
Gabriel Moore	Democratic	1829-1831	Emmett O'Neal	Democratic	1911-1915
Samuel B. Moore	Democratic	1831	Charles Henderson	Democratic	1915-1919
John Gayle	Democratic	1831-1835	Thomas Erby Kilby	Democratic	1919-1923
Clement Comer Clay	Democratic	1835-1837	William W. Brandon	Democratic	1923-1927
Hugh McVay	Democratic	1837	Bibb Graves	Democratic	1927-1931
Arthur P. Bagby	Democratic	1837-1841	Benjamin Meek Miller	Democratic	1931-1935
Benjamin Fitzpatrick	Democratic	1841-1845	Bibb Graves	Democratic	1935-1939
Joshua Lanier Martin	Democratic	1845-1847	Frank M. Dixon	Democratic	1939-1943
Reuben Chapman	Democratic	1847-1849	Chauncey Sparks	Democratic	1943-1947
Henry Watkins Collier	Democratic	1849-1853	James E. Folsom	Democratic	1947-1951
John Anthony Winston	Democratic	1853-1857	Gordon Persons	Democratic	1951-1955
Andrew Barry Moore	Democratic	1857-1861	James E. Folsom	Democratic	1955-1959
John Gill Shorter	Democratic	1861-1863	John M. Patterson	Democratic	1959-1963
Thomas Hill Watts	Democratic	1863-1865	George C. Wallace	Democratic	1963-1967
Lewis E. Parsons	Democratic	1865	Lurleen Wallace	Democratic	1967-1968
Robert Miller Patton	Republican	1865-1867	Albert P. Brewer	Democratic	1968-1971
Military rule		1867-1868	George C. Wallace	Democratic	1971-1979
William Hugh Smith	Republican	1868-1870	Forrest H. (Fob) James, Jr.	Democratic	1979-1983
Robert Burns Lindsay	Democratic	1870-1872	George C. Wallace	Democratic	1983-1987
David Peter Lewis	Republican	1872-1874	Guy Hunt	Republican	1987-1993
George Smith Houston	Democratic	1874-1878	Jim Folsom	Democratic	1993-1995
Rufus W. Cobb	Democratic	1878-1882	Fob James, Jr.	Republican	1995-1999
Edward Asbury O'Neal	Democratic	1882-1886	Donald Siegelman	Democratic	1999-2003
Thomas Seay	Democratic	1886-1890	Bob Riley	Republican	2003-2011
Thomas Goode Jones	Democratic	1890-1894	Robert Bentley	Republican	2011-2017
William Calvin Oates	Democratic	1894-1896	Kay Ivey	Republican	2017-

*Democratic-Republican

known officially as county commissions. In each county, the probate judge additionally serves as the chief election official. The probate judge is elected to a six-year term. Other county officials include the sheriff, district attorney, superintendent of education, engineer, and tax assessor.

Most Alabama municipalities have a mayor-council form of government. A few cities operate under a city-manager plan. Birmingham, Huntsville, Montgomery, and Tuscaloosa have mayor-council governments.

Revenue. Taxes provide about two-fifths of Alabama's *general revenue* (income). Most of the rest comes from federal grants. The main sources of tax revenue are personal and corporate income taxes, and general sales and use taxes. Other major sources of tax revenue include taxes on alcoholic beverages, motor fuels, property, public utilities, and tobacco. Alabama also taxes business licenses and motor vehicle licenses.

Politics. As in other Southern states, most candidates elected to national, state, and local offices in Alabama have been Democrats. Most of Alabama's major state and local political battles have traditionally been waged in primary elections for the Democratic nomination. But since the mid-1900's, Alabamians have elected a number of Republican candidates to local offices and to the Congress of the United States. In 1986, Guy Hunt became the first Republican to be elected governor of Alabama since the early 1870's.

Until the 1960's, Alabama voters usually supported Democratic presidential candidates. But in 1964, the state voted for Senator Barry M. Goldwater of Arizona, the Republican candidate. It was the first time since 1872 that the state of Alabama supported a Republican presidential candidate. Since 1964, the Republican candidate has won Alabama's electoral votes in almost every presidential election. For Alabama's electoral votes and voting record in presidential elections since 1820, see **Electoral College** (table).

History

Before European exploration. Cliff-dwelling Indians lived in the Alabama region at least 8,000 years ago. Excavations in Russell Cave, in northeastern Jackson County, have revealed details of their lives. Later, the Cherokee, Creek, Choctaw, and Chickasaw Indians lived in the region. Whites called these groups the Civilized Tribes because they adopted many European customs. See **Five Civilized Tribes.**

European exploration and settlement. Alonso Álvarez de Pineda, a Spanish explorer, sailed into Mobile Bay in 1519. In 1528, an expedition led by Pánfilo de Narváez passed through Alabama coastal waters. Álvar Núñez Cabeza de Vaca, the first European to cross North America, was a member of this expedition. Hernando de Soto, another Spaniard, led an expedition into the Alabama region from the northeast in 1540. He became the first European to explore the interior. De Soto (also called Soto) and the Indians fought a battle in southwestern Alabama. De Soto's forces defeated Chief Tuscaloosa and his warriors.

In 1559, Tristán de Luna y Arellano, a Spanish adventurer from Mexico, explored the Alabama region. He organized small, temporary settlements on the Florida Panhandle and in southern Alabama. In 1561, he was removed from his command and returned to Spain.

The first permanent group of white settlers in the Alabama region were French. In 1699, two French-Canadian brothers—Pierre Le Moyne, Sieur d'Iberville, and Jean Baptiste Le Moyne, Sieur de Bienville—sailed to Dauphin Island in Mobile Bay. They founded Fort Louis along the Mobile River in 1702. Fort Louis became the capital of the French colony known as Louisiana. In 1711, river floods forced the French to move 27 miles (43 kilometers) south to the present site of Mobile. This settlement, also called Fort Louis, became Alabama's first permanent white settlement. It was renamed Fort Condé in 1720. The settlement was the capital of French Louisiana until 1722, when New Orleans became the capital.

In 1763, the French gave most of their colony of Louisiana to the British in the Treaty of Paris. This treaty ended the French and Indian War. The Mobile area became part of West Florida, under British control. Northern Alabama was included in the Illinois country, a region in what is now the central United States.

In 1779, Spain declared war on Britain (now called the United Kingdom). In 1780, Bernardo de Gálvez captured Mobile from the British. In the Treaty of Paris, signed in 1783, Britain gave the Mobile region to Spain.

Territorial days. In 1795, Thomas Pinckney, a U.S. diplomat, negotiated the Treaty of San Lorenzo. This treaty, also called the Pinckney Treaty, fixed the southern boundary of the United States along the 31st parallel of north latitude. All of present-day Alabama except the Mobile area lay north of the line and became part of the United States. In 1798, the U.S. Congress organized the southern part of the Alabama region, except the Mobile area, into the Mississippi Territory. In 1804, Congress extended the territory north to the border of Tennessee.

Just before entering the War of 1812 against the British, U.S. forces seized Mobile from the Spanish. But it took until April 15, 1813, to drive the Spanish garrison from the fort there. Also in 1813, a Creek Indian group known as the Red Sticks fought a war against the American settlers and killed hundreds of pioneers and slaves at Fort Mims, near Tensaw. In March 1814, U.S. forces under General Andrew Jackson defeated the Red Sticks in the Battle of Horseshoe Bend on the Tallapoosa River. Chief Red Eagle (also known as William Weatherford), who had not been present at Horseshoe Bend, and other Red Stick warriors surrendered in the following weeks. Later, the Treaty of Fort Jackson required even friendly Creeks to give up their Alabama lands.

In 1817, Congress organized the Alabama Territory. St. Stephens, on the Tombigbee River, became the capital.

Early statehood. A constitutional convention met in Huntsville in 1819 and drew up the territory's first Constitution. On Dec. 14, 1819, Alabama entered the Union as the 22nd state. Huntsville served as the capital of Alabama for a little more than a year. William Wyatt Bibb, who had been governor of the Alabama Territory, became the new state's first governor. Cahaba became the capital in 1820. In 1825, floods from the Alabama River

From a painting by Alonzo Chappel, from "The Pageant of America" series. Yale University Press. United States Publishers Assoc., Inc., sole distributors.

Fort Mims, near Tensaw, was the site of a fierce battle. On Aug. 30, 1813, the Creek Indians led by Chief Red Eagle attacked the fort and killed hundreds of pioneers.

caused great damage to Cahaba. Because of the floods, the capital was moved to Tuscaloosa in 1826.

In 1838, federal troops marched into the remaining Indian territory of Alabama, in the northeast section of the state. They demanded that all the Indians move to the West. By 1840, all but a few scattered tribes had moved west beyond the Mississippi River.

Alabama suffered severe financial troubles during the 1840's and 1850's. The state bank, created during the 1820's, was poorly managed. The bank issued too much money and, as a result, the money decreased in value. The bank also loaned large amounts of money for political reasons. In 1837, a financial panic and depression swept across the United States. The Alabama state bank could not afford to pay back the money it owed to its depositors. For this reason, Governor Benjamin Fitzpatrick began to *liquidate* (close) the bank during the early 1840's. Many Alabamians lost all their savings. The state also suffered from a drought that ruined crops, and from several epidemics of yellow fever.

During the 1840's and 1850's, many Northerners wanted the federal government to outlaw slavery in the nation's Western territories. Others wanted to allow Westerners themselves to vote on the issue. In 1848, a Democratic state convention in Alabama adopted the "Alabama Platform" supported by William L. Yancey, a prominent politician. This platform demanded that the federal government protect slavery in the territories. Yancey later led the Southern delegates in walking out of the Democratic Party's 1860 presidential convention. The walkout split the Democratic Party and ensured the election of Republican Abraham Lincoln as president.

The Civil War and Reconstruction. Slavery was not the only cause of discord between the North and South. Economic rivalries between the agricultural South and the industrial North and disagreements about the rights of states also created conflicts (see **States' rights**). On Jan. 11, 1861, Alabama *seceded* (withdrew) from the Union. The Alabama secession convention then invited other seceding states to send delegates to Montgomery.

On February 8, the convention established the Confederate States of America, with Montgomery as its capital. For this reason, Montgomery became known as the *Cradle of the Confederacy.* In May 1861, the capital of the Confederate States was moved to Richmond, Virginia.

In 1863, during the Civil War, Confederate forces led by General Nathan Bedford Forrest captured a much larger Union force near Cedar Bluff. However, the most significant Civil War action in Alabama was the Battle of Mobile Bay on Aug. 5, 1864. The battle was won by Union forces under Rear Admiral David G. Farragut (see **Farragut, David G.**). Union General Lovell H. Rousseau raided eastern Alabama, also in 1864. In 1865, General James H. Wilson's Union forces wrecked ironworks across the state, burned buildings at the University of Alabama, and destroyed the Selma munitions industry.

Poverty and uncertainty marked life in Alabama after the Civil War. Former slaves were free but poor, and many white farmers were penniless. Formerly well-off planters were broken financially and had lost their leadership positions.

On June 25, 1868, Alabama was readmitted to the Union. From then until 1874, Reconstruction gave power to Northerners called *carpetbaggers,* Southern Unionists called *scalawags,* and former slaves. Fraud, corruption, and waste put the state deeply into debt. However, the government provided much-needed public schools and colleges, and it took steps to give black men full rights as citizens. Conservative Democrats took back the state government in 1874. In 1875, they adopted a new constitution that ensured that power would return to former Confederates. In 1901, Alabama rewrote its constitution yet again, denying blacks and poor whites the right to vote, and establishing racial segregation by law.

State prosperity. Alabama's railroads and iron industry expanded dramatically in the 1870's and 1880's. The Appalachian foothills of northern Alabama held large deposits of iron ore, limestone, and coal—materials used to make iron and steel. The growing town of Birmingham became home to Alabama's first blast furnace, Alice No. 1, in 1880. By 1900, Birmingham had become known as the *Pittsburgh of the South* because of its iron industry. Iron and steel works were also built in Anniston, Bessemer, Decatur, Gadsden, and Talladega. Many cities also benefited from the growth of the textile industry. In addition, the piney woods of southern Alabama provided raw materials for a growing lumber industry.

In the early 1900's, however, crop failures and labor shortages threatened Alabama's prosperity. Boll weevils devastated the state's cotton crop, and many black workers began to leave Alabama for better jobs in the North.

World War I and the Great Depression. Alabama's industry and commerce grew after the United States entered World War I in 1917. Shipbuilding became an important industry in Mobile, and steelmaking increased in Birmingham. Farmers increased production of cotton and food to meet the demands of the war effort. In the mid-1920's, the Alabama State Docks agency built new port facilities at Mobile. Alabama's trade with other countries increased greatly as a result. The state's politics during the era reflected the growth of the Ku Klux Klan, a group that opposed the advancement of blacks and other minority groups. White politicians often joined the Klan to improve their electoral opportunities.

Historic Alabama

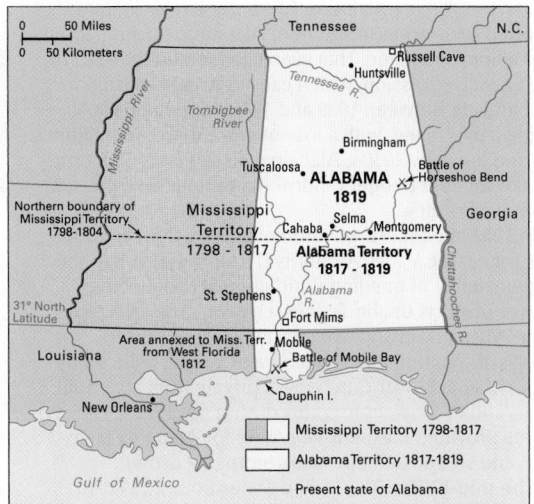

WORLD BOOK map

Russell Cave, in northeastern Jackson County, was the home of cliff-dwelling Indians 8,000 years ago. Excavations at the cave, now part of Russell Cave National Monument, have revealed details of the Indians' lives.

Alabama was part of the Mississippi Territory, formed in 1798 and expanded in 1804. The Alabama Territory was formed in 1817. Alabama became a state in 1819.

The Union won an important battle in the American Civil War at Mobile Bay on Aug. 5, 1864. During the battle, Union Commander David G. Farragut reportedly cried, "Damn the torpedoes! Full speed ahead!" Union sailors captured the forts that had defended the bay.

Important dates in Alabama

WORLD BOOK illustrations by Richard Bonson, The Art Agency

1519 Alonso Álvarez de Pineda sailed into Mobile Bay.
1540 Hernando de Soto explored much of what is now Alabama.
1559 Tristán de Luna y Arellano established several temporary settlements in what is now Alabama.
1702 French Canadians founded Fort Louis on the Mobile River. In 1711, the colony moved to what is now Mobile.
1763 France gave the Alabama region to Britain.
1783 Britain gave the United States much of what is now Alabama. It gave the Mobile region to Spain.
1795 The United States and Spain signed the Treaty of San Lorenzo, setting the southern boundary of the United States at the 31st parallel, across Alabama.
1813 The United States captured Mobile Bay from Spain.
1814 The Creek Indians surrendered nearly half the present state of Alabama to the United States.
1817 The Alabama Territory was created.
1819 Alabama became the 22nd state on Dec. 14.
1861 Alabama seceded from the Union on Jan. 11 and became the Republic of Alabama until Feb. 8, when it joined the Confederacy.
1864 Union forces, led by Commander David G. Farragut, won an important battle at Mobile Bay on Aug. 5.
1868 Alabama was readmitted to the Union on June 25.

1880 The state's first blast furnace began operating in Birmingham.
1901 The present state constitution was adopted.
1933 The federal government created the Tennessee Valley Authority.
1940's The Redstone Arsenal at Huntsville became a center of rocket and spacecraft research.
1956 A federal court ordered Montgomery to desegregate its public bus system.
1960 The George C. Marshall Space Flight Center was established in Huntsville.
1965 Civil rights leader Martin Luther King, Jr., led a march from Selma to Montgomery to demonstrate the demands of blacks for an end to discrimination in voter registration.
1974 George C. Wallace became the first Alabama governor to be elected to a third term. He won a fourth term in 1982.
1985 Completion of the Tennessee-Tombigbee Waterway linked the Alabama port of Mobile with ports on the Tennessee and Ohio rivers.
1986 Guy Hunt became Alabama's first Republican governor since Reconstruction.
2006 Sue Bell Cobb became the first woman to be elected chief justice of the Alabama Supreme Court.

Economic decline followed the prosperity of the 1920's. In 1929, the Alabama-Tombigbee river system flooded large areas in southern Alabama, causing about $6 million in damage. That year also marked the start of the Great Depression, which caused great hardship for Alabamians. Between 1929 and 1931, more than 60 Alabama banks failed, with a loss of more than $16 million. During the early 1930's, Alabama passed a state income tax law and the Budget Control Act to help save the state from bankruptcy.

In 1933, the federal government's New Deal created the Tennessee Valley Authority (TVA). The TVA had the responsibility of building flood-control and electric-power projects on the Tennessee River. The TVA took over Wilson Dam and two nitrate plants at Muscle Shoals. It also built the Wheeler and Guntersville dams. The Alabama Power Company, a private firm, also built dams and hydroelectric plants during the 1930's. These plants provided inexpensive power for Alabama factories, and so boosted the state's industrial growth.

The mid-1900's. The United States entered World War II on Dec. 8, 1941. Because of the war, the federal government expanded existing military bases in Alabama and built several new ones, including Redstone Arsenal in Huntsville. Federal money poured into the state's shipbuilding and steelmaking industries. Thousands of Alabamians served in the nation's military.

World War II helped establish new industries in Alabama—including chemicals, minerals, and rubber products—and expanded the state's textile industries. New opportunities emerged for many black and female workers. However, neither group was able to retain its advances in the years following the war.

Alabama's industrial growth slowed down during the 1950's, and many Alabamians left the state to find jobs in the North and West. Iron ore production in Alabama dropped sharply in the 1950's. By the early 1960's, most of Alabama's iron ore mines had closed. In northern Alabama, however, the space and defense industries provided an economic boost. The National Aeronautics and Space Administration (NASA) established the George C. Marshall Space Flight Center at the Redstone Arsenal in 1960. The center built much of the Saturn V rocket that carried astronauts to the moon in 1969.

Alabama's agriculture also changed in the mid-1900's. Farmers relied less on cotton and more on poultry, cattle, hogs, peanuts, and soybeans. Farmers also relied less on manual labor and more on machinery. Displaced farmworkers moved to the cities for jobs, changing Alabama from a rural to an urban state.

Social changes accompanied the economic changes. During the 1950's and 1960's, African Americans sought equality with whites in education, public accommodations, voting rights, and economic opportunities. In 1955 and 1956, the Montgomery Improvement Association and its spokesman, civil rights leader Martin Luther King, Jr., conducted the Montgomery bus boycott. Numerous blacks refused to ride in public buses until the city abandoned the requirement that they sit in the rear. In 1956, a federal court ordered Montgomery to desegregate its buses.

In 1954, the Supreme Court of the United States had ruled that compulsory segregation in public schools was unconstitutional. On June 11, 1963, Alabama Gover-

AP/Wide World

Martin Luther King, Jr., organized a boycott of the Montgomery bus system in 1955. Many blacks stopped riding buses because the law required them to sit in the rear. In 1956, a federal court ordered Montgomery to desegregate its buses.

nor George C. Wallace stood in the doorway of Foster Auditorium at the University of Alabama to block, symbolically, the admission of two black students, Vivian Malone and James Hood. President John F. Kennedy activated the National Guard to enforce the law, and the students were admitted. That September, Wallace tried to prevent public school desegregation in several cities. Again, President Kennedy called in the National Guard.

In 1963, King and fellow civil rights leader Fred Shuttlesworth led demonstrations to desegregate public facilities and businesses in Birmingham. Police Commissioner Eugene "Bull" Connor ordered that demonstrators be attacked with police dogs and fire hoses. After the events were shown on national television, the demonstrators became the focus of public sympathy. In March 1965, King led a five-day march from Selma to Montgomery to protest discrimination in voter registration. In August of that year, Congress passed the Voting Rights Act, which made thousands of Alabama blacks eligible to vote.

President Lyndon B. Johnson's support of African American civil rights sparked a reaction from Alabama's white voters, who had traditionally supported the president's Democratic Party. These voters came to support the presidential campaigns of George C. Wallace and grew separate from the national Democratic Party. The Republican Party eventually benefited from this division to become the dominant party in Alabama politics.

The late 1900's. Alabama, like other states, faced financial problems in the 1980's and early 1990's. The state government sought ways to provide sufficient funds for such services as state-supported nursing homes and public education. In 1980, the state legislature increased taxes on cigarettes and alcohol to increase funds for government services.

The rising costs of petroleum and natural gas led to increased use of coal. This action spurred further development of Alabama's coal deposits. Industry continued to grow in the state, and the population rose steadily.

African Americans came to play a more important role in local and state politics. At the same time, the Republican Party continued to gain strength. In 1986, Guy Hunt became the first Republican elected governor of Alabama since Reconstruction. But he was removed from office in 1993, after his conviction for felony ethics violations. A state parole board pardoned Hunt in 1998.

The 2000's. In 2004, Hurricane Ivan struck Alabama's popular Gulf Shores resort area, damaging many vacation homes and hotels.

Alabama began the 2000's with financial problems, but the state recovered by 2006. Because of increases in jobs in construction and at automotive plants, the unemployment rate at the end of that year was the lowest in state history. Alabama's income exceeded its budget, and the Legislature reduced taxes. For the first time, voters elected a woman, Sue Bell Cobb, a Democrat, as chief justice of the state Supreme Court.

Former Governor Donald Siegelman was convicted in 2006 on federal corruption charges and sentenced to 88 months in prison. In 2012, a federal judge threw out two charges against Siegelman and reduced his prison sentence. Siegelman was released in 2017.

In 2010, an explosion on an offshore oil rig left 11 people dead and caused about 134 million gallons (507 million liters) of oil to pour into the Gulf of Mexico. Oil from the spill polluted marshes along Alabama's coast. It harmed marine life and affected the state's fisheries and tourism industry.

In April 2011, a series of tornadoes struck Alabama. The tornadoes, which also hit several other Southern States, killed more than 230 Alabamians and caused billions of dollars in property damage. Hard-hit areas included Tuscaloosa and the suburbs of Birmingham.

In 2017, Governor Robert Bentley resigned from office after reaching a deal with prosecutors. He had stood accused of abusing his office's power while covering up an extramarital affair with an aide. Lieutenant Governor Kay Ivey then succeeded Bentley as governor.

Eric J. Fournier and Martin T. Olliff

Related articles in *World Book* include:

Biographies

Barkley, Charles	Lee, Harper	Sparkman, John J.
Black, Hugo L.	Le Moyne, Jean	Walker, Leroy P.
Carver, George	Baptiste, Sieur	Wallace, George C.
Washington	de Bienville	Washington,
De Soto, Hernando	Le Moyne, Pierre,	Booker T.
Forrest, Nathan B.	Sieur d'Iberville	Wheeler, Joseph
Gorgas, William C.	Owens, Jesse	Yancey, William L.
Keller, Helen	Parks, Rosa Louise	

Cities

Birmingham	Huntsville	Mobile	Montgomery

History

Civil War, American	Reconstruction
Confederate States of	Selma marches
America	States' rights
Hurricane Katrina	Tennessee Valley Authority

Physical features

Appalachian	Gulf Stream	Piedmont Region
Mountains	Mobile River	Tennessee River
Gulf of Mexico	Muscle Shoals	Tombigbee River

Other related articles

Alabama, University of	Fort Rucker

Outline

I. People
  A. Population
  B. Schools
  C. Libraries
  D. Museums
II. Visitor's guide
III. Land and climate
  A. Land regions
  B. Coastline
  C. Rivers and lakes
  D. Plant and animal life
  E. Climate
IV. Economy
  A. Natural resources
  B. Service industries
  C. Manufacturing
  D. Agriculture
  E. Mining
  F. Fishing industry
  G. Electric power and utilities
  H. Transportation
  I. Communication
V. Government
  A. Constitution
  B. Executive
  C. Legislature
  D. Courts
  E. Local government
  F. Revenue
  G. Politics
VI. History

Additional resources

Level I

Bass, Hester. *Seeds of Freedom: The Peaceful Integration of Huntsville, Alabama.* Candlewick Pr., 2015.
Hart, Joyce, and Bass, Elissa. *Alabama.* 3rd ed. Cavendish Square, 2016.
Heinrichs, Ann. *Alabama.* Child's World, 2018.
Kirchner, Jason. *Alabama.* Next Page Pr., 2017.

Level II

Flynt, Wayne. *Alabama in the Twentieth Century.* 2004. Reprint. Univ. of Ala. Pr., 2006.
Forner, Karlyn D. *Why the Vote Wasn't Enough for Selma.* Duke Univ. Pr., 2017.
Steponaitis, Vincas P., and Scarry, C. M., eds. *Rethinking Moundville and Its Hinterland.* Univ. Pr. of Fla., 2016.
Wills, Kenneth M., and Davenport, L. J. *Exploring Wild Alabama: A Guide to the State's Publicly Accessible Natural Areas.* Univ. of Ala. Pr., 2016.

Alabama, University of, is a state-supported educational system. Its official name is the University of Alabama System. It consists of three separate universities that report to the same board of trustees. The original and flagship campus is the University of Alabama in Tuscaloosa. The system also includes the University of Alabama at Birmingham (UAB) and the University of Alabama in Huntsville (UAH). The University of Alabama was founded in 1831. UAB and UAH were established as extensions of the University of Alabama in Tuscaloosa and began operating independently in 1969. The system was established in 1975. The university's athletic teams from the Tuscaloosa campus are called the Crimson Tide. The website at http://uasystem.edu offers additional information.   Critically reviewed by the University of Alabama

Alabama River flows through the East Gulf Coastal Plain of Alabama. It is formed where the Coosa and Tallapoosa rivers join north of Montgomery in the central part of the state (see **Alabama** [terrain map]). The Alabama follows a winding course southwest for 315 miles (507 kilometers). At a point about 45 miles (72 kilometers) north of Mobile, it unites with the Tombigbee River to form the Mobile River. The Alabama River is navigable for its entire length. Three dams lie along the river. They create three bodies of water—R. E. "Bob" Woodruff Lake, William Dannelly Reservoir, and Claiborne Lake. Power stations generated by the dams provide electric power. The lakes and reservoir are used for recreation. See also **Mobile River.**   Howard A. Clonts, Jr.

SCALA/Art Resource

An alabaster bust of King Tutankhamen dates back to the 1300's B.C. Many ancient Egyptian sculptors used alabaster.

Alabaster, *AL uh BAS tuhr,* is the name of two types of fine-grained white rocks that look similar but have different chemical compositions. Both types are used for ornamental purposes.

The Metropolitan Museum of Art, New York City, Rogers Fund, 1926

An alabaster headrest was part of the rich furnishings of an ancient Egyptian tomb.

Today, the word *alabaster* commonly refers to a type of rock composed of the mineral gypsum. Gypsum is an extremely soft mineral made of calcium sulfate and water. Its chemical formula is $CaSO_4 \cdot 2H_2O$. Craftworkers make vases, statues, and building stone from gypsum alabaster. It is soft, and workers can carve it without special tools. Deposits of gypsum alabaster occur in many parts of the world.

In ancient times, the word *alabaster* referred to a type of rock from which carvers made vases called *alabasters.* People kept ointments and perfumes in these vases. Carvers shaped alabasters from cave formations called *stalactites* and *stalagmites.* These formations are composed of calcite ($CaCO_3$), which is harder than gypsum. Calcite crystals are *hexagonal.* One kind of calcite alabaster, called *oriental alabaster,* is mined mainly near Florence, Italy. Another kind, *Egyptian alabaster,* was mined in ancient times near Thebes, Egypt.

Mark A. Helper

See also **Calcite; Gypsum.**

Aladdin, *uh LAD uhn,* is the hero of one of the most famous tales of the *Thousand and One Nights,* also known as the *Arabian Nights.* Aladdin's story is told by the Princess Scheherazade to her husband.

According to the tale, Aladdin is a poor Chinese boy who comes into the possession of a magic lamp. By rubbing the lamp, he can make a *genie* (spirit) appear who obeys Aladdin's every command. The boy becomes enormously rich and marries the sultan's daughter. However, a magician plots against their happiness and tricks Aladdin's wife into giving up the lamp. Eventually, Aladdin regains the lamp, his prosperity, and his bride. When the sultan dies, Aladdin succeeds him. The charm of the story lies as much in the humor and good will of Aladdin as in the description of fabulous events.

Dick Davis

See also **Arabian Nights; Genie.**

Alamein, El. See El Alamein.

Alamo, *AL uh moh,* is a historic structure in the center of San Antonio. A famous battle was fought there from Feb. 23 to March 6, 1836, during the war for Texan independence. The Alamo is sometimes called the *Thermopylae of America,* after the famous battle in which the ancient Greeks held off a large Persian force. No Texans escaped from the Alamo after the night of March 5. The Alamo is now a restored historic site.

Early days. The Alamo was built as a Roman Catholic mission. Antonio Olivares, a Spanish missionary, established it at San Antonio in 1718. The mission consisted of a monastery and church enclosed by high walls. The mission was originally called *San Antonio de Valero.* It was later called *Alamo,* the Spanish name for the cottonwood trees surrounding the mission. The Texans occasionally used the mission as a fort.

During the winter of 1835-1836, the people of Texas decided to sever their relations with Mexico because of dissatisfaction with the Mexican government. To prevent the success of this independence movement, General Antonio López de Santa Anna, in command of the Mexican Army, approached San Antonio with his troops. Lieutenant Colonel William Barret Travis and a force of about 150 Texans sought to defend the city. The company included the famous frontiersmen James Bowie and Davy Crockett. The quick arrival of the Mexicans surprised the Texans, who retreated to the Alamo. Over the following days, about 5,000 Mexican troops arrived in San Antonio. Travis sent out a plea for help, declaring, "I shall never surrender or retreat." A relief party from Gonzales, Texas, passed through the Mexican lines and entered the Alamo, increasing the Alamo forces to 189 men. Colonel J. W. Fannin left Goliad, Texas, with most of his 400 men to relieve the Alamo, but he had equipment trouble on the way and returned to Goliad.

The siege of the Alamo lasted 13 days. By March 5, the garrison could not return Mexican fire because ammunition was low. Early the next morning, a Mexican force of about 1,500 soldiers stormed the Alamo and succeeded in scaling the walls. At the end, the Texans fought using their rifles as clubs. Some historians believe that a few defenders, perhaps including Crockett, survived the battle only to be executed at Santa Anna's orders. Other historians accept the more familiar story that all the Texans who fought died in the battle. At 8 a.m., the Mexican general reported his victory to his government. Survivors of the battle included Susanna Dickinson, the wife of an officer; her baby; her Mexican nurse; and Colonel Travis's black slave Joe.

The Battle of the Alamo took place in a mission in San Antonio. On the morning of March 6, 1836, Mexican troops under General Santa Anna successfully stormed the mission and killed all the defenders.

Dawn at the Alamo by H. A. McArdle, Texas State Library, Austin, Texas. WORLD BOOK photo by William Malone

"Remember the Alamo" became a battle cry. The determined defense of the Alamo gave General Sam Houston time to gather the forces he needed to save the independence movement of Texas. He retreated eastward, pursued by Santa Anna. At San Jacinto, Texas, he turned on the Mexicans, surprised them during an afternoon siesta, and on April 21, in just 18 minutes, captured or killed most of the Mexican army of over 1,200 men. Houston's army captured Santa Anna the following day and forced him to sign a treaty granting Texas its independence.   Joseph A. Stout, Jr.

Related articles in *World Book* include:

Bowie, James
Crockett, Davy
Houston, Sam
Mexico (Difficulties of the early republic)
Santa Anna, Antonio López de
Texas (picture: Historic Alamo in San Antonio)
Travis, William B.

Alanbrooke, Lord (1883-1963), was one of Britain's military leaders during World War II (1939-1945). He won special distinction for his leadership during the retreat to—and, later, from—Dunkerque, France, after Belgium fell to Germany in May 1940. Alanbrooke served as chief of the Imperial General Staff from 1941 to 1946. He also fought in World War I (1914-1918). He was born on July 23, 1883, near Lourdes, France, of British parents. His given and family name was Alan Francis Brooke. In 1945, he became a nobleman and changed his name to Alanbrooke. He died on June 17, 1963.   Ian F. W. Beckett

Al-Anon, *AL uh nahn,* is a worldwide fellowship of the families and friends of alcoholics. Members learn how the disease of alcoholism affects family life so that they can solve their own problems and understand problem drinkers. Al-Anon has a teen-age division called Alateen.

Al-Anon cooperates with Alcoholics Anonymous (A.A.), an organization for alcoholics, but is not a branch of A.A. Al-Anon was incorporated in 1954. Its members, like A.A. members, use only their first names to ensure anonymity. Al-Anon groups work to follow A.A.'s 12 suggestions for better living, the Twelve Steps.

Al-Anon collects no dues but accepts members' contributions to cover expenses. It is not connected with any religious or other group. Al-Anon's world service office, the Al-Anon Family Group Headquarters, Inc., is in Virginia Beach, Virginia.   Critically reviewed by Al-Anon

See also **Alcoholics Anonymous; Alcoholism.**

Alarcón, *AH lahr KOHN,* **Pedro Antonio de** (1833-1891), was a Spanish author. He is best known today for his short novel *The Three-Cornered Hat* (1874), one of the most popular works in Spanish literature. In 1919, the Spanish composer Manuel de Falla adapted Alarcón's tale into a famous ballet of the same name.

Alarcón based *The Three-Cornered Hat* on a traditional Spanish ballad. His humorous story describes the confusion that occurs when a miller believes his wife has been having an affair with the mayor of the village. The story provides a lively picture of village life in Alarcón's native region of Andalusia. Alarcón wrote another popular short novel, *Captain Venom* (1881). One of his four novels, *The Scandal* (1875), became noted for its keen psychological insights. Alarcón also wrote travel books and short stories and essays.

Alarcón was born on March 10, 1833, in Guadix, near Granada. In 1859, he served in a Spanish military operation in Morocco. He first gained literary recognition with his account of it, *A Witness's Diary of the African War* (1859-1860). Alarcón died on July 10, 1891.

David Thatcher Gies

Alaric, *AL uhr ihk* (A.D. 370?-410), was a Visigoth king. In the early A.D. 390's, he commanded Gothic troops in the Roman army. In 395, the Roman Empire split into the East and West Roman empires. Alaric desired a high position in the eastern empire but did not receive one. He then became king of the Visigoths. In the late 390's, his forces plundered the Balkan region of the eastern empire. He invaded Italy in 401 and began attacks on the western empire. He attacked Rome in 408 and 409, but ended both sieges in exchange for huge bribes. In 410, Alaric captured and looted Rome, but did little damage to the city. He intended to move his troops to Africa, but a storm destroyed his fleet. He soon died of an illness in southern Italy.   Christopher S. Mackay

See also **Goths.**

Alarm, Burglar. See Burglar alarm.

Mark Newman, Tom Stack & Assoc.

Denali, in Denali National Park in central Alaska, has the highest summit in North America. The mountain's South Peak rises 20,310 feet (6,190 meters) above sea level. Alaska's majestic mountains and vast areas of unspoiled wilderness attract many people who love the outdoors.

Alaska *The Last Frontier*

Alaska is the largest state of the United States in area. It is almost a fifth as large as all the rest of the United States, and more than twice the size of Texas, the second largest state. But Alaska has a relatively small population. According to the 2010 census, Alaska ranks 47th among all the states in population. Only Wyoming, Vermont, and North Dakota have fewer people than Alaska. Alaska is often called the *Last Frontier* because much of the state is not fully settled. Juneau is Alaska's capital. Anchorage is the state's largest city in terms of population.

When Alaska entered the Union in 1959, it was the first new state in 47 years. About 500 miles (800 kilometers) of Canadian territory separate Alaska from the state of Washington. Alaskans often refer to the rest of the continental United States as the "lower 48." The Alaska Highway, which runs between Delta Junction, Alaska, and Dawson Creek, British Columbia, Canada, connects

---

The contributors of this article are F. Patrick Fitzgerald, former Professor of Geography and History at the University of Alaska Southeast at Juneau, and Claus-M. Naske, coauthor of Alaska: A History.

Alaska with the road systems of the other states as well as with Canada.

The Alaskan mainland's most western point is only 51 miles (82 kilometers) from Russia. Alaska's Little Diomede Island, in the Bering Strait, is about 2 ½ miles (4 kilometers) from Russia's Big Diomede Island. No other part of North America is closer to Asia.

Almost a third of Alaska lies north of the Arctic Circle. However, Point Barrow, the state's northernmost point, is almost 1,300 miles (2,090 kilometers) south of the North Pole. The state has a wide range of temperatures—as low as –80 °F (–62 °C), and as high as 100 °F (38 °C). The climate and soil as far north as the Arctic Circle permit farmers to raise livestock and grow barley, potatoes, and other crops. The summer sun shines about 20 hours a day in Alaska, and crops grow rapidly in the state. At Point Barrow, from May 10 to August 2, the sun never sets.

Alaska is famous for its towering mountains and beautiful scenery. Denali, which rises 20,310 feet (6,190 meters) above sea level, is the nation's highest peak. In the language of the Athabaskan Indians, the name *Denali* means *The Great One* or *The High One.* The mountain was once officially known as Mount McKinley. Alaska also has the 15 next highest peaks and almost all of the active volcanoes in the United States.

Interesting facts about Alaska

WORLD BOOK illustrations by Kevin Chadwick

Alaska has more inland water than any other state—20,171 square miles (52,243 square kilometers). Inland water covers an area in Alaska larger than the area of Vermont and New Hampshire combined.

The Aleutian islands of Attu and Kiska were the only parts of North America occupied by Japanese troops during World War II. The islands were captured in 1942 and recovered by the United States in 1943.

Alaska has the longest general coastline of any state. It measures 6,640 miles (10,686 kilometers), a distance greater than that of all the other states' coastlines combined. The coastline of the Alaskan mainland and all the major islands washed by tidewater measures 33,904 miles (54,563 kilometers).

Bald eagles gather in greater numbers along the Chilkat River just north of Haines than at any other place in the world. Each year, more than 3,500 of the birds come to this site to feed on late runs of salmon. The salmon are accessible because an unusual upwelling of warm water keeps the river free of ice.

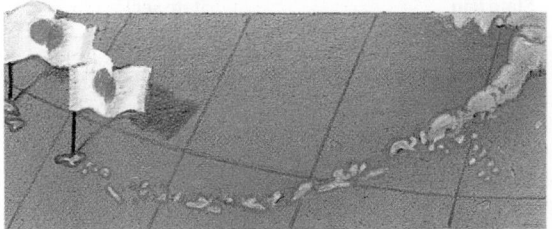

Japanese-occupied islands during World War II

Bald eagles

Keith Gunnar, West Stock

Juneau, the capital of Alaska, is situated between steep mountains and a fine, deep harbor. In addition to government operations, the city's main industries are fishing, mining, and tourism.

Denali rises in central Alaska's Denali National Park, one of a number of national parks in the state. Wrangell-St. Elias National Park in Alaska is the nation's largest national park. It covers more than 8 million acres (3 million hectares). Alaska also has the nation's largest wildlife refuge. The Yukon Delta National Wildlife Refuge covers nearly 20 million acres (8 million hectares).

Inuits, Aleuts, and Indians were living in Alaska when Russian explorers arrived. A Russian trader established the first white settlement, on Kodiak Island, in 1784.

United States Secretary of State William H. Seward bought Alaska from Russia in 1867 for $7,200,000—only about 2 cents per acre (5 cents per hectare). Some Americans thought the region was a wasteland of ice and snow. They called it *Seward's Folly, Seward's Icebox,* and *Icebergia.* However, Alaska proved to be rich in fish, minerals, timber, and potential water power. The value of resources taken from the region has paid back the purchase price thousands of times. Huge oil reserves at Prudhoe Bay along the Arctic coast rank as Alaska's chief source of wealth.

© Jane Gnass, West Stock

Downtown Anchorage includes a log cabin visitor information center, *shown here.* Anchorage is Alaska's largest city and the state's chief center of commerce and transportation.

Alaska in brief

Symbols of Alaska

The state flag, adopted in 1927, was designed by a 13-year-old schoolboy. Seven gold stars, representing Alaska's gold resources, form the Big Dipper. An eighth star in the corner is the North Star, symbolizing Alaska's location in the Far North. The state seal was adopted in 1913. It has symbols, relating to Alaska's economy, for agriculture, fishing, forestry, mining, and transportation. The rays above the mountains represent the northern lights.

State flag

Lt. Governor's Office, State of Alaska

State seal

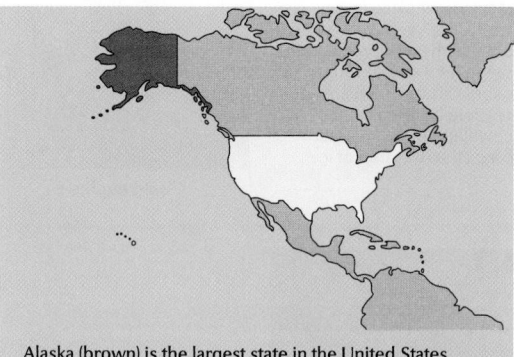

Alaska (brown) is the largest state in the United States.

General information

Statehood: Jan. 3, 1959, the 49th state.
State abbreviation: AK (postal).
State motto: *North to the Future.*
State song: "Alaska's Flag." Words by Marie Drake; music by Elinor Dusenbury.

The State Capitol is in Juneau, the capital of Alaska since 1900. Sitka served as capital from 1884 to 1900.

Land and climate

Area: 590,693 mi² (1,529,888 km²), including 20,028 mi² (51,872 km²) of inland water but excluding 28,162 mi² (72,940 km²) of coastal water.
Elevation: *Highest*—Denali, 20,310 ft (6,190 m) above sea level. *Lowest*—sea level.
Coastline: 6,640 mi (10,686 km).
Record high temperature: 100 °F (38 °C) at Fort Yukon on June 27, 1915.
Record low temperature: –80 °F (–62 °C) at Prospect Creek, near Stevens Village, on Jan. 23, 1971.
Average July temperature: 55 °F (13 °C).
Average January temperature: 5 °F (–13 °C).
Average yearly precipitation: 55 in (140 cm).

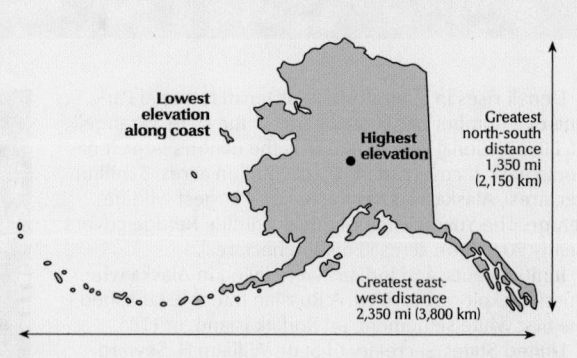

Lowest elevation along coast

Highest elevation

Greatest north-south distance 1,350 mi (2,150 km)

Greatest east-west distance 2,350 mi (3,800 km)

Important dates

Russians established the first white settlement in Alaska on Kodiak Island.

The Klondike and Alaska gold rush started.

| 1741 | 1784 | 1867 | 1897-1898 |

Captain Vitus Bering, a Danish navigator, landed on what is now Kayak Island.

The United States purchased Alaska from Russia.

State bird
Willow ptarmigan

State flower
Alpine forget-me-not

State tree
Sitka spruce

People

Population: 710,231
Rank among the states: 47th
Density: 120 per 100 mi² (46 per 100 km²),
   U.S. average 85 per mi² (33 per km²)
Distribution: 66 percent urban, 34 percent rural
Largest cities in Alaska

Anchorage	291,826
Fairbanks	31,535
Juneau	31,275
Badger*	19,482
Knik-Fairview*	14,923
College*	12,964

*Unincorporated place.
Source: 2010 census.

Population trend

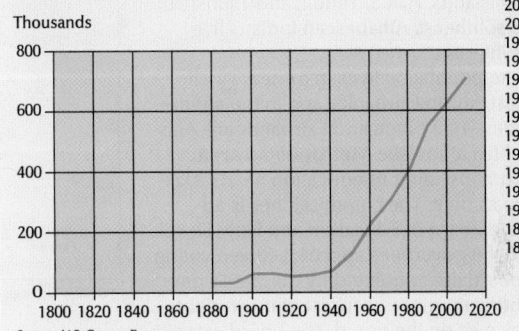

Thousands

Year	Population
2010	710,231
2000	626,932
1990	550,043
1980	401,851
1970	300,382
1960	226,167
1950	128,643
1940	72,524
1930	59,278
1920	55,036
1910	64,356
1900	63,592
1890	32,052
1880	33,426

Source: U.S. Census Bureau.

Economy

Chief products

Fishing industry: cod, crab, halibut, pollock, sablefish, salmon, sole.
Manufacturing: food products, petroleum products.
Mining: gold, lead, natural gas, petroleum, sand and gravel, silver, zinc.

Gross domestic product

Value of goods and services produced in 2016: $49,381,000,000. *Services* include community, business, and personal services; finance; government; trade; and transportation and communication. *Industry* includes construction, manufacturing, mining, and utilities. *Agriculture* includes agriculture, fishing, and forestry.

Source: U.S. Bureau of Economic Analysis.

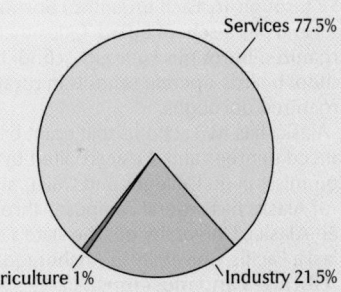

Services 77.5%

Agriculture 1%

Industry 21.5%

Government

State government

Governor: 4-year term
State senators: 20; 4-year terms
State representatives: 40; 2-year terms
Organized boroughs: 19

Federal government

United States senators: 2
United States representatives: 1
Electoral votes: 3

Sources of information

Alaska's official website at http://www.alaska.gov provides a gateway to much information on the state's government, history, and economy.

In addition, the website at https://www.travelalaska.com provides information about tourism.

Congress established Alaska as a U.S. territory.

Large oil reserves were discovered near Prudhoe Bay.

The Trans-Alaska Pipeline was completed.

A tanker in Prince William Sound caused one of the largest oil spills in U.S. history.

| 1912 | 1959 | 1968 | 1971 | 1977 | 1980 | 1989 | 1992 |

Alaska became the 49th state on January 3.

The Alaska Native Claims Settlement Act passed.

Congress passed the Alaska National Interest Lands Conservation Act.

Most oil-spill cleanup was completed at a cost of over $2 billion.

Population. The 2010 United States census reported that Alaska had 710,231 people. The population had increased 13 percent over the 2000 figure of 626,932. According to the 2010 census, Alaska ranks 47th in population among the 50 states. Only Wyoming, Vermont, and North Dakota have fewer people than Alaska.

About two-fifths of Alaska's people were born in Alaska. Many of those who were born in other states are members of the United States armed forces that are assigned to Alaska.

Alaska has about 105,000 *natives.* Of this figure, about two-thirds are Inuit and one-third are Indians. Most Inuit live in the northern and western parts of the state. Many of the Inuit are Aleuts. Aleuts live on the Alaska Peninsula and the Aleutian Islands. Haida, Tlingit, and Tsimshian Indians live in the southeast. Athabascan Indians live mainly in Alaska's interior.

Most of the white population lives in or near Anchorage, Alaska's largest city; in Fairbanks; and in the southeastern coastal cities. Anchorage and Fairbanks are Alaska's only metropolitan areas (see **Metropolitan area**).

Schools. The commissioner of education heads Alaska's education department. The commissioner is appointed by the State Board of Education and Early Development subject to the governor's approval. Seven voting members of the board are appointed by the state's governor. Two nonvoting members, representing students and the military, also sit on the board. The board establishes policies for Alaska's public school system.

Children in Alaska must attend school from the ages of 7 through 16. Each organized borough is a school district and has a school board. Cities that lie outside the organized boroughs have city school boards. Regional school boards operate schools in rural areas outside the organized boroughs.

Alaska has two schools that grant bachelor's or advanced degrees and are accredited by the Northwest Commission on Colleges and Universities. The University of Alaska has several campuses throughout the state (see **Alaska, University of**). The state's other university is Alaska Pacific University in Anchorage.

Libraries and museums. Alaska's State Library, in

Population density

Alaska is the most thinly populated state. Most Alaskans live in Anchorage or along the southeastern coast. Anchorage is the state's largest city in terms of population.

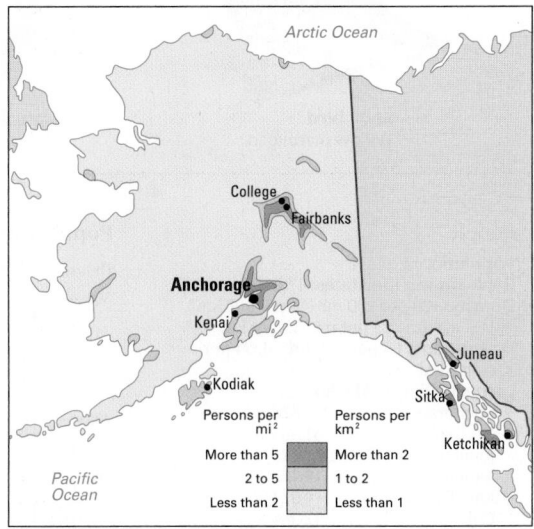

WORLD BOOK map; based on U.S. Census Bureau data.

Juneau, includes a historical section and a state archives and records management section. Academic libraries are at the University of Alaska Fairbanks, the University of Alaska Anchorage, and the University of Alaska Southeast in Juneau.

The Alaska State Museum in Juneau features exhibits of Inuit and Indian objects. It also has displays dealing with animals and minerals in the state. A branch of the state museum, the Sheldon Jackson Museum in Sitka, has Inuit and Indian collections. The University of Alaska Museum of the North in Fairbanks focuses on the state's cultural and natural history. Other cities that have museums include Anchorage, Kenai, Ketchikan, Kodiak, Palmer, Skagway, and Wasilla.

University of Alaska Fairbanks

The University of Alaska has several campuses. The Gruening Building on the Fairbanks campus, *shown here,* was named for Ernest Gruening, known as "the father of Alaskan statehood." He was governor of the Alaska Territory from 1939 to 1953 and a U.S. senator from the state from 1959 to 1969.

Alaska map index

Metropolitan areas

Anchorage 380,821
Fairbanks..............97,581

Boroughs*

Aleutians East....3,141 ..I 6
Anchorage‡§..291,826 ..F 11
Bristol Bay.........997 ..G 9
Denali ....1,826 ..D 11
Fairbanks
North Star....97,581 ..D 12
Haines...........2,508 ..G 15
Juneau§.........31,275 ..G 15
Kenai
Peninsula ....55,400 ..F 11
Ketchikan
Gateway .....13,477 ..H 16
Kodiak
Island ....13,592 ..H 10
Lake and
Peninsula .....1,631 ..H 8
Matanuska-
Susitna.......88,995 ..E 11
North Slope .....9,430 ..B 10
Northwest
Arctic ....7,523 ..C 9
Sitka§............8,881 ..H 15
Skagway‡..........968 ..F 15
Wrangell§.......2,369 ..H 16
Yakutat§ ....662 ..G 13

Cities and towns

Adak*..............326 ..I 3
Akhiok..............71 ..H 10
Akiachak† ....627 ..F 8
Akiak ....346 ..F 8
Akutan...........1,027 ..I 7
Alakanuk ....677 ..E 8
Aleknagik..........219 ..G 9
Allakaket ....105 ..C 10
Ambler ....258 ..C 9
Anaktuvuk
Pass.............324 ..C 11
Anchor
Point†.........1,930 ..G 11
Anchorage§ ...291,826 ..F 11
Anderson..........246 ..D 11
Angoon............459 ..G 15
Aniak ....501 ..F 9
Annette..................H 16
Anvik ....85 ..E 9
Arctic Village†.....152 ..C 12
Atka................61 ..I 4
Atmautluak†.......277 ..F 8
Atqasuk............233 ..A 10
Attu.......................G 1
Barrow, see Utqiagvik
Bear Creek*† ....1,956 ..G 11
Beaver† ....84 ..C 12
Bethel ....6,080 ..F 8
Big Delta† ....591 ..F 12
Big Horn*................D 11
Big Lake..................C 11
Big Lake†.........3,350 ..F 11
Birch Creek† ....33 ..D 12
Bodenburg
Butte*...................F 11
Brevig Mission, see
Teller Mission
[-Brevig Mission]
Buckland..........416 ..C 9
Buffalo
Soapstone*† ....855 ..F 11
Butte† ....3,246 ..F 11
Candle.....................D 9
Cantwell ....219 ..E 11
Cape Lisburne...........B 8
Cape Pole................H 15
Cape Yakataga...........F 13
Central† ....96 ..D 12
Chalkyitsik†.........69 ..C 12
Chefornak ....418 ..F 8
Chevak ....938 ..E 7
Chickaloon† ....272 ..F 11
Chicken† ....7 ..E 13
Chignik.............91 ..H 9
Chignik
Lagoon† ....78 ..H 9
Chignik Lake† .....73 ..H 9
Chistochina†........93 ..E 12
Chitina†............126 ..F 12
Chuathbaluk*.......118 ..F 9
Circle†.............104 ..D 12
Circle
Hot Springs...........D 12
Clam Gulch*†......176 ..F 11
Clarks Point† ....62 ..G 9
Clover Pass*.............H 16
Coffman Cove*.......176 ..H 16
Cohoe† ....1,364 ..F 11
Cold Bay............108 ..I 7
College†........12,964 ..D 11
Cooper
Landing†........289 ..F 11
Copper
Center† ....328 ..F 12
Cordova ....2,239 ..F 12
Craig............1,201 ..H 16
Crooked
Creek† ....105 ..F 9
Curry ....E 11
Deadhorse ....B 11
Deering ....122 ..C 8
Delta Junction .....958 ..E 12
Deltana*† ....2,251 ..E 12
Diamond
Ridge*† ....1,156 ..G 11
Dillingham ......2,329 ..G 9
Diomede* ....115 ..C 7
Donnelly ....E 12
Dot Lake† ....13 ..E 12
Dunbar*...................D 11
Dutch Harbor ....I 6
Eagle ....86 ..D 13
Eagle Village† ......67 ..D 13
Edna Bay† ....42 ..H 15
Eek ....296 ..F 8
Egegik†............109 ..G 9
Eielson AFB† ....2,647 ..D 12
Ekuk........................G 9
Ekwok.............115 ..G 9
Elfin Cove*†.........20 ..G 14
Elim................330 ..D 8
Emmonak..........762 ..E 8
English Bay..............G 10
Eska ....F 11
Ester†............2,422 ..D 11
Evansville*†.........15 ..D 11
Fairbanks.......31,535 ..D 11
False Pass...........35 ..I 7
Farm Loop*†.....1,028 ..F 11
Fishhook*† ......4,679 ..G 11
Flat ....E 9
Fort Greely†.......539 ..E 12
Fort Wainwright.........D 12
Fort Yukon ....583 ..C 12
Fox*† ....417 ..D 11
Fritz Creek*†.....1,932 ..G 11
Gakona†...........218 ..E 12
Galena.............470 ..D 10
Gambell ....681 ..D 6
Gateway*† ....5,552 ..F 11
Glennallen†........483 ..F 12
Golovin............156 ..D 8
Goodnews Bay ....243 ..G 8
Grayling ....194 ..E 9
Gulkana† ....119 ..E 12
Gustavus† ....442 ..G 15
Haines...........1,713 ..G 15
Halibut Cove† ......76 ..G 11
Healy†...........1,021 ..E 11
Healy Lake*†........13 ..E 12
Herring Cove............H 16
Hollis†.............112 ..H 16
Holy Cross.........178 ..E 9
Homer...........5,003 ..G 11
Hoonah............760 ..G 15
Hooper Bay .....1,093 ..E 7
Hope† ....192 ..F 11
Houston* ....1,912 ..F 11
Hughes..............77 ..D 10
Huslia..............275 ..D 10
Hydaburg..........376 ..H 16
Hyder† ....87 ..H 16
Igiugig*†............50 ..G 10
Iliamna† ....109 ..G 10
Ivanof Bay†..........7 ..H 8
Juneau§.........31,275 ..G 15
Kachemak* ....472 ..G 11
Kake...............557 ..H 15
Kaktovik...........239 ..B 12
Kalifonsky*† .....7,850 ..F 11
Kaltag..............190 ..D 9
Karluk† ....37 ..H 10
Kasaan...............49 ..H 16
Kasilof†............549 ..F 11
Kenai ....7,100 ..F 11
Ketchikan........8,050 ..H 16
Kiana ....361 ..C 9
King Cove ....938 ..I 8
King Salmon† .....374 ..G 9
Kipnuk† ....639 ..F 8
Kivalina............374 ..C 8
Klawock...........755 ..H 16
Klukwan† ....95 ..F 14
Knik-
Fairview*† ...14,923 ..F 11
Kobuk ....151 ..C 10
Kodiak...........6,130 ..H 10
Kodiak
Station*† ......1,301 ..H 10
Kokhanok ....170 ..G 10
Kokrines..................D 10
Koliganek† ....209 ..G 9
Kongiganak*†......439 ..F 8
Kotlik..............577 ..E 8
Kotzebue........3,201 ..C 9
Koyuk ....332 ..D 9
Koyukuk............96 ..D 9
Kupreanof...........27 ..H 15
Kwethluk ....721 ..F 8
Kwigillingok†......321 ..F 8
Lakes*† ....8,364 ..F 11
Larsen Bay..........87 ..H 10
Lazy
Mountain*† ...1,479 ..F 11
Levelock† ....69 ..G 9
Lime Village†.......29 ..F 10
Livengood†..........13 ..D 11
Lower Kalskag.....282 ..F 9
Lower Tonsina*..........F 12
Manley
Hot Springs†.....89 ..D 11
Manokotak ....442 ..G 9
Marshall...........414 ..E 8
McGrath...........346 ..E 10
McKinley Park† ...185 ..E 11
Meadow
Lakes*† ....7,570 ..F 11
Medfra ....E 10
Mekoryuk ....191 ..F 7
Mentasta Lake†....112 ..E 12
Metlakatla†......1,405 ..H 16
Minto†.............210 ..D 11
Montana..................E 11
Moose Creek*†....747 ..D 11
Moose Pass† ......219 ..F 11
Mountain Point..........H 16
Mountain
Village ....813 ..E 8
Murphy Dome*..........D 11
Myers Chuck............H 16
Naknek† ....544 ..G 9
Napakiak ....354 ..F 8
Napaskiak ....405 ..F 8
Nelson
Lagoon*†.........52 ..I 8
Nenana............378 ..D 11
Nenana Native
Village ....D 11
New Stuyahok.....510 ..G 9
Newhalen ....190 ..G 10
Newtok†...........354 ..F 8
Nightmute.........280 ..F 8
Nikiski*† ....4,493 ..F 11
Nikolai...............94 ..E 10
Nikolski† ....18 ..I 6
Ninilchik†..........883 ..G 11
Noatak†............514 ..C 9
Nome............3,598 ..D 8
Nondalton ....164 ..G 10
Noorvik............668 ..C 9
North Pole.......2,117 ..D 12
Northway†..........71 ..E 13
Northway
Village*† ....98 ..E 13
Nuiqsut............402 ..B 11
Nulato ....264 ..D 9
Nunam Iqua ....187 ..E 8
Old Harbor ....218 ..H 10
Oscarville*†.........70 ..F 8
Ouzinkie...........161 ..H 10
Palmer...........5,937 ..F 11
Paxson† ....40 ..E 12
Pedro Bay† ....42 ..G 10
Pelican ....88 ..G 14
Pennock Island* ....H 16
Perkinsville*.............D 8
Perryville†.........113 ..H 8
Petersburg ......2,948 ..H 15
Pilot Point† ....68 ..H 9
Pilot Station........568 ..E 8
Pitkas Point†.......109 ..E 8
Platinum.............61 ..G 8
Point Baker*†.......15 ..H 16
Point Hope ....674 ..B 8
Point Lay† ....189 ..B 9
Port Alexander .....52 ..H 15
Port Clarence*†......24 ..D 8
Port Graham† .....177 ..G 11
Port Heiden† ......102 ..H 9
Port Lions..........194 ..H 10
Portlock* ....G 11
Prudhoe Bay† ...2,174 ..B 11
Quinhagak.........669 ..F 8
Rampart†...........24 ..D 11
Red Devil†..........23 ..F 9
Ridgeway*†......2,022 ..F 11
Ruby...............166 ..D 10
Russian Mission ...312 ..E 8
St. George ....102 ..G 6
St. Marys ....507 ..E 8
St. Michael.........401 ..E 8
St. Paul............479 ..G 6
Salamatof*†........980 ..F 11
Salcha*† ....1,095 ..D 11
Sand Point.........976 ..I 8
Savoonga..........671 ..D 7
Saxman* ....411 ..H 16
Saxman East* ....H 16
Scammon Bay .....474 ..E 7
Selawik............829 ..C 9
Seldovia...........255 ..G 11
Seward ....2,693 ..G 11
Shageluk ....83 ..E 9
Shaktoolik.........251 ..D 9
Shemya Station*.........I 4
Shishmaref ....563 ..C 8
Shungnak..........262 ..C 10
Sitka§............8,881 ..H 15
Skagway†..........920 ..F 15
Slana*† ....147 ..E 12
Sleetmute† ....86 ..F 9
Soldotna.........4,163 ..F 11
South Naknek† .....79 ..G 9
Sparrevohn
Station* ....F 10
Stebbins...........556 ..E 8
Sterling†.........5,617 ..F 11
Stevens
Village† ....78 ..D 11
Stony River† ....54 ..F 9
Suntrana.................E 11
Susitna† ....18 ..F 11
Sutton
[-Alpine]† .....1,447 ..F 11
Takotna†............52 ..E 10
Talkeetna†.........876 ..E 11
Tanacross† ....136 ..E 12
Tanaina*† ....8,197 ..F 11
Tanana.............246 ..D 11
Tatitlek† ....88 ..F 12
Tazlina*†...........297 ..F 12
Teller ....229 ..D 8
Teller Mission
[Brevig
Mission]..........388 ..D 8
Tenakee
Springs ....131 ..G 15
Tetlin† ....127 ..E 13
Thorne Bay* ....471 ..H 16
Togiak ....817 ..G 8
Tok† ....1,258 ..E 13
Toksook Bay*......590 ..F 7
Tonsina*† ....78 ..F 12
Tuluksak†..........373 ..F 8
Tuntutuliak† ....408 ..F 8
Tununak†..........327 ..F 7
Twin Hills†..........74 ..G 8
Two Rivers*†.......719 ..D 11
Tyonek† ....171 ..F 11
Ugashik† ....12 ..H 9
Umiat......................B 11
Unalakleet.........688 ..D 9
Unalaska.........4,376 ..I 6
Unga........................I 8
Upper Kalskag.....210 ..F 9
Usibelli ....E 11
Usibelli Mine* ....D 11
Utqiagvik ....4,212 ..A 10
Valdez...........3,976 ..F 12
Venetie†...........166 ..C 12
Wainwright........556 ..A 9
Wales ....145 ..C 7
Wasilla ....7,831 ..F 11
White
Mountain ....190 ..D 8
Whittier ....220 ..F 11
Willow† ....2,102 ..F 11
Wiseman† ....14 ..C 11
Wrangell§.......2,369 ..H 16
Yakutat†§..........662 ..G 13

*Borough names and names of cities marked with an asterisk do not appear on the map; key shows general location.
†Census designated place—unincorporated, but recognized as a significant settled community by the U.S. Census Bureau.
‡Municipality. Municipalities have the same function as boroughs.
§City and borough/municipality have same boundary and population.
Places without population figures are unincorporated areas.
Source: 2010 census. Metropolitan area figures are based on the 2013 Office of Management and Budget reorganization of 2010 census data.

Harold E. Wilson, Warden & Associates

Atka is a remote Alaskan village in the Andreanof Islands. The Andreanof Islands are part of the Aleutian chain, which extends westward from the tip of the Alaska Peninsula.

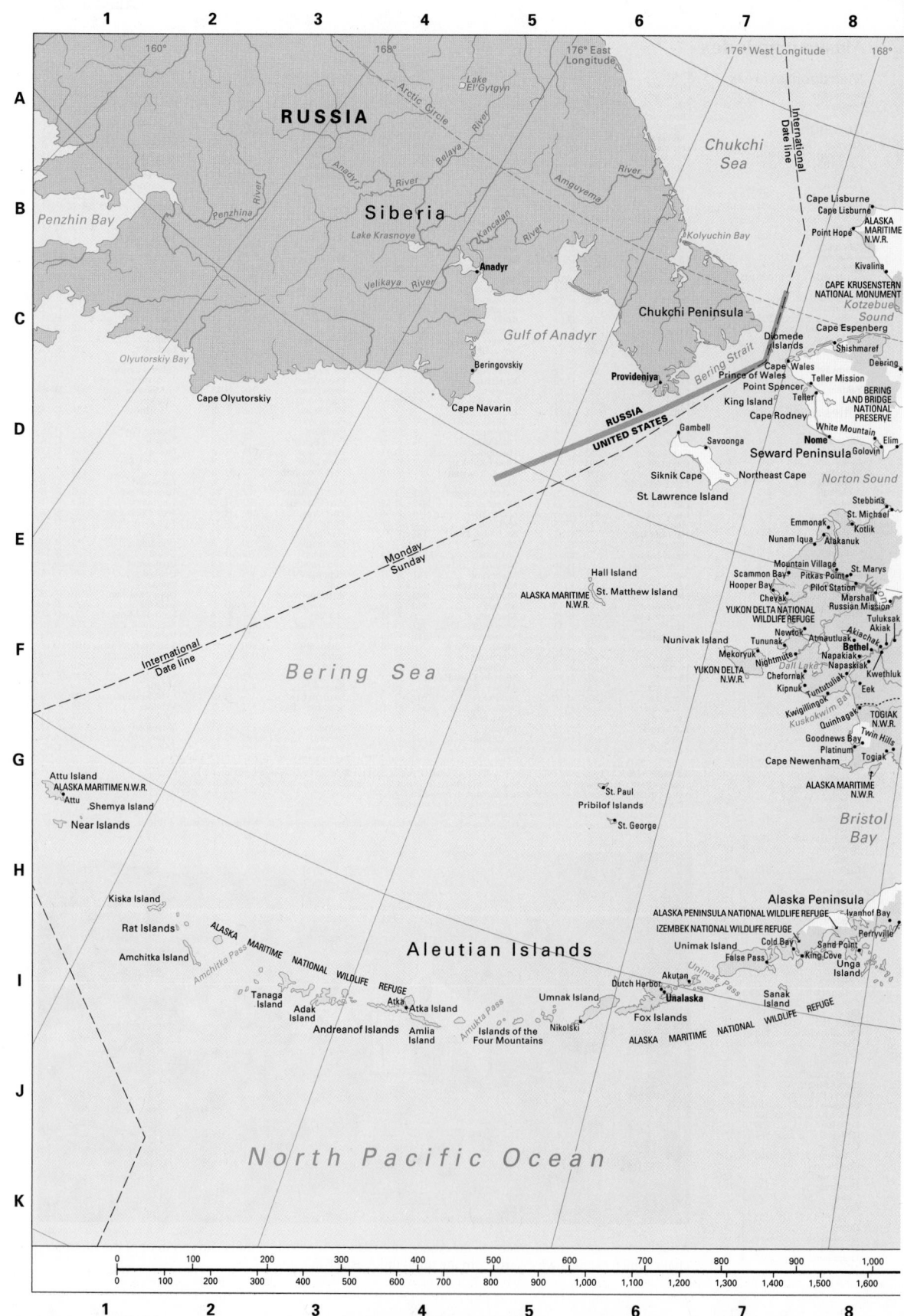

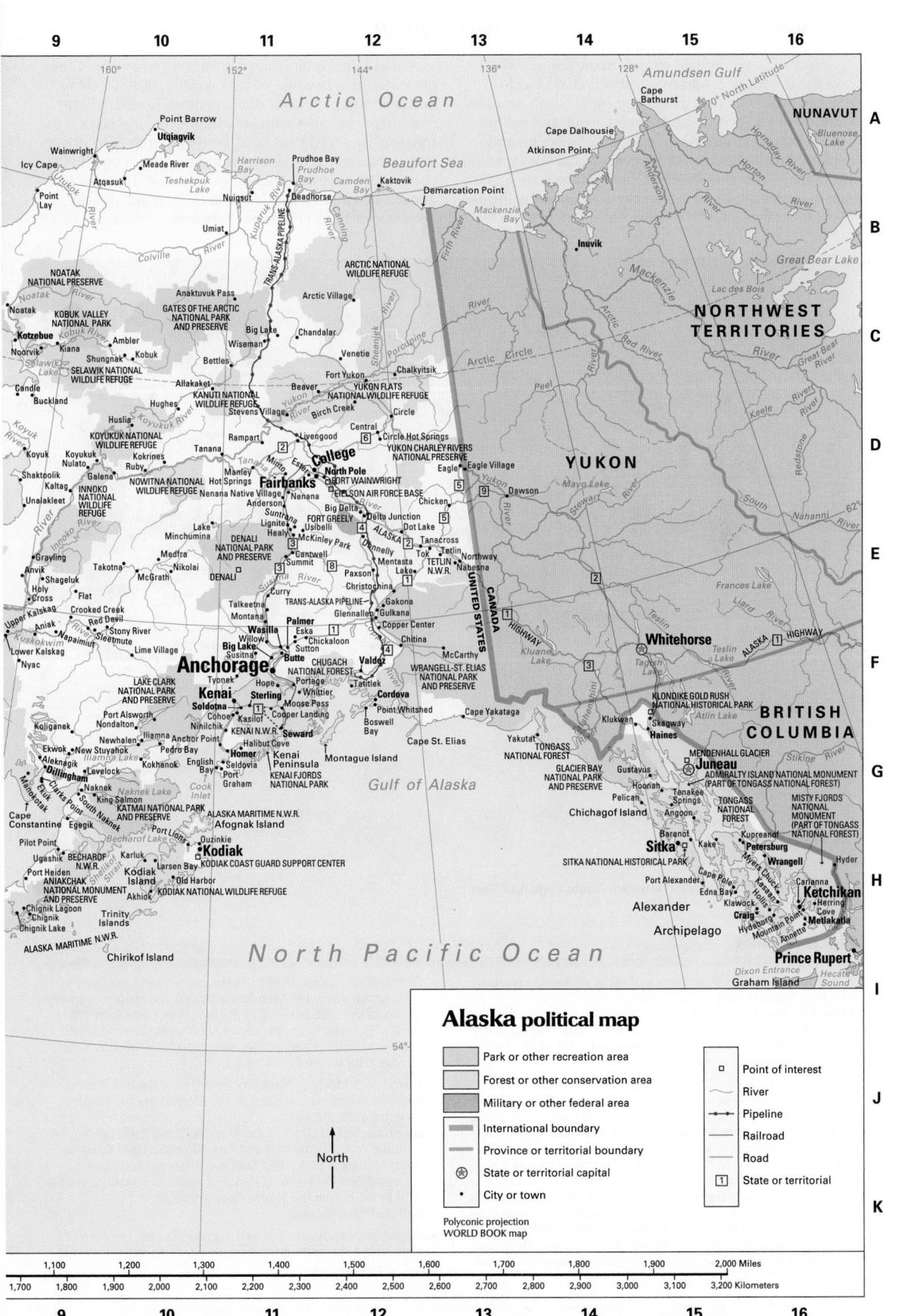

Alaska political map

	Park or other recreation area
	Forest or other conservation area
	Military or other federal area
	International boundary
	Province or territorial boundary
⊛	State or territorial capital
•	City or town

▫	Point of interest
	River
•—•—•	Pipeline
	Railroad
	Road
1	State or territorial

Polyconic projection
WORLD BOOK map

North

1,100   1,200   1,300   1,400   1,500   1,600   1,700   1,800   1,900   2,000 Miles

1,700 1,800 1,900 2,000 2,100 2,200 2,300 2,400 2,500 2,600 2,700 2,800 2,900 3,000 3,100 3,200 Kilometers

Alaska's vast wilderness attracts many people who love the outdoors. Expert mountain climbers tackle Alaskan peaks that rank as the highest in North America. People fish for record-sized salmon, trout, and halibut.

Thousands of tourists come to see Alaska's magnificent mountain scenery and historic coastal towns. Many vacationers from the "lower 48" drive to the state on the Alaska Highway or take a scenic cruise along the Inside Passage of Alaska's southeastern coast.

Alaska offers interesting activities for everyone. These activities include white-water kayaking, bird watching, and photographic tours of the famous "northern lights."

Perhaps the most popular winter event in Alaska is the Iditarod Trail Sled Dog Race, held in March. Sled drivers called mushers and their teams of dogs race over a rugged course from Anchorage to Nome. The course is about 1,000 miles (1,600 kilometers) long and usually takes about 10 to 17 days to complete.

© Jeff Schultz, Alaska Stock

Iditarod Trail Sled Dog Race between Anchorage and Nome

Places to visit

Following are brief descriptions of some of Alaska's many interesting places to visit.

Alaska Highway extends between Dawson Creek, British Columbia, and Delta Junction, Alaska. Linking highways go north to Fairbanks and south to Anchorage and other cities. See Alaska Highway.

"Marine Highway" is Alaska's state ferryliner system and the first marine highway to be designated a national scenic byway. Oceangoing ferryliners carry cars and passengers along this route from Prince Rupert, British Columbia, and Bellingham, Washington, to southeastern coastal cities. The ferryliners follow the Inside Passage running between forested islands and the steep, inlet-cut mainland coast. Each town located along this scenic route offers special attractions to visitors. Ketchikan has a large collection of authentic totem poles. Sitka, which was the capital when Alaska belonged to Russia, includes historic St. Michael's Cathedral, a Russian Orthodox church. Juneau, the state capital, offers close-up views of the

Mendenhall Glacier. Visitors to the glacier can hike nearby trails or raft down the Mendenhall River. The Haines Highway connects the northern end of the ferryliner route with the Alaska Highway. In south-central Alaska, ferryliners operate between Cordova and Kodiak, with stops at Valdez, Whittier, Seward, Homer, and Seldovia.

National parklands in Alaska include Denali National Park, which features majestic Denali, the highest peak in North America at 20,310 feet, or 6,190 meters, above sea level. Alaska is also the site of Gates of the Arctic National Park, Glacier Bay National Park, Katmai National Park, Klondike Gold Rush National Historical Park, Sitka National Historical Park, and Wrangell-St. Elias National Park. For more information, see the map and tables in the *World Book* article on National Park System.

National forests. Alaska has two national forests. They are Chugach, along the southern central coast, and Tongass, along the southeastern coast.

**Totem pole and tribal
house near Ketchikan**

Warden & Associates

© Wolfgang Kaehler, Corbis

St. Michael's Cathedral in downtown Sitka

Alaska State Fair

Alaska State Fair in Palmer

Chambers, Miller Services

Ferry line in Ketchikan Harbor

Land regions. Alaska has four main land regions:
(1) the Pacific Mountain System, (2) the Central Uplands
and Lowlands, (3) the Rocky Mountain System, and (4)
the Arctic Coastal Plain.

The Pacific Mountain System of Alaska is part of a
group of ranges that extends down the Pacific Coast to
southern California. In Alaska, the ranges curve from the
Aleutian Islands in the west through south-central Alaska and along the coast in the southeast.

The region has many subdivisions. The strip of coastal
land 400 miles (640 kilometers) long in the southeast is
called the Alaska Panhandle. It is 10 to 150 miles (16 to
241 kilometers) wide, and it includes tall mountains and
ice fields. The Saint Elias Range extends northwestward
from the Panhandle. Mount Saint Elias rises 18,008 feet
(5,489 meters) in this range. The Wrangell Mountains,
northwest of the Saint Elias Range, include Mount Bona
(16,421 feet, or 5,005 meters) and three tall peaks—
Mount Blackburn (16,390 feet, or 4,996 meters), Mount
Sanford (16,208 feet, or 4,940 meters), and Mount
Wrangell (14,005 feet, or 4,269 meters). Mount Wrangell
is an active volcano. The Chugach and Kenai mountains
border the coast from the Saint Elias Range west to the
Kenai Peninsula and Kodiak Island. Fairweather Mountain, in the Chugach Mountains, is 15,300 feet (4,663 meters) high. The Talkeetna Mountains, north of Anchorage, are a low range of rugged, glacier-cut peaks. The
Alaska Range is the most inland section of the Pacific
Mountain System. From the Canadian border, it curves
west and southwest to the Alaska Peninsula. The Alaska
Range includes Denali (20,310 feet, or 6,190 meters), the
highest peak in North America, and Mount Foraker
(17,400 feet, or 5,304 meters).

The Alaska Peninsula and the Aleutian Islands extend
southwest in a long chain from the Alaska Range. The
Aleutians include 14 large islands, about 55 small islands, and many islets. The largest islands are Unimak,
Unalaska, and Umnak. The Aleutian Range forms the
"backbone" of the peninsula and islands. It extends 1,600
miles (2,570 kilometers), from Mount Spurr, across Cook
Inlet from Anchorage, to Attu Island near the Asian con-

© Jane Gnass, West Stock

The Matanuska Valley produces most of Alaska's farm products. On the farm shown above, caps protect squash plants from
frost. The Chugach Mountains tower in the background.

Land regions of Alaska

WORLD BOOK map

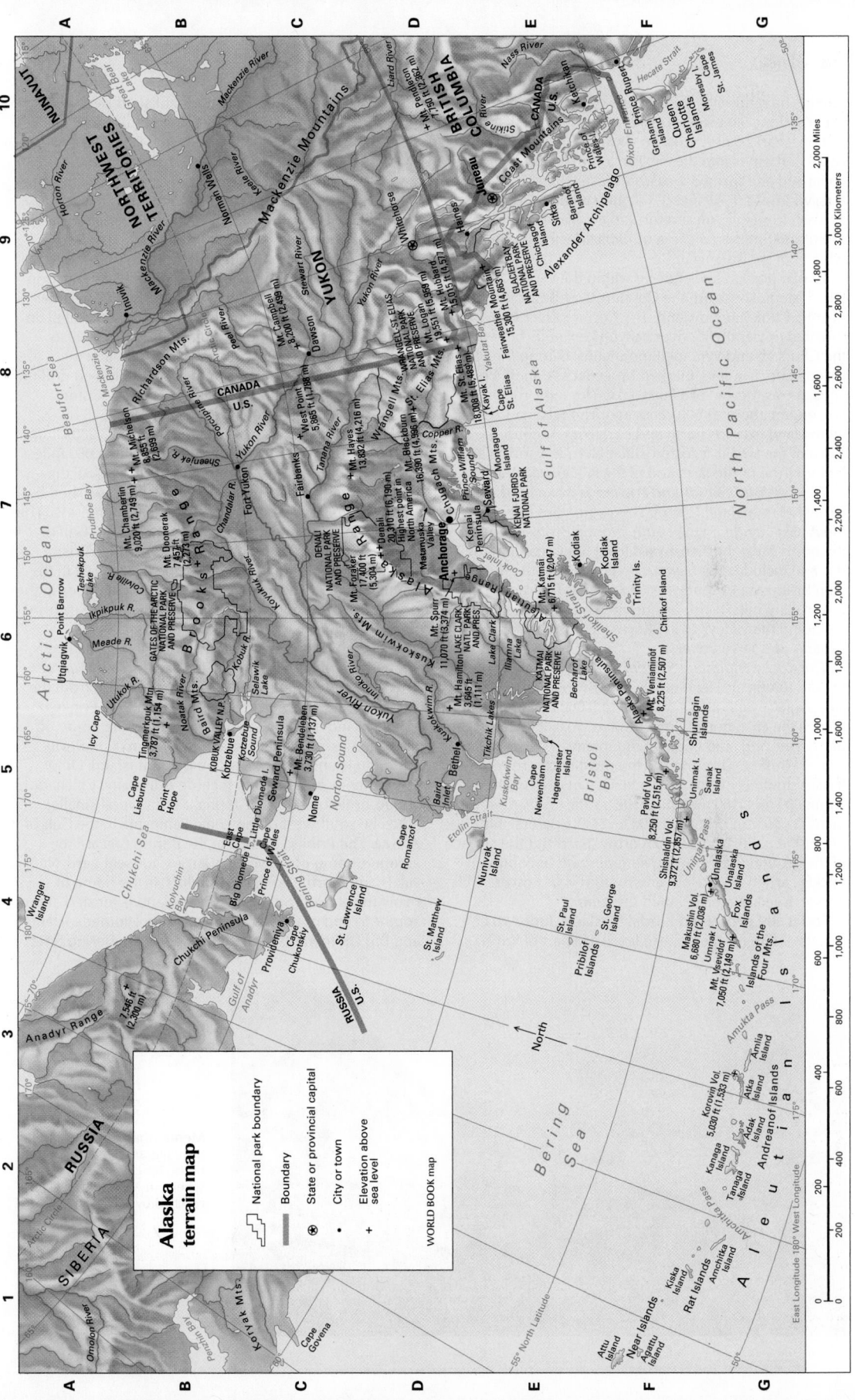

Alaska
terrain map

National park boundary

Boundary

State or provincial capital ⊛

City or town •

Elevation above + sea level

WORLD BOOK map

tinent. The range has many active volcanoes. The greatest eruptions occurred in 1912, at what is now Katmai National Park. A new volcano, Novarupta, hurled tons of rocks and ashes into the air. The top of Mount Katmai collapsed and formed a *caldera* (basin) 3 miles (5 kilometers) wide and 3,700 feet (1,130 meters) deep. The lava and ash from the volcano formed the Valley of Ten Thousand Smokes, an area of *fumaroles* (holes from which hot gas steams up).

Two important lowlands lie within the Pacific Mountain System. These are the Copper River Basin and the Susitna-Cook Inlet lowland. The Copper River Basin, a forested lowland with river canyons, extends between the Chugach and Wrangell mountains. During the Pleistocene Epoch, a time marked by a succession of ice ages, it was the site of a large lake. The most recent ice age ended about 11,500 years ago. The Susitna-Cook Inlet lowland extends north and east from Anchorage. Most of the area is forested. But it has a few towns and includes the fertile farmland of the Matanuska Valley.

The Central Uplands and Lowlands make up the largest Alaskan land region. This region lies between the Alaska Range on the south and the Brooks Range on the north. It extends westward from the Canadian border and includes the Seward Peninsula and the Kuskokwim River area of southwestern Alaska. The region has low, rolling hills. It also has broad, swampy river valleys, including the valleys of the Koyukuk, Kuskokwim, Tanana, and Yukon rivers.

The Rocky Mountain System of Alaska consists of the Brooks Range and its foothills. The Brooks Range has steep, glacier-cut peaks that rise to 9,000 feet (2,700 meters) in the east, but are lower in the west. It includes the Baird, De Long, and Endicott mountains.

The Arctic Coastal Plain is the most northern region. It rises gradually from the Arctic Ocean to a height of about 600 feet (180 meters) in the south. *Permafrost* (permanently frozen ground) 1,000 feet (300 meters) thick lies under the plain. No trees can grow there. But the surface of the ground thaws during summer and becomes thickly carpeted with low grasses and wild flowers. This grassy, treeless area is called the *tundra.*

Federally protected lands. Alaska includes 16 national wildlife refuges. These lands are part of the National Wildlife Refuge System, established by the U.S. government to protect and increase wildlife and their habitat. The system is managed by the U.S. Fish and Wildlife Service. Alaska's refuges make up more than 80 percent of the land in the system. The Yukon Delta National Wildlife Refuge, in western Alaska, ranks as the nation's largest refuge. It covers nearly 20 million acres (8 million hectares).

The Arctic National Wildlife Refuge, in northeastern Alaska, has become a topic of debate between environmentalists and the oil and gas industry. Oil companies have sought the right to drill for oil on the coastal plain in the northern part of the refuge. Environmentalists have protested that the drilling would damage the refuge. The federal government has not allowed drilling to take place. See **National Wildlife Refuge System.**

Coastline. Alaska's general coastline is 6,640 miles (10,686 kilometers) long. About 5,580 miles (8,980 kilometers) are along the Pacific Ocean, and about 1,060 miles (1,706 kilometers) are along the Arctic Ocean. All the coastline of the mainland and major islands washed by tidewater measures 33,904 miles (54,563 kilometers). The main features of the coast in the south are the Gulf of Alaska, Prince William Sound, and Cook Inlet. Bristol Bay and Norton Sound open into the Bering Sea in the southwest. Kotzebue Sound faces the Chukchi Sea in the northwest. The Arctic Ocean and the Beaufort Sea border the northern coast.

The southern coast is cut by hundreds of small bays, channels, and narrow, steep-sided inlets called *fiords.* The islands of the Alexander Archipelago rise from the Pacific off the shore of the Alaska Panhandle. Prince of Wales Island, the largest of the group, is the home of most of Alaska's Haida Indians. Ketchikan is on Revillagigedo Island, and Sitka is on Baranof Island. Other large islands in the group include Admiralty, Chichagof, and Kupreanof. Kodiak, Afognak, and several smaller islands lie southwest of the Kenai Peninsula in the Gulf of Alaska. The Pribilof Islands in the Bering Sea are the summer home of the world's largest fur seal herd. Nunivak Island, northeast of the Pribilofs, is the home of many musk oxen. Saint Lawrence Island is located at the southern end of the Bering Strait. Little Diomede Island and Big Diomede Island are located in the Bering Strait.

Artstreet

Mendenhall Glacier near Juneau fills a valley with ice and rock. This glacier is one of several in Alaska that can be reached by highway.

Little Diomede is part of Alaska. Big Diomede belongs to Russia.

Rivers and lakes. The Yukon River, Alaska's chief waterway, is the fifth-longest river in North America. It flows 1,979 miles (3,185 kilometers) through Alaska and parts of Canada. From June to October, the river is free of ice. Small boats and barges can travel from its mouth on the Bering Sea across Alaska and into Canada. The Yukon's main tributaries are the Koyukuk and the Tanana rivers. See **Yukon River.**

Alaska's second-longest river, the Kuskokwim, empties into the Bering Sea at Kuskokwim Bay. The Colville River flows into the Arctic Ocean, and the Noatak and Kobuk rivers flow into the Chukchi Sea at Kotzebue Sound. The Susitna and Matanuska rivers flow into Cook Inlet, and the Copper River empties into the Gulf of Alaska. Several rivers, including the Alsek, Stikine, and Taku, begin in Canada and flow south or west across the Alaska Panhandle to the Pacific.

Harold E. Wilson, Warden & Associates
Northern fur seals spend the summer on islands off Alaska's coast. The world's largest herd lives on the Pribilof Islands.

Alaska has thousands of lakes. The largest, Iliamna Lake on the Alaska Peninsula, is 80 miles (130 kilometers) long and 20 miles (32 kilometers) wide. Other lakes include Aleknagik, Becharof, Clark, Minchumina, Naknek, Selawik, Skilak, Teshekpuk, and Tustumena.

Glaciers. Thousands of glaciers from 1 to 30 miles (1.6 to 48 kilometers) long fill Alaska's mountain valleys and canyons. The greatest number of glaciers are along the coast in the south and southeast. Malaspina, in the Saint Elias Range, is North America's largest glacier. It measures almost 50 miles (80 kilometers) wide. Many Alaska glaciers are easy to reach, and scientists from all parts of North America come to study them. Columbia Glacier can be reached by boat from Cordova. This huge glacier ends in an ice cliff in the sea. Glaciers that can be reached by highway include Black Rapids, Canwell, Castner, Gulkana, Matanuska, Mendenhall, Portage, and Worthington.

Plant and animal life. Forests cover about a third of

Average monthly weather

	Anchorage						Barrow				
	Temperatures °F		Temperatures °C		Days of rain or snow			Temperatures °F		Temperatures °C		Days of rain or snow
	High	Low	High	Low	snow			High	Low	High	Low	snow
Jan.	23	11	-5	-12	7	Jan.	-7	-20	-22	-29	4
Feb.	27	14	-3	-10	7	Feb.	-8	-20	-22	-29	4
Mar.	34	19	1	-7	6	Mar.	-6	-19	-21	-28	3
Apr.	45	29	7	-2	5	Apr.	9	-5	-13	-21	4
May	56	40	13	4	6	May	26	17	-3	-8	4
June	63	48	17	9	8	June	41	31	5	-1	4
July	65	52	18	11	11	July	47	35	8	1	8
Aug.	64	50	18	10	14	Aug.	44	34	7	1	10
Sept.	55	42	13	6	14	Sept.	36	29	2	-2	11
Oct.	41	29	5	-2	12	Oct.	22	13	-6	-11	11
Nov.	28	17	-2	-8	9	Nov.	6	-5	-14	-21	6
Dec.	25	13	-4	-11	10	Dec.	-2	-14	-19	-26	5

WORLD BOOK maps

Average January temperatures

The southern coastal areas generally remain above freezing in winter. The rest of the state can be extremely cold.

Degrees Fahrenheit	Degrees Celsius
Above 32	Above 0
10 to 32	-12 to 0
0 to 10	-18 to -12
-10 to 0	-23 to -18
Below -10	Below -23

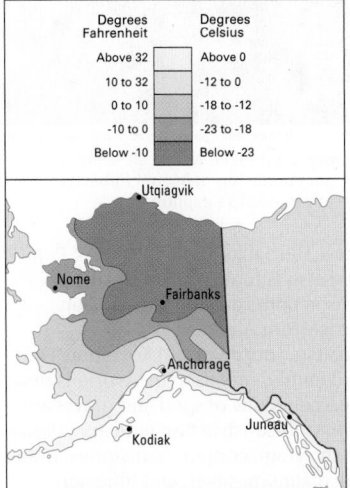

Average July temperatures

Alaska has short, cool summers with big variations in temperature between the cold north and milder southern areas.

Degrees Fahrenheit	Degrees Celsius
Above 60	Above 16
55 to 60	13 to 16
50 to 55	10 to 13
45 to 50	7 to 10
Below 45	Below 7

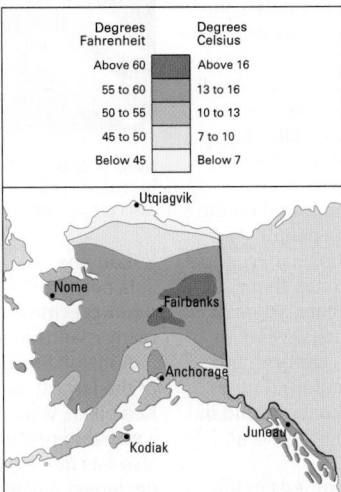

Average yearly precipitation

The southern coastal areas receive heavy precipitation. The rest of the state generally is extremely dry.

Inches	Centimeters
More than 64	More than 163
32 to 64	81 to 163
16 to 32	41 to 81
8 to 16	20 to 41
Less than 8	Less than 20

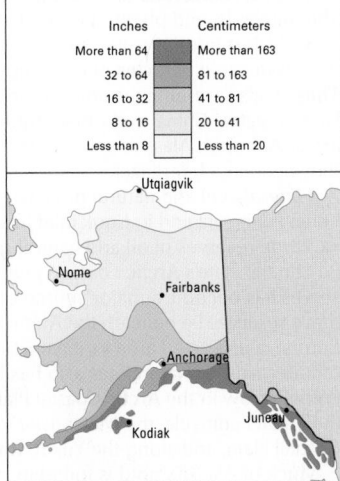

Alaska. The most important trees are birches, Sitka spruces, western hemlocks, and white spruces. Other trees include aspens, black spruces, cottonwoods, tamaracks, and willows.

Grasses, mosses, sedges, and plantlike organisms called *lichens* are found in many parts of Alaska. In the far north, they provide food for caribou and other animals. Wildflowers also grow throughout the state. Wildflowers on the tundra include asters, cinquefoils, fireweeds, forget-me-nots, larkspurs, and mountain laurels. Arctic daisies, bog laurels, cowslips, violets, wild hyacinths, and wood nymphs bloom in the mountains.

The waters off Alaska's shores are rich in salmon and halibut. They also contain great quantities of clams, cod, crabs, herring, and shrimp. The world's largest herd of fur seals is found on the Pribilof Islands in summer. A herd of musk oxen lives on Nunivak Island. Brown bears live on Kodiak Island and in other parts of south-central and southeast Alaska. Polar bears live along the Arctic Coast. Other animals include caribou, deer, elk, grizzly bears, moose, mountain goats, and mountain sheep. Game birds include ducks, geese, and grouse.

Climate. Alaska has a great variety of climates. Winds that blow eastward over the warm Kuroshio (Japan Current) give southern Alaska a fairly mild climate. Near the southern coast of Alaska, temperatures average 33 °F (1 °C) in January and 56 °F (13 °C) in July. Precipitation averages 20 inches (51 centimeters) at Cook Inlet and 95 inches (241 centimeters) in the Panhandle. Parts of the southeast coast get heavy precipitation. Port Walter, on Baranof Island, has the highest average yearly precipitation in the continental United States—225 inches (571 centimeters).

In the inland parts of Alaska, temperatures average about –7 °F (–22 °C) in January and about 61 °F (16 °C) in July. The annual precipitation averages about 15 inches (38 centimeters). Fort Yukon recorded Alaska's highest temperature, 100 °F (38 °C), on June 27, 1915. The record low, –80 °F (–62 °C), was set at Prospect Creek, near Stevens Village, on Jan. 23, 1971. This ranks as the lowest temperature ever recorded in the United States.

The Alaskan Arctic has an average January temperature of –13 °F (–25 °C). Its average July temperature is 44 °F (7 °C). Annual precipitation is low.

Economy

Alaska's economy relies heavily on government activities and petroleum production. The huge amounts of petroleum produced by Alaska's oil industry are shipped to other states in oil tankers and through the Trans-Alaska Pipeline. Although mining remains one of Alaska's most important economic activities, other industries have helped diversify the state's economy.

Service industries, which include such activities as government operations and transportation, are also important to Alaska. Tourism benefits many businesses, including hotels, shops, restaurants, and tour organizers.

Fishing is the dominant industry in many parts of the state. Alaska catches more fish than any other state.

Land use is a difficult problem in Alaska because economic development and environmental protection interests often clash. The federal government owns and controls most of the state's land, and it has set aside large areas for wildlife conservation and national parklands.

Natural resources of Alaska include rich soils, valuable minerals, and plentiful water, fish, and forests.

Soil. Most interior valley soils in Alaska are composed of *loess* (coarse particles of dust deposited by the wind). These soils resemble the soils found in the western United States, China, and other highly productive farm areas. Although Alaska's soils are naturally productive, they need much fertilizer.

Minerals. Oil and natural gas have been found on the Kenai Peninsula and in Cook Inlet in south-central Alaska. Large reserves of oil and natural gas lie near Prudhoe Bay on the state's Arctic coast. Whether to tap these reserves has become a major source of debate. Some of these reserves lie beneath the Arctic National Wildlife Refuge, a protected area for bears, birds, caribou, and other creatures. Natural gas also has been found near Point Barrow in the Arctic Coastal Plain. Coal is found in the Kenai Peninsula, the Matanuska Valley, the Arctic Coastal Plain, and along the Yukon River.

Much of Alaska's gold is found in streambeds in the

© Mark Kelley, Juneau Convention & Visitors Bureau

Mount Roberts Tramway is a popular tourist attraction in Juneau. It carries passengers to the top of Mount Roberts. Tourism contributes greatly to Alaska's economy.

Yukon River Basin near Fairbanks and the Seward Peninsula near Nome. Gold also is found in combination with other precious metals in underground deposits on many islands in southeastern Alaska.

A major zinc deposit lies northwest of Kotzebue. One of the largest molybdenum deposits in the world is near Ketchikan. Widespread deposits of sand and gravel are a valuable resource for the construction industry. Alaska also has deposits of chromite, copper, gemstones, granite, limestone, nickel, platinum, silver, and tungsten.

Alaska economy

General economy

Gross domestic product (GDP)* (2017) $51,479,000,000
    Rank among U.S. states   46th
Unemployment rate (2018)   6.7% (U.S. avg: 3.9%)

*Gross domestic product is the total value of goods and services produced in a year.
Sources: U.S. Bureau of Economic Analysis and U.S. Bureau of Labor Statistics.

Production and workers by economic activities

Economic activities	Percent of GDP produced	Employed workers	
		Number of people	Percent of total
Government	22	103,600	23
Community, business, & personal services	17	129,500	28
Transportation & communication	16	30,600	7
Finance, insurance, & real estate	14	32,200	7
Mining	13	18,600	4
Trade, restaurants, & hotels	10	88,400	19
Construction	4	23,900	5
Manufacturing	3	16,400	4
Utilities	2	2,300	1
Agriculture, forestry, & fishing	1	11,300	2
Total*	100	456,800	100

*Figures may not add up to 100 percent, due to rounding.
Figures are for 2016; employment figures include full- and part-time workers.
Source: *World Book* estimates based on data from U.S. Bureau of Economic Analysis.

Manufacturing

Value added by manufacture* $2,212,462,000
    Rank among U.S. states   49th

Leading products
Food products, petroleum products.

*Value added by manufacture is the increase in value of raw materials as they become finished products.

Mining

Nonfuel mineral production (2015) $3,030,000,000
    Rank among U.S. states   6th
Coal (tons*)   959,000
    Rank among U.S. states   20th
Crude oil (barrels†)   180,467,000
    Rank among U.S. states   3rd
Natural gas (cubic feet‡)   344,385,000,000
    Rank among U.S. states   12th

*One ton equals 0.9072 metric ton.
†Includes offshore oil production. One barrel equals 42 gallons (159 liters).
‡One cubic foot equals 0.0283 cubic meter.

Leading products

1. Petroleum   (ranks 3rd in U.S.)
2. Zinc   (ranks 1st in U.S.)
3. Gold   (ranks 2nd in U.S.)
4. Natural gas
Other products: crushed stone, lead, sand and gravel, silver.

Electric power

Natural gas	49.8%
Hydroelectric	25.3%
Petroleum	13.6%
Coal	8.6%
Wind	2.2%
Other	0.5%

Figures are for 2017, except for the manufacturing figures, which are for 2016.
Sources: U.S. Census Bureau, U.S. Energy Information Administration, U.S. Geological Survey.

continued on page 298

Economy of Alaska

This map shows the economic uses of land in Alaska and where the state's leading farm, forest, and mineral products are produced. Major manufacturing centers are shown in red.

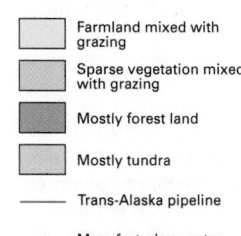

    Farmland mixed with grazing

    Sparse vegetation mixed with grazing

    Mostly forest land

    Mostly tundra

—— Trans-Alaska pipeline

• Manufacturing center

• Mineral deposit

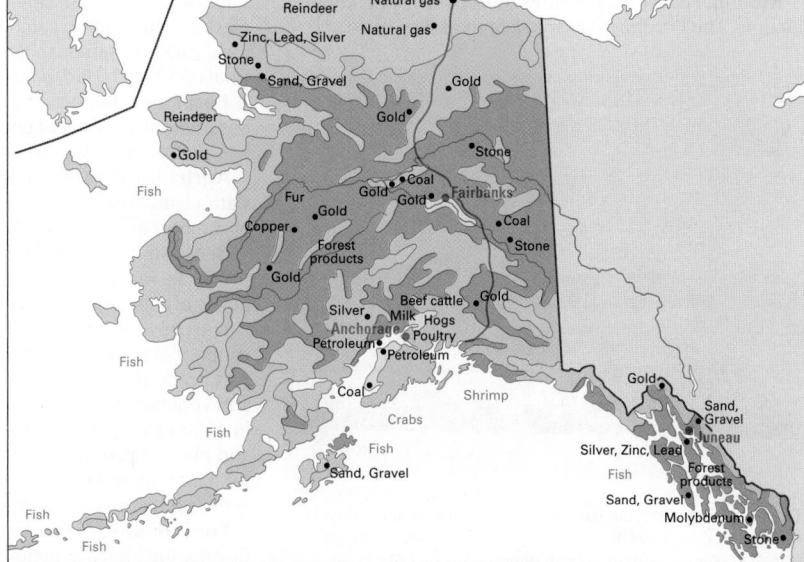

WORLD BOOK map

Agriculture

Cash receipts	$37,666,000
Rank among U.S. states	50th
Distribution	80% crops, 20% livestock
Farms	1,000
Farm acres (hectares)	850,000 (340,000)
Rank among U.S. states	44th
Farmland	0.2% of Alaska

Leading products

1. Greenhouse and nursery products
2. Hay
3. Cattle and calves
4. Mushrooms
Other products: barley, dairy products, hogs, honey, oats, potatoes, wool.

Fishing

Commercial catch	$1,550,840,000
Rank among U.S. states	1st

Leading catches

1. Pollock	(ranks 1st in U.S.)
2. Salmon	(ranks 1st in U.S.)
3. Crabs	(ranks 1st in U.S.)
4. Cod	(ranks 1st in U.S.)
5. Halibut	(ranks 1st in U.S.)
6. Sablefish	(ranks 1st in U.S.)
7. Sole	(ranks 1st in U.S.)

Other catches: herring, mackerel, rockfish.

Agricultural figures are for 2017 and the fishing figures are for 2016.
Sources: U.S. Department of Agriculture, U.S. National Marine Fisheries Service.

Service industries, taken together, account for the largest portion of Alaska's *gross domestic product*—the total value of goods and services produced in the state in a year. Most of the service industries are concentrated in the urban areas of the state.

Anchorage is Alaska's chief financial center. Many hotels, restaurants, and retail trade establishments operate in the Anchorage and Fairbanks areas. Government services are also important. An extensive network of government services is necessary because Alaska's people are spread over a large area. State government activities are concentrated in Anchorage and Juneau. Military bases are near Anchorage and Fairbanks.

Transportation is essential to Alaska's economy because the state lies far from major markets. Pipeline and shipping companies transport petroleum to processors. Ships also bring essential goods to Alaska from other states. Alaska's location between Asia and the continental United States has also helped make it an air freight transfer hub for such companies as FedEx and United Parcel Service. At Kodiak Island, the Alaska Aerospace Development Corporation (now Alaska Aerospace Corporation) created the nation's first privately operated rocket launch complex.

Mining. Petroleum provides most of Alaska's mining income. The Prudhoe Bay area is one of the world's

© Jeff Schultz, Alaska Stock Images

The Red Dog Mine, the largest U.S. zinc mine, is in northwestern Alaska, near Kotzebue. A truck hauls zinc from the mine, *shown here.* Zinc is an important mineral product of Alaska.

major petroleum-producing regions. Prudhoe Bay also contains vast natural gas reserves. The Trans-Alaska Pipeline transports petroleum south from Prudhoe Bay. Petroleum is also pumped from oil fields in the Kenai Peninsula-Cook Inlet area.

For many years, gold was Alaska's major mined product. Today, Alaska still ranks as a leading gold-mining state. Much of the gold comes from *placer deposits*—particles in streambeds—near Fairbanks and Nome.

Alaska is also a major producer of lead, silver, and zinc. The Red Dog Mine, near Kotzebue, is the largest zinc mine in the United States. The mine is also a leading producer of lead. The Greens Creek Mine, near Juneau, is a leading producer of both silver and zinc. Alaska's other mined products include coal, crushed stone, and sand and gravel.

Manufacturing. Food processing is Alaska's leading manufacturing activity. Fish products are the main source of food-processing income. Many coastal cities process salmon and other fish. Petroleum products are also important. The Fairbanks and Kenai areas have large oil refineries. Refineries also operate at Prudhoe Bay.

Fishing industry. Alaska leads the states in the value of fish caught by the commercial fishing industry. The state has a yearly fish catch valued at over $1 ½ billion. Alaska is the leading catcher of cod, crabs, halibut, pollock, rockfish, sablefish, salmon, and sole. Kodiak and Unalaska/Dutch Harbor are the chief fishing ports.

Forestry is important to Alaska's economy. Alaska has millions of acres of commercial forestland. The Panhandle has many log-processing camps and sawmills.

Agriculture. Farms cover well under 1 percent of the state's land area. The fertile Matanuska Valley northeast of Anchorage produces much of Alaska's farm products.

Beef and milk are Alaska's most valuable livestock products. Farmers also raise hogs and sheep. Inuit keep herds of reindeer as a source of meat and hides.

The growing season in Alaska is short. However, the summer sun shines about 20 hours a day in the central part of the state, and crops ripen quickly there. All fruits and vegetables that grow in a cool climate can be raised in Alaska as far north as the Arctic Circle. Greenhouse and nursery products are the leading source of agricultural income in Alaska. In addition, Alaskan farmers grow such crops as barley, hay, oats, and potatoes.

Fur industry. Alaska trappers catch many kinds of fur-bearing animals, including beavers, lynxes, martens,

Terry Domico, Earth Images

A salmon catch is unloaded at Annette Island. Fish products rank among Alaska's leading manufactured goods. Alaska leads the states in the value of fish caught by the fishing industry.

minks, wolves, and wolverines. Many Alaskans, most of them Inuit or Native Americans, hunt and fish for food. They also make clothing and other items of animal skins.

Electric power and utilities. Power plants that burn natural gas provide about half of the electric power generated in Alaska. Coal-burning plants, petroleum-burning plants, and hydroelectric plants generate most of the rest. Only a small fraction of the state's potential hydroelectric power has been developed.

Transportation. It is difficult and expensive to build roads and railroads in Alaska. The land is rugged, and the weather is often too cold for construction projects.

The Alaska Highway is the only major land route between Alaska, Canada, and the "lower 48." The highway extends between Dawson Creek, British Columbia, and Delta Junction, where it joins the Richardson Highway to Fairbanks. Alaska has an extensive system of roads and highways. Most roads link the Alaska Highway with the Kenai Peninsula, Anchorage, Valdez, and Fairbanks.

The state-owned Alaska Railroad provides freight service from Seward and Whittier to Anchorage and Fairbanks. This railroad also operates passenger trains.

Small planes flown by "bush pilots" provide the primary link between remote villages and the outside world. These pilots carry passengers, supplies, and mail across thousands of miles of rugged, remote country. Ted Stevens Anchorage International Airport is a major air terminal. It serves as one of the world's busiest cargo hubs. Other major airports are at Juneau and Fairbanks.

Alaska depends on container ship service for most of its trade with the "lower 48." The state's chief ports include Anchorage, Seward, Unalaska/Dutch Harbor, Valdez, and ports near Ketchikan and Kodiak. Nome, the main port on the Bering Sea, is blocked by ice in winter.

Alaska has an outstanding ferry liner system owned by the state. Three main routes serve the state's coastal areas. In the southeast, huge ferry liners stop at several cities between Haines and Skagway in the north and Bellingham, Washington, and Prince Rupert, British Columbia, in the south. Another route connects Cordova, Homer, Kodiak, Valdez, and Whittier. The third main route provides service between Kodiak and Unalaska/Dutch Harbor. Still another ferry route connects Juneau, Valdez, and Seward during the summer months.

Communication. Alaska's first public newspaper, the *Sitka Times,* began publication in Sitka in 1868. Today, Alaska's leading dailies include the *Anchorage Daily News, Fairbanks Daily News-Miner,* and *Juneau Empire.*

Government

Constitution. Alaska's present Constitution was adopted in 1956, three years before the territory became a state. A constitutional amendment must be approved by two-thirds of the members of each house of the State Legislature. Then it must be approved by a majority of voters in a statewide election.

Amendments may also be proposed by a constitutional convention. The convention must be approved by a majority of each house of the Legislature. All amendments proposed by the convention must be approved by the voters. If no constitutional convention has been held in a 10-year period, the question of calling a convention must be put to the voters.

Executive. Alaska's governor and lieutenant governor are the state's only elected state officials. They serve four-year terms and cannot serve more than two terms in a row.

The state's other top executive officials include the commissioners who head 12 of Alaska's 14 executive departments. Alaska also has an attorney general, who heads the Department of Law, and an adjutant general, who heads the Department of Military and Veterans Affairs. The governor appoints these 2 officials and the 12

commissioners with the approval of a majority of the legislators voting in a joint session.

Legislature consists of a 20-member Senate and a 40-member House of Representatives. Each senatorial district elects one senator. Two representative districts make up each senatorial district. Each representative district elects one representative. Senators serve four-year terms. Representatives serve two-year terms.

The Legislature holds a regular session every year. The sessions usually begin on the third Tuesday in January. The length of a session is limited to 90 days from the day it convenes. The Legislature or governor may call a 30-day special session.

Courts. The highest court in the state is the Alaska Supreme Court. It has five justices, one of whom is chosen by the other justices to serve a three-year term as chief justice. The Supreme Court concentrates on civil matters but has ultimate authority in all cases.

The Court of Appeals, which has three judges, is the second-highest court for criminal matters. The Superior Court, Alaska's second-highest court for civil cases, has 42 judges. It is divided into four districts. District courts handle civil and criminal cases. More than 20 district court judges serve in four judicial districts. The Court of Appeals reviews district court decisions.

The governor appoints the Supreme Court justices and the Superior Court and Court of Appeals judges from people nominated by the Alaska Judicial Council. The council is an independent citizens' commission that screens applicants for judicial vacancies and evaluates the performance of judges. It consists of a chief justice and six private citizens. After serving three years, a Supreme Court justice or Superior Court or Court of Appeals judge must be approved by the voters in the next general election. Each Supreme Court justice must be reapproved every 10 years. Superior Court judges must be reapproved every 6 years, and Court of Appeals judges every 8 years.

The governor appoints district court judges from candidates recommended by the Alaska Judicial Council. Voters must approve such judges in the first general election held more than two years after their appointment, and every four years thereafter.

Local government. Alaska is divided into 19 local units called *organized boroughs.* Organized boroughs are incorporated areas that may include cities, suburbs, and rural areas. They are equivalent to counties in other states. Some boroughs are called *municipalities.* Each borough is governed by an assembly of from 5 to 11 members. In most boroughs, the top administrative officer is a mayor elected by the people. A borough may instead have a manager appointed by the assembly. Other borough officials are appointed by the mayor or the manager.

Organized boroughs cover less than half of Alaska. However, they have about 90 percent of the population. The rest of the state is called the *unorganized borough.* It is governed by the Legislature. Alaska's cities use a mayor-council or city-manager form of government. All

The governors of Alaska

	Party	Term
William A. Egan	Democratic	1959-1966
Walter J. Hickel	Republican	1966-1969
Keith Miller	Republican	1969-1970
William A. Egan	Democratic	1970-1974
Jay S. Hammond	Republican	1974-1982
Bill Sheffield	Democratic	1982-1986
Steve Cowper	Democratic	1986-1990
Walter J. Hickel	Independent	1990-1994
Tony Knowles	Democratic	1994-2002
Frank Murkowski	Republican	2002-2006
Sarah Palin	Republican	2006-2009
Sean Parnell	Republican	2009-2014
Bill Walker	Independent	2014-2018
Mike Dunleavy	Republican	2018-

of the cities have elected city councils.

Revenue. Much of the income of Alaska's government comes directly from oil and gas production. Petroleum companies pay the state production taxes and *royalties,* a share of their profits. In addition, the state receives revenue from taxes on corporate income, property, and tobacco. Alaska also gets money from federal grants and other U.S. government programs. The state has no personal income tax or sales tax.

Politics. Fewer contests take place between political parties in Alaska than in most other states. Almost all of Alaska's state and local government officials are appointed or are elected on a *nonpartisan* (no-party) basis. The state's elections for governor have resulted in several victories for both Democrats and Republicans. In elections for president, Alaska's voters have favored the Republican candidate almost every time. For Alaska's electoral votes and voting record in presidential elections, see **Electoral College** (table).

History

Early days. No one knows exactly how long human beings have lived in America. But most scientists believe that the first Americans walked across a land bridge from Asia into what is now Alaska about 15,000 years ago. In the 1700's, when whites first arrived in the Alaskan region, three groups of people—Inuit, Aleuts, and Indians—were living there.

The Inuit lived in the Far North and West. From the north coast of Alaska to Greenland, Inuit hunted such large sea mammals as whales, seals, and polar bears. Some small groups of Inuit inhabited inland areas and hunted caribou.

The Aleuts, closely related to the Inuit, lived on the Aleutian Islands and the Alaska Peninsula. The Aleuts were skillful sea hunters.

The largest Indian groups, the Tlingit and Haida, lived along the coast, where fish and game were plentiful. Some Tsimshian Indians also lived there. The Athabascan Indians lived in the interior, a rugged region without the rich natural resources of the coast. The Athabascans fished and hunted caribou.

European exploration. The Russians were the first Europeans to become interested in the Alaskan region. In 1648, a group of Russians, led by Semen I. Dezhnev,

Anchorage Museum of History and Art

Totem poles carved by the Haida Indians stand at Kasaan, on Prince of Wales Island. Totem poles are a traditional Indian art form in the Pacific Northwest. They symbolize tribes or families.

sailed through the strait separating northeastern Asia and northwestern North America. In 1725, Czar Peter the Great of Russia commissioned Vitus Bering, a Danish navigator, to explore the North Pacific region. Bering and his crew traveled more than 6,000 miles (9,700 kilometers) across Russia and Asia. Then they built a ship and in 1728 sailed through the strait navigated earlier by Dezhnev. This body of water later became known as the Bering Strait. But Bering did not sight the North American mainland because of fog.

In 1741, Bering and Aleksei Chirikov, a Russian explorer, led a second expedition to the region. Bering's party sighted Mount St. Elias in southeastern Alaska and landed on what is now Kayak Island.

Expeditions from England, France, and Spain soon reached Alaskan waters. Most of these explorers sought a sea route between the Atlantic and Pacific oceans.

The Russian era. Members of the second Bering expedition returned to Russia with sea otter furs. Russian traders and hunters then developed a brisk fur trade on the Aleutian Islands and later on the mainland. Fur traders enslaved the Aleuts and, by overhunting, nearly destroyed populations of fur-bearing animals in the Aleutians. In 1784, Gregory Shelikof, a trader, established the first white settlement in Alaska, then called *Russian America,* on Kodiak Island.

In 1799, Russia chartered the Russian-American Company, a trading firm. Alexander Baranof became the firm's chief manager. Baranof moved the company's headquarters to Novo Arkhangelsk (New Archangel, now Sitka), which he captured from the Tlingit Indians. Novo Arkhangelsk became the largest town in Russian America. Baranof managed company affairs profitably for the stockholders, and he established good relations with many native groups. The Russian-American Company sent Russian Orthodox priests to convert the native Alaskans to Christianity.

In 1818, Baranof retired, and the company began to lose money. Russian naval commanders then ruled the colony.

In 1824 and 1825, Russia signed separate treaties with the United States and the United Kingdom. These pacts recognized latitude 54°40' as the southern boundary of Russian territory in America. As part of the agreements, Russia gave the United States and the United Kingdom trading rights along Alaska's Pacific Coast.

American purchase. The Russians tried to develop several industries, including coal mining, shipbuilding, and whale hunting. But by the 1850's, the fur trade had declined and the company's other enterprises had begun to fail. After the Crimean War (1853-1856) weakened Russia, the country became eager to sell Alaska. United States Secretary of State William H. Seward agreed to buy the region for $7,200,000, about 2 cents per acre (5 cents per hectare). On March 30, 1867, he signed the Treaty of Cession of Russian America to the United States. Some Americans opposed the purchase. They called Alaska such names as *Seward's Folly, Seward's Icebox,* and *Icebergia.* But many Americans favored the acquisition. Congress approved the purchase, and American troops raised the U.S. flag at Sitka on Oct. 18, 1867.

Congress did not provide for an Alaskan government during the next 17 years. Alaska was administered first by the War Department, next by the Treasury Department, and then by the Navy Department. These three agencies had little interest in the local problems of the region.

A few American companies became interested in Alaska's rich salmon fisheries. In 1878, they built the first canneries in Alaska.

In 1884, Congress passed the first Organic Act. This act established Alaska as a "civil and judicial district." It provided for a governor, a code of laws, and a federal court. But the laws were the laws of Oregon, and they were not adapted to Alaskan conditions. Congress kept the power to make laws for Alaska.

The gold rush. In 1880, Joseph Juneau and Richard T. Harris discovered gold deposits along Gastineau Channel in southeastern Alaska. This discovery led to the founding of the city of Juneau. In 1896, prospectors found rich gold deposits in the Klondike district of Canada's Yukon region, just across the border from Alaska. The discovery led to the Klondike and Alaska gold rush of 1897-1898. Miners discovered gold at what is now Nome in 1898 and in the Fairbanks area in 1902. The three gold discoveries attracted thousands of people hoping to strike it rich and aroused nationwide interest in Alaska. Alaska's population nearly doubled in 10 years, reaching 63,592 by 1900.

The early 1900's. The gold discoveries focused congressional attention on Alaska. In 1903, a group of U.S. senators toured the territory to learn of Alaska's needs. They recommended that the government construct a system of transportation routes there. Congress then created a Board of Road Commissioners for Alaska, which built and maintained wagon roads, trails, bridges, and ferries throughout the territory.

In 1906, Congress allowed Alaskans to elect their own delegate to Congress. They chose Frank H. Waskey, a Democrat. He could speak in the House of Representatives but was not allowed to vote. During this period, James W. Wickersham, a federal judge, rallied Alaskans to the cause of more self-government for Alaska. In 1908, Wickersham was elected Alaska's delegate to Congress. In 1912, Congress passed the second Organic Act, which gave Alaska a territorial legislature with limited powers.

The Alaska Native Brotherhood (ANB) was formed in 1913. It was joined by the Alaska Native Sisterhood two years later. These organizations sought to unite the native communities of the region and fought for the political interests of its members. The groups helped achieve voting rights, integrated classrooms, and other civil rights for Alaska's native peoples.

In 1929, the ANB enlisted Wickersham to pursue a settlement for native lands seized by the federal government. Wickersham failed to persuade Congress to recognize native land claims. But the work of his successors and native groups eventually led to the Alaska Native Claims Settlement Act of 1971.

World War II (1939-1945) caused great changes in Alaska. The United States recognized the military importance of the territory, which lay close to Asia, and sent thousands of workers there to build and maintain military installations. In 1942, the Japanese bombed Dutch Harbor in the Aleutian Islands and occupied Kiska and Attu, two islands in the chain. These islands were the

Historic Alaska

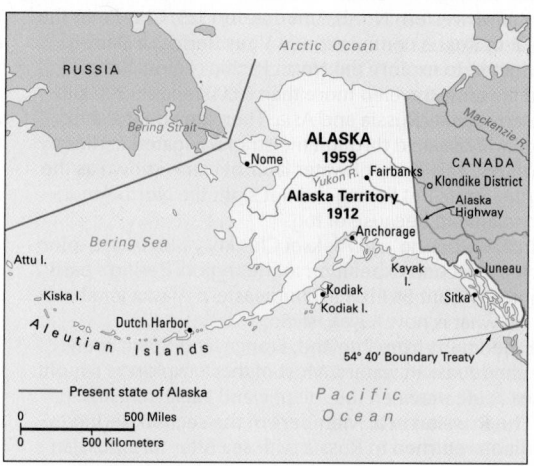

WORLD BOOK map

The Bering Strait separates Alaska from Russia. It was named after Danish navigator Captain Vitus Bering, who explored the waters around Alaska in the early 1700's.

Alaska was home to Inuit, Aleuts, and Indians before Russians arrived in the 1700's. The United States purchased the region in 1867. Alaska became a U.S. territory in 1912 and a state in 1959.

The gold rush of 1897 and 1898 began after the discovery of gold in Yukon, just across the border from Alaska. Prospectors later found gold near what are now Nome and Fairbanks.

Important dates in Alaska

WORLD BOOK illustrations by Richard Bonson, The Art Agency

1741   The second Vitus Bering expedition landed on what is now Kayak Island.

1784   Russians established the first white settlement in Alaska, on Kodiak Island.

1824-1825   Russia agreed to recognize latitude 54°40′ as the southern boundary of Alaska.

1867   The United States purchased Alaska from Russia at a cost of $7,200,000, or about 2 cents per acre (5 cents per hectare).

1884   Congress gave Alaska laws and a federal court.

1897-1898   The Klondike and Alaska gold rush started.

1906   Alaskans elected their first delegate to the U.S. Congress.

1912   Congress established Alaska as a U.S. territory.

1942   The Japanese bombed Dutch Harbor and invaded the Aleutians. The Alaska Highway was completed.

1958   Congress approved Alaskan statehood on June 30.

1959   Alaska became the 49th state on January 3.

1964   One of the largest earthquakes ever known to strike

North America occurred in the area around Anchorage and Valdez.

1968   Large oil reserves were discovered near Prudhoe Bay.

1971   Congress passed the Alaska Native Claims Settlement Act, giving 44 million acres (18 million hectares) of land to native Alaskans.

1977   Workers completed construction of a pipeline to carry oil from Prudhoe Bay to Valdez.

1980   Congress passed the Alaska National Interest Lands Conservation Act, which placed about a fourth of the state's land in the National Park System.

1989   The *Exxon Valdez* dumped nearly 11 million gallons (42 million liters) of oil into Prince William Sound in one of the largest oil spills in United States history.

1998   The Alaska SeaLife Center, a science facility devoted to the study and protection of the state's marine ecosystem, opened in Seward.

2006   Sarah Palin took office as Alaska's first woman governor.

A U.S. Treasury warrant for $7,200,000 was used to purchase Alaska from Russia in 1867. The price came to about 2 cents per acre (5 cents per hectare).

only part of North America invaded during World War II. The government built the Alaska Highway in 1942, mainly as a military supply road. In 1943, about 152,000 military personnel were stationed in Alaska. United States troops recovered Kiska and Attu later that year, and the war in Alaska ended. But the military impact altered the territory forever.

Statehood. The war led to demands that Congress admit the territory to statehood. The first Alaskan statehood bill was introduced in Congress in 1916, but it did not receive a hearing. Other statehood bills were introduced from the mid-1940's until 1958. In 1958, Congress voted to admit Alaska to the Union. On Jan. 3, 1959, President Dwight D. Eisenhower signed the proclamation declaring Alaska the 49th state. Alaska became the first new state since 1912. William A. Egan, a Democrat, became the first elected governor of Alaska.

Alaska found its first years of statehood difficult and costly. It had to take over the expenses of public services that the federal government had provided. Congress helped by giving Alaska some buildings, transition grants, and other funding. Alaska also received funds from the lease of public lands and the right to claim 103.5 million acres (41.9 million hectares) of federal land over a 25-year period. State selection of lands began soon afterward. Alaska's Inuit and Indians, however, protested the selection process. They charged that the process did not recognize their claims of ownership or their traditional way of life, in which small bands moved over large areas hunting, fishing, and gathering food. These and other issues spurred the formation of the Alaska Federation of Natives (AFN) in 1966. The organization included representatives from nearly every group of native people and helped lead the fight for a full set-

A massive earthquake rocked Alaska on March 27, 1964. In Anchorage, the city hit hardest by the quake, buildings crumbled and pavement fell 30 feet (9 meters) in a few seconds. The earthquake was one of the most powerful ever recorded on the North American continent.

tlement of Alaska native land claims.

During the 1960's, the state improved its transportation facilities. It developed a state ferry system, the "Marine Highway," to serve coastal cities.

In 1964, one of the biggest earthquakes ever known to hit North America shook the area around Anchorage and Valdez. It measured 9.2 on the moment magnitude scale. The quake and the *tsunami* (series of huge, destructive ocean waves) that it caused killed 131 people and resulted in over $300 million in property damage.

The discovery of oil. In 1968, the Atlantic Richfield Company announced the discovery of a giant oil field at Prudhoe Bay on the Arctic Coastal Plain. It was one of the greatest oil discoveries in history. This oil field has the largest reserves of oil in North America. In 1969, Alaska auctioned oil and gas leases on the field's 450,000 acres (182,000 hectares) and earned over $900 million. Construction of a pipeline to carry oil about 800 miles (1,300 kilometers) across the state, from Prudhoe Bay to the port of Valdez, began in 1974. The pipeline was completed in 1977 at a total cost of about $8 billion, and oil production began.

The development of the Prudhoe Bay oil field provided new jobs and greatly increased state revenues during the late 1970's and early 1980's. In 1976, the state's voters had approved an amendment to the state Constitution that created the Alaska Permanent Fund, a savings account that belongs to all the people of Alaska. The amendment calls for at least 25 percent of all money earned by mineral development to be deposited into this fund. In 1980, the high revenues created by the oil boom enabled the state government to abolish individual state income taxes. In 1982, every Alaskan resident of six months or more began receiving dividend payments from the Alaska Permanent Fund.

Land-use issues. From 1971 to 1980, the federal government set aside large amounts of land for native Alas-

kans and for conservation purposes. In 1971, President Richard M. Nixon signed the Alaska Native Claims Settlement Act. This revolutionary measure gave $962.5 million and about 44 million acres (18 million hectares) of land to the state's Inuit and Indians. The act created 12 regional corporations to administer the money and the land. A 13th corporation was added later. Every Alaskan Inuit and Indian received shares in the corporations.

In 1978, 56 million acres (23 million hectares) of Alaskan land were set aside as national monuments. In 1980, Congress passed the Alaska National Interest Lands Conservation Act. This act added more than 104 million acres (42 million hectares) to the conservation system in Alaska. It established the boundaries for a widespread network of federal, state, native, and private lands.

The 1980 conservation act gave rural Alaskans priority in hunting and fishing for food on federal lands. Many urban Alaskans who hunt and fish for sport complained that these provisions discriminated against them. Disputes over hunting and fishing rights led to increasing racial tensions between urban whites and rural native people. In the 1990's, when Alaskans still failed to comply with the act's provisions, the federal government took over fish and game management on these lands.

Recent developments. In 1989, an oil tanker, the *Exxon Valdez,* struck a reef in Prince William Sound in southeastern Alaska, causing one of the largest oil spills in U.S. history. Nearly 11 million gallons (42 million liters) of crude oil spilled into the sound. The oil polluted beaches and fishing waters and destroyed wildlife. Most of the cleanup work at the sound was completed in 1992 at a cost of more than $2 billion. But scientists continued to work toward restoring the ecological balance of the area. In 1998, the Alaska SeaLife Center opened in Seward, Alaska. Much of the center's construction was funded by money from a settlement in the *Exxon Valdez* case. In 2006, Sarah Palin became the first woman elected governor of Alaska. In 2008, Palin became the Republican nominee for U.S. vice president. She resigned as governor in 2009.

Falling oil prices led to a state budget crisis beginning in 2015. Lawmakers considered cuts in government positions to trim the state's deficit. In 2018, legislators moved to reduce the deficit by passing a law allowing the state to access billions of dollars from the Alaska Permanent Fund.   F. Patrick Fitzgerald and Claus-M. Naske

Related articles in *World Book* include:

Biographies

Bartlett, Edward L.	Gruening, Ernest	Palin, Sarah Heath
Bering, Vitus	Muir, John	Seward, William H.

Cities and towns

Anchorage	Juneau	Sitka
Fairbanks	Nome	

History

Gold rush	State, Department of (picture:
Haida Indians	Secretary of State William
Klondike	H. Seward)
	Tlingit Indians

Physical features

Aleutian Islands	Denali	Saint Elias
Arctic Ocean	Inside Passage	Mountains
Bering Sea	Pacific Ocean	Yukon River
Coast Ranges	Pribilof Islands	

Terry Domico, Earth Images

Construction of the Trans-Alaska Pipeline began in 1974 and was completed in 1977. The pipeline carries oil from Prudhoe Bay to the port of Valdez, a distance of about 800 miles (1,300 kilometers). It cost about $8 billion to build.

Outline

I. People
   A. Population   C. Libraries and museums
   B. Schools
II. Visitor's guide
III. Land and climate
   A. Land regions   D. Rivers and lakes
   B. Federally protected   E. Glaciers
      lands   F. Plant and animal life
   C. Coastline   G. Climate
IV. Economy
   A. Natural resources   G. Agriculture
   B. Service industries   H. Fur industry
   C. Mining   I. Electric power and utilities
   D. Manufacturing   J. Transportation
   E. Fishing industry   K. Communication
   F. Forestry
V. Government
   A. Constitution   E. Local government
   B. Executive   F. Revenue
   C. Legislature   G. Politics
   D. Courts
VI. History

Questions

What is Alaska's "Marine Highway"?
Why do summer crops ripen quickly in central Alaska?
What is Alaska's most valuable mineral? What had been the state's most valuable mineral for many years?
What three groups of people lived in Alaska before Europeans arrived?

Additional resources

Level I

Hamilton, Sue L. *Iditarod.* ABDO, 2013.
Miller, Debbie S. *Survival at 40 Below.* Walker, 2010. This book describes how Arctic animals survive the winter in northern Alaska.
Orr, Tamra B. *Alaska.* Rev. ed. Children's Pr., 2014.
Sandler, Martin W. *The Impossible Rescue: The True Story of an Amazing Arctic Adventure.* Candlewick Pr., 2012.
Seiple, Samantha. *Ghosts in the Fog: The Untold Story of Alaska's WWII Invasion.* Scholastic, 2011.

Level II

Borneman, Walter R. *Alaska.* HarperCollins, 2003.
Brinkley, Douglas. *The Quiet World: Saving Alaska's Wilderness Kingdom, 1879-1960.* Harper, 2011.
Crowell, Aron L., and others, eds. *Living Our Cultures, Sharing Our Heritage: The First Peoples of Alaska.* Smithsonian Bks., 2010.
Heacox, Kim. *John Muir and the Ice that Started a Fire: How a Visionary and the Glaciers of Alaska Changed America.* Lyons Pr., 2014.

Alaska, University of, is a state-supported system of higher education. The system includes three multicampus universities, community colleges, and a network of services for rural Alaska. The system includes the University of Alaska Anchorage (UAA), which, in addition to the Anchorage campus, includes Kenai Peninsula College, Kodiak College, Matanuska-Susitna College, and Prince William Sound College. The University of Alaska Fairbanks (UAF) includes the campuses of Bristol Bay, Chukchi, Fairbanks, Interior Alaska, Kuskokwim, and Northwest, and the Community and Technical College. The University of Alaska Southeast has campuses in Juneau, Ketchikan, and Sitka.

The university was founded in 1917 as the Alaska Agricultural College and School of Mines in Fairbanks. It was renamed the University of Alaska in 1935. The system's website at http://www.alaska.edu offers additional information.

Critically reviewed by the University of Alaska

See also **Alaska** (picture).

Alaska Highway is a 1,397-mile (2,248-kilometer) road that runs between Dawson Creek, British Columbia, and Delta Junction, Alaska. The Richardson Highway links Delta Junction and nearby Fairbanks. The Alaska Highway is the only highway that connects Alaska with the road systems of the other states and Canada.

United States Army engineers and civilian contractors built the Alaska Highway as a military supply route in 1942 and 1943, when the United States was fighting in World War II. The highway was originally known as the Alcan Highway. The highway's original length was 1,422 miles (2,288 kilometers). The southern 1,221 miles (1,965 kilometers) of the road crossed Canada and became the property of Canada on April 1, 1946. Reconstruction has shortened the length in Canada to 1,196 miles (1,925 kilometers). Nearly all of the highway has a paved surface. The region's extreme weather, however, occasionally damages the surface and can lead to uneven driving conditions.   John C. Hudson

Alaskan malamute is a strong, rugged sled dog that came originally from Alaska. The dog is large and compactly built, and its thick coat usually is wolf-gray or black and white, with darker markings on the head. The malamute carries its bushy tail over its back. When it sleeps, the Alaskan malamute curls up so that its tail covers its nose. Most malamutes weigh from 75 to 85 pounds (34 to 39 kilograms). A group of Inuit people called Malemiuts developed the breed. The Inuit were formerly known as Eskimos.

Critically reviewed by the American Kennel Club

See also **Dog** (picture: Working dogs); **Sled dog.**

Alateen. See Al-Anon.

Al-Azhar University is one of the oldest universities in the world. The university was founded about A.D. 970 in Cairo, Egypt, and it is a center of Islamic learning. The university has campuses in several Egyptian cities and branches in a number of other countries.   P. A. McGinley

Alba, *AL buh* or *AHL bah,* **Duke of** (1507-1582), also called the Duke of Alva, was a Spanish general and diplomat who served Kings Charles I and Philip II of Spain. In 1567, Philip made Alba governor of the Netherlands and ordered him to crush a revolt that had broken out there against Spain. Alba's court sentenced about 1,200 rebels to death and was called the Council of Blood. His brutality and harsh taxes only made Netherlanders more determined to be free. Patriots seized the major coastal towns and attacked Spanish shipping. They cut the dikes, and the floodwaters stopped Alba's army. Alba returned to Spain in disgrace. But in 1580, he helped Philip conquer Portugal. The duke's full name was Fernando Álvarez de Toledo. He was born on Oct. 29, 1507, and died on Dec. 11, 1582.

Carla Rahn Phillips and William D. Phillips, Jr.

Albacore. See Tuna.

Albania is a small, mountainous nation in the Balkan Peninsula of southeastern Europe. It is one of the least developed countries in Europe. Most of the people make their living through agriculture.

Albania's name in Albanian, the official language, is Shqipëria, which means *The Land of the Eagle.* The country's full, official name is Republika e Shqipërisë (Republic of Albania). Tiranë is its capital and largest city.

Albania was part of the Ottoman Empire for more than 400 years. It gained its independence in 1912. From 1944 until the early 1990's, Albania was a Communist country.

Government. A president serves as the head of state in Albania. A prime minister serves as head of government and presides over a cabinet, which helps carry out the functions of the government. The prime minister is the country's most powerful official.

Albania's parliament, called the Assembly, has one house of 140 members. The Assembly elects the president, who then appoints the prime minister. The prime minister, with parliament's approval, forms a cabinet. Members of the Assembly are elected by the people to four-year terms.

The country is divided into 12 *qarqe* (counties). A council of elected representatives governs each of these counties.

People. Albanians are divided into two major groups—the Ghegs and the Tosks—according to which Albanian dialect they speak. Most of the Ghegs live north of the Shkumbin (also spelled *Shkumbi)* River, and most of the Tosks live south of the river. A few Greeks live in the regions that adjoin Greece.

About two-fifths of the people live on farms or in rural villages. A few Albanians along the Adriatic coast earn their living by fishing. Only eight cities in Albania have populations of more than 50,000.

Living standards in Albania are extremely low compared with those of other European countries. The incomes of most Albanians are small, but health care, social services, and education are free. Bread, vegetables, and such dairy products as cheese and milk make up the daily diet of most of the people.

Approximately 70 percent of all Albanians are Muslims. Most of the rest, including the country's Greeks and some of the Tosks, belong to Eastern Orthodox Churches.

All of Albania's children must complete eight years of school. Aleksandër Xhuvani University in Elbasan and the University of Tiranë are among the country's largest universities.

Land. Mountains cover most of Albania. The North Albanian Alps tower about 8,500 feet (2,590 meters) above sea level. Mount Korab (9,068 feet, or 2,764 meters), along the country's northeastern border, is Albania's highest point. A coastal plain lies along the Adriatic Sea. Scrub forests cover approximately 30 percent of the country.

Albania's major rivers, the Bunë, Drin, Shkumbin, and Vjosë, all empty into the Adriatic Sea. But the Bunë is the only river that can be used for shipping. Albania shares Lake Scutari (also called Lake Skhodra) with Montenegro, Lake Ohrid with North Macedonia, and Lake Prespa with North Macedonia and Greece.

Along the Adriatic, the climate is mild, with hot, dry summers and rainy winters. The mountains have a mod-

Albania

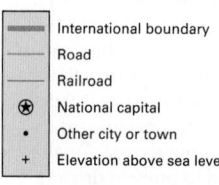

▬▬▬	International boundary
▬▬▬	Road
▬▬▬	Railroad
✪	National capital
•	Other city or town
+	Elevation above sea level

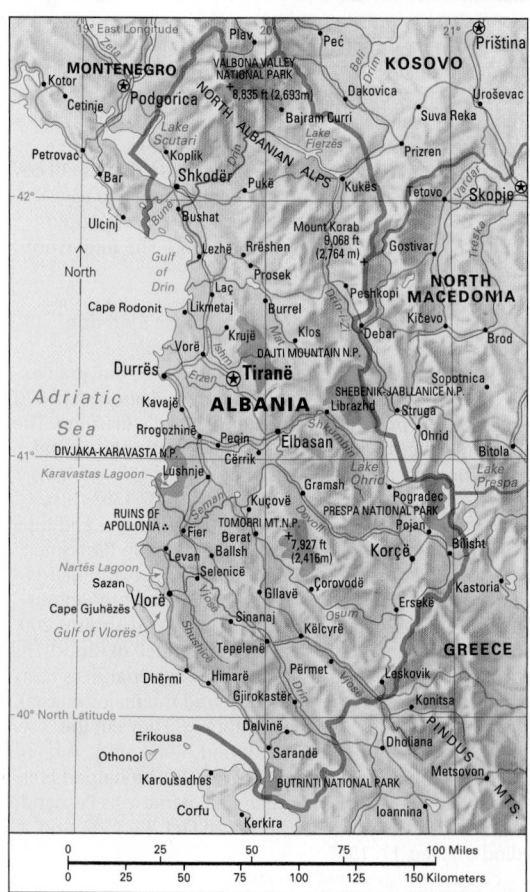

WORLD BOOK maps

Facts in brief

Capital: Tiranë.

Official language: Albanian.

Area: 11,100 mi² (28,748 km²). *Greatest distances*—north-south, 215 mi (346 km); east-west, 90 mi (145 km). *Coastline*—175 mi (282 km).

Population: *Estimated 2022 population*—2,890,000; density, 260 per mi² (101 per km²); distribution, 62 percent urban, 38 percent rural. *2020 official government estimate*—2,845,955.

Chief products: *Agriculture*—beef, corn, grapes, milk, potatoes, sheep, wheat. *Mining*—chromite, copper, natural gas, petroleum. *Manufacturing*—cement, food products, textiles.

Flag: A two-headed black eagle appears on a red field. See **Flag** (picture: Flags of Europe).

Money: *Basic unit*—lek.

erate climate. The country's average annual rainfall varies from 40 to 60 inches (100 to 150 centimeters).

Economy. Albania has been working on internal economic reform with the help of the European Union, but it remains one of the poorest countries in Europe. Agriculture is an important sector of Albania's economy, and employs more Albanians than any other economic activity. The country's chief crops include corn, grapes, olives, potatoes, tomatoes, and wheat. Farmers also raise such livestock as beef and dairy cattle, chickens, goats, and sheep.

Albania is rich in mineral resources. Albania's mines produce chromite, copper, lignite, limestone, and other minerals. The country also produces natural gas and petroleum. Albania has relatively few factories. Its factory products include cement, food products, and textiles.

Albania's exports include chromite and other minerals, footwear, fruits and vegetables, and textiles. Farm and industrial machinery and food are among its chief imports. Albania imports much more than it exports. Italy is its main trading partner. *Remittances* (money sent home) from Albanians living in Greece and Italy are also important to the economy.

Buses and trains are common means of transportation in Albania. Private ownership of automobiles was illegal until 1991. Albania's railroad network connects Tiranë and Durrës—the country's chief port—with such important industrial centers as Elbasan, Fier, Shkodër, and Vlorë. A small airport outside Tiranë links Albania with several European countries.

History. About 300 B.C., the Illyrian kingdom covered much of what is now Albania. Greece also had colonies in Albania then, and Greek civilization influenced the Illyrians. In 167 B.C., Roman forces conquered the Illyrians and spread Roman civilization into Albania. When the Roman Empire split in A.D. 395, much of Albania be-

came part of the Eastern Roman, or Byzantine, Empire. Between the 300's and 1000's, Goths, Bulgarians, Slavs, and Normans invaded Albania. Southern Albania was part of the Byzantine Empire until 1204. In the 1300's, much of Albania became part of the Serbian Empire.

Ottoman rule. The Albanians long resisted attempts by the Ottoman Empire to take over the country. The most distinguished leader against the Ottomans was Scanderbeg (also spelled Skanderbeg or Skënderbeg), who became Albania's national hero. After Scanderbeg's death in 1468, the Ottomans conquered Albania, and it became part of the Ottoman Empire. However, during more than 400 years of Ottoman rule, Albanian chiefs controlled most local matters. Many Albanians became Muslims during this period.

Independence. A number of local uprisings took place in Albania during the Ottoman rule, but a nationalist movement did not develop in the country until the 1800's. In 1878, a group of Albanian leaders organized the League of Prizren, which called for Albanian self-government within the Ottoman Empire. But Albania remained under Ottoman rule until 1912, when it gained independence during the First Balkan War. In 1913, the great European powers established Albania's borders, and the country became a self-governing principality. The European powers selected William of Wied, a German prince, as ruler. But he ruled for only a few months.

Austro-Hungarians, Italians, Serbs, and French occupied Albania during World War I (1914-1918). The Italians remained until 1920, when Albania insisted on its independence. Ahmed Beg Zogu seized power in 1925, proclaimed Albania a republic, and became the country's first president. In 1928, Zogu made himself King Zog I. He ruled until 1939.

World War II. Italy invaded Albania in April 1939 and made the nation part of the Italian Empire. World War II

Ferdinando Scianna, Magnum

Tiranë is Albania's largest city. It has been the country's capital since 1920. Tiranë's central district, *left,* has many modern stone buildings.

began later that year. When Italy surrendered to the Allies in 1943, during the war, German troops occupied Albania.

During World War II, there were three main resistance movements in Albania: (1) a nationalist movement called Balli Kombetar, led by Midhat Frashëri; (2) a royalist group called the Legality Movement, headed by Abas Kupi; and (3) a Communist organization called the National Liberation Front (NLF), led by Enver Hoxha. These groups fought against one another as well as against the German occupation forces.

Communist control. In 1944, the Germans were driven out of Albania, and the Communists gained control of the country. Hoxha established a Communist government at Tiranë during that year, and he began ruling the country as first secretary of the Communist Party. The Communists greatly restricted the people's freedom.

The Communist Party in Yugoslavia had helped the Communists of Albania organize the NLF, and relations with Albania remained close until 1948. But in that year, a split developed between the Soviet Union and Yugoslavia. The split resulted in the expulsion of Yugoslavia from the Cominform, a Soviet-dominated organization of European Communist parties. The people of Albania supported the Soviet Union to free themselves from Yugoslav influence. They also hoped to obtain Soviet aid in gaining control of a part of Yugoslavia where Albanians lived.

Albania's close relations with the Soviet Union ended in the early 1960's. At that time, a break occurred between the Soviet Union and China over the interpretations of certain Communist teachings. In particular, China rejected the Soviet Union's policy of coexistence with non-Communist countries. Albania supported China in the dispute. In 1961, Albania and the Soviet Union broke off relations. At about the same time, Albania limited its contact with most other nations.

China provided Albania with technical assistance and other aid from the 1960's to the late 1970's. Albania then became China's only ally in Europe. Albanian delegates at the United Nations (UN) played a leading role in the efforts that led to China's admission to the UN in 1971.

Relations between Albania and China became strained during the late 1970's. Albania's leaders accused China of abandoning Communist principles. They criticized China for improving relations with Yugoslavia and the United States. In 1978, China responded to these attacks by cutting off all aid to Albania. In the early 1990's, Albania restored relations with the United States, improved relations with China, and increased its contact with other nations. In addition, Albania restored relations with the Soviet Union prior to that country's breakup in 1991.

Hoxha died in 1985, after ruling Albania for more than 40 years. Ramiz Alia succeeded Hoxha as first secretary of the Communist Party. Alia had been elected president of Albania in 1982, and he continued to serve as president. Alia's government introduced some social and economic reforms in an attempt to avoid the downfall suffered by other Communist governments in Eastern Europe in 1989. The government again allowed the public practice of religion. In 1967, the government had outlawed all religious groups and seized their property. But places of worship began to reopen in 1990. Another reform called for paying workers bonuses to work harder and produce more goods as a way to ease shortages.

However, the people felt that the reforms did not go far enough. In December 1990, Albanians staged protests to try to force the Communists from power. As a result, the Communists allowed the formation of new political parties.

End of Communist rule. In March 1991, multiparty national elections were held. The Communists won a majority of seats in the National Assembly and remained in power. But anti-Communist protests continued, and the Communist prime minister and cabinet resigned in June.

Bruce Coleman Ltd.

Albanian peasants meet at a livestock market in a rural area. Farmers raise such livestock as beef and dairy cattle, chickens, goats, *shown here,* and sheep.

Hutchison Library

A statue of Scanderbeg, Albania's national hero, stands in Tiranë. Scanderbeg led a resistance movement against the Ottoman Empire during the 1400's.

Communists and non-Communists who had given up their party affiliations formed a temporary government. Parliamentary elections in March 1992 gave the Democratic Party a majority of seats. In April, Alia resigned as president. The Assembly then elected Sali Berisha of the Democratic Party as president. Berisha supported the creation of a free-enterprise economy, and his government introduced a program for economic reform.

In parliamentary elections held in 1996, the Democratic Party again won a majority of seats in the National Assembly. However, international observers criticized the elections for ballot fraud and other irregularities.

Tens of thousands of Albanians staged violent protests across the country against Berisha's government in January 1997. The protests began after the collapse of investment schemes in which hundreds of thousands of people lost their savings. Most investors blamed the government for not warning them against the risky investments, and they claimed that the government profited from the funds. Many people demanded Berisha's resignation. He remained in office but formed a coalition government. Unrest continued to spread, and Albania fell into disorder. Thousands left the country.

In April, the UN sent an international force to oversee relief efforts and help restore order. In parliamentary elections held in June and July, the Socialist Party defeated Berisha's Democratic Party by a landslide. Socialist leader Rexhep Meidani became president. Some measure of calm returned, and the UN force left in August.

Recent developments. In 1998 and 1999, almost half a million ethnic Albanian refugees streamed into Albania from the Yugoslav province of Kosovo. They were fleeing attacks by Serbian forces. With help from international organizations, Albania housed the refugees for several months until it was safe for them to return.

In 1998, Albania adopted a new constitution. The Socialist Party retained control of parliament in elections in 2001. In 2002, Meidani's term expired, and parliament chose former defense minister Alfred Moisiu as Alba-

nia's new president. Disputes arose over the results of parliamentary elections held in July 2005. That September, Albania's Central Election Commission confirmed that the Democratic Party had won the most seats.

Albania's National Assembly elected Bamir Topi as president in July 2007. Topi was the deputy leader of the Democratic Party, which continued as the governing party. In June 2012, the Assembly elected former interior minister Bujar Nishani as the republic's new president.

Sharon L. Wolchik

Related articles in *World Book* include:

Adriatic Sea	Hoxha, Enver	Tiranë
Balkans	Ionian Sea	Warsaw Pact

Albany (pop. 97,856) is the capital of New York and one of the oldest cities in the United States. It was first settled in 1624 and became a city in 1686. Albany lies on the Hudson River in eastern New York and has an active port, though it is 150 miles (241 kilometers) from the Atlantic Ocean. The Hudson River has been cleaned out and deepened so that ocean ships can reach the city. For the location of Albany, see **New York** (political map).

Description. Albany, the seat of Albany County, covers 21 square miles (54 square kilometers) on the west bank of the Hudson River. The business district lies on a slope leading down to the river. The historic and inner-city neighborhoods cluster around the downtown area. In the 1900's, the city expanded westward, and newer, more prosperous neighborhoods lie mainly to the west and southwest. Albany and two other cities—Schenectady and Troy—form a metropolitan area of 870,716 people. The area is often called the Capital Region.

The State University of New York (SUNY) has its system headquarters downtown at SUNY Plaza. The University at Albany is part of the SUNY system. Other colleges in the area include the College of St. Rose, Rensselaer Polytechnic Institute, the three Sage Colleges, Siena College, and Union University.

Points of interest in the city include the Albany Institute of History and Art; the Ten Broeck, Schuyler, and Cherry Hill mansions, all built in the 1700's; the State Capitol; and the Empire State Plaza, a large complex of government office towers and other buildings. The plaza includes the New York State Museum; the New York State Library; the Egg, an oval-shaped building with two theaters; and the 44-story Corning Tower, the tallest building in the state outside of New York City.

Economy. Albany is a center of government, education, health care, banking, insurance, and other service industries. It is also an important transportation center. Many workers commute, mainly by automobile, from other cities and towns in the Capital Region. The area is sometimes called Tech Valley owing to its research universities and high-technology companies. Albany International Airport, northwest of the city, serves the region.

Government and history. Albany has a mayor-council form of government. The voters elect the mayor to a two-year term. Council members are elected to four-year terms.

Iroquois people lived in what is now the Albany area before European settlers arrived. In 1609, the English explorer Henry Hudson and his crew became the first Europeans to reach the site, during a voyage for the Dutch East India Company, a trading firm. In 1624, Dutch settlers established Fort Orange on the west bank of the

Hudson River in what is now downtown Albany. The settlement around the fort became the Village of Beverwyck in 1652. In 1664, the English claimed the region, and the settlement was renamed Albany for the Duke of York and Albany, the English king's brother. On July 27, 1686, Albany received a charter incorporating it as a city.

Albany played an important role in the American Colonies as a river port, a fur-trading center, and a military post. The city is nicknamed *Cradle of the Union* because American statesman Benjamin Franklin presented his Plan of Union there at the Albany Congress in 1754. It was the first formal proposal to unite the American Colonies. Albany was chosen as the state capital in 1797.

Albany's most rapid period of growth followed the completion of the Erie Canal in 1825. The canal opened the way for barge traffic between Albany and Buffalo and connected the Hudson River to the Great Lakes. Albany's population grew from 12,630 in 1820 to 24,209 in 1830. New York's first railroad, the Mohawk and Hudson, began to operate between Albany and Schenectady in 1831. The city was a major railroad center during the last half of the 1800's. Transportation, commerce, and industry flourished during the late 1800's and early 1900's. Albany had 94,151 people in 1900, and 134,995 by 1950.

During the last half of the 1900's, Albany lost population to the suburbs, and many retail stores moved to suburban shopping malls. Manufacturing declined, and service industries became increasingly important to the economy. The Empire State Plaza was completed during this period, as part of a downtown renewal program.

Ray Bromley

See also **Albany Congress; New York.**

Albany Congress was a meeting that adopted the first formal proposal for a political union of the American Colonies. It was held in Albany, New York, in June 1754. Representatives from Massachusetts, New Hampshire, Connecticut, Rhode Island, New York, Pennsylvania, and Maryland met with representatives of the Iroquois tribes at the request of the British government. The purpose of the meeting was to win the loyalty of the Iroquois in view of a threatening war with France, and to work out some form of agreement with them. Colonial representatives included James DeLancey (New York), Thomas Hutchinson (Massachusetts), Stephen Hopkins (Rhode Island), William Pitkin (Connecticut), John Penn (Pennsylvania), and Benjamin Franklin (Pennsylvania).

The delegates realized the real problem was to unify the colonies, and several plans were proposed. The congress adopted Franklin's proposal, often called the Albany Plan of Union. Under it, each colony would send from two to seven representatives to a Grand Council. The council would levy taxes, raise troops, and regulate trade with the Indians. Britain and the colonies failed to seriously consider the plan. The Stamp Act Congress of 1765 marked the colonies' next big step toward an American union (see **Revolution, American** [The Quartering and Stamp acts]). Jack N. Rakove

Al Basrah. See Basra.

Albatross, *AL buh traws,* is the name for any one of several kinds of large sea birds. Albatrosses are found over nearly all oceans, except the North Atlantic. The best-known albatross is the *wandering albatross* of southern seas. It has a white body and darker wings and tail. The spread wings may be up to 11 ½ feet (3.5 meters)

Bruce Coleman Inc.
Wandering albatrosses have a white body with darker wings and tail. Like other albatrosses, they breed on remote islands.

from tip to tip. Its bill is long, heavy, and powerful.

The albatross sometimes follows a ship for days but is seldom seen resting. It feeds on scraps of food thrown from the ship, or on fish and squid. On such food-gathering flights, the wandering albatross has been known to cover more than 9,300 miles (15,000 kilometers) and to maintain an average speed of 35 miles (56 kilometers) per hour for 500 miles (800 kilometers).

Albatrosses come to land only to breed. Thousands of these birds gather on remote islands. The female albatross's single egg is white with brown spots. It is laid on bare ground or in a shallow nest and hatches after about 81 days. The young bird has dark, fluffy down. Two species of albatrosses are commonly found along the Pacific Coast of North America. George L. Hunt, Jr.

Scientific classification. Albatrosses make up the albatross family, Diomedeidae. The scientific name for the wandering albatross is *Diomedea exulans.*

See also **Animal** (picture: The courtship ritual).

Albee, Edward (1928-2016), was a major American playwright who used a wide variety of styles ranging from realism to fantasy. He wrote about the need for human contact and the illusions his characters embrace to face the meaninglessness of existence. Albee gained international fame with *Who's Afraid of Virginia Woolf?* (1962), a moving examination of power struggles and the combination of cruelty and love in marriage.

Albee won the 1967 Pulitzer Prize for *A Delicate Balance* (1966), a study of family relationships and friendships set in an emotionally sterile suburban atmosphere. He won the 1975 Pulitzer Prize for *Seascape* (1975), a fantasy about a middle-aged couple's ability to move beyond a fear of change and the unknown. He received a third Pulitzer Prize in 1994 for *Three Tall Women* (world premiere in Vienna in 1991), about an aged woman's encounter with mortality.

Albee's first plays were short, probing dramas about the materialism, complacency, and alienation he saw in American society. They were influenced by the Theater of the Absurd, a 1950's European drama movement. The plays include *The Zoo Story* (1959), *The Death of Bessie Smith* (1960), *The Sandbox* (1960), and *The American Dream* (1961). Later, he wrote *Homelife* as a companion piece to *The Zoo Story.* These two one-act plays were combined into *Peter and Jerry* (2004), later retitled *At Home at the Zoo.* Among Albee's other plays are *Tiny Alice* (1964), a symbolic religious drama; *The Play About the Baby* (1998), in which an older couple strips away the illusions of a younger couple; and *The Occupant* (2002), about the famous sculptor Louise Nevelson. *The Goat, or Who Is Sylvia?* (2002) is a dark comedy about the mysterious workings of the heart and the necessity for tolerance. *Me, Myself & I* (2008) is a farce about the shifting meanings of language. Albee's essays on the theater were collected in *Stretching My Mind* (2005). Edward Franklin Albee was born on March 12, 1928, in Washington, D.C. He died on Sept. 16, 2016.   Thomas P. Adler

Albéniz, *ahl BAY nees* or *ahl VAY neeth,* **Isaac** (1860-1909), a Spanish composer and pianist, was one of the creators of a national style for Spanish music. His most famous composition, *Iberia* (1908), consists of four books of solo piano music. His orchestral works include *Spanish Rhapsody* (1887) and *Catalonia* (1899). From 1893 to 1900, he lived in Paris, where his music influenced the French composers Claude Debussy and Maurice Ravel. Albéniz died on May 18, 1909.

Isaac Manuel Frescesco Albéniz was born on May 29, 1860, in Camprodón in Catalonia. He gave his first piano recital at the age of 4. He was a respected concert pianist throughout his life.   Vincent McDermott

Albers, Josef (1888-1976), was a German-born painter and teacher. Albers focused on the way colors are made to perform by their relationship within a picture. He limited himself for years to one form: the square. By painting squares within squares, he explored color relationships with more freedom because he was relieved of the problem of form. He called his series of square paintings *Homage to the Square.*

Albers was born on March 19, 1888, in Bottrop. He taught color theory and abstract art at the Bauhaus school of design from 1923 to 1933, then moved to the

Casein painting on Masonite (1956); Corcoran Gallery of Art, William A. Clark Fund

An Albers painting is one of a series the artist called *Homage to the Square.* These abstract works typically consist of three or four squares set inside one another and painted in flat colors.

United States. Albers taught at Black Mountain College from 1933 to 1939 and at Yale University from 1950 to 1960. Albers helped bring about the Bauhaus influence on American design. He became a U.S. citizen in 1939. Albers died on March 25, 1976.   Dore Ashton

Albert I (1875-1934), king of Belgium from 1909 to 1934, was a heroic military leader during World War I (1914-1918). As commander in chief of the Belgian army, he slowed the German advance to France in September 1914. Albert led Belgian and French troops in the final Allied assault in September 1918. After the war, he brought the leaders of Belgium's political parties together to work on the reconstruction of their country.

Albert was born on April 8, 1875, in Brussels. He was the grandson of King Leopold I, a German prince elected king of Belgium in 1831. Albert married Elizabeth, Duchess of Bavaria, in 1900. He succeeded his uncle Leopold II in 1909. As king, Albert worked for equal voting rights for all Belgians. He died on Feb. 17, 1934, mountain climbing near Namur, Belgium. His oldest son succeeded him as Leopold III.   Janet L. Polasky

Albert, Carl Bert (1908-2000), an Oklahoma Democrat, was speaker of the United States House of Representatives from 1971 until he retired in 1977. He had been majority leader of the House since 1962. Albert played an important role in the passage of President Lyndon B. Johnson's domestic program in the mid-1960's. Albert backed Johnson's civil rights proposals even though his district largely opposed them. He died on Feb. 4, 2000.

Albert was born on May 10, 1908, in McAlester, Oklahoma. He graduated from the University of Oklahoma and studied at Oxford University in England on a Rhodes scholarship. He began his first House term in 1947 and was majority whip from 1955 to 1962. Albert was chairman of the platform committee of the 1964 Democratic National Convention and was permanent chairman of the party's 1968 national convention.   Charles Bartlett

Albert, Lake. See Lake Albert.

Albert, Prince (1819-1861), married his first cousin, Queen Victoria of the United Kingdom, in 1840. As prince consort, he was respected for his industry and business sense. Some distrusted him as the queen's adviser because he was not born in England. See **Victoria.**

Albert was born on Aug. 26, 1819, near Coburg, Germany. His father, Ernest, was the Duke of Saxe-Coburg and Saalfeld (from 1826, of Saxe-Coburg and Gotha). Albert's full given name was Francis Charles Augustus Albert Emmanuel. Albert became the adviser and private secretary to the queen. He reorganized the royal household and started a study of politics. In 1841, he was appointed head of a commission to encourage the country's fine arts. He spent his leisure time in museums and art studios, and in parts of London where conditions were either being improved or in need of it. His speeches to the working people showed his ability and tact.

In 1847, Cambridge University elected Albert chancellor. His ideas on education helped alter the academic program, which was soon imitated by Oxford University. At the request of the Duke of Wellington, he helped reorganize the Army training plan during the Crimean War (1853-1856). He was interested in agricultural improvements, and he planned and landscaped Victoria's winter home on the Isle of Wight. He died of typhoid fever on Dec. 14, 1861.   Richard W. Davis

Lake Louise, in southwestern Alberta, is sheltered by the Canadian Rocky Mountains. The lake attracts many tourists.

Alberta

Alberta, the westernmost Prairie Province of Canada, is one of North America's greatest oil-producing regions. About two-thirds of Canada's petroleum comes from oil sands deposits and oil wells that dot Alberta's rolling plains. About three-fourths of Canada's natural gas is from huge deposits that lie near oil fields. Pipelines carry Alberta's oil and natural gas throughout Canada and into the United States. Alberta's major oil fields lie in the central and northern parts of the province.

Petroleum has helped make Alberta prosperous. Oil and natural gas production fees and leases make up the provincial government's greatest source of income. This income has paid a large portion of the cost of Alberta's hospitals, roads, schools, and other public works. Industries related to petroleum and natural gas production provide a large share of the personal income of Alberta's people. Service industries, however, provide the greatest source of personal income. The province's

standard of living is among the highest in Canada.

Alberta also has other resources, including more than half of the known coal deposits of Canada. Other minerals found in the province include natural gas liquids, sand and gravel, and sulfur. Alberta's mining production accounts for about half of the national total.

Alberta is also a leading province in agriculture. In many areas of the province, vast fields of golden wheat can be seen extending to the horizon. Among the provinces, Alberta ranks second, behind only Saskatchewan, in its production of canola and wheat. Alberta also produces more beef cattle than any other Canadian province.

The production of chemicals is the leading manufacturing activity in Alberta. *Petrochemicals* (chemicals made from petroleum) and fertilizer are the province's chief chemicals.

Millions of tourists visit the province yearly. The most popular attractions are the majestic, snow-capped Cana-

Interesting facts about Alberta

The world's largest Easter egg is in Vegreville. It is 26 feet (7.9 meters) long and 18 feet (5.5 meters) wide, stands 31 feet (9.4 meters) high on its base, and weighs about 5,000 pounds (2,300 kilograms). It is called the *Pysanka,* the Ukrainian term for Easter egg. The computer-designed egg has a shell composed of multicolored aluminum pieces joined together to form a colorful pattern.

WORLD BOOK illustrations by Kevin Chadwick

World's largest Easter egg

The world's largest shopping center is the West Edmonton Mall. It has more than 800 shops, the world's largest indoor amusement park, 20 movie theaters, and an ice arena.

The world's foremost dinosaur museum is the Royal Tyrrell Museum of Palaeontology in Drumheller. Opened in 1985, it has dinosaur fossils from throughout the provinces. The museum is named after Joseph Burr Tyrrell, a Canadian geologist who discovered rich beds of dinosaur fossils in Alberta in 1844.

Head-Smashed-In Buffalo Jump, near Fort Macleod, is a cliff that Native Americans used to kill large numbers of buffalo. Archaeological evidence shows that the cliff was used for this purpose during different periods between about 3,600 B.C. and the mid-1800's. Native Americans stampeded buffaloes over the 33-foot (10-meter) cliff while hunters waited below to butcher the animals for meat, hide, and bone. The native Blackfoot people gave the site its present name after a young brave's skull was crushed while he watched from below as buffaloes were being driven over the cliff. They called the place Estipah-Sikikini-kots, meaning "where he got his head smashed in."

Head-Smashed-In Buffalo Jump

© age fotostock/SuperStock

The downtown area of Calgary, Alberta's largest city

dian Rockies along the province's western border. There lie three of Alberta's five national parks—Banff, Jasper, and Waterton Lakes. Lake Louise, which is surrounded by the Canadian Rockies in Banff National Park, is one of the most popular scenic attractions in Canada. Many vacationers go to the province's northern forests to hunt bears, caribou, deer, elk, and moose, or to fish in the sparkling lakes and streams. Others stay at dude ranches in Alberta's cattle country. Tourists visit the forts, missions, and trading posts that were built during Alberta's fur-trading days. Winter skiing in the Canadian Rockies is also an attraction. Unusually clear skies give Alberta many hours of sunshine throughout the year, earning it the nickname *Sunny Alberta.*

The name of the province dates from 1882. During that time, the Canadian government decided to divide the region of land lying between Manitoba and British Columbia into four territorial districts—Alberta, Assiniboia, Athabaska, and Saskatchewan. The Alberta district was named after Princess Louise Caroline Alberta, a daughter of Queen Victoria. The princess was married to the Marquess of Lorne, the Canadian governor general. The princess's first name was given to what is now Alberta's most famous lake, Lake Louise in Banff National Park.

For Alberta's relationship to the other provinces of Canada, see the *World Book* articles on **Canada; Canada, Government of; Canada, History of.**

Alberta in brief

Symbols of Alberta

The provincial flag, adopted in 1968, bears the shield from the coat of arms. The shield has a cross of St. George, which represents Alberta's link with the United Kingdom, and a landscape with mountains, hills, a prairie, and a field of wheat. The shield was adopted as the provincial coat of arms in 1907. A lion and a pronghorn supporting the shield and a crest including a helmet, a beaver, and a crown were added in 1980.

Provincial flag

Provincial coat of arms

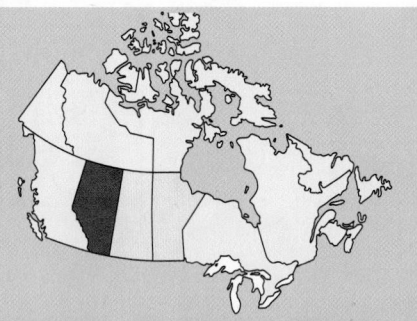

Alberta (brown) is the fourth largest province and the largest of the Prairie Provinces (yellow).

General information

Entered the Dominion: Sept. 1, 1905, with Saskatchewan, as the 8th and 9th provinces.
Provincial abbreviation: AB (postal).
Provincial motto: *Fortis et Liber* (Strong and Free).

The Legislature Building is in Edmonton, the capital of Alberta since it entered the Dominion in 1905.

Land and climate

Area: 255,541 mi² (661,848 km²), including 7,541 mi² (19,531 km²) of inland water.
Elevation: *Highest*—Mount Columbia, 12,294 ft (3,747 m) above sea level. *Lowest*—557 ft (170 m) above sea level along the Slave River in northern Alberta.
Record high temperature: 110 °F (43 °C) at Bassano Dam on July 21, 1931, and at Fort Macleod on July 18, 1941.
Record low temperature: −78 °F (−61 °C) at Fort Vermilion on Jan. 11, 1911.
Average July temperature: 63 °F (17 °C).
Average January temperature: 9 °F (−13 °C).
Average yearly precipitation: 16 in (41 cm).

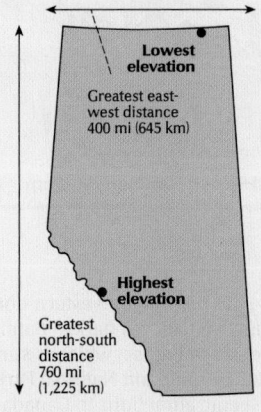

Lowest elevation

Greatest east-west distance 400 mi (645 km)

Highest elevation

Greatest north-south distance 760 mi (1,225 km)

Important dates

Peter Pond of the United States established a trading post near Lake Athabasca.

The North-West Mounted Police established Fort Macleod.

The Canadian Pacific Railway reached Calgary.

| 1754-1755 | 1778 | 1874 | 1876-1877 | 1883 |

Anthony Henday of England explored the Alberta region.

Native Americans surrendered central and southern Alberta to the government through two treaties.

Bird
Great horned owl

Tree
Lodgepole pine

Floral emblem
Prickly rose (prickly wild rose)

People

Population: 4,067,175 (2016 census)
Rank among the provinces: 4th
Density: 16 persons per mi² (6 per km²),
Canada average 10 per mi² (4 per km²)
Distribution: 84 percent urban, 16 percent rural
Largest cities and towns*

Calgary	1,239,220
Edmonton	932,546
Red Deer	100,418
Lethbridge	92,729
St. Albert	65,589
Medicine Hat	63,260

*2016 census.
Source: Statistics Canada.

Population trend

Millions

Year	Population
2016	4,067,175
2011	3,645,257
2006	3,290,350
2001	2,974,807
1996	2,696,826
1991	2,545,553
1986	2,375,278
1981	2,237,724
1976	1,838,037
1971	1,627,874
1966	1,463,203
1961	1,331,944
1951	939,501
1941	796,169
1931	731,605
1921	588,454
1911	374,295

1860 1880 1900 1920 1940 1960 1980 2000 2020
Source: Statistics Canada.

Economy

Chief products

Agriculture: beef and dairy cattle, canola, hogs, wheat.
Manufacturing: chemicals, fabricated metal products, machinery, paper products, petroleum products, processed food and beverages, wood products.
Mining: natural gas, petroleum.

Gross domestic product

Value of goods and services produced in 2018: $344,812,000,000.*
Services include community, business, and personal services; finance; government; trade; and transportation and communication. *Industry* includes construction, manufacturing, mining, and utilities. *Agriculture* includes agriculture, fishing, and forestry.

*Canadian dollars.
Source: Statistics Canada.

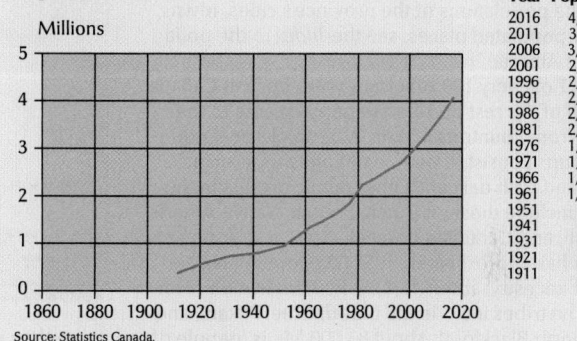

Services 55%
Agriculture 2%
Industry 43%

Government

Provincial government

Premier: term of up to 4 years
Members of the Legislative Assembly:
87; terms of up to 4 years

Federal government

Members of the House of Commons: 34
Members of the Senate: 6

Sources of information

Alberta's official website at https://www.alberta.ca provides a gateway to much information on the province's government, history, and economy.

In addition, the website at https://www.travelalberta.com provides information about tourism.

—The province's first major oil discovery was made in Turner Valley.

The Winter Olympic Games were held in Calgary.

1905   1914   1967   1988

Alberta became a province on September 1.

Alberta's first plant to remove oil from bituminous sands began operation.

Population. The 2016 Canadian census reported that Alberta had 4,067,175 people. The figure represented an increase of more than 10 percent over the 2011 census total of 3,645,257 people.

Most of Alberta's people live in the southern part of the province. Calgary is Alberta's largest city, followed by the capital, Edmonton. For more information, see the separate articles on Alberta cities and towns listed in the *Related articles* at the end of this article.

About 85 percent of Alberta's people live in urban areas. Calgary, Edmonton, and Red Deer are the only cities in Alberta with populations of more than 100,000. Calgary, Edmonton, and Lethbridge have Alberta's only Census Metropolitan Areas as defined by Statistics Canada. For the populations of the province's cities, towns, and other populated places, see the *Index* to the political map of Alberta.

About 77 of every 100 Albertans were born in Canada. About half of the rest of Alberta's people came to the province from countries in Asia. Alberta's largest population groups consist of people of English, German, Scottish, and Irish descent. Other ethnic groups in the province include those of Dutch, French, Native American, Polish, and Ukrainian descent.

Alberta has approximately 105,000 people of Native American ancestry, about 41,000 of whom live on reservations. The tribes include the Blood, Cree, Piikani, and Siksika (North Blackfoot). About 83,000 Métis (people of mixed Native American and European descent) also live in the province. About 17,000 Hutterites live in Alberta,

Population density

Most of Alberta's people live in the southern part of the province—especially in and around Calgary and Edmonton, the province's largest cities. The northern areas are thinly settled.

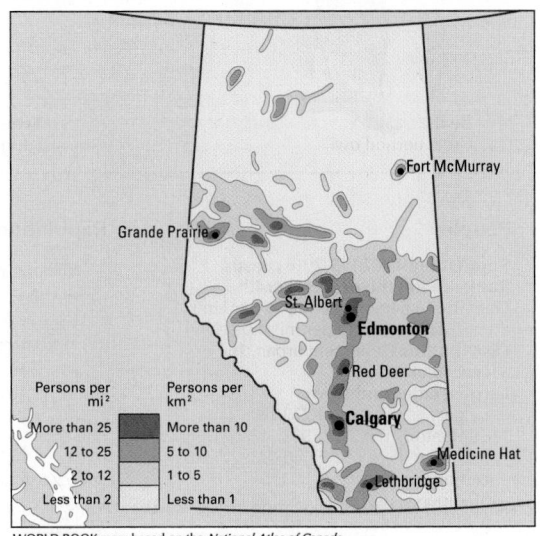

Persons per mi²	Persons per km²
More than 25	More than 10
12 to 25	5 to 10
2 to 12	1 to 5
Less than 2	Less than 1

WORLD BOOK map; based on the *National Atlas of Canada*.

more than in any other province. The members of this community-oriented religious group are successful farmers who lead simple lives. They live in about 175

Alberta map index

colonies, most in southwestern Alberta or northeast of Calgary. Many Hutterite families include nine or more children. The Hutterites came to Alberta from South Dakota in 1918. See **Hutterites.**

Schools. Missionaries established the first schools in the Alberta area during the mid-1800's. A public school system was set up in the province in 1884. Today, Alberta has public and private schools; *francophone schools,* in which French is spoken; *separate schools,* which are either Roman Catholic or Protestant; *charter schools,* which operate under local control according to special contracts called *charters;* and schools that serve Alberta's First Nations, Inuit, and Métis communities.

Elected boards of trustees administer the public, separate, and francophone school systems. Private schools are organized by private groups and offer a variety of academic, religious, special needs, or language instruction. First Nations, Inuit, and Métis schools operate under the supervision of Indigenous Services Canada, a federal agency. Public, separate, francophone, charter, and First Nations, Inuit, and Métis schools are supported by taxes. Private schools receive funding from private sources. Accredited private schools may qualify for partial provincial funding. Parents may also choose an accredited private school or home education programs supervised by a school board.

Alberta Education, which is headed by the minister of education, oversees education from early childhood through high school. Alberta law requires all children from the ages of 6 to 16 to attend school.

Libraries and museums. Alberta has many public libraries throughout the province. The University of Alberta in Edmonton, the University of Calgary, and the University of Lethbridge have large academic libraries.

The Glenbow Museum in Calgary features exhibits on the history of Alberta and western Canada. The Royal Alberta Museum in Edmonton has exhibits on Alberta's cultural and natural history. The Royal Tyrrell Museum of Palaeontology, in Drumheller, has a large collection of complete dinosaur skeletons. TELUS World of Science-Edmonton has exhibits on science, a planetarium, an observatory, and an IMAX theater. Fort Edmonton Park, in Edmonton, features re-creations of Edmonton streets from different periods in history. Heritage Park Historical Village in Calgary and the Ukrainian Cultural Heritage Village near Edmonton teach visitors about life in pioneer villages. Fort Calgary, in Calgary, has re-creations of historic buildings, including a *barracks* (living area) originally built in 1888. The Remington Carriage Museum in Cardston has horse-drawn vehicles from the 1800's and early 1900's. The Reynolds-Alberta Museum in Wetaskiwin exhibits old-time automobiles, farm equipment, and aircraft. Calgary, Edmonton, Lethbridge, Medicine Hat, and Red Deer have art galleries.

Universities and colleges

This table lists the universities and colleges in Alberta that grant bachelor's or advanced degrees and are members of Universities Canada.

Name	Mailing address
Alberta, University of	Edmonton
Athabasca University	Athabasca
Calgary, University of	Calgary
Concordia University of Edmonton	Edmonton
King's University	Edmonton
Lethbridge, University of	Lethbridge
MacEwan University	Edmonton
Mount Royal University	Calgary

Kikino		H 9
Killam	989	J 9
Kinuso		G 6
Kitscoty	925	J 10
Kneehill County*†	5,001	L 8
Lac La Biche*†	8,330	H 9
Lac Ste. Anne County*†	10,899	I 7
Lacombe	13,057	K 8
La Crete		C 5
La Glace		G 3
Lakeview*		J 7
Lake Louise		L 6
Lamont	1,774	I 8
Langdon		M 8
Lavoy		J 9
Leduc	29,993	J 8
Legal	1,345	I 8
Leslieville		K 7
Lesser Slave River*†	2,803	H 7
Lethbridge	92,729	O 9
Linden	828	L 8
Linn Valley*		K 7
Little Buffalo		F 6
Lloydminster‡	19,645	J 11
Lodgepole		J 6
Lomond	166	N 9
Longview	307	N 7
Loon Lake		E 6
Lougheed	256	K 10
Lundbreck		O 7
Magrath	2,374	O 8
Mallaig		H 9
Ma-Me-O Beach	110	J 7
Manning	1,183	E 4
Mannville	828	J 10
Manyberries		O 10
Marlboro		I 5
Marwayne	564	I 10
Mayerthorpe	1,320	I 6
McLennan	701	G 5
Medicine Hat	63,260	N 10
Metiskow		K 10
Milk River	827	O 9
Millet	1,945	J 8
Milo	91	N 8
Minburn		J 9
Monarch		O 8
Morinville	9,848	I 8
Morrin	240	L 8
Mulhurst		J 7
Mundare*	852	I 9
Munson	192	L 8
Myrnam	339	I 10
Nacmine		L 8
Nampa	364	F 5
Nanton	2,130	N 8
Neerlandia		H 7
New Norway		J 8
New Sarepta		J 8
Nobleford	1,278	N 8
Northern Lights*†	4,200	D 5
Ohaton		J 8
Okotoks	28,881	M 7
Olds	9,184	L 7
Onoway	1,029	I 7
Opportunity*†	3,181	E 7
Oyen	1,001	L 10
Paddle Prairie		C 5
Paradise Valley	179	J 10
Peace*†	1,747	F 4
Peace River	6,842	F 5
Peerless Lake		E 7
Peers		I 6
Penhold	3,277	K 7
Pibroch		I 7
Pickardville		I 7
Picture Butte	1,810	N 9
Piikani Indian Reserve	1,544	O 8
Pincher Creek	3,642	O 7
Pincher Creek*†	2,965	O 8
Ponoka	7,229	K 8
Poplar Ridge*		J 7
Provost	1,998	K 10
Provost*†	2,205	K 10
Radway		I 8
Rainbow Lake	795	C 3
Ralston		N 10
Ranchland*†	92	N 7
Ranfurly		J 9
Raymond	3,708	O 9
Red Deer	100,418	K 8
Redcliff	5,600	N 10
Redwater	2,053	I 8
Rimbey	2,567	K 7
Robb		J 5
Rochester		H 8
Rochfort Bridge		I 7
Rocky Mountain House	6,635	K 7
Rocky Rapids		J 7
Rocky View*†	39,407	M 7
Rockyford	316	M 8
Rolling Hills		N 9
Rolly View*		J 8
Rosalind	188	J 9
Rosedale		L 9
Rosemary	396	M 9
Round Hill		J 9
Rumsey		L 8
Rycroft	612	F 4
Ryley	483	J 9
Saddle Hills County*†	2,225	F 3
St. Albert	65,589	I 8
St. Isadore*		F 5
St. Paul	5,827	I 9
Samson Indian Reserve*	3,373	K 8
Sangudo		I 7
Schuler		N 11
Scot Haven*		J 8
Seba Beach	169	J 7
Sedgewick	811	J 9
Seebe		M 6
Seven Persons*		N 10
Sexsmith	2,620	G 4
Shaughnessy		O 8
Slave Lake	6,651	G 7
Smith		G 7
Smoky Lake	964	I 9
Smoky River*†	2,023	G 5
South Bailey*		I 8
Spirit River	995	F 4
Spirit River*†	700	F 3
Spring Lake*	699	I 7
Spruce Grove	34,066	J 7
Spruce View*		K 7
Standard	353	M 8
Starland County*†	2,066	L 9
Stavely	541	N 8
Stettler	5,952	K 8
Stirling	978	O 9
Stony Plain	17,189	J 7
Strathmore	13,756	M 8
Strome		J 9
Sturgeon County*†	20,495	I 8
Suffield		N 10
Sundre	2,729	L 7
Swan Hills	1,301	H 6
Sylvan Lake	14,816	K 7
Taber	8,428	O 9
Taber*†	7,098	O 9
Tangent		F 4
Tees		K 8
Thorhild*†	3,254	I 8
Thorsby	985	J 7
Three Hills	3,212	L 8
Tilley		N 9
Tofield	2,081	J 8
Tomahawk		J 7
Torrington		L 8
Trochu	1,058	L 8
Turin		N 9
Turner Valley	2,559	M 7
Two Hills	1,352	I 9
Valleyview	1,863	G 5
Vauxhall	1,222	N 9
Vegreville	5,708	I 9
Vermilion	4,084	J 10
Veteran	207	L 10
Viking	1,083	J 9
Vilna	290	I 9
Vimy*		I 7
Vulcan	1,917	N 8
Wabamun	682	J 7
Wabasca		F 7
Wainwright	6,270	J 10
Wainwright*†	4,479	J 10
Walsh		N 11
Wandering River		G 8
Wanham		F 4
Warburg	766	J 7
Warner	373	O 9
Waskatenau	186	I 8
Water Valley		L 7
Waterton Park		O 7
Wayne		L 8
Wembley	1,516	G 3
Westlock	5,101	I 7
Westlock County*†	7,220	I 7
Westward Ho		L 7
Wetaskiwin	12,655	J 8
Whitecourt	10,204	I 6
Whitelaw		F 4
Widewater*		G 7
Willingdon	319	I 9
Willow Creek*†	5,179	N 8
Winfield		J 7
Woking		G 4
Woodlands County*†	4,754	I 6
Wrentham		O 9
Wyeclif*		I 8
Yellowhead County*†	10,995	J 5
Youngstown	154	L 10
Zama City		B 4

*Does not appear on map; key shows general location.
†Municipal District.
‡City on Alberta-Saskatchewan border; total population, 31,410.
Source: 2016 census. Places without populations are unincorporated.

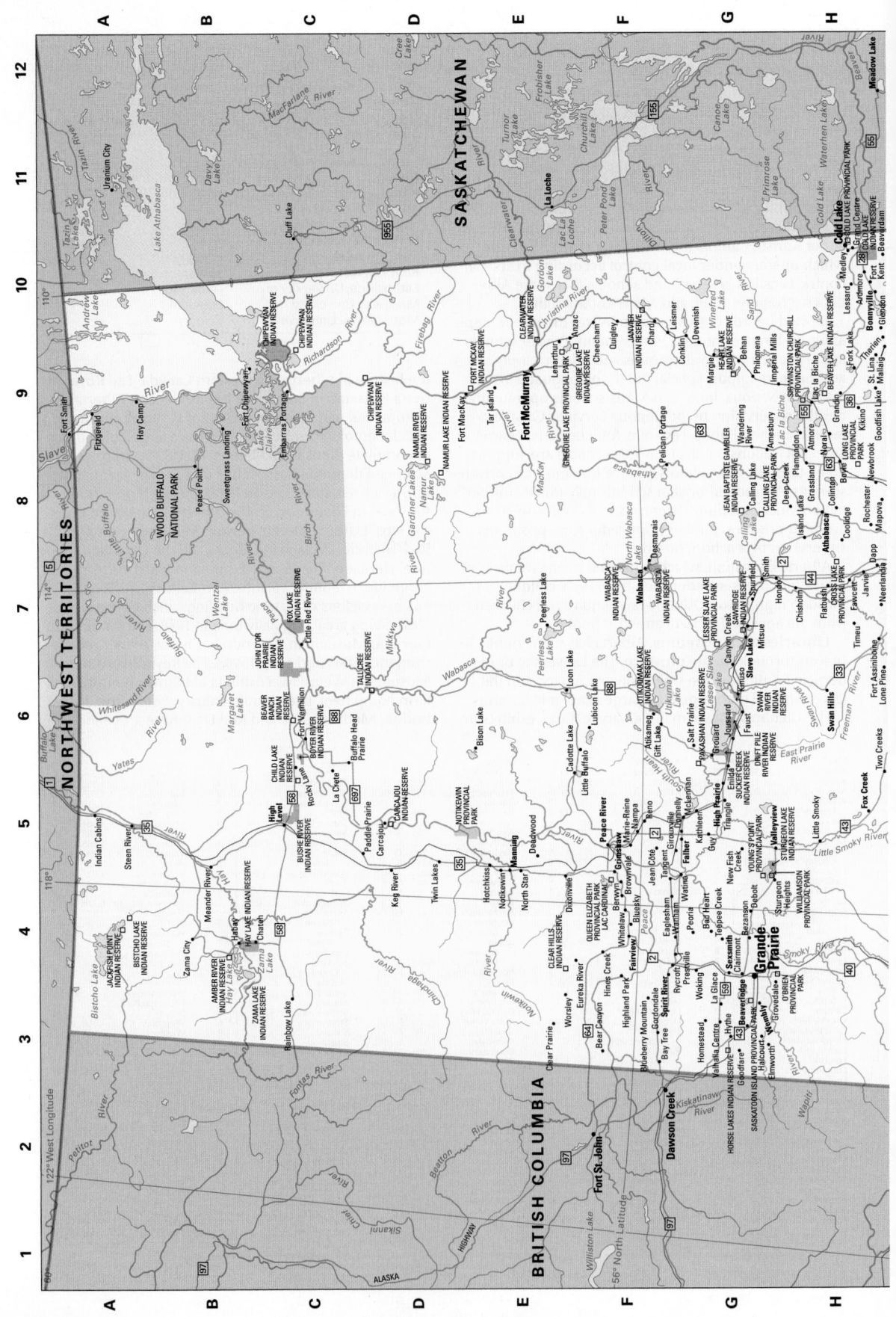

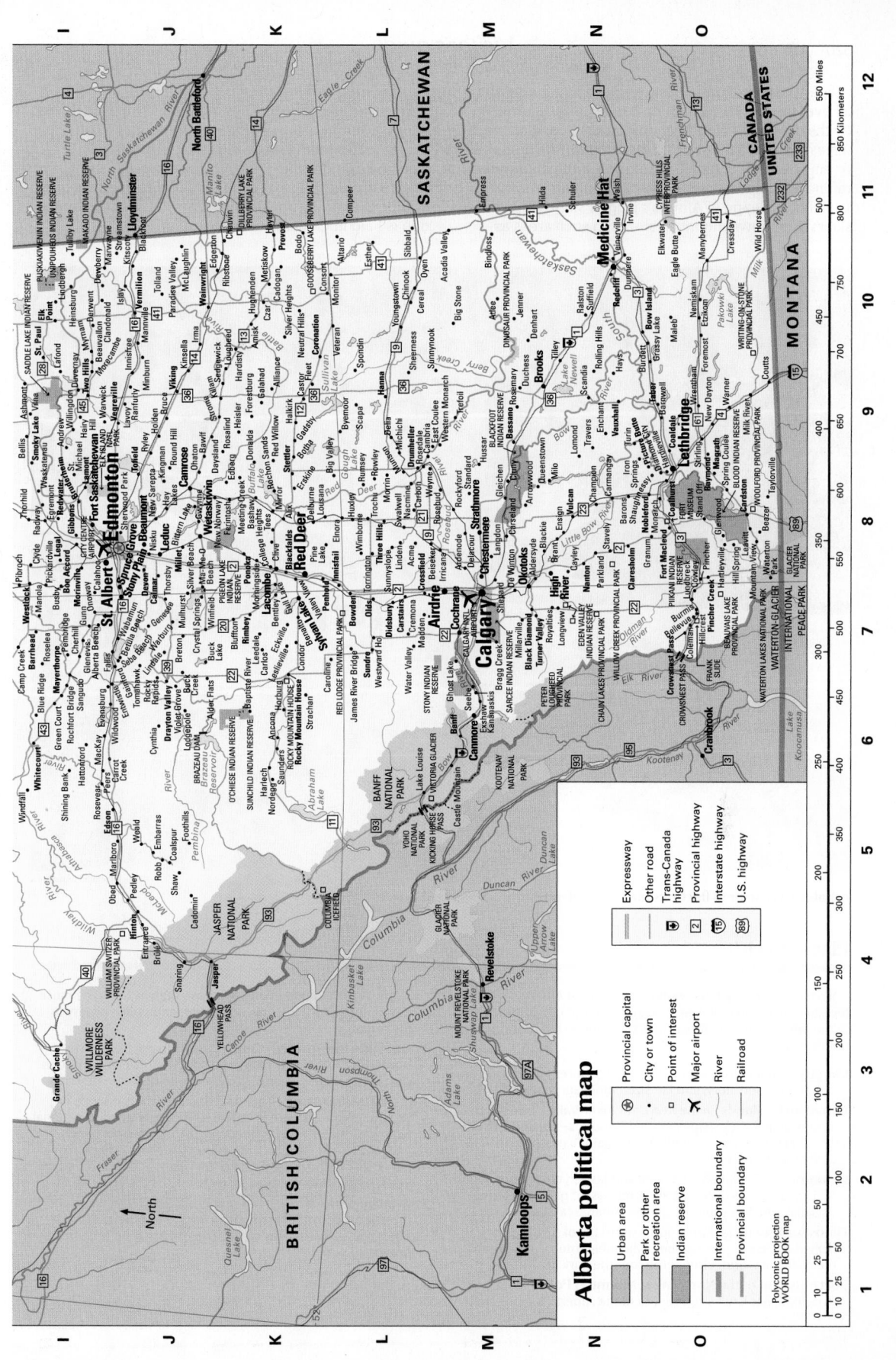

Alberta political map

Urban area

Park or other recreation area

Indian reserve

✪	Provincial capital
•	City or town
□	Point of interest
✈	Major airport
	River
	Railroad

	Expressway
	Other road
⊕	Trans-Canada highway
2	Provincial highway
15	Interstate highway
89	U.S. highway

International boundary

Provincial boundary

Polyconic projection
WORLD BOOK map

North

BRITISH COLUMBIA

SASKATCHEWAN

MONTANA

UNITED STATES

CANADA

0 10 25   50   100   150   250   300   350   450   500   550 Miles
0 10 25   50   100   150   200   250   300   350   400   450   500   600   650   700   750   800   850 Kilometers

Every year, millions of visitors come to Alberta from all over the world. Vacationers are especially attracted by the province's world-famous national parks in the majestic Canadian Rockies. Tourists may ride horseback or enjoy boating, golfing, swimming, and white water rafting amid spectacular scenery. Mountain climbers face the challenge of Alberta's jagged slopes. In winter, skiers skim down mountain slopes in such areas as Banff, Jasper, and Kananaskis.

Trails for hikers lie throughout the province. Each year, many vacationers travel to northern Alberta to fish in the province's sparkling lakes and streams for gray-ling, trout, pike, and walleye. Many other tourists stay at guest ranches and farms. The Calgary Stampede is one of Alberta's most popular annual events. This 10-day rodeo is held in Calgary each July.

© age fotostock/SuperStock

Athabasca Glacier in the Columbia Icefield, on Alberta's western border

Places to visit

Following are brief descriptions of some of Alberta's many interesting places to visit. See also entries about other attractions in the *Interesting facts about Alberta* section in the introduction of this article.

Calgary Zoo features natural habitat enclosures, a tropical aviary and conservatory, and life-sized dinosaur models.

Canadian Badlands, in the Red Deer River Valley, have weird and beautiful rock shapes—called *hoodoos*—created by wind and water erosion. The badlands contain fossils of dinosaurs and other forms of life.

Columbia Icefield, between Banff and Jasper, consists of about 125 square miles (325 square kilometers) of glacial ice. Tourists may ride in a snowcoach over Athabasca Glacier.

Dinosaur Provincial Park, northeast of Brooks, was established in 1955 to protect one of the most extensive dinosaur fields in the world. Visitors can tour the park.

Fort Museum of the North West Mounted Police, in Fort Macleod, has a full-sized replica of the Alberta region's first North-West Mounted Police outpost, built in 1874. The museum explores the early native, pioneer, and police history in the region.

Frank Slide Interpretive Centre, near Alberta's southwestern border, is the site of a 1903 rockslide. Visitors can explore the slide area and learn about early coal mining in the region.

National parks. Alberta's national parks cover thousands of square miles or square kilometers. The first Canadian national park was established in Alberta in 1885. This park is now known as Banff National Park. Alberta has four other national parks—Elk Island, Jasper, Waterton Lakes, and Wood Buffalo. See **Canada** (National park system).

Provincial parks. Alberta has numerous provincial parks and provincial recreation areas. The website of Alberta Parks at http://www.albertaparks.ca provides information on Alberta's provincial parks.

© age fotostock/SuperStock

Frank Slide near Alberta's southwestern border

© Norm Betts, Bloomberg News/Landov

Horses pulling a chuck wagon at the Calgary Stampede

Kimberly Cleary, Hot Shots

Striking rock formations in the Canadian Badlands near Drumheller, Alberta

Land regions. Alberta has four main land regions. They are (1) the Canadian Shield, (2) the Saskatchewan Plain, (3) the Alberta Plain, and (4) the Rocky Mountains and Foothills. These regions increase in altitude toward the Canadian Rockies in the southwest.

The Canadian Shield is a vast, horseshoe-shaped region that covers almost half of Canada and extends into the United States. This hilly section, made up of ancient granites and other rocks, covers a small part of the northeastern corner of Alberta. Most of the region lies less than 1,000 feet (300 meters) above sea level. The lowest point in Alberta, 557 feet (170 meters) above sea level, is along the Slave River. The region has forests of *coniferous* (cone-bearing) trees and many lakes. It is thinly populated. See **Canadian Shield.**

The Saskatchewan Plain is part of the Western Interior Plains, the Canadian section of the North American Great Plains. Pine and spruce forests cover much of this gently rolling region. Alberta's *bituminous sands* (sands that contain a substance from which oil can be obtained) are found along the lower Athabasca River. The Saskatchewan Plain lies less than 2,000 feet (610 meters) above sea level.

The Alberta Plain, another part of the Western Interior Plains, is the province's largest land region. It covers about two-thirds of Alberta. Most of this region has an altitude of more than 2,000 feet (610 meters). Pine and spruce forests cover the northern part of the Alberta Plain. Grasslands with some aspen groves lie near Grande Prairie and north of the Peace River between the North Saskatchewan River and Grimshaw. The area between the North Saskatchewan River and the Red Deer River is called the Parklands. This area has groves of aspen trees within grasslands. It is Alberta's chief farming region and one of the most productive in Canada. It has rich soils and regular rainfall. Parklands farms produce such crops as barley, canola, and wheat, as well as livestock. To the south, the Alberta Plain ranges from gently rolling to flat grassland. There, wheat and other grains grow well, and ranchers raise cattle and some sheep.

The Rocky Mountains and Foothills extend through western North America between Northern Alaska and New Mexico in the United States. They are part of the great Cordilleran mountain chain that reaches to the southern tip of South America. In Alberta, the Canadian Rockies rise along the Great Divide, which forms the province's southwestern border with British Columbia (see **Great Divide**). Mount Columbia, the highest point in Alberta, rises 12,294 feet (3,747 meters). The Twins (north peak 12,085 feet, or 3,684 meters, and south peak 11,675 feet, or 3,559 meters) tower over Jasper National Park. Thirty other mountains in the region are higher than 10,000 feet (3,000 meters).

The Canadian Rockies have some of the most spectacular scenery in the world. The snow-capped peaks consist of bare, jagged rock. Thick growths of aspens, balsam firs, pines, poplars, and spruces cover the northern foothills. They provide much lumber and pulpwood for Alberta's forest industries. The rugged Rockies attract many mountain climbers. The Rockies also appeal to people who enjoy sport fishing in the high lakes and streams or hunting mountain goats and sheep in designated areas. Banff, Jasper, and Waterton Lakes national parks are in this beautiful region. Waterton Lakes National Park and Glacier National Park of the United States together form the Waterton-Glacier International Peace Park. It was the first such park in the world.

Rivers and lakes. Northern and north-central Alberta are drained by the Athabasca, Hay, and Peace rivers and their tributaries. In warm weather, barges and tugboats operate on the Athabasca River. They can travel as far as the Arctic. The North Saskatchewan River and its branches, including the Battle and Vermilion rivers, drain the Parklands in south-central Alberta. The North Saskatchewan River rises in the Columbia Icefield, which lies in Banff and Jasper national parks and in British Columbia. The Columbia Icefield measures 100 square miles (260 square kilometers) and consists of gla-

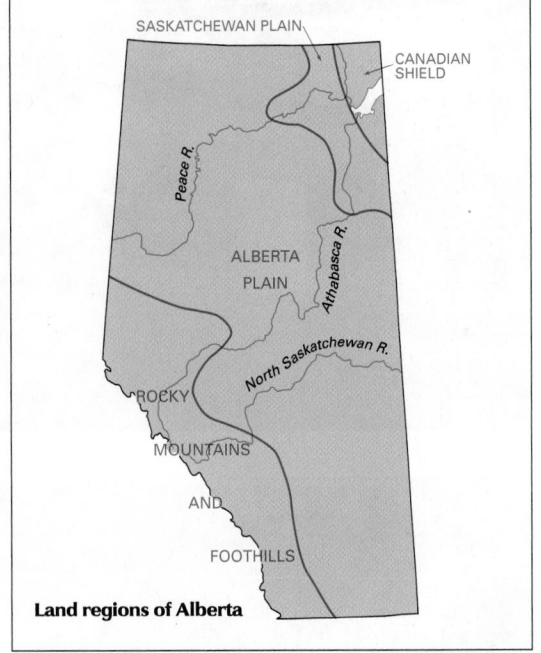

Land regions of Alberta

WORLD BOOK map

Map index

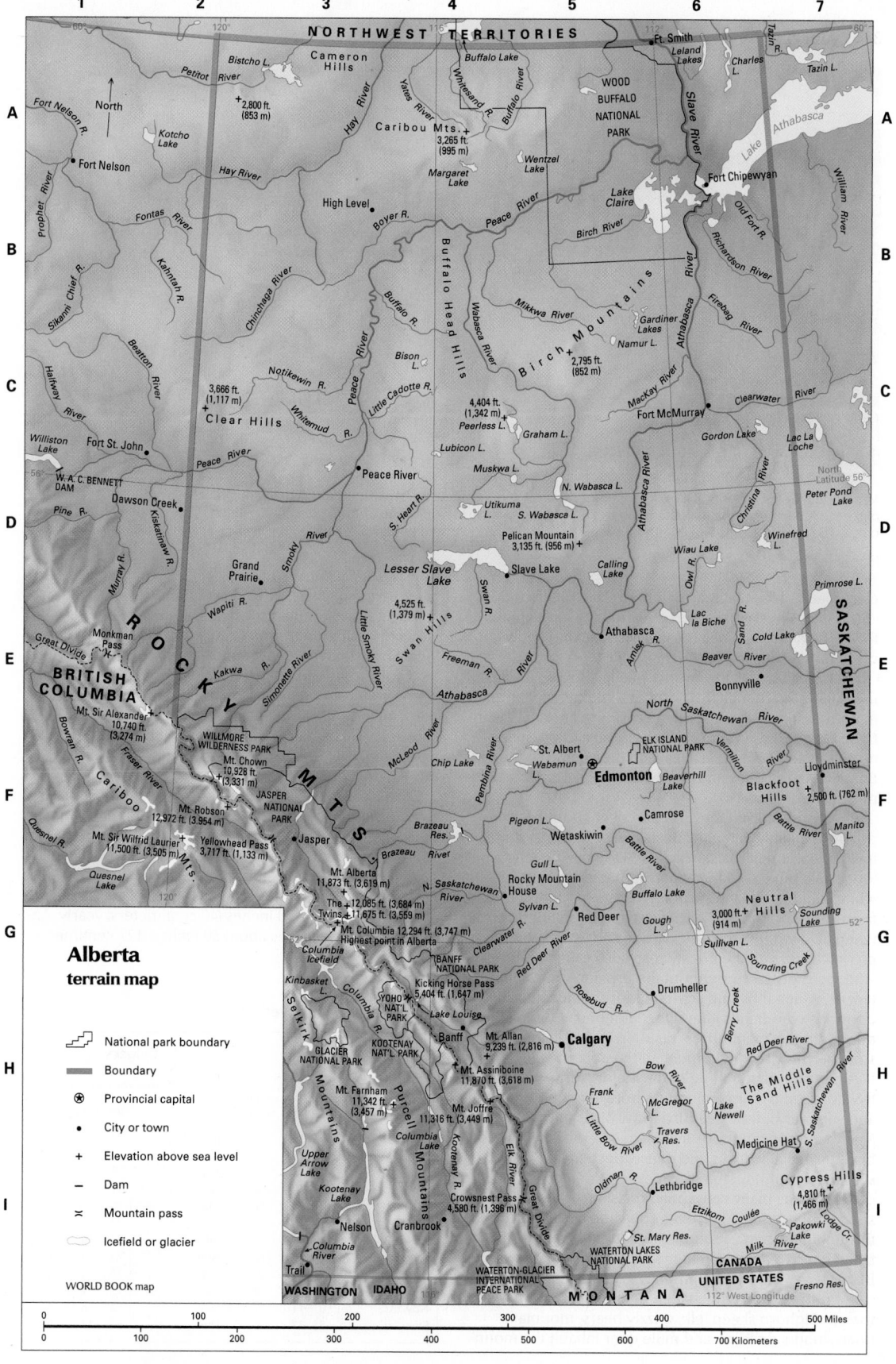

Alberta
terrain map

National park boundary
Boundary
⊛ Provincial capital
• City or town
+ Elevation above sea level
— Dam
⋈ Mountain pass
Icefield or glacier

WORLD BOOK map

NORTHWEST TERRITORIES

1   2   3   4   5   6   7

A

Fort Nelson R.
North
Bistcho L.
Petitot River
Cameron Hills
+ 2,800 ft. (853 m)
Hay River
Buffalo Lake
Whitesand
Buffalo River
Ft. Smith
Leland Lakes
Charles L.
Tazin R.
Tazin L.

Kotcho Lake
Caribou Mts. + 3,265 ft. (995 m)
Wentzel Lake
WOOD BUFFALO NATIONAL PARK
Fort Chipewyan
William River

• Fort Nelson
Hay River
High Level •
Boyer R.
Margaret Lake
Peace River
Birch River
Lake Claire
Old Fort R.
Lake Athabasca

B

Prophet River
Fontas River
Chinchaga River
Buffalo R.
Wabasca River
Mikkwa River
Gardiner Lakes
Athabasca River
Richardson River
Firebag River

Sikanni Chief R.
Kahntah R.
Beatton River
Buffalo Head Hills
Namur L.
MacKay River
Birch Mountains
2,795 ft. (852 m) +

C

Halfway River
Notikewin R.
Little Cadotte R.
Bison L.
4,404 ft. (1,342 m) +
Peerless L.
Graham L.
Fort McMurray •
Clearwater River
Gordon Lake
Lac La Loche

Williston Lake
Fort St. John •
3,666 ft. (1,117 m) +
Clear Hills
Whitemud R.
Peace River
Lubicon L.
Muskwa L.
N. Wabasca L.
Christina River
Winefred L.
Primrose L.

D

W. A. C. BENNETT DAM
Dawson Creek •
Pine R.
Peace River •
S. Heart R.
Utikuma L.
S. Wabasca L.
Pelican Mountain 3,135 ft. (956 m) +
Calling Lake
Wiau Lake
Owl R.
Cold Lake
Peter Pond Lake
North Latitude 56

56°

Murray R.
Kiskatinaw R.
Smoky River
Grand Prairie •
Lesser Slave Lake
Slave Lake •
Swan R.
Athabasca •
Lac la Biche
Sand R.
Anisk
Beaver River
Bonnyville •

E

BRITISH COLUMBIA
Great Divide
Monkman Pass
ROCKY
Wapiti R.
Kakwa
Little Smoky River
Simonette River
Swan Hills
4,525 ft. (1,379 m) +
Freeman River
Athabasca
SASKATCHEWAN

Fraser River
Bowron R.
Caribou
Mt. Sir Alexander 10,740 ft. (3,274 m) +
WILLMORE WILDERNESS PARK
McLeod River
North Saskatchewan River
Vermilion River
Lloydminster •

F

Quesnel R.
Mt. Chown 10,928 ft. (3,331 m) +
MTS.
Chip Lake
Pembina River
St. Albert •
Wabamun
ELK ISLAND NATIONAL PARK
Edmonton ⊛
Beaverhill Lake
Blackfoot Hills
2,500 ft. (762 m) +

Mt. Robson 12,972 ft. (3,954 m) +
JASPER NATIONAL PARK
Brazeau Res.
Pigeon L.
Camrose •
Battle River
Manito L.

Mt. Sir Wilfrid Laurier 11,500 ft. (3,505 m) +
Yellowhead Pass 3,717 ft. (1,133 m)
• Jasper
Brazeau River
Wetaskiwin •
Gull L.
Buffalo Lake

G

Quesnel Lake
Mt. Alberta 11,873 ft. (3,619 m) +
The Twins + 12,085 ft. (3,684 m) + 11,675 ft. (3,559 m)
N. Saskatchewan River
Rocky Mountain House •
Sylvan L.
Red Deer •
Gough
Neutral Hills 3,000 ft. (914 m) +
Sounding Lake

52°

Mt. Columbia 12,294 ft. (3,747 m) + Highest point in Alberta
Columbia Icefield
BANFF NATIONAL PARK
Clearwater R.
Red Deer River
Sullivan L.
Sounding Creek

H

Kinbasket L.
Columbia River
Kicking Horse Pass 5,404 ft. (1,647 m)
YOHO NAT'L PARK
Lake Louise
Rosebud R.
Drumheller •
Berry Creek
Red Deer River

Selkirk Mountains
KOOTENAY NAT'L PARK
Banff •
Mt. Allan 9,239 ft. (2,816 m)
Calgary •
Bow River
The Middle Sand Hills

GLACIER NATIONAL PARK
Mt. Assiniboine 11,870 ft. (3,618 m)
Frank L.
McGregor L.
Lake Newell
S. Saskatchewan River

Mt. Farnham 11,342 ft. (3,457 m) +
Purcell Mountains
Columbia Lake
Mt. Joffre 11,316 ft. (3,449 m) +
Kootenay R.
Little Bow River
Travers Res.
Medicine Hat •

I

Upper Arrow Lake
Kootenay Lake
Elk River
Great Divide
Crowsnest Pass 4,580 ft. (1,396 m)
Oldman R.
Lethbridge •
Etzikom Coulee
Cypress Hills 4,810 ft. (1,466 m) +
Pakowki Lake
Lodge Cr.

Nelson •
Cranbrook •
St. Mary Res.
Milk River
CANADA

Columbia River
Trail •
WATERTON LAKES NATIONAL PARK
WATERTON-GLACIER INTERNATIONAL PEACE PARK
UNITED STATES
Fresno Res.

WASHINGTON   IDAHO   **MONTANA**   112° West Longitude

0   100   200   300   400   500 Miles
0   100   200   300   400   500   600   700 Kilometers

Alberta Agriculture

Vast wheat fields cover much of the southern Alberta Plain. Fertile soil and regular rainfall help make the Alberta Plain the major farming region of the province. Wheat is one of Alberta's chief crops. The province is also an important producer of barley, canola, and potatoes.

ciers made of ice that may be hundreds of years old.

Most of Alberta's major rivers originate in the mountains. Their water comes mostly from melting snow and glaciers.

Lake Athabasca is the largest lake in Alberta. A third of this 3,064-square-mile (7,935-square-kilometer) lake lies in northeastern Alberta, and the rest is in Saskatchewan. Other large lakes in Alberta include Lake Claire in the northeast and Lesser Slave Lake in the central region. Beautiful Lake Louise in Banff National Park is Alberta's most famous lake.

Plant and animal life. Forests cover about half the province, mainly in the north and west. Important trees include balsam fir, balsam poplar, Douglas-fir, jack pine, lodgepole pine, quaking aspen, tamarack, and black, white, and Engelmann spruce. Flowers in Alberta bloom from early spring, when crocuses appear, to autumn, when frost withers the goldenrods and asters. The provincial flower, the prickly rose (also called the prickly wild rose), grows throughout the province. Purple fireweeds, which thrive on scorched forestlands, quickly cover the woodlands after a fire. Blueberries, chokeberries, highbush cranberries, raspberries, saskatoons, and strawberries grow over much of the countryside.

Alberta lies along three of the major North American flyways used by birds migrating between their winter and summer homes (see **Bird** [How birds migrate]). Many kinds of songbirds live in the river valleys. Game birds, especially ducks and geese, nest on lakes and sloughs throughout the province.

Alberta has many native mammals, including several species of ground squirrels. Snowshoe hares are found throughout Alberta. Pronghorns and mule and white-tailed deer are common in the grasslands of Alberta. Black bears, caribou, chipmunks, elk, moose, mule deer, tree squirrels, and white-tailed deer can be found in the forests. Bighorn sheep, elk, grizzly bears, mountain goats, mountain lions, and mule deer inhabit the moun-

tains. Bears, beavers, coyotes, ermines, fishers, foxes, lynxes, martens, minks, muskrats, squirrels, wolves, and wolverines are common in the northern half of the province. Some native people in northern Alberta make a living by trapping these animals for fur.

Important species of fish in the lakes and rivers of Alberta include grayling, pickerel, pike, trout, and whitefish. Several species of reptiles inhabit the southern parts of the province. But these animals are less common in the cooler northern areas.

Climate. Alberta has long, cold winters and short, warm summers. Temperatures in both summer and winter are generally much lower in the north than in the south. January temperatures in the province average 12 °F (–11 °C), and July temperatures average 61 °F (16 °C). *Precipitation* (rain, melted snow, and other forms of moisture) averages 18 inches (46 centimeters) yearly. Annual snowfall averages about 50 inches (127 centimeters).

Average monthly weather

	Edmonton					Calgary				
	Temperatures				Days of rain or snow		**Temperatures**			Days of rain or snow
	°F		°C				°F		°C	
	High	Low	High	Low			High	Low	High	Low	
Jan.	21	0	–6	–18	10	Jan.	30	9	–1	–13	7
Feb.	25	3	–4	–16	8	Feb.	34	12	1	–11	7
Mar.	34	14	1	–10	9	Mar.	39	18	4	–8	9
Apr.	52	27	11	–3	8	Apr.	52	28	11	–2	9
May	63	37	17	3	11	May	61	37	16	3	11
June	70	46	21	8	14	June	68	45	20	7	14
July	73	50	23	10	15	July	73	50	23	10	13
Aug.	72	46	22	8	12	Aug.	73	48	23	9	11
Sept.	63	37	17	3	10	Sept.	64	39	18	4	9
Oct.	50	27	10	–3	8	Oct.	54	30	12	–1	7
Nov.	32	12	0	–11	9	Nov.	37	18	3	–8	8
Dec.	23	1	–5	–17	9	Dec.	30	9	–1	–13	7

Average January temperatures

Alberta has long, cold winters. The province's temperatures decrease steadily from the south to the far northern region.

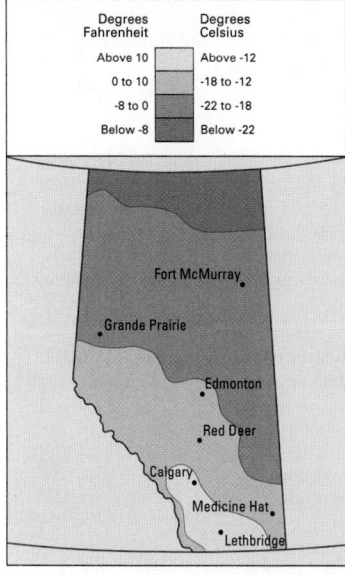

Average July temperatures

The province has short, mild summers. The southeastern part of Alberta has the warmest summertime temperatures.

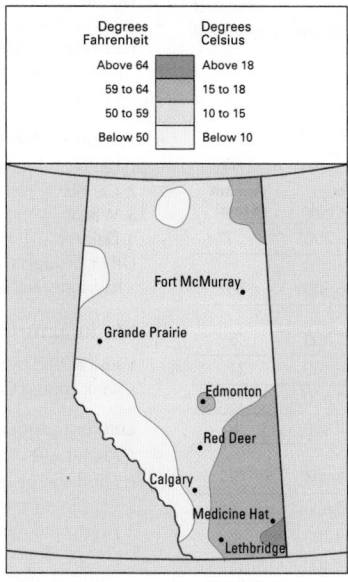

Average yearly precipitation

Precipitation varies widely throughout the province. The north and southeast are much drier than the southwestern area.

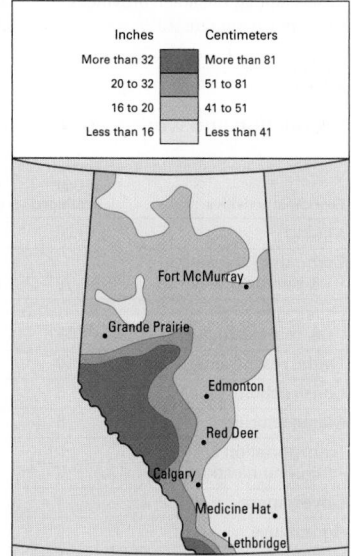

WORLD BOOK maps; based on the *National Atlas of Canada.*

Economy

As in much of Canada, the Alberta region's early economy was based chiefly on the fur trade. Agriculture became important during the early 1900's. Petroleum and natural gas became important sources of income during the late 1940's. Today, Alberta has a diversified economy built on agriculture and resource-based industries. Service industries, taken together, account for about half of Alberta's *gross domestic product* (GDP)—the total value of all goods and services produced in the province in a year.

Natural resources. Alberta's fertile soil helps produce plentiful crops. Its vast mineral deposits supply important industries. The provincial government owns most of the mineral and forest resources, and enforces strict regulations to protect them and the land.

Soil. The brown soil of Alberta's south-central and southeastern prairies, which gets little rain, requires irrigation. The rich, dark brown or black soil of the prairies farther north receives more rain and produces much of Alberta's grain. The Parklands have the richest topsoil, much of it 1 foot (30 centimeters) thick. The uplands and northern forests have gray soil.

Minerals. Alberta may have billions of barrels of oil in underground pools. After an oil well has been drilled, provincial laws require the oil companies to remove the drilling rig and restore the land to its former state.

In the Athabasca River Valley, oil sands, also called *bituminous sands* or *tar sands,* are so soaked with oil that a person gets oily handling them. Native Americans and fur traders once used these sands to make their canoes watertight. Extracting oil from the oil sands is complicated and costly. However, improved exploration methods

and extraction technology since the 1990's have made oil production there more promising. The oil sands deposits are among the world's largest known reserves. Alberta also has tens of trillions of cubic feet of natural gas underground, most of it near oil fields.

Most of Canada's known coal reserves lie in Alberta. Coal beds extend from the foothills of the Rockies through much of the central and southern plains. Most of Alberta's deposits consist of soft forms of coal called *bituminous coal* and *subbituminous coal.*

Sand and gravel are found throughout the province. Fine limestone occurs on the eastern slopes of the Rocky Mountains, and clay and shale are plentiful in the Medicine Hat area. Thick salt beds are found in the northeast and near Edmonton.

Service industries, taken together, account for about half of Alberta's gross domestic product. Alberta's service industries are concentrated in the Calgary and Edmonton metropolitan areas. Edmonton, the provincial capital, is the center of government activities. Hotels, restaurants, and other service industries benefit from the millions of tourists who visit the province each year. Banff National Park in the Rocky Mountains and the cities of Calgary and Edmonton rank among Alberta's leading tourist destinations.

Many of the service industries center around Alberta's natural resources. Finance, insurance, and real estate benefit greatly from income brought in by Alberta's petroleum and gas industries. For example, each year the provincial government collects billions of dollars in royalties from petroleum companies, which it invests in the province's financial institutions. Alberta's wholesale

Alberta economy

General economy

Gross domestic product (GDP)* (2018) $344,812,000,000
  Rank among Canadian provinces   3rd
Unemployment rate (2019)   6.9% (Canada avg: 5.7%)

*Gross domestic product is the total value of goods and services produced in a year and is in Canadian dollars.
Source: Statistics Canada.

Production and workers by economic activities

Economic activities	Percent of GDP produced	Employed workers	
		Number of people	Percent of total
Mining	26	153,200*	7*
Community, business, & personal services	19	816,600†	35†
Finance, insurance, & real estate	15†	105,700	5
Trade, restaurants, & hotels	10	480,900	21
Construction	8	245,400	11
Manufacturing	8	129,800	6
Transportation & communication	7	216,800	9
Government	4	109,600	5
Agriculture	2*	49,300	2
Utilities	1	23,400	1
Total‡	100	2,330,700	100

*Includes figures from forestry and fishing.
†Includes figures from establishments that manage other companies.
‡Figures may not add up to 100 percent, due to rounding.
Figures are for 2018.
Source: Statistics Canada.

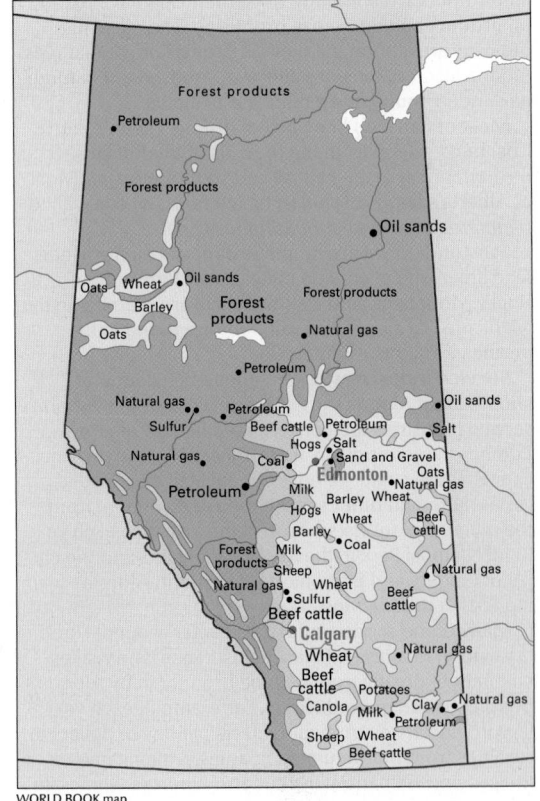

Forest products
Petroleum
Forest products
Oil sands
Oats Wheat Oil sands
Barley Forest Forest products
Oats products Natural gas
Petroleum
Natural gas Petroleum Oil sands
Sulfur Beef cattle Petroleum Salt
Hogs Salt
Natural gas Coal Sand and Gravel
Petroleum Edmonton Oats
Milk Natural gas
Hogs Barley Wheat
Barley Wheat Beef cattle
Forest Milk Coal
products Sheep Natural gas
Natural gas Wheat Beef
Sulfur cattle
Beef cattle
Calgary
Wheat Natural gas
Beef cattle Potatoes
Canola Clay Natural gas
Milk Petroleum
Sheep Wheat
Beef cattle

WORLD BOOK map

Agriculture

Cash receipts $13,570,567,000
  Rank among Canadian provinces   3rd
Distribution   50% livestock, 50% crops
Farms (2016)   40,600
Farm acres/hectares (2016)   50,250,183/20,335,527
  Rank among Canadian provinces   2nd
Farmland   31% of Alberta

Leading products

1. Cattle and calves   (ranks 1st in Canada)
2. Canola   (ranks 2nd in Canada)
3. Wheat   (ranks 2nd in Canada)
4. Dairy
Other products: barley, floriculture and nursery products, hay, hens and chickens, hogs, lentils, oats, peas, potatoes.

Manufacturing

Value added by manufacture* $28,413,670,000
  Rank among Canadian provinces   3rd

Leading products

1. Chemicals
2. Food and beverage products
3. Petroleum and coal products
4. Fabricated metals
Other products: machinery, nonmetallic minerals, paper products, plastic and rubber products, wood products.

*Value added by manufacture is the increase in value of raw materials as they become finished products.

Mining

Mineral production $2,031,743,000
  Rank among Canadian provinces   6th
Crude oil and equivalents (barrels*)   1,358,030,874
  Rank among Canadian provinces   1st
Natural gas (million cubic feet †)   4,472,972
  Rank among Canadian provinces   1st

*One barrel equals 42 gallons (159 liters).
†One cubic foot equals 0.0283 cubic meter.

Leading products

Coal (ranks 2nd in Canada), natural gas (ranks 1st in Canada), peat, petroleum (ranks 1st in Canada), quartz (ranks 1st in Canada), salt, sand and gravel (ranks 2nd in Canada), stone, sulfur (ranks 1st in Canada).

Electric power

Coal   46.4%
Natural gas   43.1%
Hydroelectric   8.7%
Other   1.8%

Figures are for 2018, except for the manufacturing and electric power figures, which are for 2017.
Dollar amounts are in Canadian dollars.
Source: Statistics Canada.

Economic map of Alberta

The map at the left shows the economic uses of land in Alberta and where the province's leading farm, mineral, and forest products are produced. Major manufacturing centers appear in red.

  Mostly cropland
  Mostly grazing land
  Forest land
  Mostly unproductive land with alpine vegetation
  Manufacturing and service industry center
  Mineral deposit

trade is based mainly on the distribution of food and mined products. The province exports large amounts of petroleum and natural gas to the United States.

Mining. Petroleum and natural gas account for the vast majority of Alberta's mining income. Alberta produces more natural gas and more oil than any other Canadian province. Alberta's major oil fields are at Judy Creek, Pembina, Rainbow Lake, Redwater, and Swan Hills.

Alberta has two large plants that produce petroleum from oil sands. These plants lie near Fort McMurray in the Athabasca River Valley. Smaller plants operate at Cold Lake and Peace River. Since the 1990's, the Fort McMurray area has grown rapidly, as major oil companies have moved in and attracted workers from Canada and around the world.

Pipelines carry natural gas and petroleum throughout Alberta and to the east, south, and west. Gathering lines transport the fuels within the province and feed them into cross-country lines. The Interprovincial Pipeline starts in Redwater, near Edmonton, and carries Alberta oil east to Montreal. The Trans Mountain Pipeline System carries oil southwest from the Edmonton area to Burnaby, British Columbia. Pipelines in Alberta feed natural gas into the Trans-Canada Pipeline, which extends from the Alberta-Saskatchewan border to Montreal. All these pipelines have branches into the United States. In addition, a network of pipelines carries natural gas from Alberta to California.

Coal, sand and gravel, and sulfur are also important mined products. Mining operations in southern Alberta produce much of Canada's yearly coal output. Most of the coal is obtainable by surface mining. Much of Alberta's sand and gravel production occurs in the south-central part of the province. Most of Alberta's sulfur comes from processing natural gas. Sulfur is used in the manufacture of paper and fertilizer.

Manufacturing. Much of Alberta's manufacturing is dedicated to processing its agricultural, forest, and mined products. Meat packing is the leading type of food processing in Alberta. The Calgary area is a major center of Canada's meat-packing industry. Other important products include baked goods, dairy products, snack foods, and soft drinks. Sawmills, which are mainly in the northern part of the province, produce lumber and other wood products.

Alberta's main chemical products are petrochemicals and fertilizers. Petrochemicals are made from petroleum and include such compounds as ethylene and methanol. Edmonton, Fort McMurray, and Scotford have oil refineries. Oil and gas industry equipment accounts for a large part of Alberta's machinery production. Fabricated metal production is also important to the province.

Agriculture. Farmland covers about a third of the land area. Beef cattle are the leading farm product in Alberta. The heaviest concentration of cattle ranches lies in a wide belt that begins north of Calgary and extends to the U.S. border. Alberta has more beef cattle than any other province. Farmers in Alberta also raise large numbers of dairy cattle, hogs, and chickens.

Canola and wheat are the leading crops in Alberta. Canola, which is used to make cooking oil, is grown throughout the province. Wheat is also grown throughout much of the province, but especially in the south. Only Saskatchewan produces more canola and wheat.

Forestry. Alberta has vast timber resources. Forests cover about 60 percent of Alberta's land area. Forests grow primarily in the northern and western parts of the province. Softwoods, such as spruce and pine, are the most valuable species. Aspen hardwoods are also important. The provincial government regulates timber harvesting.

Electric power and utilities. Coal and natural gas are the chief fuels for power plants in the province. Renewable power sources also produce small amounts of Alberta's electric power. These sources include water, wind, and organic waste products.

Transportation. Alberta has a fine highway system. The Trans-Canada Highway and the Yellowhead Highway, two branches of the Trans-Canada Highway system, cross Alberta from east to west. The North/South Trade Corridor connects northern Alberta and markets in the southern part of the province.

Major airports at Calgary and Edmonton offer both domestic and international service. Alberta also has other regional airports with scheduled service. Many small airports handle cargo traffic for northern Alberta, the Northwest Territories, and Yukon. Calgary is the headquarters for WestJet, one of Canada's largest airlines.

Alberta has an excellent system of railroads. Two transcontinental rail lines, the Canadian National Railway and the Canadian Pacific Railway, cross the province from east to west. Together with several short line railroads, they connect Alberta's exporters of grain, coal, and forest and petroleum products with western ports. The head office of the Canadian Pacific is in Calgary.

Water transportation declined after the province's fur-trading days but increased after the discovery of petroleum in Alaska and the Northwest Territories. In warm weather, barges carry freight on the Athabasca River and the Slave River, which link northern regions of Alberta with the northern part of the Northwest Territories. In winter, airplanes equipped with landing skis and other special equipment are used to haul freight on frozen lakes and rivers.

Communication. The first newspaper in the Alberta region was the *Edmonton Bulletin,* published from 1880 to 1951. Today, the *Calgary Herald* and the *Edmonton Journal* are the largest daily newspapers. The *Calgary Sun* and the *Edmonton Sun* also have large circulations.

Government

Lieutenant governor of Alberta represents the British monarch, Canada's official head of state, in the province. The lieutenant governor is appointed by Canada's *governor general in council*—the governor general of Canada acting with the advice and consent of the Cabinet—for a period of at least five years. The position of lieutenant governor is largely honorary.

Premier of Alberta is the actual head of the provincial government. Alberta, like Canada itself, has a parliamentary form of government. The premier of the province is

The Legislative Assembly of Alberta meets in the Legislature Building in Edmonton. The Assembly makes provincial laws.

an elected member of the legislature, called the Legislative Assembly. The person who serves as Alberta's premier is usually the leader of the party holding the most seats in the Legislative Assembly.

The Executive Council includes ministers chosen by the premier from among members of the premier's party in the Legislative Assembly. Each minister directs one or more departments of the provincial government. The premier and the Executive Council resign if they lose the support of a majority of the Assembly.

Legislative Assembly of Alberta is a one-house legislature that makes provincial laws. It has 87 members, each of whom is elected from a separate electoral district called a *constituency.* The members' terms may last up to four years. However, the lieutenant governor, on the advice of the premier, may call for an election before the end of the four-year period. If this is done, all Legislative Assembly members must run again for office.

Courts. The highest court in Alberta is the Court of Appeal. It hears only appeals in civil and criminal cases. The Court of Appeal has the chief justice of Alberta and 13 full-time justices of appeal. The Court of Queen's Bench hears all cases involving murder, treason, and other major crimes. This court has a chief justice, two associate chief justices, and 65 other full-time justices. Judges of Alberta's Court of Appeal and the Court of Queen's Bench are appointed by the governor general in council. Judges may serve until the age of 75.

Provincial court judges hear criminal, civil, family, traffic, and youth cases and are appointed by the lieutenant governor in council—that is, acting with the advice of the Executive Council. The Provincial Court of Alberta consists of a chief judge, a deputy chief judge, 9 assistant chief judges, and more than 100 judges.

Local government. Alberta has more than 350 rural, urban, and *specialized* municipalities. Rural municipalities cover a large majority of Alberta's area. Specialized municipalities are municipalities with a unique structure designed to meet local needs. An elected council governs each of the province's municipalities. Every council must have a chief elected officer (CEO) and a deputy CEO. The chief elected officer is appointed in some municipalities and elected in others. The deputy CEO is appointed from among the elected councilors.

Other units of local government in Alberta include *improvement districts* and *special areas.* Improvement districts exist in areas that lack enough people and tax income to support an independent local government. The Department of Municipal Affairs and local advisory councils administer the improvement districts.

The special areas consist of a region in southeastern Alberta that was badly affected by drought in the early 1900's. When many farmers left their farms, the provincial government acquired the land. It then created the Special Areas Board to govern the region. The board has many of the same responsibilities that governing councils have in Alberta's municipalities. An elected advisory council assists the Special Areas Board.

Revenue. Taxation accounts for about two-fifths of the provincial government's *general revenue* (income). About a ninth of the general revenue comes from the government's charges for rights to petroleum deposits. In the past, some of this money was invested in a special fund. Investments made with the fund's money continue to provide revenue. Like other provinces, Alberta receives financial aid from the federal government. Alberta is the only province with no sales tax.

Politics. Since Alberta became a province in 1905, four provincial parties have controlled much of its political life—the Liberal Party, the United Farmers of Alberta, the Social Credit Party, and the Progressive Conservative (PC) party. The United Farmers of Alberta won control of the government in the 1920's, when agriculture dominated the economy and prices for farm products were low. Voters frustrated by the Great Depression elected the Social Credit Party in 1935.

Today, political parties in Alberta include the Liberal Party, the New Democratic Party (NDP), and the United Conservative Party (UCP).

The premiers of Alberta

	Party	Term
Alexander C. Rutherford	Liberal	1905-1910
Arthur L. Sifton	Liberal	1910-1917
Charles Stewart	Liberal	1917-1921
Herbert Greenfield	United Farmers of Alberta	1921-1925
John E. Brownlee	United Farmers of Alberta	1925-1934
Richard G. Reid	United Farmers of Alberta	1934-1935
William Aberhart	Social Credit	1935-1943
Ernest C. Manning	Social Credit	1943-1968
Harry E. Strom	Social Credit	1968-1971
Peter Lougheed	Progressive Conservative	1971-1985
Donald R. Getty	Progressive Conservative	1985-1992
Ralph Klein	Progressive Conservative	1992-2006
Edward M. Stelmach	Progressive Conservative	2006-2011
Alison Redford	Progressive Conservative	2011-2014
Dave Hancock	Progressive Conservative	2014
Jim Prentice	Progressive Conservative	2014-2015
Rachel Notley	New Democratic	2015-2019
Jason Kenney	United Conservative	2019-

Early inhabitants. When Europeans first arrived in the Alberta region, the native Blackfoot (also called Blackfeet) Nation lived in the southern prairies and foothills. It consisted of the Blood, Piegan, and Siksika (North Blackfoot) tribes. The Sarcee, their allies, also lived in the south. The Cree lived in the northern forests. Other Native Americans—also known as First Nations—of the Alberta region included the Beaver and Gros Ventre tribes, and the Stonies, a branch of the Assiniboine tribe.

The fur trade. In 1670, King Charles II of England granted fur-trading rights in the Alberta region to an English company called the Hudson's Bay Company. The region was part of a vast territory called Rupert's Land. The first European known to visit the Alberta region was Anthony Henday, an English fur trader and explorer. In 1754, the Hudson's Bay Company sent Henday to promote trade with the Blackfoot people. He stayed with the Blackfoot that winter and returned to York Factory, on Hudson Bay, in 1755. See **Henday, Anthony; Hudson's Bay Company.**

In 1778, Peter Pond, of the United States, built a fur-trading post near Lake Athabasca. During the 1780's, the North West Company, formed by fur traders in Montreal, began to compete with the Hudson's Bay Company. The firms competed in the Alberta region until they combined in 1821. See **North West Company.**

In 1788, Roderick Mackenzie, a fur trader, established Fort Chipewyan. His cousin Alexander Mackenzie traveled from this post to the Arctic Ocean in 1789 and to the Pacific Ocean in 1793 (see **Mackenzie, Sir Alexander**). Between 1789 and 1812, the geographer David Thompson made surveys in the Alberta region that provided the first good map of the Canadian Northwest.

Missionary activity. During the mid-1800's, most of the settlers in the Alberta region were traders and Métis (people of mixed Native American and European descent). Missionaries converted many Native Americans. They also introduced schools and attempted to persuade Native Americans and Métis to settle permanently and begin farming.

Robert T. Rundle, a Methodist, was the first missionary in the region. He arrived in 1840 and stayed until 1848. Two other Methodist leaders, George McDougall and his son John McDougall, arrived in the Alberta region in 1863. A priest named Jean Thibault established Alberta's first Roman Catholic mission in 1843 in Lac Ste. Anne. In 1852, Albert Lacombe, another Catholic priest, began working among the Native Americans and Métis. Lacombe founded the town of St. Albert in 1861.

Early settlement. In 1870, the Hudson's Bay Company gave up Rupert's Land to the British government, which then transferred it to the newly formed Dominion of Canada. The dominion paid the company $1 ½ million and permitted it to keep large areas of the plains. Later in 1870, Canada established the North-West Territories, which included the Alberta region and the rest of the former Rupert's Land.

At this time, traders from Montana were carrying on an illegal liquor trade with Native Americans in the North-West Territories. To stop this trade and to prepare the way for peaceful settlement of the region, the Canadian government organized the North-West Mounted Police (see **Royal Canadian Mounted Police** [History]). The Mounties established their first post in the Alberta region in 1874 at Fort Macleod. They soon stopped the illegal trading and won the confidence and respect of the native people. Within a few years, the native people and the Canadian government signed three treaties. Treaty No. 6, signed in 1876, and Treaty No. 7, signed in 1877, gave the Canadian government the central and southern parts of Alberta in return for reservations, annual payments, and promises of future assistance for the Native Americans. Treaty No. 8, signed in 1899, gave the northern half of Alberta to Canada on similar terms.

By 1883, about 500 settlers, most of them cattle ranchers, were living in the Alberta region. That year, the Canadian Pacific Railway linked Calgary with cities in eastern Canada. The North West Rebellion of 1885, an uprising of Native Americans and Métis led by Louis Riel, caused great alarm in the Alberta region. However, the only violence in the area was the killing of nine white people by Native Americans at Frog Lake. See **North West Rebellion.**

A new province. Opportunities for settlement in the Alberta region drew thousands of farmers from eastern Canada, the United States, and Europe. In 1905, the Canadian government established the province of Alberta. Alexander C. Rutherford, a Liberal politician, became the first premier. Alberta's first major oil discovery was made in 1914, in Turner Valley.

After World War I (1914-1918), many farmers lost their land because of drought and low prices on farm products. The United Farmers of Alberta, a new political party, won control of the provincial government from the Liberal Party in 1921. The new party received support from the farmers, who felt it could best protect their interests. Prosperity returned soon. The provincial government improved and expanded education, highways, and public health programs.

Low farm prices during the Great Depression of the 1930's led to another new party taking power in Alberta. The Social Credit Party, led by William Aberhart, was elected in 1935. It had promised to solve the problems of the Depression. The new government did pass laws to control banking and credit, but the federal government declared these laws unconstitutional.

The mid-1900's. Alberta prospered during World War II (1939-1945). Farmers raised grain and livestock to help meet the food needs of the Allies. Mining and manufacturing increased with the production of war goods.

In 1947, petroleum and natural gas were discovered at Leduc, near Edmonton. The discoveries led to widespread industrialization that changed Alberta's economy. The province owned most of the mineral rights in the land and received income from leases, rentals, and *royalties* (shares of the profits). Alberta used the money to expand its hospitals, roads, schools, and other public works. In 1957, the province paid its citizens a dividend from its oil income. Every adult who had lived in Alberta for at least five years received $20. In 1958, the provincial government paid a dividend of $17.50.

In 1954, for the first time, the combined value of Alberta's mining and manufacturing became greater than that of agriculture. As industrialization increased, thousands of workers came to Alberta from other provinces, Europe, and the United States. Alberta's population increased greatly in the late 1950's and became mostly ur-

Historic Alberta

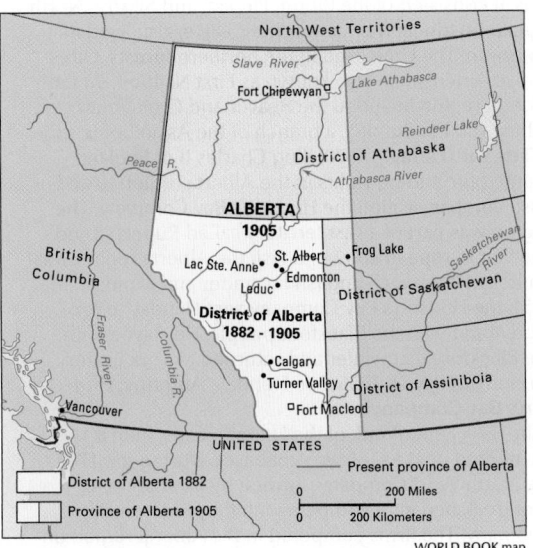

WORLD BOOK map

Sir Alexander Mackenzie led a small expedition from Fort Chipewyan in 1789. The group discovered the Mackenzie River, the longest river in Canada, and followed it to the Arctic.

The District of Alberta was established as part of the North-West Territories in 1882. In 1905, the district and other land obtained from the Native Americans became a province.

The North-West Mounted Police, also known as the Mounties, arrived in Alberta in 1874. They drove liquor traders and other outlaws out of the region. Some of them stayed in the area and became ranchers.

WORLD BOOK illustrations by Richard Bonson, The Art Agency

Important dates in Alberta

Before 1670 The Blackfeet (Blackfoot), Cree, and other First Nations lived in what is now Alberta.

1670 King Charles II of England granted trading rights in the Alberta region to the Hudson's Bay Company.

1754-1755 Anthony Henday of the Hudson's Bay Company explored the Alberta region.

1778 Peter Pond of the United States established a trading post near Lake Athabasca.

1840 Robert T. Rundle became the first missionary in the Alberta region.

1843 Jean Thibault established the region's first Roman Catholic mission at Lac Ste. Anne.

1874 The North-West Mounted Police established Fort Macleod.

1876-1877 Native Americans signed two treaties surrendering central and southern Alberta to Canada.

1883 The Canadian Pacific Railway reached Calgary.

1905 Alberta became a province on September 1.

1921 The United Farmers of Alberta, a new political party, came to power.

1935 The Social Credit Party, another new organization, took over the Alberta government.

1947 Oil and natural gas were discovered at Leduc.

1954 The combined value of Alberta's mining and manufacturing exceeded that of agriculture for the first time.

1967 Alberta's first plant to remove oil from bituminous sands began operation.

1971 The Progressive Conservative Party came to power, ending 36 years of rule by the Social Credit Party.

1988 The Winter Olympic Games were held in Calgary.

2006 Stephen Harper, a member of Parliament from Calgary, became prime minister of Canada.

2011 Alison Redford became Alberta's first woman premier.

2015 The New Democrats won a general election, following over 40 years of Progressive Conservative government.

ban instead of rural. In 1945, less than a fourth of the people lived in Calgary or Edmonton. By 1966, about half the people lived in those two cities.

In 1958, James Gladstone of Alberta became the first Native American member of the Canadian Senate. Prime Minister John G. Diefenbaker had recommended Gladstone's appointment.

The coal industry had begun to decline in the 1950's. Railroads switched from coal to diesel fuel as diesel locomotives replaced steam engines. Also, natural gas and fuel oil replaced coal in many heating systems. In 1962, coal production in Alberta dropped to a record low. But in 1967, Japan became a new market for coal, and coal production started to increase.

In 1967, Alberta's first plant to remove oil from the bituminous sands of the Athabasca River Valley was completed. The Alberta "resources railway" went into operation in 1969. This 235-mile (378-kilometer) line extends from Grande Prairie to Brûlé. It opened undeveloped land in northern Alberta so that industry could reach mineral deposits and timber. The Alberta portions of the Trans-Canada Highway and the Yellowhead Highway also were completed during the 1960's.

The late 1900's. In 1971, voters gave control of Alberta's government to the Progressive Conservative party. The win ended 36 years of Social Credit Party rule.

In the 1970's and early 1980's, Alberta experienced great industrial expansion. The province's vast oil deposits attracted many new industries, and thousands of people from other parts of Canada came to Alberta to find jobs. A second plant to remove oil from Alberta's bituminous sands opened in 1978.

Calgary and Edmonton grew rapidly due to the expansion of retail trade, tourism, and other service industries. The 1988 Winter Olympic Games were held in Calgary. Calgary also became the headquarters of the national Reform Party of Canada, founded in 1987. The Reform Party, which called for more attention to the western provinces, was dissolved in 2000.

The early 2000's. In 2006, Stephen Harper, a former leader of the Reform Party and a Conservative member of Parliament from Calgary, became prime minister of Canada. Progressive Conservative Alison Redford served as the first woman premier of Alberta from 2011 to 2014.

Heavy rainfall caused historic flooding in southern Alberta in June 2013. Over 25 communities, including Calgary, declared a local state of emergency. Several people died and tens of thousands had to leave their homes.

In 2015, the New Democratic Party (NDP), led by Rachel Notley, won a general election in Alberta for the first time. The NDP's victory followed more than 40 years of Progressive Conservative government in the province.

In May 2016, raging wildfires in northeastern Alberta forced the evacuation of nearly 90,000 people from the Fort McMurray area. Thousands of homes were destroyed. Oil sands production in the area also shut down temporarily, dealing a setback to Canada's petroleum industry.

In 2017, the Progressive Conservatives and the Wild Rose Party, another conservative party, combined to form the United Conservative Party (UCP). The UCP, led by Jason Kenney, won Alberta's next general election, held in 2019.   Glen T. Hvenegaard and Tamara Palmer Seiler

Related articles in *World Book* include:

Biographies

Bennett, Richard B.	Mackenzie, Roderick
Clark, Joe	Manning, Preston
Crowfoot	McLuhan, Marshall
Day, Stockwell	Michener, Roland
Harper, Stephen J.	Murphy, Emily Gowan
Henday, Anthony	

Cities and towns

Banff	Edmonton
Calgary	Lethbridge

Physical features

Athabasca River	Peace River
Lake Athabasca	Rocky Mountains
Lake Louise	Saskatchewan River

Other related articles

Banff National Park	Jasper National Park
Famous Five	North West Company
Hudson's Bay Company	

Outline

I. **People**
  A. Population
  B. Schools
  C. Libraries and museums
II. **Visitor's guide**
III. **Land and climate**
  A. Land regions
  B. Rivers and lakes
  C. Plant and animal life
  D. Climate
IV. **Economy**
  A. Natural resources
  B. Service industries
  C. Mining
  D. Manufacturing
  E. Agriculture
  F. Forestry
  G. Electric power and utilities
  H. Transportation
  I. Communication
V. **Government**
  A. Lieutenant governor   E. Local government
  B. Premier   F. Revenue
  C. Legislative Assembly   G. Politics
  D. Courts
VI. **History**

Alberta, University of, is a public university with its main campus in Edmonton, in the Canadian province of Alberta. The university's Faculty of Native Studies focuses on issues that affect Canadian *aboriginal* (native) peoples. In addition to the original campus, North Campus, in Edmonton, the university has three other campuses in Edmonton—South Campus, Enterprise Square, and a French-language campus called Campus Saint-Jean. The university's Augustana Campus, in Camrose, serves students in rural areas. The University of Alberta was established in 1906. It offered its first classes in 1908. The university's men's athletic teams are called the Golden Bears, and women's teams are called the Pandas. The school's website at https://www.ualberta.ca offers additional information.   Critically reviewed by the University of Alberta

Alberti, *ahl BEHR tee,* **Leon Battista,** *lay OHN baht TEES tah* (1404-1472), was an Italian Renaissance architect, painter, and scholar. He spent his early years studying ancient Greek and Roman civilizations. During this time, Alberti gained a reputation as a humanist and learned

Latin scholar as he wrote two influential books, *On Painting* (1435) and *On Architecture* (begun in the 1440's). The work on painting was the first scientific study of *perspective* (representing objects on a flat surface to give the illusion of receding distance).

From 1450 until his death, Alberti concentrated on architecture. His best-known buildings include the church of San Francesco (1450) in Rimini, the Rucellai Palace (1452) in Florence, and the *facade* (front) of the church of Santa Maria Novella (about 1456-1470) in Florence. Another of Alberti's masterpieces of architecture, the church of Sant' Andrea in Mantua, was completed in 1494, after his death.

Alberti was born on Feb. 14, 1404, in Genoa. He died on April 25, 1472.   J. William Rudd

See also **Architecture** (Early Renaissance architecture; picture); **Florence** (picture: Santa Maria Novella).

Albertosaurus, *al BUR tuh sawr uhs,* was one of the largest meat-eating dinosaurs. *Albertosaurus* grew approximately 25 to 30 feet (7.6 to 9.1 meters) long, stood about 12 feet (3.7 meters) tall at the hips, and weighed between 2 and 3 tons (1.8 and 2.7 metric tons).

Albertosaurus lived about 70 million years ago, near the end of the Cretaceous Period. The dinosaur inhabited what is now western Canada and the western United States.

The dinosaur's name means *Alberta lizard.* It got the name because its remains were first unearthed in the Canadian province of Alberta.

Albertosaurus resembled its distant relative *Tyrannosaurus rex.* It had a huge head and walked on two long, powerful hind legs. Enormous claws grew from the three toes on each foot. The animal's small forelimbs ended in two-fingered hands. Its long tail provided balance and agility for its massive body and head. The dinosaur probably could run quickly for short distances when pursuing prey.

Albertosaurus ate plant-eating dinosaurs. Its huge toe claws and curved, saw-edged teeth helped it tear apart prey. Because its teeth were not designed for chewing, *Albertosaurus* probably swallowed its food in large chunks. Scientists think *Albertosaurus* ate prey that it killed as well as animals that it found already dead.

Kenneth Carpenter

Albertus Magnus, Saint (1206?-1280), was a German-born Christian theologian, philosopher, and scientist. His importance lies in his awareness of the difference between theology and philosophy and between revealed truth and experimental science. Albertus believed that different areas of human knowledge follow different sets of laws and require different methods of investigation.

Albertus was advanced for his time in his knowledge of the sciences. He wrote about many scientific subjects, including astronomy, chemistry, geography, and physiology, using his own scientific observations.

Albertus devoted much of his time to popularizing the writings of the ancient Greek philosopher Aristotle. Albertus wrote a large number of commentaries on Aristotle's philosophy. These writings influenced Saint Thomas Aquinas, Albertus's most famous pupil, and other theologians of the 1200's known as scholastics (see **Scholasticism**).

Albertus Magnus was born into a noble family in Lauingen, near Ulm. He attended the University of Padua in Italy, where he joined the Dominican religious order in 1223. He studied and taught at several European universities but spent most of his time in Cologne, Germa-ny. Albertus served as a high-ranking Dominican official in Germany, as a bishop, and as a representative of the pope. His feast day is November 15, the date on which he died in 1280. Albertus is the patron saint of students of the natural sciences.   Marilyn J. Harran

Albigenses, *AL buh JEHN seez,* were a group named for Albi, a city in southern France. They were part of a sect called the *Cathari,* which flourished in parts of Germany, France, and Italy in the 1100's and 1200's. The Albigenses believed the principles of good and evil continually opposed each other in the world. They believed that worldly things represented the evil force, and the human spirit was the only good. The Albigenses taught that the spirit had been imprisoned in the body as punishment for sinning, and that the highest good was to free the spirit from the body. The Albigenses opposed marriage, bearing children, and eating meat and other animal products. They advocated suicide, especially by starvation.

The Albigenses grew in popularity until the church pronounced them heretics in the mid-1100's. But the nobility and the townsfolk supported them. The church conducted a crusade against the Albigenses in the early 1200's. Crusaders and the Inquisition gradually destroyed the Albigenses' power, but there were brief rebellions from time to time. By about 1350, the Albigenses had disappeared in western Europe.   Eugene TeSelle

See also **Dominic, Saint; Heresy**.

Albino, *al BY noh,* is an animal or plant that is unable to produce *pigment* (coloring substance) in some or all of its organs. As a result, the animal or plant has abnormally light coloration.

Albinism is caused by a change in the *genes* (units of heredity) and can be inherited. A person who is a *true* (complete) albino has milky-white skin and white hair. True albinos appear to have pink *irises* (colored parts of the eyes) because of the way light reflects off the eyes. The irises themselves do not have pink coloring, but instead possess a small amount of blue pigment or no pigment at all. In normal eyes, enough pigment exists in the irises to hide the pinkness. Albinism occurs about once in every 20,000 births.

Albinism may vary from the complete absence of color to the presence of nearly normal amounts of pigment in some organs. Most white horses, chickens, ducks, and geese are only *partial* albinos because these animals have pigment in their eyes, beaks, or legs. Albino animals are rarely seen in the wild because their unusual coloration makes them inviting prey.

In many partial albino plants, only the flowers have no pigment. But some albino plants also lack chlorophyll and the leaves are also white. Such plants die unless they can get food from their surroundings, because plants need chlorophyll to make food.   Lawrence C. Wit

See also **Heredity** (diagram: The transmission of albinism); **Horse** (Color types; picture).

Albright, Madeleine Korbel (1937-   ), served as secretary of state of the United States from 1997 to 2001. She was the first woman to hold the post. President Bill Clinton appointed her to the office. Albright had served as United States ambassador to the United Nations (UN) from 1993 to 1997. At the UN, Albright became known as an outspoken supporter of human rights and of the use of UN peacekeeping forces in troubled areas.

Albright was born on May 15, 1937, in Prague, Czechoslovakia (now the Czech Republic). Her maiden name was Madeleine Korbel. Her father was a Czech diplomat. In 1939, after Nazi German forces occupied Czechoslovakia, her family fled to Yugoslavia and, eventually, to the United Kingdom. The family returned to Czechoslovakia in 1945 but fled again in 1948 when Communists took over the country. They settled in the United States.

Albright received a bachelor's degree from Wellesley College in 1959 and a doctorate in government from Columbia University in 1976. She was married to Joseph Albright, a journalist, from 1959 to 1983.

Albright served as a member of President Jimmy Carter's National Security Council staff from 1978 to 1981. She was a professor of international affairs at Georgetown University from 1982 to 1993. She returned to Georgetown in the 2000's to teach in the university's school of foreign service. After leaving her Cabinet post in 2001, Albright turned to teaching and writing. Her autobiography, *Madam Secretary: A Memoir,* was published in 2003. Albright's other books include *The Mighty and the Almighty: Reflections on America, God, and World Affairs* (2006), *Memo to the President Elect* (2008), and *Read My Pins: Stories from a Diplomat's Jewel Box* (2009).   Andrew Bennett

Albumin, *al BYOO muhn,* also spelled *albumen,* is a sticky, gelatinlike substance. Its best-known form is the white of an egg. Albumin belongs to the class of foods called proteins (see **Protein**). The word is spelled *albumen* when it refers to egg whites, but *albumin* when referring to the general substance. The albumin of egg white is called *ovalbumin.* The albumin in milk is called *lactalbumin. Serum albumin* is the albumin in blood serum. It makes up over half of the protein in blood serum and helps stabilize other serum proteins. Some albumin is found in vegetable matter. All albumins contain carbon, hydrogen, nitrogen, oxygen, and sulfur.

Albumin becomes a solid mass when heated. If albumin is heated with a liquid, it either settles to the bottom as sediment or forms a scum at the top. The sediment or the scum collects foreign substances as it forms. Albumins are used to collect impurities from liquids in sugar refining, industrial dyeing, and making photographic chemicals.   Kermit L. Carraway

See also **Blood** (Regulating the volume of blood components); **Egg** (Parts of a bird egg).

Albuquerque, *AL buh KUR kee* (pop. 545,852; met. area pop. 887,077), is the largest city in New Mexico. It serves as a financial, industrial, trade, and transportation center of the Southwest. The city is also a leading center for energy, space, and defense research. For location, see **New Mexico** (political map). Albuquerque's cultural heritage shows both Pueblo Indian and Spanish influences.

Description. Albuquerque, the seat of Bernalillo County, covers 188 square miles (487 square kilometers). The skyline of Albuquerque includes a number of skyscrapers, but many low, flat-roofed, adobe houses help the city keep its Indian character. One of the city's landmarks, the Roman Catholic Church of San Felipe de Neri, served as a fortress that protected the early settlers

during Indian raids. East of the city, the Sandia Mountains provide ski slopes, an aerial tram, and other recreational facilities. Albuquerque is the home of the University of New Mexico.

Federal nuclear weapon research and defense-related research rank as the city's chief industries. Nearby Kirtland Air Force Base is a defense and energy research center. Sandia National Laboratories, on the Kirtland base, conducts energy research and development programs. Tourism is Albuquerque's most profitable nongovernment industry. Clothing and electronics factories, food-processing plants, and health care facilities employ many workers.

Government and history. Albuquerque has a mayor-council form of government. The voters elect a mayor and nine councilors to four-year terms.

Francisco Cuervo y Valdés, governor of the Spanish province of New Mexico, founded Albuquerque in 1706. It was named for the Duke of Alburquerque, a Spanish nobleman. The town became part of the United States as a result of the Mexican War (1846-1848). Albuquerque was incorporated as a city in 1891. It had about 3,785 people and was a trading center for sheep ranchers.

After World War II ended in 1945, an increase in military spending created thousands of jobs in the nuclear research centers in and near Albuquerque. The city's population more than doubled from 1950 to 1960, rising from 96,815 to 201,189. An urban renewal program in the mid-1970's included a new convention center and a public library. In the late 1900's, the city completed expansions of the convention center and the airport, called Albuquerque International Sunport.   Kelly Brewer

For the monthly weather in Albuquerque, see **New Mexico** (Climate).

Alcan Inc. was one of the world's largest producers of aluminum and aluminum products. Its headquarters were in Montreal, Canada. Alcan was involved in all aspects of the aluminum business: bauxite mining, alumina refining, aluminum smelting, manufacturing, sales, and recycling. Alcan also owned hydroelectric power plants that supplied the energy needed for aluminum smelting.

Alcan was formed in 1902 as a Canadian firm owned by the Aluminum Company of America (now Alcoa Inc.), a business based in the United States. In 1928, Alcan became an independent company and took control of most of Alcoa's business outside the United States. In 2007, Alcan was acquired by the large metal and mining conglomerate Rio Tinto. The aluminum operations of Rio Tinto were renamed Rio Tinto Alcan after the merger.   Critically reviewed by Rio Tinto Alcan Inc.

See also **Aluminum.**

Alcatraz, *AL kuh TRAZ,* was a famous federal prison on Alcatraz Island in San Francisco Bay. The name *Alcatraz* comes from a Spanish word meaning *pelican.* The island stands on 12 acres (5 hectares) of solid rock, and Alcatraz was often called "The Rock." More than 1 mile (1.6 kilometers) of water separates it from the mainland. For the location of Alcatraz, see **San Francisco** (map).

Alcatraz Island became the site of the first permanent military fort on the West Coast in 1854. A military prison was added in 1861. In 1909, the wooden prison was replaced by a more modern concrete cell block. Alcatraz became a federal prison in 1934, built to confine some of the most dangerous criminals in the United States.

Prisoners included the gangsters Al Capone and George "Machine Gun" Kelly, as well as the murderer Robert Stroud, who became known as "The Birdman of Alcatraz." In 1963, the federal government decided Alcatraz was too expensive to maintain and supply, and closed it. In 1969, a group of American Indians came to Alcatraz and symbolically claimed the island for the Indian people. They occupied the island until 1971. In 1972, Alcatraz became part of the Golden Gate National Recreation Area. Visitors may tour the prison.

James O. Finckenauer

Alcazar, *AL kuh zahr,* is the name usually given to Spanish palaces built by the Moors, a Muslim people from North Africa. Some alcazars were walled fortresses used for defense. An alcazar in Toledo, Spain, was destroyed during the Spanish Civil War (1936-1939). The Alhambra is perhaps the best-known alcazar.

William J. Hennessey

See also **Alhambra.**

Alchemy is a way of studying and experimenting with matter that includes elements of chemistry, philosophy, and spirituality. Much of alchemy deals with transforming natural materials into useful or valuable substances. Before the development of modern chemistry, alchemists sought to understand the changes they saw in metals and other materials that were exposed to fire and acids. People still practice alchemy today, but modern alchemists primarily seek spiritual transformation.

Alchemy developed from such activities as coloring and *alloying* (mixing) metals and making gems. Some alchemists tried to transform cheaper metals into silver or gold, a process called *transmutation.* Some early alchemists produced counterfeit gold, silver, and precious stones. Such activities may have given alchemy its reputation for deceptive practices.

Alchemists and metalsmiths used similar techniques. But alchemists often saw themselves as trying to speed up or perfect the workings of nature. Some alchemists searched for the *philosopher's stone,* which they thought could greatly speed up the transmutation process. Many alchemists believed that they could perfect and purify materials only if they themselves were spiritually perfected and purified in the process.

Ancient societies in Egypt, India, and China practiced alchemy. Egyptian writers later produced written works on alchemy from about 200 B.C. to A.D. 200. Arab scholars built on these works from the 640's to about 1200. Alchemy reached Europe around 1100 and flourished, especially in noble courts. At its peak in the 1600's, a number of famous scientists practiced alchemy, including Robert Boyle of Ireland and Isaac Newton of England. In the late 1700's, many learned people began to ridicule alchemy as *pseudoscientific* (falsely claiming scientific merit) and deceptive.

Alchemists based their ideas on the ancient Greek belief that matter consists of four elements: (1) water, (2) earth, (3) air, and (4) fire. Alchemists also thought that all metals could be reduced to a single type of matter and thus transformed into one another. During the 700's, Arab alchemists thought that the qualities of all metals could be explained in terms of sulfur, which burns in hot fires, and mercury, which is liquid at room temperature and has a metallic shine. During the early 1500's, the Swiss physician Philippus Paracelsus thought that

sulfur, mercury, and salt gave metals their distinctive qualities.

Alchemy played a key role in the development of modern science. The theories of alchemy gave rise to modern chemical theory. Modern experimental techniques developed from such alchemical practices as studying nature in a laboratory; observing experiments and keeping records; and measuring the ingredients and products of chemical reactions.

Pamela H. Smith

See also **Chemistry** (Alchemy).

Alcibiades, *AL suh BY uh DEEZ* (450?-404 B.C.), was an Athenian general. He became a central figure in the Peloponnesian War, which was fought between Athens and Sparta from 431 to 404 B.C.

Alcibiades was the ward of the Athenian leader Pericles and a favorite pupil of Socrates, a famous Greek philosopher. Acibiades entered politics in 420 B.C., and he soon became popular for his aggressive foreign policy.

Alcibiades's policy led Athens to a battle with Sparta in 418 B.C., which Athens lost. Later, he persuaded the Athenians to invade Sicily. In 415 B.C., just before the invasion began, citizens accused Alcibiades of defacing statues of the god Hermes and of mocking the religious rituals known as the Eleusinian Mysteries. The Athenians refused his request for an immediate trial, so he sailed on to Sicily. Shortly after arriving in Sicily, Alcibiades was called back to Athens for trial. But he escaped to Sparta. He advised the Spartans to aid the Sicilians, and the Athenians were defeated in Sicily.

Later, the Spartans grew suspicious of Alcibiades. Alcibiades then became an adviser to the Persian leader Tissaphernes. In 411 B.C., the Athenians asked Alcibiades to lead their fleet at Samos. With this navy, he defeated the Spartans in several battles and became a hero. In 406 B.C., however, the Spartan general Lysander defeated Alcibiades's fleet. After Athens's final defeat in the war, Alcibiades fled to Asia Minor (now part of Turkey). There, his enemies set fire to his house, and he died trying to escape.

Peter Krentz

Alcindor, Lew. See Abdul-Jabbar, Kareem.

Alcoa Corporation is a leading aluminum-mining company. It maintains operating facilities in numerous locations worldwide. Alcoa is engaged in the mining of aluminum ores such as *bauxite* and the refining of such ores into cast and rolled aluminum to be sold to manufacturers. Alcoa also has plants for recycling used aluminum.

The company was organized in 1888 as the Pittsburgh Reduction Company. It was formed to produce aluminum by a process discovered by the American scientist Charles M. Hall in 1886. The company's name was changed to the Aluminum Company of America in 1907. It changed its name to Alcoa Incorporated in 1998. In 2016, Alcoa spun off its aluminum manufacturing division into a separate company, called Arconic, and changed its own name to Alcoa Corporation. The company has headquarters in Pittsburgh, Pennsylvania, and in New York City, New York.

Critically reviewed by Alcoa Corporation

See also **Alcan Inc.; Aluminum** (Growth of the aluminum industry).

Alcock and Brown, *AWL kahk,* were pioneering British aviators who made the first nonstop flight across the Atlantic Ocean. Sir John William Alcock (1892-1919) was the pilot, and Sir Arthur Whitten Brown (1886-1948) was the navigator. On June 14, 1919, the two men took off from Lester's Field near St. John's, Newfoundland (now Newfoundland and Labrador), in a twin-engine Vickers *Vimy,* a converted bomber. They landed the plane in a bog near Clifden, Ireland, the next day. The aviators traveled nearly 2,000 miles (3,200 kilometers) in 16 hours and 27 minutes.

Alcock and Brown were knighted for their effort by King George V. They also received a prize of 10,000 pounds ($46,200) that the *London Daily Mail* newspaper in 1913 had offered to the crew of the first airplane to make a nonstop transatlantic crossing.

Alcock was born on Nov. 6, 1892, in Manchester, England. During World War I (1914-1918), he was considered one of the best pilots in the United Kingdom's Royal Naval Air Service. He died in an air crash on Dec. 18, 1919, six months after his transatlantic flight.

Brown was born of American parents in Glasgow, Scotland, on July 23, 1886. He became a British citizen and served in the Royal Flying Corps. He died on Oct. 4, 1948.   Timothy S. Wolters

Alcohol refers to a class of chemical compounds, all of which consist of chemically bonded atoms of carbon, hydrogen, and oxygen. All alcohol molecules contain at least one *hydroxyl group.* A hydroxyl group is a specific arrangement of atoms in which a hydrogen atom is bonded to an oxygen atom. In alcohol molecules, the oxygen atom in the hydroxyl group is, in turn, bonded to a carbon atom.

People commonly use the word *alcohol* to refer to such beverages as beer, wine, and liquors. But there are many types of alcohols, and they have a variety of uses. This article discusses the chemical properties and commercial uses of several alcohols. For information on alcoholic beverages, see **Alcoholic beverage.**

Methanol, also called *methyl alcohol* or *wood alcohol,* is the simplest of the alcohols. It has one hydroxyl group, and its chemical formula is CH_3OH. Methanol is a highly toxic, colorless liquid. It boils at 149 °F (65 °C) and freezes at −137 °F (−94 °C).

Methanol originally was produced from wood, but it is now commercially produced primarily from *methane,* the chief component of natural gas. The majority of commercially produced methanol is converted to *formaldehyde,* a chemical used to make plastics. As an industrial *solvent* (substance that dissolves other substances), methanol is important in the manufacture of paints and varnishes. Methanol also functions as a fuel-line antifreeze for automobiles, and it serves as an ingredient in the production of other chemicals. Methanol can be used as a motor fuel, but it is more expensive than other fuels. See **Methanol.**

Ethanol, also called *ethyl alcohol,* is the alcohol found in alcoholic beverages. Ethanol is also used for a variety of other purposes. It serves as a solvent for chemical reactions and for lacquers, varnishes, and stains. It is also important in the preparation of chemicals used as detergents, flavorings, and fragrances.

As a gasoline additive, ethanol improves vehicle performance and reduces emissions of dangerous pollu-

tants. Some motor vehicles are designed to run on fuels of 85 percent or more ethanol. Several automakers manufacture a number of *flexible fuel vehicles,* which can run on gasoline, fuel of 85 percent ethanol, or any mixture of the two.

Ethanol is produced by several methods. For example, ethanol used in beverages is produced by fermenting fruits, grains, or vegetables. However, most ethanol used for commercial purposes is made by heating ethylene and water under pressure in the presence of a phosphoric acid catalyst (see **Catalysis**). Ethylene is a gas that is a component of crude oil.

The United States government controls and taxes the production and distribution of ethanol in the United States and taxes ethyl alcohol used in alcoholic beverages. For this reason, ethanol manufacturers in the United States *denature* (make unfit to drink) most of the ethanol that will be used for purposes other than alcoholic drinks. Manufacturers denature ethanol by mixing it with methanol or other poisonous chemicals.

Ethanol boils at 172 °F (78 °C) and freezes at −173 °F (−114 °C). Its chemical formula is CH_3CH_2OH. It has one hydroxyl group. See **Ethanol.**

Propanol, or *propyl alcohol,* has one hydroxyl group, and its chemical formula is $CH_3CH_2CH_2OH$. There are two forms of propanol, called *isomers.* Isomers have the same kind and number of atoms. However, they have different molecular structures and therefore different chemical and physical properties. For example, one of the isomers of propanol, called *normal propanol, 1-propanol,* or *n-propyl alcohol,* boils at 208 °F (98 °C) and freezes at −195 °F (−126 °C). But the other isomer, known as *isopropanol, 2-propanol,* or *isopropyl alcohol,* boils at 181 °F (83 °C) and freezes at −126 °F (−88 °C).

Normal propanol is made commercially from ethylene and synthesis gas, a mixture of hydrogen and carbon monoxide, in the presence of a rhodium or cobalt catalyst. Propyl alcohol is used to prepare other chemicals, and it is used as a solvent for sticky substances called *resins.*

Isopropanol is produced by reaction of the gas propylene, a component of crude oil, with water in the presence of an acid or metal catalyst. Isopropanol is mainly used to produce acetone, a common industrial solvent. It is also used as a rubbing alcohol, and in cosmetics and lotions.

Ethanediol, or *ethylene glycol,* is a highly toxic alcohol that is used mainly as an antifreeze in automobile radiators. It is produced by the reaction of ethylene with water and oxygen in the presence of a silver oxide catalyst. Ethanediol has a boiling point of 388 °F (198 °C) and a freezing point of −9 °F (−13 °C). It has two hydroxyl groups and a chemical formula of $HOCH_2CH_2OH$.

Other alcohols include *plasticizer alcohols,* which have 6 to 11 carbon atoms. Plasticizers are used in the manufacture of plastics, and they give these substances flexibility.

Alcohols that have more than 11 carbon atoms are called *detergent alcohols.* Manufacturers use these alcohols to make detergents, soaps, and shampoos. In combination with other chemicals, these alcohols have the ability to dissolve dirt and grease in water in a process called *emulsification.*   Marianna A. Busch

See also **Antifreeze; Glycerol; Solvent.**

Alcohol, Tobacco, Firearms and Explosives, Bureau of, is a law enforcement agency within the United States Department of Justice dedicated to preventing terrorism and reducing violent crime. The bureau, often called the ATF, enforces federal laws involving firearms and explosives, arson and bombings, and illegal trafficking of alcohol and tobacco products.

Most ATF criminal cases involve people suspected of the illegal possession and use of firearms or explosives. Targets of investigation include killers for hire, gun smugglers, bombers, and arsonists. ATF special agents go undercover to break up illegal commerce in firearms, drug-smuggling rings, outlaw motorcycle gangs, and other criminal groups. The ATF works closely with other law enforcement agencies. The ATF also regulates the sale, possession, and transportation of firearms, ammunition, explosives, liquor, and tobacco in interstate commerce.

The ATF was chartered as the Bureau of Alcohol, Tobacco and Firearms in 1972. It acquired its present name in 2003. Its headquarters are in Washington, D.C.

Franklin E. Zimring

Alcoholic beverage is a drink containing *ethyl alcohol,* also called *ethanol,* a chemical that slows the activity of the nervous system. People often consume alcoholic beverages to celebrate and to relax at social gatherings. Such beverages are also used in cooking and in religious rituals. Many people find the effects of drinking alcohol pleasurable, but excessive drinking can cause intoxication and even death. Prolonged drinking may lead to alcoholism and other health problems. This article describes various types of alcoholic beverages and how they are made. For more information on some dangers of alcohol abuse, see **Alcoholism.**

Alcoholic beverages are made chiefly from such grains as barley, corn, and rye or from grapes and other fruits. The grain or fruit provides the sugar needed for *fermentation,* a process by which yeast converts sugar into ethyl alcohol and carbon dioxide gas.

There are two main groups of alcoholic beverages: *fermented drinks* and *distilled drinks.* Fermented drinks, such as beer and wine, are made through fermentation alone. They usually contain from 2 to 20 percent ethyl alcohol. Distilled drinks, also called *liquor, spirits,* or *hard alcohol,* are purified after fermentation through a process called *distillation.* They usually contain from 12 to 55 percent ethyl alcohol. They include brandy, gin, rum, vodka, and whiskey.

Taxes on alcoholic beverages provide a major source of revenue for many governments. Such taxes are usually much higher than taxes on foods and nonalcoholic beverages. In the United States, taxes and other fees make up about half the price of a bottle of liquor. Distilled drinks carry higher taxes than fermented drinks.

Fermented drinks

Fermented drinks are made by fermenting substances that contain sugar. The principal fermented beverages are beer and wine.

Beer is made from barley and other grains. Brewers crush the grains and mix them with water to form a *mash.* They then heat the mash to convert the starch in the grains to sugar. Dried flowers from the hops plant are added to flavor the mash, and then yeast is added to begin fermentation. After the sugar converts to alcohol, brewers age beer for several weeks to develop its taste.

Beer is a foaming, carbonated beverage that is generally served chilled. Most beer contains from 3 to 6 percent alcohol. There are two major types of beer: *lager* and *ale.* Lager is typically bubbly and golden. Ale often has a richer flavor and darker color. Beer with a high alcohol content is sometimes called *malt liquor.*

Wine is usually made from grapes, which contain more sugar than most other fruits, but it can also be made from cherries, apples, or other fruits. Winemakers crush the fruit and then ferment the juice. They then age the wine to develop its flavor.

Most wine has an alcohol content of 7 to 24 percent. Red wine comes from grapes that are fermented with their skins. For white wine, only the juice is fermented. Pink-colored *blush* or *rosé* wine is made by separating the juice and skins part way through fermentation. People traditionally serve red wines at room temperature and other wines chilled.

Other fermented beverages. *Sake,* a popular Japanese drink, is made from rice. *Mead* is made from honey. *Hard cider* comes from apples and, occasionally, other fruits. Some beverage makers sell soft-drinklike malt beverages that resemble sweetened, unhopped beer.

Distilled drinks

Distilled beverages are made chiefly from fermented grain mash or fruit juice. In the distillation process, beverage makers heat the mash or juice, causing the alcohol to become a vapor. They collect the vapor and cool it to form a liquid, which can be mixed or aged to make liquor. Some liquors are distilled several times.

The percentage of alcohol in liquor is expressed as *proof.* In the United States, proof equals twice the percentage of alcohol in the beverage. For example, a beverage that is 80 proof contains 40 percent alcohol. In Canada and the United Kingdom, the amount of alcohol is about 57 percent at 100 proof.

People can serve distilled drinks *neat* (straight from the bottle) or *on the rocks* (with ice). They can also mix them with other kinds of liquor and nonalcoholic ingredients to make *mixed drinks,* also called *cocktails.*

Brandy is distilled from grape wine or other fermented fruit juices. Brandy made from grape wine is at least 80 proof. *Cognac,* a well-known variety, comes from the area around Cognac, France. Brandy makers often age the liquor for several years to develop its flavor and color. Brandies made from other fruits are at least 70 proof.

Gin is a clear liquor flavored with juniper berries. Gin makers first distill liquor from fermented grains. They then add the berries and distill the mixture a second time. Gin varies from 80 to 94 proof.

Rum is distilled from fermented sugar cane juice or molasses. It is at least 80 proof and may be white or amber, depending largely on the aging process. Rum makers sometimes flavor the liquor with spices and caramel. Rum is often used in mixed drinks with tropical flavors.

Vodka is distilled from barley, corn, rye, or sometimes from potatoes. It varies from 80 to 100 proof. Like gin, it is not aged and has no color. Unlike gin, vodka has no flavor or smell. For this reason, people use it in a wide variety of mixed drinks. Vodka is traditionally associated with Russia and other Eastern European countries but has become popular in much of the world.

Whiskey is made chiefly from barley, corn, or rye. Most whiskey sold commercially ranges from 80 to 100 proof and consists of a blend of as many as 50 kinds of whiskey made from different grains. Distillers may age whiskey two years or more to develop its flavor and amber color. Whiskey from Scotland, called *Scotch whisky* or *Scotch,* has a distinctive smoky flavor. Distillers make it from mash that consists primarily of barley. In the United States, distillers make a type of whiskey called *bourbon* from a mash consisting chiefly of corn.

Other distilled drinks include *aquavit, tequila,* and *liqueurs.* Aquavit, also spelled *akvavit,* is a Scandinavian beverage made from grains or potatoes and flavored with caraway seeds. Distillers make tequila, a Mexican drink, from the fermented juice of the agave plant.

Liqueur makers flavor liquor by soaking it with chocolate, coffee, flowers, fruits, or other substances. Liqueurs consist of at least 2 ½ percent sugar and sometimes contain cream. They range from 20 to 110 proof and have a variety of colors.

History

The first alcoholic beverages were fermented drinks. Scenes showing fermentation appear as early as 4200 B.C. on pottery made in Mesopotamia. An ancient Sumerian tablet from the 1800's B.C. bears a hymn to the goddess of brewing that is also a recipe for making beer. The ancient Egyptians made wine and stored it in clay vessels. Wine developed an important role in the religious rituals of many groups, including Greek, Roman, and Christian traditions.

Distillation played an important role in *alchemy,* an early study that incorporated elements of chemistry and *mysticism,* the search for spiritual knowledge. The term *spirits* comes from the alchemical belief that distilled beverages contained the spirit of the fermented liquid. Brandy, probably the oldest distilled drink, may have been made as early as A.D. 100. By the 1400's, people in Ireland and Scotland were distilling whiskey. Gin originated in Holland by about 1600. Distillers first produced rum by 1650 in Barbados, an island in the West Indies. The first distillery for the production of bourbon began operating in 1789 near Georgetown, Kentucky.

Throughout history, people have attempted to prohibit or limit the drinking of alcoholic beverages. Some religions forbid their consumption. Governments have imposed various measures to limit alcohol use. These measures include rationing alcoholic beverages, taxing them heavily, and imposing legal bans against drinking. For several years during the early 1900's, for example, Canada, Finland, Norway, and the United States banned alcoholic beverages. Many people opposed or defied this *prohibition,* some of them by distilling their own crude liquor, called *moonshine.* These prohibition laws were eventually repealed. But in the United States, it remains illegal to produce liquor without a license from the state government. Other national governments also restrict the production of liquor. Michael J. Claus

Related articles in *World Book* include:

Prohibition   Wine
Whiskey

Alcoholics Anonymous (A.A.) is a worldwide organization of people who help each other solve their common problem of alcoholism. They also offer to share their recovery experiences with others who have a drinking problem and want to do something about it. The fellowship of Alcoholics Anonymous was founded in 1935. It has local groups throughout the world. The people in each group meet to share their problems and experiences. A.A. is not a medical or religious organization. It is concerned only with the personal recovery and continued sobriety of individual alcoholics who turn to A.A. for help. The General Service Office is the center of A.A. activities. The organization's headquarters are in New York City. See also **Al-Anon.**

Critically reviewed by Alcoholics Anonymous

Alcoholism is a serious disease in which people have an overwhelming desire for the mental and physical effects of drinking alcoholic beverages. The formal term for alcoholism is *alcohol dependence.* Alcohol is one of the most widely used drugs in the history of the world. Many adults drink alcoholic beverages on social or ceremonial occasions but have no wish to consume large amounts regularly. People with alcoholism, who are called *alcoholics,* feel a strong, continuing urge to drink.

Alcoholism has four main symptoms: (1) craving, (2) lack of control, (3) physical tolerance, and (4) physical dependence. Craving is a strong need to drink in spite of serious harmful consequences, such as drinking-related illnesses or job problems. Lack of control is the inability to stop drinking once a drinking episode starts. Physical tolerance is the need to consume increasing amounts of alcohol to feel its effects. Physical dependence occurs when people's bodies become so accustomed to alcohol that they have withdrawal symptoms after they stop drinking. Symptoms of withdrawal include shakiness, rapid heartbeat, nausea, sweating, and anxiety. Physical dependence does not occur in all alcoholics.

People who are not alcoholics may also have problems caused by excessive drinking. These problems include difficulties at work or school, neglect of family responsibilities, and strains in personal relationships. Drinking that causes problems but does not meet the formal definition for alcoholism is called *alcohol abuse.*

Causes of alcoholism. Scientists do not yet fully understand what causes alcoholism. Though many people use alcohol, only a small percentage develop drinking problems. Researchers are beginning to identify ways that the brains of alcoholics differ from the brains of nonalcoholics. For example, tests show that alcoholics and nonalcoholics have different patterns of brain electrical activity. Such differences may provide evidence that alcohol does not affect the brains of alcoholics the same way it affects those of nonalcoholics. Because of the way their brains respond, problem drinkers may develop an unusually strong desire for alcohol's effects.

Research shows that heredity plays an important role in alcoholism. For example, the pattern of brain electrical activity associated with alcoholism appears to be inherited. Other studies show that people with an alcoholic parent have a greater risk of developing the disease than do children of nonalcoholics. Scientists are working to identify the particular *genes* (chemical units of heredity) that increase risk. Most experts think that many genes are involved and that environment also plays a role. Environmental influences may include income level, family stability, and community acceptance of drinking. Experts think that the relative importance of genes and environment may differ among individuals.

Other research focuses on how alcohol affects *neurotransmitters*, chemicals that carry messages among nerve cells. Studies show that alcohol affects many neurotransmitters in the brain. The neurotransmitters affected include *dopamine* and *serotonin*. These chemicals carry information about pleasure, sadness, and other moods. Prolonged drinking changes levels of neurotransmitter activity. The levels do not immediately return to normal when drinking stops. Thus, problem drinkers may not "feel right" when they stop drinking because their neurotransmitters have adapted to alcohol.

Effects of alcoholism. Alcohol affects the entire body. Health problems caused by long-term drinking include damage to the brain, stomach, intestines, and heart. Liver problems, including a disorder called *cirrhosis*, are common in alcoholics. The liver plays a key role in breaking down alcohol. Excess drinking puts abnormal demands on the organ. When alcoholics stop drinking, some suffer a severe form of withdrawal called *delirium tremens*. Delirium tremens is a state of confusion sometimes accompanied by *hallucinations* (seeing or hearing things that are not present). Drinking is also a factor in many vehicle crashes, falls, and other accidents.

Treatment aims to help alcoholics stop drinking and remain sober. Behavioral treatments and medications are two important approaches that have succeeded with some alcoholics. Behavioral treatments include participation in Alcoholics Anonymous (A.A.) and various types of counseling. Medications include tranquilizers called *benzodiazepines*, sold under such trade names as Librium and Valium. Benzodiazepines are used in the first few days after a person stops drinking to help prevent symptoms of withdrawal. A medication called *disulfiram* (sold under the trade name Antabuse) discourages alcohol use. It causes nausea, vomiting, and other unpleasant symptoms when people drink. Other drugs include *naltrexone* (trade name, Revia) and *acamprosate* (trade name, Campral). For many people, these drugs lessen the craving for alcohol, thereby enabling them to stay sober.   Brett C. Plyler

Related articles in *World Book* include:

Al-Anon	Delirium tremens	Fetal alcohol syndrome
Alcoholics Anonymous	Disulfiram	drome
	Driving while intoxicated	Mental illness
Benzodiazepine		(Substance use
Breath testing	Drug abuse	disorders)
Cirrhosis		Pancreatitis

Additional resources

Bakewell, Lisa, ed. *Alcohol Information for Teens*. 2nd ed. Omnigraphics, 2009.
Gold, Mark S., and Adamec, C. A. *The Encyclopedia of Alcoholism and Alcohol Abuse*. Facts on File, 2010.

Alcott, *AWL kuht* or *AWL kaht,* **Bronson** (1799-1888), was an American social reformer and a leader of a philosophical movement called Transcendentalism. From 1834 to 1839, Alcott operated the experimental Temple School in Boston. He tried to develop the bodies and spiritual natures—as well as the minds—of his students.

Alcott was a leading abolitionist. He opposed the

Mexican War (1846-1848) because he felt it resulted from a desire by the United States government to extend slavery into Texas. In the 1840's, Alcott helped found two cooperative experimental communities—the socialist Brook Farm and the vegetarian Fruitlands.

Amos Bronson Alcott was born on Nov. 29, 1799, near Wolcott, Connecticut. He died on March 4, 1888. He was the father of Louisa May Alcott, who wrote the famous novel *Little Women* (1868-1869).   John Clendenning

See also **Brook Farm; Transcendentalism.**

Alcott, *AWL kuht* or *AWL kaht,* **Louisa May** (1832-1888), was an American author. Her famous novel *Little Women* (1868-1869) tells the story of four sisters growing up in a New England town during the mid-1800's. Alcott also worked to gain voting rights for women and was active in the *temperance* (antidrinking) movement.

Alcott was born on Nov. 29, 1832, in Germantown, Pennsylvania, but she grew up in Boston and Concord, Massachusetts. Her father, Bronson Alcott, was a social reformer. The family's friends and neighbors included the writers Ralph Waldo Emerson, Margaret Fuller, Nathaniel Hawthorne, and Henry David Thoreau. William Ellery Channing, a prominent Unitarian minister, was also a friend. All these people influenced Alcott and helped form her ideas about politics and social reform.

Alcott spent most of her childhood in poverty because her father invested in many idealistic projects that failed. At an early age, she began to help support the family by working as a seamstress, a household servant, and a teacher. Her first book, *Flower Fables* (1855), consisted of fairy stories she made up to tell one of her students. *Hospital Sketches* (1863) contains letters she wrote home while nursing soldiers during the American Civil War (1861-1865).

Alcott's first novel, *Moods,* was published in 1864. She became editor of *Merry's Museum,* a magazine for girls, in 1867. That year, a publisher urged her to write a book for girls. She wrote *Little Women,* which became an immediate success. The income from sales of *Little Women* gave her financial security. In *Little Women,* Alcott gave American juvenile fiction an enduring family story, a new kind of girl character, and a narrative style less aimed at moral teaching. The March family in the book is largely the Alcott family. Jo March, the central character, is Louisa. She continued the story of the March family in *Little Men: Life at Plumfield with Jo's Boys* (1871) and *Jo's Boys, and How They Turned Out* (1886).

Alcott's other books for young readers include *An Old-Fashioned Girl* (1870) and *Eight Cousins* (1875). She also wrote novels for adults, including *Work: A Story of Experience* (1873) and *A Modern Mephistopheles* (1877), but these books were less successful. Alcott died on March 6, 1888.   Donald G. Marshall

Alden, *AWL duhn,* **John and Priscilla,** came to America on the *Mayflower* in 1620. They became husband and wife, probably in 1622. They were among the first *Mayflower* passengers to be married in America. The Aldens had 11 children. Their descendants include President John Quincy Adams and American poets Henry Wadsworth Longfellow and William Cullen Bryant. Longfellow wrote about the couple's marriage in his fictional poem *The Courtship of Miles Standish* (1858).

John Alden (1599-1687) was a *cooper* (barrelmaker) from Harwich, in the county of Essex, England. The Pilgrims hired him to accompany them to America. When the *Mayflower* sailed from England, Alden had not yet decided if he would stay in America. But he eventually became a leader of the Plymouth Colony. Alden served as an assistant to the governor of the colony most of the time from about 1631 until he died on Sept. 12, 1687. He served as treasurer from 1656 to 1658. In 1634, authorities held Alden on a technical charge of murder because he had favored defending a Plymouth outpost against attack, and in the resulting fight two men were killed. However, he was acquitted. Alden was a stern, unyielding man, and he led in the persecution of Quakers and Baptists.

Priscilla Mullens Alden (1602?-1685?) was the daughter of William Mullens, one of the Pilgrims. The Mullenses came from Dorking, in the county of Surrey, England.

James Axtell

Alder, *AWL duhr,* is the name of a group of shrubs and trees that grow in moist ground. Alders are found in *temperate* regions of the Northern Hemisphere, which have hot summers and cool or cold winters. The trees also grow at high elevations in parts of Central and South America, Asia, and North Africa.

Alders have oval leaves with toothed edges and produce separate male and female flowers. The female flowers grow in *catkins* (clusters of stalkless flowers) that harden into scaly, woody conelike structures. The structures have nuts and are later shed by the plant.

Several species of alders grow in North America. Most are large shrubs that form dense thickets. The *speckled alder* grows throughout Canada, south to Virginia, and west to North Dakota. The *red alder* is the only alder large enough for commercial timber production. It is the most important hardwood tree in the Pacific Northwest, where it grows up to 100 feet (30 meters) high. Its wood is soft and light. It is whitish when first cut and light reddish-brown when dry. It is used mostly for inexpensive furniture.   Michael J. Baranski

Scientific classification. Alders make up the genus *Alnus.* The speckled alder's scientific name is *A. incana.* The red alder is *A. rubra.*

See also **Tree** (Broadleaf and needleleaf trees [picture]).

Aldridge, Ira (1807?-1867), was the first African American actor to win fame in the Western world. He was best known for his roles in the tragedies of William Shakespeare, especially Othello. Unlike other tragic actors of his day, Aldridge was also a skilled comic actor.

Ira Frederick Aldridge was born on July 24, probably in 1807. His birthplace was either in New York City or Senegal. He was raised in New York City. In 1825, he left the United States because racial prejudice limited opportunities for black actors. He went to the United Kingdom in 1826 and made his debut as Othello in London. He also toured other

Museum of the City of New York
Ira Aldridge

European countries and achieved success in Germany and Russia. He became a British citizen in 1863. Aldridge died on Aug. 10, 1867.   Stanley L. Glenn

Aldrin, *AWL drihn,* **Buzz** (1930-   ), a United States astronaut, was the second person to set foot on the moon. He and Neil A. Armstrong landed there in the Apollo 11 lunar module on July 20, 1969. Aldrin stepped onto the moon 19 minutes after Armstrong.

Aldrin was born in Montclair, New Jersey, on Jan. 20, 1930, and was named Edwin Eugene Aldrin, Jr. His family nicknamed him Buzz, short for Buzzer, his young sister's pronunciation of the word *brother.* He legally changed his name to Buzz Aldrin as an adult.

Aldrin graduated from the U.S. Military Academy in 1951 and became an Air Force officer. After completing pilot training in 1952, he flew 66 combat missions in the Korean War. In 1963, he received a doctor's degree in astronautics from the Massachusetts Institute of Technology. He became an astronaut later that year.

Aldrin piloted the Gemini 12 space flight in 1966. During this flight, he left the spacecraft and, drawing on his experience as a scuba diver, "walked" in space. He was partially or completely outside the spacecraft for 5 ½ hours. This experience helped prove that people can work outside an orbiting vehicle.

In 1971, Aldrin resigned from the astronaut program and returned to active duty with the Air Force. In 1998, he founded the ShareSpace Foundation, a nonprofit organization that promotes interest in space travel. Aldrin wrote two volumes of autobiography, *Return to Earth* (1973) and *Magnificent Desolation* (2009).

Frank Morring, Jr.

See also **Space exploration** (Apollo: Mission to the moon).

Aleatory music, *AY lee uh TAWR ee,* is a type of music in which the composer does not determine the specific shape of a composition. The composer does not specify pitches, rhythms, and tone colors. He or she only gives ranges of these materials and relies on chance procedures or performers to select and shape them.

There are two basic types of aleatory music. In the first type, the composer uses chance procedures, such as the tossing of dice, to determine the order and quality of sounds. After the chance operations have established the musical details, the composer creates a fixed score using traditional musical notation. In the second type, the performer largely creates a composition. The composer might specify eight measures to be played with high notes, followed by six measures of low notes. The performers then create melodies, harmonies, and rhythms of their own design.

The most important composer of aleatory music was John Cage of the United States. Other major composers have included Earle Brown, Morton Feldman, and Christian Wolff of the United States; Pierre Boulez of France; and Karlheinz Stockhausen of Germany.   Mark D. Nelson

See also **Boulez, Pierre; Cage, John; Electronic music; Stockhausen, Karlheinz.**

Aleichem, Sholem. See Sholem Aleichem.

Aleixandre, *AH layks AHN dray,* **Vicente** (1898-1984), a Spanish poet, won the 1977 Nobel Prize in literature. He influenced other Spanish poets for much of the 1900's.

Aleixandre's early poetry, which he wrote chiefly in free verse, is highly surrealistic. It also praises the beauty of nature by using symbols that represent earth and the sea. Many of Aleixandre's early poems are filled with sadness. These poems reflect his feeling that people have lost the passion and free spirit that he saw in nature. Aleixandre's early poetry collections include *Passion of the Earth* (1935) and *Destruction or Love* (1933).

In *Shadow of Paradise* (1944), Aleixandre began to concentrate on such themes as fellowship, friendliness, and spiritual unity. His later books of poetry include *History of the Heart* (1954) and *In a Vast Dominion* (1962).

Aleixandre was born on April 26, 1898, in Seville. He studied law at the University of Madrid. Selections of his work were translated into English in *Twenty Poems of Vicente Aleixandre* (1977). He died on Dec. 14, 1984.

Dick Gerdes

Aleppo, *uh LEHP oh,* is one of the largest and most important cities in Syria. The city has about 4 million people. An industrial center, it lies nestled among the hills in northwestern Syria. For location, see **Syria** (map).

Aleppo is one of the oldest continuously inhabited cities, dating to about 2000 B.C. The city's bazaar, narrow streets, and limestone buildings reflect its ancient past. A medieval *citadel* (fort) surrounds the city. Aleppo is one of Syria's most important agricultural and industrial centers. Its chief products include cotton, wool, and textiles. The city is home to the University of Aleppo.

In ancient times, Aleppo served as a gateway between Europe and the eastern Mediterranean to Asia. In the 1500's, the city flourished as a major trading center of the Ottoman Empire.   Christine Moss Helms

Aleutian Islands, *uh LOO shuhn,* are a volcanic island chain that extends 1,100 miles (1,800 kilometers) west from the tip of the Alaska Peninsula. The Aleutians, part of Alaska, separate the Bering Sea from the Pacific Ocean. They include 14 large islands, about 55 smaller islands, and many islets. The mountains on the islands are part of the Alaska Range.

The Aleutians cover an area of 6,777 square miles (17,552 square kilometers). They lie 800 to 1,000 miles (1,300 to 1,600 kilometers) south of the Arctic Circle between the 51st and 55th parallels. This places the islands in the same latitude as England.

The Aleutians have many hot springs, as well as many cool springs and swift streams, on some of the islands.

No trees grow there, but the islands have many varieties of small shrubs, flowers, grasses, and mosses. The climate is cool and foggy. The principal industry is fishing. A few sheep ranches are operated there. The population of the islands is about 8,700.

The Aleutian Islands are divided into five main groups from east to west. These include the Fox Islands, Islands of Four Mountains, Andreanof Islands, the Rat Islands, and the Near Islands. Unimak, largest of the Aleutian Islands, has the highest mountain in the chain, Shishaldin Volcano (9,372 feet, or 2,857 meters). The village of Unalaska, on the island of the same name, is the trading center of the Aleutians and one of the leading fishing ports in the United States. Unalaska is the second largest island in the chain. It is the site of Dutch Harbor, which served as a United States naval air base during World War II (1939-1945).   Claus-M. Naske

See also **Alaska** (terrain map); **Aleuts.**

Aleuts, *AL ee ootz* or *uh LOOTZ,* are people who have traditionally lived on the harsh, windswept Aleutian Islands, which lie off the mainland of Alaska. The Aleuts call themselves *Unangan,* meaning *we the people.* They descended from Inuit (formerly called Eskimos) who settled on the islands thousands of years ago. But the Aleut language differs from that of the Inuit.

The early Aleuts lived off the rich sea environment. Aleut hunters harpooned whales, seals, and other sea mammals from seagoing kayaks. They caught fish with spears and on fishhooks and also hunted birds. The Aleuts wore parkas made of furs, bird skins, or other parts of animals. Several Aleut families lived together in large homes sunk 3 to 4 feet (91 to 122 centimeters) into the ground. The frames consisted of drift logs or whale bones. The homes were covered with a layer of dry grass or skins and a layer of sod.

Russian explorers discovered the Aleutian Islands in 1741. Russian traders and fur hunters later forced the Aleuts into labor and killed many of them. Many others died from diseases brought by the Russians. The Aleut population once numbered between 12,000 and 15,000 people. By the mid-1800's, fewer than 2,000 remained.

In 1867, the United States bought the islands, along with the rest of Alaska. Japanese forces attacked the islands during World War II (1939-1945). They captured the Aleut villagers of Attu and later sent them to a prison camp in Japan. There, about half the Aleuts died of tuberculosis and malnutrition. The United States government evacuated other Aleuts to Alaska. The Aleuts returned to the islands in 1945.

In 1971, the U.S. Congress passed the Alaska Native Claims Settlement Act, and the Aleuts regained control of much of their homeland. There are about 12,000 Aleuts living in Alaska. They follow a modern way of life, but many still hunt and fish for food.   Claus-M. Naske

See also **Aleutian Islands; Inuit; Mask** (picture: Burial masks).

Alewife is a fish that lives mainly in the Great Lakes and along the Atlantic coast of North America. It has large eyes, a forked tail, silvery sides, and a grayish-green back. Freshwater alewives grow 3 to 6 inches (8 to 15 centimeters) long. Saltwater alewives grow as long as 15 inches (38 centimeters). Saltwater species are caught commercially for human food. Freshwater species are used for animal feed and fertilizer. Saltwater alewives

Location of the Aleutian Islands

WORLD BOOK illustration by James Teason

The alewife lives in the Great Lakes and along the Atlantic Coast of North America.

live along the Atlantic coast from the Canadian province of Newfoundland and Labrador to South Carolina. They swim in large schools. They are *anadromous*—that is, they migrate to freshwater rivers to lay their eggs. Each female lays approximately 10,000 to 100,000 eggs in the spring. The adults then return immediately to the ocean. The young swim to the ocean a few months later, after they have grown.

Alewives probably are not native to any of the five Great Lakes. It is not certain when they colonized Lake Ontario, but they were abundant there by the 1870's. Alewives colonized the other four lakes after 1932. Sudden die-offs of alewives often occur during the spring in the Great Lakes. Scientists believe these die-offs may be due to sudden drops in water temperature.

W. Gary Sprules

Scientific classification. The alewife's scientific name is *Alosa pseudoharengus.*

Alexander I (1777-1825) was czar of Russia from 1801 to 1825 and a member of the Romanov line of rulers. He struggled to defeat Emperor Napoleon I of France. Russia finally succeeded after France invaded Russia in 1812. Alexander was influential at the Congress of Vienna, which in 1815 approved Russian territorial gains in Poland, Finland, and Bessarabia. The same year, he led the formation of the Holy Alliance (see **Holy Alliance**).

Alexander was born on Dec. 23, 1777. At the beginning of his reign, he considered freeing Russia's serfs, introducing a constitution, and limiting the czars' powers. But nothing came of these projects. Soon after Alexander died on Dec. 1, 1825, disappointed liberal army officers tried unsuccessfully to overthrow the government.　　　　Joseph T. Fuhrmann

See also **Russia** (Alexander I); **Vienna, Congress of.**

Alexander I (1888-1934) was a Serbian ruler who presided over the creation of Yugoslavia. During World War I (1914-1918), Alexander ruled Serbia as regent for his father, King Peter I. After the war, the Kingdom of the Serbs, Croats, and Slovenes was created with Peter as its king. Alexander ruled the new country as regent, and he became king when Peter died in 1921. The other peoples thought the Serbs had too much power, and it proved difficult to unite the country. In 1929, Alexander dissolved parliament, established a royal dictatorship, and renamed the country Yugoslavia. On Oct. 9, 1934, he was assassinated by a Macedonian revolutionary supported by a Croatian group. Alexander was born on Dec. 16, 1888, in Cetinje, Montenegro.　　Thomas A. Emmert

Alexander II (1818-1881) was czar of Russia from 1855 to 1881 and a member of the Romanov line of rulers. He succeeded his father, Nicholas I. Alexander is called the "czar liberator" because he freed Russia's serfs in 1861.

He also introduced local self-government and a court system based on French models. He modernized the Russian army and defeated the Ottoman Empire in 1878. On March 13, 1881, he was assassinated by revolutionaries. Alexander was born on April 29, 1818. See also **Russia** (Alexander II).　　Joseph T. Fuhrmann

Alexander III (1845-1894) was czar of Russia from 1881 to 1894 and a member of the Romanov line of rulers. He became czar after revolutionaries assassinated his father, Alexander II, who had adopted liberal reforms. Alexander III opposed further reform and fought the revolutionaries. During his reign, Russian industry and science advanced, and culture thrived. Alexander was born on March 10, 1845, and died on Nov. 1, 1894.

Joseph T. Fuhrmann

See also **Russia** (Alexander III).

Alexander VI (1431-1503) was the most worldly of the Renaissance popes. He was elected pope in 1492 and displayed the character and ambition more typical of a *secular* (nonreligious) ruler.

Alexander was born in Játiva, Spain. His given and family name was Rodrigo Borja (Borgia in Italian). His uncle Alphonso Borgia became Pope Callistus III in 1455. He soon appointed Alexander to the profitable position of vice chancellor of the Roman Curia, the administrative arm of the pope. Alexander held the position for many years, gathering vast wealth and influence. He fathered many children, whose fortunes he worked to advance even before becoming pope.

The first years of Alexander's reign were dominated by Italian wars, which broke out when King Charles VIII of France invaded Italy in 1494. The pope managed to survive the dangers of the conflict, largely through skillful diplomatic maneuvers. After Alexander's son Juan was murdered in Rome in 1497, the grief-stricken pope decided to launch a program of church reform but never carried it out. For the rest of his reign, Alexander devoted many papal resources to furthering the ambitions of his son Cesare to control central Italy for the Borgias. The pope died on Aug. 18, 1503.　　Charles L. Stinger

See also **Borgia, Cesare; Borgia, Lucrezia; Savonarola, Girolamo.**

Alexander, Grover Cleveland (1887-1950), was one of baseball's greatest pitchers. He won 373 games and pitched 90 shutouts while playing for the Philadelphia Phillies, Chicago Cubs, and St. Louis Cardinals from 1911 through 1930. Alexander set a record in 1916 by pitching 16 shutouts for the Phillies.

Alexander was born in Elba, Nebraska, on Feb. 26, 1887. He was elected to the National Baseball Hall of Fame in 1938. He died on Nov. 4, 1950.　　Dave Nightingale

Alexander, Kwame, *KWAH mee* (1968-　　), is an American writer of books and poetry for children and young adults. He won the 2015 Newbery Medal for his *verse novel The Crossover* (2014). A verse novel is a novel-length work written in *verse* (poetry) rather than in prose. The book tells the story of 12-year-old twin brothers who share a passion for basketball but find themselves drifting apart as they enter junior high school. Alexander also wrote the verse novels *Booked* (2016), about a 12-year-old soccer player who discovers the power of reading, and *Rebound* (2018), a prequel to *The Crossover* illustrated with graphic novel panels. In 2019, *The Crossover* was published as a graphic novel.

Edward Curtis Kwame Alexander II was born on Aug. 21, 1968, in the New York City borough of Manhattan, New York. He grew up in the New York City borough of Brooklyn and in Chesapeake, Virginia. Alexander graduated in 1990 from Virginia Polytechnic Institute and State University with a B.A. degree in psychology, English, and Black studies. He also studied poetry there under the American poet Nikki Giovanni. Alexander published his first book, *Just Us: Poems & Counterpoems, 1986-1995,* a collection of poetry, in 1995.

© Kwame Alexander
Kwame Alexander

Other notable works include the poetry collection *Crush: Love Poems for Teenagers* (2007); the children's books *Indigo Blume and the Garden City* (2010, illustrated by JahSun) and *Acoustic Rooster and His Barnyard Band* (2011, illustrated by Tim Bowers); the young adult novels *Solo* (2017) and *Swing* (2018), written in free verse with Mary Rand Hess; the picture book *Surf's Up* (2016, illustrated by Daniel Miyares); and *How to Read a Book* (2019), a poetry picture book about the joy of reading.

Alexander also has written and edited nonfiction books. The poetry picture book *The Undefeated* (2019, illustrated by Kadir Nelson) pays tribute to the lives and history of African Americans. *Light for the World to See: A Thousand Words on Race and Hope* (2020) is a book of poetry that addresses the issue of racial inequality.

Alexander has owned several publishing companies. He is the founding director of Book-in-a-Day, a literacy project that teaches students the fundamentals of creative writing and book publishing.   Ebony Elizabeth Thomas

Alexander of Tunis, Earl (1891-1969), was a British military leader and statesman and the last British-born governor general of Canada. He was one of the main Allied battle commanders during World War II (1939-1945). Alexander served as governor general of Canada from 1946 to 1952. He traveled extensively in the country and was highly popular. During his term, in 1949, Newfoundland (now Newfoundland and Labrador) became Canada's 10th province.

Harold Rupert Leofric George Alexander was born on Dec. 10, 1891, in London. In 1911, he became an officer in the Irish Guards of the British Army and later commanded a battalion in France in World War I (1914-1918).

During World War II, Alexander organized the evacuation of Allied troops at Dunkerque, France, in 1940. Later, he served as British commander in Burma (now Myanmar), the Middle East, and North Africa. Alexander directed the Allied campaigns in Sicily and Italy in 1943 and 1944. In 1944, he was named supreme commander of the Allied forces in the Mediterranean area. The same year, Alexander became the youngest field marshal in the British Commonwealth. He was made a viscount in 1946 and an earl in 1952. Alexander was the United Kingdom's minister of defense from 1952 to 1954. He died on June 16, 1969.   Jacques Monet

Alexander the Great (356-323 B.C.) was king of Macedonia and one of the greatest generals in history. He conquered the Persian Empire, which stretched from the Mediterranean Sea to India and formed much of what was then considered the civilized world. Alexander's conquests furthered the spread of Greek culture in western Asia and Egypt.

His youth. Alexander was born in Pella, the capital of the Macedonian kingdom. His father was Philip II, a shrewd king and general who conquered Greece. His mother was Olympias, a strong-willed princess from Epirus in western Greece. Alexander traced his ancestry, through his mother, to the hero Achilles, made famous by the epic poem the *Iliad.* Alexander also traced his ancestry, through his father and Macedonian royalty, to the hero Hercules (also called Heracles), who in Greek mythology was a son of the god Zeus. Alexander strove to outdo both heroes.

Roman copy of marble sculpture after Lysippus, Capitolino Museum, Rome (Alinari from Art Reference Bureau)
Alexander the Great

There are many stories about Alexander's life. Some are true, but others are legends. According to one story, the boy Alexander tamed the great horse Bucephalus. This magnificent steed later carried Alexander as far as India, where it died. Alexander built a city there and named it Bucephala after the horse.

In 343 or 342 B.C., Philip hired the great philosopher Aristotle to tutor Alexander. Aristotle may have encouraged Alexander's interest in foreign places and his curiosity about animals and plants.

Alexander's education followed the Greek principle of "a sound mind in a sound body." He studied literature, philosophy, and politics and received training in sports, physical fitness, and warfare. When Alexander was 16, Philip appointed him *regent* (temporary ruler) of the kingdom while Philip was away attacking Byzantium (now Istanbul, Turkey).

In 338 B.C., the 18-year-old Alexander commanded a section of Philip's army in the Battle of Chaeronea. This battle brought Greece under Macedonian control. Philip next prepared to invade the Persian Empire in Asia, but was murdered before he could do so. Thus, at the age of 20, Alexander became king of Macedonia. There were rumors that Olympias, and even Alexander, had plotted Philip's death, but the evidence they did so is weak.

After Philip's death, some Greek cities under Macedonian rule revolted. In 335 B.C., Alexander's army stormed the walls of the rebellious city of Thebes and demolished it. About 30,000 Thebans were sold into slavery.

Invasion of Asia. With Greece under control, Alexander turned to his father's plan for attacking the Persian Empire. The official reasons for the campaign were to avenge the Persian invasion of Greece in 480-479 B.C. and to free Greeks under Persian rule. In 334 B.C., Alexander led an army of about 35,000 infantry and cavalry across the Hellespont from Europe to Asia. The Hellespont is a strait now known as the Dardanelles. The Persians sent out troops that met Alexander's forces at the Granicus River. Alexander and his cavalry charged

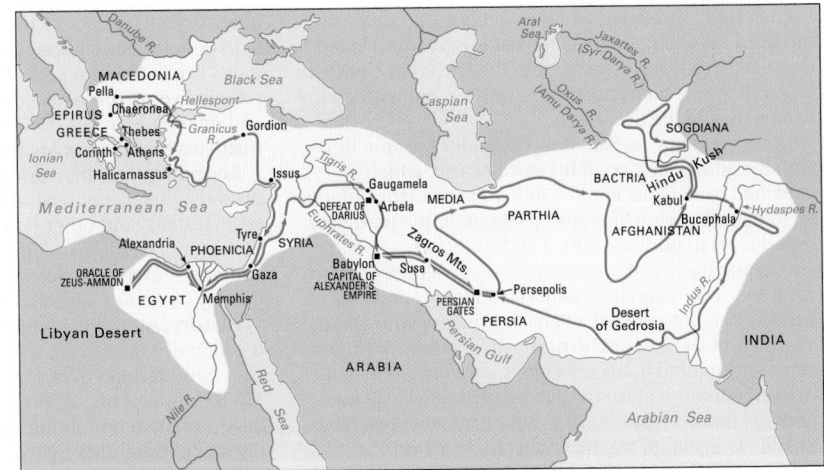

Alexander's empire extended from Greece to India, with Babylon as its capital. In 323 B.C., when Alexander died, his empire covered much of what was then considered the civilized world. Alexander's conquests helped Greek culture spread in Egypt and western Asia.

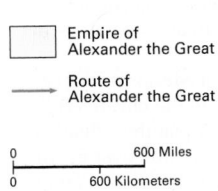

▢ Empire of Alexander the Great

→ Route of Alexander the Great

0   600 Miles

0   600 Kilometers

across the river and won the battle. This victory opened Asia Minor (now part of Turkey) to Alexander.

After marching along the southern coast of Asia Minor, Alexander and his army headed north to the city of Gordion. There, according to legend, Alexander found a wagon with an ox yoke tied by a tight, complex knot. An ancient prophecy said that whoever could untie this *Gordian knot* would become ruler of Asia. According to the most famous version of the story, Alexander first tried unsuccessfully to untie the knot and then drew his sword and cut it in a single stroke.

By 333 B.C., Alexander had reached the coast of Syria. There, in a fierce battle at Issus, he defeated the king of Persia, Darius III, but could not capture him. Alexander's army then marched south into Phoenicia to capture the naval bases of the Phoenician navy that fought for Darius. One such base was the city of Tyre, which stood on an island about ½ mile (800 meters) offshore. Unable to capture the island from the sea, Alexander had his engineers build a causeway out to the island, converting it into a peninsula that remains today. His troops used battering rams, catapults, and mobile towers in their attack. The Tyrians surrendered in 332 B.C., after seven months of fighting. Alexander's use of huge siege machines at Tyre led to a new age of warfare.

Alexander next entered Egypt. The Egyptians welcomed him as a liberator from Persian rule, and they acknowledged him as their king. On the western edge of the Nile Delta, Alexander founded a city in 331 B.C. and named it Alexandria after himself. Alexandria became a great metropolis.

From Alexandria, the Macedonian king made a long, difficult trek through the Libyan Desert, part of the Sahara, to the oasis of Siwah. He consulted the oracle of the god Zeus-Ammon, and, according to legend, the oracle pronounced Alexander the son of the god.

Victory over Darius. Alexander left Egypt in 331 B.C., traveling eastward into the Persian Empire. King Darius had formed a huge army that met Alexander's forces on a vast plain between the villages of Gaugamela and Arbela, just east of the Tigris River. The Persians far outnumbered Alexander's army, but Alexander's tactics and the training of his troops proved superior. Darius was

forced to flee and escaped across the Zagros Mountains into Media. This clash of armies, known as the Battle of Gaugamela or the Battle of Arbela, ended more than two centuries of Persian rule in Asia.

Alexander easily captured the city of Babylon and then the Persian capital at Susa. In the winter of 331-330 B.C., Alexander's army marched to Persepolis. There, Alexander seized the royal palaces and captured a vast storehouse of gold and silver. Before leaving Persepolis, Alexander had his soldiers burn down the palaces.

In the spring of 330 B.C., Alexander swung north toward the Caspian Sea to find Darius. The Persian king was killed by his own nobles, one of whom named himself King Artaxerxes (V). The capture and execution of Artaxerxes in 329 B.C. left Alexander the undisputed king of Asia.

Central Asia and the Indus. Alexander moved his army into Bactria and then across the Hindu Kush mountain range into Sogdiana, overcoming local military challenges as he went. In 327 B.C., Alexander married the Bactrian princess Roxane.

By 326 B.C., Alexander's forces had reached the upper Indus River Valley, in what is now Pakistan. Alexander wanted to continue east toward the Ganges River. But his homesick troops were tired of traveling and refused to follow him farther eastward.

During his years in central Asia, Alexander began to adopt the customs of the Persian kings. Many of his troops resented this change. They considered their king a fellow warrior, not an Asian sovereign. Plots against Alexander's life appeared, and he executed several prominent Greeks and Macedonians who he believed had conspired against him. Two of these alleged conspirators were his second-in-command, Parmenion, and Parmenion's son. In a drunken brawl, Alexander killed his veteran general Cleitus, who had saved his life at Granicus.

Return westward. After Alexander's army refused to march eastward in 326 B.C., Alexander marched down the Indus River and subdued the local population. In 325 B.C., Alexander had ships built that sailed westward from the mouth of the Indus River. Their mission was to explore the northern shore of the Arabian Sea and the

Persian Gulf. Alexander sent part of his army back along the main road to Carmania, in what is now Iran. He led the rest of his troops west across the Desert of Gedrosia. Many of the women and children who accompanied the troops died in the desert.

Upon his return to Babylon, Alexander became busy with the administration of his vast domain, which stretched from Greece to the Indus. He probably intended to make Babylon his capital. Alexander planned new expeditions to northern Africa and Arabia. He tried to encourage trade and commerce and develop a greater spirit of cooperation between Macedonians and Persians. Alexander married a Persian princess who was a daughter of Darius, and he performed a mass marriage ceremony joining thousands of his soldiers to Persian women. Alexander also tried to incorporate large numbers of Persians into his army. But he failed to establish a stable kingship to maintain what he had won.

His death. In the spring of 323 B.C., Alexander became seriously ill with a fever at Babylon. He also suffered from exhaustion and the effects of several battle wounds. He died at the age of 32 on June 10, 323 B.C. His body was placed in a golden coffin, later replaced by a glass coffin, in a tomb at Alexandria.

After Alexander died, his half-brother, Philip III Arrhidaeus, became king of Macedonia. At the time of Alexander's death, Roxane was pregnant with his son, Alexander IV, who later shared rule over the Macedonians with Philip. But Philip was murdered in 317 B.C., and young Alexander was killed about seven years later.

No one succeeded Alexander the Great in the rule of his vast empire. His leading generals became governors of various areas and fought among themselves for control of the empire. By 300 B.C., Alexander's empire had split into a number of independent states. The three most powerful states were led by Alexander's generals Antigonus, Ptolemy, and Seleucus.   Joseph Roisman

Related articles in *World Book* include:

Alexandria (pop. 4,939,093) is Egypt's busiest seaport and second largest city. Only Cairo, Egypt's capital, has more people. Alexandria is also a major industrial center. The city lies on Egypt's Mediterranean coast in the northwest corner of the Nile Delta, a fertile agricultural area. For location, see **Egypt** (political map). In ancient times, Alexandria was one of the world's most important commercial and cultural centers.

The city is built on a long *isthmus* (strip of land) between Lake Maryut and the Mediterranean Sea. A hammer-shaped peninsula extends out from the isthmus and forms two large harbors, east and west. These magnificent harbors have made Alexandria one of the Mediterranean's leading ports for thousands of years.

Hotels and beaches line the Corniche, a broad, curving road along the city's shoreline. The city is the home of Alexandria University. The Bibliotheca Alexandrina, a large research library that opened in 2002, is a revival of Alexandria's great ancient library.

People. Almost all of Alexandria's people are Egyptians. Most of the Egyptians are Muslims who speak Ar-

abic. A small number of foreigners live in the city.

In general, Alexandria's upper- and middle-class residents live in the east part of the city. Most working-class people live on the west side close to industrial areas, and on the peninsula between the two harbors. Most residents live in large apartment complexes.

Economy. Manufacturing plants in or near the city produce petroleum products, plastics, processed foods, steel, textiles, and other goods. Tourism also contributes to the city's economy. Huge numbers of vacationers come to Alexandria each summer to take advantage of the city's beaches and resorts.

History. Alexandria is named after Alexander the Great, the king of Macedonia, who founded the city in 331 B.C. after conquering Egypt. Following Alexander's death in 323 B.C., one of his generals, Ptolemy, took over Egypt's government and founded the Ptolemaic dynasty. Ptolemy made Alexandria the capital of Egypt.

Under the Ptolemies, Alexandria thrived. It was one of the great centers of trade and culture, and its population was the largest of any Mediterranean city. Many of the leading thinkers of the Greek-speaking world worked in the city. The towering Lighthouse of Alexandria was one of the Seven Wonders of the Ancient World (see **Seven Wonders of the Ancient World** [with picture]). The city had a scientific institute called the Mouseion and a library with about 500,000 scrolls made of an early form of paper called *papyrus*. These institutions conserved and developed the science, literature, philosophy, and religious culture of the ancient world.

The Ptolemaic dynasty ended when its last ruler, Cleopatra, rebelled against the growing power of Rome. After her failure to defend Egypt's independence, she killed herself in 30 B.C. Egypt was then made part of the Roman Empire. Under the Romans, Alexandria remained an important trade center. It also was a major center for the processing of gold and silver and the production of glass, jewelry, linen, and papyrus.

According to tradition, Saint Mark, a Christian missionary, founded the Egyptian (Coptic) church in Alexandria around A.D. 40. The city, which already had a large community of Jews, soon also developed a thriving Christian community. Bishops of Alexandria exercised enormous influence in defining beliefs and practices of the new Christian faith.

During Roman rule, clashes often took place between rival ethnic and religious groups in the city. In the late 200's, the Mouseion and library were destroyed during a war over control of the Roman Empire. When the Roman Empire was divided in 395, Egypt became part of the Byzantine Empire.

In 642, Arab Muslims conquered Egypt. The Arabs moved the capital from Alexandria to what is now Cairo. Alexandria's population gradually declined, and the city ceased to be a cultural center. In 1517, Egypt became part of the Ottoman Empire, which was based in what is now Turkey. Under Ottoman rule, Alexandria's population fell sharply.

Muhammad Ali, an Ottoman army officer, was appointed Egypt's governor in 1805. Under Muhammad Ali and his successors, Alexandria again became a center of business, banking, and trade. In 1820, a canal connecting Alexandria to the Nile River was completed. A railroad linking Alexandria to Cairo was built in the 1850's.

The city's population grew rapidly in the 1800's. Most of the new residents were Egyptian Muslims. But many immigrants from other countries also came to the city. Many of these foreigners became important business leaders. Tensions rose between the Egyptian and foreign communities, and bloody riots took place in 1882. Later that year, British warships bombarded the city, and British troops occupied Egypt. The British acted to crush a movement for Egyptian self-government, to protect foreigners, and to further British influence in the region. Foreign business interests strengthened their control of Alexandria in the late 1800's and early 1900's. But after Egypt gained independence from the United Kingdom in 1922, foreign control of the city weakened. By the 1950's, most foreigners had left Alexandria. In the 1950's and 1960's, the city experienced rapid industrial growth.

In the 1990's, archaeologists working in waters near Alexandria found hundreds of granite blocks, huge statues, and other stonework belonging to the ancient lighthouse, which had collapsed during an earthquake in the 1300's. The archaeologists also found about 40 sunken ships, which showed the wide range of Alexandria's early commercial activity.   Michael J. Reimer

See also **Middle East** (picture: Large cities in the Middle East).

Alexandria, Virginia (pop. 139,966), is a historic city on the west bank of the Potomac River, across from Washington, D.C. For the location, see **Virginia** (political map). During the 1730's, a warehouse was established on the site of Alexandria for the export of tobacco. The military leaders George Washington, Henry "Light-Horse Harry" Lee, and Robert E. Lee, who was Henry Lee's son, had homes in Alexandria. Their homes are preserved in a historic district that has made Alexandria a major tourist center. At Gadsby's Tavern, Washington recruited his first command in 1754 and held his last military review in 1799. The *Alexandria Gazette Packet,* founded in 1784, is one of the oldest newspapers in the United States.

Alexandria was part of the District of Columbia from 1791 to 1846. Today, it is a suburb of Washington, D.C. Alexandria has many technology and research and development firms and a large railroad freight yard. It is also the home of hundreds of national trade and professional associations. It has a council-manager form of government.   Susan L. Woodward

Alexandrite, AL ihg ZAN dryt, is a rare gem variety of the mineral chrysoberyl. The most valuable alexandrite looks emerald green in natural light but looks ruby red in most kinds of artificial light. This strong color change is rare. Most alexandrite shows a color change from blue-green to purple, or from blue to purple in artificial varieties. A tiny amount of the element chromium causes the perceived shift in color. The presence of chromium sets alexandrite apart from all other types of chrysoberyl. Alexandrite is a birthstone for the month of June.

Alexandrite was first discovered in the Ural Mountains in Russia in 1833. The stone was named after Alexander II, who later became the czar of Russia. Today, alexandrite is still mined in Russia. Other countries that produce alexandrite include Brazil, Myanmar, Sri Lanka, Zambia, and Zimbabwe.   Mark A. Helper

See also **Gem** (picture).

Alexie, Sherman (1966-   ), is an author whose writings reflect his experiences as a Native American in a white world. Alexie combines oral storytelling traditions with established literary forms to create realistic but often humorous pictures of Native American life.

Sherman Joseph Alexie, Jr., was born on Oct. 7, 1966, in Spokane, Washington. He grew up as a member of the Coeur d'Alene tribe on the Spokane Indian Reservation. Alexie received a B.A. degree from Washington State University in 1991 and began his literary career with two collections of poems, *The Business of Fancydancing* and *I Would Steal Horses* (both 1992). Later collections include *One Stick Song* (2000) and *Faces* (2009). His short stories have been collected in *The Lone Ranger and Tonto Fistfight in Heaven* (1993), *The Toughest Indian in the World* (2000), *Ten Little Indians* (2003), *War Dances* (2009), and *Blasphemy* (2012). He also co-wrote the screenplay for *Smoke Signals* (1998), a movie based on one of his stories.

Alexie's first novel was *Reservation Blues* (1995). *Flight* (2007) is a time-travel novel about a half-Native American, half-Irish teenage boy. *The Absolutely True Diary of a Part-Time Indian* (2007) is an autobiographical novel for young adults about a teenager who leaves his reservation to attend an all-white school. The picture book *Thunder Boy Jr.* (2016) is an autobiographical story about a Native American boy who is named after his father and feels that he is growing up in his father's shadow. It was illustrated by the Mexican-born children's author and illustrator Yuyi Morales. Alexie published *You Don't Have to Say You Love Me,* a memoir centering on his relationship with his mother, in 2017.

In 2018, Alexie was accused of sexual harassment by several dozen women. He apologized that he had "done things that have harmed other people" but denied some of the accusations. The Institute of American Indian Arts (IAIA), a tribal college in Santa Fe, New Mexico, removed his name from a scholarship named in his honor. Alexie had helped establish a graduate program in creative writing at the IAIA in 2013.   Donald G. Marshall

Alfalfa, also called *lucerne,* is a cloverlike plant grown mainly for *forage* (livestock feed). Livestock producers feed alfalfa to cattle, horses, sheep, and other animals. Alfalfa is sometimes called the "queen of the forages." Alfalfa produces an abundant harvest and is high in nu-

Steve Orloff

Farmers harvest alfalfa mainly for use as livestock feed. This photograph shows a farmer cutting alfalfa in California. Alfalfa gives livestock large amounts of energy, protein, and minerals.

trient quality. It provides energy, protein, and minerals that promote rapid growth and good health in animals. Farmers harvest alfalfa as hay. They also make *silage* (feed stored in silos) and alfalfa cubes or pellets. In addition, farmers grow alfalfa for grazing and for its seeds. Planting alfalfa benefits the environment by enriching the soil with nitrogen and protecting it from erosion.

The United States ranks as the leading alfalfa grower. It raises about 60 million tons (54 million metric tons) of alfalfa each year. The leading alfalfa-growing states include California, Idaho, Montana, Nebraska, South Dakota, and Wisconsin. Other major alfalfa producers include Argentina, Canada, China, Italy, and Russia. The leading alfalfa-growing provinces in Canada are Alberta, Manitoba, Ontario, and Saskatchewan.

The alfalfa plant

Alfalfa is a *perennial*—that is, it grows from year to year without being replanted. It can live as long as 25 years, but a typical lifespan is 4 to 7 years. The alfalfa plant is a *legume,* a member of the pea family.

The alfalfa plant produces many slender stems. The stems regrow readily after cutting. They reach up to about 3 feet (1 meter) high and bear compound leaves, each consisting of three leaflets. New stems grow from buds on the plant's woody *crown.* The crown is an enlarged portion of the top of the roots. Alfalfa leaves and stems are usually harvested after about four or five weeks of growth. They are used for livestock feed.

Flowers grow on the stems in clusters called *racemes.* Each raceme consists of 5 to 50 flowers. Most alfalfa flowers are purple, but some are green, white, yellow, or *variegated* (multicolored).

Alfalfa has a deep *taproot* (long main root). Alfalfa roots can reach as deep as 15 feet (4.6 meters) or more. These deep roots can reach water and nutrients far belowground. For this reason, alfalfa plants have a greater resistance to drought than do many other crops. Beneficial bacteria called *Rhizobium* live in the roots of alfalfa. These bacteria absorb nitrogen from the air. They *fix* the

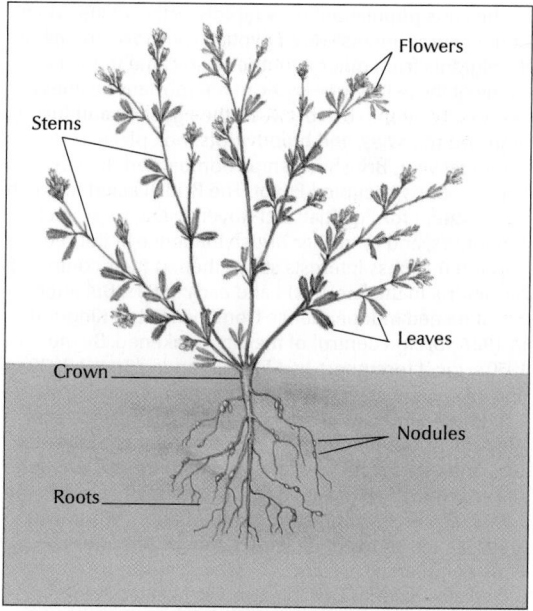

WORLD BOOK illustration by Kate Lloyd-Jones, Linden Artists Ltd.
The alfalfa plant has many slender stems, which develop from buds on the *crown* (base). Swellings called *nodules* grow on the roots. Bacteria in the nodules take nitrogen from the air. Nitrogen is essential to the plant's health and growth.

nitrogen—that is, they convert nitrogen gas from the air into nitrogen compounds that the plant can use.

Uses of alfalfa

As livestock feed. Most alfalfa grown in the United States is baled as hay or preserved as silage. Livestock may also graze directly on alfalfa or eat it freshly cut. Dairy cattle eat more than 75 percent of alfalfa. Farmers also feed alfalfa to beef cattle, goats, horses, and sheep. Alfalfa thus aids in the production of a variety of goods, including cheese, milk, yogurt, meat, and wool. Bees that feed on alfalfa nectar produce honey.

Alfalfa hay is typically stored in bales. Small rectangular bales weigh from 50 to 150 pounds (23 to 68 kilograms). Large rectangular bales weigh from 1,200 to 2,000 pounds (540 to 900 kilograms). Round bales weigh as much as 2,000 pounds (900 kilograms).

To make hay, farmers *swath* (cut) the alfalfa, rake it, and let the sun dry the plants. At the time alfalfa is cut, it contains 70 to 80 percent moisture. Before being baled, the plants should contain less than 15 percent moisture. Hay that is too dry when baled will lose its nutritious leaves. Hay that is too wet will mold. See **Hay.**

Hay can be used to feed livestock on the farm. It also may be sold to other farmers or ranchers. Hay and other alfalfa products are exported by Canada and the United States to Japan, South Korea, and the Middle East.

Some alfalfa is stored as silage. Farmers in wet areas often use silos during the spring, when the weather is unsuitable for drying hay. Silage can be preserved for many months. The key advantage of silage is that a farmer can harvest the crop more quickly. A quick harvest reduces the chance that the crop will be damaged by wet weather. See **Silo.**

J. C. Allen and Son
Alfalfa flowers attract pollinators, such as bumble bees and honey bees. The flowers grow in clusters along the alfalfa plant's many slender stems. Most alfalfa flowers are purple.

Some alfalfa is preserved in the form of thickly packed cubes or pellets. Alfalfa cubes are often used to feed horses. Pellets are commonly used to feed such pets as gerbils and rabbits. Poultry farmers often add alfalfa pellets to poultry feed. This practice helps to produce high-quality eggs and meat.

Farmers may plant alfalfa mixed with grass for grazing, especially in rainy areas with poor drainage. Growers graze their livestock for about a week. They then allow the alfalfa plants to grow back for about four weeks. This method of feeding livestock is called *rotational grazing.* Alfalfa grazing is uncommon in North America, but it is common in Argentina and other countries.

As a cover and rotation crop. Some farmers use alfalfa as a *cover crop.* A cover crop enriches the soil and protects it from erosion. *Rhizobium* bacteria living in *nodules* (swellings) on alfalfa roots fix nitrogen from the air. Like other plants, alfalfa needs nitrogen to grow. In exchange, the plant provides food to the bacteria. This relationship is an example of *symbiosis.* Symbiosis is an arrangement in which organisms live together in a way that benefits one or more of them. Alfalfa plants enrich the soil by adding more nitrogen to it than they use.

Farmers often alternate growing alfalfa with other crops. This practice is known as *crop rotation.* Corn or grain crops that cannot fix nitrogen may require less chemical fertilizer in fields where alfalfa has grown. In addition, diseases and pests that thrive on one crop may not thrive on others. By rotating crops, farmers can help to control diseases and pests.

As a seed crop. A small amount of alfalfa is grown for its seeds. Seeds are sold to farmers who grow alfalfa for livestock feed. Alfalfa cultivated for seed requires dry weather for harvesting. The seeds develop only if the flowers have been pollinated by bees. In the United States, most pollination is carried out by commercial beekeepers, who carry their bees from farm to farm.

As food for people. People consume alfalfa sprouts, alfalfa supplements, and alfalfa juice. But people directly consume only a relatively small amount of alfalfa.

Kinds of alfalfa

Farmers grow hundreds of varieties of alfalfa. Each variety is adapted to a particular kind of climate. Breeders develop varieties to improve such traits as yield, winter hardiness, resistance to disease and pests, persistence, and forage quality, among others.

As perennials, most alfalfa plants slow their growth in the fall to prepare for winter, a trait known as fall *dormancy* (inactivity). They resume growth in the spring. Alfalfa varieties differ in their degree of fall dormancy. They also differ in how well they withstand winter weather conditions. Alfalfa varieties with the greatest degree of fall dormancy and winter hardiness can be grown in such places as Canada, Wisconsin, and Minnesota. Varieties that do not become dormant are grown under irrigation in the southwestern United States, Mexico, and warm areas around the world.

Breeders have developed alfalfa varieties with resistance to a wide range of diseases, insects, and other pests. Alfalfa may have a wider resistance to pests and diseases than any other cultivated crop plant. This resistance reduces the need to use artificial chemicals.

Growing alfalfa

Alfalfa plants flourish in fertile, well-drained soil that is slightly *alkaline* (acid-neutralizing) or *neutral* (neither acidic nor alkaline). In dry regions, alfalfa needs irrigation for successful growth. Before planting alfalfa, farmers may prepare the soil by applying fertilizers, herbicides, or other chemicals. Farmers plant alfalfa seeds ¼ to ½ inch (6 to 13 millimeters) or less below the surface.

Farmers plant alfalfa in early spring to late summer or fall, depending upon the region. They harvest a new crop every four to six weeks. Harvests are timed after flower buds form but before significant flowering. Farmers must harvest at just the right time to maximize the amount and quality of the forage. Alfalfa is harvested from 2 to 4 times a year in northern climates. It is harvested from 5 to 11 times a year in the Mediterranean and desert regions of Argentina, Australia, the United States, Mexico, and the Middle East.

Diseases and pests. A number of diseases and pests damage alfalfa crops. The diseases include anthracnose, bacterial wilt, *Phytopthora* root rot, leaf spot, and spring blackstem. All of these diseases are caused by bacteria or fungi. Crown rot and root rot severely damage alfalfa that has been injured by cold weather, field traffic, insects, or poor harvesting methods (see **Rot**). Leaf diseases harm alfalfa by causing the leaves to drop off.

Weeds use up nutrients and water that alfalfa plants need. They also shade the plants, blocking the sunlight plants need to grow. Weeds in the forage also reduce its quality. Some poisonous weeds can sicken or even kill livestock. Farmers often control weeds through the use of *herbicides* (weed-killing chemicals).

Insect pests that attack alfalfa include alfalfa weevils, potato leafhoppers, and aphids. *Larval* (young) alfalfa weevils eat alfalfa leaves, reducing the yield and quality of the hay. Potato leafhoppers and aphids suck juices

J. C. Allen and Son
Farmers dry alfalfa for use as hay, often by cutting the crop and letting the sun dry it in the field. The hay can then be pressed into bales.

from alfalfa stems. This damage hinders the growth of the plants. Some *nematodes* (microscopic roundworms) also damage alfalfa. Farmers may use insecticides to control insect pests.

Beneficial insects. Alfalfa is known as an *insectary* because it supports many beneficial insects. Such helpful insects include ladybugs and various wasps. They attack and kill such pests as aphids and worms. Farmers may grow strips of alfalfa near other crops to promote beneficial insects.

Organic alfalfa, like other organic crops, is grown using little or no pesticides, synthetic fertilizers, or other artificial chemicals. Alfalfa is often used in farms making a transition from conventional to organic agriculture. Alfalfa provides many benefits to organic farms. It improves the soil structure and enriches the soil with nitrogen. It also supports beneficial insects. Certified organic dairy or beef production requires some grazing. For this reason, organic alfalfa may be grazed rather than cut. Such grazing helps to control weeds. Organic alfalfa makes up a small but expanding part of overall alfalfa production in the United States.

History

Alfalfa was one of the earliest crops grown by human beings. It probably originated in the region between the Middle East and the Caucasus, a region that includes Armenia, Azerbaijan, and Georgia. Records on brick tablets found in Turkey indicate that alfalfa was an important feed for cattle in that region by 1400 B.C. It was brought to Greece by 490 B.C. Later, it was introduced to northern Africa and present-day Italy and Spain.

During the 1500's, Portuguese and Spanish explorers brought alfalfa to Central and South America and to what is now the southwestern United States. Settlers brought alfalfa from Europe to the American Colonies. There, it was grown by George Washington and Thomas Jefferson, among others. However, it did not grow well in the East because of the acidic soils along the Atlantic Coast. Alfalfa did not become widely grown in the United States until after 1850. At that time, a variety called *Chilean clover* was brought to California from Chile. California farmers grew it successfully under irrigation. Alfalfa farming then spread rapidly through the West.

In 1900, nearly all alfalfa production in the United States took place west of the Mississippi River. About that time, new varieties of alfalfa were brought from cold climates in Europe and Asia. These varieties grew well in the upper Midwest and Northeast.

Daniel H. Putnam

Scientific classification. Alfalfa's scientific name is *Medicago sativa.*

Alfieri, *ahl FYEH ree,* **Vittorio,** *veet TAWR yoh* (1749-1803), was an Italian playwright and poet. He was born into an aristocratic family on Jan. 16, 1749, in Asti, where French was the spoken language of the nobility. The experience of writing his first play in 1774 taught him how imperfectly he knew Italian. He studied Italian language and literature so he could write tragedy, a literary form long ignored by other Italians.

From 1775 to 1787, Alfieri wrote 19 verse tragedies, most of which reflect his hatred of tyranny and his admiration of human dignity. These themes helped arouse a spirit of nationalism in Italy. All his plays have a mythical, Biblical, or historical plot. His best works include *Filippo* (1775), *Oreste* (1786), and *Mirra* (1786). Alfieri wrote many poems, a treatise in defense of liberty, and a lively two-part *Autobiography* (1790, 1803). He died on Oct. 8, 1803.

Richard H. Lansing

Alfonso XIII, *al FAHN soh* (1886-1941), was king of Spain from 1902 to 1931. Throughout his reign, Alfonso faced a number of economic, political, and social challenges. After World War I (1914-1918), Spain's economy suffered from widespread *inflation* (rising prices), poverty, and unemployment. In addition, the growing momentum of separatist movements centered in the Basque and Catalonia regions increasingly challenged the authority of Spain's central government in Madrid. The country's disastrous colonial policy in Africa between 1909 and 1921 also served to weaken the constitutional monarchy.

Alfonso, who had close ties to the military, was linked to a scandalous military defeat in Morocco at the Battle of Anwal in 1921. The defeat became a major national issue and sparked the downfall of the constitutional monarchy two years later.

Fearful that the social and political problems facing Spain would overwhelm the national government, General Primo de Rivera established a military dictatorship in 1923. Alfonso's support of Primo's antidemocratic policies between 1923 and 1930 called into question his commitment to constitutional principles. Alfonso's declining popularity was apparent in the national elections of 1931. When it became clear that Spaniards favored a republican form of government over a monarchy, Alfonso abandoned the throne.

Alfonso XIII lived in exile until his death on Feb. 28, 1941. In 1975, monarchy resumed in Spain when Alfonso's grandson, Juan Carlos de Bórbon, became king. See **Juan Carlos I.**

Alfonso XIII was born in Madrid on May 17, 1886, six months after the death of his father, King Alfonso XII. Alfonso XIII's mother, María Cristina of Austria, ruled until he came of age in 1902.   George R. Esenwein

Alfred the Great (849-899) was king of the West Saxons in southwestern England. He saved his kingdom, Wessex, from the Danish Vikings and laid the basis for the unification of England under the West Saxon monarchy. He also led a revival of learning and literature. He was such an outstanding leader in war and peace that he is the only English king known as "the Great."

Alfred was born in Wantage, now in Oxfordshire, England. He was the youngest son of King Ethelwulf of Wessex. According to the Welsh writer Asser, who wrote a biography of Alfred shortly after his death, Alfred was always eager to learn. Asser says that Alfred's mother offered a book of Anglo-Saxon poems as a prize to the first of her sons who could read it. Alfred won. As a boy, Alfred twice went to Rome, where the pope acknowledged the status of the royal house of Wessex. The journeys also showed Alfred the contrast between England and the more advanced parts of Europe.

Alfred became king in 871 at the death of his brother Ethelred. The West Saxons had been at war with the Danes for many years. After several losing battles, Alfred made peace with the invaders. But the Danes renewed their attacks and defeated Alfred at the Battle of Chippenham in 877. Alfred then defeated the Danes at the Battle of Edington in 878. The Danish leader, Guthrum, agreed to be baptized a Christian. He also agreed to stay north and east of the River Thames, in an area called the Danelaw. However, the Danes broke the peace, and Alfred renewed the war. He won London in 886. All the English people not subject to the Danes recognized Alfred as their ruler and paid him homage. The old, independent Anglo-Saxon kingdoms began to merge under the rule of Wessex.

Alfred built forts and *boroughs* (fortified towns) at strategic points. He stationed his fleet along the coast as protection against further invasions. He also issued a code of laws to restore peaceful government.

Before Alfred, education had declined in England because the Danes had looted monasteries and churches, the centers of learning. Alfred revived learning by bringing teachers and writers from Wales and continental Europe. He encouraged the translation of famous Christian books from Latin into Old English. Under his influence, the *Anglo-Saxon Chronicle* began to be compiled. It is now the main source for Anglo-Saxon history up to 1154.   Joel T. Rosenthal

See also **Anglo-Saxons; England** (The Anglo-Saxon period).

Algae, *AL jee,* are simple organisms that live in oceans, lakes, rivers, ponds, and moist soil. A single organism of this type is called an *alga.* Some algae are microscopic and consist of just one cell, but others are large and contain many cells. Some species drift or swim, and others remain attached to stones or weeds in the water. Large marine algae are called seaweeds. Algae serve as food for fish and other water animals.

A few algae live on land, growing on trees or other land plants, soil, and rocks. Other kinds live on certain animals, including sloths and turtles. Still others dwell inside plants or animals.

Algae include *dinoflagellates* and *diatoms,* most of which have only one cell. Many such algae occur with marine animals in drifting masses called *plankton.* Dinoflagellate cells swim by means of two hairlike structures called *flagella.* Diatoms have cell walls made up of silica. These "skeletons" resist decay and may accumulate on the ocean floor. In some places, they form a whitish material called *diatomite,* which has many industrial uses. See **Diatom; Plankton.**

Some algae multiply rapidly in parts of lakes, rivers, and oceans. These growing algae may form dense populations called *algal blooms.* Algal blooms often occur where such waste materials as sewage and fertilizers flow into the water and provide additional nourishment for algal growth. Algal blooms sometimes upset the natural balance of life in water. The water eventually may become extremely low in oxygen, killing fish and other water creatures. Algal blooms may also make the water unfit for use by people.

Structure of algae. All algae have cells with at least one nucleus. The cells contain a green pigment called *chlorophyll* in specialized cell parts known as *chloroplasts.* Chlorophyll helps return oxygen to the air as it absorbs energy from sunlight in the process called *photosynthesis.* Many algal cells contain other pigments besides chlorophyll. The cells grow and reproduce by cell division. Most kinds can also reproduce sexually.

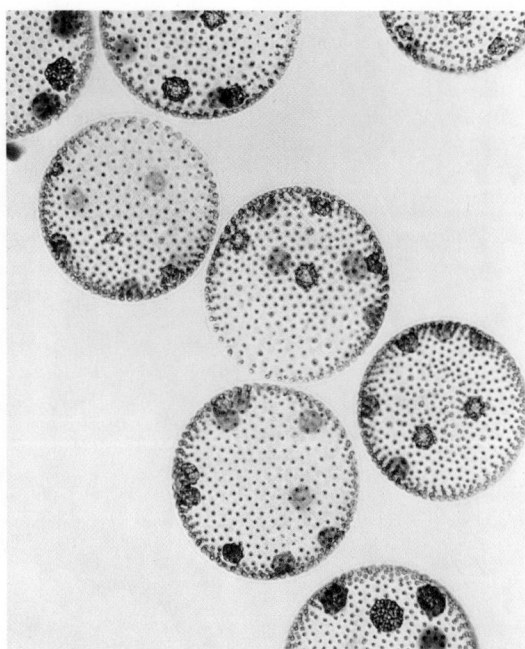

E. R. Degginger

Microscopic algae often grow in bodies of water. Spherical colonies of the green alga *Volvox, shown here,* consist of many cells. Other kinds of algae have only one cell.

Scientists classify true algae in the kingdom Protista. Another group of organisms, the *cyanobacteria* or *blue-green algae,* have algaelike characteristics. But most scientists classify these organisms in the kingdom Bacteria. See **Cyanobacteria.**

Kinds of algae. Biologists often group algae according to color—brown, green, or red. Brown algae occur plentifully along many seashores of *temperate zones—* that is, the parts of the world between the tropics and the polar regions. Some kinds, called *kelps,* grow as much as 200 feet (60 meters) long (see **Kelp**). Manufacturers use *algin,* a gummy substance obtained from kelp, to thicken cosmetics, ice cream, mayonnaise, and other products. Some brown algae are used as fertilizer.

Green algae occur in both fresh and salt water. Most species are microscopic and live in lakes, ponds, and streams. Huge quantities of such algae may color an entire lake. Larger species of green algae grow along seashores. Many tropical coral beaches consist of pieces of green seaweeds filled with lime. Some scientists are experimenting with growing varieties of green algae for food.

Red algae live mostly in subtropical and temperate seas, where they sometimes grow with corals. A few species live in fresh water. Some red algae have blue as well as green and red pigments. Certain red algae provide sources of *agar,* a gelatinlike substance used in laboratories to grow bacteria. In Japan, people eat a kind of red alga called *nori.* It is typically sold dried as papery sheets, which people often use in making sushi rolls.

David L. Garrison

 Scientific classification. Algae belong to the kingdom Protista.

See also **Eutrophication; Lichen; Seaweed.**

An algebra problem involves letters that stand for unknown numbers.

Algebra is one of the chief branches of mathematics. Mastery of mathematics depends on a sound understanding of algebra. Engineers and scientists use algebra every day. Business and industry rely on algebra to help solve many problems. Because of its importance in modern living, algebra is studied in schools and colleges in all parts of the world.

Unknown numbers in algebra are represented by letters, such as x or y. In some problems, the letter can be replaced by only one number. A simple example would be $x + 3 = 8$. For this statement to be true, x must be 5, because $5 + 3 = 8$. In other problems, the letter may be replaced by one of many numbers. For example, for the algebraic statement $x + y = 12$ to be true, x would be 6 if y is 6, or x would be 4 if y is 8. In such an algebraic statement, you can find many values for x that make true statements if you give different values to y.

People can use algebra to solve problems in ways that would be beyond the range of arithmetic alone. For example:

An airplane travels 1,710 kilometers in 4 hours flying with the wind, but it travels only 1,370 kilometers in 5 hours flying against the wind. The speed of the airplane in relation to the air is the same in both directions, and the wind speed is constant. What is (1) the speed of the airplane in relation to the air and (2) the speed of the wind?

The key to solving this problem is to use letters to represent the two unknown numbers. For example, you might use x to represent the speed of the plane relative to the air, and y to represent wind speed. Using letters in this way is not part of arithmetic, but is an essential part of algebra.

Learning algebra

Sets and variables. Letters in algebra are related to sets of numbers. Everyone is familiar with sets of objects. There are sets of books, sets of stamps, and sets of dishes. Sets of numbers are much the same. In algebra, one way to describe a set of numbers is to use a capital letter, such as N, as a name for the set. Then you list the numbers of the set within braces { }. For example, here is the set of single-digit whole numbers:

$$W = \{0, 1, 2, 3, 4, 5, 6, 7, 8, 9\}$$

Here is the set of odd numbers smaller than 20:

$$Y = \{1, 3, 5, 7, 9, 11, 13, 15, 17, 19\}$$

These are the kinds of sets used in algebra.

Imagine a group of people whose ages are 12 years, 15 years, 20 years, and 24 years. You can write these ages as a set of numbers:

$$A = \{12, 15, 20, 24\}$$

How old will these people be three years from now? One way of answering this question is to write out $12 + 3$; $15 + 3$; $20 + 3$; and $24 + 3$. However, the number 3 is the same in all four of these expressions. In algebra, you can write all four expressions as one general expression, $m + 3$, in which m can be replaced with any number of the set A. For example, you can replace m with 12, 15, 20, or 24.

The letter m is called a *variable,* and the set A is the *domain of the variable.* The number 3 in the expression $m + 3$ is called a *constant,* because 3 always has the same value. A variable in algebra is a letter that can be replaced by one or more numbers belonging to a set.

Statements and equations. In mathematics, a *statement* is a sentence that is either true or false. Mathematical statements can be illustrated in everyday language. For example, here is an incomplete statement:

"_____ was the inventor of the telephone."

As it stands, this statement is neither true nor false. Suppose you write a name in the blank:

"   Bell   was the inventor of the telephone."

Now the statement is true.

You can write a statement with a variable:

"y is a state bordered by the Pacific Ocean."

You can replace a variable with the members of its domain. That is, you can replace the variable with names that will produce a true or false statement.

"*Ohio* is a state bordered by the Pacific Ocean."

This statement is false. It is true only when you use Alaska, California, Hawaii, Oregon, or Washington:

"*Oregon* is a state bordered by the Pacific Ocean."

The replacements that make true statements are called *roots.* The set that includes all the roots is called the *solution set.* As with other sets, braces are used to enclose the solution set. The solution set of this example is {Alaska, California, Hawaii, Oregon, Washington}. In algebra, you do not use names to replace a variable. Instead, you use numbers.

Equations are one kind of sentence in algebra. They are mathematical sentences that say two things are equal. Here is a simple equation:

$$7 + x = 12$$

Terms used in algebra

Binomial is an expression in algebra consisting of two terms connected by + or − symbols.

Coefficient is the multiplier of a variable or number, usually written next to the variable.

Constant is a number or a variable whose domain is a set of one number.

Equation is a mathematical sentence that says two expressions are equal.

Exponent is a number placed at the upper right of a number or variable to show how many times it is to be used as a factor.

Expression, in algebra, is a certain number or variable, or numbers and variables, combined by operations such as addition, subtraction, multiplication, or division.

Factors are two or more expressions that are multiplied.

Monomial is an expression in algebra consisting of a product of numbers and variables.

Polynomial is an expression consisting of two or more terms.

Quadratic refers to a variable that has been *squared* (used as a factor twice).

Roots of an equation are numbers that make a true statement when they are substituted for a variable in the equation.

Term is part of an expression connected to other terms by addition or subtraction symbols.

Variable is a symbol in algebra, usually a letter, that can be replaced by one or more numerical values.

This equation means that "the sum of 7 and a number equals 12." To solve the equation, you can replace x with different numbers until you find one that will make the equation a true statement. If you replace x in this equation with 5, the equation will be a true statement. If you replace x with any other number, the equation will be false. So the solution set to this equation is {5}. The solution set consists of only one root.

Equations can have more than one root:

$$x^2 + 18 = 9x$$

The little 2 above the first x means that the number x represents is *squared.* That is, the number is multiplied once by itself (see **Square**). Also, one quantity placed next to another quantity indicates that one quantity is to be multiplied by the other quantity. Therefore, the expression $9x$ means x *multiplied by 9.*

In the above equation, you can replace x with 3:

$$3 \times 3 + 18 = 9 \times 3$$
$$9 + 18 = 27$$
$$27 = 27$$

You can also replace x with 6:

$$6 \times 6 + 18 = 9 \times 6$$
$$36 + 18 = 54$$
$$54 = 54$$

Any other replacements of x make the equation a false statement. So 3 and 6 are roots of the equation, and its solution set is {3, 6}.

Some equations do not have roots:

$$x = x + 3$$

This equation becomes a false statement for any number you use to replace x. Its solution set is called an *empty set.* An empty set is written { }.

Some equations have many roots. Some even have an *infinite* (unlimited) number of roots:

$$(x + 1)^2 = x^2 + 2x + 1$$

This equation will be a true statement if you replace x with *any* number. Its solution set consists of all numbers.

Mathematicians use a number of terms to describe parts of an equation. They call the expression on each side of the equals sign a *member* of the equation. For example, in the equation $3x + 2 = 11$, "$3x + 2$" is the left member and "11" is the right member. Each part of a member that is connected by addition or subtraction signs—or stands alone—is called a *term.* Therefore, $3x$ and 2 are the terms in the left member, and 11 is the term in the right member.

Solving equations. The goal in solving an equation with a variable is to isolate the variable on one side of the equation. It does not matter on which side of the equals sign the variable appears because $x = 5$ means $5 = x$. But most people prefer to have the variable on the left because they read from left to right.

A variable may be isolated by means of subtraction, division, addition, and multiplication. Sometimes, you must perform more than one operation to arrive at the final answer.

Subtraction. If the same number is subtracted from

each side of an equation, the new members remain equal. All roots of the original equation are also roots of the new equation. Thus, for example, you can subtract 2 from each member of the equation $3x + 2 = 11$:

$$3x + 2 - 2 = 11 - 2$$

to obtain the new equation

$$3x = 9$$

The equation $3x = 9$ is equivalent to $3x + 2 = 11$. The roots of either of these equations will solve the other. To isolate the variable of the new equation, you must perform one more operation—the operation of division.

Division. If each side of an equation is divided by the same number, except zero, the new members will be equal. The roots of the original equation are the roots of the new equation. Using this rule you can divide each side of $3x = 9$ by 3:

$$\frac{3x}{3} = \frac{9}{3}$$
$$x = 3$$

So the solution set of the equation $3x + 2 = 11$ is {3}. You can prove this by replacing x with 3 in the original equation: $3 \times 3 + 2 = 11$, or $11 = 11$.

You cannot divide members of an equation by zero. Division by zero is meaningless.

Addition. Another rule for solving algebraic equations is that if the same number is added to each member of an equation, the new members will be equal. The roots of the original equation are roots of the new equation. For example, in the equation $x - 6 = 18$, you can add 6 to each member of the equation to isolate the x on the left side of the equation. That is, $x - 6 + 6 = 18 + 6$, and $x = 24$. The solution is the set {24}.

When adding terms with identical variables, the numbers before the variables are added. For example, $5a + 2a = 7a$. When subtracting terms with identical variables, the numbers are subtracted, so that $8y - 3y = 5y$.

Multiplication. The last rule for solving simple equations is that if each member of an equation is multiplied by the same number, the new members are equal. It would not be useful to multiply by zero, however, because any number multiplied by zero equals zero.

After multiplying both sides of an equation by the same number, the roots of the original equation equal the roots of the new equation. For example, you can multiply each member of the equation $\frac{1}{4}x = 5$ by 4:

$$4 \times \frac{1}{4}x = 4 \times 5$$

to obtain

$$x = 20$$

Thus, the solution set of $\frac{1}{4}x = 5$ is {20}.

You can use all four rules to find the solution set of the equation

$$\frac{2}{3}x - 4 = \frac{1}{4}x + 6$$

First, use multiplication to produce an equation that has only whole numbers. Such an equation is easier to solve than one containing fractions. The numbers in the denominators, 3 and 4, have the *common factor* 12 (see **Factor**). Multiplying both sides of the equation by 12 therefore changes the fractions into whole numbers:

$$12\left(\tfrac{2}{3}x - 4\right) = 12\left(\tfrac{1}{4}x + 6\right)$$
$$8x - 48 = 3x + 72$$

Second, add 48 to each member of the equation to eliminate the 48 from the left side of the equation:

$$8x - 48 + 48 = 3x + 72 + 48$$
$$8x = 3x + 120$$

Third, subtract $3x$ from each member to eliminate the $3x$ from the right side of the equation:

$$8x - 3x = 3x + 120 - 3x$$
$$5x = 120$$

Finally, divide each member by 5 to isolate the variable x on the left side of the equation:

$$\frac{5x}{5} = \frac{120}{5}$$
$$x = 24$$

The solution set is therefore {24}. You can verify this by replacing x with 24 in the original equation:

$$\tfrac{2}{3} \times 24 - 4 = \tfrac{1}{4} \times 24 + 6$$
$$16 - 4 = 6 + 6$$
$$12 = 12$$

Since the equation-solving techniques did not produce any other solutions, 24 is the only solution.

Positive and negative numbers. In arithmetic, you can always add, multiply, or divide numbers. But you cannot always subtract. For example, "$3 - 5$" is meaningless in ordinary arithmetic. Algebra has an extended number system that solves this problem.

In ordinary arithmetic, numbers indicate only size. That is, they show how many or how much. However, many everyday measurements indicate both size and direction. The temperature above or below zero is a good example of this. In algebra, we use numbers that show direction.

You can show these new numbers on a scale:

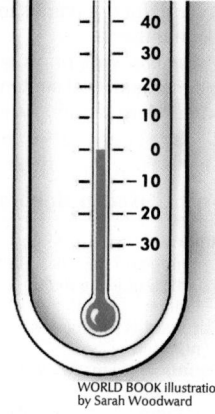

WORLD BOOK illustration by Sarah Woodward

Below zero						Above zero		
-4	-3	-2	-1	0	$+1$	$+2$	$+3$	$+4$

The origin or starting point is zero. To the right of zero, the points show positive distance or direction. These numbers are like temperatures above zero. To the left of zero, the points show negative distance or direction. These numbers are like temperatures below zero. Point A is not just 1, but $+1$ or positive one. The $+$ sign shows its direction from zero. Point B is not just 1, but -1 or negative one. The $-$ sign also shows direction. The numbers on this scale are called positive numbers and negative numbers. In everyday life, you can use these numbers to represent temperatures, distances above or below sea level, changes in stock-market prices, business earnings, and many other things. For every positive number, there is a negative number of the same arithmetical size. For example, the number 7 always means seven things, positive or negative. The arithmetical size of a number is called its *absolute value.*

You can add, subtract, multiply, and divide positive and negative numbers, but the rules of these operations are different from those in ordinary arithmetic.

Adding can be illustrated with the problem $(+5) + (-7)$, or the sum of positive five and negative seven. You can work out the solution on the following scale.

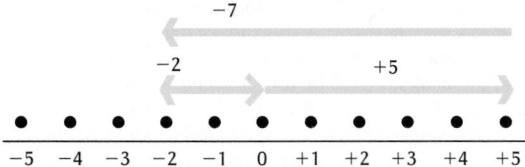

If you were adding $(+5)$ and $(+7)$ on a scale, you would count five points to the right from zero, and then count seven more to the right to $(+12)$. To add $(+5) + (-7)$, start at zero on the scale above and count off the first number to be added. This number is $+5$, so you count off 5 to the right. Next, count off in the direction indicated by the second number to be added. This number is -7, so you count off -7 to the left from $+5$. This takes you to the left of 0, to -2. You can read the sum of $(+5) + (-7)$ on the scale: -2. Therefore, $(+5) + (-7) = (-2)$. Numbers with positive or negative signs are often called *signed numbers.*

One rule for adding signed numbers has two parts. First, *if the signs are the same, add the absolute values of the numbers and give the sum the common sign.* For example,

$$(+5) + (+8) = (+13) \text{ and } (-5) + (-8) = (-13)$$

Second, *if the signs are different, subtract the smaller absolute value from the larger absolute value, and give the result the sign of the number with the larger absolute value.* For example,

$$(+5) + (-8) = (-3) \text{ and } (-5) + (+8) = (+3)$$

Subtracting. In arithmetic, subtraction is often thought of as the opposite of addition. But using negative numbers, we can think about subtraction as simply a special kind of addition. Subtracting a number is the same as adding the number with the opposite sign.

You may have noticed this rule when adding negative numbers to positive numbers. For example, take the arithmetic expression $9 - 4$. In this expression, both the 9 and the 4 are positive. By switching the sign of the number 4 from positive to negative, we can rewrite this subtraction problem as an addition problem:

$$(+9) - (+4) \quad \text{becomes} \quad (+9) + (-4).$$

Both expressions equal the same number: 5.

The idea of switching signs lets us simplify how we subtract negative numbers. Subtracting a negative number is the same as adding that number's positive. For example, the expression $(+6) - (-2)$ is the same as $(+6) + (+2)$. Both expressions equal 8.

Multiplying. The rule for multiplying signed numbers is to *multiply the absolute values. If the signs are alike, the product is positive.*

$$(+3) \times (+8) = (+24) \qquad (-3) \times (-8) = (+24)$$

If the signs are not alike, the product is negative.

$$(+3) \times (-8) = (-24) \qquad (-3) \times (+8) = (-24)$$

Dividing. The rule for dividing signed numbers is similar. *Dividing numbers with the same sign gives a positive quotient.*

$$(+24) \div (+3) = (+8) \qquad (-24) \div (-8) = (+3)$$

Dividing numbers with signs that are not alike gives a negative quotient.

$$(+24) \div (-3) = (-8) \qquad (-24) \div (+8) = (-3)$$

In algebra, you may need to use negative numbers in order to obtain a root to an equation. For example, the equation $x + 4 = 1$ has no root with positive numbers. With the extended number system, its root is -3. Operations with negative numbers can be applied to variables that represent numbers. That is, you can deal with quantities such as $-x$ or $-y$.

Writing formulas. Algebra uses general formulas to help solve many practical problems in science, engineering, and everyday life. A wide variety of arithmetic situations can be expressed in general formulas.

One example of the use of general formulas involves room dimensions. Consider a room that is 5 meters long and 4 meters wide. Its *perimeter,* or outside measurement, is $5 + 4 + 5 + 4$ meters, or $2 \times (5 + 4)$ meters. If the room is 5 meters long and the width is unknown, you can use w, a variable, to represent the width. The perimeter is then $5 + w + 5 + w$, or $2 \times (5 + w)$. Going one step further, you can write a formula for the perimeter of *any* rectangular room by using l for the length and w for the width. The formula is $2 \times (l + w)$. You can solve many problems with this kind of formula.

Some situations call for an equation. For example, a man collected a sum of money on August 1, and $\frac{1}{3}$ as much on August 2. He collected a total of $6,500. How much was each amount? If n is the amount collected on August 1, then $\frac{1}{3}n$ is the amount collected on August 2. The equation is $n + \frac{1}{3}n = 6,500$. You can solve this equation to find n. First, multiply both members of the equation by 3 to change the fraction $\frac{1}{3}$ to a whole number:

$$3 \times (n + \tfrac{1}{3}n) = 3 \times 6,500$$
$$3n + n = 19,500$$

Add the terms on the left side of the equation:

$$4n = 19,500$$

Divide both members of the equation by 4 to find n.

$$n = 4,875$$

And $\frac{1}{3}n = 4,875 \div 3$, or 1,625. Therefore, the man collected $4,875 on August 1 and $1,625 on August 2. To check this result, add the two amounts collected: $4,875 + $1,625 = $6,500.

Basic algebra

After you learn to work with variables, equations, and signed numbers, you will find that the fundamental principles of algebra are not hard to understand.

Symbols in algebra. The symbol + indicates addition. But in algebra, it also signifies a positive number. The symbol − indicates subtraction and a negative number. You usually do not use × to indicate multiplication in algebra, because it might be confused with the letter x. Instead, you use a dot · or no symbol at all. You write a multiplied by b as $a \cdot b$, $(a)(b)$, or ab. (Note that $3 \cdot 6$ and $(3)(6)$ both mean six multiplied by three, but that 36 still means 36, as in arithmetic.) The symbol ÷ for division is the same as it is in arithmetic.

Parentheses ( ), brackets [ ], and braces { } often enclose quantities or numbers. They are called *signs of aggregation* because everything within them must be treated as a single expression. You must often simplify the enclosed expression before it can be used in other parts of a problem. Here is an example using numbers:

$$\{12 + [4 + 5 - (5 - 3) + 4] - 4\}$$

First, simplify the group $(5 - 3)$:

$$\{12 + [4 + 5 - 2 + 4] - 4\}$$

Second, simplify the group $[4 + 5 - 2 + 4]$:

$$\{12 + 11 - 4\} = 19$$

You use the same method to simplify expressions with variables. Here is an example of simplifying groups of variables:

$$\{5a + 6a + [5a - a + (3a + 4a)] - a\}$$

First, simplify the group $(3a + 4a)$:

$$\{5a + 6a + [5a - a + 7a] - a\}$$

Second, simplify the group $[5a - a + 7a]$:

$$\{5a + 6a + 11a - a\} = 21a$$

Sometimes it is useful to remove the parentheses from an expression without simplifying it. You can do this by using the rules for addition and subtraction of signed numbers. For example, the expression $a + (b \ 1 \ c)$ can be rewritten $a + b + c$. To illustrate this, the expression $40 + (8 - 2)$ means that $8 - 2$, or 6, must be added to 40, or $40 + 6$. Removing the parentheses, $40 + 8 - 2$, or $48 - 2$, is the same as the simplified expression, $40 + 6$. *If an expression within parentheses has an addition or positive sign before it, you can remove the parentheses without changing the signs of the quantities within the parentheses.* Thus, $a + (-b - c)$ becomes $a - b - c$.

But, *if an expression within parentheses has a subtraction or negative sign before it, you must change the subtraction or negative sign, and you must change the sign of the quantities within the parentheses. That is, you make an addition problem out of a subtraction problem.* Thus, $6 - (-8)$ becomes $6 + (+8)$. Here is another example: $6 - (+8)$ becomes $6 + (-8)$. If there is more than one quantity within the parentheses, you must change the

sign of each quantity. For example, $6 - (-3 + 2)$ becomes $6 + 3 - 2$, or 7. For this general situation, you can rewrite $a - (b + c)$ as the formula $a - b - c$.

If you want to change the signs of expressions or numbers, you can reverse the process and put them within parentheses. For example, you can rewrite the expression $8 + 7$ as $-(-8 - 7)$. Or, you can rewrite $8 + 4 - 6$ as $8 - (-4 + 6)$.

Fundamental laws. There are five fundamental laws in algebra. These laws govern addition, subtraction, multiplication, and division. They are expressed in variables, and the variables can be replaced with any numbers. Here are the laws:

1. *The Commutative Law of Addition* is written $x + y = y + x$. This means that if you want to add two numbers, you can add them in either order, and the sum will be the same. For example, $2 + 3 = 3 + 2 = 5$, and $(-8) + (-36) = (-36) + (-8) = -44$.

2. *The Associative Law of Addition* is written $x + (y + z) = (x + y) + z$. This means that if you want to add several numbers, you can add any combination first, and the final sum will be the same. For example, $2 + (3 + 4) = (2 + 3) + 4$, or $2 + 7 = 5 + 4 = 9$.

3. *The Commutative Law of Multiplication* is written $x \cdot y = y \cdot x$. This means that if you want to multiply two numbers, you can multiply them in either order, and the product will be the same. For example, $(2)(3) = (3)(2) = 6$, and $(-8)(-36) = (-36)(-8) = 288$.

4. *The Associative Law of Multiplication* is written $x \cdot (y \cdot z) = (x \cdot y) \cdot z$. This means that if you want to multiply several numbers, you can multiply any combination first, and the final product will be the same. For example, $2(3 \cdot 4) = (2 \cdot 3)4$, or $2(12) = (6)4 = 24$.

5. *The Distributive Law of Multiplication over Addition* is written $x(y + z) = xy + xz$. This law can be illustrated with an example: $3 \cdot (4 + 5) = (3 \cdot 4) + (3 \cdot 5)$. If a number multiplies a sum, for example, $3(4 + 5)$, or $3 \cdot 9$, the result is the same as the sum of the separate products of the multiplier and each addend, $(3 \cdot 4) + (3 \cdot 5)$, or $12 + 15$. In this example, you can see that $3 \cdot 9 = 12 + 15 = 27$.

Other definitions. It is important to define some other words used in algebra. An expression consisting of a product of numbers and variables is a *monomial.* For example, $5xy$ is a monomial. This particular monomial contains three elements (5, x, and y), called *factors*, that multiply each other. An expression with two or more terms connected by addition or subtraction symbols is called a *polynomial.* For example, $x - y + z$ is a polynomial. One kind of polynomial is a binomial, an expression with two terms connected by an addition or subtraction symbol. For example, $x + y$ and $3a^2 - 4b$ are binomials.

A number, variable, or expression that acts as a multiplier is called a *coefficient.* For example, in the expression $5a$, 5 is the coefficient of a and a is the coefficient of 5. In $a(x + y)$, a is the coefficient of $(x + y)$ and $(x + y)$ is the coefficient of a.

Addition in algebra is much like that in arithmetic. In algebra, a added to a is $2a$. The expressions a and $2a$ are said to be *like* or *similar* because they contain exactly the same variables. To add two or more like quantities, you use the Distributive Law. In this way, $2x + 3x + 4x$ is $(2 + 3 + 4)x$, or $9x$. But there is no single term for the sum of unlike quantities, such as a and b. This sum must be written $a + b$. To add $3a$, $4b$, $6a$, and b, you can use the Commutative and Associative laws of addition. These laws permit you to add a series of numbers in any order. First, add the similar terms: $3a + 6a = 9a$ and $4b + b = 5b$. Then, combine the sums. Thus, $3a + 4b + 6a + b = 9a + 5b$.

You can use this form to work out the problem:

$$
\begin{array}{r}
3a + 4b \\
+ \quad 6a + b \\
\hline
9a + 5b
\end{array}
$$

To add unlike quantities that are both positive and negative, you can use the Distributive Law of Multiplication over Addition. This can be shown by adding $(2a^3 - b^2c + 6bd^2 + 2d^3)$, $(4a^3 + 3b^2c - 4bd^2 - 3d^3)$, $(3a^3 + 2b^2c + 2bd^2 - 4d^3)$, and $(-2a^3 - 8b^2c + 6bd^2 + 6d^3)$. The little 3 above such terms as $2a^3$ means that the number represented by the variable is *cubed*. That is, the number is used as a factor three times (see **Cube**). To add these terms, you should first arrange like terms in columns:

$$
\begin{array}{r}
2a^3 - b^2c + 6bd^2 + 2d^3 \\
+ \quad 4a^3 + 3b^2c - 4bd^2 - 3d^3 \\
+ \quad 3a^3 + 2b^2c + 2bd^2 - 4d^3 \\
+ \quad -2a^3 - 8b^2c + 6bd^2 + 6d^3 \\
\hline
7a^3 - 4b^2c + 10bd^2 + d^3
\end{array}
$$

An explanation of the second column illustrates this method of adding polynomials. This column is $-b^2c + 3b^2c + 2b^2c - 8b^2c$. Using the Distributive Law, you can see that these terms are the separate products of a multiplier, b^2c. The coefficients are the numbers that make up a sum. These numbers are -1, $+3$, $+2$, and -8. You can add them together to obtain $(-4)b^2c$, or $-4b^2c$. Use the same method to add the other columns.

Subtraction of products of numbers and variables follows the same rule as the subtraction of signed numbers. To subtract a number, you can simply reverse its sign and add it. In the example $8a - 3a$, the sign of both the minuend and the subtrahend is positive. That is, $(+8)a - (+3)a$. Changing this from a subtraction problem to an addition problem converts it to $(+8)a + (-3)a$. The sum of $8a$ and $-3a$ is $5a$.

The subtraction $(2a^3 - b^2c + 6bd^2 + 2d^3) - (4a^3 + 3b^2c - 4bd^2 - 3d^3)$ can be handled as an addition problem with reversed signs. First, arrange like terms in columns:

$$
\begin{array}{r}
2a^3 - b^2c + 6bd^2 + 2d^3 \\
4a^3 + 3b^2c - 4bd^2 - 3d^3
\end{array}
$$

Next, subtract the coefficients of like terms by changing the signs of the subtracted quantities and adding:

$$
\begin{array}{r}
2a^3 - b^2c + 6bd^2 + 2d^3 \\
+ \quad -4a^3 - 3b^2c + 4bd^2 + 3d^3 \\
\hline
-2a^3 - 4b^2c + 10bd^2 + 5d^3
\end{array}
$$

Multiplication in algebra is usually indicated by writing two or more expressions together without an operation symbol. For example, $a \cdot b$ is written ab.

When a variable or number is multiplied by itself, the multiplication is abbreviated. For example, abb is written ab^2 and $abbbb$ is written ab^4. The little number is called

an *exponent*. It indicates the number of times a quantity is multiplied by itself. Thus, $a \cdot a$ or aa is written a^2. It is called the *square* of a. Next, $a \cdot a \cdot a$ or aaa is written a^3. It is called the *cube* of a. And $aaaa$ is written as a^4, and $aaaaa$ is written as a^5. A variable that occurs by itself has an exponent of 1. If you are adding or subtracting exponents, you can write a as a^1.

When you multiply like variables, you add their exponents. You can see that $b^2 \cdot b^3$ is $(b \cdot b)(b \cdot b \cdot b)$, or b^5. It is easier to add the exponents: $b^2 \cdot b^3 = b^{2+3}$, and $b^{2+3} = b^5$. You cannot combine the exponents in $a^2 \cdot b^2$ because a and b could possibly represent different numbers.

To multiply $abcd$ by bc^2dy, you combine the variables that are alike. In $(abcd)(bc^2dy)$, there are one a, two b's or $b \cdot b$, three c's or $c \cdot c^2$, two d's or $d \cdot d$, and one y. So the product of $abcd$ and bc^2dy is $ab^2c^3d^2y$. The Commutative Law of Multiplication permits you to multiply variables and numbers in any order.

To multiply an expression consisting of two or more terms by a single term or expression, you can use the Distributive Law of Multiplication over Addition: $x(y + z) = xy + xz$. Multiplying $(3bd)(5b^2c + 2d)$ shows the use of this law. You can modify the form used in arithmetic for multiplication:

$$
\begin{array}{r}
5b^2c + 2d \\
\times \quad 3bd \\
\hline
15b^3cd + 6bd^2
\end{array}
$$

To find the product in this example, you multiply the terms of $(5b^2c + 2d)$ one at a time. First, multiply $5b^2c$ by $3bd$. This product is $15b^3cd$. Write $15b^3cd$ as the first term in the answer. Next, multiply $2d$ by $3bd$. This product is $6bd^2$. Write $6bd^2$ as the second term in the answer. The total product is $15b^3cd + 6bd^2$.

To multiply two expressions each consisting of two or more quantities is more difficult. Here is an example. The problem is $(a^2 - 2ab + b^2)(a - b)$.

$$
\begin{array}{r}
a^2 - 2ab + b^2 \\
\times \quad a - b \\
\hline
a^3 - 2a^2b + ab^2 \\
+ \quad\quad - a^2b + 2ab^2 - b^3 \\
\hline
a^3 - 3a^2b + 3ab^2 - b^3
\end{array}
$$

First, multiply each term in the top expression $(a^2 - 2ab + b^2)$ by a, the first term of the bottom expression $(a - b)$. Write the product of this multiplication.

Next, multiply each term in the top expression by b, the second term of bottom expression. Write this second product below the first product. Arrange like terms in columns.

Last, add the two products to obtain the total product. Arranging like terms in columns helps you to do the addition that gives the total product.

Division in algebra is the opposite of multiplication. Remember that to multiply like terms, you add their exponents. To divide like terms, you subtract the exponents. For example, $b^5 \div b^2 = b^{5-2}$ and $b^{5-2} = b^3$.

Here is a more difficult problem: $(3x^4y^2z - 9x^3yz - 6x^2zy^3) \div (3x^2y)$. In this case, you must divide each part of the first expression in turn by $(3x^2y)$. For each part, ask what multiplied by $(3x^2y)$ will give that part of the dividend. For example, what quantity, when multiplied by $(3x^2y)$, will give $(3x^4y^2z)$? The answer is (x^2yz). Using this method, $(3x^4y^2z - 9x^3yz^2 - 6x^2y^3) \div (3x^2y) = (x^2yz - 3xz^2 - 2y^2)$.

Here is another problem: $(12a^2 + 18ab + 6b^2) \div (4a + 2b)$. For a problem of this kind, you can use a form somewhat like that used in arithmetic for long division:

$$12a^2 + 18ab + 6b^2$$
$$12a^2 + 6ab$$
$$\overline{12ab + 6b^2} \quad \boxed{4a + 2b}\,\text{Divisor}$$
$$12ab + 6b^2 \quad 3a + 3b\,\text{Quotient}$$

First, divide the first term of the dividend by the first term of the divisor: $12a^2 \div 4a = 3a$. Write the result, $3a$, as the first term in the quotient to the right. Next, multiply both terms of the divisor by $3a$, the first term in the quotient: $(4a + 2b)(3a) = 12a^2 + 6ab$. Write this product below the dividend and subtract it from the dividend. You must account for the result of this subtraction, $12ab + 6b^2$, with a second term in the quotient. To do this, divide $12ab$ by the first term of the divisor: $12ab \div 4a = 3b$. And $3b$ proves to be the second term of the quotient. Multiply the divisor by $3b$: $(4a + 2b)(3b) = 12ab + 6b^2$. You can see that there is no remainder.

Factoring means to find expressions that are factors of a given product. For example, $(4a + 2b)$ and $(3a + 3b)$ are factors of $12a^2 + 18ab + 6b^2$. If you multiply $(4a + 2b)(3a + 3b)$, the product is $12a^2 + 18ab + 6b^2$. An expression can have more than one set of factors. For example, 2×12, 3×8, and 4×6 are sets of factors of 24. Factoring is important in algebra because it is used to simplify complicated expressions (see **Factor**).

Working with equations

Functions. The amount of gasoline used by an airplane is related to its speed. The amount of postage required for a parcel depends on its weight. The idea of one thing depending on another is important in mathematics. It is called the *relation* of one thing to another. In algebra, a certain relation of two variables is called a *function.*

You can learn the idea of a function from familiar things. For example, imagine a concrete foundation 16 centimeters above the level of the ground. On this foundation, you build up 6 layers of stone blocks. Each layer is 8 centimeters thick. As you add each layer of blocks, the height of the pile becomes larger. Use x to represent the number of layers and y to represent the height of the pile. Here is a table showing the relation of the number of layers of stone blocks to the height of the pile.

x	0	1	2	3	4	5	6
y	16	24	32	40	48	56	64

You can show the numbers in this table on a graph. Distances along two lines represent the values of x and y. One line is horizontal and shows values of x. The other line is vertical and shows values of y. These two lines are called *coordinates*. You can plot the number pairs from the table on the graph with 7 dots.

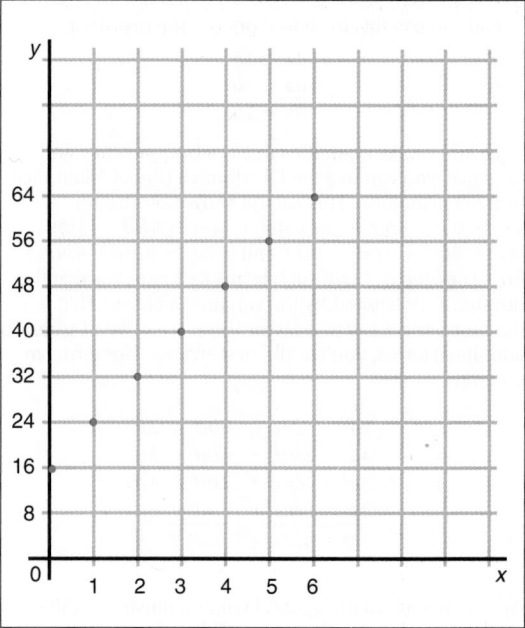

There is an equation that describes this line of dots: $y = 8x + 16$. You can see how the equation fits the table of values. For example, if $x = 2$, then $y = 8(2) + 16$, or 32. If $x = 5$, then $y = 8(5) + 16$, or 56.

In the equation, the *domain* of x is the set of numbers $\{0, 1, 2, 3, 4, 5, 6\}$. The values of y are called the *range* of

WORLD BOOK illustration by Sarah Woodward

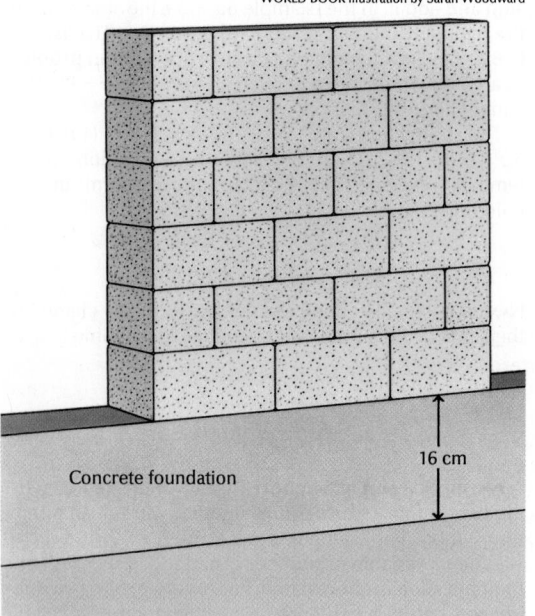

16 cm

Concrete foundation

y. The range of *y* is the set of numbers {16, 24, 32, 40, 48, 56, 64}. Mathematicians call the relation between the two sets of numbers *a set of ordered pairs*. This set is written {(*x,y*)}$\mapsto${(0, 16), (1, 24), (2, 32) … (6, 64)}. This set of pairs is a function. It is called a *discrete function* because it cannot be represented by a continuous line. On the graph that appears on page 356, the function is shown by the dots or points.

Now, imagine that the bottom of an aquarium is 20 inches above the floor. The aquarium is 36 inches high. Water flowing into the aquarium causes the level of the

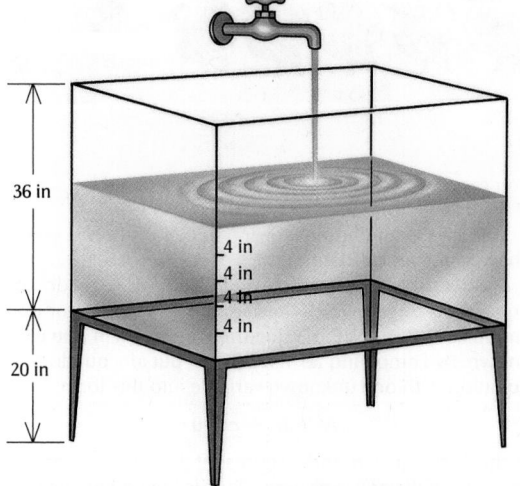

36 in

4 in
4 in
4 in
4 in

20 in

WORLD BOOK illustration by Sarah Woodward

water in the aquarium to rise 4 inches every minute. This means that the height of the water above the floor is related to the time the water has been flowing. In this example, use *x* to represent the number of minutes the water has been flowing and *y* to represent the distance of the surface of the water from the floor. Here are some of the values of *x* and *y*:

x	0	1	2	3	4	5	6	7	8	9
y	20	24	28	32	36	40	44	48	52	56

When this relation is shown on a graph, the line is solid because the height of *y* increases continuously. You can describe this line with an equation: $y = 4x + 20$. If $x = 2$, then $y = 4(2) + 20$, or 28. You can see how this equation fits the table of values. The domain of *x* is all numbers between 0 and 9, and the range of *y* is all numbers between 20 and 56. This function is called a *linear function* because it is continuous and can be represented by a solid line. The equation $y = 4x + 20$ is called a *linear equation*. The study of linear equations is one of the most important topics in algebra.

Solving linear equations in two variables. The equation $y = 4x + 20$ is linear. It has two variables, *x* and

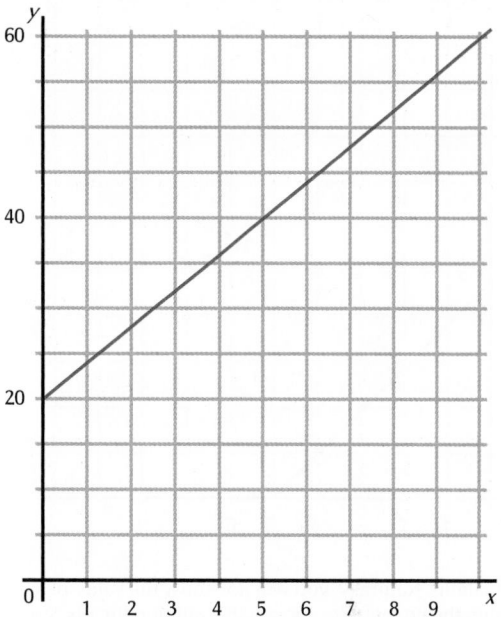

y. Every point on this line represents two numbers that count as a solution to the equation. Thus, many pairs of numbers make $y = 4x + 20$ a true statement.

Because linear equations have many solutions, it is often useful to find some sort of restriction or limit for them. For example, you might want to use a linear equation to solve a practical problem. To do this, you must find some way to restrict the equation to one set of values. One method is to use a *pair of equations* that are true for only one pair of numbers.

The equations $2y = x + 4$ and $y + x = 5$ illustrate this method. To solve these equations, you can use a graph. First, make tables of a few of the values that solve each equation.

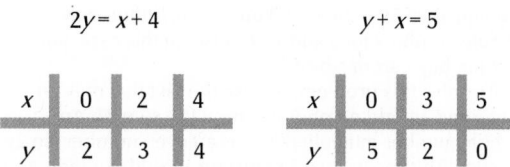

$$2y = x + 4 \qquad\qquad y + x = 5$$

x	0	2	4
y	2	3	4

x	0	3	5
y	5	2	0

Plot these points on the graph (as shown on page 358) and draw a line for each equation. The two lines cross. The point where they cross represents the numbers that will solve both equations. This point is (2, 3). That is, *x* has the value 2, and *y* has the value 3. Only these values for *x* and *y* will solve the two equations.

You can also solve a pair of linear equations in two variables by eliminating one of the variables. This results in a single equation in one variable. You can use $2y = x + 4$ and $y + x = 5$ as examples. There are various ways of eliminating a variable. The method that can be used here is called *substitution*. First, solve one of the equations for *y*. That is, find what *y* equals in one of the

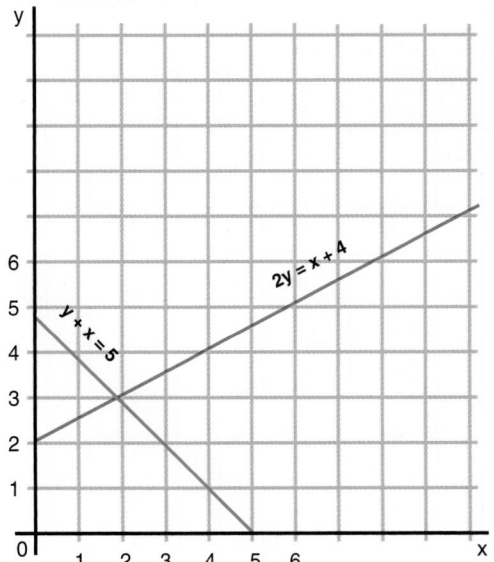

Or three turkeys and eight ducks:

$15 $16

Or five turkeys and three ducks:

$25 $6

equations. Naturally, you will not know the value of x. Using the equation $y + x = 5$, the solution for y is $5 - x$. Substitute this for y in the other equation. The other equation is $2y = x + 4$. Substituting the new value for y, you obtain $2(5 - x) = x + 4$. Simplified, this is $10 - 2x = x + 4$. Subtracting 4 from both sides of this equation produces $6 - 2x = x$. Adding $2x$ to both sides of the new equation produces $6 = 3x$. Therefore, $x = 2$. Now you can replace x with 2 in either of the two equations and find 3 as the value for y: $2y = 2 + 4$ and $y + 2 = 5$. So the solution of the two equations is $\{(2, 3)\}$.

An equation in two variables can also be solved by restricting the solution to positive whole numbers. You can see this in a problem involving a man who bought some prize turkeys and ducks. He spent $31. He paid $5 for each turkey and $2 for each duck. How many of each did he buy? Use x to represent the number of turkeys and $5x$ as their cost. Use y to represent the number of ducks and $2y$ as their cost. You can write this problem as an equation: $5x + 2y = 31$. You can substitute only whole numbers for x and y because, in this case, you cannot buy part of a bird.

To solve this problem, we use the fact that only an even and an odd number can have the sum 31. Any whole number multiplied by 2 is an even number, so $2y$ is even. This means that $5x$ must be an odd number. Any even number multiplied by 5 is an even number, so x cannot be even. Any odd number multiplied by 5 is an odd number, so x might be any odd number. Replacing x with odd numbers, you will find that the pairs of numbers that solve the equation are (1, 13), (3, 8), and (5, 3). The man could have bought 1 turkey and 13 ducks:

WORLD BOOK illustrations by Sarah Woodward

$5 $26

You cannot use 7 for x because the pair would be $(7, -2)$, and -2 ducks is not a solution.

For another method of solving equations in two variables, see **Determinant**.

Quadratic equations in one unknown. A quadratic equation is one in which the variable is squared. For example, $x^2 - 8x = -16$ is a quadratic equation in one unknown. By combining terms, you can put any quadratic equation with one unknown variable into this form:

$$ax^2 + bx + c = 0$$

In this formula, a, b, and c represent the *known* numbers or coefficients. For example, b is the coefficient of x, and x is the unknown variable. In the simplest example of this kind of equation, the coefficient $a = 1$ and $b = 0$. For instance, if $a = 1$, $b = 0$, and $c = -36$, then $x^2 - 36 = 0$. This means that $x^2 = 36$ and the solution set is $\{6, -6\}$. If b does *not* equal zero, there are three other methods for solving this type of equation.

The first method is to factor the equation after it has been put in the form $ax^2 + bx + c = 0$. You can use $x^2 + 8x + 15 = 0$ as an example. You can factor the left-hand side of this equation: $x^2 + 8x + 15 = (x + 3)(x + 5)$. So $(x + 3)(x + 5) = 0$. If the product of two numbers is zero, one of the numbers must be zero. If $x + 5 = 0$, then $x = -5$. Similarly, if $x + 3 = 0$, then $x = -3$. The solution set of $x^2 + 8x + 15$ is $\{-3, -5\}$.

The second method is called *completing the square*. An expression such as $a^2 + 2ab + b^2$ is called a *perfect square* because it can be rewritten $(a + b)^2$. You can change an equation such as $x^2 + 8x + 15 = 0$ so that the left-hand member is a perfect square. To do this, rewrite the equation $x^2 + 8x + 15 = 0$ as $x^2 + 8x = -15$. You know that $x^2 + 8x + 16$ is a perfect square because it can be rewritten $(x + 4)^2$. You can add 16 to both sides of $x^2 + 8x = -15$. This gives you $x^2 + 8x + 16 = -15 + 16$. Factoring this, you find that $(x + 4)^2 = 1$. One of two equal factors of a number is called its *square root* (see **Square root**). In the equation $(x + 4)^2 = 1$, $x + 4$ must equal the square root of 1. The square root of 1 is either 1 or -1. So $x + 4 = 1$ or $x + 4 = -1$. Then $x = -3$ or $x = -5$. This means that the solution set to $x^2 + 8x + 15 = 0$ is $\{-3, -5\}$.

The third method for solving a quadratic equation in

one unknown is to use the following formula:

$$x = \frac{-b \pm \sqrt{b^2 - 4ac}}{2a}$$

You can obtain the coefficients a, b, and c from any quadratic equation put in the form $ax^2 + bx + c = 0$. Substituting these numbers in the formula will give you the value of x. In the formula, the symbol $\pm$ means positive *or* negative. It also indicates that there will be two roots to the equation.

Here is how to apply the equation to the formula $x^2 + 8x + 15 = 0$:

$$x = \frac{-8 \pm \sqrt{(8)^2 - 4\,(1)(15)}}{2(1)}$$

$$x = \frac{-8 \pm \sqrt{4}}{2}$$

$$x = \frac{-8 \pm 2}{2}$$

$$x = \frac{-6}{2}, \frac{-10}{2}$$

The solution set to $x^2 + 8x + 15 = 0$ is $\{-3, -5\}$.

History

The ancient Egyptians and Babylonians used algebra. Evidence for its development appears in an Egyptian book that was copied by the scribe Ahmes about 1650 B.C. The Babylonians used more advanced algebra than did the Egyptians. Hundreds of years later, the Greeks, Chinese, and people of India contributed to the development of algebra. Diophantus, a mathematician who lived in the A.D. 200's, used quadratic equations and symbols for unknown quantities.

The Arabs made many contributions to the study of algebra. They adopted the number system of India, including the zero, and developed fractions much as they are used today. They helped transmit earlier mathematical ideas to the West. In the early 800's, the Persian mathematician al-Khwārizmī wrote an influential book on algebra that was used as a textbook. Most scholars consider either al-Khwārizmī or Diophantus to be the father of algebra. The English word *algebra* comes from an Arabic word meaning *restoration* or *completion* in the title of this work. The Persian astronomer and poet Omar Khayyam (c. 1048-1131) wrote a book on algebra.

There was little progress in the development of algebra during the Middle Ages, from about A.D. 400 through the 1400's. Europeans began to study the subject in the late 1400's and in the 1500's. Many mathematicians contributed to its later development.

The widespread use of computers has caused major changes in the study and use of algebra. Inexpensive software can perform most problem-solving steps studied in algebra. For example, the programs can quickly solve linear or quadratic equations. The emphasis in algebra classes has therefore begun to shift from learning basic symbol-manipulation skills to understanding algebra's underlying concepts.　　George W. Bright

Related articles in *World Book* include:

Al-Khwārizmī	Mathematics
Binomial theorem	Newton, Sir Isaac
Boolean algebra	Omar Khayyam
Descartes, René	Progression
Determinant	Series
Factor	Set theory

Outline

I. **Learning algebra**
  A. Sets and variables
  B. Statements and equations
  C. Solving equations
  D. Positive and negative numbers
  E. Writing formulas

II. **Basic algebra**
  A. Symbols in algebra
  B. Fundamental laws
  C. Other definitions
  D. Addition
  E. Subtraction
  F. Multiplication
  G. Division
  H. Factoring

III. **Working with equations**
  A. Functions
  B. Solving linear equations in two variables
  C. Quadratic equations in one unknown

IV. **History**

Questions

How does the use of a variable help solve math problems?
How may an equation be compared to a balance?
What is meant by the *root* or *roots* of an equation?
How can numbers in algebra indicate size and direction?
What is the rule for multiplying positive and negative numbers?
How are two like variables with exponents multiplied? For example, $(5y^4)(3y^2)$.
How is a function shown on a graph?
What is the Commutative Law of Multiplication?
What methods are used to solve quadratic equations in one unknown?
Where does the word *algebra* come from?

Additional resources

Bashmakova, I. G., and Smirnova, G. S. *The Beginnings and Evolution of Algebra.* Mathematical Assn. of Am., 2000.
Martin-Gay, K. E. *Algebra: A Combined Approach.* 2nd ed. Prentice Hall, 2003.
Stephens, Larry J. *Algebra for the Utterly Confused.* McGraw, 2000.
Sterling, Mary J. *Algebra for Dummies.* Hungry Minds, 2001.

Alger, *AL juhr,* **Horatio** (1832-1899), was an American author of novels for boys. He became famous for his stories about boys who rose from poverty to wealth and fame through hard work, virtuous living, and luck. Alger's works reinforced an image of the United States as a land where dreams of material prosperity, high social position, and power could come true. The name Horatio Alger is still used to describe fictional and real-life individuals who achieve "rags to riches" success through their own efforts.

Critics now consider Alger's novels poorly written and dull. But during the latter half of the 1800's, his stories made him one of the most influential writers in the United States. Alger wrote more than 130 books, which sold about 40 million copies. Many of his boy heroes appeared in series, notably *Ragged Dick* (begun in 1867), *Luck and Pluck* (begun in 1869), and *Tattered Tom* (begun in 1871).

Horatio Alger, Jr., was born in Revere, Massachusetts, on Jan. 13, 1832. From 1866 to 1896, he devoted much of his time and money to helping a home for orphans and runaway boys in New York City. He used this experience as material for his novels. Alger died on July 18, 1899.　　Ronald T. Curran

© Shutterstock

Algiers, the capital and largest city of Algeria, is often called *Algiers the White* because of its many white buildings. The city has an excellent harbor on the Mediterranean Sea. Most Algerians live in cities in the country's narrow Mediterranean coastal region.

Algeria

Algeria, *al JEER ee uh,* is the largest country in Africa. Northern Algeria stretches along the Mediterranean Sea. The country's narrow Mediterranean region has a warm climate and rich farmland. Almost all Algerians live in this region. Algiers, the country's capital and largest city, lies on the Mediterranean. To the south, the sun-scorched wastes of the Sahara cover more than four-fifths of Algeria. Beneath the surface of this desert area lie huge deposits of natural gas and petroleum.

Most Algerians are of mixed Arab and Berber descent. However, the people form two distinct cultural groups—Arab and Berber. Each group has its own customs and language. But nearly all Algerians are Muslims—that is, followers of Islam.

For about 130 years, Algeria belonged to France. In 1962, it gained independence following a bloody revolution. Algerians then formed a socialist government that began a program of rapid industrial development. The program has been financed chiefly by income from Algeria's government-owned natural gas and petroleum industries. But industry has not grown fast enough to eliminate poverty and widespread unemployment.

Government

National government. Algeria's first constitution was adopted in 1963. Since then, the constitution has

been revised several times. In 2020, voters approved a new constitution that was adopted in 2021.

A president serves as Algeria's head of state. The president is elected by the people to a five-year term. The president appoints a prime minister to head the government. The prime minister, in turn, nominates a cabinet called the Council of Ministers, which is then appointed by the president. The Council of Ministers helps in carrying out the day-to-day operations of the government.

Facts in brief

Capital: Algiers.
Official language: Arabic.
Official name: Al-Jumhuriyah al-Jaz'iriyah ad Dimuqratiyah wa ash-Sha'biyah (People's Democratic Republic of Algeria).
Area: 919,595 mi² (2,381,741 km²). *Greatest distances*—east-west, 1,500 mi (2,400 km); north-south, 1,300 mi (2,100 km). *Coastline*—750 mi (1,200 km).
Elevation: *Highest elevation*—Mount Tahat, 9,573 ft (2,918 m) above sea level. *Lowest elevation*—Chott Melrhir, 102 ft (31 m) below sea level.
Population: *Estimated 2022 population*—45,605,000; density, 50 per mi² (19 per km²); distribution, 74 percent urban, 26 percent rural. *2018 official government estimate*—42,500,000.
Chief products: *Agriculture*—barley, citrus fruits, dates, grapes, meat, milk, olives, potatoes, wheat. *Manufacturing*—construction materials, iron and steel, liquid natural gas, motor vehicles, refined petroleum products. *Mining*—iron ore, lead, natural gas, petroleum, phosphate rock, zinc.
National anthem: "Kassaman" ("We Pledge").
Money: *Basic unit*—Algerian dinar. One hundred centimes equal one Algerian dinar.

Kenneth J. Perkins, the contributor of this article, is Distinguished Professor Emeritus of History at the University of South Carolina.

Algeria has two houses in its national legislature, the National People's Assembly and the Council of the Nation. The people elect the members of the National People's Assembly to five-year terms. The members of the Council of the Nation serve six-year terms. Two-thirds of the members of the council are elected from representatives of local assemblies. The president appoints the other one-third.

Until 1989, the Front de Libération Nationale (FLN), or National Liberation Front, was Algeria's only legally permitted party. Today, Algeria is a multiparty state. But the Constitution bans the formation of political parties based on race, religion, language, sex, or regional differences. Other important political parties in Algeria today besides the FLN include the Movement of Society for Peace and the National Democratic Rally.

Local government. Algeria has 48 provinces called *wilayas.* Each wilaya has an elected assembly and a *wali* (governor), who is appointed by the president.

Courts. The Supreme Court is Algeria's highest court. It reviews cases from 48 wilaya courts. Wilaya courts hear appeals from lower courts called *tribunals.*

Armed forces. Algeria has an army, air force, and navy. Military service is required for Algerian men.

People

Ancestry. Most of Algeria's people are of mixed Arab and Berber ancestry. Berbers lived in what is now Algeria at least 5,000 years ago. Arabs began to arrive from the Arabian Peninsula during the A.D. 600's. Through the years, so many Arabs and Berbers intermarried that it is now difficult to separate the groups by ancestry. However, many Berbers in the country still maintain their own language and culture. Less than 1 percent of the people are of European descent.

Language. A large majority of Algerians speak Arabic, the country's official language and one of its two national languages. In addition to Arabic, many Algerians speak French. About a fifth of the people speak dialects of the Berber language, Tamazight, which is Algeria's other national language.

Way of life. Since Algeria gained its independence from France in 1962, the government has worked to rid the country of French cultural influences. For example, the government requires that legal proceedings be in Arabic rather than French. Arabic has also replaced French as the language used to teach elementary and high school students. Many Algerians have called for stricter observance of Islamic teachings, which regulate family and community relationships and many other aspects of daily life.

Rural life. Rural Algerians typically live in large family groups made up of several generations. Most houses are built of stone or concrete or of sun-dried bricks made of mud and straw. Most also have flat tile or tin roofs. The majority of rural Algerians make a living raising livestock or farming small plots.

City life. The architecture of Algeria's larger cities reflects Islamic and European influences. *Mosques* (Islamic houses of worship) and open-air markets are common. Older sections of the cities are called *casbahs.* In these sections, shops and houses are crowded along narrow streets. Newer sections have broad boulevards and tall office and apartment buildings.

In Algeria's cities, many men work in factories or offices. The typical household consists of only a father and mother and their children. City people have much more contact with European and American ideas than do rural Algerians. As a result, some city dwellers follow European and American customs.

Since Algeria gained independence, many rural people have moved to the cities to seek factory work. However, many of them have not been able to find jobs. The migration and a severe housing shortage have resulted in the growth of large slums in many Algerian cities.

Clothing. Many Algerians, especially in rural areas, wear traditional clothing. A woman may wear a long, white cotton outer garment called a *haik.* It covers the head and the lower part of the face and extends down as far as the feet. Traditional clothing for men includes a long, hooded cloak called a *burnoose.* Many people in urban areas wear clothing similar to that worn by North Americans and Europeans.

Foods made from such grains as wheat and barley form the chief part of the diet of most Algerians. The national dish is *couscous.* It consists of steamed wheat served with meat, vegetables, and a souplike sauce. Many city dwellers eat dishes similar to those eaten by North Americans and Europeans.

© Loveshop/Shutterstock

WORLD BOOK illustration

Algeria's flag and coat of arms display a star and crescent, symbols of Islam, partly against a background of green, a traditional Islamic color. The flag was officially adopted in 1962, when Algeria gained its independence from France. The Arabic letter *jim,* which appears twice at the top of the coat of arms, is an abbreviation for the Arabic form of *Republic of Algeria.*

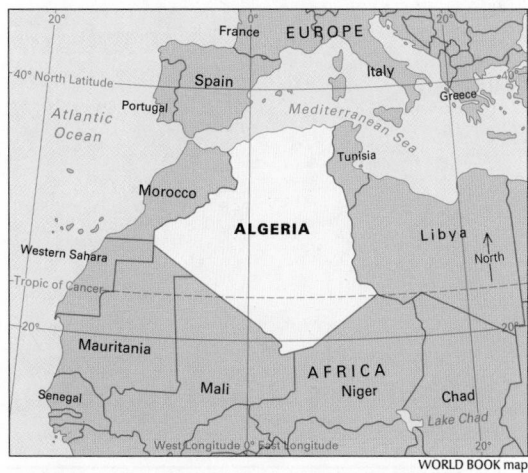

WORLD BOOK map

Algeria is a large country in northern Africa. Nearly all its people live in an area that borders the Mediterranean Sea.

Recreation. Soccer is the most popular sport in Algeria. Many Algerians enjoy playing the game or watching soccer matches. A favorite pastime in cities is going to motion pictures. Algerians celebrate several national holidays, including their country's independence day on July 5. They also enjoy a number of religious festivals.

Religion. The Constitution of Algeria declares Islam to be the country's official religion. About 99 percent of the people are Muslims, but they do not all agree about the role that Islam should play in the country's political and social life.

Education. About 80 percent of Algerians age 15 or older can read and write. Algerian law requires all children from 6 to 15 years old to attend school. More than 90 percent of all children attend elementary school. But only about a third of them go on to high school. The University of Algiers is the country's largest university.

The arts. Many of Algeria's finest works of art reflect the influence of Islam. Outstanding examples include the beautiful domed mosques found throughout the country. Algerians are also known for their superb jewelry, pottery, rugs, and other handicrafts in which they use distinct Islamic designs and traditional techniques.

Algerian painters and writers were strongly influenced by French culture during the period when Algeria belonged to France. Since then, they have increasingly drawn upon their Arabic, Berber, and Islamic cultural roots. Today, many Algerian painters use traditional Arabic or Berber designs. Numerous Algerian authors now write novels and plays in Arabic instead of in French.

Cities and towns

Adrar	68,276	.D	3
Aflou*	93,585	.B	3
Ain Beida	116,064	.B	4
Ain Defla*	55,259	.A	3
Ain Oussera*	98,107	.A	3
Ain Sefra	47,415	.B	2
Ain Témouchent	70,810	.B	2
Algiers (Alger)	2,364,230	.A	3
Annaba	342,703	.A	4
Arzew	58,162	.A	3
Barika*	98,141	.B	4
Batna	289,504	.B	4
Béchar	165,241	.C	2
Bejaia	176,139	.A	4
Berrouaghia*	55,775	.A	3
Biskra	204,661	.B	4
Blida	331,779	.A	3
Bordj Bou Arreridj	158,812	.A	4
Boufarik	57,162	.A	3
Boumerdes*	28,996	.A	3
Bouira	68,545	.A	4
Bou Saâda	111,787	.A	3
Chlef	155,134	.A	3
Constantine	448,028	.A	4
Djelfa	265,833	.B	3
El Bayadh*	85,577	.B	3
El Eulma*	145,380	.A	4
El Oued	186,525	.B	4
El Tarf*	13,346	.B	4
Ghardaïa	142,913	.B	3
Guelma	120,004	.A	4
Hassi Messaoud	44,478	.C	4
Illizi	13,029	.D	5
Jijel	131,513	.A	4
Khenchela	114,472	.B	4
Laghouat	134,372	.B	3
Maghnia	87,373	.B	2
Mascara	108,629	.B	3
Méchéria	65,043	.B	3
Médéa	145,441	.A	3
Mila*	63,251	.A	4
Mostaganem	162,885	.A	3
M'Sila*	132,975	.B	4
Naama*	14,624	.B	3
Oran	803,329	.A	3
Ouargla	169,928	.C	4
Oum El Bouaghi*	67,201	.A	3
Relizane	123,255	.A	3
Saida	142,497	.B	3
Sétif	252,127	.A	4
Sidi Bel Abbès	210,146	.B	3
Sig*	61,373	.B	2
Skikda	182,903	.A	4
Souk Ahras	153,479	.A	4
Tamanrasset	81,752	.E	4
Tébessa	194,461	.B	4
Tiaret	178,915	.B	3
Tindouf	45,610	.D	1
Tipaza*	15,180	.A	3
Tissemsilt*	66,084	.A	3
Tizi Ouzou	104,312	.A	4
Tlemcen	173,531	.B	2
Touggourt	143,270	.B	4

Physical features

Ahaggar Mountains	.E	4
Chelif River	.A	3
Chott Melrhir (lake)	.B	4
Djebel Aissa (mountain)	.B	3
Grand Erg Occidental (desert)	.C	3
Grand Erg Oriental (dune)	.C	4
Mediterranean Sea	.A	4
Mount Tahat	.E	4
Mouydir Mountains	.E	4
Plateau of Tademait	.D	3
Sahara (desert)	.D	3
Saharan Atlas (mountains)	.B	3
Sebkha Mekerrhane (lake)	.D	3
Tassili Oua-n-Ahaggar (plateau)	.F	4
Tell Atlas (mountains)	.B	2

Algeria

▨	National park
▬	International boundary
─	Road
┼┼	Railroad
╌╌	Oil pipeline
∿	Seasonal stream
✹	National capital
•	Other city or town
+	Elevation above sea level

*Name not shown on map; key shows general location.

Source: 2008 census.

WORLD BOOK map

Sarah Emington, Camerapix Hutchison Library

Algerian townspeople in Timimoun, in the country's Sahara region, wear either traditional or European-style clothing. The group at the right includes schoolchildren.

The land and climate

Algeria has three major land regions. They are, from north to south: (1) the Tell, (2) the High Plateaus, and (3) the Sahara.

The Tell stretches about 750 miles (1,200 kilometers) along the Mediterranean coast. The region is from about 80 to 200 miles (130 to 320 kilometers) wide. It consists chiefly of coastal plains and gently rolling hills. The word *Tell* is an Arabic term meaning *hill*. Much of Algeria's best farmland lies in the western and central parts of the region. Rugged mountains cover most of the eastern Tell. Many Aleppo pine, juniper, and cork oak trees grow on the mountain slopes. The Tell Atlas Mountains rise along the region's southern edge. Over 90 percent of Algeria's people live in the Tell.

Near the sea, temperatures in the Tell average 77 °F (25 °C) in summer and 52 °F (11 °C) in winter. Annual rainfall averages 16 inches (41 centimeters) in the west and 27 inches (69 centimeters) in the east.

The High Plateaus lie south of the Tell Atlas Mountains and range from about 1,300 to 4,300 feet (400 to 1,300 meters) above sea level. Herders graze cattle, sheep, and goats on the grasses and shrubs that cover much of the region. During rainy periods, shallow salt lakes called *chotts* form on the plateaus. About 7 percent of the Algerian people live in the region.

Average temperatures on the High Plateaus range from 81 °F (27 °C) in summer to 41 °F (5 °C) in winter. The region receives less than 16 inches (41 centimeters) of rain a year.

The Sahara. The Saharan Atlas Mountains form the northern border of the Algerian Sahara. This vast desert region occupies more than 80 percent of the country. Sand dunes cover much of the northern Sahara. Other parts of the region consist of bare rock, boulders, and stones. A wealth of natural gas and oil lies under the eastern part of the wasteland. In the southeast, the Ahaggar Mountains tower above the desert floor. The range includes Algeria's highest peak, Mount Tahat, which rises 9,573 feet (2,918 meters) above sea level.

Daytime temperatures in the Algerian Sahara sometimes soar above 120 °F (49 °C). During the summer, a hot, dusty wind called the *sirocco* blows northward across the region. The sirocco parches the High Plateaus about 40 days each summer and the Tell about 20 days.

Less than 3 percent of all Algerians live in the Sahara. Many of the region's people live in oases and rely on underground springs to water such crops as dates and grains. Nomads travel between grazing areas with their camels, sheep, and other livestock.

Economy

Much of Algeria's economy is controlled by the state. The economy is based largely on income from natural gas and petroleum production.

Service industries account for about one-third of the total value of Algeria's economic production and employ about three-fifths of the nation's workers. These industries include education, finance, government, health services, and wholesale and retail trade.

Mining employs only a small percentage of the nation's workers, but it accounts for much of Algeria's economic production. Algeria produces large quantities of natural gas and petroleum, chiefly from fields in the northeastern part of the Sahara region. Other important minerals produced in Algeria include iron ore, lead, phosphate rock, and zinc.

Manufacturing and construction also account for much of Algeria's economic production. They employ about 30 percent of all workers. The nation's chief manufactured products include construction materials, iron and steel, liquid natural gas, motor vehicles, and refined petroleum products. Almost all Algerian factories are on or near the coast in such cities as Algiers, Annaba,

Shostal

The High Plateaus region stretches across northern Algeria. The region's grasses and shrubs provide feed for herds of livestock. This shepherd is grazing a flock of sheep near Tiaret.

H. Kanus, Shostal

The Sahara, a hot desert region, covers over four-fifths of Algeria. Date palm trees, such as the ones shown here, grow in oases, where they are watered by underground springs.

Arzew, Constantine, and Skikda.

The government has poured much money into the construction of factories. But the industries have not grown fast enough to provide jobs for all workers. Thus, Algeria has a high rate of unemployment and many Algerians work in foreign countries.

Agriculture provides a living for about one-tenth of Algeria's workers. Most of the country's farmers own small plots on which they produce enough to feed their families. Other farmers work on large government farms. Algeria has a small amount of land that is suitable for farming and must import much of its food.

Crops are grown mainly in the northern area near the Mediterranean Sea. Grains, especially barley and wheat, are the chief crops. Other crops include citrus fruits, dates, grapes, olives, potatoes, and tomatoes. Dairy products and meat come from cattle, goats, and sheep that are herded in the High Plateaus region.

Trade. Algeria exports more than it imports. Natural gas, petroleum, and refined petroleum products account for almost all of the value of Algeria's exports. Algeria belongs to the Organization of the Petroleum Exporting Countries (OPEC), an association of countries whose economies depend heavily on oil exports. Algeria imports large amounts of food and machinery and many vehicles. Its main trading partners include China, France, Italy, Spain, and the United States.

Transportation and communication. Algeria has tens of thousands of miles of roads and thousands of miles of railroad track. Nearly all the roads and railroad track lie north of the Sahara. Camel caravans still cross the Algerian Sahara, as they have for hundreds of years. But goods and people also move across the desert by aircraft, jeeps, and trucks. Algeria's chief international airports are in Algiers, Constantine, and Oran. Algiers, Arzew, Oran, and Skikda have major seaports. The government controls some of the country's daily newspapers. Other newspapers are privately owned. Cellular phone usage has increased rapidly since the early 2000's. Internet usage has increased more slowly.

© Daniel Simon, Gamma/Liaison

A gas-processing plant in Arzew changes natural gas into a liquid so that it can be shipped overseas. Natural gas is one of Algeria's most valuable exports.

History

People have lived in what is now Algeria for at least 40,000 years. By about 3000 B.C., nomadic Berbers had begun migrating to the region. They probably came from Europe or Asia. In the 1100's B.C., the Phoenicians, who lived on the eastern shore of the Mediterranean Sea, established trading posts on the Algerian coast.

About 200 B.C., the Romans helped a Berber chieftain named Massinissa form and become ruler of the Kingdom of Numidia in northern Algeria. From 46 B.C. to the A.D. 600's, the area was controlled, in turn, by the Romans, the Vandals, and the Byzantines.

Arab conquest. In the A.D. 600's, Arabs from the Arabian Peninsula began to invade much of northern Africa, including Algeria. This invasion resulted in the spread of Arabic culture throughout northern Africa and into what is now Spain. In Algeria, most of the Berbers adopted Islam—the religion of the Arabs—and, in time, the Arabic language. Many Arabs and Berbers also intermarried.

Ottoman rule. During the early 1500's, Spanish Christians captured Algiers and other Algerian coastal cities. But in 1518, Barbarossa, a Turkish sea captain, gained control of Algiers. He later helped drive the Spanish from most other Algerian coastal areas. Barbarossa joined the areas under his control to the Ottoman Empire, an Islamic empire based in what is now Turkey. Algeria remained a part of the empire until the early 1800's. During that time, ships in the Mediterranean Sea were attacked by private warships under the command of *corsairs* (sea raiders) from Algeria and other countries. Raids by Algerian corsairs on the ships of other nations became Algeria's chief source of income.

French rule. In 1830, France invaded and gained control of northern Algeria. The French king, Charles X, hoped an overseas military victory would strengthen his rule in France. The French governed Algeria as part of France. Many French and other Europeans settled in Algeria. These settlers became known as *colons.* Non-French colons were given French citizenship. However, France made it difficult for the Muslim majority of the Algerian population to become French citizens. France gave the colons large amounts of Algerian tribal land, and the colons soon controlled Algeria's economy and government. Many native Algerians fought against French rule. In 1847, the French defeated powerful rebel forces led by Abd al-Qadir, a Muslim religious leader. By 1914, France controlled all of what is now Algeria.

As subjects of France, many Algerians fought on the Allied side in World War I (1914-1918). During World War II (1939-1945), Algeria became a battleground. In 1940, France surrendered to Germany. France, cooperating with Germany, formed a government at Vichy in central France. The Vichy government ruled Algeria until 1942, when the United Kingdom, the United States, and other Allied countries invaded and occupied Algeria (see **World War II** [The Tunisia Campaign]). After the war, the Allies returned control of Algeria to France.

The Algerian Revolution. After both world wars, native Algerians demanded greater political power. But each time, the colons blocked all reforms that would have given native Algerians a voice in the government in proportion to their population. In 1954, native Algerians formed an organization to fight for independence—the Front de Libération Nationale (FLN), or National Liberation Front. The FLN began a revolution on November 1. It carried out assassinations and bombing raids against the colons and the French forces in Algeria. The French army, in turn, destroyed orchards and cropland belonging to native Algerians, forced millions of Algerians into concentration camps, and tortured rebel leaders. By the late 1950's, the army's tactics had aroused strong opposition in France. On July 3, 1962, France finally granted Algeria independence. See **France** (History).

Independence. Most colons—about a million of them—fled Algeria during or soon after the revolution. In 1963, one of the rebel leaders, Ahmed Ben Bella, became Algeria's first president. Ben Bella proclaimed Algeria a socialist state and urged workers to take over businesses and farms abandoned by colons.

In 1965, Houari Boumedienne, the army commander, overthrew Ben Bella. Boumedienne began a program of rapid economic development based on government ownership and control of industry. He used income from natural gas and petroleum to build fertilizer plants, steel mills, oil refineries, and other factories.

Boumedienne died in 1978. In 1979, Defense Minister Chadli Bendjedid was elected president. He slowed industrial development to devote more resources to producing agricultural and consumer goods. Until 1989, the FLN was the only political party allowed by Algeria's Constitution. A 1989 revision permitted other parties to operate. The main opposition party—the Front Islamique du Salut (FIS), or Islamic Salvation Front—claimed that changes in the electoral law favored the FLN.

In 1991, the FIS won a clear majority of seats in a first round of elections for the National People's Assembly. To prevent an FIS victory, the government canceled a second round of elections scheduled for 1992. The government then dissolved the Assembly, and President Bendjedid resigned. A military-dominated High State Committee governed Algeria until 1994, when the committee was replaced by a president, Liamine Zeroual. In 1995, he was elected president in a multiparty election.

The courts banned the FIS in 1992, and thousands of FIS members were arrested. Violent protests escalated into a bloody civil war between the government and fundamentalist Islamist groups led by the FIS and the Groupe Islamique Armé (GIA), or Armed Islamic Group. The GIA staged terrorist attacks on government troops and facilities. Beginning in late 1997, the GIA killed hundreds of foreigners and Algerian civilians in brutal massacres. In mid-1999, the FIS made peace with the government, but GIA violence continued for years. From 1992 to 2006, an estimated 150,000 people died in the fighting. Portions of the GIA, now known as al-Qa`ida in the Islamic Maghreb (AQIM), remained in Algeria.

Recent developments. In 1996, Algerians approved a revised constitution that banned parties based on race, religion, sex, language, or regional differences. Multiparty elections for the National People's Assembly were held in 1997. In 1999, Abdelaziz Bouteflika, an independent candidate supported by the military and Zeroual, was elected president in a contest marred by vote fraud charges. Bouteflika was reelected in 2004 and 2009.

In 2001, clashes broke out between security forces and Berber protesters in northern Algeria. The protesters demanded greater political and cultural recognition for Berbers. The government agreed to some Berber demands. In 2002, for example, it made the Berber language, Tamazight, a national language.

Antigovernment protests erupted in Algiers and other cities in 2011. The protesters called for greater political freedom and criticized President Bouteflika.

In 2013, AQIM-linked terrorists took hundreds of people hostage at a natural gas plant in eastern Algeria. Algerian troops stormed the plant, killing or capturing the terrorists. However, about 40 of the hostages died.

Bouteflika was reelected president in 2014 despite ill health. In 2019, protests broke out when he sought a fifth term. He resigned in April. Abdelkader Bensalah, chairman of the upper house of Parliament and a Bouteflika ally, became interim president. But protesters demanded a new, civilian government. In December, voters elected former prime minister Abdelmadjid Tebboune as president. Protesters denounced Tebboune's ties to the old government. Tebboune, however, promised reforms. He signed a new constitution into law in January 2021.   Kenneth J. Perkins

Related articles in *World Book* include:

Outline

I. **Government**
 A. National government
 B. Local government
 C. Courts
 D. Armed forces
II. **People**
 A. Ancestry
 B. Language
 C. Way of life
 D. Clothing
 E. Foods
 F. Recreation
 G. Religion
 H. Education
 I. The arts
III. **The land and climate**
 A. The Tell
 B. The High Plateaus
 C. The Sahara
IV. **Economy**
 A. Service industries
 B. Mining
 C. Manufacturing and construction
 D. Agriculture
 E. Trade
 F. Transportation and communication
V. **History**

Algiers, *al JEERZ* (pop. 2,364,230), is the capital and largest city of Algeria. The city is also the nation's commercial and financial center. Algiers lies in northern Algeria, on the Mediterranean Sea (see **Algeria** [map]).

Algiers was built on top of a hill. The oldest section of the city is the Casbah in the north. The Casbah has a large population, and its many old buildings are crowded close together. This section was named for the *casbah* (fortress) that still stands on the hill. The commercial, governmental, and residential areas of Algiers are down the hill and in the suburbs. White buildings, constructed in the late 1800's, line the waterfront. Algiers has a number of museums and *mosques* (Islamic houses of worship) and is the home of the University of Algiers.

Many of the city's people work for the national government. Others are employed in banking and international trade or in industry. The city's industries include food and tobacco processing, metalworking, and the production of cement, chemicals, shoes, and soap.

The chief of the Sanhaja, a Muslim tribe, founded Algiers in the A.D. 900's. The Ottoman Empire ruled the city from the early 1500's to 1830. The French took control of Algiers that year. They brought a European culture, which blended with the city's Muslim culture. Algiers was a colonial capital for many years under Ottoman and then French rule. It became the national capital in 1962, when Algeria gained independence. The population of Algiers has greatly increased since 1954, causing severe overcrowding. The Algiers subway system—the Metro—began operating in 2011.   Malcolm C. Peck

See also **Africa** (picture); **Algeria** (picture); **World, History of the** (picture: Algerians celebrate their independence).

Algin. See Algae; Seaweed.

Algonquin Indians, *al GAHNG kihn* or *al GAHNG kwihn,* once fished and hunted in the Ottawa River region of Canada, in what is now Ontario and Quebec. They are also called the *Algonkin.* The Algonquin, Cree, and other tribes spoke Algonquian languages, a group of related languages named for the Algonquin. These tribes had strong similarities, and scholars use the term *Algonquian Indians* or *Algonquian family* to refer to all of the Algonquian-speaking tribes.

The Algonquin lived in bands of 100 to 300 members. Each band was divided into hunting groups of up to 25 close relatives. Algonquin families lived in lodges made of bent saplings covered with birchbark. Each lodge housed a husband and wife, their young children and unmarried grown-up daughters, and their married sons with their own wives and children.

In winter, the Algonquin hunted deer, moose, and other animals. During the rest of the year, they fished and also gathered wild fruits, nuts, and roots. The Algonquin were experts in building and handling canoes. They traveled by canoe during spring, summer, and fall. In winter, they used toboggans and snowshoes.

The Algonquin believed in a *great spirit,* an especially powerful god. But they believed their lives were affected mostly by ancestral spirits and the spirits of animals, plants, and other parts of their natural surroundings. Certain men and women, called *shamans,* were thought to have spiritual powers and served as advisers.

The Algonquin and their allies the Huron fought a bitter war against the Iroquois in the 1600's. About 1640, the Algonquin were defeated and driven from their territory. This war and epidemics of measles and smallpox reduced the Algonquin population from about 4,000 to 1,000 in a 10-year period. Today, there are several thousand Algonquin, most of whom live in eastern Ontario and southwestern Quebec.   Conrad E. Heidenreich

Algorithm, *AL guh rihth uhm,* is a step-by-step procedure for solving a mathematical problem in a limited number of steps. The instructions for each step are precise. Many algorithms involve repeating the same steps several times and can be carried out by a computer.

Probably the most famous algorithm is *Euclid's algorithm.* It is used to find the greatest common divisor of any two whole numbers, *a* and *b.* To use this algorithm, first divide the smaller number *(b)* into the larger number *(a): ᵃ⁄_b.* If the numbers divide evenly, with a remainder *(r)* of 0, the algorithm ends and *b* is the answer. But if the remainder is not 0, divide the remainder into the former divisor: *ᵇ⁄_r.* Keep dividing each succeeding remainder into the previous divisor until you reach a remainder of 0. Then stop. The last divisor is the greatest common divisor of the original numbers *a* and *b.*   Thomas Butts

Algren, *AWL grihn,* **Nelson** (1909-1981), an American author, is best known for fiction about life in Chicago's slums of the 1930's and 1940's. His characters constantly are defeated by their sordid environment, but the reader sympathizes with their yearning for love and dignity.

Algren's most moving and artistic novel is *The Man with the Golden Arm* (1949). It records the unsuccessful struggle of the central character, Frankie Machine, against gambling, drug addiction, and a crippled, neurotic wife. Algren's novel *A Walk on the Wild Side* (1956) has a robust comic quality. Algren also wrote a collection of stories, *The Neon Wilderness* (1947), and a book of stories and nonfiction called *The Last Carousel* (1973).

Algren was born on March 28, 1909, in Detroit, but he lived most of his life in Chicago. He died on May 9, 1981.   Victor A. Kramer

Alhambra, *ah LAHM brah* or *al HAM bruh,* is a famous palace and fortress in Granada, Spain. The Moors, a Muslim people from northern Africa, built it between 1248 and 1354 (see **Moors**). Now a monument, the Alhambra is one of the most elaborate and important examples of Islamic architecture in the Western world.

An outer wall encloses the Alhambra, which occupies 35 acres (14 hectares). Twenty-three towers rise from this wall, which is made of red bricks. *Alhambra* is an Arabic word meaning *the red.* Colorful, delicately ornamented plaster moldings cover many of the walls and ceilings of the palace. The Alhambra is also noted for its two courtyards. The Court of the Lions, in particular, is

© Madrugada Verde, Shutterstock

The Alhambra is a palace and fortress in Granada, Spain. Built by the Moors between 1248 and 1354, the Alhambra is one of the finest examples of Islamic architecture in Europe.

famous for its carved columns, its delicate screens, and its fountain (see **Spain** [picture: The Alhambra]).

The Alhambra was the last stronghold of the Moors in Spain. In 1492, it was captured by forces of the Spanish monarchs Ferdinand and Isabella.   J. William Rudd

Alhazen, *ahl HA zehn* (965-1040), also spelled *Alhacen,* an Arab scientist and mathematician, made influential contributions to the study of light and vision. His most important work, completed in the early 1000's, was the massive *Kitāb al-Manāzir (Book of Optics).* He claimed in it that vision results from rays of light passing from objects into the eye. At the time, most scholars accepted the view of the Greek thinkers Euclid and Ptolemy that the eye sends out visual rays to objects. But Alhazen said that a luminous or illuminated object gives off light rays from every point on its surface in all possible directions. Alhazen thought that the front of the eye's lens senses light. He claimed that it senses only those light rays that hit it at *right* (90°) angles and passes these rays into the eye. In this way, he thought, the eye forms images from the numerous rays striking it. Scholars accepted Alhazen's theory, revised by later thinkers, from the late 1200's to the early 1600's. But in 1604, the German scientist Johannes Kepler showed that visual images form on a layer of tissue called the *retina*, rather than on the lens.

Alhazen was born in Basra, in what is now Iraq. He is known as Ibn al-Haytham in Arabic. The name *Alhazen* is a Latin form of *al-Hasan,* his first name in Arabic. Alhazen died in Cairo, Egypt. A. Mark Smith

See also **Color** (Early theories of color vision).

Ali, Muhammad, *ah LEE, moo HAHM uhd* (1942-2016), was an American heavyweight boxing champion. He first won the championship by knocking out defending champion Sonny Liston in 1964. Some boxing groups recognized Ali as champion until 1967. But he was stripped of the World Boxing Association (WBA) title late in 1964 in a dispute over a contract. The WBA again recognized Ali as champion after he defeated defending champion Ernie Terrell in 1967.

Ali ranks as perhaps the most colorful and controversial boxing champion in the history of the sport. Early in his career, he bragged about his ability. He made up poems that scorned his opponents, at times even predicting the round in which he would win.

Early life. Ali was born Cassius Marcellus Clay on Jan. 17, 1942, in Louisville, Kentucky. He became a professional boxer after winning the light heavyweight title at the 1960 Summer Olympic Games. In 1964, after defeating Liston, he joined the Nation of Islam and changed his name to Muhammad Ali. The Nation of Islam is a religious group that combines some aspects of Islam with doctrines of black nationalism. He converted from the Nation of Islam to traditional Islam in 1975. Ali discussed his boxing career and religious views in his autobiography, *The Greatest: My Own Story* (1975).

Draft controversy and comeback. In 1967, Ali was drafted into the United States Army. However, he refused *induction*—that is, he refused to serve. The WBA and other boxing groups then stripped Ali of his title. He was also convicted on charges of refusing induction. Ali appealed his conviction and did not go to prison. But he did not box for 3 ½ years.

Ali returned to boxing in 1970 and won two fights that year. In 1971, he attempted to regain the heavyweight title from Joe Frazier but lost. The defeat was Ali's first loss after 31 straight victories in professional fights. Later in 1971, the Supreme Court of the United States reversed Ali's conviction.

Ali regained the heavyweight championship by knocking out George Foreman, the defending champion, in 1974. Early in 1978, Ali lost the title when he was upset by little-known Leon Spinks. Later in 1978, Ali won the title for the fourth time when he defeated Spinks in a 15-round decision.

Chicago Daily Defender
Muhammad Ali

Later years. In 1979, Ali gave up his title and announced his retirement. In 1980, however, he came out of retirement and fought defending champion Larry Holmes, seeking to win the World Boxing Council version of the title. Holmes defeated Ali by a technical knockout. In 1984, Ali was diagnosed with a brain illness called Parkinson disease.

Ali became one of the most recognized athletes in the world, even after his illness greatly diminished his ability to speak. At the 1996 Summer Olympic Games in Atlanta, he was the final carrier of the Olympic torch. For Olympic Games, runners transport the Olympic flame in a torch relay from Greece to the site of the games. To be the final carrier of the torch is a high honor.

In 1999, Ali was named Sportsman of the Century by *Sports Illustrated* magazine and Sports Personality of the Century by the British Broadcasting Corporation. Ali's daughter Laila became a professional boxer in 1999, fighting other women. In 2005, Muhammad Ali received the Presidential Medal of Freedom, one of the country's highest civilian honors. Also in 2005, the Muhammad Ali Center opened in Louisville. This museum and cultural center is dedicated to Ali's life in and out of boxing. Ali died on June 3, 2016. Michael Hirsley

See also **Boxing** (pictures).

Ali, Muhammad, ruler of Egypt. See Muhammad Ali.

Alice in Wonderland, by the English author Lewis Carroll, is a classic children's fantasy story. Its full title is *Alice's Adventures in Wonderland.* Lewis Carroll was the pen name of Charles Lutwidge Dodgson, an Oxford University mathematics professor and an early expert in photography.

Carroll began the book as a short story in 1862 under the title *Alice's Adventures under Ground.* He expanded it to a full-length book that was published in 1865 and again in 1866 with the now famous illustrations by Sir John Tenniel. *Alice in Wonderland* tells about the adventures of a little girl named Alice in a make-believe world under the ground. Alice enters this "wonderland" after she falls down a hole while following a nervous and fashionably dressed white rabbit. She meets many strange characters, including the March Hare, Mad Hatter, Cheshire Cat, Queen of Hearts, and Mock Turtle.

Carroll continued the story in *Through the Looking-Glass and What Alice Found There* (1872). This book introduced new characters, including Humpty Dumpty, dragonlike Jabberwock, the silly twins Tweedledum and Tweedledee, and the Walrus and the Carpenter.

Carroll created the character of Alice to amuse a little girl named Alice Liddell and her two sisters. Carroll wrote both books to give pleasure to children, but adults also enjoy the humor, fantastic characters, word games, puzzles, and absurd moments in the stories. Scholars study the books to find intricate and elevated meanings in what seems to be nonsense. Michael Seidel

See also **Carroll, Lewis.**

Alien, *AYL yuhn* or *AY lee uhn,* is a person who is not a citizen or national of the country in which he or she is living. Legal and social rights of aliens differ by country.

The United States recognizes two kinds of aliens, *temporary visitors* and *resident aliens.* An individual in the United States as a tourist or on business is a temporary visitor. Temporary visitors may not travel or accept employment without permission from the U.S. government.

They are protected under the Bill of Rights. Resident aliens live in the United States on a permanent basis. They generally enjoy the same rights as citizens, but cannot vote or hold public office. *Illegal aliens* are noncitizens living in a country without the proper documents. They may be deported if they are discovered.

The Alien Enemies Act of 1798 gives the president the power to apprehend, restrain, secure, and remove alien enemies in wartime. The U.S. government first registered aliens in 1940.   Thomas M. DeFrank

See also **Citizenship; Deportation; Immigration; Naturalization; Smith Act.**

Alien and Sedition Acts, *AYL yuhn* or *AY lee uhn, sih DIHSH uhn,* were a series of laws passed by Congress in 1798 to silence opposition to an expected war with France. Neither France nor the United States had declared war, but French and American ships had fought many battles.

The Alien and Sedition Acts consisted of three laws dealing with *aliens* (foreigners) and one dealing with *sedition* (inciting rebellion). The Alien Enemies Act authorized the president to imprison or deport citizens of enemy nations. The Alien Friends Act allowed even citizens of friendly nations to be deported if the president considered them dangerous. The Naturalization Act required a foreigner to live in the United States for 14 years before becoming a citizen. The Sedition Act was used to fine or imprison anyone who encouraged resistance to federal laws or who criticized the government.

The chief supporters of the Alien and Sedition Acts were members of the Federalist Party, which controlled Congress. The Federalists generally supported Great Britain (now also called the United Kingdom) in international disputes. Their opponents were members of the Democratic-Republican Party, which usually sided with France. The Democratic-Republican Party gained much support from recent immigrants to the United States, most of whom were from France or Ireland.

By passing the Alien and Sedition Acts, the Federalists hoped to silence their critics. The plan failed, however. Many people objected to the Alien and Sedition Acts as a violation of freedom. Thomas Jefferson and James Madison, two Democratic-Republican leaders, challenged the constitutionality of the acts in the Kentucky and Virginia Resolutions. The Democratic-Republicans went on to defeat the Federalists in the 1800 presidential election. The Alien Friends Act expired that year, and the Sedition Act expired in 1801. Congress repealed the Naturalization Act and amended the Alien Enemies Act. In 1800, after two years of naval conflict, the Americans and French signed a peace agreement.   Jerald A. Combs

See also **Kentucky and Virginia Resolutions.**

Alien Registration Act of 1940. See Smith Act.

Alienation, also known as *estrangement,* is a breakdown in relations between an individual or group and others. Alienation may also be a breakdown in relations between an individual or group and an idea or concept. People who feel alienated may describe it as *apathy* (lack of feeling), *indifference* (loss of caring), loss of affection, disrespect, or even hostility toward the object of their alienation. Objects of alienation may include another person, group, institution, or religion.

Alienation may arise from a variety of circumstances. For example, alienation may occur when a group loses a leader who represented its hopes or when a child discovers the shortcomings of an adult the child has admired. Or it may result when persons believe that a political, economic, or social institution does not share their values, beliefs, or practices.

Actions resulting from alienation may range from withdrawal within oneself to violence toward society. Social and political scientists have studied alienation as a factor in voter apathy, criminal behavior, and mental illness. But alienation sometimes has such positive consequences as artistic creation, invention, and discovery. Alienation has been a topic of philosophical and political writing and a theme in literature.   Timothy J. Bruce

Alimentary canal is a long tube through which food is taken into the body and digested. In human beings, this passage is about 30 feet (9 meters) long. Animals that eat meat usually have shorter alimentary canals than animals that eat grass. The alimentary canal begins at the mouth, and includes the pharynx, esophagus, stomach, small and large intestines, and rectum.

When a person swallows food, muscles of the pharynx push the food into the esophagus. The muscles in the esophagus walls respond with a wavelike contraction called *peristalsis.* At the same time, the *lower esophageal sphincter* relaxes, allowing the food to pass down to the stomach. In the stomach, fluids lubricate and partially digest the food. The partially digested food is called *chyme.* Stomach contractions mix and grind the

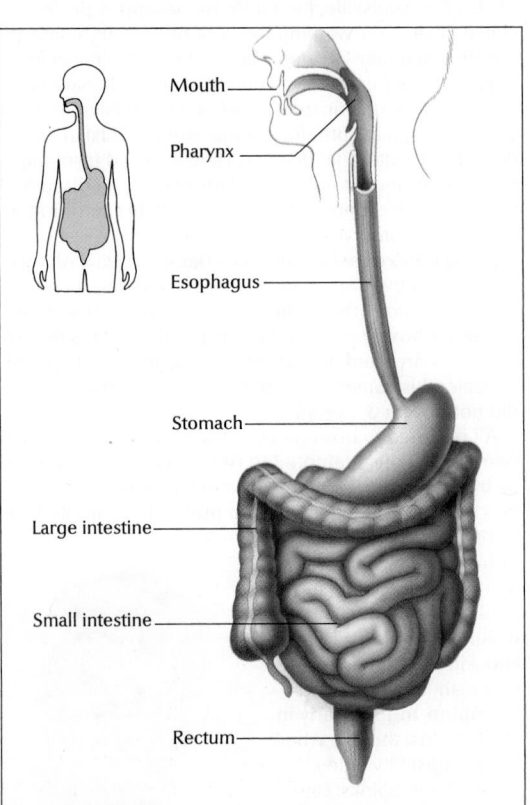

WORLD BOOK illustration by Charles Wellek

The alimentary canal is a tube through which food is taken into the body and digested. It is about 30 feet (9 meters) long in an adult, beginning at the mouth and ending at the rectum.

food into a liquidlike mixture that contains small particles. This mixture is emptied into the small intestine. There, juices from the pancreas, liver, and intestine wall continue the process of digestion. The small intestine squeezes the chyme back and forth to mix it thoroughly. The frequency and pressure of these contractions varies and keeps the chyme moving through the intestine.

Most of the food elements in the digested food are absorbed into the bloodstream through the small intestine. The intestine is lined with a mucous membrane made up of tiny fingerlike projections called *villi.* The villi increase the area through which absorption can take place. Soluble parts of the chyme pass through the small intestine into the bloodstream and are carried to all parts of the body. The water and salts that remain are absorbed in the large intestine. The remaining solid wastes, called *feces,* are mixed with bacteria. The feces pass out of the body through the rectum in a process called *defecation.*   André Dubois

Related articles in *World Book* include:

Digestive system	Intestine
Esophagus	Mouth
Human body (Anatomy of the human body)	Pharynx
	Stomach

Alimony, *AL uh* MOH *nee,* is support money paid by one *spouse* (husband or wife) to the other during a legal separation or after a divorce. A court sets the amount and orders that it be paid in a lump sum or in installments. A person may also be ordered to pay alimony while waiting for a separation or divorce to be granted.

In many cases in the past, a divorce was granted to one spouse because of misconduct by the other. The marriage partner who was found at fault would not receive alimony. Today, however, courts can grant a divorce without finding either person guilty. These courts base alimony decisions on the spouses' financial condition. A court may order that no alimony be paid, or that it be paid only temporarily. If the wife has a higher income than her husband, she may have to pay alimony.

People who fail to pay alimony may have payments taken out of their wages, or they may be imprisoned. An alimony order may be changed if either spouse's financial or marital condition changes.   Michael J. Broyde

See also **Divorce.**

Alinsky, *uh LIHN skee,* **Saul David** (1909-1972), won fame for helping poor people help themselves. A professional organizer, he helped the poor in more than 40 U.S. communities form groups to gain a voice in local affairs and improve their economic and social positions. These groups used various methods of protest, including boycotts, picketing, rent strikes, and sit-down strikes.

Alinsky's first community action project was the "Back-of-the-Yards" program in the stockyards area of Chicago in 1939. In 1940, several wealthy Chicagoans gave him money to establish the Industrial Areas Foundation. Alinsky continued his work through this organization. One of his best-known achievements was the creation in 1960 of The Woodlawn Organization (TWO) in a predominantly black neighborhood in Chicago. In 1969, Alinsky founded a school in Chicago to train organizers for work in poor and middle-class neighborhoods.

Alinsky was born in Chicago on Jan. 30, 1909. He graduated from the University of Chicago in 1930. He died on June 12, 1972.   Robert A. Pratt

Alito, Samuel Anthony, Jr. (1950-   ), became an associate justice of the Supreme Court of the United States in 2006. President George W. Bush named him to fill the vacancy created by the retirement of Justice Sandra Day O'Connor.

Prior to his appointment to the court, Alito served as a judge on the U.S. Court of Appeals for the Third Circuit. He had previously worked as an attorney in President Ronald Reagan's administration and as a federal *prosecutor,* who argues the government's case against a defendant in a trial. Alito was known as a conservative.

Alito was born on April 1, 1950, in Trenton, New Jersey. He graduated from Princeton University in 1972 and from Yale Law School in 1975. He served as a law clerk to a federal judge from 1976 to 1977. From 1977 to 1981, he served as assistant U.S. attorney for the District of New Jersey. In 1981, he became assistant to the U.S. solicitor general in the Reagan administration. As assistant to the solicitor general, Alito successfully argued 12 cases before the Supreme Court. In 1985, he became deputy assistant attorney general in the U.S. Department of Justice. From 1987 to 1990, he served as U.S. attorney for the New Jersey District. He was appointed a federal appeals court judge in 1990.   Dennis J. Hutchinson

Alkali. See Base.

Alkali metal, *AL kuh ly,* in chemistry, refers to six chemical elements: lithium, sodium, potassium, rubidium, cesium, and francium. These elements make up group 1 of the periodic table. Compounds of alkali metals rank among the most common and most useful of all chemicals. Millions of tons of alkali metal salts are used by industry each year. The salts come from mines and wells. Sodium and potassium salts are raw materials for sodium hydroxide and potassium hydroxide. These alkali metal compounds and others made from them are used in making glass, paper, soap, and textiles; in refining petroleum; and in preparing leather.

The word *alkali* comes from the Arabic word *al-qili,* meaning *plant ashes.* Plant ashes were the first source of alkali metal compounds.

When used alone, the word *alkali* can refer to alkali metal hydroxides, and sometimes to alkali metal carbonates. An *alkali metal hydroxide* is a compound that contains an alkali metal positive ion (such as Na^+) and a negative *hydroxide* (OH^-) ion. Sodium hydroxide (NaOH) and potassium hydroxide (KOH) are alkalis. When the term *alkali metal* precedes another word, as in *alkali metal halide,* it refers to the presence of a positive ion of an alkali metal. The salt sodium chloride (NaCl) is an alkali metal halide. Sodium chloride is made of the positive ion of the alkali metal sodium, and the negative ion of the halogen chlorine.

In nature, alkali metals always occur in compounds. A process called electrolysis can separate the metals from their salts and hydroxides. An average sample of Earth's crust is about 2.8 percent sodium, 2.6 percent potassium, 0.034 percent rubidium, 0.034 percent cesium, and 0.007 percent lithium. Francium, a radioactive alkali metal, occurs in nature only briefly when uranium decays.

With the exception of minerals known as common silicates, most alkali compounds dissolve easily in water. Rain washes these compounds from the soil. The compounds then collect in the ocean and in lakes that have no outlets, such as Great Salt Lake in Utah. The evaporation of ancient seas and lakes left vast deposits of alkali salts throughout the world.

The alkali metals all form singly charged positive ions and are extremely reactive chemically. They react violently with water, forming hydroxides and releasing hydrogen gas and heat.   Duward F. Shriver

Related articles in *World Book* include:

Base	Francium	Rubidium
Cesium	Lithium	Sodium
Element, Chemical	Potassium	Sodium hydroxide

Alkaloid, *AL kuh loyd,* is any of a group of organic bases found in plants. Alkaloids contain carbon, hydrogen, nitrogen, and oxygen. Small amounts of many alkaloids can have a powerful effect on people and animals, and are used as medicines or poisons. Some useful alkaloids are *synthesized* (artificially put together) in chemical factories, as well as taken from plants.

Alkaloids with medicinal value include codeine and morphine from the poppy plant, and quinine and quinidine from the cinchona. Others are caffeine from coffee and tea, cocaine from coca, ephedrine from the *Ephedra* genus of plants, reserpine from *Rauwolfia serpentina,* and tubocurarine from curare.

Poisonous alkaloids from such plants as curare are used on arrowheads by peoples who hunt chiefly with bow and arrow. The hemlock plant, which was used to kill the Greek philosopher Socrates, contains lethal amounts of conine and other alkaloids. Aconitine from the aconite plant is also highly poisonous. Nicotine, an alkaloid of the tobacco plant, is toxic to human beings and is also used to kill insects.   Patrice C. Bélanger

Related articles in *World Book* include:

Aconite	Caffeine	Morphine	Quinine
Base	Cocaine	Nicotine	

Al-Khwārizmī, *al KWAHR ihz MEE* (780?-850?), a Persian mathematician, wrote one of the first algebra texts. He also wrote a book that helped popularize a system of numbering originally used in India. This system, later known as the *Hindu-Arabic system,* is in common use throughout the world today (see **Arabic numerals**). Translations of al-Khwārizmī's works helped spread mathematical knowledge from India and the Middle East into Europe.

Al-Khwārizmī's book on algebra provided systematic methods for solving *quadratic equations,* mathematical statements using squared variables, such as x^2 or y^2. It also applied algebra to geometry and problems of inheritance. The word *algebra* comes from the book's title. The title contains the word *al-jabr,* Arabic for *completion* or *restoration,* which over time became *algebra.*

Al-Khwārizmī's name suggests he or his family came from Khorezm, now western Uzbekistan. At that time, Khorezm lay within the historic region of Persia and was ruled by the Abbasid caliphate, an Islamic empire. His full name was Muhammad ibn Mūsā al-Khwārizmī. He did much of his writing at the House of Wisdom, a Baghdad library and research center founded by the Abbasid ruler al-Ma'mūn around 815.   Victor J. Katz

See also **Algebra** (History); **Mathematics** (In the Middle East).

All Fools' Day. See April Fools' Day.

All Saints' Day is a Christian holy day observed by Western Christians on November 1 and by Eastern Christians on the first Sunday of Pentecost (see **Pente–**

cost). It honors all Christian saints, especially those who do not have days named for them. All Saints' Day was also called All Hallows. *Hallow* means *saint* or *one who is holy.* The evening before All Hallows was known as All Hallows' Eve or All Hallow e'en. This name eventually was shortened to Halloween.

In A.D. 609 or 610, Emperor Phocas gave the Roman temple called the Pantheon to Pope Boniface IV as a church. The pope rededicated it to the Virgin Mary and Christian martyrs. The anniversary of this event may have been the origin of All Saints' Day among Western Christians. In the early 700's, Pope Gregory III dedicated a chapel to all saints on November 1 in St. Peter's church. Some historians think the celebration of that event may have established the date of the feast. The celebration of the feast day by Christians throughout western Europe probably began in the 800's.   Richard L. Schebera

See also **Halloween; Saint.**

All-terrain vehicle (ATV) is a motorized off-road vehicle typically designed to be ridden by one person. ATV's can climb steep hills and handle rough terrain. An ATV is typically equipped with four fat, low-pressure tires. ATV's are also called *quads.*

Many people race ATV's or use them for recreation. Farmers, rescue workers, and law enforcement and military personnel use ATV's in their work.

The basic parts of an ATV are the engine, transmission, wheels, suspension system, brakes, and a metal frame. An ATV has either a one- or two- cylinder gasoline engine. The engine operates on either a two- or four-stroke cycle. The transmission may be automatic or manual. An ATV may have either rear-wheel or all-wheel drive. The rider steers using handlebars. Levers on the handlebars control the throttle and brakes. On some ATV's, foot controls are used to select gears and brake.

ATV's weigh from about 150 pounds (70 kilograms) for some youth models to 850 pounds (385 kilograms) for heavy utility models. The fastest ATV's modified for racing may approach 100 miles (160 kilometers) per hour.

The 1970 Honda ATC90, a vehicle with three wheels, is generally considered the first ATV. Nearly all ATV's sold today have four wheels. ATV's can be hazardous. Manufacturers include warnings that riders should wear helmets, avoid paved roads, and not carry passengers unless the ATV is designed to do so.   Bill Lanphier

Allah, *AL uh* or *AH luh,* is the Arabic word for God or the Supreme Being. The word is used by Muslims as well as Arabic-speaking Christians. The word is a compound of *al* (the) and *ilah* (god). It denotes the Supreme Being in the Qur'ān, the holy book of Islam. Muslims recite the creed: "There is no god but Allah; and Muhammad is the Messenger of Allah."   Richard C. Martin

Allahabad, *AL uh huh BAD* (pop. 1,112,544; met. area pop. 1,216,719), is a holy city of India. The name means *City of God.* Allahabad lies in the state of Uttar Pradesh, where the Ganges and Yamuna rivers meet (see **India** [political map]). Hindus consider these rivers sacred.

Allahabad is a trade center for cotton, sugar, and other products of nearby farms. The business and market district lies at the main crossroads of the city.

Allahabad was founded in the 200's B.C. Its old buildings include a famous mosque called the Jama Musjid and an ancient palace and fort built by the Mughal emperor Akbar in 1583. Jawaharlal Nehru, India's first prime minister, was born in Allahabad in 1889. His daughter, Indira Gandhi—who also served as prime minister—was born in the city in 1917.   P. P. Karan

Allegheny Mountains, AL uh GAY nee, form part of the Appalachian Mountain system of the eastern United States. They extend southwest from central Pennsylvania through western Maryland, eastern West Virginia, and western Virginia.

The Alleghenies vary in height from about 2,000 feet (610 meters) above sea level in the north to over 4,800 feet (1,460 meters) in the south. Spruce Knob, the tallest peak in the Alleghenies, rises 4,861 feet (1,482 meters) in West Virginia. The mountains form a divide between streams that flow into the Atlantic Ocean and those that empty into the Gulf of Mexico. The Alleghenies are the eastern edge of the Allegheny Plateau, the major source of coal used by iron and steel plants in Pittsburgh and nearby industrial areas. Trees from the mountains, including hickories and maples, are shipped to pulp and paper mills and sawmills in the Allegheny region.

The Alleghenies are one of the most thinly populated regions in the East. Most of the people live in valleys east of the mountains or on the Allegheny Plateau.

The Alleghenies were created about 230 million years ago by disturbances in Earth's crust. Before then, the region made up part of an ocean trough. About 40,000 feet (12,000 meters) of *sediment* (loose pieces of minerals and rock) had piled up in the trough. The upper layers of sediment once formed the floor of swampy forests. The remains of plants from the forests created the thick coal deposits of the Alleghenies and the Allegheny Plateau.

In pioneer times, the Alleghenies were major barriers to transportation. In 1755, the British general Edward Braddock built a road through a mountain pass called Cumberland Narrows, near Cumberland, Maryland. Part of this road, called Braddock's Road, became part of the National Road, which linked the East Coast and the Ohio River Valley. Today, the pass is the heart of major routes through the Alleghenies.   John Edwin Coffman

See also **West Virginia** (picture).

Location of the Allegheny Mountains

Allegheny River, AL uh GAY nee, is a major stream of western Pennsylvania and a principal headwater of the Ohio River. It rises in the hilly plateau country of north-central Pennsylvania, curves across the southwest corner of New York, and returns to Pennsylvania. It then continues south to Pittsburgh, where it joins the Monongahela River to form the Ohio. The Allegheny is about 325 miles (523 kilometers) long and drains about 11,400 square miles (29,530 square kilometers). Its branches include the Kiskiminetas, Clarion, and Conemaugh rivers and Red Bank, Oil, and French creeks. Major deposits of coal, oil, and natural gas lie in the drainage basin. The river is navigable with a channel for 70 miles (110 kilometers), from Pittsburgh to East Brady.   William C. Rense

Allegory, AL uh GAWR ee, is a story with more than one meaning. Most allegories have moral or religious meanings. Famous allegories include the *fables* attributed to Aesop, an ancient Greek writer. Aesop's fables seem to describe the adventures of animals and human beings. But the author actually wanted to teach his readers something about human nature.

Allegories had their greatest popularity during medieval and Renaissance times in Europe. *The Divine Comedy,* written by the Italian author Dante Alighieri in the early 1300's, literally tells of a man's journey to heaven through hell and purgatory. Allegorically, the poem describes a Christian soul rising from a state of sin to a state of blessedness. Other allegories include the *parables* of Jesus, and *The Faerie Queene,* written by the English poet Edmund Spenser in the late 1500's.

Allegories lost popularity in Europe after about 1600, but some, such as *Pilgrim's Progress* (1678, 1684) gained recognition in later times. Allegory also exists in other ways. Many novels include allegorical suggestions of an additional level of meaning. Examples include *Moby-Dick* (1851), a whaling adventure that raises issues of human struggle and fate in a mysterious universe, and *Lord of the Flies* (1954), a story about shipwrecked boys that examines the persistence of evil.   Paul Strohm

Related articles in *World Book* include:

Aesop's fables	Fable	Morality play
Bunyan, John	Golding, William	Parable
Divine Comedy	Melville, Herman	Spenser, Edmund

Allen, Ethan (1738-1789), a fiery patriot and soldier, led the Green Mountain Boys in the capture of Fort Ticonderoga from the British in 1775. It was one of the first important American victories of the American Revolution.

Allen was born on Jan. 21, 1738, in Litchfield, Connecticut. Historians know little of his early life. He served briefly in the French and Indian War in 1757, and then settled in the New Hampshire Grants, now Vermont.

New Hampshire granted land to settlers to the west, but in 1764 the British decreed the land belonged to New York. In 1770, New York courts ruled that land titles in Vermont were not good unless purchased from New York. The settlers resisted this ruling by force. Allen and Seth Warner organized the Green Mountain Boys. They terrorized settlers from New York and fought off officials. New York's governor offered a reward of 20 pounds and later, 100 pounds, for Allen's arrest.

With the outbreak of the American Revolution in 1775, Allen and the Green Mountain Boys supported the patriot cause. On May 10, 1775, Allen and Colonel Benedict Arnold led a force of 83 men in the attack on Fort Ticonderoga. They subdued the British garrison and captured cannon and other weapons for the American cause.

In 1775, Allen tried to seize Montreal, Canada. Captured by the British and held prisoner until 1778, he wrote *A Narrative of Col. Ethan Allen's Captivity* (1779). After his release, he petitioned the Continental Congress for Vermont's statehood. When Congress refused, he attempted to make Vermont a British province. He was accused of treason, but no one could prove his guilt. He settled in Burlington, Vermont. He died on Feb. 12, 1789. A statue of Allen represents Vermont in Statuary Hall in the U.S. Capitol in Washington, D.C. Gregory J. W. Urwin

See also **Fort Ticonderoga; Green Mountain Boys.**

Allen, Richard (1760-1831), founded the African Methodist Episcopal Church (A.M.E.), the first African American denomination in the United States. Allen was born a slave on Feb. 14, 1760, in Philadelphia and grew up on a plantation in Delaware. He later bought his freedom and moved to Philadelphia in 1786. In 1787, Allen helped form the Free African Society, a self-help organization for African Americans. A leader in the independent black church movement, he believed African Americans should have control over their religious worship. In 1794, he founded Bethel African Methodist Church. He was ordained a minister in 1799. In 1816, Bethel ended its ties to the Methodist Church. That year, Allen helped set up the African Methodist Episcopal Church. He was elected bishop of the new church. Allen died on March 26, 1831. See also **Jones, Absalom.** Lawrence S. Little

Allen, William (1803-1879), served as an Ohio Democrat in the United States House of Representatives from 1833 to 1835 and in the U.S. Senate from 1837 to 1849. During the Mexican War (1846-1848), he was a Senate spokesman for President James K. Polk. Allen, known as the "Ohio Foghorn" because of his loud voice, supported westward expansion. He threatened war with the United Kingdom to secure the Oregon Country, a large area between California and Alaska, for the United States. Allen was a critic of President Abraham Lincoln during the American Civil War (1861-1865). He was governor of Ohio from 1874 to 1876. Allen was born in Edenton, North Carolina, on Dec. 18, 1803. He died on July 11, 1879. Michael F. Holt

Allen, Woody (1935-), is an American actor, filmmaker, author, and comedian. He won Academy Awards for directing and co-writing *Annie Hall* (1977). The film also won the Oscar as best picture. Allen won best original screenplay Oscars for *Hannah and Her Sisters* (1986) and *Midnight in Paris* (2011). He also directed both films.

Allen is skilled at depicting the American character in a satirical light. He often satirizes the anxieties and romantic difficulties of intellectual, urban people. In some of his films, Allen portrays a witty but insecure, self-conscious individual troubled by the lack of values in modern society and by his relationship with women.

Allen was born on Dec. 1, 1935, in New York City. His real name is Allen Stewart Konigsberg. He began his career writing jokes for magazines, newspapers, and television. During the early 1960's, Allen was a popular nightclub comedian. He made his film debut as an actor in *What's New, Pussycat?* (1965), which he wrote.

Allen wrote, directed, and starred in such films as *Take the Money and Run* (1969), *Bananas* (1971), *Sleeper* (1973), *Love and Death* (1975), *Manhattan* (1979), *Zelig* (1983), *Broadway Danny Rose* (1984), *Crimes and Misdemeanors* (1989), *Husbands and Wives* (1992), *Manhattan Murder Mystery* (1993), *Mighty Aphrodite* (1995), *Everyone Says I Love You* (1996), and *Deconstructing Harry* (1997). He also wrote and directed *Interiors* (1978), *The Purple Rose of Cairo* (1985), *Radio Days* (1987), *Another Woman* (1988), *Bullets over Broadway* (1994), *Sweet and Lowdown* (1999), *Match Point* (2005), *Cassandra's Dream* (2007), *Vicky Cristina Barcelona* (2008), *Whatever Works* (2009), *Blue Jasmine* (2013), *Irrational Man* (2015), *Café Society* (2016), and other movies. Allen acted in *Fading Gigolo* (2013). He wrote, directed, and acted in the television miniseries *Crisis in Six Scenes* (2016).

Allen wrote three full-length comic plays, *Don't Drink the Water* (1966), *Play It Again, Sam* (1969), and *The Floating Light Bulb* (1981). He has also written humorous essays and stories. Many were published in the collections *Getting Even* (1971), *Without Feathers* (1975), *Side Effects* (1980), and *Mere Anarchy* (2007). In addition, Allen wrote the memoir *Apropos of Nothing* (2020). Gene D. Phillips

Allenby, Lord (1861-1936), was a British military leader. During World War I (1914-1918), he led British forces in Egypt and Palestine. By skillfully combining attacks by his own forces with those of Arab guerrillas led by Major T. E. Lawrence (Lawrence of Arabia), he defeated the troops of the Ottoman Empire in 1917 and 1918 (see **Lawrence, T. E.**). His victory at Megiddo in Palestine on Sept. 18, 1918, gave the British control of Syria and Palestine. Allenby was British high commissioner for Egypt from 1919 to 1925. Edmund Henry Hynman Allenby was born on April 23, 1861, in Suffolk, England. When World War I began, he commanded first a cavalry division and then a corps of the British Expeditionary Force in France. He became an Army commander in Paris in 1915. His full title was Viscount Allenby of Megiddo and Felixstowe. He died on May 14, 1936. Ian F. W. Beckett

Allende, *ah YEHN day,* **Isabel,** *IHZ uh behl* (1942-   ), is one of the leading novelists and journalists from Chile.

Allende was born on Aug. 2, 1942, in Lima, Peru, where her father was a diplomat. In 1970, her cousin and godfather Salvador Allende Gossens, a socialist politician, was democratically elected president of Chile (see **Allende Gossens, Salvador**). In 1973, Salvador was overthrown and died in a right-wing military coup led by army general Augusto Pinochet Ugarte (see **Pinochet Ugarte, Augusto**). The Allende family fled Chile, and Isabel went to Venezuela, where she worked as a journalist. In 1983, she moved to the United States.

Allende's first novel, *The House of Spirits* (1982), is a reflection of her experiences in Chile during the time of the Pinochet coup and her later separation from her family. Her other works steeped in Chile's turbulent history include two more novels, *Of Love and Shadows* (1984) and *Eva Luna* (1989), and the short-story collections *Tales of Eva Luna* (1990) and *The Infinite Plan* (1992). *Portrait in Sepia* (2001) is a family chronicle set in Chile and California from 1862 to 1910. It draws on characters from *The House of Spirits* and from another of Allende's novels, *Daughter of Fortune* (2000).

Allende's historical novel *Inés of My Soul* (2006) is set during the Spanish conquest of the Inca Empire in South America during the 1530's. Her novel *Island Beneath the Sea* (2010) portrays a slave revolt in Haiti. *Ripper* (2014) is a mystery novel that features a child detective. *The Japanese Lover* (2015) is a love story about a Polish-born woman and her one-time Japanese gardener over a period of 70 years. *In the Midst of Winter* (2017) deals with three troubled characters with roots in Latin America whose lives intermingle in Brooklyn, New York. *Long Petal of the Sea* (2020) tells of refugees who flee to Chile to escape the civil war in Spain during the 1930's.

Allende wrote *Paula* (1995) as a letter to her daughter, who was dying of a blood disease. She wrote a trilogy of young adult novels, *City of the Beasts* (2002), *Kingdom of the Golden Dragon* (2004), and *Forest of the Pygmies* (2005). She also wrote the memoirs *My Invented Country* (2003) and *The Sum of Our Days* (2008). She received the U.S. Presidential Medal of Freedom, one of the country's highest civilian honors, in 2014.   Naomi Lindstrom

Allende Gossens, *ah YEHN day GOH sehns,* **Salvador** (1908-1973), was elected president of Chile in 1970. In 1973, military leaders overthrew his government. They reported that Allende committed suicide on Sept. 11, 1973, during the revolt, after refusing to resign from office. Allende was the first freely elected Marxist to lead a nation of the Western Hemisphere. As president, he nationalized Chile's banks and copper mines.

Allende was born on July 26, 1908, in Valparaíso, Chile. He earned an M.D. degree from the University of Chile in 1932. In 1933, he helped organize Chile's Socialist Party. Allende was elected to the Chamber of Deputies, a house of the Chilean legislature, in 1937. He later served as Chile's minister of health. From 1945 to 1970, Allende served in the Senate.   Lois Hecht Oppenheim

See also **Chile** (Socialism and military rule).

Allentown (pop. 118,032) is a city in eastern Pennsylvania. It lies on the Lehigh River (see **Pennsylvania** [political map]). Allentown, Bethlehem, and Easton form a metropolitan area with 821,173 people.

Allentown was once an important manufacturing center. But by the late 1900's, many of the factories had shut down. Today, health care and other services are major sources of employment in Allentown. The city also makes cryogenic equipment and gases, which are used to produce extreme cold for scientific and industrial purposes. Allentown is a center for pipeline transportation and tank storage of petroleum and natural gas. Airlines, truck lines, and freight railroads serve the city.

Allentown's downtown business district is laid out around a central square near the Lehigh River. Brick row houses, many of which were built during the 1800's, are the most common type of housing. Many of the people are descendants of Germans who moved to Pennsylvania during the 1600's and 1700's. They are often called Pennsylvania Dutch. Allentown is an important center of Pennsylvania Dutch culture. See **Pennsylvania Dutch.**

Allentown is home to Cedar Crest College and Muhlenberg College. The city has a symphony orchestra, a professional theater company, and an art museum. The Allentown Band is the oldest U.S. civilian concert band.

Allentown, originally called Northampton Town, was founded in 1762 by William Allen, chief justice of Pennsylvania. British troops captured Philadelphia in September 1777, during the American Revolution. The Liberty Bell was then moved from Philadelphia to Allentown for safety. It remained concealed in Allentown in Zion's Reformed Church until the summer of 1778, when it was returned to Philadelphia. Allentown became an incorporated city in 1867. In the late 1900's, it carried out development projects to preserve historical districts and rehabilitate housing. Allentown is the seat of Lehigh County. It has a mayor-council government.   William C. Rense

Allergy is an abnormal bodily reaction to a particular substance. An otherwise harmless substance may cause mild to extremely severe symptoms in a person who is allergic to it. Such symptoms range from sneezing and breathing difficulty to irritation of the skin, eyes, and stomach. Few people die from allergies. But allergies can significantly reduce quality of life.

Allergies rank among the most common causes of *chronic* (ongoing) medical disease in the United States and other developed countries. The most common allergic diseases include *allergic rhinitis,* known as *nasal allergies* or *hay fever,* and *allergic conjunctivitis,* an irritation of the eye. Physicians consider asthma an allergic disease of the respiratory system. Other disorders often associated with allergies include digestive disturbances, headaches, itchy skin patches called *hives,* and *eczema,* a skin disorder marked by itching and inflammation. The incidence of most allergic diseases has increased steadily in the United States and many other countries. Physicians who treat allergies are called *allergists.*

An otherwise harmless substance that causes an allergy is called an *allergen.* A relatively small number of allergens account for most allergies in people. The most common allergens found indoors include dust mites, mold spores, and pet *dander* (bits of dried skin and hair or feathers). Outdoor allergens include many substances in the air we breathe, such as pollen from grass, trees, and weeds, as well as mold spores. The most common food allergens for children are eggs, fish, milk, nuts that grow on trees, peanuts, soybeans, and wheat. In adults, common food allergens include fish, peanuts, shellfish, and tree nuts. Medications can also cause allergies. Certain antibiotic drugs, especially antibiotics in the penicillin family, are a common cause of medication allergies. The venom of such stinging insects as bees, fire ants, hornets, and wasps can also cause allergies.

Allergens may enter the body through several routes. Food and medicine allergens gain entry through the mouth. Inhaled allergens—such as animal dander, dust mites, mold spores, and plant pollens—enter through the nose and mouth and into the respiratory system. Other allergens may enter through the skin, either by contact with its surface or through an injection or sting.

Allergies are reactions of the immune system. A major function of the immune system is to detect and respond to foreign substances that enter the body. If a foreign substance is a harmful one, such as a bacterium or virus, the immune system attacks to counter the threat. However, some substances, such as food, are needed by the body, and others, such as dust, are harmless. These substances are typically ignored or *tolerated* by the immune system. An allergy develops when the immune system attacks rather than tolerates a harmless substance.

Allergic reactions. There are many different types of allergic reactions. The most common type is called the *type I* allergic reaction or *IgE-mediated* allergic reaction. *IgE* stands for *immunoglobulin E.* IgE is an *antibody* produced by the immune system. Antibodies are proteins that protect the body from infection and from *toxins* (poisons) secreted by some bacteria.

The immune system produces a different form of IgE for every allergen it encounters. Some IgE circulates in the blood, but most IgE is bound to the surface of *mast cells*. Mast cells are protective cells found in almost every organ of the body.

Allergens that enter the body are taken up by nearby immune cells and eventually transported to mast cells. The allergen binds to the corresponding IgE on the mast cell's surface. The binding sets off a series of events. First, mast cells release a chemical called *histamine*. Histamine, in turn, triggers many of the symptoms of allergic reactions, such as sneezing, itching, and swelling. Next, mast cells produce other chemicals called *mediators*. Mediators make an allergic reaction last longer by directly causing allergic symptoms and by attracting other immune cells that prolong and intensify the reaction.

Allergic reactions can occur in many different organs of the human body. Scientists do not know why the same allergen entering in the same way will cause a skin rash in one person, breathing difficulty in another person, and intestinal problems in still another person. They do know that the immune cells involved are attracted to different parts of the body by signals from both the immune system and the target organs. This process is called *cell trafficking*. However, scientists know little about how cell trafficking actually works.

Occasionally, an allergen will trigger a sudden and overwhelming reaction that affects several parts of the body at the same time. This reaction is called *anaphylaxis* (AN uh fuh LAK sihs). Symptoms of anaphylaxis can include the swelling and closing of the throat, spasms of the airways in the lungs, and a drop in blood pressure. If severe, anaphylaxis can lead to shock and even death. Many allergies can lead to anaphylaxis, but the condition most commonly results from allergies to certain foods, medicines, and insect stings.

The development of allergies. Scientists know little about why people develop allergies. But they do know that the development of allergies is influenced by both *genetic* (hereditary) and environmental factors.

Scientists know that *atopy,* the tendency to develop allergies, runs in families. They have identified many different genes that play a role in the development of allergies. These genes include those that control the production of IgE and IgE *receptors,* proteins on the surface of cells to which IgE binds. The genes involved also include genes that govern production of mediators. Despite being able to identify these genes, scientists cannot predict who will develop allergies.

The risk of developing allergies can increase with exposure to many substances in the environment. Exposure to cigarette smoke, for example, ranks as a strong risk factor for allergies. Common infections, especially respiratory infections, can increase a child's chance of developing allergies. People who live in homes with pets, excessive dust, or mold are exposed to potential allergens, which can increase the risk of developing allergies. However, scientists believe that some exposure to certain substances in the environment may actually decrease the risk of allergies. Similarly, they think that a lack of exposure to certain substances may increase the risk of developing allergies. Scientists call this idea the *hygiene hypothesis.* According to the hygiene hypothesis, children who are exposed to relatively high levels of bacteria products, such as those who grow up on farms, may be protected against developing allergies. The hypothesis may explain why allergic diseases are more prevalent in urban areas than rural areas. It also may explain why scientists have seen an increase in allergies in many regions as overall sanitation has improved.

Diagnosis. Often, observation can reveal the cause of an allergic reaction. In many cases, however, the cause of the reaction is not apparent. Doctors often diagnose such allergies using *skin testing*. In this procedure, a health care professional places extracts of purified allergens as drops on the skin. A small pointed device is used to push the liquid into the skin. For each substance to which the person is allergic, a small bump surrounded by a ring of red skin will appear within minutes.

Blood tests can also be used to diagnose allergies. Such tests measure concentrations of specific forms of IgE. For example, a person allergic to ragweed will have a form of IgE in the blood that binds only to ragweed pollen. The allergy's severity is related to the concentration of the IgE in the blood.

Treatment. The most effective way to treat an allergic disease is to avoid exposure to the allergens that trigger it. Certain allergens, such as foods and pets, can be avoided entirely. However, it is usually impossible to totally eliminate indoor allergens. The only way to completely avoid outdoor allergens is to stay indoors, which is often impossible.

Common drugs used to relieve allergy symptoms include *antihistamines.* These drugs block histamine from binding to histamine receptors on the body's cells. Doctors also treat allergy symptoms using drugs that fight inflammation. Anti-inflammatory drugs called *glucocorticoids* block the action of mediators. In the treatment of allergies, such drugs are often referred to simply as *steroids.* Some allergy drugs are swallowed as tablets. Others include skin creams and ointments, eye drops, nasal sprays, and inhaled sprays. Still other allergy medications can be injected. Such drugs are usually used to treat emergency cases of anaphylaxis.

Doctors also treat allergies using *desensitization* or *specific allergen immunotherapy.* In this process, the doctor combines concentrated extracts of a patient's known allergens to make a vaccine for that patient. At first, an extremely dilute solution is injected. The concentration is gradually increased. The patient becomes less sensitive to the allergens as the course of shots reaches the highest concentration. More shots are given every one to four weeks for several years to maintain the effect. After treatment, many people no longer suffer reactions when exposed to allergens. Ronald M. Ferdman

Related articles in *World Book* include:

Anaphylactic shock	Asthma	Hay fever
Antibiotic (Allergic reactions)	Conjunctivitis	Hives
Antihistamine	Dust mite	Immune system (Allergies)
	Eczema	

Alliance. See International relations.

Alliance for Progress, or, in Spanish, Alianza para el Progreso, was a cooperative program that promoted economic and social development in Latin America. It involved the United States and more than 20 Latin American nations. The program began in 1961 and ended during the early 1970's.

In 1961, President John F. Kennedy called for the establishment of the Alliance for Progress. Kennedy proposed the cooperative program to replace previous efforts by the United States to help Latin American countries on an individual basis. The United States and 19 Latin American countries signed the charter of the Alliance for Progress on Aug. 17, 1961, in Punta del Este, Uruguay. Other Latin American countries later joined the program.

Under the alliance's charter, the participating Latin American countries provided 80 percent of the funds for the program. The remainder was furnished by the United States, other wealthy countries, and a variety of public and private groups. During the 1960's, the United States provided nearly $10 billion for projects connected with the Alliance for Progress program. These projects included housing developments, power plants, and roads.

The Organization of American States, an association of Latin American countries and the United States, coordinated the activities of the Alliance for Progress. United States participation was directed by the Agency for International Development, which was then a part of the United States Department of State. Other United States government agencies involved in the program included the Export-Import Bank and the Peace Corps. International lending agencies, such as the Inter-American Development Bank and the World Bank, also worked with the alliance.

One of the goals of the Alliance for Progress was an annual economic growth rate of at least 2 ½ percent per nation. Almost all the Latin American countries exceeded this goal during the 1960's. They also improved their educational systems and programs to benefit the poor. But the alliance was less successful in providing more jobs. Unemployment in much of Latin America remained high, though the alliance had pledged to reduce it. Critics charged that the alliance failed to deal realistically with Latin America's overpopulation problem. Others said the program's goals had been too ambitious. Still others blamed the U.S. Congress, which began to cut funds for the alliance in the late 1960's.

During the early 1970's, the U.S. government began to emphasize increased trade, rather than direct aid, as a means of solving Latin America's economic problems. Also, Latin American nations were providing more and more of their own development resources. In addition, international lending agencies, especially the World Bank, provided more money for development projects in Latin America.   Nathan A. Haverstock

See also **Organization of American States.**

Allies. See **World War I** (introduction); **World War II** (table: The Allies; Strategy).

Alligator is the name for two kinds of reptiles related to crocodiles. The *American alligator* lives in waters and lowlands of the southeastern United States. The *Chinese alligator* inhabits the lower Yangtze River Valley in China. Alligators and crocodiles belong to a group of reptiles known as *crocodilians*. This group also includes caimans and gavials. Caimans live in Central America and South America, and people frequently refer to them as alligators.

Body. Alligators resemble lizards in their shape, but their bodies and tails are thicker than those of most lizards. Alligators' jaws are set with many sharp teeth. Their eyes stick up above their skulls so that alligators can see above the water while their bodies are beneath it. They use their short legs for walking, and they can run quickly for short distances. Alligators swim by moving their tails from side to side.

The tough skin on an alligator's back is ridged with dozens of small bones called *osteoderms*. The skin lower on the body is smooth. People have used the smooth alligator skin to make leather for handbags, shoes, and other products. A young American alligator has yellow marks across its body, but these fade after a time. When grown, the American alligator is dull gray and dark olive in color.

Alligators in the past grew to be 18 feet (5.5 meters) long or longer. Today, few can be found that have reached even a length of 12 feet (3.7 meters). Male alligators from 11 to 12 feet (3.4 to 3.7 meters) long weigh from 450 to 550 pounds (204 to 249 kilograms). Females seldom measure more than 9 feet (2.7 meters) long, or weigh over 160 pounds (73 kilograms).

Habits. The female alligator makes her nest of rotting leaves and other plant materials, which she forms into a pile about 3 feet (0.9 meter) high and 7 feet (2.1 meters) across. She lays 20 to 60 eggs in the center of the pile, where the nest is moist. The eggs are white, hard-shelled, and slightly larger than hens' eggs. The young emerge from the eggs after about nine weeks.

Treat Davidson, NAS

An alligator's body is suited for life on land and in water. The alligator uses its short, stocky legs for walking. In the water, it swims by sweeping its tail from side to side.

Bruce Coleman Inc.

The alligator's powerful jaws can crack cattle bones. But if the jaws are shut, they can be held closed by a person's hands.

© Shutterstock

A swimming alligator can keep its eyes and nostrils above the water because of the shape of its skull.

Alligators provide more care for their young than do most reptiles. After laying eggs, the female stays near the nest, guarding the eggs against predators. When the young hatch, they give high-pitched yelps, and the mother comes to scratch open the nest and free them. The mother alligator protects her young for a year or more.

When first hatched, young alligators measure about 9 inches (23 centimeters) long. During the first six years of their lives, both males and females grow about 1 foot (30 centimeters) in length each year. After this time, the females grow more slowly. But the males continue to grow at the same rate for several years more. Alligators probably live 50 to 60 years.

In winter, alligators remain resting underwater, bury themselves in mud, or go into deep holes that they have made with their bodies. These holes are often called 'gator holes. During droughts, 'gator holes may provide the only refuge for aquatic animals. When rains return, the fish, frogs, turtles, and other animals that have survived in 'gator holes repopulate the swamps and marshy lakes.

Alligators eat many kinds of small animals that live in or near the water, including birds, fish, frogs, small mammals, snakes, and turtles. Pits along the sides of an alligator's jaws act as sense organs, helping the animal detect movements of its prey in water. Large male alligators sometimes attack dogs, pigs, or even cattle. They drag these animals underwater to drown them, and then tear them to pieces. Alligators tear their prey apart by grabbing a part of the animal with their jaws. They then spin the prey's body until the held part twists off.

Fortunately, even the largest alligators seldom attack human beings. The muscles that close an alligator's jaws are very strong. But once the jaws are shut, they can easily be held closed by a person's bare hands. People have sometimes captured alligators in this way, without using any weapons.

Alligators and crocodiles. People often mistake alligators for crocodiles, but these animals differ in various ways. The fourth tooth of the alligator's lower jaw fits into a pocket of the upper jaw. The same tooth in the crocodile fits into a groove in the side of the upper jaw, making it visible when the animal's mouth is closed. Also, the snout of an alligator is broader than that of a crocodile.

Where alligators live. Alligators were once common in lakes, swamps, and rivers along the Gulf of Mexico and on the Atlantic Coast as far north as North Carolina. They also occurred far up the Mississippi River. But so many alligators were killed for their hides or for food and sport that they became scarce.

In 1967, the United States Fish and Wildlife Service classified the alligator as an endangered species. This designation gave the animal almost complete protection. But by 1977, alligator populations had increased so much in Florida and other southern coastal regions that the animals were reclassified as threatened. By 1987, the agency had declared the species to be recovered throughout its range.   D. Bruce Means

Scientific classification. Alligators belong to the alligator and caiman family, Alligatoridae. The American alligator is *Alligator mississippiensis,* and the Chinese alligator is *A. sinensis.*

See also **Crocodile; Gavial.**

Alliteration, *uh* LIHT *uh* RAY *shuhn,* occurs when the same sound starts succeeding accented syllables. In "Peter Piper picked a peck of pickled peppers," for example, alliteration is created by the occurrence of a *p* sound at the beginning of every accented syllable. The first sentence of this paragraph has alliteration of *s* sounds. Old English poetry had no rhyme, but was held together by a pattern of alliteration. Alliteration, like rhyme, assonance, and consonance, is a device of repetition that helps express the feelings and ideas of a poem. See also **Poetry** (Sounds).   Paul B. Diehl

Allosaurus, AL *uh* SAWR *uhs,* was a large, meat-eating dinosaur that lived about 150 million years ago. *Allosaurus* inhabited what is now the western United States. It grew about 36 feet (11 meters) long, stood about 7 feet (2 meters) high at the hips, and weighed about 2 tons (1.8 metric tons).

The head of *Allosaurus* was 3 feet (0.9 meter) long. Its jaws had about 70 teeth, each 3 inches (8 centimeters) long with jagged edges for slicing flesh. Holes in the skull lightened the weight of the dinosaur's large head. A pair of distinctive low, bony bumps rose in front of the eyes. The short front legs had three strong, curved claws on each hand. The hind feet were birdlike, with three toes pointing forward and a small inner toe pointing backward. *Allosaurus* walked on two legs with its body parallel to the ground and held its long tail out behind for balance. The animal could rear up to a height of 12 feet (3.7 meters) or more.

Allosaurus preyed on other dinosaurs. Many dinosaurs, including *Apatosaurus* and *Diplodocus,* were much larger, and so *Allosaurus* may have eaten mostly smaller dinosaurs. When *Allosaurus* did eat larger dinosaurs, it may have attacked only the weaker ones, such as the young or the sick. It may also have eaten dinosaurs that had already died.   Peter Dodson

See also **Dinosaur** (Allosaurs).

Allotropy, *uh LAHT ruh pee,* in chemistry, is the ability of an element to exist in more than one form. These forms are called *allotropes.* For example, three common allotropes of carbon are (1) hard, transparent diamond crystals, (2) soft, steel-gray or black graphite crystals, and (3) black, sooty, uncrystallized carbon black (see **Carbon**). The word *allotropy* comes from two Greek words meaning *another* and *way.*

Solid allotropes differ in their crystal structures. But allotropic gases differ in their molecular structures. For example, each molecule of ordinary oxygen is made of two oxygen atoms. Each molecule of the allotrope *ozone* is made of three oxygen atoms. Ordinary oxygen has no odor. But ozone has a peculiar sharp odor (see **Ozone**).

Robert J. Ouellette

Alloy is a material made up of a metal and at least one other element. Most alloys contain a large amount of the main metal, or *base metal,* and smaller amounts of other components. These components can be metals, such as iron; metalloids, such as silicon; or nonmetals, such as carbon. Many pure metals are too soft, rust too easily, or have other disadvantages. But often these disadvantages can be overcome if the metals are combined with other elements. Three, four, or more different substances may be present in a single alloy.

People usually make alloys by melting a base metal and adding other components. This liquid alloy then cools and solidifies. Many alloys need to be worked into a final shape after cooling. Other alloys can be made without melting the base metal. For example, manufacturers can blend metal powders together and heat them under pressure. The solid powder particles then bond to form the alloy.

Characteristics of alloys

Alloys consist of tiny crystals called *grains.* In every grain, the atoms are packed together in a particular geometric arrangement. Each grain is tilted differently from those next to it. Manufacturers can control grain size by the way they heat, form, and cool the material. Grain size determines particular characteristics in alloys. For example, smaller grains make stronger alloys. Boundaries between the grains also help determine alloy characteristics. Boundaries can become sources of weakness when an alloy has impurities, or when people use the alloy at high temperatures or with damaging chemicals.

There are two types of alloys: (1) *single phase alloys* and (2) *polyphase alloys.* Single phase alloys consist of grains that all have the same composition. In these alloys, one metal dissolves into another in the same way that salt dissolves into water. A mixture of copper and nickel in any proportion forms a single phase alloy.

Polyphase alloys have different types of grains mixed together. In these alloys, the different atoms bond together in various ways to form strong, stable compounds. The proportion of metals in polyphase alloys is

Carpenter Technology Corporation

The structure of an alloy consists of tiny crystals called *grains.* This photograph, taken with a microscope, shows the different grains of a kind of steel. Steels are iron alloys.

the same in all grains of a particular type. But this proportion can vary significantly from one grain type to another. Steels are polyphase alloys that include some grains of iron containing small amounts of carbon and other grains of a chemical compound called *iron carbide.* Iron carbide has one atom of carbon to every three atoms of iron.

Most alloys are stronger and harder than the pure metals from which they are made. Alloys also usually have lower melting temperatures than pure metals. Most alloys are less *ductile* than pure metals—that is, they are more difficult to hammer into shape, roll into sheets, or draw into wires. But some special *superplastic alloys* are extremely ductile. Few alloys can conduct electricity as well as pure metals. But there are some *superconducting alloys* that are excellent conductors.

Kinds of alloys

The first alloys. People first discovered alloys in nature during prehistoric times. Such alloys included meteorites of iron and nickel and mixtures of gold and silver in river beds. The first alloy made by people was bronze. The oldest bronzes consisted of copper and arsenic. Prehistoric copper smelters first produced them accidentally in about 3500 B.C. Over the next few hundred years, people discovered that mixing tin with copper produced a more useful bronze. They began to make tools, ornaments, and weapons out of this bronze. Bronze is much harder than pure copper, and it is easier to melt and cast into useful shapes.

Alloys of iron. Iron is the most important industrial metal. Manufacturers have almost always used it as an alloy rather than as a pure metal. Iron-based alloys are called *ferrous alloys.*

The most widely used ferrous alloys are the steels. Steels vary both in the way people make them and in their composition. All steels, however, contain small amounts of carbon and manganese and large amounts of iron.

Each variety of steel has certain advantages. *Carbon steels* rank as the most widely used steels. Most carbon steels contain less than 1 percent carbon. Their strength and durability make them popular materials for structural beams, automobile bodies, and food cans. *Alloy steels* contain nickel, chromium, and molybdenum. They are strong enough for such products as bicycle frames and aircraft landing gear. *Stainless steels* contain more than 12 percent chromium, and many varieties also use nickel. Stainless steels can resist *corrosion* (rust and other chemical damage) extremely well. They are common materials for kitchen utensils, pots and pans, and hospital equipment. *Tool steels* are ferrous alloys used to work and shape other materials. They contain such components as tungsten, chromium, and molybdenum. Machines used to shape metal are made with special tool steels that keep their hardness and sharp cutting edges, even when they become red-hot in use.

Alloys for strength and lightness. Many alloys used in vehicles, and especially aircraft, must be strong and light. Aluminum is a common base metal for many of these alloys. Pure aluminum is too light and weak for construction purposes. But manufacturers can mix the metal with other components to make strong, durable, alloys. Some common aluminum alloys contain small amounts of copper, manganese, and magnesium. These alloys are only slightly heavier than pure aluminum and are as strong as some steels. Other aluminum alloys contain zinc, magnesium, and lithium and are even stronger materials. People make aluminum alloys into many different products, including beverage cans, bicycle rims, and house siding.

Magnesium is only about two-thirds as heavy as aluminum. It is not strong enough by itself for most structural purposes, but it serves as the base metal in many useful alloys. Products using magnesium alloys include aircraft and automobile parts, as well as various tools and equipment. Titanium is another base metal for many strong, light alloys. Industries use titanium alloys to make jet engines, aircraft parts, and corrosion-resistant equipment in chemical plants.

Costly and ornamental alloys. People have long used gold and silver as alloys rather than as pure metals. Manufacturers usually add cheaper metals to the gold or silver. This reduces the cost of the alloy while keeping the appearance of the precious metal. Alloying also hardens the gold or silver and keeps it from wearing away rapidly through use. *Yellow gold* is a gold alloy containing copper and silver. It is common in jewelry and other ornamental items. Dentists use similar gold alloys as fillings for teeth. Jewelry and tableware are often made of alloys that contain silver and copper.

Several cheaper alloys make attractive but inexpensive household articles. *German silver* is a blue-white, copper-based alloy containing nickel and zinc. People use German silver for such objects as candlesticks and hardware. *Pewter,* a silver-colored, tin-based alloy, is easy to work and can be highly polished. Plates, mugs, and vases are often made of pewter. Coins are commonly made of copper-nickel alloys.

Other alloys. Among the most common alloys are the brasses. These copper-based alloys contain up to about 40 percent zinc and small amounts of tin, lead, or other elements. Plumbing materials, locks, fasteners,

and other hardware are among the many products containing brass. *Monel* is a nickel-copper alloy. Manufacturers often use this alloy for materials that must resist corrosion in sea water, such as pump fittings and boat propellers.

Many alloys have specialized applications. *Stellite,* an extremely hard alloy, consists chiefly of cobalt, chromium, and tungsten. People use stellite as a surface layer on steel to improve its resistance to wear. *Solder,* which has a low melting point, is used to join metal surfaces. *Wood's metal,* another alloy with a low melting point, is employed in fuses for automatic fire alarms and sprinkler systems. *Invar,* an iron-nickel alloy, barely expands or contracts when its temperature changes. It is used in products that must remain at a constant size, such as measuring devices and pendulum rods.

Several alloys make excellent magnets. One example is *Alnico,* a group of alloys containing aluminum, nickel, cobalt, iron, and copper. These alloys can lift up to 60 times their own weight. However, alloys containing large amounts of metallic elements called *lanthanide elements,* such as samarium, produce magnets hundreds of times more powerful than Alnico.

Scientists are developing many alloys that offer greater strength and durability than older alloys. For example, *superalloys* can resist extremely high temperatures and severely corrosive conditions. They contain the base metals nickel or cobalt alloyed with chromium and many other elements. These superalloys are key components of jet engines and spacecraft.   Michael L. Wayman

Related articles in *World Book* include:

Babbitt metals	Lead (Properties)	Permalloy
Brass	Metal	Pewter
Britannia metal	Monel metal	Silver
Bronze	Money (Modern	Solder
Gold (Gold alloys)	U.S. currency)	Stainless steel
Iron and steel		

Allston, Washington (1779-1843), was one of the first American artists to paint in a Romantic style. He became famous for imaginative, dramatic works, many of which had supernatural themes.

Allston based many of his early paintings on the Bible and other literature. One of his finest early pictures was the Biblical work *The Dead Man Revived by Touching the Bones of the Prophet Elijah* (1813). He also painted idealized landscapes.

Allston later abandoned elaborate and dramatic themes and concentrated on simpler subjects, particularly graceful, dreamlike women in dim landscapes. Allston's *Moonlit Landscape* (1819) and other night scenes are noted for their delicate tones. Allston died before completing his last major painting, *Belshazzar's Feast,* which he began in 1817.

Allston was born on Nov. 5, 1779, in Georgetown County, South Carolina. In 1801, he went to London, where he studied with the American painter Benjamin West. While in Europe, Allston came into contact with English Romantic literature and paintings by Venetian artists of the 1500's that influenced his best work. Allston returned to the United States in 1818. He died on July 9, 1843.   Sarah Burns

Alma-Ata. See Almaty.

Alma mater, *AL muh MAH tuhr* or *AHL muh MAH tuhr,* is an expression used by students or graduates to refer to their university or college. The Latin words mean *fostering mother.* The Romans often used the words in speaking of some of their goddesses, such as Ceres and Cybele. In the 1300's and 1400's, the expression was applied to the universities in Paris; Oxford, England; and Bologna, Italy.   Michaelangelo F. Allocca

Almagro, *ahl MAHG roh,* **Diego de,** *DYAY goh deh* (1474 or 1475-1538), was a Spanish *conquistador* (conqueror) and explorer of South America. He accompanied another Spanish conquistador, Francisco Pizarro, on various expeditions.

By the early 1520's, Spanish settlers in Panama had heard reports of a rich American Indian empire somewhere to the south. In 1524, Pizarro set out to find this empire. Almagro stayed in Panama at first to obtain more soldiers and supplies for the expedition. He later joined Pizarro. However, the explorers made it only as far south as what is now Colombia before they returned to Panama. During a second expedition in 1526, Pizarro reached the coast of Ecuador with difficulty. Almagro then brought reinforcements to Ecuador from Panama, allowing the expedition to continue.

By 1528, Pizarro's group had found the Inca Empire, centered in what is now Peru. Pizarro then traveled to Spain to obtain a royal license to conquer the area. The Spanish king, Charles I (Holy Roman Emperor Charles V), granted Pizarro the license and named him commander of the expedition. The powers that Pizarro acquired from Charles I displeased Almagro.

Pizarro invaded Peru in 1532. Almagro stayed in Panama to gather more recruits and equipment. He joined Pizarro in Peru after the Battle of Cajamarca, which took place in 1532. In the battle, the Spaniards captured the Inca ruler Atahualpa and killed thousands of Inca. Almagro served as one of the leaders of the special court that condemned Atahualpa to death in 1533. Following Atahualpa's execution, Pizarro and Almagro seized the Inca city of Cusco and worked together to occupy Peru.

In 1534, Charles I assigned Almagro to explore and conquer the region of New Toledo (now southern Peru and Chile). From July 1535 to September 1536, Almagro explored parts of what are now Bolivia and Argentina and crossed the Andes Mountains into Chile. Almagro and his expedition hoped to find gold and silver. They traveled as far south as central Chile, but they found only scattered settlements with no riches. They also met strong resistance from the local people.

In 1537, Almagro returned to Peru. In the late 1530's, a dispute between Almagro and Pizarro over who would rule the area around Cusco led to war. Pizarro's forces won the conflict, and they executed Almagro in 1538.

Martin Malcolm Elbl

See also **Pizarro, Francisco.**

Almanac, *AWL muh nak,* is a book or pamphlet, usually published once a year, that contains many kinds of information. An almanac often includes a calendar, outstanding dates and events, movements of heavenly bodies, and facts about governments, history, geography, and weather. It may also give figures on population, industry, and farm production.

Almanacs originally provided a calendar of the months, with eclipses, the movements of the planets, and the rising and setting times of the sun, moon, and stars. People believed that this information would be useful to farmers and to navigators.

Many scholars believe that the earliest almanacs contained predictions made by ancient Persian astrologers. Later, almanacs appeared in Rome. The oldest existing copies of almanacs today were written in the 1300's and 1400's. Publishers issued almanacs in England in the 1600's to give information about the calendar. These included the *Nautical Almanac,* for sailors.

Almanacs appeared in colonial America in the 1600's. Most were pamphlets giving calendars, the dates of religious feasts, weather forecasts, and signs of the zodiac (see **Zodiac**). *Poor Richard's Almanac* was the best known of these early books. Benjamin Franklin first published it for the year 1733. The book had poetry, astronomy information, and lists of court justices and roads. Franklin contributed many *proverbs* (short sayings) that became widely quoted. See **Poor Richard's Almanac.**

In the 1800's, many governments and newspapers began issuing almanacs. These included food recipes, first-aid advice for injuries and snake bite, weather predictions, and *conundrums* (short, humorous questions and answers). Gradually, publishers stopped predicting the weather, except in the *Old Farmer's Almanac,* the *Farmers' Almanac,* and several local almanacs.

Almanacs today, such as *The World Almanac and Book of Facts,* contain general information. Almanacs published by groups, such as the United Nations, contain facts, statistics, and documents about many countries. Newspapers, religious groups, business organizations, and certain trades or professions publish almanacs with specialized information.

Navigators and astronomers value *The Astronomical Almanac,* published by the United States Naval Observatory and Her Majesty's Nautical Almanac Office in the United Kingdom. This almanac includes tables and charts about stars, tides, eclipses, latitude, longitude, and weather. Two almanacs published in the United Kingdom are *Whitaker's Almanack* and *The Statesman's Yearbook.* They provide general information about all countries in the world. By the 2000's, certain almanacs began publishing both an online and a print edition. Almanacs on the Internet included *The Astronomical Almanac* and *The Statesman's Yearbook.*   Michael H. Harris

See also **Banneker, Benjamin; Calendar** (picture: An American calendar of 1841).

Almandine. See Garnet.

Almaty, *ahl mah TIH* (pop. 1,129,400), also spelled *Alma-Ata,* is the largest city and the economic and cultural center of Kazakhstan. It lies in the southeastern part of the country, in an irrigated valley at the foot of the Tian Shan mountain range. For the location of Almaty, see **Kazakhstan** (map).

Almaty has many treelined boulevards and large parks. It is the home of Al-Farabi Kazakh National University. The Medeo ice rink hosts international sports competitions. Industries in Almaty produce food products, metal products, printed material, and textiles.

Almaty was founded in 1854. It was originally called Verny. In 1921, it was renamed Almaty, which means *father of apples.* The name refers to nearby apple orchards. In 1929, it became the capital of Kazakhstan, then an autonomous republic of the Soviet Union. Almaty remained the capital after Kazakhstan became an independent nation in 1991. In 1997, Akmola (now called Nur-Sultan) replaced Almaty as the capital.   Nancy Lubin

Almodóvar, *ahl moh DOH vahr,* **Pedro,** *PAY droh* (1951-   ), is a Spanish motion-picture director, screenwriter, and actor. He became a leading personality in the newly liberated Spanish cinema that emerged after the death of the dictator General Francisco Franco in 1975. Almodóvar has gained a reputation for making movies that are whimsical, shocking, and comic. Many of his movies center on social issues, including sex, homosexuality, and male violence toward women. Almodóvar won an Academy Award for best foreign language film for *All About My Mother* (1999) and for best original screenplay for *Talk to Her* (2002).

Almodóvar was born on Sept. 25, 1951, in Calzada de Calatrava, La Mancha, Spain. In 1967, he moved to Madrid. In the early 1970's, he began acting with a drama group called Los Goliardos. In 1974, he directed his first movie, *Two Whores, or a Love Story That Ends with a Wedding.* His first feature film was *Pepi, Luci, Bom, and Lots of Other Girls* (1980). Almodóvar's first movie to gain widespread international acclaim was *What Have I Done to Deserve This?* (1984). His 1988 film *Women on the Verge of a Nervous Breakdown* also received critical praise and won several awards at film festivals. In 1987, he founded his own production company.

Almodóvar also wrote and directed *Matador* (1986); *Law of Desire* (1987); *Tie Me Up! Tie Me Down!* (1990); *High Heels* (1991); *Kika* (1993); *The Flower of My Secret* (1995); *Live Flesh* (1997); *Bad Education* (2004); *Volver* (2006); *Broken Embraces* (2009); *The Skin I Live In* (2011); *I'm So Excited* (2013); and *Julieta* (2016), based on short stories by the Canadian writer Alice Munro. He also writes the music for many of his movies.   Philip Wuntch

Almond, *AH muhnd* or *AHL muhnd,* is a delicious nut. The nuts are the seeds of the beautiful almond tree. Each nut grows in a thin shell that looks somewhat like a peach stone. A green leathery hull covers the shell. The hull splits open when the almond is ripe.

Some almond trees produce sweet nuts; others have bitter ones. Sweet almonds are a popular delicacy when toasted, salted, and eaten whole, or added to candies and rich pastries. Bitter almonds are not edible. Growers cultivate bitter almond trees only for the almond's oil, al-

though people also extract oil from the sweet nuts. Oil of bitter almonds contains the poisonous hydrocyanic (prussic) acid (see **Prussic acid**). After the acid is removed, the oil is used in flavoring extracts.

The almond tree is native to southwestern Asia. But today it is widely grown in the countries that border the Mediterranean Sea. The trees also thrive in California, where commercial groves produce large annual crops of almond nuts.

Almond trees are well-proportioned and may grow 40 feet (12 meters) high. They have long, pointed leaves that curl, and showy pink blossoms that reach about 1 ½ inches (3.8 centimeters) across. The blossoms open early in spring, long before the leaves appear. For this reason, almonds are grown commercially only in regions that do not have early spring frosts. In other regions, people grow the trees as ornamentals.   Walter S. Judd

Scientific classification. The almond's scientific name is *Prunus dulcis.*

Aloe, *AL oh,* is the name of a group of hundreds of fleshy-leaved plants native to the Middle East, Madagascar, and southern Africa. They are often cultivated in regions with warm climates.

Aloe plants range in height from a few inches or centimeters to 30 feet (9 meters) or more. The leaves of many species become large. They are lance-shaped and sharp-pointed, with jagged edges that end in sharp hooks. The leaves usually grow directly from the ground in the form of a large rosette. From the center of this rosette springs the flowering stalk that ends in a dense cluster of yellow or reddish tube-shaped flowers. The century plant, also called *American aloe,* is similar in appearance but unrelated.

Farmers in southern Texas raise large quantities of the *Barbados aloe,* also known as *aloe vera.* This species also is a common houseplant. Its leaves contain a bitter juice. Manufacturers heat the juice at low temperatures to produce a powder and a gel. Aloe powder is used as a laxative and in some dietary supplements.

Aloe gel is colorless and feels cool on the skin. It is used to make various cosmetics, including skin creams, shampoos, and suntan lotions. Research has shown that aloe gel is effective in treating burns and frostbite.

Certain African species of aloe have fibers in their leaves that are used for making rope, fishing nets, and coarse cloth. Others

David M. Stone, Photo/Nats

Barbados aloe

have a finer fiber that is used to make lace, and some species are used to make violet dye.   Alwyn H. Gentry

Scientific classification. Aloes make up the genus *Aloe.* The Barbados aloe's scientific name is *Aloe vera* or *A. barbadensis.*

Alpaca, *al PAK uh,* is a grazing animal of South America that is related to the camel. It is raised usually for its fine wool. Sometimes the young, known as *crias (KREE ahz),* are killed for meat. The alpaca lives in mountain regions of Bolivia, Chile, and Peru. It thrives at heights from 12,000 to 16,000 feet (3,660 to 4,880 meters) above

WORLD BOOK illustration by Kate Lloyd-Jones, Linden Artists Ltd.

The almond is the seed of the almond tree and a delicious nut. Each nut grows in a shell that resembles a peach stone.

Francisco Erize, Bruce Coleman Ltd.

The alpaca is a South American animal valued for its thick, straight hair, which is used to make warm, soft material.

sea level. The alpaca's blood is especially efficient in carrying oxygen, which is less abundant at high elevations.

The alpaca resembles the vicuña, a wild animal of the Andes Mountains. Scientists believe the alpaca is descended from the vicuña. The alpaca has wool that is longer and of lower quality than that of the vicuña. Alpacas are also close relatives of domesticated llamas and wild guanacos, which also live in the Andes.

The alpaca stands a little less than 4 feet (1.2 meters) high at the shoulder. It has a thick coat of black, white, or brown hair that grows from 8 to 24 inches (20 to 61 centimeters) long. This hair is much straighter and finer than sheep's wool. It provides one of the best fibers known for making warm, soft material. Owners usually shear their alpacas every year. They get as much as 7 pounds (3 kilograms) of wool from some of them.

Bolivia and Peru have become the world's most important producers of alpaca wool. They export much of the wool to the United States and Europe to be manufactured into cloth. They weave the rest at home and often make shawls out of it. Indians of Peru raised alpacas, and made the wool into cloth for centuries before Europeans came to South America. Alpacas are also raised for their wool in the United States. Kenneth J. Raedeke

Scientific classification. The alpaca's scientific name is *Lama pacos.*

See also **Guanaco; Llama; Vicuña.**

Alpenhorn. See **Alphorn.**

Alpha Centauri, *AL fuh sehn TAWR eye,* is a multiple star system in the constellation Centaurus. It is an extremely bright star system that astronomers classify as a zero magnitude system (see **Star** [Brightness of stars]). It can be seen from the Southern Hemisphere and just north of the equator. It consists of Centauri A, a –0.01 magnitude yellow star similar to the sun, and the smaller 1.33 magnitude orange star Centauri B. These two stars make up a *binary star* (pair of stars) that orbit each other every 80 years (see **Binary star**). About 0.1 *light-year* away is the magnitude 11 small reddish star Proxima Centauri. One light-year equals the distance light travels in a vacuum in a year, about 9.46 trillion kilometers. Proxima is the closest star to Earth besides the sun. Many astronomers believe Proxima Centauri orbits Centauri A

and B about once every 1 million years. This orbit would make Alpha Centauri a triple star system. Centauri A and B are 4.3 light-years from Earth. Proxima is 4.2 light-years from Earth. Alpha Centauri is approaching Earth at 12 miles (23 kilometers) per second. In 2016, astronomers announced evidence of a roughly Earth-sized planet orbiting Proxima Centauri within its *habitable zone,* the region around a star in which liquid water could exist on a planet's surface. James B. Kaler

Alpha Orionis. See **Betelgeuse.**

Alpha particle is an atomic nucleus of two protons and two neutrons. An alpha particle can become the nucleus of a helium atom by capturing two electrons.

Two processes create alpha particles—(1) *radioactive decay* and (2) *nuclear fusion.* In the decay process, a larger nucleus *emits* (gives off) an alpha particle. For example, nuclei of heavy chemical elements, such as uranium and thorium, decay by emitting alpha particles. Almost all the helium on Earth is formed by radioactive decay.

In the fusion process, hydrogen atoms *fuse* (join) to create alpha particles. The amount of helium measured in stars and galaxies agrees with the big bang theory of the beginning of the universe. In that theory, most of the helium in the universe was produced by nuclear fusion within the first thousand seconds of the big bang.

Fusion also creates alpha particles inside stars. For example, a series of fusion reactions produces most of the sun's energy. These reactions consume four protons and make one alpha particle; a single proton is the same as the nucleus of the simplest form of hydrogen. The alpha particle has less matter than the protons had. The missing matter is converted to energy. William Karl Pitts

See also **Big bang; Helium; Radiation** (Sources of radiation); **Star** (Fusion in stars).

Alphabet is a series of letters in a specific order representing the speech sounds of a language. *Linguists* (scholars who study language) have defined an alphabet as having letters representing both the consonants and vowels of a language. But, for the purposes of this article, a series of letters that are all consonants may also be considered an alphabet. The word *alphabet* comes from the names of the first two letters of the Greek alphabet, *alpha* and *beta.* The alphabet for English is called the Roman alphabet, but the history of this alphabet began long before ancient Rome. For writing before the invention of letters, see **Writing system.**

The earliest alphabets

Semitic scripts. The earliest known alphabet had letters only for consonants. This earliest alphabet is called Proto-Sinaitic. In the early 1900's, the British archaeologist Flinders Petrie found examples of Proto-Sinaitic writing at an Egyptian outpost in the Sinai Peninsula called Serabit el-Khadim. The writing at this site, where the ancient Egyptians mined turquoise, dates to around 1500 B.C. In the 1990's, other archaeologists found similar writing in limestone inscriptions in Egypt at Wadi el-Hol. This writing is dated to around 1900 to 1800 B.C.

Scholars have deciphered only a few words of Proto-Sinaitic, that of Serabit el-Khadim. But language experts think the letters record a Semitic language, an early relative of Hebrew and Arabic. The pictograms used in Proto-Sinaitic letters are adapted from Egyptian writing, but the letters do not stand for the same sounds in Se-

Development of the English alphabet

The alphabet used for the modern English language developed from a number of early writing systems, beginning with the hieroglyphs of ancient Egypt. These were adapted into an alphabet known as Proto-Sinaitic by around 1500 B.C. By around 1100 B.C., the Phoenician alphabet had developed from Proto-Sinaitic. The ancient Greek alphabet was adapted from the Phoenician around 800 B.C., Etruscan from the Greek around 700 B.C., and Roman from the Etruscan by around 650 B.C. The dates in this table give the periods for which the hieroglyphs and letters were formed as shown.

Egyptian* About 3000 B.C.	Proto-Sinaitic About 1500 B.C.	Phoenician About 900 B.C.	Greek§ About 800-600 B.C.	Etruscan About 200 B.C.	Latin A.D. 114	Modern English††
(bull)	'alp†	'alp (ox)	alpha		A	A
(house)	b	bayt (house)	beta		B	B
(throwstick)	g	gaml (stick)	gamma		C,G	C,G
(door)	d	dalt (door)	delta		D	D
(high, joy)	h	he (Lo!)	epsilon		E	E
(mace)	w	waw‡ (peg)	[digamma]# upsilon		F V,Y	F U,V,W,Y
(fence)	ch	chet (?)	eta		H	H
(hand)	y	yod (hand)	iota		I	I,J
(hand)	k	kap (palm of hand)	kappa		K	K
(rope)	l	lamd (oxgoad)	lambda		L	L
(water)	m	maym (water)	mu		M	M
(viper)	n	nun (fish)	nu		N	N
(eye)	'ayn†	'ayn (eye)	omicron		O	O
(corner)	p	pe (mouth)	pi		P	P
(baboon)	q	qop (monkey)	[qoppa]#		Q	Q
(head)	r	resh (head)	rho		R	R
(papyrus)	ts	tsad (cricket)	sigma		S	S
(ax)	t	taw (mark)	tau		T	T
			chi**		X	X
(ax)	z	zayn (weapon)	zeta		Z	Z

*The first column gives scholars' suggestions for those Egyptian hieroglyphs that were imitated by Proto-Sinaitic letters.

†The sounds represented by the Proto-Sinaitic letters that became the Phoenician 'alp and 'ayn do not occur in the English language. The former ('alp) represented the sound made by English speakers in the middle of the phrase "Uh-oh!" The latter ('ayn) has been referred to as a gargling noise.

‡The letters F, U, V, W, and Y all evolved from the Phoenician letter waw.

§Because certain sounds were not used in certain languages, the letters representing those sounds dropped out of some alphabets. For example, the Greek letters theta (Θ), xi (Ξ), phi (Φ), psi (Ψ), and omega (Ω) did not continue into the Roman alphabet.

#The Greek letters digamma (F) and qoppa (Ϙ) were not in the standard Greek alphabet used for the classical texts of ancient Greece, but these letters did appear in some dialects of Greek. They were then adapted by the Etruscans.

**For many Greek dialects, chi (X) represented the sound kh. The dialect that the Etruscans borrowed their alphabet from, however, used chi to represent the sound ks. The Romans continued to use the letter X for this sound.

††The letters J, U, and W did not appear in the alphabet of the ancient Romans. These letters were added to the English alphabet in the Middle Ages (A.D. 400's through the 1400's).

mitic as they stand for in Egyptian. See **Pictogram.**

For scholars, the surprising thing about Proto-Sinaitic writing is who developed it. The people at these sites would have been foreign workers living in Egypt. With no formal training, these workers created a writing system using 27 symbols to represent the sounds of their language. They adapted this system from the Egyptian writing system, which required years of study to master and which had hundreds of symbols.

Proto-Canaanite and Phoenician. In about the 1400's B.C., the people in an area centered on modern-day Israel used another alphabet system, Proto-Canaanite. Proto-Canaanite adopted the pictograms used in Proto-Sinaitic. By around 1000 B.C., Proto-Canaanite letters had developed into what scholars call Phoenician. The Phoenician script had a set of 22 letters.

The Phoenicians lived along the coast of the Mediterranean Sea, in an area centered on modern-day Lebanon. The Phoenicians were seafaring merchants and traders. Their letter system became important because it was the Phoenicians who introduced the Greeks to writing. Thus, the Phoenician letters spread indirectly, through the Greek alphabet, to many languages.

Aramaic, Hebrew, and Arabic all developed writing systems based either directly or indirectly upon Phoenician letters. Aramaic was the most important language of the ancient Middle East for centuries, starting in about 900 B.C., and its script developed many local varieties across the region. The Israelites, for example, wrote Hebrew with a form of Phoenician letters until about the 500's B.C. After that time, they wrote Hebrew in one of the local varieties of Aramaic.

Arab scribes first wrote down Arabic shortly before the Qur'ān was composed in the A.D. 600's. Arabic writing developed out of another variety of Aramaic.

Scripts of Asia. Farther east, varieties of Aramaic writing provided the foundation of many scripts. Aramaic was the basis of Brahmi scripts in India. In these scripts, vowels are written with marks attached to the consonant letters. Hundreds of regional scripts of this kind developed across South and Southeast Asia. Another group of scripts developed in Central Asia, out of yet another variety of Aramaic script. The best known of this group is Mongolian.

The Greek alphabet

The Greeks came in contact with Phoenician traders and learned writing from them around 800 B.C. The Greeks borrowed Phoenician symbols to form the Greek alphabet. The Phoenician language had more consonants than the Greek (such as *H, W,* and *Y*), and the Greeks used the extra letters to represent vowel sounds.

The Greeks also adapted their letter names from Phoenician. In Phoenician, the names of letters were actual words, but in Greek the letter names have no meaning. For example, the first letter in Phoenician, *alp,* meant *ox,* and the letter represented an ox head. *Alp* became *alpha* in Greek. The second letter, *bayt,* meant *house* in Phoenician, and the letter portrayed a simplified house with an entrance. This letter became *beta* in Greek. The letters' shapes changed gradually over the centuries, and some were added and some dropped.

With Greek, for the first time, a script read from left to right. Previously, the reader read from right to left.

The Roman alphabet

The Etruscans, in what is now central Italy, learned the Greek alphabet from Greek colonists near Naples in around 700 B.C. The Etruscans did not use *B, C, D,* or *O* in writing their own language, but they kept these letters in their alphabet. Consequently, when the Romans learned the alphabet from the Etruscans, they took over 20 letters. They gradually added *G, Y,* and *Z.* Other peoples in ancient Italy used about a dozen similar alphabets for languages about which scholars know little.

Capital letters, known as *majuscules,* are the Roman letter forms that developed from Etruscan letters. The most beautiful Roman capitals are often said to be those used in the inscriptions on the column built in A.D. 113 to honor the emperor Trajan. These letters probably have their thick-and-thin strokes and their *serifs* (small finishing strokes) because the stonecarvers followed the shapes written by a writing master with an edged pen or brush. The word *capital* comes from a Latin word that meant *concerning the head.* The term *capital* letter refers to the use of this set of letters at the head of a page or sentence.

Small letters, known as *minuscules,* gradually developed from capitals. Scribes in the court of the emperor Charlemagne perfected the shapes used in modern small letters early in the A.D. 800's.

The names *upper case* and *lower case* for capitals and small letters are based upon how printers once stored the individual pieces of type. They kept the minuscules in a case below the case for capital letters.

The English alphabet added three letters to the alphabet used by the Romans: *J, U,* and *W.* English does not have a separate character for every distinctive sound in the language. Instead, it uses *digraphs* (pairs of letters) for some sounds, such as *ch, sh, th.* English also has several characters that represent more than one sound.

Other alphabets

Scripts have often followed religions. For example, the early Christian church was centered in Rome. Wherever early Christian missionaries traveled, they brought the Latin language and its Roman alphabet with them. In time, the local languages also came to be written with the Roman alphabet.

Similarly, Islamic missionaries brought Arabic writing with them. Persian is written in the Arabic script, as was Turkish at one time.

Missionaries from the Eastern Orthodox Churches did not insist on using Greek but translated their sacred books into local languages. Because of this practice, the Egyptian language Coptic used a version of the Greek alphabet that also has seven letters from an older Egyptian writing, demotic.

Saint Mesrop, an Armenian monk of the A.D. 400's, is said to have created alphabets for the Armenian and Georgian languages. Letters in these alphabets come in the same order as in the Greek alphabet, but the shapes are entirely different from the Greek letters. Extra Armenian letters are inserted within the Greek order, but extra Georgian letters are added at the end.

In the late 800's, Saints Cyril and Methodius, two Greek monks who were missionaries among the Slavs, invented the Glagolitic alphabet. They based Glagolitic on Greek and used it to write the language of the Slavs, called Old Church Slavonic. Before 900, the Cyrillic alphabet was modeled on a more formal Greek alphabet with extra letters borrowed from Glagolitic. Cyrillic is still used for Russian, Serbian, Bulgarian, Macedonian, and many minority languages in Russia and in many countries formerly in the Soviet Union.

In the 1400's, the king of Korea, Sejong, began an alphabet project. Sejong wanted a simple form of Korean writing to introduce Buddhist scripture and ideas to the common people. At this time, the Korean writing system used Chinese characters and was difficult to learn. King Sejong's alphabet was first published in 1446. The alphabet had 28 letters, of which 24 are still in use. Today, the alphabet is known as Han'gul (also spelled Hangeul). In Han'gul, letters are not written in a row as they are in such languages as English. Instead, the letters for each syllable are combined into a square shape that looks something like a Chinese character.   Peter T. Daniels

Related articles. See the articles on each letter of the alphabet. See also the following articles:

Braille	Handwriting	Russian language
Codes and ciphers	Hebrew language	(Alphabet)
(Substitution)	Hieroglyphics	Semaphore
Cuneiform	Manuscript	Sequoyah
Egypt, Ancient (The	Morse code	Shorthand
people)	Pictogram	Sign language
Greek language	Pronunciation	(picture)
(Alphabet)	Rebus	Spelling
	Rune	Writing system

Alphonsus Liguori, *al FAHN suhs lee GWAW ree,* **Saint** (1696-1787), was an Italian Roman Catholic religious teacher. In 1732, he founded the Congregation of the Most Holy Redeemer, also known as the Redemptorists, to do religious work among the rural poor. Alphonsus wrote books on moral problems and for devotional and educational purposes. He emphasized the power of prayer. Alphonsus also composed many popular hymns. He was born on Sept. 27, 1696, near Naples, Italy. He died on Aug. 1, 1787. He was *canonized* (proclaimed a saint) in 1839. His feast day is August 2.
          Marvin R. O'Connell

Alphorn, also called *alpenhorn,* is a long tube-shaped instrument used chiefly by herders to call cattle in mountain regions of Switzerland. It is made of long

Swiss National Tourist Office

The alphorn is a long, tube-shaped musical instrument used in Switzerland and other mountainous countries.

wooden staves tightly bound together with birchbark strips to form an airtight tube. Alphorns are from 7 to 12 feet (2.1 to 3.7 meters) long. Their crude construction causes certain irregularities of pitch. The alphorn is played with a cup-shaped wooden mouthpiece. Gioachino Rossini included an alphorn in his opera *William Tell* (1829). The alphorn has been used since prehistoric times.   Melvin Berger

Alpinism. See Mountain climbing.

Alps are the largest mountain system in Europe. The snow-capped peaks and deep valleys of the Alps are among Europe's most spectacular sights.

The Alps stretch across south-central Europe in a broad arc. The mountains extend from the Mediterranean Sea and run along the border between France and Italy. The Alps then stretch northward and eastward through northern Italy, Switzerland, Liechtenstein, southern Germany, Austria, and Slovenia. The mountain system forms a chain about 660 miles (1,060 kilometers) long and covers an area of about 80,000 square miles (210,000 square kilometers). The broadest part of the Alps is about 160 miles (260 kilometers) wide, and the narrowest part is less than 100 miles (160 kilometers). The highest Alpine peak, Mont Blanc, rises 15,771 feet (4,807 meters) on the border between France, Italy, and Switzerland. Other famous peaks in the Alps include the Matterhorn, at 14,692 feet (4,478 meters); Monte Rosa, at 15,203 feet (4,634 meters); Jungfrau, at 13,642 feet (4,158 meters); and Grossglockner, at 12,461 feet (3,798 meters).

The Alps form a natural barrier between central and southern Europe. The Romans gained control of the Alpine region between 58 and 15 B.C. and built roads through several Alpine passes. The roads allowed communication and trade between people on opposite sides of the Alps. Today, highways and railroads enable people to travel easily through the mountains. The two St. Gotthard tunnels, a highway and a railroad tunnel, run through the Alps in south-central Switzerland.

How the Alps were formed. Geologists believe that a large sea once covered what is now the Alpine region. More than 100 million years ago, the land masses north and south of this sea began to move closer together. The great pressure placed on the seabed layers forced the land masses to fold gradually and to tilt, so that ridges and valleys formed. Rock that once lay deep below the seabed was pushed to the top of ridges. The central parts of the Alps include such rocks as gneiss, granite, schist, and shale. The southern and northern Alps consist chiefly of rugged limestone formations.

Glaciers covered most of the Alps until about 10,000 years ago. Since then, the ice has slowly retreated to the highest mountain parts. As the glaciers moved downhill and outward from the mountain core, they gouged the earth and rock, creating U-shaped valleys, *cirques,* and *cols.* Cirques are bowl-shaped hollows near mountain peaks. A col is a high pass between two cirques.

The Alpine glaciers also moved earth and rock that had collected along the edges and top of the ice. As the ice melted, rock debris piled up along the glacier's path in bands called *moraines.* Some of these moraines formed natural dams across valleys, creating lakes as water collected behind the dams. The major Alpine lakes that were created by the erosive force of glaciers include Lake Como, Lake Constance, Lake Garda, Lake

Peter Baker

Three famous Alpine peaks—the Eiger, the Mönch, and the Jungfrau, *left to right*—form part of the majestic Bernese Alps in southern Switzerland. Glaciers lie near the mountaintops.

Geneva, Lake Maggiore, the Lake of Lucerne, and Lake Zurich. Today, there are more than 1,000 small glaciers in the Alps. The largest is the Aletsch Glacier in southern Switzerland. However, most of the glaciers have thinned out or retreated considerably. Many of the smaller icefields have disappeared completely. See **Glacier; Moraine.**

Chief ranges of the Alps. Most geographers divide the Alpine region into the western, central, and eastern Alps. The western Alps include the ranges west of the Great St. Bernard Pass, which is between northwestern Italy and southwestern Switzerland. The Cottian, Dauphiné, Graian, Ligurian, Maritime, and Savoy Alps are considered western Alps. The central Alps lie between the Great St. Bernard Pass and Lake Constance. They include the Bernese, Lepontine, Pennine (also called Valais), and Rhaetian Alps. The eastern Alps ex-

tend east of Lake Constance. They consist of the Bavarian, Carnic, Julian, and Noric Alps; the Dolomites; Karawanken; and the Tauern.

Climate. In general, the Alps have a temperate mountain climate. Such a climate is typically cooler and wetter than that of surrounding areas. The Alps are affected by the humid, temperate influences of the North Atlantic in the west and the drier continental influences, with greater seasonal temperature variations, in the east.

The Alps form a divide between the climate of central Europe to the north and west and the climate of the Mediterranean to the south. The land to the north and west of the Alps has a temperate climate with warm summers, cool winters, and precipitation throughout the year. The regions south of the Alps have hot and dry summers, mild winters, and precipitation mainly during the winter.

The Alps frequently experience warm, dry, violent winds, called *foehns,* that blow downward from the mountains into the valleys. These winds melt snow and ice on the mountainsides, often causing avalanches.

Plant and animal life. Vegetation varies at different locations and elevations in the Alps. The valleys at the base of the Alps are filled mainly with grasslands. Beech and oak trees grow on the lower slopes. Fir, pine, and spruce trees cover the higher slopes. Alpine meadows appear at high elevations where trees cannot grow. Lichens, mosses, rock, shrubs, and ice and snow cover the highest elevations of the Alps.

Many species of animals live in Alpine forests and meadows. They include *chamois,* sometimes called *goat antelopes;* deer; foxes; and *ibexes,* a type of wild goat. Eagles and falcons live among the highest peaks.

Agriculture and industry. Most farming is done in the valleys and on the sunny lower slopes of the Alps. Small family-owned farms are most common. The chief crops include such grains as barley, oats, and rye. Traditional Alpine farmers raise cattle, goats, and sheep. Dairy farming is also an important economic activity.

A variety of industries operate in the foothills and valleys of the Alps. Factories manufacture chemicals, electrical machinery, and other equipment. Traditional

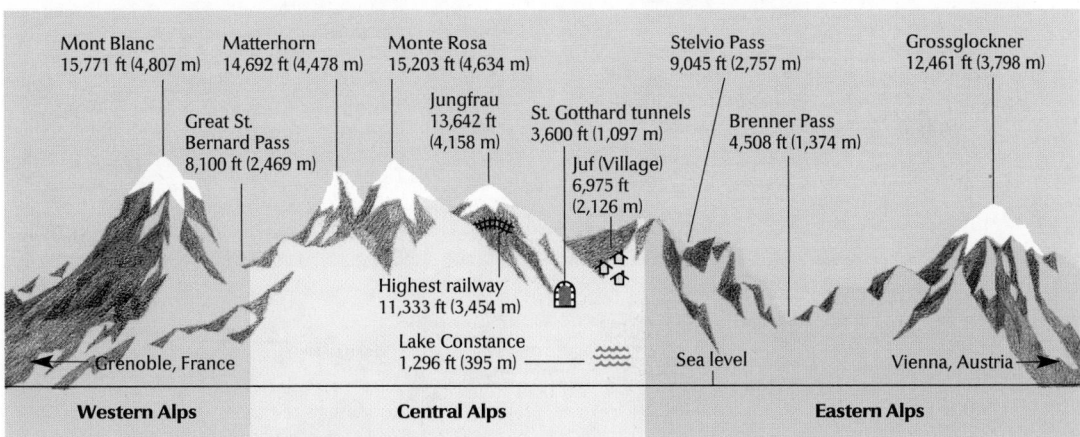

WORLD BOOK diagram by George Suyeoka

Some features of the Alps are shown in the above illustration. Most of these features are in the mountain ranges that include Italy's border with Austria, France, or Switzerland. Lake Constance lies in both Switzerland and Germany. The measurements show height above sea level.

handicrafts still produced in the region include ceramics, shoes and other leather goods, and textiles.

Natural resources found in the Alps include bauxite, iron ore, stone, and timber. Many factories run on hydroelectric power that is generated by waterfalls in the mountains. Hydroelectric power also runs most railroads in the region. Power plants in the Alps transmit some electric power to other parts of Europe.

Tourism is important to the economy of the Alps. Well-known Alpine resort communities include Chamonix in France, Lucerne and St. Moritz in Switzerland, Berchtesgaden in Germany, Cortina d'Ampezzo in Italy, and Innsbruck and Salzburg in Austria.

Alpine travel. More than 40 passes occur naturally in the Alps. Highways and railroads have been built through many of these passes. The Brenner Pass, 4,508 feet (1,374 meters) high, is the most widely used pass in the eastern Alps. It lies between western Austria and northern Italy and has both a major highway and a railroad.

In addition, tunnels have been built through the mountains beneath several of the passes. The St. Gotthard Road Tunnel in south-central Switzerland is 10.5 miles (16.9 kilometers) long and is one of the longest highway tunnels in the world. It is part of the St. Gotthard Road, the most-traveled route through the central Alps running between western Germany and Italy. The Gotthard Base Tunnel is the longest railroad tunnel in the world. It extends 35 miles (57 kilometers) beneath the Swiss Alps. The Simplon Tunnel, another railroad tunnel, links Switzerland and northwest Italy. The Great St. Bernard Tunnel was the first major highway tunnel to connect Italy and Switzerland. The Fréjus Tunnels and the Mont Blanc Road Tunnel link France and Italy.

Climbing the Alps. Few people attempted mountaineering in the Alps until the 1700's, when scientists began to study the ecology, geography, and geology of the region. In 1786, two Frenchmen, physician Michel G. Paccard and his guide, Jacques Balmat, became the first to reach the top of Mont Blanc. They recorded scientific observations along the way.

Many of the Alpine peaks were climbed for the first

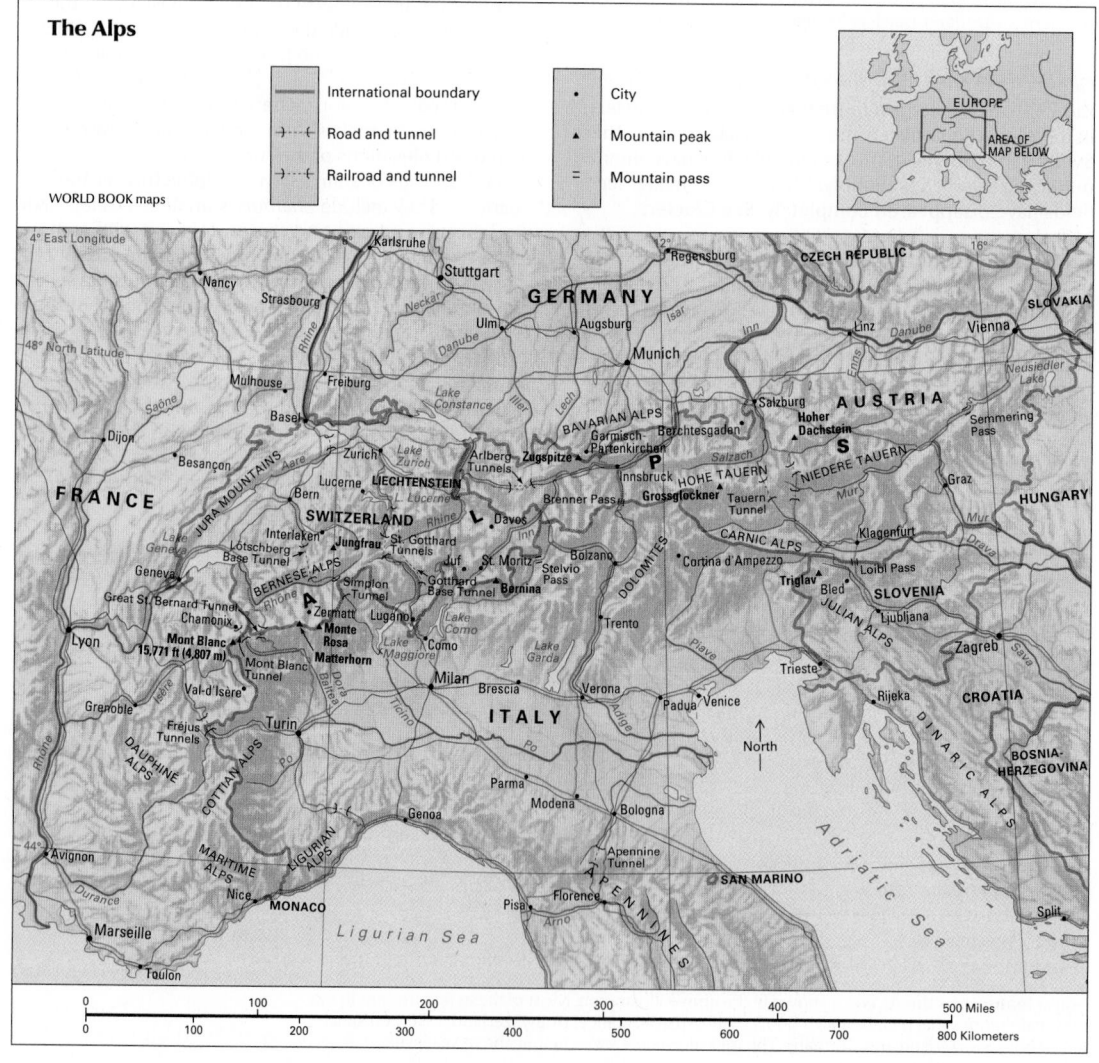

The Alps

International boundary

Road and tunnel

Railroad and tunnel

City

Mountain peak

Mountain pass

WORLD BOOK maps

EUROPE

AREA OF MAP BELOW

time during the mid-1800's, when mountaineering gained popularity as a sport. In 1855, a group of Swiss and British climbers made the first successful climb to the top of Monte Rosa. In 1865, climbers reached the top of the Matterhorn for the first time. Most Alpine summits were conquered by 1900.

Mountain climbing in the Alps became even more popular in the 1900's. Today, professional guides use modern equipment to help people scale the highest peaks. Each year, thousands of people climb to the top of the Matterhorn.

History. People have lived in the Alps for thousands of years. By the 500's B.C., Celtic tribes controlled much of the region. From 58 to 15 B.C., the Romans conquered the Alpine Celts. The Romans established settlements and engaged in agriculture, forestry, and mining. The Romans also built roads through various Alpine passes to link Rome with its northern provinces. The roads enabled the Romans to expand their influence into parts of northern Europe. These roads came to rank among the busiest in Europe as a result of Roman trade with the north.

The Roman Empire collapsed in western Europe during the A.D. 400's. Through the centuries, the Alpine region came under the control of a number of empires and states. Travel in the Alps gradually became more difficult after the Romans lost control of it. However, government officials, merchants, religious leaders, and soldiers continued to use Roman roadways to cross the mountains.

During the late 1800's, the first railroads crossed the Alps. This service led to the rapid growth of tourism in the region. Today, travelers can cross the Alps in less than eight hours by highway or train. Trans-Alpine routes have increased trade among the Alpine countries and between northern and southern Europe. But environmental pollution and overdevelopment caused by growth in highway traffic and tourism are a concern.

Christoph Stadel

Related articles in *World Book* include:

Austria (Land regions)	Glacier
Brenner Pass	Italy (The Alpine Slope)
Europe (The Alpine Mountain	Matterhorn
System)	Mont Blanc
France (The land)	Saint Bernard passes
Fréjus Tunnels	Saint Gotthard Pass
Germany (The Bavarian Alps)	Switzerland (The Swiss Alps)

**Al-Qa`ida.** See Qa`ida, Al-.

ALS. See Amyotrophic lateral sclerosis.

Alsace-Lorraine, *AL sas loh RAYN,* is a historical region in northeastern France, on the French-German border. It covers about 12,000 square miles (31,000 square kilometers). Switzerland lies to the south of this historic region and Luxembourg and Belgium lie to the north. Today, Alsace and Lorraine form the eastern part of France's Grand Est *region* (main administrative district).

Approximately 4 million people live in Alsace and Lorraine. Most of them belong to the Roman Catholic Church. Important products of these two regions include barley, oats, rye, textiles, wheat, and wine. Mineral products include iron ore from Lorraine and potash from Alsace. The Vosges Mountains area supplies timber, coal, and salt; and the streams of this area provide hydroelectric power. Alsace and Lorraine also support

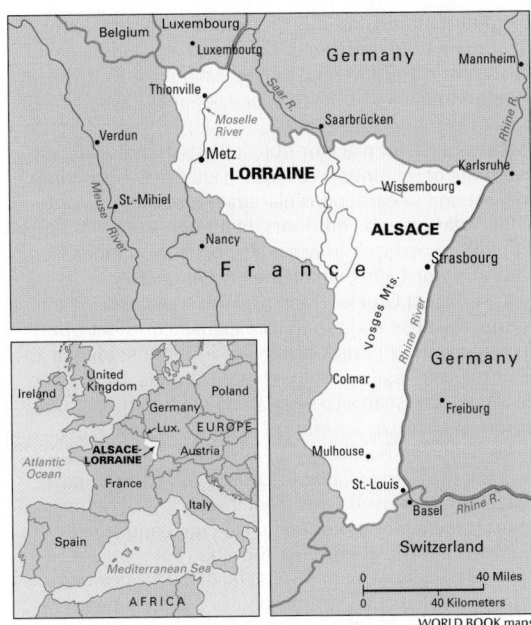

WORLD BOOK maps

Alsace-Lorraine is a historical region in France.

an important automobile industry.

For hundreds of years, the inhabitants of Alsace and Lorraine have been part German and part French. Alsace and Lorraine were often a prize in wars between France and Germany. In the A.D. 300's and 400's, Teutonic bands drove out the Celtic tribes then living in the region. In the late 700's, the area became part of Charlemagne's empire. The area fell to the middle kingdom between France and Germany when Charlemagne's grandsons divided the empire. But before long Alsace and Lorraine came under German rule.

Alsace and Lorraine remained under German rule until the 1500's, when France gained control of them by slow stages. The people resisted efforts to turn them into French people. But the French Revolution (1789-1799) brought a change of heart. The Alsatian people became so French in spirit that more than 50,000 moved to France when Germany won most of Alsace in 1871 after the Franco-Prussian War. The map with this article shows the parts of Alsace and Lorraine annexed by Germany in 1871.

The Germans resented the loss of Alsace-Lorraine after World War I (1914-1918). They regained the area in World War II (1939-1945). The Germans moved thousands of people out of the region and replaced them with Germans, Poles, and Russians. The Allies drove the Germans out of Alsace-Lorraine in 1944-1945, and France again reclaimed the region.

William M. Reddy

Alsatian dog, *al SAY shuhn,* is the term used in the United Kingdom and Commonwealth countries for a German shepherd dog. See **German shepherd dog.**

Altai Mountains, *AL ty,* form a lofty range that runs about 1,200 miles (1,900 kilometers) northwest across the borders of western Mongolia and Kazakhstan. For location, see **China** (terrain map). The Altai are among the oldest mountains in Asia. They contain rich deposits of copper, gold, iron, lead, silver, and zinc. Some have pastureland and forests. The highest peak is Belukha, or White Mountain (14,783 feet, or 4,506 meters).

James A. Hafner

Altar is a raised place or object that serves as the central point of religious worship. An altar may be as simple as a mound of earth or as elaborate as a carved stone table. Altars may be outdoors, in homes, or in buildings of public worship. The word *altar* probably comes from the Latin word *altus,* which means *high place.*

The ancient Greeks, Romans, and Israelites used altars to burn incense and to sacrifice animals or other offerings to a god or gods. Christians adopted the idea of an altar for sacrificial worship by the A.D. 100's. By the Middle Ages, Christian altars had been moved from a more central position in the church to the back wall. The priest stood at the altar, with his back to the worshipers. In 1964, the Roman Catholic Church issued a directive that altars be moved away from the back wall of the church so that the priest could face the congregation. In Eastern Orthodox Churches, the altar is behind a screen called an *iconostasis.* In the 1500's, many Protestants converted altars into simple tables on which the sacrament of the Lord's Supper is celebrated.   Jill Raitt

For pictures of an altar, see **Buddhism** (Buddhist monks); **Hinduism; Religion** (pictures: Salvation from eternal punishment; Confucius's birthday).

Alternating current. See Electric current; Electric generator; Tesla, Nikola.

Alternation of generations is a term that describes the life cycle of most plants and some algae. The term *generations* is misleading since it refers to two different phases that make up a single life cycle.

In one phase, the plant is known as a *gametophyte* or *gamete-bearing plant* and produces sex cells called *gametes.* Gametophytes can produce male sperm cells, female egg cells, or both. When a sperm cell and an egg cell unite, they form a *zygote* (fertilized egg). The zygote develops into the next phase of the reproductive cycle. In this phase, the plant is known as a *sporophyte* or *spore-bearing plant* and produces reproductive cells called *spores.* Then spores develop into gamete-producing plants, and the cycle begins again.

In most plants, the gametophyte and the sporophyte differ in size and appearance. For example, the phase that people recognize in ferns is the sporophyte. The familiar phase of mosses is the gametophyte. The sporophyte is the familiar phase of all flowering and cone-bearing plants.   Joseph E. Armstrong

See also **Fern; Liverwort; Moss; Plant** (The reproduction of plants); **Seed** (How seeds develop); **Spore.**

Alternative medicine refers to a wide range of healing practices that generally are not considered part of conventional medicine. In general, practitioners of alternative medicine use natural remedies and believe that the body can heal itself if given a chance. They feel that "invasive" treatments, such as drugs and surgery, should only be used as a last resort.

Some forms of alternative medicine—such as acupuncture, chiropractic, and *naturopathy* (use of natural agents, such as fresh air, massage, and exercise)—are well-established professions with standard training and licensing of practitioners. Other forms are less organized as professions. These include *herbalism* (use of remedies derived from plants) and *homeopathy* (use of minute amounts of substances that, in a healthy person, produce the same symptoms as those of the disorder). Still other forms of alternative medicine—including faith healing and psychic healing—are even further removed from the world of scientific and professional medicine.

During the second half of the 1900's, growing numbers of people became disillusioned with conventional medicine, particularly its expense, risks, and inability to cure certain common serious diseases. Many patients complain that conventional doctors too readily prescribe drugs as treatment. Others complain that conventional medicine is too impersonal—that it focuses on the disorder rather than the patient. Such disillusioned patients often seek out alternative practitioners.

Most doctors have regarded alternative medicine as unscientific. But an increasing number of doctors are trying to combine the best ideas and practices of both conventional and alternative medicine. This use of alternative medicine as a potentially helpful supplement to conventional treatments is often called *complementary and alternative medicine.*   Andrew Weil

See also **Acupuncture; Cancer** (Alternative medicine); **Chiropractic; Herbal medicine; Homeopathy; Pioneer life in America** (Health).

Alternative school is a public or private school that differs from traditional schools in curriculum, purpose, or teaching methods. Most alternative schools try to establish a less formal relationship between teachers and pupils. They try to make greater use of community facilities outside the school and involve parents in the educational process. These schools developed due to dissatisfaction with the quality and aims of traditional schools.

Alternative schools have voluntary enrollments. A typical alternative school has 30 to 40 students. A school of this size can easily adjust its program to fit individual needs and desires. Some alternative schools work only with children of elementary-school age. Others accept only teen-agers. Many alternative schools put students of several ages into classes based on subject interest.

Many alternative schools in the United States operate independently of the public school system. These schools, which are privately run, are usually called *free schools.* The word *free* refers to the independence of such schools. It also describes the emphasis of the schools in allowing students to make their own decisions. Other alternative schools operate as part of the public school system. Such schools may be in one area of a public school building or in a separate building provided by the school system. The separate buildings are often called *magnet schools* or *specialty schools.* They attempt to attract students from a wider attendance area than a traditional neighborhood school.

Features of alternative schools

The basic principle followed by alternative schools is that not all children have the same goals and the same ways of learning. Many of the people involved in operating these schools do not want to convert the whole school system to their methods. They want to provide the opportunity for a different kind of education for children who would benefit from it.

The major feature of many alternative schools is the

open space classroom, sometimes called an *open classroom.* The teacher of an open space classroom, instead of lecturing most of the time, helps students find interesting ways to learn on their own. Many kinds of educational materials are kept in the classroom. The students work with these materials alone or in groups. The teacher gives the students more individual help than in traditional schools. Time with students has always been an important element in alternative schools.

Most alternative schools lack adequate funds and such facilities as gymnasiums, laboratories, and shops. Parents and volunteers provide most of the finances, help run the classes, and help maintain the buildings.

Many forms of alternative schools have developed. *Street academies* and *dropout centers,* which function in the poor sections of big cities, help high school dropouts continue their education. *Storefront schools* have developed from child-care and kindergarten facilities. *Work schools* hold classes part of the day, and the students work at regular jobs the rest of the day.

The *school without walls* plan, used in some large cities, takes advantage of the educational opportunities provided by businesses and institutions of the community. Students may spend part of the day at an artist's studio, a factory, a museum, a newspaper office, a repair shop, a theater, or a government or private agency. The purpose of this method is to make learning more realistic and enjoyable, and to broaden the experiences offered high school students.

Some alternative schools emphasize the study of the culture and history of a certain minority group. Some accept only students from one such group. Others seek students from several cultures and ethnic groups.

A number of alternative schools have been designed for children from middle- or upper-class families. Usually such schools are in suburban or rural areas. Most of them stress the independence of each student and have no required subjects.

A trend in the development of alternative schools has been the establishment of such schools within the public school system. One plan offers a variety of learning environments from which students, parents, and teachers may choose. At the elementary school level, parents can choose to place their children in a traditional classroom or in one of several kinds of open space classrooms. High school students decide whether to enter a free school with few course requirements, or one of several programs in the regular high school program.

History

Experimental schools similar to alternative schools have been set up throughout the history of public education. But the term *alternative school* first came into common use during the 1960's. It referred to a variety of programs and institutions that differed greatly from private schools and special programs within public schools. Most private schools were established for children of wealthy families. Most special programs worked only with students who had special problems or exceptional ability. However, most alternative schools welcomed any student.

African Americans in the Southern States set up some of the first alternative schools. During the 1960's, these people established *freedom schools* in communities where public schools refused to admit their children based on skin color. In many Northern cities, African Americans set up alternative schools because of dissatisfaction with the treatment of their children in public schools. Other groups, such as Hispanic Americans and American Indians, also set up alternative schools.

Many people began to realize that a public school system could hurt, rather than help, some children. They declared that parents and educators should have the freedom to set up alternative education methods.

During the late 1960's, several groups created open space classrooms modeled on the United Kingdom's *infant schools.* Such schools are attended by children from age 5 to 7. In the United States, similar classrooms were set up in a number of public schools. Their success contributed to the growth of the alternative school movement.   David A. Bolin and Jesus Garcia

See also **EdisonLearning, Inc.**

Alternator. See Electric generator.

Altgeld, John Peter (1847-1902), was a reformer who served as governor of Illinois from 1893 to 1897. Under his leadership, Illinois established a board to help settle strikes, gave prisoners the right to parole and probation, and also improved its public school system.

Shortly after taking office, Altgeld, a Democrat, pardoned three of the men who had been convicted of a bombing during the Haymarket Riot of 1866 (see **Haymarket Riot**). He believed they had not received a fair trial. However, he was widely criticized for his action.

In 1894, President Grover Cleveland sent federal troops to Chicago during the Pullman Strike (see **Pullman Strike**). Altgeld opposed what he considered interference in a state matter. He protested to Cleveland but again received wide criticism.

Altgeld was born on Dec. 30, 1847, in Niederselters, Germany, near Wiesbaden. His family moved to the United States and settled in Ohio in 1848. At 16, Altgeld joined the Union Army during the American Civil War (1861-1865). He became a lawyer in 1871 and served as a superior court judge in Cook County, Illinois, from 1886 to 1891. His book *Our Penal Machinery and Its Victims* (1884) criticized the U.S. court system for discriminating against the poor. He died on March 12, 1902.

Clyde C. Walton

Altimeter, *al TIHM uh tuhr* or *AL tuh MEE tuhr,* is an instrument that measures altitude. Aircraft and some satellites are equipped with altimeters. Mountain climbers, surveyors, and scientists also use altimeters.

There are three main kinds of altimeters: (1) pressure altimeters, (2) radar altimeters, and (3) laser altimeters. Pressure altimeters are standard equipment on aircraft. Some planes also carry radar altimeters. Earth satellites carry radar and laser altimeters to measure the height of the oceans, land, and icecaps. Scientists have used radar and laser altimeters mounted on space probes to map the surfaces of other planets and the moon.

A pressure altimeter resembles a type of gauge known as an *aneroid barometer.* Both devices measure the effect of air pressure on a metal chamber from which most of the air has been removed. A pressure altimeter determines an aircraft's distance above sea level by measuring the pressure of Earth's atmosphere. This pressure decreases as altitude increases.

A radar altimeter measures the time a radio signal

takes to travel from a plane or satellite to Earth's surface and back. A laser altimeter works in the same way, but uses pulses of laser light rather than radio waves.

To use a satellite-based altimeter to measure the height of features on Earth's surface, scientists must first measure the satellite's distance above sea level. They do this by tracking the satellite by lasers and radio from ground-based stations and from satellites of the Global Positioning System (GPS). The GPS is a worldwide navigation system of radio signals from satellites. The altitudes of the stations and satellites are precisely known. Thus, scientists can use those altitudes and the tracking data to determine a satellite's distance above sea level.

Researchers have used measurements from satellite-based altimeters to determine how the ocean shrinks and expands as its temperature changes. They have also used satellite data to measure the speed and direction of ocean currents. In addition, satellite-based altimeters have measured the height of the icecaps covering large areas of land in the polar regions. Researchers can use the information about the icecaps to determine whether the caps are growing or shrinking.   George H. Born

See also **Barometer; Global Positioning System.**

Altitude is the height of an object above the surface of Earth, the moon, or some other reference body. In geography, the height of a physical feature or place is commonly called elevation. In astronomy, altitude is the angle between a line from an observer to, for example, a star and a line from the observer to the horizon. See also **Air; Altimeter; Mountain; Navigation.**

Altitude sickness, often called high-altitude sickness, is an illness caused by a lack of oxygen in the blood or body tissue at high altitudes. Air pressure decreases with altitude, thereby forcing a person's body to function with lower levels of oxygen than those found at or near sea level. In most cases, symptoms of altitude sickness begin at altitudes over 7,000 feet (2,100 meters).

Physicians recognize three forms of altitude sickness: (1) *acute mountain sickness* (AMS), (2) *high-altitude cerebral edema* (HACE), and (3) *high-altitude pulmonary edema* (HAPE). Medical experts do not fully understand the cause of AMS, but they believe it is related to swelling that occurs in the brain at high altitudes. Common symptoms include nausea, poor sleep, headache, and drowsiness. With HACE, the symptoms may become more severe and include loss of balance and changes in mental condition. Individuals suffering from HAPE experience a build-up of fluid in the lungs. They typically have a cough, gurgling breaths, chest congestion, and difficulty breathing. Most deaths from high-altitude sickness can be attributed to HAPE.

Descent to lower elevation will normally eliminate the symptoms of altitude sickness, and some medications are also effective. A gradual ascent to high elevation allowing the body to adjust to lower oxygen levels is the most effective way to avoid altitude sickness.

George Rodway

See also **Anoxia.**

Altman, Robert (1925-2006), was an American motion-picture director known for his unusual, offbeat films. His movies have a documentary visual style that seems as if the camera just happened to catch revealing moments in the characters' lives. He often used ensemble casts, with many equally important performers, rather than casts dominated by a few stars. His films tend to favor character analysis over plot. They reflect an ironic skepticism toward traditional American values and institutions. Many of his films have pessimistic, unhappy endings, though they employ eccentric humor and raunchy comedy. In 2006, Altman received an honorary Academy Award for lifetime achievement.

Robert Bernard Altman was born on Feb. 20, 1925, in Kansas City, Missouri. He began his career directing industrial films and then TV in the 1950's. Altman gained prominence with *M*A*S*H* (1970), a darkly comic movie about a battlefield hospital. In the 1970's, he directed a series of offbeat films praised by critics, including *McCabe and Mrs. Miller* (1971), a quirky Western; *Thieves Like Us* (1974), a rural gangster film; and *Nashville* (1975), about the country music industry.

Altman's output fell in the 1980's, but he made a comeback in the 1990's with *The Player* (1992), a satire on the movie industry; *Short Cuts* (1993), based on stories by the American author Raymond Carver; *Kansas City* (1996), set during the Great Depression of the 1930's; and *Cookie's Fortune* (1999), a comedy about eccentric characters in a Mississippi town. *Dr. T & the Women* (2000) portrays the life of a *gynecologist* (women's doctor). Altman's other films include *Brewster McCloud* (1971), *California Split* (1974), *A Wedding* (1978), *Popeye* (1980), *Fool for Love* (1985), *The Gingerbread Man* (1998), *Gosford Park* (2001), and *A Prairie Home Companion* (2006). Altman died on Nov. 20, 2006.   Louis Giannetti

Alum, *AL uhm,* is the name of a group of double salts. Double salts consist of two simple salts that form crystals together in fixed amounts. Common alum is a double salt of *hydrated* (water-containing) potassium sulfate and aluminum sulfate. It is also called potash alum or potassium alum. Its formula is $K_2SO_4 \cdot Al_2(SO_4)_3 \cdot 24H_2O$. Other alums are ammonium alum, sodium alum, and potassium chrome alum. Most are manufactured from *bauxite* (aluminum oxide ore). Alums are used to make glue, dyes, baking powder, flame retardants, and leather tanning agents. Industry also uses alums to purify water, to harden plaster of Paris, and to preserve fruits and vegetables. Potassium alum helps stop bleeding.

Scott W. Waite

See also **Salt, Chemical.**

Alumina, *uh LOO muh nuh,* also called *aluminum oxide,* is a compound composed of aluminum and oxygen. It has the chemical formula Al_2O_3. Alumina occurs in nature as a mineral called *corundum.* Alumina and water occur in different combinations in the minerals boehmite, diaspore, and gibbsite. These minerals are found in *bauxite,* the chief source of the alumina from which aluminum is made. Refined alumina has wide use as an *abrasive,* a material used for grinding and polishing. Alumina resists high temperatures and is a poor conductor of electric current, so it is used in furnace linings and electrical insulators. A white clay called *kaolin,* which contains alumina, is used to make porcelain.

Alumina occurs in several crystal forms called *isomers.* These forms have the same chemical formula but differ in the arrangement of their aluminum and oxygen atoms. The various isomers can be changed by heating them to certain temperatures.   David F. Hess

See also **Aluminum; Corundum; Kaolin.**

Aluminium. See Aluminum.

Aluminum Company of America

Recycling aluminum cans

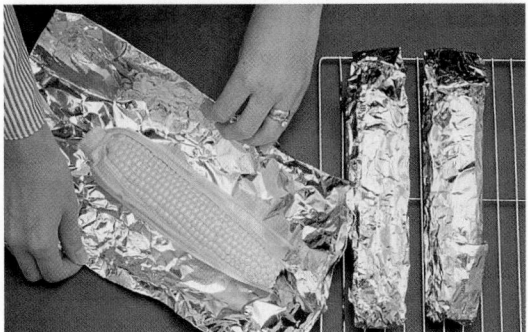

WORLD BOOK photo

Boeing

Building airplanes of aluminum

Roasting corn on the cob in aluminum foil

Aluminum alloys have a variety of uses because of their valuable properties. For example, the metals are lightweight but strong and so are used in the construction of airplanes. Aluminum cans chill quickly and can be recycled. Flexible aluminum foil is used in storing and cooking food.

Aluminum

Aluminum, *uh LOO muh nuhm,* is a lightweight, silver-colored metal that can be formed into almost any shape. It can be rolled into thick plates for armored tanks or into thin foil for chewing gum wrappers. It may be drawn into wire or made into cans. Aluminum does not rust, and it resists wear from weather and chemicals. Aluminum is called *aluminium (AL yuh MIHN ee uhm)* in English-speaking countries outside North America.

Pure aluminum is soft and has little strength. For this reason, aluminum producers generally *alloy* (mix) it with small amounts of copper, magnesium, zinc, and other elements to form *aluminum alloys.* The added elements give aluminum strength and other properties that make it one of the most useful metals. The world uses more aluminum than any other metal except iron and steel.

The largest share of aluminum alloy production goes to the packaging industry for use in such items as beverage cans, bottle caps, foil pouches, foil wrappers, and food containers. The construction industry uses aluminum alloys in such items as gutters, panels, residential siding, roofing, tubes for electric wires, and window frames. Manufacturers of transportation equipment use huge amounts of aluminum in airplanes, automobiles, boats, railroad cars, and trucks. Aluminum is used in

Kenneth A. Bowman, the contributor of this article, is a technical specialist at Alcoa Laboratories.

much electrical equipment, including light bulbs, power lines, and telephone wires. Thousands of other products also contain aluminum. These products include air conditioners, cookware, golf clubs, knitting needles, lawn furniture, license plates, paints, refrigerators, rocket fuel, and zippers.

Aluminum is the most plentiful metallic element in Earth's crust and the third most common of all the elements, after oxygen and silicon. Aluminum makes up about 8 percent of Earth's crust. But unlike some other metals, such as gold and silver, aluminum metal never occurs *free* (uncombined) in nature. It is always chemically combined with other elements in minerals. People had no way of separating aluminum from these elements until the 1800's. Scientists then developed processes for separating the minerals and producing aluminum. These processes have been used to make aluminum ever since.

Properties of aluminum alloys

Only a small percentage of aluminum is used in pure form. It is made into such items as electrical conductors,

Properties of pure aluminum

Al		
	Atomic number	13
	Relative atomic mass	26.981538
	Density (at 20° C)	2.70 (g/cm³)
	Melting point	660.2 °C
Chemical symbol	**Boiling point**	2500 °C

jewelry, and decorative trim for appliances and cars.

Almost all aluminum is used commercially in alloy form with up to 15 percent of one or more other elements. The chief elements are copper, magnesium, manganese, silicon, tin, and zinc. Copper and magnesium increase the strength and hardness of aluminum. Magnesium also makes aluminum easier to weld. Manganese helps aluminum resist corrosion and also provides strength. Silicon lowers the melting point of aluminum and makes it easier to cast. Tin makes aluminum easier to shape with metalworking tools. Zinc, especially when combined with magnesium, gives added strength. Other elements may also be alloyed with aluminum for special purposes. These elements include bismuth, boron, cadmium, chromium, cobalt, iron, lead, lithium, nickel, sodium, titanium, vanadium, and zirconium.

Aluminum, with its alloys, has many valuable properties that make it an exceptionally useful metal. These properties include (1) light weight, (2) strength, (3) corrosion resistance, (4) electrical conduction, (5) heat conduction, and (6) light and heat reflection.

Light weight. Aluminum is one of the lightest metals. It weighs about 170 pounds per cubic foot (2,720 kilograms per cubic meter)—about a third as much as steel. As a result, aluminum has replaced steel for many uses. For example, some parts of airplanes, automobiles, and trucks are now made of aluminum rather than of steel because lighter vehicles use less fuel. Products packed in aluminum containers cost less to ship because the containers weigh less than those made of other metals. To make aluminum alloys even lighter, the lightest metal, lithium, is added to the aluminum.

Strength. Although pure aluminum is weak, certain aluminum alloys are as strong as steel. Such alloys are used in airplanes and trucks, in guardrails along highways, and in other products that require strength. Aluminum alloys lose some strength at high temperatures. But unlike many other metals, they get stronger at extremely low temperatures. Aluminum alloys are widely used in equipment for processing, transporting, and storing liquefied natural gas, which can have a temperature of –260 °F (–162 °C).

Corrosion resistance. Some metals *corrode* (wear away) if exposed to oxygen, water, or various chemicals. A chemical reaction occurs that causes the metals to rust or become discolored. When aluminum reacts with oxygen, however, the metal forms an invisible layer of a chemical compound called *aluminum oxide*. This layer protects aluminum from corrosion by oxygen, water, and many chemicals. It makes aluminum especially valuable for use outdoors, where the metal resists the effects of wind, rain, and pollution.

Electrical conduction. Aluminum and copper are the only common metals suitable for use as electrical conductors. Aluminum conducts electric current about 62 percent as well as copper. But aluminum weighs a third as much. Aluminum wire can therefore carry the same amount of electric power as copper wire that weighs twice as much. In addition, aluminum is more *ductile* than copper, which means it can more easily be drawn into wires. Aluminum wire reinforced with steel is used for nearly all high-voltage power lines.

Heat conduction. The first large commercial use of aluminum was in cookware. Aluminum cookware heats quickly and evenly. Aluminum also cools quickly, which helps make it popular for such items as beverage cans and radiators.

Light and heat reflection. Aluminum reflects about 80 percent of the light that strikes it. Because of this property, aluminum is widely used in lighting fixtures. Aluminum also reflects heat well. Buildings with aluminum roofs reflect much of the sun's heat and so stay cooler in hot weather. When firefighters must walk through flames, they wear special protective suits coated with aluminum.

Other properties. Aluminum is nonmagnetic, which makes it valuable for protecting electrical equipment from magnetic interference. Aluminum does not produce sparks when struck and so can be used near flammable or explosive materials. The metal is not poisonous, and so food can be safely wrapped in aluminum foil and cooked in aluminum pots. Aluminum can be shaped by almost any metalworking process. It can also be bolted, glued, riveted, soldered, welded, and otherwise joined by most methods used for other metals. Finally, aluminum can be recycled.

Sources of aluminum

Most minerals, rocks, and soils contain aluminum compounds. But aluminum can be made economically

Where bauxite is mined

This map shows the most important bauxite-mining areas of the world. The richest bauxite deposits lie in tropical and near-tropical regions.

• Major bauxite-mining area

○ Other bauxite-mining area

Leading bauxite-mining countries

Tons of bauxite mined in a year

Australia	●●●●●●●●●●●●●●	95,200,000 tons (86,400,000 metric tons)
China	●●●●●●●●●●●●●	87,100,000 tons (79,000,000 metric tons)
Guinea	●●●●●●●●●(	62,800,000 tons (57,000,000 metric tons)
Brazil	●●●●◖	32,000,000 tons (29,000,000 metric tons)
India	●●●◖	25,400,000 tons (23,000,000 metric tons)
Indonesia	●◖	12,100,000 tons (11,000,000 metric tons)
Jamaica	●◖	11,100,000 tons (10,100,000 metric tons)
Russia	●	6,200,000 tons (5,600,000 metric tons)
Kazakhstan	◖	5,300,000 tons (4,800,000 metric tons)
Vietnam	◖	4,500,000 tons (4,100,000 metric tons)

Figures are for 2018.
Source: U.S. Geological Survey.

only from *bauxite.* Bauxite is the name for any ore that has a large amount of *aluminum hydroxide*—a chemical combination of aluminum oxide and water. Aluminum oxide, also called *alumina,* is the compound from which aluminum is made.

Most bauxite consists of 30 to 60 percent alumina and 12 to 30 percent water. It also contains iron oxide, silica, and titanium oxide. The color of bauxite depends chiefly on how much iron oxide the ore contains. The more iron oxide it has, the darker the color. Bauxite may be white, cream, gray, pink, yellow, red, or brown. Most bauxite is as hard as rock, but some is as soft as clay.

The richest deposits of bauxite lie in tropical and near-tropical regions. Enough bauxite deposits have been found to last several hundred years. The leading bauxite-mining countries include Australia, Brazil, China, Guinea, India, Indonesia, and Jamaica.

Most bauxite deposits lie near the surface of Earth and are mined by the *open-pit method,* also called the *opencast method.* In this process, bulldozers and other earthmoving machines first clear away the *overburden*—the soil, rocks, and trees that cover the deposits. Next, explosives are used to blast the ore loose. Huge power shovels scoop up the bauxite, and trucks or railroad cars carry it to a processing plant.

At the processing plant, the bauxite is crushed and then washed to remove clay and dirt. Some of the water in the bauxite is removed by drying the ore in *kilns* (ovens). The bauxite is then ground into a powder and shipped to a refining plant.

How aluminum is produced

There are two chief steps in producing aluminum: (1) refining the bauxite to obtain alumina and (2) smelting the alumina to obtain aluminum. After smelting, the molten aluminum is cast into blocks called *ingots* or other forms that will be shaped into finished products. It takes 4 to 6 pounds (1.8 to 2.7 kilograms) of bauxite to make 1 pound (0.5 kilogram) of aluminum.

Refining the bauxite separates the alumina in the ore from the iron oxide, silica, and titanium oxide. To separate the alumina, aluminum producers use the *Bayer process.* This technique was patented by Karl Joseph Bayer, an Austrian chemist, in 1888.

The first step of the Bayer process is mixing powdered bauxite with a solution of *sodium hydroxide* (also called caustic soda, or lye). Machines pump the mixture into large tanks called *digesters.* The digesters heat the mixture under pressure at 300 to 480 °F (150 to 250 °C) for about 30 minutes. The alumina dissolves in the sodium hydroxide solution, forming a solution of *sodium aluminate.* The other materials in the bauxite remain as solids and are called *red mud* because of their color.

The mixture of sodium aluminate solution and red mud next passes through a series of tanks in which cloth filters separate the liquid from the solids. The red mud is discarded. The sodium aluminate solution is cooled slightly and sent to tanks called *precipitators.* Crystals of aluminum hydroxide are then added to the solution, which is *agitated* (stirred) for several days. This process causes most of the alumina in the solution to *precipitate* (come out of solution) and collect on the crystals.

After the alumina has precipitated, the solution is filtered to separate the aluminum hydroxide crystals from the liquid. The crystals are washed to remove any impurities and then heated at 2000 to 2200 °F (1090 to 1200 °C). The heat drives out water, leaving a fine white powder of alumina. The alumina is composed of aluminum and oxygen. To recover the alumina that did not precipitate, manufacturers take the liquid and refine it with a new batch of bauxite and sodium hydroxide. Small amounts of lime and soda ash may also be added.

Smelting the alumina separates the aluminum in the powder from the oxygen. The smelting is done by the *Hall-Héroult process.* Two scientists, Charles Martin Hall of the United States and Paul L. T. Héroult of France, developed this method independently in 1886.

Aluminum producers begin the Hall-Héroult process by dissolving the alumina in a chemical bath composed mainly of *cryolite* (sodium aluminum fluoride). The bath also contains a little aluminum fluoride and calcium fluoride. The bath is held in large rectangular steel containers and heated to about 1740 °F (950 °C). The containers, called *pots* or *cells,* have a carbon lining.

In a process called *electrolytic reduction,* one or more carbon blocks suspended in each pot send an electric current through the bath. The current flows to the carbon lining, completing the electric circuit. The blocks act as the *anode,* or positive pole of the circuit, and the lining acts as the *cathode,* or negative pole. As the current flows through the bath, the alumina breaks apart. The oxygen in the alumina combines with the carbon in the anode and is released as carbon dioxide gas. The aluminum metal collects at the cathode at the bottom of the pot. See **Electrolysis.**

An aluminum plant may have as many as 200 pots electrically connected to one another in long rows called *potlines.* The reduction of alumina to aluminum goes on continuously. Alumina is added to the pots regularly, and the electric current keeps the bath at the proper temperature. A large pot may produce more than 2 tons (1.8 metric tons) of aluminum daily.

How aluminum is made

Aluminum comes from *bauxite,* an ore that has a large amount of a compound called *alumina.* Aluminum making involves separating the alumina and then obtaining aluminum from it.

WORLD BOOK diagram by Arthur Grebetz

Bauxite is crushed and then mixed with a solution of *caustic soda.* A tank called a *digester* heats the mixture under pressure. The heat and pressure cause the alumina in the bauxite to dissolve in the caustic soda, forming a solution of *sodium aluminate.* The other materials in the bauxite, which are called *red mud,* remain as solids and are filtered out.

Alumina comes out of the sodium aluminate solution in a tank called a *precipitator.* The solution is *agitated* (stirred) in the precipitator after crystals of aluminum hydroxide have been added. The stirring causes alumina in the solution to collect on the crystals. The solution is then filtered to separate the crystals, which are heated in a *kiln* (oven). The heat drives the water out of the aluminum hydroxide, leaving a fine white powder of alumina.

Aluminum is made in a carbon-lined pot. The alumina is first dissolved in a chemical bath in the pot. Carbon blocks suspended in the pot send an electric current through the bath. The current breaks the alumina apart, and molten aluminum collects at the bottom of the pot. The aluminum is siphoned into a pot called a *crucible* and later cast into forms called *ingots* and *billets.*

Casting the molten aluminum. About once a day, molten aluminum from the potlines is drawn off into pots called *crucibles.* Each crucible holds 4,000 to 8,000 pounds (1,800 to 3,600 kilograms) of aluminum. Most of the aluminum is cast into ingots. There are two types of ingots: (1) fabricating ingots and (2) foundry ingots. Aluminum is also cast into forms called *billets* and into thin slabs.

Fabricating ingots, or *rolling ingots,* are used by aluminum producers to make plates, sheets, and foil. The ingots may be 30 feet (9 meters) long, 6 feet (1.8 meters) wide, and 2 feet (0.6 meter) thick. They may weigh up to 18 tons (16 metric tons).

To make fabricating ingots, producers alloy other metals with the molten aluminum in a furnace and then purify the mixture. Scrap aluminum and recycled aluminum may also be added. The purification process, called *fluxing,* usually consists of pumping chlorine, or a mixture of chlorine with argon and nitrogen, through the liquid. The gas causes impurities to float to the surface, where they are skimmed off. Water vapor in the air reacts with aluminum metal to produce hydrogen gas along with oxides and hydroxides of aluminum. Some of this hydrogen gas becomes trapped in the molten aluminum. *Degassing* involves the addition of one or more gases to the liquid to remove the hydrogen. Gases used in this process include argon, chlorine, and nitrogen, either alone or in various combinations.

After fluxing and degassing, the molten aluminum alloy is filtered to remove solid impurities. It is then cast into ingots, usually by the *direct chill method,* also known as *direct chill casting.* In this process, the alloy is poured into a cooled mold. The mold helps solidify the outside of the ingot, but the core remains molten. The ingot then passes through a spray of cold water. The water quickly cools and hardens the entire alloy.

Foundry ingots, also called *alloy ingots* or *remelt ingots,* weigh 4 to 50 pounds (1.8 to 23 kilograms). In most cases, the molten aluminum is poured from the crucibles directly into molds, where it cools and hardens gradually. Aluminum producers sell foundry ingots to plants called *foundries.* The foundries remelt the ingots with scrap and recycled aluminum and perform the alloying, fluxing, and degassing operations themselves. The alloyed aluminum is then recast and turned into parts for appliances, automobiles, and other products. Aluminum producers supply some foundry ingots in alloy form. Foundries near aluminum plants may buy molten aluminum that comes directly from the potlines to eliminate the need for remelting.

Billets are made either in long rectangular shapes that look like railroad ties or in the shape of logs. They are produced in the same way as fabricating ingots. Billets can be made into *bars, rods,* and parts for thousands of items. Bars look like small rectangular billets. Bars may also be hexagonal or octagonal. Rods look like small pole-shaped billets. Bars and rods are made into tubing, wire, and various other products.

Thin slabs are made by *roll casting*—that is, by feeding molten aluminum alloy between two cooled rolls. The aluminum solidifies into a slab less than 1 inch (2.5 centimeters) thick. Roll-cast slabs are then further rolled to produce aluminum plates, sheets, strips, or foil.

How aluminum is shaped and finished

Aluminum ingots and billets can be shaped by any of the metalworking processes. These processes include (1) rolling, (2) casting, (3) extruding, (4) drawing, (5) deep drawing, (6) forging, and (7) machining. After the aluminum is shaped, various finishes may be applied.

Rolling consists of reducing the thickness of fabricating ingots by squeezing them between pairs of heavy rollers. The ingots are heated and then rolled to a thickness of 1 to 3 inches (2.5 to 7.6 centimeters). After cooling, the metal is rolled again to form plates, sheets, or foil. Aluminum plates are ¼ inch (6.4 millimeters) thick or more. They are used in applications in which heavy construction is required, such as in railroad cars, ships, and storage tanks. Aluminum sheets measure ⁶⁄₁₀₀₀ to ¼ inch (0.15 to 6.4 millimeters) thick. They are used for the "skins" of airplanes and in such products as awnings and body panels for motor vehicles. Aluminum foil is less than ⁶⁄₁₀,₀₀₀ inch (0.15 millimeter) thick. It has many household uses, especially in cooking and in wrapping food. Rolling may be used to shape aluminum billets into bars and rods.

Casting is a process in which alloyed foundry ingots are melted and then poured or forced into molds of a desired shape. The aluminum is removed from the molds after it hardens. Casting is used to make parts of particular items, such as the bottoms of electric irons or parts for automobile engines. See **Cast and casting.**

Some shapes of aluminum

Reynolds Aluminum

Aluminum sheeting is made by squeezing ingots between pairs of heavy rollers. The sheeting shown above will be used for the *siding* (outside walls) of buildings.

Aluminum Company of America

Aluminum tubing is formed by forcing a billet or rod through an opening in a tool called a *die.* The tubing above will be used in air-conditioning units.

Aluminum Company of America

An aluminum forging is made by hammering an ingot or billet into the desired shape. This forging will be installed in the tail section of an airplane.

Extruding consists of forcing a heated billet through an opening in a tool called a *die.* A ram at one end of a cylinder forces the billet through a die opening at the other end. The aluminum comes out shaped like the die opening. The extrusion process is used to make rods and tubing, trim for automobiles, and frames for doors and windows. See **Extrusion.**

Drawing produces aluminum wire and tubing. To make wire, a pointed aluminum rod is pulled through a series of successively smaller dies. The aluminum rod becomes wire when it reaches a diameter of less than ⅜ inch (9.5 millimeters). Tubing is made by pulling an aluminum rod through one die. A steel bar called a *mandrel* extends through the center of the die and hollows out the rod.

Deep drawing forms aluminum into beverage cans, beer barrels, pots and pans, and various other containers. In this process, a ram forces aluminum plate or an aluminum sheet into a cavity of the desired shape.

Forging is the process of hammering or pressing heated aluminum ingots or billets into the desired shape. Forging produces exceptionally strong parts for use in aircraft landing gear, truck wheels, tools, and various other items. See **Forging.**

Machining. Aluminum can be shaped with a variety of machine tools, including drills, grinders, saws, and shears. Such tools shape aluminum bars and rods into bolts, screws, and other small items. Machining may also be used to put final touches on products that have been cast or forged. See **Machine tool.**

Other shaping processes produce aluminum in such forms as powders and pastes, which consist of finely ground particles of aluminum. Aluminum powder goes into such products as explosives and inks. In paste form, aluminum is used in paints and in metallic finishes for automobiles.

Aluminum powder is also used to produce gears and other small parts by a process called *powder metallurgy.* In this process, the aluminum powder is pressed into the desired shape and then heated to bond the particles together. Powders of other metals also may be mixed with the aluminum. Powders of aluminum alloys also may be used. The item is further shaped by forging or some other process. See **Powder metallurgy.**

Finishing aluminum. Aluminum has an attractive natural appearance and so is often used without a special finish. However, various finishes may be used for decoration or to improve resistance to corrosion and wear. More kinds of finishes can be applied to aluminum than to any other metal. There are four types of finishes. They are (1) mechanical, (2) chemical, (3) electrochemical, and (4) applied.

Mechanical finishes include such processes as *embossing* and polishing. In embossing, a raised pattern is made on aluminum sheets by passing them between rollers that have been engraved with a design. A method called *barrel burnishing* polishes aluminum articles in a revolving or vibrating barrel that contains an *abrasive* (gritty) substance.

Chemical finishes include acid and alkaline *etches,* which eat designs into aluminum. Acid etches are also used to remove stains from the metal and to prepare it for further finishing. Alkaline etches may be used to give aluminum a dull finish.

Electrochemical finishes include *anodizing* and *electroplating.* Anodizing thickens aluminum's natural coating of aluminum oxide and thus increases resistance to corrosion, scratching, and wear. It also makes aluminum easy to dye. Electroplating involves coating aluminum with another metal. Certain coatings improve aluminum's corrosion resistance, electrical conduction, or other properties. See **Anodizing; Electroplating.**

Applied finishes include such coatings as enamel, lacquer, paint, and plastic film. They may be applied by dipping, spraying, rolling, or other methods.

The aluminum industry

About 40 countries produce aluminum. The world's annual aluminum production totals about 71 million tons (64 million metric tons). China, the leading aluminum producer, accounts for about half of the world total.

The *primary aluminum industry* consists of companies that produce aluminum ingots and billets and shape them into such forms as plates, sheets, foil, bars, rods, and wires. The firms also sell the ingots and billets to foundries in the *secondary aluminum industry,* which specializes in shaping aluminum. Specialized workers in the primary aluminum industry include engineers, geologists, and metallurgists.

In China, the primary aluminum industry produces about 39 million tons (36 million metric tons) of metal a year. Aluminum Corporation of China Limited (Chalco) is the country's leading aluminum producer.

In Russia, the primary aluminum industry produces approximately 4 million tons (3.6 million metric tons) of metal annually. Russia's leading aluminum producer is United Company Rusal, which was formed by the merger of the Russian Aluminum Company (Rusal), the Siberian Ural Aluminum Company (SUAL), and Glencore International AG.

In the United States, the primary aluminum industry produces about 980,000 tons (890,000 metric tons) of the metal yearly. The leading aluminum companies in the United States are Alcoa Corporation and Century Aluminum Company. Aluminum producers in the United States import almost all of their bauxite, chiefly from Brazil and Jamaica. Aluminum producers also import alumina from such countries as Australia, Brazil, and Jamaica.

In Canada, the primary aluminum industry produces about 3 ¼ million tons (2.9 million metric tons) of the

Leading aluminum-producing countries

Tons of aluminum produced in a year

China	●●●●●●●●●●●●●● 39,500,000 tons (35,800,000 metric tons)
India	●◖ 4,100,000 tons (3,700,000 metric tons)
Russia	●◖ 4,000,000 tons (3,600,000 metric tons)
Canada	●◖ 3,200,000 tons (2,900,000) metric tons)
United Arab Emirates	● 2,900,000 tons (2,600,000 metric tons)

Figures are for 2018.
Source: U.S. Geological Survey.

Leading aluminum-producing states and provinces

Annual aluminum-producing capacity*

Quebec	●●●●●●●●●●●●●●
	2,712,000 tons (2,460,000 metric tons)
Kentucky	●●◖
	518,000 tons (470,000 metric tons)
Washington	●●◖
	468,000 tons (425,000 metric tons)
British Columbia	●●
	424,000 tons (385,000 metric tons)
Indiana	●◖
	297,000 tons (269,000 metric tons)

*Capacity may be greater than actual production.
Figures are for 2018.
Sources: U.S. Geological Survey; Natural Resources Canada.

metal yearly. The vast majority of Canada's aluminum is made in Quebec. The country's leading aluminum manufacturer is Rio Tinto Alcan. Alcoa Corporation, based in the United States, also produces a significant amount of aluminum in Canada. Canada produces no bauxite. It imports most of this ore from Australia, Guinea, Guyana, and Suriname.

In other countries. Only about a third of the aluminum-producing countries perform each step in aluminum production—mining the bauxite, refining the ore, and smelting the alumina. In some countries, such as Guinea and Jamaica, the industry mines and refines bauxite for export but produces no aluminum. Germany and some other countries import bauxite and then refine it and smelt the alumina. Some countries, including Norway and Tajikistan, import alumina but not bauxite. Countries that perform each step in the production process include Australia, Brazil, and Suriname.

Recycling

Recycling has become an important aspect of the aluminum industry in many countries. Heavily recycled items include used beverage cans, parts from old automobiles, and scrap accumulated during the manufacture of aluminum products.

One benefit of recycling aluminum is that it conserves natural resources. The most important natural resource saved is energy. Recycling saves about 95 percent of the energy required to make aluminum from bauxite. One recycled aluminum can saves enough energy to keep a 100-watt light bulb burning for about 3 ½ hours. In addition, recycling reduces the amount of garbage sent to sanitary landfills.

History

The word *aluminum* comes from the term *alumen*. Alumen is the Latin name for alum, a group of aluminum compounds that occur in nature and which ancient peoples used in dyeing textiles. In 1746, Johann Heinrich Pott, a Prussian chemist, prepared alumina from alum. Scientists believed that alumina was a chemical compound that consisted of oxygen and an unknown metal. The British chemist Sir Humphry Davy called this metal *alumium* and later changed the name to *aluminum*. In 1809, Davy formed an alloy of iron and aluminum by electrically melting alumina with iron and carbon.

The first aluminum. In 1825, Hans Christian Oersted, a Danish physicist, produced the first aluminum. Oersted prepared aluminum chloride from alumina. He then heated the aluminum chloride with an alloy of potassium and mercury, and a small lump of impure aluminum formed in the alloy.

In 1827, Friedrich Wöhler, a German chemist, produced aluminum in the form of a gray powder by heating aluminum chloride with potassium. In 1845, Wöhler produced aluminum particles large enough to be weighed. He discovered that aluminum was lightweight. Wöhler was the first scientist to describe several other properties of aluminum.

In 1854, Henri Étienne Sainte-Claire Deville, a French chemist, improved on Wöhler's method. Deville used sodium instead of potassium to break down aluminum chloride. This process produced larger quantities of aluminum. Commercial aluminum plants using Deville's method soon opened in France. The price of aluminum dropped from $115 (U.S.) a pound ($254 a kilogram) in 1855 to $17 a pound in 1859. However, it was still too costly for widespread use.

Growth of the aluminum industry. In 1886, two scientists—Charles Martin Hall of the United States and Paul L. T. Héroult of France—developed an inexpensive way to make aluminum. Neither scientist knew that the other was working on the problem. However, each thought of dissolving alumina in the mineral cryolite and separating aluminum from the mixture by electrolytic reduction. Today, the Hall-Héroult process is used to produce nearly all the aluminum in the world.

Karl Joseph Bayer, an Austrian chemist, further reduced the cost of aluminum production. In 1888, he patented an inexpensive method for obtaining alumina from bauxite. The aluminum industry still uses the Bayer process to produce alumina. The Hall-Héroult and Bayer processes are described in the section *How aluminum is produced*.

Hall and several business associates organized the Pittsburgh Reduction Company in 1888. The company began producing 50 pounds (23 kilograms) of aluminum a day. The firm changed its name to the Aluminum Company of America (Alcoa) in 1907. By 1909, Alcoa was producing 16,500 tons (14,970 metric tons) a year. The price of aluminum dropped to less than 30 cents a pound (66 cents a kilogram).

Héroult formed a Swiss aluminum company in 1888, but it did not begin production immediately. In 1902, the Northern Aluminium Company, Limited (now Rio Tinto Alcan), was founded in Canada.

Aluminum production soared during World War I (1914-1918) as the fighting nations increased output to help fill their military needs. During the 1920's, the development of new aluminum alloys and of improved methods of turning aluminum into useful products continued to boost production. The Great Depression of the 1930's cut world aluminum output almost in half. But the start of World War II (1939-1945) brought tremendous expansion in production.

After World War II, the aluminum industry developed many products that have become commonplace. The first successful aluminum foil wrap appeared in 1947. Also in the 1940's, aluminum began to replace brass in the base of light bulbs. High-strength aluminum wire for power lines was introduced in 1957. Aluminum cans became popular in the 1960's. Today, nearly all beverage cans are made completely of aluminum.

Recent developments. In the late 1900's, such developing nations as India, Brazil, and China experienced great industrial growth and an increased standard of living. This growth has created new demand for aluminum packaging for foods and beverages, electric transmission cable, automobiles and trucks, and building construction materials.

Increased competition and supply issues have led a number of aluminum countries to join together. In some instances, large companies have bought smaller companies to gain their products and customers. In others, two or more large companies have merged to create even larger corporations. Such corporations can more efficiently supply a wide range of products to customers around the world. Government agencies study merger plans and must give permission for the completion of a merger to avoid creating monopolies.

Kenneth A. Bowman

Questions

What is the Hall-Héroult process? What is the Bayer process?
Why is aluminum wire used for most high-voltage power lines?
Into what forms is molten aluminum cast?
What are some benefits of recycling aluminum?
Why is aluminum usually alloyed with other elements?
How are aluminum plates, sheets, and foil made?

How much bauxite does it take to produce 1 pound (0.5 kilogram) of aluminum?
What factors have contributed to the growth of the aluminum industry in some developing countries?
What is the purpose of anodizing aluminum?
How does aluminum resist corrosion?

Aluminum Company of America (Alcoa). See Alcoa Corporation
Alva, Duke of. See Alba, Duke of.
Alvarado, AHL vah RAH thoh, **Pedro de** (1485?-1541), helped Hernán Cortés subdue the Aztec people in Mexico and later conquered Guatemala. Born in Badajoz, Spain, Alvarado went to the Caribbean in 1510. In 1518, he joined an expedition led by Juan de Grijalva to southern Mexico. Alvarado accompanied Cortés to Mexico in 1519. After Cortés conquered Mexico in 1521, he sent Alvarado to seize Guatemala. Alvarado succeeded in 1524 with American Indian allies. In 1525, he conquered El Salvador for Spain and directed the founding of the capital city, San Salvador. Alvarado became governor of Guatemala. He died on July 4, 1541.   Helen Delpar

See also **Cortés, Hernán; Guatemala** (History); **Latin America** (map: Early exploration of Latin America).
Alyssum, Sweet. See Sweet alyssum.
Alzheimer's disease, AWLTS hy muhrz, often abbreviated as AD, is the most common cause of *dementia* late in life. Dementia is characterized by loss of the ability to think clearly. AD attacks few people younger than age 60, but it becomes increasingly common with age.

Scientists know that changes in the brain occur up to 10 years before symptoms of Alzheimer's disease become apparent. Later, people with AD may forget names, conversations, or recent events. As the disease progresses, memory loss increases, and patients begin to lose other mental functions. Patients can become confused or disoriented, easily getting lost even in familiar locations. In later stages, patients lose the ability to remember or talk meaningfully. Eventually, they cannot care for themselves and become bedridden, requiring constant care. In their weakened condition, patients are vulnerable to pneumonia and other infectious diseases. Most patients die from such infections 10 to 12 years after developing AD.

In the past, elderly adults suffering from severe memory loss were often labeled *senile,* but they were probably suffering from what doctors now recognize as AD. Today, AD affects about half of all people over age 85.

The disease is named for Alois Alzheimer, a German psychiatrist and neurologist. Alzheimer first described the disease at a medical meeting in Europe in 1907.

Diagnosis. There is no single test used to identify people with AD. Patients, or their family members, may first notice increasing forgetfulness, often accompanied by reduced interest in, or awareness of, ongoing activities. Physicians suspect AD if no other disease or disorder is found to explain the symptoms.

An autopsy performed after the patient dies can confirm the diagnosis of AD. In patients with AD, the nerve cells of the parts of the brain responsible for thinking, remembering, and reasoning appear distorted. Examination of brain tissue with a microscope reveals many deposits of a protein called *amyloid.* These abnormal deposits, called *plaques,* are surrounded by damaged and dead nerve cells. Clumps of abnormal, wiry protein, called *neurofibrillary tangles,* are also seen inside the nerve cells. Affected areas of the brain become severely shrunken.

In 2004, scientists developed a method of using *positron emission tomography* (PET) to detect amyloid plaques in the brain before a person shows symptoms of AD. PET produces images of the chemical activity of the brain. The technique uses a radioactive dye that finds and sticks to amyloid deposits and is visible in PET scans. Scientists believe the technique can eventually be used to detect AD and to measure the effectiveness of drugs used to treat it.

Causes. The amyloid plaques and neurofibrillary tangles that characterize AD are rarely found in the brains of healthy people. Therefore, researchers believe that AD results from the development of these abnormal structures. Scientific studies have provided evidence that genetic and environmental factors linked to the formation of amyloid plaques constitute the primary causes of AD.

The plaques found in AD patients are almost entirely made up of *peptides* (protein fragments) called *amyloid-beta peptides* (Aß). In 1986, biologists discovered that Aß is produced from the breakdown of a larger, normally occurring protein called *amyloid precursor protein* (APP). The production of this protein in the body is controlled by a specific gene. Geneticists discovered that mutations in the APP gene could lead to the formation of abnormal Aß protein. Cell biologists found that when mutant APP breaks down, it produces Aß peptides that are especially sticky and prone to forming plaques.

Scientists have also discovered another protein, called *presenilin,* that controls the breakdown of APP in the brain. They found that mutations in the presenilin gene can also lead to AD. Mutated forms of presenilin also enhance the accumulation of amyloid plaques in the brain.

An additional gene associated with the development of AD controls production of a protein called *apolipo-protein E* (apoE). A person inherits two genes for apoE production. There are three variants of the gene: apoE epsilon-2, apoE epsilon-3, and apoE epsilon-4. People who have one or two apoE epsilon-4 genes have a higher risk of developing AD after the age of 60 than people who do not have that variant. However, scientists do not think the apoE epsilon-4 gene alone can cause AD. Some people with two copies of the apoE epsilon-4 gene do not develop AD, while others who do not have the gene at all go on to develop AD.

The neurofibrillary tangles characteristic of AD are composed of an abnormal nerve cell structural protein called *tau.* Scientists have observed a type of dementia caused by mutations in the tau gene. This dementia, called *Pick's disease,* or *fronto-temporal dementia,* is similar to AD. The mutations lead to the development of neurofibrillary tangles, but amyloid plaques characteristic of AD are absent.

Not all instances of AD in people can be linked to genetic causes. Scientists have been successful in discovering some specific environmental factors that are connected to the development of AD, such as head injuries.

Treatment. There is no cure for Alzheimer's disease. Drugs called *cholinesterase inhibitors* (ChEI's) can temporarily relieve symptoms of AD. These drugs block the action of the enzyme *cholinesterase,* which breaks down acetylcholine in the brain. Acetylcholine, a chemical that transmits nerve impulses, is reduced in AD patients as brain cells die. However, ChEI's provide only modest and temporary improvement of symptoms, because they do nothing to stop the death of nerve cells. The drugs do not alter the course of the disease.

Scientists are experimenting with a number of treatments for delaying, halting, or reversing the course of Alzheimer's disease. Some researchers are investigating drugs that prevent amyloid from accumulating and forming plaques. Scientists are also working to develop a vaccine against AD. The vaccine would spur the immune system to attack and destroy Aß protein, preventing the accumulation of amyloid plaques.

Proper nutrition, good hygiene, and reassurance can help preserve the comfort and dignity of AD patients. Several organizations, including the Alzheimer's Association in the United States, the Alzheimer Society of Canada, and Alzheimer's Australia, offer support and information to patients and their families.   Sam Gandy

See also **Senility.**

A.M. stands for the Latin words *ante meridiem,* which mean *before noon.* See **Hour.**

AMA. See **American Medical Association.**

Amadís of Gaul, *AM uh dihs,* is a famous Spanish romance of chivalry. It may have appeared in Spain in the 1300's, but the first preserved version, *The Four Books of the Virtuous Knight Amadís of Gaul,* was published in 1508. At least part of the work is attributed to Garci Ordóñez (or Rodríguez) de Montalvo.

The story describes the adventures of a romantic, brave, modest hero named Amadís. His aristocratic manners and his strict sense of justice reveal a Renaissance interpretation of the ideal medieval knight. The story is marked by flowery prose. The episodes deal with spectacular and fantastic events, including knightly duels, magic spells, and fierce combat with giants and dragons. Young Amadís loves Princess Oriana and, despite many obstacles and temptations, he remains faithful to her until they are married. The Spanish author Miguel de Cervantes was influenced by *Amadís* when he created *Don Quixote.*   Harry Sieber

Amado, *ah MAH doh,* **Jorge,** *ZHAWR zhay* (1912-2001), was a Brazilian novelist. Amado was born on Aug. 10, 1912, in Ilhéus in the state of Bahia, along the northeastern coast of Brazil. He wrote mainly about the people of Brazil's lower classes living in his native region, especially the area around the port of Salvador. In a style that is both poetic and realistic, Amado used the language of these people to portray their infectious zest for life.

Before 1958, Amado wrote essentially Marxist novels, such as *Jubiaba* (1935) and *The Violent Land* (1942), which reflected his sympathy for victims of social injustice. Between 1937 and 1952, he was exiled several times because of his political views. Beginning with *Gabriela, Clove and Cinnamon* (1958), he wrote in a more sophisticated style that emphasized satirical humor. Many critics regard *The Two Deaths of Quincas Wateryell* (1961) as his masterpiece.

Amado made an important contribution to Brazilian literature by becoming the first major writer to praise his nation's extensive African heritage. This theme dominates one of his finest works, *Tent of Miracles* (1969). Among his other novels are *Dona Flor and Her Two Husbands* (1966), *Tieta* (1977), *Pen, Sword, Camisole* (1979), *Showdown* (1984), and *The War of the Saints* (1993). Amado died on Aug. 6, 2001.   Earl E. Fitz

Amalekites, *uh MAL uh kyts,* were a desert people who lived south of Canaan in biblical times. Canaan consisted roughly of an area extending east of the Jordan River to the Mediterranean Sea. The Israelites considered the Amalekites their oldest enemies. Joshua defeated the Amalekites in the late 1200's B.C. King Saul defeated them 200 years later. Afterward, the Amalekites destroyed Ziklag, the town where David and his followers lived. David found them celebrating this victory. He killed many, but 400 escaped.   H. Darrell Lance

Amalgamated Clothing and Textile Workers Union. See UNITE HERE.

Amanites, *uh MAN nyts,* are members of a religious group called the Amana Church Society. The word *Amana* comes from the Song of Solomon 4:8. It is the name of a mountain, and means *true* or *fixed.*

Eberhard Gruber and Johann Rock founded the society in Germany in 1714. It was originally called the Community of True Inspiration. Members led simple lives according to the word of God, revealed in the Bible and in the "true inspiration" of their prophets. The last leader believed to be inspired died in 1885. But the group continued to read and study the testimonies of their past prophets. Christian Metz and Barbara Heinemann led the group to the United States in 1842. It settled near Buffalo, New York, and was called the Ebenezer Society. Members owned villages and lands in common. They moved near Cedar Rapids, Iowa, in 1855. They founded seven villages: Amana, East Amana, High Amana, Homestead, Middle Amana, South Amana, and West Amana. They farmed and made woolen goods and drugs.

The society gave up its communal economic life in 1932, during the Great Depression. But the villagers continue to live a simple life, making crafts and operating restaurants that serve traditional foods. The society became a cooperative stock company that manufactured household appliances. The religious members organized the Amana Church Society.   Charles H. Lippy

See also **Iowa** (Places to visit).

Amaranth, *AM uh ranth,* is the common name of a *genus* (group) of plants that includes weeds, garden flowers, and crops. This genus is made up chiefly of herbs. Amaranths grow widely, especially in warm climates. The name *amaranth* comes from a Greek word meaning *unfading.* It was given to amaranths because their flowers retain their color even when dried.

Among the weeds that belong to the amaranth genus are *giant pigweed* (often called *redroot), spreading pigweed,* and a kind of tumbleweed. *Love-lies-bleeding* is an ornamental amaranth with long, drooping, crimson flower clusters. The *purple amaranth* is a tall plant with late-blooming, pinkish-purple flower clusters. Amaranths cultivated for their edible seeds are called *grain amaranths.* Amaranth seeds were an important food for the Aztec and Inca Indians.   Anton A. Reznicek

Scientific classification. Amaranths make up the genus *Amaranthus.* The scientific name for the love-lies-bleeding is *A. caudatus.* Purple amaranth is *A. cruentus.*

See also **Tumbleweed.**

Amarillo, *AM uh RIHL oh* (pop. 190,695; met. area pop. 251,933), is the largest city and commercial center of the Panhandle of northern Texas. It serves as a major distribution and processing center for cattle, oil, and other products. For its location, see **Texas** (political map).

Cattle auctions held by the Amarillo Livestock Auction rank among the largest in the state. Several large beef-processing plants operate in Amarillo. Large deposits of oil and natural gas lie in the Panhandle, and Amarillo has many petrochemical plants. The city lies in one of the world's chief helium-producing areas. An assembly and disassembly plant for United States nuclear weapons is northeast of the city. Other industries produce aviation equipment, copper, and fiberglass.

Amarillo's cultural attractions include an art museum, a community theater, and a symphony orchestra. Downtown Amarillo has a Civic Center with convention and entertainment facilities. The Amarillo area is home to West Texas A&M University and a branch of the Texas Tech University medical school. The American Quarter Horse Association, the world's largest horse registry, is based in Amarillo. Palo Duro Canyon, a major tourist attraction, is just southeast of the city.

In 1887, construction crews of the Fort Worth and Denver City Railway founded the settlement of Ragtown near what is now Amarillo. In the same year, a land developer laid out the site of Amarillo near the settlement. Settlers called the town *Amarillo,* which means *yellow* in Spanish. The name may refer to the yellowish soil that borders nearby Amarillo Creek.

Amarillo grew rapidly during the early 1900's, when other railroads began to serve the community and oil and natural gas were discovered in the area. Today, manufacturing and such service industries as education, government, and health care support Amarillo's economy. The city has a commission-manager form of government and is the seat of Potter County.

Carol Roark

Amaryllis, *AM uh RIHL ihs,* is a small group of plants native to western South Africa that have beautiful, funnel-shaped flowers. Two *species* (kinds) of amaryllis exist. Both are grown as bulbs. Both have long stems and long, narrow leaves. Their flowers are made up of three petals and three petallike structures called *sepals.*

WORLD BOOK illustration by Christabel King

An ornamental amaranth called *love-lies-bleeding* has a number of long, drooping clusters of crimson flowers.

WORLD BOOK illustration by Richard Lewington, The Garden Studio

An amaryllis has a long stem and trumpet-shaped flowers. The belladonna lily, *pictured here*, is a popular species.

The *belladonna lily* is the better-known species of amaryllis. It is a popular garden plant. Although it resembles a lily in many ways, most scientists do not consider the belladonna lily to be a true lily. The stalk of the belladonna lily is 18 to 30 inches (46 to 76 centimeters) high. It is topped by a cluster of 6 to 10 flowers. The fragrant blossoms are usually 3 inches (8 centimeters) long and vary in color from rose-red to white.

The other species of amaryllis was discovered in the late 1900's. It is so rare that it does not have a common name. Its flowers are typically pink-colored.

The word *amaryllis* is also used as the name of the plant family to which the two species of amaryllis belong. *Amaryllis* is also sometimes used to describe flowers that look like those of the belladonna lily but are not true amaryllises.   August A. De Hertogh

Scientific classification. Amaryllises make up the genus *Amaryllis,* in the amaryllis family, Amaryliidaceae. The belladonna lily is *Amaryllis belladonna.* The other species of amaryllis is *A. paradisicola.*

Amateur Athletic Union (AAU) is an organization that promotes and develops amateur sports and physical fitness programs in the United States. The AAU is a nonprofit, volunteer group.

The largest program sponsored by the organization is the Junior Olympic Games. In this annual competition, young people compete in such sports as basketball, gymnastics, swimming, track and field, and wrestling. The AAU sponsors other athletic competitions at the local, state, regional, and national level. The organization also conducts adult sports programs and physical fitness programs for youth and adults. In addition, the AAU annually presents the James E. Sullivan Award to the nation's outstanding amateur athlete. The award is named for an early AAU executive.

The AAU was founded in 1888. It has headquarters in Lake Buena Vista, Florida.

Critically reviewed by the Amateur Athletic Union of the United States

Amateur radio. See Radio, Amateur.

Amati family, *ah MAH tee,* was a family of violin makers who worked in Cremona, Italy, from the 1500's to the 1700's. Amati violins come in a variety of varnish tones

ranging from dark red to light yellow. The violins have refined proportions and curves, and a high-arched shaping of the top. The arch helps produce a sweet, somewhat restrained soprano sound that was preferred for the intimate ensemble music popular in the 1600's.

Andrea Amati (about 1511-1579) was one of the first violin makers to give the instrument its distinctive shape and features. His work was carried on by his sons, Antonio (born about 1540) and Girolamo (1561-1630). Girolamo's son Nicolo (1596-1684) was the most famous and influential Amati. Nicolo trained many instrument makers, including Andrea Guarneri and Antonio Stradivari. Nicolo's son, Girolamo II (1649-1740), was the last violin maker in the family.   Abram Loft

Amazon. See Amazons.

Amazon rain forest, *AM uh zahn,* is the world's largest tropical rain forest. It covers approximately 2 million square miles (5.2 million square kilometers) in South America's Amazon River Basin. About two-thirds of the forest lies in Brazil. The forest also occupies parts of eight other countries, with the largest areas in Bolivia, Colombia, Peru, and Venezuela. The Amazon rain forest receives an average annual rainfall of 60 to 175 inches (152 to 445 centimeters). Temperatures average about 80 °F (27 °C).

Trees in most of the Amazon rain forest grow in several distinct layers. Some trees, called *emergents,* tower above the rest of the forest and may reach heights of more than 130 feet (40 meters). The *upper canopy* generally grows 80 to 130 feet (24 to 40 meters) high. Plants called *epiphytes,* or *air plants,* thrive in this layer. Aroids, bromeliads, ferns, liverworts, mosses, and orchids grow on high branches and tree trunks in the upper canopy. One or two *lower canopies* consist of saplings of the trees in the upper canopy, plus smaller trees and shrubs. *Lianas* (woody vines) wind around tree trunks and branches, extending from the ground to the upper canopy. The canopies get sunlight, but they prevent much light from reaching the forest floor. Most of the Amazon rain forest has soil with low fertility.

The Amazon rain forest contains a wider variety of

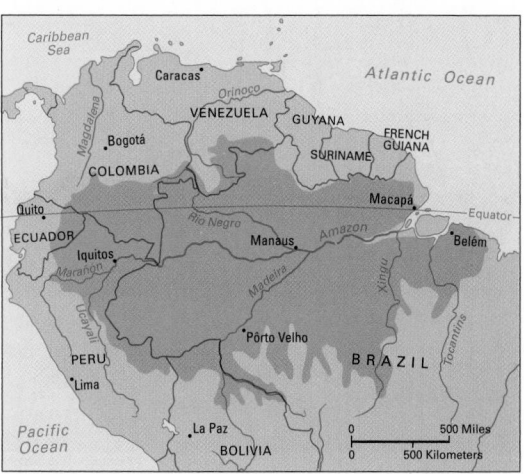

WORLD BOOK map

Amazon rain forest covers much of northern South America. About two-thirds of the rain forest lies in Brazil. The rain forest also occupies parts of several other countries.

Trees in the Amazon rain forest grow in several different layers, including the *upper canopy* and *lower canopies.* The tallest trees, called *emergents,* may reach heights of more than 130 feet (40 meters). The canopies block much sunlight from reaching the floor of the rain forest. This picture shows part of the rain forest in Peru.

© Andrew McLachlan, age fotostock

plant and animal life than any other place in the world. Tens of thousands of different *species* (kinds) of plants live there. A 2 ½-acre (1-hectare) area of the rain forest may contain up to 280 or more species of trees. Many economically important plants live in the rain forest. They yield such products as Brazil nuts, cocoa, *curare* (an important drug), dyes, pineapples, and rubber. More than 1,300 species of birds make their homes in the rain forest. The region's rivers contain as many as 3,000 species of fish. Millions of different insect species live in the forest.

Increasing demands for land and natural resources have seriously threatened the Amazon rain forest. Loggers cut down trees for wood products. Ranchers and farmers clear land to graze beef cattle and to grow such crops as soybeans.

Areas of the rain forest that have been cleared can regenerate. However, regenerated areas are much less diverse than the original forest. Large areas of the Amazon rain forest have been destroyed. Development, *deforestation* (the destruction of forests), disease, and gold mining also threaten the cultures of the few remaining native peoples of the Amazon rain forest. Many of these people depend on the forest to support themselves.

Oliver T. Coomes

See also **Forest** (Deforestation); **Rain forest; Yanomami Indians.**

Amazon River, *AM uh zahn,* is the world's second longest river and the chief river of South America. Only the Nile River in Africa is longer. The Amazon is 4,000 miles (6,437 kilometers) long. It carries more water than any other river and more than the Mississippi, Nile, and Yangtze rivers together. Each year, the Amazon delivers 15 percent of the fresh water that enters the ocean.

The Amazon is too wide at many points for a person on one bank to see the opposite shore. The river ranges from 1 ½ to 6 miles (2.4 to 10 kilometers) wide for most of its course. It widens to about 90 miles (140 kilometers) at its mouth. The Amazon's depth averages about 40 feet (12 meters) and increases to more than 300 feet (90 meters) in some places. The Amazon has a vast flood plain that covers 38,200 square miles (98,938 square kilometers) and is under water for up to half the year. Water levels fluctuate from 13 to 43 feet (4 to 13 meters) between low and high water.

The Amazon River Basin covers about 2,700,000 square miles (7,000,000 square kilometers) and includes the world's largest tropical rain forest. The temperature averages about 80° F (27° C) and varies little throughout the year. Rainfall in the Amazon region ranges from 60 inches (152 centimeters) in low-lying areas to 175 inches (445 centimeters) near the Andes Mountains in Peru.

Most ships enter the Amazon River via the Pará River, south of Marajó Island. Ocean vessels can sail about 2,300 miles (3,700 kilometers) up the Amazon to Iquitos, Peru. Belém, on the Pará River about 90 miles (140 kilometers) from the Atlantic coast, and Manaus, 1,000 miles (1,600 kilometers) upstream from the mouth of the Amazon, are important ports. Ships bring in clothing, food, equipment, machinery, oil, and other products. They pick up such raw materials as Brazil nuts, cattle, soy-

© Frontpage/Shutterstock

Deforestation is a serious threat to the natural environment and *Indigenous* (native) peoples of the Amazon rain forest. Loggers, farmers, and ranchers clear large areas of the forest, sometimes illegally, to obtain wood, grow crops, and graze cattle.

Amazon River

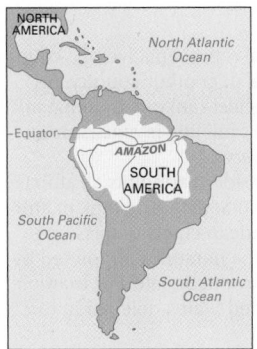

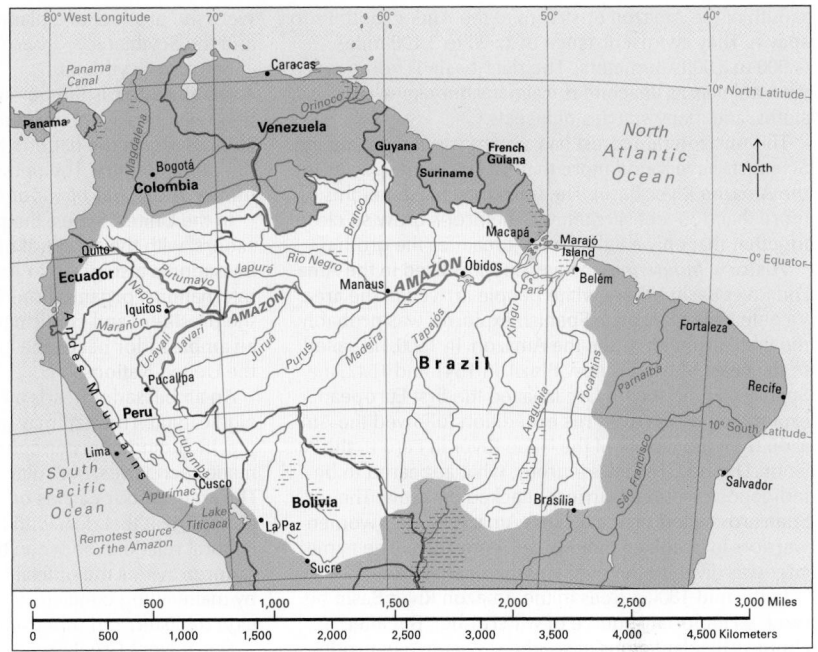

Amazon River drainage basin

International boundary

• City

Swamp

WORLD BOOK maps

beans, and other agricultural products; lumber; and rubber. They also take aboard live birds, fish, and other animals for pet shops and zoos.

The course of the Amazon begins high in the Andes of Peru as a small stream that flows into the Apurímac River. The Apurímac is 17,200 feet (5,240 meters) above sea level. It flows northwest into the Ucayali River, the southern branch of the Amazon in Peru. The Ucayali flows north, down through the Andean foothills, then turns east and joins the Marañón River, the Amazon's northern branch. This junction occurs near Iquitos and forms the main channel of the Amazon. The river continues eastward across Brazil and flows into the Atlantic Ocean north of Marajó Island.

The rivers that form the Amazon tumble rapidly through the Andes and fall about 16,400 feet (5,000 meters) in the first 600 miles (970 kilometers). The Amazon itself falls about 340 feet (100 meters) between Iquitos and the Atlantic Ocean, which lies about 2,300 miles

(3,700 kilometers) east. The river flows at about 1 ½ miles (2.4 kilometers) per hour during the dry season. Its flow increases to about 3 miles (5 kilometers) per hour when it is swollen by rain, during the annual flood.

More than 1,000 tributaries flow into the Amazon. They include the Japurá, Juruá, Madeira, Purus, Tapajós, Xingu, and Rio Negro rivers. Few of the tributaries have dams that help generate electricity, and no dam or bridge spans the Amazon.

An unusually high ocean tide occasionally overpowers the current at the mouth of the Amazon. This creates a wall of water called a *bore* that typically measures up to 6.5 feet (2 meters) high and rushes upstream.

Animal and plant life. Many kinds of fish live in the Amazon River and the lakes on its flood plain. They include the fierce, flesh-eating piranha and the arapaima, one of South America's largest freshwater fish. Many aquarium fish sold in pet shops come from the Amazon. Some species of river catfish migrate from near the

© DeAgostini/Getty Images

The Amazon is the world's second longest river and carries more water than any other river. It originates in Peru, in western South America. It then flows eastward through Brazil and empties into the Atlantic Ocean. This picture shows bends in the Amazon in Peru.

mouth of the Amazon upstream to the Andes foothills to spawn. They swim a distance of 2,500 to 3,100 miles (4,000 to 5,000 kilometers). The river basin is home to such animals as anacondas, caimans, monkeys, parrots, sloths, and many species of insects.

The Amazon rain forest has a great variety of plant life. Scientists have found more than 40,000 plant species in the Amazon River Basin. The trees may reach heights of more than 130 feet (40 meters). Their tops grow so close together that only a little sunlight reaches the ground.

History. *Indigenous* (native) peoples lived in the Amazon River Basin before white people arrived in the area. Vicente Yañez Pinzón, a Spanish explorer, was probably the first European to see the Amazon. In 1500, he sailed to the coast of what is now Brazil. In 1541 and 1542, the Spaniard Francisco de Orellana led the first European exploration of the river. His expedition followed the Amazon from the mouth of the Napo River in Peru to the Atlantic. During Orellana's journey, what appeared to be Indigenous women warriors attacked his crew. The Spaniards called their attackers Amazons, after women warriors in Greek mythology (see **Amazons**). The name later was given to the river and the nearby area.

In the mid-1800's, trees in the Amazon River Basin became an important source of wild rubber. But after about 1910, plantations in southern Asia began producing rubber more cheaply. The demand for Amazon rubber fell, and the regional economy collapsed. Since the 1960's, Brazil's government has built more and more highways and airports in the Amazon River Basin. New towns and farms have been established in this region, and its population has grown. Today, more than half of the Amazon's people live in towns and cities.

Increasing demands for natural resources threaten the Amazon rain forest. Forest fires, mining, and the clearing of land for agriculture and industry have caused rapid destruction of the local plant and animal life.   Oliver T. Coomes

See also **Amazon rain forest; Brazil** (The Amazon Region); **Orellana, Francisco de.**

Amazons, *AM uh zahnz,* were a tribe of warrior women in Greek mythology. To the male-centered Greeks of the 400's B.C., the Amazons symbolized all that was barbaric and non-Greek. The Greeks believed that the Amazons inhabited a remote region of Asia Minor and maintained their female culture by mating periodically with men of neighboring tribes. The women sent their sons back to the tribes of their fathers, or enslaved them, rearing only the girls.

The name *Amazon* is usually taken to mean *breastless.* The women, according to some sources, seared off the right breast of each daughter so she could shoot the bow and arrow more easily.

Many references to Amazons appear in ancient Greek literature. For example, the Amazon queen Penthesileia aided the Trojans against the Greeks in the Trojan War. After killing many Greeks, she was killed by the Greek warrior Achilles.

Some scholars believe that the concept of a race of women warriors originated when the Greeks fought the Scythians, a people who lived north of the Black Sea. Scythian women sometimes fought alongside the men and had masculine habits. The Greek historian Herodotus believed the Sarmatians, who replaced the Scythians,

were the product of a planned union of the Amazons and the Scythians.   Nancy Felson

See also **Scythians.**

Ambassador is the personal representative of a country's head of state at the capital of another country. An ambassador is the nation's highest-ranking diplomat in the other country. The person's full title is *ambassador extraordinary and plenipotentiary.*

In the United States, the president appoints all ambassadors, with the approval of the Senate. The rank of ambassador is also given to American chiefs of mission to international organizations if the person is appointed by the president and confirmed by the Senate. For example, an ambassador heads the United States delegation to the United Nations.

An ambassador heads a country's embassy in the foreign capital. The staff may number several hundred people, including minister-counselors, counselors, diplomatic secretaries, consular officers, attachés, and clerks. The ambassador carries on negotiations with the foreign government that deal with the political, economic, and cultural relations between the two nations. The ambassador provides the official channel of communications by maintaining contacts with the head of state, the foreign minister, and other officials.

The ancient Greeks were among the first people to exchange diplomatic representatives. The Congress of Vienna in 1814 and 1815 and the Congress of Aix-la-Chapelle in 1818 placed diplomacy on a systematic basis by creating four classes of representatives. These classes consisted of ambassadors (the highest rank), ministers, ministers resident, and chargés d'affaires. During its early history, the United States appointed representatives of the three lower ranks. In 1893, the United States appointed its first ambassadors—to France, Germany, Italy, and the United Kingdom. Today, the United States assigns ambassadors to all countries with which it has diplomatic relations.   Michael P. Sullivan

See also **Address, Forms of; Consul; Diplomacy; Minister; State, Department of.**

Amber is a hard, yellowish-brown fossilized resin. It comes chiefly from the resins of pine trees that grew in northern Europe millions of years ago. These resins were gummy materials mixed with oils in the trees. When the oils became *oxidized* (combined with oxygen), hard resins were left. These pine trees were buried underground or underwater, and the resins slowly changed into irregularly shaped lumps of amber. Lumps of amber often contain insects that were trapped as the resins flowed from the trees. Some lumps of amber have air bubbles.

The largest supply of amber lies in the Baltic Sea area. It comes from a species of pine tree that is now extinct. Some experts consider this amber the only true amber. Central America has important deposits of amber from other sources. Most amber is mined from a claylike soil called *blue earth.* Amber is used to make beads, mouthpieces for pipes, and other ornaments.

The ancient Greeks called amber *elektron.* When they rubbed amber with cloth, it became electrically charged and attracted bits of lightweight material, such as straw and feathers. The word *electricity* comes from the Greek word *elektron.*   Roger D. Barry

See also **Electricity** (History); **Gem** (picture); **Resin.**

Ambergris, *AM buhr grees* or *AM buhr grihs,* is a waxy substance found in the intestines of some sperm whales. It has a musky smell when dried and was once used in expensive perfumes. Ambergris was added to perfume because its odor made the odor of the perfume last longer. Today, artificial substitutes have almost entirely replaced natural ambergris in perfume making.

Ambergris was once collected chiefly from the bodies of dead sperm whales. The whales also pass ambergris as a waste product, and clumps of it can sometimes be found in the water or on shore.   John K. B. Ford

See also **Sperm whale.**

Amberjack is a large, fast-swimming game fish found in warm and tropical oceans. People who fish for sport prize the amberjack for its fierce fighting ability when hooked. Amberjacks have a streamlined body and a sharply forked tail. They are variously colored. Some

WORLD BOOK illustration by John D. Dawson

The greater amberjack is the largest species of this fast-swimming game fish. It may weigh more than 175 pounds (80 kilograms). The greater amberjack lives in tropical seas.

species have a brownish, gray-green, or blue back. Some have silvery sides and deeply colored fins.

There are about a dozen *species* (kinds) of amberjacks. The largest species is the greater amberjack. It may grow more than 6 feet (1.8 meters) in length and may weigh more than 175 pounds (80 kilograms). It lives in tropical seas throughout the world. A species of amberjack called the yellowtail has a bright yellow tail and

Gemological Institute of America

Amber is the fossilized resin of pine trees. Amber is used to make pipestems and jewelry, such as the pendant shown here. Most amber comes from the Baltic Sea area in northern Europe.

a yellowish stripe along the side of the body. It lives in coastal areas of the Pacific Ocean.   Theodore W. Pietsch

Scientific classification. Amberjacks make up the genus *Seriola.* The greater amberjack is *Seriola dumerili.* The yellowtail is *S. lalandei.*

Ambler, Eric (1909-1998), an English author, won fame for his well-constructed novels of intrigue and international adventure. He also wrote screenplays for motion pictures. Ambler's novels include *A Coffin for Dimitrios* (1939), *Journey into Fear* (1940), *The Light of Day* (1963), *The Levanter* (1972), and *The Care of Time* (1981). During World War II (1939-1945), Ambler made educational films for the British Army. He continued writing for motion pictures after the war. His screenplays include *The Cruel Sea* (1953) and *The Wreck of the Mary Deare* (1959). His autobiography, *Here Lies,* was published in 1986. Ambler was born on June 28, 1909, in London and died on Oct. 22, 1998.   David Geherin

Ambrose, Saint (A.D. 340?-397), was a bishop of Milan and one of the most influential people of his time. As bishop, he acted as an adviser for three Roman emperors and defended the freedom of the Christian church from government interference.

Ambrose preached widely. He also wrote essays promoting Christian ethics and upholding the ideal of virginity. In *Concerning Faith* (377), Ambrose defended the belief in the divinity of Jesus Christ against the ideas of the Arians, who believed only God the Father was completely divine (see **Arianism**). Ambrose also helped defeat an attempt to regain government approval of the ancient Roman religion. Historians believe that Ambrose popularized the practice of singing hymns in church. His sermons and piety inspired Saint Augustine to convert to Christianity. Ambrose baptized Augustine in 387.

Ambrose was born in what is now Trier, in western Germany. He pursued a career as a lawyer and provincial governor. The people of Milan chose him as bishop in 374. His feast day is December 7.   Marilyn J. Harran

Ambrosia, *am BROH zhuh,* was a magical substance eaten by the gods of Greek and Roman mythology. Ambrosia was eaten with nectar, the drink of the gods. A human being who ate ambrosia and drank nectar became immortal. The word *ambrosial* means *sweet-smelling* or *delicious.*   Mary R. Lefkowitz

Ambrozic, Aloysius Matthew (1930-2011), was appointed a cardinal of the Roman Catholic Church by Pope John Paul II in 1998. The pope had appointed him archbishop of Toronto in 1990. In 2007, Thomas Collins replaced Ambrozic as archbishop.

Ambrozic was born in Gabrje, Slovenia, then part of Yugoslavia, on Jan. 27, 1930. He settled in Canada in 1948 and studied for the priesthood at St. Augustine's Seminary in Scarborough, Ontario (now part of Toronto). He was ordained a priest in 1955. He served as a professor at St. Augustine's from 1960 to 1967 and dean from 1971 to 1976. He also taught at the Toronto School of Theology from 1970 to 1976.

Ambrozic became auxiliary bishop of the archdiocese of Toronto in 1976 and coadjutor archbishop in 1986. He wrote *The Hidden Kingdom* (1972) and *Remarks on the Canadian Catechism* (1974). Ambrozic died on Aug. 26, 2011.   Robert P. Imbelli

Ambulance is a vehicle designed to transport sick or injured people. Many types of vehicles serve as ambu-

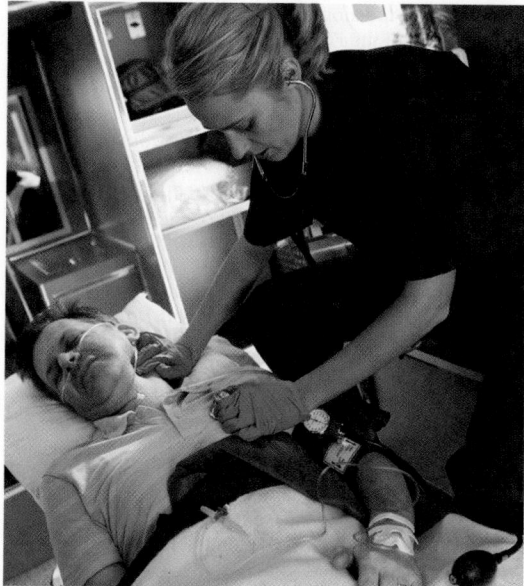

© Shutterstock

Ambulances are staffed by trained medical workers called *paramedics*. Paramedics provide emergency care to patients before they reach the hospital.

lances. Ambulances for ground transport are specially built versions of trucks or vans. They are equipped with flashing lights and sirens for alerting drivers and pedestrians of their approach. Helicopters or airplanes serve as fast transport for the seriously ill or injured. Modern ambulances carry a variety of emergency equipment, including bandages, splints, heart monitors and *defibrillators* (devices to correct abnormal heart rhythms), oxygen machines, and medicines. Highly trained professionals working in ambulances can respond to a wide variety of situations involving serious illness or *trauma* (injury). Ambulances and the professionals that staff them are essential parts of a health care system.

Horses, mules, and camels were used in early times to transport injured people. In the late 1700's, a French military surgeon, Dominique-Jean Larrey, created the earliest vehicles called ambulances. Larrey developed these lightweight wagons to transport wounded soldiers from battlefields.

During the American Civil War (1861-1865), the United States Congress formally established an ambulance system for U.S. armies under the Ambulance Corps Act of 1864. In the late 1860's, Commercial Hospital in Cincinnati, Ohio, and Bellevue Hospital in New York City became the first U.S. hospitals to operate ambulance services for the general public.

Until the late 1950's and the 1960's, ambulances mainly just transported patients to a hospital. Then ambulance design changed greatly to enable the vehicles to carry more medical equipment. The development of such emergency lifesaving measures as cardiopulmonary resuscitation (CPR) and artificial respiration changed how care was provided outside the hospital setting (see **Cardiopulmonary resuscitation**). The development of emergency health-care systems, such as the Emergency Medical Service in the United States, resulted in im-

provements in the design of ambulances and the capabilities of their attendants. Walt Alan Stoy

Ameba, *uh MEE buh,* also spelled amoeba, is a tiny, one-celled organism that usually can only be seen under a microscope. Amebas vary in size from about ⅟₁₀₀ inch (0.25 millimeter) to ⅟₁₀ inch (2.5 millimeters) across. Some amebas live in water and moist soil. Others live in the bodies of animals and human beings.

Only one cell makes up an ameba's whole body. The cell contains a *nucleus,* the structure that directs the cell's activities, and the *cytoplasm,* material around the nucleus. An elastic membrane surrounds the cytoplasm and nucleus and holds them together. Water and gases pass in and out of the ameba through the membrane.

To move about, an ameba must change its body shape. The cytoplasm pushes out the membrane to form a fingerlike *pseudopod* (false foot), and all of the cytoplasm seems to flow into it. For every "step," another pseudopod must form. Cells that move in this way are called *ameboid cells*. The white blood cells of human beings are ameboid cells.

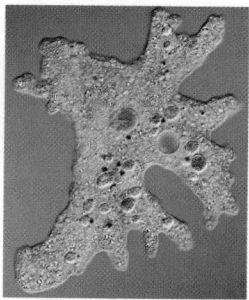

© Shutterstock

Ameba

Amebas eat tiny living organisms and particles of dead and decaying matter. They engulf their food by slowly wrapping pseudopods around a food particle. In this way, the food gets inside the cell. The section of the cell that contains the food is called a *food vacuole*. It floats in the cytoplasm until the food is digested. All undigested food passes out as the ameba slowly moves away. Amebas in fresh water must control water taken into their bodies or they will burst. They have a *contractile vacuole* to collect the extra water that builds up in the cell. When the contractile vacuole is filled, it empties through the cell membrane.

Amebas reproduce by *fission* (splitting apart) when they reach a certain size. The nucleus divides first. Then the rest of the body divides. The division results in two *daughter cells,* which can also grow, feed, and divide.

Most amebas are harmless to people. But one type causes a serious ailment called *amebic dysentery* when it gets into the large intestine. Lawrence C. Wit

Scientific classification. Amebas belong to the kingdom Protista. A common ameba is *Amoeba proteus.* The ameba that causes dysentery is *Entamoeba histolytica.*

See also **Dysentery; Protoplasm; Protozoan.**

Amendment, in legislation, is a change in a law, or in a bill before it becomes a law. Bills often have amendments attached before a legislature votes on them.

Amendments to the Constitution of the United States may be proposed in two ways:

(1) If two-thirds of both houses approve, Congress may propose an amendment. The amendment becomes a law when ratified either by legislatures or by conventions in three-fourths of the states.

(2) If the legislatures of two-thirds of the states ask for an amendment, Congress must call a convention to propose it. The amendment becomes a law when ratified

either by the legislatures or by conventions in three-fourths of the states. This method has never been used.

For the text of amendments to the U.S. Constitution, see **Constitution of the United States.**　Rebecca E. Zietlow

See also **Parliamentary procedure.**

Amenhotep IV. See **Egypt, Ancient** (The New Kingdom).

America is the great land mass of the Western Hemisphere. For location, see **World** (map). It is made up of North and South America. The mainland of America is the longest north-to-south land mass on Earth. The greatest distance of its mainland from north to south is about 8,700 miles (14,000 kilometers), from the Boothia Peninsula in Canada to Cape Froward in Chile. The westernmost point of mainland America is at the Seward Peninsula on the west coast of Alaska. Northeastern Brazil is the easternmost point.

America also includes many islands north, south, east, and west of the mainland. North and South America are connected by a land bridge that is narrowest at the Isthmus of Panama.

Many scientists believe that America was connected to the western edge of Africa and Eurasia from about 250 million years ago until about 200 million years ago. Volcanic formations in Brazil are similar to such formations in South Africa. Likewise, the Appalachian Mountains of North America may be related to the Caledonian Mountains of Scotland.

The word *America* is believed to be in honor of the Italian explorer Amerigo Vespucci. It was first used only for South America but was later applied to the whole Western Hemisphere. Today, the term is often used to refer to the United States of America.

John Edwin Coffman

Related articles in *World Book* include:

Central America
Exploration
Latin America
North America
South America
United States
Vespucci, Amerigo

America, also known as "My Country 'Tis of Thee," is one of the national hymns of the United States. The words were written in 1831 for a church school in Boston by Samuel Francis Smith, who was then studying for the ministry. The song was first sung at the school's Fourth of July celebration that year.

Smith wrote the words to a melody that was popular in many European countries. He found the tune in a collection of German melodies. "God Save the Queen," the British national anthem, uses the same melody. Smith wrote five stanzas. The third stanza, which called the British "tyrants," is not sung today.

Valerie Woodring Goertzen

See also **God Save the Queen.**

America First Committee, founded in September 1940, was the most powerful isolationist group in the United States before the country entered World War II in 1941. It had more than 800,000 members, who wanted to keep the United States neutral. It tried to influence public opinion through publications and speeches.

America First disagreed with another powerful group, the Committee to Defend America by Aiding the Allies. Both of the groups wanted to build American defenses and keep the United States out of the war. However, the Committee to Defend America by Aiding the Allies argued that the best way to keep the country neutral was to aid the United Kingdom. America First thought it more important to stay out of the war than to assure a British victory. America First was dissolved four days after the Japanese attacked Pearl Harbor on Dec. 7, 1941.

David A. Shannon

America the Beautiful, also called "O Beautiful for Spacious Skies," is one of the most familiar and popular American patriotic songs. Katharine Lee Bates, a college professor, wrote the words as a poem during a visit to Colorado in 1893. She was inspired by the view from Pikes Peak.

The poem, which describes the wonders of the United States, was published on July 4, 1895. Sometime after that, the words became associated with the hymn tune "Materna" (also called "O Mother Dear, Jerusalem"), written by the American composer Samuel Augustus Ward in 1882. The music and text were published together in 1910.　Katherine K. Preston

See **Bates, Katharine Lee.**

American Academy of Arts and Letters is an organization that promotes literature and the fine arts in the United States. It gives awards and prizes to notable artists, writers, and composers. The academy maintains an archive and library. It also organizes exhibitions of art and manuscripts, sponsors stage readings and performances of new works, and buys works by American artists to donate to U.S. museums.

A maximum of 250 U.S. citizens may be members of the academy. They serve for life and belong to one of three departments—art, literature, or music. Membership openings result from the death of a member. After a vacancy occurs, members nominate replacements. The membership votes on these nominees for election to the academy. The academy also grants honorary membership to 75 artists, composers, and writers from other countries. In addition, 10 Americans are granted honorary membership from cultural fields other than art, literature, and music.

The organization was founded in 1898. It grew out of the American Social Science Association and became known as the National Institute of Arts and Letters. Members of the institute created the American Academy of Arts and Letters in 1904. The institute and the academy merged in 1976 into the American Academy and Institute of Arts and Letters. In 1993, the organization assumed its present name. Its headquarters are in New York City.

Critically reviewed by the American Academy of Arts and Letters

American Academy of Arts and Sciences is one of the oldest learned societies in the United States. It was founded in 1780 to advance research and to promote the study of national and international problems. Members are chosen for achievements in scholarship, the arts, the professions, or public affairs.

The American Academy of Arts and Sciences administers funds for research and awards prizes for outstanding achievement, including the Rumford Prize in the physical and biological sciences and the Emerson-Thoreau Medal in literature. One of the academy's main activities is to appraise current and emerging issues in such areas as arms control, education, and economic development. Headquarters of the academy are in Cambridge, Massachusetts.

American Association for the Advancement of Science (AAAS) is the world's largest federation of scientific organizations. AAAS has approximately 260 affiliated societies and academies of science, which cover the physical, life, and social sciences. Individual members of AAAS number about 140,000. Membership is open to anyone interested in achieving the objectives of the association.

Main objectives of AAAS are to further the progress of science, make it easy for scientists to cooperate with one another, help increase scientific freedom and responsibility, make science more effective in the promotion of human welfare, and advance education in science. AAAS publishes a weekly journal called *Science.* The association was founded in 1848. Its headquarters are in Washington, D.C.

American Association of Retired Persons. See **AARP.**

American Baptist Association (ABA) is an international organization of self-governing Baptist churches. Members work together in charitable, educational, evangelical, and missionary activities worldwide. The American Baptist Association includes congregations in many countries. Local churches sponsor a number of seminaries and support missionary work in many parts of the world.

ABA members believe in member churches' equality and independence. They do not accept baptism by non-Baptist churches or take part in shared services with other denominations. They believe in a direct line of Baptist churches from the time of Jesus Christ to the present. Their social positions generally are conservative.

The ABA originated in the southern United States with the Landmark movement of the 1850's. This movement stressed the role of individual congregations. In 1924, two Landmark associations joined to form the ABA. The group has offices and a publishing house in Texarkana, Texas.

American Baptist Churches in the U.S.A. is an organization of Baptist associations, churches, and mission agencies. It is a member of the Baptist World Alliance and Christian Churches Together in the USA. The organization has relationships with a number of colleges, hospitals, retirement homes, theological seminaries, and other institutions. It supports agricultural, educational, evangelistic, and medical missions in many countries. The organization's headquarters are in Valley Forge, Pennsylvania.

American Baptist Churches in the U.S.A. was formed as the Northern Baptist Convention in 1907. Its purpose was partly to help coordinate the work of national educational and missionary bodies established by Baptist churches in the early 1800's. For more information about Baptist doctrine and history, see **Baptists.**

American Bar Association is a voluntary organization of lawyers, judges, law students, and law teachers of the United States and its possessions. The organization's goals include promoting the administration of justice and upholding high standards of legal education and ethics.

The American Bar Association, which is often called the ABA, gives *accreditation* (official approval) to law schools. The association also publishes studies on subjects of legal and public interest, such as legal aid and prison reform. In addition, the organization provides opportunities for continuing legal education in these subjects. Many members of Congress ask the ABA for its views on current legislation. The ABA publishes the monthly *ABA Journal,* plus numerous books and pamphlets yearly on topics including business, criminal, and taxation law. The ABA was founded in 1878 and has headquarters in Chicago.

American Battle Monuments Commission is an independent federal agency that commemorates the achievements and sacrifices of United States armed forces. The commission designs, constructs, operates, and maintains U.S. military cemeteries and memorials in foreign countries. It also maintains certain monuments in the United States. The commission controls the design and construction of military monuments and markers erected in other countries by U.S. citizens and by private and public organizations. It also encourages the sponsors to maintain these sites. Congress established the commission in 1923. Private citizens and members of the armed forces serve on the commission.

American Cancer Society is a voluntary health organization dedicated to the control and elimination of cancer. It supports research through grants to individuals and institutions. The organization also supports service and rehabilitation programs for cancer patients and their families. It develops and directs educational programs for the public and for health professionals.

The society is governed by a national board of volunteer directors. Half the directors are laypersons, and half are doctors and scientists. Most society funds are raised in its annual community crusade during April, designated as Cancer Control Month by the United States Congress in 1938.

American Chemical Society is an organization of chemists and chemical engineers. It has more than 150,000 members and is one of the world's largest scientific societies. It consists of more than 30 professional divisions. Local groups meet throughout the world.

The American Chemical Society was founded in 1876. The society's headquarters are in Washington, D.C. Some of the American Chemical Society's best-known publications are the *Journal of the American Chemical Society, Chemical Reviews,* and *Chemical and Engineering News.*

American Civil Liberties Union (ACLU) is a nonpartisan organization devoted to defending the rights and freedoms of people in the United States. It works mainly by providing lawyers and legal advice for individuals and groups in local, state, and federal courts. Officials of the ACLU also testify before state and federal legislative committees, advise government officials, and conduct educational programs. The chief goal of the ACLU is to protect the fundamental rights of individuals as described in the Constitution of the United States. These basic rights include freedom of speech and protection against unfair punishment for people accused of crimes.

The ACLU has defended the constitutional rights of a wide range of individuals and groups. It played an important part in Supreme Court rulings that guaranteed legal aid to poor people. The group has supported fair treatment of *conscientious objectors,* people whose conscience does not allow them to take part in war. The ACLU has urged desegregation of schools and promoted the black civil rights movement. In 1978, the organization defended the right of a group of American Nazis to march in Skokie, Illinois.

One of the current goals of the ACLU is the abolition of capital punishment. The group also calls for further restrictions on government investigative agencies and for stricter separation of church and state. In addition, it seeks greater protection for the rights of immigrants who enter the United States without the required papers, and for the rights of homosexuals and mental patients. The ACLU also supports the rights of women to have abortions.

The ACLU was founded in 1920. It has more than 500,000 members. Its headquarters are in New York City.

Harvey Glickman

American colonies. See Colonial life in America.

American Council on Education is an alliance of nearly 1,800 institutions and organizations of higher education. Most members are colleges, universities, community colleges, and technical schools. But many national, regional, and state associations also belong. The council was organized in 1918. It tries to advance education through the cooperation of member institutions. The council's prime interest has been education beyond high school.

The council has sponsored national programs of research and development to improve testing, guidance, and the quality of teaching. The council represents American higher education in dealing with the government on matters of public policy that affect higher education. Its headquarters are in Washington, D.C.

Critically reviewed by the American Council on Education

American Dental Association is a national organization of dentists. Its purpose is to promote oral health care and the art and science of dentistry. The association has more than 500 local dental societies in the United States and its possessions. The American Dental Association was founded in 1859. Its headquarters are in Chicago. Critically reviewed by the American Dental Association

American Education Week. See Education Week, American.

American Enterprise Institute for Public Policy Research sponsors research on government policy, the United States economy, and American and world politics. The institute, called AEI for short, is home to renowned economists, legal scholars, political scientists, and foreign policy specialists.

AEI was founded in 1943 mainly to conduct economic policy research, which remains the core of its work. Its program in foreign and defense policy examines how American interests can be advanced and how political and economic freedom can be promoted. The institute is financed by contributions from corporations, founda-

tions, and individuals. AEI is based in Washington, D.C.

Critically reviewed by the American Enterprise Institute for Public Policy Research

American Eskimo dog is a small dog known for its fluffy, white coat. Breeders in the United States developed the dog during the early 1900's. It is descended from European spitz breeds. American Eskimo dogs are often called "Eskies." There are three varieties—the standard, the miniature, and the toy. Standard Eskies measure 15 to 19 inches (38 to 48 centimeters) tall at the shoulder, miniature Eskies stand 12 to 15 (30 to 38 centimeters) inches tall, and toy Eskies are 9 to 12 inches (23 to 30 centimeters) tall.

© Shutterstock

The American Eskimo dog has a fluffy, white coat.

American Eskimo dogs are intelligent, alert, and energetic. They once performed tricks in many American circuses but are now kept chiefly as pets and show dogs.

Critically reviewed by the American Eskimo Dog Club of America

American Federation of Arts. See Arts, American Federation of.

American Federation of Government Employees (AFGE) is a union of civilian employees of the United States government and the District of Columbia. The AFGE represents general office workers, janitors, lawyers, mechanics, and scientists. It is associated with the American Federation of Labor and Congress of Industrial Organizations (AFL-CIO).

The AFGE was formed in 1932 by workers who withdrew from a similar union, the National Federation of Federal Employees (NFFE). In 1931, the NFFE had broken its ties with what was then the AFL. NFFE members who wanted to have an association with the AFL then founded the AFGE. AFGE headquarters are in Washington, D.C. For membership, see **Labor movement** (table: Important U.S. labor unions). James G. Scoville

American Federation of Labor and Congress of Industrial Organizations (AFL-CIO) is a federation of labor unions. The AFL-CIO consists of many national and international craft and industrial unions that together have millions of members. The national unions are self-governing, but cooperate with one another within the federation. Each national union has local unions in the United States and its territories. The international unions also have local unions in Canada and in Puerto Rico, Panama, and other Caribbean lands. Altogether, the national and international labor unions have tens of thousands of local unions. AFL-CIO headquarters are in Washington, D.C.

Organization. All the affiliated unions are represented at the AFL-CIO's conventions, held every two years. The convention is the supreme governing body of the organization. It elects the president, secretary-treasurer, executive vice president, and vice presidents who make up the executive council. The council determines AFL-CIO policy between conventions and carries out policies established by the convention. The AFL-CIO has *central bodies* (federations) in all 50 states and Puerto Rico, and hundreds of local central bodies. In addition, it has a number of directly affiliated local unions.

Six trade and industrial departments are affiliated with the AFL-CIO. They are the Building and Construction Trades, Metal Trades, Union Label and Service Trades, Maritime Trades, Professional Employees, and Transportation Trades departments. National and international unions affiliate with the department or departments that represent their interests.

The AFL-CIO also has a number of other departments and committees. These groups deal with such matters as organizing, legislation, civil rights, ethical practices, international affairs, education, economic policy, community services, and occupational safety and health.

Activities of the AFL-CIO include working with unions to increase their membership, informing union members about legislative and political matters, providing legal assistance, and representing the interests of workers' families. In the legislative field, the AFL-CIO works for enactment of desired legislation on national and state levels. The organization promotes the activity of union members in such projects as campaigns for voter registration and for improvements in education and training. In addition, the AFL-CIO works to resolve certain types of disputes among its member unions.

History. In 1881, in Pittsburgh, a group of trade unionists representing about 50,000 members founded the Federation of Organized Trades and Labor Unions of the United States and Canada. The group reorganized in 1886, changing its name to the American Federation of Labor. It organized workers by crafts and skills.

In 1935, eight leaders of AFL unions set up the Committee for Industrial Organization to carry on an organizing drive in mass-production industries. The CIO tried to sign up all workers in a plant, unskilled as well as skilled. Because of a disagreement over this type of organizing, the AFL suspended 10 national unions participating in the CIO in 1936. The CIO then formed its own labor federation in 1938 and changed its name to the Congress of Industrial Organizations. The AFL and the CIO formally merged in 1955.

The Teamsters Union, then the largest union in the United States, was expelled from the AFL-CIO in 1957, after its leaders were accused of unethical practices. The Teamsters rejoined in 1987. Another of the country's largest unions, the United Automobile Workers, disaffiliated in 1968 but rejoined in 1981.

In 2001, the United Brotherhood of Carpenters and Joiners of America (UBC) ended its affiliation with the AFL-CIO. In 2005, five other large unions—the Laborers International Union of North America (LIUNA), the Service Employees International Union (SEIU), the Teamsters Union, UNITE HERE, and the United Food and Commercial Workers (UFCW)—joined with the UBC and the United Farm Workers of America (UFW) to found a new labor alliance called the Change to Win Coalition. Later in 2005, the SEIU, the Teamsters, the UFCW, and UNITE HERE withdrew from the AFL-CIO. In 2006, the LIUNA and the UFW left the AFL-CIO. The move reflected a desire on the part of some unions to have more of the dues money paid to the AFL-CIO be devoted to labor organizing instead of to political contributions. The loss of these unions meant a serious reduction in funding for the AFL-CIO. Some of the breakaway unions later rejoined the AFL-CIO.   James G. Scoville

Related articles in *World Book* include:

American Federation of Government Employees
Congress of Industrial Organizations
Gompers, Samuel

Kirkland, Lane
Labor movement
Meany, George
Sweeney, John J.

American Federation of Musicians. See Musicians, American Federation of.

American Federation of State, County, and Municipal Employees is one of the largest unions in the United States. The union, often called AFSCME, represents public employees and health care workers. It seeks to improve working conditions and achieve dignity for its members through collective bargaining with employers. The union is affiliated with the American Federation of Labor and Congress of Industrial Organizations. It has local unions throughout the country.

AFSCME's members include employees of state, county, and municipal governments; school districts; public and private hospitals; universities; and nonprofit agencies. Health and hospital workers form the largest part of the union's membership.

The organization was founded in 1936. Its headquarters are in Washington, D.C. For membership, see **Labor movement** (table: Important U.S. labor unions).

Critically reviewed by the American Federation of State, County, and Municipal Employees

American Federation of Teachers is a union affiliated with the American Federation of Labor and Congress of Industrial Organizations (AFL-CIO). The union is made up of educational workers, including teachers, counselors, school custodians, and school-bus drivers. It also represents state employees, faculty at colleges and universities, and nurses. The American Federation of Teachers has local unions throughout the United States.

The union's chief objectives are to promote professionalism in teaching and to secure appropriate wages, better working conditions, and job security for its members. The union supports school-based management, better school construction, and equal educational opportunities for people of all races. The federation upholds the rights of teachers to help form school policies and programs. Its members believe it can achieve its goals through democratic discussions between teacher representatives and school administrators, and through collective bargaining.

The American Federation of Teachers was founded in 1916. Its headquarters are in Washington, D.C. For membership, see **Labor movement** (table: Important U.S. labor unions).

American foxhound is a medium-sized hunting dog. It is trained to hunt foxes by following the scent they leave on the ground. Hounds can be trained to hunt singly or in packs of 15 or 20. Most hunt clubs use packs of foxhounds. American foxhounds are trained to run competitively at field trials. They are well known for their speed, endurance, and stamina in the field.

Foxhounds are usually white, with different-sized

An American foxhound is a medium-sized hunting dog. Most foxhounds have a white, black, and tan coat. The dog uses its speed, endurance, and sensitive nose to help people hunt foxes.

patches of black or tan or both. But a foxhound can be almost any color. The American foxhound stands from 21 to 25 inches (53 to 64 centimeters) tall at the shoulder and weighs 60 to 70 pounds (27 to 32 kilograms). It has well-shaped legs, hard muscles, a long tail, ears that hang down, and a distinctive bark.

See also **Dog** (picture: Hounds); **English foxhound**.

American Friends Service Committee (AFSC) is a Quaker organization committed to nonviolence and social equality. AFSC promotes peaceful policies that respect human rights and the rights of nations to choose their own future. AFSC has played a prominent role in efforts to end racial separation in South Africa and to build peace in Angola. In addition, AFSC has carried out programs in developing countries that help people raise food and improve health conditions.

Quakers, who started AFSC, believe in the equality of all people. In the United States, AFSC works for fair treatment of Native Americans, farm laborers, people of color, gay and lesbian individuals, immigrants, and others who experience poverty or discrimination.

AFSC was founded in 1917 with the aim of caring for civilian victims of World War I. In 1947, AFSC received the Nobel Peace Prize for Quaker relief work after World War I, which ended in 1918, and World War II, which ended in 1945. AFSC is privately funded by individuals from many religious backgrounds. It operates

assistance programs in more than 20 countries. The organization's headquarters are in Philadelphia.

See also **Quakers.**

American GI Forum of the United States is a civil rights organization for Mexican American military veterans and their families. It fights discrimination against Mexican Americans in education, employment, and housing.

Héctor P. García, a World War II (1939-1945) Army medical officer, founded the organization in 1948 in Corpus Christi, Texas. He and other veterans organized the American GI Forum to aid needy and disabled veterans who encountered prejudice after the war. The group sponsors programs to help Mexican Americans obtain employment, medical services, and scholarships. Its national headquarters are in Denver and local chapters are throughout the United States.   Feliciano M. Ribera

American Heart Association is a national voluntary health agency organized to fight diseases of the heart and blood vessels. It sponsors research, community services, and professional and public education on heart disease. The American Heart Association has offices throughout the United States and Puerto Rico.

The American Heart Association gains financial support for its program from the general public through contributions made to the association or to its Heart Fund. The association has its national headquarters in Dallas.

American Historical Association. See Historical Association, American.

American history. See United States, History of the.

American Indian. See Indian, American.

American Indian Movement (AIM) was a civil rights organization in the United States and Canada that was founded to protect equal rights for American Indians and improve their living conditions. The group participated in efforts to establish Indian land ownership rights. AIM was founded in 1968. In 1993, the organization split into two main factions, with each group claiming to be the true inheritor of AIM's founding principles.

AIM was often critical of the Bureau of Indian Affairs, a United States government agency that works to promote the welfare of the nation's Indians. AIM believed the bureau had failed to eliminate widespread job and housing discrimination and poverty among Native Americans. The organization also demanded the return of property rights guaranteed by treaties between the United States and Canadian governments and various Indian tribes.

AIM was founded in Minneapolis in 1968 by Dennis Banks, George Mitchell, and Clyde H. Bellecourt. Its original goals were to help improve the lives of the city's Indians and to protect them from police actions that AIM considered brutality. AIM chapters began to be formed in other cities in 1970. AIM carried out several protests to call national attention to the problems of Indians. In 1972, members occupied the headquarters of the Bureau of Indian Affairs in Washington, D.C., for seven days. The following year, AIM members and other Indians seized the village of Wounded Knee, South Dakota, where the U.S. Cavalry massacred as many as 300 Sioux in 1890 (see **Wounded Knee**).

During the 1970's, AIM established and operated a

number of organizations to help Indians develop a sense of self-determination. These groups, consisting only of Indians, worked to improve schools, legal services, employment programs, and health services for Native Americans.

In the mid-1970's, the U.S. government brought many of AIM's leaders to trial for their activities. In response, AIM decentralized. The national chairmanship disbanded, but local chapters continued to function. Problems among AIM leaders contributed to the group's decline in the 1980's.

In 1993, AIM split into two main groups, the American Indian Movement Grand Governing Council (AIMGGC) and the International Confederation of Autonomous Chapters of the American Indian Movement (Autonomous AIM). AIMGGC—led by Banks, Bellecourt, and Bellecourt's brother Vernon Bellecourt—formed a centralized organization with local chapters. Its national headquarters is in Minneapolis. Autonomous AIM opposed any centralized decision-making body or national headquarters. It consists of *autonomous* (self-governing) local chapters. Russell Means, the first national director of AIM, was an important spokesperson for Autonomous AIM's chapters.   Dorene P. Wiese

American Institute of Aeronautics and Astronautics, often called the AIAA, is a professional society for engineers and scientists engaged in aviation and space work. The AIAA addresses the needs of professionals who design, develop, build, test, and operate air and space vehicles and equipment. It operates regional sections throughout the United States as well as several sections overseas. It sponsors conferences and publishes books, journals, a monthly magazine, and a number of electronic products. The AIAA was established in 1963 through the consolidation of the American Rocket Society and the Institute of the Aerospace Sciences. Headquarters are in Reston, Virginia.   Critically reviewed by the American Institute of Aeronautics and Astronautics

American Kennel Club (AKC) maintains the largest registry for purebred dogs in the world. The club registers more than 1 million dogs a year. It maintains a file called the Stud Book, which contains a family history of every dog ever registered with the AKC.

The AKC is made up of several thousand licensed and member dog clubs and affiliated organizations in the United States. The national member breed clubs set the standards by which dogs are judged at AKC shows. Representatives from the clubs carry out the AKC's activities. The AKC makes rules for dog shows and such competitions as obedience trials, field trials, and hunting tests. The AKC also approves dog show judges and maintains a staff to assist at competitions.

The AKC supports the ownership of purebred dogs as family companions, advances canine health and well-being, and promotes responsible dog ownership. The club publishes a number of periodicals, including *AKC Gazette* and *AKC Family Dog* magazines. Its reference books include *The Complete Dog Book* and *The American Kennel Club Dog Care and Training.*

The AKC produces videos on each breed and on other subjects of interest to dog owners. It also sells products to help owners care for their dogs. In addition, the AKC maintains a library and a museum. The AKC was founded in 1884.   Critically reviewed by the American Kennel Club

American League. See Baseball.

American Legion, The, is the largest veterans' organization in the United States. It seeks to advance the interests of veterans, to continue friendships formed during military service, and to see that disabled veterans get the care and help they need. It also takes part in programs that promote the American way of life at the local, state, and national levels and sponsors patriotic community projects and educational and charitable programs.

Members of the American Legion include members of the U.S. armed forces who are on active duty, and veterans who have been honorably discharged from federal active duty. The Legion has thousands of local posts in the United States and other countries. It holds a national convention each year to determine policies and programs and to elect national officers, including a national commander. The national adjutant heads the national headquarters staff in Indianapolis, Indiana. The Legion also has a national office in Washington, D.C. The Legion publishes *The American Legion Magazine.*

Activities. Legion posts have built community houses, swimming pools, playgrounds, and many parks throughout the United States. They have supplied ambulances and equipment for community hospitals and for hospitals operated by the U.S. Department of Veterans Affairs and the U.S. Department of Defense. The Legion also provides cash grants to veterans who suffer severe losses following natural disasters, and operates a nationwide blood donation program.

The American Legion has actively opposed Communism, fascism, and all forms of totalitarianism. In national defense, the Legion has always favored adequate military preparedness.

Legion youth programs work to build American ideals and promote responsible citizenship. The Legion sponsors youth baseball and marksmanship programs and other athletic activities. It also sponsors Scouting troops and Junior Reserve Officers Training Corps (ROTC) units. Each year, the Legion holds a national high school oratory contest to promote the study of the U.S. Constitution and the Bill of Rights. It awards scholarships to the finalists. The Legion also helped create and sponsors American Education Week (see **Education Week, American**).

© The American Legion
Legion emblem

The Legion conducts an annual Boys State. Under this program, boys selected by local Legion posts and civic, religious, and educational organizations take part in a one-week course on the practical operation of state government. Some Boys State participants are chosen to attend the Legion's annual Boys Nation, a program in the study of national government. See **Boys State**.

History. A group of 20 officers who served in the American Expeditionary Forces (A.E.F.) in France in World War I (1914-1918) is credited with planning the Legion. A.E.F. headquarters asked these officers for ideas on how to improve troop morale. One officer,

Lieutenant Colonel Theodore Roosevelt, Jr., proposed an organization of veterans. In early 1919, two *caucuses* (meetings) were held in Paris, France, and St. Louis, Missouri, to plan the new organization. Later that year, the U.S. Congress granted the American Legion a national charter. The first national convention, held in Minneapolis, Minnesota, adopted a permanent constitution and elected officers to head the organization.

The Legion began its work at once. In 1919, it organized a rehabilitation service to help disabled veterans make claims for compensation and get medical care. This rehabilitation service became a nationwide corps of trained, accredited service officers. In 1921, the country plunged into a sharp economic depression. Millions of people lost their jobs. In addition, about 4 million troops had returned to civilian life after World War I. To address this situation, the Legion acted as a nationwide employment service and helped more than 1 million veterans find jobs. Additionally, the Legion won recognition for keeping many schools running during the economic depressions of the early 1920's and early 1930's.

During World War II (1939-1945), the Legion helped write the Servicemen's Readjustment Act of 1944, better known as the GI Bill, and worked for its adoption by Congress. During and after the Vietnam War, the Legion promoted job opportunities for returning veterans. It also worked to increase veterans' benefits under the GI Bill to meet rising educational costs.

Following the Vietnam War, the Legion commissioned studies about and lobbied for federal recognition of post-traumatic stress disorder (PTSD) connected with military service, as well as harmful medical conditions caused by wartime exposure to the chemical Agent Orange. These efforts resulted in affected veterans being able to seek care and disability compensation from the Department of Veterans Affairs.

In 1989, the U.S. Supreme Court ruled that the First Amendment to the U.S. Constitution protected the right of citizens to damage the American flag intentionally. The Legion then established a Citizens Flag Alliance and has supported efforts to protect the flag by law.

Following the Sept. 11, 2001, terrorist attacks on the United States, the American Legion has worked with Congress and the Department of Veterans Affairs on updating and strengthening the GI Bill to better meet veterans' needs. The Harry W. Colmery Veterans Educational Assistance Act of 2017, also called the Forever GI Bill, was named for the former national commander of the Legion credited with drafting the original GI Bill in 1944.

The American Legion has established thousands of military and veterans memorials worldwide. It also has opposed the removal of such public monuments that contain religious symbolism. In 2019, the U.S. Supreme Court ruled in favor of the Legion's suit to protect the cross-shaped Bladensburg World War I Veterans Memorial in Bladensburg, Maryland, after certain groups argued that it violated the separation of church and state.

Critically reviewed by The American Legion

American Legion Auxiliary is the largest women's patriotic organization in the United States. It is affiliated with the American Legion. Women eligible for membership in the Auxiliary are (1) wives, mothers, sisters, and female descendants of Legion members; (2) wives, mothers, sisters, and female descendants of men and women who died in World War I (1914-1918), World War II (1939-1945), the Korean War (1950-1953), the Vietnam War (1957-1975), military actions in Grenada, Lebanon, and Panama in the 1980's and 1990, the Persian Gulf War of 1991, the "war on terror" of the early 2000's, and other conflicts, or of men and women who died after they were honorably discharged from the U.S. armed services; (3) female military veterans eligible for membership in the American Legion; and (4) female members of the Legion.

Auxiliary emblem

The Auxiliary conducts programs to benefit veterans, their families, and the community. It sponsors Girls State, an annual program that educates high school girls about the U.S. government and citizenship (see **Girls State**). The Auxiliary also helps sponsor the National Veterans Creative Arts Festival. The first national American Legion convention in 1919 authorized the creation of the Auxiliary. The Auxiliary held its first convention in Kansas City, Missouri, in 1921. The group's headquarters are in Indianapolis, Indiana.

Critically reviewed by the American Legion Auxiliary

American Liberty League. See Liberty League.

American Library Association (ALA) is an organization founded in 1876 for libraries, librarians, library trustees, and other people interested in libraries. It works closely with organizations in education, recreation, and public service. The ALA's 50,000 members include individuals and libraries from across the world.

The ALA aims to improve the quality and effectiveness of libraries. It seeks to make libraries accessible to all people, to improve professional standards of libraries and librarians, and to promote the distribution of books and other library materials without censorship. The ALA presents several awards and citations for outstanding achievements in librarianship and related fields. Its Association for Library Service to Children awards the Caldecott and Newbery medals for children's books (see **Caldecott Medal; Newbery Medal**).

The association works for legislation to increase the availability or to improve the quality of library service. It urged passage of the Library Services Act of 1956, which was designed to aid the development of public libraries in rural areas. In 1964, the act was amended and became known as the Library Services and Construction Act. This and later amendments authorized aid to both urban and rural libraries. After a new copyright law was enacted in 1976, the association helped librarians and library users understand the law's provisions.

The ALA publishes books and periodicals. Its official bulletin, *American Libraries,* is published 11 times a year. Other periodicals include *Booklist, Choice, College and Research Libraries,* and *Library Resources and Technical Services.* The ALA publishes a yearbook on library and information services. It also provides information about library careers. ALA headquarters are in Chicago, Illinois.

Critically reviewed by the American Library Association

See also **Library** (School library standards).

American literature reflects the many religious, historical, and cultural traditions of the American people, one of the world's most varied populations. Mark Twain, shown in this photograph from about 1900, was one of the most popular and influential writers in American literature.

American literature

American literature cannot be captured in a simple definition. It reflects the many religious, historical, and cultural traditions of the American people, one of the world's most varied populations. It includes poetry, fiction, drama, and other kinds of writing by authors in what is now the United States. It also includes unwritten material, such as the oral literature of Native Americans and folk tales and legends. In addition, American literature includes accounts of America written by immigrants and visitors from other countries, as well as works by American writers who spent some or all of their lives abroad.

This article discusses the literature of what is now the United States. For information on the literature of Canada and Latin America, see the articles **Canadian literature** and **Latin American literature**.

Beginnings of American literature

American literature begins with the legends, myths, and poetry of Native American peoples. Native Americans were the first people to live in what is now the United States. Native legends include stories about the origin of the world, tribal histories, and tales of heroes. With rare exceptions, this oral literature was not written down until the 1800's.

The earliest writing in America consisted of the journals and reports of European explorers and missionaries. These early authors left a rich literature describing their encounters with new lands and new civilizations. They publicized their adventures, described the New World, and tried to attract settlers in works that sometimes mixed facts with propaganda.

Colonial literature (1608-1764)

Colonists from England and other European countries began settling along the eastern coast of North America in the early 1600's and created the first American colonial literature. The colonies in Virginia and New England produced the most important writings in the 1600's. In the 1700's, Philadelphia emerged as the literary center of the American Colonies.

Virginia. Captain John Smith wrote one of the first American books in English, *A True Relation of ... Virginia* (1608). It describes how he and other colonists established the first permanent English settlement in America at Jamestown, Virginia, in 1607. Smith told a version of the famous story of Pocahontas in *The Generall Historie of Virginia, New England, and the Summer Isles* (1624). The story claims that Pocahontas, the daughter of Powhatan, a Native American leader, saved Smith's life when her father was about to have him killed.

In *The History and Present State of Virginia* (1705), historian Robert Beverley wrote about the tragic destruction of the *indigenous* (native) people of Virginia. To Beverley, Native Americans represented possibilities for happiness, innocence, harmony, and freedom. William Byrd II, a Virginia planter, told about a 1728 surveying expedition in *The History of the Dividing Line* (published in 1841). The "line" divides the orderly society of Virginia from the less polished settlers of North Carolina.

New England. In 1620, the Pilgrims founded Plymouth Colony. It was the second permanent English settlement in America. Many Pilgrims belonged to a group of English Protestants called Puritans. The Puritans were followers of the religious reformer John Calvin. The Puritans faced persecution in England. They came to America mainly to seek refuge where they could practice their religion. The Puritans were an intensely intellectual people. Soon after arriving, they began founding schools and colleges and writing and printing books.

They wrote histories, sermons and other religious writings, and poetry.

Histories. The Puritans recorded their own history out of a desire to communicate with fellow believers in England. They also wanted to attract new colonists and to justify their bold move to a new country. In their histories, the Puritans portrayed their successes as evidence of God's favor and their hardships as signs of God's disapproval.

William Bradford, the second governor of Plymouth Colony, told the story of the colony in *Of Plimoth Plantation.* It was written between 1630 and 1651 and published in 1856 as *History of Plymouth Plantation.*

Cotton Mather was the greatest of the Puritan historians. He wrote about 450 works on many subjects, including a defense of the witchcraft trials of the 1690's in Salem, Massachusetts. But he poured his heart into *Magnalia Christi Americana* (1702), a religious history of New England that upholds traditional Puritan beliefs.

Religious writings. The Puritans based their religion on constant study of the Bible. Sermons began with a passage from the Bible, followed by an analysis of its meaning, and then its application to personal and community life. The greatest Puritan preacher and theologian was Jonathan Edwards. He wrote learned essays reformulating traditional Calvinist doctrines, but also defending them. Edwards's famous sermon "Sinners in the Hands of an Angry God" (1741) emphasizes the distance between an all-powerful God and helpless human beings. The sermon expressed the values of the Great Awakening, a religious movement that encouraged American Christians to take their faith more seriously.

Poetry. Although life as a settler was hard, Anne Bradstreet found time to write beautiful and philosophical poems. Her work was printed in London as *The Tenth Muse* (1650), the first volume of American poetry ever published. The resulting publicity encouraged Bradstreet to experiment with meter, imagery, structure, and theme. A revised second edition of her poetry appeared in 1678, after her death. It includes the critically acclaimed "Contemplations," a nature poem on the brief length of human life.

Edward Taylor, a clergyman, composed a series of meditative poems on Scripture readings. He intended the poems to prepare his mind to preach and to celebrate Communion. His verse followed the learned style of the English metaphysical poets of the 1600's. Like them, he mingled everyday words and incidents with Biblical language and complex metaphors. Taylor's poems were not discovered until the 1930's.

Philadelphia was the largest city in the American Colonies by 1710. It replaced Virginia and New England as the cultural center of the emerging nation.

During the 1700's, a greater number of people learned to read, and a growing press served new literary tastes. Literature addressed such interests as politics and science. The essay, satire, and novel became important literary forms.

The publisher, statesman, and scientist Benjamin Franklin helped make Philadelphia a center of intellectual life. His *Autobiography* tells the story of how he ran away from Boston to Philadelphia at the age of 17. His rise from "rags to riches" through hard work and self-improvement became a model for American success.

Franklin's writings emphasized practical intelligence and material success, balanced by charity and public service. His worldliness differed greatly from the earnest spirituality of the Puritans. His witty and often satiric proverbs made *Poor Richard's Almanac* one of his most popular publications. It was published for each year from 1733 to 1758.

The revolutionary period (1765-1787)

During the 1760's, a movement to end British rule in the American Colonies began to gain strength. The United States became an independent nation by winning the American Revolution (1775-1783). Much of the literature of this period addressed issues relating to American independence.

Thomas Paine, a poor and largely self-taught Englishman, immigrated to Philadelphia in 1774. He soon became famous for his fiery essays in support of the American patriots. His pamphlet *Common Sense* (1776) called for complete independence from Great Britain (now also called the United Kingdom). In a series of pamphlets called *The American Crisis* (1776-1783), he encouraged the rebels to persist during the darkest days of the American Revolution.

The French-born essayist Michel-Guillaume Jean de Crèvecoeur, also an immigrant to America, helped the colonists think of themselves as Americans rather than Europeans. One of the letters in his *Letters from an American Farmer* (1782) begins with the question "What is an American?" Crèvecoeur saw America as a new land where individuals could throw off old prejudices, suffocating social customs, and tyrannical government. Yet he also showed the harsh reality of slavery.

Like many writers of the 1700's, Franklin, Paine, and Crèvecoeur wrote in dignified, but plain and clear, prose. This style reached its peak in the ringing eloquence of the Declaration of Independence written by Thomas Jefferson. The same type of writing appears in the sober language of the Constitution of the United States. Alexander Hamilton, James Madison, and John Jay used this clear style in *The Federalist* (1787-1788), a series of public letters that persuaded New Yorkers to ratify the Constitution.

Literature of a young nation (1788-1830)

In the early years of United States independence, many American writers still patterned their writing after Europe's latest literary styles and forms. Gradually, however, American literature began to reflect American experiences.

The most successful American writer of the early 1800's was Washington Irving. He rose to fame with humorous and satiric writing about New York City and its past. These writings appeared in the magazine *Salmagundi* (1807-1808) and in a book, *A History of New York from the Beginning of the World to the End of the Dutch Dynasty* (1809). The book is also called *Knickerbocker's History of New York* because Irving wrote it under the name Diedrich Knickerbocker. In *The Sketch Book of Geoffrey Crayon, Gent.* (1819-1820), Irving combined the style of the essay and the sketch to create the first short stories in American literature. The book includes "Rip Van Winkle" and "The Legend of Sleepy Hollow," two of Irving's most famous tales. In "Rip Van Winkle," the title character awakens from a 20-year sleep to find everything changed by the American Revolution. Irving's doubts about American independence, his hostility toward New England culture, and his desire to maintain cultural ties with England run through all his early writing.

The poet William Cullen Bryant adapted the style of English Romantic poetry to describe the American landscape and to find moral significance in its beauty. Such poems as "Thanatopsis" (1817), "To a Waterfowl" (1818), and "To the Fringed Gentian" (1832) reflect Bryant's admiration of nature.

The Era of Expansion (1831-1870)

During the mid-1800's, the United States gained control of Texas, California, Oregon, and other Western lands. By the 1850's, the nation stretched from coast to coast. Americans moved westward by the thousands. Native American groups who occupied many of these lands were forced to surrender their claims and to resettle on reservations. During this period, many American writers glorified the frontier or praised the beauty of nature. Much American literature reflected the optimism of a rapidly growing nation. But other American literature focused on the country's problems, including slavery. In 1861, the American Civil War broke out between the North and South chiefly over this issue. The North won the war in 1865, and slavery was soon outlawed throughout the United States.

Two main forms of fiction were practiced by American writers in the mid-1800's: (1) the sentimental novel and (2) the romance. Other important literary forms included nonfiction prose and poetry.

Brown Bros.   Library of Congress

Harriet Beecher Stowe   **Louisa May Alcott**

The sentimental novel had been developed by the English author Samuel Richardson in the mid-1700's. It became immensely popular in the United States in the mid-1800's. This type of novel emphasized feelings and such values as religious faith, moral virtue, and family closeness. Its stress on traditional values appealed to many people during a period of rapid social and political change.

The sentimental novel also urged reform. It became the means for rousing concern about the plight of black slaves, poor people, and other unfortunate members of society. Harriet Beecher Stowe's *Uncle Tom's Cabin* (serialized in a newspaper in 1851 and 1852 and published in book form in 1852) is a powerful description of the evils of slavery. It was the best-selling novel of the 1800's, combining an exciting plot, memorable characters, stirring appeals to the emotions, and humor. Stage adaptations of the book also drew large audiences.

Louisa May Alcott's novel *Little Women* (1868-1869) was another best-selling sentimental novel. Based loosely on the author's own life, it tells the story of four sisters growing up. The story centers on the girls' home and personal life. Two of the sisters fall in love, while Jo, the heroine, develops a career as a writer.

The romance. Most people use the term *novel* to refer to any long fictional story in prose. Critics of the 1800's, however, distinguished a novel from a *romance*. A romance is a long work of fiction that is less realistic than a novel. Instead of everyday events, a romance describes exciting adventures or strange events. Writers often use the romance to explore dark passions or to examine the problem of evil.

James Fenimore Cooper wrote historical romances that explored the moral uncertainties of Americans' push westward. In Cooper's romances, such as *The Last of the Mohicans* (1826) and *The Deerslayer* (1841), the beauty and majesty of nature inspire a nearly religious feeling of awe. But civilization intrudes, and settlers turn the wilderness into property that they selfishly or thoughtlessly misuse.

Nathaniel Hawthorne used the romance to study the depths of human nature. Many of his romances show the psychological effects of the Puritan focus on sin and evil. *The Scarlet Letter* (1850), set in Puritan New England, dramatizes the suffering caused by the concealment of sin.

Herman Melville's *Moby-Dick* (1851) is one of the greatest American romances. Most of the story is set on

Nathaniel Hawthorne

Herman Melville

a whaling ship. It describes the hunt for Moby Dick, a fierce white whale. Ahab, the ship's captain, has lost his leg in an earlier encounter with Moby Dick and is determined to kill the whale. Ahab eventually loses his life in the pursuit. On a symbolic level, the book describes one man's struggle against fate.

A type of romance called the *Gothic novel* influenced the American poet and short-story writer Edgar Allan Poe. The Gothic novel featured exotic settings and mysterious or supernatural happenings. These novels were called *Gothic* because they often took place in gloomy medieval castles. Poe adapted these elements in shortened form in the Gothic horror story. He filled his powerful tales with decaying castles, forbidden passions, and guilt-ridden and insane criminals. With "The Murders in the Rue Morgue" (1841), Poe invented the modern detective story.

Nonfiction prose. During the 1830's and 1840's, a literary and philosophical movement called *Transcendentalism* developed in New England. The Transcendentalists believed that God was present in nature. They also believed that human intuition can lead to truth, and so they stressed self-reliance and individuality. The transcendentalists included Ralph Waldo Emerson; Henry David Thoreau; George Ripley; Margaret Fuller; and Bronson Alcott, Louisa May Alcott's father.

Emerson was the leader of the movement. He kept a journal in which he recorded incidents, ideas, and reactions to his wide reading. Emerson drew on his journal in such essays as *Nature* (1836) and "Self-Reliance" (1841). He achieved a prose style that was personal and conversational.

Edgar Allan Poe

Ralph Waldo Emerson

Emerson caught the mood of Americans at the time, a buoyant optimism and sense that the United States was an exciting new beginning in human history. He urged Americans to be independent thinkers and to study life directly. Emerson declared that individuals had access to the eternal and ideal truths of nature. He therefore urged Americans to trust their own creative instincts and not look to Europe for models.

In *Walden* (1854), Thoreau described his experiences living close to nature. The book tells how Thoreau built a cabin in the woods on the shore of Walden Pond in Massachusetts and lived there alone. He read, entertained visitors, worked the land, and recorded his observations in journals. Thoreau's style shows his sensitive response to the root meanings, sounds, images, and nuances of words.

In 1838, Frederick Douglass escaped from slavery and fled north. During the early 1840's, he joined the abolitionists. His fiery attacks on slavery made him a famous speaker. In the first edition of his autobiography, the *Narrative of the Life of Frederick Douglass* (1845), Douglass vividly describes his life as a slave.

Poetry. During the 1800's, the most famous American poets were William Cullen Bryant, Henry Wadsworth Longfellow, James Russell Lowell, John Greenleaf Whittier, and Oliver Wendell Holmes. They were called the "Fireside Poets" or the "Schoolroom Poets" because their works were most often read "by the fireside" at home or in school in *anthologies* (collections of literary works). Like the sentimental novelists, these poets concerned themselves with feelings and called for social reform.

Edgar Allan Poe wrote haunting, often mournful poems. "The Raven" (1845) and "Annabel Lee" (1849) express despair over the death of a woman. Poe's poetry did not make an immediate impact on American poets. But he gained a great following in Europe after two important French poets, Charles Baudelaire and Stéphane Mallarmé, praised and translated his work. Influenced by Poe, they in turn inspired several modern American poets, including T. S. Eliot and Wallace Stevens.

Henry W. Longfellow

Walt Whitman and Emily Dickinson were the two greatest American poets of the 1800's. Whitman took inspiration from Emerson's call for a self-confident American literature. He expressed the variety of American life in long lines that caught the flow of operatic singing. His verse often takes the form of rhythmic lists.

Walt Whitman

It sprawls, seeming impro- vised. But Whitman also packed his poems with vivid images and memo- rable phrases. He wrote in *free verse,* a style of poetry that avoids regular meter and rhyme. Whit- man published the first edition of his masterpiece, *Leaves of Grass,* in 1855. Five more enlarged and revised editions of the col- lection appeared between 1856 and 1882. *Leaves of Grass* describes the best

Emily Dickinson

and worst of American life, from exuberant democracy to suffering slaves. The longest poem in the collection, "Song of Myself," glorifies a spiritual life grounded in the body and everyday life.

Dickinson wrote more than 1,700 short, puzzling poems in the mid-1800's. Her subjects were love, death, nature, and immortality. Only 11 of Dickinson's poems were printed in her lifetime. After an accurate, complete edition of her poems appeared in 1955, Dickinson's reputation and influence rapidly grew. Critics admired her precise observations, her complex and unexpected images, and her questioning of established religion and authority.

The Age of Realism (1871-1913)

The Civil War marked a dramatic change in American life. The war ended slavery, but it left the deeper prob- lem of race relations. After the conflict, the United States turned its energies to economic concerns. Machines re- placed hand labor as the chief means of manufacturing. Industry grew enormously. The new business activity centered in cities, and people moved to them in huge numbers. While some people made fortunes in busi- ness, others lived in poverty.

Realists. Many American writers of the late 1800's were inspired by an international literary movement called *Realism.* Realism was in part a revolt against Ro- manticism and its idealized portrayal of life. The Realists sought to show life as it is. Realism encouraged writers to examine the problems and conditions around them. They wanted to use the language of ordinary people, including dialects. In this way, Realism encouraged the emergence of a distinctively American literature.

The Realists explored the new economic conditions and often called for social reforms. The American dream of "rags to riches" success was captured in popular nov- els by Horatio Alger. But the American Realists focused on the harsh underside of this dream. They feared that success brought greed, materialism, and corruption.

William Dean Howells, an influential magazine editor, vigorously argued for Realism against Romanticism and sentimentalism. In such novels as *The Rise of Silas Lapham* (1885) and *A Hazard of New Fortunes* (1890), he explored the impact of commercial success and failure.

Many of the Realists focused on particular regions of the United States. Bret Harte portrayed the West of the gold rush in such short stories as "The Luck of Roaring Camp" (1868) and "The Outcasts of Poker Flat" (1869).

Sarah Orne Jewett's *The Country of the Pointed Firs* (1896) shows the changes in small-town life in coastal Maine caused by economic development.

Mark Twain was one of the most popular writers of the late 1800's. His *Adventures of Tom Sawyer* (1876) de- scribes the actions of a clever and mischievous boy and his friend Huckleberry Finn. *Adventures of Huckleberry Finn* (1884) is recognized as an American classic. It con- tinues the story of the first novel. The book narrates the adventures of Huck and the runaway slave Jim as they float down the Mississippi River on a raft. In this novel, Twain contrasted nature—where a white boy and a black man can become friends—with the hypocrisy of civiliza- tion along the shore. Twain also captured southwestern dialects and satirized the writing that dominated earlier American literature.

Henry James is often regarded as one of the greatest American novelists. James left the United States in his 30's, settling in England in 1876. In his study of Nathaniel Hawthorne, published in 1879, James argued that the lack of a rich cultural tradition made American novels thin and unrealistic. In many of James's works, charac- ters travel to Europe, where their innocence and integri- ty clash with a culture that is attractive but sometimes corrupt. In *The Portrait of a Lady* (1881), a young Ameri- can discovers the immorality of her husband. James's style grew more complex in later novels. He traced with increasing detail the psychological and moral problems of his intelligent and self-conscious characters.

Early Southern realists included George Washington Cable and Joel Chandler Harris. Cable's *The Grandis- simes* (1880) portrays the tragic clash of races and cul- tures in Louisiana. Harris's *Uncle Remus: His Songs and His Sayings* (1881) and later collections of stories were immensely popular. Charles Waddell Chesnutt's *The Conjure Woman* (1899) is also a collection of African American folk tales in dialect.

Naturalists were the most extreme and pessimistic Realists. Unlike other Realists, the Naturalists believed that people could not make moral choices. They showed their characters as completely controlled by economic, social, or biological forces.

Hamlin Garland wrote bitterly of the hardships of Midwestern farmers in *Main-Travelled Roads* (1891). In *The Awakening* (1899), Kate Chopin powerfully portrayed a woman's psychological and sexual development and eventual suicide. Frank Norris described the struggle of California farmers against the powerful railroads in *The Octopus* (1901). Up- ton Sinclair's *The Jungle* (1906) exposed unsanitary conditions in the Chicago meat-packing industry and helped bring about federal regulation.

In such stories as "The Open Boat" (1897) and "The Blue Hotel" (1898), Stephen Crane stressed the need for courage and generosi- ty in a universe indifferent to human life. His most famous work, *The Red Badge of Courage* (1895),

Henry James

shows a young soldier in the American Civil War, wandering in a state of shock and confusion through scenes of battle.

Jack London became one of the most popular American authors in the world by writing tales of fierce competition for survival in hostile environments. An example is his famous novel about a dog in the Yukon, *The Call of the Wild* (1903). Theodore Dreiser has been especially praised for such novels as *Sister Carrie* (1900). The story traces a young woman's rise to success and social prominence despite her violation of society's moral codes. Her fate contrasts with her first lover's decline into poverty and, finally, suicide.

Edith Wharton was a close friend of James's. Like him, she wrote novels of manners. But many of them have American, instead of European, settings. Wharton became known for her keen moral and psychological examination of characters. *The House of Mirth* (1905) exposes the selfishness and materialism of upper-class society in New York City.

Nonfiction writers also flourished in the United States after the Civil War. The philosopher William James, brother of Henry James, wrote powerfully on many subjects, including religion and psychology. In *The Principles of Psychology* (1890), James invented the phrase *stream-of-consciousness* and thus sparked the development of a new fictional technique. In this technique, the writer tracks the shifting feelings and thoughts flowing through the mind of a character.

The economist Thorstein Veblen explored social and economic issues with biting satire in *The Theory of the Leisure Class* (1899). In *The Story of My Life* (1903), Helen Keller told how she had been helped to overcome blindness and deafness. Jane Addams's *Twenty Years at Hull House* (1912) tells of her work among Chicago's Italian, Greek, Russian, and other immigrants. As settlement in the West became more widespread, many Americans wanted to preserve the unspoiled wilderness. In *The Mountains of California* (1894) and other books, the naturalist John Muir described the American wilderness as God's temple and attacked threats to its preservation.

One of the most notable nonfiction prose writers of this period was the historian Henry Adams. His autobiography, *The Education of Henry Adams,* was privately printed in 1907 and published in 1918. In it, Adams contrasted the power of religion in the Middle Ages with the power of science in the modern world.

Two prominent black leaders disagreed on the best course for African American advancement. In his autobiography, *Up from Slavery* (1901), educator Booker T. Washington urged African Americans to temporarily suspend their demands for equal rights in exchange for vocational education and jobs. He predicted that blacks would achieve equal rights once they gained economic power. But historian and sociologist W. E. B. Du Bois challenged what he regarded as Washington's surrender of rights for economic gain. Du Bois refused all compromises. In *The Souls of Black Folk* (1903), he insisted that "the problem of the twentieth century is the problem of the color line."

Sarah Winnemucca described the plight of the Native Americans in the West in her memoir, *Life Among the Paiutes* (1883). In the early 1900's, the Sioux author Zitkála-Šá wrote eloquently about Native American identity and heritage.

The World Wars and Depression (1914-1945)

In 1914, World War I broke out in Europe. In 1917, the United States entered the war against Germany, which was defeated in 1918. After the war, the U.S. economy boomed. But prosperity did not last. A stock market crash in 1929 led to the Great Depression, a deep economic slump in the 1930's.

In 1939, World War II began in Europe. The United States fought in the war from 1941 to 1945 and played an important role in defeating Germany and Japan.

About the time of World War I, an international artistic movement called Modernism emerged in Europe. Modernist artists believed that the traditional social, religious, and political order had broken down. They felt that Realism could not adequately describe how greatly modern life differed from the past. As a result, they sought stylistic innovations that could better portray new realities.

The American writers who lived in Europe around the time of World War I made important contributions to Modernism. Their influence extended to writers in the United States. The Great Depression led some writers of the period to focus on social or economic issues.

Modernist poetry leaves out the explanations and narrative connections that provide unity and clarity in traditional writing. It mixes everyday language with elegant phrases and short quotations from earlier poems. Modernist poets placed contradictory feelings and events side by side to evoke the disconnectedness of modern life.

Brown Bros.
Jack London

Public Domain
Edith Wharton

Library of Congress
Booker T. Washington

Public Domain
Sarah Winnemucca

Schaal, Pix   Lofman-Pix

Carl Sandburg   **Robert Frost**

Modernism was influenced by a poetic movement called *Imagism,* which lasted from 1908 to 1917. Imagist poetry was characterized by precise images and a spareness of expression. The most important Imagist poets were Ezra Pound, Amy Lowell, and Hilda Doolittle, who wrote under the initials H. D.

T. S. Eliot, one of the first Modernists, moved to London in 1914. There, he became friends with Pound, who had already settled in Europe. Together, Eliot and Pound discovered and absorbed a wide range of poetic traditions. They developed many of the features of Modernist poetry and made them well known.

Eliot mastered the Modernist style in "The Love Song of J. Alfred Prufrock" (1915). His long poem *The Waste Land* (1922) created an uproar. This complex, pessimistic reflection on the emptiness of modern life seemed a masterpiece to some but bewildered others. Eliot gradually gained a widespread influence in modern poetry. In many critical essays, he redefined the way people thought about literature.

Pound's long poem *Cantos* was published in several installments from 1925 to 1968. It reflects on poetry and the course of European and American history. Pound was also important as a critic, vigorously promoting a wide range of ancient and modern poets.

Several important Modernist poets emerged in the United States. Hart Crane's *The Bridge* (1930) weaves American images and themes, such as the Brooklyn Bridge, into a visionary Modernist poem. Wallace Stevens's philosophical poems explore the relation of imagination to reality.

William Carlos Williams celebrated everyday objects and experiences in short poems and an epic, *Paterson* (1946-1958). He favored a clean, direct style that would capture the individuality of the subject matter. E. E. Cummings experimented with the physical form of poems, particularly punctuation, capitalization, and spacing on the page. Marianne Moore was known for her unconventional uses of meter.

Realist poetry. Some poets of the early and mid-1900's practiced Realism rather than Modernism. In Edgar Lee Masters's *Spoon River Anthology* (1915), the now-dead inhabitants of an imaginary Midwestern town tell their life stories. Carl Sandburg was influenced by Whitman in his use of plain, everyday language. He aimed to help readers understand the lives of common people.

The poems of Robert Frost, such as "Mending Wall" (1914) and "Stopping by Woods on a Snowy Evening"

(1923), are simple and readable on the surface. But they reveal complex feelings, often through subtle irony and dry wit. Frost expressed in ordinary language the puzzling hints of doubt and uncertainty that haunt everyday incidents. These feelings connect him to Modernism, despite his traditional meter, rhyme, and verse forms.

The African American writer Paul Laurence Dunbar achieved international recognition for his poetry and his fiction. Many of his poems use standard English and traditional meter, but he received greater acclaim for his portraits in dialect of black lives in the South.

The Lost Generation. A number of writers joined the flourishing arts community in Paris after World War I. Many of these newcomers to Paris gathered around the novelist and critic Gertrude Stein, who had settled there before the war. She described these disillusioned writers as a "lost generation." Her experiments with prose rhythm, fractured sentence structure, and disconnected narrative were challenging and influential.

Two of the most important writers of the Lost Generation were Ernest Hemingway and F. Scott Fitzgerald. Hemingway's *The Sun Also Rises* (1926) describes these uprooted Americans. His characters desperately search for something to believe in after the destruction caused by the war. Some critics consider Hemingway's short stories to be his finest work. In them, Hemingway crafted a bare, blunt prose that sought to clear away the emptiness of old ideas and values. His prose style has inspired many imitators.

Fitzgerald focused on American life in the Roaring Twenties, also called the Jazz Age. In short stories and in such novels as *The Great Gatsby* (1925) and *Tender Is the Night* (1934), he showed how the values of the American dream had been corrupted by materialism and class divisions. Fitzgerald's strong visual sense and way of composing a story into scenes showed the influence of early motion pictures.

Modernist fiction. Modernism led writers of fiction to reexamine the techniques of storytelling. Writers began to strip away descriptions of scenes and characters, explanations, direct statements of theme, and summaries of the plot. A few writers experimented with prose styles as fragmented and difficult as some poetry.

William Faulkner is one of the most highly regarded American novelists of the 1900's. Faulkner set most of his novels, such as *The Sound and the Fury* (1929) and *As I Lay Dying* (1930), in the imaginary Mississippi county of Yoknapatawpha. He saw slavery and racism as the great

Karsh, Ottawa   United Press Int.

Ernest Hemingway   **William Faulkner**

sins haunting Southern history. He believed the South fought heroically in the Civil War but for an evil cause. Faulkner's Southerners live with this heritage of guilt and useless, misguided nobility. Faulkner absorbed all the techniques of Modernist storytelling. His style is symbolic, lyric, and sometimes eloquent. He evoked the contradictory feelings of his characters through fragmented and difficult plots. Faulkner often employed the stream-of-consciousness technique.

The Harlem Renaissance. During the early 1900's, particularly in the 1920's, African American literature began to flourish in Harlem, a district of New York City. This movement became known as the Harlem Renaissance. It was also called the New Negro after the title of an anthology collected by educator and writer Alain Locke. The major writers of the Harlem Renaissance included Sterling A. Brown, Countee Cullen, Jessie Redmon Fauset, and Langston Hughes. Other important writers were Zora Neale Hurston, James Weldon Johnson, Alain Locke, Claude McKay, and Jean Toomer.

Johnson's *God's Trombones* (1927) consists of seven black sermons set in verse. His poetry's dramatic and musical qualities also reflect his experience writing songs for the musical theater. McKay was one of the most powerful African American poets. He began with poems in dialect. Later, he wrote highly formal but emotional verse, often on explosive topics. Hughes made a deliberate effort to bring the rhythms of African American music into poetry. Brown used dialect in subtly varied ways both to protest against racial prejudice and to express pride in the distinctive cultural tradition of African Americans. Cullen was mainly a lyric poet, but he sometimes used verse to protest racism.

African American prose writers also flourished during the Harlem Renaissance. Toomer's *Cane* (1923) is a sophisticated mixture of short stories, sketches, poetry, and a play. Hurston collected African American folk tales and became well known as a skilled oral storyteller. Her best-known novel, *Their Eyes Were Watching God* (1937), traces a black woman's steady growth in insight and spiritual strength. Her characters are vivid, realistic mixtures of strength and weakness. Locke wrote several nonfiction works on African American culture.

Realist fiction. In *O Pioneers!* (1913) and *My Ántonia* (1918), Willa Cather described frontier life in Nebraska. Each story in Sherwood Anderson's *Winesburg, Ohio* (1919) explores, from a psychological viewpoint, a different personality in a small Ohio town. Thomas Wolfe

studied American morals and values in four huge, poetic novels. Each novel, beginning with *Look Homeward, Angel* (1929), is based on Wolfe's own life. John Steinbeck's *The Grapes of Wrath* (1939) depicts the sufferings of Dust Bowl farmers who migrate from Oklahoma to California during the Great Depression. One of the most powerful Realist novels is Richard Wright's *Native Son* (1940). It tells the story of a poor young black man driven to brutal violence by the hatred and prejudice he meets in a white world.

Library of Congress

Willa Cather

During the 1920's and 1930's, many writers and critics debated the relation between literature and social or political change. Particularly because of the Depression, many writers felt a responsibility to address economic and social problems. These authors often used journalistic techniques to educate a wide audience about needed reforms. Other writers, such as John Dos Passos, experimented with new forms and styles. In his trilogy *U.S.A.* (1930-1936), Dos Passos aimed to portray American society fully and realistically. His novels include what he called Newsreels, which use newspaper headlines, words from popular songs, and advertisements to surround characters and action.

Popular forms. Many novels in the mid-1900's were written in established patterns called "genre" or "formula" fiction. They included Westerns and detective stories. These literary forms often became extremely popular. Owen Wister's *The Virginian* (1902) and Zane Grey's many novels, including *Riders of the Purple Sage* (1912), had established the Western novel.

A distinctive American contribution to detective fiction was the "hard-boiled" detective story, featuring a tough, cynical hero with a sarcastic sense of humor. Dashiell Hammett and Raymond Chandler popularized the hard-boiled detective story.

H. P. Lovecraft became a pioneer in horror fiction in the 1920's. The magazine *Weird Tales* published many of his stories.

Drama. Most American plays of the 1700's and 1800's were sentimental comedies or melodramatic tragedies. Eugene O'Neill broke from this tradition in the 1920's. Early in his career, he created highly realistic plays. He wrote about the criminals, homeless, alcoholics, laborers, artists, and radicals he had encountered in several years of drifting. These characters spoke in crude, slangy, but lively language. Gradually, O'Neill's plays grew longer, and he experimented more boldly with artistic techniques. He moved toward a more symbolic, stylized theater that could express his characters' inner emotions. He turned toward autobiographical material for his final plays. They include *Long Day's Journey into Night,* written from 1939 to 1941 and first performed in 1956.

During the 1930's, vigorous debates took place over the purpose of drama. Some playwrights wanted the

Library of Congress

Zora Neale Hurston

Library of Congress

Langston Hughes

Random House

Eugene O'Neill

Public Domain

Lillian Hellman

© AP Images

Robert Lowell

theater to serve as a force for social reform. Others concentrated on experimental technique, and still others aimed at frankly escapist and commercially successful work. Clifford Odets's *Waiting for Lefty* (1935) and *Awake and Sing!* (1935) attack social problems of the time. Lillian Hellman's plays, such as *The Children's Hour* (1934) and *The Little Foxes* (1939), explore the destructiveness of greed, materialism, and sexual repression in American life. In *Our Town* (1938), Thornton Wilder used uncommon staging techniques, such as the absence of scenery or a curtain, to balance a somewhat sentimental picture of small-town New England life.

Literature from 1945 to 2000

From the end of World War II in 1945 to the late 1900's, the United States took on a central role in global affairs. The national economy prospered, and American culture, especially popular culture, became influential worldwide. Massive immigration brought new ethnic groups into the United States and influenced popular culture. During these postwar decades, strong social movements fought for full and equal rights for African Americans, women, and gays and lesbians. The involvement of the United States in the Vietnam War (1957-1975) was controversial at home and abroad. The collapse of Communist governments in Eastern Europe in the late 1980's left the United States the dominant world power. These social changes influenced many writers during the second half of the 1900's.

Poetry. American poetry after World War II was characterized by its diversity of voices. A wide variety of poetic styles appealed to readers. By the 1950's, Modernism was the dominant influence. Modernist poets experimented with new arrangements of language and expression. The personal identity of the poet became more prominent. However, many poets still defended traditional meter and forms.

"Confessional" poetry. Some poets of the 1950's began to write directly about their own lives and feelings. Their work became known as "confessional" poetry. Robert Lowell's *Life Studies* (1959) and John Berryman's *The Dream Songs* (1969) speak frankly of each poet's troubled life. Theodore Roethke explored the themes of growth and childhood in elegantly written poems. Sylvia Plath sometimes used the Holocaust, the mass murder of European Jews and others by the Nazis during World War II, as a metaphor for personal crisis. Anne Sexton wrote about her mental illness in a direct and open style.

Variations on Modernist poetry. A group of writers called the Black Mountain poets gathered around

Charles Olson at Black Mountain College, an experimental arts school in Black Mountain, North Carolina. Olson sought to give poetry a physical immediacy. In *The Maximus Poems* (1953-1975), he let the rhythm of his own breathing determine the length of his verse lines. He called the technique "projective verse." Robert Creeley, Robert Duncan, and Denise Levertov carried forward Olson's style of verse. They sought an "open" form that could admit a range of experiences, feelings, and insights.

Several authors known as the *Beat poets* condemned what they considered the failings of American society and turned poetry into a powerful tool of social protest. One of the most important Beat poets was Allen Ginsberg. His "Howl" (1956) describes spiritual ecstasy and the torments of urban life in long verse lines influenced by Whitman and William Carlos Williams.

Frank O'Hara led a group of poets centered in New York City. His poems, especially his *Lunch Poems* (1964), read like improvised and casual records of quickly changing and scattered moments of urban life. John Ashbery, a member of the New York group, wrote poems that reflect the influence of Modern art and music. Many of his poems, such as those collected in his *Self-Portrait in a Convex Mirror* (1975), hint at their subject only indirectly and vaguely.

James Merrill wrote polished formal verse, often autobiographical but highly restrained. His long poem *The Changing Light at Sandover* (1982) describes the structure of the universe and shares thoughts with spirits of dead family, friends, and poets.

Elizabeth Bishop's poems are formal and self-restrained. But they express powerful personal feelings and experiences. *Questions of Travel* (1965) explores themes of travel, exile, and response to exotic landscapes. The poems of Gary Snyder, collected in such works as *Turtle Island* (1974), reflect a widespread interest in Asian cultures and in the relationship of human beings to their environment. Snyder had also been involved with the Beat movement. W. S. Merwin became known for poetry influenced by Buddhism and ecology. Adrienne Rich became a significant voice of feminist poetry, most notably in *Diving into the Wreck* (1973). Thom Gunn, an openly gay poet, lamented the AIDS epidemic in *The Man with Night Sweats* (1992).

The African American experience became the subject of many poets beginning in the later 1940's. Gwendolyn Brooks drew on oral black preaching and street talk. She described the ordinary lives of African Americans and the injustices they suffered in such collections as *A Street in Bronzeville.*

In the 1960's, with the growing visibility of the civil rights movement, many African Americans rejected earlier hopes for an integrated society and began to call for a separate black culture. LeRoi Jones's early poems express the personal agonies of living in a racist world.

But he increasingly saw the problem as social, not personal. He began to write plays and helped start the Black Arts Movement. The movement rejected the literary forms and values of white culture. As Jones became more politically active, he changed his name to Imamu Ameer Baraka, then to Amiri Baraka, to reflect his African heritage. Many poets associated with the Black Arts Movement collaborated with musicians, and their spoken-word performances can be considered the forerunners of hip-hop. These poets included Nikki Giovanni, Jayne Cortez, and Gil Scott-Heron.

Bob Black, *Chicago Daily News*
Gwendolyn Brooks

Jill Krementz
Joyce Carol Oates

© Monica Morgan, Getty Images
Alice Walker

In her poems, Audre Lorde fought against racism and sexism. In *Coal* (1976), she rose to national prominence by drawing on her experiences as a black lesbian.

Fiction. The attempt to capture human experience in a realistic tone remained popular after World War II. Several authors drew their subjects from World War II, including James Jones, Norman Mailer, Irwin Shaw, and Herman Wouk. Others focused on regions of the country or on more personal experiences. John Cheever and John O'Hara wrote about suburban life in the northeastern United States. J. D. Salinger exposed the shortcomings of the adult world as seen through the eyes of a New York teenager in *The Catcher in the Rye* (1951). Ralph Ellison, in *Invisible Man* (1952), drew a haunting picture of African American life in the United States. Joyce Carol Oates produced a large body of fiction that ranged from realistic stories of urban life to nightmarish novels.

A number of Southern writers, influenced by Faulkner, focused on the poor, outcasts, or grotesque characters. Carson McCullers depicted the pain of loneliness in many of her works, including *The Member of the Wedding* (1946). Flannery O'Connor wrote about strange characters and disturbed behavior that nevertheless reflected spiritual yearning. Her brilliant short stories were published in such collections as *A Good Man Is Hard to Find* (1955). The poet and novelist Alice Walker told the story of a Southern black woman in her novel *The Color Purple* (1982). Other notable Southern writers include Walker Percy and Eudora Welty.

Many postwar writers, such as Henry Miller and Gore Vidal, became known for their use of sexually explicit material. *Lolita* (published in France, 1955; United States, 1958), a controversial novel by the Russian-born Vladimir Nabokov, concerns an affair between a 12-year-old girl and an older man. John Updike examined the materialism of middle-class American life in many novels and short stories. He achieved fame for his realistic accounts of marital infidelity in *Couples* (1968) and in his four-volume "Rabbit" series (1960-1990). Philip Roth wrote biting satires that often focus on Jewish family life, notably *Portnoy's Complaint* (1969), which became controversial for its graphic sexual content.

Postwar novelists tried to express American experiences through the natural voices of colorful leading characters. Much of Saul Bellow's fiction, such as *The Adventures of Augie March* (1953), features exuberant narration by such characters. The Beat novelist Jack Kerouac's *On the Road* (1957) tells of young men who rebel against the boredom and pointlessness they saw in daily life as they wandered across the United States in a search for meaning. Kerouac's strongly rhythmic flow of words creates an impression of spontaneity and improvisation, like that in jazz. In contrast, Raymond Carver used a blunt, spare style in his moving short stories about lower-class characters.

Cormac McCarthy described the often harsh and violent, but darkly comic, world of the Old West in his "Border Crossing" trilogy—*All the Pretty Horses* (1992), *The Crossing* (1994), and *Cities of the Plain* (1998). Don DeLillo often interweaves historical facts with fictional characters in his novels. His themes include mass culture, the excesses of consumer consumption, and politics in American society. His notable novels include *White Noise* (1985) and *Underworld* (1997).

Experimental styles. The stylistic experiments of the Modernists opened the way for the Postmodernists of the 1960's and 1970's. Postmodern fiction is sometimes written in a style called *self-reflexive* that calls attention to the act of writing itself. For example, it may comment on or even argue with itself, address or mock the read-

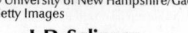

© University of New Hampshire/Gado/ Getty Images
J. D. Salinger

Jill Krementz
Ralph Ellison

Jill Krementz
Saul Bellow

er, or include the author as a character in the story. Short fiction by Robert Coover and Donald Barthelme has been especially influential in this style. William S. Burroughs used what he called the "cut-up method," which involved physically clipping and pasting together random pieces of prose.

Postmodern fiction often concerns themes of madness and conspiracy. Ken Kesey's *One Flew over the Cuckoo's Nest* (1962) uses a mental hospital and a confidence-man hero as symbols of modern American society. Thomas Pynchon's massive *Gravity's Rainbow* (1973) is a nightmarish reimagining of the end of World War II, with heavy undertones of confusion and paranoia. Kurt Vonnegut's *Slaughterhouse-Five* (1969) uses time travel and dark humor to express the stress of wartime experiences and their aftermath.

Authors used experimental styles to describe experiences of racism in the United States. In *Mumbo Jumbo* (1972) and other works, the black writer Ishmael Reed drew a satiric and disorienting picture of race relations and other aspects of modern life.

N. Scott Momaday, of Kiowa and Cherokee ancestry, used various modern narrative techniques in *House Made of Dawn* (1968). The novel is the story of an alienated Native American veteran of World War II. *Ceremony* (1977), by Pueblo novelist Leslie Marmon Silko, tells about another Native American World War II veteran. Torn by conflict between ancient Native American ways and the modern white world, he is gradually healed by Pueblo ritual.

By the 1980's, Toni Morrison was recognized as one of the most significant American novelists since World War II. She crafted a powerful and unique interior voice for her novels, especially *Sula* (1973) and *Beloved* (1987). These works feature strong African American women. The influence of her work on other American writers and on readers has been tremendous. She received the Nobel Prize in literature in 1993.

Maxine Hong Kingston's *The Woman Warrior* (1976) blends fiction with fact to express the complex experience of growing up as a Chinese-American woman. Amy Tan also addressed the lives of Chinese-American families in *The Joy Luck Club* (1989). In the 1980's, Sandra Cisneros emerged as a pioneer writer of Chicano themes. A Chicano or Chicana is a male or female, respectively, of Mexican heritage who was born in the United States or who identifies with that group. Her novel *The House on Mango Street* (1984) deals with questions about identity and belonging.

Popular genres. Many writers continued to work in the established patterns of popular fiction. Louis L'Amour wrote many Western novels and short stories that sold millions of copies. The "hard-boiled" detective story style continued in Elmore Leonard's novels, which combine dark humor, lively prose, and quirky characters. Science fiction flourished in the imaginative works of Isaac Asimov, Octavia Butler, Philip K. Dick, and Ursula K. Le Guin. Stephen King became the most successful writer in the genre of horror fiction.

Nonfiction prose. The "New Journalism" of the 1960's and 1970's promoted the reporting of facts with a narrative voice more common to works of fiction. Tom Wolfe used an exuberant, inventive, and often satiric style to report on popular culture in such works as *The Electric Kool-Aid Acid Test* (1968). Truman Capote's *In Cold Blood* (1965) employs powerful narrative skills to tell the story of the brutal murder of a family in Kansas. Joan Didion wrote sharp, observant essays about modern life, especially in California. Many of her essays were collected in *Slouching Towards Bethlehem* (1968) and *The White Album* (1979).

The civil rights movement of the 1960's inspired a number of important works of literary nonfiction. The most famous include Martin Luther King, Jr.'s "Letter from Birmingham Jail" (1963), and *The Autobiography of Malcolm X* (1965, edited by Alex Haley). James Baldwin established himself as one of America's leading essayists with his forceful writings of cultural criticism in *Notes of a Native Son* (1955) and other collections. Baldwin was also an outstanding fiction writer.

Among other notable nonfiction writers of the time, Susan Sontag stands out for her expert writing on a variety of subjects, such as photography, war, AIDS, art, and politics. Sontag's best-known books include *Against Interpretation* (1966) and *Illness as Metaphor* (1978). Annie Dillard's wide-ranging observations on religion, philosophy, and natural history were published in *Pilgrim at Tinker Creek* (1974). Edward Abbey earned praise as a nature writer with such works as *Desert Solitaire* (1968). John McPhee was influential for his writings on the geological history of America in such works as *Basin and Range* (1981).

Drama. The leading playwrights after World War II included Tennessee Willliams and Arthur Miller. Williams's dramas often show a conflict between sensitive individuals and the brutality and coarseness of modern life. This theme appears in his two best-known plays, *A Streetcar Named Desire* (1947) and *Cat on a Hot Tin Roof* (1955). Miller's *Death of a Salesman* (1949) lends tragic dignity to the anguish of Willy Loman, a traveling salesman. Loman is destroyed by accepting popularity and material success as the highest values in life. In *The Crucible* (1953), Miller uses the Salem Witch Trials of the 1600's in colonial America as a metaphor for government anti-Communist investigations of the 1950's.

Kurt Vonnegut

Toni Morrison

James Baldwin

Edward Albee became one of the leading American playwrights of his generation. Albee adapted the style of the Theater of the Absurd in plays that probed social and personal problems, such as *The Zoo Story* (1959). Theater of the Absurd was a largely European drama movement of the 1950's and 1960's that stressed the absurdity and lack of meaning the playwrights saw in modern life. Albee's *Who's Afraid of Virginia Woolf?* (1962) explored with biting wit how love and cruelty are entangled within marital relationships.

Lorraine Hansberry's *A Raisin in the Sun* (1959) realistically portrays a black family living in Chicago who decide to move to an all-white neighborhood. They must find the courage to resist the racism in society and claim the right to realize their hopes. August Wilson became famous for his cycle of 10 plays about African American life, one for each decade of the 1900's. Wilson set most of the plays in a black neighborhood in Pittsburgh, Pennsylvania. The best-known plays in the cycle are *Fences* (1985) and *The Piano Lesson* (1987).

Sam Shepard's long career as a playwright began with experimental works in the 1960's and 1970's. His *Buried Child* (1978) cemented his reputation with its dark portrayal of family relations in the modern West. David Mamet became a star in American drama in the 1980's with plays noted for their vigorous, explosive, and often profane dialogue. His best-known dramas include *Glengarry Glen Ross* (1984) and *Speed-the-Plow* (1988).

Recent American literature

The early 2000's became a time of concern and anxiety in American society. Such subjects as terrorism, nationalism, and political and economic instability were reflected in American literature. Many works have featured a tension between a national past and a global future.

Poetry. Much poetry since the late 1900's has been political in content. The poets have often dealt with issues of identity, whether personal or within a community. For example, Li-Young Lee, whose family was exiled from China, produced carefully crafted poems of great emotional depth. Lee wrote about his life and spiritual insights in *Book of My Nights* (2001).

Jimmy Santiago Baca, a poet of Apache and Chicano descent, was abandoned as a child and served several years in prison as a young man. His poems express spiritual triumph over adversity in richly lyric language. *Winter Poems Along the Rio Grande* (2004) celebrates nature in the area along the U.S.-Mexico border and Baca's later

life and dreams. In 2015, Juan Felipe Herrera became the first Chicano poet laureate of the United States. He described the Chicano experience in his poems, especially those collected in *Half the World in Light* (2008).

African American voices and experiences are central to American poetry of the 2000's. Such poets as Rita Dove, Tracy K. Smith, and Kevin Young have become prominent forces shaping the current direction of American poetry. Major contemporary works include Jamaican-born Claudia Rankine's *Citizen: An American Lyric* (2014) and Terrance Hayes's *How to Be Drawn* (2015).

Literary critics of the early 2000's have increasingly considered popular lyricists as major contributors to American poetry. Bob Dylan was awarded the Nobel Prize for literature in 2017 for poetic expressions of his songs. Hip-hop music has produced a number of gifted lyricists, including Jay-Z and Kanye West.

Fiction. The Postmodern movement continued to influence American novels and short stories. Paul Auster was recognized for narratives, including *4321* (2017), that feature the unstable identities of leading characters and strange coincidences. David Foster Wallace's long novel *Infinite Jest* (1996) is set in the near future and addresses issues of terrorism and substance abuse in a shifting style that includes many footnotes.

Much critically acclaimed fiction combined traditional literary fiction with genre fiction. Walter Mosley gained popularity for detective fiction centered on an African American named Easy Rawlins living in Los Angeles, California, during the 1940's. Rawlins first appeared in *Devil in a Blue Dress* (1990). Michael Chabon and Colson Whitehead included themes and plot devices common in science fiction, such as alternative history and murderous zombies, respectively.

A number of writers gained praise with a diverse range of styles and perspectives that had previously received little attention. Sherman Alexie, a Spokane-Coeur d'Alene writer, described life on a Native American reservation in many stories. Louise Erdrich drew upon Chippewa culture in novels that explore problems facing Native Americans in the modern world. Junot Díaz wrote absorbing stories about the lives of immigrants from the Dominican Republic, especially in his novel *The Brief Wondrous Life of Oscar Wao* (2007). Edwidge Danticat, a Haitian-American author, wrote powerfully about the immigrant experience, as well as about relationships between mothers and daughters.

Graphic novels emerged as a notable segment of American fiction. A graphic novel combines lengthy

Jill Krementz
Edward Albee

UPI/Bettmann
Lorraine Hansberry

Denise Applewhite, Princeton University
Tracy K. Smith

© Ulf Andersen, Getty Images
Michael Chabon

narrative with comic book-style illustrations. Leading graphic novelists include Alison Bechdel, Art Spiegelman, and Chris Ware.

Nonfiction prose. The status of literary nonfiction, especially essays, rose considerably during the early 2000's. Phillip Lopate's personal essays, published in *Portrait Inside My Head* (2013) and other collections, became influential. David Sedaris became known for his humorous short personal essays. David Shields analyzed the state of modern literature in *Reality Hunger* (2010). John D'Agata discussed the idea of conflict between truth and accuracy in literary nonfiction in *The Lifespan of a Fact* (2012).

Much of the leading nonfiction of the early 2000's was related to political activism. In *The Will to Change* (2004), Gloria Jean Watkins, who wrote under the pen name bell hooks, wrote powerfully about racism and oppression. Rebecca Solnit's travel writings often focus on the environment. Roxane Gay gained attention with her essays on feminism, such as those in *Bad Feminist* (2014). Leslie Jamison earned recognition with essays in *The Empathy Exams* (2014) that explore how to enter into the feelings and motives of other people.

Drama. New works for the stage in the early 2000's challenged the beliefs of mainstream society and dealt with previously underrepresented characters. Tony Kushner wrote an early example of the trend in *Angels in America* (two parts, 1991, 1992). The seven-hour work is an epic about gay characters and the AIDS epidemic. In *Topdog/Underdog* (2001), Suzan-Lori Parks examined the quarrelsome relationship between two African American brothers who live together. Sarah Ruhl's plays deal with issues of women's sexuality. Paula Vogel and Tracy Letts wrote powerful accounts of troublesome romantic relationships. The plays of Annie Baker, especially *The Flick* (2013), are known for their witty dialogue. Lin-Manuel Miranda gained tremendous success with Broadway musicals, especially *Hamilton* (2015). This work incorporates hip-hop music and casts non-white actors to play the Founding Fathers of the United States.

The study of American literature

Starting in the 1920's, American literature became an accepted field of study in higher education. Scholars wrote histories of American literature. They also designated some books as "classics" of superior value. Some scholars sought common themes that unified and distinguished American literature. These themes included the Puritan origins of the United States, the shared interest in a democratic constitutional government, and the exploration and conquest of frontier lands. Other scholars stressed conflicting themes, such as the individual versus the community, or uneasy relations between different races and ethnic groups.

Today, educators seek to broaden the definition and scope of American literature and to place it in a global setting. They promote the diversity, rather than the unity, of American literature. Teachers and critics today display greater interest in texts and authors that would have been considered marginal or nontraditional in the past.   John Hay

Related articles. See Literature for children and its list of *Related articles.* See also the following:

Colonial literature (1608-1764)

Bay Psalm Book	Mather, Cotton
Bradford, William (1590-1657)	Mather, Richard
Bradstreet, Anne	Poor Richard's Almanac
Byrd, William, II	Smith, John
Edwards, Jonathan	Taylor, Edward
Franklin, Benjamin	Wigglesworth, Michael
Great Awakening	

The revolutionary period (1765-1787)

Crèvecoeur, Michel-Guillaume Jean de	Paine, Thomas
Federalist, The	Warren, Mercy Otis
Freneau, Philip	Wheatley, Phillis
	Woolman, John

Literature of a young nation (1788-1830)

Brown, Charles Brockden	Payne, John Howard
Bryant, William Cullen	Rip Van Winkle
Dunlap, William	Tyler, Royall
Irving, Washington	Weems, Mason Locke

The Era of Expansion (1831-1870)

Alcott, Louisa May	Longfellow, Henry Wadsworth
Cooper, James Fenimore	Lowell, James Russell
Dana, Richard Henry, Jr.	Melville, Herman
Dickinson, Emily	Poe, Edgar Allan
Douglass, Frederick	Stowe, Harriet Beecher
Emerson, Ralph Waldo	Thoreau, Henry David
Frietchie, Barbara	Transcendentalism
Fuller, Margaret	Uncle Tom's Cabin
Hale, Edward Everett	Whitman, Walt
Hawthorne, Nathaniel	Whittier, John Greenleaf

The Age of Realism (1871-1913)
Short-story and prose writers

Adams, Henry	Holmes, Oliver Wendell
Addams, Jane	James, William
Ade, George	Jewett, Sarah Orne
Bierce, Ambrose	Keller, Helen
Du Bois, W. E. B.	Muir, John
Dunne, Finley Peter	Nye, Bill
Freeman, Mary E. Wilkins	Stockton, Frank R.
Garland, Hamlin	Tyler, Moses Coit
Hale, Edward Everett	Veblen, Thorstein
Harris, Joel Chandler	Ward, Artemus
Harte, Bret	Washington, Booker T.
Henry, O.	Winnemucca, Sarah

Novelists

Alger, Horatio	Frederic, Harold
Bellamy, Edward	Grey, Zane
Cable, George Washington	Hough, Emerson
Chesnutt, Charles Waddell	Howells, William Dean
Chopin, Kate	James, Henry
Crane, Stephen	London, Jack
Dreiser, Theodore	Norris, Frank
Eggleston, Edward	Sinclair, Upton

© Walter McBride, Getty Images

Annie Baker

© Ga Fullner, Shutterstock

Lin-Manuel Miranda

Twain, Mark

Wharton, Edith

Dramatists

Cohan, George M.
Fitch, Clyde
Herne, James A.
Moody, William Vaughn

Poets

Bates, Katharine Lee	Lanier, Sidney	Miller, Joaquin
Field, Eugene	Lazarus, Emma	Riley, James
Kilmer, Joyce	Markham, Edwin	Whitcomb

The World Wars and Depression (1914-1945)
Short-story and prose writers

Anderson, Sherwood	Runyon, Damon
Barzun, Jacques	Santayana, George
Bradford, Roark	Saroyan, William
De Voto, Bernard	Stein, Gertrude
Dobie, J. Frank	Tate, Allen
Lardner, Ring	Thurber, James
Locke, Alain LeRoy	Toomer, Jean
Lovecraft, H. P.	Welty, Eudora
Marquis, Don	White, E. B.
Mencken, H. L.	Wilson, Edmund
Parker, Dorothy	Woolrich, Cornell
Porter, Katherine Anne	

Novelists

Adams, Samuel Hopkins	La Farge, Oliver
Algren, Nelson	Lewis, Sinclair
Bromfield, Louis	Marquand, John P.
Buck, Pearl	McKay, Claude
Burroughs, Edgar Rice	Miller, Henry
Cabell, James Branch	Mitchell, Margaret
Cain, James	Nordhoff and Hall
Caldwell, Erskine	Norris, Frank
Cather, Willa	O'Hara, John
Chandler, Raymond	Queen, Ellery
Cozzens, James Gould	Rawlings, Marjorie Kinnan
Dos Passos, John	Richter, Conrad
Dreiser, Theodore	Roth, Henry
Farrell, James T.	Sinclair, Upton
Faulkner, William	Steinbeck, John
Ferber, Edna	Stout, Rex
Fitzgerald, F. Scott	Stuart, Jesse
Gardner, Erle Stanley	Tarkington, Booth
Glasgow, Ellen	Van Dine, S. S.
Hammett, Dashiell	West, Nathanael
Hecht, Ben	Wharton, Edith
Hemingway, Ernest	Wolfe, Thomas
Heyward, DuBose	Wright, Richard
Hurston, Zora Neale	

Dramatists

Anderson, Maxwell	Kelly, George
Barry, Philip	Kingsley, Sidney
Behrman, S. N.	Lindsay, Howard
Connelly, Marc	Luce, Clare Boothe
Glaspell, Susan	Odets, Clifford
Hart, Moss	O'Neill, Eugene
Hecht, Ben	Rice, Elmer
Hellman, Lillian	Van Druten, John
Howard, Sidney	Wilder, Thornton
Kaufman, George S.	

Poets

Aiken, Conrad	Eliot, T. S.
Benét, Stephen Vincent	Frost, Robert
Coffin, Robert P. T.	Guest, Edgar
Crane, Hart	Hughes, Langston
Cullen, Countee	Jeffers, Robinson
Cummings, E. E.	Johnson, James Weldon
Doolittle, Hilda	Lindsay, Vachel
Dunbar, Paul Laurence	Lowell, Amy

MacLeish, Archibald	Ransom, John Crowe
Masters, Edgar Lee	Robinson, Edwin Arlington
Millay, Edna St. Vincent	Sandburg, Carl
Monroe, Harriet	Stevens, Wallace
Moore, Marianne	Tate, Allen
Nash, Ogden	Teasdale, Sara
Neihardt, John	Van Doren, Mark
Pound, Ezra	Williams, William Carlos

Literature from 1945 to 2000
Short-story and prose writers

Alexie, Sherman	King, Martin Luther, Jr.
Angelou, Maya	McCarthy, Mary
Asimov, Isaac	O'Connor, Flannery
Bradbury, Ray	Parker, Robert B.
Carver, Raymond	Perelman, S. J.
Cheever, John	Singer, Isaac B.
Cleaver, Eldridge	Sontag, Susan
Didion, Joan	Stafford, Jean
Ellison, Harlan	Sturgeon, Theodore
Haley, Alex	Wolfe, Tom
Jackson, Shirley	

Novelists

Auchincloss, Louis	Mailer, Norman
Baldwin, James	Malamud, Bernard
Barth, John	McBain, Ed
Bellow, Saul	McCarthy, Cormac
Cain, James M.	McCullers, Carson
Capote, Truman	McKay, Claude
Clark, Mary Higgins	McMurtry, Larry
Cornwell, Patricia	Michener, James A.
Crichton, Michael	Miller, Henry
Derleth, August	Morrison, Toni
Doctorow, E. L.	Mosley, Walter
Eisner, Will	Muller, Marcia
Ellison, Ralph	Nabokov, Vladimir
Faulkner, William	Norton, Andre
George, Elizabeth	Oates, Joyce Carol
Grafton, Sue	O'Hara, John
Grimes, Martha	Ozick, Cynthia
Grisham, John	Paretsky, Sara
Guthrie, A. B., Jr.	Puzo, Mario
Heinlein, Robert A.	Pynchon, Thomas
Heller, Joseph	Rand, Ayn
Herbert, Frank	Roth, Philip
Hersey, John	Salinger, J. D.
Highsmith, Patricia	Shaw, Irwin
Hillerman, Tony	Spiegelman, Art
Himes, Chester	Stegner, Wallace
Hobson, Laura Z.	Styron, William
Irving, John	Theroux, Paul
Kerouac, Jack	Tyler, Anne
Kesey, Ken	Updike, John
King, Stephen	Uris, Leon
Koontz, Dean	Vidal, Gore
L'Amour, Louis	Vonnegut, Kurt
Lee, Harper	Walker, Alice
Le Guin, Ursula K.	Welty, Eudora
Leonard, Elmore	West, Jessamyn
MacDonald, John D.	Wiesel, Elie
Macdonald, Ross	Wouk, Herman

Dramatists

Albee, Edward	Norman, Marsha
Baraka, Amiri	Parks, Suzan-Lori
Hansberry, Lorraine	Shepard, Sam
Inge, William	Simon, Neil
Mamet, David	Wasserstein, Wendy
McNally, Terrence	Williams, Tennessee
Miller, Arthur	Wilson, August

Poets

Ashbery, John	Bishop, Elizabeth
Berryman, John	Brodsky, Joseph

Brooks, Gwendolyn
Ciardi, John
Creeley, Robert
Dickey, James
Duncan, Robert
Ferlinghetti, Lawrence
Ginsberg, Allen
Giovanni, Nikki
Jarrell, Randall
Lindbergh, Anne Morrow
Lowell, Robert
McGinley, Phyllis

Merrill, James
Merwin, W. S.
Olson, Charles
Plath, Sylvia
Rich, Adrienne
Roethke, Theodore
Schwartz, Delmore
Sexton, Anne
Shapiro, Karl Jay
Warren, Robert Penn
Wilbur, Richard

Recent American literature

Novelists

Alexie, Sherman
Collins, Suzanne
Erdrich, Louise
George, Elizabeth
Grafton, Sue
Green, John

Grisham, John
Koontz, Dean
Meyer, Stephenie
Mosley, Walter
Paolini, Christopher

Dramatists

Miranda, Lin-Manuel

Parks, Suzan-Lori

Poets

Ashbery, John
Dove, Rita

Glück, Louise
Rich, Adrienne

Other related articles

African American literature
Beat movement
Biography
Colonial life in America
  (Literature)
Criticism
Detective story
Drama
Essay
Gone with the Wind
Grapes of Wrath, The
Harlem Renaissance
Huckleberry Finn

Lost Generation
Muckrakers
Nobel Prizes
Novel
Poetry
Pulitzer Prizes
Satire
Science fiction
Short story
Western frontier life in
  America (Literature)
Westerns
Writing

American Lung Association is the oldest nation-wide voluntary public health agency in the United States. The agency was founded in 1904 to fight tuberculosis. Today, the association and its state and local affiliates work to control and prevent all lung diseases. The association and its affiliates also work to combat some of the related causes of breathing problems, including smoking, air pollution, and occupational lung hazards.

The American Lung Association provides public health education programs and materials on such diseases as asthma, emphysema, influenza, lung cancer, pneumonia, and tuberculosis, as well as lung disorders in infants. It supports medical research and awards grants to encourage young medical professionals to specialize in lung health. The work of the association is funded in part by public contributions to its annual Christmas Seal Campaign. Headquarters of the American Lung Association are in Washington, D.C.

Critically reviewed by the American Lung Association

American Medical Association (AMA) is a professional society of physicians. Its purpose is "to promote the art and science of medicine and the betterment of public health." The association's membership includes physicians, resident physicians, and medical students.

The AMA publishes a weekly scientific journal, *JAMA: The Journal of the American Medical Association;* a weekly newspaper, *American Medical News;* monthly specialty journals; and other publications on medical subjects. The AMA was founded in 1847. Its headquarters are in Chicago.

Critically reviewed by the American Medical Association

American Museum of Natural History, in New York City, is a museum that works to educate the public and advance the study of natural science. The museum's scientific departments conduct research in such areas as anthropology, paleontology, zoology, and the physical sciences. The museum also has departments of education and exhibition, a research library, and the Rose Center for Earth and Space, which includes the Hayden Planetarium. The museum was incorporated in 1869.

The American Museum of Natural History includes exhibits on animals and plants, including dinosaurs and other fossil life, as well as rare gems, minerals, and meteorites. Other exhibits illustrate human cultures and biology, and the origin of life.

Critically reviewed by the American Museum of Natural History

American Party is a conservative political party in the United States. It was set up in 1968 under the name American Independent Party to support former Governor George C. Wallace of Alabama in his campaign for president. Wallace had been governor of Alabama from 1963 to 1967 and had run unsuccessfully for the Democratic nomination for president in 1964. Wallace had gained national attention by resisting the U.S. government's efforts to desegregate Alabama public schools.

The roots of the American Independent Party can be traced to the 1960 presidential election. Six of Alabama's 11 Democratic electors in the Electoral College rejected the national Democratic candidate, John F. Kennedy. Instead, the six voted for Senator Harry F. Byrd of Virginia.

In 1968, Wallace's supporters succeeded in placing the American Independent Party on the ballot in every state. That year, Wallace chose retired General Curtis E. LeMay as his running mate. The party platform condemned government welfare programs, the Civil Rights Act of 1964, and what the party considered a "no-win" policy in the Vietnam War (1957-1975). Republican Richard M. Nixon won the 1968 election. Wallace ran far behind the Democratic candidate, Hubert H. Humphrey. However, Wallace got 13 ½ percent of the popular vote and 46 electoral votes.

In 1969, representatives from 38 states established the American Party as the successor to the American Independent Party. In 1976, the party split into the American Party and the American Independent Party. Both parties have nominated candidates for the presidency and other offices. But neither party has achieved the strength of the American Independent Party under Wallace. The Know-Nothing Party of the 1850's also used the name American Party (see **Know-Nothings**).   Peter N. Carroll

See also **Wallace, George C.**

American Revolution. See Revolution, American.

American Samoa is a United States territory about 2,300 miles (3,700 kilometers) southwest of Hawaii. Six of the territory's seven islands are divided among three groups—Tutuila and Aunuu; Ofu, Olosega, and Tau (the Manua group); and Rose. These islands are in the Samoan chain. The seventh, Swains Island, lies 200 miles (320 kilometers) north. The Jennings family has owned Swains Island since 1856. That year, Eli Jennings, an American, and his Samoan wife settled there.

The largest and most important island is Tutuila. Pago Pago (pronounced *PAHNG oh PAHNG oh)*, the capital of American Samoa, lies on Tutuila on one of the best and most beautiful harbors in the South Pacific. Pago Pago is the territory's only port and urban center.

American Samoa's 53,000 people are nationals, but not citizens, of the United States. As nationals, they do not vote in U.S. elections but may freely enter the country at any time. Many people of Samoan descent live in Hawaii and the continental United States.

Government. American Samoa is administered by the U.S. Department of the Interior. It is classified as an *unorganized and unincorporated territory.* For details, see **Territory** (Territories in the United States). The Constitution of American Samoa took effect in 1967. American Samoans elect a governor to a four-year term. The territory has a legislature with a Senate and a House of Representatives. The Senate has 18 members chosen by county councils to serve four-year terms. The House has 20 members elected by the people to two-year terms and 1 nonvoting delegate from Swains Island. Samoans who are 18 years old or older may vote. Samoans elect a delegate to the U.S. House of Representatives. The delegate may only vote in House committees.

People. Almost all American Samoans are Polynesians. Samoan, a Polynesian language, is the main language, but many people also speak English. Most of the people live in villages, and their lives center around their families. Each family group is headed by a chief who controls the family's property, represents it in the village council, and takes care of its sick or aged. Most American Samoans are Christians.

In 1961, the United States began an economic development program in American Samoa. Many people left their villages to work in industries around Pago Pago. Thatch-roofed *fale* (houses) were replaced by hurricane-proof concrete buildings. New schools were built, and teaching by television was introduced. Children between the ages of 5 and 18 must attend school.

Land. The islands of American Samoa have a total area of 77 square miles (200 square kilometers). Only a third of the land can be cultivated. Rose and Swains islands consist of coral. The others are remains of extinct volcanoes. Most of the land is mountainous, with some fertile soil in the valleys. Coconuts, bananas, and taro are grown (see **Taro**). There are few natural resources. The islands have a wet tropical climate. Yearly rainfall

Cameramann International, Ltd.

Pago Pago, American Samoa's capital, lies on one of the most beautiful harbors in the South Pacific. Pago Pago is the territory's only port and urban center.

averages about 125 inches (320 centimeters) in drier areas and 200 inches (510 centimeters) in wetter locations. Temperatures range from 70 to 90 °F (21 to 32 °C).

Economy. The leading industry is tuna canning and canned tuna is the territory's main export. Leading crops include bananas, coconuts, taro, and yams. Tourism has become an important source of income. The U.S. government has provided large amounts of money to American Samoa's economy.

History. The Samoa Islands have been occupied by Polynesian peoples for at least 2,000 years. These peoples probably migrated from eastern Melanesia. European explorers first reached the Samoa Islands in 1722 (see **Samoa** [History]). In 1872, the Samoans agreed to let the United States use Pago Pago Bay as a naval coaling station. Later, the United States was given trading rights in the islands.

In 1899, the United States, Germany, and the United Kingdom signed a treaty dividing the Samoa Islands between the United States and Germany. Germany took control of the western islands in 1900. The United States took control of Tutuila, Aunuu, and Rose Island in 1900, and the Manua group in 1904. Swains Island was annexed in 1925. The islands were administered by the U.S. Navy until 1951, when they were transferred to the Department of the Interior. Afterward, the governor of

American Samoa

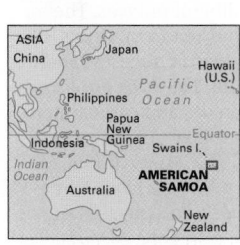

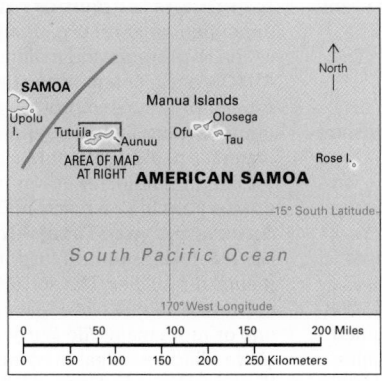

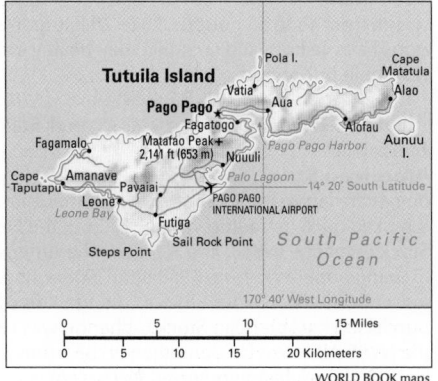

Road

★ Government center

• Village or settlement

+ Elevation above sea level

WORLD BOOK maps

American Samoa was appointed by the secretary of the interior. In the early 1970's, the United States proposed that the territory elect its governor. But Samoan voters rejected the proposal three times. Many believed the change would weaken their ties to the United States. American Samoans approved the proposal in 1976 and first elected a governor in 1977.   Donald H. Rubinstein

See also **American Samoa, National Park of.**

American Samoa, National Park of, lies in the United States territory of American Samoa in the South Pacific Ocean. The park was established primarily to protect the area's tropical rain forest on the islands of Tutuila and Tau. The rain forest is home to many kinds of plants and animals, including two species of large bats called *flying foxes.* A white sand beach and a coral reef on the island of Ofu are also protected.

The national park also protects the way of life of the Samoan people. The people practice traditional methods of farming and reef fishing in certain areas of the park. The park was established in 1988. For its area, see **National Park System** (table: National parks).

Critically reviewed by the National Park Service

American Society of Composers, Authors and Publishers (ASCAP) is an association of writers and publishers of music. Composer Victor Herbert helped found ASCAP in 1914. The federal copyright law states that no musical work may be performed publicly without permission of the copyright owner. ASCAP is a clearinghouse between users and creators of music. Its license permits users to perform any member's music at any time without separate clearance. It collects license fees from music users and distributes it to members and to associated societies. Royalties are distributed to members based on the nature of the performance and how often the music is used. ASCAP has mutual agreements with other performing rights societies in many other countries. Its headquarters are in New York City.

Critically reviewed by the American Society of Composers, Authors and Publishers

American Staffordshire terrier is a breed of dog that originated in the United States. It descended from the Staffordshire bull terrier, a breed brought from England in the late 1800's. By the early 1900's, American breeders had developed a dog taller and heavier than its British ancestors. The American Staffordshire terrier has been called *Yankee terrier* and *pit bull.* It was once used in vicious dog fights in pits. The dog is still popularly called pit bull. American Staffordshire terriers stand from 17 to 19 inches (43 to 48 centimeters) tall and weigh from 45 to 65 pounds (20 to 29 kilograms). The dogs have a short, stiff coat that may be any color. They resemble bull terriers.

Critically reviewed by the American Kennel Club

See also **Dog** (picture: Terriers); **Pit bull; Staffordshire bull terrier.**

American Stock Exchange, also called *AMEX,* was one of the largest stock exchanges in the United States. It ranked third in trading volume behind the New York Stock Exchange (NYSE) and Nasdaq. The American Stock Exchange operated from 1953 until 2008, when it was acquired by the New York Stock Exchange. After the 2008 purchase, the American Stock Exchange was renamed the NYSE Alternext U.S., and then NYSE Amex Equities. In 2012, the exchange received its current name, NYSE

MKT LLC. After the acquisition, the NYSE closed AMEX's equities trading floor and moved it to the NYSE trading floor. In addition to stocks, the exchange also traded in *options*—that is, it was also a marketplace for stock-buying rights. It was a leader in *exchange-traded funds* (ETF's), publicly traded investments similar to mutual funds.

The American Stock Exchange began in the mid-1800's as the New York Curb Exchange. This organization was composed of New York City brokers who met outdoors at the curbside to buy and sell stocks. They were called *curbstone brokers.* In 1921, trading moved indoors to an Art Deco building in Manhattan. The organization changed its name to the American Stock Exchange in 1953, a name it kept until its acquisition in 2008.

Critically reviewed by NYSE MKT LLC

See also **Stock exchange.**

American System. See **Clay, Henry; Monroe, James** ("The American System").

American water spaniel is a hunting dog that was developed in the United States. The dog is especially helpful to pheasant and duck hunters. It *flushes* birds (forces them to fly out of their hiding place) so the hunter can shoot the birds. The dog then brings the dead bird back to the hunter. The dog's thick, curly coat protects it from both cold water and thorny bushes. Its coat may be *liver* (reddish-brown), brown, or dark chocolate-brown in color. Some American water spaniels have white markings on the chest or toes. Most of the dogs weigh from 25 to 45 pounds (11 to 20 kilograms) and stand 15 to 18 inches (38 to 46 centimeters) at the shoulder.   Critically reviewed by the American Kennel Club

See also **Dog** (picture: American water spaniel).

American's Creed won a nationwide contest for William Tyler Page of Maryland in 1917 as "the best summary of the political faith of America." It follows:

"I believe in the United States of America as a government of the people, by the people, for the people; whose just powers are derived from the consent of the governed; a democracy in a Republic; a sovereign Nation of many sovereign States; a perfect Union, one and inseparable; established upon those principles of freedom, equality, justice, and humanity for which American patriots sacrificed their lives and fortunes.

"I therefore believe it is my duty to my country to love it; to support its Constitution; to obey its laws; to respect its flag; and to defend it against all enemies."

Kenneth Janda

Americans for Democratic Action (ADA) is an independent political organization that urges government action to promote and maintain liberal policies. The ADA favors action to protect and extend civil rights, to expand programs to provide economic security, and to improve international cooperation. The ADA publishes materials to influence public opinion, and campaigns for liberal candidates. It was founded in 1947. Its headquarters are in Washington, D.C.   Murray Clark Havens

Americans with Disabilities Act is a United States law that forbids discrimination based on physical or mental disabilities. The act, often called the ADA, seeks to protect people with disabilities that significantly limit one or more major life activities. Such disabilities include blindness, deafness, muscular and nervous disorders, paralysis, and loss of limbs. The ADA's chief goal is to ensure that people with disabilities are not denied basic rights and have an opportunity to lead fulfilling lives.

The first right protected by the ADA is the freedom to seek employment. The law bans discrimination in hiring, pay, and promotion. It also requires that employers make efforts to accommodate the workplace needs and limitations of employees with disabilities.

A second section of the ADA states that people with disabilities must have equal opportunities to benefit from all government-run activities, programs, and services. This provision requires many public buildings to have wheelchair-accessible entrances and ramps. It also requires government organizations to make special efforts to communicate with people who have hearing, vision, or speech disabilities.

Other issues addressed by the ADA include the accessibility of buses, trains, hotels, motion-picture theaters, restaurants, and stores. Many transit services and other establishments must provide ramps or lifts for people in wheelchairs, and signs in braille for customers who are blind. The act also requires telephone companies to provide telephone relay services for people with speech or hearing disabilities. A victim of employer discrimination can file a complaint with the Equal Employment Opportunity Commission, which will take the case to court. The U.S. Department of Justice handles other complaints of discrimination under the ADA.

The National Council on Disability, an independent federal agency, developed the ADA in the mid-1980's. Congress passed it in 1990. In 2008, Congress expanded the ADA's protections to people who can compensate for their disabilities by the use of medication, medical devices, or prosthetics. Earlier decisions by the U.S. Supreme Court had limited the scope of the act's protections.   Critically reviewed by the National Council on Disability

See also **Disability**.

America's Cup is the oldest trophy in international sports. It is awarded to the winner of the world's best-known sailboat competition. A yacht from a defending country races against a yacht from a challenging country. The first yacht to win a certain number of races wins the cup. Races are held on a course off the coast of the defending nation every three or four years.

The cup gets its name from the American schooner *America*. In 1851, *America* defeated 14 British yachts in a race around the Isle of Wight to win a silver trophy. The yacht's owners gave the trophy to the New York Yacht Club in New York City in 1857. That yacht club successfully defended the cup in 16 challenges before the outbreak of World War II in 1939. In the final three prewar

America's Cup winners*

Year	Winner	Country
1992	*America*[3]	United States
1995	*Black Magic*	New Zealand
2000	*Black Magic*	New Zealand
2003	*Alinghi*	Switzerland
2007	*Alinghi*	Switzerland
2010	*BMW Oracle*	United States
2013	*Oracle Team USA*	United States
2017	*Emirates Team New Zealand*	New Zealand
2021	*Emirates Team New Zealand*	New Zealand

*The America's Cup race began in 1851. However, a code of conduct and yacht design specifications were only established beginning with the 1992 race. See article text for a history of the race prior to 1992.

© Steve Todd, Shutterstock

In the America's Cup competition in 2021, *Emirates Team New Zealand, right,* won its second consecutive America's Cup, defeating the Italian yacht *Luna Rossa, left.* The New Zealand yacht won seven of the ten races.

races, the competitors sailed large yachts called J-Class. Competition resumed in 1958 in a match sailed on 12-Meter yachts, which were much smaller than the J-Class.

In 1970, two countries challenged for the cup for the first time, requiring selection trials to determine who would race the defender. In 1983, *Australia II* defeated the New York Yacht Club *Liberty* and became the first challenger ever to win the America's Cup. In 1987, the United States yacht *Stars & Stripes* defeated Australia's *Kookaburra III* to return the cup to the United States.

Since 1992, competition has operated under a code of conduct and design specifications that are intended to ensure races between evenly matched competitors. The current class is called *AC75* (America's Cup 75). The yachts are designed with specific lengths, weights, and sail areas. They are about 75 feet (23 meters) long, made of lightweight carbon fiber, and have a crew of 11. The first challenge in AC75 yachts took place in 2021 when the New Zealand yacht *Emirates Team New Zealand* defeated the Italian challenger *Luna Rossa*.   Charles Mason

See also **Sailing** (America's Cup).

Americium, *AM uh RIHSH ee uhm* or *AM uh REES ee uhm*, is an artificially created radioactive element. Its chemical symbol is Am, and its *atomic number* (number of protons) is 95. Americium has 15 known *isotopes,* forms of the element that have the same number of protons but different numbers of neutrons. The most stable isotope has an *atomic mass number* (total number of protons and neutrons) of 243. That isotope has a *half-life* of 7,370 years—that is, due to radioactive decay, only half the atoms in a sample of Americium 243 would still be atoms of that isotope after 7,370 years. Only this isotope and one that has a mass number of 241 and a half-life of 432 years can be produced in large amounts. At 20 °C, americium has a density of 13.67 grams per cubic centimeter (see **Density**). The metal melts at 1173 °C. It is an important part of some household smoke detectors, where it gives off so little radiation that it is considered safe for people.

Americium was discovered in 1944 by the American scientists Glenn T. Seaborg, Ralph A. James, Leon O. Morgan, and Albert Ghiorso when they bombarded plutonium with neutrons. It was named for its place of discovery, the United States of America. Americium becomes *superconductive* (see **Superconductivity**) when cooled to –272.36 °C.   Marianna A. Busch

See also **Seaborg, Glenn T.; Transuranium element.**
Amerigo Vespucci. See **Vespucci, Amerigo.**
Amethyst, *AM uh thihst,* is a purple or bluish-violet gem. It is used to make rings, necklaces, and brooches. The amethyst is a variety of quartz. The color of the amethyst is believed to be caused by impurities such as iron and manganese. Amethysts have been mined in Brazil, Canada, India, Madagascar, Mexico, Siberia, Sri Lanka, and Uruguay. Amethyst is the birthstone for February.   Willis Hames

See also **Birthstone; Gem** (picture).
Amex. See **American Stock Exchange.**
Amherst, *AM uhrst,* **Lord Jeffery** (1717-1797), was a British general who helped Britain win Canada from France. In 1758, during the Seven Years' War (also called the French and Indian War), he captured the French fort of Louisbourg in what is now Nova Scotia. Amherst was made commander in chief of the British army in North America after that victory. In 1759, he captured Crown Point and Fort Ticonderoga, both in what is now New York. In 1760, he directed an advance on Montreal, and the city surrendered. Amherst then administered Canada until his return to England in 1763. He was made a baron in 1776 and commander in chief of the British Army in 1778. Amherst was born on Jan. 29, 1717, in Riverhead, near Tonbridge, England. He died on Aug. 3, 1797.   Phillip Buckner

Amiens, *AM ee uhnz,* or in French *ah MYAN* (pop. 133,755; met. area pop. 297,468), is a city in northern France. The city lies along the Somme River (see **France** [political map]). The old section of Amiens has numerous buildings that date from the Middle Ages. This section is dominated by one of the world's largest and most famous Gothic cathedrals, which was built during the 1200's and 1300's. Much of the modern section of the city was built after World War II (1939-1945).

Amiens is the capital of the Somme department within the Hauts-de-France region. It is a center of commerce, communications, and education. Its industries include food processing, metalworking, and the manufacture of agricultural machinery, textiles, and tires. The University of Picardy Jules Verne is in the city.

Julius Caesar had headquarters at the site of what is now Amiens in 54 B.C., during the Gallic Wars. The city grew during the Middle Ages, when it became a center of the textile trade. It was badly damaged in World War I (1914-1918) and World War II.   Mark Kesselman

See also **Architecture** (picture: Gothic cathedrals).

Amin Dada, *ah MEEN DAH dah,* **Idi,** *EE dee* (1925?-2003), was the ruler of Uganda from 1971 to 1979. Amin, an army officer, came to power after leading the army in overthrowing Uganda's civilian government. His rule ended when Ugandans who opposed his policies and troops from neighboring Tanzania overthrew his government. Amin then fled the country.

Amin was a controversial leader. In 1972, he forced an estimated 40,000 to 50,000 Asians living in Uganda to leave the country. He said that he did so to put control of the nation's economy in the hands of Ugandans. Many thousands of Ugandans who opposed Amin's policies were killed, at Amin's order or by order of his supporters. Amin also called for the "extinction of Israel" and praised Nazi dictator Adolf Hitler for murdering Jews.

Amin was born in northern Uganda. Amin enlisted in the army in 1944. He was appointed to the rank of deputy commander of the armed forces in 1964. From 1951 to 1960, Amin was the heavyweight boxing champion of Uganda. Amin died on Aug. 16, 2003, in Saudi Arabia, where he had been living in exile.   Robert I. Rotberg

Amino acid, *uh MEE noh,* is the name for the type of organic acids that make up all the proteins in living things. Scientists call amino acids the *building blocks of proteins.* All amino acids contain carbon, hydrogen, oxygen, and nitrogen. Some amino acids contain sulfur.

Green plants and some microorganisms can make all the amino acids they need. But human beings and higher animals cannot make all 20 amino acids needed to build tissues. Human beings must get at least nine amino acids from food. Protein foods, such as eggs, meat, milk products, and some vegetables, provide amino acids. The body breaks down these foods into amino acids. It then links the amino acids to form new proteins.

The body can make many kinds of proteins. A protein may consist of several hundred amino acid units linked by chemical bonds. Also, the order of the amino acids may vary, producing different proteins. These amino acid sequences determine the functions of the proteins.

Some simple proteins may be made up of only four different kinds of amino acids. Most of the more complex proteins contain about 20 amino acids. All amino acids contain one or more groups of one nitrogen and two hydrogen atoms called *amino,* or NH_2, groups. Amino acids are made up of amino groups and certain organic acids.   Kermit L. Carraway

See also **Cell** (The work of a cell); **Hormone** (How hormones work); **Protein.**

Amis, *AY mihs,* **Kingsley** (1922-1995), was an English novelist best known for his witty, satirical stories about British society. His most famous work is his first novel, *Lucky Jim* (1954). In it, Jim Dixon, a young university instructor, is disgusted by the falseness of his colleagues and their work. *The Old Devils* (1986), about a group of aging friends in Wales, won the 1986 Booker Prize, the United Kingdom's highest literary award. Amis's other novels include *That Uncertain Feeling* (1955), *Take a Girl Like You* (1960), *One Fat Englishman* (1964), *The Green Man* (1970), *Jake's Thing* (1979), *Difficulties with Girls* (1989), and *The Folks That Live on the Hill* (1990).

Kingsley William Amis was born on April 16, 1922, in London. In the 1950's, he became identified with the Angry Young Men, a group of writers who ridiculed middle-class society. Later, he began writing detective and spy fiction under the name Robert Markham. Amis was also a noted poet. His *Collected Poems: 1944-1979* was published in 1979. *Memoirs* (1991) is a book of autobiographical essays. Amis was knighted by Queen Elizabeth II in 1990. Martin Amis, his son, is a noted English novelist. Kingsley Amis died on Oct. 22, 1995.   Michael Seidel

Amish, *AM ihsh* or *AH mihsh,* are members of an Anabaptist Protestant group that teaches separation from the world. The Amish religion stresses hard work, humility, nonviolence, and simplicity. Members may not go to war, hold public office, or swear oaths. The men wear dark clothes and wide-brimmed hats. After marry-

© Shutterstock

An Amish carriage travels through the countryside. The Amish do not believe in owning cars.

ing, they grow a beard. The women wear plain dresses and bonnets. The children attend rural Amish schools.

The Amish live in farming communities, but a minority make a living as farmers. Others are engaged in cottage industries, in which they make goods at home; own small businesses; or work for wages. The Amish do not buy insurance or pay social security taxes, and they do not participate in government social programs. They support the rights of private property and individual economic freedom. In addition, they willingly help one another and non-Amish people in times of financial need as part of their religious commitments.

The Amish religion originated in Switzerland among the Swiss and immigrants from southwestern Germany. It was named for Jacob Ammann. In 1693, Ammann led his followers in breaking away from the Swiss Mennonites because of disagreements over church discipline.

The Amish first traveled to North America in the early 1700's. They settled in eastern Pennsylvania and spoke a German dialect that became known as Pennsylvania Dutch. Today, several groups of Old Order Amish and New Order Amish live in rural communities in the United States and Canada. The largest Amish communities are in Illinois, Indiana, Iowa, Ohio, and Pennsylvania. Central and South America also have some Amish communities, but there are none remaining in Europe.

Barbara J. Dilly

See also **Anabaptists; Mennonites; Pennsylvania Dutch.**

Amistad Rebellion was a revolt in 1839 by black slaves against Spaniards who had bought them. The re-

bellion took place on a ship called *La Amistad.* Joseph Cinque, a member of the Mende people of what is now Sierra Leone, led the uprising. The slaves were later tried in courts in the United States for their rebellion and were found not guilty. This legal decision was a landmark because blacks had few rights at the time.

The slaves who became the Amistad rebels were captured in western Africa. Early in 1839, Spanish slave traders brought them to Cuba illegally on a Portuguese ship. In Havana, two Spaniards, Pedro Montes and José Ruiz, bought Cinque and 52 other captives from the traders. Montes and Ruiz intended to resell the 53 slaves in the Cuban town of Puerto Principe (now Camagüey). They set sail in the Caribbean Sea on the schooner *La Amistad.* They hired a ship captain and two crewmen. The captain brought a cook and a cabin boy with him.

The slaves were chained to a wall below the deck of the ship. One night, Cinque saw an opportunity to escape. He used a nail to break his wrist chains and iron collar. He helped other slaves get free and they, in turn, helped others. The slaves attacked the crew and took control of the ship. They killed the captain and his cook. The two crewmen jumped ship and escaped. Montes, Ruiz, and the cabin boy were captured by the slaves. Two slaves died during the rebellion.

The rebels did not know how to sail the ship. Cinque ordered Montes and Ruiz to sail it to Africa. During the day, the Spaniards sailed slowly eastward, the direction of Africa. At night, they secretly changed to a northwest course and moved rapidly. The ship ended up at Long Island, New York. Eight more rebels had died by then.

When *La Amistad* reached New York, Montes and Ruiz reported the killings. The rebels were arrested and taken to Connecticut, where they were put on trial.

United States district and circuit courts ruled that the rebels had been free people who were illegally enslaved and thus were justified in rebelling. The case went to the U.S. Supreme Court in 1841. John Quincy Adams, who had been president of the United States from 1825 to 1829, defended the rebels in the Supreme Court. He based his defense on the right of every person to be free. The court ruled in favor of the rebels. Cinque and most of the other remaining Amistad rebels returned to Africa in January 1842.   Nudie Eugene Williams

Amman, *AHM mahn* (pop. 1,155,000), is the capital and largest city of Jordan. It lies 25 miles (40 kilometers) northeast of the Dead Sea (see **Jordan** [map]).

Most of Amman's buildings stand on several hills. The main streets run between the hills. Amman has many government buildings, churches, and *mosques* (Muslim houses of worship). The city lies on old trade routes and still is a major trading center. Its factories produce more than half of Jordan's manufactured goods.

About 1000 B.C., Amman, then called Rabbath-Ammon, was the capital of the Ammonites. The Bible describes how the Israelites, led by David and Joab, captured it. Greeks, Arab Muslims, and Turks later controlled the city. In 1921, Amman became the capital of the new state of Transjordan. Transjordan changed its name to Jordan in 1949.   Bernard Reich

See also **Jordan** (picture).

Ammonia, *uh MOHN yuh* or *uh MOH nee uh* (chemical formula NH_3), is a colorless gas made up of one part nitrogen and three parts hydrogen. Ammonia is lighter than air and has a sharp, stinging odor. Ammonia can be inhaled safely if it is greatly diluted in air, but concentrated ammonia gas can cause suffocation and death. Ammonia does not burn in air, but it burns in oxygen with a weak yellow flame. Chemists classify ammonia as a base.

Properties of ammonia. Ammonia is highly soluble in water and forms a solution known as *ammonium hydroxide* (ammonia water). Ammonia is not very reactive when dry, but it reacts with many chemicals when dissolved in water. Ammonium hydroxide neutralizes acids and forms the corresponding ammonium salts. For example, hydrochloric acid (HCl) added to ammonium hydroxide (NH_4OH) produces a solution of ammonium chloride (NH_4Cl). When combined with some metals, ammonium hydroxide forms complex compounds called *ammines.* For example, the addition of ammonium hydroxide to a pale blue solution of cupric sulfate ($CuSO_4$) produces a deep blue solution of cupric ammine sulfate [$Cu(NH_3)_4SO_4$].

Ammonia gas changes to a liquid at -33.35 °C. Liquid ammonia boils at the same temperature. It freezes to a clear solid at -77.7 °C. In going from a liquid back to a gas, ammonia absorbs a large amount of heat from its surroundings. Upon evaporation, one gram of ammonia absorbs 327 calories of heat. For this reason, ammonia is widely used in refrigeration equipment.

Preparing ammonia. In the laboratory, ammonia is prepared by heating an ammonium salt with sodium hydroxide. Commercially, ammonia is made by the Haber process, which combines free nitrogen and hydrogen gases, both of which can be obtained easily and cheaply (see **Haber process**). One volume of nitrogen is mixed with three volumes of hydrogen under high pressure and temperature in the presence of an iron catalyst (see **Catalysis**). Ammonia is also obtained as a by-product in the production of coal and coke gas.

Uses. Ammonia is widely used as a fertilizer. Ammonium nitrate and other ammonium salts help to increase crop production because they have a high percentage of nitrogen. In some farming areas, anhydrous ammonia is now applied directly to the fields from large tanks that contain the compressed gas.

Large quantities of ammonia are oxidized to make nitric acid, which is needed to make such explosives as TNT (trinitrotoluene), nitroglycerin, and ammonium nitrate. The textile industry uses ammonia in the production of synthetic fibers such as nylon and cuprammonium rayon. Ammonia is also used in dyeing and scouring cotton, wool, and other fibers. Ammonia water sometimes serves as a cleaning fluid and can be used to restore fabrics that have been stained by acids. Ammonia is also vital in the manufacture of many chemicals, plastics, vitamins, and drugs.   David C. Armbruster

Related articles in *World Book* include:

Anhydrous ammonia	Gas	Refrigeration
	Ice	Smelling salts
Base	Nitrogen	

Ammons, A. R. (1926-2001), was an American poet whose verse explores natural processes, from the cosmic to the microscopic. Trained in science, he brought to his poetry a subtle understanding of how organisms and events interact in nature to produce endless complexity. In "Cascadilla Falls," he contemplated a single stone while trying to imagine all the forces that affect it:

gravity, the spinning of Earth and its orbit around the sun, and the movement of the solar system and galaxy.

The form and language of Ammons's poems often reflect the complexity he saw in nature. Some of his poems adopt a loose, wandering format with lines and phrases scattered across the page in patterns that suggest the uneven beauty of a wild landscape. Others unroll in regular groups of lines that resemble the rapid flowing of a stream.

Archie Randolph Ammons was born on Feb. 18, 1926, in Whiteville, North Carolina. His *Selected Poems* were published in 1969, 1977, and 1986. A late collection, *Bosh and Flapdoodle*, was published in 2005, after his death on Feb. 25, 2001. *The Complete Poems of A. R. Ammons* was published in two volumes in 2017.

Roger Gilbert

Ammunition is any object fired or launched from a gun or some other weapon. Such objects, also called *projectiles,* include cartridges, shells, and rockets. Weapons that fire projectiles include handguns, cannons, and rocket launchers. Guided missiles and torpedos are also examples of ammunition, but this article does not discuss them. For information on these two

Kinds of bullets

Bullets consist of a metal core that is either fully or partly covered by a metal jacket. Bullets with a full metal jacket keep their shape when they strike a target. However, partly jacketed bullets, called *soft-point bullets,* expand on impact, *shown here.*

WORLD BOOK diagram by Steven Liska

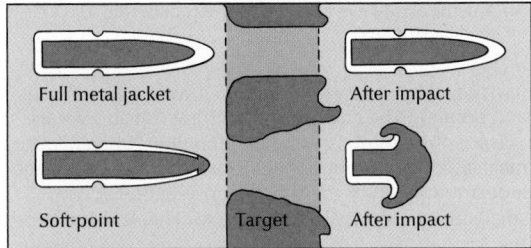

Full metal jacket   After impact

Soft-point   Target   After impact

Common calibers of cartridges

Caliber (bullet diameter) is given in decimal fractions of an inch or in millimeters (mm). For example, the diameter of a .30-06 Springfield cartridge, *shown here,* is $\frac{30}{100}$ inch. This is the same diameter as that of the 7.62 mm Soviet Model 1943. The illustrations are not drawn to the same scale.

WORLD BOOK illustrations by Bensen Studios

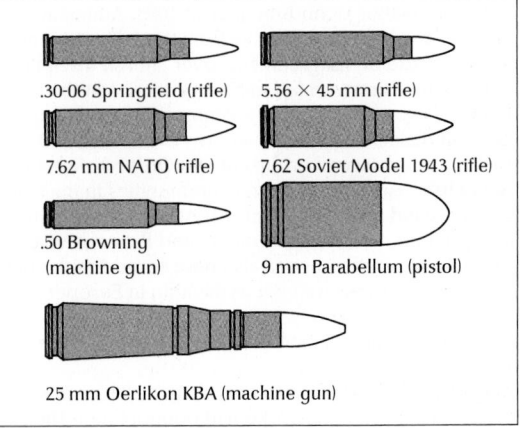

.30-06 Springfield (rifle)   5.56 × 45 mm (rifle)

7.62 mm NATO (rifle)   7.62 Soviet Model 1943 (rifle)

.50 Browning (machine gun)   9 mm Parabellum (pistol)

25 mm Oerlikon KBA (machine gun)

Kinds of small-arms ammunition The various small-arms cartridges differ in the type of projectile they contain. Most cartridges include a bullet, *left.* But shotgun cartridges contain a number of metal pellets called *shot, right.*

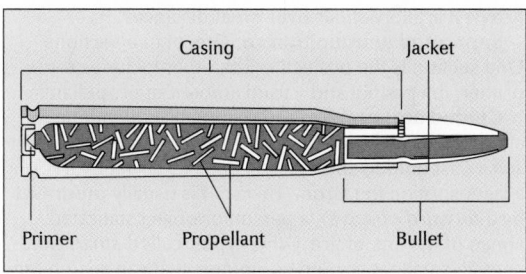

Casing   Jacket

Primer   Propellant   Bullet

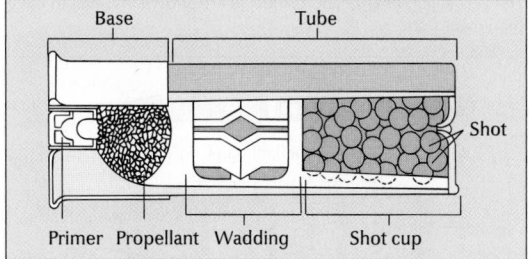

Base   Tube   Shot

Primer   Propellant   Wadding   Shot cup

kinds of ammunition, see the **Guided missile** and **Torpedo** articles.

Most kinds of ammunition contain a *propellant,* an explosive or a fuel that provides the force to send the projectile to its target. Nearly all ammunition also has a *primer,* a small amount of an explosive that *detonates* (explodes) and ignites the propellant. Some types of ammunition contain an additional explosive that shatters the projectile when it reaches the target, thus increasing the damage.

Ammunition can be classified into three types, according to its effects: (1) *penetrators,* (2) *high explosives,* and (3) *carrier projectiles.* Penetrators pierce targets using a single bullet. High explosives burst before hitting their target, fragmenting into thousands of penetrating pieces or becoming a high-speed jet of molten metal. Carrier projectiles break open near the target to deliver leaflets, radar-deceiving materials, or *submunitions* (small ammunition).

Ammunition can also be categorized by the kind of weapon from which it is fired. Categorized this way, the main types of ammunition are (1) small-arms, (2) artillery, and (3) armored-vehicle ammunition.

Small-arms ammunition

Small arms include light weapons such as pistols, rifles, and shotguns. Most kinds of small arms fire penetrators called cartridges. A single cartridge is known as a *round.*

Cartridges are called *fixed ammunition* because they are manufactured as completely assembled units. Nearly all types of cartridges have a propellant, a primer, and a casing. However, cartridges differ in the type of projectile they contain. Most cartridges contain a bullet. Cartridges fired by shotguns hold metal pellets called *shot.*

The bullet is the projectile part of a cartridge. Most bullets have a steel or lead core covered by a jacket of hard metal. Some types of bullets expand when they strike their target, causing additional damage. International law forbids the military use of such bullets. Military forces use bullets that have a jacket of *gilding metal,* an alloy of copper and zinc that prevents expansion. Cartridges used in weapons other than shotguns are measured by *caliber* (the diameter of the bullet). Manufacturers and users of ammunition in the United States have traditionally specified caliber in decimal fractions of an inch. For example, a .30-caliber cartridge has a diameter of $^{30}/_{100}$ inch (7.6 millimeters). However, it is becoming customary to use millimeters instead. The U.S. armed forces

specify caliber in millimeters. Small-arms cartridges are less than 20 millimeters or .78 caliber.

The propellant drives the bullet from the gun and propels it to the target. Propellants used in guns are called *low explosives.* Low explosives *deflagrate* (burn rapidly). This accelerates the bullet through the gun's barrel. All small-arms ammunition has a propellant of smokeless powder, which consists of nitrocellulose or a mixture of nitrocellulose and nitroglycerin. This powder is also used in firing projectiles from cannons.

The primer explodes when struck by the *firing pin,* a hammerlike device inside a gun. Lead styphnate is a common primer material.

The casing holds the propellant and the primer and also grips the base of the projectile. It remains in the gun or falls out when the bullet is fired. Most casings are made of aluminum alloys or brass. Some cartridges have no casing. The propellant in caseless cartridges is molded to the base of the bullet. *Cased, telescoped cartridges* hide the bullet inside the propellant.

Shotgun cartridges consist of a plastic or paper tube with a brass or steel case at one end. They contain lead or steel shot instead of bullets.

Riot control ammunition is used by law enforcement officials to subdue rioters without causing serious injury. Most of this ammunition consists of hard rubber bullets. Another type is made of soft rubber rings that look like doughnuts and may contain tear gas. These rings cause less damage than do rubber bullets.

Artillery ammunition

Artillery includes rocket launchers and such mounted guns as howitzers, mortars, antiaircraft guns, and naval guns. Most types of field and naval artillery ammunition are called *shells.* A single shell, like a single cartridge, is known as a round. Field artillery projectiles range in size from tens of millimeters to a few hundred millimeters, and they can weigh from a few pounds (1 kilogram) to hundreds of pounds (hundreds of kilograms). Most artillery shells taper to the rear, a shape that gives them greater range. Some have streamlined *ogives* (nose shields). Others, known as *base-burner shells,* have a small amount of propellant burning in the tail during flight. This reduces *drag* (air resistance).

Some shells are high explosives, which detonate on impact and damage or destroy the target. Detonating the shell's explosive filler shatters the shell into thousands of fragments. High explosives include TNT; RDX, also known as cyclonite or hexogen; composition B, a

Artillery ammunition

Separate loading ammunition consists of separate sections for the projectile, the primer, and a propelling charge, *upper figure*. The propelling charge and projectile are shown in detail in the two lower figures.

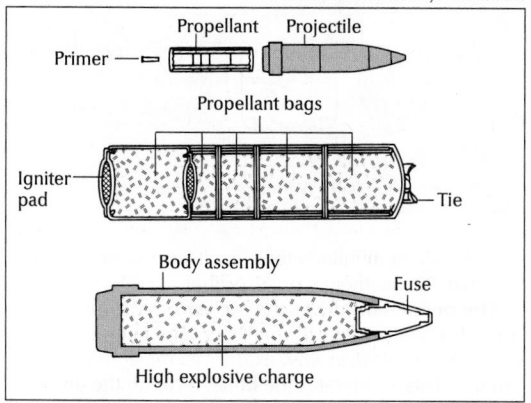

WORLD BOOK illustrations by Bensen Studios

mixture of RDX and TNT; PETN; and pentolite, a combination of PETN and TNT. Other shells contain mines or small shells that can be expelled at intervals over a specified area or during a certain period of time.

Still other shells are filled with nonexplosive substances, such as chemicals that are poisonous or that produce smoke or fire. *Illuminating,* or *star, shells* light up the battlefield or seascape. A shell with a *chaff warhead* expels strips of aluminum, which produce images on a radar screen similar to those caused by aircraft. Such images confuse radar operators and thus help protect aircraft from enemy attack.

There are five main types of artillery shells: (1) fixed ammunition; (2) semifixed ammunition; (3) separate loading, or bag, ammunition; (4) separated ammunition; and (5) guided ammunition. The word *shell* often refers not only to the entire unit of ammunition but also to the actual projectile part of the unit.

Fixed ammunition fired by artillery consists of a projectile, a casing, a primer, and a propellant. Like small-arms cartridges, fixed artillery ammunition shells are manufactured as complete units.

Semifixed ammunition resembles fixed ammunition. However, the projectile fits loosely into the casing so that the sections can be separated. Thus, the amount of propellant in the casing can be increased or decreased, depending on how far the shell is from the target.

Separate loading ammunition, also called *bag ammunition,* consists of separate sections for the projectile, the primer, and the propellant. The propellant is packed

into bags that are placed behind the projectile. The number of bags used depends on the distance the shell must travel. This type of ammunition is used to fire the heaviest artillery shells over great distances.

Separated ammunition consists of two sections. One section is the projectile. The other includes the primer, the casing, and a fixed amount of propellant.

Guided ammunition can correct its flight in the air after being fired. It often uses pop-out tail fins to steer itself. Most guided ammunition finds its target by tracking a laser spot on the target. This spot is usually produced by a *forward observer,* a person or object stationed ahead of the line of fire. Other types, called *smart shells,* contain small radars and computers that can search for and find such targets as armored vehicles or trucks.

How shells explode. A shell explodes by means of a process called the *explosive train*. This process consists of a series of explosions that detonate the shell after the projectile has been fired.

The explosive train begins with the explosion of the *fuse* (triggering device). The fuse may explode the instant the shell hits the target, or it may detonate a few seconds earlier or later. Some armor-piercing shells have a delayed fuse, which enables the projectile to penetrate before exploding. Most fuses operate mechanically or electronically. Mechanical fuses are activated by the movement of the shell during launch from the weapon, and the rotation of the shell as it travels through the air. Electronic *proximity fuses* are activated by devices inside the shell that use radar waves to determine when the projectile is near the target.

In most shells, the fuse ignites the primer and thus sets off the first charge in the explosive train. Each successive charge in the process is more powerful than the previous one. The amount of force generated by the explosion of the charges increases until enough power has been created to detonate the main charge.

Armored-vehicle ammunition

Armored-vehicle ammunition consists of projectiles fired by guns mounted on tanks and other armored vehicles. They have diameters from 20 to 125 millimeters.

A common armored-vehicle penetrator is a projectile with a nose cap of tungsten or another heavy metal. The cap helps the projectile penetrate opposing vehicles. A high explosive projectile is a *hollow-charge warhead.* This warhead is hollow in the front and has an explosive charge in the back. Its explosion converts a copper cone in the warhead to a molten, high-speed jet. The jet penetrates the target. Another armored vehicle projectile is a long dart made of tungsten or *depleted uranium* (uranium with most of its radioactivity removed). The dart trav-

Armored-vehicle ammunition — A *hollow-charge warhead* is hollow in front with an explosive charge in the back. Upon impact, the copper liner collapses, creating a shock wave and a jet of molten metal that penetrates the target.

WORLD BOOK illustrations by Bensen Studios

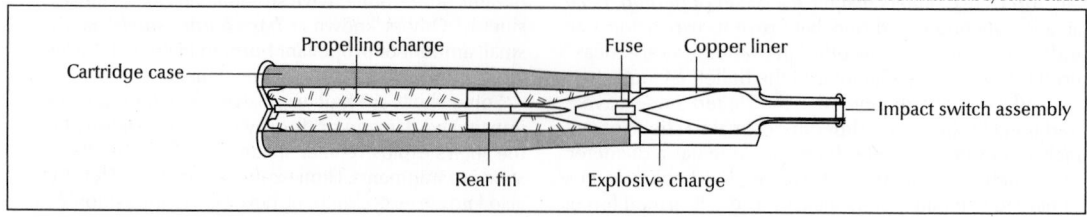

els on a device called a *sabot,* which breaks away after the dart leaves the gun's barrel.

History

Stones, which people hurled from slings and other small weapons, were the first form of ammunition. The ancient Romans flung stones from huge siege weapons, such as the ballista and catapult. Arrows fired by longbows were effective ammunition against armored knights during the European Middle Ages (about the A.D. 400's through the 1400's). By the mid-1300's, gunpowder was used to fire stones from cannons. By the 1400's, iron and lead balls were also used as artillery ammunition.

During the 1400's, people began to use handheld weapons that fired lead balls by the use of a trigger. By the 1500's, the Dutch had developed powder-filled metal bombs that were fired from mortars. Cartridges became common in Europe in the early 1600's. During the 1800's, people began using paper fuses and shotguns that fired lead shot enclosed in paper shells. Smokeless powder also was invented in the 1800's.

During World War I (1914-1918), high explosive shells, *incendiary* (fire-producing) bullets and shells, and chemical shells became common. In 1953, the United States Army fired the first shell with a nuclear charge. In the 1960's and 1970's, developments included the production of shells and cartridges made of plastics and lighter, stronger metals. Increasingly powerful propellants and more sophisticated guidance systems also came into use. In the 1980's, weapons experts improved ammunition by increasing its range. Multiple-rocket launchers took the place of many big guns. Weapons experts continue to work on inventing more powerful projectiles that can disable several targets, such as an entire tank column, at once.   Amy Sue Bix

Related articles in *World Book* include:

Artillery	Cartridge	Grenade
Ballistics	Depth charge	Magazine (military)
Bullet	Explosive	Rocket
Cannon	Firearm	Shrapnel

Amnesia, *am NEE zhuh,* is a partial or, in rare cases, a complete loss of memory. Everyone forgets minor daily incidents as time goes by, but a person with amnesia has large gaps in memory. People who suffer from amnesia lose the ability to recall past or recent experiences (see **Memory** [Uncommon memory conditions]). They may even leave their homes, wander for a while, and start a new life somewhere else. This wandering while experiencing amnesia is called *psychogenic fugue.* Amnesia may be caused by emotional shock, disease, or physical injury. In emotional shock, amnesia is usually restricted to experiences closely related to the cause of the shock. Doctors treat amnesia of emotional origin by hypnosis or with such drugs as sodium amytal or thiopental. Diseases and injuries may cause changes in the brain, making recall impossible.   Nancy C. Andreasen

Amnesty, *AM nuh stee,* is forgiveness by a government for crimes against it. Amnesty restores wrongdoers to the legal status they had before committing the crimes. The term comes from the Greek word *amnestia,* which means *a forgetting.*

Throughout history, governments have granted amnesty to restore unity after a war or an internal uprising.

One of the earliest recorded amnesties took place in 403 B.C., when the people of the ancient Greek city of Athens overthrew their rulers, the Thirty Tyrants, and established a democracy. The new leader, Thrasybulus, declared amnesty for all citizens except the Thirty Tyrants and a few other officials.

The Constitution of the United States gives the president authority "to grant reprieves and pardons for offenses against the United States." Those words establish the president's power to declare amnesty because there is no actual difference between an amnesty and a pardon. However, a pardon is granted to an individual, and an amnesty is granted to a group of people. In addition, most pardons are issued after the offender has been convicted. Most amnesties are granted before trial. Congress also can grant amnesties.

During the late 1700's and early 1800's, several presidents used their amnesty powers. In 1795, for example, President George Washington granted amnesty to Pennsylvania residents who had participated in an uprising called the Whiskey Rebellion (see **Whiskey Rebellion**). In 1807, President Thomas Jefferson offered amnesty to all Army deserters who returned to their posts within four months. President James Madison extended similar amnesty before and during the War of 1812.

The Civil War brought a number of amnesty declarations. In 1863, President Abraham Lincoln granted amnesty to Confederates who swore to support the Union. Thousands of soldiers accepted his offer. Lincoln and his successor, Andrew Johnson, issued several more conditional amnesties. In 1898, Congress extended unconditional amnesty to all former Confederates.

Since the early 1900's, most amnesties have involved people who opposed the nation's involvement in a war. In 1917 and 1918, many Americans criticized the U.S. role in World War I. Nearly 2,000 persons were imprisoned for their protests. During the 1920's, Presidents Warren G. Harding and Calvin Coolidge pardoned many individuals on a case-by-case basis. In 1933, President Franklin D. Roosevelt issued an amnesty that restored the voting rights of more than 1,500 of the protesters. They had lost these rights by being convicted of certain crimes in connection with their protests.

After World War II ended in 1945, President Harry S. Truman established a panel to study the individual cases of men who had evaded the draft or had deserted. The board suggested pardons for 1,523 individuals. But it refused to recommend amnesty for men who, according to the board, had "set themselves up as wiser and more competent than society to determine their duty."

In the 1960's and early 1970's, many Americans opposed the Vietnam War. The government estimated that about 93,000 U.S. servicemen deserted or were discharged for going *AWOL* (absent without leave), and about 13,000 men evaded the draft. Many fled to foreign countries or went into hiding in the United States. After U.S. involvement in the war ended in 1973, many people demanded amnesty for the entire group. The demand increased in 1974 after President Gerald R. Ford pardoned former President Richard M. Nixon for all federal crimes he may have committed as chief executive. Ford offered conditional amnesty to deserters and draft evaders who agreed to take public-service jobs. Only about 22,000 men applied for amnesty. In 1977, President

Jimmy Carter granted a pardon to nearly everyone who violated draft laws between 1964 and 1973. The pardon covered all except employees of the draft system and those who used violence in breaking draft laws.

In 1987, the U.S. government began an amnesty program for aliens who had entered the country illegally before Jan. 1, 1982, and had resided in the United States since then. The program was part of the Immigration Reform and Control Act of 1986.   Stanley I. Kutler

See also **Pardon.**

Amnesty International, *AM nuh stee,* is an independent, worldwide human-rights organization. It works to free people imprisoned "for their beliefs, color, ethnic origin, sex, religion, or language, provided they have neither used nor advocated violence." The organization also works for fair and speedy trials for political prisoners and for an end to torture and executions. It received the Nobel Peace Prize in 1977.

Amnesty International has hundreds of thousands of members in over 150 nations and includes thousands of volunteer groups. Each local group "adopts" prisoners in foreign countries. It works for their release by pressuring government officials and arousing public opinion. The organization also sends observers to political trials and on missions to investigate human rights abuses. The organization was founded in 1961. Its headquarters are in London.   Critically reviewed by Amnesty International USA

See also **Political prisoner.**

Amniocentesis, *AM nee oh sehn TEE sihs,* is a medical procedure performed during pregnancy to help determine the health and maturity of an unborn baby. It involves the withdrawal and study of a small amount of the *amniotic fluid* that surrounds the fetus in the mother's uterus. With this procedure, physicians can accurately diagnose any of more than 150 serious disorders that may affect the fetus. Such disorders include Down syndrome and Tay-Sachs disease. Amniocentesis involves little risk to either the mother or the fetus.

Amniocentesis is usually performed either late in the fourth month of pregnancy or during the last three months. In the fourth month, its purpose is to detect genetic disorders. The physician can then immediately treat the fetus for certain diseases or plan to treat other disorders right after birth. Some parents choose to end the pregnancy if amniocentesis reveals an incurable disorder. Amniocentesis is performed during the last three months of pregnancy primarily to determine whether the fetus has reached a normal stage of development.

A physician performs amniocentesis with the aid of *ultrasound* (high frequency sound waves). The ultrasonic waves produce an image of the fetus on a special screen. The physician monitors the position of the fetus while inserting a long hollow needle through the mother's abdominal wall and into the uterus. The physician then withdraws a small amount of amniotic fluid, which contains cells shed by the fetus. These cells are allowed to grow under controlled laboratory conditions for a few weeks and are then examined.   Henry L. Nadler

See also **Genetic counseling.**

Amoeba. See Ameba.

Amon. See Amun.

Amos, Book of, is a book of the Old Testament, or Hebrew Bible, named for an Israelite prophet. Amos was the first prophet to have his sayings collected into a single work. He expressed for the first time in the prophetic literature the idea that there is one God for all humanity, for both Israel and the other nations.

Amos was a native of the southern kingdom of Judah and was active at the shrine of Bethel in the northern kingdom of Israel. Amos prophesied from about 750 to 740 B.C. Most of his statements are announcements of judgment or prophecies of punishment. He stated that God was about to intervene in history to punish Israel for its sins. Amos criticized the excesses in the outward expression of religion. He declared that the Israelites' religion had no worth without demonstrating righteousness and social justice. He pointed out that Israel should suffer more for its sins than the surrounding nations because the Hebrews knew the true God.   Eric M. Meyers

Ampere, *AM pihr,* or *amp* for short, is the unit used to measure the rate of flow of an electric current. It is one of seven base units in the metric system. There is an electric current of 1 ampere when 1 unit of electric charge flows past a cross section of an electric circuit in 1 second. The unit of electric charge is called a *coulomb* (see **Coulomb**). Thus, 1 ampere equals 1 coulomb per second. Physicists also define amperes in terms of elementary electric charge (e), the smallest possible unit of electric charge. This is the electric charge carried by a single proton or the magnitude of charge carried by a single electron.

A 100-watt light bulb requires about 1 ampere of current at 100 volts. Calculators and computers use currents so tiny they are measured in *milliamperes* (thousandths of amperes) or *microamperes* (millionths of amperes). Large industrial equipment uses currents measured in *kiloamperes* (thousands of amperes). The ampere was named for the French physicist André-Marie Ampère. He was the first person to show that currents flowing through parallel wires cause magnetic forces between the wires.   Raymond D. Findlay

See also **Ampère, André-Marie; Ohm's law.**

Ampère, *ahn PAIR* or *AM peer,* **André-Marie,** *ahn DRAY mah REE* (1775-1836), a French mathematician and physicist, discovered the laws of electromagnetism in the 1820's. He showed that parallel electric currents attract each other if they move in the same direction, and repel if their directions are opposite. His mathematical theory describing these phenomena provided the foundation for the development of electrodynamics. He found that an electric current flowing through a coiled wire acts like a magnet. This led to the invention of the galvanometer, an instrument for detecting and measuring electric currents. Ampère used the galvanometer to show that an electric current completes a circuit through the battery which produces the current.

Ampère was born in Lyon on Jan. 22, 1775. He showed early promise as a mathematician. He taught at the École Polytechnique in Paris. His classic work, *Mathematical Theory of Electrodynamic Phenomena,* was published in 1827. Ampère died on June 10, 1836.   Richard G. Olson

See also **Ampere; Electromagnetism.**

Amphetamine, *am FEHT uh meen,* is one of several drugs that increase physical and mental activity, prevent sleep, and decrease appetite. Many people become psychologically dependent on amphetamines, and some scientists believe these drugs can also cause addiction. The United States and many other countries ban the use of amphetamines unless prescribed by a physician. But many people take them illegally for energy or pleasure.

Amphetamines include such drugs as Benzedrine, Dexedrine, and methamphetamine. They are sometimes called "bennies," "pep pills," "uppers," or "wakeups." Methamphetamine is also called "speed."

Medical uses. Doctors prescribe amphetamines for three purposes. The drugs decrease appetite, but they lose this effect in a few weeks. They also control *narcolepsy,* an illness that causes sudden, uncontrollable attacks of sleep. In addition, amphetamines calm children with *hyperkinesis,* a brain disorder that causes constant activity and inability to concentrate. Physicians do not know why amphetamines have an effect on hyperkinetic children that is opposite to the effect on other patients.

Amphetamine abuse. Some people occasionally take amphetamines to stay awake or to increase their confidence and energy for such activities as study or athletics. But amphetamines do little to speed learning, and they may slow it down. In athletics, the drugs increase alertness and may quicken reflex actions. But amphetamines have an unpredictable effect on strength, and they may cause poor judgment.

A person who uses amphetamines regularly must take increasingly large doses to get the same effects. In time, the person may feel dizzy, irritable, nervous, or shaky. Some people take large, repeated doses of amphetamines. Most of these users inject the drugs, but some sniff or swallow them. Such doses produce a sense of joyous excitement. The user becomes extremely active and talkative and feels able to do anything.

When the effects of amphetamines wear off, users sleep for hours. After awakening, they feel hungry, sluggish, and depressed. To feel better, they may start to take amphetamines again. Some users feel so depressed that they attempt suicide.

Persons who take large, repeated doses of amphetamines may become overly alert, tense, and suspicious. These users may believe that others want to hurt them, and they may try to injure these "enemies." Such beliefs and actions resemble those of some persons with the mental illness called *paranoia.* Amphetamine users may also *hallucinate* (see, hear, or feel things that are not present). If a person stops using the drugs, the paranoid feelings and hallucinations will probably disappear.

Continued use of large amounts of amphetamines may cause physical collapse and even death. Constant supervision, and group discussions with former amphetamine users, have helped many users break their drug habit.   Donald J. Wolk

See also **Attention deficit disorder; Doping; Drug abuse; Ecstasy; Methamphetamine.**

Amphibian. See Airplane (Seaplanes).

Amphibian, *am FIHB ee uhn,* is an animal with scaleless skin that—with some exceptions—lives part of its life in water and part on land. There are thousands of kinds of amphibians. They make up one of the classes of *vertebrates* (animals with backbones) and include frogs, salamanders, and the wormlike caecilians.

Most amphibians hatch from eggs laid in water or moist ground, and they begin life as water-dwelling *larvae* (young). Through a gradual process called *metamorphosis,* the larvae change into adults. The adults of most amphibians look much different from larvae. Some

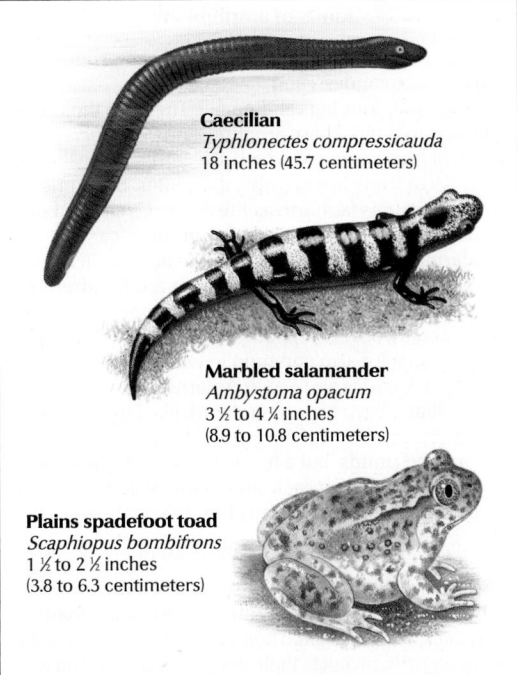

Caecilian
Typhlonectes compressicauda
18 inches (45.7 centimeters)

Marbled salamander
Ambystoma opacum
3 ½ to 4 ¼ inches
(8.9 to 10.8 centimeters)

Plains spadefoot toad
Scaphiopus bombifrons
1 ½ to 2 ½ inches
(3.8 to 6.3 centimeters)

WORLD BOOK illustration by Richard Lewington

Amphibians are divided into three main groups: (1) caecilians, (2) salamanders, and (3) frogs (including toads). These drawings show representatives from each of the three groups.

adults continue to live in water, but most spend their lives on land. Almost all return to water to find mates and produce young, often returning to the same pond or stream each year.

Amphibians generally grow smaller than such other vertebrates as fish, birds, and mammals. Most amphibians measure no more than 6 inches (15 centimeters) long and weigh less than 2 ounces (60 grams). The smallest amphibians are frogs that can sit on a person's thumbnail. The largest, the Chinese giant salamander, may grow up to about 6 feet (1.8 meters) long.

Amphibians are cold-blooded—that is, their body temperature stays about the same as the temperature of their surroundings. Those that live in regions with harsh winters hibernate during the cold weather. Some amphibians, including the gray tree frog of North America, have evolved substances similar to antifreeze in their blood and tissues. These substances enable the animals to freeze solid and then thaw without suffering harm. Many amphibians that live in warm, dry climates *estivate* (become inactive in summer). Several kinds, including the Australian water-holding frog, produce a cocoon and may remain in estivation for months at a time.

Amphibians live on every continent except Antarctica. They generally live in moist habitats near ponds, lakes, or streams. Certain tropical tree frogs never leave the trees. They lay their eggs in rainwater that collects at the base of leaves. Some amphibians live in dry regions. They survive for weeks or months in moist places underground, waiting for rain. After a rainfall, they gather at puddles to mate and lay eggs. The eggs hatch and the larvae develop quickly, before the puddles dry up.

Kinds of amphibians

Zoologists divide amphibians into three groups: (1) frogs, (2) salamanders, and (3) caecilians.

Frogs have four legs and no tail. They use their long hind legs to jump. There are thousands of *species* (kinds) of frogs, some of which are commonly called *toads*. Most frogs live in tropical climates. But some species occur as far north as the Arctic Circle, and others inhabit the southern tip of South America.

Salamanders have long tails and four—or in a few species, two—short, weak legs. There are hundreds of species of salamanders. Most live in *temperate zones*— that is, areas between the polar regions and the tropics. Salamanders are also common in warm, humid regions of Central America and South America.

Caecilians have no legs and look like large earthworms. Most inhabit underground burrows next to streams and ponds, but a few live in water. They use sensitive tentacles on each side of the head to navigate their environments. Caecilians live only in the tropics.

The bodies of amphibians

Skin. Amphibians have no external scales, hair, or feathers. Most possess smooth skin, but some toads have thick, leathery skin. Their outer layer of skin, called the *epidermis,* protects their deeper tissues. Adult amphibians shed the outermost portion of the epidermis several times a year. The inner layer of skin, called the *dermis,* contains many nerves and blood vessels. It also has many glands, which open onto the skin surface. Many amphibians produce *mucus,* a thick, slimy substance that moistens and protects the skin. Other glands produce poisons that can hurt or kill a predator.

Most amphibians have color patterns that make them difficult to see against their normal background. Some frogs and salamanders have poisonous skin with bright colors to warn predators. Skin color results from *pigments* (coloring matter) found in special cells that lie just below the epidermis. Movement of the pigments in the cells enables some species to change color rapidly. For example, some change color when the temperature goes up or down, or when the animal is under stress.

Breathing. Most land-dwelling adult amphibians breathe with lungs. Water-dwelling adults and larvae breathe by means of gills, as do fish. Some aquatic adults have both lungs and gills. In addition, all amphibians take in oxygen through the skin and through the lining of the mouth and throat. More than half of the world's salamanders belong to a group that has no lungs and breathes only through the skin and mouth.

Digestive system. Amphibians eat and digest food with the mouth, *esophagus* (tube to the stomach), stomach, and intestines. Food is mixed and partially digested in the stomach, but most digestion takes place in the small intestine. The stomach walls contain glands that secrete digestive juices, which break food down into substances that can be absorbed and used by the animal's body. Two large glands—the liver and pancreas— pour digestive juices into the small intestine. Digested food is absorbed from the small intestine, and the remaining wastes travel down the large intestine to the *cloaca,* a chamber that opens to the outside of the body. Waste products exit the body through the cloaca.

Sense organs. Most frogs and salamanders have good eyesight, which helps them catch insects. Caecilians' eyes are either extremely small or completely absent. Most caecilians have little use for eyes in their underground burrows. Water-dwelling amphibians also have a *lateral line system,* a set of sensitive organs along the sides of the body. This system enables an animal to sense movement in the surrounding water.

Frogs can hear a wider range of sounds than can salamanders and caecilians. Frogs have well-developed voices. They use their calls in mating. Caecilians and most salamanders have no voices, and their external ears have been lost. To locate and identify mates, they rely primarily on their sense of smell and taste. In addition to the specialized cells in their nasal passage, amphibians also smell and taste by means of the *Jacobson's organ,* a pair of tiny cavities in the roof of the mouth. The tissues that line these cavities respond to chemical changes in the mouth or nose.

Ways of life

Reproduction. Amphibians generally mate during a rainy period. They gather at night into large groups to find partners. In most species of frogs, *fertilization* (the joining of egg and sperm) takes place outside the female's body. Among most salamanders and all caecilians, fertilization occurs inside the female's body, before the eggs are laid. In most amphibians, the females lay many eggs at one time. The eggs generally develop and hatch in water or another moist place.

Amphibian eggs have a jellylike covering. The adults usually leave eggs unguarded. But some frogs carry the eggs until they hatch, and many salamanders and caecilians wrap their bodies around the eggs and guard them throughout development. In most species, eggs hatch into larvae with gills, a flattened tail, and tiny limbs or no limbs. Frog larvae are known as *tadpoles* or *polliwogs.* Metamorphosis into an adult takes from two weeks to as long as three years, depending on the species. During metamorphosis, larvae slowly lose their gills and develop lungs. Among tadpoles, the hind legs develop before the front legs do. The eyes, digestive system, and other organs must also undergo changes to prepare the animal for life on land.

Food and predators. Most frog tadpoles eat algae and plants, but salamander larvae feed on tiny aquatic animals. Adult amphibians prey on insects and other small animals. Bullfrogs and other large amphibians may eat snakes, small mammals, and birds. One group of South American frogs feeds mainly on other frogs. Most amphibians use their tongue to capture prey. Some salamanders can shoot out their tongue a distance of more than half their body length to catch food.

Adult amphibians have many predators, including snakes, birds, and mammals. Numerous birds, snakes, fish, and small aquatic animals prey on amphibian larvae. Amphibians use many methods to protect themselves. Some have coloring that enables them to blend into their surroundings. Tree frogs are often green, and ground-dwelling salamanders may be dull gray or brown. Salamanders and caecilians avoid enemies simply by staying out of sight. Caecilians are so well hidden in their burrows that even scientists know little about them. Poisons from the skin glands of some frogs and

Interesting facts about amphibians

WORLD BOOK illustrations by James Teason

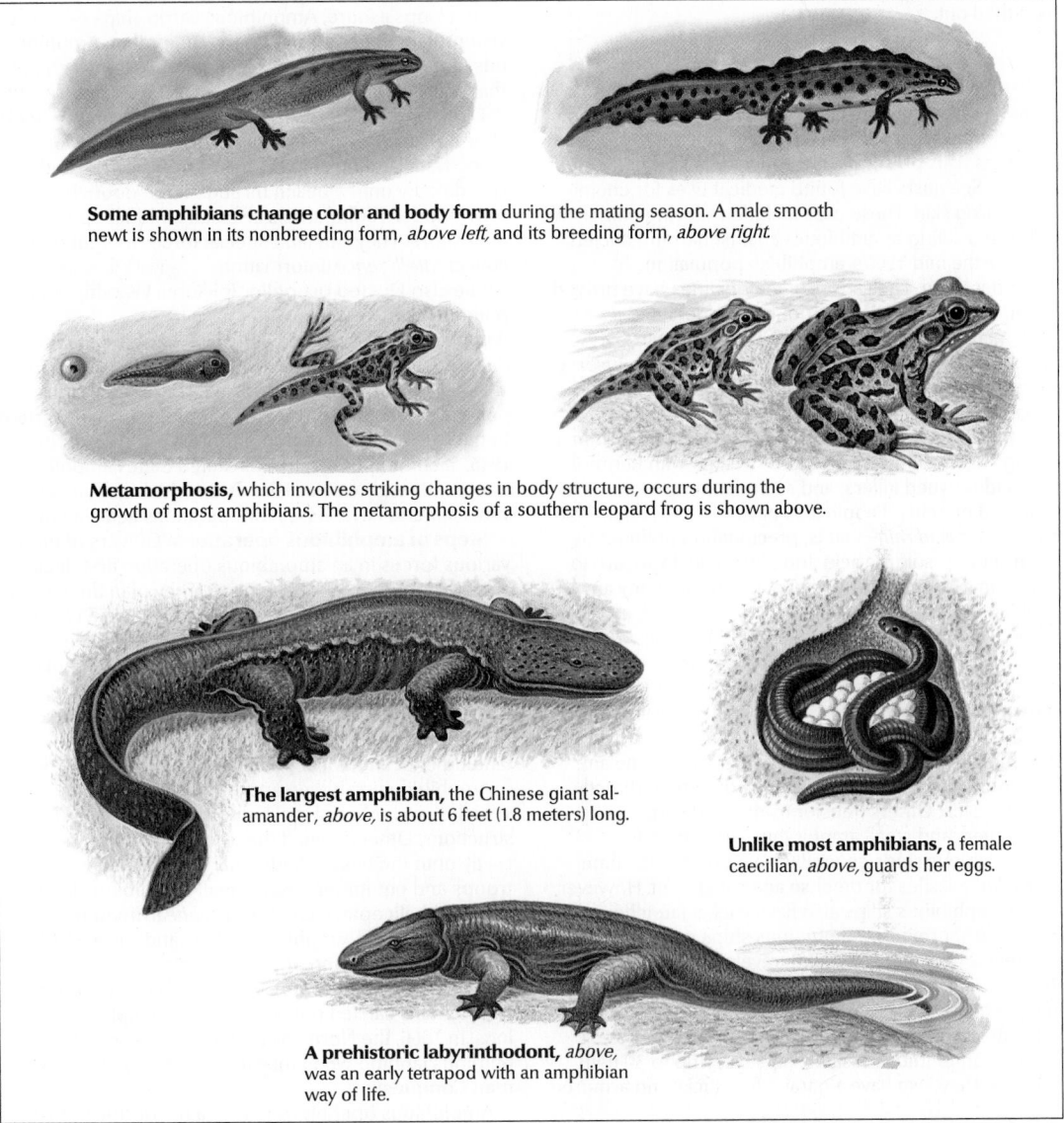

Some amphibians change color and body form during the mating season. A male smooth newt is shown in its nonbreeding form, *above left,* and its breeding form, *above right.*

Metamorphosis, which involves striking changes in body structure, occurs during the growth of most amphibians. The metamorphosis of a southern leopard frog is shown above.

The largest amphibian, the Chinese giant salamander, *above,* is about 6 feet (1.8 meters) long.

Unlike most amphibians, a female caecilian, *above,* guards her eggs.

A prehistoric labyrinthodont, *above,* was an early tetrapod with an amphibian way of life.

salamanders irritate the mouths of the animals' attackers.

The history of amphibians

The first *tetrapods* (four-legged animals) to emerge from water and live on land were somewhat like amphibians. These early tetrapods resembled modern amphibians in some respects, especially in their need to return to the water to lay their eggs. In other respects, they somewhat resembled crocodiles. Fossils of these early tetrapods date from the end of the Devonian Period—about 370 million years ago. Scientists believe that tetrapods *evolved* (changed over many generations) from lobe-finned fish. Lobe-finned fish had lungs and enlarged fins supported by a bony skeleton. They could use their fins as legs to come out of water for brief periods. These fins evolved into legs with *digits* (fingers or

toes). A variety of early tetrapods with an amphibian way of life flourished in the Carboniferous Period—from about 360 million to 300 million years ago.

Most early tetrapods left no descendants. But some early tetrapods gave rise to the ancestors of modern amphibians and *amniotes.* Amniotes did not depend so much on water because they produced eggs with shells that would not dry out on land. Amniotes had appeared by about 320 million years ago. Early amniotes were the ancestors of reptiles and mammals. Amniotes became the most important large land animals during the Permian Period, from about 300 million to 250 million years ago. The world's climate became drier during this time, which put tetrapods with an amphibian way of life at a disadvantage. The groups to which modern amphibians belong did not appear until the Mesozoic Era—from approximately 250 million to 65 million years ago. By then, most other animals with an amphibian way of life had died out.

Amphibians and people

People have long hunted frogs as a source of food. Some South American cultures have used a secretion from the skin of poisonous frogs to coat the tips of hunting darts. This poisonous secretion attacks the nervous system. Scientists have found medical uses for chemicals in frog skin. These uses include relieving pain in animals and acting as antibiotics against harmful bacteria.

Since the mid-1900's, amphibian populations have been declining. The causes of the declines have proved complex, and scientists do not fully understand them.

In many regions of the world, including parts of Australia, Central America, and the United States, a disease-causing fungus has killed large numbers of frogs. But most of the declines have resulted from human activities, including habitat destruction and pollution. Human beings have polluted rivers and streams with harmful pesticides, weed killers, and such dangerous metals as lead and mercury. People also have released chemicals that create *acid rain*—that is, precipitation polluted by such acids as sulfuric acid and nitric acid. Exposure to acid rain causes reproductive problems in many amphibians.   Don C. Forester

See **Frog, Salamander,** and **Toad** with their *Related article* lists. See also **Caecilian; Eryops; Heart** (Amphibians and reptiles); **Tetrapod; Tiktaalik.**

Amphibious ship, *am FIHB ee uhs,* is a warship that lands troops, weapons, and vehicles on beaches during amphibious assaults or special operations. Some amphibious ships unload troops and equipment directly onto a beach. Others transfer troops and cargo using helicopters and small amphibious landing craft.

Amphibious ships generally have only short-range guns and missiles for defense against aircraft. However, some amphibious ships also have rocket launchers for bombing shorelines. Amphibious ships measure up to 820 feet (245 meters) long and travel at speeds of about 20 knots (nautical miles per hour). Most are equipped to handle helicopter take-offs and landings. Both the United States and Russia have many amphibious ships.

Large amphibious assault ships carry up to 30 helicopters. They also have a garage for trucks and armored

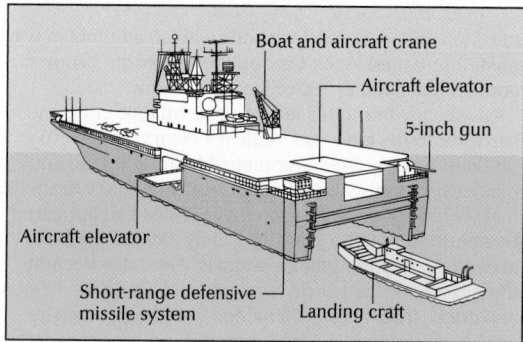

Boat and aircraft crane

Aircraft elevator

5-inch gun

Aircraft elevator

Short-range defensive missile system

Landing craft

WORLD BOOK diagram by George Suyeoka

Amphibious ships, such as the USS *Tarawa,* land troops, weapons, and vehicles for amphibious attacks. The *Tarawa,* as seen from the stern, is shown in this diagram.

vehicles. Some assault ships have a *docking well* that can be flooded, enabling landing craft to float out and carry troops ashore. Amphibious cargo ships carry provisions, landing craft, and heavy equipment. Amphibious command ships serve as communications centers that coordinate air, surface, and shore operations.

Dock landing ships serve as both ships and dry docks. They transport landing craft and dry-dock them for repairs. Tank landing ships unload troops, cargo, and vehicles directly onto a beach through large doors in the bow. Modern submarines also can conduct operations near shore. They can land special forces to fight or to collect *intelligence* (information).   Paul F. Johnston

See also **Ducted propeller** (picture); **Warship** (Amphibious warfare ships).

Amphibious warfare, *am FIHB ee uhs,* is the conduct of military operations by naval, air, and land forces to enter or seize a beach or coast. These operations are generally considered the most complex form of warfare. In the Pacific Ocean region during World War II (1939-1945), a common objective of United States amphibious operations was to seize islands on which to build advance air and naval bases for operations against Japan.

Steps in amphibious operations. Officers of the various forces in an amphibious operation first decide where the landing will take place. They plan the number and kinds of ships, planes, and troops that will take part. They also plan the equipment the troops will need.

The first step in an amphibious landing is to gain complete mastery of the skies over the area to be seized. Planes and warships then bombard the landing beach to prevent defenders from shooting at the approaching landing craft and helicopters.

Amphibious craft then arrive with troops, weapons, vehicles, and other cargo. Some clear the area of obstructions. Others unload the troops and equipment directly onto the beach. Additional vessels transfer the troops and equipment using small amphibious landing craft and helicopters. Once a *beachhead* (foothold) has been established, amphibious ships and cargo ships send more troops and equipment ashore.

History of amphibious warfare. The ancient Greeks and Romans carried out early forms of amphibious landings. In 1066, the Normans undertook a successful amphibious landing when they invaded England (see **Norman Conquest**).

Amphibious operations played a major role in World War II. The Japanese carried out amphibious assaults on the Philippines, Malaya, and the East Indies. American forces counterattacked with amphibious landings in the Central Pacific. Beginning at Guadalcanal in the Solomon Islands, they worked their way toward Japan by landing on numerous Pacific islands. Allied troops also made amphibious invasions of North Africa and Italy. The Allied landing at Normandy in northern France on June 6, 1944—known as D-Day—was the largest amphibious invasion in history. German and Soviet forces also made amphibious landings during the war.

In the Korean War (1950-1953), U.S. marines made a difficult but successful landing at Incheon (also called Inchon), a Korean port on the Yellow Sea. In 1982, British forces made a major amphibious landing in the Falkland Islands after Argentine troops invaded and occupied the islands. United States troops undertook an amphibious invasion of the Caribbean island of Grenada in 1983 after Communists took control of Grenada's government.

After World War II, American and British forces developed techniques for moving troops by helicopter from ship to shore. Today, inflatable watercraft and air cushion vehicles (ACV's) are also used. ACV's can move troops and equipment at high speeds from amphibious ships to the beach. These craft travel on a cushion of air and can move over land or water (see **Air cushion vehicle**). Following the Cold War, submarines have broadened their amphibious capabilities. Such submarines can land special forces in secret to fight or to collect *intelligence* (information).   Paul F. Johnston

See also **Airborne troops; D-Day; Warship** (Amphibious warfare ships); **World War II**.

Amphibole, *AM fuh bohl,* is any one of a large group of relatively hard minerals found in many igneous and metamorphic rocks (see **Rock**). Many amphiboles are shaped like blades. Many are black, brown, or green, though they can be almost any color.

An amphibole called nephrite is the chief source of jade, which is widely used for fine carvings and jewelry. Amphibole asbestos is used in cement pipe and in filters that are resistant to harsh chemicals.

The general chemical formula for amphiboles is $A_{0-1}X_2Y_5Z_8O_{22}(OH)_2$, in which A can be potassium or sodium; X can be calcium, magnesium, manganese, or sodium; Y can be aluminum, iron, magnesium, manganese, or titanium; and Z can be aluminum or silicon. Amphibole crystals form in the monoclinic or the orthorhombic system (see **Crystal** [Classifying crystals]). They have pyramid-shaped units of silicon and oxygen that are linked in double chains.   David L. Bish

See also **Asbestos; Jade; Silicate**.

Amphioxus, *AM fee AHK suhs,* also called the lancelet, *LANS liht,* is a group of small sea animals that live in shallow water. The amphioxus is a link between *vertebrates* and *invertebrates*—that is, animals with backbones and animals without backbones. It has no distinct

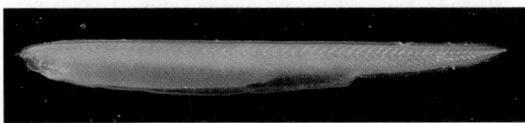

S. Stammers, Science Photo Library

The amphioxus is a slender, fishlike sea animal that lives in shallow water. The amphioxus is also known as the lancelet.

brain, but it has a nerve cord running along its back that is somewhat like the spinal cord of vertebrates. Instead of the hard, jointed backbone of the vertebrates, the amphioxus has an organ called the *notochord.* This is a fairly stiff rod of cartilage, found along the back just under the nerve cord. This primitive form of backbone makes the amphioxus more like a vertebrate than an invertebrate.   L. Muscatine

Scientific classification. Amphioxi are in the family Branchiostomidae. A typical amphioxus is *Branchiostoma costa.*

Amphisbaenian, *AM fihs BAY nee uhn,* also known as a worm lizard, is any of a group of wormlike, burrowing reptiles that are related to lizards and snakes. Dozens of amphisbaenian *species* (kinds) live in warm regions around the world. Most species live in Africa, South

© Jany Sauvanet, Photo Researchers

An amphisbaenian has a long, wormlike body and tiny eyes. It spends most of its life underground in tunnels that it digs through the soil. Amphisbaenians inhabit many warm regions.

America, and southern North America.

Adult amphisbaenians range from about 3 to 30 inches (8 to 76 centimeters) long. All species have long bodies with tiny eyes. An amphisbaenian's thick, bony skull helps it dig tunnels. Its loose skin enables it to travel underground by *rectilinear motion.* In this motion, the reptile moves part of its skin forward and anchors it against the tunnel walls. It then uses muscles to move the rest of its body forward with the skin. Most amphisbaenians have no limbs. But a few Mexican species have well-developed front limbs with toes and claws for digging.

Most amphisbaenians lay eggs, but a few kinds give birth to live young. All species are effective *predators* (hunting animals), using good hearing and strong jaws to find and capture prey. The reptiles feed on such small animals as worms and insects.   D. Bruce Means

Scientific classification. Amphisbaenians make up the suborder Amphisbaenia.

Ampicillin, *AM puh SIHL ihn,* is a drug used to treat infections caused by certain bacteria. It is an *antibiotic* (drug produced by microbes). It belongs to the penicillin group of drugs and is a *semisynthetic penicillin.*

Ampicillin can kill some bacteria that are not effectively killed by *penicillin G,* one of the most widely used forms of penicillin. For example, ampicillin is used against *Salmonella* bacteria, which cause a form of food poisoning. The drug is also effective in treating severe ear and sinus infections, meningitis in children, and urinary and respiratory tract infections.

Some people who take ampicillin suffer side effects. In most cases, the side effects are minor, such as rashes. But some people who take the drug by mouth develop diarrhea. In such cases, physicians prescribe a semisynthetic penicillin called *amoxicillin,* which produces fewer side effects involving the stomach and intestines.

Ampicillin was introduced in 1961. Its effectiveness has decreased as some bacteria once killed by the drug have developed a resistance to it.   Eugene M. Johnson, Jr.

See also **Penicillin**.

Amputation, *AM pyuh TAY shuhn,* is the process of cutting off a limb, part of a limb, or another part of the body. Amputation may be necessary as a result of severe injury, infection, tumor, or other diseases.

Before surgery, the patient is given an anesthetic. The

body part to receive the incision is cleaned, disinfected, and protected with a drape. The surgeon uses a *tourniquet* (tight cloth wrapped around the limb) to stop the flow of blood through the large vessels of the limb (see **Tourniquet**). The soft tissues are cut apart in a way they can be used to cover the end of the bone.

Before cutting through the bone, the surgeon severs and ties the blood vessels to prevent bleeding. The surgeon then saws through the bone. After this, the tourniquet is released. In most amputations done under war conditions, the wound cannot be closed immediately because of danger of infection. In such cases, healing takes many weeks. In most cases resulting from injury in civilian life, the wound can be sewed up right after the amputation. The most common dangers are infection, hemorrhage, and shock.   James A. Hill

See also **Artificial limb.**

Amritsar, *uhm RIHT suhr* (pop. 1,132,383; met. area pop. 1,183,705), is a manufacturing center in Punjab, a state in northern India (see **India** [political map]). It was founded in 1577. It is the holy city of Sikhism, an Indian religion. The city grew up around the famous Golden Temple, the main center of Sikh devotion. The temple stands in a *tank* (pool) of constantly changing fresh water. The city was named for the tank, which was called *Amritsar,* meaning *the tank of nectar or immortality.* Hindus and Sikhs live in Amritsar. Factories include cement plants, steel mills, spinning mills, silk-weaving and carpet firms, and factories that make electrical and chemical products. See also **Sikhism** (picture).   P. P. Karan

Amsterdam (pop. 810,937) is the capital and largest city of the Netherlands. It lies at the junction of the Amstel River and the IJ, an arm of a large lake called the IJsselmeer (see **Netherlands** [political map]). The city's name means *dam of the Amstel* and refers to a dam built there in the 1200's. Amsterdam is the national capital, but the seat of government is in The Hague, 34 miles (55 kilometers) away. Amsterdam's residents come from more than 150 different countries.

The city lies on marshy land slightly below sea level. Most of its buildings stand on large wooden or concrete *piles* (posts) driven into the soggy ground. More than 100 canals crisscross the city and help drain the land. The canals and attractive buildings help make Amsterdam one of Europe's most charming cities.

The old section of Amsterdam lies at the heart of the city. This section is a jumble of narrow streets, many of which are closed to automobile traffic. Some of its buildings date from the Middle Ages, from about the A.D. 400's through the 1400's. The Royal Palace, built in the mid-1600's, overlooks Dam Square at the center of the old section. Next to the palace stands the Nieuwe Kerk (New Church), where the nation's monarchs are inaugurated. The church was built in the 1400's. The city's stock exchange, founded in 1612, is nearby.

The IJ and the port area are just north of the old section. Three canals—the Herengracht, the Keizersgracht, and the Prinsengracht—border the old section on the east, south, and west. Impressive mansions, built during the 1600's by the city's merchants, line the canals. Many of the mansions are now banks or office buildings. Beyond the canals are large neighborhoods and suburbs built during the 1800's and 1900's.

Amsterdam's major cultural attractions include the

Photri

Handsome mansions line the Keizersgracht, *shown here,* one of the main canals of Amsterdam. The city's merchants built the mansions during the 1600's. Boats take visitors on canal tours.

Rijksmuseum, Amsterdam's principal art museum; the Stedelijk Museum, a municipal museum of modern art; and the Van Gogh Museum, which features many works by the famous Dutch painter Vincent van Gogh. Amsterdam also has a municipal theater, two universities, and the world-famous Royal Concertgebouw Orchestra.

Economy. Amsterdam's economy is based on financial services, manufacturing, tourism, and foreign trade. The city is the headquarters of the Netherlands Central Bank, the nation's major commercial banks, and many insurance and investment companies. Amsterdam's stock exchange is part of Euronext, an exchange that serves all of Europe. The city's industries include aircraft manufacturing, electronics, food processing, publishing, ship repairing, and chemical and steel production.

Canals link the city to the North Sea and to the Rhine River. Schiphol Airport lies south of Amsterdam.

History. Amsterdam was founded about 1200 as a fishing village. A dam was built there during the 1200's. The village then became the point for cargo transfers between seagoing ships on the IJ and boats on the Amstel River. By the 1400's, Amsterdam had developed into a prosperous center of European trade.

The city began to grow rapidly in the 1580's. During that period, and for about the next 100 years, thousands of political and religious refugees fled to Amsterdam to escape persecution. They included Jews from Portugal and Protestant merchants from Antwerp and other cities in Flanders. They helped establish a variety of industries and trade links. The city's trade spread to Africa, the Americas, the East Indies, and elsewhere. Amsterdam was Europe's greatest trading center during the 1600's, and the city's cultural life also flourished.

During the 1700's, Amsterdam developed into a great financial center. Its bankers lent money throughout Europe, especially to foreign governments. France took control of the Netherlands in 1795 and made Amsterdam the capital in 1808. But the Dutch restored their government in The Hague after they regained independence in 1813. Amsterdam's economy was ruined during the period of French rule, but the opening of the North

Sea Canal in 1876 helped revive it. The city's population doubled between 1850 and 1900.

Amsterdam's people suffered greatly during World War II (1939-1945). The city was occupied by German troops, and its Jewish community was almost wiped out in Nazi concentration camps. Roughly 60,000 of the city's 75,000 Jews died during the war, including the young diarist Anne Frank. The city also suffered a severe famine during the winter of 1944, and thousands starved.

Amsterdam had a housing shortage for many years after World War II. To relieve overcrowding, several carefully planned residential areas were built on the outskirts of the city. One apartment complex, constructed in the 1970's, houses 100,000 people. A subway connects the complex to the old section of the city.   Inez Hollander

See also **Architecture** (picture: The Euronext Amsterdam stock exchange).

Amtrak, also known as the National Railroad Passenger Corporation, is a semipublic corporation that operates intercity passenger trains in the United States. It was created by Congress in 1970 and took over the operation of trains in 1971. It is partly financed by the U.S. government. Amtrak's board of directors is nominated by the president or by the Department of Transportation.

When Amtrak was created, *subsidies* (grants) from Congress covered about half of its operating costs. But financial support has decreased as new equipment has made Amtrak more efficient. Amtrak owns and maintains the tracks on the busy "Northeast Corridor" linking Boston, New York City, and Washington, D.C. Elsewhere, it pays freight railroads for the use of their tracks. Amtrak hires its own train crews, operates its own stations, and buys its own locomotives and cars. Amtrak also establishes routes and schedules, and handles ticket sales. It receives income from ticket sales and from carrying mail and express parcels.   Richard Saunders, Jr.

See also **Railroad** (map: Railroad passenger routes).

Amulet, *AM yuh liht,* is a charm that is often worn around the neck. Some people believe that amulets protect them from evil, sickness, misfortune, and witchcraft. Amulets may be made of any material, but many are made of stone or metal. Others are small cloth bags filled with objects the wearers believe to be powerful. A tooth or a piece of horn or wood can also serve as an amulet. Some amulets have a symbolic shape, such as a crescent. See also **Birthstone; Evil eye; Magic** (Magical objects); **Superstition.**   Sarah M. Pike

Amun, *AH muhn,* became the most important god in ancient Egyptian mythology. His name is sometimes spelled *Amon.* He was worshiped mainly in the city of Thebes and was specially honored by the kings of Thebes. Amun's temples at Karnak and Luxor were the wealthiest in the country. Amun gained his greatest importance during the period of the New Kingdom (about 1539-1075 B.C.), when Thebes was the capital of Egypt. The Egyptians eventually identified Amun with the sun god Re to create a new deity called Amun-Re, who was known as King of the Gods.

Amun first appeared in Egyptian mythology about 2100 B.C. At Thebes, Amun's wife was the goddess Mut. Their child was Khons, a moon god. The three became known as the *Theban triad.* Amun was usually portrayed in human form, wearing a double plumed crown. He sometimes appeared as a goose or a ram.   R. F. G. Sweet

See also **Mythology** (Egyptian mythology); **Thebes.**

Amundsen, *AH muhn suhn* or *AH muhnd suhn,* **Roald,** *ROH ahl* (1872-1928), a Norwegian explorer, led the first expedition to reach the South Pole. Amundsen and four companions discovered the pole on Dec. 14, 1911. They beat a British expedition led by Robert F. Scott by five weeks.

Amundsen is also noted for his many Arctic explorations.

The race to the South Pole. Amundsen had originally planned on discovering the North Pole. He organized an Arctic expedition and was about to leave when he heard that Commander Robert E. Peary, an American explorer, had just reached the pole (see **Peary, Robert E.**). Amundsen changed his plans and decided to lead an expedition to the South Pole instead.

Bettmann Archive

Roald Amundsen

Amundsen left Norway secretly in June 1910 aboard the ship *Fram*. At about the same time, Scott, unaware of Amundsen's expedition, also was on his way to the Antarctic. While stopping in Melbourne, Australia, in October 1910, Scott received a message from Amundsen informing him that Amundsen was proceeding to Antarctica. The race to the South Pole was on.

Amundsen and his crew arrived at the eastern edge of the Ross Ice Shelf in January 1911. They spent an Antarctic winter there, making short trips inland to set

Roald Amundsen explored in the Arctic and Antarctic regions. During a voyage from 1903 to 1906, he sailed his ship, the *Gjøa,* along the water route called the Northwest Passage. In 1911, Amundsen crossed the Ross Ice Shelf of Antarctica and discovered the South Pole. In 1926, he flew over the North Pole in a dirigible, the *Norge.*

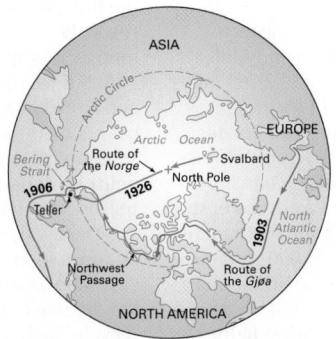

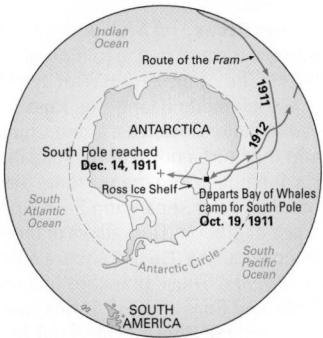

up stores of food and fuel. On Oct. 19, 1911, after spring had arrived, Amundsen and his men set off for the pole in four sleds pulled by 52 dogs. Near the journey's end, when they were no longer needed to pull the sleds, the weaker dogs were killed. They were fed to the surviving animals and to the men.

Scott's expedition met with disaster. Instead of using dogs all the way, Scott relied mainly on ponies to pull the sledges. However, the ponies became exhausted and had to be shot. Without ponies, the men had to pull the sledges, carrying the supplies. The men also had to fight severe cold and fierce winds, and they lacked the proper clothes for such conditions. See **Scott, Robert F.**

Amundsen had a smooth journey by comparison. The route he had chosen was shorter than Scott's and covered flatter terrain. The dogs withstood the hard work and cold well, and the weather was clear.

On Dec. 14, 1911, Amundsen and his companions calculated that they had reached the South Pole. They began their return journey three days later, leaving behind them a tent and a Norwegian flag. Five weeks later, Scott and his men finally reached the pole, only to discover that Amundsen had been there first. Weary and disappointed, they began their return. But injuries, fatigue, and continued bad weather slowed them down. The entire party soon died of cold and hunger.

Other achievements. Roald Engelbregt Gravning Amundsen was born on July 16, 1872, in Borge, near Oslo. He studied medicine for two years before going to sea in 1897 aboard the *Belgica.* During this voyage, Amundsen's efforts helped to combat scurvy among the crew. In 1898, the *Belgica,* with Amundsen aboard, became the first ship to winter in Antarctic waters.

In 1906, Amundsen completed the first voyage from the Atlantic to the Pacific through the Arctic waters of Canada. During this voyage through the Northwest Passage, Amundsen determined the precise position of the north magnetic pole. From 1918 to 1920, he sailed the Northeast Passage. He traveled from Norway through the Arctic Ocean to the Bering Sea. Amundsen was the first person to sail both the Northwest and Northeast passages.

In 1926, Amundsen made history by flying over the North Pole in an airship called the *Norge.* The aircraft was piloted by Umberto Nobile, an Italian explorer. In June 1928, Amundsen and his crew vanished in the Arctic while searching for Nobile, who had disappeared in May. Nobile was eventually rescued. Amundsen's body was never found.   Barry M. Gough

See also **Antarctica** (The "Heroic Era"); **Exploration** (picture).

Amur River, *uh MOOR,* is a huge river in eastern Siberia, formed by the joining of the Argun and Shilka rivers. The Amur-Argun river system is about 2,760 miles (4,440 kilometers) long (see **Russia** [terrain map]).

The Amur flows east along China's northern border and then turns north into the Khabarovsk region of Russia. It empties into the northern Tatar Strait, a narrow band of water separating Sakhalin Island from the east coast of Siberia. The valleys of the Amur and its branches cover about 716,000 square miles (1,855,000 square kilometers). These branches include the Ussuri, Sungari, Zeya, and Bureya rivers. Dams have been built on the Zeya and the Bureya. The Amur becomes wide in the

Khabarovsk Region, and it often floods there during the summer monsoon season.

Boats operate on the Amur for most of its length from April to November. The cities of Khabarovsk and Komsomolsk stand on the banks of the Amur. Railroads link both cities with the port of Vladivostok to the south.
Craig ZumBrunnen

Amusement park is a permanent outdoor entertainment complex that typically offers games, rides, and shows. There are amusement parks in many countries, but most of the biggest parks are in the United States.

Amusement parks developed in the United States in the late 1800's. One of the earliest types was the *trolley park.* Railways built these at the end of their lines to encourage the weekend use of trolleys. The World's Columbian Exposition, held in Chicago in 1893, stimulated the development of the amusement park. The first important park, and the model for all later parks, was opened in the late 1800's at Coney Island, a beach resort in the Brooklyn area of New York City.

Amusement parks flourished from about 1900 until World War II (1939-1945). Since then, their popularity has declined, and many parks have closed. In the United States, *theme parks* have replaced many amusement parks. They are organized around such themes as local historical events, pioneer life, and wildlife. They emphasize cleanliness, courtesy, and family entertainment. The first theme park, Disneyland Park, opened in 1955 in Anaheim, California. Its theme is the cartoon characters created by Walt Disney.   Don B. Wilmeth

Related articles in *World Book* include:

California (Places to visit) | Merry-go-round
Denmark (picture: Tivoli Gardens) | Roller coaster
Texas (Places to visit)
Ferris wheel | Walt Disney Company
Florida (Places to visit)

Amusements. See **Recreation.**

AMVETS is an organization of veterans who have served honorably in the United States military. It was founded in 1944 during World War II (1939-1945) and chartered by Congress in 1947. Its major aims are to promote world peace, to preserve the American way of life, and to help veterans help themselves. The headquarters of AMVETS is in Lanham, Maryland.
Critically reviewed by AMVETS

Amyotrophic lateral sclerosis, *uh MY uh TRAHF ihk LAT uhr uhl sklih ROH sihs,* also called ALS, is a rare, incurable disease of the nervous system. It is also called *Lou Gehrig's disease,* after a baseball player who died from it. ALS gradually destroys the nerves that control the muscles. Weakness, paralysis, and eventually death result. Physicians advise patients to remain active as long as possible. No treatment can halt ALS.

ALS develops when certain nerve cells in the brain and spinal cord *degenerate* (break down) and die. These cells, called *motor neurons,* make the muscles work by sending them *impulses* (nerve messages). As the motor neurons degenerate, they lose the ability to transmit impulses. The muscles they control gradually stop working and then waste away. Physicians believe that there may be more than one cause of ALS. In 2011, medical researchers discovered the cause of ALS. They found that the disease occurs when nerve cells lose the ability to recycle the building blocks of proteins necessary for proper nerve function. Over time, the nerve cells become damaged and can no longer carry signals from the brain to the muscles that move the body.

Small twitches occur in ALS patients as the dying neurons send irregular impulses to the muscles. The arms and legs grow increasingly weak. Patients find it hard to walk and to do simple tasks with their hands. They lose weight and gradually become paralyzed as their muscles grow useless. Talking and swallowing may become hard. Death occurs when the muscles that control breathing stop working. In most cases, this happens within two to five years after the first symptoms appear.

ALS is painless and does not affect the mind. It afflicts slightly more men than women. Most patients develop the symptoms in their 50's.   William J. Weiner

See also **Gehrig, Lou.**

Anabaptists were one form of what has been called the radical wing of the Reformation of the 1500's. The Anabaptists believed that the church was a gathering of people united by faith, repentance, obedience, and discipline. Therefore, baptism as an entrance to this community should be limited to believers old enough to choose membership. People called them *anabaptists* (rebaptizers) because they baptized adults who had been baptized in infancy. The Anabaptists condemned government involvement in religion, which eventually led to the idea of the separation of church and state.

Many Anabaptists were persecuted in both Protestant and Roman Catholic countries. Their movement was concentrated in Switzerland, southern Germany, Austria, and the Netherlands. The Anabaptists' beliefs survive today in Mennonite and Hutterite religious communities (see **Hutterites; Mennonites**).   Stanley K. Stowers

See also **Reformation** (Zwingli and the Anabaptists).

WORLD BOOK illustration by Harry McNaught

The anableps swims with its eyes projecting partway into the air. Both eyes are divided into two parts. The top part can see above water, while the bottom part can see underwater.

Anableps, *AN uh blehps,* also called *four-eyed fish,* is a small fish that lives in freshwater streams of tropical America. This fish swims at the top of the water with its eyes projecting partway into the air. The upper half of each eye can see threatening birds of prey in the air. The lower half, different in structure, can see underwater and enables the fish to find food.   John E. McCosker

Scientific classification. The scientific name of the anableps is *Anableps anableps.*

See also **Fish** (Interesting facts about fish).

Anaconda, *AN uh KAHN duh,* is the name of a group of large snakes found in tropical South America. Anacon-

das are also called *water boas.* The green anaconda can reach about 30 feet (9 meters) long and weigh nearly 450 pounds (205 kilograms). No other South American snake approaches this length or weight.

WORLD BOOK illustration by Richard Lewington, The Garden Studio

The green anaconda ranks as the largest snake in the Western Hemisphere. It has olive-green skin with black rings or spots. The snake lives in tropical forests and rivers of South America.

Anacondas have greenish, yellowish, or brownish skin, often with many black rings or spots. These snakes live near water, usually swimming in rivers. Anacondas bear live young. Their main food is fish, but they also will eat birds, small mammals, and other reptiles. The largest snakes may attack large mammals. Anacondas kill by wrapping their coils tightly around prey to keep it from breathing. Like other snakes, anacondas defend themselves from enemies by retreating or, if cornered, by biting. Their bite is not poisonous, but their many teeth can inflict deep wounds.   Albert F. Bennett

Scientific classification. Anacondas make up the genus *Eunectes.* The green anaconda is *E. murinas.*

See also **Boa; Boa constrictor; Python.**

Anacreon, *uh NAK ree uhn* (572?-487 B.C.), a Greek lyric poet, made wine and love his main themes. Little of his work has survived. Most of the so-called *Anacreontics,* poems popular in the 1700's, are imitations. The tune of a drinking song about him, "To Anacreon in Heaven" (1760's), was adopted in 1814 for "The Star-Spangled Banner" (see **Star-Spangled Banner**). He is called "the Teian bard" because he was born in Teos, in Ionia. The emphasis on wit and pleasure in his poems is probably due to the taste and demands of his royal patrons.   Cynthia W. Shelmerdine

Anaheim, *AN uh HYM* (pop. 336,265), is a residential and light-industrial city and tourist center in southern California. It lies 28 miles (45 kilometers) southeast of Los Angeles and 16 miles (26 kilometers) from the Pacific Ocean (see **California** [political map]). It is part of the Los Angeles-Long Beach-Anaheim metropolitan area, which has a population of 12,828,837. Anaheim's industries include aircraft, automotive, electronics, engineering, and hardware plants. Disneyland Park, an amusement park that opened in 1955, is the largest employer. A second park, Disney California Adventure Park, opened in 2001. The Los Angeles Angels of Anaheim baseball team competes in the American League. The Anaheim Ducks play in the National Hockey League.

Anaheim was originally part of a Spanish land grant to the San Gabriel Mission. The city was founded in 1857 as a farming community by a group of former Forty-Niners —miners who came during the 1849 gold rush—mostly of German descent (see **Forty-Niners**). The name *Anaheim* means *home by the Santa Ana River.* Anaheim has a council-manager form of government.   James J. Rawls

Analgesic, AN *uhl JEE zihk,* is any drug that relieves pain without causing unconsciousness. People use various analgesics to eliminate or reduce many types of pain. Aspirin, a relatively mild analgesic, relieves headaches, muscle pains, and some discomforts of a cold. A doctor may prescribe more powerful analgesics, such as codeine, for the severe pain caused by back injuries, serious burns, and such illnesses as cancer. Analgesics relieve pain by acting on the nervous system or by blocking the formation of *prostaglandins,* hormonelike chemicals found throughout the body. However, scientists do not know exactly how analgesics work.

There are two kinds of analgesics, *narcotic* and *non-narcotic.* Narcotic analgesics, also known as *opioid analgesics,* relieve severe pain but are addictive. Nonnarcotic analgesics relieve only minor pain but are not addictive. The most commonly used nonnarcotic analgesics include *acetylsalicylic acid,* or aspirin; and acetaminophen, used by many people who cannot take aspirin without suffering side effects. Acetaminophen is sold under many trade names, the best known probably being Tylenol. Narcotic analgesics include codeine, morphine, and meperidine, a drug that is often referred to by the trade name Demerol.

The misuse of any analgesic can cause severe illness or death. Narcotic analgesics are especially dangerous because they are addictive. For this reason, narcotic analgesics can be legally obtained only with a prescription from a physician or dentist.   N. E. Sladek

Related articles in *World Book* include:

Acetaminophen	Drug	Morphine
Aspirin	Drug abuse	Narcotic
Codeine	Ibuprofen	

Analog computer is a device that uses continuously changing quantities to model the behavior of a system being studied. Analog computers are contrasted with *digital* computers, which use quantities that change in noncontinuous "jumps" (see **Digital technology**).

Some analog computers are physical systems that behave in a similar way to a more complex system. For example, the 1949 Phillips Economics Computer, also called the Moniac, used flowing water to represent aspects of a nation's economy, such as the money supply. Other analog computers are more versatile and can solve mathematical equations that describe the behavior of various systems.

Before electronics, the most common analog computers were mechanical. Such a computer may have included rotating disks, gears, and levers. The motions and positions of these parts could be measured, for example, to solve mathematical equations describing the flight path of an artillery shell.

Beginning in the mid-1900's, as electronics became more common, most analog computers used electrical voltages. The voltages could represent such physical properties as force, temperature, motion, or pressure.

Electronic analog computers have largely been re-placed by digital computers. But they are still used in some specialized applications. Analog computers are particularly useful when the system they model is harder to study than a model of that system. They are also useful when mathematical equations describing such systems are difficult to solve.   Doron D. Swade

Analogous structures. See Homology.

Analytic geometry. See Geometry.

Anaphylactic shock, an uh fu LAK tihk, also called *anaphylaxis,* is a rare, life-threatening allergic reaction that affects the whole body. The reaction develops rapidly after two or more exposures to an *allergen* (substance that causes an allergy). The allergens that cause most anaphylactic reactions include bee and wasp venom, antibiotics, latex rubber, and such foods as eggs, nuts, and shellfish.

Symptoms of anaphylactic shock include skin rashes, wheezing, chest tightness, and nausea. The blood pressure drops, and the person may collapse. Without immediate medical attention, death may occur. Doctors treat anaphylactic shock with epinephrine or certain other drugs and oxygen to help restore normal blood pressure and breathing.

Usually, the speed of an anaphylactic reaction makes the allergen that caused the attack obvious. If there is any doubt, blood and skin tests can help people identify and avoid the allergen. People also should wear a medical bracelet identifying the allergen and carry an emergency epinephrine injection for use should another attack occur.   Carol A. Hirshman

Anarchism, AN uhr kihz uhm, is a belief that every form of regulation or government is immoral, and that restraint of one person by another is an evil which must be destroyed. *Anarchism* comes from a Greek word meaning *without government.*

Anarchism dates back to ancient times. The legends of many countries tell of a "golden age" of freedom which preceded organized governments. Anarchism also appeared among early Christian groups.

Later anarchism proposed a social organization that was based on common ownership and free agreements, but its disciples differed among themselves in methods and forms. The French socialist Pierre Joseph Proudhon, often called the father of anarchism, became the first to make anarchism a mass movement. Proudhon's *philosophical,* or *individualistic,* anarchism urged the willing cooperation of free individuals without any regulation or government.

Terroristic anarchism began under the leadership of Mikhail Bakunin (1814-1876) in Russia during the 1800's. Followers of this type of anarchism believed in the destruction of the government by violence and terror. They believed that land and other means of production should be owned in common.

Many anarchists throughout the world resorted to revolution and assassination in the belief that terror would correct what they thought to be evil. They murdered heads of governments, including Czar Alexander II of Russia and President William McKinley of the United States. After the death of McKinley, the United States government passed a law barring anarchists from entering the country.

Anarchism under the leadership of Prince Peter Kropotkin of Russia, during the late 1800's, assumed a more rigid communistic form. Kropotkin rejected the terroristic methods of Bakunin. However, he also opposed the authoritative type of communism. Under Kropotkin's kind of anarchism, the state would be eliminated and society would be built on the *communes,* or *village communities,* which had existed in feudal Russian society. Each commune would be a self-sufficient group.

The strength of anarchism declined throughout the world in the 1900's. Anarchists played a part in the Spanish Civil War (1936-1939). Anarchism also influenced such radical groups as Students for a Democratic Society (SDS) in the United States in the 1960's, and the Baader-Meinhof gang in West Germany in the 1970's. Some groups in Europe practice terroristic anarchism.

James D. Forman

See also **Goldman, Emma; Nihilism; Proudhon, Pierre Joseph; Sacco-Vanzetti case.**

Anatolia. See Asia Minor; Turkey.

Anatolian shepherd is a breed of large, rugged working dog. It stands about 30 inches (76 centimeters) tall at the shoulders and weighs from 80 to 150 pounds (36 to 68 kilograms). The breed has an outer coat that varies from short to medium long and a thick undercoat. Coat colors include *fawn* (light beige), white, *brindle* (black body with brown stripes), and *pinto* (white body with beige to dark gray spots).

Mary Bloom © American Kennel Club

The Anatolian shepherd has a strong, sturdy body.

The Anatolian shepherd originated in Turkey during ancient times. Shepherds developed the breed to guard their sheep. The breed can make an excellent family pet, and is protective of children and property. But it must undergo obedience training and become accustomed to the people and surroundings outside its home.

Critically reviewed by the Anatolian Shepherd Dog Club of America

Anatomy is the study of the biological structure of living things. The term comes from the Greek words meaning *to cut up,* because knowledge of anatomy was first obtained through dissection. The bodies of human beings and animals are so complex that scientists divide anatomy into many branches. *Gross anatomy* is the study of structures that can be seen with the unaided eye. *Microscopic anatomy,* or *histology,* is the study of tissues under a microscope. *Comparative anatomy* compares the structure of different animals. *Embryology* is the study of the development of plants and animals in their earliest stages.

Human anatomy includes the study of the structure of the skeleton, muscles, nerves, and the various organs of the human body. A knowledge of the structure of the body is essential for an understanding of its function in health and disease. Health care professionals must know the structure of the part of the body they expect to treat. Physical education and health science teachers also need to know how the body is built.

In ancient times, people believed the dead body was sacred. Cutting it up was a serious crime. After 400 B.C., the Greeks allowed occasional dissections. The physician Galen, in the A.D. 100's, described many anatomical structures. But he based his work mainly on dissections of animals and treatment of injured gladiators. After A.D. 1300, dissection and anatomy became a recognized part of medical education in western Europe. In 1543, the Flemish physician Andreas Vesalius wrote his classic work on anatomy, which was based on human dissections. Since then, steady progress has made possible such discoveries as that of the English physician William Harvey on blood circulation. Because of present knowledge of the body's structure and function, a surgeon can operate on every part of the body.   Delmas J. Allen

Related articles in *World Book* include:

Developmental biology	Human body
Galen	Physiology
Harvey, William	Vesalius, Andreas
Histology	

Anaxagoras, *AN ak SAG uhr uhs* (500?-428 B.C.), was an early Greek philosopher. He argued that, in the beginning, the world was a uniform mixture of all the things that would later emerge during its development. Thus, nothing really comes to be or perishes, and all change is merely rearrangement of the original components. He also argued that matter is infinitely divisible and that everything has a tiny portion of everything else in it. A thing appears to be the thing that makes up its largest part. Anaxagoras introduced *Mind* as a cosmic principle. He regarded Mind as composed of exceptionally fine and pure matter. Its primary function was to initiate a rotary motion in the original mixture of the world. The rotary motion led to the separation of the various parts. Anaxagoras was born in Clazomenae in Asia Minor (now part of Turkey) but spent much of his life in Athens.

Carl A. Huffman

See also **Pre-Socratic philosophy.**

Anaximander, *uh NAK suh MAN duhr* (611?-547? B.C.), was an early Greek philosopher. He was one of the first people to describe the world as governed by systematic laws rather than by the actions of the gods. Only one fragment survives from a book he wrote on nature, but we know his views from other ancient authors.

Anaximander believed that the world originated from what he called the *indefinite* or *unlimited.* He probably imagined the indefinite as a substance of no definite character that was unlimited in extent. Opposites such as hot and cold and dry and wet emerged from the indefinite and came into conflict with one another, thus producing the world. None of the opposites gains the upper hand. This balancing of opposites in part explains such phenomena as the seasons. He anticipated aspects of the theory of evolution by stating that animals came from a moist environment and that human beings originally had fishlike forms. Anaximander was born in Miletus in Asia Minor (now part of Turkey).   Carl A. Huffman

See also **Pre-Socratic philosophy.**

Anaximenes, *an ak SIHM uh neez,* was an early Greek philosopher who lived in Miletus in Asia Minor (now part of Turkey) during the 500's B.C. Like other Greek philosophers, Anaximenes was interested in giving an account of the natural world. He did so by describing how he believed the universe had begun, followed by a discussion of astronomy and meteorology. Little remains of a book he wrote on nature. Our knowledge of his work comes from reports by other ancient authors.

Anaximenes believed that the world developed out of air. He argued that air turned into such substances as water and earth through condensation, and into fire through a process called *rarefaction.* Anaximenes's theory may be partly based on his observation of evaporation. He also believed that human souls consisted of air, and he may have chosen air as the original substance of the universe because of this belief.   Carl A. Huffman

See also **Pre-Socratic philosophy.**

Ancestor worship refers to certain beliefs and practices of families with regard to ancestors who have been dead for many years. In some cultures, deceased ancestors are worshiped as gods. Such worship may involve rituals performed at a shrine decorated with objects that symbolize the ancestor. In many cultures, people believe that the spirits of ancestors are angered by violations of law or custom, and they use rituals to pacify them. These rituals commonly include offerings of food and other items. Ancestor worship forms a part of many religions, especially in Asia and Africa. In general, it serves to uphold the authority and honor of elders, to keep the family together, and to maintain the society's traditions.   Edward O. Henry

Ancestral Pueblo, once called the Anasazi *(AH nuh SAH zee),* were the ancestors of the modern-day Pueblo, a native people of the American Southwest. Modern Pueblo prefer the terms Ancestral Pueblo or Hisatsinom *(hih SAHT sih nohm)* to describe their ancestors. The term Anasazi was once widely used for these people. But the modern Pueblo point out that *Anasazi* is a Navajo term meaning *enemy of long ago.*

The Ancestral Pueblo culture was centered in the southwestern United States, especially in what is now the Four Corners area, where Colorado, Utah, New Mexico, and Arizona meet. In that region, about A.D. 1100, the Ancestral Pueblo built homes called *cliff dwellings* in canyon walls or under rocky overhangs.

History. The Ancestral Pueblo culture developed from Basketmaker ancestors in the Southwest about A.D. 1. They lived in villages of *pit houses,* underground pits with roofs formed by a wooden framework covered with earth. They farmed and gathered food in the wild. Around 750, they began building *pueblos,* aboveground structures resembling modern apartment buildings. By that time, the Ancestral Pueblo traded extensively with peoples in what are now Mexico and California.

The Ancestral Pueblo built their first large pueblos about 900, in the area known today as Chaco Canyon, New Mexico. This broad valley in northern New Mexico held many large pueblos made of shaped stone. The pueblos were two or three stories high with many rooms. The largest, Pueblo Bonito, had about 800 rooms and may have housed as many as 1,200 people. The Ancestral Pueblo in Chaco Canyon produced turquoise beads and figurines. They traded with peoples in what is now Mexico for such items as copper bells, shell trumpets, and macaws. The Chaco Canyon culture ended about 1150, perhaps due to drought, warfare, or disease.

Some of the Chaco Canyon peoples settled in the Four Corners area, the location of the famous cliff dwellings seen at Mesa Verde National Park in Colorado. These buildings consist of many levels of rooms built one above another. The largest cliff dwellings, constructed of sandstone, could house as many as 2,500 people.

The Ancestral Pueblo abandoned the area about 1300. Scientists have developed several theories to explain why the sites were abandoned, including drought, invasion, plague, and resource depletion, but no theory has completely answered the question. Some of the people moved to northern New Mexico, while others settled on *mesas* (flat-topped hills) in eastern Arizona. There they built large multistory surface pueblos and developed the traits of Puebloan culture seen today in the peoples known as Hopi and Zuni.

© James P. Rowan

A multilevel Ancestral Pueblo home known as the Cliff Palace is the largest cliff dwelling in Mesa Verde National Park in southwestern Colorado. Some sections of the Cliff Palace are four stories high. The Ancestral Pueblo (once known as the Anasazi) began building cliff dwellings at this site after A.D. 1150.

Way of life. The Ancestral Pueblo built large permanent structures because their agricultural lifestyle allowed them to stay in one place for long periods. In valleys and on top of mesas, they grew corn, beans, squash, cotton, and tobacco. They raised turkeys, but they also hunted both deer and mountain sheep to add to their diet. Hunters and warriors launched stone-tipped spears using a device called an *atlatl (AHT laht uhl),* a stick with a spur at one end to hold the butt of the spear. Between 400 and 700, Ancestral Pueblo hunters had begun to use the bow and arrow. Ancestral Pueblo warfare may have included cannibalism.

In the winter, the Ancestral Pueblo wore robes and blankets made from rabbit fur and turkey feathers. In the summer, both men and women wore skirts made from cotton and other materials. The men held social and religious ceremonies in *kivas,* underground pits about 25 feet (7.6 meters) in diameter. Colorful symbolic paintings decorated the walls of the kivas.

The dry climate of the Southwest and the protection of the cliffs and canyons preserved many items made by the Ancestral Pueblo. Archaeologists have found many artifacts that the Indians used in everyday life, including clothing and stone tools. Ancestral Pueblo potters created fine ceramics, the earliest of which were in a black-on-white style. Later, pottery featured black-and-red patterns painted on bowls, jars, and pitchers. As pottery techniques improved, these designs became more complex. By studying the patterns on fragments of pottery, archaeologists can determine the age of Ancestral Pueblo ruins.   Thomas R. Hester

Related articles in *World Book* include:

Canyon de Chelly National
  Monument
Chaco Culture National
  Historical Park

Mesa Verde National Park
New Mexico (Indian peoples)
Pueblo Indians
Zuni Indians

Additional resources

Lourie, Peter. *The Lost World of the Anasazi.* Boyds Mills, 2003. Younger readers.
Roberts, David. *In Search of the Old Ones.* 1996. Reprint. Simon & Schuster, 1997.
Stuart, David E., and Moczygemba-McKinsey, S. B. *Anasazi America.* 2000. Reprint. Univ. of N. Mex. Pr., 2004.

Ancestry. See Genealogy.

Anchor is a heavy weight used to hold a ship or boat in place. A rope or chain is fastened to the anchor and tied to the ship. When the anchor is lowered, it generally catches at the bottom of the water to keep the vessel in place. An anchor may be as simple as a rock tied to the end of a line. The most common kinds of anchors are made of iron or steel.

Anchors come in a wide variety of shapes and sizes. The shape depends in part upon the expected composition of the land at the bottom of the water. For example, when the bottom is mud, a small boat may be held in place by a *mushroom anchor,* a cast-iron bowl on the end of a rod. For a rock bottom, however, the boat would be secured with a *grapnel,* an anchor with several hooks on its end. The size of the anchor depends mainly on the size of the craft. An enormous aircraft carrier may use an anchor weighing more than 60,000 pounds (27,200 kilograms).

Anchors are essential for navigation buoys, which must remain in one place at all times and in all kinds of weather. Buoys are held to the bottom by anchors made of concrete.   Robert L. Scheina

Anchorage (pop. 291,826; met. area pop. 380,821) is Alaska's largest city and the state's main center of commerce and transportation. Its metropolitan area, which includes the fast-growing Matanuska Valley, is home to about half of the state's population. It is also a chief United States defense center. The city covers 1,961 square miles (5,079 square kilometers) of land and water on upper Cook Inlet in south-central Alaska, west of the Chugach Mountains (see **Alaska** [political map]).

Anchorage has high-rise buildings, hotels, and shopping malls. A system of bicycle and ski trails extends in and around the city. Ted Stevens Anchorage International Airport, one of the busiest in the United States, is a regional transfer hub for air freight bound for Asia. The city is a chief Alaskan port and headquarters of the Alaska Railroad. Cultural attractions include the Anchorage Museum at Rasmuson Center, the Alaska Native Heritage Center, the Anchorage Symphony Orchestra, and the Anchorage Opera. The University of Alaska Anchor-

Some common anchors

These illustrations show four common kinds of anchors: the *stock anchor,* the *stockless anchor,* the *mushroom anchor,* and the *grapnel.* The stock and stockless anchors are used chiefly on large vessels. The mushroom anchor and the grapnel are used to hold small boats in place.

WORLD BOOK illustrations by Arthur Grebetz

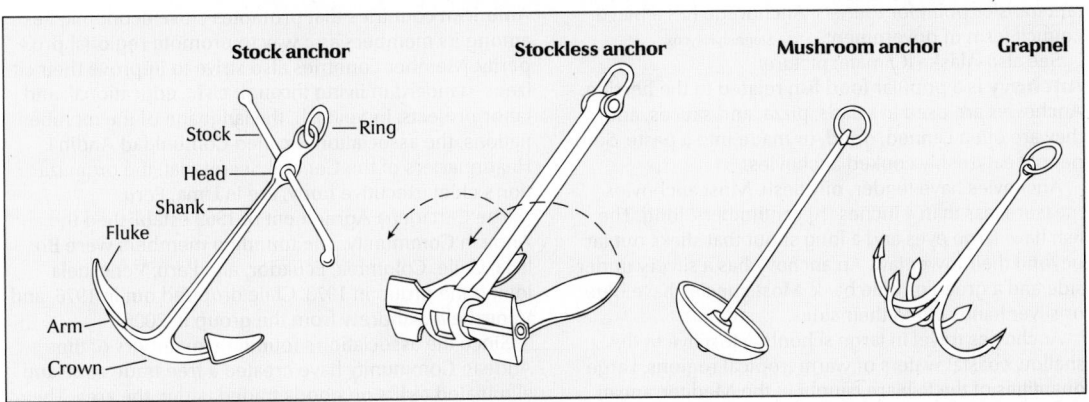

Stock anchor

Stockless anchor

Mushroom anchor

Grapnel

Stock — Ring
Head
Shank
Fluke
Arm
Crown

Anchorage, one of Alaska's chief ports, lies on Cook Inlet in the south-central part of the state. The Chugach Mountains rise behind the downtown skyline, *shown here.*

© Danny Daniels, Alaska Stock

WORLD BOOK illustration by John F. Eggert

The anchovy is a popular food fish.

age is the largest campus in the state university system. Alaska Pacific University is a small, private school in the city. Joint Base Elmendorf-Richardson, a combined Air Force and Army post, borders Anchorage to the north.

Prior to white settlement, Athabascan Indians inhabited the region, harvesting salmon and moose. In 1914, the U.S. Congress authorized construction of the Alaska Railroad. Engineers selected the mouth of Ship Creek as the railroad staging and construction center and laid out the town. In 1915, the town was formally named Anchorage, because ships anchored there with supplies for the railroad. The city was incorporated in 1920.

Anchorage grew slowly until World War II (1939-1945), when service personnel and civilian military employees swelled its population from 2,500 to 70,000. Modest oil finds on the nearby Kenai Peninsula in 1957 aided development. On March 27, 1964, one of the worst earthquakes in North America's history hit the Anchorage area, killing 131 people. However, the city quickly rebuilt.

In 1975, Anchorage merged with several other communities to form the Municipality of Anchorage. The construction of the Trans-Alaska Pipeline in 1977 provided a strong boost to the economy. The city is an important transfer point for tourists. Anchorage has a mayor-council form of government. Stephen Haycox

See also **Alaska** (Climate; picture).

Anchovy is a popular food fish related to the herring. Anchovies are used in salads, pizza, and sauces, and they are often canned, dried, or made into a paste. Some people eat freshly cooked anchovies.

Anchovies have tender, oily flesh. Most anchovies measure less than 4 inches (10 centimeters) long. The fish have large eyes and a long snout that sticks out far beyond their lower jaw. An anchovy has a silvery underside and a green or blue back. Most species have blue or silver bands along their sides.

Anchovies travel in large schools. Most live in the shallow coastal waters of warm tropical regions. Large quantities of the fish are caught in the Mediterranean

Sea and along the coast of Peru in South America. The type of anchovy caught along the Peruvian coast is sometimes called an *anchoveta.* It is used mainly in animal feed or as fish bait. John E. McCosker

Scientific classification. Anchovies belong to the family Engraulidae. The scientific name of the European anchovy is *Engraulis encrasicholus,* and the Peruvian anchovy is *E. ringens.* The northern anchovy that lives off the west coast of North America is *E. mordax.* The bay anchovy that ranges from Cape Cod, Massachusetts, to the Yucatán Peninsula in Mexico is *Anchoa mitchelli.*

Ancient civilization refers to civilizations that flourished long ago. The term is used especially for the way of life that existed around the Mediterranean Sea beginning before 3000 B.C. and ending with the fall of Rome in A.D. 476. It includes great civilizations developed by the Assyrians, Egyptians, Israelites, and Persians. The cultures of ancient Greece and Rome are also considered part of it. But great early civilizations also grew in the Far East, India, central and southern Africa, and North and South America. Barbara Mertz

Related articles in *World Book* include:

Aegean civilization	Indus Valley civilization
Aksum	Jews
Assyria	Kush
Babylonia	Media
Carthage	Mesopotamia
Chaldeans	Mitanni
China (History)	Nok
Ebla	Persia, Ancient
Egypt, Ancient	Phoenicia
Etruscans	Rome, Ancient
Greece, Ancient	Sumer
Hittites	World, History of the
Indian, American (The first Americans)	

Andean Community is an association of South American countries that promotes close economic ties among its members as a way to promote regional prosperity. Member countries also strive to improve their citizens' standard of living through civic, educational, and labor projects. In Spanish, the language of the member nations, the association is called Comunidad Andina. Headquarters of the General Secretariat, the organization's chief executive body, are in Lima, Peru.

The Cartagena Agreement of 1969 established the Andean Community. The founding members were Bolivia, Chile, Colombia, Ecuador, and Peru. Venezuela joined the group in 1973. Chile dropped out in 1976, and Venezuela withdrew from the group in 2006.

Since the association's founding, members of the Andean Community have created a free trade zone and eliminated tariffs on goods traded within the area. They have also tried to develop a common foreign policy to guide their dealings with nations outside the group.

Eliza J. Willis

Andersen, Hans Christian (1805-1875), was Denmark's most famous author. His fairy tales are among the most widely read works in world literature. His stories of make-believe have enchanted young readers around the world for generations.

Andersen wrote with wisdom, with deliberate simplicity, and often with sly humor. His fairy tales can be considered both children's literature and adult literature. Many of Andersen's fairy tales have serious moral meanings that are intended for adults.

Anderson gave each tale its own style, but they can be roughly classified into four groups: (1) imitations of folk tales—"The Tinder Box," "Little Claus and Big Claus," and "The Traveling Companion" (all 1835); (2) tales based on Andersen's life—"The Ugly Duckling" (1844) and "She Was Good for Nothing" (1853); (3) tales that make fun of human faults—"The Emperor's New Clothes" (1837) and "The Rags" (1874); and (4) philosophical tales—"The Shadow" (1847) and "The Story of a Mother" (1848). Some tales use settings in Denmark—"Holger Danske" (1845) and "The Wind Tells About Valdemar Daae and His Daughters" (1859). But others can take place anywhere.

Andersen was born on April 2, 1805, in Odense, Denmark. He was the son of a poor shoemaker who died when Hans was 11 years old. After attending the city school for poor children, Andersen left Odense at the age of 14 to seek a career as an artist in Copenhagen. He nearly starved while trying to earn a living as an actor, singer, and dancer. In Copenhagen, he received help from Jonas Collin, a wealthy businessman who became his lifelong friend. Collin got Andersen a royal scholarship, which permitted Andersen to continue his education from 1822 to 1828. In 1829, Andersen's first play, *Love in St. Nicolai Church Tower,* was produced. For several years, his reputation as a writer rested on his many plays and novels. But his plays are no longer produced. His novels, the best of which is *The Improvisation* (1835), are seldom read outside of Scandinavia.

Andersen wrote the first of his 156 fairy tales in 1835 and continued writing them until he died. They first appeared in a series of pamphlets and later were collected and published in books. The stories became popular in the early 1840's and made Andersen famous. His acquaintances included royalty and such fellow artists as the composer Franz Liszt, the poet Heinrich Heine, and the novelists Charles Dickens and Victor Hugo.

Andersen traveled throughout Europe and wrote many lively books about his experiences. *A Poet's Bazaar* (1842) and *In Sweden* (1851) are probably his best travel books. He also wrote an autobiography called *The Fairy Tale of My Life* (1855). Andersen never married, though he fell in love with three women, including the Swedish singer Jenny Lind and Louise Collin, the daughter of Jonas Collin. But none of the women returned his love. Anderson died on Aug. 4, 1875.   Niels Ingwersen

Additional resources

Andersen, Hans Christian. *Fairy Tales of Hans Christian Andersen.* Ed. by Neil Philip. Viking, 1995. Younger readers.
Langley, Andrew. *Hans Christian Andersen.* Oxford, 1998. Younger readers.
Wullschlager, Jackie. *Hans Christian Andersen.* Knopf, 2001.

Anderson, Carl David (1905-1991), an American physicist, discovered two subatomic particles—the *positron* and the *muon.* He identified these particles while studying cosmic rays with the aid of a Wilson cloud chamber (see **Cosmic rays**). For his discovery of the positron in 1932, Anderson shared the 1936 Nobel Prize in physics with Victor F. Hess.

The positron was the first known antiparticle (see **Antimatter**). The British physicist Paul Dirac had predicted its existence in 1931. The positron has a mass equal to that of the negatively charged electron, but its electric charge is positive. In 1937, Anderson discovered the particle known as the mu-meson, or muon. Muons have positive or negative charges and closely resemble positrons and electrons. However, a muon's mass is about 207 times as great as that of an electron.

Anderson was born on Sept. 3, 1905, in New York City. In 1930, he received a Ph.D. degree in physics from the California Institute of Technology. He died on Jan. 11, 1991.   Matthew Stanley

See also **Meson.**

Anderson, Judith (1898-1992), ranked among the leading English-speaking actresses of the 1900's. Anderson was a character actress and interpreter of intensely emotional roles. Her greatest stage successes included *Strange Interlude* (1928), *Mourning Becomes Electra* (1931), *Macbeth* (1941), and *Medea* (1947). She appeared in more than 25 motion pictures, including *Rebecca* (1940), *King's Row* (1941), *Laura* (1944), *The Ten Commandments* (1956), and *Cat on a Hot Tin Roof* (1958). Anderson was born on Feb. 10, 1898, in Adelaide, Australia. Her real name was Frances Margaret Anderson. Queen Elizabeth II named her dame commander of the Order of the British Empire in 1960, and she became Dame Judith Anderson. She was the first Australian actress so honored. She died on Jan. 3, 1992.   Don B. Wilmeth

Anderson, Marian (1897-1993), was an African American contralto. She gained fame primarily as a concert singer. In 1955, Anderson became the first black soloist to sing with the Metropolitan Opera of New York City. The famous conductor Arturo Toscanini praised her voice as one "that comes once in a hundred years."

Anderson was born on Feb. 27, 1897, in Philadelphia and sang in church choirs as a child. After graduating from high school, she studied voice and began to make concert tours. She spent several years studying and performing in Europe, where her singing won wide praise. She became a top concert singer in the United States after performing at Town Hall in New York City in 1935.

Racism affected Anderson's career. In 1939, the Daughters of the American Revolution would not let her perform in Constitution Hall in Washington, D.C., because she was black. She sang instead at the Lincoln Memorial for over 75,000 people. Anderson won the Spingarn Medal that year. She was a U.S. delegate to the United Nations (UN) in 1958 and won the UN peace prize in

Franz Rupp

Marian Anderson

1977. *My Lord, What a Morning* (1956) is her autobiography. She died on April 8, 1993.   Thomas A. Bauman

See also **African Americans** (The Great Depression; picture).

Anderson, Maxwell (1888-1959), an American playwright, brought seriousness and idealism to the theater. He wrote several realistic plays, including the war drama *What Price Glory?* (with Laurence Stallings, 1924) and the psychological melodrama *The Bad Seed* (1955). But his major contributions were historical plays, verse dramas, and his attempts to revive traditional heroic tragedy in the modern theater.

Among Anderson's historical plays, *Elizabeth the Queen* (1930) is one of the most significant. This tragedy in verse is based on the romance of Queen Elizabeth and Lord Essex. Like many of Anderson's works, it pictures the defeat of good by the inevitable forces of evil, but it also praises the counterforces of nobility and love in humanity. *Winterset* (1935), his most enduring play, is based on the Sacco-Vanzetti case (see **Sacco-Vanzetti case**). But it mainly deals with the dilemma created when love conflicts with a crusade for justice against evil. Another verse tragedy, *Key Largo* (1939), explores the difficulties of deciding to fight evil, as symbolized by a gangster. Anderson won the 1933 Pulitzer Prize for his political satire *Both Your Houses* (1933).

Anderson was born on Dec. 15, 1888, in Atlantic, Pennsylvania. In 1938, he helped found the Playwrights' Company, which produced many notable plays. He died on Feb. 28, 1959.   Thomas P. Adler

Anderson, Sherwood (1876-1941), was an American short-story writer and novelist. Although none of his novels was wholly successful, several of his short stories have become classics.

Anderson was a major influence on the generation of American writers who came after him. These writers included Ernest Hemingway, F. Scott Fitzgerald, and William Faulkner. Anderson thus occupies a place in literary history that cannot be fully explained by the literary quality of his work.

Anderson was born on Sept. 13, 1876, in Camden, Ohio. He never finished

Schaal Pix; Harcourt, Brace
Sherwood Anderson

high school because he had to work to support his family. By 1912, he was the successful manager of a paint factory in Elyria, Ohio, and the father of three children by the first of his four wives. In 1912, Anderson deserted his family and job. In early 1913, he moved to Chicago, where he devoted more time to his imaginative writing. He became a heroic model for younger writers because he broke with what they considered to be American materialism and convention to commit himself to art.

Anderson's most important book is *Winesburg, Ohio* (1919), a collection of 23 stories and sketches. The stories and sketches explore the lives of inhabitants of Winesburg, a fictional version of Clyde, Ohio, the small farm town where Anderson lived for about 12 years of his early life. These tales made a significant break with the traditional American short story. Instead of emphasizing plot and action, Anderson used a simple, precise, unsentimental style to reveal the frustration, loneliness, and longing in the lives of his characters. They are stunted by the narrowness of Midwestern small-town life and by their own limitations.

In *Winesburg, Ohio,* Anderson became one of the first American writers to use modern psychological insights, especially those of the Austrian psychiatrist Sigmund Freud. Anderson's characters tend to make themselves into what the author called *grotesques.* Anderson believed there were once hundreds of truths, all of them beautiful. But people tended to adopt only one truth and call it theirs. According to Anderson, the moment "one of the people took one of the truths to himself, called it his truth, and tried to live his life by it, he became a grotesque and the truth he embraced became a falsehood."

Anderson's most important book after *Winesburg, Ohio* is the short-story collection *The Triumph of the Egg* (1921). His many novels include *Poor White* (1920) and *Dark Laughter* (1925). He also wrote several volumes of revealing autobiography. He died on March 8, 1941.

Daniel Mark Fogel

Andes Mountains, *AN deez,* are a group of mountain ranges in South America. The Andes are the world's longest *cordillera*—Spanish for *mountain chain*—above sea level. They extend for about 4,500 miles (7,200 kilometers) along the west coast of South America, from Cape Horn, Chile, in the south to Panama and Venezuela in the north. The Andes are about 400 miles (645 kilometers) wide across their widest part, in Bolivia. Many Andean peaks rise higher than 20,000 feet (6,100 meters). Only the Himalaya of Asia are higher than the Andes.

Physical features. The Andes may be divided into three segments—southern, central, and northern.

The southern Andes are less than 10,000 feet (3,000 meters) high near the tip of South America. Farther north, the southern Andes rise higher. Aconcagua (22,841 feet, or 6,962 meters) is the highest peak in the Americas. It stands in Mendoza, Argentina, about 65 miles (105 kilometers) west of Santiago, Chile.

The central Andes are broad twin ranges running from northwest to southeast. Between these ranges lies the Altiplano, a highland plateau region, of southern Peru and western Bolivia. This section of the Altiplano is about 13,000 feet (4,000 meters) above sea level. Farther north, the two ranges draw closer together. The highest peaks of the central Andes include Pissis (22,241 feet, or 6,779 meters), Huascarán (22,205 feet, or 6,768 meters), Llullaillaco (22,057 feet, or 6,723 meters), Illampu (21,276 feet, or 6,485 meters), Sajama (21,463 feet, or 6,542 meters), Illimani (21,004 feet, or 6,402 meters), Chimborazo (20,702 feet, or 6,310 meters), and Cotopaxi (19,347 feet, or 5,897 meters).

The northern Andes have three parallel mountain ranges with a lower altitude than the cordillera's other segments. The western range runs along the coast through Colombia and into Panama. The central range stands between the valleys of the Cauca and Magdalena rivers. It includes the Tolima volcano (17,110 feet, or 5,215 meters). The third range, to the east, runs into Venezuela. Many mountain peaks in the northern Andes reach 15,000 feet (4,570 meters) or more. The Sierra Nevada de Santa Marta, a mountain in northern Colombia, has the two highest peaks in the northern Andes, Bolívar and Colón, both 18,947 feet (5,775 meters) high.

Volcanoes and earthquakes. Many Andean mountains are volcanoes, and some are active. The most famous of these volcanoes are Cotopaxi, Tungurahua, and Sangay in Ecuador; Nevado del Ruiz and Nevado del Huila in Colombia; El Misti in Peru; Pomerape in Bolivia; Parinacotoa and Chaitén in Chile; and Ojos del Salado in Argentina. Ojos del Salado is the tallest volcano in the world, measuring 22,664 feet (6,908 meters).

Earthquakes are common in the Andes. They have caused great damage and even wiped out many towns.

Glaciers, lakes, and rivers. Glaciers cover many high Andean peaks, including those near the equator. The largest glaciers are in southern Chile. Others reach down to the Pacific Coast. Many of the glaciers in the southern Andes have cut deep valleys into the rocky coastline. These *fiords* go far below the water level and make the coastline ragged, like Norway's. Many deep inlets and rocky islands dot the coastline. Such rivers as the Guayas and the Esmeraldas flow into the Pacific Ocean through gaps in the mountains. Many more rivers in the Andes flow toward the Atlantic Ocean.

Many of the Amazon River's main tributaries rise on the Andes' eastern slopes. The Paraná and Orinoco rivers also receive tributaries from the Andes. Rainfall is light on the western slopes of the Andes, except in the Chocó region, north of the equator in western Colombia, and in the Araucanía region of southern Chile.

Between the two ranges of the central Andes in Peru, Bolivia, and northern Argentina, water from the Altiplano does not flow to the Atlantic or the Pacific. Instead, it collects in Lake Titicaca and when water levels are high enough flows into the *ephemeral* Lake Poopó. An ephemeral lake usually is dry, but has water during the wet season or for certain periods of time.

Natural resources. The name *Andes* may come from Spanish explorers' descriptions of the *andenes* (terraced farms) that they saw in the mountains. The name may also come from the *indigenous* (native) word *anta,* meaning *copper.* The mountains contain an abundance of copper. The Andes also contain gold, iron, lead, mercury, platinum, silver, and tin.

Many kinds of wild animals live in the mountains, including bears, chinchillas, condors, cougars, deer, and *vicuñas* (animals that look like small camels without a hump). Tame llamas and alpacas graze in the central Andes in high grasslands called *jalca, puna,* or *páramos.* Below the grasslands, farmers have removed many *cloud forests* (forests almost constantly covered by clouds). They have created large terraces and irrigation systems, and they grow such crops as corn, potatoes, and wheat.

Transportation. Passes in the Andes Mountains are narrow, steep, and winding. The mountains are so high and rise so sharply that they divide the continent into Pacific and Atlantic South America.

It is difficult to build railroads in the Andes. Engineers may climb more than 10,000 feet (3,000 meters) to find a pass suitable for a railroad. Several railroads run up the west slope to the rich mineral beds on the plateaus of Peru and Bolivia. One of these, the Central Railway, climbs to over 15,800 feet (4,816 meters) above sea level. It is the highest standard-gauge railroad in the world.

In Peru, a paved highway runs from Callao, on the west coast, to Cerro de Pasco, over 100 miles (160 kilometers) inland. From there, an all-weather road continues down a deep canyon in the eastern Andes to a branch of the Amazon River. Other highways lead over the Andes into the eastern lowlands. One of these highways, the Yungas Road in Bolivia, is called the "Road of Death" because it is the site of so many fatal accidents. The Pan American Highway extends along the entire length of the Andes cordillera from north to south.

Flying provides another important means of travel in the Andes. Regular flights link capital cities in the Andes with national capitals elsewhere. Large passenger airplanes fly through foggy Uspallata Pass to connect Santi-

© Shutterstock

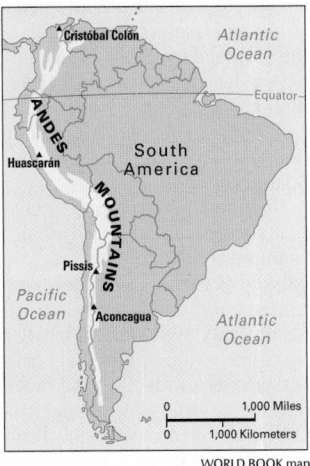

The Andes Mountains stretch along the west coast of South America. Many Andean peaks rise more than 20,000 feet (6,100 meters) above sea level.

WORLD BOOK map

ago, Chile, with Mendoza, Argentina. The pass is 12,674 feet (3,863 meters) above sea level. *Fausto Sarmiento*

Related articles in *World Book* include:

Aconcagua	Mountain (picture: A moun-
Chile (The land)	tain range)
Chimborazo	Pichincha
Cotopaxi	

Andorra, one of the smallest countries in the world, lies high in the Pyrenees mountains between France and Spain. The official name of Andorra in Catalan, a language that closely resembles the Provençal spoken in southern France, is Valls d'Andorra (Valleys of Andorra). Andorra la Vella (Andorra the Old) is the capital. Many tourists visit Andorra. Many people also go to Andorra to buy goods that are relatively inexpensive because Andorra charges almost no tax on them.

The steep, rocky mountains that surround Andorra cut the country off from the rest of the world for hundreds of years. As a result, Andorra's boundaries have changed little since the Middle Ages (about A.D. 400 through the 1400's). Andorra's legal system is based on ancient laws and *common law* (rules based on customs) that date from the Roman Empire.

Government. Andorra is a parliamentary coprincipality. Until 1993, the bishop of Urgel, Spain, and the president of France ruled Andorra jointly under treaties signed in the 1200's. Both rulers, known as the "princes of Andorra," had to agree before any changes could be made in Andorra's government. Each prince had the right to veto laws made by the parliament.

In 1993, Andorra's citizens adopted their first constitution. It made elected officials responsible for governing Andorra. The role of the princes became mostly ceremonial. But the princes still must approve international treaties with France and Spain, and some other matters concerning boundaries, defense, and internal security.

A 28-member parliament known as the General Council of the Valleys makes the nation's laws. Two members are elected from each of Andorra's seven *parishes* (districts). The other 14 members are elected nationwide. The General Council elects a head of government from among its members. The head then appoints a cabinet, the Executive Council, to help run the government.

People. From the 1100's to the 1930's, life in Andorra changed little. The people worked as farmers and shepherds. The villages and parishes owned the grazing lands, and farmers owned their own cropland. To keep the cropland from being divided into tiny plots, farmers gave at least three-fourths of their inheritance to one of their children, usually the oldest son. Many of the other children had to move out of Andorra. As a result, more people of Andorran descent now live in France and Spain than in Andorra.

The opening of roads to France and Spain in the 1930's and the sudden growth of tourism in the 1950's changed some of the old ways of living. Many who had worked as farmers, shepherds, and smugglers became storekeepers and hotel owners. Tourists brought new wealth, and fewer people had to move out of the country. Some people from Spain have moved into Andorra. Today, only about one-third of the country's people are Andorran citizens. More than half are citizens of Spain. Other inhabitants are mainly from France and Portugal. Citizenship is given to the children of Andorran citizens

Facts in brief

Capital: Andorra la Vella.
Official language: Catalan.
Area: 181 mi² (468 km²). *Greatest distances*—north-south, about 16 mi (26 km); east-west, about 19 mi (31 km).
Elevation: *Highest*—Coma Pedrosa, 9,665 ft (2,946 m) above sea level. *Lowest*—2,756 ft (840 m) above sea level.
Population: *Estimated 2022 population*—77,000; density, 425 per mi² (165 per km²); distribution, 88 percent urban, 12 percent rural. *2019 official government estimate*—77,543.
Chief products: *Agriculture*—cattle, oats, potatoes, rye, sheep, tobacco, wheat. *Manufacturing*—tobacco products.
Flag: The national flag, used by the people, has blue, yellow, and red vertical stripes. The state flag, used by the government, has a coat of arms on the yellow stripe. See **Flag** (picture: Flags of Europe).
Money: *Basic unit*—euro. One hundred cents equal one euro.

and to legal residents after 25 years of residency. Dual citizenship is not permitted.

These changes weakened the strong control Andorran fathers had always held over their families. But in other ways life has changed little. Life for the average Andorran still centers around the family. Many Andorrans still live in big farmhouses with stone walls and rough slate roofs. Most of these houses are three stories high with a barn to house livestock or a tool shed on the ground floor, a living room and kitchen on the second floor, and bedrooms opening onto wooden or iron balconies on the third floor. The people speak Catalan, but most Andorrans also understand French and Spanish. The government prints its official documents in Catalan.

Almost all Andorrans are Roman Catholics, and their religion greatly influences their social life. All public

Andorra

▬▬	International boundary
───	Road
─┼─	Railroad
⊛	National capital
•	Other city or town
+	Elevation above sea level

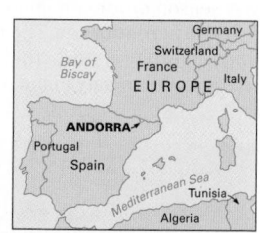

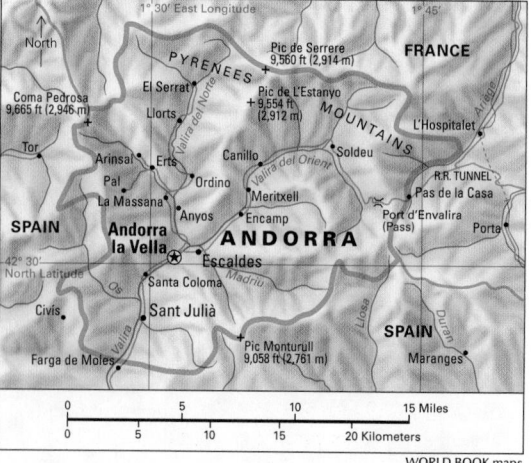

WORLD BOOK maps

records are kept by the church, and only Roman Catholics can get married in Andorra. On their national holiday, September 8, Andorrans make a *pilgrimage* (journey) to the shrine of Our Lady of Meritxell, patron saint of Andorra. Children in Andorra must attend school from ages 6 to 16. Andorra has Andorran, French, and Spanish schools.

Land. Steep mountain peaks as high as 9,665 feet (2,946 meters) above sea level tower over the valleys of Andorra. Fields and meadows lie in the valleys, and oak, pine, and fir trees cover the lower mountain slopes. Only grass grows farther up the mountainsides. The Valira del Norte (Northern Valira) and the Valira del Orient (Eastern Valira) rivers meet near the town of Andorra la Vella to form the Valira River, which flows into Spain. The main roads in Andorra follow the Valira del Norte toward France and the Valira into Spain.

Andorra has a dry, sunny climate. Three or four heavy snows fall each year, and even powerful snowplows cannot keep the mountain road between Andorra and France open all winter. However, in the valleys south of Escaldes, the snows melt in a few days. Winter temperatures at Escaldes range between 20 and 30 °F (-7 and -1 °C). In the summer, the valleys are warm during the day and cool at night. Temperatures at Escaldes reach 70 to 80 °F (21 to 27 °C).

Economy. Tourism is one of Andorra's chief sources of income. Andorra's beautiful mountains and ancient buildings are the main attractions. Ski slopes have been opened at Pas de la Casa and Soldeu, where the snow lasts until the end of April. Tourists can buy many goods at low prices in Andorra because import *duties* (charges) are low. The banking industry is also important to the country's economy.

Andorra has a small amount of arable land, and few Andorrans farm. The country must import most of its food. Tobacco is Andorra's main crop, and cigarettes and cigars are among the country's leading manufactured products. Other crops include oats, potatoes, rye, and wheat. Farmers also raise cattle and sheep.

History. According to legends, Charlemagne either founded or freed Andorra. The first known ruler of Andorra was a Spanish noble, the Count of Urgel. He controlled the region in the A.D. 800's, and then gave it to the diocese of Urgel. In the 1000's, the bishop of Urgel could not control Andorra by himself, and he asked a Spanish noble, the Lord of Caboet, to defend the region. A French noble, the Count of Foix, inherited the lord's duties through marriages. The French count and the bishop fought over Andorra. They finally ended their disputes by signing treaties in 1278 and 1288. The treaties made them joint rulers.

Through marriages, the king of France inherited the count's rights. During the French Revolution, France refused to rule Andorra. But the Andorrans later asked Napoleon I to rule them, and he accepted in 1806. France's head of state has been a prince of Andorra since then. Today, the French president serves as prince. Until 1993, as the old treaties required, Andorra paid about $2 every other year to the president of France and about $8 to the Spanish bishop.

Until the 1930's, only male citizens who were the heads of households could vote in Andorra. In 1933, youths stormed the General Council and forced it to

Cameramann International, Ltd. from Marilyn Gartman

Andorra's capital, called Andorra la Vella, nestles among the rocky peaks of the Pyrenees mountains. The quaint old town has become a leading tourist center.

give male citizens over 25 years old the right to vote. In 1970, the voting age was reduced to 21 and female citizens won the right to vote. In 1984, a woman was elected to the General Council for the first time. In 1985, the voting age was lowered to 18. The people of Andorra adopted their first constitution in 1993.

Fiona M. Davidson

See also **Andorra la Vella.**

Andorra la Vella, *an DAWR uh lah VEHL yah* (pop. 19,156), is the capital and largest town of Andorra. About one-fourth of Andorra's people live in Andorra la Vella. The town lies beside the Valira River in a valley high amid the Pyrenees. For location, see **Andorra** (map).

The economy of Andorra la Vella depends on tourism. Many visitors come from neighboring Spain and France. The town has numerous medieval structures, including the Santa Coloma church. Andorra's parliament meets in the Casa de la Vall, which dates from the 1500's.

For hundreds of years, the Pyrenees kept Andorra la Vella isolated from the outside world. After the mid-1900's, however, modernization proceeded rapidly. Today, the city bustles with commercial activity, and air pollution sometimes clouds the valley. William M. Reddy

Andrada e Silva, *an DRAH duh ee SEEL vuh,* **José Bonifácio de,** *zhoh ZEH вон nee FAH syoo duh* (1763-1838), was a Brazilian statesman known as the "architect of Brazilian independence." He supported land reform, an end to slavery, and rule by a monarchy. In 1822, he guided Brazil out of the Portuguese empire. He then served Pedro I, the first emperor of an independent Brazil. He fell from favor and was banished temporarily. Pedro later named him guardian of his son, the future Pedro II (see **Pedro I; Pedro II**).

Andrada was also an accomplished scientist. In 1783, he went to Portugal to study philosophy and law at the University of Coimbra. In 1790, the king sent Andrada on a 10-year tour. He studied chemistry in Paris, and mining and metallurgy in Germany, Norway, Switzerland, and

England. Andrada taught at the University of Coimbra and held important government posts. He returned to Brazil in 1819.

Andrada was born in Santos, Brazil, on June 13, 1763. He died on April 6, 1838.   Robert M. Levine

André, *AHN dray,* **John** (1751-1780), a British officer, was hanged as a spy by the Americans during the American Revolution (1775-1783). He was the messenger of the British general, Sir Henry Clinton, who, with Benedict Arnold, had concocted a plot for taking the vital American fort at West Point (see **Arnold, Benedict**).

André was Clinton's personal aide and adjutant general of the British forces in America. Clinton chose him to meet Arnold and arrange the final details of the plot for taking West Point. Clinton sent him up the Hudson River on a British sloop. The men met on shore on the night of Sept. 21, 1780.

At dawn, the Americans opened fire on the sloop and forced it to retreat. André, caught inside the American lines, was forced to go overland to New York. Disobeying Clinton's instructions, he discarded his military uniform for civilian clothes. By this action, André lost his chance, if captured, to be considered an officer instead of a spy. Not far from the British outposts, André was stopped by American militia, who searched him and found papers that Arnold had given him. He was taken to the nearest officer, who notified Arnold. This gave Arnold a chance to escape. André was tried by a military court and sentenced to death. In spite of Clinton's efforts to save him, he was hanged on October 2.

André was born in London, probably on May 2, 1751. He was handsome, witty, interested in literature and music, and popular in the British Army. While in prison, André won the affection even of his American captors. His youth, charm, and courage in facing death make his story one of the tragedies of the American Revolution.

Paul David Nelson

Andretti, *an DREHT tee,* **Mario** (1940-   ), became a top race car driver. Andretti won the Grand Prix world driving championship in 1978. He won the Daytona 500 race for stock cars in 1967 and the Indianapolis 500 race in 1969. Andretti won the United States Auto Club national driving championship in 1965 and 1966. In 1966, he finished first in eight of the races that made up the U.S. championship circuit. He won the national championship in 1969 and 1984. Andretti is the only driver who has won the Grand Prix world driving championship, the Daytona 500 race, and the Indianapolis 500 race. He retired from racing in 1994.

Andretti was born on Feb. 28, 1940, near Trieste, a city on the Adriatic Sea. He spent seven years in a displaced persons camp after World War II and moved to the United States in 1955. Michael Andretti, his son, was also a leading race car driver.   Sylvia Wilkinson

Andrew, Saint, was the first of the 12 apostles of Jesus Christ. He was the brother of the apostle Peter. Andrew was a fisherman from Bethsaida, a village on the north shore of the Sea of Galilee. In Matthew 4:19, Jesus calls Andrew and Peter to become his followers.

The Gospel of John says that before Andrew became a disciple of Jesus, he was a follower of Saint John the Baptist. It also tells that Andrew was present at the feeding of the multitude and received a request from some Greeks who wanted to meet with Jesus.

According to later tradition, Andrew preached in Asia Minor and Greece, and he may have preached in what is now Ukraine. He was martyred in Greece by being crucified on an X-shaped cross. Andrew became the patron saint of Greece, Russia, and Scotland. The X on the Scottish flag is a symbol of his crucifixion. His feast day is November 30.   Richard A. Edwards

See also **Apostles**.

Andrews, Julie
(1935-   ), is a British-born star of stage and motion-picture musical comedies known for her clear, well-trained soprano voice. She gained international fame as Eliza Doolittle in the Broadway musical hit *My Fair Lady* (1956). She won the Academy Award as best actress in the title role of the movie musical *Mary Poppins* (1964), her first film.

© Volker Dornberger, dpa/Landov
Julie Andrews

Andrews was born on Oct. 1, 1935, in Walton-on-Thames in Surrey, England. Her real name was Julia Elizabeth Wells. Andrews began her show-business career as a child singing in English stage shows. She received her first recognition in 1954 in the New York City production of the English musical *The Boy Friend.* After her success in *My Fair Lady,* Andrews starred in the Broadway musical hit *Camelot* (1960). She then devoted herself to motion pictures, most of them directed by Blake Edwards, her second husband, whom she married in 1969.

Andrews's films include *The Americanization of Emily* (1964), the movie version of *The Sound of Music* (1965), *Thoroughly Modern Millie* (1967), *Victor/Victoria* (1982), *A Fine Romance* (1992), *The Princess Diaries* (2001), and *The Princess Diaries 2: Royal Engagement* (2004). She returned to the stage as the star of the musical adaptation of *Victor/Victoria* (1995).

In 2000, Andrews was made dame commander in the Order of the British Empire and thus became known as Dame Julie Andrews. In 2005, Andrews directed a revival of *The Boy Friend.* Andrews also is a published author. She has written or co-written a number of children's books and personal memoirs.   Dan Zeff

Andrews, Roy Chapman (1884-1960), was well known as an author and explorer, and as a leader of expeditions for the American Museum of Natural History. As a result of work from 1908 to 1914 in Alaska and Asia, he became an authority on whales. Between 1916 and 1930, Andrews led expeditions to central and eastern Asia. In the desert known as the Gobi, he and his co-workers found the remains of *Baluchitherium,* the largest land mammal that ever lived. They also discovered the first dinosaur eggs ever found and unearthed evidence of a prehistoric civilization.

Andrews was born in Beloit, Wisconsin, on Jan. 26, 1884, and he graduated from Beloit College. He served as director of the American Museum of Natural History from 1935 to 1942. He wrote several books, including *Whale Hunting with Gun and Camera* (1916), *The New Conquest of Central Asia* (1932), and *Beyond Adventure* (1954). Andrews died on March 11, 1960.   G. J. Kenagy

Andromeda, *an DRAHM uh duh,* is a constellation of the northern celestial hemisphere. It extends from the constellation Perseus to the northeast corner of the great square of the constellation Pegasus. The brightest star of Andromeda, called Alpheratz, completes the square of Pegasus. The Andromeda Galaxy, which is a spiral galaxy close to our solar system, is visible as a faint, misty spot in the Andromeda constellation.

David H. Levy

See also **Andromeda Galaxy.**

Andromeda, *an DRAHM uh duh,* in Greek mythology, was the daughter of Cassiopeia and Cepheus, rulers of Ethiopia. Cassiopeia dared to compare her own beauty to that of the Nereids (sea nymphs) who attended Poseidon. In anger, Poseidon sent a sea monster to attack Ethiopia. An oracle said Andromeda should be sacrificed to the serpent to save the land. Perseus saw Andromeda chained to a rock, fell in love with her, and killed the monster. He then married Andromeda. Among their descendants was Hercules. After her death, Andromeda became a constellation. Jon D. Mikalson

Andromeda Galaxy, also known as M31, is the closest large galaxy to our home galaxy, the Milky Way. It lies about 2.5 million *light-years* from Earth. A light-year is the distance that light travels in a vacuum in a year—about 5.88 trillion miles (9.46 trillion kilometers). The Andromeda Galaxy is one of the farthest objects visible to the unaided eye. It appears on fall and winter nights in the Northern Hemisphere, northwest of the Great Square of Pegasus in the constellation Andromeda.

The Andromeda Galaxy appears as a thin disk tilted to our line of sight. Like the Milky Way, it is a *spiral galaxy,* with sweeping arms of stars wrapped about a distinct center. The Andromeda Galaxy's *mass* (amount of matter) measures from hundreds of billions to more than 1 tril-

The Andromeda Galaxy, *shown in this photograph,* is the nearest large galaxy to our home galaxy, the Milky Way. Like the Milky Way, the Andromeda Galaxy has a bright central bulge surrounded by a thin disk made up of spiraling arms of stars.

Bill Schoening, Vanessa Harvey/REU program/NOAO/AURA/NSF

lion times that of the sun, comparable to the mass of the Milky Way. But the Andromeda Galaxy is larger and gives off more light than the Milky Way. These two galaxies account for the vast majority of the mass and light of the Local Group of galaxies. See **Local Group.**

The Andromeda Galaxy consists of a bright central bulge surrounded by a flat spiral disk and a vast *halo* of material. Its core contains a *supermassive black hole.* A black hole is a region of space whose gravitational pull is so strong that nothing can escape from it. This particular black hole has a mass about 140 million times that of the sun. The bulge extends thousands of light-years from the core. The disk measures more than 200,000 light-years in diameter but only about 1,000 light-years thick. The halo reaches more than 1 million light-years across. It contains most of the galaxy's mass in the form of unidentified material called *dark matter* (see **Dark matter**). Many small *satellite galaxies* called *dwarf galaxies* orbit the Andromeda Galaxy within the halo. The halo also contains *tidal streams,* or *tidal tails,* the remains of satellite galaxies shredded by the Andromeda Galaxy's *tidal forces.* Tidal forces are strains caused by the uneven pull of gravity near a massive body.

The mutual gravitational pull of the Andromeda Galaxy and the Milky Way is causing them to move toward each other. In a few billion years, they will probably collide and form a single large galaxy. Mario Mateo

Anemia, *uh NEE mee uh,* is a condition in which the number of healthy red blood cells falls below normal. Red blood cells pick up oxygen in the lungs and carry it to tissues throughout the body. There, the oxygen is combined with food to release energy. In an anemic person, the blood cannot provide the tissues with enough oxygen. Thus, the person feels weak or tired. Other symptoms are dizziness, headaches, pale or cool skin, rapid heartbeat, and shortness of breath.

Anemia, which is not a disease itself, is caused by a variety of diseases and disorders. The main causes are (1) insufficient production of red blood cells, (2) loss of blood, and (3) excessive destruction of red blood cells.

Insufficient production of red blood cells. Each day, about 0.8 percent of the body's red blood cells wear out and are destroyed. If the body fails to replace these cells at the same rate, anemia results. Red blood cells are produced in the *bone marrow,* a tissue in the center of certain bones. This process requires the intake of various minerals and vitamins, and the proper functioning of certain hormones in the body.

Deficiency anemias develop if the diet lacks sufficient iron, vitamin B_{12}, or folic acid (also called folate). These nutrients are essential for the production of red blood cells. Deficiency anemias also result if the body cannot absorb these nutrients properly. For example, *pernicious anemia* occurs when vitamin B_{12} cannot be absorbed. Physicians treat deficiency anemias by adding the missing nutrient to the diet or by administering it through injections or in tablets.

Aplastic anemias occur if the bone marrow loses its ability to produce red blood cells. Some cases are due to diseases that affect the marrow, such as leukemia in its early stages. Other cases result from exposure to chemicals or radiation. Many cases have no apparent cause. Victims of aplastic anemia may receive a bone marrow transplant if they are young and if an appropriate donor is available. Chances of recovery are good if rejection of the transplant and infection do not occur. Other victims receive regular blood transfusions until their bone marrow begins to function again. In many cases, the marrow never regains function, and the victim requires a bone marrow transplant to survive.

Anemia of renal disease occurs as a result of the kidney's lost ability to produce a hormone called *erythropoietin.* This hormone stimulates bone marrow to make red blood cells. People whose kidneys have failed or have been removed, as well as some cancer and AIDS patients, suffer from this anemia. In 1989, the Food and Drug Administration approved *Epoetin alfa,* a drug that is a genetically engineered form of erythropoietin. The drug stimulates bone marrow to make red blood cells.

Loss of blood. The body responds to excessive blood loss by retaining water to replace the fluid part of the blood. As a result, the percentage of red cells in the blood decreases, and anemia develops. The blood loss may occur rapidly, as from a wound, or slowly, as from a bleeding ulcer in the stomach. Treatment involves stopping the bleeding and, if necessary, providing blood transfusions.

Excessive destruction of red blood cells. Old red blood cells are destroyed in the liver and spleen by a process called *hemolysis.* If hemolysis occurs faster than the production of new red blood cells, anemia results. Such *hemolytic anemia* may be caused by inherited defects in the red blood cells, or it may be acquired.

Hereditary causes of hemolytic anemia include sickle cell anemia and thalassemia, disorders that affect the *hemoglobin* portion of red blood cells. Hemoglobin is the molecule that enables red blood cells to carry oxygen. Other hereditary defects may involve the *cell membrane*—the envelope that encloses a red blood cell—or the enzymes of the red blood cell. All of these hereditary disorders produce abnormal red blood cells, which are destroyed faster than normal.

Acquired hemolytic anemia can occur if the red blood cells are damaged by severe burns or freezing. It also sometimes follows infections. Normally, infections cause the body to produce *antibodies,* which attack the invading germs. In some cases, the body produces abnormal antibodies, called *autoantibodies,* which attack the person's own red blood cells.

Treatment of hemolytic anemia varies according to the cause and severity. Treatments may include drugs, blood transfusions, removal of the spleen, or a bone marrow transplant. Edward E. Morse

See also **Blood** (Red blood cells); **Hodgkin, Dorothy Crowfoot; Sickle cell anemia; Thalassemia.**

Anemometer, *AN uh MAHM uh tuhr,* is an instrument that measures wind speed. There are several types of anemometers. The most common type has three or four cone-shaped cups at the end of rods that are from 2 to 8 inches (5 to 20 centimeters) long. This unit rotates on a vertical spindle. The wind pressure is greater on the *concave* (inward curving) side of the cups, than on the *convex* (outward curving) side of the cups. Because of this, the wind makes the cups rotate regardless of wind direction. The faster the wind blows, the faster the cups rotate. The wind speed is measured by the number of revolutions that the cups make in a given period. This information is often registered on a dial on the anemome-

ter. However, it can also be transmitted by electrical means to display devices that are some distance from the anemometer itself. Brian Nicklas

Anemone, *uh NEHM uh nee,* is any of dozens of species of spring flowers that grow mainly in northern regions with cold winters and warm summers. The flowers' name comes from the Greek word for *wind.* They are also called windflowers.

The best-known anemone is the wood anemone, a delicate plant with white blossoms. Other species grow much taller and may be tinted with pink, purple, or blue. J. Massey

Scientific classification. Anemones make up the genus *Anemone.* The wood anemone's scientific name is *Anemone quinquefolia.*

Anemone, Sea. See Sea anemone.

Anesthesia, *an uhs THEE zhuh,* is the loss of sensation—particularly that of pain—in all or part of the body. Drugs called *anesthetics* are used to produce temporary anesthesia for medical purposes. Anesthesia is also produced by hypnosis and by *acupuncture*—the insertion of needles at certain points on the body. Some injuries and diseases, especially those of the nervous system, also can lead to loss of sensation.

Without anesthesia, doctors could not perform most surgical operations. Because an anesthetic makes the patient insensitive to pain, it greatly reduces the physical shock and emotional stress of the operation. The use of anesthetics gives the surgeon time to perform complicated operations safely.

General anesthesia is the loss of feeling in the entire body. It is accompanied by unconsciousness. General anesthetics are inhaled, injected, or swallowed. The blood carries them to the brain, where they block pain impulses in the nervous system. Common general anesthetics include enflurane, halothane, isoflurane, nitrous oxide (laughing gas), and thiopental (sodium pentothal).

A person under general anesthesia shows various signs that indicate the depth of unconsciousness. In deep levels of anesthesia, the patient loses such reflex actions as coughing, and heart and respiration rates slow. In surgery, the patient's reactions to the anesthetic and to the stress of the operation are monitored by the anesthetist to maintain a safe level of anesthesia.

Local anesthesia involves the loss of pain sensation in only a part of the body. The individual remains conscious. Local anesthetics may be applied to body surfaces or injected around nerves. Doctors frequently use them when they operate on the eyes, nose, mouth, or skin. Dentists also use local anesthetics during painful procedures. Common local anesthetics include lidocaine, tetracaine, and procainelike drugs. They additionally may be used to treat the pain associated with injuries or diseases.

One type of local anesthesia, called *regional nerve block,* involves injecting an anesthetic around large nerves. With this technique, only the pain impulses from a particular region of the body are blocked. *Spinal anesthesia* occurs when the anesthetic is injected into the fluid within the coverings of the spinal cord. *Peridural anesthesia* is caused by injecting the anesthetic into the space just outside the covering of the spinal cord. Both spinal and peridural anesthesia render the lower parts of the body insensitive to pain, but the patient remains conscious. They are commonly used during childbirth.

History. Before the discovery of an effective anesthetic, the great pain and shock of operations severely limited the usefulness of surgery. In 1800, Humphry Davy, a British chemist, suggested that nitrous oxide be used as an anesthetic. However, no one tried this until 1844, when Horace Wells, an American dentist, used it on himself while having a tooth pulled.

In 1842, Crawford W. Long, a Georgia doctor, performed an operation after he had his patient breathe ether vapor until he was unconscious. In 1845, Long used ether for the first time in delivering a child. He did not publish the facts of his discoveries until 1849, by which time credit for the discovery of ether anesthesia had been given to W. T. G. Morton, a Boston dentist. At the recommendation of Charles T. Jackson, a Boston chemist, Morton used ether during a tooth extraction in the mid-1840's. In 1846, he administered ether during a surgical operation at Massachusetts General Hospital. In 1847 and 1848, Sir James Y. Simpson, a Scottish physician, used chloroform to ease the pain of childbirth. Queen Victoria was one of the first women to be anesthetized during childbirth. The use of local anesthetics did not begin until the mid-1880's.

During the early 1930's, medical schools began offering formal training in anesthesia. Over the following decade, the study of anesthesia and the administration of anesthetics was recognized as a separate medical specialty called *anesthesiology.*   Edwin S. Munson

Related articles in *World Book* include:

Acupuncture	Ether	Morton,
Anesthesiology	Halothane	William T. G.
Apgar, Virginia	Hypnosis	Nitrous oxide
Benzocaine	Lidocaine	Thiopental
Cocaine	Long, Crawford W.	

Anesthesiology, *AN uhs THEE zee AHL uh jee,* is a branch of medicine that deals with the administration of drugs for the relief of pain and anxiety during surgery and childbirth. Doctors in this field are called *anesthesiologists.* They administer drugs called *anesthetics.*

Before a surgical operation, an anesthesiologist supervises the preparation of the patient, recommends tests or medications, and selects the appropriate anesthetic. During surgery, the anesthesiologist uses various techniques to anesthetize all, or part, of the patient's body. The anesthesiologist carefully monitors the patient's important body functions and administers oxygen, drugs, and fluids to keep these functions normal.

Anesthesiologists also have special knowledge in obstetrics, pediatrics, internal medicine, and pain management. They frequently treat patients with lung problems and supervise intensive care units. They also teach specialized breathing therapies to other health workers. Many anesthesiologists operate pain clinics and conduct research to improve the care of patients during anesthesia and surgery.   Edwin S. Munson

Aneurysm, *AN yuh rihz uhm,* is a balloonlike bulge that forms in a weakened area of the wall of an artery or vein. The most dangerous aneurysms are those that form in arteries, especially the arteries of the brain and the *aorta,* the main artery leading from the heart. Most aneurysms result from *atherosclerosis,* which is a disease caused by cholesterol build-up in artery walls. Other causes of aneurysms include genetic disorders or other defects that are present at birth.

The symptoms of an aneurysm vary with its location and size. There may be no symptoms, or pain may develop at the site of the aneurysm. Shortness of breath occurs if the aneurysm interferes with the heart's pumping ability. Some aneurysms press on nearby structures, producing a cough, hoarseness, or difficulty in swallowing. An aneurysm may worsen without the patient knowing and then suddenly rupture, causing a coma, paralysis, or death. Many strokes result from the rupture of an aneurysm in an artery of the brain (see **Stroke**).

Physicians can detect aneurysms with X rays and, in many cases, can repair them surgically. Surgeons remove the diseased portion of the blood vessel. If it is a minor vessel, they tie off the loose ends. In a major artery or vein, they replace the diseased portion with a plastic tube, a fabric patch, or a piece of another blood vessel.   Toby R. Engel

Angel, according to many religions, is a spiritual being created by God. The word *angel* comes from a Greek word meaning *messenger* or *one who is sent.* According to religious tradition, angels live in heaven and act as God's servants and as messengers between God and human beings. They also serve as guardians of individuals and nations. Angels traditionally are pictured as having a human body and wings. Poets and artists have portrayed angels as symbols of innocence or virtue.

Many religions have teachings about angels or similar beings. In some early religions, legends tell of bright, powerful spirits that appear in dreams and visions and protect people or tribes. In Hinduism and Buddhism, many major gods are accompanied by a band or court of spiritual beings.

Judaism, Christianity, and Islam developed the most elaborate doctrines about angels. These religions recognize an order of beings in which angels rank above human beings but under God. God is all-powerful, and the human is sometimes portrayed as created in God's image. In some traditions, Satan and other "fallen angels" rebel against this order. According to other traditions, they fell because of their lust for women.

The concept of angels with a human body and wings began in the Hebrew Bible, or Old Testament, and in Christianity. Later tradition refers to many *archangels* (angels of high rank), including Saint Michael.

Christian doctrine regarding angels reached full development during the A.D. 1100's and 1200's, especially in the teachings of Saint Thomas Aquinas. Thomas believed angels were necessary to fill the gap between God and human beings. He taught that countless numbers of angels existed and that they were immortal. According to Thomas, angels knew everything except what depended on human choice and what was known only to God. The concept of angels strongly influenced *Paradise Lost* (1667), a famous epic by the English poet John Milton. *Paradise Lost* includes a version of Satan's fall and of Adam and Eve's expulsion from Paradise.

The Islamic belief in angels resembles that of Judaism and Christianity. These three faiths place angels near God and give special duties to some.   J. H. Charlesworth

See also **Michael, Saint.**

Angel Falls is the highest waterfall in the world. It drains into the Churún River in eastern Venezuela. For location, see **Venezuela** (terrain map). Angel Falls has a total height of 3,212 feet (979 meters). Its longest unbroken drop is 2,648 feet (807 meters).

Angel Falls plunges down a cliff in a highland area called La Gran Sabana. This region has many huge, colorful *mesas* (flat-topped hills) with sandstone surfaces. Grasslands and tropical rain forests cover much of the mesas. Some of the mesas are more than 2,500 feet (760 meters) high. There are many steep cliffs in the area. Angel Falls is on the Auyán-Tepuí mountain, which rises 8,400 feet (2,560 meters) above sea level.

The waterfall is named for Jimmy Angel, an American pilot. Angel became the first known white person to see the falls, when he flew over it in 1935. He was searching for gold in the area. Today, small planes carry tourists over Angel Falls and its surroundings.   Robert C. Eidt

See also **South America** (picture); **Waterfall** (picture).

Angelfish is a type of fish with a thin, oval body and long, pointed fins. Marine angelfish also have stripes or patterns on the body and patches of vivid color. There are dozens of marine *species* (kinds). A species commonly called the freshwater angelfish is only distantly related to the marine angelfishes.

Marine angelfishes live mainly around coral reefs in warm and tropical seas. Most feed on animals attached to the sea floor. The juveniles of some species clean parasites off larger fish. Most species live in male-female pairs or small social groups. Individuals in some species can change sex from female to male. Many species are kept in commercial aquariums and are highly valued for their colorful patterns.

WORLD BOOK illustration
by Colin Newman, Linden Artists Ltd.

The freshwater angelfish of South America's Amazon River is popular in many home aquariums.

The freshwater angelfish is among the most popular fishes for home aquariums. It is native to the Amazon River Basin in South America.   Mark A. Hixon

Scientific classification. Marine angelfish are in the family Pomacanthidae. The freshwater angelfish is in the family Cichlidae. It is *Pterophyllum scalare.*

See also **Fish** (pictures: Fish of coral reefs).

Angelico, *an JAY lee koh* or *an JEHL uh koh,* **Fra** (1400?-1455), was an Italian painter. He combined the clarity of form, linear perspective, and light and shade of the new Renaissance style with the flowing line, brilliant color, and symbolism of earlier medieval painting.

Fra Angelico was born in Vicchio, Italy, near Florence. He was born Guido di Pietro. He became a Dominican monk in Fiesole about 1418 and took the name Fra Giovanni da Fiesole. He was a man of legendary piety and came to be called Fra Angelico (angelic brother).

In 1450, Fra Angelico became prior of the Dominican convent of San Marco in Florence. Some of his most famous altarpieces, painted in the 1430's, can be seen in the museum of his work in San Marco. He and his assistants also painted the monks' cells in San Marco with religious images using a technique called *fresco.*

In 1445, Fra Angelico was called to Rome, where he painted in the Vatican for two popes during the next five years. He also worked in Orvieto and again in Florence before his death on Feb. 18, 1455.   David Summers

See also **Painting** (The 1400's; picture: *The Annunciation).*

Angelou, *AN juh loh,* **Maya,** *MY uh* (1928-2014), an American writer, drew from the African American storytelling tradition. She wove humor, wisdom, and folk sayings into her writing. Her works celebrate womanhood, the human spirit, and the will to overcome hardship. Angelou was also a performer and theater director.

Angelou was best known for her series of autobiographical writings. The first and most acclaimed installment is *I Know Why the Caged Bird Sings* (1970). It recounts the author's childhood in the segregated rural South and her transition to urban life. Angelou continued to chronicle her life in *Gather Together in My Name* (1974), *Singin' and Swingin' and Getting Merry Like Christmas* (1976), *The Heart of a Woman* (1981), *All God's Children Need Traveling Shoes* (1986), *A Song Flung Up to Heaven* (2002), and *Mom & Me & Mom* (2013).

Angelou's poetry is compiled in *The Complete Poetry* (published in 2015, after her death). Several of her essays are collected in *Wouldn't Take Nothing for My Journey Now* (1993), *Even the Stars Look Lonesome* (1997), and *Letter to My Daughter* (2008).

Angelou was born on April 4, 1928, in St. Louis but spent much of her early life in Stamps, Arkansas. Her given name was Marguerite Johnson. She adopted the name Maya Angelou in 1953. Angelou died on May 28, 2014.   Andreá N. Williams

Monastery of San Marco, Florence, Italy (SCALA/Art Resource)

Annunciation **by Fra Angelico** shows the Italian artist's skill in combining delicate colors with simple, graceful figures.

Angina pectoris, *an JY nuh PEHK tuhr ihs,* is chest discomfort or pain that occurs when the blood flow to the heart is limited. The word *angina* means *to strangle,* and angina pectoris feels like a pressing or squeezing sensation in the area of the breastbone. The pain may travel to the shoulders, especially the left shoulder, and down the arms. The pain is usually called simply *angina.*

An attack of angina can occur any time the heart works harder than usual and requires more blood. For example, an attack may occur after physical exertion or at a time of emotional stress. Blood flowing through the coronary arteries carries oxygen to the heart. The coronary arteries can become narrowed by accumulations of fatty deposits, called *plaque,* and scar tissue. These conditions result in *arteriosclerosis* (hardening of the arteries), the primary cause of angina pectoris. If the coronary arteries are narrowed, extra blood cannot reach the heart. Part of the heart muscle is temporarily deprived of oxygen carried by the blood, causing pain. Angina can also be caused by a spasm in the coronary artery.

Most people who experience angina are middle-aged or older. Many are overweight, have high blood pressure, eat foods high in cholesterol, smoke cigarettes, and get little exercise. Resting and taking a medication called *nitroglycerin* can relieve most attacks of angina. Doctors may also prescribe drugs called *beta-blockers* and *calcium channel blockers.* These drugs help keep the heart from working harder under stress.

When medication can no longer control angina, other treatments are necessary. Physicians may perform a procedure called *angioplasty* to clear the narrowed arteries. Angioplasty involves threading a balloon-tipped *catheter* (slender tube) into the blocked artery. The balloon is then inflated, flattening the blockage against the artery wall. In severe cases of angina, narrowed coronary arteries may also be bypassed by grafts of vessels taken from the leg or chest. Surgeons may use lasers to create channels in the heart muscle to increase blood flow. Scientists are also investigating ways to increase blood flow to the heart by stimulating *angiogenesis*—that is, the growth of new blood vessels.   James W. Jones

See also **Angiogenesis; Calcium channel blocker; Heart** (Coronary artery disease); **Nitroglycerin** (As a medication).

Angiogenesis, *AN jee oh JEHN uh sihs,* is the formation and growth of new blood vessels in the body. It plays an important role in tissue growth and tissue repair from wounds or infection. Abnormal angiogenesis occurs in a variety of diseases. Excessive angiogenesis occurs in cancer and *macular degeneration,* an eye condition. Insufficient angiogenesis can occur after stroke.

Substances called *angiogenesis-stimulating growth factors* cause angiogenesis. One, called *vascular endothelial growth factor* (VEGF), is produced during growth or by injury or disease. Lack of oxygen in tissue not receiving enough blood stimulates VEGF production in wounds. VEGF can also be used as a drug to stimulate blood vessel growth to help heal damaged tissues.

Cancer cells secrete chemicals that promote angiogenesis. The new blood vessels support the growth of the abnormal, rapidly dividing cells into larger tumors. The new blood vessels also allow cancer cells to spread to other sites in the body. Scientists are testing chemicals that *inhibit* (block) or promote angiogenesis to

develop drugs to treat diseases in which abnormal angiogenesis occurs. In 2004, the United States Food and Drug Administration approved an angiogenesis-inhibiting drug, marketed under the name Avastin, to treat colon cancer.   Christian M. Becker and Bruce R. Zetter

See also **Cancer** (Molecular medicine); **Macular degeneration; Thalidomide.**

Angioplasty, *AN jee oh PLAS tee,* is a technique used to open arteries that have become blocked by deposits of cholesterol, calcium, and other substances. Such deposits are called *plaques.* Angioplasty is especially important for patients whose coronary arteries have become critically narrowed and who have *angina* (chest pain that occurs during exertion) or a high risk of heart attack. Angioplasty provides an alternative to surgery.

In coronary angioplasty, a *catheter* (long tube) with a balloon attached to it is inserted into the blocked artery. After the catheter enters the narrowed part of the vessel, the balloon is inflated. The balloon then pushes the plaque against the artery wall and expands the artery. In most cases, slight injury to the wall of the artery accompanies the widening of the vessel's inside diameter. This damage may benefit the patient, however, because further widening can occur as the artery wall heals.

Most angioplasties are successful. In about 30 percent of patients, however, the cleared vessel soon renarrows, requiring another angioplasty or surgery. In a small number of cases, the procedure severely tears the artery. In those cases, the patient must undergo immediate surgery and repair. Doctors have prevented tears and abrupt closures of arteries by inserting an expandable metal mesh called a *stent* into the vessel. The stent prevents collapse of the artery wall without blocking

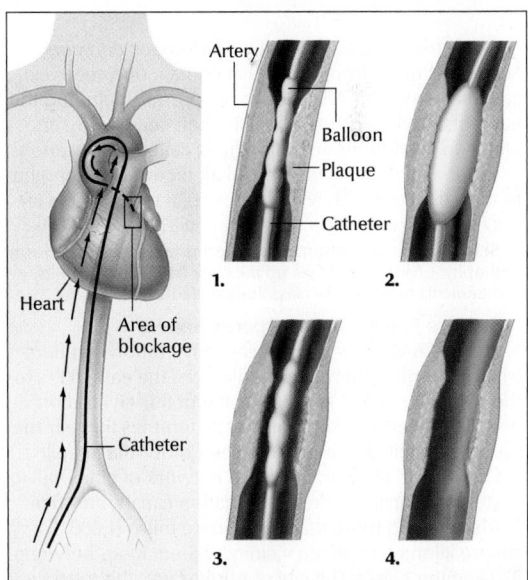

WORLD BOOK illustrations by Charles Wellek and Tom Rolain

In coronary angioplasty, surgeons insert a long tube called a *catheter* through the patient's groin and guide the catheter to a blocked artery in the heart. The close-ups show the interior of the artery during the procedure. A balloon on the catheter is positioned in the artery (1) and inflated (2) to crush deposits called *plaques* and expand the artery. The balloon is then deflated (3) and removed, leaving the inside diameter of the artery wider (4).

blood flow. In some cases, a stent can also reduce the chance the artery will renarrow.   Michael H. Crawford

Angiosperm, *AN jee uh spurm,* is the technical name for flowering plants. Angiosperms make up the vast majority of all plant *species* (kinds). They also occur in most of the world's environments, including Arctic tundra, deserts, and rain forests. Among the most important angiosperms are broadleaf trees and crop plants.

Angiosperm flowers contain both male reproductive organs called *stamens* and female reproductive organs called *carpels.* Stamens produce pollen grains that carry *sperm* (male sex cells) to the carpels. Carpels contain *ovules,* or eggs, that become seeds after fertilization by sperm. The carpels develop into fruits.

Scientists divide the angiosperms into several groups called *classes.* The two largest classes are *monocotyle-*

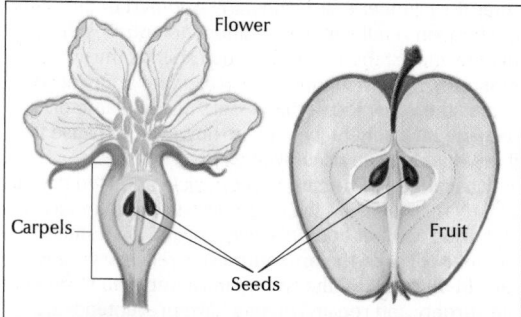

WORLD BOOK illustration by Lorraine Moseley Epstein
The flower and fruit of an angiosperm contain a plant's seeds. The seeds develop in the flower's carpels, which grow into the fruit. The flower and fruit of an apple tree are shown here.

dons, or *monocots,* and *eudicotyledons,* or *eudicots.* Monocots grow from seeds that contain one seed leaf called a *cotyledon.* All other angiosperms, including the eudicots, have two cotyledons in their seeds. Flowers with two cotyledons are sometimes called *dicotyledons,* or *dicots.* Scientists once treated all dicots as belonging to their own class. They now know that many dicots are only distantly related to others.   Bruce H. Tiffney

Scientific classification. Angiosperms make up the division Anthophyta. Monocots make up the class Monocotyledones, and eudicots make up the class Eudicotyledones.

See also **Flower; Gymnosperm; Seed.**

Angkor, *ANG kohr,* was an early civilization that flourished in northwestern Cambodia from the early 800's to the 1400's. The most famous capital of this civilization was also called Angkor. Ruins of its temples lie near the present-day city of Siem Reap (see **Cambodia** [map]).

Cambodian kings built a large network of cities, villages, temples, artificial ponds, irrigation canals, and rice fields covering more than 386 square miles (1,000 square kilometers) in the vicinity of Siem Reap between 820 and the 1100's. The city of Angkor was the most magnificent. It may have had a million people, more than any European city at that time. The city included Angkor Thom, which was actually a city within the city of Angkor, and covered 4 square miles (10 square kilometers). The city of Angkor also contained many temples and palaces. The city and its temples rank as one of the artistic and architectural wonders of the world. Carved

scenes of Cambodian life and Buddhist or Hindu mythology decorate the walls of the temples.

One of the temples, Angkor Wat, is probably Cambodia's finest architectural monument. It covers nearly 1 square mile (2.6 square kilometers) and has a pyramidal form. This form imitates the mythological home of the Hindu gods. Angkor Wat was built in the 1100's to honor the Hindu god Vishnu. It was also used as an astronomical observatory. Angkor Wat later became the tomb of the Cambodian king who had it built. Another temple, the Bayon, stands at the center of Angkor Thom. It was dedicated to Buddha and the reigning king. More than 200 giant stone faces adorn its towers.

The civilization of Angkor reached its peak in the 1100's and then began to decline. Invasions from neighboring Thailand, epidemics of malaria, deforestation and environmental degradation, and disputes within the royal Cambodian family may have caused this decline. Thai forces captured the city of Angkor in 1431 but soon abandoned it. Forest growth gradually covered most of the city. In 1860, Henri Mouhot, a French naturalist, discovered the city's ruins. From the 1860's to the mid-1900's, French and Cambodian archaeologists restored and rebuilt many of its temples.   David P. Chandler

See also **Architecture** (picture: Angkor).

Angle, in plane geometry, is a figure formed by two *rays* with the same end point. A ray is a part of a line extending indefinitely in one direction from a point. The point where the rays of an angle meet is called the *vertex,* and the rays themselves are known as the *sides.*

The size of an angle is usually measured in *degrees.* When the rays make a square corner, the angle is called a *right angle.* A right angle has 90 degrees (90°). An *acute angle* has less than 90°. An *obtuse angle* has between 90° and 180°. An angle of 180° is a *straight angle* because its sides form a straight line. Two angles are *complementary* if the sum of the angles is 90°. They are *supplementary* if their sum is 180°. People use a simple device called a *protractor* to measure angles. Angles can also be measured in units called *radians* (see **Radian**).

In trigonometry, an angle is considered to consist of a fixed, or *initial,* side and a rotating, or *terminal,* side. The amount and direction of rotation of the terminal side determine the size of an angle and whether it is *positive* or *negative.* Positive angles are formed when the rotation of the terminal side is counterclockwise. Negative angles are formed when the rotation is clockwise. If one clock hand is fixed at 3 and the other hand starts at 3 and turns counterclockwise until it reaches 12, an angle of 90° results. This rotation is a *quarter turn.* A *half turn* results in a 180° angle; a *three-quarter turn,* in a 270° angle; and a *full turn,* in a 360° angle. A second complete rotation of the terminal side generates angles between 360° and 720°, a third rotation produces angles between 720° and 1,080°, and so forth for all positive angles.

Negative angles are formed when the terminal side

Kinds of angles

WORLD BOOK illustrations

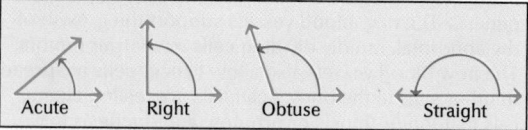

Acute   Right   Obtuse   Straight

moves clockwise. Compass directions in naval naviga-tion are given by means of angles measured in the clockwise direction from 12. But the measurements are given in positive numbers. Eli Maor

See also **Degree; Protractor.**

Anglerfish is a fish that uses a spine on its snout to "fish" for food. Anglerfish live in many parts of the ocean, including the deep sea. There are hundreds of *species* (kinds). Some species are colorful, but other species are drab or even completely black. Anglerfish of different species range from about 1 inch (2.5 centimeters) to 6 feet (2 meters) in length.

The anglerfish gets its name from the fin spine on its snout. It uses this spine somewhat as an angler uses a fishing pole. The spine's tip features a small, colorful tag of skin that serves as a lure. The anglerfish moves the spine back and forth to attract other fish and shrimp, which it eats. In deep-sea species, the tag even glows.

Deep-sea anglerfish reproduce in an unusual way. Males are much smaller than females. When a male finds a female, he attaches by mouth to her body. The female's blood feeds the male, who fertilizes the fe-male's eggs with his sperm. Theodore W. Pietsch

Scientific classification. Anglerfish belong to the order Lophiiformes.

Angles made up one of the Germanic peoples who in-vaded Britain during the A.D. 400's and 500's. The best known of the other invaders were the Saxons and Jutes, to whom the Angles were closely related. The invaders established small kingdoms, some of which lasted until the Norman Conquest in 1066. See **Anglo-Saxons.**

The Angles came from Angeln, a district in what is now Schleswig-Holstein state in Germany, and from the southern part of the Danish peninsula. They conquered the Britons who lived along the east coast, and founded the kingdoms of Northumbria, Mercia, and East Anglia in what is now north, central, and east England. The name *England* came from an Anglo-Saxon word that meant *Angle folk* or *land of the Angles.* John Gillingham

See also **England** (History).

Angleworm. See Earthworm.

Anglican Communion is one of the world's largest Christian denominations. The Communion is made up of 46 self-governing regional or national churches. They include the Church of England and the churches that de-veloped from it, such as the Episcopal Church in the United States, the Anglican Church of Canada, and the Anglican Church of Australia. The Communion has about 85 million members in more than 165 countries.

Beliefs and worship. Anglicans base their faith pri-marily on the Bible. They emphasize the importance of human reason in interpreting the Bible. They turn for guidance to the ways in which earlier Christians, espe-cially in the ancient church, interpreted the Bible and conducted worship. Anglicans uphold the beliefs ex-pressed in the Apostles' and Nicene *creeds* (statements of faith) of the ancient Christian church.

Anglican worship is anchored in the sacraments of baptism and the Eucharist (also called Holy Communion) and is guided by the Book of Common Prayer. Archbish-op of Canterbury Thomas Cranmer first produced this book in 1549, during the religious movement known as the Protestant Reformation. Anglicanism combines ele-ments of both Roman Catholicism and Protestantism.

Organization. The Anglican clergy consists of bish-ops, priests, and deacons. Anglicans consider the arch-bishop of Canterbury, head of the Church of England, to be the symbolic head of the Anglican Communion. The Communion was one of the first major Christian denom-inations to ordain women as priests and bishops.

The leadership of the archbishop and three interna-tional gatherings of church leaders make up the four In-struments of Communion. The three meetings are the Lambeth Conference, the Anglican Consultative Council, and the Primates Meetings. The Lambeth Conference is a meeting of all Anglican bishops. They consult one an-other but do not make official rules for one another's churches. The conference meets every 10 years. The An-glican Consultative Council meets every 2 or 3 years. It includes bishops, other clergy, and *laity* (regular church members). It works to promote cooperation and the ex-change of information between churches. The Primates Meetings bring together the *primates* (head bishops) of each regional or national church in the Communion.

Christian unity. Anglicans have played a major role in developing the modern *ecumenical* movement, which seeks unity among Christian churches. Several archbishops of Canterbury played a key role in found-ing international ecumenical bodies, such as the World Council of Churches. The Anglican Communion has close ties with several Protestant churches, including Lu-theran, Congregational, Methodist, Presbyterian, and Reformed churches. It also has formal relationships with the Roman Catholic and Eastern Orthodox churches.

History. In the 1500's, the Christian Church in England asserted its independence from the Church in Rome, becoming a *peer* (equal) church in its own right. In the 1700's and 1800's, Anglicanism spread rapidly to other countries with the growth of the British colonial empire.

In the late 1900's and early 2000's, the Anglican Com-munion entered into difficult debates about human sex-uality. These debates led to larger, unresolved questions about the nature of church authority and organization.

Historically, the arts have held a special place in Angli-canism. The Book of Common Prayer and the King James Bible and such Anglican writers as John Donne, George Herbert, and Jeremy Taylor helped shape the English language. Anglicans also have produced many beautiful works of architecture, church music, painting, sculpture, and stained glass. Christopher A. Beeley

Related articles in *World Book* include:

Apostles' Creed	England (The Eng-	Nicene Councils
Church of England	lish Reformation)	Reformation (In
	Episcopal Church	England)

Anglo-Boer Wars, *ANG gloh bawr,* were fought in what is now South Africa from 1880 to 1881 and from 1899 to 1902. They were struggles between the British and the Boers (now called Afrikaners) of the northern South African regions of the Orange Free State and the South African Republic (also called Transvaal). Most of the Boers were farmers of Dutch ancestry. The main cause of the wars was the United Kingdom's desire for supremacy in South Africa. In the war of 1880-1881, the Boers regained the independence of the South African Republic, which the British had annexed in 1877. That struggle is often called the Anglo-Transvaal War. The Anglo-Boer War of 1899-1902 was a longer and larger conflict. It is also called simply the Anglo-Boer War and sometimes the Boer War or the South African War.

Many Uitlanders (foreigners), most of whom were British, rushed into the South African Republic after the discovery of the Witwatersrand gold fields there in 1886. The republic's government denied them full political rights and power. In 1895, some Uitlanders plotted to overthrow the government. Leander Jameson, a British colonial administrator, led a failed Uitlander raid into the republic from the British-controlled Cape Colony. The Orange Free State joined the South African Republic in declaring war on the United Kingdom in October 1899.

The Boers won victories in the early stages of the war. In January 1900, Lord Roberts and Lord Kitchener took command of the British troops. The British captured the capitals of the two republics in April and June of that year, and a Boer army surrendered to Roberts in September. But the remaining Boer forces took to the countryside, where they carried on guerrilla warfare. The war ended when the Treaty of Vereeniging was signed on May 31, 1902. As a result of the war, the two defeated republics became British colonies.   Christopher Saunders

Related articles in *World Book* include:

Afrikaners	Rhodes, Cecil John
Botha, Louis	Smuts, Jan Christiaan
Hertzog, James Barry Munnik	South Africa (Discovery of
Kitchener, Horatio H.	diamonds and gold)
Kruger, Paul	

Anglo-Saxon Chronicle, *ANG gloh SAK suhn,* is the first great work of English prose and the most important source for English history from about 800 to 1066. No other European land has a history in its own language as old as the *Chronicle.*

The *Chronicle* was begun as part of a cultural renewal by King Alfred the Great following destructive raids by Danish invaders (see **Alfred the Great**). The *Chronicle's* first part, covering events up to 891, was adapted from earlier English historical sources, now lost. After about 892, a number of writers contributed to the *Chronicle* in copies circulated among several English cathedrals.

The *Chronicle* consists of short yearly descriptions of major events, especially warfare, and the activities of kings and bishops. Many entries consist of only one line. The longest entry runs over 100 lines and deals with William the Conqueror's death in 1087. Many years have no entries. The earliest important entry in the *Chronicle* refers to events in A.D. 449. The final entry was made in 1154.   David S. Chamberlain

Anglo-Saxons, *ANG gloh SAK suhnz,* were members of the Germanic tribes that settled in what is now England in the A.D. 400's and 500's. These tribes included primarily the Angles, the Saxons, and the Jutes. According to tradition, a British king named Vortigern invited the Germanic tribes to help him drive back the invading Picts and Scots. But the allies quarreled, and soon the Germanic tribes began to drive out the native Britons. By the end of the 500's, the Angles, Saxons, and Jutes had occupied nearly all of southern and eastern Britain.

At first there were many Anglo-Saxon kingdoms, and wars between them were frequent. By the 700's, there were seven principal kingdoms: East Anglia, Essex, Kent, Mercia, Northumbria, Sussex, and Wessex. Together, they are known as the Heptarchy, which means *rule of seven.* In the early 800's, Egbert of Wessex became the first king to establish control over the entire Heptarchy.

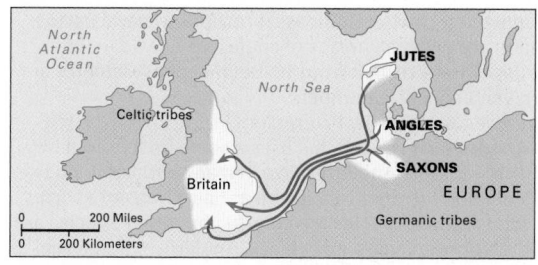

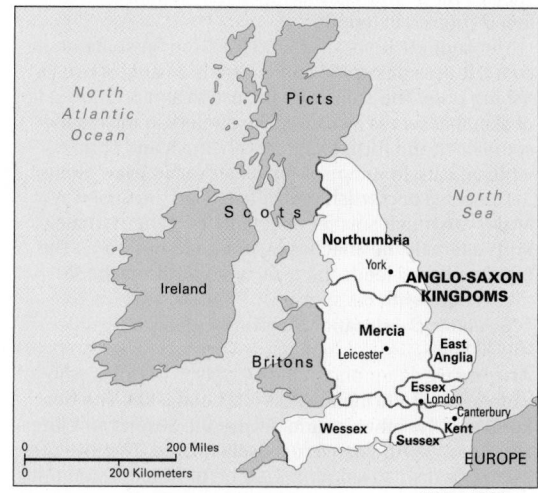

WORLD BOOK maps

The seafaring Jutes, Angles, and Saxons who invaded Britain in the A.D. 400's, *smaller map,* became known as Anglo-Saxons. They eventually formed seven main kingdoms, *larger map.*

In the late 800's, all the kingdoms came under attack from Danish Vikings. Only Wessex, under Alfred the Great, survived the invasion. Alfred eventually captured London and other areas. In the 900's, Alfred's descendants defeated the Vikings and incorporated the Viking territory into their kingdom. This new, larger kingdom was called England, a word that came from Anglo-Saxon words meaning *Angle folk* or *land of the Angles.*

The Anglo-Saxons influenced the English language in its grammar and in thousands of its words, including perhaps a fifth of the words we use today.   John Gilling

Related articles in *World Book* include:

Alfred the Great	English language	Jutes
Angles	English literature	Saxons
Egbert	(Old English	Teutons
England (History)	literature)	

Angola is a country on Africa's southwest coast. Its official name is the Republic of Angola. Cabinda, in the northwest, is a district of Angola. The Congo River and the Democratic Republic of the Congo separate it from the rest of the country.

About one-third of Angola's people live in rural areas and work on farms. Angola produces various crops, including bananas, coffee, corn, sugar cane, and a starchy root called *cassava.* Angola has many natural resources, including diamonds, iron ore, and petroleum. Luanda, the capital and largest city, is a major African seaport.

Angola became independent in November 1975. Parts of it had been ruled by Portugal for most of the period since the 1500's. Between 1975 and 2002, Angola was torn apart by a brutal civil war.

Government. A president is the most powerful official in Angola's government. The National Assembly, the country's legislature, makes the laws. The people of Angola elect the National Assembly. The head of the party with a majority in the National Assembly becomes president. The president appoints a vice president to help run the day-to-day affairs of the government.

People. Angola's people belong to several ethnic groups, including the Ovimbundu, the Mbundu, the Kongo, and the Luanda-Chokwe. Before the country became independent, more than 400,000 Europeans and *mestizos* (people of mixed African and European ancestry) lived in Angola. Most Europeans fled during the civil war that began in 1975.

People in Angola's rural areas work as farmers and herders. Many of them raise just enough food for their own use. Most Europeans and mestizos who did not leave the country live in cities. They own small businesses or hold other jobs that require technical and management skills. Most Angolans speak a Bantu language (see **Bantu**). Some Angolans speak Portuguese, the official language. About half of the people are Christians, mostly Roman Catholics. Many Angolans have traditional beliefs based on the worship of ancestors and spirits. The majority of Angola's adults can read and write.

Land and climate. Angola forms part of the large inland plateau of southern Africa. The country consists chiefly of hilly grasslands, but a rocky desert covers the south. The land gradually rises from the interior to the west, where it drops sharply to a narrow coastal plain. Most of the coastal plain has little natural vegetation. Tropical forests grow in the north.

Angola has many rivers and more than 900 miles (1,400 kilometers) of coastline. Some of the rivers flow north into the Congo River, and others flow west into the Atlantic Ocean. A few, including the Cunene and the Cuanza, serve as waterways to the interior.

Temperatures in the coastal plain region average about 70 °F (21 °C) in January and about 60 °F (16 °C) in June. Most of the inland region has slightly higher temperatures. From 40 to 60 inches (100 to 150 centimeters) of rain falls annually on the northern coast and in most of the interior. Only about 2 inches (5 centimeters) of rain falls yearly in the desert.

Economy. Mining and agriculture are the most important sectors of Angola's economy. The country has vast deposits of petroleum and diamonds. Petroleum accounts for almost all of Angola's exports. Angola is one of the world's leading diamond producers.

Over half of Angola's workers are employed in agriculture. The main crops include bananas, cassava, corn, pineapples, sugar cane, and sweet potatoes. Farmers raise cattle for beef and milk. Fishing is important in coastal areas. Angolan industries produce cement, chemicals, petroleum products, processed foods, and textiles.

Many of Angola's roads are unpaved. Luanda has an international airport. Major ports are at Lobito, Luanda, and Namibe.

History. Prehistoric peoples lived in what is now Angola as early as 50,000 B.C. Bantu-speaking peoples settled there about 2,000 years ago. The Portuguese

established bases in Angola during the 1500's. By the early 1600's, Angola had become a major source of slave labor for Portugal's colony in Brazil. In 1641, the Dutch forced the Portuguese out of Angola and took over the slave trade. Portugal regained control in 1648. During the 1800's, after the decline of the slave trade, Portuguese planters began to grow corn, sugar cane, and tobacco in Angola. Angola was sometimes called Portuguese West Africa during Portuguese rule.

Portugal began to improve Angola's economy after the Portuguese dictator António de Oliveira Salazar came to power in the late 1920's. During this time, thousands of Portuguese moved to Angola and started businesses there.

In the 1950's, many Angolans began to demand freedom from Portuguese rule. In 1956, the Popular Movement for the Liberation of Angola (MPLA) was organized. MPLA members revolted in Luanda in 1961. Rioting spread throughout the country and developed into a bloody war. A Portuguese army that included many Angolans put down the uprising. The MPLA rebels then set up guerrilla bases in neighboring countries.

Facts in brief

Capital: Luanda.
Official language: Portuguese.
Area: 481,354 mi² (1,246,700 km²). *Greatest distances*—north-south, 850 mi (1,368 km); east-west, 800 mi (1,287 km). *Coastline*—928 mi (1,493 km).
Elevation: *Highest*—Môco, 8,596 ft (2,620 m). *Lowest*—sea level.
Population: *Estimated 2022 population*—34,872,000; density, 72 per mi² (28 per km²); distribution, 66 percent urban, 34 percent rural. *2014 census*—24,383,301.
Chief products: *Agriculture*—bananas, cassava, corn, sugar cane. *Manufacturing*—cement, petroleum products, processed foods, textiles. *Mining*—diamonds, petroleum.
Flag: The top half is red, and the bottom half is black. A yellow emblem in the center has a five-pointed star that stands for socialism, a half cogwheel for industry, and a machete for agriculture. Adopted in 1975. See **Flag** (picture: Flags of Africa).
Money: *Basic unit*—kwanza. One hundred centavos equal one kwanza.

Hutchison Library

An Angolan village lies in the rocky desert terrain of the southern part of the country. Many of Angola's people live in rural areas and work as farmers and herders.

Cultural and political differences soon divided the rebels. In 1962, a group of northern rebels formed the National Front for the Liberation of Angola (FNLA). Southern rebels organized the National Union for the Total Independence of Angola (UNITA) in 1966. In 1974, Portuguese military officers overthrew the government of Portugal. They decided to grant independence to Angola in January 1975. At first, the Angolans agreed to set up a government with representatives from all three rebel groups. But each group wanted to head the government. A civil war broke out over which would rule.

Angola gained independence from Portugal on Nov. 11, 1975. But the civil war continued between the MPLA and the FNLA and UNITA, whose forces had united. The MPLA received much aid from two Communist nations, the Soviet Union and Cuba. The United States and South Africa assisted UNITA. The MPLA largely defeated its enemies in April 1976 and formed a Marxist government, based on the philosophy of Karl Marx, the founder of revolutionary Communism.

Angola's new government faced major problems. Members of UNITA waged guerrilla warfare against the government. The FNLA did too until 1984, when it became inactive. The sudden departure of most of Angola's Europeans caused a shortage of executives and

Hutchison Library

Luanda, the capital and largest city of Angola, has many modern buildings and broad, treelined streets.

Angola

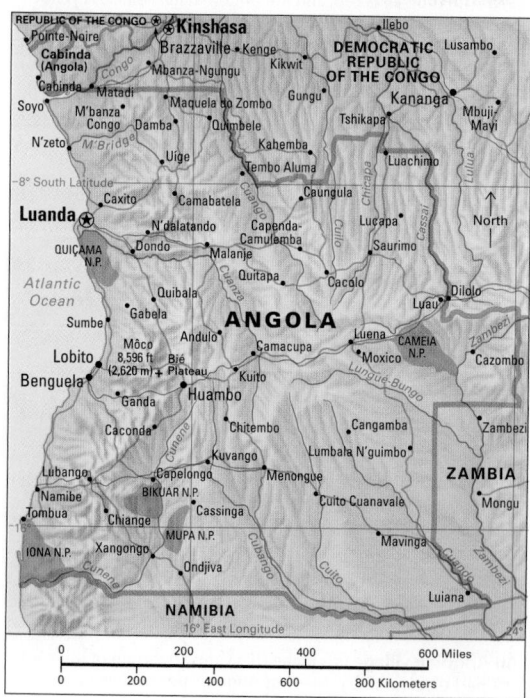

	National park (N.P.)
	International boundary
	Road
	Railroad
⊛	National capital
•	Other city or town
+	Elevation above sea level

WORLD BOOK maps

technicians. Many industries and large farms could not be managed properly, and production declined.

The government began several programs to overcome the effects of the civil war. It took control of many businesses and started to train teachers and technicians. The Soviet Union, Cuba, and other Communist countries provided financial and technical aid. But the government also encouraged non-Communist nations to invest in Angolan businesses. Cuba kept troops in Angola to aid the government in its fight against the guerrillas.

Under an agreement signed by Angola, Cuba, and South Africa in late 1988, South Africa stopped sending aid to UNITA, and Cuba began withdrawing its troops. In 1989, the government and UNITA agreed to a ceasefire. The two sides signed a peace treaty in May 1991. Violence continued in the Cabinda area, where guerrillas demanded Cabinda's independence from Angola.

In 1990, the MPLA renounced Marxism, and in 1991, it legalized all political parties. Multiparty elections were held in September 1992. The head of the MPLA government, José Eduardo dos Santos, won the first round of the elections. But UNITA protested that the elections were fraudulent, and civil war erupted again. The second round of the elections did not take place, but dos Santos continued as president.

The two sides signed a peace agreement in November 1994. However, in 1998 and early 1999, violence increased, and the peace agreement broke down. The fighting continued, mainly in northwestern Angola. In February 2002, government troops shot and killed UNITA's longtime leader, Jonas Malheiro Savimbi. In April, the two sides signed a cease-fire agreement.

In 2010, Angola's government enacted a new constitution. The Constitution eliminated direct presidential elections and gave the presidency to the head of the party with a majority of seats in the National Assembly. In 2012, the MPLA again won the most seats in the Assembly. Dos Santos remained in office as president. In 2017, João Lourenço of the MPLA was elected president.

Louis A. Picard

See also **Bantu; Cabinda; Kongo; Luanda.**

Angora, *ang GAWR uh* or *ang GOHR uh,* is a hair fiber made from the fur of the Angora rabbit. The term is sometimes used for hair fiber made from the Angora goat, but the goat fiber is correctly called *mohair.* Both animals are native to the Turkish province of Ankara (formerly Angora). Pure angora is used to make soft fabrics. It is usually blended with other fibers and then spun into yarn. Angora is also the name of a type of cat. See also **Cat** (Long-haired breeds); **Rabbit** (picture).

Keith Slater

Angstrom, *ANG struhm,* is a unit of length used to measure very small distances. For example, the atoms in a salt crystal are only several angstroms apart. Wavelengths of light are sometimes measured in angstroms. The wavelength of visible light measures several thousand angstroms. One angstrom equals $\frac{1}{10}$ nanometer, or $\frac{1}{10,000,000}$ millimeter ($\frac{1}{254,000,000}$ inch). The symbol for angstrom is Å. It is named in honor of the Swedish physicist Anders Jonas Ångström, who made important studies of light.

Lawrence P. Brehm

Anguilla, *ang GWIHL uh,* is a coral island in the Caribbean Sea. It is an overseas territory of the United Kingdom. Anguilla covers about 35 square miles (91 square kilometers) and has a population of about 17,000 (see **West Indies** [map]). It has a dry, hot climate and is covered by low-lying plant life. Tourism has replaced fishing and salt processing as Anguilla's major industry. A community called The Valley is the island's capital.

The Italian navigator Christopher Columbus may have sighted the island in 1493 on his second voyage to the New World. Explorers named it Anguilla (Latin for *eel)* because of its long, narrow shape. It became a British colony in 1650. In 1883, the United Kingdom made Anguilla and the Caribbean islands of St. Kitts and Nevis a single colony. The three islands became an associated state of the United Kingdom in 1967. But most Anguillans favored separation from St. Kitts and Nevis. In 1980, Anguilla officially became a separate British dependency (see **West Indies** [History]).

Hilary Beckles

Anhinga, *an HIHNG guh,* also called the American darter, is a large bird that lives in swamps, ponds, and rivers in warm regions of the Western Hemisphere. It is found from the south-central and southeastern United States to Argentina. The anhinga measures about 3 feet (91 centimeters) in length, with a long, thin neck; a small head and pointed bill; and webbed feet. It has glossy black feathers, with silver markings on the back of the wings and neck, and a broad, brown-tipped tail. The anhinga feeds on fish and other water animals, which it spears with its bill. It is an excellent swimmer and a strong flier. The anhinga is sometimes called the *snakebird* because it often swims with only its head and snakelike neck visible above the surface.

The Old World darters, which resemble the anhinga, live in tropical and subtropical regions of Africa, Asia, New Guinea, and Australia. Most experts recognize three species of Old World darters: the African, Oriental, and Australian darters.

James J. Dinsmore

Scientific classification. The anhinga's scientific name is *Anhinga anhinga.* The African darter is *A. rufa;* the Oriental darter is *A. melanogaster;* and the Australian darter is *A. novaehollandiae.*

See also **Bird** (picture: How birds feed).

Anhydride, *an HY dryd,* is a chemical substance that forms acids or bases when combined with water. For example, water and acetic anhydride, an acid anhydride, make acetic acid. Water and calcium oxide, a basic anhydride, make basic calcium hydroxide. Anhydrides can be formed by *dehydrating* (removing the water from) compounds or by *synthesizing* (making) them directly from other substances. Anhydrides are used in the manufacture of artificial fibers, medicines, photographic films, and plastics. See also **Acid; Base.**

Marianna A. Busch

Anhydrous ammonia, *an HY druhs uh MOHN yuh,* is the liquid form of pure ammonia gas. Because of its high nitrogen content—about 82 percent—farmers use anhydrous ammonia as a fertilizer. It may be used alone or in a commercial mixture containing compounds of phosphorus and potassium. It may be combined with water to form a solution for making a mixed fertilizer. Anhydrous ammonia is also used as a refrigerant in cold-storage and ice-manufacturing plants. It is made by compressing dry ammonia gas (NH_3). See also **Ammonia; Ice; Refrigeration.**

Taylor J. Johnston

Ani, *AH nee,* is the name of three *species* (kinds) of birds that resemble the cuckoo. Anis live in open, brushy country, from the Caribbean region and Mexico to southern South America. Two species are also found in the extreme southern United States. The *smooth-billed ani* nests in southern Florida, and the *groove-billed ani* lives in southern Texas. The third species, the *greater ani,* ranges only as far north as central Panama.

Anis measure from 12 to 15 inches (30 to 40 centimeters) in length, about half of which is tail. They have a huge bill with a high arched ridge and black feathers that shine with a purple, green, or bronze luster. Anis feed chiefly on insects. They often gather in pastures where cattle are grazing. There, they seize large ground-dwelling insects that are stirred up by the cattle. Anis sometimes perch on the cattle's backs.

Anis live in noisy flocks of up to about 20 birds. Each flock consists of one to four mated pairs and a number of younger, unmated birds. During the breeding season, the flock claims a territory and prevents other anis from entering it. All of the birds in the flock build a single nest of twigs in a tree or thorny bush. Each mated female lays three to five eggs in the nest. The entire flock helps care for the eggs and the young.

Sandra L. Vehrencamp

Scientific classification. The scientific name for the smooth-billed ani is *Crotophaga ani.* The groove-billed ani is *C. sulcirostris,* and the greater ani is *C. major.*

Aniline, *AN uh lihn,* is a chemical best known for its use in making dyes. Aniline became important in 1856, when the British chemist William Perkin accidentally made a violet dye from aniline. Industries use aniline dyes to color textiles and in making inks, paints, and varnishes. Bacteriologists use the dyes to stain bacteria and other organisms. Industries also use aniline in making drugs, explosives, rocket fuels, and other products.

In the laboratory, chemists prepare aniline through a chemical reaction involving nitrobenzene, iron filings, and hydrochloric acid. In industry, aniline is prepared by heating chlorobenzene and ammonia under high pressure, or by a process using nitrobenzene.

Aniline is a colorless, oily liquid that is only slightly soluble in water. It has a strong, pleasing odor but is highly poisonous. Aniline boils at 184 °C. Its chemical formula is $C_6H_5NH_2$.

Howard L. Needles

See also **Coal tar; Dye; Indigo.**

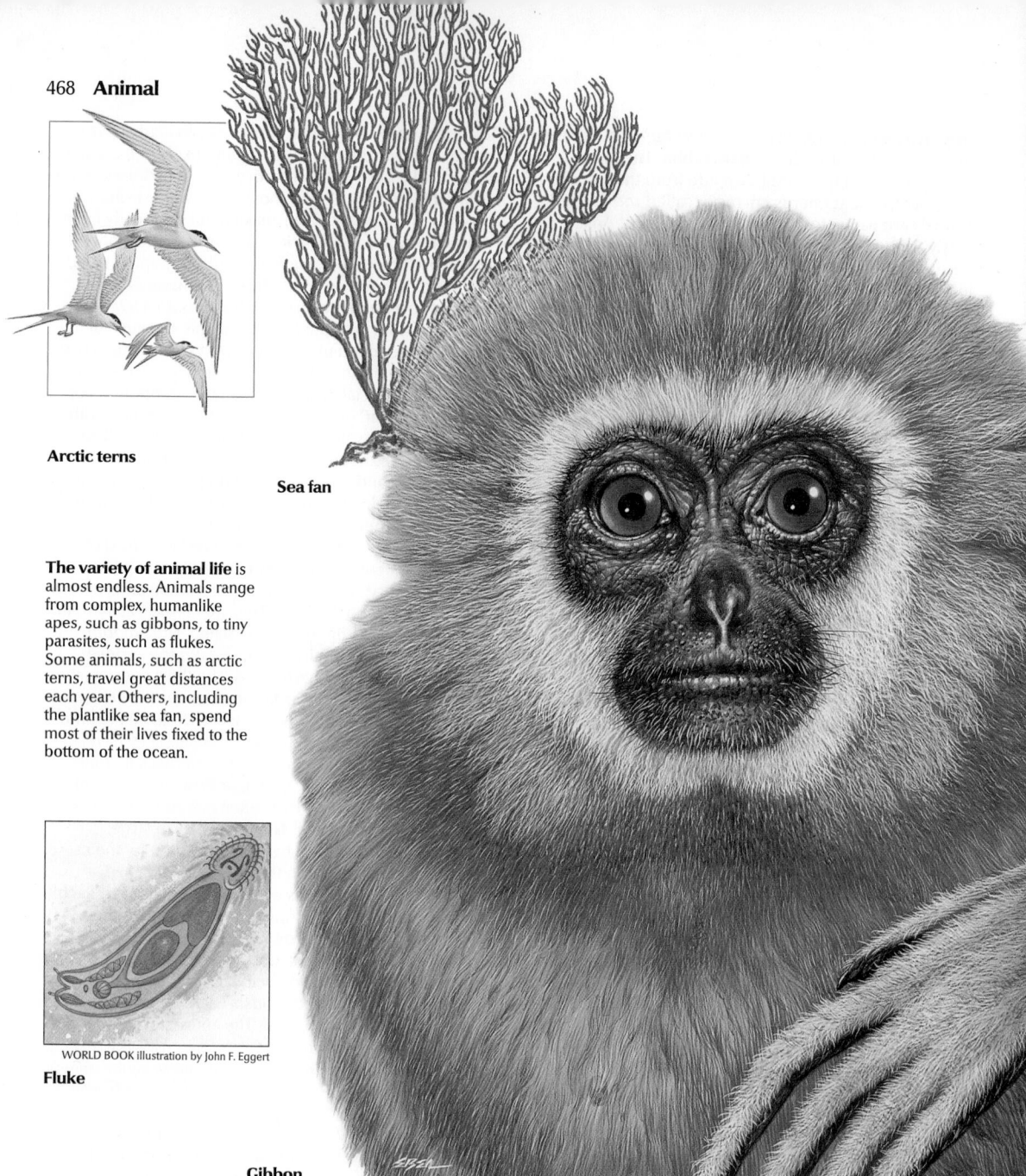

Arctic terns

Sea fan

The variety of animal life is almost endless. Animals range from complex, humanlike apes, such as gibbons, to tiny parasites, such as flukes. Some animals, such as arctic terns, travel great distances each year. Others, including the plantlike sea fan, spend most of their lives fixed to the bottom of the ocean.

WORLD BOOK illustration by John F. Eggert

Fluke

Gibbon

WORLD BOOK illustrations by Alex Ebel except where noted

Animal

Animal. Animals come in many shapes and sizes. They live throughout the world. Animals walk or crawl on land and dig through the soil. They swim in the water and fly through the air. They even live inside the bodies of other animals. Bats, dogs, horses, kangaroos, and moles are all animals. So are butterflies, frogs, jellyfish, pigeons, sharks, snakes, and worms.

Most kinds of animals are less than 1 inch (2.5 centimeters) long. Many are so tiny that they can be seen only with a microscope. The largest animal is the blue whale. It is about as long as five elephants in a row.

Animals are not the only living things. Scientists divide living things into six main *kingdoms* (groups)—animals, plants, fungi, protists, archaea, and bacteria. *Fungi* include molds, mushrooms, and yeasts. *Protists,* such as amebas, cannot be seen without a microscope. *Archaea* and *bacteria,* collectively known as *prokaryotes,* rank as some of the smallest, simplest forms of life.

Interesting facts about animals

Kinds of animals. No one knows exactly how many kinds of animals there are. New kinds are found every year. So far, scientists have identified more than 1 ½ million types of animals. About 1 million of these are insects, and there are thousands of kinds of fish, amphibians, reptiles, birds, and mammals.

Largest ears and eyes. The largest ears of all animals are those of the African elephant. Elephant ears grow as large as 4 feet (1.2 meters) across. The largest eyes of all animals are those of the giant squid. They measure about 10 inches (25 centimeters) wide.

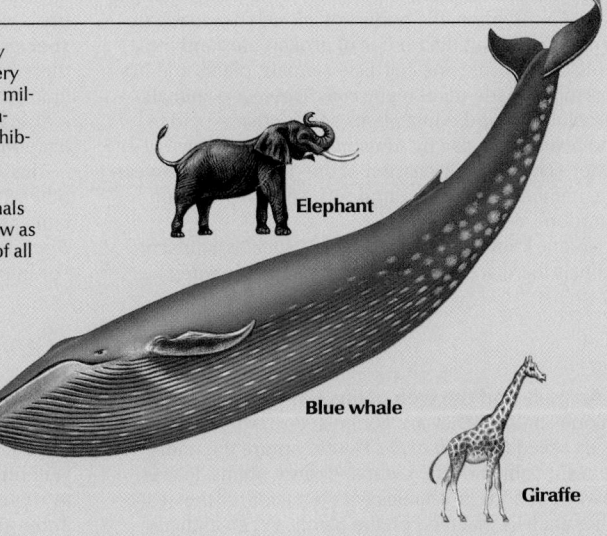

Elephant

Blue whale

Giraffe

The flying dragon is another name for the draco lizard. This lizard can spread out folds of skin to form "wings" that it uses to glide through the air from tree to tree. It lives in Asia and the East Indies.

The huge blue whale is far bigger than the elephant, the biggest land animal, or the giraffe, tallest of all the animals.

Mayfly

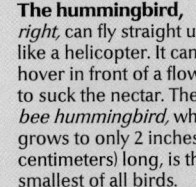

The hummingbird, *right,* can fly straight up like a helicopter. It can hover in front of a flower to suck the nectar. The *bee hummingbird,* which grows to only 2 inches (5 centimeters) long, is the smallest of all birds.

The chameleon's tongue is as long as its body. This lizard swiftly shoots out its tongue to capture insects for food. Certain chameleons can quickly change color and even develop spots and streaks that make them seem to be part of their background.

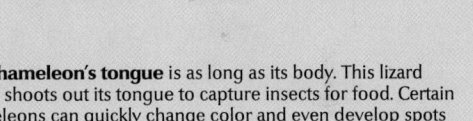

A tree-climbing crab lives on many tropical islands. It is called the *coconut crab* because it cracks coconuts with its powerful claws and eats the sweet meat.

Giant tortoise

Lives of animals range from several hours to many years. An adult mayfly survives only a few hours or days. Some giant tortoises have lived more than 100 years.

The world's only known poisonous bird is the hooded pitohui, which lives on the island of New Guinea. This brilliantly colored orange-and-black bird has poison on its feathers and skin. This poison serves as a defense against hawks, snakes, and other enemies. It is the same type of poison as that carried by the deadly poison-dart frog of South America.

The platypus, a mammal, has a bill like a duck and lays eggs as birds do, *right.* But it nurses its young with milk as do other mammals. It lives only on mainland Australia and the island of Tasmania.

WORLD BOOK illustrations by Alex Ebel and Robert Kuhn

Animals are different from other living things in many ways. For example, the bodies of animals are made up of many cells. But the bodies of prokaryotes and most protists have only one cell. Like animals, plants and fungi also are made up of many cells. However, animals can move around. Most plants and fungi are held to one place in the soil by roots or rootlike structures. For a more complete discussion of the differences between the members of the six kingdoms, see the article on **Kingdom.**

No one knows exactly how many *species* (kinds) of animals there are. So far, scientists have *classified* (grouped) and named more than 1 ½ million kinds of animals. Over half of these are types of insects. Many new species are discovered each year. Scientists believe there may be from 2 million to as many as 50 million kinds of animals alive today. Many other kinds of animals used to live on the earth but have died out. They include dinosaurs and dodos.

This article provides general information on animals other than human beings. It includes a classification table and pictures of many animals. Separate *World Book* articles give details about hundreds of animals. For information on human beings, see **Human being.**

Importance of animals

Animals and the web of life. Living things depend on one another. They are connected in what is sometimes called the *web of life.* Plants capture the energy from sunlight and use it to make roots, stems, leaves, flowers, and fruits. Animals eat the plants, or they eat other animals that feed on the plants. When animals die, their bodies decay and release materials that help fertilize the soil for plants.

Animals and plants are also connected in other ways. When animals breathe, they take in oxygen from the air and give off carbon dioxide. Green plants take in carbon dioxide and give off oxygen in a food-making process called *photosynthesis.* Many plants with flowers need insects or birds to carry their pollen from plant to plant. Without this transfer of pollen, these plants are not able to *reproduce* (create new individuals of their own kind). Some seeds are prickly and cling to the fur or feathers of animals. When the animals move from place to place, they take the seeds with them. In this way, the seeds get dropped in new areas where they can grow into plants.

The web of life relies on balance among its parts. A change in one part may mean disaster for others. For

WORLD BOOK illustration by John F. Eggert

Animals and plants are linked in a pattern of nature often called the *web of life.* This pattern can be seen in a garden or backyard. There, many kinds of animals keep themselves alive by eating some of the plants. Likewise, much of the food that plants need comes from the body wastes of animals. In most cases, natural forces keep the total number of living things in balance.

example, if all the trees in an area are cut down, then many animals that depend on them will die. For more information on how living things are linked, see **Ecology.**

Animals and people. Animals have provided people with food and clothing since prehistoric times. Without animals, people would not have such things as meat, honey, eggs, wool, leather, or silk.

At least 10,000 years ago, people began *domesticating* (taming) animals. Some of these animals provide food and clothing. For example, cattle supply meat, milk, and leather. Chickens lay eggs. Sheep supply wool and meat.

Some domesticated animals help people work. Water buffaloes pull plows in Asian rice fields. Horses and camels carry people from one place to another. In the past, people kept cats in their houses to catch rats and mice. They raised dogs to help them hunt. Today, cats and dogs are kept largely as pets.

Certain insects are useful to people. Bees make honey, which people harvest for food. Bees also pollinate many food crops, including fruits and vegetables. Silk comes from fiber made by silkworms.

Some animals harm people. On rare occasions, croc-

Melissa Grimes-Guy, Photo Researchers

Some animals make wonderful pets. Cats and dogs are favorite pets around the world. They are affectionate and loyal, and they provide companionship to people of all ages.

Larry Stessin, Photo Researchers

Some animals can be dangerous to people. A great white shark, *above,* usually feeds on tuna and other large sea animals. But sharks sometimes kill and eat people.

Anna E. Zuckerman, Tom Stack & Assoc.

Some animals help people work. Through the centuries, cattle and horses have pulled plows, carts, and wagons and carried products and riders on their backs. The water buffaloes shown at the left are helping a farmer plow a rice field in Southeast Asia.

Animal facts
worldbook.com/an-14

odiles, lions, and tigers attack and kill people. So do grizzly bears and polar bears. Sharks sometimes kill and eat human beings. Bites from such poisonous snakes as rattlesnakes and cobras can cause death. The black widow spiders have a poison that makes people extremely sick.

Some animals pass diseases along from person to person. Certain mosquitoes transmit malaria and yellow fever. Some ticks carry the bacteria that cause Lyme disease and Rocky Mountain spotted fever. Some animals cause disease themselves. Worms called *flukes,* which live in human organs, can cause *schistosomiasis.* This disease infects millions of people in many African, Asian, and Latin American countries.

Kinds of animals

People often divide animals into various groups based on certain similarities the animals share. For example, some animals can be kept as pets, but others are wild. Arranging animals according to their similarities is a handy way of remembering and understanding them.

Some common ways of grouping animals. Animals can be grouped in many ways. They can be arranged according to whether they live on land or in water. Animals that live on land are known as *terrestrial animals.* They include cats, dogs, lizards, mice, and worms. Animals that live in water are called *aquatic animals.* They include eels, fish, lobsters, octopuses, and whales.

Animals can be arranged by the number of legs they have. Dogs, frogs, and lizards have four legs. Bats and birds have two legs. Insects have six legs, and spiders have eight. Snakes and worms have no legs.

Another way to group animals is according to how they move. Bats, most birds, and many insects fly. Whales, fish, and squid swim. Snakes and worms crawl. Antelope and cheetahs run. Frogs, kangaroos, and rabbits hop.

Some animals are *cold-blooded,* and others are *warm-blooded.* The bodies of cold-blooded animals are warm when their surroundings are warm and cool when their surroundings are cool. Warm-blooded animals, on the other hand, almost always have the same body temperature, regardless of the warmth of their surroundings. Birds, *mammals* (animals whose babies drink the mother's milk), and a few species of fish and insects are warm-blooded. All other kinds of animals are cold-blooded.

Animals are also commonly divided into groups according to whether they have backbones. *Invertebrates* do not have backbones, but *vertebrates* do. The vast majority of animals are invertebrates. They include clams, insects, jellyfish, sea urchins, snails, spiders, sponges, and worms. Birds, fish, mammals, and reptiles are vertebrates. So are *amphibians*—frogs, salamanders, and other animals that spend part of their lives in water and part on land.

The scientific classification of animals involves grouping animals according to the biological relationships among them. This orderly arrangement of animals depends in part on the features the animals share. In general, the more features they share, the more closely they are related. However, the scientific classification of animals is based mainly on the belief that certain animals share a common ancestor. Animals with a more recent common ancestor are more closely related than those who share an ancestor further back in time. In a somewhat similar way, brothers and sisters are more closely related than are cousins. Brothers and sisters share parents. First cousins share grandparents.

In classifying animals, *zoologists* (scientists who study animals) divide them into ever-smaller groups that have more and more features in common. All animals belong to one large group, the kingdom Animalia. This kingdom consists of a number of smaller groups called *phyla.* Each phylum is further divided into groups called

The cat and its relatives

Domestic cat

Lion

Tiger

Snow leopard

The cat family includes many kinds of wild animals with similar body characteristics. Most members of the cat family have many of the same habits. They are clever hunters and stalk their prey on padded feet. They use their sharp claws and teeth to tear their food. Some also use their claws to climb trees to seek food or escape enemies.

Leopard

Ocelot

Lynx

Jaguar

Cheetah

Mountain lion

Length of life of animals

Figures in this list are average life spans in years for animals in the wild, unless otherwise noted.

Mammals				Birds			
Buffalo, American	20	Horse	20-30*	Blue jay	6-9	Owl (snowy)	10
Cat	14*	Lion	13	Canada goose	12-23	Penguin (emperor)	20
Chimpanzee	30-40	Monkey (rhesus)	27-28	Canary	6-8	Pigeon	6
Deer (fallow)	20	Mouse (field)	1	Cardinal	13	Raven	5
Dog	12-20*	Sheep	10-20	Chickadee	6-8	Robin, American	17
Elephant	50-70	Squirrel	7	Condor	35-40	Sky lark	9
Goat, Mountain	14-18	Tiger	20	Heron	10-20	Sparrow	2 ½-7
Grizzly bear	25	Wolf (gray)	12-16	Macaw	64	Starling	9-16
Hippopotamus	41	Zebra	22	Ostrich (African)	40		

Fish				Reptiles and amphibians			
Dogfish (lesser spotted)	8	Perch	3-10	Bullfrog	5	Rattlesnake (diamondback)	14-15
Goldfish	10	Pike	60-70	Chameleon	4-5	Salamander (spotted)	20
Halibut	25	Salmon (Pacific)	4-5	Cottonmouth	18-20	Turtle (box)	80
Lamprey	7	Seahorse	4 ½	Crocodile (Nile)	25-50	Water snake	11
Lungfish (African)	18	Sturgeon	50	Garter snake	3-4		
		Trout (rainbow)	11	King snake	3		
				Puff adder	14		

*Domesticated animal; life span in captivity.

classes. The classes are broken down into *orders,* and the orders into *families.* The families are split into *genera,* and the genera into *species.* The singular form of *genera* is *genus,* but the word *species* may be either singular or plural.

Scientists have classified more than 1 ½ million kinds of animals. They continue to discover and classify new species. Scientists believe that they have classified most of the members of some groups. For example, scientists have classified about 4,500 species of mammals, and it is unlikely that a large number of mammals remain undiscovered. For other groups, scientists believe they have classified only a fraction of the actual number of species. For instance, scientists have classified more than 1 million species of insects. But most scientists believe another 5 to 30 million insects have not yet been classified. As these numbers illustrate, there are great differences between the numbers of species in each group of animals.

Each species of animal belongs to one phylum, one class, one order, one family, and one genus. For example, tigers belong to the kingdom Animalia, the phylum Chordata, the class Mammalia, the order Carnivora, the family Felidae, and the genus *Panthera.* They are members of the species *Panthera tigris.* Lions are related to tigers. They belong to the same kingdom (Animalia), phylum (Chordata), class (Mammalia), order (Carnivora), family (Felidae), and genus *(Panthera)* as tigers. But lions are classified in a different species—*Panthera leo,* also written simply as *P. leo.*

A *table* of animal classification, showing some of the major groups of animals, appears at the end of this article. See also **Classification, Scientific.**

Where animals live

Animals live in many kinds of places. The kind of place where an animal lives is called its *habitat.* Each type of habitat presents a special challenge to animals. For example, animals that live in polar regions must withstand bitter cold. Those that inhabit the tropics face extreme heat. In spite of these challenges, animals can be found everywhere on Earth. They live on the highest mountains and in the deepest oceans. They roam the driest deserts and the wettest rain forests. They swim in fresh water and salt water.

Each habitat supports many kinds of animals. In most cases, the animals are the same kinds that have lived in those surroundings for thousands of years. As a result, the animals have developed bodies and ways of life that suit them to that particular habitat. No single species of animal can survive everywhere. For example, tropical fish from the Amazon River thrive in warm water but cannot withstand the cold streams of the Andes Mountains. On the other hand, many kinds of fish that live in the Arctic Ocean would die if they were exposed to the warm waters of the Caribbean Sea. However, some animals may travel between habitats from time to time. For example, African elephants eat both grass and tree parts and so move between grassland and forest. But these animals would not be able to withstand the freezing temperatures of the polar regions.

Some habitats, including many forests and grasslands, are being destroyed by human beings. The destruction of these habitats usually causes the death of many animals. When people convert grassland to farmland, for example, they destroy the homes and source of food of many species. Without these necessities, some animals will die immediately. Others may try moving to another grassland. But the new area may not have enough food and shelter to support the additional wildlife. As a result, many more animals will die.

This section tells about some of the major animals, grouped according to seven types of habitats: (1) mountains, (2) grasslands, (3) temperate forests, (4) tropical forests, (5) deserts, (6) polar regions, and (7) oceans. For descriptions and pictures of animals grouped according to the continent on which they live, see the articles on **Africa; Antarctica; Asia; Australia; Europe; North America; South America.**

Animals of the mountains

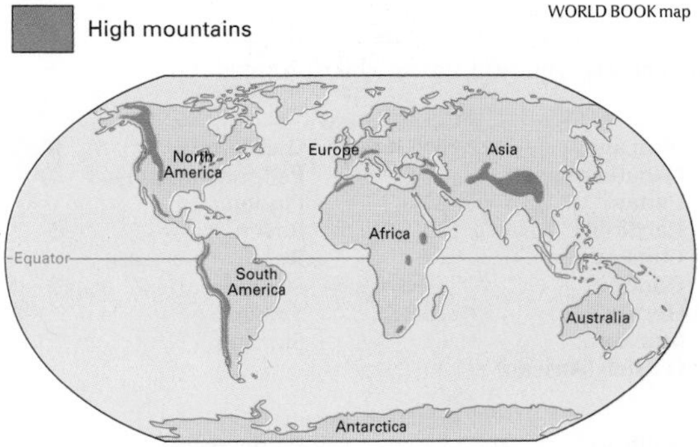

High mountains

(map showing high mountain regions: North America, Europe, Asia, Africa, South America, Australia, Antarctica, Equator)

Mountains support a variety of animal life. The numbers and kinds of animals found on mountains vary with altitude. More animals and more kinds of animals live at lower altitudes than at higher ones, largely because of the differences in climate between elevations. Generally, mountain climates become colder, wetter, and windier with increasing altitude. The air also gets thinner and has less oxygen. In addition, fewer plants are found at higher elevations, and therefore less food is available for animals.

Bears, deer, elk, and mink make their homes on the forested lower slopes and in the wooded or grassy valleys of mountains. Rainbow trout and graylings swim in mountain streams. Many mountains have meadows of grasses and herbs. These meadows are home to chinchillas, ibexes, llamas, vicuñas, and yaks. Butterflies, grasshoppers, and spiders also live there.

Above the *timber line*—that is, the line beyond which trees will not grow because of the cold—stand rocky cliffs and peaks dotted with shrubs, mosses, and other plants. Small meadows are also found there. Sure-footed bighorn sheep and mountain goats dwell among the windswept rocks, as do furry marmots and pikas. High on the snow-capped peaks, only a few insects, spiders, and ice worms can survive. Golden eagles and some other birds fly above the mountains. A large African vulture, Rüppell's griffon, has been known to soar as high as 36,600 feet (11,150 meters).

© Thinkstock

Vicuña   South America

Jane Burton, Bruce Coleman Ltd.

Chinchilla   South America

Bighorn sheep
North America

Rocky Mountain goat
North America

Rocky Mountain pika
North America

House swift
Asia

Wolf spider
North America

© Shutterstock

Yak Asia

Giant panda Asia

Russ Kinne, Photo Researchers

Himalayan ibex
Asia

Marco Polo sheep
Asia

Snow leopard Asia

WORLD BOOK illustrations by Margaret L. Estey

Animals of the grasslands

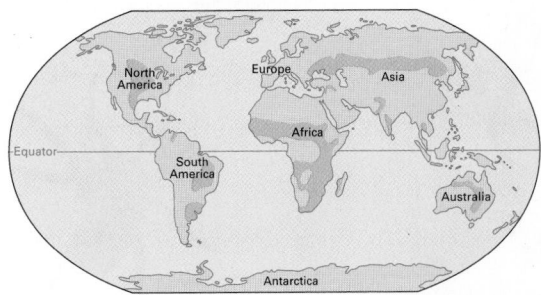

Grassland

WORLD BOOK map

Grasslands include the prairies of North America, the Pampas of South America, the plains of Europe, and the steppes of Asia. The savannas of east Africa have more grassland animals than any other area.

Rainfall in grasslands is seasonal, and animals sometimes travel great distances to find green grass. Gazelles, wildebeests, and zebras migrate by the thousands through the African savannas. Smaller groups of ele-

phants and rhinoceroses also feed on the grasses there. Such meat-eating mammals as cheetahs, hyenas, and lions roam the savannas in search of prey. The savannas are also home to giraffes, jackals, ostriches, secretary birds, and termites. In addition, hippopotamuses live in and near bodies of water in African grasslands. Animals of other grasslands include the kangaroos and wombats of Australia, the cavies and rheas of South America, and the coyotes and prairie dogs of North America.

Many animals of the grasslands have become endangered due to loss of their habitat and to overhunting. The rich soils of grasslands are ideal for farming, and people have converted many such areas to farmland. Many of the large grassland animals are favorite big game for hunters. For example, the once-plentiful pampas deer of South America have become extremely rare. As the Pampas are converted to farmland, the tall grass that grows there disappears. Without this grass, the pampas deer have no shelter and become easy prey. Bison once grazed in huge herds in the Great Plains of North America. But so many of these animals were killed by hunters or died as their grassland habitat was converted to farmland that they were nearly wiped out.

Giraffe

Ostrich

Zebra

Termite mound

Aardvark

Wildebeest

Africa

Pronghorn
North America

Blackbuck
Asia

Eland
Africa

Indian rhinoceros Asia

Ylla, Rapho Guillumette

African elephant

Secretary bird Africa

Guggisberg, Photo Researchers

Hippopotamus Africa

Conzett & Huber

© Shutterstock

African lion

Kangaroo
Australia

Prairie dog
North America

Peterson, Photo Researchers

African vulture

WORLD BOOK illustrations by John F. Eggert and René Martin

Animals of the temperate forests

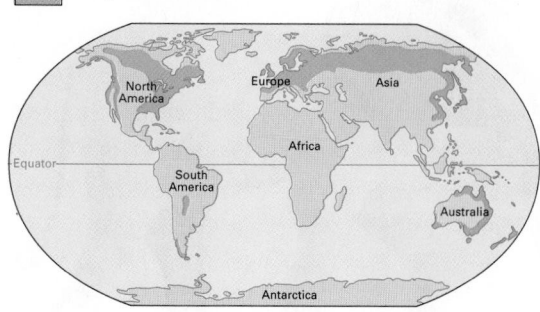

Temperate forest

WORLD BOOK map

Many forest animals have small bodies that allow them to move easily through the underbrush. Forest mammals include chipmunks, mice, opossums, porcupines, raccoons, skunks, and squirrels. Bears, deer, and wild boars also live in temperate forests. Bobcats and wolves were once common in woodland areas. However, so many of these predators have been hunted and trapped through the years that they have become rare.

Salamanders are often plentiful in temperate forests. They hide in the leaf litter or under rocks, where they feed on insects and other small organisms. In wet forests, slugs and other snails are common. Beavers, fish, frogs, muskrats, otters, salamanders, and turtles live in or near woodland streams, ponds, and lakes. Great numbers of birds nest in the trees and shrubs.

Temperate forests consist largely of *deciduous trees* and *evergreen trees*. Deciduous trees shed their leaves in the fall and grow new ones in the spring. Evergreen trees have leaves that live two or more years. Some evergreens have needle-shaped leaves. Most temperate forests are in Asia, Europe, and North America. Australia also has some temperate forests.

Many temperate forests have been cleared for farms and cities, and many others have been cut down for fuel and lumber. This *deforestation* (destruction of forests) places woodland animals in danger. Extensive logging in the Pacific Northwest of the United States, for example, has destroyed much of the habitat of the spotted owl, threatening the existence of that species.

Redstart
North America

Gray squirrel
North America

European brown bear

Russ Kinne, Photo Researchers

Moose   North America

FPG

Spotted owl
North America

Otter   North America

Red-backed salamander
North America

Wood frog
North America

Beaver
North America

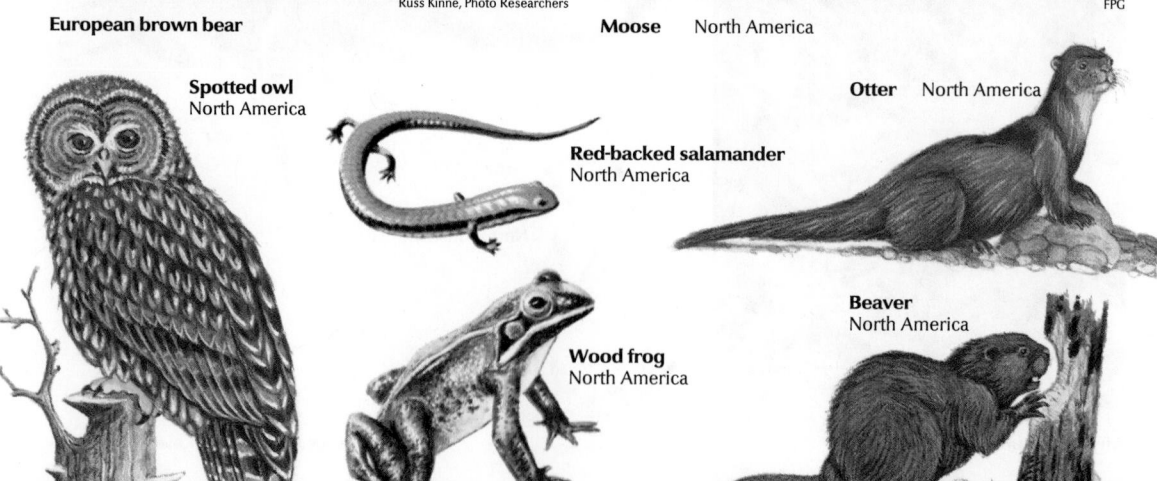

Downy woodpecker

Ovenbird

Raccoon

White-tailed deer

Chipmunk

Muskrat

Woodchuck

Skunk

Porcupine

Snapping turtle

Opossum

Okapia, Publix

Wild boar Europe

Geoffroy Kinns, Photo Researchers

Red deer Europe

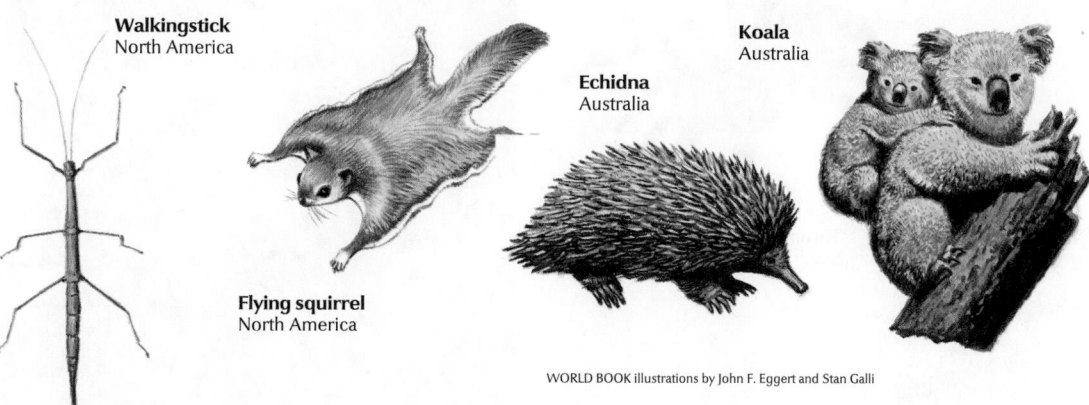

Walkingstick
North America

Koala
Australia

Echidna
Australia

Flying squirrel
North America

WORLD BOOK illustrations by John F. Eggert and Stan Galli

Tropical forest
WORLD BOOK map

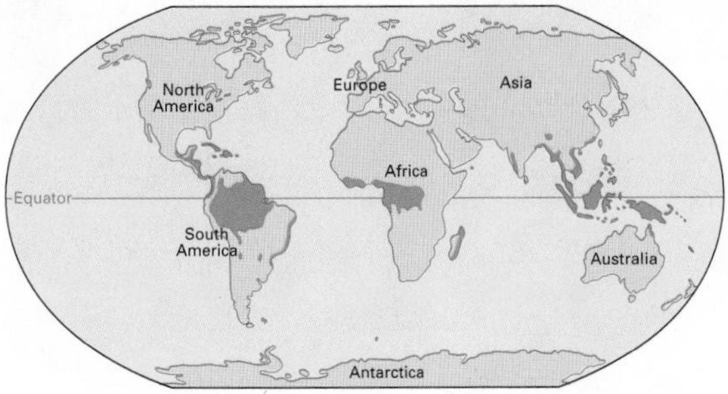

North America
Europe
Asia
Africa
Equator
South America
Australia
Antarctica

Tropical forests stay warm all year and receive plentiful rainfall. These forests are found in Africa, Asia, Australia, Central and South America, and the Pacific Islands. More kinds of animals live in tropical forests than in any other habitat. Scientists estimate that perhaps as many as 30 million species of tropical animals have not even been discovered yet.

Insects make up the largest single group of animals that live in tropical forests. They include brightly colored butterflies, huge colonies of ants, mosquitoes, and camouflaged stick insects. Spiders are also plentiful. Many tropical birds, such as quetzals and parrots, are spectacularly colored.

The broad leaves of trees in tropical forests form a thick overhead covering called a *canopy* that blocks nearly all sunlight from reaching the forest floor. Many kinds of animals live in the canopies of tropical forests. They include harpy eagles and toucans; tree frogs; flying dragons; spider monkeys and howlers; gibbons and orangutans; sloths; slow lorises; tree boa constrictors; bats; and wasps, beetles, and leaf-cutting ants.

Jaguars, tapirs, and bushmaster snakes live on the ground in tropical forests. Chimpanzees and lowland gorillas alternate between the ground and the trees. Crocodiles, fish, and turtles inhabit rivers and ponds.

People are rapidly destroying tropical forests for wood and for farming. The continuing destruction of this habitat means that many animals will disappear forever. Scientists believe countless species have already been wiped out.

Tarantula
South America

Driver ant
South America

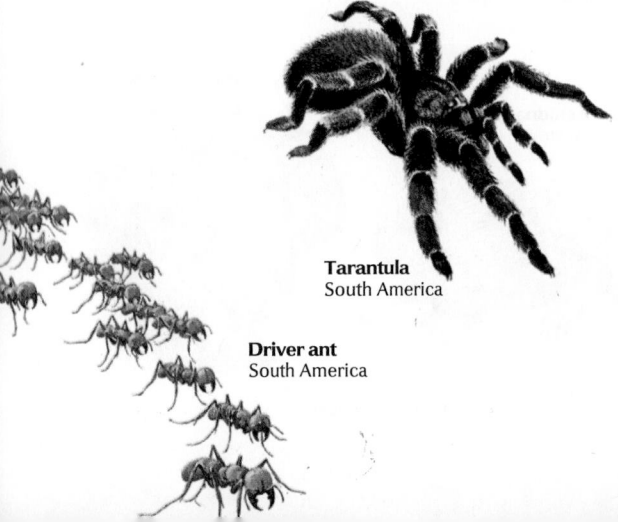

Black howler monkey

Common marmoset

Macaw

Spider monkey

Coati

Iguana

Two-toed sloth

Parasol ant

Ocelot

Tree frog

Tree boa constrictor

South American rain forest

Axis deer
Asia

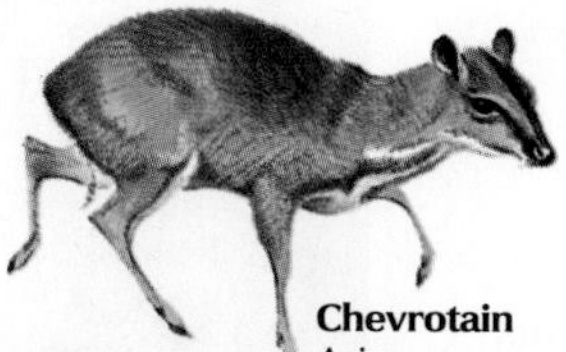

South American tapir

Malayan tapir
Asia

Chevrotain
Asia

Des Bartlett, Photo Researchers

Bongo   Africa

Nancy Adams, Tom Stack & Assoc.

Gorilla   Africa

Orangutan
Asia

James Simon, Photo Researchers

Woolly monkey   South America

James Simon, Photo Researchers

Giant anteater   South America

Leopard   Africa, Asia

Tiger   Asia

Ylla, Rapho Guillumette

Jaguar
Central and South
America, Mexico

WORLD BOOK illustrations by John F. Eggert and Robert Kuhn

Animals of the deserts

Desert
WORLD BOOK map

Most deserts lie near the edges of the tropics. Food and water are often scarce in deserts, and temperatures in the summer can be scorching. Despite these conditions, many kinds of animals live there. They include geckos, iguanas, and skinks; bees, butterflies, and moths; spiders; elf owls and roadrunners; sidewinders; dorcas gazelles and mule deer; and bobcats, coyotes, and dingoes.

Animals of the deserts have developed special bodies and ways of life that enable them to survive the extreme heat. Centipedes, kangaroo rats, rattlesnakes, and scorpions spend the day in burrows. They come out to search for food only when temperatures drop at night. Many insects, lizards, and tortoises can tolerate high desert temperatures and are active in the daytime. But even they must retreat underground or find the shade of a tree during the hottest part of the day. Some snails, insects, frogs, lizards, mice, and ground squirrels *estivate* (sleep through the summer).

Many desert dwellers have light-colored skin, which helps keep them cool by reflecting sunlight. Desert foxes and hares have long ears. When overheated, these animals move to a cool cave or burrow where they can get rid of excess body heat through their ears. The Cape ground squirrel makes its own shade by using its fluffy tail like a parasol. Fairy shrimp and spadefoot toads may spend months or years underground waiting for rain to create ponds. Then they quickly feed and reproduce before the ponds dry again.

Southwestern United States

Dingo Australia
© Shutterstock

Roadrunner North America
© Jerry L. Ferrara, Photo Researchers

Scorpion North America
Bob McKeever, Tom Stack & Assoc.

WORLD BOOK illustration by Rudolf Freund

Pallid bat

Coyote

Bobcat

Mule deer

Antelope
jack rabbit

Cactus wren

Kit fox

Gila monster

© Shutterstock

© Shutterstock

Shovel-nosed snake North America

Saiga Asia

Elf owl North America

Addax Africa

Lewis W. Walker, Photo Researchers

© Gail Rubin, Photo Researchers

Animals of the polar regions

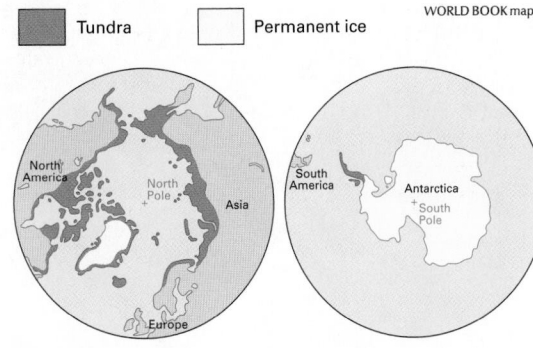

■ Tundra □ Permanent ice

WORLD BOOK maps

Animals that live in polar regions must withstand extremely cold temperatures. No land animals except ice worms and a few species of insects live in polar regions that have ice and snow the year around. But the seas of the Arctic and Antarctic have large numbers of wildlife, including fish, giant sponges, whales, and tiny shrimp-like creatures called *krill.* In addition, polar bears, sea lions, and walruses spend much of their time on floating sheets of ice in the Arctic. Penguins and seals live on the Antarctic coast.

Many animals inhabit the vast arctic *tundras* (cold treeless plains) of northern Asia, North America, and Europe. They include caribou, ermine, musk oxen, reindeer, lemmings, snowy owls, and wolves. Shallow ponds in the region provide a place for mosquitoes and many other insects to lay their eggs. These insects serve as food for the birds that migrate to the tundra each summer to nest.

Animals that live in polar regions have developed bodies and ways of life that enable them to deal with the frigid winter weather. Caribou, musk oxen, and polar bears have thick fur, which helps them stay warm. The Arctic fox and Arctic hare have short ears and tails that keep them from losing much body heat. Arctic ground squirrels *hibernate* (sleep through the winter). They curl up in a burrow, and their body temperature drops, saving energy during the long winter. They also do not eat in the winter. They live off fat stored in their bodies.

Musk ox

Snowy owl

Arctic hare

Rock ptarmigan

Ermine

Arctic winter

Emil Schulthess, Black Star

Polar bear   Arctic

© Thinkstock

Arctic bumble bee

Emperor penguin   Antarctica

Kodiak bear North America

St. Meyers/Okapia, Photo Researchers

Sandhill crane

Arctic loon

Golden plover

Caribou

Arctic fox

Arctic summer

WORLD BOOK illustrations by John F. Eggert and Guy Tudor

Krill
Polar seas

Collared lemming
Arctic

Walrus Arctic

© Thinkstock

Animals of the oceans

Animals of many kinds are found everywhere in the vast oceans. Some of the smallest animals live in the sea, as does the world's largest, the blue whale. Cod, halibut, seals, and whales swim the frigid waters of the polar regions. Lobsters, sea urchins, and many types of brightly colored fish inhabit coral reefs in warm tropical seas. Some ocean animals live near the shore—in shallow water, in tide pools, and on rocks. They include anemones, barnacles, mussels, octopuses, and starfish. Other marine animals—mostly such tiny shrimplike creatures as krill and copepods—are found in the open sea. Krill and some species of copepods form part of the group of or-

ganisms called *plankton*. Many fish and some whales feed on plankton.

The great depths of the ocean are completely dark, and the water there is bitterly cold. Even so, anglerfish, clams, and certain other creatures live there. On the other hand, flyingfish, manta rays, marlins, and porpoises generally swim near the ocean surface. Albatrosses, gulls, and petrels fly above the sea.

Oceans provide people with such foods as crab, fish, lobster, and shrimp. However, the demand for seafood has led to the overfishing of halibut, herring, and some other marine animals. Millions of dolphins, which are mammals, have drowned in fishing nets that were intended to catch cod, tuna, and other fish. In addition, spills of toxic materials and other forms of pollution have reduced the numbers of some ocean species.

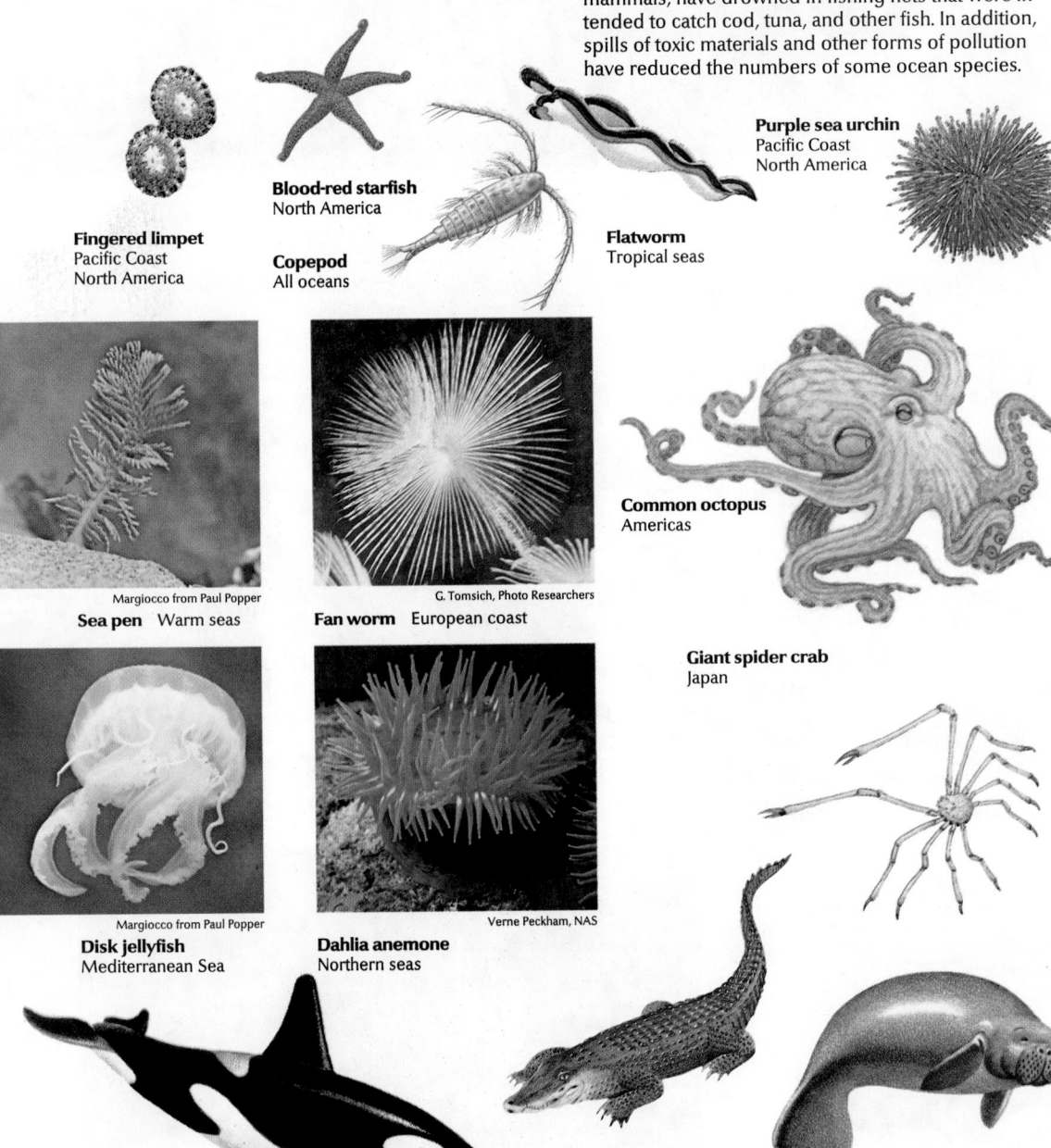

Fingered limpet
Pacific Coast
North America

Blood-red starfish
North America

Copepod
All oceans

Flatworm
Tropical seas

Purple sea urchin
Pacific Coast
North America

Margiocco from Paul Popper
Sea pen Warm seas

G. Tomsich, Photo Researchers
Fan worm European coast

Common octopus
Americas

Giant spider crab
Japan

Margiocco from Paul Popper
Disk jellyfish
Mediterranean Sea

Verne Peckham, NAS
Dahlia anemone
Northern seas

Killer whale
Pacific

Saltwater crocodile
Southeastern Asia

Manatee
Tropical Atlantic

Mike Bacon, Tom Stack & Assoc.

Raccoon butterflyfish and coral Red Sea

Flyingfish Warm seas

Deep-sea angler Atlantic and Pacific

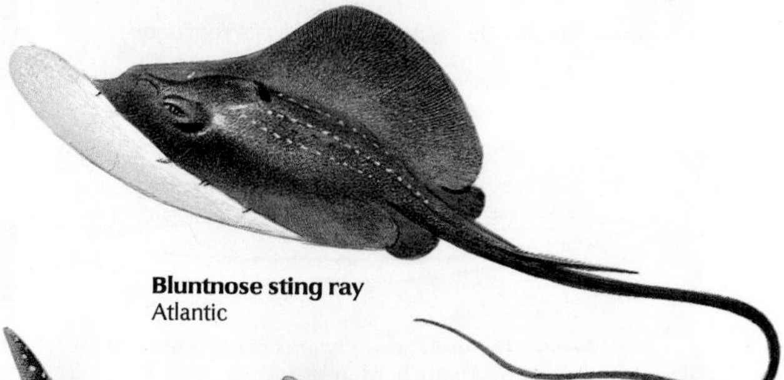

Bluntnose sting ray
Atlantic

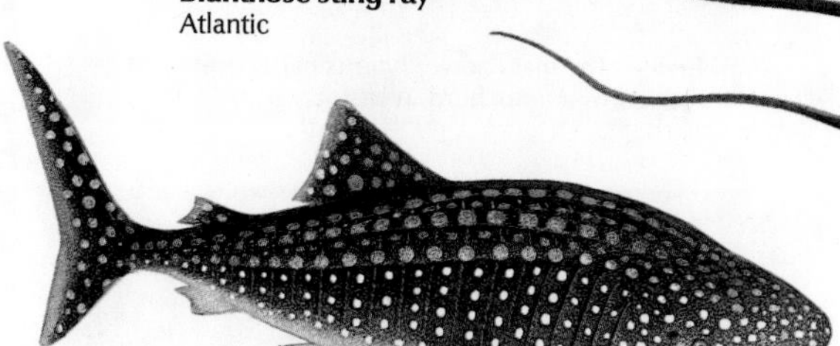

Whale shark
Warm seas

WORLD BOOK illustrations by Tom Dolan, Alex Ebel, and John F. Eggert

The bodies of animals

Animals have special body features that enable them to survive in their environment. These special features, called *adaptations,* result from the ability animal species have to *adapt* (adjust) over time to changes in their surroundings. Adaptations for survival enable animals to move about, to eat, to breathe, and to sense their environment. Legs, wings, and fins help animals move. Teeth and jaws help them eat. Lungs and gills help them obtain oxygen. Eyes and ears help them find food and detect predators.

Animals live in many kinds of environments. The body features of an animal that work well in one type of environment may not work in others. For example, the adaptations that enable fish to breathe in water do not let them breathe on land. Even in the same environment, animals may have different adaptations for survival. Shrimp, fish, and sea turtles can all swim in the ocean, but they have different body features for doing so.

Invertebrates and vertebrates

The animal kingdom is often divided into two main groups—animals without backbones, called *invertebrates,* and animals with backbones, called *vertebrates.* Invertebrates include sponges, worms, centipedes, starfish, mollusks, and insects. Vertebrates include fish, amphibians, reptiles, birds, and mammals. Invertebrates are commonly known as the *lower animals.* Vertebrates are known as the *higher animals.* The backbone of a vertebrate helps protect the *spinal* (main nerve) *cord.* The main nerve cord of invertebrates is unprotected. A small sea animal, the amphioxus, has a *notochord,* which is a rod of cartilage that serves as a backbone and partly protects the animal's main nerve. The amphioxus is considered to be a link between the lower animals and the higher animals.

WORLD BOOK illustrations by Patricia Wynne

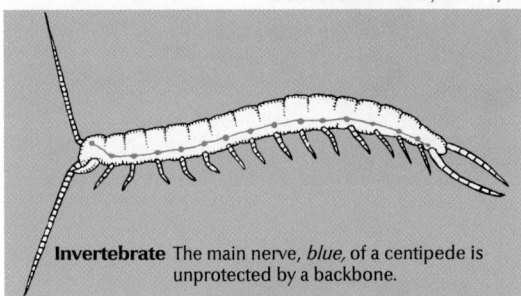

Invertebrate The main nerve, *blue,* of a centipede is unprotected by a backbone.

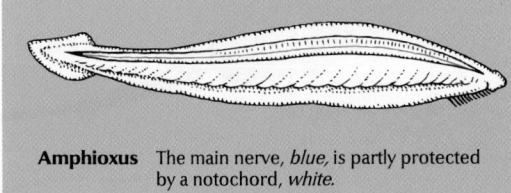

Amphioxus The main nerve, *blue,* is partly protected by a notochord, *white.*

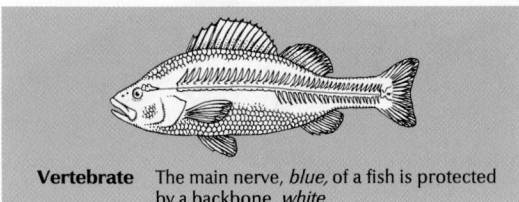

Vertebrate The main nerve, *blue,* of a fish is protected by a backbone, *white.*

Shrimp have tiny swimming legs, fish have fins and muscular tails, and turtles have flippers. Because animals adapt to their surroundings in many ways, there is a wide diversity of animals in any environment.

This section describes some of the ways animal bodies are adapted for moving, eating, breathing, and sensing the environment. For information on the basic process of adaptation, see **Adaptation.**

Adaptations for moving about

Legs and feet. Mammals, birds, insects, and many reptiles and amphibians have legs with feet that enable them to walk or run on land. Most amphibians, mammals, and reptiles walk on four legs. Birds and people walk on two. Insects have six legs, and spiders have eight. Millipedes may have up to 200 legs.

Animals can crawl without legs and feet. Such tiny creatures as planarians and other flatworms slide by moving many small hairlike structures, called *cilia,* back and forth like miniature oars. Snails move by coating the ground with a sticky fluid from their bodies. They then crawl through the fluid using a muscular organ called a *foot.* Most snakes slide along the ground by bending their bodies from side to side. An earthworm crawls through the soil by alternately lengthening and shortening parts of its body.

Many walking and crawling organisms live in water. Crabs and lobsters have legs that enable them to walk across the bottom of a body of water.

Wings. Three groups of animals have the ability to fly under their own power: (1) insects, (2) bats, and (3) birds. Most insects have two pairs of wings. Muscles inside the *thorax* (middle section of an insect's body) move the wings up and down.

Bats are the only mammals with wings. Batwings are

Jacana

Long, powerful legs and a stride of 15 feet (4.6 meters) make the ostrich one of the fastest land animals. Ostriches can reach speeds as high as 40 miles (64 kilometers) per hour.

Comparative speeds of animals

The speeds of animals vary greatly. Birds are the fastest of all animals, with flying speeds of more than 200 miles (320 kilometers) per hour. The speediest land animals outstrip the fastest water animals. Many of the figures given in the table below are estimates because scientists have difficulty measuring the speeds of wild animals. In addition, the maximum speed of an animal may differ widely from its usual speed. A rabbit runs faster than a greyhound for a short time. But the greyhound can keep up its speed for longer distances.

WORLD BOOK illustrations by Linda Kinnaman and Robert Klunder

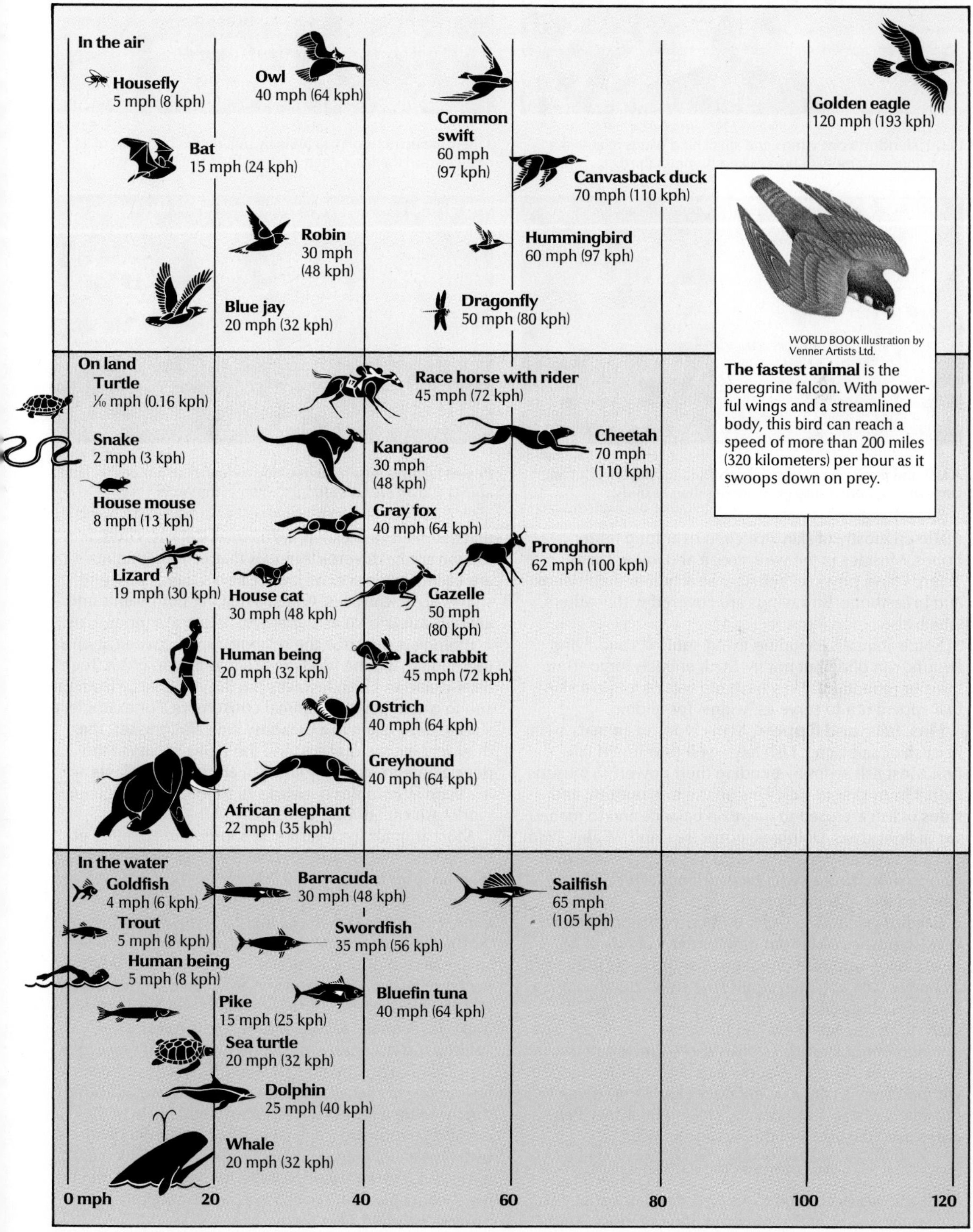

In the air

Housefly 5 mph (8 kph)
Owl 40 mph (64 kph)
Golden eagle 120 mph (193 kph)
Bat 15 mph (24 kph)
Common swift 60 mph (97 kph)
Canvasback duck 70 mph (110 kph)
Robin 30 mph (48 kph)
Hummingbird 60 mph (97 kph)
Blue jay 20 mph (32 kph)
Dragonfly 50 mph (80 kph)

WORLD BOOK illustration by Venner Artists Ltd.

The fastest animal is the peregrine falcon. With powerful wings and a streamlined body, this bird can reach a speed of more than 200 miles (320 kilometers) per hour as it swoops down on prey.

On land

Turtle 1/10 mph (0.16 kph)
Race horse with rider 45 mph (72 kph)
Cheetah 70 mph (110 kph)
Snake 2 mph (3 kph)
Kangaroo 30 mph (48 kph)
House mouse 8 mph (13 kph)
Gray fox 40 mph (64 kph)
Pronghorn 62 mph (100 kph)
Lizard 19 mph (30 kph)
House cat 30 mph (48 kph)
Gazelle 50 mph (80 kph)
Human being 20 mph (32 kph)
Jack rabbit 45 mph (72 kph)
Ostrich 40 mph (64 kph)
Greyhound 40 mph (64 kph)
African elephant 22 mph (35 kph)

In the water

Goldfish 4 mph (6 kph)
Barracuda 30 mph (48 kph)
Sailfish 65 mph (105 kph)
Trout 5 mph (8 kph)
Swordfish 35 mph (56 kph)
Human being 5 mph (8 kph)
Bluefin tuna 40 mph (64 kph)
Pike 15 mph (25 kph)
Sea turtle 20 mph (32 kph)
Dolphin 25 mph (40 kph)
Whale 20 mph (32 kph)

0 mph   20   40   60   80   100   120

Long, slender front wings and small hind wings enable the fast-flying hawk moth to hover like a hummingbird.

The measuring worm crawls by pulling the back part of its body toward the front, then pushing the front part forward.

A tail and fins serve most fish in swimming. The tail of a male fancy guppy, *above,* may grow longer than its body.

Powerful hind legs make the frog a champion jumper on land, *above,* and an expert swimmer when in the water.

made up mostly of skin stretched over long finger bones. Muscles in the wings raise and lower them.

Birds have powerful muscles attached to their wings and breastbone. Bird wings are covered with feathers, which also aid in flight.

Some animals, including flying squirrels and flying lemurs, can glide but not fly. Such animals jump from trees or mountains. They have big feet or folds of skin that spread out to serve as "wings" for gliding.

Fins, tails, and flippers. Many types of animals swim in fresh or salt water. Fish have well-developed tails and fins. Most fish swim by bending their powerful, muscular tail from side to side. Fins on the top, bottom, and sides of fish are used to maintain balance and to maneuver in tight areas. Dolphins, porpoises, and whales swim by moving their massive tails up and down rather than side to side. Turtles swim by paddling with their webbed feet or their flippers.

Jellyfish and squids swim by jet propulsion. When a jellyfish pushes water out from under its body, it is thrust in the opposite direction. A squid takes water into its body cavity and then squirts the water out through a small opening called a *funnel.* This action repeated many times pushes the squid forward.

A number of species of birds can swim. Some ducks and gulls paddle on the surface of the water using their webbed feet as oars. Torrent ducks and loons dive underwater, where they swim by kicking their feet. Penguins use their feet and their wings to swim.

Adaptations for eating

All animals need food to survive. Animals eat plants, other animals, or both plants and other animals. Animals that eat plants are called *herbivores.* Zebras, cows, and moose are herbivores. Animals that eat other animals are called *carnivores* or *meat-eaters.* Dogs, lions, and sharks are carnivores. Animals that eat both plants and animals are known as *omnivores.* Bears are omnivores.

Biologists describe the relationships between animals in a habitat and the foods they eat as a *food chain.* Technically, a food chain involves the flow of energy from the sun to green plants to animal consumers. For example, a simple food chain in a meadow links the grasses, the deer that eat the grasses, and the wolves that eat the deer. Sometimes, many kinds of animals and plants are involved in complex networks of food chains. Such networks are called *food webs.*

Most animals eat a variety of foods. For example, pigeons eat fruits, grains, and nuts, and they sometimes feed on insects, snails, and worms.

Some animals eat only a few foods. A snail called a cone shell preys only on a single species of marine worm. Several kinds of snakes eat only slugs or other snails. Hummingbirds and honey possums live on the nectar of flowers. A sapsucker drills holes in trees and eats the sap that flows from the holes. The koala of Australia dines on the leaves of eucalyptus trees.

Filtering mechanisms. Huge numbers of tiny organisms called plankton float or swim slowly near the surface of oceans, lakes, and other bodies of water. Plankton make up a part of an important food chain in the ocean. Plankton are too small to be captured individually by animals that feed on them. Some animals, such as barnacles, sweep water past themselves while straining out the tiny plankton, which are thereby captured. This process is called *filter feeding.*

© Shutterstock

A gray whale filters food from water by squeezing the water out of its mouth through thin plates called *baleen*.

E. R. Degginger

A snake swallows food whole. It has loose jaws that enable it to swallow eggs or animals much larger than its own head.

Alan Root/Okapia, Photo Researchers

A lion has long, razor-sharp *canine* (pointed) teeth for killing and tearing such prey as antelope and zebras. It does not have teeth for chewing, however. It swallows its food in chunks.

Baleen whales are probably the best-known filter feeders. These animals, which do not have teeth, feed by gulping huge mouthfuls of water containing plankton, small fish, and other marine organisms. They then force the water out of their mouths through a series of strainers called *baleen*. The food is captured on the baleen and then swallowed. A baleen whale can consume as much as 4 tons (3.6 metric tons) of food a day.

Teeth and jaws. A large number of animals eat food that they need to tear into pieces small enough to be swallowed and digested easily. Teeth and jaws are adaptations for tearing food. Teeth may also be used to kill prey.

Teeth are adapted for the particular type of food an animal eats. Deer, giraffes, and other herbivores have teeth with broad surfaces for grinding grasses and plants into small bits. The powerful front teeth of beavers enable these animals to cut down trees for food and shelter. Lions have razor-sharp *canine* (pointed) teeth for killing and then tearing prey.

Birds have bills that are adapted for certain types of feeding. A hawk has a sharp, hooked beak for tearing prey. A woodpecker uses its long, pointed bill to drill into the bark of trees to find insects.

Insects have jaws and movable mouthparts that act like teeth. The jaws of grasshoppers are adapted for cutting and chewing plants. Mosquitoes have needle-shaped mouthparts for piercing skin and sucking blood.

Adaptations for breathing

Most animals need a continuous supply of oxygen to survive. The entire process of obtaining and using oxygen is called *respiration*. That part of the process that involves how an animal takes oxygen from its environment and gives off carbon dioxide is known as *breathing*. This section focuses on breathing. For a complete description of how oxygen flows to various cells of an animal's body and how it is used by those cells, see **Respiration**.

The way that animals breathe depends on where they live. Land animals get oxygen from the air. Aquatic animals obtain oxygen from water.

Many land animals have lungs for breathing. As blood flows through the lungs, it picks up oxygen from the air

Oxford Scientific Films from Animals Animals

A European water spider breathes underwater by carrying air bubbles on its abdomen. The spider fills its web with air bubbles, which gradually push all the water out of the web.

and releases carbon dioxide. The blood then carries oxygen to the rest of the body. See **Lung.**

Many aquatic organisms, such as fish and tadpoles, use gills to obtain oxygen that is dissolved in water. Some animals pump water across their gills to increase the efficiency of breathing. Sharks do this by swimming continuously.

Tiny tubes called *tracheae* allow insects to breathe in air. Tracheae branch throughout an insect's body. They open to the outside air through holes called *spiracles.* When air enters the tracheae, oxygen is carried to every cell in the body.

Some animals that live in damp environments have unusual ways of breathing. For example, many salamanders have no lungs or gills. They breathe through their moist skin.

Adaptations for sensing the environment

Most kinds of animals have special body parts that respond to changes in the animal's environment. Such a

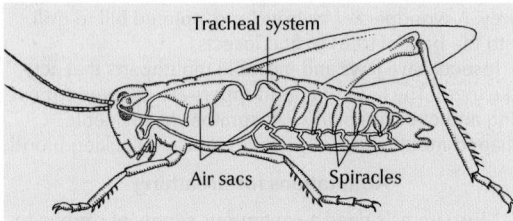

Spiracles are openings on the outside of an insect's body. Air enters the body through these openings and flows into air sacs. A *tracheal* (air tube) system distributes the air.

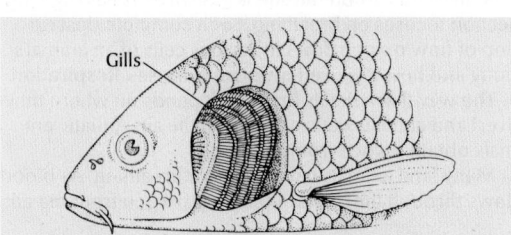

Gills are the breathing organs of most fish. The thin tissues of the gills absorb oxygen from the water. A fish gulps in water, and then forces it out through the gill openings.

WORLD BOOK illustrations by Patricia Wynne

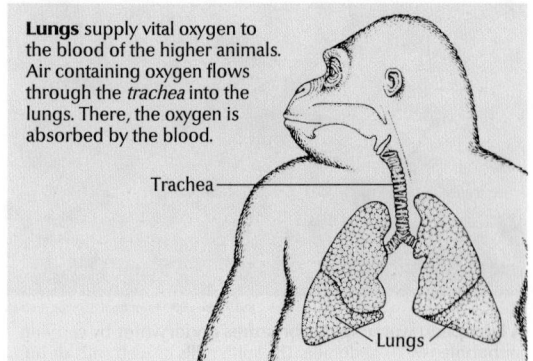

Lungs supply vital oxygen to the blood of the higher animals. Air containing oxygen flows through the *trachea* into the lungs. There, the oxygen is absorbed by the blood.

Touch. Woodcocks and many other birds can use the tips of their beaks to locate worms underground.

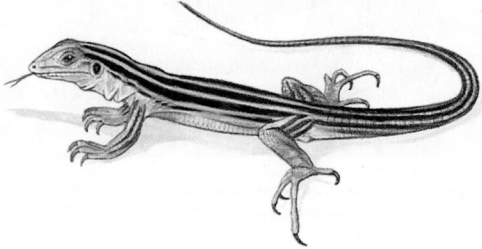

Smell. The forked tongues of snakes and some lizards are used to smell as well as to touch.

Taste. Catfish and certain other fish have cells called *taste buds* in the skin that covers their bodies.

Hearing. Bats hunt insects by the echoes that result from their high-pitched sounds striking their prey.

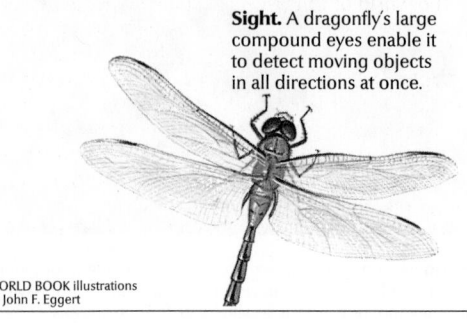

Sight. A dragonfly's large compound eyes enable it to detect moving objects in all directions at once.

WORLD BOOK illustrations by John F. Eggert

A table of animal intelligence

Many animals can learn to do some tricks if they are carefully trained. But the ability to do tricks is not a sign of intelligence. Even fleas can be trained as circus performers.

Scientists measure the intelligence of animals by giving them problems to solve and by studying their behavior. In the past, most animals were studied in isolation from other animals. They were tested for how they performed tasks when given food as a reward.

Today, however, many studies of animal intelligence focus on animals in group settings. Such research concentrates on the intelligence animals use in their dealing with others of their kind and in solving group problems. Scientists believe this *social intelligence* may be closely related to the development of communication skills. The ability to communicate represents a high degree of intelligence.

The following table provides information on the intelligence of a number of types of animals, based on various scientific studies.

Apes and monkeys have the most humanlike intelligence. Chimpanzees seem to be the most advanced. They can make tools, plan complicated searches for food, and even count. They can also communicate by means of symbols. For example, they may use certain gestures to symbolize particular objects, actions, or states of being.

Large aquatic mammals, such as dolphins, whales, and sea lions, have brains much like those of human beings. They are capable of learning sophisticated symbolic communication.

For example, dolphins seem to recognize differences in meaning based on the order in which the symbols are presented.

Carnivorous mammals in the cat and dog families show learning ability as good as, or better than, all animals except apes, some monkeys, and large aquatic mammals. Lions, tigers, and wolves probably can learn more rapidly than domesticated cats or dogs can.

Hoofed animals. Elephants and pigs are the best problem solvers among the hoofed animals.

Rodents are generally good at solving problems that involve finding their way through complicated pathways.

Birds, such as the raven and the pigeon, can solve simple counting problems. Parrots can learn to say human words and use them meaningfully in naming and counting objects.

Amphibians and reptiles are difficult to test, but alligators, crocodiles, turtles, and large monitor lizards may rival mammals and birds in locating sources of food and in some other forms of nonsocial learning.

Fish. Salmon and some other kinds of fish can remember odors for as long as several years. Sharks have brains as large as those of some birds and mammals. They have keen senses, and they are surprisingly clever at finding food and avoiding danger.

Animals without backbones often seem to learn very little. But some have remarkable and specialized abilities involving communication, food, and place learning. Many scientists consider octopuses to have the most complex brains of all the invertebrates. Octopuses learn rapidly and have distinct personalities.

stimulus (change) might come from an odor, a sight, a sound, a taste, or a touch. The simplest kinds of animals, such as sponges, have no special body parts and react to stimuli with their body cells. Animals with more complex physical structures, especially vertebrates, have highly developed organs for reacting to stimuli. These organs are described in the articles on **Brain** and **Nervous system.**

Some simple animals, such as hydras, react to stimuli with special cells. These sensory cells are scattered among the outermost cells of the body. The reactions of most other kinds of animals depend largely on one or more of the major senses. These senses are sight, hearing, smell, taste, and touch. See **Senses.**

Some senses are more important to one kind of animal than to another. Most birds cannot find food if they

cannot see it. Hearing is vital to bats. If the ears of a bat are covered, the animal will crash into objects when it tries to fly. A keen sense of smell enables dogs and wolves to find food, follow trails, and recognize danger. Taste is highly important to many insects. Some butterflies can taste the sweetness of flowers with their feet. A cat's long whiskers serve as touch organs. They enable the cat to feel its way through underbrush and avoid bumping into objects.

A number of animals have special senses. A rattlesnake has *pit organs* on the side of its face that sense heat. These organs enable the snake to tell if a mouse or some other warm-blooded prey is nearby, even in total darkness. Many scientists believe that some birds and insects can detect the direction of Earth's magnetic field. This ability may help these animals navigate.

How animals protect themselves

The world of an animal is filled with danger from predators. This section describes some of the many ways animals protect themselves from such danger.

Hiding in a safe place. The best protection against a predator is to avoid being seen by it. Many animals rest or sleep in a safe hiding place. Some desert toads crawl down a crack in the mud. A cricket hides under a large rock or under the loose bark of a tree. Worms and moles dig underground tunnels.

Many species, such as rabbits, leave their nests mainly or only at night, when they are harder for predators to spot. Other species become active for only short periods so they are not exposed to predators for long.

Camouflage. Many animals are difficult for predators to see because they resemble their surroundings. The various ways animals blend with their surroundings are called *camouflage.* For camouflage to be effective, the animals must remain motionless or nearly so.

Protective coloration is coloring that helps animals to hide. A dark moth lying against the brown or black bark of a tree is hard to see. However, that same moth would be clearly visible if it sat on a green leaf.

Many animals can change their colors and thus remain camouflaged even when moving among backgrounds of different colors. The chameleon, a lizard, is green when surrounded by leaves but turns brown

Animals defend themselves from predators by a variety of means. Some use such weapons as sharp teeth and claws. Others simply run from attackers. In some cases, the weapons an animal uses for defense are the same ones it uses to capture prey.

© Thinkstock

A lobster's claws are powerful weapons. The animal uses its claws to seize crabs, fish, snails, and other prey. The strong, toothed claws then crush the prey and tear it into pieces.

Leonard Lee Rue III

The armadillo's armor protects the animal from harm. The bony plates of the armor fit together so well that the armadillo can roll up tightly into a ball when an enemy comes near.

© Thinkstock

Sharp claws called *talons* are used by owls to defend their nests from intruders and to capture prey.

E. R. Degginger

Speed is the impala's main defense. An impala can run as fast as 50 miles (80 kilometers) per hour in bounding leaps.

A. J. Deane, Bruce Coleman Ltd.

Large, heavy horns protect the slow-moving Cape buffalo of southern Africa from predators. A fierce and powerful fighter, this animal can kill even an attacking lion.

E. R. Degginger

Sharp quills help protect a porcupine from attack. When touched, the barbed quills come off the porcupine and hook into the attacker's flesh, where they can cause painful wounds.

Alan Blank, Bruce Coleman Inc.

Rattlesnake fangs inject deadly poison. The needlelike fangs fold back against the roof of the mouth when not in use. They move forward when the snake opens its mouth to strike.

Animal camouflage

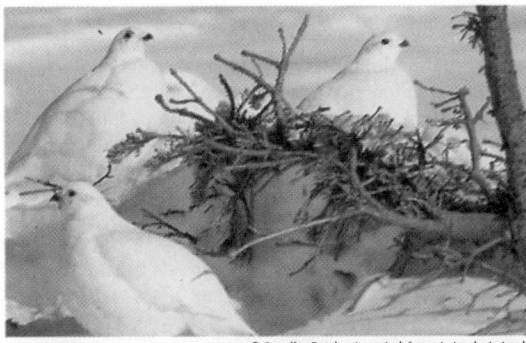

© Stouffer Productions, Ltd. from Animals Animals

Eric A. Soder, Tom Stack & Assoc.

© Shutterstock

© Shutterstock

Pierre Labout, Jacana

Protective coloration helps many animals hide from predators. In winter, ptarmigan feathers match the snow, *top left.* The roe deer is hard to see because its colors resemble those of its woodland home. The engrailed is typical of many moths whose coloring makes them seem to disappear when they rest on certain trees. The pheasant's colors make it seem part of its surroundings.

Denise Tackett, Tom Stack & Assoc.

E. R. Degginger

© Animals Animals/SuperStock

Mimicry helps many animals avoid predators. Some animals *mimic* (resemble) other objects in their environment or other animals. The wings of a dead-leaf insect mantis, *above,* resemble leaves. Some robber flies look so much like a bumble bee that predators often avoid them. The razor fish has a long, slender body that resembles the long, thin leaves of a sea plant. A treehopper on the stem of a rosebush looks so much like a thorn that birds often overlook the insect.

when moving slowly on bark or on the ground. The ptarmigan, an arctic bird, is brown in summer but becomes white in winter, when snow covers the ground.

Mimicry helps many animals avoid predators. Some animals *mimic* (resemble) other objects in their environment. For example, many green insects are shaped like leaves. Some caterpillars look like lizards or bird droppings. Walkingstick insects are shaped and colored like twigs. Anglerfish resemble rocks on the ocean floor.

Batesian mimicry is a form of mimicry in which an otherwise harmless animal strongly mimics an offensive animal. This type of mimicry was named after the English naturalist Henry W. Bates, who studied it in the 1800's. Bates observed that some harmless species have coloring and behavior that make them look like a dangerous or bad-tasting animal. A predator spotting such a species may mistake it for the undesirable animal and leave it alone. For example, some species of harmless king snakes feature coloration that helps them to resemble poisonous coral snakes. For this reason, birds and other predators may avoid the harmless snakes. See **Protective coloration.**

Escaping by flight. Many animals run away from an attacker. Antelope sprint away at high speed when charged by a lion or a cheetah. Many animals stay near safe places, such as burrows, and run to them if attacked. The octopus squirts a black inky fluid to conceal itself and then quickly swims for safety.

Armor. Some species have a hard shell or covering that is used as armor against predators. Clams pull back into their shells when a predator approaches. Many turtles can pull in their head, legs, and tail when attacked. Armadillos and pangolins are covered by hard, bony plates. When frightened, these animals roll into a tight ball that is difficult for attackers to penetrate.

Playing dead. A few species sometimes fool predators by lying motionless and appearing to be dead. If the predator does not deliver a killing blow or bite, then the animal may have a chance to escape. A threatened opossum goes limp. The hognose snake flips onto its back when a predator approaches.

Giving up a body part. Many animals break off a nonessential part of their body when attacked. The glass lizard breaks off its tail, which flops about and attracts the attention of the predator. While the attacker struggles with the tail, the lizard escapes. In most cases, the lost body part grows back quickly.

Fighting. Many animals have special weapons for fighting predators. The sharp hooves of a moose or the claws of an ostrich can rip open an attacker. Porcupines have long, sharp quills on their back, sides, and tail. These animals strike attackers with their quilled tails. The quills come out easily and stick in the attackers. Bees and wasps sting animals that approach their nests.

Chemical defenses. A number of animals use special chemicals for defense. Hagfish and one kind of starfish give off huge quantities of slime when disturbed. The bombardier beetle squirts irritating chemicals at an attacker. Some cobras spit blinding venom at the eyes of attackers. Skunks spray foul-smelling chemicals. Birds from New Guinea called hooded pitohuis have poisonous feathers and skin.

How animals reproduce

All types of animals reproduce. Many animals have special organs that are used in reproduction. These organs are called *gonads.* Some simple animals do not have gonads, but they are still able to reproduce. The various methods used by living things to reproduce are described in detail in the **Reproduction** article.

There are two general forms of animal reproduction: (1) *asexual reproduction* and (2) *sexual reproduction.* In asexual reproduction, only one parent produces the offspring. In sexual reproduction, two parents of opposite sexes are needed to produce the offspring. Many of the simplest animals, including sponges, sea anemones, and some flatworms, reproduce asexually most of the time. Sometimes, they reproduce sexually as well. Most other kinds of animals reproduce only sexually.

Asexual reproduction. Planarians and some other flatworms can reproduce by *fragmentation,* the division of the body into two or more pieces. When a planarian reproduces asexually, it typically divides into two sections, one with the head and the other with the tail. Each section then grows the parts that are missing and becomes a complete new individual.

Hydras and some sea anemones reproduce by *budding.* The animal produces small projections, called *buds,* from its side. These buds develop into miniature copies of the parent. The buds eventually detach from the parent, and the individuals produced by budding grow to be as large as their parents. Then they can put forth buds to create their own offspring.

Sexual reproduction. Most animals that reproduce only sexually do so with special sex cells known as *gametes.* Female sex cells are called *eggs* and are produced in the female gonads, the *ovaries.* The male sex cells are known as *sperm* and are made in the male gonads, the *testes.* Sperm are much smaller than eggs and have a tail that enables them to swim toward eggs. When a sperm cell unites with an egg cell, a new animal starts to form. The process in which the sperm unites with the egg is called *fertilization.*

External fertilization occurs outside an animal's body. Many aquatic animals reproduce sexually without ever meeting. Female sea urchins release millions of egg cells directly into the water. About the same time, the males release their sperm. The sperm swim through the water, and some unite with eggs, leading to fertilization. The fertilized eggs develop into swimming offspring, which are called *larvae.* The larvae grow and eventually sink to the bottom of the sea, where they become small sea urchins with bodies similar to those of their parents.

Internal fertilization occurs within an animal's body. If gametes are released on land, they dry up and die. Consequently, land-dwelling animals that reproduce sexually have developed ways for fertilization to take place inside their bodies.

Animals mate in many ways. Males of such species as snakes, lizards, birds, and mammals mate by releasing sperm directly into an opening in the female's body. Fertilization occurs in the female's reproductive organs.

Male salamanders do not release sperm directly into the female's body. Instead, they deposit a packet of sperm at the bottom of a stream or pond. When the female passes over the sperm, she draws them into an opening in her body that leads to her reproductive organs. Several other animals, including mites and scorpions, mate in a manner similar to that of salamanders. Males deposit packets of sperm on the ground, which are then picked up by females.

In almost all mammals and some reptiles, the *embryo* (undeveloped animal) grows inside the female's body after fertilization. However, in birds and some reptiles, the embryo develops outside the body. The female lays an egg in which the embryo develops. See **Fertilization.**

Courtship behavior consists of actions that help animals find and choose suitable mates. This behavior tends to follow a specific pattern according to species. As a result, courtship behavior helps ensure that animals mate with members of their own species. If two different species mate, they may not produce young, or their offspring may be unhealthy or unable to reproduce. Such courtship behaviors as singing and displaying colors help animals recognize their own species.

Animal mates find each other in a number of ways. Female birds are attracted to the beautiful songs and bright feathers of males. Female grasshoppers, cicadas, bullfrogs, and toads also are attracted to the calls made by males of their species. Female silkworm moths release into the air a perfumelike chemical called a *pheromone* to attract males from as far away as several miles or kilometers. At certain times of the year, female dogs give off a pheromone that attracts male dogs. Female fireflies watch for male fireflies that flash their lights in a certain rhythmic pattern. Male fence lizards bob their heads rhythmically when a female approaches. Siamese fightingfish perform a complicated courtship dance, followed by the release of eggs and sperm into the water.

Some animals choose particular mates. The female anole lizard typically prefers to mate with the largest

Animal reproduction

Animal	Approximate gestation period	Typical number of newborn
Alligator (American)	9 weeks*	50-60†
Bat (common vampire)	210 days	1
Cat	65 days	4
Dog	9 weeks	1-10
Elephant	21-22 months	1
Frog (bullfrog)	5-20 days*	20,000†
Gerbil	19-21 days	4-7
Guinea pig	68 days	1-5
Hamster (golden)	16 days	6-9
Horse	332-342 days	1
Lion	100-119 days	3-4
Monkey (spider)	226-232 days	1
Mouse (field)	21-23 days	5-6
Rabbit (cottontail)	25-40 days	3-6
Robin, American	12-14 days*	4†
Sheep	150-180 days	1-2
Squirrel (red)	33-35 days	4-6
Tiger	104-106 days	2-3

*Approximate incubation period.
†Approximate number of eggs a female lays. Not all of them hatch into newborns.

male. The peacock spreads his fantastic tail feathers, hoping to coax a peahen into becoming his mate. Peahens choose males with many spots on their tail feathers. Male birds of paradise gather in a tree. When a female appears, the brilliantly colored males strut and dance to show off their bright feathers. If a female chooses to watch this display, she will usually mate with the male that has the brightest colors.

Male bowerbirds build chambers or runways, called *bowers,* made of sticks or other material. They decorate these structures with brightly colored stones, bones, or other objects. The male dances and bows in front of his bower, hoping that a passing female will accept him as a mate. If one does, she enters the bower with him, and they mate there.

Some male animals give food to possible mates. A male tern catches a fish and places it into the mouth of

Animal reproduction   Animal reproduction may be *asexual* or *sexual.* Planarians and hydras can reproduce asexually. Planarians, *left,* split into two worms. Hydras, *middle,* grow from projections called *buds* on the parent. In sexual reproduction, *right,* a sperm cell fertilizes an egg, which develops into a new animal.

WORLD BOOK illustrations by Patricia Wynne

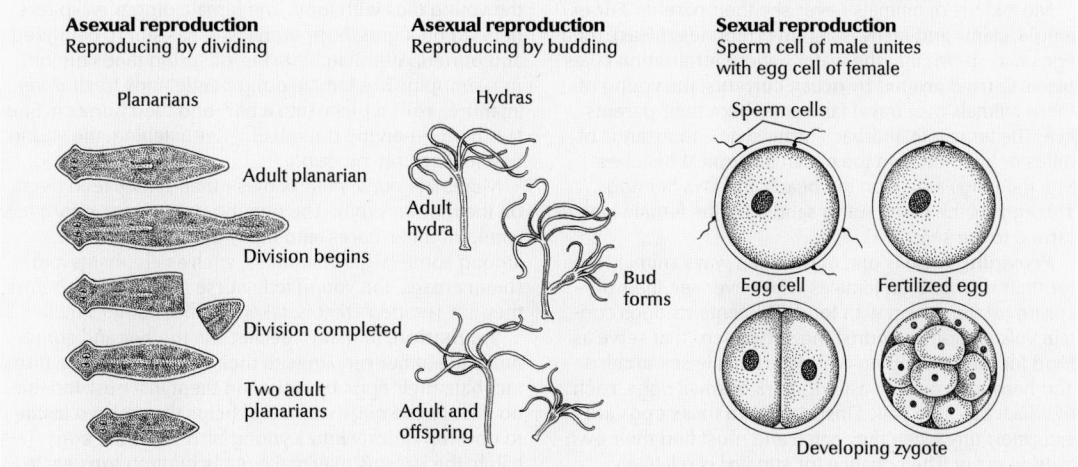

Asexual reproduction
Reproducing by dividing

Planarians

Adult planarian

Division begins

Division completed

Two adult planarians

Asexual reproduction
Reproducing by budding

Hydras

Adult hydra

Bud forms

Adult and offspring

Sexual reproduction
Sperm cell of male unites with egg cell of female

Sperm cells

Egg cell   Fertilized egg

Developing zygote

The courtship ritual of the albatross involves an elaborate dance between a male and female, *left*, before they mate. Through courtship rituals, animals can identify members of their own species for mating. In some cases, such rituals help them choose specific mates.

Frans Lanting, Photo Researchers

the female he wants for his mate. A male dance fly brings a dead insect to a female. She eats the insect while mating with the male. A male that does not bring a dead insect risks being eaten by the female.

Mating is dangerous for some male spiders and insects. In certain species of black widow spiders, females sometimes eat the males after mating. A female praying mantis may pounce unexpectedly on a male in her vicinity. Sometimes, she mates with a male and then eats him.

Regeneration. Some kinds of animals, mostly simple animals, can replace lost body parts by *regeneration.* If a sponge is broken into small pieces, some of the frag-

ments will grow into new sponges. Earthworms and their marine relatives can regenerate their heads or tails if those parts are broken off. Crabs and lobsters can grow new claws. Sea cucumbers sometimes throw out their intestines and other internal body parts to distract attackers. New parts grow back quickly.

Even some vertebrates can regenerate parts of their bodies. A salamander that loses a leg will grow a new one. Many salamanders can break off their tails to escape the grip of an enemy. These animals soon grow new tails. Mammals can regenerate hair, nails, and some other body tissues.

How animals raise their young

The newborn young of many species need no care from their parents. Even from birth, they can move about and find food on their own. The young of other species need parental care for some time after birth. One or both parents provide them with food and protection until they are old enough to manage for themselves.

Most kinds of animals never see their parents. For example, clams and many other invertebrates release their eggs and sperm into the water, where fertilization takes place. Carried around by ocean currents, the young of these animals may travel far from where their parents live. The female leatherback turtle swims thousands of miles or kilometers in the ocean to tropical beaches. She then digs a hole on the beach and lays her eggs. The eggs hatch in the warm sand after the female has returned to the sea.

Providing food is one of the main ways animals care for their young. Even females who never see their offspring provide them with food. The female's eggs contain yolk and other nourishing substances that serve as food for the developing embryos. Female sea urchins and herring produce vast numbers of small eggs, each of which has little yolk. Offspring from these eggs are extremely tiny when they hatch and must find their own food to grow. Their chance for survival is relatively

small. Female birds, on the other hand, lay only a few eggs, each with large amounts of yolk. Offspring from these eggs are relatively large and have a higher chance of survival.

Some animals that do not see their offspring provide their young with food in addition to that in the egg. Many flies lay their eggs on rotting fruits, which supply the young flies with food. The female digger wasp lays her egg on a grasshopper that she has stung, paralyzed, and buried. After hatching, her offspring feeds on the grasshopper. The female dung beetle finds fresh *dung* (manure), rolls a piece into a ball, and then buries it. She lays her egg on the dung ball. After hatching, the young beetle feeds on the dung.

Mammals *nurse* their babies—that is, they feed them on the mother's milk. The nursing period lasts only a few weeks in mice, hares, and many other species. But among some larger mammals, such as elephants and rhinoceroses, the young may nurse several years before they are *weaned*—that is, taken off the mother's milk.

Incubation. In many species, the mother and sometimes the father remain with their eggs and young. Birds incubate their eggs by sitting on them in a nest. Incubation keeps the eggs warm and helps the embryo inside to develop quickly into a young bird. After the eggs hatch, the parents may make many hunting trips each

Monkeys take good care of their babies. These crab-eating macaques show great affection for their young and train them carefully. Most monkeys fight fiercely to protect their babies.

B. Amadeus Rubel, Shostal

A baby wallaby stays in its mother's pouch until it can care for itself. Wallabies belong to a group of animals called *marsupials,* which give birth to extremely undeveloped young.

David Fleay

A male emperor penguin incubates an egg by holding it between his feet, protecting it from the Antarctic chill. Another male shelters a newly hatched chick between his feet.

© Fred Olivier, Nature Picture Library

day, trying to catch enough insects to feed the hungry *nestlings* (young birds). When the young are old enough to hunt, they leave the nest and fly away.

Among many species of birds, including pigeons and starlings, the parents take turns incubating the eggs. Among ducks, geese, and some other birds, the females are the only incubators. In most species of hornbills, the

Names of animals and their young

Animal	Male	Female	Young
Ant		queen	antling
Antelope	bull	doe	kid
Bear	boar	sow	cub
Cat*	tom	tabby	kitten
Cattle*	bull	cow	calf
Chicken	cock, rooster	hen	chick
Deer	buck, stag	doe	fawn
Dog	dog	bitch, dam	puppy, whelp
Dolphin	bull	cow	calf
Duck	drake	duck	duckling
Elephant	bull	cow	calf
Fox	renard, dog	vixen, bitch	kit, cub
Goat	billy, buck	nanny, doe	kid
Hog	boar	sow	piglet, shoat
Kangaroo	buck, boomer	doe, flier	joey
Lion	lion	lioness	cub
Sheep	buck, ram	dam, ewe	lamb, lambkin
Swan	cob	pen	cygnet
Tiger	tiger	tigress	cub
Turkey	cock, tom	hen	poult

*There are numerous alternate names for this animal and its young.

Fur seals start life in a group with many other pups and their mothers. Mother seals divide their time between eating at sea and nursing their pups on land. Each mother seal nurses and tends only her own young.

Karl W. Kenyon, NAS

female even imprisons herself inside a walled-up nest chamber to incubate eggs. The male passes food to the female through a tiny slit in the wall. In a few species of birds, the male does all the incubating. For example, a female emperor penguin lays a single egg, which the male then incubates on top of his toes. He tucks his toes and the egg under the fluffy feathers of his belly. When the egg hatches, the little penguin stays warm and grows in this cozy "nest."

Female pythons also incubate their eggs. They produce the heat to warm their eggs by twitching their muscles, much as people do when shivering. After the baby pythons hatch, they must find food and shelter on their own.

Providing shelter. Some species provide shelter for their young. A female lizard may lay her eggs in an underground nest, where they are hidden from predators. The huge nests of sociable weavers, a type of African bird, protect the baby birds from bad weather and enemies. Some frogs and fish build nests for their eggs and young. A few tropical frogs carry their tadpoles around on their backs until they find a safe pool of water for the young frogs.

Parents sometimes provide shelter for their offspring within their own bodies. The male seahorse carries the female's eggs in a pouch. When the young seahorses hatch, the male releases them from the pouch. Female kangaroos, koalas, opossums, wallabies, and other *marsupials* give birth to tiny, poorly developed offspring. The babies mature in a pouch on the mother's abdomen. There, they nurse and are protected by the mother. One kind of Australian frog swallows her eggs into her stomach, where they develop. After the eggs hatch, the female opens her mouth, and tadpoles and small froglets come out.

Providing protection. Parents often protect their young from enemies. A male stickleback fish will attack any predatory fish or insect that approaches its young. A female scorpion carries her babies on her back and defends them with the poisonous sting on the tip of her long tail. Female crocodiles guard their nests and will fight any predator that comes near. As young crocodiles begin to hatch, they cry out, and the female helps them dig out of the nest. She then gently picks them up in her jaws and carries them to a nearby pond. A female bear

Names of groups of animals

Animal	Group	Animal	Group
Bear	sloth	**Lion**	pride
Cat	clowder		troop
Dog	kennel	**Monkey**	troop
Donkey	pace	**Quail**	covey
Fox	skulk	**Seal**	herd
Frog	army		trip
Goose (in flight)	skein	**Toad**	knot
(on land or		**Whale**	herd
in water)	gaggle		pod
Kangaroo	herd	**Wolf**	pack
	mob		

will sometimes attack hikers who venture too close to her cubs. A female pet dog may attack even her owner if she fears that her puppies are threatened.

Group care. Some animals live together in groups of several families. As many as a hundred pairs of sociable weavers raise their chicks together in a large nest. Several female lions may care for their young cubs together. Naked mole rats live in underground colonies. One female produces offspring. Most of the other females help tend the young. Many monkeys and baboons live in small groups. All the adults in a group will work together to defend their young from an attacking leopard. When attacked by a wolf, a herd of musk oxen will protect their calves by placing them between adults.

Learning and play. Young animals may learn many things about the world from their parents. By watching what foods its parents eat and reject, a young animal can learn to recognize the kinds of foods that are safe. If young animals see their mother show fear of another type of animal or of certain locations, they learn to avoid those animals and places. Thus, they learn which types of animals, foods, and environments are safe and which are dangerous.

Many animals play while they are young. Lion cubs may try to pounce on the twitching tail of an adult lion. They also play with one another as though they were fighting. Such games help young animals develop coordination and strength. Play also helps them learn how to defend themselves and to fight effectively. In addition, it enables some animals to learn how to stalk and capture prey.

Animals' homes provide shelter from harsh weather or protection against enemies. Some animals have shelters that they use only once. Others make homes where they live for many years. However, a number of animals, such as fish that live in the ocean, spend their whole lives moving about. They never have homes.

A number of animals use caves, cracks in the ground, logs, plants, or rocks as temporary shelter. Garter snakes and many insects spend the night under rocks but leave this shelter the next day to hunt for food.

Some animals build their homes. Field mice collect dried grass and then construct a small nest under a protective log. Many birds and squirrels collect grass and twigs to build nests in the trees or on the ground. Gophers and moles dig burrows in the soil.

Home ranges. Most animals live within certain areas that form their *home range.* An animal's home range includes all the resources an animal needs to survive. By living within a specific area, an animal can learn where best to find food or shelter there.

The size of an animal's home range depends typically on the animal's size. Crickets and sea urchins have small home ranges. But elephants and lions may have home ranges that cover vast distances. Big animals require extensive home ranges to obtain the large amounts of food they need to survive.

Some animals defend their home ranges from other animals. A defended home range is called a *territory.* The song of a warbler, the hoot of an owl, or the roar of a lion warns other animals of their kind to stay away. Some animals use chemical warnings rather than sounds to ward off invaders from their own species. Intruders can easily smell the urine of wolves and the scent marks of cats and hyenas and know that a territory is already occupied. Often the intruder leaves without a

Dennis Green, Bruce Coleman Ltd.

A raven's nest is usually built on a cliff in late winter. The bird makes its nest out of sticks and lines it with bark, moss, cattle hair, wool, seaweed, grasses, or rabbit fur.

E. R. Degginger

A mountain lion's den is usually in a hidden, protected place. The animal may use a cave, a thicket, or a group of rocks.

Anthony Bannister, Animals Animals

A male antelope marks his territory by rubbing his face on plants within its borders. His facial glands release a fluid with a scent that warns other males to stay away.

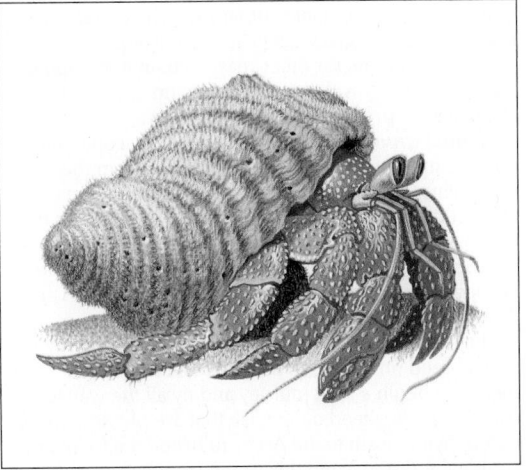

WORLD BOOK illustration by James Teason

A hermit crab's home is an empty sea snail shell. When the crab grows too large for the shell, it hunts for a larger one.

Meerkats live in colonies of up to 30 individuals. These burrowing animals of southern Africa leave their underground homes only during the day. Meerkats stand upright to watch for large birds that may attack them, *left*.

© Charles G. Summers, Jr., Tom Stack & Assoc.

fight. Sometimes, however, fights break out over territory, resulting in injury or death.

Group living. Many animals live in groups. Some groups, such as herds of elephants, remain together for many years. Others are small families that come together only during the breeding season. A mother and father bird may cooperate in raising their nestlings but may separate when the young leave the nest.

Wolf packs and some other animal groups have a social order called a *dominance hierarchy.* In such groups, every member has a certain rank in the hierarchy. High-ranking members are called *dominant individuals,* and low-ranking ones are known as *subordinate individuals.*

The dominant individuals have first choice of such resources as food and water. They also have their pick of mates. See **Dominance.**

Some groups are large and complex. Ants, bees, and termites live in huge colonies that consist of many thousands or even millions of individuals. The individuals in these colonies often have specific tasks. With honey bees, the *queen bee* is responsible for producing eggs. *Workers* search for pollen, make honey, and feed and care for the queen and her offspring. *Drones* do little but fertilize the queen's eggs.

Fish may form large schools in the open ocean. Herring schools may consist of hundreds of millions of fish.

Animal migration

Why animals migrate. The environment of some animals becomes extremely harsh at certain times of the year. In winter, for example, high mountains become bitterly cold. Snow and ice cover the peaks, and food becomes hard for animals to find. Some animals survive by hibernating. Others travel to places where the weather is milder and more food is available. The next spring, these animals return home. This type of regular round-trip journey is called a *migration.* Many animals that migrate live in the mountains or far from the equator. Migrating animals usually travel in large groups.

Animals migrate for other reasons than to escape cold weather. Some travel to favorite feeding areas or to special places to produce their young.

Animal travelers. Many birds make seasonal migrations. Some simply move short distances from the mountains to the valleys below. Others make remarkable long-distance journeys. In the fall, huge flocks of ducks and geese fly south for the winter. European white storks spend the spring and summer in northern Europe, where they breed and raise their young. They fly as far south as southern Africa for the winter.

The arctic tern is the champion long-distance traveler. Terns breed on islands in the Arctic Ocean. In late summer, they begin a long journey and fly all the way to Antarctica. They feed on the fish that are plentiful there before flying north to the Arctic to breed the following summer. A tern making this round trip may fly as many as 22,000 miles (35,400 kilometers).

Humpback whales and blue whales also make long

WORLD BOOK map

Repeated round-trip migrations are made by the European white stork. This bird lives in northern Europe in spring and summer. Every fall it flies to Africa over one of the routes on the map. The white stork returns to Europe by the same route.

migrations. They spend the summer in polar oceans, which have plentiful food. In the autumn, they swim toward the equator until they reach the warm tropical seas. There, the females that are pregnant give birth. Others mate and then give birth the next year. The warm waters provide a comfortable environment for the babies. The whales spend the winter in the tropics before returning to the polar feeding area in the spring.

Monarch butterflies and many other insects also migrate. When winter approaches, swarms of monarch butterflies travel from Canada and the northern United States to California and Florida. Some even fly as far south as southern Mexico. The butterflies begin the return trip in the spring, but few of the adults that flew south live long enough to complete it. Female monarchs lay eggs along the way back. The offspring, after maturing, continue the northward journey.

Some animals travel long distances to find a breeding site. The green sea turtle feeds along the east coast of South America. It then swims 1,200 miles (1,900 kilome-

ters) of open ocean to breed on Ascension Island, a small island in the middle of the Atlantic Ocean. When the baby turtles hatch, they swim to South America, where they may remain for many years. When they are mature, they swim back to Ascension Island and breed.

Most salmon live for years in ocean waters. When the time comes for them to *spawn* (lay their eggs), they travel thousands of miles or kilometers. The salmon swim to inland waters, where they produce their young. The adult salmon die before the young hatch.

Dangers of migration. Migrating animals may face a number of dangers, including new predators, during their long journeys. Some dangers come from human beings. For example, the fences that farmers use to corral their livestock prevent antelope from making their seasonal migrations. Farmers often shoot migrating animals that stop to feed on their crops. The draining of wetlands makes it harder for ducks and geese to find a safe place to rest and feed during migration. Some winter feeding areas are also being destroyed.

The origin and development of animals

Most scientists believe that all plant and animal species probably developed from a single form of life that arose about 3 ½ billion years ago. The basic life form gradually changed so that through the centuries, millions of kinds of animals have come into being. Some kinds are still alive. Others are *extinct* (no longer living). All animals, whether living or extinct, are related to one another.

This set of ideas about how species change over time is called the theory of evolution. The theory is supported by a vast amount of evidence from many fields, and nearly all scientists consider the occurrence of evolution to be a scientific fact. However, many people reject the concept of evolution because it conflicts with their religious beliefs. The Biblical account of the Creation, for example, says that God took only a few days to create all living things essentially as they exist today.

This section uses evolutionary theory as the basis of a discussion of when some animals originated and how species undergo change. For a discussion of religion and evolution and for more information on evolution, see **Evolution**. For more information on creationism, see **Creationism**.

When animals appeared on the earth. Most scientists believe that Earth formed as a planet at least 4 ½ billion years ago. The first life forms were simple, single-celled organisms that appeared about 1 billion years later. More complex animals and plants gradually evolved from these simple organisms. Many groups of invertebrates arose about 650 million years ago. The first vertebrates—fish—developed about 500 million years ago, and the first mammals appeared more than 200 million years ago.

Another way of looking at these times is to imagine the history of life on Earth in terms of a single year. Start with the formation of Earth on New Year's Day, January 1. Simple single-celled organisms were the first types of living things. They would not appear until March 22. Many invertebrates would not show up until November 9. Fish would evolve from their invertebrate ancestors

about November 20. Mammals would appear on December 16. Monkeys and apes would not be found until December 28. Human beings would appear only a few minutes before the end of the year, on December 31.

For more information on when various types of animals appeared on Earth, see **Earth** (History of Earth).

How new species are formed. Scientists consider groups of animals to represent distinct species when they become so different that they cannot produce fertile offspring together. Imagine a group of birds that lived only on one island. Then imagine that a few individuals got lost in a storm and landed on a different island. The two groups, now separated from each other, may gradually develop different traits as they adapt to different environments. If they become dissimilar enough, they cannot produce fertile offspring if they mate. They are then two separate species. This process can repeat itself many times over many millions of years, resulting in great numbers of species.

How species change. The individuals of any given species are not the same. Some individuals are larger, some are darker, some tolerate heat better, and some are stronger. Some individuals have traits that make them better able than others of their species to survive and reproduce in their environment. Over long periods, those animals will produce more young that survive than will individuals with less desirable traits. The offspring of the better-suited species will probably share some of the desirable traits of their parents. For example, dark moths will be well hidden in a shady forest. More of their offspring will probably survive than will those of lighter moths, which may be easily seen and eaten by hungry predators. In the next generation, more moths in the forest will be dark. This process, which causes the traits of animal groups in nature to change through time, is called *natural selection*. See **Natural selection**.

Why species become extinct. Scientists estimate that, left to natural processes, most species of animals live 1 million to 10 million years before becoming extinct. Natural causes that lead to the extinction of animals include drastic changes in climate and failure of a species to compete with other animals for food. For example, the dinosaurs died out rather suddenly about 65 million years ago. Many scientists believe that dinosaurs became extinct because of a rapid change in climate caused by the impact of a large asteroid. The dinosaurs were unable to survive in these new conditions.

Some human activities also cause animals to become extinct. Such activities are discussed in the next section of this article. For more information on why animals become extinct, see **Extinction.**

The future of animals

Most scientists believe that we are living in a period of mass extinction. Hundreds of species of vertebrate animals have become extinct during the last 200 years. Most of these species became extinct as a result of human activities. Thousands of other species have become *endangered* (in danger of going extinct). But today, more and more people around the world are working to preserve the variety of animal life for future generations.

How human beings endanger animals

Destruction of habitat. When people build cities or cut down forests to obtain wood or to clear land for farming or grazing, they destroy the habitats that animals need to survive. For example, grizzly bears and mountain lions once roamed freely where the city of San Francisco now stands. But a wild grizzly bear or mountain lion could not survive in San Francisco today.

The habitats of animals in tropical forests are particularly threatened today. People are rapidly cutting down these forests to obtain such valuable hardwoods as mahogany and teak. They also are clearing the land to plant crops or to create rangeland. However, soils in such areas are not very fertile, and farms there produce crops for only a few years. To continue farming in such areas, people have to keep cutting down more of the forests to create new farmland. By the early 2000's, much of the world's tropical forests had already been destroyed.

Many scientists and other people are especially concerned about the destruction of tropical forests. They point out that these forests have more *biodiversity*—that is, a greater variety of plant and animal species—than

any other place. One square mile (2.6 square kilometers) of forest in South America may have more species of birds and insects than many countries do. In fact, biologists discovered a single tree in a tropical forest in Brazil that supported 82 species of ants. That is about twice as many ant species as live in the entire United Kingdom.

Even though many types of plant and animal life can be found in one place in the tropics, the total range of some tropical species is extremely small. As a result, when a large area of forest is cleared, all the members of some species are killed.

Pollution can also destroy animals and their habitats. Agricultural chemicals and industrial wastes sometimes drain into ponds and streams and kill the plants and animals there. Factories, power plants, and vehicles create air pollution by burning such fossil fuels as coal and oil. Such pollution has seriously damaged forests and wildlife. *Acid rain*—rainfall with a high concentration of sulfuric and nitric acids due to air pollution—kills fish and other animals.

An increase in carbon dioxide in the atmosphere presents a long-term threat to animals and habitats. Many factories, power plants, and vehicles release carbon dioxide into the air. Forest trees and plants help absorb this gas, but as more of them are cut down, carbon dioxide levels rise. Most scientists believe that higher amounts of carbon dioxide in the atmosphere speed up global warming caused by the phenomenon called the *greenhouse effect.* Rapid global warming could destroy many kinds of plants and animals and flood large areas. See **Global warming.**

W. K. Fletcher, Photo Researchers

Destroying a forest results in the loss of habitat for many animal species. Animals that live in tropical forests have become especially threatened today. People cut down these forests to obtain wood and fuel and to clear land for farms, rangeland, and cities. This photograph shows a logging operation in a tropical rain forest in Malaysia.

Introduction of new species into an area can have harmful consequences. Such species may spread rapidly in their new environment and become *invasive.* In the mid-1800's, for example, people introduced rabbits into the wild in Australia for hunting. But the rabbits had no natural enemies there, and their population grew quickly, spreading over most of the continent. Partly because of the rapid spread of rabbits, rabbit-eared bandicoots, which are native to Australia, disappeared from many areas of the continent. These bandicoots had to compete with rabbits for burrow space. The traps and poisons people set out for rabbits also killed the bandicoots.

Humans may unintentionally introduce invasive species to an area. Zebra mussels are shellfish native to the Caspian Sea region between Europe and Asia. During the late 1900's, zebra mussel larvae were unintentionally released into the North American Great Lakes in *ballast water,* the water kept in a ship's hold to keep the vessel stable. Today, the mussels are a major pest in North America. The explosive growth of zebra mussels may threaten the food supply of many fish and shellfish species native to the Great Lakes. See **Zebra mussel.**

Hunting and fishing. In many parts of the world, people depend on native animals for food or medicine. However, overhunting and overfishing has led to the decline and even extinction of various animal species. Such activities have proven especially destructive during the past 200 years. Overhunting contributed to the extinction of such animals as the great auk, the passenger pigeon, and the Steller's sea cow. Formerly plentiful fish species, such as the Atlantic cod, have become threatened partly due to overfishing.

Human population growth. The human population is growing rapidly. Such growth may place additional pressure on natural habitats and their species. People will need more land for food and housing. Industrial activities will probably increase to process the food and manufacture the goods needed by the growing population. Many such activities cause pollution that can damage or destroy habitats. Also, increased global trade and travel will spread more and more invasive species. For more information on why animals become endangered, see **Endangered species.**

How human beings protect animals

Since the late 1800's, people have become increasingly concerned about vanishing wildlife. Such concerns have resulted in part from a growing awareness of the interconnectedness of species—the web of life. More people now recognize that the disappearance of large numbers of species threatens the survival of other living things, including human beings. People who help protect habitats and animals are called *conservationists.*

Protected areas. Many countries have created national parks, game reserves, and wildlife refuges. In these areas, habitats are protected from development and hunting is banned. Many conservationists believe such areas may represent the last hope for saving some threatened species in the wild. Yellowstone National Park in the United States provides a home for rare grizzly bears, bison, bald eagles, and trumpeter swans. The African elephant and black rhinoceros are protected in parks and reserves in African savannas. Unfortunately, however, many protected areas are too small to ensure

Stephen J. Krasemann, Nature Conservancy from Photo Researchers

People protect some animals by raising them in captivity. The peregrine falcon chick in this picture is receiving a meal. Peregrine falcons are rare or absent in many of their former habitats.

the survival of certain large species within their borders. Large animals often need lots of room to roam.

Laws protect wildlife in many countries. Under the U.S. Endangered Species Act of 1973, officials keep an up-to-date list of species in danger of extinction. The act prohibits federal projects that would destroy the habitat of an endangered species. This act was later amended to require anyone who wants to develop or change a habitat occupied by an endangered species to show that the planned changes will not harm that species.

Government agencies also determine the number of certain game animals that can be hunted and fished each season. If an animal starts to become rare, the agencies can reduce the number of that species that can be taken legally. The population of the species then has an opportunity to recover.

Habitat restoration. Human beings destroy habitats, but they also try to restore them. Trees cleared by logging can be replanted, re-creating habitat for forest creatures. People can remove dams from rivers and restore wetlands. Parks in cities can provide homes for wildlife.

Breeding in captivity. Some species have become so rare that scientists believe the only hope of saving them is to breed them in captivity. For example, many of the surviving California condors live in zoos in the United States. A condor chick raised in captivity has a better chance of survival than one in nature does. As the number of condors has grown, biologists have reintroduced some of the birds back into the wild. Other endangered species being bred in captivity include the Arabian oryx and the whooping crane.

Despite conservation efforts, the future of wildlife remains uncertain. The human population continues to grow. Forests and grasslands are still being destroyed. People continue to hunt African elephants, snow leopards, and other vanishing species. Air pollution, acid rain, water pollution, and climate change also still threaten wild animals.   Raymond B. Huey and W. Herbert Wilson, Jr.

A classification of the animal kingdom

Scientists classify animals chiefly according to the animals' ancestry. Those with a common ancestor nearer in time are more closely related than those who share an ancestor further back in time. Closely related animals share certain unique features, some of which occur only during early stages in their life cycle. Scientists arrange animals into major groups called *phyla* (singular *phylum)*. The table below lists some of the phyla and certain important features of their members. See **Classification, Scientific** (table: How animals are classified).

Phylum	Characteristics	Example
Porifera (Sponges)	Sponges attach themselves to rocks and other objects at the bottom of oceans, lakes, or rivers. Many take the shape of such objects. Sponges have cells called *choanocytes* or *collar cells* that trap food particles within chambers in their bodies.	 Vase sponge
Cnidaria (Cnidarians or coelenterates)	Cnidarians may be shaped like a cylinder, a bell, or an umbrella. Their bodies contain a jellylike material between two layers of cells. This phylum includes jellyfish, sea fans, sea anemones, and corals.	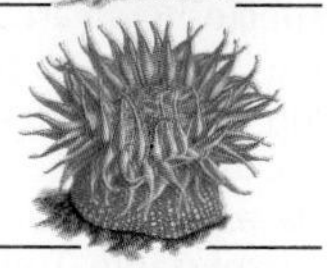 Sea anemone
Ctenophora (Comb jellies or sea walnuts)	These transparent animals live in oceans. They have eight bands of comblike organs on the side of their bodies. Most are pea-sized to thimble-sized. Comb jellies of a group called *Venus' girdle* can measure over 3 feet (90 centimeters) long.	Venus' girdle 
Platyhelminthes (Flatworms)	Many flatworms live as parasites in other animals. Flatworms have soft, thin, flattened bodies with three layers of cells. Most are less than 1 inch (2.5 centimeters) long. The largest flatworms, called *tapeworms*, grow as long as 100 feet (30 meters). Some flatworms cause such diseases as schistosomiasis.	 Planarian
Nemertea (Ribbon worms or proboscis worms)	Almost all ribbon worms live in the oceans. They have a slender, often flattened, body. The worms shoot out a *proboscis* (tubelike structure) from their head to capture prey. Some species can inject poison from the proboscis into their prey. Most of these worms range from less than 1 inch (2.5 centimeters) to 8 inches (20 centimeters) long, but one species can reach a length of 100 feet (30 meters).	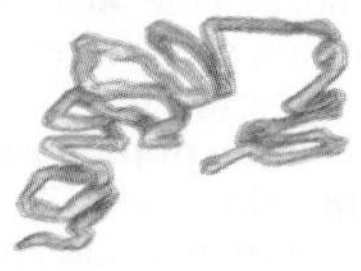 Bootlace worm
Rotifera (Rotifers or "wheel animals")	Rotifers live in lakes, rivers, streams, and the oceans. They have cylinder- or vase-shaped bodies. On their heads are circles of hairlike projections known as *cilia.* The largest rotifers are about $\frac{1}{10}$ inch (3 millimeters) long.	*Brachionus calyciflorus* 
Acanthocephala (Spiny-headed worms)	These parasites live in many animals. They have a spiny, tubelike proboscis on their head that attaches them to the wall of their hosts' intestines. Most species measure about ¾ inch (2 centimeters) or less in length.	 *Leptorynchoides thecatus*
Nematoda (Roundworms or nematodes)	Many roundworms live in soil, water, or dead tissue. Some are parasites that are found in living plants and animals. Roundworms range from microscopic to about 3 feet (90 centimeters) long. The phylum includes filariae, hookworms, pinworms, and trichinae. Parasitic species cause such human diseases as trichinosis, elephantiasis, and filariasis.	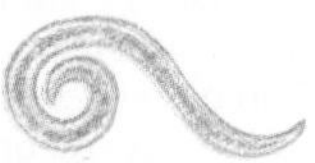 Hookworm
Mollusca (Mollusks)	Mollusks make up the largest group of water animals, though some species live on land. Most mollusks have a hard shell that protects a soft body. The phylum includes clams, mussels, octopuses, oysters, snails, and squids.	 Snail
Annelida (Segmented worms)	The bodies of these worms consist of segments. Many of these worms have tentacles on their head and a pair of leglike projections called *parapodia* on each body segment. Earthworms and leeches belong to this phylum.	Earthworm 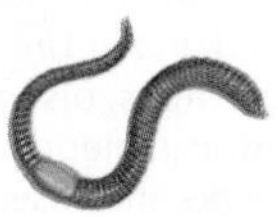

Arthropoda
(Arthropods)

Arthropods have jointed legs, segmented bodies, and an outside shell called an *exoskeleton*. This phylum includes insects, such as ants, bees, beetles, and butterflies; crustaceans, such as crabs, lobsters, and shrimps; arachnids, such as mites, ticks, and spiders; centipedes; and millipedes.

Beetle

Bryozoa
(Bryozoans)

Bryozoans live in water, and most form colonies. Some colonies are jellylike masses. Others form branchlike networks on water plants. Bryozoans have a boxlike or tube-shaped body that holds fluid. *Tentacles* (feelers) cluster on the head.

Bowing
ectoproct

Brachiopoda
(Lamp shells)

Lamp shells have two hard shells that cover a soft body. They live in the oceans. Some attach themselves to rocks and other hard surfaces. Others burrow or lie loose in sand or mud.

Lamp shell

Chaetognatha
(Arrow worms)

These worms have an arrow shape. They range from about ¼ to 6 inches (0.5 to 15 centimeters) long. They have movable hooks on their heads that they use to catch prey. They live in open seas, particularly in warm waters.

Arrow worm

Echinodermata
(Echinoderms)

Echinoderms are spiny-skinned animals that have an internal skeleton made of calcium. They are the only animals that possess tiny tubelike structures called tube feet. This phylum includes brittle stars, sand dollars, sea cucumbers, sea urchins, and starfish.

Starfish

Chordata
(Chordates)

At some point in their life cycle, all chordates have a *notochord* (a rodlike, flexible cord that runs down the back of the body). A hollow nerve tube runs above the notochord. This phylum is the one to which human beings and many familiar animals belong. It includes amphibians, birds, mammals, and reptiles, as well as hagfishes, lampreys, and bony fishes.

WORLD BOOK illustrations by John D. Dawson; Alex Ebel; John F. Eggert; Alan Male, Linden Artists Ltd.; Donald Moss; Peter Snowball; James Teason

Coelacanth

Trout

Manta ray

Hagfish

Lamprey

Frog

Turtle

Parrot

Bear, seal, monkey

Related articles in *World Book* include:

The study of animals

Biology	Ecology	Marine biology
Classification,	Entomology	Ornithology
Scientific	Ethology	Paleontology
Comparative	Gnotobiotics	Sociobiology
psychology	Herpetology	Zoology
Developmental	Ichthyology	
biology		

Groups of animals

Amphibian	Fish	Reptile
Arachnid	Herbivore	Rotifer
Arthropod	Insect	Ruminant
Bird	Invertebrate	Sponge
Carnivore	Mammal	Vertebrate
Cnidarian	Mollusk	Viviparous animal
Cold-blooded	Omnivore	Warm-blooded
animal	Oviparous animal	animal
Crustacean	Parasite	Worm
Echinoderm	Primate	

Individual animals

World Book has hundreds of separate articles on specific animals. Many are listed below.

Cnidarians

Coral	Portuguese man-of-war
Hydra	Sea anemone
Jellyfish	

Worms

Earthworm	Horsehair worm	Ribbon worm
Eelworm	Leech	Roundworm
Filaria	Lugworm	Tapeworm
Flatworm	Pinworm	Trichina
Fluke	Planarian	Vinegar eel
Hookworm		

Echinoderms

Brittle star	Sea lily
Sand dollar	Sea urchin
Sea cucumber	Starfish

Mollusks

Abalone	Geoduck	Periwinkle
Argonaut	Giant squid	Scallop
Chiton	Limpet	Shipworm
Clam	Mussel	Slug
Cockle	Nautilus	Snail
Conch	Octopus	Squid
Cowrie	Oyster	Whelk
Cuttlefish		

Crustaceans

Barnacle	Fiddler crab	Shrimp
Blue crab	Hermit crab	Water flea
Crab	Krill	Wood louse
Crayfish	Lobster	

Arachnids

Black widow	Mite	
Brown recluse	Scorpion	
Chigger	Spider	
Daddy longlegs	Tarantula	
Deer tick	Tick	
House spider	Trap-door spider	

Insects

For a list of separate articles on insects, see the *Related articles* at the end of the **Insect** article.

Fish

For a list of separate articles on fishes, see the *Related articles* at the end of the **Fish** article.

Amphibians

Bullfrog	Mudpuppy	Tadpole
Caecilian	Newt	Toad
Frog	Salamander	Tree frog
Midwife toad	Surinam toad	

Reptiles

See **Lizard** and **Snake**, with their lists of *Related articles*. See also the following articles:

Alligator	Terrapin
Crocodile	Tortoise
Gavial	Turtle

Birds

For a list of separate articles on birds, see the *Related articles* at the end of the **Bird** article.

Mammals

See the following general articles and the lists of *Related articles* at the ends of these articles:

Antelope	Horse
Ape	Human being
Bat	Marsupial
Bear	Monkey
Camel	Ox
Cat	Rabbit
Cattle	Raccoon
Cetacean	Rodent
Deer	Sheep
Dog	Sirenia
Edentate	Ungulate
Goat	Weasel
Hog	Whale

Extinct and prehistoric animals

See **Dinosaur**, with its list of *Related articles*. See also the following articles:

Archaeopteryx	Mastodon
Dodo	Moa
Elephant bird	Passenger pigeon
Eryops	Prehistoric animal
Extinction	Pterosaur
Ground sloth	Saber-toothed cat
Hesperornis	Trilobite
Mammoth	

The history of animal life

Adaptation
Earth (History of Earth)
Endangered species
Evolution
Fossil
Heredity
Life
Natural selection

Animal habitats

For a general discussion of animal habitats, see the articles on **Biome**, **Environment**, and **Habitat**. See also:

Desert	Prairie	Steppe
Forest	Rain forest	Swamp
Marsh	Savanna	Tundra
Mountain	Seashore	Wetland
Ocean		

Animal traits and behavior

Biological clock	Mimicry
Dominance	Pheromone
Estivation	Play (behavior)
Growth	Protective coloration
Hibernation	Reproduction
Instinct	Sleep (Sleep in animals)
Metamorphosis	Sound (Animal sounds)
Migration	Territoriality

Additional resources

Level I
Animals: A Visual Encyclopedia. DK Pub., 2008. *Animals Alive.* 2011.
Burton, Maurice and Robert. *International Wildlife Encyclopedia.* 22 vols. 3rd ed. Cavendish, 2002.
McGhee, Karen, and McKay, George. *Encyclopedia of Animals.* National Geographic Soc., 2007.
Wild Animal Atlas. National Geographic Soc., 2010.

Level II
Bambaradeniya, Channa, and others. *The Illustrated Atlas of Wildlife.* Univ. of Calif. Pr., 2009.
Breed, Michael D., and Moore, Janice, eds. *Encyclopedia of Animal Behavior.* 3 vols. Elsevier, 2010.
Grzimek's Animal Life Encyclopedia. 17 vols. 2nd ed. Gale Group, 2003-2004.
Macdonald, David W., ed. *The Princeton Encyclopedia of Mammals.* Princeton, 2009.

Animal, Extinct. See Extinction.

Animal, Prehistoric. See Prehistoric animal.

Animal experimentation is the use of animals in biological, medical, and psychological studies. Human beings and many animals have similar organ systems and body processes. Experiments on animals thus help scientists learn how the human body works. Animal experimentation has played a part in many major medical advances. These advances include the development of antibiotics, vaccines, and surgical techniques.

People have experimented with animals for hundreds of years. But the practice did not become widespread until the late 1800's.

Animal experimentation produces considerable benefits to people. But it often results in the suffering and death of animals. Because of this, animal experimentation is a highly controversial issue. Animal experimentation that involves performing surgery on live animals is called *vivisection.* People opposed to this and other forms of animal experimentation are sometimes called *antivivisectionists.*

Mice and rats account for about 85 percent of the animals used. Scientists also use amphibians, birds, cats, dogs, fish, guinea pigs, hamsters, insects, monkeys, and rabbits. In addition, educators use animals to teach students about anatomy, biology, *physiology* (how living things function), and surgery.

Reasons for experimentation. Medical researchers study animals to gain a better understanding of body processes in humans and animals. They use animals to study the causes and effects of illnesses, such as cancer and heart disease. In addition, they use animals to develop and test drugs, surgical techniques, and other medical therapies. Scientists use animals to test the safety of ingredients in products that come into close contact with people. Such products include cosmetics, disinfectants, and food additives. In many countries, the law requires that new chemicals be tested for safety using animals. Psychologists observe the behavior of animals under a variety of conditions. They study animal learning and memory to better understand how the brain works.

Controversy. Some people have called for an end to all animal experimentation. They believe either that such research is morally wrong or that the benefits gained are trivial compared with the costs in animal suffering. Some also claim that humans and animals are not comparable, so the results of animal experiments are meaningless. Others accept the need to use animals in research but oppose animal testing of products with no scientific value, such as cosmetics and perfumes. Many people argue for stricter laws to prevent the mistreatment of laboratory animals. Critics of animal experimentation also believe that scientists should more thoroughly investigate other research methods. These methods include test-tube experiments on bacteria or on bits of human or animal tissue. Other alternatives include the use of computer models of living systems.

Most scientists, on the other hand, argue that without animal experimentation, they could not continue to make significant progress in medicine and other sciences. They claim that experiments are designed to keep animal suffering to a minimum. Studies are planned so that researchers use only the minimum number of animals needed. Experiments are carried out without using animals whenever possible. However, methods that do not involve animals are not always adequate. For example, testing a drug on isolated tissues or organs will not show how it affects the body as a whole.

The "three R's." Most researchers who use animals in experiments follow principles called the "three R's." The three R's are (1) reduction, (2) refinement, and (3) replacement. Reduction refers to the use of as few animals as possible. Refinement refers to efforts to minimize the pain and distress of animals. Replacement refers to the use of alternatives to animal experimentation when possible. The three R's have been widely adopted internationally. They have been incorporated into the laws and regulations of many countries.

Laws and regulations. In the United States, the Animal Welfare Act of 1966 requires scientists to provide adequate food and shelter for certain kinds of laboratory animals. Many private and government agencies that provide funds to research institutions regulate experimentation. For example, the National Institutes of Health, a federal agency, requires each institution it funds to set up a committee to oversee the use and care of the animals. In Australia, Canada, and many European countries, such animal ethics committees are required by law. They usually consist of researchers, experts on laboratory animals, and in some cases, animal rights advocates.   Paul Flecknell

Animal husbandry. See Livestock.

Animal rights movement refers to organized efforts opposing the use of animals for research, food, clothing, and human entertainment. People who support animal rights point out that most animals feel pain and distress and many show reasoning ability. They argue that, because of these qualities, animals deserve greater moral consideration and legal protections than human beings generally give them.

Most people agree that human beings have some obligations to animals, but they also believe that people can use animals for certain purposes. For example, they argue that research on a few animals can save many human lives.

Animal rights activists, also called animal rightists, focus on various projects. Some work to outlaw laboratory experiments on animals. Others teach that human beings do not need to eat animals for survival. Many activists protest the use of fur coats or leather products. They also oppose hunting and spectator sports in which animals may be treated inhumanely, such as bullfighting and dog racing.

The animal rights movement developed out of the animal protection, or animal welfare, movement. These movements have slightly different opinions on how animals may be used. The animal protection movement tends to accept the need to raise animals for food and to use them in some research as long as they receive proper care and do not suffer. In contrast, the animal rights movement opposes any use of animals that causes suffering or death. Public opinion polls show that most people agree with the less radical animal protection movement.

Organizations that protect animals typically run local shelters and rescue groups. They also raise millions of dollars each year. People for the Ethical Treatment of Animals (PETA) ranks as the world's largest animal rights group. PETA has recruited many celebrities to help it challenge the use of animals for food, clothing, and research. Major animal protection organizations include the Humane Society of the United States and the World Society for the Protection of Animals.

The animal protection movement began to attract large numbers of supporters at the end of the 1800's. It declined during and after World War I (1914-1918) but began to reemerge after World War II (1939-1945). The 1950's saw the establishment of several new animal protection organizations, as well as the expansion of existing groups. During the 1970's, the animal rights movement grew out of the animal protection movement. Both movements have expanded dramatically since the 1980's.

Andrew N. Rowan

See also **Animal experimentation; Humane society; People for the Ethical Treatment of Animals; Society for the Prevention of Cruelty to Animals.**

Animal worship is the practice of worshiping or honoring animals. Many societies worship animals because they believe that everything in nature has a soul. This belief is called *animism*. A hunting society may worship an animal to gain its good will, to apologize for killing it, or to get the animal's qualities, such as speed or strength.

Many Indians of northern North America worshiped animals as part of a belief known as *totemism*. Each group had its own sacred symbol called a *totem*. Most totems were animals. Many groups considered themselves descendants of their totem animal. Some people worship a god believed to have taken the form of an animal. For example, the ancient Egyptian god Thoth sometimes appeared as a baboon and sometimes as a wading bird called an ibis.   Sarah M. Pike

See also **Animism; Totem.**

Shrek (2001) is one of the most popular animated motion pictures ever made. The computer-generated comedy tells about a green ogre named Shrek, who falls in love with the Princess Fiona. Other characters are Shrek's wisecracking donkey and the ogre's rival for Fiona, Lord Farquaad.

Animation

Animation is a visual technique that creates the illusion of motion, rather than recording motion through live action. The technique is used mainly for motion pictures and video games. Animation can be created by illustrators, filmmakers, video makers, and computer specialists. Advertisers also employ animation to develop commercials for television. In addition, producers of instructional films may use animation to help explain a difficult idea or one that could not be shown in live action. Animation can also be combined with live action in a movie.

In the past, in making an animated film, a filmmaker would photograph a series of drawings or objects one by one. Each drawing or object takes up one frame of the film. The position of a character or scene changes slightly from frame to frame. When the film is shown through a projector, the pictures appear to move.

Animation can exist with little technology. One simple animation device is the *flip book*, a group of sketches in sequence placed one on top of the other. When a viewer flips the pages rapidly, the images appear to move.

Since the late 1900's, however, *digital technology* has dominated animation. Digital technology includes computers and other types of electronic equipment and ap-

The contributors of this article, John Canemaker and Peter Weishar, are animators who have both written widely on the art of animation. Canemaker is head of the animation program at New York University's Tisch School of the Arts. Weishar is Dean of Film and Digital Media at the Savannah College of Art and Design.

plications that use information in the form of numeric code. Digital technology can add to or replace traditional techniques by creating animation partly or entirely using a computer. Computers have become so common in film, video, and animation production that almost every moving image made today is generated on a computer to some extent.

Through the digital revolution, animators have many technical choices available when they create a movie. Digital technology has made possible greater realism, more exciting special effects, and more elaborate fantasy stories. However, technology alone does not attract or entertain audiences. An interesting story and appealing characters will always be necessary.

This article will discuss the preliminary steps in creating an animated film, the different paths followed by traditional hand-drawn animation and by computer animation, and the history of animation.

Preliminary steps in animation

The use of computers has brought great changes to animation production. But several processes remain the same in both traditional and digital methods.

The first step in making any animated film is creating a story. After a story has been established, an artist and writer prepare a *storyboard*, which serves as the film's script. The storyboard resembles a giant comic strip. It consists of rough sketches that portray the action of the story, with the dialogue accompanying each sketch.

After the director and other key personnel approve the storyboard, performers make a recording of the dialogue and any music that must be *synchronized* (matched) with the action. The composer and performers carefully follow the storyboard to make sure the music and dialogue match each sequence of the action.

Animators synchronize animation to sound using a guide called an *exposure sheet*. The sheet indicates the number of frames needed to express each movement and each word of the recorded dialogue. In computer animation, the artist "digitizes" the sounds so they can be played back as well as visually graphed on the computer screen. Material is digitized by translating it from its original form into a format that a computer can read, electric charges representing numbers.

Up to this point, both computer-animated and traditionally drawn animated productions follow a similar path. But now traditional animation and computer animation diverge.

Traditional animation

In traditional animation, layout artists work with the director to determine what settings will be drawn, how each character will act and look, and how the action can best be broken down into scenes. After these decisions have been made, the layout artists prepare drawings to guide two other groups of artists, called *background artists* and *animators*.

The background artists draw all the backgrounds for the film—that is, everything that will appear on the screen except the characters. The animators make separate drawings of the characters. Working from the exposure sheet, the animators must create the exact number of drawings required by the action and dialogue. In one episode, for example, a character may answer the telephone by saying "Hello." The exposure sheet shows that the word "Hello" requires eight frames. The animators thus must make eight drawings in which the character's mouth moves in sequence to form the word. They must also include all the character's body movements.

In the past, after the animators completed their drawings, another group of artists traced the drawings onto clear sheets of celluloid acetate called *cels*. Tens of thousands of separate cels in sequence were required for a feature-length animation movie, and a lesser number were needed for many television cartoons.

A painting department applied colors to the reverse

Traditional animation Groups of artists, each with separate responsibilities, develop an animated film through thousands of drawings that create the backgrounds and characters which will make up the completed movie.

An artist called an *animator* makes separate drawings of each character, creating the exact number of drawings required to portray all the movements required by the action and dialogue.

Other artists trace the animator's drawings onto clear sheets of celluloid acetate called *cels*. A painting department then applies the necessary colors to the reverse side of the cels, *shown here*.

The finished cels are placed over backgrounds drawn by background artists, *shown here*. Backgrounds also can be scanned and painted on a computer and combined with the characters.

WORLD BOOK photos by John R. Hamilton, Globe Photos

The completed cels are sent to the camera department, where camera operators photograph the cels frame by frame over the proper background, *shown here*. Then the sound track is added.

side of the cels. The completed cels were then sent to the camera department, where camera operators photographed the cels frame by frame over the proper background. The exposure sheets told the camera operator which cels and backgrounds were needed for each frame. After the camera operators completed the photography, the sound track was added. Finally, the studio made prints of the film and released it.

Today, most hand-drawn animated productions use photoelectric devices called *scanners* to translate the drawings from their original form into a format that a computer can read. Artists can then ink and paint the drawings on the computer. The backgrounds are also scanned and painted on the computer and combined with the characters.

Computer animation

The most popular form of animation is called a *computer-generated image* (CGI) or just *computer graphics* (CG). Almost every modern film, video, and animation production uses computers to create at least some images. CGI can create the illusion of entire three-dimensional worlds as models inside a computer. These models can include trees, grass, and even weather that interact with believable, but entirely digital, characters.

Generating animation on a computer can be complex. Since the 1980's, the artists in the computer animation and effects industry have become more specialized. Some artists concentrate on modeling figures on the computer and designing *virtual* sets—that is, artificial sets created on a computer. Others concentrate on special effects, such as fire, rain, smoke, and even hair. A computer animator can create such effects by running *dynamic simulation* software. In a dynamic simulation, software calculates the physics of how objects or characters would move and react in the real world and then turns them into computer animation. For example, in a dynamic simulation of marbles pouring out of a cup, the software would figure out the collisions, bouncing, and rolling of the marbles. Without dynamic simulation, an animator would have to spend many hours determining the movement of each marble.

Modeling. To create a character using CGI animation, most designers start with a series of detailed sketches, often along with a small-scale physical model known as a *maquette*. Animators use these aids to study and refine the character from all angles. A CGI artist will then use computer software to create a digital model of the character. This model is not a photograph. It is a three-dimensional computer "sculpture," made of data, that can be viewed from all sides. The digital modeling process can be relatively quick for simple objects. However, a professional computer modeler can spend three or four months building a single character model for a feature production.

Making the model move. After the digital character model is approved, it goes to the *rigging department*. Just as a boat is "rigged" so a sailor can pull ropes to turn and unfurl the sails, a CGI character is rigged so it will move correctly. An artist called a *rigger* creates a computer model called a *skeleton* with "bones" connecting pivot points, called *joints*. The joints are placed wherever the model is expected to rotate or bend. The rigger also sets up a series of restraints on these pivots

so the joints move correctly. For example, the fingers on a hand should curl forward, not backward or sideways. The fingers should also stop when they meet the palm of the hand. The rigger often creates dozens of controls to make it easier for the animators to manipulate the character. The skeletons, restraints, and controls are invisible when the final image is generated.

If the character has a speaking part, a rigger poses the face into many different expressions. The rigger labels the expressions (such as "happy" or "sad") and then saves them on the computer. Mouth shapes are saved as well. When people speak, they make many distinct mouth shapes, such as a circle for an "oh" sound or closed lips for an "em." These shapes correspond to basic sounds of language called *phonemes*. An animator will then *lip-synch,* using the library of phonemes and expressions to match the digitized dialogue track. The correct shapes and expressions create a realistic speaking character.

A common method of computer animation called *keyframe animation* begins when the animator poses the model at different points along a timeline. These poses are known as "key poses" or "keyframes." Each keyframe pose will take up a single frame in the final animation. The computer then *interpolates* (inserts) directions for how the character will move between the frames. The interpolation will determine the smoothest path between the two poses. To make an animation look lifelike, an animator may rework a sequence of keyframes hundreds of times until the final animation looks right.

Another approach to computer modeling and animation is known as *motion capture*. Typically, small reflective dots (also called *pick ups)* are placed along many of a live actor's joints and other key body parts. The actor then moves within a circle of specialized cameras. These cameras record the actor's motion by tracking the dots through space and send the information, in digital form, to a computer. The animator applies the motion data to a computer-generated character, who will then move in the same general way as the live actor. Many video game makers use motion capture for character movement. Filmmakers often use the technique for creatures with humanlike facial expressions, such as Gollum in the trilogy "The Lord of the Rings" (2001-2003) and Caesar the chimpanzee in *Rise of the Planet of the Apes* (2011). *The Polar Express* (2004) and *The Adventures of Tintin* (2011) used motion capture for all of the movies' characters.

Lighting and rendering. The next steps in the computer animation production process are lighting and creating texture. An artist assigns a *shader* to every object in a computer-generated image. A shader is software code that determines the properties of a surface, such as color, transparency, or reflectivity, or whether it is shiny or dull, smooth or rough. Once the textures are applied to the objects, the frames are lit and *rendered*. In the rendering process, the computer calculates the effects of light, shadow, and color on each object and generates a digital picture of each frame. Rendering can require a lot of processing time on the computer. All major CGI animation studios have a network of computers known as *render farms* that can consist of hundreds of processors, all devoted to rendering. Computers also assist in editing the final images and the sound track.

Compositing. Computer-animated characters can be combined with live action or with other computer-

Computer animation   Computer animation is the leading animation technique. The photo sequence from the film *The Lord of the Rings: The Return of the King* shown here illustrates some of the steps required to create a single frame.

An actor stands on a partial set in front of a blue wall called a *blue screen*. The computer artist can select the blue in a software application and remove that color from the image, thus removing unwanted parts of the scene.

The actor and the set are *composited* (combined) with a computer-generated background.

The Lord of the Rings: The Return of the King © MMIII, New Line Productions, Inc. The Lord of the Rings characters, names, and places therein. ™ The Saul Zaentz Co. d/b/a Tolkien Enterprises under license to New Line Productions, Inc.

The final composited shot includes a model boat enlarged to look like a real sailing ship. Additional actors have been placed in the scene. Deeper shadows and a golden glow have also been added to make the shot appear outdoors at sunset.

animated characters and sets in a process called *compositing.* In compositing, two or more images are combined on one piece of film by photographic or digital means. Compositing can also be used to combine real actors with computer-generated sets and special effects. To do so, actors perform in front of a solid-color green or blue background called a *green screen* or a *blue screen.* A computer removes that single color around the actor's silhouette. The actor can then be *composited* (placed) onto another background, either a digital set that exists only in a computer or a "real" location.

Other kinds of animation

There are several kinds of animation besides hand-drawn and computer-generated animation. They include (1) stop-motion animation, (2) pixilation, (3) pin screen animation, and (4) drawing on film.

Stop-motion animation, also called *puppet animation,* uses three-dimensional figures or objects. To make puppet animation possible, a special camera is stopped after a single frame is photographed. Each time the camera stops, animators make slight adjustments in the positions of the figures or objects. When the frames are projected in rapid succession, the models appear to move. This type of animation is frequently used in making short animated films and sometimes in making feature-length films. Puppet animation also appears in live-action features, such as *King Kong* (1933) and the *Star Wars* movies (1977-2005).

Clay animation is a type of stop-motion animation that uses figures or objects made of clay or plastic. This technique is often used for commercials and short animated films. The American animator Will Vinton patented a form of the technique under the name Claymation.

Pixilation is a way of animating live action. When the camera is stopped, the actors slightly alter their positions. Pixilation makes people look cartoonlike in films.

Pin screen animation is a seldom-used technique that employs a large screen with about 1 million pinholes. Animators place headless pins into the holes and light the screen from the side so that shadows cast by the pins create images. Animators move the pins to change the images. After each change, they photograph the screen to produce a series of frames.

Drawing on film is an inexpensive technique that requires little equipment. The animator draws, paints, stencils, or scratches the sequence of images directly on the film stock, instead of photographing them.

History

Early animation. The first examples of animation were toys developed in the 1800's. One of the earliest devices was the *phenakistoscope,* invented by the Belgian scientist Joseph Antoine Plateau in 1832. It was a notched wheel attached to a handle. One side of the wheel had a series of drawings. The viewer held the wheel up to a mirror, with the drawings facing the mirror. When the viewer spun the wheel and looked through the notches on the blank side of the wheel, the images appeared to move. The phenakistoscope and similar devices contributed to the invention of motion pictures.

Arthur Melbourne-Cooper of England was one of the first to make motion pictures using animation. In 1899,

Photofest

A gorilla puppet was used in the famous motion-picture thriller *King Kong* (1933). Animators used *stop motion,* creating a small model of a gorilla that appeared as a giant on the screen.

Melbourne-Cooper moved matchsticks in different sequences and photographed them frame by frame to produce an advertisement called *Matches: An Appeal.*

J. Stuart Blackton, a British-born American newspaper cartoonist, was the first person to film drawings frame by frame. In 1906, Blackton made *Humorous Phases of Funny Faces* by filming a series of faces drawn on a blackboard.

Émile Cohl of France was another important early animator. Cohl made about 250 short animated films from 1908 to 1918.

Pioneers of American animation. Winsor McCay exhibited his first animated film, *Little Nemo,* in 1911 in

© John Canemaker Collection

An early animated film by Winsor McCay in 1914 starred Gertie the dinosaur. McCay pioneered in creating cartoon characters with flexible movements and distinct personality traits.

New York City. McCay produced films that featured cartoon characters with graceful movements and distinct personality traits. He established the techniques and visual approaches that set the standard for character animation. McCay's work became influential because of its fluid motion, high-quality draftsmanship, and feeling of weight. McCay's most famous animated short film was called *Gertie the Dinosaur* (1914), a story about a trained dinosaur.

In 1914, the American animator John Randolph Bray began streamlining the production processes involved in animation. Under Bray, studios hired large staffs and operated like assembly lines, making cartoons cheaper and faster to produce. Bray collaborated with the animator Earl Hurd, who had patented the cel technique. Together, Bray and Hurd revolutionized the process of animation. Before cels were used, animators had to completely redraw both the characters and the background for each frame in a scene. With cels, however, animators draw the background only once, which saves work.

About 1915, American movie studios began to create cartoon characters who appeared regularly in series of animated films. The *Felix the Cat* series, which debuted in 1919, was produced by cartoonist Pat Sullivan. Felix was the first internationally popular animated character. Animator Otto Messmer created and directed about 175 short Felix films during the 1920's.

Max Fleischer, a former newspaper cartoonist, and his brother Dave produced animated series featuring Koko the Clown, Betty Boop, and Popeye the Sailor. Other well-known cartoon characters of the early 1900's included Krazy Kat and Mutt and Jeff. Some of the characters first appeared in newspaper comic strips.

Animation in Europe. While animators in the United States concentrated on developing cartoon characters, animators in Europe experimented with creative techniques. From 1910 through the 1920's, for example, the Polish-born artist Ladislas Starevitch (also spelled Władysław Starewicz) used puppet animation. Germany's Lotte Reiniger produced short animated films with black silhouettes and created the first feature-length animated film, *Adventures of Prince Achmed* (1926).

Some European artists experimented with abstract animation. The German artists Walter Ruttmann and Oskar Fischinger created animated short films with abstract geometric shapes. In France, Russian-born Alexandre Alexeieff and American-born Claire Parker developed pin screen animation in the early 1930's.

Walt Disney became the most famous producer of animated films. He created such popular cartoon characters as Mickey Mouse, Donald Duck, Goofy, and Pluto. Disney produced *Steamboat Willie,* starring Mickey Mouse, in 1928. It was the first animated cartoon with a synchronized sound track that creatively integrated music, voices, and sound effects. From 1928 to 1939, Disney perfected the character animation film, mainly through his popular cartoon series called "Silly Symphonies."

In 1937, Disney issued *Snow White and the Seven Dwarfs*, his first full-length animated film. It became one of the most popular films in movie history. Disney died in 1966, but his influence on animated storytelling, design, and artistic theory continues to be felt throughout the animation industry.

© The Walt Disney Company from The Ronald Grant Archive

Snow White and the Seven Dwarfs was the first feature-length animated film issued by Walt Disney. This frame shows Snow White, the heroine, and Dopey, one of the seven dwarfs.

Animation in the mid-1900's. Along with Disney, several other major film studios dominated the animation industry from the 1930's to the early 1950's. At Metro-Goldwyn-Mayer (MGM), William Hanna and Joseph Barbera made short animated features starring Tom and Jerry, a cat and mouse team. Walter Lantz of Universal Studios produced animated shorts featuring Oswald the Rabbit and later Woody Woodpecker. At Warner Bros., Tex Avery, Chuck Jones, Bob Clampett, and Friz Freleng directed animated shorts starring Bugs Bunny, Daffy Duck, Elmer Fudd, and Porky Pig.

In 1945, a group of former Disney animation artists established United Productions of America (UPA). This group broke away from Disney's emphasis on realism. Instead, they stressed a bold, flat, modernist style. Famous UPA cartoon characters included Gerald McBoing Boing and Mr. Magoo. UPA also popularized a technique called *limited animation* that differed from the full-figure animation done by Disney. In limited animation, only certain simple movements of a character are animated, allowing portions of the figure to be reused.

The UPA style proved less expensive than full-figure animation and influenced many other studios. The low cost of limited animation made it popular for children's television cartoons, such as "The Flintstones" and "Yogi Bear" by Hanna-Barbera Productions. In 1960, "The Flintstones" became the first animated series to appear on prime-time television.

Over time, some animators left UPA to form their own production companies. Among the most talented was John Hubley. He and his wife, Faith, created films whose playful images and sense of fantasy expanded the content and style of character animation. The Hubleys produced cartoons for the "Sesame Street" TV series and won three Academy Awards for their animated short films *Moonbird* (1959), *The Hole* (1962), and *Herb Alpert and the Tijuana Brass Double Feature* (1966).

During the mid-1950's, the Scottish-born animator Norman McLaren made acclaimed animated films for the National Film Board of Canada. McLaren became known for his technique of drawing directly on film in such productions as *Blinkity Blank* (1955).

The animation revival. Production of feature-length animated cartoons declined from the mid-1950's through the 1960's, partly because of the rising popularity of television. However, a revival of feature-length cartoons began during the 1970's. The American filmmaker Steven Spielberg released his first animated cartoon feature, *An American Tail,* in 1986. The Disney and Spielberg studios jointly produced *Who Framed Roger Rabbit* (1988), which combined live action and animation. Disney followed with several creative and popular features, including *Beauty and the Beast* (1991), *Aladdin* (1992), and *The Lion King* (1994). In 2001, the Academy of Motion Picture Arts and Sciences created a new category for feature-length animated films to receive an Academy Award.

The computer revolution. Computer scientists and artists had begun to experiment with computer visualization in the 1960's. In the early 1970's, a few academic institutions, such as the University of Utah, animated simple shapes with computers. Disney's *TRON* (1982) was the first feature film to use significant amounts of CGI animation. The film was a major technical achievement that proved computers could be used to create imagery.

The science-fiction film *Jurassic Park* (1993), directed by Spielberg, expanded the use of computer animation. The film combined actual actors and sets with dinosaurs created by Industrial Light & Magic (ILM), a company that develops special visual effects for motion pictures. The computer-generated dinosaurs moved across the screen as realistically as live animals. *Jurassic Park* was a

© Walt Disney Pictures from Shooting Star

Toy Story, released in 1995, was the first feature-length animated motion picture that was entirely computer generated. The movie follows the adventures of toys living in a boy's bedroom.

breakthrough event in the entertainment industry. It proved that computer animation could help filmmakers achieve almost any effect.

In 1995, John Lasseter and Pixar Animation Studios produced an all-CGI feature film, *Toy Story.* The film became a blockbuster hit and elevated CGI from a tool for creating special effects to a unique artistic medium. *Toy Story* was followed by several successful sequels. Pixar produced many other box-office hits, including *A Bug's Life* (1998); *Monsters, Inc.* (2001); *Finding Nemo* (2003) and its sequel, *Finding Dory* (2016); *The Incredibles* (2004); *Ratatouille* (2007); *WALL·E* (2008); and *Up* (2009).

New diversity. In the 1990's and early 2000's, animators used a great variety of methods and styles of animation. Two-dimensional animation continued to thrive, especially on TV. Although earlier animation was aimed mainly at children, new animated TV series proved to be popular with older audiences. Such series as "The Simpsons," which began in 1989, and "King of the Hill" (1997-2010) gained high audience ratings.

A Japanese style of two-dimensional animation called *anime* also became popular. Anime uses some of the traditions of limited animation, such as characters who speak by moving only their mouths. Many anime characters have large, saucerlike eyes. In 2003, the Japanese motion picture *Spirited Away* became the first anime production to win the Academy Award as best animated feature film.

A new studio, DreamWorks SKG, began releasing animated features that employed both traditional methods and CGI. DreamWorks issued such films as *Antz* and *The Prince of Egypt* (both 1998), *Shrek* (2001) and its sequel *Shrek 2* (2004), and *Over the Hedge* (2006). Aardman Animations, a British studio, made feature-length films in the clay puppet animation style, including *Chicken Run* (2000). DreamWorks and Aardman collaborated on *Wallace & Gromit: The Curse of the Were-Rabbit* (2005) and *Flushed Away* (2006). The American director Tim Bur-

© Warner Bros. Inc.

Bugs Bunny and Daffy Duck are two of the most popular characters in animation history. Like many cartoon characters, they are animals who speak, dress, and behave like human beings.

© DreamWorks Animation from ZUMA Press

Stop-motion animation using clay puppets was used to create the popular English animated motion picture *Wallace & Gromit: The Curse of the Were-Rabbit* (2005). The feature-length film portrays the adventures of an inventor named Wallace and his pet dog, Gromit.

Early animation
worldbook.com/gd-16

ton used stop-motion animation in making *The Nightmare Before Christmas* (1993) and *Corpse Bride* (2005).

International cooperation increased among animation studios in different countries. An example of such cooperation was *The Spongebob Squarepants Movie* (2004), based on a popular TV series. Filmmakers in the United States created storyboards and layouts for the film. They then sent them to South Korea, where artists animated the characters by hand. The film returned to the United States for digital coloring and compositing.

Animation today. Thousands of artists work in animation houses in such countries as South Korea and Japan. They turn out feature-length films as well as cartoons and commercials for television. Many Canadian, U.S., and Russian animators operate smaller studios.

Many movie theaters today have digital projectors that allow a feature to be shot and screened without using film. Many filmmakers choose to shoot their features using high-end digital cameras. They use all digital production to create a feature without developing any film. This enables them to streamline production and better integrate digital sets and characters.

John Canemaker and Peter Weishar

Related articles in *World Book* include:
Advertising (Production)
Bugs Bunny
Cartoon
Computer graphics
Disney, Walt
Motion picture
Pixar Animation Studios
Schulz, Charles M.

Outline

I. Preliminary steps in animation
II. Traditional animation
III. Computer animation
   A. Modeling
   B. Making the model move
   C. Lighting and rendering
   D. Compositing
IV. Other kinds of animation
   A. Stop-motion animation
   B. Pixilation
   C. Pin screen animation
   D. Drawing on film
V. History

Questions

What is a *storyboard?*
Who starred in *Steamboat Willie?*
How does a *flip book* work?
What was a *phenakistoscope?*
How does puppet animation work?
What is the role of animators in cel animation?
What is CGI?
How did Winsor McCay influence animation?
What is *rendering* in computer animation?
What animation process was used in *The Polar Express?*

Additional resources

Canemaker, John. *Paper Dreams: The Art and Artists of Disney Storyboards.* Hyperion, 1999.
Grant, John. *Masters of Animation.* Watson-Guptill, 2001.
Kanfer, Stefan. *Serious Business: The Art and Commerce of Animation in America from Betty Boop to Toy Story.* Scribner, 1997.
Laybourne, Kit. *The Animation Book.* Rev. ed. Three Rivers Pr., 1998.
Weishar, Peter. *Digital Space: Designing Virtual Environments.* McGraw, 1998.
Woods, Samuel G. *Computer Animation.* Blackbirch Pr., 2000. Younger readers.

Animism, *AN uh mihz uhm,* is a term used to describe certain religious beliefs based upon the concept of a soul that departs the body after death. The British anthropologist Edward Burnett Tylor introduced the term in 1871, from the Latin word *animae* meaning *souls* or *spirits*. He argued that early people first developed the idea of the soul from dreams about the dead.

Scholars today have rejected Tylor's theory. However, many of them believe that animism is the basis of later religions, including Judaism, Christianity, and Islam.

Elliot Fratkin

See also **Mythology** (Anthropological approaches); **Religion** (Earlier theories).

Anise, *AN ihs,* is an annual herb related to caraway and dill. It is grown mainly for its seeds, which have a spicy taste and are used to give candy a licorice flavor. Cooks also use the seeds to flavor pastries, cookies, and certain kinds of cheese. The oil extracted from the seeds is used to make absinthe, an alcoholic beverage. The oil is also used in medicines, especially those for treating children's stomach troubles. Many cooks use anise leaves as a garnish or for seasoning soups and sauces.

Anise grows wild in the Mediterranean region. It needs warm, dry summers to grow well. Egypt, Germany, Italy, Mexico, Spain, and Turkey are important anise-producing countries.   Albert Liptay

Scientific classification. Anise is *Pimpinella anisum.*

Ankara, *ANG kuh ruh,* is one of the largest cities in Turkey. The metropolitan municipality of Ankara has a population of 4,630,735. A metropolitan municipality may include rural areas as well as the urban center. Ankara lies at the center of Anatolia in west-central Turkey. For location, see **Turkey** (political map).

Ankara has an old section and a modern section. The old section is on a hill and consists of a fortress that is hundreds of years old. After Ankara became Turkey's capital in 1923, a modern section began to grow at the base of the hill. It has merged with the old section. The Museum of Anatolian Civilizations in Ankara has an outstanding collection of Hittite art. Many Turks and other travelers come to the city to visit the tomb of Kemal Atatürk, founder of the Republic of Turkey. Ankara is the home of Ankara University, the Middle East Technical University, Bilkent University, and Hacettepe University. The National Library of Turkey is also in the city.

The Turkish government employs more of Ankara's people than does any other kind of business. The city serves as a market for the grain, Angora wool and mohair, and other farm products of the area. Ankara's industries process food and produce building materials, farm equipment, and various kinds of machinery.

People probably lived in what is now the Ankara area during the Stone Age, which began about 2 ½ million years ago. By about 700 B.C., Ankara had become an important town of Phrygia (now central Turkey). Alexander the Great of Macedonia conquered Ankara in the 330's B.C. The Romans took over the town in 25 B.C. In the Middle Ages (about the A.D. 400's through the 1400's), several groups gained and lost control of Ankara.

By 1360, the Ottomans had captured the city and made it part of the Ottoman Empire. The empire was defeated in World War I (1914-1918). Kemal Atatürk established a nationalist government in Ankara in 1920. Ankara became the capital of the Republic of Turkey in 1923, replacing Istanbul, the old Ottoman capital.

F. Muge Gocek

See also **Turkey** (picture).

Ankle is the joint where the leg and the foot meet. The

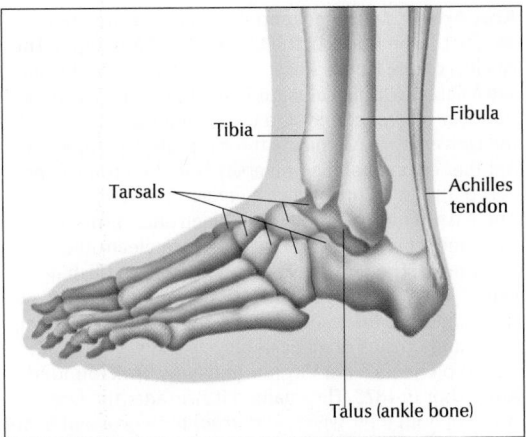

Tibia

Fibula

Tarsals

Achilles tendon

Talus (ankle bone)

WORLD BOOK illustration by Leonard Morgan

The ankle joint allows movement of the foot. The talus, one of seven tarsal bones, fits between the lower ends of the tibia and fibula and moves between them like a hinge.

ankle joint enables the foot to move up and down.

Each leg has two bony bumps—one on each side—that we commonly call the *ankles.* These bumps are formed by the ends of the lower leg bones, the *tibia* and the *fibula.* Below the leg bones are seven *tarsal bones,* which extend about halfway down the foot. The top of the *talus,* the highest tarsal bone, fits between the ends of the tibia and the fibula and moves between them like a hinge. The *Achilles tendon* links the heel bone—the largest tarsal bone—to the calf muscles and helps move the ankle joint.

Three small joints among the tarsal bones enable the foot to move sideways. Many strong, cordlike tissues called *ligaments* connect the tarsal bones to the leg bones, to the bones lower in the foot, and to one another. If one of these ligaments is torn, a sprained ankle results.   John F. Waller

See also **Achilles tendon; Ligament; Sprain.**

Ankylosaurus, *ANG kuh luh SAWR uhs,* was a large, armored dinosaur that lived between 68 million years and 65 million years ago in what is now western North America. The name *Ankylosaurus* means *fused lizard* and describes the dinosaur's armor, which consisted of bony pieces that had *fused,* or grown together. The *Ankylosaurus's* heavy armor protected the exposed parts of its body, including the head, back, and tail.

Ankylosaurus was one of the largest of the armored dinosaurs. It was about 25 feet (7.6 meters) long and weighed about 4 to 5 tons (3.6 to 4.5 metric tons). It was a plant-eater with small teeth. The dinosaur's triangular skull was 2 ½ feet (76 centimeters) long and equally wide. A spike stuck out from each cheek, and two more stuck out from the back of the head. Short, thick legs supported the weight of the dinosaur's low, broad body. The tail ended in a big, heavy ball of bone.

When attacked, *Ankylosaurus* may have crouched down and pressed itself to the ground. In this position, the attacker could only bite or claw at the thick, hard armor. *Ankylosaurus* also may have defended itself by swinging its tail and hitting an attacker with the bony club at the end.   Peter Dodson

See also **Dinosaur** (Ankylosaurs).

Ann Arbor, Michigan (pop. 113,934; met. area pop. 344,791), is the home of the University of Michigan. The city lies on the Huron River, west of Detroit. For location, see **Michigan** (political map). Downtown Ann Arbor is home to several county and civic buildings and part of the University of Michigan, the city's largest employer. Another campus of the university is in the northeastern part of the city. Concordia University is also in Ann Arbor. Many computer and other electronics firms in the city conduct research and manufacture electronic equipment. The city is also a printing and publishing center. Detroit Metropolitan Wayne County Airport, railroads, and bus lines serve the city. Ann Arbor has many parks and dozens of miles of bicycle trails.

Two pioneers from Virginia and New York founded Ann Arbor in 1823. They named it *Ann* after the first name of both their wives, and *arbor* for a grove of beautiful oak trees there. Ann Arbor was incorporated as a city in 1851. It is the seat of Washtenaw County and has a council-manager government. Peter Gavrilovich

Annan, *AN uhn,* **Kofi Atta,** *KOH fee AT uh* (1938-2018), was a diplomat from Ghana who served as the seventh secretary-general of the United Nations (UN) from 1997 to 2006. He replaced Boutros Boutros-Ghali of Egypt, who held the office from 1992 to 1996. Annan was the first secretary-general from sub-Saharan Africa. He was praised for his support of human rights and for his campaigns against AIDS and international terrorism. He and the UN won the 2001 Nobel Peace Prize for their efforts in building peace and security.

Annan was born in Kumasi, Ghana, on April 8, 1938. He studied at the University of Science and Technology in Kumasi. He completed undergraduate work in economics at Macalester College in St. Paul, Minnesota, in 1961. From 1961 to 1962, he attended the Graduate Institute of International Studies in Geneva, Switzerland. He received a master's degree in management from Massachusetts Institute of Technology in 1972.

Annan began his career with the UN as an administrative and budget officer at the World Health Organization in 1962. He steadily advanced at the UN, holding posts in budget, personnel, and refugee affairs. He served as assistant secretary-general for peace-keeping operations in 1992 and 1993. He then served as undersecretary-general for peacekeeping operations until 1996. In addition to his peacekeeping work, Annan was also responsible for carrying out difficult diplomatic assignments. In 1991, he negotiated the release of UN staff members held in Iraq during the Persian Gulf War of 1991. In 1995 and 1996, he supervised the turnover of the UN peacekeeping mission in Bosnia-Herzegovina to troops of the North Atlantic Treaty Organization (NATO).

As secretary-general, Annan faced difficult political situations. He worked to promote the transition to civilian rule in Nigeria. He helped develop an international response to the violence that erupted in East Timor after

Milton Grant, United Nations
Kofi Atta Annan

its vote for independence from Indonesia. He also took an active role in the Middle East, encouraging Israelis and Palestinians to try to resolve their differences peacefully. Annan died on Aug. 18, 2018. Michael G. Schechter

Annapolis, *uh NAP uh lihs* (pop. 38,394), is the capital of Maryland and the home of the United States Naval Academy. It lies along the Severn River on the western shore of Chesapeake Bay (see **Maryland** [political map]).

The layout of the city features two central circles, with narrow streets branching off in all directions. Colonial buildings give Annapolis a historic charm. They include Paca House, built in 1763 by Governor William Paca; and the red brick State House, built in 1772. The State House is the oldest state capitol still actively used by a legislature. The Continental Congress met in the State House when Annapolis was the United States capital, from Nov. 26, 1783, to June 3, 1784. St. John's College was founded as an academy in Annapolis in 1696.

The city is a yachting center. Its economy is based heavily on tourism and government activities. Puritans founded Annapolis in 1649. Annapolis was named for Queen Anne of Britain, who gave the city its charter in 1708. It has a mayor-council government. The city is the seat of Anne Arundel County. Thomas L. Marquardt

See also **Maryland** (picture: State Capitol); **United States Naval Academy.**

Annapolis Convention, *uh NAP uh lihs,* was a meeting held in Annapolis, Maryland, in 1786 to discuss changes in the Articles of Confederation, which had served as the basic law of the United States since 1781. The proposed changes referred especially to commercial issues. Virginia invited all the states to the convention, but only New York, New Jersey, Pennsylvania, Delaware, and Virginia attended. Many political leaders, including Alexander Hamilton and James Madison, urged that all the states send delegates to a second convention. Meeting in Philadelphia in 1787, this second convention abandoned the Articles and wrote the Constitution of the United States. Donna J. Spindel

See also **Constitution of the United States.**

Annapolis Royal, *uh NAP uh lihs,* Nova Scotia (pop. 491), is one of the oldest communities in North America. It lies along the Annapolis Basin, an inlet of the Bay of Fundy (see **Nova Scotia** [political map]). French colonists founded the settlement of Port-Royal near what is now Annapolis Royal in 1605. English raiders captured and burned the colony in 1613. In the 1630's, the French reestablished the settlement at the present site of Annapolis Royal. Port-Royal became a military outpost and often changed hands during continual fighting between French and English forces in the area.

In 1710, the British captured the settlement and renamed it Annapolis Royal. The town served as the capital of Nova Scotia until Halifax became the capital in 1749. Annapolis Royal prospered as a shipping center in the 1800's. Today, it is a popular tourist resort. The nearby Port-Royal National Historic Site features a replica of the original French settlement. D. A. Sutherland

Annapurna, *AN uh PUR nuh,* a small range of mountains within the Himalaya, includes some of the highest peaks in the world. It stands in north-central Nepal. Its highest peak, known as Annapurna I, rises 26,504 feet (8,078 meters). The Nepalese call this snowy peak the *Goddess of the Harvests* because they believe it watches over the farms below. In 1950, a French expedition led by Maurice Herzog climbed it. Until the conquest of Mount Everest in 1953, Annapurna was the highest mountain people had climbed. See also **Mountain** (diagram: Major mountains). James A. Hafner

Anne (1665-1714) was the first queen of Great Britain, which was formed when the Kingdom of Scotland united with the Kingdom of England and Wales in 1707. She was also queen of Ireland. Anne was the last monarch of the royal family called the House of Stuart. She became pregnant at least 17 times and had 5 children, but none survived her. She was succeeded by her distant cousin George, Elector of Hanover.

Anne was born on Feb. 6, 1665, at Twickenham, near London. She was the second daughter of King James II and married Prince George of Denmark in 1683. She became queen in 1702, after the death of her brother-in-law William III, who left no heirs. During most of her reign, John Churchill, Duke of Marlborough, wielded much power. He was captain-general in the War of the Spanish Succession (1701-1714). His wife, Sarah, dominated Anne for years. Their interference made the court a scene of political intrigue.

Although Anne's health was never good, she took an active part in public affairs. She often attended debates in the House of Lords and was particularly concerned with religious legislation. Anne died on Aug. 4, 1714. Anne's reign

Detail of portrait by M. Dahl (1699).
National Portrait Gallery, London
Queen Anne

is often said to mark the start of the Augustan Age, because the leaders of the times tried to reproduce in England the political stability and classical art of Rome under the Emperor Augustus. These leaders included the writers Joseph Addison, Alexander Pope, Richard Steele, and Jonathan Swift. James J. Sack

See also **Furniture** (The Queen Anne style); **Marlborough, Duke of; Stuart, House of.**

Anne, Saint, is a Christian saint who is traditionally regarded as the mother of the Virgin Mary. Stories about her life appear only in the *apocryphal* books of the New Testament, a group of early Christian writings not included in the Bible. According to these stories, an angel appeared to Anne and her husband, Joachim. The angel announced that their child would be blessed by the whole world. There are many shrines built in honor of Saint Anne. One of the best-known is the shrine of Ste.-Anne-de-Beaupré, near Quebec City, in Canada. See also **Sainte-Anne-de-Beaupré.** J. H. Charlesworth

Anne of Austria (1601-1666) was the wife of King Louis XIII of France and the mother of King Louis XIV. After her husband's death in 1643, she ruled France as queen *regent* (temporary ruler) for her young son. Anne governed during the difficult end of the Thirty Years' War (1618-1648) and the civil disruptions in France known as the *Fronde* (1648-1653). In 1651, in response to criticism of Anne's regency by rebellious nobles of the Fronde, 13-year-old Louis XIV was formally declared old

enough to rule. But Anne continued to play a dominant role in government policy during his teenage years and beyond. Anne's chief minister and principal adviser throughout this time was Cardinal Jules Mazarin.

Anne was born on Sept. 22, 1601, in Valladolid, Spain. Her parents were King Philip III of Spain and Margaret of Austria. Anne died on Jan. 20, 1666. Donald A. Bailey

See also **Louis XIV; Mazarin, Jules.**

Annexation, *AN uhk SAY shuhn,* is the process that governments use to acquire and establish sovereignty over new territory. Annexation can occur through military force or by other means, such as *cession, purchase,* and *discovery* and *occupation.* Many cities and other municipalities in the United States have annexed nearby areas by referendum and other legal means.

An annexed territory becomes an integral part of the annexing country. Protectorates, leased territories, and areas under military occupation are not annexed lands, because they do not become integral to the country controlling them. The citizens of an annexed territory must become citizens of the annexing country. Laws of the annexed territory that are not in conflict with those of the annexing country may be retained, and special arrangements for limited self-government may also be made. The annexing country also inherits treaty obligations the territory may have had prior to its annexation.

Many annexations caused or resulted from wars. For example, Italy annexed Ethiopia in 1936, and Germany annexed Austria in 1938. These events helped create the tensions that led to World War II (1939-1945). During and after the war, the Soviet Union annexed territories in eastern Europe and eastern Asia covering about 270,000 square miles (699,000 square kilometers). After the Spanish-American War, in 1898, Spain ceded Puerto Rico, the Philippines, and Guam to the United States. Many annexations have been peaceful. The United States annexed Texas in 1845 following consent by the governing authority. France ceded the Louisiana Territory to the United States in 1803 for about $15 million. Thomas S. Vontz

Anning, Mary (1799-1847), a British scientist, found and identified important fossils of prehistoric animals. Anning was an early leader in *paleontology,* the study of prehistoric life. But Anning received little recognition in her lifetime, largely because she was a woman.

Anning made her first major fossil discovery when she was only 12 years old. The fossil belonged to an *ichthyosaur,* a prehistoric marine reptile. Anning went on to find the first *plesiosaur,* another marine reptile. She discovered one of the first *pterosaurs,* a type of flying reptile, and the first *Squaloraja,* a prehistoric fish. Anning also found many other fossils.

Anning made many important contributions to science. She helped to prove that many animals have become extinct. This idea was once controversial because many people held religious beliefs that life did not change over time. Anning's work helped to lay the foundation for the theory of evolution (see **Evolution**).

Anning lived at a time when the work of female scientists was hardly ever recognized. Also, Anning grew up in extreme poverty. She was able to attend school for only a few years. Anning taught herself anatomy, geology, paleontology, and scientific illustration. She often borrowed scientific papers and copied them by hand. Many of the fossils Anning found became important parts of museum collections without being credited to her. Male scientists sometimes used Anning's discoveries in their work without acknowledging her contribution. Today, scientists recognize Anning as one of the most important paleontologists of her time.

Mary Anning was born on May 21, 1799, in Lyme Regis, England. She died of breast cancer on March 9, 1847. Shelley Emling

Anniversary, Wedding. See Wedding anniversary.

Anno Domini. See A.D.

Annual is a plant that grows, blossoms, produces seed, and dies within one growing season. Plants called *biennials* require two growing seasons to complete their life cycles. Other plants, called *perennials,* can live for many years. Many garden vegetables and flowers are annuals. Such plants, which include beans, peas, petunias, squash, and zinnias, must be raised from seed each year. See also **Biennial; Flower** (Garden annuals); **Gardening; Perennial.** Joseph E. Armstrong

Annuity, *uh NOO uh tee,* is a sum of money paid out at regular times, usually monthly or yearly. The word comes from the Latin word *annus,* meaning *year.* Insurance policies, wills, and other documents provide for annuities. People may leave money to an heir in the form of an annuity. The inheritance will then be paid in installments instead of in a lump sum.

Usually the term *annuity* refers to a type of insurance. Individuals pay the insurance company a certain amount of money. They receive in return income payments that begin at a certain time and continue on a regular basis for a certain period. For instance, payments may begin when a person reaches 60 and continue until the person's death. Pension plans also provide for annuities. The most common use of annuities is to provide regular payments during the retirement years. James R. Barth

See also **Insurance** (Annuities); **Pension; Social security.**

Annulment is the declaration that a marriage never really existed, or was void from the beginning. Most states of the United States, as well as many religious groups, have strict laws saying that first cousins may not marry each other. If two persons are found to be within the forbidden degree of *consanguinity* (blood relationship), their marriage can be annulled.

Annulments are sometimes granted for other reasons, such as fraud or undue force against one of the parties. A marriage can also be annulled if either party is under age, or if both parties declare that they considered the ceremony a joke when it was performed. An annulment differs from a divorce, which has the effect of dissolving a valid marriage for some cause arising after the ceremony. The Roman Catholic Church does not recognize divorce, but it recognizes annulment. Michael J. Broyde

See also **Divorce; Marriage.**

Annunciation, *uh NUHN see AY shuhn,* is the announcement, according to Luke 1:26–38, which the angel Gabriel made to Mary. He told her that she was to be the mother of Jesus, who was to be called "the Christ."

The Annunciation should not be confused with the Immaculate Conception of Mary. In Roman Catholic belief, the Immaculate Conception means that Mary, at the instant of her existence in her mother's womb, was free from original sin.

Beginning in medieval times, Gabriel's words at the

Annunciation, "Hail, full of grace, the Lord is with thee," gradually became the opening words of the "Hail Mary" prayer, though that prayer did not receive its full form until the 1500's. Another devotion honoring the Annunciation developed into the Angelus prayer (see **Angelus**). Traditionally, the Angelus is recited three times daily—in the morning, at noon, and in the evening, when church bells also are rung to commemorate the birth of Jesus.

The Annunciation has been the subject of paintings by great artists, including the Italian painters Fra Angelico and Andrea del Sarto and the Flemish painter Jan van Eyck. Artists usually show Mary holding a book or some needlework, and Gabriel carries an olive branch or a flower. J. H. Charlesworth

See also **Angelico, Fra** (picture); **Mary.**

Annunzio, Gabriele d'. See D'Annunzio, Gabriele.

Anodizing, *AN uh DYZ ihng,* is a process used to thicken the natural coatings on metal surfaces, called *oxides.* During the process, the metal acts as a positive pole, called an *anode,* for electric current. The metal is submerged in a liquid that conducts electric current. As current runs through the liquid, negatively charged oxygen *ions* collect on the surface of the metal. There, they react with the metal to create the oxide coating. The coating's thickness depends on the amount of electric current passed through the liquid. Thicknesses usually range from 0.0001 to 0.0008 inch (0.003 to 0.02 millimeter).

Anodizing serves several uses. For example, it forms a hard coating on the metal that resists corrosion. Special anodizing treatments create a porous oxide layer that can absorb colors from dyes that do not rub or scratch off. Anodized aluminum or magnesium can be used in airplanes and on the outsides of buildings. Aluminum and magnesium are often anodized. But the process is not used on steel because the oxide (commonly called rust) flakes off. Rose M. Torielli and Robert C. Voigt

See also **Aluminum** (Finishing aluminum); **Electrolysis.**

Anointing of the sick is a sacrament of the Roman Catholic and Eastern Orthodox churches. A priest administers it to a person who is aged, seriously ill, or in danger of death from sickness or an accident. The sacrament also may be administered to a group, such as patients in a hospital. In the Roman Catholic Church, the sacrament formerly was called *extreme unction.* In administering the sacrament, the priest anoints a person's hands and forehead with holy oil. At the same time, prayers are said for the person's spiritual and physical healing. The prayers are based on the Epistle of James (5:13-15). See also **Sacrament.** Richard L. Schebera

Anole, *uh NOH lee,* is a group of lizards that live in the Caribbean region and in Central and South America. There are hundreds of *species* (kinds). One species, the green anole, is native to the southern United States. This species is also called the American chameleon, but it is not a true chameleon (see **Chameleon**).

Most anoles grow to 8 inches (20 centimeters) long. They are generally green or brown and may have bright colors. Many species can change colors. Anoles have a throat flap called a *dewlap.* The dewlap of a male anole is large and colorful. Males fan their dewlap when they want to attract females or scare off rival males. Anoles live in shrubs, grasses, and trees and have toes suited for climbing. Each toe ends with an enlarged pad and a

© Michael Fogden, DRK

Male anoles have large, colorful dewlaps.

sharp claw. The pad has thousands of hairlike bristles that stick to bark. Anoles eat mainly insects. A few species eat fruit. Most female anoles lay one egg every few weeks during the breeding season.   Raymond B. Huey

Scientific classification. Anoles make up the genus *Anolis.* The green anole is *A. carolinensis.*

Anorexia nervosa, *AN uh REHK see uh nur VOH suh,* is an emotional illness in which a person refuses to eat. It occurs chiefly among adolescent girls and young women. The word *anorexia* means *without appetite,* but people with anorexia may be extremely hungry most of the time. They avoid food for psychological reasons.

Some people with anorexia experience bouts of *bulimia*—an overwhelming craving for food—during which they consume large amounts of food. Afterward, they may make themselves vomit. Some of them use laxatives or diuretics to eliminate food from the body. Others may exercise excessively to burn off the calories consumed.

The chief physical symptom of anorexia is severe weight loss, involving more than 25 percent of the body weight. Other symptoms include low blood pressure, slow heartbeat, and growth of fine hair on the body. In adolescents, puberty may be delayed. Females with anorexia may not begin to menstruate, or their menstrual periods may stop. The disorder also affects the personality. Many people with anorexia isolate themselves from family and friends and may appear depressed. Most sufferers seem unaware of their condition. They consider themselves healthy, or even overweight.

Physicians disagree about the cause of anorexia nervosa. Some psychiatrists believe that sufferers try to starve themselves to avoid growing into adults. Other experts suggest that sufferers may want to gain attention and a sense of being special.

Treatment for anorexia may include psychotherapy and medication. People with anorexia should be hospitalized if they suffer malnutrition. Some physicians recommend that the family also undergo therapy. Most patients can be cured if they receive prompt treatment. But the disease is fatal in some cases.   Charles Michael Wuhl

See also **Adolescent** (Eating disorders); **Bulimia; Eating disorder.**

Anouilh, *ah NOO yuh,* **Jean,** *zhahn* (1910-1987), was a French playwright. Anouilh's plays explore matters of illusion and reality and conflicts between the individual and society. Many of them feature a sensitive and articulate young woman struggling to preserve her integrity in a corrupt, greedy world. His works are noted for polished dialogue and tight dramatic action.

Anouilh classified his plays according to their dominant mood. He called his tragic plays "black." One of his most famous "black" plays is *Antigone* (1944), a modern version of an ancient Greek myth. Anouilh used "grating" to describe his bitterly comic plays *Poor Bitos* (1956) and *The Waltz of the Toreadors* (1952). His lighter comedies were labeled "rose" or "pink" and "sparkling." They include *Thieves' Carnival* (completed in 1932, first produced in 1938), *Ring Round the Moon* (1947), and *The Rehearsal* (1950). Anouilh called his historical dramas "costumed" plays. His best-known "costumed" plays are *The Lark* (1953) and *Becket* (1959).

Anouilh was born near Bordeaux on June 23, 1910. He died on Oct. 3, 1987.   Felicia Hardison Londré

Anoxia, *an AHK see uh,* is the lack of a normal supply of oxygen to body tissues, or the inability of the tissues to use the oxygen. It is also called *hypoxia.*

Anoxic anoxia occurs when blood flowing through the lungs does not pick up enough oxygen. This can happen when there is a reduced amount of oxygen in the air, such as at altitudes above 10,000 feet (3,000 meters). The blood also can fail to pick up sufficient oxygen because of defects in the lungs or because of obstruction of the air passages involved in breathing. Rapid, deep breathing is a common symptom of anoxic anoxia. The condition is often accompanied by *cyanosis,* a bluish coloration of the skin. Severe cases may lead to loss of consciousness and even death.

Anemic anoxia occurs when the blood cannot carry its normal load of oxygen. This happens when the blood has insufficient amounts of *hemoglobin* (the substance that transports oxygen in the blood), or when the hemoglobin is altered by carbon monoxide or other poisons.

Stagnant anoxia develops when the blood flows so slowly that it loses most of its oxygen before completing its course through a tissue. Part of the tissue thus receives little or no oxygen. An example of stagnant anoxia occurs during cold temperatures when blood vessels under the fingernails and in the lips constrict, causing cyanosis in those body parts. *Histotoxic anoxia* is caused by poisons that make the tissues incapable of using the oxygen supplied. Cyanide is such a poison.   K. E. Money

See also **Altitude sickness; Oxygen.**

Anselm, Saint (1033-1109), was an influential Christian theologian and church leader. He became famous for his long essays *Monologion* and *Proslogion.* In both works, Anselm attempted to prove the existence of God through reason. His best-known argument, which appears in *Proslogion,* states that the existence of the idea of God necessarily means that God exists. Anselm also wrote *Cur Deus Homo.* This book argues that only the death of a God-man like Jesus Christ could fulfill the debt that sinful humanity owed to God.

Anselm was born in Aosta, Italy. He joined the Benedictine monastery of Bec in France in about 1060. There he studied with Lanfranc, a noted Italian monk and scholar. Anselm rose rapidly in the organization of the monastery and became the abbot in 1078. In 1093, he was appointed archbishop of Canterbury, the most important religious position in England. He held the post until his death on April 21, 1109. Anselm went into exile from 1097 to 1100 and again from 1103 to 1107 because he opposed the king's power to select church officials. Anselm's feast day is April 21.   Marilyn J. Harran

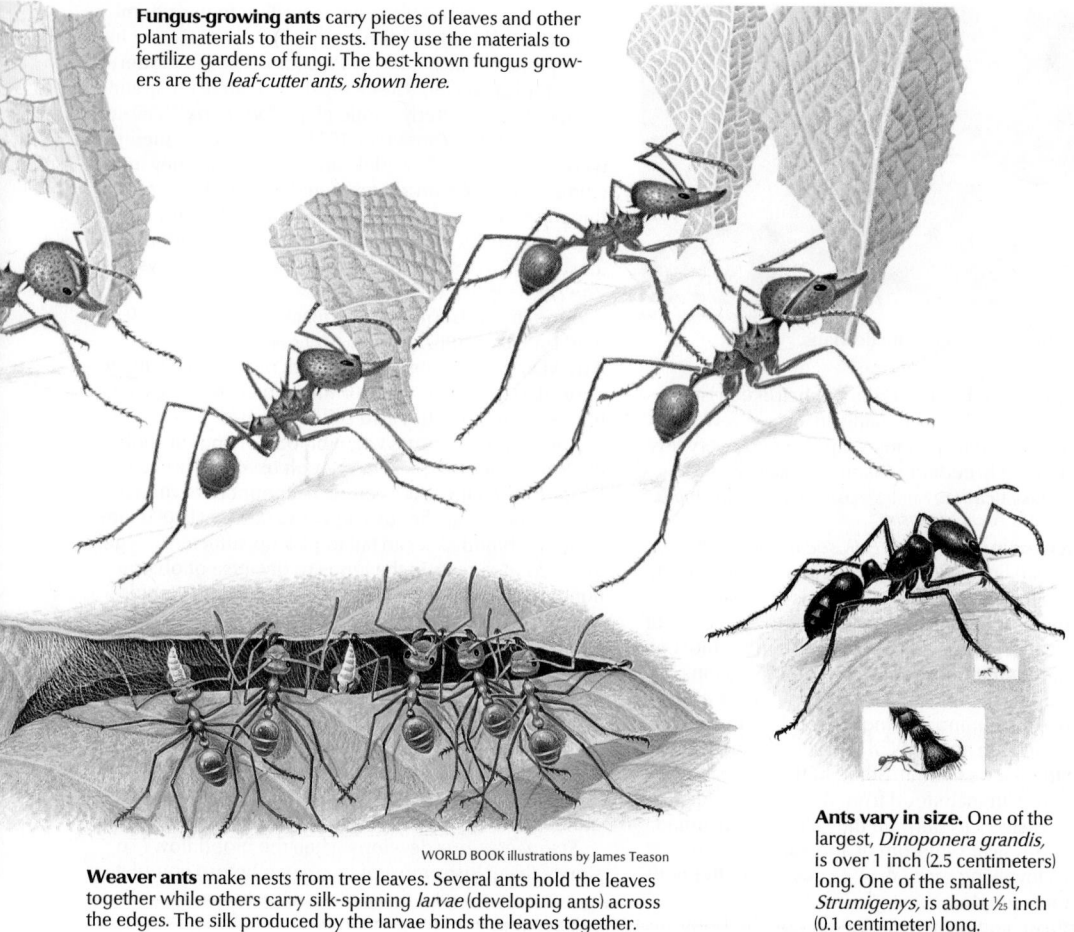

Fungus-growing ants carry pieces of leaves and other plant materials to their nests. They use the materials to fertilize gardens of fungi. The best-known fungus growers are the *leaf-cutter ants, shown here.*

WORLD BOOK illustrations by James Teason

Weaver ants make nests from tree leaves. Several ants hold the leaves together while others carry silk-spinning *larvae* (developing ants) across the edges. The silk produced by the larvae binds the leaves together.

Ants vary in size. One of the largest, *Dinoponera grandis,* is over 1 inch (2.5 centimeters) long. One of the smallest, *Strumigenys,* is about ⅖ inch (0.1 centimeter) long.

Ant

Ant is a small insect—usually black, brown, red, or yellow in color—that lives in organized communities called *colonies.* Ants somewhat resemble termites but can be distinguished by their narrow waists and *elbowed* (bent) antennae. Because ants depend on their colonies for survival, scientists classify them as *social insects.* Ants belong to the same *order* (related group) of insects as bees and wasps.

Ants vary in color and size. Besides black, brown, red, and yellow, they can be orange, blue, green, or even purple. The largest ants measure over 1 inch (2.5 centimeters) long. The smallest ants are about ⅖ inch (0.1 centimeter) long—barely visible to the unaided eye.

Ant colonies differ enormously in size. A colony may have a dozen, hundreds, thousands, or in rare cases, even millions of members. Regardless of size, most ant colonies share the same general structure. A colony usually has one or more *queens,* females whose chief

Linda M. Hooper-Bui, the contributor of this article, is Associate Professor of Entomology at the Louisiana State University Agricultural Center.

job is to lay eggs. The rest of the colony consists mostly of *workers.* These wingless female ants do not lay fertile eggs but instead build the nest, search for food, care for the queen and the young, and protect the colony. Unlike queens, workers commonly leave the nest and can often be seen walking about on the ground or in trees. An ant colony also includes the ant young or *larvae.* The worm-like larvae hatch from eggs laid by the queen. Male ants, who have wings, live in the colony only at certain times of the year. Their only job is to mate with young queens, who also have wings.

Scientists have identified more than 10,000 ant species, and they name new species every year. Most experts estimate that 20,000 to 30,000 ant species exist. Ants live almost everywhere on land, except in extremely cold areas. Most inhabit regions with warm climates, including deserts. Mild regions of Europe, North America, Japan, and China also have large ant populations. Some ant species live in underground tunnels, and some build earthen mounds. Others live inside trees or in hollow parts of certain other plants. Still other species construct their nests from tree leaves. Some ants do not build permanent nests.

Scientists think that ants gradually developed from wasp ancestors over 100 million years ago. Ants closely resemble wasps in the structure of their bodies. How-

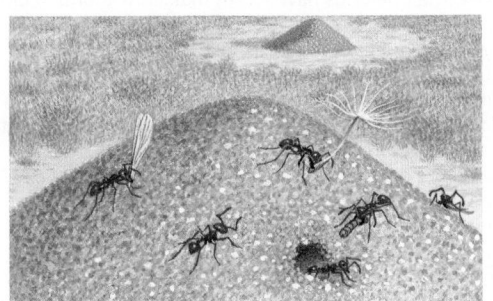

Some ants build earthen mounds over their underground nests. The mounds of harvester ants, *above,* are a common sight in the southwestern United States.

Ants use their antennae to smell one another. In this way, ants recognize nestmates. The antennae are organs of touch and taste as well as smell.

Many ants share food by *regurgitation.* Two ants stand mouth to mouth, and one spits up food for the other. Food is shared among all members of a colony.

Some carpenter ants nest in tunnels in tree branches. Large workers are called *soldiers.* A soldier blocks the nest entrance with its pluglike head, *above,* to keep out enemies.

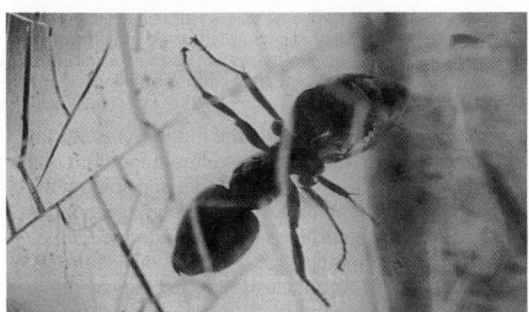

Fossils of ants indicate that ants have lived on Earth for more than 100 million years. This fossil ant, which became preserved in amber, is about 30 million years old.

ever, an ant has a *node* (knotlike growth) on top of its waist that distinguishes it from most antlike   wasps.

The bodies of ants

Among most ant species, the queens, workers, and males differ in size. In many cases, the queens grow several times larger than the workers. The males usually appear larger than the workers, but smaller than the queens. The workers of a particular species may also differ in size. Scientists call the largest workers *soldiers.*

Like all insects, ants have a hard, shell-like covering called an *exoskeleton* that protects their internal organs. An ant's muscles attach to the inside of the exoskeleton.

An ant's body features three main sections: (1) the head, (2) the thorax, and (3) the abdomen. The internal organs and sense organs of an ant resemble those of many other insects.

The head of an ant has the antennae, eyes, and mouthparts. The mouthparts include the *mandibles* and the *maxillae.* The mandibles consist of a pair of jaws attached to the front of the head that move from side to side rather than up and down. Ants use them to grasp food, carry their young, construct nests, and fight enemies. A pair of maxillae lie behind the mandibles and enable an ant to chew food into small particles. The ant then laps up the particles with its tongue and passes

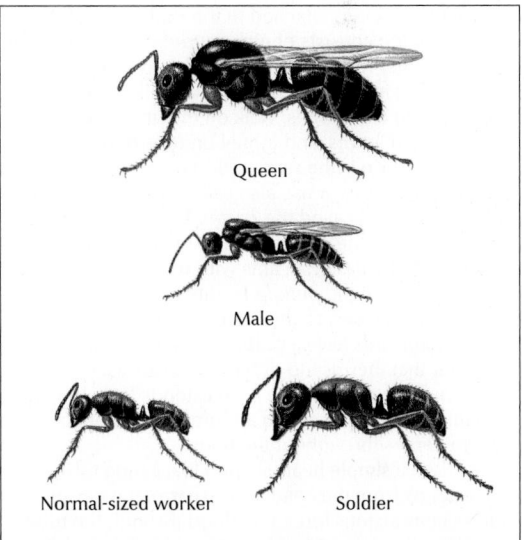

Queen

Male

Normal-sized worker   Soldier

WORLD BOOK illustrations by James Teason

The classes of ants—queens, males, and workers—differ in size. In most cases, queens are the largest, followed by males and workers. Among carpenter ants, *above,* some workers are larger than males. These large workers are called *soldiers.*

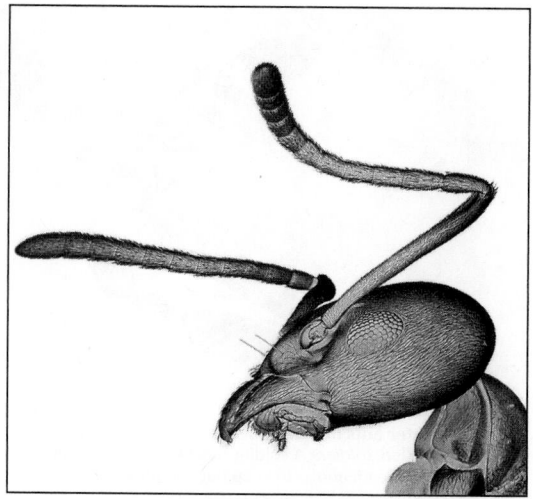

© David Scharf from Peter Arnold, Inc.

An ant's head includes two antennae, a pair of many-lensed *compound eyes,* and a pair of jaws called *mandibles.* This highly magnified view shows the tiny lenses that make up a compound eye and the fine hairs and spines that cover the antennae.

them into a small pouch inside the mouth. Muscles that line the pouch contract, squeezing liquid food out of the solid particles. Ants swallow the liquid and spit out the remaining solids as a pellet. They sometimes feed this pellet to larvae, who process it into liquid food.

Each of an ant's maxillae has a comb, which consists of a row of tiny hairs. An ant cleans its front legs by drawing them across the combs.

The thorax is the middle section of an ant's body. Among most species, the males and young queens have two pairs of wings attached to the thorax. The thorax holds the muscles that enable ants to beat their wings and fly at mating time. Worker ants do not have wings.

An ant has six legs attached to the underside of the thorax. Each leg consists of nine segments connected by movable joints. The foot of each leg has two hooked claws that dig into a surface as an ant walks. The claws enable ants to climb trees, walk on the undersides of tree limbs and leaves, and tunnel underground.

The abdomen is the rear section of an ant's body. It includes the narrow waist, also called the *pedicel,* and a bulblike hind part called the *gaster.* The waist consists of one or two movable, beadlike segments that connect the thorax to the gaster. In ants with one such segment, the waist is called the *petiole.* In ants with two, the second segment, closest to the gaster, is called the *postpetiole.* Some ants have a poisonous sting at the tip of the gaster that they use to defend themselves.

Internal organs. A nerve cord extends from the ant's head through the thorax and abdomen. It connects the brain to nerves throughout the body.

Ants have a simple heart shaped like a long tube. The tube extends from the head to the rear of the gaster. Muscle contractions force the blood through the tube toward the head. The blood empties out of the tube near the brain. An ant does not have blood vessels. Instead, the blood flows from the head back through the body cavity, bathing all the tissues and organs. It then reenters the tube through small openings along the

sides. The openings have valves that allow blood to enter the tube but prevent it from leaking out.

Ants do not have lungs. Instead, they have many air tubes that branch out to all parts of the body. Oxygen enters the tubes through tiny openings along the sides of the body called *spiracles.* Carbon dioxide passes out of the body through the spiracles as well.

An ant's digestive system consists of a tube that extends from the mouth to the end of the gaster. This tube connects the insect's two stomachs, both in the gaster. The first stomach, called the *crop* or *social stomach,* stores liquid food without digesting it. The crop can expand greatly to hold food. An ant frequently *regurgitates* (spits up) some of the stored food and shares it with other ants. A valve separates the crop from the ant's second stomach. When the ant is hungry, it moves food from the crop to the second stomach for digestion.

Sense organs. An ant's chief sense organs are its antennae. Ants have two antennae attached to the front of the head. The antennae serve as organs of smell, touch, and taste. When an ant engages in activity, its antennae move constantly. Ants use their antennae to feel the ground, detect scents in the air, examine food, and stroke one another. Antennae also help ants to find their way about, search for food, and recognize nestmates, who share a similar odor.

Ants have taste organs on their mouthparts in addition to those on the antennae. These taste organs lie between the mandibles. Ants have touch organs not only on the antennae but also on almost all other parts of the body. The touch organs consist of tiny hairs and spurs.

Most ants have two *compound eyes,* one on each side of the head. A compound eye consists of tiny lenses set close together. The number of lenses varies from 6 to more than 1,000, depending on the ant species. Usually, the males and queens have more lenses than the workers do. Each lens sees only a small part of whatever an ant looks at. Impressions from all the lenses together form a picture composed of tiny bits. Compound eyes enable ants to see movements easily. However, ants can clearly see only nearby objects. In addition to compound eyes, some ant species have three simple eyes, called *ocelli,* on the top of the head. Ocelli can sense only light or dark. Some ants that live their entire lives underground have no eyes.

Ants lack ears, but they can detect vibrations by means of sense cells called *chordotonal organs* on their antennae, legs, and body. These organs register vibrations that pass through the ground or other solid material. Researchers do not know for certain whether ants can hear sounds that pass through the air.

Some ants can make sounds by means of a *stridulatory organ* on the abdomen. In most cases, this organ consists of a row of ridges on one segment of the abdomen and a hard point on another segment. Ants make squeaky or buzzing sounds by rubbing the segments together, much as a person might make noise by running a fingernail over the teeth of a comb. Some ant sounds can be heard by people.

Life in an ant colony

All ants live in groups, but different ant species vary in their ways of life. This section discusses the general features of life in an ant colony. The section *Kinds of ants*

The body of an ant

The external anatomy

An ant's body has three main parts: (1) the head, (2) the thorax, and (3) the abdomen. The main features of the head are the eyes, antennae, and mandibles. Three pairs of legs extend from the bottom of the thorax. The narrow front part of the abdomen is called the *waist,* and the large back part is called the *gaster.* Some ants have a sting at the tip of the gaster.

The internal anatomy

An ant's internal organs include a brain and nerve cord and a tube-shaped heart. Tiny openings called *spiracles* let oxygen into the body and carbon dioxide out. The ant's system includes a food pouch that squeezes the liquid out of food. The liquid moves through a food passage to the *crop* and then to the second stomach, where digestion occurs. Wastes pass through the rectum and out of the body.

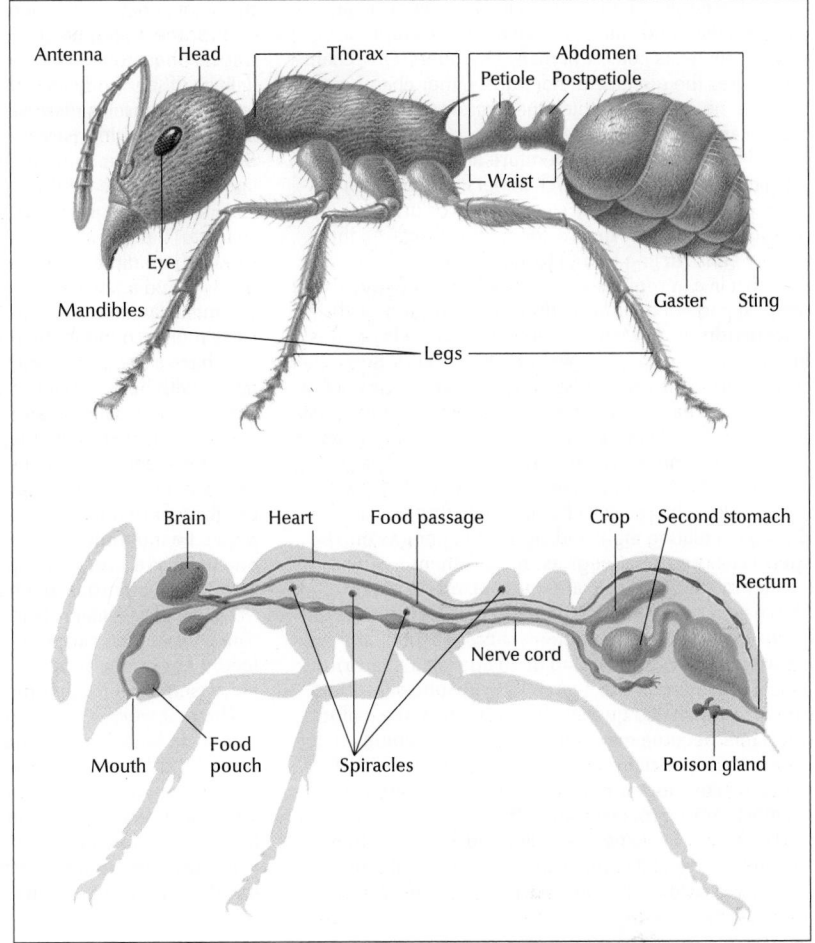

WORLD BOOK illustration by James Teason

describes some of the many ways of life among ants.

Castes. Most ant colonies share the same basic structure. It divides the colony into three distinct *castes* (classes): (1) the queen, (2) the males, and (3) the workers.

In most cases, a young queen starts a new colony after mating with one or several males. After establishing a colony, the queen lays eggs for the rest of her life. The other ants protect, feed, and tend the queen because her eggs help ensure the survival of the colony. However, the queen does not "rule" the colony. Some colonies have only one queen. However, in some species, thousands of queens may reside in a single colony.

Males do not do any work in the colony. They live only a short time, and their only purpose is to mate with young queens. The workers feed and lick the queen, as they do one another. Besides caring for the queen, the workers enlarge, repair, clean, and defend the nest; care for the young; gather food; and even remove dead or sick ants from the colony. A worker may do chiefly one job all its life or may change jobs from time to time.

The workers among many species of ants vary in size and shape but are always female. The largest workers, the soldiers, have a big head and large mandibles. In some species, the soldier's chief job is to defend the colony. Among certain *carpenter ants,* ants that nest in

wood, the soldiers have a blunt, plug-shaped head. These soldiers serve as doorkeepers. To keep enemies out, the soldier blocks a tunnel with its head. The soldier will stand aside to allow a nestmate to pass, recognizing the member by its odor. Among *harvester ants,* ants that collect seeds for food, the soldiers crack open the seeds that smaller workers collect. The small workers then feed on the soft, inner contents of the seeds.

Nests. Most ant species make their nests underground by carving tunnels and chambers in the soil. Some of these species build large mounds of soil, twigs, and pine needles over their underground nests.

Many ants nest in other places. For example, carpenter ants make nests in the trunks and branches of trees and in the wooden beams of houses. These ants, unlike termites, do not eat wood. They chew tunnels in wood only to make nesting space. Other kinds of ants make their homes beneath the bark of trees, in hollow twigs, or in the thorns of certain plants. Some species chew up plant fibers and use the material to make "cardboard" nests. Ants may even nest in old acorns and hickory nuts that beetles have hollowed out.

Tropical *weaver ants* construct nests from tree leaves. Some workers hold the edges of leaves together, while other workers carry silk-spinning larvae back and forth across the edges. The result is a thick sheet of silken webbing that binds the edges of the leaves together.

Most ant nests consist of many chambers. One chamber houses the queen and her eggs. Other chambers serve as "nurseries" in which the workers keep the immature ants. Ants move their young among chambers to keep them at the ideal temperature and humidity. Workers gather and rest in other chambers. The nests of some ants have rooms for storing food or growing fungi for food. As a colony grows, the workers enlarge the nest by constructing more chambers and passageways. Ants that live in regions with cold winters move to the deepest parts of their nests during that season.

Reproduction. Many queens lay thousands of eggs in a lifetime. Most eggs develop into workers. Some become males and young queens that leave the nest a few weeks after reaching adulthood. These ants go on a *mating flight.* They fly in a swarm high in the air and mate.

During mating, a male deposits sperm inside a queen's body. A young queen may mate with one or more males. She receives her lifetime supply of sperm during the mating flight and stores it in her gaster. The sperm later enter her eggs as she lays them.

After mating, the male and queen land on the ground. The male wanders off and dies. The queen removes her wings by knocking them off with her legs, pulling them off with her jaws, or rubbing them against a nearby object. She then begins to search for a nesting site. Sometimes, newly mated queens do not begin a new colony but rather become members of an existing colony of the same species or return to their original colony. In other cases, two or more unrelated queens may start a colony together. Among parasitic ants, the queen takes over the nest of another ant species, called the *host.* She then rids the colony of its queen and depends on the host workers to care for her and her eggs. However, among most ant species, the queen establishes a new nest.

After the queen prepares a nest, she seals the entrance. She soon begins to lay eggs. The queen primarily lives off her body fat during this time. Her now useless wing muscles dissolve into nourishing substances that enter the bloodstream and provide her with energy. She may also eat some of her eggs. Queens of most species do not leave the nest to search for food.

Ants go through four stages of development: (1) egg, (2) larva, (3) pupa, and (4) adult. The small size of ant eggs makes them difficult to see without a microscope. They hatch within a few days and become larvae. The white, wormlike larvae cannot move, and the workers often carry them around in their jaws. The larvae lack legs, but they have a head and a mouth. The queen feeds her first larvae with her saliva and sometimes with her eggs. The larval stage usually lasts a few weeks. After the larvae complete their growth, they become pupae. The larvae of some species spin a fine silk cocoon around themselves before becoming pupae. In other species, only a tough layer of transparent skin covers the pupae. The pupae lie motionless and do not eat. Over a period of one to several weeks, the pupae transform into adult ants, which emerge from the cocoon or skin.

Larvae play a vital role in feeding most colonies because they alone can process solid food. The workers feed them solids, and the larvae regurgitate a nutritious fluid used to feed other members of the colony.

The first worker ants to become adults leave the nest and bring back food for the queen. They take over the care of the *brood*—the eggs, larvae, and pupae—and the queen continues to lay eggs. As the colony increases in size, it produces more young queens and males who leave the nest to mate and repeat the cycle.

Protection against enemies. Anteaters, birds, frogs, lizards, spiders, toads, and many insects prey on ants. In

Inside an ant nest

This drawing shows the nest of a colony of harvester ants. The nest consists of various rooms and connecting tunnels. The tunnels extend through the mound and deep underground. One chamber houses the queen and her eggs. Several rooms serve as "nurseries," where the workers care for the growing young. Some chambers are gathering or resting places for the workers. Harvester ants also have rooms for storing seeds, which they gather outside the nest. As a colony grows, the workers make more rooms and tunnels. The ants spend the winter in the deepest rooms of the nest.

WORLD BOOK illustration
by James Teason

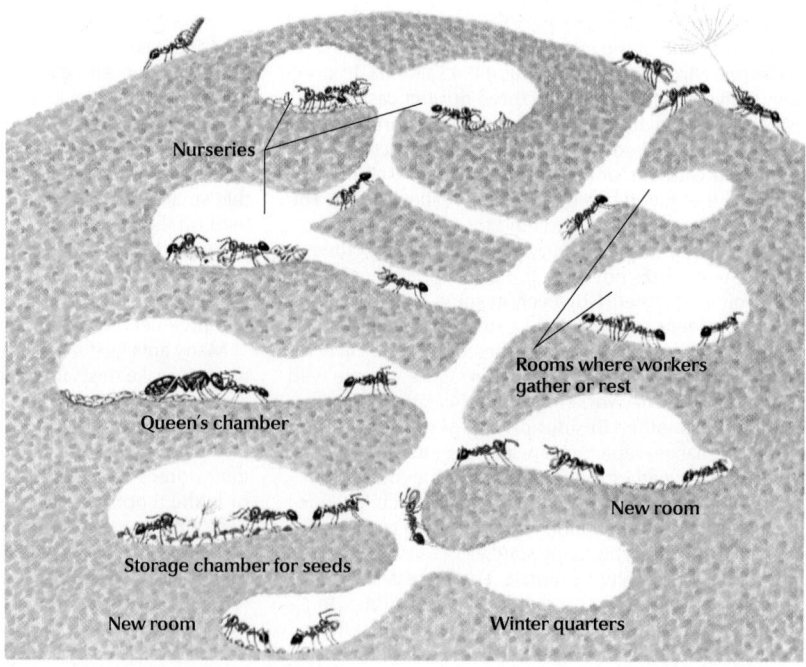

Nurseries

Rooms where workers gather or rest

Queen's chamber

New room

Storage chamber for seeds

New room

Winter quarters

most cases, ants from different colonies, even those from the same species, treat one another as enemies.

About half of all ant species have a sting that serves as an effective defense against other insects. The sting releases a poison that can damage or destroy tissue. Some ants that lack a sting can spray poison from the tip of the gaster. Ants can only defend themselves against larger predators by attacking in a massive swarm.

Battles between worker ants from different colonies occur often. Sometimes these battles do not result in serious injuries. For example, *honey ants,* ants that collect and store liquid food, often engage in shoving matches between workers from rival colonies. The workers do not hurt one another, but the victors sometimes take over the nest of the defeated colony. Some ants fight huge, grim wars in which thousands of ants kill one another. The ants may use their jaws to grab enemies by a leg or an antenna. Often, several nestmates grab the legs and antennae of an enemy ant and hold the victim stretched out. Other nestmates may join the fight and tear the victim apart with their jaws. The winners may invade the nest of the defeated colony and carry off the brood, which they eat. Certain ant species live entirely by robbing the nests of other ants in this way.

Communication. Coordinating the activities of an ant colony requires efficient methods of communication. The release of chemicals called *pheromones* serves as the basic means of communication among ants. An ant's body contains about a dozen glands that open at certain places in the head, thorax, and abdomen. These glands produce pheromone signals that other ants can smell and taste, enabling nestmates to communicate. The various kinds of pheromones communicate different information. By releasing pheromones from the tip of the gaster, for example, an ant may lay a scent trail from a new food supply to its nest. Nestmates then follow the trail to the food. To immediately warn nestmates of danger, ants can release airborne "alarm" pheromones.

Ants recognize nestmates by their familiar odor. When two ants meet, they smell each other with their antennae. Ants can even distinguish between the different castes within the colony and identify the queen by her unique chemical signals.

Ants also communicate by touch and vibrations. Ants that live inside plants or in leaf nests may tap their gasters against the outside walls of the nest when they

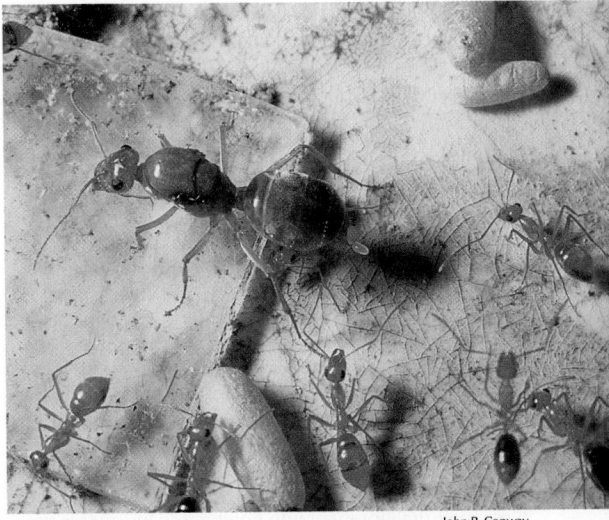

John R. Conway

Reproduction. This large queen honey ant is laying eggs, which the nearby workers will care for. In time, the developing young will be enclosed in cocoons like the three shown here.

discover food or an enemy nearby. The taps send vibrations through the nest walls to alert the ants inside. Ants with a stridulatory organ arouse their nestmates by producing squeaky or buzzing sounds.

Life span. Among insects, ants have a long life span. Queens, workers, and males live for different lengths of time. Queens live the longest, usually from about 5 to 15 years. However, some queens have lived more than 20 years. Workers live from less than 1 year to more than 5 years. Males live only a few weeks or months before the mating flight and die soon after mating.

Kinds of ants

Entomologists (scientists who study insects) sometimes group ants according to their ways of life, which vary greatly. This section discusses six groups of ants that live in different ways. They include: (1) army ants, (2) slave-making ants, (3) harvester ants, (4) dairying ants, (5) honey ants, and (6) fungus-growing ants.

Army ants prey ferociously on insects and spiders. Some feed primarily on other ants and their young.

The life cycle of ants   Ants develop in four stages: (1) egg, (2) larva, (3) pupa, and (4) adult. Ant eggs hatch within a few days into larvae. The larval stage lasts a few weeks. In some species, the larvae spin a cocoon before becoming pupae. The pupal stage lasts from one to several weeks. The adult ant then emerges.

WORLD BOOK illustration by James Teason

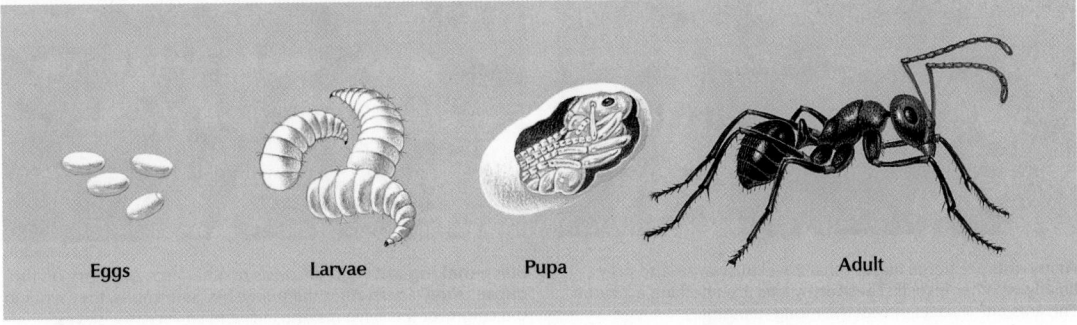

Eggs   Larvae   Pupa   Adult

While most species of army ants travel across the land in narrow columns, some species in desert regions live primarily underground. Army ants live in immense colonies numbering from 10,000 to several million members. Each colony includes a single large queen. Army ant colonies do not build permanent nests but instead establish temporary nests called *bivouacs.*

Many army ant species follow complex patterns of movement based around the reproductive cycle. In one common pattern, the colony remains in the same location for two to three weeks while the queen lays thousands of eggs. Once the eggs hatch, the colony has many hungry larvae to feed. At that time, the colony migrates to a different bivouac nearly every night and sends out raiding columns of worker ants to hunt for food for the young. This period of *migration* (wandering) continues until the larvae mature into pupae and no longer require feeding. The demand for food within the colony drops suddenly, and the colony remains in a single location for a couple of weeks while the pupae complete their development into adult ants. During this time, the colony sends out small raids to secure food, and the queen lays a new batch of eggs. The pupae and the newly laid eggs hatch at about the same time, and the colony begins another cycle of migration in search of food for the larvae.

Most army ants inhabit the tropical regions and rain forests of Central America, South America, Africa, and Asia. However, some species live in milder climates in North America. Army ants generally do not present a danger to people or large animals, although their sting is extremely painful.

Slave-making ants invade the nests of other ants, kidnap the pupae, and bring them back to the invaders' colony. When the pupae develop into adults, they act as members of the slave-making colony. The "slaves" help to build the nest, care for the young, and hunt for food.

Some kinds of slave-making ants depend on slaves for their survival. For example, *Amazon ants* have long, curved, swordlike mandibles that serve well for fighting and carrying home pupae but interfere with hunting and eating, digging nests, and caring for young. These ants rely on slaves to perform these tasks.

After the mating flight, the young slave-making queen takes over the nest of a slave species to establish a new colony. She kills or drives away many of the colony's workers and their queen. The slave-making queen then stays with the colony's brood until some of them reach adulthood. These new worker ants treat the slave-making queen as they would their own queen. They care for her eggs, which develop into slave-making adults, who will raid other nests and bring back more slaves. Slave-making ants most commonly live in the cool regions of North America, Europe, and Asia.

Harvester ants collect seeds and store them in special chambers in their nests. In doing so, they always have a supply of food available in case food outside the nest becomes scarce. The ants remove the husks from the seeds and chew the kernels into a soft paste called *ant bread.* They feed this paste to one another and to their young. Most harvester ants will also eat insects when available, especially termites.

Harvester ants live throughout much of the world, primarily in deserts and other regions with a distinct dry season. They build their nest in exposed areas in the form of a mound.

Dairying ants live chiefly on a sugary liquid called *honeydew* produced by other insects. In addition to sugar, honeydew contains small amounts of protein and other nutrients. Dairying ants obtain honeydew from insects that suck juices from plants. These juices contain more sugar and water than the insects need, and they discharge the excess as honeydew. Dairying ants visit the plants on which the insects feed so that they can lick up the honeydew. In most cases, the insect will wait for an ant to come by and "milk" it before releasing its honeydew. The ant does so by stroking the insect with its antennae. The best-known dairying ants feed on *aphids* (plant lice). Other ants obtain honeydew from scale insects called *mealy bugs* or other insect species.

Many dairying ants collect the eggs of aphids and store them in their nests in winter. When spring arrives, the eggs hatch, and the ants carry the aphids out of the nest and place them back on plants. The ants then begin

Edward S. Ross

Army ants are fierce hunters that travel in swarms and prey chiefly on other insects. These army ants are attacking a katydid. The ants bite the victim with their long mandibles.

Slave-making ants raid the nests of other ants and carry off the pupae, *shown here.* After the pupae become adults, they work in the colony of the slave-making ants and so serve as "slaves."

to collect honeydew from the aphids again.

Certain species of dairying ants tend underground "herds" of aphids that feed on plant roots inside the ant nest. Among these species, the young queen carries an egg-laying aphid between her jaws when she leaves the nest to go on the mating flight. After the queen digs her new nest, she places the aphid on a root and starts a new herd. Other species of dairying ants tend aphids aboveground on stems, leaves, and flowers.

Dairying ants protect honeydew-producing insects by fighting off predators. Because the insects they protect can feed on crops and cause great damage, farmers consider dairying ants to be agricultural pests.

Honey ants, also called *honeypot ants,* gather honeydew from aphids and other insects or directly from plants and store it in their nests. Inside the nest, certain workers, called *repletes,* serve as living storage tanks for the colony. After returning to the nest, the workers that gather the honeydew feed it to the repletes. The replete stores the food in its crop. Over time, the gaster of the replete becomes so swollen with honeydew that the ant cannot walk. It hangs motionless from the ceiling of a special chamber in the nest. The replete feeds its nestmates by regurgitating some honeydew whenever a nestmate taps it with its antennae. Honey ants most commonly inhabit deserts and other dry, warm regions, particularly in Australasia and North America.

Fungus-growing ants cultivate gardens of fungi in their nests. Each colony of fungus growers raises one particular type of fungus. The fungi grow tiny, nourishing knobs that provide the ants with their only source of food. The ants in a colony fertilize their garden with plant materials—including seeds and parts of flowers and leaves—that they gather from outside the nest. Some fungus growers use insect waste, such as caterpillar droppings, for fertilizer. The ants tend carefully to their garden, controlling the temperature and humidity in the nest and removing fungi that may grow as weeds. The ants also produce chemicals in their glands that they can apply to the garden to prevent the wrong fungi from taking over. When a young fungus-growing queen leaves the nest to mate and establish a new colony, she

Edward S. Ross

Dairying ants "milk" honeydew from aphids, *shown here.* The aphids release drops of honeydew whenever the ants stroke them with their antennae. The ants then lap up the sugary liquid.

carries a little pellet of fungus in a special chamber under her head. After the queen prepares her nest, she starts a new garden with the pellet. Most fungus growers reside in the tropical and subtropical regions of North and South America.

Perhaps the best known fungus growers are the *leaf-cutter ants.* These ants build huge underground nests in which millions of ants may live. At night, they send out columns of workers to cut pieces of leaves from trees, shrubs, and other plants. The workers carry the leaf fragments back to the nest, holding them over their heads. The ants look as though they are carrying parasols, and so people sometimes call them *parasol ants* or *umbrella ants.* Inside the nest, the ants chew the leaf fragments to a pulp, which they use to grow fungi. In parts of Central and South America, leaf-cutters cause severe damage to crops by stripping away their leaves. For example, in Brazil, colonies of leaf-cutter ants sometimes strip all the leaves from an orange grove in one night.

Ross E. Hutchins

Harvester ants store seeds in special rooms inside their nests, *shown here.* The ants tear off the husks and chew the kernels into a soft pulp. They then squeeze out the liquid and swallow it.

John R. Conway

Honey ant workers called repletes serve as storage tanks. They store honeydew in their gasters, which expand greatly. The repletes feed the liquid to nestmates.

Keeping an ant farm

You can study a colony of ants as they work, eat, and care for their young by keeping an artificial nest called an *ant farm*. An ant farm consists of a container made of transparent plastic or glass through which you can view the chambers of the ants' nest. You can purchase a commercial ant farm that comes with a certificate to exchange for live ants. To help prevent the spread of nonnative ant species, many countries prohibit the shipping of queen ants in the mail. For this reason, the ants you receive will likely consist entirely of workers. Without a queen to lay eggs, your ant colony will not last long. The worker ants will only live for a month or two.

You can also make your own ant farm. A large, clean glass jar or plastic container with clear sides and a lid makes the simplest ant farm. First, fill the jar with slightly wet soil and pack the soil down lightly. Next, collect the eggs, larvae, pupae, and ants from a single colony. This will take some practice and skill. You can find ant colonies under rocks or by digging up a nest in the soil. You may recognize the colony's queen by her large size. Gather the ants in a plastic bag. Then put the bag of ants in the refrigerator for half an hour to slow them down, which will help you transfer them to the jar more easily. Once the ants have dug a nest in the jar, they will become less eager to leave and easier to observe. Ants typically need little or no light, so wrap dark paper around the walls of the jar to keep out the light. Take the paper off only when you wish to watch the ants. However, you may allow light to pass through the top of the jar. When handling the jar, be careful not to shake it.

Feed the ants every few days with a little honey mixed with water and soaked into a cotton ball. You may also feed them small pieces of nuts, dead insects, and cookie crumbs, among other things. You may be surprised to learn all of the things that ants will eat. Remove unused food from the ant farm promptly, or it will become moldy. Moisten the soil in the jar when it starts to become dry. Do not forget to release the ants outside when you have completed your observations.

The importance of ants

Ants play an important role in the balance of nature. They eat large numbers of insects and keep them from becoming too plentiful. Ants themselves serve as an important food source for birds, frogs, lizards, and many other animals. See **Balance of nature.**

The activities of ants can both benefit and interfere with agriculture. Some ant species aid farmers by eating insects that damage crops. Ants that dig underground also help to break up, loosen, and mix the soil. In doing so, they enable the soil to absorb water more easily. However, some species, such as dairying ants, protect aphids and other insects that harm crops. *Fire ants,* stinging ants common in the southern United States, build large mounds that interfere with the cutting of hay.

Some ants act as household pests. For example, carpenter ants damage houses by tunneling through their wooden beams. *Pharaoh's ants* and *thief ants* invade houses, restaurants, and other buildings and eat stored food. Certain species, such as the fire ant, also have a painful sting, which can cause an allergic reaction in some people.

Occasionally, people introduce ant species into areas where the insects do not naturally occur. The ants grow in number and destroy native ants and other insects in the area. Once a nonnative ant species has established itself in an area, getting rid of it becomes difficult.

Ants play an important role in maintaining many *ecosystems.* An ecosystem consists of a community of living things along with its natural environment. Tunneling by ants adds air to the soil and distributes *nutrients* (nourishing substances) near plant roots. Ants also consume dead plants and animals and animal wastes and break down fallen leaves and wood. These activities help recycle nutrients and the element carbon, making them available for use by growing plants.

Linda M. Hooper-Bui

Scientific classification. Ants make up the family Formicidae in the order Hymenoptera.

Edward S. Ross

Leaf-cutter ants are major agricultural pests in parts of South America because they strip the leaves from crops. This leaf-cutter ant is using its mandibles to cut a piece of a leaf from a plant. The ant will then carry the fragment to its colony's nest, where it will be used to fertilize a garden of fungi.

Additional resources

Level I
Fleisher, Paul. *Ants.* Benchmark Bks., 2002.
Greenaway, Theresa. *Ants.* Raintree Steck-Vaughn, 2000.
Hoyt, Erich. *The Earth Dwellers: Adventures in the Land of Ants.* 1996. Reprint. Simon & Schuster, 1997.

Level II
Bolton, Barry. *Identification Guide to the Ant Genera of the World.* Harvard Univ. Pr., 1994.
Gordon, Deborah. *Ants at Work.* 1999. Reprint. Norton, 2000.
Holldobler, Bert, and Wilson, E. O. *The Ants.* Belknap, 1990. *Journey to the Ants.* 1994.

Ant bear. See Anteater.

Ant lion is an insect whose *larva* (young) digs a pit in the soil to trap ants and other small insects for its food. The adult ant lion looks like a dragonfly. The ant lion larva is often called the *doodlebug.*

The ant lion has a plump, hairy body. A pair of sword-shaped *mandibles* (jaws) extends from its narrow head. Three pairs of legs are found on its *thorax* (midsection). The ant lion can walk only backward.

The ant lion usually chooses a place with dry, sandy soil for its pit. It starts to work by walking around and around backward, pushing its tail like a shovel down into the sand behind it. The sand slides up over the ant lion's broad back and toward its head. By jerking its head suddenly, the ant lion throws the sand to one side. It moves in smaller and smaller circles until it reaches the center of the circle. Then it has formed a funnel-shaped hole in the earth. This pit sometimes reaches as much as 2 inches (5 centimeters) across and 1 inch (2.5 centimeters) deep or deeper.

© Shutterstock
Ant lion

The ant lion traps its prey by hiding under the sand at the bottom of the pit. If an ant crawls close to the edge of the pit, the soft sand slides away under its feet, and the ant falls into the pit. The ant lion then kills the ant with its jaws and sucks the juices from the ant's body. Frank G. Zalom

Scientific classification. Ant lions make up the ant lion family, Myrmeleontidae. There are hundreds of species.

Antabuse. See Disulfiram.

Antacid is any of a group of drugs that neutralize acid in the digestive system. Hydrochloric acid, produced in the stomach, is important to digestion. However, it can cause pain when it comes in contact with *peptic ulcers,* sores that can occur in the lining of the esophagus, stomach, or *duodenum* (first part of the small intestine). Antacids help relieve or prevent pain associated with peptic ulcers by neutralizing this acid. In addition, people take antacids to stop the pain of heartburn and indigestion.

Many antacid products contain compounds of aluminum, magnesium, or, often, both. These chemicals react with acids to form more neutral compounds that do not irritate peptic ulcers. By relieving irritation, antacids also can help promote healing of the ulcers. Many doctors recommend their use along with other antiulcer drugs, such as antibiotics and histamine H2-receptor antagonists (for example, cimetidine).

Antacids come in tablet, capsule, and liquid form. Commonly used antacids include such brand-name products as Maalox and Mylanta. Tums, another common antacid, contains a compound of calcium that is helpful for digestion but not recommended for ulcer treatment.

These drugs ordinarily do not cause harmful side effects, and a doctor's prescription is not needed to purchase them. However, antacids that contain magnesium hydroxide can cause diarrhea, while those with aluminum hydroxide can cause constipation. Problems also may develop when antacids are used for long periods. For example, extensive use of antacids that contain calcium carbonate can cause too much calcium to accumulate in the body. High calcium levels can lead to kidney damage and other problems. N. E. Sladek

Antakya. See Antioch.

Antananarivo, *AHN tuh NAH nuh REE voh,* is the capital and largest city of Madagascar, which includes the island of Madagascar and small nearby islands. About 1 ½ million people live in the city. Antananarivo, formerly called Tananarive, is near the center of the island of Madagascar. For location, see **Madagascar** (map). The city lies on a mountain ridge that runs across the island from north to south. Railroads running along the ridge link Antananarivo with the rest of the island and bring crops to the city for processing.

The majority of people who live in Antananarivo are of Indonesian descent. They are members of the Merina and Betsileo ethnic groups. Some of Antananarivo's residents are French. Madagascar was once a French colony. The French work with the local people in government, university education, and international trade. The University of Antananarivo and several scientific research institutes are in the city.

Antananarivo's most famous building is the palace of the last queen of Madagascar's Merina kingdom. Built in the 1800's, the palace was destroyed by fire in 1995. Restoration began on the building shortly after the fire. Bruce Fetter

See also **Madagascar** (picture).

Antarctic. See Antarctica.

Antarctic Circle, *ant AHRK tihk* or *ant AHR tihk,* is an imaginary line that encloses almost all of Antarctica. Points on the Antarctic Circle lie at 66° 33′ south latitude, about 1,624 miles (2,613 kilometers) from the south geographic pole (see **Antarctica** [map]).

The Antarctic Circle marks the edge of an area where the sun stays above the horizon one or more days each year. The sun never sets on the Antarctic Circle during the longest day of summer, about December 21. The sun never rises on the shortest day of winter, about June 21. If the South Pole at 90° south latitude were at sea level instead of nearly 10,000 feet (3,000 meters) above sea level, and if no atmospheric phenomena or other obstacles affected observations, the sun would be visible 90 days before and 90 days after the longest day of summer. It would stay below the horizon for the same time before and after the shortest day of winter. Leslie Duram

Antarctic Ocean. See Southern Ocean.

© Rod Planck, Photo Researchers

Antarctica's rugged coast features jagged mountain peaks and glacier-filled valleys. Ice and snow cover 98 percent of the continent. Antarctica is the world's coldest region.

Antarctica

Antarctica, *ant AHRK tih kuh* or *ant AHR tih kuh,* is the coldest, highest, brightest, driest, and windiest continent on Earth. Temperatures there almost never rise above 32 °F (0 °C). Antarctica is colder than the icy region of the Arctic Ocean centered on the North Pole. Bright ice and snow cover nearly the entire continent. Antarctica has the highest average elevation of the continents, at about 7,500 feet (2,300 meters). The South Pole, Earth's southernmost point, lies near the center of Antarctica on a high, windy plateau.

Antarctica covers about 5,400,000 square miles (14,000,000 square kilometers). It is larger in area than either Europe or Australia. Surrounding Antarctica is the Southern Ocean, which connects the Pacific, Atlantic, and Indian oceans.

Only a few small plants and insects can survive in Antarctica's interior. But many animals thrive in and near the surrounding waters, including fish, tiny shellfish called *krill,* seals, whales, penguins, and other sea birds.

Long before Antarctica was discovered, ancient Greek philosophers believed that a continent covered the southern end of Earth. Antarctica was first sighted in 1820. During the mid-1800's, explorers sailed along its coast and learned that it was large enough to be considered a continent. Inland exploration began in the early 1900's. The Norwegian explorer Roald Amundsen reached the South Pole in 1911. In what turned out to be a dramatic race, he arrived there five weeks ahead of a British expedition led by Captain Robert F. Scott.

During the mid-1900's, United States Navy officer Richard Byrd led air expeditions that increased scientific

Facts in brief

Area: About 5,400,000 mi² (14,000,000 km²). *Greatest distance*— Antarctic Peninsula to Wilhelm II Coast, about 3,450 mi (5,550 km). *Coastline*—about 19,800 mi (31,900 km).

Elevation: *Highest*—Vinson Massif, 16,067 ft (4,897 m) above sea level. *Lowest*—sea level.

Physical features: *Chief mountain ranges*—Antarctic Peninsula, Ellsworth, Prince Charles, Transantarctic, Whitmore. *Chief glaciers*—Beardmore, Lambert, Rennick, Support Force. *Chief ice shelves*—Amery, Filchner, Larsen, Ronne, Ross.

Interesting facts about Antarctica

The krill—a small, shrimplike animal—is a key source of food in the Antarctic region. Such animals as fish, birds, and seals feed on krill and are, in turn, eaten by larger animals. Swarms of krill form huge red masses in coastal waters during the day and glow bluish-green at night.

Antarctica's wandering pole, officially called the *south magnetic pole,* moves at least 5 miles (8 kilometers) a year. This is the South Pole indicated by compass needles.

Thick ice buries most of Antarctica. The continent's deepest ice is more than 10 times the height of the Willis Tower, one of the world's tallest buildings.

First to reach the South Pole was Roald Amundsen, a Norwegian explorer. His expedition set off from Antarctica's Bay of Whales on Oct. 19, 1911, and reached the pole on Dec. 14, 1911.

Plant fossils found in Antarctica reveal that the continent once had a warm, ice-free climate with trees and other leafy plants.

WORLD BOOK illustrations by Paul D. Turnbaugh

interest in Antarctica. In 1959, officials of 12 countries signed an international agreement called the Antarctic Treaty. This treaty provides that the continent be used mainly for research and other peaceful purposes.

Today, scientists maintain year-round research stations in Antarctica. Activities on the continent encourage international cooperation and the sharing of scientific knowledge. Several countries have claimed parts of the continent. But the Antarctic Treaty places a freeze on existing claims and prohibits new ones.

Geography

Ice and snow cover 98 percent of Antarctica. High mountain peaks and a few other bare rocky areas make up the only visible land. Underneath the ice lie features similar to those on other continents, including mountains, lowlands, valleys, and even lakes and rivers.

Land. If all Antarctica's ice were removed, the continent would be only about half its size. Much of the continent's mass lies below sea level.

Volcanoes are common in Antarctica. Some are active, and others are hidden beneath the ice. Mount Erebus, Antarctica's most active volcano, lies on Ross Island and rises 12,448 feet (3,794 meters) above sea level.

One prominent feature of the continent is the Antarc-

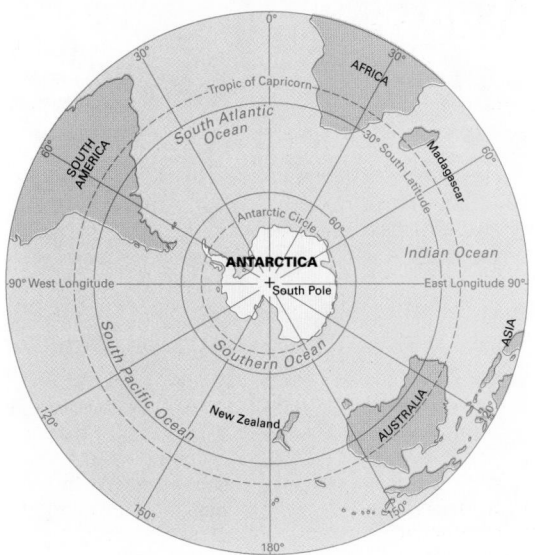

WORLD BOOK map

Antarctica is the continent that covers the South Pole. The Southern Ocean surrounds the continent.

tic Peninsula. The peninsula is an S-shaped mountain chain that stretches northward toward South America. It forms a continuation of South America's Andes Mountains. Several islands lie near the peninsula. The South Shetland Islands to the west include Deception Island, an active volcano with a well-protected harbor. The harbor is the result of a violent eruption 10,000 years ago that blew out the summit crater.

A mountain chain called the Transantarctic Mountains crosses the entire continent. These mountains contain the oldest Antarctic rocks, some over 570 million years old. Several ranges make up the Transantarctic chain.

Vinson Massif, the highest point in Antarctica at 16,067 feet (4,897 meters), stands in the Ellsworth Mountains near the Antarctic Peninsula. The Transantarctic chain has the largest of the rocky, ice-free areas known as *dry valleys*. The valleys were carved by glaciers that once occupied them. Snow that falls in dry valleys is swept away by winds. Some of the valleys have lakes. Most of the lakes remain frozen the year around.

Ice. Antarctica has about 90 percent of the world's ice. This ice, with a volume of 7.25 million cubic miles (30 million cubic kilometers), represents about 70 percent of the world's fresh water. If the ice melted, Earth's oceans would rise nearly 230 feet (70 meters), flooding coastal cities around the world. The weight of the ice causes it to spread outward and flow toward the coasts. The average thickness of the ice is over 7,100 feet (2,200 meters). The thickest ice measures 15,700 feet (4,790 meters) thick. The Transantarctic Mountains separate Antarctica's ice into two giant ice sheets.

The East Antarctic ice sheet lies mainly in the Eastern Hemisphere. It is the larger, thicker, slower flowing, and colder of the two ice sheets. It covers 90 percent of the continent, including the South Pole. The East Antarctic ice sheet is a high-elevation polar desert about 10,000

feet (3,000 meters) above sea level. Less than 1 inch (2.5 centimeters) of snow falls there each year.

The West Antarctic ice sheet lies primarily in the Western Hemisphere. It contains Antarctica's fastest flowing ice. The ice's speed results from its warmer temperatures and underlying terrain that is an average of 3,300 feet (1,000 meters) below sea level. If the ice sheet melted, all that would remain of West Antarctica would be a group of islands.

Ice near the center of the Antarctic ice sheets moves only a few feet or meters per year. But ice speeds up to many hundreds of feet or meters per year as it nears the coast. In many places, ice from the interior flows into faster-moving glaciers. Large outlet glaciers can be 250 miles (400 kilometers) long and more than 30 miles (50 kilometers) wide. They can move more than 2.5 miles (4 kilometers) per year. Fast-moving ice often breaks, forming deep *crevasses* (cracks). When the ice reaches the coast, it breaks off to form icebergs that are then carried out to sea. This process is called *calving*.

Ocean

The Southern Ocean surrounds Antarctica. The northern boundary of the ocean is 60° south latitude. Farther north, at about 55° south latitude, lies the center of an irregular band of water about 25 miles (40 kilometers) wide called the Antarctic Convergence. Within the band, cold southern waters meet warmer, saltier northern waters. At about 50° south latitude is the massive Antarctic

© Shutterstock

Mount Erebus is the most active volcano in Antarctica. It is located on Ross Island, a small island just off the Antarctic mainland in the Ross Sea.

© Guy Mannering, Bruce Coleman Inc.

Ice-free areas called *dry valleys* appear where Antarctica's glaciers have retreated and wind prevents snow from collecting. About 98 percent of the continent lies beneath ice and snow.

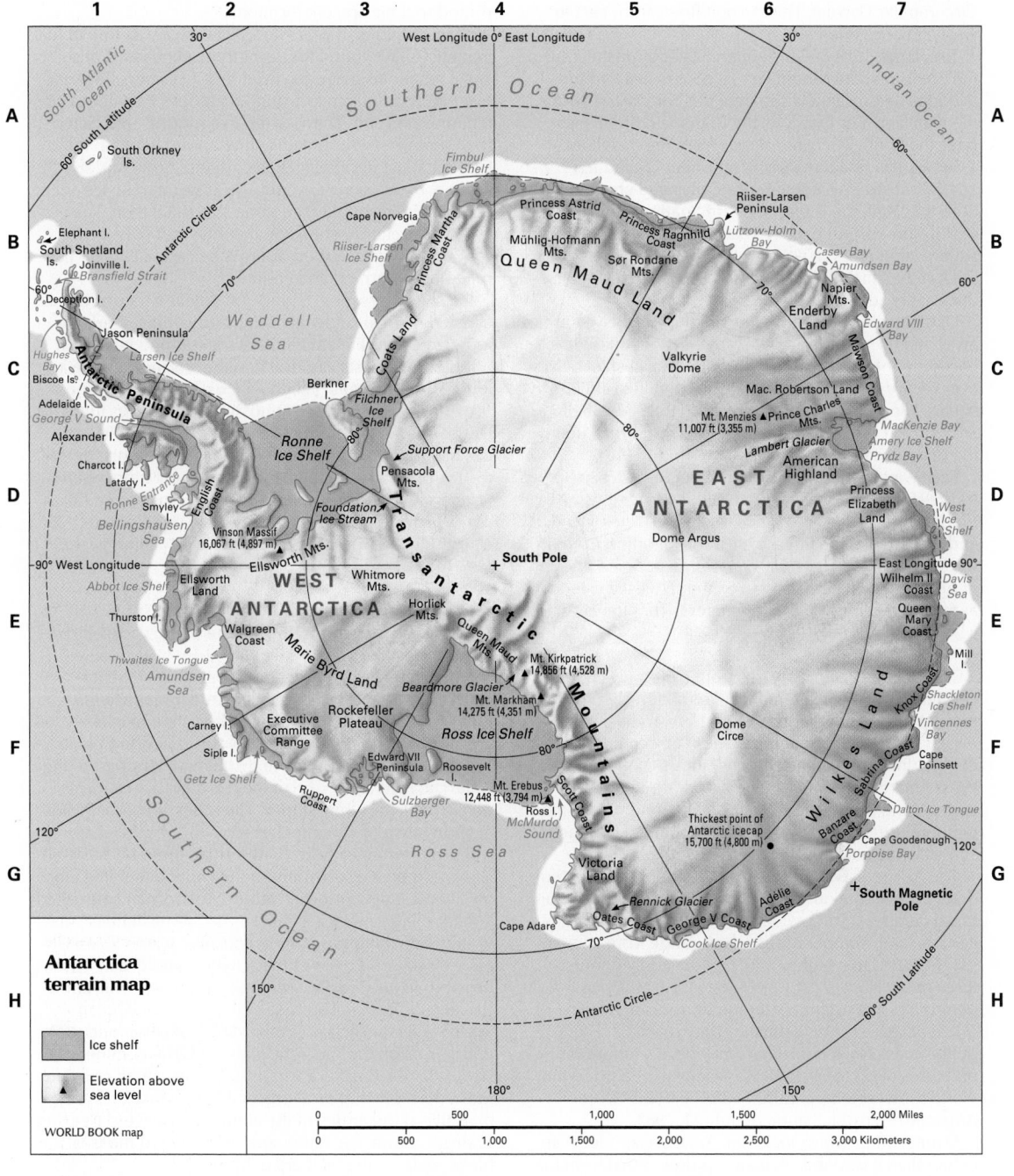

Antarctica terrain map

Ice shelf

▲ Elevation above sea level

WORLD BOOK map

0 500 1,000 1,500 2,000 Miles
0 500 1,000 1,500 2,000 2,500 3,000 Kilometers

Physical features

Circumpolar Current. This current flows from east to west, circling Antarctica.

Two large gulfs cut into Antarctica at opposite ends of the Transantarctic Mountains—the Ross Sea and the Weddell Sea. Channels separate offshore islands from the mainland. For example, the Bransfield Strait separates the South Shetland Islands from the mainland.

Broad, flat, floating parts of ice sheets called *ice shelves* fill several of Antarctica's bays and channels. The Ross Ice Shelf, the largest mass of floating ice in the world, spreads out over 190,000 square miles (490,000 square kilometers). It is about 2,300 feet (700 meters) thick at the inner edge and about 660 feet (200 meters) thick at the seaward edge.

Occasionally, the outer edges of the ice shelves break away and form immense *tabular icebergs*. Antarctic icebergs are the largest in the world. The largest iceberg ever recorded was about 4,200 square miles (11,000 square kilometers). It calved from the Ross Ice Shelf in March 2000. Icebergs eventually melt and break up in the open ocean.

Each winter, the surface of the Southern Ocean freezes into a sheet of salty ice called *sea ice*. In summer, this ice breaks into pieces called *ice floes*. Wind and waves push the floes against one another, forming thick masses known as *pack ice*. Some pack ice piles up in ridges against the shore. In winter, pack ice extends as far as 1,000 miles (1,600 kilometers) from the coast.

Climate

The Antarctic climate varies from extremely cold, dry conditions on the inland plateau to milder, slightly moister conditions along the coasts. Average snowfalls in East Antarctica range from 1 inch (2.5 centimeters) in the interior to 24 inches (61 centimeters) at the coast. In West Antarctica, annual snowfalls are three times this large. Along the Antarctic Peninsula, strong winds, mild temperatures, and nearby water combine to produce snowfall rates of many feet per year.

The Antarctic winter lasts from May through September. For several months, most of the continent is in continual darkness. Summer lasts from November through February. July temperatures inland range from a low of –94 °F (–70 °C) to a high of –40 °F (–40 °C). July temperatures range from –22 °F (–30 °C) to –5 °F (–21 °C) on the peninsula's coast. January temperatures range from –31 °F (–35 °C) to 5 °F (–15 °C) inland. They reach 32 °F (0 °C) on the coast. Northern islands may have summer temperatures of up to 50 °F (10 °C). Scientists recorded the world's lowest temperature, –128.6 °F (–89.2 °C), at Antarctica's Vostok Station on July 21, 1983.

Strong, bitter winds make the Antarctic air feel even colder than it is. Winds that sweep downward from the plateau can average 44 miles (70 kilometers) per hour. Gusts often reach the coast at 120 miles (190 kilometers) per hour. On the plateau, winds blow the snow into ridgelike snow dunes called *sastrugi*. The sastrugi measure up to 6 feet (1.8 meters) tall.

Antarctica's climate has not always been so cold. Geologists think Antarctica was once part of a giant supercontinent called Gondwanaland. This huge landmass also included what are now Africa, Australia, India, and South America. By about 140 million years ago, Gondwanaland had begun to break apart. The parts slowly drifted to their present locations.

Many millions of years ago, Antarctica was free of ice. Scientists have found fossils of trees, dinosaurs, and small mammals that once lived there. Glaciers began to form in East Antarctica around the South Pole about 38 million years ago. They started in a rugged area called the Gamburtsev Mountains, now buried beneath the East Antarctic ice sheet. These glaciers grew rapidly around 13 million years ago. The East Antarctic ice sheet has remained roughly the same size since then. The West Antarctic ice sheet, on the other hand, has advanced and retreated many times as Earth's climate has repeatedly warmed and cooled.

Ice sheets preserve a long and detailed record of past climate. As fresh snow is buried and compressed into ice, samples of the atmosphere are trapped in tiny air bubbles. Scientists can drill into the ice and remove a long, vertical sample called an *ice core*. Such a sample provides a record of the atmosphere at various times. Deeper parts of the core represent the more distant past. Slight differences in the chemical composition of the ice provide additional information on atmospheric temperature and ancient weather patterns. Antarctic ice cores provide an important way of learning about changes in Earth's climate over the past million years.

Living things

Only a few small plants and insects can survive in Antarctica's dry interior. But various living things thrive in and near the surrounding waters.

Few plants grow in Antarctica because of the ice-covered land and the harsh climate. Mosses are the most common Antarctic plants. They cling to rocky areas, mostly on the coasts. Only two flowering plants grow in Antarctica. Both live on the northern part of the Antarctic Peninsula. One of them is a grass that forms dense mats on sunny slopes. The other, an herb, grows in short, cushionlike bunches.

Simpler organisms known as algae grow on snow, in lakes, and on ice surrounding the continent. Some algae give snow a pink or green tinge. Other organisms called lichens cling to rocks as mosses do. Some lichens survive by bunching together to conserve water. Scientists have discovered rows of black, white, and green lichens growing in tiny cracks in dry valleys. Small plants and algae also drift on the surface of the Southern Ocean.

Only a few insects and other tiny animals spend their entire lives on the Antarctic mainland. The continent's largest land animal is a wingless midge, a type of fly no more than ½ inch (12 millimeters) long. Most land animals live at the edges of the continent. To avoid freezing to death, some lice, mites, and ticks cling to mosses, the fur of seals, or the feathers of birds.

Unlike the continent, the Southern Ocean has abundant wildlife. The most common ocean animal is *krill*, a small, shrimplike creature that feeds on tiny floating organisms. Many Antarctic animals depend on krill for food. Several countries also catch krill as a protein-rich food for people. Many Antarctic animals also eat squid. In addition, about 100 kinds of fish live in the ocean, including Antarctic cod, icefish, and plunderfish.

Several kinds of whales migrate to Antarctica for the summer. Blue whales, fin whales, humpback whales, minke whales, right whales, and sei whales feed on krill.

Animal life in Antarctica Antarctica's coastal waters have plentiful wildlife, though only tiny animals can survive in the harsh interior. Seals and birds nest on the coast and nearby islands, and whales migrate to the area for the summer. Many of these animals have extra layers of fat to keep warm in the cold, icy climate.

WORLD BOOK illustration by Paul D. Turnbaugh

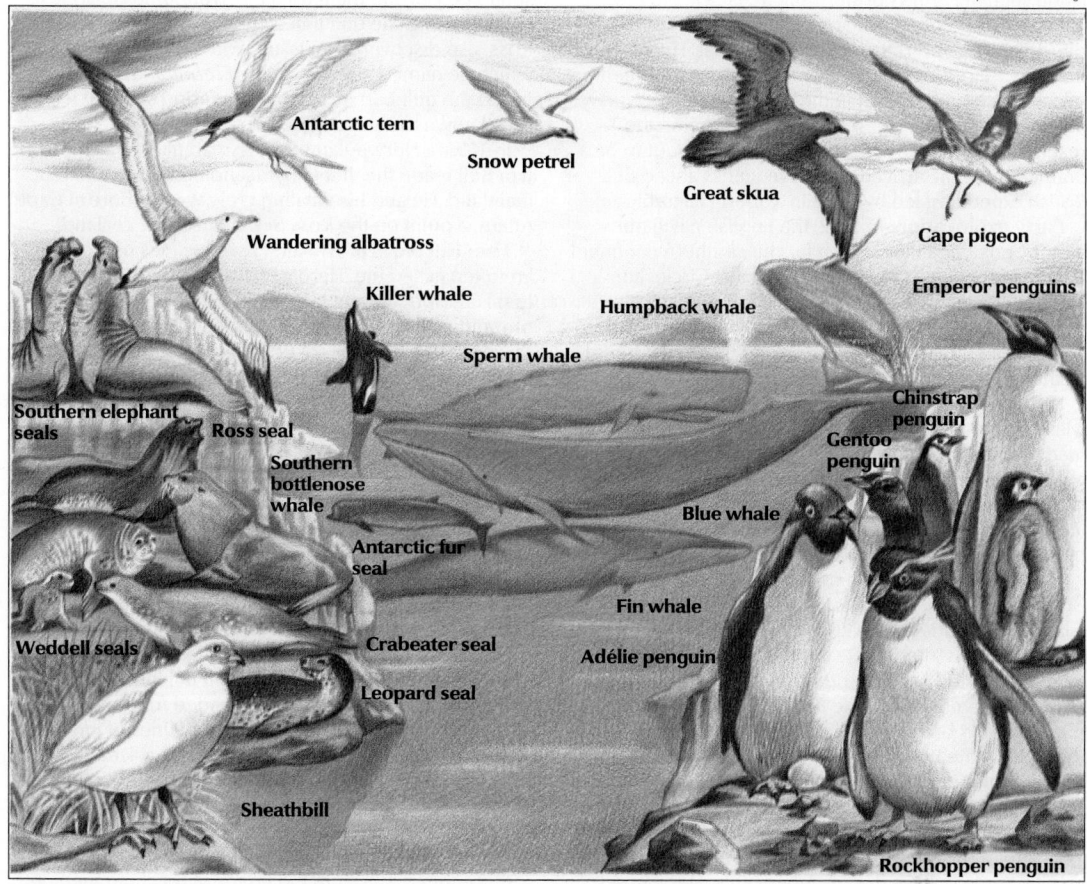

The blue whale is the largest animal ever. This rare giant grows up to 100 feet (30 meters) long. Antarctic whales that eat fish and squid include killer whales—also called *orcas*—and southern bottlenose whales, southern four-tooth whales, and sperm whales. Killer whales also hunt seals, penguins, and smaller whales.

Various kinds of seals live in Antarctica. They spend most of their lives in the water. Many of them nest on the coasts. The Antarctic fur seal nests on nearby islands. The largest seal in the world, the southern elephant seal, feeds on squid and may reach a length of 16 feet (5 meters). Ross seals and Weddell seals eat fish and squid. Antarctic fur seals and crabeater seals eat krill. Leopard seals hunt other seals and penguins.

During the 1800's and early 1900's, hunters greatly reduced the number of whales and Antarctic fur seals. Today, international wildlife laws prohibit or restrict the killing of these animals.

Penguins are the animals most often associated with Antarctica. These birds cannot fly, and they waddle awkwardly on land. But they are skillful swimmers. Six kinds of penguins breed on the continent. Adélie penguins, the most common kind, build nests of pebbles on the coasts. The tall, quieter emperor penguin usually grows

to about 3 feet (1 meter). After the female emperor penguin lays an egg, the male rests the egg on his feet and warms it with the lower part of his belly. Chinstrap, gentoo, king, and macaroni penguins nest on the Antarctic Peninsula and on islands. Rockhopper penguins nest only on islands north of Antarctica.

More than 40 kinds of flying birds spend the summer in Antarctica. Many types nest on land but spend most of their time diving for food. These birds include albatrosses, prions, and a large group of sea birds known as petrels. Other birds, such as cormorants, gulls, skuas, and terns, return to land more frequently. Some of them steal food from the nests of other birds. Some land birds, such as sheathbills, nest on the peninsula. Others, including pintails and pipits, nest on islands.

Exploration

People wrote about a southern continent centuries before Antarctica was discovered. Ancient Greek philosophers supposed that a landmass at Earth's southern end was needed to balance the weight of the northern lands. During the A.D. 100's, the Greek geographer Ptolemy gave this undiscovered continent the Latin name Terra Australis Incognita, meaning *unknown southern land.* He believed the land was populated and fertile. The name *Antarctica* later came from two Greek words meaning *opposite the bear.* The Bear is a constellation seen in Earth's northern sky.

People first sighted Antarctica in 1820. During the mid-1800's, explorers sailed along its coast. They learned that it was large enough to be considered a continent. Inland exploration began in the early 1900's. The Norwegian explorer Roald Amundsen became the first to reach the South Pole in 1911. In what turned out to be a dramatic race, he arrived there five weeks ahead of a British expedition led by Captain Robert F. Scott.

Early exploration. In 1772, the English navigator James Cook began his search for the southern continent. In January 1773, he crossed the Antarctic Circle, an imaginary line circling Earth at 66° 33' south latitude. A year later, Cook reached 71° 10' south latitude. Huge icebergs and thick ice floes prevented him from going farther, however, and he never sighted land.

Nobody knows who first saw the Antarctic continent. Many historians divide the credit among three men who made separate voyages in 1820. In January of that year, Captain Fabian von Bellingshausen of the Russian Imperial Navy reported reaching a point only 20 miles (32 kilometers) from the Antarctic Peninsula. Some historians believe that he saw land but thought it was ice.

That same month, Captain Edward Bransfield of the British Navy journeyed south of the South Shetland Islands and probably saw the Antarctic Peninsula. In November, an American sealer named Nathaniel Brown Palmer reported seeing land during a sealing expedition in the same area. Some geographers later called the peninsula Graham Land in honor of James Graham, the head of the British Navy in Bransfield's time. Others called it Palmer Land. The United States and the members of the Commonwealth of Nations finally agreed to the term *Antarctic Peninsula* in 1964.

Historians also are unsure of who first set foot on Antarctica. Some believe that an American sealer named John Davis went ashore at Hughes Bay on the tip of the peninsula in 1821. But Davis did not know if he had reached the continent or an island.

In 1823, a British sealer named James Weddell sailed south in search of hunting waters. He reached about 74° south latitude, farther than earlier voyagers had sailed, and found what is now called the Weddell Sea.

In 1831, the English whaler John Biscoe became the first to spot land in East Antarctica. He named it Enderby Land after the whaling company that owned his ship.

In 1837, the king of France sent Lieutenant Jules Dumont d'Urville to claim some southern lands for France. D'Urville's first attempt led him to discover what is now called Joinville Island, off the tip of the Antarctic Peninsula. He began his next Antarctic voyage from Tasmania, an island south of the Australian mainland. In January 1840, he sighted icy cliffs rising along the East Antarctic coastline. Many small penguins dotted the pack ice that blocked his way to the land. D'Urville named both the land and the penguins after his wife, Adélie.

About the time that d'Urville sighted land, U.S. Navy Lieutenant Charles Wilkes headed an expedition to perform scientific research. Wilkes's greatest contribution to Antarctic studies was his coastal exploration. His ship moved from the Adélie Coast toward Enderby Land,

tracing over 1,500 miles (2,400 kilometers) of coastline.

From 1839 to 1843, the British explorer James Clark Ross made several discoveries. Ross was the first person to go beyond the pack ice surrounding Antarctica. He sailed into the gulf that is now called the Ross Sea. Ross also discovered an island with two volcanoes, which he named after his ships, *Erebus* and *Terror.* He found the gulf barricaded by a towering sheet of ice, now known as the Ross Ice Shelf.

In 1895, a Norwegian businessman named Henryk Johan Bull made the first known landing on the Antarctic mainland. He and his whaling crew went ashore at Cape Adare, a point on the Ross Sea facing New Zealand.

The "Heroic Era." The first two decades of the 1900's are often called the "Heroic Era" of Antarctic exploration. In this period, people learned much about the geography and environment of the continent. It was also during this period that explorers first reached the South Pole.

The first inland exploration of Antarctica took place from 1901 to 1904. Robert Falcon Scott of the British Navy led a team of explorers and scientists to the Ross Sea. In November 1902, Scott and two other men headed south across the Ross Ice Shelf. But illness, harsh weather, and lack of food forced them to rejoin the team earlier than planned. Another group moved up a glacier through the Transantarctic Mountains and reached the edge of the harsh inland plateau.

Ernest Shackleton, a member of Scott's team, returned to Antarctica in 1907. Part of his expedition searched for the south magnetic pole in a remote area of East Antarctica, nearly reaching it in January 1909. At the same time, the main group headed for the south geographic pole, the meeting point of lines of longitude. Food shortages forced the men to turn back early. But they had come within about 110 miles (180 kilometers) of the pole, close enough to prove that the pole was on land rather than beneath a frozen sea.

In June 1910, Captain Scott left London, hoping to win for the United Kingdom the honor of reaching the South Pole first. In October, while Scott was in Australia, he received a telegram from the Norwegian explorer Roald Amundsen. The telegram informed Scott that Amundsen, too, was going to Antarctica. Amundsen originally had hoped to be the first to reach the North Pole. He switched his goal when he heard that the North Pole had been reached. The race to the South Pole became one of the most famous events in Antarctica's history.

Amundsen and his four assistants began crossing the Ross Ice Shelf from its northeastern corner, at the Bay of Whales, on Oct. 19, 1911. To reach the inland plateau, they had to carve their own route along an unexplored glacier in the Queen Maud Mountains, a part of the Transantarctic Mountains at the southern edge of the ice shelf. The men journeyed on skis, while 52 dogs pulled their four sleds of supplies. Amundsen marked his route and food storage areas with mounds of snow. He shot the weakest dogs for food when they were no longer needed to pull the sleds.

Scott set out with 15 other men on Nov. 1, 1911, from Cape Evans, Ross Island, at the northwestern corner of the Ross Ice Shelf. This location was about 800 miles (1,300 kilometers) from the pole, about 60 miles (100 kilometers) farther than Amundsen's starting point. However, Scott's expedition reached the plateau by way of the

Bettmann Archive

Hulton Getty from Liaison Agency

A dramatic race to the South Pole began in late 1911. British Navy Captain Robert F. Scott, *standing in the group photograph,* and the Norwegian explorer Roald Amundsen, *standing next to the flag of Norway,* each hoped to be the first to arrive at the pole. Amundsen reached the South Pole on December 14, five weeks before Scott. Amundsen's group returned safely. Scott and his men died on the way back, not long after this photograph was taken.

Beardmore Glacier, a known route. Scott tried using motorized sleds to carry some supplies and using ponies as well as dogs to pull other sleds. But the ponies and motor sleds bogged down in the soft snow. Eventually, the men had to drag the sleds, and food soon ran low. Scott crossed the plateau accompanied by four men.

Amundsen's group arrived at the South Pole on Dec. 14, 1911. They used special navigating instruments to calculate their position. Amundsen left behind his tent, a Norwegian flag, and a message for Scott. The group then headed back to their base, which they reached on Jan. 25, 1912. By that time, only 11 dogs remained, but all five men were in good health.

Scott's group reached the pole on Jan. 17, 1912, finding Amundsen's flag. Cold, hunger, and exhaustion had severely weakened the explorers. They photographed themselves at the pole and began their return. All five men perished on the way. Two of them died after they

were injured on the trail. Late in March, a long blizzard forced Scott and his two remaining assistants to make camp only 11 miles (18 kilometers) away from food and supplies. A search party found their frozen bodies inside the tent eight months later.

Exploration by air provided a new way to study Antarctica. In 1928, the Australian explorer Sir Hubert Wilkins surveyed the Antarctic Peninsula and nearby islands in the first airplane voyage over the continent.

In November 1929, the U.S. Navy officer Richard E. Byrd led the first flight over the South Pole. A Norwegian-American pilot, Bernt Balchen, flew Byrd's crew from the Bay of Whales to the pole and back. The flight lasted less than 16 hours. This journey was part of an expedition that Byrd supervised from 1928 to 1930. In a second expedition from 1933 to 1935, Byrd and his assistants traveled by plane and tractor over the Antarctic interior. They studied the ice, Earth's magnetism, cosmic

© Bettmann/Corbis/AP Images

Exploration by air greatly expanded knowledge of Antarctica's geography. In 1929, Richard E. Byrd of the United States Navy first flew over the South Pole. Byrd later led expeditions for the U.S. government in this Fokker trimotor plane.

rays, weather, and geology.

In 1935, the U.S. engineer Lincoln Ellsworth and the English-born pilot Herbert Hollick-Kenyon took off from Dundee Island, north of the Antarctic Peninsula, hoping to make the first flight across the continent. Near the Weddell Sea, they discovered what are now called the Ellsworth Mountains. Their plane had to land four times because of storms and a fuel shortage. They finally completed the crossing on foot at the Bay of Whales.

In 1946 and 1947, Byrd commanded the U.S. Navy's Operation Highjump, the largest Antarctic expedition by a single country. Operation Highjump sent 4,700 men, 13 ships, and 23 airplanes and helicopters to Antarctica. The expedition members discovered new land, including 26 islands. They photographed about 1,400 miles (2,300 kilometers) of previously unexplored coastline.

That same year, Captain Finn Ronne led a private U.S. air expedition to West Antarctica. Ronne explored areas of the Weddell Sea that had never been seen. The crew included Ronne's wife, Edith, and Jennie Darlington, the wife of his chief pilot. They were the first women to spend a winter on the continent.

The International Geophysical Year. Scientific knowledge of Antarctica increased rapidly during the International Geophysical Year (IGY). The IGY was a global program in which scientists coordinated observations and shared their findings. It began on July 1, 1957, and ended on Dec. 31, 1958.

As part of the IGY, 12 countries established over 50 scientific stations on Antarctica and nearby islands. These countries were Argentina, Australia, Belgium, Chile, France, Japan, New Zealand, Norway, South

Africa, the Soviet Union, the United Kingdom, and the United States. The United States set up a station at the South Pole, five coastal stations, and one inland station. The Soviet Union built a station at a point it named the Pole of Inaccessibility. This station, called Vostok, lies in East Antarctica, far inland from all coasts.

IGY researchers in Antarctica studied such topics as earthquakes, gravity, magnetism, oceanography, and solar activity. *Meteorologists* (scientists who study weather) determined air pressure, humidity, temperature, and wind direction and prepared Antarctica's first complete weather charts. *Glaciologists* (scientists who study ice) measured the thickness of the ice. Geologists studied the land formations.

During the IGY, the British geologist Vivian Fuchs headed the first land crossing of the continent. The Commonwealth of Nations organized the expedition, which covered 2,158 miles (3,473 kilometers). Fuchs left on Nov. 24, 1957, from the shore of the Weddell Sea, with dogs and snow tractors. A team led by the New Zealand explorer Sir Edmund Hillary placed food and supplies along the second part of the trail. Hillary met Fuchs at the South Pole in January 1958. Fuchs reached McMurdo Sound in the Ross Sea on March 2, 1958.

Seven of the 12 countries that built Antarctic bases for the IGY claim parts of Antarctica as their national territory. The parts are shaped like pie slices, with the South Pole at the center. Many nations, including the United States, do not recognize these claims.

International agreements. In 1959, at the end of the IGY, officials of the 12 countries signed the Antarctic Treaty. This agreement freezes all current territorial

Antarctica exploration

This map shows the routes of major expeditions in the Antarctic region. The continent was first sighted in 1820. Inland exploration of Antarctica began in the 1900's.

——— Cook (U.K.) 1773-74

-·-·- Bellingshausen (Russia) 1819-21

——— Weddell (U.K.) 1823

- - - - Wilkes (U.S.) 1840

········· d'Urville (France) 1840

-··-··- Ross (U.K.) 1840-41

——— Amundsen (Norway) 1911

- - - - Scott (U.K.) 1911-12

········· Byrd (U.S.) 1929

-··-··- Ellsworth (U.S.) 1935

-··-··- Fuchs (U.K.) 1957-58

○ Historic base camp

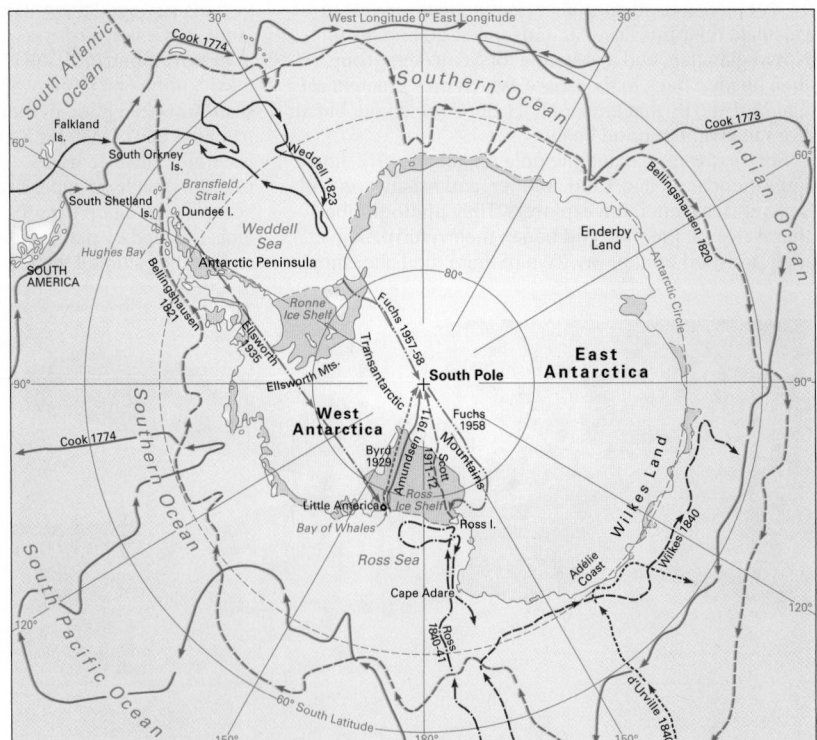

WORLD BOOK map

McMurdo Station, a United States research base on Ross Island, has Antarctica's largest community. About 1,200 people live there during the warmer months. A number of other nations—including Argentina, Australia, Chile, New Zealand, Russia, and the United Kingdom—also maintain research stations in Antarctica.

© David Ball, Corbis Stock Market

claims and prohibits new claims. It allows people to use Antarctica only for peaceful purposes, such as scientific research and tourism. It also requires scientists to share the results of their studies. The treaty forbids military forces in Antarctica, except those assisting scientific expeditions. It also outlaws the use of nuclear weapons and the disposal of radioactive wastes in Antarctica.

Since 1961, when the Antarctic Treaty took effect, a number of other nations have joined the treaty. Many of these nations have set up scientific programs in Antarctica. In 1991, the Antarctic Treaty nations signed the Madrid Protocol. This agreement, which went into effect in 1998, establishes Antarctica as a natural reserve devoted to peace and science. The protocol prohibits mineral exploitation in Antarctica and establishes strict rules

designed to protect the Antarctic environment.

Scientific research. Today, more than 40 year-round scientific stations operate on the continent and nearby islands. The National Science Foundation maintains three year-round U.S. stations: (1) Amundsen-Scott South Pole Station, (2) McMurdo Station on Ross Island, and (3) Palmer Station on Anvers Island near the Antarctic Peninsula. Other research stations are maintained by Argentina, Australia, Brazil, Bulgaria, Chile, China, Finland, France, Germany, India, Italy, Japan, New Zealand, Norway, Poland, Russia, South Africa, South Korea, Spain, Ukraine, the United Kingdom, and Uruguay.

McMurdo Station has Antarctica's largest community. About 1,200 scientists, pilots, and other specialists live there each summer. About 250 people stay through the

Antarctica territorial claims

Seven countries claim areas in Antarctica. This map shows the boundaries of these areas, some of which overlap. The map also pinpoints major Antarctic research stations and indicates the country that operates each station.

● Year-round research station

Areas claimed by:

☐ Argentina
☐ Australia
☐ Chile
☐ France
☐ New Zealand
☐ Norway
☐ United Kingdom

| 0 | 1,000 Miles |
| 0 | 1,000 Kilometers |

WORLD BOOK map

West Longitude 0° East Longitude

ARGENTINE CLAIM
NORWEGIAN CLAIM
Boundary undefined

10 Stations
Argentina, Brazil, Chile (3), China, Poland, Russia, South Korea, and Uruguay

South Atlantic Ocean
Southern Ocean
Indian Ocean

Falkland Is. (U.K.)
Orcadas (Argentina)
Neumayer (Germany)
SANAE IV (South Africa)
Russia and India

ARGENTINA
Argentina
Troll (Norway)
Syowa (Japan)

Chile Chile
Halley (U.K.)
Mawson (Australia)

CHILE
Palmer (U.S.) Ukraine
Belgrano II (Argentina)

BRITISH CLAIM
U.K. Argentina
Davis (Australia)

Russia and China

CHILEAN CLAIM
South Pole Amundsen-Scott (U.S.)
Mirny (Russia)
Vostok (Russia)

Southern Ocean
France and Italy
Casey (Australia)

McMurdo (U.S.)
Scott (N.Z.)

South Pacific Ocean
Antarctic Circle
60° South Latitude
80°
Dumont d'Urville (France)

NEW ZEALAND CLAIM
FRENCH CLAIM
AUSTRALIAN CLAIM

dark, frigid winter. A water plant collects and desalts seawater from McMurdo Sound. An aggressive recycling program minimizes unusable waste. Powerful ships called *icebreakers* plow through the ice, arrive with people and supplies, and leave with waste materials and scientific samples. The station also has runways and a helicopter pad.

South Pole Station is smaller. It has a summer population of about 200. Its winter crew is about 12. Cargo planes with skis from McMurdo Station service it.

Palmer Station supports an even smaller population. Its population shrinks to just four during the winter. It is serviced by ship during the summer.

Summer activities in Antarctica vary. Geologists collect rock samples from the ice-free dry valleys of the Transantarctic Mountains. Glaciologists measure the speed of ice flow, ice thickness, and properties beneath the ice at many of the most rapidly moving and changing locations. Physicists at the South Pole have converted a cubic kilometer of the ice into a vast detector of high-energy particles. They did this by placing over 1,000 sensitive detectors within the ice. Astronomers have many specialized telescopes at the South Pole. These telescopes take advantage of the six-month-long days and nights and the thin, stable atmosphere. On the coasts and at sea, biologists observe how animals adapt to their environment. Winter restricts scientists to such activities as recording weather data and studying earthquakes and solar radiation.

One important area of research in the Antarctic has been *ozone* in the atmosphere. Ozone is a form of oxygen. It is concentrated in an atmospheric layer that ranges in altitude from about 9 to 18 miles (15 to 30 kilometers). This layer protects all living things from certain harmful rays from the sun. In the mid-1980's, scientists discovered that the ozone layer over Antarctica was thinning. Evidence pointed to manufactured compounds called fluorocarbons as a major cause of this "ozone hole." Prompted by these findings, nations around the globe signed the Montreal Protocol in 1987, banning the use of chlorofluorocarbons, a major cause of ozone loss. See **Ozone hole.**

Research in Antarctica can answer important questions about the past, present, and future of Earth. Much scientific work there focuses on issues related to global climate change, in particular *global warming.* Global warming is an ongoing increase in average global surface temperatures. Some of this research focuses on the causes and effects of ice loss in Antarctica. Rates at which ice flows into the sea are increasing in many locations, causing sea level to rise. This rise in sea level threatens coastal regions around the world. Predicting the fate of the ice sheet as temperatures continue to increase will help people anticipate and manage coastal changes around the world.

In 2007, scientists from dozens of nations launched a two-year study of the Arctic and Antarctic called the International Polar Year. The investigation involved more than 200 research projects. They focused on assessing the status of the polar regions and determining how global warming will affect the polar and global climate and the inhabitants of the polar regions.

Since the late 1900's, it has become easier to travel to Antarctica. The number of tourists visiting the continent has increased rapidly. Researchers face challenges in managing the Antarctic environment as the continent's human population increases.

During the early decades of the 2000's, scientists' concern about rising temperatures—and the resulting melting of ice in Antarctica—continued to grow. On Feb. 6, 2020, the temperature at the Esperanza Research Station, an Argentine scientific site on the Antarctic Peninsula, reached 64.9 °F (18.3 °C). It was the highest temperature ever recorded on Antarctica.   Robert Bindschadler

Related articles in *World Book* include:

Amundsen, Roald	Global warming
Antarctic Circle	Hillary, Sir Edmund Percival
Biscoe, John	Iceberg
Byrd, Richard Evelyn	Ozone hole
Cook, James	Ross, Sir James Clark
Ellsworth, Lincoln	Scott, Robert Falcon
Enderby Land	Shackleton, Sir Ernest Henry
Exploration (The exploration	South Pole
of Antarctica)	Southern Ocean
Fuchs, Sir Vivian Ernest	Wilkes, Charles
Glacier	Wilkins, Sir Hubert

Anteater is the name of a group of mammals that lack teeth and feed mostly on ants and termites. The largest and best-known *species* (kind) of anteater is the *giant anteater.* It lives in tropical forests and grassy plains from Panama to Argentina. The animal has become rare in some areas as human settlers push into its range.

The giant anteater has a tube-shaped head with a long, slender snout. Its coarse, brittle hair is mostly gray and forms a bushy mass on the tail and sides. A black band of hair bordered by white bands runs from the throat to the middle of the back. Some giant anteaters grow more than 6 feet (1.8 meters) in length, including a tail

National Science Foundation

The South Pole Telescope is a microwave observatory located at the Amundsen-Scott South Pole Station in Antarctica. The South Pole's high altitude and dry, stable atmosphere allow the telescope an especially clear view of the microwave sky.

measuring about 3 feet (0.9 meter) in length.

The giant anteater lives on the ground. It walks with its front feet turned on their sides to protect the claws. When feeding, the animal uses the large second and third claws of its front foot to rip open ant nests. It then flits its tongue, which is about 2 feet (60 centimeters) long, into the nest in rapid in-and-out movements to lick up the ants.

A female giant anteater gives birth to one baby each year. The newborn rides on the mother's back for up to a year.

Two species of anteaters are called *tamanduas,* or *collared anteaters.* Both live in tropical forests and grassy plains. The *northern tamandua* is found from southern Mexico to Peru. The *southern tamandua* lives only in

© Shutterstock

The giant anteater has a tube-shaped head and snout. The animal licks up ants and termites with its long tongue.

South America. Tamanduas can live both in trees and on the ground. They use their hairless, *prehensile* (grasping) tail for climbing. Tamanduas have short, stiff, tan to brown hair. Some have darker hair around the neck and on other areas of the body. The animals can reach more than 4 feet (1.2 meters) in length.

The squirrel-sized *silky anteater* resembles a small tamandua but is covered with soft, golden-yellow or gray fur. This anteater can grow about 20 inches (50 centimeters) long. It lives in trees in the tropical forests of southern Mexico, Central America, and South America.

Aardvarks, pangolins, and echidnas are also sometimes called *anteaters.* These animals feed on termites and ants and have other characteristics in common with anteaters, but they belong to different *orders* (scientific groups).   Duane A. Schlitter

Scientific classification. Anteaters belong to the family Myrmecophagidae in the order Xenarthra. The giant anteater is *Myrmecophaga tridactyla.* The northern tamandua is *Tamandua mexicana,* the southern tamandua is *T. tetradactyla,* and the silky anteater is *Cyclopes didactylus.*

Antecedent, *AN tuh SEE duhnt,* is a word or group of words to which a pronoun refers in a sentence. An antecedent may come before or after the pronoun. In the sentence *Venice is famous for its canals,* the antecedent *Venice* comes before the pronoun *its.* In the sentence *At*

her best, Jill was unbeatable, the antecedent *Jill* comes after the pronoun *her.*

Personal pronouns, such as *I, you, he, she,* and *it,* must agree with their antecedents in *gender, number,* and *person.* The pronoun's *case* is determined by its use in the sentence. For example, the sentence *The children, after seeing the movie, were asked what they remembered about it* contains two personal pronouns, *they* and *it.* The pronoun *they* agrees with its antecedent *children* in gender (common), number (plural), and person (third). *They* is the subjective case because the pronoun is the subject of the verb *remembered.* *It* agrees with its antecedent *movie* because both are neuter in gender, singular in number, and in the third person. But *it* is the object of *about* and so is in the objective case.

Special problems in agreement arise in cases where the antecedent is an indefinite pronoun, such as *all, each, none,* and *some.* Some indefinite pronouns, such as *everyone* and *somebody,* have a singular form but are plural in meaning. In formal usage, singular pronouns are used: *Everyone did his or her share.* Informal usage, especially in speaking, favors the plural: *Everyone did their share.*

The pronouns *all, any, each, none,* and *some* can be either singular or plural, depending on their use. For example, *Some of the crop is now at its best* (singular); *Some of the apples are now at their best* (plural).

Agreement problems may develop when the antecedent is a collective noun, such as *crew* or *jury.* The use of singular or plural pronouns with collective nouns depends on the intention of the speaker or writer. The use of the singular emphasizes the entire unit: *The jury was unanimous in its decision.* The use of the plural stresses the parts of the unit: *The judge told the jury they were dismissed.*

Confusion can result from the careless use of relative pronouns—*that, what, which,* or *who.* In the sentence *The club adopted a new constitution, which we thought was a good idea,* the relative pronoun could refer either to *adopted* or to *constitution.* For clarity, the statement should be divided into two sentences: *The club adopted a new constitution. We thought the adoption was a good idea.*   Patricia A. Moody

See also **Case; Gender; Number; Pronoun.**

Antelope is the name of a large group of animals that have hoofs and hollow horns. They belong to the same animal family as goats and oxen. But antelope more closely resemble deer because most of them are slender and graceful. Antelope, like cattle, are *ruminants* (see **Ruminant**).

Antelope keep their horns as long as they live. Among many kinds of antelope, both the males and the females have horns. The horns of the males usually grow larger. Some antelope have short, straight horns. The horns of others are long and curved, sometimes in a spiral twist. Some antelope horns are smooth, while others have ring-shaped ridges along their length. Antelope horns form around a single bony core. The horns are never forked like tree branches, as are deer antlers.

Most antelope live in Africa, but a few *species* (kinds) are found in Asia. The North American *pronghorn* is not a true antelope, though it resembles antelope (see **Pronghorn**). Some antelope, such as the *duiker* and the *bongo,* live in forests. Others live on mountainsides and

Thomas Nebbia, DPI

A group of impalas bounds across a grassland in Kenya. The females, which lack horns, often move together in large herds.

Mark Boulton, NAS

The eland can jump an obstacle 6 feet (1.8 meters) high from a standing start. This antelope lives in small or large herds.

© Shutterstock

Greater kudus live in small groups in open woodlands. Their coloring provides excellent camouflage in grasses and bushes.

desert plateaus. A few, such as the *sitatunga* and the *lechwe* of central Africa, live in marshes. However, more kinds and greater numbers of antelope live on the dry or grassy plains of eastern and southern Africa than anywhere else.

Habits and appearance. Most antelope are timid and run away from their enemies. The *gazelle* and the *blackbuck* are among the fastest runners in the world. A few antelope defend themselves when they must. They are the *wildebeest* or *gnu,* the *roan* antelope, and the *sable* antelope, all found in Africa. Sometimes other animals warn antelope of danger.

Most species of antelope are territorial. The male defends a territory during the breeding season so that other males may not enter it. The females visit the territories and mate with the males of their choice.

Antelope vary in size. Some, such as the *dik-dik* and the *steenbok,* are not much larger than jack rabbits. Others, notably the *eland,* grow about the size of an ox.

A smooth coat of hair covers the skin of most antelope, except a few, such as the shaggy-haired *waterbuck.* This coat may appear in various shades and patterns. Brown and gray are the most common colors.

Kinds of antelope. Separate articles in *World Book* describe several kinds of antelope. See the list of *Related articles* at the end of this article. There are many other kinds, all in the Eastern Hemisphere. One of these is

the *four-horned antelope.* The males of this Indian antelope have two pairs of horns instead of the usual single pair. Several kinds of *harnessed antelope* live in central and southern Africa. The stripes on their bodies make them appear to be wearing a harness. Only the males of this kind have horns.

The *klipspringer,* a small antelope that resembles the European chamois, lives in rocky places from southern Africa north to the Sahara. This animal walks on the tips of its narrow, round hoofs, which give it sure footing.

A large bluish-gray antelope of India is called the *nilgai.* The male has short horns and long hair under its chin. Several large African antelope, including the *gemsbok,* are named oryx. Both the males and females have long horns that are nearly straight.

The *roan antelope* is a large, light-colored animal that lives from South Africa north to Ethiopia and Gambia. The *sable antelope,* related to the roan but slightly smaller, lives in southern Africa. It has large curved horns and a coat of black or rich brown with white underparts. Two kinds of antelope of the southern half of Africa are called *waterbuck.* The *defassa waterbuck* may be trained as a pet, when it is caught young.

Antelope and people. People have long hunted antelope both for sport and for their meat and skins. In much of Africa, people still hunt antelope for food.

The gemsbok can live in desert areas where there are few plants and no standing water. It is found in southern Africa.

Game ranches also raise many kinds of antelope for meat. Antelope make good meat animals in tropical areas because herds of several species feed on more kinds of tropical plants than do cattle or sheep. In addition, antelope have better resistance to tropical diseases.

Unregulated hunting, habitat loss, and shooting of antelope by settlers have reduced the numbers of some wild antelope species. Many of the kinds of antelope considered most handsome, such as the *bontebok,* the *giant sable antelope,* and the *white oryx,* have become scarce.   Kenneth J. Raedeke

Scientific classification. Antelope belong to the bovid family, Bovidae. There are numerous species.

Related articles in *World Book* include:

Addax	Gazelle	Impala	Springbok
Blackbuck	Gemsbok	Kudu	Steenbok
Dik-dik	Hartebeest	Mountain goat	Wildebeest
Eland			

Antenna is a device used in an electronic system to help information pass from a transmitting location to a receiving location. An antenna takes in or sends information in the form of waves of energy, known as *electromagnetic signals,* via cable, wire, the air, or another medium. Antennas are used in nearly all electronic communication and navigation systems.

The signals sent out from an antenna travel via a *carrier wave.* The frequency of this wave is called the *center frequency* or *carrier frequency.* The wave begins as a continuous wave pattern but is *modulated* (altered) in one or more of three ways to include a representation of the information. The three main forms of modulation are *amplitude, frequency,* and *phase.* In amplitude modulation (AM), changes in the *amplitude* (strength) of the carrier wave represent the information. Frequency modulation (FM) varies the number of cycles per second of the carrier wave (see **Frequency modulation**). Phase modulation (PM) alters the *phase* (timing) of the carrier wave. In PM transmissions, the relative starting point of the carrier wave periodically readjusts as signals fall out of phase.

Antenna systems are designed with different *directivities*—that is, they do not all send out or pick up signals equally in all directions. A radar antenna, for example, transmits electromagnetic signals in a narrow beam and in a specific direction. On the other hand, an antenna in a Global Positioning System (GPS) receiver must be able

to receive signals from any of several navigation satellites in orbit above Earth.

Types of antennas. Different applications require different types of antennas. The length of a *resonant antenna* is proportional to the wavelength of its system's center frequency. Resonant antennas include *dipoles, monopoles,* and *patch antennas.* A dipole consists of a straight metal rod or wire that is split in the center. A monopole is simply a straight metal rod or wire. A patch antenna is basically a flat square of metal foil. Resonant antennas are inexpensive to produce, and they can receive from, and transmit to, a wide area. They are used in such devices as cellular telephones, wireless computer network equipment, and GPS navigation systems. A resonant antenna is physically small when its system's center frequency is high.

Electrically short antennas are antennas that work well for low-frequency applications. Such applications include long-range communication, commercial broadcasting, and navigation. *Aperture antennas* are often shaped like horns. They are typically used in directional high-frequency applications, as in police radar systems for measuring the speeds of automobiles. *Dish antennas* are somewhat bowl-shaped. Their uses include relaying electromagnetic signals to and from artificial satellites. One well-known purpose of dish antennas is to receive television programming from satellites in *geostationary orbit,* an orbit that matches the rate of rotation of Earth. Another is to communicate with deep-space probes. *Ar-*

Kinds of receiving antennas

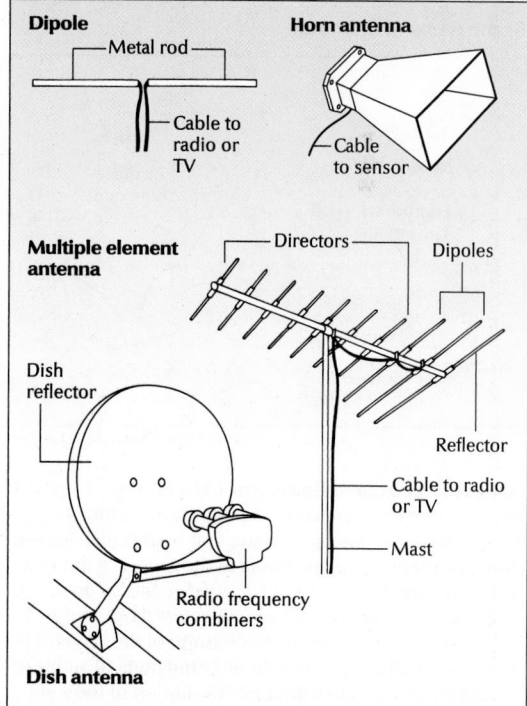

WORLD BOOK diagrams by Arthur Grebetz and Adam Weiskind

Antennas take in or send information in the form of waves of energy called *electromagnetic signals.* These illustrations show four common types of antennas.

ray antennas combine two or more specially positioned antennas that vary in amplitude, phase, or both, to increase the overall performance.

History. Heinrich Rudolf Hertz, a German physicist, invented the first antenna around 1887. In the early 1860's, James Clerk Maxwell, a Scottish scientist, had predicted the existence of electromagnetic waves that can travel through space. Hertz used his antenna to confirm Maxwell's prediction. Hertz's device was able to transmit and receive radio waves, a type of electromagnetic signal.　　Chris G. Bartone

See also **Radar** (The antenna); **Radio** (Transmitting radio waves; The antenna).

Antennae, *an TEHN ee,* are long, delicate sensory organs on the heads of almost all insects and most other arthropods (see **Arthropod**). Insects, centipedes, and millipedes have a single pair of antennae. Crustaceans, such as lobsters and crabs, have two pairs of antennae. Spiders and their relatives have none.

The antennae contain many nerves and may be sensitive to heat, vibrations, water vapor, and certain chemicals and gases. Fine hairlike parts that cover the antennae serve as touch receptors. Tiny pits in the antennae of some insects make them useful in smelling. A Junebug has nearly 80,000 such smelling pits. The antennae of male mosquitoes have hairlike parts that are sensitive to sound. These mosquitoes can use their antennae to detect the sound of female mosquitoes as much as ¼ mile (0.4 kilometer) away.　　E. W. Cupp

See also **Ant** (Sense organs); **Bee** (The body of the honey bee); **Beetle** (The bodies of beetles); **Butterfly** (The head); **Insect** (The senses of insects).

Some types of antennae

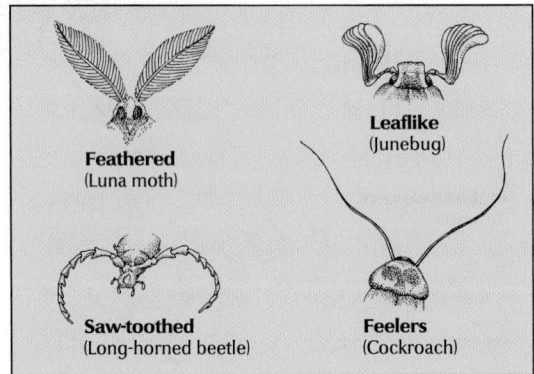

Feathered
(Luna moth)

Leaflike
(Junebug)

Saw-toothed
(Long-horned beetle)

Feelers
(Cockroach)

WORLD BOOK illustration by Marion Pahl

Anterior cruciate ligament (ACL) is one of the four main *ligaments* of the knee. Ligaments are bands of strong fibrous connective tissue that hold bones in position. The other three ligaments of the knee are the *posterior cruciate ligament* (PCL), *medial collateral ligament* (MCL), and the *lateral collateral ligament* (LCL). The ACL helps connect the *tibia* (the large bone of the lower leg) to the *femur* (thigh bone). The ACL functions to stabilize the knee and prevent front-to-back motion of the joint so that the knee moves like a hinge.

ACL injuries usually occur when an athlete twists the knee while making a sudden stop and turn, such as in basketball, football, or soccer. Injuries include stretch-

ing and partial or full tears of the ligament. Physicians often use physical examination and magnetic resonance imaging (MRI) to diagnose and confirm an ACL tear.

Initial treatment of an ACL tear includes applying ice to reduce inflammation and a knee brace to provide support, using pain medication, and keeping the knee elevated. However, ACL tears will not heal on their own. Surgery is required to repair the ACL, and physical therapy is needed to restore full function to the knee. A patient can often return to normal activities in five to six months following surgery.　　James M. Nieman

See also **Knee.**

Anthem. See National anthem; Hymn.

Anther. See Flower (The stamens; diagram: Parts of a flower).

Anthony, Susan Brownell (1820-1906), was a reformer and one of the first leaders of the campaign for women's rights. She helped organize the woman suffrage movement, which worked to get women the right to vote.

Anthony was born on Feb. 15, 1820, in Adams, Massachusetts. Her family were Quakers, who believed in the equality of men and women. Anthony's family supported major reforms, such as antislavery and *temperance,* the campaign to abolish alcoholic beverages.

From 1839 to 1849, Anthony taught school. She then joined the temperance movement. But most temperance groups consisted of men who did not allow women to help the movement. In 1852, she attended a temperance rally in Albany, New York, but was not allowed to speak because she was a woman. Soon after, she formed the Woman's State Temperance Society of New York.

Through her temperance work, Anthony became increasingly aware that women did not have the same rights as men. In 1851, she met Elizabeth Cady Stanton, a leader of the women's rights movement. The two women became close friends and co-workers. Soon, Anthony devoted herself completely to women's rights and became a leader of the movement. She supported dress reform and, for a time, wore bloomers, which became a symbol of the women's rights movement. She also worked in support of equal educational opportunities and property rights for women.

Before and during the American Civil War (1861-1865), Anthony and Stanton supported abolitionism. But after the war, they broke away from the abolitionists, many of whom showed little interest in woman suffrage and supported the 15th Amendment to the United States Constitution. This amendment gave the vote to black men, but not to women. In 1869, Anthony and Stanton formed the National Woman Suffrage Association to add a woman suffrage amendment to the Constitution. From 1868 to 1870, Anthony published a weekly journal that demanded equal rights for women. She voted in the 1872 presidential election and was ar-

© Everett Historical/Shutterstock

Susan B. Anthony

rested and fined $100 for voting illegally. Anthony never paid the fine, but no further action was taken against her. From 1881 to 1886, Anthony and Stanton coedited three volumes of a book called *History of Woman Suffrage.* Anthony completed a fourth volume of the book in 1902. In 1904, she established the International Woman Suffrage Alliance with Carrie Chapman Catt, another leader of the suffrage movement.

In 1890, the National Woman Suffrage Association and the American Woman Suffrage Association united to form the National American Woman Suffrage Association. Anthony served as the group's president from 1892 until 1900. She died on March 13, 1906, 14 years before the 19th Amendment to the Constitution became law and gave women the right to vote. In 1979 and 1980, the United States minted for circulation $1 coins bearing Anthony's picture. She was the first woman to be pictured on a U.S. coin in general circulation.   June Sochen

See also **Woman suffrage** (Growth of the movement).

Additional resources

Boothroyd, Jennifer. *Susan B. Anthony.* Lerner, 2006. Younger readers.
McPherson, Stephanie S. *Susan B. Anthony.* Lerner, 2006. Younger readers.
Orr, Tamra. *The Life and Times of Susan B. Anthony.* Mitchell Lane, 2007. Younger readers.

Anthony of Padua, *PAJ oo uh,* **Saint** (1195-1231), was a Christian religious leader and a popular preacher of his time. Many miracles have been attributed to Anthony, both during his lifetime and after his death. Anthony's body lies in a church built in his honor in Padua, Italy. The church has become a shrine, attracting thousands of pilgrims seeking the saint's aid.

Anthony was born in Lisbon, Portugal, probably on Aug. 15, 1195. His original name was Ferdinand. He entered the Augustinian canons, a religious order, about 1210 and joined the Franciscan order in 1220, taking the name Anthony. He traveled to Morocco to convert the Muslims, but became ill and returned to Europe. Anthony's ship landed in Sicily, and he settled in Italy. After leading a solitary life for a short time, Anthony began to preach. He amazed his listeners with his skill as a speaker and his knowledge of the Bible. Anthony delivered sermons before huge crowds in Florence and Padua. He showed deep concern for the common people, who loved him as their protector. He died on June 13, 1231, and his feast day is June 13.   Marilyn J. Harran

Anthony of Thebes, Saint (250?-356), was the founder of Christian monasticism. Anthony spent much of his life as a hermit in the Egyptian desert. He established religious communities of hermits that became models for monastic life.

Anthony was born in a village in Egypt. At about age 20, he gave away his belongings and began living a hermit's life of *asceticism* (self-denial). He studied with another hermit and later lived in empty tombs near his home for about 15 years. There he practiced spiritual discipline alone. He later lived in an abandoned desert fort for 20 years, where he fasted, prayed, and worked. During that time, his reputation as a holy man grew, and eventually he left his solitude to teach others the ascetic life. He spent his last years in solitude on a mountain.

Saint Athanasius wrote the influential *Life of Anthony* in 357. It described Anthony's piety and his legendary battles against temptations sent by the Devil. Anthony's feast day is January 17.   Marilyn J. Harran

Anthracite. See Coal (Coal rank; Coal as a fuel; How coal was formed; map).

Anthrax is a serious infectious disease that chiefly affects animals but can also occur in people. It is caused by the bacterium *Bacillus anthracis.* Anthrax usually affects plant-eating animals infected by eating anthrax *spores* (inactive bacteria) from the soil. Anthrax spores can survive harsh conditions and occur in soil throughout the world, including the United States. People can get anthrax through contact with infected animals or contaminated animal products. But, naturally occurring anthrax is rare in human beings today.

In people, anthrax infection can occur in three main forms: *inhalational,* caused by breathing in spores; *cutaneous,* caused by spores infecting skin sores; and *gastrointestinal,* caused by swallowing spores. Inhalational anthrax causes a severe illness that begins in the chest and rapidly spreads through the body. Cutaneous anthrax, the most common form, can cause a severe skin infection. Gastrointestinal anthrax results from eating undercooked, contaminated meat. Symptoms include fever, vomiting, abdominal pain, and bloody diarrhea. Anthrax can be cured with antibiotics if patients receive treatment early. However, inhalational and gastrointestinal anthrax are often fatal if not rapidly treated.

Some nations and international terrorist groups are known to have developed or are suspected of having developed anthrax as a biological weapon. In 1979, the accidental release of anthrax spores from a military facility in the Soviet Union caused 68 deaths. In the 1990's, Russia—which had been part of the Soviet Union—announced it had ended all biological weapons programs. Many nations are now working to end the development and use of biological weapons, including anthrax.

In 2001, anthrax spores were used as a weapon when they were sent through the United States mail to several business and government offices. As a result, a number of office buildings and post office facilities were contaminated. Some people became ill with inhalational anthrax, and several died. Others contracted cutaneous anthrax. In 2008, the U.S. Federal Bureau of Investigation declared that a government scientist had carried out the attack. However, the scientist committed suicide before he could be charged with the crime.   Thomas V. Inglesby

Anthropoid. See Primate.

Anthropology is the scientific study of humanity and of human culture. It is unique among the social sciences in that it focuses on all societies and all aspects of human physical, social, and cultural life. Anthropologists investigate *culture,* the strategies for living that people learn and share as members of social groups.

Anthropologists also examine the characteristics that human beings share as members of a single species and the diverse ways that people live in different environments. They also analyze the products of social groups—both material objects and less material creations, such as beliefs and values.

Like other social scientists, anthropologists look sys-

John W. Burton, the contributor of this article, is Professor of Anthropology at Connecticut College.

tematically for general patterns in human behavior. They develop theories and use scientific methods to test them. Anthropologists study and try to understand cultures different from their own, and describe them to members of their own society.

Anthropologists are interested in understanding all human societies. Their research is *cross-cultural*, meaning that they focus on those aspects of human experience found in all cultures. But anthropology is also *comparative*, meaning that anthropologists are interested in how the particular features of cultures are alike and how they are different. For example, marriage in Western societies is a union between one man and one woman. But marriages are different in other parts of the world. In many African and Islamic societies, a man may be married to more than one woman at a time. Among the Nyinba people and other groups of Nepal, however, a woman typically marries several men who are brothers.

Another important feature of anthropology is its emphasis on an insider's view of a society. Anthropologists try to determine how people who share a culture view their world. Anthropology can make major contributions to international harmony because it helps provide an understanding of various cultures.

Because different cultures and societies have different habits and customs, anthropologists use the term *cultural relativism* to describe and understand different cultures. This concept suggests that one culture is not better or worse than any other—it is merely different.

The concept of cultural relativism in anthropology is closely related to the concept of *ethnocentrism*. Ethnocentrism refers to the idea that one's own culture is inherently superior to a different culture. Such an assertion is a form of racism, and anthropologists strive to show that racist claims have no scientific proof. They are instead a form of ethnocentrism. See **Ethnocentrism.**

Branches of anthropology

The chief branches of anthropology include *physical anthropology, archaeology, linguistic anthropology,* and *social anthropology,* also called *cultural anthropology.* These branches often overlap. For example, archaeologists and cultural anthropologists study many of the same cultural features. But archaeologists concentrate on past civilizations, and cultural anthropologists work mainly on present ones.

Physical anthropology, also called *biological anthropology* or *bioanthropology,* is the study of human physical characteristics. Physical anthropologists, called *paleoanthropologists,* search for fossil remains from prehistoric times to trace the development of human physical characteristics. They also seek remains, such as stone tools and evidence of fires, to analyze the links among physical traits and cultural development.

Some physical anthropologists study primates—the animals that are most closely related to human beings, including chimpanzees and other apes. By observing these animals, the scientists try to understand what our prehuman ancestors were like and how human beings have changed through millions of years. Advances in the study of human and animal genes help scientists discover how closely different species and different groups of people are related to one another.

Other physical anthropologists study physical differences among human beings, including blood types, skin colors, and hereditary diseases. They also analyze the effect of nutrition and environmental factors, such as altitude and climate, on human growth and development. For example, studies have shown that people who spend their entire lives in the high-altitude Andes Mountains have larger hearts and lungs than people who live at lower altitudes. The enlarged organs are an adaptation to the lower oxygen concentration of high-altitude environments.

Archaeology is the study of objects left by earlier peoples, including artwork, buildings, clothing, pottery, and tools. Archaeologists trace the development of cultures by studying the things those people made and used. Such objects help them determine what early social life may have been like. For example, the size of

© Fernando Morales, Agence France-Presse

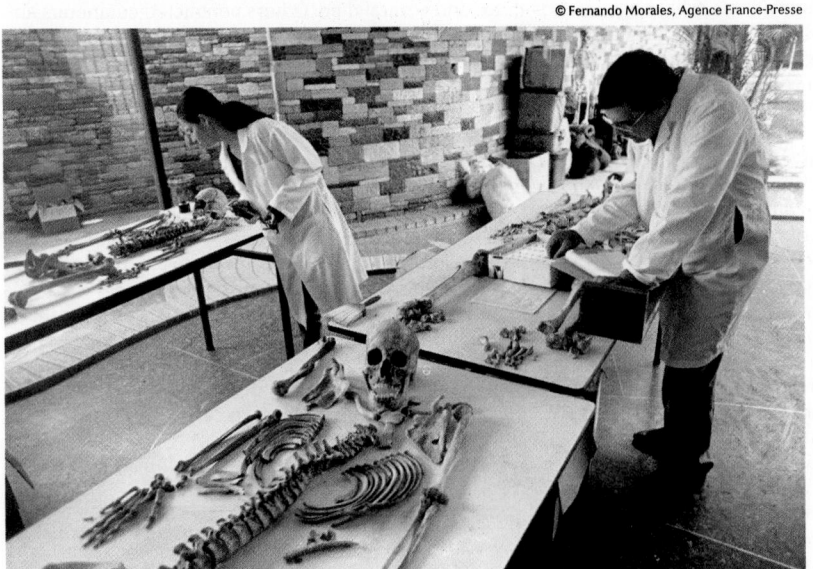

Physical anthropologists examine skeletal remains in a Guatemalan laboratory to identify victims of a civil war. Physical anthropologists are often called to help law enforcement agencies identify human remains in cases of crime, war, or natural disaster.

houses and the number of cooking hearths may show how many people lived together in a household. Differences in the number and value of objects put in graves may indicate differences in social class. Animal bones and plant pollen show whether people raised animals or hunted them and whether they grew crops or gathered wild plants for food. See **Archaeology.**

Linguistic anthropology analyzes the ways that language is used by people of different societies. Anthropological linguists try to find connections between people's language and other aspects of their culture. In the Indonesian language, for example, many statements include a reference to the social status of the person addressed. Houses and other objects have various names, depending on the rank of the listener. This use of language reflects the great importance of social class in Indonesian culture.

Other topics of study for anthropological linguists include formal and informal speech, forms of address, insults, and jokes. These experts also analyze the structure of unwritten languages. Some anthropological linguists study how words and their definitions and classifications reflect people's views of their environment and society. The Nuer, a herding people of eastern Africa, have many words for the colors and markings of cattle. Their vocabulary shows the importance of livestock in their way of life.

The ways that different cultures classify such things as animals, plants, and relatives show how they view the world. The English language uses the same word—*uncle*—for a mother's brother, a father's brother, and the husband of either parent's sister. But some languages have a word for each of these relatives. Such words suggest differences in the roles and behavior expected of such relatives.

Cultural anthropology is the study of human culture. Cultural anthropologists study the artwork, houses, tools, and other material products of a culture. They also study a culture's nonmaterial creations, including its music, religious beliefs, symbols, and values.

Some anthropologists specialize in various fields of cultural anthropology. *Ecological anthropologists* investigate the way a society fits into its environment and how the environment affects the society's culture. *Psychological anthropologists* study how individual personalities are shaped by different cultures and how children learn to share in their culture. *Medical anthropology* examines the ways in which different people and cultures experience, describe, and understand illness.

Social anthropology deals with social relationships in groups. Such relationships include marriage, family life, authority, and conflict. Social anthropologists devote much research into how social life is organized in different societies. A researcher might study a community to see how people are divided into groups within it and to learn about relationships among these groups.

Many studies examine such human characteristics as age, sex, and kinship, which are universal but have different functions in various societies. In some communities, these characteristics determine what society expects from an individual. In others, such characteristics as education, income, and occupation help define how people are expected to behave.

Early social anthropologists often studied an entire community, including all aspects of its life. Today, however, these scientists practice several specialties. For example, *economic anthropologists* concentrate on how food and other goods are produced and distributed. *Political anthropologists* analyze how decisions are made and how conflicts are resolved within communities.

Social and cultural anthropologists do not study only non-Western societies. Many anthropologists also work in Europe and North America. They point out that no human society is isolated from other societies.

How anthropologists work

The primary method used by anthropologists to collect and understand information on human cultures is known as *fieldwork.* The first anthropological researchers worked in isolated societies about which little was known. They attempted to describe the culture of the people they studied as completely as possible. The research and description of a culture, called *ethnography,* describes details on the people's values, daily life, material culture, and social relationships. See **Ethnography.**

To study societies, anthropologists developed a method called *participant observation.* The researcher, called a *participant-observer,* learned about a people by living among them and taking part in their daily lives. Although it is impossible to record information on every aspect of a culture during fieldwork, anthropologists try to learn all that they can from local people. Today, participant observation is still the most characteristic technique of anthropology, but anthropologists use many other methods as well.

Like all scientists, anthropologists begin their research by asking questions and formulating possible answers called *hypotheses.* Then they collect evidence with which to evaluate the hypotheses.

Entering the community. Most anthropologists have interests in a particular geographic area of the world but also look to answer specific questions about human culture. For example, in the 1930's, the British anthropologist E. E. Evans-Pritchard lived among the Nuer in Sudan. At the time, the Nuer did not have chiefs or kings or any kind of government. Evans-Pritchard stud-

WORLD BOOK photo

A cultural anthropologist, *left,* conducts fieldwork in a rural village in Uzbekistan. He is listening to a grandmother talk about life in the village and how village life has changed over time.

ied the problem of how a society without a political system could hold together and work.

Before anthropologists begin their fieldwork, they read about and try to gain knowledge about the region where they will conduct their research. If possible, they learn the language that is spoken there before they arrive at a fieldwork site.

After arriving at a field site, the anthropologist must find a place to live and try to blend into the local society. Local people often take in and house such researchers and befriend them. Over time, the scientist begins to learn the language, values, sentiments, and other *norms* (standards) of the culture. Fieldwork usually takes at least one year. It is important for an anthropologist to see how seasonal changes affect the way people live and what they do to gain their livelihood.

At first, the researcher gathers information mainly through observation and conversations with members of the community. Many researchers conduct a community census to collect basic information. Most field workers take notes every day and type them up at night. Some anthropologists revisit the same community many times over many years, while others carry out fieldwork in a number of different societies.

Developing hypotheses. An anthropologist must decide what information he or she wishes to gather about the community. Then the researcher asks questions and forms hypotheses to answer them. Many new questions will arise from what the scientist has already learned about the community.

Collecting evidence. After developing specific hypotheses, the anthropologist gathers information to test them. The researcher may conduct a survey by distributing questionnaires to everyone in the community or to a selected group of individuals. He or she may take inventories of household possessions or obtain life histories from a number of people. An anthropologist may record interviews, music, or special events, and make motion pictures or photographs of various activities.

Drawing conclusions. The researcher must organize all the information that has been collected so it can be used easily and efficiently. The anthropologist, like other scientists, may use a computer to analyze large amounts of information. Finally, the researcher evaluates the hypotheses that have been formulated and writes up his or her conclusions for scientific journals or in books.

History

Early anthropological thought. As long as human beings have been aware of other human beings, they have compared one society to another. In the past, myth and imagination often inspired the observation of other peoples. Some European travelers in the 1600's and 1700's reported that they had seen human beings in different parts of the world with one eye, with four legs, or with three heads. Many people were not even aware that there was a single species of human being.

Anthropology did not become a separate area of study until the mid-1800's. In 1859, the British naturalist Charles R. Darwin presented some key ideas in *The Origin of Species,* one of the most influential science books ever written. In it, Darwin explained his theory of *natural selection,* the process in nature by which the people, other animals, and plants best adapted to their environ-

ment tend to leave the most offspring. The theory of natural selection helped explain the workings of *evolution,* the process by which all living things developed from a few simple forms of life through a series of changes.

Early anthropologists came to the conclusion that all members of the human species shared a common past. They tried to determine how different societies were related and how they had evolved. They viewed the history of human culture as a process of evolution from lower to higher forms. For example, the American scholar Lewis Henry Morgan imagined that all human societies evolved through a fixed series of stages, from savagery, to barbarism, to civilization.

According to Morgan and other early anthropologists, this process climaxed with the cultures of Europe and North America. So-called primitive peoples, whose technology was less advanced than that of the West, supposedly represented earlier stages of development.

Development of field research. By the late 1800's, many anthropologists began to criticize the evolutionary theories of Morgan and others. To support their criticism, such anthropologists as Adolf Bastian of Germany, Franz Boas of the United States, and William H. R. Rivers of the United Kingdom organized expeditions to observe the cultures of other societies firsthand.

In 1899, at Columbia University in New York City, Boas founded the first major department for the teaching of anthropology. His students included Ruth F. Benedict, Alfred L. Kroeber, Robert H. Lowie, and Margaret Mead, all of whom became famous anthropologists. Boas trained them to conduct intensive eyewitness studies of individual cultures. The resulting field studies highlighted many differences among societies.

The early 1900's. During the 1920's, the Polish-born British anthropologist Bronisław Malinowski developed an approach called *functionalism.* Functionalism stressed the ways that different cultural traits function to

AP Images

Margaret Mead, an American anthropologist, lived among the Samoans in 1925 and 1926 to observe their ways of life. Her research resulted in the book *Coming of Age in Samoa* (1928).

satisfy basic human needs, both biological and psychological. Malinowski's students included the prominent British anthropologists E. E. Evans-Pritchard, Raymond Firth, Max Gluckman, and Isaac Schapera, and an American, Hortense Powdermaker.

By the late 1920's, anthropologists from Europe and North America had carried out fieldwork throughout the world. The results of their research changed the nature of anthropology and also revolutionized the Western view of "primitive" people. The new method of participant observation questioned and dramatically changed the idea that such people were less highly evolved than European or American society.

Anthropologists realized that every society had its own history, and that these histories did not conform to the evolutionary schemes of Morgan and others. Fieldwork showed that human cultures grew, changed, and adapted through human invention and creativity, and through contact with different cultures. Many anthropologists recognized that peoples around the world had been dramatically affected by contact with Europeans over the past 300 years. The scientists felt that information about various groups should be gathered before the cultures of those groups were further transformed by contact with the West.

The middle and late 1900's. Rapid and extensive changes in many societies during the middle and late 1900's stimulated a shift in anthropological thought. Instead of studying a society at a specific point in time, anthropologists began to study the culture at intervals. They wanted to learn how the society had changed and to analyze the process of change itself. For example, Clifford J. Geertz of the United States studied economic development in Indonesia. Abner Cohen of the United Kingdom investigated the changing role of religion among the Hausa cattle traders of Africa.

Nearly all early anthropologists were Europeans or North Americans who studied societies in Africa or other distant areas. During the mid-1900's, African and Asian anthropologists began to study societies in the West that formerly had sent researchers to their countries. The Nigerian anthropologist John Ogbu investigated a suburban school in California. Another Nigerian anthropologist, E. U. Essien-Udom, studied the Nation of Islam, also known as the Black Muslims, a religious group in the United States.

Modern anthropology. Early anthropologists mainly studied small communities in technologically simple societies. But modern anthropologists work in a wide range of settings. An anthropologist may study how a small community responds to contact with modern society, as George Foster of the United States did in the Mexican village of Tzintzuntzan.

Anthropologists continue to find new problems and topics to study as societies continue to change throughout the world. Today, many anthropologists are interested in issues related to globalization and a growing population of people termed *transnationals*. These people are born in one part of the world but later migrate to a different region and live in a different culture. Such people carry with them elements of two cultures.

Careers in anthropology

Most careers in anthropology require either a master's degree or a doctor's degree. Many anthropologists teach and carry out research in colleges and universities. Some collect and supervise the display of items for museums.

An increasing number of anthropologists enter the growing field of *applied anthropology,* the use of anthropological research to achieve a practical goal. They may work for government-sponsored development projects or relief agencies helping to assist refugee populations throughout the world. Applied anthropologists also work in advertising and other corporate jobs, where they can apply their knowledge about social systems to specific problems.

John W. Burton

Related articles. See **Indian, American** and the articles on Indian groups listed in the tables with that article; and the *People* section of the various country and continent articles, such as **Argentina** (People) and **North America** (People). See also the following articles:

Anthropologists

Benedict, Ruth Fulton	Leakey, Meave Gillian
Boas, Franz	Leakey, Richard Erskine Frere
Dubois, Eugene	Lévi-Strauss, Claude
Frazer, Sir James George	Linton, Ralph
Galdikas, Biruté	Malinowski, Bronisław
Gamio, Manuel	Mead, Margaret
Johanson, Donald Carl	Morgan, Lewis Henry
Kingsley, Mary Henrietta	Parsons, Elsie Clews
Kroeber, Alfred Louis	Radcliffe-Brown, A. R.
La Farge, Oliver	Tylor, Sir Edward Burnett
Leakey, Louis Seymour Bazett	Westermarck, Edward
Leakey, Mary Douglas	Alexander

Archaeology

See the **Archaeology** article and its list of *Related articles.*

Physical anthropology

Ardipithecus	Homo floresiensis	Peking fossils
Australopithecus	Homo habilis	Piltdown hoax
Cave dwellers	Java fossils	Prehistoric people
Cro-Magnons	Neandertals	Races, Human
Homo erectus	Olduvai Gorge	

Cultural and social anthropology

Barbarian	Ethnography	Mores
Cannibal	Family	Mythology
Caste	Folklore	Nomad
Civilization	Food (Customs)	Religion
Clan	Funeral customs	Shelter
Clothing	Headhunter	Social class
Culture	Language	Superstition
Custom	Magic	Taboo
Ethnocentrism	Marriage	Tribe

Peoples of Africa and Asia

Afrikaners	Gurkhas	Pashtuns
Ainu	Hausa	Pygmies
Arabs	Khoikhoi	San
Aryans	Luba	Semites
Ashanti	Lunda	Swahili
Bantu	Maasai	Tatars
Bedouins	Malays	Turks
Berbers	Mandinka	Xhosa
Dinka	Moors	Yoruba
Druses	Nuer	Zulu
Fulani	Palestinians	

Peoples of Europe

Anglo-Saxons	Cossacks	Roma
Basques	Gaels	Slavs
Celts	Magyars	

Other peoples

Aboriginal people of Australia	Cajuns Dayaks	Māori Negritos
Aleuts	Inuit	

Additional resources

Barfield, Thomas J., ed. *The Dictionary of Anthropology.* Blackwell, 1997.
Barnard, Alan, and Spencer, Jonathan, eds. *Encyclopedia of Social and Cultural Anthropology.* Routledge, 1998.
Batten, Mary. *Anthropologist.* Houghton, 2001. Younger readers.
Eriksen, Thomas H. *Small Places, Large Issues: An Introduction to Social and Cultural Anthropology.* 2nd ed. Pluto Pr., 2001.

Anthurium, *an THUR ee um,* is the name of a large *genus* (group) of flowering plants native to tropical regions in North and South America. There are hundreds of *species* (kinds) of anthuriums. They grow wild chiefly in rain forests. They are also cultivated in greenhouses and gardens.

Many wild anthuriums wrap around tree trunks and branches, though some grow along the ground. Most anthuriums have large evergreen leaves shaped like hearts. In some species, the leaves are lobed or separated into fingerlike leaflets. Anthuriums bear small flowers tightly packed on a cylindrical, fleshy stalk called a *spadix.* The spadix rises from a shiny, leaflike *spathe,* which is often brightly colored.

A commonly cultivated anthurium is the *pink flamingo,* also called the *flamingo lily.* This plant has a bright pink spathe that lasts several weeks. Gardeners also grow anthuriums for their attractive leaves. The leaf veins of some species are outlined in pale green to silvery white against a dark green or purple background.

David H. Wagner

Scientific classification. Anthuriums make up the genus *Anthurium.* The scientific name for the pink flamingo is *A. andraeanum.*

Antibiotic, *AN tee by AHT ihk* or *AN tih by AHT ihk,* is a substance produced by certain bacteria or fungi that kills other cells or interferes with their growth. In nature, these substances help some microbes survive by limiting the multiplication of other microbes that share the same environment. Antibiotics that attack *pathogenic* (disease-causing) microbes without severely harming normal body cells are useful as drugs.

Antibiotics are especially useful for treating infections caused by bacteria. Antibiotics came into widespread use during the 1940's. At that time, they were often called "wonder drugs" because they cured many bacterial diseases that were once fatal. The number of deaths caused by meningitis, pneumonia, tuberculosis, and scarlet fever declined drastically after antibiotics became available. Today, physicians prescribe antibiotics to treat many diseases caused by bacteria.

In addition, some antibiotics are effective against infections caused by fungi and protozoa, and a few are useful in treating cancer. Antibiotics are also used to treat infectious diseases in animals. Farmers sometimes add small amounts of antibiotics to livestock feed. The antibiotics support the animals' growth for reasons that are not entirely understood.

Antibiotics are not effective against colds, influenza, or other viral diseases. In addition, the effectiveness of antibiotics is limited because both pathogenic microbes and cancer cells can become resistant to them.

Kinds of antibiotics

Antibiotics are *selectively toxic*—that is, they damage some types of cells without harming others. Medically useful antibiotics attack infectious microbes or cancer cells without excessively hurting human cells. Antibiotics fight different types of illnesses in a variety of ways.

Antibacterial antibiotics. Antibiotics are selectively toxic against bacteria because bacterial cells differ greatly from human cells. One of the chief differences is that bacteria, unlike animal cells, have a *cell wall.* This wall is a rigid structure that forms the cell's outer boundary.

The type of cell wall a bacterium has is one factor that determines which antibiotics can kill it. Scientists use a process called *Gram staining* to classify cell walls of bacteria. Hans C. J. Gram, a Danish bacteriologist of the late 1800's, developed the process. This method classifies bacteria as *gram-positive* (G+) or *gram-negative* (G−).

Some antibiotics selectively kill either gram-positive bacteria or gram-negative bacteria. These substances are called *narrow spectrum antibiotics.* The antibiotic Vancomycin *(VAN koh MY sihn)* selectively kills such gram-positive bacteria as *Staphylococcus (STAF uh luh KAHK uhs), Streptococcus (STREHP tuh KAHK uhs),* and *Enterococcus (EHN tuhr oh KAHK uhs).* Aztreonam *(az TREE oh nahm)* is a narrow spectrum antibiotic that kills only gram-negative bacteria, such as *Escherichia coli (EHSH uh RIHK ee uh KOH ly)* and *Pseudomonas aeruginosa (SOO duh MOH nas ih ROO juh NOH suh).* Other antibiotics can kill both gram-positive and gram-negative bacteria. These drugs are called *broad spectrum antibiotics.* Ceftriaxone *(sehf try AHKS ohn)* is one example of a broad spectrum antibiotic. No broad spectrum antibiotic can kill all bacteria, and no narrow spectrum antibiotic can kill all gram-positive or all gram-negative bacteria.

Other kinds of antibiotics. Some antibiotics are effective against infections caused by fungi and protozoans, whose cells differ from human cells. Antibiotics that fight fungi include miconazole *(mih KAHN ah zohl)* and amphotericin *(AM fuh TEHR uh sihn).* Paromomycin *(PAR oh moh MY sihn)* is used to treat amebiasis *(AM uh BY uh sihs),* an intestinal disease caused by a protozoan.

Anticancer antibiotics attack cells while they are dividing. These drugs are somewhat selectively toxic because cancer cells generally divide much more frequently than do normal cells. But some normal cells—such as blood-forming cells—divide rapidly. Anticancer antibiotics also affect these cells. The antibiotic doxorubicin *(DAHK soh ROO buh sihn)* is used to treat certain types of leukemia, breast cancer, and other tumors.

How antibiotics work

Antibiotics fight microbes and cancer cells by interfering with normal cell functions. In most cases, this interference occurs in one of three ways: (1) prevention of cell wall formation, (2) disruption of the cell *membrane* (covering), and (3) disruption of chemical processes.

Prevention of cell wall formation. Penicillins and some other antibiotics destroy microbes by interfering with their cell wall formation. Animal cells do not form walls. As a result, these antibiotics do not damage them.

Disruption of the cell membrane. All cells have a membrane that controls the movement of substances in and out of the cell. Some antibiotics, including amphotericin B and nystatin, disrupt the cell membrane of certain microbes. A damaged membrane might allow vital nutrients to escape or poisonous substances to enter and kill the cell. These antibiotics do not harm human cells because the drugs affect membrane components found only in microbial cells.

Disruption of chemical processes. All cells produce proteins and nucleic acids, which are vital to life. Human cells produce these substances in much the same way as microbial cells do. But in some cases, these processes differ enough so that antibiotics interfere with the chemical activities in microbial cells, but not in human cells. For example, streptomycin *(STREHP tuh MY sihn)* and tetracycline *(TEHT ruh SY klihn)* prevent certain kinds of microbes from producing proteins, and rifampin *(RIHF am pihn)* interferes with the formation of nucleic acids.

Dangers of antibiotics

Many antibiotics are regarded among the safest drugs when properly used. But antibiotics can sometimes cause unpleasant or dangerous side effects. The three main dangers are (1) allergic reactions, (2) destruction of helpful microbes, and (3) damage to organs and tissues.

Allergic reactions, in most cases, are mild and produce only a rash or fever. But severe reactions can occur, and can even cause death. All antibiotics are able to produce allergic reactions, but such reactions occur most often with penicillins. A physician usually asks if a patient has ever had an allergic reaction to an antibiotic before prescribing that drug. Most people who are allergic to one antibiotic can take other antibiotics that have significantly different chemical compositions.

Destruction of helpful microbes. Certain areas of the body commonly harbor both harmless and pathogenic microbes. These two types of microbes compete for food, and so the harmless microorganisms help restrain the growth of those that cause disease. Many an-

Some widely used antibiotics

Antibiotic	Some infections and diseases treated
Ampicillin	G+ and G– infections, including respiratory infections and urinary tract infections.
Ceftriaxone	G+ and G– infections, including gonorrhea.
Chloram-phenicol	Rocky Mountain spotted fever and G+ and G– infections, including meningitis.
Ciprofloxacin	Urinary tract infections and acute diarrheal diseases caused by certain G– infections.
Dicloxacillin	Penicillin-G resistant, methicillin-sensitive staphylococcal infections.
Doxycycline	Pneumonia, G+ and G– infections, bite wounds, acne.
Azithromycin	Many kinds of pneumonia, and certain other G+ infections.
Gentamicin	Serious infections, especially G- infections.
Neomycin	G+ and G– infections, especially skin infections and those resulting from burns.
Fluconazole	Fungus infections of the skin, mucous membranes, blood, and brain.
Penicillin G	Syphilis, strep throat, and other G+ infections.
Rifampin	Tuberculosis.
Streptomycin	Tuberculosis and bubonic plague.
Vancomycin	Serious staphylococcal, enterococcal, and streptococcal infections that resist other drugs.

tibiotics—especially broad spectrum drugs—do not always distinguish between harmless and dangerous microbes. If a drug destroys too many harmless microorganisms, the pathogenic ones will have a greater chance to multiply. This situation can lead to a new infection called a *superinfection*. Physicians usually prescribe a second drug to combat a superinfection.

Damage to organs and tissues is rare in people using antibiotics that act only against the cells of pathogenic microbes. Extensive use of some antibiotics, however, may damage tissues and organs. For example, streptomycin has caused kidney damage and deafness. Physicians prescribe drugs with such known risks only if no other drug is effective.

Anticancer antibiotics act against all cells that divide rapidly, and so can affect normal cells as well as cancer cells. For example, cells in the bone marrow divide constantly to produce fresh blood cells. Anticancer antibiotics can damage the bone marrow. Such damage increases the risk of infection by reducing the number of white blood cells, which help the body fight disease.

Resistance to antibiotics

Some pathogenic microbes develop an ability to resist the effects of certain antibiotics. The most widespread and worrisome resistance in pathogenic microbes occurs in bacteria.

Bacteria can become resistant to antibiotics through a type of evolution. In bacteria—as in other living things—genes carry instructions controlling life processes. Occasionally, a gene in a bacterium naturally changes in a way that enables the microbe to resist the effects of an antibiotic. Such a change is called a *mutation.* The change may provide resistance to one specific antibiotic or to a group of chemically similar antibiotics—for example, the penicillins. Bacteria can also acquire resistance from other bacteria by transferring genetic material. In some cases, these exchanges enable bacteria to acquire resistance to more than one type or more than one group of antibiotics.

Bacteria also can become resistant to antibiotics by producing an enzyme that breaks down the drug. This occurs with *Staphylococcus,* which may resist penicillins and cephalosporins *(SEHF uh luh SPAWR ihnz).* Bacteria can also change their cell membranes so that antibiotics can not penetrate them. An example of this kind of bacteria is *Pseudomonas. Pseudomonas* may develop resistance to the quinolone antibiotics this way. *Enterococcus,* a gram-positive bacteria, can become resistant to vancomycin by changing the proteins to which vancomycin usually binds. *Streptococcus* can resist penicillins and cephalosporins in this way.

Testing and producing antibiotics

Testing. Every year, scientists test thousands of natural and chemically modified microbial substances for potential use as antibiotics. First, they test these substances against harmful microbes or cancer cells that have been grown either in test tubes or on laboratory plates.

A substance that shows strong antibiotic activity against pathogenic microbes or cancer cells undergoes extensive tests in laboratory animals. If it produces no harmful effects in the animals, scientists test the antibiotic in human beings. In the United States, the Food and

Drug Administration (FDA) must approve human testing. If the drug proves to be safe and effective, it is referred to the FDA for approval. Finally, if the FDA approves the antibiotic, the developer begins to produce it for sale.

Production of antibiotics involves several steps. First, cultures of antibiotic-producing microbes are grown in flasks and then transferred to huge fermentation vats (see **Fermentation**). The microbes multiply rapidly in the vats because the environment is controlled to stimulate their growth. After fermentation, the antibiotic substance is extracted from the culture and purified.

Some natural antibiotic substances are modified chemically to produce semisynthetic antibiotics. Many such drugs are more effective than the natural antibiotics from which they were developed.

Drug companies conduct special tests on antibiotics during and after production to ensure their quality. Finally, manufacturers make the purified antibiotic substances into pills, liquids, and ointments for medical use.

History

For more than 2,500 years, people have treated certain skin infections with molds that form antibiotics. However, modern scientific study of these substances did not begin until the late 1800's. At that time, the French chemist Louis Pasteur discovered that bacteria spread infectious diseases. Then Robert Koch, a German bacteriologist, developed methods of isolating and growing various kinds of bacteria. Koch also identified specific bacteria that cause certain diseases.

Scientists then began working to develop drugs that could destroy pathogenic microbes, but the substances they produced proved either ineffective or dangerous. A historic breakthrough came in 1928, when British bacteriologist Alexander Fleming observed that a mold of the genus *Penicillium* produced a substance that destroyed bacteria. He called the substance *penicillin*.

In the early 1940's, American bacteriologist Selman A. Waksman tested about 10,000 types of soil bacteria for antibiotic activity. In 1943, he discovered that some

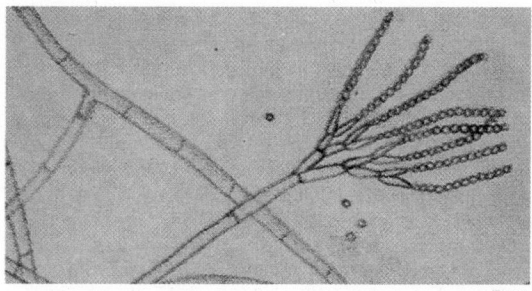

Taurus

Penicillin became the first effective antibiotic. It is obtained from *Penicillium* mold and then purified and crystallized. This photo gives a microscopic view of *Penicillium* mold.

Streptomyces (strehp tuh MY seez), a type of fungi, produced a substance that had potent antibiotic properties. A new antibiotic called *streptomycin* resulted from Waksman's research. Thousands of antibiotic substances have been found in nature or have been produced chemically. Relatively few antibiotic substances, however, have proved safe and effective.

Since the 1990's, resistance to antibiotics has been a growing threat to public health. Widespread use of antibiotics to treat human infections increases the number of resistant bacteria. Antibiotic use in livestock promotes the development of resistant bacteria that can spread to humans. For example, studies in the Netherlands, Spain, the United States, and the United Kingdom in the late 1990's revealed that many chickens were infected with antibiotic resistant strains of a bacterium called *Campylobacter (KAM py loh BAK tur)*. When people cooked the meat of these chickens, some of the *Campylobacter* microbes survived, and the people became infected.

Certain kinds of *Enterococcus* bacteria are especially troublesome because of their resistance. In Europe, drug-resistant *strains* (types) of *Enterococcus* that originated in livestock have spread to people. In the United States, *Enterococcus* resistant to multiple antibiotics has

How antibiotics are produced   Drug manufacturers produce millions of tons of antibiotics yearly, and the production process varies among companies. Some drug firms use the process shown here. The companies conduct extensive tests during and after production to make sure the antibiotics are safe and effective.

WORLD BOOK diagram by Arthur Grebetz

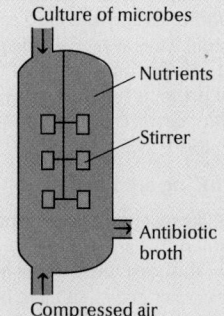

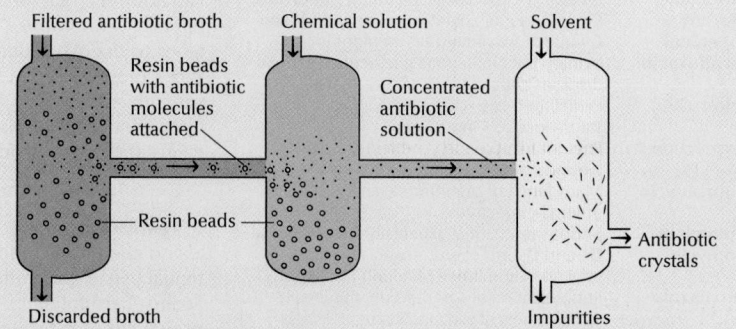

Fermentation causes a culture of microbes to grow rapidly and produce antibiotic broth. Stirring, air, and nutrients help stimulate growth.

Purification. Antibiotic broth is filtered into a tank containing substances called *resin beads*. Antibiotic molecules separate from impure elements in the broth and attach onto the resin beads. The remaining broth is flushed from the tank. A chemical solution is added to force the beads to the bottom of the tank, and the concentrated antibiotic solution flows into another tank. There, a solvent causes the solution to form pure antibiotic crystals.

caused human infections that are difficult or impossible to treat. Infections caused by antibiotic-resistant varieties of *Enterococcus* occur mostly in patients who are already seriously ill.

In the 1990's, scientists combined the antibiotics quinupristin and dalfopristin to create a drug that works against resistant strains of *Enterococcus.* In 2000, the FDA approved *linezolid (lyn AY zoh lihd),* the first entirely new type of antibiotic developed in more than 30 years. The antibiotic, sold under the brand name Zyvox, is effective against gram-positive bacteria, including *Enterococcus,* that have become resistant to all other antibiotics. In 2005, the FDA approved a new antibiotic marketed under the name Tygacil. The drug is a new class of antibiotics that work by defeating mechanisms that some bacteria use to resist existing drugs. But experts believe antibiotic-resistant *Enterococcus* remains a major threat to public health.

Melanie Johns Cupp

Related articles in *World Book* include:

Ampicillin	Fleming, Sir Alexander
Bacteria	Florey, Lord
Cephalosporin	Koch, Robert
Chain, Ernst Boris	Pasteur, Louis
Chloramphenicol	Penicillin
Disease	Streptomycin
Dubos, René Jules	Tetracycline
Erythromycin	Waksman, Selman Abraham

Antibody. See Immune system.

Antichrist is a power or person opposed to Jesus Christ. According to the Bible, the Antichrist will rise to power before the Last Judgment but will then be defeated by Christ. The idea of such a final war between good and evil occurred among Babylonians, Persians, and Jews before being adopted by Christians.

In the Bible, the term *Antichrist* appears only in the First and Second Epistles (Letters) of John. However, the concept of the Antichrist appears in various passages in the New Testament. For example, it is symbolized in the Book of Revelation as a beast—a form of Satan.

Joseph M. Hallman

Anticoagulant, *AN tee koh AG yuh luhnt,* is a chemical substance used to prevent the normal *coagulation* (clotting) of blood. The chief types are (1) drugs that slow clotting in a person's bloodstream and (2) substances that prevent the clotting of blood in a test tube.

Anticoagulant drugs are administered to treat and prevent blood clots. They frequently are used in the treatment of *thrombophlebitis,* the formation of a clot in a damaged vein. When a vein is damaged, a series of reactions changes the inactive blood chemical *prothrombin* into *thrombin.* Thrombin helps cause the formation of *fibrin,* the protein that makes up the most important part of a blood clot. Anticoagulant drugs slow the speed of one of these steps. For example, *dicoumarol* slows the conversion of prothrombin into thrombin.

Certain anticoagulants are added to blood stored for transfusions and to blood samples used for laboratory tests. These anticoagulants work by joining with calcium ions in the blood. Free calcium ions must be in the blood for clotting to occur.

Edward E. Morse

See also **Blood** (Controlling bleeding).

Anticonvulsant is a type of drug used to treat or prevent seizures. Seizures are episodes of overactive brain function in which people may lose consciousness or experience sensory or emotional disturbances. Convulsions are a type of seizure during which violent, involuntary muscle contractions occur. Anticonvulsants are the primary drugs for treating epilepsy, a disease that involves recurring seizures.

Scientists do not know exactly how anticonvulsants work. During a seizure, excessive electrical activity takes place in the brain. This electrical activity can begin in widespread areas of the brain, or it can start in limited parts of the brain and spread to other parts. Scientists think anticonvulsants may prevent the electrical activity from starting or reduce its spread to other parts of the brain.

Throughout history, people have used many magical, religious, or medicinal agents to attempt to prevent seizures. During the 1800's, drugs called *bromides* were found to be somewhat effective against seizures. However, bromides often caused mental disturbances and other harmful side effects. The use of bromides as anticonvulsants ended in the first half of the 1900's, when safer and more effective drugs were introduced. These drugs included phenobarbital (Luminal) and phenytoin (Dilantin). Other anticonvulsants widely used today include carbamazepine, clonazepam, and valproic acid.

Some anticonvulsants are taken only by mouth. Others are usually taken by mouth but also may be injected into a vein. All anticonvulsants are powerful and should only be used under the supervision of a doctor.

N. E. Sladek

Anticosti, *AN tuh KAW stee,* is a rocky island in the Gulf of Saint Lawrence, off the southern coast of Quebec. Anticosti has an area of 3,071 square miles (7,953 square kilometers) and a population of about 220. The French explorer Jacques Cartier reached Anticosti in 1534. The government of Quebec owns Anticosti. The island is used for hunting, fishing, and vacationing. The island's large herd of white-tailed deer attracts many hunters. Roger Nadeau

Antidepressant is the name of a group of drugs used to treat major depression, a severe mental illness. Antidepressants also help treat other disorders, including chronic pain, anxiety disorders, and obsessive-compulsive disorder. See **Depression; Mental illness.**

Antidepressants are thought to work by regulating the brain's neurotransmission system. Chemicals called *neurotransmitters* carry messages from one nerve cell in the brain to another. These chemicals attach to special molecules on nerve cells called *receptors,* both in sending and receiving messages. Antidepressants first increase the concentration of neurotransmitters in the brain. After several weeks of treatment, the receptors become less sensitive, and depression lifts.

The three main types of antidepressants are (1) *selective serotonin reuptake inhibitors* (SSRI's), (2) *tricyclic antidepressants* (TCA's), and (3) *monoamine oxidase inhibitors* (MAOI's). SSRI's and TCA's prevent brain cells from reabsorbing excess neurotransmitters after the chemicals have delivered their messages. SSRI's block the reabsorption of the neurotransmitter called *serotonin.* SSRI's include the most widely prescribed antidepressant, fluoxetine (Prozac). TCA's, such as the drug amitriptyline (for example, Elavil), block the reabsorption of several neurotransmitters, including serotonin and norepinephrine. MAOI's, which include the drug phenelzine (Nardil), inactivate a protein that breaks down excess neurotransmitters.

Most antidepressants are taken by mouth, and all require the prescription of a doctor. The drugs may cause various side effects. For example, SSRI's can cause increased anxiety, poor sleep, nausea, and loss of sexual interest. TCA's can cause *hypotension* (low blood pressure), irregular heartbeat, and constipation. MAOI's may combine with certain foods or drugs to create life-threatening *hypertension* (high blood pressure). In addition, the United States Food and Drug Administration (FDA) requires warning labels to indicate that antidepressants could lead some patients, particularly teenagers and children, to become suicidal. Antidepressants should be taken only under the supervision of a physician.   Alan M. Gruenberg

Antidote, *AN tee doht* or *AN tih DOHT,* is a substance that fights the harmful action of a poison in the body. Some antidotes act chemically on poisons to make them harmless. Other antidotes produce an action that works against the poison's action. Still other antidotes can stop certain body cells from reacting to the poison's effects. *Antitoxins* are a special kind of antidote (see **Antitoxin**). Most antidotes are effective against only one kind of poison. But they usually have either a worsening effect or no effect at all when used against another type of poison. For this reason, a doctor should be called immediately in any case of poisoning. See also **First aid** (Swallowed poisons); **Poison; Snakebite.**   David R. Boyd

Antietam, Battle of. See **Civil War, American** (Battle of Antietam).

Anti-Federalists were a political group in the United States in the late 1780's that feared a strong national government. Many opposed the adoption of the U.S. Constitution. Others voted for it but said it should be interpreted to give the national government the least possible power. In the 1790's, the name *Anti-Federalist* was sometimes applied to Thomas Jefferson's followers, who wanted to limit the growth of the central government's power. See also **Democratic-Republican Party; Federalist Party.**   Donald R. McCoy

Antifreeze is a substance that is added to a liquid to lower its freezing point. Antifreezes are used in compounds that remove ice or prevent it from forming, and in refrigerants and heat-transfer fluids. This article discusses automotive antifreezes, which are added to an automobile engine's cooling system.

An automobile engine operates at extremely high temperatures. It is cooled by fluid circulating through a cooling system. This prevents the engine from overheating, which can result in engine damage. Previously, water alone was used in the cooling system during the summer, and antifreeze was added to the water during the winter. Today, however, automobiles are designed to use a mixture of equal parts of water and antifreeze as the coolant the year around. Antifreeze prevents the water from freezing in cold temperatures. Modern antifreezes also raise the boiling point of the water. The cooling system therefore can operate at higher temperatures without the risk of boiling. The cooling system also operates more efficiently at higher temperatures.

Such materials as kerosene, honey, salt water, and methyl alcohol were once used as antifreezes, but these substances can damage a car's engine. Today, most automotive antifreezes are composed chiefly of a liquid compound called *ethylene glycol* (see **Glycol**). Automotive antifreezes also contain chemicals that protect the metal parts of the engine's cooling system from corrosion.   Kathleen C. Taylor

Antigen. See **Immune system.**

Antigone, *an TIHG uh nee,* in Greek mythology, was the daughter of King Oedipus and Queen Jocasta, the rulers of Thebes. Oedipus had unknowingly killed his father and married his mother. When he discovered what he had done, he blinded himself and was banished from Thebes. Antigone accompanied her father and served as his guide during his exile (see **Oedipus**).

Following Oedipus's death, Antigone returned to Thebes, where her brothers Eteocles and Polynices were struggling for the throne. The brothers had agreed to share rule, but Eteocles broke the agreement. Polynices tried to regain his share of the throne by attacking the city in what was called the Seven Against Thebes. In the battle, the brothers killed each other. Creon, the new king, buried Eteocles with great honor. But he consid-

Antigone was a princess in Greek mythology. She gave her brother Polynices an honorable burial against the wishes of King Creon of Thebes. This painting on a Greek vase shows Creon, *left,* sentencing Antigone, *right,* to death for her disobedience.

ered Polynices a rebel and a traitor and forbade anyone to give him a proper burial. Antigone felt that this order violated divine law, and so she buried her brother.

Creon sentenced Antigone to death for her disobedience, despite the pleas of his son Haemon, whom Antigone was to marry. Ancient sources differ on what finally happened to her. One says she and Haemon committed suicide. Others say she was killed by Creon or went into exile. Antigone has come to represent personal courage and conscience, especially in opposing the unjust use of power by the state.   Nancy Felson

Antigonid dynasty, *an TIHG oh nihd,* was the name of a line of kings who ruled ancient Macedonia, certain strongholds in Greece, and parts of the Near East. The dynasty began with Antigonus I, a general under Alexander the Great. After Alexander died in 323 B.C., Antigonus seized part of his empire in what are now Iraq, Syria, and Turkey. While fighting to extend his rule, Antigonus was defeated and killed at the Battle of Ipsus in 301 B.C. His son Demetrius I won control of Macedonia in 294 B.C. but lost it in 288 B.C. Demetrius's son Antigonus II regained control of Macedonia in 276 B.C., after defeating Celtic invaders. Philip V, a grandson of Antigonus II, became an ally of Hannibal, a great general of Carthage. Together, they fought two wars against Rome. The Romans ended Antigonid rule by defeating Perseus, Philip's son, in 168 B.C.   George E. Pesely

Antigravity is a hypothetical force of repulsion. It is described in some science-fiction stories but has not been observed by scientists. In theory, antigravity would resemble gravity except that it would cause objects to repel, rather than be attracted to, one another. For example, gravity on Earth pulls objects toward the planet's center. But antigravity, if it existed, would push objects away from Earth's center.

Some people have speculated that, because electric forces can be attractive or repulsive, gravitational force also may be either attractive or repulsive. However, electric force can be attractive or repulsive because it is proportional to electric charge, which is either positive or negative. For this reason, like charges repel and unlike charges attract. Gravitational force, on the other hand, is proportional to *mass* (the amount of matter that makes up an object). Mass is always positive and has no known negative counterpart. Therefore, it seems that gravitational force must always be attractive.

It is possible, however, that evidence of antigravity will be provided by observations of *antimatter* (see **Antimatter**). A few scientists have speculated that antimatter will fall *up*. No one has yet been able to observe freely falling antimatter. But other experiments have led most physicists to conclude that antimatter, just like matter, must fall toward the center of Earth.   Joel R. Primack

Antigua, *ahn TEE gwuh* (pop. 46,148), formerly Antigua Guatemala, was the capital of Guatemala in colonial days. The city was founded in 1543. It is west of the present capital, Guatemala City (see **Guatemala** [map]). In 1773, an earthquake destroyed Antigua. The capital was moved to its present site in 1776. Antigua's colonial ruins attract many tourists.   Gary S. Elbow

Antigua and Barbuda, *an TEE gah* and *bahr BYOO dah,* is an island country in the Caribbean Sea. It consists

Antigua and Barbuda

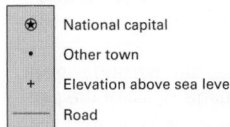

⊛ National capital

• Other town

+ Elevation above sea level

▓ Road

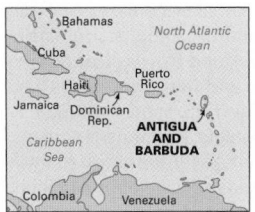

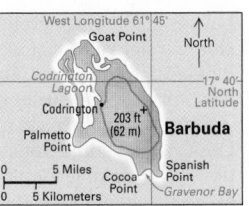

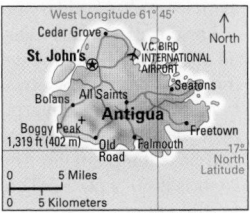

WORLD BOOK maps

of three islands—Antigua, Barbuda, and Redonda. They lie about 430 miles (692 kilometers) north of Venezuela.

Antigua and Barbuda has a total land area of 171 square miles (442 square kilometers) and a population of about 100,000. The island of Antigua covers 108 square miles (280 square kilometers); Barbuda, 62 square miles (161 square kilometers); and Redonda, only ½ square mile (1.3 square kilometers). About 98 percent of the people live on Antigua and 2 percent on Barbuda. Redonda is uninhabited. St. John's (pop. 22,000), on the northwest coast of Antigua, is the country's capital and largest city. The East Caribbean dollar is the country's basic unit of currency. For a picture of the flag of Antigua and Barbuda, see **Flag** (Flags of the Americas).

Government. Antigua and Barbuda is a constitutional monarchy and a member of the Commonwealth of Nations, an association of nations that includes the United Kingdom and many of its former possessions. A prime minister heads the government. The prime minister and a Cabinet conduct government operations. The country's Parliament consists of a House of Representatives with mostly elected members and a Senate that is appointed. The head of the majority party of the House of Representatives serves as prime minister. The prime minister appoints the Cabinet members.

People. The vast majority of the people of Antigua and Barbuda are descendants of Africans. About half of the people live in St. John's, and most of the rest live in rural areas. Most of the nation's people live in one-story

J. Alex Langley, DPI

Antigua and Barbuda is a nation in the Caribbean Sea that consists of three islands. Many tourists visit the islands to enjoy the beautiful beaches, clear water, and warm, sunny climate.

houses made of concrete blocks or wood. They wear clothing similar to that worn in the United States and other Western nations. Their main foods include beans, fish, lobsters, and sweet potatoes.

Almost all the people of Antigua and Barbuda speak English, the nation's official language. Most of the people are Protestants. Anglicans make up the largest Protestant group. Antigua and Barbuda has well-developed primary and secondary educational systems.

Land and climate. The islands of Antigua and Barbuda are mostly flat. They were formed from volcanoes that were worn down by wind and rain. The islands have beautiful beaches covered with white sand. Antigua's coast has numerous bays and inlets. Redonda is rocky and has little plant life. The average temperature of the islands is 80 °F (27 °C). The islands receive about 45 inches (114 centimeters) of rain annually. However, long periods of drought strike the area from time to time.

Economy. Tourism ranks as Antigua and Barbuda's major economic activity. The country's beaches, resorts, and sunny climate attract tourists from the United Kingdom, the United States, and other countries. The tourist industry employs many of Antigua and Barbuda's people. Agriculture is also important to the country's economy. Farmers raise cotton, fruit, livestock, and vegetables. The country's crop production is often harmed by droughts. As a result, the government encourages the development of small industries to strengthen the economy. Many of the country's people work in construction.

History. Carib Indians were the first inhabitants of Antigua and Barbuda. In 1493, Christopher Columbus became the first European to reach Antigua. British settlers established a colony on Antigua in 1632. The colony, which later included Barbuda and Redonda, was called Antigua. The British brought Africans to the islands to work as slaves on sugar cane plantations. The slaves were freed in 1834, the year after slavery was abolished in the British Empire. Most of the British people eventually left, but the British retained control of the colony.

In 1967, the colony of Antigua became part of the West Indies Associated States and gained control of its internal affairs. It became the independent nation of Antigua and Barbuda on Nov. 1, 1981. In 1989, Hurricane Hugo struck Antigua and Barbuda, causing two deaths and $80 million in property damage. Another powerful hurricane, Hurricane Luis, hit the islands in 1995, killing two people and causing $300 million in damage. In 2017, Hurricane Irma destroyed much of Barbuda, killing three people and forcing a temporary evacuation of the island's population.　　　Bert J. Thomas

Antihistamine, *AN tee HIHS tuh meen,* is the name of a group of drugs used to treat allergy symptoms, including irritated eyes, runny nose, sneezing, and hives. Antihistamines work by counteracting the effects of *histamine,* a substance found in many body cells. Excessive or inappropriate release of histamine into body fluids can cause allergies, such as hay fever, and contribute to dangerous reactions to insect bites and certain medications. Antihistamines are also used to treat motion sickness, to promote sleep, and to relieve cold symptoms.

Chemists in France developed the first useful antihistamines in the early 1940's. Diphenhydramine, a common antihistamine, was developed in the United States in 1946. People can purchase diphenhydramine, known by such trade names as AllerMax and Benadryl, and many other antihistamines without a doctor's prescription.

A common side effect of many antihistamines is drowsiness. People are advised not to drive or operate heavy machinery while using the drugs. In the 1970's and 1980's, scientists developed the first antihistamines that did not cause drowsiness. The first such drug available in the United States was terfenadine, sold until 1998 under the trade name Seldane. A similar drug, astemizole, was sold under the name Hismanal until 1999. In rare cases, these drugs have caused irregular heartbeats. Newer antihistamines, including fexofenadine, marketed under the name Allegra, do not cause such side effects. Many antihistamines are available only with a doctor's prescription, but others are sold over the counter.
　　　Richard W. Sloan

Antilles. See West Indies.

Anti-Masonic Party, *AN tee muh SAHN ihk,* was an American political party active in the late 1820's and early 1830's. It was one of the earliest American third party movements. The movement began in 1826 when William Morgan, a New York Mason, disappeared mysteriously after threatening to reveal Masonic secrets. Many people believed Masons had kidnapped and murdered him. Anti-Masonic feelings swept through New York and nearby states, and a political party was organized.

In 1831, the Anti-Masonic Party held the first national nominating convention in United States history. The party's presidential candidate, William Wirt, received only seven electoral votes in the 1832 election. But the party won the Vermont governorship and elected several congressmen. The party then declined. Most of its members joined the Whig Party.　　　Richard E. Ellis

Antimatter resembles ordinary matter but with certain properties of its particles, such as electric charge, reversed. Both kinds of matter consist of elementary particles. The elementary particles of antimatter have the same mass as their counterparts in ordinary matter. For example, the *positron* is the antimatter counterpart to the electron. It has the same mass as an electron but a positive charge, rather than a negative one.

Antimatter particles can bind together just like ordinary particles. For example, a positron and *antiproton* (the antimatter counterpart of a proton) can combine to form an antihydrogen atom. In principle, particles of antimatter can combine to form *antiatoms* and *antimolecules* of all the ordinary atoms and molecules. However, only one type of antiatom, antihydrogen, and a few types of antinuclei have been created in experiments.

When matter and antimatter particles come into contact, they can convert into energetic photons or other particles in a process called *pair annihilation.* For this reason, antimatter on Earth is usually destroyed instantly, through contact with ordinary matter. The reverse process can also take place, in which a particle-antiparticle pair is created. In either case, antimatter and ordinary matter are created or destroyed in equal amounts.

The British physicist Paul Dirac predicted the existence of antimatter in 1931, based on an equation he discovered in 1928, describing how electrons behave. In 1932, the American physicist Carl D. Anderson discovered evidence for antiparticles. Although Dirac's theory was incomplete, modern particle physics predicts that all elementary particles have antiparticle counterparts.

Some electrically neutral particles serve as their own antiparticles.

The existence of antimatter raises questions regarding the *big bang*. The big bang was the massive cosmic explosion that marked the birth of our universe. Most matter was created in the first few seconds after the big bang. If identical quantities of ordinary matter and antimatter were created then, they would have destroyed each other entirely, leaving nothing but energy behind. However, we know that ordinary matter remains in the universe. This fact suggests that more matter than antimatter was present in the first fraction of a second following the big bang. Scientists do not yet know why more matter than antimatter was created.

Doctors use antimatter in *positron emission tomography* (PET). A PET scan uses gamma rays given off by electron-positron pair annihilation to produce images of the brain or other organs (see **Positron emission tomography**). Scientists have also observed gamma rays produced by pair annihilation during thunderstorms. Some observers suspect that the antimatter created during the storms is a product of lightning strikes.   Dan Hooper

See also **Anderson, Carl David; Matter** (Antimatter).

Anti-Monopoly Party was active in United States politics in 1884. The party opposed monopolies in business. In 1884, it joined with the Greenback Party in backing Benjamin F. Butler of Massachusetts for president. The party broke up after Butler received only 175,000 votes.   Donald R. McCoy

See also **Butler, Benjamin F.**

Antimony, *AN tuh MOH nee,* a chemical element, is a bluish-white, brittle metalloid. It is used to strengthen and harden lead. Antimony-lead alloys are used in electric cables and batteries. Compounds containing antimony are used in producing refrigerants, air conditioners, aerosol sprays, paints, and flame-proofing agents.

Antimony is most commonly found combined with sulfur in the mineral *stibnite.* Pure antimony can exist as metallic antimony—the more common form—and as a black powder, known as black or gray antimony.

Antimony has the chemical symbol Sb, from *stibium,* the old name for the element. Its *atomic number* (number of protons in its nucleus) is 51. Its *relative atomic mass* is 121.760. An element's relative atomic mass equals its *mass* (amount of matter) divided by $\frac{1}{12}$ of the mass of carbon 12, the most abundant form of carbon. The density of antimony is 6.691 grams per cubic centimeter at 20 °C. Antimony melts at 630.74 °C and boils at 1586.85 °C. It *conducts* (carries) electric current better as a liquid than as a solid.

Antimony has been used for thousands of years. The ancient Egyptians used substances containing antimony as cosmetics and medicines. The Bible and ancient writings from China, India, and Mexico also refer to medical uses of antimony preparations.   Marianna A. Busch

See also **Element, Chemical** (tables).

Antioch, *AN tee AHK* (pop. 216,960), is an ancient city in southern Turkey near the Syrian border. Its name in Turkish is Antakya (pronounced *ANT uh KYAH).* Antioch lies along the Orontes River near the Mediterranean Sea. The city was founded about 300 B.C. by Seleucus, the ruler of the area. It became one of ancient Rome's great cities and was later a center of early Christianity. Saints Peter and Paul both preached there. Antioch was the capital of Syria during the A.D. 900's and 1000's. The Ottoman Empire captured Antioch in 1516. France took control of the city after the Ottoman Empire was defeated in World War I (1914-1918). In 1939, Antioch became a part of the Republic of Turkey.   F. Muge Gocek

Antioxidant, *AN tee AHK suh duhnt,* is any of a group of chemical compounds that may prevent certain types of cell damage. Antioxidants block the effects of *oxidation,* a chemical reaction in which a substance loses electrons, often while combining with oxygen. Antioxidants are important because they protect cells from the effects of *free radicals,* unstable molecules produced by oxidation. Scientists believe free radicals may be involved in the aging process as well as in many diseases.

In the body, cells create free radicals when oxygen combines with food molecules to produce energy. Radiation, cigarette smoke, and air pollution also trigger the production of free radicals. Free radicals can attract and "steal" electrons from almost any nearby molecule to replace the electrons they lost during oxidation. Such attacks can damage cells and can cause changes in genes. Antioxidants are the body's defense against free radicals. An antioxidant can provide an electron to a free radical before the free radical attacks important cell structures.

The body naturally produces enzymes that are antioxidants. In addition, vitamins C and E and certain plant chemicals, such as *carotenoids* and *flavonoids* (often called *bioflavonoids),* are antioxidants. Fruits and vegetables are rich sources of flavonoids and other antioxidants (see **Flavonoid**). Citrus fruits are a rich source of vitamin C. Vitamin E is found in vegetable oils and nuts. Foods plentiful in carotenoids tend to be deep yellow or green, such as carrots and spinach. Some studies have connected a diet rich in antioxidants with a reduced risk of cancer, heart disease, cataracts, and other diseases. Scientists are trying to determine if these reduced risks are due to the antioxidants or other factors.

Antioxidants also have commercial uses. They are added to foods to prevent spoilage. Synthetic antioxidants are used to prevent oxidation in gasoline, rubber, and other products.   Jeffrey B. Blumberg

Antiperspirant. See Deodorant.

Antique is an object from the past that has artistic or historical value. Antiques are commonly called *decorative arts.* They range from everyday household items to commissioned pieces not intended for personal use.

Opinions differ as to what is an antique. Experts consider three factors in judging an antique—its age, its artistic value, and its historical importance. The United States government, which levies no import tax on antiques, says an item must be more than 100 years old to be an antique. Most collectors also use this standard.

Antiques differ from *antiquities* and the *fine arts.* Antiquities are items created by ancient cultures. The fine arts include architecture, painting, and sculpture. However, the lines separating antiques, antiquities, and the fine arts are not always clear. Objects known as *collectibles*—such as advertising items, postcards, and baseball cards—are not considered antiques.

The variety of antiques is enormous. For example, people collect arms and armor, clocks, dolls, embroidery, musical instruments, needlework, quilts, and toys. However, antiques generally fall into four major categories—ceramics, furniture, glass, and metalwork.

Hancock Shaker Village, Inc.,
Pittsfield, Mass.

A Shaker rocking chair made about 1890 is valued for its functional design, quality materials, and craftsmanship.

Amethyst cologne bottle (1769-1774);
The Toledo Museum of Art

A glass bottle with a distinctive diamond and daisy pattern was made in the glass factory of Henry William Stiegel.

Clock (about 1820) probably made by Eli Terry or
Seth Thomas; Shelburne Museum, Shelburne, Vt.

A shelf clock made in New England in the early 1800's had a scroll top and thin pillars on the sides.

Ceramic antiques usually are divided into two categories—pottery and porcelain. Porcelain, commonly called china, is hard, thin, and usually white. Pottery is any type of ware made from baked clay. Porcelain was not made in America until the late 1700's. Until then, the colonies imported pieces from China and Europe. Colonists began making pottery in the 1600's because pottery making required simpler technology and clay was available. Many early pieces are decorated with painted flowers, animals, and other designs. Many of these pieces have a delightful simplicity and are collected by folk art enthusiasts.

Furniture was made by some of the earliest European settlers in America. These settlers brought their homeland traditions in *joinery* (skilled woodworking) and cabinetmaking with them. Few pieces remain from the 1600's. Surviving pieces from the 1600's and 1700's often can be linked to a particular region. For example, the *kas* (large wardrobe) was made by the Dutch in New York and New Jersey. Furniture makers worked in such urban centers as Baltimore; Boston; Charleston, South Carolina; New York City; Newport, Rhode Island; and Philadelphia. The showy, highly decorated pieces from the Victorian Age (1837-1901) have become valuable. However, folk art collectors also prize pieces crafted in rural areas in a highly individual style that often includes paint decoration.

Glass. In the 1600's, several glassmaking factories opened in what is now the United States. But they all soon failed. The first successful factory to produce blown glass opened in 1739. In the mid-1700's, colonial factories also began making *blown-molded glass,* which was glass shaped by being blown into a mold. During the 1820's, American glassmakers invented the method of making *pressed glass.* Pressed glass was liquid glass that was pressed into a mold by a mechanical plunger.

Metalwork. Antique American gold is extremely rare, but antique silver is not. Silversmiths were well established in the colonies, and silver was a symbol of wealth. Many silver *tankards* (large drinking mugs) bear en-

graved decorations, such as coats of arms, monograms, designs, and inscriptions. In the British tradition, most silversmiths labeled their wares with their own unique mark. Because of its affordability, pewter was made in America in large quantities. Pewterers, too, often marked their wares. These marks enable collectors to trace the origins and dates of particular pieces. Other metal antiques include brass, copper, and wrought-iron household items. Painted tin called *toleware* was popular in the 1800's. Allison Eckardt Ledes

Related articles in *World Book* include:

Collectibles	Glass (History of	Pottery
Colonial life in	glass)	Quilt
America	Jewelry	Sampler
Doll	Lace	Stoneware
Folk art	Pewter	Watch
Furniture	Porcelain	

Anti-Semitism is prejudice against Jews. However, the term is misleading because the root word *Semites* properly refers to all people who speak Semitic languages, including Arabs and some other non-Jewish peoples (see **Semites**).

Since ancient times, the Jews have lived as a minority group in many countries. Both Christian and Muslim nations often persecuted Jews for not accepting the religion of the majority. When economic or other conditions were bad, Jews were blamed for causing the troubles of society.

During the Middle Ages, Jews in many European countries were forced to pay special taxes and to live in segregated areas called *ghettos.* Jews also were denied the right to own land and to enter certain occupations. Some countries even expelled many Jews. In 1492, for example, the Jews were driven out of Spain.

Wilhelm Marr, a German author, coined the term *anti-Semitism* in the anti-Jewish pamphlet "The Victory of Jewry Over Germandom" (1879). The new word indicated that many people had begun to discriminate against Jews on ethnic rather than religious grounds. In the late 1800's and early 1900's, many Jews in Poland and Russia were killed in organized massacres called *pogroms.* A Jewish movement called Zionism developed partly in response to such persecution. The Zionists hoped to establish an independent Jewish nation in Palestine, where Jews could escape anti-Semitism. See **Zionism.**

In 1933, the Nazi dictator Adolf Hitler came to power in Germany and made anti-Semitism an official government policy. The German government stripped the Jews of their citizenship, seized their property, and sent thousands to concentration camps. By the end of World War II in 1945, the Nazis had killed about 6 million Jews in a campaign of mass murder known as the Holocaust.

Anti-Semitism still exists in many countries. In some countries, it affects government policies.   Yosef Levanon

Related articles in *World Book* include:

Concentration	Ghetto	Jews
camp	Hate crime	Mein Kampf
Genocide	Holocaust	Racism

Antiseptic is a substance that destroys or stops the growth of germs on living tissue. Antiseptics are applied to skin and mucous membranes to help prevent infection. They must be strong enough to fight germs but mild enough not to irritate sensitive tissues. Antiseptics differ from disinfectants and antibiotics. Disinfectants are chemicals that destroy germs on nonliving objects. Antibiotics are drugs that treat infection after it occurs.

Kinds of antiseptics. There are hundreds of antiseptic products, including creams, mouthwashes, ointments, powders, shampoos, soaps, solutions, and sprays. Each type contains a germ-fighting chemical that carries out the antiseptic action. Such chemicals include alcohols, dyes, iodophors, mercurials, phenols, and salicylamides. The kinds and amounts of chemicals that are used depend chiefly on the type of product.

The use of antiseptics. Physicians use special antiseptic cleansers to scrub their hands and to wash the skin of their patients before performing surgery. Doctors also spray serious wounds with antiseptics in order to keep the wounds from becoming infected.

The germ-fighting chemicals in antiseptics can cause serious side effects. These effects include a rash or some other allergic reaction, or damage to the skin. But medical experts generally believe antiseptics are safe if used as directed by the manufacturer. In the United States, the Food and Drug Administration (FDA), an agency of the federal government, regulates the manufacture and sale of antiseptics.

History. People used vinegar and wine as antiseptics as early as 2,500 years ago, long before the discovery that germs cause disease. Several hundred years ago, surgeons noticed that untreated battle wounds and surgical incisions quickly began to smell like rotting flesh. To prevent this odor, they treated the tissues with a variety of substances that became known as *antiseptics.* The word comes from two Greek words—*anti,* meaning *against,* and *sepsis,* meaning *decay.*

Through the centuries, a number of fluids and potions were used as antiseptics. In addition to vinegar and wine, they included brandy, mercury, pitch, tar, and turpentine. Some were powerful germ killers but would also harm living tissue. As a result, many patients were saved from infection but died from the treatment.

In the mid-1800's, Ignaz P. Semmelweis, a Hungarian physician, showed that a mild solution of lime chloride helped prevent infection during childbirth. Doctors who rinsed their hands in the solution kept infection from spreading among their patients. In the mid-1860's, Sir Joseph Lister, an English surgeon, pioneered the use of antiseptics in surgery. He used carbolic acid to help prevent infection in incisions. The work of Semmelweis and Lister led to the creation of many mild but effective antiseptics. Some of these products, such as alcohol and iodine, are still widely used.   Christopher A. Rodowskas, Jr.

Related articles in *World Book* include:

Alcohol	Iodine
Disinfectant	Lister, Sir Joseph
Hydrogen peroxide	Medicine (Antiseptic surgery)

Antislavery movement. See Abolition movement.

Antitoxin, *AN tee TAHK sihn,* is a substance made by living cells that counteracts illness caused by a *toxin.* Toxins are poisons produced by living organisms, such as bacteria. Doctors use antitoxins to treat diseases, including *tetanus* (lockjaw) and diphtheria. Antitoxins are a kind of *antibody* that can cure or prevent diseases or make them milder (see Immune system).

Many commercial antitoxins come from animals, such as horses and rabbits. Toxin is injected into an animal's bloodstream, and the animal produces an antitoxin that circulates in its blood serum. A nonpoisonous, chemically modified toxin called a *toxoid* is sometimes used to cause the body to produce antitoxin. The blood serum can be removed and then injected into patients. Most animal antitoxins are cheaper and easier to make than human antitoxins. However, animal antitoxins are less effective and may cause bad reactions.

Injected antitoxins usually do not make a patient permanently *immune* (safe from disease). The antitoxins produced by the body when a person is exposed to a particular toxin are the most effective. In addition, body tissues produce these antitoxins again in future poisonings by the toxin. A reasonable concentration of the antitoxin usually will prevent poisoning. Antitoxins that are produced by another person also are effective in neutralizing a toxin but do not give permanent protection. Permanent immunity can be stimulated in the body by injecting toxoids.   Alan R. Hinman

See also **Diphtheria** (Treatment); **Immunization; Serum; Tetanus; Toxin.**

Antitrust laws are designed to protect competition and consumers. They prohibit *price fixing agreements,* in which business firms agree on the price they will charge for products or services. They also outlaw *mergers*—that is, the joining of business firms—that interfere with competition. In addition, antitrust laws prohibit firms from using their economic power to gain or maintain a monopoly. While the United States pioneered antitrust laws, some other nations have adopted such laws, along with freer world trade policies. Both the U.S. government and state governments have antitrust laws. This article discusses federal antitrust legislation.

During the late 1800's, business leaders, such as John D. Rockefeller, bought up or stamped out many of their competitors. They then brought their surviving competitors under informal common control in organizations called *trusts.* The trusts limited production and raised prices. A public outcry against abuses by the trusts led to passage of the Sherman Antitrust Act in 1890. The act outlaws any contract, combination, or conspiracy in restraint of trade. In addition, it prohibits any person or business from monopolizing or trying to monopolize any market.

During the early 1900's, the U.S. government sued and broke up existing oil, tobacco, and farm machinery trusts, as well as several others. But many companies continued to grow by merging with or buying competing firms. Also, many businesses sought to eliminate competition by buying the stocks of their competitors and by forcing their customers to sign exclusive dealing contracts. Some businesses required customers to buy goods they did not want to acquire the goods they needed. The courts allowed many of these practices.

In 1914, Congress responded to these practices by passing two laws that give support to the Sherman Antitrust Act. These laws were the Clayton Antitrust Act and the Federal Trade Commission Act. The Clayton Act outlaws price discrimination that gives favored buyers an advantage over their competitors. It also forbids anticompetitive agreements in which manufacturers sell only to dealers who agree not to handle the products of a rival manufacturer. In addition, the act prohibits mergers that lessen competition. The Federal Trade Commission Act established the Federal Trade Commission (FTC). This government agency works to prevent unfair and anticompetitive business practices.

Despite the Clayton Act and the Federal Trade Commission Act, companies continued to make anticompetitive mergers and acquisitions. The Celler-Kefauver Act of 1950 strengthened the Clayton Act by tightening control over mergers that reduce competition.

In 2000, a U.S. district court judge ruled that Microsoft Corporation had violated antitrust laws by abusing its monopoly in personal computer operating systems. In 2002, Microsoft and the U.S. Department of Justice agreed to a settlement that a federal judge determined to be agreeable to the company, the government, and the public. In 2004, the European Union (EU) found Microsoft guilty of additional antitrust violations. The EU fined Microsoft and required the company to change its business practices.

The late 1900's and early 2000's marked a lowering of trade barriers worldwide. As a result, opportunities for competition grew. But an increase in the number of large corporate mergers also occurred. Debate continues over whether a successful global economy requires more or less antitrust control. Some people argue that business can best respond to consumer needs if left alone. Others feel that strict enforcement of antitrust laws is necessary to protect competition and consumers.

Eleanor M. Fox

See also **Monopoly and competition** (History).

Antiviral drug is the term for a group of chemical compounds used to treat diseases caused by viruses. Antiviral drugs usually do not cure viral diseases but can shorten the duration of the disease and lessen the severity of symptoms. But many antiviral drugs can cause side effects, such as anemia or kidney damage.

Many viral diseases can be prevented by using vaccines. But vaccines have not been developed for all viral diseases, and vaccines are not useful for treating people once they become ill. Other drugs, including antibiotics such as penicillin, have no effect on viruses.

Viruses use substances in the cells of living organisms, called *host cells,* to manufacture enzymes and other materials they need to reproduce. Antiviral drugs interfere with parts of the viral life cycle that are different from steps completed by the hosts. This allows drugs to attack viruses while not harming host cells. But since viruses rely on substances made by hosts to carry out many steps in their life cycles, the drugs can target only a few viral materials. Getting drugs into infected cells is also an obstacle. Despite these difficulties, researchers have developed many successful antiviral drugs.

Many antiviral drugs are chemical compounds that bind to viral enzymes, changing the structure so the enzymes cannot be used by the viruses. The drugs bind only to viral enzymes, while enzymes used by the host cell are not impaired. The virus, however, cannot reproduce to infect other host cells. The progression of the disease is thus slowed or halted by the drugs.

The first antiviral drugs were developed in the 1960's. One of the earliest, *acyclovir,* is widely used to treat infections of *herpesviruses,* a group of viruses that cause chickenpox, mononucleosis, shingles, and cold sores. This drug mimics a building block of the genetic material *DNA* (deoxyribonucleic acid), which herpesviruses need to reproduce. Viral enzymes mistakenly add this drug into a growing strand of DNA and stop its production. Acyclovir is given to patients by injection, as a pill, or in ointment applied to the skin. Other drugs, such as *zanamivir,* used to treat influenza, can be inhaled. Many antiviral drugs available today have been developed to treat HIV, the virus that causes AIDS. Nelson M. Gantz

See also **AIDS** (Treatment); **Interferon; Virus.**

Antler. See **Deer; Horn; Reindeer** (picture).

Antoinette, Marie. See **Marie Antoinette.**

Antoninus Pius, *an tuh NY nuhs PY uhs* (A.D. 86-161), was Roman emperor from A.D. 138 until his death on March 7, 161. He was open-minded and just, and his reign was probably the calmest in Roman history.

Antoninus was born into a rich and influential family on Sept. 19, A.D. 86. He had a distinguished senatorial career. He also administered a court of appeals in Italy and served as *proconsul* (governor) of the province of Asia in western Asia Minor.

Antoninus's legal experience, his wealth and reputation, and his popularity with the Senate influenced Emperor Hadrian to choose him as successor. As emperor, Antoninus built the Antonine Wall in northern Britain, the empire's chief trouble spot. F. G. B. Millar

Antony, *AN tuh nee,* **Mark** (83?-30 B.C.), a Roman senator and general, was one of Rome's rulers from 43 B.C. until his death. Antony's reputation has suffered because of his relationship with Queen Cleopatra of Egypt, and because his rival Octavian defeated him to become Rome's sole ruler.

Marcus Antonius, known in English as Mark Antony, was born into a distinguished family with a history of service in the Roman Senate. He served as an officer under Julius Caesar during Caesar's military campaigns in Gaul. As a *tribune* of the people (elected representative) in 49 B.C., Antony unsuccessfully advised the Senate against provoking Caesar into civil war. In 48 B.C., he commanded part of the army with which Caesar defeated Pompey, defender of the Roman Republic, at the Battle of Pharsalus.

In 44 B.C., Antony and Caesar were fellow *consuls*

(joint heads of the republic). That year, members of the Senate assassinated Caesar. Afterward, Antony's efforts to reach a compromise with the Senate failed to satisfy hostile public opinion regarding Caesar's death. In addition, Antony never imagined that Caesar would make Octavian, his great-nephew, his principal heir. Nor did Antony imagine that Octavian, a weak teenager, would sway public opinion and gather military support against him as effectively as he did. In 43 B.C., after a failed attempt to establish himself as governor of Cisalpine Gaul in northern Italy, Antony agreed to join Octavian and Marcus Aemilius Lepidus in a partnership to rule the Roman world (see **Triumvirate**). The trio ruthlessly executed opponents and seized their property. Antony took the lead in avenging Caesar's murder for Octavian. Because of Antony's generalship, Caesar's principal assassins— Marcus Junius Brutus and Gaius Cassius Longinus—were defeated in battle at Philippi in 42 B.C.

After the battles at Philippi, Antony oversaw Rome's eastern territories, and Octavian worked at settling veterans on seized land in Italy. Antony's wife and brother stirred up resistance to Octavian. Antony might have supported them, but he decided not to turn against Octavian. The gravest threat to the joint rulers' partnership was the growing seaborne power of Sextus Pompey, the son of Pompey, in the west. Antony dared not refuse Octavian's pleas for aid, especially for ships, to fight Sextus. In 40 B.C., Antony's wife died and he married Octavian's sister Octavia, thus strengthening the two men's partnership. Octavian finally defeated Sextus Pompey at Naulochus, Sicily, in 36 B.C. with support from both Antony and Lepidus. Then, after Lepidus tried to take control of Sicily and Octavian's forces, Octavian exiled him from Rome.

In 41 B.C., Antony had sought support from Cleopatra, queen of the wealthy kingdom of Egypt. Antony and Cleopatra's relationship became personal. Cleopatra bore Antony twins—a girl and a boy—in 40 B.C., and another son in 36 B.C. Antony and Cleopatra seemed to be husband and wife. But Roman law did not recognize marriage with foreigners, and Antony did not divorce Octavia until 32 B.C. Octavia bore him two daughters in 39 and 36 B.C.

A major military campaign by Antony against the kingdom of Parthia in 36 B.C. failed badly. In 34 B.C., however, Antony succeeded in occupying Armenia, and extravagant celebrations were held in Alexandria, Egypt. Octavian, who wished to eliminate Antony, publicized the celebrations as proof that Antony no longer was Roman, but enchanted by Cleopatra's ambitions. Antony, who still had many friends in Rome, probably wished to continue his partnership with Octavian. But he could not ignore Octavian's attack, so he called up troops for battle. Octavian defeated Antony and Cleopatra at the Battle of Actium in 31 B.C. Octavian then laid siege to Alexandria, and Antony soon took his own life.   Richard J. A. Talbert

Related articles in *World Book* include:

Actium, Battle of	Caesar, Julius	Octavia
Augustus	Cleopatra	Pompey the Great

Antwerp, *ANT wuhrp* (pop. 513,570), is Belgium's largest city and its main port. Antwerp is one of the major ports of Europe. It is called Antwerpen (pronounced *AHNT vehr puhn)* in Flemish and Anvers (pronounced *ahn VEHR)* in French.

Antwerp lies on the Schelde River, 55 miles (89 kilometers) from the North Sea (see **Belgium** [political map]). The city's waterways and railways serve all Belgium and industrial cities in Germany and France. The harbor at Antwerp is one of the world's largest. Besides its vast trade, the city has many industries, including sugar refining, lace making, brewing, distilling, and shipbuilding. It is also the world's largest diamond-trading center.

Chief buildings. Antwerp's Cathedral of Our Lady is the largest Gothic church in Belgium and often considered the most beautiful. Its graceful tower rises over 400 feet (120 meters) above its surrounding plain. The cathedral was constructed in sections from 1352 to 1520 and houses masterpieces by the Flemish artist Peter Paul Rubens. The large Renaissance town hall, or *Stadhuis,* was built in the 1560's as a monument to the city's wealth. It stands on the main square, *Grote Markt,* facing the elaborate, Gothic facades of the guild houses. Most of these were also built in the 1500's. Antwerp's fine arts museum includes priceless works by Rubens, Anthony Van Dyck, and Jacob Jordaens. The beautiful mansion and gardens of the Rubens House contain more of the artist's works and the studio where he created them.

History. Antwerp became a great port of trade between the European mainland and England in the 1400's. In the 1500's, Antwerp was one of the world's richest cities and Europe's chief money market. The first stock exchange was set up there in 1531. Antwerp reached the height of its prosperity about 1560. The Eighty Years' War (1568-1648) then plunged the city and the surrounding country into turmoil, as the Dutch provinces fought for—and gained—independence from Spain.

Antwerp declined steadily until 1800, when its population fell below 40,000. The French ruler Napoleon I, realizing its strategic and commercial value, decided to open and improve its harbor and to set it up as a rival to London. The trade of Antwerp grew rapidly until 1830, when Belgium separated from Holland. The Dutch, who controlled the Schelde estuary upon which Antwerp is located, imposed heavy tolls upon shipping. These tolls were abolished in 1863, and the city's trade recovered.

Antwerp was for a long time the key fortress in the national defense of Belgium and one of the strongest fortresses in Europe. But modern artillery enabled the Germans to capture and occupy Antwerp in World War I (1914-1918). In May 1940, during World War II (1939-1945), German troops occupied the city. They mined the harbor, planning to destroy the installations upon retreating. But daring Belgian underground workers prevented the explosions when the Allies liberated Antwerp in September 1944. The city was heavily damaged in the fighting, but the port's survival was key to European recovery after the war.   Aristide R. Zolberg

See also **Belgium** (picture); **Rubens, Peter Paul; Van Dyck, Sir Anthony.**

Anubis, *uh NOO bihs,* in Egyptian mythology, served as the god of *mummification,* the ancient Egyptian technique of embalming the dead. The jackal—and later the dog—served as his sacred animal. In Egyptian art, Anubis often appears as a crouching jackal or dog or as a man with a jackal's head. His main center of worship was at Kynopolis, which means *Dog City* in Greek. In the myth of Osiris, Anubis invents embalming and helps restore Osiris to life after he is murdered by Seth. With

Thoth, Anubis weighed the hearts of the dead on the scales of justice in the underworld, judging the merit of their souls. Robert K. Ritner

See also **Mythology** (Egyptian mythology; pictures).

Anvers. See Antwerp.

Anxiety disorder is any one of several mental disorders in which the sufferer repeatedly experiences mild to severe fear or dread, thereby causing undue distress or disability. Anxiety is a common emotion, often accompanied by physical feelings of nervousness and urges to escape or avoid a seemingly threatening situation. Anxiety becomes a problem when it interferes with life or occurs in response to objects or situations that are not dangerous or in response to nothing at all.

Mental health professionals recognize six primary types of anxiety disorders. *Phobias* involve excessive fear and avoidance of objects or situations that pose little or no threat. *Social anxiety disorder* is an excessive fear and avoidance of social situations where people unrealistically fear they may be embarrassed or humiliated. *Panic disorder* is characterized by sudden surges of fear, called *panic attacks,* that occur unexpectedly and without apparent reason. *Generalized anxiety disorder* (GAD) involves excessive uncontrollable worry about everyday life activities. People with *obsessive-compulsive disorder* (OCD) experience intrusive and unwanted fearful thoughts, images, or impulses that they find distressing even while recognizing that such thoughts or impulses are highly unrealistic. Many OCD sufferers engage in *compulsions,* which are mental or behavioral rituals that they feel help relieve the anxiety. *Post-traumatic stress disorder* (PTSD) involves a distressing and disabling response to experiencing a trauma, such as an automobile accident or an assault.

Treatment of anxiety disorders may involve medication and *cognitive behavioral therapy* (CBT). CBT involves gradually facing and overcoming fears. Timothy J. Bruce

Anzac Day is a patriotic holiday in Australia and New Zealand. It is a day to honor people who have served in the armed forces of those countries.

During World War I (1914-1918), the Australian and New Zealand Army Corps (ANZAC)—fighting on the side of the Allies—was sent to attack the Ottoman Empire, which was allied with Germany. The ANZAC troops landed on the Gallipoli Peninsula in what is now Turkey on April 25, 1915. Although the ANZAC and British forces fought with great courage, the Ottoman defense held firm. Australia lost more than 8,000 men, and New Zealand lost more than 2,700. The Allied troops withdrew in December 1915 and January 1916.

Anzac Day was first observed on April 25, 1916, to commemorate the anniversary of the Gallipoli landing. By the 1920's, the day had become a day to remember all Australians and New Zealanders who had died in World War I. In 1920, New Zealand officially declared April 25 a national holiday. During a 1921 premiers' conference, Australian leaders agreed that April 25 should be the day on which to hold Anzac Day celebrations. By the end of the 1920's, all the states had passed legislation to make Anzac Day a legal holiday. After World War II (1939-1945), Anzac Day became a time to remember people who died in that war as well. Since then, the holiday has come to be a day of remembrance to honor Australians and New Zealanders who died in wars, as well as an oc-

casion to honor veterans and those currently serving in the armed forces.

Anzac Day is observed with dawn services at war memorials and other public places, as well as with parades and other memorial ceremonies. Many Australians and New Zealanders travel to what is now known as Anzac Cove on the Gallipoli Peninsula to participate in Anzac Day memorial services there. Giselle M. Byrnes

Aorta, *ay AWR tuh,* is the body's longest and largest artery. Its many branches distribute purified blood to all parts of the body. The first part of the aorta is the *ascending aorta.* It rises from the left ventricle of the heart almost to the top of the breastbone. The aorta's first branches are the coronary arteries, which supply blood to the heart. From near the top of the breastbone, the aorta arches backward and slightly to the left to form the *arch of the aorta.* Branches from the arch supply blood to the head and neck. The section after the arch, the *descending aorta,* passes downward through the chest and abdomen. It supplies the bones, organs, and muscles with blood. In the chest, or *thorax,* the aorta is called the *thoracic aorta;* in the abdomen, the *abdominal aorta.* At the hips, the aorta divides into two large arteries, the *common iliac arteries,* which carry blood to the pelvis and legs. See also **Aneurysm; Heart** (pictures); **Human body** (Anatomy of the human body). Joseph V. Simone

Apache Indians, *uh PACH ee,* belong to a number of tribes of the southwestern United States and northern Mexico. According to the 2010 census, there are about 63,000 Apache in the United States. Many Apache live on reservations in Arizona and New Mexico. Apache tribes include the Jicarilla, the Mescalero, the San Carlos, and the White Mountain Apache. In the late 1800's, the Apache became known for their resistance to U.S. government attempts to restrict them to reservations.

The Apache once hunted game and gathered wild plants for food. They wore animal skins and lived in thatched houses or in tipis. They became known for their raids against early Spanish settlers and other *indigenous* (native) groups in the area.

The Apache were placed on reservations in the 1870's after being defeated by the United States Army. However, several Apache bands fled from their reservations and resumed their raids. In 1885, Geronimo led the most famous outbreak from an Apache reservation. He surrendered in 1886. The Army imprisoned many peaceful Apache along with Geronimo and his followers.

Today, many Apache work for tribal-owned lumber or cattle companies. The Jicarilla of New Mexico earn most of their income from mineral deposits on their reservations. In 1982, the Supreme Court of the United States upheld the right of the Jicarilla to tax the production of oil and natural gas on their lands. Keith H. Basso

See also **Cochise; Geronimo; Indian, American** (Indians of the Southwest); **Indian wars** (Apache warfare).

Apartheid, *ah PAHRT hayt* or *ah PAHRT hyt,* was, from 1948 until 1991, the South African government's policy of rigid racial segregation. The word *apartheid* means *separateness* in Afrikaans, one of South Africa's official languages.

Built on earlier South African laws and customs, apartheid classified every South African person by race as either (1) Black, (2) white, (3) Coloured (mixed race), or (4) Asian. Apartheid required segregation in housing, education, employment, public accommodations, and transportation. It segregated not only almost all white and nonwhite people, but also major groups of non-white people from one another. It also limited the rights of nonwhite people to own and occupy land, and to enter white neighborhoods.

The South African government tried to justify apartheid by claiming that peaceful coexistence of the races was possible only if the races were separated from one another. However, white South Africans used apartheid chiefly as a way to control the vast nonwhite majority.

Most South Africans strongly opposed apartheid. Leading opposition groups included the African National Congress (ANC). Most ANC members were Black. Between 1948 and 1991, large numbers of people protested apartheid by staging boycotts, demonstrations, and strikes. Violence often broke out, and thousands of people, most of them Black, were killed.

Many countries also opposed apartheid. As a result, South Africa grew increasingly isolated in the world community. In 1962, the United Nations General Assembly urged its members to break diplomatic and economic ties with South Africa until apartheid was abolished. In the 1980's, an economic boycott of South Africa took hold. In response to the pressure, South Africa began repealing apartheid laws in the 1970's. By 1991, it had repealed most of the remaining laws that had formed the legal basis of apartheid. But apartheid's effects continued after the laws were repealed. Many Black and other nonwhite people still face unofficial segregation and discrimination in South Africa today.   Thomas F. Pettigrew

Related articles in *World Book* include:

African National Congress
Biko, Steve
Malan, Daniel François
South Africa (History)
Verwoerd, Hendrik

Apatosaurus, *uh PAT oh SAWR uhs* or *AP uh toh SAWR uhs,* was a gigantic dinosaur with a long neck. It belonged to the group of plant-eating dinosaurs called *sauropods. Apatosaurus* lived about 150 million years ago in what is now the western United States.

Apatosaurus grew to about 75 feet (23 meters) long and 15 feet (4.5 meters) tall at the hip. It weighed about 20 to 30 tons (18 to 27 metric tons). Some individuals may have grown to be much larger and heavier.

Apatosaurus had a small, narrow head at the end of its long, muscular neck. The neck made up over a quarter of the animal's length. It was far thicker and more solidly built than the necks of other sauropods. *Apatosaurus* may have used the neck to club *predators* (hunting animals) or rivals. *Apatosaurus* had a relatively short body, with its back sloping gently down from hips to shoulders. Its long tail was thick at the base but narrowed to a thin, whiplike tip. A pair of massive hind limbs bore most of the animal's weight. They had padded feet with large claws. The forelimbs of *Apatosaurus* were relatively short, and each forefoot had only one small claw.

Since its discovery, *Apatosaurus* has been linked to another sauropod, *Brontosaurus.* The American *paleontologist* (scientist who studies prehistoric life) Othniel C. Marsh first described an incomplete fossil skeleton of *Apatosaurus* in 1877. Two years later, he found a more complete skeleton and named it *Brontosaurus.* But in the 1900's, scientists concluded that *Apatosaurus* and *Brontosaurus* were the same kind of dinosaur. The *Apato-*

saurus name was kept because it came first, but the name *Brontosaurus* remained in popular use. In 2015, scientists again studied the fossil skeletons and concluded that *Brontosaurus* and *Apatosaurus* may be two distinct kinds of dinosaurs after all.   Michael P. Taylor

See also **Dinosaur** (Diplodocids).

Ape is a member of the group of animals that look most like human beings. There are five main kinds of apes—bonobos, chimpanzees, gibbons, gorillas, and orangutans. These animals have hairy, tailless bodies; longer arms than legs; and long fingers and toes. They have large brains and are the smartest animals after humans.

Scientists believe apes and humans *evolved* (developed gradually) from a common ancestor. Apes resemble humans in body structure more than any other animals do. For example, they have similar bones, muscles, and organs. They also have similar *genomes.* A genome is the complete set of hereditary information for a particular organism. But humans also differ from apes in many ways. Humans walk on two legs and have longer legs and less body hair than apes. They also have a larger brain than apes. For more information on human beings and apes, see **Human being** (Physical characteristics).

Scientists divide the apes into two groups, based chiefly on size. Gibbons, the smallest apes, are called *lesser apes* and consist of many different *species* (kinds). Bonobos, chimpanzees, gorillas, and orangutans are called *great apes.* Gorillas are the largest, followed by orangutans, chimpanzees, and bonobos. Each of the great apes consists of one species.

Differences between apes and monkeys. Many people confuse apes with monkeys, but the two groups of animals differ in many ways. Monkeys have tails and smaller brains in relation to their body size. The great apes are much larger and have longer fingers and toes. Apes are skillful tree climbers. On the ground, bonobos, chimpanzees, and gorillas walk in a semiupright posture, supporting the front part of their bodies on their knuckles. Orangutans walk infrequently on the ground, but when they do, they support themselves on their fists. Gibbons spend almost all their time in trees but often walk on two legs on branches. By contrast, monkeys run and jump on all fours, both in trees and on the ground.

Way of life. Apes live in tropical Africa and Asia. All apes prefer to eat fruit. When fruit is unavailable, gorillas eat leafy plants, such as wild celery and bamboo shoots.

Gibbons live in the tropical forests of Southeast Asia. They spend much time hanging from tree branches or swinging from branch to branch. Gibbons form family groups of a male and a female and their young.

Chimpanzees live in a wide range of habitats in Africa. They are found in rain forests as well as dry grasslands, and they live both in trees and on the ground. Chimpanzee groups may vary from 10 to over 50 members. Often, the females leave their group and join another.

Bonobos, also called pygmy chimpanzees, strongly resemble chimpanzees. Bonobos live in a section of rain forest in the Democratic Republic of the Congo. They live both in trees and on the ground, in small groups that are part of larger bonobo communities.

Gorillas live in the lowland forests of western and central Africa and in the mountain forests of eastern Africa. They normally make nests and sleep on the ground. Gorillas travel in groups of up to 20 individuals. Older

The five types of apes There are five major kinds of apes: gorillas, bonobos, chimpanzees, gibbons, and orangutans. Gorillas, bonobos, chimpanzees, and orangutans are known as *great apes*. Gibbons, the smallest apes, are called *lesser apes*. These illustrations include average weight figures for adult males.

WORLD BOOK illustrations by James Teason
WORLD BOOK illustration (Bonobo) by Robin Bouttell, Wildlife Art Ltd.

Gibbon (Lar gibbon)
Hylobates lar
Weight: about 13 pounds
(6 kilograms)

Gorilla
Gorilla gorilla
Weight: about 450
pounds (204 kilograms)

Bonobo
Pan paniscus
Weight: about 100
pounds (45 kilograms)

Chimpanzee
Pan troglodytes
Weight: about 110
pounds (50 kilograms)

Orangutan
Pongo pygmaeus
Weight: about 180
pounds (82 kilograms)

males develop a patch of white or silvery hair on their backs and are called *silverbacks*. One or two of these males lead each group.

Orangutans live in the tropical forests of Borneo and Sumatra. They spend most of the time in trees, though large males are often seen on the ground. Orangutans usually travel alone, but a female and her offspring travel together.

The number of apes is decreasing because people hunt them for food and for pets and to sell to zoos and research centers. In addition, roads, farms, and the forest industry have destroyed much of the forests where apes once lived. Craig B. Stanford

Scientific classification. Apes belong to the order Primates. The great apes make up the family Pongidae. Gibbons make up the family Hylobatidae. Bonobos and chimpanzees are in the genus *Pan,* gorillas are genus *Gorilla,* and orangutans are genus *Pongo.*

Related articles in *World Book* include:

Bonobo	Gigantopithecus	Orangutan
Chimpanzee	Gorilla	Siamang
Gibbon		

Apelles, *uh PEHL eez,* was one of the most famous ancient Greek painters. He lived during the 300's B.C. Although none of his paintings has survived, their subjects are known from ancient authors who praised the artist for the amazing realism of his work. Apelles was court painter to Philip II and Alexander the Great of Macedonia. Apelles painted a portrait of Philip and another of Alexander holding a thunderbolt. Apelles was also famous for his painting of the goddess Aphrodite rising from the sea. Marjorie S. Venit

Apennines, *AP uh NYNZ,* is a mountain range in Italy that extends from the Gulf of Genoa to the Strait of Messina, about 840 miles (1,350 kilometers). The range varies from about 25 to 80 miles (40 to 130 kilometers) in width.

The mountains have been worn down by wind and rain for millions of years and are among the lowest in Europe. Corno Grande, the highest peak, rises 9,554 feet (2,912 meters). Vesuvius, a famous peak, is the only active volcano in mainland Europe. Many types of vegetation grow in the Apennines. Shrubs and rough pastures grow above about 6,000 feet (1,800 meters). Below them are forests of beech, chestnut, conifers, and oak. Olive groves and farms spread across the lowest elevations. The mountains consist mainly of limestone and marble. Quarries near Carrara are noted for their marble. See also Italy (The Apennines; terrain map). Howell C. Lloyd

Apgar, Virginia (1909-1974), was an American physician who developed a system for evaluating the physical condition of a baby immediately after birth. The system, known as the Apgar score, assigns a numerical score to five vital functions measured one and five minutes after birth. Doctors worldwide use the score to determine the short-term health care needs of newborn babies.

Apgar was born in Westfield, New Jersey, on June 7, 1909. She studied zoology, chemistry, and physiology at Mount Holyoke College in Massachusetts, graduating in 1929. She studied medicine at Columbia University, receiving her M.D. in 1933. Apgar specialized in anesthesiology, which deals with the administration of drugs for the relief of pain, especially during surgery. In 1938, she was appointed the first director of anesthesiology at Columbia-Presbyterian Medical Center in New York City. In 1949, she became the first female professor at Columbia's College of Physicians and Surgeons. That same year, she began to study the use of anesthesia during childbirth. This research led to the development of the Apgar score, introduced in 1952.

In 1959, Apgar joined the National Foundation-March of Dimes, where she helped raise public support and funds for research on birth defects. She coauthored *Is*

My Baby All Right? (1972), which dealt with birth defects. Apgar died on Aug. 7, 1974.

See also **Apgar score.**

Apgar score is a system for evaluating the physical condition of a baby immediately after birth. An Apgar score is given to most babies born in the United States and to newborns in many other parts of the world. The score measures five vital functions: (1) appearance (skin color), (2) pulse (heart rate), (3) grimace (reflex response), (4) activity (muscle tone), and (5) respiration. The first letters of these functions form the word *Apgar.* The Apgar score is obtained at one minute and, in most cases, at five minutes after birth.

A newborn baby can score from a low value of 0 to a normal value of 2 for each function. The scores are then added, for a maximum total of 10. A baby who scores 7 or higher receives routine care. A score of less than 7 indicates that the baby may need emergency respiratory treatment to survive. In such cases, the five-minute score can demonstrate the success of the treatment. If the five-minute score remains below 7, the doctor may continue treatment and retest the baby every five minutes until a score of 7 or higher is obtained.

Doctors use the Apgar score with other measures of a newborn's condition to help predict the baby's short-term health prospects. The Apgar score was developed by the American physician Virginia Apgar and introduced in 1952.   Gerald B. Merenstein

See also **Apgar, Virginia.**

Aphasia, *uh FAY zhuh,* is the loss or partial loss of the ability to use and understand spoken and written language. It results from damage to the language centers of the brain. Many cases result from a stroke, which occurs when part of the brain does not receive sufficient oxygen-carrying blood. Aphasia also may result from a brain tumor, an infection, or a blow to the head.

Aphasia may affect some types of communication more than others, depending on the site and extent of the brain injury. Most people with aphasia have difficulty reading, writing, speaking, and understanding words and sentences. Their ability to use numbers and gestures also may be impaired. Some types of aphasia may affect only reading or writing. People with such reading disabilities as *alexia* and *dyslexia* can see written material but cannot read it. People with *agraphia* cannot write even though their fingers and hands are undamaged.

Two speech disorders, *dysarthria* and *apraxia,* are often associated with aphasia. Dysarthria results from damage to the nerves that control the muscles used for speech, such as the tongue. In patients with this disorder, speech sounds are slurred. Patients with apraxia have forgotten how to make certain sounds, though they may have normal use of the speech muscles.

Some aphasia patients can regain part or most of their ability to understand language. Working with speech-language pathologists can help most patients. But if no improvement occurs within several months, complete recovery is unlikely.   Angela N. Burda

See also **Brain** (Language).

Aphid, *AY fihd* or *AF ihd,* also called *plant louse,* is a tiny, soft-bodied insect that feeds on plant juices. Many kinds of aphids are harmful to gardens, orchards, and farm crops. They have plump bodies, small heads, and tube-shaped mouths. They use the tubes to pierce plant stems or leaves and feed on the juices. Aphids may be green, black, whitish, or other colors. Many aphids have four wings. Others are wingless.

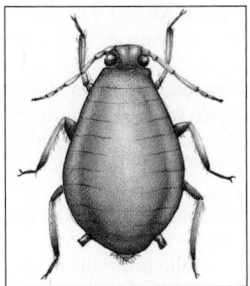

WORLD BOOK illustration by Shirley Hooper, Oxford Illustrators Limited
Aphid

Most kinds of aphids make a sweet fluid called *honeydew.* This fluid is one of the favorite foods of the ant. The ant licks up the honeydew as it pours out of tube-shaped organs called *cornicles* at the tip of the aphid's body. In order to have plenty of honeydew, ants take good care of some kinds of aphids. They move the aphids from one plant to another and may infest an entire garden.

Aphids multiply rapidly. The males and females mate in the fall. The females lay fertilized eggs that hatch the next spring. These young do not mate and lay eggs. They give birth to living young hatched from unfertilized eggs within their bodies. During summer, many generations of fatherless aphids are born by this process, called *parthenogenesis.* In fall, adult males and females appear, and the life process repeats. Spiders, ladybugs, and lacewings prey on aphids.   Candace Martinson

Scientific classification. Aphids are in the superfamily Aphidoidea.

See also **Ant** (Dairying ants); **Mosaic disease; Phylloxera; Whitefly.**

Aphrodite, *AF roh DY tee,* was a major Greek goddess. She was the Greek version of an Asian goddess of life similar to Astarte. Many artists and poets have restricted Aphrodite's role to goddess of love and beauty, but her functions in ancient Greece were varied and complex. The Greeks worshiped Aphrodite as a universal goddess called Urania (queen of heaven) and as a goddess of civic life called Pandemos (goddess of all people). In some parts of Greece, Aphrodite was considered a goddess of seafaring and warfare. She was also associated with the myths and ceremonies surrounding Adonis, a fertility god who died and was reborn annually. Many myths report that she instigated human love affairs. The Roman goddess Venus was identified with Aphrodite.

In the works attributed to the Greek poet Homer, Aphrodite was the daughter of the goddess Dione and Zeus, the king of the gods. In earlier myths, Aphrodite rose full-grown from sea foam. The name *Aphrodite* may come from *aphros,* the Greek word for *foam.*

According to Homer, Aphrodite was married to Hephaestus, the blacksmith of the gods. But many stories give her other lovers, including Ares, the god of war, and the Trojan prince Anchises. In later myths, she was the mother of Eros, the god of love.   F. Carter Philips

See also **Adonis; Ares; Astarte; Hephaestus; Mythology** (Greek divinities); **Venus.**

Apia, *ah PEE ah* or *AH pee AH* (pop. 37,391), is the capital of Samoa. It lies on the northern coast of Upolu Island (see **Samoa** [map]). Apia is the country's commercial center and only international port. A large Roman Catholic cathedral, begun in 1885, stands on the main road. A modern government building sits on the waterfront. The Scottish author Robert Louis Stevenson is buried on nearby Mount Vaea. His last home, built on a hill over-looking Apia, is now a museum. See also **Samoa** (picture). Scott Kroeker

Apnea. See **Sleep apnea.**

Apocalypse. See **Revelation, Book of.**

Apocrypha. See **Bible** (The Christian Old Testament).

Apollo, *uh PAHL oh,* was a major god in Greek mythology. He was the son of Zeus, the king of the gods, and the goddess Leto. The goddess Artemis was Apollo's twin.

Apollo probably originated in Asia Minor (now part of Turkey). At one time, he was known as a god of shepherds. Apollo also became associated with archery, healing, music, poetry, prophecy, purification, and seafaring. Under the name Phoebus Apollo, he became the god of light. He was also considered the god of the sun. Only Zeus was more widely worshiped than Apollo.

Apollo killed a dragon named Python at Delphi and established his temple there. The Greeks believed Apollo foretold the future through an *oracle* (prophet) at Delphi. Temple priests asked questions of this oracle, an elderly woman named the Pythia, who responded in the words of Apollo. The priests interpreted her responses. Delphi became the greatest of Apollo's many oracles throughout the ancient world. See **Delphi; Oracle.**

The Greeks sometimes blamed Apollo and Artemis for sudden deaths. The two gods killed the children of Niobe, queen of Thebes, who had boasted that she had more children and was superior to Leto (see **Niobe**).

Apollo had trouble in many of his love affairs. For example, he loved the *nymph* (minor goddess) Daphne, but she fled from him. When Apollo was finally about to catch her, Daphne called out for help and was changed into a laurel tree (see **Daphne**). Apollo also loved Coronis, a mortal woman. But Coronis was unfaithful, and either Apollo or Artemis killed her and her lover.

The Romans worshiped Apollo primarily as a god of healing and prophecy. His influence increased when the Roman emperor Augustus made him his *patron* (protector). In art, Apollo is depicted as a beardless young man, the Greek ideal of male beauty. He is often shown with a bow or lyre. F. Carter Philips

See also **Artemis; Asclepius; Cassandra; Midas.**

Apollo was the United States space program that carried people to the moon. The program lasted from 1961 to 1975. It was conducted by the National Aeronautics and Space Administration (NASA). Each Apollo mission carried three astronauts. In moon-landing missions, two of the astronauts landed on the lunar surface. The third astronaut stayed with the orbiting capsule. The program landed a total of 12 astronauts on the lunar surface.

Apollo's rocket, the Saturn V, had to produce enough power to propel three astronauts on the roughly 250,000-mile (400,000-kilometer) journey from Earth to the moon. The rocket measured 363 feet (111 meters) in height, taller than a 30-story building. It weighed 6.2 million pounds (2.8 million kilograms). The rocket had three stages, each with its own engines and fuel supply. The first stage lifted the rocket and its payload to an Earth orbit of about 40 miles (64 kilometers). The two remaining stages accelerated the capsule to a speed needed to break free of Earth's gravitation and reach the moon.

At its top, the Saturn V carried a craft consisting of three parts or modules. They were (1) the command

module, (2) the service module, and (3) the lunar module. The command module was a small, three-seat capsule. It was the living quarters and control center for the astronauts. It was also the module that returned the astronauts to Earth's surface. The service module sat directly behind the capsule. It carried engines along with thrusters to control the craft's flight. The service module would also provide such things as electricity, oxygen, and water to the command module, as well as carry communications equipment and fuel. The lunar module was built to take two astronauts down to the lunar surface and back to the orbiting command and service modules. Three of the missions carried a lunar roving vehicle (LRV). The LRV was a lightweight, four-wheeled "moon buggy" that enabled the astronauts to explore more of the moon's surface.

Three Apollo missions circled the moon without landing. The first landing occurred during Apollo 11 on July 20, 1969. Astronauts Neil Armstrong and Buzz Aldrin set down on the flat feature known as the Sea of Tranquility. The third Apollo 11 astronaut, Michael Collins, stayed aboard the orbiting command module.

Over the course of the Apollo missions, lunar explorers took photographs and made measurements of the moon's airless environment. The astronauts installed scientific instruments and left them behind to keep transmitting data. The astronauts collected a total of about 842 pounds (382 kilograms) of rocks and other samples. Scientists continue to study the samples for clues to the origins of Earth, the moon, and the solar system.

The Apollo program suffered two major disasters. Apollo 1 was scheduled for launch on Feb. 21, 1967. On January 27, however, a fire during a launch pad test took the lives of astronauts Roger B. Chaffee, Virgil I. (Gus) Grissom, and Edward H. White II. The second disaster occurred during Apollo 13. On April 14, 1970, about 56 hours after launch, a short circuit caused an explosion in one of the service module's two oxygen tanks. The blast severely damaged the systems that supplied electricity and oxygen to the command module. The astronauts—Fred W. Haise, Jr., James A. Lovell, Jr., and John L. Swigert, Jr.—had to move into the lunar lander for the oxygen they needed to return to Earth. During the flight, the crew, with considerable help from NASA engineers on the ground, overcame the lack of power, a shortage of water, the loss of cabin heat, and the build up of carbon dioxide in the vehicle to return safely to Earth.

The last Apollo flight was not a mission to the moon. In 1972, the United States and the Soviet Union agreed to participate in the first international piloted space mission. They planned to perform an orbital rendezvous between a Soviet Soyuz capsule and a U.S. Apollo capsule. The Apollo-Soyuz Test Project launched on July 15, 1975. The Apollo capsule, commanded by astronaut Thomas P. Stafford, linked up with the Soyuz capsule, commanded by cosmonaut Alexei A. Leonov. Frank Morring, Jr.

Apostles, in the New Testament, are the 12 men chosen by Jesus Christ to be his close companions. The term is also used to identify other early missionaries, such as Paul and Barnabas. The word is used once in the Bible to refer to Jesus himself. The term *apostle* should be distinguished from *disciple,* a New Testament term for any follower of Jesus.

There are four lists of the 12 apostles in the New Testament. The lists agree on Peter (also called Simon Peter), Andrew, James, John, Philip, Bartholomew, Thomas, Matthew, James the son of Alphaeus, Simon, and Judas Iscariot. The gospels of Matthew and Mark list Thaddeus, and the gospel of Luke and Acts of the Apostles list Judas the son of James (or the brother of James in some versions of the Bible). Judas Iscariot died after betraying Jesus, and Matthias was chosen to take his place among the 12. This story, told in Acts 1: 21-26, states that an apostle must have accompanied Jesus from the time of Jesus's Baptism until his Ascension into heaven.

Richard A. Edwards

There is a separate article in *World Book* for each apostle. See also **Acts of the Apostles; Barnabas; Jesus Christ; Paul, Saint.**

Apostles' Creed is a statement of the main Western Christian beliefs. It contains three sections, dealing with God the Father, Jesus Christ, and the Holy Spirit. Both Roman Catholic and Protestant churches use it today. Here is the basic Catholic form of the Apostles' Creed:

I believe in God, the Father Almighty, Creator of heaven and earth; and in Jesus Christ, His only Son, our Lord; who was conceived by the Holy Spirit, born of the Virgin Mary, suffered under Pontius Pilate, was crucified, died, and was buried. He descended into hell; the third day He rose again from the dead; He ascended into heaven; sits at the right hand of God, the Father Almighty; from thence He shall come to judge the living and the dead. I believe in the Holy Spirit, the holy Catholic Church, the communion of saints, the forgiveness of sins, the resurrection of the body, and life everlasting. Amen.

The Protestant form generally substitutes the word *Maker* for *Creator* and uses *catholic* or *Christian* instead of *Catholic.*

The earliest version of the Apostles' Creed can be traced back to about the late A.D. 100's. A legend arose stating that the 12 apostles composed the creed, but this has not been proven. It is more likely that the creed simply grew out of Christian church life. The creed probably was derived from an earlier Roman Creed, which was a baptismal confession. Richard L. Schebera

Apostolic succession. See Bishop.

Apostrophe. See Punctuation.

Apothecaries' weight, *uh PAHTH uh KEHR eez,* is a system of weights once widely used by druggists for prescriptions. The metric system has replaced it. Apothecaries' weight divides the pound into 12 ounces, the ounce into 8 drams, the dram into 3 scruples, and the scruple into 20 grains. In the apothecaries' system, 5,760 grains make 1 pound (0.373 kilogram) and 480 grains make 1 ounce (31 grams). See also **Metric system; Ounce; Pound; Weights and measures.** Leland F. Webb

Apothecary. See Pharmacy.

Appalachian Mountains, *AP uh LAY chuhn* or *AP uh LACH uhn,* are the second largest mountain system of North America. Only the Rocky Mountain system is larger. The Appalachians extend about 1,500 miles (2,400 kilometers) between the Gaspé Peninsula in the Canadian province of Quebec and Birmingham, in central Alabama. The valleys of these mountains include important agricultural and recreational regions. The Appa-

Appalachian Mountains

The Appalachian system extends about 1,500 miles (2,400 kilometers) across eastern North America, between central Alabama and the Gaspé Peninsula in Canada. The region includes important agricultural and mining areas and offers many recreational opportunities.

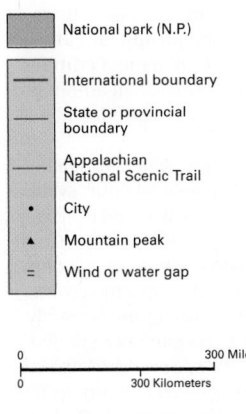

	National park (N.P.)
	International boundary
	State or provincial boundary
	Appalachian National Scenic Trail
•	City
▲	Mountain peak
=	Wind or water gap

0   300 Miles
0   300 Kilometers

WORLD BOOK map

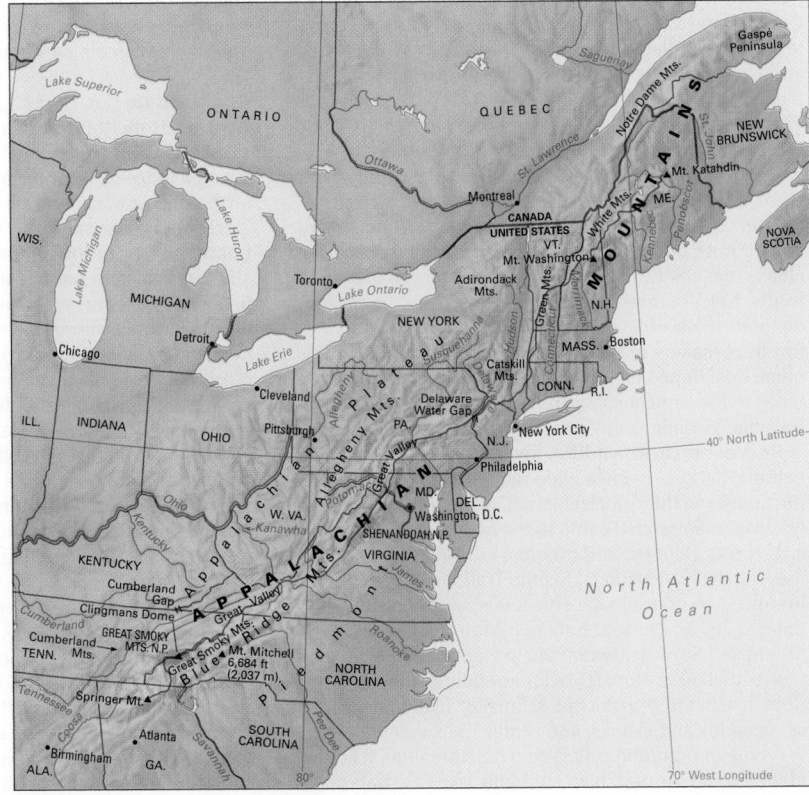

lachians are also a major source of mineral deposits.

The Appalachian Mountains were formed between about 435 million and 250 million years ago. The Appalachians are the oldest mountains in North America. The name *Appalachian* comes from the Apalachee Indians.

Physical features. The chief ranges of the northern Appalachians include the Notre Dame Mountains in Quebec, the White Mountains in New Hampshire, the Green Mountains in Vermont, and the Catskill Mountains in New York.

Southwest of the Hudson River, the Appalachians are divided into three sections—the Blue Ridge, the Great Valley, and the Ridge-and-Valley Province. The Blue Ridge has most of the tallest mountains, including the tallest, Mount Mitchell. This peak rises 6,684 feet (2,037 meters) near Asheville, North Carolina.

North of Virginia, the Blue Ridge Mountains are separated into small sections by major valleys called *water gaps* and *wind gaps*. A water gap, such as the Delaware Water Gap in Pennsylvania and New Jersey, is a valley that has a river flowing through it. A wind gap is a dry valley. An example of a wind gap is the Cumberland Gap on the borders of Kentucky, Tennessee, and Virginia.

Immediately west of the Blue Ridge is the Great Valley, which extends from the Hudson River Valley to Alabama. The Great Valley includes the Cumberland, Lebanon, and Lehigh valleys in Pennsylvania; the Cumberland Valley in Maryland; the Shenandoah Valley and the Valley of Virginia in Virginia; the Valley of East Tennessee; and the Coosa River Valley in Alabama.

West of the Great Valley is the Ridge-and-Valley Province, which consists of long, sharp ridges separated by narrow valleys. This area is bordered on the west by the Cumberland and Allegheny mountains. North of central Virginia, the Alleghenies in the north and the Blue Ridge and Great Smoky mountains in the south make the Appalachians one of the great divides of North America. This region separates rivers that empty into the Atlantic Ocean from those flowing into the Gulf of Mexico.

Economic importance. Thousands of people in the Appalachians make their living in farming or mining. Farmers in the southern sections grow corn and tobacco and raise poultry. In the northern part of the Appalachians, the chief valley products are apples, barley, dairy foods, hay, potatoes, and wheat. Trees from the region, including hickories, maples, and oaks, are shipped to furniture makers in Hickory and High Point, North Carolina. Coal deposits cover tens of thousands of square miles in the Appalachians in Alabama, Kentucky, Pennsylvania, Virginia, and West Virginia.

Recreation and wildlife. Rivers, lakes, and state and national parks provide a wide range of recreational opportunities in the Appalachians. During the winter, skiers from many states come to the northern Appalachians. Throughout the summer and fall, hikers walk along the Appalachian National Scenic Trail, the nation's longest marked footpath. This trail extends about 2,000 miles (3,200 kilometers) between Mount Katahdin in Maine and Springer Mountain in Georgia.

Many large mammals, including bears, bobcats, and deer, live in the Appalachians. Smaller mammals, such as raccoons and skunks, and reptiles are also plentiful.

A type of pollution called *acid rain* threatens wildlife in the region. Appalachian soils and lakes are naturally highly acidic because of the kinds of vegetation and *bedrock* (solid rock beneath the soil) found there. This acidic environment has been compounded by rain carrying sulfuric and nitric acid, which can harm plants and fish. The region is more seriously affected by acid rain than any other area in North America.

History. The Appalachians were formed between about 435 million and 250 million years ago by a folding in Earth's crust. During the late 1700's, pioneers followed the Great Valley southward through the Appalachians to the Cumberland Gap and the Wilderness Road. Railroads began to transport settlers across the mountains in the 1840's. In 1933, Congress created the Tennessee Valley Authority (TVA) to control flooding and provide electric power to the southern Appalachians. The TVA has built dams and power plants and has planted forests to halt soil erosion. John Edwin Coffman

Related articles in *World Book* include:

Allegheny Mountains	Cumberland Mountains
Appalachian National Scenic	Great Smoky Mountains
Trail	Green Mountains
Blue Ridge Mountains	Mount Washington
Catskill Mountains	White Mountains
Clingmans Dome	Wilderness Road
Cumberland Gap	

Appalachian National Scenic Trail, *AP uh LAY chuhn* or *AP uh LACH uhn,* is a footpath that extends about 2,000 miles (3,200 kilometers) from Mount Katahdin in Maine to Springer Mountain in Georgia. The trail passes through 14 states, 2 national parks, and 8 national forests. It follows the crests of the White and Green mountains and the Berkshires of New England, the Blue Ridge Mountains from Pennsylvania to North Carolina, and the Unakas and Great Smokies of North Carolina. Volunteers constructed the trail in the 1920's and 1930's. The trail became a part of the National Park System in 1968. Critically reviewed by the National Park Service

Appaloosa. See Horse (Color types; picture).

Appeal is the transfer of a legal action to a higher, or superior, court for review. The court may review the decision of a lower, or inferior, court; a government board; or the officer of an administrative hearing. The *appellant* (person who appeals) seeks to have the decision of the board, officer, or lower court reversed or modified. Usually, a dissatisfied party to a suit must file a notice of appeal with the court within a specified time and show why the appeal should be granted. The discovery of new evidence or of an error in the trial or hearing are reasons frequently given for seeking an appeal. However, there is an absolute right of appeal in most criminal cases. In addition, many states provide for an automatic appeal in criminal cases where a death sentence has been imposed.

Every state has at least one court to which appeals may be taken from trial courts. The federal court system includes 13 Courts of Appeals to review cases tried in lower federal courts. In some cases, the Supreme Court of the United States considers and reverses cases decided by a Court of Appeals or by a state supreme court.

A party in a state court action cannot appeal directly to the U.S. Supreme Court. He or she can only ask that court for a writ of certiorari. A *writ of certiorari* is an order from a higher court to a lower court to send up the records of a case for review (see **Certiorari, Writ of**). The court can refuse such an "appeal" unless it feels there has been a violation of federal law or of the party's constitutional rights.   Jack M. Kress

See also **Bonding; Court of appeals.**

Appellate court. See Court (Trial and appellate courts); Trial (The criminal defendant's rights).

Appendicitis, *uh* PEHN *duh* SY *tihs,* is an inflammation of the *vermiform appendix* (see **Appendix**). It results from an infection caused by bacteria. The appendix becomes swollen and fills with pus. The pus may be walled off and form an abscess. Or the appendix may break, allowing the infection to spread to surrounding body organs. It may also cause *peritonitis,* an inflammation of the membrane that lines the abdominal cavity (see **Peritonitis**).

Symptoms. An attack of appendicitis usually begins with pain in the region of the navel. Then it moves to the right lower side of the abdomen. At first the pain is not constant—it comes and goes. But soon it becomes continuous, and soreness develops over the appendix region. The abdominal muscles tighten, and the patient becomes nauseated and usually has a fever. A blood count shows an increase in white blood cells.

Treatment. It is very important that no laxatives, such as castor oil, be given to a person with appendicitis. Laxatives should never be given to a person with an abdominal disorder that might be appendicitis. Any such medicines may cause the appendix to rupture, spreading bacteria through the abdomen. The patient should remain quiet. A doctor should be called immediately. The usual treatment for acute appendicitis is surgical removal of the appendix, an operation known as an *appendectomy.* In mild cases, the inflammation may subside by itself. Some people may have recurrent appendicitis.

Andrew G. Plaut

See also **Surgery** (A typical operation).

Appendix, in anatomy, is a structure attached to a larger or more important part. The term usually refers to the *vermiform* (wormlike) *appendix,* a slender, closed tube that extends from the *cecum,* the first part of the large intestine. The vermiform appendix lies in the lower right part of the abdomen in human beings. It is also found in the higher apes, some rodents, and various other animals. Rats and certain other rodents have a long appendix that functions in digestion. Scientists are not certain what function the appendix has in human beings. Some believe that the appendix may have a role in the devel-

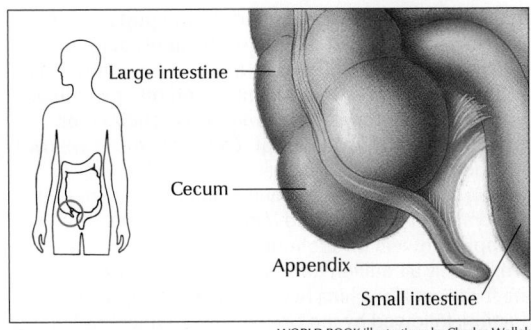

WORLD BOOK illustrations by Charles Wellek

The appendix is a narrow tube that extends from the cecum of the large intestine. A normal appendix, *above,* resembles a worm. Infection of the appendix produces appendicitis, *right,* a condition in which the appendix becomes swollen and filled with pus.

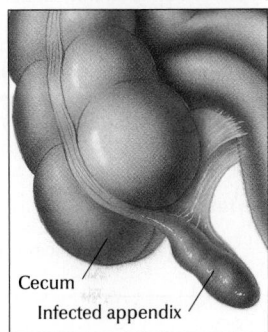

opment of the immune system or that it may store beneficial bacteria in the digestive system. When inflamed, it causes a disease known as appendicitis (see **Appendicitis**).   Laurence H. Beck

Appetite. See Hunger.

Apperson, Elmer and Edgar. See Haynes, Elwood.

Appian Way, AP *ee uhn,* was the first and most famous military highway built by the ancient Romans. Also called Via Appia, it is still used today. It was named for Appius Claudius Caecus, a Roman official who began its construction in 312 B.C.

The road originally led 132 miles (212 kilometers) from Rome southeastward to Capua, linking Rome to some of its early conquests. It was extended 234 miles (377 kilometers) to Brundisium (now Brindisi) on Italy's southeast coast. Early Christians met in tombs and catacombs along the road.   Arthur M. Eckstein

© Ray Manley from Shostal

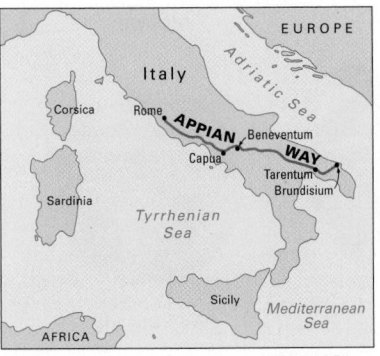

WORLD BOOK map

Location of the Appian Way

The Appian Way is an ancient Roman highway that was named for Appius Claudius Caecus, who began its construction in 312 B.C. The highway, lined with the ruins of the tombs of prominent Romans, is still in use.

Apple is one of the most important and popular fruits that grow on trees. Since prehistoric times, people have enjoyed the delicious flavor of apples. Apples also serve as a source of fiber, some vitamins, and other nutrients.

Thousands of varieties of apples exist. Their color ranges from various shades of red to green and yellow, and their flavor varies from tart to sweet. Apple trees belong to the rose family. Their beautiful white to pink flowers open in spring and look like tiny roses.

Apple growers throughout the world produce approximately 94 million tons (85 million metric tons) of the fruit annually. China leads the world in apple production, followed by the United States. Other leading apple-growing countries include India, Iran, Italy, Poland, and Turkey.

Apples rank as an important crop in several U.S. regions, especially the Pacific Northwest. Washington produces the most apples, followed by New York, Michigan, Pennsylvania, and California. The U.S. apple crop totals about 5 million tons (4.5 million metric tons) each year, with a wholesale value of about $3 billion.

In Canada, apples rank as one of the chief fruit crops. They are grown commercially in British Columbia, New Brunswick, Nova Scotia, Ontario, Prince Edward Island, and Quebec. Canadian growers produce about 420,000 tons (380,000 metric tons) of apples yearly.

People eat more than half of all apples fresh. They bake many of the rest into pies and other dishes. Apples serve as the main ingredient in applesauce, apple butter, apple juice, and apple jelly. Apple juice can be made into vinegar or wine. Apple products may come canned, bottled, dried, or frozen. Apples consist of about 85 percent water. They also contain calcium, fiber, folate, iron, pectin, phosphorus, potassium, and vitamins A and C.

Through the ages, apples have appeared in legends, poems, and religious books. In the Swiss legend of William Tell, a tyrant arrests an archer but promises to free him if he shoots an apple off his son's head. Many people believe an apple was the fruit that, according to the Bible, Adam and Eve ate in the Garden of Eden.

Varieties of apples Thousands of kinds of apples exist. They differ in color, flavor, shape, size, and texture. Different varieties also serve different purposes. For example, people usually eat Delicious apples fresh, but they reserve Golden Delicious apples primarily for baking pies.

WORLD BOOK illustrations by James Teason and Paul D. Turnbaugh

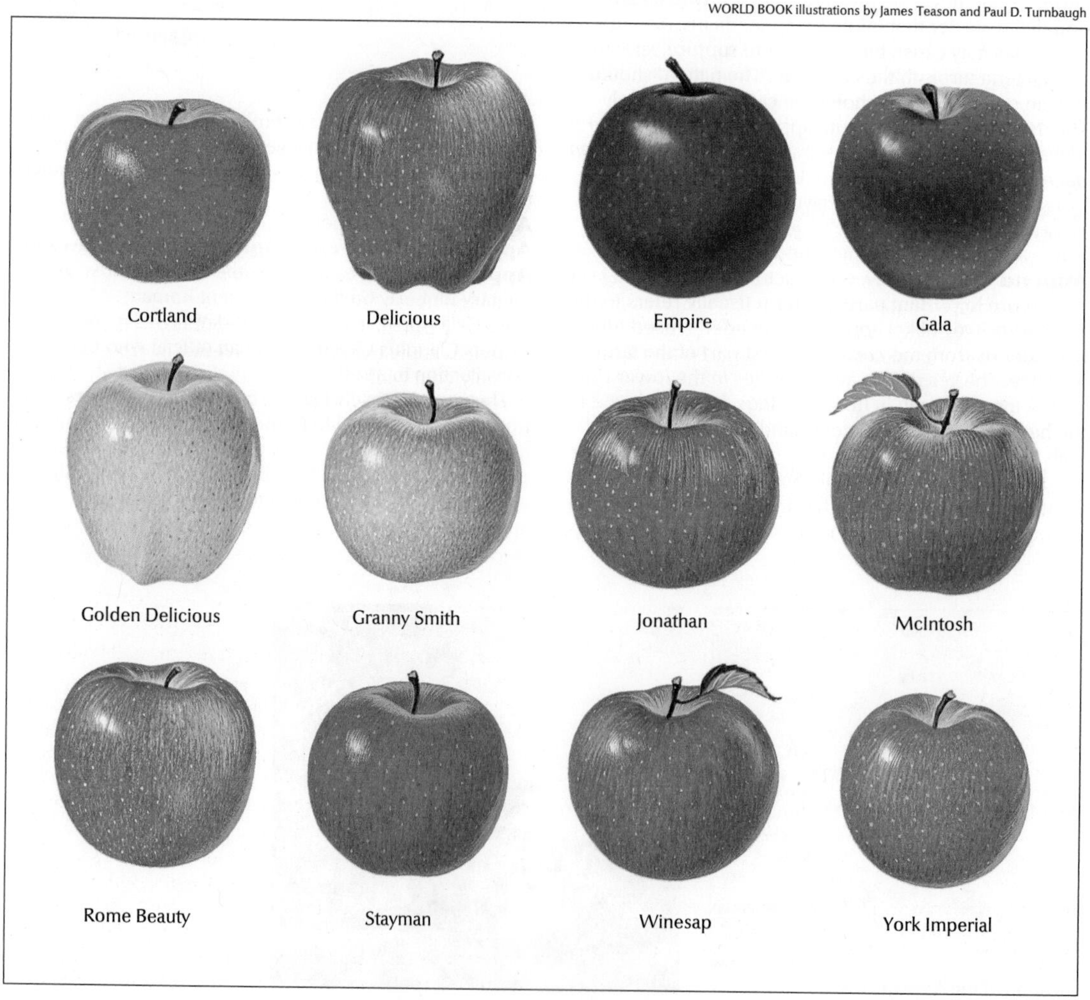

| Cortland | Delicious | Empire | Gala |

| Golden Delicious | Granny Smith | Jonathan | McIntosh |

| Rome Beauty | Stayman | Winesap | York Imperial |

Varieties of apples

Although thousands of kinds of apples exist, only about 100 varieties appear commonly in commercial orchards and in home gardens. Six varieties of apples—Delicious, Fuji, Gala, Golden Delicious, Granny Smith, and Honeycrisp—are among the leading varieties produced in the United States. Ambrosia and Gala apples are among the chief varieties grown in Canada. Growers around the world have introduced disease-resistant varieties, such as Liberty, Gold Rush, and Enterprise.

The many kinds of apples differ in color, flavor, shape, size, and texture. Apple skin may appear green, yellow, or various shades of red. Colors of apple flesh include cream, greenish-white, white, and yellow. An apple's texture may be soft or firm and its flavor tart or sweet. Generally, people eat sweet apples fresh and use tart varieties to make such products as applesauce, apple butter, and vinegar. Flavorful applesauces and ciders often consist of a blend of several varieties.

A number of species of wild apples exist. Most wild apples are crab apples (see **Crab apple**).

Apple growers in other countries raise several varieties that are seldom cultivated in the United States. For example, the Cox's Orange Pippin is grown in Denmark,

Leading apple-growing countries

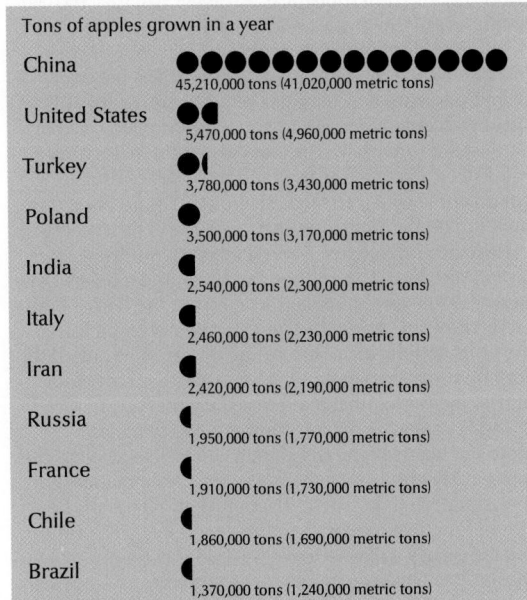

Tons of apples grown in a year

China	45,210,000 tons (41,020,000 metric tons)
United States	5,470,000 tons (4,960,000 metric tons)
Turkey	3,780,000 tons (3,430,000 metric tons)
Poland	3,500,000 tons (3,170,000 metric tons)
India	2,540,000 tons (2,300,000 metric tons)
Italy	2,460,000 tons (2,230,000 metric tons)
Iran	2,420,000 tons (2,190,000 metric tons)
Russia	1,950,000 tons (1,770,000 metric tons)
France	1,910,000 tons (1,730,000 metric tons)
Chile	1,860,000 tons (1,690,000 metric tons)
Brazil	1,370,000 tons (1,240,000 metric tons)

Figures are for a three-year average, 2017-2019.
Source: FAOSTAT, Statistics Division, Food and Agriculture Organization of the UN.
http://www.fao.org. Data accessed in 2021.

Varieties of apples

Cortland, a dark red apple with red stripes, is large and has flat ends. It tastes mildly acid to sweet and is tender and juicy. It is eaten fresh and used for cooking. Its white flesh makes it an excellent salad apple.

Delicious has a solid dark red color or is dark red with darker stripes. It is medium to large and has an oval shape with five knobs on the bottom. This sweet-tasting apple is firm, crisp, and juicy and is usually eaten fresh.

Empire is a dark red apple. It has crisp, juicy, slightly tart flesh and is eaten fresh.

Gala is a yellowish-orange to red apple. Its yellow to cream-colored flesh is crisp and sweet.

Golden Delicious has a golden-yellow skin and an oval shape. Its juicy, firm flesh has a sweet flavor. It ranges from medium to large and is a good all-purpose apple.

Granny Smith is a bright green apple. It ranges from medium to large and has an almost round shape. Its firm flesh tastes tart and is eaten fresh and used for cooking.

Jonathan is bright red, touched with yellow and green. This apple varies from small to medium and has a tart flavor and juicy, firm flesh. Its shape is round to oval, and it is eaten fresh and baked in pies.

McIntosh, a bright red apple, is medium-sized and round or oval. It tastes mildly acid to sweet. It has tender flesh and is usually eaten fresh.

Rome Beauty is red with yellow or green markings. It is large and has a round to oval shape. The crisp, firm flesh has a mildly acid flavor. This apple is used for cooking, baking, and processing.

Stayman is dull red with darker red stripes. This apple varies from medium to large and has a roundish shape. Its firm flesh has a mildly acid flavor and is eaten fresh and used for processing.

Winesap is bright red and roundish. It ranges from small to medium and has a mildly acid flavor. Its flesh is firm and juicy and is eaten fresh and used for processing.

York Imperial is green or yellow with red stripes. This medium to large apple is round to oval and has a slightly lopsided appearance. Its firm flesh tastes mildly acid to sweet. It is used mainly for processing.

the Netherlands, and the United Kingdom. The Bramley ranks as a favorite cooking apple in the United Kingdom.

Raising apples

Apples belong to a group of fruits called *pomes* that have a fleshy outer layer and a paperlike core. An apple's core usually encloses from 5 to 10 seeds.

Apple trees may grow more than 40 feet (12 meters) tall. Most apple trees do not grow well in areas with extremely cold winters or long, hot summers. They thrive in regions with moderately cold winters, requiring exposure to cool temperatures for part of the year to flourish. Flowers bloom on apple trees in late spring. The flowers rely on insects for pollination. For this reason, some growers place hives of honey bees in their orchards while the trees blossom. The blossoms must be cross-pollinated with pollen from a different apple variety to form fruit.

Seeds grow in a pollinated flower's ovary. The ovary and other parts of the flower form the tree's fruit. Most apple varieties ripen 140 to 200 days after pollination.

Apple trees can bear fruit for as long as 100 years. But most of the apple trees grown in orchards are replaced every 12 to 30 years.

Planting and caring for apple trees. Seeds from an apple will not produce trees of the same variety. Therefore, most apple trees are grown from buds. Growers cut the buds from a healthy tree that has produced the kind of fruit desired and graft them to *rootstocks.* A rootstock is a root or a root plus a stem (see **Grafting**). The resulting trees will bear apples of the same variety as those of the tree from which the buds were cut. Apple growers select rootstocks for characteristics such as resistance to pests, tolerance of cold and other environmental factors, and ability to produce dwarf trees. By choosing different rootstocks, growers can vary the height of the tree from 3 to 30 feet (0.9 to 9 meters).

Apple trees in orchards are planted in rows from 14 to 24 feet (4 to 7 meters) apart. Within rows, growers plant trees from 6 to 18 feet (2 to 5 meters) apart. This spacing enables growers to spray the orchards and to harvest the fruit easily. Growers prune the trees to improve the quality of the fruit and to control pests. A young apple tree starts to bear fruit in 3 to 5 years, depending on the rootstock, the variety, and other factors.

Pests and diseases. Several insects and diseases attack apple trees. The codling moth, the most destructive pest that attacks apples, lays its eggs on the leaves and on the fruits in spring. *Larvae* (caterpillars) hatch from the eggs and bore into the young apples. Growers fight codling moths by spraying the trees with insecticides during the period that the females lay their eggs.

The European red mite, another pest, feeds on the leaves of plants in the rose family, including apples. The females lay eggs on the bark of the trees in the fall, and the young hatch in spring just before the trees bloom. The mites consume the contents of the leaf cells, reducing the plant's ability to make its food through photosynthesis. Apple growers control the mites by using pesticides or by introducing other mites, and certain beetles, that prey on the pest mites without harming the trees.

Growers control the apple maggot, an insect that attacks the fruit, by spraying apple trees with an insecticide several times in midsummer, when the adult flies emerge and begin to lay eggs. Two species of sucking insects, aphids and San Jose scales, also harm apple trees. See **Aphid; Apple maggot; San Jose scale.**

A fungus causes apple scab, the most damaging disease that attacks apple trees. Apple scab is most severe in cool, humid areas. The fungus spends the winter on the ground in the dead apple leaves. In spring, rain re-

Leading apple-growing states and provinces

Tons of apples produced in a year

Washington	●●●●●●●●●●●●◖
	3,634,000 tons (3,296,000 metric tons)
New York	●●◖
	678,000 tons (615,000 metric tons)
Michigan	●◖
	480,000 tons (435,000 metric tons)
Pennsylvania	●
	254,000 tons (230,000 metric tons)
Ontario	◖
	155,000 tons (141,000 metric tons)

Figures are a three-year average, for 2017-2019.
Source: U.S. Department of Agriculture; Statistics Canada.

leases spores from the fungus, and they infect the flowers, fruit, and leaves. Growers control apple scab by spraying the trees with fungicides.

Fire blight, a bacterial disease, kills blossoms, leaves, twigs, and sometimes entire trees. Leaves on infected branches take on a scorched appearance. To combat fire blight, growers prune infected wood and spray trees with an antibiotic. Some growers avoid the disease by planting apple varieties that can resist the bacteria.

Harvesting and processing. Apple growers start to harvest their crop in late summer or early fall. Harvest dates vary according to the variety of apples and the geographical location. Workers pick apples by hand.

Some newly harvested apples are soon sold fresh to consumers. But a significant portion of the annual crop is stored in cold rooms with a controlled atmosphere. The fruit stays fresh in these rooms for up to 12 months, and so consumers can buy the apples the year around. A large percentage of the apple crop is processed, including apples that are canned, dried, or frozen.

History

Apples have served as a favorite fruit of people for tens of thousands of years. Archaeologists studying the ruins of Stone Age villages in Europe have found the charcoal remains of apples. By the 300's B.C., the Greeks were growing several varieties of apples. The ancient Romans also cultivated the fruit. The Romans spread various kinds of apples throughout much of England and other parts of Europe during their numerous military conquests. The early American colonists brought both apple seeds and apple trees with them from England. The colonists dried their apples or used them in making cider, vinegar, and apple butter.

As the settlers moved westward across America, they took apple seeds and seedling trees with them. Some settlers found that American Indians had already planted apple seeds brought from the east.

During the early 1800's, a pioneer apple planter named John Chapman distributed apple seeds and apple trees to settlers in Ohio and Indiana. He became known as Johnny Appleseed. See **Appleseed, Johnny.**

Through the years, American apple growers have developed new and improved varieties of the fruit. In addition, researchers have introduced new ways to grow, store, preserve, and use apples. Richard Marini

© Thinkstock

An apple harvester empties the fruit from a bag into a large bin. Tractors equipped with lifting devices take the full bins to trucks or warehouses.

Scientific classification. The scientific name for the wild apple of Europe and Asia is *Malus pumila.* All cultivated apples belong to the species *Malus domestica.*

See also **Cider; Codling moth** (with picture); **Tree** (Broadleaf and needleleaf trees [picture]).

Apple butter is a spread for bread made by cooking apples to a thick, pasty consistency and seasoning them with spices. Sometimes, cider is added.

Apple Inc. is a major international firm that manufactures innovative computers, cell phones, and other electronic devices. The company also develops and publishes computer software and distributes music, books, videos, and other media over the internet. Apple runs a chain of retail stores around the world.

Apple was founded in 1976 as Apple Computer, Inc., by Steve Jobs and Steve Wozniak, two computer enthusiasts in their 20's. That year, the company introduced the Apple I microcomputer. The machine became popular with hobbyists, but it had little commercial use. Wozniak redesigned the computer, which the company produced in 1977 as a home and small-business machine called the Apple II. It was an immediate success.

In 1983, Apple introduced the Lisa, the first commercial computer to feature a mouse. In 1984, Apple followed up with the Macintosh. This popular home computer used a *graphical user interface* (GUI), a feature that enables people to issue commands by pointing to on-screen symbols and clicking a mouse. Before GUI's, people operated home computers using typed commands.

In 1986, Apple introduced the Mac Plus computer and LaserWriter printer, two devices that became popular tools in *desktop publishing,* in which editors and designers use computers to edit text and lay out pages. In 1994, Apple brought to market the Power Macintosh, a high-powered personal computer. The iMac, a computer designed to be especially easy to set up and use, was introduced in 1998.

In 2001, Apple introduced the iPod, a peripheral device for storing and playing digital music. In 2003, Apple launched the iTunes Music Store, which allowed users to buy and download digital music online. The iTunes store offered not only songs but also podcasts, audiobooks, television shows, and movies for purchase. A version of the iPod capable of storing and playing digital video was released in 2005. The iPod line proved profitable for Apple, which introduced various accessories for the device. The success of the line led the company to change its name in 2007, from Apple Computer, Inc., to Apple Inc. The new name reflected the widening of the company's focus from computers to other kinds of consumer electronics. In 2019, Apple replaced iTunes with three different *apps* (applications): Apple Music, Apple Podcasts, and Apple TV.

Apple released the iPhone in 2007. It featured a touch-sensitive screen and combined a wireless phone, a music and video player, and mobile internet and e-mail capabilities. In 2010, Apple unveiled the iPad, a lightweight, touch-sensitive tablet computer. The iPad also works as an e-book reader, a music and video player, and a game console. In 2015, Apple released the Apple Watch, a "smart watch" that links to a user's iPhone. Apple's headquarters are in Cupertino, California.

Jarice Hanson

See also **Jobs, Steve.**

Apple maggot is the wormlike *larva* (young) of the apple fly. Apple maggots sometimes do serious damage to apple crops. These insects are also called *railroad worms* because they make long, winding trails under the apple skin. Apple maggots are especially harmful in New England and northern New York.

The adult fly is a kind of fruit fly. It is slightly smaller than the common house fly and has wings marked with four black bands. Eight to ten days after appearing in midsummer, the female fly begins laying eggs just under the skin of apples. Sometimes as many as 15 eggs are laid in one apple. The maggots that hatch burrow through the flesh of the apple, leaving rusty streaks in it. After feeding on the apple from four to six weeks, the maggots drop to the ground and enter the soil. Apple maggots change to the pupal stage there and stay all winter. They emerge the next summer as adult flies.

Scientists have discovered that apple maggots can be controlled by hanging sticky traps of yellow panels or red spheres in the apple orchard. Adult flies are attracted to the shape and color of these traps, and they become entangled and die in the special adhesive.

John R. Meyer

Scientific classification. The apple maggot's scientific name is *Rhagoletis pomonella.*

See also **Codling moth; Fruit fly.**

Appleseed, Johnny (1774-1845), was the name given to John Chapman, an American pioneer who planted large numbers of apple trees along the early frontier. He became a folk hero as the result of many novels, short stories, and poems about his deeds. However, most of these deeds were probably imaginary.

Chapman was born on Sept. 26, 1774, in Leominster, Massachusetts. Nothing is known about his childhood.

Engraving from *History of Ashland County, Ohio,* frontispiece, J. B. Lippincott & Co., Philadelphia; Chicago History Museum

Johnny Appleseed was a pioneer planter.

From about 1800 until his death on March 10, 1845, he traveled alone through Ohio and Indiana, planting orchards as settlers moved westward. Chapman eventually owned about 1,200 acres (490 hectares) of orchards.

The most famous story about John Chapman tells of his giving apple seeds and apple saplings to everybody he met. He supposedly traveled hundreds of miles to tend one of his orchards. Some people said he wore a tin pot as a hat, a coffee sack as a shirt, and no shoes. Various tales describe him serving as a medicine man to the Indians.

None of the folk stories about Chapman has ever been proved true. The tales became widely known after an article describing his deeds appeared in *Harper's New Monthly Magazine* in 1871. The article, called "Johnny Appleseed, a Pioneer Hero," was written by an author named W. D. Haley.   Harry Oster

Applied science. See Agriculture; Engineering; Medicine; Science; Technology.

Appliqué, *AP lih KAY,* is a decorative process used in sewing and dressmaking. It consists of sewing cut-out

© Richard Nowitz, Corbis

Appliqué is a method of decorating objects by sewing cut-out pieces of such materials as cloth or leather onto a larger piece.

designed pieces of cloth onto a larger piece. The edges of the designed piece are usually tucked under. Then it is sewed onto the larger piece with small, hidden stitches or ornamental stitches.   Patrick H. Ela

Appomattox Court House, *AP uh MAT uhks,* was a little country settlement in central Virginia. It was the scene of Robert E. Lee's surrender to Ulysses S. Grant on April 9, 1865, which led to the end of the American Civil War (1861-1865). Appomattox became a national historical park in 1954. The park is near the town of Appomattox, Virginia. Points of interest include a visitor center; the McLean House, site of the agreement on the surrender terms; and a Confederate cemetery. For the area of the park, see **National Park System** (table: National historical parks). See also **Civil War, American** (The South surrenders).   Critically reviewed by the National Park Service

Apportionment is the process by which representation in legislative bodies is distributed among the people. It may involve the assignment of a number of seats to specified areas, such as states or counties. Each area may then be divided into districts, from which representatives are elected. The reassignment of seats in a legislature among the areas represented is usually called *reapportionment.* The division of an area into new election districts is called *redistricting.* However, these terms are often used interchangeably to mean any change in an area's representation.

Representation has been apportioned in various ways. Two common bases have been (1) population and (2) political units, such as states, counties, or townships. In *bicameral* (two-house) legislatures, one house may be based on population and the other on political units. For example, in the United States Congress, each state still is allowed two senators regardless of population. States are apportioned seats in the House of Representatives according to population, with each state guaranteed at least one seat. In most states, the state legislature draws up its state's congressional election districts.

Great differences in the population of districts occur when representation is not based on population. Differences may arise even when population is the apportionment base. As people move from rural areas to urban areas, some districts become more heavily populated than others. People in overpopulated districts have less influence in the legislature than people in underpopulated areas. But legislatures often do not redistrict because they wish to protect the seats of some members. In the United States as late as 1962, the population of many state legislative districts varied by as much as 30 to 1.

Initial efforts to get U.S. courts to order redistricting failed. The Supreme Court of the United States held that the issue was of a "political nature" and thus could not be decided by the courts. The Supreme Court reversed this ruling in the 1962 case of *Baker v. Carr.* In this case, the court held that voters could bring questions of unfair apportionment before federal courts. Since this ruling, legislatures have been undergoing a major redistricting upheaval. Based on 1963 and 1964 rulings, the Supreme Court developed the "one-person, one-vote" principle. As a result, all congressional districts must be "substantially equal" in population, and districts for electing both houses of state legislatures must meet the

National Park Service

Appomattox Court House in Virginia was the site of Robert E. Lee's surrender to Ulysses S. Grant in 1865. The surrender took place in the McLean House, *shown here.*

same requirement. The principle was extended to local governments in 1968. In 1969, the court demanded that the states try to make their congressional districts precisely equal in population. In 1973, the court clarified its position on state legislative districts. It ruled that the populations of these districts need not be exactly equal if the districts were drawn to reflect legitimate considerations, such as following political subdivisions or equalizing political opportunity.   Robert Agranoff

See also **Gerrymander; House of Representatives** (Size); **Senate** (Size); **State government** (Legislative branch).

Apposition extends the meaning of a word or a phrase next to it. Words that are in apposition refer to each other. Most appositive units can be considered nonrestrictive clauses with the relative pronoun and the verb deleted. Appositive units may be classified as nouns, adjectives, or adverbs. "Abraham Lincoln, (who was) *the 16th president of the United States,* was assassinated" is a noun appositive. "The crowd, (which was) *anxious to escape danger,* began to panic" is an adjective appositive. "The man shouted loudly, (which was) *even frantically,* to calm the crowd" is an adverb appositive.

A few appositives, called *restrictive appositives,* are an inseparable part of the word to which they are joined. Examples include "Alexander *the Great"* and "Winnie-*the-Pooh."*   Sara Garnes

Appraisal is an opinion of value, usually the *market value* of a piece of property. Market value is the most probable price at which a property would be bought or sold by knowledgeable people. Specialists called *appraisers* make appraisals. They are trained by professional appraisal societies, and many colleges and universities offer courses in appraising.

Lending companies have real estate appraised before they grant a mortgage on it. Government agencies use appraisals to help determine assessments, property taxes, and the price at which they buy private property for public use. Many people have private property appraised before they buy it or sell it.

Appraisers consider several factors in arriving at their estimates. These include the sale price of similar property, reproduction cost less depreciation, and estimated future income from property use. Market prices usually provide the best estimate of market value. Property location often affects real estate value more than physical improvements made on property.   John M. Clapp

Apprentice is a person who learns a trade by working under the guidance of a skilled master. Apprentices serve in construction, metalworking, printing, and other skilled trades. Many employers and unions jointly direct apprenticeship programs. Usually, apprentices must be high-school graduates. Most apprentices earn wages and work regular hours. People who finish apprenticeships become *journeyworkers,* also called *journeymen.*

Apprenticeship dates from ancient times. But it reached its most developed form in Europe between about A.D. 1000 and 1600, under organizations of workers called *craft guilds.* Apprentices served in almost every occupation, including medicine, painting, and brewing. Some girls were apprenticed to learn domestic skills, but most apprentices were boys. Ordinarily, a boy in his early teens went to live with a master, who taught him a craft and fed, housed, and clothed him. In return, the boy worked for the master about seven years. Once the training ended, the boy was a journeyman. He could sell his labor to any master.

Between the late 1700's and mid-1800's, apprenticeship changed greatly as power-driven machinery allowed unskilled workers to perform tasks of skilled hands, such as sewing and weaving. But new areas for apprenticeship opened, especially among machinists, electricians, and tool-and-die makers.   Warren Van Tine

See also **Colonial life in America** (Education); **Education** (History); **Guild; Labor movement** (Conducting apprenticeship programs; Craft guilds); **Vocational education** (History).

Apricot, *AY pruh kaht* or *AP ruh kaht,* is a golden, peachlike fruit with a pit. Apricots are smaller than peaches, and they have a smoother skin. Some have a reddish blush on one side. Fresh and dried apricots are eaten raw or are cooked to make jams, pies, and puddings. A liqueur is made from the *kernels* (seeds) found inside the pits. Most kernels are bitter, but some apricots have sweet kernels that can be eaten like almonds.

Apricot trees grow as tall as 30 feet (9 meters). They grow best in dry, mild climates. The trees blossom in early spring, so fruit production is poor if spring frosts occur. Apricots are native to eastern Asia and were brought to North America from Europe. Iran and Turkey are the chief world producers of apricots. California is the leading United States producer of apricots.

Most apricot trees are grown by grafting buds onto the roots of plum, peach, or apricot seedlings. When the trees reach 1 year of age, they are transplanted from the nursery to orchards. Apricot trees are pruned more heavily than most other trees that bear their fruit on *spurs* (short side shoots). Larger fruit is produced by *thinning* (removing) some fruit from the tree when the fruit is about 1 inch (2.5 centimeters) in diameter. Most apricots are harvested by hand, though some mechanical harvesting is done in California.   Fenton E. Larsen

Scientific classification. The scientific name of apricot trees is *Prunus armeniaca.*

WORLD BOOK illustration by Kate Lloyd-Jones, Linden Artists Ltd.

The apricot is a golden fruit with a large pit. The apricot tree has delicate white or pink blossoms in the springtime.

April is the fourth month of the year, according to the Gregorian calendar, which is used by most of the world today. The Romans called the month *Aprilis*. This name might have come from a word meaning *to open,* or from the name of *Aphrodite*, the Greek goddess of love. April was the second month in an early Roman calendar. However, it became the fourth month when the ancient Romans moved the beginning of the year to January. On the first of April, April Fools' Day, people all over the world cause mischief and play tricks on each other.

Many cultures celebrate the arrival of spring, or other aspects of the natural world, in April. Walpurgis Night is a spring celebration held in Sweden and Finland on April 30. People there welcome spring with bonfires, singing, and parties. The Japanese hold Sakura Matsuri, the Cherry Blossom Festival, in April. In the Netherlands,

flower parades are held toward the end of April, when the tulips are blooming. Many people plant trees on Arbor Day, which occurs on different dates in different countries. Many nations celebrate Earth Day on April 22. This holiday was organized in 1970 to raise awareness of the environment. The Angolan Feast of Nganja, a celebration of the corn harvest, has no specific date, but always falls in April.

Some cultures welcome the New Year in this month. Nava Varsha, the Nepalese New Year, falls on or near April 13. Several countries in Southeast Asia, including Cambodia, Laos, Myanmar, and Thailand, also celebrate the new year at this time. In Thailand, the holiday is called Songkran.

Chakri Day, April 6, marks the date in 1782 when King Rama I took control of Siam's (now Thailand's) govern-

Important April events

1 April Fools' Day in many countries.
— William Harvey, English physician, born 1578.
— Otto von Bismarck, Prussian statesman, born 1815.
— Edmond Rostand, French dramatist, born 1868.
— Sergei Rachmaninoff, Russian composer, born 1873.
2 First federal U.S. mint established, 1792.
— Hans Christian Andersen, Danish fairy-tale writer, born 1805.
— Émile Zola, French novelist, born 1840.
— Walter P. Chrysler, American automaker, born 1875.
3 Washington Irving, American author, born 1783.
— John Burroughs, American naturalist, born 1837.
— First pony express service began in the United States, 1860.
4 National Day, Senegal.
— Dorothea Lynde Dix, American prison and asylum reformer, born 1802.
— United States Congress adopted the flag with 13 stripes and with 1 star for each state, 1818.
— Robert E. Sherwood, American playwright, born 1896.
— North Atlantic Treaty signed, 1949.
5 Pocahontas married John Rolfe, 1614.
— Sir Joseph Lister, English surgeon, born 1827.
— Algernon Swinburne, English poet, born 1837.
— Booker T. Washington, American educator, born 1856.
6 Chakri Day, Thailand.
— Joseph Smith founded the Church of Jesus Christ of Latter-day Saints, 1830.
— Robert Peary, American explorer, reached what he claimed was the North Pole, 1909.
— United States declared war on Germany, World War I, 1917.
7 William Wordsworth, English poet, born 1770.
8 Hana Matsuri (Flower Festival) in Japan celebrates the birth of the Buddha.
— Henry Aaron broke Babe Ruth's career major-league

home run record, 1974.
9 Isambard Kingdom Brunel, British engineer, born 1806.
— General Robert E. Lee surrendered to General Ulysses S. Grant in the American Civil War, 1865.
— Charles P. Steinmetz, German American physicist and electrical engineer, born 1865.
— Bataan Peninsula in the Philippines fell to Japan, 1942.
10 King James I chartered the Virginia companies of London and Plymouth, 1606.
— United States patent system established, 1790.
— Matthew C. Perry, American officer who opened Japan to world trade, born 1794.
— William Booth, English reformer and founder of the Salvation Army, born 1829.
— Joseph Pulitzer, Hungarian American publisher, born 1847.
— Clare Boothe Luce, American diplomat and playwright, born 1903.
11 Charles Evans Hughes, chief justice of the United States, born 1862.
12 Henry Clay, American statesman, born 1777.
— The American Civil War began at Fort Sumter, 1861.
— U.S. President Franklin D. Roosevelt died, 1945.
— Yuri Gagarin, Soviet astronaut, became the first person to orbit the earth, 1961.
13 The Edict of Nantes gave religious toleration to Huguenots in France, 1598.
— Thomas Jefferson, third U.S. president, born 1743.
— F. W. Woolworth, American merchant, born 1852.
— Samuel Beckett, Irish playwright, born 1906.
14 Christiaan Huygens, Dutch physicist, born 1629.
— Noah Webster copyrighted the first edition of his dictionary, 1828.
— John Wilkes Booth shot U.S. President Abraham Lincoln, 1865.
15 Leonardo da Vinci, Italian artist and scientist, born 1452.
— American Revolutionary War declared over, 1783.

April birthstone— diamond

April flower— daisy

April 5—Booker T. Washington born

April 6—Robert E. Peary reaches what he claims to be North Pole

ment. Matatirtha Aunsi, Nepalese Mothers' Day, also falls in April. The Christian celebration of Easter often occurs in this month, as does the Jewish festival of Pesah, also known as Passover.

April's flowers are the daisy and the sweet pea. The birthstone for April is the diamond. Carole S. Angell

Quotations

April cold with dropping rain
Willows and lilacs brings again,
The whistle of returning birds
And trumpet-lowing of the herds.
Ralph Waldo Emerson

When proud-pied April, dressed in all his trim
Has put a spirit of youth in everything.
William Shakespeare

The first of April, some do say
Is set apart for All Fools' Day;
But why the people call it so
Nor I, nor they themselves, do know.
From *Poor Robin's Almanac, 1760*

Related articles in *World Book* include:

April Fools' Day	Calendar	Earth Day	Holy Week
Arbor Day	Daisy	Easter	Palm Sunday
	Diamond	Good Friday	Passover
			Spring

April Fools' Day, or All Fools' Day, is the first day of April. In many countries, including the United States, it is the custom on this day to play tricks on people. A favorite joke is to send someone on a *fool's errand,* a search for something that does not exist. In the United States, the victim is called an *April Fool.*

Important April events

15 Henry James, American novelist, born 1843.
— Thomas Hart Benton, American painter, born 1889.
— British ocean liner *Titanic* sank after striking an iceberg, 1912.
16 Anatole France, French novelist, born 1844.
— Wilbur Wright, American inventor, born 1867.
17 Independence Day, Syria.
— Samuel Chase, American jurist, born 1741.
— J. P. Morgan, American financier, born 1837.
— Nikita Khrushchev, Soviet premier, born 1894.
— Queen Elizabeth II signed Constitution Act, making Canada completely independent of the United Kingdom, 1982.
18 Independence Day, Zimbabwe.
— Famous ride of Paul Revere, American patriot, 1775.
— San Francisco earthquake and fire began, 1906.
— Lieutenant Colonel James Doolittle led carrier-based planes in a raid on Tokyo in World War II, 1942.
19 Independence Day, Venezuela.
— The American Revolution began, 1775.
20 Adolf Hitler, dictator of Germany, born 1889.
21 Rome founded, according to tradition, 753 B.C.
— Friedrich Fröbel, German founder of the kindergarten system, born 1782.
— Charlotte Brontë, English novelist, born 1816.
— Hippolyte Taine, French historian and critic, born 1828.
— Texans routed the Mexicans in Battle of San Jacinto, 1836.
— The Spanish-American War began, 1898.
— Queen Elizabeth II of the United Kingdom born in 1926.
22 Earth Day celebrated in many countries.
— Isabella I, Spanish queen, born 1451.
— Henry Fielding, English novelist, born 1707.
— Immanuel Kant, German philosopher, born 1724.
— V. I. Lenin, first dictator of the Soviet Union, born 1870. (April 10 on the Russian calendar then in use).
— Sidney Nolan, Australian artist, born 1917.
23 Traditional birth date of William Shakespeare, 1564.

23 James Buchanan, 15th U.S. president, born 1791.
— Sergei Prokofiev, Russian composer, born 1891.
— First public showing of a motion picture, in New York City, 1896.
— Lester Pearson, Canadian Prime Minister, born 1897.
24 American Library of Congress established, 1800.
25 William I, Prince of Orange, born 1533 (April 16 by the calendar then in use).
— Oliver Cromwell, English general, born 1599.
— Guglielmo Marconi, Italian inventor, born 1874.
— San Francisco Conference to establish the United Nations began, 1945.
26 Union Day, Tanzania.
— John James Audubon, American ornithologist and painter, born 1785.
— Alfred Krupp, German industrialist, born 1812.
27 Samuel Morse, inventor of the telegraph, born 1791.
— Ulysses S. Grant, 18th U.S. president, born 1822.
— Togo became independent in 1960.
— Sierra Leone became independent in 1961.
28 James Monroe, fifth U.S. president, born 1758.
— Maryland ratified the U.S. Constitution, 1788.
— Mutiny on the British ship *Bounty,* 1789.
— Charles Sturt, British explorer of Australia, born 1795.
29 Lorado Taft, American sculptor, born 1860.
— William Randolph Hearst, American publisher, born 1863.
— Sir Thomas Beecham, British conductor, born 1879.
30 Washington inaugurated as first U.S. president, 1789.
— Louisiana Territory purchased from France by U.S., 1803 (treaty was signed May 2, but dated April 30).
— Louisiana became the 18th U.S. state, 1812.
— Television first publicly broadcast, from the Empire State Building in New York City, 1939.
— Adolf Hitler committed suicide, 1945.
— Vietnam War ended, 1975.
— Walpurgis Night (Feast of Valborg), Sweden.

WORLD BOOK illustrations by Mike Hagel

April 8—Henry Aaron breaks Babe Ruth's home run record

April 12—Civil War begins at Fort Sumter

April 15—Ocean liner *Titanic* sinks

April 18—Paul Revere's famous ride

No one knows where the April Fools' custom began. But some historians believe it may have started in France. There, the old New Year's festival was observed from March 25 to April 1 and ended with an exchange of gifts. In the mid-1560's, King Charles IX changed the New Year to January 1. People who still celebrated the New Year in April were called *April fish* and sent mock presents. April Fools' Day may be related to the ancient Roman spring festival Hilaria, which celebrates the resurrection of the god Attis. Jack Santino

Aquaculture, *AK wuh* KUHL *chuhr,* is the controlled raising of aquatic animals and plants. The word comes from Latin words meaning *water* and *cultivation.* The primary goal of the aquaculture industry is to produce food. About half of the world's annual fish harvest comes from aquaculture. Some fish are raised for aquariums, or for release into the wild. In addition, some plants grown through aquaculture yield substances that are used as thickeners or gelling agents in foods and other products.

Aquaculture takes place in natural bodies of water, in enclosures built on land, or in artificial ponds or reservoirs. In natural bodies of water, aquaculturists may grow the crop in nets or cages, attached to rafts, or seeded on the bottom. The animals or plants may be raised in fresh, *brackish* (slightly salty), or salt water. By controlling environment, nutrition, breeding, and life cycle, aquaculturists can improve the quality and productivity of their crops.

By weight, fish account for about 50 percent of the annual worldwide aquaculture production. Seaweeds account for about 25 percent. Mollusks—mainly oysters, mussels, and clams—make up over 15 percent. Crustaceans—mainly shrimp and prawns—account for over 5 percent of aquaculture production.

Aquaculture is an ancient occupation. Chinese people practiced aquaculture more than 2,500 years ago. The aquaculture industry expanded rapidly during the 1980's and 1990's. Worldwide production more than doubled from 1985 to 1995. Production in the United States nearly doubled during the same period. Today, China still ranks as the world leader in raising aquatic plants and animals. It accounts for about 60 percent of the world's production. David Berlinsky

Aquamarine, *AK wuh muh REEN,* is a light blue or bluish-green gem variety of the mineral *beryl.* The most popular color is a clear sky-blue. Aquamarine is often treated with heat to improve its color. Almost all aquamarine is transparent. Aquamarine is cut in *facets* (polished flat surfaces) and used in all types of jewelry. Aquamarine and bloodstone are the two birthstones for March.

Aquamarines have been known since ancient times. The ancient Romans believed the gem could cure laziness and produce courage.

The most important source of aquamarines is Brazil. The gem is also found in Argentina, China, India, Madagascar, Myanmar, Namibia, Northern Ireland, Norway, Russia, and the United States. Mark A. Helper

See also **Beryl; Birthstone** (table); **Gem** (picture).

Aquarium, Home, is a place where people keep their collections of fish and other water animals. A majority of such aquariums are in people's homes, but some individuals have aquariums at work or other loca-

tions. The word *aquarium* additionally refers to large institutions that maintain extensive exhibits of fish and other creatures. For information on these places, see **Aquarium, Public.**

A person who has an aquarium is called an *aquarist.* Most home aquarists have freshwater aquariums rather than marine aquariums. The freshwater type requires less expense and work to set up and maintain.

Basic equipment for a home aquarium includes (1) a tank and tank cover, (2) one or more filters, (3) a heater, and (4) a thermometer.

A rectangular tank that holds 10 to 20 gallons (38 to 76 liters) is good for a beginning aquarist. Most aquariums are made of glass and are held together with silicone sealant to make them watertight. A decorative plastic strip covers the top and bottom edges. Most tank covers include an incandescent or fluorescent lamp that shines into the tank. Such covers, called *light reflectors,* make it easy to see the fish. Lids that cover the entire top prevent fish from jumping out of the tank and reduce the amount of heat loss.

The aquarium filter removes dirt suspended in the water and keeps the water clean. Some filters are connected to an electrically operated air pump. The pump produces a stream of air that pushes water through the filter.

An aquarium may have an *external filter,* an *undergravel filter,* or both. External filters pump the water through activated carbon, filter pads, or filter floss, which remove particles and some impurities. Undergravel filters suck potentially harmful wastes into the gravel at the bottom of the tank. Bacteria in the gravel use the wastes as food and convert them into less harmful substances.

The electric heater warms the water to the proper temperature to keep fish healthy. For most fish, the water must be kept between 72 and 80 °F (22 and 27 °C). Most heaters hang on the tank's edge and extend into the water. Place the thermometer away from the heater where you can easily read it.

Setting up an aquarium. After acquiring a new tank, wash the tank inside and out with lukewarm, salty water and rinse it thoroughly. Place the tank on a level, strong surface near an electrical outlet. The aquarium should sit away from direct sunlight, drafts, and radiators. If only an external filter is used, the gravel should be rinsed and put into the tank in a layer about 1 inch (2.5 centimeters) deep. An undergravel filter should be covered with 2 to 3 inches (5 to 7.6 centimeters) of gravel.

Use tap water in your aquarium tank. Be sure to fill the tank a little at a time and to watch for leaks. When the tank is about two-thirds full, put in plants that can root in the gravel. Put the filter and heater in just before the aquarium is completely filled.

In most cases, the water should become suitable for fish two to three days after you fill the tank and start the electrical equipment. The water will look cloudy at first due to unsettled particles of dirt. Bubbles of gas may also appear. The cloudiness and bubbles will disappear in a day or two. After that time, a new cloudiness might appear, caused by bacteria. This condition should clear up in a few days.

Choosing fish and plants. Beginners should choose hardy, inexpensive fish that do not tend to fight or chase

A home aquarium should have an air pump and one or more filters to keep the water clean. A heater keeps the water at the desired temperature, and a cover reduces the amount of heat lost.

WORLD BOOK illustration by John F. Eggert

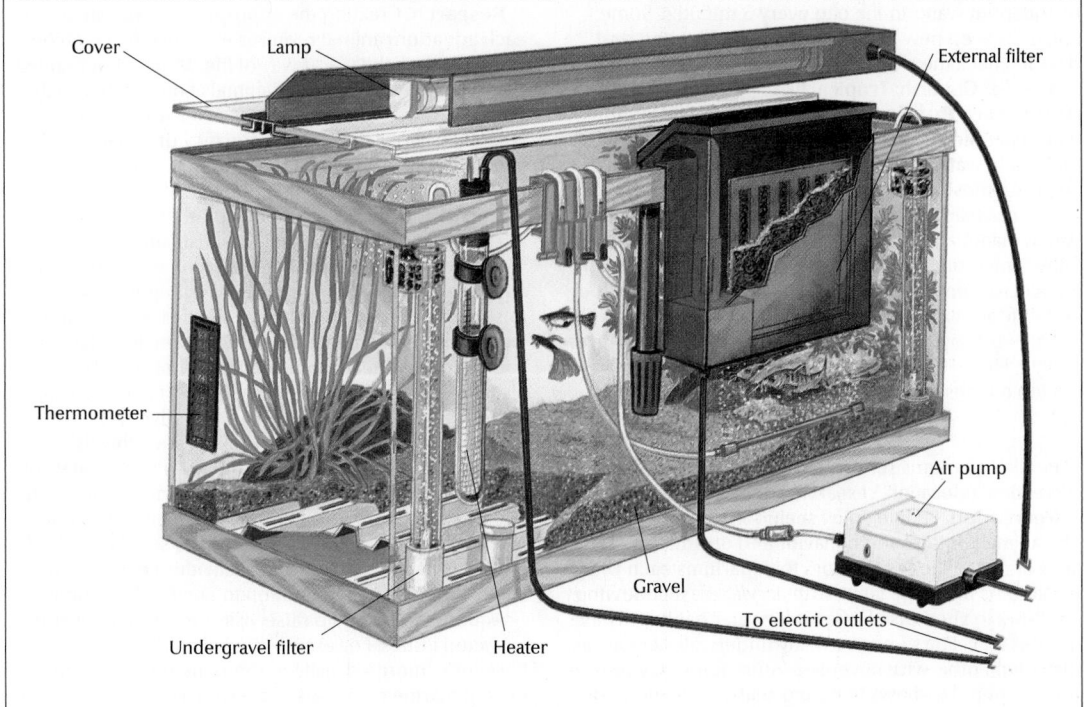

other fish. Popular fish for beginners include angelfish, cardinal tetras, guppies, mollies, neon tetras, and platies. Place only a few fish in the tank at first. You may add more fish gradually over several weeks. The aquarist must be careful not to put too many fish in the tank. The total length of all the fish in inches should be no greater than the number of gallons in the tank.

Most aquarists begin with fish that give birth to fully formed young that are able to swim. These fish, called *live-bearers,* include guppies and platies. Most female live-bearers will produce young about every six weeks when the water is kept at about 75 °F (24 °C).

A live-bearer about to give birth has a bulging belly and a dark spot on the bottom of her body. Keep the *fry* (young fish) separate until they get big enough to live among adult fish without being eaten.

©Zig Leszczynski, Animals Animals
Neon tetras are popular aquarium fish.

Some kinds of fish, called *egglayers,* hatch their young from eggs. Good egglayers for beginners include cardinal tetras, neon tetras, white clouds, and small angelfish. To breed, a female egglayer swollen with eggs should live in a separate tank with a male. Babies of egglayers are harder to raise than those of live-bearers. Live-bearers and egglayers can live in the same tank.

Plants make the aquarium more attractive and provide some food and shelter for the fish. They also give off oxygen, which the fish breathe, and take in carbon dioxide given off by the fish. Good aquarium plants include *Elodea,* which can be stuck in the gravel or floated on the surface; and *Vallisneria,* which takes root in the gravel. Many aquarists use lifelike plastic plants, further reducing tank maintenance.

Keeping the fish healthy. Most aquarium fish should eat once or twice a day. At each feeding, fish should get no more than they can consume in 10 minutes. Most tropical fish will eat any good-quality commercial fish food. They also may have live and processed brine shrimp, shellfish called *Daphnia,* and red worms called *Tubifex.* Some fish can find particles of food overlooked by others, and so help clean the tank. These fish include catfish and algae eaters.

Many fish diseases can spread quickly and kill all the fish in an aquarium. Signs of illness include change of color, funguslike growths, poor appetite, slow or unusual movement, and spots. If any of these signs appear, place the affected fish into a separate tank. A tropical fish dealer can provide information on treatment.

Do not place new fish in the aquarium water until they

have adjusted to the water's temperature. To help the fish adjust, float the plastic bag containing the new fish in the aquarium for 15 minutes, adding a small amount of aquarium water to the bag every 5 minutes. Some aquarists keep new fish in a separate tank for several days to check them for disease.   Louis E. Garibaldi

See also **Goldfish; Tropical fish.**

Aquarium, Public, or *aquatic zoo,* is an institution where people keep and display fish and other animals that live in water. Some public aquariums are parts of zoos, but most are independent institutions. Aquariums called *oceanariums* primarily display large *marine* (saltwater) mammals, including dolphins, seals, and whales. Other aquariums combine a traditional aquarium with an oceanarium. Such institutions may have large indoor and outdoor exhibits.

The word *aquarium* also refers to small collections of aquatic life that people keep in their homes. For information on these aquariums, see **Aquarium, Home.**

The purpose of aquariums

Public aquariums serve many purposes. They include recreation, education, research, and conservation.

Recreation. People enjoy seeing live aquatic animals. The animals' interesting behavior and unusual appearance attract millions of visitors to aquariums each year. Aquariums use huge tanks with *acrylic* (plastic) viewing windows to showcase large underwater habitats. These exhibits let visitors observe many underwater creatures they might otherwise never see. Aquariums may also present popular shows featuring seals, dolphins, and other trained marine mammals.

Education. Aquarium visitors learn many interesting facts about aquatic life from viewing the exhibits, which usually display information about the animals. Students

© Sydney Aquarium

A public aquarium displays fish and other animals in colorful exhibit tanks. Such exhibits often resemble particular marine environments, such as a coral reef. This aquarium exhibit in Sydney, Australia, includes information about its animals in lighted panels above the tank.

take school field trips to aquariums to learn more about the animals they study in class. Most aquariums provide tours and lectures for schoolchildren and other groups.

Research. Creating the appropriate environment for each aquarium animal requires extensive research on that animal's habitat and way of life. Much of our knowledge of the lives of aquatic animals comes from such research. For example, biologists have learned most of what they know about the pregnancy of certain whale species by studying the animals in aquariums. Aquariums also have advanced the practice of *aquaculture* (the raising of aquatic life for food and other uses) by studying the diets and diseases of food fish and shellfish.

Conservation. Aquariums help conserve threatened aquatic animals in many ways. For example, they may raise populations of threatened species whose natural habitats have been damaged. Such animals include a species of steelhead from central California. Water levels in the Carmel River, the steelhead's native habitat, periodically become low because the river is heavily used as a human water source. To protect this fish from extinction, the Monterey Bay Aquarium continually collects the fish's eggs from the river and raises the fish to maturity. When the river's level is high enough, aquarium workers release the captive-raised steelheads back into their natural habitat. Such activities keep river populations of the fish high enough to ensure their survival.

Aquariums also help raise visitor awareness of conservation issues. For example, whale and dolphin shows have long informed visitors about the declining numbers of marine mammals. Increased awareness of this issue has led to the passage of government legislation protecting marine mammals and their habitats.

How aquariums operate

Obtaining animals. Aquariums often rely on their own breeding programs to provide them with many of their exhibit animals. To expand the range of their collections, however, aquariums must purchase animals from outside sources. Public aquariums buy many of their exhibit animals from the suppliers that sell aquatic life to fish markets and pet shops. Aquariums also exchange animals among one another. On occasion, aquariums acquire specimens from individual fish collectors, or they may collect species directly from nature. Public aquariums must obtain permits to acquire and display threatened species, or species considered harmful to local water habitats.

Displaying exhibits. Aquarium exhibits range from small 10-gallon (38-liter) glass tanks to huge habitat exhibits in excess of 2 million gallons (7.6 million liters). Public aquariums display different animals for different reasons. Some creatures, such as blind cavefish, represent animals that have developed specialized adaptations for unusual habitats. Others, including lobsters and groupers, represent animals that provide people with important sources of food.

Aquarium exhibits place together animals that live together in nature. Most exhibits attempt to re-create particular environments, such as coral reefs, rocky shores, or tide pools. Aquarium workers add rocks, plants, and other features of an environment to each exhibit. These additions help satisfy the animals' ecological needs. They also make the exhibits more realistic for viewers.

© Ross Denotter, Vancouver Aquarium Marine Science Center

An aquarium worker can help teach people about the animals that live in the world's lakes, rivers, and oceans. This employee at the Vancouver Aquarium in Canada is introducing a beluga whale to a child visitor.

Most large public aquariums display habitats from around the world. Smaller, regional ones often emphasize local environments. Many aquariums use one or more tanks to present exhibits that last only 12 to 18 months. These presentations might focus on one region, such as Mexico's Gulf of California. Or they might present a group of animals, such as sea horses or sharks.

Some aquariums have created presentations called *immersion experiences.* These presentations show an unusual perspective of aquatic environments. For example, certain aquariums take guests through shark-inhabited tanks on moving sidewalks in acrylic tunnels.

Caring for animals involves many tasks. They include feeding, maintaining life support systems, and providing medical care.

Feeding. Aquarium animals require a variety of specialized diets. Most aquarium inhabitants will eat a wide range of frozen natural foods, such as fish, shrimp, and squid. But many species will consume only live animals. Aquariums raise and maintain a number of live foods, including algae, crabs, and small bait fish.

Life support systems. An aquarium's exhibit tank must always have clean water processed through life support systems. These systems maintain a safe environment for the animals. They circulate the water and maintain high levels of dissolved oxygen for animals to breathe. Filters remove particles of dirt and animal waste. Water treatments eliminate dissolved poisonous materials. Life support systems also keep the water at an appropriate and stable temperature.

Medical care. Nearly all aquariums employ a veterinarian to help care for their animals. When a new animal arrives, the aquarium at first keeps it quarantined. During quarantine, aquarium workers clean the animal of parasites and check for diseases. Daily observations of the animals help identify medical problems that may require treatment.

Jobs. Many aquarium jobs require a college degree, experience working with animals, or both. These aquarium professions include veterinarians, biologists, and laboratory technicians. Workers called *aquarists* take care of exhibits. Trainers work with animals in shows. Other aquarium employees help educate tour groups and maintain the life support systems.

History

Archaeological records indicate that the ancient Sumerians, in what is now Iraq, kept food fish in ponds over 4,500 years ago. About 2,000 years ago, ancient Romans kept both food fish and pet fish in shallow ponds and pools. The Chinese probably bred the first domestic goldfish more than 1,000 years ago. They displayed these fish in porcelain vessels.

During the mid-1800's, the invention of relatively clear glass tanks led to the development of modern aquariums. In 1853, the Zoological Society of London opened the first true public aquarium. This aquarium, called the "Fish House," was part of the zoological gardens in London. The exhibition became popular. Other aquariums opened in cities across Europe over the next 20 years. The first true public aquarium in North America, the Boston Aquarial Gardens, opened in 1859.

Marine Studios was founded near St. Augustine in 1938 for filming underwater motion-picture scenes. This park, later called Marineland Dolphin Adventure, soon became a popular tourist attraction. It developed a trained animal show with dolphins and other sea mammals. Marineland's success led to the foundation of other similar theme parks, including the popular SeaWorld parks. Such places, in turn, helped promote the development of oceanariums.

During the late 1900's, aquariums became both more numerous and more controversial. The invention of large acrylic viewing panels in the 1970's enabled aquariums to showcase large aquatic habitats. Improved technology increased the popularity of aquariums. But some animal welfare groups raised concerns about oceanariums. Such groups oppose keeping large sea mammals in captivity. They argue that aquarium environments are too restrictive for these creatures. The animals' natural habitats often cover large areas of the oceans. Despite such criticism, an unprecedented number of oceanariums and other aquariums were built worldwide in the late 1900's and early 2000's.   Louis E. Garibaldi

See also **Atlanta** (picture: The Georgia Aquarium); **Zoo** (picture: An underwater viewing exhibit).

Aquarius, *uh KWAIR ee uhs,* is the 11th sign of the zodiac. It is symbolized by a person carrying a pitcher of water. Astrologers believe that Aquarius is ruled by two planets—Saturn, which they consider a stern planet; and Uranus, the planet of change and disturbance. Aquarius is an air sign. Astrologers believe that people born under the sign, from January 20 to February 18, show the influence of Saturn by being serious-minded. However, their independence and love of freedom reflect the influence of Uranus. Aquarians do not respect tradition and enjoy shocking people by their behavior.

Aquarians have powerful, logical, and scientific minds. They are always open to new ideas. Aquarians have many friends but are hard to get to know deeply. They usually avoid close personal relationships. Aquari-

Aquarius—The Water Bearer

Symbol

Birth dates: Jan. 20–Feb. 18.
Group: Air.
Characteristics: Curious, independent, modern, open-minded, outgoing, serious.

Signs of the Zodiac

Aries
Mar. 21–Apr. 19

Taurus
Apr. 20–May 20

Gemini
May 21–June 20

Cancer
June 21–July 22

Leo
July 23–Aug. 22

Virgo
Aug. 23–Sept. 22

Libra
Sept. 23–Oct. 22

Scorpio
Oct. 23–Nov. 21

Sagittarius
Nov. 22–Dec. 21

Capricorn
Dec. 22–Jan. 19

**Aquarius
Jan. 21–Feb. 18**

Pisces
Feb. 19–Mar. 20

WORLD BOOK illustration by Robert Keys

ans support social and political causes with great enthusiasm.   Charles W. Clark

See also **Astrology; Horoscope; Zodiac.**

Aquatic plant. See Water plant.

Aqueduct, *AK wuh duhkt,* is an artificial channel through which water is conducted to the place where it is used. The materials used for aqueduct construction may be masonry, concrete, cast iron, steel, or wood. Some aqueducts are tunnels dug through rocks, and others are canals in the earth. In many aqueducts, the outlet is so much lower than the water source that gravity alone carries the water. Where gravity is insufficient, the water is forced through the aqueduct by pumps.

As cities and industries grow, they require more water, and more aqueducts must be built. Such modern conveniences as commercial air conditioners require large quantities of water. Aqueducts also supply water to dry lands that must be irrigated to produce crops.

Ancient aqueducts. It is not known when or where the first aqueducts were built. In ancient times, Jerusalem used a leaky aqueduct made of a series of limestone blocks in which 15-inch (38-centimeter) holes had been drilled by hand. The Greeks built masonry conduits to bring water to their cities, and even bored tunnels by hand. One of these tunnels, 4,200 feet (1,280 meters) long, was built by Athens 2,500 years ago. Most aqueducts of ancient times were built of stone, brick, or *pozzuolana,* a mixture of limestone and volcanic dust.

The city of Rome had many aqueducts and was the only ancient city reasonably supplied with water. The first person in charge of the Roman waterworks was Marcus Agrippa, who was appointed water commissioner in 33 B.C. By A.D. 97, nine aqueducts brought about 85 million gallons (322 million liters) of water a day from mountain springs. Later, five additional aqueducts were built. About 200 cities in the Roman colonies had aqueducts. One famous Roman aqueduct, the Pont du Gard, still stands across a river near Nîmes, France.

Later aqueducts. Only a few new aqueducts were built until the Middle Ages. Late in the 1500's, an aqueduct was built for the English town of Plymouth by Sir

Francis Drake, then mayor. It was called the River Leet and was an open channel 24 miles (39 kilometers) long. London had no aqueduct until 1609 when the aqueduct called New River was built, bringing water 38 miles (61 kilometers) to London.

Present-day aqueducts. Costly bridges to carry water across rivers and valleys are no longer necessary. They have been replaced by pipe through which water is carried across hilly country. Sections of pipe called *inverted siphons* curve downward to pass beneath streams and other low places in the aqueduct's course.

One of the first great modern aqueducts was the first Croton Aqueduct, built by New York City in 1842. It was made of masonry lined with brick. Iron pipes carried water across the Harlem River over a viaduct. During the late 1800's, other cities, especially those of the United Kingdom, built large aqueducts. These cities included Birmingham, Glasgow, Liverpool, and Manchester.

Many of the world's greatest aqueducts were built in the early 1900's. The Catskill Aqueduct, completed in 1913 for New York City, extends 120 miles (193 kilometers). The Colorado Aqueduct, in southern California, was completed in 1939. It carries water through 29 tunnels across the desert from the Colorado River.

In 1973, a 685-mile (1,102-kilometer) aqueduct was completed in California. Other noted aqueducts in the United States include the Hetch-Hetchy (O'Shaughnessy), which supplies San Francisco, and those of Denver, Boston, and Tulsa. One of the most noted aqueducts is the Apulian Aqueduct of southern Italy. Other major aqueducts include those of Winnipeg, Canada, and Rio de Janeiro, Brazil.   Amy Sue Bix

See also **Rome, Ancient** (picture: Aqueduct construction).

Aquinas, *uh KWY nuhs,* **Saint Thomas** (1225?-1274), was one of the greatest medieval philosophers and theologians. Through the centuries, he has influenced Christian—especially Roman Catholic—thought.

His life. Thomas was born of a noble family in Roccasecca, Italy, near Cassino. He attended the University of Naples from 1239 until 1244, when he joined the Dominican order. He was ordained a priest in 1250. From 1245 to 1252, he studied philosophy and theology under the German theologian Saint Albertus Magnus. In 1256, Thomas was named professor of theology at the University of Paris. There, he became famous because he developed his intellect in the service of the Christian faith.

In 1258, Thomas began to write the *Summa contra Gentiles.* In this work, he tried to convince non-Christians that Christianity's doctrines were not contrary to reason. From 1259 to 1268, Thomas wrote commentaries on many writings of the ancient Greek philosopher Aristotle. In 1265, he began to write his most famous work, *Summa Theologica,* in which he tried to systematically explain Christian theology. But Thomas had a mystical experience in 1273 that caused him to stop writing. He said that all he had written seemed like straw compared with what he had seen in this experience. He died on March 7, 1274. Thomas's feast day is January 28.

His thought. Thomas combined Aristotle's teachings with Christian doctrine. For example, Thomas argued that no conflict exists between reason and faith. Philosophy is based on reason, he declared, and theology comes from faith in divine revelation, yet both come from God. So Thomas believed that any differences between divine revelation and the conclusions of philosophy result from faulty reasoning. He also maintained that reason can support faith. Thomas accepted—on faith—the idea that God exists. However, he formulated five proofs of God's existence to support such a belief.

According to Thomas, all people desire happiness, but they can satisfy this desire only through direct communion with God. He believed that God gives grace to help humanity overcome the influence of sin and gain this communion. Thomas taught that the sacraments are important in communicating God's grace to people.

Thomas believed that governments have a moral responsibility to serve people and to help them lead virtuous lives. He declared that governments must not violate what he considered human rights—life, education, religion, and reproduction. Thomas also taught that if human laws were to be just, they must not contradict divine law.　　David B. Burrell

See also **Scholasticism**.

Aquino, Benigno Simeon Cojuangco, III

(1960-2021), also known as Noynoy, was president of the Philippines from 2010 to 2016. He had previously served in the Philippine Senate and House of Representatives.

Aquino was born on Feb. 8, 1960, in Manila, the capital of the Philippines. His father, Benigno "Ninoy" Aquino, was then vice governor of Tarlac province on the northern Philippine island of Luzon. Ninoy Aquino later became the main political rival of President Ferdinand Marcos. From 1972 to 1980, Ninoy was imprisoned for his opposition to the Marcos regime. Marcos released Ninoy in 1980 so he could undergo a heart operation in the United States. Ninoy was joined there by his wife and children. Noynoy completed his degree in economics at Ateneo de Manila University in Quezon City in 1981 and then joined his family in the United States.

In 1983, Ninoy Aquino returned to the Philippines and was assassinated. The killing shocked the people and strengthened opponents of the government. The Aquino family also soon returned. Noynoy worked as a businessman. His mother, Corazon "Cory" Aquino, became the first woman president of the Philippines in 1986.

Noynoy entered politics in the 1990's. He was elected to represent Tarlac in the Philippine House of Representatives in 1998. He was reelected in 2001 and 2004. From 1999 to 2002 and from 2004 to 2006, he served as secretary general of the Liberal Party of the Philippines. He became the party's vice chairman in 2006 and was elected to the Senate in 2007. In 2010, he was elected president. In 2014, his government signed a peace agreement with Muslim separatists of the Moro rebellion and pledged to create an autonomous Muslim region. Aquino died on June 24, 2021.　　S. Thomas Richardson

See also **Aquino, Corazon**.

Aquino, uh KEE noh, Corazon, KAWR uh ZOHN

(1933-2009), also known as Cory, was the first woman president of the Philippines. She held the office from 1986 to 1992. Aquino succeeded Ferdinand E. Marcos. Both Aquino and Marcos claimed victory in an election marked by fraud and violence. But Marcos fled abroad when large numbers of Filipinos backed military officers who demanded his resignation. Aquino then became president. She did not run for reelection in 1992.

Maria Corazon Sumulong Cojuangco was born on

Jan. 25, 1933, in Tarlac into a wealthy and politically influential family. She studied in the United States and graduated from the College of Mount St. Vincent in New York City in 1953. In 1954, she married Benigno S. "Ninoy" Aquino, Jr., who became the chief political rival of Ferdinand Marcos. Benigno Aquino was assassinated in 1983, and Corazon Aquino blamed the Marcos government for the murder. In 1985, Marcos called for a presidential election, and Aquino rallied opposition to end his 20-year rule.

In 1986, Aquino appointed a commission to draft a new constitution, which was approved the following year. Members of the military tried several times to overthrow Aquino's government but failed to do so. Aquino died on Aug. 1, 2009. Cory and Ninoy's son, Benigno "Noynoy" Aquino, served as president from 2010 to 2016.　　Henry S. Bradsher

See also **Philippines** (The Philippines today).

Arab Americans are Americans who have roots in the Arab world—that is, the areas where people speak the Arabic language and share other cultural traditions. The Arab world includes much of the Middle East, the region that spreads across southwestern Asia and northern Africa. Countries of the Arab world include Algeria, Bahrain, Egypt, Iraq, Jordan, Kuwait, Lebanon, Libya, Mauritania, Morocco, Oman, Qatar, Saudi Arabia, Sudan, Syria, Tunisia, the United Arab Emirates, and Yemen. The Arab world also includes the historic region of Palestine. Palestine today consists of the state of Israel and two Palestinian territories, the West Bank and the Gaza Strip.

Who Arab Americans are. According to the U.S. Census Bureau, about 1 ¾ million Arab Americans live in the United States. About half of them have roots in either Egypt, Lebanon, or Syria. Large numbers also come from Iraq, Jordan, Morocco, and Palestine.

In the Middle East, more than 95 percent of Arabs are Muslims—that is, followers of the religion of Islam. However, less than half of all Arab Americans practice Islam. Many Arab Americans belong to Eastern Rite Churches, such as the Antiochian Orthodox, Coptic, and Maronite churches. Eastern Rite Churches are independent but related Christian churches with roots in eastern Europe, Africa, and Asia. Other Arab American Christians belong to Roman Catholic and Protestant churches.

Ethnic background of Arab Americans

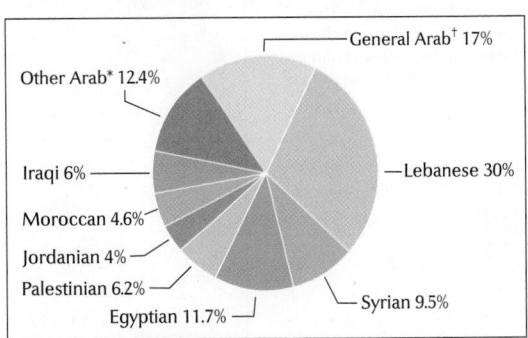

General Arab[†] 17%
Other Arab* 12.4%
Iraqi 6%
Moroccan 4.6%
Jordanian 4%
Palestinian 6.2%
Egyptian 11.7%
Lebanese 30%
Syrian 9.5%

*Includes Yemeni, Kurdish, Algerian, Saudi, Tunisian, Kuwaiti, Libyan, Berber, and other specific Arab ancestries.
†Those who responded Arab, Arabic, Middle Eastern, or North African.
Figures are for 2009 and do not add up to 100 percent, due to respondents who identified with more than one Arab ancestry group.
Source: U.S. Census Bureau.

Arab Americans, like other Americans, value family and education. The parents shown here read a storybook to their daughter. Many Arab American children grow up speaking both Arabic and English.

© Amy Etra, PhotoEdit

Many Arab Americans speak the Arabic language and emphasize the teaching of Arabic to children. Arab American Muslims especially stress the importance of Arabic, since it is the language of the Qur'ān, the sacred book of Islam, and the language in which Muslims pray.

Arab Americans typically hold the same values that other Americans hold. They emphasize education, family, faith, and hospitality. In most cases, the lifestyles of Arab Americans are not different from those of other Americans. Some Arab American immigrants keep certain customs, habits, and traditions from their homelands. For example, an Arab American girl from a Muslim family might cover her hair with a headscarf and still wear jeans and sneakers like other American girls.

Where Arab Americans live. Arab Americans live in all 50 states. The states with the largest Arab American populations are California, Michigan, and New York.

About 90 percent of Arab Americans live in urban areas. For many years, New York City was the main center for Arab immigrants in the United States. But during the late 1900's, the Detroit area emerged as the major hub of Arab American life and culture. Numerous Arab American cultural, business, and human service organizations are based in Detroit. Other major centers of Arab American life include Chicago; Los Angeles and other parts of southern California; Washington, D.C.; and parts of northeastern New Jersey.

Arab American accomplishments, as well as the traditions of the Arab world, have strongly influenced life and culture in the United States. Americans of Arab descent have made significant contributions to virtually every field and profession.

Michael E. DeBakey, a surgeon of Lebanese descent, won fame for his groundbreaking work with the heart and blood vessels. He also worked on the development of an artificial heart. Arab American scientists Elias J. Corey and Ahmed H. Zewail won the Nobel Prize in chemistry in 1990 and 1999, respectively. Steve Jobs, the son of a Syrian immigrant father, cofounded the computer company Apple Inc. in 1976.

George A. Kasem was the first Arab American to serve in the Congress of the United States. Kasem, who represented California in the House of Representatives, was elected in 1958. Donna E. Shalala was the first Arab American to serve in a U.S. president's Cabinet. She served as secretary of health and human services from 1993 to 2001. Ralph Nader, the son of Lebanese immigrants, is well known as a consumer advocate and presidential candidate.

Well-known Arab American entertainers have includ-

Where Arab Americans live

This map shows the state-by-state distribution of the Arab American population according to the 2010 census. The numbers on the map indicate the percentage of Arab Americans in the total population of each state.

Percent of total population by state

- More than 1.50
- 0.75 to 1.50
- 0.50 to 0.75
- 0.25 to 0.50
- Less than 0.25

Wash. 0.32
Montana 0.25
N. Dak. 0.14
Minn. 0.37
Vt. 0.47
N.H. 0.56
Me. 0.21
Oregon 0.51
Idaho 0.15
Wyoming 0.04
S. Dak. 0.37
Wis. 0.19
Mich. 1.69
N.Y. 0.82
Mass. 1.04
R.I. 0.79
Conn. 0.51
Nevada 0.54
Utah 0.24
Colorado 0.36
Nebraska 0.38
Iowa 0.18
Illinois 0.61
Ind. 0.29
Ohio 0.58
Penn. 0.53
N.J. 1.04
Del. 0.29
California 0.71
Kansas 0.27
Missouri 0.34
Ken. 0.23
W.Va. 0.38
D.C. 0.52
Va. 0.62
Md. 0.50
Arizona 0.54
New Mexico 0.21
Oklahoma 0.27
Arkansas 0.24
Tenn. 0.43
N.C. 0.38
S.C. 0.35
Texas 0.44
Miss. 0.27
Ala. 0.26
Georgia 0.27
La. 0.40
Florida 0.49
Alaska 0.05
Hawaii 0.13

ed the comedian and philanthropist Danny Thomas; the Emmy Award-winning actor Tony Shalhoub; and the "American Top 40" disk jockey Casey Kasem. Notable Arab American athletes have included football players John Elway and Doug Flutie, race car driver Bobby Rahal, and the Moroccan-born marathon runner Khalid Khannouchi.

Traditional aspects of Arab culture have become part of the daily life of many Americans. For instance, "pita" bread and chickpea dishes—such as *hummus* and *felafel*—are familiar foods for many people in the United States. In addition, some people use *couscous* (steamed cracked wheat) instead of rice in many dishes. Couscous originated in northern Africa.

Henna (a reddish dye) and *kohl* (powder worn around the eyes) are common cosmetic products that have roots in the Arab world. *Raqs sharqi*—commonly known as *belly dancing*—is a Middle Eastern dance style that many people in the United States use as a form of exercise or entertainment. Many Americans also listen to Arab popular music or to regional styles, such as *raï* (pronounced *ry)* music. Raï music originated in Algeria and combines Arabic love poetry and Bedouin folk music. Modern raï has also been influenced by such genres as rock, flamenco, soul, and reggae.

History of Arab immigration. Arab immigrants began settling in the United States in the 1880's. The first immigrants were mainly Christian Arabs from the lands that are now Lebanon and Syria, then part of the Ottoman Empire. They came to the United States in search of economic opportunity and freedom from famine and other harsh conditions. Most early Arab immigrants settled in commercial and industrial areas. By 1925, an estimated 200,000 Arabs were living in the United States.

During the late 1800's and early 1900's, many Arab immigrants faced challenges to their eligibility for U.S. citizenship. Many of these challenges involved special restrictions the U.S. government had placed on Asian immigration. Some judges denied Arab immigrants—

© Corbis/Bettmann

Many Arab immigrants opened shops and other businesses in the United States during the late 1800's and early 1900's. The grocery store shown here offered traditional Syrian food.

most of whom came from southwestern Asia—the same rights granted to "white" immigrants at the time. Eventually, after many years of dispute, the Arab immigrants' eligibility for citizenship was confirmed.

Arab immigrants faced additional obstacles in the early 1900's, when *quotas* (limits) were placed on immigration from countries outside of northern Europe. Under the National Origins Act of 1924, the United States admitted only a few hundred Arab immigrants annually.

During the mid-1900's, a cultural transformation took place among many Arab Americans. They continued to organize around their Arab heritage, establishing Arab cultural organizations, charity groups, Eastern Rite Churches, and mosques. But they increasingly identified themselves as Americans. In the years surrounding World War II (1939-1945), Arab Americans were strongly patriotic, served in the military, and took pride in their U.S. citizenship. Most Arab American families focused heavily on education and economic advancement.

A new wave of Arab immigrants came to the United States after the government lifted nationality-based immigration quotas in the 1960's. Many immigrants came to avoid instability and violence associated with conflicts in newly independent Arab states. The Arab-Israeli wars of 1948 and 1967, for instance, displaced hundreds of thousands of Palestinians.

This second wave of immigrants came primarily from Egypt, Iraq, Jordan, Lebanon, Syria, and Palestine. The first wave of immigrants had been mainly Christians, but the new wave included large numbers of Muslims. Many of these Muslims faced unique challenges in balancing their religious lives with American culture. Many Americans knew little about—and sometimes were hostile to—Muslim beliefs and traditions.

The second wave of immigrants placed a heavy emphasis on ethnic identity and on the continuation of Arab traditions. Since the 1960's, numerous Arab American organizations have sought to assist Arab immigrants, foster ties with the Arab world, and promote use of the Arabic language. Some organizations specifically address the needs of Arab Americans of a particular religious sect or country of origin.

By the 1990's, more than 10,000 Arab immigrants arrived in the United States each year. In the late 1990's and early 2000's, however, changes in immigration law made it more difficult for Arabs to come to the United States.

Arab Americans today. The Arab American community has been directly affected by political instability in the Middle East; the terrorist attacks of Sept. 11, 2001; and hostilities between the United States and parts of the Arab world. Because the terrorists responsible for the September 11 attacks were Arab Muslims, some Americans began to treat Arab Americans with suspicion and hostility. Many innocent Arab Americans faced discrimination, harassment, threats, and violence in the months and years following the attacks. Many people argued that certain government actions unfairly targeted Arabs and Muslims in the United States. The Iraq War (2003-2011) caused further difficulties for Arab Americans, especially those of Iraqi descent. The U.S. government and numerous Arab American organizations have worked to address these concerns and to eliminate discrimination.

Since 2001, the Arab American community has actively sought to promote cultural understanding between Arab Americans and their fellow citizens. Many Arab Americans have also assisted the U.S. government by providing expertise on Arab culture and politics, and by working to build friendly relations between the United States and the Arab world. Helen Hatab Samhan

See also **Arabic language; Arabic literature; Arabs; Muslims.**

Arab-Israeli conflict is a struggle between the Jewish state of Israel and the Arabs of the Middle East. About 90 percent of all Arabs are Muslims. The conflict has included several wars between Israel and certain Arab countries that have opposed Israel's existence. Israel was formed in 1948. The conflict has also involved a struggle by Palestinian Arabs to establish their own country in some or all of the land occupied by Israel.

The Arab-Israeli conflict is the continuation of an Arab-Jewish struggle that began in the early 1900's for control of Palestine. Palestine today consists of Israel and the areas known as the Gaza Strip and the West Bank. The Arab people known as the Palestinians lived in the region long before Jews began moving there in large numbers in the late 1800's.

The Arab-Israeli conflict has been hard to resolve. In 1979, Egypt became the first Arab country to sign a peace treaty with Israel. Jordan, another Arab country, signed a peace treaty with Israel in 1994. But Israel has not made final peace agreements with Syria or with the Palestine Liberation Organization (PLO). The PLO is a political body that represents the Palestinian people.

Historical background. In the mid-1800's, Jewish intellectuals in Europe began to support the idea that Jews should settle in Palestine, which the Bible describes as the Jews' ancient homeland. The word *Palestine* does not appear in the Bible. But it has long been used to refer to the area the Bible describes. The idea that Jews should settle in Palestine became known as Zionism. In the 1800's, Palestine was controlled by the Ottoman Empire, which was centered in present-day Turkey.

Zionism became an important political movement among Jews in Europe because of increasing *anti-Semitism* (prejudice against Jews) there. The anti-Semitism resulted in violent attacks on Jews and their property. In the 1800's, the immigration of European Jews to Palestine accelerated. At first, many of the immigrants and the Palestinians lived together peacefully. But as more Jews arrived, conflicts increased.

In 1917 and 1918, at the end of World War I, the United Kingdom gained control of Palestine from the Ottoman Empire. In the Balfour Declaration of 1917, the United Kingdom had supported creating a national homeland for the Jews. Under British rule, the Jewish population of Palestine continued to grow.

During World War II (1939-1945), German dictator Adolf Hitler tried to kill all of Europe's Jews. About 6 million Jews were murdered. After the war, many countries supported the idea of creating a new Jewish state where Jews would be safe from persecution.

The 1948 war. In November 1947, the United Nations (UN) approved a plan to divide Palestine into two states, one Jewish and the other Palestinian. Zionist leaders accepted the plan. But Arab governments and the Palestinians saw the division as the theft of Arab land by Zionists and the governments that supported them.

British rule over Palestine ended when Zionists proclaimed the state of Israel on May 14, 1948. The next day, armies of Egypt, Syria, Lebanon, Transjordan (which became known as Jordan in 1949), and Iraq attacked Israel. Israel fought back. In the war, Israel absorbed much of the land the UN had set aside for the Palestinians. Egypt and Jordan occupied the rest of the area assigned to the Palestinians. Egypt held the Gaza Strip, a small area between Israel and the Mediterranean Sea. Jordan held the West Bank, a territory between Israel and the Jordan River. By August 1949, Israel and all five Arab states had agreed to end the fighting. Because of the war, more than 700,000 Palestinians became refugees. Most fled to Jordan—including the West Bank—or to the Gaza Strip. Other Palestinians went to Lebanon and Syria.

The Suez crisis of 1956. During the 1950's, nationalism spread among the Arab countries of the Middle East. Egyptian President Gamal Abdel Nasser and his followers sought to rid Arab lands of the influence of Western nations. On July 26, 1956, Nasser took control of the Suez Canal from its British and French owners. The canal connects the Mediterranean and Red seas and is a key shipping route between Europe and Asia.

Many countries protested Nasser's action. France, Israel, and the United Kingdom secretly plotted to end Egypt's control of the canal. On October 29, Israel attacked Egyptian forces in Egypt's Sinai Peninsula and quickly defeated them. The Sinai lies between Israel and the canal. Israel, with British and French help, occupied most of the peninsula. The UN called a cease-fire on November 6. By early 1957, Israel, under international pressure, returned the Sinai to Egypt. The canal reopened under Egyptian management in April of that year.

After the Suez crisis, Arab guerrillas launched small-scale attacks inside Israel, and Israel responded with raids into Arab territory. At the same time, the Arab nationalist movement began receiving financial and military support from the Soviet Union. The United States, fearing the spread of Soviet-sponsored Communism, gave financial and military aid to Israel.

In 1964, the PLO was formed to represent the Palestinians. It included guerrilla groups dedicated to defeating Israel and creating an independent Palestinian state.

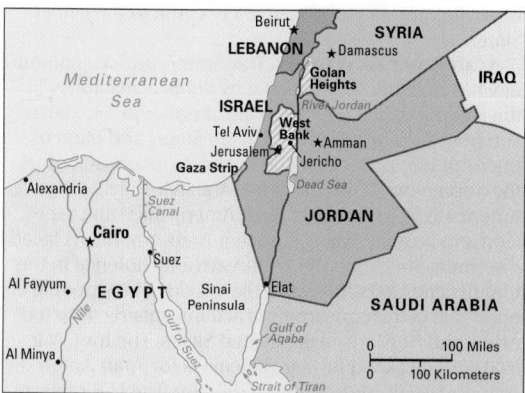

WORLD BOOK map

Israel and its Arab neighbors lie at the eastern end of the Mediterranean Sea. Arab countries that have fought wars against Israel include Egypt, Iraq, Jordan, and Syria.

The 1967 war. In May 1967, Nasser closed the Gulf of Aqaba to Israeli shipping. The gulf was Israel's only access to the Red Sea. By June 5, Egypt had signed defense agreements with Syria, Jordan, and Iraq, creating a joint military command. These apparent preparations for war alarmed the Israelis. On June 5, they launched a surprise attack on Egypt. Syria, Jordan, and Iraq joined Egypt in fighting Israel. Within hours, Israeli warplanes destroyed almost all the Arab air forces. Israeli tanks then retook the Sinai Peninsula. Israel also captured the West Bank, the Gaza Strip, and East Jerusalem. It had taken West Jerusalem in the 1948 war. In the north, Israel took Syria's Golan Heights, an area bordering Israel. The fighting ended on June 10. Israelis call this conflict the Six-Day War. Arabs call it the June War. After the war, Israel decided it would return the territories it had taken only if the Arab countries recognized its right to exist.

Also after the 1967 war, the PLO sought to become the representative of the Palestinians in world politics. It developed educational and social service organizations for Palestinians, mainly in the West Bank and Gaza Strip and in refugee camps in Lebanon and Jordan.

The PLO also began to take independent military action. In the late 1960's, PLO groups began to attack Israelis both inside and outside Israel. In response, Israel attacked Palestinian refugee camps in Jordan and Lebanon, in which many guerrillas were based. The Israelis also assassinated a number of PLO leaders.

The 1973 war. After the 1967 war, Egyptian and Israeli troops continued to clash along the western border of the Sinai Peninsula. On Oct. 6, 1973, Egypt and Syria launched a massive assault on Israeli forces in the Sinai Peninsula and Golan Heights. The attack took Israel by surprise, in part because it came on Yom Kippur, Judaism's holiest day. At first, Egypt drove Israel out of the western Sinai, and Syria pushed Israeli troops from the eastern Golan Heights. But the United States gave Israel large amounts of military equipment. By October 24, Israeli forces crossed the Suez Canal and surrounded the Egyptian army. They also defeated the Syrian army in the Golan Heights. Israelis call this war the Yom Kippur War. Arabs call it the October War or the Ramadan War.

The Camp David Accords. In 1978, Egyptian President Anwar el-Sadat joined Israeli Prime Minister Menachem Begin and U.S. President Jimmy Carter in signing the Camp David Accords. Under these agreements, Egypt recognized Israel's right to exist. In return, Israel agreed to give back to Egypt the part of the Sinai it still occupied. Israel had returned the far western part of the Sinai in 1975. In talks leading up to the accords, Egypt and Israel were promised large amounts of U.S. economic and military aid. In 1979, Egypt and Israel signed a treaty that confirmed their new peaceful relationship.

Most Arab leaders strongly opposed the Camp David Accords and the 1979 treaty. The Arab League, an organization of Arab countries, expelled Egypt in 1979.

The Israeli invasion of Lebanon. After the signing of the Camp David Accords, the PLO continued to launch guerrilla attacks on Israel, especially from southern Lebanon. In 1982, Israel invaded Lebanon and drove the PLO out of the southern part of the country. Israeli forces remained in southern Lebanon until 2000.

The first intifada. In 1987, Palestinians in the West Bank and Gaza Strip began an uprising against Israel's military rule of these territories. During this *intifada* (an Arabic term meaning *uprising* or *shaking off*), demonstrations occurred. Most of them were peaceful, but a few became violent. The intifada grabbed international attention and triggered criticism of Israel for its extensive use of force in trying to control the Palestinians.

Peacemaking. In 1988, the PLO recognized Israel's right to exist. It also declared its readiness to negotiate with Israel for peace in return for the creation of an independent Palestinian state. In addition, it declared it would no longer use violence against Israel. But some PLO members continued to attack Israeli targets.

In 1993, Israel and the PLO, aided by Norway, began secret peace talks. In September, the PLO and Israel signed an agreement in Washington, D.C. Under the agreement, the PLO again recognized Israel's right to exist, and Israel recognized the PLO as the representative of the Palestinians. It also promised to withdraw from part or all of the West Bank and Gaza Strip. In 1994, Israel gave the PLO control of the Gaza Strip and the West Bank city of Jericho. In 1995 and 1996, Israel gave the Palestinians control of most West Bank cities and towns.

Jordan signed a peace treaty with Israel in 1994. Peace talks between Israel and Syria, however, broke down in 1996. Talks resumed in 1999 but quickly ended because of continuing disagreement over the Golan Heights.

The second intifada. Peace talks between Israeli and Palestinian leaders continued in 2000. But the two sides were unable to agree on key remaining issues, especially those involving the final status of Jerusalem. In September, Palestinians began a second intifada. Attacks by Palestinian militias and suicide bombers took place in Israel, the West Bank, and Gaza, killing hundreds of Israelis. Israeli forces repeatedly bombed and invaded the West Bank and Gaza Strip, killing thousands of Palestinians and demolishing hundreds of houses. In 2002, Israel reoccupied most West Bank cities. It began building a barrier to separate most of the West Bank from Israel. In 2005, Israel withdrew from the Gaza Strip.

Conflict continues. In 2006, Palestinian militants captured an Israeli soldier. Fighting increased, with Israel bombing parts of Gaza and militants firing rockets into Israel. That same year, the radical Lebanese Islamic group Hezbollah captured two more Israeli soldiers. Israel bombed Lebanon, and Hezbollah fired missiles into Israel. Israel and Lebanon later accepted a cease-fire agreement drafted by the UN Security Council. The conflict caused over 1,000 Lebanese and Israeli deaths.

In 2008, Israel launched air attacks on Gaza, calling the air strikes a response to rocket attacks from Hamas. The next year, Israel sent troops into Gaza. The fighting caused over 1,300 deaths, almost all Palestinian. Despite a cease-fire, fighting continued.

In 2012, violence in Gaza erupted again as Hamas rocket attacks met with Israeli naval and air strikes. In about one week, some 170 people were killed, all but 6 of them Palestinians. Israeli soldiers again entered Gaza in 2014, after cross-border violence increased. More than 2,000 Palestinians and dozens of Israelis were killed over several weeks. In 2015, violence flared up in the occupied Palestinian territories, resulting in the deaths of dozens of people, most of them Palestinian. In 2018, Israeli security forces killed more than 120 Palestinians during protests along the Gaza Strip's border with Israel.

New peace plan. In 2017, the United States officially recognized Jerusalem as Israel's capital. The U.S. Embassy moved from Tel Aviv to Jerusalem in 2018. The move sparked protests in Gaza, where Israeli security forces killed 62 Palestinians and injured about 2,700 others.

In 2020, the administration of U.S. President Donald J. Trump proposed a Middle East peace plan. The plan acknowledged the right of Palestinians to form an independent state. But it allowed Israel to annex 30 percent of the West Bank, including all Israeli settlements there. The Palestinians would receive some territory near Gaza. The plan proposed a unified Jerusalem as Israel's capital and the establishment of a Palestinian capital northeast of the city. Israel supported the plan and agreed to temporarily halt its expansion of West Bank settlements. The Palestinians, who had no role in drafting the plan, rejected it. Later in 2020, the United Arab Emirates (UAE) and Israel agreed to establish official diplomatic ties. The UAE became only the third Arab nation, after Egypt and Jordan, to agree to such ties. The deal required Israel to suspend annexation of settlements in the West Bank.

In 2021, Israeli police actions sparked violence in East Jerusalem. Hamas and Israel exchanged airstrikes during which over 260 people, mostly Palestinians, were killed. Hamas and Israel later agreed to a cease-fire.

William B. Vogele

Related articles in *World Book.* See the *History* sections of the articles on countries involved in the struggle. See also:

Fatah	Palestine	Suez Canal
Hamas	Palestine	United Nations
Hezbollah	Liberation	(Working for
Intifada	Organization	peace and
Olympic Games	Palestinian	security)
(Terrorism in	Authority	Zionism
Munich)	Palestinians	

Arab League is an organization of 22 Middle Eastern and African countries where Arabic is the main spoken language. Its official name is the League of Arab States. The league regards Palestine, represented by the Palestinian Authority, as a country. The Pact of the League of Arab States says that the league promotes political, economic, cultural, and social ties among its members.

A council of representatives from the member states works to settle disputes peacefully. It can also decide how to repel aggression against a member.

The league's charter was signed in 1945 by seven countries—Egypt, Iraq, Lebanon, Saudi Arabia, Syria, Transjordan (now Jordan), and Yemen (Sanaa). Since then, 16 other members have joined—Algeria, Bahrain, Comoros, Djibouti, Kuwait, Libya, Mauritania, Morocco, Oman, Palestine, Qatar, Somalia, Sudan, Tunisia, United Arab Emirates, and Yemen (Aden). In 1990, Yemen (Aden) and Yemen (Sanaa) united as Yemen.

The Arab League has had difficulty living up to the aspirations of its founders. Political differences, suspicions, and rivalries have made the league's political and defense agreements largely ineffective. However, the league has had some success in expressing the rights of Palestinians. In 1974, it helped Palestinians attain observer status at the United Nations (UN). Observers have the right to speak at UN meetings but not to vote.

The Arab League's greatest accomplishments have been in the social, cultural, and communications fields. The 1976 formation of ARABSAT, an Arab communications satellite system, helped foster cooperation among Arab countries. The league has also worked to preserve Arabic language and heritage and improve education.

The Arab League has often reflected rather than settled disputes among its members. In 1979, Egypt signed a peace treaty with Israel. Because Arab countries at that time had no diplomatic relations with Israel, the league suspended Egypt's membership. It also transferred its headquarters from Cairo, Egypt, to Tunis, Tunisia. The league readmitted Egypt in 1989 and returned its headquarters to Cairo in 1990. In 1994, Jordan signed a treaty with Israel but was not punished by the league.

After Iraq invaded Kuwait in 1990, most league members approved of the use of military force to expel Iraq from Kuwait. But in 2003, only Kuwait supported a United States-led war against Iraq. Some other members, including Bahrain and Qatar, allowed their territory to be used for planning and staging the war effort.

In 2002, the Arab League approved a peace plan, sponsored by Saudi Arabia, between its members and Israel. However, Israel did not agree with many of the plan's terms. In 2005 and 2007, the league revived the plan, but Israel has not accepted it.   Imad Harb

Arabia. See Arabian Peninsula; Saudi Arabia.

Arabian Desert, *uh RAY bee uhn,* is a desert that covers most of the Arabian Peninsula. It occupies about 1 million square miles (2.6 million square kilometers). Countries entirely in the desert are Saudi Arabia, Kuwait, Qatar, the United Arab Emirates, Oman, and Yemen. Parts of Jordan, Syria, and Iraq also lie within the desert. The northwestern Arabian Desert is also known as the Syrian Desert. For location, see **Desert** (map).

Most of the Arabian Desert consists of barren, stony highlands and plains, but sand in the form of dunes and thin sheets is common. An area in the southeast called Rub al Khali is the largest continuous area of desert sand on Earth. It covers about 250,000 square miles (647,500 square kilometers).

Average annual rainfall in most of the Arabian Desert is less than 4 inches (10 centimeters). Mountainous areas in the southwest get up to 20 inches (50 centimeters). Most of the desert is hot all year, but freezing temperatures occur in some areas in winter.   Wayne Lambert

See also **Syrian Desert.**

Arabian Nights, a collection of about 200 stories, is probably the most famous piece of Arabic literature in the West. It includes the adventures of such well-known characters as Aladdin, Ali Baba, and Sinbad.

The *Arabian Nights,* also called *The Thousand and One Nights,* begins with the story of King Shahriyar, whose wife has been unfaithful. He orders her killed and vows to marry a new maiden each night and have her beheaded the next morning. One of the king's officials has a beautiful and talented daughter, Scheherazade, who insists on being the ruler's bride. Her sister comes to the bedchamber on the wedding night and requests permission for Scheherazade to tell one last story. The king agrees, and Scheherazade tells a tale so entertaining that he allows her to live another day to finish it. One story leads to another, and Scheherazade tells tales for 1,001 nights. By then, the king has fallen in love with her.

The stories of the *Arabian Nights* are folk tales from Arabia, Egypt, India, Persia, and other countries. The work in its present form was written in Arabic about 1500. In the early 1700's, Jean Antoine Galland translated the *Arabian Nights* into French. John Payne and Sir Richard Francis Burton wrote English translations of the collection in the 1880's.   Dick Davis

See also **Burton, Sir Richard Francis; Genie.**

Arabian Peninsula, in southwestern Asia, is a vast land that is largely desert. Saudi Arabia covers most of the peninsula. The other countries on the peninsula are Yemen, Oman, United Arab Emirates, Qatar, and Kuwait. Bahrain, an island country, lies just east of the peninsula.

The Arabian Peninsula has an area of about 1,000,000 square miles (2,600,000 square kilometers). Most of it is dry wasteland. Rain seldom falls in some parts, and temperatures in the interior may rise to 130 °F (54 °C). But in parts of Oman, Saudi Arabia, the United Arab Emirates, and Yemen, rainfall and irrigation support farming. The peninsula is an area of great economic importance because it has large deposits of petroleum.

For detailed information on the Arabian Peninsula, see **Saudi Arabia** and the articles on the region's other countries. See also **Arabs.**   Malcolm C. Peck

Arabian Sea, part of the Indian Ocean, lies between the Arabian Peninsula and India. Iran and Pakistan border it on the north. For location, see **Asia** (map). The Red Sea, Gulf of Aden, Persian Gulf, and Gulf of Oman are arms of the Arabian Sea. Along the Indian coast are the gulfs of Kutch and Khambhat. The Indus, Narmada, and Tapi (or Tapti) rivers empty into the Arabian Sea. The chief islands in the sea are the Laccadive Islands, off the west coast of India; Socotra, northeast of Somalia; and Masira and the Kuria Muria Islands, off Oman's coast. In ancient times, the Arabian Sea was an important shipping route. Goods from the Far East were brought by ship to its western shores and carried inland by camel caravans. Today, tankers pass through the sea to and from the Persian Gulf, where they take on cargoes of crude oil and petroleum products.   Malcolm C. Peck

Arabic language is one of the world's most widely used languages. It is the official language of many Arab countries in the Middle East and northern Africa, including Egypt, Iraq, Jordan, Lebanon, Saudi Arabia, and Syria (see **Language** [map]). It is also a major language in international business and politics.

There are two types of Arabic, *spoken* and *written.* Spoken Arabic, sometimes called vernacular Arabic, consists of *dialects* in different areas of the Arabic-speaking world. These dialects can be roughly divided into Gulf, Iraqi, Levantine, Maghrebi, North Egyptian, Saudi, South Egyptian and Sudanese, and Tunisian. These dialect areas can be subdivided further. Written Arabic, sometimes called classical Arabic, serves as the standard written language of all Arab countries. It is the descendant of the language of the Qur'ān, the sacred book of Islam. Arabs use a spoken form of written Arabic for radio and TV news broadcasts, and in plays and motion pictures. This form also serves as a common spoken language for Arabs who speak different dialects.

Arabic belongs to the Semitic language groups, and is thus related to Aramaic, Hebrew, and Ethiopic. The Arabic alphabet has 28 symbols. The alphabet is written from right to left or from the top of the page to the bottom. Many English words come from the Arabic language. They include *algebra, check, checkmate, lute, magazine,* and *tariff.*

No one knows when Arabic originally developed, but people of the Arabian Peninsula were the first to use it. During the A.D. 600's, Islam spread throughout southwestern Asia and northern Africa, and the Arabic language was introduced in these areas.   Richard W. Hallett

See also **Arabic literature; Arabs** (Language); **Qur'ān; Semitic languages.**

Arabic literature is the literature of people who speak the Arabic language. Arabic is widely spoken in the Middle East and North Africa. Because it is also the language of the Qur'ān, the holy book of Islam, Arabic is read and chanted by millions of Muslims worldwide.

The earliest examples of Arabic literature date from the A.D. 500's, though they were not written down until up to 200 years later. Likewise, the Qur'ān originally had no written form. When the Muslim community in the mid-600's felt the need for a recorded version of the sacred text, the Qur'ān and other memorized texts from the earlier period were written down.

From its origin in the Arabian Peninsula, Islam spread to the west and east from the 600's to the 900's. With the spread of Islam, Arabic literature became known over a vast area, which, at its height, stretched from Spain across North Africa, through the Middle East, and to India. Today, the Arabic-speaking area still extends across North Africa and the Middle East.

Since its beginnings in the 500's, poetry has been the most important form of literary expression. In the 1800's, increased contacts with the West introduced Arab authors to new ideas and forms, including the novel, short story, and drama. Poetry still has a special place in people's hearts and minds, but fiction, and its transfer to motion pictures and videos, has become more popular.

Poetry is described as the "register of the Arabs" in their literary tradition. Poetry is a powerful source of identity within Arab culture. From the beginning, it has been a public form, to be recited and sung. Tribal poets celebrated the qualities of their tribe: courage, loyalty, the beauty of their women, the speed of their horses, and the hardiness of their camels. With the spread of Islam, poetry moved from the tribe in the desert to the court of the ruler in various Islamic cities, such as Damascus and Aleppo, Syria; Cairo, Egypt; Baghdad, Iraq; Fez, Morocco; and Córdoba, Spain. New themes were added, including wine, hunting, philosophical reflections on the individual's role in life, and the glory of the ruler. These themes were mostly expressed in the ancient poetic forms. But new poetic forms emerged, particularly in Spain starting in the 900's, which combined aspects of both Arabic and Spanish poetry. Among the most famous classical poets are Imru' al-Qays, Abu Nuwas, Abu Tammam, al-Mutanabbi, and al-Ma'arri.

In the 1900's, Arab poets imported Western forms, such as free verse and the prose poem. Perhaps most significantly, they felt free to break with tradition and compose their poems in various forms and on a range of topics unavailable to their predecessors. Major poets of the 1900's included Kahlil Gibran and Khalil Hawi from Lebanon; the Syrian-born Lebanese poet Ali Ahmad Said (also known as Adunis or Adonis); Badr Shakir al-Sayyab from Iraq; and Salah 'Abd al-Sabur from Egypt.

Fiction. Several types of stories are found in early Arabic literature. For example, the *maqamah* usually contains short, witty narratives in which two characters visit cities through the Middle East. They observe the way people behave and play tricks on them. From the 1300's, the famous collection of stories called *The Thousand and One Nights,* or *Arabian Nights,* was gathered. These tales were mostly performed in public by storytellers. Written versions were fairly rare until they were translated into Western languages.

In the 1900's, the novel and short story became popular in Arabic literature. The most famous modern fiction writer is Naguib Mahfouz, an Egyptian who in 1988 became the first Arab author to win the Nobel Prize in literature. Other important modern fiction writers include Yusuf Idris and Gamal al-Ghitani from Egypt, al-Tayyib Salih from the Sudan, Emile Habibi from Palestine, Hanan al-Shaykh from Lebanon, and Zakariyah Tamir from Syria.

Drama. Before the 1800's, there were several types of dramatic performances in the Arab world, though few of them were written down. In the 1800's, Arab writers visited Europe, where they saw plays performed. They began the process of transferring the form to the Arab world. One of the first major dramatists was Tawfiq al-Hakim of Egypt. He wrote many plays, ranging from one-act comedies of manners to long tragedies.

Since the 1950's, drama has flourished in many Arab countries. The most famous playwrights include Alfred Farag and Yusuf Idris of Egypt, Sa'dallah Wannus of Syria, Al-Tayyib al-Siddiqi of Morocco, and Yusuf al-'Ani of Iraq.   Roger Allen

Related articles in *World Book* include:

Arabian Nights
Arabic language
Arabs (Literature and the arts)
Avicenna
Egypt (The arts)
Gibran, Kahlil
Ibn Battūta
Qur'ān
Syria (The arts)

Arabic numerals, *AR uh bihk,* also called *Hindu-Arabic numerals,* are the most common symbols used to represent numbers. Every counting number can be expressed in Arabic numerals by using 10 basic symbols, alone or in combination. The basic symbols, called *digits,* are 0, 1, 2, 3, 4, 5, 6, 7, 8, and 9. The position of a digit in an Arabic numeral determines its value—that is, what number each digit represents in terms of ones, tens, hundreds, and so on. For example, the Arabic numeral 237 means 2 hundreds, 3 tens, and 7 ones. The Arabic numeral 7,003 means 7 thousands, no hundreds, no tens, and 3 ones. The digit 0 (zero) fills empty positions so that the other digits have their proper values. See **Decimal system.**

Scholars do not know how Arabic numerals originated. But the symbols for all the digits except zero probably originated with the Hindus in India, possibly as early as the 200's B.C. The Hindus developed the zero sometime after A.D. 600. The word *zero* probably comes from the Arabic form of the Sanskrit word *sunya,* which means *empty* (see **Zero**).

Traders and merchants helped spread the Arabic numeral system across the Mediterranean region, especially into Spain. Beginning in the 800's, merchants and scholars introduced it throughout the rest of Europe. The system came into general use in Europe when the digit symbols were standardized. This was brought about by the invention of the printing press in the mid-1400's.   Nadine L. Verderber

See also **Roman numerals.**

Arabs

Arabs are a large group of people whose native language is Arabic. Arabs also share a common history and culture. Most Arabs live in the Middle East. The Middle East is a large region that spreads across southwestern Asia and northern Africa. Arabs have also migrated to other countries. European countries with large Arab populations include Belgium, France, Germany, the Netherlands, Sweden, and the United Kingdom. In South America,. Argentina and Brazil have many Arab people. So do Canada and the United States.

This article discusses the approximately 250 million Arabs who live in the Arab world. One is a political definition. The other is a *linguistic* (language-related) one. Politically, the Arab world is usually said to include 18 states. In Asia, these states are Iraq, Jordan, Kuwait, Lebanon, Oman, Qatar, Saudi Arabia, Syria, the United Arab Emirates, and Yemen. The Arab states in Africa are Algeria, Bahrain, Egypt, Libya, Mauritania, Morocco, Sudan, and Tunisia. All 18 states are called Arab states because a majority of their people are Arabs and their governments regard themselves as Arab. Three other African countries—Djibouti, Somalia, and Comoros—have only small Arab populations. However, they are sometimes included in this political definition because they belong to an organization of Arab states called the Arab League.

The Palestine Liberation Organization (PLO) is also a member of the Arab League. The organization represents Arabs who are working to establish an Arab state in the West Bank and Gaza areas of historic Palestine. The PLO is a group approved by Arab countries to represent the Palestinians.

In a linguistic sense, the term *Arab world* refers to those areas where most people speak Arabic as their native language. This linguistic definition differs from the political one because some Arab countries include large areas populated by non-Arabs. Some non-Arab countries also have significant Arab minorities. For example, the Kurds of Iraq and the Berbers of northern Africa are non-Arabs living in Arab states. At the same time, many Arabs live within the borders of such non-Arab nations as Iran and Israel. In this article, the term *Arab world* chiefly refers to the countries usually considered Arab in a political sense.

The word *Arab* was probably originally associated with tribes of the Arabian Peninsula and nearby Middle East. These tribes lived a nomadic lifestyle herding camels. By approximately 400 B.C., the word was additionally applied to the settled people in these areas who spoke the Arabic language. The number of Arabs who follow a nomadic way of life gradually shrank over the centuries. By A.D. 850, many settled people in the region identified themselves as Arabs. Arabic had become the standard language of trade and religious discussions by this time. Today, almost all Arabs live in cities, towns, and villages.

Arabs today are united by their culture. Important aspects of that culture include the Arabic language and shared social values. The Arabs also share traditions in literature, art, and music. Religious and historical factors also bind the Arabs together. Most Arabs are Muslims,

Arabs throughout the world are united by language, shared social values, and common cultural traditions. Religious and historical factors also bind the Arabs together. Most Arabs, such as the Iraqis shown worshiping here, are Muslims.

© Martin Adler, Panos Pictures

followers of a religion called Islam. The Arabs' rise to political and cultural importance during the A.D. 600's and 700's was closely associated with the rise of Islam. Another bond among all Arabs is their shared pride in classical Arab and Islamic civilization. The modern Arab identity emerged during the 1800's and 1900's. During that period, most Arab lands were colonies of European powers. Thus, Arabs also share a sense of themselves as former subjects of European rule.

Despite this common heritage, deep differences exist among the Arab countries. For example, many Arab countries possess valuable petroleum deposits. The export of oil has made some countries, such as Kuwait and Qatar, rich. But such countries as Sudan and Yemen remain poor. Some countries, including Jordan and Lebanon, have highly urban societies. Many people in those countries work in industry or commerce. Others, such as Mauritania and Yemen, have largely rural societies.

There many people are farmers or herders. Some countries, such as Lebanon and Tunisia, have been heavily influenced by European and American culture. Others, such as Saudi Arabia, have chosen to maintain traditional culture in many areas of life. These and other differences have caused conflicts, and even wars, within the Arab world.

Land of the Arabs

The Arab world extends over about 5 million square miles (13 million square kilometers). It covers roughly three main regions. These regions are the Arabian Peninsula (sometimes called Arabia); northern Africa; and part of an area called the Fertile Crescent. The Fertile Crescent includes Iraq, Jordan, Lebanon, Syria, and historical Palestine. Palestine today consists of the non-Arab state of Israel and the Arab areas of the Gaza Strip and the West Bank.

The Arab world is made up of 18 countries in the Middle East and across northern Africa. The term usually refers to those areas where people speak Arabic as their native language. Other aspects of culture are also shared.

—— Arab country boundary

▢ Arabic language area

0 ————— 1,000 Miles
0 ————— 1,000 Kilometers

WORLD BOOK map

An Arab designer and television host illustrate the mix of traditional custom and Western influence in modern Arab society. The designer, *on the left,* works with traditional Arab fashions, such as the *hijāb* (headscarf). The TV host, however, has adopted fashions like those worn in Europe and North America.

© Getty Images

Despite the vast area of the Arab world, only a small percentage of it is suitable for settlement. Much of the region is extremely hot and dry, and it has large deserts. These include the Sahara of northern Africa, the deserts of the Arabian Peninsula, and the Syrian Desert. At the other extreme are snow-capped mountains, such as Mount Lebanon in Lebanon and the High Atlas range in Morocco. The vast majority of Arabs live in well-watered hilly regions, fertile river valleys, and coastal areas. The most densely settled area is the Nile Valley and Nile River Delta of Egypt. Virtually all the people of Egypt—almost a third of all Arabs—live in this area. Many of Iraq's people live in the fertile area between the Tigris and Euphrates rivers. The Orontes River valley in Syria is likewise densely populated. Other population centers include the coastal and hill zones of northwestern Africa and of Lebanon, Syria, and parts of Palestine.

Historically, a scarcity of water and the resulting limited farming capacity hampered population growth and economic development in the dry areas of the Middle East. Irrigation has substantially expanded the amount of land that can be farmed in many regions. However, sizable Arab cities have long existed even in dry areas. Cities of the Arab world thrived in the desert climate mainly because they lay at the crossroads of major trade routes that supported urban commercial centers.

Life in the Arab world

About half of all Arabs live in cities and large towns. Many of these people work in factories or in such fields as business, government, and health care. Most other Arabs live in villages or small towns and work as farmers or in local trades. In many Arab countries, the creation of modern road networks has enabled industries to spread to rural areas, and some villagers have jobs in nearby factories. In the oil-producing countries of the Arab world, a large percentage of the male population work in the petroleum industry.

In the past, many Arabs were nomadic herders, or Bedouins, who lived in tents and crossed the desert with their camels, sheep, goats, or cattle in search of water and grazing land. Today, few Arabs are nomads. Livestock herding now resembles ranching rather than nomadic life, and herders usually transport their animals—even camels—by truck.

Language. Arabic belongs to the Semitic group of languages, which also includes Hebrew and Aramaic. Virtually all people who consider themselves Arab speak Arabic as their native language. But different forms of spoken Arabic, called *dialects,* vary considerably from one region to another. A common form of Arabic taught in schools, called Modern Standard Arabic (MSA) in English or *Fus-hā* in Arabic, is often used to communicate across different dialects. MSA is a modernized and simplified version of the classical Arabic of the Qur'ān, the sacred book of Islam. MSA serves as the chief form of written Arabic. It is also the language used in mosques and universities, in public speeches and at other formal events, and in radio and television broadcasts throughout the Arab world. Most Arabs know and use two different forms of Arabic, their own native dialect used in informal settings and MSA for formal occasions and also written communication. Arabs today are increasingly familiar with MSA because of a rise in literacy and exposure to television and other media.

Many other languages are used in the Arab world. For example, many people speak French in the former French colonies of Algeria, Morocco, and Tunisia, where French became the chief language in cultural and political life. Many Arabs also learn English. Many large businesses use English for commercial purposes.

Religion. More than 90 percent of Arabs are Muslims. Most belong to the Sunni branch of Islam. However, significant Shī'ite Muslim communities exist in Iraq, the eastern Arabian Peninsula, Bahrain, and Lebanon. Some Shī'ites live in most other Arab countries. Small numbers of Arabs belong to other Muslim groups. Druses, who follow a religion related to Islam, live mainly in Lebanon, Syria, and Palestine.

Most non-Muslim Arabs are Christians. The Copts of

Egypt belong to one of the oldest Christian groups. Other Christian Arabs belong to various Eastern Orthodox, Roman Catholic, or Protestant churches. They live mainly in Iraq, Jordan, Lebanon, Syria, and Palestine. Most of the Christians in Palestine and adjoining areas are the descendants of the oldest Christian communities in the world. However, in some of these areas their numbers are shrinking, as families move seeking to escape from economic and political hardship.

Family life. Arabs strongly value family ties. Traditionally, Arabs have placed great importance on belonging to family or kinship groups, including the *extended family, clan,* and *tribe.* An extended family includes members of two or more generations, many of them sharing one home. A clan consists of several adjoining families. A tribe might include hundreds of families. In the past, most social and even many business activities took place within these groups. In traditional Arab society, the role of the family is to take care of all its members, including the sick, the elderly, and people with disabilities. In exchange, individuals were expected to be loyal to, and protect, the reputation of their kinship group by behaving properly and maintaining the family honor.

The traditional Arab kinship system emphasizes hospitality as a source of honor. A host who richly entertained a guest raised the reputation of the entire tribe. In the past, parents often sought marriage partners for their children within their own clan or tribe. Even after marriage, men and women remained close to the family into which they were born. If a woman divorced, she could return to her family, who supported her until she remarried. A divorced man returned to his family, and his parents cared for his children.

Today, many traditional kinship ties have loosened, especially among Arabs in cities. The need for some people to move away from the extended family to earn a living has weakened family relationships. Among the poorer countries of the Arab world, many men must find work abroad and leave their homes for long periods. Women now make up a significant part of the labor force in many Arab countries. Increased educational opportunities have also led a number of women to work outside the home. Arab culture has also been affected by European and American ideas about individualism that influence the life and career choices of some men and women. Most Arab states have developed social welfare programs that now provide some of the services formerly provided by the family.

Today, for many Arabs the family continues to be the main source of social and often economic support. Many rural Arabs still live in extended families with several generations in a single household. Arabs in cities often choose to live near their relatives. Many Arab children are raised by grandparents, aunts, uncles, and other relatives in addition to their parents.

Women formed the focus of family life in traditional Arab culture. They supervised the raising of children, the preparation of meals, and family celebrations. An Arab wife was responsible for the running of the household and was usually consulted by her husband, brothers, and sons on important decisions. Today, the role of the mother in the Arab family remains strong.

Education. Arab institutions of higher learning have existed for centuries. For example, al-Azhar University in Cairo, Egypt, was founded in A.D. 970 and is one of the oldest universities in the world. It predates European universities by several hundred years.

Until the 1800's, religious authorities operated most schools in the Arab world. Today, all Arab countries also have free, nonreligious primary and secondary schools that provide public schooling. In most Arab countries, about 90 percent of all children receive at least a primary education. Most Arab governments regard education as key to national development, and they devote large portions of their national budgets to fund education. However, in many poorer Arab states, schools and universities are badly maintained and the level of education remains low. As a result, literacy rates differ from country to country in the Arab world.

Traditionally, some people in the Arab world considered education to be less important for girls than for boys. However, enrollment rates for girls have steadily increased in primary schools and also at the secondary and higher levels across the Arab world. Today, an increasing number of Arab women are studying professional fields, such as engineering, law, and the sciences.

Literature and the arts. Arabic literature began about 1,600 years ago with pre-Islamic poetry that glorified the ideals of tribal customs in the Arabian Desert. This was an oral literature that was not written down until much later. The first major Arabic written work was the Qur'ān, the holy book of Islam, which dates from the 600's. Many scholars regard the Qur'ān as the greatest masterpiece of Arabic literary style. Many Muslims memorized the Qur'ān completely, and it became the model for the classical Arabic language. See Qur'ān.

Classical Arabic literature extends from the time of the Qur'ān to about the mid-1800's and includes a rich tradition in poetry and prose. A highly developed poetic tradition flourished in the Arab world beginning in the 700's. Arabic poets produced works of great lyrical beauty. Some poetic works expressed deep philosophical and religious thought, and others were political in nature. Still others were celebrations of the beauties of nature and the joy of life. Poetry remains especially beloved in modern Arab culture. Nearly all Arabs enjoy reciting and listening to classical and modern verses, and many compose their own poetry. Modern Arab poetry often deals with political themes.

Arabic prose literature covers a wide range of forms and styles. Scholarly works, written in classical Arabic, range from witty essays of social commentary to large volumes on history and philosophy. For example, the *Muqaddimah* of Ibn Khaldun, a historian of the 1300's, examines the rise and fall of civilizations. Prose literature also includes scholarly writings in the fields of theology, interpretation of the Qur'ān, and legal and political theory. Popular prose, usually composed in various local Arab dialects, includes folk epics about heroic figures of the past and the popular tales of the *Arabian Nights.* It also includes proverbs, many of which are still used by Arabs today. Arabic novels and plays have become increasingly popular since the 1900's.

Arabs were important in the flowering of art and architecture throughout the Muslim world from the mid-700's (see **Islamic art**). Traditional crafts, such as metalworking, woodworking, pottery, and glass blowing, still flourish today. Weaving, lacework, and embroidery are also common. Since about 1900, painting and sculpture have become popular in many Arab lands. *Calligraphy,* the art of beautiful handwriting, has long been a favorite form of art in the Arab world.

Traditional Arab music, with its strong rhythmic patterns, is closely linked with the poetic tradition. Arab music is both vocal and instrumental. Many of the musical instruments found in European and American orchestras, including castanets, guitars, lutes, oboes, and tambourines, are derived from Arab instruments. Today, many Arab musicians experiment with new styles, mixing aspects of Arab and non-Arab music or combining styles from different parts of the Arab world. Arab rap music, popular in both Europe and the Arab world, is one example of the globalization of Arab music.

Sciences. Arab culture has made great contributions to world civilization in the sciences. From the 700's through the 1500's, the Arab world was a leading center for scientific learning and discovery. Arabs preserved and studied ancient manuscripts from Greece and Rome and carefully translated them into Arabic. Arab conquests in India and Iran introduced Arab scientists to other scientific developments and to the Indian system of numbers and the decimal numeral system. Arab scholars then added their own new calculations, discoveries, and theories. Arab scientists were especially skilled in the fields of mathematics, including geometry, arithmetic, and algebra. They also made many advances in astronomy, geography, and medicine.

Many major Arabic scientific works were introduced into Europe during the later Middle Ages, the period from about the A.D. 800's through the 1400's. Scholars translated these works into Latin, the language of learning in western Europe. These introductions contributed to the beginnings of the scientific revolution in Europe in the 1500's. Arabs today continue to feel a shared pride in the contributions of Arab culture to science. See **Science** (The Middle Ages).

Food and drink. Arab *cuisine* (style of cooking) varies among regions. In some areas, such as Yemen, the food can be spicy, while in others, such as Egypt, it can be quite bland. Basic foods in the Arab world include beans, chickpeas, lentils, vegetables, and rice. In northern Africa, *couscous* (steamed cracked wheat) replaces rice as a staple. Beans, chickpeas, or eggplants are often cooked into dips. Arabs eat these dips by scooping up mouthfuls with thin bread, called *pita* in Western countries. People also eat eggs; various milk products, especially feta and other cheeses and yogurt; and a wide variety of salads and cooked vegetables. A specialty of Arab cuisine is to stuff vegetables with rice or a mixture of rice, meat, and pine nuts. Olive oil, sesame seed oil, or sesame seed paste add flavor to many dishes. Arabs also enjoy chicken, lamb, beef, and fish that are either baked, grilled, or made into a stew.

Fresh and dried fruits are the main desserts. On special occasions, Arabs serve cookies, cakes, puddings, honey-soaked pastries, such as *baklava,* preserved fruits, and sugared almonds. Water, coffee, and tea—especially mint tea—are the most popular beverages.

Clothing. Because of the hot climate of most Arab lands, both men and women have traditionally worn loose-fitting garments that cover most of the body and head, shielding them from the sun. Traditional Arab clothing for men consists of a full-length robe, or a cloak over some combination of shirt, vest, and skirt. Traditional headcovers for men were the turban, skullcap, or *kaffiyeh*—a loose, folded headscarf, often held in place by a decorative cord. In the Arab countries surrounding the Persian Gulf, most men dress for work or for public occasions in *kaffiyehs* (which they call *ghutrahs)* and traditional robes called *dishdashahs.* In Egypt, a man's traditional robe is called a *galabiyyah,* which is usually worn with a skullcap. Some men combine elements of modern and traditional dress, such as wearing a sports jacket over a robe. However, in the towns and cities, many men today wear clothing like that worn in Europe and the Americas, such as pants, shirt, coat, and a tie.

In most Arab countries, women have a choice of wearing clothing like that worn in Europe and the Americas, or a combination of a modest floor-length garment and a headscarf. This traditional style of dressing is usually known as *Islamic dress* or the *hijāb,* from a word that in some regions means *headscarf.* Since the 1970's, many Arab women have preferred to wear the hijāb and rejected European and American styles. In Saudi Arabia, women are required by law to wear the `*abbāyah,* a black mantle and head covering, in public.

Architecture. Arabs developed new forms and styles of architecture. The mosque form originated from the style of the prophet Muhammad's house, built in the 600's in Medina, now in Saudi Arabia. Arabs developed new technologies for building mosques, castles, fortresses, and private dwellings. The traditional Arab house was a mud-walled structure with an enclosed courtyard. Today, many modern Arab homes, both urban and rural, open to a private or semiprivate central courtyard, with blank walls that face the street. The dwellings are constructed in this way to ensure the privacy of the inhabitants.

Most rural Arabs live in one- or two-story houses of brick, mud brick, or stone. Mud-brick architecture, in particular, takes a wide variety of forms, from simple rectangular structures to the beehive-shaped houses of northern Syria (see **Syria** [picture]). Mud brick is cheap and easy to use, and it provides excellent insulation

© Wendy Chan, Getty Images

Traditional Arab architecture places great importance on privacy. Many houses are constructed around a central courtyard, like the homes in this neighborhood in Muscat, Oman.

against heat and cold. However, concrete and cinder blocks are increasingly replacing mud brick as building materials in Arab countries.

Traditional forms of Arab architecture still exist in large cities. The distinctive many-storied mud-brick or stone buildings in Yemen and southern Saudi Arabia rank among the world's first "skyscrapers" (see **Yemen** [picture]). However, most modern buildings in Arab cities use new materials and styles. Apartment buildings are more common in towns and cities. Office buildings made of cement, metal, and glass stand in all large cities.

Economy. For centuries, the Arab world was a crossroads of international commerce. Arab and other merchants carried such goods as spices, textiles, porcelain, metalwork, and glasswork between Asia, Africa, and Europe. Beginning in the 1700's, the expansion of European commerce and industry led to economic decline in the Arab world. Then, during the 1900's, petroleum became one of the world's most important economic resources. Together, the petroleum-producing Arab countries hold about three-fifths of the world's reserves of oil. Petroleum has brought enormous prosperity to some Arab governments, permitting rapid improvement in education, health care, transportation, and other services.

The Arab countries rich in petroleum include Iraq, Kuwait, Libya, Oman, Qatar, Saudi Arabia, and the United Arab Emirates. In addition to petroleum and natural gas, most of these countries also export petroleum-derived chemical products. Port cities in Kuwait, Qatar, Saudi Arabia, and especially the United Arab Emirates are hubs of international commerce. Other Arab countries have smaller oil reserves and petroleum industries, and some have none at all. Their exports consist mainly of raw materials and agricultural products. Several Arab countries are members of the World Trade Organization (WTO), which works to promote freer trade in goods and services throughout the world.

Manufacturing is developing in the Arab world. Jordan, Lebanon, Morocco, Tunisia, and Egypt receive a significant amount of income from manufacturing. In some of the poorer Arab countries, individuals must go abroad to other Arab countries or to Europe to work and send money to their families at home. This money makes up a significant portion of the economies of some Arab countries.

A scarcity of fresh water has limited the development of the agricultural economy throughout the Arab world. Large-scale irrigation projects have increased the amount of fresh water for agricultural use, allowing formerly dry regions to be turned into farmland. However, these large projects can be harmful to the environment by depleting natural *aquifers* (underground water resources). Modern *desalinization* technologies that process seawater to remove salt have also increased the supply of fresh water. But these technologies are expensive and sometimes unreliable.

History

The Arabs before Islam. References to Arabs as nomads and camel herders of northern Arabia appear in writings dating back to the 800's B.C. The name *Arab* was later applied to all inhabitants of the Arabian Peninsula, and others in Syria and Iraq who spoke Arabic. Arabs at this time were a tribal society with groups organized by family lineages that all traced their origins back to a common ancestor. Politically, tribal society in the Arabian Peninsula was fragmented. Tribes typically broke up into smaller clans that roamed the desert, occasionally stopping at oases and wells for food and water. About the 400's B.C., some Arab families established several small states in the border regions of the Arabian Peninsula at centers for the overland caravan trade. One of these states centered in Petra, in what is now Jordan, founded by Arabs known as Nabataeans. The Roman Empire conquered Petra in A.D. 106, but it continued to flourish until the early A.D. 200's. Another state centered around the oasis of Palmyra in the Syrian Desert. Palmyra also fell under Roman domination by about A.D. 160.

The rise of Islam and the Arab empire. The prophet Muhammad, one of history's most important

AP/Wide World

The petroleum industry has brought enormous prosperity to some Arab governments and employs a large portion of the Arab population. Arab lands hold about three-fifths of the world's reserves of oil.

figures, was born in the Arab city of Mecca about A.D. 570. Muslims believe that God revealed the teachings of Islam to Muhammad, who began preaching about 610. *Islam* is an Arabic word that means *surrender* or *submission*. Today, Islam is the world's second largest religion, next to Christianity.

Muhammad preached a *monotheistic religion* (belief in one God), like that of Jews and Christians. He fled with his followers north to Medina, then called Yathrib, in 622 when pagan Arabs of Mecca opposed him. This year became known as the year of the *Hijra* or *Hijrah* (migration), and later became the first year of the Islamic calendar. In Medina, Muhammad organized his followers into a community. This community quickly grew into a state that controlled much of the Arabian Peninsula. Today, Mecca and Medina are Islam's two holiest cities.

After Muhammad's death in 632, Muslim rulers called *caliphs* headed the Islamic state. Armies under the caliphs soon seized the rest of Arabia and an area stretching from Egypt to Iran. The result was a vast and expanding new empire dominated by Arabian Muslims. Islam was the official religion of the empire, and Arabic was its official language.

For several hundred years, the empire was dominated politically by three families from Muhammad's tribe of Quraysh: the Umayyads, the `Abbāsids, and the `Ālids. A sense of Arab identity seems to have emerged in connection with the spread of Islam. This sense of "Arabness" resulted partly from use of the Arabic language and partly from pride in the Islamic empire. It also stemmed from identification with the rich culture that developed under the Umayyads and `Abbāsids.

From the 1000's to the 1500's, parts of the eastern Arab lands were conquered by several waves of non-Arab invaders. Chief among these were the Seljuk Turks and the Mongols, who executed the last `Abbāsid caliph in Baghdad in 1258. Northern Africa remained in the hands of local groups, mainly Arabs and Berbers.

Ottoman and European rule. By the mid-1500's, nearly all Arab territories had come under the control of the Ottoman Empire, centered in what is now Turkey. Even though the Ottoman Empire stretched far into Europe, the Arab lands were an important part of it. Many high-ranking Ottoman officials were of Arab origin, and these Arabs regarded themselves as Ottomans and Muslims, not as Arabs.

Beginning in the mid-1700's, the rapid economic and military development of much of Europe gave European states an advantage over the Ottomans. In their efforts to modernize their economies, the Ottomans often developed large debts to European financiers. The financiers then sometimes persuaded their governments to seize economic or political control of Ottoman possessions to ensure repayment of the debts. In other cases, European nations simply invaded Ottoman territories. France began its occupation of Algeria in 1830, and it controlled Tunisia and Morocco by the early 1900's. Beginning in the late 1800's, the United Kingdom took over Egypt and Sudan. Italy gained control of Libya in 1912. By the start of World War I (1914-1918), all of northern Africa was under European control. The United Kingdom also controlled many of the affairs of the small Arab states surrounding the Persian Gulf.

After the Ottoman Empire entered World War I on the side of Germany in 1914, the United Kingdom helped stir up an Arab nationalist revolt against the Ottomans. The United Kingdom promised the leaders of the revolt that it would recognize an independent Arab government in former Ottoman territories after the war. But the United Kingdom also made a secret agreement with France to divide these territories into British and French spheres of influence after the war. When World War I ended in 1918, the League of Nations—a forerunner of the United Nations—divided the Arab areas still held by the Ottomans between the United Kingdom and France. In turn, the United Kingdom and France were expected to supervise these lands—known as *mandated territories*—and help them attain self-government. The United Kingdom received mandates over Iraq and Palestine, which included present-day Jordan and Israel. France received what are now Syria and Lebanon.

Arab nationalism was part of a nationalist idea that spread through much of the world during the 1800's and 1900's. Its central belief was that humanity was divided into distinct nations or peoples. The members of each nation shared a common history and language, and had a historic claim to a particular homeland.

Among most Arabs, Islam remained the main binding force for many years. Significant Arab nationalist movements did not develop until the early 1900's. The movements took two forms. In some cases, nationalist feeling arose around particular areas or regions as a form of patriotism. In others, it centered on factors of common descent and the shared Arabic language as sources of unity. This form of nationalism later grew into a movement for Arab political unification called *Pan-Arabism*.

Struggles for independence. By the early 1920's, the population of the Arab world had been split into more than 15 European colonies and *protectorates* (territories under partial control). The influence of the colonial powers divided these colonies politically, economically, and, increasingly, culturally. Because of these divisions, the goal of Pan-Arab unification became less important than that of independence within each colony.

Most of the Arab lands won their independence in stages after World War II ended in 1945. Some did so peacefully, others after a struggle. The last colonies to become independent—British-controlled Bahrain, Qatar, and the states that now make up the United Arab Emirates—did so in 1971.

Arabs today

Arab countries emerged from colonial rule as free and independent states, but most continue to struggle with many problems. Modern Arab countries face significant challenges that include a lack of unity in the Arab world, economic inequality between and within Arab states, the Arab-Israeli conflict, religious and ethnic conflicts, and a lack of democratically elected governments. The Arab world has a significant role in world affairs due to its location and the petroleum reserves that it owns. As a result, foreign interest and foreign involvement in Arab politics represent another challenge that modern Arabs must face. Many conflicts arise between Islamic tradition and the influence of the West—that is, Europe and the United States.

The search for unity among all Arab countries has not been successful. Several times, two or three Arab countries have attempted to unite into a single state. For example, Syria and Egypt joined to form the United Arab Republic in 1958, but the union ended when Syria withdrew in 1961. In 1945, seven countries founded the Arab League. Today, 21 countries and the Palestine Liberation Organization (PLO) belong to the league. The organization works to promote closer political, economic, and social relations among its members.

The Arab-Israeli conflict can best be understood as a struggle between two nationalist movements. Both movements claim Palestine as their homeland. During World War I, British officials had suggested to Arab leaders that Palestine would be included in areas to be granted Arab self-determination. The British, however, also promised Palestine to leaders of the Zionist movement. The Zionists sought to make Palestine an independent Jewish nation. The conflicting promises to Arabs and Zionists regarding Palestine contributed to a struggle between the two nationalist movements.

More than 700,000 Arabs were forced to flee historic Palestine following the creation of the Jewish state of Israel in 1948. This set off hostilities that led to five wars between Israel and Arab countries from 1948 to 1982. The conflict continues today. Egypt and Israel signed a peace treaty in 1979. In 1994, Jordan and Israel signed a declaration that formally ended a state of war between the two countries. But Israel has not made final peace agreements with Syria or with the PLO. The long and bloody struggle between the Palestinian people and the state of Israel has brought great suffering, especially to the Palestinians. It remains a problem of major importance to world peace.

Economic inequality. The different economic needs and political goals of Arab states have at times made them bitter rivals. The wealth of some Arab countries from petroleum exports has contributed to tension. Petroleum-poor states resent the wealth of their richer neighbors and seek to share in the oil income. Disagreements have also occurred among petroleum exporters over pricing and production policies.

Disagreements regarding petroleum wealth helped set off an invasion of Kuwait by Iraq in 1990. Iraq's president, Saddam Hussein, wished to gain control of Kuwait's vast oil reserves. The subsequent war severely divided Arab states. Several Arab countries, including Saudi Arabia and Egypt, took part in a coalition led by the United States that fought the Persian Gulf War of 1991 and expelled Iraqi forces from Kuwait.

Religious and ethnic clashes. Territorial ambitions or religious differences between Arab countries or between groups within the countries themselves have led to other clashes in the Arab world. For example, a long and bloody conflict in Lebanon began in 1975. It reflected the struggle for political power between Christian and Muslim religious communities. Both the Christian groups and the Muslim groups also began fighting among themselves. The civil war in Lebanon did not end until 1991.

In Iraq, old ethnic hostilities between Iraqi Arabs and Kurds emerged after the Persian Gulf War of 1991 and the Iraq War (2003-2011). The Kurds are Iraq's largest non-Arab ethnic minority. Old religious tensions between Iraqi Sunni and Shi`ite Muslims also erupted following the war.

Lack of democracy. A small number of powerful people dominate political life in most Arab lands. The ruling group may consist of military leaders or wealthy individuals of prominent tribal background. The European powers took some limited steps toward developing institutions of democratic government in their Arab colonies. But they kept such institutions from becoming strong enough to threaten their colonial rule. They also failed to create economic or educational systems that would stimulate the growth of a middle class. As a result, most independent Arab states lack strong institutions of multiparty, civilian government.

In late 2010 and 2011, antigovernment protests erupted in several Arab countries. The protests were fueled in part by poor economic conditions and accusations of government corruption. Protesters clashed with government forces in Bahrain, Egypt, Libya, Syria, Tunisia, and Yemen. The presidents of Egypt, Tunisia, and Yemen stepped down. In Libya, the protests led to an armed rebellion that overthrew Mu'ammar al-Qadhāfī.

Relations with Europe and the United States. In 2003, the United States led a coalition of nations in a war that toppled the Iraqi regime of Saddam Hussein. Coalition troops invaded the country from Kuwait in the south. However, most other Arab countries opposed this war. Many Arabs saw the war as an intervention by the United States in Arab affairs. The war contributed to widespread feelings of anti-Americanism among citizens of Arab countries and other, non-Arab Islamic states. Many nationalist Arabs blame their current lack of political rights on the long periods of oppressive European colonialism. They also blame the United States for its support of Saudi Arabia and other undemocratic regimes, and for its support of Israel.

Activist Islamist movements in the Arab world have long seen European and American influences on traditional Arab Islamic culture as a threat. Such movements have also expressed frustration with the lack of democracy and the economic inequality in the Arab world. They also are frustrated with the ongoing Arab-Israeli conflict. Islamist movement groups often blame foreign powers, especially the United States, as the source of many or most of the problems Arabs face today.

Activist Islamist movements seek political, social, and economic reform. The goal of many movement groups is to ensure that Arab governments represent and uphold Islamic morality and Islamic values of social and economic justice. Some groups, however, have engaged in armed attacks against their own governments and sometimes against foreigners. Americans and Europeans often refer to activist Islamist movements as *militant Islam* or *radical Islam*. Some government leaders and media have tended to label all Islamist movement groups as terrorist organizations. Others point out, however, that only a small number of such groups use violence or terrorism to achieve their goals.

One terrorist network, known as *al-Qāʿida*, also spelled *al-Qāʿidah* or *al-Qaeda*, supports the worldwide activities of Muslim extremists. Al-Qāʿida is an Arabic term that means *the base.* Its founder and leader was Osama bin Laden, a Saudi-born millionaire. Al-Qāʿida believes in the overthrow of governments of Muslim countries that fail to follow Islamic law. It also considers the United States to be a primary enemy of Islam.

In 2001, members of al-Qā'ida launched terrorist attacks that destroyed the World Trade Center in New York City and damaged the Pentagon Building near Washington, D.C. Other terrorist attacks attributed to al-Qā'ida have occurred since. Most leaders in the Arab world have denounced these crimes and promised cooperation in helping bring the terrorists to justice. Many prominent Muslim clerics also issued *fatwās* (legal opinions) that these attacks violated Islamic law. Bin Laden was killed in a U.S. military raid in Pakistan in 2011.

Other challenges. Arabs today take great pride in their cultural heritage but face major challenges. The problems of poverty, overpopulation, poor health care, and inadequate educational facilities are severe in some Arab states. In addition, the oil-rich states must plan carefully for the day when oil reserves run dry. Many of these countries are working to develop other economic activities that can help maintain their growth in the post-petroleum age. Finally, Arabs also must deal with powerful conflicts between Islamic tradition and the challenges of modernity.   Barbara R. F. Stowasser

Related articles. See the separate articles on the countries where Arabs live. See also the following articles:

Biographies

Other related articles

Outline

I. **Land of the Arabs**
II. **Life in the Arab world**
   A. Language
   B. Religion
   C. Family life
   D. Education
   E. Literature and the arts
   F. Sciences
   G. Food and drink
   H. Clothing
   I. Architecture
   J. Economy
III. **History**
IV. **Arabs today**

Additional resources

Baali, Fuad. *Arab Unity and Disunity: Past and Present.* Univ. Pr. of Am., 2004.
Hammond, Andrew. *Pop Culture Arab World!* ABC-CLIO, 2004.
Rubin, Barry. *The Long War for Freedom: The Arab Struggle for Democracy in the Middle East.* Wiley, 2006.
Sowell, Kirk H. *The Arab World: An Illustrated History.* Hippocrene, 2004.

Arachne, *uh RAK nee,* was a skilled weaver in Greek mythology. She boasted that she could weave fabrics more beautiful than those woven by Athena, the goddess of arts and crafts. Athena, disguised as an old woman, warned Arachne not to be so boastful. When Arachne scorned her advice, Athena revealed herself as a goddess and accepted Arachne's challenge to a weaving contest.

Athena wove a tapestry that pictured mortals being punished by the gods for their pride. Arachne's work showed the shocking misbehavior of gods and goddesses. When Athena saw that Arachne's work was as beautiful as her own, the goddess angrily ripped the fabric. As Arachne attempted to hang herself in terror, Athena took pity on her and transformed her into a spider. Arachne's skill survived in the spinning of webs by spiders.   Nancy Felson

Arachnid, *uh RAK nihd,* is the name of any member of a class of small, insectlike, land animals. The best-known arachnids are spiders, ticks, mites, scorpions, and daddy longlegs, or harvestmen. Arachnids, unlike insects, have no wings. Their bodies are divided into two main parts, the abdomen and the *cephalothorax,* which consists of the head and the thorax joined together. Insects, however, have three main body parts: the head, the thorax, and the abdomen. Arachnids have four pairs of legs but have no *antennae* (feelers). Insects have antennae, but only three pairs of legs.

Arachnids have from one to six pairs of simple eyes. Some species are eyeless. Unlike insects, arachnids have no *compound eyes* (eyes that are made up of many smaller eyes crowded together). Some arachnids breathe like insects by means of air tubes. Others have breathing organs somewhat like lungs, called *book lungs.* These are small sacs within the abdomen, connected with the outer air by small openings. Within each sac are many layers of tissue resembling the leaves of a book. The air enters the sac through the small openings and furnishes oxygen to the blood flowing through the leaves. Most spiders have air tubes and book lungs.

Some arachnids are harmful to people. Certain of them can inflict poisonous bites or stings. Others suck the blood of human beings and animals, and may carry serious diseases. Many arachnids are helpful to people because they eat harmful insects.   James E. Carico

Scientific classification. Arachnids make up the class Arachnida.

Related articles in *World Book* include:

Arafat, *AHR uh FAT,* **Yasir,** *YAHS uhr* (1929-2004), was head of the Palestine Liberation Organization (PLO) from 1969 to 2004 and president of the Palestinian Authority (PA) from 1996 to 2004. His first name was also spelled Yasser. The PLO is a political body that represents the Palestinian people. Its goal is to establish an independent Palestinian state in the West Bank and Gaza Strip, territories fully or partly occupied by Israel since 1967. Israel, the Gaza Strip, and the West Bank make up the historic region of Palestine in southwest Asia. The PA was created in 1994 to govern Palestinian-controlled parts of the West Bank and Gaza Strip.

Arafat probably was born on Aug. 24, 1929, in Cairo, Egypt, to Palestinian parents. He claimed he was born in Jerusalem. His full name was Mohammed Abdel-Raouf Arafat al-Qudwa al-Husseini. He acquired the nickname Yasir, which means *easygoing,* as a teenager. In 1956, he earned a degree in civil engineering at King Fuad I University (later Cairo University). In the 1950's, he helped organize Fatah, a guerrilla group that opposed Israeli control of territory in Palestine. Arab leaders established the PLO in 1964 to represent the Palestinians. In 1967, Israel defeated Arab countries in a war and began occupying the West Bank and Gaza Strip. After the war, Palestinian guerrilla groups gained control of the PLO. The largest was Fatah, led by Arafat. In 1969, Arafat was elected chairman of the PLO Executive Committee, the highest PLO post. Fatah and other PLO groups repeatedly attacked Israeli targets and, in turn, Israel attacked PLO and guerrilla bases.

In 1974, Arafat became the first person to address the United Nations (UN) General Assembly as a leader of a liberation movement rather than a UN member state. That year, the UN recognized the PLO as the representative of the Palestinians.

In 1982, Israel invaded Lebanon, where the PLO was based. Arafat and his supporters were forced to leave their bases in Lebanon. They then moved to Tunisia.

The PLO and Israel agreed in 1993 to the creation of the Palestinian Authority to govern parts of the West Bank and Gaza Strip. In the 1990's, Israeli-PLO agreements led to the withdrawal of Israeli troops from most of the Gaza Strip and many cities and towns of the West Bank. As the Israelis withdrew, the PA took control of these areas. In 1994, Arafat moved to the Gaza Strip, marking the end of a 27-year exile from Palestine. That year, Arafat and the Israeli leaders Yitzhak Rabin and Shimon Peres shared the Nobel Peace Prize for their peace efforts. In 1996, Arafat was elected president of the PA.

In 2000, Israeli-PLO peace talks broke down, and a period of violence began between Israelis and Palestinians. Arafat's position was weakened. In 2003, he agreed to appoint a prime minister to assume some of his executive duties. Arafat died on Nov. 11, 2004.   Jamal R. Nassar

See also **Fatah; Palestine Liberation Organization; Palestinian Authority.**

Aragon. See **Castile and Aragon.**

Aral Sea, *AR uhl,* is a large saltwater lake in Kazakhstan and Uzbekistan. It is one of the world's largest inland bodies of water. Since the early 1960's, however, irrigation has caused the lake to shrink to about a tenth of its former size. The lake now covers about 2,600 square miles (6,700 square kilometers). It contains many islands.

Leslie Dienes

Aramaic language, *AR uh MAY ihk,* is a language of the Middle East. It is a Semitic language and belongs to

© Barthelemy, Sipa Press
Yasir Arafat

the Afro-Asian family of languages, along with Hebrew and Arabic. The earliest evidence of Aramaic dates from about 900 B.C. Jesus Christ and his disciples spoke Aramaic. Aramaic is still spoken by Assyrian Christians in isolated areas of Syria, Turkey, Iraq, and Iran. The long history of Aramaic and the wide extent of its use have resulted in many dialects.

The earliest samples of Aramaic writing date from about 900 B.C. Parts of the Biblical books of Ezra and Daniel and some of the ancient manuscripts known as the Dead Sea Scrolls were written in Aramaic. A number of major Jewish works of the period from A.D. 1 to 600 were composed in Aramaic.   Richard W. Hallett

See also **Hebrew language; Semitic languages.**

Aramid is a manufactured fiber that is chemically similar to nylon but is stronger by weight than steel. Like nylon fibers, aramids are made of chemical compounds called *amides.* The amides are linked to *aromatic rings* (rings of six carbon atoms) to form long, chainlike molecules called *polymers.* But unlike the amides in nylons, at least 85 percent of the amides in aramids are attached directly to two aromatic rings. This arrangement results in a stronger and more heat-resistant fiber than nylon.

Aramids are used in many products, including tires, parachutes, reinforced tape, and bulletproof vests. They are also used as a reinforcing material in boat hulls and the bodies of aircraft. Aramids are manufactured under the trade names Kevlar and Nomex.   Richard V. Gregory

Arapaho Indians, *uh RAP uh hoh,* are a tribe who once hunted on the Great Plains of North America. They moved about frequently, living in tipis and following the buffalo herds, their major source of food. At first, the Arapaho fought to keep white settlers from taking their hunting lands. But the Arapaho made peace in the 1860's and 1870's and moved to reservations.

The Arapaho religion involved belief in a powerful spirit world. The most important religious ceremony was the *sun dance* (see **Sun dance**). The Arapaho also had two sacred objects, a ceremonial pipe called the *flat pipe* and a wooden hoop called the *wheel.* The men belonged to special clubs that performed sacred ceremo-

The Aral Sea lies in Kazakhstan and Uzbekistan. The diversion, from feeder rivers, of water for irrigation has caused the sea to shrink greatly since the 1960's.

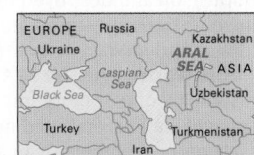

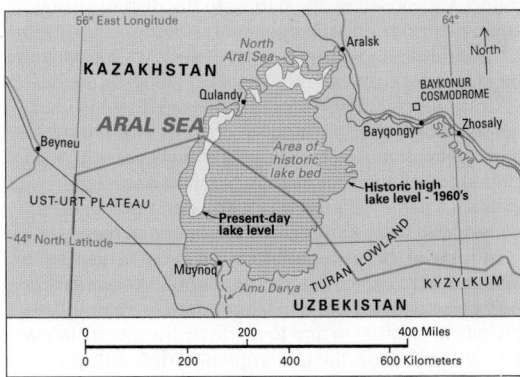

WORLD BOOK maps

nies and enforced tribal laws. A women's group that was called the Buffalo Society also carried out certain rituals.

Today, there are about 8,000 Arapaho. They have split into three groups: (1) the Southern Arapaho of Oklahoma; (2) the Northern Arapaho of Wyoming; and (3) the Gros Ventre (see **Gros Ventre Indians**). The Arapaho work in farming, ranching, and other occupations. The Northern Arapaho also receive income from oil and natural gas obtained from their land.   Stanton K. Tefft

Ararat, *AR uh rat,* was the country where, according to the Bible, Noah's ark landed after the Deluge. The Biblical story is told in Genesis 6-8. Ararat was the area surrounding Lake Van in ancient Armenia, now part of Turkey. Many people believe that Noah's ark came to rest on Mount Massis, the tallest mountain in Ararat, known today as Mount Ararat. However, the Aramaic and Syriac translations of the story speak of the ark landing in the mountains of Kurdistan, southeast of Lake Van. The land of Ararat is also mentioned in II Kings 19:37 and Isaiah 37:38. These passages tell that the sons of the Assyrian king Sennacherib fled to Ararat after they killed their father. See also **Armenia** (map); **Noah.**   Jacob Neusner

Araucanian Indians. See Mapuche.

Arawak Indians, *AH rah wahk,* were the first Indians that Christopher Columbus met in the Americas in 1492. The Arawak lived on the Caribbean Islands. Arawak who lived in a broad region of the northern Caribbean—including much of what is now Cuba and the islands of the Bahamas, Hispaniola, Jamaica, and Puerto Rico—are also called Taíno Indians. Other groups of Indians speaking Arawakan languages lived in the Amazon River Basin and other parts of South America.

The villages were organized into larger units and ruled by chiefs called *caciques* (pronounced *kuh SEEKS).* The Arawak grew corn, yams, cotton, and *cassava,* a root crop. Their diet included fish, shellfish, and the meat of iguanas, sea turtles, and a rodent called the *hutia.*

Many Arawak died from diseases brought to the Americas by European explorers. Spanish colonists forced the Arawak to mine gold or perform other physical labor. This forced labor further reduced the Arawak population and destroyed their traditional way of life. By the mid-1500's, nearly all the Arawak Indians of the Caribbean had died.   Samuel M. Wilson

Arbitration, *AHR buh TRAY shuhn,* is the judging of a dispute by one or more impartial people whose decision will be final and binding. The judges are called *arbitrators* or members of an *arbitration board.* The arbitrators are chosen by the parties to the dispute, or by some neutral agency designated by them. The decision of the arbitrators is known as an *award.* Arbitration may be employed between individuals, groups, or nations.

Commercial arbitration is a process in which businesses submit their disputes to one or more arbitrators. It has been practiced in Europe for many years. In the United States, the American Arbitration Association maintains panels of arbitrators. The decisions of these panels have been enforced by the courts of many states.

Industrial, or labor, arbitration is the settlement of disputes between employers and labor. In *voluntary arbitration,* management and labor agree to submit the dispute to arbitration and to abide by the award. In *compulsory arbitration,* the government orders a dispute to be submitted to arbitration because the dispute affects the public interest. Compulsory arbitration is usually ordered only after voluntary methods have failed. Most industrial disputes involve fixing wages, hours, and conditions of labor. Arbitration is sometimes a way of settling grievances and avoiding or ending strikes and lockouts.

In the United States, arbitration has been used most widely in disputes over existing contracts, especially in the railroad industry. In 1963, Congress prevented a national railroad strike over work rules by requiring compulsory arbitration. It was the first compulsory arbitration law ever passed in peacetime.

International arbitration is the settlement of disputes that arise between two or more nations. The dispute is submitted to judges chosen because of their knowledge of international affairs. These judges may be members of the Permanent Court of Arbitration. Their decisions are regarded as binding.   Daniel Quinn Mills

See also **International relations; Labor movement** (Handling labor disputes); **Peace.**

Arbor Day is a day set apart for planting trees. It is observed especially by schoolchildren. All states in the United States celebrate it. Most states in the southern part of the country celebrate it at various times from November to March. Northern states celebrate it in April or May. National Arbor Day is the last Friday in April. Many other countries also celebrate Arbor Day by planting trees, or they have other special days or weeks for tree planting. In Canada, Maple Leaf Day falls on the last Wednesday in September during National Forest Week.

Arbor Day began in Nebraska. Julius Sterling Morton, a newspaper publisher, realized that trees would enrich the soil and conserve moisture in it. Through his efforts, April 10, 1872, was set aside as Nebraska's first Arbor Day. The Nebraska Legislature later made Arbor Day a legal holiday and changed its date to April 22, Morton's birthday.   Jack Santino

See also **Morton, Julius Sterling; Nebraska** (Places to visit); **Tree** (Planting and caring for trees).

Arboretum, *AHR buh REE tuhm,* is an outdoor laboratory where trees, shrubs, and other woody plants are grown under natural conditions. Most arboretums are open to the public and have been the means of developing a widespread appreciation of this kind of landscaped botanical garden. Research at arboretums has led to improved methods of growing hardier and more beautiful trees and shrubs. Most arboretums also have trial sections where experiments are made in raising new and rare plants. Arboretums are dedicated mainly to trees, but sometimes special sections are devoted to such plants as vines and shrubs.   Richard C. Schlesinger

Arbus, Diane, *dee AN* (1923-1971), was an American photographer known for her powerful pictures of society's outsiders. Arbus photographed people on the streets of New York City, sideshow freaks, and people who dress in the clothing of the opposite sex. The often grotesque black-and-white images created a feeling in the viewer that was both sympathetic to the subjects and eerie.

Arbus was born Diane Nemerov on March 14, 1923, into a wealthy family in New York City. Her brother was the American poet and critic Howard Nemerov. Diane married photographer Allan Arbus in 1941. She suffered from depression late in her life and committed suicide on July 26, 1971, at the age of 48.   John Pultz

Arbutus. See Trailing arbutus.

Arc, in geometry. See **Circle** (Parts of a circle).

Arc, Joan of. See Joan of Arc, Saint.

Arc de Triomphe, *ahrk duh tree AWNF,* in Paris, is the largest triumphal arch in the world. The arch stands 162 feet (49.5 meters) high. It is known as the Arch of Triumph in English. It stands at the western end of the broad avenue called the Champs Élysées. See **Paris** (picture: The Arc de Triomphe; map: Central Paris).

Emperor Napoleon I commissioned the arch in 1806 as a memorial to his imperial armies. It was designed by the architect Jean-François Chalgrin, who patterned it after the triumphal arches of ancient Rome. The arch was left unfinished when Napoleon lost power in 1814. It was completed in 1836. The structure is an example of the Neoclassical style of the late 1700's and early 1800's. The arch is decorated with relief sculpture, notably the group of figures called *La Marseillaise* (1836) by François Rude. The grave of France's Unknown Soldier of World War I lies beneath the arch.   Leland M. Roth

Arcadia, *ahr KAY dee uh,* a *prefecture* (political division) of present-day Greece, was an important region in ancient times. About 90,000 people live in this region of mountains and fertile valleys in the Peloponnesus (Greece's southern peninsula). Arcadia was the only part of the Peloponnesus not overrun by Dorians in the 1100's B.C. In the 500's B.C., Arcadia joined the Peloponnesian League, a military alliance of Peloponnesian cities led by Sparta. Arcadian cities were loyal to Sparta until 369 B.C., when they formed their own defensive league. The Arcadian League soon split, but Macedonia and then the Achaean and Aetolian leagues protected Arcadia.   John J. Baxevanis

Arcaro, *ahr KAIR oh,* **Eddie** (1916-1997), an American jockey, rode 4,779 winners in 31 years of racing. Arcaro became the first jockey to win the Kentucky Derby five times (see **Kentucky Derby**). He was also the first to win the Triple Crown (Kentucky Derby, Preakness, and Belmont Stakes) twice. He won it riding Whirlaway in 1941 and Citation in 1948. Edward Arcaro was born on Feb. 19, 1916, in Newport, Kentucky. He retired in 1962. His purses totaled $30,039,543, a record until 1964. Arcaro died on Nov. 14, 1997.   William F. Reed

Arch is a curved structure that supports or strengthens a building. Almost all arches span openings and support weight above them. Others are enclosed in walls.

Most arches are made of stone, brick, concrete, or steel. Arches of stone or brick consist of wedge-shaped blocks called *voussoirs.* During the construction of most such arches, the blocks are supported by a wooden frame. The last block to be inserted is the *keystone,* the center stone at the top. The pressure of each side of the arc against the keystone supports the arch when the frame is removed. In addition, the arch is supported on both sides by masonry or by other arches to keep it from collapsing under the weight above.

The first people to fully utilize the arch were architects of ancient Rome. During the 300's B.C., they began to use semicircular arches to build aqueducts and bridges. Later, they also constructed *triumphal arches* to honor their leaders. Pointed arches were developed during the Middle Ages. Medieval architects arranged arches in rows to form passageways called *arcades.* They also built arched roofs called *vaults.* Arches shaped like

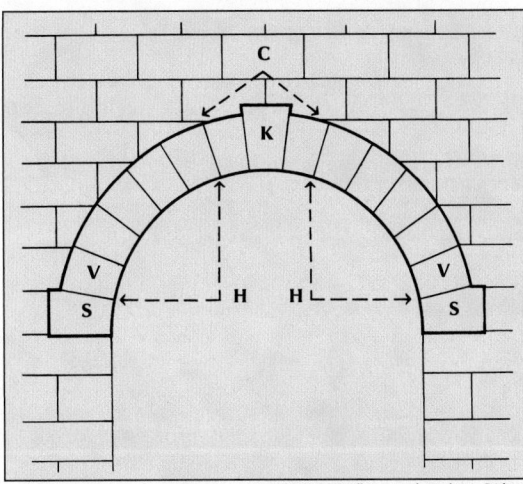

WORLD BOOK illustration by Arthur L. Grebetz

An arch is made up of parts that support one another. Wedge-shaped arch stones called *voussoirs* (labeled *V*) make up most of the arch, rising from *springers (S)* to the *keystone (K)* at the top. The *crown (C)* is the highest part of the arch. The *haunches (H)* are the sides of the arch, from the crown to the springers.

horseshoes are common in Islamic architecture.

William J. Hennessey

Related articles in *World Book* include:

Arc de Triomphe	Romanesque architecture
Architecture (pictures)	Spain (picture: Ancient Roman structures)
Bridge (Arch bridges)	
Gateway Arch National Park	Vault

Archaea, *ahr KEE uh,* sometimes called *archaebacteria,* are a group of single-celled organisms that make up one of three basic divisions of life. Scientists often call these basic divisions *domains.* The other two domains of living organisms are Eukaryota, which includes animals and plants, and Bacteria, which includes all true bacteria and the algaelike cyanobacteria. Eukaryotes have *eukaryotic cells,* or cells with a nucleus, while bacteria and archaea have *prokaryotic cells,* or cells that lack a nucleus. Scientists had traditionally classified archaea with bacteria because of their similar cell structures. But beginning in the 1970's, close analyses of their genes revealed that archaea and bacteria are too different to be grouped together. In many respects, archaea more closely resemble eukaryotes than they do bacteria.

Archaea rank among the oldest forms of life on Earth. Some scientists believe these organisms are similar to the original ancestors of all modern life. Archaea have developed unusual properties. For example, various kinds of archaea can consume acetic acid, hydrogen, or sulfur. Some archaea can even produce the gas methane. Other kinds have developed an unusual form of *photosynthesis,* a process by which they make food. Unlike photosynthesis in plants and bacteria, archaeal photosynthesis does not use the green pigment chlorophyll.

Archaea live in a wide variety of habitats. Many live in such harsh conditions as oil wells, deep-sea *hydrothermal vents* (hot springs), and *anaerobic* (oxygen-free) environments. Other archaea grow in soils and within various living organisms. People have archaea living harmlessly in their digestive system.   Gary J. Olsen

See also **Cell** (Inside a living cell); **Extremophile.**

Archaeologists excavate ruins of the ancient city of Ubar in Oman searching for remains of past human activities. Modern archaeology often combines hard work, such as digging with hand tools, with complex technology. These ruins were found in 1981 using radar images obtained from space.

Archaeology

Archaeology, *AHR kee AHL uh jee,* is the scientific study of the remains of past human cultures. Archaeological research is the chief method available for learning about societies that existed before the invention of writing about 5,500 years ago. It also provides an important supplement to our knowledge of ancient societies that left written records.

Archaeologists investigate the lives of early people by studying the cultural remains they left behind. Such remains can include buildings, artwork, tools, weapons,. or pottery. Archaeologists also examine the context and associations of the cultural remains, which can provide information about how the remains were used. The preserved residues from food items, such as bones and plant parts, can also reveal much about how ancient people lived.

Archaeology in North and South America and in Europe is considered a branch of *anthropology,* the scientific study of human culture. Some archaeological investigations are closely linked to history, though historians mainly study events in the past recorded in written documents.

Archaeologists look for information about how, where, and when cultures developed. Like other social scientists, they search for reasons why major changes have occurred in certain cultures. Some archaeologists try to understand why ancient people stopped hunting and started farming. Others develop theories about what caused people to build cities and to set up trade routes. In addition, some archaeologists look for reasons behind the fall of early civilizations, such as the Roman Empire, or examine why large cities of the Maya civilization were abandoned around A.D. 850.

What archaeologists study

Archaeologists examine any evidence that can help explain how people lived in the past. Such evidence ranges from the ruins of a large city to a few stone flakes left by someone making a stone tool long ago.

The three basic kinds of archaeological evidence are (1) artifacts, (2) features, and (3) ecofacts. *Artifacts* are any objects made by human hands. An artifact can be a pyramid, a point chipped from flint, a ceramic pot, or a variety of other items made from a wide range of materials.

Features are evidence of past human activities visible as disturbances in the earth. Such disturbances can be produced by people digging pits for storage, building a house or tomb, or constructing canals for irrigation. Unlike artifacts, features cannot be separated from their surroundings.

Ecofacts are natural objects found with artifacts or features. Ecofacts reveal clues about past environments and how ancient people utilized the resources available to them. For example, charred seeds and animal bones tell archaeologists about the foods of ancient peoples, while preserved pollen can provide evidence about vegetation and climate changes over time.

Any place where archaeological evidence is found is called an *archaeological site*. To understand the behavior of the people who occupied a site, archaeologists must study the relationships among the artifacts, features, and ecofacts found there. For example, American archaeologists discovered flint spearpoints among the bones of extinct, Ice Age buffalo at the Folsom site in

An army of life-sized statues of soldiers and horses form an amazing collection of *artifacts* (objects made by people). The earthenware figures were first discovered in 1974 in burial pits near Xi'an, China, close to the tomb of Shi Huangdi, who ruled China in the 200's B.C.

Archaeology questions
worldbook.com/ar-14

© SuperStock

New Mexico. These artifacts demonstrated that ancient peoples had reached the New World at least 10,000 years ago.

If objects are buried in the ground, their position in the earth is also of interest to archaeologists. The scientists study the layers of earth and rock in which objects are found to understand the conditions that existed when the objects were placed there. In some places, archaeologists find many levels of deposits called *strata*. The archaeological study of strata, called *stratigraphy*, developed from the study of rock layers in geology.

How archaeologists gather information

Archaeologists use special techniques and equipment to gather archaeological evidence precisely and accurately. They also maintain detailed written records, photographs, maps, and plans of sites because archaeological research actually destroys much of the site.

Locating sites is the first job of the archaeologist. Sites may be aboveground, underground, or underwater. Underwater sites include sunken ships as well as entire towns that have been submerged because of shifts in land or water level.

© Phil Degginger, Bruce Coleman Inc.

The foundation of a Roman bath at Caesarea, near Hadera, Israel, is an example of an archaeological *feature*. Features are evidence of human activities often visible as changes in the earth.

National Museum of Man, Ottawa, Canada

Whale bones, *foreground,* were among the *ecofacts* found in diggings on Bathurst Island in the Canadian Arctic. Such natural objects reveal how ancient people related to their surroundings.

Some large sites are located easily because they are clearly visible or can be traced from descriptions in ancient stories or other historical records. Such sites include the pyramids in Egypt and the ancient city of Athens in Greece. Some less obvious sites have been discovered accidentally by nonarchaeologists. In 1940, for example, four children in search of their dog found the Lascaux Cave in southwestern France, which has prehistoric wall paintings. Many important discoveries have been made by archaeologists who searched tirelessly over many years for a specific site or type of site. Working in this way, an English archaeologist named Howard Carter discovered the treasure-filled tomb of the ancient Egyptian king Tutankhamun in 1922.

Archaeologists use systematic methods to discover sites. The traditional way to find all the sites in a region is through a *foot survey.* In this method, archaeologists space themselves at measured distances and walk in preset directions. Each person looks for archaeological evidence, such as bits of flint or pottery fragments, while walking. Archaeologists use this method when they want to know where sites do not occur as well as where they do. For example, they might use it to confirm that sites in a particular region occur on hilltops but never in valleys.

Archaeologists use a variety of scientific methods to help discover sites that have been covered over by natural forces, such as floods or blowing sand, or obscured by human activities, such as farming. *Remote sensing,* the use of instruments to observe and record information from a distance, is a common technique used by archaeologists. Aerial photography, for example, can reveal variations in vegetation that indicate the presence of an archaeological site. Plants that are taller in one area of a field may be growing over an ancient grave or irrigation ditch. Plants that are shorter in another area may be growing in shallow ground over an ancient building or road. Today, archaeologists may locate sites with *infrared* (heat detecting) imaging or even photographs tak-

Aerofilms Ltd.

Aerial photography can reveal unsuspected sites. The outlines of a royal Celtic monument were discovered in County Meath, Ireland. The monument, called Tara, dates from about 2,000 B.C.

en from orbiting satellites. On the ground, remote sensing techniques, such as *ground-penetrating radar,* can reveal buried structures or graves. Even simple metal detectors can be used to detect buried metal artifacts.

Surveying sites. Archaeologists begin to study a site by describing it and plotting the location on a *topographic map* (map showing surface features). Handheld tools called Global Positioning System (GPS) devices enable archaeologists to determine precise locations through readings obtained from satellites. Archaeologists make detailed notes about the condition of the site and the kinds of evidence visible on its surface. They also take photographs of the site.

Pat Baker, Western Australian Maritime Museum

An underwater site may contain cargo from sunken ships. Such cargo has added to our knowledge of ancient Greek and Roman times. Archaeologists working off the west coast of Australia use a vacuum device to scoop up coins and other small objects, as shown here.

Archaeologists make maps of most sites they find. The type of map drawn depends on the importance of the site, the study's goals, and the amount of time and money available. In some cases, simple maps are made after pacing off distances or using a measuring tape. In other cases, a special instrument called a *transit* is used to survey the site carefully. Today, many archaeologists use a *total data station*, a device utilizing laser and computer technology, to rapidly survey and map a site.

After making a map, the scientists collect artifacts from the surface of the site. They divide the surface into a grid pattern of squares and examine one square at a time. The locations where artifacts are found are recorded on the map. Some surface artifacts can give information about when or how a site was used.

Excavating sites. Archaeologists dig carefully for buried remains in a process called *excavation.* The method of excavation depends partly on the type of site. The archaeologist must use precise techniques and careful observation to determine the context and association of buried artifacts and features. For example, archaeologists working in a cave might divide the floor and the area in front of the cave into square units and then excavate each unit separately. Archaeologists working on a temple platform might dig a trench into the front part of the platform and extend the trench into the ground next to the platform. At large sites, excavation may be limited to certain areas. Other considerations that frequently determine the excavation method include the climate and soil at the site. Today, archaeologists often expose broad areas of a site in a technique called *open area* or *block excavation* so the patterns of an ancient settlement can be detected.

Tools used in excavation range from backhoes and other heavy equipment to shovels and paintbrushes. The most common tool used is the *trowel,* a small, flat, pointed implement often used in bricklaying. A trowel is used to carefully remove earth so that artifacts and features can be found in place, carefully exposed, and documented. In most excavations, archaeologists screen excavated deposits through wire-mesh sieves to recover small artifacts and ecofacts. They also collect soil samples to be analyzed in a laboratory to detect microscopic pollen grains or charred plant remains. Chemical analysis of soil can also detect evidence of human activities.

Working underwater. Archaeologists who work underwater use many methods adopted from land archaeology. Aerial photography over clear water may reveal the outlines of sunken harbors and towns. A method called *sonar scanning* helps detect underwater objects by the reflection of sound waves. In addition, divers use metal detectors to uncover metal objects. Photographic maps of sites can be made from submarines or by divers carrying underwater cameras. Archaeologists work at underwater sites in submersible decompression chambers. They sometimes use balloons to raise large objects to the surface for further study.

Some underwater sites require extraordinary measures. Archaeologists working in rough waters to examine the French ship *La Belle,* which had sunk off the Texas coast in the 1700's, exposed the site by building a giant steel enclosure around it. After the ocean water was pumped out, they could begin excavation on the fragile wreck.

Douglas Gann/Homol'ovi Research Program, Arizona State Museum

A rendering of an Ancestral Pueblo ceremonial center called a *kiva* was produced by archaeologists using computer software. Archaeologists frequently use computers to evaluate information.

Recording and preserving evidence. Archaeologists describe, photograph, and count the objects they find. They group the objects according to type and location. For example, broken pieces of pottery, called *potsherds,* are bagged together by excavation unit and level. This collection then goes to the field laboratory to be cleaned and labeled. Some artifacts, such as knives or spearpoints, should not be washed. Washing removes residues, such as fat or blood, that can be identified through microscopic or chemical analysis. Identification of the residues can indicate how the artifact was used.

At the field laboratory, archaeologists must take special care to preserve objects made of such materials as metal and wood. For example, rust on a metal object must be removed without damaging the surface. Water-soaked wooden objects may crack or lose their shape when exposed to the air. These objects must be kept wet until specialists called *conservators* can preserve them.

How archaeologists interpret findings

Archaeologists follow three basic steps in interpreting the evidence they find: (1) classification, (2) dating, and (3) evaluation.

Classification. Archaeologists can interpret their findings only if they can detect patterns of distribution of artifacts in space or through time. To find these patterns, archaeologists must first classify artifacts into groups of similar objects.

Typology is the most common approach in classification. Artifacts are usually first sorted into groups based on their shape, known as *morphological types.* If the shape and manufacturing methods found among morphological types are distinctive during certain periods, they may represent *temporal types.* Archaeologists use temporal types to construct a sequence that reflects changes in the style or manufacture of artifacts over time. A sequence of different temporal types from a region reflects cultural change through the years. More detailed studies, such as the microscopic examination of a flint blade or the analysis of residues on a potsherd, can lead to the recognition of *functional types.* Some types are defined by the archaeologist, while other typological classifications actually reveal the designs and shapes intentionally developed by ancient peoples.

Dating of archaeological objects is called *archaeometry.* The methods of archaeometry are divided into two major types: (1) *relative dating* and (2) *absolute dating.*

Relative dating gives information about the age of an object in relation to other objects. Thus, relative dating methods produce only comparisons, not actual dates. For example, archaeologists can determine the relative ages of bones found at a site by measuring their fluorine content. Fluorine from underground water gradually replaces other elements in bones, and so older bones contain more fluorine.

Christopher Cunningham, Stratford Hall Plantation

A reconstructed slave cabin stands at Stratford Hall, the birthplace of Robert E. Lee in Virginia. Historical archaeologists work with historians and architects to re-create such historic buildings

Absolute dating determines the age of an object in years. There are many absolute dating methods. The method used in a specific case depends mainly on the type of object being dated.

The most widely used dating method is *radiocarbon dating.* This method requires *organic material*—that is, something that was once living, such as plant parts, charcoal from cooking pits, bone, or shells. Two types of radiocarbon dating are available to archaeologists today. *Traditional* radiocarbon dating is less expensive to perform but it requires several grams of organic material. *Accelerator mass spectrometry* dating is used when only a small amount of organic material can be recovered from a site, or if only a tiny sample can be removed from a fragile artifact. See **Radiocarbon.**

Other absolute dating techniques have more narrow applications. *Potassium-argon dating* is used mainly in Africa to determine the age of rocks associated with fossils of early human ancestors. Other techniques, such as *electron spin resonance, uranium-series dating,* and *obsidian-hydration dating,* are used in special circumstances or when radiocarbon dating is not possible.

The best-known method for dating wood is called *dendrochronology.* This technique is used mainly in the southwestern United States. It involves counting the yearly growth rings on cross sections of cut trees used to construct ancient *pueblos* (houses). Archaeologists match tree ring patterns with overlapping patterns to a reference sample that extends back at least 8,000 years.

Evaluation. Archaeologists evaluate artifacts and features to learn such information as how and where the objects were made and used. In some cases, the scientists learn by direct experimentation. *Flintknapping* (chipping stone to make a tool) is one widely used form of experimentation. Many archaeologists are skilled at producing exact duplicates of the flint tools found in archaeological sites. Flintknapping helps archaeologists

Christopher Cunningham, Stratford Hall Plantation

Historical archaeologists often study the everyday lives of people in the recent past not recorded in historical documents. These archaeologists have uncovered evidence of a small building and other articles left by former residents at Stratford Hall near Montross, Virginia. The statesman Richard Henry Lee and the military leader Robert E. Lee were born at Stratford Hall, a large plantation built between 1730 and 1738.

understand ancient tool manufacturing techniques and interpret the broken artifacts and flint chips found in excavations. Artifacts and features can also help explain the social lives of ancient people. For example, the size of houses can show how many people lived in one household. The number and value of objects found in graves can indicate differences in social class.

The evaluation of ecofacts reveals such information as what food people ate and whether they grew crops or gathered wild plants. Ecofacts can even explain ancient migration patterns. A seed of grain not native to the area where it is found may reveal how and when eating habits spread from one place to another.

Archaeologists evaluate evidence with the help of specialists from other fields. Zoologists help identify animal bones and butchering techniques. Botanists analyze seeds to learn about ancient agricultural practices. Such specialists as geologists, architects, and engineers also work with archaeologists.

Computers are extremely valuable in evaluating archaeological information. Archaeologists use computer software to produce site maps, plot the distribution artifact types throughout a site, and perform the many statistical analyses necessary to interpret the huge numbers of artifacts and ecofacts recovered in an excavation.

History

Beginnings. The idea of studying the past through ancient objects has developed gradually. But the most intense interest has occurred in the past 200 years. During the 1700's, some wealthy Europeans began to study and collect art objects from the times of ancient Greece and Rome. This interest in classical art is called *antiquarianism.* These first diggers looked only for treasures and threw away ordinary objects.

Also during the 1700's, European scholars began to debate how long human beings had lived on Earth. Their interest resulted partly from discoveries of primitive stone tools together with the bones of extinct animals. These scholars also knew about the huge mounds and ruined cities in the Americas that pointed to ancient human life there. They realized that human beings had a prehistoric past, but they could not decide when and where this past had begun.

The 1800's brought a more scientific approach to the study of the past. The great length of human prehistory became widely accepted due to advances in geology and biology. By the early 1800's, geologists had determined that rock formation resulted from extremely slow processes, such as erosion and volcanic activity. This view, known as *uniformitarianism,* led most scholars to believe that Earth was much older than previously thought. Then, in 1859, the British biologist Charles R. Darwin proposed the theory of biological evolution in his book *The Origin of Species.* This theory suggested that human beings, like other animals and Earth itself, had developed slowly over a vast time.

By the mid-1800's, archaeology had become a separate field of study, and evidence of human prehistory was accumulating rapidly. Important discoveries included prehistoric lake dwellings in Switzerland, ancient cave paintings in France and Spain, and part of a prehistoric human skull found in Germany. In the late 1800's, archaeologists began to use techniques of excavation

that made it possible to determine sequences of cultural development. In an excavation at Naqada, near Qus, Egypt, the British scholar Sir Flinders Petrie became one of the first diggers to look carefully for all remains, not just for treasures. Others who undertook major excavations at that time included the British nobleman Sir Austen Henry Layard, at Nineveh in what is now Iraq, and the German businessman Heinrich Schliemann, at Troy in what is now Turkey.

European archaeologists of the late 1800's focused their studies on the ancient European and Middle Eastern civilizations described by classical and Biblical authors. American archaeologists, however, could find almost no written records of the civilizations they studied. Partly for this reason, they turned to anthropology for methods of interpreting their discoveries. For example, they studied artifacts produced by contemporary American Indians to help interpret objects from past societies.

The 1900's. The scope of archaeology expanded greatly during the 1900's. Archaeologists began to explore the past civilizations of Central and South America, China, Japan, Southeast Asia, and other areas. By the early 1900's, archaeologists were using stratigraphy to date their finds. During the mid-1900's, new techniques made dating much easier and more accurate. The most significant of these techniques was radiocarbon dating, developed in the 1940's by an American chemist named Willard F. Libby.

Great advances in underwater archaeology also occurred during the mid-1900's. Previously, underwater excavation had been both difficult and expensive. The aqualung and other diving devices invented during the 1940's enabled divers to move more freely.

Beginning in the 1970's, space satellites began to provide valuable sources of data. Photographs taken from satellites helped locate archaeological sites. In 1995, Global Positioning System (GPS) satellites became fully

The Griffith Institute, Ashmolean Museum, Oxford

The tomb of King Tutankhamun of Egypt was discovered in 1922 by the English archaeologist Howard Carter. Carter, *left,* and his sponsor, Lord Carnarvon, stand at the tomb's entrance.

Important dates in archaeology

1797 British geologist John Frere found flint tools at Hoxne, England, and reported that they belonged to a period "beyond that of the present world."

1837 Christian J. Thomsen, a Danish curator, proposed that the history of humankind, before written records began, could be divided into Stone, Bronze, and Iron ages.

1853-1854 A drought revealed Swiss lake villages dating back at least 5,000 years.

1870 Heinrich Schliemann, a German businessman, began excavations on the site of Troy in what is now Turkey.

1879 Prehistoric wallpaintings were found in a cave at Altamira, Spain.

1884 French archaeologist Marcel-Auguste Dieulafoy uncovered the palace of Persian King Darius I in what is now Iran.

1900 British archaeologist Arthur J. Evans began excavating Knossos, capital of the Minoan civilization of Crete.

1922 Howard Carter of the United Kingdom created worldwide interest in archaeology after finding King Tutankhamun's tomb in Egypt.

1925 Flint points found at Folsom, New Mexico, showed that people lived in Ice Age North America more than 10,000 years ago.

1952 British archaeologist Kathleen Mary Kenyon led excavations at Jericho, Jordan, that proved it to be one of the oldest known communities.

1977-1985 Excavations by American archaeologist Thomas D. Dillehay at Monte Verde, Chile, revealed the earliest known occupation of the New World, more than 12,000 years old.

1991 Hikers in the Alps discovered the frozen, preserved body of a man who lived more than 5,000 years ago. Nicknamed Ötzi, this accidental find provided archaeologists with many new insights into pre-Bronze Age life.

operational. The GPS satellites produce signals that can be used to calculate exact locations on Earth (see **Global Positioning System**).

Archaeology today. A major concern among archaeologists today is the preservation of archaeological sites that have not yet been studied. Many such sites are threatened by construction projects, the expansion of agriculture, and other types of development, or by theft. Several countries, including the United States, have enacted laws that require government agencies to identify and preserve places that might be of historic or archaeological importance. Today, governments and private consulting businesses employ many archaeologists to survey, excavate, and protect endangered sites in a process called *cultural resource management.*

Another major concern is protecting the rights of local peoples whose ancestors left the remains unearthed by archaeologists. Many local peoples argue that the skeletal remains of their ancestors deserve a proper burial and should not be considered specimens for research. They also say that many artifacts were sacred objects used for religious purposes and should be treated with reverence. In the United States, the Native American Graves Protection and Repatriation Act of 1990 deals with the ownership of remains and artifacts. The law requires archaeologists to consult with Native American tribes when ancient burials are found in excavations on public lands or at sites where federal funds or permits have been issued. If the archaeologists find human remains or artifacts and a tribe can prove that it has a valid claim to the items, the scientists must return them to the tribe. Australia, New Zealand, and other countries have similar laws protecting the grave sites of local peoples.

On an international scale, archaeologists seek to halt the illegal sale of archaeological objects. They urge developed nations to enact and enforce laws to prohibit the import of ancient objects unless an export certificate has been obtained from the country of origin.

Careers in archaeology

Most careers in archaeology require a master's or doctoral degree. In college, most students who wish to become archaeologists major in anthropology but also take courses in history, languages, biology, computer science, statistics, and geology. In addition, their studies should include experience in excavation. In graduate school, students generally select a geographic area that becomes their research specialty.

Archaeologists are employed in three main fields: (1) academic, (2) museum work, and (3) government service. Most archaeologists who teach at colleges and universities also carry out research and publish their findings. Archaeologists who work in museums conduct research, publish articles, preserve and restore ancient objects, and use those objects to educate the public. Today, the largest number of archaeologists have jobs in the field of cultural resource management. They often work directly for a government agency or for a private business that is hired by the government or by other private companies.   Thomas R. Hester

Related articles in *World Book* include:

Biographies

Breasted, James H.	Stephens, John Lloyd
Carter, Howard	Ventris, Michael G. F.
Evans, Sir Arthur J.	Winckelmann, Johann J.
Leakey, Mary Douglas	Woolley, Sir Leonard
Piranesi, Giovanni B.	

Egypt

Egypt, Ancient	Necropolis	Rosetta stone
Hieroglyphics	Obelisk	Sphinx
Mummy	Pyramids	Valley of the Kings

Greece

Acropolis	Corinth	Knossos	Parthenon
Aegean civilization	Elgin Marbles	Mycenae	Sparta
	Ephesus	Olympia	Troy

Italy

Appian Way	Pantheon
Forum, Roman	Pompeii
Herculaneum	Rome (Ancient city)

Middle East

Babylonia	Ebla	Nineveh	Sumer
Dead Sea Scrolls	Mesopotamia	Persia, Ancient	Ur
	Moabite stone	Phoenicia	

The Americas

Ancestral Pueblo	Indian, American (The first Americans)	Maya
Aztec		Monte Albán
Chichén Itzá		Mound builders
Copán	Kensington rune stone	Tenochtitlan
Easter Island	Machu Picchu	Teotihuacán
Folsom point		Tikal
Inca		

Other related articles

Angkor	India (History)
Anthropology	Lake dwelling
Carthage (picture)	Lascaux Cave
Civilization	Megalithic monuments

Metal detector
Paleontology
Prehistoric people

Radiocarbon
Stonehenge

Archaeopteryx, AHR *kee AHP tuhr ihks,* was a feathered animal that lived about 150 million years ago, near the end of the Jurassic Period. This crow-sized creature had a skeleton closely resembling that of a small dinosaur. However, it also had fully developed feathers and birdlike wings. As a result, *Archaeopteryx* has traditionally been classified as a bird. The first *Archaeopteryx* fossils were discovered during the 1860's in Bavaria, a state in Germany. These fossils provided the first solid evidence that birds descended from reptiles.

Unlike modern birds, *Archaeopteryx* had teeth; a long, reptilelike tail lined with feathers; and three "fingers" with claws on its wings. Many scientists believe that the animal used its claws to climb trees. *Archaeopteryx* was most likely an excellent glider. The animal could probably fly, though scientists do not know how well. The word *Archaeopteryx* is Greek for *ancient wing.*

Peter Dodson

See also **Bird** (The first birds).

Archangel. See Arkhangelsk.

Archbishop is the chief bishop of a religious province in the Roman Catholic Church and other churches. A province consists of a number of *dioceses* (districts). An archbishop usually governs a diocese, called an *archdiocese.* He has limited authority over the bishops of the other dioceses in his province.   Ralph W. Quere

See also **Address, Forms of; Bishop.**

Archbishop of Canterbury is the spiritual leader of the Anglican Communion, one of the largest bodies of Christians in the world. The archbishop is also the senior bishop of the Church of England. He is sometimes called the *primate of all England.* He oversees the Diocese of Canterbury, a district of the church. He and the archbishop of York preside over the General Synod, the Church of England's ruling body. The archbishop of Canterbury also heads international Anglican gatherings, such as the Lambeth Conference and the Anglican Consultative Council. He lives at Lambeth Palace in London.

The title of archbishop of Canterbury dates back to 597. That year, Pope Gregory I sent missionaries led by a monk named Augustine from Rome to England to convert its people to Christianity. Augustine and his missionary monks converted thousands of people. The pope named Augustine, now known as Saint Augustine of Canterbury, archbishop of Canterbury in 601. Today, the British prime minister chooses the archbishop in the name of the British monarch.   Sheryl A. Kujawa-Holbrook

See also **Anglican Communion; Church of England.**

Archerfish is a group of large-eyed fish that can shoot drops of water from the mouth into the air with force and accuracy. Archerfish are found in southeastern Asia

WORLD BOOK illustration by John F. Eggert
An archerfish hunts insects at the water surface.

from India to Indonesia and the Philippines, and in Australia. They live in fresh or slightly salty water, often among the roots of mangrove trees. They grow as long as 16 inches (41 centimeters), but most are about 6 inches (15 centimeters) long.

An archerfish shoots water drops by squeezing its gill covers and forcing water forward along a groove within the bones of the roof of its mouth. It can shoot water more than 3 feet (90 centimeters) into the air. Archerfish aim at insects on the stems and leaves of plants hanging over the water surface. They also shoot at spiders in webs above the water. When hit, the insects or spiders fall to the water, where the archerfish eats them.

John E. McCosker

Scientific classification. Archerfish make up the genus *Toxotes.* The best-known species is *Toxotes jaculatrix.*

See **Fish** (picture: An archerfish).

Archery is the sport of shooting with a bow and arrow. Archers may participate in several forms of the sport. The most popular versions are *bow hunting, target archery, field archery, indoor archery,* and *flight archery.* In bow hunting, the archer hunts game with a bow and arrow. In target, field, and indoor archery, archers compete in shooting at targets. In flight archery, competitors shoot for distance.

Millions of people take part in archery. The sport is especially popular in schools and summer camps. All the states in the United States and most provinces in Canada have special hunting seasons for archers, who shoot such animals as bear, deer, and rabbits. Some archers shoot fish in the shallow waters of lakes and streams. Archers participate in international archery competitions. In addition, archery is an event of the Summer Olympic Games.

Archery equipment

Bows. Three main kinds of bows are used in archery —the *recurve bow,* the *compound bow,* and the *longbow.* The recurve bow, the most common type used by target archers, has tips that curve away from the archer. A compound bow has a system of two cables and from two to six pulleys built into it. The cables and pulleys make this kind of bow easier to hold at the fully *drawn* (pulled back) position than other types. Compound bows are popular with bow hunters and field archers, but they may not be used in Olympic archery competition. The longbow, once the most popular type of bow, is now used only by a small number of archers. An unstrung longbow looks somewhat like a straight line.

Most bows are made of aluminum, carbon-reinforced plastics, or wood. The core consists of several layers of wood that have been *laminated* (glued together). Some bows can be separated into two or three pieces for carrying or storage. They are commonly called "take-down" bows.

Bowstrings are made of plastics or polyethylene cord, and have a wrapping of nylon thread opposite the handle of the bow. This wrapping protects the string at the *nocking point,* the place where the notch of the arrow fits. Each end of the string has a loop that is used in stringing the bow. In recurve bows and longbows, the loop fits into a notch at each bow tip. In compound bows, the loop is attached to one of the two cables or to wheels called *cams* at each end of the bow.

The amount of pull required to bring a 28-inch (71-centimeter) arrow to full draw is called the *draw weight* of the bow. For example, a 40-pound (18-kilogram) bow requires 40 pounds of force to draw a 28-inch arrow. Some bows have a draw weight of more than 60 pounds (27 kilograms). A beginning archer should use a bow with a draw weight of 20 pounds (9 kilograms) or less.

Bows vary in length, depending on their use. Archers also choose a bow that is comfortable for their draw length. Many recurve target archers use bows 68 to 70 inches (173 to 180 centimeters) long. Compound bows average about 35 to 45 inches (89 to 114 centimeters) in length.

Arrows are made of carbon, aluminum, fiberglass, or wood. Target archers prefer lightweight carbon composite or aluminum arrows, which travel especially fast and are more uniform. Hunters and other archers who sometimes shoot on rough land generally use aluminum arrows, which can withstand rough treatment. Beginners should shoot with aluminum or wooden arrows.

All arrows have three main parts—the *point,* which in most cases is made of metal; the *shaft;* and the *nock,* which attaches to the string. Points vary in shape and size. Bow hunters use points that have blades with two or more cutting edges. Target and field archers use a conical, bullet-shaped point. The nock has a notch for the bowstring. Three *fletches* on the shaft help provide accuracy in shooting. An arrow may be *fletched* with plastic vanes or turkey feathers.

Arrow length varies from about 24 to 32 inches (61 to 81 centimeters). An archer can estimate the proper length to use by holding an arrow perpendicular to the chest and extending the other arm straight out. The arrow should reach just beyond the fingertips.

Most archers carry their arrows in a holder called a

Archery safety

Archers should observe the following rules to avoid injuring themselves or others:

Never point a drawn bow at any object or animal you do not want to hit.

Never shoot an arrow unless the area is free of people or animals.

Never shoot an arrow straight up.

Keep all archery equipment in good condition.

quiver. The quiver may be attached to the bow or a belt, or placed on the ground.

Other equipment includes an armguard of leather or plastic. The guard is worn on the forearm of the hand that holds the bow. It protects the forearm when the bowstring snaps forward after being released. Archers also wear a *shooting glove* or, most commonly, a leather *tab* to protect the fingers that draw the bowstring.

Many bows are equipped with a *sight* used for aiming. Sights range from simple metal pins to telescopic eyepieces. Most target archers use one or two composite or metal rods called *stabilizers* to reduce the vibrations in a bow after the bowstring is released. These rods, manufactured in various lengths and weights, are usually attached to the back of the bow handle.

Archery competition

Archers take part in many types of competition. The most popular contests include those in *target archery, field archery, flight archery, indoor archery,* and *3-D archery.*

Target archery is the most common form of competition. The archers shoot down a long course at woven straw or foam mats called *buttresses.* The buttresses are covered with a target that is divided into five colored circles. A thin line divides every color into two rings, each of which counts for a different score. The colors

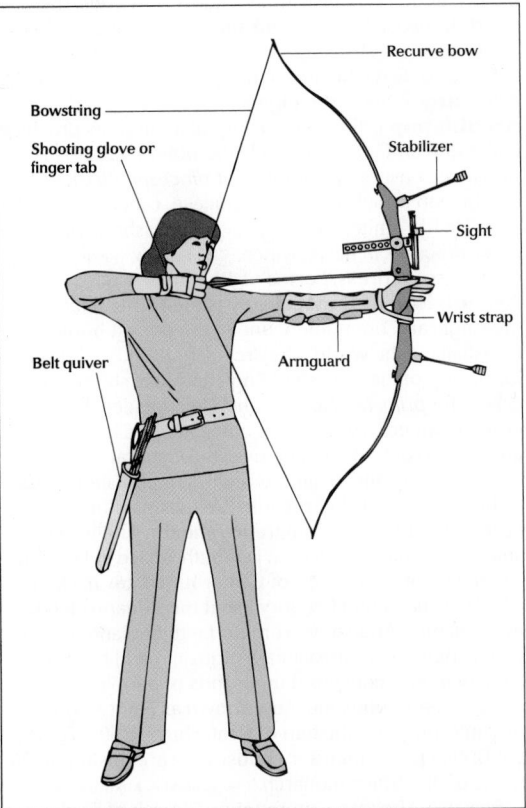

WORLD BOOK illustration by David Cunningham

Archery equipment includes accessories that help an archer shoot better and more comfortably. Most target archers use recurve bows equipped with a *sight* and one or two *stabilizers.*

and their value in points are: gold, 10 and 9; red, 8 and 7; blue, 6 and 5; black, 4 and 3; and white, 2 and 1.

The number of shots allowed each archer is called a *round.* In the United States, the National Archery Association has established many kinds of rounds for men, women, and children. Olympic archery competition and all international tournaments are held under the rules of the International Archery Federation. These rules call for men and women to shoot from varying distances, 90 meters (98 yards) being the maximum distance for men and 70 meters (77 yards) the maximum for women. The types of rounds that the archers shoot vary according to the level of competition, such as the World Championships or the Olympic Games. In the 90-, 70-, and 60-meter (66-yard) distances, and in all competition in the United States, archers shoot at targets 122 centimeters (48 inches) in diameter. The 50-and 30-meter (55- and 33-yard) distances use a target 80 centimeters (31 inches) in diameter.

Field archery involves walking across a course set out in an open field or wooded area shooting at buttresses from various distances. The basic contest, called a *field round,* consists of 24 buttresses. They are covered with black-and-gold targets that measure 20, 40, 60, or 80 centimeters (8, 16, 24, or 31 inches) in diameter. Each target has five circular scoring rings—a gold center ring worth 5 points and four black rings worth 4, 3, 2, and 1

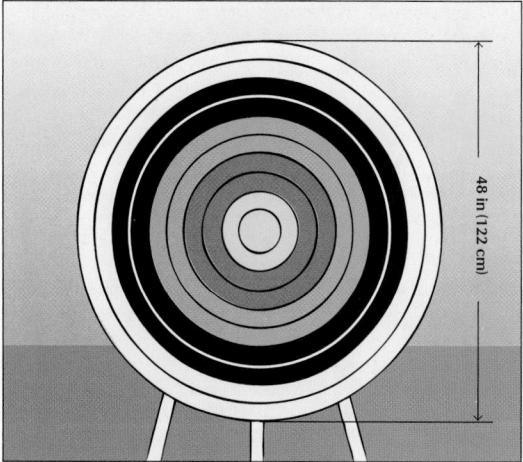

48 in (122 cm)

WORLD BOOK diagram by Richard Fickle

The target used in target archery competition in the United States has 10 scoring rings and 5 colored circles. An archer scores 10 points by hitting the bull's-eye.

points.The archers shoot two rounds of three arrows at every target. The distance to the targets ranges from about 6 to 72 meters (7 to 80 yards).

Flight archery is competition in which archers try only for distance, not accuracy. They use special bows with a draw weight of up to 200 pounds (91 kilograms), and small, lightweight arrows. In regular flight archery, the archers shoot while standing. In *freestyle* flight archery, they lie on their back with the bow strapped to their feet. They use both hands to draw the bow. An archer can shoot farther than 700 yards (640 meters).

Indoor archery involves shooting at a distance of 18 meters (20 yards). The archer generally shoots 12 *ends* (rounds) of five arrows or 20 ends of three arrows. Many archers compete indoors during the winter months to keep in shape for outdoor competitions or hunting.

3-D archery consists of shooting arrows at lifelike foam models of game animals, such as deer and elk. The archer must correctly estimate the distance of the target. The model animal has scoring rings that can only be seen from a short distance. Because 3-D archery has many of the same challenges as hunting, it is a popular off-season activity for bow hunters.

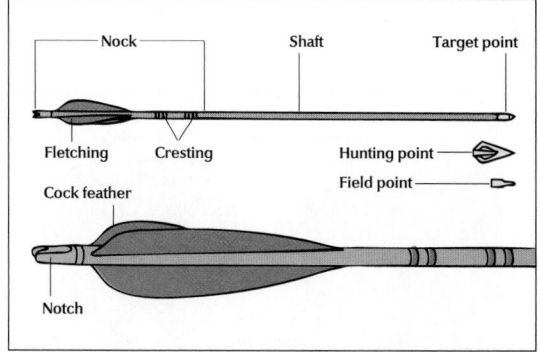

Nock   Shaft   Target point

Fletching   Cresting   Hunting point

Cock feather   Field point

Notch

WORLD BOOK diagram by Richard Fickle

The main parts of an arrow are the point, the shaft, and the nock. The nock includes a notch for the bowstring and three or four feathers that help provide shooting accuracy.

History

Prehistoric people invented the bow and arrow thousands of years ago. The weapon revolutionized early hunting methods by enabling people to kill animals from a distance. The ancient Egyptians were the first people known to use the bow and arrow extensively. They used the weapon for hunting and in war as early as 5000 B.C. Other early peoples who used bows and arrows included the Assyrians and the Persians.

By the A.D. 900's, the Turks had developed advanced archery equipment. They used laminated bows made of a combination of wood and animal horns and tendons. The tips of their bows curved outward like modern recurve bows. By the 1100's, the crossbow had become a popular weapon in Europe (see **Crossbow**).

The *longbow* ranked as the chief weapon of the English army when the Hundred Years' War began in 1337.

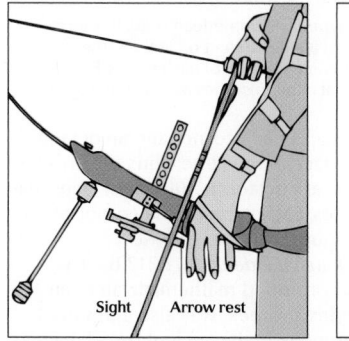
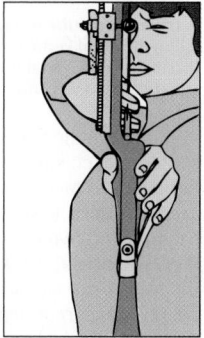

Sight   Arrow rest

WORLD BOOK illustration by David Cunningham

Notching an arrow, a process called *nocking, left,* is the first step in drawing the bowstring. The archer grasps the string with three fingers. Many archers aim by using a sight, *right.*

© Jason Vaccarello, National Archery Association

Target archery is the most common type of archery contest. An archer tries to score points by shooting arrows from several distances at a circular target divided into 10 scoring rings.

In 1346, in the Battle of Crécy, 7,000 English archers routed a much larger French force that included more than 1,000 armor-clad knights. In 1415, in the Battle of Agincourt, about 6,000 English troops with longbows defeated a French force of about 20,000 to 30,000.

By about 1500, firearms had replaced the bow and arrow as the chief weapon of English infantry. In the 1540's, English author Roger Ascham wrote *Toxophilus*, the first book to describe the proper way to shoot a bow and arrow. The Royal Toxophilite Society was set up in England in 1781 to promote archery as a sport.

The first archery organization in the United States was the United Bowmen of Philadelphia, founded in 1828. The National Archery Association was established in 1879 and held its first tournament that year. In 1931, the International Archery Federation (FITA) was founded to conduct international tournaments. The National Field Archery Association was organized in 1939 by a group of American hunters. In 1969, FITA added field archery to the events in world championship archery competition. In 1991, the federation added indoor archery.

Compound bows came into use during the 1970's. They soon gained wide popularity because they are so easy to hold.   Critically reviewed by USA Archery

See also **Arrowhead; Indian, American** (Hunting, gathering, and fishing; Weapons).

Additional resources

Bolnick, Helen, and others. *Archery Instruction Manual.* Ed. by Donald W. Campbell. 4th ed. National Archery Assn. of the United States, 1993.
McKinney, Wayne C. and Mike W. *Archery.* 8th ed. Brown & Benchmark, 1997.

Arches National Park lies near Moab in southeastern Utah (see **Utah** [physical map]). Its unusual sandstone rock formations look like huge arches, windows, and towers. Landscape Arch is one of the world's longest natural arches. It has a 306-foot (93-meter) span. The park became a national monument in 1929 and a national park in 1971. See **National Park System** (table: National parks).   Critically reviewed by the National Park Service

Archimedean screw, *AHR kuh MEE dee uhn,* is a device for raising water. It consists of a screw or a pattern of blades sealed to the inside of a cylinder. The lower end is placed in the water. The upper end has a crank that turns the cylinder. The threads of the screw or the blades slowly raise the water until it flows out the upper end. This device was used in the Nile Valley for draining and irrigating land and is still used for some tasks. Some scholars believe it was invented by the ancient Greek mathematician Archimedes.   Gregory S. Chirikjian

See also **Invention** (The legacies of inventors).

Archimedean solid, *AHR kuh MEE dee uhn,* is any of 13 solid figures. These figures were first described by the ancient Greek mathematician Archimedes.

Archimedean solids are *semiregular convex polyhedrons* (see **Polyhedron**). The *faces* (surfaces) of any Archimedean solid represent more than one kind of regular polygon. However, all the *polyhedral angles* are identical. A polyhedral angle is a figure formed at a *vertex* (point) where three or more faces meet.

One example of an Archimedean solid is the *truncated cube.* This figure is formed when each corner of a cube is *truncated* (cut off) at the same angle. An equilat-

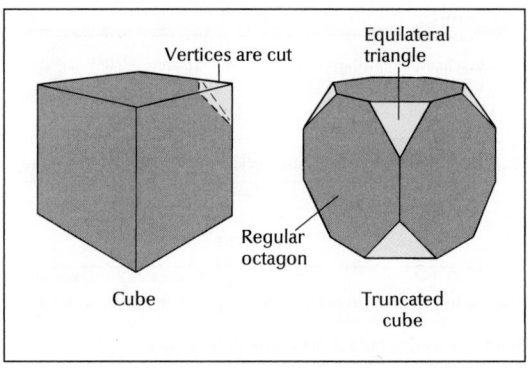

WORLD BOOK illustrations by Zorica Dabich

A truncated cube is a type of Archimedean solid. It is formed when the eight vertices of a cube are cut off at the same angle, leaving an equilateral triangle in place of each vertex. Each square face of the original cube becomes a regular octagon.

eral triangle then replaces each corner and an octagon replaces each square face of the cube. Thus, a truncated cube has six faces that are octagons, and eight faces that are equilateral triangles. Each vertex is the corner of one triangle and two octagons.   Blake E. Peterson

Archimedes, *AHR kuh MEE deez* (287?-212 B.C.), was the most original and profound mathematician of ancient times. Archimedes, a Greek, was also a physicist and a mechanical engineer. In the ancient world, he was best known as an inventor. His surviving writings rank among the masterpieces of scientific literature, especially *On the Sphere and Cylinder.*

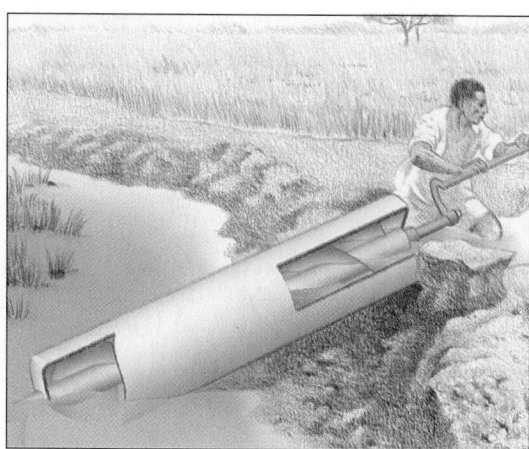

The Archimedean screw raises water as the handle is turned. The water is carried upward within the spiral chambers as the screw revolves. The water comes out of the screw's upper end.

WORLD BOOK illustration by Oxford Illustrators Limited

His life. Archimedes was born in Syracuse, the largest Greek settlement in Sicily. He probably went to study in Alexandria, Egypt, then the chief center of Greek learning. There, Archimedes studied with disciples of Euclid, a famous Greek mathematician. Archimedes spent the rest of his life in Syracuse. When the Romans captured Syracuse, the Roman commander Marcellus ordered that citizens of Syracuse be left unharmed. But according to one story, Archimedes was killed by a soldier while working on a geometry problem.

His discoveries. Archimedes proved the law of the lever and invented the compound pulley. With these machines, it is possible to move a great weight with a small force. Archimedes reportedly once boasted to Hiero II, king of Syracuse: "Give me a place to stand on, and I will move the entire Earth." He was referring to the way levers and pulleys can help people move objects many times their own size. The king challenged him to prove his boast. Archimedes is said to have used a system of pulleys to move a ship fully loaded with passengers and freight (see **Lever; Pulley**). In his investigations of force and motion, Archimedes also discovered that every object has a *center of gravity.* This is a single point at which the force of gravity appears to act on the object (see **Gravity, Center of**).

Archimedes did much of his work for King Hiero. In one famous story, the king suspected that a goldsmith had not made a new crown of pure gold but had mixed in some less costly silver. The king asked Archimedes to find out if the goldsmith had cheated.

Archimedes found the answer to this problem while taking a bath. His solution rested on *volume* (the amount of space occupied by an object). Archimedes noticed that water spilled out of the bath as he placed his body into it. By measuring the amount of water his body displaced, he could measure its volume. Archimedes was so excited when he found the answer that he ran into the street without dressing, shouting "Eureka!" (I have found it!). Archimedes compared the amount of water displaced by the crown with the amount of water displaced by an equal weight of pure gold. The crown dis-

placed more water, and so it was not pure gold. The goldsmith had cheated.

Archimedes discovered other basic laws of *hydrostatics,* the branch of physics that deals with liquids at rest. One of the major laws, called *Archimedes's principle,* describes *buoyancy.* Buoyancy is the loss in weight an object seems to undergo when placed in a liquid, as compared to its weight in air. Archimedes's principle states that an object fully or partly immersed in a liquid is buoyed upward by a force equal to the weight of the liquid displaced by that object. From this principle, he concluded that a floating object displaces an amount of liquid equal to its own weight.

His inventions. Archimedes is credited with inventing a device used in ancient Egypt to drain and irrigate the land in the Nile Valley. This device, known as the Archimedean screw, is still used today. Archimedes also invented devices used to defend Syracuse against Roman attacks. These devices included cranes that could pull Roman ships out of the water and twirl them around, and *catapults,* weapons that shot heavy rocks at the enemy. Some writers of ancient times reported that Archimedes designed a system of mirrors that reflected the sun's rays to set Roman ships on fire. However, historians doubt if the fire mirrors ever existed.

His mathematics. Archimedes made significant contributions to *pure mathematics* (mathematical knowledge for its own sake). He was the first to find the area under a segment of the *parabola,* a kind of curved shape in geometry. Archimedes also devised an *algorithm* (procedure) to approximate the value of *pi,* the ratio of a circle's circumference to its diameter. He showed that the value of pi is greater than $3\frac{10}{71}$ but less than $3\frac{1}{7}$. Archimedes felt that his greatest discoveries were the formulas for the surface and volume of a sphere. He also devised a system of notation for expressing numbers far larger than those represented in the alphabetic numeration system then used. Eli Maor

See also **Archimedean screw; Archimedean solid; Calculus; Hydraulics.**

Archipelago, AHR *kuh PEHL uh goh,* is a Greek word that means *chief sea.* It now applies to any broad expanse of water containing islands, and is often used for the islands themselves. The best-known examples are the Malay and Lofoten archipelagos. See also **Island; Pacific Islands.** Peter P. Sakalowsky

Archipenko, AHR *kuh PEHNG koh,* **Alexander** (1887-1964), was a pioneer Cubist sculptor. He was one of the first sculptors to show that spaces can be as important to a work as the solids. This view was a basic element in Archipenko's style throughout his career. His use of solids and hollows influenced many modern sculptors. Archipenko's forms are *concave* (curving inward) and *convex* (curving outward) with angular shapes and openings. Typical examples include *Seated Woman* (1916) and *Dual* (1955). He was also one of the first artists to adapt the new technique of *collage* to sculpture, mixing a wide variety of materials (see **Collage**).

Archipenko was born on May 30, 1887, in Kiev, Ukraine. He moved to the United States in 1923 and became a citizen in 1928. He founded art schools in Europe and America and taught at several universities in the United States. Archipenko died on Feb. 25, 1964. Joseph F. Lamb

The Heydar Aliyev Center, a cultural complex in Baku, Azerbaijan, was designed by the Iraqi-British architect Zaha Hadid (2012). Hadid used concrete to create a flowing, curved style that harmonizes with the surrounding landscape. Throughout history, architects have sought to reflect their society's values and ideals as they practiced one of the world's oldest art forms.

Architecture

Architecture is a term with several meanings. It may refer to the art and science of building, which is practiced by artists called architects. Or, *architecture* may mean the buildings themselves. The term may also have a historical meaning referring either to the building style of a particular culture or to an artistic movement. For example, we speak of Greek architecture, Gothic architecture, or Islamic architecture.

Architects create many kinds of structures. For instance, they design houses, schools, hotels, hospitals, stadiums, factories, office buildings, theaters, and houses of worship. Architects also design monuments dedicated to the memory of important events and people. The beauty of a city or town is largely influenced by the quality of its architecture.

Although architecture has artistic qualities, it must also satisfy a number of important practical requirements. For example, an architect may design an office building that looks beautiful. However, if people cannot work comfortably and efficiently in it, the building fails architecturally.

There are unique features of architecture that set it apart from other arts. In most cases, painters, writers, composers, and other artists create their works and then try to sell them. But a building may cost millions or billions of dollars to construct. In nearly all instances, architects must have a buyer for their work before they create it. Rarely can an architect design an office building, afford to have it constructed, and then try to find someone who will buy it.

Unlike some other artists, architects must work with other people to produce their designs. Novelists, for example, can create their stories alone from their own inspiration. But almost all architects design a building for a client and must observe the client's wishes and needs. Within the limits of those wishes and needs, architects can make their personal artistic contributions.

Architects work closely with the client throughout the development of a building. They decide how best to fulfill the client's requirements and give advice on probable costs. They make drawings and models that show how the building will look after it is completed. They also work with the many different types of contractors who actually build the structure. Architects supervise the construction and, in many cases, receive a percentage of the construction budget as their fee.

Architecture is one of the oldest art forms. It dates from prehistoric times and is found in almost all societies. A society's architecture reflects the values and ideals of its people. For example, the ancient Greeks stressed discipline and harmony in life, and so they created an architectural style that was balanced and orderly. The beautifully proportioned Greek temple reflects this emphasis on harmony. The Middle Ages was a period of deep religious faith in Europe. Architects designed majestic cathedrals with *vaults* (arched ceilings) and towers that seemed to soar toward heaven. Like the Greek temple, the medieval cathedral was intended to inspire a mood of reverence among worshipers.

Architects rank among the greatest figures in the history of art. Many architectural masterpieces, however, were created by skilled builders who probably did not consider themselves artists and did not intend to build important works of architecture. During the 1600's, for example, colonists in New England built houses that were not primarily designed to be beautiful. Some of these houses have been preserved and are admired today for their skilled carpentry and handsome outlines.

This article describes the basic elements of architecture and discusses the history of architecture throughout the world from its beginnings to the present. The article also surveys the education and training needed to become an architect as well as the various careers available in architecture.

Elements of architecture

In designing a building, architects think in terms of *space, planes,* and *openings.* They consider a building as space enclosed by planes—that is, by the surface of walls, floors, and ceilings. Openings include doorways, windows, and archways. An architect's basic task is to "shape" space into appropriate and practical forms through the arrangement of openings and planes. At various times in history, architects have considered certain shapes more beautiful than others and have emphasized them in their designs. The most popular shapes have included the square, rectangle, and sphere. Architects often combine two or more shapes in one design.

A building should be pleasing to look at, but it should also enable people to live or work in it comfortably and efficiently. In addition, the structure should be well built so that it can stand a long time without expensive maintenance. To create an attractive and efficient building, an architect must balance three major elements: (1) function, (2) appearance, and (3) durability.

Function. Every building is designed for certain purposes. A functional building—whether a small house or a gigantic office building—fulfills those purposes by serving the needs of its users in a pleasant and convenient way. The building is also designed to provide lighting, electricity, and climate control.

Today, energy conservation has become an important consideration in architectural planning. For example, architects may use large windows or even entire walls made of glass to help heat a building with solar energy.

Many activities may take place within a building. In a house, common activities include eating, sleeping, bathing, and entertaining. Each activity has different requirements in regard to the location, size, lighting, and accessibility of the rooms in which the activity occurs. For example, a bedroom is a private room and should be set off from the rest of the living spaces. But everyone in a house uses the dining room, and so it should be more centrally located.

An office building involves a much more complex arrangement of space than a house. The architect must make sure that hundreds or perhaps thousands of workers can move quickly through the various parts of the building. In addition, visitors should be able to enter and leave the building easily. Parts of the structure may house special equipment, and a large amount of storage space may be required. The architect must also consider the activities that take place outside the building. For example, the building may require parking facilities. In addition, the architect may have to plan traffic patterns so that automobiles and other vehicles can approach and leave the building without crossing many lanes of traffic. Driveways must be wide enough for fire trucks to enter, and loading docks must be the proper height for delivery trucks.

Appearance. An architect determines the exterior appearance of the building not only by its shape but also by the choice of materials. The natural colors of stone, brick, and wood have always been popular, alone or in combinations. During the 1900's, tinted glass played an important role in exterior building design. Many architects give special attention to texture in their designs. Some architects choose rough-textured wood or stone. Others prefer the sleek, elegant quality of highly polished glass and metal.

Many architects have created dramatic or pleasing patterns through the skillful arrangement of materials. For example, architects have used glass and concrete, various combinations of brickwork, or contrasting kinds of stone.

Proportion is vital to a building's appearance. All the parts of a building should be in proper relation to one another, neither too large nor too small. In addition, the size and shape of the building should blend with its site and surroundings. A tall glass-and-metal building would be appropriate in the downtown area of a large city, but it would be out of place in a neighborhood of single-family houses.

Durability. Most architecture is intended to stand a long time. To last many years without costly maintenance, a building must have a strong foundation. In addition, the exterior must be able to resist wear from the weather, and high-quality materials must be used in the interior.

Architectural terms

Ambulatory is a continuous aisle in a circular building. In a church, the ambulatory serves as a semicircular aisle that encloses the apse.

Apse is a semicircular area. In most churches, the apse is at the far end of the building and contains the main altar.

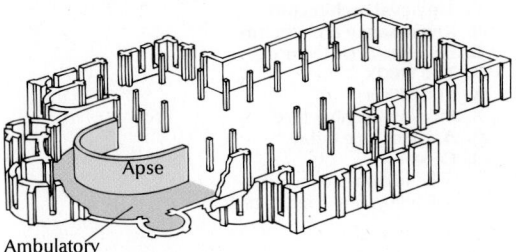

Apse

Ambulatory

Arcade refers to a series of arches supported by columns or piers. A passageway formed by the arches is also called an arcade.

Arch is a curved structure used to support the weight of the material above it. The stone at the top of an arch is called the *keystone.*

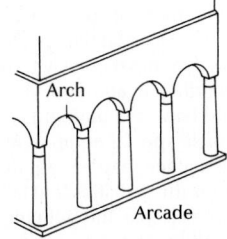

Arch

Arcade

Architrave makes up the lowest part of an entablature. It rests on the capital of a column. For a drawing of an architrave, see Entablature on the opposite page.

Buttress is a support built against an outside wall of a building. A *flying buttress* is an arched support that extends from a column or pier to the wall.

Buttress   Flying buttress

Cantilever is a horizontal projection, such as a balcony or a beam, which is supported only at one end.

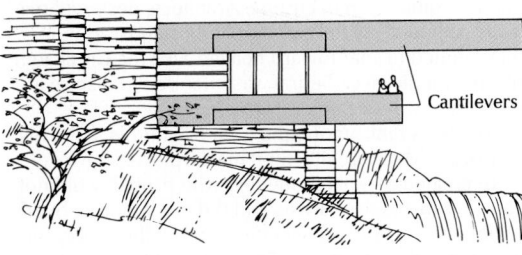

Cantilevers

Capital, in an order, forms the upper part of a column. It separates the shaft from the entablature.

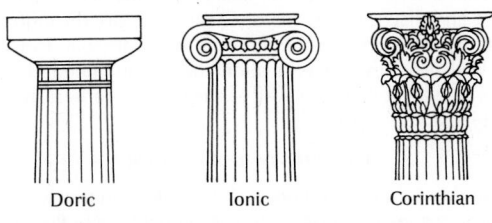

Doric   Ionic   Corinthian

Colonnade means a row of columns, usually set an equal distance from each other.

Column is a vertical support. In an order, it consists of a shaft and a capital and often rests on a base.

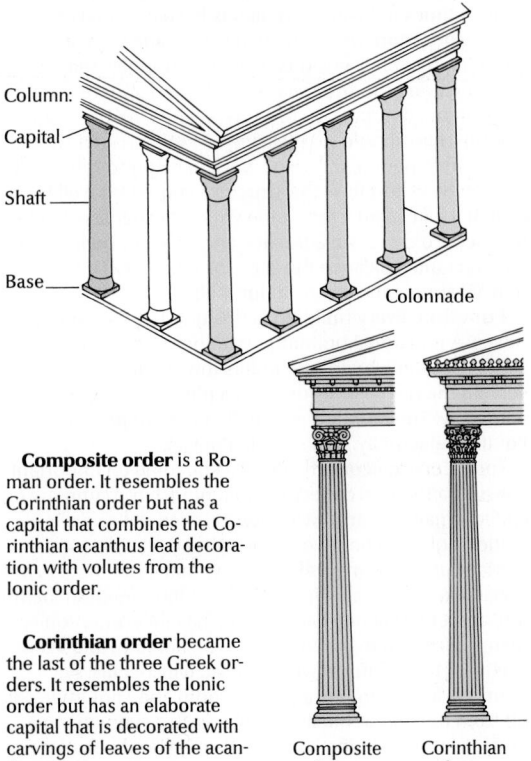

Column:

Capital

Shaft

Base

Colonnade

Composite order is a Roman order. It resembles the Corinthian order but has a capital that combines the Corinthian acanthus leaf decoration with volutes from the Ionic order.

Corinthian order became the last of the three Greek orders. It resembles the Ionic order but has an elaborate capital that is decorated with carvings of leaves of the acanthus plant.

Composite order

Corinthian order

Cornice forms the upper part of an entablature and extends beyond the frieze.

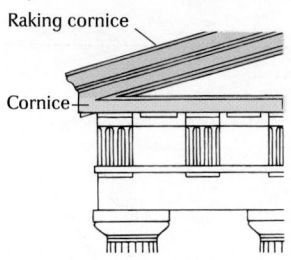

Raking cornice

Cornice

Doric order

Doric order was the first and simplest of the three Greek orders. The Doric is the only order that normally has no base.

Entablature refers to the upper horizontal part of an order between a capital and the roof. It consists of three major parts—the architrave, frieze, and cornice.

Entablature:

Cornice

Frieze

Architrave

Facade is the front of a building. Most facades contain an entrance.

Frieze forms the middle part of an entablature and is often decorated with a horizontal band of relief sculpture.

Ionic order was the second of the three Greek orders. It has a capital decorated with carved spiral scrolls called *volutes.*

Module is a measurement, such as the diameter of a column, which architects use to establish the proportions of an entire structure.

Ionic order

Nave is the chief area within a church. It extends from the main entrance to the transept.

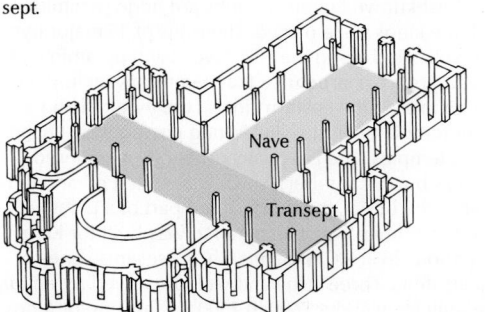

Nave

Transept

Order, in classical architecture, consisted of a type of column and entablature. Orders served as the basic elements of Greek and Roman architecture and influenced many later styles.

Pediment is a triangular area between the horizontal entablature and the sloping roof at the front of a classical-style building.

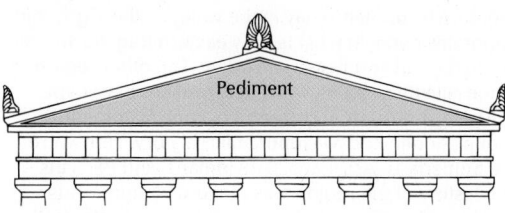

Pediment

Pendentive is a curved support shaped like an inverted triangle. Pendentives hold up a dome.

Dome

Pendentive

Pier refers to a supporting element other than a wall or column.

Post and lintel is a method of construction in which vertical beams (posts) support a horizontal beam (lintel).

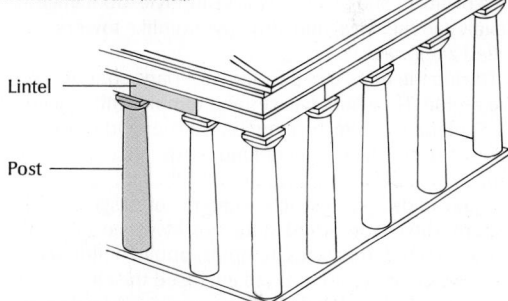

Lintel

Post

Shaft is the main part of a column below the capital. Many shafts have shallow vertical grooves called *fluting.*

Transept forms the arms in a T- or cross-shaped church.

Tuscan order, a Roman order, resembles the Doric order, but the shaft has no fluting.

Vault is an arched ceiling commonly made of brick, concrete, or stone. A *barrel vault,* the simplest form of vault, is a single continuous arch. A *groined vault* is formed by joining two barrel vaults at right angles. A *ribbed vault* has diagonal arches that project from the inner surface.

Tuscan order

WORLD BOOK illustrations by Robert Keys

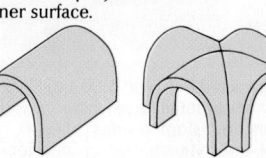

Barrel vault   Groined vault   Ribbed vault

Early architecture

The first significant architecture appeared in two regions of the Middle East more than 5,000 years ago. One region, Mesopotamia, lay in the valley of the Tigris and Euphrates rivers in what is now eastern Iraq, northeastern Syria, and southeastern Turkey. The other region lay in the Nile River Valley in what is present-day Egypt.

Mesopotamian architecture. Four major culture groups dominated Mesopotamian history. They were the Sumerians, Assyrians, Babylonians, and Persians. The history of the region was marked by numerous wars and invasions. Thus, the various cultures constructed many fortified buildings.

Most Mesopotamian buildings were made of brick and clay, which are not highly durable materials. As a result, no complete example of Mesopotamian architecture has survived. However, archaeologists have been able to reconstruct the plans of some buildings.

A Sumerian civilization developed in Mesopotamia in the 3000's B.C. The first important Sumerian structures were temples. An early example was the White Temple (late 3000's B.C.) in the city of Uruk. The temple was made of whitewashed brick. Architects built the temple on a platform known as a *plinth.* Later Mesopotamians developed this form into large pyramidlike towers called *ziggurats.*

During the mid-700's B.C., the Assyrians conquered the region. They built palaces and temples influenced by Sumerian architecture but on a larger and more magnificent scale. The citadel of King Sargon II, which was built in the city of Khorsabad during the late 700's B.C., was one of the greatest achievements of Assyrian architecture. The citadel stood in the northwest corner of the city and included palaces, temples, public buildings, and a ziggurat. A fortified wall enclosed the city.

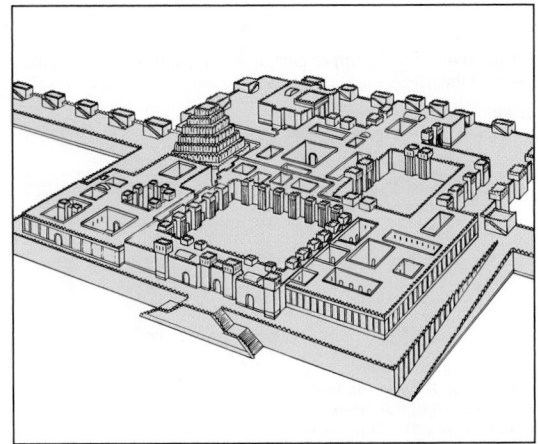

The citadel of King Sargon II was built in the Assyrian capital of Khorsabad during the late 700's B.C. The citadel included palaces, temples, public buildings, and a stepped pyramid called a *ziggurat,* which rose above the other structures.

After the Assyrians fell in the 600's B.C., the Babylonians rose to power. They built a large ziggurat in their capital city of Babylon (early 500's B.C.). Babylon also included the famous Hanging Gardens and the Ishtar Gate, which was decorated with colored glazed brick. The gate is now preserved in the State Museums in Berlin, Germany.

In 539 B.C., the Persians conquered Mesopotamia. The Persian religion, Zoroastrianism, did not require temples. But the Persians built many palaces, most notably a palace complex in the religious capital of Persepolis. This group of adjoining buildings, which was completed in the mid-400's B.C., consisted of several palaces, halls, chambers, and courtyards. The Persian king received visitors in a huge room known as the Hall of One Hundred Columns. This room was 250 feet (76 meters) square with a vast beamed ceiling supported by columns perhaps 60 feet (18 meters) high.

For illustrations of Mesopotamian architecture, see **Babylon; Persia, Ancient.**

Egyptian architecture centered on the king, who was the religious and political ruler of ancient Egypt. The Egyptians considered their kings to be gods, and they built stone tombs, temples, and palaces as monuments to them.

The best-known Egyptian tombs are huge pyramids in which the kings were buried. The ruins of 35 major pyramids still stand along the Nile River. Each pyramid was part of a group of structures that commonly included a large temple on the eastern side of the pyramid and a smaller temple near the Nile. A long passageway linked the two temples. The Egyptians probably considered the king's burial chamber, which was sealed off and hidden after the burial, the most sacred part of a pyramid.

The first known Egyptian pyramid was built for King Zoser about 2650 B.C. at Saqqarah. It rises in a series of six giant steps. Three large and well-preserved pyramids were built from about 2600 to 2500 B.C. at Giza for Kings Khufu, Khafre, and Menkaure. These massive works originally had smooth sides.

A great period of Egyptian architecture began in the

The White Temple was constructed between 3500 and 3100 B.C. at Uruk, a city in southern Mesopotamia, in what is now Iraq. It was built atop a platform with four sloping sides called a *plinth,* as shown in this model. Later Mesopotamians developed this form into the pyramidlike towers called *ziggurats* that stood in a city center as part of a temple complex.

Queen Hatshepsut's temple was built about 1480 B.C. at Deir el-Bahri, Egypt. The Egyptians erected the temple at the foot of a huge cliff. Rows of columns supported a series of limestone terraces. A ramp provided access to each terrace.

© Nestor Noci, Shutterstock

1500's B.C. and lasted for about 500 years. Architects during this time mainly designed temples rather than pyramids. The temples were huge structures supported by columns. Ramps and halls connected the various rooms. People entered most temples through gateways formed by two huge towers called *pylons*. One unusual masterpiece of the period is the temple built for Queen Hatshepsut at Deir el-Bahri about 1480 B.C. Her subjects erected it along the foot of a huge cliff, vividly uniting architecture with nature.

For illustrations of Egyptian architecture, see **Egypt, Ancient; Pyramids.**

Asian and pre-Columbian architecture

Asian architecture has four main branches—Chinese, Japanese, Indian, and Islamic. Indian and Islamic architecture have had especially widespread influence. Indian architecture includes the architecture of Bangladesh,

Cambodia, Indonesia, Myanmar (also called Burma), Nepal, Pakistan, Sri Lanka, Thailand, and Tibet as well as that of India. Islamic architecture refers to buildings designed by Muslims. Muslims are followers of Islam, the religion based on the life and teaching of the Prophet Muhammad. Islamic architecture can be found primarily in the Middle East, northern Africa, Spain, and Asia.

Thousands of years ago, the ancestors of Native Americans migrated from Asia to the Americas. By 100 B.C., several Native American groups, particularly in what is now Latin America, had developed advanced cultures and produced magnificent architecture. Native American art and architecture created before A.D. 1492 is called *pre-Columbian* because it was produced before Christopher Columbus arrived in the Americas.

Chinese architecture. Chinese architecture began to develop in ancient times. The Chinese constructed a variety of buildings, but the chief structures were Bud-

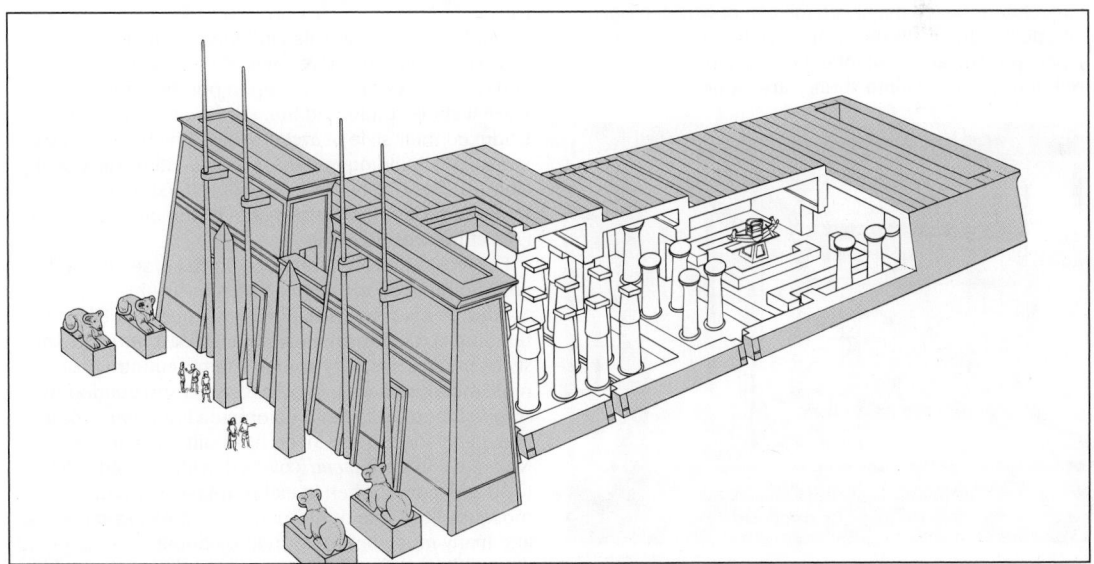

WORLD BOOK illustration by Kevin Maddison

The Temple of Khons was built in Karnak, Egypt, during the 1100's B.C. Two large towers called *pylons, left,* guarded the entrance. This cutaway drawing shows the columns within the temple that supported the roof. A sacred chamber at the right was dedicated to the moon god Khons.

Traditional Chinese architecture featured roofs that curved upward at the end. The roofs were supported by wooden columns connected to the ceiling beams by wooden brackets known as *dougong.* The structure shown here is part of the famous Forbidden City in Beijing.

© Sean Pavone, Shutterstock

dhist temples and many-storied towers called *pagodas.*

Chinese temples consisted of rectangular wooden halls that featured an elaborate and beautiful arrangement of timber beams in the ceiling. Walls did not support the roof but served simply as screens for privacy and for protection against the weather. The roof support came from posts connected to the ceiling beams by wooden brackets called *dougong,* many of which were carved, painted red, and coated with gold. The dougong allowed the roof to curve gracefully upward. The Chinese covered many of their roofs with blue, green, or yellow glazed tiles.

For illustrations of Chinese architecture, see **Beijing; Pagoda.**

Japanese architecture has been strongly influenced by Chinese architecture. Thus, traditional Japanese architecture is based mainly on the use of wooden beams and posts. Shinto shrines, which are found throughout Japan, provide an excellent example. Shinto is the native religion of Japan. Shinto shrines are wooden frame

Japanese architecture became noted for its simplicity, elegance, and sense of proportion. In a traditional house, thin walls are used to provide privacy rather than support. Partitions can be moved to change the room size.

© SenSeHi/Shutterstock

structures built on posts that raise the shrine above the ground. Ceiling beams project beyond the walls and give the roofs a deep overhang.

Traditional Japanese houses, whether large or small, have the same design. Upright posts support the roof. Sliding doors are built into the lightweight walls. The interior walls provide privacy rather than support. Many of the houses are set within walled gardens. For a picture of a traditional house, see **Japan** (Way of life).

Indian architecture had developed by the 200's B.C. The first great influence on Indian architecture was Buddhism, a major religion in India. Buddhism inspired the building of temples called *chaityas,* monasteries, and *stupas.* A stupa is a dome-shaped monument that houses relics of Buddha, who founded the religion in the 500's B.C. Many of the temples were carved from solid rock.

Hinduism and Islam also influenced Indian architecture. Hindu temples have rows of sculptured columns and richly carved exteriors, open porches, and spires. The Muslims conquered India during the 1500's and introduced their style of architecture. The most outstanding Islamic building in India is the beautiful Taj Mahal (about 1630-1650) in Agra. Angkor (1100's), a group of temples in Cambodia, shows the Hindu influence on architecture outside India.

For illustrations of Indian architecture, see **India** (The arts); **Sculpture** (As part of architecture).

Islamic architecture. The most important Islamic building is the house of worship called a *mosque.* The styles of mosques vary among Islamic countries, but most mosques have a large courtyard surrounded by *colonnades* or *arcades.* A colonnade is a row of columns, and an arcade is a row of arches built on columns. Mosque walls are *faced* (covered) with colored brick, tiles, and stucco, often in elaborate patterns. All mosques have one or more towers known as *minarets,* and many mosques are topped by domes.

In addition to mosques, Muslim architects have designed palaces, tombs, and religious schools called *madrasahs.* The typical madrasah is a four-sided building surrounding a courtyard. In most cases, a large arched

Angkor is a group of temples in Cambodia. The temples, built of richly carved sandstone, were begun in the A.D. 1100's and show the Hindu influence on architecture outside India. The main entrance, pictured at the left, is a long ceremonial gateway topped by three towers.

© Oleskaus/Shutterstock

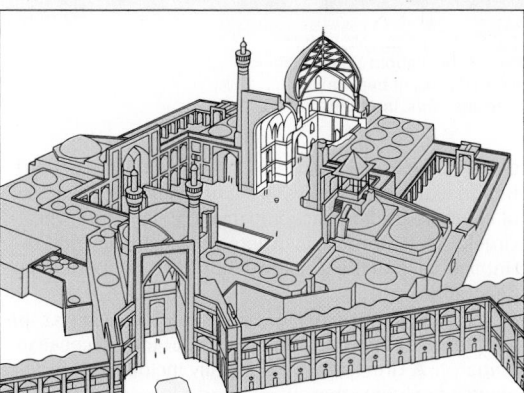

WORLD BOOK illustration by Trevor Hill, Venner Artists Ltd.

Islamic architecture has produced many beautiful houses of worship called *mosques*. The drawing above shows the Imperial Mosque in Isfahan, Iran. The domed sanctuary appears at the top. Four *iwans* (halls) with arched entrances surround the main courtyard. The slender towers are called *minarets*.

hall called an *iwan* is in the middle of each side of the building. Students hear lectures held in the iwans.

For illustrations of Islamic architecture, see **Islamic art; Jerusalem; Spain** (The arts).

Pre-Columbian architecture. The Aztec, Toltec,

Maya, and Inca developed the most influential ancient cultures in what is now Latin America. The Aztec and Toltec flourished in central Mexico. The Maya lived in Mexico and Central America, and the Inca built a huge empire in western South America.

Nearly all the surviving Aztec, Toltec, and Maya structures had a religious purpose. The most impressive of these structures were stone pyramids topped by small temples. The pyramids were part of ceremonial centers that also included altars, palaces, and plazas. The Inca built large temples, fortresses, and public buildings on mountainsides. Some of the best-known Inca ruins are at Machu Picchu, a site that lies in the Andes Mountains about 8,000 feet (2,400 meters) above sea level.

A number of Native American cultures developed in North America. The Ancestral Pueblo people of what is now the Southwestern United States created the most significant architecture. Their architecture consisted primarily of housing that rose next to cliffs like apartment houses. They built their cliff dwellings of stone, adobe, or timber. Social and religious ceremonies were held in circular chambers called *kivas,* which were constructed underground.

For illustrations of pre-Columbian architecture, see **Aztec; Colorado** (Visitor's guide); **Indian, American** (Indians of Middle America); **Maya; Mexico** (History); **Pyramids.**

© GoodShoot/SuperStock

Maya architecture was noted for magnificent stone pyramids. Most of the pyramids had a flat top on which one or more small temples stood. Priests climbed the stairs of the pyramids and performed ceremonies in the temples. This picture shows the ruins of a pyramid in the Maya city of Chichén Itzá in northern Yucatán, Mexico.

© Thinkstock   © Thinkstock

Greek architecture can be traced back to palaces built on the island of Crete by a people known as the Minoans. Short wooden columns supported the Palace of Minos, *left,* built about 1500 B.C. in Knossos, Crete. By the mid-400's B.C., classical Greek architecture featured rows of beautifully proportioned stone columns in such structures as the Temple of Hephaestus, *right,* in Athens.

Classical architecture

The term *classical architecture* refers to the building styles developed by the ancient Greeks and Romans. But the roots of classical architecture can be traced to buildings created by two early Greek peoples—the Minoans and the Mycenaeans. Classical Greek architecture, in turn, greatly influenced Roman architecture.

Minoan architecture. The Minoans developed the first important European civilization. They lived on the island of Crete in the Mediterranean Sea. The great age of Minoan architecture lasted from approximately 2000 to 1450 B.C.

The finest Minoan architectural achievement was the Palace of Minos (about 1500 B.C.) in the town of Knossos. This complex and sprawling structure had dozens of rooms built around a courtyard. Wooden columns supported the beams of the ceiling. Architects divided these beams into three horizontal bands. They were the *architrave* on the bottom, the *frieze* in the middle, and the *cornice* on top. The three sections together are called the *entablature.* The entablature became a vital part of later Greek architecture.

The Minoans also built palaces in the towns of Kato Zakro, Mallia, and Phaistos. All Minoan palaces served as administrative and commercial centers as well as royal residences.

Mycenaean architecture. The main center of the Mycenaeans was the city of Mycenae in southern Greece. After about 1600 B.C., they built beautifully cut stone tombs that resemble the shape of beehives. The finest example of a beehive tomb is called the Treasury of Atreus (about 1300-1250 B.C.).

The Mycenaeans constructed fortresslike palaces of huge stone blocks. The heart of the palace was a rectangular royal audience hall known as the *megaron.* A porch, which was supported by two columns, and a vestibule led to the megaron. The megaron had a hearth in the middle for an open fire. A hole in the ceiling allowed the smoke to escape. Four columns around the hearth supported the roof.

Classical Greek architecture has been imitated down to the present day. The best-known Greek contribution to architecture was a set of styles, called *orders,* of columns and their accompanying entablature. The Greeks used three basic orders—Doric, Ionic, and Corinthian. Each of the three orders had its own distinctive decoration.

The principal type of classical Greek building was the temple. Its design followed the plan of the Mycenaean megaron. A Greek temple generally included arrangements of columns that surrounded a long chamber for a statue of the god or goddess to whom the temple was dedicated. Many Greek temples were built on a hill that overlooked a city. Such a hill was known as an *acropolis.*

The Greeks developed formulas for the various styles of temples. The formulas set forth the order; the number, height, width, and spacing of the columns; and even the details of the smallest carvings. A typical formula was *Doric peripteral hexastyle. Doric* meant that the building would be erected in the Doric order with standard Doric ornamentation. *Peripteral* indicated that the building would be surrounded by a single row of columns. *Hexastyle* meant that the front entrance, or *portico,* would be six columns wide. Greek architects used the diameter of the column at its base as the unit of measurement for determining the proportions of the entire building. This unit is called the *module.*

In spite of the use of formulas, Greek temple designs had great flexibility and variety. A temple could be low and long or high and short. It might be simple or highly decorative. The number of columns could vary from 2 to more than 100.

For illustrations of Greek architecture, see **Athens; Column; Drama** (Greek drama); **Greece; Greece, Ancient.**

Roman architecture. The Romans ruled the largest empire of ancient times. At its peak, the Roman Empire included all the lands bordering the Mediterranean Sea. It also extended as far north as Scotland and as far east as the Persian Gulf. Numerous architectural styles were used throughout the empire because many regions had developed their own building traditions. Nevertheless, Roman architecture had a great deal of stylistic unity.

Houses built by aristocrats of ancient Rome often featured a large central hall called an *atrium* and a courtyard called a *peristyle*. A covered walkway enclosed the peristyle, which included a garden, fountains, and statues. The atrium shown here in the foreground and the peristyle in the background were part of a residence called the House of the Vettii. The residence was excavated and restored at Pompeii, which was buried by the eruption of Mount Vesuvius in A.D. 79.

© Thinkstock

The Romans built more kinds of structures than did the people of any earlier civilization. In addition to houses, temples, and palaces, the Romans constructed such projects as aqueducts, public baths, shops, theaters, and gigantic outdoor arenas. Most of these structures were built during the period from about 100 B.C. to the A.D. 300's.

The Romans were the first to fully utilize two structural forms, the *arch* and the *vault.* A vault is an arched ceiling. The dome was a common form of vault in Roman architecture. The use of the arch and vault reduced or eliminated the need for columns to support the roof. Instead, the roof could rest solely on the outer walls. The Romans often used columns simply as sculptural decoration attached to walls.

A splendid example of Roman vault design is the Baths of Caracalla (A.D. 217) in Rome. The ruins of the building still stand. The baths had a system of vaults that

© Bojan Pavlukovic, Shutterstock

A vault is an arched ceiling that can cover a large space or building. The Romans invented the vault. The Basilica of Constantine in Rome, *shown here,* had a vaulted ceiling.

covered vast areas of interior space. This space was so high and so deep that the Romans admired it as an extraordinary new form of architectural beauty.

For illustrations of Roman architecture, see **Rome; Rome, Ancient; Forum, Roman; Spain** (History); **Colosseum.**

Medieval architecture

Medieval architecture refers to structures built in Europe during the Middle Ages. This historical period lasted from about the A.D. 400's through the 1400's. The intellectual and spiritual life of medieval Europe centered on the Christian church, and so nearly all architects designed churches, monasteries, and other religious

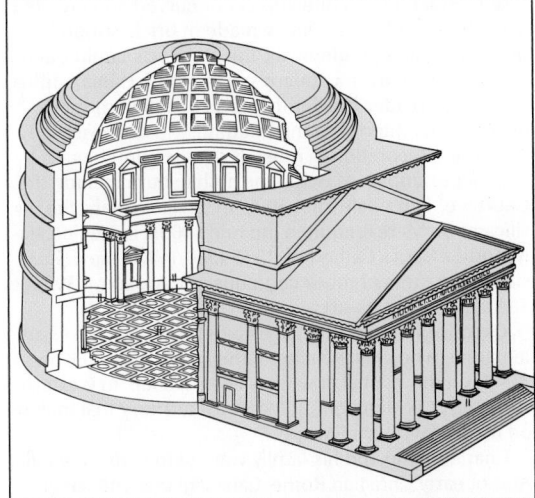

WORLD BOOK illustration by Trevor Hill, Venner Artists Ltd.

The Pantheon, built as a temple in Rome about A.D. 126, still stands. This cutaway drawing shows the interior of the domed, circular building. Corinthian columns support the porch roof.

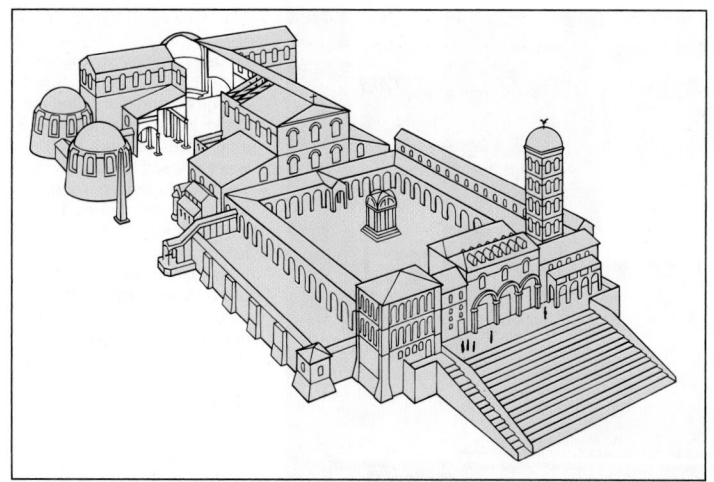 

WORLD BOOK illustrations by Trevor Hill, Venner Artists Ltd.

Early churches were built, in most cases, on the oblong *basilica* plan or the round or many-sided *centralized* plan. Old St. Peter's, *left,* which stood on the site of the present St. Peter's in Rome, was the best-known early Christian basilica. It was begun about 330. San Vitale, *right,* is a centralized church in the Byzantine style. It was built in Ravenna, Italy, in the mid-500's.

buildings. However, castles, fortresses, and other nonreligious structures were also built.

Medieval architects developed a number of styles. The *Byzantine* style became dominant in eastern Europe. In western Europe, the leading styles were the *Carolingian,* the *Romanesque,* and the *Gothic.* All four styles were preceded by early Christian architecture, which flourished from the 300's to the 500's.

Early Christian architecture. During the early centuries of Christianity, a number of regional cultures—and regional architectural styles—developed in Europe and the Middle East. But most early Christian architects borrowed heavily from the Romans. They based their primary church design, the *basilica,* on large Roman halls that were used for public meetings.

Old St. Peter's Church (begun about 330) was probably the first important early Christian basilica. It stood on the site of the present St. Peter's Basilica in Rome. Worshipers entered Old St. Peter's through a large open courtyard called the *atrium* and a vestibule called the *narthex.* The atrium and narthex separated the noisy city from the quiet church. The plan of the interior resembled the shape of a T. The stem of the T was the *nave.* Two aisles ran along each side of the nave. The *transept* formed the arms of the T. A semicircular space called the *apse* opened from the center of the transept at the far end of the church. The apse, which was covered by a half dome, contained the main altar.

In many basilicas, colonnades and arcades separated the interior into a nave and side aisles. The exteriors of most basilicas were plain brick or stone, but the interiors glowed with brilliant *mosaics* and *frescoes.* Mosaics consist of small pieces of glass, marble, or stone arranged to form an image. Frescoes are paintings created by applying paint to fresh plaster.

Byzantine architecture. In 330, the Roman emperor Constantine the Great established a new capital of the Roman Empire at the city of Byzantium in what is now Turkey. Byzantium was renamed *Constantinople.* In 395, the Roman Empire split into two parts—the East Roman Empire, which had its capital in Constantinople, and the West Roman Empire, which had its capital in Rome. The West Roman Empire fell to Germanic tribes in the 400's. But the East Roman Empire thrived. It later became known as the Byzantine Empire.

By the 500's, a distinct Byzantine style of art had developed. The finest achievement of Byzantine architecture was the great domed cathedral Hagia Sophia (532-537) in Constantinople. It was designed by Anthemius of Tralles and Isidorus of Miletus. The Ottoman Turks captured Constantinople in 1453 and later renamed the city *Istanbul.* They converted Hagia Sophia into a mosque. But the only change they made to the exterior of the building was to add four minarets.

Hagia Sophia has a huge central dome that tops a square space. This arrangement became a common feature of Byzantine architecture. Four curved and inverted triangles called *pendentives,* made of brick, support the dome. By using pendentives, the architects could build a round dome over a square space. Inside Hagia Sophia, two-story arcades border the nave. Beautiful mosaics decorate the interior of the building. Mosaics were an important decoration in most Byzantine churches.

Other examples of Byzantine architecture include the Church of San Vitale (mid-500's) in Ravenna, Italy; the Basilica of St. Mark (begun in the mid-1000's) in Venice, Italy; and St. Basil's Cathedral (1555-1560) in Moscow, Russia. For pictures of these churches, see **Moscow; Venice.** See also **Byzantine art.**

Carolingian architecture takes its name from Charlemagne, who was the king of the Franks from 768 to 814. From his capital at what is now Aachen, in western Germany, Charlemagne ruled a vast territory that included most of western Europe.

Charlemagne and his family wanted to revive the culture of early Christian Rome. Carolingian architects claimed that they copied early Christian architecture, but they changed the models to suit their needs. In particular, they made outstanding contributions to church and monastery design. The architects followed the plan

Hagia Sophia is the finest example of Byzantine architecture. It was built from 532 to 537 as a cathedral in Constantinople (now Istanbul), Turkey. It is noted for its great interior space.

© Artur Bogacki, Shutterstock

of the basilica but added chapels, elaborate tombs, and high towers. They also invented an entrance known as a *westwork,* which included a porch, chapels, and small towers called *turrets.* Carolingian monks developed a monastery plan in which *cloisters* (covered walks) joined the church, library, kitchen, and other facilities.

Romanesque architecture began in the late 800's and achieved its greatest importance during the 1000's and 1100's. The most significant Romanesque buildings were churches designed in Italy, France, Germany, Spain, and England.

Scholars of the 1800's originated the term *Romanesque,* which means *like the Roman.* These scholars believed that Romanesque architecture chiefly reflected Roman designs. However, Romanesque architecture actually combined Roman with Byzantine styles and many new features.

Romanesque churches differed from country to country, but many of the churches shared certain features. The typical Romanesque church had thick walls, columns built close together, and heavy curved arches. A tower rose from the roof over the point where the transept crossed the nave. Four large supports called *piers* held up the tower. An arcade separated the nave from the side aisles. A gallery was built above the arcade. The *clerestory,* made up of a row of windows set in arches, topped the gallery.

During the Romanesque period, many people made *pilgrimages*—that is, journeys to sacred places. Groups of pilgrims traveled throughout Europe and Palestine to visit *pilgrimage churches,* which housed the bones or possessions of certain saints. Important pilgrimage churches were extremely large to accommodate the many visitors. An example is the enormous Church of St. Sernin (about 1080-1120) in Toulouse, France. The church has two aisles on each side of the nave. Small chapels open into the *ambulatory,* a semicircular aisle enclosing the apse. This plan permitted pilgrims to

© Gian Berto Vanni, Art Resource

© Vorm in Beeld/Shutterstock

Romanesque architecture flourished in the 1000's and 1100's. Maria Laach Abbey Church in Germany, *above,* is dominated by a square tower and two turrets. The interior of Worms Cathedral, *right,* in Germany has rounded arches typical of the Romanesque style.

move along the aisles without disturbing services at the main altar. See **Romanesque architecture**.

Gothic architecture flourished from the mid-1100's to as late as the 1600's in some parts of Europe. The word *Gothic* originated as a term of disapproval. It was used by artists and writers of the 1500's who wanted to revive the classical architecture of ancient Greece and Rome in Europe. They associated the Gothic style with the Goths, a Germanic people who had invaded Rome during the 400's. The artists and writers objected to the complicated Gothic designs, which differed so greatly from the harmonious classical style.

A new system of construction enabled Gothic architects to design churches with thinner walls and lighter piers than was possible in Romanesque churches. Many piers consisted of clusters of columns several stories high. Gothic architects extended the piers into the roof area and then curved out the individual columns like the ribs of an open umbrella. The space between the ribs was filled in with masonry. These *ribbed vaults* were among the most distinctive characteristics of Gothic architecture. Other common features of the style included pointed arches and the substitution of stained-glass windows for large portions of the walls. Many churches also had *flying buttresses,* which were brick or stone arched supports built against the exterior walls.

Sculptors carved the figures of saints and heroes of Christianity on church doorways. Medieval Christians believed that, in a symbolic sense, these saints and heroes inhabited and strengthened the church building.

For illustrations of Gothic churches, see **Chartres Cathedral; Gothic art; Notre Dame, Cathedral of; Reims; Rouen; Strasbourg**.

Renaissance architecture

The word *renaissance* means *rebirth*. In European history, it refers to the great rebirth of interest in classical culture, especially that of ancient Rome.

Renaissance architecture started in Italy in the early 1400's and spread throughout Europe during the 1500's. A group of Italian scholars and architects greatly influenced Renaissance architecture. These individuals knew classical culture well and considered it superior to the culture of their time. They studied Roman ruins and modeled their designs on classical buildings. They adopted the classical orders as well as Roman and Byzantine vaults and domes.

Early Renaissance architecture began during the 1400's. The originator of the new Renaissance style was Filippo Brunelleschi of Florence. Brunelleschi's first great project was the dome (1420-1436) for the Cathedral of Florence. The cathedral was begun in 1296 in the Gothic style of the late Middle Ages. Brunelleschi followed this style in designing the octagonal dome, but he also used a vault technique inspired by the Romans. Italians considered the Brunelleschi dome to be the greatest engineering accomplishment of their time.

Brunelleschi also designed other notable structures in Florence. They include the Foundling Hospital (begun in 1421), the Church of San Lorenzo (begun in 1421), and the Church of Santo Spirito (begun in 1436). The two churches were not completed until the second half of the 1400's, after Brunelleschi's death. In all of these buildings, the architect revived the classical forms that became basic elements of the Italian Renaissance style. For example, he used Corinthian columns in the Church of San Lorenzo. The church has geometric balance, and harmony typical of Renaissance architecture.

Leon Battista Alberti was another leading Italian Renaissance architect. Alberti wrote an influential book about classical architecture titled *On Architecture* (begun in the 1440's). The book stimulated scholars to discuss architectural theory for its own sake apart from its application in actual buildings.

© Ivan Vdovin, Alamy Images   © Photo Golfer/Shutterstock

Gothic cathedrals dominated French architecture from about 1150 to 1500. Arched supports called *flying buttresses* brace the exterior of the cathedral at Bourges, *left.* An arched ceiling called a *ribbed vault* covers the nave of the cathedral at Amiens, *right.* Ribbed vaults were one of the distinctive characteristics of Gothic architecture.

© Kavalenkava/Shutterstock

The dome of the Cathedral of Florence was an early achievement of Italian Renaissance architecture. Filippo Brunelleschi designed the dome, which was completed in 1436, partly on the principles of Roman vaults.

© Karin Wabro, Shutterstock

The Church of Sant' Andrea in Mantua, Italy, was designed by Leon Battista Alberti in the mid-1400's. The front resembles a Roman temple with an arch.

Alberti completed only a few designs, but they had great impact on later architects. He designed the *facade* (front) of the Church of Santa Maria Novella (about 1456-1470) in Florence. He decorated the facade with black and white marble, arranging a pattern of circles, squares, and rectangles in the upper stories. These patterns were taken from classical decorations and gave the impression of mathematical proportion and harmony. Alberti also designed the Church of Sant' Andrea (begun in 1470) in Mantua. The church's exterior has none of the sculptured Christian figures and other features typical of Gothic architecture. Instead, Alberti designed the facade to resemble a classical temple with a large arch in the center.

Later Renaissance architecture. The greatest building project of the later Renaissance was the reconstruction of St. Peter's Basilica in Rome. The project began in 1506, when Pope Julius II decided to demolish Old St. Peter's Church and build a new church on the site. The reconstruction was completed in the late 1600's. Altogether, 10 Italian architects worked on the church during that time, including Donato Bramante, Michelangelo, and Gian Lorenzo Bernini.

Bramante was the original architect of St. Peter's. He designed the structure as a combination of square, circular, and *Greek cross* forms. A Greek cross has four arms of equal length. Michelangelo designed the great ribbed dome (completed in 1591, after his death) as a Renaissance version of Brunelleschi's Gothic-style dome on the Cathedral of Florence.

Another great Italian Renaissance architect was Andrea Palladio. During the middle and late 1500's, Palladio designed Roman-inspired villas and palaces, which he published in a book that made him one of the most influential architects in history. His Villa Rotonda (begun about 1567) near Vicenza particularly influenced

© Andre Nantel, Shutterstock

St. Peter's Basilica stands in Rome on the site of Old St. Peter's. Construction began in 1506 and took about 150 years to complete. Ten architects worked on the project. The view shown here looks down the nave toward the main altar, which was designed by Gian Lorenzo Bernini, one of the church's most important architects.

The Villa Rotonda, designed by Andrea Palladio in the mid-1500's, is a classic of Renaissance architecture. It stands on a hill near Vicenza, Italy. A porch based on classical Roman temple designs extends from each of the building's four sides. A low dome covers the circular central hall.

© Photo MDP/Shutterstock

English and American architects of the 1700's.

From Italy, Renaissance architecture spread to France in the early 1500's and then to other European countries. At first, architects in these countries followed Italian models. However, they rapidly developed distinct national styles.

The finest French Renaissance buildings are magnificent *châteaux* (castles), such as those built at Fontainebleau, Chambord, and Azay-le-Rideau mainly during the early 1500's. In Spain, Juan de Herrera designed much of the Escorial (1563-1584) near Madrid. This enormous building consists of a church, a monastery, a palace, and a college. Inigo Jones produced the most notable early examples of Renaissance architecture in England during the early 1600's. He based his superb Banqueting House (1622) in London on Palladio's designs.

For illustrations of Renaissance architecture, see **Bramante, Donato; Jones, Inigo; Vatican City.**

© Richie Chan, Shutterstock

The château of Fontainebleau is an early example of Renaissance architecture in France. A horseshoe-shaped staircase, completed in the early 1500's, dominates the building's entrance.

Baroque architecture

Baroque architecture began in Rome during the early 1600's. It soon spread throughout Italy and to other parts of Europe. Baroque architects sought to produce highly dramatic effects in their works. The typical Baroque building featured curved forms, an extravagant use of columns, and ornate decoration.

The leading supporters of Baroque architecture were the Roman Catholic Church and powerful European monarchs. Church support resulted from the Counter Reformation of the 1500's and 1600's. This movement of renewal within the church stimulated a great outpouring of religious enthusiasm in Catholic countries. Architects designed elaborate Baroque churches and monasteries that reflected the drama and emotion of this religious spirit. At the same time, strong monarchs wanted architecture that would glorify their reigns. Magnificent Baroque palaces expressed the authority of these rulers.

The most spectacular examples of the Baroque style appeared in Italy, Austria, Spain, and southern Germany. Gian Lorenzo Bernini, Francesco Borromini, and Guarino Guarini rank as the most outstanding Baroque architects in Italy. The Baroque fascination with columns is reflected in the keyhole-shaped colonnade (begun 1657) that Bernini designed to enclose the courtyard of St. Peter's Basilica. Borromini's curves and twisted shapes characterize the famous Church of Sant' Agnese in Piazza Navona (1666) in Rome. The Church of San Lorenzo (1668-1687), located in Turin, is one of Guarini's finest designs.

Johann Bernhard Fischer von Erlach of Austria and Balthasar Neumann of Germany designed many fine Baroque churches and palaces in their countries. The extremely elaborate Spanish Baroque style is often called *Churrigueresque.* The name comes from three brothers—Alberto, Joaquín, and José Churriguera—who were early leaders of the style.

In France and England, the Baroque style was far less extravagant than it was in other European countries.

St. Paul's Cathedral in London is a masterpiece of English Baroque architecture. Sir Christopher Wren designed the church in the late 1600's. He included columns and other elements of classical Greek and Roman architecture.

French and English architects retained the Renaissance square, rectangle, and circle as basic forms of decoration. They designed enormous buildings with simple lines and row after row of columns or windows.

Perhaps the greatest French Baroque building is the magnificent Palace of Versailles (begun about 1661). Its major architects were Louis Le Vau and Jules Hardouin-Mansart. The palace is more than ¼ mile (0.4 kilometer) long and has about 1,300 rooms.

Sir John Vanbrugh designed the most extravagant English Baroque palace, Blenheim Palace (1705-1724) in Oxfordshire. The leading English architect of the Baroque style, however, was Sir Christopher Wren. His design for St. Paul's Cathedral (1675-1710) in London is a masterpiece of the style.

For pictures of Baroque architecture, see **Versailles, Palace of; Wren, Sir Christopher.**

The 1700's

During the 1700's, three major architectural styles appeared in Europe: (1) Rococo architecture, (2) the Palladian Revival, and (3) Neoclassical architecture. In addition, colonial architecture in America began to flourish in the 1700's. Colonial architecture was heavily influenced by European styles.

Rococo architecture was the final phase of the Baroque style. It developed in France about 1720 and spread to other countries during the next 60 years. Compared with the monumental Baroque style, Rococo architecture was light and delicate. However, Rococo buildings had even more elaborate decorations than did Baroque structures. In France, the most outstanding Rococo buildings were elegant houses built in Paris for the nobility. But the most impressive Rococo structures were palaces, churches, and monasteries erected in southern Germany and Austria. Dominikus Zimmer-

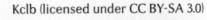

Rococo architecture was highly decorative. The refined, ornamental character of the Rococo style can be seen in the Hall of Mirrors in the Amalienburg Pavilion in southern Germany, near Munich. The Flemish-born architect François Cuvilliés designed the graceful building in the 1730's.

mann created a Rococo masterpiece in his design for Die Wies pilgrimage church (1754) in southern Germany.

The Palladian Revival mainly reflected the classical designs of the Renaissance architect Andrea Palladio. The style began in the early 1700's and was most prominent in England, though it also appeared in northern Italy and North America. Most Palladian Revival buildings were country houses.

Colen Campbell, a Scottish architect, introduced the Palladian Revival style. However, the leader of the movement was Lord Burlington, an English amateur architect. Burlington and his friend William Kent designed the first great Palladian Revival building, Chiswick House (1726) in London. It was modeled on Palladio's Villa Rotonda and set in a large garden based on Roman garden design. Such gardens became a common feature of Palladian Revival architecture.

Neoclassical architecture reflected a renewed interest in the architecture of ancient Greece and Rome. The prefix *neo* means *new.* Neoclassical architecture was inspired by buildings discovered in the ancient Roman cities of Pompeii and Herculaneum. The cities had been buried by an eruption of Mount Vesuvius in A.D. 79. Archaeologists began excavating the cities in the mid-1700's.

Neoclassical architects followed Greek and Roman styles more closely than Renaissance architects had done. Like Baroque architects, the Neoclassicists designed colonnades and large structures, especially public buildings. In their designs, however, they used simpler geometric forms, such as the square and sphere, rather than the Baroque swirls and curves.

The most important Neoclassical architects in England were Sir William Chambers and Robert Adam. Chambers designed many public buildings, notably Somerset House (1780) in London. Adam became an influential interior designer and furniture designer as well as a leading architect. He made Roman designs fashionable in such country houses as Osterley Park House (1763-1780) in London.

Pietro Bianchi, an Italian architect, designed one of the major Neoclassical buildings of the early 1800's, the Church of San Francesco di Paola (begun about 1816) in Naples. The design of the church is based on that of the Pantheon. However, the curved exterior colonnade shows the influence of Bernini's St. Peter's Basilica.

French architects designed many Neoclassical buildings. One of the most famous is the Panthéon (about 1757-1790) in Paris, designed by Jacques Soufflot. The Panthéon was originally a church named after Sainte Geneviève, but the building is now a public monument.

In the United States, Neoclassical architecture became known as the *Federal* style. The leading Federal style architects were Benjamin Latrobe and Charles Bulfinch. Latrobe is best known for his designs for the United States Capitol in Washington, D.C. Bulfinch's most important projects included the statehouses of Maine and Massachusetts.

Colonial architecture in America developed mainly from European styles of the Middle Ages and the Renaissance. In Latin America, the Baroque and Spanish Renaissance styles dominated in the Spanish and Portuguese colonies. In the Spanish colonies in what is now the Southwestern United States, missionaries built adobe churches that combined Native American and Spanish architectural styles. In time, however, the colonists adapted European influences to suit regional tastes and needs.

In the Northern Colonies, the colonists built wooden houses designed to withstand the cold winters. Most of the houses were small, with one or two rooms that could be heated easily. The houses had sloping roofs to shed snow. Architecture in the Middle Colonies showed the influence of a number of European styles. In New York, for example, many Dutch colonists followed architectural styles in the Netherlands and built houses of brick with wooden shutters. In the two Chesapeake Colonies of Virginia and Maryland and in the Southern Colonies, wealthy planters constructed the largest colonial residences, modeling some of these buildings on English country houses. Thomas Jefferson designed several buildings in Virginia that reflected Neoclassicism and the Palladian Revival.

For pictures of colonial architecture, see the *Visitor's guide* section in the articles **Arizona; New Mexico; Virginia.** See also **Colonial life in America; Jefferson, Thomas; Williamsburg.**

The 1800's

By the early 1800's, the development of architecture was greatly affected by the rapid growth of industrialization in western Europe and eastern North America. This *Industrial Revolution* created a demand for architects to plan new types of buildings and to devise new construction techniques. At the same time, many architects revived various styles of the past. The most important revivals were the *Greek Revival* and the *Gothic Revival.* A number of architects combined two or more earlier styles into one design.

The Industrial Revolution began in Britain during the 1700's and spread to other European countries and to North America by the early 1800's. For centuries, architects had concentrated on designing religious buildings, castles, palaces, and country houses. The Industrial Revolution required such structures as factories, railroad stations, warehouses, and office buildings. Architects used new materials and new methods to

His Grace the Duke of Northumberland

Neoclassical architecture followed Greek and Roman designs. Robert Adam used Ionic columns and classical-style sculpture in Syon House (1769), built in London.

Early American architecture reflected European styles. The timber frame design of the Parson Capen House, *above,* shows the influence of medieval English architecture. Colonial settlers in Topsfield, Massachusetts, built the house in 1683. The State House in Boston, *right,* resembles an English Neoclassical building. It was designed by Charles Bulfinch and completed in 1798.

design the new structures.

The Industrial Revolution led to the first commercial and industrial world's fair, the Great Exhibition of 1851 in London. The fair was housed in the Crystal Palace (1851), a revolutionary glass and iron structure designed by Sir Joseph Paxton. The building covered almost 19 acres (8 hectares) and looked much like a giant greenhouse. Paxton's Crystal Palace was also the first important *prefabricated* structure. The iron frame and glass panels were manufactured in a factory and then assembled at the site of the exhibition.

The success of the Great Exhibition brought about similar fairs in other cities in Europe and in the United States. These exhibitions required special facilities and gave architects an opportunity to test new ideas. The Crystal Palace and later glass and iron exhibition halls influenced the development of the glass and metal skyscrapers of the 1900's.

The Crystal Palace did not resemble any earlier style of architecture. However, many structures built with the new technology preserved associations with historical styles. For example, the English architects John Dobson

and Philip Hardwick designed a number of railroad stations with Neoclassical facades. Hardwick also used cast-iron Doric columns to support his St. Katherine's Dock warehouses (1828) in London. The French architect Henri Labrouste combined new building techniques with the Renaissance style in the library of Sainte Geneviève (1850) in Paris. The library has walls of traditional masonry, but the vaults and columns are made of iron. Labrouste allowed the iron to show, making the library the first major public building to use iron as part of the architectural style.

The Greek Revival began in the late 1700's. It ended as a distinct movement in the mid-1800's, though buildings in the Greek style are still being built. The Greek Revival style was considered especially appropriate for such buildings as museums, stock exchanges, banks, and government offices. Advances in classical scholarship enabled architects to re-create Greek designs with great accuracy.

A leading Greek Revival architect in England was Sir Robert Smirke. He designed the British Museum (1823-1847) in London to resemble a huge Greek temple of the

The Crystal Palace was designed by Sir Joseph Paxton for a London exhibition in 1851. The iron frame and glass panels were made in a factory and assembled at the building site.

The Gothic Revival of the 1800's reflected a renewed interest in medieval Gothic architecture. In the 1860's, William Butterfield designed these buildings at Oxford University in Oxford, England, in the Revival style, including Keble College Chapel, *shown here*. Butterfield's use of stone and colored brick shows his interpretation of the Gothic architectural style.

Ionic order. William Strickland designed the first important Greek Revival building in the United States, the Second Bank of the United States (1824) in Philadelphia. The front of the structure resembles a Greek temple of the Doric order.

The Gothic Revival. The Gothic style never went completely out of fashion. In the centuries after the Middle Ages, various architects used elements of the Gothic style. But the revival of Gothic as a deliberate architectural movement began in the 1700's and reached its peak during the mid-1800's. By the 1880's, the movement was in decline.

During the early and mid-1800's, the English architect A. W. N. Pugin wrote several influential books supporting the Gothic style. Pugin urged architects to design churches in the Gothic style because it best expressed the Christian faith. The most ambitious project of the Gothic Revival was the Houses of Parliament (1840-1860) in London, designed by Pugin and Sir Charles Barry. William Butterfield, another English architect, created a number of highly individual designs in the Gothic style. One of his best-known Gothic buildings is All Saints' Church, Margaret Street (1849-1859) in London. Among Butterfield's most important projects was his design for Keble College (1860's) at Oxford University in Oxford, England. Butterfield designed the entire college, including the library, chapel, and residence halls, in the Gothic Revival style.

For a picture of the Gothic Revival, see **Parliament**.

Combined styles. Some architects of the 1800's combined what they considered to be the best features of two or more historical styles. The Paris opera house known as the Palais Garnier (1861-1875) is a masterpiece of this approach, called the *eclectic* approach. The building's designer, Charles Garnier, planned the huge structure chiefly in the elaborate Baroque style. For example, the spectacular Grand Staircase features a lavish use of colored marble. However, Garnier also included classical orders and elements from the designs of French and Italian Renaissance palaces.

Modern architecture

The period from the late 1800's to the present has been one of the most creative and productive times in the history of architecture. Architects have used new materials and new building methods to develop the first completely new styles in centuries.

During the Modern era, American architects made an international impact on architecture for the first time.

The Palais Garnier, a famous opera house in Paris, features a number of architectural styles. The Grand Staircase, *pictured here,* shows strong Baroque influences. Charles Garnier designed the building in 1861.

The Machine Hall was built for the 1889 World's Fair in Paris, France. It was designed by Ferdinand Dutert. The arches of steel girders and glass panels enclosed a vast amount of space used for a machinery exhibit.

Public Domain

For example, the skyscraper, perhaps the best-known symbol of Modern architecture, was first developed in the United States.

The remarkable changes in architecture since the late 1800's have emerged from the theories and works of a few individuals and small groups. Many masterpieces of Modern architecture were designed or influenced by four men—Frank Lloyd Wright of the United States; Walter Gropius and Ludwig Mies van der Rohe of Germany; and Charles Jeanneret-Gris, generally known as Le Corbusier, of France.

Early Modern architecture in Europe. Modern architecture in Europe originated as a reaction against the historical revivals and combined styles of the 1800's. Young architects tried to find fresh approaches that would reflect their time.

One of the first important influences on Modern architecture was the Arts and Crafts Movement, founded in the mid-1800's by William Morris in England. Morris had studied to be an architect, but he decided to concentrate on interior design. Morris criticized the poor artistic quality that he saw in the machine-made products of the Industrial Revolution. With other artists in the Arts and Crafts Movement, Morris created original and high-quality designs for furniture, stained glass, textiles, and wallpaper. Although Morris did not design buildings, his influence encouraged a new artistic freedom and spirit of experimentation that played an important part in Modern European architecture.

Most of the first Modern architects worked in the Netherlands, Austria, and Germany. In the Netherlands, Hendrik Petrus Berlage used an unusual red brick design for his masterpiece, the Amsterdam Stock Exchange (1903), now called the Euronext Amsterdam stock exchange. The building's simple, spare design marked a departure from the highly decorative revival structures and pointed toward more modern styles.

Otto Wagner founded Modern architecture in Austria during the 1890's. Wagner was a teacher and theorist as well as an architect. His most important designs were

Ernst Heyer, Burkhard-Verlag

The Euronext Amsterdam stock exchange in Amsterdam, the Netherlands, is noted for its simple lines and an extensive use of brick. Hendrik Petrus Berlage designed the building in 1896.

The Secession Building in Vienna, Austria, was designed in 1898 by Josef Olbrich as an exhibition gallery for a group of artists and architects called the Vienna Secession. The building's simple, cubelike form and flat, undecorated walls became common characteristics of Modern architecture.

houses with horizontal lines and little ornamentation. The structures had flat, slablike roofs that projected beyond the walls. These features characterized much architecture of the early 1900's.

Josef Olbrich and Josef Hoffmann, two of Wagner's students, joined with other Austrian artists and architects to found a group known as the Vienna Secession. The group was united by its rebellion against the revival styles. Olbrich designed the Secession Building (1898), an exhibition gallery in Vienna, for the group. He took the Renaissance and Neoclassical style of the domed villa and redesigned it in modern terms. Wagner's influence appears in the building's projecting slab roof and undecorated walls. Hoffmann designed a house called the Palais Stoclet (1911) in Brussels, Belgium. The plain white walls and cubelike geometric outlines of the house made it one of the most advanced architectural works of the early 1900's.

Adolf Loos, another Austrian, fiercely opposed ornamentation in architecture. He believed that the decorative qualities of a building would emerge naturally from the structure's materials and form. Loos designed Steiner House (1910) in Vienna and other buildings with cubelike forms and no decorative details.

In Germany, Peter Behrens designed some of the first factories to reflect Modern architectural ideas. His most significant design was the AEG Turbine Factory (1909), a glass, steel, and concrete building in Berlin. Behrens also influenced the theories of Mies van der Rohe, Gropius, and Le Corbusier, all of whom worked in his office during the early 1900's.

Early Modern architecture in America. Henry Hobson Richardson became the first important architect in the United States to include Modern elements in his designs. He was a leading American architect from about 1870 to his death in 1886. He worked in a variety of medi-

Steiner House in Vienna has a cubelike shape and no decoration. Adolf Loos, who designed the building in 1910, fiercely opposed any ornamentation in architecture.

The AEG Turbine Factory, with simple lines and glass walls, was one of the first factories to reflect Modern design principles. It was designed in 1909 in Berlin by Peter Behrens.

eval styles, especially Romanesque. However, he often used features of Modern design, from simplified geometric forms to the absence of exterior ornamentation, in his later works. Richardson designed a number of buildings with both Romanesque and Modern elements, including the Glessner House (1887) and the Marshall Field Wholesale Store (1887), both in Chicago.

Chicago became the center of Modern architecture in the United States during the late 1800's and early 1900's. The Great Chicago Fire destroyed much of the city in 1871, giving architects an opportunity to test new ideas as the city was rebuilt.

William Le Baron Jenney designed the 10-story Home Insurance Building (1885) in downtown Chicago. The building is often considered the world's first metal-framed skyscraper. Instead of thick walls, a steel frame supported the building. The walls provided no support but hung like curtains on the frame. The steel frame and *curtain wall* became fundamental to Modern design.

Jenney trained a number of architects in his Chicago office, including Louis Sullivan and Daniel Burnham. Sullivan became the leader of a style of architecture called the *Chicago School.* Other Chicago School architects included Dankmar Adler and John Wellborn Root. These architects gained fame for their steel-frame stores and office buildings. Sullivan designed the Carson, Pirie, Scott and Company Building (1906), now called the Sullivan Center, which is famous for its horizontal bands of windows and skillful use of light-colored brick. Sullivan also designed skyscraper office buildings, such as the Wainwright Building (1891) in St. Louis, Missouri, and the Guaranty Building (1895) in Buffalo, New York.

Burnham became better known as a city planner than as an architect. However, he designed several significant commercial buildings. His Railway Exchange Building (1904) in Chicago is noted especially for its many windows.

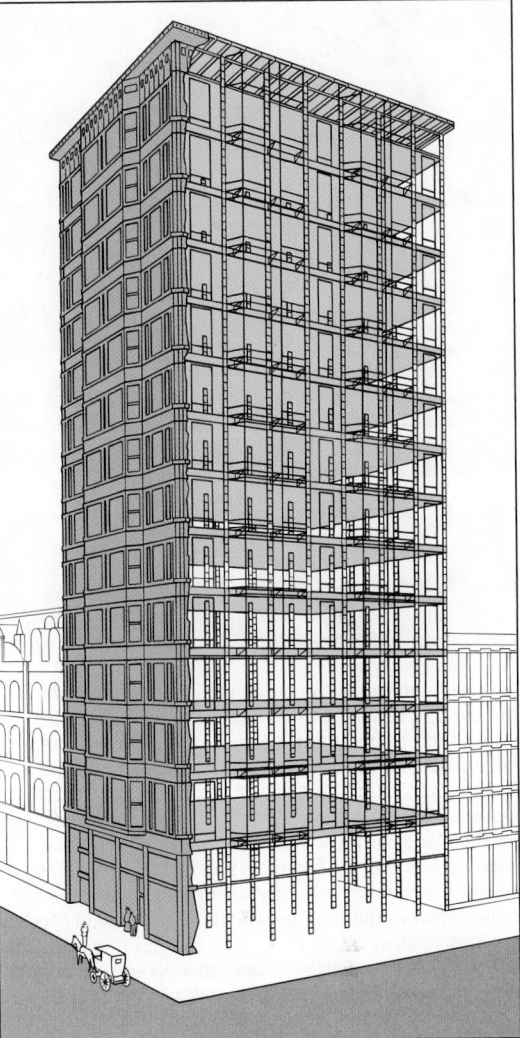

WORLD BOOK illustration by Trevor Hill, Venner Artists Ltd.

The Reliance Building in Chicago was one of the first Modern skyscrapers. The firm of Daniel Burnham and Company designed the building, which was completed in 1894. This cutaway drawing shows the building's steel-frame construction.

For pictures of early Modern architecture in America, see **Burnham, Daniel Hudson; Richardson, Henry Hobson; Sullivan, Louis Henri.**

Frank Lloyd Wright was the greatest figure in Modern American architecture. Wright worked in Chicago for the firm of Adler and Sullivan from 1887 to 1893, when he began his own practice. Wright gained international attention for a series of houses he designed from about 1900 to 1910 in the *prairie style.* The houses had low, horizontal shapes because Wright believed that such a design blended with the open Midwestern prairies. He said that a building should "grow" from its site. Wright selected materials in earth colors and emphasized the natural appearance of those materials.

Wright revolutionized the arrangement of interior space in his prairie style houses. In traditional American houses of the late 1800's, walls divided the interior into

Hedrich-Blessing

The Carson, Pirie, Scott and Company Building, now called the Sullivan Center, is a masterpiece of the Chicago School of architecture. The Chicago School was a pioneering group of Modern American architects based in Chicago. The building was designed by Louis Sullivan and completed in 1906. It features horizontal bands of windows separated by light-colored stone. Sullivan decorated the first two stories with ornamental black cast iron.

The prairie style created by Frank Lloyd Wright revolutionized American domestic architecture. The houses he designed in this style emphasize horizontal lines and natural materials that harmonize with the landscape. Wright designed this prairie style house in 1902 in Oak Park, Illinois.

boxlike rooms. In his houses, however, Wright reduced the number of walls so that one room flowed into another. This flexible use of interior space and the horizontal outlines of the houses greatly influenced European architects. Wright's best-known prairie house is Robie House (1910) in Chicago. Wright also designed large projects, such as the Larkin Building (1906) in Buffalo, New York, and Unity Temple (1908) in Oak Park, Illinois. His bold and imaginative use of concrete in these buildings helped popularize the use of the material in Modern architecture.

Wright's most impressive later project was perhaps the buildings that he designed for the Johnson Wax Company in Racine, Wisconsin. The main administration building (1939) has a smooth exterior of brick and glass. Inside the building, the chief office area is a large windowless room lined with balconies. Soft light enters the area through strips of glass tubing at the edges of the ceiling. Thin concrete columns rise from the floor of the building and support large concrete disks at the ceiling level.

For other pictures of Wright's work, see **Furniture** (The Bauhaus); **United States** (The arts); **Wright, Frank Lloyd.**

Walter Gropius influenced Modern architecture both as an architect and as a teacher. In 1919, he founded the Bauhaus, a school of design in Weimar, Germany. The school was dedicated to uniting the arts and architecture with modern industrial technology. In 1925, the Bauhaus moved to Dessau. Gropius designed the buildings for the Dessau campus. The geometric concrete and glass structures rank among the finest designs of the period.

Gropius came to the United States in 1937. The next year, he became chairman of the Department of Architecture at Harvard University. Gropius's architectural theories spread throughout the United States as a result of his work as an architect and teacher. In 1946, Gropius and some of his former students, along with other young architects, formed the Architects Collaborative. The group designed many projects in the United States and other countries, beginning with the Graduate Center (1950) at Harvard.

The International Style dominated architecture until about 1950. The name came from the title of a book, *The International Style* (1932), written by two Americans—the architect Philip Johnson and the architectural historian Henry-Russell Hitchcock. In the book, the authors reviewed architecture of the previous 10 years and stated that a new and distinct "international" style had developed in many countries.

The Bauhaus was a German art school that greatly influenced Modern architecture. Walter Gropius designed the Dessau campus in 1925. His buildings emphasized cubic shapes and the use of the transparent and reflective qualities of glass.

The International Style became one of the dominant architectural movements of the 1900's. The Swiss architect Le Corbusier, the leader of the movement, designed the Villa Savoye, *shown here,* in Poissy, France. The residence, completed in 1931, includes the major elements of the International Style. The structure has a geometric shape, white concrete walls, a flat roof, and a continuous band of windows. It stands on pillars called *pilotis.*

The International Style actually summarized many of the ideas of such pioneer modern architects as Hoffmann, Loos, Wright, and Gropius. Typical buildings in the style have geometric shapes, white walls, and a flat roof with a garden. Most are constructed of *reinforced concrete,* which has embedded metal rods for added strength. Typical International Style buildings also have large windows to create a light, airy feeling. The exteriors of buildings in this style have little or no ornamentation.

Le Corbusier was probably the greatest architect to work in the International Style. Most of his early works were houses that resembled white boxes. The houses were built of white reinforced concrete and stood above the ground on pillars called *pilotis.* One of Le Corbusier's most important houses in this style was the Villa Savoye (1931) in Poissy, France.

Le Corbusier's later works showed more variety than his cubelike houses. One of his most famous later proj- ects is the Unité d'Habitation (1952), a 337-unit apartment building in Marseille, France. As in his earlier works, Le Corbusier had this building constructed of reinforced concrete and raised on pilotis. But he honeycombed the exterior with balconies to shield the apartments from the strong sun. The balconies created a lively pattern of dark and light rectangles in the sunlight. Le Corbusier had the walls at the sides of the balconies painted in bright colors to provide vivid contrasts with the white concrete.

Ludwig Mies van der Rohe was the master of glass and steel architecture. He designed skyscrapers that had a steel frame and thin metal and glass walls. The style became popular for commercial buildings after World War II (1939-1945).

Mies, as he was generally called, became director of the Bauhaus in 1930 and served in that position until the school closed in 1933. In 1937, he immigrated to the United States. The next year, he became head of the ar-

The works of Ludwig Mies van der Rohe, a German architect, are noted for his skillful use of steel and glass. In 1939, Mies began designing the campus for what became the Illinois Institute of Technology in Chicago. The large areas of tinted glass in Crown Hall (1956), *shown here,* are typical of his style.

chitecture department at the Armour Institute (now the Illinois Institute of Technology) in Chicago. In 1939, Mies began to design the buildings for a new Armour Institute campus. His designs stressed rectangular, cubelike structures of brick, exposed steel columns, and huge windows.

Mies designed several apartment and office building skyscrapers in the United States. His Lake Shore Drive apartment complex (1951) in Chicago resembles two gigantic glass rectangles. Perhaps his most praised project is the Seagram Building (1958), an office skyscraper in New York City designed with Philip Johnson. The building has walls of bronze and bronze-tinted glass.

Architecture today

By about 1950, younger architects had begun to react against the International Style. These architects believed that the style lacked variety in design, because of the emphasis on simple geometric shapes and the lack of decorative elements. Since then, many architectural movements have developed around the world. Some of these movements have made significant impacts. Others merely became popular among a small group of architects. The introduction of computers into the process of design in the late 1900's greatly expanded the possibilities for architects in all aspects of their work.

Brutalism and Metabolism. The attack against the International Style was first led by a group of architects often called the Brutalists. The Brutalists based their designs on the later work of Le Corbusier. They created plain, massive buildings with rough reinforced concrete exteriors. Leading members of this movement included the British husband-and-wife team of Alison and Peter Smithson, and the American architects Walter Netsch and Paul Rudolph. Like the Brutalists, the American architect Louis Kahn made imaginative use of concrete. Kahn's major designs include the Salk Institute for Biological Studies (1965) in La Jolla, California, and the Kimbell Art Museum (1972) in Fort Worth, Texas.

After the catastrophic destruction of World War II, a group of prominent architects in Japan responded to the need to rebuild by forming a group known as the Metabolists. The leader of the group, Kenzo Tange, was interested in the ability of cities to develop in new ways and at speeds that reflected the modern era. The Metabolists believed that buildings and cities should be constructed and grow the way that a living organism does, through a process based on replaceable, cell-like structures. Tange's St. Mary's Cathedral (1964) in Tokyo, Japan, reflects those principles. Other prominent Metabolists include Kiyonori Kikutake, who designed the Expo Tower (1970) for the 1970 World's Fair in Osaka, and Fumihiko Maki, who designed Steinberg Hall (1960) for Washington University in St. Louis, Missouri.

Postmodernism. Perhaps the best-known architectural movement of the late 1900's was Postmodernism. It

© Andriy Blokhin, Shutterstock

Brutalist architects made skillful use of geometric shapes and concrete walls. Like the Brutalists, the American architect Louis Kahn made imaginative use of concrete, as in his Salk Institute for Biological Studies (1965) in La Jolla, California.

Tokyo Cathedral (1965), designed by Kenzo Tange; Orion Press

St. Mary's Cathedral, built in Tokyo, Japan, in 1964, was designed by Kenzo Tange to replace a wooden cathedral destroyed on the site during World War II (1939-1945). The new structure mimics the traditional shape of a cross. But its dramatic roof lines and modern materials reflect Tange's shift to a new architectural style that came to be called Metabolism.

began during the 1960's in the United States. The Postmodernists had no style or theories in common, but they were united by their rejection of the International Style. One of the leading American Postmodern theorists and designers was Robert Venturi. Other American architects generally grouped as Postmodernists include Michael Graves, Charles Moore, and Stanley Tigerman.

Many Postmodernists revived historical styles that had been ignored by earlier Modern architects. For example, Venturi often used traditional styles, borrowing from the Italian Renaissance and other periods. Venturi became one of the first Postmodern architects to add ornamentation to building exteriors, such as in his Sainsbury Wing (1991) for the National Gallery in London, England. A number of Postmodernists incorporated arches, columns, domes, and other classical elements into their designs.

In 1978, Philip Johnson, coauthor of *The International Style,* unveiled the design he created with John Burgee for the first Postmodern skyscraper. This building, originally the headquarters of the American Telephone and Telegraph Company and now called the 550 Madison building in New York City, has a base like the Pazzi Chapel of the Renaissance.

The interest of Postmodernists in historical styles was accompanied by concern for preserving old buildings and adapting them to new uses. Many government

© David Falconer, West Stock

Postmodern architects adopted elements from earlier architectural styles. In the Portland Building, Michael Graves featured colored facades of browns and reds on a sandy background. Small square windows dominate the exterior of the 15-story building. The building was completed in Portland, Oregon, in 1982.

agencies were created at this time to preserve buildings of architectural value. These agencies continue today to have the power to grant *landmark status* to such buildings. Buildings with landmark status may not be destroyed or significantly altered. Historic preservation has become a significant part of architecture as many prominent buildings age and require restoration.

Deconstructivism was a style that developed in response to Modernism. Deconstructivists sought to change traditional ways of looking at form and space and to disrupt customary expectations of harmony and unity. A building reflecting Deconstructivist ideas might feature sharp, clashing angles and shapes, along with incomplete forms. Startling contrasts could exist between a building's interior and exterior. A famous example is the American architect Frank Gehry's Guggenheim Museum (1997) in Bilbao, Spain. Other prominent Deconstructivist architects include Peter Eisenman and Thom Mayne of the United States and Bernard Tschumi of Switzerland.

Computers revolutionize design. In the late 1900's, the widespread availability of personal computers led to a revolution in architectural design. Computer-aided design (CAD) software replaced manual drafting with an automated process. The advance allowed architects to design with more freedom and precision. Forms previously unavailable to architecture became constructible options. Two-dimensional and three-dimensional software programs have greatly enlarged the architect's

toolbox. Today, most architecture firms design structures by creating digital models and computer graphics of their projects rather than by hand drawing. Some firms produce videos and animations of their work.

Starchitects. So many new architectural styles have developed since the 1960's that architects today are generally classified into small groups of similarly minded designers rather than into large movements. Many of these groups focus around the work of a particularly prominent architect who has built many projects throughout the world. Such international architects have come to be called star architects, or *starchitects*. Many of them have received the Pritzker Architecture Prize, the most distinguished architectural award in the world. The most famous starchitects include Frank Gehry, Rem Koolhaas of the Netherlands, and Iraqi-born Zaha Hadid of the United Kingdom.

Since the late 1980's, Gehry has been a pioneer of CAD software use in architecture design. His designs are often characterized by free-form shapes, extreme curves, and metallic surfaces. Gehry's most famous buildings include the Guggenheim Museum and the Walt Disney Concert Hall (2003) in Los Angeles, California. In addition to his architectural practice, he founded Gehry Technologies, a company that pioneered the development of Building Information Modeling (BIM). BIM software allows architects, engineers, and contractors to work together on drawings, three-dimensional models, and construction plans online.

© Sean Pavone, Shutterstock

Deconstructivists sought to disrupt customary expectations of harmony and unity, as in the Walt Disney Concert Hall (2003) in Los Angeles, California, by the American architect Frank Gehry. Gehry has been a pioneer of computer-aided design (CAD) software, which allows him to build the free-form shapes and extreme curves that have become his trademark.

CCTV Headquarters in Beijing, China, is a 44-story skyscraper completed in 2012. The distinctively shaped tower was designed by the Dutch *starchitect* (star architect) Rem Koolhaas.

Koolhaas first became known in the late 1970's for his *conceptual* (idea-based) design projects in London and New York City. These projects, which were often massive structures, were never built. However, they remain an important part of architecture history. Since that time, Koolhaas has designed dozens of buildings that have been constructed around the world, including the Seattle Public Library (2004) in Washington and the China Central Television Headquarters (2012) in Beijing.

Hadid was a student of Koolhaas at the Architectural Association School of Architecture in London. In 2004, she became the first woman to be awarded the Pritzker Architecture Prize. Hadid was influenced by a Russian style of the early 1900's called *Suprematism*. She later became a leader of the movement called *Parametricism*. Suprematism involves fragmented geometric forms. Parametricism relies on the ability of CAD software to digitally create structures with more fluid lines and less rigid forms than those of previous styles. It is considered particularly suited for large-scale urban environments. Hadid's most prominent projects include the Heydar Aliyev cultural center (2012) in Baku, Azerbaijan, and the Dongdaemun Design Plaza (2014) in Seoul, South Korea.

Although the field of architecture is constantly changing, history continues to play a major role in its development. The designs of Gehry, Koolhaas, Hadid, and many other starchitects reveal a deep understanding and passion for history. Their work contains glimpses of traditions that date back to the first architects.

Careers

Young people who want to become architects face a difficult, yet engaging, training period. Training begins with instruction in design and ultimately leads to expert knowledge of building codes, regulations, and construction management. The following discussion deals with the training and licensing of architects in the United States.

Education and training. High school students interested in becoming architects should take courses in art, history, foreign languages, mechanical drafting in CAD,

© Pep Daude, Construction Board of the Temple of the Sagrada Família

Architects develop detailed plans of their ideas for building projects. The architect above is making a drawing, which will be translated into a model of the building. A three-dimensional model, *at right in this photo,* aids in both design and construction.

mathematics, and computer programming. Because contemporary architecture work is based so heavily on digital representations of physical structures, spatial reasoning is one of the most valuable skills a student can develop. In addition, students should seek an internship in a local architecture office, or consider one of a fast-growing assortment of summer design programs for high school students. A list of such programs can be found at the American Institute of Architecture Students website (www.aias.org).

After graduating from high school, future architects must attend college. The current standard for becoming licensed as an architect in the United States is to earn either a five-year professional bachelor of architecture degree, or a three-year professional master of architecture program after graduating from college. A list of accredited schools can be found on the National Architecture Accrediting Board (NAAB) website (www.naab.org). In addition, several hundred colleges and trade schools offer some technical courses in architectural drawing and engineering. Such courses can lead to a license after an extended time as an apprentice. However, a person can become a licensed architect faster by attending an accredited school.

In addition to professional degrees in architecture, a wide variety of post-professional degrees can be earned. These degrees include advanced design; computational methods; data analysis of populations; urban design; and the history, theory, and criticism of architecture. Most architecture schools stress practical design and

the *precedent method,* in which the class solves problems related to an actual building.

Many college students work as an *intern* in the office of a licensed architect or in the office of an engineer or contractor. Upon graduation, an apprenticeship can take the form of a full-time job devoted to acquiring the Architecture Experience Program hours required by the licensing organization, the National Council of Architecture Registration Boards (NCARB). During this time, apprentice architects are also required to complete the Architecture Records Examinations (ARE).

Information about architecture schools can also be obtained from the American Institute of Architects (AIA) in Washington, D.C. The institute also publishes literature on architecture, holds meetings, and awards prizes for excellence in architectural design.

Employment opportunities. Licensed architects may open their own office or join an architectural firm. City, state, and federal agencies also employ architects. Most architects work for an architecture or engineering firm. Most young architects specialize in a certain phase of the profession, such as designing houses, schools, or office buildings.

People with training in architecture can also work in related fields. Such fields include city planning, furniture design, industrial design, and interior design. There also is an increasing demand for architects who can recondition existing buildings of artistic or historical value, and for specialists in laws governing architectural preservation. In addition, architects with the necessary computer skills are in high demand to work for motion picture studios and social media companies.

Zachariah Michielli

Study aids

Related articles in *World Book*. Many city, state, country, and continent articles show notable structures. See also:

American architects

Adler, Dankmar
Bulfinch, Charles
Burnham, Daniel Hudson
Fuller, Buckminster
Gehry, Frank
Graves, Michael
Hunt, Richard Morris
Jahn, Helmut
Jefferson, Thomas
Jenney, William Le Baron
Johnson, Philip Cortelyou
Kahn, Louis Isadore
Latrobe, Benjamin
Mayne, Thom

Mies van der Rohe, Ludwig
Mills, Robert
Morgan, Julia
Neutra, Richard Joseph
Pei, I. M.
Richardson, Henry Hobson
Root, John Wellborn
Rudolph, Paul
Saarinen, Eero
Stone, Edward Durell
Sullivan, Louis Henri
Venturi, Robert
White, Stanford
Wright, Frank Lloyd

Italian architects

Alberti, Leon Battista
Bernini, Gian Lorenzo
Borromini, Francesco
Bramante, Donato
Brunelleschi, Filippo
Giotto
Michelangelo
Nervi, Pier Luigi
Palladio, Andrea
Soleri, Paolo

Other architects

Aalto, Alvar
Adam (Robert; James)
Behrens, Peter
Breuer, Marcel Lajos
Erickson, Arthur Charles
Gaudí, Antoni
Gropius, Walter
Hadid, Zaha
Jones, Inigo
Le Corbusier
L'Enfant, Pierre Charles
Lutyens, Sir Edwin Landseer
Niemeyer, Oscar
Safdie, Moshe
Vanbrugh, Sir John
Wren, Sir Christopher

Famous structures

Abu Simbel, Temples of
Alhambra
Arc de Triomphe
Capitol, United States
Chartres Cathedral
Colosseum
Eiffel Tower
Empire State Building
Escorial
Federal Hall
Gateway Arch National Park
Guggenheim Museum
Hagia Sophia
Independence Hall
Jefferson Memorial
Kremlin
Leaning Tower of Pisa
Lincoln Memorial
Louvre
Milan Cathedral

Monte Cassino
Montserrat
National Gallery of Art
National Gallery of Canada
Notre Dame, Cathedral of
Old North Church
Pantheon
Parthenon
Petronas Towers
Pyramids
Saint Mark, Basilica of
Saint Patrick's Cathedral
Saint Peter's Basilica
Sainte-Anne-de-Beaupré
Seven Wonders of the
 Ancient World
Statue of Liberty
Sydney Opera House
Taj Mahal
Tower of London

Tuileries
Versailles, Palace of
Washington National
 Cathedral

White House
Willis Tower
Windsor Castle
World Trade Center

Kinds of buildings

Basilica
Campanile
Castle
Cathedral
Church
Hospital
Hotel
House
Library
Monument
Mosque

Motel
Museum
Pagoda
Pyramids
Skyscraper
Synagogue
Temple
Tomb
Tower
Ziggurat

Parts of buildings

Arch
Atrium
Cantilever
Clerestory
Column
Gargoyle
Minaret

Roof
Spire
Stained glass
Tracery
Vault
Window

Styles of architecture

Baroque
Byzantine art
Classicism
Georgian architecture
Gothic art
Islamic art

Norman architecture
Postmodernism
Renaissance
Rococo
Romanesque architecture

Other related articles

Acropolis
Bauhaus
Building construction
Building trade
City
City planning

Furniture
Housing
Interior design
Landscape architecture
Sculpture
Shelter

Archives, National. See National Archives and Records Administration.

Arcology. See Soleri, Paolo.

Arctic is the northernmost region of Earth. It surrounds the North Pole and includes the northern areas of North America, Europe, and Asia.

Some parts of the Arctic are freezing, barren landscapes that cannot support much life. During winter, the sun never rises above the horizon in much of the Arctic. But during the brief Arctic summer, the sun never sets, and life flourishes in some places. The word *Arctic* comes from *Arktos* (bear), the ancient Greek name for a constellation that appears in the northern sky.

The southernmost parts of the Arctic border a vast band of evergreen forests called the *taiga*. Farther north, trees cannot grow, and the landscape consists of dry, frozen plains called the *tundra*. Herds of caribou migrate seasonally between the tundra and the taiga. In the rocky, windswept lands north of the tundra, few plants can survive.

Arctic lands encircle the Arctic Ocean, which remains mostly frozen all year. The North Pole lies in the Arctic Ocean.

Despite the challenging environment, people have found ways to adapt to life in the Arctic since ancient times. The *indigenous* (native) peoples of the Arctic include the Inuit (sometimes called Eskimos) of North America and the Sami of Europe. English, Dutch, and

The Arctic landscape is mostly dry and treeless. In this photograph, an Inuit stone marker overlooks a glacier valley on Baffin Island, Canada. Mosses and lichens grow on the rocks.

© Robert Huberman, SuperStock

Arctic wildlife are adapted for living in cold, harsh conditions. Caribou, shown in this photograph, migrate vast distances to find food in the winter, sometimes traveling thousands of miles.

© All Canada Photos/Alamy Images

Russian explorers arrived in the Arctic later.

Underground, the Arctic is rich in minerals, natural gas, and petroleum. Today, global demand for petroleum and gas drives much Arctic exploration.

This article will discuss the Arctic's land, climate, and natural resources; the traditional ways of life of Arctic peoples; and the history of Arctic exploration. The final section of the article deals with challenges facing the region today.

Land and climate

Scientists and governments define the Arctic in several different ways. Politically and culturally, the Arctic can be defined as the lands north of the taiga. Defined this way, it includes the northern parts of Alaska and Canada; northern Scandinavia (Norway and Sweden); northern Finland; and Russia's Siberia region. It also includes Greenland and most of Iceland.

Another common definition limits the Arctic to the region north of the Arctic Circle, an imaginary line that circles the globe at 66°33′ north latitude. The Arctic Circle marks the edge of an area where the sun stays above the horizon one or more full days each year, a phenomenon known as the *midnight sun.*

Many scientists define the Arctic as the northern region with an average July temperature lower than 50 °F (10 °C). The boundary of this region is called the 50 °F (10 °C) July *isotherm.* An isotherm is an imaginary line defined by a common temperature. Under this definition, the Arctic includes some lands south of the Arctic Circle, but not some lands north of the Arctic Circle.

Climate. The Arctic climate is cold because the area receives relatively little energy from sunlight. In winter, the sun never rises during the day in some places. Even when the sun is shining, the sunlight is less direct and thus less intense than that farther south. Without sunlight, winter temperatures may drop below −76 °F (−60 °C). But in the constant sunlight of summer, temper-

atures in some regions can rise above 86 °F (30 °C).

The Arctic is a dry region. Most of the Arctic receives only 2 to 10 inches (5 to 25 centimeters) of precipitation each year, much of which falls as snow. Some parts of the Arctic are as dry as many deserts in other regions.

Land regions. The Arctic can be divided into three land regions: (1) the polar deserts, (2) the tundra, and (3) the subarctic.

Polar deserts make up the northernmost lands on Earth. Like warmer deserts, they receive little precipitation and have thin, rocky soil. Strong, cold winds blow frequently in the polar deserts. Few plants can survive the extreme conditions, but *lichens*—algae and fungi that live together—grow on the rocky surfaces (see Lichen).

The tundra lies south of the polar deserts. The tundra receives more precipitation than the polar deserts and is therefore more favorable for plant growth. In addition to mosses and lichens, grasses and other flowering plants grow in the tundra. Shrubs also grow there, but trees cannot survive in the tundra.

The subarctic includes lands south of the 50 °F (10 °C) July isotherm and thus is excluded from some definitions of the Arctic. The subarctic climate is warmer and less dry than that of the tundra and so can support trees. The subarctic includes the northern fringes of the taiga.

Environment and natural resources

The Arctic includes vast areas of wilderness largely untouched by industry and development. Other areas have long served as an important source of food and raw materials.

Soil conditions in the Arctic are shaped by the presence of *permafrost,* a layer of permanently frozen soil beneath the ground. Only the top layer of soil, called the *active layer,* thaws during summer. In some areas, the active layer can extend about 10 feet (300 centimeters) deep. In other areas, the top layer may only thaw to a depth of about 8 to 12 inches (20 to 30 centimeters).

Despite the dry climate, Arctic soils tend to be moist because the permafrost prevents drainage. But plants grow slowly because cold temperatures slow biological processes in the soil, limiting the availability of nutrients.

Plant life in the Arctic is limited by the cold and the short growing season. In the polar deserts, mosses and lichens dominate. The tundra supports a variety of grasses and such shrubs as dwarf birch, Labrador tea, lingonberry, and willow. In the subarctic, birch, larch, and spruce trees may dominate the landscape.

Arctic plants have adapted to the harsh climate and soil conditions in several ways. Some plants have extensive root systems. They use the extra roots to better absorb scarce nutrients from the soil. Because the growing season in the Arctic is only 6 to 12 weeks long, most Arctic plants are *perennials*—that is, they take several years to complete their life cycle. Some plants can keep their delicate leaves and flower buds alive under the cover of winter snow. When the snow melts, these structures quickly develop to take full advantage of the short growing season. Some Arctic plants can even sprout from seeds under the snow.

Animal life in the Arctic depends on cycles of plant life for food. In general, food for animals is abundant in the summer and scarce in the winter. During the growing season, such *herbivores* (plant-eating animals) as lemmings, hares, and caribou flourish. The large population of herbivores in the summer, in turn, supports such predators as snowy owls, Arctic foxes, and wolves.

Both herbivores and predators respond to the changing availability of food in a variety of ways. Some Arctic animals simply leave during the winter. Arctic birds migrate in large numbers to warmer regions in the south. Caribou migrate overland from the tundra to the taiga, where more plants grow during the winter. Some groups of caribou travel more than 3,000 miles (4,800 kilometers) in their migrations.

Other animals survive the winter by living off fat they build up during the summer. Musk oxen restrict their activity in the winter to conserve energy. Their thick, warm undercoats help insulate against the cold. Such predators as foxes, lynxes, and wolves also grow thick fur coats in the winter. Smaller hunters, such as weasels, spend their time under the snow, which reduces their exposure to the cold winds above. They also hunt for lemmings, voles, and other prey beneath the snow. Ground squirrels and bears move into underground dens during the winter and enter a sleeplike state.

Many of the world's most important fishing waters lie around the edge of the Arctic. Indigenous people also hunt seals and whales in Arctic waters.

Minerals, oil, and natural gas are abundant in the Arctic, and mining ranks as an important industrial activ-

The Arctic

Scientists define the boundaries of the Arctic in several ways. The *tree line* is the northern limit of tree growth. The climatic boundary of the Arctic is the 50 °F (10 °C) July isotherm. This imaginary line connects areas where the average July temperature is 50 °F (10 °C). Both lines are shown on this map.

Polar ice

50°F (10°C) summer isotherm

Tree line

International boundary

• City or town

0   1,000 Miles

0   1,000 Kilometers

WORLD BOOK map

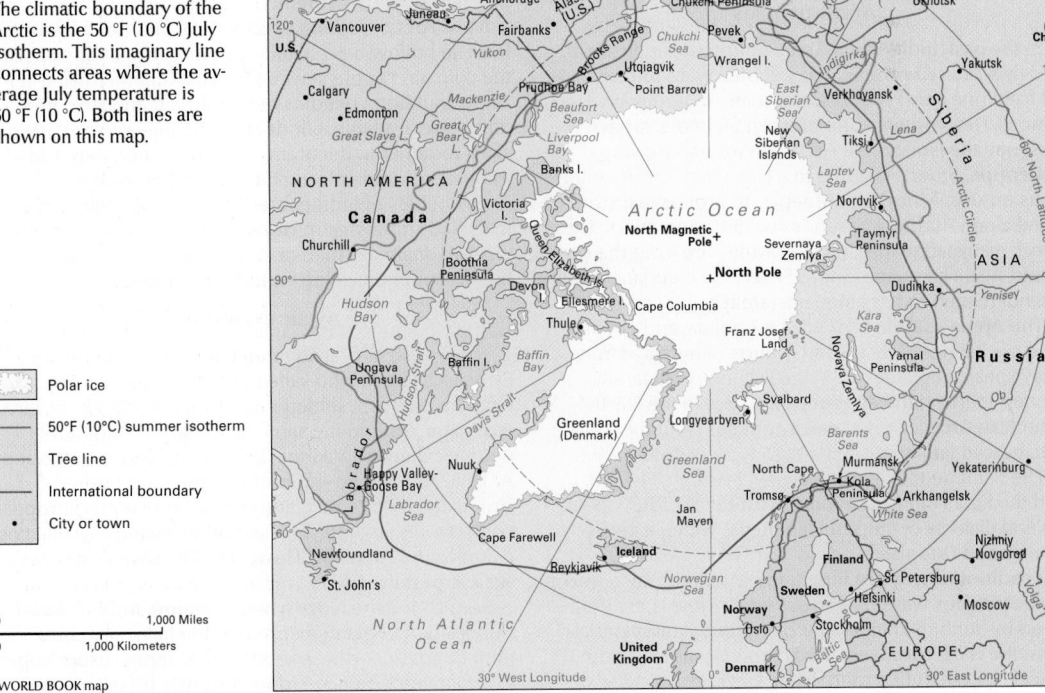

Housing in the Arctic consists mostly of modern buildings specially adapted to the extreme cold. In this photograph, for example, heated corridors hold the pipes that carry water and sewage to and from homes. A layer of permanently frozen soil, called *permafrost,* prevents pipes and home foundations from being dug into the ground.

© John Sylvester, Alamy Images

ity throughout the region. Coal deposits are found in Alaska, Siberia, Canada, and Greenland, as well as on Svalbard, a group of Norwegian islands. Subarctic areas of Alaska and Canada support large mining operations for such minerals as copper, gold, lead, silver, and zinc. Several areas in the Canadian Arctic have active diamond mines. The Arctic has large reserves of oil and natural gas, most of them in Russia. Production of oil and gas forms a major part of the economy of Alaska, Norway, and Russia.

Arctic peoples

In the past, indigenous Arctic peoples lived in small, widely scattered groups. The peoples were often isolated from one another and spoke many different languages. Development and modern technology have lessened the isolation of Arctic life for many groups.

Groups. Siberia is home to a large number of indigenous groups. More than 20 separate groups live scattered along northern Siberia's coastline and rivers. They speak many languages, most of which are from the Uralic and Altaic language family. Several of their languages are not related to any language family.

The Arctic coastlines of Alaska, Canada, and Greenland are inhabited by several groups of Inuit and Yuit. They speak languages from the Eskimo-Aleut family. Some American Indian groups also live in the North American Arctic. They speak languages from the Athabascan family.

The Sami people live in Norway, Sweden, Finland, and the Kola Peninsula in northwest Russia. They speak several dialects of the Sami language, which is related to Finnish and Estonian.

Traditional ways of life. Before modernization, most Arctic peoples were *hunter-gatherers*—that is, they survived by hunting animals and gathering plant materials from the wild. They were *seminomadic,* moving from place to place to find food. Their diet consisted of fish,

game, roots, and berries. Before firearms, Arctic peoples used a variety of devices to hunt, such as snares, traps, harpoons, spears, and bows and arrows. In the winter, they rode sleds pulled by dogs or reindeer.

In winter, many Arctic peoples lived together in small communities. They built underground winter houses made of stone or sod. In summer, smaller bands moved about in search of game. Each band consisted of an *extended family*—parents, married children and their offspring, and other relatives. Portable tents made of animal skin served as summer housing.

Most Arctic clothing was made of caribou or reindeer fur. The hollow hairs acted as a good insulation against the cold air. People sewed the skins together using sinew and bone needles before thread and steel needles were available. For decoration, they sewed various skins together in decorative patterns. Later, they added trade beads and colored threads to their outfits.

The beliefs of indigenous Arctic people held that animals had spirits that must be respected. Most communities had *shamans,* men or women who were responsible for communicating with the spirit world.

Arctic exploration

The first written account of the Arctic comes from Pytheas, a Greek who sailed to the Far North around 325 B.C. The Inuit first settled much of the Arctic about 1,000 years ago, around the same time that a Scandinavian people called the Vikings began to explore there. About A.D. 982, the Viking explorer Erik the Red reached Greenland, where he made the earliest known European contact with the Inuit. Erik and other Vikings established colonies in Greenland. However, the colonies did not survive past the 1400's.

Search for the Northwest Passage. In 1497, King Henry VII of England dispatched the Italian explorer John Cabot to northeastern North America. Cabot hoped to find a quick passage to eastern Asia by sailing west through North America—a "Northwest Passage." At the time, Europeans did not realize the size of the North American continent and the extent to which it blocked their path. Though Cabot believed he had reached Asia, in actuality he probably landed in Newfoundland.

Europeans continued to explore the Arctic. In the 1570's, the English navigator Martin Frobisher sailed around Greenland to Baffin Island, where he had several hostile meetings with the Inuit. In 1590, the Dutch explorer Willem Barents reached the far northern islands of Svalbard and Novaya Zemlya, which later became whaling centers. In the early 1600's, the English explorer Henry Hudson sailed farther north than any European explorer before him. He helped to establish the North American fur trade.

In 1648, the Russian explorer Semyon Dezhnev sailed through what is now known as the Bering Strait. Vitus Bering, the Danish navigator for whom the strait is named, made several voyages between 1725 and 1742, exploring the strait and southeastern Alaska. He encountered the Aleuts when he landed on the Shumagin Islands. In 1778, the British navigator James Cook explored North America's northwestern coast, continuing the search for the Northwest Passage. He passed through the Bering Strait and on to Cape Prince of Wales.

In the early 1800's, the British Navy sent several expeditions to try to find the Northwest Passage, despite centuries of exploration without success. William Edward Parry, a British naval officer, led three expeditions and went farther north than any previous explorer.

In 1845, the British Navy launched the most ambitious—and ultimately the most disastrous—Northwest Passage expedition. Its leader was John Franklin, who had previously led two Arctic expeditions. In 1847, Franklin's ships became icebound, and he and his crew died of starvation. Search parties charted much of the remaining stretches of Arctic coast while looking for his stranded expedition. The first explorer to actually sail through the Northwest Passage was the Norwegian adventurer Roald Amundsen in 1906.

Race to the pole. During the 1860's, attention turned to reaching the North Pole. To get there, explorers had to cross the treacherous, frozen Arctic Ocean.

After numerous attempts, the American explorer Robert E. Peary claimed to be the first person to reach the pole in 1909. That same week, the American physician Frederick A. Cook claimed that he had reached the pole a year before Peary, in 1908. Peary disputed Cook's claim, and the controversy over who actually first reached the pole continues today.

The Arctic today

The Arctic, once protected by its remoteness and harsh climate, faces many challenges today. Moderniza-

Arctic exploration

Europeans began widespread exploration of the Arctic during the 1500's. This map shows the routes taken by some of the most important Arctic explorers since then.

——— Frobisher (Britain) 1576

– – – Barents (Netherlands) 1596-97

------- Bering (Netherlands) 1728-29

——— Franklin (Britain) 1845-47

–·–·– McClure (Britain) 1850-54

,,,,,,, Nordenskjöld (Sweden) 1878-79

—··—·· Nansen (Norway) 1893-96

——— Amundsen (Norway) 1903-06

– – – Peary (U.S.) 1908-09

------- Nobile (Italy) 1926

—·—·— U.S.S. Nautilus 1958

0   1,000 Miles

0   1,000 Kilometers

WORLD BOOK map

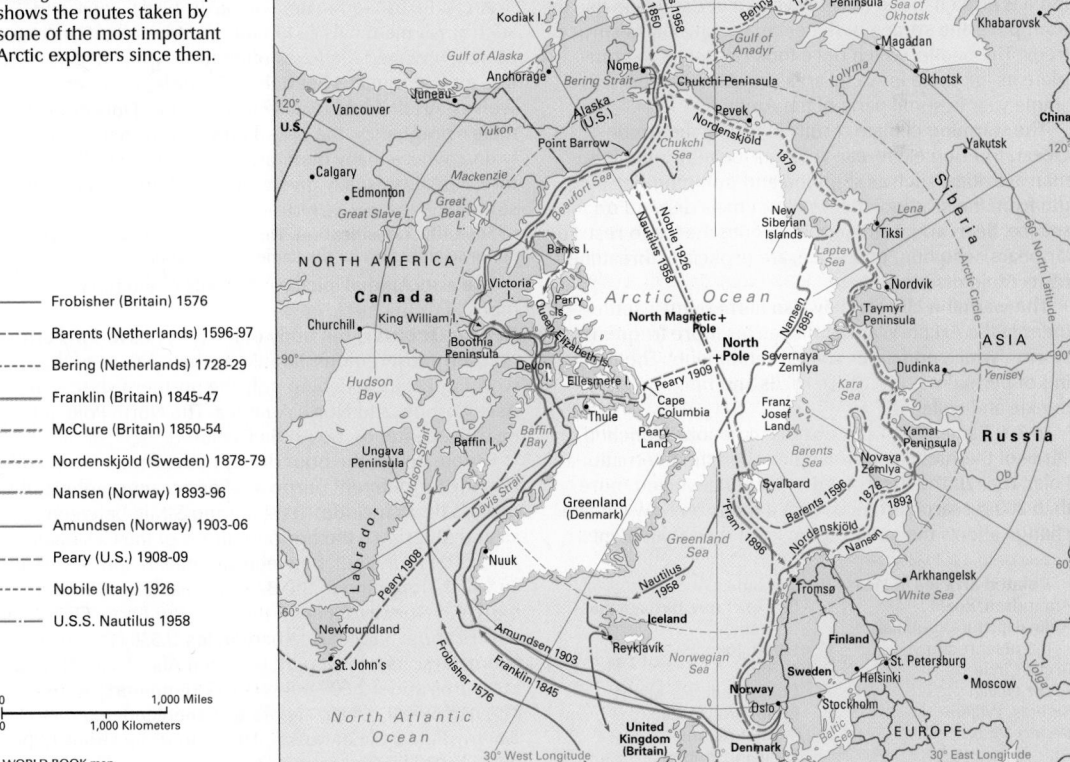

tion has upset traditional Arctic ways of life, and many indigenous peoples have struggled to preserve their culture. Further, a warming climate threatens the landscape and environment of the region.

Modernization. Today, the Arctic is governed by Canada, Denmark, Finland, Iceland, Greenland, Russia, and the United States. These countries have worked to develop the region, largely for its natural resources. As a result, the lifestyles of most indigenous peoples have changed dramatically. Many Arctic people speak English or another European language instead of their native language, and many Arctic languages are in danger of being forgotten. Many Arctic peoples have converted from their traditional religions to Christianity.

Most indigenous peoples have settled towns and cities and use modern technology. Many live in *prefabricated* housing, housing built in sections at a factory and assembled at the building site. Arctic hunters drive snowmobiles and four-wheeled all-terrain vehicles. The modern Arctic diet includes fewer traditional foods and more imported goods, such as frozen meals, soft drinks, and candy.

The removal of minerals, natural gas, and petroleum from Arctic lands has damaged hunting and fishing in many areas. Rapid modernization has also led to serious social problems among indigenous people, such as alcoholism, drug use, domestic violence, and suicide.

Climate change. The Arctic climate has warmed significantly in the past few decades, causing the ranges of various Arctic plants to shift northward. Shrubs have become dominant in some areas of the tundra, crowding out mosses and lichens. Along with plants, a number of animals have extended their ranges northward. Warming has also changed the life cycle of certain animals. An example is the spruce bark beetle, which attacks spruce trees. The beetle, which once took two years to complete its life cycle in Arctic areas, now completes it in a single year in some parts of the Arctic.

The warming climate results in less of the Arctic Ocean freezing each year. Less sea ice may benefit human activities, such as shipping and pumping petroleum from the sea floor. But many animals depend on the sea ice. Seals and walruses climb onto the ice to rest. Polar bears, who hunt on the ice, are especially threatened by its rapid disappearance.

The warming climate may also harm human settlement in the Arctic. Warmer air causes more frequent storms, which endanger coastal settlements. The thawing of permafrost can cause roads and buildings to buckle and collapse.

In 2007, scientists from dozens of nations launched a study of the Arctic and Antarctic called the International Polar Year 2007-2008. The investigation involved more than 200 research projects, with a focus on how climate change affects the polar regions and their inhabitants.

Knut Kielland and Molly Lee

Related articles in *World Book* include:

Arctic Circle, *AHRK tihk* or *AHR tihk,* is an imaginary line that runs through the northern parts of Canada, Alaska, Russia, and Scandinavia. All points on the Arctic Circle lie at 66° 33′ north latitude, 1,624 miles (2,613 kilometers) from the north geographic pole (see **Arctic Ocean** [map]).

The Arctic Circle marks the edge of an area where the sun stays above the horizon one or more days each year. The sun never sets there on the longest day of summer, about June 21. The sun never rises on the Arctic Circle during the shortest day of winter, about December 21. At the North Pole itself, the sun is visible 90 days before and 90 days after June 21 if the sky is clear. It stays below the horizon for the same amount of time before and after December 21. See **Midnight sun.**   Leslie Duram

Arctic fox is a small fox that lives on the treeless coastal areas and islands of the Arctic Ocean. It grows approximately 20 inches (50 centimeters) long, not including its tail, and weighs from 2 to 20 pounds (1 to 9 kilograms).

Arctic foxes have long, thick winter fur to protect them from the extreme cold. Their relatively small ears also keep them from losing too much body heat. Most Arctic foxes change color from brown or gray in summer to white in winter. This change camouflages the foxes, enabling them to sneak up on prey. One kind of Arctic fox has a light gray or blue winter coat.

Arctic foxes feed mainly on birds, birds' eggs, and such small mammals as lemmings. When food becomes scarce in winter, the foxes often travel great distances to find animal remains left behind by polar bears or wolves. Arctic foxes usually mate for life. During the female's pregnancy, the breeding pair return to their family den, where many generations of foxes have lived before. Females usually give birth to 5 to 10 young each summer.   Thomas L. Poulson

Scientific classification. The Arctic fox is *Vulpes lagopus.* Some scientists prefer the name *Alopex lagopus.*

See also **Animal** (picture: Animals of the polar regions); **Fox** (picture).

Arctic Ocean is the body of icy water covering Earth's northernmost regions. It ranks as the smallest of the world's oceans, touching only the northern shores of Asia, Europe, and North America. The North Pole lies near the center of the Arctic Ocean.

People define the boundaries of the Arctic Ocean differently for different purposes. For oceanographers, the ocean's limits include: (1) the Bering Strait, between Alaska and Siberia; (2) the northern limits of the Canadian islands; (3) Fram Strait, between Greenland and Svalbard; and (4) the opening to the Barents Sea, between Svalbard and Norway. Defined this way, the Arctic Ocean covers about 3,680,000 square miles (9,530,000 square kilometers). Its widest part, between Alaska and Norway, measures about 2,630 miles (4,235 kilometers) across. The narrowest stretch separates Greenland and the Taymyr Peninsula of Russia. These areas lie about 1,200 miles (1,930 kilometers) apart.

The Arctic Ocean is bitterly cold. At its surface, thick chunks of floating ice form a treacherous, shifting landscape. In winter, the sun does not rise for weeks over the Arctic Ocean. In summer, the sun remains above the horizon for several weeks, and some of the ice melts.

The Greek explorer Pytheas sailed near the Arctic Ocean in the late 300's B.C. He reported that a frozen sea lay a six-day voyage north of Britain. The name *Arctic* comes from *Arktos* (bear), the ancient Greek name for a constellation that appears in the northern sky.

Groups of islands divide the coastal waters of the Arctic Ocean into seven seas. These seas, from Greenland eastward, are (1) the Barents Sea; (2) the Kara Sea; (3) the Laptev Sea; (4) the East Siberian Sea; (5) the Chukchi Sea; (6) the Beaufort Sea; and (7) the Lincoln Sea.

Far northern lands extend into the Arctic Ocean. They include most of Greenland and parts of Norway, Russia, and Canada, as well as Alaska. For more information on the land and people of the Arctic region, see **Arctic.**

Climate

In January, surface water temperatures in the Arctic Ocean drop to as low as about 28 °F (-2 °C), the freezing point of seawater. In summer, the waters warm to only a few degrees above freezing—and only in limited areas.

A high-pressure dome of cold, dry air generally covers the Arctic region. It prevents moist, warmer air from the south from reaching the central Arctic Ocean. As a result, rain and snowfall tend to be light over the Arctic Ocean. However, fog commonly forms over coastal waters in the summer, when humid, warm air from the land blows out over the ocean.

Arctic weather varies dramatically. In winter, violent storms form rapidly and unexpectedly in some areas. Such storms are sometimes called *Arctic hurricanes.*

Since the late 1900's, the patterns of air pressure that drive Arctic weather have been changing. The changes result from a combination of natural cycles and *global warming.* Global warming is an average increase in Earth's surface temperature, thought to be caused in part by human activities (see **Global warming**). Scientists have linked changing air pressure patterns to other changes, such as increases in the frequency of storms and the strength of waves. These changes, in turn, contribute to increased erosion along lengthy stretches of Arctic coastline.

Ice

Much of the Arctic Ocean is covered in a thick layer of floating ice. Most of the ice is *sea ice* or frozen seawa-

ter. The rest is *glacial ice,* which breaks off from glaciers along the coasts of Arctic lands.

Sea ice. Seawater freezes at a lower temperature than does fresh water because seawater has a higher salt content. When sea ice forms on the ocean surface, much of the salt sinks into the water below.

In winter, the cover of sea ice spreads beyond the Arctic Ocean's boundaries. But in the summer, the sea ice melts to less than half the ocean's area. The ice that remains in the Arctic Ocean throughout the summer can be up to 15 feet (5 meters) thick. The ice sometimes piles up into ridges and becomes thicker.

Arctic sea ice is constantly on the move. Winds and currents push the floating ice at speeds of up to about a mile or a couple kilometers per day. On the North American side of the ocean, the ice tends to drift in a clockwise motion called the Beaufort Gyre. On the European side, it flows along a path from the New Siberian Islands toward Fram Strait, called the Transpolar Drift.

Because sea ice is always moving, there are always areas of open water throughout the ice cover, called *leads.* Leads range from extremely thin cracks to huge breaks in the ice as wide as rivers.

Some areas of the ice cover tend to have thin ice or open water in the same place each winter. These areas, called *polynias,* serve as seasonal homes to many living things in the Arctic Ocean.

Glacial ice, unlike sea ice, is frozen fresh water from glaciers on land. Chunks of glacial ice break off along the coasts of Greenland, northern Canada, Svalbard, and other lands to form *icebergs.* Some icebergs become part of the Arctic sea ice cover. Many other icebergs float into the North Atlantic Ocean, where they eventually melt in the warm waters of the Gulf Stream.

Icebergs can be extremely dangerous to ships. Some icebergs are so large and thick that they are called *ice islands.* Scientists have even been able to set up research stations on some ice islands.

Disappearance of ice. The Arctic Ocean's summer sea ice cover has decreased by about 10 percent each

Facts in brief

Area: About 3,680,000 mi² (9,530,000 km²).
Greatest distance: About 2,630 mi² (4,235 km²), between Alaska and Norway.
Average depth: 4,465 ft (1,361 m).
Greatest depth: 18,399 ft (5,608 m), Molloy Hole, northwest of Svalbard.
Surface temperature: *Lowest,* 28 °F (-2 °C), in January. *Highest,* 29 °F (-1.5 °C), in July.

Floating ice covers much of the Arctic Ocean's surface. Most of the ice is *sea ice* (frozen seawater) that drifts with the currents. The rest is freshwater *glacial ice,* which breaks off from glaciers along the coasts of Arctic lands. Chunks of glacial ice form *icebergs,* seen in the distance in this photo.

decade since 1978, when satellite measurements were first gathered. Global warming may be contributing to this trend in a number of ways. For example, more sea ice may melt each year as a result of warming air temperatures over Siberia and North America. The ice cover may also be affected by changing weather and ocean circulation patterns related to global warming.

Declining sea ice cover could accelerate warming across the planet. White snow and ice reflect the sun's heat back into space, in much the same way that white clothing helps people stay cool in the summer sun. Darker areas of open water, on the other hand, absorb the sun's heat in much the same way dark clothing does. Thus, the more the ice melts, the more heat Earth absorbs. The heat can, in turn, cause even more ice to melt, creating a dangerous, escalating cycle.

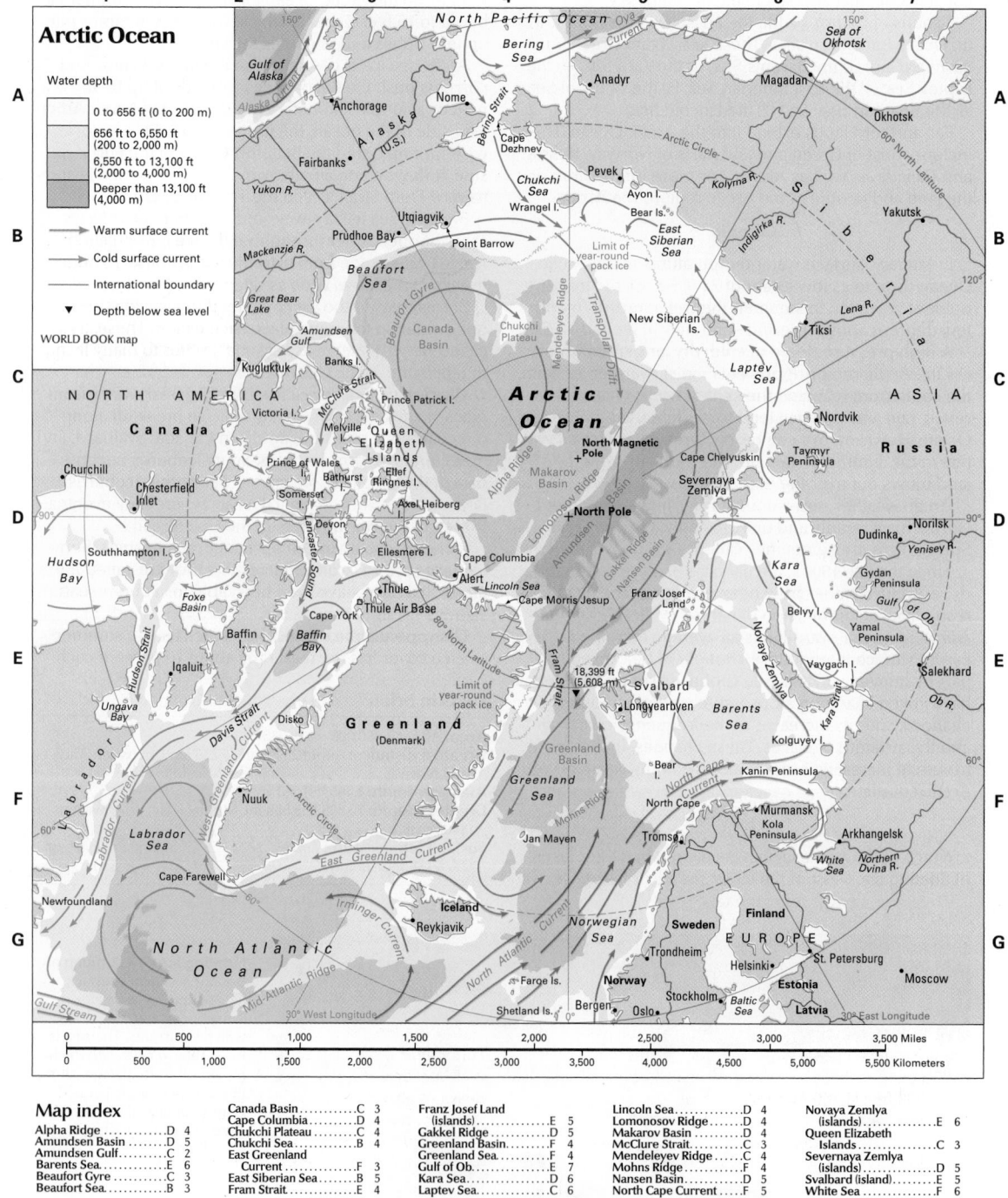

Map index

NASA

The disappearance of sea ice poses a threat to the wildlife of the Arctic Ocean. These satellite photographs show the extent of summer sea ice in 1979 *(left)* and 2005 *(right)*. The ice covering has decreased as a result of *global warming,* an increase in the average temperature at Earth's surface.

Ocean life

Despite its icy cover, the Arctic Ocean supports a diversity of wildlife. Seals and whales feed on fish and tiny floating organisms called *plankton.* Large numbers of diatoms, a type of plantlike *phytoplankton,* thrive near the surface of waters along the edges of the sea ice. Some whales eat huge amounts of shrimplike *zooplankton* called *krill.* Shellfish serve as an important source of food for walruses, bearded seals, and sperm whales. Halibut and other bottom-dwelling fish are plentiful in shallow seas along the ocean's coasts.

Polar bears live on top of the sea ice. They use it as a platform from which to hunt seals in the water below.

The ocean floor

The floor of the Arctic Ocean includes a shallow area along the coasts—called the *continental shelf*—and a central area called the *deep basin.* The Arctic Ocean's average depth is 4,465 feet (1,361 meters).

The continental shelf is a gently sloping band of underwater land at the edges of the continents. In the Arctic Ocean, it is mostly less than 500 feet (150 meters) deep. North of Greenland and North America, it extends about 45 to 120 miles (70 to 200 kilometers) from shore. Off the Russian coast, it extends much farther into the ocean—up to 1,000 miles (1,600 kilometers) from shore.

The deep basin. Several underwater ridges crisscross the deep basin of the Arctic Ocean. These ridges divide the deep basin into several smaller basins.

The Lomonosov Ridge, the tallest of the dividing ridges, rises about 10,000 feet (3,000 meters) from the surrounding floor. It extends about 1,100 miles (1,800 kilometers), stretching from a point near Ellesmere Island to an area north of the New Siberian Islands. The Lomonosov Ridge divides the deep basin into two main areas—the Canadian Basin and the Eurasian Basin. The Canadian Basin has an average depth of 12,500 feet (3,800 meters). The Eurasian Basin has an average depth of 13,800 feet (4,200 meters).

Several other ridges run parallel to the Lomonosov Ridge. On the Canadian side, the Alpha Ridge and the Mendeleyev Ridge form a ridge system that stretches from north of Ellesmere Island to the East Siberian Sea.

The ridge system separates the Canadian Basin into two smaller parts—the Canada Basin and the Makarov Basin.

In the European Basin, the Nansen-Gakkel Ridge stretches from the tip of Greenland toward the Laptev Sea. It separates the Amundsen Basin from the Nansen Basin. The Amundsen Basin includes the deepest areas of the Arctic Ocean, dropping in places to more than 18,000 feet (5,500 meters) below the ocean surface.

Waters

Water constantly flows into, out of, and around the Arctic Ocean, pushed along by currents and winds. In addition, about 10 percent of Earth's river water flows into the Arctic Ocean.

Currents. The North Atlantic Current brings a large amount of relatively warm, salty water from the Atlantic Ocean into the Arctic Ocean. The rest of the seawater flowing into the Arctic Ocean comes from the Pacific Ocean. This water is colder and less salty.

Ice and water flow out of the Arctic Ocean through the Fram Strait and along the East Greenland Current. Some of this water flows all the way around Greenland into Baffin Bay. There, it circles in a counterclockwise motion before flowing south. It is joined by water flowing out of the Arctic Ocean through passages between Canadian islands, where it forms the Labrador Current of the northwestern Atlantic Ocean.

Water masses. The Arctic Ocean's waters are not uniform in temperature or salt content. As in other oceans, the different layers of the water form distinct *water masses* with unique properties.

The Arctic Ocean's surface waters tend to be less salty than those of other oceans. Rivers and precipitation bring much fresh water to the ocean's surface. Also, the formation of sea ice causes much salt to sink to lower levels. The surface waters circulate in a pattern similar to that of sea ice, following the Beaufort Gyre and the Transpolar Drift. These motions vary somewhat, depending on wind patterns. The surface waters extend down to about 80 to 250 feet (25 to 75 meters) of depth.

Below the surface waters lies a near-freezing, nutrient-rich mass of Pacific water. This layer reaches about 500 feet (150 meters) deep and is generally found only in basins in the ocean's Canadian side.

A warmer mass of Atlantic water lies deeper, reaching 2,625 feet (800 meters) below the surface. This water enters the Arctic Ocean from the Fram Strait, where it starts out several degrees above freezing. It circulates in the smaller basins in counterclockwise patterns.

The deepest water mass, called Arctic bottom water, is saltier and colder than the Atlantic water mass. The Arctic bottom water is slightly warmer and saltier in the Canadian Basin than in it is in the Eurasian Basin. Little is known about how the Arctic bottom water circulates.

Tides. The Arctic Ocean has smaller tides overall than the other oceans do, probably due to its small size and nearly landlocked geography. Most of the tides in the Arctic Ocean rise and fall less than 1 foot (0.3 meter).

The Arctic Ocean and people

The Arctic Ocean has long provided fishing waters and hunting platforms for Arctic peoples. For many centuries, Europeans tried to find a sea route through the Arctic Ocean, referred to as the Northwest Passage. The ocean continues to provide many natural resources. But it also faces threats from pollution and global warming.

Use. The Arctic Ocean provides a water route to distant Arctic ports. It enables ships to deliver fuel, manufactured goods, and other products to Arctic settlements and carry back such goods as fish, fur, and lumber. Special *icebreaker* ships clear routes for these ships, and aircraft help guide them through the ice.

Major petroleum deposits lie off the north coast of Russia and Alaska, and oil wells operate in these areas. The continental shelf near Canada and Russia is also believed to hold large reserves of oil and natural gas.

Russian and Nordic fishing crews catch such fish as cod and halibut in the Barents and Kara seas. Arctic people from several nations hunt whales in the ocean.

Threats. Pollution is limited in the Arctic Ocean because there is little development in the region. But the disposal of wastes from military bases in the Arctic has resulted in some local pollution, as has oil production on the Alaskan shelf. Air pollution sometimes drifts over the region from factories in China, Russia, the United States, and other northern countries. This pollution contributes to the *Arctic haze* sometimes reported by airplane pilots. Some toxic chemicals used in low latitudes end up in the Arctic because they repeatedly evaporate, redepositing in colder areas. These chemicals tend to accumulate in animal fat, reaching higher concentrations in animals high on the food chain.

Global warming causes the Arctic Ocean's sea ice to decrease. The ice's disappearance threatens polar bears and other animals that depend on it.   Kelly K. Falkner

Related articles in *World Book* include:

Arctic	Iceberg	North Pole
Barents Sea	Kara Sea	Northwest Passage
Ice formation	Labrador Current	White Sea

Arctic tern, *AHRK tihk* or *AHR tihk,* is a sea bird that migrates over a greater distance than any other bird. The Arctic tern grows about 17 inches (43 centimeters) long; has bluish-gray, black, and white feathers; and has red feet and a red bill. Arctic terns breed on Atlantic seacoasts from New England to Greenland and the northernmost islands of the Arctic Ocean, and on the coasts of the northern North Pacific Ocean and Bering Sea. Late in August, the birds and their young begin a long jour-

ney to the shores of Antarctica and nearby islands. Later, the birds fly north once more, arriving in the Arctic about mid-June.   George L. Hunt, Jr.

Scientific classification. The scientific name of the Arctic tern is *Sterna paradisaea.*

See also **Bird** (Interesting facts about birds [Greatest traveler]; picture: Birds of the Arctic); **Tern.**

Ardennes Mountains and Forest, *ahr DEHN,* extend from northern France into Belgium and Luxembourg. They have some of the largest oak and beech forests in Europe. The Ardennes Mountains average about 1,600 feet (488 meters) in height. Fighting occurred in the Belgian and French Ardennes in World War I (1914-1918). The Battle of the Bulge took place in the Ardennes in 1944, near the end of World War II.   Hugh D. Clout

See also **Belgium** (The Ardennes); **Bulge, Battle of the.**

Ardern, Jacinda (1980-   ), became prime minister of New Zealand in 2017. She belongs to New Zealand's Labour Party, a center-left political party that favors socially liberal policies.

Jacinda Kate Laurell Ardern was born in Hamilton, New Zealand, on July 26, 1980. She earned a bachelor's degree in communications studies from the University of Waikato in 1999. She was first elected to New Zealand's Parliament in 2008. In March 2017, Labour elected Ardern as its deputy leader. She replaced Andrew Little as Labour leader in July.

In the 2017 election, no party won a majority of parliamentary seats. Labour formed a government with support from the New Zealand First Party and the Green Party. Ardern became prime minister. In 2020, Ardern won praise for her leadership in New Zealand's rapid and effective response to the COVID-19 pandemic. She remained prime minister after Labour won a majority in the 2020 elections. See **COVID-19.**   S. Thomas Richardson

Ardipithecus is an early humanlike creature known from fossils found in northern Ethiopia. The fossils are about 4.4 million to 5.8 million years old. Scientists recognize two *species* (kinds) of *Ardipithecus, Ardipithecus ramidus* and *Ardipithecus kadabba. Ardipithecus* is a type of *hominin.* In scientific classification, hominins are the group that includes human beings and early humanlike ancestors. Scientists think that hominins *evolved* (developed over time) from an apelike common ancestor, shared with modern African apes, between 10 million and 7 million years ago. *Ardipithecus* lived soon after this evolutionary split. The first *Ardipithecus* fossils were discovered in 1992.   Holly M. Dunsworth

See also **Human being** (Prehuman ancestors); **Prehistoric people** (The earliest hominins).

Area, in plane geometry, is the amount of surface contained within the boundaries of a plane figure. It is generally expressed in square units. For example, a square inch is a square whose sides are each 1 inch long. Other units of area include square feet, square miles, and square meters. The area of most common plane figures can be calculated from certain of their dimensions. Thus, a rectangle's area can be found by multiplying the lengths of two adjoining sides. *Area* can also mean the measure of a curved surface or the surface of a solid figure, in which case it is called *surface area.* See also **Calculus** (Finding areas); **Metric system** (Use of related units; Non-SI metric units); **Square measure; Weights and measures** (table: Surface or area).   Blake E. Peterson

Area 51 is the unofficial name for a United States military installation popular in UFO folklore. UFO stands for unidentified *f*lying *o*bject. Some people think UFO's are alien spacecraft (see **Unidentified flying object**). Area 51 is about 85 miles (137 kilometers) northwest of Las Vegas. It lies within the Nevada Test and Training Range, a U.S. Air Force installation.

Government officials have long been reluctant to discuss Area 51, stating that highly classified activities have taken place near there. In 2013, the Central Intelligence Agency acknowledged that top-secret aircraft, including the U-2 spy plane, were developed at Area 51. Such planes fly faster than normal planes and have unusual shapes. These aircraft may account for some UFO reports. Such reports, and Area 51's secrecy, have led to conspiracy theories about it. A popular one claims Area 51 houses the wreckage—and possibly the alien crew—of a spacecraft that supposedly crashed near Roswell, New Mexico, in 1947 (see **Roswell**).   Robert Hodierne

Arecibo Observatory, *AHR uh SEE boh,* is an astronomical observatory in Puerto Rico, 50 miles (80 kilometers) west of San Juan. When the observatory opened, in 1963, it had the world's most powerful *radio telescope* (telescope that collects and measures radio waves given off by objects in space). In 2020, the telescope was *decommissioned* (retired) after a structural collapse. Scientists now use other instruments for research at Arecibo.

Arecibo's radio telescope had the world's second largest *dish* (bowl-shaped reflector). Only the dish of the Five-hundred-meter Aperture Spherical radio Telescope (FAST) in Guizhou Province, China, is larger. The Arecibo dish was built into a basin-shaped valley and was 1,000 feet (305 meters) in diameter. The dish focused radio waves onto receivers above it. Radio waves come from such distant objects as *pulsars* (rapidly spinning stars whose waves arrive on Earth as regular pulses). Arecibo astronomers discovered the first *binary pulsar* (pulsar in orbit around a companion star) in 1974. In the 1990's, astronomers at the observatory discovered planets beyond the solar system and ice at the poles of Mercury.

In 1996, special mirrors were added to sharpen the telescope's focus. Astronomers could track an object for several hours by repositioning the mirrors. The telescope was also used as a giant radar system to map the surfaces of planets, comets, and asteroids. In addition, scientists studied the *ionosphere* with the telescope. The ionosphere is made up of regions of Earth's atmosphere with many *ions* (electrically charged atoms and groups of atoms).   B. M. Lewis

See also **Telescope** (Radio and microwave telescopes).

Arendt, *uh REHNT,* **Hannah** (1906-1975), was a German-born American historian and political philosopher. She gained international fame for her writings on *totalitarianism* (government by dictatorship) and Jewish affairs.

Arendt's first notable book was *Origins of Totalitarianism* (1951, revised and expanded 1968, 1973). In it, Arendt linked the rise of totalitarian government in the 1900's to anti-Semitism and imperialism in the 1800's. She blamed its growth on the disappearance of the traditional *nation-state.* A nation-state is an area of land where the people share a common culture, history, or language, and also have an independent government.

Arendt's *Eichmann in Jerusalem* (1963) is an analysis of the trial of the German war criminal Adolf Eichmann, held in Jerusalem in 1961. The book created controversy because it advanced the opinion that Jewish community leaders had played a cooperative role in the Nazi extermination of Jews during World War II (1939-1945). But critics generally consider the book a major contribution to Holocaust studies. Arendt's many other books include *The Human Condition* (1958), *On Revolution* (1963), *On Violence* (1970), *Crises of the Republic* (1972), and the unfinished *The Life of the Mind* (1978). Her letters to the American writer Mary McCarthy, a close friend, were published as *Between Friends* (1995).

Arendt was born on Oct. 14, 1906, in Hanover, Germany, into a family of Jewish descent. She earned a Ph.D. in philosophy from the University of Heidelberg in 1929. In 1933, when the Nazis took control of Germany, she fled to France. In 1941, she again fled from the Nazis, this time to the United States. Settling in New York City, Arendt worked for several Jewish organizations. In 1951, she became a U.S. citizen. During the 1950's and 1960's, she taught at the University of California at Berkeley and at the University of Chicago. From 1967 until her death, she was a professor at the New School for Social Research (now simply the New School) in New York City. Arendt died on Dec. 4, 1975.   Richard E. Rupp

Areopagus, *AR ee AHP uh guhs,* was the oldest and most respected council of ancient Athens. Prominent citizens who were *archons,* one of the highest offices in the city-state, were members of the Areopagus for life.

In early Athenian history, the Areopagus had administrative and constitutional powers. About 600 B.C., a new group, the Council of the Four Hundred, took over many duties of the Areopagus. About 450 B.C., most of the remaining duties and privileges of the Areopagus were transferred to large people's courts. But it continued to try murder cases and retained the power to fine citizens found guilty of extravagance, insolence, or intemperance. The council was named for the Areopagus, or Hill of Ares, where it held meetings.   Jennifer Tolbert Roberts

See also **Solon.**

Arequipa, *AR uh KEE pah* (pop. 969,284), is the commercial center of southern Peru and one of Peru's largest cities. It lies 8,100 feet (2,470 meters) above sea level in the Andes Mountains (see **Peru** [map]). Ancient ruins and American Indian villages around Arequipa attract many tourists. The Spaniards began settlements at Arequipa in 1540. The city has some of the best examples of Spanish colonial architecture in Peru.   Jerry R. Williams

Ares, *AIR eez,* was a god of war in Greek mythology. He was the son of Zeus and Hera, the king and queen of the gods. Ares fathered many children, most of whom were warlike or were associated with war. The Romans identified Mars, their god of war, with Ares. See **Mars.**

Ares was associated with the Greek goddess Aphrodite. Aphrodite was married to the Greek god Hephaestus, but she had a love affair with Ares. According to some myths, Aphrodite bore some of Ares's children, including Eros, the god of love. In poetry, Ares's name has often been used as a synonym for war. However, he was often portrayed as an incompetent warrior. The epic poem the *Iliad,* also attributed to Homer, mocks Ares for being wounded in battle by the mortal hero Diomedes with the help of the goddess Athena.   F. Carter Philips

The Obelisco monument, *on the right,* stands at the intersection of Avenida 9 de Julio and Avenida Corrientes in Buenos Aires, Argentina's capital. It was erected in 1936 to mark the 400th anniversary of the city's original founding. The broad Avenida 9 de Julio, *shown here,* is named for the date in 1816 when Argentina declared its independence from Spain.

Argentina

Argentina is the second largest country in area in South America, after Brazil, and the eighth largest in the world. It lies in the southern part of South America and covers an area of 1,073,519 square miles (2,780,400 square kilometers). Chile, Bolivia, Paraguay, Brazil, Uruguay, and the Atlantic Ocean form Argentina's borders.

Argentina's landscape varies dramatically throughout the country. The rugged Andes Mountains stretch along the country's western border. A bare, windswept plateau called Patagonia extends across the south. The Pampas, a fertile, grassy plain, lies near the center of the country. Scrub forests cover much of the north.

Argentina has a republican form of government. The country is divided into 23 provinces and Buenos Aires Federal District. The city of Buenos Aires, in the federal district, is Argentina's capital, largest city, main port, and center of business, culture, and trade.

Most Argentines are of Italian or Spanish ancestry. The *indigenous* (Native American) groups that occupied the territory before the arrival of the Spanish today represent only a small portion of the population. Nearly all Argentines speak Spanish and are Roman Catholics.

Argentina is rich in natural resources. Most of its farm exports come from the Pampas region. Beef, corn, soybeans, and wheat are the chief agricultural products. Manufacturing became important in the 1900's, yet much of the manufacturing involves processing farm products. Argentina's petroleum industry produces enough oil to meet local demand and also export oil to other countries.

For almost 300 years, Argentina was a Spanish colony. Argentines declared their independence in 1816. Dis-

putes between the capital and the provinces marked most of the 1800's. Unification and stability in the 1880's brought prosperity and growth to Argentina. The exporting of meat and grain to Europe made the country wealthy. By the late 1920's, Argentina had become one of the richest nations in the world.

Today, Argentina no longer ranks among the world's economic giants. It has an advanced level of industrialization, but economic decline, political instability, social conflict, and violence hampered Argentina's progress during the last half of the 1900's.

Government

National government. Argentina's Constitution, adopted in 1853, established the country as a democratic republic with independent executive, legislative, and judicial branches. In practice, the executive branch is the strongest. It consists of a president, a vice president, and a Cabinet appointed by the president. The president serves as chief of state and head of government. The people elect the president and vice president to four-year terms. The president and vice president may serve no more than two terms in a row.

The legislature consists of a two-house National Congress. The two houses are a 72-member Senate and a 257-member Chamber of Deputies. Every two years, citizens elect one-third the number of senators, who serve six-year terms. They also elect about half the number of deputies, who serve four-year terms.

Local government. Each of the 23 provinces of Argentina has an elected governor and legislature as well as its own constitution. The constitutions of the prov-

Larry Lee Photography/Corbis/Getty Images

The Casa Rosada (Pink House) contains the offices of the president of Argentina and other government officials. It faces the Plaza de Mayo, the historic center and heart of Buenos Aires.

inces resemble the national Constitution. An elected mayor and city council govern Buenos Aires Federal District. Since the mid-1990's, the federal government has passed reforms to give more responsibilities to local governments.

Politics. The Justicialist Party (PJ), founded in 1945, historically has been one of Argentina's largest and strongest political parties. The Radical Civic Union (UCR), founded in 1891, is one of the oldest parties. Traditionally, the PJ has represented labor interests, and the UCR has represented urban middle-class voters. Citizens from 18 to 70 years old are required to vote. Those who are 16 and 17 years old may vote, but voting is optional.

Courts. The Supreme Court of Justice is Argentina's highest court. The president appoints the judges of the Supreme Court with the Senate's approval. The Supreme Court may declare acts of the legislature uncon-

© Rusalam Ma-teeyoh, Shutterstock

Symbols of Argentina. The national flag, adopted in 1818, and the coat of arms bear a sun, which represents Argentina's freedom from Spain. The blue and white of the flag are the colors worn by patriots who fought off British invaders in 1806 and 1807. The coat of arms also bears a liberty cap.

Facts in brief

Capital: Buenos Aires.
Official language: Spanish.
Official name: República Argentina (Argentine Republic).
Area: 1,073,519 mi² (2,780,400 km²). *Greatest distances*—north-south, 2,300 mi (3,700 km); east-west, 980 mi (1,577 km). *Coastline*—2,940 mi (4,731 km).
Elevation: *Highest*—Aconcagua, 22,841 ft (6,962 m) above sea level. *Lowest*—Valdés Peninsula, 131 ft (40 m) below sea level.
Population: *Estimated 2022 population*—46,068,000; density, 43 per mi² (17 per km²); distribution, 92 percent urban, 8 percent rural. *2020 official government estimate*—45,376,763.
Chief products: *Agriculture*—apples, beef, corn, grapes, milk, poultry, soybeans, sugar cane, sunflower seeds, wheat, wool. *Manufacturing*—chemicals, machinery, meat and other food products, motor vehicles, oil. *Mining*—natural gas, petroleum.
Money: *Basic unit*—Argentine peso. One hundred centavos equal one peso.

WORLD BOOK map

Argentina occupies most of the southern part of South America. It borders five other countries and the South Atlantic Ocean.

stitutional. The president also appoints judges to the federal courts of appeals upon the recommendation of a Magistrates' Council. Each province has its own supreme court and lower court system. Provincial governors appoint provincial court judges.

Armed forces. The three main branches of Argentina's armed forces are the Air Force, the Army, and the Navy. Other branches include the Coast Guard and the National Gendarmerie (border police). Military service is voluntary.

People

Population. Some parts of Argentina are heavily populated, and others have few people. For example, about two-fifths of the country's population lives in Buenos Aires and its suburbs. Large regions of the country have an unfavorable climate and terrain, and so are sparsely populated. Such regions include the high Andes Mountains in the west, the dry Patagonian plateau in the south, and the wooded area called the Chaco in the north.

Ancestry. Most Argentines are of European ancestry, chiefly Italian and Spanish. Spaniards colonized Argentina in the 1500's. After Argentina became independent, several waves of European immigration occurred. The largest wave occurred from the late 1800's to the early 1900's and was encouraged by a government plan to attract European settlers. The indigenous population is small compared to that of other Latin American countries and is concentrated mainly in isolated areas in the north and the southwest. Argentina has one of the largest Jewish populations in the Americas. In addition, many people are from Bolivia, Paraguay, and other South American countries.

Language. The official language of Argentina is Spanish. Many people understand Italian, even if they do not speak it fluently. Argentina's urban population has become increasingly familiar with English, and English and French are part of the high school curriculum. The main indigenous languages spoken today are Guaraní, Quechua, and Tehuelche.

Way of life

City life. Most Argentines, especially middle-class Argentines, live in urban centers, which offer the highest standard of living. Buenos Aires, the capital, is a center of art and culture, as well as the country's main harbor and a hub of commerce, government, and industry.

Since 1940, industrialization has drawn people to urban centers, where business opportunities, education, and jobs are more readily available than in the countryside. This migration resulted in the development of a large middle-class population in Argentine cities. But

Argentina map index

Provinces

Map key	Name	Area In mi²	Area In km²	Population
E 4	**Buenos Aires**	118,754	307,571	15,625,084
B 3	**Catamarca**	39,615	102,602	367,828
B 5	**Chaco**	38,469	99,633	1,055,259
G 3	**Chubut**	86,752	224,686	509,108
D 4	**Córdoba**	65,161	168,766	3,308,876
C 5	**Corrientes**	34,054	88,199	992,595
D 5	**Entre Ríos**	30,418	78,781	1,235,994
A 5	**Formosa**	27,825	72,066	530,162
A 3	**Jujuy**	20,548	53,219	673,307
E 3	**La Pampa**	55,382	143,440	318,951
C 3	**La Rioja**	34,626	89,680	333,642
D 3	**Mendoza**	57,462	148,827	1,738,929
B 6	**Misiones**	11,506	29,801	1,101,593
E 2	**Neuquén**	36,324	94,078	551,266
F 3	**Río Negro**	78,384	203,013	638,645
B 4	**Salta**	59,759	154,775	1,214,441
C 3	**San Juan**	34,614	89,651	681,055
D 3	**San Luis**	29,633	76,748	432,310
H 3	**Santa Cruz**	94,187	243,943	273,964
C 5	**Santa Fe**	51,354	133,007	3,194,537
B 4	**Santiago del Estero**	52,222	135,254	874,006
B 3	**Tucumán**	8,697	22,524	1,448,188

Other political units

Map key	Name	Area In mi²	Area In km²	Population
D 5	**Federal District**	78	203	2,890,151
J 3	**Tierra del Fuego (territory)**	8,329	21,571	127,205

Cities and towns

Name	Population	Map key
Aguilares	32,908	B 3
Almirante Brown*†	552,139	D 5
Allen*	22,859	E 3
Alta Gracia	48,140	C 4
Añatuya	23,286	C 4
Arrecifes*	26,400	D 5
Avellaneda*†	342,677	D 5
Azul	55,728	E 5
Bahía Blanca	291,327	E 4
Balcarce	38,376	E 5
Baradero*	28,537	D 5
Barranqueras*	54,698	B 5
Bell Ville	33,835	D 4
Bella Vista	29,071	C 5
Berazategui*†	324,156	D 5
Berisso*	87,698	E 5
Bolívar*	26,242	E 5
Bragado	33,222	D 5
Buenos Aires	2,890,151	D 5
Caleta Olivia	51,733	H 3
Campana*	86,860	D 5
Cañada de Gómez	29,205	D 4
Cañuelas*	29,974	D 5
Casilda*	34,703	D 5
Catamarca	159,139	C 3
Caucete	28,222	C 3
Centenario*	32,928	F 3
Chacabuco*	38,418	D 5
Chajarí*	32,734	D 5
Chascomús	33,607	E 5
Chilecito	33,724	C 3
Chimbas*	87,258	C 3
Chivilcoy	58,152	D 5
Cinco Saltos	22,790	E 3
Cipolleti	77,713	E 3
Clorinda	52,837	B 6
Comodoro Rivadavia	175,196	G 3
Concepcíon	49,782	B 3
Concepcíon del Uruguay	72,528	D 5
Concordia	149,450	C 5
Córdoba	1,317,298	C 4
Coronel Pringles	20,263	E 4
Coronel Rosales (Punta Alta)	58,315	E 4
Corrientes	346,334	B 5
Cruz del Eje	30,680	C 4
Curuzú Cuatiá	34,470	C 5
Cutral-Có	35,465	F 3
Deán Funes	21,211	C 4
Dolores	25,940	E 5
Eldorado	57,323	B 6
Ensenada*	54,463	E 5
Esperanza*	40,125	C 5
Esquel	32,343	G 2
Esteban Echeverría*†	300,745	D 5
Ezeiza*†	162,475	D 5
Famailla*	22,924	B 3
Florencio Varela*†	426,005	D 5
Formosa	222,226	B 5
Frías	26,649	C 4
General Acha	12,184	E 4
General Alvear	29,909	D 3
General Güemes	31,494	A 4
General Pico	56,795	E 4
General Roca	81,534	F 3
General San Martín*†	414,196	D 5
Godoy Cruz	191,299	D 3
Goya	71,606	C 5
Gualequay	40,507	D 5
Guale-guaychú	80,614	D 5
Guaymallén*	252,618	D 3
Hurlingham*†	181,241	D 5
Ituzaingó†	167,284	D 5
Jesus Maria	31,602	C 4
José C. Paz*†	265,981	D 5
Junín	87,509	D 5
La Banda	106,441	B 4
La Matanza (San Justo)*†	1,775,272	D 5
Lanús*†	459,263	D 5
La Paz	24,307	C 5
La Plata	643,133	D 5
La Rioja	178,872	C 3
Las Flores	21,455	E 5
Las Heras	17,821	H 3
Las Heras*	189,067	D 3
Libertador General San Martín	46,642	A 4
Lomas de Zamora*†	616,279	D 5
Luján*	97,363	D 5
Lules*	21,088	B 3
Machagi*	21,997	B 5
Maipú*	106,662	D 3
Malvinas Argentinas*†	322,375	D 5
Mar del Plata	593,337	E 5
Marcos Juárez*	27,004	D 5
Mendoza	114,893	D 3
Mercedes	111,391	D 3
Mercedes	56,116	D 5
Mercedes	33,551	C 5
Merlo*†	527,658	D 5
Metán	28,295	B 4
Miramar*	29,433	D 5
Monte Caseros	23,470	C 5
Monteros*	23,274	B 4
Moreno*†	452,505	D 5
Morón*†	321,109	D 5
Necochea	84,784	E 5
Neuquén	231,198	E 3
Nueve de Julio	36,494	E 5
Oberá	63,960	B 6
Olavarría	89,721	E 5
Palpalá*	50,183	A 3
Paraná	247,139	C 5
Paso de los Libres	43,251	C 6
Pehuajó	31,553	E 4
Pergamino	91,399	D 5
Plottier*	32,390	F 3
Posadas	275,028	B 6
Presidencía Rogue Sáenz Peña	89,882	B 5
Puerto Deseado	14,183	H 4
Puerto Madryn	81,315	G 4
Puerto San Julián	7,894	I 3
Puerto Santa Cruz	4,431	I 3
Punta Alta, see Coronel Rosales		
Quilmes*†	582,943	D 5
Quitilipi*	24,517	B 5
Rafaela	91,571	C 4
Rawson	24,616	G 4
Rawson*	114,368	C 3
Reconquista	70,549	C 5
Resistencia	290,723	B 5
Río Cuarto	157,010	D 4
Río Gallegos	95,796	I 3
Río Grande	66,425	J 3
Río Tercero	46,421	D 4
Rivadavia*	82,582	C 3
Rosario	948,312	D 5
Rufino	18,727	D 4
Saladillo*	26,763	E 5
Salta	520,683	A 3
San Antonio Oeste	16,265	F 4
San Carlos de Bariloche	109,305	F 2
San Cristóbal	14,389	C 5
San Fernando*†	160,284	D 5
San Francisco	61,750	C 4
San Isidro*†	292,878	D 5
San Juan	109,123	C 3
San Justo*	21,624	C 5
San Luis	169,947	D 3
San Martín	79,476	D 3
San Miguel*†	276,190	D 5
San Nicolás	133,602	D 5
San Pedro*	47,452	D 5
San Pedro	75,037	A 4
San Rafael	118,009	D 3
San Ramón de la Nueva Orán	76,070	A 3
San Salvador de Jujuy	257,970	A 3
Santa Fe	391,164	C 5
Santa Rosa	102,880	E 4
Santiago del Estero	252,192	B 4
Santo Tomé	65,684	C 5
Santo Tomé	23,299	C 6
Sarmiento	10,858	G 3
Tafi Viejo*	39,601	B 4
Tandil	116,916	E 5
Tartagal	63,196	A 4
Termas de Río Hondo	32,166	B 4
Tigre*†	370,913	D 5
Trelew	97,915	G 4
Trenque Lauquén	33,442	E 4
Tres Arroyos	46,867	E 5
Tres de Febrero*†	340,071	D 5
Tucumán (San Miguel de Tucumán)	548,866	B 4
Tunuyán*	28,859	D 3
Ushuaia	56,593	J 3
Venado Tuerto	75,437	D 4
Vicente López†	269,420	D 5
Victoria	30,623	D 5
Viedma	52,789	F 4
Villa Ángela	41,403	B 5
Villa Carlos Paz	62,423	C 4
Villa Constitución	47,374	D 5
Villa Dolores	29,854	D 4
Villa María	79,351	D 4
Villa Regina*	30,028	E 3
Villaguay*	32,881	C 5
Yacimiento Río Turbio	8,814	I 2
Zapala	32,097	F 3
Zárate	98,522	D 5

*Does not appear on map; key shows general location.
†One of the 24 political divisions within Greater Buenos Aires.

Source: 2010 census.

Argentina
political map

	National park (N.P.)
	International boundary
	Provincial boundary
	Expressway
	Road
	Railroad
⊛	National capital
★	Provincial capital
•	Other city or town

0   200   400   600   800   1,000 Miles

0   200   400   600   800   1,000   1,200   1,400   1,600 Kilometers

WORLD BOOK map

the cities are also places of striking contrasts. Wealthy Argentines live in mansions and luxury apartment buildings, while poor workers and a large unemployed population live in suburban slums. Economic problems in the late 1900's led to the expansion of *shantytowns* (roughly built areas outside a city).

Many Argentine cities resemble Spanish ones. They are centered around a main square called a *plaza*. A cathedral and official buildings usually stand near the plaza. Buenos Aires resembles a European capital with attractive parks, balconied apartment buildings, impressive government buildings, and wide boulevards.

Rural life. As in the cities, there is a large gap between the rich and poor. Wealthy landowners live in elegant homes on huge ranches called *estancias,* especially on the Pampas and in Patagonia. Some of these homes resemble Spanish houses, with rooms surrounding a patio. Poor rural workers live on small farms with modest houses built of *adobe* (packed mud) or in huts with adobe walls, dirt floors, and roofs of straw and mud.

In the 1800's, cowboys called *gauchos* caught wild cattle and horses on the Pampas for their hides. Many gauchos were *mestizos* (people of mixed European and indigenous ancestry). The romantic figure of the gaucho became part of Argentine folklore. Today, the few remaining gauchos work chiefly as ranch hands on estancias.

Clothing. Argentines have a reputation for being well-dressed. Wealthy city dwellers closely follow international fashion trends. In some rural areas, people wear distinctive clothing. For example, workers on estancias wear at least part of the traditional gaucho costume. These garments include loose trousers tucked into low boots, a *poncho* (blanket with a slit in the middle for the head), and a wide-brimmed hat. In northwestern Argentina, where Andean culture is strong, clothing sometimes resembles that of Bolivian and Peruvian indigenous people. For example, some people wear derby hats and ponchos.

Food and drink. Argentina is known for the excellent quality of its beef. The *asado* (barbecue or roast) is perhaps the most typical Argentine method of cooking meat. An asado may include chicken, pork, prime ribs of beef, sausages, and various glands and organs of animals roasted on an open-air grill called a *parrilla* or on large spits over a fire. *Empanadas,* pastries usually filled with ground meat, cheese, vegetables, or other fillings, are a traditional appetizer or snack. High-quality ice cream, pasta, and pizza reflect the influence of Italian cooking. Typical desserts are *dulce de leche* (a milky caramel) and *alfajores* (two cookies with a filling, often dulce de leche, sandwiched between them).

In general, Argentines dine at a late hour. Typically, they eat breakfast until 10 a.m., lunch between noon and 2:30 p.m., and dinner after 9 p.m.

The high quality of Argentine wine is recognized worldwide. La Rioja, Mendoza, Salta, and San Juan are notable wine-growing regions. Malbec is a unique Argentine red wine. A tea called *mate* (pronounced *MAH tay)* is a popular drink. It is made from the yerba mate plant. People gather and pass a gourd filled with mate around the table, each person sipping through a metal straw. The sharing of mate is an expression of friendship. Yerba mate tea also can be made with tea bags.

Recreation. Soccer is the most popular sport in Argentina. Other popular sports include basketball, rugby, and automobile and horse racing. The Atlantic coast south of Buenos Aires and the hilly country around Córdoba province are popular vacation spots. The southern Andes is an important tourist destination, attracting hikers, hunters, and skiers.

Argentines observe a number of regional festivals. Northwesterners celebrate Inti Raymi, the Quechua Festival of the Sun, in June. During the festival, they give thanks for the year's harvest. Two important national holidays are July 9, Independence Day; and May 25, the anniversary of the 1810 revolution, when citizens of Buenos Aires set up an independent government.

Education. Almost all Argentines age 15 or older can read and write. The government provides free public elementary and high school education. Argentina also has many privately funded schools that charge tuition. Children from 5 to 14 years old must attend school.

Argentina has about 80 universities. About half of them are free public universities run by the government. The University of Buenos Aires is Argentina's largest uni-

Eitan Abramovich/AFP/Getty Images

Soccer, known as *fútbol* in Spanish, is an extremely popular sport in Argentina. Many Argentines enjoy the game not only as spectators but also as participants. These children are playing soccer in a shantytown in Buenos Aires.

Asados are a popular way of cooking meat in Argentina. The Spanish word *asado* means *roast* or *barbecue*. An asado may include chicken, pork, prime ribs of beef, sausages, and various glands and organs of animals. Such foods are roasted on an open-air grill called a *parrilla* or on large spits around a fire, as shown.

A. Garozzo/DEA/Getty Images

versity. Other prominent universities include the Catholic University of Argentina, the National Technological University, and the National University of Córdoba. The country also has a number of public and private technical and vocational schools.

Religion. More than 90 percent of Argentines are Roman Catholic. However, fewer than 20 percent of urban Catholics regularly practice their religion. Argentina also has small populations of Protestant Christians, Jews, and Muslims.

The arts. Argentina's urban centers have many artistic and cultural offerings. European influences are evident in Argentine architecture, motion pictures, fine arts, and music. The Colón Theater, in Buenos Aires, is home to the National Ballet, National Opera, and National Symphony. Buenos Aires also has numerous professional theaters that present plays and musical revues.

Music and dance. Tango, the national music and dance of Argentina, combines African and European influences. Tango originated in the late 1800's in the Buenos Aires area. Initially considered a low-class art form,

tango eventually spread to such fashionable cities as Paris and New York City, where it gained in popularity and refinement. A sometimes-dramatic dance for couples, tango may be danced socially at events called *milongas,* or as performance. It incorporates elegant, intentional walking, intertwining leg movements, and other steps, mostly danced in an embrace.

Tango music may be performed by as few as two musicians or a whole orchestra. A piano, a violin, and a *bandoneón,* a kind of accordion, are usually included. The lyrics are typically sad and nostalgic. One of the music's most famous composers was Enrique Santos Discépolo. He wrote many popular tangos from the 1920's to 1940's. Carlos Gardel was an important tango singer in the 1920's and 1930's. During the second half of the 1900's, Astor Piazzolla developed a *genre* (style) of music called *tango nuevo* (new tango). Piazzolla introduced elements of classical and jazz music into the tango. Argentina also has a strong tradition of folk dances and music, including styles known as chacarera, zamba, and malambo.

Literature. Unlike many former Spanish colonies, Ar-

Jeff Greenberg/UIG/Getty Images

Tango is the national dance and music of Argentina. These couples are dancing at a *milonga* in Plaza Dorrego, in the San Telmo neighborhood of Buenos Aires. Milongas are social events for dancing tango. They have their own special etiquette. For example, couples circulate around the dance floor in a counterclockwise direction.

gentina lacks a significant body of colonial literature. About 1776, Alonso Carrió de la Vandera's travel guide titled *The Guide for Blind Wayfarers* was published. Filled with details about everyday colonial life, it is a rare and important historical source. *Gauchesca* poetry, which developed in the mid-1800's, describes gaucho life and satirizes politics of that time. *El gaucho Martín Fierro* (1872) and *La vuelta de Martín Fierro (The Return of Martín Fierro,* 1879), by José Hernández, are the most famous examples of gauchesca poetry. A genre known as *criollismo,* which originated in the 1800's and continued into the early 1900's, describes the lives of rural *criollos,* people of Spanish descent born in Latin America. Important authors of criollo literature include Benito Lynch and Roberto Jorge Payró.

Historical and political writing characterized much Argentine literature from the middle and late 1800's. Important writers of this period include Bartolomé Mitre and Domingo Faustino Sarmiento.

Jorge Luis Borges, an Argentine essayist, poet, and short-story writer of the 1900's, won broad praise for his brilliant use of language and original observations on the meaning of human existence. Other important authors of the period include Adolfo Bioy Casares, Julio Cortázar, Marta Lynch, Alejandra Pizarnik, Manuel Puig, Ernesto Sábato, Osvaldo Soriano, and Luisa Valenzuela. Important writers of the early 2000's include the novelists César Aria, Andrés Neuman, and Ricardo Piglia. See **Latin American literature.**

Painting did not develop much before the late 1800's in Argentina. During the 1800's, rural life and gaucho legends inspired such Argentine painters as Carlos Morel and Prilidiano Pueyrredón. During the 1900's, the painter Benito Quinquela Martín portrayed the lives of immigrants and workers in Buenos Aires. Emilio Pettoruti and Alfredo Guttero introduced European avant-garde painting to Argentina in the 1920's. Since then, various regional and international trends have caught on. Today, Argentina is a major center for Latin American painting. Artists thrive especially in Buenos Aires and the other provincial capitals.

The land

Argentina stretches about 2,300 miles (3,700 kilometers) from north to south. The southernmost tip of Argentina lies only about 600 miles (970 kilometers) from Antarctica. The northernmost part has a nearly tropical climate. Argentina's landscape includes lofty mountains, vast deserts, fertile plains, and swampy forests.

Argentina can be divided into four main land regions. They are (1) Northern Argentina; (2) the Pampas; (3) the Andean region; and (4) Patagonia.

Northern Argentina is a lowland plain that lies east of the Andes Mountains and north of the Córdoba Mountains. It consists of two subregions: (1) the Gran Chaco and (2) Mesopotamia.

The Gran Chaco, also called simply *Chaco,* lies between the Paraná River on the east and the lower ranges of the Andes on the west. It spreads northward across Paraguay and into Bolivia. Scrub forests cover much of the Chaco, and few people live in the region. The land is dry for most of the year, but heavy rains fall in summer, causing riverbeds to overflow. Farmers plant mostly cotton, soybeans, and sunflowers. They also plant corn,

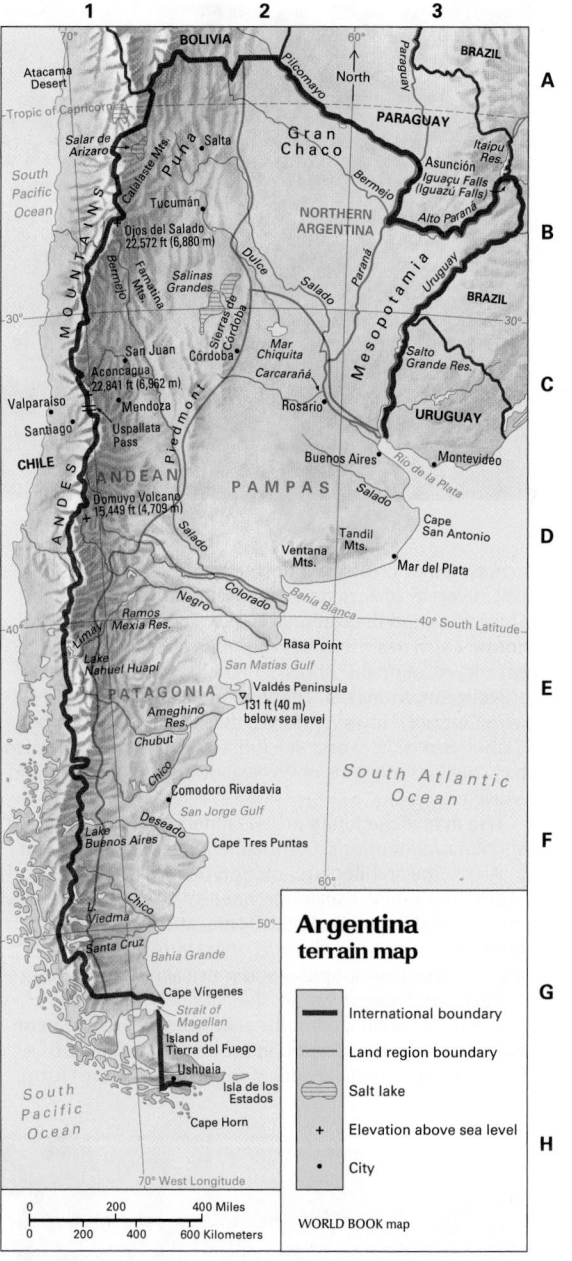

Argentina terrain map

▬▬	International boundary
—	Land region boundary
⬭	Salt lake
+	Elevation above sea level
•	City

WORLD BOOK map

Physical features

Perito Moreno National Park lies in southwestern Argentina, on the border with Chile. It is in the country's mountainous Andean Region. Guanacos, which resemble small camels, live in the park.

Javier Etcheverry/VW PICS/UIG/Getty Images

wheat, and other crops after the summer rains.

Quebracho trees grow in the Chaco, and harvesting the trees is an important economic activity. *Quebracho* means *ax breaker* in Spanish. The name comes from the tree's hard wood, which is used to make telephone poles and railroad ties. The tree is also a source of *tannin,* a chemical used in the leather industry.

Mesopotamia, like its ancient Middle Eastern namesake, is a fertile region between two rivers. The Argentine Mesopotamia lies between the Paraná and Uruguay rivers. The Paraná River basin is the second largest in South America, after the Amazon basin. Rivers from Bolivia, Brazil, and Paraguay enter the Paraná River. The river originates in Brazil and flows 2,485 miles (3,999 kilometers), emptying into the Atlantic Ocean near Buenos Aires. Along the region's northern border, the Iguazú (spelled *Iguaçu* in the Portuguese language) River empties into the Paraná. Near the junction of the two rivers, 275 waterfalls form the spectacular Iguazú Falls.

Mesopotamia has hot, humid summers and cool winters. Rolling, grass-covered plains spread across parts of the region. Farmers graze cattle, sheep, and horses on the plains and grow corn, soybeans, wheat, and some citrus fruits and rice. Swampy forests cover the extreme northeast. The holly tree whose leaves are used to make the tea called mate grows wild in the region.

The Pampas is a fertile plain that fans out around Buenos Aires. It extends from the Atlantic Ocean to the Andes and covers about a fifth of Argentina. The Pampas has some of the world's richest topsoil and is Argentina's most important agricultural region. Fields of corn, soybeans, and wheat cover much of the land. Great herds of cattle graze on the pastures of the Pampas.

The Pampas has about two-thirds of Argentina's people and most of its urban centers, industries, and transportation facilities. Buenos Aires and Rosario, Argentina's third largest city, stand at the edge of the Pampas. Beyond these cities, plains stretch as far as the eye can see. Large estates owned by wealthy ranchers cover much of the thinly settled rural Pampas. Westward toward the Andes, the land grows drier.

The Andean Region is the mountainous western region of Argentina. It consists of two subregions: (1) the Andes Mountains and (2) the Piedmont.

The Andes Mountains separate Argentina from Chile. Their highest peaks include the tallest mountain in the Western Hemisphere, Aconcagua. It towers 22,841 feet (6,962 meters) above sea level just inside the Argentine border. A small indigenous population raises sheep in an area of broad plateaus called the Puna in the northern part of the Argentine Andes. In the south, snow-capped peaks, active glaciers, and beautiful lakes attract crowds of vacationers who come to ski and hike.

The Piedmont is a region of low mountains and desert valleys east of the Andes. Mountain streams provide water for irrigation and make the Piedmont a productive farming area. Farmers grow sugar cane and corn near Tucumán and alfalfa and cotton near Córdoba. Vineyards in Mendoza and San Juan provinces produce grapes for most Argentine wines, which are exported around the world. Argentina is one of the largest producers of wine in the world. The cities of the Piedmont are some of the oldest Spanish settlements in Argentina.

Patagonia is a dry, windswept plateau in the south. It occupies more than a quarter of Argentina but has only about 5 percent of the population. Poor soil and scarce rainfall make most of Patagonia unsuitable for crop farming. The extraction of oil and natural gas and sheep ranching are the major economic activities.

Most Patagonians live near the region's two northern rivers—the Colorado and the Negro. Farmers grow alfalfa, apples, and pears in the river valleys. Wildlife enthusiasts visit Patagonia's rugged coast to see penguins, sea lions, whales, and other animals.

The island of Tierra del Fuego lies at the southern tip of South America. The Strait of Magellan separates it from the mainland. The island is divided between Argentina and Chile. Ushuaia, one of the southernmost towns in the world, is on Argentina's part of the island.

Climate

Argentina's climate is mild. The north has the highest temperatures, and the south the lowest. Argentina lies south of the equator, and so its seasons are opposite

Argentina's gross domestic product

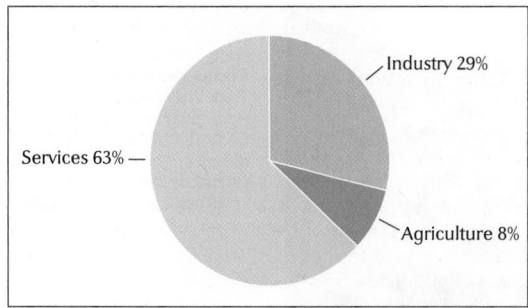

Industry 29%

Services 63%

Agriculture 8%

Argentina's gross domestic product (GDP) was $543,061,000,000 in United States dollars in 2014. The GDP is the total value of goods and services produced within a country in a year. *Services* include community, government, and personal services; finance, insurance, real estate, and business services; trade, restaurants, and hotels; and transportation and communication. *Industry* includes construction, manufacturing, mining, and utilities. *Agriculture* includes agriculture, forestry, and fishing.

Production and workers by economic activities

Economic activities	Percent of GDP produced	Employed workers	
		Number of people	Percent of total
Community, government, & personal services	28	5,685,500	37
Finance, insurance, real estate, & business services	16	1,282,500	8
Manufacturing	15	1,999,200	13
Trade, restaurants, & hotels	13	3,252,000	21
Agriculture, forestry, & fishing	8	*	*
Construction	6	1,603,700	10
Transportation & communication	6	1,203,100	8
Mining	5	81,100	1
Utilities	4	167,900	1
Total†	100	15,275,000	100

*Agricultural employment figures unavailable.
†Figures do not add up to 100 percent, due to rounding.
Figures are for 2014. Employment figures are for urban areas only.
Sources: Argentina National Institute of Statistics and Censuses; International Labour Organization; International Monetary Fund.

those in the Northern Hemisphere. Summer lasts from late December to late March, and winter from late June to late September. January temperatures average about 80 °F (27 °C) in the north and about 60 °F (16 °C) in the far south. Average July temperatures range from about 60 °F (16 °C) in the north to about 40 °F (4 °C) in the south.

Rainfall is plentiful in the northeast but decreases toward the west and south. Mesopotamia may receive over 60 inches (150 centimeters) of rain annually, mostly in the summer. Areas of the Piedmont and most of Patagonia get less than 10 inches (25 centimeters), making them deserts or slightly less dry *semiarid* regions. Nearly two-thirds of Argentina is desert or seimarid.

Ocean currents and winds strongly affect Argentina's climate. Warm, moist air from the Atlantic can make summers uncomfortably humid in Mesopotamia and the Pampas. Winds from the Pacific lose most of their moisture over the Andes, leaving the Piedmont and Patagonia dry. Winds from both oceans howl continuously

over Patagonia. They warm the plateau in winter and cool it in summer. In winter, air from Antarctica sometimes brings cold weather and light snow to Patagonia and the Pampas.

Economy

In the first few decades of the 1900's, Argentina was one of the richest countries in the world. However, since about 1930, Argentina has had many economic problems. Today, Argentina is no longer one of the world's economic giants.

Argentina's economic activity is concentrated mainly in Buenos Aires, Córdoba, and Santa Fe provinces and in the city of Buenos Aires. Traditionally, the economy was based on agricultural exports. Although agricultural exports remain important, service industries and manufacturing now account for about 90 percent of the *gross domestic product* (GDP)—that is, the total value of goods and services produced in a country in one year.

Service industries account for about two-thirds of Argentina's GDP. These include financial and insurance services, government services, retail trade, tourism, and transportation. International tourism has gained importance since the early 2000's. The increase in tourism has helped hotels, restaurants, and other service industries.

Manufacturing accounts for about 15 percent of Argentina's GDP. The chief industrial areas include Buenos Aires, Córdoba, and Rosario. The country manufactures automobiles and other transportation equipment, chemicals, machinery, oil, and processed foods.

Mining accounts for only a small portion of Argentina's GDP. Petroleum is the country's chief mineral resource. Patagonia and the Piedmont yield nearly all the oil that Argentina uses, plus a relatively small amount for export. These regions produce natural gas as well. Most of the country's metal deposits lie in the Andes Mountains and the Piedmont. The deposits include copper, gold, lead, silver, and zinc.

Electric power and utilities. Plants that burn natural gas are the leading supplier of Argentina's electric pow-

Lalito/Alamy Stock Photo

Argentina's petroleum industry produces enough oil to meet local demand, plus more for export. This refining facility is in Patagonia, a chief oil-producing region in the south.

er. Hydroelectric plants supply most of the rest, while nuclear plants provide a small amount. In the 1990's, the government turned over many public utilities to private owners.

Agriculture. Fertile farmland is Argentina's most important natural resource. The Pampas and Mesopotamia produce most of Argentina's leading farm products, such as beef, corn, soybeans, and wheat. Farmers raise sheep, mainly for wool, in dry areas throughout the country. Argentina is among the world's leading producers of beef, corn, soybeans, and wool. Much of the country's soybean harvest is exported to China. Other farm products include apples, citrus fruits, eggs, grapes, milk, potatoes, poultry, sorghum, sugar cane, sunflower seeds, and tea.

Argentine farms vary greatly in size. Huge estates spread over much of the Pampas and make use of modern equipment. In the north, many families farm small plots and raise only enough food to feed themselves. These small farmers often use horse-drawn equipment.

Fishing. Argentina's long coastline and *continental shelf* (submerged land along the coast) provide a great volume and variety of fish. Leading fishing catches include croaker, hake, shrimp, and squid. Fishing crews export most of their catch. China, Italy, Spain, and the United States are among the leading buyers of Argentina's seafood exports. Since the late 1990's, laws against overfishing have led to a decrease in Argentina's commercial catch.

International trade. Argentina exports more than it imports. Argentina's main trading partners include Brazil, China, and the United States. Important exports include cars and trucks; corn, soybeans, wheat, and other agricultural products; and petroleum and natural gas. Argentina imports chemicals, machinery, petroleum products, plastics, and transportation equipment.

In 1991, Argentina, Brazil, Paraguay, and Uruguay created a trade association known as Mercosur, which stands for Southern Common Market. Venezuela later became a member of the group. Other South American countries have become associate members of, or signed preferential trade agreements with, Mercosur. The Mercosur nations seek to integrate their economies and form one common South American market.

Transportation and communication. Air routes, highways, and railroads spread out from Buenos Aires, linking most Argentine cities and towns with the capital. The country's busiest airports are in Buenos Aires. Argentina's rail network is the largest in South America, but much of it is out-of-date and inefficient.

Dozens of television stations operate in Argentina. A majority are privately owned. There are hundreds of radio stations, including private, national, provincial, municipal, and university stations. Argentines also have access to cable and satellite television services. Internet cafes are widely available in major cities. More than 150 newspapers are published in Argentina. *Clarín* and *La Nación,* dailies that are published in Buenos Aires, have the largest circulations.

History

Early inhabitants. Many nomadic tribes roamed the Pampas and Patagonia before Europeans arrived in the 1500's. Two of the main indigenous groups in what is now Argentina were the Diaguita, in the northwest, and the Guaraní, in the northeastern and north-central regions of the country. The Diaguita and Guaraní were the first people to settle down and farm in Argentina. They cultivated corn, also called *maize,* and other crops.

Arrival of the Spanish. In 1516, a Spanish expedition led by Juan Díaz de Solís landed on the shores of the Río de la Plata and claimed the area for Spain. Solís was seeking a southern passage to the Pacific Ocean. The expedition failed after indigenous people captured and killed Solís and some of his men. The indigenous population strongly resisted colonization, and it was not until 1580 that the Spanish securely established the city of Buenos Aires. Spanish colonists who traveled over the Andes Mountains from Peru founded such northwestern settlements as Santiago del Estero and Tucumán.

Gauchos herd cattle on a ranch in the Mesopotamia region in northeastern Argentina. Mesopotamia and the Pampas region together produce most of the country's leading farm products, including beef.

Important dates in Argentina

1580 Spaniards established Buenos Aires.
1776 Spain created the Viceroyalty of the Río de la Plata.
1810 Buenos Aires formed an independent government.
1816 Argentina declared its independence from Spain.
1853 Argentina adopted a federal Constitution.
1912 The Sáenz Peña Law reformed national elections.
1930 Army officers overthrew the elected government.
1943 Juan Domingo Perón began his rise to power.
1955 A military revolt overthrew Perón's government. Perón fled the country.
1973 Perón returned to Argentina and was elected president.
1974 Perón died. His third wife, Isabel, became president.
1976 A military coup removed Isabel Perón from office.
1982 Argentina lost a war with the United Kingdom over control of the Falkland Islands.
1983 Civilian rule was restored following free elections.
1991 Argentina joined the Mercosur trade association.
2001 Argentina suffered the worst economic crisis in its history.

Settlement and colonial life. Spanish military campaigns and the introduction of European diseases weakened indigenous resistance to colonization. Some indigenous people and Spaniards intermarried, creating a *mestizo* population of mixed descent. Spain, busy exploiting Peru's gold and silver, largely neglected Argentina, which lacked such riches.

At first, settlements in the northwest grew more rapidly than Buenos Aires and other coastal towns. Spanish colonists forced the indigenous people to work for them, farming the land and weaving wool into cloth. Soon, these settlements began to supply mining towns in Peru with animals, cloth, and food.

For many years, the Spanish government limited trade through Buenos Aires because they thought the city was vulnerable to attacks by pirates and rival European nations. The city grew slowly, and smuggling became common. In 1680, Portuguese settlers established a trading post across the Río de la Plata from Buenos Aires. Spain then encouraged the city's growth to protect its colony from Portuguese expansion.

In 1776, Spain combined its American colonies into the Viceroyalty of the Río de la Plata. The viceroyalty included present-day Argentina, Paraguay, and Uruguay, and parts of Bolivia, Brazil, and Chile. Buenos Aires became the capital of the viceroyalty and a flourishing port.

Road to becoming a nation. During the early 1800's, the people of Buenos Aires grew increasingly dissatisfied with Spanish rule. In 1806 and 1807, British troops tried to seize Buenos Aires to establish a foothold in the region for British trade. The city's residents fought them off without help from Spain, which increased their confidence in gaining freedom from the mother country.

In 1807 and 1808, during the Napoleonic Wars in Europe, France invaded Spain. While the Spanish were busy fighting against Napoleon, Buenos Aires made a move toward independence. On May 25, 1810, citizens of the port city set up their own government to administer the Viceroyalty of the Río de la Plata. But the viceroyal provinces outside Argentina eventually broke away.

Beginning in 1812, the Argentine General José de San Martín led the fight against Spain. At his urging, representatives of the Argentine provinces met at the Congress of Tucumán on July 9, 1816, and officially declared their independence. The new nation became known as the United Provinces of the Río de la Plata. San Martín wanted to expel the Spanish from all of South America. In 1817, he led an expedition into Chile, where he defeated the Spanish. Then, his forces helped Peru win freedom from Spain.

Early independence in Argentina was marked by a struggle between two political groups—the Unitarists and the Federalists. The Unitarists wanted to set up a strong central government in Buenos Aires. The Federalists represented the large rural landowners of the interior and sought greater local self-rule.

In 1826, a national assembly drew up a constitution for Argentina. The assembly named Bernardino de Rivadavia as the nation's first president. But Rivadavia resigned in 1827, after failing to create a strong national government. Juan Manuel de Rosas, a landowner from the Pampas, ruled Argentina as a dictator from 1829 to 1852. Rosas created a network of secret police to spy on his enemies and led violent campaigns against the indigenous people of the Pampas. He quarreled in his

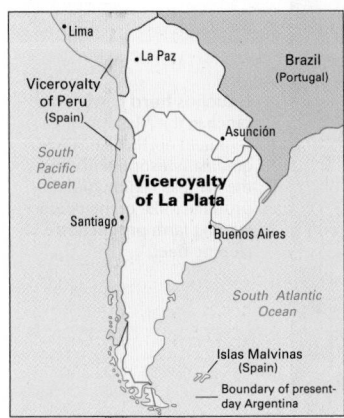
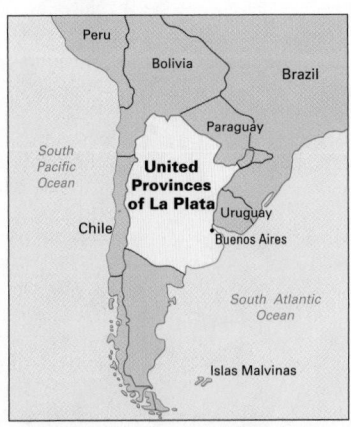

WORLD BOOK maps

In 1776, Spain created the Viceroyalty of the Río de la Plata, made up of what are now Argentina, Paraguay, Uruguay, and parts of Bolivia, Brazil, and Chile.

In 1816, what is now northern Argentina declared independence from Spain. The new country was called the United Provinces of the Río de la Plata.

In 1860, Argentina took its present name. It gained territory in the northeast in 1874 after a war with Paraguay. Patagonia became part of Argentina in 1881.

José de San Martín became the hero of Argentina's fight for independence from Spain. The great Argentine general also helped win independence for Chile and Peru. In this painting, San Martín, *center right,* is greeted by Chilean General Bernardo O'Higgins after their victory over Spanish forces at the Maipo (also spelled Maipú) River in Chile in 1818.

The Embrace at Maipú (1908), detail of an oil painting by Pedro Subercaseaux; Public Domain

dealings with other nations. In 1852, General Justo José de Urquiza led an army revolt that overthrew Rosas.

The Constitution of 1853. Delegates from all the provinces except Buenos Aires met in Santa Fe in 1852 to organize a national government. They drew up a new constitution based largely on that of the United States. The Constitution, proclaimed in 1853, established a confederation of provinces.

The province of Buenos Aires refused to join the confederation. It prospered as an independent state, aided by good government, high immigration, and European investment. But the confederated provinces fared worse. Urquiza tried to force Buenos Aires to join the confederation. In 1859, he defeated a Buenos Aires army led by General Bartolomé Mitre. But in 1861, Mitre defeated Urquiza in another war. In 1862, Buenos Aires Province agreed to enter the confederation on its own terms. The city of Buenos Aires became the nation's capital, and Mitre was elected president. In 1860, the country had taken the name Argentina from the Latin word for *silver.*

With the election of Mitre, Argentina entered a prosperous and stable period that lasted nearly 70 years. Domingo Faustino Sarmiento succeeded Mitre in 1868 and served until 1874. Both men tried to attract European immigrants and investment to speed national growth. Sarmiento also promoted public education.

By the late 1800's, the Pampas had become the heart of Argentina. Few indigenous people remained in the region, and thousands of European farmers worked the land. British investment helped build railroads to carry farm products from the Pampas to Buenos Aires for shipment overseas. Between 1880 and 1930, Argentina ranked as one of the world's wealthiest nations.

Reform movements. During the late 1800's, conservative forces dominated Argentine politics, often using fraud to win elections. By that time, a new working-class population had grown up in Argentine cities. In 1889, dissatisfied Argentines formed the Civic Union, an organization that demanded election reform. The Civic Union, which later became the Radical Civic Union, appealed to many immigrants and middle-class business people.

In 1910, Roque Sáenz Peña became president. Although a conservative, Sáenz Peña pushed election reforms through Congress. The reforms, known collectively as the Sáenz Peña Law of 1912, provided for the secret ballot and required every Argentine man 18 years old and older to vote and to register for Army service. The law prevented large landholders from controlling elections and enabled the expanding working and middle classes to participate directly in politics. In 1916, voters elected Radical Civic Union leader Hipólito Yrigoyen president. Marcelo Torcuato de Alvear, also of the Radical Civic Union, succeeded Yrigoyen in 1922.

The first military coup. Yrigoyen was elected president again in 1928, but he was too ill to govern effectively. The next year, the Great Depression began to shatter the nation's economy. In 1930, a military *coup d'état* (unconstitutional seizure of the government) abruptly ended Yrigoyen's presidency. The Supreme Court declared the coup lawful, clearing the way for military regimes to rule the country on and off for the next 50 years.

Argentina under Perón. Following a military coup in 1943, Colonel Juan Domingo Perón rose to power. As head of the Department of Labor and Social Welfare, Perón strengthened Argentina's unions. Perón's efforts to improve labor conditions won him the support of urban workers.

Perón was elected president in 1946 and founded the Justicialist Party, also known as the Peronist Party. He helped the working class by promoting union growth and workers' rights legislation. Perón also promoted industrialization, government control of industry, and Argentine self-determination in foreign affairs. Federal spending rose greatly under Perón. The government taxed farm products to raise money for manufacturing endeavors. As a result, farm production and national income fell.

Perón's government established strict control over the press. In 1949, he modified the Constitution to increase his powers and allow himself a second term. His second wife, Eva Duarte de Perón, played a key role in developing support for her husband. Known popularly as Evita, she worked to strengthen the voice of Argen-

Bettmann/Getty Images

Juan Perón rides in triumph with his second wife, Eva, after being reelected president of Argentina in 1952. Perón was overthrown in 1955 but again served as president in 1973 and 1974.

tine women and the poor until her death in 1952.

Social conflict and economic trouble marked Perón's second term as president, which began in 1952. He lost the support of the Roman Catholic Church in 1955, after limiting its authority. Perón's policies resulted in large debts, high inflation, and stagnant productivity levels. In 1955, the Army and Navy revolted against the government. Perón then resigned and went into exile in Spain. But he maintained a base of supporters, especially among labor unions.

Military leaders took control of the government after Perón's overthrow. In 1956, they reversed Perón's modifications to the Constitution. In 1958, Arturo Frondizi of the Intransigent Radical Party was elected president. Frondizi cut government spending, limited wage hikes, and introduced other measures to curb inflation and reduce the nation's debt. Argentines, however, disliked these actions, which called for financial sacrifices.

Army leaders feared that Frondizi would yield to pressure from the Peronistas (supporters of Perón) and restore Perón's economic policies. They removed Frondizi from office in 1962, and a series of civilian presidents and military dictators ruled until 1972.

During this period, poor management of national finances and military corruption harmed the economy. Public strikes, violence, and antigovernment protests broke out. Military leaders finally allowed Perón's supporters to return to power in the hope that they could restore order. The people elected Héctor José Cámpora of the Justicialist Party president in 1973. Perón returned to Argentina later that year, and Cámpora resigned. Voters then elected Perón president by a wide margin, and his third wife, Isabel, became vice president. After Perón died in 1974, Isabel became the first woman president in the Western Hemisphere.

The 1970's military dictatorship. Argentina's problems increased after Isabel Perón took office. Inflation soared to over 300 percent per year. Many people died

in terrorist attacks by political extremists of both the right and the left. In 1976, military leaders arrested Isabel Perón and took control of the government. The new military dictatorship, led by General Jorge Videla, became known as the Process of National Reorganization, or simply the Process (*el Proceso* in Spanish). El Proceso closed Congress, imposed censorship, and banned labor unions. A paramilitary death squad, unopposed by the state, silenced critics and opponents of the regime. Many experts estimate that the dictatorship imprisoned, tortured, and executed about 30,000 people without trials. Many victims went missing and never were found. They are known as *los desaparecidos* (the disappeared). The government named the campaign against its enemies the "dirty war."

Meanwhile, government corruption and the mismanagement of funds caused foreign debt to increase dramatically. The Falklands War of 1982 further strained national finances. Argentina has long claimed the Falkland Islands, which lie about 310 miles (499 kilometers) east of the Strait of Magellan. But since 1833, the United Kingdom has ruled the islands, which Argentines call the Islas Malvinas. In April 1982, Argentine troops seized the Falklands and battled British forces for control of the territory. Argentina surrendered in June but maintained its claim to the islands.

The defeat in the Falklands, public disapproval, and continued economic woes, as well as denunciations of human rights violations by such groups as the Mothers of the Plaza de Mayo, forced the military government to call free elections. In 1983, voters elected Radical Civic Union leader Raúl Alfonsín president.

The late 1900's. President Alfonsín launched a series of measures that aimed to improve the economy, renegotiate the terms of Argentina's debt, investigate and punish past human rights abuses, and bring the armed forces under civilian control. However, the economy continued to deteriorate, military rebellions occurred, and public confidence in the administration declined.

In 1989, Carlos Saúl Menem of the Justicialist Party won the presidency. Almost immediately after taking office, Menem attempted to stimulate the economy by removing certain restrictions on economic activity. In 1991, in an effort to slow inflation, Menem's government linked the value of the Argentine peso to that of the U.S. dollar at a rate of one peso to one dollar.

Although Menem's policies resulted in lower inflation, the return of foreign capital, and economic growth, they had social repercussions. Poverty rose, standards for education and health fell, and the unemployment rate neared 20 percent. In 1994, a constitutional reform shortened the term of the presidency from six to four years and made it possible for Menem to run for reelection.

Menem was reelected in 1995. During his second term, government spending increased and Argentina's deficit discouraged foreign investment. Domestic interest rates rose, making it more expensive for companies to do business. Many companies closed, resulting in a loss of jobs. Additionally, the transfer of many government-owned businesses to private owners put many more people out of work.

During the late 1990's, financial crises in other countries and a drop in world prices for farm products contributed to a recession in Argentina that lasted nearly

© Enrique Marcarian, Reuters

Depositors lined up to remove their money from a Buenos Aires bank during a major economic crisis in 2001. The government limited bank withdrawals until 2003.

four years. In addition, Argentina's exports and foreign investment declined. The fixed peso-dollar exchange rate meant that foreign buyers and investors could get more for the same price in other countries.

A coalition of the Radical Civic Union and other center-left parties, running on an anticorruption platform, won the 1999 election. Fernando de la Rúa became president. He raised taxes and slashed spending, but these measures impaired economic growth. Fighting within the coalition also prevented the passage of needed reforms. The political situation declined when Vice President Carlos Álvarez resigned over a lack of support for investigation into government corruption.

The early 2000's. Argentina experienced an economic crisis in 2001. In December of that year, many people feared that the government would reduce the value of the peso. Large investors withdrew their money from banks and transferred it to accounts overseas. The general population rushed to banks to withdraw their money and convert it to dollars. The government then limited the amount that people could withdraw each week. Violent demonstrations broke out, and more than 25 people were killed. Soon afterward, de la Rúa resigned. In the two weeks following de la Rúa's resignation, two acting presidents and one interim president held office. President Adolfo Rodríguez Saá stopped payment of Argentina's huge foreign debt.

In January 2002, Congress named Justicialist Senator Eduardo Duhalde president. Duhalde ended the peso's fixed exchange rate. As a result, the peso fell sharply in value and inflation rose. Poor and middle-class Argentines continued to protest, while the government continued to limit bank withdrawals to keep money in Argentina. Duhalde's policies eventually stabilized the economy, and the government ended limits on withdrawals.

Néstor Kirchner of the Justicialist Party was elected president in 2003. Kirchner had governed Santa Cruz Province for 12 years. As president, he showed a commitment to reorganizing the police and armed forces, ending corruption, reviewing past human rights abuses, and negotiating terms for repayment of the foreign debt.

Argentine first lady and legislator Cristina Fernández de Kirchner was elected president in 2007 and 2011. Like her husband, she was a Peronist. Fernández de Kirchner gained popularity for her social welfare programs. But her policies eventually led to high inflation, weak economic growth, and a large budget *deficit* (shortage). Charges of corruption also troubled her presidency.

In 2015, Argentines elected Mauricio Macri of the center-right Cambiemos coalition as president. Macri, a former mayor of Buenos Aires, failed to improve Argentina's economy as promised. He lost the 2019 presidential election to Alberto Fernández of the Peronist coalition Frente de Todos. Fernández's vice presidential running mate was Cristina Fernández de Kirchner.

Beginning in 2020, a global outbreak of the disease COVID-19 greatly impacted Argentina's public health and strained its economy. Efforts to control the outbreak included restricting many public activities and, later, vaccinating people. By mid-2021, however, millions of people in Argentina had been infected and tens of thousands had died from the disease. See **COVID-19.**

Brad D. Jokisch and Natalia Milanesio

Related articles in *World Book* include:

Biographies

Borges, Jorge Luis	Perón, Juan D.
Drago, Luis M.	San Martín, José de
Perón, Eva Duarte de	

Cities

Buenos Aires	Paraná
Córdoba	Rosario
Mar del Plata	Santa Fe

Physical features

Aconcagua	Magellan, Strait of	Patagonia
Andes Mountains	Pampas	Río de la Plata
Gran Chaco	Paraguay River	Tierra del Fuego
Iguaçu Falls	Paraná River	Uruguay River

Other related articles

Gaucho	National park (Argentina)
Latin America	South America

Outline

I. Government
  A. National government   D. Courts
  B. Local government   E. Armed forces
  C. Politics
II. People
  A. Population   C. Language
  B. Ancestry
III. Way of life
  A. City life   E. Recreation
  B. Rural life   F. Education
  C. Clothing   G. Religion
  D. Food and drink   H. The arts
IV. The land
  A. Northern Argentina   C. The Andean region
  B. The Pampas   D. Patagonia
V. Climate
VI. Economy
  A. Service industries   E. Agriculture
  B. Manufacturing   F. Fishing
  C. Mining   G. International trade
  D. Electric power and   H. Transportation and
     utilities   communication
VII. History

Argon, *AHR gahn,* is a chemical element that forms 0.94 percent of Earth's atmosphere. Most light bulbs are filled with argon and a little nitrogen. Argon is also used as a shielding gas in arc welding to protect the metal from oxygen in the air. Only one compound of the element is known to exist. The compound, called argon fluorohydride, is only stable below –256 °C. Argon is classed as a *noble gas* (see **Noble gas**). It is colorless, odorless, and tasteless. It does not react readily with other chemicals. Lord Rayleigh and Sir William Ramsay discovered it in 1894.

Argon's symbol is Ar. Its *atomic number* (number of protons in its nucleus) is 18. It has a *relative atomic mass* of 39.948. An element's relative atomic mass equals its *mass* (amount of matter) divided by $\frac{1}{12}$ of the mass of carbon 12, the most abundant form of carbon. The freezing point of argon is –189.2 °C. Its boiling point is –185.7 °C. The density is 0.00178 gram per cubic centimeter at 0 °C and one atmosphere of pressure (see **Atmosphere**). Argon is continuously released into the atmosphere through the *decay* (breaking down) of radioactive potassium in Earth's crust. When the potassium decays, it changes into argon.   Marianna A. Busch

Argonaut, *AHR guh nawt,* is an eight-armed animal that lives near the surface of warm seas worldwide. It feeds on such animals as small fish. The argonaut swims slowly by forcing a jet of water through its *siphon,* a tube-shaped organ under its head. Female argonauts may reach more than 18 inches (45 centimeters) long. Males rarely grow more than 1 inch (2.5 centimeters) long. The female argonaut builds a fragile, paper-thin

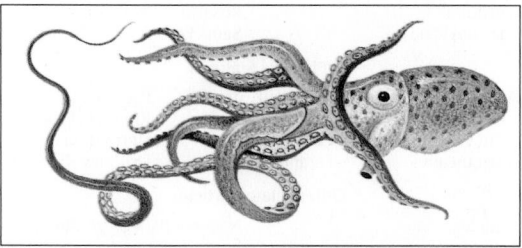

WORLD BOOK illustration by James Teason

The argonaut is an eight-armed animal that lives in warm sea waters. The male, *shown here,* is much smaller than the female.

shell. Two of the female's arms have broad flaps of skin that release liquid shell material. The shell quickly hardens and is covered by the flaps. Female argonauts live in the shell and store their eggs there. The name *paper nautilus,* often used for the argonaut, comes from this shell. Male argonauts make no shell.

People once believed that the argonaut sailed on water by using two enlarged arms as sails. It was named after the sailors on the *Argo,* a ship described in the Greek myth of the Golden Fleece.   Brian Hartwick

Scientific classification. Argonauts make up the genus *Argonauta.* The scientific name of the greater argonaut, a common species, is *Argonauta argo.*

Argonauts, *AHR guh nawts,* in Greek mythology, were the companions of Jason, a famous hero. They sailed with Jason on a voyage to capture the Golden Fleece, the golden wool of a flying ram. About 50 of the greatest Greek heroes took part, including Castor and

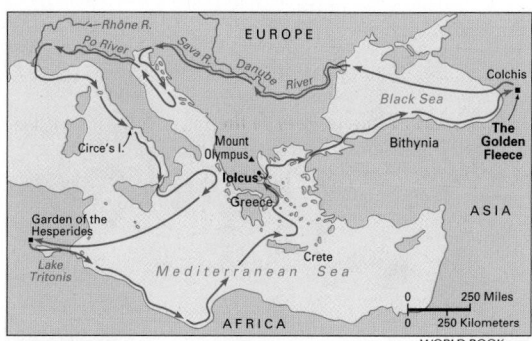

WORLD BOOK map

The voyage of the Argonauts began at Iolcus. They sailed to Colchis, where they captured the Golden Fleece. On the return trip, they traveled through much of the Mediterranean area.

Pollux, Hercules, Orpheus, Peleus, and Telamon.

The Argonauts took their name from their ship, the *Argo.* The ship had been named for its builder, Argos, a famous craftsman. The *Argo* was the longest ship built until that time. The goddess Athena helped build it.

After many adventures, the Argonauts found the Golden Fleece in the far-off land of Colchis. They brought it back to Greece after surviving many dangers. Because of their successful quest, the Argonauts were honored above all other men. In ancient times, it was a mark of great honor to have an ancestor who had sailed with Jason to find the Golden Fleece.   John Hamilton

See also **Golden Fleece; Jason; Medea.**

Argonne National Laboratory, *AHR gahn,* is one of the largest centers in the United States for research and development in energy technologies. It is 27 miles (43 kilometers) southwest of Chicago. Argonne has contributed greatly to the development of nuclear reactors, including boiling water reactors and breeder reactors (see **Nuclear energy**).

Scientists at Argonne conduct research in biology, chemistry, materials science, mathematics and computer science, and physics. They work to develop energy technologies, such as batteries and fuel cells. Environmental scientists at Argonne work on managing and solving the nation's environmental problems. Other researchers are developing technologies to protect national security, such as instruments that detect chemical, biological, and radioactive weapons.

Argonne began in 1942 as the University of Chicago's Metallurgical Laboratory, part of the World War II Manhattan Project to produce the first atomic bomb. In 1946, the laboratory was moved to its present location and renamed Argonne National Laboratory. The University of Chicago operates Argonne for the United States Department of Energy.   Toni Grayson Joseph

Argus, *AHR guhs,* was a gigantic monster in Greek mythology. He had 100 eyes and was called *Panoptes,* which means *all-seeing.* The goddess Hera assigned Argus to guard her hated rival, the beautiful Princess Io, a mistress of her husband Zeus (see **Io**). For this reason, the term *argus* is sometimes used to describe a watchful guardian. Acting on orders from Zeus, the god Hermes killed Argus, thus winning the title *Argeiphontes* (the Slayer of Argus). According to one story, Hera used Argus's 100 eyes to decorate the tail of her peacock.

Argus, or Argos, was also the name of the faithful hunting dog of the hero Ulysses in the epic poem the *Odyssey.* The dog recognized his master when Ulysses returned home after an absence of 20 years. Argus, or Argos, was also the builder of the *Argo,* the ship commanded by the hero Jason. Justin M. Glenn

Århus, *AWR hoos,* also spelled *Aarhus,* is one of the largest cities in Denmark. The municipality of Århus has a population of 319,094. A municipality may include rural areas as well as the urban center. Only Copenhagen has more people. Århus lies on the east coast of the peninsula of Jutland (see **Denmark** [map]). Århus is a busy seaport and a center of industry and commerce. Its major industries include the production of chemicals, clothing, iron, machines, and timber.

Århus developed from a settlement founded in the A.D. 800's. The Cathedral of St. Clemens, built in the 1100's, is a major landmark. An open-air museum on the outskirts of Århus—called Den Gamle By (The Old Town)—displays town houses dating from the 1500's to the 1800's. Other sites in Århus include a marble city hall and Aarhus University. The city also has schools of art, music, dentistry, and journalism. M. Donald Hancock

Arianism, *AIR ee uh NIHZ uhm,* was an early departure from generally accepted Christian teaching about the nature of the Trinity. It takes its name from its chief promoter, Arius, a priest in Alexandria, Egypt.

About A.D. 318, Arius and his disciples rejected the Christian doctrine that the three Persons of the Trinity—the Father, the Son, and the Holy Spirit—are equal. In particular, Arius denied that the Son (Jesus Christ) shared the same eternal, divine nature as the Father. Arius instead taught that the Son was created by the Father to redeem the human race. Jesus thus was not eternal because he had not always existed. The Son, according to Arius, was "of like substance" rather than "of the same substance" as the Father. Arius further taught that both the Father and the Son were superior to the Holy Spirit.

In 325, the Council of Nicaea condemned the teachings of Arius as *heresy*—that is, opposed to basic Christian beliefs. But many preachers and missionaries in the eastern Roman Empire continued throughout the 300's to teach that Jesus Christ was not truly God. Church leaders vigorously opposed this teaching. The First Council of Constantinople reasserted the Nicene condemnation of Arianism as heresy in 381, and Arianism soon disappeared from the Roman Empire. However, its supporters remained active outside the empire. Arian teachings continued to circulate until the 600's.

Neil J. Roy

See also **Arius; Nicene Councils; Trinity.**

Arias Sánchez, *AH ryahs SAHN chehz,* **Oscar** (1941-), served as president of Costa Rica from 1986 to 1990 and from 2006 to 2010. He became best known for his work for peace in Central America. As president, Arias also promoted environmentally friendly development and free-trade economic policies.

During the 1980's, widespread fighting took place between rebel forces and the governments of Nicaragua and El Salvador. Arias negotiated with other Central American presidents on a plan to promote peace in the region. Their 1987 plan, which was known as the Arias Peace Initiative, called for an end to the fighting in Central America. Arias won the 1987 Nobel Peace Prize for his leadership in developing the plan. However, some Costa Ricans accused him of paying too much attention to foreign affairs while neglecting the problems of his own country.

Arias was born on Sept. 13, 1941, in Heredia. He attended the University of Costa Rica, and he taught there from 1969 to 1972. A member of the National Liberation Party, Arias served in the legislature of Costa Rica from 1978 to 1981. Steve C. Ropp

Aries, *AIR eez,* is the first sign of the zodiac. It is symbolized by a ram. Astrologers believe that Aries is ruled by the planet Mars, which is named for the ancient Roman god of war. Aries is a fire sign.

Astrologers regard people born under the sign of Aries, from March 21 to April 19, as active, strong, and fierce-tempered. Arians often seem to be in a hurry. They like excitement and variety, and they tend to lose interest in tasks that require much time. Arians also like to compete and are excellent athletes. They also do well as firefighters, soldiers, and surgeons and in other occupations that require physical skill. Charles W. Clark

See also **Astrology; Horoscope; Zodiac.**

WORLD BOOK illustration by Robert Keys

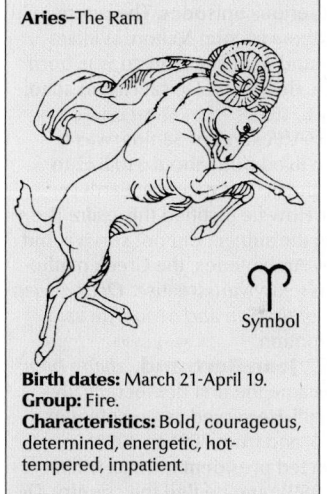

Aries–The Ram

Symbol

Birth dates: March 21-April 19.
Group: Fire.
Characteristics: Bold, courageous, determined, energetic, hot-tempered, impatient.

Signs of the Zodiac

Aries
March 21-April 19

Taurus
April 20-May 20

Gemini
May 21-June 20

Cancer
June 21-July 22

Leo
July 23-Aug. 22

Virgo
Aug. 23-Sept. 22

Libra
Sept. 23-Oct. 22

Scorpio
Oct. 23-Nov. 21

Sagittarius
Nov. 22-Dec. 21

Capricorn
Dec. 22-Jan. 19

Aquarius
Jan. 20-Feb. 18

Pisces
Feb. 19-March 20

Arikara Indians, *uh RIHK uh ruh,* are a tribe that once lived in villages along the Missouri River. They were farmers and buffalo hunters. Today, about 3,000 descendants of the Arikara, the Mandan, and the Hidatsa live on the Fort Berthold Reservation in North Dakota. The three tribes have intermarried so much that they now call themselves the Three Affiliated Tribes.

The name *Arikara* comes from an Indian word meaning *horns.* The term refers to the Arikara's custom of wrapping their hair around two pieces of bone so that it stood up like horns. The tribe's name in sign language was *corn eaters.* The Arikara grew corn and traded it to neighboring tribes for buffalo robes and furs.

Corn played an important role in the Arikara religion. The tribe held ceremonies throughout the growing season to ensure a plentiful harvest. They preserved some of the finest ears of corn for many years and honored them as sacred objects. The Arikara lived in earth-covered lodges, each of which housed several families.

In the mid-1700's, French explorers became the first Europeans to encounter the Arikara. The Arikara were numerous and powerful. They fought frequently with French and American traders and settlers. During the late 1700's, many Arikara died in battles with the Sioux, who finally drove them from their home. Smallpox killed many more members of the tribe in 1837. In 1862, the remaining Arikara settled with the Mandan and the Hidatsa near Fort Berthold in what is now North Dakota. The United States government established the area as a reservation for the three tribes in 1870.　　Douglas H. Ubelaker

See also **Mandan Indians**.

Ariosto, *AH ree AWS toh,* **Ludovico,** *LOO doh VEE koh* (1474-1533), was a poet of the Italian Renaissance. His masterpiece, *Orlando Furioso* (published in 1516, revised in 1521 and 1532), is a long narrative poem about the struggle between Christians and Arab-Muslim tribes called the Saracens. Its complicated plot tells of knights who travel the world seeking adventure, defending their religion, and aiding victims in distress. In the poem, Ariosto perfected the strict eight-line stanza called *ottava rima.* He also perfected the chivalric romance that combines stories about Charlemagne's knights with those about King Arthur's. Ariosto wrote with a robust humor that is present even in serious episodes. The poem influenced such English authors as John Milton, William Shakespeare, and Edmund Spenser. Ariosto was born Sept. 8, 1474, in Reggio. He also wrote satire and scholarly plays. He died July 6, 1533.　　Richard H. Lansing

Aristarchus, *AR ih STAHR kuhs,* of Samos, was a Greek astronomer who lived from about 310 B.C. to about 230 B.C. He was the first to state that Earth revolves around the sun. How he justified this claim is unknown. His writings on the subject did not survive, but his idea was quoted by Archimedes, the Greek mathematician. In Aristarchus's surviving treatise, *On the Magnitudes and Distances of the Sun and Moon,* he said nothing about Earth's motion.　　A. Mark Smith

Aristide, *AR uh STEED,* **Jean-Bertrand,** *zhahn behr TRAHN* (1953-　　), became the first democratically elected president of Haiti. He served as president in 1991, from 1994 to 1996, and from 2001 to 2004.

Aristide was first elected president in 1990. Military leaders ousted him in 1991, and he fled the country. Despite international pressure, the military leaders refused to permit Aristide to return. In 1994, the United States began sending troops to Haiti as part of a United Nations (UN) mission designed to force Haiti's military government to restore democracy. The military leaders soon gave up their power and Aristide returned to Haiti as president.

Aristide left office in 1996, at the end of his term. He remained active in politics and was reelected president in 2000. In 2004, he resigned and fled to Africa after months of protests and several weeks of violent rebellion in northern Haiti. Aristide's opponents claimed the 2000 elections had been fraudulent. Aristide said the United States had forced him to resign, but U.S. officials denied the charge. He returned to Haiti in 2011.

Aristide was born in poverty on July 15, 1953, in Port-Salut, Haiti. He became a Roman Catholic priest in 1982. He won popularity by speaking out against President Jean-Claude Duvalier's dictatorship, particularly the oppression of the poor. Duvalier's government tried to assassinate Aristide several times. In 1988, the Salesian religious order banned Aristide from preaching, claiming that his teachings advocated violence. Aristide resigned from the priesthood in 1994.　　Patrick Bellegarde-Smith

Aristides, *AR ih STY deez* (530?-468? B.C.), called the "Just," was an Athenian statesman and military leader. He was a rival of Themistocles, who wanted to make Athens a naval power. Aristides thought it best to maintain a powerful land force because the army, rather than the naval forces, had defeated the Persians at the Battle of Marathon in 490 B.C. The people of Athens resolved the dispute about 483 B.C. According to custom, the Athenians voted on whether Aristides or Themistocles should be *ostracized* (banished). Each voter wrote one of the names on an *ostracon* (piece of pottery). Because of Themistocles's great influence with the people, Aristides lost the vote and was exiled.

Aristides remained loyal to Athens. In 480 B.C., he warned the city that the armies of King Xerxes of Persia were coming. He joined Themistocles at the Battle of Salamis and helped the Greek victory there by forcing the Persians off Psyttalea, an island near Salamis, with troops he had raised (see **Salamis**). He was called back from exile and appointed general in 479. From then on, Aristides was the most powerful leader in Athens. In 477 B.C., the Delian League was formed to free and protect Greek colonies in Asia Minor from Persian rule. Aristides determined the amount of money and number of ships each city should give the league. He decided that each should give according to its ability to pay. Aristides himself served without pay. When Aristides died, the state paid for his burial.　　Jennifer Tolbert Roberts

See also **Themistocles**.

Aristocracy, *AR uh STAHK ruh see,* is a high social class that often used to include the government leaders of a state or nation. Its members claim to be, or are considered to be, superior to others owing to family ties, social rank, wealth, or ability. Historically, the word *aristocracy* referred to a form of government controlled by a few wealthy or socially prominent citizens. The word comes from the Greek term meaning *rule by the best.*

Many aristocrats have inherited titles of nobility, such as *duke* or *baron.* These titles were usually given to their ancestors by monarchs because of their wealth or service to the state. In most cases, people were accepted into aristocracy because they owned much land.

In ancient times, aristocracies controlled the governments of Greece and Rome. In modern times, they ruled theUnited Kingdom, Japan, Russia, and Germany. By the early 1900's, the idea that all people are equal had gained influence in many nations through democracy and socialism. As a result, the role of aristocracies in government declined sharply.　　Alexander J. Groth

Aristophanes, *AR ih STAHF uh NEEZ* (445?-385? B.C.), was the greatest ancient Greek writer of comedy. His plays combine fantasy, rollicking wit, and graceful lyrics with serious criticism of politics, manners, education, music, and literature. He was a master of song and rhythm, and he had a rich imagination.

Aristophanes's comedies provide the best picture we have of Athenian life during its most interesting period. They also provide some of the earliest and best examples of political and social satire. Aristophanes began to produce comedies before he was 20. He wrote more than 40 plays, and 11 have survived. They are *Acharnians* (425 B.C.), *Knights* (424), *Clouds* (423), *Wasps* (422), *Peace* (421), *Birds* (414), *Lysistrata* (411), *Thesmophoriazusae* (411), *Frogs* (405), *Ecclesiazusae* (393 or 392?), and *Plutus* (388).

Aristophanes's most popular plays are *Frogs,* which criticized Euripides; *Clouds,* which satirized Socrates; *Birds,* a fantasy about a city in the sky; and *Lysistrata,* a partly farcical play in which the women of Greece force their husbands to stop warring against each other.

Luci Berkowitz

See also **Drama** (Old comedy); **Euripides; Socrates.**

Aristotle, *AR ih STAHT uhl* (384-322 B.C.), a Greek philosopher, educator, and scientist, was one of the greatest and most influential thinkers in Western culture. Aristotle was probably the most scholarly and learned of the *classical* or *ancient* Greek philosophers. He familiarized himself with the entire development of Greek thought preceding him. In his own writings, Aristotle considered, summarized, criticized, and further developed all the intellectual tradition that he had inherited. Aristotle and his teacher Plato are usually considered to be the most important ancient Greek philosophers.

Aristotle's life

Aristotle was born in Stagira, a small town in northern Greece. His father, Nichomachus, was the personal physician of Amyntas II, the king of nearby Macedonia. Amyntas was the father of Philip of Macedonia and the grandfather of Alexander the Great. Aristotle's parents died when he was a boy, and he was then raised by a guardian named Proxenus.

When Aristotle was about 18 years old, he entered Plato's school in Athens, known as the Academy. He remained there for about 20 years. Plato recognized Aristotle as the Academy's brightest and most learned student, and called him the "intelligence of the school" and the "reader."

When Plato died in 347 B.C., Aristotle left the Academy to join a group of Plato's disciples living with Hermeias, a former student at the Academy. Hermeias had become ruler of the towns of Atarneus and Assos in Asia Minor. Aristotle stayed with Hermeias for about three years and married the ruler's adopted daughter, Pithias.

In 343 or 342 B.C., Philip II, king of Macedonia, invited Aristotle to supervise the education of his young son Alexander. Alexander later conquered all of Greece, overthrew the Persian Empire, and became known as Alexander the Great. Alexander studied under Aristotle until 336 B.C., when the youth became ruler of Macedonia after his father was assassinated (see **Alexander the Great** [His youth]).

Aristotle returned to Athens, and in 335 B.C., he founded a school called the Lyceum. Aristotle's school, philosophy, and followers were called *peripatetic.* This word probably came from the Greek term meaning *covered walkway.* Lyceum students often were taught on such a walkway. See **Lyceum; Peripatetic philosophy.**

Soon after Alexander died in 323 B.C., Aristotle was charged with *impiety* (lack of reverence for the gods) by the Athenians. They probably resented his friendship with Alexander, the man who had conquered them. Aristotle had not forgotten the fate of the philosopher

Aristotle Contemplating the Bust of Homer (1653), an oil painting on canvas; the Metropolitan Museum of Art, New York City

Aristotle, a Greek philosopher, gazes at a statue of the Greek poet Homer in this painting by the Dutch artist Rembrandt.

Socrates, condemned to death on a similar charge by the Athenians in 399 B.C. He fled to the city of Chalcis so the Athenians would not, as he said, "sin twice against philosophy." He died in Chalcis a year later.

Aristotle's writings

Aristotle's writings are usually divided into three groups: (1) popular writings, (2) memoranda, and (3) treatises.

The popular writings were mostly dialogues modeled on Plato's dialogues and produced while Aristotle was still at Plato's Academy. These works were intended for a general audience *outside* the school, rather than for philosophers at the school. For this reason, Aristotle referred to them as his *exoteric* writings (*exo-* means *outside* in Greek). These writings have not survived, but the works of later writers include many references to them and quotations from them.

The memoranda were largely collections of research materials and historical records. Prepared by Aristotle and his students, they were intended as sources of information for scholars. With few exceptions, the memoranda, like the popular writings, were lost.

The treatises make up nearly all of Aristotle's surviving writings. They were probably written for use either as lecture notes or as textbooks at the Lyceum. Unlike the popular works, the treatises were intended only for students *in* the school. Thus, the treatises are called Aristotle's *esoteric* works (*eso-* means *inside* in Greek).

Aristotle's philosophy

Logic. Aristotle's works on logic are collectively called the *Organon,* which means *instrument,* because they investigate thought, which is the instrument of knowledge. The *Organon* includes *The Categories, The Prior and Posterior Analytics, The Topics,* and *On Interpretation.* Aristotle was the first philosopher to analyze the process whereby certain propositions can be logically inferred to be true from the fact that certain other propositions are true. He believed that this process of logical inference was based on a form of argument he called the *syllogism*. In a syllogism, a proposition is argued or logically inferred to be true from the fact that two other propositions are true. For example, from the facts that (1) all people are mortal and (2) Socrates is a person, it can be logically argued that (3) Socrates is mortal. The syllogism continued to play an important role in later philosophy. See **Logic**.

Philosophy of nature. For Aristotle, the most striking aspect of nature was change. He even defined the philosophy of nature in his *Physics* as the study of things that change. Aristotle argued that to understand change, a distinction must be made between the *form* and *matter* of a thing. For example, a sculpture might have the form of a human being, and bronze as its matter. Aristotle believed that change essentially consists of the same matter acquiring new form. In our example, change occurs if the bronze sculpture is molded into a new form.

To better understand change, Aristotle studied its causes. He distinguished four kinds of causes: (1) *material*, (2) *efficient*, (3) *formal*, and (4) *final*. The material cause of the sculpture is the material of which it is made. Its efficient cause is the activity of the sculptor who made it. Its formal cause is the form in which the bronze is molded. Its final cause is the plan or design in the sculptor's mind.

Aristotle studied movement as a kind of change and wrote about the movement of the heavenly bodies in *On the Heavens*. In *On Coming-to-be and Passing-away*, he investigated the changes that occur when something seems to be created or destroyed.

Aristotle's philosophy of nature includes psychology and biology. In *On the Soul*, he investigated the functions of the soul and the relationship between the soul and the body. Aristotle was the world's first great biologist. He gathered vast amounts of information about the variety, structure, and behavior of animals and plants. Aristotle analyzed the parts of living organisms *teleologically*, that is, in terms of the purposes they serve.

Metaphysics. In his *Metaphysics*, Aristotle tried to develop a science of things that never change and to investigate the most general and basic principles of reality and knowledge. Because the most important of these unchanging things is God, Aristotle sometimes called this science *theology*, the study of God. He also called this branch of his philosophy *first philosophy*, because of its fundamental importance. Aristotle himself never used the name *metaphysics*, which literally means *after the physics*. This name was given to the work centuries later simply because it followed the *Physics* in the written edition of Aristotle's works. But the word *metaphysics* has now come to mean any philosophic study of the basic principles of reality and knowledge.

Ethics and politics. For Aristotle, ethics and politics both study *practical knowledge*, that is, knowledge that enables people to act properly and live happily. Aristotle's works on this subject include the *Nicomachean Ethics* and the *Politics*.

Aristotle argued that the goal of human beings is happiness, and that we achieve happiness when we fulfill our function. Therefore, it is necessary to determine what our function is. The function of a thing is what it alone can do, or what it can do best. For example, the function of the eye is to see, and the function of a knife is to cut. Aristotle declared that a human being is "the rational animal" whose function is to reason. Thus, according to Aristotle, a happy life for human beings is a life governed by reason.

Aristotle believed that a person who has difficulty behaving ethically is morally imperfect. His ideal person practices behaving reasonably and properly until he or she can do so naturally and without effort. Aristotle believed that moral virtue is a matter of avoiding extremes in behavior and finding instead the *mean* between the extremes. For example, the virtue of courage is the mean between the vices of cowardice at one extreme and foolhardiness at the other. Similarly, generosity is the mean between stinginess and wastefulness.

Literary criticism. Aristotle's *Poetics* has probably been the single most influential work in all literary criticism. The *Poetics* examines the nature of tragedy, and takes as its prime example Sophocles's tragedy *Oedipus Rex*. Aristotle believed that tragedy affects the spectator by arousing the emotions of pity and fear, and then purifying and cleansing the spectator of these emotions. He called this process of purifying and cleansing *catharsis*.

Aristotle's place in Western thought

After Aristotle's death, his philosophy continued to be taught at the Peripatetic school by a long line of successors. One of these philosophers, Critolaus, went to Rome in 155 B.C. and gave the Romans their first contact with Greek philosophy. About 50 B.C., Andronicus of Rhodes edited Aristotle's works. This edition stimulated much scholarly analysis of Aristotle's philosophy, particularly in Alexandria. From about A.D. 500 to 1100, knowledge of his philosophy was almost completely lost in the West. During this period, it was preserved by Arab and Syrian scholars who reintroduced it to the Christian culture of Western Europe in the 1100's and 1200's.

Aristotle enjoyed tremendous prestige during this time. To some leading Christian, Jewish, and Arab scholars of the Middle Ages, which lasted from about A.D. 400 through the 1400's, his writings seemed to contain the sum total of human knowledge. Saint Thomas Aquinas, one of the most influential philosophers of the Middle Ages, considered Aristotle "the philosopher." Dante Alighieri, perhaps the greatest poet of the Middle Ages, called Aristotle the "master of those who know."

Aristotle's authority has declined since the Middle Ages, but many modern philosophers owe much to him. The extent of Aristotle's influence is difficult to judge, because many of his ideas have been absorbed into the language of science and philosophy.   Ivan Soll

Related articles in *World Book* include:

Boethius, Anicius Manlius Severinus
Encyclopedia (The first reference works)
Ethics (Plato)
Philosophy (Ancient philosophy)
Scholasticism

Additional resources

Anderson, Margaret J., and Stephenson, K. F. *Aristotle*. Enslow, 2004. Younger readers.
Höffe, Otfried. *Aristotle*. State Univ. of N. Y. Pr., 2003.
Hughes, Gerard J. *Routledge Philosophy Guidebook to Aristotle on Ethics*. Routledge, 2001.

A calculator can help us with such difficult tasks as filling out a tax return. It is especially helpful in the addition of long strings of numbers and in such operations as multiplication and division.

A pen or pencil remains the instrument of choice for many people when it comes to simple arithmetic, such as the addition and subtraction operations that keep a checkbook up to date.

Arithmetic is the process of calculating by means of symbols called *numerals*. It is the part of mathematics that concerns how to get answers to addition, subtraction, multiplication, and division problems. The word *arithmetic* comes from the Greek word *arithmos*, which means *number*.

Mathematicians use the term *number* to mean an idea having to do with the amount or quantity of a thing or things. They use *numeral* to mean a symbol that represents a number. For example, the numerals 6 and VI stand for the number also represented by the word *six*. But in everyday language, *number* is also used to mean *numeral*. The rest of this article uses *number* in the everyday way.

Many people use computers and calculators to do most of their arithmetic, but much arithmetic is still done with pencil and paper. Both methods of calculating rely on a *numeration system* (a system of counting and naming numbers) that determines the value of a digit by its position in a number.

The numeration system used by most people is called the *decimal* system, or *base 10* system. In this system, a *digit* is any one of the symbols 0, 1, 2, 3, 4, 5, 6, 7, 8, and 9. Each position in a number with two or more digits has a value 10 times greater than the position to its right. And each position has a name that corresponds to its value. The positions, from right to left, are called the *ones'* position, the *tens'* position, the *hundreds'* position, the *thousands'* position, and so on. Each position has only one digit.

A computer or calculator does the actual arithmetic with another numeration system, the *binary system*. However, in this approach, the user enters the problem in the decimal system, and the results are shown in the decimal system. This article describes various pencil-and-paper procedures for calculating with the decimal system.

Addition

Several methods of addition are in use today. Methods A through C shown here work from right to left. In the United States and Japan, many people use method A. When a column of numerals adds up to 10 or more, write the digit in the tens' place above the column to the left. In the example, in the ones' column, 7 + 6 = 13. Take one 10 from the 13 and write it as 1 above the tens' column. In the hundreds' column, when you add 8 hundreds and 6 hundreds, you get 14 hundreds. Because 10 hundreds equals 1 thousand, take 10 from the 14 hundreds and add 1 above the thousands' column.

Method B is similar to method A except that you add the 1 to the top number instead of just writing the 1 above the column. Then you have to add only two numbers, which for most people is much easier than adding three. In the tens' column, the 4 becomes a 5 when you add the one 10 from the ones' column.

In method C, all the answer is kept together on or below the line instead of part of it moving above the columns. If the sum of a column is 10 or more, write 1 on the line and then add it to the sum of the next column. In this example, you move one 10 from the 13 in the ones' column into the tens' column on the line. In the tens' column, after adding 4 and 3 for a sum of 7,

Addition methods (A to C)

$$
\textbf{A.} \quad \overset{1\quad1}{2\,8\,4\,7} \qquad \textbf{B.} \quad \overset{3\quad5}{2\,8\,4\,7} \qquad \textbf{C.} \; 2\,8\,4\,7
$$
$$
\quad\;\;\, +3\,6\,3\,6 \qquad\qquad\;\; +3\,6\,3\,6 \qquad\qquad\; +3\,6\,3\,6
$$
$$
\quad\;\;\, \overline{6\,4\,8\,3} \qquad\qquad\quad\;\; \overline{6\,4\,8\,3} \qquad\qquad\quad \overline{6\,4\,8\,3}
$$

you add the 1 to the 7 for a total of 8. Method C is easier than method A because you add the two numbers you see above the line and then just increase the sum by 1.

Method D does not require working from right to left. First, add each column. Write the sum at the bottom of each column. Next, modify any two-digit sum by adding the number in the tens' position into the position to the left. For example, take 1 thousand—that is, 10 hundreds—from the 14 hundreds and add it to the thousands' column. The total in the thousands' column becomes 6.

In method E, you add from left to right without writing the numbers carried to the next column. Many Europeans learn method E. Before writing a sum in a column, they look at the next column to the right to see whether it adds up to 10 or more. If it does, they increase the sum of the column on which they are working by 1.

Methods F through H are commonly used by people who have not learned formal calculation techniques. Many people use these methods without writing down any of the steps. In method F, you first add the values in each position—the ones, tens, and so on. Then add the sums for all the positions to get the final answer.

Method G breaks down the process further. You add the numbers in the position of highest value first. In this case, add the 40 from the 47 and the 30 from the 35: $40 + 30 = 70$. Then add the 7 from the 47 for a total of 77. Finally, count on the remaining 5 from the 35. People sometimes use equal signs instead of arrows to indicate the accumulating total, but that usage is not correct.

In method H, you adjust numbers to make them easier to add. Increase the 47 by 3 to 50. To balance the increase, decrease the 35 by 3 to 32. Then add 50 to 32.

Subtraction

In method A shown here, you change top numbers to make them larger than bottom numbers. Then you can easily subtract all the bottom numbers from the top numbers. In the example shown, the bottom number in the ones' column, 7, cannot be subtracted from the top number, 3. So you take one 10 from the top number in the tens' column and add it to the ones' position in that number. This addition changes the number in the ones' position from 3 to 13. In the hundreds' column, you cannot subtract 8 hundreds from 4 hundreds. So you make the 4 hundreds bigger by adding to it one of the thousands, or 10 hundreds, to make 14 hundreds.

Method A can be used in two ways. In the easier way, you adjust top numbers so that every top number is larger than the number below it. Then you do all the subtraction. You can work from left to right or from right to left. In a more difficult technique, you work one column at a time, starting at the right. You adjust the top number if necessary, then subtract. Schools in the United States commonly teach this technique.

A comparison of subtraction method A and addition method D shows how addition and subtraction are opposite procedures. When doing addition, you can get too many digits in one position and therefore have to add one 10 of the quantity corresponding to that position to the place to the left. When doing subtraction, if you do not have a large enough number from which to subtract, you have to take one 10 of the quantity corresponding to that position from the place to the left.

Method B is similar to method A, but when you take

Addition methods (D to H)

D.
```
  2 8 4 7
+ 3 6 3 6
─────────
  5 14 7 13
  6 4 8 3
```

E.
```
  2 8 4 7
+ 3 6 3 6
─────────
  6 4 8 3
```

F. $47 + 35 = 70 + 12 = 82$

G. $47 + 35 \rightarrow 40 + 30 \rightarrow 70 \rightarrow 77 \rightarrow 78, 79, 80, 81, 82$

H. $47 + 35 = 50 + 32 = 82$

10 from the left position, you write it as 10. There are two ways to use method B. In the example shown, if you split the 7 in the ones' column into 3 and 4, you can easily subtract 3 from the 3 to get 0. Then you can subtract the 4 from the 10, which leaves 6. Another approach is to take the entire bottom number from the 10: $10 - 7 = 3$. Then add the difference from that subtraction to the top number: $3 + 3 = 6$. Method B comes from Korea.

Method C uses *equal additions*. You add the same amount to the top and bottom numbers so the difference between them stays the same. Schools in Latin America and many European countries teach method C. However, students in some countries do not write the 1's in the top number.

In this method, you add 10 ones to the ones' position in the top number to make 13. Then you subtract 7 from 13 to get 6. To balance the 10 ones that you added, you add one 10 to the bottom number in the tens' column. Write a 1 representing the 10 beside the 4 in the tens' position. In the tens' column, first subtract 4 from 8: $8 - 4 = 4$. Then subtract the 1: $4 - 1 = 3$. In the hundreds' column, add 10 hundreds to the 4 hundreds in the top number to get 14 hundreds. Then add 1 thousand to the 2 thousands in the thousands' column.

Methods D and E involve working with numbers that have the same value positions. In method D, you subtract the 200 of the 278 from the 600 of the 634 to get 400. Then, you subtract the remaining 78 from 400 to get 322. Finally, you add to the 322 the 34 left over from the 634 for an answer of 356.

Method E is similar to addition method H. You adjust the numbers to make them easier to use. Adding the same amount to both numbers does not change the difference between them. By adding 2 to both numbers,

Subtraction methods (A to E)

A.
```
  5 14 7 13
  6 4 8 3
- 2 8 4 7
─────────
  3 6 3 6
```

B.
```
  5 10 7 10
  6 4 8 3
- 2 8 4 7
─────────
  3 6 3 6
```

C.
```
  6 4 8 3
- 2 8 4 7
─────────
  3 6 3 6
```

D. $634 - 278 \rightarrow 400 - 78 \rightarrow 322 + 34 = 356$

E. $634 - 278 = 636 - 280 = 20 + 300 + 36 = 356$

you get 636 and 280. The number 280 is easier to work with than 278. To count up from 280 to 636, you first count 20 to get to 300, then 300 to get to 600, and then 36 to get to 636. Then add the numbers 20, 300, and 36 for the total difference.

Multiplication

You can multiply by adding repeated copies of a number. Method A requires only that you multiply by 10, 100, or 1,000, and so on, and then add the resulting multiples. Multiplying by 10 moves a number one value position to the left. So 10 times 486 is 4,860. Multiplying by 100 moves each number two value places to the left. So 100 times 486 is 48,600. So 324 × 486 is just four copies of 486, two copies of 4,860, and three copies of 48,600. Add all of these copies together to find the final answer, called the *product.*

In method B, you multiply each digit in the top number, called the *multiplicand,* by each digit in the bottom number, called the *multiplier.* In this example, 486 is the multiplicand and 324 is the multiplier.

Method C is a shortcut of method B in which you multiply the entire multiplicand by each number in the multiplier. You begin on the right. In the example shown, first multiply 486 by 4. Then multiply 486 by the number in the tens' position in the multiplier: 20 × 486. And then multiply 486 by the number in the hundreds' position in the multiplier: 300 × 486. Schools in the United States teach method C.

Egyptians used method D more than 2,000 years ago. To use this doubling method, sketch a table with two columns. In the right column, write the multiplicand on top, double it, and write the doubled figure below it. Double this second number and write it as the third number in the column. In the left column, write 1 on top, double it to 2, and write the 2 below the 1. Then double the 2 to 4 and write the 4 below the 2. Continue in this manner until the next number you would write in the left column is bigger than the multiplier.

Then, choose the numbers in the left column that add up to the multiplier. Finally, add the corresponding values from the right column. For example, to multiply 486 by 324, add the values for 256, 64, and 4 because 256 + 64 + 4 = 324. The result is the following: 124,416 + 31,104 + 1,944 = 157,464.

Method E has been used in Arab nations, China, India, Japan, and Western Europe. First, draw a rectangle and divide it into rows and columns. Divide each resulting square by a diagonal line running from top right to bottom left. Write the multiplicand, 486, across the top, and the multiplier, 324, down the right side. Write the product of each row and column in the square for that row and column. Place the tens part of the product in the top triangle and the ones part in the bottom triangle.

Then add from right to left. Begin by writing below the square the number in the lower right triangle—in this case, a 4. Then, add the numbers in the diagonally arranged group of triangles that are above and to the

Multiplication methods

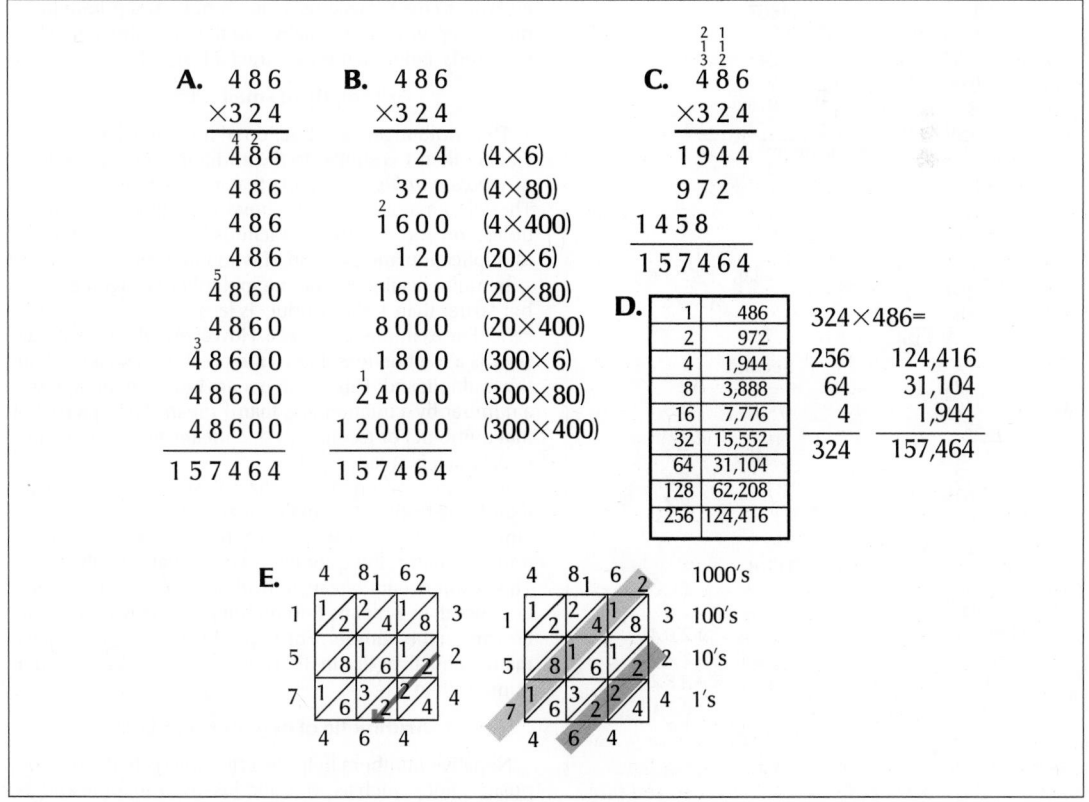

left—in the example, the three 2's. You continue in this manner. If a sum has two digits, write the tens' digit above the top triangle of the next group. Include that digit when you calculate the sum for that next group.

In the example, the shaded 2 + 2 + 2 = 6 consists of the first group of triangles and its sum. The shaded 2 + 1 + 4 + 1 + 8 + 1 = 7 consists of the tens' digit from the second group (the 2), the numbers in the entire third group (the 1, 4, 1, 8, and 1), and the ones' digit of the sum of those six numbers (the 7). The answer to the problem runs from the square's top left side to its bottom right.

Division

Method A shows the basic method of division. In this method, you take away copies of the *divisor* (the number by which you are dividing) in multiples of 1, 10, 100, and so on. You continue taking away copies until you use up the *dividend* (the number you are dividing) and therefore cannot take away any more copies. The answer is called the *quotient.* There is also usually an amount left over called the *remainder.* Method A for division is the opposite of method A for multiplication.

Division methods

```
A. 486/157467
       48600   100
      108867
       48600   100
       60267
       48600   100
       11667
        4860    10
        6807
        4860    10
        1947
         486     1
        1451
         486     1
         975
         486     1
         489
         486     1
remainder  3   324
```

```
B. 486/157467
       97200   200
       60267
       48600   100
       11667
        9720    20
        1947
         972     2
         975
         972     2
 remainder  3   324
```

```
                        324
C. 486/157467
       1458
       1166
        972
       1947
       1944
           3 remainder
```

```
D. 157464 |486
    1166   324
    1944
       0
```

```
E. First          1
                 1⟋2 6
      486  ⟋4⟋8⟋7⟋4 6 4   3
             ⟋4⟋4⟋5⟋8

   Second         1
                  ⟋2
                 ⟋4 9
                ⟋4⟋2⟋8 4
      486  ⟋4⟋8⟋7⟋4⟋8 4   32
             ⟋4⟋4⟋5⟋8⟋2
                 ⟋8⟋7

   Third          ⟋4
                  ⟋2
                 ⟋4 ⟋8
                ⟋4⟋2⟋8⟋4
      486  ⟋4⟋8⟋7⟋4⟋8⟋4   324
             ⟋4⟋4⟋5⟋8⟋2⟋4
                 ⟋8⟋7 ⟋4
                 ⟋4 ⟋8
```

Method B resembles division method A, but you take away more than one set of each multiple at a time. You do not need to take away all the sets of a given size in the first try. In the example shown, 3 sets of 100 copies of the divisor could have been taken away in the first try. But actually, 2 sets of 100 copies, then 1 set of 100 copies, were taken away.

In method C, you must take away all the sets of a given size in the first try. In the example, you must begin by taking away 3 sets of 100 copies of the divisor. Schools in the United States usually teach method C.

Method D is an abbreviation of method C. It comes from Argentina and other Latin American countries. Write the divisor on the right, the dividend on the left, and the quotient below the divisor. When you subtract from the dividend, write down only the answer to that subtraction.

Method E became widespread in Europe in the 1400's. It began in India, where the calculations were written in sand. Method E resembles method C, except that you write the results of subtraction above the dividend instead of below. This method is shown in three steps to show how it works. The work for each step is shaded. Each number is scratched out as it is used.

In the first step, multiply 486 by 3. Write the first part of the quotient—3—to the right and the answer—1,458—below the dividend. Then subtract 1,458 from 1,574. Work from left to right (5 − 4 =1 and 7 −5 = 2), writing the remainder above the dividend. To make a subtraction in the hundreds' column, you need to change the thousands' column. Take 1 from the 2, crossing out the 2 and writing the resulting 1 above it. The 1 that you took away from the thousands' column becomes a 10 in the hundreds' column. Mentally add the 10 to the 4 in the hundreds' column, then subtract 8 from 14.

Arithmetic of small fractions

The addition and subtraction of fractions that are smaller than 1 is similar to the addition and subtraction of *whole numbers* (numbers that are not fractions). There is a major difference, however, between the multiplication and division of fractions less than 1 and the multiplication and division of whole numbers.

In multiplication, when the multiplier is a whole number larger than 1, the product is larger than the multiplicand. For example, 2 × 3 = 6. However, when the multiplier is a fraction less than 1, the product is smaller than the multiplicand. This result occurs because multiplying a number by a fraction less than 1 means taking a part of that number. For example, $\frac{1}{2}$ × 3 means taking one-half of 3, which is smaller than 3.

In division, when the divisor is a whole number larger than 1, the quotient is smaller than the dividend. For example, 6 ÷ 3 = 2. However, when the divisor is a fraction less than 1, the quotient is larger than the dividend. This result occurs because dividing a number by a fraction less than 1 means finding out how many of that fraction are in the number. For example, 3 ÷ $\frac{1}{2}$ means, "How many one-halves are in 3?" There are 6, and 6 is a bigger number than 3.

Arithmetic of negative numbers

Negative numbers help describe things that have opposite values, such as wins and losses or income and expenses. Negative numbers also help describe measurements whose amounts are opposite in direction—temperatures above and below zero degrees or heights above and below sea level. One value or direction is considered to be positive and the opposite value or direction negative. Positive numbers have a plus sign; negative numbers, a minus sign.

Because negative numbers are the opposite of positive numbers, the arithmetic of negative numbers differs from that of positive numbers. Adding two positive numbers makes a bigger positive number, and adding two negative numbers makes a bigger negative number. But when a positive number and a negative number are added, the smaller number cancels that much of the bigger number. Whether the sum is positive or negative depends on the sign of the bigger number. If the bigger number is positive, the sum is positive. If the bigger number is negative, the sum is negative. Adding a negative number is equivalent to subtracting a positive number of the same size.

Subtracting a negative or a positive number from a number of opposite sign is the same as adding the opposite kind of number. For example, $10 - (-5) = 15$ just as $10 + 5 = 15$. And $-10 - (+5) = -15$ just as $-10 + (-5) = -15$. Therefore, subtraction does not always result in a smaller number. If you subtract a negative number from a positive number, you will get a larger number because taking away the negative value provides that much more of the positive value.

Multiplying by a positive number can be thought of as repeated addition. Repeatedly adding a negative number results in a larger negative number: $8 \times (-3) = -24$. Multiplying by a negative number can be thought of as repeated subtraction. Repeatedly subtracting a positive number also gives a larger negative number: $-3 \times (+8) = -24$. However, repeatedly subtracting a negative number gives a positive number. Thus, when the signs of the numbers are opposite, a negative number results. When the signs are the same, a positive number results.

Division is the opposite of multiplication. Therefore, to determine the sign of a quotient, you can convert the division problem to a multiplication problem. For example, you can convert $-24 \div 8 = ?$ to $8 \times ? = -24$. You know that multiplying a positive number by a negative number results in a negative number. Thus, the number represented by the question mark in the multiplication problem—and the division problem—must be negative.

General rules for division are: Dividing opposite kinds of numbers, one positive and one negative, results in a negative quotient. Dividing like kinds of numbers, both positive or both negative, yields a positive quotient.

History

Calculation tools. During most of human history, few people used written numbers to calculate. Many numeration systems were difficult to use, especially for multiplication and division. Writing materials were also expensive until the mid-1800's, when machine-made wood pulp paper became available.

Most ancient people used calculating objects, such as pebbles and sticks. An individual manipulated the objects on a board, a cloth, or some other surface. Lines drawn on the surface helped the individual distinguish columns or rows that had different numerical values.

People living in western Africa used a type of small seashell called a *cowrie shell* for their calculations. The Inca of South America calculated with kernels of wheat on a board. The ancient Greeks and Romans used stones on wood or marble tables. The Chinese and Japanese used small bamboo or wooden reckoning sticks on a board divided into columns. Later, the use of an *abacus*, a counting device with beads fastened on rods, became widespread in Asia and Russia.

Mechanical calculators that used gears began to appear in Europe in the 1600's. In the 1940's, scientists and engineers built electronic calculators using vacuum tubes. As smaller electronic components were developed, electronic calculators became smaller, faster, and cheaper. By the late 1900's, inexpensive handheld calculators were available throughout the world.

Written arithmetic methods. The decimal system of numeration made written calculations easy to perform. This system evolved in India sometime between A.D. 600 and 900. Indian and Arabic scientists and mathematicians devised a variety of arithmetic methods based on the decimal system. By 1000, the Arabs had spread these methods throughout their empire, and the methods had begun to filter into Europe.

The development of the printing press in Europe in the mid-1400's enabled printers to produce inexpensive books. Arithmetic books written in the languages of the common people soon became available. Prior to that time, arithmetic was taught mostly at universities in the Latin language. By the 1800's, young children were learning arithmetic in school in their own language.

Today, calculators make it seem unnecessary for older students to memorize and practice arithmetic. But it is important to know whether an answer obtained on a calculator is reasonable.   Karen Connors Fuson

Related articles in *World Book*. See **Mathematics** and its list of *Related articles*. See also:

Abacus	Decimal system	Number
Addition	Division	Subtraction
Cuisenaire	Fraction	Zero
Method	Multiplication	

Arithmetic progression. See Progression (Arithmetic progression); Series.

Arius, *AIR ee uhs* or *uh RY uhs* (A.D. 256?-336), was a priest of Alexandria, Egypt, who gave his name to a movement that challenged the Christian doctrine of the Holy Trinity. The movement became known as *Arianism.* Orthodox Christianity taught that the three Persons of the Holy Trinity—the Father, the Son, and the Holy Spirit—were all equal and eternal. Arius argued that the Father was superior to the Son (Jesus Christ), and that both the Father and the Son were superior to the Holy Spirit.

About A.D. 318, Alexander, bishop of Alexandria, condemned Arius's teachings as *heresy* (beliefs contrary to those of the church) and *excommunicated* him—that is, expelled h im from the church. Arius continued to promote his views and had many followers. Constantine the Great, the first Christian emperor, tried to settle the dispute. In A.D. 325, he convened a general church council in Nicaea in present-day Turkey. The council condemned the teachings of Arius and issued the earliest version of a statement of orthodox belief now known as the Nicene Creed.   Neil J. Roy

See also **Arianism; Nicene Councils; Trinity.**

Bill Ross, West Light

Organ-pipe cactus, *right foreground,* grows in a desert in southern Arizona. The desert, part of Organ Pipe Cactus National Monument, has plant and animal life found nowhere else in the United States. Arizona's natural beauty is preserved in numerous national parks and monuments.

Arizona *The Grand Canyon State*

Arizona, once thought to be an almost worthless desert, has become a prosperous state of the United States. It is rich in farm and mineral products, and it is growing rapidly in manufacturing and population. Vast irrigation systems transform Arizona's desert soil into rich farmland. Dams built by the government or with federal funds provide water to irrigate large areas of land. These dams also generate electric power for the state's cities and industries.

Although the desert summers are hot, Arizonans stay comfortable. They live in air-cooled homes, work in air-conditioned factories, and travel in air-conditioned automobiles.

The desert winters are warm and pleasant. Arizonans, along with thousands of vacationers, enjoy the desert

The contributors of this article are Lay James Gibson, Professor of Geography and Regional Development and Director of the Economic Development Research Program at the University of Arizona, and Thomas E. Sheridan, author of Arizona: A History.

sun while winter chills other parts of the United States.

Arizona's climate attracts so many people that the state has become one of the nation's fastest-growing areas. Between 1950 and 2010, Arizona's population grew by almost nine times.

Most of Arizona's people live in desert areas, but more than half the state is mountain and plateau country. These higher, cooler areas have the largest ponderosa pine forest in the United States. Large herds of cattle graze in these regions.

The northwestern part of the state has one of the greatest scenic attractions in the United States—the mighty Grand Canyon of the Colorado River. Arizona's other scenic wonders include the Painted Desert, the Petrified Forest, and numerous national parklands. These areas attract millions of tourists to the state each year.

Arizona has the third-largest Indian population in the United States. Only Oklahoma and California have more Indians. Indian reservations cover more than a fourth of Arizona's land. Nearly 300,000 Indians live in Arizona.

Interesting facts about Arizona

The dwarf planet Pluto was discovered from the Lowell Observatory in Flagstaff by Clyde W. Tombaugh in 1930.

Tucson is known as the *Astronomy Capital of the World.* No other place has as many telescopes concentrated in one area. About 30 telescopes are placed on mountain peaks near the city. Most are operated by three major observatories. Kitt Peak has the McMath-Pierce Solar Telescope, the largest solar telescope in the world. It produces an image of the sun that has a diameter of about 30 inches (75 centimeters).

WORLD BOOK illustration by Kevin Chadwick
Astronomy Capital of the World

Casa Grande, an ancient "skyscraper" dating from about A.D. 1350, represents an engineering achievement in adobe construction. The four-story tower, in Coolidge, contains an 11-room house. It is 38 feet (11.6 meters) high. The Hohokam Indians built the structure by gradually tapering it toward the top.

WORLD BOOK illustration by Stephen Brayfield
Casa Grande

Four states meet at Four Corners, the junction of Arizona, New Mexico, Colorado, and Utah. Highway U.S. 160 in Arizona leads directly to the site, which is marked by a low concrete monument that bears the seals of the four states.

The first organized rodeo to charge admission and award prizes was held at Prescott on July 4, 1888. Called a "Cowboy Tournament" at that time, the competition marked the beginning of the modern rodeo as an organized spectator sport. The Prescott Rodeo has been held each year since then.

Tom Campbell, West Light

Phoenix is the capital and largest city of Arizona. It lies in a desert valley surrounded by mountains. A corridor of high-rise buildings, *shown here,* extends along Central Avenue in the city's business district.

More than half of them live on 21 reservations in the state.

Indians have contributed much to Arizona's history. Some Indians still live in communities built more than 800 years ago. Hundreds of years before Europeans arrived on the continent, Hohokam Indians in what is now central Arizona built the largest irrigation system in North America. After Europeans arrived in Arizona, the Indians fought to keep their rugged, beautiful land. Cochise and Geronimo, leaders of the Chiricahua Apache Indians, led war parties in Arizona long after most other Indians had surrendered.

Arizona's history also includes many years of rule by Spanish conquerors, and by Mexicans who freed the region from Spanish control. Today, a large number of Americans of Mexican ancestry live in Arizona. Their influence is apparent in the customs, foods, and place names found in the state.

Arizona derives its nickname, the *Grand Canyon State,* from its most famous physical feature. Phoenix is the state's capital and largest city.

© Thinkstock

The San Francisco mountains rise near Flagstaff. Arizona's landscape provides vivid contrasts of rugged mountains, barren deserts, broad valleys, and deep canyons.

Arizona in brief

Symbols of Arizona

On the state flag, adopted in 1917, red and yellow rays represent the setting sun. These are the colors of Spain, carried by Coronado's expedition into the region in 1540. A copper-colored star represents the state's chief mineral product. The state seal, adopted in 1911, has symbols relating to important economic activities, including mining, cattle-raising, and farming. A dam and reservoir in the background show the importance of water resources.

State flag

Secretary of State's Office
State seal

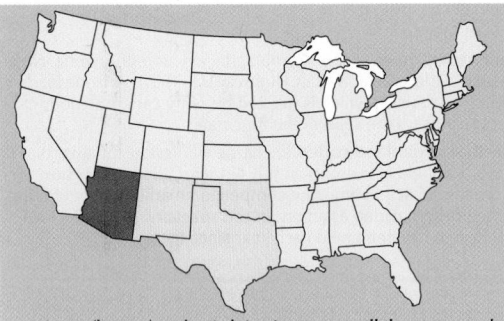

Arizona (brown) ranks sixth in size among all the states and third in size among the Southwestern States (yellow).

General information

Statehood: Feb. 14, 1912, the 48th state.
State abbreviations: Ariz. (traditional), AZ (postal).
State motto: *Ditat Deus* (God Enriches).
State songs: "Arizona March Song." Words by Margaret Rowe Clifford; music by Maurice Blumenthal. "Arizona." Words and music by Rex Allen, Jr.

The State Capitol is in Phoenix, the capital of Arizona since 1889. Earlier capitals were Fort Whipple (1864), Prescott (1864-1867 and 1877-1889), and Tucson (1867-1877).

Land and climate

Area: 113,991 mi² (295,235 km²), including 396 mi² (1,026 km²) of inland water.
Elevation: *Highest*—Humphreys Peak, 12,633 ft (3,851 m) above sea level. *Lowest*—70 ft (21 m) above sea level along the Colorado River in Yuma County.
Record high temperature: 128 °F (53 °C) at Lake Havasu City on June 29, 1994.
Record low temperature: –40 °F (–40 °C) at Hawley Lake, near McNary, on Jan. 7, 1971.
Average July temperature: 80 °F (27 °C).
Average January temperature: 41 °F (5 °C).
Average yearly precipitation: 13 in (33 cm).

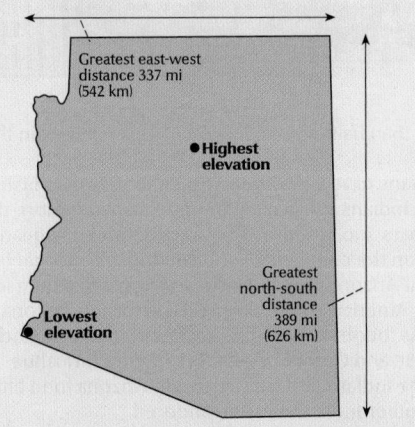

Greatest east-west distance 337 mi (542 km)

●**Highest elevation**

Greatest north-south distance 389 mi (626 km)

●**Lowest elevation**

Important dates

Spaniards established a military outpost at Tucson.

1540

Coronado led a Spanish expedition into the Arizona region.

1776

1848

Mexico ceded most of present-day Arizona to the United States following the Mexican War.

State bird
Cactus wren

State flower
Saguaro cactus blossom

State tree
Paloverde

People

Population: 6,392,017
Rank among the states: 16th
Density: 56 per mi² (22 per km²), U.S.
   average 85 per mi² (33 per km²)
Distribution: 90 percent urban, 10
   percent rural
Largest cities in Arizona

Phoenix	1,445,632
Tucson	520,116
Mesa	439,041
Chandler	236,123
Glendale	226,721
Scottsdale	217,385

Source: 2010 census.

Population trend

Millions

(Line graph showing population growth from 1800 to 2020)

1800 1820 1840 1860 1880 1900 1920 1940 1960 1980 2000 2020

Source: U.S. Census Bureau.

Year	Population
2010	6,392,017
2000	5,130,632
1990	3,665,228
1980	2,718,215
1970	1,770,900
1960	1,302,161
1950	749,587
1940	499,261
1930	435,573
1920	334,162
1910	204,354
1900	122,931
1890	88,243
1880	40,440
1870	9,658

Economy

Chief products

Agriculture: beef cattle, cotton,
   hay, lettuce, melons, milk.
Manufacturing: chemicals, computer and electronic equipment,
   fabricated metal products,
   nonmetallic mineral products,
   processed foods, transportation
   equipment.
Mining: copper, molybdenum,
   sand and gravel.

Gross domestic product

Value of goods and services produced in 2016: $310,929,000,000.
Services include community,
business, and personal services;
finance; government; trade; and
transportation and communication.
Industry includes construction,
manufacturing, mining, and utilities.
Agriculture includes agriculture,
fishing, and forestry.

Source: U.S. Bureau of Economic Analysis.

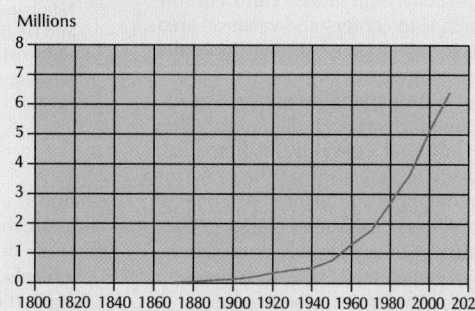

Services 83%

Agriculture 1%   Industry 16%

Government

State government

Governor: 4-year term
State senators: 30; 2-year terms
State representatives: 60; 2-year terms
Counties: 15

Federal government

United States senators: 2
United States representatives: 9
Electoral votes: 11

Sources of information

Arizona's official website at https://az.gov provides a gateway to
much information on the state's government, history, and economy.

In addition, the website at https://www.visitarizona.com provides
information about tourism.

Arizona became the 48th
state on February 14.

Construction began on the Central Arizona Project,
designed to provide water to needy areas of the state.

Central Arizona
Project completed.

1853   1912   1936   1974   1981   1991

The United States and Mexico signed the Gadsden Purchase, which added more land to Arizona.

Hoover Dam was
completed.

Arizona judge Sandra Day O'Connor became the first
woman appointed to serve on the U.S. Supreme Court.

Population. The 2010 United States census reported that Arizona had 6,392,017 people. The population had increased 25 percent over the 2000 figure, 5,130,632. According to the 2010 census, Arizona ranks 16th in population among the 50 states.

Approximately 95 percent of Arizona's people live in metropolitan areas (see **Metropolitan area**). About 65 percent live in the Phoenix-Mesa-Scottsdale metropolitan area. About 15 percent live in the Tucson metropolitan area. For the populations of the state's metropolitan areas, see the *Index* to the political map of Arizona.

Phoenix, the largest city in Arizona, is a trading and shipping center for a rich agricultural district. Tucson is Arizona's second largest city. Both Phoenix and Tucson are important manufacturing centers and vacation areas. Arizona's other large cities include Chandler, Glendale, Mesa, Scottsdale, and Tempe.

Approximately 5 out of 100 Arizonans are American Indians. Arizona has the third largest Indian population in the United States. Only California and Oklahoma have more Indians. The Navajo are the largest tribe in Arizona. The Indian settlement of Oraibi, in northern Arizona, is one of the oldest continuously inhabited places in the United States. Hopi Indians built the settlement in the 1100's. Arizona has 16 tribal councils. These councils help govern the various tribes and supervise their property.

Approximately 30 percent of Arizona's people are Hispanics. People of Mexican ancestry account for 90 percent of the state's Hispanic population. Many families in these groups speak Spanish at home. However, the children in these families learn English at school. Mexi-

can foods and customs are popular among Arizonans. In addition, the state has many people of German, English, and Irish descent.

Schools. The first schools in Arizona were established in the 1700's by Spanish missionary priests. These schools taught little except religion. By the 1840's, missions were abandoned. The first public school in Arizona opened in Tucson in 1871.

The state's school system is headed by an elected superintendent of public instruction. This official is a member of, and carries out policy made by, the State Board of Education. Other members of the board are appointed by the governor. Schools in Arizona are financed chiefly by taxes. Children in Arizona are required to attend school from the age of 6 to 16, or until they complete grade 10.

Navajo Community College (now Diné College), with its main campus in Tsaile, was the first tribally controlled community college in the United States. It was established in 1968.

Libraries and museums. Mission libraries were the first libraries in Arizona. In the 1860's, Samuel Colt, the famous pistol maker, provided books for workers at his mine in Arivaca. Tucson had a rental library in the 1870's. By 1878, both Phoenix and Prescott had small libraries. The Arizona Territorial Library, which was founded in 1864, became the Arizona State Library, Archives and Public Records.

Arizona museums feature art, science, history, and Indian cultures. The Arizona State Museum at the University of Arizona and the Arizona Historical Society's Tucson museums are among the oldest in the state. The Arizona-Sonora Desert Museum, the Pima Air & Space Museum, and the International Wildlife Museum are also in the Tucson area. The Museum of Northern Arizona, near Flagstaff, exhibits Indian arts and crafts. Museums in the Phoenix area include the Phoenix Art Museum; the Musical Instrument Museum; the Heard Museum, which features Indian art; the Pueblo Grande Museum and Archaeological Park, with remains of a prehistoric Indian village; and the Arizona Capitol Museum, with exhibits on state government history.

Universities and colleges	
This table lists the nonprofit universities and colleges based in Arizona that grant bachelor's or advanced degrees and are accredited by the Higher Learning Commission.	
Name	**Mailing address**
Arizona, University of	Tucson
Arizona Christian University	Phoenix
Arizona State University	*
Diné College	Tsaile
Grand Canyon University	Phoenix
Northern Arizona University	Flagstaff
Phoenix Seminary	Phoenix
Prescott College	Prescott
Southwest College of Naturopathic Medicine and Health Sciences	Tempe
Southwest University of Visual Arts	Tucson

*For campuses, see **Arizona State University**.

Population density

Most of the people live in southern Arizona—especially in and around Phoenix and Tucson, the state's largest cities. The northern areas are thinly populated.

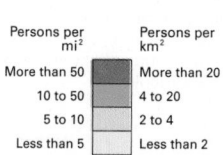

Persons per mi²	Persons per km²
More than 50	More than 20
10 to 50	4 to 20
5 to 10	2 to 4
Less than 5	Less than 2

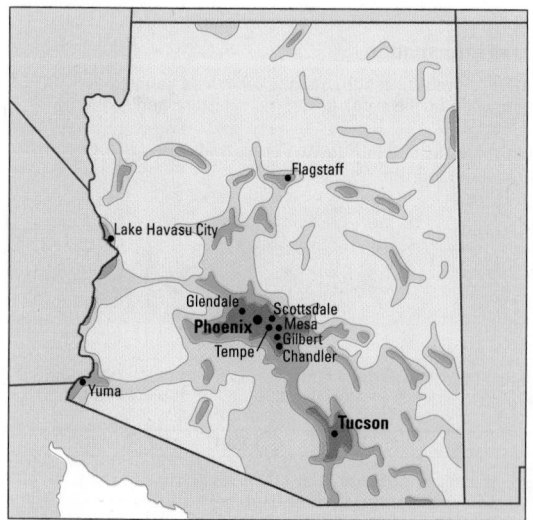

WORLD BOOK map; based on U.S. Census Bureau data.

Arizona map index

Metropolitan areas

Flagstaff ... 134,421
Lake Havasu City-Kingman ... 200,186
Phoenix-Mesa-Scottsdale ... 4,192,887
Prescott ... 211,033
Sierra Vista-Douglas ... 131,346
Tucson ... 980,263
Yuma ... 195,751

Counties

Apache ... 71,518 .. G 11
Cochise ... 131,346 .. L 11
Coconino ... 134,421 .. E 7
Gila ... 53,597 .. H 8
Graham ... 37,220 .. I 10
Greenlee ... 8,437 .. I 11
La Paz ... 20,489 .. H 3
Maricopa ... 3,817,117 .. I 5
Mohave ... 200,186 .. F 3
Navajo ... 107,449 .. E 9
Pima ... 980,263 .. K 7
Pinal ... 375,770 .. J 8
Santa Cruz ... 47,420 .. M 8
Yavapai ... 211,033 .. F 5
Yuma ... 195,751 .. J 3

Cities, towns, and other populated places

Aguila† ... 798 .. H 4
Ajo† ... 3,304 .. K 5
Ak Chin† ... 862 .. J 6
Alpine† ... 145 .. H 11
Amado† ... 295 .. L 8
Apache ... L 11
Apache Grove ... J 11
Apache Junction ... 35,840 .. I 7
Arivaca† ... 695 .. M 7
Arivaca Junction ... 1,090 .. L 8
Arizona City† ... 10,475 .. J 7
Arlington† ... 194 .. I 5
Artesia ... J 10
Ash Fork† ... 396 .. E 5
Avondale ... 76,238 .. I 6
Avra Valley*† ... 6,050 .. K 8
Aztec† ... 47 .. J 4
Bacavi ... D 9
see Hotevilla [-Bacavi]
Bagdad† ... 1,876 .. F 4
Bapchule ... I 7
Beardsley ... H 6
Bellemont ... E 7
Benson ... 5,105 .. L 9
Bisbee° ... 5,575 .. M 10
Black Canyon City† ... 2,837 .. G 6
Blackwater*† ... 1,062 .. J 7
Bluewater*† ... 725 .. G 2
Borree Corner ... J 7
Bosque ... J 5
Bouse† ... 996 .. H 3
Bowie† ... 449 .. K 11
Brenda† ... 676 .. H 3
Bryce† ... 175 .. J 10
Buckeye ... 50,876 .. I 5
Bullhead City ... 39,540 .. E 2
Bumble Bee ... G 6
Bylas† ... 1,962 .. I 10
Cactus Flat† ... 1,518 .. J 10
Cameron† ... 885 .. D 7
Camp Verde ... 10,873 .. G 7
Camp Verde Indian Reservation ... G 7
Cane Beds† ... 448 .. B 5
Cane Springs ... F 3
Canyon Diablo ... E 8
Canyon Day*† ... 1,209 .. H 10
Carefree ... 3,363 .. H 7
Carmen ... M 8
Carrizo ... F 10
Casa Grande ... 48,571 .. J 7
Casas Adobes*† ... 66,795 .. K 8
Cascabel ... K 9
Castle Butte ... E 9
Catalina† ... 7,569 .. K 8
Catalina Foothills*† ... 50,796 .. K 8
Cave Creek ... 5,015 .. H 6
Cedar Creek† ... 318 .. H 9
Cedar Ridge ... C 7
Central† ... 645 .. J 10
Central Heights [-Midland City]† ... 2,534 .. I 8
Chambers ... E 11
Chandler ... 236,123 .. I 6
Chandler Heights ... I 7
Charleston ... M 10
Cherry ... F 6
Chiapuk ... K 6
Chiawuli Tak† ... 78 .. L 7
Childs ... K 5
Chinle† ... 4,518 .. C 10
Chino Valley ... 10,817 .. F 5
Christmas ... J 9
Chuichu† ... 269 .. J 7
Cibecue† ... 1,713 .. H 9
Cibola† ... 250 .. I 2
Clarkdale ... 4,097 .. F 6
Claypool† ... 1,538 .. I 8
Clifton° ... 3,311 .. I 11
Clints Well ... G 8
Cochise ... L 10
Cocopah Indian Reservation ... 817 .. J 1
Colorado City ... 4,821 .. A 5
Colorado River Indian Reservation ... H 2
Congress† ... 1,975 .. G 5
Continental ... L 8
Coolidge ... 11,825 .. J 7
Coolidge Dam ... I 9
Cordes ... G 6
Cornville† ... 3,280 .. F 6
Corona de Tucson*† ... 5,675 .. L 8
Cortaro ... K 8
Cotton Center ... J 5
Cottonwood ... 11,265 .. F 6
Courtland ... L 10
Cowlic† ... 135 .. L 6
Cross Canyon ... D 11
Curtiss ... L 10
Cutter† ... 74 .. I 9
Date Creek ... G 5
Dateland† ... 416 .. J 4
Davis-Monthan AFB ... L 8
Dennehotso† ... 746 .. B 10
Desert Hills*† ... 2,245 .. G 2
Dewey [-Humboldt]† ... 3,894 .. G 6
Dilkon† ... 1,184 .. E 9
Dolan Springs† ... 2,033 .. D 3
Dome ... J 2
Don Luis ... M 10
Douglas ... 17,378 .. M 11
Dragoon† ... 209 .. L 10
Drake ... F 6
Drexel Heights*† ... 27,749 .. L 8
Dudleyville† ... 959 .. J 9
Duncan ... 696 .. J 11
Duquesne ... M 9
Eagar ... 4,885 .. G 11
Eden ... J 10
Ehrenberg† ... 1,470 .. H 2
Elfrida† ... 459 .. L 10
Elgin† ... 161 .. L 9
El Mirage ... 31,797 .. H 6
Eloy ... 16,631 .. J 7
Fairbank ... L 10
Flagstaff° ... 65,870 .. E 7
Florence° ... 25,536 .. J 7
Florence Junction ... I 7
Flowing Wells*† ... 16,419 .. K 8
Forbing Park ... F 5
Fort Apache† ... 143 .. H 10
Fort Apache Indian Reservation ... 13,409 .. H 9
Fort Defiance† ... 3,624 .. D 11
Fort Grant ... J 10
Fort McDowell ... H 7
Fort McDowell Indian Reservation ... 971 .. H 7
Fort Mohave Indian Reservation ... 1,004 .. F 2
Fort Thomas† ... 374 .. J 10
Fortuna Foothills*† ... 26,265 .. J 3
Fountain Hills ... 22,489 .. H 7
Franklin† ... 92 .. J 11
Fredonia ... 1,314 .. B 5
Freeman ... J 6
Gadsden† ... 678 .. K 1
Ganado† ... 1,210 .. D 10
Gap, The ... C 7
Geronimo ... J 10
Gila Bend ... 1,922 .. J 5
Gila Center ... J 2
Gila River Indian Reservation ... G 7
Gilbert ... 208,453 .. I 7
Gillespie ... I 4
Glenbar ... J 10
Glendale ... 226,721 .. I 6
Globe° ... 7,532 .. I 8
Gold Canyon*† ... 10,159 .. I 7
Golden Valley*† ... 8,370 .. E 3
Goodyear ... 65,275 .. I 5
Grand Canyon Village† ... 2,004 .. C 6
Granville ... I 11
Gray Mountain ... D 7
Greasewood† ... 547 .. D 10
Greaterville ... L 9
Green Valley† ... 21,391 .. L 8
Greer† ... 41 .. H 11
Griffith ... E 3
Growler Pass ... K 5
Gu Oidak† ... 188 .. L 6
Gu Vo ... L 5
Guadalupe ... 5,523 .. I 6
Guthrie ... J 11
Hackberry† ... 68 .. E 3
Hannagan Meadow ... H 11
Harcuvar ... H 3
Harris ... E 3
Hassayampa ... I 5
Havasupai Indian Reservation ... 465 .. C 5
Hayden ... 662 .. J 8
Heber [-Overgaard]† ... 2,822 .. G 9
Hickiwan ... K 5
Higley ... I 7
Hillside ... G 5
Holbrook° ... 5,053 .. F 9
Hope ... H 3
Hopi Indian Reservation ... 7,106 .. D 9
Horn ... J 4
Hotason Vo ... K 5
Hotevilla [-Bacavi]† ... 957 .. D 8
Houck† ... 1,024 .. E 11
House Rock ... B 6
Huachuca City ... 1,853 .. M 9
Hualapai Indian Reservation ... D 4
Humboldt ... G 6
see Dewey [-Humboldt]
Hunt ... F 10
Inspiration ... I 8
Jacob Lake ... B 6
Jerome ... 444 .. F 6
Johnson ... L 10
Joseph City† ... 1,386 .. F 9
Kachina Village*† ... 2,622 .. E 7
Kaibab† ... 124 .. B 5
Kaibab Indian Reservation ... G 7
Kaibito† ... 1,522 .. B 8
Kayenta† ... 5,189 .. B 9
Keams Canyon† ... 304 .. D 9
Kearny ... 1,950 .. J 8
Kelvin ... I 8
Kingman° ... 28,068 .. E 3
Kirkland ... G 5
Kirkland Junction ... G 5
Klagetoh† ... 242 .. D 10
Ko Vaya† ... 46 .. L 6
Kom Vo ... L 6
Komatke*† ... 821 .. I 6
Kykotsmovi Village† ... 746 .. D 9
Laguna ... J 2
Lake Havasu City ... 52,527 .. G 2
Lake Montezuma† ... 4,706 .. F 7
Lakeside, see Pinetop-Lakeside
La Palma ... J 7
Lees Ferry ... B 7
Leupp† ... 951 .. E 8
Lewis Springs ... M 10
Ligurta ... J 2
Linden† ... 2,597 .. G 9
Litchfield Park* ... 5,476 .. I 6
Littlefield† ... 308 .. B 3
Lochiel ... M 9
Lower Miami ... I 8
Lukachukai† ... 1,701 .. C 11
Luke AFB ... I 5
Magma ... I 7
Mammoth ... 1,426 .. J 9
Many Farms† ... 1,348 .. C 10
Marana ... 34,961 .. K 8
Marble Canyon ... B 7
Maricopa ... 43,482 .. J 6
Maricopa-Ak Chin Indian Reservation ... J 6
Mayer† ... 1,497 .. G 6
McConnico† ... 70 .. E 3
McGuireville ... F 7
McNary† ... 528 .. G 10
McNeal† ... 238 .. M 11
Mesa ... 439,041 .. I 7
Mescal† ... 1,812 .. L 9
Mexican Water ... A 10
Miami ... 1,837 .. I 8
Midland City ... I 8
see Central Heights [-Midland City]
Miracle Valley† ... 644 .. M 10
Mobile ... J 6
Moccasin† ... 89 .. B 5
Moenkopi† ... 964 .. C 8
Mohave Valley*† ... 2,616 .. E 2
Mohawk ... J 3
Morenci† ... 1,489 .. I 11
Mormon Lake ... F 7
Morristown† ... 227 .. H 5
Naco† ... 1,046 .. M 10
Navajo ... E 11
Navajo Indian Reservation ... 101,816 .. B 10
New Kingman-Butler*† ... 12,134 .. E 3
New River† ... 14,952 .. H 6
Nogales° ... 20,837 .. M 8
Nolia ... L 6
North Rim ... C 6
Nutrioso† ... 26 .. H 11
Oatman† ... 135 .. E 2
Olberg ... J 7
Old Columbine ... J 10
Oracle† ... 3,686 .. J 8
Oracle Junction ... K 8
Oraibi ... D 9
Oro Blanco ... M 8
Oro Valley ... 41,011 .. K 8
Overgaard ... G 9
see Heber [-Overgaard]
Page ... 7,247 .. B 7
Page Springs ... F 6
Palo Verde ... I 5
Palominas† ... 212 .. M 10
Pantano ... L 9
Papago (Tohono O'odham) Indian Reservation ... 10,201 .. K 6
Paradise ... L 11
Paradise Valley* ... 12,820 .. I 6
Parker° ... 3,083 .. G 2
Parks† ... 1,188 .. E 6
Pascua Yaqui Indian Reservation* ... 3,484 .. K 8
Patagonia ... 913 .. M 9
Paul Spur ... M 10
Paulden† ... 5,231 .. F 5
Payson ... 15,301 .. G 8
Payson Community Indian Reservation ... G 8
Peach Springs† ... 1,090 .. D 4
Pearce ... L 10
Peoria ... 154,065 .. I 6
Peridot† ... 1,350 .. I 9
Perkinsville ... F 6
Phoenix° ... 1,445,632 .. I 6
Pica ... E 4
Picacho† ... 471 .. J 7
Picture Rocks*† ... 9,563 .. K 8
Pima ... 2,387 .. J 10
Pine† ... 1,963 .. G 7
Pine Springs Ranch ... E 6
Pinetop-Lakeside ... 4,282 .. G 10
Piñon† ... 904 .. C 9
Pinta ... E 10
Pirtleville† ... 1,744 .. M 11
Pisinemo† ... 321 .. L 6
Plantsite ... I 11
Polacca ... D 9
Poland Junction ... G 6
Pomerene ... L 9
Poston† ... 285 .. H 2
Prescott° ... 39,843 .. G 5
Prescott Valley ... 38,822 .. F 6
Quartzsite ... 3,677 .. H 2
Queen ... I 8
Queen Creek ... 26,381 .. I 7
Quijotoa ... L 6
Quivero ... D 6
Randolph ... J 7
Ray ... I 8
Red Lake ... E 6
Red Rock† ... 2,169 .. K 8
Redington ... K 9
Rice ... I 8
Rillito† ... 97 .. K 8
Rimrock ... F 7
Rio Rico*† ... 18,962 .. M 8
Rock Point† ... 642 .. B 10
Rock Springs ... H 6
Roll ... J 3
Roosevelt† ... 28 .. H 8
Rough Rock† ... 414 .. C 10
Round Rock† ... 789 .. B 11
Ruby ... M 8
Sacaton† ... 2,672 .. J 7
Saddlebrooke*† ... 9,614 .. K 8
Safford° ... 9,566 .. J 10
Sahuarita ... 25,259 .. L 8
St. David† ... 1,699 .. L 9
St. Johns° ... 3,480 .. G 11
St. Michaels† ... 1,443 .. D 11
Salome† ... 1,530 .. H 3
Salt River Indian Reservation* ... 6,289 .. I 7
San Carlos† ... 4,038 .. I 9
San Carlos Indian Reservation ... 10,068 .. I 9
San Jose† ... 506 .. J 11
San Luis ... 25,505 .. K 1
San Luis ... L 6
San Manuel† ... 3,551 .. K 9
San Miguel† ... 197 .. M 7
San Pedro ... L 7
San Tan Valley*† ... 81,321 .. J 7
San Xavier ... L 8
San Xavier Indian Reservation ... L 8
Sanders† ... 630 .. E 11
Santa Claus ... E 2
Santa Cruz† ... 37 .. I 6
Santa Rosa† ... 628 .. K 6
Sasabe ... M 7
Sawmill ... 748 .. D 11
Sawmill ... H 9
Schuchuli ... K 5
Scottsdale ... 217,385 .. I 6
Second Mesa† ... 962 .. D 9
Sedona ... 10,031 .. F 7
Seligman† ... 445 .. E 5
Sells† ... 2,495 .. L 6
Sentinel ... J 4
Sheldon ... J 11
Shongopovi† ... 831 .. D 9
Shonto† ... 591 .. B 9
Show Low ... 10,660 .. G 10
Sierra Vista ... 43,888 .. M 9
Sierra Vista Southeast*† ... 14,797 .. M 10
Sil Nakya ... K 7
Silver Bell ... K 7
Simmons ... F 5
Skull Valley ... G 5
Snowflake ... 5,590 .. F 10
Solomon† ... 426 .. J 11
Somerton ... 14,287 .. J 2
South Tucson ... 5,652 .. K 8
Springerville ... 1,961 .. G 11
Stanfield† ... 740 .. J 6
Stargo ... J 11
Strawberry† ... 961 .. G 7
Sun City† ... 37,499 .. H 6
Sun City West† ... 24,535 .. H 6
Sun Lakes† ... 13,975 .. I 7
Sunizona† ... 281 .. L 11
Sunrise ... D 10
Sunset ... K 10
Supai† ... 208 .. C 5
Superior ... 2,837 .. I 8
Surprise ... 117,517 .. H 6
Swansea ... G 3
Swift Trail Junction† ... 2,935 .. J 10
Tacna† ... 602 .. J 3
Tanque Verde† ... 16,901 .. K 9
Taylor ... 4,112 .. G 10
Teec Nos Pos† ... 730 .. B 11
Tees Toh† ... 448 .. D 9
Tempe ... 161,719 .. I 6
Temple Bar ... C 2
Thatcher ... 4,865 .. J 10
Theba† ... 158 .. J 5
Three Points† ... 5,581 .. L 8
Tolleson* ... 6,545 .. I 6
Toltec ... J 7
Tombstone ... 1,380 .. L 10
Tonalea† ... 549 .. C 8
Tonopah† ... 60 .. I 5
Tonto Basin† ... 1,424 .. H 8
Topawa† ... 299 .. L 7
Topock† ... 10 .. F 2
Tortilla Flat ... I 7
Truxton† ... 134 .. E 3
Tsaile† ... 1,205 .. C 11
Tuba City† ... 8,611 .. C 7
Tubac† ... 1,191 .. M 8
Tucson° ... 520,116 .. K 8
Tucson Estates*† ... 12,192 .. K 8
Tumacacori ... M 8
Tusayan† ... 558 .. D 6
Tuweep ... C 5
Two Guns ... E 8
Utting† ... 126 .. H 3
Vail† ... 10,208 .. L 9
Vaiva Vo† ... 128 .. J 6
Valencia ... I 5
Valencia West*† ... 9,355 .. L 8
Valentine† ... 38 .. E 4
Valle† ... 832 .. D 6
Valley Farms ... J 7
Vamori ... L 6
Vaya Chin ... K 6
Vernon† ... 122 .. G 10
Vicksburg† ... 597 .. H 3
Wahak Hotrontk† ... 114 .. K 6
Walker ... G 6
Washington Camp ... M 9
Webb ... L 10
Wellton ... 2,882 .. J 3
Wenden† ... 728 .. H 4
West Yuma ... J 1
Whetstone*† ... 2,617 .. M 9
Whiteriver† ... 4,104 .. H 10
Why† ... 167 .. K 5
Wickenburg ... 6,363 .. H 5
Wide Ruins† ... 176 .. E 11
Wikieup† ... 133 .. F 3
Willcox ... 3,757 .. K 10
Williams ... 3,023 .. E 6
Willow Valley*† ... 1,062 .. E 2
Window Rock† ... 2,712 .. D 11
Winkelman ... 353 .. J 8
Winona ... E 7
Winslow ... 9,655 .. F 8
Witch Well ... F 11
Wittmann† ... 763 .. H 5
Yampai ... D 4
Yarnell† ... 649 .. G 5
Yavapai Indian Reservation ... F 5
Youngtown ... 6,156 .. H 6
Yucca† ... 126 .. F 3
Yuma° ... 93,064 .. J 2
Zuni Indian Reservation ... F 11

*Does not appear on map; key shows general location.
†Census designated place—unincorporated, but recognized as a significant settled community by the U.S. Census Bureau.
°County seat.
Places without population figures are unincorporated areas.
Source: 2010 census. Metropolitan area figures are based on the 2013 Office of Management and Budget reorganization of 2010 census data.

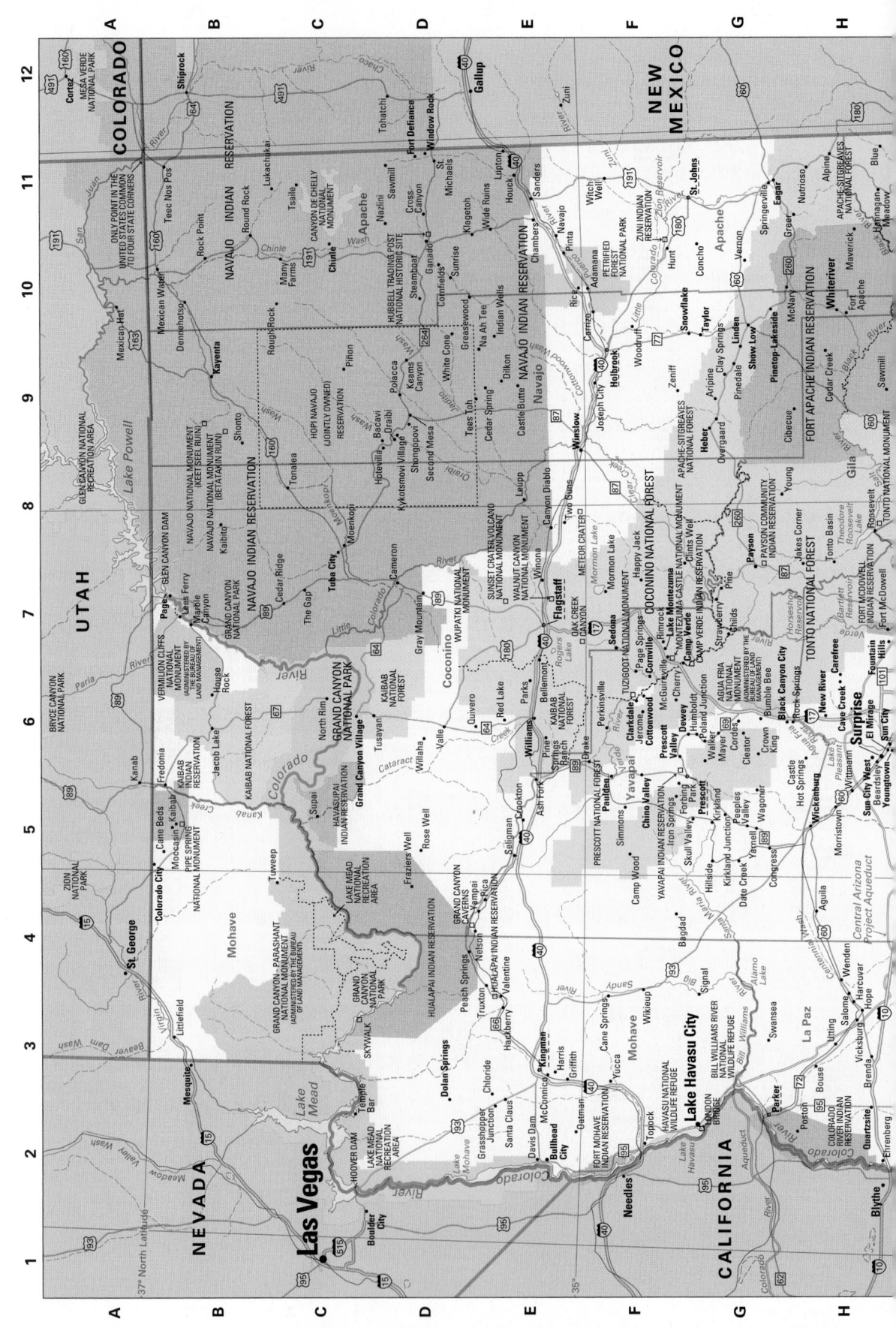

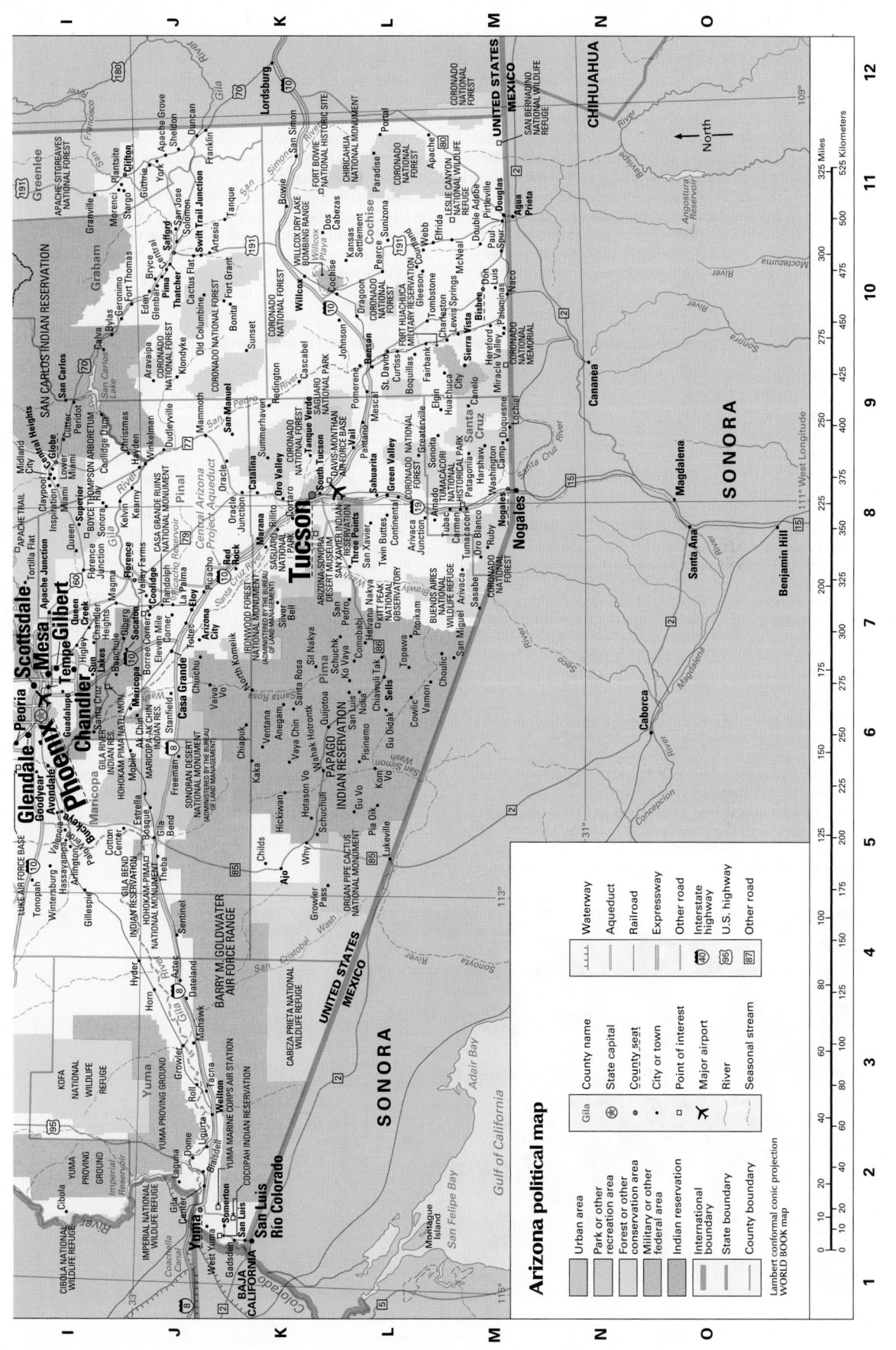

Arizona political map

	Urban area
	Park or other recreation area
	Forest or other conservation area
	Military or other federal area
	Indian reservation

	International boundary
	State boundary
	County boundary

Gila	County name
✹	State capital
○	County seat
□	City or town
✈	Point of interest
✈	Major airport
〰	River
	Seasonal stream

	Waterway
	Aqueduct
	Railroad
	Expressway
	Other road
40	Interstate highway
95	U.S. highway
87	Other road

Lambert conformal conic projection
WORLD BOOK map

Visitor's guide

Arizona attracts visitors throughout the year. But its winter season has become nationally famous. Thousands of vacationers flock to the sunny desert playgrounds when other parts of the country are cold. At the same time, ski resorts in the mountains of northern Arizona lure winter sports lovers. Dude ranches, historic sites, and magnificent scenery draw other travelers to the state. The outstanding scenic feature is the world-famous Grand Canyon, one of the natural wonders of the world. This giant gorge, 277 miles (446 kilometers) long and 1 mile (1.6 kilometers) deep, cuts through the rock of northwestern Arizona. Every year, millions of visitors gaze at its splendor. The Petrified Forest in northeastern Arizona is made up of ancient logs that were buried in mud, sand, or volcanic ash years ago and have turned to stone. Grand Canyon National Park and Petrified Forest National Park are among Arizona's many national parklands.

Arizona's popular annual events include rodeos, county fairs, and Indian ceremonials. These events are held throughout the year. On May 5, Arizona communities celebrate *Cinco de Mayo.* This Mexican holiday honors the victory of a Mexican army over an invading French force at Puebla, Mexico, in 1862.

Places to visit

Following are brief descriptions of some of Arizona's many interesting places to visit.

Apache Trail, a scenic mountain highway, passes American Indian ruins in the rugged Tonto National Forest.

Arizona-Sonora Desert Museum, west of Tucson, features a zoo, natural history museum, and botanical garden.

Canyon de Chelly National Monument, in Chinle, features colorful, steep-walled canyons that house the ancient ruins of Indian villages, including White House and Standing Rock.

Kitt Peak National Observatory, southwest of Tucson on the Tohono O'odham Indian reservation, has telescopes mounted on the 6,875-foot (2,096-meter) peak.

London Bridge, at Lake Havasu City, is a stone bridge first built in London in the early 1800's. The bridge opened at Lake Havasu City in 1971 after its stones were disassembled, shipped to the United States, and reassembled in their original form.

Meteor Crater, in Coconino County, is a large hole that measures 4,180 feet (1,275 meters) wide and 570 feet (175 meters) deep. The crater was created when a huge object from space struck the earth. Fragments of meteorite material have been found nearby. See **Meteor** (picture).

Monument Valley Navajo Tribal Park is on the Navajo Indian reservation in northeastern Arizona. The tribal council has a tourist center there.

Oak Creek Canyon, near Sedona, has red-rock formations that some people consider second in beauty and coloring only to those of the Grand Canyon.

Painted Desert, with colorful rock and sand, extends about 200 miles (320 kilometers) along the Little Colorado River in northern Arizona.

San Xavier del Bac Mission, near Tucson, is the best preserved of Arizona's early missions. It features numerous beautiful and unusual carvings and paintings.

Tombstone, a famous Western boom town, is in Cochise County. Many tourists visit the area, where Wyatt Earp won fame as a gunfighter.

National parklands are among Arizona's chief attractions. Grand Canyon National Park is a famous scenic wonder. The state's other national parks are Petrified Forest, site of the world's greatest concentration of petrified wood, and Saguaro, noted for giant cactuses. Arizona has six national forests. Coconino, Kaibab, Prescott, and Tonto lie completely in Arizona. Apache-Sitgreaves and Coronado lie partly in New Mexico. Some national forest areas are national wildernesses. Arizona's many national monuments include Agua Fria, Canyon de Chelly, Casa Grande Ruins, Chiricahua, Hohokam Pima, Montezuma Castle, Navajo, Organ Pipe Cactus, Parashant, Pipe Spring, Sunset Crater Volcano, Tonto, Tuzigoot, Walnut Canyon, and Wupatki. Other parklands in the state include Coronado National Memorial, Fort Bowie National Historic Site, Hubbell Trading Post National Historic Site, and Tumacácori National Historical Park. Glen Canyon National Recreation Area lies partly in Arizona and partly in Utah. Lake Mead National Recreation Area lies partly in Arizona and partly in Nevada.

State parks. Arizona has a number of state parks. For more information, visit the official website of Arizona State Parks at https://azstateparks.com.

Eddie Goldbaum Rios, Metropolitan Tucson Convention & Visitors Bureau

La Fiesta de los Vaqueros rodeo in Tucson

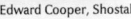

World-famous Grand Canyon National Park

Edward Cooper, Shostal

William D. McKinney, Shostal

San Xavier del Bac Mission near Tucson

Navajo Nation Fair Office

Navajo Tribal Fair parade in Window Rock

Land and climate

David A. Barnes, Stock Market

Monument Valley in Arizona's Colorado Plateau has beautiful rock formations. The Colorado Plateau, in northern Arizona, also includes the Grand Canyon and the Painted Desert.

Land regions. Arizona has three main land regions: (1) the Colorado Plateau, (2) the Transition Zone, and (3) the Basin and Range Region.

The Colorado Plateau, in northern Arizona, covers about two-fifths of the state. The region consists of a series of plateaus with fairly level surfaces. This pattern is broken here and there by a few mountains and canyons. Humphreys Peak, the highest mountain in the state, rises 12,633 feet (3,851 meters) near Flagstaff. The deepest canyon is the famous Grand Canyon on the Colorado River. Tributaries of the Colorado have cut other beautiful canyons into the flatland. These include Canyon de Chelly and Oak Creek Canyon.

Many of the mountains are forested, but the region also has dry deserts with little vegetation. Along the Arizona-Utah border in the northeast, strange and beautiful rock formations rise from the floor of a broad valley. They gave the valley the name Monument Valley. The colorful Painted Desert and the Petrified Forest are two well-known parts of the region. The series of level plateaus that makes up the region ends in the Mogollon

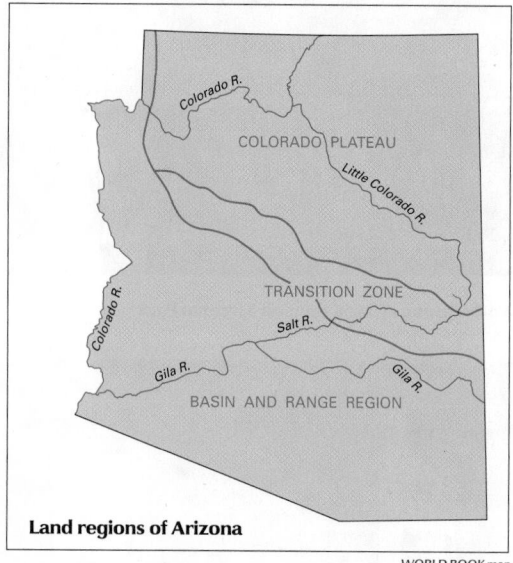

Land regions of Arizona

WORLD BOOK map

Map index

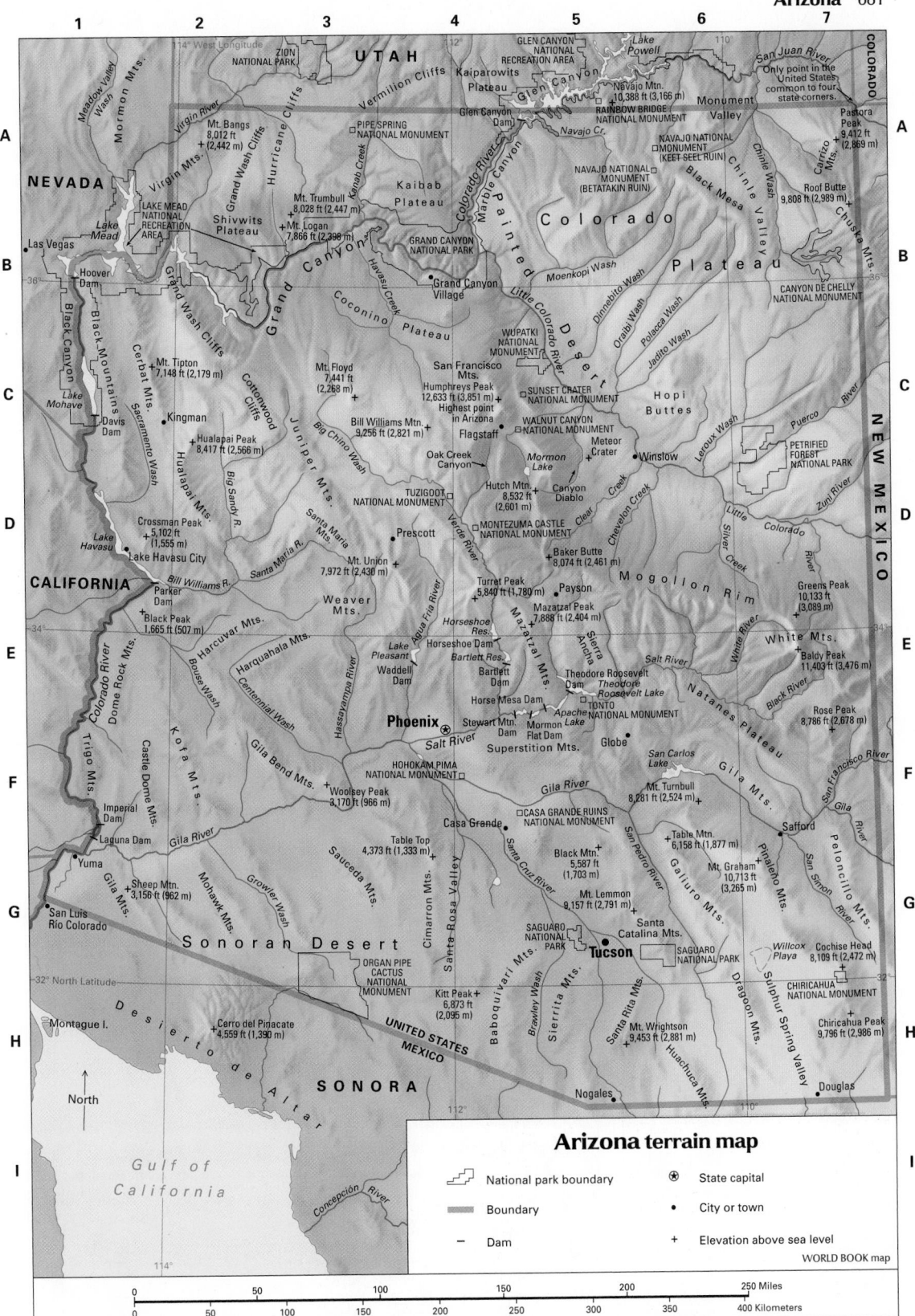

Arizona terrain map

National park boundary   State capital

Boundary   City or town

Dam   + Elevation above sea level

WORLD BOOK map

Rim on the south. The Mogollon Rim is a steep rock wall almost 2,000 feet (610 meters) high. It extends from central Arizona to the Mogollon Mountains in southwestern New Mexico. The principal industries of Arizona's Colorado Plateau are livestock raising, lumbering, and tourism.

The Transition Zone is a narrow strip of land that lies just south of the Colorado Plateau. This region has a number of mountain ranges. The ranges are close together in an area of rugged peaks and narrow valleys. This rough country in Arizona includes the Mazatzal, Santa Maria, Sierra Ancha, and White mountain ranges.

The Basin and Range Region includes most of the southern part of the state and a narrow strip in the west. Mountain ranges run through the Basin and Range Region from northwest to southeast. The most important mountain ranges are the Chiricahua, Gila, Huachuca, Hualapai, Pinaleño, Santa Catalina, Santa Rita, and Superstition ranges. The mountain valleys are broad and fertile. This part of the Basin and Range Region produces excellent crops when the soil is irrigated. The state's largest cities developed in this area.

In the extreme west and south of the Basin and Range Region, the mountains are low and barren. Broad desert basins lie between the ranges. This area of the state gets little rain, and it has almost no vegetation. Along the western border of Arizona, water from the Colorado River is used to irrigate the dry land. The irrigated land produces excellent crops.

Rivers, waterfalls, and lakes. Arizona's most important river is the Colorado. In Arizona, the river is 688 miles (1,107 kilometers) long. It enters the state from Utah almost in the middle of the northern border. Then it winds west through the Grand Canyon and turns south. The river forms almost the entire western boundary of Arizona.

The Colorado and its tributaries drain most of the state. Before 1935, the muddy Colorado carried about a million tons of rich soil to the Gulf of California every day. Irrigation and power dams on the great river and its branches have helped control the flow, and the river is much clearer today.

Few small streams in Arizona flow all year. Some mountain creeks have a steady flow, but most streams often seem dry. Rushing water fills the riverbeds of the Bill Williams, Little Colorado, San Pedro, and Santa Cruz rivers after a rain. At other times, these rivers appear to be dry. However, water always flows beneath their sandy beds. Many mountain streams tumble down cliffs and canyon walls in waterfalls and cascades. The best-known falls include Beaver, Bridal Veil, Havasu, Mooney, and Navajo. All of these falls are on Havasu Creek in the Supai Canyon area of the Grand Canyon.

Average monthly weather

	Phoenix						Yuma				
	Temperatures °F		Temperatures °C		Days of rain or snow		Temperatures °F		Temperatures °C		Days of rain or snow
	High	Low	High	Low			High	Low	High	Low	
Jan.	67	46	19	8	3	Jan.	69	43	21	6	3
Feb.	71	49	22	9	4	Feb.	72	45	22	7	2
Mar.	77	54	25	12	3	Mar.	78	48	26	9	2
Apr.	85	60	29	16	1	Apr.	85	55	29	13	1
May	95	69	35	21	0	May	94	62	34	17	0
June	104	78	40	26	0	June	103	70	39	21	0
July	106	84	41	29	4	July	106	79	41	26	1
Aug.	104	83	40	28	4	Aug.	105	79	41	26	2
Sept.	100	77	38	25	2	Sept.	100	72	38	22	1
Oct.	89	65	32	18	2	Oct.	89	59	32	15	1
Nov.	76	53	24	12	2	Nov.	76	48	24	9	1
Dec.	66	45	19	7	3	Dec.	67	41	19	5	2

Average January temperatures

In winter, southern Arizona has a mild climate. Mountain areas of central and northern Arizona are much colder.

Average July temperatures

In summer, Arizona's southern deserts have extremely hot, dry weather. Higher elevations are considerably cooler.

Average yearly precipitation

Little rain falls in desert areas. The mountains receive much heavier rainfall. Snow is abundant in some mountain areas.

WORLD BOOK maps

Degrees Fahrenheit	Degrees Celsius
Above 48	Above 9
40 to 48	4 to 9
32 to 40	0 to 4
Below 32	Below 0

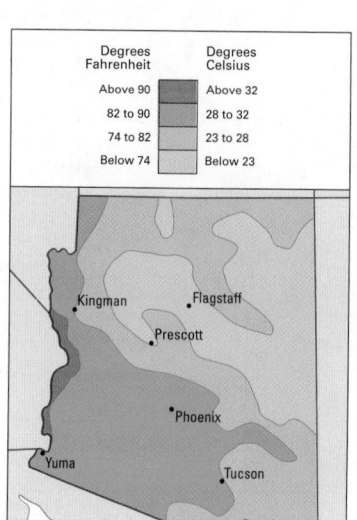

Degrees Fahrenheit	Degrees Celsius
Above 90	Above 32
82 to 90	28 to 32
74 to 82	23 to 28
Below 74	Below 23

Inches	Centimeters
More than 16	More than 41
12 to 16	30 to 41
8 to 12	20 to 30
Less than 8	Less than 20

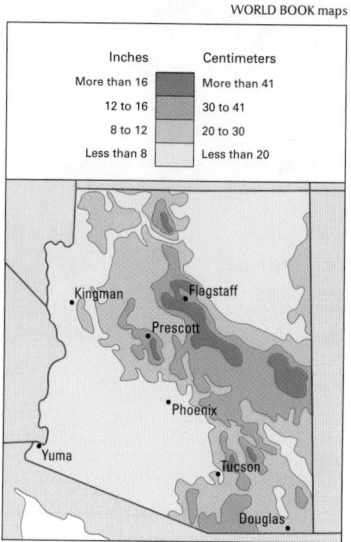

Saguaro National Park in southern Arizona's Basin and Range Region is named for its giant saguaro cactuses. Many kinds of cactuses thrive in the broad desert areas of the region.

Several small natural lakes lie in the mountain areas of the state, but all the largest lakes are artificially created. Many artificial lakes have been made by damming streams for irrigation and for water conservation. The largest of these lakes include Theodore Roosevelt Lake and San Carlos Lake. Lake Mead, behind Hoover Dam, lies partly in Nevada. Part of Lake Havasu, formed by Parker Dam, is in California. Lake Powell, which was created by Glen Canyon Dam, lies partly in Arizona and partly in Utah.

Plant and animal life. Forests cover more than one-fourth of Arizona's land. The mountain regions of the state have the largest area of ponderosa pine in the United States. Other trees in the state include aspen, blue spruce, cottonwood, Douglas-fir, juniper, piñon, walnut, and white fir.

Arizona is famous for its cactus plants. The sharp-spined cholla cactus is common in the hot desert areas. Creosote bushes and prickly pear cactuses also grow in the desert. The organ-pipe cactus is found in desert areas near sea level. The saguaro, which is common in southern Arizona, grows larger than any other cactus in the United States. The saguaro blossom is the state flower.

Other unusual plants that grow in Arizona include the night-blooming cereus and several varieties of the yucca plant. Arizona wildflowers include the geranium, golden columbine, paintbrush, phlox, pink, poppy, and sand verbena.

Animal life in Arizona includes large numbers of mule deer and white-tailed deer. Other big-game animals include black bears, elk, bighorn sheep, and pronghorns.

Several members of the cat family, including bobcats and mountain lions, prowl in the forested areas. Jaguars are occasionally sighted in southern Arizona.

Other Arizona animals include badgers, beavers, foxes, raccoons, skunks, squirrels, and weasels. The state is also home to the collared peccary or javelina, an animal distantly related to the wild hog.

Arizona has more than 40 kinds of lizards, including the poisonous Gila monster. Rattlesnakes live in most parts of the state, and the rare, poisonous coral snake is found in the desert. The state's hotter areas have scorpions and tarantulas.

Arizona's game birds include doves, grouse, quail, wild turkeys, and various waterfowl. Trout swim in the Colorado River and in the mountain streams. Other fishes include bass, bluegills, and crappies.

Climate. Temperatures vary greatly in Arizona. Mountain areas often have winter temperatures below 0 °F (–18 °C). The southern deserts may not have freezing weather for years. The dry air in the deserts makes cold or heat seem more comfortable there than in humid regions.

The state's highest temperature, 128 °F (53 °C), was recorded at Lake Havasu City on June 29, 1994. Hawley Lake, near McNary, had the record low, –40 °F (–40 °C), on Jan. 7, 1971. In Phoenix, temperatures average about 95 °F (35 °C) in July and about 56 °F (13 °C) in January.

Precipitation varies greatly throughout the state. The deserts of the southwest get only 2 to 5 inches (5 to 13 centimeters) of moisture a year. Arizona's high mountain areas may receive as much as 30 inches (76 centimeters) a year.

Service industries provide the vast majority of jobs for residents of this rapidly growing state. Many service industries benefit from spending by tourists and by retired people who live in the state all or part of the year.

Arizona's manufacturing is based on high-technology products, such as computer components and aerospace vehicles. Agriculture and mining are also important in Arizona. The state has many cattle ranches and is the nation's leading copper producer.

Natural resources. Arizona's leading natural resources are its warm climate and its mineral deposits.

Water is a scarce resource in Arizona. Expanding urban areas require more water. Farmers must bring water to their land to make crops grow. A system of canals supplies the water. The canals follow ancient canals built by the Hohokam Indians hundreds of years before Europeans came to the area. The water comes from mountain reservoirs fed by winter snow and spring rain. But Arizona uses more water than it can get from its streams and storage reservoirs. The state's underground water supply is being used up faster than nature can replace it.

In 1968, the United States Congress approved funding for the Central Arizona Project, a system of canals, tunnels, and pipelines. The system, completed in 1991, provides for pumping large quantities of water from the Colorado River to the Phoenix and Tucson areas for agricultural and other purposes. Arizona has also put in place a statewide water management and water reclamation program to meet current water needs while replenishing the state's supply of underground water.

Minerals. Arizona's mountains and plains contain large deposits of minerals and other materials, the most valuable of which is copper. Sand and gravel come from almost all of the counties in the state. Molybdenum, which is used in hardening steel, is also present. Other mined products in Arizona include coal, gemstones, gold, lime, perlite, pumice, silver, and stone.

Soil. Only about an eighth of Arizona's soil is suitable for farming because of the limited amount of water available for irrigation. Soils of the plateau region in northern and eastern Arizona are thin and gray. The mountain soils also are thin and are brown or gray. The lowlands of southwestern Arizona have red soils. In some parts of this region, the soil lies over another layer of soil called *caliche.* This concretelike soil may be so hard that power tools may be needed to dig holes.

Service industries account for the majority of both Arizona's employment and its *gross domestic product*— the total value of goods and services produced in a year. Most of the service industries are concentrated in the Phoenix and Tucson areas.

Phoenix, the state capital, is the center of government activities. Several financial institutions are in Phoenix and its surrounding area. The majority of hotels, restaurants, and retail trade establishments are in the Phoenix and Tucson areas. Hotels and restaurants especially benefit from the tens of millions of tourists who visit Arizona each year.

The state's rapidly growing population has created a strong demand for new housing. Since the early 1990's, many office buildings and resorts have opened. The operation of military bases and American Indian reservations are important government services in Arizona. Military bases include Davis-Monthan Air Force Base, Fort Huachuca, Luke Air Force Base, and the Yuma Proving Ground. The state has several large Indian reservations. The Navajo reservation, the nation's largest reservation, covers most of northeastern Arizona.

Manufacturing. Arizona's leading manufactured products are computer and electronic products and transportation equipment. Factories in the Phoenix area produce most of the electronic products. Electronic products include search, detection, and navigation instruments, and semiconductors. Both the Phoenix and Tucson areas turn out large amounts of transportation equipment. Most of the transportation equipment is aerospace products, including aircraft and aircraft parts, guided missiles, helicopters, and space vehicles.

Other manufactured products include chemicals, fabricated metal products, nonmetallic minerals, and processed foods. All of these products are primarily manufactured in the Phoenix and Tucson areas. Cleaning products and *pharmaceuticals* (medicinal drugs) are the leading chemical products. Important fabricated metal products include structural metals, including sheet metal and frames for windows and doors. Concrete is the leading nonmetallic mineral product. Food products include baked goods and dairy products.

Agriculture. Farmland covers more than a third of the state. All of Arizona's 15 counties have some irrigated land.

Crops account for over half of Arizona's total farm income, even though less than 5 percent of its land is used for growing crops. Lettuce is the most valuable crop. Most lettuce is produced in Yuma County. Cotton and hay are also valuable crops. Cotton and hay production are concentrated in southern Arizona, especially in Maricopa and Pinal counties. Arizona ranks as a leading producer of citrus fruits, melons, and vegetables.

Livestock accounts for less than half of Arizona's farm income. Beef and dairy cattle are among the leading sources of farm income in the state. Ranchers raise beef cattle in many parts of the state. Most of the state's dairy cows are in Maricopa and Pinal counties. Angora goats, hogs, and sheep are also raised in Arizona.

Mining. Copper provides most of Arizona's mining income, and Arizona is the leading copper-producing

© Bloomberg/Getty Images

Construction workers assemble a building west of Phoenix. The construction of new homes and businesses is an important part of Arizona's economy.

Arizona economy

General economy

Gross domestic product (GDP)* (2017) $326,446,000,000
  Rank among U.S. states 20th
Unemployment rate (2018) 4.7% (U.S. avg: 3.9%)

*Gross domestic product is the total value of goods and services produced in a year.
Sources: U.S. Bureau of Economic Analysis and U.S. Bureau of Labor Statistics.

Agriculture

Cash receipts $4,741,177,000
  Rank among U.S. states 29th
Distribution 63% crops, 37% livestock
Farms 19,100
Farm acres (hectares) 26,100,000 (10,560,000)
  Rank among U.S. states 14th
Farmland 36% of Arizona

Leading products

1. Lettuce (ranks 2nd in U.S.)
2. Dairy products
3. Cattle and calves
Other products: broccoli, cantaloupe, cauliflower, cotton, dates, greenhouse and nursery products, hay, hogs, lemons, pecans, spinach, watermelons, wheat.

Manufacturing

Value added by manufacture* $29,122,054,000
  Rank among U.S. states 27th

Leading products

1. Transportation equipment
2. Computer and electronic products
3. Food and beverage products
4. Fabricated metal products
5. Medical equipment
Other products: chemicals, machinery, nonmetallic minerals, plastics and rubber products.

*Value added by manufacture is the increase in value of raw materials as they become finished products.

Mining

Nonfuel mineral production (2015) $6,470,000,000
  Rank among U.S. states 2nd
Coal (tons*) 6,221,000
  Rank among U.S. states 16th
Crude oil (barrels†) 13,000
  Rank among U.S. states 31st
Natural gas (cubic feet‡) 56,000,000
  Rank among U.S. states 31st

*One ton equals 0.9072 metric ton.
†One barrel equals 42 gallons (159 liters).
‡One cubic foot equals 0.0283 cubic meter.

Leading product

Copper (ranks 1st in U.S.)
Other products: gemstones, gold, granite, lime, limestone, molybdenum, perlite, portland cement, pumice, sand and gravel, silver.

Electric power

Nuclear 30.6%
Coal 29.7%
Natural gas 28.0%
Hydroelectric 6.5%
Solar 4.7%
Other 0.5%

Figures are for 2017, except for the manufacturing figures, which are for 2016.
Sources: U.S. Census Bureau, U.S. Department of Agriculture, U.S. Energy Information Administration, U.S. Geological Survey.

Production and workers by economic activities

Economic activities	Percent of GDP produced	Employed workers	
		Number of people	Percent of total
Finance, insurance, & real estate	24	484,800	13
Community, business, & personal services	23	1,286,800	35
Trade, restaurants, & hotels	17	791,300	22
Government	13	445,800	12
Manufacturing	8	175,200	5
Transportation & communication	6	185,300	5
Construction	4	191,400	5
Utilities	2	13,300	*
Agriculture	1	50,400	1
Mining	1	22,700	1
Total†	100	3,647,000	100

*Less than one-half of 1 percent.
†Figures do not add up to 100 percent, due to rounding.
Figures are for 2016; employment figures include full- and part-time workers.
Source: *World Book* estimates based on data from U.S. Bureau of Economic Analysis.

Map of Arizona's economy

This map shows the economic uses of land in Arizona and where the state's leading farm and mineral products are produced. Major manufacturing centers are shown in red.

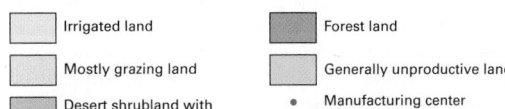

- Irrigated land
- Mostly grazing land
- Desert shrubland with grazing
- Forest land
- Generally unproductive land
- • Manufacturing center
- • Mineral deposit

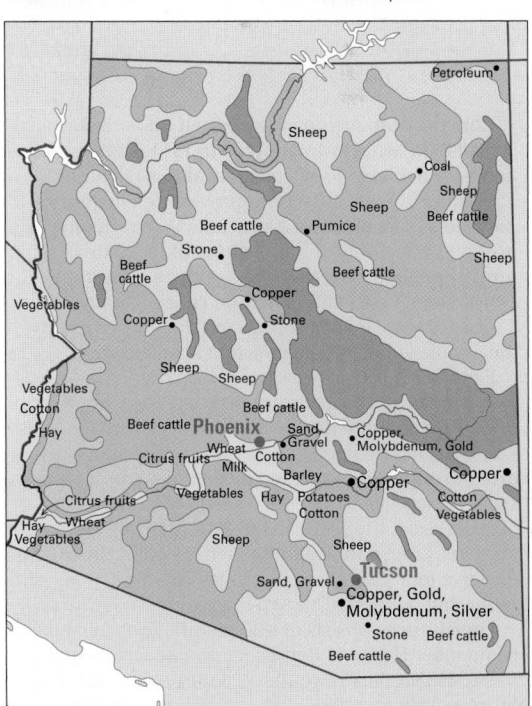

WORLD BOOK map

Glen Canyon Dam, on the Colorado River in northern Arizona, was completed in 1964. It helps regulate the river flow, and its huge generators produce hydroelectric power.

Manley Features from Shostal

state. Greenlee, Pima, and Pinal counties supply most of the copper. Gila and Yavapai counties also have major copper mines. Large amounts of gold, molybdenum, and silver are recovered as by-products of mining copper ore. Freeport-McMoRan Copper & Gold Inc., a major mining company, is headquartered in Phoenix.

Crushed stone, molybdenum, and sand and gravel are also important mined products in Arizona. Granite and limestone are the leading crushed-stone products.

Electric power and utilities. Nuclear plants and power plants that burn natural gas supply most of Arizona's electric power. Hydroelectric plants and solar installations produce most of the remaining power. Cheaper prices for natural gas and renewable energy sources led to the decline of coal power in Arizona in the 2010's.

Transportation. Arizona has an extensive system of roads and highways. Interstate 10 connects Tucson, Phoenix, and Los Angeles. Interstate 40 passes through Flagstaff. The part of Arizona north of the Colorado River is isolated from the rest of the state by the Grand Canyon. No roads cross the canyon.

Phoenix Sky Harbor International Airport is the state's busiest commercial airport. Tucson International Airport is also a major airport. In 1919, Tucson became the first U.S. city to have its own municipal airport.

Rail lines provide freight service, and passenger trains serve several cities in the state. The Southern Pacific (now part of the Union Pacific) became the first railroad to enter the region, reaching Yuma in 1877.

Communication. Arizona's first newspaper, the *Weekly Arizonian,* began publication in Tubac in 1859. Today, Arizona's leading newspapers include *The Arizona Republic* of Phoenix and the *Arizona Daily Star* of Tucson.

Government

Constitution. Arizona is governed under its original constitution, which was adopted in 1911. The Constitution has been *amended* (changed) about 150 times.

All amendments must be approved by a majority of the voters in an election. Amendments may be proposed by a majority of both houses of the State Legislature, by petition from the voters, or by a constitutional convention. A convention may be called if approved by a majority vote of both houses and then by a majority of the people voting on the question in an election.

Executive. The governor of Arizona is elected to a four-year term. The governor may serve any number of terms, but no more than two terms in a row.

Arizona has no lieutenant governor. A governor who dies or resigns is succeeded by one of the other four state officials elected by the voters. These are, in order of succession, the secretary of state, attorney general, state treasurer, and superintendent of public instruction. All serve four-year terms. They may serve any number of terms, but no more than two in a row.

Legislature consists of a 30-member Senate and a 60-member House of Representatives. Each of Arizona's 30 legislative districts elects one senator and two representatives to two-year terms. These officials may serve any number of terms, but no more than four in a row. The Legislature meets each year starting on the second Monday in January. Rules have been adopted to end the sessions no later than the Saturday after the 100th day. But the president of the Senate and the speaker of the House may extend a session for no longer than seven days. After that, the session can be extended only by a majority vote of the Legislature. The governor may call a special session, which has no time limit.

Courts. Arizona's highest court is the state Supreme Court. Its seven justices are appointed to six-year terms by the governor from a list of candidates submitted by a judicial nominating commission. At the end of each justice's term, the judge runs unopposed as a nonpartisan candidate, and the voters decide whether the judge should be retained. The justices elect one of their members as chief justice for a five-year term.

A state Court of Appeals was created in 1964. This court has two divisions, one centered in Phoenix and the other in Tucson. The Phoenix division has 16 judges, and the Tucson division has 6 judges. These judges serve six-year terms and are selected and retained in the same way as are Arizona Supreme Court justices. Superior Courts in each county handle most major criminal and civil cases. Superior Court judges in Maricopa and Pima counties are appointed by the governor to four-year terms. In other counties, Superior Court judges are elected to four-year terms. After that, voters decide whether they are retained. Justice-of-the-peace courts and municipal courts deal with less important cases.

Local government in Arizona is carried on through 15 counties and about 90 incorporated cities and towns. Counties are governed by a three- or five-member board of supervisors. Supervisors are elected to four-year terms. Counties have either a county-manager or an administrator who conducts the daily business of the county and is guided by the board of supervisors.

Communities with more than 1,500 people may vote to incorporate their community as a town. Cities must have at least 3,000 people. Depending on their size, towns are governed by councils of five or seven members. A council elects one of its members as mayor. Some Arizona cities also use this same system. But a city may adopt a *home rule* charter, which allows it to change the form of its government. Many cities, including most of the largest ones, have city managers.

Revenue. Taxes provide about two-fifths of the Arizona state government's *general revenue* (income). Four taxes produce almost all the tax money. These taxes are (1) a sales tax, (2) income taxes on corporations and individuals, (3) a tax on motor fuels, and (4) property taxes. Federal grants and federal and local government programs also provide much of the general revenue. Most of the rest of the state government's revenue comes from taxes on licenses and tobacco.

Politics. For many years, Democrats controlled Arizona politics, particularly on the local level. In the second half of the 1900's, however, Republicans won the sup-

The governors of Arizona

	Party	Term
George W. P. Hunt	Democratic	1912-1917
Thomas E. Campbell	Republican	1917
George W. P. Hunt	Democratic	1917-1919
Thomas E. Campbell	Republican	1919-1923
George W. P. Hunt	Democratic	1923-1929
John C. Phillips	Republican	1929-1931
George W. P. Hunt	Democratic	1931-1933
Benjamin B. Moeur	Democratic	1933-1937
Rawghlie C. Stanford	Democratic	1937-1939
Robert T. Jones	Democratic	1939-1941
Sidney P. Osborn	Democratic	1941-1948
Dan E. Garvey	Democratic	1948-1951
J. Howard Pyle	Republican	1951-1955
Ernest W. McFarland	Democratic	1955-1959
Paul Fannin	Republican	1959-1965
Samuel P. Goddard, Jr.	Democratic	1965-1967
John R. Williams	Republican	1967-1975
Raul H. Castro	Democratic	1975-1977
Wesley Bolin	Democratic	1977-1978
Bruce E. Babbitt	Democratic	1978-1987
Evan Mecham	Republican	1987-1988
Rose Mofford	Democratic	1988-1991
Fife Symington	Republican	1991-1997
Jane Dee Hull	Republican	1997-2003
Janet Napolitano	Democratic	2003-2009
Jan Brewer	Republican	2009-2015
Doug Ducey	Republican	2015-

© Shutterstock

Arizona's State Capitol building is in Phoenix. The building housed the state Legislature until 1960. Today, it is the site of the Arizona Capitol Museum.

port of many voters in Arizona's rapidly growing cities. Among the Republican leaders who helped make Arizona a two-party state was U.S. Senator Barry M. Goldwater, the Republican candidate for president in 1964.

Maricopa County, which includes Phoenix, Mesa, and several large suburbs, has a majority of the state's voters. As a result, that county is extremely important in elections. The state's largest city, Phoenix, has leaned Democratic since the late 1900's. Democratic support is also strong in Apache and Pima counties. Republican strength is greater in rural areas and small towns.

In presidential elections, Arizona has voted for Republican candidates about two-thirds of the time, including most of the presidential elections since 1952. For Arizona's electoral votes and voting record in presidential elections, see **Electoral College** (table).

History

Early days. Indians have lived in Arizona for at least 12,000 years. Over the centuries, many of them built large settlements and developed civilizations known as the Ancestral Pueblo (once called the Anasazi); Hohokam; and Mogollon. The Ancestral Pueblo, who lived in the north, were the ancestors of the present-day Pueblo Indians. The Hohokam, who settled in the Gila and Salt river valleys, constructed the largest irrigation systems in North America before Europeans arrived. Their descendants are the Pima Indians and the Tohono O'odham, also known as the Papago Indians. The Mogollon lived in what are now eastern Arizona and western New Mexico. Apache and Navajo Indians moved into the Arizona area shortly before the Spaniards arrived.

Spanish exploration. During the 1530's, stories reached the Spaniards in Mexico telling about the great wealth of the Seven Cities of Cíbola. Spanish authorities sent a small group headed by Franciscan priest Marcos de Niza to find the cities. Niza, in 1539, became the first European known to enter the Arizona region. He reported seeing one of the seven cities from a distance. In 1540, a much larger expedition led by explorer Francisco Vásquez de Coronado traveled to Zuni pueblos and other Pueblo Indian settlements in what is now northern New Mexico. Lieutenants of Coronado visited Hopi pueblos and the Grand Canyon in what is now northern Arizona. The expedition found neither gold nor silver and returned to Mexico disappointed.

Spanish settlement of Arizona began in 1629, when Franciscan priests established missions among the Hopi. In 1680, however, the Hopi killed their missionaries and threw off Spanish rule. In the late 1600's and early 1700's, Jesuit missionary Eusebio Kino founded a number of missions among the O'odham Indians in what are now northern Mexico and southern Arizona.

Because Spanish and mission Indian settlements had cattle, horses, sheep, and goats, they became targets of raids by Apache Indians. The threat of Apache attacks limited permanent Spanish settlement to the Santa Cruz river valley. There, in 1752, Spanish troops established the state's first white settlement, a military post at Tubac. During 1775 and 1776, the soldiers moved to Tucson. They built a fort there with high, thick adobe walls to protect themselves and the settlers from Apache attacks.

Mexico won its independence from Spain in 1821, and the land that is now Arizona became part of the new country. In 1846, the United States went to war with Mexico. U.S. forces took control of the region. Under the terms of the Treaty of Guadalupe Hidalgo, which ended the war in 1848, the United States took possession of

Lauren Freudmann, Woodfin Camp, Inc.

Ancient rock carvings offer evidence of Arizona's early Indian inhabitants. The carvings shown here, on Newspaper Rock in Petrified Forest National Park, have never been translated.

Historic Arizona

Oraibi is one of the oldest continuously inhabited settlements in the United States. It was built by Hopi Indians in northeastern Arizona during the 1100's.

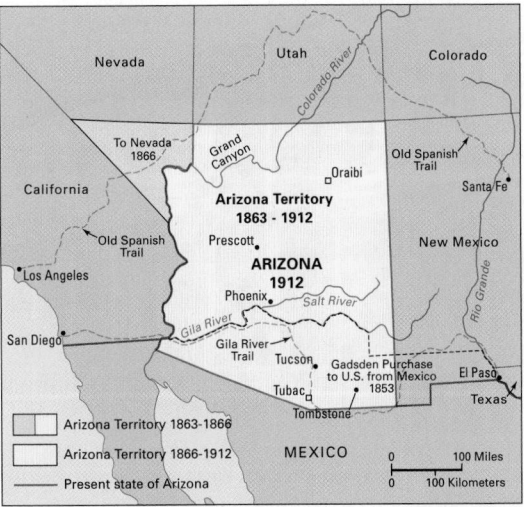

WORLD BOOK map

Arizona was home to a number of Indian groups before the Spanish first arrived in the 1500's. The area became part of the Arizona Territory in 1863. Arizona became a U.S. state in 1912.

Hoover Dam, completed in 1936, provides water for generating power and irrigating land. Lake Mead, the dam's reservoir, is one of the world's largest artificially created bodies of water. Arizona's other large dams include Coolidge, Glen Canyon, Parker, and Roosevelt.

Important dates in Arizona

WORLD BOOK illustrations by Richard Bonson, The Art Agency

c. 10,000 B.C. The first American Indians came to the Arizona area. In the centuries that followed, the Ancestral Pueblo (once called the Anasazi), Hohokam, and Mogollon built civilizations there.

1539 Marcos de Niza, a Franciscan priest, entered what is now Arizona.

1540 Francisco Coronado led a Spanish expedition into the region.

1776 Tucson was established as a military outpost.

1821 Arizona became part of Mexico.

1848 Following the Mexican War (1846-1848), Mexico ceded to the United States most of what is now Arizona.

1853 The United States and Mexico signed the Gadsden Purchase, which added territory to Arizona.

1863 Congress created the Arizona Territory.

1912 Arizona became the 48th state on February 14.

1936 Hoover Dam was completed.

1948 Arizona Indians received the right to vote.

1974 Construction began on the Central Arizona Project to provide water from the Colorado River to the state's needy areas. The project was completed in 1991.

1975 Raul H. Castro became the first Mexican American governor of Arizona.

1981 Arizona Judge Sandra Day O'Connor became the first woman appointed to the U.S. Supreme Court.

1988 Governor Evan Mecham was removed from office. He was replaced by Secretary of State Rose Mofford, the first woman to serve as Arizona's governor.

1980's-1990's Drawn by a warm, dry climate and a strong economy, newcomers to Arizona helped make the state one of the fastest-growing areas in the United States.

1997 Arizona Governor Fife Symington resigned.

1998 Jane Dee Hull, who had replaced Symington, was elected to a full term. She became the first woman to be elected governor of Arizona.

Arizona Historical Society Library

Tombstone, shown above in 1882, sprang up because of a silver-mining boom nearby. Gold and silver discoveries brought many people to the Arizona Territory. Lawlessness was widespread in Tombstone. The famous gunfight at the O.K. Corral took place there in 1881.

New Mexico. At that time, New Mexico included Arizona as far south as the Gila River. Many Easterners opposed the treaty because they feared that slavery would be established in the newly acquired land. But the U.S. Senate approved the treaty.

In 1853, the United States and Mexico signed the Gadsden Purchase. Through this treaty, the United States acquired the region south of the Gila River that forms the present boundary between the United States and Mexico.

Territorial days. The American Civil War (1861-1865) brought great political changes to Arizona. In the 1850's, the settlers had asked Congress to create an Arizona Territory, but their requests were ignored. After the Confederacy was formed, many Arizona settlers wanted to join it because they had come from the South. They chose a delegate to the Confederate Congress.

In 1862, the Confederacy sent troops to occupy the New Mexico and Arizona areas. Union forces defeated the Southerners. In 1863, the Confederate government created the Confederate Territory of Arizona. The action had little meaning because of the earlier military defeat.

The Confederate activity led to action by the United States. Congress created the Arizona Territory with boundaries about the same as those of the present state. On Dec. 27, 1863, John N. Goodwin officially took control of the area as territorial governor. Goodwin established his headquarters at Fort Whipple. A log house was built for him not far from the fort. The town of Prescott grew up around this house.

Indian fighting. Arizona's few settlers lived in fear of hostile Indians. The Navajo were defeated in 1864 in a campaign led by the famous scout Kit Carson. But the Apache continued to fight. Small bands of warriors

made hundreds of raids on lonely ranches and outposts throughout the Southwest. Under such leaders as Cochise and Geronimo, the Apache even attacked forts and towns. The last raiding party under Geronimo finally surrendered on Sept. 4, 1886.

Territorial progress. In spite of almost constant Indian fighting, Arizona made great progress. Gold and silver discoveries brought many miners to the territory. As early as 1867, farmers in the Salt River Valley near present-day Phoenix began irrigating their fields. Ranching became a large-scale business during the 1880's. The rich copper mines of Arizona became highly developed in the 1880's and 1890's. The Southern Pacific Railroad entered Arizona from California on Sept. 30, 1877.

Statehood. In 1910, Congress permitted Arizona to draw up a Constitution and apply for statehood. But President William Howard Taft vetoed the bill because the proposed state constitution would have permitted the voters to remove judges from office by a process known as *recall* (see **Recall**). This clause was taken out of the Constitution, and statehood was approved. Arizona became the 48th state on Feb. 14, 1912. The people soon changed their Constitution to allow the recall of judges.

Progress as a state. George W. P. Hunt, a Democrat, greatly influenced Arizona's early history. He became the state's first governor and served seven terms. Hunt supported the development of dams and irrigation systems, and he worked for laws favorable to the ranching and mining industries.

Federal projects helped the new state in water development and tourism. The first big dam providing irrigation water was the Theodore Roosevelt Dam, completed in 1911 on the Salt River above Phoenix. More dams were built during the next 25 years. Coolidge Dam on the Gila River, Bartlett Dam on the Verde River, and three more dams on the Salt River added greatly to the state's irrigated area. The biggest dam, Hoover Dam on the Colorado River, was completed in 1935. The warm, dry climate attracted health seekers and winter visitors.

During World War I (1914-1918), cotton became an important crop. The amount of irrigated land expanded rapidly, and agricultural production increased. Farmers became reliant on water pumped from the ground. Arizona's copper production increased through the 1920's. The Great Depression of the 1930's forced workers in many parts of the nation to seek new jobs. Some of them settled in Arizona. Between 1920 and 1940, the population grew from 334,162 to 499,261.

The mid-1900's. During World War II (1939-1945), the government built many air bases in Arizona because the large number of sunny days provided ideal flying weather. The demand for Arizona's chief products—cattle, copper, and cotton—increased rapidly during the wartime boom. Phoenix doubled in size.

The boom continued into the 1950's. Thousands of veterans who had been stationed in Arizona returned with their families to live there. Air conditioning became widespread and made life pleasant in the desert region. As a result, many people, including large numbers of retired persons, moved to Arizona from the East. The state's population rose by about 50 percent during the 1940's and by about 74 percent in the 1950's.

In 1948, Arizona's Indians won the right to vote. The Arizona Supreme Court struck down parts of the state Constitution that had kept Indians from voting.

Arizona shifted from an agricultural to a manufacturing economy during the 1950's and 1960's. By 1967, the value of industrial production had reached $1 billion, compared with about $600 million for agricultural products. New factories produced a wide variety of electrical and electronic goods. Tourism became an even larger industry.

Growth in agriculture, manufacturing, and population during the 1940's and 1950's strained Arizona's water resources. By the 1960's, the state was pumping more water from its underground supply than it was getting from rainfall. In 1963, the Supreme Court of the United States gave Arizona rights to 2,800,000 acre-feet (3.5 billion cubic meters) of water a year from the Colorado River. One acre-foot (1,233 cubic meters) is equal to 1 acre (0.4 hectare) of water 1 foot (30 centimeters) deep and will supply about five city dwellers for one year.

In 1965, Judge Lorna Lockwood was elected chief justice of the Arizona Supreme Court. Her election by her fellow judges made her the first woman in the United States to head a state supreme court.

Arizona's Indians made economic gains during the 1960's. Several tribes started to operate business companies, factories, and industrial and recreational areas on their reservations. Navajo Community College, the first college ever built on an Indian reservation, opened at Many Farms, on the Navajo reservation in northeastern Arizona, in 1969. The college moved to Tsaile in 1973.

The late 1900's. In 1974, construction began on the Central Arizona Project, a system of canals, tunnels, and pipelines designed to ensure the state a sufficient supply of water. The project was completed in 1991. The system covers 336 miles (541 kilometers) and extends from Lake Havasu on the Colorado River to the San Xavier Indian Reservation southwest of Tucson.

In 1975, Raul H. Castro became governor. He was the first Mexican American to be elected to the office.

Museum of New Mexico

Geronimo and his band of Apache surrendered to U.S. troops at Skeleton Canyon in 1886. Geronimo was captured several times and placed on reservations, but he escaped and returned to fight again and again. Apache fought throughout the Southwest from the late 1600's until 1886.

President Ronald Reagan appointed Arizona Judge Sandra Day O'Connor to the U.S. Supreme Court in 1981. She became the first woman member of the court.

In the late 1900's, casino gambling became an important source of revenue for many Arizona Indian tribes, funding health, education, and housing programs on reservations. Tribes also used their allotments of Central Arizona Project water to create new agricultural projects or to sell to cities.

The state Legislature removed Governor Evan Mecham from office in 1988. He had been charged with illegally lending state money to his automobile dealership and trying to block an investigation into charges that one of his aides had made a death threat against a grand jury witness. The state House of Representatives impeached him. The Senate convicted Mecham on the charges, and he was removed from office. Secretary of State Rose Mofford finished his term, becoming the first woman to serve as Arizona's governor.

In 1997, Governor Fife Symington resigned after being convicted of fraud for filing false financial statements to banks. The actions occurred while he was a real estate developer, and before he was governor. Symington appealed his conviction in 1998. In 1999, the federal appeals court overturned the conviction. Secretary of State Jane Dee Hull, who had replaced Symington, ran in 1998 for a full term as governor. Her election victory made her the first woman to be elected governor of the state.

The early 2000's. The state's economy remained strong through the late 1900's and into the 2000's. But declining copper prices and long labor disputes had led to severe economic problems in several mining areas.

Arizona continued to be one of the nation's fastest-growing states. Its population increased by 40 percent between 1990 and 2000 and by 25 percent between 2000 and 2010. The population growth shifted to cities and away from rural areas.

In 2010, Governor Jan Brewer signed a controversial state law designed to discourage illegal immigration. Before the law took effect, however, a federal judge blocked some of its key elements, ruling that they conflicted with federal authority. Two of the provisions blocked would have required police to question people about their immigration status and would have demanded that immigrants carry papers. In June 2012, the U.S. Supreme Court rejected most parts of the controversial law. But the court upheld the provision requiring police to check the immigration status of people they detain.

In January 2011, a gunman killed 6 people and wounded 13 at an event held by U.S. Representative Gabrielle Giffords in Tucson. Giffords, a Democrat representing a district in southeastern Arizona, was shot in the head. Doctors expected her to need lengthy rehabilitation. Jared Loughner of Tucson was charged with the shootings. A federal judge ruled Loughner unfit to stand trial and sent him to a federal mental health facility for treatment. In August 2012, a federal judge ruled Loughner competent to stand trial. Loughner pleaded guilty to 19 counts, including murder and attempted murder. In November, a judge sentenced Loughner to seven consecutive life sentences, plus 140 years, in federal prison.

Several major wildfires raged in eastern Arizona from May through July 2011. One called the Wallow Fire charred more than 800 square miles (2,070 square kilo-

meters) of land in the White Mountains and the Apache-Sitgreaves National Forest. Officials said the fire was the largest in state history. On June 30, 2013, 19 firefighters from Prescott, Arizona, were killed while fighting the Yarnell Hill Fire, northwest of Phoenix. Officials said that the wildfire was the deadliest in state history.

Lay James Gibson and Thomas E. Sheridan

Related articles in *World Book* include:

Biographies

Castro, Raul Hector	Geronimo	Kino, Eusebio F.
Cochise	Goldwater, Barry M.	Lowell, Percival
Coronado, Francisco Vásquez de	Greenway, John Campbell	McCain, John
Earp, Wyatt	Hayden, Carl T.	O'Connor, Sandra Day

Cities

Mesa	Scottsdale	Tucson
Phoenix	Tombstone	Yuma

History

Ancestral Pueblo	Guadalupe Hidalgo, Treaty of	Mission life in America
Cíbola, Seven Cities of	Indian, American	Mogollon
Gadsden Purchase	Indian wars	Western frontier life in America
	Mexican War	

Physical features

Colorado River	Meteor Crater	Salt River
Grand Canyon	Painted Desert	Sonoran Desert
Lake Powell	Petrified Forest	

Other related articles

Cactus	Grand Canyon National Park	Hopi Indians
Glen Canyon Dam	Hoover Dam	Navajo Indians
		Pima Indians

Outline

I. People
  A. Population
  B. Schools
  C. Libraries and museums
II. Visitor's guide
III. Land and climate
  A. Land regions
  B. Rivers, waterfalls, and lakes
  C. Plant and animal life
  D. Climate
IV. Economy
  A. Natural resources
  B. Service industries
  C. Manufacturing
  D. Agriculture
  E. Mining
  F. Electric power and utilities
  G. Transportation
  H. Communication
V. Government
  A. Constitution
  B. Executive
  C. Legislature
  D. Courts
  E. Local government
  F. Revenue
  G. Politics
VI. History

Additional resources

Level I

Craats, Rennay. *Arizona.* AV2 by Weigl, 2012.
Derzipilski, Kathleen, and Hudson, Amanda. *Arizona.* 2nd ed. Marshall Cavendish Benchmark, 2012.
Frisch, Nate. *Grand Canyon National Park.* Creative Education, 2013.
Somervill, Barbara A. *Arizona.* Children's Pr., 2009.

Level II

Ffolliott, Peter F., and Davis, O. K., eds. *Natural Environments of Arizona.* Univ. of Ariz. Pr., 2008.
Sheridan, Thomas E. *Arizona.* Rev. ed. Univ. of Ariz. Pr., 2012.
Truett, Samuel. *Fugitive Landscapes: The Forgotten History of the U.S.-Mexico Borderlands.* Yale, 2006.
VanderMeer, Philip R. *Desert Visions and the Making of Phoenix, 1860-2009.* Univ. of N. Mex. Pr., 2010.

Arizona (ship). See **Pearl Harbor** (The war memorials).

Arizona, University of, is a state-supported coeducational institution in Tucson, Arizona. It has colleges of agriculture, architecture, education, engineering, fine arts, humanities, law, management, medicine, nursing, optical sciences, pharmacy, science, and social and behavioral sciences. It also has a graduate college and a number of specialized schools. Courses at the University of Arizona lead to bachelor's, master's, and doctor's degrees.

The university's Lunar and Planetary Laboratory, Steward Observatory, and astronomy department operate several observatories. The University Museum of Art includes the Samuel H. Kress Collection of Renaissance paintings and the C. Leonard Pfeiffer Collection of contemporary American art.

The University of Arizona was chartered in 1885. The university opened in 1891.

Critically reviewed by the University of Arizona

Arizona State University is a coeducational state-supported university with campuses in Tempe, Phoenix, and Mesa. The university offers programs in architecture, business, education, engineering, fine arts, law, liberal arts and sciences, nursing, social work, and technology. Arizona State University grants bachelor's, master's, and doctor's degrees. The Center for Meteorite Studies, which is in Tempe, houses one of the world's largest collections of meteorites.

Arizona State University was founded in 1885. It became a university in 1958.

Critically reviewed by Arizona State University

Ark usually refers to the vessel that sheltered Noah and his family during the *Deluge* (great flood) described in the Bible (Genesis 6). In addition, the word applies to the basket in which Moses's mother hid him. In Jewish synagogues, the ark is the cabinet that holds the scrolls of the Torah, the first five books of the Old Testament. *Ark* comes from the Latin word *arca,* meaning *chest, box,* or *coffer.* In Europe, *ark* used to mean a chest or closed basket for storing valuables or other goods. In the United States, *ark* referred to a large flatboat used on western rivers during the expansion of the country.

H. Darrell Lance

See also **Ark of the Covenant; Deluge; Noah.**

Josh Young, University of Arizona

The University of Arizona campus in Tucson includes Bear Down Gymnasium, *left,* and the main library, *right.*

Ark of the Covenant was a sacred wooden chest described in the Bible as representing God's presence. It was called the Ark of the Covenant because it symbolized the *covenant,* a special agreement that the Israelites made with God at Mount Sinai.

Descriptions of the Ark appear in chapters 25 and 37 of the Book of Exodus. A craftworker named Bezalel built the Ark in the wilderness while the Israelites wandered from Egypt toward the Promised Land (present-day Israel). The Ark was kept in a tent and equipped with poles for carrying. It enclosed the tablets inscribed with the Ten Commandments. See **Tabernacle.**

The Israelite leader Moses communicated with God before the Ark, and the Israelites carried it into battle to ensure victory. When the Israelites entered the land of Israel, their priests carried the Ark before them over the Jordan River. The Philistines captured the Ark during a battle, but returned it seven months later. King David eventually brought the Ark to Jerusalem in a great procession. His son, King Solomon, installed it permanently in his new Temple in Jerusalem. By the time the Babylonians destroyed the Temple in 587 or 586 B.C., the Ark had disappeared and was no longer mentioned in the Bible. The Ark does appear in later legends. Some people assume the Ark was destroyed by a conquering army. Others claim it is hidden.   Lawrence H. Schiffman

Detail (about A.D. 239) from the west wall of the Second Synagogue, Dura Europas, Syria; National Museum of Damascus (Art Resource)

The Ark of the Covenant held the tablets inscribed with the Ten Commandments. The Israelites carried it during their wanderings. The Philistines captured the Ark after the Israelites entered the land of Israel. This fresco shows the Philistines returning the Ark.

National Park Service

The Buffalo National River flows past massive limestone bluffs in the Ozark Mountains in northern Arkansas. The state's natural beauty and recreational facilities attract large numbers of visitors.

Arkansas *The Natural State*

Arkansas, *AHR kuhn* SAW, one of the Southern States of the United States, is almost evenly divided between the Highlands and the Lowlands. The Highlands area, in northern and western Arkansas, has scenic mountains, forests, free-flowing streams, and land suitable for raising livestock. The Lowlands area includes a plain along the Mississippi River in eastern Arkansas, sometimes called the Delta, and a plain in southern Arkansas. The Delta has some of the richest farmland in the United States, and the southern plain has extensive pine forests. Arkansas is known as *The Natural State* because of its natural beauty and abundant wildlife.

Little Rock is the capital and largest city of Arkansas. The name *Arkansas* comes from an Indian term for the Quapaw tribe, known as *the downstream people.*

Millions of tourists visit Arkansas every year. Its clear lakes and streams attract many vacationers who enjoy boating and fishing. Arkansas is famous for its spring waters, which many people believe help cure certain ailments. Mammoth Spring is one of the largest springs in the United States. Hot Springs is a famous health center and a national park. Crater of Diamonds State Park, near Murfreesboro, has a diamond mine open to the public. Tourists sometimes find valuable diamonds there and are permitted to keep their finds.

Food processing is the leading manufacturing industry in the state. The production of primary metal products and transportation equipment is also important. The Fort Smith and the Little Rock areas are the leading manufacturing centers. Service industries employ most of the state's workers. These industries include such activities as education, health care, real estate, retail trade, and transportation. Several large store chains and two leading trucking firms are headquartered in the state.

Farming and mining are also important parts of the economy. Arkansas produces more rice than any other state. It is one of the leading states in raising chickens. Among Arkansas's mineral products, natural gas and petroleum bring in the most income.

Arkansas belonged first to France, then to Spain, and then to France again. The United States acquired the region in 1803. Arkansas was part of the Louisiana Territory until 1812. Then, it belonged to the Missouri Territory until 1819, when the Arkansaw Territory was established. In 1836, Arkansas became the 25th state of the Union.

The contributors of this article are Michael B. Dougan, Emeritus Professor of History at Arkansas State University and author of Arkansas Odyssey: The Saga of Arkansas from Prehistoric Times to Present; *and John G. Hehr, Professor and Associate Dean of the J. William Fulbright College of Arts and Sciences at the University of Arkansas.*

Interesting facts about Arkansas

Pivot Rock, near Eureka Springs, balances on a base only one-fifteenth as large as its top.

The Basin Park Hotel in Eureka Springs is seven stories tall, but every floor is a "ground" floor. The hotel is built against a hillside, and each story opens onto the hill at a different height.

"The Hanging Judge," Isaac Parker, brought law and order to the frontier from his courtroom in Fort Smith. He served from 1875 until his death in 1896 as judge of the federal court's Western District of Arkansas. Parker was widely known for his harshness. He sentenced 160 men to death, 79 of whom were hanged.

The city of Texarkana is divided by the Arkansas-Texas state line. Texarkana has two city governments—one for the Arkansas side and one for the Texas side. The Texarkana post office building stands in both states. Its address is "Texarkana, Arkansas-Texas."

The largest federal trout hatchery in the United States is the Norfork National Fish Hatchery in Mountain Home. Each year, this hatchery raises over 2 million trout from eggs until they are about 9 inches (23 centimeters) long. The fish are placed in streams in Arkansas, Missouri, and Oklahoma.

The first jockey to win 100 stakes races worth $100,000 or more was Bill Shoemaker. He won his 100th stakes race at Oaklawn Park in Hot Springs on March 30, 1974.

Pivot Rock

Texarkana post office

© Shutterstock

Little Rock, the capital and largest city of Arkansas, ranks as the state's main center of transportation and trade. It lies on the south bank of the Arkansas River.

Matt Bradley

Rice is harvested on many Arkansas farms. The state is the nation's leading producer of rice. Cotton and soybeans also rank among Arkansas's chief crops.

Arkansas in brief

Symbols of Arkansas

On the state flag, adopted in 1913, the diamond-shaped design represents Arkansas as a major diamond-producing state. On the state seal, adopted in 1907, a shield against the breast of an American eagle displays a steamboat, a beehive, a plow, and a sheaf of wheat—all symbols of industrial and agricultural wealth. The Goddess of Liberty stands above the eagle. The Angel of Mercy and the Sword of Justice stand on the sides.

State flag

Secretary of State's Office
State seal

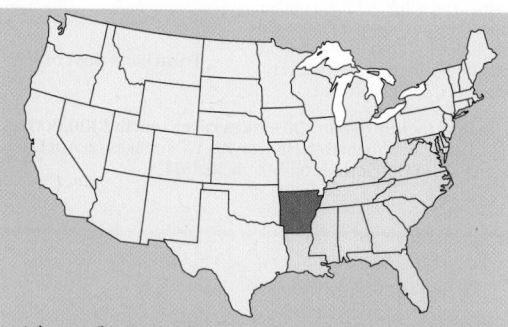

Arkansas (brown) ranks 27th in size among all the states and 3rd in size among the Southern States (yellow).

The State Capitol is in Little Rock, the capital of Arkansas since 1821. It is modeled after the U.S. Capitol. Arkansas Post was the capital from 1819 to 1821.

General information

Statehood: June 15, 1836, the 25th state.
State abbreviations: Ark. (traditional); AR (postal).
State motto: *Regnat Populus* (The People Rule).
State anthem: "Arkansas." Words and music by Mrs. Eva Ware Barnett.

Land and climate

Area: 53,179 mi² (137,733 km²), including 1,149 mi² (2,976 km²) of inland water.
Elevation: *Highest*—Magazine Mountain, 2,753 ft (839 m) above sea level. *Lowest*—Ouachita River in Ashley and Union counties, 55 ft (17 m) above sea level.
Record high temperature: 120 °F (49 °C) at Ozark on Aug. 10, 1936.
Record low temperature: –29 °F (–34 °C) in Benton County on Feb. 13, 1905.
Average July temperature: 81 °F (27 °C).
Average January temperature: 40 °F (4 °C).
Average yearly precipitation: 49 in (124 cm).

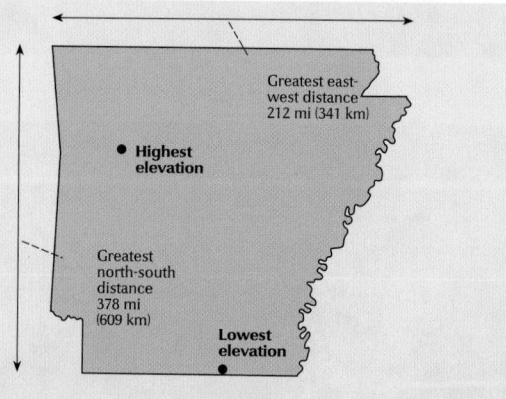

Greatest east-west distance 212 mi (341 km)

● Highest elevation

Greatest north-south distance 378 mi (609 km)

Lowest elevation

Important dates

René-Robert Cavalier, Sieur de La Salle, claimed the Mississippi Valley for France.

Arkansas became the 25th state on June 15.

| 1541 | 1682 | 1803 | 1836 |

Hernando de Soto of Spain explored the region.

The United States acquired Arkansas as part of the Louisiana Purchase.

State bird
Northern mockingbird

State flower
Apple blossom

State tree
Pine tree

People

Population: 2,915,918

Rank among the states: 32nd

Density: 55 per mi^2 (21 per km^2), U.S. average 85 per mi^2 (33 per km^2)

Distribution: 56 percent urban, 44 percent rural

Largest cities in Arkansas

Little Rock	193,524
Fort Smith	86,209
Fayetteville	73,580
Springdale	69,797
Jonesboro	67,263
North Little Rock	62,304

Source: 2010 census.

Population trend

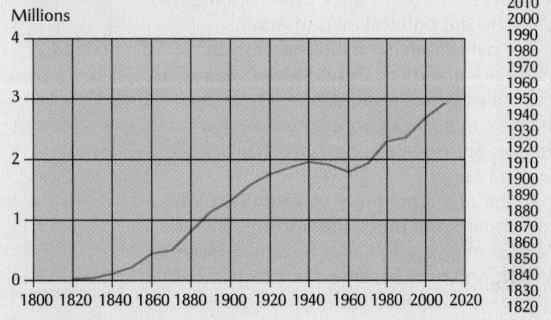

Millions

Source: U.S. Census Bureau.

Year	Population
2010	2,915,918
2000	2,673,400
1990	2,350,725
1980	2,286,435
1970	1,923,295
1960	1,786,272
1950	1,909,511
1940	1,949,387
1930	1,854,482
1920	1,752,204
1910	1,574,449
1900	1,311,564
1890	1,128,211
1880	802,525
1870	484,471
1860	435,450
1850	209,897
1840	97,574
1830	30,388
1820	14,273

Economy

Chief products

Agriculture: beef cattle, broilers, cotton, eggs, rice, soybeans.

Manufacturing: fabricated metal products, food products, machinery, paper products, primary metal products, transportation equipment.

Mining: bromine, crushed stone, natural gas, petroleum.

Gross domestic product

Value of goods and services produced in 2016: $119,947,000,000. *Services* include community, business, and personal services; finance; government; trade; and transportation and communication. *Industry* includes construction, manufacturing, mining, and utilities. *Agriculture* includes agriculture, fishing, and forestry.

Source: U.S. Bureau of Economic Analysis.

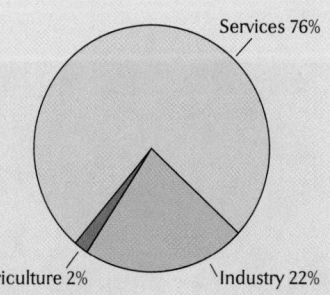

Services 76%

Agriculture 2%

Industry 22%

Government

State government

Governor: 4-year term
State senators: 35; 4-year terms
State representatives: 100; 2-year terms
Counties: 75

Federal government

United States senators: 2
United States representatives: 4
Electoral votes: 6

Sources of information

The official website of the state of Arkansas at https://portal.arkansas.gov/ provides a gateway to much information on the state's government, history, and economy.

In addition, the website at https://www.arkansas.com provides information about tourism.

The state adopted its present constitution.

The National Guard helped enforce a court order to integrate Little Rock's Central High School.

Former Arkansas Governor Bill Clinton was president of the United States.

| 1874 | 1921 | 1957 | 1970 | 1993-2001 |

Oil was discovered near El Dorado.

The Arkansas River Development program opened the river to navigation from the Mississippi River to Oklahoma.

Population. The 2010 United States census reported that Arkansas had 2,915,918 people. The state's population had increased about 9 percent over the 2000 census figure, 2,673,400. According to the 2010 census, Arkansas ranks 32nd in population among the 50 states.

About 60 percent of the people of Arkansas live in metropolitan areas (see **Metropolitan area**). Four metropolitan areas lie entirely in Arkansas—Hot Springs, Jonesboro, Little Rock-North Little Rock-Conway, and Pine Bluff. The Fayetteville-Springdale-Rogers metropolitan area lies mainly in Arkansas and extends into Missouri. The Fort Smith metropolitan area extends into Oklahoma. The Memphis (Tennessee) and Texarkana (Texas) areas lie mainly in Tennessee and Texas, respectively. For the populations of the state's metropolitan areas, see the *Index* to the political map of Arkansas.

Little Rock, the state capital, is the largest city in Arkansas. It has a population of about 194,000. Arkansas has seven other cities with a population of more than 50,000. These cities, in order of population, are Fort Smith, Fayetteville, Springdale, Jonesboro, North Little Rock, Conway, and Rogers.

About 15 percent of the people of Arkansas are African Americans. Other large population groups include people of Irish, German, English, and Hispanic descent.

Schools. When Arkansas became a territory in 1819, Congress set aside land in each county for a general school system. In 1820, the Reverend Cephas Washburn established Dwight Mission, the territory's first school, in Russellville. Washburn and other missionaries taught

Population density

About 60 percent of the people in Arkansas live in one of the state's eight metropolitan areas. Little Rock is the largest city and the state capital.

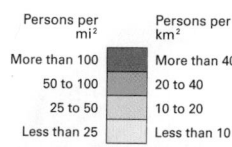

	Persons per mi²	Persons per km²
	More than 100	More than 40
	50 to 100	20 to 40
	25 to 50	10 to 20
	Less than 25	Less than 10

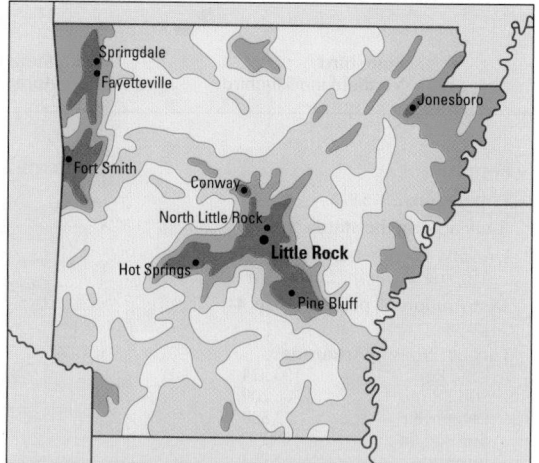

WORLD BOOK map; based on U.S. Census Bureau data.

Arkansas Department of Parks and Tourism

A fisherman on the White River in northern Arkansas displays his catch. The state's rivers and lakes attract many people who enjoy fishing, boating, canoeing, and water-skiing.

Matt Bradley

Woodcarvers work in a home craft shop near Mountain View. Woodcarving is a traditional craft among people of the Ozark Plateau region of northern Arkansas.

The University of Arkansas has several campuses throughout the state. The main campus, in Fayetteville, includes Vol Walker Hall, *shown here,* the headquarters for the Department of Architecture.

University of Arkansas at Fayetteville

Universities and colleges

This table lists the nonprofit universities and colleges based in Arkansas that grant bachelor's or advanced degrees and are accredited by the Higher Learning Commission.

Name	Mailing address
Arkansas, University of	*
Arkansas Baptist College	Little Rock
Arkansas State University	Jonesboro
Arkansas Tech University	Russellville
Central Arkansas, University of	Conway
Central Baptist College	Conway
Crowley's Ridge College	Paragould
Harding University	Searcy
Henderson State University	Arkadelphia
Hendrix College	Conway
John Brown University	Siloam Springs
Lyon College	Batesville
Ouachita Baptist University	Arkadelphia
Ozarks, University of the	Clarksville
Philander Smith College	Little Rock
Southern Arkansas University	Magnolia
Williams Baptist University	Walnut Ridge

*For campuses, see Arkansas, University of.

Cherokee Indian children in Russellville. In 1829, the territorial legislature provided for construction of schools.

In 1843, seven years after Arkansas became a state, the legislature provided for a public school system. The 1868 Constitution provided for a system of schools for those between the ages of 5 and 21. A law passed in 1909 required all children between the ages of 8 and 16 to attend school. This law now affects children from 5 through 16. In 1948, voters approved a plan to consolidate the state's school districts. As a result of this plan, the number of districts was reduced from about 1,600

to a little more than 300.

The state Department of Education administers Arkansas's public school system. The department is governed by the Board of Education. The governor appoints the members of the board. Their appointments are subject to the approval of the state Senate. The Board of Education, with the approval of the governor, appoints the commissioner of education.

Libraries. In 1843, William Woodruff founded the state's first subscription library, in Little Rock. Members of this library contributed money to purchase books, which they could then use without charge. The Helena Public Library, established in 1888, became the first tax-supported library in the state. Jefferson County established the state's first countywide library service in 1926. In 1935, the Arkansas Library Commission was created by the state legislature. In 1979, the legislature changed the name of the commission to the Arkansas State Library.

Today, Arkansas's public library system includes county libraries and regional libraries. A number of Arkansas cities also operate their own public libraries. The University of Arkansas in Fayetteville has a large collection of materials on Arkansas and the American Civil War (1861-1865).

Museums. A number of fine museums are in Little Rock. They include the Arkansas Arts Center, the Historic Arkansas Museum, the Museum of Discovery, and the Old State House Museum.

Other museums in the state are the Arkansas State University Museum in Jonesboro, the Arts & Science Center for Southeast Arkansas in Pine Bluff, Crystal Bridges Museum of American Art in Bentonville, and the Shiloh Museum of Ozark History in Springdale. The William J. Clinton Presidential Center in Little Rock contains many objects and documents relating to Bill Clinton's presidency.

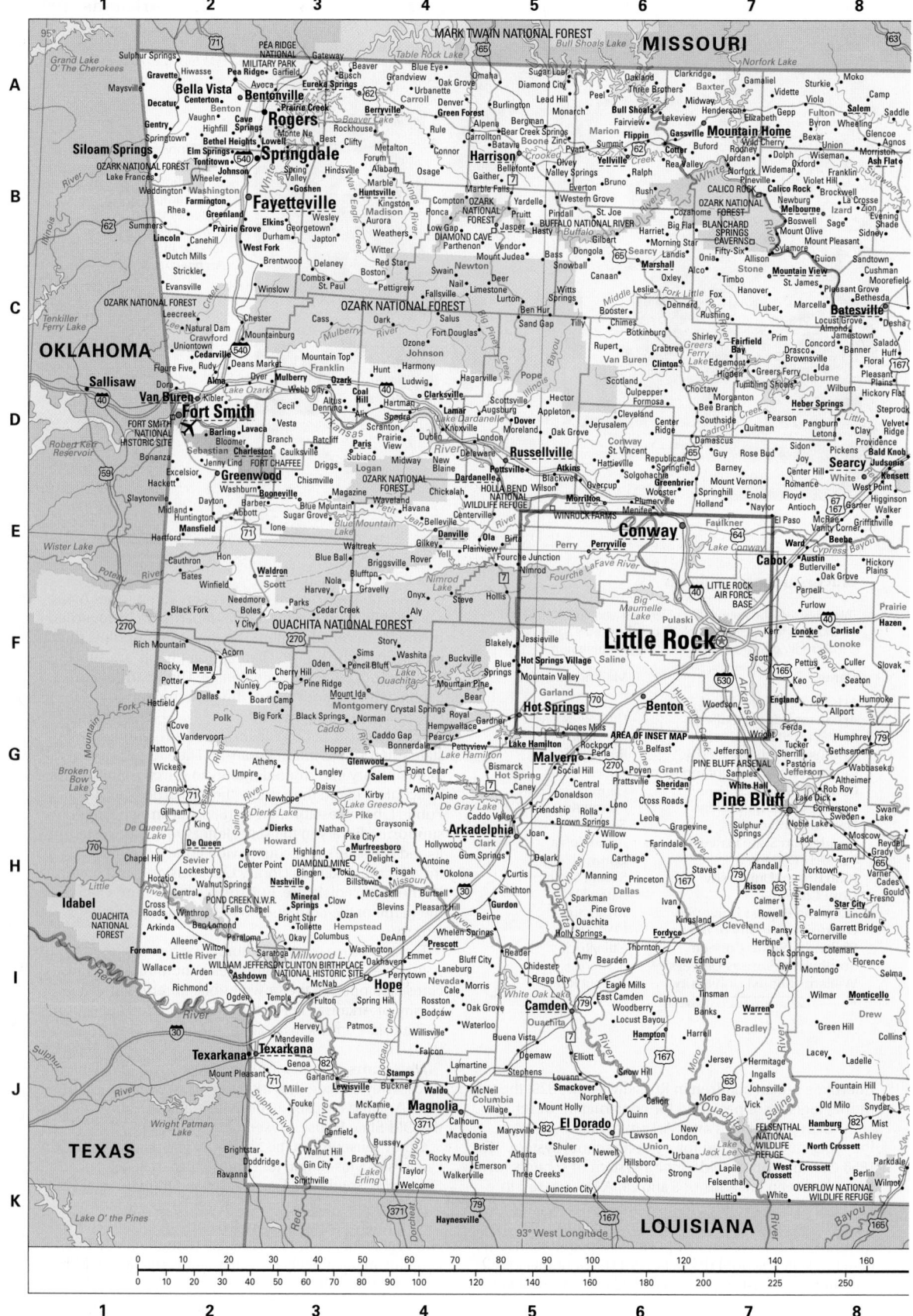

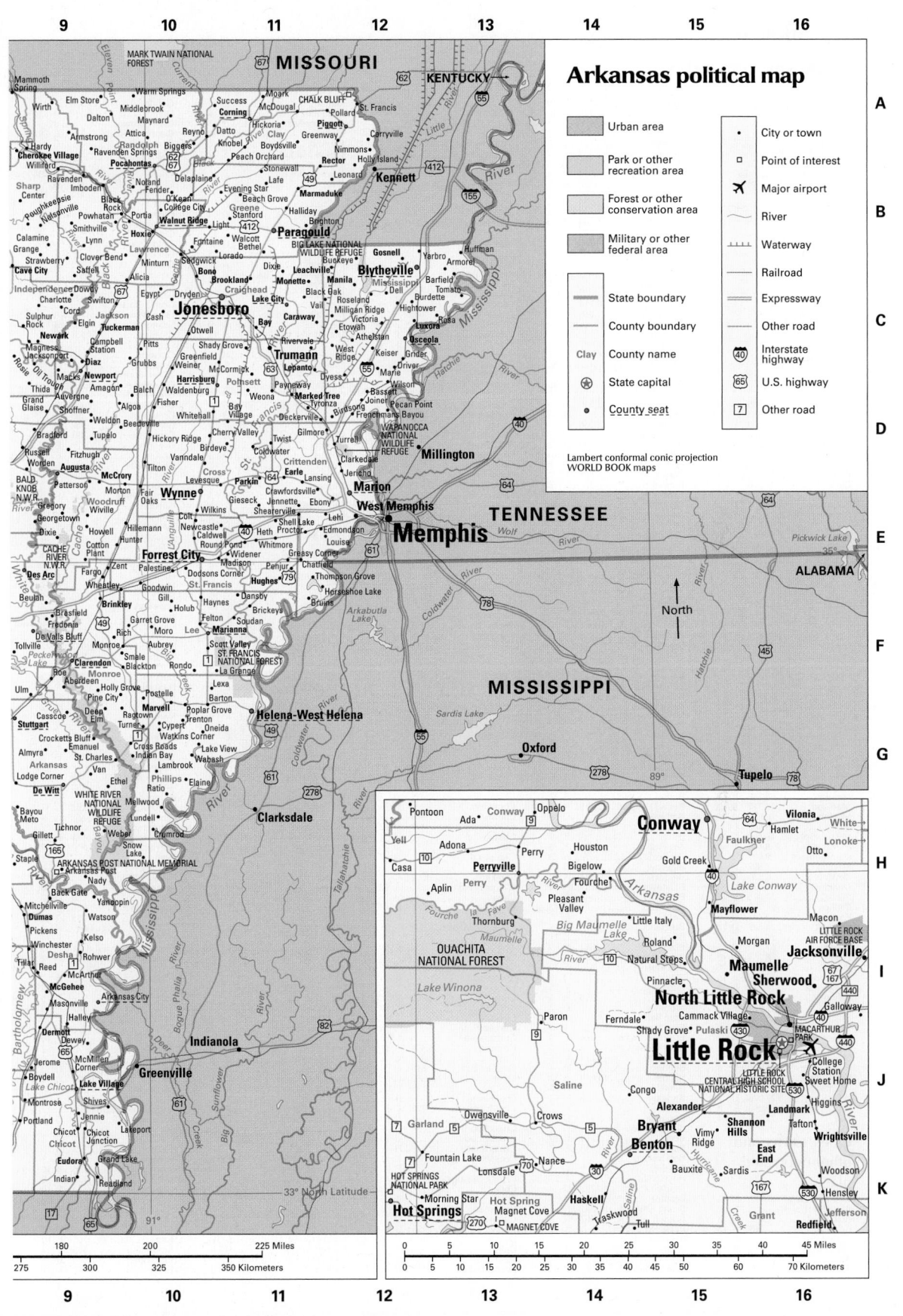

Arkansas political map

Legend

- Urban area
- Park or other recreation area
- Forest or other conservation area
- Military or other federal area

State boundary
County boundary
Clay — County name
State capital
County seat

- City or town
- Point of interest
- Major airport
- River
- Waterway
- Railroad
- Expressway
- Other road
- 40 Interstate highway
- 65 U.S. highway
- 7 Other road

Lambert conformal conic projection
WORLD BOOK maps

MISSOURI

KENTUCKY

Mammoth Spring, Warm Springs, Wirth, Elm Store, Middlebrook, Dalton, Maynard, Armstrong, Reyno, Success, McDougal, Moark, Corning, Hardy, Cherokee Village, Williford, Ravenden Springs, Biggers, Pocahontas, Datto, Knobel, Peach Orchard, Hickoria, Clay, Corrville, Piggott, Greenway, Nimmons, Pollard, St. Francis, CHALK BLUFF

Sharp Center, Ravenden, Imboden, Poughkeepsie, Nalsonville, Black Rock, Portia, Walnut Ridge, Hoxie, **Paragould**, Gosnell, Huffman, Yarbro

Calamine, Grange, Strawberry, Cave City, Swifton, Lynn, Clover Bend, Saffell, Alicia, Light, Fontaine, Walcott, Bethel, Dixie, Leachville, Monette, Manila, **Blytheville**

Jonesboro

Memphis

TENNESSEE

MISSISSIPPI

ALABAMA

North

Conway

Little Rock

North Little Rock

Hot Springs

225 Miles
350 Kilometers

Arkansas map index

Ida ....D 8
Imboden ....677 ..B 9
Indian Bay ....G 10
Ingalls ....J 7
Ivan ....H 6
Jacksonport ....212 ..C 9
Jacksonville ....28,364 ..I 16
Jamestown ....C 8
Japton ....B 3
Jasper○ ....466 ..B 5
Jefferson ....G 7
Jennette ....115 ..E 11
Jennie ....J 9
Jenny Lind ....D 2
Jericho ....119 ..D 12
Jerome ....39 ..J 9
Jersey ....J 7
Jerusalem ....D 6
Jessieville ....F 5
Johnson ....3,354 ..B 2
Joiner ....576 ..D 12
Jones Mills ....G 5
Jonesboro○ ....67,263 ..C 11
Jordan ....B 7
Judsonia ....2,019 ..D 8
Junction City ....581 ..K 6
Keiser ....759 ..C 12
Kelso ....I 9
Kensett ....1,648 ..D 8
Keo ....256 ..F 7
Kerr ....F 7
Kibler ....961 ..D 2
King ....H 2
Kingsland ....447 ..H 7
Kingston ....B 4
Kirby† ....786 ..G 3
Knobel ....287 ..A 11
Knoxville ....731 ..D 4
La Crosse ....B 8
Ladelle ....J 8
Lafe ....458 ..B 11
La Grange ....89 ..F 10
Lake City ....2,082 ..C 11
Lake Dick ....G 8
Lake Frances ....B 1
Lake Hamilton† ..2,135 ..G 5
Lake View ....443 ..G 10
Lake Village○ ....2,575 ..J 9
Lakeport ....J 10
Lakeview ....741 ..A 6
Lamar ....1,605 ..D 4
Lamartine ....J 4
Landis ....B 6
Landmark*† ....3,555 ..J 16
Laneburg ....I 4
Langley ....G 3
Lapile ....K 7
Lavaca ....2,289 ..D 2
Lawson ....J 6
Leachville ....1,993 ..C 11
Lead Hill ....271 ..A 5
Leola ....501 ..H 6
Leonard ....B 12
Lepanto ....1,893 ..C 11
Leslie ....441 ..C 6
Letona ....255 ..D 8
Levesque ....D 10
Lewisville○ ....1,280 ..J 3
Lexa ....286 ..F 10
Light ....B 10
Lincoln ....2,249 ..B 2
Little Flock* ....2,585 ..A 2
Little Italy ....I 14
Little Rock○ ....193,524 ..F 7
Lockesburg ....739 ..H 2
Locust Bayou ....I 6
Locust Grove ....C 8
London ....1,039 ..D 4
Lonoke○ ....4,245 ..F 8
Lonsdale ....94 ..K 13
Lorado ....B 10
Louann ....164 ..J 5
Lowell ....7,327 ..A 2
Luber ....C 7
Ludwig ....D 4
Lumber ....J 4
Lundell ....H 10
Lurton ....C 5
Luxora ....1,178 ..C 12
Lynn ....288 ..B 9
Macedonia ....J 4
Macks ....C 9
Madison ....769 ..E 10
Magazine ....847 ..E 3
Magness ....202 ..C 9
Magnet Cove ....5 ..K 13
Magnolia○ ....11,577 ..J 4
Malvern○ ....10,318 ..G 5
Mammoth
  Spring ....977 ..A 9
Mandeville ....J 3
Manila ....3,342 ..C 12
Manning ....H 5
Mansfield ....1,139 ..E 2
Marble ....B 4
Marble Falls ....B 5
Marcella ....C 8
Marianna○ ....4,115 ..F 10
Marie ....84 ..C 12
Marion○ ....12,345 ..E 12
Marked Tree ....2,566 ..D 11
Marmaduke ....1,111 ..B 11
Marshall○ ....1,355 ..C 6
Marvell ....1,186 ..F 10
Masonville ....I 9
Maumelle ....17,163 ..I 15
Mayflower ....2,234 ..H 15
Maynard ....426 ..A 10
Maysville ....A 1
McAlmont*† ....1,873 ..I 16
McArthur ....I 9
McCaskill ....96 ..H 3
McCrory ....1,729 ..D 9
McDougal ....186 ..A 11
McGehee ....4,219 ..I 9
McKamie ....J 4
McNab ....68 ..I 3
McNeil ....516 ..J 4
McRae ....682 ..E 8
Melbourne○ ....1,848 ..B 8
Mellwood ....G 10
Mena○ ....5,737 ..F 2
Menifee ....302 ..E 6
Middlebrook ....A 10
Midland ....325 ..E 2
Midway† ....1,084 ..A 6
Midway ....D 4
Midway* ....389 ..G 5
Milligan Ridge ....C 12
Mineral
  Springs ....1,208 ..H 3
Minturn ....109 ..B 10
Mist ....J 8
Mitchellville ....360 ..H 9
Moark ....A 11
Moko ....A 8
Monette ....1,501 ..C 11
Monroe ....F 10
Monticello○ ....9,467 ..I 8
Montrose ....354 ..J 9
Moorefield ....137 ..C 8
Moreland ....D 5
Morgan ....I 15
Morganton ....D 7
Morning Star ....B 6
Morning Star ....K 12
Moro ....216 ..F 10
Moro Bay ....J 7
Morrilton○ ....6,767 ..E 6
Morrison Bluff* ....64 ..D 4
Morriston ....B 8
Morton ....E 10
Moscow ....H 8
Mount Holly ....J 5
Mount Ida○ ....1,076 ..F 3
Mount Judea ....C 5
Mount Olive ....B 7
Mount Pleasant ....414 ..B 8
Mount Vernon ....145 ..E 7
Mountain
  Home○ ....12,448 ..A 7
Mountain Pine ....770 ..F 5
Mountain Top ....C 3
Mountain Valley ....F 5
Mountain
  View○ ....2,748 ..C 7
Mountainburg ....631 ..C 2
Mulberry ....1,655 ..D 3
Murfreesboro○ ..1,641 ..H 3
Nail ....C 4
Nance ....K 13
Nashville○ ....4,627 ..H 3
Nathan ....H 3
Natural Steps† ....426 ..I 15
Naylor ....E 7
Nelsonville ....B 9
New Blaine† ....174 ..D 4
New Edinburg† ....127 ..I 7
New London ....J 7
Newark ....1,176 ..C 9
Newburg ....B 8
Newell ....J 6
Newhope ....G 3
Newport○ ....7,879 ..C 9
Nimmons ....69 ..A 12
Noble Lake ....H 8
Nola ....E 3
Norfork ....511 ..B 7
Norman ....378 ..G 3
Norphlet ....844 ..J 6
North
  Crossett† ....3,119 ..J 8
North Little
  Rock ....62,304 ..I 16
Nunley ....F 2
Oak Grove ....369 ..A 4
Oak Grove ....D 5
Oak Grove ....E 8
Oak Grove ....I 4
Oak Grove
  Heights* ....889 ..B 11
Oakhaven ....63 ..I 3
Oark ....C 4
Oden ....232 ..F 3
Ogden ....180 ..I 2
Ogemaw ....J 5
Oil Trough ....260 ..C 9
Okay ....I 3
O'Kean ....194 ..B 10
Okolona ....147 ..H 4
Ola ....1,281 ..E 5
Olvey ....B 5
Omaha ....169 ..A 5
Oneida ....G 10
Onia ....C 7
Onyx ....F 4
Oppelo ....781 ..H 13
Osage ....B 4
Osceola ....7,757 ..C 12
Otwell ....C 10
Ouachita ....H 5
Owensville ....J 13
Oxford ....670 ..B 8
Ozan ....85 ..H 3
Ozark○ ....3,684 ..D 3
Ozone ....C 4
Palestine ....681 ..E 10
Palmyra ....H 8
Pangburn ....601 ..D 8
Pansy ....I 7
Paragould○ ....26,113 ..B 11
Paraloma ....I 2
Paris○ ....3,532 ..D 3
Parkdale ....277 ..K 8
Parkin ....1,105 ..D 11
Parks ....F 3
Parnell ....E 7
Paron ....I 14
Parthenon ....B 4
Patmos ....64 ..I 4
Patterson ....452 ..E 9
Payneway ....D 11
Pea Ridge ....4,794 ..A 2
Peach Orchard ....135 ..A 11
Pearcy ....G 4
Pearson ....D 7
Peel ....A 6
Pencil Bluff ....F 3
Perla ....241 ..G 6
Perry ....270 ..H 13
Perrytown ....272 ..I 4
Perryville○ ....1,460 ..E 6
Pettigrew ....C 4
Pettyview ....G 5
Pickens ....D 8
Pickens ....I 9
Piggott○ ....3,849 ..A 12
Pike City ....H 4
Pindall ....112 ..B 5
Pine Bluff○ ....49,083 ..H 7
Pine City ....F 9
Pine Ridge ....F 3
Pineville ....238 ..B 7
Piney*† ....4,699 ..G 5
Pinnacle ....I 15
Plainview ....608 ..E 4
Pleasant Hill ....H 4
Pleasant Plains ....349 ..D 8
Pleasant Valley ....H 14
Plumerville ....826 ..E 6
Pocahontas○ ....6,608 ..B 10
Point Cedar ....G 4
Pollard ....222 ..A 12
Ponca ....B 4
Poplar Grove ....G 10
Portia ....437 ..B 10
Portland ....430 ..J 9
Postelle ....F 10
Potter ....F 2
Pottsville ....2,838 ..D 5
Poughkeepsie ....B 9
Powhatan ....72 ..B 9
Poyen ....290 ..G 6
Prairie Creek† ..2,066 ..A 3
Prairie Grove ....4,380 ..B 2
Prairie View ....D 4
Prattsville ....305 ..G 6
Prescott○ ....3,296 ..I 4
Prim ....C 7
Princeton ....H 6
Proctor ....E 11
Provo ....H 2
Pruitt ....B 5
Pyatt ....221 ..B 5
Quinn ....J 6
Quitman ....762 ..D 7
Ragtown ....G 10
Ralph ....B 6
Randall ....H 7
Ratcliff ....202 ..D 3
Ravana ....K 2
Ravenden ....470 ..B 9
Ravenden
  Springs ....118 ..A 9
Reader† ....66 ..I 5
Readland ....K 9
Rector ....1,977 ..B 11
Redfield ....1,297 ..K 16
Reed ....141 ..I 9
Republican ....D 6
Reydell ....H 8
Reyno ....456 ..A 10
Rhea ....B 2
Rich ....F 9
Rich Mountain ....F 2
Richmond ....I 2
Rison○ ....1,344 ..H 7
Rivervale ....C 11
Rockhouse ....A 4
Rockport ....755 ..G 5
Rockwell*† ....3,780 ..G 5
Roe ....114 ..F 9
Rogers ....55,964 ..A 3
Rohwer ....I 9
Roland† ....746 ..I 15
Rolla ....G 6
Romance ....D 7
Rondo ....198 ..F 10
Rosa ....C 13
Rose Bud ....482 ..D 7
Roseland ....C 12
Rosston ....261 ..I 4
Round Pond ....E 11
Rover ....E 4
Rowell ....H 7
Royal ....G 4
Rudy ....61 ..D 2
Rushing ....C 7
Russell ....216 ..D 9
Russellville○ ....27,920 ..D 5
Rye† ....146 ..I 7
Saffell ....C 9
Sage ....B 8
St. Charles ....230 ..G 9
St. Francis ....250 ..A 12
St. James ....C 8
St. Joe ....132 ..B 6
St. Paul ....113 ..C 3
St. Vincent ....D 6
Salado ....C 8
Salem○ ....1,635 ..A 8
Salem† ....2,607 ..G 4
Salesville* ....450 ..B 7
Samples ....G 7
Sand Gap ....C 5
Saratoga ....I 3
Scotland ....D 6
Scott† ....72 ..F 7
Scott Valley ....F 10
Scottsville ....D 5
Scranton ....224 ..D 4
Searcy○ ....22,858 ..D 8
Sedgwick ....152 ..B 10
Selma ....I 8
Shady Grove ....J 15
Shannon Hills ....3,143 ..J 15
Shearerville ....E 11
Sheridan○ ....4,603 ..G 6
Sherrill ....84 ..G 7
Sherwood ....29,523 ..I 16
Shirley ....291 ..C 7
Shives ....J 9
Shoffner ....D 9
Sidney ....181 ..B 8
Sidon ....D 8
Siloam
  Springs ....15,039 ..B 1
Sims ....F 3
Slovak ....F 8
Smackover ....1,865 ..J 6
Smale ....F 10
Smithton ....H 5
Smithville ....78 ..B 9
Smithville ....K 3
Snow Hill ....J 6
Snow Lake ....H 10
Snowball ....C 6
Snyder ....J 8
Social Hill ....G 5
Solgohachia ....D 6
South Lead Hill* ....102 ..A 5
Southside ....D 7
Sparkman ....427 ..H 5
Spring Hill ....I 3
Spring Valley ....B 3
Springdale ....69,797 ..B 2
Springfield ....D 6
Springhill ....E 7
Springtown ....87 ..A 2
Stamps ....1,693 ..J 4
Stanford ....B 11
Staple ....H 9
Star City○ ....2,274 ..H 8
Staves† ....116 ..H 7
Stephens ....891 ..J 5
Stonewall ....B 11
Story ....F 4
Strawberry ....302 ..B 9
Strong ....558 ..K 6
Stuttgart○ ....9,326 ..G 9
Subiaco ....572 ..D 4
Success ....149 ..A 10
Sugar Grove ....E 3
Sugar Loaf ....A 5
Sulphur Rock ....456 ..C 9
Sulphur
  Springs ....511 ..A 2
Sulphur
  Springs† ....1,101 ..H 7
Summers ....B 2
Summit ....604 ..B 6
Sunset* ....198 ..E 12
Swain ....C 4
Swan Lake ....H 8
Sweet Home† ....849 ..J 16
Swifton ....798 ..C 9
Tafton ....J 16
Tamo ....H 8
Tarry ....H 8
Taylor ....566 ..K 4
Temple ....I 3
Texarkana○ ....29,919 ..J 2
Thebes ....J 8
Thida ....D 9
Thompson Grove ....E 11
Thornburg ....I 13
Thornton ....407 ..I 6
Tichnor ....H 9
Tillar ....225 ..I 9
Tilton ....D 10
Timbo ....C 7
Tinsman ....54 ..I 7
Tokio ....H 3
Tollette ....240 ..I 3
Tomato ....C 13
Tontitown ....2,460 ..B 2
Traskwood ....518 ..K 14
Trenton ....G 10
Trumann ....7,243 ..C 11
Tucker ....G 8
Tuckerman ....1,862 ..C 9
Tull ....448 ..K 14
Tumbling
  Shoals† ....978 ..D 7
Tupelo ....180 ..D 9
Turner ....G 10
Turrell ....615 ..D 12
Twin Groves* ....335 ..D 6
Twist ....D 11
Tyronza ....762 ..D 11
Ulm ....170 ..F 9
Umpire ....G 2
Union ....B 8
Uniontown ....C 2
Urbana ....K 6
Urbanette ....A 4
Valley Springs ....183 ..B 5
Van Buren○ ....22,791 ..D 2
Vandervoort ....87 ..G 2
Vanndale ....D 10
Vaughn ....A 2
Vesta ....D 3
Vick ....J 7
Victoria ....37 ..C 12
Village ....J 5
Vilonia ....3,815 ..H 16
Vimy Ridge ....J 15
Viola ....337 ..A 8
Violet Hill ....B 8
Wabash ....G 10
Wabbaseka ....255 ..G 8
Walcott ....B 11
Waldenburg ....61 ..D 10
Waldo ....1,372 ..J 4
Waldron○ ....3,618 ..E 2
Walker ....E 8
Wallace ....I 2
Walnut Ridge○ ..4,890 ..B 10
Waltreak ....E 4
Ward ....4,067 ..E 8
Warm Springs ....A 10
Warren○ ....6,003 ..I 7
Washburn ....E 2
Washington ....180 ..I 3
Waterloo ....I 4
Watson ....211 ..H 9
Waveland ....E 4
Weathers ....B 4
Webb City ....D 3
Weber ....H 9
Wedington ....B 2
Weiner ....716 ..C 10
Welcome ....K 4
Weldon ....75 ..D 9
Weona ....D 11
Wesley ....B 3
Wesson ....K 5
West
  Crossett† ....1,256 ..K 7
West Fork ....2,317 ..B 2
West Helena, see
  Helena
  [-West Helena]
West
  Memphis ....26,245 ..E 12
West Point ....185 ..E 8
West Ridge ....C 12
Western Grove ....384 ..B 5
Wheatley ....355 ..E 9
Wheeler ....B 2
Whelen Springs ....92 ..I 5
White ....K 7
White Hall ....5,526 ..G 7
Whitehall ....D 10
Wickes ....754 ..G 2
Wideman ....B 7
Widener ....273 ..E 11
Wiederkehr
  Village* ....38 ..D 3
Wilburn ....D 8
Wild Cherry ....B 7
Wilkins ....E 10
Williford ....75 ..B 9
Willisville ....152 ..I 4
Willow ....H 6
Wilmar ....511 ..I 8
Wilmot ....550 ..K 8
Wilson ....903 ..D 12
Wilton ....374 ..I 2
Winchester ....167 ..I 9
Winslow ....391 ..C 2
Winthrop ....192 ..H 2
Wiseman ....B 8
Witter ....B 4
Witts Springs ....C 5
Wiville ....E 9
Woodberry ....I 6
Woodson† ....403 ..K 16
Wooster ....860 ..E 6
Worden ....D 9
Wright ....G 7
Wrightsville ....2,114 ..J 16
Wynne○ ....8,367 ..E 10
Y City ....F 2
Yarbro ....B 12
Yellville○ ....1,204 ..B 6
Yorktown ....H 8
Zent ....E 9
Zinc ....103 ..B 5
Zion ....B 8

*Does not appear on map; key shows general location.
†Census designated place—unincorporated, but recognized as a significant settled community by the U.S. Census Bureau.

○County seat.
Source: 2010 census. Metropolitan area figures are based on the 2013 Office of Management and Budget reorganization of 2010 census data.

Places without population figures are unincorporated areas.

Millions of tourists visit Arkansas every year. They enjoy the state's natural beauty, its many recreational facilities, and its historic sites. Nature lovers are drawn to beautiful caverns, limestone cliffs, forests, mountains, and streams. The state's mineral and hot spring waters are considered helpful in treating persons with certain illnesses. Hot Springs has the most famous of these springs. The lakes and streams of Arkansas attract people who like fishing, boating, canoeing, and water-skiing. Hunters track black bears, deer, opossum, and raccoons in the southeastern lowlands and elk in the Ozarks. They stalk game birds and waterfowl in the rice marshes near Stuttgart. The Ouachita and Ozark mountain ranges are popular tourist attractions.

The most popular annual events in Arkansas include folk festivals and county fairs. One of the best-known events is the Arkansas State Fair, held in Little Rock in October.

Fishing on an artificially created lake in central Arkansas

Wesley Hitt, Alamy Images

Places to visit

Following are brief descriptions of some of Arkansas's many interesting places to visit.

Blanchard Springs Caverns, near Mountain View, features beautiful limestone formations. Camping, picnicking, and swimming are available nearby.

Crater of Diamonds State Park, near Murfreesboro, has a diamond mine open to the public. Visitors may hunt for diamonds in the mine and keep what they find. Thousands of diamonds have been found in the Crater of Diamonds.

Crystal Bridges Museum of American Art, in Bentonville, is known for its architecture and comprehensive collection of American art.

Delta Cultural Center, in downtown Helena, offers exhibits in a Visitors' Center and in a restored 1912 train depot on the culture and heritage of the Arkansas Delta.

Eureka Springs, a Victorian resort town high in the Ozarks, is a favorite spot for tourists. Attractions include a Passion Play, Beaver Lake, a botanical garden, museums, musical entertainment, and a steam-powered train.

MacArthur Park, in Little Rock, honors Douglas MacArthur, commander of Allied forces in the Southwest Pacific during World War II (1939-1945). MacArthur's birthplace, in the park, is now the MacArthur Museum of Arkansas Military History. The Arkansas Arts Center is also in MacArthur Park.

Ozark Folk Center, in Mountain View, offers traditional American folk culture, crafts, music, and festivals. The complex has an auditorium, craft shops, a restaurant, cabins, and a conference center.

National forests and parklands. Arkansas has three national forests: Ouachita in western Arkansas, which the state shares with Oklahoma; Ozark in northern Arkansas; and St. Francis in eastern Arkansas. Next to Ozark National Forest, the Buffalo National River preserves one of the last free-flowing streams in mid-America. Hot Springs National Park, in Hot Springs, includes many thermal springs. The park also features a historic bathhouse, hiking trails through the Ouachita Mountains, and a variety of recreational activities. Pea Ridge National Military Park in the northwest was the site of a major Civil War battle in March 1862. Arkansas Post National Memorial near Gillett marks the first permanent white settlement in Arkansas. Fort Smith National Historic Site in western Arkansas honors one of the first military posts in the American West. Central High School National Historic Site, in Little Rock, is an important civil rights landmark. It was the site of a 1957 confrontation in the struggle to integrate U.S. public schools.

State parks. Arkansas has a number of state parks. For more information, visit the official website of the State Parks of Arkansas at http://www.arkansasstateparks.com.

© Getty Images

Oaklawn Park in Hot Springs

Arkansas Department of Parks and Tourism

Crater of Diamonds State Park near Murfreesboro

© Don Smetzer, Alamy Images

Fiddle competition in Mountain View

© Shutterstock

Blanchard Springs Caverns near Mountain View

Land regions. Arkansas has five main land regions: (1) the Ozark Plateau, (2) the Ouachita Mountains, (3) the Arkansas Valley, (4) the Mississippi Alluvial Plain, and (5) the West Gulf Coastal Plain. The Ozark Plateau and the Ouachita Mountains make up the portion of Arkansas known as the *Highlands*. The Arkansas Valley divides these two highland regions. The Mississippi Alluvial Plain and the West Gulf Coastal Plain make up the *Lowlands* portion of the state.

The Ozark Plateau is a land region that covers parts of Arkansas, Illinois, Missouri, and Oklahoma. This region is often called the *Ozark Mountains.* In Arkansas, it extends across the northwestern and north-central parts of the state. Rugged hills, deep valleys, and swift streams give the region great beauty. Thick forests and underbrush cover much of the region. Many fruit, livestock, and poultry farms are located in the northeast and northwest sections of the Ozarks. The southern edge of the region has a series of steep, wooded hills called the Boston Mountains. River gorges, 500 to 1,500 feet (150 to 457 meters) deep, wind through these hills.

The Ouachita Mountains region stretches from eastern Oklahoma to central Arkansas. In Arkansas, it consists of a series of parallel ridges and valleys. Blue Mountain rises 2,623 feet (799 meters). Farmers cultivate some of the land. But the Ouachita region is best known for its timber and mineral resources, and for its hot springs. The Ouachita River flows through the central part of the region before curving south to Louisiana. Dams built along the river have created a chain of lakes.

The Arkansas Valley, a broad, rolling valley region, lies between the Ozark Plateau and the Ouachita Moun-

tains. The Arkansas Valley is lower than the highland regions to the north and south, but it has several mountain peaks of its own. Magazine Mountain, the highest point in the state, rises 2,753 feet (839 meters) in the Arkansas Valley. The Arkansas River flows through the center of the region southeast into the Mississippi River. Deposits of coal and natural gas lie beneath the region's fertile fields and pastures.

The Mississippi Alluvial Plain lies along the Mississippi River. This region extends from Missouri south to Louisiana, and it is sometimes called the Delta. It covers the eastern third of Arkansas. Much of the plain is low, level land, covered with rich deposits of soils carried to the region by the Mississippi River and its tributaries. Most of Arkansas's major crops are grown in this region. An excellent system of levees and drainage ditches protects the plain from flooding (see **Levee**). A narrow strip of hills called Crowleys Ridge stretches from north to south through the central part of the Mississippi Alluvial Plain. The ridge is formed of gravel deposits and of wind-blown, yellow mineral particles called *loess.*

The West Gulf Coastal Plain covers sizable parts of Arkansas, Louisiana, and Texas. In Arkansas, it is a large, low region in the southwestern and south-central parts of the state. The coastal plain has pine forests, natural gas and petroleum deposits, and beds of bromine salts. Farmers raise livestock and poultry, and grow fruits and vegetables. The lowest point in the state—55 feet (17 meters) above sea level—is near the Ouachita River at the Arkansas-Louisiana border.

Rivers and lakes. The Mississippi River forms the eastern border of Arkansas. The Arkansas River, the

© Shutterstock

Fertile farmland lies at the foot of Petit Jean Mountain, one of several peaks in the Arkansas Valley region.

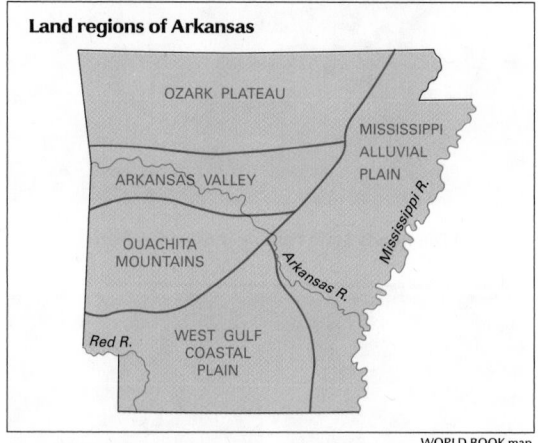

Land regions of Arkansas

OZARK PLATEAU

MISSISSIPPI ALLUVIAL PLAIN

ARKANSAS VALLEY

OUACHITA MOUNTAINS

Mississippi R.

Arkansas R.

Red R.

WEST GULF COASTAL PLAIN

WORLD BOOK map

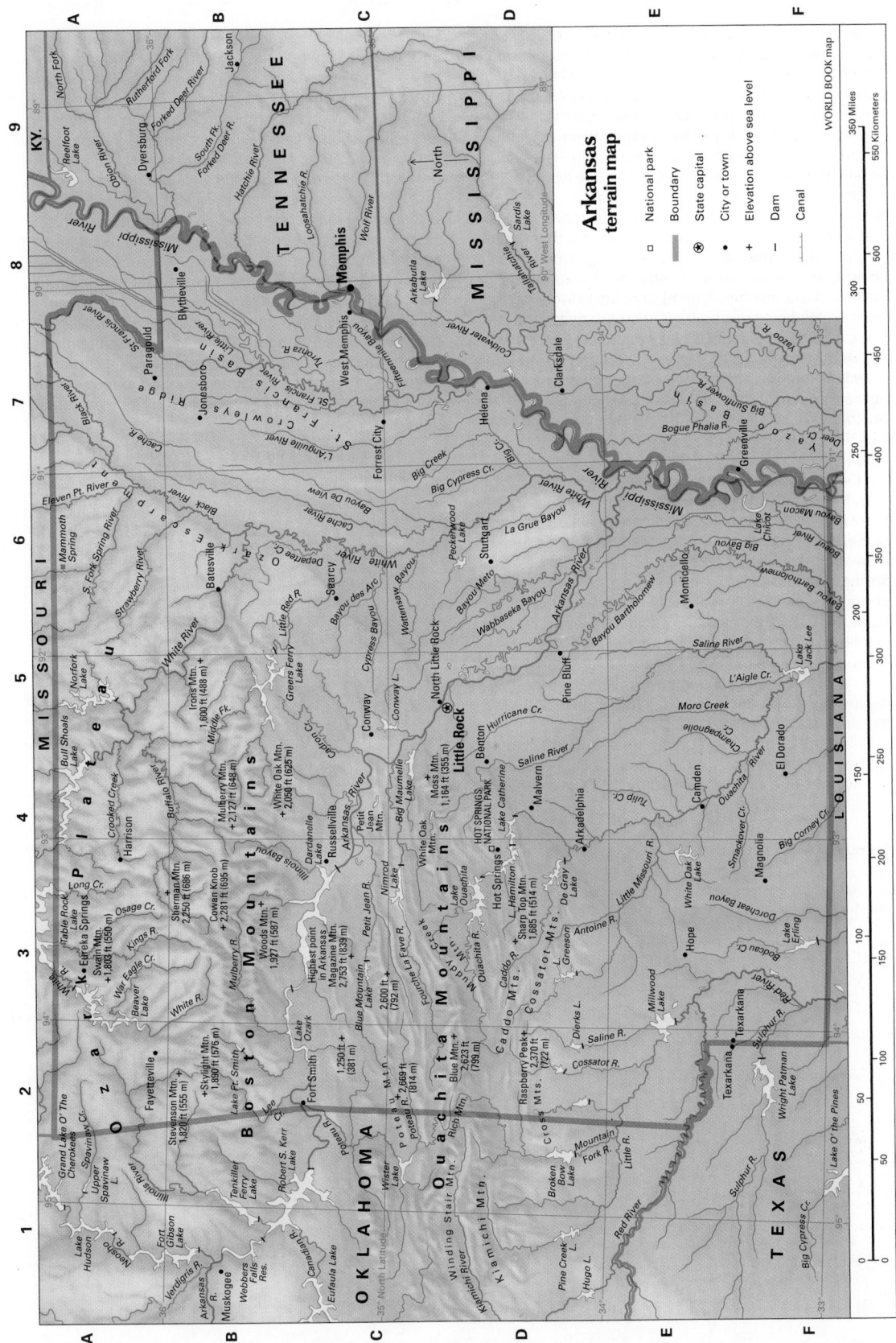

Arkansas
terrain map

▫	National park
▬	Boundary
⊛	State capital
•	City or town
+	Elevation above sea level
—	Dam
～	Canal

WORLD BOOK map

350 Miles
550 Kilometers

largest river within the state, flows southeast across Arkansas. The McClellan-Kerr Arkansas River Navigation System was completed in 1970. The system allows boats to travel up the Arkansas River from its mouth at the Mississippi River to Tulsa, Oklahoma. Other important rivers in the state include the Ouachita River in south-central Arkansas, the St. Francis River in the east, the Red River in the southwest, and the White River in northern and eastern Arkansas. The unpolluted, free-flowing Buffalo National River is in the Ozarks.

Lake Chicot, the largest natural lake in the state, is an *oxbow lake,* formed by a river's changing its course (see **Oxbow lake**). Several smaller Arkansas lakes were also formed in this manner. A number of large lakes have been created by dams built on Arkansas rivers and streams. A chain of artificially created lakes nestles in the Ouachita Mountains. These include Lakes Catherine, Hamilton, and Ouachita. Lakes along the White River in northern Arkansas include Beaver Lake, Bull Shoals Lake, Norfork Lake, and Table Rock Lake. Big Maumelle Lake and Nimrod Lake lie west of Little Rock.

Springs in Arkansas are especially plentiful around the foothills of the Ouachita and Ozark mountains. Every year, thousands of people visit the state's springs in hope that the waters will relieve certain illnesses. Some of the springs contain minerals. Many, however, are known for their purity and their lack of minerals. Eureka Springs in the Ozarks has nearly 65 springs. Mammoth Spring, also in the Ozarks, is one of the largest springs in the United States. About 235 million gallons (890 million liters) of cold water gush from the earth each day. The state's famous Hot Springs consists of 47 different springs that together yield about 1 million gallons (3.8 million liters) of water a day. The temperature of the water remains constant at about 143 °F (62 °C).

Plant and animal life. Forests cover about half of Arkansas. The state's most common trees include ashes, basswoods, buckeyes, elms, hackberries, hawthorns, hickories, hollies, maples, oaks, plums, wild cherries, and willows. Flowering trees include the dogwood, locust, magnolia, red haw, and redbud.

Arkansas has many kinds of wildflowers, including American bellflowers, orchids, passionflowers, water lilies, wild verbenas, and yellow jasmines. Ferns and herbs are plentiful. The fern *Woodsia scopulina,* which grows on Magazine Mountain, is found nowhere else between the Allegheny and Rocky mountains.

Animal life in Arkansas's fields and forests includes black bears, bobcats, deer, foxes, gray and red squirrels, and rabbits. Mountainous regions have minks, muskrats, opossums, raccoons, skunks, weasels, and woodchucks. Arkansas has many varieties of game birds, including pheasants, quail, wild ducks, wild geese, wild turkeys, and woodcocks. Common songbirds include the blue jay, brown-headed nuthatch, brown thrasher, cardinal, goldfinch, mockingbird, painted bunting, phoebe, robin, warbler, and whip-poor-will. Reptiles include lizards,

Average monthly weather

Fort Smith						Little Rock				
	Temperatures				Days of		Temperatures			Days of
	°F		°C		rain or		°F		°C	rain or
	High	Low	High	Low	snow		High	Low	High Low	snow
Jan.	50	29	10	−2	7	Jan.	51	31	11 −1	9
Feb.	55	33	13	1	7	Feb.	55	35	13 2	9
Mar.	65	41	18	5	9	Mar.	64	43	18 6	10
Apr.	74	50	23	10	9	Apr.	73	51	23 11	9
May	81	59	27	15	10	May	81	61	27 16	10
June	88	68	31	20	8	June	89	69	32 21	8
July	93	72	34	22	7	July	93	73	34 22	8
Aug.	93	71	34	22	6	Aug.	93	72	34 22	6
Sept.	85	62	29	17	7	Sept.	86	65	30 18	7
Oct.	75	51	24	11	7	Oct.	75	53	24 12	7
Nov.	63	40	17	4	7	Nov.	63	42	17 6	8
Dec.	52	31	11	−1	7	Dec.	52	34	11 1	9

Average January temperatures

Arkansas has cool winters. The northern area has the coolest temperatures, which rise steadily to the south.

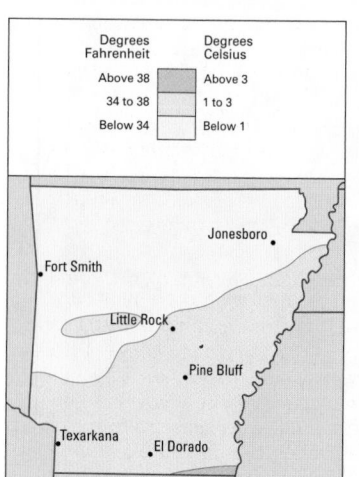

Average July temperatures

The state has warm to hot summers, with most of Arkansas averaging above 80 °F (27 °C). The far north is cooler.

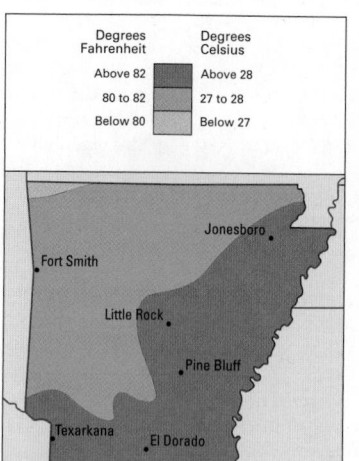

Average yearly precipitation

Arkansas has a rainy climate. The heaviest precipitation generally falls in the southern section of the state.

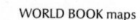

WORLD BOOK maps

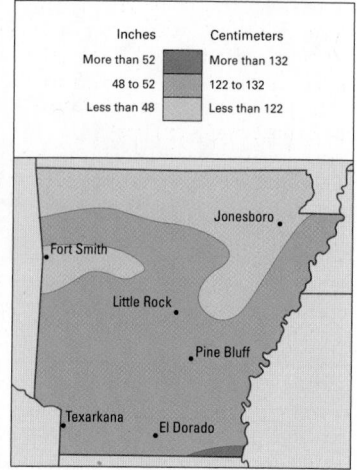

turtles, and many kinds of snakes. The lakes, rivers, and streams are filled with bass, bream, catfish, crappies, drum, perch, pickerel, sturgeon, and trout.

Climate. Arkansas has a warm, moist climate with warm to hot summers and cool winters. The highlands of northern and western Arkansas are cooler than the lower regions to the south and east.

July temperatures average 77 °F (25 °C) in northwestern Arkansas and 82 °F (28 °C) in the lowlands. Even in summer, the highland regions are cool at night. In January, temperatures average from 36 °F (2 °C) in the northwest to 44 °F (7 °C) in the south and east. The lowlands often have warm, sunny days, even in winter. The state's highest recorded temperature, 120 °F (49 °C), was at Ozark on Aug. 10, 1936. The lowest recorded temperature, –29 °F (–34 °C), was in Benton County on Feb. 13, 1905.

Yearly precipitation averages about 50 inches (127 centimeters). It ranges from about 42 inches (107 centimeters) in the far north-central region to about 56 inches (142 centimeters) in the core of the Ouachita mountain region. Snowfall in Arkansas averages about 6 inches (15 centimeters) a year. The snow occurs mostly in the highlands.

Economy

Service industries of Arkansas, taken together, account for the largest portion of the *gross domestic product*—the total value of all goods and services produced in the state in a year. Manufacturing is one of the most important economic activities in Arkansas.

Natural resources of Arkansas include fertile soils and rich mineral deposits. The state also has thick forests and abundant water.

Soil. Much of Arkansas has fertile soil. The best farmland lies in the Mississippi Alluvial Plain and the Arkansas and Red river valleys. The northern part of the Ozark Plateau has good loamy soils. The southern Ozarks and Ouachita region have silty and sandy soils. Clay loams mixed with gravel are found in southwest Arkansas. The Crowleys Ridge section of eastern Arkansas has wind-deposited *loess* (fine-grained topsoil).

Minerals. The West Gulf Coastal Plain has petroleum deposits. *Bituminous* (soft) coal and a harder coal called *semianthracite* come from the Arkansas Valley. Natural gas is also found in parts of the valley. Other mined products include bromine, cement, clays, gemstones, gypsum, limestone, sand and gravel, and tripoli.

Forests cover about half of the state. Northwest Arkansas has shortleaf pine and hardwood forests. The southwest has forests of loblolly and shortleaf pines. Most of the eastern forests are hardwood.

Service industries account for the majority of both Arkansas's employment and its gross domestic product. Most of the service industries are concentrated in the Little Rock area and in other metropolitan areas.

Little Rock, the state capital, is the center of state government activities. Many financial companies and insurance companies also have offices in Little Rock. Many hotels, restaurants, and retail trade establishments operate in the Little Rock area and in northwestern Arkansas. Large hospitals provide medical care in Fayetteville, Fort Smith, Jonesboro, and Little Rock. Little Rock Air Force Base is the largest military installation in Arkansas.

Dillard's, Inc., a chain of department stores, is based in Little Rock. Walmart Inc., the nation's largest discount-store chain, is based in Bentonville. Two leading U.S. trucking companies have headquarters in the state. They are J. B. Hunt, in Lowell, and ABF Freight System, Inc., in Fort Smith.

Manufacturing. Food products are the state's leading manufactured items. Poultry processing is the leading food-processing activity. Tyson Foods, Inc., based in Springdale, is one of the world's largest poultry producers and processors. Food-processing plants are in Fort Smith, Jonesboro, Little Rock, and other cities.

Fabricated metal products, primary metals products, and transportation equipment are also important manufactured items. Architectural and structural metals are the most valuable types of fabricated metal products made in the state. Aluminum, iron, and steel are the leading types of primary metals. Aircraft parts, motor vehicle parts, and railroad cars are made in Arkansas.

Agriculture. Farmland covers about two-fifths of the state's land area. Livestock products provide about three-fifths of the farm income. *Broilers* (young, tender chickens) are the leading farm product. Arkansas is one of the leading states in the production of broilers. Most broilers are raised in the western part of the state.

Beef cattle, dairy products, eggs, hogs, and turkeys are also important livestock products. Beef cattle are raised in most parts of the state. Dairy farming is centered in the Ozark Plateau and near Little Rock. Egg production is heaviest in the northwest corner of the state. Hogs are raised mainly in the western part of the state. Arkansas is a leading state in turkey production.

Crops account for much of the farm income. Cotton, rice, and soybeans are among the state's most valuable crops. Arkansas ranks among the leading states in both cotton and soybean production. Both cotton and soybeans are primarily grown in the east. Arkansas is the leading U.S. producer of rice. Rice is grown mainly in the Mississippi Alluvial Plain region. Some farmers flood their rice fields and raise fish in them. Other leading crops include corn, hay, and wheat. Corn and wheat are primarily grown in the east, and hay is important in northwestern Arkansas.

Mining. Natural gas is the leading mined product of Arkansas. Petroleum ranks second. Much of the state's natural gas is found in an area called the Arkoma Basin. The Arkoma Basin extends from western Arkansas into Oklahoma. The largest oil fields in Arkansas lie near the southern border.

Bromine and crushed stone are also major mined products. Arkansas is the only bromine-mining state. Bromine is obtained from underground *brines* (salty waters) in the south-central part of the state. Several areas in Arkansas have stone quarries. Arkansas is the only state to produce novaculite, a dense, silica-rich stone.

Electric power and utilities. Plants that burn coal, plants that burn natural gas, and nuclear plants are the leading producers of electric power. Hydroelectric

Arkansas economy

General economy

Gross domestic product (GDP)* (2017) $122,704,000,000
    Rank among U.S. states   34th
Unemployment rate (2018)   3.7% (U.S. avg: 3.9%)

*Gross domestic product is the total value of goods and services produced in a year.
Sources: U.S. Bureau of Economic Analysis and U.S. Bureau of Labor Statistics.

Agriculture

Cash receipts $8,917,844,000
    Rank among U.S. states   14th
Distribution   60% livestock, 40% crops
Farms   42,600
Farm acres (hectares)   13,900,000 (5,630,000)
    Rank among U.S. states   22nd
Farmland   41% of Arkansas

Leading products

1. Broilers   (ranks 2nd in U.S.)
2. Soybeans
3. Rice   (ranks 1st in U.S.)
4. Cattle and calves
5. Chicken eggs   (ranks 4th in U.S.)
Other products: corn, cotton, greenhouse and nursery
  products, hay, hogs, peanuts, sorghum, turkeys, wheat.

Manufacturing

Value added by manufacture* $25,095,630,000
    Rank among U.S. states   30th

Leading products

1. Food and beverage products
2. Paper products
3. Fabricated metal products
4. Transportation equipment
5. Machinery
Other products: chemicals, plastics and rubber products,
  primary metal products wood products.

*Value added by manufacture is the increase in value of raw materials as they
 become finished products.

Production and workers by economic activities

Economic activities	Percent of GDP produced	Employed workers	
		Number of people	Percent of total
Finance, insurance, & real estate	19	156,000	10
Community, business, & personal services	18	479,400	29
Trade, restaurants, & hotels	18	336,100	21
Manufacturing	15	161,000	10
Government	13	228,300	14
Transportation & communication	7	85,900	5
Construction	4	88,700	5
Utilities	3	8,200	1
Agriculture	2	69,300	4
Mining	1	15,800	1
Total	100	1,628,700	100

Figures are for 2016; employment figures include full- and part-time workers.
Source: *World Book* estimates based on data from U.S. Bureau of Economic Analysis.

Mining

Nonfuel mineral production (2015) $849,000,000
    Rank among U.S. states   26th
Coal (tons*)   43,000
    Rank among U.S. states   24th
Crude oil (barrels†)   5,288,000
    Rank among U.S. states   20th
Natural gas (cubic feet‡)   707,292,000,000
    Rank among U.S. states   10th

*One ton equals 0.9072 metric ton.
†One barrel equals 42 gallons (159 liters).
‡One cubic foot equals 0.0283 cubic meter.

Leading product

Natural gas
Other products: bromine, crushed stone, portland cement,
  sand and gravel.

Figures are for 2017, except for the manufacturing figures, which are for 2016.
Sources: U.S. Census Bureau, U.S. Department of Agriculture, U.S. Geological Survey.

continued on page 711

Economy of Arkansas

This map shows the economic uses of land in Arkansas
and where the state's leading
farm, mineral, and forest
products are produced. Major manufacturing centers are
shown in red.

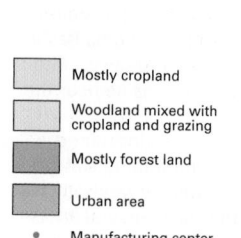

   Mostly cropland

   Woodland mixed with
   cropland and grazing

   Mostly forest land

   Urban area

•   Manufacturing center

•   Mineral deposit

WORLD BOOK map

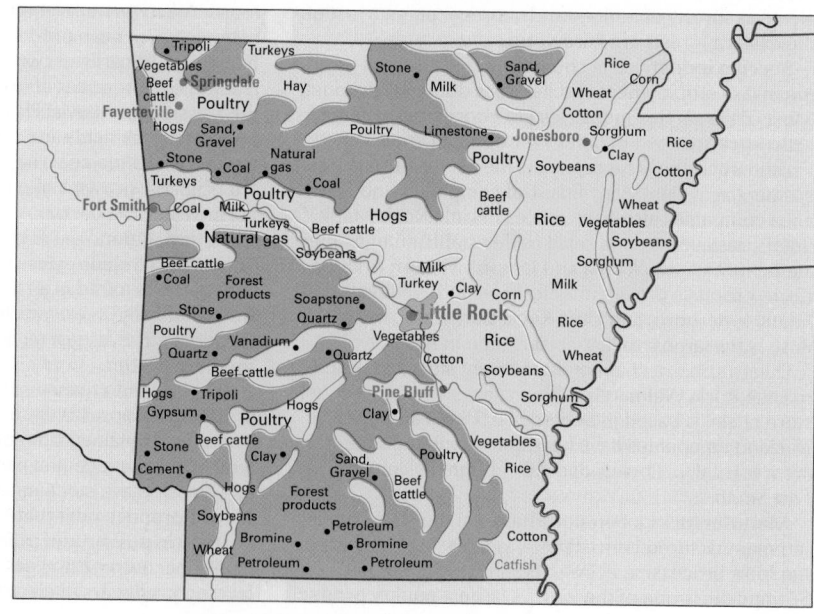

Electric power	
Coal	43.3%
Natural gas	28.5%
Nuclear	20.9%
Hydroelectric	4.8%
Other	2.5%

Figures are for 2017.   Source: U.S. Energy Information Administration.

plants and other renewable energy sources produce most of the rest of the electric power in Arkansas.

Transportation. The earliest settlements in Arkansas were built along rivers. Flatboats and keelboats provided early links with New Orleans, St. Louis, and other market centers. Steamboats appeared in the 1820's. Paths and trails were built from the river settlements to other parts of the region.

Stagecoach lines were established in the state in the 1830's. The main early road in Arkansas ran between Memphis and Little Rock and Van Buren. Railroad building in Arkansas began in the 1850's. The earliest railroads were the Memphis and Little Rock, and the Mis-sissippi, Ouachita & Red River. Water transportation in Arkansas declined in the late 1800's, but railroad construction increased. A state highway commission was created in 1913.

Today, Arkansas has an extensive system of roads and highways. Interstate 40, which links Little Rock with Fort Smith and Memphis, and Interstate 30, which runs between Little Rock and Texas, are the busiest highways. Freight railroads operate on thousands of miles of rail line in the state. Little Rock has the state's largest airport.

Waterways connect Arkansas with cities in adjoining states. In 1970, the Arkansas River opened to barge traffic from the Mississippi River to Oklahoma. Fort Smith, Little Rock, and Pine Bluff became river ports.

Communication. The *Arkansas Gazette,* the state's first newspaper, was founded in Arkansas Post in 1819. It moved to Little Rock in 1821. In 1991, the *Arkansas Democrat* of Little Rock bought the *Gazette* and became the *Arkansas Democrat-Gazette,* now the state's leading paper. Other major papers include *The Jonesboro Sun,* the *Texarkana Gazette,* and the *Times Record* of Fort Smith.

Government

Constitution. The present Constitution of Arkansas was adopted in 1874, after the Reconstruction period ended in the state. Earlier constitutions had been adopted in 1836, 1861, 1864, and 1868.

Amendments (changes) to the Constitution may be proposed in several ways. *Legislative amendments* are introduced by members of the state legislature. They must be approved by a majority of each house of the legislature. *Initiative amendments* are introduced through petitions signed by a specified number of voters. Every amendment must be approved in an election by a majority of the voters who cast ballots on the amendment.

Executive. The governor of Arkansas serves a four-year term and may serve no more than two terms. Other elected state officers are the lieutenant governor, secretary of state, attorney general, treasurer, auditor, and land commissioner. They are also elected to four-year terms and may serve no more than two terms. The governor appoints the *adjutant general* (commander) of the Arkansas National Guard and the heads and members of various departments and commissions. Many of these appointments must be approved by the state Senate.

Legislature, called the General Assembly, consists of a 35-member Senate and a 100-member House of Representatives. Each of the state's 35 senatorial districts elects one senator. Each of the 100 representative districts elects one representative. Senators are elected to four-year terms. Representatives are elected to two-year terms. Legislators can serve no more than 16 years in the General Assembly.

Regular legislative sessions begin on the second Monday in January of odd-numbered years. These sessions last up to 60 calendar days unless extended by a two-thirds vote of both houses of the legislature. Fiscal legislative sessions begin on the second Monday in February of even-numbered years. Fiscal sessions last up to 30 calendar days unless extended by a three-fourths vote of both houses of the legislature. The governor may call the legislature into special session, which has no time limit.

In 1965, a federal district court ordered the state Board of Apportionment to *reapportion* (redivide) the legislature to provide equal representation based on population. The governor, secretary of state, and attorney general make up the Board of Apportionment. The board drew reapportionment plans for the House and Senate. The federal district court and the Supreme Court of the United States approved the plans. The state Board of Apportionment has reapportioned the Arkansas legislature after every federal census since 1970.

Courts. The highest court in Arkansas is the state Supreme Court. It consists of a chief justice and six associate justices, all elected to eight-year terms. The Court of Appeals hears appeals from circuit courts. It has a chief judge and 11 associate judges, all elected to eight-year terms. The state is divided into 23 circuit court districts that elect circuit court judges to six-year terms. Other Arkansas courts include district and city courts. These courts hear minor civil and criminal cases.

Local government. Each of the state's 75 counties is administered by the county judge. The judge approves county expenditures and is the chief executive officer of the county. The judge also presides over the Quorum Court, a legislative group whose duties include approving the county budget. The county judge, Quorum Court members, and county constitutional officers are elected to two-year terms. County constitutional officials include the assessor, the circuit clerk, the county clerk, the medical examiner or coroner, the sheriff, the surveyor, the treasurer, and the collector. Some counties have various combinations of these offices. For example, some counties combine the offices of the county and circuit clerks or those of the sheriff and collector. Counties may reorganize their governments by vote of the people.

The majority of Arkansas cities follow the mayor-council form of government. Some cities run according to the council-manager or city administrator forms.

Revenue. Taxes are the largest source of the state government's *general revenue* (income). They account for about half of the state's general revenue. They include corporate and individual income taxes, a general sales tax, license fees, and taxes on alcoholic beverages, motor fuels, and tobacco products. Federal grants are the second largest source of revenue. They account for about a third of the state's general revenue.

Politics. The Democratic Party controlled Arkansas politics from the late 1800's until the 1960's. From 1874 until 1966, no Republican was elected governor of the state nor elected to a seat in the U.S. Congress. However, Republicans have steadily gained strength in the state since the 1960's. Voters supported Democratic Arkansas native Bill Clinton, however, in his successful campaigns for president in the 1990's. For Arkansas's voting record in presidential elections, see **Electoral College** (table).

The governors of Arkansas

	Party	Term		Party	Term
James Sevier Conway	Democratic	1836-1840	Joseph Taylor Robinson	Democratic	1913
Archibald Yell	Democratic	1840-1844	George Washington Hays	Democratic	1913-1917
Thomas S. Drew	Democratic	1844-1849	Charles Hillman Brough	Democratic	1917-1921
John Seldon Roane	Democratic	1849-1852	Thomas Chipman McRae	Democratic	1921-1925
Elias Nelson Conway	Democratic	1852-1860	Thomas J. Terral	Democratic	1925-1927
Henry Massey Rector	Democratic	1860-1862	John Ellis Martineau	Democratic	1927-1928
Harris Flanagin			Harvey Parnell	Democratic	1928-1933
(Confederate governor)	Democratic	1862-1865*	Junius Marion Futrell	Democratic	1933-1937
Isaac Murphy			Carl E. Bailey	Democratic	1937-1941
(Union governor)	Union	1864-1868*	Homer Martin Adkins	Democratic	1941-1945
Powell Clayton	Republican	1868-1871	Benjamin T. Laney	Democratic	1945-1949
Ozra A. Hadley	Republican	1871-1873	Sidney Sanders McMath	Democratic	1949-1953
Elisha Baxter	Republican	1873-1874	Francis Cherry	Democratic	1953-1955
Augustus Hill Garland	Democratic	1874-1877	Orval E. Faubus	Democratic	1955-1967
William R. Miller	Democratic	1877-1881	Winthrop Rockefeller	Republican	1967-1971
Thomas J. Churchill	Democratic	1881-1883	Dale L. Bumpers	Democratic	1971-1975
James Henderson Berry	Democratic	1883-1885	David H. Pryor	Democratic	1975-1979
Simon P. Hughes	Democratic	1885-1889	Bill Clinton	Democratic	1979-1981
James Philip Eagle	Democratic	1889-1893	Frank D. White	Republican	1981-1983
William Meade Fishback	Democratic	1893-1895	Bill Clinton	Democratic	1983-1992
James P. Clarke	Democratic	1895-1897	Jim Guy Tucker	Democratic	1992-1996
Daniel Webster Jones	Democratic	1897-1901	Mike Huckabee	Republican	1996-2007
Jeff Davis	Democratic	1901-1907	Mike Beebe	Democratic	2007-2015
John Sebastian Little	Democratic	1907-1909	Asa Hutchinson	Republican	2015-
George Washington Donaghey	Democratic	1909-1913			

*In 1864 and 1865, Arkansas had two governors—one for the Confederate State of Arkansas, one for the Union State of Arkansas.

History

Early days. American Indians lived in the Arkansas region about 12,000 years ago. Early European explorers found three principal tribes—the Caddo, Osage, and Quapaw—in the region.

Exploration and settlement. In 1541, Hernando de Soto, a Spanish explorer, led an expedition that reached Arkansas. The Europeans failed to find the gold they were searching for, but historians believe the expedition introduced diseases that killed much of the population. In 1673, Father Jacques Marquette and Louis Jolliet of France traveled down the Mississippi to the mouth of the Arkansas River, where they met Quapaw Indians. In 1682, René-Robert Cavelier, Sieur de La Salle, claimed the Mississippi Valley for France. La Salle made a grant of land to Henri de Tonty, who built a trading station called the Post of Arkansas (also known as Arkansas Post) near the mouth of the Arkansas River in 1686.

In 1717, France gave exclusive trading rights in Louisiana to Scottish banker John Law. To finance his company, Law developed a plan called the "Mississippi Scheme" (see **Mississippi Scheme**). Law's company eventually collapsed in a financial disaster called the "Mississippi Bubble." But the scheme brought many set-tlers to Louisiana. About 100 Europeans and a few African slaves settled near the Post. Most of the settlers left, but some farmers remained.

In 1762, during the French and Indian War (1754-1763), France ceded Spain the land west of the Mississippi River. This land included the Louisiana Territory. In 1800, Spain transferred the Louisiana Territory back to France. In 1803, the United States bought the Louisiana Territory from France. See **Louisiana Purchase.**

Territorial years. In 1812, the southern part of the Louisiana Territory was made the state of Louisiana. The northern part, including Arkansas, became the Missouri Territory. In 1817, the U.S. government established Fort Smith in what is now northwestern Arkansas to keep peace among Indian tribes in the region. In 1819, the government created the Arkansaw Territory. It included present-day Arkansas and part of what is now Oklahoma. The town of Fort Smith grew up around the fort. Van Buren developed nearby. The town of Washington (now a state park) became an important stopping point on the route to Texas.

In the early 1800's, northwestern Arkansas became a temporary home to large numbers of Cherokee Indians.

Historic Arkansas

Louis Jolliet and Jacques Marquette explored the Mississippi River as far south as the mouth of the Arkansas River in 1673. Jolliet, a French-Canadian fur trader, and Marquette, a French missionary, traveled in birchbark canoes.

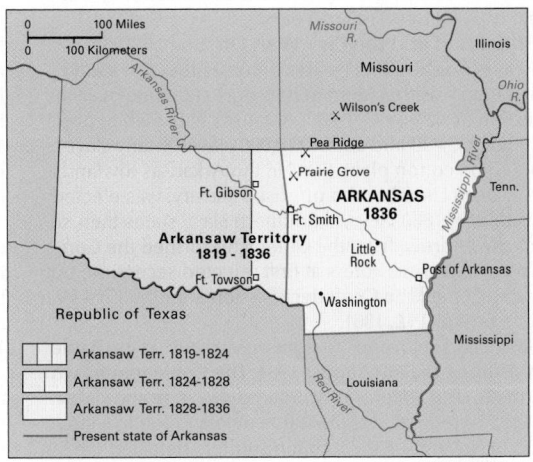

WORLD BOOK map

Arkansas became part of the Louisiana Territory when the United States purchased the land from France in 1803. In 1812, the area became part of the new Missouri Territory. The U.S. Congress created the Arkansaw Territory in 1819. Arkansas became a U.S. state in 1836.

Hattie Caraway of Arkansas, a Democrat, in 1932 became the first woman elected to the United States Senate.

WORLD BOOK illustrations by Richard Bonson, The Art Agency

Important dates in Arkansas

1541 Hernando de Soto of Spain led an expedition to the region.

1673 Jacques Marquette and Louis Jolliet of France explored the Mississippi River in the region.

1682 René-Robert Cavelier, Sieur de La Salle, claimed the Mississippi Valley for France.

1686 Henri de Tonty, a friend of La Salle, established a trading station at the mouth of the Arkansas River.

1803 The United States acquired Arkansas as part of the Louisiana Purchase.

1819 The Arkansaw Territory was formed from the Missouri Territory.

1836 Arkansas became the 25th state on June 15.

1861 Arkansas seceded from the Union.

1868 Arkansas was readmitted to the Union.

1874 Arkansas adopted its present constitution.

1921 The first oil well was drilled in the El Dorado field.

1957 National Guard units and federal troops helped enforce a court order to integrate Little Rock's Central High School.

1964 Orval E. Faubus became the first Arkansas governor to be elected to a sixth consecutive term.

1970 The Arkansas River Development Program opened the river to navigation from the Mississippi River to Oklahoma.

1993-2001 Former Arkansas Governor Bill Clinton served as the 42nd president of the United States.

But the Cherokee and other eastern tribes were forcibly moved to Indian Territory (present-day Oklahoma) during the 1830's (see **Trail of Tears**).

Statehood and the Civil War. On June 15, 1836, Arkansas was admitted to the Union as the 25th state. The nation was then engaged in a great debate over the question of slavery. By 1860, Arkansas had a white population of 435,450 and about 110,000 slaves. Many slaves worked on cotton plantations in the Arkansas lowlands.

Abraham Lincoln, who opposed slavery, was elected president in 1860. Several Southern slave states then *seceded* (withdrew) from the Union and formed the Confederacy. Arkansas voters at first rejected secession, but the state joined the Confederacy soon after the Civil War began on April 12, 1861.

Arkansas sent troops to fight in Missouri at the Battle of Wilson's Creek in August 1861. The Confederates won the battle. The Union Army entered the state and defeated the Confederates at the Battle of Pea Ridge in March 1862. In November 1862, Union soldiers defeated the Confederates at the Battle of Prairie Grove.

On Sept. 10, 1863, the Union Army took Little Rock. The Confederates then moved their capital to Washington in southwestern Arkansas. In 1864, Arkansans loyal to the Union wrote a new state constitution, establishing a Union government in Little Rock and abolishing slavery. But much of the state was not controlled by either the Union or the Confederacy. Lawless *bushwhackers* robbed and murdered many people.

Reconstruction. During the Reconstruction period that followed the war, ex-Confederates dominating the Arkansas legislature refused to rejoin the Union. The U.S. Congress put Arkansas under military control. Federal troops occupied the state from 1867 to 1874.

Arkansas was readmitted to the Union in 1868. In that year, the state adopted a new constitution, giving black men the right to vote but denying it to ex-Confederates. The Republican government tried to speed economic development, establish schools, and protect the civil rights of ex-slaves. Violence broke out between Republicans and Democrats and between whites and blacks.

Arkansas Gazette

Conflict over school integration occurred at Central High School in Little Rock in 1957. President Dwight D. Eisenhower sent United States Army troops to the school to enforce a federal court order to integrate the school.

Antiblack groups such as the Ku Klux Klan spread terror.

In 1872, two Republicans clashed in the contest for governor. Elisha Baxter defeated Joseph Brooks, but Brooks charged fraud and claimed that he had won. On April 15, 1874, Brooks forced Baxter to leave the Statehouse at gunpoint. Rival supporters of the men clashed in what was called the Brooks-Baxter War. On May 15, 1874, President Ulysses S. Grant proclaimed Baxter the governor. Later in 1874, the state adopted a new constitution, which, though much amended, is still in use.

The late 1800's. New railroads crisscrossed Arkansas in the late 1800's. Timber companies moved to the state to harvest the rich forest resources. New levees along the rivers and drainage ditches produced a land boom in the Delta. Bauxite was discovered near Little Rock in 1887, and mines opened.

The early 1900's brought continued development. Improved schools, medical care, and other government services were available at least in the towns. Rice growing was introduced in eastern Arkansas and began to replace cotton. In 1921, oil was found near El Dorado. The state's first large hydroelectric dam was built in 1924.

However, agricultural prices fell after 1920, and many Arkansans lost their farms. The state was also affected by a destructive Mississippi flood in 1927, by a drought in 1930, and by the Great Depression of the 1930's. In 1934, after the price of cotton fell below the cost of production, some rebellious Arkansas farmers organized the short-lived Southern Tenant Farmers Union at Tyronza. But conditions remained poor for tenant farmers and sharecroppers.

In 1932, an Arkansas woman, Hattie Caraway, became the first woman elected to the United States Senate. She won a special election held shortly after the death of her husband, U.S. Senator Thaddeus Caraway.

The mid-1900's. Farming and mining expanded in Arkansas during World War II (1939-1945). Soon after the war, the state began to shift from an agricultural to an industrial economy. Many farmworkers were replaced by the increased use of farm machinery. Manufacturing grew, but not fast enough to provide jobs for all these unskilled workers. Many left Arkansas to find jobs in other states. In spite of these problems, the number of Arkansas manufacturing plants more than doubled during the 1940's and 1950's. A number of plants were attracted to the state by the Arkansas Industrial Development Commission, which was established in 1955.

In 1957, Arkansas became a center of the controversy over school integration. The Supreme Court of the United States had ruled in 1954 that compulsory segregation in public schools is unconstitutional. In 1957, a federal court ordered Central High School in Little Rock to integrate. Governor Orval E. Faubus sent the Arkansas National Guard to block integration. President Dwight D. Eisenhower then put the National Guard under federal control and sent U.S. Army troops to enforce the court order. By 1970, most Arkansas schools and other public facilities were integrated to a degree.

In the early 1960's, Arkansas's manufacturing income passed its farm income for the first time. Faubus was re-elected governor in 1964 to a sixth consecutive term. No other Arkansas governor had served more than three terms. In 1967, Winthrop Rockefeller became Arkansas's first Republican governor since Reconstruction days.

The late 1900's. The Arkansas River Development Program was completed in 1970. The development, renamed the McClellan-Kerr Arkansas River Navigation System, opened the river to navigation across the state from the Mississippi River into Oklahoma.

Bill Clinton, a Democrat who had been elected governor of Arkansas five times, was elected president of the United States in 1992 and reelected in 1996.

In May 1996, Governor Jim Guy Tucker of Arkansas was convicted of conspiring to defraud financial institutions and win illegal loans. He resigned from office. He was sentenced to probation and community service.

The early 2000's. Today, Arkansas faces such tasks as reducing air and water pollution, providing enough energy for the state, improving its public education, and strengthening its unstable farm economy. State officials have succeeded in some attempts to promote trade with other countries and to attract new industry. The northwest part of the state has thrived, and retirees have found this region attractive. However, many Delta counties have lost population.

Arkansas has made repeated attempts to bring its schools up to the national average, but problems of funding remain. Private schools and home-schooling have increased in popularity. New junior colleges and new branches of existing colleges have expanded educational opportunities.   Michael B. Dougan and John G. Hehr

Related articles in *World Book* include:

Biographies

Caraway, Hattie O. W.	La Salle, René-Robert
Clinton, Bill	Cavelier, Sieur de
De Soto, Hernando	MacArthur, Douglas
Fulbright, J. William	Marquette, Jacques
	Robinson, Joseph T.

Cities

Fort Smith	Hot Springs	Little Rock

History

Caddo Indians	Civil War, American	Mound builders
Carpetbaggers	Little Rock Nine	Osage Indians
Cherokee Indians	Louisiana Purchase	Reconstruction

Physical features

Arkansas River	Ouachita River
Hot Springs National Park	Ozark Mountains
Lake Ouachita	Red River
Mississippi River	

Outline

I. **People**
  A. Population
  B. Schools
  C. Libraries
  D. Museums
II. **Visitor's guide**
III. **Land and climate**
  A. Land regions
  B. Rivers and lakes
  C. Springs
  D. Plant and animal life
  E. Climate
IV. **Economy**
  A. Natural resources
  B. Service industries
  C. Manufacturing
  D. Agriculture
  E. Mining
  F. Electric power and utilities
  G. Transportation
  H. Communication
V. **Government**
  A. Constitution
  B. Executive
  C. Legislature
  D. Courts
  E. Local government
  F. Revenue
  G. Politics
VI. **History**

Additional resources

Level I
Altman, Linda J., and others. *Arkansas.* 2nd ed. Benchmark Bks., 2009.
Levy, Janey. *Arkansas: Past and Present.* Rosen Central, 2011.
Prentzas, G. S. *Arkansas.* Children's Pr., 2009.
Tieck, Sarah. *Arkansas.* ABDO, 2013.

Level II
Christ, Mark K. *Civil War Arkansas, 1863: The Battle for a State.* Univ. of Okla. Pr., 2010.
Dougan, Michael B. *Arkansas Odyssey: The Saga of Arkansas from Prehistoric Times to the Present.* Rose Pub. Co., 1994.
Margolick, David. *Elizabeth and Hazel: Two Women of Little Rock.* Yale, 2011.
Whayne, Jeannie M., and others. *Arkansas.* 2nd ed. Univ. of Ark. Pr., 2013.

Arkansas, University of, is a system of higher education with its main campus in Fayetteville. Other major campuses are in Fort Smith, Little Rock, Monticello, and Pine Bluff, and graduate campuses of medicine and public service are in Little Rock. The campuses in Fayetteville and Pine Bluff are *land-grant universities,* which means they are partly endowed by the United States government under the Morrill Acts of 1862 and 1890. The main campus was founded in 1871. The Pine Bluff campus, a historically black university, was founded in 1873. The medical campus was founded in 1879. The Clinton School of Public Service was founded in 2004. Athletic teams at the main campus in Fayetteville are called the Razorbacks. The university system's website at http://www.uasys.edu offers additional information.

Critically reviewed by the University of Arkansas

Arkansas River, *AHR kuhn SAW* or *ahr KAN zuhs,* is a stream of the south-central United States. It is the longest river that flows into the Mississippi-Missouri river system. The total length of the Arkansas is 1,459 miles (2,348 kilometers). The river rises on the east slope of the Rocky Mountains, in the central part of Colorado near Leadville. It flows southeast through Kansas, Oklahoma, and Arkansas. The Cimarron, Canadian, and White rivers flow into the Arkansas. They drain parts of New Mexico, Texas, Oklahoma, Arkansas, and Missouri.

The Arkansas has a rapid current as it flows through mountain valleys and canyons. A rocky canyon worn by the Arkansas is the Royal Gorge. Its walls rise more than 1,000 feet (300 meters). Cities on the banks of the river include Pueblo, Colorado; Wichita, Kansas; Tulsa and Muskogee, Oklahoma; and Fort Smith and Little Rock, Arkansas. The river is named for the Arkansas Indians.

The Arkansas River makes up the main section of the

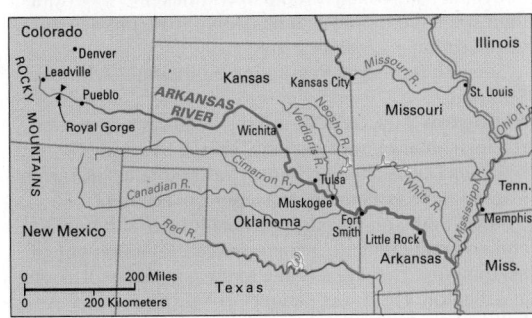

WORLD BOOK map

Location of the Arkansas River

McClellan-Kerr Arkansas River Navigation System. The flow of water on much of the river system is controlled by 18 dam and reservoir projects. These projects control flooding and generate water power. John G. Hehr

See also **Oklahoma** (Rivers and lakes); **Royal Gorge.**

Arkhangelsk, *ahr KHAHN gehlsk* (pop. 348,716), is one of the largest far-northern cities in the world. It is also called Archangel (pronounced *AHRK AYN juhl).* Arkhangelsk lies about 140 miles (225 kilometers) below the Arctic Circle in Russia, where the Dvina River flows into the White Sea. The city extends about 25 miles (40 kilometers) along the shores of the islands in the river's delta. For location, see **Russia** (political map).

Arkhangelsk is a center for the lumber industry and a major port, though the harbor is frozen from November through May, and icebreakers must be used. The city's port exports lumber, metals, and oil products. A railroad connects Arkhangelsk with Russian cities in the south.

Arkhangelsk was founded as Novo-Kholmogory, in 1583. Its Cathedral of the Archangel Michael was built between 1685 and 1699. The city declined during the 1700's and 1800's but regained importance after the railroad was built in 1897. During World War II (1939-1945), Arkhangelsk was an important northern port for receiving supplies from the Allies. Zvi Gitelman

Arkwright, Sir Richard (1732-1792), was a British inventor and manufacturer. In 1769, he patented a spinning machine, called the *water frame* because water powered it. Sets of rollers turning at different speeds drew cotton from the carding machine, which straightened out the fibers. Spindles then twisted the cotton into thread. The water frame made hard, firm, and rather coarse thread.

Arkwright and two manufacturers started cotton mills that combined the various manufacturing processes of machine carding, drawing, roving, and spinning in one operation. Such organization of manufacturing processes contributed to the development of modern factories.

In 1781, Arkwright's patent was challenged and finally canceled on the grounds of previous invention and deliberately vague and confusing specifications. It is now generally agreed that while Arkwright knew of earlier work on the machine, he added mechanical details that made it work. But his prosperity did not suffer seriously when he lost his patent. His experience and business ability helped him keep his advantage. He was knighted in 1786 and died a wealthy man on Aug. 3, 1792.

Arkwright was born on Dec. 23, 1732, in Preston. He became a barber's apprentice and developed a method of dyeing hair, which he sold to wigmakers. Arkwright then spent the money that he gained from this sale on his invention. Richard F. Hirsh

See also **Industrial Revolution** (Spinning machines); **Spinning.**

Arlington (pop. 365,438) is a residential city and recreation center in northeastern Texas. It lies midway between Dallas and Fort Worth. Arlington lies in Tarrant County and has a council-manager government.

Retail trade, manufacturing, health care, and hotels and entertainment are leading sources of employment in Arlington. The city is home to the University of Texas at Arlington. The Texas Rangers of Major League Baseball and the Dallas Cowboys of the National Football League play in the city.

The Arlington area was home to the Caddo people and other Native American groups before white settlers arrived around 1840. In 1848, the Texas Rangers, a frontier defense organization, assigned Colonel Middleton Tate Johnson to a trading post in the area. A community that grew there became known as Johnson's Station. During the 1870's, Andrew Hayter, a Presbyterian minister, helped establish a town near a rail line being built in the area. He named this settlement Arlington, after the Virginia home of Confederate General Robert E. Lee. Arlington was incorporated as a town in 1884. It became known as a market town for products, such as cotton, from nearby farms.

During the 1930's, Arlington gained fame as a center for entertainment. A casino and horse racetrack drew visitors to the city. The city's population boomed after 1950, and rapid growth continued into the first decades of the 2000's. In 2020, Arlington hosted baseball's first neutral-site World Series, a result of precautions taken during the COVID-19 pandemic. Kenneth J. Shenkman

Arlington National Cemetery is one of the largest and most famous national cemeteries in the United States. It covers 639 acres (259 hectares) in Arlington, Virginia, across the Potomac River from Washington, D.C. The cemetery surrounds Arlington House, The Robert E. Lee Memorial, which was the home of General Robert E. Lee of the Confederate Army. It occupies land that was once a part of the estate of Lee's wife, Mary Custis Lee. The United States government made Arlington a national cemetery in 1864. The Department of the Army administers it.

Space in the cemetery is available for honorably discharged winners of the Air Force Cross, Distinguished Service Cross, Distinguished Service Medal, Medal of Honor, Navy Cross, Purple Heart, or Silver Star; members of the armed services who die on active duty; certain disabled veterans; members of the armed forces who have served long enough to be officially retired; and honorably discharged veterans who have held a federal elective office or a Cabinet-level position, or who have served on the Supreme Court of the United States. Their wives or husbands and dependent children

Kurt Scholz, Shostal

The Tomb of the Unknowns in Arlington, Virginia, honors members of the U.S. armed forces who have given their lives in war. A sentry guards this famous memorial day and night.

are also eligible. Until 1967, all honorably discharged veterans could be buried in the cemetery.

The Tomb of the Unknowns of World Wars I and II, the Korean War, and the Vietnam War is in Arlington (see **Unknown soldier**). Wreaths are placed at this tomb on national holidays and during visits of dignitaries. The grave of President John F. Kennedy, marked by an eternal flame, lies on a hillside near Arlington House. Kennedy and William Howard Taft are the only presidents buried in Arlington.

Critically reviewed by Arlington National Cemetery

See also **National cemetery; Washington, D.C.** (picture).

Arm is the upper limb of a human being. Properly, the arm is only the part between the shoulder and elbow. The portion of the arm below the elbow is the *forearm.*

The arm contains one large bone, the *humerus.* Shoulder muscles are attached to its upper portion. Two flexor muscles bend the upper limb at the elbow. These are the *biceps brachii* and the *brachialis.* Two extensor muscles, the *triceps brachii* and the *anconeus,* straighten the upper limb. The forearm contains two bones, the *radius* and the *ulna.* Attached to these are 19 muscles that move the wrist and fingers.

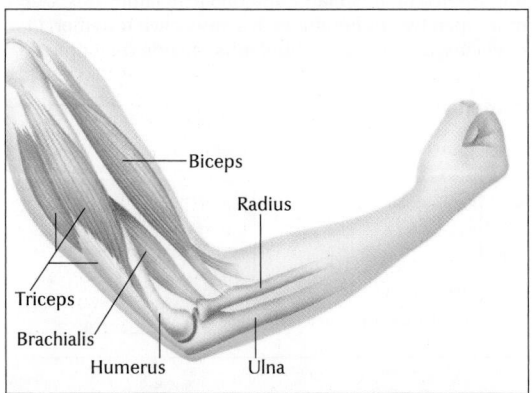

Biceps

Radius

Triceps

Brachialis

Humerus   Ulna

WORLD BOOK illustration by Leonard Morgan

The arm contains three bones—the humerus, the radius, and the ulna. It also contains the biceps and triceps muscles.

Scientists sometimes call the forelimbs of animals arms. Each kind of animal has arms suited to its own needs. However, all arms follow the same basic pattern. The wings of birds and bats, the flippers of seals and whales, and the fins of some fish are all variations of the arm. Because of the complex functional capabilities of their hands, human beings can use their arms for more purposes than can any other animal.   Leslie S. Matthews

See also **Bone; Elbow; Human body** (Anatomy of the human body).

Armada. See Spanish Armada.

Armadillo, *AHR muh DIHL oh,* is any of several small mammals with bony plates in the upper body skin. Armadillos live from Argentina to the southern United States. The animals have strong claws, which they use to dig burrows and to search for food. They use their long, narrow tongue to lick up beetles and other insects. Armadillos may also eat fruit, snails, spiders, and worms. Because an armadillo has only small teeth well back in its mouth, it cannot bite in self-defense.

Francisco Erize, Bruce Coleman Ltd.

The nine-banded armadillo has a protective shell of nine narrow bands of bony plates that slide upon one another.

An armadillo's shell is its best protection. The shell consists of many small plates of bony armor fitted closely together. It is hard and stiff, but is jointed across the animal's back. This jointing enables South American *three-banded armadillos* to curl up into a hard, tight ball with the shell on the outside and the head and feet tucked in, out of harm's way. Few animals can then get a grip on these armadillos with their teeth or claws. But most armadillos hide in their shell only as a last resort. They usually hurry into their burrow at the first sign of danger. When an armadillo is too far from its burrow to hide there, it may dig itself rapidly into the ground if it has time.

Most kinds of armadillos live in South America. They include the *pink fairy armadillo,* which grows about 6 inches (15 centimeters) long, and the *giant armadillo,* which measures approximately 5 feet (1.5 meters) in length. The most widespread type, the *nine-banded armadillo,* ranges from the southern United States to Uruguay. It grows about 2 feet (61 centimeters) long. The female usually gives birth to four young at a time, always identical quadruplets.

Armadillos are the only known animal host for the bacterium that causes leprosy (Hansen's disease) in human beings. For this reason, armadillos prove important in leprosy research.   Duane A. Schlitter

Scientific classification. Armadillos make up the family Dasypodidae. The nine-banded armadillo is *Dasypus novemcinctus.* The pink fairy armadillo is *Chlamyphorus truncatus,* and the giant armadillo is *Priodontes maximus.* Three-banded armadillos make up the genus *Tolypeutes.*

See also **Animal** (How animals protect themselves [picture]); **Edentate; Giant armadillo; Shell** (picture).

Armageddon, *AHR muh GEHD uhn,* is a Greek word taken from the Hebrew *Har-Megiddo,* which probably means *Mount Megiddo.* In the Bible, the Book of Revelation names Armageddon as the place where the rulers of the world will fight a great battle between good and evil.

No Mount Megiddo has been identified. However, an ancient city called *Megiddo* was in the mountains of northern Israel, across the Plain of Esdraelon from Nazareth. Many battles were fought on this plain in Biblical times. Archaeologists from the Oriental Institute in Chicago have found temples, jewelry, art objects, and many other valuable archaeological items at Megiddo.

Joseph M. Hallman

Armaments. See Weapon.

Armani, *ahr MAH nee,* **Giorgio,** *JAWR jee oh*
(1934-   ), is a leading Italian fashion designer. He designs for both men and women. His clothes have a soft, fluid silhouette that became his signature and one of the most important fashion trends of the late 1900's. He uses beautiful textiles to give special distinction to his clothes.

Armani was born in Piacenza, Italy, on July 11, 1934. He began his career as an assistant buyer for a major Italian department store. He then worked with the Italian designer Nino Cerruti in 1961. After free-lancing for a number of manufacturers, Armani introduced his first menswear collection in 1974. The collection created a sensation with a style known as the *unconstructed jacket*—a loose-fitting jacket with no lining or shoulder pads. Armani adapted his style for a line of women's clothes in 1975 when he formed his own company with Italian businessman Sergio Galeotti. Armani's company brought to ready-to-wear clothing exceptional fabric quality, elegance, and a revolutionary emphasis on comfort and informality in tailoring.   Jean L. Druesedow

Armed forces. See Air force; Air Force, United States; Army; Army, United States; Canadian Armed Forces; Coast Guard, United States; Marine; Marine Corps, United States; Navy; Navy, United States.

Armenia is a country in the Caucasus Mountain region in southwestern Asia. It is a rugged land with many mountains and gorges. Yerevan is the country's capital and largest city.

Present-day Armenia and what is now eastern Turkey make up historic Armenia, the original homeland of the Armenian people. This land was conquered many times in its long history. By 1915, the Turks had driven most Armenians out of western Armenia, which became eastern Turkey. In 1920, Russian Communists took control of eastern Armenia. This area became part of the Transcaucasian Republic of the Soviet Union in 1922. In 1936, it became the Armenian Soviet Socialist Republic. Armenia remained under Soviet control until 1991, when the people voted to become an independent nation.

Several million Armenians live outside Armenia. The strong national identity of Armenians worldwide helped keep Armenian culture alive during the Soviet years.

Government. A one-house legislature called the National Assembly makes Armenia's laws. Members are elected by the people to five-year terms. The assembly elects a president, who serves as head of state. The assembly nominates a prime minister, who is formally appointed by the president. The prime minister serves as head of government. The president also appoints a cabinet on the advice of the prime minister.

Armenia's main units of local government are provinces *(marzer)* and communities *(hamainkner)*. Each community has a governing council elected by the people. All Armenians 18 years old or older may vote.

Armenia's highest court is called the Court of Cassation. There are also courts of appeal for criminal, military, civil, and economic cases.

Armenia's armed forces consist of an army, air force, air defense force, and border guard. All males must serve two years in the armed forces, starting at age 18.

People. About 90 percent of Armenia's people are Armenians. Kurds and Russians make up the country's largest minority ethnic groups.

Facts in brief

Capital: Yerevan.
Official language: Armenian.
Official name: Haikakan Hanrapetoutioun (Republic of Armenia).
Area: 11,484 mi² (29,743 km²). *Greatest distances*—north-south, 170 mi (275 km); east-west, 130 mi (210 km).
Elevation: *Highest*—Mount Aragats, 13,419 ft (4,090 m) above sea level. *Lowest*—Aras River at the southeastern border, 1,475 ft (450 m) above sea level.
Population: *Estimated 2022 population*—2,978,000; density, 259 per mi² (100 per km²); distribution, 63 percent urban, 37 percent rural. *2020 official government estimate*—2,961,300.
Chief products: *Agriculture*—barley, cattle, potatoes, sheep, tomatoes, wheat, wine grapes. *Manufacturing*—chemicals, clothing, diamonds, electronics, machinery, processed foods and beverages, tobacco products. *Mining*—copper, gold, lead, zinc.
Flag: Armenia's flag has three horizontal stripes. From top to bottom, the stripes are red, blue, and orange. See Flag (picture: Flags of Asia and the Pacific).
Money: *Basic unit*—dram. One hundred luma equal one dram.

Most of Armenia's people live in urban areas, in apartment buildings. Many people in smaller cities and villages live in single-family houses. Armenians place great importance on hospitality and on close family ties. Often, more than two generations of a family live together. In the cities, many women hold jobs outside the home,

Armenia

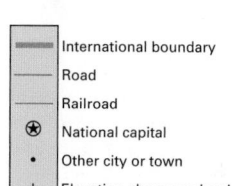

International boundary
Road
Railroad
National capital
Other city or town
Elevation above sea level

WORLD BOOK maps

© Bob Krist, Getty Images

Armenian shoppers examine produce at a market in Yerevan, the nation's capital. The country's farmers raise a variety of fruits and vegetables for local markets.

© Shutterstock

Armenia's rugged land includes mountains and gorges. The country lies on the Armenian Plateau and has an average altitude of 5,000 feet (1,500 meters) above sea level.

but they still do most of the housework and shopping.

Most Armenians speak the Armenian language. It is unlike any other language and has its own alphabet.

Armenia was the first country in the world to make Christianity its official religion. It did so in the early 300's. Today, most Armenians belong to the Armenian Church, an independent church that is close to the Eastern Orthodox Churches in its beliefs.

Armenians enjoy such foods as barbecued shish kebab, bean salads, a thin bread called *lavash,* and *dolma* (cabbage or grape leaves stuffed with rice and meat). Fruit juices, wine and cognac, and *tan* (a mixture of water, yogurt, and salt) are popular beverages.

Chess and backgammon are popular forms of recreation in Armenia. Yerevan has many theaters for motion pictures, concerts, and drama. It also has an opera house and a symphony hall.

Armenians enjoy such sports as basketball, tennis, and soccer. During the summer, many Armenians vacation at Lake Sevan—a popular resort area—or at summer homes in the countryside.

Armenia has a rich artistic tradition. Its people have excelled at such crafts as rug weaving and metalwork. The making of decorative carved stone monuments called *khatchkars* is a purely Armenian art form. Armenian architecture through the ages has produced beautiful stone churches, many with domed roofs. Armenia also has a highly developed tradition of religious music dating to the Middle Ages (from about A.D. 400 through the 1400's). Many Armenian craftworkers and artists carry on old traditions today.

Nearly all adults in Armenia can read and write. The government requires children to attend school from the ages of 6 to 16. A student may then attend a technical school or go on to higher education at a university or specialized institute. Armenia has a number of schools of higher education.

Land and climate. Armenia lies on the Armenian Plateau, a rugged highland that extends from the Little Caucasus Mountains southwest into Turkey. The land is broken by mountains and deep gorges. Armenia has an average altitude of 5,000 feet (1,500 meters) above sea level. The highest mountain ranges stand in central Armenia. The country's highest point, Mount Aragats, rises 13,419 feet (4,090 meters). The lowest altitudes are in the northeast and southeast.

Much of the Armenian Plateau was formed millions of years ago by volcanic activity. For this reason, most of Armenia is covered with volcanic stones. *Faults*—fractures in Earth's rocky outer shell—crisscross the plateau, and earthquakes sometimes occur in Armenia.

Armenia has about 100 mountain lakes. Lake Sevan, in the east, is the largest. It covers about 5 percent of Armenia. The country also has many small, fast-flowing rivers and streams. The longest river, the Aras, separates Armenia from Turkey on the west and from Iran on the south. The streams and rivers serve as a source for irrigation and energy. A chain of hydroelectric power stations stands along the Razdan River, between Lake Sevan and Yerevan.

Most of Armenia's vegetation consists of grasses and shrubs. Some forests of beech, hornbeam, juniper, and oak are found in the northeast and southeast.

Armenia's climate is dry, with long cold winters and short hot summers. January temperatures usually range from 10 to 23 °F (–12 to –5 °C) and can fall below –22 °F (–30 °C). July temperatures average about 50 °F (10 °C) in the mountains and about 77 °F (25 °C) elsewhere.

Armenia receives a yearly rainfall of about 8 to 31 inches (20 to 80 centimeters), rising with elevation. The highest peaks are snow-covered all year.

Economy. Manufacturing and mining are important to Armenia's economy. The chief industries process diamonds and make chemicals, clothing, computer and electronic products, metal products, processed foods, and tobacco products. Armenia is a leading distiller of a type of brandy called *cognac.* The country's main industrial centers include Alaverdi, Kapan, Vanadzor, and

Yerevan. Armenian mines produce copper, gold, molybdenum, silver, and zinc. Construction is also a major contributor to Armenia's economy.

Agriculture employs about a third of the country's workers. Farm products include barley, potatoes, tomatoes, wheat, and wine grapes. Crop production benefits from Armenia's many areas of fertile black topsoils called *chernozem* soils. The Aras River Valley is the chief farming region. Herders raise cattle and sheep on mountain slopes.

Armenia imports more than it exports. The country imports diamonds, food, machinery, natural gas, and petroleum. Leading exports include beverages, copper, diamonds, food, and iron. China, Germany, Iran, Russia, Ukraine, and the United States are among Armenia's chief trading partners.

Armenia has several railways and an extensive road and highway system. Car ownership is steadily increasing in Armenia. Yerevan has a subway. An international airport also operates at Yerevan.

History. People lived in historic Armenia by 6000 B.C. The earliest societies in the region were probably tribal groups that lived by farming or raising cattle. In the 800's B.C., a coalition of several tribes formed the kingdom of Urartu. The Urartians introduced irrigation and built fortresses, palaces, and temples. In the 600's B.C., ancestors of the Armenians migrated—probably from the west—to the Armenian Plateau. They settled with the native population. In the 500's B.C., Urartu was conquered by the Medes, a people from what is now Iran.

Soon after Urartu fell to the Medes, the Medes were conquered by the Persians. Armenia was under Persian and then Greek rule for hundreds of years. But it maintained a degree of independence.

King Tigran II, who came to power in 95 B.C., built an independent Armenian empire that reached from the Caspian Sea to the Mediterranean Sea. The Romans defeated Tigran in 55 B.C., and Armenia became part of the Roman Empire.

In the early A.D. 300's, Armenia became the first nation to adopt Christianity as its state religion. The Armenian alphabet was developed in the early 400's by an Armenian cleric. In 451, Armenians under Vartan Mamikonian defended their religion against the Persians in the Battle of Avarair.

Arabs conquered Armenia in the 600's. In 884, Armenians created an independent kingdom in the northern part of the region. Seljuk Turks conquered Armenia in the mid-1000's, but Armenians established a new state in Cilicia on the Mediterranean coast. This last Armenian kingdom fell to Mamluk invaders in 1375.

Ottoman rule. By 1514, the Ottoman Empire had gained control of Armenia. The Ottomans ruled western Armenia until their defeat in World War I in 1918. Persians gained control of eastern Armenia in 1639. They ruled it until 1828, when Russia annexed eastern Armenia. During the 1800's, the growth of nationalism among Turks, Armenians, and other peoples caused conflicts.

During the late 1800's, Armenians under Ottoman rule suffered increasingly from discrimination, heavy taxation, and armed attacks. From 1894 through 1896, the Ottomans and Kurds, under Sultan Abdülhamit II, carried out a campaign to wipe out Armenians. Hundreds of thousands of Armenians were killed.

Armenia became a battleground between the Ottoman Empire and Russia during World War I (1914-1918). The Ottomans feared that the Armenians would support the Russians. In 1915, the Ottoman government deported Armenians who were living in western Armenia into the deserts of what is now Syria. About 1 ½ million Armenians died from lack of water and starvation or were killed by Ottoman soldiers or Arabs and Kurds. The mass deaths of the Armenians are often referred to as the Armenian Genocide. The term *genocide* refers to the systematic extermination of an ethnic or racial group. See **Armenian Genocide.**

A large number of survivors fled to Russian Armenia. There, in 1918, an Armenian republic was established.

Soviet rule. Conflicts resurfaced between the Armenian republic and the Ottoman Empire. Armenia's leaders reluctantly turned to Communist Russia for protection. In December 1920, eastern Armenia became a Communist republic. The Ottoman Empire kept the rest of Armenia. In early 1922, Armenia joined Azerbaijan and Georgia to form the Transcaucasian Republic. This republic was one of four that joined to form the Soviet Union in late 1922. In 1936, Armenia, Azerbaijan, and Georgia became separate republics of the Soviet Union.

Joseph Stalin became Soviet dictator in 1929. He allowed little expression by nationalists and had many political and cultural leaders killed. After Stalin's death in 1953, the Soviet Union became more tolerant of national differences. Armenia began to develop into a more European-style society while keeping its ethnic culture.

Before the beginning of Soviet rule in the 1920's, most Armenians had lived in rural areas and worked as farmers or herders. Also, because the region lies on ancient trade routes, many Armenians had become merchants or traders. Under Soviet rule, Armenia became industrialized. The Soviet government built many factories and modern apartment buildings in Armenia's cities. Many rural people moved to the cities.

Nagorno-Karabakh, an *autonomous* (self-governing) region in neighboring Azerbaijan, has long been a source of dispute between Armenia and Azerbaijan. Until the late 1980's, a large majority of the people of Nagorno-Karabakh were Armenians. In 1988, large numbers of Armenians demonstrated in Yerevan and other cities, demanding that Nagorno-Karabakh be made part of Armenia. The protests soon led to fighting between Armenians and Azerbaijanis. After the fighting began, about 400,000 Armenians fled to Armenia from Azerbaijan. About 200,000 Azerbaijanis—almost all those who lived in Armenia—fled to Azerbaijan.

On Dec. 7, 1988, a severe earthquake struck Armenia. It killed about 25,000 people and destroyed much property. The destruction caused by the earthquake, along with the large number of refugees from Azerbaijan, led to a severe shortage of housing and jobs in Armenia.

Independence. In 1990, non-Communists won control of Armenia's government. Armenia's legislature then declared that Armenia's laws took precedence over those of the Soviet Union. In August 1991, conservative Communist officials failed in an attempt to overthrow the Soviet Union's president, Mikhail S. Gorbachev. In the upheaval that followed, several republics declared their independence. In a September referendum, the Armenian people voted for independence from the Soviet

Union. In October, Levon Ter-Petrosyan was elected president. The Soviet Union was formally dissolved on December 25. Armenia joined other former republics in an association called the Commonwealth of Independent States.

During the Soviet era, the government owned most businesses, factories, and farmland. In 1991, the government began introducing elements of a free-enterprise system and sold about three-fourths of the farmland to private owners. Through the 1990's, the government converted many other businesses to private ownership.

Recent developments. In 1994, Armenia and Azerbaijan declared a cease-fire in the fighting over Nagorno-Karabakh. However, sporadic fighting continued. Ethnic Armenian forces controlled Nagorno-Karabakh and some surrounding Azerbaijani territory.

In 1996, Ter-Petrosyan was reelected president. Many Armenians protested that the election had been marred by fraud. Ter-Petrosyan resigned in February 1998. The prime minister, Robert Kocharian, became acting president. He was elected later in 1998 and reelected in 2003.

In 1999, gunmen assassinated Prime Minister Vazgen Sargsyan and several other government officials. The gunmen were soon arrested. In 2008, Prime Minister Serzh Sargsyan (no relation to Vazgen) succeeded Kocharian as president. Serzh Sargsyan was reelected in 2013.

In a 2015 referendum, Armenians approved constitutional changes to weaken the presidency. In 2018, the National Assembly elected former Prime Minister Armen Sargsyan (also no relation) president and elected outgoing president Serzh Sargsyan prime minister. Popular protests against Serzh Sargsyan led him to resign and pressured the National Assembly into electing Nikol Pashinyan, the protest leader, as prime minister.

Fighting between Armenia and Azerbaijan flared again in 2020. Azerbaijan seized some areas in and near Nagorno-Karabakh. A truce arranged by Russia allowed Azerbaijan to keep those lands and some other areas.

Nancy Lubin

See also **Armenian Genocide; Azerbaijan; Caucasus; Commonwealth of Independent States; Kurds; Yerevan.**

Armenian Genocide refers to the mass deaths of about 1 ½ million Armenians in the Ottoman Empire during World War I (1914-1918). At the time, the Ottoman Empire covered what is now Turkey, plus some other lands in western Asia. The term *genocide* refers to the systematic extermination of an ethnic or racial group. Historians generally agree that the Armenian deaths were the result of genocide. However, the Turkish government has disputed the details of the deaths and claimed that the incident did not constitute genocide.

From 1514 to 1918, most of Armenia was part of the Ottoman Empire. In the second half of the 1800's, the growth of nationalism among Turks, Armenians, and other peoples began to cause conflicts within the empire. Russia's defeat of the Ottomans in the Russo-Turkish War of 1877-1878 led to the reorganization of parts of the Ottoman Empire. The question of Armenian independence soon drew international interest—and a threat to the stability of a weakened Ottoman Empire.

Ottoman authorities moved to suppress any expressions of Armenian national identity. During the late 1800's, Armenians under Ottoman rule suffered increasingly from ethnic and religious discrimination, heavy taxation, and armed attacks. From 1894 through 1896, and again in 1909 and 1912, Ottoman Turks and Kurds carried out campaigns to wipe out the Armenian population. Many thousands of Armenians were killed.

During World War I, Armenia was a battleground between the Ottoman and Russian empires, and the Ottoman government became concerned with Armenian support for Russia. In 1915, the Ottoman government deported Armenians from western Armenia into a desert area in what is now part of Syria. In what many consider to be genocide, about 1 ½ million Armenians were killed or died from lack of water and food.

The Turkish government, which replaced Ottoman authority after World War I, has claimed that the number of Armenian dead was exaggerated and that the Armenians were casualties of war—not the victims of systematic genocide. But dozens of countries around the world have formally recognized the mass deaths as genocide.

Many survivors fled to Russian Armenia, where the Republic of Armenia was founded in 1918. Further violence against Armenians occurred in Turkey from 1920 to 1923, as the Turks fought to expel the Greek army that was placed there after World War I.

Ronald Bruce St John

See also **Armenia** (Ottoman rule); **Turkey** (After World War I).

Armey, Dick (1940-   ), a Republican from Texas, was a member of the United States House of Representatives from 1985 to 2003, when he retired from office. He was House majority leader from 1995 to 2003.

Armey helped wage an aggressive campaign against policies of the Democratic Party. This campaign helped the Republicans win control of both houses of Congress from the Democrats in the elections of 1994. Armey became a strong supporter of free-market capitalism and an opponent of many government social programs.

Richard Keith Armey was born on July 7, 1940, in Cando, North Dakota. He earned a Ph.D. degree in economics from the University of Oklahoma in 1968. He was a professor of economics at North Texas State University from 1972 to 1983. Armey first won election to the House in 1984.   Jackie Koszczuk

Armor is a covering used primarily for protection in battle. Through the centuries, such materials as animal skins, bronze, and steel have been used to make armor. Until the invention of firearms, armor was designed to match advances in weapons. Today, armor is worn by members of the military and law enforcement. It is also used on ships, tanks, and other military vehicles.

In early times, people wore layers of animal hides to soften blows from clubs and axes. The Assyrians and people of other early civilizations carried shields and wore helmets and body armor made chiefly of leather strengthened with bronze. The Greeks and later the Romans wore helmets, *cuirasses* (short body armor), and *greaves* (leg armor), and they carried large shields. Greek and Roman armor was constructed mainly of bronze or steel, and it served as protection against arrows, spears, and swords.

During the Middle Ages, from about the A.D. 400's through the 1400's, the use of armor reached its peak. During the 1200's, *chain mail* (tiny rings of metal linked together) served as the major form of protection. Suits of chain mail covered a knight's body from head to

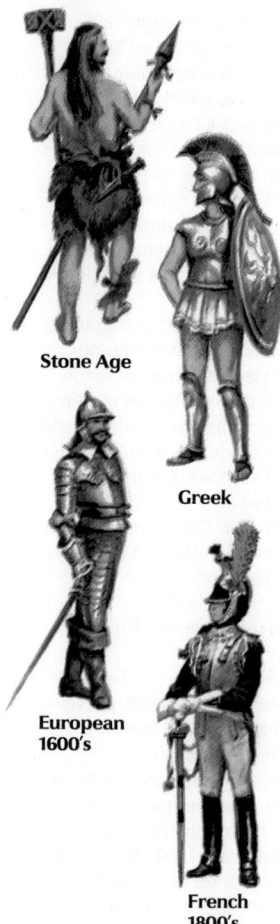

Stone Age

Greek

European 1600's

French 1800's

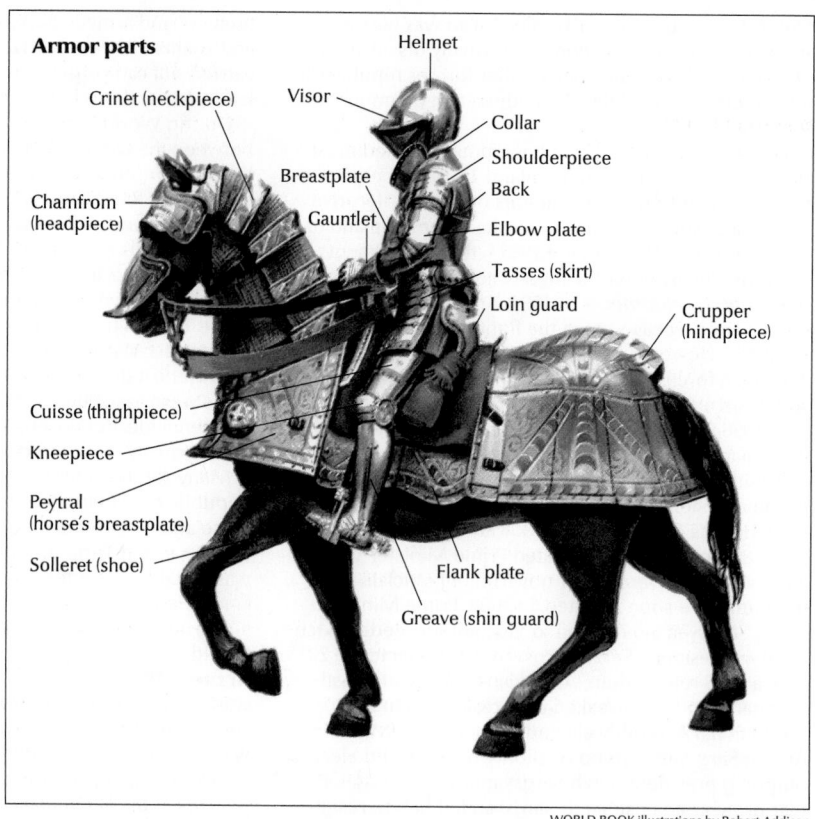

Armor parts

Crinet (neckpiece)

Chamfrom (headpiece)

Breastplate

Gauntlet

Visor

Helmet

Collar

Shoulderpiece

Back

Elbow plate

Tasses (skirt)

Loin guard

Crupper (hindpiece)

Cuisse (thighpiece)

Kneepiece

Peytral (horse's breastplate)

Solleret (shoe)

Flank plate

Greave (shin guard)

WORLD BOOK illustrations by Robert Addison

People have used armor to protect themselves in battle since prehistoric times. The armor worn through the centuries, *left,* was made from such materials as animal skins, bronze, and steel. In the 1400's—during the late Middle Ages—metal armor covered a soldier's entire body, as well as his horse, *above.*

foot and provided protection against arrows, lances, and swords. The crusaders and many other knights also wore metal helmets that covered the face.

By the 1300's, foot soldiers fought with such weapons as crossbows, longbows, maces, and axes. Arrows fired from a longbow or crossbow could pierce chain mail, and blows from an ax or a mace would crush it. As a result, *armorers* (armor makers) began to produce *plate armor* consisting of large pieces of steel. By the 1400's, suits of plate armor were designed to cover the entire body. Helmets, *gauntlets* (gloves), and shoes—all of steel—completed the outfit. Horses wore armor as well. Plate armor was highly effective, but it was extremely heavy and hot to wear. A suit of armor was also expensive, costing as much as a small farm.

Armorers were highly skilled craftworkers. Their job was to preserve lives, particularly those of leaders. After armor became a safe defense, armorers concentrated on decorating armor for tournaments and parades. *Gothic armor* produced in northern Italy and southern Germany became especially well known for its gracefulness and elegance. German *Maximilian armor* of the early 1500's was *fluted* (grooved) to give it extra strength and a glancing surface. By the mid-1500's, armor was etched or engraved with designs or scenes, and was of-

ten gilded or silvered. Later examples imitated current fashions in dress, or were exaggerated and grotesque.

Guns changed the ways of waging war. Armor, made ever thicker and heavier to be bulletproof, became too

© Peter Chartrand, Liaison Agency

Police officers use armor in situations that involve armed suspects. These police officers, equipped with riot shields and bulletproof vests and helmets, are performing a training exercise.

heavy to wear. By the mid-1600's, only helmets and breastplates continued to be used.

Later developments. By the 1900's, the only armor soldiers wore was a helmet. Engineers began to work on group protection, armoring trains, ships, and other vehicles. During World War I (1914-1918), the British developed the tank. The tank became one of the most important weapons in World War II (1939-1945) and later conflicts. During the Korean War (1950-1953) and the Vietnam War (1957-1975), soldiers wore bulletproof body armor made of light, strong synthetic material. Today, some body armor is lined with pockets holding ceramic plates that can break up bullets.

Besides its use in warfare, armor is also worn by some people in their jobs. For example, police officers sometimes wear bulletproof vests and helmets and carry riot shields. Helmets are part of hockey and football players' uniforms.   Robert Powell Smith

See also **Aramid; Knights and knighthood** (Armor); **Gauntlet; Helmet; Shield.**

Arms control is the limiting, regulating, reducing, or eliminating of a nation's armed forces and weapons. Most arms-control agreements are treaties approved by many nations.

Arms-control proposals have ranged from general and complete disarmament to forms of limited arms control. General and complete disarmament would allow nations to keep only those weapons and forces necessary to provide police services and support international peacekeeping units. Limited arms-control measures call for restrictions on testing, production, distribution, or possession of certain types of weapons. The restrictions may ban the weapons entirely or only forbid their presence in certain areas. In addition, nations may limit or ban the distribution of equipment or information that can be used to produce certain kinds of weapons.

Working out an arms-control agreement is a difficult process, especially if relations between the negotiating countries are unstable. Countries negotiating an agreement may be critical and suspicious of each other and therefore may tend to disagree over proposals. Also, it is often hard to compare the military strength of powerful nations because of differences in the types and numbers of weapons. The combined strength of allied nations also makes comparisons difficult.

The current arms-control debate

The argument for arms control. Today, many nations have the ability to make *weapons of mass destruction*—that is, chemical, biological, and nuclear weapons. The existence of such weapons has helped encourage support for arms control. People who favor arms control use the following arguments:

The overwhelming power of modern weapons exceeds any reasonable purpose. Today, one submarine can carry missiles and nuclear warheads that contain more destructive power than all the weapons used in World War II (1939-1945). The use of all existing nuclear warheads in an attack would almost certainly destroy the countries attacked. Similarly, the use of chemical or biological weapons against troops or civilian populations would cause large numbers of deaths.

The threat to use such weapons against a country might itself cause a war. A threatened country might question its ability to survive an attack. As a result, it might strike first if it feared that it was about to be attacked. Arms control is intended to reduce such fears.

Arms control reduces the need for countries to acquire nuclear weapons or increase their supply of other weapons. Arms control thus eases world tension and limits other conditions that might lead to nuclear war.

The argument against arms control. Some nations want to build or acquire sophisticated weapons because they regard them as a symbol of achievement, prestige, and modernness. Also, many people feel more secure if their country is militarily strong. Opponents of arms control use the following arguments:

Armed forces and weapons by themselves do not cause international disputes or tension. They merely reflect political, economic, and other disputes, which must be settled before nations can agree on arms control.

Arms-control agreements between an open, free society and a secret, authoritarian society are risky. The authoritarian nation often will not permit adequate inspection to assure that it is keeping its part of the agreement.

Arms control may damage a nation's military defense. Agreements may call for the destruction of some needed weapons and may also prevent the replacement or improvement of other necessary weapons systems.

History of arms control

Early efforts in arms control. Until the 1900's, there were only a few limited arms-control agreements. One was the Rush-Bagot Agreement of 1817 between the United States and the United Kingdom. This agreement limited each nation's armed forces along the Great Lakes. The peace treaty signed after World War I (1914-1918) disarmed Germany and limited the size of its army. In 1922, the Washington Conference led to an arms-control agreement among France, Italy, Japan, the United Kingdom, and the United States. These nations agreed to destroy some of their battleships and ban construction of others for 10 years. At the London Naval Conference in 1930, Japan, the United Kingdom, and the United States consented to limit the size and guns of their cruisers, destroyers, and submarines. This agreement lasted until 1936.

Arms control in the mid-1900's. Agreements at the end of World War II (1939-1945) provided for the disarmament of Germany and Japan. After the war, the United Nations (UN) tried to obtain an agreement limiting arms for all nations.

In 1952, a 12-nation Disarmament Commission set up by the UN General Assembly began to meet. In 1959, it took in all UN members. In 1961, a treaty to keep Antarctica free of military weapons took effect. In 1963, the Limited Test Ban Treaty was ratified by the United States, the Soviet Union, and the United Kingdom. It prohibited testing of nuclear weapons in the atmosphere, in space, or underwater. A treaty often called the Outer Space Treaty, which took effect in 1967, limited military activity in space. That same year, 21 Latin American states signed the Treaty of Tlatelolco, which banned nuclear weapons in Latin America. Today, most Latin American countries participate in the treaty. In 1968, the UN approved the Treaty on the Non-Proliferation of Nuclear Weapons, which prohibited countries from giving nuclear weapons to other nations. It took effect in 1970.

Several more UN arms-control treaties won approval during the early 1970's. The Seabed Arms Control Treaty, which took effect in 1972, prohibited countries from putting nuclear weapons on the ocean floor more than 12 nautical miles (23 kilometers) from their coastlines. The Biological Weapons Convention, a UN treaty signed in 1972, banned the production and stockpiling of biological weapons. It went into effect in 1975.

Meetings between the Soviet Union and the United States to discuss the possibility of limiting *strategic* (long-range offensive) nuclear weapons led to two agreements in 1972. The first agreement, called the ABM (antiballistic missile) Treaty, limited each nation's defensive missile systems. The other agreement restricted U.S. and Soviet production of certain kinds of offensive nuclear weapons. Both agreements went into force in 1972. The United States withdrew from the ABM Treaty in 2002. See **Strategic Arms Limitation Talks.**

Arms control in the late 1900's and early 2000's.
From the late 1980's, improved relations between the United States and the Soviet Union led to a number of arms-control agreements. A U.S.-Soviet treaty that took effect in 1988 eliminated all of the two nations' ground-launched nuclear missiles with ranges of 500 to 5,500 kilometers (310 to 3,420 miles). It also provided for the first inspection procedures on national territory to support verification. But the United States withdrew from the treaty in 2019, after accusing Russia of violating it.

In 1990, the United States, the Soviet Union, and 20 other nations signed a treaty to destroy large numbers of their tanks and other nonnuclear weapons in Europe. This agreement, called the Treaty on Conventional Armed Forces in Europe, went into effect in 1992.

In July 1991, U.S. President George H. W. Bush and Soviet President Mikhail Gorbachev signed the Strategic Arms Reduction Treaty, or START. This treaty, now known as START I, was designed to reduce U.S. and Soviet long-range nuclear missiles and bombers by about a third. Final approval of the treaty required legislative ratification by both countries. Later in 1991, the United States and the Soviet Union stated that they would destroy many of their short-range nuclear weapons.

The future of START I and many other arms-control agreements became uncertain when the Soviet Union was dissolved in late 1991. This event raised questions about who would be responsible for ratifying and carrying out agreements entered into by the Soviet Union. In 1992, however, officials of Belarus, Kazakhstan, Russia, and Ukraine—the four former Soviet states that possessed nuclear weapons—signed an agreement upholding START I. The agreement also committed Belarus, Kazakhstan, and Ukraine to eliminating their nuclear weapons. The United States and the four former Soviet states ratified the agreement. It went into effect in 1994.

In 1993, Bush and Russian President Boris Yeltsin signed START II. This treaty called for cutting the number of U.S. and former Soviet long-range nuclear weapons to less than half the number proposed by START I. However, START II never went into effect, due to disputes over later amendments to the treaty.

Also in 1993, over 120 nations signed a UN-sponsored treaty banning the manufacture, use, transfer, and stockpiling of chemical weapons. The pact took effect in 1997.

The UN in 1996 approved the Comprehensive Nuclear-Test-Ban Treaty, designed to end the testing of nuclear weapons. To go into effect, the pact must be ratified by all countries that have *nuclear reactors* (devices for producing nuclear energy). Three of these countries—India, Pakistan, and North Korea—have not signed the treaty, and several others—including the United States—have not ratified it. But experts expect that countries that have approved the treaty will abide by it, even though it has not gone into effect.

Since 1997, more than 160 countries have signed a treaty to ban the use of land mines designed to kill or injure soldiers. The treaty went into effect in 1999. It was adopted mainly to eliminate civilian deaths and injuries caused by mines. But some countries consider the devices im-portant defensive weapons and refuse to sign the treaty.

In 2002, U.S. President George W. Bush and Russian President Vladimir Putin signed a treaty to reduce the U.S. and Russian nuclear forces by about two-thirds over 10 years. The agreement, commonly known as the Treaty of Moscow, took effect in 2003.

The START I agreement expired in December 2009. In 2010, Russian President Dmitry Medvedev and U.S. President Barack Obama signed a new START agreement that aimed to reduce long-range nuclear weapons by 30 percent over seven years. The treaty took effect in early 2011 following ratification by the U.S. Senate and the Russian parliament.

In 2013, the UN General Assembly overwhelmingly adopted the landmark Arms Trade Treaty (ATT). The treaty is aimed at regulating the international trade in conventional arms by stemming the flow of arms to conflict zones worldwide. These weapons range from small arms to battle tanks, combat aircraft, and warships. The treaty seeks to prevent such weapons from being supplied to human rights abusers, warlords, pirates, and gangs. The treaty went into effect on Dec. 24, 2014, after it was ratified by more than 50 UN member nations.

Richard E. Rupp

Related articles in *World Book* include:

Biological Weapons Convention	Organization for Security and Co-operation in Europe
Chemical Weapons Convention	Strategic Arms Reduction Treaty
Nuclear Nonproliferation Treaty	United Nations (Arms control) Washington Conference

Armstrong, Edwin Howard (1890-1954), an American electrical engineer and inventor, made important contributions to electronics and radio communication. In 1933, he introduced the *frequency modulation* (FM) broadcasting system that is still in use today. This system provided better sound reproduction and less static interference than the older *amplitude modulation* (AM) system (see **Frequency modulation**). Earlier, in 1918, Armstrong developed the superheterodyne radio receiver, which became widely used. In 1921, Armstrong developed the superregenerative receiver that came into use in mobile radio and other systems. Armstrong was born on Dec. 18, 1890, in New York City. He died there on Jan. 31, 1954.　James E. Brittain

Armstrong, Lance (1971-　), an American cyclist, gained international fame by winning the Tour de France from 1999 through 2005. The Tour de France is the world's most prestigious bicycle race. Armstrong became the first cyclist to win the race seven consecutive times. His victories capped a comeback in a fight against cancer. He retired after the 2005 Tour de France but returned to racing in 2008. In 2011, he again retired.

Throughout his racing career, Armstrong faced charges that he took illegal drugs to improve his performance in races. Armstrong denied the claims, stating he had passed every drug test administered to detect doping. In 2010, the United States Anti-Doping Agency (USADA) began an investigation of Armstrong that led to accusations of illegal doping. After fighting the USADA's investigation for many months, Armstrong announced on Aug. 23, 2012, that he would end his fight against the drug charges. But he still insisted he was innocent of all doping violations. The USADA immediately announced it would strip Armstrong of his seven Tour de France titles and the bronze medal he won at the 2000 Summer Olympic Games, as well as other awards and titles, and banned him from cycling for life. In October 2012, the International Cycling Union (ICU), the international governing body for cycling, accepted the USADA action. In a television interview in January 2013, Armstrong admitted he had been involved in doping during his career.

Lance Edward Gunderson was born on Sept. 18, 1971, in Plano, Texas. In 1974, his mother married Terry Armstrong, who adopted Lance. Lance Armstrong began his professional cycling career in 1992. In 1993, he won the World Cycling Championships in Oslo, Norway. He captured the Tour DuPont, the best-known bicycle race in the United States, in 1995 and 1996.   Dave Nightingale

Armstrong, Louis (1901-1971), was one of the most famous and influential performers in the history of jazz. Armstrong gained recognition as the world's greatest jazz cornet and trumpet player in the 1920's and early 1930's. He also became famous for his gravelly singing voice. He was known by the nickname "Satchmo" (short for "Satchel Mouth," referring to his large mouth).

Armstrong was born on Aug. 4, 1901, in New Orleans. He learned to play the cornet while serving a sentence for delinquency in the Home for Colored Waifs. In 1922, Armstrong left New Orleans to join King Oliver's Creole Jazz Band in Chicago. His first recorded solo appears on the band's recording of "Chimes Blues" (1923). Armstrong was coached by Lil Hardin, the band's classically trained pianist. They were married in 1924. In that year, with Hardin's encouragement, Armstrong left Oliver to join the Fletcher Henderson band in New York City.

In 1925, Armstrong returned to Chicago. There, in the next three years, he made a series of small band recordings that rank among the masterpieces of jazz. Many of these recordings were issued under the names Hot Five and Hot Seven. They showed his brilliant tone and tremendous range.

In the Hot Five recording of "Heebie Jeebies" (1926), Armstrong first employed *scat singing,* a form of rhythmic wordless singing. Many singers adopted the style. In this

Wide World
Louis Armstrong

period, he switched from the cornet to the trumpet.

Starting in 1929, Armstrong appeared in musical shows, often as a featured soloist with a big band. By the mid-1930's, he had become less a jazz artist than a popular entertainer, on the advice of his managers. But he retained his brilliance as a trumpeter. In 1947, he formed the first in a series of small bands called the All-Stars. As time passed and his health declined, he played less and sang more. A new generation of fans in the 1950's and 1960's knew him mainly as an outgoing singer and entertainer. Armstrong made several hit vocal recordings, including "Hello, Dolly!" (1964) and "What a Wonderful World" (1967). He wrote an autobiography, *Satchmo: My Life in New Orleans* (1954). A selection of his writings was published as *Louis Armstrong: In His Own Words* (1999). Armstrong died on July 6, 1971.   Eddie Cook

See also **Jazz** (picture: Louis Armstrong).

Armstrong, Neil Alden (1930-2012), a United States astronaut, was the first person to set foot on the moon. On July 20, 1969, Armstrong and Buzz Aldrin landed the Apollo 11 lunar module *Eagle* on the moon. Armstrong, the mission commander, left the module to explore. Taking his first step onto the moon, Armstrong said: "That's one small step for a man, one giant leap for mankind." But the word *a* was lost in radio transmission.

Armstrong was born on his grandparents' farm in Auglaize County, Ohio, on Aug. 5, 1930. His family settled in Wapakoneta, Ohio, when Neil was 13 years old. A love of airplanes grew when he went for his first plane ride in a Ford Tri-Motor, a "Tin Goose," at the age of 6.

In 1947, Armstrong entered Purdue University. He began studies in aeronautical engineering. But in 1949, the U.S. Navy called him to active duty. Armstrong became a Navy pilot and was sent to Korea in 1950, near the start of the Korean War (1950-1953). In Korea, he flew 78 combat missions. In 1952, he returned to Purdue to complete his bachelor's degree in aeronautical engineering.

Armstrong was a civilian test pilot assigned to test the X-15 rocket airplane before becoming an astronaut in 1962. He made his first space flight in 1966 on Gemini 8 with David R. Scott. The two men performed the first successful docking of two vehicles in space—the Gemini 8 and an uninhabited Agena rocket.

Armstrong resigned from the United States astronaut program in 1970. Also in 1970, he earned a master's degree in aerospace engineering at the University of Southern California. From 1971 to 1979, Armstrong was a professor of aerospace engineering at the University of Cincinnati. In 1986, he was named vice chairman of a presidential commission investigating the breakup of the space shuttle Challenger. From 1982 to 1992, he was chairman of the board of Computing Technologies for Aviation, a company that develops software for flight scheduling. Armstrong died on Aug. 25, 2012.

James R. Hansen

See also **Space exploration** (Apollo: Mission to the moon).

NASA
Neil A. Armstrong

United States Army soldiers from Charlie Company patrol a stream in Chabar, Afghanistan.
Army soldiers are trained to fight on land, defend territory, and help establish security.

Army

Army is the branch of a nation's armed forces that is trained to fight on land. An army consists of ground troops, their weapons and equipment, and military bases. It includes infantry, armored vehicles, and artillery, plus support troops who handle transportation, medical care, and other responsibilities.

Almost every nation in the world has an army. Armies vary greatly in size and strength, depending on several factors. The economy of a nation plays a major role because wealthy nations can afford to buy expensive weapons and pay large numbers of soldiers. Nearly all developed nations maintain armies with large numbers of tanks, armored personnel carriers, helicopters, and even ships. Less developed nations that cannot afford advanced weapons often depend on specially trained light infantry, small ground attack aircraft, and armored cars.

Potential threats also shape the army of a country. For example, Switzerland, which has few potential enemies, does not have a standing army of professional soldiers. Instead, Switzerland maintains a large national militia made up of men who can be called into service at any time. Nations with extensive foreign commitments, such as France, the United Kingdom, and the United States, need a large standing army to meet their needs outside the country.

Countries also differ in how they raise and maintain their army. Some nations use a military draft, in which certain individuals are selected for duty. Others have universal military service, which requires all qualified men and women in a certain age range to serve. Still other nations have a completely volunteer army. Today, almost all armies include women.

Most nations divide their army into a *regular army* and an *army reserve*. The regular army consists of professional soldiers. They continually receive training and are always on active duty and ready for combat. No nation, however, can afford to support a regular army large enough to meet any crisis. Even nations that rely on large regular forces generally maintain an extensive army reserve. Such a reserve, also called a *national guard* or *militia,* trains citizens for immediate active duty in an emergency. Except during training, reservists remain on inactive duty, living as civilians but prepared to respond to a call to duty.

For thousands of years, warfare consisted almost entirely of battles between armies. Often, a single land battle would decide the fate of nations and empires. Beginning in the 1600's, the importance of navies rose to equal that of land forces. In the early 1900's, military aircraft first appeared and changed warfare forever. Armies still formed the largest part of the military power of most nations. However, nations began to use their armies in combination with air and naval units in *joint operations,* which involve more than one branch of the armed forces. The rise of military alliances beginning in the 1700's led to the growth of *combined* or *coalition* warfare, which involves the military forces of a number of nations.

Every army has a specific set of ideas, plans, and training practices that determines how it fights. For example, a nation in a mountainous or jungle region will have substantially different plans and practices than an industrialized nation with an advanced highway system.

The organization of armies

How a country organizes its army depends on the nation's customs, its history, and the tasks it expects the army to accomplish. But there is a general similarity in the organization of armies throughout the world.

The largest units of some armies are called *army groups* and may have several hundred thousand soldiers. Army groups usually consist of several organizations themselves known as *armies*. Each army is made up of several *corps* (pronounced *kawrz* or *kohrz*). A corps (pronounced *kawr* or *kohr*) normally has from 50,000 to 100,000 soldiers. A corps consists of two or more *divisions* and any necessary support troops.

The division is the basic fighting unit of many armies. Divisions include such combat troops as infantry, armored forces, and artillery; and engineers, who are sometimes considered as combat troops. Divisions also have support troops who handle transportation, medical care, and other responsibilities. Divisions usually are identified according to their equipment, training, and function. Types of divisions include infantry, mechanized, armored, and airborne divisions.

The size of a division varies from about 10,000 to 18,000 soldiers. Most divisions have three or more *brigades* of roughly equal size, and each brigade has three to five *battalions*. The battalion, a combat unit of 500 to 800 soldiers, is further divided into groups of 100 to 200 soldiers. Infantry and armored units of this size are called *companies*. Artillery groups are known as *batteries*, and groups of *cavalry* (highly mobile forces used for scouting and surprise attacks) are called *troops*.

The role of armies

In war, a nation uses its army to conquer enemy territory and to defend itself from attack. In peacetime, an army can help prevent war. It also aids civilians in certain emergencies.

Attack. A nation may seek to take over territory held by an enemy by conducting offensive operations. The attacker's tanks and other armored vehicles invade the enemy's territory, with planes and artillery supporting the advance. Other planes drop airborne troops behind enemy lines, and helicopters carry in specially trained soldiers, sometimes called *special forces* or *commandos,* to seize certain key positions. Later, mechanized infantry sweeps in and occupies the conquered territory.

Defense. An army is trained for both offensive and defensive combat operations. But some units may be assigned to fight only in case of an enemy attack. In the past, fortifications along borders formed the main line of defense for many countries. But modern armies do not rely nearly as much on fortifications, which can often be bypassed with airborne assaults or by the combined action of land, sea, and air forces.

Prevention of war. A powerful nation may sometimes station troops in politically troubled regions or in areas threatened by attack. Such a show of military strength may help prevent war. In 1991, for example, French and Belgian troops went to Zaire—now Congo (Kinshasa)—to restore order after Zairian soldiers rioted.

The development of *tactical nuclear weapons* in the

Embassy of Pakistan

Soldiers from Pakistan's army aim a mortar before firing. Mortars, which fire shells in a high arc, can reach targets that are protected by hills or other obstacles.

Thierry Campion, Gamma/Liaison

Armies wear protective clothing to prevent injury from chemical, biological, or radiological weapons. These soldiers from the French Army are outfitted for a chemical attack.

1950's gave armies an important defensive strategy. These weapons are designed to be used in areas where a conventional war is being fought. An army that massed its men and equipment was vulnerable to a nuclear attack. The fear of such an attack could prevent a nation from invading an enemy. This idea, known as *deterrence,* was used by the Soviet Union and Western nations from the end of World War II in 1945 to the late 1980's, a period of hostility known as the Cold War.

Internal security and civilian aid. Armies may be used by a nation for roles other than combat. In some countries, armies serve as an internal police force. In others, regular or reserve forces may serve in a multitude of roles that include disaster relief, humanitarian

Ricki Rosen, SABA

A country may use its army to maintain order within its own borders during periods of internal unrest. This Israeli soldier is checking the identification of civilians in Jerusalem.

aid to foreign nations, and peacekeeping functions. They may respond to major disasters, such as forest fires or hurricanes, to provide emergency medical aid and food and water distribution, or to prevent looting.

The world's major armies

An army's ranking among the armies of the world is based on its overall fighting strength. In general, fighting strength depends on the number of troops on active duty. However, an army's size does not necessarily reflect its actual strength. Well-trained soldiers and modern weapons are also important. A small army with tactical nuclear weapons may have greater striking power than a large army with outdated weapons.

The world's major armies include those of China, India, North Korea, Russia, the United States, France, and the United Kingdom. All of these armies except India's and North Korea's have tactical nuclear weapons. However, both India and North Korea have the capability to produce such weapons.

The Chinese Army has about 1 ½ million troops on active duty. Many of the forces are assigned to defensive positions near the Russian border in northeastern China. The Chinese Army has about 500,000 people in its reserve and armed militia. China uses a military draft.

The Indian Army has about 1,200,000 men on active duty, about 300,000 in the reserve, and about 40,000 in the Territorial Army. Only a few hundred women serve in the Indian Army, many as doctors and nurses. All members of India's Army are volunteers.

The North Korean Army has about 1,100,000 troops on active duty and about 600,000 in the reserve. Men from the ages of 20 to 25 are drafted to serve in the Army for 5 to 12 years. After service, they serve part-time in local militias until the age of 40 and then in the Red Guard until the age of 60. Women may join the army on a volunteer basis.

The Russian army, officially called the Ground Forces of the Russian Federation, has about 280,000 troops on active duty. Many troops are posted along Russia's border with China. Russia began organizing its army in 1992, following the breakup of the Soviet Union in 1991. The Russian army has small forces in the former Soviet republics of Georgia, Moldova, and Tajikistan. The army has both volunteers and draftees. After 18 months of active duty, Russian soldiers serve in the reserve until the age of 50.

The United States Army has about 475,000 troops on active duty and about 525,000 in the reserve and the National Guard. Army troops serve in the United States, Western Europe, Japan, South Korea, and parts of Latin America and the Middle East. All members of the United States Army are volunteers. See **Army, United States; National Guard.**

The French Army has about 115,000 members on active duty and 22,000 in the reserve. French troops serve in Western Europe, in several African countries, and in France's overseas territories. The French Army has both volunteers and draftees.

The British Army has about 84,000 troops on active duty and about 30,000 members of the Territorial Army. British troops serve in Germany, Northern Ireland, and many other parts of the world. All members of the British Army are volunteers.

Other major armies include those of Egypt, Iran, Myanmar, Pakistan, South Korea, and Vietnam. Each of these armies has 300,000 or more troops on active duty. The armies have purchased weapons and equipment from the world's major powers. None has tactical nuclear weapons, though Pakistan has the capability to produce them.

History

Ancient armies developed as civilizations grew in Mesopotamia—the region between the Tigris and Euphrates rivers in what is now Iraq—and in the Nile Valley of Egypt. As early as 3200 B.C., the Mesopotamians had built a regular army of spear throwers and archers. About 2500 B.C., the Sumerians used the first war chariots. Small wild asses and, later, horses drew these chariots. By the 700's B.C., the Assyrians had organized armies that were equipped with spears and battering rams.

In the 600's B.C., the ancient Greeks introduced the *phalanx,* which was probably the first important tactical formation in history. In this formation, soldiers with spears and heavy armor stood from 4 to 50 rows deep in a solid rectangle. The phalanx was primarily a defensive formation. It could withstand the shock of a cavalry charge, but it could neither move rapidly nor attack across rough ground.

The mightiest conqueror of the period was Cyrus the Great of Persia. During the mid-500's B.C., Cyrus extended the Persian Empire to include most of southwestern Asia. In the 300's B.C., Alexander the Great of Macedonia, the next world conqueror, organized the first known military supply system.

The ancient Romans developed the next great tactical formation. During the early 300's B.C., they devised the *legion.* This rectangular formation had greater flexibility than the phalanx. It consisted of three lines of small phalanxes called *maniples* or, later, *cohorts.* The Romans conquered Carthage in 146 B.C. and built a great empire overseas. They were also skilled military engineers. The armies of the Roman general Julius Caesar built roads, bridges, and forts in much of Europe. See **Legion**.

China's civilization grew up in isolation from the empires of Europe and western Asia. The Chinese had knowledge of gunpowder long before the A.D. 1300's, when Europeans began to use it in guns. But gunpowder did not become an important weapon of war for the Chinese because they did not use it in artillery, except possibly in rockets.

Armies in the Middle Ages. After the Roman Empire collapsed in the A.D. 400's, Europe had no large regular armies for several centuries. All able-bodied free men in the tribes that overran the empire were warriors. The tradition of a militia developed at this time (see **Militia**).

During the Middle Ages, military relationships were central to the organization of Western Europe's society. A king ruled this society and was, in turn, supported by nobles. These nobles ruled their own estates, and their education normally included training as knights. The nobles exercised political, economic, judicial, and military power. The lower classes, known as *serfs* or *peasants,* labored on the estates. The nobles used the wealth provided by the serfs' labor to arm and equip themselves and their loyal soldiers, who were called *men-at-arms.* A knight's equipment included broadswords, lances, and armor, and it was expensive. The entire agricultural output of a knight's holdings for several years could only pay for a single warrior's armor, horses, and weapons. Due to this expense, the armies of the Middle Ages were small.

The cost of medieval armies led some rulers to turn to *mercenaries* (hired soldiers) to fight for their nations. Some mercenaries specialized in siege weaponry, such as the stone-throwing weapons called *catapults,* while others used crossbows or long spears known as *pikes.* Among the best-known mercenaries of the late Middle Ages were the Swiss pikemen. They would form large phalanxes to prevent heavily armored, mounted knights from overrunning them. The Swiss mercenaries, along with hired soldiers from England, Germany, and Italy, formed groups called *companies.* The company still forms the basic unit of most armies.

During the 1300's, the Ottoman Empire, which ruled what are now Turkey, the Middle East, Greece, and most of southeastern Europe, established the first full-time professional national army since the Roman Empire. These soldiers, known as Janissaries, were mostly slave soldiers taken from the Balkan provinces. They were much feared on the battlefield because they were loyal only to the sultan, who ruled the Ottoman Empire, and to their fellow Janissaries.

Western European nations copied the Ottoman example of a permanent army. By 1500, most major European nations had a permanent army, usually called the Royal Army or King's Army. Some nations, such as the independent states in Germany, developed the first permanent *quartermaster* organizations to find quarters and food for their armies.

Gunpowder had a dramatic impact on the organization and tactics of armies, and it played a major role in changing medieval warfare and society. Castles built by nobles could not stand up to bombardment by cannons. Rulers who could afford gunpowder-based artillery became much more powerful. The nobles lost their military function because armies of commoners with muskets could shoot them off their horses.

The rise of modern armies. By the late 1600's, infantry armed with bayonets mounted on muskets could defend themselves against cavalry charges. They did not have to rely on troops armed with pikes. Three rows of soldiers stood in ranks, shoulder to shoulder, in a formation called *the line.* A line of infantry could fire many shots at the same time at close range.

The obligation of all men to serve in wartime had disappeared almost everywhere by the early 1600's. But Sweden kept this custom throughout the Middle Ages, and King Gustavus Adolphus used a military draft to recruit troops for the Thirty Years' War (1618-1648). He gave his army greater mobility by equipping it with lighter weapons and increased firepower. His force is sometimes called the first modern army. See **Gustavus Adolphus; Thirty Years' War.**

During the 1700's, most governments continued to build their armies by recruiting volunteers, especially among the poor and unemployed. Armies became pro-

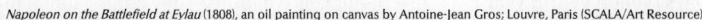

Napoleon on the Battlefield at Eylau (1808), an oil painting on canvas by Antoine-Jean Gros; Louvre, Paris (SCALA/Art Resource)

Napoleon I was one of history's greatest military leaders. This painting depicts Napoleon commanding French cavalry and infantry troops in 1807 during the Battle of Eylau near what is now the Russian city of Kaliningrad.

fessional groups of well-trained foot soldiers supported by artillery and cavalry. Most countries followed certain rules in warfare. Campaigns took place only in good weather. The troops went into quarters in winter and did not fight again until spring. They tried to gain a favorable position before they attacked the enemy. Commanders who were caught in a poor position often withdrew instead of fighting to the finish.

In the mid-1700's, Frederick the Great of Prussia introduced greater mobility to warfare. When his enemies outnumbered him, he struck quickly and unexpectedly. Frederick was forced to fight wars on several fronts at the same time. He moved rapidly to attack a single army before it could unite with others and attack his forces.

The French government adopted a military draft system in 1793. Napoleon I drafted huge armies for his conquests. He divided his armies into divisions that marched separately but joined to fight. Napoleon often massed all his heavy guns together into a *grande batterie* (big battery). He poured a tremendous amount of fire into one point in the enemy's lines, then sent forward his heavy formations of cavalry and infantry at that point. To defeat him, Napoleon's enemies had to adopt draft systems and develop national armies.

The growth in the size of armies made necessary an organization to control troops from a distance. Only a military genius such as Napoleon could personally direct so many military units in the field. From 1840 on, railroads began to spread across Europe. The Prussians realized that they could move armies much more quickly by rail, and that this made possible more accurate long-range planning. Gerhard von Scharnhorst of the Prussian Army developed the modern general staff that planned military operations.

During the 1800's, the Industrial Revolution, a period of rapid industrialization and technological advances, dramatically changed the size and strength of armies. Mass production enabled armies to equip more soldiers than ever before. Technology improved weapons and helped provide such supplies as canned food and rifles. As technology changed, so did the way armies were organized and how they fought.

Armies in the two world wars. When World War I began in 1914, the machine gun and artillery became the dominant weapons on the battlefield. The use of these weapons made free movement impossible on the Western Front, where the United Kingdom and France battled Germany. Both sides adopted trench warfare. Infantry dug in to hold their positions when they could not advance against the enemy. Railroads carried millions of soldiers to the fighting fronts. Motor trucks hauled supplies from railroads to the front lines. See **World War I.**

Field commanders tried to end trench warfare and regain tactical mobility. They shelled and bombed enemy lines, and followed with mass bayonet attacks. Sometimes they used poison gas against enemy lines. But most assaults—even those that used poison gas—failed to break through enemy lines during more than three years of intense fighting. The trenches of the Western Front repelled almost all attacks. Army commanders found a solution, but they used it improperly and too late. The United Kingdom built an armored tracked vehicle with a gasoline engine and created the first military tank. Tanks soon replaced horse cavalry. During World

War I, airplanes were used for the first time in support of ground fighting. See **Tank; Air force** (World War I).

In World War II (1939-1945), tanks and airplanes restored mobility to warfare. In the war, the Allies, who included Canada, the Soviet Union, the United Kingdom, and the United States, fought the Axis powers, who included Germany and Japan. The Germans developed a type of warfare called *blitzkrieg* (lightning war). Tanks and bombers blasted great holes in enemy defenses. Then infantry poured through the gaps and carried the war deep into enemy territory. See **World War II** (The invasion of Poland).

World War II also saw the first use of armies in large-scale airborne operations. The Germans launched the first successful paratroop invasion in May 1941, when they seized the island of Crete. The largest airborne operation took place in September 1944, when three divisions of Allied paratroops dropped behind the German lines in an unsuccessful attempt to capture bridges across the Rhine River. The largest combined land, sea, and air attack in history occurred on June 6, 1944, when Allied armies landed in Normandy, in northern France.

During World War II, armies brought the military art of *logistics* (supply and services) to a high point of development. They organized huge commands that provided food, clothing, fuel, ammunition, weapons, supplies, and transportation for combat troops. The Allied victory in World War II resulted partly from superiority in logistics and in civilian industrial production. See **Logistics.**

Armies in the nuclear age. World War II ended shortly after United States warplanes dropped atomic bombs on two Japanese cities, Hiroshima and Nagasaki. Development of the atomic bomb marked the beginning of the nuclear age.

The earliest nuclear warheads could be delivered only by bomber planes flying at high altitudes. Such a delivery could not be used on the battlefield and could be considered only for *strategic targets*—that is, facilities that supported the war effort, such as weapons factories and transportation systems. By the 1950's, armies had developed nuclear cannons and missiles. These weapons changed the thinking of many experts about the tactical use of nuclear weapons. They could launch nuclear warheads at a large body of troops, a supply dump, or any other target within the weapons' range.

Since World War II, the fear of starting a nuclear war has helped prevent major armies from using nuclear weapons. As a result, only conventional weapons have been used in wars fought during the nuclear age. The first major conflict was the Korean War, which began in 1950. Large armies did most of the fighting in this war. See **Korean War.**

Armies have continued to use conventional tactics and weapons in war. For example, the U.S. Army relied heavily on conventional warfare tactics during its involvement in the Vietnam War, from 1965 to 1973. At the time, these tactics were considered the most effective way to fight Communist guerrillas in the jungles of Vietnam. However, Vietnamese guerrillas avoided major battles in the open, where heavy U.S. firepower could be decisive. They relied on surprise and mobility instead (see **Vietnam War**). Arab and Israeli forces fought wars with conventional weapons in 1956, 1967, and 1973. The tactics used by both sides resembled those of World

War II, in which aircraft and tanks spearheaded attacks and were followed into battle by infantry.

Since the mid-1970's, armies of developed nations have tended to fight brief, intense wars that usually decide a conflict quickly. Advances in computer technology and other electronics have had a massive impact on armies. Today, many armies have access to instant satellite photographs, real-time images of battlefields, and worldwide communications with political and military leaders. Armies have begun to concentrate on *strategic mobility,* the ability to quickly move troops, supplies, and equipment anywhere on short notice. This can be done using fast troop transport ships and large, troop-carrying jet airplanes. For example, during Operation Desert Storm in 1990, the United States *deployed* (positioned for combat) nearly 200,000 troops and their equipment to Saudi Arabia in only two months. Technology will continue to advance, and armies will likely change with each new development.   Robert R. Mackey

Related articles in *World Book.* See **War** and its list of *Related articles.* See also:

Battles

Agincourt, Battle of	Iwo Jima, Battle of
Austerlitz, Battle of	Louisbourg
Balaklava, Battle of	Marathon, Battle of
Bannockburn, Battle of	Okinawa
Bataan Death March	Poitiers, Battle of
Blenheim, Battle of	Quebec, Battle of
Boyne, Battle of the	Saipan
Bunker Hill, Battle of	Stalingrad, Battle of
Corregidor	Thermopylae
Crécy, Battle of	Verdun, Battles of
Dunkerque	Vimy Ridge, Battle of
Gettysburg, Battle of	Waterloo, Battle of
Hastings, Battle of	

History

Archery	Foreign Legion	Musket
Battering ram	Greek fire	Powder horn
Blunderbuss	Gunpowder	Sling
Boomerang	Harquebus	Spear
Catapult	Janissaries	Swiss Guard
Commando	Legion	Tomahawk
Flintlock	Mercenary	Zouaves

Organization

Airborne troops	Infantry
Armor	Inspector general
Artillery	Intelligence service
Cavalry	Military police
Engineers, Corps of	

Weapons

Ammunition	Grenade
Bayonet	Guided missile
Bazooka	Gun
Bullet	Handgun
Cannon	Machine gun
Carbine	Mortar
Cartridge	Night vision systems
Explosive	Nuclear weapon
Firearm	Rifle
Flame thrower	Rocket
Garand rifle	Tank

Other related articles

Army, U.S.
Camouflage
Canadian armed forces
Chemical-biological-radiological warfare
Court-martial

Desertion
Helmet
Insignia
Logistics
Medals, decorations, and orders
Military school
Military training
Militia
Mine warfare
National Guard

Outline

I. The organization of armies
II. The role of armies
  A. Attack
  B. Defense
  C. Prevention of war
  D. Internal security and civilian aid
III. The world's major armies
  A. The Chinese Army   E. The United States Army
  B. The Indian Army   F. The French Army
  C. The North Korean Army   G. The British Army
  D. The Russian army   H. Other major armies
IV. History

Questions

What country first used a military draft?
Who organized the first modern regular army?
How does a *regular army* differ from an *army reserve?*
What was history's largest combined land, sea, and air attack?
Why did rulers begin hiring *mercenaries* in the 1000's?
What was probably history's first important tactical formation?
What is the basic fighting unit of many armies?
How did armies get food before quartermaster offices were established?
What are the four chief roles of armies?
What are some of the ways in which the development of nuclear weapons changed the role of armies?

Army, Department of the, is a military department within the Department of Defense of the United States government. It serves as headquarters of the United States Army and is in Washington, D.C. The Department of the Army organizes, trains, and equips land forces to support the national and international policies of the United States.

The *secretary of the Army* heads the department, under the supervision of the secretary of defense, and ranks equally with the secretaries of the Air Force and the Navy. This official's principal civilian aides include an undersecretary and five assistant secretaries.

The *chief of staff of the United States Army* serves as the main military adviser of the secretary and supervises all members and organizations of the Army. The chief of staff is assisted by the vice chief of staff and the Army General Staff. This staff includes the director of the Army staff and deputy chiefs of staff for intelligence, logistics, military operations and plans, and personnel.

Congress established the Department of War in 1789 as an executive agency. In 1903, Congress approved the adoption of a general staff system for the Army. Congress set up the National Military Establishment (NME) with a secretary of defense in 1947. At that time, the Department of War was renamed the Department of the Army and made part of the NME. In 1949, Congress replaced the NME with the Department of Defense. The Department of the Army came under the authority of the Department of Defense.

Critically reviewed by the Department of Defense

See also **Army, United States; Defense, Department of.**

The United States Army depends on both highly trained soldiers and specialized equipment to protect the nation and its interests. In this photograph, armed soldiers wait in loose formation as a Black Hawk utility helicopter lands nearby. The helicopter will carry the soldiers as they participate in patrol operations to locate and destroy enemy forces.

United States Army

Army, United States, is the branch of the armed services responsible for military land operations. The Army must be prepared to use swift, forceful action to overcome any enemy that might threaten the United States or its interests in other parts of the world. It also helps train the military forces of many nations that have friendly relations with the United States.

The Army is often called upon to help in disasters, such as epidemics, floods, forest fires, and storms. In addition, the Army constructs and operates a large number of public works, including flood control projects. It also improves inland waterways and harbors.

The Army is the oldest branch of the U.S. armed services. It dates back to June 14, 1775, when the Continental Congress created the Continental Army. Army history includes the deeds of such leaders as George Washington, Ulysses S. Grant, John J. Pershing, George C. Marshall, and Douglas MacArthur, as well as the heroism of countless soldiers. Army history also covers changes brought about by science, inventions, and discoveries. Its weapons have grown from muzzle-loading muskets to nuclear blasts delivered by guns and missiles. Army transport has changed from horses and wagons to trucks and aircraft. The radio, telegraph, and television

revolutionized communications. The use of aircraft and airborne troops added new strength on the battlefield.

The U.S. Army operates under the Department of Defense. Army strength varies according to the nation's needs. The Army has about 475,000 men and women on active duty throughout the world. About 525,000 people serve in the Army Reserve and National Guard. The Army also has about 300,000 civilian employees.

The official Army flag is blue, white, and red, with yellow fringes. It carries about 190 streamers. Each streamer represents a battle or campaign fought by the Army.

In all wars that have involved the United States, about 500,000 soldiers have died in battle. About 1,400,000 soldiers have been wounded in battle.

Life in the Army

People in the Army perform many different duties. *Enlisted soldiers* form the main fighting force of the Army. They take orders from officers. The leaders of the Army are *commissioned officers.*

Training a soldier. After entering the Army, trainees undergo basic training at various Army training centers. There, trainees learn a number of fundamental military skills, such as marksmanship, drill and ceremony, first aid, and land navigation. Trainees also undergo intensive physical training and are taught to act as part of a disciplined team.

After basic training, most soldiers attend a school to learn the techniques of the *military occupational specialty* (line of work) that they agreed to perform when they enlisted. These schools are on military posts throughout the country. In school, soldiers may learn to repair a truck, rifle, or missile. They may learn to program a computer or be a military police officer. Some schools require only a few weeks of training. Other schools give technical training that requires several months.

Soldiers may become eligible for other schools throughout their term of service. *Noncommissioned officers* (corporals and sergeants) who are making a career of Army service receive continued training through a special educational system.

Training an officer. To become a United States Army officer, men and women may follow one of several paths: (1) the United States Military Academy at West

U.S. Army

Physical training builds a soldier's strength and endurance. This photograph shows a drill sergeant supervising recruits as they crawl through an obstacle course.

U.S. Army

Drills and marching help reinforce order and discipline, which are essential to the Army's operation. In this photograph, recruits practice patrol tactics while marching in combat uniform.

U.S. Army

Urban tactics have become an increasingly important part of Army basic training. In this photograph, recruits infiltrate a mock house as part of a training exercise.

Uniforms and insignia of the United States Army

The Army Service Uniform has an iconic Army green color that was originally worn during World War II (1939-1945). Shown here are a version of the uniform for male officers, *above,* and a version for female enlisted soldiers, *below.*

U.S. Army

Grade insignia for officers

General of the Army

General

Lieutenant General

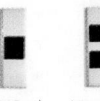
Major General

Brigadier General

Colonel

Lieutenant Colonel

Major

Captain

First Lieutenant

Second Lieutenant

| (WO-1) | (CW-2) | (CW-3) | (CW-4) | (CW-5) |
| Warrant Officer | Chief Warrant Officer | | | |

Grade insignia for enlisted men and women

Sergeant Major of the Army (E-9)

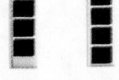
Command Sergeant Major (E-9)

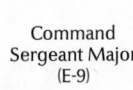
Sergeant Major (E-9)

First Sergeant (E-8)

Master Sergeant (E-8)

Sergeant First Class (E-7)

Staff Sergeant (E-6)

Sergeant (E-5)

Specialist Four (E-4)

Corporal (E-4)

Private First Class (E-3)

Private (E-2)

Branch of service insignia*

Armor

Air Defense
Artillery

Field
Artillery

Infantry

Corps of
Engineers

Ordnance
Corps

Signal
Corps

Chemical
Corps

Army
Aviation

Transportation
Corps

Quartermaster
Corps

Military Police
Corps

Medical
Corps

Judge Advocate
General's Corps

Finance
Corps

Chaplain
(Christian)

Chaplain
(Jewish)

Civil
Affairs

Inspector
General

General
Staff

Adjutant General's
Corps

Special
Forces

Military
Intelligence

Badges*

Expert (rifle)

Explosive
Ordnance Disposal

Driver and Mechanic
(driver)

Master Diver

Senior
Parachutist

Combat
Infantryman

Combat Medical

Senior
Army Aviator

Organization insignia*

First
Army

Second
Army
(inactive)

Third
Army

Fourth
Army
(inactive)

Fifth
Army

Sixth
Army
(inactive)

Seventh
Army

Eighth
Army

First Infantry
Division

Second Infantry
Division

Third Infantry
Division

Fourth Infantry
Division

Eighth Infantry
Division

Ninth Infantry
Division
(inactive)

25th Infantry
Division

Second Armored
Division
(inactive)

Third Armored
Division

First Cavalry
Division

82nd Airborne
Division

101st Airborne
Division
(Air Assault)

*Some branch of service insignia, badges, and organization insignia are not shown.

Point, (2) Reserve Officers Training Corps (ROTC) at many universities and colleges, (3) officer candidate schools conducted by the United States Army and by state national guards, and (4) direct commissions to civilians with special skills in such professions as law and medicine.

All Army officers receive basic and advanced training in their assigned branches. The United States Army Command and General Staff College, at Fort Leavenworth, Kansas, teaches officers how to use the various units of the Army as a team. The United States Army War College at Carlisle Barracks, Pennsylvania, prepares officers for senior command and staff positions.

Warrant officers rank higher than noncommissioned officers and lower than commissioned officers. They work in such specialized fields as data processing, electronics, and law enforcement. Many warrant officers are former enlisted men and women who became experts in their specialty and applied for a warrant from the secretary of the Army.

A typical day for soldiers depends on their assignments. Soldiers assigned to a unit develop the skills that they learned in basic and advanced training. They train with their unit and function as team members. They may participate in a sports program and use educational facilities provided by the Army. The squad leader, a noncommissioned officer, guides soldiers in their normal routine. The food service manager supervises the dining facility. The supply sergeant cares for and issues clothing and equipment. The unit commander is responsible for formulating and supervising unit training.

The normal daily routine begins early on weekdays and ends by 5 p.m. Soldiers' evenings and weekends are their own, except when they are on field-training exercises. During these exercises, or "practice wars," soldiers sometimes cannot eat a normal meal because of maneuver requirements. Then they receive packages of ready-to-eat food that provides the nourishment they need in easy-to-carry form.

Careers in the Army offer job security and opportunities for travel to many parts of the world. But soldiers must make sacrifices, because they must go wherever the Army assigns them.

The Army has hundreds of jobs that require special skill or experience. A man or woman who enlists has a choice of careers and can often use skill or training gained in civilian life. Professional men and women, such as doctors and lawyers, may receive direct commissions. Soldiers who have leadership abilities usually become noncommissioned officers. Soldiers who demonstrate high technical ability may become warrant officers. Army training often prepares a person for a civilian job later.

Applicants for enlistment must be at least 17 years of age and younger than 42. In addition, applicants must be able to pass the Army's physical examination and written examinations. Enlistments range from 15 months to 6 years.

Enlisted personnel receive pay increases with each promotion, and extra pay according to *longevity* (length of service). They also receive extra pay for some overseas duty. The Army pays extra amounts for *quarters* (housing) and *subsistence* (food). Soldiers earn 30 days' *leave* (vacation) every year. They also are entitled to free medical care. In certain areas overseas, soldiers receive *station allowances* to cover the increased cost of living. The Army also grants extra pay to various specialists and to soldiers who serve in combat or perform hazardous duty, such as demolition work. Army personnel may retire with half pay after 20 years' service, or with higher pay for longer service.

In 2013, the Defense Department announced that it would no longer ban women from serving in direct combat. The announcement reversed a 1994 rule officially banning women from serving in such units and positions as infantry, artillery, and armor. Many women had fought in combat despite the official ban.

Weapons and equipment of the Army

Combat units of the Army consist of soldiers trained and equipped to fight enemy forces. Infantry, artillery, armored units, Army aviation, and various specialized units are called the *combat arms* because they do the direct fighting. Other units, called the *combat support* and *combat service support,* aid the combat arms.

Infantry is the Army's largest arm. Infantrymen must seize, occupy, and defend land areas. They bear the heaviest share of close combat. Infantrymen throw grenades and fire rifles, machine guns, mortars, pistols, and various types of rockets and missiles. They enter battle on foot or by helicopter, parachute, or infantry fighting vehicle.

Artillery provides the firepower necessary for a heavy and successful attack by infantry or armored units. It protects troops holding defensive positions, and it can neutralize enemy fire.

Artillery travels by heavy trucks, helicopters, or other means. Its weapons include the Army's heaviest howitzers and guns. The highly mobile howitzers can fire to a maximum range of about 18 ½ miles (30 kilometers). Certain rocket-fired weapons have an even greater range. See **Artillery.**

Armor in the Army usually means tanks and other armored vehicles. The Army uses M-1 Abrams Main Battle Tanks. The M-1 tank has a 120-millimeter gun. The Army's armored units can move swiftly and advance deep into enemy territory. They also have strong firepower. See **Tank.**

Army aviation bolsters the Army's battlefield mobility. Army aircraft can spot enemy targets for artillery units. They provide rapid transportation to and from the front lines. They lay communication wires and take aerial photographs. In addition, Army aircraft transport troops and supplies, and rush wounded soldiers to hospitals that are in the rear areas.

Army aviators fly airplanes and helicopters. Airplanes are used for surveillance, observation, and command transport. Helicopters are classified as scout, utility, lift, or attack types. Attack helicopters are more mobile than airplanes and can rapidly attack targets throughout an area of operations.

The Army classifies its aircraft by letters and numbers. For example, the UH-60 is a utility aircraft (U) and a helicopter (H). Other symbols used to indicate the type or purpose of the aircraft include: A, attack; C, cargo transport; O, observation; and V, short take-off and landing. The Army traditionally names its aircraft after American Indian tribes.

Special units. The Army has several kinds of specialized units. These units include Special Forces and Rangers.

Special Forces, popularly known as *Green Berets,* are trained in various specialized operations. An important peacetime activity is helping other governments train forces that can oppose guerrillas and other rebel groups. Special forces are also trained to take part in raiding operations, antiterrorist actions, and *reconnaissance* (information gathering).

Special Forces personnel are organized into groups. Each group has responsibility for a specific region of the world. The group's members learn about the languages, customs, and cultures of the region. This training equips them to operate deep behind enemy lines.

Rangers are specialized units that can move quickly to any area of the world and that are prepared to strike by land, sea, or air. Ranger units are trained to make surprise raids behind enemy lines and to participate in other similarly daring operations. The Army has three Ranger battalions.

Missiles. The Army's arsenal includes both free rockets and guided missiles. *Rockets* provide fire support for troops on the battlefield. Some rockets can be equipped with nuclear warheads. Missiles may be fired from ground to ground in support of troops. The same missiles also can be fired from ground to air to destroy enemy aircraft. The guidance and control systems of the Army's air defense guided missiles, such as the Patriot and the Avenger, enable these missiles to track down and destroy enemy aircraft. See **Guided missile; Rocket.**

Communications and observation. Various types of electronic equipment are used to send and receive messages. Electronic "eyes and ears" enable the Army to survey the battlefield day and night in all kinds of weather. The Army uses portable radar sets to detect troop movements in darkness. Remote-controlled drone aircraft carry cameras, infrared devices, and radar to spot enemy positions. Computers prepare weather reports, using information sent from instruments mounted on balloons.

Transportation by various types of vehicles gives the Army mobility. These include passenger and cargo vehicles, helicopters, rail equipment, watercraft, amphibious vehicles, and air cushion vehicles.

Engineers of the Army build bridges, repair roads, and construct landing strips, mine fields, and fortifications. These units must often work under direct enemy fire. Their equipment includes bulldozers, mine-clearing vehicles, and a scissors-type bridge, which is pushed into place by a tank or other tracked vehicle and extended to cross a stream or ravine. To cross rivers, the engineers also use floating bridges, inflatable assault boats, and aluminum rafts.

Equipment can be delivered to Army engineers by aircraft, or it can be dropped by parachute. Air-dropped equipment includes cranes, tractors, air compressors, and dump trucks.

Logistic units package and move supplies by air, bulk containers, and pipelines. To save time, food for combat troops is prepackaged in individual ready-to-eat servings. Special clothing developed by the Army includes protective armored vests, rubber-coated fabric clothing for handlers of missile fuels, and cold-weather clothing and boots for arctic wear. Soldiers also have special uniforms for use in desert and jungle regions.

Chemical equipment provides defense against chemical agents (gas), biological agents (germs), and the effects of radiation. Other chemical equipment includes smoke-generating devices to conceal troop movements and flame throwers to attack fortifications. Special chemical instruments detect contamination. The Army uses such equipment as protective gas masks, airtight clothing, and first-aid kits to counteract the effects of chemical, biological, or radiological warfare.

Organization of the Army

In peacetime, the U.S. Army is made up of men and women who have volunteered for service in the Regular Army, the Army Reserve, and the Army National Guard. Regular Army personnel are professional soldiers and are always on active duty. The Army Reserve and National Guard consist of citizens who are trained to conduct active duty tasks and missions. Except during training, or during emergency or wartime activation, most members of these reserve forces remain on inactive duty. The

U.S. Army

Nonmilitary assistance is part of the Army's mission both at home and abroad. When not caring for U.S. soldiers, Army doctors and nurses overseas sometimes provide care for local residents. In this photograph, an Army medic checks the blood pressure of an Afghan woman.

Army Chinook helicopters can transport jeeps, trucks, artillery, and supplies to remote military outposts. This photograph shows a Chinook carrying emergency supplies to victims of an earthquake in the mountains of Pakistan.

U.S. Army

Armored transports carry soldiers onto the battlefield. This photograph shows two Stryker Infantry Carrier Vehicles. These eight-wheeled, heavily armored transports also carry a variety of tools and artillery.

U.S. Army

president may call to active duty members of the Army Reserve and National Guard. State governors may call to active duty members of the National Guard.

The United States Army operates under the Department of the Army, which is a part of the Department of Defense. The Army consists of Department of the Army headquarters, Army commands, Army service component commands, and direct reporting units.

Army Department headquarters are in Washington, D.C. The secretary of the Army, a civilian appointed by the president, heads the Army organization. The chief of staff of the U.S. Army serves as the principal military adviser to the secretary. The Army chief of staff also represents the Army on the Joint Chiefs of Staff.

The Army headquarters include the Army secretariat and the Army staff. The secretariat consists of agencies that report directly to the secretary of the Army. The Army staff consists of agencies that report to the secretary through the chief of staff. The secretariat and the Army staff provide professional advice and administrative and technical assistance to the Office of the Secretary. See **Army, Department of the; Joint Chiefs of Staff.**

Army commands. Units that are designated simply as Army commands have a global role and a variety of functions. The U.S. Army Forces Command, with headquarters at Fort Bragg, North Carolina, is responsible for

the combat readiness of the Army's active and reserve forces. The command trains, mobilizes, and deploys forces to wherever they are needed in the world. Forces Command executes its responsibilities for the Army Reserve and National Guard through the First U.S. Army, headquartered at Rock Island Arsenal, Illinois.

The U.S. Army Training and Doctrine Command, with headquarters at Fort Eustis, Virginia, controls all Army individual schooling and training. It sets the Army's standards and requirements. The command also manages the Army ROTC program. In addition, it develops plans for organizing Army forces and assists in the development of combat equipment.

The U.S. Army Materiel Command has headquarters in Redstone Arsenal, Alabama. It is responsible for the development, procurement, delivery, supply, and maintenance of equipment, supplies, and weapons.

The U.S. Army Futures Command is headquartered in Austin, Texas. The command is responsible for modernizing the Army so that future soldiers will have the weapons and organization needed to win future battles.

Army service component commands are Army units that are part of the unified commands of the United States armed forces. The U.S. Army Special Operations Command, headquartered at Fort Bragg, North Carolina, oversees the operation of Special Forces,

Rangers, and other units. It is part of the U.S. Special Operations Command, which coordinates the special units from the different military branches.

The Military Surface Deployment and Distribution Command, headquartered at Scott Air Force Base, Illinois, handles land transportation of military cargo and personnel. It also operates ocean terminals to move military cargo. It is part of the U.S. Transportation Command, which provides air, land, and sea transportation for the armed forces. The U.S. Army Space and Missile Defense Command has headquarters at Redstone Arsenal, Alabama. It is part of the U.S. Strategic Command, which coordinates the military's space operations, missile defense, information and intelligence activities, and strategic deterrence. The U.S. Army Cyber Command, headquartered at Fort Gordon, Georgia, conducts electronic warfare. It defends Army networks from cyber threats and fights adversaries through cyberspace.

Other Army service component commands are part of regional unified commands, which coordinate the activities of U.S. armed forces in a specified region of the world. United States Army Europe is part of the U.S. European Command, which covers Europe, Russia, and part of southwest Asia, including Israel and Turkey. United States Army Central is part of the U.S. Central Command, which covers most of southwest and central Asia and northeast Africa. This region includes the Middle East—with the exceptions of Turkey and Israel—as well as such countries as Afghanistan and Pakistan. United States Army Africa is part of the U.S. Africa Command, which covers most of Africa. United States Army North is part of the U.S. Northern Command, which covers most of North America. United States Army South is part of the U.S. Southern Command, which covers Central America, South America, and the Caribbean. United States Army Pacific is part of the U.S. Indo-Pacific Command, which covers eastern and southern Asia, Australia, and the Pacific. The Eighth U.S. Army is part of U.S. Forces Korea, which is a subordinate command of the U.S. Indo-Pacific Command.

Army levels of command

Unit and approximate strength	Rank of leader	Organizational elements of each unit
Field Army*	General	Headquarters, two or more corps, support troops.
Corps 20,000-45,000	Lieutenant general	Headquarters, two or more divisions, support troops.
Division 10,000-15,000	Major general	Headquarters, three tactical maneuver brigades, support troops. Five types of divisions: Airborne, Air Assault, Armor, Light Infantry, Mechanized Infantry.
Brigade, group, or regiment 1,500-5,000	Brigadier general or colonel	Headquarters, two or more battalions, support troops.
Battalion or squadron 300-1,000	Lieutenant colonel	Headquarters, three or more companies.
Company, troop, or battery 60-200	Captain	Headquarters, three or more platoons.
Platoon 16-44	Lieutenant	Two to four squads.
Squad 8-16	Staff sergeant	Two to four teams.
Team 4	Sergeant	Smallest unit.

*Strength varies to meet situation.

United States Army Europe has headquarters in Wiesbaden, Germany. United States Army Central, also called the Third U.S. Army, has headquarters at Shaw Air Force Base, South Carolina. United States Army Africa has headquarters in Vicenza, Italy. United States Army North, also called the Fifth U.S. Army, and United States Army South both have headquarters at Fort Sam Houston, Texas. United States Army Pacific has headquarters at Fort Shafter, Hawaii. The Eighth U.S. Army has headquarters near Seoul, South Korea.

Direct reporting units provide institutional support and usually have a single, unique function. These units, and their headquarters, include the U.S. Army Acquisition Support Center, Fort Belvoir; the U.S. Army Corps of Engineers, Washington, D.C.; the U.S. Army Criminal Investigation Command, Quantico, Virginia; the U.S. Army Human Resources Command, Fort Knox; the U.S. Army Intelligence and Security Command, Fort Belvoir; the U.S. Army Medical Command, Fort Sam Houston; the U.S. Army Military District of Washington, D.C.; the U.S. Army Test and Evaluation Command, Aberdeen Proving Ground, Maryland; the U.S. Army War College, Carlisle, Pennsylvania; and the U.S. Military Academy, West Point, New York. See **Engineers, Corps of; United States Military Academy.**

History

The Continental Army, which grew into the U.S. Army, began before the American Revolution (1775-1783). All 13 English colonies had militia that fought in the French and Indian wars (1689-1763). All colonies except Pennsylvania had a standing militia that able-bodied men from 16 to 60 had to join. Every colony also had a volunteer militia. These forces, along with troops re-

© Gary P. Bonaccorso, Getty Images

Information and communications systems enable Army command personnel to monitor and control operations in the field. The temporary command center shown in this photograph uses laptop computers connected through a network.

cruited by the British as *regulars,* fought in the French and Indian War (1754-1763).

On June 14, 1775, the Continental Congress voted to raise 10 companies of riflemen for service in the Revolutionary War and to take charge of colonial militias that were then besieging the British in Boston. The next day, the Congress appointed George Washington "general and commander in chief" of the Continental Army.

In 1776, the Continental Congress established a Board of War and Ordnance to administer the Army. It abolished the board in 1781, and assigned its duties to a secretary at war, who directed the Army and Navy. The U.S. Congress set up a Department of War in 1789.

The Army probably never had more than 30,000 men at any time. But by the late 1780's, the regular forces had been cut to about 800 men. In 1802, Congress set up the U.S. Military Academy at West Point, New York, the nation's first military school.

The War of 1812 (1812-1815). The United States had an army of nearly 12,000 men when it went to war against Britain in 1812. This force reached a peak strength of 38,000 men. Artillery units made important contributions to American victories. Military leaders who won fame in the war included Jacob Brown, Andrew Jackson, and Winfield Scott.

At various times after the war, Congress authorized an army of from 6,000 to 12,000 men. The government used this army to fight two wars against the Seminole Indians and the Black Hawk War against the Sauk and Fox Indians. The Army also forced the Cherokee to move to lands west of the Mississippi River.

The Mexican War (1846-1848) was chiefly a ground war. About two-thirds of the soldiers were members of militia and volunteer units. The Army had to rely mainly on regular army soldiers and 12-month volunteers because of the continual turnover of short-term militiamen. About 104,000 men served during the war, which saw a number of Army "firsts." For the first time, the Army fought far beyond the frontiers of the United States. It used steam vessels as troop transports. American soldiers fought in unaccustomed climate and terrain, and in combat in the streets of Monterrey. Also for the first time, the Army administered a military government over a conquered area.

The American Civil War (1861-1865). The United States adopted its first federal military draft law during the Civil War. Both the North and the South called for volunteers, but not enough men enlisted. On March 3, 1863, Congress passed the Enrollment Act. This law required all men in the North between the ages of 20 and 45 to register for military service.

The Union Army had about 16,000 men under arms in 1860 and reached a peak strength of about 1 million in 1865. Ulysses S. Grant, the Union commander, later became the first person to hold the rank of General of the Army. During the war, the Union Army made wide use of railroads, telegraph, photography, observation balloons, and rifled artillery.

Within 10 years after the Civil War, the Army had been reduced to about 25,000 men. Its soldiers were toughened by years of Indian fighting. However, few had experience handling problems of war mobilization and large-scale command.

The Spanish-American War (1898). The regular Army had only 28,000 men when war broke out with Spain. The National Guard numbered about 100,000. Congress authorized a twofold increase in the size of the Army, and an initial enlistment of 125,000 volunteers. As the war progressed, inadequacies in Army organization and preparedness became apparent. The problems of supply, health, and sanitation in the tropics were as dangerous as the Spanish troops in Cuba and the Philippines. More soldiers died from disease than were killed in battle.

After the war, the Army helped establish American authority in the Philippines. It also fought in the Boxer Rebellion in China (see **Boxer Rebellion**).

The early 1900's were a period of reorganization for the Army. Through the efforts of Secretary of War Elihu Root, Congress approved the adoption of the general staff system and the appointment of a chief of staff to replace the commanding general of the Army. On Aug. 15, 1903, Lieutenant General Samuel B. M. Young became the first chief of staff.

On Aug. 1, 1907, the Army set up an aeronautical division within its signal corps. This force of one officer and two enlisted men slowly grew until it became an independent military service 40 years later (see **Air Force, United States**).

World War I (1914-1918). The United States had a Regular Army of only 128,000 men when it declared war on Germany on April 6, 1917. But the National Guard had

Important dates in Army history

1775 The Continental Congress created the Continental Army to fight in the Revolutionary War.

1789 Congress established the Department of War to direct military affairs.

1802 The U.S. Military Academy, first military school in the United States, opened at West Point.

1847 During the Mexican War, the U.S. Army administered a military government over an occupied area for the first time.

1863 Congress passed the first federal draft law in the United States, the Enrollment Act.

1903 The Army adopted the general staff system and set up the Office of the Chief of Staff, United States Army.

1914 The Panama Canal, a project of the Army engineers, was completed, linking the Atlantic and Pacific oceans.

1917 (April 6) The United States declared war on Germany.

1944 Army troops and other Allied forces stormed Normandy, France, in the greatest amphibious attack in history.

1945 Atomic bombs, developed by U.S. Army and by civilian scientists, were dropped on Hiroshima and Nagasaki in Japan.

1965 The Army's first air mobile division was activated at Fort Benning, Georgia, and shipped to Vietnam.

1973 All U.S. combat troops withdrew from Vietnam after a cease-fire agreement was signed.

1974 The Army achieved all-volunteer status at full authorized strength.

1976 Women were admitted to the U.S. Military Academy.

1991 The Army led a land attack on Iraqi forces in the Persian Gulf War of 1991, resulting in Iraq's defeat in a few days.

2001 The Army began participation in the Afghanistan War and helped end the Taliban's rule over the country.

2003 The Army began participation in the Iraq War, helping to end the rule of Iraqi dictator Saddam Hussein.

developed into a military organization far superior to the state militias of earlier wars. However, with the need for a larger army, Congress passed a Selective Service Act that made all able-bodied men between the ages of 21 and 30 (later, 18 and 45) subject to military service. The government sent nearly 2 million soldiers overseas in the American Expeditionary Forces. By the summer of 1918, American manpower and arms had helped turn the tide of battle in favor of the Allies. General John J. Pershing commanded the American doughboys who fought in France. The Meuse-Argonne offensive marked the Army's largest battle up to that time. But, with the signing of the armistice in 1918, the Army again faced a cutback in strength. Within two years, it had been reduced to about 204,000 men, and it was reduced to even fewer in the following postwar years.

After World War I, U.S. Army troops came to the aid of anti-Communist forces in the Russian civil war. But they accomplished little and soon were brought home.

World War II (1939-1945) witnessed the mobilization of the largest American army ever to take the field. The Army expanded from about 190,000 men in 1939 to almost 8,270,000 in 1945. The Selective Service Act of 1940 required all male citizens age 21 through 35 to register for a year of military service. Later amendments to the law extended the age limits to 18 and 44 and increased the length of service to the duration of the war. The first drafted men entered the Army on Nov. 18, 1940. The Army multiplied its units by means of the cadre system. A certain number of key men were removed from a unit as it became ready for service. This group of men, or *cadre,* formed the basis of new units.

General George C. Marshall became Army chief of staff on Sept. 1, 1939, the day that Germany attacked Poland. Japan's attack at Pearl Harbor on Dec. 7, 1941, plunged the United States into World War II.

The Army underwent several reorganizations during the war to cope with the complexities of fighting on many battlefronts. Lieutenant General Lesley J. McNair became commander of U.S. Army Ground Forces. General Henry H. Arnold commanded the Army Air Forces.

The Army took part in the largest amphibious attack in history when the Allies landed in Normandy, France, in 1944. It organized airborne divisions that added a new dimension to warfare (see **Airborne troops**). Its engineers cooperated with civilian scientists to develop the atomic bomb (see **Nuclear weapon**).

In May 1942, the Army established the Women's Army Auxiliary Corps (WAAC). In 1943, the WAAC became a part of the United States Army, and the name was changed to Women's Army Corps (WAC). Women in the Army became known as *Wacs.* More than 17,000 Wacs served overseas during the war. In 1945, the last year of the war, the WAC reached a peak strength of about 100,000 enlisted women and officers. The WAC was dissolved in 1978.

At the end of the war, the Army faced the huge problem of *demobilization* (releasing millions of soldiers from active duty). By 1948, it had about 554,000 soldiers. The government discontinued the draft in 1947, but resumed it in 1948.

The Korean War (1950-1953). In response to a United Nations (UN) request, President Harry S. Truman in June 1950 ordered U.S. Army troops on occupation duty in Japan to aid South Korea. General of the Army Douglas MacArthur headed the UN Command in Korea. Generals Matthew B. Ridgway and Mark W. Clark later succeeded MacArthur.

During the war, the Army gained considerable experience in training and outfitting troops of many nationalities. The Army, which had 593,000 soldiers before war broke out, had 1,596,000 by June 1952. But its strength was less than 1 million by June 1957.

The atomic age Army. In 1953, the first atomic artillery shell was fired in a test at Frenchman Flat, Nevada.

In the early 1960's, the Army completed several reorganizations. For example, it completed the Reorganization Objectives, Army Division (ROAD) plan to increase the flexibility of its fighting forces in limited wars. In 1962, the reorganization added a *mechanized* division to the three existing types: infantry, airborne, and armored.

In 1965, the Army added an *airmobile* division. This division was to use helicopters and airplanes to support its ground units in combat.

The Vietnam War (1957-1975). United States involvement in the struggle to prevent Communist forces from taking control of South Vietnam began in the mid-1950's. At first, the Army contributed only advisers to South Vietnamese government forces. But by 1965, the U.S. commitment to South Vietnam had grown, and large Army units went into action. The airmobile division proved very effective in a war that required the ability to strike with surprise. The helicopter was a major weapon. It was used as an armed attack troop and cargo carrier, as well as an ambulance.

The peak of U.S. Army strength in Vietnam reached about 363,000 in April 1969. In the early 1970's, the South Vietnamese assumed increasing responsibility for their own defense. By December 1972, about 14,000 U.S. Army troops remained. An agreement for a cease-fire in Vietnam was signed in Paris on Jan. 27, 1973. All U.S. ground troops left Vietnam shortly after the agreement was signed. But the war did not end until 1975.

Reorganizations. In 1973, the U.S. government ended the military draft, and the armed services began recruiting all-volunteer forces. The same year, the Army began a reorganization designed to cut personnel and operating costs and improve readiness and efficiency. It included the establishment of the Forces Command and the Training and Doctrine Command.

In the mid-1980's, the Army worked to reduce the amount of equipment and number of soldiers of its heavy divisions while keeping their combat abilities intact. Light infantry forces were redesigned so they could move rapidly anywhere. Army corps were provided with more artillery, aviation, and air defense capabilities.

The Persian Gulf War of 1991. In August 1990, Iraq invaded neighboring Kuwait. The United States, to prevent further aggression in the area by Iraq, began sending troops to Saudi Arabia. The United Kingdom, Egypt, and other nations also sent troops. By November, over one-third the total forces of the U.S. Army, including about 149,000 soldiers of the Army Reserve and National Guard, had been mobilized for war.

War began on Jan. 16, 1991, United States time, which was January 17 in Iraq. At first, allied air forces bombed military targets. On February 23 U.S. time (February 24 in the war area), allied land forces began moving into

© Erik S. Lesser, Getty Images

Army combat uniforms have camouflage colors and patterns designed to help soldiers avoid detection by the enemy.

Kuwait and Iraq. The allies quickly defeated the Iraqi forces there, suffering few casualties. Two days later, the Iraqi troops began withdrawing from Kuwait.

The Iraq War (2003-2011) ended the rule of Iraqi dictator Saddam Hussein. After the war began in March 2003, the Army participated in a U.S.-led invasion of Iraq, mainly from Kuwait. Other Army troops parachuted into northern Iraq and joined forces there with Kurdish rebels. In April, the Army helped capture Baghdad, Iraq's capital, ending Hussein's rule. In December, Army forces captured Hussein in Ad Dawr, north of Baghdad.

Following the fall of Hussein's regime, Army troops sought to provide security and training for Iraqis. But U.S. soldiers continued to meet resistance from militant groups in Iraq. Militants used crude bombs called *improvised explosive devices* (IED's) to kill and wound thousands of Army soldiers. In 2006, Army troops faced violence between Iraqi Sunnis and Shi'ites—the two main Muslim sects—after Sunni militants bombed the al-Askari shrine in Samarra, considered holy to Shi'ites.

In 2011, U.S. troops withdrew from Iraq, but the country remained troubled by violence. In 2014, Sunni militants seized much of Iraq's north and west. A small number of Army special forces returned to aid Iraq's government, the Kurds, and other groups threatened by the militants, who called themselves the Islamic State.

The Afghanistan War (2001-2021) began in response to the terrorist attacks of Sept. 11, 2001. The attacks, launched by the extremist group al-Qa'ida, killed about 3,000 people. Beginning in October 2001, an inter-national force led by the United States attacked the Taliban, the Sunni fundamentalist group that had ruled Afghanistan and sheltered al-Qa'ida. The force quickly overthrew the Taliban. However, the Taliban and other militant groups mounted a long-lasting *insurgency* (uprising) against Afghanistan's new government. The United States supported the new government. The U.S. Army often fought insurgent forces in harsh terrain, facing ambushes and deadly improvised explosive devices.

In 2011, U.S. special forces killed Osama bin Laden, the leader of al-Qa'ida, in neighboring Pakistan. A ceremony in Afghanistan's capital in 2014 marked the official end of the war, even as the Taliban insurgency continued. Thousands of additional U.S. troops were sent to Afghanistan in 2017. In 2021, as the United States and its allies withdrew their military forces from Afghanistan, the Taliban took over the country once again.

Critically reviewed by the United States Army

Related articles in *World Book.* See Army and its list of *Related articles.* See also the following articles:

Army installations

History

Other related articles

Outline

I. **Life in the Army**
   A. Training a soldier   C. A typical day
   B. Training an officer   D. Careers in the Army
II. **Weapons and equipment of the Army**
   A. Infantry   G. Communications
   B. Artillery   and observation
   C. Armor   H. Transportation
   D. Army aviation   I. Engineers
   E. Special units   J. Logistic units
   F. Missiles
III. **Organization of the Army**
IV. **History**

Armyworm is a caterpillar especially harmful to corn, other grains, and garden crops east of the Rocky Mountains in the United States and Canada. It is the *larva* (young) of a night-flying moth (see **Larva**). Sometimes large numbers of these caterpillars march like an army across fields. They stick together in dense patches and sometimes form processions 12 or 14 feet (3.7 or 4.3 meters) long and 2 or 3 inches (5 or 8 centimeters) wide. They apparently band together to search for new feeding grounds.

The armyworm is hairless and fleshy. It is about 1 ½ inches (3.8 centimeters) long, and it has green and yellow stripes. When full grown, it burrows into the soil and transforms into a *pupa* (see **Pupa**). The pupa changes into a pale brown moth that emerges in the spring. The female moth deposits strings of eggs on the lower leaves of grasses. The caterpillars hatch from these eggs. They usually feed at night and hide during the day. There are two or three broods per year.

Farmers fight armyworms with various insecticide sprays. Dust *furrows* (narrow grooves) may be dug as barriers against them. The natural enemies of the armyworm include parasitic flies and wasps, and the fiery ground beetle.   Charles V. Covell, Jr.

Scientific classification. The armyworm's scientific name is *Pseudaletia unipuncta.*

See also **Moth.**

Arnaz, Desi (1917-1986), was a Cuban-born actor, musician, and bandleader. He was the husband of the actress Lucille Ball and co-starred with her in one of the most popular series in television history, "I Love Lucy" (1951-1957). In the series, Arnaz played Ricky Ricardo, the husband of the zany Lucy. Arnaz was the first Hispanic American to co-star on a network TV series.

Arnaz was born in Santiago, Cuba, on March 2, 1917. His full name was Desiderio Alberto Arnaz y de Acha. He moved to the United States at age 16 and joined a Cuban music combo. He eventually formed his own band, singing in an exuberant style and playing the bongo drums. Arnaz made his motion-picture debut in *Too Many Girls* (1940), co-starring Lucille Ball. They married in 1940. He appeared in several other movie musicals in the 1940's and co-starred with Ball in two film comedies, *The Long Long Trailer* (1954) and *Forever Darling* (1956).

In 1950, Arnaz and Ball formed Desilu Productions, which produced "I Love Lucy" and many other TV shows. They divorced in 1960. Ball bought out Arnaz's share of Desilu Productions, and Arnaz became an independent television producer. Arnaz and Ball had two children, Lucie and Desi, Jr. Both developed successful careers in movies and TV. Arnaz wrote an autobiography, *A Book* (1976). He died on Dec. 2, 1986.   Dan Zeff

Arnica, *AHR nuh kuh,* is the name of several kinds of plants of the Northern Hemisphere that yield a juice used to drive away the blood that collects in bruises. The *common,* or *mountain, arnica* is the source of commercial arnica. Its twisted root lives from year to year. Its stem is about 2 feet (61 centimeters) high and bears heads of golden-yellow flowers. Every part of the plant contains *arnicin,* which is used to make the medicine. Mountain arnica is native to the mountain meadows and moors of northern and central Europe.   W. Dennis Clark

Scientific classification. Arnicas make up the genus *Arnica.* The mountain arnica's scientific name is *Arnica montana.*

Arno River rises in the Etruscan section of the Apennine Mountains in northwestern Italy. It flows west for about 150 miles (241 kilometers) and empties into the Ligurian Sea (see **Italy** [terrain map]). Florence and Pisa

lie along the river. The fertile Arno Valley has vineyards and olive groves and is noted for its scenic beauty. See also **Florence; Pisa.**   Hugh D. Clout

Arnold, Benedict (1741-1801), was an American general of the Revolutionary War period. Once trusted and admired, he became the most famous traitor in United States history.

Arnold was born on Jan. 14, 1741, in Norwich, Connecticut. He learned the *apothecary* (pharmacy) trade and, in 1762, opened a book and drug store in New Haven, Connecticut. Arnold also carried on trade with the Caribbean Islands. By 1774, he was one of the wealthiest citizens in New Haven. In 1767, Arnold married Margaret Mansfield, who was the daughter of the sheriff of New Haven County. She died in 1775.

A courageous soldier. In 1774, Arnold became a captain in the Connecticut militia. Soon after the American Revolution began in 1775, he was commissioned as a colonel in the patriot forces. Arnold and Ethan Allen led the capture of Fort Ticonderoga, in New York, on May 10, 1775.

Later that same year, Arnold led 1,100 soldiers into Canada. He cooperated with Brigadier General Richard Montgomery in an unsuccessful assault on Quebec. Arnold's leg was severely wounded in the assault, and his courage won him a promotion to brigadier general. In October 1776, he distinguished himself in the Battle of Valcour Island, a naval battle on Lake Champlain.

A disappointed officer. Arnold had several disappointments. He was passed over for promotion in February 1777, when Congress appointed five new major generals. Arnold, who had more seniority than any of the men promoted, was talked out of leaving the army by General George Washington. In May 1777, Congress promoted Arnold to major general as a reward for his bravery in helping drive a British raiding party out of Connecticut.

Later that year, Arnold served under Major General Horatio Gates against British Lieutenant General John Burgoyne. Burgoyne hoped to cut New York in half during an advance from Canada. In October 1777, at the Second Battle of Freeman's Farm, Arnold showed ex-

WORLD BOOK illustration by Christabel King
The mountain arnica bears heads of golden-yellow flowers from its stem. The plant grows in northern and central Europe.

traordinary courage and leadership against Burgoyne's army and was again seriously wounded. This battle, won by the patriots, is also known as the Battle of Bemis Heights. It led to Burgoyne's surrender at Saratoga several days later. Gates took credit for the victory. Congress voted Arnold the country's thanks and had Washington restore his seniority over the other generals.

In 1778, Arnold took command of Philadelphia. There he married Margaret Shippen, a young woman from a prominent family. Arnold was not a good administrator, and he drew criticism for living extravagantly. The executive council of Pennsylvania accused him of being too gentle with Americans who opposed independence from Britain (now also called the United Kingdom). The council also accused him of using military personnel to do personal favors. A court-martial cleared Arnold, but it ordered General Washington to reprimand him.

Turns traitor. Arnold brooded over what he considered his country's ingratitude and injustice, and he began corresponding with the enemy. Arnold was in command of West Point in 1780, and he worked out a plan to surrender that important military base to the British commander General Sir Henry Clinton.

The capture of British Major John André, who was carrying papers sent by Arnold to Clinton, exposed Arnold's treachery (see **André, John**). Arnold escaped to New York City and became a brigadier general in the British Army. He demanded 20,000 pounds from the British for the losses he incurred in joining them. But he received only 6,315 pounds. As a British officer, he led expeditions that raided Richmond, Virginia, and burned New London, Connecticut.

Scorned in England. Arnold was received warmly by King George III when he went to England in 1782, but others there scorned him. In 1797, the British government granted him 13,400 acres (5,423 hectares) in Canada, but the land was of little use to him. He spent most of his remaining years as a merchant in the Caribbean Islands trade. In his last days, Arnold was burdened with debt, became discouraged, and was generally distrusted. He died on June 14, 1801.   Gregory J. W. Urwin

See also **Fort Ticonderoga.**

Arnold, Eddy (1918-2008), an American singer, was a leading performer in country music from the mid-1940's through the 1960's. He was a pioneer in gaining a mass audience for country music. His best-known songs include "That's How Much I Love You" (1946), "I'll Hold You in My Heart (Till I Hold You in My Arms)" (1947), "Any Time" (1948), "Don't Rob Another Man's Castle" (1949), "Kentucky Waltz" (1951), "Eddy's Song" (1953), "I Really Don't Want to Know" (1954), "Cattle Call" (1955), "You Don't Know Me" (1956), "Tennessee Stud" (1959), "Make the World Go Away" (1965), "I Wish I Had Loved You Better" (1974), and "Cowboy" (1976).

Richard Edward Arnold, known as "the Tennessee

Engraving by H. B. Hall,
Historical Pictures Service

Benedict Arnold

Plowboy," was born on May 15, 1918, near Henderson, Tennessee. His mother taught him to play the guitar. In 1936, Arnold became a radio performer. His increasing popularity as a singer on the radio gained him a recording contract with RCA Victor in 1943. Arnold hosted several country music shows on television from 1952 to 1956. He was elected to the Country Music Hall of Fame in 1966. Arnold died on May 8, 2008.   Lee Rector

Arnold, Henry Harley (1886-1950), developed the small United States Army Air Corps into a large, powerful U.S. Air Force. Arnold commanded the Army Air Forces during World War II (1939-1945). He was the only person to serve as both General of the Army and General of the Air Force.

Arnold was born on June 25, 1886, in Gladwyne, Pennsylvania. He was nicknamed "Hap." He graduated from the U.S. Military Academy (West Point) in 1907 and took flying lessons from the Wright brothers. In World War I (1914-1918), he organized the air defense of the Canal Zone. After the war, he transferred to the newly formed Air Service. He made many experimental flights, including the first mass flight of B-10 bombers. He helped start air mail flights, air refueling, and air forest fire patrols.

Before and during World War II, Arnold fought for expansion of U.S. air power. He became chief of the Army Air Corps in 1938 and United States deputy chief of staff for air in 1940. Arnold was made chief of the new Army Air Forces in 1941. He became commanding general in 1942. As a member of the Joint Chiefs of Staff, Arnold successfully asked for daylight precision bombing against Germany. Previous bombing raids had been staged at night because they were thought to be safer. Daylight bombing increased accuracy because the targets could be seen. Arnold retired in 1946 and died on Jan. 15, 1950.   Maurice Matloff

Arnold, Matthew (1822-1888), was one of the intellectual leaders of Victorian England. He ranks with Lord Tennyson, Robert Browning, and Gerard Manley Hopkins among the greatest Victorian poets. Arnold was also the most important English literary critic of his time. He was a major social critic and wrote important works on religion and education.

Arnold's poetry expresses his experience during an age when traditional religious beliefs and certainties were being questioned without new beliefs to take their place. As he wrote in "Stanzas from the Grande Chartreuse" (1855), he felt himself to be

Wandering between two worlds, one dead,
The other powerless to be born ...

Arnold's most famous poem, "Dover Beach," describes the "melancholy, long, withdrawing roar" of the "Sea of Faith." His poetry resembles the poetry of our own time in its yearning for peace and its portrayal of personal loneliness. Faced with these difficulties, Arnold often counseled resignation and endurance.

Arnold's prose includes the literary criticism in *Essays in Criticism* (1865, second series 1888) and the social criticism of *Culture and Anarchy* (1869). Arnold judged both literature and Victorian society according to the standard of "the best that is known and thought in the world." He found writers of his time, such as Percy Bysshe Shelley, William Wordsworth, or Robert Burns, inadequate when measured against Homer, Dante, or William Shakespeare. Arnold condemned what he felt was the tendency toward *anarchy* (lawlessness) in Victorian culture. He criticized his society for resisting the new ideas that come from a "free play of the mind." Arnold hoped that maintaining high standards of judgment would aid the return of better literature and a better society.

Arnold was born on Dec. 24, 1822, in Laleham. His father was Thomas Arnold, headmaster of Rugby, the famous English secondary school. Arnold attended Rugby and Oxford University. In 1851, he became an inspector of schools for the British government, a post at which he worked hard for the next 35 years. Most of his poems were published between 1849 and 1855. His prose appeared after 1855. He was professor of poetry at Oxford from 1857 to 1867. He died April 15, 1888.　　K. K. Collins

See also **English literature** (Later Victorian literature).

Arp, *ahrp,* **Jean,** *zhahn* (1887-1966), was a French sculptor. He was also called Hans Arp. He worked with many materials, including wood, bronze, and polished stone. Arp became famous for his reliefs, free-standing sculptures, and collages (see **Collage**). While Arp's works may at first seem abstract, many of them suggest plants, animals, and human anatomy. These organic forms capture the life, vitality, and sense of growth found in nature, rather than specific physical appearances.

Arp avoided preconceived plans when creating his works. He let the sculpture "create itself" in such works as *Shepherd of the Clouds* (1953).

Arp was born on Sept. 16, 1887, in Strasbourg. He was also a painter, a poet, and a graphic artist. He exhibited with the German Expressionist artists just before World War I (1914-1918). In 1916, he helped found Dadaism. He was later associated with the Surrealists (see **Dadaism; Surrealism**). He died on June 7, 1966.　　Joseph F. Lamb

Árpád. See **Hungary** (History).

Arpino, *ahr PEEN oh,* **Gerald** (1928-2008), was an important American ballet *choreographer* (dance creator). Arpino's career was closely identified with the American choreographer Robert Joffrey. Arpino and Joffrey cofounded the Joffrey Ballet in 1956 in New York City. Arpino was a principal dancer with the company until 1964 and then served as its chief choreographer. After Joffrey died in 1988, Arpino became the company's artistic director. He held this position until 2007. Arpino moved the company to Chicago in 1995.

Gennaro Peter Arpino was born on Jan. 14, 1928, in the New York City borough of Staten Island. He made his debut as a choreographer in 1961 with *Ropes.* His other works include *Partita for Four* (1961), *Sea Shadow* (1963), *Viva Vivaldi!* (1965), *Olympics* (1966), *Trinity* (1969), *Kettentanz* (1971), *Celebration* (1980), *Light Rain* (1981), *Billboards* (1993), and *Ruth: Ricordi per Due* (2007). He died on Oct. 29, 2008.　　Dan Zeff

Arquebus. See **Harquebus.**

Arrest is the act of taking a person into the custody of the law and depriving the person of liberty. The term comes from the French word *arrêter,* which means *to stop.* Any police officer may make arrests. Agents of the United States Federal Bureau of Investigation also have the power to make some types of arrests. Private citizens have the right to make an arrest if a serious crime is committed in their presence. People may be arrested after they are accused of murder, theft, or other criminal offenses. For some crimes, and under certain conditions, a police officer must get a court order called a *warrant*

before making an arrest. But an officer does not need a warrant to arrest a person in the act of committing a crime. Ordinarily police may arrest anyone whom they reasonably believe to be guilty of a serious crime.

Usually only those people accused of such serious crimes as murder are forced to stay in jail until they are brought to trial. Other people may go free until trial if they can provide a sum of money called *bail.* This money is a pledge to appear for trial. In 1991, the Supreme Court of the United States ruled that a person arrested without a warrant has the right to be heard before a judge within 48 hours after the arrest.　　George T. Felkenes

See also **Bail; Habeas corpus; Warrant.**

Arrhythmia, *uh RIHTH mee uh,* is an abnormal heart rhythm. Arrhythmias often are extra heartbeats that cause no serious problems. However, sometimes the heart rhythm can become dangerously slow or fast.

Abnormally slow heart rhythms often are a sign of *heart block,* in which the electrical impulses started by the heart's natural "pacemaker" fail to be conducted to the *ventricles,* the heart's main pumping chambers. The heart rate becomes very slow, which may cause loss of consciousness, heart failure, or death. A doctor can correct the condition by implanting an electronic *pacemaker* in the body. This device transmits an electric impulse to the heart, stimulating it to beat in a normal rhythm.

Abnormally fast heart rhythms are the chief cause of disabling symptoms or death from heart disease. Such arrhythmias can occur unexpectedly in the months or years after a heart attack. Many can be controlled with medication. In serious emergencies, they can be treated by applying a strong electric shock, but the shock must be administered within minutes to prevent severe heart damage or death. In some cases, doctors implant a device called a *defibrillator* to detect and treat abnormally fast heart rhythms. The defibrillator monitors the heart and automatically delivers electric shocks before the arrhythmia causes permanent damage.　　Toby R. Engel

See also **Defibrillator; Digitalis.**

Arrow. See **Archery.**

Arrow, Kenneth Joseph (1921-2017), an American economist, shared the 1972 Nobel Prize in economics with Sir John Hicks of the United Kingdom. They won the award for their contributions to *general equilibrium theory* and to *welfare economics.* General equilibrium theory examines the relationship between the processes of production, distribution, and consumption in the total economy. Welfare economics is a branch of economics concerned with how an economic system might achieve the greatest possible welfare for its people.

Arrow is best known for his *impossibility theorem,* an idea that revolutionized welfare economics. The theorem proves mathematically that a perfect form of government can never be possible. Arrow also did pioneering research on the theory of business risks.

Arrow was born on Aug. 23, 1921, in New York City. He taught economics at Stanford University from 1949 to 1968 and at Harvard University from 1968 to 1979. He returned to Stanford in 1979 and taught there until his retirement in 1991. His books include *Essays in the Theory of Risk Bearing* (1971) and *The Limits of Organization* (1974). Arrow died on Feb. 21, 2017.　　Barry W. Poulson

Arrowhead is a sharp point on the striking end of an arrow. It is usually a separate piece attached to the

Prehistoric arrowheads used by Stone Age Europeans were chipped into leaf shapes and triangular shapes.

A bronze arrowhead from Iran dates to about 1000 to 500 B.C.

Obsidian

Quartzite

Agate

Jasper

Quartz

Chert

Flint

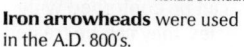

Iron arrowheads were used in the A.D. 800's.

American Indian arrowheads were fashioned in many shapes and sizes and from a variety of materials. The Indians sharpened such minerals as jasper, quartz, and flint into deadly points.

arrow shaft. Prehistoric people first made arrowheads of stone or bone, and later of metal. Stone points that may have been arrowheads have been found at sites in southern Africa that are up to 71,000 years old. Stone arrowheads are especially common in the Americas, where the bow and arrow appeared by about A.D. 500. Older, larger stone points found in the Americas were used as knives or spear points.

Stone arrowheads were made by chipping, or *knapping,* stones such as flint, chert, obsidian, jasper, chalcedony, and quartz. An arrowhead maker began by breaking a piece off a stone using another stone as a hammer. The maker then removed small chips from the underside of the arrowhead by pressing with an antler, bone, or ivory tool. A skillful knapper can make an arrowhead in only a few minutes.

Arrowheads differ in size and shape. Most are less than 2 inches (5 centimeters) long. Many are triangular, while others are oval or leaf-shaped. They often have notches for attaching them to the arrow shaft. Archaeologists recognize various types of arrowheads made by Indians of different time periods or geographic regions. Stone arrowheads are sharp, but they are not as strong as metal. Indians stopped making stone arrowheads after European traders brought iron.   John C. Whittaker

See also **Flint.**

Arrowroot is a plant cultivated in many tropical countries. People use the *rhizomes* (underground stems) of the arrowroot plant to make a light starch that is used in puddings, pie fillings, and other dessert mixtures. The starch obtained from the plant is also called arrowroot.

See also **Starch.**   Michael J. Tanabe

Scientific classification. The arrowroot's scientific name is *Maranta arundinacea.*

Arroyo. See Desert (Desert climate and land).

Arsenic, *AHR suh nihk* or *AHRS nihk,* is a chemical element classified as a metalloid. It is a deadly poison, and prolonged low-dose exposure to arsenic causes cancer in human beings. Many rat poisons, insecticides, and weedkillers contain arsenic. It is also used to manufacture lead gun shot and certain types of electrical equipment, and to increase the strength of certain alloys.

There are three chief *allotropes* (solid forms) of arsenic: (1) gray arsenic, (2) yellow arsenic, and (3) black arsenic. Gray arsenic is the ordinary, stable form of the element. It has a shiny appearance and is a moderately good conductor of heat and electricity. But gray arsenic is brittle and breaks easily. When heated to 1135 °F (613 °C), gray arsenic *sublimes*—that is, it passes directly into a vapor without melting (see **Sublimation**).

Arsenic occasionally occurs in its pure form in nature. But it is most commonly found in chemical combination with sulfur or oxygen, or with such metals as cobalt, copper, iron, nickel, silver, and tin. The principal arsenic-containing mineral is arsenopyrite. The most widely used arsenic compound is *white arsenic,* also called *arsenic trioxide.* It is usually produced as a by-product of the *smelting* (melting) of copper or lead.

Compounds of arsenic have been used since ancient times for many purposes, including medicines and poisons. The German scholar Albertus Magnus is often credited with first isolating the element about 1250. Arsenic has the chemical symbol As. Its *atomic number* (number of protons in its nucleus) is 33. Its *relative atomic mass* is 74.92159. An element's relative atomic mass equals its *mass* (amount of matter) divided by $\frac{1}{12}$ of the mass of an atom of carbon 12, the most abundant form of carbon. Marianna A. Busch

See also **Arsenical; Insecticide.**

Arsenical, *ahr SEHN uh kuhl,* is one of a group of drugs that contain arsenic and have been used as a medicine. *Carbarsone* is an arsenical used in treating amebic dysentery. Arsenic is a deadly poison. Arsenicals are being replaced by other drugs. See also **Arsenic.**

Christopher A. Rodowskas, Jr.

Arson, *AHR suhn,* is the crime of maliciously and willfully damaging or destroying a building or other property by fire or explosion. In most of the United States, arson includes burning one's own property to collect insurance payments on it. In some cases, arson is committed for revenge against a building owner or occupant. Other fires are set to destroy evidence of another crime, such as murder or burglary. Still other arson cases result from vandalism or *pyromania,* an uncontrollable urge to set fires (see **Pyromania**). Arson is difficult to prove because fire can destroy almost all evidence of the crime, and most cities lack enough trained arson investigators.

The police and fire departments of most major cities have arson squads and are training their members to investigate cases of suspected arson. Insurance companies have become increasingly unwilling to pay for losses due to fire unless a thorough investigation has been made. Many fire departments have called for the adoption of stronger laws against arson. Charles F. Wellford

See also **Fire department** (Arson investigations).

Art, Commercial. See **Commercial art.**

Art and the arts. In a broad sense, art is skill in making or doing. We can say that someone knows and practices the art of basket-weaving, of tuning a piano, or even of hitting a home run. In this sense, there are many arts—as many as there are kinds of deliberate, specialized activities for human beings to engage in.

The word *art* is used in many other ways. Some people speak of *the useful arts* as those that produce beautiful objects for everyday use, and *the decorative arts* as those that produce beautiful objects for their own sakes. Schools offer *liberal arts* courses in such topics as history and philosophy, and *applied arts* courses in such subjects as architecture and mechanical drawing. *Language arts* are the related skills of reading, writing, speaking, and spelling. Many people speak of *the graphic arts* as those involved in printing and bookmaking.

The word *art* is often used in a more specialized way to mean *fine arts,* such as painting pictures, writing novels, or composing music. Things created as the result of such activity are supposed to be different from, and more valuable than, things that require mere craftsmanship or technical skill. Some traditional fine arts are poetry, fiction, opera, painting, sculpture, drama, and ballet. Today architecture, motion pictures, photographs, pottery, weaving, and some forms of modern dancing are also considered art in this special sense.

The reasons for art

Human beings are makers of many things, and they make them for many purposes. Some creations serve obvious practical needs. For example, people have always made tools for cutting, digging, killing, and eating. But in all cultures, people also seem to have two less obvious purposes for some of the objects they make. First, they want to make things in forms that give pleasure when seen or heard. Second, people want to make objects that will remind them, and also teach other people, about their most important discoveries regarding fundamental realities. We call these reasons for making and valuing art *formal* and *cognitive* interests.

Formal interest. People have always had an interest in order. Most of us enjoy experiencing patterns that display balance and contrast. Prehistoric people carved the handles of their hunting knives in regular, pleasing patterns. In the 1800's, American cowboys liked to have guns and saddles decorated with patterns. We experience the same delight in form or design when we buy clothes or automobiles for their appearance rather than their warmth or efficiency. Perceiving works of art has long been considered a little like understanding mathematics because both involve patterns or forms.

Cognitive interest refers to meaning. Certain events and ideas take on the highest importance in our religious, social, moral, political, and personal lives. People have always used formal symbols or performances to make such events meaningful or to signify such ideas so they can be transmitted from person to person and from generation to generation. Prehistoric people used dances and paintings to communicate the idea of success in planting, harvesting, and hunting. The ancient Greeks gave their ideas about such ideal human qualities as wisdom and courage visual form in their beautiful statues of gods and goddesses. Today, we still give occasions like graduations or weddings importance through music and song. We also try to understand the meaning of important personal events, such as falling in love, and important public events, such as wars, by composing music, writing novels and poetry, painting pictures, or making films about them.

The work of art

The aesthetic experience. Works of art result when the formal interest and the cognitive interest come together in the creative process through which artists make art. In general, art presents us with forms we enjoy perceiving and invites us to recall or learn something important. But we do not feel these interests separately when we appreciate art. Art gives us a special kind of experience that unites pleasure in perceiving orderly forms and in learning. Scholars call this the *aesthetic experience.*

The Greek epic poem the *Odyssey* appeals to us in a way that joins the two interests. It is a story about basic human problems and a study of the resourcefulness and adaptability of human nature. It is also a well-formed story, with episodes following each other in a way that builds toward the climax. The poem's words form images in our minds and tell us about the feelings that go with the story. As we read or listen to the *Odyssey,* our experiencing of the formal features enriches our understanding of the meaning. In the same way, Vincent van Gogh's painting *Sunflowers* is more than a formal composition of shapes and colors. It has a bright vividness that stays in our experience as a symbol of how nature

"Site Unseen" (1998), a performance by Julie Laffin, Glasgow, Scotland,
from "Streetworks Festival of Live Art." © Steve Bottoms

A performance artist on a city street

Assumption of the Virgin (1577) by El Greco; WORLD BOOK photo

Students examining a painting by El Greco

Gianfranco Gorgoni

American painter Frank Stella working in his studio

Creating and enjoying art rank among humanity's most important activities. Some people like to express themselves through art as a form of recreation, *above left.* Others become professional artists, *lower left.* Art masterpieces can be studied, *right,* for pleasure and to learn how artists throughout history have felt about such subjects as love, religion, and social justice.

bursts with life. For other examples of the way formal and cognitive interests come together, see **Painting** (What do painters paint?).

Works of art differ widely in how they combine formal features with meaning. Toward one end of the scale, where the cognitive interest is strongest, are such works as the tragedies of Shakespeare. These works explore fundamental human situations and move us profoundly. They reward us with the discovery of more subtle and complex meaning as we read them or see them performed again and again. Similarly, we enjoy experiencing the religious paintings of the Italian Renaissance, the great novels of Charles Dickens, and Johann Sebastian Bach's Mass in B minor. These works of art do more than convey religious and moral beliefs and attitudes. They convey these meanings through delightful design and pleasurable patterns of perception.

Toward the other end of the scale is art that evokes strong formal interest but weak cognitive interest. This is true of the paintings of the modern American painter

Frank Stella. It is also true of Bach's Preludes and Fugues and Joseph Haydn's chamber music, where the melody and counterpoint emphasize musical form. The formal patterns of classical music, as well as ballet and even the freer forms of modern dance, produce pleasure by satisfying our interest in experiencing orderly shapes and sequences. Most such works are not vehicles for philosophical themes. Yet, even here, some critics give interpretations of highly formal art that show how such works are meaningful. They point out that Stella's paintings contrast with El Greco's to show how curved shapes can define a painting's perceived surface as depicting stillness or motion (see the illustrations with this article). The formal patterns of music have qualities like joy, sadness, and vitality, which reflect features found in human life.

Beauty. Some people identify the formal interest with our desire to make and enjoy beautiful things. But others prefer to use the word *beauty* in a fuller sense. They say that the sheer satisfaction we feel when we perceive complex but balanced design, and the profound satisfaction we experience in understanding complex but clear meaning, both contribute to beauty.

Even in the fuller sense, whether a thing is beautiful does not depend on its being useful. Many paintings, poems, and musical compositions have no use apart from their value as works of art. Of course, we could use van Gogh's *Sunflowers* as a sign for a florist's shop, or we could use a piece of sculpture to hold a door open, but their real function is to be art. Such objects as chairs, dishes, and vases have useful functions. Yet some of these works are considered art and displayed in museums because they illustrate something of aesthetic importance in their design.

Grouping the arts

Generally speaking, works of art have certain things in common. Each presents something to our sense-perception, such as the music we hear, or to our imaginative contemplation, like the story we read. Each one is set off from other things in some way. For example, a statue stands on a pedestal, and a play takes place on a stage. This way of setting the work off helps us grasp it as a whole. The work is always more or less complicated. For instance, the play has several characters, the painting consists of several shapes or colors, and the music contains a variety of sounds. The work is always organized to some degree into a unified whole.

At the same time, works of art differ in important ways. Some, such as operas and novels, can tell a story. Others, like chamber music, do not. Some, such as music and poetry, take time to unfold. Still others, like painting, are presented all at once. But this difference should not be stressed too much, because it takes time to see a painting fully, just as it does to listen to a symphony. Some kinds of art, such as sculpture, come to us just as they left the hands of their creators. Other kinds are performed or interpreted. The orchestra plays music or the actors perform the play.

But perhaps the most fundamental way of classifying works of art is in terms of the kinds of elements that make them up. Arts that use words differ from those that

Herman Miller Inc. (WORLD BOOK photo)

The useful arts bring beauty and imaginative design to many everyday objects. The chairs shown above are considered works of art as well as practical pieces of furniture.

do not, because words introduce a special sort of reference into the arts.

Verbal art is literature, which can be divided into poetry, fiction, and the essay. Literary critics have suggested a number of ways by which to distinguish literary works from other kinds of writing, such as science or history. See Literature.

Nonverbal arts include two main types: (1) musical composition and (2) visual design. Works that consist of patterns of sound, pitch, or rhythm are *musical compositions*. Even a simple melody, or a drum solo with no melody, can be considered music. Works that consist of patterns of line, shape, and color are *visual designs*.

The arts can be divided even further. For example, we can divide visual designs according to the kinds of materials that are used and the way the designs are produced. In this way, we can distinguish photographs and prints from paintings. In a group of prints, we can separate etchings from lithographs. Pictures may be painted with oils or water colors.

WORLD BOOK photo by Alexander Sobelewski

Nonverbal arts communicate without using words. Music is one of the most important of these arts. A musical composition may express emotions or ideas as strongly as a work of literature.

A third group of nonverbal arts, which some experts consider part of the second group, produces *three-dimensional objects* that we can see from several points of view and also can touch. There is no general name for them, but they include sculpture, architecture, ceramics, weaving, fine glassware, jewelry, and furniture.

Mixed arts are combinations of the basic arts. For example, songs and oratorios consist of music and poetry. Dance is a combination of music and action. Drama combines action, words, and stage scenery. Films combine visual design with storytelling. Performance art is a live performance that combines elements from such art forms as literature, music, dance, video, and the theater.

Scholars often wonder whether other senses besides sight and hearing might be used for works of art. Should a dinner that is made of gourmet dishes be considered a work of art? Could a series of different odors be considered a work of art?

Enjoying the arts

People who love music, who can lose themselves in a book, or who can spend hours painting a picture of a barn know the deep satisfaction that can be found in art. It is not easy to express this satisfaction in words. But, in some partly mysterious way, works of art are among the things of highest value in our lives.

A fine piece of music, a masterpiece of painting, or a first-rate play has the power to capture and hold our fullest and most concentrated attention. We are completely wrapped up in it, and everything works out right. The music comes to the right close at the right time and in the right way. The play ends, not necessarily on a happy note, but in a way that seems inevitable and appropriate. As we grow more and more aware of the painting, its parts seem to belong together and to be made for each other. We perceive harmony in the object and feel harmony within ourselves.

When the aesthetic experience has ended, we often feel uplifted and refreshed. Our eyes and ears, our insight into other persons, or our understanding of moral values may be sharpened and refined. We may feel more at home with ourselves. Works of art have value for us in some such ways as these.

It is this value that marks the difference between great art and simple entertainment. A work that is fairly easy to understand and appreciate takes little effort on our part. It may give us pleasure. But it does not deeply involve our emotions or our attention. It may take our minds off our troubles for a time, but it does not give us the spiritually enriching experience of vital and orderly design.

Studying the arts

To enjoy the special value of works of art, we must be ready to give a great deal to them. The greatest works of music and poetry often present difficulties. We cannot expect to master them all at once. And we cannot always find what is worthy in them at a glance. It is possible to get some satisfaction out of music while reading a newspaper or peeling potatoes. But we must listen with full attention to find the riches in great works of music.

Some of us feel that we cannot find much to enjoy in one art or another. But most of us can find aesthetic satisfaction in some of the arts—if we know how to go about it. In addition, many of us find that music, painting, or poetry provides an inexhaustible source of joy.

At the same time, we may discover that we have the ability to create art. If we do, we have a source of satisfaction we do not want to miss. Children take music lessons, learn to sing, and study drawing. Many persons try amateur acting or write stories and poems. Some have great talent and become professional artists. Even those of us who conclude that we do not have much creative ability find that trying to paint or write sharpens our perceptions and adds to our enjoyment of the arts.

There is also a more theoretical approach to the arts. We may think about some of the more complex matters connected with appreciating artworks. This is the study of aesthetics. It tries to find what makes one work of art better than another, and if there are objective standards of criticism. It considers how our interest in art is connected with our other great philosophic interests such as science and religion. Philosophers have studied such questions. In asking and trying to answer them, we become philosophers ourselves.   Anita Silvers

Related articles in *World Book* include:

Kinds of art

Architecture	Interior design	Photography
Ballet	Jewelry	Poetry
Body art	Landscape	Pottery
Bookbinding	architecture	Printing
Commercial art	Literature	Sculpture
Dance	Mosaic	Tapestry
Drama	Motion picture	Theater
Drawing	Music	Video art
Graphic arts	Painting	Weaving
Handicraft	Performance art	

Styles of art

Abstract art	Avant-garde
Abstract Expressionism	Baroque
Art Deco	Byzantine art
Art Nouveau	Carolingian art

© ITAR-TASS Photo Agency/Alamy Images

Mixed arts blend several art forms. The ballet *The Sleeping Beauty,* shown here, by the Russian composer Peter Ilich Tchaikovsky, combines dancing, drama, music, and costume and scenery design.

Classicism	Pop Art
Folk art	Realism
Gothic art	Rococo
Islamic art	Romanticism
Naturalism	Surrealism

Elements of art

Aesthetics	Perspective
Design	Rhythm

Art Deco was a style of design that became popular during the 1920's and 1930's. It was used chiefly in furniture, jewelry, pottery, and textiles. Most Art Deco designers created objects that could be mass-produced,

Mahogany cabinet with kingwood veneer and ivory inlay (about 1923) by Émile-Jacques Ruhlmann; Brooklyn Museum

Art Deco furniture, such as the cabinet shown here, has a look of sleek elegance that was characteristic of the style.

rather than such individual works as paintings and sculptures. The term *Art Deco* comes from *Exposition Internationale des Arts Décoratifs et Industriels Modernes,* the title of a design exhibition held in Paris in 1925.

Art Deco was characterized by geometric shapes, smooth lines, and streamlined forms. It featured a look of sleek elegance that was associated with wealth and sophistication. Many works were made of chrome, plastics, and other industrial materials. Art Deco designers also used such expensive materials as crystal, ivory, and silver. The style was inspired by a variety of sources, including Cubism and the art of ancient America.

Art Deco also influenced architecture. Many buildings in New York City have the metal ornamentation and geometric patterns typical of the style. One such structure is the Chrysler Building, with its soaring tower formed by bands of stainless steel arches. Radio City Music Hall's curving stairways and round chandeliers also show the influence of Art Deco.   Alison McNeil Kettering

See also **Furniture** (Art Deco; picture).

Art Institute of Chicago is one of the world's leading cultural and educational institutions. The museum's vast permanent collection includes paintings and sculpture, prints and drawings, decorative arts, photography,

and textiles from different cultures that span 5,000 years of art history.

The European painting collection, with examples from the Middle Ages to the present, is best known for its works by French Impressionists and Postimpressionists. The large collection of prints at the Art Institute contains unique examples by masters of the 1400's and important series by French artists of the 1800's. The Asian galleries show arts of the Far East, with notable collections of bronzes, sculpture, and Japanese prints. Furniture, glass, porcelain, and metalwork are displayed in the galleries of the museum's Department of European Decorative Arts and Sculpture in the Rice Building.

The American art collection includes two of the most famous paintings in art, Edward Hopper's *Nighthawks* and Grant Wood's *American Gothic.* The Modern Wing, designed by the Italian architect Renzo Piano, opened in May 2009. The building houses the museum's collection of modern and contemporary art, architecture and design, and photography.

The Art Institute was founded in 1879 as a museum and school called the Chicago Academy of Fine Arts. It took its present name in 1882. The Art Institute moved to its current site in downtown Chicago in 1893. It is governed by a board of trustees and supported mainly by private funds. The School of the Art Institute grants degrees in the visual and related arts.

Critically reviewed by the Art Institute of Chicago

See also **Chicago** (map; picture); **Illinois** (picture).

Art museum. See Museum (Art museums).

Art Nouveau, *noo VOH,* was a decorative style of design that flourished from the 1890's until about 1910. *Art Nouveau* means *New Art* in French. It comes from the name of a Paris art gallery, Maison de l'Art Nouveau, which exhibited works created in this style of design.

Art Nouveau was an ornate style, characterized by long, flowing lines and wavelike contours often influenced by forms in nature. The style developed in part as

Enamel paintings on crystal vases (about 1896) by Alphonse Mucha; Fly By Nite Gallery, Chicago (WORLD BOOK photo)

Art Nouveau is characterized by long, flowing lines that twist in snakelike fashion. The images on the vases shown here were painted in this style, which was popular about 1900.

a protest against the mass production of the industrial age. It was used mainly for interior decoration and in the design of glassware, jewelry, and other ornamental objects. Some artists used the Art Nouveau style for such graphic-design works as book illustrations and posters.

The drawings of the English artist Aubrey Beardsley and the posters of Henri de Toulouse-Lautrec of France are outstanding examples of Art Nouveau graphic design. Other leading figures in the Art Nouveau movement included Emile Gallé of France and Louis Comfort Tiffany of the United States, both of whom created colorful glassware. Such architects as Antoni Gaudí of Spain and Victor Horta of Belgium also incorporated elements of the style in their work.   Alison McNeil Kettering

See also **Beardsley, Aubrey V.** (with picture); **Furniture** (Art Nouveau; picture).

Artemis, *AHR tuh mihs,* was a goddess in Greek mythology. She was the daughter of Zeus, the king of the gods, and the goddess Leto. The god Apollo was her twin. Artemis was sometimes identified with the moon goddess Selene. The Roman fertility goddess Diana closely resembled her.

Artemis was the goddess of childbirth and female maturation. Young girls about to be married prayed to her and sometimes dedicated their dolls or a lock of hair to her. But Artemis could be cruel and destructive. She and Apollo killed the children of Niobe, queen of Thebes, after Niobe boasted that she had more children than Leto. The Greeks often blamed Artemis for the sudden death of women.

Artemis was a virgin goddess who demanded that her followers dedicate themselves to lives of purity. According to one myth, Artemis shot one of her followers, the nymph Callisto, with an arrow after Callisto became pregnant by Zeus. Other sources say Artemis transformed Callisto into a bear. Several myths tell of attempts to rape Artemis and of her successful defense.

Artemis was the goddess of wild animals and hunting. Artists showed her as a beautiful young huntress carrying a bow and a quiver of arrows, often with a deer at her side.   Nancy Felson

See also **Diana; Iphigenia; Niobe; Orion; Selene.**

Arteriosclerosis, *ahr TIHR ee oh skluh ROH sihs,* is a disease of the arteries. It is often called "hardening of the arteries" because it involves hardening, thickening, and loss of elasticity in the artery walls.

There are several forms of arteriosclerosis. Two types are *Mönckeberg's arteriosclerosis,* in which the middle layer of the arteries becomes stiffened by calcium deposits, and *arteriolar sclerosis,* which affects the body's smaller arteries. But by far the most widespread form of arteriosclerosis is the type called *atherosclerosis.* Atherosclerosis affects medium and large arteries, especially those that carry blood to the heart, brain, kidneys, and legs. The effects of the disease appear mainly in middle-aged or older people, but they may also strike young people. Atherosclerosis ranks as a major health problem in the United States and other developed countries. The remainder of this article discusses atherosclerosis.

Causes. Atherosclerosis begins when certain fatty substances in the bloodstream—particularly cholesterol—form deposits on the inner lining of the arteries. Over a period of years, these deposits, called fatty streaks, enlarge and thicken to form *plaques.* The plaques cause inflammation of the smooth lining of the arteries, causing cells to die and scars to form. The build-up of dead cells, calcium, and scar tissue in the plaques makes the arteries hard and narrow, decreasing the flow of blood. Over time, the plaque deposit may be covered with a fibrous lining. A tear or rupture of this lining may cause a *thrombus* (blood clot) to form on the arterial wall. A thrombus can block an artery suddenly.

Certain risk factors are associated with the development of atherosclerosis. Three major risk factors are *hypertension* (high blood pressure), cigarette smoking, and high blood levels of cholesterol. Others include obesity, physical inactivity, and diabetes mellitus.

Effects of atherosclerosis result from the decreased flow of blood through the diseased arteries. Tissues nourished by these arteries do not receive enough oxygen. A decrease in the blood supply to the brain can cause dizziness, numbness, slurred speech, and other symptoms. In the heart, decreased blood supply can produce severe chest pain called *angina pectoris.* The complete blockage of an artery supplying the heart or brain results in a heart attack or a stroke, respectively. A reduced flow of blood to the kidneys may cause hypertension or kidney damage. In the legs, it may cause pain while walking, skin sores, or *gangrene* (death of tissue).

Prevention and treatment. Most physicians believe that many cases of atherosclerosis can be prevented by reducing exposure to risk factors. Therefore, doctors advise people to avoid cigarette smoking, to reduce if overweight, and to exercise regularly. Detection and control of hypertension and diabetes mellitus are especially important. Many physicians also recommend a diet low in cholesterol and saturated fats.

Treatment of atherosclerosis, like prevention, centers on reducing risk factors. Some patients also get drugs that lower the blood levels of cholesterol. If a major artery becomes obstructed, surgery may be needed. In severe cases, diseased arteries may be replaced or bypassed by grafts of natural or artificial vessels. Another technique, called *angioplasty,* involves threading a balloon-tipped *catheter* (slender tube) into the blocked artery. The balloon is then inflated, flattening the blockage against the artery wall.

Toby R. Engel

Related articles in *World Book* include:

Aneurysm	Cerebral hemorrhage
Angina pectoris	Heart (Coronary artery
Angioplasty	disease)
Artery	Hypertension
C-reactive protein	Stroke

Artery, *AHR tuhr ee,* is the name of the tubes or blood vessels through which blood is pumped away from the heart to the various parts of the body. The blood carried by most arteries is bright red because it has picked up oxygen while passing through the lungs. However, the blood that flows through the arteries connecting the right side of the heart with the lungs has not yet picked up oxygen. This blood has a brownish color. If an artery is cut, blood gushes out in spurts timed with the heartbeats. Veins differ from arteries because they carry the blood back to the heart instead of away from the heart. If a vein is cut, blood flows from it in an even stream.

When a large blood vessel has been cut by accident, the difference in the color and flow of the blood from the vessel makes it possible to tell whether an artery or a vein has been injured.

The walls of arteries are made up of three layers. The outer layer consists of elastic tissue, and the middle layer is muscle. The inner layer, or lining, of the arteries is made of thin, smooth cells of the same kind that line the other blood vessels and the heart. Each time the heart beats, the elastic walls of the arteries swell to make room for the blood forced into them. Then their muscular tissues slowly contract again. This squeezes the blood farther along the length of the arteries and toward the capillaries. In this way, the arteries do a considerable share of the work that keeps the blood circulating through the body. If the arteries had rigid instead of elastic walls, the heart would have to pump all the blood without the arteries' assistance. As a result, the heart would work much harder than it does. This is what happens to persons who suffer from *arteriosclerosis* (hardening of the arteries).

Principal arteries. The largest of all the arteries is the *aorta.* It is directly connected with a chamber of the heart. The heart pumps oxygenated blood through the aorta and its many branches to nearly all parts of the body. Two small but important branches of the aorta are the *coronary* arteries. They supply the blood by which the heart muscle itself is nourished. The right and left *carotid* arteries carry blood to the two sides of the head and neck. Blood flows through the right and left *subclavian* arteries to the shoulders and arms. Numerous other branches of the aorta furnish blood to the internal organs. In the abdominal region the aorta divides into two large branches, the right and left *iliac* arteries. These arteries have branches that supply the organs in the pelvis. The iliac arteries then continue downward into the legs, where they become known as the *femoral* arteries.

After the arterial blood has passed through the body and has picked up impurities, the veins collect it and return it to another chamber of the heart. The heart pumps this blood through the *pulmonary* artery to the lungs. Here the blood takes on a new store of oxygen. It then returns to the heart, where it is once more pumped out through the aorta.   Joseph V. Simone

Related articles in *World Book* include:

Aneurysm	Aorta	Heart
Angiogenesis	Arteriosclerosis	Vein
Angioplasty	Blood	

Artesian well, *ahr TEE zhuhn,* is a well that taps ground water which is under pressure. Such water can rise to the surface without the aid of a pump if enough pressure exists. The term *artesian well* also refers to any extremely deep water well.

Most artesian wells tap a layer of porous material filled with ground water. This layer, called an *aquifer,* may lie between two layers of clay or some other material that does not let water through. The aquifer may be tilted, allowing rainfall to refill it at its upper end. This water seeps down in the aquifer, supplying the reservoir of ground water. An artesian well flows naturally

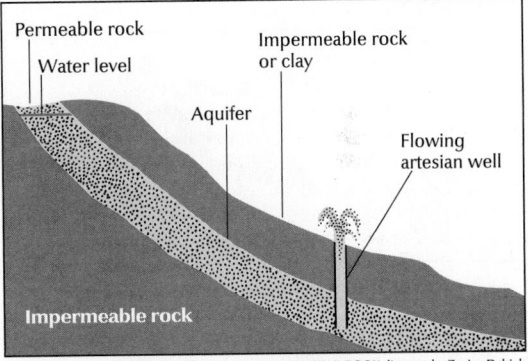

WORLD BOOK diagram by Zorica Dabich

An artesian well, as shown in this cross-section drawing, taps a layer of permeable rock filled with ground water. This *aquifer,* which lies between layers of impermeable material, is refilled from the rainfall at its upper end. Pressure exerted by the inflowing water causes the water in the aquifer to rise.

because of the pressure exerted on water in the aquifer by water entering at the aquifer's upper end.

Areas where artesian wells can be drilled are called *artesian basins.* The word *artesian* comes from *Artois,* a province in France, where artesian wells were first drilled during the 1100's.   Douglas S. Cherkauer

See also **Australia** (Underground water); **Ground water.**

Arthritis, *ahr THRY tihs,* is any of more than 100 diseases of the joints. People with arthritis often experience pain, stiffness, and swelling in their joints. Many people are crippled by arthritis. Individuals of all ages and backgrounds can be affected by the disease.

The terms *arthritis* and *rheumatism* are often used interchangeably. However, rheumatism is a more general term that refers to a variety of disorders of the joints, muscles, and connecting tissues. The two chief forms of arthritis are *osteoarthritis* and *rheumatoid arthritis.*

Osteoarthritis, also called *degenerative joint disease,* occurs when a joint wears out. Many elderly people have osteoarthritis, and the disease may also occur if a joint has been injured many times. The joints most frequently affected are those of the hands, hips, knees, lower back, and neck. Severe disability may result,

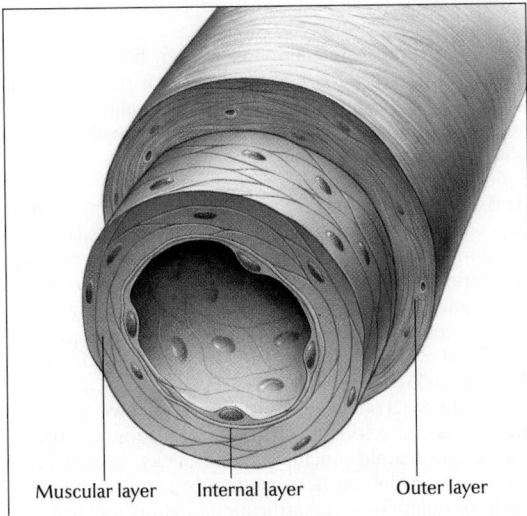

Muscular layer   Internal layer   Outer layer

WORLD BOOK illustration by Robert Demarest

Cross section of an artery

The two main types of arthritis

Many forms of arthritis can disable the joints. In a healthy joint, cartilage covers the ends of the bones. In *osteoarthritis,* the cartilage disintegrates and the bones rub against one another. In *rheumatoid arthritis,* inflamed tissue in a joint leads to erosion of the cartilage and the bones. Joints affected by severe cases of rheumatoid arthritis may stiffen in deformed positions.

Healthy joints

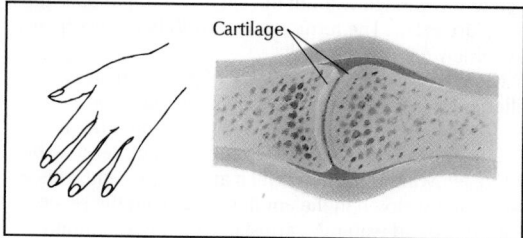

Cartilage

Osteoarthritis

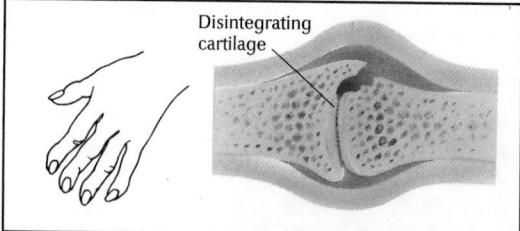

Disintegrating cartilage

Rheumatoid arthritis

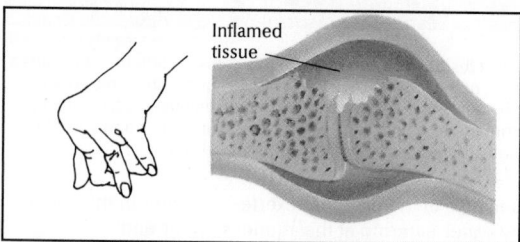

Inflamed tissue

WORLD BOOK illustrations by Charles Wellek

especially if the hips or knees are badly diseased.

People with osteoarthritis have pain in the affected area and may feel a grating sensation when they move. In advanced osteoarthritis, the cartilage between bones breaks down, so the bones rub against each other. Knobs of bone and of hardened bits of cartilage may develop in the joint, causing swelling and deformity.

Physicians treat patients to relieve pain and prevent disability from osteoarthritis. Treatment usually includes drugs, such a aspirin or ibuprofen, and special programs of exercise. Surgeons may repair or replace some severely damaged joints. A new class of drugs called *Cox-2 inhibitors* are also effective in relieving the pain and inflammation of osteoarthritis. However, scientists have found that high dosages of these drugs may increase the risk for heart attack and stroke. Medical experts recommend that people consult a physician before taking any medication to treat osteoarthritis.

Rheumatoid arthritis is one of the more common chronic illnesses in adults. People usually develop rheumatoid arthritis between the ages of 20 and 40, but children or elderly people can also develop rheumatoid arthritis.

Joints affected by rheumatoid arthritis are warm, painful, red, and swollen. The disorder commonly affects the wrists and knuckles, but it may occur in any joint. In some cases, rheumatoid arthritis spreads throughout the body, damaging organs and connective tissue. If it remains unchecked, the diseased joints eventually stiffen in deformed positions. Inflamed tissue and other substances in a joint can erode the bone and cartilage. The disorder may remain throughout the patient's life or disappear for varying periods. Physicians believe rheumatoid arthritis is caused by *autoimmunity* (the body's attack on its own tissues) (see **Immune system**). Some people inherit a tendency toward rheumatoid arthritis.

Effective drug treatments have been developed for rheumatoid arthritis. Some medications treat the immediate symptoms of pain and joint inflammation, while others work to slow the progression of the disease. It is important to treat rheumatoid arthritis early. Additional treatments include exercise programs, rest, physical and occupational therapy, and surgery.

Other forms of arthritis include *gout, ankylosing spondylitis,* and *septic arthritis.* Gout victims suffer repeated flare-ups of painful swelling, but they feel well between attacks. The bunion joint, which connects the big toe and the foot, is affected first in most cases. Gout is caused by the presence of too much uric acid in the blood. During an attack, this chemical takes the form of needle-shaped crystals in the joints. Some people inherit gout. Alcoholic beverages and rich food can lead to an attack in people who have gout, but they do not cause the disease. Doctors prescribe drugs to reduce inflammation and prevent further attacks. See **Gout.**

Ankylosing spondylitis attacks the spine. It mainly affects people between the ages of 17 and 35, and males are affected more than females. The spinal joints become inflamed, and the patient may develop a rigid, stooped back. Treatment consists of physical therapy and drugs.

Septic arthritis is infection of a joint by bacteria. Its most common forms occur after a lung or skin infection, surgery on the joint, or any of several sexually transmitted diseases. In most cases, early treatment with antibiotic drugs prevents crippling.   Daniel J. Lovell

See also **Rheumatology.**

Arthropod, *AHR thruh pahd,* is an animal with jointed legs and no backbone. Arthropods make up the largest division, or *phylum,* of the animal kingdom—the phylum Arthropoda. The term *arthropoda* comes from Greek words meaning *jointed feet,* though it is the legs rather than the feet that are jointed. Among the most important groups of arthropods are the following: (1) insects, including cockroaches, beetles, bees, butterflies, and many others; (2) crustaceans, including such well-known animals as crabs, lobsters, shrimps, sowbugs, and barnacles; (3) arachnids, including mites, ticks, spiders, and scorpions; (4) chilopods, or centipedes; and (5) diplopods, or millipedes. The arthropod phylum contains more than three-fourths of all the different kinds of animals. Arthropods outnumber people 200 million to one.

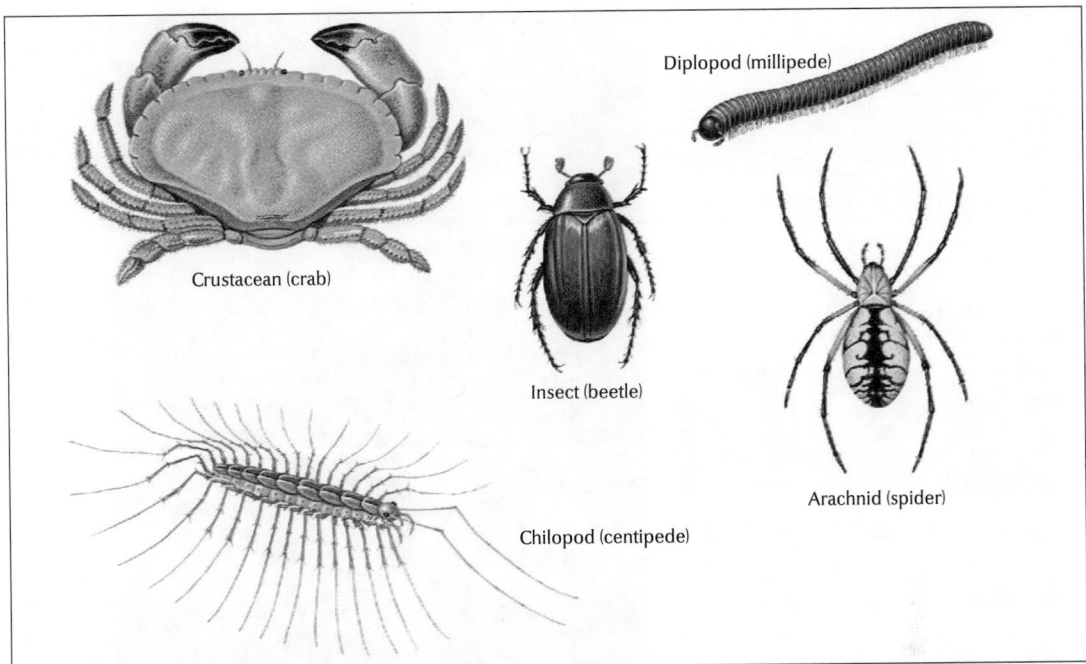

Arthropods form a major division of the animal kingdom. All of these animals have jointed legs. Examples of some of the most important groups of arthropods are shown above.

Insects make up the largest class of arthropods in terms of the number of *species* (kinds).

The bodies of arthropods, as well as their legs, are made up of sections. Among some arthropods, each section of the body has its own pair of legs. Most of these legs are used for swimming or walking. In some types of arthropods, certain legs have developed special shapes and uses. Some serve as sucking organs, some are jaws, some serve as weapons, and some are sense organs. Insects lack most of the pairs of legs found in other arthropods. They have only three pair. One pair is attached to each segment of an insect's chest or thorax. Insects also may have one or two pairs of wings.

Arthropods have an outside shell, or *exoskeleton,* that contains a stiff, horny material called *chitin.* Certain arthropods, such as flies and moths, have only thin, weak shells. Others, including crabs and lobsters, have thick, strong shells. Nearly all arthropods have a kind of heart and blood system and usually a well-organized nervous system. Some arthropods have simple eyes, some have compound eyes, and some (including many insects) have eyes of both types.   Frank G. Zalom

See also **Arachnid; Centipede; Crustacean; Insect; Millipede.**

Arthroscopy, *ahr THRAHS kuh pee,* is the technique of using an *arthroscope* to examine a joint of the body. An arthroscope is a straight, tubelike instrument with a series of lenses and optical-fiber bundles. It comes in sizes from ½ to ⅕ inch (2 to 5 millimeters) in diameter. It can be inserted into a joint through a small incision. A light transmitted by the optical fibers to the tip of the arthroscope illuminates the joint. Using an arthroscope, a doctor can thoroughly examine a joint and perform certain surgical operations.

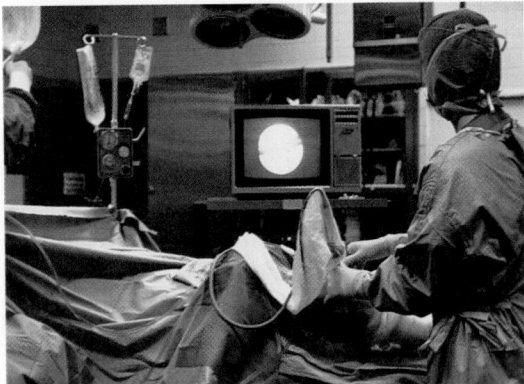

Arthroscopy allows a physician to examine and treat joint problems. In the picture above, the tubelike arthroscope has been inserted into a patient's knee joint.

Doctors use arthroscopy mainly on shoulder, elbow, hip, knee, and ankle joints. The problem most commonly treated by arthroscopy is torn cartilage in the knee. The doctor diagnoses this problem by looking into the knee joint through the arthroscope. Then the cartilage is removed with other instruments through a second incision.

The main advantage of arthroscopic surgery is that the operation can be performed through a small incision at the joint. As a result, a patient can sometimes have the surgery and leave the hospital the same day. Also, the patient experiences a minimum amount of discomfort, and healing time is much shorter than for other methods of surgery.   James A. Hill

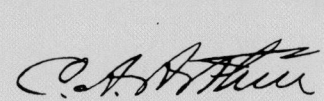

**21st president of
the United States 1881-1885**

Garfield
20th president
1881
Republican

Arthur
21st president
1881-1885
Republican

Cleveland
22nd president
1885-1889
Democrat

Oil painting on canvas (1884) by G.P.A. Healey, Corcoran Gallery of Art, Washington, D.C., gift of William Willson Corcoran

Arthur, Chester Alan (1829-1886), became president after James A. Garfield died from an assassin's bullet. Arthur was the fourth vice president to succeed to the presidency upon the death of a chief executive.

Arthur had risen rapidly in the Republican Party *machine* (organization) of New York City. In 1871, he became collector of the New York Custom House, then the largest single federal office in the United States. Widespread dishonesty in government occurred during this period, and Arthur used his office to reward Republicans and strengthen the party. These actions contributed to graft and waste in the Custom House and led to his removal in 1878.

As president, however, Arthur surprised the nation by the honesty and efficiency shown by his administration. Protests by reformers about the dishonesty of previous administrations in the appointment of government officials caused Congress to pass the Civil Service Act. Arthur signed the law and administered it faithfully.

Arthur enjoyed fashionable surroundings and fine clothes. He also liked to entertain friends. Tall, ruddy, and handsome, Arthur was sometimes called the "Gentleman Boss." He traveled widely as president, attending the opening of the Brooklyn Bridge in New York City and touring Florida and Yellowstone National Park.

Important dates in Arthur's life

1829	(Oct. 5) Born in Fairfield, Vermont.
1859	(Oct. 25) Married Ellen Lewis Herndon.
1871	Named collector of the New York Custom House.
1880	(Jan. 12) Mrs. Ellen Arthur died.
	Elected vice president of the United States.
1881	(Sept. 20) Sworn in as president.
1886	(Nov. 18) Died in New York City.

While Arthur was president, the United States celebrated the 100th anniversary of the British surrender at Yorktown. New books included *The Adventures of Huckleberry Finn* and *Life on the Mississippi* by Mark Twain. Cities and towns throughout the United States and Canada began to adopt standard time after the railroads devised time zones to aid travelers.

Early life

Boyhood. Chester Alan Arthur was born on Oct. 5, 1829, in Fairfield, Vermont. He was the first son in a family of six girls and three boys. His father, William, had come to the United States from Northern Ireland. The elder Arthur was a teacher and Baptist minister. Chester's mother, Malvina Stone Arthur, grew up on her father's Vermont farm. Like many other rural ministers, William Arthur seldom stayed long at any one post. The family moved to various villages in Vermont and upstate New York.

Chester was a good student and developed an early interest in politics. In 1844, at the age of 14, he supported Henry Clay, the Whig Party's presidential candidate, and got into a fight with some young opponents of Clay. "I have been in many a political battle since then," Arthur later recalled, "but none livelier, or that more thoroughly enlisted me."

Legal career. At the age of 18, Arthur graduated from Union College in Schenectady, New York. He began studying law and at the same time taught school. In 1854, he became a partner in a New York City law firm. Arthur soon became known as a defender of the civil rights of blacks. The young lawyer won a case in 1855 that established the right of blacks to ride on any streetcar in New York City.

Marvels of engineering were erected in the 1880's. The Brooklyn Bridge, *above,* was the world's longest suspension bridge when it opened in 1883. The Home Insurance Building in Chicago, *left,* is often considered the first metal-frame skyscraper. The structure was built in 1884 and 1885.

The world of President Arthur

Trade unionists led by Samuel Gompers founded the Federation of Organized Trades and Labor Unions of the United States and Canada in November 1881. The group later reorganized as the American Federation of Labor.

The Standard Oil Trust was formed in 1882 by John D. Rockefeller and his associates in the oil industry. The trust controlled about 90 percent of the oil refining capacity in the United States until it was forced to disband in 1892.

The germ that causes tuberculosis was discovered by German physician Robert Koch in 1882.

Jesse James, a notorious bank and train robber, was killed by one of his own gang members, Robert Ford, in 1882. Ford shot James in order to receive a $5,000 reward.

Popular entertainment took various forms in the early 1880's. In 1883, William Frederick Cody, known as Buffalo Bill, organized his "Wild West Circus" to tour the United States and Europe. That same year, the first vaudeville theater in the United States opened in Boston, and the Metropolitan Opera House opened in New York City.

Standard time was adopted by the railroads in 1883. The four time zones in the United States replaced about 100 different "railroad times."

The linotype machine was patented by German-born inventor Ottmar Mergenthaler in 1884. The machine greatly increased the speed of typesetting.

The Adventures of Huckleberry Finn by Mark Twain was published in England in 1884 and in the United States in 1885. The novel became known as an American masterpiece.

Leslie's Illustrated Weekly, Newberry Library, Chicago; Brown Brothers

Arthur's family. On Oct. 25, 1859, Arthur married Ellen Lewis Herndon (Aug. 30, 1837-Jan. 12, 1880), the daughter of a naval officer. The couple had two sons and a daughter, but the older boy died at the age of $2\frac{1}{2}$. Mrs. Arthur died about 10 months before Arthur was elected vice president, leaving him with their children, Chester, Jr., and Ellen.

Political and public career

Political growth. In 1854, Arthur attended a meeting that led to the creation of a Republican Party in New York. Edwin D. Morgan, a Republican, became governor of New York in 1859, and Republican friends of Arthur's got him a position on Morgan's staff. Morgan soon named Arthur state engineer-in-chief with the rank of brigadier general. After the Civil War began in 1861, Morgan put Arthur in charge of outfitting the New York militia for federal service. The governor appointed Arthur inspector general of the militia early in 1862 and later that year appointed him state quartermaster-general.

Custom house collector. During the late 1860's, Arthur became an associate of Senator Roscoe Conkling of New York. Conkling was the leader of the New York Republican organization. To help this machine, President Ulysses S. Grant in 1871 appointed Arthur collector of the New York Custom House. The custom house, with more than 1,000 employees, was then the largest federal office in the nation. Officially, Arthur supervised the collection of import duties. But politically, he used the position to strengthen the Republican Party, largely by giving jobs to party workers.

Arthur soon became the leader of the party machine in New York City, and eventually became chairman of the Republican state committee. All the customs employees paid a portion of their salaries into Republican campaign funds. Some money collected for customs violations also ended up in the treasury of the Republican Party. Politicians in all parts of the country took similar advantage of this so-called spoils system (see **Spoils system**). Reformers protested that such appointments resulted in incompetent and dishonest officials. After Rutherford B. Hayes became president of the United States in 1877, he issued an order forbidding government employees from taking part in the management of a political party.

Vermont Division of Historic Preservation

A replica of Arthur's birthplace stands in Fairfield, Vt. The state maintains the house and a small park as a memorial.

Library of Congress;
© White House Historical Association
(National Geographic Society)

Ellen Herndon Arthur,
above, died about 20 months
before her husband became
president. Arthur's youngest
sister, Mary Arthur McElroy,
right, was his White House
hostess.

Hayes appointed a commission to investigate the New York Custom House. The commission uncovered evidence of corruption, inefficiency, and waste. It also found continued involvement by the top custom house officials in Republican Party affairs. In 1877, Hayes asked Arthur and two chief aides to resign. They replied that they would not give up their offices until, as then required by law, the Senate had confirmed new appointees. Hayes suspended Arthur and one of the aides in 1878. Senator Conkling temporarily blocked the confirmation of new appointees. The Senate approved the new officials early in 1879.

Election of 1880. At the Republican National Convention of 1880, Conkling's machine supported former President Grant for a third term. However, the convention nominated Senator-elect James A. Garfield of Ohio. The delegates then nominated Arthur for vice president in hope of receiving support from Grant's followers. Garfield and Arthur defeated their Democratic opponents, General Winfield Scott Hancock and former Congressman William H. English of Indiana (see **Garfield, James A.** [Election of 1880]).

Opposition to Garfield. Arthur soon found himself in the middle of a quarrel between President Garfield and Senator Conkling. Conkling demanded that Garfield consult him on all federal appointments in New York. He became furious when Garfield named James G. Blaine, Conkling's chief political enemy, as secretary of state

and another old political opponent as collector of the New York Custom House.

Conkling and Thomas C. Platt, the other New York senator, both resigned. They asked the New York Legislature to show its disapproval of Garfield by reelecting them to the Senate. Arthur shocked many political observers by campaigning for his friends, but they were defeated.

Assassination of Garfield. Garfield never had a chance to enjoy the benefits of his victory over Senator Conkling. He was shot by Charles J. Guiteau on July 2, 1881, and died on September 19. Arthur took the presidential oath in his home in New York City at 2:15 a.m. the next day.

Arthur's administration (1881-1885)

Life in the White House. Arthur thought the White House looked like "a badly kept barracks," and ordered it renovated. During his first months as president, he lived in the Washington home of Senator John P. Jones of Nevada. Arthur moved into the redecorated White House on Dec. 7, 1881. The president, whose wife had died in 1880, asked his youngest sister, Mrs. Mary A. McElroy, to serve as his hostess. She won wide praise for her warm hospitality.

About a year after Arthur became president, he learned that he was dying of a kidney disease called *glomerulonephritis,* or *Bright's disease.* Arthur often suffered great pain but kept his illness a secret.

Civil service reform. Most Americans regarded Arthur as a machine politician. They believed he would oppose civil service reform. But the assassination of Garfield led to a great popular demand for a better system of filling public offices. In response to this demand, Congress passed the Pendleton Civil Service Act. Arthur signed the bill on Jan. 16, 1883. He named attorney Dorman B. Eaton, the author of the bill, as chairman of the first Civil Service Commission. See **Civil service** (History).

The star route frauds. During Garfield's term, two of Arthur's close political allies had been charged with fraud. They were accused of obtaining money by giving false estimates on the cost of operating postal star routes. Arthur renewed the prosecutions, and his administration worked vigorously for convictions. A jury acquitted the accused men after two trials. But the postal frauds were halted.

The fight for lower tariffs. American consumers exerted pressure on the Arthur administration to lower

Arthur's Cabinet

Secretary of state	.Frederick T. Frelinghuysen
Secretary of the treasury	.Charles J. Folger
	Walter Q. Gresham (1884)
	Hugh McCulloch (1884)
Secretary of war	.Robert Todd Lincoln
Attorney general	.Benjamin H. Brewster
Postmaster general	.Timothy O. Howe
	Walter Q. Gresham (1883)
	Frank Hatton (1884)
Secretary of the Navy	.William H. Hunt
	William E. Chandler (1882)
Secretary of the interior	.Samuel J. Kirkwood
	Henry M. Teller (1882)

*Has a separate biography in WORLD BOOK.

import tariffs. In 1882, the president appointed a commission to study tariff rates. It urged sharp tariff cuts, but Congress ignored the commission and passed a law in 1883 that lowered rates only slightly.

Other legislation. In 1882, Congress authorized $18,743,875 to be spent on improvements for waterways. Arthur knew many of the improvements were extravagant, and he vetoed the bill. But Congress passed the bill over Arthur's veto.

The Edmunds Anti-Polygamy Act of 1882, aimed at the Mormons of Utah, made it illegal for a man to have more than one wife. Congress also passed a bill in 1882 to prohibit Chinese immigration for 20 years. Arthur vetoed the bill, saying it violated a treaty with China. Congress amended the bill to limit the suspension of Chinese immigration to 10 years, and it became law. Arthur also fought with some success to modernize the United States Navy.

Election of 1884. Arthur worked hard to avoid major involvement in Republican Party affairs during his presidency. But in 1882, he was blamed for the defeat of Charles J. Folger, his secretary of the treasury, in the race for governor of New York. Folger lost to Democrat Grover Cleveland. High-ranking Republicans in the Arthur administration tried to build Republican strength in the South but achieved little.

Because of his illness, Arthur quietly discouraged friends from working to help him win the Republican presidential nomination in 1884. He received about a third of the votes for the nomination at the Republican National Convention in Chicago. Former Secretary of State James G. Blaine won the nomination, but he lost the presidential election to Cleveland.

Later years

Arthur returned to New York City after leaving the presidency. His health steadily declined, and he died of a cerebral hemorrhage on Nov. 18, 1886. Arthur was buried beside his wife in the Rural Cemetery at Albany, New York.   Thomas C. Reeves

Related articles in *World Book* include:

Civil service	President of the United States
Garfield, James A.	Vice president of the United
Oriental Exclusion Acts	States (Tyler takes over)

Outline

I. Early life
   A. Boyhood
   B. Legal career
   C. Arthur's family

II. Political and public career
   A. Political growth   D. Opposition to Garfield
   B. Custom house collector   E. Assassination of Garfield
   C. Election of 1880

III. Arthur's administration (1881-1885)
   A. Life in the White House D. The fight for lower tariffs
   B. Civil service reform   E. Other legislation
   C. The star route frauds   F. Election of 1884

IV. Later years

Additional resources

Elish, Dan. *Chester A. Arthur.* Children's Pr., 2004. Younger readers.

Karabell, Zachary. *Chester Alan Arthur.* Times Bks., 2004.

Reeves, Thomas C. *Gentleman Boss: The Life of Chester Alan Arthur.* 1975. Reprint. Am. Political Biography Pr., 1991.

Santella, Andrew. *Chester A. Arthur.* Compass Point, 2004. Younger readers.

Arthur, King, was a legendary king of medieval Britain. He became the main character in some of the most popular stories in world literature. For almost 1,000 years, writers have told of Arthur's brave deeds and the adventures of his knights of the Round Table.

A real Arthur probably existed, but historians know little about him. Storytellers passed on the earliest tales about Arthur by word of mouth. They may have based the tales on an actual British leader who won minor victories over German invaders in the early A.D. 500's.

The earliest accounts of Arthur were from Celtic, Latin, and French sources. In Latin sources, Arthur's father was King Uther Pendragon, who fell in love with Igrayne, the wife of the Duke of Cornwall. With the aid of Merlin, a Celtic magician, Uther took the form of the duke and so conceived Arthur. Arthur was raised without knowledge of his royal ancestry. But when he pulled the magic sword Excalibur from a block of stone, he proved himself the rightful heir to the throne of Britain and became king. Later, Arthur married Princess Guenevere. Arthur had several residences. His favorite was Camelot, a castle in southern England.

There are two versions of the events that led to Arthur's death. Both say he fought a war against the Roman emperor Lucius and conquered much of western Europe. Latin chronicles said he was called home before completing his conquest. He had heard that Modred, a knight who was either his nephew or his son, had seized his kingdom and queen. Arthur killed Modred but died from wounds received in the fight.

Later authors wrote that Arthur had completed his victory over the Romans. After he returned to Britain, Arthur and his court began the quest for the Holy Grail, sometimes depicted as the cup or dish that Jesus used at the Last Supper. After the quest ended, a love affair developed between Queen Guenevere and Sir Lancelot, the greatest knight of the Round Table. While fighting a war of revenge against Lancelot, Arthur learned of Modred's treachery. Then followed the battle that resulted in the death of Arthur and Modred. Many people believed that Arthur had gone to the otherworldly island of Avalon to be healed and that someday he would return to help his country.

Sir Thomas Malory compiled his famous prose romance *Le Morte Darthur* (about 1470) from much earlier French and English romances about Arthur. Many authors have based their novels or poems on Malory's work.   Edmund Reiss

Related articles in *World Book* include:

Camelot	Literature for chil-	Merlin
Excalibur	dren (picture:	Round Table
Holy Grail	Great illustra-	Tristan
	tors of the	
	1900's)	

Additional resources

For fictional accounts for younger readers, see **Literature for children** *(Books to read* [Traditional literature/Epics, ballads, and fables]).

Crossley-Holland, Kevin. *The World of King Arthur and His Court.* 1999. Reprint. Dutton, 2004. Younger readers.

Lacy, Norris J., and others. *The Arthurian Handbook.* 2nd ed. Garland, 1997.

Lupack, Alan. *The Oxford Guide to Arthurian Literature and Legend.* Oxford, 2005.

Matthews, John. *King Arthur.* Gramercy, 2004.

WORLD BOOK illustration by Jill Coombs

The artichoke has prickly leaves and an edible bud.

Artichoke is a large, thistlelike plant that produces edible flower buds. The scales and *hearts* (centers) of the buds are eaten as vegetables. Artichokes provide a number of vitamins and minerals. Artichokes are sometimes called *globe artichokes.* They originated in the Mediterranean region. In the United States, artichokes are grown commercially chiefly in California.

Artichoke plants stand 3 to 5 feet (0.9 to 1.5 meters) tall and may spread over an area 5 to 6 feet (1.5 to 1.8 meters) in diameter. In the spring, the *crown* (top of the root) sprouts stems surrounded by large, coarse leaves. Round or oblong buds develop at the tips of the stems and branches. The buds are immature flowers and may range from light to dark green and may have a red or purple tint. Buds weigh up to 1 pound (0.45 kilogram).

Artichokes thrive in frost-free climates with cool, foggy summers. Commercial growers usually plant artichoke seedlings, though the plants can grow from seeds. Artichoke plants may live over 15 years. But commercial growers usually replant their fields every three or four years to ensure strong, active growth. The buds are harvested before they mature—otherwise, they become inedible. Some harvesting occurs in late summer and into the fall, but most of it is done the next spring.

The plant called *Jerusalem artichoke* is related to the sunflower. It is not a true artichoke. See **Jerusalem artichoke.** Anusuya Rangarajan

Scientific classification. The scientific name for the artichoke is *Cynara scolymus.*

Article, in English grammar, is the name given to one of three words—*a, an,* and *the.* They are classified as determiners and sometimes considered a separate part of speech. Determiners are used before nouns. They place limits on the noun rather than adding description.

The definite article is the word *the.* Speakers and writers use *the* before a noun when they believe their audience knows the identity of the noun that follows. The identity of the noun may be known because it refers to a unique person, place, object, action, quality, or idea. For example, in the sentence "She visited the Statue of Liberty," *the Statue of Liberty* refers to a unique object.

The identity of the noun may also have been stated or may somehow have been made clear. From the sentence "Nancy bought two TV sets and a radio but had to return the TV's," *the TV's* clearly refers to the two that Nancy bought. "Hand me the hammer" makes sense only if the listener knows which hammer. The definite article can also be used with proper names to distinguish one person from others that may have the same name: "Is that *the* Michael Jordan?"

The indefinite articles are *a* and *an.* They are only used before singular nouns. Writers and speakers use the indefinite article when they believe their audience does not know the identity of the following noun. In the sentence "Mary handed the book to a boy," the writer does not believe that the reader knows which boy.

The article *an* is used before words beginning with a vowel sound, as in *an elephant.* It is also correct to say *an heir,* because the *h* at the beginning of *heir* is silent. However, *a* is used in the expression *a one-sided argument* because *one* begins with a *w* sound.

General use of articles. Sometimes, articles refer to an entire class of objects instead of particular ones. For example, it is possible to talk of elephants in general in each of the following ways: *"The* elephant has long tusks." *"An* elephant has long tusks." "Elephants have long tusks." But when the idea of the sentence only applies to an entire class, *a* and *an* cannot be used. For this reason, one cannot say *"An* elephant is in danger of extinction."

Usage of articles is often inconsistent. For example, we say *to school* but *to the library.* Such nouns as *flour* and *milk,* which are thought of collectively, do not require articles: "Milk is good for you."

Using or omitting the article often changes the meaning of a sentence. The following three sentences are examples: "A revolution changed the government." "The revolution changed the government." "Revolution changed the government." The first sentence mentions a revolution, but does not specify any particular one. The second sentence refers to a particular revolution previously mentioned or known to the reader. The third sentence refers to revolution as a process. Unnecessary articles often appear after such expressions as *kind of* or *sort of.* For example, *that kind of hat,* not *that kind of a hat,* is standard usage. Susan M. Gass

Articles of Confederation was the agreement under which the 13 original states established a federal government in 1781. The states called their confederation the United States of America, continuing the name used in the Declaration of Independence. The Articles of Confederation served as the new nation's basic charter of government until the first government under the Constitution of the United States was formed in 1789. The *Congress of the Confederation* operated the government under the Articles of Confederation.

The Articles tried to balance the need for an effective national government with the traditional independence of each state. The document guaranteed each state sovereignty and granted each state one vote in Congress. Under the Articles, Congress could not levy taxes, regulate trade, or force states to fulfill their obligations. However, the Articles did allow Congress to declare war and peace, manage foreign relations, establish and command an army and navy, and issue and borrow money.

The Second Continental Congress drafted the Articles

of Confederation. Richard Henry Lee of Virginia first proposed the establishment of a confederation in the Congress on June 7, 1776. Congress appointed a committee to draw up a plan of union. Within a month, John Dickinson of Pennsylvania prepared a first draft. On Nov. 15, 1777, Congress adopted a final version. By 1779, all the states except Maryland had *ratified* (approved) it. Maryland withheld its approval until Virginia, New York, and other states had agreed to give Congress title to lands the states had claimed northwest of the Ohio River. The states promised to do so, and Maryland approved the Articles on March 1, 1781. The Articles went into effect on that date.

Even after the Articles of Confederation went into effect, many national leaders thought that the agreement did not give Congress enough power to operate effectively. But amendments were difficult to pass because all 13 states had to approve them. By 1786, James Madison, Alexander Hamilton, and others were convinced that a general convention was needed to make changes in the Articles. In September 1786, delegates from five states met at Annapolis, Maryland, and proposed that such a convention meet in Philadelphia in May 1787. Eventually, every state approved the proposal except Rhode Island.

The Constitutional Convention quickly agreed that the Articles had to be abandoned. The convention delegates wrote a new document to replace the Articles—the U.S. Constitution. The Constitution increased the power of Congress. It was ratified in June 1788.   Jack N. Rakove

See also **Annapolis Convention; Congress of the Confederation; Constitution of the United States; Continental Congress.**

Articles of War governed the conduct of United States Army personnel until 1951, when the Uniform Code of Military Justice became effective. The Continental Congress adopted the articles in 1775 to administer justice and enforce discipline in the Continental Army. The articles were based on a British Army Code adopted in the English Mutiny Act of 1689. They were revised in 1776, 1786, 1806, and 1916. Congress also revised them after both World War I (1914-1918) and World War II (1939-1945), chiefly to assure more leniency. In 1950, it adopted the Uniform Code of Military Justice and ap-

plied it to all branches of the U.S. armed services. The code replaced the Articles of War.   Joel D. Meyerson

See also **Uniform Code of Military Justice.**

Artificial eye, also called a *prosthetic eye,* is worn by a person who has lost an eye to disease or injury. In removing the eye, a surgeon cuts the optic nerve and the muscles that hold and move the eyeball. The surgeon then places a plastic, metal, or ceramic ball into the cavity and sews the muscles and the surrounding *conjunctival tissue* together in front of the ball. The artificial eye that is visible from the outside consists of a curved shell of lightweight plastic or glass painted to match the normal eye. It fits between the eyelids and the conjunctival tissue covering the ball. The eye muscles can move the ball and shell just like the normal eye.

An artificial eye requires little care. In most cases, people cannot easily distinguish the artificial eye from a normal eye by appearance. The wearer, however, cannot see with it. Scientists are working to develop genuine artificial eyes that provide vision.   Gislin Dagnelie

Artificial heart is a machine that pumps blood and is designed to replace a natural heart. The first use of an artificial heart in a human being occurred in 1969. That year, a team of surgeons headed by Denton A. Cooley of the Texas Heart Institute used a device to temporarily support blood circulation in a patient awaiting a heart transplant. The patient was kept alive for 64 hours until a natural heart transplant was performed.

Scientists have since worked to develop an artificial heart that can permanently replace a diseased human heart. In 1982, a surgical team led by William C. DeVries of the University of Utah implanted an air-powered device as the first permanent artificial heart. The device, called the Jarvik-7, was designed by the American physician Robert K. Jarvik. The recipient, Barney B. Clark, survived for 112 days. Several other patients also received Jarvik hearts, and one survived for 620 days.

The Jarvik-7 had several features that limited the quality of life for patients. The device had a large, heavy, external power unit that hindered movement and air tubes that passed through the skin of the patient. Complications from the device, including bleeding and stroke in some patients, forced physicians to abandon it as a pos-

WORLD BOOK illustration by Barbara Cousins

Replacement heart

Internal controller

Energy transfer system

Rechargeable internal battery

External battery

The AbioCor artificial heart uses a computer-controlled electric motor to pump blood throughout the body. The energy transfer system supplies power to the heart without wires that penetrate the skin. Thus, patients have enough mobility to participate in most activities of daily life.

sible long-term heart replacement. But it is still used today for sustaining patients temporarily until a natural heart transplant can be performed.

In the 1990's, teams of scientists in the United States developed the AbioCor artificial heart. This device is made up of an electric pump implanted within the patient. Power is supplied to the device through an internal *transcutaneous energy transmission* (TET) coil. Energy passes from an external TET coil, which is attached to a small battery pack, through the skin to the internal TET coil. The two coils are not connected to each other by any wires that penetrate the skin, thereby reducing the risk of infection. With the AbioCor heart, patients can participate in most activities of daily living without being connected to a large power supply.

In July 2001, Robert Tools became the first patient to be implanted with the AbioCor artificial heart. He died 151 days later from complications unrelated to the function of the heart. Since then, other patients have had the AbioCor implanted. Several were able to make short trips from the hospital, and two patients lived outside the hospital for a time. The longest a patient has survived with the AbioCor artificial heart is 512 days.

In 2013, doctors in France implanted a new type of artificial heart in a patient suffering heart failure. The patient lived for 74 days. The device, made by the French company Carmat, includes a combination of artificial materials and tissues obtained from cattle, which help prevent blood clots and other medical complications. In 2014, doctors implanted a Carmat heart in another patient. This patient became healthy enough to leave the hospital and resume a normal lifestyle.   Louis Samuels

Artificial intelligence (AI) is the ability of a computer system to process information in a manner similar to human thought or to exhibit humanlike behavior. AI is also a branch of computer science that strives to design systems with such capabilities. A computer with AI could perform such tasks as learning, understanding language, working toward goals, and perceiving the world through vision, hearing, and other senses.

AI as a scientific field began at a workshop at Dartmouth College in 1956. Dartmouth professor John McCarthy, with four colleagues, organized the workshop and coined the name of the new discipline. At the meeting, scientists presented the first computer programs capable of logical reasoning, learning, and playing board games. AI research can be divided into several major topics. These include: (1) knowledge representation and reasoning, (2) planning and problem solving, (3) speech and natural language processing, (4) machine learning, (5) computer vision, and (6) robotics.

Knowledge representation and reasoning are two core challenges in AI. They can be handled in various ways. In one type of approach, called a *logical* approach, knowledge is represented by precise logical rules. Such a rule might take the form, "If x is true and y is true, then z is true," where x, y, and z represent various statements. In this approach, reasoning involves computing the consequences implied by such rules. The logical approach has led to the development of *expert systems,* software systems that solve problems in narrow fields of expertise, such as the diagnosis of disease. In a *probabilistic* approach, knowledge is represented using numerical probabilities. Reasoning involves computing the proba-

bility of various conclusions given specific evidence. In a *neural network* approach, knowledge is represented as a network of interconnected units that perform certain tasks by exchanging information. This approach mimics the behavior of *neurons* (nerve cells) in the brain.

Planning and problem solving require programs to identify sequences of actions that accomplish specified goals. Such programs often search a large number of alternative plans guided by *heuristics*, rules that direct the search toward promising solutions. A common type of problem solving involves playing board games. AI programs can play many games at the level of the best human players. In 1997, Deep Blue, a chess-playing computer developed by International Business Machines Corporation (IBM), won a match against Garry Kasparov, the reigning world chess champion. Programmers developed an unbeatable AI checkers program in 2007. In 2011, an IBM-developed computer called Watson demonstrated an advanced ability to understand human language. Watson defeated two human champions on "Jeopardy!," a question-and-answer quiz show.

Speech and natural language processing involves developing computer programs that communicate in a human language, such as English, instead of a specialized programming language. Scientists have developed logical, probabilistic, and neural network systems for processing natural language. Modern systems can successfully carry on conversations about a narrow topic—for example, taking an airline reservation—and can translate Web pages from one human language to another.

Machine learning involves computer programs that learn from examples and from experience. The 1956 Dartmouth workshop presented the first program that learned to play checkers by competing against a copy of itself. Other programs have learned to play backgammon and to recognize human speech and handwriting.

Computer vision attempts to build computers that can recognize patterns and objects in visual images. Vision systems first extract image features, such as edges and textures, then use rules or neural networks to identify objects in the scene.

Robotics studies the control of mechanical robots. Robots must control their motion to manipulate objects and avoid obstacles. Robotics enables machines to perform complicated tasks by combining motion planning, interpretation of visual and sound information, and artificial speech. AI robots developed to operate without human supervision could be used in space exploration or in driverless military vehicles.   Diane J. Litman

See also **Robot; Turing, Alan M.**

Artificial limb is a synthetic replacement for an arm or leg lost as the result of injury, disease, or a birth defect. An artificial limb is also called a *prosthesis*. No artificial limb can perform all the functions of a human limb, but a well-fitted prosthesis can help a person participate in most everyday activities.

Preparation of an artificial limb. A prosthesis must be custom made for each patient. In most cases involving an amputated limb, the remaining stump must heal and shrink before it can be fitted with a permanent prosthesis. For several weeks, the stump may be wrapped tightly with elastic bandages to help it shrink to a firm, smooth surface. In some cases, the person wears a rigid plaster cast, to which a temporary prosthesis can be at-

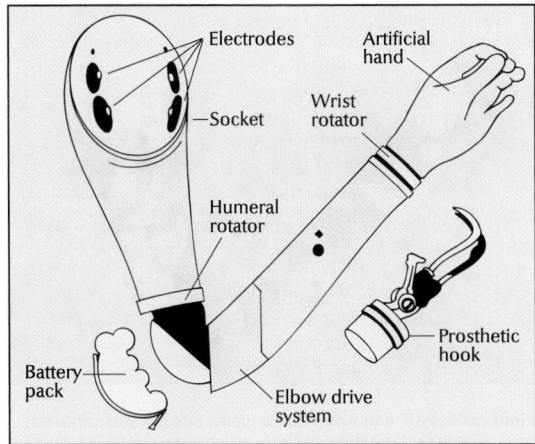

WORLD BOOK diagram by Bill Anderson

A myoelectric artificial arm responds to muscle contractions in the remaining upper arm or shoulder. The contractions generate a tiny electric current, which is picked up by electrodes in the socket of the artificial arm. The current controls the output of the battery pack, which powers a motor that bends the elbow. The arm can be fitted with an artificial hand or a prosthetic hook.

tached. During this time, the person exercises the remaining limb muscles to preserve their strength and movement, and to promote circulation.

The next step in preparing a prosthesis involves making a plastic socket that will fit over the stump snugly and comfortably. A cast for the socket may be obtained by wrapping the stump with bandages soaked in wet plaster and letting them harden. After the bandages are removed, they form a mold. Liquid plaster poured into this mold provides a model of the stump. A plastic socket is then formed over the model.

An artificial arm or leg is attached to the socket. Materials used in making artificial limbs include plastic, fiberglass, metal, and wood. Light metal supports attached to the socket may contain an artificial joint to replace an elbow or a knee. The prosthesis ends in a substitute hand or foot. Hand substitutes look like a real hand. A foot substitute has the same general shape as a normal foot. Most prostheses stay on the body with straps or suction.

Control of artificial limbs. Most artificial arms are controlled by a cable that loops around the opposite shoulder. Movements of that shoulder produce movement in the arm prosthesis. Artificial legs are chiefly controlled by the body's normal walking movements.

In the early 1960's, researchers developed a type of prosthesis that was controlled by *myoelectricity*—the electric current produced when a muscle contracts. Metal disks inside the socket rest against the skin of the stump. The disks pick up myoelectric impulses, which are then amplified and used to control an electric motor in the prosthesis. In most myoelectric arms, impulses from one muscle bend the arm, and those from another muscle straighten it. Similarly, impulses from one arm muscle open a myoelectric hand, and those from another muscle close it. These actions are somewhat like an arm's natural muscle contractions.   Dudley S. Childress

See also **Disability** (picture: People with disabilities); **Engineering** (picture: Biomedical engineers); **Occupational therapy; Prosthetics.**

Artificial respiration. See First aid (Giving artificial respiration).

Artificial satellite. See Satellite, Artificial.

Artificial sweetener is a synthetic substance used in food and beverages in place of sugar. Artificial sweeteners are sweeter and have fewer calories than *sucrose* (table sugar). Excess sucrose can cause weight gain and raise blood sugar levels. Artificial sweeteners are used as an alternative to sugar by people dieting to lose weight and by people with diabetes.

In the United States, the Food and Drug Administration (FDA) regulates the use of artificial sweeteners. The FDA has prohibited the use of several of the substances because experiments indicated they could cause cancer in people. For example, artificial sweeteners called cyclamates were banned in the United States in 1970. However, they are still used in other countries. The artificial sweeteners approved for use in the United States are aspartame, saccharin, acesulfame-K, and sucralose.

Aspartame is the most widely used artificial sweetener. It is derived from aspartic acid and phenylalanine, chemicals that occur in some foods. It is about 200 times as sweet as sucrose. Aspartame was first produced in 1965. Early experiments suggested that large amounts of it might cause brain damage. But in 1981, the FDA concluded that it posed no significant health risk. The FDA approved it for use in breakfast cereals, soft drinks, chewing gum, and other products. Aspartame is sold under the brand names NutraSweet and SugarTwin.

Saccharin is about 300 times as sweet as sucrose. It is made from toluene and petroleum. It is the oldest artificial sweetener and one of the most studied food ingredients. Several countries have banned saccharin over concerns that it may cause cancer. In 1981, the National Toxicology Program (NTP), a part of the U.S. Department of Health and Human Services, added saccharin to its list of known human *carcinogens* (substances that can cause cancer). In 2000, however, the NTP removed saccharin from the list, saying that the links to cancer in tests do not apply to human beings. Sweet'N Low and SugarTwin are brand names for saccharin. See **Saccharin.**

Acesulfame-K, also called acesulfame-potassium, is derived from acetoacetic acid. It is about 200 times as sweet as sucrose. The FDA approved the use of acesulfame-K in dry goods in 1988. The sweetener is now used in many other products, including yogurt, baked goods, and soft drinks, and as a sugar substitute. Its brand names are Sunett and Sweet One.

Sucralose is about 600 times as sweet as sucrose. It is made from modified sugar molecules. The body does not recognize it as a sugar and so does not absorb it. Thus, sucralose supplies no calories. The FDA approved the sweetener in 1998 for use in the same foods for which aspartame has been approved. Canada has also approved the use of sucralose. Splenda is a brand name for sucralose.   Janet Waters

See also **Food additive.**

Artificial turf is a manufactured product that looks like grass. Athletic stadiums and recreation departments use it as a playing surface for indoor and outdoor activities. Artificial turf is also used in landscaping, patios, highway medians, and doormats. Manufacturers have developed many varieties of artificial turf since it first came into use in the early 1960's.

The surface of artificial turf consists of tough nylon fibers or similar material woven into a base pad of the same material like a household carpet. The base pad is glued to a rubber pad about 1 inch (2.5 centimeters) thick. The rubber pad is glued to a foundation consisting of a layer of asphalt about 5 inches (12.5 centimeters) thick that covers a layer of gravel or other porous material about 18 inches (46 centimeters) thick. Modern foundations have special drainage systems that prevent water from accumulating on the playing surface.

Unlike grass, artificial turf does not require costly care and is not damaged by hard use in sports. Its surface stays smooth and even, and weather does not affect it. Artificial turf also has some disadvantages. Some athletes and doctors believe that the additional traction and the hard subsurface cause knee injuries. The turf also becomes hot in warm weather because the asphalt absorbs heat.   John L. O'Donnell

Artigas, *ahr TEE gahs,* **José Gervasio,** *hoh SAY hehr VAH syoh* (1764-1850), was a leader in Uruguay's struggle for independence. In the early 1800's, he raised an army to free Uruguay from Spain. In 1814, however, troops from Argentina captured Montevideo, Uruguay's chief city. In 1815, Artigas gained control of Montevideo for Uruguay. For a short time that year, he governed most of Uruguay and parts of Argentina. But Portuguese troops from Brazil captured Montevideo in 1817, and Artigas fled to Paraguay in 1820. Uruguay did not gain its independence until 1828. Artigas was born in Montevideo on June 19, 1764, and died on Sept. 23, 1850. See **Uruguay** (Independence).   Michael L. Conniff

Artillery, *ahr TIHL uhr ee,* is a class of weapon made up of heavy guns that fire large ammunition. Artillery includes the big guns once called *cannon* in addition to mounted guns and rocket launchers. The term *artillery* is generally reserved for weapons that are not fired from the hand or shoulder.

Parts of an artillery weapon

An artillery weapon, also known as an *artillery piece,* consists largely of a tube called the *barrel.* The barrel has two openings. The *breech* is the opening where the

A mortar is a type of artillery that is loaded from the muzzle. It launches shells in high, arcing trajectories. The shells can thus sail over hills or other obstacles.
Department of Defense

U.S. Army

Field artillery like this howitzer support infantry and armored forces. Light and medium artillery, which range from 75 to 155 millimeters, can be transported by truck or helicopter.

ammunition is inserted. The opening where the shell comes out is the *muzzle.* The inner surface of the barrel is known as the *bore.* The bore's diameter determines the weapon's size, or *caliber,* and that of its ammunition. The *breechblock* closes the breech and usually holds the firing pin or firing mechanism.

An artillery piece may have a bore that is smooth or one that is *rifled.* Rifled bores have spiraled grooves that spin and steady the shell, so it will travel nose-first to the target. *Smoothbore* artillery use ammunition with fins, which steady the shell in flight.

The firing mechanism contains a *primer* for large-caliber guns, or a firing pin for smaller weapons. The primer ignites a substance in the ammunition called the *propellant.* The propellant develops an extremely high pressure that shoots the ammunition out of the muzzle.

Kinds of artillery

Artillery is classified according to size as light, medium, or heavy artillery. It may also be classified by the *trajectory* (curved path of flight) of its ammunition. Artillery *guns* use ammunition that follows a low, flat trajectory with high speed at the muzzle. *Howitzers* use a high, arcing trajectory to hit targets hidden behind obstacles.

Some other weapons are often considered artillery, including rocket launchers, *mortars,* and *recoilless rifles.* Mortars usually have a smooth bore and are typically loaded from the muzzle. They send shells in higher arc trajectories than do howitzers. Recoilless rifles fire small-caliber artillery shells. They are much lighter than other artillery and may be mounted on vehicles or carried by hand. A rocket launcher starts an explosive rocket on its flight.

Field artillery is used to support infantry and armored forces. The guns may be towed by heavy tracked vehicles or trucks or mounted on vehicles so they can be brought into battle quickly. Field artillery guns vary in size—some fire shells weighing a few pounds, while others fire shells weighing hundreds of pounds or kilograms. Other kinds of field artillery are mounted on tanks and vehicles designed to destroy tanks.

Ammunition trailers and tracked support vehicles have replaced the *caissons* (ammunition wagons) that used to carry ammunition for field artillery. Powerful

A self-propelled howitzer, *shown here,* can be driven without being towed. This 155-millimeter howitzer can fire 95-pound (43-kilogram) shells about 9 miles (14 kilometers).

artillery can be mounted on tanks and tank destroyers. Particularly large weapons can be mounted on specially designed *chassis* (frames) with tracks. Surface-to-surface guided missiles supplement field artillery.

Antiaircraft artillery fire shells rapidly at high angles. They are usually aimed at the target by electronic automatic fire control systems. Generally, special fuses are used to explode the shells in the area of the target. Surface-to-air missiles support antiaircraft guns in many armies and have completely replaced them in others.

Other artillery. Guns mounted in airplanes and helicopters are sometimes called artillery. So are guns mounted on naval vessels.

How artillery is made

Until after the American Civil War (1861-1865), almost all cannon were cast in brass, bronze, or cast iron. To make the cannon stronger, manufacturers added more metal to make the walls of the barrel thicker.

Later in the 1800's, manufacturers made larger guns by *forging.* Forging is a process in which heated metal is shaped and then hammered or pressed.

The monobloc process is used to make most bar-

Antiaircraft artillery fires rapidly at high angles. In this photograph, Libyan rebels fire a scavenged antiaircraft gun mounted on the back of a pickup truck.

rels today. It takes advantage of modern, high-strength steels. In this process, manufacturers make the tube stronger by expanding it under internal pressure until the interior diameter of the tube has been permanently enlarged. The outer layers of metal tend to shrink to their original dimensions when the pressure is released, but the inner layers tend to keep their enlarged diameter. This compresses the inner layers. This process is also called *cold working* or *autofrettage.* After the tube has been formed, it is *annealed* (tempered) by being heated and slowly cooled. Workers then use powered machine tools to shape it to final specifications.

Rifling. During or after the final shaping, the gun may be rifled. In this process, workers cut or impress grooves in the finished bore. Alternatively, they may cut them into a separate tube called a *liner,* which can be inserted into the barrel. Rifled liners can be replaced if they become worn, but high construction costs have limited their use.

History

Artillery was first used during the 1300's. The French used small cannon against the English in 1450. The Ottomans under Mehmet II used artillery in their final campaign to capture Constantinople in 1453. From that time, artillery increased enormously in size, firepower, and accuracy and played an ever-increasing part in battles. Napoleon was the first general to collect his artillery in a *grande batterie* (big battery). He concentrated his artillery fire on one point in the enemy's line, and then sent troops against that point.

During World War I (1914-1918), troops on the Western Front dug great mazes of trenches and fought from fairly fixed positions. Much of the fighting consisted of exchanges of fire between big-gun batteries. In 1918, the Germans attacked Paris with huge, specially built guns known as "Paris Guns." The guns hurled shells to heights of about 25 miles (40 kilometers) above the ground to reach a target roughly 75 miles (120 kilometers) away.

But giant guns had little place in World War II (1939-1945). They could not move fast enough to keep up with the war's rapid changes in battle lines. Airplanes could easily destroy fixed batteries of large guns. The greatest artillery advances during the war were in the power and mobility of smaller weapons. Helicopters can now carry some artillery pieces into battle.   Frances M. Lussier

Related articles in *World Book* include:

Ammunition (Artillery ammunition)	Firearm
	Mortar
Army, United States (Artillery)	Shrapnel
Cannon	

Artist. See Advertising (Careers); **Clothing** (Careers); **Commercial art; Map** (Planning and graphic design). See also **Drawing; Painting; Sculpture.**

Arts. See Art and the arts.

Arts, American Federation of (AFA), is a nonprofit service organization that aims to broaden public knowledge and appreciation of historical and contemporary art. Each year, the AFA organizes or circulates many art exhibitions to member museums, university art galleries, and cultural centers throughout the United States and other countries. It also organizes exhibitions of fine art, decorative art, architecture and design, photography, and film and video. Hundreds of art institutions be-

long to the organization, founded in 1909. The headquarters of the AFA are in New York City.

Critically reviewed by the American Federation of Arts

Arts and crafts. See the *Arts* section in various country and continent articles. See also **Handicraft; Hobby;
Indian, American** (Arts and crafts).

Arts and Sciences, American Academy of. See
American Academy of Arts and Sciences.

Aruba, *ah ROO bah,* is an island in the Caribbean Sea
that is part of the Lesser Antilles island group. Since
1986, Aruba has been an *autonomous* (self-governing)
country within the Kingdom of the Netherlands. Previously, it was part of the Netherlands Antilles, which
was a largely independent part of the Kingdom of the
Netherlands. For location, see **West Indies** (map). Aruba
covers 69 square miles (180 square kilometers) and has
a population of about 112,000. Oranjestad is the capital
and largest city.

Aruba is a hilly, rocky island that supports little agriculture. But it has coral reefs, white sand beaches, and
a warm, dry climate that attract many tourists. The population is chiefly *mestizo*—that is, of mixed *Indigenous*
(native) and European ancestry. Dutch and Papiamento,
the local Creole language, are the official languages.

Aruba is one of the most prosperous islands in the
Caribbean. Its chief industries include tourism, financial
services, and oil refining.

Indigenous people were the first inhabitants of Aruba.
The Spanish explorer Alonso de Ojeda claimed Aruba
for Spain in 1499. The Dutch gained control of the island
in 1636. A gold rush in the 1820's and the opening of
an oil refinery in the 1920's contributed to Aruba's prosperity. After World War II (1939-1945), Arubans became
increasingly uncomfortable as part of the Netherlands
Antilles. There were constant disputes between Aruba
and the nearby island of Curaçao. Arubans began seeking independence from both the Netherlands and the
other islands of the Netherlands Antilles. An agreement
between Aruba and the Netherlands resulted in Aruba's
separation from the Netherlands Antilles in 1986. Aruba
has local self-government, but the Netherlands retains
responsibility for its defense and foreign affairs.

Jeroen Dewulf

See also **Netherlands Antilles.**

Arum, *AIR uhm,* is the name of a large family of plants.
There are thousands of *species* (kinds) of arums. Most
grow in tropical and subtropical regions, but some are
found in temperate areas. Many arums are poisonous.

The arum plant bears a flower cluster made up of tiny
blossoms. The blossoms grow at the tip of a slender
stalk called the *spadix* and are surrounded by a colorful,
leaflike *spathe.* Arums that grow wild in North America
include the *water arum, jack-in-the-pulpit, skunk cabbage,* and *sweet flag.* True arums are native to the Eastern Hemisphere and make up a small group in the arum
family. The *cuckoopint,* also known as *lords-and-ladies,*
is a true arum that grows in Europe. It resembles the
jack-in-the-pulpit.   Kenneth R. Robertson

Scientific classification. Arums make up the arum family,
Araceae. The cuckoopint is *Arum maculatum.*

Related articles in *World Book* include:

Caladium	Jack-in-the-pulpit	Skunk cabbage
Calla	Monstera	Sweet flag
Elephant's-ear	Philodendron	Taro

Aryans, *AIR ee uhnz,* is a term used both for a group
of Asian languages and for certain Asian peoples.
Indo-Aryan is a group of languages spoken mainly on
the Indian subcontinent. Some of these languages date
back to as long ago as about 1500 B.C. Indo-Aryan includes the ancient Sanskrit language and the modern
Hindi. In Sanskrit, the term *arya* referred to a group of
people in ancient India. These Aryans were Brahmans,
members of the highest Hindu caste, who followed the
traditionally accepted religious practices and used Sanskrit. In Sanskrit, *arya* also means *kinsmen* or *nobles.*

Other peoples that referred to themselves as Aryans
were the Iranians, including the Persian family of rulers
known as the Achaemenids. The Indo-Iranians settled
about 1500 B.C. in what are now Afghanistan, northern
India, Iran, and Pakistan. The Achaemenid family ruled
what is now Iran from about 550 B.C. to 331 B.C. The
name *Iran* comes from the word *Aryan.*

In the mid-1900's, the rulers of Nazi Germany used the
term *Aryan* to refer to Germans and certain other northern Europeans, whom they considered racially superior
to all other peoples. This racist use of the term has continued among certain white supremacist groups in the
United States.   George Cardona

See also **Asia** (The Indus Valley); **India** (The Aryans);
Mythology (Comparing myths); **Nazism; Races, Human**
(Race and discrimination).

Asante. See Ashanti.

Asbestos, *as BEHS tuhs,* is any of a group of soft,
threadlike mineral fibers. Asbestos has many properties
that make it commercially valuable. It does not burn or
easily conduct heat or electric current. Asbestos fibers
are also flexible and strong and are not affected by most
chemicals. Asbestos occurs in certain types of rocks,
which are mined and then processed to remove the
asbestos fibers.

Asbestos can cause health problems if it is inhaled. It
is thought to present no health hazard so long as it remains intact. It is believed to become dangerous only
after it crumbles and releases its tiny fibers into the air.
Asbestos that is dry and capable of crumbling with the
slightest pressure is said to be *friable.* Inhaling asbestos

WORLD BOOK illustration by Christabel King

The cuckoopint is a type of arum that grows in Europe. It bears
tiny flowers surrounded by a leaflike *spathe.*

is associated with a disease called *asbestosis.* It is also associated with certain types of cancer.

Manufacturers once used asbestos to reinforce thousands of products, many of which could release high concentrations of breathable asbestos fibers. Today, manufacturers mainly use asbestos in high-density building materials that do not release large amounts of breathable fibers. These include cement and asphalt-based roofing materials.

Types of asbestos. Geologists use the word *asbestos* to refer to the fibrous varieties of certain *hydrated silicates.* Hydrated silicates are minerals that are composed of silica and a metallic element, which are chemically combined with water. The fibrous hydrated silicates that make up commercially used asbestos belong to either the *serpentine group* of minerals or to the *amphibole group* of minerals.

The serpentine mineral group includes *chrysotile,* the best known, most abundant, and most widely used type of asbestos. Its chemical formula is $Mg_3Si_2(OH)_4O_5$. The crystal structure of chrysotile consists of alternate sheets of magnesia and silica. These sheets are rolled into tubes called *fibrils* that resemble a rolled newspaper.

The amphibole mineral group consists of several types of asbestos. The most abundant types are *crocidolite* and *amosite.* Amphibole asbestos has coarser fibers than does chrysotile. These types of asbestos also consist of hydrated silicates plus other elements. The crystal structure of amphibole asbestos is made up of a double chain of silicon and oxygen atoms that is coordinated with atoms of other elements. The strands of amphibole fibers lie parallel to the double chain of atoms.

Uses of asbestos. Each type of asbestos has certain qualities, and so each kind is used for different purposes. For example, most chrysotile has fine, curly fibers that are strong and resist heat. Manufacturers use chrysotile for such products as roof coatings and roof cements, asbestos cement sheets, and siding and shingles for houses. Chrysotile is also used for asbestos cement water pipes and for packings and gaskets used in the automotive and petrochemical industries. Short chrysotile fibers are used to make materials that can

WORLD BOOK photo, courtesy Field Museum

Asbestos is a soft, threadlike mineral fiber in certain types of rock, as shown here. The rock is mined and hauled to a plant where a series of machines crush it to free the asbestos fibers.

withstand heat generated by friction, such as brake linings for motor vehicles.

Amphibole asbestos is noted for its high resistance to heat and acids. Crocidolite is used in asbestos cement pipes and in diaphragms used in chlorine production.

Sources of asbestos. Most asbestos is found in *metamorphic rocks* (see **Metamorphic rock**). Chrysotile develops mainly as deposits in the cracks and seams of such rocks. Amosite and crocidolite, the most abundant types of amphibole asbestos, occur chiefly in highly folded metamorphic rocks.

Russia and China produce most of the world's asbestos. Other leading producers include Brazil, Canada, Kazakhstan, and Zimbabwe.

How asbestos is mined and processed. Most asbestos is obtained from enormous pits dug in the ground. This process is called *open-pit mining.* But some asbestos deposits are mined underground.

After the rocks have been mined, trucks take them to a plant called a *mill.* There, a series of machines crush the rocks into progressively smaller pieces with little damage to the fibers. In one common method, the loose fibers are *aspirated* (drawn by suction) through screens that allow only the asbestos to pass through. Special equipment divides the fibers according to length. The asbestos is then shipped to manufacturers.

Hazards of asbestos. People who mine asbestos, manufacture asbestos products, install asbestos insulation, or remove asbestos may inhale the fibers. People who hold such jobs in countries that do not limit exposure to asbestos are at high risk of contracting a disease related to asbestos. Also at high risk are workers who held such jobs for many years before exposure was limited by law. Asbestos can also be a hazard to the families of asbestos workers, who may carry asbestos dust home on their clothing. Asbestos dust may also affect people who live near asbestos mines or processing plants.

Asbestosis is a disease in which scar tissue blocks the exchange of gases in the lungs. This condition causes shortness of breath. Another disease associated with asbestos is lung cancer. Asbestos workers who smoke are at an even higher risk for lung cancer. Asbestos also causes *mesothelioma,* a rare and fatal cancer of the lining of the chest or abdomen.

Scientists do not know exactly how asbestos causes disease. Many researchers say that inhaling fibers longer than 5 to 10 micrometers (0.0002 to 0.0004 inch) and less than 2 micrometers (0.00008 inch) wide increases the risk of illness. Inhaling fibers for even a short amount of time may result in mesothelioma.

In the United States, government regulations established by the Occupational Safety and Health Administration (OSHA) limit the hazard of asbestos among workers. Government regulations also protect consumers from certain products containing asbestos.

History. The properties of asbestos have been known since ancient times. The Egyptians used asbestos cloth to prepare bodies for burial. The Romans collected the ashes of the dead by wrapping the bodies in asbestos cloth before cremation.

In 1774, Abraham G. Werner, a German mineralogist, wrote the first comprehensive scientific description of asbestos. People did not become aware of the health hazards of asbestos until the early 1900's. The United

Kingdom, in 1931, was probably the first country to set up health laws regulating exposure to asbestos. In 1935, the Canadian province of British Columbia passed a law requiring asbestos workers to wear protective equipment when working with asbestos. The United States enacted similar standards into law in 1972. In 1973, the U.S. Environmental Protection Agency (EPA) banned the use of sprayed asbestos for insulation or fireproofing. In 1975, this ban was expanded to include wet applications of asbestos, such as application with a trowel, and the use of molded asbestos that could become friable.

In 1986, the EPA began a program to reduce the danger of asbestos in all public and private school buildings. These structures must be inspected to determine the amount of asbestos in them, and its location and condition. If a building contains asbestos, the school must develop and implement an asbestos management plan. The EPA also ordered that any removal, encapsulation, or enclosure of asbestos be followed by tests to ensure that the amount of asbestos has been reduced to a safe level. Synthetic fibers of fiberglass and plastics are used as a substitute for asbestos fibers.   Robert P. Nolan

Asbjørnsen, *AHS byurn suhn,* **Peter Christen,** *PAY tuhr KRIHS tuhn* (1812-1885), was a collector of Norwegian folk tales and a naturalist. He won fame for his work with Jørgen Moe in immortalizing the tales told by the people of Norway. Their collection, *Norwegian Folk Tales* (1842-1843), became a literary classic. It includes such diverse stories as "The Three Billy Goats Gruff," "Mastermaid," and "Little Per and Big Per."

Asbjørnsen was born on Jan. 15, 1812, in Christiania (now Oslo). He explored the coasts of Norway and made important contributions to botany and zoology. Asbjørnsen died on Jan. 5, 1885.   Niels Ingwersen

Asbury, *AZ buh ree,* **Francis** (1745-1816), was the most important Methodist leader in America during the late 1700's and early 1800's. Asbury was born in England, but he lived in America from 1771 until his death. When Asbury arrived in America, there were only a few hundred Methodists in scattered, disorganized groups. Under his leadership, the Methodists increased in number until they ranked second only to the Baptists as the largest Protestant denomination in America.

Asbury was born on Aug. 20, 1745, near Birmingham, England. He became a Methodist while a teen-ager. He was a traveling preacher from 1767 to 1771, when he volunteered to go to America as a missionary. The other Methodist missionaries returned to Britain after the colonists rebelled. But Asbury stayed in America.

In 1784, Asbury became a superintendent, or bishop, of the newly founded Methodist Episcopal Church. He gained this position by order of the Methodist leader John Wesley and by a vote of the Methodist preachers in America. The church lacked enough formally educated ministers to serve the growing American population, and so Asbury expanded the Methodist technique of enlisting laymen to lead local congregations. From these laymen, he recruited many young preachers to travel on horseback among frontier congregations, overseeing local meetings and conducting public worship. These preachers were called *circuit riders.* They were supervised by more experienced preachers called *presiding elders.* Asbury supervised the system.

Asbury traveled almost constantly, riding from 4,000 to 6,000 miles (6,400 to 9,700 kilometers) a year on horseback. He planned a many religious gatherings, especially camp meetings where thousands of people gathered outdoors in order to sing hymns and hear sermons. Asbury died on March 31, 1816.   Mark A. Noll

See also **Methodists; Circuit rider.**

ASCAP. See **American Society of Composers, Authors and Publishers.**

Ascension, *uh SEHN shuhn,* is an island in the South Atlantic about 700 miles (1,100 kilometers) northwest of Saint Helena and 500 miles (800 kilometers) south of the equator. It belongs to the United Kingdom and is under the administration of Saint Helena (see **Saint Helena**). It has an area of 34 square miles (88 square kilometers), and a population of about 1,000. The island is a breeding ground for sea turtles and the sooty tern. For location, see **Atlantic Ocean** (map).   Hartmut S. Walter

Asceticism, *uh SEHT uh sihz uhm,* is the practice of self-denial or self-punishment, often for religious purposes. Those who practice asceticism are called *ascetics.* They may go for long periods without food or sleep, wear rough clothing, expose themselves to extreme heat or cold, or refrain from sexual relations. Some even whip themselves or stick sharp objects in their skin.

Ascetics believe a person's physical life conflicts with his or her spiritual life. Ascetics strive to become more spiritual by denying themselves physical pleasures and necessities. Sometimes, ascetic practices produce religious visions, which ascetics regard as a sign of their increasing spirituality. Asceticism has long been a part of religious traditions. Many early Christians gave up physical comforts to become closer to God. Asceticism has been especially important in Roman Catholicism and certain religions of India and Japan.   Nancy E. Auer Falk

See also **Hermit.**

Asch, *ash,* **Sholem,** *SHAW luhm* (1880-1957), a Polish-born author, was the first person to achieve international renown writing in Yiddish. His heroes search for faith and yearn for an ideal. A key theme of his works is that the individual, no matter how sinful, strives for holiness.

Asch first gained fame for his novel *A Shtetl (A Town,* 1904), which introduced a new romantic tone to Yiddish literature. Earlier Yiddish writers had portrayed Jewish life in eastern Europe in a grim way. In *A Shtetl,* Asch stressed its harmony, strength, and respect for tradition.

Asch was fascinated with the relation between Christianity and Judaism. He wrote three related biographical novels about the founders of Christianity—*The Nazarene* (1939), *The Apostle* (1943), and *Mary* (1949). He hoped that his presentation of Christianity's Jewish heritage would reduce prejudice against Jews. But many Jewish critics attacked Asch for what they believed was a move toward Christianity. He also became known for his plays, most notably *God of Vengeance* (1907). Asch was born in Kutno, Poland, on Nov. 1, 1880. He moved to the United States in 1914. He died July 10, 1957.   Eugene V. Orenstein

Ascidian. See **Sea squirt.**

Asclepius, *uh SKLEE pee uhs,* was the god of healing in Greek mythology. The Romans called him Aesculapius. The Greeks prayed to Asclepius during plagues and in times of illness. His best-known child was Hygeia, the goddess of health. Epidaurus in Greece was the special site of his followers, the Asclepiads, the first physicians. Asclepius's symbol, a snake entwined around a staff, is often used as a symbol of the medical profession. Asclepius's father was the god Apollo, who taught his son the art of health. But Asclepius misused this gift by trying to revive a dead man. Zeus, ruler of the gods, therefore killed him with a thunderbolt and sent him to Hades, god of the underworld. See also **Epidaurus; Greece, Ancient** (picture: Asclepius).   Nancy Felson

ASEAN. See **Association of Southeast Asian Nations.**

Asexual reproduction. See Reproduction (How genes are transferred).

Ash is a group of hardwood trees found in North America, Europe, and Asia. Some *species* (kinds) of ash are commercially valuable. Ashes may be planted as shade trees to prevent soil erosion. White ash and red ash are common in the eastern United States. Black ash is found in the northeastern United States.

Ash leaves and branches form in pairs. Each leaf has 5 to 11 pointed leaflets. Small male and female flowers usually grow on separate trees. The *keys* (winged fruit) look like canoe paddles. They develop late in the season and fall to the ground in autumn. Ash wood is hard, strong, and stiff and is used mainly for shovel, hoe, and rake handles and for baseball bats. Ash is also used for furniture, oars, and skis.

A major pest of ash trees is the *emerald ash borer,* an Asian beetle that first spread to North America on ships during the late 1900's. Ash borer *larvae* (young) feed on the inner bark of the tree, eventually killing it. Emerald ash borers have killed tens of millions of ash trees in North America.

Certain other trees and shrubs are called *ash,* but they are not true ashes. They include mountain ashes and prickly-ashes.   Norman L. Christensen, Jr.

Scientific classification. Ash trees make up the genus *Fraxinus.* White ash is *Fraxinus americana.* Red ash is *F. pennsylvanica.* Black ash is *F. nigra.*

See also **Emerald ash borer; Mountain ash; Prickly-ash; Tree** (Broadleaf and needleleaf trees [picture]).

Ash is the substance that remains after an organic substance has been burned. The word *ashes* usually refers to the minerals obtained from burning coal, wood, or other fuels. An analysis of the ashes of burned foods and other substances can determine the minerals they contain. For example, chemical tests of the ashes of burnt milk show that they contain calcium. Some kinds of ashes can be used for various purposes. For example, *fly ash,* the dust produced by power plants that burn coal, is used as a soil fertilizer.   Clark L. Fields

Ash Wednesday is the first day of Lent, a season observed in the spring by most Christians. The day marks the start of a period of discipline and penitence that precedes Easter. Ash Wednesday is observed by Western Christian churches, especially Roman Catholic, Anglican, and Lutheran churches. In many churches, the observance of Ash Wednesday centers on ashes from burned palms used in the previous year's Palm Sunday procession. A priest or pastor blesses the ashes and uses them to mark the foreheads of worshipers. This blessing is based on the Biblical passage "you are dust, and to dust you shall return" (Genesis 3: 19). Ashes also serve as a symbol of purification and penitence.   David G. Truemper

See also **Easter** (The beginning of Lent); **Lent; Mardi Gras; Palm Sunday; Shrove Tuesday.**

Ashanti, *ah SHAN tee,* refers both to a region in the western African nation of Ghana and to a people who live there. The people call themselves Asante. Historically, Ashanti was a powerful military and political state, and Asante influence extended far beyond the boundaries of modern Ghana. Today, Ashanti is one of 10 local administrative regions that make up Ghana. It includes only about 10 percent of Ghana's land area, but it ranks as the most populous region of the country.

The Asante people are largely farmers, raising cacao, which is used to make chocolate, and other crops. The region also has important timber resources and gold deposits. Asante artisans, specializing in goldsmithing and woodcarving, and Asante weavers, famous for their colorful *kente cloth,* attract tourists to the region.

The Ashanti state first developed in the late 1600's, when a leader named Osei Tutu unified a federation of independent kingdoms. Tutu became the first *asantehene* (king) of the unified nation and made his capital at Kumasi. The asantehene was a constitutional ruler whose power was balanced by a council of chiefs. The king made decisions after discussions with the council, and he could be removed from his position if he ruled poorly. The queen mother, the senior female of the ruling family, held political power equal to that of a chief.

In the early 1700's, the Ashanti state expanded by conquering neighboring kingdoms. During the 1800's, the Asante increased trade with Muslims in the north and with European traders on the coast. In the late 1800's, the Asante and the British fought for control of trade in West Africa. The British defeated the Asante in 1901 and colonized the Ashanti lands. In 1957, Ashanti and other nearby areas under British control became the independent country of Ghana. Since then, traditional Asante rulers have played a major role in Ghana's economic and political development.   David Owusu-Ansah

See also **Africa** (pictures); **Ghana** (People; History).

Ashbery, John (1927-2017), was an influential American poet. His poems are admired for their blending of humor and seriousness, their experimental freedom, and their quirky, unpredictable use of language. The themes of Ashbery's poems include the nature of time and the difficulty of achieving true knowledge.

Ashbery said that his poems attempt to capture the wandering movements of the mind as it drifts from one idea or image to another. This can make his work difficult to follow. Some of Ashbery's poems seem almost random in their relationships. He enjoyed mixing unlikely elements, including figures from pop culture. For example, he used such cartoon characters as Popeye and Daffy Duck. Ashbery's poems also refer to classical works of art and literature. One of his most famous poems, "Self-Portrait in a Convex Mirror," is an extended meditation on a painting by the Italian Renaissance master Parmigianino. It is the title poem in a collection that won the 1976 Pulitzer Prize for poetry.

Ashbery was born on July 28, 1927, in Rochester, New York. The best introduction to his work is *Collected Poems, 1956-1987* (2008) and *Collected Poems 1991-2000* (2017). Later poems were collected in *Notes from the Air: Selected Later Poems (2007), Planisphere* (2009), *Quick Question* (2012), *Breezeway* (2015), and *Commotion of the Birds* (2016). Ashbery's literary and art criticism has been collected in *Reported Sightings* (1991) and *Selected Prose* (2004). His translation of the French poet Arthur

Rimbaud's *Illuminations* was published in 2011. Ashbery died on Sept. 3, 2017. Roger Gilbert

See also **Postmodernism**.

Ashcan School was a group of American artists of the early 1900's known mainly for their realistic paintings of city life. The group revolted against the traditional, sentimental subject matter then fashionable in American art. It helped establish Realism as an acceptable art style in the United States. The Ashcan School consisted of Arthur Bowen Davies, William Glackens, Robert Henri, Ernest Lawson, George Luks, Maurice Prendergast, Everett Shinn, and John Sloan.

The Ashcan School was originally called *The Eight.* It was formed by Henri in 1907 in New York City to oppose the conservative exhibition policies of many of the city's art galleries. In 1908, the group held an exhibit that included paintings by Glackens, Henri, Luks, Shinn, and Sloan. Their works realistically showed city scenes, such as factories, slums, crowded streets, and night life. Critics called the group the Ashcan School because of the "down-to-earth" realistic subject matter. Three members did not paint in a Realistic style. Davies painted dreamlike scenes. Lawson was an Impressionist, and Prendergast painted in a partially abstract style. Sarah Burns

Ashcroft, John David (1942-   ), was attorney general of the United States from 2001 to 2005, during President George W. Bush's first administration. Before serving in the Cabinet, Ashcroft was a Republican senator, representing Missouri from 1995 to 2001.

After Sept. 11, 2001, when the United States suffered the worst terrorist attack in its history, Ashcroft helped to coordinate a massive investigation to find those responsible for the attack. He successfully pressed Congress for broadened powers for the Justice Department to prevent future attacks. But he received criticism from people who felt such powers would limit civil liberties.

As a senator, Ashcroft worked on legislation designed to give states control over more government programs. He was a strong advocate for the pro-life cause, which opposes abortion. He supported the idea of limits on the number of terms members of Congress may serve.

Ashcroft was born in Chicago on May 9, 1942. He later moved with his family to Springfield, Missouri, where he graduated from high school. He received a bachelor's degree from Yale University in 1964 and a law degree from the University of Chicago in 1967.

Ashcroft ran for Congress in 1972 but lost. From 1973 to 1975, he served as Missouri state auditor. Ashcroft was Missouri state assistant attorney general in 1975 and 1976 and state attorney general from 1976 to 1985. He served as Missouri's governor from 1985 to 1993. Ashcroft won election to the U.S. Senate in 1994 but narrowly lost a bid for reelection in 2000. In 2005, Ashcroft opened the Ashcroft Group, a lobbying firm based in Washington, D.C. That same year, Regent University hired Ashcroft to teach law and government courses at its Washington, D.C., campus. Jeremy D. Mayer

Ashe, ash, Arthur (1943-1993), a tennis player, became the first African American to win the U.S. men's national singles championship. He won the title in 1968. In that same year, he played on the winning U.S. Davis Cup team (see **Davis Cup**). In 1975, he became the first Black man to win the Wimbledon singles title in England. Ashe retired from competition in 1980.

Oil painting on canvas; the Cleveland Museum of Art, Gift of Amelia Elizabeth White

An Ashcan School painting called *Woman's Work* shows a realistic scene of urban life in New York City. John Sloan, one of the group's most important artists, painted the scene in 1911.

Arthur Robert Ashe, Jr., was born in Richmond, Virginia, on July 10, 1943. In 1966, while a student at the University of California at Los Angeles, he won the National Collegiate Athletic Association singles and doubles championships. He wrote a history of Black athletes in America called *A Hard Road to Glory* (1987). Ashe died from pneumonia brought on by AIDS on Feb. 6, 1993. He probably contracted HIV, the virus that causes AIDS, from a blood transfusion. Ashe's memoir, *Days of Grace,* was published in 1993, after his death. Chris Evert

AP/Wide World
Arthur Ashe

Asheville (pop. 83,393; met. area pop. 424,858) is the economic and cultural center of 18 counties in western North Carolina. It is set in the midst of recreational areas covering more than 1 million acres (400,000 hectares). Asheville is next to Pisgah National Forest and serves as the eastern gateway to Great Smoky Mountains National Park. The scenic Blue Ridge Parkway passes nearby the city (see **North Carolina** [political map]).

The Asheville area's manufactured products include electrical equipment, engine components, laboratory equipment, paper products, and plastics products. The city serves as the agricultural wholesale center for the surrounding area.

Author Thomas Wolfe was born and raised in Asheville. The boarding house his mother ran, called "Dixieland" in his novel *Look Homeward, Angel* (1929), is open to the public. A branch of the University of North Carolina is in the city. Asheville was incorporated as a town in 1797. It is the seat of Buncombe County and has a council-manager government.　　Jerry L. Surratt

Ashgabat, *ASH guh BAHT* (pop. 407,000), is the capital of Turkmenistan. About 700,000 people live in the city. Ashgabat, also called Ashkhabad, lies in an oasis in the Karakum desert in southern Turkmenistan (see **Turkmenistan** [map]). An earthquake destroyed much of Ashgabat in 1948. The city was rebuilt with low buildings. The Karakum Canal supplies the city with water from the Amu Darya, a river more than 250 miles (400 kilometers) away in eastern Turkmenistan. Irrigation ditches called *aryks* line both sides of roads in Ashgabat. Economic activities in Ashgabat include carpet, textile, metal, and glass manufacturing.

Ashgabat was founded in 1881 as a military outpost for the Russian Empire. It was called Poltoratsk from 1919 to 1927. Already a regional center, Ashgabat became the capital of Turkmenistan in 1924, when Turkmenistan was made a republic of the Soviet Union. It remained the capital after Turkmenistan became an independent nation in 1991.　　Nancy Lubin

Ashkenazim, *ASH kuh NAZ ihm,* are a Jewish people who trace their cultural and ethnic ancestry through northern and central Europe. The term *Ashkenazim* comes from *Ashkenaz,* a Biblical name later used to refer to what is now Germany. Scholars think the ancestors of the Ashkenazim originated in the Middle East and migrated to Italy, moving to the Rhine Valley region around the 900's. Over time, the Ashkenazim developed distinct religious customs and their own language, called Yiddish.

In the 1200's, large numbers of Ashkenazim migrated to what is now Poland, Ukraine, and surrounding areas. There, many worked as legal scholars, teachers, moneylenders, and merchants. For centuries, these eastern European Ashkenazim dominated Jewish religious and intellectual life. At times, however, they faced terrible persecution.

Beginning in the late 1700's, many Ashkenazim in western Europe adopted the language, customs, and occupations of their host countries. In the 1800's, Ashkenazim in Germany founded the Reform, Conservative, and Orthodox branches of Judaism. In the late 1800's, millions of Ashkenazim from eastern Europe began to migrate to Argentina, Australia, Canada, South Africa, the United Kingdom, and the United States. In the early 1900's, many migrated to Palestine, helping to establish the state of Israel. In the 1940's, millions of European Ashkenazim were killed as part of the Holocaust, the Nazi campaign to exterminate the Jews. See **Holocaust.**

Today, Ashkenazim make up about 80 percent of all Jews in the world. They live in many parts of the world, in particular the United States and Israel.

Barry Trachtenberg

See also **Israel** (Jews); **Jews; Yiddish language.**

Ashkenazy, Vladimir (1937-　　), a Soviet-born pianist and conductor, ranks among the finest piano soloists of his generation. He gained fame for the warmth and delicacy of his style. Ashkenazy has been praised for his interpretation of such Russian composers as Sergei

Prokofiev, Sergei Rachmaninoff, and Alexander Scriabin.

Ashkenazy was music director of the Royal Philharmonic Orchestra in London from 1987 to 1994 and principal guest conductor of the Cleveland Orchestra from 1987 to 1994. He was music director of the German Symphony Orchestra Berlin (formerly the Berlin Radio Symphony Orchestra) from 1989 to 1999. He served as director of the Czech Philharmonic from 1998 to 2003. Ashkenazy became music director of the European Union Youth Orchestra in 2000. In 2004, he became music director of the NHK Symphony Orchestra in Japan.

Vladimir Davidovich Ashkenazy was born on July 6, 1937, in Gorki in the Soviet Union (now Nizhniy Novgorod, Russia). He made his performing debut when he was 8 years old and attended the Moscow Conservatory. Ashkenazy married Thorunn Johannsdottir, an Icelandic pianist, in 1961. He left the Soviet Union in 1963 and lived in England until 1968, when he settled in Iceland. He became an Icelandic citizen in 1972.　　John H. Baron

Ashoka, *uh SHOH kuh* (?-232 B.C.), ruled the Mauryan Empire from about 272 B.C. until his death. Under his rule, the empire covered much of what are now Afghanistan, Bangladesh, India, and Pakistan.

In 261 B.C., Ashoka conquered Kalinga, a region on the east coast of India. After he saw the bloodshed his conquest had caused, Ashoka declared that he was filled with sorrow and regret. He rejected war as a way of gaining political power. Ashoka had many public announcements inscribed on rocks, stone pillars, and cave walls. His inscriptions recommended Buddhist ideals as the highest moral code, but also urged toleration of all peoples and beliefs. He instructed his officials to preach religion and obedience to his laws. He also sent diplomats and Buddhist missionaries to Ceylon (now Sri Lanka), Egypt, Greece, Persia, and Syria.　　Michael H. Fisher

See also **Mauryan Empire.**

Ashton, Sir Frederick (1904-1988), was an English *choreographer* (creator of dances). His gracious, refined, and tasteful dances helped establish today's English national style in classical ballet.

Ashton was born in Guayaquil, Ecuador, on Sept. 17, 1904. In 1935, he joined the Vic-Wells Ballet as a choreographer. He was knighted in 1962. In 1963, he became director of the company, now the Royal Ballet. He retired as director in 1970 but continued to choreograph. His major works include *Façade* (1931), *Symphonic Variations* (1946), *Ondine* (1958), and *A Month in the Country* (1976). Ashton died on Aug. 18, 1988.　　Dorothy Lourdou

Ashtoreth. See **Astarte.**

Ashurbanipal, *AH shoor BAH nee PAHL,* also spelled *Assurbanipal,* was the last great king of the Assyrians. During his reign (668-627 B.C.), Assyria became a leading world power. His empire included Babylonia, Persia, Syria, and Egypt. But it was also during his reign that Assyria's power began to decline. In 651 B.C., the Assyrians were expelled from Egypt. A civil war with Babylonia further weakened his empire, even though Assyria won the war in 648 B.C. Ashurbanipal was a dreaded warrior and a great patron of the arts. At his royal palace, he gathered a huge collection of Sumerian, Babylonian, and Assyrian writings. This famous library of clay tablets, now mainly in the British Museum, is a valuable guide to Mesopotamian history.　　Norman Yoffee

See also **Assyria** (Language and literature).

© Philip Lange, Shutterstock

Asia has some of the world's most heavily populated areas. Many of the largest cities in the world are there, and even many rural areas of the continent are densely populated. Dubai, *shown here,* in the United Arab Emirates, is one of Asia's fastest-growing cities.

Asia

Asia is the largest continent in both size and population. It covers about 30 percent of the world's land area and has about 60 percent of its people. Asia extends from Africa and Europe in the west to the Pacific Ocean in the east. The northernmost part of the continent lies within the frozen Arctic. But in the south, Asia ends in the steaming tropics near the equator.

Asia has some of the world's longest rivers, largest deserts, and thickest forests and jungles. The highest and lowest places on Earth are in Asia. Mount Everest, the highest, rises 29,032 feet (8,849 meters) above sea level along the Nepal-Tibet border. The Dead Sea shore, the world's lowest land, lies about 1,411 feet (430 meters) below sea level between Israel and Jordan.

The 50 countries of Asia include some of the world's largest and smallest countries in population. China, the world's most populated nation, has about 1.4 billion people. But about 25 percent of Asia's countries have populations of less than 5 million people.

Asia also contains some of the world's largest and smallest countries in area. Russia, which lies partly in Europe but mostly in Asia, is the world's largest country in area. It covers more than 6 ½ million square miles (17 million square kilometers). But three Asian nations—Bahrain, the Maldives, and Singapore—each cover less than 400 square miles (1,000 square kilometers).

The nations of Asia have a variety of political systems. Different types of Communist governments rule China, North Korea, and Vietnam. Such nations as Bhutan and Saudi Arabia have kings. Sheikhs control Bahrain, Qatar, and the United Arab Emirates. Asian nations that operate under democratic principles include India, Israel, and Japan. Military leaders have taken control of many Asian countries in times of trouble.

The people who inhabit Asia are as varied as everything else about the continent. The people differ greatly in their ancestry, customs, languages, religious beliefs, and ways of life. Because of these differences, this article

Facts in brief

Area: 17,029,000 mi² (44,104,000 km²). *Greatest distances*—east-west, about 6,000 mi (9,700 km); north-south, about 5,400 mi (8,690 km). *Coastline*—80,205 mi (129,077 km).

Population: *Estimated 2022 population*—4,645,057,000; density, 273 per mi² (105 per km²).

Elevation: *Highest*—Mount Everest, 29,032 ft (8,849 m) above sea level. *Lowest*—shore of the Dead Sea, about 1,411 feet (430 meters) below sea level.

Physical features: *Chief mountain ranges*—Altai, Elburz, Himalaya, Hindu Kush, Karakoram, Kunlun, Qilian, Qinling, Stanovoy, Tian Shan, Yablonovyy, Zagros. *Chief rivers*—Amur, Brahmaputra, Euphrates, Ganges, Huang, Indus, Irrawaddy, Lena, Mekong, Menam, Ob, Salween, Tigris, Xi, Yangtze, Yenisey. *Chief deserts*—Gobi, Karakum, Kyzylkum, Rub al Khali, Taklimakan.

Number of independent countries: 50

discusses the life of the people of Asia in six separate *Way of life* sections. The article also describes the land, climate, animals, plants, agriculture, and industry of Asia. A final section traces the history of the continent.

Civilization in Asia began about 5,500 years ago, long before it began in Europe. During ancient and medieval times, Asia moved ahead of Europe in economic, cultural, and scientific development. Asians founded the first cities, set up the first systems of law, and became the first farmers and merchants. Asians invented writing and created the earliest literatures. All the world's major religions originated in Asia. In addition, Asians invented paper, the magnetic compass, and movable type.

In the 1500's and 1600's, Europeans began to establish trading outposts in Asia, some of which gradually became colonies. From about 1750, Western European nations began conquering large parts of Asia.

In the 1800's, when European colonizers ruled much of Asia, the economic gap between Asia and the West widened. European colonies in Asia became sources of raw materials to fuel development for European industry. The colonies served as markets for European manufactured products. They also began commercial production for the European market. Asian nations remained largely agricultural, and their farmers continued to use traditional tools and farming methods. Almost all colonial Asia gained independence during the mid-1900's.

After World War II (1939-1945), Asia became a center of the struggle between Communist and non-Communist countries, and fighting broke out in many Asian nations. The Communists succeeded in China and Vietnam, and achieved partial success in Korea.

Tensions between the Communists and their democratic rivals have eased in some places but remain high in others. The non-Communist Chinese Nationalists retreated to the island of Taiwan. Today, China and Taiwan struggle over the issue of Taiwanese independence. Korea was divided into Communist North Korea and democratic South Korea. The two sides never signed a formal truce, and a 487-square-mile (1,262-square-kilometer)

© Digital Vision/SuperStock

Most of the world's tea comes from Asia. These women are picking tea in Sri Lanka, a leading tea-producing nation.

area called the Demilitarized Zone (DMZ) still divides them.

Other disputes have brought about fighting between many groups of people in Asia. For example, India and Pakistan have never resolved which country controls the territory of Kashmir. As a result of such disputes, some areas of Asia almost continually face wars and threats of

© Trix1428/Dreamstime

Asian art includes huge Chinese sculptures of Buddhist figures. These sculptures of protectors of the Buddha were carved in the A.D. 600's for a cliffside chapel at Longmen Grottoes, caves near Luoyang in east-central China. Buddhism is one of Asia's chief religions.

The Taj Mahal, in Agra, India, is the tomb of an Indian ruler and his wife. Built in the 1600's, the magnificent marble structure is an example of Islamic architecture, seen in many parts of Asia.

© Holger Mette, Shutterstock

wars while trying to solve their other problems.

Meanwhile, a worldwide population explosion sent the number of people in Asia and elsewhere soaring. The growing populations created a need for more food, jobs, schools, and other necessities. In the 1960's, there were fears that food production could not keep up with Asia's rapidly growing population. However, family planning policies in some countries helped to curb population growth, and the introduction of new farming technologies increased agricultural production. Slowing population growth, improving agriculture, and increasing industry have raised living standards. Beginning in the 1980's and 1990's, increased foreign investment in the industries of China, India, and other Asian nations has greatly improved their economies.

People

About 4 ⅔ billion people, or about 60 percent of the world's population, live in Asia. China has more people than any other country in the world, and India has the second largest population. More than one-third of all the people in the world live in these two countries.

This section gives a broad overview of the population distribution in Asia. It also discusses, in general terms, Asia's *ethnic* (cultural) groups, religions, and languages. The article's six *Way of life* sections then provide more detailed information about Asian peoples who live in various regions of the continent.

Population distribution. If Asia's people were distributed evenly throughout the continent, there would be 273 per square mile (105 per square kilometer). But many areas are so cold, so hot, so dry, or so mountainous that few people live there. The vast majority of Asians live in river or mountain valleys or near seacoasts, where many of them live by farming or fishing.

Parts of Asia rank among the world's most densely populated areas. They include Bangladesh; Hong Kong, Macau, and eastern China; Singapore; the Ganges Valley of India; most of Japan; and the island of Java in Indonesia. In these regions, millions of people pack the big cities. Even many rural areas in these places are densely populated.

Peoples of Asia. The peoples of Asia have rich and varied cultures and ancestries. Asia has dozens of ethnic groups—both large and small. A single country may have several groups. The largest ethnic groups on the continent include the Arabs of Southwest Asia and the Chinese of East Asia.

The members of an ethnic group may be united by language, religion, common ancestry, or other characteristics. Ethnic groups establish rules of conduct for their members and preserve artistic, religious, and other traditions. Many members of ethnic groups feel a strong sense of identification or belonging.

Asia has often been divided by religious and ethnic tensions. Sometimes, these tensions have led to violent

Emil Schulthess, Black Star

The land of North Asia is snow-covered and frozen for much of the year. The people of Siberia, in North Asia, raise reindeer for food, clothing, and transportation.

conflict. For example, there have been wars between Arabs and Jews, Greeks and Turks, Hindus and Muslims, and Armenians and Azerbaijanis. Some conflicts arise from a minority religious or ethnic group's desire to achieve self-determination within a country. In other cases, the conflict is between two or more countries.

Religions. All the world's major religions began in Asia—Buddhism, Christianity, Confucianism, Hinduism, Islam, and Judaism. The history and beliefs of these religions are discussed in separate articles and in the **Religion** article.

More Asians practice Hinduism than any other religion. Hinduism is the major faith in India and Nepal.

Islam has the second largest number of Asian followers. Geographically, it is the most widespread religion on the continent. In Southwest Asia, in much of Central Asia, and in such countries as Bangladesh, Indonesia, and Pakistan, most of the people are Muslims (followers of Islam).

Buddhism is the chief religion of mainland Southeast Asia and also has many followers in East Asia. Lamaism, a branch of Buddhism, is the chief religion of Mongolia and other parts of Central Asia. Confucianism and Taoism (also spelled *Daoism)* also have many followers in China, and Shinto is important in Japan. Many Asian people combine Buddhism with other beliefs.

Most people in Cyprus and the Philippines and many in Lebanon, Armenia, Georgia, and Russia practice Christianity. It is also spreading quickly in China. Judaism is the chief religion in only one nation—Israel.

Languages. The many languages and *dialects* (local forms of languages) spoken in Asia present a major barrier to communication. In some parts of the continent, the people of one village cannot speak to their neighbors in a village a few miles away. For example, in Madhya Pradesh, one of India's states, the people speak more than 375 languages and dialects.

Arabic and Hebrew, the chief languages of far southwestern Asia, belong to the Afro-Asiatic family of languages. Russian and the chief languages of Afghanistan, northern India, Iran, Pakistan, and Sri Lanka are Indo-European languages. The major languages of southern India are in the Dravidian family. Languages of the Uralic

and Altaic families are spoken in Kazakhstan, Mongolia, Siberia, Turkey, Turkmenistan, and Uzbekistan. Some linguists include Japanese and Korean in the Altaic family. Chinese is the major language of the Sino-Tibetan family, which also includes Burmese, Lao, Thai, and Tibetan. Such southeastern Asian languages as Khmer and Vietnamese are in the Mon-Khmer family. Most people on Southeast Asian islands speak Austronesian languages, including Indonesian, Malay, and Filipino. See **Language** (Language families).

Way of life in Southwest Asia

Southwest Asia covers about 2,755,000 square miles (7,137,000 square kilometers), or 16 percent of the continent. It includes the 7 nations of the Arabian Peninsula and 12 nations north and east of the peninsula.

Saudi Arabia, which is the region's largest nation in size, covers about two-thirds of the Arabian Peninsula. The other peninsular nations are Bahrain, Kuwait, Oman,

Qatar, the United Arab Emirates, and Yemen. The nations that lie outside the peninsula include Afghanistan, Armenia, Azerbaijan, Cyprus, Georgia, Iran, Iraq, Israel, Jordan, Lebanon, Syria, and Turkey. Small parts of Azerbaijan, Georgia, and Turkey are in Europe, but these countries lie mainly in Asia. Southwest Asia also includes the Sinai Peninsula, which is the northeast corner of the African country of Egypt, and the disputed regions known as the Gaza Strip and the West Bank.

Where the people of Asia live

More people live in Asia than on any other continent. This map shows where they live and where the largest Asian cities are. The heavily populated areas are shown in the darkest color. Most of the people live in areas where the climate is favorable and the land is suitable for farming.

Persons per mi²	Persons per km²
More than 250	More than 97
125 to 250	48 to 97
25 to 125	10 to 48
2 to 25	1 to 10
Less than 2	Less than 1

Major urban centers

● More than 10 million inhabitants

● 5 million to 10 million inhabitants

○ Less than 5 million inhabitants

WORLD BOOK map

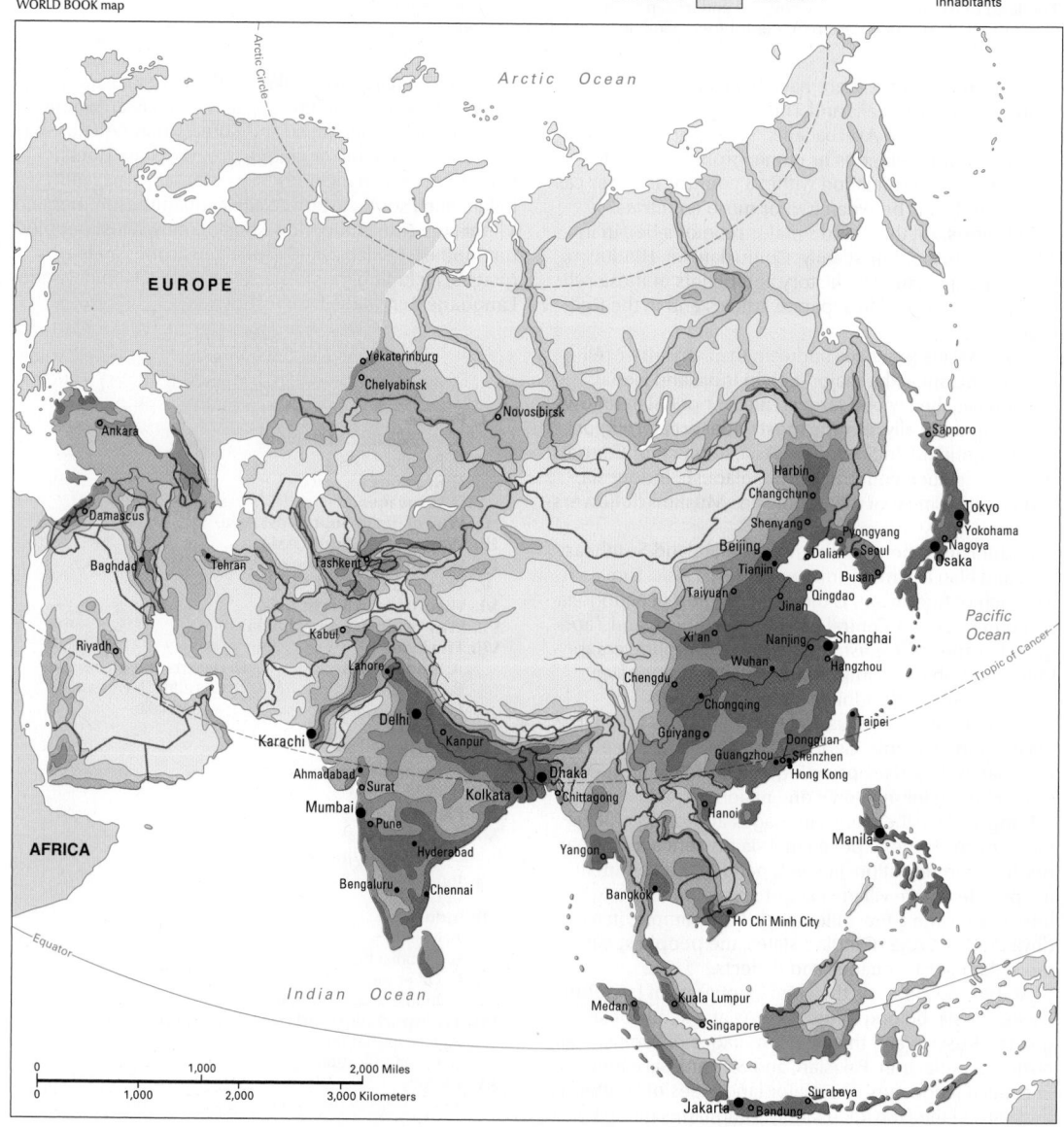

Independent countries of Asia*

Map key	Name	Area In mi²	Area In km²	Population[†]	Capital	Date of independence
G 6	Afghanistan	251,827	652,230	40,803,000	Kabul	‡
E 5	Armenia	11,484	29,743	2,978,000	Yerevan	1991
E 5	Azerbaijan (Asian)	27,915	72,300	7,196,000	Baku	1991
G 5	Bahrain	300	778	1,632,000	Manama	1971
H 8	Bangladesh	56,977	147,570	168,166,000	Dhaka	1971
H 8	Bhutan	14,824	38,394	765,000	Thimphu	‡
J 11	Brunei	2,226	5,765	469,000	Bandar Seri Begawan	1984
I 10	Cambodia	69,898	181,035	17,221,000	Phnom Penh	1953
G 10	China	3,697,002	9,575,191	1,421,566,000	Beijing	‡
F 4	Cyprus	3,572	9,251	1,226,000	Nicosia	1960
K 13	East Timor	5,774	14,954	1,376,000	Dili	2002
F 3	Egypt (Asian)	23,442	60,714	548,000	Cairo	‡
E 5	Georgia (Asian)	21,260	55,063	3,345,000	Tbilisi	1991
H 7	India	1,222,548	3,166,384	1,355,491,000	New Delhi	1947
K 11	Indonesia (Asian)	572,479	1,482,714	271,506,000	Jakarta	1949
G 5	Iran	636,372	1,648,195	86,021,000	Tehran	‡
F 4	Iraq	167,975	435,052	42,053,000	Baghdad	‡
F 4	Israel	8,522	22,072	9,521,000	Jerusalem	1948
F 12	Japan	145,937	377,974	125,291,000	Tokyo	‡
F 4	Jordan	34,495	89,342	10,852,000	Amman	1946
E 7	Kazakhstan (Asian)	1,005,487	2,604,200	18,702,000	Nur-Sultan	1991
F 11	Korea, North	46,540	120,538	26,022,000	Pyongyang	1948
F 11	Korea, South	38,741	100,339	51,967,000	Seoul	1948
G 5	Kuwait	6,880	17,818	4,591,000	Kuwait	1961
F 7	Kyrgyzstan	77,201	199,949	6,762,000	Bishkek	1991
I 10	Laos	91,429	236,800	7,455,000	Vientiane	1953
F 4	Lebanon	4,036	10,452	5,566,000	Beirut	‡
J 10	Malaysia	127,724	330,803	33,505,000	Kuala Lumpur	1957
J 6	Maldives	115	298	557,000	Male	1965
F 9	Mongolia	603,909	1,564,116	3,464,000	Ulaanbaatar	‡
H 9	Myanmar	261,228	676,577	55,273,000	Naypyidaw	1948
H 8	Nepal	56,827	147,181	30,972,000	Kathmandu	‡
H 5	Oman	119,499	309,500	4,895,000	Muscat	‡
G 6	Pakistan	341,311	883,992	230,041,000	Islamabad	1947
I 12	Philippines	115,831	300,000	111,861,000	Manila	1946
G 5	Qatar	4,473	11,586	2,809,000	Doha	1971
D 8	Russia (Asian)	4,937,801	12,788,846	32,181,000	Moscow	1991
G 4	Saudi Arabia	830,000	2,149,690	35,937,000	Riyadh	‡
K 10	Singapore	278	719	5,793,000	Singapore	1965
J 7	Sri Lanka	25,332	65,610	22,2577,000	Sri Jayewardene-pura Kotte	1948
F 4	Syria	71,498	185,180	19,774,000	Damascus	1946
H 11	Taiwan[§]	13,905	36,015	23,681,000	Taipei	‡
F 7	Tajikistan	54,810	141,958	9,728,000	Dushanbe	1991
I 10	Thailand	198,117	513,120	70,223,000	Bangkok	‡
E 4	Turkey (Asian)	293,415	759,941	76,423,000	Ankara	‡
F 6	Turkmenistan	188,456	488,100	6,135,000	Ashgabat	1991
G 5	United Arab Emirates	32,278	83,600	10,151,000	Abu Dhabi	1971
F 6	Uzbekistan	172,742	447,400	34,985,000	Tashkent	1991
I 10	Vietnam	127,891	331,236	99,256,000	Hanoi	1954
H 4	Yemen	203,850	527,968	31,055,000	Sanaa	‡

Dependencies in Asia*

Map key	Name	Area In mi²	Area In km²	Population[†]	Capital	Status
F 4[#]	Gaza Strip	139	360	2,050,000	Gaza	Transitional**
F 4[#]	West Bank	2,263	5,860	2,950,000	—	Transitional††

*Each country and dependency listed has a separate article in *World Book.*
†Populations are current estimates based on the latest figures from official government, United Nations, and other sources.
‡See the article on this country for details of its history. Dates are shown only for those countries that gained independence after World War II.

§Claimed by China.
#Not on map; key shows general location.
**Administered by the Palestinian Authority; Israel controls Gaza's borders and airspace.

††Part of the West Bank administered by the Palestinian Authority; external security and foreign affairs controlled by Israel; other parts occupied by Israel.

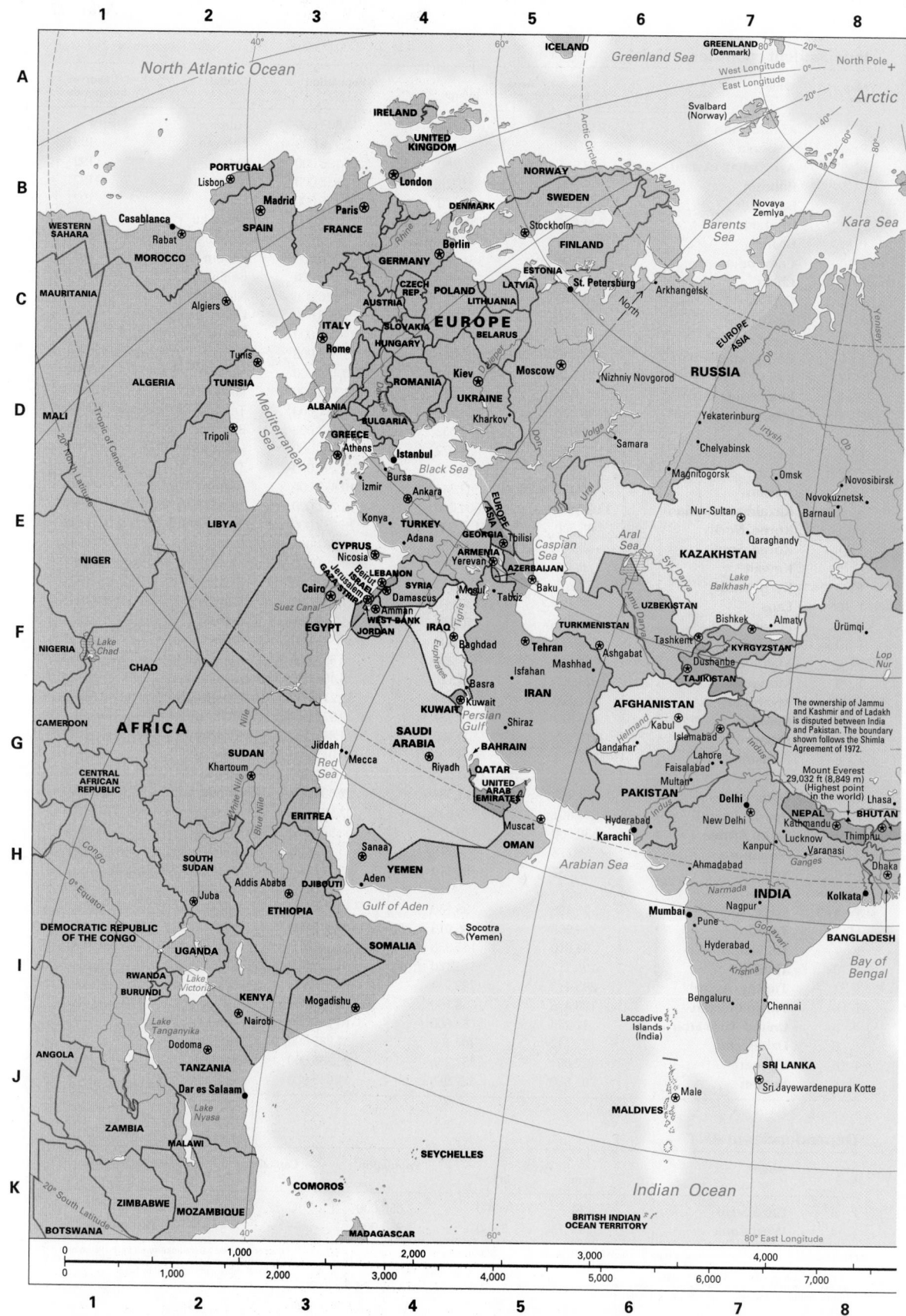

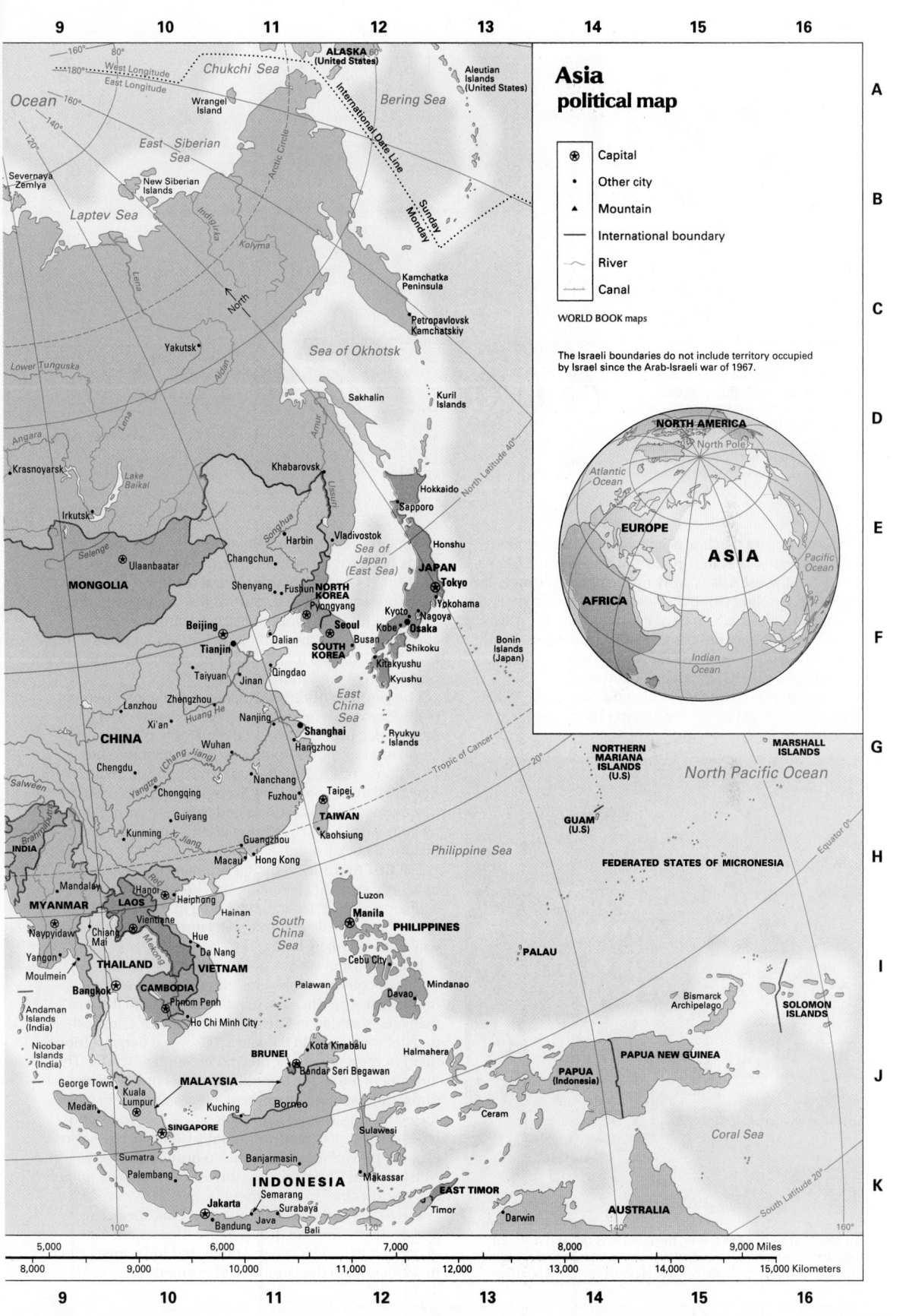

9 **10** **11** **12** **13** **14** **15** **16**

Ocean 160° West Longitude 80° 60° *Chukchi Sea* ALASKA (United States) Aleutian Islands (United States) **A**
180° East Longitude International Date Line *Bering Sea*
140° Wrangel Island
160° *East Siberian Sea* New Siberian Islands Sunday Monday **B**
Severnaya Zemlya 120° Arctic Circle
Laptev Sea Indigirka Kolyma Kamchatka Peninsula **C**
Lower Tunguska Lena North Petropavlovsk Kamchatskiy
Angara Yakutsk *Sea of Okhotsk* **D**
Krasnoyarsk Lake Baikal Aldan Amur Sakhalin Khabarovsk Kuril Islands

9 **10** **11** **12** **13** **14** **15** **16**

Asia
political map

⊛ Capital
• Other city
▲ Mountain
— International boundary
〜 River
〜 Canal

WORLD BOOK maps

The Israeli boundaries do not include territory occupied
by Israel since the Arab-Israeli war of 1967.

NORTH AMERICA
North Pole
Atlantic Ocean
EUROPE
ASIA
Pacific Ocean
AFRICA
Indian Ocean

Irkutsk Selenge Songhua Harbin Vladivostok Hokkaido Sapporo Honshu **E**
Ulaanbaatar Changchun *Sea of Japan (East Sea)* JAPAN Tokyo
MONGOLIA Shenyang Fushun NORTH KOREA Kyoto Nagoya Yokohama **F**
Beijing Dalian Pyongyang Kobe Osaka
Tianjin Taiyuan Jinan Seoul Busan Shikoku
Lanzhou Zhengzhou Qingdao SOUTH KOREA Kitakyushu Bonin Islands (Japan)
Xi'an Huang He Nanjing Kyushu
CHINA Wuhan Shanghai *East China Sea* **G**
Chengdu Yangtze (Chang Jiang) Hangzhou Ryukyu Islands MARSHALL ISLANDS
Salween Chongqing Nanchang Tropic of Cancer 20° NORTHERN MARIANA ISLANDS (U.S) *North Pacific Ocean*
Guiyang Fuzhou Taipei
Brahmaputra Kunming Xi Jiang Guangzhou TAIWAN GUAM (U.S) **H**
INDIA Macau Hong Kong Kaohsiung *Philippine Sea* FEDERATED STATES OF MICRONESIA
Mandalay Hanoi Hainan Luzon
MYANMAR LAOS Haiphong *South China Sea* Manila PALAU Equator 0°
Naypyidaw Vientiane Hue Da Nang **PHILIPPINES** **I**
Yangon Chiang Mai **THAILAND** **VIETNAM** Cebu City Bismarck Archipelago SOLOMON ISLANDS
Moulmein Mekong Palawan Davao Mindanao
Andaman Islands (India) Bangkok **CAMBODIA** Phnom Penh Kota Kinabalu
Nicobar Islands (India) Ho Chi Minh City BRUNEI Halmahera PAPUA NEW GUINEA **J**
George Town Kuala Lumpur **MALAYSIA** Bandar Seri Begawan PAPUA (Indonesia)
Medan Kuching Borneo Ceram *Coral Sea*
Sumatra SINGAPORE Sulawesi
Palembang Banjarmasin Makassar EAST TIMOR **K**
Jakarta Semarang **INDONESIA** Timor AUSTRALIA South Latitude 20°
100° Bandung Surabaya Java Bali 120° Darwin 140° 160°

5,000 6,000 7,000 8,000 9,000 Miles
8,000 9,000 10,000 11,000 12,000 13,000 14,000 15,000 Kilometers

9 **10** **11** **12** **13** **14** **15** **16**

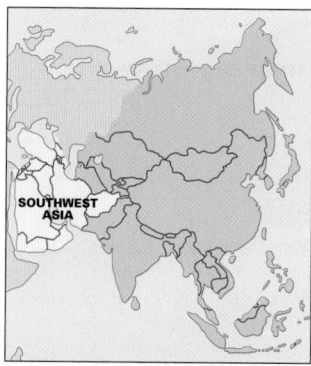

Deserts, such as this one in Kuwait, cover much of Southwest Asia. These dry lands are difficult to farm, but much oil lies under them. Income from oil raises living standards and helps modernize the region. But many peoples still follow traditional ways of life and, like their ancestors, travel the deserts with their animals.

WORLD BOOK map; photo from John Lewis Stage, Photo Researchers

Desert covers much of Southwest Asia. Little rain falls, and water is scarce in most of the region. Even so, many Southwest Asians work on farms. The farmers live crowded together along the seacoasts and in river and mountain valleys, which have enough water for growing crops. The region's deserts are thinly populated. Southwest Asia has a population density of only 146 people per square mile (56 per square kilometer).

A shortage of good farmland and a lack of big industrial cities in most of Southwest Asia have made economic progress difficult. But the land—even the desert—holds hope for the future. It yields huge quantities of oil, the region's most valuable natural resource. Southwest Asian governments use some of the oil income to fight poverty. They also work to increase farm production and to bring industry to their nations. Rapid population growth has forced many countries of the region to import much of their food.

The people. About 400 million people, or 9 percent of all Asians, live in Southwest Asia. Members of the Arab ethnic group make up the majority of the population in 11 of the 19 Southwest Asian nations. These 11 nations are the 7 of the Arabian Peninsula, plus Iraq, Jordan, Lebanon, and Syria. The millions of Arabs throughout Southwest Asia and North Africa are united by language (Arabic), religion (Islam), and cultural and historical background.

The first Arabs lived on the Arabian Peninsula and in nearby areas in ancient times. The Islamic prophet Muhammad was an Arab who died in A.D. 632. His followers spread Islam, the Arabic language, and the Arab way of life to many lands.

Israel, most of whose people are Jews, lies among the Arab countries. Like the Arabs, Jews have lived in Southwest Asia since ancient times. Through the years, many Jews settled in Europe, North America, and other parts of the world. In the late 1800's, Jews began a movement to reestablish a homeland in Southwest Asia. This movement led to the founding of Israel in 1948. The Arabs opposed the creation of a Jewish nation in what they considered Arab land. Ever since, the Arabs and Israelis have quarreled and fought. Conflicts have also erupted between various Muslim groups and between Muslims and Christians. Southwest Asia remains one of the world's chief trouble spots.

The Arabs and Jews of Southwest Asia speak languages in the Semitic group of the Afro-Asiatic language family. Arabs speak Arabic, and Jews speak Hebrew. People in the countries of northern Southwest

Sid Latham, Photo Researchers

In much of Southwest Asia, the climate is hot and dry, and large areas of land are sandy desert. Many Arabs in the region use camels to carry them over the shifting sands of the desert.

Asia—Afghanistan, Armenia, Azerbaijan, Cyprus, Georgia, Iran, and Turkey—speak Indo-European and Turkic languages.

The ancestors of the Afghans, Azerbaijanis, Iranians, and Turks came mainly from Central Asia. The Armenians and Georgians are descended from ancient peoples of the Caucasus Mountain region. About 80 percent of the people on the island of Cyprus are Greeks, and Turks make up the other 20 percent of the population of Cyprus.

Religions. Christianity, Islam, and Judaism began in Southwest Asia. Today, the majority of people in most of the Southwest Asian nations practice Islam. However, Christianity is the chief religion of Armenia, Cyprus, and Georgia. Judaism is the chief religion of Israel.

Country life. About a fourth of Southwest Asia's people work on farms. Also, thousands of nomads move through the deserts and mountains of Asia herding camels, goats, and sheep. Most farmers and nomads follow ways of life that have roots deep in the past. Many people wear clothing similar to that of their ancestors. For example, many Arab men wear long, flowing robes and a draping cloth that covers the head and neck.

Like their ancestors, most of the farmers do not own the land they work. Instead, they rent it from wealthy landlords or the state. Machinery is gradually replacing traditional tools, and farmers grow cash crops in addition to crops for their family. Farm families eat foods made from such grain crops as barley and wheat. Other important foods include dates, olives, and other fruits.

Some Southwest Asian farmers live on the outskirts of urban areas. Many others live in small villages near the land they work. A typical village consists of about 50 houses crowded together along narrow streets. Dried mud and adobe are traditional building materials, but modern materials are increasingly used. Some villages have a public bathhouse, and a teahouse where men gather to discuss community affairs. But many villages have only one public building—a *mosque* (Islamic house of worship).

Southwest Asian nomads rely almost entirely on their animals for the necessities of life. They live in tents made from camel or goat hair. Their food includes cheese, meat, and milk, all of which come from their animals. Many nomads make their clothing from animal hair and skins. The nomads move about, looking for pasture for their herds. Occasionally—perhaps once a year—a nomad visits a city or town to sell cheese, meat, skins, and wool and to buy supplies. The number of nomads has declined as many have settled in villages and towns, sometimes under pressure from their governments.

Many rural Southwest Asian women—especially Arab women—remain at home most of the time, as their female ancestors did. These women both keep house and take part in outdoor chores, such as harvesting crops or milking animals. When they appear in public, they cover their faces with a veil.

Social relationships in rural Southwest Asia are also based on traditions. Most farm and nomad families live in *extended families*. Grandparents, parents, unmarried children, and married sons and their families all live together. The oldest male in the family has authority over the rest of the family. He also has the responsibility for the well-being of the entire group.

Outside the family, a farmer's strongest ties are to the village, and a nomad's are to the tribe. A chief and a council of elders govern most villages. These officials settle disputes between families. Most nomad tribes consist of many families related on the male side. The tribal leader, called a *sheikh* in Arab countries, is usually the wealthiest member of the group. The leader settles disputes between families and often provides aid for needy members of the tribe.

In the past, many farmers and most nomads had little or nothing to do with their national government. They viewed government officials as outsiders without power in village or tribal matters. Many Southwest Asian gov-

© Mian Kursheed, Reuters

Muslims make up the largest religious group in Southwest Asia. A Muslim's religious life centers around a house of worship called a *mosque*. Some mosques, including this one in Islamabad, Pakistan, are famous for their beautiful decorations.

ernments have worked to establish more contact with their rural people and to teach modern agricultural techniques to farmers. They have also established schools and medical clinics in rural communities.

In rural Southwest Asia, radios and televisions have become more common. However, in these remote corners, people must use satellite dishes to receive TV signals beamed from satellites high above Earth.

Rural life in Israel differs greatly from that in other nations of Southwest Asia. Many Israeli farmers live in a collective community called a *kibbutz,* in which the farmers share all property and combine their labor. Other Israeli farmers belong to a cooperative community called a *moshav.* On a moshav, the farmers own their own land and homes but purchase equipment and other goods as a group.

City life. Since the 1950's, the cities of Southwest Asia have grown tremendously. The three largest cities of Southwest Asia are Baghdad, Iraq; Tehran, Iran; and Is-

tanbul, Turkey. However, most of the city of Istanbul lies in Europe. Riyadh, Saudi Arabia, is the largest city of the Arabian Peninsula. There are more urban people than rural people in each of the countries of Southwest Asia, except Afghanistan and Yemen.

Many Southwest Asian cities present a sharp contrast between the old and the new. They include an old section, which dates back hundreds of years, and a modern section. The old sections have long been trading centers where farmers, nomads, and merchants exchange goods and where craftworkers make and sell handcrafted articles. Much of this activity takes place in crowded trading and shopping centers called *bazaars* or *suqs.* Some of these are open-air markets, while others are covered. The covered bazaar in Istanbul, which was built in the mid-1400's, contains more than 4,000 shops. The houses in the old sections are small and jammed tightly together. Old sections of Muslim cities feature beautiful mosques.

In the modern sections of Southwest Asian cities, tall apartment and office buildings rise along wide streets. Some cities have industrial plants, such as factories and oil refineries.

Social changes have also come to the cities of Southwest Asia. New jobs have opened up for business people, factory workers, government workers, physicians, teachers, and others. Most of the governments have expanded their school systems to train people for new job opportunities. The extended family has become much less common in the cities than in rural areas.

Women in cities have more freedom than do women in rural areas. In most countries, old customs—such as wearing a veil in public—have been challenged. In Iran and Saudi Arabia, however, conservative Muslims continue to enforce old customs.

Education. The *literacy rate* (percentage of people over 15 years old who can read and write) varies widely from country to country in Southwest Asia. In Armenia, Azerbaijan, Georgia, and Israel, almost all adults can read and write.

Historically, most Southwest Asian children received little or no schooling. Boys learned a craft, farming, or herding from their fathers, and girls learned housekeeping and craft skills from their mothers. But during the mid-1900's, most Southwest Asian nations built many new schools, especially in the cities. Today, almost all city children attend primary school and many go to secondary school. More children than ever go on to a college or technical school. Educational progress has been much slower in rural Southwest Asia than in the cities, though most children attend primary school. In much of Southwest Asia, education is encouraged more for males than for females.

The arts. The best-known art of Southwest Asia is Islamic art. This term refers to an art style developed by the Arabs and adopted by the many peoples they conquered. Islamic art flourished from the mid-700's to about 1700 and then declined. However, since the late 1900's, interest in Islamic art has increased.

Architectural works—especially mosques—rank as the most famous examples of Islamic art. Islamic artists also created beautiful bookbindings and illustrations, ceramics, glassware, metalware, rugs, textiles, and sculptures. Islamic religious leaders prohibited artists from depict-

Photographic Library of Australia

Skilled craftworkers in Southwest Asia produce a variety of goods that are prized by people in many parts of the world. These craftworkers in Jordan weave an Oriental rug, a kind of rug that is valued for its high quality and beauty. The rug has elaborate designs, for which Islamic art is famous.

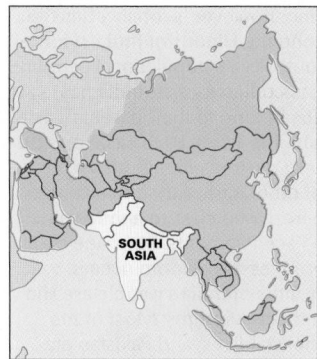

A South Asian farmer gets advice from a government farm expert. In an effort to reduce the widespread poverty that exists in their countries, South Asian governments try to teach farmers about new seeds and fertilizers and improved agricultural methods. This scene is in India, South Asia's largest country.

WORLD BOOK map; WORLD BOOK photo

ing human beings and animals. Instead of drawing people and animals, artists developed a style of decoration that consisted of elaborate patterns of winding stems, leaves, and other objects. See **Islamic art.**

Many Southwest Asian decorative artists, including potters and rug makers, still use the traditional Islamic style. But authors have modernized Southwest Asian literature. In the past, most authors wrote about life among the nobility and royalty. Today, however, many writers deal with life among the common people. In 2006, the Turkish writer Orhan Pamuk won the Nobel Prize in literature for his novels set in Turkey.

Way of life in South Asia

South Asia covers about 1,720,000 square miles (4,450,000 square kilometers), or 10 percent of the continent. India occupies about 70 percent of this region, and Pakistan makes up about 20 percent. Pakistan borders India to the northwest. South Asia also includes five smaller nations. These nations are Bangladesh, along India's eastern border; Bhutan and Nepal, high in the mountains along India's northeast border; and Sri Lanka and the Maldives, island countries that lie south of India in the Indian Ocean.

South Asia ranks among the world's most crowded places. About 1 ⅖ billion people live there—nearly two-fifths of all Asians and about one-fourth of all the people in the world. The region's population density of 1,053 people per square mile (406 per square kilometer) is about 8 times the world average. The Indian cities of Kolkata and Mumbai are two of the most densely populated cities in the world. The population density is high even in many rural regions, particularly in the northern plains of India, South Asia's chief farming area.

South Asia has much fertile farmland. In addition, there are many large cities, which are thriving and growing fast. In the 1990's and early 2000's, many South Asian countries had a surge in economic growth. However, hundreds of millions of people still live in poverty,

particularly in the lower Ganges Valley and Bangladesh.

The people. About 75 percent of South Asia's people live in India. More than 10 percent live in Pakistan, and a similar percentage also live in Bangladesh.

India's two largest groups are the Indo-Aryans and the Dravidians. Most of the Indo-Aryans live in northern India. The majority of the Dravidians live in the south. The ancestors of the Indo-Aryans invaded India from Central Asia about 1500 B.C. These people are known as the Aryans. The Aryans conquered the Dravidians in northern India and drove some of them south.

The many groups that make up Pakistan's population include people of Afghan, Arabic, Aryan, Dravidian, Persian, and Turkish origin. Other South Asian peoples include the Sinhalese of Sri Lanka, whose ancestors came from northern India, and the Maldivians, a people whose ancestors came from southern India, Sri Lanka, eastern Africa, and Arabia. The Tamils of Sri Lanka are descendants of people from southern India. The Nepalese have ancestors who include both Aryans and people from Tibet and Mongolia.

The people of South Asia are divided along the lines of religion, language, and social class. Differences between Hindus and Muslims—the region's two major religious groups—have often led to conflict and violence. These differences even led to the creation in 1947 of a new nation, Pakistan. In an attempt to end the bloodshed between Hindus and Muslims, the United Kingdom, which then controlled India, divided it into two nations—India for Hindus and Pakistan for Muslims. East Pakistan became the independent nation of Bangladesh in 1971.

Language differences also have far-reaching effects among the people of South Asia. Most states of India, for example, consist chiefly of people who speak the same language. The Indian government changed state boundaries and created new states to give certain language groups their own states.

In general, social class divides people throughout

South Asia. Social standing, however, probably has the greatest importance among the Hindus of India, who make up a majority of South Asia's population. Each Hindu belongs to a social class called a *caste*. India has about 3,000 castes. Hindus belong to their parents' caste and find it hard to join a higher caste. Each caste in India has its own customs. These customs limit both social contact with members of other castes and the extent to which people can move from one class to another through their actions and achievements. Marriage between members of different castes seldom occurs.

Religions. About four-fifths of India's people are Hindus, and more than a tenth are Muslims. Most of the people of Bangladesh, the Maldives, and Pakistan are Muslims. Sri Lanka has a mixture of Buddhists, Christians, Hindus, and Muslims. In Nepal, about 90 percent of the people are Hindus, and most of the others are Buddhists. About two-thirds of Bhutan's people are Buddhists, and a majority of the rest are Hindus.

Country life. About two-thirds of the people of South Asia live in villages and work on nearby farms. The majority of South Asian farmers own a small piece of land, but some rent land from wealthy landlords.

Some farms in South Asia employ modern agricultural tools and methods, but many of the farmers still use the same kinds of tools and farming methods as their ancestors used hundreds of years ago. Large numbers of South Asian farmers must struggle just to raise enough to feed their own families. Most South Asian farm families include not only several children but also the other members of an extended family.

South Asians get most of their food from rice, wheat, millet, barley, and other grains, and from such vegetables as beans and peas. Many Hindus eat no meat. They believe all animals have a soul and must not be killed.

The clothing worn by rural South Asians varies from region to region. Many people wear a large piece of cloth wrapped around the body. Women's garments of this kind are called *saris*. Some men cover their heads with a turban.

The houses of a typical South Asian village stand close together. Most of them are small and made of sun-dried bricks or mud. A wall surrounds each house in many villages, giving the people a little extra privacy.

There is much contact between rural and urban South Asia. Government officials often go to villages to teach the people how to use modern fertilizers, plows, and seeds. The government also sets up health clinics, schools, roads, and irrigation systems in rural areas.

The struggle to improve the people's lives faces many difficulties. South Asian governments lack great wealth. But even if they had much wealth, they would be hard-pressed to end poverty quickly. In addition, many rural South Asians are proud of their customs and traditions and feel reluctant to change the way they live and work. However, the economic growth and modernization of urban areas holds promise for the future of the region.

City life. Although South Asia is chiefly a rural region, it has many large cities. Delhi, Kolkata, and Mumbai in India; Karachi in Pakistan; and Dhaka in Bangladesh rank as the biggest. Many other cities in India and Pakistan also have more than a million people.

Few places present so sharp a contrast between old and new—and between the wealthy and the poor—as do

© Jeremy Richards, Dreamstime

Hindus bathe in the Ganges River at Varanasi, India. Hindus consider the Ganges River sacred. They believe they purify themselves spiritually by bathing in its waters.

WORLD BOOK photo

An Indian schoolroom is used by two groups of children at the same time. The teacher instructs older children in writing while younger children play with educational toys.

the cities of South Asia. The United Kingdom ruled most of the region from the late 1700's to the mid-1900's. During this colonial period, British citizens occupied much of the housing in the sections they had built.

South Asian governments continued to build up the cities after the various nations became independent. Today, middle-class and wealthy South Asians, including business people, doctors, government officials, and lawyers, live primarily in the newest sections.

South Asia's cities include many slums. Millions of people in these slums live in cheap, crowded apartments and in shacks made of pieces of metal, wood, or cloth. The slums in some cities are so crowded and poverty is so widespread that thousands of people have nowhere to live at all. They sleep in doorways, on sidewalks, or in any other place they can find.

South Asian governments are trying to improve city life as well as rural life. Their efforts include slum clearance and construction programs to provide better housing. However, sometimes these slum clearance programs do not benefit those people living there. The governments also sponsor programs to expand industry and provide more jobs—and to train unskilled workers for those jobs. But the cost of improving any city is high, and the problems are many. High birth rates rank among the major problems. Also, thousands of rural people move to the cities each year in search of a better life. Many end up no better off than they were before.

Education. More than 90 percent of Sri Lanka's adults can read and write. However, some countries in the region have low literacy rates. Large numbers of children never go to school at all, either because no school is nearby or because they must work to help support their families.

Since the mid-1900's, the South Asian governments have built many new schools. More children now attend school than ever before, and literacy rates are improving. But the governments have found it difficult to build enough schools and to train enough teachers to serve their enormous populations.

The arts. South Asia has a rich and varied artistic tradition. In ancient times, the Aryans produced outstanding literature. Numerous Aryan literary works contributed to the development of Hinduism. Such writings included the epics the *Mahabharata* and the *Ramayana* and the philosophical works called the Vedas and the Upanishads. The Aryans composed their works in Sanskrit, the first Indo-European language with a literature.

Three religions—Buddhism, Islam, and Hinduism—influenced the arts of South Asia. Major Buddhist works include many beautiful sculptures of Buddha, founder of the religion. The Muslims made their major contribution in the field of Islamic architecture. A giant tomb in this style, the magnificent Taj Mahal, is one of the world's most beautiful buildings. Many Hindu stone temples are richly decorated with sculptures of gods.

Other important arts in South Asia include dance and music. The highly symbolic movements in South Asian dances tell stories and are included in many dramas. South Asian music sounds strange to many Western people because it uses a different scale than does music of the West. South Asian people play much of their music on stringed instruments, such as the lute, sitar, and vina. The flute and the *tabla*, a type of drum, are also

T. S. Satyan, Black Star

Whirling Bhutanese dancers perform in colorful costumes. Dance ranks among South Asia's major arts. The highly symbolic movements in the dances tell stories, usually religious ones.

important instruments in the music of South Asia.

During the colonial period, the British introduced forms of Western art—including Western architecture and the novel—into South Asia. Today, the art of the region shows the influence of both traditional South Asian art and Western art.

A reversal of the West's influence on South Asian culture occurred during the mid-1900's. At that time, South Asian art and philosophy began to attract many people in the West. Sitar music, a physical and mental exercise called *yoga*, and Hindu religious teachers called *gurus* became especially popular. The attraction to South Asian culture was most widespread among young people of the West.

Way of life in Southeast Asia

Southeast Asia covers about 1,573,000 square miles (4,073,000 square kilometers), or 9 percent of the continent. The area has an average of 428 people per square mile (165 per square kilometer)—about three times the world average. The region includes the peninsula east of India and south of China, and thousands of islands south and east of the peninsula.

Eleven independent nations make up Southeast Asia. Five of them—Cambodia, Laos, Myanmar, Thailand, and Vietnam—lie on the peninsula. Malaysia lies partly on the peninsula and partly on the island of Borneo. Brunei also lies on Borneo. Indonesia and the Philippines both consist of thousands of islands, and Singapore is made up of one large island and about 50 smaller islands. East Timor takes up about half of Timor Island, the rest of which is part of Indonesia. Geographers consider far eastern Indonesia to be part of Oceania rather than part of Asia.

Southeast Asia has a wealth of natural resources. Forests cover much of the land, valuable minerals lie be-

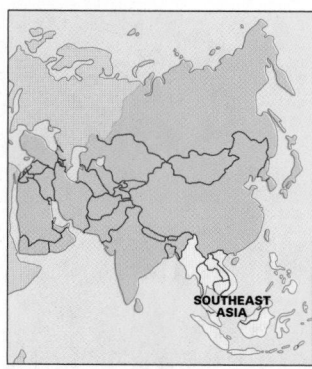

Fields of rice—such as these in Indonesia—cover a large part of the Southeast Asian countryside. Southeast Asia has much fertile soil and plenty of water from rivers and rainfall. The soil and water are natural resources that help farmers in the region grow large amounts of rice and other agricultural products.

WORLD BOOK map; photo from Herta Newton, Van Cleve Photography

neath it, and fish are plentiful in the coastal waters. Much of the soil is fertile, and the rivers and rainfall provide plenty of water.

Europeans had established trading outposts in Southeast Asia as early as the 1500's. In the 1700's, Europeans began taking control of Southeast Asia. By the late 1800's, only Thailand remained free of European rule. Many Southeast Asians resented colonialism and fought for independence. These nations began to win independence after World War II ended in 1945.

The people. About 675 million people, or 15 percent of all Asians, live in Southeast Asia. About half live in rural areas, but millions live in large, crowded cities.

The ancestors of most Southeast Asians came to the region from Central Asia and southern China during prehistoric and ancient times. They drove the original inhabitants of the region into the mountains and other remote areas. Today, descendants of the original inhabitants live in those remote areas. Through the years, thousands of people from China and India settled in Southeast Asia. These people control much of the region's business activity.

Fighting has taken place within and between nations in Southeast Asia, especially as groups there have battled over control of the best land. Through much of the 1900's, political differences between Communists and non-Communists caused sharp divisions and even fighting among Southeast Asians. The fighting divided the people and stalled economic progress. In 1954, for example, Communists came to power in North Vietnam. A United States-backed government ruled South Vietnam. In 1975—after years of bitter fighting—the Communists took over South Vietnam, Cambodia, and Laos. In 1976, North and South Vietnam united as Vietnam.

In the 1980's, relations between Southeast Asian nations—both Communist and non-Communist—began to improve. By 2000, all of the nations of the region belonged to an economic and political organization known as the Association of Southeast Asian Nations (ASEAN).

Religions. Buddhism is the chief religion on the peninsula. Islam began in Arabia and spread all the way to Southeast Asia. Today, it ranks as the chief religion in Indonesia, Malaysia, and Brunei. Christianity became the major faith of the Philippines during the period of Spanish rule, and it remains so today.

Many Southeast Asians, especially rural people, mix these religious beliefs and practices with *animism,* the belief that everything in nature has a spirit. These people believe that good and bad spirits cause good and bad fortune. Some farmers perform traditional religious ceremonies in the hope that the spirits will bring a bountiful harvest. Some of these farmers build small boxes resembling birdhouses on the tops of poles in their rice fields. In the boxes, they put cloth, food, incense, paper, and other offerings to the spirits.

Country life. The majority of Southeast Asians live in small villages and work on farms. Many Southeast Asian farmers, like farmers elsewhere in Asia, use traditional agricultural methods. They plant by hand and harvest with sickles and other hand tools. Many use water buffaloes to pull large rakelike tools that plow the *paddies* (rice fields). However, the use of modern farm machines, high-yielding seeds, and chemical fertilizers and pesticides is becoming more common. Rice is the major crop and chief food throughout the majority of Southeast Asia.

A typical farm village in this region has from 25 to 30 houses, made mostly of bamboo and wood. Many rural Southeast Asians build their houses on raised platforms for protection against insects, wild animals, and heavy rains. The space under the platforms provides shelter for household animals. Almost all villages on the Southeast Asian peninsula include a pagoda or some other Buddhist shrine.

The clothing of Southeast Asia varies widely. Traditionally, farmers wore straw hats to protect them from the sun. Burmese, Indonesians, Malaysians, and Thais wore colorful *sarongs* (skirts). Although traditional clothing is still popular, many Southeast Asians wear clothing like that of North Americans and Europeans.

Some Southeast Asians, especially islanders, work on large plantations owned by corporations, the government, or wealthy landowners. The plantations produce large quantities of coffee, copra, fruits and vegetables, palm oil, rubber, sugar cane, tea, and tobacco. Most of these products are exported.

Most of the mainland farmers own a small plot of land. Much of the land is fertile and, in good times, almost all the farmers can raise enough food to feed their families. Many have food left over that they sell. Some have begun planting cash crops, such as cashews, cotton, and jute. In general, farmers on the peninsula are better off than those on the islands. Good farmland is scarce on the islands, and a large number of farmers work on land that is owned by others.

Rural Southeast Asians maintain the custom of the extended family. But compared with Southwest Asia and South Asia, relationships between older and younger generations are less rigidly patterned. Social change has led to an increase in *nuclear families,* which consist only of parents and their children.

City life. Most of the nations of Southeast Asia have at least one big city, and some nations have several. Jakarta, in Indonesia, and Manila, in the Philippines, are two of the largest cities in the region.

Southeast Asian cities serve as centers of government and manufacturing and as links between the rural areas and the rest of the world. Farm products, lumber, minerals, and other goods go from the rural areas to the cities to be shipped abroad. Goods from other countries pass through the cities before being sent on to the rural areas. Manufacturing takes place in many of the region's cities. Such large cities as Manila in the Philippines, Jakarta in Indonesia, Bangkok in Thailand, Ho Chi Minh City in Vietnam, and Kuala Lumpur in Malaysia are centers of manufacturing. Singapore is an important financial center.

Outsiders have long played important roles in Southeast Asian cities. During the 1800's, Chinese and Indian immigrants began taking over a large part of the retail trade in the cities. Today, in some countries, they are still retail leaders. The European colonial rulers also established businesses and governments in the cities and modernized cities with European-style buildings, services, and facilities.

Southeast Asians continued the modernization process after becoming independent. Many of the cities have luxury hotels, high-rise apartment and office buildings, and other modern features. But like cities everywhere, they include slums and other run-down areas.

Education varies widely in Southeast Asia, but the region as a whole has a high literacy rate. Since independence, governments have established many new schools and set up special programs to increase literacy. Indonesia, for example, has raised its literacy rate from less than 10 percent in 1945 to about 90 percent today.

The arts. Precolonial Southeast Asian art reveals much Indian and some Chinese influence. A large part of the art is religious and includes many Hindu and Buddhist monuments. Examples include the Hindu temples at Prambanan and the Buddhist temple Borobudur on the Indonesian island of Java, as well as small Buddhist temple-monasteries called *wats* in Thailand. Bali has a rich tradition of music, dance, and drama. The art of

Hermann Schlenker, Photo Researchers

A Buddhist monk in Thailand collects money from people at a religious celebration. He hangs it on a money tree. Buddhism is the major religion on the Southeast Asian peninsula.

batik—a decorative method of dyeing cloth—is a distinctive art form of Indonesia and Malaysia.

Way of life in East Asia

East Asia covers about 2,556,000 square miles (6,621,000 square kilometers), or 15 percent of the continent. The region includes most of China, the world's largest nation in population. Tibet, Qinghai, and Xinjiang, three thinly populated parts of western China, are in Central Asia.

China covers about 90 percent of East Asia, and it has about 85 percent of East Asia's people. Japan, North Korea, South Korea, and Taiwan are also part of East Asia.

More than 1 ⅔ billion people, or about 35 percent of all Asians and 20 percent of all the people in the world, live in East Asia. The region is one of the world's most crowded places. The population density of East Asia, 632 people per square mile (244 per square kilometer), is about five times the world average.

Off and on throughout history, China has ruled much of East Asia. The Chinese influence spread through the places the Chinese ruled and even to areas they did not rule. Chinese art strongly influenced art throughout East Asia. People throughout the region adopted Chinese religious and philosophical beliefs to some degree.

The Confucian system of ethics is probably the most important Chinese contribution to everyday life in East Asia. This system teaches the duties and manners of rulers and subjects toward each other, of family members toward one another, and of friends toward friends. The Confucian system emphasizes polite behavior and obe-

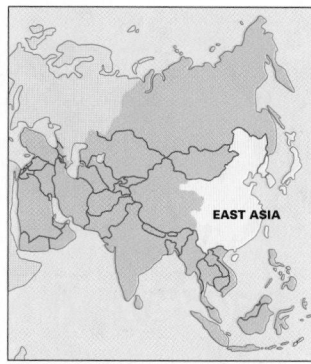

The Great Wall of China, built to keep out invaders, stretches thousands of miles across northern China. China covers about 90 percent of East Asia. Japan, North Korea, South Korea, and Taiwan make up the rest of the region.

WORLD BOOK map; photo © Susan Zheng from Peter Arnold, Inc.

dience to proper authority, two lasting characteristics of East Asian society.

The influence of China brought some unity to life in East Asia. However, the region has been sharply divided along political lines. China and Japan, the two largest nations in East Asia, have different political systems. A Communist government rules China, and the people have limited political freedom. Japan operates under democratic principles of government, and its people have much freedom.

Political differences divide China and Taiwan and also North Korea and South Korea. The Chinese Communists drove the Chinese Nationalists out of China in 1949. The Nationalists then established their government in Taiwan. Before World War II broke out in 1939, North Korea and South Korea were a single country. Today, Communists rule the north, and non-Communists govern the south. Troops have patrolled both sides of the border between North Korea and South Korea since the two countries fought each other during the Korean War (1950-1953).

The people. The first East Asian civilization began in China. Today, the Han ethnic group—many of whom are descendants of the early Chinese—make up a majority of China's people, except in the far north and west. In addition, Han people form a majority in Taiwan. The Koreans are an ancient people who have frequently come under Chinese rule.

People called the Ainu were among the first inhabitants of some of the islands that now make up Japan. But almost all of the people of Japan today are descended from Asian peoples who settled the country about 2,000 years ago.

Religions. The Chinese government tolerates religious activity, with some restrictions. Many Chinese still practice the traditional religion of their country. This religion—Buddhism combined with teachings of Confucianism and Taoism—is also the chief faith in Taiwan. Many Koreans practice Buddhism, but their religion also shows Confucian influences. Buddhism and Christianity

rank as the leading religions in South Korea. The North Korean government strongly discourages religion. Buddhism and Shinto are Japan's major faiths, and many Japanese combine the two. Confucianism influences religion in Japan, as it does elsewhere in East Asia.

Life in China. China has many large cities, including over 150 with a population of 1 million or more. Even so, it has always been an agricultural nation. About half of the people work on farms.

Most Chinese farm families live in two- or three-room houses. These homes are made of mud or clay brick and have a roof of tile or straw. Many city dwellers live in large apartment buildings. However, other city residents live in crowded apartments above stores or behind workshops. Still others live in old neighborhoods where the houses resemble those in rural areas. The Chinese eat mainly rice, wheat, and other grains—often made into such foods as noodles and dumplings—and many vegetables. Fish, pork, and poultry are their main sources of animal protein.

Only about 5 percent of China's people belong to the Communist Party. However, the party has almost complete control of the country—and it has the power to order sweeping changes in the people's way of life. In the early 1980's, for example, the Communists decreed that each married couple should have no more than one child. They hoped to limit China's population growth by this measure. Other major Communist goals include the elimination of social classes and the modernization of China's economy.

Property. After the Communists came to power in 1949, they took over most businesses and factories in China. They also *collectivized* China's agriculture—that is, they organized the peasants into groups who owned and farmed the land cooperatively. Initially, the farmers were required to give part of their crop to their collective and to sell a quota of farm products to the government at a fixed price. The government has gradually relaxed its requirements. Now many farm families are free to raise and sell crops as they choose. They can also

A fish market in Busan (also spelled *Pusan*), South Korea, operates in a way that is common in many parts of Asia. Sellers display their goods out-of-doors, and the customers inspect the goods carefully before buying. Fish markets are common throughout East Asia.

pass the rights to work a specific piece of land on to their descendants.

The government also encourages families to establish small businesses, such as stores, repair shops, and restaurants. Though the government still owns many large businesses, it has sold many other state-owned enterprises to individuals or companies, and large private corporations have grown rapidly.

Family life has always been important in Chinese society. In pre-Communist China, extended families were widespread. In such families, the oldest male had authority. Husbands ruled their wives, and parents expect-

ed obedience from their children. Today, most family units consist only of parents and children, though some also include grandparents. Relationships within families have become much less rigid, though many of the traditional rules are still followed.

In pre-Communist days, relatively few women worked outside the home. Today, nearly all adults have a job. In many families, a grandparent cares for the children during the day. Many other children stay in day-care centers while their parents work.

Social class. Confucian teachings gave the Chinese a respect for educated people. In pre-Communist China, a

A Japanese factory produces automobiles that will be exported to countries throughout the world. Factory workers in Japan manufacture a wide variety of goods for export and for use at home, helping to provide the Japanese people with one of the highest standards of living in the world.

© SuperStock

Hong Kong's skyline, crowded with skyscrapers and other commercial buildings, reflects the city's prosperity. Hong Kong is China's leading center of international trade and finance.

© Michele Burgess, The Stock Market

Rural houses in China are built of mud bricks, clay bricks, or stone. The majority of the Chinese people work on farms and live in rural villages, such as this one in Yunnan Province.

group of scholars who served as government officials ranked just below the emperor and his family in social importance. To become a scholar-official, a person had to learn Confucian philosophy thoroughly and pass difficult civil-service examinations. Other well-educated Chinese, including doctors, lawyers, and teachers, also had high social rank. The Communists, however, teach the principle of *egalitarianism.* According to this principle, all people, no matter what their occupation, have equal social rank. In practice, though, some groups of people—such as government officials—have much more power, wealth, and prestige than others.

The economy. China has some areas of good farmland, and it ranks among the leading producers of many crops. But China has such a large population that it must struggle to raise enough food for everyone.

The Chinese government has made great strides in reducing poverty through the modernization of the country's agriculture and industry. Chinese agricultural production has increased, but most farmers still use traditional tools and farming methods.

China's economy began to grow rapidly in the 1980's. Since then, China has greatly increased industrial production, and the country's standard of living has improved rapidly. But further growth will depend on China's acquiring new technology and training highly skilled workers and technicians.

Life in Japan differs greatly from that in most of the rest of Asia. About 90 percent of its people live in urban areas. Japan's cities are busy, modern centers of commerce and industry. Tokyo, the capital of Japan, is one of the world's largest cities. Tokyo is also the chief city in the heavily populated Tokyo-Yokohama urban area.

Japan ranks among the world's main industrial nations. Manufacturing has made the country an industrial giant. The Japanese have one of the world's highest standards of living. Most Japanese are employed in the industrial and service sectors. But Japan also has many small family farms, which the government protects with laws and *subsidies* (payments).

Japan's farms also reflect a modern way of life. Almost all Japanese farmers own their own land. The use of chemical fertilizers, farm machinery, and other advanced agricultural methods is more common in Japan than anywhere else in Asia. But most farms are small, and the government must provide financial assistance for many farms. Even so, many Japanese farmers have to seek part-time work outside the farm.

The Japanese, more than many other Asian peoples, have adopted features of Western life, especially American life. For example, baseball ranks as Japan's favorite sport, and neon signs light up many city streets. Some Japanese, especially older people, wear the traditional *kimono* (loose robe) at home and for special occasions. But most people in Japan wear clothing similar to that worn by North Americans and Europeans.

The Japanese have also kept many old traditions, including their deep respect for beauty. Shinto, once Japan's state religion, teaches love of nature's beauty. Zen, a branch of Buddhism chiefly practiced in Japan, is famous for its emphasis on beauty in even simple things. Long ago, monks in Zen monasteries made art forms of everyday functions, including bathing, flower arranging, gardening, and tea drinking. These and other artistic tra-

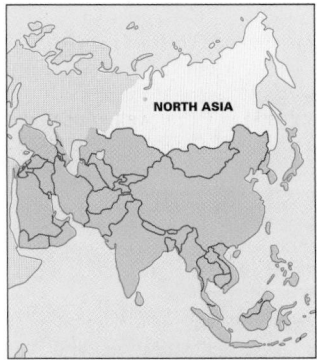

The Trans-Siberian Railroad winds through a bleak and frozen part of North Asia. North Asia is the continent's largest region in area but its smallest in population. Much of the region is undeveloped, partly because of its cold climate. Ice and snow cover most of North Asia about half the year.

WORLD BOOK map; photo © John Warburton Lee, SuperStock

ditions became—and remain—part of the way of life for people in Japan.

Many people in Japan, including the wealthy, live in a traditional plain, wooden Japanese house. Most of these homes have a garden and a high surrounding wall. Almost every Japanese family that can afford it owns at least one brush painting mounted on a scroll. At many meals, the Japanese serve each food in a separate bowl to emphasize the food's color, shape, and texture. Rice remains the chief food.

The extended family is not nearly so common in Japan as it was before the 1900's. But the Japanese still have strong family ties and a deep respect for authority. They expect individuals to obey all people who have authority over them, including their father and older brothers, and government officials. At the same time, persons in authority must act courteously toward others. This rule comes from an old belief that one person should never embarrass another.

Economic growth and modernization began in Japan in the mid-1800's. Before that time, Japan's rulers worked to keep the country free from outside influences. Japan ended its isolation when it began trading with the United States during the 1850's. It adopted Western economic ways and made itself a world power while maintaining its social and cultural distinctiveness.

Japan's economic progress suffered a major setback with the nation's defeat in World War II. But the Japanese, with help from the United States and its allies, rebuilt their country and its economy with astonishing speed.

Korea and Taiwan. North Korea modeled its economic, political, and social systems on those of other Communist countries. Rural people, who make up about a third of the population, live on collective farms operated by the government. Most of the country's industrial workers live in city apartments and work in factories owned and operated by the government.

Agriculture is still important in South Korea and Tai-

wan, but both countries have rapidly developed into industrial states since the 1950's. Their economies expanded, and living standards rose greatly.

Education. Japan, Taiwan, and North and South Korea have high literacy rates. Almost all people 15 years of age or older in those countries can read and write. All Japanese attend elementary school and high school, and a high percentage go on to college.

In China, the government has expanded elementary education. During the 1940's, only a small percentage of the people could read and write. Today, about 95 percent of all Chinese 15 years of age or older can do so. The country is also expanding higher education.

The arts. East Asia has one of the world's oldest and richest artistic traditions. The Chinese created artworks before the beginning of written history. Through the years, Chinese artists became masters in many art forms, including architecture, painted porcelain, carving, scroll painting, and sculpture. Much Chinese art shows Buddhist or other religious subject matter. Chinese artists also portrayed people, animals, and nature, and created beautiful designs and rich colors. Chinese art has influenced artists throughout East Asia.

In China today, artists strive for self-expression. But the government discourages art that is critical of Communism. Both Japan and South Korea have continued their rich artistic traditions but have also adopted some Western art forms. For example, the people of both countries enjoy Western plays, television dramas, and motion pictures. Filmmakers in Japan and Hong Kong, which returned to Chinese control in 1997, produce hundreds of movies yearly, many of which have won international awards.

Way of life in North Asia

North Asia covers about 5 million square miles (12,800,000 square kilometers), or about 30 percent of the continent. It is the largest region in Asia, extending from the Ural Mountains to the Pacific Ocean. North

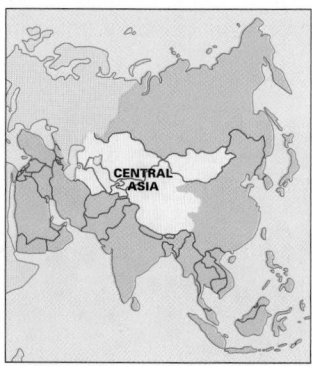

Central Asia's grassy plains are the home of many livestock herders. Raising livestock is the major economic activity in Central Asia. In Mongolia, the herders live in tents called *yurts*. Except for the plains, Central Asia is largely an area of huge deserts and high mountains and plateaus.

WORLD BOOK map; photo from George Holton, Photo Researchers

Asia consists entirely of Siberia, which makes up about 75 percent of Russia. The rest of Russia lies west of the Urals, in Europe.

North Asia covers more land than any other region in Asia but has the smallest population. About 32 million people live in the region, or about 1 percent of Asia's total. North Asia has a population density of only 6 ½ people per square mile (2.5 per square kilometer).

A harsh climate has limited North Asia's development and population growth. The region has an abundance of natural resources, including many minerals, vast oil fields, rich forests, and grasslands in the extreme southwest that are good for farming. But the winters are long and bitter. Ice and snow cover most of the region about six months of the year. The temperature can drop below −90 °F (−68 °C). Most of the coastal waters, lakes, and rivers freeze for much of the year.

Because of North Asia's isolation, imperial Russia and the Soviet Union used it as a place of exile and imprisonment. The Soviet Union was a Communist country that covered nearly two-fifths of Asia from 1922 until the country broke apart in 1991. Russia was the most important republic in the Soviet Union. Soviet rulers sent millions of criminal and political prisoners to isolated parts of Siberia. Many prisoners were forced to work building factories, mines, and railroads. The large-scale use of forced labor for Siberian construction projects ended soon after the death of Soviet dictator Joseph Stalin in 1953.

The people. Most Siberians are Russians. Ethnic Russians are descended from Slavs who lived in Eastern Europe several thousand years ago. Such Mongol and Turkic groups as Buryats, Tuvinians, and Yakuts lived in Siberia originally, and descendants of these peoples still live there.

Religion. Russian Orthodoxy, a branch of Christianity, is the chief religion among North Asians of European descent. Many descendants of the original North Asians practice Buddhism or Islam.

Life of the people. Many North Asians farm, fish, or work in factories or mines. Most North Asian factories operate in cities along the Trans-Siberian Railroad.

About 70 percent of Siberia's people live in cities. Most city people are crowded into small apartments. Many people in rural areas live in simple, but more spacious, log houses. Novosibirsk is the largest city in Siberia. It has a population of about 1 ½ million.

Education. Almost all Russians can read and write. Public education is free for all citizens. Children attend school for 11 years, from ages 6 to 17.

The arts. Much art of North Asia shows Chinese and Islamic influence. Some art shows Christian influence.

Way of life in Central Asia

Central Asia covers about 3,489,000 square miles (9,035,000 square kilometers), or about 20 percent of the continent. It is the second largest region in Asia. Only North Asia has more land. Central Asia includes Tibet, Qinghai, and Xinjiang, which lie in western China, and the independent nations of Kazakhstan, Kyrgyzstan, Mongolia, Tajikistan, Turkmenistan, and Uzbekistan. Qinghai is a province of China. China calls Tibet and Xinjiang *autonomous* (self-governing) regions, but the Chinese government actually rules them. A tiny part of Kazakhstan lies west of the Ural River, on the continent of Europe.

Except Mongolia and the Chinese-controlled areas, the lands of Central Asia were once part of the Communist-led Soviet Union, which broke up in 1991. These nations have moved away from the Communist system to other forms of government. However, most have retained close ties to Russia.

Central Asia is a region of high plateaus and mountains, vast deserts, and treeless, grassy plains. Much of the land is too dry or too rugged for farming. Many people earn a living by herding livestock. Industrial activity centers in the region's few cities.

About 112 million people, or about 3 percent of Asia's

population, live in Central Asia. Of the regions of Asia, only North Asia has fewer people. Central Asia has a population density of 32 people per square mile (12 per square kilometer).

The people. The people of Mongolia are called Mongols. The great conqueror Genghis Khan united various Mongol tribes in the early 1200's. He and his grandson Kublai Khan built the largest land empire in history. It extended from China and Korea, across much of Central and Southwest Asia, and into Europe. The people of Central Asia's other independent nations include the Kazakhs, the Kyrgyz ethnic group, and ethnic Tajiks, Turkmen, and Uzbeks.

Even though Qinghai, Tibet, and Xinjiang are part of China, most of their people are not Han Chinese. Tibetans make up the population of Tibet and much of the population of Qinghai. Tibetans have lived in the area since ancient times. Uyghurs (also spelled Uighurs), a people of Turkic origin, make up about half of Xinjiang's population. Tibet and Xinjiang are also home to increasing numbers of Han Chinese, who have moved there from other regions of China.

Religion. Most Central Asians are Muslims. Islam is the chief religion in Kazakhstan, Kyrgyzstan, Tajikistan, Turkmenistan, and Uzbekistan. When these areas were part of the Soviet Union, the Communist government discouraged religion, but people continued to practice their faith. These nations now allow religious freedom.

Islam is also the chief religion in the Chinese region of Xinjiang. Lamaism, a branch of Buddhism, is the chief religion in Mongolia, Tibet, and Qinghai. The Chinese Communists tolerate religion but attempt to maintain control over religious groups. The Communists recognize several religions but restrict the practice of others. The Chinese government has at times persecuted religious believers.

Life of the people. All of Central Asia was once under Communist control. Today, only Qinghai, Tibet, and Xinjiang continue to be ruled by a Communist government. The six independent nations of Central Asia have

moved to other forms of government, and they have removed controls that existed in such areas as religion, education, and the arts.

Tashkent, the capital of Uzbekistan, is the largest city in Central Asia. It has about 2 million people. Most city dwellers live in single-story houses or apartment buildings. The majority of the people of Central Asia live in rural areas. Most of them farm or raise livestock.

In much of Central Asia, people in rural areas live in mud-brick houses in villages. Many rural villages do not have electric power or running water. Most families are large, and many members of an extended family may live together in one household. Such a household might include parents, married children and their offspring, and other relatives. Some rural people live in traditional tentlike dwellings called *yurts*. These portable homes are constructed of a circular wooden frame covered with felt.

Many of Mongolia's people live on livestock farms. The farms are like huge ranches with small towns in the center. The central buildings include houses, offices, shops, and medical centers.

In Xinjiang, large numbers of people are herders who live near oases. Many people farm on the oases.

The Chinese Communists seized Tibet in 1950. Before that time, few parts of the world were so completely controlled by religious leaders as was Tibet. Buddhist monks ruled the country and owned most of the land. The monks and a small group of nobles made up Tibet's upper class. Farmers and wandering herders formed Tibet's lower class. The farmers worked the land, and most nomads tended the flocks of monks and nobles.

The Chinese government reduced the power and wealth of the monks and nobles. They broke up many large estates and took over the land or distributed it among the people. They also reduced the importance of religion. The work of farmers and herders has changed little since the Chinese take-over. But the farmers and herders give much of what they produce to the government rather than to landowners.

Mount Everest, the highest place on Earth, towers 29,032 feet (8,849 meters) in the Himalaya range on the Nepal-Tibet border. Several other Asian peaks are also more than 25,000 feet (7,620 meters) high.

Education. Most of the people in Central Asia can read and write. Most children attend school for 11 years, from ages 6 to 17. Teaching Communist principles is an important part of the curriculum in Qinghai, Tibet, and Xinjiang.

The arts. Carpet making is an important craft in Central Asia. Other important crafts include embroidery and jewelry making. In Kazakhstan and Kyrgyzstan, the recitation of *epics* (poems about heroic events) is an important part of the culture. In the Chinese regions of Central Asia, the arts, like education, formerly centered around religion but today are intended to serve Communism. However, the Chinese have relaxed many controls on artistic expression.

The land

Asia, the world's largest continent, covers about 17 million square miles (44 million square kilometers), or about 30 percent of the world's land area. It extends from the Arabian Peninsula, Turkey, and the Ural Mountains eastward to the Pacific Ocean. From the Arctic Ocean, it reaches south to the Indian Ocean. Geographers consider thousands of islands off the mainland as part of Asia. These islands include—roughly from west to east—Cyprus, the Maldives, Sri Lanka, most of Indonesia, the Philippines, Taiwan, and Japan.

Asia and Europe are part of the same mass of land. No body of water separates the two completely, and so some geographers consider them as a single continent called Eurasia. Certain physical features mark the division between Asia and Europe. The Ural Mountains, Ural River, and Caspian Sea act as a northern boundary between east and west. The Dardanelles, Sea of Marmara, Bosporus Straight, Black Sea, and Caucasus Mountains link to form a border between north and south in the west.

Asia has some of the world's highest mountains, largest deserts and plains, most important rivers, and best—and worst—soil. This section describes each land region of Asia. It also tells about Asia's major natural features and how they affect the lives of the people.

Land regions. Asia has six major land regions, as discussed in the *Way of life* sections of this article. Southwest Asia is a land of desert in the south and of mountains and plateaus in the north. Dry soil makes farming difficult in most of the region. But Southwest Asia's land contains much oil, one of the world's most valuable natural resources. The northern border of South Asia includes the Himalaya, the world's highest mountain range. Much fertile soil lies south of the mountains. Southeast Asia is rich in natural resources, including fertile soil, forests, and mineral deposits. East Asia also has much fertile soil and other valuable resources.

Forests cover a large part of North Asia, and areas of good farmland lie in the southwestern section of this region. But much of northern North Asia is so cold that the land stays frozen throughout most of the year. Central Asia has much of the continent's poorest land. Its main features include deserts, mountains, and rocky plateaus.

Mountains. Asia has more mountains than any other continent. The mountains make transportation difficult in many places. They also separate people from each other and have hindered the exchange of ideas. Over the centuries, some mountain areas, such as in Lebanon, have

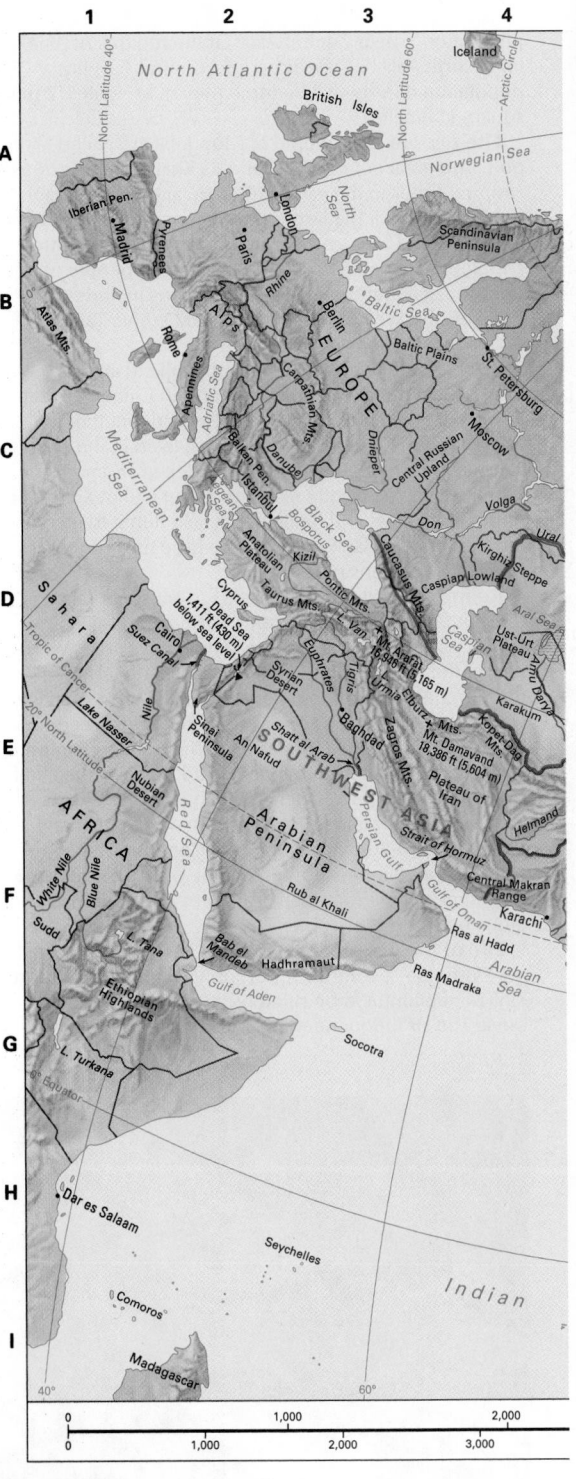

Physical features

Altai Mountains	E	6	Caspian Sea	D 4
Andaman Islands	H	7	Caucasus	
Amur River	C	9	Mountains	D 4
Arabian Sea	G	4	Celebes Sea	H 10
Aral Sea	D	4	Dead Sea	D 2
Banda Sea	I	10	Deccan	G 5
Bay of Bengal	G	6	East Siberian Sea	A 8
Bering Strait	A	9	Euphrates River	D 3
Brahmaputra River	F	7	Formosa Strait	F 9
			Ganges River	F 6

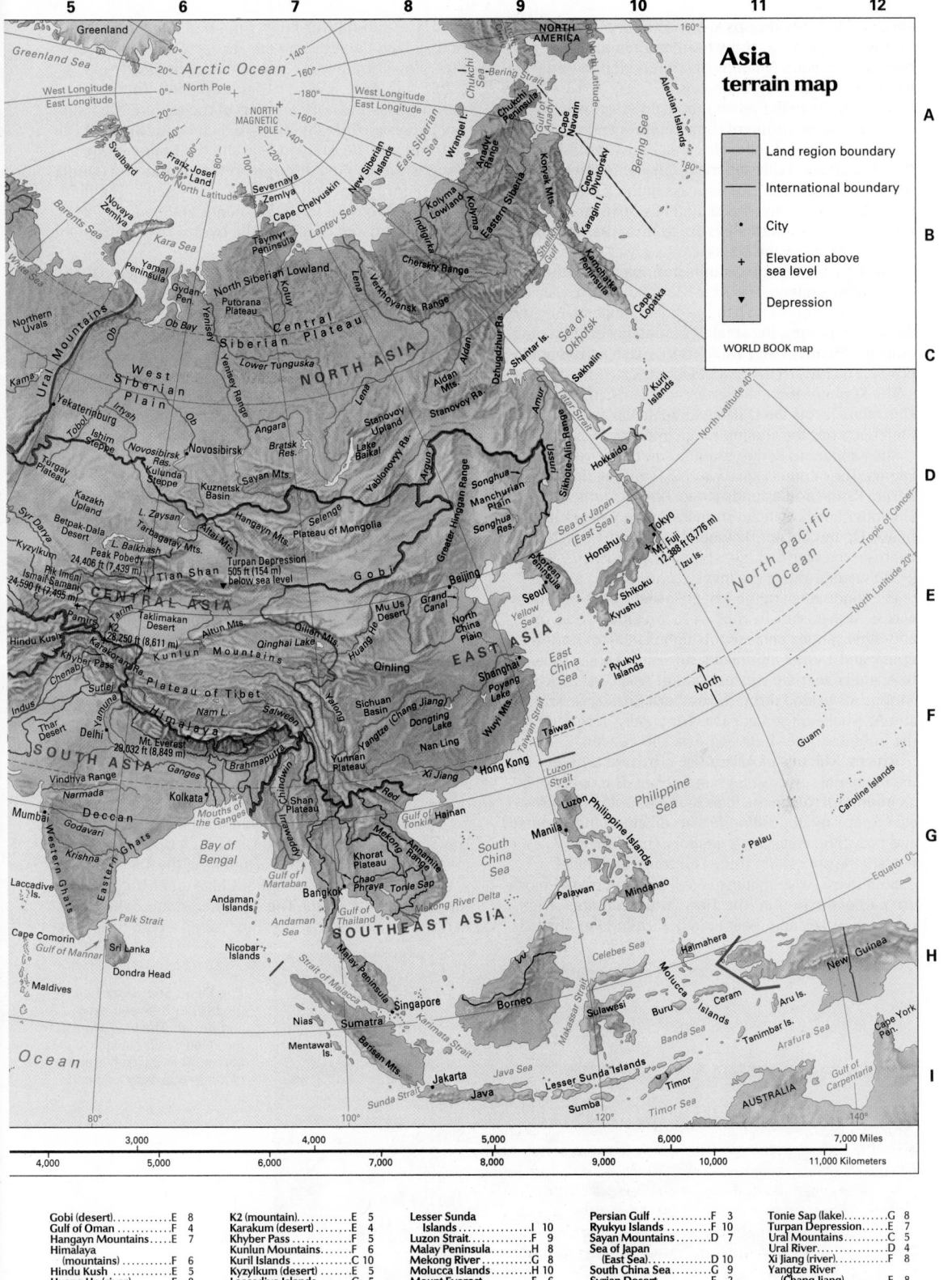

Asia
terrain map

	Land region boundary
	International boundary
•	City
+	Elevation above sea level
▼	Depression

WORLD BOOK map

attracted minority groups seeking shelter from persecution. Melting ice and snow from mountaintops feed many Asian rivers. Millions of farmers depend on water from these rivers to grow crops.

Many of the major Asian mountain systems branch out from a large group of rugged peaks and deep valleys called the Pamirs. This area lies where Afghanistan, China, and Tajikistan meet. It is sometimes called the *roof of the world.* Some peaks in the Pamirs tower more than 25,000 feet (7,620 meters) above sea level. The floors of some of the valleys are as much as 4 miles (6 kilometers) below the peaks.

The Tian Shan range extends northeast from the Pamirs into Xinjiang. The Altai Mountains form part of the boundary between Mongolia and Xinjiang. Beyond these high ranges, the smaller mountains of such ranges as the Stanovoy and Yablonovyy reach across southern Siberia toward the Sea of Okhotsk.

The Kunlun Mountains extend east from the Pamirs. This range forms the Qilian Mountains in eastern Tibet, then becomes the Qinling range in central China.

The Karakoram Range extends southeast from the Pamirs. The famous Himalaya rises south of the Karakoram Range and extends along Tibet's southern border. The lofty Himalaya includes many of the world's highest peaks. On the border between Nepal and Tibet, Mount Everest—the world's highest mountain—rises 29,032 feet (8,849 meters) above sea level.

The Hindu Kush range extends west from the Pamirs across Afghanistan. Farther west, the Elburz, Zagros, and other ranges enclose the high Plateau of Iran. The Pontic and Taurus mountains surround Turkey's Plateau of Anatolia near the western end of Asia. The Caucasus Mountains extend through southern Russia, Georgia, and Azerbaijan. The Caucasus Mountains form one of the boundary lines between Asia and Europe.

Rivers. Millions of Asians live crowded together in the continent's river valleys and deltas. The rivers play an important role in the lives of the people. Many rivers aid farmers by depositing fertile soil along their courses and providing water for irrigation. They also serve as important transportation routes for trade and travel.

Southwest Asia's major rivers flow through the northern part of the region. The Tigris and Euphrates rivers begin in Turkey and meet in Iraq, forming the Shatt al Arab. The Karun River flows from Iran into the Shatt al Arab, which empties into the Persian Gulf. The Jordan River flows south from Lebanon into the Dead Sea.

In South Asia, several rivers flow south from the mountains in the northern part of the region. The main waterways include the Indus, which winds through Pakistan and into the Arabian Sea; and the Brahmaputra and Ganges, which flow through northern India and Bangladesh before emptying into the Bay of Bengal. The delta, a low plain formed from sediments, at the mouth of the Brahmaputra and Ganges is the largest river delta in the world.

Four important Southeast Asian rivers begin in the mountains that are in and near Tibet. There, the Irrawaddy, Mekong, Menam (Chao Phraya), and Salween rivers start their long routes through Southeast Asia to the sea.

East Asia's major rivers, the Huang He (Yellow River) and Yangtze River (also called Chang Jiang), begin in the Tibetan Highlands and flow east across China. The Huang He empties into the Yellow Sea, and the Yangtze empties into the East China Sea. The Yangtze, which measures 3,900 miles (6,275 kilometers) long, is Asia's longest river. The Xi Jiang (West River), southern China's chief river, flows from south-central China into the South China Sea.

The major rivers of North Asia—the Lena, Ob, and Yenisey—flow from south to north through northern Siberia. They empty into the Arctic Ocean. The Amur River is the major waterway of far eastern Siberia.

Large parts of Central Asia have no rivers. But important rivers rise in the mountains of that region.

Deserts and plains. Deserts extend diagonally across Asia from the Arabian Peninsula northeast to China and Mongolia. These huge deserts are unsuitable for farming, and few people live there.

The Arabian Desert makes up most of the Arabian Peninsula. Other deserts cover much of the rest of Southwest Asia. A desert called Karakum occupies most of Turkmenistan. Kyzylkum is a desert that spreads across southern Kazakhstan and northern Uzbekistan. The Thar Desert stretches across much of the border between India and Pakistan. Farther east, the Taklimakan of western China and the Gobi of China and Mongolia form huge wastelands. The frozen tundra region that is in northern Russia is sometimes called a cold desert be-

The Dead Sea shore lies on the border between Israel and Jordan. The land around the Dead Sea is rocky and barren. The sea itself is about nine times as salty as the ocean.

cause so few plants can grow there.

Plains are flatlands. Rivers cut through most plains and rain falls on them, helping make the soil fertile. The major Asian plains include those that lie across northern India, eastern China, northern Kazakhstan, and central Russia.

Coastline, bays, seas, and lakes. Asia's coastline measures about 80,205 miles (129,077 kilometers)—over three times the distance around Earth's equator. Many

harbors along the coast are shallow. Through the years, mud and silt carried downstream by rivers have partly filled the harbors. Asia's northern harbors, on the Arctic Ocean, stay frozen much of the year.

Two huge bays of the Indian Ocean indent Asia's southern coast. These are the Bay of Bengal east of India, and the Arabian Sea west of India.

Along Asia's east coast, islands and peninsulas block

Climate regions in Asia

Tropical wet–Always hot and wet. Heavy precipitation well distributed throughout year.

Tropical wet and dry–Always hot, with alternate wet and dry seasons. Heavy precipitation in wet season.

Semiarid–Hot to cold. Great changes in temperature from day to night except in coastal areas. Light precipitation.

Desert–Hot to cool. Great changes in temperature from day to night except in coastal areas. Very little precipitation.

Subtropical dry summer–Hot, dry summers and mild, rainy winters. Moderate precipitation in winter.

Humid subtropical–Warm to hot summers and cool winters. Moderate precipitation in all seasons.

Humid continental–Mild summers and cold winters. Moderate precipitation in all seasons.

Subarctic–Short, cool summers and long, cold winters. Light to moderate precipitation, mostly in summer.

Tundra–Always cold, with a brief, chilly summer. Little precipitation in all seasons.

Highland–Climate depends on altitude. Climates at various altitudes are like those found in flat terrain.

WORLD BOOK map

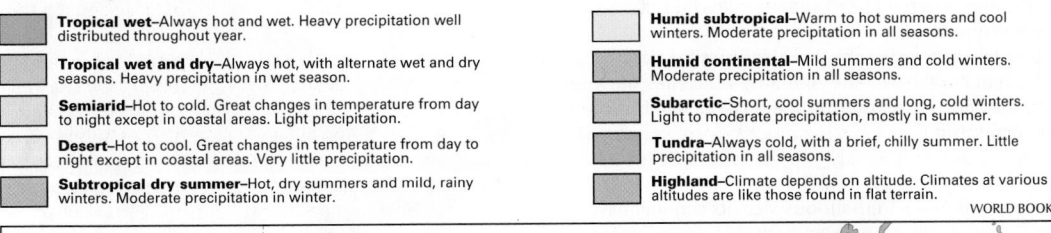

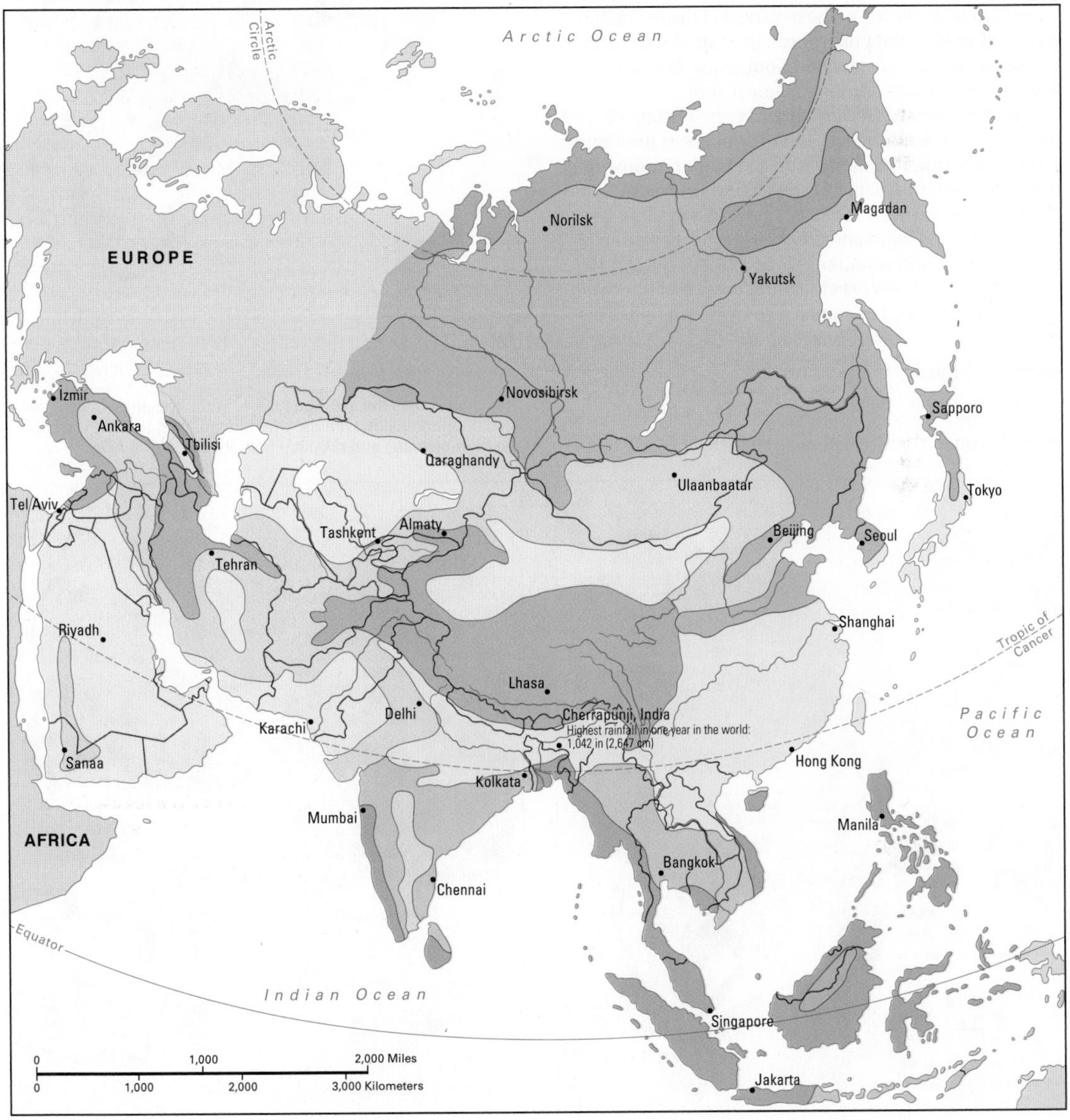

off parts of the Pacific Ocean into a series of seas. These seas include—from north to south—the Bering and Okhotsk seas, the Sea of Japan (also called the East Sea), and the Yellow, East China, and South China seas. The Philippine Sea lies east and north of the Philippines.

The Red Sea lies between the continents of Asia and Africa. The Aegean, Black, and Caspian seas make up part of the boundary between Asia and Europe. The Caspian Sea, which lies north of Iran, is the world's largest inland body of water. It is not really a sea but a salt lake that covers 143,250 square miles (371,000 square kilometers).

Other lakes include Lake Baikal in Russia; Lake Balkhash in Kazakhstan; the Aral Sea, which lies between Kazakhstan and Uzbekistan; and the Dead Sea, between Israel and Jordan.

Climate

Because of Asia's tremendous size, its regions have a wide variety of climates. These varied climates include the bitter cold of the polar north; the hot, dry desert environment of Central Asia and Southwest Asia; and the hot, humid conditions of the tropical south.

Winds called *monsoons* influence the climate of much of Asia. A monsoon blows regularly in the same direction during definite seasons. In winter, monsoons from the north move into East Asia and cause cold, dry weather. The wind switches in summer and blows from the seas that lie south and southeast of that region. It causes hot, humid weather.

Most of East Asia's precipitation falls as rain between April and October. The rainfall is heaviest in the east,

Average yearly precipitation
(Rain, melted snow, and other moisture)
Most of the rainfall in Asia is caused by the summer monsoon, a warm and moist southerly wind. The monsoon does not reach the central part of Asia, which is dry throughout the year.

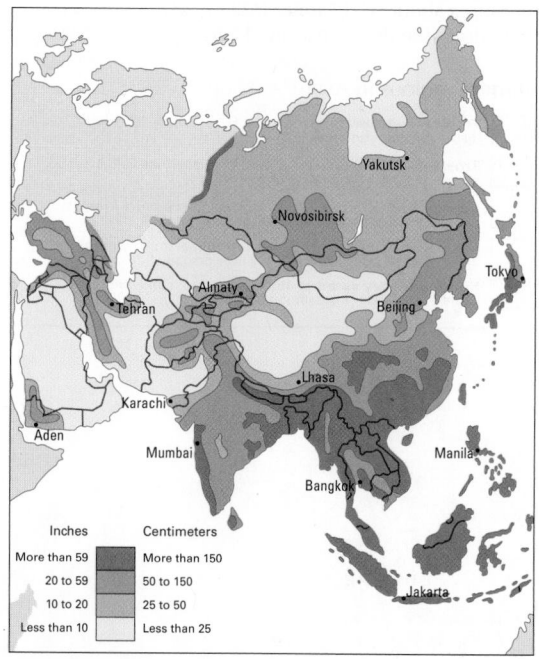

Inches	Centimeters
More than 59	More than 150
20 to 59	50 to 150
10 to 20	25 to 50
Less than 10	Less than 25

Average January temperatures
This map shows the average January temperatures in Asia. The Himalaya forms a barrier against the cold northerly winds and protects southern Asia from freezing temperatures.

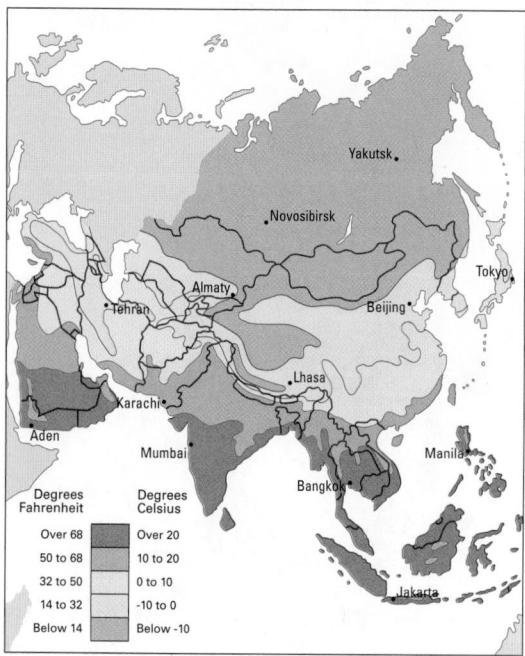

Degrees Fahrenheit	Degrees Celsius
Over 68	Over 20
50 to 68	10 to 20
32 to 50	0 to 10
14 to 32	-10 to 0
Below 14	Below -10

Average July temperatures
This map shows the average July temperatures in Asia. Most of the continent is hot, with the exception of northern Siberia and the high plateaus and mountain ranges of Central Asia.

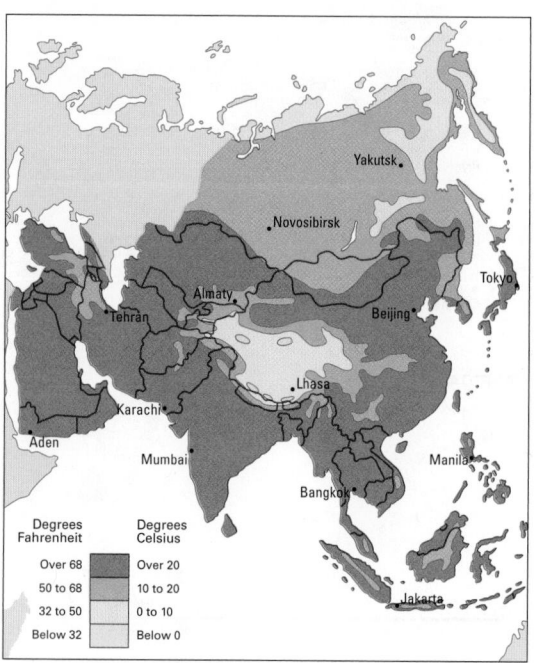

Degrees Fahrenheit	Degrees Celsius
Over 68	Over 20
50 to 68	10 to 20
32 to 50	0 to 10
Below 32	Below 0

and the amount of rain decreases away from the sea.

Monsoons pass through South Asia and Southeast Asia from November to March. They cause the coolest weather in those two regions. Beginning in April, monsoons from the southwest send temperatures soaring. From May to October, wet monsoons bring heavy rains from the south seas. Many of these monsoons cause floods.

In Southwest Asia, monsoons affect only the southern and southwestern coasts of the Arabian Peninsula. Most of Southwest Asia has long, hot summers and mild winters. Inland, temperatures often climb above 115 °F (46 °C) in summer. But there are no clouds to keep the daytime heat close to Earth at night. A warm but comfortable night may follow an extremely hot day. The region's

heaviest rains fall in Turkey near the Black Sea and in the Caucasus region between the Black and Caspian seas. Some parts of the Arabian Peninsula receive no rain for several years at a time.

Bitter cold polar weather keeps part of northern Siberia's land frozen the year around. In the grasslands in the southwest, the temperatures vary from 3 °F (–16 °C) in January to 64 °F (18 °C) in July. Central Asia's climate ranges from extremely cold in its mountain regions to hot and dry in the deserts in the summer.

Animals

Domesticated animals. Many Asian people use *domesticated* (tamed) animals to do work and as sources of food, clothing, and shelter. Useful domesticated animals

Animals of Asia   This map provides a general idea of where some animals of Asia live. Most of the animals shown are wild. People have trained others, including camels, reindeer, and water buffaloes, to do work.

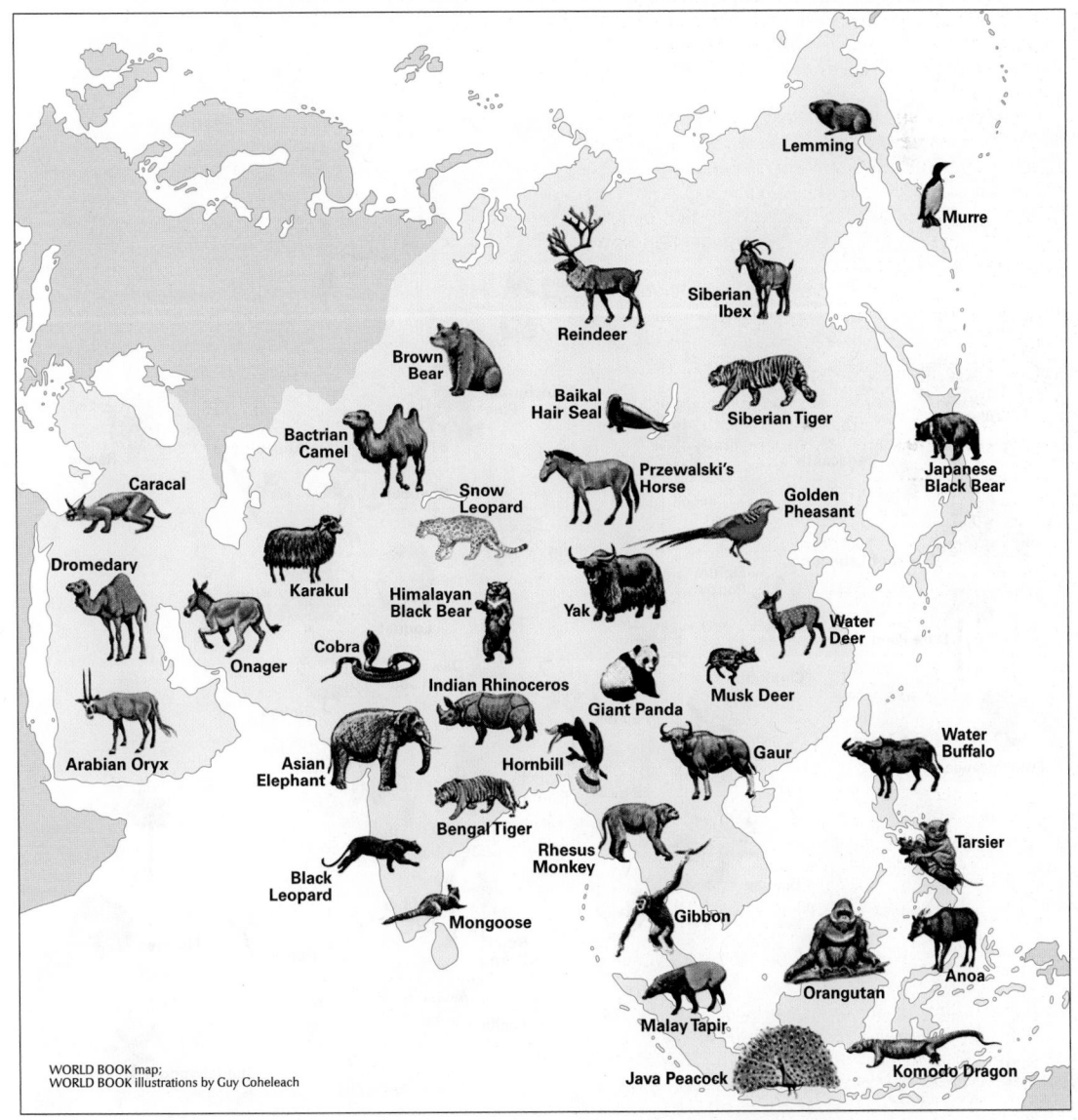

WORLD BOOK map;
WORLD BOOK illustrations by Guy Coheleach

include the dromedary and other camels of Southwest Asia, and the elephant and the ox or bullock of South Asia. Other domesticated animals used by Asian people are the yak and Bactrian camel of Central Asia, the water buffalo of Southeast and East Asia, and the reindeer of North Asia.

Wild animals. Arctic foxes, Arctic hares, lemmings, and reindeer live in the Arctic. Lemmings live under the snow in the winter. Many animals in North Asia south of the Arctic are highly valued for their fur. They include brown bears, elks, ermines, lynxes, martens, otters, and sables.

Antelopes, burrowing rodents, and locusts live in Mongolia and northwestern China. From time to time, swarms of locusts attack the fields of northern China, eating the crops in their paths. The giant panda, a black-

and-white bear, lives in the wild only in China.

China's industrial boom has created significant pollution that threatens some of its wildlife. For example, water pollution, heavy river traffic, and dam building have caused the Yangtze river dolphin to become critically endangered and possibly extinct.

South and Southeast Asia have the continent's greatest variety of wild animals. Apes and monkeys and beautiful tropical birds are plentiful in these regions. Some animals—including elephants, crocodiles, leopards, rhinoceroses, scorpions, tigers, and poisonous snakes—can endanger the rural people.

Wild animals that live in Southwest Asia include antelopes, caracals, onagers, and ibexes and other wild goats. The region's deserts support many insects and reptiles.

Plants of Asia   This map provides a general idea of where some plants of Asia grow. Little plant life grows in the cold of the Far North. Warm and wet South and Southeast Asia have a wide variety of plant life.

WORLD BOOK map;
WORLD BOOK illustrations by Guy Coheleach

How the land of Asia is used

This map shows the different uses of land in Asia. The most important crops—such as wheat in Russia, rice in southern China, and rubber in Southeast Asia—are shown in larger type. Large areas of Asian land are generally unproductive because they are either extremely cold or too dry and not irrigated.

WORLD BOOK map

Mostly cropland

Grazing land

Forest land

Generally unproductive land

Plants

Few kinds of plants can survive in the Arctic area of North Asia. But the world's largest fir and pine forest lies south of the Arctic. Its trees supply lumber, pulpwood, and other products.

The dry land of most of Central Asia supports little plant life except for grasses. But grass serves as the food for livestock, the basis of Central Asia's economy.

Valuable plant life grows in eastern East Asia, which has plentiful rain. Trees supply East Asians with fruit,

lumber, and paper. The people use the leaves of the mulberry tree to feed silkworms, which produce silk thread for clothing.

Much valuable plant life also grows in the warm, wet climate of Southeast Asia and parts of South Asia. Products from plants account for a large part of the exports of these regions. People in many parts of the world use products from the nutmeg, rubber, and teak trees, the tea bush, and bamboo grass.

Few plants grow in the dry parts of Southwest Asia. But date palms and olive trees of desert oases provide many people with a large amount of the food they eat and export.

Agriculture

Agriculture is still the most important economic activity in Asia in terms of people's livelihoods. About half of the people make a living from farming. Farm products also account for a large part of Asia's exports.

In many Asian countries, most of the farmers use hand tools, and many have animals that pull plows and do other work. Such countries as China and Bangladesh produce high crop yields, largely through intensive hand labor and the use of every bit of available land. Even so, these nations have so many people that there is barely enough food to go around.

The use of modern farm tools and chemical fertilizers has become widespread in some Asian nations, including Israel, Japan, and the countries that were formerly part of the Soviet Union. Some Asian nations have increased farm productivity by the use of irrigation and new, higher-yielding rice and wheat seeds. These countries include China, India, South Korea, and Thailand.

This section gives an overview of how farms are organized in Asia and of Asia's major crops and livestock animals. The six *Way of life* sections of this article provide more information on how rural Asians live and work.

Farm organization in Asia follows three chief systems: *private ownership, tenant farming,* and *collective farming.*

Some farmers in all parts of Asia own their own farms. Private farm ownership is most common, however, in South Asia and on the mainland of Southeast Asia. Many farmers in these areas own a small plot of land.

Tenant farming is also practiced in many parts of the continent but is probably most common in Southwest Asia. Many farmers in that region work on land they rent from wealthy landlords. They pay the landlords with crops or money.

Few collective farms still exist. Israel has many collective farming communities called *kibbutzim,* and there are still some collective farms in China.

The Communist countries of Asia formerly practiced collective farming, but it proved inefficient and unpopular. The Chinese government introduced collective farming communities called *communes* in 1958 but began abandoning them in 1979. The government then tried a system similar to tenant farming. Farm families produced a certain amount of crops for the state. They could sell whatever excess they produced on the open market. The Chinese government gradually relaxed its crop requirements. Now many farm families raise and sell crops as they choose.

Crops. South Asia, Southeast Asia, East Asia, and southwestern North Asia rank as the continent's main crop-growing regions. The land and climate of most of Southwest Asia, Central Asia, and North Asia are poorly suited to farming.

The chief crops of Asia are rice and wheat. The countries of Asia—led by China and India—produce more than 90 percent of the world's supply of rice, and Thailand is the world's largest rice exporter. Asia's leading wheat-producing countries include China, India, Russia, and Turkey.

Most of the world's natural rubber and tea come from Asia. Indonesia, Malaysia, and Thailand are the top natural-rubber producers in the world. Asia's leading tea-growing countries include India, China, Sri Lanka, and Indonesia.

Other important Asian crops include cotton, jute (fiber from which burlap is made), and sugar cane. China, India, Pakistan, Turkey, Turkmenistan, and Uzbekistan stand among the leading cotton-growing nations. Jute comes chiefly from Bangladesh, China, and India. India

Marc Riboud, Magnum

Agriculture provides a living for more than half of all Asians. Most Asian farmers, like the Chinese rice growers shown here wading in water, perform many tasks by hand.

ranks second in the world in the production of sugar cane. Only Brazil produces more.

The opium poppy is grown in parts of Asia, including Afghanistan and Myanmar. Such powerful drugs as heroin, morphine, and opium are made from this flower. Doctors prescribe such drugs to ease pain. However, millions of people around the world abuse the drugs, often becoming addicted to them.

Livestock. In South Asia, Hindu farmers who raise cattle use the animals to obtain milk and *ghee* (a clarified, liquid form of butter) and for work. Because cows are sacred to Hindus, the farmers do not slaughter the

animals at the end of their working lives. India has the largest population of cattle of any nation. In the less fertile parts of Central, North, and Southwest Asia, many people raise livestock for a living. They get cheese, milk, and meat from their animals, as well as fur and hides for clothing and shelter. Manure from livestock is used as fertilizer and sometimes as a cooking fuel.

Some of the animals are used for transportation. Livestock farmers also sell animals or products made from them to buy supplies.

Hogs and poultry are raised for food throughout most of East Asia and Southeast Asia. Camels, goats, and

Mining and manufacturing in Asia

This map shows the sources of Asia's leading mined products. Products of outstanding economic importance in each area—such as petroleum in the Persian Gulf area, coal in China, and tin in Malaysia—are shown in larger type. The map shows major manufacturing centers in red.

WORLD BOOK map

● Gold   Major mineral deposit

• Lead   Other mineral deposit

·   Manufacturing center

© Superstock

Heavy manufacturing takes place chiefly in technologically advanced countries, such as China, India, Japan, Russia, South Korea, and Taiwan. The factory shown here is in China. Many Asian nations, however, have relatively little manufacturing.

Bernard Wolf, DPI

The handicrafts industry provides work for many Asians. Women in Sri Lanka, *shown here,* make beautiful designs on textiles. People throughout the world buy Asian handicrafts.

sheep are the most important livestock in Southwest Asia. Central Asians herd Bactrian camels, cattle, goats, horses, pigs, sheep, and yaks. Reindeer herding is a major activity in the northern part of North Asia.

Industry

Industry is growing rapidly in many East, South, and Southeast Asian nations. These countries have prospered as their industries have expanded. Japan, China, and India rank among the largest economies in the world. But most other Asian nations have relatively little manufacturing and depend heavily on agriculture.

Mining. Raw mined materials rank among Asia's most important exports. Southwest Asia supplies a large part of the world's oil. Southeast Asia provides much of the world's tin. China's exports include antimony, barite, fluorite, graphite, granite, and tungsten. India's exports include bauxite, iron ore, and zinc. Chromite mined in Turkey and the Philippines is exported to many parts of the world.

Asia used to export most of its raw mined materials to industrialized nations on other continents. But because of rapid economic growth, Asia is becoming a major importer of raw materials from other regions.

Manufacturing. During colonial days, Asia served as a source of food for Europe's people and as a source of raw materials for its industries. The processing of food and other products became important in Asia, and it still is today. Such industries as sugar refining and the processing of fish, rice, and tobacco have major economic importance in some parts of the continent.

Most of Asia's heavy manufacturing takes place in such countries as China, India, Japan, Russia, South Korea, and Taiwan, all of which have large, modern factories. Industries in these countries make such products as automobiles, electronic equipment, factory machinery, iron and steel, military weapons, and ships. Israel, North Korea, Singapore, and Turkey also have some heavy industry.

Other industries. Light industries play an important role in the economies of such countries as Indonesia, Malaysia, and Thailand. Many Southeast Asian countries manufacture textiles, footwear, personal electronic products, and other consumer goods, primarily for export.

Millions of Asians who live along the seacoasts and rivers catch fish for a living. The countries of China, India, Indonesia, Japan, Russia, and Thailand rank among the most important fishing nations of the world.

Tourism and a related industry, handicrafts, have great economic importance in many parts of Asia. Large numbers of non-Asians visit the continent each year, and many Asians travel outside their home countries within Asia. The tourists spend money on food, transportation, lodging, and such handicrafts as carvings, leather goods, metalware, pottery, rugs, and textiles. The tourist industry is especially active in South, Southeast, and East Asia.

Industrial development. Many Asian governments are trying to improve the economies of their nations by creating new industries and by expanding old ones. Some countries offer low tax rates to non-Asian business people to set up businesses in Asia. Asian governments have also used their own funds and aid from other countries to establish industries. The governments sold some of these industries to Asian business people at low cost. Many changes in Asian education have been aimed at training people in industrial skills.

A number of Asian countries have succeeded in increasing their industry. Japan is one of the world's leading industrial nations. It exports cars, electronics, and other consumer goods throughout the world. China and India have huge factories and manufacture a wide variety of goods. Israel, South Korea, and Taiwan have also made great progress in industrial development. Such other Asian nations as Malaysia, Pakistan, the Philippines, Thailand, and Turkey are developing modern industry. Since the late 1900's, the governments of Asia's Communist countries have begun to loosen government controls and to encourage private enterprise and foreign investment.

Most other Asian countries have little industry other than the processing of agricultural products and raw materials. Saudi Arabia and other oil-producing nations have large oil refineries. The Asian countries that were once part of the Soviet Union face the need to replace old industrial equipment and develop new markets for their goods.

Transportation and communication

The transportation and communication systems of Asia's cities are more advanced than those of the rural areas. The cities have many of the same modern devices that Western cities have. But in some rural areas, transportation and communication differ little from what they were hundreds of years ago.

Transportation. Many kinds of vehicles transport people and goods in Asian cities. Automobiles, buses, motor scooters, and trucks speed by vehicles powered by people or animals. People supply the power for such vehicles as bicycles and *pedicabs*. The pedicab, a taxicab operated like a bicycle, has largely replaced the *jinrikisha* and other taxis pulled by runners. Oxen, water buffaloes, and other animals pull carts through the streets of some cities. Many cities have mass transit systems.

Motor vehicles are less common in rural Asia. Buses travel along the rural roads, many of which are unpaved. Some people share the ownership of a jeep. Many villagers transport goods in carts pulled by animals or people. Others travel by foot—to save wear and tear on their animals. Carts get stuck in the soft sands of the deserts, and so many people use the sure-footed camel for desert transportation.

Rivers rank among the chief transportation routes of rural Asia. The people use barges, canoelike vessels, *junks, sampans,* and other small boats for travel and to transport goods. Junks and some other boats of rural Asia have sails and are moved by the wind. But many Asians must paddle their boats or move them by pushing a long pole against the river bottom. Sometimes, people on shore pull heavy barges by means of long ropes attached to the barges. People in Iraq sail an unusual boat called a *kufa* that looks like a huge bowl.

Airlines link most large Asian cities with one another and with other parts of the world. But railroads are still the continent's chief means of long-distance transportation. Colonial rulers built a large network of railroads during the late 1800's. They used trains to carry raw

© Lincoln Potter, Liaison Agency

Motor vehicle transportation is common in much of Asia. These residents of Bangkok, Thailand, face thoroughfares crowded with traffic.

materials from inland areas to coastal cities and ports. Today, almost all Asian countries have at least one railroad. More trains are needed, however, to handle increased passenger and cargo loads. Asia also has a shortage of railroad managers, train repair personnel, and replacement parts for old trains. Japan has one of the world's most modern railroad systems.

The colonial rulers also built up Asia's highway system between inland areas and coastal cities. Since the end of colonial rule, Asian nations have continued to build or improve highways so that more trucks and buses can use them.

Oceangoing vessels carry much cargo to and from Asia's ports. These huge modern ships tower above the small, old-fashioned sampans and other boats that dockworkers use while loading and unloading them.

Communication in some Asian countries is much the same as in Western countries. Many people read newspapers. Radio and television stations broadcast from most cities. Most households have radios, many households own television sets, and most of the population has internet access.

In other Asian countries, newspapers, radio stations, and television stations are less numerous. Radio and TV broadcasts do not reach some rural areas. Some families own radios, but few own television sets, and only a small portion of the population has access to the internet.

Shi Huangdi's tomb is surrounded by an army of life-sized terra cotta statues of soldiers. In the 200's B.C., Shi Huangdi united China for the first time and began the famous Great Wall of China.

© Lawrence Migdale, Photo Researchers

Satellite television receivers and mobile telephones enable some rural communities to stay in touch with the rest of the world.

History

Four areas of the world are sometimes called the *cradles of civilization* because of the important early civilizations that began there. One of these areas is in Egypt and the other three are in Asia. The Asian cradles of civilization are (1) the Tigris-Euphrates Valley, now mostly Iraq, in Southwest Asia; (2) the Indus Valley of South Asia; and (3) the Huang He and Yangtze valleys of China, in East Asia.

The Tigris-Euphrates Valley, near the head of the Persian Gulf, was the site of the world's first civilization, in the area known as Mesopotamia. This valley forms the center of a larger historic region called the Fertile Crescent. This region, named for its rich farmland, follows the Tigris and Euphrates rivers north and west from the Persian Gulf. Then it curves south through the valley of the Jordan River. The region includes parts of what are now Iraq, Israel, Jordan, Lebanon, and Syria.

Ruins of old cities dot the Fertile Crescent. Archaeologists have discovered much about the ancient civilizations that existed in the area between about 3500 B.C. and the 200's B.C. These civilizations included the Sumerian, Babylonian, and Assyrian civilizations.

The Sumerians developed the world's first civilization about 3500 B.C. They invented a method of writing, called *cuneiform,* and used it to inscribe clay tablets. The Sumerians traded widely with other peoples, including the Egyptians. Sumerian armies had war chariots a thousand years before the Egyptians did. The Sumerians also developed a complicated system of laws governing weights, measures, and trading.

No one really knows why Sumer declined. But by about 1900 B.C., the first of several great Babylonian dynasties appeared in the region north of Sumer. Babylon

Asian civilizations and empires of ancient times   These maps show the locations of some of the most important civilizations and empires of Asia during ancient times. The map at the left locates the Asian *cradles of civilization*—areas where important early civilizations developed. The other maps show the extent of some of the major early empires in Asia.

Cradles of civilization

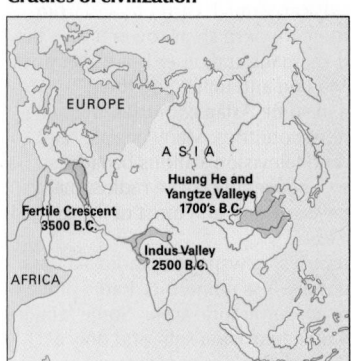

EUROPE

A S I A

Huang He and Yangtze Valleys 1700's B.C.

Fertile Crescent 3500 B.C.

Indus Valley 2500 B.C.

AFRICA

300's and 200's B.C.

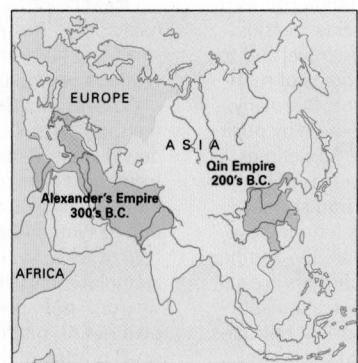

EUROPE

A S I A

Qin Empire 200's B.C.

Alexander's Empire 300's B.C.

AFRICA

A.D. 100's to 300's

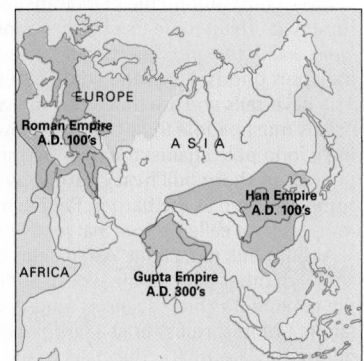

EUROPE

Roman Empire A.D. 100's

A S I A

Han Empire A.D. 100's

AFRICA

Gupta Empire A.D. 300's

WORLD BOOK maps

became the capital city of an advanced civilization that gained fame for its laws, religion, and walled cities.

The Assyrian Empire, north of Babylonia, began to expand after 883 B.C. For about 100 years, between 728 and 626 B.C., Assyria controlled Babylonia. Babylonia regained its independence after King Ashurbanipal of Assyria died in 627 B.C. But the Persians conquered the empire in 539 B.C.

The Persian Empire reached its height about 520 B.C. At that time, it included much of Southwest Asia and parts of South Asia, the southern part of Russia, and North Africa. Persia's importance lasted nearly 200 years. Alexander the Great conquered the Persian Empire in 331 B.C.

The Indus Valley. From about 2600 B.C. to about 1900 B.C., an advanced Bronze Age culture developed in South Asia. This civilization spread through the valley of the Indus River and included hundreds of settlements in what are now Pakistan and northwestern India. Scholars do not know how the Indus society began, nor if its people were related to the peoples of Southwest Asia.

About 1500 B.C., nomadic tribes called Aryans invaded India. The Aryans probably came from the plains north of the Caspian Sea. They gradually spread their culture eastward to the Ganges Valley. The Aryans developed the religious and social practices that formed the basis of later Hindu cultures. By 517 B.C., the Persian Empire had started to overrun the Indus Valley.

From 327 to 325 B.C., Alexander the Great conquered the Indus area. But he soon gave up his rule over the area, and India came under the control of Buddhist rulers. Buddhist dynasties controlled much of the Indian subcontinent for hundreds of years. The greatest empire in this period was that of Ashoka. He united nearly two-thirds of South Asia during his rule, which lasted from about 272 to 232 B.C. Art and literature thrived during Ashoka's reign.

The Huang He and Yangtze valleys of north and central China make up the third early center of Asian culture. In the Huang He Valley, during the 1700's B.C., the Shang dynasty became the first major civilization of East Asia. Palaces filled the Shang capital of Anyang. Shang priests used *pictograms* (simple drawings representing words) to report events and keep records. This early picture writing formed the basis of the written Chinese language.

The Zhou (also spelled Chou) dynasty replaced Shang rule about 1045 B.C. The Zhou dynasty was centered in the Yangtze Valley. During Zhou rule, Chinese art and learning flourished. Great thinkers, such as Confucius and Laozi (also spelled Lao Tzu), laid the basis of East Asian philosophy. Internal wars weakened the Zhou dynasty after 403 B.C., and the dynasty ended in 256 B.C. Several large states controlled China until 221 B.C., when the Qin (also spelled Ch'in) dynasty took over.

Qin rulers created the first united Chinese empire. The first Qin ruler, Shi Huangdi, ordered major construction on the Great Wall of China in an attempt to protect the empire from the nomadic peoples of the north. But rebel warriors overthrew the Qin rulers in the late 200's B.C. China's next dynasty, the Han, ruled a large empire from 202 B.C. to A.D. 220.

Nomadic invasions destroyed ancient civilizations in all parts of Asia after A.D. 300. For centuries, nomads poured out of Central Asia and southern North Asia. In East Asia, during the 300's, the Huns of Mongolia conquered northern China. Then they turned west and invaded Europe, where they contributed to the fall of the Roman Empire. In about 500, Huns ended India's 180-year-old Gupta Empire.

From the early 600's to the 1100's, when nomadic invasions and religious wars weakened western Asia, East Asia had peace. The Tang and Song (also spelled Sung) dynasties ruled China during that period. They developed gunpowder, printing, paper money, and porcelain.

Muslim peoples conquered Southwest Asia during the 600's and built an empire that included North Africa and most of Spain and Portugal. From the 300's to the 1100's, the Byzantine Empire in the eastern Mediterranean area was the only Christian power in Asia. That Christian influence eroded as the empire fell to the Ottomans, Muslim nomadic Turkish tribes that had migrated to the Middle East from Central Asia. Over several centuries, the Ottomans steadily occupied Byzantine territories and established the expansive Ottoman Empire.

Asian empires in medieval and modern times These maps show the locations of some of the major empires in Asia from the A.D. 700's to the 1700's. The Mongol Empire, *center,* was the largest land empire in history. It extended all the way from China and Korea to the Danube River in Europe.

A.D. 700's

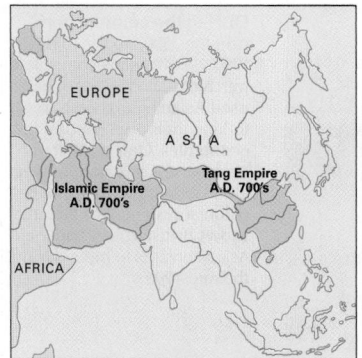

A.D. 1200's

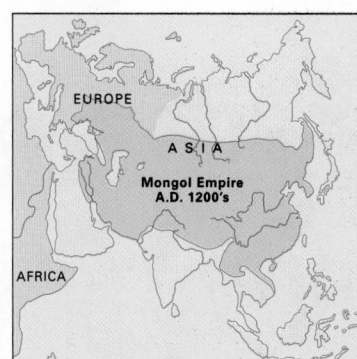

A.D. 1500's to 1700's

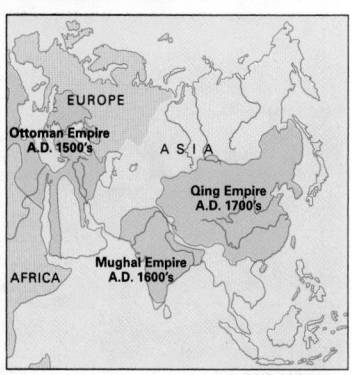

WORLD BOOK maps

In 1453, they captured the Byzantine capital, Constantinople, which then became known as Istanbul.

New invasions came from the center of Asia after 1206, when Genghis Khan united Mongol tribes and conquered northern China, northern India, Persia (now Iran), and parts of Europe. The Mongol Empire extended from China and Korea to the Danube River in Europe. It was the largest land empire in history. The empire lasted until 1368, but it achieved its greatest importance during the mid-1200's under Kublai Khan.

After the fall of the Mongol Empire, the Ming dynasty gained control of China and spread its power throughout most of East Asia. During the nearly 300 years of Ming rule, Chinese art and literature flourished.

In 1526, Mongols again invaded India and established the Mughal Empire. About the same time, the Ottoman Empire reached its height in Southwest Asia. Ottoman rule also extended to North Africa and southeastern Europe. But none of these empires remained powerful. Europeans had entered a period of cultural and economic expansion that resulted in their conquest of Asia.

The Western conquest of Asia began during the early 1500's. The desire for Asia's riches—especially control of the spice trade—excited Europe, and an age of colonial expansion followed. In the 1500's, the Portuguese took control of Indian Ocean trade routes and obtained Macau and Melaka as ports for trade. The Spanish began trading in the Philippines about 1565. The English and Dutch entered the Asian trade after 1600. The Dutch gained a foothold in Java in 1619. They took Melaka from the Portuguese in 1641 to control the spice trade.

In Japan, the strong Tokugawa rulers forced the Spanish and Portuguese to leave the country in 1639. Japan allowed only the Dutch to send a ship to trade at Nagasaki once a year. China, under the Qing dynasty of the Manchus, also closed its doors to the West. Foreign traders were permitted only at Guangzhou (Canton).

The British and Dutch, stopped from trading with China and Japan, turned to South and Southeast Asia. The British gradually conquered most of India, and the Dutch took over the East Indies (now Indonesia). At about the same time, European Russians pushed into Siberia from the west.

The age of colonialism. Europe and the United States brought their economic and military strength to bear on Asia during the 1800's. In 1839, China and the United Kingdom began the First Anglo-Chinese War (also called the First Opium War), a battle over opening China to imports. China lost and, in 1842, agreed to British trade at five Chinese ports. Two years later, China began trading with the United States and France. In 1854, Matthew C. Perry, the leader of an American naval mission, signed a treaty that opened Japan to limited U.S. trade.

A period of fierce competition began among Western powers seeking Asian trade and colonial expansion. The United Kingdom became a powerful force in Southwest Asia, India, Southeast Asia, and southern China. Russia expanded into Central Asia and Manchuria. The French colonized Indochina (the area that is now Cambodia, Laos, and Vietnam). The United States acquired the Philippines from Spain in 1898, after the Spanish-American War.

By the 1900's, Western influence had produced great changes throughout Asia. Western art influenced Asian art, and the colonials built large parts of Asian cities in a Western style. The colonials played the leading part in the economic and political life of much of Asia. However, many people in rural areas remained unaffected by Western influence.

During World War I (1914-1918), the United Kingdom, France, and other Allied nations occupied the Ottoman Empire, which collapsed during the war. After the war, several of the new countries created from the empire were placed under the administration of the United Kingdom or France. This system, called the *mandate system,* lasted until the 1940's.

The colonials made great profits through their control of Asia. At the same time, large numbers of Asians lived in poverty and had no voice in their government. Many Asians were dissatisfied with colonialism and demanded that Asians rule Asia. New feelings of nationalism grew up in many parts of the continent. In time, these nationalist movements ended colonialism in Asia.

The rise of the Japanese Empire. Japan overthrew the Tokugawa system of government in 1867. After adopting a constitutional monarchy in 1889, Japan quickly rose to great power in eastern Asia. From 1894 to 1905, in wars with China and Russia, Japan won the island of Taiwan and a foothold in Manchuria and Korea.

A new republic replaced China's Qin dynasty in 1912. However, the country found it difficult to build a strong new government. For many years, warlords

Bombay Green in 1767, a woodcut by an unknown artist; Radio Times Hulton Picture Library, London

During the colonial period—the 1500's to the mid-1900's—Europeans controlled much of Asia. The Europeans used Asian natural resources to help their own nations' economies. Only a small percentage of Asia's people benefited economically from the colonial system. This picture shows British rulers and their Asian servants in India during the mid-1700's.

fought for control of the country. Finally, in 1928, the Chinese Nationalists united China under one government. But the Nationalists still had to contend with rival Communist groups, which left the nation open to attack.

In 1931, Japanese troops invaded Manchuria. Six years later, they swept into central China. The troops left China only partly conquered and began to drive toward Southeast Asia and the Pacific Islands.

In 1941, Japan joined Germany and Italy in World War II. At the height of its power, in 1942, the Japanese Empire extended from the Aleutian Islands of Alaska, south to the Netherlands Indies, and as far west as Burma (now also called Myanmar). The huge empire collapsed with Japan's defeat in 1945.

The end of colonialism. The Allied victory in World War II returned most of the colonies to the Western powers, but only for a short time. Feelings of nationalism in Asia had grown during the war. Mohandas K. Gandhi, who led India's movement for independence from the United Kingdom, was perhaps the most famous Asian nationalist.

Between 1943 and 1949, Burma, Ceylon (now called Sri Lanka), India, Indonesia, Pakistan, and the Philippines changed from colonies into nations. A number of Southwest Asian colonies and territories also became independent nations. In addition, a new nation, Israel, was formed in 1948 as a homeland for Jews. In 1949, Indochina was the only part of Asia that still had major Western colonies. However, that region gained independence five years later.

Results of colonialism. With the end of colonialism, most Asian nations again controlled their own development. But years of colonial rule had left Asia poorly prepared in some ways to face the modern world.

Economically, Asia lagged far behind the West. An industrial boom in the West, which began during the 1700's, provided jobs for the rapidly increasing population. The boom enriched governments and business people and gradually raised the living standard of most of the population. The West also made major improvements in farm tools and methods.

Under colonial rule, Asia provided raw materials needed for Western industry. But most of Asia did not become industrialized. Nor did the continent experience much agricultural improvement. As a result, poverty became more widespread in Asia than in the West.

Colonialism also slowed Asia's political and military development. At the same time Western nations ruled Asia, they developed a tradition of strong central government that their colonial possessions lacked. After the Europeans left, various groups in many Asian nations struggled for political power. In many cases, Asians who came to power had difficulty establishing their authority over all the people in their countries. Political factions divided many nations.

Western nations developed militarily during the colonial period. But in Asia, the colonial rulers—not the Asians—were responsible for the military defense of the lands they governed. After the colonial rulers left, many Asian nations found themselves without suitable military protection. This military weakness added to Asia's problems.

Colonial rule also left a deep impact on Asian culture. Many Asians adopted Western dress, architecture, edu-

United Press Int.

Mohandas K. Gandhi, *center,* was an Asian leader in the struggle for independence. He led India's movement for independence from British rule.

cation, and ideas, often blending their traditions with Western ways. In many countries, colonial rulers created an elite Westernized class. The elite took power after colonial rule ended.

The spread of Communism. Two Asian nations—the Soviet Union and Mongolia—turned Communist in the 1920's, long before World War II. By the time the war began in 1939, Communist parties had gained strength in many other parts of the continent. The Communists spoke out against colonial rule and used their stand against colonialism to gain followers. During World War II, many Communists fought alongside the Allies, some of which were colonial powers. But after the war, the Communists called for an end to colonialism and sought power for themselves.

In 1949, the Chinese Communists defeated the Chinese Nationalists. Mao Zedong led the Communists during most of their 22-year struggle for control of China. With this victory, Communists controlled Asia's two largest nations—China and the Soviet Union.

At the end of World War II, Korean Communists took control of North Korea, and non-Communist Koreans took over South Korea. In 1950, the North Koreans invaded South Korea, touching off the first international war between Communists and non-Communists. The United States and other non-Communist nations fought on the side of the South Koreans. North Korea's allies included China, which sent troops, and the Soviet Union, which sent supplies. The Korean War ended in 1953. But Korea still remains divided between a Communist north and a non-Communist south.

Communism also gained a foothold in Southeast Asia. In 1946, Communists in Vietnam, which was then a colony of French Indochina, began a long war against the French forces there. A nationalist group called the Vietminh, headed by the Communist leader Ho Chi Minh, led the movement. The Communists finally defeated the French in 1954. Indochina was then divided into four independent nations—Cambodia, Laos, North Vietnam, and South Vietnam.

The fighting did not end when the French left. Communists in Cambodia, Laos, and South Vietnam continued to fight the new non-Communist governments. North Vietnam sent troops and supplies to help them, and China and the Soviet Union sent supplies. The United States sent supplies to the non-Communist countries.

In the early 1960's, South Vietnam seemed about to fall to the Communists. The United States sent troops to help defend South Vietnam. A cease-fire agreement ended U.S. participation in the fighting in 1973. But

clashes continued between the Vietnamese Communists and non-Communists. Battles also flared up in Cambodia and Laos during the 1960's and early 1970's. In 1975, Communists took control of South Vietnam, Cambodia, and Laos. North and South Vietnam were reunited in 1976. Communist rebels have fought against the governments of several other Asian countries, including Myanmar, the Philippines, and Thailand.

The decline of Communism. In 1978, leftist military leaders gained control of the government of Afghanistan. Many Afghans rebelled against the new government. At the end of 1979, the Soviet Union began send-

Foreign influence in Asia—1914

This map shows Asia in 1914. Cities under colonial rule are shown by circles. Treaty ports, which handled international commerce, are shown by black dots. Pink stripes show the sphere of British influence, green stripes the Russian sphere.

British	Portuguese	Independent countries	
Dutch	Russian		
French	United States		

Abbreviations on Map
(Fr.) . . . . France   (U.K.) . . . United Kingdom
(Port.) . . . . . Portugal   (U.S.) . . . . . United States

WORLD BOOK map

ing troops to help the Afghan government crush the rebels, called *mujahideen*. Muslims from Saudi Arabia and other Arab countries supported the rebels in their struggle against Soviet control. The Afghanistan government and its Soviet allies could not defeat the rebels. The Soviet Union withdrew its troops in 1988 and 1989. The war between the rebels and the government in Afghanistan continued until 1992, when the rebels overthrew the government. Some supporters of the rebels later joined the terrorist organization al-Qa'ida.

Also in 1979, Vietnamese troops crossed into neighboring Cambodia and overthrew the Communist Khmer Rouge regime. The Khmer Rouge had seized control of Cambodia in 1975 and enforced its rule by torture and terror. Members of the Khmer Rouge retreated into the jungles of northern Cambodia and carried out attacks on the new Vietnam-backed government. The Khmer Rouge movement gradually weakened before coming to an end in the late 1990's.

Communism went into retreat across much of Asia beginning in the 1980's. Mongolia changed from a Communist system of government to a democratic one in 1990. By the end of 1991, the Soviet Union had ceased to exist as a country. First, Communist rule ended there after conservative Communist officials failed in an attempt to overthrow Soviet leader Mikhail S. Gorbachev. After

Pix
Communists battled Nationalists in China for 22 years before finally gaining control of the country in 1949. The spread of Communism led to much fighting in Asia during the 1900's.

When the countries of Asia became independent

More than 30 Asian nations have become independent since World War II ended in 1945. This map shows when the various countries of Asia gained their independence. Yemen (Aden) and Yemen (Sanaa) merged into the country of Yemen in 1990.

Countries independent before World War I
Countries independent after World War II
Countries independent between World War I and World War II
Countries independent from former Soviet Union in 1991
WORLD BOOK map

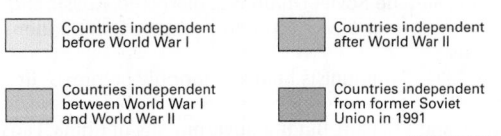

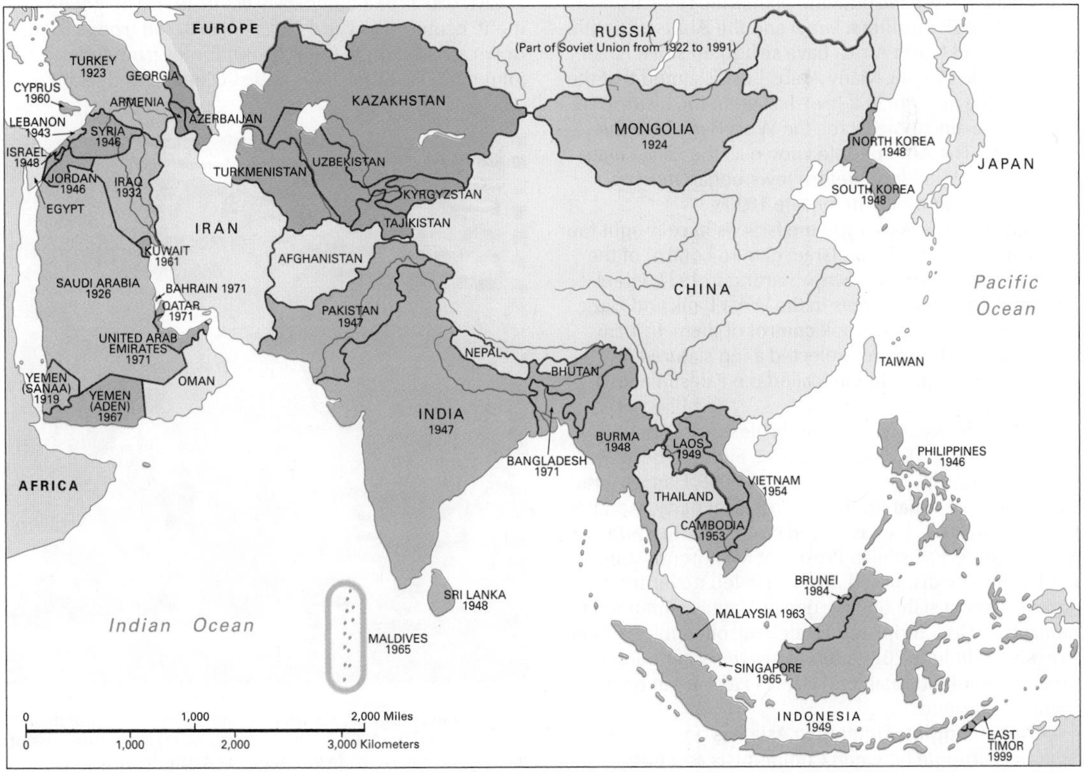

Wide World

War raged in Vietnam for almost 30 years as Vietnamese Communists struggled to control the country. Beginning in 1965, United States troops fought as allies of the non-Communists.

the failed attempt, most of the Soviet republics declared their independence. In December 1991, Gorbachev resigned, and the Soviet Union was dissolved. Russia and the other former Soviet republics became independent nations.

By 1992, Communists held a monopoly on power in only a few Asian countries, including China, Laos, North Korea, and Vietnam. But the governments of China, Laos, and Vietnam were introducing economic reforms.

Arab-Israeli conflicts. Israel and the Arabs of Southwest Asia and North Africa have struggled since Israel was founded in 1948. Many Arabs have claimed that the Israelis have no right to a Jewish state in the historic region of Palestine (now Israel, the West Bank, and the Gaza Strip). The Arab people known as the Palestinians lived in the region long before Jews began moving there in large numbers in the late 1800's.

Since 1948, the Arabs and the Israelis have fought four major wars. In a 1967 war, Israel gained control of the West Bank and the Gaza Strip. Starting in 1994, Israel withdrew from some areas in the West Bank and Gaza, and Palestinian officials took control of them. In 1996, Palestinians in these areas elected a legislature and president for a government called the Palestinian Authority (PA).

Violence between Israelis and Palestinians increased briefly in 2006, 2008, 2009, and 2012. Fighting between Palestinian groups also increased. In 2006, Hamas, a radical Palestinian organization and political party, won PA elections. In 2007, Hamas seized control of the Gaza Strip by force. Palestinian President Mahmoud Abbas of the Fatah party dismissed the Hamas-led government and declared a state of emergency. Hamas continued to control the Gaza Strip, and Fatah controlled the PA in the West Bank. In June 2014, after many years of negotiations, a combined Fatah and Hamas Palestinian government was formed.

Other struggles. Fighting in Asia has not been limited to the struggle between Communists and non-

Communists and between Arabs and Israelis. Ethnic friction, power struggles within nations, border disputes, and other causes have led to fighting among many Asian peoples.

Chinese forces took control of neighboring Tibet in 1950. Since then, native Tibetans have sought independence a number of times but have been unsuccessful. In 1959, Chinese troops put down a Tibetan uprising against its harsh rule. The Dalai Lama, Tibet's spiritual leader, fled into exile in India.

Conflicts have also erupted between various groups of Muslims in Southwest Asia. In the 1950's and 1960's, rebels battled government forces in Iraq, Jordan, Lebanon, Oman, Syria, and North Yemen (with its capital in Sanaa), now part of a united Yemen. Iran and Iraq fought a war against each other from 1980 to 1988. In Lebanon, fighting broke out between Muslims and Christians in the mid-1970's, and among various Muslim groups in the 1980's. A peace plan ended most of the fighting in Lebanon in 1991. In 1990, Iraq invaded and occupied Kuwait. Many Southwest Asian nations and Western nations joined forces to drive Iraqi troops out of Kuwait in 1991.

The Kurds are a Muslim people whose homeland extends across the mountainous border regions of several Southwest Asian nations. In the late 1900's, the Kurds often battled the governments of those countries for the right to establish their own government.

India and Pakistan have disputed control of Kashmir since the two countries were formed in the late 1940's. Fighting has erupted many times. In 2005, fighting eased as India and Pakistan cooperated to help aid reach Kashmir, which had been devastated by an earthquake.

Civil war broke out in Pakistan in 1971. The government, centered in West Pakistan, ordered troops to put down a rebellion in the east. But forces from India joined the East Pakistanis and succeeded in defeating

United Nations

Palestinian refugees, *shown here,* were forced to leave their homes during the 1967 Arab-Israeli war. Wars in various parts of the continent have made thousands of Asians homeless.

Important dates in Asia

c. 3500 B.C. Civilization began in Southwest Asia.

c. 2600 B.C. Civilization developed in South Asia.

1700's B.C. Civilization developed in East Asia.

c. 563 B.C. Buddha was born in what is now Nepal.

c. 551 B.C. Confucius was born in China.

c. 4 B.C. Jesus Christ was born in Bethlehem in Southwest Asia.

A.D. 317 The Huns from Mongolia conquered northern China, starting a series of nomadic invasions of Asia.

c. 570 Muhammad was born in Arabia.

661-750 Arab civilization spread in Southwest Asia.

1200's The Mongols conquered much of Asia.

1500's European nations began conquests in Asia.

1526 The Mongols set up the Mughal Empire in India.

1639 Japan closed its doors to influences from Europe.

1842 After a war with the United Kingdom, China opened five ports to trade with Western nations.

1905 Japan defeated Russia and took control of Russian interests in Korea and Manchuria.

1912 The Chinese overthrew their emperor.

1931 Japan invaded and occupied Manchuria.

1937-1938 Japan invaded and occupied central China.

1941-1945 Japan fought the Allies in the Pacific area during World War II—and lost all its possessions.

1940's-1950's Most colonial Asian nations won independence.

1946-1954 Vietnamese Communists fought France for control of Vietnam and gained control of North Vietnam.

1948 Israel was established as a Jewish homeland. The Arabs and the Israelis fought the first of four wars.

1949 The Chinese Communists conquered mainland China.

1950-1953 The Korean War pitted Communists in the northern part of Korea against non-Communists in the south.

1957 The Vietnam War began as a Communist rebellion.

1965 The United States began sending troops to Vietnam.

1975 The Communist North won the Vietnam War. Communists also took control of Cambodia and Laos.

1980-1988 Iran and Iraq engaged in a war.

1990-1991 Iraq invaded and occupied Kuwait. An international force led by the United States drove Iraq out of Kuwait.

1991 Most republics of the Soviet Union declared their independence. The Soviet Union was dissolved.

1997 The United Kingdom returned Hong Kong to China.

2000 The leaders of North and South Korea met for the first time since Korea was divided.

2001 The United States and its allies drove the ruling Taliban from power in Afghanistan.

2003 Forces led by the United States attacked Iraq and drove the Iraqi government from power.

2004 A *tsunami* (series of huge ocean waves) killed about 228,000 people in coastal South and Southeast Asia.

West Pakistan in December 1971. East Pakistan then became the independent nation of Bangladesh.

Indonesia occupied East Timor in 1975, after Portugal ended its colonial rule there. Many East Timorese opposed Indonesian control, and the United Nations refused to recognize Indonesia's claim. In 1999, the East Timorese voted overwhelmingly for independence, and East Timor became an independent country in 2002.

In several Asian nations, Muslim militants have fought to gain power. In the late 1970's, Muslim revolutionaries overthrew the shah of Iran and established a conservative Islamic government. Muslim rebels have fought the

governments of the Philippines and several other Asian nations. An Islamic group called the Taliban gained control of most of Afghanistan by the mid-1990's. The Taliban imposed a harsh interpretation of Islamic law on that country. The Taliban also allowed al-Qa'ida, the organization behind the terrorist attacks in the United States on Sept. 11, 2001, to remain in Afghanistan. Later in 2001, the United States helped Afghan anti-Taliban forces drive the Taliban from power.

In 2003, forces led by the United States attacked Iraq and overthrew the Iraqi government of President Saddam Hussein. Afterward, U.S. and allied forces in Iraq

© Olivier Rebbot, Woodfin Camp, Inc.

The Iranian revolution, led by Ayatollah Ruhollah Khomeini, made Iran an Islamic republic. Muslims gained greater political power in many of the nations of Asia during the 1900's.

© Lana Slivar, Reuters

The tsunami of December 2004 killed about 228,000 people in South and Southeast Asia. The damaged buildings shown here are on the coast of one of Thailand's Phi Phi Islands.

© Jim Steinberg, Photo Researchers

The Petronas Towers, among the world's tallest buildings, rise above Kuala Lumpur, Malaysia. Many East and Southeast Asian cities showed rapid growth in the late 1900's and early 2000's.

tried to rebuild the country. However, Iraqi and foreign militants carried out many attacks against the coalition forces and against nonmilitary targets. There were also a number of attacks between followers of the two main branches of Islam, the Sunnis and the Shi`ites. Over 2 million Iraqis fled their country to escape the violence.

Natural disasters struck Asia numerous times in the late 1900's and early 2000's. In 1988, for example, floodwaters from the Brahmaputra, Ganges, and Meghna rivers covered most of Bangladesh, killing more than 1,600 people. The Huang He has been called China's Sorrow because of its destructive floods.

Cyclones often strike South and Southeast Asia at the end of the monsoon season. The deadliest cyclones create giant rushes of seawater called *storm surges* that sweep across low-lying coastal areas. In 1970, a cyclone and storm surge in the Bay of Bengal caused the worst coastal flooding in history. Huge waves swept over the coast of Bangladesh (then called East Pakistan) and killed from 300,000 to 500,000 people. In 2008, a cyclone and storm surge hit the coast of Myanmar, leaving more than 130,000 people dead or missing.

Earthquakes are common in much of East Asia and Southwest Asia. In 1976, an earthquake hit the city of Tangshan, in northeastern China. It left at least 240,000 people dead. Some estimates run as high as 655,000. Un-

dersea quakes sometimes cause a *tsunami* (a series of huge waves) that may strike coastlines. In 2004, a quake in the Indian Ocean caused a tsunami that killed about 228,000 people in coastal South and Southeast Asia and left millions of people homeless. The hardest hit nations were Indonesia, Sri Lanka, India, and Thailand.

A new era. Asia still faces many problems. Millions of people in Asia are poor and illiterate. Disputes continue to threaten peace in many areas. Nevertheless, in much of Asia, an era of development began in the late 1900's.

Parts of East Asia and Southeast Asia have progressed rapidly. In the 1990's, some states, including Singapore, South Korea, and Taiwan, became known as "Asian tigers" because their economies were so strong. These economies are based largely on high-technology businesses, such as computer manufacturing. In the 2000's, reforms in the world's two most populous nations, China and India, stimulated rapid economic growth. In Southwest Asia, Israel developed a strong economy. Earnings from oil improved the economies of other nations. In 2020, the 10 members of ASEAN, along with Australia, China, Japan, South Korea, and New Zealand, formed the Regional Comprehensive Economic Partnership (RCEP) to encourage mutual trade.

Economic progress has enabled governments to build new schools and train new teachers. Today, a larger percentage of Asians than ever before attend school.

Rapid economic growth and industrialization have introduced challenges, including high levels of environmental pollution, especially in South and East Asia. Economic progress in Asia has also been uneven. In some nations, including Cambodia and Laos, development has been slow. In other nations, including Bangladesh, Sri Lanka, and Pakistan, parts of the country have gained greater prosperity, while other parts remain poor.

Fewer Asians suffer malnutrition today, but millions still do not have enough to eat. The development of new, high-yielding varieties of rice and wheat has helped reduce hunger in parts of the continent.

In 2020 and 2021, Asia faced a public health emergency and great financial strain caused by the worldwide COVID-19 pandemic. The contagious respiratory disease was first identified in Wuhan, China, in late 2019. It spread quickly. Many Asian nations limited travel, as well as business, school, and social activities, to try to contain the disease. Vaccination programs began in most nations in 2021. See **COVID-19.**   Graham P. Chapman, Richard Louis Edmonds, Abraham Marcus, and Jonathan Rigg

Related articles. See the separate articles on Asian countries and other political units listed in the table with this article. See also the articles on Asian cities listed at the end of each country article. Other related articles include:

Biographies

Alexander the Great	Gandhi, Mohandas Karamchand	Kublai Khan
Ashurbanipal		Mao Zedong
Cyrus the Great		Polo, Marco
Darius I	Genghis Khan	Timur
Darius III	Hammurabi	Xerxes I

History

See the *History* section of each Asian country, such as **China** (History). See also:

Afghanistan War	Assyria	Chaldeans
	Babylonia	Cold War

Asia Minor is a peninsula of western Asia between the Black Sea and the Mediterranean Sea. Some people call it Anatolia. The Aegean Sea separates Asia Minor from Greece on the west. On the east, the peninsula extends to the upper Euphrates River. *Asia Minor* is the geographical name for the region. Turkey occupies all the land on the peninsula.

Asia Minor was one of the first places in the world to become civilized. It may have been here that people first learned the use of iron over 3,500 years ago. Archaeologists have found evidence of an advanced society that lived in the south-central area of Asia Minor before 7000

Location of Asia Minor

WORLD BOOK map

B.C. The Hittite kingdom developed on the peninsula in 1900 B.C., and the Aegean peoples settled there in about 1200 B.C. The civilization of classical Greece had its beginnings among the Ionian Greeks of Asia Minor. The Romans took over the western part of Asia Minor in 133 B.C. The Romans gained the rest of the peninsula around 50 B.C.

People from central Asia invaded Asia Minor in the A.D. 200's. Arabs attacked the cities of Asia Minor in the 600's, when the peninsula was part of the Byzantine Empire. The long period of Turkish control began in 1071. The Crusades and Mongol invasions of the 1200's and 1300's caused the breakup of the government set up by the Seljuk Turks and prepared the way for the rise of the Ottoman Empire. The resources of Asia Minor were developed after the Turkish Republic was formed in 1923 (see **Turkey** [The Republic of Turkey]).

F. Muge Gocek

Related articles in *World Book* include:

Aegean civilization	İzmir
Byzantine Empire	Lydia
Ephesus	Phrygia
Galatia	Tarsus
Hittites	Troy
Ionians	

Asia-Pacific Economic Cooperation (APEC) is an organization created to strengthen economic relations among its members. The organization achieves this primarily through reducing legal barriers to trade and investment between members. APEC encourages policies that allow goods, services, and people to move easily between member economies.

APEC members are concerned with a broad range of economic issues, and officials from member economies frequently consult on these issues. APEC members have developed cooperative approaches to regional energy and environmental issues.

At its founding in 1989, APEC had 12 members—Australia, Brunei, Canada, Indonesia, Japan, Malaysia, New Zealand, the Philippines, Singapore, South Korea, Thailand, and the United States. In 1991, China, Hong Kong, and Taiwan joined the group. Hong Kong became a special administrative region of China in 1997 but kept its separate membership in APEC. Mexico and Papua New Guinea were added in 1993; Chile in 1994; and Peru, Russia, and Vietnam, in 1998.

Since 1993, Asia-Pacific Economic Cooperation has hosted annual summit meetings of the heads of state of its members (and an official representative of Taiwan). The location of these summits rotates among APEC member economies. The host government organizes the sessions with assistance from the APEC Secretariat based in Singapore.

At the 2014 APEC summit in Beijing, China, the 21-nation organization endorsed a plan that called for the establishment of a Free Trade Area of the Asia-Pacific (FTAAP). A trans-Pacific free trade agreement would boost the weak global economic recovery and lower tariffs, making trade among APEC nations easier and cheaper. In 2016, APEC leaders meeting in Lima, Peru, reaffirmed their commitment to work toward a new regional free trade agreement that would include all 21 members of APEC.

Ken Rebeck

Asian Americans add their many different ethnic and cultural groups to the blend of American life. Asian markets, such as this dry goods store in New York City's Chinatown, are popular in many American cities.

© dbimages/Alamy Images

Asian Americans

Asian Americans are Americans of Asian descent. They or their ancestors came from Asian countries, particularly Cambodia, China, India, Indonesia, Japan, Korea, Laos, Pakistan, the Philippines, Thailand, and Vietnam. About 15 million people of Asian descent live in the United States. Asian Americans make up the country's third largest minority group, after Hispanic Americans and African Americans.

The first Asian immigrants who arrived in large numbers in the United States came from southeastern China. They immigrated to Hawaii and California beginning in the 1840's. In 1882, however, the U.S. government began placing restrictions on Asian immigration because of pressure from white Americans. Many white Americans feared job competition from the newcomers and resented their "foreign" customs. It was not until 1965 that all restrictions against Asian immigration to the United States were lifted. Today, their high rate of immigration makes Asian Americans one of the country's fastest-growing minority groups.

Who Asian Americans are

According to the 2010 U.S. census, nearly 5 percent of the United States population is of Asian descent. Asia, the world's largest continent, has 50 countries, so the Asian American population consists of many different ethnic and cultural groups. Chinese Americans form the largest Asian group, making up about 3 ⅓ million of the approximately 15 million Asian Americans. Asian Indians are the second largest group, with about 3 million people. The next largest groups are Americans of Filipino, Vietnamese, Korean, and Japanese ancestry.

The languages of the many Asian American groups include Chinese, Hindi, Japanese, Javanese, Korean, Tagalog, Thai, and Vietnamese. Asian Americans practice several major religions, including Buddhism, Christianity, Hinduism, Islam, and Shinto.

Asian American groups differ in physical appearance, language, and culture from one another as well as from other Americans. But Asian Americans have many of the same values most other Americans cherish. For example, most Asian Americans strongly believe in the importance of family. They believe that family members should work together for everyone's benefit and that relatives should protect and take care of one another. Success through hard work and self-discipline is another value emphasized in Asian American families. Children are encouraged to work hard in and out of school to be worthy of the sacrifices their parents make for them. Self-control is also an important value. Children are taught that mature people do not show their feelings too readily.

Where Asian Americans live

Most Asian Americans live in the western United States. According to the 2010 census, only about one-fourth of the total U.S. population lives in the West, but nearly half of the Asian American population make their homes there. About one-third of Asian Americans live in California.

More than 95 percent of Asian Americans live in urban areas. About half of them have homes in cities, and about half in suburbs. Many of the larger cities have neighborhoods known by such names as Chinatown,

Koreatown, Little Manila, Little Saigon, or Little Tokyo. These neighborhoods feature many ethnic restaurants and other businesses.

Asian influences on American culture

Although Asians have been in the New World since the 1500's, large numbers of Asians first came to the United States in the 1840's. Since then, they have influenced many areas of American culture. *Tai chi ch'uan* is a form of exercise that the Chinese have practiced for centuries. It has become especially popular among older Americans of many ethnicities. Its slow, gentle movements provide good exercise for aging bodies. *Taekwondo* is a traditional Korean *martial art* (style of fighting). Korean immigrants popularized it, and many of them now teach it to American youth. *Judo* is a traditional Japanese form of wrestling. Many U.S. colleges offer it in physical education programs. Both judo and taekwondo are Olympic sports.

Many Asian foods have become a regular part of American meals. Americans of all races are familiar with many Chinese foods, such as dumplings and *kung pao* chicken, spicy deep-fried chicken cubes with nuts. *Dim sum,* a variety of dumplings and other bite-size morsels, is another popular Chinese dish. A favorite for some Americans is *sushi,* a Japanese dish of vinegar-flavored rice and raw fish or vegetables. Many U.S. restaurants and groceries offer sushi. Restaurants that serve spicy Thai or Indian food are also popular. Some U.S. grocery stores carry *naan,* an Indian flat bread. Many supermarkets carry *tofu,* soybean curd that can be sautéed, braised, or grilled. Tofu originated in China more than 1,000 years ago. Many Americans enjoy the Korean dish *kimchi* (also spelled *gimchi*), a highly seasoned mix of pickled cabbage, radishes, and other vegetables. Korean beef barbecue is also popular with many Americans. Many U.S. groceries sell soy milk, a traditional drink in

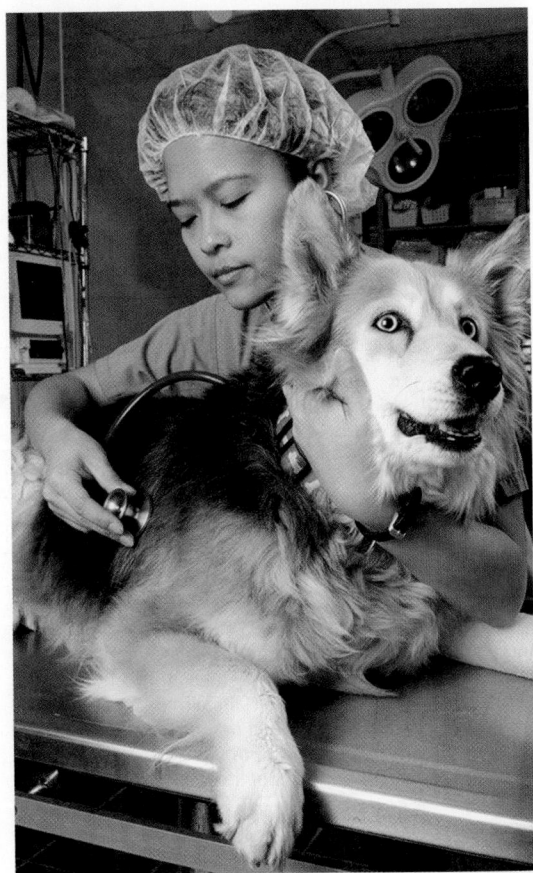

© Flirt/Superstock

An Asian American veterinarian examines a dog. Asian Americans have distinguished themselves in a number of professions.

AP Images

Ancient Chinese exercises called *t'ai chi ch'uan* have become especially popular among older Americans of many ethnic heritages. The slow, gentle movements of t'ai chi provide good exercise for bodies of all ages.

Where Asian Americans live

This map shows the state-by-state distribution of the U.S. Asian population according to the 2010 census. The numbers on the map indicate the percentage of Asians in the total population of each state.

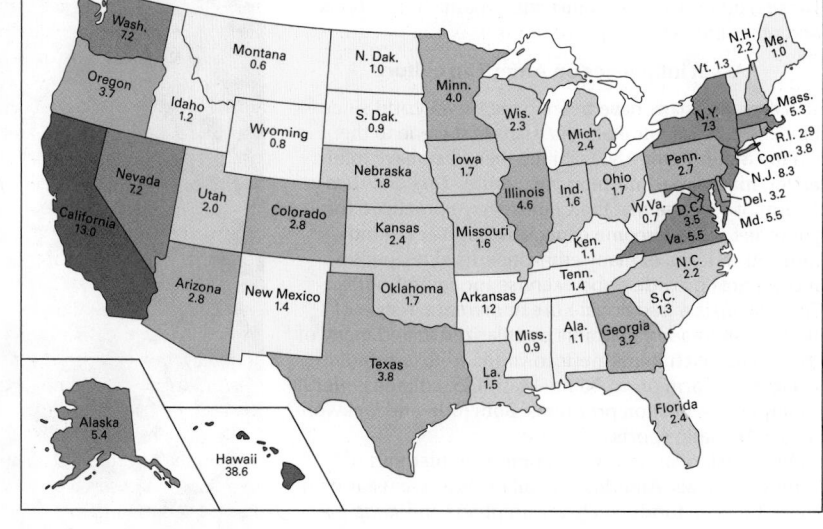

Percent of total population by state

- More than 10.0
- 5.0 to 10.0
- 2.5 to 5.0
- 1.5 to 2.5
- Less than 1.5

WORLD BOOK map

many Asian countries, as an alternative to cow's milk.

Acupuncture is a traditional Chinese method of relieving pain and treating disease by inserting needles in the body. It has become accepted by the American medical profession as a way to treat certain ailments. Yoga is a traditional South Asian spiritual practice of meditation and exercise. It has become a popular form of exercise for Americans from all walks of life.

History of Asian immigration

In 1763, a small group of Filipinos settled in what is now Louisiana. However, the first wave of Asian immigration to the United States did not begin until the mid-1800's, more than 200 years after the first wave of European immigration.

One major reason that Asians did not leave their homelands was that their societies were relatively stable. Asia did not experience the revolutions that brought political, economic, and social changes to Europe. The people had little reason to leave in search of a better life. But by the mid-1800's, the traditional Asian systems began to prove ineffective in the face of increasing social problems.

The first major social crises erupted in China. The government began to weaken under repeated foreign invasions, domestic revolts, and problems caused by overpopulation. The rulers could no longer control people who wanted to leave the country.

The first wave of Asian immigration. The news in 1848 that gold had been discovered on John Sutter's California property attracted many people to the state. In 1849, about 700 Chinese arrived hoping to find work mining gold. They were poor peasants from southeastern China. Most of them could not even pay their fare to the United States. They got loans from merchants in their own country and promised to pay off their debts after they found work in America.

By the end of 1850, there were 4,000 Chinese in California. By 1860, the United States had a Chinese population of about 35,000, most of whom lived in California. By then, Chinese laborers were well known to industri-

Ethnic background of Asian Americans

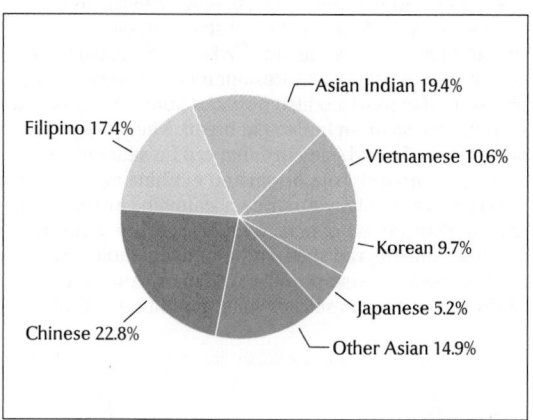

Asian Indian 19.4%

Filipino 17.4%

Vietnamese 10.6%

Korean 9.7%

Japanese 5.2%

Other Asian 14.9%

Chinese 22.8%

Figures are for 2010.
Source: U.S. Census Bureau.

alists and plantation owners in both North and South America. Sugar plantation owners in Hawaii recruited Chinese laborers, and railroads sent labor recruiters to China. Chinese laborers were the primary work force for the western half of the Transcontinental Railroad, which connects California and other settlements and territories in the West with the eastern United States.

California civic leaders and industrialists greeted the first arrivals of Chinese laborers with enthusiasm. But soon, white workers came to believe that Chinese workers were rivals for jobs. The U.S. Democratic Party and labor unions campaigned against Chinese immigration. The general American public became fearful that Chinese would overrun the United States. In numerous instances, mobs attacked and killed Chinese immigrants. In 1882, Congress passed the Chinese Exclusion Act, which prohibited all Chinese laborers from immigrating to the United States. The act permitted only merchants, teachers, and certain other groups from China to come.

The act was the first of numerous restrictions the U.S.

government placed on Asian immigration. The restrictions resulted in part because many white American workers feared job competition from Asian immigrants, many of whom were forced to work for low wages. In addition, some Americans argued that Asians could not be *assimilated* (incorporated) into American society because of their physical and cultural differences.

The second wave. Hawaii did not become a state until 1959. But by the late 1800's and early 1900's, it was the destination for several Asian immigrant groups. The first group were Chinese workers. Between 1852 and 1900, some 50,000 came to work on sugar plantations. The second group consisted of Japanese workers. Like the Chinese, they were recruited by an association of owners of Hawaiian sugar plantations. Between 1885 and 1894, the association recruited almost 29,000 Japanese as *contract laborers,* workers imported under an agreement to work for a particular employer.

After the Japanese fulfilled their contracts, most of them settled in Hawaii or in the Pacific Coast States of California, Oregon, and Washington. They worked first as farm hands and later grew vegetables on land they purchased or rented.

In the early 1900's, the Japanese population in the Pacific Coast States began to face the same opposition that Chinese workers had. In 1905, an organization that later became the Asiatic Exclusion League was established in California to work toward halting the immigration of Japanese people and other Asians. In 1908, the United States and Japan reached an understanding that became known as the *gentlemen's agreement.* The agreement restricted new Japanese immigration to the relatives of immigrants who had already settled in the United States. The gentlemen's agreement was not a law, and it was never put into writing. Japan cooperated voluntarily to avoid the fate of China, which was specifically excluded from immigration into the United States.

Arrivals of the early 1900's. The Hawaiian plantation owners began looking for other sources of labor in the

early 1900's. Their Japanese workers had organized labor unions and frequently went on strike, demanding higher wages and better living conditions. The plantation owners turned to Korea, where the people had recently suffered through war and famine. During the early 1900's, the Hawaiians recruited more than 7,000 Korean laborers. But Korean immigration halted in 1905. Japanese workers had complained to their government that Korean workers were being used as strikebreakers. Japan, then in the process of taking control of Korea, put pressure on the Korean government to stop immigration to Hawaii. Most Koreans in Hawaii remained there. A small group migrated to the U.S. Pacific Coast.

In 1906, the plantation owners began bringing in workers from the Philippines. By 1931, about 110,000 Filipino laborers had arrived. During the early 1900's, a small number of Filipinos went to Alaska for seasonal work in the fishing industry. Others found agricultural work in such states as California and Oregon.

Groups of immigrants from India began arriving in the United States in the early 1900's. Most of the immigrants were young men from farm households in search of job opportunities. They arrived by ship in British Columbia, Canada. Many made their way south into the United States. Most of them found work in lumber mills in Washington state or on farms in central California. Like other Asians before them, they faced opposition from local citizens. In 1907, a mob in Bellingham, Washington, rioted against Asian Indian sawmill workers. The mob attacked the homes of the Asians and drove the immigrants out of town. Most of the immigrants fled to Canada.

Asian immigration halted. In 1917, Congress passed one of the country's most restrictive immigration laws. The law prohibited immigrants from an area known as the Asiatic Barred Zone from coming to the United States. This area included most of Asia and a majority of islands in the Pacific Ocean.

The Immigration Act of 1924 excluded any Asians who

Visual Communications

Filipino farm laborers, *above,* were among Asian immigrants of the early 1900's. During that period, thousands of Filipinos arrived to do agricultural work.

Ansel Adams, Library of Congress

Japanese Americans detained during World War II lived in barracks in internment camps. West Coast residents of Japanese ancestry were forced into such camps in the 1940's.

An Indian restaurant is an example of the many small business-es owned and operated by Asian Americans today. Often, sever-al members of a family work long hours to run the business.

had not been barred by the 1917 law. The legislation closed the doors of the country to Asians—with one ex-ception. People from the Philippines were allowed entry. At that time, the Philippines was a U.S. colony, so Filipi-nos could freely enter the country. But the Tydings-Mc-Duffie Act of 1934 limited immigration from the Philip-pines to an annual quota of 50.

World War II and Japanese Americans. Japan's at-tack on the U.S. military base at Pearl Harbor, Hawaii, on Dec. 7, 1941, brought the United States into World War II (1939-1945). The attack also stirred hostility against Jap-anese Americans. Many people associated Japanese Americans with the enemy who had destroyed United States Navy ships.

In February 1942, President Franklin D. Roosevelt signed Executive Order 9066. It authorized designation of military areas from which "any or all persons may be excluded." This act permitted the government to bypass the constitutional safeguards of immigrants and Ameri-can citizens for the reason of "military necessity." With as little as one week's warning, the Army removed all peo-ple of Japanese ancestry from the West Coast and south-ern Arizona, and confined them in detention camps. Two-thirds of the people held in the camps were U.S. citizens. Detainees lost not only their freedom but also their homes and jobs. The authorities branded them as "disloyal" and barred them from serving in the military.

Over 110,000 Japanese Americans were confined. The Army sent them to 10 main camps in Arizona, Arkansas, California, Colorado, Idaho, Utah, and Wyoming, as well as to other detention facilities. Many of the camps stood in deserts or swamps. Barbed wire fences surrounded the camps, and armed guards kept watch. Each family lived in a single room in Army-style barracks. In 1944, the Supreme Court of the United States accepted the government's claim of "military necessity" and upheld the mass confinement. Then the court ruled that loyal citizens could not be detained. The government used a questionnaire and background checks to determine who was loyal. It released the Japanese Americans it considered loyal to live in cities far from the Pacific Coast. The government also began to draft Japanese American men into the U.S. military.

Thousands of Japanese Americans served in the U.S. armed forces during World War II. Most fought in the Army's 442nd Regimental Combat Unit. The unit served bravely in Europe and suffered many casualties. Its com-bat record improved public opinion about the loyalty of Japanese Americans.

In 1980, Representative Norman Y. Mineta of Califor-nia and Senator Daniel Inouye of Hawaii sponsored a bill that established the Commission on Wartime Relo-cation and Internment of Civilians. The commission ex-amined the circumstances surrounding Executive Order 9066 and its impact on those affected. The commission's two-year study concluded that Japanese Americans were innocent victims. The true reasons for the mass de-tention, it said, were racism, war hysteria, and failed

Notable Asian American "firsts"

1922 Anna May Wong, Chinese American, first Asian Ameri-can to star in a Hollywood motion picture, *The Toll of the Sea*

1948 Sammy Lee, Korean American diver, first Asian American to win an Olympic gold medal for the United States

1957 Dalip Singh Saund, Indian-born Democrat from Califor-nia, first Asian American in the U.S. Congress

1957 Chen Ning Yang and Tsung Dao Lee, Chinese-born American physicists, first Asian Americans to win the Nobel Prize in physics

1959 Hiram L. Fong, Chinese American Republican from Ha-waii, first Asian American to serve in the U.S. Senate

1963 Daniel K. Inouye, Japanese American Democrat from Ha-waii, first Asian American to serve in both houses of Congress

1964 Hiram L. Fong, Chinese American Republican from Ha-waii, first Asian American to run for president of the United States

1965 Patsy T. Mink, Japanese American Democrat from Hawaii, first Asian American woman in Congress

1974 George R. Ariyoshi, Japanese American Democratic gov-ernor of Hawaii, first Asian American governor of a U.S. state

1976 Samuel Chao Chung Ting, first U.S.-born Chinese physi-cist to win the Nobel Prize in physics

1984 Haing S. Ngor, Cambodian-born American actor and phy-sician, first Asian American to win an Academy Award, as best supporting actor for his role in *The Killing Fields*

1985 Ellison Onizuka, Japanese American astronaut, first Asian American in space

1992 Kristi Yamaguchi, Japanese American figure skater, first Asian American to win an Olympic gold medal in skating

1997 Eric Shinseki, Japanese American military officer, first Asian American four-star general in the U.S. Army

2001 Norman Y. Mineta, Japanese American secretary of transportation, first Asian American in the U.S. Cabinet

2001 Elaine Lan Chao, Chinese American secretary of labor, first Asian American woman in the Cabinet

2007 Bobby Jindal, Republican governor of Louisiana, first person of Asian Indian ancestry elected governor of a U.S. state

2008 Don Wakamatsu, Japanese American baseball manager, first Asian American manager of a major league baseball team, the Seattle Mariners

2009 Steven Chu, Chinese American physicist, first Asian American se cretary of energy and first person appointed to the Cabinet after winning a Nobel Prize

2010 Apolo Anton Ohno, Japanese American speed skater, first Asian American to win eight medals in the Winter Olym-pic Games

2010 Nikki Haley, Republican governor of South Carolina, first Asian American woman elected governor of a U.S. state

2020 Kamala Harris, U.S. senator from California, first person of South Asian ancestry to be elected vice president of the United States

leadership. The commission recommended that the president offer a national apology to Japanese Americans. It also called for a compensatory payment of $20,000 to surviving Japanese Americans sent to the camps. These and other recommendations of the commission became law under the Civil Liberties Act of 1988.

Restrictions lifted. Although World War II brought suffering to many Japanese Americans, it also brought about the first easing of U.S. restrictions on Asian immigration. Because China was fighting as an ally of the United States, many people felt that Chinese immigrants should no longer be barred. In 1943, the government lifted the ban on Chinese immigration and also allowed Chinese immigrants to become citizens. This was the first time that foreign-born Asians were granted the right to United States citizenship. In 1946, the government extended similar rights to Filipino and Asian Indian immigrants.

In 1952, Congress passed the Immigration and Nationality Act, also called the McCarran-Walter Act. This law essentially retained the Asiatic Barred Zone provision, but it did allow limited immigration from the countries within the zone. It extended to all Asian immigrants the right to become U.S. citizens.

The Immigration Act of 1965 eliminated the Asiatic Barred Zone and set higher immigration quotas per nation. After 1965, large numbers of Asians started moving to the United States, particularly from China, South Korea, and the Philippines.

Arrivals of the late 1900's. Millions of Southeast Asians have come to the United States since the mid-1970's. Most of them fled their homelands as a result of the Vietnam War (1957-1975). The first wave of Southeast Asians to arrive in the United States were Vietnamese political refugees who had worked for the U.S. government or U.S. companies. For the most part, they were educated, skilled workers. Most of the second wave were rural people from Cambodia and Laos, who had less education and fewer job skills.

About three-fourths of the Southeast Asian immigrants settled in 10 states: California, Florida, Massachusetts, Minnesota, New York, Pennsylvania, Texas, Virginia, Washington, and Wisconsin. The initial response in most communities where the refugees settled was sympathetic. However, in some cases, conflicts arose with local residents when the newcomers began to move into the labor force. Many Vietnamese refugees, for example, found jobs in the shrimp fishing industry in Mississippi, Texas, and other Gulf Coast states. Local fishing crews accused the Southeast Asians of setting too many traps, fishing in areas claimed by American crews, and other offenses. Fighting often broke out, and vandals on both sides damaged their rivals' boats and fishing nets.

Asian Americans today

Between 2000 and 2010, the number of Asian Americans increased by 43 percent. Asian Americans and Hispanic Americans, whose numbers also increased by 43 percent, were the fastest growing minority groups in the United States. In spite of their growth, however, Asian Americans still make up less than 5 percent of the population.

Like other members of minority groups, Asian Americans face problems of acceptance in American society. Also like other minorities, Asians struggle against inaccurate images that many people have of them. On the one hand, for example, many books and motion pictures have portrayed Asian Americans as either sinister villains or meek servants. But on the other hand, sociologists have referred to Asian Americans as the "model minority." The label implies that all Asian Americans have achieved success through discipline and hard work and thus other minority groups should imitate them. However, although many Asian Americans succeed, many others do not.

Education levels of Asian Americans vary widely, for example. A higher percentage of Asian Americans receive doctorates every year than either African Americans or Hispanics. Yet many recent Southeast Asian immigrants have little or no formal education and few job skills. Lack of English language skills is a major problem facing many recent Asian immigrants, for whom jobs are hard to find.

Income levels also vary greatly. The median household income among Asian Americans is higher than that for the population of the United States as a whole. However, a higher percentage of Asians than whites live in poverty. Also, Asian American household income often includes the wages of several people. Many Asian Americans operate small businesses, primarily restaurants, grocery stores, and dry cleaners. Often, the whole family is involved in the business, and some members may work 12 to 14 hours a day.

Ji-Yeon Yuh

Related articles in *World Book* include:

Biographies

Chandrasekhar, Subrahmanyan
Fong, Hiram Leong
Lee, Bruce
Mehta, Zubin
Mineta, Norman Yoshio
Noguchi, Isamu
Pei, I. M.
Woods, Tiger
Wu, Chien-shiung
Yang, Chen Ning

History

California (Early statehood)
Gentlemen's agreement
Hawaii (World War II)
Immigration (Immigration to the United States)
Japanese American internment
Oriental Exclusion Acts
Riot (During the 1800's)
Roosevelt, Theodore (Friction with Japan)
World War II (Treatment of enemy aliens)

Other related articles

City (Neighborhoods)
Hmong
Judo
Karate
Martial arts
Minority group (Asian Americans)
Racism
Sushi
Taekwondo
Tai chi ch'uan
Yoga

Asian Development Bank (ADB) lends money to developing countries of Asia and the Pacific to promote their economic growth. A country must be an ADB member to borrow from the bank. The ADB also lends to—and invests in—private enterprises in Asia. The bank was established by the United Nations Economic Commission for Asia and the Far East (now called the United Nations Economic and Social Commission for Asia and the Pacific). Membership is open to countries that belong to the United Nations or to one of its specialized agencies. A non-Asian nation must be economically developed to become a member of the ADB.

When a country joins the ADB, it pledges a sum of money to the bank. Money also comes from donations by member nations. The ADB has loaned money for the development of agriculture, energy resources, and industry and for many other programs.

The ADB started operations in 1966. It has headquarters in Manila, the Philippines.

Critically reviewed by the Asian Development Bank

Asimov, *AZ ih mahf,* **Isaac** (1920-1992), was an American author. He wrote about 400 books for young people and adults, mostly nonfiction emphasizing science and technology. However, he became best known for his science fiction. Many of Asimov's short stories and novels feature robots as characters. Several were collected in *I, Robot* (1950). His popular *Foundation* series of science-fiction novels includes *Foundation* (1951), *Foundation and Empire* (1952), *Second Foundation* (1953), *Foundation's Edge* (1982), *Foundation and Earth* (1986), *Prelude to Foundation* (1988), and *Forward the Foundation* (published in 1993, after his death). He also wrote *Fantastic Voyage* (1966) and *The Gods Themselves* (1972).

Asimov's nonfiction is notable for making complicated material understandable to the general reader. These works include *Asimov's New Guide to Science* (1984). He also wrote on history, humor, William Shakespeare, and the Bible. Asimov wrote two volumes of autobiography, *In Memory Yet Green* (1979) and *In Joy Still Felt* (1980).

Asimov was born on Jan. 2, 1920, in Petrovichi, Russia, near Smolensk. When he was 3 years old, his family moved to New York City. Asimov became a United States citizen in 1928. He taught biochemistry at Boston University from 1949 to 1958 before becoming a full-time writer. He died on April 6, 1992.   Neil Barron

Askia Muhammad, *AS kee ah moo HAM uhd* (1441?-1538), also called Askia I or Askia the Great, ruled the Songhai Empire in western Africa during its height. He was the first of several Songhai kings named Askia. Askia Muhammad became king in 1493 when he overthrew Bakori Da'a, the son of Sunni Ali (see **Songhai Empire**). He seized territories from the Mali Empire, conquered the Hausa states, and turned Saharan Berber towns into Songhai colonies. He encouraged the spread of Islam in West Africa and modeled his empire's laws on those of Islam. His eldest son, Askia Musa, overthrew him in 1528.

Askia Muhammad died on March 2, 1538, in Gao, the Songhai capital. Many people visit his huge tomb in Gao, in present-day Mali.   Kevin C. MacDonald

Asmara, *az MAHR uh,* is the capital and largest city of Eritrea. About 800,000 people live there. It lies in central Eritrea, about 40 miles (64 kilometers) west of the Red Sea. For the location of Asmara, see **Eritrea** (map). The city has areas of treelined streets, expensive homes called *villas,* and large public buildings. Asmara also has slum areas. A Roman Catholic cathedral, a large Eastern Orthodox church, and a major mosque stand near the center of the city. Many buildings in Asmara date from the early 1900's, when Eritrea was a colonial possession of Italy.

The city's industries include tanning, textile production, and processing of agricultural goods. A railroad connects Asmara with Massawa, a port on the Red Sea.

The site of Asmara was a small village until the late 1800's. It became the center for the Italian colonial government in 1897. The United Kingdom occupied Asmara from 1941 to 1952, when Eritrea became part of Ethiopia. In 1993, following a 30-year civil war between Eritrean rebels and the Ethiopian government, Eritrea gained formal independence.   Stephen K. Commins

See also **Eritrea** (picture).

Asoka. See Ashoka.

Asp is a cobra found in Egypt. It is also known as the *Egyptian cobra.* The hood of this *venomous* (poisonous) snake lacks the spectacular markings of the Indian cobra. The asp served as an important religious symbol for the ancient Egyptians. It is believed that Cleopatra committed suicide by holding an asp against her body. Others claim the snake was the horned viper, sometimes called an asp. See also **Cleopatra; Cobra; Snake.**

Kenneth L. Krysko

WORLD BOOK illustration by Richard Lewington, The Garden Studio

Asp

Scientific classification. The scientific name of the asp is *Naja haje.*

Asparagus is a nutritious green vegetable. People eat the young *shoots* (stems) of the asparagus plant. These shoots are called *spears.* Asparagus is an excellent source of protein, vitamins, and minerals. For the best taste and highest nutritional value, fresh asparagus should be cooked gently until soft, but it should remain a brilliant green in color.

Asparagus plants originated in the Mediterranean region and in Africa. They grow best in moderate climates and in loose, moist, sandy soil. In the United States, most asparagus is produced in California, Michigan, and Washington.

Asparagus is a *perennial* plant—that is, it can live for several years without replanting. Most of the commercial asparagus crop is grown from seedlings planted in early spring. As the plants grow, they develop a root system called the *crown.* The crown consists of fleshy roots that store food and underground stems called *rhizomes.* As the soil temperature rises, buds on the rhizomes grow through the soil and become the spears. If the spears are not harvested, they develop into tall, mature plants with feathery leaves. Generally, asparagus plantings are first harvested during the second or third year, depending on the area in which they are grown, when

WORLD BOOK illustration by Kate Lloyd-Jones, Linden Artists Ltd.
Two types of asparagus. People eat edible asparagus, *left.* Florists use asparagus fern, *right,* in decorations.

the roots are able to store large amounts of food. In some cases, properly established plantings may continue to produce well for 15 to 25 years.

Asparagus fern is a kind of asparagus used in floral arrangements. It is also a good house plant.　　Albert Liptay

Scientific classification. The scientific name of edible asparagus is *Asparagus officinalis.* The asparagus fern is *A. plumosus.*

Aspartame. See Artificial sweetener.

Aspen, Colorado (pop. 6,658), once a rich silver-mining center, is now a year-round resort. It lies at an altitude of 7,930 feet (2,417 meters) on the Roaring Fork River in west-central Colorado (see Colorado [political map]).

Aspen is one of the most popular ski centers in the western United States, with four mountains for downhill skiing and about 60 miles (97 kilometers) of trails for cross-country skiing. Throughout the year, the Aspen Institute holds seminars that foster leadership skills. The Aspen Music Festival and School runs for eight weeks. Aspen Santa Fe Ballet hosts dance performances.

　　Mary Eshbaugh Hayes

Aspen is the name of a group of medium-sized poplar trees in North America, Europe, Asia, and Africa. Aspens have smooth, light-colored bark. Their leaves have long, flattened stalks and may be triangular, heart-shaped, or round. In fall, the leaves turn brilliant yellow.

The most common type of aspen in North America is the *quaking aspen,* also known as the *trembling aspen.* It is found from eastern Canada to Alaska, across the Northeastern and Great Lakes states, and in western mountains south into Mexico. Its nearly round leaves have fine-toothed edges. The *bigtooth aspen* grows throughout southeastern Canada and eastward from Minnesota and Iowa in the United States. It is found primarily in low-lying areas with sandy soils. Its leaves are egg-shaped and have coarse-toothed edges. The *European aspen* is found in Europe, North Africa, western Asia, and Siberia. Its leaves are round or oval with notched edges.

Aspens require open, sunny places to reproduce. In forest areas that have been opened up by fire, disease, or other disturbances, aspens grow rapidly and often become the dominant species in a few years. Later, they are generally replaced by trees that grow well in shade.

Aspen wood is used primarily to make pulp for paper. The wood is also used to make matchsticks, boxes, and crates.　　Michael J. Baranski

Scientific classification. Aspens are in the genus *Populus.* The quaking aspen is *Populus tremuloides.* The bigtooth aspen is *P. grandidentata.* The European aspen is *P. tremula.*

See also **Poplar; Tree** (Broadleaf and needleleaf trees [picture]).

Asphalt, *AS fawlt,* is a black cementlike substance that is found in most crude petroleum. It has hundreds of uses. It is used to pave streets, highways, and airfields; to make floor tiles and roofing, waterproofing, and insulating materials; and to line reservoirs, waste storage ponds, dams, and irrigation canals. Asphalt is also used in varnish and inks. In addition, asphalt coatings protect underground pipelines from corrosion.

Asphalt is *thermoplastic*—that is, it softens and becomes a liquid when heated, and it returns to a solid when cooled. Asphalt wears well, is highly waterproof, and is unharmed by most acids and salts.

Asphalt production. Asphalt is separated from crude petroleum by refining methods that also produce gasoline, kerosene, and other products. Usually, a *distillation* (boiling) process removes gasoline and other products with low boiling points. The oil that remains is commonly called *topped crude.* Topped crude may be used as a fuel oil, or it may be further refined to asphalt or other products. By varying the refining processes, refineries may obtain different kinds of asphalt. For example, they make *blown* or *oxidized* asphalts by blowing hot air through topped crude. These asphalts are widely used for roofing, enamels, and other industrial applications. Most topped crude is refined to produce *asphalt cement,* a semisolid asphalt used for paving.

Asphalt also occurs in natural deposits in pits, lakes, and rocks. But only a small part of the asphalt used in the world comes from natural deposits. Some natural deposits found in pits and lakes are pure, but most have become mixed with mineral matter, water, and other substances. One of the best-known deposits is Pitch Lake on the island of Trinidad in the Caribbean Sea. The English explorer Sir Walter Raleigh discovered this 114-acre (46-hectare) bed in 1595. One of the largest deposits of asphalt is in Lake Guanoco in Venezuela, near the Gulf of Paria. The deposit covers about 1,000 acres (400 hectares). *Uintaite* or *gilsonite,* a solid form of asphalt, is found in Utah and Colorado in the United States.

Paving with asphalt. Asphalt is used mainly to pave streets, highways, and airports. *Blacktop* is the common name for many types of asphalt paving. Asphalt pavements are made in several ways. But usually, asphalt cement is mixed with *mineral aggregates,* such as crushed stone, gravel, and sand. These aggregates vary in size. The largest particles are usually about ¾ inch (19 millimeters) in diameter.

The aggregates are blended, dried, and heated to about 300 °F (149 °C) in a paving plant. *Hot mixes* are prepared by adding hot asphalt cement. Paddles mix the asphalt with the aggregates in a *pugmill mixer.* The mix contains only about 5 to 10 percent asphalt by weight. Sometimes, ground rubber from recycled tires is added to the mix to improve a pavement's heat resistance and flexibility. At the job site, a paving machine spreads the mixture evenly on the roadbed, and a roller flattens it into a smooth, hard pavement. *Cold mixes* are made with liquid asphalt. Liquid asphalt is a blend of asphalt cement and a light petroleum *solvent* (substance that can dissolve other substances). Cold mixes can also be made by blending asphalt cement with water. Cold mixes often can be prepared directly on the roadbed because little or no heating is needed in their preparation.

Surface treatment is used to resurface pavements or to pave lightly traveled roads. Hot asphalt cement or liquid asphalt is sprayed evenly over the roadway surface. Mineral aggregates are then spread over the surface and rolled into the asphalt.   Michael A. Adewumi

See also **Bitumen; Petroleum; Road** (picture: Blacktopping).

Asphyxiation, *as* FIHK *see AY shuhn,* is a condition that occurs when there is a lack of oxygen in the air or in the blood or the tissues of the body. During breathing, the lungs provide the blood with oxygen from the air needed to sustain life. Without oxygen, the brain, heart, and other vital organs fail to function. A person loses consciousness when too little oxygen reaches the brain. The heart stops beating if it receives too little oxygen.

Common causes of asphyxiation include drowning, choking, receiving an electric shock, and inhaling poisonous fumes. A person who is not breathing often requires the mouth-to-mouth form of *artificial respiration,* also called *rescue breathing* (see **First aid** [Restoring breathing]). First aid for a person choking on food or other objects includes the application of upward thrusts to the middle of the abdomen. This technique is known as the *Heimlich maneuver* (see **First aid** [Choking]). A person whose heart has stopped beating requires *cardiopulmonary resuscitation,* or *CPR* (see **Cardiopulmonary resuscitation**).   Ryland P. Byrd, Jr.

Aspirin, also known as *acetylsalicylic acid,* is one of the most commonly used drugs in the world. Chemists classify aspirin in a group of chemical compounds called *salicylates.* It is a white, odorless powder with a bitter taste. Aspirin helps relieve pain, lowers fever arising from infections, and helps reduce inflammation due to illness or injury. It also interferes with blood clotting, and thus it is useful in preventing heart attacks, strokes, and other disorders that involve blood clots.

Aspirin is relatively safe if taken at the recommended dosage. But it can irritate the stomach lining and cause stomach bleeding, a serious side effect in some people, particularly the elderly. Children with chickenpox or influenza should not take aspirin. Its use during such viral illnesses is associated with a serious complication called *Reye's syndrome* (see **Reye's syndrome**).

How aspirin works. Aspirin is one of a class of drugs called *nonsteroidal anti-inflammatory drugs* (NSAID's). These drugs include other pain relievers, such as *ibuprofen.* NSAID's work mainly by blocking the formation in the body of *prostaglandins,* biochemical compounds similar to hormones. Aspirin inactivates two enzymes, *cyclooxygenase-1* and *cyclooxygenase-2,* that are necessary for the formation of prostaglandins.

Aspirin's reactions with the two enzymes have different effects in the human body. When aspirin blocks cyclooxygenase-1, the main effects are reduced blood clotting and irritation of the stomach lining. In contrast, the inactivation of cyclooxygenase-2 reduces fever and inflammation. By the late 1990's, scientists had developed new drugs called *COX-2 inhibitors* that act only on cyclooxygenase-2. These so-called *superaspirins,* such as Celebrex, relieve pain and reduce inflammation and fever without the stomach irritation that aspirin can cause. However, scientists have found that high dosages of these drugs may increase the risk for heart attack and stroke. Medical experts recommend that people consult with a physician before taking these medications.

Health benefits. Many doctors advise their adult patients to take one aspirin tablet a day to reduce the risk of heart attacks and strokes. Scientists also have observed that people who use aspirin regularly have a lower incidence of breast, colon, and rectal cancer. They believe that aspirin's effects on the cyclooxygenase-2 enzyme block inflammation and other processes necessary for cancer to develop. Scientists are investigating other health benefits of aspirin. But people should use aspirin to prevent disease only under the care of a physician.

History. For centuries, people used willow bark to relieve pain and fever. The bark contains a chemical that the body converts to a salicylate. Charles F. Gerhardt, a French chemist, first made aspirin in a laboratory in 1853. The drug's medicinal value was not fully recognized until 1899, when Heinrich Dreser, a German drug researcher, wrote about it.   R. Michael Garavito

See also **Analgesic; Prostaglandin.**

Asquith, *AS kwihth,* **Herbert Henry** (1852-1928), served as prime minister of the United Kingdom from 1908 to 1916. His ministry was significant for the Old Age Pension Act (1908), the National Insurance Act (1911), and the Parliamentary Act (1911), which restricted the power of the House of Lords. David Lloyd George replaced Asquith as both Liberal Party leader and as prime minister in 1916. A breach between the two men helped bring about a decline of the Liberal Party after World War I ended in 1918 (see **Lloyd George, David**).

Asquith was born on Sept. 12, 1852, in Morley, Yorkshire. He served as the U.K. chancellor of the exchequer from 1905 to 1908. In 1925, he became the Earl of Oxford and Asquith. He died on Feb. 15, 1928.   Keith Robbins

Ass. See Donkey; Onager.

Assad, *ah SAHD,* **Bashar al-,** *bah SHAHR uhl* (1965-   ), became president of Syria in July 2000. His name is also spelled *Bashar al-Asad.* He took over the presidency following the death of his father, Hafez al-Assad (also spelled *Hafiz al-Asad),* Syria's leader since 1970. Hafez al-Assad had begun preparing Bashar to be his successor after the death in 1994 of Bashar's older brother, Basil. For information on Syria during Bashar's presidency, see **Syria** (The early 2000's).

Bashar al-Assad was born on Sept. 11, 1965, in Damascus. He received a medical degree from the University of Damascus in 1988. He trained in *ophthalmology* (the study of diseases of the eye) at the Tishrin military hospital in Damascus from 1988 until 1992. He moved to England in 1992 to complete a medical residency program.

After Basil's death in a car accident, Bashar returned to Syria. He attended the military academy at Homs, north of Damascus, earning the rank of colonel. After his father died, Bashar was promoted to lieutenant general and made commander in chief of the armed forces. He also became head of the Baath Party.   As'ad AbuKhalil

Assad, *ah SAHD,* **Hafez al-,** *HAH fehz uhl* (1930-2000), was president of Syria from 1971 until his death in 2000. A military leader, he seized power from Syria's radical government in 1970. He was elected president the next year. His name is also spelled *Hafiz al-Asad.*

Assad sought to make Syria the leader of the Arab struggle against Israel. In 1973, Syria and Egypt fought a war against Israel in an unsuccessful attempt to regain Arab land Israel had occupied in 1967. In 1976, Syria sent troops to help end a civil war in Lebanon. In 1982, Assad's government crushed a rebellion by militant Sunni Islamic opposition. Syrian troops helped allied forces defeat Iraq in the Persian Gulf War of 1991. Assad was a member of the Baath socialist party and of Syria's minority Alawite Muslim sect.

Assad was born on Oct. 6, 1930, in Al Qardahah, near Latakia. He attended the military academy in Homs and graduated from the air force academy in Aleppo. He was commander of the Syrian Air Force and minister of defense when he seized power in 1970. Assad died on June 10, 2000. His son Bashar al-Assad succeeded him as president.   Michel Le Gall

See also **Syria** (Recent developments).

Assange, *ah SAHNJ,* **Julian** (1971-   ), is an Australian internet activist and the founder of WikiLeaks. WikiLeaks is a website that posts secret government and business information. Assange founded WikiLeaks as an expression of his political ideas. He believes that publishing secrets can force governments and corporations to become more open and just.

Assange was born in Townsville, in Queensland, Australia, on July 3, 1971. As a teenager, he learned how to *hack* into computer networks—that is, gain unauthorized access to them. In 1991, after Assange was caught hacking into a computer system, Australian federal police raided his home. He pleaded guilty and paid a small fine to the government. In the 1990's, he wrote computer programs, most of them for *open-source* (free) software.

Assange founded WikiLeaks in 2006. Early leaks on the organization's website revealed United States military policies at a detention camp in Guantánamo Bay, the site of a U.S. naval base in Cuba. In 2010, WikiLeaks published a video filmed in Iraq in 2007, during the Iraq War (2003-2011), that showed a U.S. Army helicopter killing civilians. The controversy surrounding the video made Assange a public figure.

While Assange was living in the United Kingdom in 2010, Swedish authorities issued a warrant for his arrest. He was wanted for questioning over claims of sexual misconduct. In 2012, the British Supreme Court ruled that Assange should be *extradited* (handed over) to Sweden. He then *jumped bail* (failed to appear in court) and was granted *asylum* (safe shelter) at Ecuador's embassy in London. Assange remained there for years, fearing that if he left, British authorities would arrest him and turn him over to Sweden. Sweden, in turn, could extradite him to the United States, where he could face charges for leaking top-secret government documents. In 2017, Swedish prosecutors suspended the investigation against Assange. British police still had a warrant to arrest him for jumping bail, so he stayed at the embassy.

Assange continued to publish millions of secret documents and communications from a number of governments and corporations. In 2016, WikiLeaks published numerous hacked internal emails linked to U.S. Democratic presidential nominee Hillary Clinton. Some political analysts believe the leaked emails may have played a role in Clinton's defeat in the 2016 election.

In 2019, Ecuador *revoked* (withdrew) its asylum offer. Assange had to leave the embassy, and British authorities took him into custody. A British court sentenced him to 50 weeks in prison for jumping bail in 2012. In 2019 and 2020, the U.S. government charged him with espionage. He remained in custody awaiting decisions on extradition by British authorities.   Steve Jones

Assassination is the murder of a person who holds a position of public importance. Ordinarily, assassinations are committed for one or more of three reasons: to gain revenge, to earn a reward, or to remove a political enemy from office. The assassination of a ruler has often been applauded. Brutus, one of the assassins of Julius Caesar, was considered a hero by many Romans.

The assassination of Archduke Franz Ferdinand of Austria, in 1914, was one cause of World War I. The series of assassinations committed by the Black Dragon Society in Japan in the 1930's threw control of the government into the hands of the Japanese Army. Four presidents of the United States have been assassinated: Abraham Lincoln in 1865, James A. Garfield in 1881, William McKinley in 1901, and John F. Kennedy in 1963.

The word *assassination* comes from *assassins* or *hashshashin* (hemp-eaters), a band of Muslims in Persia and Asia Minor in the 1100's. They smoked a drug called *hashish,* which is made from the hemp plant, and killed their enemies while under its influence.   Stephen Goode

Assault and battery is a legal term for a physical threat and act. An act of assault puts the victim in fear of bodily harm. Spoken threats are not assaults, because there must be a physical act. Raising a club or drawing back a fist is assault, even if no actual blow follows. One who levels a gun at a crowd may be found guilty of assault against every person in the crowd. Battery refers to the actual blow, or other physical injury. The two offenses usually occur together and are usually punished as one. No assault results if a person has a right to threaten or inflict harm. People can legally remove intruders from their homes with force if necessary.

Parents may use force in punishing children. But they become guilty of assault and battery if they punish too roughly. Assault and battery are crimes punishable by fine or imprisonment. The offender may also be sued for damages by the victim.   Charles F. Wellford

Assemblies of God is a fellowship of Pentecostal churches based in the United States. Its official name is the General Council of the Assemblies of God. It grew from a revival movement that began in the late 1800's. It was organized in Hot Springs, Arkansas, in 1914.

Churches in the Assemblies of God teach that the Bible is the inspired word of God. They also teach the fall and redemption of human beings, divine healing through prayer, the return of Jesus Christ and his reign, and eternal punishment for the unsaved. The churches teach that Christians should seek to be filled with the Holy Spirit. The initial evidence of this comes when people *speak in tongues* (speak in a language they never learned). Believers are baptized by *immersion* (dipping into water). Assemblies of God churches also observe Holy Communion, sometimes called the Lord's Supper.

A General Council supervises the educational, missionary, and publishing activities of the Assemblies of God in the United States. Elected pastors and boards of deacons are responsible for the affairs of local congregations. All affiliated churches must adhere to the Statement of Fundamental Truths of the Assemblies of God and to a Biblical code of conduct. The Assemblies of God has millions of followers worldwide. Its headquarters are in Springfield, Missouri.

Critically reviewed by the General Council of the Assemblies of God

Assembly, Freedom of. See Freedom of assembly.

Assembly line is a manufacturing method that divides production into separate tasks, turning out large quantities of goods at low prices. Workers repeatedly perform a single step in an assembly process, such as inserting, tightening, or inspecting a part. Assembly lines reflect the principle of *division of labor,* which breaks up complex manufacturing jobs into smaller, specialized tasks.

Before assembly lines, skilled workers made items and parts by hand. No two finished products were exactly alike. The 1800's brought the development of identical, *interchangeable parts.* Standardizing the parts of manufactured items was a key step toward assembly-line production. Henry Ford, an American automobile manufacturer, helped popularize assembly lines in the early 1900's. He refined the use of conveyor belts to carry parts between workstations. New cars rolled out of Ford's factory every few minutes.

Assembly lines allowed unskilled workers to quickly learn and perform jobs. Efficient manufacturing made complex products cheap and raised living standards. But some workers complained about constantly having to repeat the same motions. Modern assembly lines often involve the use of industrial robots.   Amy Sue Bix

Related articles in *World Book* include:

Automobile (Manufacturing; diagram)	Ford, Henry
Conveyor belt	Mass production
Factory	Robot

Assessment is the process of assigning a cash value to property for taxation. Assessed property may include land, buildings, business equipment, and inventory. The term *assessment* also refers to the amount of tax levied on a property. The amount of tax is based on the assessed value of the property (see **Property tax**). In most cases, assessments are determined by state or local officials called *assessors.* Assessors may be elected by the voters or appointed by the state or local government.

Assigning a fair and uniform value to property is the chief goal of assessment. Assessors try to determine what property would sell for if it were offered on the open market for a reasonable time and if both buyer and seller were well informed. Assessors make such determinations largely by collecting information about the sales prices of similar property recently sold.

Several problems make it difficult to make a fair estimate of value. One problem is that nearly all properties are different. For example, a large house on the corner differs from a small house in the middle of the block. If recent sales involve only small houses, the assessor must use that information to estimate the value of a large house. Another problem is that sales information quickly grows out of date. Prices more than a year old are probably not a useful guide to current values.

Still another problem is that much property, such as office and medical buildings, is rented rather than sold. The assessor must use information on rental income and expenses to estimate what the building is worth to the owner. Some property—such as factories, power plants, and railroad tracks—is neither rented nor sold. To assess such property, the assessor must collect information on the cost of buying vacant land and building a similar structure.   John M. Clapp

Assignment is the legal term for the transfer of rights to property or money from one person to another. The person who makes the transfer is the *assignor.* The *assignee* receives whatever rights the assignor had. For example, if the assignor has the right to possess a piece of land, the assignee receives the right. If the assignor has only the right to collect rents from the land, the assignee receives only that right. People usually make assignments in writing. In some cases, a person may assign property that he or she expects to own. See also **Loan company.**   Linda Henry Elrod

Assimilation, *uh SIHM uh LAY shuhn,* is the process by which cells convert food into living tissues. This process makes possible the growth and repair of living organisms. In human beings, assimilation begins when food is broken down into simple molecules in the stomach. This process is called digestion. The bloodstream absorbs the digested food and carries it to all parts of the body. The cells then assimilate the food for use in the growth and repair of the body. See also **Absorption and adsorption; Cell; Digestive system.**   George B. Johnson

Assimilation, *uh SIHM uh LAY shuhn,* is the process through which one social and cultural group becomes part of another social and cultural group. For example, groups of people from many countries have settled in the United States. Most of these people gradually abandoned the way of life of their homeland and adopted an American way of life. They learned the language, adopted the customs, and followed the traditions.

Assimilation may also occur when people move from one part of a country to another part. For example, farm people who move to a city become assimilated into the way of life of the city. An assimilated group does not necessarily adopt the new way of life fully. It may keep some old customs or modify some of the new customs.

Sometimes, assimilation is prevented or slowed down because a majority group does not want contact with a minority group. Black people, Jewish people, and other minority groups have often been forced to remain in *ghettos* (segregated living areas). In other cases, minorities have held to their way of life and have deliberately avoided assimilation into the majority. The Amish of U.S. farm communities are an example (see **Amish**). In industrial countries, minorities almost always assimilate into the majority's way of life. But in developing countries, majorities sometimes become assimilated into a minority. This occurs when a minority is socially and economically more advanced or powerful than the majority.

Russell Zanca

Assiniboia, *uh SIHN uh BOY uh,* was the name of two territorial districts in what are now the United States and Canada. One district lay on either side of the Red River in both countries. The other district was mainly in the present-day province of Saskatchewan.

In 1811, the district along the Red River was granted

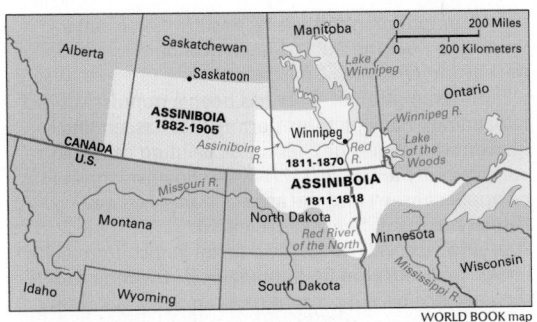

Assiniboia was the name of two historic areas of southern Canada and the northern United States.

to the Earl of Selkirk, a Scottish colonizer in Canada. He named the area after local Indians. Part of the district, including much of what are now North Dakota and Minnesota, was cut off when the 49th parallel became the U.S.-Canadian boundary in 1818. The rest disappeared when the province of Manitoba was created in 1870. See **Manitoba** (The Red River Colony); **Selkirk, Earl of.**

In 1882, a district in what was then the Canadian North-West Territories was named Assiniboia. In 1905, it became part of Alberta and Saskatchewan. See **Saskatchewan** (North-West Territories).   J. M. Bumsted

Assiniboine Indians, *uh SIHN uh BOYN,* are a large Plains tribe who live in parts of Canada and the United States. Before Europeans came to North America, the Assiniboine lived near Lake Superior in what is now Ontario. During the late 1600's and the 1700's, they moved to what became Saskatchewan, Montana, and North Dakota. The name *Assiniboine* probably comes from a Chippewa word that means *one who cooks by the use of stones.* They boiled soup by dropping hot stones into a pot. In Canada, they are often called Stonies.

The Assiniboine were a nomadic people who moved about following buffalo herds. They lived in tipis made of buffalo hides and wore buckskin clothing. The men hunted game, especially buffalo and antelope, and the women gathered berries, fruits, and plants to eat. The Assiniboine formed bands of related families who camped and hunted together. Each band was headed by a chief and a council of elders. The tribe's religion centered on the pursuit of visions and on a ceremony called the *sun dance* (see **Sun dance**). The Assiniboine believed visions brought help from the gods.

The Assiniboine were originally a division of the Sioux Indians but separated from them before 1640. They then became allies of the Cree, who were enemies of the Sioux. During the late 1700's and early 1800's, smallpox wiped out nearly half the Assiniboine.

Today, a few thousand Assiniboine live on the Fort Peck and Fort Belknap reservations in Montana and on small reserves in Alberta and Saskatchewan. Each reservation or reserve is governed by an elected tribal council. Some Assiniboine are farmers or ranchers. Many members of the tribe are poor and depend on economic aid from the government of the United States or Canada. Despite these problems, the people are proud of being Assiniboine, and many still speak their native language.   Raymond J. DeMallie

Assisi, Francis of. See **Francis of Assisi, Saint.**

Associated Press (AP) is one of the world's largest news-gathering services. The AP distributes international, regional, and local news to media worldwide.

The AP is a nonprofit organization. It is owned and controlled by about 1,500 United States daily newspapers. Thousands of U.S. newspapers, radio and TV stations, and online providers receive news from the AP. News media in over 120 other countries also subscribe to the service. The AP provides news in four languages.

The AP offers daily news reports, features, photographs, *graphics* (artwork), audio, video, and interactive online content. Most AP subscribers receive news around the clock. Some radio stations receive AP audio newscasts. AP photographs are sent digitally via satellite or communications lines. Digital transmission is a method of sending sounds or pictures by converting them into electrical signals in the form of a *digital* (numerical) code. Some television stations also receive AP video graphics in digital form.

Five New York City newspapers founded the Associated Press in 1846. They began the service to save money on the gathering of news by telegraph. Today, the AP has about 240 news bureaus worldwide. Its headquarters are in New York City.   Rich Gordon

Association, in psychology, refers to one theory of how people learn things. The theory's three laws of association attempt to explain how a person *associates* (relates) experiences. These laws are (1) the law of contiguity, (2) the law of similarity, and (3) the law of contrast.

The law of contiguity states that mental associations occur when two events take place close to each other in time or space. For example, teachers try to grade an examination soon after students take it. This helps students associate the correct answers with the questions while the examination is fresh in their minds.

The law of similarity states that a person is more likely to connect two things that are almost the same. For example, a child is more likely to associate a wagon with an automobile than with an airplane.

The law of contrast states that greatly differing things are likely to be associated. For example, it is easier to learn the differences between "hot" and "cold" than between "hot" and "warm."

Critics of the theory say it puts too much emphasis on the events associated and not enough emphasis on the person. Psychologists holding other views think that the ability of a person to understand the similarity or difference between things is also important in learning.

Few psychologists accept the associationist point of view completely. Most of them realize association takes place but doubt it explains all learning.   Allen Frances

See also **Behavior; Learning; Psychology.**

Association for the Study of African American Life and History, often called the ASALH, conducts and promotes research and study of the black person's role in world history. The association collects writings and materials relating to African Americans and other ethnic groups. It promotes harmony and understanding among all people. The association's members include historians, scholars, and students. It sponsors Black History Month and sets the national theme for the celebration. It also publishes *Black History Bulletin* and *The Journal of African American History.* The American historian Carter G. Woodson founded the Association for the

Study of Negro Life and History in 1915. The association received its present name in 1998. Headquarters are in Washington, D.C. See also **Black History Month; Woodson, Carter Godwin.** Critically reviewed by the Association for the Study of African American Life and History

Association of Southeast Asian Nations

(ASEAN) is an organization of 10 Southeast Asian countries—Brunei, Cambodia, Indonesia, Laos, Malaysia, Myanmar, the Philippines, Singapore, Thailand, and Vietnam. It promotes political, economic, cultural, and social cooperation among its members. Although ASEAN works for peace and stability in Southeast Asia, it is not a defense organization.

The members of ASEAN cooperate in such fields as population control, prevention of drug abuse, scientific research, and combating terrorism. Teachers, students, and artists of the member nations exchange visits. In addition, the organization develops plans to promote tourism in ASEAN countries and to encourage programs of Southeast Asian studies. It works to reduce trade barriers among the members.

The foreign ministers of the member countries meet annually to determine ASEAN policy and to consider projects recommended by ASEAN committees. These committees consist of experts and officials from the member countries and are responsible for putting ASEAN projects into effect. ASEAN's administrative body, the ASEAN Secretariat, is in Jakarta, Indonesia.

ASEAN was established in 1967 by Indonesia, Malaysia, the Philippines, Singapore, and Thailand. The ASEAN heads of government met first in 1976 and made several important agreements. The member nations agreed to share basic products during shortages and to gradually remove trade restrictions. They also decided to build an industrial project in each country. The leaders established the organization's Secretariat, as well as a council to settle disputes among the member nations.

In 1994, the members of ASEAN established the ASEAN Regional Forum (ARF). The ARF promotes cooperation and diplomacy on security matters throughout Southeast Asia. Participants in the ARF include the members of ASEAN plus China, Japan, the United States, and other major countries.

Brunei became a member of ASEAN in 1984. Vietnam was admitted in 1995, Laos and Myanmar in 1997, and Cambodia in 1999. David P. Chandler

Assumption is the religious belief that a certain person was taken bodily into heaven. The belief is part of both Jewish and Christian tradition.

In Judaism, an assumption is called an *aliyah,* which means *ascent* or *going up.* In the Old Testament, or Hebrew Bible, there is only one specific reference to an assumption. In 2 Kings 2:1-13, God takes the prophet Elijah into heaven in a whirlwind. Other traditions based on Bible stories state that Enoch, the father of Methuselah, and the Israelite leader Moses ascended into heaven.

Belief in assumption is not found in the New Testament, but it became significant during the late Middle Ages (the A.D. 1300's and 1400's), especially in the Western church. The Assumption of the Blessed Virgin is a doctrine of the Roman Catholic Church. It states that the body and soul of the Virgin Mary were taken into heaven. Pope Pius XII proclaimed the Assumption a church doctrine in 1950. Roman Catholics celebrate the Feast of the Assumption on August 15. Assumption is not a Protestant doctrine but has been accepted as a belief in the Eastern Orthodox Churches.

The Assumption of Mary has been a popular subject in painting. Many pictures portray Mary ascending to heaven with angels or cherubs. A painting called *Assumption of the Virgin* (1577) by the Spanish artist El Greco appears in **Art and the arts.** Stanley K. Stowers

Assurbanipal. See Ashurbanipal.

Assyria, *uh SIHR ee uh,* was an ancient country on the upper Tigris River in Mesopotamia. It covered roughly the northern part of present-day Iraq. Assyria's civilization was similar to that of ancient Babylonia, its southern neighbor. People began settling in Assyria about 8500 B.C. In the 800's B.C., the Assyrians started to build an empire that lasted until the end of the 600's B.C.

The Assyrians have been called the *Romans of Asia* because they were great conquerors. During the days of their empire, they won their victories in the Roman way—by superb organization, weapons, and equipment.

The land

Assyria was a land of rolling hills. The Tigris and the small streams that fed it kept the valleys fertile. To the north rose the steep Armenian Mountains. On the east were the Zagros Mountains and the high hills of Iran. The Assyrians were more interested in the rich lands of Babylonia and the fertile plains of western Mesopotamia and Syria. Assyria had a better natural climate for agriculture than Babylonia did. It was cooler there, and the rainfall was heavier. But irrigation was much easier on the Babylonian plain than in the Assyrian hills. Once started on the path of conquest, the Assyrians took much more than the fertile farmland nearby. Their empire came to include forests, areas with mineral resources, and other kinds of land. Assyria itself remained a farming country. It also had plenty of good building stone, some timber, and a small amount of minerals.

Way of life

The Assyrian people dressed in coatlike garments called *tunics* and wore sandals. The men often wore their hair long, and many grew beards. Many high-ranking officials wore long, squared-off beards. Most other men had short beards. Married women often wore veils outside their homes.

Most Assyrians worked for Assyrian rulers or other powerful people. Farmers lived in small villages on estates and worked the land. They lived in houses with thatched roofs and walls made of intertwined branches and mud. Farmers raised livestock and produced milk and other dairy products. The chief crop was barley.

Assyria had few large cities. The most important were Assur, Nineveh, and Kalhu (also spelled Calah, but now called Nimrud). Most city dwellers were craftworkers or traders. Craftworkers made pottery as well as objects of bronze, gold, ivory, silver, and wood. High walls, guarded by archers, encircled the cities to protect residents from attack. Citizens tended gardens and orchards just outside the city walls.

Some Assyrians roamed the countryside in seminomadic groups. These groups consisted mostly of runaway slaves, unsuccessful farmers, and people who had been expelled from the cities. Relations between the city dwellers and the seminomads often were tense.

Most slaves in Assyria were prisoners of war or people who could not pay their debts. The slaves' owners probably treated them fairly well. Some Assyrians sold their wives and children into slavery to clear their debts.

Language and literature. A variety of peoples lived in Assyria, and they spoke various languages. The most important of these languages was Assyrian, a Semitic language related to modern Hebrew and Arabic and similar to the ancient Babylonian language.

The Assyrians used a writing system called *cuneiform* that was developed by the Sumerians in Babylonia. It consisted of wedge-shaped symbols on clay tablets. Assyrian *scribes* (writers) wrote letters and contracts, as well as texts that dealt with religion, literature, medicine, history, and other subjects. A few Assyrian kings collected the clay tablets in libraries. There, librarians carefully indexed the tablets and kept them on shelves.

In the 1850's, archaeologists discovered two major libraries in Nineveh, each containing thousands of clay tablets. King Sennacherib, who reigned in Assyria from 704 to 681 B.C., assembled one of the libraries. His grandson King Ashurbanipal assembled the other, which included Assyrian, Babylonian, and Sumerian tablets. Most of the tablets from Ashurbanipal's library are now in the British Museum in London.

The Assyrians also wrote legal texts. The *Middle Assyrian Laws* date from the 1300's B.C. Like the Babylonian Code of Hammurabi, these laws consist of examples of cases, each with its judgment. But the Assyrians' penalties for lawbreakers were harsher than the Babylonians'.

Many later Assyrians probably spoke Aramaic and did much of their writing in the Aramaic script with ink on papyrus. Aramaic did not completely replace the cuneiform script, however. Both scripts survived until the end of the Assyrian Empire, but they were used for different purposes. The historical and religious texts were written in cuneiform, and Aramaic was used for everyday business. Most of the Aramaic papyrus documents decayed long ago, so scholars know little about later Assyrian business affairs.

Religion. Assyrian religion was related closely to the earlier Sumerian and Babylonian religions. Assyrians believed that many gods directed human destiny and controlled the sky, earth, water, storms, and fire. The Assyrians also believed in good and evil spirits, and in magic.

Assyrian religion differed from the earlier religions in some ways. The chief god of Assyria was Ashur, or Assur, whose name was the same as the Assyrians' name for their country and most important city. The chief Babylonian god was Marduk. Babylonian kings were not religious leaders. However, Assyrian kings served as both rulers and head priests, and the people considered them Ashur's governors on earth.

Assyrians worshiped other gods, including Nabu, the god of learning and patron of scribes; Ninurta, the god of war and agriculture; and Ishtar, the goddess of love and war. Ishtar was so famous that the Assyrians sent a statue of her from Nineveh to Egypt to help cure an ailing Egyptian king. Assyrians offered food and precious objects to the gods. Priests tried to foretell the future by examining sacrificed animals and by observing and interpreting such natural things as the weather and animals' behavior.

The Metropolitan Museum of Art, New York City, Gift of John D. Rockefeller, Jr., 1932

A winged lion of the 800's B.C. stood in front of the palace of Ashurnasirpal II. It was supposed to ward off evil.

Art and architecture. The earliest Assyrian art was similar to the art of Babylonia and other nearby cultures. A separate style of Assyrian art developed between 1400 and 1000 B.C. Assyrian craftworkers made some of the finest cylindrical seals ever produced in Mesopotamia. These seals were rolled over soft clay to seal documents and other objects.

The early Assyrians decorated their buildings with wallpaintings and colorful bricks. Later, between 900 and 600 B.C., they decorated palace walls with carved stone slabs showing religious ceremonies or military victories. The wall carvings became the most familiar of all Assyrian artworks. Some of the finest carvings, found at the palace of Ashurbanipal in Nineveh, show hunting scenes. Human figures in Assyrian art never display emotion, but the carvings at Ashurbanipal's palace show vividly the ferocity and suffering of the hunted lions.

Assyrian sculptors were skilled at making *reliefs* (raised carvings), and they experimented with different *perspectives*—that is, ways to create illusions of three-dimensional space and solid shapes on flat surfaces. They also created enormous statues of human-headed bulls and lions to guard palace gates. Assyrian statues of humans and gods are rare, however.

Assyrians usually made their buildings of unbaked mud bricks. Some of the foundations and wall decorations were stone. All the buildings had flat roofs. Some palaces had rooms with ceilings as high as 30 feet (9 meters). The magnificent palace courts, chambers, and hallways spread over several acres or hectares. Great temples and palaces as well as numerous smaller buildings filled the cities of Assur, Nineveh, and Kalhu.

Assyrian craftworkers excelled in decorating small objects made of ivory, metal, stone, and wood. Some art

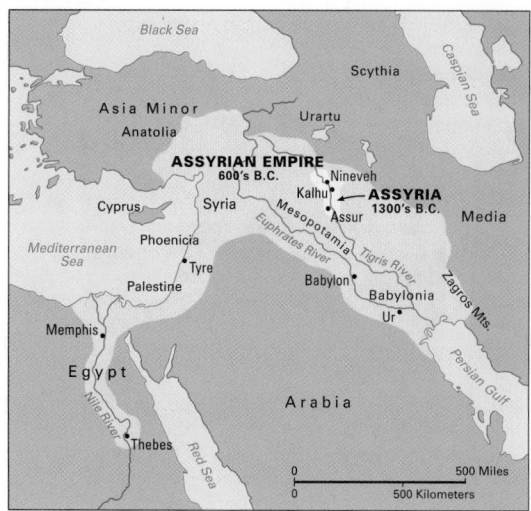

Location of the Assyrian Empire

WORLD BOOK map

objects were imported from Phoenicia and Egypt.

In the late 1980's, Iraqi archaeologists uncovered royal tombs at Kalhu containing exquisite examples of Assyrian goldwork. The tombs held hundreds of beautifully crafted gold vessels and pieces of jewelry, including bracelets, crowns, earrings, and necklaces.

Government

Kings of the Assyrian Empire period were called "the great king, the legitimate king, the king of the world, king of Assyria, king of all the four corners of the earth, king of kings, prince without rival, who rules from the Upper Sea to the Lower Sea." The king was the supreme head of the Assyrian Empire and chief priest of the god Ashur. He often led the army personally in military campaigns to parts of the empire. These campaigns brought in *tribute* (forced payments), and defeated enemies were made to pay taxes. During the late period of the empire, the crown prince, the heir to the throne, usually handled administrative affairs. The prince lived in the Palace of Administration when the king was away on campaigns.

The Assyrian Empire was divided into provinces, each administered by a governor responsible to the central government. Residents of some of the older cities, such as Assur and Nineveh, enjoyed special privileges, including low taxes and freedom from military service. Landlords had to pay taxes and provide young men from their estates to serve in the army.

Written records and relief sculptures indicate that the Assyrians treated conquered peoples cruelly. But sometimes the Assyrians only threatened to be cruel to frighten other peoples into surrendering. The Assyrians sometimes allowed conquered peoples to keep their own rulers. But if the people rebelled or refused to pay taxes, the Assyrians often destroyed their cities and sent the people to distant parts of the empire.

History

People began to settle in farming villages in Assyria about 8500 B.C. The villagers cultivated plants and do-

mesticated sheep and goats. They traded goods with both nearby and distant towns and villages. As the population grew, villages in Assyria developed into small towns, and trade increased. Some Assyrians became wealthy and powerful, while others lived in simple homes with few possessions. By about 3000 B.C., many different peoples lived in Assyria.

From about 2000 to 1700 B.C., Assyrian traders from the city of Assur established colonies in Anatolia (now part of Turkey) to acquire the silver and gold that were plentiful there. They traded tin and Babylonian cloth for the metals. Toward the end of the 1800's B.C., Shamshi-Adad, a forceful leader belonging to a desert people called the Amorites, took control of Assyria. He extended its powers and boundaries to western Syria, northern Mesopotamia, and the borders of Babylonia.

Few records have been found of the next few hundred years of Assyria's history. Historians believe that the country was ruled for part of the period by Mitanni, a kingdom in northern Syria. Records show that Assyria had shaken off foreign control by the mid-1300's B.C.

Assyria enjoyed brief periods of expansion in the 1200's and 1100's, before it began to build its empire in the 800's B.C. Shalmaneser III, who reigned from 858 to 824 B.C., gained control of some of the trade routes from Mesopotamia to the Mediterranean. Tiglath-pileser III, the king from 744 to 727 B.C., conquered large parts of Syria and Israel and became king of Babylonia. Sennacherib, who reigned from 704 to 681 B.C., attacked Jerusalem. He turned Judah into an Assyrian *vassal state*—that is, a state controlled by Assyria. Esarhaddon, who held the throne from 680 to 669 B.C., added Egypt to the empire. Assyria declined after the mid-600's B.C., and Median and Babylonian attacks in 614 and 612 B.C. ended the empire.

Eckart Frahm

Related articles in *World Book* include:
Aramaic language
Architecture
    (Mesopotamian architecture)
Ashurbanipal
Babylonia
Cuneiform
Gilgamesh, Epic of
Hittites
Iraq
Mesopotamia
Mitanni
Nineveh
Phoenicia (Decline)
Sargon of Akkad
Semiramis
Semites
Sennacherib
Syria
Tiglath-pileser III
Tigris River

Astaire, *uh STAIR,* **Fred** (1899-1987), an American dancer and actor, became a popular star of musical motion pictures. He was best known for his graceful, imaginative dancing and his lively portrayals of charming, sophisticated gentlemen.

Astaire, whose real name was Frederick Austerlitz, was born on May 10, 1899, in Omaha, Nebraska. From 1916 to 1932, he and his sister, Adele, starred as a dance team in many Broadway musicals. Astaire made his film debut in 1933 in *Dancing Lady.* Later that year, he and

Scene from *Swing Time* (1936) from © Corbis/Bettmann

Ginger Rogers and Fred Astaire gained fame as dancing partners in a popular series of motion-picture musicals during the 1930's. Rogers also won recognition as a dramatic actress.

dancer Ginger Rogers teamed up in *Flying Down to Rio.* Their graceful dancing and the chemistry between the two led to nine more musicals. They were *The Gay Divorcee* (1934), *Roberta* and *Top Hat* (both 1935), *Follow the Fleet* and *Swing Time* (both 1936), *Shall We Dance?* (1937), *Carefree* (1938), *The Story of Vernon and Irene Castle* (1939), and *The Barkleys of Broadway* (1949).

Astaire appeared in over 35 movies, including the musicals *Holiday Inn* (1942), *Easter Parade* (1948), *Royal Wedding* (1951), *The Band Wagon* (1953), *Funny Face* (1957), and *Finian's Rainbow* (1968). He also played straight dramatic roles in such films as *On the Beach* (1959) and *The Towering Inferno* (1974). Astaire wrote an autobiography, *Steps in Time* (1960). He died on June 22, 1987.   Roger Ebert

See also **Rogers, Ginger.**

Astana. See Nur-Sultan.

Astarte, *as TAHR tee,* is the Greek name for one of the most important goddesses of the ancient Middle East. Astarte was worshiped in Syria, Egypt, and the Phoenician colonies of the western Mediterranean.

The first mention of Astarte appeared about 1430 B.C. in Egyptian records that called her a war goddess. She was also a goddess of sexual love. The Greeks later identified her with Aphrodite, their goddess of love. Astarte was also related to the important Mesopotamian goddess Ishtar. An Egyptian myth about Astarte was found in a papyrus fragment that dates from about 1300 B.C. In this myth, Astarte apparently persuaded the sea not to impose *tribute* (forced payments) on the deities of Egypt. As a reward, the deities accepted her into their circle. In the Bible, Astarte is called "Ashtoreth the goddess of the Sidonians" and Ashtaroth, the plural form of

the name, is used to mean *pagan goddesses.*

R. F. G. Sweet

Astatine, *AS tuh teen* or *AS tuh tihn,* is the heaviest member found in nature of the halogen family of chemical elements. It is radioactive and has the chemical symbol At and an *atomic number* (number of protons) of 85. Chemists think astatine may be the rarest naturally occurring element on Earth, with less than 1 ounce (28 grams) existing at any one time. Astatine has more than 30 known *isotopes,* forms with the same number of protons but different numbers of neutrons. The most stable isotope has an *atomic mass number* (total number of protons and neutrons) of 210. That isotope has a *half-life* of 8.1 hours—that is, due to radioactive decay, only half the atoms in a sample of isotope 210 would still be atoms of that isotope after 8.1 hours. The chemical properties of astatine resemble those of iodine.

Astatine was first prepared in 1940 by Dale R. Corson, K. R. MacKenzie, and Emilio Segrè at Berkeley, California. It was made in a cyclotron by bombarding bismuth with high-energy alpha particles. It was named for the Greek word meaning *unstable,* in reference to its short half-life. Small amounts of the element exist in uranium ores, but most astatine is created artificially.

Marianna A. Busch

Aster is the common name of various plants valued for their colorful flowers. Most asters are *perennials,* which means they live more than two years. Some are *annuals* that die after one growing season. Hundreds of *species* (kinds) of asters grow in North America, and lesser numbers are found in Europe, Asia, and South America. *Aster* is the Greek word for *star.*

The leaves of asters are positioned alternately along the stem. The blossoms consist of small *disk flowers* in the center surrounded by petallike *ray flowers.* The disk flowers range in color from white to dark purple. The ray flowers are most commonly white but also may be blue or purple. Most asters bloom late in summer. Some bloom until late fall.

The *New England aster* is a popular garden flower that blooms in the fall and has purple flowers. Its long narrow leaves grow on a hairy stem. Because these asters bloom at the time of the feast of Michaelmas, they are known as Michaelmas daisies in England.

Most asters are difficult to grow from seed. They can be broken into several pieces and transplanted in the spring. Asters thrive in almost any type of soil. The *China aster,* an annual, is grown from seed.   James S. Miller

Scientific classification. Asters are in the composite family, Asteraceae or Compositae. The New England aster's scientific name is *Symphyotrichum novae-angliae.* The China aster is *Callistephus chinensis.*

See also **Flower** (picture: Garden perennials).

Asteroid is a rocky or metallic object smaller than a planet that orbits a star. Most asteroids in our solar system orbit between Mars and Jupiter in a region called the Main Belt. Millions of asteroids may exist, but astronomers think most of them measure less than 6 miles (10 kilometers) in diameter. Most asteroids are rocky, but some consist of metal or a mixture of metal and rock.

People often call the asteroids *minor planets,* but that term has no formal definition in astronomy. According to the International Astronomical Union (IAU), a widely recognized authority in naming heavenly bodies, no

NASA/JPL/Galileo Project

The asteroid Ida and its tiny moon Dactyl appear in a photograph taken by the U.S. spacecraft Galileo. Dactyl may be a piece of Ida that broke away during a collision with another asteroid.

asteroid is large enough to be considered a planet. The IAU classifies Ceres, the largest asteroid, as a nearly planet-sized object called a *dwarf planet.*

Scientists think that asteroids consist of material left over from the formation of the solar system. Much of this material is relatively unchanged by such processes as erosion and volcanic activity, which have altered the planets and moons. Much of our knowledge of asteroids comes from studying *meteorites,* pieces of matter that have fallen to Earth from asteroids.

Sizes and shapes. Ceres's longest diameter measures 605 miles (975 kilometers). Ceres makes up more than one-fourth of the total *mass* (amount of matter) of the Main Belt asteroids. The next largest asteroids, Pallas and Vesta, each stretch slightly over 300 miles (500 kilometers) in diameter. The smallest asteroids known measure only about 20 feet (6 meters) across. The tiniest asteroids may be pebble-sized—too small to be seen by Earth-based telescopes. Occasionally, a large asteroid will break apart into many smaller ones, usually as the result of a collision. For this reason, smaller asteroids are far more common than larger ones. Astronomers estimate that only about 1,000 Main Belt asteroids have diameters of over 18 miles (30 kilometers).

Asteroids have a variety of shapes. A large object's gravitational pull tends to compact its mass into a ball. The largest asteroids, therefore, appear roughly spherical. Smaller asteroids have gravitational pulls that are too weak to significantly alter their shapes. They tend to take on irregular, *elongated* (long and thin) forms. The Main Belt asteroid Kleopatra, for example, has a "dog bone" shape, with two rounded knobs connected by a thin center. Kleopatra measures about 135 miles (217 kilometers) long and 58 miles (94 kilometers) wide.

The irregular shapes of small asteroids may result from collisions. Also, scientists think some oddly shaped asteroids may be piles of *rubble* (broken fragments) only loosely held together by gravity. The asteroid Itokawa, for example, appears to consist of two physically distinct, weakly bound pieces. Itokawa measures about 0.3 mile (0.5 kilometer) long and about half as wide.

Composition. Astronomers analyze the light that asteroids reflect to determine the objects' composition, a technique called *spectroscopy.* They also study meteorites thought to be fragments of asteroid material. Astronomers have identified several distinct classes of as-

teroids. Most asteroids belong to one of three major types: (1) C-type, (2) S-type, and (3) M-type.

C-type asteroids make up about 75 percent of all known asteroids. They have a rocky composition and appear darker than coal, resembling a group of carbon-rich meteorites known as *carbonaceous chondrites.* C-type asteroids have a chemical composition similar to that of the sun except they lack the lightest elements, hydrogen and helium.

S-type asteroids. Scientists classify roughly 15 percent of asteroids as S-type asteroids, bright rocky bodies that also contain some metal. The metal is an *alloy* (mixture) of nickel and iron called *nickel-iron.* S-type asteroids consist of nickel-iron and *silicates* (rock-forming compounds) of iron and magnesium.

M-type asteroids. Most of the remaining asteroids belong to the third major group, the M-type asteroids. These bright objects consist of nearly pure nickel-iron. They may be fragments of the metallic core of a larger body that broke apart.

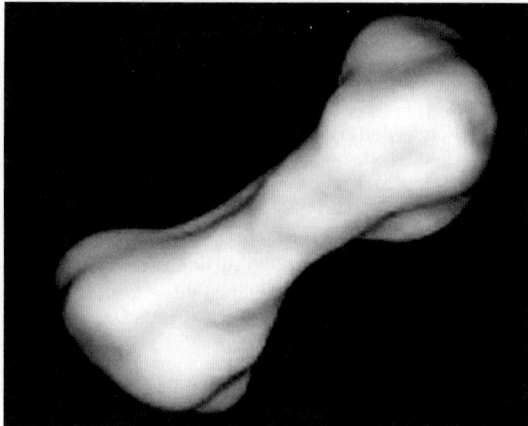

NASA/JPL/NSF/Arecibo Radio Telescope

The asteroid Kleopatra ranks among the most oddly shaped asteroids. This radar image reveals Kleopatra's "dog bone" shape, with two rounded knobs connected by a slender center.

NASA/ISAS/JAXA

The asteroid Itokawa appears to consist of two physically distinct pieces loosely held together by gravity. Japan's Hayabusa probe captured this image when it visited the asteroid in 2005.

Other asteroid types are relatively rare. One group, the D-type asteroids, occurs more frequently in the outer solar system. They appear more primitive—that is, unchanged—than inner solar system asteroids, whose compositions have been modified by the sun's heat.

Orbital groups. The vast majority of asteroids lie in the Main Belt, which stretches more than 100 million miles (160 million kilometers) in width. Most asteroids in the Main Belt orbit the sun at distances between roughly 2 and 3 *astronomical units.* An astronomical unit (AU) equals the average distance between Earth and the sun, about 93 million miles (150 million kilometers).

Main Belt asteroids occur in *families,* groups of tens to hundreds of asteroids that have similar orbits. Some groups, such as the Eos family, share a similar composition, suggesting that their members are broken fragments of a larger body or group of bodies. Other families exhibit a variety of characteristics, which suggests that their members do not share a common origin.

An important class of asteroids called *near-Earth asteroids* follow orbits that can bring them close to our planet. Evidence suggests that near-Earth asteroids were ejected from the Main Belt, most likely by collisions with one another and by the gravitational influence of Jupiter. Astronomers classify near-Earth asteroids into three orbital groups: (1) Amors, (2) Apollos, and (3) Atens. The orbits of Amors lie between those of Earth and Mars. Apollos have orbits that cross that of Earth. Atens follow orbits that lie mostly between Earth's orbit and the sun. Astronomers have discovered more than 800 near-Earth asteroids larger than 0.6 mile (1 kilometer) in diameter. They estimate that about 1,000 such asteroids may exist.

Other asteroid groups lie in the outer solar system. Two groups known as the Trojan asteroids or Jovian Trojans are found in Jupiter's orbit, one group about 60 degrees ahead of the planet and the other group about 60 degrees behind it. The Centaurs, another group of objects, have orbits that lie between those of Jupiter and Neptune, typically about 5 to 30 AU from the sun. Centaurs share some traits with both asteroids and comets, suggesting that Centaurs and comets may be related.

Origin and development. Because most asteroids lie in a single belt, scientists once thought the objects were fragments of a planet that was destroyed by a massive collision. Today, scientists believe that asteroids are chunks of material left over from the solar system's formation. The gravitational pull of Jupiter probably prevented these pieces from coming together to form a full-sized planet. Some asteroids may represent the *nuclei* (cores) of comets that are no longer active.

Asteroids are relatively small and widely scattered. However, their large numbers make collisions inevitable. Repeated collisions can break an asteroid into successively smaller fragments, eventually grinding it to dust. Observations of asteroids by spacecraft show surfaces battered by countless impacts.

A collision usually blasts material from an asteroid's surface, leaving a circular depression called an *impact crater.* In rare cases, a powerful collision can smash the asteroid to pieces. The asteroid fragments may then spread apart to form a family of smaller asteroids, or the larger pieces may recombine under gravitational attraction to make a loose rubble pile. Rubble piles can also form when an asteroid passes too close to a planet and

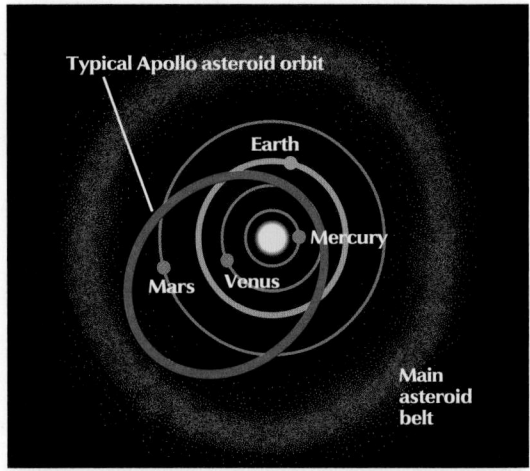

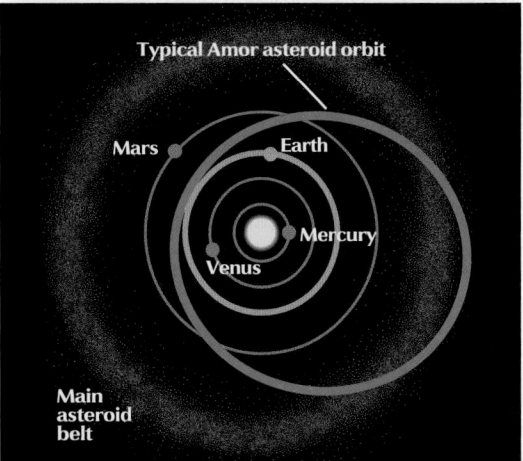

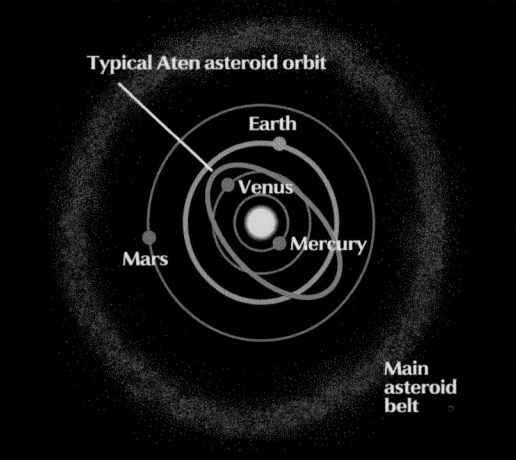

WORLD BOOK illustrations by Steve Karp

Near-Earth asteroids follow orbits that occasionally carry them close to our planet. Scientists divide near-Earth asteroids into three groups: (1) Apollos, (2) Amors, and (3) Atens. Apollos have orbits that lie mostly outside Earth's, *top.* Amors cross the orbit of Mars but do not cross that of Earth, *middle.* Atens have orbits that lie mostly inside Earth's orbit, *bottom.*

so becomes torn to pieces by gravitational stresses.

Impacts on Earth. Earth's atmosphere protects the planet from most asteroid strikes. Air friction will disintegrate an asteroid smaller than about 160 feet (50 meters) in diameter before it can reach the surface. Objects near the upper end of this size range can still cause some damage. In 1908, such an object exploded just above the ground in the Tunguska River area of Siberia. The explosion flattened nearby forests and burned an area roughly 50 miles (80 kilometers) across.

Larger asteroids can harm the global environment. The impact of an asteroid with a diameter of around 0.6 mile (1 kilometer) would kick large amounts of dust into the atmosphere. The dust could block sunlight and cool the air for many months. It might even cause widespread loss of crops and starvation.

Even larger impacts may trigger mass extinctions. One such strike occurred about 65 million years ago on Mexico's Yucatán Peninsula. The impact made the Chicxulub (pronounced *CHEEK shoo loob)* Crater. This giant impact crater has a diameter of about 112 miles (180 kilometers). Many scientists think environmental damage caused by the collision led to a mass extinction. The extinction eliminated many species, including the dinosaurs.

Asteroids large enough to cause global damage strike Earth only about once every million years. The chances of such a strike in any person's lifetime are extremely small. Several teams of astronomers are conducting surveys to identify near-Earth asteroids. No asteroids yet discovered currently present an impact danger.

History of study. In the late 1700's, astronomers began attempting to prove *Bode's law.* The law is named for the German astronomer Johann Bode, who popularized it in 1772. It states that the sizes of the planets' orbits follow a certain mathematical progression. Bode's law predicted that an unknown planet existed between the orbits of Mars and Jupiter. In 1801, the Italian astronomer Giuseppe Piazzi identified the first asteroid, Ceres. Ceres's orbit closely matched that predicted by Bode's law. Scientists initially considered Ceres to be the "missing" planet. Over the next few years, astronomers found three other large bodies in the same region: Pallas, Juno, and Vesta. Scientists began referring to these objects as asteroids. By the late 1800's, astronomers had discovered hundreds of asteroids.

In 1891, the German astronomer Max Wolf introduced a new method for finding asteroids. He used a telescope to take long-exposure photographs of the

night sky. Asteroids move across the sky so quickly that they appear in the photographs as blurred streaks. Later, astronomers began to search for asteroids by taking two photographs of the same area of the sky about an hour apart. When such a pair of images is viewed with a device called a *stereoscope,* any asteroids stand out from the background stars.

In the late 1900's and early 2000's, scientists became more interested in asteroids. They saw them as clues to the solar system's history and as a suspected cause of past and future disasters on Earth. Through spectroscopy and studies of meteorites, astronomers determined the makeup of asteroids in new detail. In 1996, the Hubble Space Telescope mapped the asteroid Vesta. The mapping revealed a giant impact crater formed a billion years ago. The impact may have created some of the meteorites found on Earth. Astronomers have also studied the shape of asteroids using radio telescopes.

On its way to Jupiter, the United States spacecraft Galileo flew by the asteroids Gaspra in 1991 and Ida in 1993, enabling scientists to study asteroids up close for the first time. The fly-bys led to the discovery that Ida has a tiny moon, later named Dactyl. Dactyl may be a piece of Ida that broke away during a collision. Astronomers have since discovered satellites around dozens of other asteroids, suggesting that such moons may be common.

In 1996, the United States launched the Near Earth Asteroid Rendezvous (NEAR) spacecraft. The NEAR probe flew by the C-type asteroid Mathilde to the S-type asteroid Eros. In 2000, the craft, later renamed NEAR-Shoemaker, began orbiting Eros. It studied the asteroid's surface, orbit, mass, composition, and *magnetic field.* An object's magnetic field is the region surrounding the object in which its magnetic influence can be detected. In 2001, NEAR-Shoemaker's controllers guided the spacecraft to the first-ever landing on an asteroid's surface.

Japan's Hayabusa probe visited Itokawa in 2005. Despite several system failures, the craft transmitted detailed pictures of the asteroid and landed on its surface. In 2010, Hayabusa returned samples of the surface material to Earth for analysis. The samples were used to determine how the sun's radiation affects S-type asteroids.

NASA's Dawn spacecraft, launched in 2007, reached the asteroid Vesta in 2011. Dawn orbited Vesta for one year and then traveled to Ceres, arriving in 2015. In 2016, NASA launched the probe OSIRIS-REx to the asteroid Bennu. The probe's name stands for *O*rigins *S*pectral *In*terpretation *R*esource *I*dentification *S*ecurity *R*egolith *Ex*plorer. The probe reached Bennu in late 2018 and will return a sample of it to Earth in 2023.

In 2014, Japan launched the Hayabusa2 spacecraft. In 2019, the probe touched down on its target asteroid, called Ryugu, about 1.9 billion miles (3 billion kilometers) from Earth. Hayabusa2 collected samples of the asteroid and was to return them to Earth for study in late 2020.   Louise M. Prockter

Related articles in *World Book* include:

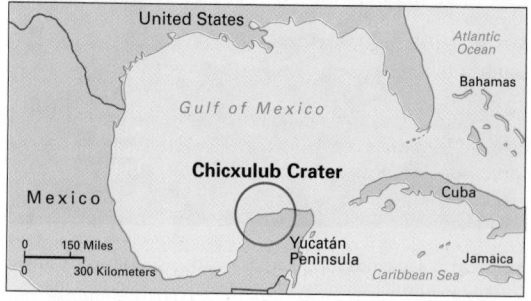

The Chicxulub Crater in Mexico's Yucatán Peninsula formed when an asteroid hit Earth about 65 million years ago. Debris from the impact may have led to the extinction of the dinosaurs.

Asthma, *AZ muh,* is a chronic lung disease characterized by periods of breathlessness, wheezing, and coughing. People with asthma suffer from chronic inflammation of the *bronchi* (airways to the lungs). The inflamed airways react to irritation by swelling, constricting, and filling with mucus. These changes obstruct *airflow* (the ability to force air in and out of the lungs). An asthmatic person may feel short of breath or have difficulty breathing. Severe attacks may involve *spasms* (sudden constriction) of the airways, making sufferers gasp for air and feel that they are suffocating. These attacks require immediate medical attention and can be fatal.

A variety of environmental or emotional stimuli, called triggers, may irritate the sensitive airways of asthma sufferers and cause an attack. Triggers include respiratory infections, pollen, mold spores, chemical irritants, tobacco smoke, animal dandruff, dust mites, exercise, or breathing cold air. An attack usually begins within minutes after exposure to a trigger and can last a few minutes, several hours, or even days.

Physicians diagnose asthma by studying the patient's history of symptoms, physical examination, and tests of lung function. Recurring episodes of breathlessness caused by one or more triggers usually indicate asthma. Physicians use a device called a *spirometer* to determine the amount of air patients can breathe out of their lungs. Another device called a *peak flow meter* measures airflow. People with asthma often have reduced airflow when exposed to triggering substances, or after vigorous exercise.

Asthma affects both children and adults. Some children with asthma experience fewer symptoms as they get older, while others develop more. Despite advances in the treatment of asthma, the incidence of the disease is increasing, especially among children living in cities.

Causes. Scientists are not certain what causes asthma or why it is becoming more common. Research shows that infants exposed to indoor air pollution, especially tobacco smoke, have a much higher risk of developing asthma than infants who are not exposed.

Asthma tends to run in families and is often accompanied by allergies. People with asthma, or members of their family, often have respiratory allergies, such as hay fever, or they are allergic to certain foods. Asthmatic persons and their family members also have a higher incidence of an allergy called atopic eczema that causes itchy red swellings on the skin. Researchers are working to discover genetic markers that can identify people at risk of developing asthma.

Treatment. There is currently no cure for asthma, but the disease can be controlled. Sudden attacks can be prevented by avoiding substances that trigger them. But it is not possible to avoid all asthma triggers all the time, so asthma sufferers usually require medication.

Medications are divided between those used for quick relief from sudden attacks, and others used for long-term control of symptoms. Quick-relief medicines are usually *bronchodilators,* drugs that decrease the constriction in the airways by relaxing small muscles in and around the lungs. These medicines are inhaled from small aerosol canisters at the onset of a sudden asthma attack. Long-term control medications include *corticosteroids,* which are *anti-inflammatories* (substances that reduce inflammation) that can be inhaled or taken orally.

Most people with asthma can lead normal, even active, lives. With proper treatment, people with asthma can participate in sports, even those that require intensive breathing, such as football, track and field, or swimming. Mark H. Moss and Robert F. Lemanske, Jr.

See also **Allergy; Bronchitis; Bronchodilator; Dust mite; Hay fever.**

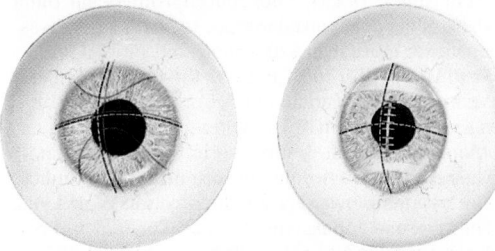

Lisa Schonemen, University of Illinois at Chicago Eye Center

Astigmatism is usually caused by an abnormally shaped cornea. A normal cornea is shaped like a basketball and has equal curvatures, *left.* In a person with astigmatism, the cornea has unequal curvatures, like those of a football, *right.*

Astigmatism, *uh STIHG muh tihz uhm,* is a visual defect in which both nearby and distant objects appear blurred. It is usually found in both eyes. In most cases, astigmatism is caused by the shape of the cornea.

A normal cornea has a spherical shape, somewhat like a basketball cut in half. As light rays pass through a normal cornea, they are bent so they focus at a single point on the retina. In people with astigmatism, the cornea is shaped somewhat like a football cut in half lengthwise. The length and the width of the football-shaped cornea have unequal *curvatures* (degrees of curve), and the difference between these curves determines how much astigmatism the person has. Light rays entering an eye with astigmatism cannot focus on a single point on the retina. Instead, the rays meet at two points, one or neither of which is on the retina.

Many cases of astigmatism are present at birth. Some result from injury or disease. Astigmatism may develop or change as a person ages, and it is often associated with *myopia* (nearsightedness) or *hyperopia* (farsightedness). Mild cases of astigmatism may come and go.

The symptoms of astigmatism include blurred vision, double vision in one eye, eyestrain, fatigue, and headaches. People with astigmatism may squint in an effort to see clearly. Doctors treat it by prescribing glasses or contact lenses. In some cases, surgical or laser treatment of the cornea may restore a more spherical shape and reduce or eliminate astigmatism. Ronald A. Krefman

See also **Contact lens; Eye** (Astigmatism); **LASIK surgery.**

Astor, John Jacob (1763-1848), was a famous American businessman. He built a large fortune through his involvement in the fur trade and through his extensive real estate investments in New York. The investments increased in value over the years, and Astor's family became one of the wealthiest in the United States.

Astor was born on July 17, 1763, in Walldorf, Germany, near Heidelberg. He came to New York City when he was 20 years old. He worked as a baker's boy and peddler and ran a music store before entering the fur trade in about 1787. He shipped furs overseas, often in his own vessels.

Astor's Pacific Fur Company established the trading post of Astoria, Oregon, in 1811, but the company lost the post during the War of 1812 (1812-1815). His fur companies won an almost complete monopoly of the trade in the United States. Astor invested his profits principally in Manhattan Island farmland, which became the heart of New York City. Astor retired from the fur trade in 1834. At his death on March 29, 1848, his estate was estimated at more than $20 million.　　John Elgin Foster

Astor, Lady (1879-1964), became the first woman to serve in the British Parliament. A Conservative, Astor was a witty champion of temperance and of the rights of women and children. Before World War II began in 1939, she became a prominent supporter of the policy of appeasement toward Nazi Germany (see **World War II** [The failure of appeasement]).

Astor was born Nancy Langhorne on May 19, 1879, in Danville, Virginia. She went to England in 1903 and, in 1906, married Waldorf Astor, a great-great-grandson of the wealthy American businessman John Jacob Astor. Waldorf Astor served in the British House of Commons, where he represented the Sutton district of Plymouth. In 1919, he gave up his seat in the House, and Lady Astor was elected to replace him. Ten years later, after the election of 1929, Lady Astor tried unsuccessfully to form a women's party in the House under her leadership. She retired from the House in 1945. Lady Astor died on May 2, 1964.　　Keith Robbins

Astoria, a STOHR ee uh (pop. 9,477), is a historic seaport at the mouth of the Columbia River in the northwest corner of Oregon. It is the seat of Clatsop County. For location, see **Oregon** (political map). The chief industries in the area are fishing, forest products, shipping, and tourism.

The city got its name from a fur-trading post established in 1811 by a party sent out by John Jacob Astor. It was the first American settlement west of the Rocky Mountains. The post was near the site of Fort Clatsop, where the Lewis and Clark expedition spent the winter of 1805-1806.

The Clatsop County Historical Society museums and the Columbia River Maritime Museum are in Astoria. The city has a council-manager government.

Katrine Barber

See also **Astor, John Jacob; Lewis and Clark expedition.**

Astrobiology is the search for and study of life in the universe. It combines elements of astronomy, biology, geology, and other sciences to study the origin, distribution, and *evolution* (development) of life, including life on Earth and any life that may exist elsewhere. Although human beings know of no life besides that on Earth, astrobiology provides a scientific means of determining whether and where such life might exist. It involves analyzing the effect cosmic events and circumstances had on life on Earth. It also helps us understand humanity's role, and Earth's place, in the universe.

The scientific search for life beyond Earth relies on the study of known life and the conditions that make life possible. For example, scientists have found that no known life can exist without liquid water. However, they have also discovered organisms called *extremophiles* that can exist in surprisingly extreme conditions. For example, some organisms can live at high temperatures of about 250 °F (121 °C). Scientists have also realized that not all life needs light or food as a direct energy source.

Some organisms get their energy from other sources, such as chemical reactions between water and rock.

The exploration of our solar system has helped scientists learn which planets and moons might support life. Many astrobiologists rank the planet Mars and Europa, a moon of Jupiter, as two of the most likely candidates. Both bodies have or once had liquid water beneath their surfaces, and both have chemical energy sources that could support life.

Astronomers have also identified planets orbiting other stars. They suspect that there are some planets around other stars that might support life. On Earth, life has altered the composition of the atmosphere through the release of certain gases, such as oxygen and methane. Astrobiologists hope to detect such biological indicators or *biosignatures* in the atmospheres of distant planets using space-based telescopes.　　Bruce Jakosky

See also **Extraterrestrial intelligence; Extremophile; Life** (The search for life on other planets); **Mars** (Possibility of life); **Planet** (Extrasolar planets); **SETI Institute.**

Astrolabe, AS truh layb, is an instrument used by early astronomers and navigators to measure the angles of celestial bodies above the horizon. It consists of a metal disk mounted on a circular frame. The astrolabe is suspended so that it remains vertical. The disk has sights for observing a star. The frame has a set of marks for measuring the star's elevation. The astrolabe was replaced by the sextant and other more accurate instruments. See also **Exploration** (picture); **Navigation** (History); **Sextant.**

Raymond E. White

Astrology, uh STRAHL uh jee, is the study of how the sun, moon, planets, and stars are supposedly related to life and events on Earth. Astrology is based on the belief that the stars and planets in the sky influence events on Earth through their mathematical relationships to one another and to Earth. An *astrologer* is a person who claims to read the patterns of the stars and planets and to tell people's fortunes and characters from them. Many people around the world believe in astrology, though scientists have found no evidence that it is valid. Many other people see astrology as a form of entertainment.

Principles of astrology

Astrologers learn about the influence of heavenly bodies on Earth by *casting* (drawing) a circular chart called a *horoscope* or *birth chart.* A horoscope shows the position of the planets in relation to both Earth and the stars at a certain time. In most cases, it shows the position of these bodies at the time of a person's birth. See **Horoscope.**

The system used by astrologers to cast a horoscope is based on a special view of the universe. This view involves four elements: (1) Earth, (2) the planets, (3) the zodiac, and (4) the houses.

Earth. In casting a horoscope, astrologers place Earth at the center of the solar system. Therefore, all heavenly bodies revolve around Earth rather than around the sun. Astrologers use this arrangement to determine the positions of the heavenly bodies in relation to Earth. They believe that the study of the positions of the heavenly bodies can reveal a person's character and future.

The planets. In astrology, the moon, Pluto, and the sun are considered planets, along with Jupiter, Mars, Mercury, Neptune, Saturn, Uranus, and Venus. Each planet supposedly represents a force that affects people in a certain way. Astrologers believe the planets influence a person more than do any other heavenly bodies.

The zodiac is a band of stars that appears to encircle Earth. It is divided into 12 equal parts called *signs*. Each sign of the zodiac has certain characteristics, which are determined by a particular planet and other factors. Astrologers believe the signs determine how the planets affect a person's character. See **Zodiac;** and the articles on the signs of the zodiac, such as **Aries.**

The houses. Like the zodiac, Earth's surface is divided into 12 parts. Each of these parts, called *houses,* supposedly represents certain characteristics of an individual's life. Astrologers believe the houses determine how the planets and the signs influence a person's daily life. See **House** (in astrology).

History

People have observed the motions of the heavens for thousands of years, and astrology developed independently in several ancient cultures. In ancient Babylonia, in what is now southeastern Iraq, the Sumerians identified specific groups of stars called *constellations* through which the sun, moon, and planets seemed to travel. Astrologers of that time knew of five planets—Jupiter, Mars, Mercury, Saturn, and Venus. By 3000 B.C., Babylonian astrologers had developed a system that linked seasonal changes with certain constellations. At that time, for example, heavy rainfall occurred in the Middle East when the sun was in a certain constellation. As a result, astrologers named the constellation Aquarius, the water bearer. The constellations Taurus, Leo, Sagittarius, and Scorpio were probably identified by this time and associated with the seasons.

Ancient Egypt developed a similar tradition. Egyptians observed that the annual flooding of the Nile River occurred following the reappearance of the star Sirius on the eastern horizon after months of being hidden. The 12-sign zodiac was probably developed in Egypt during the 1000's B.C. and adopted by the Babylonians. They believed that the gods revealed omens or the fortunes of kings through the positions of the constellations and planets. Between 600 B.C. and 200 B.C., Babylonian astrologers began the casting of individual horoscopes.

By about 400 B.C., Babylonian astrology was introduced to the Greeks, who regarded it as a science and greatly influenced its development. They used precise mathematical calculations of the positions of the stars, planets, sun, and moon to cast horoscopes. The Greeks believed that the positions of the stars and planets determined the fate of human beings, which could be revealed through the horoscope. The Romans later adopted the astrology of the Greeks. The Roman names for the planets and the signs of the zodiac are still used today in Western culture.

Interest in astrology declined in Europe with the coming of Christianity but regained popularity during the A.D. 1100's, following the Crusades, a series of Christian military expeditions to the Holy Land. Returning Crusaders introduced scientific, medical, and astrological works from the Islamic world to Europe. Interest in astrology increased again during the Renaissance, as European scholars and artists studied the learning and art of ancient Greece and Rome. By the 1600's, several astrological almanacs were published.

By the late 1800's and early 1900's, interest in astrology had spread to many other nations. Newspapers in England began publishing horoscope columns during the 1930's. Such columns soon appeared in newspapers throughout the world.

Astrology today

Many people believe astrology is simply a superstition, and scientists declare that its whole basis is unscientific. Scientists point out that Earth's position has changed in space since ancient times. As a result, the dates astrologers associate with the signs of the zodiac no longer match the positions of the constellations for which they were named.

Other people, though they believe in astrology, claim that it cannot be supported scientifically. They consider it a set of powerful symbols that can provide a deep understanding of human beings. Today, more people follow astrology than ever before. 　　Charles W. Clark

A horoscope and astrological symbols

Astrologers study charts called *horoscopes* or *birth charts* to foretell the future. A person's chart shows the position of the planets in relation to Earth and the stars at his or her birth. Astrologers believe that these patterns reveal the person's character and future. The chart shown here is the horoscope of President Thomas Jefferson.

WORLD BOOK illustration adapted from *Horoscopes of the U.S. Presidents* by Doris Chase Doane

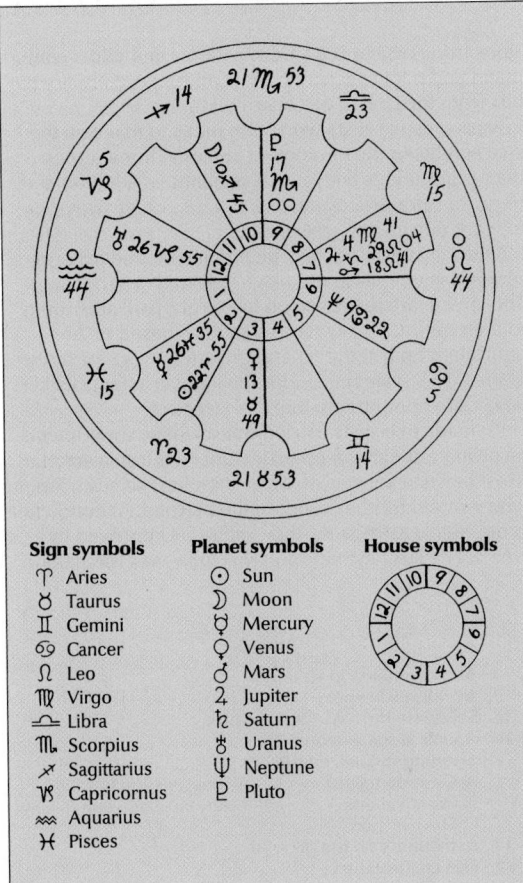

Sign symbols
♈ Aries
♉ Taurus
♊ Gemini
♋ Cancer
♌ Leo
♍ Virgo
♎ Libra
♏ Scorpius
♐ Sagittarius
♑ Capricornus
♒ Aquarius
♓ Pisces

Planet symbols
☉ Sun
☽ Moon
☿ Mercury
♀ Venus
♂ Mars
♃ Jupiter
♄ Saturn
♅ Uranus
♆ Neptune
♇ Pluto

House symbols

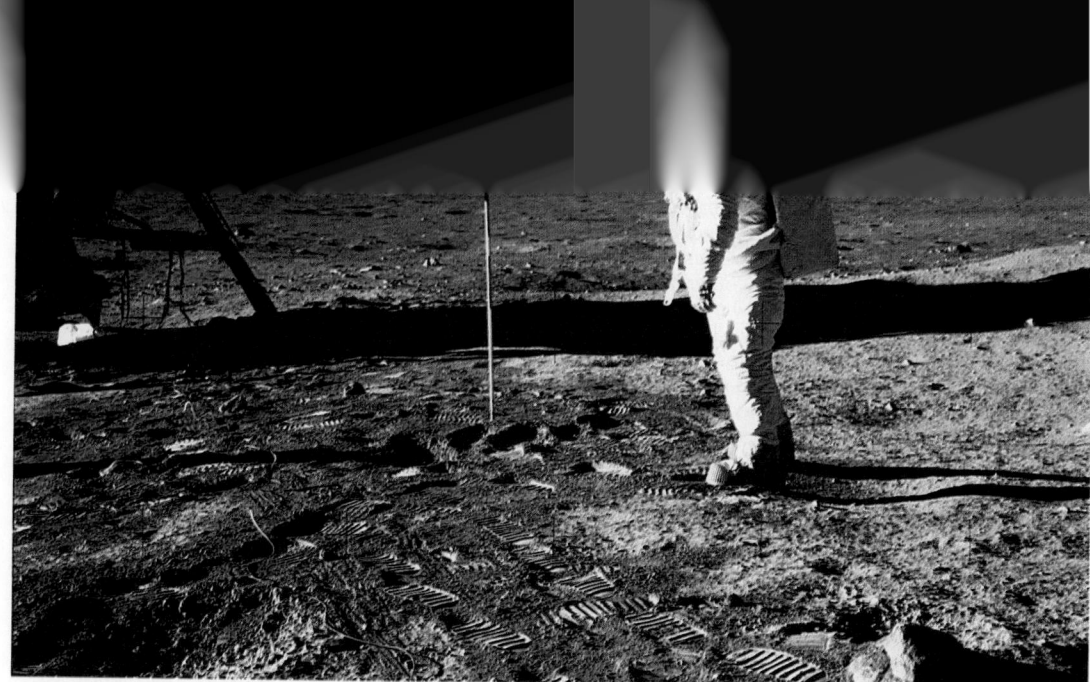

An astronaut on the moon. Buzz Aldrin, *shown here,* and Neil A. Armstrong landed on the moon on July 20, 1969. The flag, which they left on the windless lunar surface, was stiffened by a wire to give it the appearance of waving.

NASA

Astronaut

Astronaut is a person who pilots a spacecraft or works in space, particularly in the space program of the United States. In Russia and the other former republics of the Soviet Union, such men and women are called *cosmonauts.* The cosmonaut program was a project of the Soviet Union until the country broke up in 1991. Russia then took over the program. China sent its first astronaut into space in 2003.

Astronauts and cosmonauts operate spacecraft and space stations, launch and recapture satellites, and conduct scientific experiments. The word *astronaut* comes from Greek words meaning *sailor among the stars. Cosmonaut* means *sailor of the universe.* Astronauts in the Chinese space program are called *taikonauts. Taikonaut* comes from the Chinese words *tai kong* (outer space).

Most U.S. astronauts work for the National Aeronautics and Space Administration (NASA). Most of their training happens at the Lyndon B. Johnson Space Center in Houston. Specialized training also takes place at other NASA facilities, such as the Kennedy Space Center near Cape Canaveral, Florida, and the Goddard Space Flight Center in Greenbelt, Maryland. Cosmonauts train at the Yuri A. Gagarin Russian State Science Research and Test Cosmonaut Training Center, in Star City, near Moscow.

The term *astronaut* also has a meaning that is not connected with NASA activities. In the 1960's, the United States Department of Defense awarded the rating of *astronaut* to military and civilian pilots who flew aircraft higher than 50 miles (80 kilometers). Seven test pilots received this rating for flights in the X-15 rocket plane. Flights of the X-15 ended in 1968.

NASA selects two major kinds of astronauts for space flights: (1) *commander/pilot astronauts* and (2) *mission specialists.* A third type, *payload specialists,* flew on mis-

sions from 1983 to 2003. Commanders and pilots command and pilot spacecraft. Most pilot astronauts are pilots from the United States armed forces.

Mission specialists work with pilots to maintain the spacecraft and the equipment aboard. They also conduct experiments and launch satellites. In addition, they perform *extravehicular activities* (EVA), or "spacewalks," to work outside the spacecraft.

Mission specialists may be engineers, scientists, or physicians who have extensive research experience. Those who are in the armed forces are paid according to their rank. Civilians receive salaries based on an equivalent rank in the federal government's *civil service system.* This system includes most government workers who were appointed rather than elected.

Payload specialists carried out scientific experiments involving a specific *payload* (cargo) on the spacecraft. Most payload specialists were engineers or scientists who worked for the owner of the payload. Although not professional astronauts, they had to be approved by NASA. The last payload specialist to fly was Ilan Ramon from Israel, who was killed with the rest of the crew in the Columbia space shuttle disaster in 2003.

Astronauts and cosmonauts travel into space aboard Russian Soyuz spacecraft. A Soyuz carries two or three people. The commander is almost always a Russian military pilot. Many flights include a civilian flight engineer. On other flights, a third cosmonaut, usually called the cosmonaut researcher, is aboard. Still other Soyuz flights carry a Russian commander and two American astronauts. Crews lift off from the Baykonur Cosmodrome, near the Aral Sea in south-central Kazakhstan. Landings take place in remote, flat areas of Kazakhstan.

A spacecraft called the Shenzhou carries China's astronauts. The craft lifts off from Jiuquan Space Launch Center in northern China. Landings take place in remote areas of Inner Mongolia.

Achievements in space

On April 12, 1961, Yuri A. Gagarin of the Soviet Union became the first person to travel in space. He orbited Earth once in a Vostok capsule. *Vostok* is Russian for *east.* Gagarin's flight lasted 1 hour 48 minutes. Twenty-three days later, on May 5, Alan B. Shepard, Jr., became the first American space traveler. He made a 15-minute flight in a Mercury capsule but did not go into orbit. John H. Glenn, Jr., the first American in orbit, circled Earth three times on Feb. 20, 1962.

The first woman in space, the cosmonaut Valentina Tereshkova, was in space for three days in 1963. Twenty years later, the astronaut Sally K. Ride became the first American woman in space. In June 1983, Ride orbited Earth with four other crew members on a six-day mission aboard the space shuttle Challenger.

In 1964, the Soviet Union placed the first three-person spacecraft in orbit. This design was called Voskhod, which is Russian for *sunrise.* In 1965 and 1966, the United States conducted a series of 10 two-person flights in Gemini spacecraft. During those flights, the astronauts practiced maneuvering their craft and joining it to other orbiting space vehicles.

On March 18, 1965, the cosmonaut Alexei A. Leonov became the first human being to step outside a spacecraft and float freely in space. Less than three months later, on June 3, the astronaut Edward H. White II made the first spacewalk for the United States.

In 1967, cosmonauts began flying the Soyuz series of spacecraft. These are three-seat vehicles, but the first crewed flight carried only one cosmonaut, and other early flights carried two. The Soviet Union also tested spacecraft to send cosmonauts to the moon and land them there. After many failures, however, the Soviets canceled their moon-trip projects.

Space flights of the Apollo program, the U.S. project to land astronauts on the moon, began in October 1968. On December 24 and 25 of that year, Frank Borman, James A. Lovell, Jr., and William A. Anders orbited the moon 10 times in 20 hours. In doing so, they became the first people to orbit a celestial body other than Earth.

Yuri A. Gagarin of the Soviet Union was the first person in space. He rocketed into orbit on April 12, 1961, in the Vostok 1 spacecraft. Gagarin made one orbit of Earth.

John H. Glenn, Jr., America's first orbiting astronaut, circled Earth three times on Feb. 20, 1962. Glenn took control of his space capsule, Friendship 7, after its automatic controls failed.

Sovfoto

Wide World

NASA

Astronauts on a space shuttle mission work in a pressurized laboratory called Spacelab. The shuttle carried Spacelab within its cargo bay, and a tunnel connected the laboratory to the crew compartment. Each Spacelab mission focused on research in a particular area of science or technology, such as life sciences or materials processing.

On July 20, 1969, the astronauts Neil A. Armstrong and Buzz Aldrin became the first people to set foot on the moon. They landed the Apollo 11 lunar module, called the Eagle, and performed scientific experiments and collected rock samples. Other astronauts made five more moon landings from 1969 to 1972. They also left behind five scientific stations and brought back lunar dust.

In June 1971, cosmonauts established the first space station, Salyut 1. In 1973, the United States sent up a team of astronauts to operate its first space station, Skylab. The astronauts Charles Conrad, Jr., Joseph P. Kerwin, and Paul J. Weitz lived in Skylab for almost a month.

In 1975, the United States and the Soviet Union undertook their first joint space mission, the Apollo-Soyuz Test Project. On July 17, an Apollo spacecraft docked with a Soyuz craft. The Apollo craft carried the astronauts Thomas P. Stafford, Vance D. Brand, and Donald K. Slayton. Aboard the Soyuz were the cosmonauts Alexei A. Leonov and Valery N. Kubasov. For two days, the five spacefarers conducted experiments in the docked craft.

On April 12, 1981, the United States launched the space shuttle Columbia, the first reusable spacecraft to carry a crew. The astronauts John W. Young and Robert L. Crippen orbited Earth more than 36 times during a flight lasting about 2 days 6 hours. On Nov. 28, 1983, Columbia carried the first European-built research laboratory, called Spacelab, into space.

The cosmonaut Valery Polyakov completed a record 438 days in space on March 22, 1995. Polyakov spent this time aboard Russia's Mir space station. His mission helped scientists study how long periods of weightlessness affect the human body.

Astronauts first recovered, repaired, and relaunched a disabled satellite in April 1984. Traveling aboard Chal-lenger, they used a Canadian-made robot arm to capture the satellite. In May 1992, astronauts aboard the shuttle Endeavour captured a satellite using only their gloved hands. They then attached a special tool to the satellite so that a robot arm could hold it. In December 1993, astronauts aboard Endeavour repaired the Hubble Space Telescope (HST). They installed a device that corrected a problem caused by a defect in the telescope's main mirror. Four more servicing missions were flown to upgrade and extend the life of HST.

Cosmonauts began making guest flights aboard U.S. space shuttles in 1994. Astronauts began visiting Mir in 1995. Both astronauts and cosmonauts helped build, and then worked aboard, the International Space Station.

On Oct. 15, 2003, Yang Liwei became the first astronaut sent into space by China. He orbited Earth aboard a Shenzhou spacecraft for 21 hours before landing safely.

On June 21, 2004, the American test pilot Michael Melvill became the first astronaut to be launched into space by a private company. Melvill piloted a rocket called SpaceShipOne, which was built and operated by Scaled Composites of Mojave, California. The craft carried Melvill more than 62 miles (100 kilometers) above Earth on a brief suborbital flight.

Accidents in space

Space travel is risky, and a number of astronauts and cosmonauts have lost their lives in training or on space flights. The first fatality in a space program occurred on March 23, 1961. Valentin V. Bondarenko, a Soviet cosmonaut trainee, died in a fire in a pressure chamber.

During a ground test on Jan. 27, 1967, an Apollo spacecraft caught fire, killing the three astronauts inside. The astronauts—Virgil I. Grissom, Edward H. White II,

Important astronaut and cosmonaut "firsts"

Date	Name	Achievement
April 12, 1961	Cosmonaut Yuri A. Gagarin	First person in Earth orbit
May 5, 1961	Astronaut Alan B. Shepard, Jr.	First American in space
Feb. 20, 1962	Astronaut John H. Glenn, Jr.	First American in Earth orbit
June 16, 1963	Cosmonaut Valentina Tereshkova	First woman in space
March 18, 1965	Cosmonaut Alexei A. Leonov	First person to "walk" in space
July 20, 1969	Astronauts Neil A. Armstrong and Buzz Aldrin	First crew to land on the moon
June 7, 1971	Cosmonauts Georgi T. Dobrovolsky, Victor I. Patsayev, and Vladislav N. Volkov	First crew of an orbiting space station
May 25, 1973	Astronauts Charles Conrad, Jr., Joseph P. Kerwin, and Paul J. Weitz	First crew of a U.S. space station
March 2, 1978	Cosmonaut Vladimir Remek (Czechoslovak)	First non-Soviet cosmonaut
July 23, 1980	Cosmonaut Pham Tuan (Vietnamese)	First Asian in space
April 12, 1981	Astronauts John W. Young and Robert L. Crippen	First space shuttle flight
June 18, 1983	Astronaut Sally K. Ride	First American woman in space
Aug. 30, 1983	Astronaut Guion S. Bluford, Jr.	First African American in space
Oct. 5, 1984	Astronaut Marc Garneau	First Canadian in space
Oct. 5-13, 1984	Astronaut Paul D. Scully-Power	First Australian-born astronaut
Jan. 24, 1985	Astronaut Ellison Shoji Onizuka	First Asian American in space
Jan. 12, 1986	Astronaut Franklin R. Chang-Diaz	First Hispanic American in space
Jan. 22, 1992	Astronaut Roberta Bondar	First Canadian woman in space
Sept. 12, 1992	Astronaut Mae C. Jemison	First African American woman in space
April 8, 1993	Astronaut Ellen Ochoa	First Hispanic American woman in space
March 22, 1995	Cosmonaut Valery Polyakov	Completed record 438 consecutive days in space
May 19-29, 1996	Astronaut Andrew S. W. Thomas	First Australian astronaut
Sept. 26, 1996	Astronaut Shannon Wells Lucid	Completed 188 days in a row in space, a record for women
July 23-28, 1999	Astronaut Eileen M. Collins	First woman to command a shuttle
June 19, 2002	Astronauts Daniel Bursch and Carl Walz	196 consecutive days in space, a new record for Americans
Nov. 23, 2002	Astronaut John Bennett Herrington	First tribally registered Native American in space
Oct. 15, 2003	Astronaut Yang Liwei	First astronaut sent into space by China
June 21, 2004	Astronaut Michael Melvill	First astronaut launched into space by a private company

and Roger B. Chaffee—had been scheduled to fly the first Apollo spacecraft.

On April 24, 1967, the cosmonaut Vladimir Komarov became the first person to die on a space flight. Komarov's flight was the first in which a Soyuz vehicle carried a cosmonaut into space. When Komarov tried to land the vehicle, its parachutes failed to open properly. Komarov died when the Soyuz crashed to Earth.

The first mission in which people occupied a space station also ended in disaster. In June 1971, Georgi T. Dobrovolsky, Victor I. Patsayev, and Vladislav N. Volkov boarded the experimental station Salyut 1 from their Soyuz 11 spacecraft. During their 23-day mission, they conducted medical examinations of one another and carried out scientific studies. On the return flight, all three cosmonauts died because of a sudden loss of cabin pressure in the Soyuz.

On Jan. 28, 1986, Challenger broke apart shortly after launch. All seven crew members were killed. They included Christa McAuliffe, a teacher, who was aboard as part of a program to make the experience of space flight better known to the public. After the Challenger disaster, NASA canceled this program and suspended all shuttle flights. Astronauts returned to space on Sept. 29, 1988, aboard the shuttle Discovery. Discovery's rocket boosters and many other features of the craft had been redesigned as a result of the Challenger disaster.

On Feb. 1, 2003, the shuttle Columbia broke apart as it reentered Earth's atmosphere. All seven astronauts on board were killed. Officials at NASA worked for more than two years to improve the safety of the shuttle. The next shuttle launched was Discovery in July 2005.

Selecting the NASA astronauts

NASA accepts applications for pilot astronauts and mission specialist astronauts on a continuing basis. A selection board normally picks a group of about 15 to 25 candidates every two years. An applicant must be a U.S. citizen and must hold a bachelor's degree or higher in engineering, a biological science, a physical science, or mathematics. There is no age limit, but every candidate must pass the NASA space flight physical examination.

Pilot astronaut candidates must have flown for 1,000 hours as a command pilot in high-performance jet aircraft. They must be between 5 feet 4 inches and 6 feet 4 inches (163 and 193 centimeters) tall. Candidates for mission specialist do not need flight experience, but they must have at least three years of related professional experience. They must be between 5 feet and 6 feet 4 inches (152 and 193 centimeters) tall.

A look at the astronauts

Since 1959, several hundred people have flown in space. NASA chose seven test pilots as the first group of astronauts and introduced them to the public on April 9, 1959. The group consisted of the Air Force officers Gordon Cooper, Virgil I. Grissom, and Donald K. Slayton; the Navy pilots M. Scott Carpenter, Walter M. Schirra, Jr., and Alan B. Shepard, Jr.; and the Marine Corps pilot John H. Glenn, Jr. In the 1960's, NASA selected an additional 49 experienced jet pilots. From 1965 to 1967, NASA picked 17 scientist astronauts.

In 1978, NASA announced the selection of astronauts for upcoming flights of the space shuttle. In this group were 15 pilot astronauts and the first 20 mission specialists. Among the mission specialists were the first six women selected to become astronauts. All six held doctor's degrees. They were the physician Anna L. Fisher, the biochemist Shannon Wells Lucid, the electrical engineer Judith A. Resnik, the physicist Sally K. Ride, the physician Margaret R. Seddon, and the geologist Kathryn D. Sullivan. In 1990, NASA chose the first woman to become a pilot astronaut, Eileen Marie Collins.

In 1983, Canada selected six of its citizens to receive training for NASA missions. The next year, Marc Garneau, a commander in the Canadian Navy, flew aboard Challenger. He thereby became the first Canadian astronaut to travel in space. NASA has also flown payload specialists from Belgium, France, Germany, Israel, Italy, Japan, Mexico, the Netherlands, Saudi Arabia, Ukraine, and the former West Germany.

In 1985, Senator Edwin J. (Jake) Garn of Utah became the first elected official to fly in space. He was chairman of the Senate committee that had oversight responsibilities for the NASA budget. Garn flew aboard Discovery. The next year, Congressman C. William Nelson of Florida flew aboard Columbia. In 1998, John Glenn, then a U.S. senator, returned to space aboard Discovery. He was 77 years old at the time of the flight, making him the oldest person ever to travel in space.

NASA

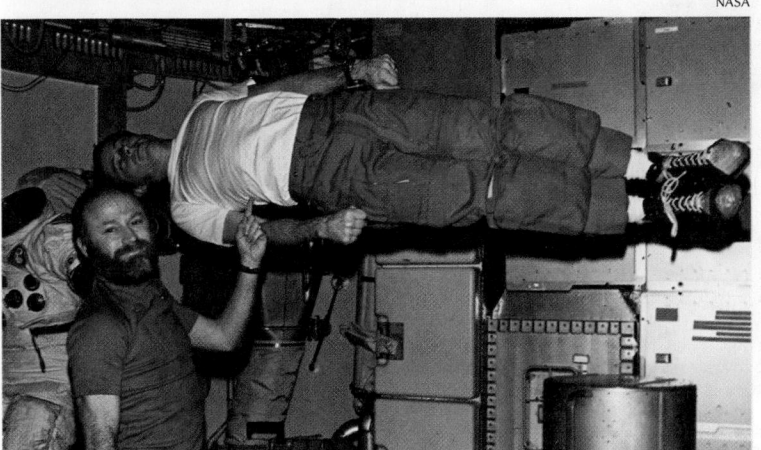

Astronauts are weightless in space, and so they must anchor themselves with straps and other devices to keep from floating about. Aboard the Skylab space station, *shown here,* Gerald P. Carr appears to be supporting a weightless Edward Gibson with one finger.

Astronaut travels
worldbook.com/ut-14

Training the astronauts

Candidates for pilot and mission specialist undergo one year of general training at Johnson Space Center. After successfully completing this training, they become astronauts. The training involves two major phases: (1) a general phase, involving classroom work, flight training, and survival training; and then (2) more specific basic mission training and advanced mission training.

Classroom work. NASA brings in instructors from its research centers and from universities to teach aerodynamics, physics, physiology, computer science, and other subjects. Experienced astronauts lecture on such topics as how to communicate with astronauts in space. Other NASA personnel discuss the people, equipment, and funding that make space flight possible.

Mercury and Gemini astronauts took courses in rocket engines, flight mechanics, and navigation. In addition to those subjects, Apollo astronauts studied the geology of the moon. They also traveled to Hawaii, Iceland, Alaska, and other places to study volcanic rocks similar to those on the moon. Skylab crews took classes in astronomy, geology, and life sciences to enable them to perform experiments and make observations.

Flight training takes place in T-38 jet aircraft. Once mission specialist candidates learn to operate the aircraft, they fly about 4 hours per month. Pilot candidates must fly 15 hours. Space shuttle pilots also trained on special airplanes called Shuttle Training Aircraft (STA), designed to land as a space shuttle did.

Survival training teaches candidates how to survive after an unplanned landing in water or in a forest. For example, astronaut candidates are towed through the water in a parachute harness to simulate being dragged by a parachute in a wind. In addition, candidates practice survival training in the wilderness.

Basic mission training involves the study of cockpit layout and flight-control systems. During such training, candidates also prepare for the actual conditions of space flight.

Candidates for pilot and mission specialist train for weightlessness in two ways. They experience the near absence of gravity as large airplanes fly through a series of arcing climbs and dives. For up to 25 seconds at the top of each arc, they float weightlessly in the body of the aircraft. Floating in water also reproduces the conditions of weightlessness. The pool used for EVA training, the Neutral Buoyancy Laboratory at the Johnson Space Center, is better suited than the airplane flights for training the astronauts to move large objects in space.

After successful completion of the training program, new astronauts continue to develop their skill while they wait for crew assignments. Some become experts in several support or operational areas.

Advanced mission training. Once assigned to a crew, astronauts spend most of their time training in simulators. For example, shuttle astronauts trained in the Shuttle Mission Simulator, a device that could reproduce the events of an entire mission.

Training in simulators is valuable preparation for what the astronauts may later face on actual flights. For example, in 1970, the Apollo 13 astronauts used the oxygen and power supply of their lunar module to return home safely after an explosion damaged their main spacecraft. This task was less difficult to carry out because the crew was knowledgeable about all systems on board. Instructors continually give the crew problems to solve to prepare them for emergency situations.

Astronauts also train with mock-ups—that is, full-sized models of the spacecraft. Mock-ups are used to practice

NASA

Training in a simulator, an astronaut learns about the instruments and controls of a space shuttle. When an astronaut operates the controls, the simulator shows how an actual shuttle would react.

working and living in the close quarters of spacecraft. The astronauts store items, prepare foods, and check equipment in the mock-ups. They also practice entering and leaving the spacecraft.

Advanced training prepares astronauts for tasks that are not part of all missions. For example, astronauts who work in the International Space Station study the Russian language. Astronauts preparing for an EVA receive extra training in the Neutral Buoyancy Laboratory and work with virtual reality systems.

Astronauts on the ground

Astronauts taking part in a space mission work on the ground as well as in space. Those on the ground relay information and instructions from flight controllers, engineers, and scientists to the crew. If problems develop, other astronauts help engineers find solutions.

Astronauts have helped change the design of spacecraft and their operating systems. For example, Mercury astronauts insisted on a window in the capsule and a hatch that opened from the inside. Also, skill displayed by the astronauts led designers to give them more control over flying the craft. Shuttle astronauts worked on the location of instruments and the modification of space suits. They also helped develop special equipment, such as satellite repair tools.

The cosmonauts

The first cosmonauts were military pilots. Most were in their middle 20's, and many were sent to college after returning from space. Since 1964, crews of cosmonauts could include civilian engineers and physicians.

The first cosmonauts spent less than two years in training. The original training program involved constant athletic activity. It included swimming, running, cycling, and parachute jumping over land and water. The U.S. program did not require such activities, but the astronauts were expected to get into good physical condition on their own.

The early Soviet program also included training in heat chambers and an isolation cell. The trainees also sat in a spinning, swinging chair that was designed to test for motion sickness.

As the Soviets became more experienced in space travel, they learned that training did not need to be so

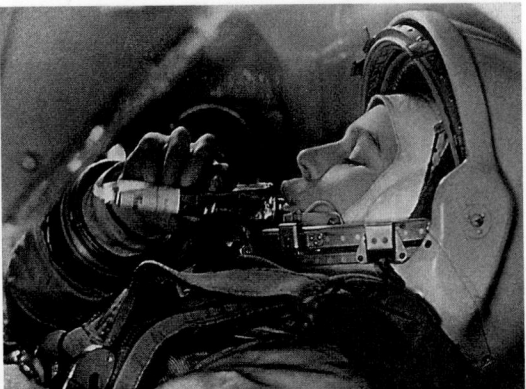

Sovfoto
First woman in space, Valentina Tereshkova, ate food from a tube before her flight in Vostok 6 on June 16-19, 1963.

demanding. They eliminated the heat and isolation chambers, and required less parachute jumping. In addition, motion sickness training became easier. Today, cosmonauts spend most of their time studying complex spacecraft systems and working in simulators. They now spend several years preparing for space flight.

The Soviet Union and Russia have sent guest cosmonauts into space since 1978. These cosmonauts' home countries include Afghanistan, Austria, Belgium, Bulgaria, Cuba, Czechoslovakia (now the Czech Republic and Slovakia), the former East Germany, France, Germany, Hungary, India, Italy, Japan, Kazakhstan, Mongolia, Poland, Romania, Slovakia, South Africa, Syria, Ukraine, the United Kingdom, the United States, and Vietnam.

Edward J. Rezac

Related articles in *World Book* include:

American astronauts

Aldrin, Buzz	Lawrence, Robert Henry, Jr.
Armstrong, Neil Alden	Lovell, James Arthur, Jr.
Bluford, Guion Stewart, Jr.	Lucid, Shannon Wells
Borman, Frank	McAuliffe, Christa
Carpenter, M. Scott	Onizuka, Ellison Shoji
Collins, Eileen Marie	Ride, Sally Kristen
Conrad, Charles, Jr.	Schirra, Walter Marty, Jr.
Cooper, Gordon	Shepard, Alan Bartlett, Jr.
Glenn, John Herschel, Jr.	Slayton, Donald Kent
Grissom, Virgil Ivan	Swigert, John Leonard, Jr.
Haise, Fred Wallace, Jr.	White, Edward Higgins, II
Irwin, James Benson	Worden, Alfred Merrill
Jemison, Mae Carol	Young, John Watts

Other astronauts and cosmonauts

Bondar, Roberta	Payette, Julie
Gagarin, Yuri Alekseyevich	Tereshkova, Valentina Vladi-
Garneau, Marc	mirovna

Other related articles

Aerospace medicine	International Space Station
Cape Canaveral	Johnson Space Center
Challenger disaster	Kennedy Space Center
Columbia disaster	Space exploration

Astronautics is the scientific study of space flight. Scientists from many countries working on the problems of space flight are united in the International Astronautical Federation. See also **Space exploration.**

Astronomical unit. See Astronomy (Units of distance).

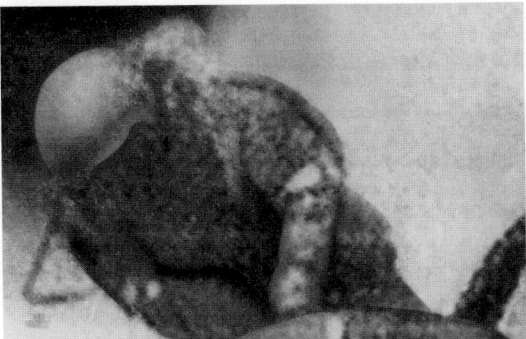

Wide World
The first spacewalk. Alexei A. Leonov climbed from the Voskhod 2 on March 18, 1965, to test the space suit and hatch. Pavel I. Belyayev controlled the two-person spacecraft.

© Tony & Daphne Hallas, Astro Photo

Stars fill the sky in the large photograph, which shows what can be seen with the unaided eye. The familiar Big Dipper tilts downward toward the mountain at the left. The inset photo, taken by the powerful Hubble Space Telescope, shows how much more astronomers can see with telescopes. It reveals galaxies filling a tiny speck of sky near the Dipper's "handle."

NASA

Astronomy

Astronomy is the study of the universe and the objects in it. Astronomers observe the sky with telescopes of different kinds that gather not only visible light but also invisible forms of energy, such as radio waves. Astronomers investigate nearby bodies, such as the sun, planets, and comets, as well as distant galaxies and other faraway objects. They also study the structure of space and the past and future of the universe.

Astronomers seek answers to such questions as: How did the universe begin? What processes release energy deep inside stars? How does one star "steal" matter from another? How do storms as big as Earth arise on Jupiter and last for hundreds of years?

To answer such questions, astronomers must study several subjects besides astronomy. Almost all astronomers are also astrophysicists because the use of physics is essential to most branches of astronomy. For example, some parts of *cosmology,* the study of the structure of the universe, require an understanding of the physics of elementary particles, such as the bits of matter called *quarks* that make up protons and neutrons. Astronomers use chemistry to analyze the dusty, gaseous matter between the stars. Specialists in the structure of planets use geology.

Astronomy is not only a modern but also an ancient science. Like today's researchers, ancient scholars based their ideas of the universe on what they observed and measured and on their understanding of why objects move as they do. However, the ancients developed some incorrect ideas about the relationships between Earth and the objects they saw in the heavens. One reason for their errors was that they did not understand the laws of motion. For example, they did not know that a force—which we know as gravitation—controls the movements of the planets. Another reason was that their measurements, made without telescopes, revealed little detail about the movements of the planets.

The ancients noted that the positions of the sun, moon, and planets change from night to night. We now know that these movements are a result of the revolution of the moon about Earth and the revolution of Earth and the other planets about the sun. The ancients, however, concluded that the sun, moon, and planets orbit a motionless Earth. In many places, religious teachings seemed to support this conclusion until the 1600's.

Although ancient people misinterpreted much of what they saw in the heavens, they put their knowledge of astronomy to practical use. Farmers in Egypt planted their crops each year when certain stars first became visible before dawn. Many civilizations used the stars as navigational aids. For example, the Polynesians used the positions of the stars to guide them as they sailed from island to island over much of the Pacific Ocean.

Observing the sky

If you look at the night sky without a telescope or a pair of binoculars, you will see what the ancients saw. If the night is clear and you are far from city lights, you will see about 3,000 stars. Stretching across the sky will be a splotchy band of bright and dark areas called the Milky Way. In addition, a few fuzzy spots will be visible.

Ancient people in the Western world noticed that certain stars are arranged in patterns shaped somewhat like human beings, animals, or common objects. Many ancient civilizations associated such patterns, called *constellations,* with mythology. Many names of constellations have come to us from Greek myths. In one myth, Artemis, goddess of hunting, was greatly saddened by the death of a human hunter named Orion. In her sorrow, she placed Orion in the sky as a constellation.

How the stars move. If you map or photograph the location of several stars for a few hours, you will observe a regular motion. The stars move relative to Earth because of Earth's rotation about its own axis. All stars move in circles around a point in the sky known as a *celestial pole.* Stars rotate counterclockwise around the ce-

lestial north pole and clockwise around the celestial south pole. Stars that are far from the pole rise from below the horizon in the east, move upward, and then set in the west.

One faint star, Polaris, is so close to the celestial north pole that it moves little. Because of its location, Polaris is also known as the North Star. It is only the 49th brightest star in the sky, but it is in an important location. There is no "South Star," but the constellation Octans (Octant) includes the celestial south pole.

The sun, like the other stars, rises in the east and sets in the west. But the sun also moves eastward relative to the other stars about 1° each day. By noting which stars are visible above the horizon just before sunrise and just after sunset, people have mapped the path of the sun among the stars for thousands of years. This path is known as the *ecliptic.* The band of constellations near this path is called the *zodiac.*

How the planets move. Without a telescope, you can see the planets Mercury, Venus, Mars, Jupiter, and Saturn. They move every night within the constellations of the zodiac. That is, when viewed at the same time on successive nights, the planets move relative to the stars. Most of the year, they move from west to east.

The planets also have a motion that differs from that of any other celestial object. In their night-to-night movement relative to the stars, they occasionally slow down and then move westward in what is known as *retrograde motion.* They then slow down again, stop, and resume their eastward motion in what are called *retrograde loops.*

How the moon moves. The moon is the brightest and most easily seen object in the night sky. As a result, the most familiar observation is of the moon's phases, such as the full moon, quarter moon, and crescent. The moon moves from east to west as it rises and sets. From night to night, the moon moves eastward about 13° relative to the stars, rising about 50 minutes later each night.

Earth-centered theories. Ancient scholars produced elaborate schemes to account for the observed movements of the stars, sun, moon, and planets. In the 300's B.C., the Greek philosopher Aristotle developed a system of 56 spheres, all with the same center. The innermost sphere, which did not move, was Earth. Around Earth were 55 transparent, rotating spherical shells. The outermost shell carried the stars, believed to be merely points of light. Other shells carried the sun, moon, and planets. These shells rotated inside other shells that rotated within still other shells in ways that accounted for almost all the observed movements.

During the A.D. 100's, Ptolemy, a Greek astronomer who lived in Alexandria, Egypt, offered an explanation that better accounted for retrograde motion. Ptolemy said that the planets moved in small circles called *epicycles.* The epicycles moved on large circles called *deferents.* Earth was near the center of all the deferents.

Sun-centered theories. By the early 1500's, the Polish astronomer Nicolaus Copernicus had developed a theory in which the sun was at the center of the universe. This theory correctly explained retrograde motion as the changing view of the planets seen from a moving Earth. The theory also correctly explained the east-to-west motion of the sun and stars across the sky. This movement is due to the west-to-east rotation of Earth about its own axis, rather than an actual motion of the sun and stars.

Several decades later, the Danish astronomer Tycho Brahe built gigantic instruments that he used to make precise measurements of planetary movements. The German mathematician Johannes Kepler analyzed Tycho's measurements of the movement of Mars. He discovered that Mars moves in an *ellipse* (oval) with the sun at a key point inside the ellipse. Kepler also found a relationship between how far Mars is from the sun and how rapidly it moves. He concluded that all planets have elliptical orbits and that the relationship between distance from the sun and speed applies to all the planets. These findings, which became known as Kepler's first two laws of planetary motion, were published in 1609. In 1619, Kepler announced his third law of planetary motion. This law shows the relation between the sizes of the planets'

orbits and the time they take to orbit the sun.

Thus, by the early 1600's, astronomers had used observations made with the unaided eye to map the movement of the planets. However, in 1609, the Italian astronomer Galileo ushered in the era of modern astronomy by using the newly invented optical telescope to observe the heavens.

Modern astronomy

Today's astronomers gather information in many ways. Perhaps most importantly, astronomers use telescopes and other instruments to detect visible light and other forms of radiation that are *emitted* (sent out) by celestial objects. Instruments also detect particles called neutrinos and cosmic rays from outer space. In addition, astronomers study chunks of matter that originated in outer space. They send spacecraft to land on other ob-

The stars and constellations of the Northern Hemisphere

This map shows the sky as it appears from the North Pole with Polaris, the North Star, directly overhead. To use the map, face south and turn the map so that the current month appears at the bottom. The stars in about the bottom two-thirds of the map will be visible at some time of the night from most areas of the United States and southern Canada.

WORLD BOOK illustration by W. J. M. Tirion

jects or to study them close-up. They also search for a type of radiation called *gravitational waves.* Gravitational waves arise in giant explosions or from the merging of extremely dense and compact objects, such as *black holes.* A black hole is an object whose gravitation pull is so strong that nothing—not even light—can escape.

Using modern techniques, astronomers have made discoveries beyond the imagination of the ancients. They have discovered two planets outside the orbit of Saturn—Uranus and Neptune—and many other distant bodies, including smaller round objects known as *dwarf planets.* Astonomers have found that millions of smaller bodies called *asteroids* revolve about the sun, most of them between the orbits of Mars and Jupiter. Astronomers have learned that the sun is merely one of hundreds of billions of stars in a vast, disk-shaped galaxy, the Milky Way. They now understand that many fuzzy spots visible with telescopes in the night sky are other galaxies.

In addition, astronomers have discovered exotic objects called *pulsars,* rapidly spinning collapsed stars from which regular bursts of radiation are received, and *quasars* that emit vast amounts of energy. They have found evidence of black holes and studied exploding stars called *supernovae.*

Units of distance. Many distances involved in astronomy are so huge that they are measured in special units. One such unit is the *light-year,* the distance that light travels in a vacuum in a year. This distance equals about 5.88 trillion miles (9.46 trillion kilometers). The star nearest the sun, Proxima Centauri, is about 4 light-years from Earth. The Milky Way is about 100,000 light-years across. The sun is roughly 25,000 light-years from its center. The nearest large galaxy is the Andromeda Galaxy. It is about

The stars and constellations of the Southern Hemisphere

This map shows the sky as it appears from the South Pole. There is no "South Star," but the constellation Octans would be almost directly overhead if you were at the South Pole. To use the map, an observer in the Southern Hemisphere would face north and turn the map so that the current month appears at the bottom.

WORLD BOOK illustration by W. J. M. Tirion

2 million light-years away. Some galaxies are more than 10 billion light-years distant.

Astronomers measure distances in the solar system in *astronomical units* (AU). One AU is the average distance from Earth to the sun—about 93,000,000 miles (150,000,000 kilometers). This distance equals about 8 light-minutes. The average distance from the sun to Neptune, the farthest planet, is about 30 AU.

In their technical work with extremely long distances, astronomers use a unit called a *parsec,* rather than the light-year. The parsec is based on *parallax,* an angular measurement. One parsec equals about 3.26 light-years.

Locating objects in space. Astronomers still use two concepts developed by the ancients to specify locations of celestial objects: (1) an imaginary *celestial sphere* and (2) the constellations.

The celestial coordinate system. Astronomers specify locations in terms of the *celestial coordinate system,* a set of imaginary lines drawn on the *celestial sphere.* The celestial sphere is similar to the outermost shell in Aristotle's system—the shell that was thought to carry the stars. The lines are similar to the lines of longitude and latitude used by geographers. The poles of the celestial sphere are the *celestial north pole* and the *celestial south pole,* which lie over Earth's north and south geographic poles. The sphere also has a *celestial equator* over the earthly equator.

Longitude in the sky, marked by half-circles going from the north celestial pole to the south celestial pole, is called *right ascension.* Latitude in the sky, marked by circles parallel to the celestial equator, is known as *declination.* Declination north of the celestial equator is positive, while declination south of the equator is negative.

Using the constellations. To locate and assign names to stars, astronomers have divided the sky into 88 parts, each associated with a constellation. Astronomers still use a system developed in the early 1600's to identify the brightest stars in the constellations. The brightest star of all in a constellation is usually designated by alpha, the first letter of the Greek alphabet; the second brightest by beta, the second letter; and so forth. The brightest star in the constellation Lyra (the Harp) is thus Alpha Lyrae. *Lyrae* is Latin for *of Lyra.*

Because the Greek alphabet has only 24 letters, this system is limited to 24 stars per constellation. Later astronomers developed naming systems in which numbers are assigned to fainter stars and Roman letters to *variable stars* (stars that vary in brightness).

Electromagnetic radiation is the most plentiful source of information about heavenly bodies. Its name comes from the fact that it consists of waves of electric and magnetic energy. Visible light is electromagnetic radiation, and objects in space also emit many kinds of invisible electromagnetic radiation. Scientists can identify the various forms of this radiation by their wavelength, frequency, or energy.

Units of astronomical distance

1 astronomical unit	=	150.0 million kilometers	=	93.0 million miles	=	0.0000158 light-years	=	0.00000485 parsecs
1 light-year	=	9.46 trillion kilometers	=	5.88 trillion miles	=	63,200 astronomical units	=	0.307 parsecs
1 parsec	=	30.9 trillion kilometers	=	19.2 trillion miles	=	206,000 astronomical units	=	3.26 light-years

Sizes of astronomical objects   The photographs on this page and the next illustrate the great variation in the size of objects that many astronomers investigate—planets, stars, galaxies, and groups of galaxies. Other astronomers study bits of matter as small as the grains of dust and the molecules of gases between stars, while specialists known as *cosmologists* study the structure of the universe as a whole.

NASA/NSSDC
Earth has a diameter of about 7,900 miles (12,700 kilometers). The diameter of Jupiter, the biggest planet in our solar system, is more than 11 times as large as the diameter of Earth.

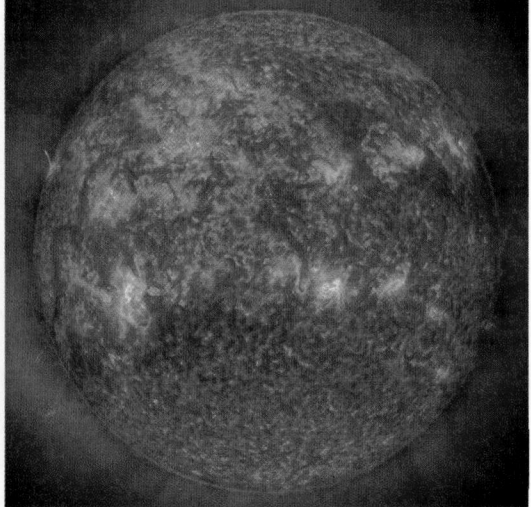

NASA/NSSDC
The sun is a star with a diameter of approximately 864,000 miles (1,390,000 kilometers), about 109 times that of Earth. The largest known stars have a diameter about 1,500 times that of the sun.

The electromagnetic spectrum

	Wavelength*	Frequency, hertz[†]	Sources
Radio waves	1 millimeter and up	Up to 3.00×10^{11}[‡]	Pulsars; quasars; gas clouds orbiting the center of the Milky Way
Infrared rays	700 nanometers[§] to 1 millimeter	3.00×10^{11} to 4.29×10^{14}	Stars in the process of forming; relatively cool stars; planets
Visible light	400 to 700 nanometers	4.29×10^{14} to 7.50×10^{14}	Planets; stars; galaxies; asteroids; comets
Ultraviolet rays	10 to 400 nanometers	7.50×10^{14} to 3.00×10^{16}	Hydrogen gas between the stars; the sun
X rays	0.1 to 10 nanometers	3.00×10^{16} to 3.00×10^{18}	The sun's corona; disks of material around black holes; quasars
Gamma rays	Up to 0.1 nanometer	3.00×10^{18} and up	Collapsed stars; matter-antimatter annihilations

* The ranges indicated are typically used by astronomers to distinguish between forms of electromagnetic radiation. Scientists working in other fields may use slightly different numbers.
† One hertz is one cycle of vibration per second.
‡ The small numeral next to the 10 indicates how many places the decimal point is moved to the right when the number is written out. For example, 3.00×10^{11} equals 300,000,000,000.
§ One nanometer is 1 billionth of a meter.

Wavelength is the distance between successive crests of a wave. From the shortest wavelength to the longest, the forms of electromagnetic radiation are gamma rays, X rays, ultraviolet rays, visible light, infrared rays, microwaves, and radio waves. These forms together make up the *electromagnetic spectrum.*

Frequency. All electromagnetic radiation travels at the same speed in a vacuum. Therefore, a short wave passes a given point more quickly than does a long wave. Thus, more of the shorter waves pass the point each second. Scientists say that a shorter wave has a higher *frequency.* The unit used to measure frequency is the *hertz* (symbol Hz). One hertz represents the passing of one wave past a point in one second.

Energy. According to quantum theory, a cornerstone of modern physics, electromagnetic radiation can also be thought of as particles of energy called *photons.* The amount of energy of a given photon depends on the wavelength—or frequency—of the corresponding wave.

Radiation that has a short wavelength and therefore a high frequency also has high energy. Radiation with a long wavelength has a low frequency and low energy.

Optical astronomy is the study of the heavens by detecting and analyzing visible light. Visible light of different wavelengths has different colors. The wavelengths range from about 400 *nanometers* for deep violet to 700 nanometers for deep red. One nanometer equals a billionth of a meter, or $\frac{1}{25,400,000}$ inch.

Modern astronomy began with observations of the sky through optical telescopes. Today, astronomers often use not only observations made with visible light but also observations made in other parts of the electromagnetic spectrum.

An optical telescope gathers and focuses light with a lens or mirror. For the faintest objects, a large light-collecting area is needed. The largest all-purpose telescopes now in general use include the twin Keck Telescopes on Mauna Kea, an extinct volcano on the island

NOAO/AURA/NSF

The galaxy M83 is shaped much like our home galaxy, the Milky Way. The diameter of the Milky Way is approximately 100,000 light-years—roughly 700 billion times the sun's diameter.

© Jerry Lodriguss

Markarian's Chain of galaxies is about 70 million light-years away. At that distance, the width of the space shown in this photo is 2 ½ million light-years—25 times the Milky Way's diameter.

The Very Large Array (VLA) radio observatory near Socorro, New Mexico, consists of 27 movable dish antennas, each 82 feet (25 meters) across. The arrangement of dishes can extend up to 22 miles (35 kilometers). Computers can combine signals from the antennas to produce images with the detail that would be provided by a single telescope 22 miles across. The VLA's full name is the Karl G. Jansky Very Large Array.

National Radio Astronomy Observatory

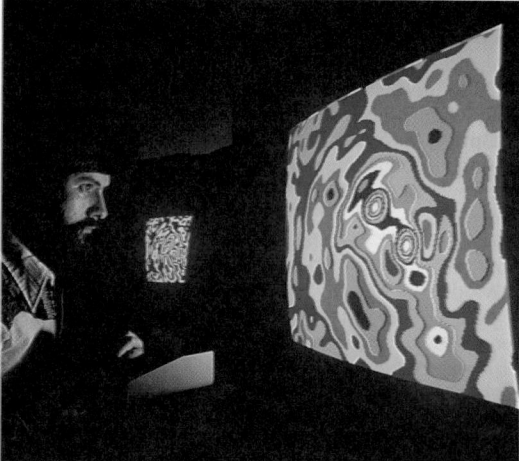

National Radio Astronomy Observatory

An astronomer studies an image produced by the Very Large Array of radio telescopes. The colors in the image represent different amounts of radio energy sent out by objects in the sky.

of Hawaii. Each telescope has a mirror 33 feet (10 meters) in diameter. Telescopes are now being constructed with much larger compound mirrors, up to 75 feet (22 meters) and 130 feet (42 meters) in diameter.

Major optical telescopes are installed on mountains so that starlight does not have to travel far through the atmosphere or so that the telescope can take advantage of smoothly flowing air. These locations minimize blurring caused by the atmosphere. The atmosphere bends light due to a phenomenon known as *refraction,* and the atmosphere is constantly moving. As a result, starlight jiggles and changes in brightness as it passes through the air. Thus, stars appear to twinkle. Twinkling blurs telescope images.

Only a telescope operating in space can avoid blurring entirely. The best-known orbiting telescope is NASA's Hubble Space Telescope, launched in 1990 to observe infrared, visible, and ultraviolet radiation. The Hubble provided images of astronomical objects in detail never before observed. These images included pictures of galaxies on the edge of the universe and what appear to be stars in the process of forming planets.

Professional astronomers rarely look through telescopes. Instead, they study recorded images. Astronomers began to photograph images through telescopes in the 1850's. The use of long exposure times revealed faint objects that the eye could not see through a telescope. Film has been replaced by electronic devices that can detect and record even fainter light. The *charge-coupled device* (CCD), for example, is about 50 times or more sensitive to light than film is.

Optical astronomers have developed three special techniques that have also been used in other kinds of astronomy. They are (1) *spectroscopy,* (2) *interferometry,* and (3) *adaptive optics.*

Spectroscopy is the breaking down of incoming radiation into a spectrum of its parts. The spectrum of visible light, for example, is a rainbowlike band of colors. At one end is red, which has the longest wavelength. At the other end is violet, with the shortest wavelength. Spectroscopy is based on a discovery made in 1814 by the German optician Joseph von Fraunhofer. He found that the spectrum of sunlight contains dark lines where specific colors are absent. Later, scientists discovered that light from other stars also has such dark lines. When the object emitting the light is a hot gas without a central star or a star behind it, the spectrum has bright lines. Other kinds of electromagnetic radiation from celestial objects also have spectral lines.

Studies of spectral lines reveal the temperature, density, and chemical composition of the object emitting the radiation. The spectral lines arise in energy processes in atoms. An electron orbiting an atomic nucleus can have only certain definite levels of energy. These levels can be thought of as stair-steps. When light energy passes through a group of atoms, the electrons can absorb just the right amount of energy to jump from a lower step to a higher one. Because the energy is absorbed from the passing light, a kind of spectral line called an *absorption line* appears in the spectrum. The dark lines discovered by Fraunhofer were absorption lines. Each kind of atom has its own pattern of absorption lines for a given range of temperature.

Bright spectral lines called *emission lines* occur when electrons in atoms of hot objects "jump down the stairs" by emitting energy. In the early 1940's, an analysis of emission lines seen when gas on the edge of the sun was silhouetted against a dark sky confirmed an earlier

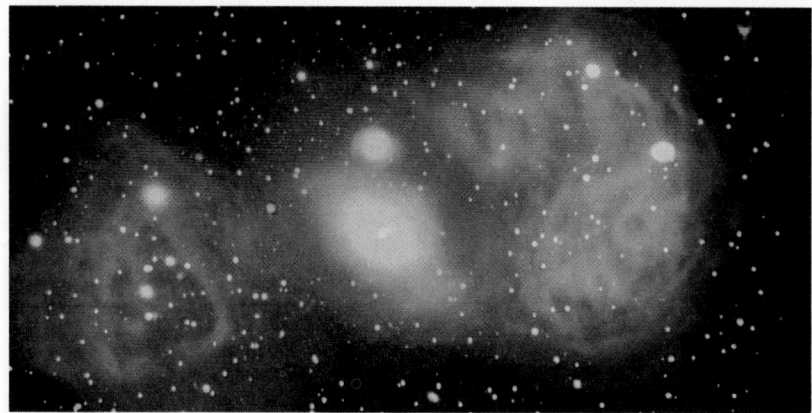

A combined optical and radio image shows radiation produced by what is probably a huge black hole in the center of a galaxy. Objects fall into the black hole, generating energy. The galaxy sends out the energy as visible light, shown in blue, and as radio waves, artificially colored red. The total distance from left to right is about 2 million light-years.

National Radio Astronomy Observatory

discovery about the temperature of the sun's *corona.* The corona, the outer edge of the sun's atmosphere, has a temperature of millions of degrees. The entire band of radiation emitted by the surface of a star also contains information about the star's temperature. Cooler stars are red-hot and can appear slightly reddish to the eye. Hotter stars can become blue-white.

Spectroscopy can even reveal the speed and direction of motion of a star. In the spectrum of any moving object, the spectral lines shift from where they would appear in the spectrum of a stationary object. An object's motion can produce a *Doppler effect.* One familiar example of this effect is a change in the pitch of sound waves emitted by a vehicle. For example, when a car approaches you, the pitch of the sound made by the engine is higher than it is when the car is going away. The shift of spectral lines also depends on whether the object is becoming farther away or closer. If the lines shift toward the blue (shorter-wavelength) end of the spectrum, the object is becoming closer. If they shift toward the red (longer-wavelength) end, the object is drawing farther away. This effect is called the *Doppler redshift.*

In 1929, the American astronomer Edwin Hubble discovered that distant galaxies show redshifts in their spectra. Other scientists interpreted the redshifts as showing that the galaxies are *receding* (becoming farther away) from our own galaxy. Hubble also found that farther galaxies have higher redshifts, indicating that they are receding at higher rates. Unlike the Doppler redshift, this *cosmological redshift*—which applies only to faraway objects— occurs because the universe is expanding. That is, every point in the universe is receding from every other point. Thus, astronomers can determine the distance of a galaxy by measuring its redshift.

Cosmic questions
worldbook.com/as-14

Interferometry uses a phenomenon called *interference* in which rays of light combine. Astronomers use the resulting patterns, with the aid of computers, to produce extremely detailed images. In the simplest example in optical astronomy, a ray of light emitted by a star strikes the mirror of a telescope, and another ray emitted by the same star strikes the mirror of a nearby telescope. Optical and mechanical devices combine the rays so that a series of bright and dark bands of light called an *interference pattern* appears. The pattern reveals any difference in the routes taken by the rays as they travel from the star to the telescopes. For example, if the rays

University of Manchester/NASA
WORLD BOOK diagram by Precision Graphics

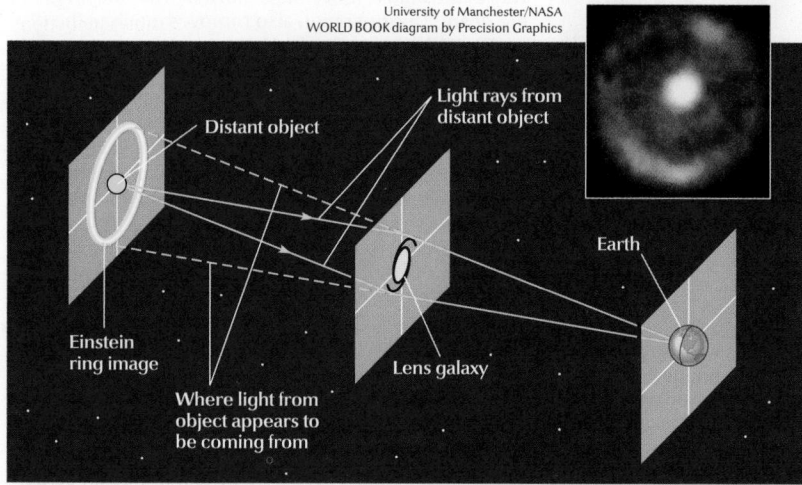

Gravitational lensing occurs when the gravitational force of a massive galaxy apparently acts as a lens, bending light rays sent out by an object on the other side of the galaxy. The light from the distant object appears to come from an arc or, as shown in the inset photo, a ring. Such rings are called Einstein rings—named after physicist Albert Einstein, who described how gravitation seems to bend light.

Locating a star by declination and right ascension

Astronomers locate objects in the sky by means of a *celestial coordinate system*. All the objects are considered to lie on an imaginary sphere surrounding Earth. Astronomers specify a location in terms of an angle measured from a horizontal circle and an angle measured from a vertical circle.

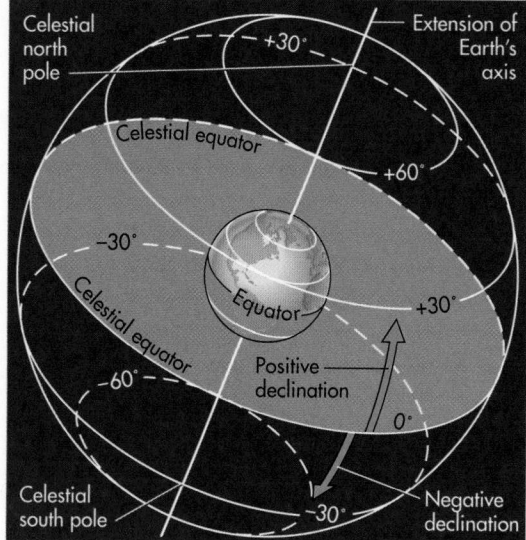

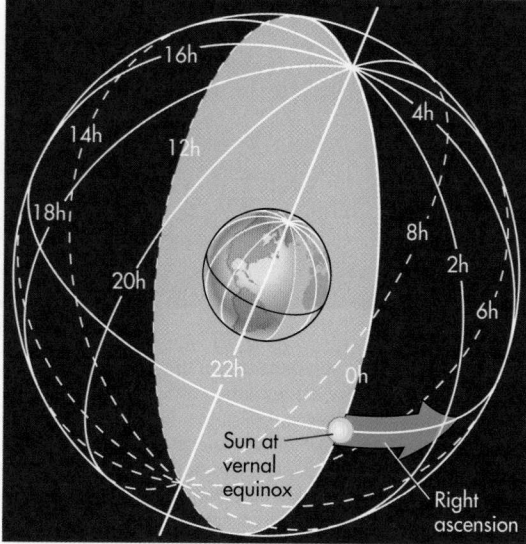

Vertical angles are measured northward and southward from the *celestial equator*, which lies above Earth's equator. A vertical angle is known as a *declination* and can be positive or negative.

Horizontal angles are measured eastward from the *vernal equinox*, where the sun crosses the celestial equator. An angle, or *right ascension*, is given in hours, minutes, and seconds.

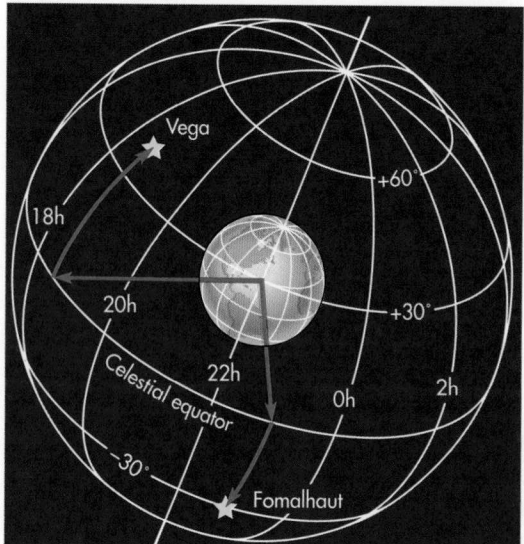

WORLD BOOK diagrams by Precision Graphics

Celestial coordinates locate the star Vega at right ascension (RA) 18 hours 36 minutes 56.3 seconds and at declination (Dec) +38 degrees 47 minutes 1 second. Astronomers give the coordinates of the star Fomalhaut as RA 22^{h}57^{m}39.1^s, Dec −29°37′20″.

were emitted at opposite edges of the star, the pattern could reveal the diameter of the star. A computer helps astronomers analyze the interference pattern and use the results to produce an image.

Adaptive optics can make up for atmospheric blurring in ground-based telescopes. In this technique, light reflects from a telescope's main mirror to a special deformable mirror, then to a CCD. Pistons mounted on the underside of the deformable mirror can change its shape several hundred times a second to make up for atmospheric blurring. A special control system senses the amount of blurring and operates the pistons.

In one arrangement, the deformable mirror is in the main telescope and the control signals come from a smaller auxiliary telescope. A laser beam emitted by the auxiliary telescope reflects off atoms in the atmosphere and returns to the auxiliary telescope. As the beam travels, the atmosphere distorts it slightly. A computer analyzes the reflected beam, then operates the pistons in a way that would remove the distortion from the image of the beam. This operation also removes much of the distortion in the image viewed by the main telescope.

Infrared astronomy deals with invisible electromagnetic waves whose wavelengths are longer than those of visible light. Objects that are bright in infrared wavelengths include cool stars and stars in the process of forming. Planets and other objects that glow by reflecting sunlight or starlight are also best studied in the infrared spectrum.

The infrared spectrum covers a range from about 700 nanometers to 1 millimeter. Infrared astronomers commonly express wavelengths in *micrometers* (thousandths of a millimeter), specifying the overall range as about 0.7 to 1,000 micrometers.

A photon of infrared radiation has less energy than a photon of visible light. Most infrared photons do not have enough energy to cause the chemical reaction that produces images on film. Infrared astronomy therefore did not develop fully until about the 1960's, when better electronic sensors could produce infrared images.

One problem with infrared astronomy is that Earth's atmosphere absorbs rays of most wavelengths in the infrared spectrum. However, some of the shorter waves can be detected at mountaintop observatories. Notable infrared telescopes include the Infrared Telescope Facility of the National Aeronautics and Space Administration (NASA) of the United States and the United Kingdom Infrared Telescope. Both are on Mauna Kea. The telescopes are above most of the water vapor in Earth's atmosphere, one of the main absorbers of infrared rays.

An orbiting infrared telescope has a limited useful life because it must be cooled artificially. Its lifetime is limited by the amount of coolant it carries. Cooling is necessary to prevent the telescope's own infrared radiation from overwhelming the faint rays coming from outer space. The telescope must be cooled to the temperature of liquid helium—about 4 Celsius degrees above *absolute zero* (-459.67 °F or -273.15 °C). Absolute zero is the theoretical temperature at which atoms and molecules would have the least possible energy.

The largest telescope in space was an infrared telescope, the Herschel Space Observatory, launched in 2009. The Herschel telescope collected light from the far-infrared part of the spectrum using a mirror 11 ½ feet (3.5 meters) in diameter. It ran out of coolant and was decommissioned in 2013.

Radio and microwave astronomy. Astronomers use radio waves emitted by celestial objects to produce images of the objects and to study the objects spectroscopically. These are the same kinds of waves that radio and television broadcasters create to transmit programs—astronomers just use them differently.

The radio spectrum includes all electromagnetic waves longer than about 1 millimeter. Microwaves are often included as part of the radio spectrum. Waves longer than about 1 millimeter and shorter than about 10 meters pass readily through Earth's atmosphere. Astronomers receive radio signals from a wide variety of objects, including pulsars, distant galaxies, quasars, particles swirling in Jupiter's magnetic field, and gas clouds orbiting the center of the Milky Way.

Karl G. Jansky, an American engineer, discovered radio waves from outer space in the early 1930's. However, the science of radio astronomy was not established until after World War II (1939-1945).

A radio telescope is essentially a large dish antenna. Unlike the reflecting surfaces of other kinds of telescopes, the dish surface does not have to be extremely smooth. The smoothness required of a reflecting surface depends on the length of the waves to be reflected. The shorter the wavelength is, the smoother the surface must be. Because radio waves are long, some dish surfaces are even made of metal mesh.

The largest radio telescopes that can be steered to point anywhere in the sky are 328 feet (100 meters) in diameter. One is in Effelsberg, Germany, near Bonn. The other is in Green Bank, West Virginia. The most powerful radio telescope of all is a nonsteerable telescope in Guizhou Province, China. Its reflecting dish measures about 1,600 feet (500 meters) in diameter.

Radio astronomy is the field in which interferometry is most useful. To use separate telescopes as an interferometer, the distance between them must be controlled

NASA/JPL

The Mars Odyssey probe, launched in 2001, found evidence of water ice beneath the surface of Mars in 2002. The probe also analyzed the chemical composition of the Martian surface.

to a fraction of the wavelength of the radiation to be detected. This requirement severely limits the use of interferometry in the other branches of observational astronomy, where wavelengths are shorter. Because radio waves are so long, however, the dishes of radio interferometers can be tens, hundreds, or even thousands of miles or kilometers apart.

The Very Large Array (VLA) near Socorro, New Mexico, links 27 movable dishes, each 82 feet (25 meters) in diameter. The telescopes move along railroad tracks built in the shape of a Y. Individual dishes can be moved as far as 22 miles (35 kilometers) from the center of the Y. In 2014, the VLA was upgraded to detect short burst radio emissions from astronomical objects. The VLA's full name is the Karl G. Jansky Very Large Array. The Very Long Baseline Array (VLBA) consists of 10 telescopes, each 82 feet across, spread across one side of Earth. Their locations range from the Virgin Islands north to New Hampshire, northwest to Washington, and west to Hawaii. As an interferometer, the VLBA is equivalent to a single telescope with a diameter roughly that of Earth.

Spacecraft orbiting between Earth and the sun have mapped the sky at microwave wavelengths. These orbiting spacecraft included the Wilkinson Microwave Anisotropy Probe (WMAP), launched by NASA in 2001, and the Planck spacecraft, launched by the European Space Agency (ESA) in 2009. Both measured tiny variations in the *cosmic microwave background radiation,* a type of energy left over from the early universe. By studying the maps, astronomers can "see" the conditions in the early universe.

Radio astronomers have learned much by studying redshifts and blueshifts of spectral lines. Because the radio spectrum is not visible, astronomers see these "lines" as low and high points in a graph of radio brightness versus wavelength. The low points represent wavelengths of radiation absorbed by celestial objects. The

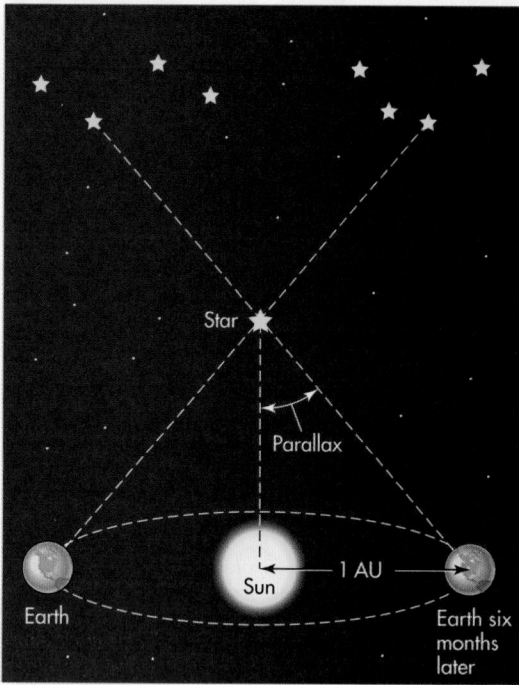

Parallax is the angle by which a star's location relative to background stars differs when measured from two points 1 astronomical unit (AU) apart and on a line perpendicular to the line from the star. One AU is the average distance from Earth to the sun—about 93 million miles (150 million kilometers). Parallax is thus half the difference seen from opposite sides of Earth's orbit.

high points represent wavelengths of radiation emitted by strong radio sources.

Redshift and blueshift work with radio waves exactly as they work with waves of visible light: If the lines in the spectrum of radiation emitted by an object shift toward the shorter-wavelength end, the object is approaching and is said to be blueshifted. If the lines shift toward the longer-wavelength end, the object is receding and is said to be redshifted. The amounts of the shifts are usually so small that no actual change in color occurs.

Astronomers have analyzed redshifts and blueshifts in radio radiation emitted by gas clouds in the Milky Way.

Their analysis showed how rapidly the galaxy is rotating and how the speed of the revolution of its stars changes with the stars' distance from the galactic center. The astronomers then applied a formula relating the speed of the stars' revolution to the stars' masses. They discovered that the amount of mass in the galaxy is about 1 trillion times the mass of the sun.

Both radio astronomers and optical astronomers have studied a phenomenon known as *gravitational lensing.* This phenomenon occurs, for example, where radiation emitted by a small, distant galaxy passes near a massive galaxy that is between the object and Earth. The gravitational force of the galaxy apparently bends the radiation much as an ordinary optical lens bends light rays that pass through it. Gravitational lensing can produce an image of the small galaxy in the shape of an arc or even a ring. Astronomers can study the radiation in the arc or ring to learn about the small galaxy.

Ultraviolet astronomy. The ultraviolet part of the electromagnetic spectrum has wavelengths shorter than those of visible light. Wavelengths of ultraviolet light range from near the limit of the shortest waves that the eye can see, about 400 nanometers, down to about 10 nanometers. Radiation from 400 to 300 nanometers, called *near ultraviolet,* passes through Earth's atmosphere and therefore can be detected on the ground. But ultraviolet astronomers get much of their information from shorter wavelengths—in the *far ultraviolet,* from 300 to about 100 nanometers; and in the part of the *extreme ultraviolet* from 100 to 10 nanometers.

Studies in the far and extreme ranges must be carried out by satellites. From 1992 to 2001, the Extreme Ultraviolet Explorer, launched by NASA, studied wavelengths from 76 down to 7 nanometers. In 1999, NASA launched the Far Ultraviolet Spectroscopic Explorer to observe wavelengths of 120 to 90 nanometers.

Another major ultraviolet telescope is the Solar and Heliospheric Observatory (SOHO), which orbits between Earth and the sun. The ESA launched SOHO in 1995 to monitor the sun with visible-light and ultraviolet cameras and spectrographs. NASA provided some of this equipment. Highly detailed images from SOHO show the sun in, for example, the ultraviolet light of helium gas at 60,000 °C or iron gas at 1,500,000 °C. NASA's pair of Solar Terrestrial Relations Observatory (STEREO) spacecraft are sending ultraviolet images that are even

Detecting redshift and blueshift

Astronomers can learn about a star's motion by comparing the spectral lines in its visible light with those in a spectrum produced in a laboratory. If the star's spectral lines are shifted toward the red end of the rainbow-like spectrum of colors, the star is moving away from Earth. If the lines are shifted toward the blue end, the star is approaching. Astronomers use a similar technique to analyze shifts in the spectral "lines" of invisible forms of radiation, such as infrared and ultraviolet rays.

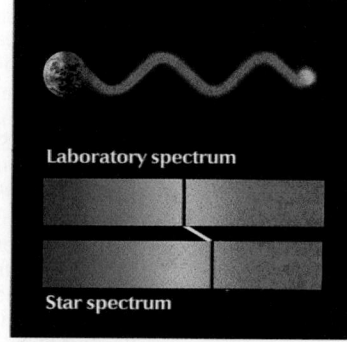

Redshift

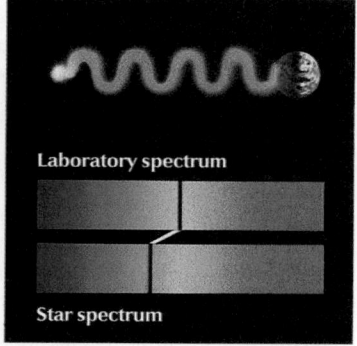

Blueshift

more detailed than SOHO's. The Solar Dynamics Observatory (SDO), launched in 2010, is giving the most detailed ultraviolet images yet.

X-ray astronomy. X rays have wavelengths from about 10 nanometers down to about 0.1 nanometer. The hottest regions in space produce X rays. These regions include the sun's corona and disks of material around black holes. The material in these disks heats up due to friction as it spirals into the black holes. As the material heats up, it emits X rays. The hot gas at the center of clusters of galaxies also emits X rays. Quasars are another source of X rays.

Celestial X rays do not penetrate Earth's atmosphere and therefore can be studied only from spacecraft. X rays would pass through ordinary telescope mirrors and lenses, so one kind of X-ray telescope has specially designed mirrors. X rays strike these mirrors at low angles, then skip away like stones skipping off water. Rays from all the mirrors meet at a single focal point.

Other X-ray telescopes do not have mirrors. The rays enter the telescope through openings between lead or iron slats, then strike special detectors.

An American X-ray telescope on the Japanese Hinode spacecraft, launched in 2006, produced detailed images of the sun. These images show the corona and eruptions on the sun's surface called *solar flares.*

In 1999, NASA launched the Chandra X-ray Observatory. Chandra produces much more detailed images than any other X-ray telescope. It has observed a wide range of astronomical objects, including especially hot or violent ones. Also in 1999, the ESA launched an X-ray observatory called XMM-Newton. This satellite's telescopes can detect much fainter X rays than Chandra can, though with lower resolution. The main mission of XMM-Newton is to investigate the spectra of X-ray sources.

Gamma-ray astronomy. Electromagnetic waves that have the shortest wavelengths—about 0.1 nanometer and shorter—are known as gamma rays. Gamma-ray photons have the highest energy in the electromagnetic spectrum. Thus, they form in the regions of the highest energy in the universe.

Gamma-ray sources include places where matter and *antimatter* are annihilating each other. Antimatter is matter composed of particles called *antiparticles.* Each antiparticle has the same mass as a corresponding particle of ordinary matter but with electric charge or certain other properties reversed. If a particle and its antiparticle collide, they annihilate each other, releasing gamma rays and other energy.

Astronomers have observed that matter-antimatter annihilation occasionally occurs near the center of the Milky Way. Other gamma-ray sources include the Crab Nebula, in the constellation Taurus, and a nearby collapsed star known as Geminga. The Crab Nebula consists of matter that was thrown out into space during a supernova observed in A.D. 1054.

In 2000, an international team of research centers launched the High Energy Transient Explorer-2 (HETE-2) satellite to detect and locate gamma-ray bursts. HETE-2 carried gamma-ray and X-ray detectors. When the satellite detected a gamma-ray burst, it located the source and relayed this information to a control center at the Massachusetts Institute of Technology in Cambridge. The center quickly sent the data to ground-based ob-

servers so that they could study the source with optical telescopes.

In 2003, HETE-2 sensed a bright gamma-ray burst in the direction of the constellation Leo that lasted 25 seconds. Telescopes on the ground spotted leftover light from the burst, which showed evidence that the burst had come from an extremely powerful supernova 2 billion light-years from Earth. Astronomers believe that many gamma-ray bursts may come from supernovae.

In 2002, the ESA's INTEGRAL (*Inter*national *G*amma-*Ray* Astrophysics *Laboratory*) satellite went into orbit. Researchers have used INTEGRAL to study black holes, *neutron stars* (collapsed stars without enough mass to become black holes), the highly energetic centers of certain galaxies, and supernovae.

INTEGRAL has an unusual orbit—its distance from Earth varies from 5,600 to 96,000 miles (9,000 to 155,000 kilometers). Scientists selected that orbit so that INTEGRAL would spend most of its time far above the *Van Allen belts,* bands of charged particles that surround Earth. INTEGRAL needs to be above the belts because their particles emit radiation that could interfere with the satellite's sensitive detectors.

In 2004, an international team led by scientists from the United States, the United Kingdom, and Italy launched a satellite called Swift. It was designed to help astronomers determine the origins of gamma-ray bursts. It uses a wide-angle telescope to detect gamma-ray bursts, then quickly adjusts its position to point more precise instruments directly at the source of the burst.

In 2005, four teams of astronomers led by scientists from the United States and Denmark reported that they had discovered the origin of short gamma-ray bursts lasting less than 2 seconds. The scientists used the HETE-2 and Swift satellites to determine that the bursts were caused by the collisions of two collapsed stars, such as black holes or neutron stars.

In 2008, NASA launched the Fermi Gamma-ray Space Telescope. This orbiting observatory was designed to be more sensitive and to gather data faster than previous gamma-ray instruments. Fermi has discovered a number of pulsars emitting gamma rays along with many gamma-ray bursts. In 2009, scientists announced that Fermi had detected the presence of antimatter particles coming from lightning strikes on Earth.

Neutrino astronomy. A type of particle that arrives from outer space is the neutrino. Neutrinos rarely interact with particles on Earth. Neutrino detectors therefore use large amounts of matter as targets for the neutrinos. One detector, known as Super-Kamiokande, is deep underground in a mine in Japan. Its main part is a cylindrical tank of water 131 feet (40 meters) deep and 131 feet in diameter. Electronic devices in the detector can sense flashes of light produced when a neutrino collides with an atomic nucleus or an electron in the water. Super-Kamiokande began operating in 1996, but all its phototubes that detect the bursts of light had to be replaced after an accident in 2001 destroyed all the detectors.

The most sensitive neutrino detector is the Sudbury Neutrino Observatory (SNO), in a mine near Greater Sudbury, Ontario. The facility uses 1,000 metric tons (1,100 tons) of *heavy water.* In heavy water, the nucleus of each hydrogen atom consists of a proton and a neutron, instead of only a proton. SNO began taking measurements in 1999. Other neutrino detectors operate in Italy and in Russia.

In the 1960's, scientists discovered that certain neutrinos were "missing." These neutrinos were *electron-neutrinos* created by nuclear reactions in the sun. Electron-neutrinos are one of three known neutrinos. The others are *muon-neutrinos* and *tau-neutrinos.* Scientists measured only about one-half to one-third of the expected number of electron-neutrinos from the sun.

Physicists suspected that the missing electron-neutrinos turn into muon-neutrinos and tau-neutrinos on their way to Earth. In 2001, scientists at Sudbury claimed that a comparison of measurements made there and at Super-Kamiokande shows that the transformation does occur. For such a transformation to occur, neutrinos, previously thought to be without mass, must have mass. Thus, this result led to a major change in physics.

Cosmic-ray astronomy. Cosmic rays are electrically charged, high-energy particles. There are two kinds of cosmic rays: (1) *primary cosmic rays,* often called *primaries,* which begin in outer space; and (2) *secondary cosmic rays,* or *secondaries,* which form in Earth's atmosphere. Secondaries originate when primaries collide with atoms at the top of the atmosphere.

Most primaries are protons or other nuclei of atoms. They do not usually penetrate the atmosphere. Astronomers therefore use instruments aboard high-flying airplanes or satellites to detect them. Secondaries can reach low altitudes. A small fraction of them even strike Earth's surface, where special sensors can detect them.

Some primary cosmic rays come from the sun, but most of them are *galactic cosmic rays,* which originate outside the solar system. Many galactic cosmic rays have tremendous energy. Astronomers do not know how they acquire this energy—though it may come from supernova explosions.

Gravitational-wave astronomy. Astronomers have built equipment to detect another type of radiation, gravitational waves. These waves are predicted by the general theory of relativity announced in 1915 by German-born American physicist Albert Einstein. Researchers have found indirect evidence for them in certain variations in the orbits of two dense stars that revolve about each other. In 2016 gravitational waves were detected for the first time by the Laser Interferometer Gravitational-wave Observatory (LIGO), a pair of detectors located in Louisiana and in Washington state.

Direct sampling is the examination of pieces of material from celestial objects. In their examinations, scientists frequently use techniques of geology, including chemical analysis. The most common samples are *meteorites,* rocks that fell through the atmosphere from farther out in our solar system. Thousands of meteorites have been found. Most come from asteroids. A handful come from the moon or Mars. The best place to find meteorites is Antarctica. They show up on the polar ice much more clearly than they do among ordinary rocks elsewhere.

Scientists have also studied hundreds of kilograms of moon rocks brought to Earth by astronauts from 1969 to 1972. In 1970, the Soviet Union's Luna 16 spacecraft, a remotely controlled vehicle, returned small samples of soil from the moon. In addition, researchers have analyzed bits of space dust collected by devices on high-

altitude aircraft. They have determined that some of the dust came from beyond our solar system.

From 2001 to 2004, NASA's Genesis spacecraft gathered samples of the *solar wind,* a continuous flow of particles from the sun. Genesis returned to Earth in September 2004. Also in 2004, NASA's Stardust spacecraft passed near Comet Wild 2 and captured particles from its *coma,* a cloud of gas and dust surrounding the comet's core. Stardust dropped a capsule containing the samples to Earth in 2006.

Computer modeling. Astronomers use computers to construct *scientific models* (sets of mathematical equations) that represent certain processes, such as the formation of a star. After entering the equations into a computer, an astronomer inserts numbers into the equations. The computer then *simulates* (represents) how the process would develop. In some cases, the computer produces a moving picture on a computer screen. The picture can run much faster than the actual process. This kind of model can help astronomers because many important processes occur much too slowly for astronomers to observe. Other important processes that can be simulated occur in inaccessible places, such as the interiors of stars.

Space probes launched from Earth have explored the sun, the moon, and all the other planets in the solar system. They have also visited asteroids, comets, and the other planets' satellites. The probes carry scientific instruments that gather information and transmit data back to Earth. Probes have landed on the surface of the moon, Venus, Mars, and Saturn's moon Titan. See **Space exploration** (Space probes).

Learning about astronomy

It is easy for students and the general public to take part in astronomy. Amateur astronomers range from individuals who make casual nighttime or solar observations to people for whom astronomy is a serious pursuit. Amateur astronomers have their own associations and local and regional clubs. Some of the larger clubs hold "star parties" at which members set up their own telescopes and observe the skies.

Amateur astronomers make major contributions to various branches of astronomy. For example, the American Association of Variable Star Observers, whose headquarters are in Cambridge, Massachusetts, collects observations from amateurs throughout the world and puts them together. The association shares the data with professional observers. Other amateur astronomers search for new comets or supernovae.

Much technical information is available to amateur astronomers. Books on observing the heavens contain tables that indicate where stars and planets can be found each month. Many cities have planetariums, which can present shows demonstrating the movements of celestial objects. Some planetariums sponsor lectures by professional astronomers. Computer programs available on DVD or over the Internet simulate sky conditions for any location, date, and time. Maps and images of the sky are also available on the Internet.

History

The roots of astronomy extend back to the dawn of civilization. More than 4,000 years ago, in what is now

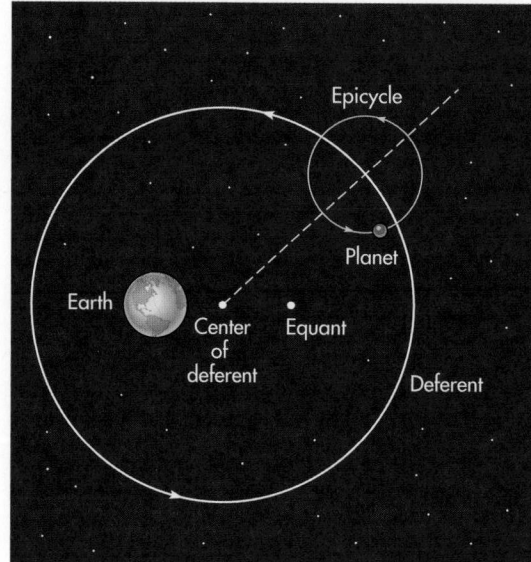

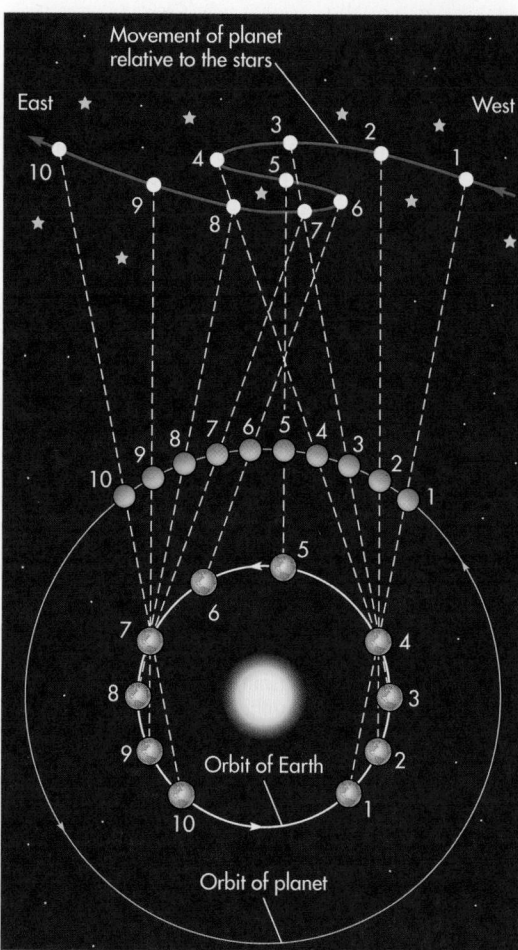

The old theory of Ptolemy put Earth at the center of the universe. Each of the other planets revolved in a circle called an *epicycle,* which revolved along a *deferent.* The epicycle's center moved at a constant speed about a point called an *equant.* This complex movement, *right,* explained why the planets sometimes appear to change direction relative to the stars.

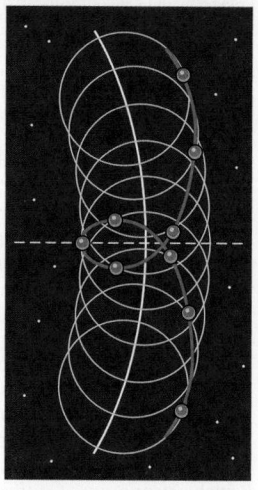

The modern explanation is that the planets appear to change direction because of differences in orbital speed as one planet passes another. A planet close to the sun orbits the sun more rapidly than does a more distant planet. In this diagram, each set of three numbers—for example, the three 5's—represents the same moment of time.

the United Kingdom, several generations of people built Stonehenge, an "observatory" consisting of huge, cut stones arranged in circles. Certain stones and alignments of stones appear to mark locations of astronomical importance, such as the point at which the sun rose on the longest day of the year. Stonehenge was apparently also a place of worship.

Some of today's constellations have their roots in patterns in the sky noted by the Sumerians in perhaps 2000 B.C. Chinese constellation patterns, which are largely different from those used in Europe, may also date from that time. Babylonian tablets show that astronomers there were noting the positions of the moon and planets by 700 B.C. The Babylonians also noted eclipses.

The ancient Greeks carried forward ideas from the Babylonians and invented some of their own. Aristotle's system of physics and astronomy, developed in the 300's B.C., survived for almost 2,000 years. In his system, Earth was the center of the universe. In the A.D. 100's, Ptolemy

modified Aristotle's system to account for the retrograde motion of the planets. Ptolemy also maintained that Earth was the center of the universe, however.

Developing the modern view. By the early 1500's, Nicolaus Copernicus had developed a theory in which Earth and the other planets revolved about the sun. In the early 1600's, Johannes Kepler analyzed precise measurements of planetary positions that had been made by Tycho Brahe. Kepler then developed three laws that correctly describe the shapes of the orbits of planets, indicate how rapidly a planet moves at various times of its year, and account for the length of the planet's year.

Kepler based his laws of planetary motion on observations, but the English astronomer and mathematician Isaac Newton proved them mathematically. Newton's work, usually called *Principia mathematica* (1687), set forth not only laws of motion but also the law of gravity that is still in general use.

By Newton's time, the field of optical astronomy had

already begun. In 1609, Galileo heard that an optical device had been built that made distant objects appear closer. He soon built his own telescope. The discoveries Galileo made with this instrument backed the Copernican theory over the theories of Aristotle and Ptolemy. In 1616, however, the Roman Catholic Church warned Galileo not to teach that Earth revolves about the sun. A book of Galileo's published in 1632 was interpreted as a violation of the ban, and Galileo was put under house arrest. Only in 1992 did the Catholic Church confirm that Galileo should not have been tried or convicted, though he was not pardoned.

Finding new objects. The British astronomer William Herschel discovered a new object in the sky in 1781. At first, he thought the object was a comet. It turned out to be a planet—later named Uranus. It was the first planet discovered since ancient times.

In 1845, astronomers John C. Adams of the United Kingdom and Urbain Le Verrier of France declared that the gravitational influence of an unknown planet was affecting the orbit of Uranus. Using one of their predictions the next year, the German astronomer Johann G. Galle found the planet, Neptune.

The American astronomer Clyde W. Tombaugh discovered Pluto in the 1930's. Tombaugh found Pluto on photos he had taken using a wide-angle telescope at Lowell Observatory in Flagstaff, Arizona. Astronomers considered Pluto a planet until 2006. Then, the discovery of Eris, an object about the same size as Pluto in the outer solar system, led to a new class of nearly planet-sized objects called dwarf planets. The first bodies to be classified as dwarf planets include Pluto, Eris, Haumea, and Makemake. A team led by the American astronomer Michael E. Brown announced the discovery of Eris, Makemake, and Haumea in 2005. Ceres, the largest asteroid, is also called a dwarf planet.

In the early 2000's, Brown and other astronomers began to discover an increasing number of large objects whose orbits lay beyond the orbit of Neptune. Some of these bodies are similar in size to Pluto. They appear to be part of a region of objects called the *Kuiper belt.*

Discovering other galaxies. In the early days of optical astronomy, the fuzzy regions of the sky became known as *nebulae*—Latin for *clouds.* When viewed through the telescopes then available, the nebulae resembled comets. Someone who was trying to discover comets could easily mistake a nebula for a comet. To prevent such errors, the French astronomer Charles Messier made a list from the 1750's to 1784 of the most prominent nebulae. This *Messier catalog* now contains 110 objects, known by their *Messier numbers.*

In Messier's time, no one knew what the nebulae were. But in the mid-1800's, Lord Rosse of Ireland built a telescope whose superior light-gathering power enabled him to discover that many nebulae have spiral shapes. The telescope's mirror measured about 6 feet (1.8 meters) across—gigantic for that time.

It took decades to discover what the spiral nebulae were. The answer came only in 1924 with the discovery by Edwin Hubble that the nebulae are so far away that they must be beyond the Milky Way. Astronomers concluded that they are independent galaxies. The "nebula" with Messier number M31, for example, is actually the Andromeda Galaxy. Astronomers now use *nebula* to

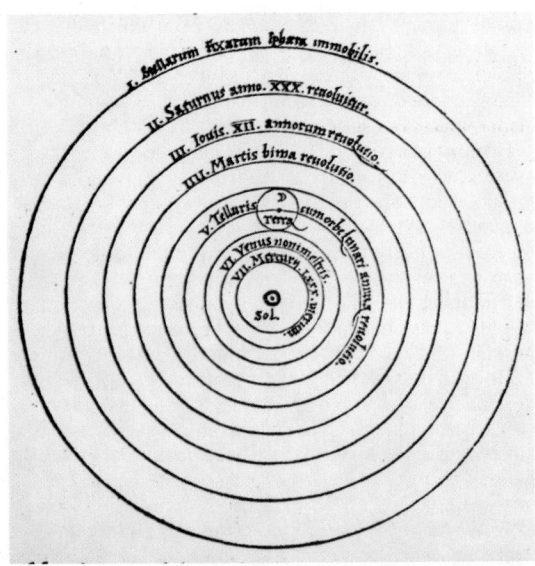

© Science Source, Getty Images

The sun-centered theory proposed by Nicolaus Copernicus of Poland in 1543 revolutionized astronomy. This diagram is from his book *On the Revolutions of the Heavenly Spheres* (1543).

mean a cloud of dust and gas. The remaining objects in the Messier catalog are *star clusters,* groups of closely placed stars.

Advances in astrophysics. By the end of the 1930's, the German-born physicist Hans Bethe, working at Cornell University in Ithaca, New York, had suggested how nuclear fusion powers the stars. For example, a process known as the *proton-proton* chain powers the sun. In this process, six protons come together in several steps to produce a helium nucleus and two protons. The final products contain slightly less mass than the original ingredients. The missing matter is converted to energy according to Albert Einstein's formula $E = mc^2$. In the formula, E is energy, m is the mass that is no longer present, and c^2 is the speed of light multiplied by itself.

The American physicist William A. Fowler and the British astronomers Geoffrey Burbidge, Margaret Burbidge, and Fred Hoyle showed in the 1950's how nuclear reactions could have built up all but the lightest chemical elements. Astronomers now know that the lighter elements formed minutes after the *big bang,* the event that began the universe. Moderately heavy elements formed inside stars. The heaviest elements formed in supernova explosions.

In 1965, the American physicists Arno Penzias and Robert Wilson discovered faint radio radiation coming equally from all directions in space. Scientists showed that the radiation was emitted about 300,000 years after the big bang and has been cooling ever since. Its temperature is now about 3 Kelvin (3 Celsius degrees above absolute zero).

For four years starting in 1989, instruments aboard the Cosmic Background Explorer (COBE) satellite measured more precisely the temperature of the radiation detected by Penzias and Wilson. Another instrument aboard the satellite found small variations in the temperature from one location in the sky to another. These so-called ripples in space may be the "seeds" from which the galaxies and clusters of galaxies grew long ago. These ripples were mapped in more detail by the Wilkinson Microwave Anisotropy Probe starting in 2001 and the Planck spacecraft starting in 2009.

Finding quasars. In 1963, the Dutch-born American astronomer Maarten Schmidt identified the starlike objects now known as quasars. He showed that the spectra of quasars have huge redshifts, indicating that the spectra are produced by powerful energy sources in distant galaxies. Most of them are billions of light-years away. Astronomers have since identified quasars as extremely bright regions that appear to get their energy from supermassive black holes in the centers of distant galaxies.

Finding pulsars. On a much smaller scale, in 1967, the British astronomer Jocelyn Bell Burnell identified a new type of object in radio observations she was making as part of her Ph.D. thesis. These objects emit radio waves that arrive at Earth in regular pulses about 1 second apart. The objects came to be known as pulsars. Later work showed that pulsars are rapidly spinning neutron stars. With every spin, a narrow beam of radio waves sweeps over Earth, producing a pulse. Astronomers have found pulsars that pulse as often as 600 times per second.

Advances in cosmology. Perhaps the biggest discovery in cosmology since Edwin Hubble's expanding universe was the discovery in the late 1990's by two teams that the expansion of the universe is speeding up. Many scientists had thought that the expansion was slowing down due to the gravity of all the objects in the universe. But studies of distant supernovae have showed them to be fainter than expected, a sign that they are farther away than predicted. An unknown force that is transmitted in an unknown way makes the universe expand more rapidly. Scientists have given this force the name *dark energy* and are trying to determine its nature. At least two-thirds of the energy in the universe consists of dark energy.

Careers

What astronomers do. Most professional astronomers work at observatories or research institutes or teach and conduct research at colleges and universities. Planetariums employ astronomers to lecture and conduct classes for the public. A few astronomers work for companies that build equipment for scientific satellites and space probes. Others work for firms that do such work as monitoring the environment from space.

Becoming an astronomer. The most important characteristic for a person who wishes to become an astronomer is a powerful spirit of inquiry. The person should also have a strong ability to learn mathematics.

High-school students who are interested in becoming astronomers should take as many math courses as they can to prepare for college mathematics and physics. A high-school physics course is also useful. Some branches of astronomy deal more with chemistry or geology than physics, so courses in those subjects can also help. Visits to planetariums and science museums as well as participation in an amateur astronomy club can help prepare a student for a career in astronomy.

To conduct research and teach astronomy at the college level requires a Ph.D. degree. Students usually take

J. R. Eyerman, *Life* magazine, © 1950 Time Inc.

Edwin Hubble, an American astronomer, demonstrated that the universe is expanding. He is shown in the observer's cage of the Hale Telescope at the Palomar Observatory near San Diego.

about six years to obtain this degree after receiving their bachelor's degree. During most of this time, Ph.D. students perform research. After obtaining their degree, most astronomers take postdoctoral positions for two or more years before searching for permanent jobs.

Astronomy associations. Astronomers from throughout the world gather every three years at the General Assembly of the International Astronomical Union. Professionals in the United States and Canada belong to the American Astronomical Society. Both professional and amateur astronomers may join the Astronomical Society of the Pacific, which has a major function in education. Many countries also have organizations devoted to astronomy, such as the Astronomical Society of India, the Royal Astronomical Society of Canada, and the United Kingdom's Royal Astronomical Society.

Jay M. Pasachoff

Related articles in *World Book.* See Solar system and Star and their lists of *Related articles.* See also the following articles:

American astronomers

Banneker, Benjamin	Langley, Samuel P.
Barnard, Edward E.	Leavitt, Henrietta S.
Bowditch, Nathaniel	Lowell, Percival
Cannon, Annie J.	Mitchell, Maria
Chandrasekhar, Subrahmanyan	Russell, Henry N.
	Sagan, Carl
Hale, George E.	Shapley, Harlow
Hogg, Helen S.	Shoemaker, Eugene Merle
Hubble, Edwin P.	Spitzer, Lyman, Jr.
Jansky, Karl G.	

British astronomers

Bell Burnell, Jocelyn	Eddington, Sir Arthur S.
Bradley, James	Halley, Edmond

Herschel, Caroline L.
Herschel, Sir John F. W.
Herschel, Sir William
Hoyle, Fred
Lovell, Sir Bernard
Newton, Sir Isaac

Other astronomers

Aristarchus
Brahe, Tycho
Cassini, Giovanni Domenico
Celsius, Anders
Copernicus, Nicolaus
De Sitter, Willem
Galileo
Hipparchus
Huygens, Christiaan
Kepler, Johannes
Laplace, Marquis de
Messier, Charles
Omar Khayyam
Ptolemy

Instruments

Astrolabe	Hubble Space Telescope
Bolometer	Spectrometer
Cassini	Telescope

Terms

Azimuth	Parallax
Corona	Redshift
Evening star	Spectrum
Horizon	Sunspot
Magnitude	Transit
Opposition	Zenith
Orbit	

Time and astronomy

Blue moon	Sidereal time
Day and night	Solstice
Equinox	Sundial
Hour	Time
International date line	Twilight
Leap year	Year
Midnight sun	
Month	
Season	

Other related articles

Andromeda Galaxy	Milky Way
Antimatter	Nebula
Astrobiology	Nebular hypothesis
Astrology	Observatory
Astrophysics	Oort cloud
Big bang	Planetarium
Black hole	Quasar
Bode's law	Refraction
Brown dwarf	Relativity
Constellation	Satellite, Artificial
Cosmology	SETI Institute
Dark energy	Solar wind
Galaxy	Space exploration
Gravitational wave	Spectroscopy
Halley's Comet	Star cluster
Halo	Tidal forces
Inflation theory	Universe
Interstellar medium	X rays (In astronomy)
Local Group	Zodiac
Magellanic Clouds	

Astrophysics is a science that applies principles of physics to many fields of astronomy. Astrophysicists try to determine the physical nature, origin, and development of the solar system, galaxies, and the universe. Almost all astronomers are also astrophysicists.

Astrophysicists use optical telescopes to view celestial objects that give off electromagnetic waves in the form of visible light. They use other kinds of telescopes to study the other forms of electromagnetic radiation—radio waves, infrared rays, ultraviolet rays, X rays, and gamma rays. One of their major techniques is the study of patterns of *wavelength* (distance between successive wave crests) of the radiation emitted by celestial objects. For example, analysis of the pattern of wavelengths in the light from a star provides information about the star's density and temperature.   Harding E. Smith

See also **Astronomy; Cosmology; Spectrometer; Telescope** (Radio and microwave telescopes).

Asturias, *ahs TOO ryahs,* **Miguel Angel,** *mee GEHL AHNG hehl* (1899-1974), a Guatemalan author and diplomat, won the Nobel Prize in literature in 1967. His early work *Legends of Guatemala* (1930) displays a creative use of Central American Indian traditions. His novel *Mr. President* (1946) condemns political dictatorship while experimenting with narrative techniques. His novel *Men of Corn* (1949) combines mythological narrative from Indian sources with social criticism. The trilogy of novels *Strong Wind* (1950), *The Green Pope* (1954), and *The Eyes of the Interred* (1960) focuses on unjust conditions of agricultural work in Central America.

Asturias was born on Oct. 19, 1899, in Guatemala City. He was his country's ambassador to France from 1966 to 1970. Asturias died on June 9, 1974.   Naomi Lindstrom

Asunción, *AH soon SYAWN* (pop. 526,408), is the capital, largest city, and chief port of Paraguay. It is in central Paraguay, on a bay of the Paraguay River, near Argentina's northeastern border. For the location of Asunción, see **Paraguay** (map).

Downtown Asunción consists of rectangular blocks in which older, lower buildings stand alongside modern skyscrapers. Treelined plazas provide relief from the hot sun and busy streets. The Pantheon of Heroes, which honors Paraguay's war heroes, is on the Plaza of Heroes, one of the main plazas. Nearer the river are the Metropolitan Cathedral; the Government Palace, also called the Palace of López, which houses the Paraguayan president's office; and the National Congress building. One of the few remaining buildings from Spanish colonial times is the House of Independence, where Paraguayan nationalists plotted their independence in 1811. There are many buildings from the late 1800's and early 1900's. The ornate central post office dates from about 1900.

Modern homes have replaced most Spanish-style houses in and around Asunción. The city has some slums on the banks of the Paraguay River. Most of Asunción's residents are of mixed European and *indigenous* (native) ancestry. Most also speak both Spanish and Guaraní, an indigenous language.

Asunción's chief industries include the processing of such agricultural and forest products as soya, sugar, and wood for export; and the production of food products, footwear, and textiles. Many people also work in commerce, for the national government, and as vendors and artisans in the *informal economy* that exists outside government control and taxation structures.

The Spanish founded Asunción in 1537. The city became the seat of government for all of Spain's territory in southeastern South America and remained so until 1617. Asunción has been Paraguay's capital since the nation gained independence in 1811.   Peter Lambert

Aswan, *AS wahn* or *ahs WAHN* (pop. 1,482, 981), is an important commercial, mining, and resort city in southeastern Egypt. It lies on the east bank of the Nile River, about 430 miles (692 kilometers) south of Cairo. For location, see **Egypt** (political map).

Aswan serves as a major market center for farmers of the Nile Valley, traders from Sudan, and Arab nomads called Bedouins. The city also ranks as a leading transportation center. A principal line of Egypt's chief railroad extends from Aswan to Cairo. The Aswan High Dam, which has revolutionized the Egyptian economy, stands about 5 miles (8 kilometers) south of Aswan (see **Aswan High Dam**). Red granite mined near Aswan has been used to build many of Egypt's most famous monuments since ancient times. Aswan's hot, dry climate makes the city a popular health resort. For the monthly weather in Aswan, see **Egypt** (Climate).   Robert L. Tignor

Aswan High Dam, *AS wahn* or *ahs WAHN,* on the Nile River in southeastern Egypt, ranks as one of the largest *rock-fill* dams in the world. Rock-fill dams consist of coarse rocks and boulders often sealed with a watertight coating—in this case, clay. The dam measures 364 feet (111 meters) high and about 2 ⅓ miles (3.7 kilometers) long. It lies south of the city of Aswan, on the northern shore of Lake Nasser. When the dam was built, it formed the lake, which extends about 300 miles (500 kilometers) from the dam into Sudan.

The Aswan High Dam provides flood control, hydroelectric power, and water for irrigation. Since the dam's construction, it has protected most of Egypt's population against the Nile River's floodwaters. With a generating capacity of about 2.1 million kilowatts, the dam supplies about 15 percent of Egypt's electric power. The dam also has increased the amount of irrigated land in Egypt, enabling the country to double its agricultural production.

While the dam has created many advantages, its operation has also caused significant harm. For thousands of years, *silt* (fine-grained particles) deposited by floodwaters had fertilized farmland along the Nile. Today, the dam prevents the water from spreading silt over the land, so farmers must enrich the soil with expensive chemical fertilizers. The absence of silt also has increased the *erosion* (wearing away) of land along the Mediterranean coast near the Nile. In addition, the dam has hindered drainage in nearby soils.

Scientists have blamed the dam for an increase in the disease *schistosomiasis,* which causes intestinal and urinary infections. Microscopic worms that cause the disease breed in snails living in the Nile and its canals. The filling of Lake Nasser displaced many people from their homes and flooded many ancient churches and temples.

Construction of the dam began in 1960 and cost about $1 billion. The dam began operating in 1968. The Soviet Union provided technical assistance and more than $300 million in loans for the project. The dam largely replaced the smaller Aswan Dam, which stands nearby and is used chiefly to generate electric power.

Katherine Kao Cushing

Asylum, in international law, is shelter and protection given by a nation to a person who is fleeing another nation. Asylum is an ancient idea. Early Israelite and Greek societies offered asylum for certain crimes. In modern times, the granting of asylum is guided by national laws and international laws and treaties. According to the United Nations, people may seek asylum if they fear persecution based on race, religion, nationality, or social or political beliefs. Asylum seekers are typically required to submit formal applications. Many countries are reluctant to accept refugees and have strict standards for asylum.

The two main types of asylum are *territorial* and *nonterritorial.* Territorial asylum is granted within a nation's boundaries. Nonterritorial asylum, commonly called *diplomatic asylum,* is given in foreign diplomatic missions—such as embassies—and on ships.

The United States bases its asylum policy on international law and the federal Refugee Act of 1980. A number of U.S. agencies work with people seeking asylum in the United States. In Canada, a federal agency dealing with refugees, Citizenship and Immigration Canada, handles requests for political asylum. In the United Kingdom, the agency that processes asylum requests is the UK Border Agency. In Australia, it is the Department of Immigration and Citizenship.   Richard E. Rupp

AT&T Inc. is a major telecommunications company in the United States and one of the world's largest. The company is a leading provider of local, long-distance, and cellular phone services. It is also a leading provider of high-speed DSL (digital subscriber line) Internet service. DSL is a technology that increases the data-carrying capacity of copper phone lines. In addition, AT&T provides Web hosting and other communication services to businesses, government, and residential customers.

The company's roots can be traced to Alexander Graham Bell's invention of the telephone in 1876. By 1877, Bell; his father-in-law, Gardiner Hubbard; and the American businessman Thomas Sanders established the Bell Telephone Company, later known as the American Bell Telephone Company. In 1882, American Bell acquired a controlling interest in the Western Electric Company, which manufactured telephone receivers and equipment. Collectively, the enterprise became known as the Bell System.

The American Telephone and Telegraph Company (AT&T) incorporated in 1885 to build and operate a long-distance wired telephone network. As the company grew, it established four divisions. One division, Western Electric, supported telephone manufacturing. Another division, AT&T Long Lines, handled long-distance services. Bell Labs was responsible for innovation. A fourth division known as Bell Companies—split into 22 separate companies—handled business operations.

In 1913, the U.S. government granted monopoly status to AT&T for national phone service. Besides domestic and international telephony, AT&T was instrumental in developing technologies that would eventually be used for TV transmission and satellite communications.

Starting in the mid-1960's, other telephone manufacturers and service providers filed challenges to AT&T's monopoly status. In 1974, the U.S. government supported the filers' claim and charged AT&T with anticompetitive practices. The lawsuit resulted in AT&T's *divestiture* (breakup of company holdings) in 1982. The Bell Companies separated from AT&T in 1984. They were grouped into seven regional firms. Each firm provided local service in a particular U.S. region. The firms were allowed to compete in different areas of the telecommunications business. One of these firms was Southwestern Bell Corporation, which changed its name to SBC Communications Inc. in 1995. In 1996, AT&T divided its operations among three separate companies. Its communication services continued to operate under the AT&T name. NCR Corporation, a computer manufacturer that AT&T had absorbed in 1991, separated from the company. AT&T also created a third company, Lucent Technologies Inc., to run its communications equipment business.

Shortly after the division, SBC merged with two of the other regional firms that had been formed in 1984. SBC acquired Pacific Telesis Group in 1997 and Ameritech Corporation in 1999. SBC also acquired the Southern New England Telecommunications Corporation, an independent company, in 1998. In 2000, BellSouth Corporation—another regional firm that had been formed in 1984—entered a joint partnership with SBC to create Cingular Wireless, a provider of cellular phone service and other wireless services.

In the 2000's, AT&T reorganized once again to streamline its wireless telephone and broadband delivery services. By 2002, Comcast Corporation acquired AT&T Broadband. In 2004, Cingular Wireless acquired AT&T Wireless. AT&T moved its headquarters to Dallas, Texas, in 2008. In 2015, AT&T acquired the satellite television provider DIRECTV. In 2018, AT&T acquired Time Warner, one of the world's largest media and communications companies.　　　Jarice Hanson

Atacama Desert, *AT uh KAM uh* or *AH tah KAH mah,* is a barren, mineral-rich region in northern Chile and the southern tip of Peru. The desert begins near Tacna, Chile, and extends southward about 600 miles (970 kilometers). It is bordered on the west by the Pacific Ocean and on the east by the Andes Mountains. The Atacama Desert averages less than 0.5 inch (1.3 centimeters) of rain yearly. Its surface contains much sand and gravel. Beds of salt are scattered throughout. For location of the Atacama Desert, see **Chile** (terrain map).

The Atacama is the world's only source of natural sodium nitrate, a mineral used in making fertilizers and gunpowder. Until the 1920's, when the production of synthetic sodium nitrate began, the desert was the world's only producer of the mineral. The desert also yields copper, iron ore, lithium, and silver.

Chile defeated Bolivia and Peru in the War of the Pacific (1879-1883). As a result of its victory, Chile took possession of all parts of the Atacama Desert that had been controlled by Bolivia and Peru. In 1929, Chile returned the northern end of the desert to Peru.　　　Robert C. Eidt

See also **Chile** (The Northern Desert; picture).

Atahualpa, *AH tah WAHL pah* (1500?-1533), also called Atabalipa, was the last ruler of the Inca Empire in Peru. In 1532, soon after Atahualpa took the throne, Francisco Pizarro and his men landed in Peru (see **Pizarro, Francisco**). Atahualpa refused to recognize King Charles I of Spain as his overlord or to accept Christianity. Pizarro's men then killed over 4,000 unarmed Inca nobles and imprisoned Atahualpa. Although he had one room filled with gold and another room filled twice with silver in ransom, Atahualpa was not released. He was executed on Aug. 29, 1533. See also **Inca** (History).　　　Brian S. Bauer

Atatürk, *AT uh TURK* or *ah tah TURK,* **Kemal,** *keh MAHL* (1881-1938), was the founder and first president of the Republic of Turkey. He served as president from 1923 until his death. Under his leadership, Turkey adopted sweeping political, economic, and social reforms.

Atatürk helped create a parliamentary form of government and adopted European law codes. His government founded new industries and banks, gave women the right to vote, and improved education. The Roman alphabet was also introduced for the Turkish language.

Atatürk also ordered all Turks to choose family names. He was given the name *Atatürk,* meaning *father of the Turks,* by the Turkish National Assembly in 1935.

Mustafa Kemal was born in 1881 in Thessaloniki, Greece (then part of the Ottoman Empire). He attended military schools. During World War I (1914-1918), he rose to the rank of general. He became famous for his role in defeating the Allies at Gallipoli Peninsula. After the war ended, he organized a Turkish nationalist movement and resisted Allied plans to break up Asia Minor. His forces drove Armenian, Greek, and French troops from the area, forcing the Allies to negotiate the Treaty of Lausanne and to recognize Turkish independence in 1923. He died on Nov. 10, 1938.　　　Justin McCarthy

See also **Turkey** (History).

Ataxia, *uh TAK see uh,* is a lack of coordination in the muscles. It is a symptom of damage to part of the central nervous system. Ataxia involves a lack of balance, or equilibrium. Patients must stand on a broad base, eyes open, or they will sway or even fall. The swaying may increase if they shut their eyes.

Many diseases that damage the central nervous system may cause ataxia. They include tumors of the brain's cerebrum and cerebellum, some deficiency diseases, and diseases of the spinal cord. Ataxia may also result from overuse of such drugs as barbiturates or alcohol. In addition, ataxia may be due to syphilis, especially if the patient's unsteadiness occurs or increases when the eyes are closed (see **Syphilis**).　　　Marianne Schuelein

Atchison, David Rice (1807-1886), was a United States senator from Missouri. Some people claim that he was president of the United States for one day— March 4, 1849. This was to be Zachary Taylor's inauguration day. But it was postponed one day because it fell on Sunday. Technically, there was no president that day. Atchison, as president *pro tempore* of the Senate, was next in line for the office. He was elected president *pro tempore* of the Senate 16 times between 1846 and 1854.

Atchison was born on Aug. 11, 1807, in Frogtown, Kentucky. He died on Jan. 26, 1886.　　　Robert F. Dalzell, Jr.

Atget, *aht ZHAY,* **Eugène,** *oo ZHEHN* (1857-1927), a French photographer, earned fame for his poetic pictures of France, particularly Paris, during the late 1800's and early 1900's. Atget took nearly 10,000 pictures. He made a historical record of the monuments of old Paris, including its houses, churches, streets, and courtyards, thus preserving the city's historic art and architecture. Atget also captured the street scenes, bars, and markets of Paris, as well as the gardens of Paris suburbs. Atget intended to record his subjects in a straightforward documentary way, but his skill in capturing light and mood elevated his photographs into art.

Jean-Eugène-Auguste Atget was born on Feb. 12, 1857, in Libourne, France. He was an actor for several years until he turned to photography in the late 1880's. In 1925, Atget met the American photographer Berenice Abbott. After his death on Aug. 4, 1927, she bought nearly half his remaining negatives and most of his prints. Abbott was largely responsible for preserving his work

Rue Luxembourg (Art Resource)

An Eugène Atget photograph shows a street scene in Paris in the late 1800's or early 1900's. Atget's pictures form a historical record of Parisian life and architecture during this period.

and winning international recognition for him as a great photographer. Michael Plante

Athabasca, Lake. See Lake Athabasca.

Athabasca River, *ATH uh BAS kuh,* is one of the most important rivers in western Canada. It begins in the Rocky Mountains with water that melts from the Columbia Icefield and empties into Lake Athabasca. For location, see **Alberta** (terrain map). The Athabasca River, which forms the southernmost part of the Mackenzie River system, is 765 miles (1,231 kilometers) long and flows entirely within Alberta. The river drains approximately 36,800 square miles (95,300 square kilometers) of land. Oil-soaked sands along the Athabasca, north of Fort McMurray, form one of the largest known oil deposits. The river was an important transportation route used by fur traders during the 1700's and 1800's.

G. Peter Kershaw

Athanasius, *ath uh NAY shuhs,* **Saint** (295?-373), was the leading Christian churchman of his time. He gained importance for his many writings that defended orthodox Christianity against attacks by the Arians. The Arians were a religious sect who believed that only God the Father was completely divine. Athanasius also introduced Eastern Christian religious community life called *monasticism* to Western Christianity.

Athanasius was probably born in Alexandria. He was ordained a deacon about 318 by Bishop Alexander of Alexandria. In 325, Athanasius attended the Council of Nicaea, which helped establish the doctrines of orthodox Christianity. In 328, Alexander died and Athanasius succeeded him as bishop. Athanasius strongly defended the decrees of the council against Arianism. His defense of Nicaea cost him five different periods of exile. During one such period, Athanasius took refuge in the Egyptian desert. There, he wrote *Life of Anthony* (about 357), a biography of Saint Anthony of Thebes, the founder of Christian monasticism. This book influenced the establishment of monastic orders in the Western church. Athanasius died on May 2, 373. His feast day is May 2.

Marilyn J. Harran

Atheism, *AY thee ihz uhm,* is the belief that there is no God. Atheism is the opposite of *theism,* the belief that God exists. Atheism is also distinguished from *agnosticism,* a belief which states that human beings do not, and cannot, know whether any gods exist.

Atheists argue that God is never encountered in human experience. They believe that nothing in human experience needs to be explained by the existence of a deity. Atheists also reject the arguments that various thinkers have advanced to prove the existence of God.

Atheists point to the presence of serious imperfections in the world, such as widespread suffering and injustice. They argue that such imperfections show that the world could not have been created by a deity who was perfect in power and goodness. Atheism conflicts with most religions.

Some prominent thinkers have been advocates of atheism. They include Baron Paul d'Holbach and Voltaire of France in the 1700's; Arthur Schopenhauer, Karl Marx, and Friedrich Nietzsche of Germany in the 1800's; Bertrand Russell of England; and Albert Camus and Jean-Paul Sartre of France in the 1900's.

Ivan Soll

See also **Agnosticism; Dawkins, Richard; God; Theism.**

Athena, *uh THEE nuh,* in Greek mythology, was the goddess of warfare, wisdom, and arts and crafts. She also was the patron goddess of Athens. The Athenians called Athena *Parthenos* (Virgin) because of her chosen state of virginity. In the 400's B.C., they dedicated a temple called the Parthenon to Athena. Athena represented strategic war planning rather than the raw violence of war. The Romans identified their goddess Minerva with Athena.

According to some ancient sources, Athena was born full-grown and dressed in armor from the head of Zeus, the king of the gods. Zeus had swallowed the goddess Metis when Metis was pregnant with Athena. From her mother, Athena inherited cunning and, according to some sources, an ability to change shape and assume disguises. In addition, Athena embodied the ancient Greek ideal of self-restraint. Athena assisted and inspired such Greek heroes as Heracles, Odysseus, and Perseus.

As the goddess of arts and crafts, Athena was skilled at weaving, embroidery, and spinning. According to one myth, a woman named Arachne once boastfully challenged Athena to a weaving contest. After the contest, Athena turned Arachne into a spider so she would have to spend the rest of her life spinning.

Athena is depicted in art as a tall, stately woman wearing a crested helmet and carrying a spear and shield. On her shield, called the *aegis,* was the head of Medusa, which could paralyze Athena's foes (see **Medusa**). Athena is often shown accompanied by a snake and carrying an owl on her shoulder. Nancy Felson

See also **Arachne; Minerva; Mythology** (picture: The gods and goddesses).

The ruins of ancient Athens are surrounded by the modern city. The remains of the Parthenon and other temples stand on a fortified hill called the Acropolis, *center.* The Odeon theater, *foreground,* has been partially restored and is used for plays and concerts.

Athens, *ATH ihnz* or *ATH uhnz* (pop. 664,046; met. area pop. 3,089,698), is one of the world's most famous and historic cities. It became the capital of Greece in 1833, after the Greeks freed themselves from Ottoman rule. But Athens's greatest fame dates from the 400's B.C., when it was the world's most powerful and most highly civilized city. The city's name in Greek is *Athinai.*

Athens lies on a plain near the southern end of Attica, a peninsula that extends from southeastern Greece into the Aegean Sea. A crescent of mountains up to 4,600 feet (1,400 meters) high bounds Athens on the west, north, and east. Athens is about 5 miles (8 kilometers) from Piraeus, Greece's largest seaport.

When Greece gained independence in 1829, Athens had only a few thousand people. The city evolved dramatically during the reign of Otto I, a Bavarian prince who became the first ruler of the new Greek kingdom. Otto was king of Greece from 1832 to 1862. Under his direction, German architects planned and built modern Athens.

Ancient Athens was the leading cultural center of the Greek world. Many of the most gifted writers of Greece lived there. They wrote works of drama, history, lyric poetry, and philosophy that have influenced literature for hundreds of years. Athenian architects built master-

John J. Baxevanis, the contributor of this article, is the author of Economy and Population Movements in the Peloponnesos of Greece.

pieces of classical beauty, and the ruins of many of these structures may still be seen. The government of ancient Athens provided an example of democracy that has inspired lawmakers ever since. The ancient Athenian statesman Pericles called Athens the "school of Greece." In many ways, the city was the birthplace of Western civilization.

The modern city

Landmarks. The bustling life of modern Athens centers around the city's three main squares—Syntagma, Omonoia, and Monastiraki. Syntagma Square, or Constitution Square, is the administrative center of Athens. The Parliament Building, formerly the royal palace, faces Syntagma. In 1843, the new Greek Constitution was proclaimed from the balcony of this building. A special corps of Greek soldiers, called *evzones,* guards the Tomb of the Unknown Soldier and the Parliament Building. The evzones wear a colorful traditional uniform including a red tasseled cap, embroidered vest, white kilt, and red leather slippers. Hotels and office buildings also face Syntagma.

Omonoia Square, also known as Concord Square, lies about ½ mile (0.8 kilometer) northwest of Syntagma. The area between Omonoia Square and Syntagma Square is Athens's chief shopping center. Omonoia Square has numerous department stores, restaurants, and other businesses. Main streets and trolley lines branch out from Omonoia.

South of Omonoia lies Monastiraki Square, the heart

of an old market district. Numerous small shops, open-air stalls, and street vendors surround Monastiraki. To the southeast is the Plaka, a district that dates from the time when the Ottoman Empire, based in what is now Turkey, controlled Greece. The Plaka still shows Ottoman influence in its winding, cobblestoned alleys. But today it also hosts many nightclubs and hotels.

In northeastern Athens, the cone-shaped hill of Lycabettus rises steeply to a height of about 910 feet (277 meters). It offers a dramatic view of the city. Directly south of Lycabettus lies the fashionable residential district of Kolonaki. The large, flat hill of the Acropolis, to the southwest, was the original center of life in ancient Athens. Here lie the remains of the Erechtheum, the Parthenon, the Propylaea, the Temple of Athena Nike, and other reminders of the glorious past.

People. Athens ranks as the cultural center of Greece, and large numbers of foreigners live in the city or visit it. As a result, Athens has an international atmosphere and a more modern style of life than any other Greek city.

The great majority of Athenians, like more than 95 percent of all Greeks, belong to the Greek Orthodox Church. Athens has many churches. The largest is the Cathedral, begun in 1840 and completed in 1855. The church of Saint Nicodemus dates from the early 1000's.

Athenian food is similar to food served in other eastern Mediterranean regions. The people of Athens eat lamb prepared in many different ways, as well as a wide variety of fish and other seafood. Other popular Greek specialties include *feta*, a cheese made from sheep's or goat's milk, and *retsina*, a wine flavored with pine resin.

© Dallas and John Heaton, Stock, Boston

The Parliament Building is the center of the Greek government. It faces Syntagma Square, the administrative center of modern Athens. The building once served as the royal palace.

Most Athenians live in small apartments or inexpensive houses. Many of the people own an automobile, but most of them ride the city's buses and trolleys or the subway that serves Athens and surrounding areas.

Education and cultural life. Athens has many public schools and several institutions of higher learning. The University of Athens, founded in 1837, has schools of law, medicine, philosophy, theology, and mathematics and the physical sciences. At the National Technical University of Athens, students study engineering and other subjects not taught at the University of Athens.

WORLD BOOK maps

Athens

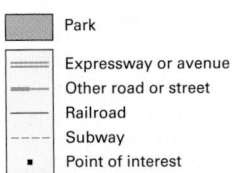

Park

▤ Expressway or avenue
═ Other road or street
── Railroad
╍╍ Subway
▪ Point of interest

Location of Athens

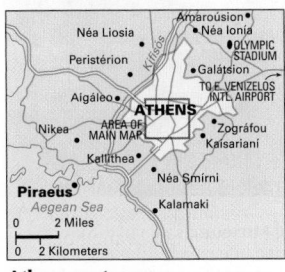

Athens metro area

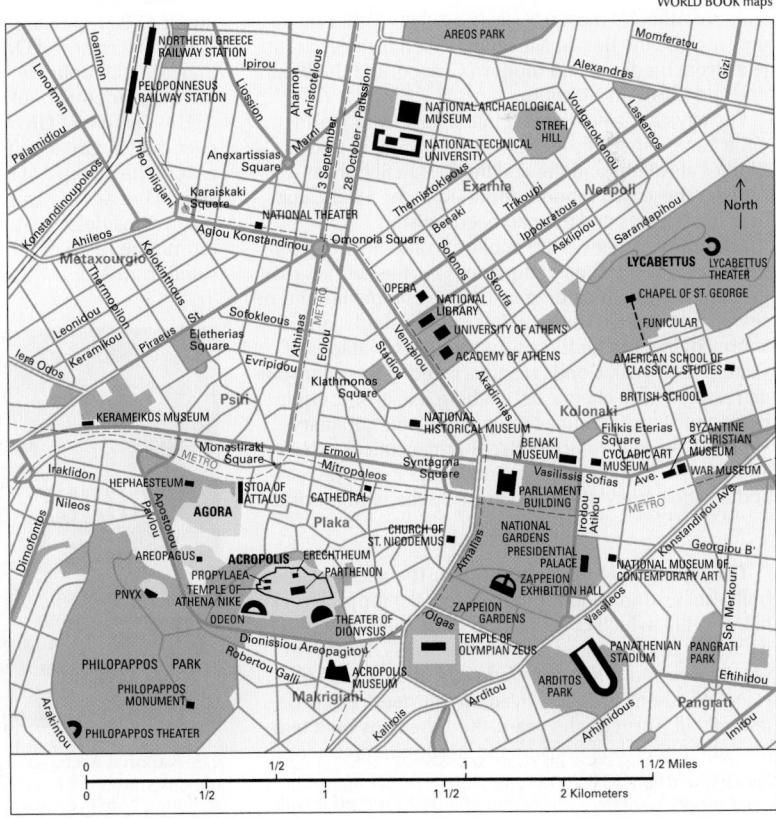

© Margot Granitsas, The Image Works

Downtown Athens is a busy center of shops, offices, and hotels. Many tourists visit Athens, the cultural center of Greece, and large numbers of foreigners live and work there.

Next door to the National Technical University stands the National Archaeological Museum, one of the world's greatest museums. It houses masterpieces of jewelry, pottery, and sculpture from all areas and every period of ancient Greece. The Acropolis Museum is home to some of Athens's most treasured artifacts. Other museums include the Benaki Museum, which features art objects from medieval and modern Greece, and the Byzantine and Christian Museum.

The city's archaeological schools have won worldwide fame, especially the American School of Classical Studies at Athens and the and the British School at Athens. These two schools, founded in the 1880's, conduct excavations and train archaeologists.

Economy. Athens is the economic and financial center of Greece. It is the headquarters for the nation's major corporations, including insurance companies and research institutions. Tourism ranks as the single largest source of income for the city, which hosts millions of visitors each year. Goods manufactured in the metropolitan area include chemicals, clothing, electronic equipment, food products, machinery, medicines, military supplies, petroleum products, pharmaceuticals, ships, and textiles. The city also produces brassware, jewelry, and a wide variety of other items popular with tourists.

The ancient city

The Acropolis and its buildings. The ancient Greeks built Athens upon and around a great flat-topped, rocky hill. This hill, which covers a little more than 10 acres (4 hectares), became known as the Acropolis. The Greek words *akro* and *polis* mean *high city,* and the early rulers of Athens probably lived on the steep, easily defended hill. Through the years, the Athenians built temples and public buildings on the Acropolis, and people stopped living there.

By about 1200 B.C., the Athenians had erected a wall around most of the Acropolis. Parts of the wall still stand, but a series of larger walls replaced it during the 400's B.C. About 530 B.C., the Athenians built a temple on the Acropolis and dedicated it to Athena, the patron goddess of the city. The temple was Athens's largest building until 480 B.C. That year, a Persian army captured the city and destroyed most of the buildings on the Acropolis. In 447 B.C., the people of Athens began to rebuild the Acropolis site under the leadership of the great statesman Pericles. They erected many new structures, including the magnificent Parthenon, a marble temple dedicated to Athena (see **Parthenon**).

Pericles also began the Propylaea, the huge monumental entrance to the Acropolis. In 431 B.C., the Peloponnesian War interrupted its construction, and the Propylaea was never completed. To its right stands the small temple of Athena Nike. The Erechtheum, a temple built in several joining sections, stands about 60 yards (55 meters) from the Parthenon. It was completed about 400 B.C. The Athenians dedicated it to Athena, the god Poseidon, and Erechtheus, a legendary king of early Athens. The most famous part of the Erechtheum is the south porch, where six columns in the form of standing maidens hold up the roof. Cement copies have replaced the original marble figures. Most of the original figures were moved to the Acropolis Museum in the early 1980's for protection from air pollution.

Other buildings. Southeast of the Acropolis stands the Theater of Dionysus, where the playwrights of ancient Athens staged their dramas. The surviving structure dates from the 300's B.C., but it includes many changes made in later times. The theater could seat about 15,000 spectators. Southwest of the Acropolis stands the restored Odeon, a theater that seats more than 5,000 people. Herodes Atticus, a wealthy Greek, built the Odeon about A.D. 160.

The Temple of Olympian Zeus, the largest temple ever built in Greece, stood about 400 yards (370 meters) east of the Theater of Dionysus. The Athenian tyrant Pisistratus began the structure about 530 B.C., but many interruptions delayed it. The temple was finally completed during the reign of the Roman emperor Hadrian, who ruled from A.D. 117 to 138. The building had 104 col-

© Thinkstock

The National Archaeological Museum is one of the world's greatest museums. Its exhibits include jewelry, pottery, and sculpture from every period of ancient Greek civilization.

umns, each 56 feet (17 meters) high, but only 16 remain.

Northwest of the Acropolis was the Agora, the marketplace of ancient Athens. Archaeologists have uncovered the ruins of many of the Agora's public buildings. Along the east side of the Agora stood the Stoa of Attalus, a long, roofed *colonnade* (row of marble columns) that housed many shops. It was built between 159 and 138 B.C. and was restored in the A.D. 1950's. Today, the Stoa of Attalus serves as a museum and as headquarters for excavations of the Agora. See **Greece, Ancient** (illustration: A bustling marketplace).

Just outside the Agora stands the Temple of Hephaestus (also called the Hephaesteum or Theseum), built about 449 B.C. It remains the best-preserved temple in Greece.

History

Earliest times. Scholars know little about the history of Athens before about 1900 B.C., when Greeks first occupied Attica. Later invaders never drove out the Greek settlers, as they did in other parts of Greece.

Athens was one of the first *city-states.* Each of these independent states consisted of a city and the region that surrounded it. Athens had a king, as did other Greek states. According to tradition, the first king of Athens was named Cecrops. Kings ruled the city-state until 682 B.C. Beginning that year, elected officials called *archons* headed the government of Athens. The general assembly, which consisted of all adult male citizens of Athens, elected the archons to one-year terms. At first, a group of three archons managed the affairs of Athens. In time, the people increased the group to nine.

After their term of office, the archons joined the Areopagus, a council of elder statesmen. The Areopagus judged murder trials and prepared political matters for the vote of the general assembly. See **Areopagus**.

As Athens's population grew, the farmers of Attica could not produce enough food for all the people and for themselves. The ruling aristocracy gradually acquired the best farmlands. Many small farmers went into debt and borrowed food that they promised to pay back out of the next year's crop. Some, who could not pay their debts, even lost their land and became slaves. Civil war threatened to break out between the lower classes and the wealthy Athenians.

Solon, one of the archons of 594 B.C., made several important reforms. First he canceled all debts, thus freeing the people who had fallen into slavery. But they did not get their land back. Solon also set up qualifications for public office based on wealth. Any qualified citizen could become a public official, regardless of whether he belonged to the traditional ruling class. In addition, Solon reorganized and published all the laws of Athens.

Solon's work did not solve the problem of poverty in Attica. Around 561 B.C., Pisistratus, a respected army commander, seized power and made himself tyrant (see **Tyranny**). He fell from power twice but ruled firmly from about 546 B.C. until his death in 528 or 527 B.C. The lower classes supported Pisistratus, and he repaid his followers by distributing land taken from his wealthy opponents. He thus continued the work of Solon in sharply reducing the power of the traditional ruling class. Pisistratus controlled, but did not suspend, the regular government and the archons. He made himself popular by making various improvements in the city, including construction of the first stages of the Temple to Zeus. After Pisistratus's death, his son Hippias ruled as tyrant.

Democracy. Hippias fell from power in 510 B.C., and Cleisthenes, the head of a leading family, became the most powerful statesman in Athens. About 508 B.C., the Athenians adopted a new constitution proposed by Cleisthenes, which made the state a democracy. This constitution was an unwritten one, but it stayed in effect with little change for hundreds of years. The constitution kept the ideas of Solon, but it also provided for new conditions that had developed since Solon's rule.

Until Cleisthenes's time, citizenship had been based on blood relationship to the four Ionic tribes that had originally settled Attica. A man had to belong to a *phratry* (brotherhood) to be a citizen. Under Cleisthenes's system, all men 18 years of age and older were registered as citizens and as members of the *deme* (village or town) in which they lived. In time, membership in the demes became hereditary, and so a man might belong to a deme in which he did not actually live. Cleisthenes organized the demes into 30 groups called *trittyes,* which, in turn, were grouped into 10 new tribes. Each of the 10 tribes was made up of 3 trittyes from different regions of Athens. Thus, members of each tribe came from various families and different parts of the city-state.

Cleisthenes's most important reform was the creation of a council of 500 members who were chosen each year by drawing lots. The council prepared business for the general assembly. The new political system provided every citizen of Athens with a chance to help run the city government. All citizens were eligible for the council and for other offices. Women were not considered citizens and could not vote or hold office. In time, all public officials except generals were chosen annually by drawing lots. Generals were elected. Individuals who were considered to be a threat to the government could be banished for 10 years by a vote of the people.

Era of achievement. Athens played a leading role in the Greek victories over Persia in the two Persian Wars (490 B.C. and 480-479 B.C.). Athens soon became head of the Delian League, a group of Greek states organized to continue to wage war against Persia. The league quickly became an Athenian empire. The period from 477 to 431 B.C. was perhaps the most brilliant in Athenian history. During this time, Athens was led by the great statesman Pericles. He increased Athens's power in Greece and reformed its government. Pericles also funded many great works of art and architecture. Athens became famous as the literary and artistic center of Greece.

War and decline. Athens led the empire into the Peloponnesian War (431-404 B.C.) against Sparta and its allies. Sparta won the war and remained the most powerful Greek state until 371 B.C., when Thebes defeated it.

Although Athens never regained its political leadership, it remained Greece's intellectual center. People came to Athens as a center of culture under Macedonian rule, and later under Roman rule. For hundreds of years, wealthy Romans sent their sons to Athens to complete their education. However, Athens lost its position as a cultural center in A.D. 529, when the Byzantine emperor Justinian closed the city's schools of philosophy.

From about 1100 to 1400, during the Middle Ages, Athens declined even further. As the power of Byzantium weakened, various Italian and other European rulers occupied the neglected city. In 1456, Athens fell to the Ottoman Empire. The Islamic Ottomans did little to restore the Christian city to its former glory.

In 1833, after the Greek War of Independence, Athens became the capital of the new kingdom of Greece. The first king, Otto I, and his advisers were German. They applied modern Western European designs—such as public squares and straight streets—to the urban landscape along the northern and eastern slopes of the Acropolis. The population grew to about 500,000 by the mid-1920's.

During World War II (1939-1945), Athens was an *open city*—that is, the Greeks agreed to neither fortify nor defend Athens. They made this agreement to protect the city's historic buildings and works of art against bomb attacks. However, it did nothing to protect Athenians from harsh treatment at the hands of the Germans, who occupied Athens in April 1941. The following winter, thousands of Athenians died of starvation. German troops abandoned the city in 1944.

Renewal. After the war, archaeologists again began to restore the ruins of ancient Athens. New buildings began to replace structures that had been erected during the reign of Otto I in the mid-1800's. The historic skyline of three-story buildings is now dotted with modern skyscrapers. In 2004, Athens hosted the Summer Olympic Games.   John J. Baxevanis

Related articles in *World Book* include:

Biographies

Aeschylus	Epicurus	Socrates
Alcibiades	Euripides	Solon
Aristides	Lysias	Sophocles
Aristophanes	Miltiades	Themistocles
Aristotle	Pericles	Thespis
Cimon	Phidias	Thucydides
Cleisthenes	Pisistratus	Xenophon
Demosthenes	Plato	Zeno of Citium
Draco	Praxiteles	

Other related articles

Acropolis	Greece, Ancient (Education;
Areopagus	Athens; History)
Athena	Law (The influence of ancient
Ballot (Older customs)	Greece)
City-state	Lyceum
Democracy (Origins of	Marathon, Battle of
democracy)	Oratory (Beginnings)
Drama (Greek drama)	Parthenon
Education (Ancient Greek ed-	Peloponnesian War
ucation)	Theseus
Europe (picture: Ancient	Thirty Tyrants
Greek drama)	Women's movement (In an-
Greece (pictures)	cient societies)

For the monthly weather in Athens, see **Greece** (Climate).

Atherosclerosis. See Arteriosclerosis.

Athlete's foot is an infectious skin disease that involves itching and scaling between the toes and on the soles of the feet. It is caused by a microscopic fungus. Nearly everyone comes into contact with this fungus, but some people are infected easier than others. The fungi thrive on warm, moist skin surfaces. For this reason, the disease affects many athletes and other people whose feet regularly become hot and sweaty.

Athlete's foot starts between the toes and then makes the bottoms of the feet red and scaly. In some cases, it causes blisters. It may spread to other parts of the body. It is then known as *ringworm* (see **Ringworm**). Athlete's

foot is also called *ringworm of the feet* or *tinea pedis.*

The disease is treated by—and can be prevented by—washing and drying the feet thoroughly; wearing socks and shoes that provide proper ventilation; using talcum powder to absorb the moisture; and, if needed, applying medicine that kills the fungus. The fungus is hard to get rid of completely if the toenails become infected. Repeated attacks of athlete's foot may occur in such cases. In severe or long-lasting cases, a physician may prescribe antifungal drugs.   Yelva Liptzin Lynfield

Athletics means sports in the United States (see **Sports**). In the United Kingdom and Commonwealth countries, it refers to track and field events (see **Track and field**).

Athlone, Earl of (1874-1957), a member of the British royal family and a military officer, served as governor general of South Africa from 1923 to 1930 and governor general of Canada from 1940 to 1946. In South Africa, he worked to unite English speakers and Afrikaners around a common theme of South African patriotism. In Canada, during World War II (1939-1945), he devoted himself to maintaining the war effort. In 1943 and 1944, he hosted President Franklin D. Roosevelt of the United States and Prime Minister Winston Churchill of the United Kingdom during two historic wartime conferences at his residence in Quebec.

The Earl of Athlone was born on April 14, 1874, in London. His full name was Alexander Augustus Frederick William Alfred George Cambridge. He was the younger brother of Queen Mary, wife of King George V. In 1904, he married Princess Alice, a granddaughter of Queen Victoria. He was an officer in the British Army and served in the Anglo-Boer War of 1899-1902 and in World War I (1914-1918). He became Earl of Athlone in 1917. He died on Jan. 16, 1957.   Christopher Saunders

See also **King, William Lyon Mackenzie** (picture: King hosted meetings).

Athos, Mount. See Greece (Macedonia); **Religious life** (The Eastern Orthodox Churches).

Atkins, Chet (1924-2001), was one of the most influential individuals in the development of modern country music in the United States. Atkins helped shape country music as a guitarist, record producer, and recording company executive. Atkins is credited with being a major force behind the creation of the *Nashville sound.* The Nashville sound brought a smooth, pop-oriented style to country music. It broadened the audience for country music internationally in the late 1950's and 1960's.

Chester Burton Atkins was born on June 20, 1924, near Luttrell, Tennessee. As a young guitarist, he greatly admired the playing of Merle Travis, who he heard on the radio. Travis played rhythm on the lower strings with his thumb, while playing melody on the higher strings with his index finger. Atkins developed the style further, often using two or even three fingers instead of one. Atkins toured with country bands and played on various radio shows during the 1940's. He first performed at the Grand Ole Opry in Nashville in 1946. Atkins settled permanently in Nashville in 1950.

Atkins made his first solo recording in 1946 and recorded over 100 albums. He served as vice president of Nashville operations for RCA Victor Records from 1968 to 1982. Atkins was elected to the Country Music Hall of Fame in 1973. He died on June 30, 2001.   Paul F. Wells

Atlanta's skyline has many prominent buildings. The three tallest pictured here are, *left to right,* the stair-shaped Georgia-Pacific Tower, 191 Peachtree, and the Westin Peachtree Plaza.

Atlanta

Atlanta is the capital and largest city of Georgia. It is a center of trade and transportation for the southeastern United States. The city is the historic core of a metropolitan area of 5 ¼ million people. It lies in northern Georgia, in the foothills of the Blue Ridge Mountains.

In 1837, a town called Terminus emerged at a railroad intersection. In 1845, it was renamed Atlanta and soon developed into a busy trade and transportation center. During the American Civil War (1861-1865), Union troops led by General William T. Sherman destroyed Atlanta.

In the late 1800's and early 1900's, Atlanta leaders promoted its transportation advantages at the center of the Southeastern rail network. Today, with excellent rail, air, and interstate highway links, it is the center of one of the fastest-growing metropolitan areas in the United States.

The city

Layout of Atlanta. The Chattahoochee, one of Georgia's major rivers, forms part of the city's western border. Most of Atlanta lies in Fulton County, but its easternmost section extends into DeKalb County.

Downtown Atlanta, in the east-central part of the city, has excellent transportation connections. At its center, the Five Points MARTA (Metropolitan Atlanta Rapid Transit Authority) Station connects two major lines of a commuter rail system. To its south is an interstate highway junction, where I-75/85 connects with I-20.

The Downtown area begins on Atlanta's south side with a complex of city, county, state, and federal government buildings. The State Capitol dates from 1889 and stands in a group of mid-rise buildings that date from the early 1900's. These buildings largely are dwarfed by 30- to 50-story skyscrapers built in the late 1900's.

East of the Five Points Station lies Underground Atlanta, a 22-acre (9-hectare) shopping and entertainment complex. To the west are major sports and convention complexes. To the northeast is Auburn Avenue, one of two famous streets in the city. From the late 1800's to the early 1960's, when the city was legally segregated, this street served as the heart of the black business community. It is now the location of the Martin Luther King, Jr., National Historical Park. It includes King's birthplace; the Ebenezer Baptist Church, where King preached; and the King Center, which houses his tomb.

Atlanta's other famous street, Peachtree, runs north from Downtown, through the Midtown area, to the Buckhead area. It is the site of Peachtree Center, a modern business complex that includes hotels, offices, restaurants, and shops. In Midtown, a commercial and residential area north of Downtown, the street is home to Atlanta's tallest building, the 1,023-foot (312-meter) Bank of America Plaza, and the Fox Theatre, a grand movie house that dates from 1929. In Buckhead, the street joins Lenox Square and Phipps Plaza, the premier shopping centers of the region.

High-rise residential buildings on Peachtree Street overlook historic neighborhoods. Middle-class bunga-

Facts in brief

Population: *City*—420,003. *Metropolitan statistical area*—5,286,728.

Area: *City*—133 mi² (344 km²). *Metropolitan statistical area*—8,686 mi² (22,497 km²). Area figures exclude inland water.

Altitude: 1,050 ft (320 m) above sea level.

Climate: *Average temperature*—January, 43 °F (6 °C); July, 80 °F (27 °C). *Average annual precipitation* (rainfall, melted snow, and other forms of moisture)—50 in (127 cm). For the monthly weather in Atlanta, see **Georgia** (Climate).

Government: Mayor-council. *Terms*—Four years for the mayor, the council president, and the 15 council members.

Founded: 1837. Incorporated as a city, 1847.

Largest communities in the Atlanta area

Name	Population	Name	Population
Atlanta	420,003	Marietta	56,579
Sandy Springs	93,853	Smyrna	51,271
Roswell	88,346	Dunwoody	46,267
Johns Creek	76,728	North Atlanta*	40,456
Alpharetta	57,551	Mableton	37,115

*Unincorporated.
Source: 2010 census.

Symbols of Atlanta. The flag, *left,* and the seal, *right,* feature the phoenix and the dates 1847 and 1865. Atlanta was chartered as a city in 1847. Atlanta adopted the phoenix as a symbol because, like that bird of Greek mythology, the city rose from its own ashes. Rebuilding began in 1865.

© William Manning Photography/Alamy Images

The birthplace of Martin Luther King, Jr., is part of the Martin Luther King, Jr., National Historical Park in Atlanta. The civil rights leader was a minister in Atlanta, his hometown.

Atlanta Convention and Visitors Bureau

Underground Atlanta is a shopping and entertainment complex that lies beneath street level in the heart of downtown. The mall spans 22 acres (9 hectares) and is mostly enclosed.

low neighborhoods circle Downtown. These neighborhoods include Virginia Highland to the east and the historic black community of Washington Park to the west.

The metropolitan area. Atlanta's metropolitan area spreads out over 29 counties. It is home to about half of Georgia's people.

Most of the metropolitan area population is concentrated in the urban areas of 10 counties organized under the Atlanta Regional Commission—Cherokee, Clayton, Cobb, DeKalb, Douglas, Fayette, Fulton, Gwinnett, Henry, and Rockdale. The majority of this population resides outside I-285, which circles the city at a distance of 12 miles (19 kilometers). Older towns, many of which are county seats, serve as subcenters in the region. These towns include Conyers, Cumming, Douglasville, Griffin, Lawrenceville, Marietta, and McDonough.

Atlanta's suburban areas offer many historical sites as well as new housing developments and large business districts. Expressway development in the late 1900's helped generate suburban "downtowns" anchored by major shopping malls. The malls attracted high-rise office towers, condominiums, and hotels. These developments include complexes around Cumberland Mall/Galleria Mall in Cobb County, Perimeter Mall in DeKalb County, and Gwinnett Place Mall in Gwinnett County.

People

Ethnic groups. African Americans make up Atlanta's largest single ethnic group. They account for about 55 percent of the city's population. In the entire metropolitan area, whites make up about 55 percent of the population and African Americans over 30 percent. Asians and Hispanics represent small but growing parts of the area's population.

Housing. Atlanta is famous for its tree-covered neighborhoods. Druid Hills is one of the nation's best-preserved planned suburban neighborhoods. Its plan was based on a design by the American landscape architect Frederick Law Olmsted. The neighborhood is known for

City of Atlanta

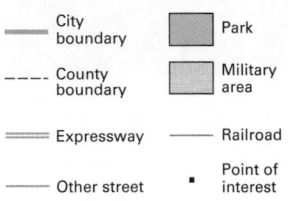

Atlanta lies in northwestern Georgia. The larger map shows the city and some of its points of interest. The smaller map shows the Atlanta area.

City boundary	Park
County boundary	Military area
Expressway	Railroad
Other street	Point of interest

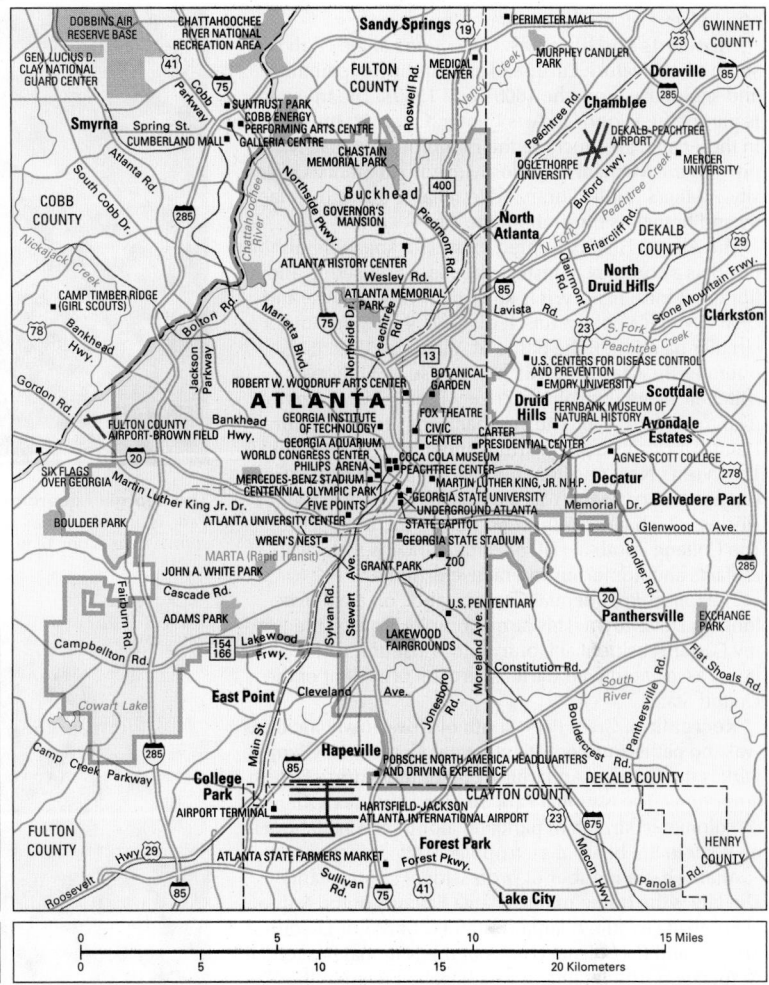

WORLD BOOK maps

---

its large houses, broad lawns, and curving streets shaded by towering trees. Other historic Atlanta neighborhoods also follow Olmsted-inspired design principles.

Education. An elected Board of Education supervises the Atlanta public school system. The Atlanta area also has many church-supported and other private schools.

Atlanta has many accredited colleges and universities. The largest are Georgia State University and the Georgia Institute of Technology, often called Georgia Tech. Atlanta has the largest complex of predominantly African American colleges and universities in the United States. The complex includes Clark Atlanta University, Morehouse College, Spelman College, and the Interdenominational Theological Center. Outside the city limits are Emory University in DeKalb County, Agnes Scott College and Columbia Theological Seminary in Decatur, Kennesaw State University in Kennesaw, and the University of West Georgia in Carrollton.

Social problems. Atlanta faces many social problems experienced by other large urban areas. Major problems include crime and homelessness. Much of the crime is associated with the problems of poverty and drug abuse. Rising housing costs have contributed to homelessness. Substandard housing is a problem in some older neighborhoods in poor areas of the central city. A number of private organizations, including Georgia-based Habitat for Humanity, run programs to assist in renovating or building houses for the poor.

Between 1995 and 2010, the Atlanta Housing Authority (AHA) tore down nearly all its large public housing projects. Instead, the AHA housed tenants in privately owned buildings. The agency issued housing vouchers that permitted tenants to choose where they would live.

Cultural life

The arts. The Atlanta Ballet, founded in 1929, and the Atlanta Opera, founded in 1979, perform at the Cobb Energy Performing Arts Centre. This facility also hosts Broadway shows, concerts, and other events. The Fox Theatre hosts Broadway shows, Atlanta Ballet performances, concerts, and films. The Woodruff Arts Center supports the Alliance Theatre and the Atlanta Symphony Orchestra. Other theaters include Downtown's Balzer Theater and the 7 Stages Theatre in Little Five Points. Arts centers at area universities include the Rialto Center for the Arts at Georgia State University, the Ferst Center for the Arts at Georgia Tech, the Donna and Marvin Schwartz Center for Performing Arts at Emory University, and Spivey Hall at Clayton State University.

Museums and libraries. Collections at the High Museum of Art feature European and American paintings and sculptures from the 1800's and 1900's. The museum is part of the Woodruff Arts Center. Other art museums in the Atlanta area include the Hammonds House Museum and the Michael C. Carlos Museum at Emory University. Atlanta's public library system has a downtown facility and branches throughout the city.

The Atlanta History Center, in the Buckhead neighborhood, is a complex of historic houses, a museum, and a library of local history. It is known for its Civil War and 1996 Olympics collections. It displays the Cyclorama, a circular painting of the Battle of Atlanta of 1864. It also operates the Margaret Mitchell House in Midtown. Mitchell wrote the Pulitzer Prize-winning novel *Gone with the Wind* (1936). The Fernbank Museum of Natural History includes a planetarium and a forest preserve. The Wren's Nest museum honors the journalist Joel Chandler Harris, who was famous for his "Uncle Remus" stories, which were published during the late 1800's. The College Football Hall of Fame contains historical artifacts and numerous interactive exhibits.

The Carter Presidential Center stands on a hill overlooking Downtown. This large complex houses the Jimmy Carter Presidential Library and Museum, which has items associated with Carter's term as president of the United States.

Recreation. Grant Park, south of Downtown, includes walking paths and Zoo Atlanta. Near Centennial Olympic Park is the Georgia Aquarium, one of the world's largest aquariums. The National Park Service manages a 48-mile (77-kilometer) stretch of parkland along the Chattahoochee River in the heart of metropolitan Atlanta.

Atlanta has a number of professional sports teams. The city is the home of the Atlanta Falcons of the National Football League, Atlanta United FC of Major League Soccer, and the Atlanta Hawks of the National Basketball Association. The Atlanta Braves baseball team of the National League plays in nearby Cobb County.

Economy

The Atlanta metropolitan area is a center for service industries. It ranks as a leader in trade, transportation, and communication. Service-related jobs employ about 80 percent of the area's people. Manufacturing employs about 10 percent. The remainder work in such industries as construction, agriculture, mining, and utilities.

Service industries. Atlanta has a thriving wholesale trade industry. Much of this trade takes place in the huge downtown AmericasMart.

Atlanta is a transportation and communication hub. Hartsfield-Jackson Atlanta International Airport in College Park ranks among the world's busiest airports for passenger and cargo flights. Delta Air Lines is headquartered in Atlanta. The city is also the chief railroad center of the Southeast. United Parcel Service, Inc., the largest U.S. package delivery company, has its headquarters in Atlanta. The Cable News Network (CNN) also is based in the city. Many newspapers serve the metropolitan area. The major paper is *The Atlanta Journal-Constitution.*

Government services also contribute to the economy of Atlanta. A number of state and federal government agencies have offices in the area. The United States

The Georgia Aquarium, near the edge of Centennial Olympic Park, is one of Atlanta's leading attractions. A whale shark, *shown here,* is one of hundreds of *species* (kinds) on display.

The Coca-Cola Company has headquarters and a museum in Atlanta. A giant Coca-Cola bottle and logo stand above the entrance of the World of Coca-Cola museum, *shown here.*

Centers for Disease Control and Prevention (CDC) maintains its headquarters just outside the city limits. The CDC also operates many laboratories in Atlanta. Military installations in the Atlanta area include Dobbins Air Reserve Base near Marietta.

Manufacturing. The chief manufactured products of the Atlanta area include food, electronics, textiles, and transportation equipment. The Coca-Cola Company has its headquarters in Atlanta. Lockheed Martin Aeronautics, which makes military planes, has a manufacturing and design facility in Marietta.

Government

Atlanta has a mayor-council form of government. The city's voters elect the mayor, the City Council president, and the 15 council members to four-year terms. The Atlanta area has over 60 other local government bodies, including county and city governments, local boards of education, and a regional transportation authority.

History

Early days. The Creek Indians inhabited the Atlanta area before whites reached the region. In 1813, the U.S. Army sent troops to the area to build a fort along the Chattahoochee River to protect farmers who were coming to the area. The site, known as Standing Peachtree, became an important trading post. But because the Chattahoochee River was not navigable, there was little chance for a city to develop in the region.

Railroads brought the potential for urban growth. In 1837, surveyor Stephen Long set the eastern *terminus* (end) for the Western and Atlantic Railroad at the site of what is now the Georgia World Congress Center. There the Western and Atlantic joined lines linking to the Atlantic Coast cities of Charleston, South Carolina, and Savannah, Georgia. A town called Terminus was founded at the site. In 1845, the town sought a new name. J. Edgar Thompson, a railroad engineer, suggested *Atlanta.*

Destruction and redevelopment. Atlanta was chartered as a city in 1847. Fulton County was established in 1853, with Atlanta as the county seat. After the American Civil War began in 1861, Atlanta's railroad connections made it a strategic target for the Union Army. In 1864, Union troops led by General William T. Sherman captured Atlanta and burned most of it to the ground.

After the Civil War ended in 1865, Atlanta was quickly rebuilt. It replaced Milledgeville as the state capital in 1868. By 1880, Atlanta had over 37,000 residents and ranked as Georgia's largest city.

In 1881, Atlanta held the International Cotton Exposition to focus attention on its potential as a manufacturing center. The city's Cotton States and International Exposition of 1895 promoted Atlanta's potential as a regional transportation center. The popular soft drink Coca-Cola was invented in Atlanta in 1886. By 1900, Atlanta had become an important manufacturing and retailing center and had nearly 90,000 residents.

As a result of laws passed by the Georgia General Assembly, the city began to impose segregation in streetcars and other public facilities at the end of the 1800's. In a 1906 race riot, white mobs roamed Downtown streets, attacking and beating blacks. The riot resulted in numerous injuries and at least 12 deaths. It led black businesses to move to Auburn Avenue, which became an important street for black businesses and black churches.

Gate City of the South. By 1920, Atlanta's 14 rail lines and 4 major railroads earned it the name *Gate City of the South.* Through a promotional campaign in the late 1920's, the Atlanta area attracted regional offices of national corporations. In 1936, one of the nation's first federally funded low-income housing projects, Techwood Homes, was opened for whites. A separate complex, University Homes, was opened for blacks in 1938.

The mid-1900's. World War II brought new military installations and industries to Atlanta. In 1943, the area's first naval air station opened on the site of what is now DeKalb-Peachtree Airport, near Chamblee. Many farmworkers moved to the Atlanta area to work in war industries and remained after the war ended in 1945. In 1952, Atlanta annexed 81 square miles (210 square kilometers) of suburban land to the north, west, and south of the

city, adding about 100,000 residents to its population.

The 1960's were a period of major growth and social change in Atlanta. The area's first expressways were completed in the late 1950's and early 1960's. Atlanta-Fulton County Stadium, finished in 1965, became the home of the city's first major league sports team, the Braves.

Auburn Avenue was the site of an early struggle for civil rights that had begun to emerge in the 1940's and 1950's. In 1957, Martin Luther King, Jr., returned to Atlanta, his hometown, after rising to prominence as a leader of the Montgomery, Alabama, bus boycott. In Atlanta, King joined with other ministers to found the Southern Christian Leadership Conference (SCLC). The SCLC coordinated the work of civil rights groups that demonstrated against segregation in the South.

By 1960, African Americans in Atlanta had regained the right to vote and were having some influence on public policy. But Atlanta remained a segregated city, and no African Americans held elective office. In May 1960, students started a public protest by holding sit-ins at restaurants in the Capitol, City Hall, and other public buildings after they were denied service. White political and civic leaders scrambled to develop a desegregation plan, and their actions helped to prevent violent racial unrest. Atlanta peacefully integrated its public schools in 1961. Also during the 1960's, many whites moved to the suburbs, and the number of registered black voters in the city increased. Maynard Jackson was elected mayor in 1973, becoming the first black mayor of a major Southern city. He was reelected in 1977.

The late 1900's. Atlanta's population reached its highest level, about 495,000, in 1970. It fell to about 394,000 by 1990 but rose in the 1990's and the first decade of the 2000's. Employment opportunities in the Atlanta area attracted workers from other parts of the United States. Most settled in the suburbs. The metropolitan population soared from about 1½ million in 1970 to about 5¼ million in 2010. Atlanta hosted the Summer Olympic Games in 1996.

The early 2000's. Voters elected Shirley Franklin mayor in 2001. Franklin became the city's first woman mayor. She won reelection in 2005. In 2009, former state Senator Kasim Reed won election as mayor. Keisha Lance Bottoms succeeded Reed as mayor in 2018.

The Atlanta area faces traffic congestion and air quality problems. Such projects as Atlantic Station, a complex of offices, stores, and homes in Midtown, were designed to reduce the area's dependence on automobiles. In 2005, Atlanta worked with private companies and community groups to move forward on a project called the Atlanta BeltLine. The project, built largely along unused rail lines, will connect dozens of Atlanta neighborhoods. The BeltLine, when completed, is expected to include a 22-mile (35-kilometer) ring of parks, trails, light rail, and economic and housing developments. From 2007 to 2009, a drought led to record low water levels in the reservoirs supplying Atlanta. Government officials imposed limits on water usage.   Timothy J. Crimmins

Related articles in *World Book* include:

Centers for Disease Control and Prevention	Jordan, Vernon E., Jr.
	King, Martin Luther, Jr.
Coca-Cola Company	Marino, Eugene A.
Georgia (pictures)	Mitchell, Margaret
Georgia Institute of Technology	

Atlantic Charter expressed the post-World War II (1939-1945) aims of the United States and the United Kingdom. President Franklin D. Roosevelt of the United States and British Prime Minister Winston Churchill adopted the declaration in August 1941 during a conference aboard the USS *Augusta* off the coast of the Canadian island of Newfoundland. Churchill had hoped to convince Roosevelt of the need for U.S. intervention in the war, but Roosevelt still faced strong opposition at home to American involvement. Nonetheless, the charter solidified the Anglo-American alliance and outlined the goals following an Allied victory. The charter maintained some of the basic principles of President Woodrow Wilson's Fourteen Points, proposed near the end of World War I (1914-1918). The United States entered World War II after the Japanese attack on the U.S. naval base at Pearl Harbor, Hawaii, on Dec. 7, 1941.

The Atlantic Charter was eventually supported by 26 countries and formed the basis of the Declaration of the United Nations in January 1942. The complete text of the charter is given in the table with this article.

Michael E. Donoghue

See also **Fourteen Points; United Nations; World War II.**

Atlantic City, New Jersey (pop. 39,558), is one of the world's largest seaside resorts. It lies on Absecon Island, on the southeast coast of New Jersey (see **New Jersey** [political map]). Roadways connect Absecon Island to the mainland. Atlantic City and another city—Hammonton—form a metropolitan area of 274,549 people.

Atlantic City is famous for its gambling casinos and its Boardwalk. The Boardwalk—made of wood, steel, and

Rudi VonBriel

Atlantic City's famous Boardwalk stretches along the Atlantic Ocean for 4 ½ miles (7.2 kilometers). It is lined with restaurants, shops, and hotels with gambling casinos.

UPI/Bettmann

The Atlantic Charter was adopted at a 1941 meeting between United States President Franklin D. Roosevelt, *seated left,* and British Prime Minister Winston Churchill, *seated right.*

Text of the Atlantic Charter

The President of the United States of America and the Prime Minister, Mr. Churchill, representing His Majesty's Government in the United Kingdom, being met together, deem it right to make known certain common principles in the national policies of their respective countries on which they base their hopes for a better future for the world.

First, their countries seek no aggrandizement, territorial or other;

Second, they desire to see no territorial changes that do not accord with the freely expressed wishes of the peoples concerned;

Third, they respect the right of all peoples to choose the form of government under which they will live; and they wish to see sovereign rights and self-government restored to those who have been forcibly deprived of them;

Fourth, they will endeavor, with due respect for their existing obligations, to further the enjoyment by all states, great or small, victor or vanquished, of access, on equal terms, to the trade and to the raw materials of the world which are needed for their economic prosperity;

Fifth, they desire to bring about the fullest collaboration be-

tween all nations in the economic field with the object of securing, for all, improved labor standards, economic advancement, and social security;

Sixth, after the final destruction of the Nazi tyranny, they hope to see established a peace which will afford to all nations the means of dwelling in safety within their own boundaries, and which will afford assurance that all the men in all the lands may live out their lives in freedom from fear and want;

Seventh, such a peace should enable all men to traverse the high seas and oceans without hindrance;

Eighth, they believe that all of the nations of the world, for realistic as well as spiritual reasons, must come to the abandonment of the use of force. Since no future peace can be maintained if land, sea, or air armaments continue to be employed by nations which threaten, or may threaten, aggression outside of their frontiers, they believe, pending the establishment of a wider and permanent system of general security, that the disarmament of such nations is essential. They will likewise aid and encourage all other practicable measures which will lighten for peace-loving peoples the crushing burden of armaments.

concrete—is 60 feet (18 meters) wide. It stretches along the Atlantic Ocean for 4 ½ miles (7.2 kilometers) in Atlantic City. It continues for 2 more miles (3.2 kilometers) in Ventnor City, a community southwest of Atlantic City. The Boardwalk is lined with restaurants, shops, and hotels with gambling casinos.

Also on the Boardwalk is Boardwalk Hall. The 1929 landmark building, formerly called the Convention Center, is a sports stadium and concert hall. It was the site of the Miss America Pageant from 1921 to 2004, and again for several years beginning in the 2010's. Five piers extend into the Atlantic Ocean from the Boardwalk, and include an art center and a shopping mall.

Tourism is Atlantic City's chief economic activity. The city attracts many vacationers and weekend and holiday visitors. Its first gambling casino opened in 1978. Casinos attract large numbers of visitors to the city. Besides tourism, the city's economic activities include fishing.

Atlantic City has a mayor-council form of government. The city was incorporated in 1854. A Boardwalk was completed in the city in 1870. The present one dates from 1896. In 1976, New Jersey voters approved a referendum to allow gambling casinos in Atlantic City. The casinos were originally promoted as a way for the city to finance urban renewal. In the late 1900's, after the arrival of the casinos, some areas of the city were rebuilt. By the mid-2010's, however, a number of casinos in the city had closed, shrinking the tax base and leaving the city deeply in debt. In November 2016, the state approved a plan that gave state leaders control of many of the city's local government functions for five years.

In October 2012, Hurricane Sandy struck the Atlantic Coast, killing more than 100 people and causing widespread damage. Floodwaters covered much of Atlantic City, and sections of the city's famed Boardwalk were washed away.   Critically reviewed by Martin DeAngelis

See also **New Jersey** (picture).

Atlantic Coastal Plain. See United States (The Coastal Lowlands).

Atlantic Intracoastal Waterway is a sheltered water route used by boats along the Atlantic Coast of the United States. It is a series of rivers, estuaries, inland bays, sounds, and inlets, nearly all linked by canals.

United States Army engineers continually dredge the 1,200-mile (1,930-kilometer) waterway. Its channel has a depth of 12 feet (3.7 meters) or more. Barges and small pleasure boats travel on the waterway. They are exposed to the open ocean for only about 50 miles (80 kilometers) south from Boston, along the Rhode Island coast, and for 37 miles (60 kilometers) along the New Jersey coast. A canal extends from Philadelphia to Chesapeake Bay. The rest of the waterway lies back from the shoreline or is protected by islands and sand bars.

About 175 bridges cross the Atlantic Intracoastal Waterway. Twenty-two lighthouses help guide the vessels. Water locks lift and lower boats to different levels in the Dismal Swamp Canal in eastern Virginia and in eastern North Carolina.

A one-way voyage on the waterway takes about 10 days for small vessels. The trip presents scenery that ranges from the busy shipping environment of New York Harbor to the lonely wilderness along the Carolina coast and the colorful resorts in Florida. Many colonists in America established settlements on streams and bays of the Atlantic seaboard. They were among the first to use the coastal and inland waterways for travel, trade, and communication along the coast.   John Edwin Coffman

See also **Canal; Inland waterway.**

Shostal

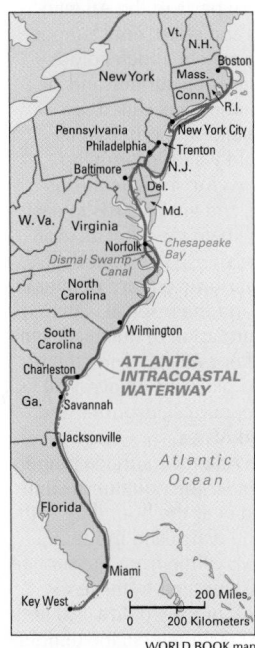

The Atlantic Intracoastal Waterway provides a sheltered route for small boats.

WORLD BOOK map

Atlantic Ocean is the world's second largest ocean. Only the Pacific Ocean is bigger. The Atlantic makes up about 26 percent of Earth's ocean area and 17 percent of its total surface area. The Atlantic Ocean contains a large number of habitats for marine life. The ocean is a rich source of seafood as well as other valuable resources. The Atlantic has been a major avenue for commerce and an active site for exploration for hundreds of years. The islands and coastal regions of the Atlantic are valuable sites for marine recreation and tourism.

The ancient Romans named the Atlantic after the Atlas Mountains. Those mountains rise at the western end of the Mediterranean Sea and, in ancient times, marked one limit of the known world. *Atlantic* probably referred to the fact that the ocean lies beyond the Atlas range.

Boundaries and size

The Atlantic Ocean is bordered by North America and South America on the west and by Europe and Africa on the east. The Atlantic connects to the Arctic Ocean, the Greenland Sea, and the Norwegian Sea through the Davis Strait. It joins the Southern Ocean between 40° and 60° south latitude. The equator separates the Atlantic Ocean into the North Atlantic and the South Atlantic. The North Atlantic has a number of seas opening into it. These seas, called marginal seas, include the Caribbean, Labrador, Mediterranean, and North seas and the Gulf of Mexico. Some scientists regard the Arctic Ocean as a marginal sea of the North Atlantic. The South Atlantic has no marginal seas.

The widest part of the Atlantic, between Spain and Mexico, extends about 5,500 miles (8,800 kilometers). The narrowest part spans about 1,800 miles (2,900 kilometers), between Brazil and western Africa. The Atlantic is about 9,000 miles (14,500 kilometers) long from north to south, and its area is about 34 million square miles (88 million square kilometers).

The Atlantic sea floor

The continental margin is the part of the Atlantic sea floor that borders the continents. The continental margin consists of (1) the *continental shelf,* (2) the *continental slope,* and (3) the *continental rise.*

The continental shelf slopes gently from the coastline to a depth of approximately 330 feet (100 meters). The width of the continental shelf varies from a few miles or kilometers to about 250 miles (400 kilometers). Beyond the continental shelf, the sea floor drops steeply to about 9,800 feet (3,000 meters). This region is called the continental slope. At the base of this slope is the continental rise, a region of sediments that have washed from the continents. From there, the sea floor drops gradually to the *abyssal depths* of about 13,100 feet (4,000 meters).

At some places along the continental shelf, continental slope, and continental rise, erosion has formed submarine canyons and channels. Some of these features occur off rivers. Others may represent ancient patterns of drainage from the continents.

The ocean's large islands lie close to the mainland of the continents and are called continental islands. They include Cuba, Great Britain, Ireland, and Newfoundland in the North Atlantic, and the Falkland Islands in the South Atlantic. The marginal seas have many more islands than the ocean itself.

The Mid-Atlantic Ridge is the most striking feature on the Atlantic Ocean's floor. The ridge is a submarine mountain range that extends from north of Iceland to the Southern Ocean. It forms the boundary between the *tectonic plates,* rigid slabs of Earth's rocky outer shell that support the continents and make up the sea floor. New sea floor is created in the gap between the plates, called a *rift,* by a process known as *sea-floor spreading.* In this process, the plates move away from the rift at about 1 inch (2.5 centimeters) per year. Melted rock rises into the rift and hardens to form the new sea floor.

The Mid-Atlantic Ridge is part of a midocean ridge system that circles Earth. This great mountain range is the site of earthquakes, volcanoes, and *hydrothermal vents.* Hydrothermal vents occur when water seeps through cracks in the sea floor and is then heated by underlying volcanic molten rock. The water then rises back to the ocean floor as mineral-rich hot water springs.

The Mid-Atlantic Ridge rises above the ocean surface in several places, forming islands. These islands include Ascension, the Azores, Iceland, and St. Helena. Volcanic islands—that is, those created by the eruption of volcanoes—include Bermuda, the Canary Islands, Cape Verde, Iceland, the Madeira Islands, the South Sandwich Islands, St. Helena, and Tristan da Cunha.

The sea floor slopes gradually away from the Mid-Atlantic Ridge to the *abyssal plains,* which lie mainly at about 14,000 to 18,000 feet (4,300 to 5,500 meters) below sea level. Trenches form the deepest parts of the Atlantic. A small number of trenches occur near the West Indies and off the southern tip of South America. The deepest point of the Atlantic Ocean is in the Puerto Rico Trench, 28,232 feet (8,605 meters) below the surface.

Climate

The far northern and southern parts of the Atlantic Ocean have long, cold winters and short, cool summers. In these regions, the winter air may be much colder than the water. The variation between surface and air temperature causes low fog, sometimes called *sea smoke,* to form. In the Grand Banks and other areas, warm, moist air moves over cold water, producing heavy fog that may be dangerous for ships. Icebergs float in the far north and south, and are hazards to navigation. Near the equator, the climate stays hot all year.

Cyclical events also affect weather patterns and climate. For example, El Niño, a periodic pattern of interaction between the atmosphere and the tropical waters of the Pacific Ocean, affects the formation of hurricanes in the Atlantic (see **El Niño**). Another cyclical event, the North Atlantic Oscillation, takes place about every 10 years. It may affect temperature, rainfall, drought, and storm conditions in Europe and Africa.

Water temperatures at the Atlantic's surface range from about 86 °F (30 °C) at and near the equator in summer to about 28 °F (–2 °C) at and near the boundary with the Southern Ocean in winter. In warm and moderate regions, the temperature may vary little from the surface to a depth of about 330 feet (100 meters). In these regions, the temperature drops off quickly below 330 feet. At a depth of about 3,300 feet (1,000 meters), the temperature is about 41 °F (5 °C) and varies little to the ocean floor. In cold regions, temperatures change little between surface and deep waters.

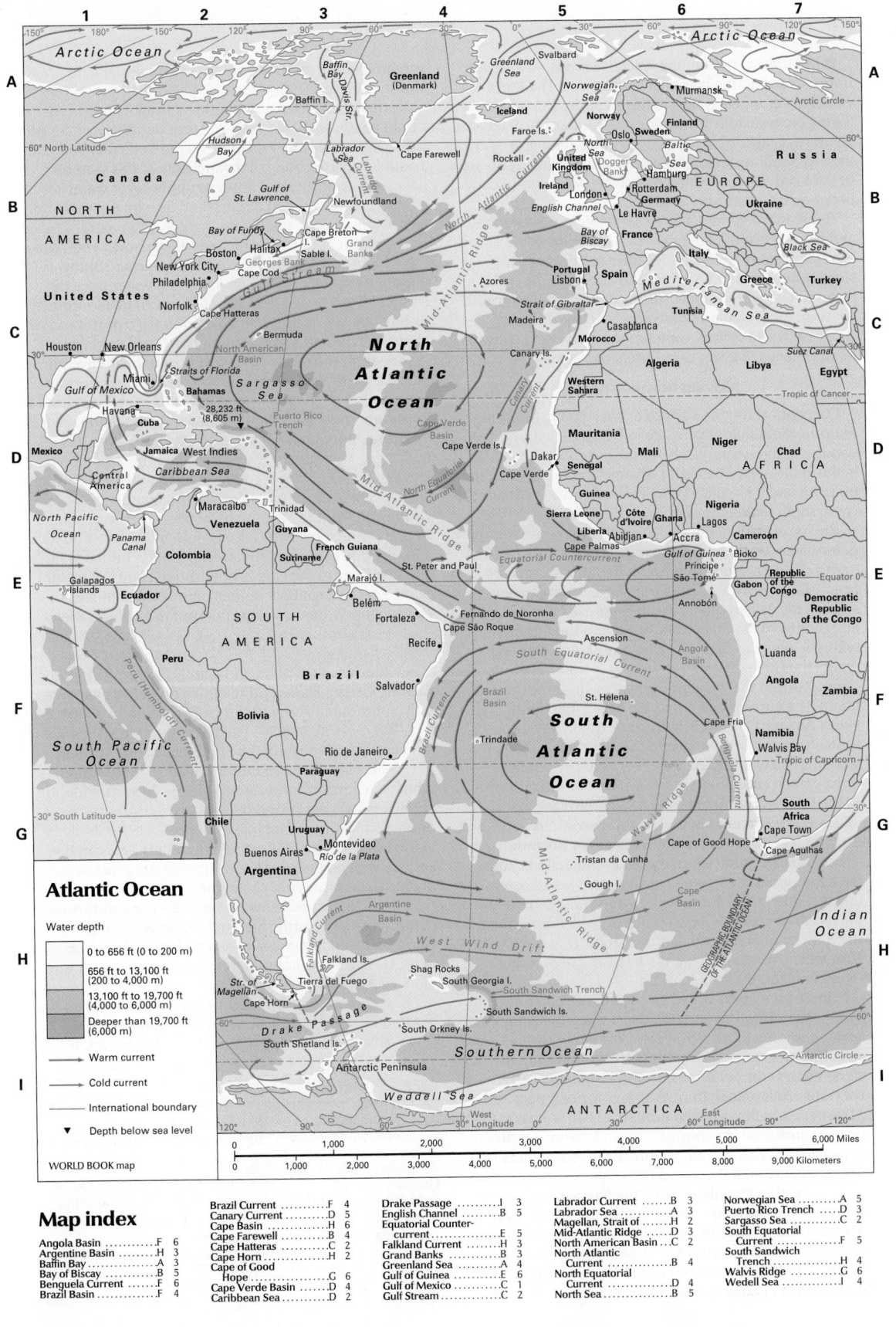

Atlantic Ocean

Water depth

	0 to 656 ft (0 to 200 m)
	656 ft to 13,100 ft (200 to 4,000 m)
	13,100 ft to 19,700 ft (4,000 to 6,000 m)
	Deeper than 19,700 ft (6,000 m)

→ Warm current
→ Cold current
— International boundary
▼ Depth below sea level

WORLD BOOK map

Scale:
0 — 1,000 — 2,000 — 3,000 — 4,000 — 5,000 — 6,000 Miles
0 — 1,000 — 2,000 — 3,000 — 4,000 — 5,000 — 6,000 — 7,000 — 8,000 — 9,000 Kilometers

Winds. Wind belts in the Atlantic Ocean include the *trade winds* and the prevailing *westerlies*. The trade winds occur on each side of the equator. The northeast trades blow steadily from Africa to the Caribbean at 5° to 30° north latitude. The southeast trades blow from Africa toward South America at 5° to 30° south latitude. An area of light and variable winds called the *doldrums* occurs between the two trade wind belts.

The westerlies extend from 35° to 60° north latitude and 35° to 60° south latitude. The westerlies in the Northern Hemisphere influence weather patterns across North America and the Atlantic to Europe. From July through October, tropical storms develop in the area of 10° to 20° north latitude between Africa and Central America. These storms sometimes intensify into powerful hurricanes that can cause great destruction.

Moving ocean waters

Currents along the surface of the Atlantic move in enormous circular patterns called *gyres*. The trade winds and the westerlies drive the gyres, which center in the subtropics. The North Atlantic Gyre is north of the equator, and it circulates clockwise. The South Atlantic Gyre, south of the equator, circulates counterclockwise.

The movement of the trade winds and the westerlies determines the direction of currents in the Atlantic. The trades drive the North and South Equatorial currents from Africa westward. The South Equatorial Current splits at the eastern tip of South America. One part travels southward, and the other flows into the Caribbean, where it joins the North Equatorial Current. This water enters the Gulf of Mexico, resulting in the Gulf Stream, a strong current that sweeps up the North American continent. The current then flows eastward, becoming the North Atlantic Current. This current splits into several routes carrying waters toward the United Kingdom, Iceland, the Norwegian Sea, and Portugal. The southernmost branch continues southward off the coast of Africa as the Canary Current. The South Atlantic Gyre consists of the South Equatorial Current, the Brazil Current, the South Atlantic Current, and the Benguela Current.

Other major surface currents in the Atlantic include the Labrador Current, which brings cold water down the east side of North America to about Cape Hatteras; the North Equatorial Countercurrent, which flows toward Africa near 5° north latitude; and the Falkland Current, which brings cold waters into the South Atlantic Gyre circulation.

Subsurface currents of the Atlantic Ocean originate from water forced down from the surface by wintertime cooling, and by inflows of water from other oceans and seas. The layers of water at the lowest depths are called *deep waters* and *bottom waters*. The densest and coldest water, Antarctic Bottom Water, is formed near Antarctica and flows below around 13,000 feet (4,000 meters) northward to about 45° north latitude. North Atlantic Deep Water lies above this layer from depths of 3,000 to 13,000 feet (1,000 to 4,000 meters). This deep water is formed by overflows from the Norwegian, Greenland, and Labrador seas. In addition, salty water from the Mediterranean flows out through the Straits of Gibraltar, sinks, and spreads across the Atlantic at depths of 3,000 to 10,000 feet (1,000 to 3,000 meters). Lying above these deep waters is Subantarctic Intermediate Water, which

spreads northward from the South Atlantic at a depth of about 2,300 feet (700 meters).

North Atlantic Deep Water flows from its northern origin southward along the western boundary of the Atlantic and across the equator into the South Atlantic and Southern Ocean. The southward flow of this water is balanced by northward flows of upper-layer water above 3,000 feet (1,000 meters) and also by Antarctic Bottom Water.

The warm upper layer of water flows northward, sinks into cold deep water in the north, and flows southward as cold deep water. This movement of water from the surface to the ocean depths makes up an ocean "conveyor belt" known as the *Atlantic meridional overturning circulation*. The warm water going north and cold water going south causes a northward flow of heat through the Atlantic Ocean. Scientists believe the meridional overturning circulation and northward heat flow play important roles in climate regulation and change.

Tides. Along most of the Atlantic coast, tides reach their maximum height twice each day. The Atlantic's—and the world's—largest difference in high and low tides takes place in eastern Canada. There, in both the Bay of Fundy and Ungava Bay, the daily tidal range can exceed 50 feet (15 meters). The Gulf of Mexico has only one high and low tide each day. The average range between high and low tides in the Gulf is only about 2 feet (0.6 meters). Some places have tidal ranges of only a few inches or centimeters. Tides are also small in the Mediterranean.

Ocean life

A wide variety of plant and animal life thrives in the Atlantic Ocean. Plants and plantlike organisms can live only in the sunlit surface waters, to a depth of about 330 feet (100 meters). Animals live throughout the Atlantic.

The surface waters of the continental shelf support one-celled plantlike organisms called *phytoplankton*, which are a major food for marine life. In winter months, surface waters are mixed by strong winds to greater depths. This process increases nutrient concentrations in the upper waters. When spring begins to warm the surface waters, the ocean experiences the year's largest phytoplankton growth, called the *spring bloom*.

The hydrothermal vents on the sea floor support vast communities of marine life. Near these vents, bacteria thrive by using mineral substances from the vents as food. The bacteria, in turn, are consumed by other forms of marine life.

Coral communities live only in warm waters. They are common in the Caribbean and in Bermuda.

Whales migrate over long distances between the

Facts in brief

Area: About 34 million mi² (88 million km²).
Greatest distances: *North-south*—9,000 mi (14,500 km). *East-west*—5,500 mi (8,800 km).
Average depth: 12,100 ft (3,700 m).
Greatest depth: 28,232 ft (8,605 m), in the Puerto Rico Trench.
Surface temperatures: *Highest,* about 86 °F (30 °C), near the equator in summer. *Lowest,* 28 °F (–2 °C), at and near the boundary with the Southern Ocean in winter.
Tides: *Highest*—Over 50 ft (15 m), in the Bay of Fundy and Ungava Bay, Canada. *Lowest*—Less than 1.5 ft (0.5 m) in areas of the Gulf of Mexico and the Mediterranean Sea.

warm waters of the tropics and the cooler, plankton-rich waters in coastal and high-latitude areas. In the North Atlantic, whales live in the Caribbean and in the waters around Greenland and the Norwegian Sea. In the South Atlantic, they swim along the coasts of Africa and Brazil and in the waters of the Antarctic Ocean.

Ocean resources

The Atlantic Ocean provides about a fourth of the world's annual catch of fish and shellfish. People also raise fish and shellfish on coastal fish farms using a process called *aquaculture*.

Petroleum and natural gas are the Atlantic's most valuable mineral resources. About a fourth of the world's petroleum comes from sediments in the Atlantic's continental shelf. About 70 percent of this petroleum comes from marginal seas, especially the Gulf of Mexico and the North Sea. Other valuable mineral products of the Atlantic include gems, sand and gravel, and sulfur.

Pollution

Pollutants enter the ocean from many sources. Rivers and runoff from land bring many wastes to the sea. Many coastal cities discharge treated and untreated wastes into the ocean. Some pollutants are transported through the atmosphere to the ocean. Some wastes enter the ocean from ships. Spills of petroleum and hazardous wastes occur when ships run aground or are damaged by storms. Before the 1980's, factories and power plants commonly discarded industrial and radioactive wastes into the ocean. Ships also incinerated hazardous wastes at sea.

Phytoplankton thrives on nutrients produced by the decay of organic matter. Thus, organic pollution can lead to a huge increase in the population of phytoplankton off the continental shelf. The phytoplankton eventually decomposes, consuming more oxygen than normal in the process. The increase in the loss of oxygen can make the waters unfit for marine animals. Under some conditions, the populations of certain *species* (kinds) of phytoplankton can increase rapidly within a few days. These thick growths of phytoplankton, called *blooms,* can kill fish. Some species produce toxins that are absorbed by the fish and shellfish that eat them. Such contaminated seafood can cause poisoning and paralysis in human beings.

Since the 1970's, governments have begun to regulate most uses of the ocean for waste disposal. Governments have also taken steps to ban the use of certain pollutants, such as lead, which was once used as an additive in gasoline, and the pesticide DDT.

Exploration

Early explorers. Phoenician traders began to explore the Atlantic by the 700's B.C. They probably reached the islands of Great Britain and Ireland and the southern part of the continent of Africa by about 600 B.C. Vikings started to explore the North Atlantic in the A.D. 800's. During the next 200 years, they colonized Greenland and Iceland and sailed as far as North America.

During the 1300's and 1400's, exploration of the Atlantic increased rapidly. Many merchants sought new routes from Europe to the Spice Islands, a group of Indonesian islands in the East Indies. People learned to build better ships, and navigation methods improved. Europeans explored most of the west coast of Africa by the late 1400's. The Portuguese navigator Bartolomeu Dias sailed around the southern tip of Africa in 1488. In 1492, Christopher Columbus, an Italian navigator in the service of Spain, made the first of his historic voyages from Europe to the Americas. His voyages raised great interest in exploration, brought knowledge of the New World to Europe, and proved that ships could safely travel the western Atlantic. During the next 50 years, explorers from such nations as England, France, Portugal, and Spain sailed through most of the Atlantic Ocean.

The beginnings of scientific oceanography. Oceanographers aboard the British research ship *Challenger* made the first major study of the Atlantic floor. In 1873 and 1876, they obtained samples of the Atlantic seabed, of the ocean's water, and of many deep-sea animals and plants.

During the German expedition of the *Meteor* from 1925 to 1927, scientists performed the first extensive survey of the South Atlantic Ocean below the surface. They gathered conclusive evidence for the existence of the Mid-Atlantic Ridge and charted the surface and deep currents of the South Atlantic Ocean.

New techniques. By the mid-1960's, sonar and other electronic devices enabled geologists to chart much of the Atlantic floor. Beginning in 1968, deep sea drilling of sediments and rocks from the ocean floor provided new information about the ocean basins. Scientists found evidence to support the theory that the Atlantic formed by sea-floor spreading over the past 180 million years. They also learned more about the geology and mineral resources of the continental shelf.

During the late 1900's and early 2000's, oceanographic studies of the Atlantic assembled large teams of scientists from many countries. Important scientific studies included the Geochemical Ocean Section Studies (GEOSECS), an international project begun in 1971 to investigate the chemical properties of ocean water. From 1987 to 2003, the Joint Global Ocean Flux Study (JGOFS) analyzed the role of carbon in the world's oceans. The World Ocean Circulation Experiment (WOCE), which ran from 1990 to 2002, was a 40-nation effort to understand ocean circulation.

The technologies developed for oceanic studies created new opportunities in the area of submarine archaeology. Explorers located many shipwrecks at the bottom of the Atlantic, including the *Titanic,* in the late 1900's. Underwater archaeologists also explored sites from Roman times in the Mediterranean, offering new opportunities to learn about the past.   Philip L. Richardson

Related articles in *World Book* include:

Arctic Ocean	Dias, Bartolomeu	North Sea
Atlantis	Fishing industry	Ocean
Baltic Sea	Grand Banks	Plate tectonics
Bermuda Triangle	Gulf Stream	(Plate move-
Black Sea	Iceberg	ment)
Columbus,	Labrador Current	Sargasso Sea
Christopher	Mediterranean	Southern Ocean
Deep	Sea	

Atlantic Provinces are the four Canadian provinces of New Brunswick, Newfoundland and Labrador, Nova Scotia, and Prince Edward Island. Three of the provinces—New Brunswick, Nova Scotia, and Prince Edward Island—are sometimes called the Maritime Provinces.

New Brunswick and Nova Scotia form part of the Canadian mainland. Newfoundland and Labrador consists of the island of Newfoundland and the coast of Labrador, a part of the mainland. The Atlantic Provinces cover 208,133 square miles (539,064 square kilometers), or about 5 percent of the total area of Canada.

About 7 percent of Canada's people live in the Atlantic Provinces. The 2016 Canadian census reported that the region had a population of 2,333,322. Most of the people have some English or Scottish ancestry. Other large ethnic groups include French, Irish, and Germans. First Nations people make up 6 percent of the population.

Over half the people of the Atlantic Provinces live in urban areas. The three largest communities of the region are, in order of size, Halifax, Nova Scotia; St. John's, in Newfoundland and Labrador; and Cape Breton, Nova Scotia.   Simon M. Evans

See also the articles on each of the Atlantic Provinces and their lists of *Related articles.*

Atlantic States are states of the United States that lie south of New England and which border on the Atlantic Ocean or are closely tied to it economically. The Middle Atlantic States are New York, New Jersey, and Pennsylvania. The South Atlantic States are Delaware, Maryland, Virginia, North Carolina, South Carolina, Georgia, and Florida. West Virginia is sometimes included in the South Atlantic States.

Atlantis was a legendary continent that many people believe sank into the Atlantic Ocean thousands of years ago. The first mention of Atlantis appeared during the 300's B.C. in *Critias* and *Timaeus,* two works by the Greek philosopher Plato. According to Plato, a brilliant civilization once existed on Atlantis. But its people became corrupt and greedy, and so the gods punished them. During one day and night, great explosions shook Atlantis, and the continent sank into the sea.

Plato's tale of Atlantis fascinated many people of later times. They developed various theories about the location of the continent and how it disappeared. Many scholars and amateurs have tried to discover the remains of Atlantis. Some people have claimed that Atlantis was the basis of all later civilizations.

Today, many scholars believe Atlantis was actually the island of Thira in the Aegean Sea, about 70 miles (110 kilometers) north of the larger island of Crete. Volcanic eruptions destroyed most of Thira about 1470 B.C. and largely wiped out the Minoan civilization, which had thrived on Thira and Crete. Scholars think these events inspired Plato's description of Atlantis.   C. Scott Littleton

Atlas is a collection of maps usually displayed in a printed book or viewed on a computer. Most printed atlases also contain charts and tables. Many atlases have photographs, including images taken by cameras on satellites. Most atlases show places on Earth. However, there are also atlases of the moon, other planets, and the stars.

Typical maps in atlases show countries, cities, and towns as well as land features, such as rivers and mountains. Some maps show the distribution of a particular feature, such as population or rainfall, over an area. An index lists the place names shown on the maps. The index also tells where to find the places on the maps.

Many atlases contain text related to information given in maps, charts, tables, and photographs. An atlas that

WORLD BOOK photo by Steinkamp/Ballogg

An atlas aids the study of geography. Many atlases have large pages so the maps can show areas in detail.

covers a small area, such as a state or country, or a special subject, such as agriculture, often has a relatively large amount of text. A general atlas of the world has little text.

Electronic atlases provide rapid access to maps. The user of an electronic atlas can type in a place name, and a map will show the location of the place. Some electronic atlases have audio clips that describe the location.

History. In the A.D. 100's, Ptolemy, an astronomer and geographer who lived in Egypt, published what some historians consider the first atlas. This work contained a variety of maps as well as information on *cartography,* the study and making of maps.

In the late 1500's, the Dutch cartographer Abraham Ortelius and the Flemish cartographer Gerardus Mercator developed more accurate atlases. These books contained maps of vast regions that were unknown to Ptolemy. Ortelius's work, published in 1570, is considered the first modern atlas. Mercator's work, which followed, was the first to use the title *Atlas* for a collection of maps. The first part of Mercator's *Atlas* was published in 1578. At the front of the book was an illustration of the Greek god Atlas supporting Earth on his shoulders.

Before printing was invented, cartographers drew all the maps in each atlas by hand. The invention of printing boosted atlas production. But cartographers still had to make by hand the woodcuts and metal engravings for the maps. Later, cartographers hand-drew maps that were photographically transferred to printing plates. Today, they use computers to create maps.   Judy M. Olson

See also **Map.**

Atlas, in Greek mythology, was one of a group of gods known as Titans. He was the son of the Titan Iapetus and a sea nymph named Clymene, and the brother of Prometheus. Atlas and the other Titans fought an unsuccessful war against Zeus and the other Olympian gods. Zeus punished Atlas by forcing him to stand and support the sky on his shoulders forever.

The famous Greek hero Hercules asked Atlas for help

Cape Rhir on the Atlantic Ocean to Cape Bon on the Mediterranean Sea, and cross parts of Morocco, Algeria, and Tunisia (see **Africa** [terrain map]). They were named for Atlas, the Greek Titan (see **Atlas**). The Atlas Mountains are made up of several chains that run from southwest to northeast. The southern chains are the High, or Haut, Atlas; the Middle, or Moyen, Atlas; and the Anti Atlas in Morocco and the Saharan Atlas in Algeria. The southern and northern chains are separated by high plateaus. The northern chains, which rise along the Mediterranean coast, are the Tell Atlas in Algeria and the Tunisian Atlas. The highest peaks in the Atlas Mountains include Jebel Toubkal (13,665 feet, or 4,165 meters) and Irhil M'Goun (13,356 feet, or 4,071 meters) in Morocco's High Atlas.

Phosphate rock, iron ore, and manganese are mined in the Atlas Mountains. Plant life of the northern regions resembles that of Mediterranean Europe. *Esparto* (alfa grass) grows on the high plateaus. It is used to make fiber, paper, and rope. Only scrubby vegetation grows on the southern slopes.   Ulrich Kamp

ATM. See Automated teller machine.

Atmosphere is a unit of measure equal to the average atmospheric pressure at sea level. In the metric system, an atmosphere is measured in newtons per square meter (N/m^2), called a *pascal* (Pa). One atmosphere (atm) equals 101,325 Pa or 14.696 pounds per square inch (lbs/in^2). The atmosphere has been largely replaced by the *bar,* defined as 100,000 Pa. Another common unit of pressure is millimeters of mercury (mm Hg) at 0 °C, called a *torr.* One torr equals 1 mm Hg or 133.3 Pa. See also **Barometer; Boiling point; Pascal; Pressure.**

Robert B. Prigo

Atmosphere is the mass of gases that surrounds a planet or other heavenly body. Scientists divide Earth's atmosphere by temperature into four layers: the *troposphere,* the *stratosphere,* the *mesosphere,* and the *thermosphere.* For information on the atmospheres of other planets, see the separate articles such as **Venus.**

Matthew H. Hitchman

See also **Air; Earth** (The atmosphere; Early development); **Mesosphere; Planet** (Solar system planets); **Stratosphere; Thermosphere; Troposphere.**

Atoll, *AT ahl,* is a circular ring of coral in the open sea, built up on a sunken bank, or formed on the crater of a

© Shutterstock

Atlas was forced by Zeus, king of the gods, to support the sky forever. Many works of art show Atlas holding Earth, rather than the sky, on his shoulders.

in taking the apples of the Hesperides (see **Hesperides**). Atlas went to get the apples, leaving Hercules to hold up the sky. When he returned with the apples, Atlas refused to take back the sky, hoping to force Hercules to support it permanently. But Hercules outwitted Atlas and deceived him into taking up the sky again.

Atlas stood in the northwest region of what is now Africa. The Atlas Mountains in northwestern Africa were named for him. Books of maps also are named for Atlas. Many works of art show Atlas supporting Earth, rather than the sky, on his shoulders.   William F. Hansen

Atlas Mountains extend for about 1,500 miles (2,400 kilometers) across northwestern Africa. They run from

© Karen Lukas, Photo Researchers

WORLD BOOK illustration

An atoll, such as the one shown in this photograph, is a circular island that surrounds a body of water called a *lagoon.* The cross-section drawing shows that the ring-shaped coral reef making up an atoll completely encloses the lagoon, *dark area.*

volcano that has sunk below the surface of the sea. A thin layer of soil generally lodges on the reef, and vegetation springs up. Tropical plants thrive on the atoll, and it becomes a coral island. Atolls enclose shallow pools or lagoons. One or more channels usually connect the lagoon of most atolls to the surrounding sea, on the windward side. Atolls are found chiefly in the Pacific Ocean.   Peter P. Sakalowsky, Jr.

See also **Coral; Coral reef.**

Atom is one of the basic units of matter. Everything around us is made up of atoms. An atom is incredibly tiny—more than a million times smaller than the thickness of a human hair. The smallest speck that can be seen under an ordinary microscope contains more than 10 billion atoms. The diameter of an atom ranges from about 0.1 to 0.5 nanometer. A nanometer is a billionth of a meter, or $\frac{1}{25,400,000}$ inch.

Atoms form the building blocks of the simplest substances, the *chemical elements*. Familiar elements include hydrogen, oxygen, iron, and lead. Each element consists of one basic kind of atom. *Compounds* are more complex substances made of two or more kinds of atoms linked in units called *molecules*. Water, for example, is a compound in which each molecule consists of two atoms of hydrogen linked to one atom of oxygen.

Atoms vary greatly in weight, but they are all about the same size. For example, an atom of plutonium, the heaviest element found in nature, weighs more than 200 times as much as an atom of hydrogen, the lightest known element. However, the diameter of a plutonium atom is only about 3 times that of a hydrogen atom.

The parts of an atom

Tiny as atoms are, they consist of even more minute particles. The three basic types are *protons, neutrons,* and *electrons.* Each atom has a definite number of these *subatomic* particles. The protons and neutrons are crowded into the *nucleus,* an exceedingly tiny region at

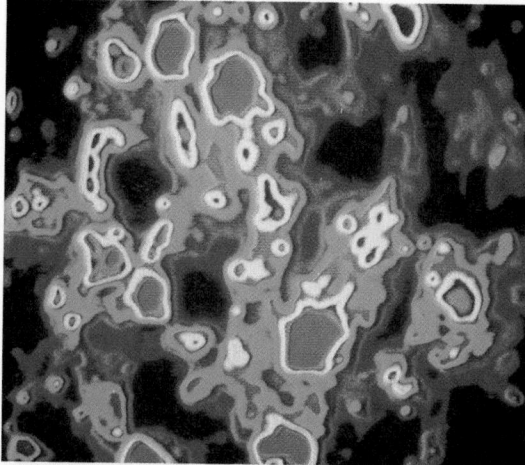

A. V. Crewe, M. Ohtsuki, and M. Utlaut,
Enrico Fermi Institute, University of Chicago

Individual atoms of the metals platinum and palladium magnified about 3 million times appear as yellow dots in this photo made with an electron microscope. The yellow areas with red or purple centers are clusters of atoms. Color was added electronically to improve the image. Atoms themselves have no color.

the center of the atom. If a hydrogen atom were about 4 miles (6.4 kilometers) in diameter, its nucleus would be no bigger than a tennis ball. The rest of an atom outside the nucleus is mostly empty space. The electrons whirl through this space, completing billions of trips around the nucleus each millionth of a second. The fantastic speed of the electrons makes atoms behave as if they were solid, much as the fast-moving blades of a fan prevent a pencil from being pushed through them.

Atoms are often compared to the solar system, with the nucleus corresponding to the sun and the electrons corresponding to the planets that orbit the sun. This

The parts of an atom

An atom consists of three basic types of particles called *protons, neutrons,* and *electrons.* Protons have a positive electric charge, and electrons have a negative charge. Neutrons are electrically neutral. The protons and neutrons are clustered in the *nucleus,* a tiny region near the center of the atom. The electrons whirl at fantastic speeds through the empty space outside the atom's nucleus.

WORLD BOOK illustration by Leonard E. Morgan

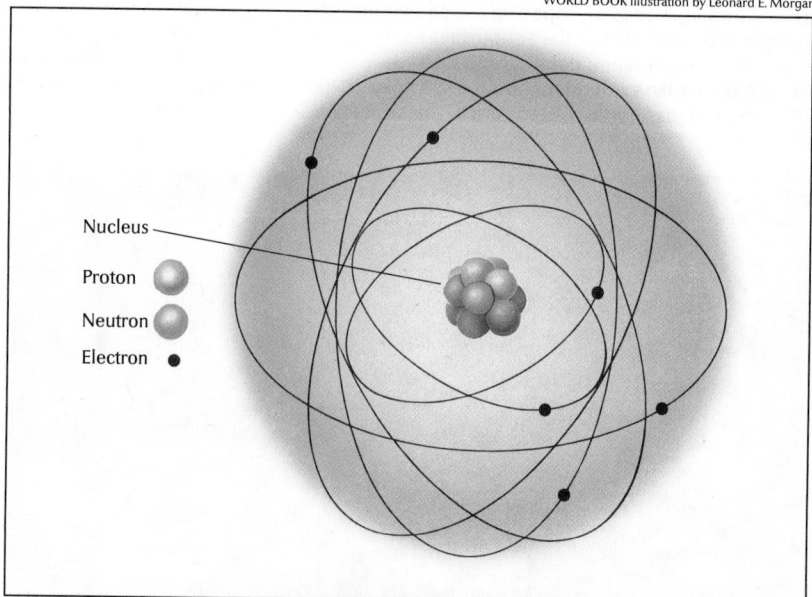

Nucleus

Proton

Neutron

Electron

comparison is not completely accurate, however. Unlike the planets, the electrons do not follow regular, orderly paths. In addition, the protons and neutrons constantly move about at random inside the nucleus.

The nucleus makes up nearly all the *mass* of an atom. Mass is the quantity of matter in an atom. Each proton has a mass roughly equal to that of 1,836 electrons. It would take 1,839 electrons to equal a neutron's mass. Each proton carries one unit of positive electric charge. Each electron carries one unit of negative charge. Neutrons have no charge. Under most conditions, an atom has the same number of protons and electrons, and so the atom is electrically neutral.

Protons and neutrons are about 100,000 times smaller than atoms, but they are in turn made up of even smaller particles called *quarks.* Each proton and neutron consists of three quarks. In the laboratory, scientists can cause quarks to combine and form other kinds of subatomic particles besides protons and neutrons. All these other particles break down and change into ordinary particles in a small fraction of a second. Thus, none of

them is found in ordinary atoms. However, scientists first learned that protons and neutrons consist of quarks through the study of other subatomic particles. For information on these other particles, see **Subatomic particle** and the separate articles on subatomic particles listed in the *Related articles* at the end of this article.

The electrons, unlike the protons and neutrons, do not seem to have smaller parts. Electrons have almost no mass. The mass of an electron in grams may be written with a decimal point followed by 27 zeros and a 9.

Opposite electric charges attract. The positively charged nucleus therefore exerts a force on the negatively charged electrons that keeps them within the atom. However, each electron has energy and so is able to resist the attraction of the nucleus. The more energy an electron has, the farther from the nucleus it will be. Thus, electrons are arranged in *shells* at various distances from the nucleus according to how much energy they have. Electrons with the least energy are in inner shells, and those with more energy are in outer shells.

Each electron shell is labeled with a number. The shell closest to the nucleus is called shell 1. The other shells, in order of increasing distance from the nucleus, are shells 2, 3, 4, 5, 6, and 7. The shells are sometimes named by the letters K, L, M, N, O, P, and Q. Each shell can hold only a limited number of electrons. Shell 1 can hold no more than 2 electrons. Shell 2 can hold 8 electrons, shell 3 can hold 18, and shell 4 can hold 32. In theory, shell 5 can hold 50 electrons, shell 6 can hold 72, and shell 7 can hold 98. However, these outer shells are never completely filled.

The properties of atoms

The atomic number tells how many protons an atom has. All atoms of an element have the same number of protons. For example, every hydrogen atom has a single proton, and so the atomic number of hydrogen is 1. The atomic numbers for other natural elements range up to

How atoms compare in weight and size

Atoms vary greatly in weight, but they are all about the same size. The smallest and lightest atom is the hydrogen atom. It consists of 1 proton and 1 electron. The largest and heaviest atom found in nature is the plutonium atom. It has 94 protons, 150 neutrons, and 94 electrons. An atom of plutonium weighs more than 200 times as much as an atom of hydrogen. However, a plutonium atom is only about 3 times as large in diameter as a hydrogen atom.

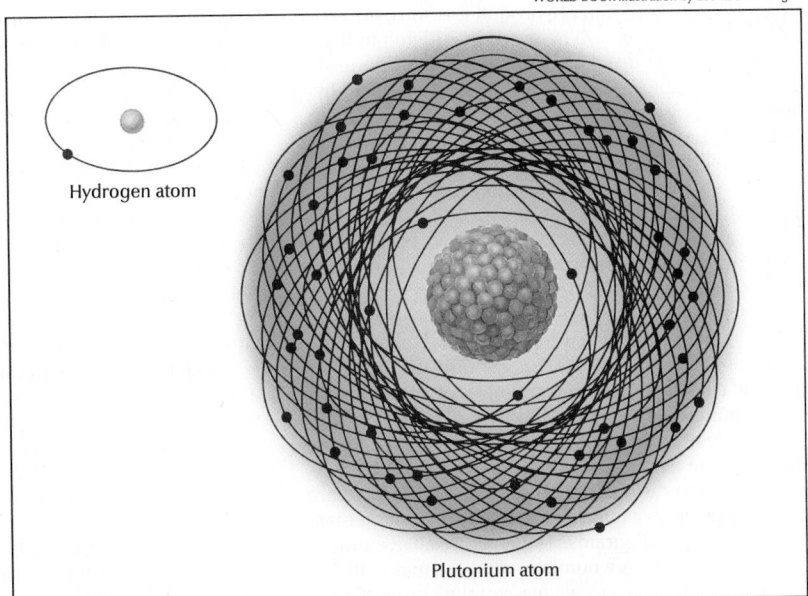

Hydrogen atom

Plutonium atom

Electron shells and chemical behavior

An atom's electrons are arranged in *shells*. Starting with the innermost, the shells are numbered 1 through 7. Each shell can hold only a certain number of electrons. For example, shell 2 can hold eight. In chemical reactions, the outermost shell gains, loses, or shares electrons.

WORLD BOOK diagrams by Zorica Dabich

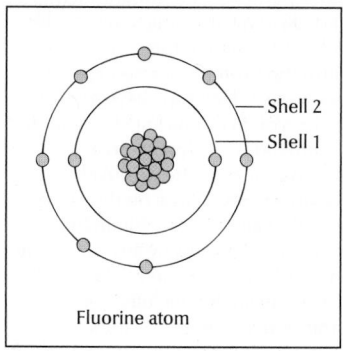

Shell 2
Shell 1

Fluorine atom

Shell 2
Shell 1

Neon atom

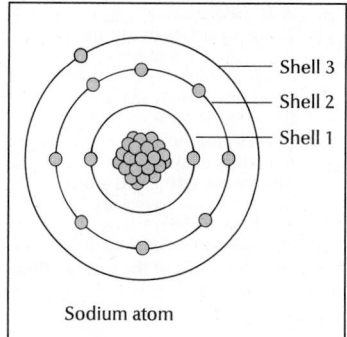

Shell 3
Shell 2
Shell 1

Sodium atom

A fluorine atom has seven electrons in shell 2. The atom fills the shell by accepting one electron from another atom.

In a neon atom, shell 2 is filled. As a result, neon generally does not enter into chemical reactions with other atoms.

A sodium atom tends to lose its single electron in shell 3. The filled shell 2 then becomes the outermost shell.

92 for uranium, which has 92 protons in each atom. Tiny amounts of plutonium, which has an atomic number of 94, also occur naturally. Elements whose atoms have more than 92 protons can be created in the laboratory. The atomic number determines an element's place in the periodic table. This table organizes the elements into groups with similar chemical properties. For a reproduction of the table, see Element, Chemical.

The atomic mass number is the sum of the protons and neutrons in an atom. Although all atoms of an element have the same number of protons, they may have different numbers of neutrons. Atoms that have the same number of protons but different numbers of neutrons are called *isotopes*.

Most of the elements in nature have more than one isotope. Hydrogen, for example, has three. In the most common hydrogen isotope, the nucleus consists only of a proton. In the two other hydrogen isotopes, the nucleus consists of one or two neutrons in addition to the proton. Scientists use the mass number to distinguish the three isotopes as hydrogen 1, hydrogen 2, and hydrogen 3. They also refer to hydrogen 1 as *protium*, to hydrogen 2 as *deuterium*, and to hydrogen 3 as *tritium*.

In most lighter atoms, the nucleus of each atom contains about an equal number of protons and neutrons. Most heavier elements, however, have more neutrons than protons. The heaviest elements have about 3 neutrons for every 2 protons. For example, uranium 238 has 146 neutrons and 92 protons.

Atoms that have the same mass number but different atomic numbers are called *isobars*. Thus, isobars are atoms of different elements. For example, the isobars argon and calcium have a mass number of 40, but argon's atomic number is 18 and calcium's is 20.

Relative atomic mass is a measure of how heavy an isotope or an element is. Relative atomic mass is expressed in an unusual way. Measurements of mass are normally given as a number followed by a unit of mass—for example, "18 kilograms." However, relative atomic mass is expressed as a number without a mass unit. For example, the relative atomic mass of the copper 63 iso-

tope, rounded to four digits, is simply "62.93."

The number that represents a relative atomic mass is based on a measurement that consists of a number followed by a unit of mass known as the *unified atomic mass unit* (u). In fact, the two numbers are identical.

Therefore, if you know the mass of an isotope or an element in unified atomic mass units, you can express the relative atomic mass by dropping the *u*. For example, the mass of the copper 65 isotope is 64.93 u, and so the relative atomic mass of that isotope is 64.93.

By definition, 1 u equals $\frac{1}{12}$ of the mass of an atom of carbon 12. Unified atomic mass units are so tiny that 1 kilogram equals about 6.02×10^{26} u. That number would be written out as 602 followed by 24 zeros.

Calculating the mass of an element. The mass of an element with only one isotope is simply the mass of that isotope. Scientists determine the mass of an element with more than one isotope by taking into account the proportions in which those isotopes occur in nature.

For example, copper has two naturally occurring isotopes. These isotopes are copper 63 and copper 65. Copper 63, with a mass of 62.93 u, represents 69.17 percent of all natural copper. Copper 65, with a mass of 64.93 u, represents the remaining 30.83 percent. The calculation for the mass of the element is (62.93 u × 0.6917) + (64.93 u × 0.3083) = 63.55 u. Dropping the *u* gives the relative atomic mass of the element, 63.55.

Other terms for mass. In some branches of science, the unified atomic mass unit is called the *dalton*, represented by the symbol Da. An older term for relative atomic mass is *atomic weight*.

Electric charge. An atom is normally electrically neutral. But it can lose or gain a few electrons in some chemical reactions, in a collision with an electron or another atom, or when exposed to extremely bright light. Such a gain or loss of electrons produces an electrically charged atom called an *ion*. An atom that loses electrons becomes a *positive ion*. One that gains electrons is a *negative ion*. The gain or loss of electrons is *ionization*.

Chemical behavior of an atom is determined largely by the number of electrons in its outermost shell. When atoms combine and form molecules, electrons in the outermost shell are either transferred from one atom to another or shared between atoms.

The number of electrons involved in this process is called the *valence.* The atoms of some elements can have more than one valence, depending on the number and kind of atoms with which they combine.

If an atom tends to lose electrons to other atoms, its valence is positive. If an atom tends to gain electrons, its valence is negative. For example, sodium tends to lose one electron from its outermost shell and thus has a valence of +1. Chlorine tends to accept one electron from another atom and so has a valence of −1. A molecule of ordinary table salt consists of one atom of sodium linked to one atom of chlorine. The sodium atom donates the electron that chlorine is able to accept.

Radioactivity. In some atoms, the nucleus can change naturally. Such an atom is called *radioactive.* The change in the nucleus may be only in the arrangement of the protons and neutrons. Or the actual number of protons and neutrons may change. When a nucleus changes, it gives off radiation. This radiation consists of *alpha particles, beta particles,* or gamma rays. Alpha particles consist of two protons and two neutrons bound together. A beta particle consists of an electron or the oppositely charged positron. Atoms of uranium, radium, and all other elements heavier than bismuth are radioactive. Some isotopes of lighter elements are also radioactive. Physicists can also create radioactive isotopes of nearly all elements in a laboratory by bombarding atoms with subatomic particles.

The type of radiation given off by a radioactive nucleus depends on the way the nucleus changes. Gamma rays are given off if only the arrangement of the protons and neutrons in the nucleus changes. But alpha or beta radiation is given off if the number of protons and neutrons in the nucleus changes. The atom then becomes an atom of a different element. This process is called *transmutation.* See **Transmutation of elements.**

The forces within an atom

The field of physics called *quantum mechanics* deals with the forces inside an atom and the motions of subatomic particles. This field began in 1900 when the German physicist Max Planck introduced the idea that radiant energy exists only in specific amounts, later called a *quantum* or the plural *quanta.* In 1913, the Danish physicist Niels Bohr used the *quantum theory* to explain the motion of electrons in atoms. See **Quantum mechanics.**

Electron energy levels. According to quantum mechanics, electrons cannot have just any amount of energy. Instead, electrons are restricted to a limited set of motions, each of which has a specific value of energy. These motions are called *quantum states* or *energy levels.* When an electron is in a given quantum state, it does not absorb or give off energy. For this reason, an atom can gain or lose energy only if one or more electrons change their quantum state.

Just as water always seeks its lowest possible level, electrons seek the state of lowest energy. However, only one electron at a time can occupy each quantum state. If the lower states are filled, other electrons are forced to occupy higher states. If all electrons are in the lowest possible state, the atom is in its *ground state.* This condi-

tion is normal for atoms at ordinary temperatures.

When matter is heated to temperatures higher than a few hundred degrees, energy is then available to raise one or more electrons to a higher energy level. The atom is then in an *excited state.* However, atoms rarely remain in an excited state for more than a fraction of a second. An excited electron almost immediately drops to a lower state and continues dropping until the atom returns to its ground state. At each succeeding drop, the electron gives off a tiny packet of radiant energy called a *photon.* The energy of the photon equals the difference between the two energy levels of the electron. The photons given off by electrons are detected as visible light and other forms of electromagnetic radiation.

Bohr originally described the quantum states of electrons as orbits like those of the planets around the sun. However, physicists now know that this description is incorrect because an electron is not simply a particle. An electron also has some characteristics of a wave. It is difficult to imagine how something could be both a par-

Electron energy levels in an atom

An electron in an atom cannot have just any amount of energy. Instead, it is restricted to a limited set of motions, each with a specific value of energy. These motions are called *energy levels* or *quantum states.* An electron absorbs or gives off energy only when it changes from one energy level to another.

WORLD BOOK diagrams by Zorica Dabich

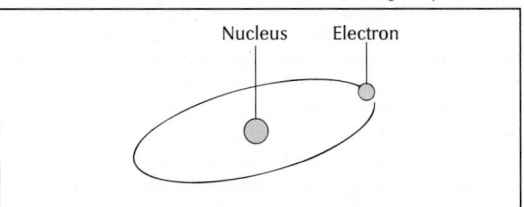

In this atom, the electron is in its lowest possible energy level. Physicists say that such an atom is in its *ground state.*

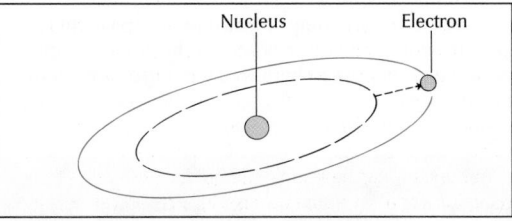

Heating the atom provides energy to raise the electron to a higher energy level. The atom is now in an *excited state.*

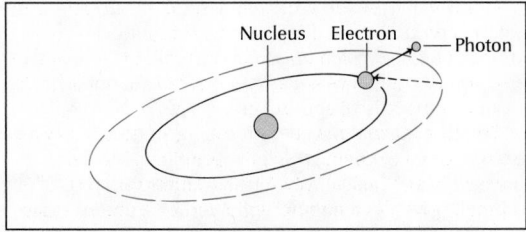

The electron drops back almost immediately. As it does so, it gives off energy in the form of a *photon* (particle of light).

ticle and a wave. This difficulty is one of the problems scientists have in trying to describe the atom to nonscientists. To do so, scientists must use familiar ideas based on our knowledge of the world as we observe it. But conditions inside the tiny atom differ greatly from those in our everyday world. For this reason, physicists can describe the motions of electrons accurately and completely only in mathematical terms.

Forces in the nucleus. The quantum rules that govern the motions of electrons also apply to the motion of protons and neutrons clustered inside the nucleus. However, the force that keeps the nuclear particles together differs greatly from the electrical attraction that holds the electrons within the atom. Each nuclear particle is attracted to its nearest neighbor by what is called the *strong nuclear force* or *strong interaction.* Like electric charges repel each other. However, the powerful nuclear force overcomes the mutual repulsion of the positively charged protons. It thus keeps the nucleus from flying apart. This force dies off quickly, however, unless the nuclear particles are extremely close together. Electrons are immune to the nuclear force.

The nuclear force is highly complicated, and no exact mathematical description of it has been formulated. Nevertheless, a theory known as the *nuclear shell model* provides reasonably accurate estimates of the energy levels in the nucleus.

One neutron and one proton can occupy each quantum state in the nucleus. For this reason, a light nucleus has a nearly equal number of protons and neutrons. But a proton and a neutron in the same state do not have the same amount of energy. Each proton is electrically repelled by all other protons in the nucleus, which increases its energy. In a nucleus with many protons, the difference in energy levels between protons and neutrons is considerable, and more low-energy states are available for neutrons than for protons. This is why a heavy nucleus has more neutrons than protons.

How scientists study atoms

Scientists use a variety of instruments and techniques to study atoms. The devices and methods used depend on whether the researchers are studying atoms themselves, electrons, nuclear particles, or quarks.

Researchers use X rays to study the arrangements of atoms in regular, repeated patterns, such as in crystals. When X rays pass through a crystal, the atoms in the crystal *diffract* (spread out) the X rays in a certain way. These diffracted rays produce patterns on photographic film that reveal how far apart the atoms are and how they are arranged. Extremely powerful *scanning electron microscopes, scanning tunneling microscopes,* and *field-emission microscopes* enable scientists to observe the positions of individual atoms. But these instruments cannot reveal any details of the structure of atoms.

Scientists study the energies of electrons chiefly by analyzing the light given off by atoms in heated gases. Instruments called *spectrometers* break up the light into a spectrum with a separate line for each wavelength of light. Each wavelength is related to the difference in energy between two quantum states in the atom. After determining the wavelengths, scientists can draw up a complete list of energy levels. With the aid of quantum mechanics, they can then obtain a description of the electron motion in the atom.

Most of what scientists know about nuclear structure has come from experiments with *particle accelerators.* These devices bombard the nucleus with beams of high-energy electrons or protons. The swift-moving electrons or protons can disrupt the motion of particles in the nucleus and occasionally even knock some of them loose. In some experiments, whole nuclei are accelerated and smashed into stationary nuclei. Nuclear physicists have developed a wide variety of detectors for observing the particles that emerge from these collisions. Most of the detectors produce an electric signal when a particle passes through them.

Particle accelerators are additionally used to study the behavior of quarks. But such studies require particles with much greater energies than those used to study atomic nuclei. Thus, much more powerful accelerators are required.

Development of the atomic theory

The idea that everything is made up of a few simple parts originated during the 400's B.C. in the philosophy

Fermilab Visual Media Services

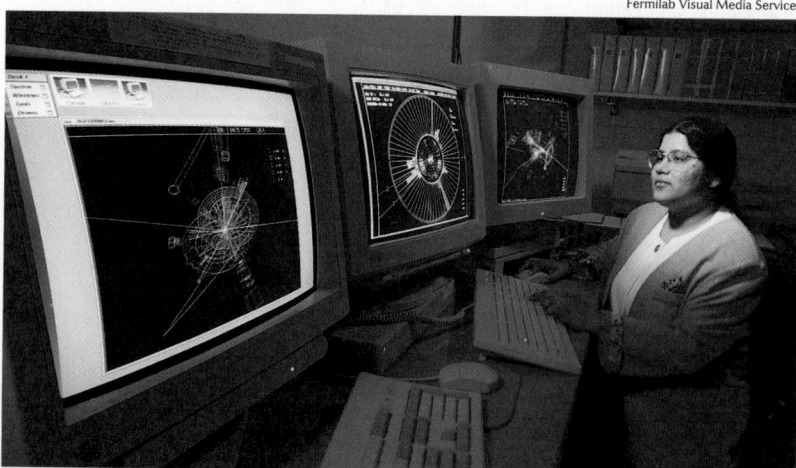

Tracks of particles that make up atoms and other bits of matter are displayed on computers at a research laboratory, *left.* At this lab, a machine called a *particle accelerator* collides particles at almost the speed of light. The collisions produce other particles whose tracks are recorded by computerized detectors. Researchers use computer displays and printouts to study the particles.

of atomism. Atomism was founded by the Greek philosopher Leucippus, but his disciple Democritus developed the philosophy more fully. Democritus gave his basic particle the name atom, which means uncuttable. He imagined atoms as small, hard particles, all composed of the same substance but of different sizes and shapes.

During the 300's B.C., a Greek philosopher named Epicurus incorporated Democritus's ideas about atoms into his philosophy. About 50 B.C., the Roman philosopher and poet Lucretius presented the fundamental principles of atomism in his long poem, *On the Nature of Things*. See **Atomism.**

During the Middle Ages, from about the A.D. 400's through the 1400's, the idea of atoms was largely ignored. This neglect resulted partly because atomism had been rejected by Aristotle, an ancient Greek philosopher whose theories dominated medieval philosophy and science. But the idea that atoms form the basic units of all matter did survive. During the 1500's and 1600's, such founders of modern science as Francis Bacon and Isaac Newton of England and Galileo of Italy believed in atoms. But those scientists could add little more to the atomic theory than Democritus had described.

The birth of the modern atomic theory. In 1750, Rudjer Boscovich, a scientist born in what is now Croatia, suggested that Democritus might have been wrong in believing that atoms are "uncuttable." Boscovich thought that atoms contain smaller parts, which in turn contain still smaller parts, and so forth down to the fundamental building blocks of matter. He felt that these building blocks must be geometric points with no size at all. Today, most atomic physicists accept a modern form of this idea.

The development of the atomic theory advanced greatly when chemistry became an exact science during the late 1700's. Chemists discovered that they could combine elements to form compounds only in certain fixed proportions according to mass. In 1803, a British chemist named John Dalton developed an atomic theory to explain this discovery. Dalton proposed that each element consists of a particular kind of atom and that the varying properties of the elements result from differences in their atoms. He further suggested that all atoms of a given element are identical in size, shape, and mass. According to Dalton's theory, when atoms combine and form a particular compound, they always combine in a specific numerical ratio. As a result, the composition by

Models of the atom   During the 1900's, physicists proposed various models of atomic structure. These diagrams show the three most important early models and a present-day model.

WORLD BOOK diagrams by Zorica Dabich

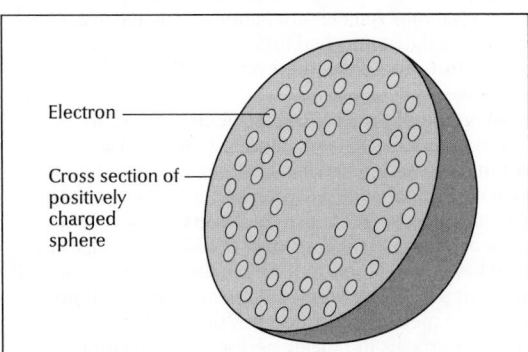

The Thomson model was proposed by the British physicist Joseph John Thomson in 1904. It showed the electrons embedded in a positively charged sphere like seeds in a watermelon.

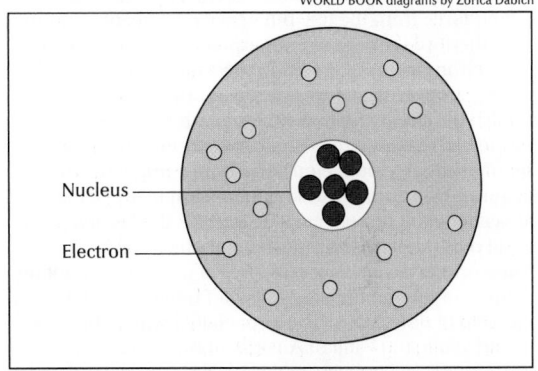

The Rutherford model showed the atom's mass in a positively charged nucleus surrounded by electrons. Ernest Rutherford, a New Zealand-born physicist, proposed this model in 1911.

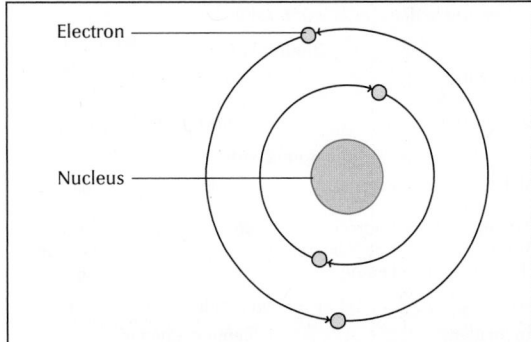

The Bohr model, proposed in 1913 by the Danish physicist Niels Bohr, described the electron structure. It showed the electrons traveling in fixed orbits around the nucleus.

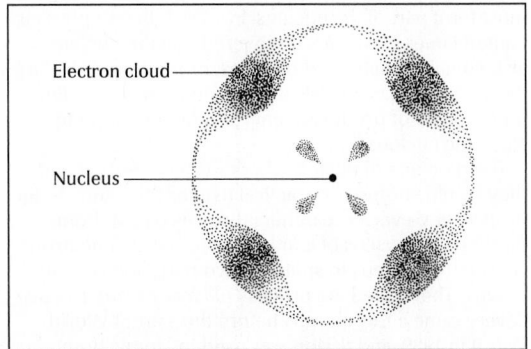

The electron cloud model, a currently accepted model, indicates the regions within the atom where electrons may be found. Electrons are most likely to be where a cloud is darkest.

mass of a particular compound is always the same.

The first descriptions of atomic structure. In 1897, a British physicist named Joseph John Thomson discovered that atoms are "cuttable." He made this discovery while studying the rays that travel between charged metal plates in a vacuum tube. Thomson determined that the rays consisted of lightweight, negatively charged particles. He had thus discovered electrons. Thomson immediately realized that the electrons must be part of the atom. He proposed a model of the atom in which negatively charged electrons were embedded in a positively charged sphere. Although Thomson's description was far from correct, his work encouraged other scientists to investigate the structure of the atom.

In 1911, the New Zealand-born physicist Ernest Rutherford presented his theory of atomic structure. Rutherford, a former student of Thomson's, declared that nearly all the mass of an atom is concentrated in a tiny nucleus. He also stated that the nucleus is surrounded by electrons traveling at tremendous speeds through the atom's outer regions.

Rutherford based his theory on the results of experiments in which he bombarded thin sheets of gold with alpha particles. Most of the particles passed through the sheets, which showed that the gold atoms must consist chiefly of empty space. But some particles bounced back as if they had hit something solid. Rutherford concluded that these particles had been reflected by a strong force from the tiny but heavy nucleus of an atom.

Rutherford's theory did not explain the arrangement of electrons in atoms. In 1913, however, a description of the electron structure was proposed by Niels Bohr, a Danish physicist who had worked with Rutherford. Bohr suggested that electrons could travel only in a certain set of orbits around the nucleus. Bohr's original, crude picture of the atom was inadequate, but many of the ideas behind it proved correct. In 1924, the French physicist Louis de Broglie proposed that electrons have some properties of waves. By 1928, a correct description of the arrangement of electrons had been obtained with the help of other physicists, especially Erwin Schrödinger and Wolfgang Pauli of Austria, Max Born and Werner Heisenberg of Germany, and Paul Dirac of England.

Studying the nucleus. Although physicists understood the motions of electrons by 1928, the nucleus remained largely a mystery. Protons had been identified in 1902, and Rutherford had proposed in 1914 that they must form part of the nucleus. In 1932, a British physicist named James Chadwick discovered that the nucleus also contains uncharged particles, or neutrons. Also in the early 1930's, scientists developed particle accelerators capable of producing energies high enough to study the nucleus.

The pioneers of nuclear physics did not expect that they would soon see a practical use for their knowledge. In 1938, however, researchers discovered that bombarding the nucleus of a uranium atom with a neutron caused the nucleus to split into two parts and release energy. They called the process *nuclear fission.* The discovery came a few months before the start of World War II in 1939, and fission was used in atomic bombs that helped end the war in 1945.

The development of atomic weapons made governments aware of the importance of nuclear physics. As a result, they provided great sums of money for nuclear research after the war. The funds made possible the construction of accelerators of increasing size and energy. As these accelerators revealed more and more details of the nucleus, researchers realized that the proton and neutron could not be simple objects. They also found that the neutron did not completely lack an electric charge. Instead, it contained equal amounts of positive and negative charge. In addition, researchers discovered hundreds of new particles. These particles were sufficiently similar to one another and to protons and neutrons to suggest that all nuclear particles might be merely different arrangements of a few simple parts.

Recent discoveries. By 1964, researchers had turned up enough clues to indicate what the fundamental parts of protons, neutrons, and other nuclear particles might be like. Two California Institute of Technology physicists, the American Murray Gell-Mann and Russian-born George Zweig, thus proposed a theory describing these parts. Gell-Mann named the parts *quarks.* According to this theory, quarks are always combined in groups of two or three. The original theory required only three kinds of quarks, *up* (or *u*), *down* (or *d*), and *strange* (or *s*), to make up protons, neutrons, and the other particles. But by 1977, experimenters had found not only the u, d, and s, but also a *charm* (or *c*) and a *bottom* (or *b*) quark.

Physicists concluded that a sixth quark, which they named the *top* (or *t*), must also exist. In 1995, scientists at Fermi National Accelerator Laboratory in Batavia, Illinois, announced that they had found the top quark. Physicists are almost certain that there are no more quarks to discover.

Although the atom's basic structure is well understood, new ways of using atoms continue to be found. Atoms are used to make *atomic clocks,* the most accurate clocks in the world. The most advanced of these clocks are so accurate that they lose only one second of time over tens of millions of years. Many scientists are also looking to atoms to improve the power and speed of computers. *Quantum computers* make use of the quantum mechanical properties of atoms or of subatomic particles to quickly perform certain computations. Some such computations might take classical computers thousands or millions of years to complete. Quantum effects are difficult to harness for computing, but researchers continue to create more powerful and stable quantum computer prototypes.   Mark Saffman

Related articles in *World Book* include:

Biographies

Bohr, Niels	Democritus
Chadwick, Sir James	Rutherford, Ernest
Dalton, John	Thomson, Sir Joseph J.

Subatomic particles

Alpha	Fermion	Meson	Psi particle
particle	Gluon	Muon	Quark
Baryon	Hadron	Neutrino	Subatomic
Boson	Higgs boson	Neutron	particle
Electron	Lepton	Proton	Tachyon

Other related articles

Antimatter	Element, Chemical
Atomic clock	Fission
Atomism	Fusion
Electricity (Atoms)	Ion

Isotope
Magnetism (Magnetism in atoms)
Molecule
Nanotechnology
Nuclear energy
Nuclear physics

Nuclear weapon
Particle accelerator
Particle detector
Quantum mechanics
Radiation
Transmutation of elements
Valence

Atomic bomb. See Nuclear weapon.

Atomic clock is the most accurate type of clock. The best atomic clocks would not lose or gain more than a second in tens of millions of years. An atomic clock keeps time by counting the energy changes of *atoms* (basic units of matter). When an atom of a certain element gains or loses energy, it vibrates at a certain *frequency* (rate). This frequency is identical from atom to atom. Thus, timekeeping based on the frequency is nearly perfect. The first experimental atomic clock was built by the United States National Bureau of Standards in 1949. In 1967, atomic clocks became the basis for world timekeeping when the second was defined as the amount of time a cesium atom takes to make 9,192,631,770 energy transitions. Global Positioning System (GPS) satellites carry atomic clocks.

Michael A. Lombardi

See also **Time.**

Atomic energy. See Nuclear energy.

Atomic Energy Commission (AEC) was a United States government agency that directed the development and use of atomic energy. Created by Congress in 1946, the AEC emphasized military over civilian operations. In 1954, however, it began to allow private companies to develop technologies that make use of atomic energy, such as nuclear power plants. Congress abolished the commission in 1974. Its research operations were transferred to the Energy Research and Development Administration and later to the Department of Energy. A new body, the Nuclear Regulatory Commission, took over the AEC functions of licensing and regulating nuclear power plants. Richard F. Hirsh

See also **Nuclear Regulatory Commission.**

Atomic fission. See Nuclear energy (introduction; Nuclear fission); Fission.

Atomic fusion. See Nuclear energy (Nuclear fusion); Fusion.

Atomic reactor. See Nuclear energy.

Atomic weapon. See Nuclear weapon.

Atomism, *AT uh mihz uhm,* was a philosophical view that developed in Greece during the 400's B.C. The atomists asserted that reality consisted of two things: atoms and void. The term *atom* comes from the Greek word *atomos,* which means *uncuttable.* According to the atomists, atoms were invisible bits of matter that were indestructible and *indivisible*—that is, they could not be divided. They were unlimited in number and varied in size, shape, and arrangement. Atoms came together by chance to form our world and the things in it as well as innumerable other worlds.

The atomists believed the motion of the atoms was governed by necessity. They also believed that every event was the result of a series of collisions. The atomists theorized that events could be predicted. The philosopher Epicurus introduced a major revision with the idea that atoms were subject to an occasional swerve. Epicurus thought the swerve broke the pattern of predetermined events and provided a basis for free will.

The atomistic philosophy was formulated by Leucippus during the second half of the 400's B.C. It was developed in detail by Democritus, taken over and modified somewhat by Epicurus, and popularized by the Roman poet Lucretius. The best source for knowledge of Greek atomism comes from Lucretius's poem *On the Nature of Things.* Carl A. Huffman

See also **Democritus; Epicurus; Leucippus; Lucretius; Materialism.**

Atrium, *AY tree uhm,* was the central room of early Roman houses. The atrium contained the hearth and was used for cooking, sleeping, and entertaining. A hole in the center of the roof allowed the smoke to escape. As the design of Roman houses became more advanced, the kitchen and hearth were removed to other locations. The atrium remained as a formal reception area and center of family life. Rain falling through the roof opening was caught in a central marble basin called the *impluvium.* A typical later Roman atrium was richly decorated. See **Rome, Ancient** (picture: An upper-class house in a Roman city).

In later times, the word *atrium* came to refer to any open courtyard surrounded by an arcade. An atrium led to the entrance of many early Christian churches from the 300's to the 500's. See **Architecture** (Early Christian architecture; picture). William J. Hennessey

SCALA/Art Resource

The atrium was a courtlike reception room in Roman houses. This ruined atrium was part of the House of the Faun at Pompeii.

Atrocity. See Concentration camp; Genocide; Nuremberg trials; Torture; War crime.

Atrophy, *AT ruh fee,* is the normal or abnormal shrinking of any part of the body. Some body tissues may shrink in size as a result of disease. For example, progressive muscular atrophy, a disease of a part of the spinal cord, causes certain muscles to atrophy. People with this disease lose the ability to move their arms and legs. The name *atrophy* comes from two Greek words meaning *not nourished.* Mary Frances Picciano

Atropine, *AT roh peen,* is a drug derived from several plants in the nightshade family, especially from a bushy plant called *belladonna* or *deadly nightshade*. Physicians now also use numerous synthetic versions of atropine because they provide shorter-lasting effects and work more selectively on specific organs of the body.

Physicians use atropine and its synthetic versions during eye examinations to relax the muscles of the eye and to cause the pupil to *dilate* (expand). The drug also relieves certain types of noninfectious diarrhea and is useful as a remedy for poisoning by certain pesticides and nerve gases. A common side effect of atropine is dry mouth.

Atropine works by counteracting the effect of *acetylcholine*, a body chemical that transmits nerve impulses. The drug is extremely powerful and should never be taken without a prescription and supervision by a physician. High doses can cause *hallucinations* (seeing, hearing, or feeling things that do not exist), rapid heartbeat, and coma. Frank Welsch

See also **Belladonna**.

Atropos. See Fates.

Atsina Indians. See Gros Ventre Indians.

Attaché, *AT uh SHAY,* is an officer attached to a diplomatic office. The word is French for *attached*. An attaché is usually an officer of the army, navy, or air force, and is called a military, naval, or air attaché. The United States often sends officers from the Departments of Commerce, Agriculture, or Labor as attachés to an ambassador. This officer is called a commercial, agricultural, or labor attaché. Most large countries send attachés of some kind. The United Kingdom assigns scientific-research attachés to important embassies.

Cultural and social-welfare officers have attaché status. Attachés usually accompany ambassadors or other high officials on missions of state. Their duties are similar to those of secretaries. Some attachés of the U.S. government are assigned to consular offices, particularly in larger cities of the world. Most are appointed from the list of foreign-service officers in the Department of State. But many attachés with special skills and experience are selected from private industry. Michael P. Sullivan

Attachment is the legal term for a court order to seize a person or a person's property. Attachment was used in England so long ago that no record of its beginnings exists. In early times, attachment provided a way of forcing a person to come to court. An officer would take the person's horse, plow, or furniture. The owner had to go to court to get these goods back. Today, attachment is chiefly used against debtors. When a person claims to be owed a debt by someone who owns property, the property can be attached and held against the debt. If the person who claims to be owed sues and wins, the attached property is sold to satisfy the claim. In addition to attaching property, courts can issue orders to attach the wages of people who owe judgments ordered by the court. This form of attachment is also known as *garnishment*. For instance, a worker's employer can be ordered to reduce the worker's paycheck by a specific amount each check to pay such judgments as child support, taxes, or outstanding court fines. Writs of attachment can also be issued. They are usually used in this way to seize a person who is in contempt of court. See also **Contempt; Debt; Garnishment**. Steven R. Probst

Attainder, *uh TAYN duhr,* is a legal term for the loss of civil rights by an outlawed person or a person sentenced to death. According to old English law, such people lost their rights to property. Their land and personal belongings were taken from them. Because they were judged to have suffered *tainting* (corruption of blood), they could not inherit property or leave property to anyone. Parliament put an end to attainder in the United KIngdom in 1870, and now almost all countries have abolished it. In the United States, people may lose their civil rights for the crime of treason, but the Constitution (Article III, Section 3 [2]) states their punishment may not affect their families, who may inherit their property.

A *bill of attainder* is an act passed by a legislature which *attaints* some person or group and thus takes away property and civil rights without a trial. To be classified as a bill of attainder, the act must punish. Mere regulations are not considered bills of attainder. Bills of attainder are not legal in most countries. In the United States, the Constitution (Article I, Section 9 [3]) prohibits the nation or any state from passing such a bill.

After the American Civil War (1861-1865), Congress passed a law taking away the property of some people it called rebels. But the courts held that Congress could only take the rents or income from such property during the lifetime of the rebels and could not deprive their heirs of the property. Jean Appleman

Attar, *AT uhr,* is a sweet-smelling oil obtained from rose petals. It gives a rose odor to perfumes. The most fragrant attar comes from a kind of red rose grown in Bulgaria and is used only in expensive women's fragrances. A less fragrant attar is taken from a white rose grown in Bulgaria. Attar also comes from roses grown in China, France, Iran, Morocco, Turkey, and Ukraine.

Producers obtain attar by placing rose petals in a tank and passing steam through them. The steam is collected in large flasks, where it cools and *condenses* (changes to a liquid). The attar floats to the top of the liquid and can then be removed. Scott W. Waite

Attention deficit disorder, often abbreviated ADD, is a behavior problem in which people have unusual difficulty paying attention, sitting still, or controlling their impulses. The formal term for attention deficit disorder is *attention-deficit/hyperactivity disorder* (ADHD). ADHD is the most common behavior problem in children. The disorder is diagnosed in boys more than twice as often as in girls. A significant number of teenagers and adults also have ADHD.

Most experts recognize three types of ADHD. The *hyperactive-impulsive type* is also called *hyperactivity*. Children with this type of ADHD are excessively fidgety and restless. They often cannot wait their turn to speak in class or to take part in a group activity. People with the *inattentive type* of ADHD are not physically restless, but they have trouble concentrating. They are forgetful and disorganized and often fail to finish schoolwork or other tasks. The inattentive type of ADHD occurs more often in girls than does the hyperactive type. Most patients with ADHD have the *combined type*, which includes symptoms of both the hyperactive and inattentive types.

Most experts think ADHD has a physical cause that has not yet been identified. Scientists now study brain function using *magnetic resonance imaging* and other techniques that produce images of the living brain. Such studies show that the brains of children with ADHD differ from those of children without the condition. Some differences occur in areas of the brain called the *frontal lobes* that control planning and setting limits on behavior. Other studies suggest that certain *genes* (the hereditary material in cells) play a role in many cases of ADHD.

Most physicians believe that certain medications help people with ADHD. The drug most often prescribed is *methylphenidate,* known by the trade name Ritalin. Ritalin and similar drugs appear to improve self-control by stimulating parts of the brain that regulate brain activity. Children with ADHD also benefit from *behavior modification.* In this therapy, adults help children gain self-control by providing close supervision and frequent rewards for appropriate behavior.   F. Xavier Castellanos

See also **Ritalin.**

Attica. See Athens.

Attila, *AT uh luh* or *uh TIHL uh* (? -A.D. 453), was a leader of the Huns, a central Asian people. The Huns settled in central Europe, north of the Roman Empire, in the late A.D. 300's and then began to raid Roman territory. Attila inherited the Hunnish kingdom, which was centered roughly in present-day Hungary. He conquered the surrounding areas, until the Huns controlled a region extending from the Danube River to the Baltic Sea, and from the Rhine River to the Caspian Sea.

About 434, Attila and his older brother, Bleda, became the leaders of the Huns. Attila murdered Bleda around 445 and became the sole leader of his people. From 435 to 439, Attila conquered many Germanic peoples in eastern and central Europe. He forced the East Roman Empire to pay him a yearly fee so he would not attack. But he looted its provinces in southeastern Europe from 441 to 443, and again in 447.

Attila then turned his attention to the West Roman Empire. In 450, he demanded Honoria, sister of Emperor Valentinian III, as his bride, and half the West Roman Empire. Valentinian refused, and Attila invaded Gaul (now mainly France). A combined army of Roman and Germanic forces stopped Attila in the Battle of Châlons-sur-Marne, near Troyes, in 451. He then retreated east of the Rhine River. Attila invaded Italy in 452, capturing and destroying many cities north of the Po River. However, famine and disease forced his troops to withdraw. Attila died in 453, and the various peoples under Hunnish control rose up in revolt. In time, the Huns were absorbed into the peoples of southeastern Europe.

Scholars question Attila's historical significance. Although Attila seriously threatened the East and West Roman empires during periods when they were weak, he was unable to conquer them permanently. Attila's kingdom collapsed soon after his death. Perhaps his greatest importance was his ability to unite the Huns for a short time.   Christopher S. Mackay

See also **Huns.**

Attlee, Clement Richard (1883-1967), was the leader of the British Labour Party from 1935 to 1955 and prime minister of the United Kingdom from 1945 to 1951. During those years, the British government nationalized various industries and established tax-supported health and welfare services. It also granted independence to India, a cause Attlee had long supported.

Attlee was born on Jan. 3, 1883, in London. He studied at Oxford University. After four years of law practice, from 1905 to 1909, he did social-service work in the Limehouse district of London. In 1910, he became secretary of Toynbee Hall, a famous settlement center. He lectured in social science at the London School of Economics and Political Science from 1913 to 1923. In 1919 and 1920, he was mayor of the Stepney district in London.

Attlee served as a major in the British Army in World War I (1914-1918). He entered the House of Commons in 1922 as a member for Limehouse. Attlee served as the United Kingdom's deputy prime minister from 1942 to 1945 and as *lord privy seal* (the keeper of one of the United Kingdom's official seals) from 1940 to 1942. Queen Elizabeth II made Attlee an earl in 1955. He died on Oct. 8, 1967.   Keith Robbins

Attorney. See Lawyer.

Attorney, District. See District attorney.

Attorney, Power of. See Power of attorney.

Attorney general is the chief law officer for the governments of many countries. In the United States, the attorney general is appointed by the president, with the approval of the Senate, and serves in the Cabinet. The attorney general heads the Department of Justice and represents the government in legal matters (see **Justice, Department of**). The responsibilities of the U.S. attorney general include advising the president and executive agencies and enforcing federal laws, particularly criminal statutes. Each U.S. state government also has an attorney general. In the United Kingdom and Australia, the

Attila's empire stretched from the Danube River on the south to the Baltic Sea on the north, and from the Rhine River on the west to the Caspian Sea on the east. In the 400's, Attila attacked the East and West Roman empires.

Empire of Attila

Roman Empire

→ Route of the Huns

0   800 Miles
0   800 Kilometers

chief law officer for the government is called the attorney general. In Canada, the minister of justice acts as the attorney general. Richard E. Rupp

See also **Flag** (picture: Flags of the United States government).

Attucks, *AT uhks,* **Crispus** (1723?-1770), was a leader of the patriot crowd that British troops fired upon in the so-called "Boston Massacre" of 1770. The British had stationed four regiments in Boston in 1768. On March 5, 1770, about 400 Bostonians surrounded a detachment of British troops and goaded them into firing. Attucks and two other men were killed instantly. Two others died later of their wounds. See **Boston Massacre.**

Little is known of Attucks, but several historians believe he had been born into slavery and later escaped. He was probably of mixed Black and white descent. In 1888, Boston erected a monument to honor the patriots who died in the incident. James Kirby Martin

See also **African Americans** (picture).

ATV. See **All-terrain vehicle.**

Atwood, Margaret (1939-   ), is a Canadian poet, novelist, and critic. She has twice won the Booker Prize, the United Kingdom's most important literary award. Atwood won the prize in 2000 for *The Blind Assassin* (2000), a complex family chronicle that includes a science-fiction novel within the main story. She won the prize in 2019 for *The Testaments* (2019), a sequel to her hugely popular novel *The Handmaid's Tale* (1985).

Atwood first gained recognition for her collection of poems *The Circle Game* (1966). Her many other books of poetry include *The Journals of Susanna Moodie* (1970), a verse biography of an early Canadian writer; *Power Politics* (1971), an investigation of the limits of male-female relationships; and *Two-Headed Poems* (1978), which includes poems about a mother and child. Atwood's poetry collections also include *Selected Poems* (1978), *Selected Poems II* (1986), and *Dearly: New Poems* (2020).

Atwood gained a wide reputation as a novelist with *Surfacing* (1972), the story of a woman who searches in the world of nature for the meaning of her life. *The Edible Woman* (1969) is a satiric comedy about a woman whose personality is being destroyed by her relationship with her fiancé. *Lady Oracle* (1976) is a mix of social satire, psychological analysis, and fantasy. *Bodily Harm* (1981) deals with a Canadian journalist and her experiences during a revolution in the Caribbean.

Atwood has written several *dystopian* novels—that is, novels that describe imaginary societies much worse than the real world. The novels are set in the future. In *The Handmaid's Tale,* women living in a country called Gilead, formerly the United States, are stripped of all rights. The novel's sequel, *The Testaments,* is set about 15 years later. Atwood also wrote a trilogy about a future civilization that is almost wiped out by a human-created plague. The trilogy consists of *Oryx and Crake* (2003), *The Year of the Flood* (2009), and *MaddAddam* (2013). In *The Heart Goes Last* (2015), a young married couple tries to survive in a nightmarish society of the near future.

Cat's Eye (1988) examines forms of autobiography. *The Robber Bride* (1993) puckishly analyzes feminist politics by rewriting a Grimm's fairy tale. *Alias Grace* (1996) is a psychological mystery. *The Penelopiad* (2005) is based on the Greek epic poem *The Odyssey. Rude Ramsay and the Roaring Radishes* (2004) is a children's picture book.

Atwood's stories have been collected in *Dancing Girls* (1977), *Bluebeard's Egg* (1983), *Wilderness Tips* (1991), *Good Bones and Simple Murders* (1994), *The Tent* and *Moral Disorder* (both 2006), and *Stone Mattress: Nine Tales* (2014). She has written a book of criticism called *Survival: A Thematic Guide to Canadian Literature* (1972). She discusses culture, economics, and politics in *Payback: Debt and the Shadow Side of Wealth* (2008). *Hag-Seed* (2016) retells William Shakespeare's play *The Tempest.* Margaret Eleanor Atwood was born on Nov. 18, 1939, in Ottawa, Ontario. Laurie R. Ricou

See also **Canadian literature** (Canadian literature in English; picture).

Auburn University is a state university with campuses in Auburn and Montgomery, Alabama. The campus in Auburn was chartered in 1856 as the East Alabama Male College of the Methodist Church. In 1872, it became a state-supported school and was renamed Agricultural and Mechanical College of Alabama. Women students were first admitted in 1892. The school became Alabama Polytechnic Institute in 1899 and was renamed Auburn University in 1960. In 1964, Auburn began admitting African American students. The Montgomery campus opened in 1969. Auburn's athletic teams are called the Tigers. Its website at https://www.auburn.edu offers more information. Critically reviewed by Auburn University

Auchincloss, *AW kihn klahs,* **Louis** (1917-2010), was an American author and one of the finest literary observers of the American "upper class" of his time. He was also a lawyer in New York City from 1941 until he retired in 1986. Many characters in his novels are attorneys.

Auchincloss recognized the influence of American authors Henry James and Edith Wharton. Like them, he saw that traditions of family, social position, and wealth can decline into snobbishness and materialism. *The Great World and Timothy Colt* (1956) shows a lawyer's desire for success and his struggle to satisfy his principles. Auchincloss's novel *The Rector of Justin* (1964) is a study of a headmaster of a New England prep school. His other novels include *I Come As a Thief* (1972), *The Partners* (1974), *The House of the Prophet* (1980), *The Golden Calves* (1988), *The Scarlet Letters* (2003), and *East Side Story* (2004). Auchincloss's stories were collected in *The Winthrop Covenant* (1976), *Narcissa and Other Fables* (1983), *Skinny Island* (1987), and *The Anniversary* (1999). His essays were collected in *The Style's the Man* (1994).

Louis Stanton Auchincloss was born on Sept. 27, 1917, in Lawrence, New York. He attended Groton, a private school; Yale University; and the University of Virginia. He wrote an autobiography, *A Writer's Capital* (1974). Auchincloss died on Jan. 26, 2010. Victor A. Kramer

Auckland, *AWK luhnd* (pop. 1,571,718), is New Zealand's largest city and chief port. About a third of the nation's people live in Auckland, which covers about 2,200 square miles (5,600 square kilometers). Auckland occupies a strip of land between Waitemata Harbour and Manukau Harbour in the country's North Island. For location, see **New Zealand** (political map). Auckland is a market center for nearby agricultural and timber areas. It is also New Zealand's chief business and transportation center. Auckland's industries produce food, machinery, metal products, printed materials, and other items. The Auckland Harbour Bridge, which links the central city and the suburbs to the north, is an important landmark.

© Wolfgang Kaehler

Auckland is the largest city and chief port of New Zealand. Nearly one-third of the nation's people live in Auckland. Auckland is also the country's main center for business and transportation.

Auckland is known as the *City of Sails* because of the many yachts in its harbors. It has spacious parks and many beaches. Auckland's cultural institutions include the University of Auckland, the Auckland War Memorial Museum, and a number of art galleries.

New Zealand's Māori people had lived in the Auckland area for hundreds of years before British settlers arrived in the 1800's. Auckland was chosen as the nation's capital in 1840. The capital was moved to Wellington in 1865.   Robin A. Kearns

See also **New Zealand** (picture: Downtown Auckland).

Auction is a type of sale in which an item is sold to the person who bids, or offers, the most money for it. An *auctioneer* takes the bids and conducts the sale. Goods often sold at auctions include fine and decorative arts, antiques, collectibles, farm products, livestock, and real estate. Thoroughbred horse auctions are also popular.

Many bidders set maximum price levels, often called *limits* or *stop prices*, above which they will not bid. Similarly, many sellers establish minimum price figures known as *reserves*, below which they will not sell. In an *auction with reserve*, the seller has the right to withhold an article from sale if he or she has decided that the highest bid is too low. Reserves are usually confidential and determined before the auction between the seller and the auctioneer or auction company. In an *auction without reserve*, the seller agrees to sell the article to the highest bidder regardless of the price.

Many auctioneers speak in a quick, rhythmic chant to inform participants of an item's bidding status. Some use the famous call of "Going once, going twice, sold!" to warn bidders that the end of the auction seems near. When one bidder outbids all the others—and exceeds the seller's reserve—the dropping of the auctioneer's hammer signals a sale. At this point, the final bid creates a binding contract between the seller and the highest bidder. The selling price is called the *hammer price*.

After an auction, the seller usually pays a *selling commission* and the buyer often pays a *buyer's premium* to the auctioneer or the auction company. Most auction organizations require auctioneers to have official licenses.

In the 1990's, certain computer websites introduced *online auctions* over the internet. The largest and most popular auction website is called eBay. Online auctions closely follow the procedures of live auctions, except that bidders can enter bids from their computers at any time. Another advantage is that the internet allows sellers to offer a wide variety of items to a vastly expanded international audience. The most reliable auction websites guarantee both the authenticity and the condition of their offerings.   C. Hugh Hildesley

See also **E-commerce; Fur** (Marketing fur); **Internet** (Business transactions); **Livestock** (Marketing livestock).

Auden, *AW duhn,* **W. H.** (1907-1973), an English-born poet, is best known for the remarkable variety of his works. He wrote ballads, blues, limericks, sonnets, nonsense verse, oratorios, free verse, *librettos* (words) for operas, and dramas. Auden won the Pulitzer Prize in 1948 for his book-length poem *The Age of Anxiety.*

Wystan Hugh Auden was born Feb. 21, 1907, in York. As a student at Oxford University, he was the leader of a group of writers. In the 1940's, he turned to Christianity and psychoanalysis as partial solutions to civilization's problems. He moved to the United States in 1939 and became a U.S. citizen. In 1972, he moved back to Oxford.

Auden collaborated with Christopher Isherwood on travel books and some symbolic and satirical plays in the 1930's, including *The Dog Beneath the Skin* (1935) and *The Ascent of F6* (1936). He helped write the libretto for the Russian composer Igor Stravinsky's opera *The Rake's Progress* (1951). Many of Auden's critical essays appear in *The Dyer's Hand* (1963). He died on Sept. 29, 1973.   William Harmon

Audiobook is a recording of a book or other piece of writing made for distribution to the public. Such recordings include works of fiction and nonfiction. Audiobooks are recorded on cassette tapes, on compact discs (CD's), and on electronic files that can be downloaded onto a computer or an iPod or other MP3 player.

Some audiobooks are *abridged*—that is, they are shortened versions of works. Some feature authors reading their own work. Many others, especially works of fiction, are read by actors. Actors often help stories come alive by using different voices and accents for different characters. Some Internet sites feature free audio-books that can be downloaded. Volunteers usually read these works.

Recordings of historical and literary works were made in the United States as early as the 1930's for blind people. These recordings—known as Talking Books—were made on long-playing records. The U.S. Library of Congress and a nonprofit organization called the American Foundation for the Blind distributed them.

The growth of portable music players from the 1970's to the 1990's led to the rise of audiobooks for the general population. Today, many people besides those who are blind or have another visual disability use audiobooks. Many people listen to audiobooks when they are doing something else, such as driving a car or walking. Audiobooks are also popular with people who cannot read and individuals who are learning a new language.

Christine Sullivan

Audiology, *AW dee AHL uh jee,* is the profession of providing nonmedical assistance to people with hearing loss or with balance problems related to the ear. Professionals called *audiologists* are trained to diagnose such problems. Audiologists can also help patients manage these conditions to reduce their effect on communication and function. If hearing loss or balance problems result from medical conditions or require surgery, audiologists can refer patients to physicians.

Audiologists use *behavioral* and *electrophysiological* tests to determine a person's ability to hear. Behavioral tests measure how the person responds to a variety of sounds and vibrations. Electrophysiological tests measure the electrical activity of a person's nervous system in response to sound. Hearing tests can also help diagnose problems in the inner ear that cause balance disorders.

Audiologists determine if a hearing aid or other assistive listening devices could help a patient hear in everyday situations. In some cases, audiologists make use of counseling, support groups, and lip reading programs to help patients deal with hearing problems.

Practicing audiology often requires a special license. In the United States, for example, a person must be licensed by the state in which they are practicing. Audiologists typically hold a Doctor of Audiology (Au.D.) degree. College requirements for a degree in audiology include courses in hearing, speech, and language. Audiologists work in such settings as hospitals, medical clinics, private offices, community speech and hearing centers, and schools.   Ruth A. Bentler

See also **Deafness.**

Audio-visual materials, also known as *instructional media,* are educational devices that work through sight, sound, or both. Any combination of seeing and hearing information can greatly increase a person's ability to remember what he or she learns. Teachers use a great variety of audio-visual materials in daily instruction. The materials range from simple devices like chalkboards to complicated digital multimedia systems.

The computer has become an increasingly influential educational tool. Originally, computers were used only to assist with regular learning programs, such as mathematics exercises. But today, a multimedia computer can blend text, pictures, moving images, and sound to create instructional packages. PowerPoint is the trade name of one of the most popular multimedia applications. In addition, the Internet makes a vast amount of visual and audio information available to students in a matter of seconds.

Visual materials are primarily for seeing. Such materials include pictures, maps, charts, models, or actual objects being discussed. They also include images projected onto screens or displayed on computers. But even with the increased capacity of computers to assist in education, the most popular visual aids continue to be devices upon which the instructor can write information. Chalkboards, dry-erase boards, and flip charts are the most commonly used of these devices.

Chalkboards, dry-erase boards, and flip charts. Chalkboards are probably the most widely used visual aid. They are smooth, dark boards made of slate, glass, or wood. Users write or draw on the boards with chalk or crayon. Other accessories used with chalkboards include large protractors to measure angles and devices to draw the five lines of a musical staff.

A *dry-erase board* is a steel surface coated with white enamel on which the user writes with special felt markers. Some dry-erase boards include a device that scans what is written on the board and makes paper copies to give to the audience.

Flip charts consist of large pads of paper mounted on a frame. The user writes information on the pad during a presentation or prepares it in advance to display while speaking. Material on a regular sheet of paper can be enlarged by a special machine for use on a flip chart. Compared to most chalkboards and dry-erase boards, flip charts are relatively small and portable. In addition, an instructor can display individual sheets of paper around the room so that the group can refer to important points presented earlier in the lesson. Business and industrial trainers frequently use flip charts.

Projection devices. Many teachers supplement their lessons with material that can be projected onto a screen. Projectors display both solid and transparent objects. The most widely used projectors include opaque projectors, overhead projectors, filmstrip and slide projectors, and liquid crystal display projectors.

Opaque projectors show materials that cannot let light through them. These projectors can display on a screen an enlarged image of a book, document, or small object. Light from the projector lamp shines on the object. A tilted mirror reflects an image of the object and enlarges it through a lens onto a screen.

Overhead projectors project *transparencies* on a screen. A transparency is a clear plastic sheet with material printed on it. The transparency is placed on a clear flat surface over a projector lamp. A mirror reflects the image through a lens onto the screen. Transparencies can be made by several methods, including drawing or writing on a clear plastic sheet. They may also be made using photocopying machines, computer printers, and other devices.

Filmstrip projectors and *slide projectors* also project images onto a screen. A filmstrip is a strip of 35-millimeter film with a series of related still images that are displayed by a projector. Some filmstrip projectors have built-in tape players to provide sound to accompany the images. A 35-millimeter slide projector is used to show individual transparent photographs called *slides.* Slides are arranged in a tray from which they individually drop between a light and the lens that projects them. In many classrooms, computers and other devices have replaced filmstrip and slide projectors.

Liquid crystal display (LCD) *projectors* pick up information using a substance called *liquid crystal,* which changes color when an electric charge is applied to it. When attached to a computer, an LCD panel picks up and displays an image of what appears on the computer screen. With LCD projectors, teachers and other people can present computer images, as well as play video clips and display computerized slide presentations. In addition, they can present information from the Internet. Many LCD projectors can project images from television systems.

Digital light processing (DLP) *projectors* create images using a special type of electronic circuit that contains up to 2 million tiny pivoting mirrors. Like LCD projectors, DLP projectors display computer images.

Audio materials are primarily for hearing. They include audio cassette tapes, audio compact discs (CD's), and the machines on which they are played. These materials are often used to present music, stories, poetry readings, dramatic performances, and speeches. With tape recorders and similar devices, students can record and listen to themselves. Music and foreign-language students, for example, often record themselves as they practice. They can then play the tape to hear how well they did. People also record lectures to review later.

Audio cassette tapes store sound information on magnetic tape and can be played on tape players. Audio compact discs store information in *digital* (numerical) code. Compact discs last longer and offer better sound quality than cassette tapes. They also allow the user to skip easily to any part of the recording. Audio compact discs can be played on CD players and on many computers as well.

Multisensory materials are designed for both seeing and hearing. As the availability of multimedia technology has grown, teachers have expanded the use of multisensory materials in instruction. Multisensory aids include video presentations, computer systems, and telecommunications equipment.

Video presentations. Films, especially 16-millimeter films, were once a major multisensory instructional tool. In the late 1900's, videotapes became more common. Videotape is easier to use, more durable than film, and less expensive. Videocassettes are a common form of videotape. Videocassette recorders (VCR's) play back the tapes, which students usually view on television sets. The tapes can present motion pictures, TV programming, or other presentations. But in many schools, multimedia computers perform many of the duties of VCR's.

Like videocassettes, discs called DVD's store materials that combine visuals and sound. The discs store information in digital code and are played using a computer or a DVD player connected to a television set. DVD's offer high picture quality and the ability to skip easily to any part of the disc. Most DVD's provide an on-screen table of contents that allows the user to select desired information.

Many schools have a video-production system, which includes equipment to produce and play back video presentations. More sophisticated systems may have various cameras, editing software and equipment, and audio equipment. They may also have *computer graphics* devices to create visual effects in producing videos. Computer graphics is a term that refers both to the use of computers to create pictures and to the pictures themselves. School video-production systems are used by teachers to produce educational material, as well as by students learning to work with television.

Other computerized tools. As multimedia technology has improved, teachers have greatly expanded the use of computers in audio-visual instruction. The availability of content from the Internet has dramatically enhanced the ability of teachers to provide audio-visual materials to students. With high-speed access to the Internet, a teacher can present information—including text, photos, sounds, and videos—found on a website to a class. Students also can use computers and the Internet for research projects.

Computer tutorials are educational programs that lead students through study exercises and provide more assistance if they give incorrect answers. In addition, some publishers offer electronic books, also called *e-books,* that present textbook information through computers.

Computer *simulations* (representations that respond to changing conditions) enable students to experience realistic situations. For example, pilots in training use *flight simulators,* which imitate an airplane in flight. Computer simulations can also be used by an entire class. The scene for the simulation may be projected onto a screen for the class to see. The computer manages the input and output, while the class tries to work through the situation presented in the simulation. For example, a simulation program may present political problems facing a mayor and city council, with the class discussing possible solutions. An advantage of such programs is that a whole class can use one computer, which is less costly for schools than providing individual computers.

Computers and various *telecommunications systems* (systems that transmit information throughout the world)

© David Young-Wolff, Photo Edit

A videotape recording project allows students to produce their own videotapes, which can then be played back on a TV set. The students shown here are using a video camera to create a videotape about skateboarding.

have allowed a development in educational media known as *distance learning.* Such technology enables students to work on the same project from two or more separate locations. Using computers, students may connect through e-mail, electronic chat rooms, or direct Internet video connections. Teachers may use satellites or cable TV to transmit a lecture or other educational presentation to many locations. This technique enables many schools to share a class taught by one teacher. Distance education provides many students with instruction that would not be available to them otherwise. For example, a small college with limited resources could show on television a class taught by a well-known professor at a large university.   Lawrence O. Picus

Related articles in *World Book* include:

Audiobook	Library (School libraries)
Chalkboard	Phonograph
Compact disc	Projector
Computer	Tape recorder
Distance learning	Telecommunications
DVD	Videotape recorder
Filmstrip	Virtual reality

Audubon, *AW duh BAHN,* **John James** (1785-1851), was one of the first people to study and paint the birds of North America. Audubon's lifelike water-color paintings of birds in their natural surroundings brought him fame and fortune.

His life. Audubon's diaries and letters created a mystery about his background and parentage, but records indicate that he was born Jean Rabin on April 26, 1785, at Les Cayes, Santo Domingo (now Haiti). His mother, a French chambermaid, died soon after his birth. Records show that his father, a French sea captain named Jean Audubon, remarried in France, and Jean Rabin soon joined him.

Audubon and his wife legally adopted the boy when he was 8 years old. These records disprove claims by Audubon's descendants, derived from passages in his diaries and letters, that Audubon was the *lost dauphin*—that is, the missing heir to the throne of France.

In 1803, Captain Audubon sent the youth to live at Mill Grove, his estate near Philadelphia. There, young John James, as he was now called, spent much time drawing birds. He and Ferdinand Rozier opened a general store in Louisville, Kentucky, in 1807. Audubon married a Mill Grove neighbor, Lucy Bakewell, the next year. He failed in several business ventures. While Rozier conducted their business, Audubon wandered through the countryside looking for birds. His business career ended in 1819 when he was jailed for debt. He entered a plea of bankruptcy to gain his freedom.

In 1820, Audubon conceived the idea of publishing a collection of paintings of North American birds. His family followed him to Louisiana, where he painted birds in their natural surroundings. His wife worked as a governess and teacher to support the family. Audubon drew portraits and taught music and drawing.

His works. Unable to find an American publisher, Audubon went to England and Scotland in 1826. His pictures created a sensation, and a British publisher brought out *Birds of America* (1827-1838), which was a work of 87 parts containing 435 life-sized, colored engravings made from his water colors. Audubon and William MacGillivray, a Scottish naturalist, wrote a text, *Ornithological Biography* (1831-1839).

Courtesy of the New-York Historical Society, New York City

An Audubon painting of passenger pigeons shows the realistic, colorful style of the artist and naturalist. This water color by John James Audubon was published in 1829.

Audubon returned to the United States in 1839 and worked on American editions of his bird paintings. Later, he worked with John Bachman on *The Viviparous Quadrupeds of North America* (1842-1854). Audubon made his last collecting trip, along the Missouri River, in 1843. He died on Jan. 27, 1851.   Donald F. Bruning

Audubon Society, *AW duh BAHN,* **National,** is one of the oldest and largest national conservation organizations in the world. It was founded in 1905 and took the name of the American bird artist and naturalist John James Audubon. The society conserves and restores natural habitats for birds and other wildlife. It was founded by conservationists alarmed by the slaughter of thousands of birds to provide feather plumes for hats.

The Audubon Society has chapters throughout the United States. Its network of nature centers and sanctuaries celebrates the natural world and the importance of conservation. The society works to encourage sound public policy. These efforts focus on renewable energy, wildlife conservation, safeguarding clean air and water, and preserving and restoring natural places. Audubon also operates citizen science programs, such as the Christmas Bird Count, a survey of bird populations first done in 1900. The count has provided data on declining bird populations and changes in the migration of birds caused by global warming, an increase in the average temperature of Earth's surface.

Audubon publishes *Audubon,* a magazine. In 2009, the society's new headquarters in New York City achieved the highest level of certification under the Leadership in Energy and Environmental Design (LEED) program. This certification recognizes energy-saving and environmentally friendly buildings.

Critically reviewed by the National Audubon Society

See also **Audubon, John James; Bird** (Bird study and protection).

Auerbach, OW uhr bahk, **Red** (1917-2006), was one of the greatest coaches in the history of the National Basketball Association (NBA). In his 20 years as a professional basketball coach, Auerbach's teams won 938 regular-season games. This mark stood as a league record until Lenny Wilkens broke it during the 1994-1995 season.

Auerbach coached the Boston Celtics from the 1950-1951 season through the 1965-1966 season. He led the Celtics to nine NBA championships, eight in a row from the 1958-1959 season through the 1965-1966 season. In 1966, he retired as Celtics coach and became the team's president and general manager. He retired as general manager in 1984 but remained as the team's president until 1997, when he became a vice president.

Arnold Jacob Auerbach was born on Sept. 20, 1917, in the Brooklyn borough of New York City. He began his professional career in 1946, coaching the Washington Capitols for three seasons. He coached the Tri-Cities Blackhawks for a season before joining the Celtics. Auerbach died on Oct. 28, 2006.   Bob Logan

See also **Basketball** (picture).

Augmented reality, also known as AR, is the addition of artificial visual, auditory, or other sensory information to the physical world, so that it appears to be part of the actual environment. AR additions to the environment are called *augmentations* or *annotations*. Augmentations are usually computer-generated graphics or sounds that are three-dimensionally (3-D) *registered* with the real world. 3-D registration keeps the augmentation matched to the physical environment in real time, even as the user moves around.

People can experience AR through various display technologies. For example, special eyewear overlays information on top of the user's perception of the physical environment. Smartphones and tablets can act as devices through which the user can see a live image of the real world with augmentations added to it. Projectors can display imagery directly on top of real-world objects to give the appearance of different materials or moving parts. Additional display hardware is needed when other sensory information, such as sound or touch sensation, is part of an augmentation.

AR systems consist of several components. A *tracking component* determines the user's position and orientation within the physical environment. A *rendering component* creates the augmentation. A *registration component* and a *spatial world model* match up and align the augmentation with the physical environment.

In 1968, the American computer scientist Ivan Sutherland demonstrated the first AR system. It consisted of a head-mounted display suspended from the ceiling that allowed the wearer to see a virtual image superimposed on the room around them. The Boeing Company coined the term "augmented reality" in the early 1990's to describe a display used for aircraft assembly. Today, many smartphone apps use AR. AR is increasingly used in medical and industrial fields, as well as in architecture,

tourism, education, entertainment, sports, and personal information management.   Tobias Höllerer

Augsburg, AWGZ burg or OWKS boork (pop. 267,767), is a commercial and industrial city in southern Germany. For location, see **Germany** (political map). Augsburg is known for its well-preserved medieval and Renaissance buildings. Its many landmarks include the Augsburg Cathedral, which dates from the 900's, and the town hall, completed in 1620. A number of beautiful Renaissance buildings stand on Maximilianstrasse and Karolinenstrasse, two famous streets in the city center. Factories in Augsburg manufacture such products as chemicals, electronics, machinery, and textiles.

The Romans founded Augsburg in 15 B.C. and later made it a provincial capital of their empire. The city became a thriving commercial and trade center during the 1300's and 1400's. Protestant and Roman Catholic leaders met in Augsburg in 1530 to try to settle their differences (see **Augsburg Confession**). During World War II (1939-1945), Allied bombing damaged much of the city. The damaged areas were soon rebuilt.   John W. Boyer

Augsburg Confession, AWGZ burg or OWKS boork, was a short summary of the religious teachings of Martin Luther. It was written mainly by Philipp Melanchthon, Luther's chief associate in starting and leading the Protestant Reformation. The Confession was prepared in 1530 for Charles V, the Holy Roman emperor. It was named for Augsburg, Germany, the scene of a *diet* (meeting) called by Charles to end religious divisions within the empire.

Melanchthon wrote the Confession to prove that Lutherans supported the historic tradition of the Christian church. He tried to compromise on some controversial issues, hoping for the reunification of Christendom. Luther was not permitted to attend the diet. He admired the Confession for "treading lightly" over disputed issues but insisted that no more concessions be made. The Confession was too Protestant in tone for the emperor, and he rejected it. Melanchthon continued to make changes to the Confession over the years, and conservative Lutherans objected to the altered versions. The original version became the basic statement of faith of the Lutheran Church.   M. U. Edwards

See also **Luther, Martin; Melanchthon, Philipp; Reformation** (picture).

Augur, AW guhr, was the title given to priests in ancient Rome who interpreted signs, such as thunder and lightning, the flight and cries of birds, and the movement of snakes and mice. Romans believed that the gods revealed their wishes through these signs. Augurs did not predict the future. Instead, they read the signs to see if the gods approved of human actions. Augurs wore a *trabea* (white garment with a purple border).

Roman officials sought the advice of augurs before beginning elections, wars, and other important public activities. The officials might delay or cancel great ventures if the augurs reported unfavorable signs. Because augurs controlled the doctrine and practice of interpreting signs, they had great power in Roman politics.

Early Rome had 3 augurs, all from the *patrician* (aristocratic) class. By the late Roman Republic, the priesthood had 16 members, both patricians and *plebeians* (commoners).   C. J. Bannon

See also **Omen; Oracle.**

August is the eighth month of the year according to the Gregorian calendar, which is used in almost all the world today. The month has 31 days. The Romans called the month Sextilis, which means *sixth*. It was the sixth month in their early calendar, but later became the eighth month. The Romans also later renamed the month for Augustus, who ruled as the first Roman emperor from 27 B.C. to A.D. 14.

In early August, much of the Caribbean celebrates Emancipation Day. In Barbados, it is also called Kadooment Day. On this day and the weeks leading up to it, people in Barbados celebrate the end of the sugar cane harvest and also commemorate the abolition of slavery. The holiday is observed with parades, music, feasting, and dancing. Native American harvest celebrations called green corn dances often fall in August.

Lammas Day, August 1, is an ancient British festival. This celebration of the harvest became associated with the Christian Church, and loaves of bread made from the season's first grains were taken to church to be blessed. The Feast of the Assumption, August 15, is celebrated by Roman Catholic and Eastern Orthodox churches. It is based on the belief that the Virgin Mary was taken up to heaven in body and soul. The feast may be related to harvest festivals of pre-Christian times. In some parts of Europe, it is called the Feast of Our Lady of the Harvest.

In Nepal, Gokarne Aunsi (Father's Day) usually falls in

Important August events

1 National Day, Switzerland.
— William Clark, American explorer, born 1770.
— Francis Scott Key, American lawyer and author of "The Star-Spangled Banner," born 1779.
— Richard Henry Dana, Jr., American author, born 1815.
— Maria Mitchell, American astronomer, born 1818.
— Herman Melville, American author, born 1819.
— Colorado became the 38th U.S. state, 1876.
— Germany declared war on Russia, World War I, 1914.
— U.S. Congress passed the Atomic Energy Act, providing for civilian control of nuclear energy, 1946.
2 First United States census began, 1790.
— John Tyndall, British physicist, born 1820.
— First Lincoln penny issued in United States, 1909.
3 Christopher Columbus set sail from Palos, Spain, on his first voyage across the Atlantic, 1492.
— Ernie Pyle, American newspaper columnist, born 1900.
4 German American publisher John Peter Zenger acquitted of libel in 1735, helping to establish American freedom of the press.
— Percy Bysshe Shelley, English poet, born 1792.
— Barack Obama, the 44th U.S. president and the nation's first African American president, born 1961.
5 Guy de Maupassant, French novelist and short-story writer, born 1850.
— Union forces won the Battle of Mobile Bay in the American Civil War, 1864.
6 Independence Day, Jamaica.
— Daniel O'Connell, Irish patriot, born 1775.
— Alfred, Lord Tennyson, English poet, born 1809.
— Bolivia became independent in 1825.
— Alexander Fleming, British discoverer of penicillin, born 1881.
— Gertrude Ederle became the first woman to swim the English Channel, 1926.
— Atomic bomb dropped on Hiroshima, Japan, 1945.
7 Louis S. B. Leakey, British anthropologist, born 1903.

— Ralph J. Bunche, American statesman, born 1904.
— United States troops landed on Guadalcanal in the Solomon Islands in World War II, 1942.
8 English fleet attacked the Spanish Armada, 1588 (July 29 by calendar then in use).
— Ernest Orlando Lawrence, American physicist, born 1901.
9 Izaak Walton, English author, born 1593.
— John Dryden, English poet and dramatist, born 1631.
— Richard M. Nixon became first U.S. president ever to resign from office, 1974.
10 The *Columbia* completed the first voyage around the world by an American ship, 1790.
— Missouri became the 24th U.S. state, 1821.
— Smithsonian Institution founded, 1846.
— Herbert Hoover, 31st U.S. president, born 1874.
11 Gifford Pinchot, American conservationist and statesman, born 1865.
12 Julius Rosenwald, American philanthropist, born 1862.
— George Bellows, American artist, born 1882.
— The United States annexed Hawaii, 1898.
13 Spanish conquerors won Mexico City from the Aztec, 1521.
— Lucy Stone, American women's rights leader, born 1818.
— Annie Oakley, American sharpshooter, born 1860.
— East Germans began building the Berlin Wall, 1961.
14 John Galsworthy, English novelist, born 1867.
— U.S. Social Security Act approved, 1935.
— Pakistan became independent, 1947.
15 Napoleon Bonaparte born 1769.
— Sir Walter Scott, Scottish author, born 1771.
— Native Americans attacked soldiers and settlers of Fort Dearborn (now Chicago) in 1812.
— Panama Canal opened to traffic, 1914.
— India became independent in 1947.
— South Korea was established in 1948.
— Republic of the Congo became independent in 1960.
16 Patriots defeated the British in the Battle of Bennington in the American Revolution, 1777.

Aug. birthstone—
sardonyx

Aug. flower—
poppy

Aug. 6—first woman
to swim English Channel

Aug. 6—atomic bomb
dropped on Hiroshima

August or early September. Fathers, both living and dead, are honored on this day.

August flowers are the poppy and gladiolus. August gemstones are the sardonyx and peridot.

Carole S. Angell

Quotations

The brilliant poppy flaunts her head
  Amidst the ripening grain,
And adds her voice to swell the song
  That August's here again.
      Helen Maria Winslow

All the long August afternoon,
The little drowsy stream

Whispers a melancholy tune
As if it dreamed of June,
  And whispered in its dream.
      William Dean Howells

Dry August and warm
Doth harvest no harm.
      Thomas Tusser

If the twenty-fourth of August
  be fair and clear,
Then hope for a prosperous Autumn that year.
      John Ray, English Proverbs

See also **Assumption; Augustus; Calendar.**

Important August events

17 Davy Crockett, American frontiersman, born 1786.
— United States and Canada arranged for joint defense of North America, 1940.
— Indonesia declared independence in 1945.
18 Virginia Dare, first English child born in America, born 1587.
— Meriwether Lewis, American explorer, born 1774.
19 The British warship *Guerrière* surrendered to the U.S.S. *Constitution* in 1812, during the War of 1812.
— Bernard Baruch, American financier and statesman, born 1870.
— Orville Wright, pioneer American aviator and airplane designer, born 1871.
— Manuel Quezon, first president of the Commonwealth of the Philippines, born 1878.
— Philo T. Farnsworth, American inventor who discovered a system for electronic television, born 1906.
— Bill Clinton, 42nd U.S. president, born 1946 in Hope, Arkansas.
20 Bernardo O'Higgins, Chilean patriot, born 1778.
— Benjamin Harrison, 23rd U.S. president, born 1833.
21 Lincoln-Douglas debates began in United States, 1858.
— Hawaii became the 50th U.S. state, 1959.
22 John Fitch successfully demonstrated his side-paddle steamboat, 1787.
— The *Savannah,* first steamship to cross the Atlantic, launched 1818.
— Claude Debussy, French composer, born 1862.
— Clara Barton founded first local chapter of the American National Red Cross, 1881.
23 Baron de Cuvier, French naturalist, born 1769.
— Oliver Hazard Perry, American naval officer, born 1785.
— Edgar Lee Masters, American poet and biographer, born 1868.
24 Massacre of St. Bartholomew's Day began in Paris, 1572.
— William Wilberforce, British statesman and crusader against slavery, born 1759.
— British troops captured Washington, D.C., and burned

the Capitol and the White House in 1814, during the War of 1812.
25 Bret Harte, American author of stories about the Western United States, born 1836.
— Leonard Bernstein, American composer, conductor, and pianist, born 1918.
26 Antoine Lavoisier, French chemist, born 1743.
— Lee De Forest, American inventor, born 1873.
— Ottmar Mergenthaler received a patent for his Linotype machine, 1884.
— Amendment 19 to the U.S. Constitution, giving women the right to vote, proclaimed 1920.
27 Georg Wilhelm Friedrich Hegel, German philosopher, born 1770.
— Commercial oil production began in the United States when Edwin Laurentine Drake struck oil, 1859.
— Theodore Dreiser, American novelist, born 1871.
— Lyndon B. Johnson, 36th U.S. president, born 1908.
28 Spanish explorers landed in Florida where St. Augustine now stands, 1565.
— Johann Wolfgang von Goethe, German poet and dramatist, born 1749.
— The United Kingdom ended slavery in its colonies, 1833.
— More than 200,000 civil rights demonstrators staged a march on Washington, D.C., 1963.
29 Oliver Wendell Holmes, American physician and man of letters, born 1809.
— Charles F. Kettering, American inventor and automobile pioneer, born 1876.
30 Mary Wollstonecraft Shelley, English author of *Frankenstein,* born 1797.
— Second Battle of Bull Run, or Manassas, ended in Confederate victory, American Civil War, 1862.
— Ernest Rutherford, British physicist, born 1871.
— Huey Long, American political leader, born 1893.
31 Queen Wilhelmina of the Netherlands born 1880.
— Federation of Malaya (now part of Malaysia) became independent, 1957.

WORLD BOOK illustrations by Mike Hagel

Aug. 15—Napoleon Bonaparte born

Aug. 15—Panama Canal opened

Aug. 22—side-paddle steamboat demonstrated

Aug. 24—British troops burn White House

Augusta, *aw GUHS tuh,* Georgia (pop. 195,844; met. area pop. 564,873), lies on the state's eastern boundary, about 125 miles (201 kilometers) from the mouth of the Savannah River. Augusta's metropolitan area includes nearby Aiken, South Carolina. For location, see **Georgia** (political map).

Augusta's chief industries produce brick, detergents, fertilizer, food products, golf carts, hospital products, newsprint, and paper products. Augusta is on the eastern edge of one of the world's greatest *kaolin* belts. Several plants near Augusta process kaolin, a white clay used for making fine pottery and as a coating on high-quality paper. Nearby Fort Gordon, a United States Army training center, has a larger payroll than that of the combined industries of metropolitan Augusta (see **Fort Gordon**).

Augusta is the home of Paine College and Augusta University. The city is a medical center and has several large hospitals. The Masters Tournament, one of the world's major golf competitions, is held every spring at the Augusta National Golf Club.

James Oglethorpe, who founded the Georgia colony, ordered Augusta established in 1736. The Georgia legislature made Augusta capital of the state from 1786 to 1795. During the American Civil War (1861-1865), Augusta served as ordnance center of the Confederacy. In 1996, Augusta and Richmond County were merged under a mayor-commission-administrator form of government. James O. Wheeler

Augusta, *aw GUHS tuh* (pop. 19,136), is the capital of Maine. The city lies on both sides of the Kennebec River in the central part of the state. For location, see **Maine** (political map).

Augusta's major buildings include the State Capitol and other state buildings; the Maine State Library; the governor's residence, called Blaine House; and Old Fort Western, a restored colonial-era fort. The University of Maine has a campus in Augusta. The state government is the city's largest employer. Other employers include health care services and utility companies.

In 1628, Pilgrims from Plymouth Colony in Massachusetts established a trading post on the site of Augusta, then an American Indian village called Cushnoc. Beginning in the 1660's, Indian wars brought trade in the area to a halt. In 1754, Fort Western was built on the site of the old trading post. The settlements that grew up around the fort were then part of the present town of Hallowell. In 1797, Augusta became a separate town. It replaced Portland as Maine's capital in 1832, due to its more central location. Augusta has a council-manager form of government. It is the seat of Kennebec County.

Patty Ammons

See also **Maine** (pictures: The State Capitol; Maine's House of Representatives).

Augustine, *AW guh STEEN* or *aw GUHS tihn,* **Saint** (354-430), was one of the greatest leaders of the early Christian church. His writings had a strong influence on medieval religious thought. Augustine's ideas also appeared in the teachings of John Calvin, Martin Luther, and other Protestant reformers. He influenced such philosophers as Immanuel Kant of Germany and Blaise Pascal of France.

His life. Augustine was born on Nov. 13, 354, in Tagaste, a city near what is now Constantine, Algeria.

His name in Latin was Aurelius Augustinus. Augustine's mother, Saint Monica, was a devout Christian. His father was a pagan. As a young man, Augustine pursued worldly success and was attracted to several non-Christian movements. He described his early life and spiritual struggles in *Confessions* (397-398), one of the first great autobiographies.

In the early 380's, Augustine taught rhetoric in Carthage and Rome and then in Milan, Italy. Some friends in Milan encouraged him to read the works of the Greek philosophers called Neoplatonists (see **Neoplatonism**). These writings and the sermons of Saint Ambrose, the bishop of Milan, helped him overcome the intellectual obstacles to accepting Christianity. In 386, Augustine decided to devote himself to the faith, and Ambrose baptized him the next year.

Soon afterward, Augustine returned to Tagaste, where he organized a community of believers. In 391, he traveled to nearby Hippo. The Christian congregation there persuaded him to stay. He was ordained as a priest in Hippo in 391. From 396 until his death on Aug. 28, 430, he served as bishop of Hippo. Augustine's feast day is August 28, the date of his death.

His beliefs can be divided into three main groups: (1) God and the soul, (2) sin and grace, and (3) the church and the sacraments.

God and the soul. Augustine's study of Neoplatonism convinced him that God is present in the soul of every human being. He believed that people should direct their attention to God and not be distracted by the cares and pleasures of the world.

Sin and grace. Augustine preached that people could not change their sinful ways unless helped by the grace of God. He believed that God chose only certain individuals to receive his grace. This belief forms part of a doctrine called *predestination* or *election.*

The church and the sacraments. Augustine believed that people could not receive God's grace unless they belonged to the church and received the sacraments. A group of clergymen in northern Africa said grace could not be given unless the clergy itself was perfect. But Augustine declared that God could bypass human weaknesses through the sacraments. Augustine's book *The City of God* (413-426) presents the history of humanity as a struggle between people who depend on God and those who rely on themselves. David B. Burrell

See also **Philosophy** (picture).

Augustine of Canterbury, *AW guh STEEN* or *aw GUHS tihn,* **Saint** (? -604), was the first archbishop of Canterbury. Pope Saint Gregory I commissioned Augustine to lead a team of 30 missionary monks from Rome to England. The group arrived in 597 and were welcomed by Ethelbert, king of Kent. Although the king was not a Christian, he invited Augustine and his monks to preach in his kingdom. Their preaching converted thousands of the English, including Ethelbert, to Christianity, and so Augustine is known as the *apostle to the English nation.*

Augustine established a cathedral at Canterbury. Pope Gregory appointed Augustine archbishop of Canterbury in 601.

Augustine's feast day in England and Wales is May 26, the date of his death. His feast day is May 27 on the general church calendar. Neil J. Roy

Augustus, *aw GUHS tuhs* (63 B.C.-A.D.14), meaning *the revered,* was the name given to Gaius Julius Caesar Octavianus, also called Octavian, when he became the first emperor of Rome in 27 B.C. That year, the era of the Roman Empire began.

Octavian was born in Rome on Sept. 23, 63 B.C. His father was Gaius Octavius, a wealthy banker. Julius Caesar was his great-uncle. In his will, Caesar adopted Octavian and made him his heir. After Caesar was assassinated in 44 B.C., Octavian took the name Gaius Julius Caesar Octavianus. He was 19 years old. The famous orator Cicero helped Octavian legalize his adoption over the objections of Mark Antony, Caesar's chief lieutenant.

Rise to power. After Caesar's death, Mark Antony had taken control of Rome. Octavian raised an army of Caesar's veterans to fight Antony and defeated him in 43 B.C. Octavian forced the Roman Senate to elect him one of Rome's two *consuls* (chief government officials).

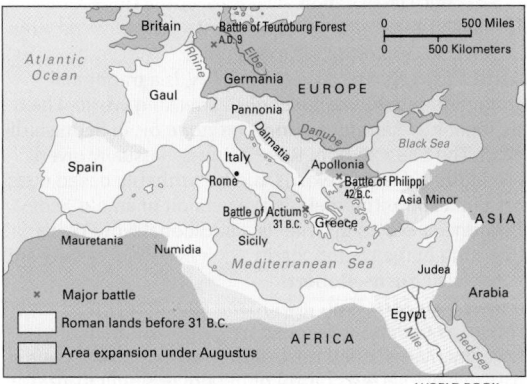

WORLD BOOK map

Roman lands under Augustus expanded greatly. In 31 B.C., before Octavian became the Emperor Augustus, his forces conquered Egypt for Rome.

He then came to an agreement with Antony. The two men formed a political alliance, known as the Second Triumvirate, with Marcus Aemilius Lepidus, the *pontifex maximus* (chief priest) of Rome's state religion. The First Triumvirate had consisted of Julius Caesar, Pompey the Great, and Marcus Licinius Crassus. Under the Second Triumvirate, Antony ruled Rome's eastern provinces, and Octavian ruled the western ones. Lepidus controlled Rome's territories in Africa.

The Triumvirate had more than 2,000 of its opponents killed. In 42 B.C., Octavian and Antony fought and defeated Marcus Junius Brutus and Gaius Cassius Longinus, Caesar's chief assassins, at Philippi, in Macedonia. Sextus Pompey, the son of Pompey the Great, posed another threat. Octavian's chief adviser and general, Marcus Agrippa, fought and defeated Sextus Pompey's military forces in 36 B.C. That same year, Octavian and Antony removed Lepidus from the Triumvirate. Octavian and Antony then turned their armies against one another.

Since about 41 B.C., Antony and Queen Cleopatra of Egypt had been lovers and allies. Octavian portrayed this relationship as a threat to Rome and used it to turn public opinion against Antony. In 32 B.C., he went to war against Antony for control of the Roman world. Marcus Agrippa defeated Antony and Cleopatra's forces at sea

at the Battle of Actium, off the west coast of Greece, on Sept. 2, 31 B.C. The pair fled to Alexandria, Egypt, where they both committed suicide. Egypt became a Roman province in 30 B.C.

Emperor of Rome. In 27 B.C., the Senate gave Octavian the name *Augustus.* Three arrangements with the Senate, in 27, 23, and 19 B.C., gave Augustus legal power to direct Rome's civil and military affairs as the *princeps* (leading citizen). In 12 B.C., Augustus also became pontifex maximus. The Senate served as an advisory body and governed Rome's more peaceful provinces. Through governors, Augustus controlled provinces that required extra troops or that, like Egypt, were very wealthy.

Augustus divided the city of Rome into 14 administrative areas. He allowed Rome's *equites* (business class) more influence in the running of the city and the empire. He also established the *Praetorian Guard,* his bodyguard.

Augustus used coins, monuments, and statues as propaganda to emphasize his high position. He claimed to be descended from the god Mars and the goddess Venus. His ancestors included the Trojan hero Aeneas. Some Romans in the provinces worshiped Augustus.

Expansion of the empire. Under Augustus, the empire doubled in size. He finally brought all of Spain under Roman control. In southeastern Europe, he advanced the empire's frontier north to the Danube River. In Germany, his army strove to push the frontier north to the Elbe River. But Germans defeated the army at the Battle of Teutoburg Forest in A.D. 9.

To better manage Roman lands, Augustus extended Rome's highway system to the remotest parts of the em-

Vatican Museums (SCALA/Art Resource)

Augustus was the first Roman emperor. This statue shows Augustus as a victorious Roman general.

pire. Colonies made up of veteran troops brought Roman civilization to newly conquered territories and helped maintain loyalty to Rome.

Other achievements. The reign of Augustus is sometimes called the Augustan Age. It ushered in a period of peace and prosperity after years of civil unrest.

Augustus restored monuments and buildings that had fallen into disrepair. He ordered the construction of aqueducts, bridges, roads, and a new *forum* (center of government). Sculptors created beautiful works in marble to decorate the city. Augustus had the Tiber River dredged to prevent flooding and improved Rome's supply of grain. These acts provided jobs for poor Romans and improved their living conditions. Augustus revived ancient religious rituals and built new temples. He promoted the growth of the senatorial and business classes by passing laws against adultery and rewarding those who married and had children.

Augustus and other statesmen of his time patronized the arts and literature and helped them flourish. Famous Roman authors of the Augustan Age included Horace, Livy, Ovid, Propertius, Tibullus, and Virgil. Augustus was also a writer himself, known for his simple, direct style.

The reign of Augustus was successful partly because of his patience in acquiring power and partly because of his diplomacy with his friends and enemies. He died on Aug. 19, A.D. 14. His remains were placed inside a great tomb called the Mausoleum. After his death, Augustus was made a god and worshiped in Rome.   Alex T. Nice

Related articles in *World Book* include:

Actium, Battle of	Caesar, Julius	Library (Libraries
Agrippa, Marcus	Calendar	of papyrus)
Antony, Mark	Cicero, Marcus	Pompey the Great
Brutus, Marcus	Tullius	Rome, Ancient
Junius	Cleopatra	

Auk, *awk,* a family of sea birds, includes auklets, dovekies, guillemots, murres, and puffins. Auks are also known as *alcids.* They live in the North Pacific, North Atlantic, and Arctic oceans. Auks look and behave somewhat like penguins, but the two types of birds are not closely related. Unlike penguins, auks can fly. Like penguins, auks are excellent underwater swimmers. They

Jacana
A dovekie, like most other auks, has black and white feathers. Auks live in the northern half of the world. They make their homes at sea and on rocky islands.

propel themselves rapidly through the water with their strong wings, steering with their webbed feet. Auks feed on fish and other marine animals.

Auks have thick bodies and short legs. They range in size from 5 to 30 inches (13 to 75 centimeters) long. Most auks have black and white feathers, but some auks have gray or brown feathers. Certain species have brightly colored legs and feet. The bills of puffins become brightly colored during the breeding season.

Auks spend all the year except the breeding season at sea. They tend to nest in colonies of thousands of birds on rocky islands and return to the same nesting sites every year. Most make their nests among rocks, in burrows in the ground, or on ledges of cliffs. The female lays one or two eggs, which hatch in four to six weeks.

The great auk, the first bird to be called a penguin, is an extinct member of the auk family. This goose-sized bird, the largest auk, could not fly. Hunters killed the last great auk in 1844.   Kevin J. McGowan

Scientific classification. Auks make up the family Alcidae. The great auk is *Pinguinus impennis.*

See also **Guillemot; Murre; Puffin.**

Auld Lang Syne, *AWLD lang SYN,* is a traditional song of friendship in the English-speaking world. The title means *old long since,* or *days gone by,* in Scottish dialect. The Scottish poet Robert Burns is usually given credit for the song's words, but he probably based them on a folk song. The melody is a version of an old Scottish tune. "Auld Lang Syne" is a traditional New Year's Eve song in the United States.   Valerie Woodring Goertzen

See also **Burns, Robert.**

Aung San Suu Kyi, *awng sahn soo chee* (1945-   ), served as the unofficial head of the government of Myanmar (also called Burma) from 2016 until the country's military seized control of the government in 2021. She is known for leading the opposition to the military dictatorship that ruled the country from 1988 to 2011. She was awarded the 1991 Nobel Peace Prize for her nonviolent efforts to bring democracy to Myanmar.

Aung San Suu Kyi was born in Yangon, Burma, on June 19, 1945. Her father, Aung San, was a leader of Burma's independence movement. He was assassinated in 1947. Her mother, Daw Khin Kyi, served as Burma's ambassador to India. Aung San Suu Kyi studied in Burma, India, and the United Kingdom. She graduated from Oxford University and earned a Ph.D. degree in Oriental and African studies at the University of London.

Aung San Suu Kyi became involved in politics in 1988, after Burma's military government killed thousands of prodemocracy protesters. That year, she cofounded the National League for Democracy (NLD) and became the group's secretary general. In 1990, the NLD won 392 of 492 seats in parliamentary elections. The military refused to yield power and arrested many of the party leaders.

From 1989 to 1995, Aung San Suu Kyi was held under house arrest. She was confined to her

© Candace Scharsu, Archive Photos
Aung San Suu Kyi

home again from 2000 to 2002. In May 2003, after a violent clash between her supporters and progovernment demonstrators, the military took her into custody. She was again placed under house arrest in September 2003. The NLD disbanded in 2010. Aung San Suu Kyi was released from house arrest later that year. In 2011, the NLD was allowed to re-register as an official political party. In 2012, Aung San Suu Kyi traveled to Europe for the first time since 1988. During the trip, she collected her 1991 Nobel Peace Prize.

Aung San Suu Kyi was elected to parliament in 2012 and continued fighting for increased democracy in Myanmar. Under her leadership, the NLD won a controlling majority in parliamentary elections in 2015 and in 2020. Aung San Suu Kyi is not eligible to serve as Myanmar's president because the Constitution prohibits anyone whose children are citizens of another country from holding that office. Her sons are British citizens. Aung San Suu Kyi said she would lead the country unofficially. In 2016, Myanmar's parliament elected one of her allies to the presidency. The new government appointed Aung San Suu Kyi to serve as state counselor, a role above that of president created specifically for her.

In 2017, more than half a million Rohingya, a Muslim people, fled Myanmar after clashes with the military. Aung San Suu Kyi faced international criticism for failure to protect the Rohingya against atrocities reportedly committed by the military and for later defending Myanmar in an international court. In February 2021, the military took control of Myanmar's government and again placed Aung San Suu Kyi under arrest.　　Neil A. Englehart

Aurangzeb, *AWR uhng ZEHB* (1618-1707), was an emperor who ruled what is now India and Pakistan from 1658 until his death. His reign over the Mughal Empire was marked by wars of expansion in southern India and wars to put down rebellions in the north. A devout Muslim, he tried to make all his people follow his religion, Islam. Aurangzeb placed special taxes on Hindus, who made up the majority of the population, and destroyed Hindu temples and images. He also destroyed many artworks, fearing they might be worshiped as idols. His policies led to much political and religious discontent, which helped weaken the empire. The empire declined rapidly after his death on March 3, 1707. Aurangzeb was born on Nov. 3, 1618, in Dohad, near Ahmadabad. In a struggle for the throne, he defeated three of his brothers in battle and executed two of them. He imprisoned his father and became emperor.　　Patricia Risso

Aurelian, *aw REE lee uhn* (A.D. 215?-275), was a Roman emperor who reunited the empire, which seemed to be breaking up when he came to power. Aurelian stamped his coins with the words *Restorer of the World.* He won victories over Germanic invaders near the Danube River; over Zenobia, queen of Palmyra in Syria; and over Tetricus, a semi-independent ruler of Gaul (now mainly France). Aurelian was born Lucius Domitius Aurelianus, probably in Illyricum, a Roman province on the northeastern coast of the Adriatic Sea. He became emperor in 270 and ruled until October or November 275, when a group of officers murdered him. Most of the wall he started to build around Rome still stands.　　F. G. B. Millar

Aurelius, Marcus. See Marcus Aurelius.

Aurora, *aw RAWR uh,* was the Roman name for Eos, the Greek goddess of the dawn. She was the sister of

Detail of the Aurora Crater (300's B.C.), a vase painting by an unknown Greek artist; Villa Giulio, Rome (SCALA/Art Resource)

Aurora was the Roman name for Eos, the Greek goddess of the dawn. The goddess often carried off handsome men to be her lovers, including the prince Cephalus, *shown here.*

Helios, the sun, and Selene, the moon. Aurora abducted several lovers. The most famous was Tithonus, a brother of King Priam of Troy. Aurora and Tithonus had a son named Memnon, who was killed by the Greek hero Achilles in the Trojan War. Aurora prayed to Jupiter, the king of the gods in Roman mythology, to make Tithonus immortal. But she forgot to ask for eternal youth for him as well. And so Tithonus, though immortal, grew older and older and shriveled up. Aurora had him locked up. He slowly became only a voice. According to one story, Tithonus turned into a grasshopper.　　F. Carter Philips

Aurora is a natural display of light in the sky, usually limited to Earth's polar regions. Auroras can be seen with the unaided eye only at night. They commonly appear as arcs, clouds, and bands of moving light that can extend across the sky for thousands of miles. An auroral display in the Northern Hemisphere is called the *aurora borealis* or *northern lights.* An auroral display in the Southern Hemisphere is called the *aurora australis.*

Most auroras occur about 60 to 250 miles (100 to 400 kilometers) above Earth. The most common color is green, but displays high in the sky may be red or purple.

Auroras result in part from Earth's *magnetic field,* the area of magnetic influence that surrounds the planet. The magnetic field dominates a region of space known as the *magnetosphere.* Above Earth's atmosphere, the magnetosphere contains both neutral and charged particles. The charged particles are produced when the

Hopkins Observatory, Williams College (Kevin Reardon)

An aurora glows in the night sky. Most auroras occur in the far northern and far southern regions. But occasionally, strong auroras like this one appear at lower latitudes.

planet's atmosphere absorbs radiation from the sun.

The magnetosphere is continuously buffeted by a flow of electrically charged particles from the sun, called the *solar wind*. This buffeting squeezes the magnetosphere and causes the charged particles already in the magnetosphere to move along the magnetic field toward the North and South poles. There, the energetic particles collide with particles in the atmosphere, releasing energy in the form of light.

Auroras are most intense during *solar maximum,* the most active phase in the 11-year sunspot cycle. During this period, violent eruptions on the sun's surface occur most frequently. These eruptions are known as *solar flares* and *coronal mass ejections*. They release additional material into the solar wind. The added material helps compress Earth's magnetosphere, producing extremely bright auroras. It also creates sharp variations in Earth's magnetic field, called *magnetic storms*. During these storms, auroras may expand toward the equator, making them visible beyond the polar regions.   Roderick A. Heelis

See also **Seven natural wonders of the world** (The aurora borealis).

Auschwitz, *OWSH vihts,* was the largest concentration camp run by Nazi Germany during World War II (1939-1945). A concentration camp is a place where people are kept against their will, usually by a government or other powerful group. The camp was in the town of Oświęcim in German-occupied Poland. The Nazis used Auschwitz as a killing center, where prisoners were murdered, and as a center for forced labor. About 1 ¼ million people, mostly Jews, were killed at Auschwitz. Other victims included Poles, Roma (sometimes called Gypsies), and Soviet prisoners of war.

Auschwitz was a group of three main camps and more than 40 smaller camps. The first camp, Auschwitz I, began in 1940 as a camp for Polish political prisoners. Many of the prisoners died from starvation, disease, or harsh treatment. In March 1942, Auschwitz II, or Birkenau, opened. It was primarily an *extermination* (mass killing) facility, and eventually had four large *gas chambers*—rooms where people were killed with poisonous hydrogen cyanide gas. In October 1942, Auschwitz III, or Monowitz, opened primarily as a slave labor camp. The camp produced *synthetic rubber* (rubber manufactured from chemicals).

In November 1944, as German forces retreated from advancing Soviet troops, the Nazis closed the gas chambers at Birkenau. In January 1945, the Nazis forced about 60,000 prisoners to march westward toward Germany. Many people died on these "death marches." In an effort to remove evidence of their crimes, the Nazis destroyed the gas chambers and *crematoriums* (buildings with furnaces for burning dead bodies) at Auschwitz before abandoning the camps. Soviet troops eventually found about 7,000 surviving prisoners at Auschwitz.

Today, the Auschwitz-Birkenau Memorial and Museum pays tribute to the camp's many victims. Auschwitz has been designated a World Heritage Site by the United Nations Educational, Scientific and Cultural Organization (UNESCO).   David Engel

See also **Concentration camp; Holocaust**.

Austen, Jane (1775-1817), is one of the best-loved English novelists. Austen wrote with a keen sense of irony about the social institutions of her time. In each of Austen's six novels, a woman meets and marries an eligible man after a series of usually comic difficulties. Overcoming these obstacles helps one or both of the characters gain the self-knowledge required for a happy marriage. Few authors have matched Austen's sure eye for human weakness. She has also been praised for her affectionate description of everyday life and her witty, elegant prose.

Austen's first novel, *Sense and Sensibility* (1811), follows Elinor and Marianne Dashwood, two sisters with differing temperaments. Elinor possesses careful self-control, or "sense." Marianne permits hasty emotions, or "sensibility," to rule her decisions. *Pride and Prejudice* (1813) is Austen's most famous work. In the novel, the lively Elizabeth Bennet dislikes Fitzwilliam Darcy's proud behavior and is blind to his better qualities. Their marriage can take place only after he humbles his pride and she loses her prejudice. In *Mansfield Park* (1814), the long-suffering and modest Fanny Price grows up mistreated by rich relatives. Her character may seem uninteresting compared with Austen's more flawed women. But Fanny is a successful portrait of personal integrity.

The self-satisfied and overly imaginative heroine of *Emma* (1816) almost ruins her chances for happiness with matchmaking schemes. *Northanger Abbey,* begun in 1797 and published in 1818, makes fun of the Gothic tales of romance and terror popular in Austen's time (see **Gothic novel**). In *Persuasion* (1818), Anne Elliot and Frederick Wentworth find love that survives an earlier parting and a disapproving family.

Austen was born in Steventon, a village in Hampshire, on Dec. 16, 1775. Her father was a clergyman. Austen received a better education than most women of her time. She began writing novels in her early 20's but did not publish them until late in life. Austen never married. She lived in the rural, upper middle class society described in her books. She died on July 18, 1817.   K. K. Collins

Austerlitz, *AW stuhr lihts,* **Battle of,** was a major battle of the Napoleonic Wars. It was fought on Dec. 2, 1805, near the Moravian town of Austerlitz (now in the Czech Republic). Napoleon I and his Grand Army, in a brilliantly fought battle, defeated the larger, combined armies of Austria and Russia. The Battle of Austerlitz led to the Treaty of Pressburg, by which Austria lost Istria and Dalmatia to Italy, and the Tyrol to Bavaria. The Holy Roman Empire was dissolved, and the way opened for Napoleon to rule central Europe.   Eric A. Arnold, Jr.

See also **Napoleon I** (Dominates Europe).

Austin (pop. 790,390; met. area pop. 1,716,289) is the capital of Texas and the state's educational center. The city of Austin lies on the Colorado River in south-central Texas (see **Texas** [political map]). In 1839, Austin was founded and became the capital of the Republic of Texas. Officials of the republic chose the site, on bluffs overlooking the Colorado River, for its beauty and central location. The city was named for pioneer Stephen F. Austin, often called the father of Texas.

Description. Austin, the county seat of Travis County, covers 254 square miles (658 square kilometers). The Austin-Round Rock metropolitan area, which consists of Bastrop, Caldwell, Hays, Travis, and Williamson counties, occupies about 4,282 square miles (11,090 square kilometers).

The State Capitol, Austin's chief landmark, is near the center of the city. State government agencies and institutions are throughout the city. The main campus of the University of Texas lies near the Capitol. Many athletic and entertainment events take place at the university's Frank Erwin Center. Other institutions of higher learning include Austin Graduate School of Theology, Austin Presbyterian Theological Seminary, Concordia University Texas, Seminary of the Southwest, Huston-Tillotson University, and St. Edward's University.

The Lyndon Baines Johnson Library and Museum on the University of Texas campus houses documents from the public career of the 36th president. The Texas Memorial Museum, also on campus, has exhibits on natural history. The Contemporary Austin exhibits works of art at its downtown site and at an estate called Laguna Gloria. Austin has a ballet association and symphony orchestra.

Economy. The state, local, and federal governments employ a large percentage of Austin's work force. The University of Texas, a state institution, ranks as the largest single employer.

Austin is the market center of a region that raises beef cattle and other farm products. Many trade organizations and associations have headquarters in Austin. The city is a center of the country music industry. Austin is famous for its parks, many of which are linked by *greenbelts* (belts of woodland or parkland).

The Austin metropolitan area has hundreds of manufacturing plants. The area is an important center for electronics and other high-technology industry. Many plants work with research institutions based in Austin. Other major industries include publishing and tourism.

Government. Austin has a council-manager form of government. The voters elect a mayor and 10 other council members to three-year terms. The council hires a city manager to carry out its policies.

History. When white settlers first arrived in the early 1800's, Tonkawa Indians lived in what is now the Austin area. The settlers named their community Waterloo. In 1839, Waterloo was renamed Austin and incorporated as a city.

In 1900, when Austin had 22,258 people, the Colorado River flooded the lower part of the city and burst a dam. Since then, seven new dams have been built. They have created seven artificial lakes near Austin. These lakes provide recreation facilities.

In 1920, Austin had 34,876 people. Every 10 years from 1920 to 2000, Austin's population increased by more than a third. During the 1970's, the increases resulted

mainly from the growth of the University of Texas and from Austin's development as a center of business and government. During the 1970's and early 1980's, many large construction projects were undertaken in the Austin area. These included many office buildings, apartments, hotels, shopping centers, and university and state government buildings. In 1992, a new convention center opened in Austin. By 2010, Austin's population had reached 790,390.

Richard A. Oppel

See also **Texas** (pictures).

Austin, Stephen Fuller (1793-1836), was an American colonizer and pioneer. He started the first American colony in Texas, then part of Mexico. His father, Moses Austin, had obtained a grant of land on the Brazos River from Spanish authorities in Mexico in 1821. Moses planned to bring 300 families to settle the land but died before starting the colony. Stephen got permission to continue the project—first from Spain, then from Mexico after it won independence from Spain in 1821. The main settlement was named San Felipe de Austin in Stephen's honor. Austin, Texas, was also named for him.

Austin managed the affairs of the colony wisely. By 1830, there were over 20,000 Americans in Texas. That year, the Mexican government prohibited further immigration of Americans to Texas. This action increased the desire of many Texans for a more independent government. In 1833, when Austin asked Mexico for a separate state government for Texas, he was accused of trying to annex Texas to the United States. He was sent to prison, but never received a trial. He returned to Texas in 1835. There he found the people ready to fight for freedom from Mexico. Austin took command of the Texan army, but soon resigned. He went to the United States for money and supplies for the Texans.

Texas became a republic in 1836. Austin was a candidate for president, but Sam Houston was elected. Austin was named secretary of state. He worked secretly for the U.S. annexation of Texas but died on Dec. 27, 1836, nine years before it happened. He was born on Nov. 3, 1793, in Wythe County, Virginia. A statue of Austin is in the United States Capitol. Joseph A. Stout, Jr.

See also **Texas** (American settlement); **Texas Rangers.**

Australasia, *AW struh LAY zhuh,* refers to Australia, New Guinea, New Zealand, and other nearby islands. New Guinea and New Zealand are also considered as part of the Pacific Islands, or Oceania. See **Australia; New Guinea; New Zealand; Pacific Islands.**

Shostal

Austin, a leading educational center of the Southwest, is the home of the Lyndon Baines Johnson Library and Museum, *shown here.* The library stands on the campus of the University of Texas.

The vast interior of Australia, often called the *outback,* consists mainly of deserts and dry grassland. Spinifex grass, *foreground,* is a common plant in the outback.

Australia

Australia is the only country that is also a continent. In area, Australia ranks as the sixth largest country and the smallest continent. It lies between the South Pacific Ocean and the Indian Ocean, about 7,000 miles (11,000 kilometers) southwest of North America and about 2,000 miles (3,200 kilometers) southeast of mainland Asia. Australia is often referred to as being "down under" because it lies entirely within the Southern Hemisphere. The name *Australia* comes from the Latin word *australis,* which means *southern.* The official name of the country is the Commonwealth of Australia.

Australia has many different kinds of environments and climates, from tropical in the north to *temperate* (with warm summers and cool winters) in the south. The huge interior of Australia, called the *outback,* is mostly desert or dry grassland and has few settlements. Kangaroos, koalas, platypuses, and wombats are only a few of the many unusual animals that are unique to Australia. The southeastern coastal region has Australia's two largest cities—Sydney and Melbourne. Canberra, the national capital, lies a short distance inland.

Australia has a strong economy that makes it one of the world's developed countries. It has busy cities, modern factories, and highly productive farms and mines. Australia is among the world's leading producers of copper, diamonds, gold, iron ore, silver, tin, and zinc.

Australia also produces and exports other minerals and farm goods. Income from these exports and other industries makes it possible for most Australians to have a high standard of living.

The Aboriginal peoples of Australia were the first people to live in Australia. Aboriginal people had lived in Australia for more than 65,000 years before the first Europeans arrived. The Torres Strait Islands are the home of the Torres Strait Islander peoples, Australia's other collective group of *Indigenous* (native) peoples.

Great Britain (later also called the United Kingdom) established a prison colony in Australia in 1788. After the British arrived, the number of people of European descent steadily increased while the Indigenous population plummeted. The Indigenous population slowed its decline in the early 1900's and has been increasing since the mid-1900's. Today, the majority of Australians have mixed European ancestry, although there are now also many Australians from Asian and Middle Eastern backgrounds. Australia considers itself a multicultural nation.

Government

Australia is a federation of six states, two self-governing mainland territories, and eight other territories. The six states, each with its own government, are New South Wales, Queensland, South Australia, Tasmania, Victoria, and Western Australia. The two self-governing mainland territories are the Australian Capital Territory (ACT) and the Northern Territory.

Australia is a constitutional monarchy like the United Kingdom. The British monarch is recognized as ruler of Australia but has little power. A governor general represents the monarch at the federal level, and a state governor represents the monarch at the state level.

Australia has a *parliamentary* system of government. Under this system, the national government is controlled by the political party or the *coalition* (alliance) of parties with a majority of seats in the lower house of Parliament. The leader of the majority party or coalition heads the government as prime minister.

The federal government of Australia is officially headed by the governor general. The monarch appoints the governor general on the recommendation of the Australian prime minister. The role of governor general is for the most part symbolic. In 1975, however, the governor general used his power to remove the prime minister from office. See the *History* section of this article for details.

The prime minister. The governor general appoints as prime minister the leader of the majority party or coalition in the House of Representatives. Prime ministers remain in office as long as their party has a majority in the House of Representatives, unless they retire, are replaced as party leader, or leave office. The prime minister is the chief spokesperson of the government. He or she leads the federal Cabinet, a group of senior ministers who make major decisions on government policy.

The federal Parliament has an upper house, called the Senate, and a lower house, called the House of Repre-

sentatives. Most bills are introduced in the House, but both houses must approve a bill before it becomes law. *Money bills* (bills authorizing taxation and spending) must be introduced in the House. The Senate may reject, but not amend, money bills. The Senate's main work is revising rather than initiating legislation.

The House of Representatives has 151 members. Membership in the House is divided among the states and mainland territories according to population. The representatives are elected every three years unless Parliament is dissolved before its three-year term is over.

The Senate has 76 members. Each state elects 12 senators, and each mainland territory elects 2. Elections to the Senate are held every three years, at the same time as general elections to the House. Voters elect half of the senators at each election.

All Australian citizens over the age of 18 who are eligible to vote are required to cast their ballots in federal and state elections. Those who do not vote may be fined.

The federal courts. The High Court of Australia decides constitutional questions. It also serves as the nation's court of final appeals. Other federal courts deal with bankruptcy cases, family law, industrial disputes, and violations of federal law.

State government. Each state has its own parliament, court system, head of government, and governor. The heads of state government are called *premiers.* The states' governors represent the monarch.

The federal Parliament has power to make laws on particular topics, including defense and foreign affairs, overseas trade, and finance. Each state government has the power to pass laws on most matters that apply to that state, such as police and legal services, road mainte-

© Creatas

Sydney is the largest city in Australia. Founded in 1788, it is also the country's oldest city. The sail-like Sydney Opera House, *center,* is a city landmark. Sydney lies on a huge, deep harbor, officially called Port Jackson but commonly known as Sydney Harbour.

Australia in brief

General information

Capital: Canberra.
Official language: English.
Official name: Commonwealth of Australia.
Anthems: "Advance Australia Fair" (national); "God Save the Queen" (royal).
Largest cities: (2016 census)
Sydney (4,321,535)
Melbourne (4,196,198)
Brisbane (2,054,614)
Perth (1,907,833)
Adelaide (1,165,632)

Australia's flag has a British Union flag, five stars that represent the constellation known as the Southern Cross, and a large star for the country's states and territories.

Australia's coat of arms features a kangaroo and an emu; golden wattle blossoms (the national floral emblem); a shield with the coats of arms of the six states of Australia; and a star for the states and territories.

Land and climate

Land: Australia is the only country that is also a continent. It lies between the South Pacific and Indian oceans. Australia is mostly flat, except for the Great Dividing Range in the east and several smaller mountainous regions. The major rivers include the Murray and the Darling.

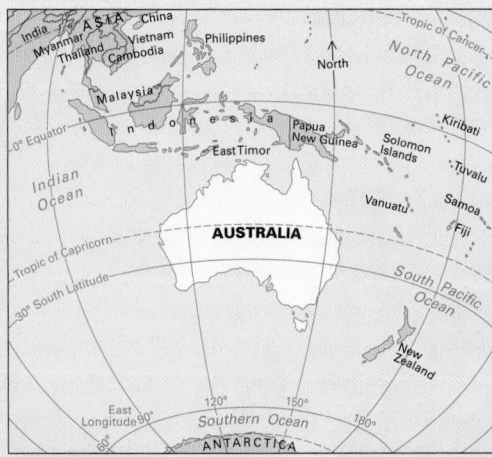

Area: 2,969,907 mi^2 (7,692,024 km^2), including 26,000 mi^2 (67,800 km^2) for Tasmania. *Greatest distances* (mainland)—east-west, 2,475 mi (3,983 km); north-south, 1,950 mi (3,138 km). *Coastline*—37,118 mi (59,736 km), including 1,760 mi (2,833 km) for Tasmania and 14,825 mi (23,859 km) for offshore islands.
Elevation: *Highest*—Mount Kosciuszko, 7,310 ft (2,228 m) above sea level. *Lowest*—Lake Eyre, 52 ft (16 m) below sea level.
Climate: The northern third of Australia lies in the tropics and is warm the year around. The rest of the country has warm summers and cool winters. About a third of the country is desert. Australia lies south of the equator, and so its seasons are opposite those in the Northern Hemisphere.

Government

Form of government: Constitutional monarchy; in practice, a parliamentary democracy.
Head of state: The United Kingdom's monarch is Australia's official head of state. A governor general, recommended by Australia's prime minister, represents the monarch.
Head of government: Prime minister, the leader of the party or coalition of parties holding a majority in the House of Representatives.
Parliament: *Senate*—76 members; *House of Representatives*—151 members.
Executive: Prime minister and Cabinet.
Political subdivisions: Six states, two self-governing mainland territories, and eight other territories.

People

Population: *Estimated 2022 population*—26,152,000. *2016 census*—23,401,892.
Population density: 9 per mi^2 (3 per km^2).
Distribution: 86 percent urban, 14 percent rural.
Major ethnic/national groups: More than 90 percent of European descent, chiefly British and Irish, but also Italian, German, Greek, and others. About 7 percent Asian. About 3 percent Aboriginal and Torres Strait Islander peoples.
Religion: About 25 percent Roman Catholic, 15 percent Anglican, and 5 percent Uniting Church in Australia, a union of Australia's Methodists and a majority of its Congregationalists and Presbyterians.

Population trend*

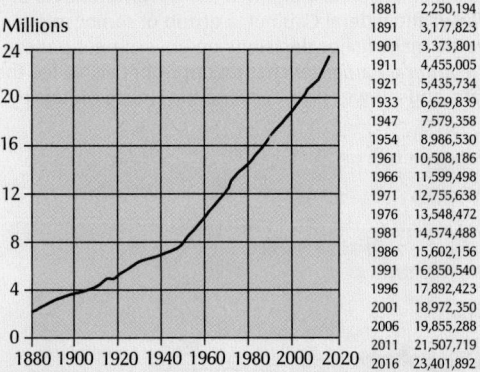

Year	Population
1881	2,250,194
1891	3,177,823
1901	3,373,801
1911	4,455,005
1921	5,435,734
1933	6,629,839
1947	7,579,358
1954	8,986,530
1961	10,508,186
1966	11,599,498
1971	12,755,638
1976	13,548,472
1981	14,574,488
1986	15,602,156
1991	16,850,540
1996	17,892,423
2001	18,972,350
2006	19,855,288
2011	21,507,719
2016	23,401,892

*Graph is based on official government estimates. Table shows census figures.

Economy

Chief products: *Agriculture*—apples, barley, beef and dairy cattle, chickens and eggs, cotton, grapes, oranges, potatoes, sheep, sugar cane, wheat, wool. *Fishing*—abalones, lobsters, oysters, sardines, tuna. *Forestry*—eucalyptus and Monterey pine. *Manufacturing*—iron, steel, and other metals; machinery; petroleum, coal and chemical products; processed foods and beverages; transportation equipment. *Mining*—bauxite, coal, copper, diamonds, gold, iron ore, lead, manganese, natural gas, nickel, opals, petroleum, silver, tin, uranium, zinc, zirconium.
Money: *Basic unit*—Australian dollar. One hundred cents equal one dollar.
International trade: *Major exports*—alumina (processed aluminum ore), beef, coal, copper, gold, iron ore, petroleum products, wheat, wool. *Major imports*—automobiles, electrical appliances, industrial machinery, petroleum products, pharmaceuticals. *Major trading partners*—China, Germany, Japan, Malaysia, New Zealand, Singapore, South Korea, Thailand, United States.

nance, and industrial and agricultural production. If a federal law conflicts with a state law, the federal law prevails, but only over the specific area of conflict.

Because the federal Parliament can impose forms of taxation that the states cannot, it has financial power over the states. Australia's federal government collects about 80 percent of all of the nation's taxes. Each state receives a share of the federal tax income, and the states depend on such federal grants for part of their annual revenue.

Local government. Victoria, Tasmania, and the more densely settled areas of the other states are divided into local government areas. *Shire* (county), city, and town councils are responsible for such services as street building, public works, and garbage collection.

Vast areas of outback Australia are thinly populated and have no local government. Community councils govern the small Aboriginal groups living in the sparsely populated interior areas of the Northern Territory.

Political parties. Australia has two main political parties—the Australian Labor Party (ALP) and the Liberal Party of Australia. The Nationals and the Australian Greens are smaller parties that regularly win seats in federal and state parliaments. The ALP promotes government action in economic and social affairs, especially to improve

National Capitol Development Commission

Parliament House in Canberra is the meeting place of the Australian Parliament. The unusual structure is set into a hill overlooking the city. The building was dedicated in 1988.

Australia map index

(Map appears on following pages.)

States and mainland territories

Map key	Name	Area In mi²	Area In km²	Population
I 13	Australian Capital Territory (Canberra)	910	2,358	397,397
I 14	Jervis Bay Territory	28	73	391
H 12	New South Wales	309,130	800,642	7,480,228
D 9	Northern Territory	520,902	1,349,129	228,833
E 12	Queensland	668,207	1,730,648	4,703,193
G 9	South Australia	379,725	983,482	1,676,653
K 12	Tasmania	26,410	68,401	509,965
I 11	Victoria	87,806	227,416	5,926,624
F 5	Western Australia	976,790	2,529,875	2,474,410

Source: Australian Bureau of Statistics, 2016 census.

External territories*

Name	Area In mi²	Area In km²	Population
Ashmore and Cartier Islands	77	199	0
Australian Antarctic Territory†	2,362,875	6,119,818	0
Christmas Island	52	135	1,843
Cocos (Keeling) Islands	5	13	544
Coral Sea Islands Territory	‡	‡	0
Heard and McDonald Islands	183	474	0
Norfolk Island	14	36	§1,748

*Not shown on map.
†Claimed by Australia.
‡400,000 square miles (1,035,995 square kilometers), including about 1 square mile (3 square kilometers) of land.
§*World Book* estimate.

Cities and towns*

Adelaide.....1,165,632
  ‡1,295,714 ..H 10
Albany...........29,373 ..I 5
Albury..........47,974 ..I 12
Alice Springs ..23,726 ..E 9
Ararat...........6,925 ..I 11
Armidale ....20,386 ..G 13
Atherton.........6,871 ..C 12
Ayr..............8,281 ..D 13
Bacchus
  Marsh†....17,302 ..I 11
Bairnsdale†...12,952 ..J 12
Ballarat........93,759 ..I 11
Ballina.........16,506 ..G 14
Batemans Bay ..11,294 ..I 13
Bathurst........33,587 ..H 13
Benalla†.........9,298 ..I 12
Bendigo........92,379 ..I 11
Biloela..........5,727 ..F 14
Blue
  Mountains†..29,319 ..H 13
Bourke...........1,824 ..G 12
Bowen...........8,854 ..D 13
Brisbane.....2,054,614
  ‡2,270,800 ..G 14
Broken Hill....17,589 ..H 11
Bunbury........71,090 ..H 4
Bundaberg.....50,148 ..F 14
Burnie
  [-Somerset]...19,385 ..K 12
Busselton......25,329 ..H 4
Cairns........144,730 ..C 12
Caloundra§.....80,512 ..F 14
Campbell-
  town§.......158,401 ..H 13
Canberra....395,790 ..I 13
Carnarvon......4,426 ..F 3

Casino...........9,982 ..G 14
Cessnock.......21,725 ..H 13
Charters
  Towers........8,120 ..D 12
Clare............3,327 ..H 10
Cobar............3,748 ..H 12
Coffs Harbour ..48,225 ..G 14
Colac†..........11,891 ..J 11
Collie...........7,192 ..H 4
Coonat...........6,379 ..I 13
Cootamundra....5,669 ..I 12
Cowra...........8,225 ..H 13
Crystal Brook...1,324 ..H 10
Cunnamulla......1,022 ..F 12
Dalby..........12,005 ..F 14
Dampier.........1,104 ..D 4
Darwin 118,456
  ‡136,828 ..A 8
Deniliquin......6,833 ..I 12
Derby...........3,325 ..C 6
Dubbo..........34,339 ..H 13
Echuca.........12,906 ..I 11
Elizabeth§.....10,376 ..H 10
Emerald........13,532 ..E 13
Esperance......10,421 ..H 6
Exmouth.........2,486 ..E 3
Forbes..........7,035 ..H 12
Fremantle§.....36,605 ..H 4
Gawler.........26,472 ..H 10
Geelong.......157,104 ..J 11
George Town.....4,257 ..K 12
Geraldton......31,982 ..G 3
Gladstone......33,418 ..E 14
Glen Innes......5,161 ..G 14
Gold Coast....540,559 ..G 14
Goondiwindi.....5,527 ..G 13
Gordonvale......5,974 ..C 12

Gosford§.....169,053 ..H 13
Goulburn.......22,419 ..I 13
Grafton........16,787 ..G 14
Griffith........18,874 ..H 12
Gunnedah.......7,984 ..G 13
Gympie.........18,267 ..F 14
Hamilton........8,888 ..I 11
Hervey Bay.....52,073 ..F 14
Hobart........178,009
  ‡222,356 ..K 12
Horsham........15,627 ..I 11
Innisfail........7,236 ..C 12
Inverell.........9,547 ..G 13
Ipswich§......193,733 ..G 14
Kalgoorlie
  [-Boulder]...29,875 ..G 5
Karratha.......15,828 ..D 4
Katherine.......6,303 ..B 8
Kempsey........10,648 ..H 14
Kiamat.........13,453 ..I 13
Kingaroy.......10,066 ..F 14
Kwinana§.......38,918 ..H 4
Launceston.....75,329 ..K 12
Leeton..........6,931 ..H 12
Lismore........27,569 ..G 14
Lithgow........11,530 ..H 13
Mackay.........75,710 ..D 13
Maitland.......78,015 ..H 14
Mandurah§.....96,736 ..H 4
Mareeba.........7,741 ..C 12
Maryborough ..22,206 ..F 14
Melbourne ..4,196,198
  ‡4,485,211 ..I 12
Mildura........33,444 ..H 11
Millicent........4,734 ..I 10
Moe-New-
  borough.....15,059 ..J 12

Moree...........7,383 ..G 13
Morwell........13,540 ..J 12
Mount
  Gambier.....26,148 ..I 10
Mount Isa......18,342 ..D 10
Mudgee.........10,966 ..H 13
Murray Bridge ..16,804 ..I 10
Muswellbrook. .10,404 ..H 13
Nambour.......18,181 ..F 14
Naracoorte......5,074 ..I 10
Narrabri.........5,903 ..G 13
Narrogin........4,274 ..H 4
New Norfolk.....5,834 ..K 12
Newcastle ....322,278 ..H 13
Northam........6,548 ..H 4
Nowra-
  Bomaderry ..30,853 ..I 13
Nyngan.........1,988 ..H 12
Orbost..........2,014 ..J 13
Paraburdoo.....1,359 ..E 4
Parkes..........9,964 ..H 12
Penrith§......139,692 ..H 13
Perth.......1,907,833
  ‡1,943,858 ..H 4
Pinjarra.........3,896 ..H 4
Port Augusta ..12,896 ..H 10
Port Hedland ..13,828 ..D 4
Port Lincoln ...14,064 ..H 9
Port
  Macquarie...44,814 ..H 14
Port Pirie.....13,740 ..H 10
Portland.......10,061 ..J 11
Queanbeyan† ..36,348 ..I 13
Quorn..........1,131 ..H 10
Rockhampton ..61,214 ..E 14
Rockingham§..125,114 ..H 4
Roma...........6,848 ..F 13

Sale†..........13,511 ..J 12
Salisbury§.....136,635 ..H 10
Shell-
  harbour†§....68,460 ..I 13
Shepparton§....63,649 ..I 12
Singleton†.....13,214 ..H 14
Stawell..........5,520 ..I 11
Sunbury†.......34,425 ..I 12
Swan Hill.......10,600 ..I 11
Sydney 4,321,535
  ‡4,823,991 ..H 13
Tamworth ......33,885 ..H 13
Taree..........18,117 ..H 14
Tenterfield......2,914 ..G 14
Tom Price......2,956 ..E 4
Toowoomba...100,032 ..F 14
Townsville....168,729 ..D 13
Traralgont......25,485 ..J 12
Tumut..........6,154 ..I 12
Tweed Heads...59,776 ..G 14
Wagga-
  Wagga.......48,263 ..I 12
Wagin..........1,358 ..H 4
Walgett.........1,546 ..G 13
Wangaratta....18,566 ..I 12
Warrnam-
  bool.........30,709 ..J 11
Warwick........13,862 ..G 14
Wellington† .....4,519 ..H 13
Wentworth†.....1,221 ..H 14
Weston
  Creek†§......22,988 ..H 13
Whyalla........21,501 ..H 10
Wodonga.......35,130 ..I 12
Wollongong§..128,301 ..I 13
Yeppoon........16,350 ..E 14
Young ....7,170 ..H 12

*Populations not labeled § are for urban centers. The Australian government does not report the populations for individual cities and towns.
†Does not appear on map; key shows general location.
‡Population of metropolitan area, including suburbs.
§Population of statistical area.
Source: Australian Bureau of Statistics, 2016 census.

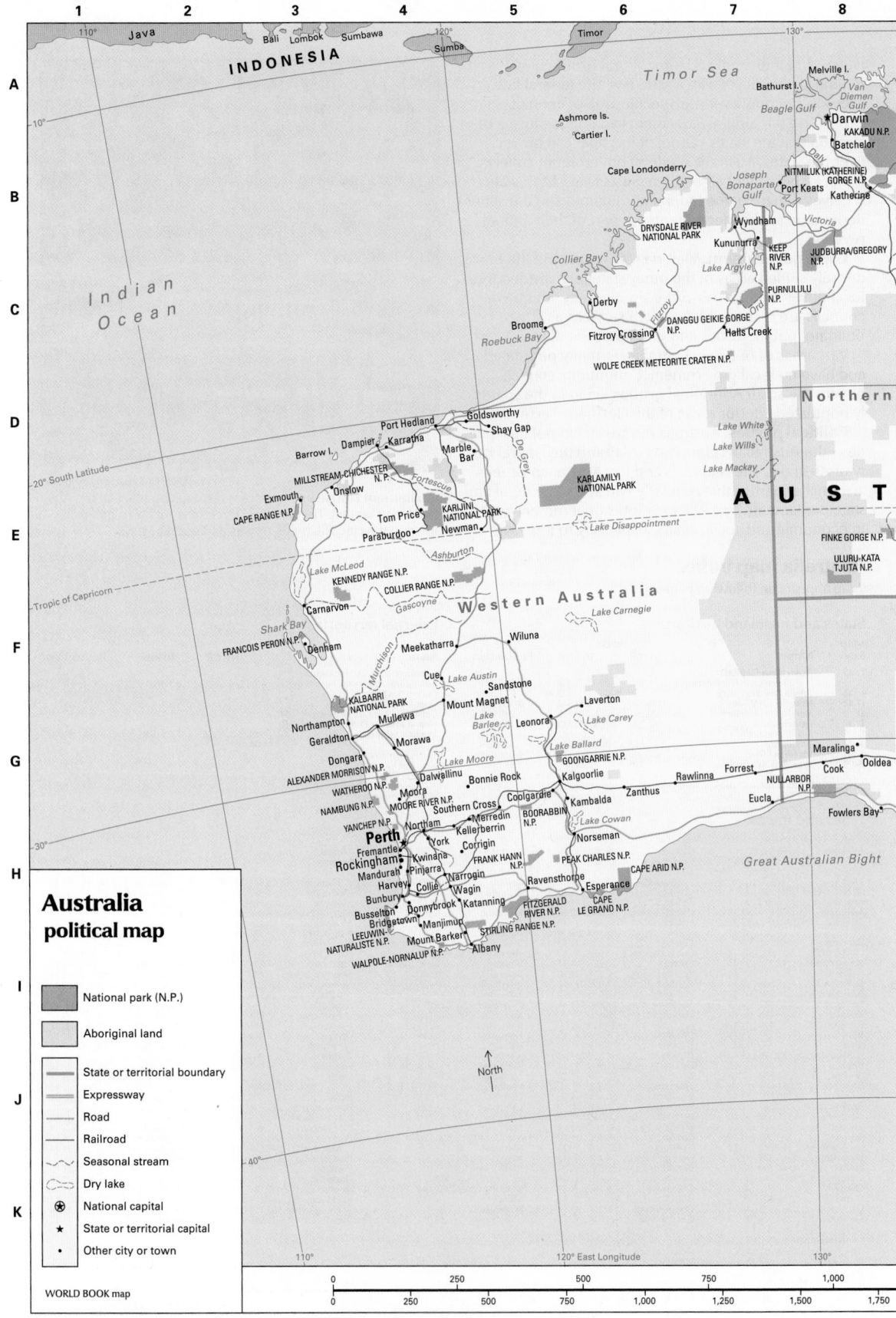

Australia
political map

| National park (N.P.) |
| Aboriginal land |
| State or territorial boundary |
| Expressway |
| Road |
| Railroad |
| Seasonal stream |
| Dry lake |
| ⊛ National capital |
| ★ State or territorial capital |
| • Other city or town |

WORLD BOOK map

North

0   250   500   750   1,000
0   250   500   750   1,000   1,250   1,500   1,750

1   2   3   4   5   6   7   8

A B C D E F G H I J K

INDONESIA
Java   Bali   Lombok   Sumbawa   Timor
Sumba

Timor Sea

Melville I.
Bathurst I.   Van Diemen Gulf
Beagle Gulf   ★Darwin   KAKADU N.P.
Batchelor

Ashmore Is.
ºCartier I.

Cape Londonderry   Joseph Bonaparte Gulf   NITMILUK (KATHERINE) GORGE N.P.
Port Keats   Katherine

DRYSDALE RIVER NATIONAL PARK   Wyndham   Victoria
Kununurra   KEEP RIVER N.P.
JUDBURRA/GREGORY N.P.
Lake Argyle

Collier Bay   PURNULULU N.P.
Derby   DANGGU GEIKIE GORGE N.P.
Broome   Fitzroy Crossing   Halls Creek
Roebuck Bay
WOLFE CREEK METEORITE CRATER N.P.

Northern

Indian Ocean

Port Hedland   Goldsworthy
Barrow I.   Dampier   Karratha   Shay Gap   Lake White
MILLSTREAM-CHICHESTER N.P.   Marble Bar   De Grey   Lake Wills
Exmouth   Onslow   Lake Mackay
CAPE RANGE N.P.   Fortescue   KARLAMILYI NATIONAL PARK
Tom Price   KARIJINI NATIONAL PARK   AUST
Paraburdoo   Newman
Lake Disappointment   FINKE GORGE N.P.
ULURU-KATA TJUTA N.P.

Lake McLeod   Ashburton
KENNEDY RANGE N.P.
COLLIER RANGE N.P.
Carnarvon   Gascoyne   Western Australia   Lake Carnegie
Shark Bay
FRANCOIS PERON N.P.   Denham   Murchison   Meekatharra   Wiluna
Cue   Lake Austin
Sandstone
KALBARRI NATIONAL PARK   Mount Magnet   Laverton
Northampton   Mullewa   Leonora   Lake Carey
Geraldton   Morawa   Lake Barlee   Lake Ballard
Dongara   Lake Moore   GOONGARRIE N.P.   Maralinga
ALEXANDER MORRISON N.P.   Dalwallinu   Bonnie Rock   Kalgoorlie   Rawlinna   Forrest   Cook   Ooldea
WATHEROO N.P.   Moora   Kambalda   NULLARBOR N.P.
NAMBUNG N.P.   MOORE RIVER N.P.   Southern Cross   Coolgardie   Zanthus   Eucla   Fowlers Bay
YANCHEP N.P.   Northam   Merredin   BOORABBIN N.P.   Norseman
Perth   York   Kellerberrin   Lake Cowan
Fremantle   Kwinana   Corrigin   PEAK CHARLES N.P.   Great Australian Bight
Rockingham   Pinjarra   Narrogin   FRANK HANN N.P.
Mandurah   Wagin   Ravensthorpe   CAPE ARID N.P.
Harvey   Collie   Esperance
Bunbury   Narrogin   CAPE LE GRAND N.P.
Busselton   Donnybrook   Katanning   FITZGERALD RIVER N.P.
Bridgetown   Manjimup   STIRLING RANGE N.P.
LEEUWIN-NATURALISTE N.P.   Mount Barker   Albany
WALPOLE-NORNALUP N.P.

110°   120° East Longitude   130°

10°
20° South Latitude
Tropic of Capricorn
30°
40°

120°   130°

working conditions. Many ALP members belong to labor unions. The Liberal Party favors the free enterprise system with little government interference. Many merchants and business executives support the Liberals. The Nationals represent the interests of farmers and other rural Australians. In Parliament, the Liberal Party and the Nationals often form a coalition in opposition to the ALP. The Greens favor protection of the environment and progressive social policies.

The armed forces of Australia are called the Australian Defence Force (ADF). They consist of the Australian Army, the Royal Australian Navy, and the Royal Australian Air Force. All military service is voluntary. About 51,000 men and women serve in the ADF full-time, and about 21,000 serve as reservists.

People

Population and ancestry. Approximately 80 percent of Australia's people live in the southeastern quarter of the country, mainly in large coastal cities. Australia's three largest cities—Sydney, Melbourne, and Brisbane—lie on the east coast. Most of the rest of the people live along the northeast and extreme southwest coasts. Canberra is the largest inland city, about 80 miles (130 kilometers) from the coasts.

Most Australians are European immigrants or descendants of European immigrants. About 30 percent of all Australians were born in other countries. Australia has admitted about 7 million immigrants since World War II ended in 1945. Many have come from the United Kingdom and Ireland. Most of the rest of the immigrants have come from mainland Europe. Immigration from Asia has greatly increased since the 1970's, and European migration has declined. During the late 1900's and early 2000's, the number of immigrants from New Zealand and Southeast Asia increased rapidly. Indigenous people make up about 3 percent of the population.

Language. English is the official language of Australia. However, about 25 percent of the people speak a language other than English at home. The most common languages after English are Chinese, Arabic, Vietnamese, and Italian.

Australians have an accent that is different from accents in other English-speaking countries. Australian English differs from British English in certain ways. The British who colonized Australia had to develop a vocabulary to describe the many unfamiliar animals and plants they found. In some cases, they used existing English words. For example, they gave the name *magpie* to a bird that resembles the British magpie but is unrelated to any bird in the United Kingdom. The British also borrowed Aboriginal words, such as *kangaroo* and *koala.*

Australian English has also produced many colorful figures of speech. For example, a brave person is said to be "as game as Ned Kelly." Ned Kelly was a famous Australian outlaw of the 1870's. "Waltzing Matilda," the title of Australia's most famous song, refers neither to a dance nor to a woman. A *matilda* is a blanket roll. "To waltz matilda" means "to tramp the roads."

The Indigenous peoples of Australia include the Aboriginal peoples and the Torres Strait Islander peoples. Each is a collection of many *peoples* (groups). Indigenous people were the first inhabitants of Australia. Most were displaced after Europeans arrived. The majority of them now live in cities and towns. Today, they are also called First Australians or First Nations peoples.

Where the people of Australia live

This map shows how Australia's population is distributed. Most of the people live along the southeast, northeast, and extreme southwest coasts. The vast, dry interior of the country has few settlements.

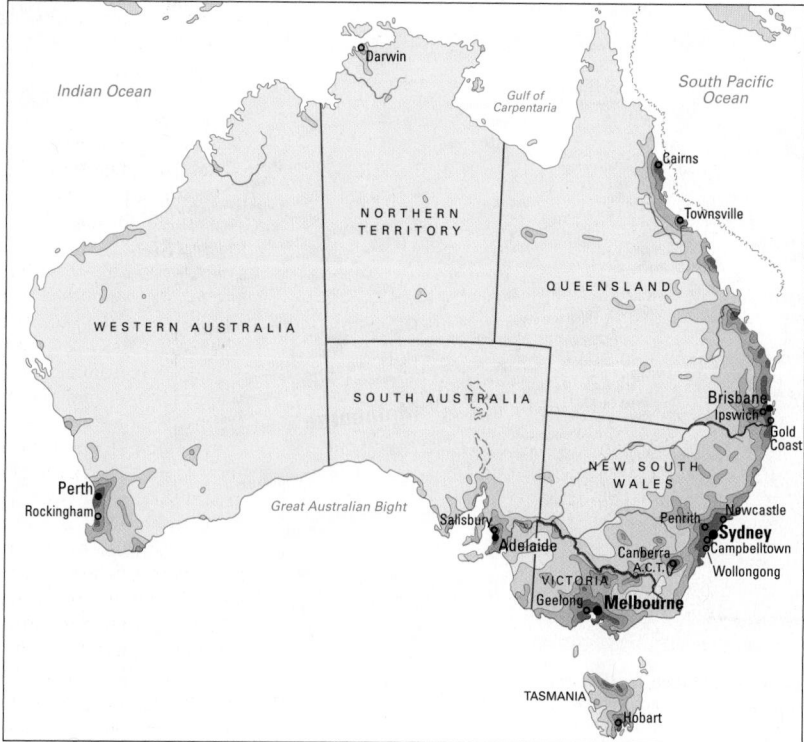

Major urban centers

● More than 3 million inhabitants

• 500,000 to 3 million inhabitants

○ Less than 500,000 inhabitants

Persons per mi²	Persons per km²
More than 15	More than 6
10 to 15	4 to 6
5 to 10	2 to 4
2 to 5	1 to 2
Less than 2	Less than 1

Since the late 1900's, some Aboriginal people in central and northern Australia have stayed on or returned to their ancestral lands. There, they often live in communities that seek to preserve some traditional ways of life, especially languages, religious beliefs, and styles of painting and craftwork. City and outback communities also nurture new areas of Aboriginal culture. Contemporary styles of Aboriginal painting and music, such as the rock group Yothu Yindi, have flourished. Contemporary Aboriginal painting is now one of the most important and internationally recognized forms of Australian art.

For more information, see the *History* section of this article and the article **Aboriginal peoples of Australia**.

Ways of life

Lifestyles in rural Australia are different from those in the cities. Many rural regions are poorer than city areas. The rural areas have higher levels of unemployment, less access to cultural and educational institutions, and fewer government or commercial services. Rural and urban voting patterns in elections differ as well. Rural voters support conservative candidates more often.

City life. About 86 of every 100 Australians live in cities and towns, making Australia one of the world's most urbanized countries. About three-fourths of all Australians live in cities of more than 100,000 people. These cities include the federal capital, Canberra, and the six state capitals. The state capitals, in order of size, are Sydney, New South Wales; Melbourne, Victoria; Brisbane, Queensland; Perth, Western Australia; Adelaide, South Australia; and Hobart, Tasmania. Canberra is smaller than all the state capitals except Hobart.

Each of Australia's state capitals serves as the political, commercial, industrial, and cultural hub of its state. The main business district of each state capital is its oldest section, the area nearest the waterfront. In the largest cities, modern structures, including high-rise office buildings, have replaced most of the original buildings in this section. In addition to office buildings, the city-center areas have fine shops, theaters, and restaurants.

Most city dwellers in Australia live in the suburbs, which have their own schools, shopping centers, and recreational facilities. Some suburbs, especially those around Sydney and Melbourne, also have industrial districts. Since the late 1900's, developers have built new high-rise apartment buildings in the central areas of the large cities. Older buildings, such as factories and warehouses, have been converted to modern apartments.

Most families live in single-story houses, each with its own garden. About three-fourths of families own their houses. There are differences in the older style of housing in the different cities. In Queensland, the older houses are made of wood, have *verandas* (wide porches), and are built above the ground on poles called *stumps.* In Melbourne and Sydney, many of the older houses are made of brick or stone and built in rows called *terraces.*

Australia's cities have problems common to big cities everywhere, including air pollution and rush-hour traffic jams. Before the 1950's, the *inner suburbs,* those closest to the city, were the poorest residential areas. These areas had high rates of unemployment and crime. But during the 1950's, many non-British immigrants began settling in the inner suburbs and helped to regenerate them. Now many middle-class and wealthy residents

© Robert Frerck

A street scene in Perth reflects the strongly European ancestry of the Australian people. The great majority of Australians are descendants of British or Irish immigrants.

© Walter Bibikow, Viesti Associates

Salamanca Place, on Hobart's waterfront, draws crowds to its outdoor market each weekend. Tasmania's scenic variety and historic sites attract many tourists.

Housing in Australia varies from city to city. Most families live in single-story dwellings, such as these in Port Macquarie, New South Wales. Each house typically has its own garden.

Rural communities in Australia serve mainly as marketing and shopping centers for farmers. This community, Tanunda, lies in a grape-growing and winemaking region northeast of Adelaide in South Australia.

have moved to these areas, and many poorer families live in the outer suburbs.

Country life. Only about 14 of every 100 Australians live in rural areas. Australians call the remote countryside *the bush.* The term *outback* refers to the interior. The outback consists mainly of open countryside and vast expanses of grazing land. Most of its few, widely scattered settlements are mining towns.

Nearly all farms in the outback are wheat farms or cattle and sheep *stations* (farms or ranches). Life on the stations tends to be extremely isolated. The largest stations cover over 1,000 square miles (2,600 square kilometers) and so may be 100 miles (160 kilometers) or more from the nearest town. The outback has few paved roads, and so travel by automobile is difficult or impossible. Many prosperous farm families have a light airplane, which they use for transportation to and from town. Families who do not own a plane may get to town only a few times a year. In farming regions nearer the coasts, the towns are larger and closer together. But even there, farm families may feel far from the life of the cities.

Rural Australians' sense of community is reflected in the fact that they have long had their own political party, the National Party. Many rural communities in Australia

have their own traditional *shows* (fairs), festivals, and sports competitions.

Poverty is a problem in some rural areas due to the lack of local employment. However, most farm families own their farms and live comfortably. Older farmhouses are built of wood and surrounded by a veranda. Newer farmhouses are constructed of bricks. Nearly all the houses have electric power, and a growing number of them have air conditioning.

All rural areas in Australia have such natural disasters as droughts, floods, and bushfires. Fires can even come close to the major cities in such areas as the Blue Mountains, north of Sydney, or the Dandenong Ranges, near Melbourne. In the early 2000's, fires damaged suburban neighborhoods in Sydney and Canberra.

Food and drink. Meat is plentiful in Australia and makes up a large part of the people's diet. Beef is the most popular meat, followed by poultry, pork, and lamb and mutton. British customs strongly influenced Australian food choices until the mid-1900's. Since then, European immigrants have introduced Italian, Greek, and other European styles of cooking to Australia. Australian food also shows the strong influence of Indian and Southeast Asian cooking.

Tea remains the favorite hot drink of older Australians. However, younger Australians prefer coffee. Coffee consumption has more than tripled since the mid-1900's, while tea consumption has declined. Beer is the most popular alcoholic drink. However, its consumption is declining in relation to the consumption of wine, which has increased rapidly since the 1980's. Australia is an important wine-producing country, and many Australians drink red or white wine regularly.

Recreation. Most Australians enjoy such recreation as visiting friends, going for a drive or walk, or watching television. Outdoor sports are extremely popular. Many people enjoy skin diving, surfing, swimming, or boating. Many also play golf and tennis. Team sports are a national pastime. The nation's professional sports teams have large and enthusiastic followings, and Australians often view athletes as national heroes.

The most popular team sports in Australia are cricket, Australian Rules football, Rugby League, Rugby Union, basketball, soccer, and netball. Cricket is a favorite summer sport. The Australian national cricket team regularly plays against teams from England, India, New Zealand, Pakistan, South Africa, and the Caribbean.

Australian Rules football, Rugby League, Rugby Union, and soccer are mainly winter sports. Australian Rules football was invented in Australia and is played there and in Papua New Guinea, a former Australian possession. The sport is especially popular in southern Australia. Rugby League and Rugby Union are forms of football invented in England. Australia plays Rugby League and Rugby Union chiefly against France, New Zealand, South Africa, and the United Kingdom. Soccer is the fastest-growing team sport. Australia's national soccer team plays teams from many other countries.

Netball is a goal-scoring game that is played mainly by women. It is popular in the Commonwealth countries. Australia has often been the world champion. In terms of the number of people playing the sport, netball is the most popular team sport in Australia. However, it does not attract the media attention or large crowds of Australian Rules football and cricket.

Australia has produced many world-famous athletes, especially in tennis, golf, swimming, and track and field. Australians have won numerous Olympic medals in swimming, track and field, rowing, cycling, and yachting. Australians also compete successfully in the international sport of surfing.

Australian tennis stars include Evonne Goolagong Cawley, Margaret Smith Court, Lleyton Hewitt, Rod Laver, John Newcombe, Patrick Rafter, and Ken Rosewall. Australian golf champions include Greg Norman, Peter Thomson, and Karrie Webb. Well-known Australian swimmers include Dawn Fraser, Shane Gould, Grant Hackett, Susie O'Neill, Kieren Perkins, Stephanie Rice, Murray Rose, and Ian Thorpe. Famous Australian track and field athletes include Ron Clarke, Herb Elliott, John Landy, and the Aboriginal track star Cathy Freeman.

Some of Australia's traditional sporting events receive worldwide attention. Probably the most famous event is the annual Melbourne Cup, a horse race eagerly followed by racing fans throughout the world.

Education. Each Australian state and mainland territory has its own laws concerning education. The federal government regulates education in the other territories.

© Tony Lewis, Getty Images

Australian Rules football was invented in Australia and is played mainly there and in Papua New Guinea. It is especially popular in southern Australia. This match is in Adelaide.

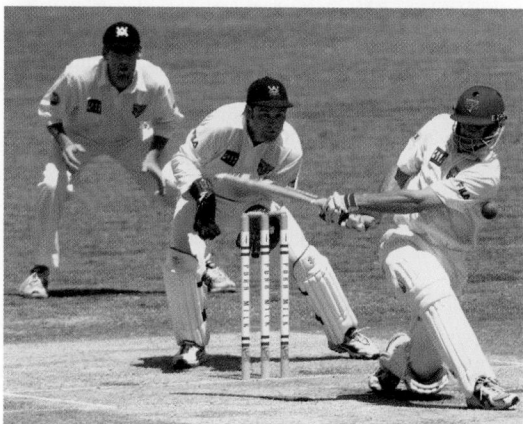

© Darren England, Getty Images

Cricket, an English game played with bats and a ball, is a favorite summer sport in Australia. Teams from each Australian state play each year in a championship series.

Children must attend school from about age 6 to age16, depending upon where they live, but those leaving school before age 17 typically must enroll in a vocational program or work full time. The majority of Australian students attend state or territory schools. Other students go to Roman Catholic schools or other independent schools.

Each Australian state operates its own state school system. However, the state systems use some funding from the federal government to support their school system. The Roman Catholic Church owns and operates most of Australia's independent schools. Unlike the state schools, most of the independent schools in Australia

Surfing, diving, swimming, and boating are some of the many outdoor sports enjoyed in Australia. Manly Beach, north of Sydney, *shown here,* is one of Australia's most popular beaches.

© Robert Francis, Alamy

charge a tuition fee. The federal government supplies funds to assist independent schools.

Australian primary schools provide six to eight years of study. Australian secondary schools offer five or six years of education. The vast majority of the students continue beyond the required years of schooling, and most of them graduate from secondary school. Most graduating students go on to a university or college.

Many Australian children in remote areas of the outback receive their primary and secondary education at home by means of traveling teachers and correspondence schools, often called *schools of the air.* Each state operates a correspondence school for children in isolated areas. The students receive and turn in their assignments by mail or through the internet.

Australia has more than 40 universities and colleges. Most of Australia's universities are publicly owned. Each university offers undergraduate and graduate studies. Australia also has several publicly owned colleges or institutes that specialize in particular areas, such as the Australian Maritime College. Students at publicly owned universities and colleges pay tuition fees that cover part of the cost of their education, and the federal government pays the rest. Tuition fees at Australia's private universities are considerably higher.

Australia has many public and school libraries. For information about Australia's libraries, see **Library** (Australia and the Far East).

Religion. The Australian Constitution forbids a state religion and guarantees religious freedom. More than half of all Australians are Christians, but many do not attend church regularly. The Anglican Church and the Roman Catholic Church have the most members.

Smaller numbers of Australians belong to the Baptist, Eastern Orthodox, Lutheran, and Uniting churches. In 1977, the Methodist Church of Australasia joined with a majority of the country's Congregationalists and Presbyterians to form the Uniting Church in Australia. The Uniting Church is now Australia's third largest religious denomination. Buddhists and Muslims each make up about 5 percent of the population. Australia has small Hindu and Jewish minorities. About 30 percent of the population claim no specific religion. The religions growing most rapidly in Australia are Buddhism, Hinduism, and Islam. The proportion of Christians is declining.

The arts

The federal government helps fund the major opera, ballet, and theater companies; the major symphony orchestras; and the motion-picture industry. It gives financial help to writers, painters, musicians, and composers.

Literature. Australia's Aboriginal and Torres Strait Islander peoples draw on a vast oral literary tradition, but no written record of their cultures existed prior to the arrival of the British. The first Europeans in Australia

© Australian Picture Library

Schools of the air help children in remote areas of Australia obtain an education at home. Teachers communicate with students using two-way radios, computers, and other equipment.

wrote extensively and often beautifully about the new environment and society. After about the 1820's, settlers began to create poetry and literature that was uniquely Australian. Poets of the time include Charles Harpur and Henry Kendall. British explorers, such as Thomas Livingston Mitchell and Charles Sturt, published their journals, which provided details of the land's interior.

The first significant novels in Australia were by British immigrants. These include *The Recollections of Geoffry Hamlyn* (1859), a romance by the novelist Henry Kingsley, and *Clara Morison* (1854), a novel by the writer, preacher, and feminist Catherine Helen Spence. One of the most important novels of the colonial period was *For the Term of His Natural Life* (1870-1872) by the novelist and journalist Marcus Clarke, based on his idea of the sufferings of convicts in Tasmania. Thomas Alexander Browne, writing under the pen name Rolf Boldrewood, wrote *Robbery Under Arms* (1882-1883), an adventure tale about a gang of *bushrangers* (outlaws in the remote countryside). The authors Ada Cambridge, Rosa Campbell Praed, and Tasma (the pen name of Jessie Couvreur) were prominent women writers of this period.

In the late 1800's, many Australian writers mythologized adventurous life in the bush. Important writers include the novelists Joseph Furphy, Henry Lawson, and Steele Rudd. Adam Lindsay, Breaker Morant, Will Ogilvie, and Banjo Paterson represented the bush tradition in poetry. Paterson's ballad "The Man from Snowy River" is one of Australia's most famous and best-loved poems.

Novelists of the early 1900's told stories of the past and celebrated the achievements of the explorers and pioneers who opened up the land. Important writers in this period include the novelists and short-story writers Frank Dalby Davison, Miles Franklin, and Vance Palmer, and the Australian author Katharine Susannah Prichard.

In the 1930's, more complex novels began to emerge in Australian literature. Christina Stead, one of the greatest Australian novelists, wrote *Seven Poor Men of Sydney* (1934), which describes radical workers and their struggle to live in Sydney, and *The Man Who Loved Children* (1940), about a demanding, tyrannical father.

The most important literary figure of the mid-1900's in Australia was Patrick White, a novelist who received the Nobel Prize in literature in 1973. His major novels include *The Tree of Man* (1955) and *Voss* (1957). Australian drama from this period includes Ray Lawler's *Summer of the Seventeenth Doll* (1955) and Alan Seymour's *The One Day of the Year* (1961).

Recent novelists have been highly successful internationally. Thomas Keneally explores themes of goodness, guilt, and sin. His most famous work is *Schindler's Ark* (1982; U.S. title *Schindler's List*). The novelist and short-story writer Thea Astley creates sharp, humorous portraits of small-town life. The Booker Prize-winning author Peter Carey's novels include *Oscar and Lucinda* (1988) and *True History of the Kelly Gang* (2001). Richard Flanagan received a Booker for *Narrow Road to the Deep North* (2014). Important women writers of the late 1900's and early 2000's include Jessica Anderson, Helen Garner, Kate Grenville, Barbara Hanrahan, and Elizabeth Jolley. Playwright David Williamson has dominated Australian drama since the early 1970's with entertaining satires of Australian life and manners. Important nonfiction authors include the feminist Germaine Greer and the Aboriginal author Sally Morgan, who tells in *My Place* (1987) of coming to terms with her Aboriginal heritage.

Painting. Aboriginal rock art is one of the world's oldest continuous art traditions, dating back at least 40,000 years. Archaeologists believe Aboriginal people may have been painting earlier. Aboriginal people also painted elaborate designs of people and animals on bark. In the late 1930's, some Aboriginal artists in central Australia developed a style of water-color landscape painting. The best-known of them was Albert Namatjira.

The first works by European painters in Australia recorded scientific and geographical information, beginning with the voyage led by the British navigator James Cook in 1768. Early artists provided colonists in Australia

© Shutterstock

Aboriginal art, such as this painting on bark, often depicted human and animal figures and geometric patterns.

National Gallery of Australia

The National Gallery of Australia in Canberra exhibits a variety of artworks, including Australian paintings and sculpture from the 1900's, *shown here.*

with portraits and landscapes to send to Britain.

In the 1880's, a group of Australian artists began to paint in the Impressionist style, showing the ever-changing effects of nature. They are often referred to as the Heidelberg School, after Heidelberg, a suburban village near Melbourne where they worked. Leaders of this school included Charles Conder, Frederick McCubbin, Tom Roberts, Clara Southern, and Arthur Streeton.

During the 1900's, a number of Australian painters developed unique styles. The portrait painter William Dobell became famous for his revealing character studies. Russell Drysdale became known for his haunting pictures of the outback. Sidney Nolan created fantastic, dreamlike paintings based on themes from Australian folklore. During the middle and late 1900's, paintings of the outback by Frederick Williams won admiration. Such painters as Margaret Preston and Grace Cossington Smith pioneered modern art in Australia.

The National Gallery of Australia in Canberra houses the country's national art collection. The National Gallery of Victoria, in Melbourne, and the Art Gallery of New South Wales, in Sydney, also have major collections of artworks.

Music and dance. Australia has a national opera company, Opera Australia, and a national ballet company, the Australian Ballet. State companies, such as the Sydney Dance Company and Opera Queensland, are well known. Each state capital has a professional symphony orchestra. A number of world-famous singers and composers were born in Australia. They include opera singers Marjorie Lawrence, Dame Nellie Melba, and Dame Joan Sutherland and composers Percy Grainger and Peter Sculthorpe. Modern composer Richard Meale is known for his stage and instrumental works, including the opera *Voss* (1986).

Theater and motion pictures. Each of Australia's state capitals has a permanent company of professional actors and actresses. Each company offers a yearlong season of classical and modern plays.

My Brilliant Career, a 1979 film based on a 1901 novel by Miles Franklin, showed the frustrations of youth in the outback of New South Wales. It starred Judy Davis and Sam Neill, *shown here.*

Australia was one of the first countries to develop a motion-picture industry. Australian filmmakers produced their first feature film in 1901. The Australian film industry nearly died out after the late 1930's because of competition from American and British movies. But Australian filmmaking revived during the late 1960's. Today, Australian film and television production are high-profile export industries. Such motion-picture stars as Cate Blanchett, Russell Crowe, Mel Gibson, and Nicole Kidman have gained international acclaim for their work. The diverse films of directors Bruce Beresford, Baz Luhrmann, George Miller, and Peter Weir show the growing importance and creativity of the Australian filmmaking industry.

Architecture. During the 1800's, many public buildings and private houses in Australia were built in the Georgian or Victorian style of architecture. Both these styles originated in England. The Georgian style featured a simple square or rectangular design and classical ornaments, especially columns. The Australian version of the Georgian style introduced the veranda as a basic element of the country's architecture. Most Victorian buildings had an irregular shape and elaborate ornaments, such as spires and pointed domes. The railings and roof supports for Victorian verandas were made of showy iron grillwork. Australia has a state-supported movement to preserve historic buildings.

Today, Australia's architecture is international in style. The large cities have towering structures of concrete, steel, and glass similar to those in other countries. However, some modern Australian architecture is highly unusual. The Sydney Opera House, a spectacular structure with saillike roofs, has attracted worldwide attention since its completion in 1973. It was designed by the Danish architect Jørn Utzon.

Aboriginal artists perform traditional dance and musical pieces. The seated musician is playing the *didgeridoo,* a musical instrument made from hollowed-out pieces of wood.

The Eastern Highlands extend in a narrow band along Australia's east coast. They are sometimes called the Great Dividing Range because their slopes divide the flow of rivers in the region. The highlands are the most fertile land region in Australia.

The land

Australia is surrounded by water, like an island. But geographers class it as a continent rather than as an island because of its great size. It is sometimes referred to as an "island continent."

Australia covers about 5 percent of Earth's land area. The island of Tasmania, which lies about 130 miles (209 kilometers) south of the Australian mainland, is considered part of the continent. Tasmania was part of the mainland until the ocean rose over a period of several thousand years at the end of the last ice age. Tasmania became a separate island about 12,000 years ago.

Most of Australia is low and flat. The highest and most mountainous land lies along the east coast. Nearly all the land west of this region—about 90 percent of the total land area—consists of level plains and plateaus.

Land regions. Australia can be divided into three major land regions. They are, from east to west: (1) the Eastern Highlands, (2) the Central Lowlands, and (3) the Western Plateau.

The Eastern Highlands include the highest elevations in Australia. The region extends from Cape York Peninsula in extreme northeastern Australia to the south coast of Tasmania. A low plain bordered by sandy beaches and rocky cliffs stretches along the Pacific coast. This coastal plain is the rainiest area in the country. The southeastern section of the plain, from Brisbane to Melbourne, is the most heavily populated part of Australia.

The Eastern Highlands are sometimes called the *Great Dividing Range* because their slopes divide the flow of the rivers in the region. Rivers that flow down the eastern slopes empty into the ocean. Rivers that run down the western slopes flow to the Central Lowlands. However, the highlands are not a single range, nor are they especially mountainous. They consist mainly of high plateaus that are broken in many places by gorges, hills, and low mountain ranges.

Many of the plateaus in the Eastern Highlands have fertile soils and are used as cropland. Grass or forests cover other plateaus. At one time, forests also covered much of the coastal plain. Except in the far north, however, people have cleared most of the coastal forests.

The Central Lowlands have the lowest elevations in Australia. The region is generally flat. Many rivers flow through the lowlands after heavy rains. Rains are infrequent, however, except along the region's north and south coasts and near the Eastern Highlands. Riverbeds farther inland are dry most of the year.

Farmers in the southern part of the Central Lowlands grow wheat. Most of the rest of the region is too dry or hot for most crops and is used to graze livestock. The west-central part of the region is a barren, sandy desert. Lake Eyre, Australia's lowest point, is 52 feet (16 meters) below sea level along the southern edge of this desert.

The region has no large cities. The two biggest cities—Mount Isa and Broken Hill—have fewer than 30,000 people each. Both cities are mining centers.

The Western Plateau covers the western two-thirds of Australia. The region has a higher average elevation than the Central Lowlands but is mostly flat.

Deserts cover the central part of the Western Plateau. Except in the south and northeast, the deserts gradually give way to land covered by grass and shrubs. Farmers use much of this land to graze livestock. Low mountain ranges rise above the plateau in the grazing areas. Rainfall is heaviest in the extreme north and southwest. These areas have most of the region's cropland. A vast, dry, treeless plateau called the Nullarbor Plain extends about 400 miles (640 kilometers) along the southern edge of the region. The name *Nullarbor* comes from the Latin words *nulla* and *arbor,* which mean *no tree.*

The Western Plateau region has two large cities, Adelaide and Perth. Both cities lie on coastal plains, Adelaide in the extreme southeastern part of the region and Perth in the extreme southwest.

Australia terrain map

Land region boundary
State boundary
+ Elevation above sea level
• City

WORLD BOOK map

Physical features

Mountains. Australia's highest mountains rise in the Australian Alps in the southern part of the Eastern Highlands. The Australian Alps consist of several ranges. The Snowy Mountains are the best known. Australia's highest peak, Mount Kosciuszko, rises 7,310 feet (2,228 meters) above sea level in the Snowy Mountains. Mount Kosciuszko and other tall peaks in the Australian Alps are snow covered in winter and attract many skiers.

The ranges in the Western Plateau are lower than those in the Australian Alps. The highest peaks are in the MacDonnell and Musgrave ranges in central Australia. Uluru (also known as Ayers Rock) is a huge loaf-shaped formation just south of the MacDonnell Ranges in Uluru-Kata Tjuta National Park. It is a popular tourist attraction and a sacred area for Aboriginal peoples.

Deserts cover about one-third of Australia. The country has four major deserts. The Simpson Desert lies along the western edge of the Central Lowlands. The three other deserts—the Gibson, Great Sandy, and Great Victoria deserts—cover the central part of the Western Plateau. All the deserts except the Gibson consist of swirling sands that often drift into giant dunes. Some dunes measure more than 200 miles (320 kilometers) long. The Gibson Desert lies outside the path of the general wind direction and of wind-blown sands. Its surface consists of a mass of small stones and pebbles.

Rivers are one of Australia's most vital resources. Rivers provide the towns and cities with drinking water and supply farmers with much-needed water for irrigation. However, many of Australia's rivers are dry at least part of the year. They fill with water only during the rainy season. Dams and reservoirs on all the largest rivers store water for use during the dry season.

The Murray River is Australia's longest permanently flowing river. The Murray starts in the Snowy Mountains in New South Wales and winds west 1,609 miles (2,589 kilometers). Its mouth lies southeast of Adelaide in South Australia. However, drought and irrigation demands have at times caused the mouth of the river to dry up. During the southern dry season, the Murray is fed by the country's longest river, the Darling. The Darling River begins in the central part of the Eastern Highlands and flows southwest 1,702 miles (2,739 kilometers) to the Murray. The Darling is dry along most of its course in the winter. Its flow increases in summer, when parts of the Eastern Highlands receive most of their rain.

Australia's biggest water conservation project is the Snowy Mountains Scheme. It consists of an extensive system of dams, aqueducts, and tunnels. Some carry water from melting snows in the Snowy Mountains to nearby dams that store the water. Other aqueducts and tunnels channel water from the dams into the Murray and Murrumbidgee rivers. The increased water in these rivers is used to irrigate cropland in New South Wales and Victoria. This irrigation is crucial to agriculture in many parts of Australia. But it has also caused serious problems of *salinization* (accumulation of salt in the soil). The salts in the soil have been brought to the surface by the water, making the land unsuitable for crops.

Hydroelectric plants at the dams supply New South Wales, Victoria, and the Capital Territory with a little of their electric power. Tasmania draws almost all of its electric power from hydroelectric facilities.

Lakes. Australia's only large permanent lakes have been artificially created. They include Lake Argyle in

© Minden Pictures, Super Stock

Irrigation projects have greatly increased farm productivity in Australia. The irrigated farmlands shown above are in the Murray River irrigation area.

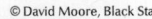

© David Moore, Black Star

Dry grazing land covers much of Australia west of the Eastern Highlands. This sheep-grazing area in South Australia is part of the Western Plateau land region.

Uluru (also called Ayers Rock), a popular tourist attraction, stands in Uluru-Kata Tjuta National Park in central Australia. The rock is about 1 ½ miles (2.4 kilometers) long. It rises 1,142 feet (348 meters) above the desert floor and 2,844 feet (867 meters) above sea level. It has many small caves. The walls of many caves are covered with rock paintings made long ago by Aboriginal artists.

© Australian Picture Library from Corbis

Western Australia and Lake Gordon in Tasmania. Both are reservoirs for water conservation projects.

Most of Australia's natural lakes are dry for months or years at a time. Dry lakes called *playas* are common in South Australia and Western Australia. Most of the time, a playa is simply a dry bed of salt or clay. It fills with water only after heavy rains. The largest playas are in South Australia. They include Lake Eyre, Lake Torrens, Lake Gairdner, and Lake Frome.

Underground water. Australia has fairly plentiful underground water. But most of it is too salty for people to drink or use as irrigation water. In many areas, however, the water is not too salty for livestock to drink. On many large cattle and sheep stations, underground wells supply all the drinking water for the animals.

Much of Australia's underground water is *artesian water*. Artesian water is trapped under such great pressure that it gushes to the surface through any opening. The

water can thus be brought to the surface merely by digging a well. It does not have to be pumped.

Australia's chief source of artesian water is a vast underground rock formation called the Great Artesian Basin. The basin extends across much of eastern Australia. Other artesian basins lie near the northwest, west, and south coasts. Most of the water in the Great Artesian Basin is quite salty and so can be drunk only by livestock. In general, the water in the coastal basins has less salt. Farmers use some of this water for irrigation. Adelaide, Perth, and many small communities get some drinking water from coastal basins.

The Great Barrier Reef is the world's largest coral reef and one of Australia's most popular tourist attractions. Although its name suggests one reef, the Great Barrier Reef is a chain of thousands of individual reefs. The reefs and islands extend in a nearly unbroken chain along Australia's northeast coast. The reefs are composed of about 400 species of corals of many shapes and colors.

The waters around the Great Barrier Reef are always warm. The Great Barrier Reef is protected because of its environmental importance. It is one of Australia's 14 World Heritage areas, areas on an international registry of sites that have great natural or cultural value. Others include Kakadu National Park and Uluru-Kata Tjuta National Park in the Northern Territory.

Climate

The northern third of Australia lies in the tropics and so is warm or hot the year around. The rest of the country lies south of the tropics and has warm summers and mild or cool winters.

In winter, many parts of the south may have frosts. But the Australian Alps and the interior of Tasmania are the only areas of the country where temperatures remain below freezing for more than a day or so at a time.

Australia receives most of its moisture as rain. Snow falls in Tasmania, the Australian Alps, and occasionally in the central western part of New South Wales. About two-thirds of the country receives less than 10 inches (25 centimeters) of rain a year. Much of the rest of Australia has less than 20 inches (51 centimeters) of rainfall annually. These regions require irrigation for farming. The heaviest rainfall occurs along the north, east, southeast, and extreme southwest coasts.

© Great Barrier Reef Marine Park Authority

The Great Barrier Reef, the world's largest coral reef, supports a fascinating variety of life, including fish and colorful water animals called *polyps.* The reef's beauty attracts many divers.

The east coast of Queensland is the wettest part of the continent. Some places along this coast receive as much as 150 inches (381 centimeters) of rain a year. Parts of the southeast coast and of Tasmania are the only areas of the continent that get uniform amounts of rainfall throughout the year. Rainfall is seasonal throughout the rest of Australia.

Australia lies south of the equator, and so its seasons are opposite those in the Northern Hemisphere. The southern part of the continent has four distinct seasons. Winter, the wettest and coolest season in Australia, lasts from June to August. Summer, the hottest and driest season, lasts from December to February.

Tropical northern Australia has only two seasons—a wet season and a dry one. The wet season corresponds with summer and lasts from November to April. The dry season corresponds with winter and lasts from May to October. The wet season brings heavy downpours and violent storms, especially on Australia's north coast. In 1974, for example, a cyclone destroyed much of the northern coastal city of Darwin. Floods plague many parts of Australia during the wet season. However, droughts are usually a far more serious problem. Nearly every section of Australia has a drought during the country's annual dry season. Water conservation prevents these droughts from doing serious harm in most cases, but they can cause severe water shortages.

Animals and plants

Native animals. At one time, all the continents were part of one huge land mass. Australia became separated from this land mass about 200 million years ago. As a result, its animals developed differently from those on oth-

er continents. Australia's most famous native animals include kangaroos, koalas, wallabies, wombats, and other *marsupials.* Marsupials are mammals that give birth to tiny, poorly developed offspring. In most species, the babies mature in a pouch on the mother's abdomen. Australia has about 200 species of marsupials.

The platypus and the echidna are among the unique Australian animals. They are the only mammals that hatch their young from eggs. Platypuses live only in Australia. Echidnas live in Australia and on New Guinea and a number of other neighboring islands.

Australia has about 700 species of native birds. They include the world's only black swans and about 60 kinds of cockatoos, parakeets, and other parrots. Two large flightless birds, the emu and the cassowary, are also native to Australia. The kookaburra, a member of the kingfisher family, is one of Australia's best-known birds. Its loud call sounds like laughter.

Australia has about 140 species of snakes and about 500 species of lizards. The lizards are nonpoisonous. Most of the snakes are poisonous. Taipans and tiger snakes are among the deadliest groups of snakes in the world.

Native plants. Two main kinds of native plants, acacias and eucalyptuses, dominate Australia's landscape. They are the most common shrubs in the dry lands and the most common trees in the moister areas. Acacias, which Australians call *wattles,* bear their seeds in pods. Australia has about 700 species of acacias. Many of them have brightly colored flowers. Common shrubby species include the mulga and the myall. The silver wattle and the blackwood are tall trees.

Eucalyptuses—or *eucalypts,* as they are known in Aus-

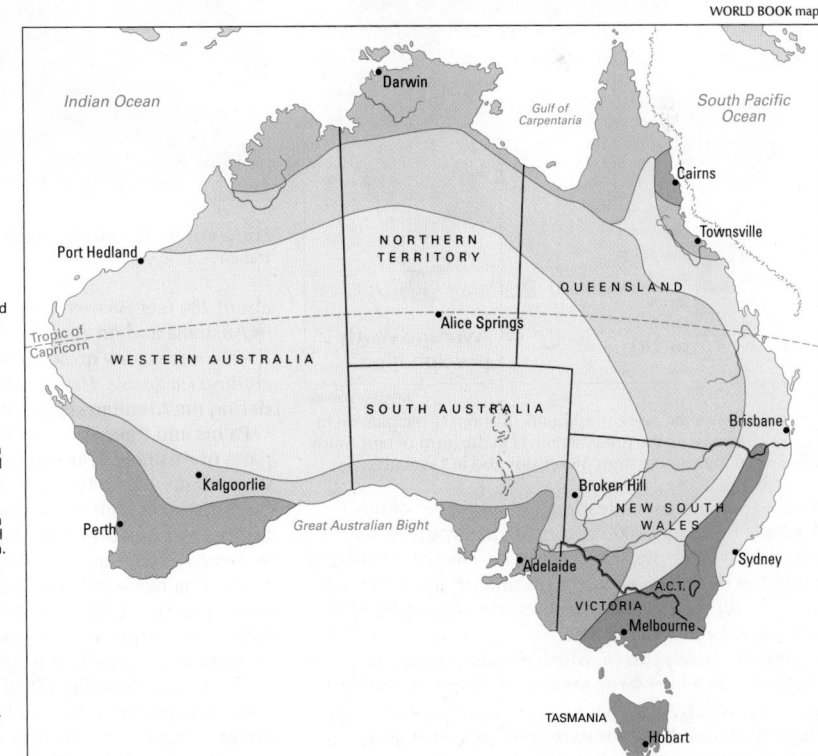

WORLD BOOK map

What Australia's climate is like

In general, Australia has a warm, dry climate. But the climate differs from one part of the country to another, as this map shows. Australia lies south of the equator, and so its seasons are opposite those in the Northern Hemisphere.

Tropical wet-Always hot and wet. Heavy precipitation well distributed throughout year.

Tropical wet and dry-Always hot, with alternate wet and dry seasons. Heavy precipitation in wet season.

Semiarid-Hot to cold. Great changes in temperature from day to night except in coastal areas. Light precipitation.

Desert-Hot to cool. Great changes in temperature from day to night except in coastal areas. Very little precipitation.

Subtropical dry summer-Hot, dry summers and mild, rainy winters. Moderate precipitation in winter.

Humid subtropical-Warm to hot summers and cool winters. Moderate precipitation in all seasons.

Humid oceanic-Moderately warm summers and generally cool winters. Moderate precipitation in all seasons.

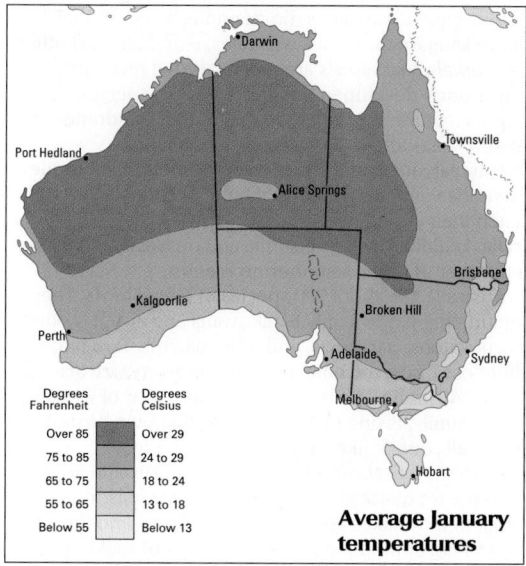

Degrees Fahrenheit	Degrees Celsius
Over 85	Over 29
75 to 85	24 to 29
65 to 75	18 to 24
55 to 65	13 to 18
Below 55	Below 13

Average January temperatures

WORLD BOOK map

This map shows the average temperatures in Australia during January, midway through the country's summer. Australia's summers are hottest in the northwest and coolest in the southeast.

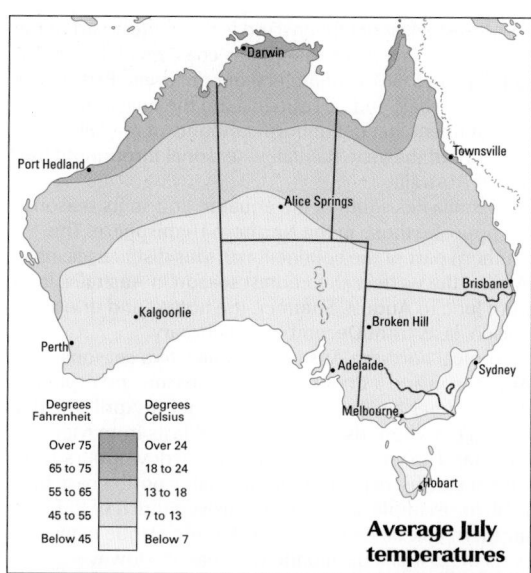

Degrees Fahrenheit	Degrees Celsius
Over 75	Over 24
65 to 75	18 to 24
55 to 65	13 to 18
45 to 55	7 to 13
Below 45	Below 7

Average July temperatures

WORLD BOOK map

July is the coolest month in every part of Australia. Light frosts are common in the south during July. But the extreme southeastern highlands are the only areas that ever have cold weather.

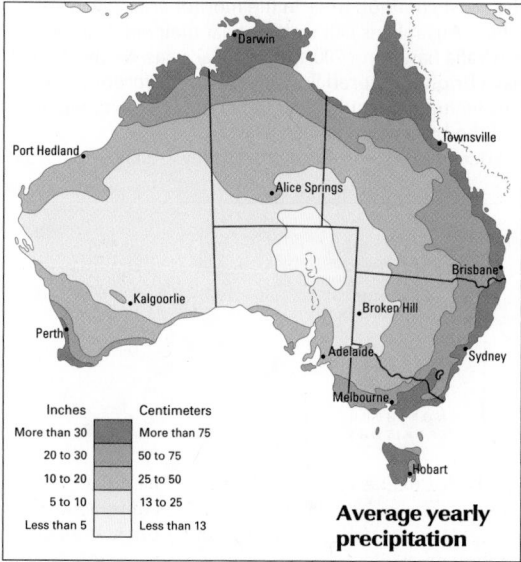

Inches	Centimeters
More than 30	More than 75
20 to 30	50 to 75
10 to 20	25 to 50
5 to 10	13 to 25
Less than 5	Less than 13

Average yearly precipitation

WORLD BOOK map

This map shows the average amounts of annual precipitation in Australia. Almost all the precipitation is in the form of rain. Snow falls only in the southeastern mountains and in Tasmania.

tralia—are the most widespread plants in the country. Australia has about 500 species of eucalyptuses. Most species have narrow, leathery leaves. The leaves contain a fragrant oil that gives the tree a unique smell. In bushfires, the oil can heat up and burst into flames even before the fire reaches the tree.

Scrubby eucalyptuses, which are also known as *mallee scrub,* cover large areas of the interior. Eucalyptus trees, which Australians call *gum trees* or *gums,* include the tallest hardwood trees in the world. Two species, the mountain ash and the karri, may grow to

© David Moore, Black Star

Snow covers Mount Kosciuszko and other peaks in the Australian Alps in winter. The area attracts many skiers.

about 280 feet (85 meters). Eucalyptuses once grew only in Australia and on a few islands to the north. However, eucalyptuses now grow in many other warm areas, including California, Hawaii, and Africa and countries bordering the Mediterranean Sea.

Palms and trees that resemble palms grow in many parts of Australia. Grass trees are palmlike trees of the western dry lands. They are related to the yucca trees of the American Southwest. Macrozamia trees grow throughout Australia. They have palmlike or fernlike leaves and bear cones, as needleleaf trees do. Australia has few native needleleaf trees, other than kauri pines and bunya pines. Shrubs called *saltbushes* are common in the dry grazing areas of southern Australia. They are so named because their leaves have a salty taste. The leaves provide excellent feed for livestock.

Australia has thousands of wildflowers. Many of them are desert species whose seeds lie buried until brought to life by a heavy rain. Then, for a few days or weeks, the

Animals of Australia Some of the many mammals, birds, and reptiles of Australia are pictured on this map. The animals live in various other areas on the continent in addition to those indicated. For example, emus live everywhere in Australia except the rain forests.

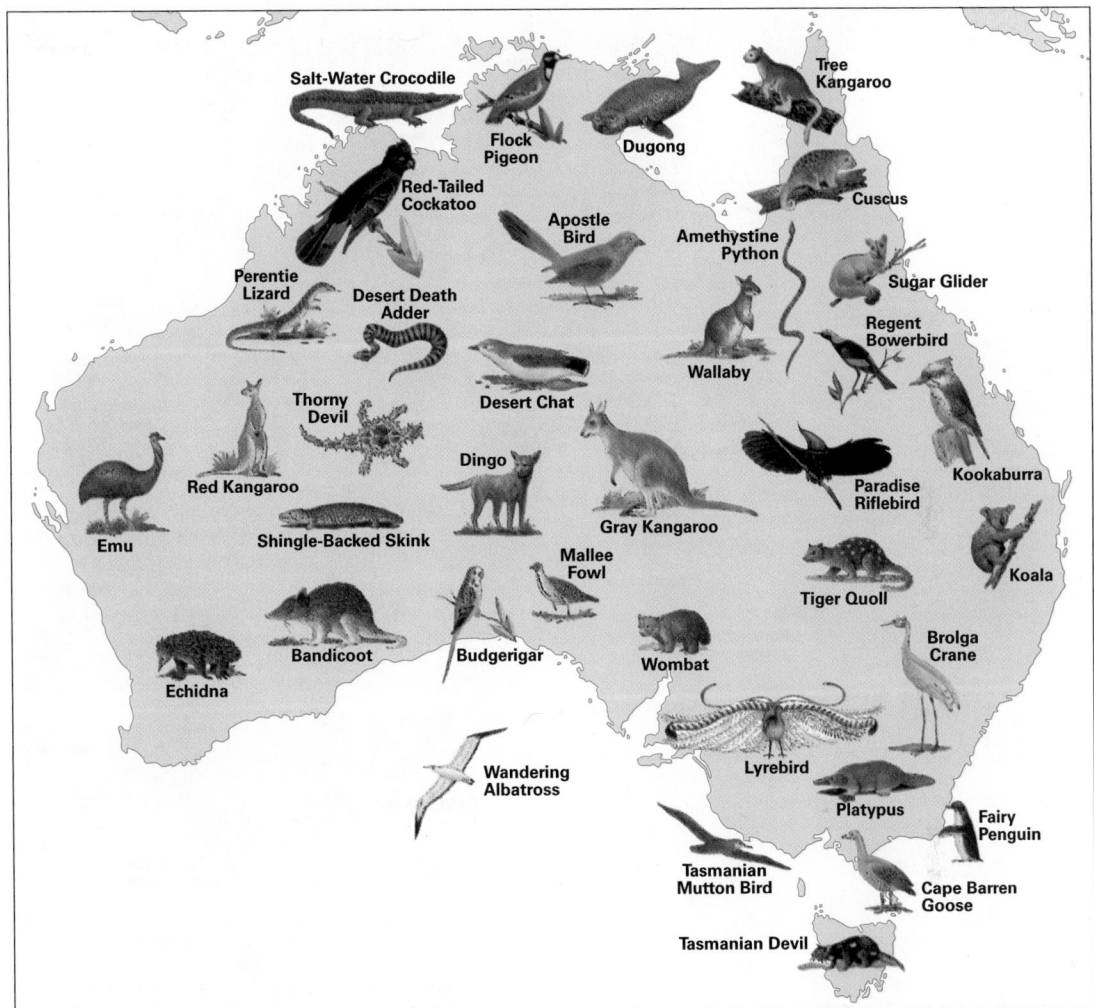

desert bursts into bloom with flowers of every color.

Introduced species. The mammals that lived in Australia before the first people lived there were bats, echidnas, mice, platypuses, rats, and the various kinds of marsupials. Aboriginal people introduced a type of dog known as a *dingo.* Some dingoes escaped into the wild. Today, their descendants are Australia's chief beasts of prey. Europeans introduced into Australia many mammals, including cats, dogs, cattle, deer, foxes, goats, hogs, horses, rabbits, and sheep. They also introduced camels, water buffaloes, various kinds of birds, and many species of plants.

Camels, cane toads, water buffaloes, and certain other introduced species have become wild and are pests. Some domestic cats have gone wild and pose a great risk to native birds and small animals. In some cases, species have had to be exterminated. Wild rabbits caused extensive damage to crops and grazing lands. In the 1950's, Australian officials attempted to wipe them

out with a deliberately introduced disease called *myxo- matosis.* This policy was successful until the rabbits developed *immunity* (natural protection from the disease). In the mid-1990's, scientists released a new virus that has helped to control the number of rabbits.

Economy

Australia is one of the world's rich, developed countries. Most developed countries have become rich through the production and export of manufactured goods. Australia's wealth, however, has come chiefly from farming and mining.

The processing of farm and mineral products makes up a major part of Australia's manufacturing industry. Manufacturing was once the leading employer in Australia. But during the late 1900's, manufacturing declined in importance, while *service industries* increased in importance. Service industries are economic activities that provide services, rather than produce goods.

Plants of Australia

This map pictures some of the trees, shrubs, and other plants of Australia. Many of the plants, such as wallaby grass and golden wattles, grow in other areas of the continent in addition to those shown. However, forest trees grow only in the moist coastal regions.

WORLD BOOK map; illustrations by Tom Dolan and James Teason

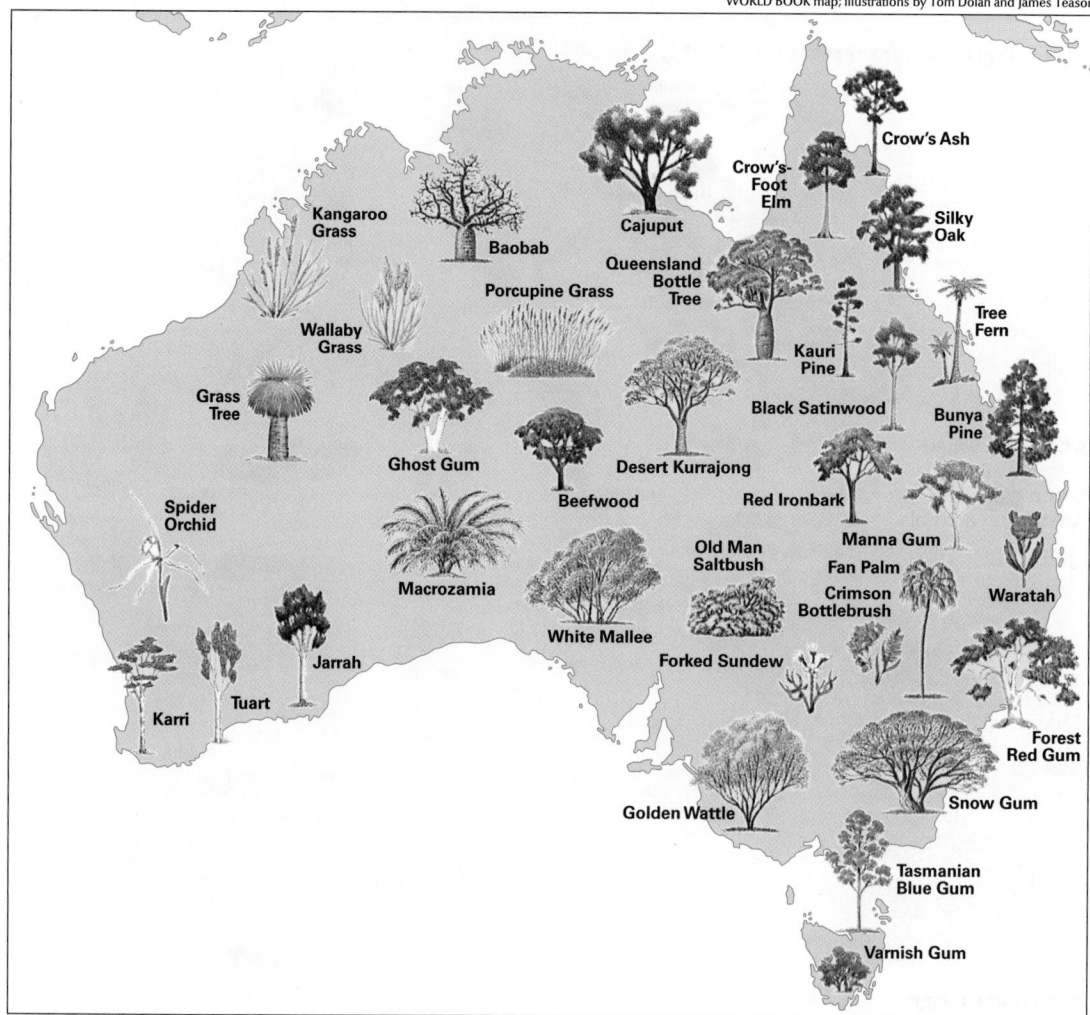

Crow's Ash

Crow's-Foot Elm

Kangaroo Grass

Cajuput

Silky Oak

Baobab

Queensland Bottle Tree

Porcupine Grass

Tree Fern

Wallaby Grass

Kauri Pine

Grass Tree

Black Satinwood

Bunya Pine

Ghost Gum

Desert Kurrajong

Spider Orchid

Beefwood

Red Ironbark

Manna Gum

Old Man Saltbush

Fan Palm

Waratah

Macrozamia

Crimson Bottlebrush

White Mallee

Jarrah

Forked Sundew

Tuart

Karri

Forest Red Gum

Golden Wattle

Snow Gum

Tasmanian Blue Gum

Varnish Gum

Australia relies on its farms and mines for export goods. By selling farm products and minerals abroad, Australia earns the export income that most other developed countries earn from the sale of manufactured products. But only part of Australia's export income goes to the farmers and mining companies that produce the goods originally. Much of it goes to firms that process and distribute the goods. Thus, Australia's agricultural and mineral exports benefit the economy as a whole.

Australia has traditionally been limited by a lack of *capital*—that is, money to finance business and industrial development. As a result, the country has had to borrow capital from other nations and has become heavily indebted to them. American, British, Japanese, and other foreign investors own or control many mining companies, factories, and other businesses in Australia.

Service industries provide about three-quarters of Australia's jobs and make up more than two-thirds of its *gross domestic product*—the total value of goods and services produced within the country annually.

Community, social, personal, business, and financial services make up the leading service industry group in terms of both employment and gross domestic product. Trade, restaurants, and hotels combine to employ about a fifth of Australia's total workforce. Transportation and communication is also important.

Manufacturing. Unlike most other developed countries, Australia imports more manufactured goods than it exports. Australian factories produce many of the *consumer goods*, such as processed foods and household articles, that the people require. But the nation has to import most of its *producer goods*—that is, factory machinery, construction equipment, and other goods used in production. Iron and steel are the chief exceptions. Australia's iron and steel industry produces enough of the metals to mostly meet the needs of other industries.

Some typical Australian plants   These pictures show three common kinds of Australian plants. Acacias, or *wattles,* have attractive flowers. Eucalyptus trees are among the world's tallest trees. Grass trees resemble palms.

© G. R. Roberts

A flowering wattle

© David R. Frazier Photolibrary

Eucalyptus trees

© Robert Frerck

Grass trees

Some typical Australian animals   These pictures show four common kinds of Australian animals. Emus are big, flightless birds. Platypuses are egg-laying mammals. Kangaroos and koalas are marsupials.

© Robert Frerck

An emu and its eggs

© Dave Watts, A.N.T. Photo Library

A platypus in water

© G. R. Roberts

A koala eating eucalyptus leaves

Australian Information Service

A red kangaroo

Australia's factories depend heavily on foreign capital.

Most of Australia's factories specialize in assembly work and light manufacturing. Many plants process farm products or minerals for export. The leading manufactured products include machinery; metals, including iron and steel; petroleum, coal, and chemical products; processed foods and beverages; and transportation equipment. New South Wales and Victoria are the chief manufacturing states. These two states produce over half of the country's manufactured goods and employ over half of the factory workers. Most of the factories operate in and around Sydney and Melbourne.

Mining. Australia has rich mineral resources. But many of the deposits lie in the dry areas, far from major settlements. Such deposits are extremely expensive to mine. Workers must construct roads and railways to the mining sites. Some settlements have been built near mines so that the miners and their families have housing. The costs of mining development in Australia are so high that the mining industry depends heavily on for-

© Carla Gottgens, Bloomberg/Getty Images

Australia's thriving mining industry makes it one of the world's leading mining countries. This huge, open-pit gold mine at Kalgoorlie, Western Australia, is known as the Super Pit.

eign capital. Foreign investors own or control much of the mining industry.

Australia began to develop its mineral resources during the 1800's. By the end of the century, it was exporting large amounts of copper, gold, lead, silver, tin, and zinc. These minerals remained the chief products of the mining industry until the mid-1900's. During the 1950's, geologists discovered huge deposits of bauxite, coal, and iron ore in Australia. They discovered manganese, natural gas, nickel, and petroleum during the 1960's.

Australia has become one of the world's major mining countries. It ranks first in the production of iron ore and zirconium. The country is a leading producer of bauxite, coal, copper, diamonds, gold, lead, manganese, nickel, silver, tin, and zinc. Nearly all the world's high-quality opals are mined in Australia.

New South Wales, Queensland, and Western Australia are the leading mining states. Western Australia produces most of the bauxite, gold, iron ore, and nickel and all of Australia's diamonds. Queensland is the chief producer of lead and silver. It also produces much of Australia's coal. New South Wales mines coal, copper, gold, and zinc. Most of the manganese comes from the Northern Territory and Western Australia. South Australia mines copper, gold, and iron ore. Tasmania produces copper, gold, and zinc. Offshore fields along the northwest coast of Western Australia are Australia's main source of petroleum. Victoria is also a major petroleum producer. Natural gas is produced in Victoria and in Western Australia's northwest coastal shelf. The country is among the world's largest producers of uranium. Australia's richest uranium deposits lie in the Northern Territory and South Australia.

Agriculture in Australia is highly mechanized, requiring minimal human labor. Only about 3 percent of the workers are farmers, but they produce nearly all the food the people need. Agriculture provides only 2 percent of Australia's gross domestic product.

Farmland covers about half of Australia. However, most of this land is dry grazing land. Farmers grow crops on less than 10 percent of the farmland. They irrigate about 5 percent of the cropland.

Australia's leading farm products include beef cattle, dairy products, and wheat. Leading crops include barley,

cotton, grapes, potatoes, and sugar cane. Farmers also raise chickens for both meat and eggs, hogs, and sheep for both meat and wool. Australia is one of the world's largest producers of barley, wheat, and wool. Another rapidly growing industry is winemaking. Australia is a leading wine-producing nation. All the Australian states produce wine, but New South Wales and South Australia produce the best vintages. In regions suitable for growing grapes, winemakers are turning old farms and orchards into vineyards to produce grapes for wine.

Farmers raise sheep and cattle in all the Australian states. New South Wales, South Australia, Victoria, and Western Australia together raise almost all of the country's sheep and produce almost all of its wool. New South Wales and Queensland are Australia's leading beef cattle producers. Victoria is the leading producer of dairy products. Farmers grow wheat in all areas of the country that have adequate rainfall and climate. But production is heavily concentrated in New South Wales and Western Australia. Farms on the east coast of Queensland grow bananas, pineapples, sugar cane, and other

Australia's gross domestic product

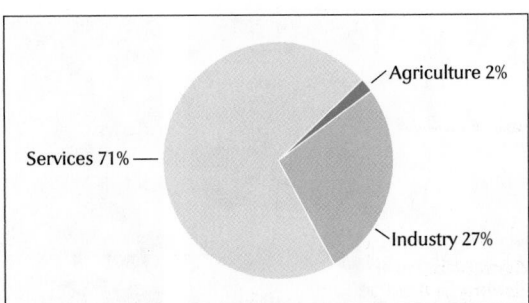

- Agriculture 2%
- Services 71%
- Industry 27%

Australia's gross domestic product (GDP) was $1,375,260,000,000 in U.S. dollars in 2019. The GDP is the total value of goods and services produced within a country in a year. *Services* include community, social, personal, business, and financial services; government; trade, restaurants, and hotels; and transportation and communication. *Industry* includes construction, manufacturing, mining, and utilities. *Agriculture* includes agriculture, forestry, and fishing.

Production and workers by economic activities

Economic activities	Percent of GDP produced	Employed workers Number of people	Percent of total
Community, social, personal, business, & financial services	47	5,804,800	45
Trade, restaurants, & hotels	11	2,594,700	20
Mining	10	247,100	2
Construction	8	1,174,600	9
Transportation & communication	7	871,600	7
Manufacturing	6	893,900	7
Government	6	836,300	6
Utilities	3	155,300	1
Agriculture, forestry, & fishing	2	326,100	3
Total	100	12,904,400	100

Figures are for 2019.
Sources: Australian Bureau of Statistics; International Monetary Fund.

Mining and manufacturing in Australia

This map shows the location of Australia's chief mineral deposits and manufacturing centers. Most of the mineral deposits are mined, and so they are the centers of Australia's mining industry. Major deposits are shown in large type, and lesser ones in small type. Manufacturing centers are in red.

• Perth   Manufacturing center

● Coal   Major mineral deposit

• Tin   Other mineral deposit

WORLD BOOK map

Agriculture and fishing in Australia

This map shows Australia's chief agricultural and fishing regions. The most fertile cropland lies along the east, southeast, and extreme southwest coasts. Dry grasslands cover much of the interior and are used to graze livestock. Shellfish are Australia's leading fishery products.

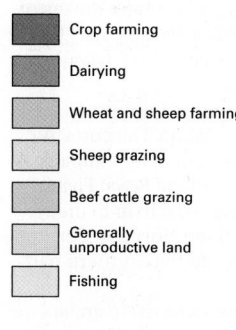

Crop farming

Dairying

Wheat and sheep farming

Sheep grazing

Beef cattle grazing

Generally unproductive land

Fishing

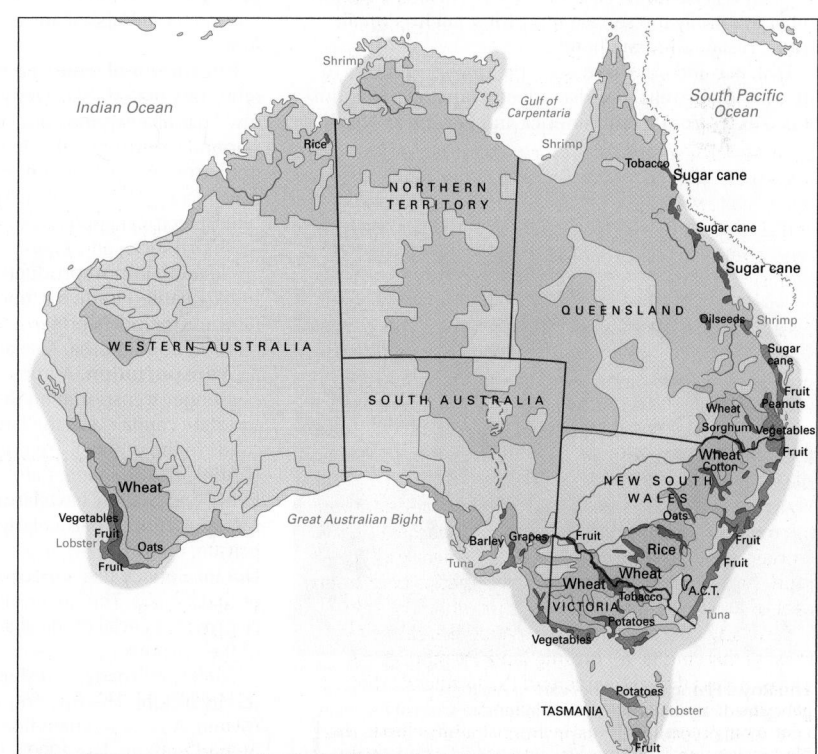

WORLD BOOK map

crops that need a wet tropical climate. Such fruit as apples and pears are common in all the states. New South Wales and South Australia are the leading orange-producing states.

Forestry and fishing. Forests cover about 15 percent of Australia, mostly in the Eastern Highlands and moist coastal areas. The northeast coast has tropical rain forests. The vast majority of Australia's forest trees are eucalyptuses. Industries use the wood of some eucalyptus species for making paper and such items as floorboards and furniture. But eucalyptus wood is too hard for most other purposes, including most types of housing construction. Therefore, tree farms plant imported species of softwoods. Monterey pines, originally from California, have become one of Australia's most important timber trees.

Although Australia is surrounded by water, its fishing resources are limited. Thousands of species of fishes live in the coastal waters, and Australia has developed a small but profitable fishing industry. The industry earns most of its income from the catch of shellfish, especially abalones, lobsters, prawns, and scallops. The fishing fleet also brings in fairly large catches of sardines and tuna. Australia exports much of the shellfish catch. Divers collect some pearls from oysters. *Aquaculture,* the commercial raising of plants and animals that live in water, is a growing industry in Australia. Australia's aquaculture industry raises oysters for pearls and for food, as well as salmon and tuna.

Tourism. Australia has a variety of tourist attractions. They include wildlife sanctuaries, sandy beaches, the Great Barrier Reef, the Australian Alps, Uluru, and numerous points of historical interest. Millions of foreign tourists visit Australia each year. Tourism aids the economy, especially the service industries, such as retail trade, restaurants, and hotels.

Distance and cost have been the major obstacles to growth of Australia's tourist industry. Australia is about twice as far from North America and Europe as North

© Ashley Cooper, Alamy Images

The Snowy Mountains Scheme is a vast irrigation and hydroelectric power project in Australia's southeastern highlands. Pipelines such as these carry water from mountain streams to a nearby series of dams and hydroelectric plants. The runoff from the dams flows into the Murray and Murrumbidgee rivers for use in irrigation.

America and Europe are from each other, so travel to Australia is costly for North American and European vacationers. About half of Australia's visitors come from less distant places, especially New Zealand and other Pacific islands, China, Japan, and Southeast Asia. These places are also the ones most visited by Australians, although many Australians also visit Europe and North America.

International trade. Farm products, minerals, and other raw materials are important to the nation's economy. Australia exports about as much as it imports. Important exports include alumina, beef, coal, copper, gold, iron ore, petroleum products, wheat, and wool. Australia imports mainly manufactured goods. Automobiles, electrical appliances, industrial machinery, petroleum products, and *pharmaceuticals* (medicinal drugs) are leading import products. China and Japan are Australia's leading trade partners. Other important trade partners include Germany, Malaysia, New Zealand, Singapore, South Korea, Thailand, and the United States.

Transportation. Automobiles are the chief means of passenger transportation in Australia. Paved roads link the state capitals and the largest inland cities. Many roads in the outback are unpaved.

Adelaide, Brisbane, Cairns, Darwin, Melbourne, Perth, and Sydney have large international airports. Air transportation is particularly important in the outback. A private, nonprofit organization called the Royal Flying Doctor Service flies emergency medical help to many outback areas. The government of the Northern Territory provides aerial medical services to the northern part of the territory.

Trucks, railroads, and ships haul most of Australia's intercity freight. The trucking industry is mainly privately owned. Australia's main-line railroads were all publicly owned until the late 1900's, but many are now privately

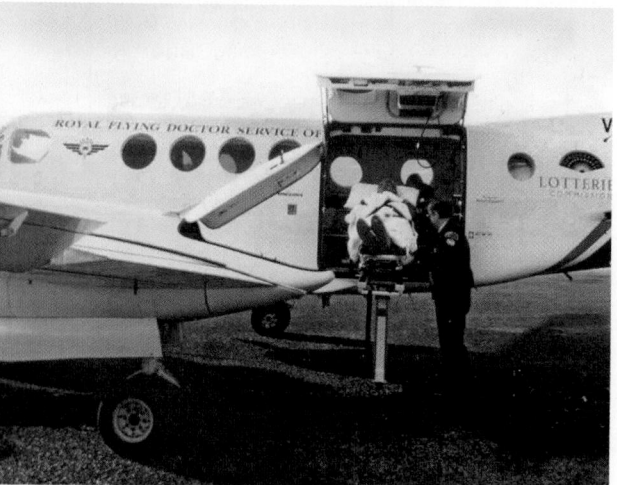

© Royal Flying Doctor Service of Australia

The Royal Flying Doctor Service of Australia provides emergency medical services to people in remote areas of the continent. Air transportation is vital in the Australian outback. This photograph shows a doctor loading a patient onto a small plane.

Golden wheat fields, such as this one in New South Wales, are important to the Australian economy. Australia exports great quantities of wheat to China, Indonesia, and other Asian countries.

© Lance Nelson, Stock Photos

owned. Rail lines link Darwin, Kalgoorlie, Melbourne, Sydney, and many other cities. The main-line railroads chiefly haul farm goods and minerals from the producing areas to the coastal cities and ports. In addition to the main rail lines, Australia has several small private railroads. These lines largely haul minerals from out-of-the-way mines to the main-line railroads. Sydney and Melbourne have extensive commuter rail systems.

Ships carry large amounts of minerals between Australian coastal ports and haul nearly all the country's overseas freight. However, Australia has only a small merchant fleet. Foreign vessels carry most of its inter-coastal freight and almost all its overseas cargo. The busiest eastern ports include Brisbane, Geelong, Melbourne, Newcastle, Port Kembla, and Sydney. Dampier, Fremantle, and Port Hedland are among Western Australia's busiest ports. Adelaide also has a large port.

Communication. Australia's postal and telephone systems are partly or fully owned by the federal government and operated by independent government agencies. The Australian Postal Corporation runs the postal system. The telephone system was fully government-owned until the 1990's. The telecommunications industry now operates in a fully competitive market. Nearly every household has a telephone. Both internet and mobile phone usage have increased rapidly since the mid-1990's. In the remotest parts of the outback, many people use two-way radios in place of telephones.

Almost all Australian families own one or more television sets and radios. Commercial broadcasters own and operate many radio stations and free TV stations. Almost all the rest are owned and financed by the federal government and operated by the Australian Broadcasting Corporation (ABC), an independent government agency.

Almost all cable and satellite TV is privately owned. The federal government owns the Special Broadcasting Service (SBS), a public broadcaster that receives most of its funding from the federal government. It provides radio, TV, and online services in dozens of languages.

Australia has experienced rapid expansion of new electronic and telecommunications technologies, in industry, government, education, and private household use. Most Australian homes have computer and internet service.

Australia has dozens of daily newspapers, all privately owned. The most widely read daily newspapers include the *Herald-Sun* and *The Age* in Melbourne, and *The Sydney Morning Herald* and *The Daily Telegraph* in Sydney. A national daily, *The Australian,* is published in Adelaide, Brisbane, Hobart, Melbourne, Perth, and Sydney. There are also many foreign-language newspapers published in Australia's cities.

History

The earliest Australians were the ancestors of today's Aboriginal and Torres Strait Islander peoples. According to some Aboriginal traditions, Aboriginal people have always lived in Australia. Archaeological findings indicate their presence more than 65,000 years ago. Archaeologists estimate that Aboriginal people came by boat from Southeast Asia, and that they lived throughout Australia by about 40,000 years ago. People may have lived on some of the Torres Strait Islands as many as 9,000 years ago.

© Robert Frerck

Beef cattle are raised throughout Australia, except in the deserts. But cattle production is greatest in New South Wales and Queensland. This cattle auction is in Rockhampton, Queensland.

Over time, Australia's inhabitants developed food gathering methods, fishing techniques, and shelters suited to the different parts of the continent, from tropical rain forests to the central desert. Their social systems and beliefs also varied. They made tools and weapons from stone, shell, bone, wood, fiber, and natural gums. They were active traders of such goods as shells, stone, and tools. They also exchanged ideas and news.

Scholars estimate that 500,000 to 1 million people lived in Australia by the time Europeans arrived in 1788. These First Australians spoke about 250 distinct languages. The Europeans often assumed that the Aboriginal and Torres Strait Islander peoples had primitive cultures. However, those cultures were rich in spirituality, art, languages, and knowledge of the Australian environment. See **Aboriginal peoples of Australia.**

Ships from Asia reached Australia's northern shores in the 1400's. These visitors included Chinese, Pacific Islanders, and Arabs. Asian visitors included fishing crews from the Indonesian port of Makassar (also spelled *Macassar),* who stayed several months each year and influenced Aboriginal culture.

European explorations. Some historians believe that Portuguese navigators sighted the coast of Australia in the 1500's. The first recorded date for a European sighting of Australia is 1606, when the Dutch explorer Willem Jansz and the Spanish navigator Luis Vaez de Torres explored the waters off northeastern Australia. The Torres Strait is named for the Spanish explorer.

Throughout the 1600's, the Dutch explored and roughly mapped every Australian coastline except the eastern seaboard. In 1642, the Dutch sea captain Abel Tasman sailed around the southern part of Tasmania. He named it *Van Diemen's Land,* in honor of a Dutch governor, and claimed it for the Netherlands. In 1855, the island was renamed *Tasmania* in Tasman's honor. The Dutch found Australia harsh and forbidding, with no trading possibilities. They made no settlements there.

Cook's voyage. In 1768, the British Admiralty appointed the British navigator James Cook to find and take possession of what it called the *southern continent.*

Cook landed at Botany Bay on the southeast coast of Australia on April 29, 1770. The fertile land and comfortable climate of Botany Bay left a good impression on Cook. He did not understand the Aboriginal ways of land management and assumed the land was free for British settlement. Cook claimed the east coast of the continent for Britain, naming it *New South Wales.*

British settlement. Until the American Revolution (1775-1783), Britain regularly sent convicts to the American Colonies. This practice, called *transportation,* helped to relieve overcrowded jails in Britain. After the war for independence began, the Americans would not accept any more British convicts. British officials needed a new prison colony. They also wanted to establish a new colony in the east as a strategic post. They chose Australia.

The First Fleet, under the command of Captain Arthur Phillip, left for Australia in May 1787. Of the more than 1,000 people who sailed, about 750 were convicts and their families, with more than 200 marines to guard them. The fleet reached Botany Bay in January 1788, but Phillip found the area unsuitable for settlement. He sailed north into the large inlet of Port Jackson and selected Sydney Cove as the site for the settlement. On Jan. 26, 1788, he unfurled the British flag there, over the lands of an Aboriginal people called the Cadigal.

The convicts sent to Australia were mainly from the working classes of England and Ireland. They provided the skilled and unskilled labor to build the colony. Convicts worked on government projects, such as constructing roads, bridges, and buildings. They also labored on government farms. Although the colony was established as a kind of jail, the convicts did not live in jail conditions. In the early years, the colony operated much like a village in England. Convicts wore their own clothes, lived in their own homes, and could run their own businesses. Free husbands, wives, and children came to the colony to join convict spouses or parents.

The New South Wales Corps. Phillip, who had served as the first governor of New South Wales, left the colony in 1792. The marines who had accompanied him were replaced by the New South Wales Corps, a

The First Fleet in Sydney Cove, January 27, 1788 (1938), an oil painting on canvas by John Allcot; National Library of Australia, Canberra

The First Fleet sailed into Sydney Cove on Jan. 26, 1788, to establish the first permanent European settlement in Australia. The fleet consisted of 11 ships carrying more than 1,000 people, of whom about 750 were British convicts, their spouses, and their children. More than 200 others were marines guarding the convicts and their families.

Important dates in Australia

c. 65,000 years ago Archaeological evidence suggests Aboriginal people were living on the continent of Australia.

A.D. 1606 Willem Jansz became the first European known to sight Australia and land there.

1642 Abel Janszoon Tasman sighted Van Diemen's Land. It was renamed Tasmania in 1855.

1770 James Cook explored Australia's east coast. He claimed the area for the United Kingdom and named it New South Wales.

1788 Great Britain (later the United Kingdom) established New South Wales as a prison colony.

1801-1803 Matthew Flinders sailed completely around Australia, proving it to be one large land mass.

1829 Charles Fremantle claimed the entire western part of the Australian continent for the United Kingdom.

1851 Gold was discovered in New South Wales and Victoria.

1868 The United Kingdom ended the transportation of convicts to Australia.

1901 Australia became an independent nation. Melbourne was named the temporary capital.

1927 The federal capital was transferred to Canberra.

1967 The Australian Constitution was amended to permit the establishment of federal programs to aid Indigenous peoples.

1978 The Northern Territory became responsible for its own administration, the first step toward Australian statehood.

1999 Voters rejected a plan to make Australia a republic and chose to keep the British monarch as Australia's head of state.

2003 A transcontinental rail line was completed, linking Adelaide in South Australia with Darwin in the Northern Territory.

Australia exploration and discovery

Sea Explorers

——— Jansz 1606 (Neth.)

—·—· Tasman 1642, 1644 (Neth.)

------ Cook 1770 (U.K.)

— — — Bass and Flinders 1798-1799 (U.K.)

—··—·· Flinders 1801-1803 (U.K.)

Land Explorers

——— Blaxland 1813

—·—· Hume and Hovell 1824

------ Sturt 1829-1830

— — — Mitchell 1835

—·—· Eyre 1840-1841

——— Leichhardt 1844-1845

—·—· Burke and Wills 1860-1861

------ Stuart 1861-1862

— — — Warburton 1873

—··—·· Forrest 1874

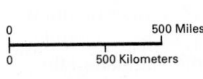

| 0 | 500 Miles |
| 0 | 500 Kilometers |

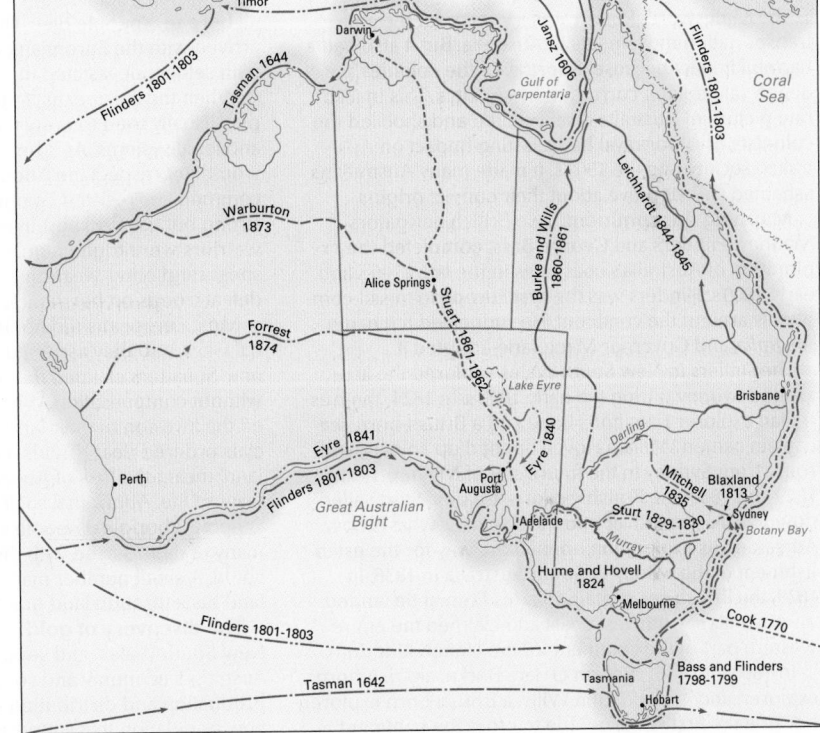

WORLD BOOK map

British infantry regiment. The corps soon gained much power in the colony. In 1806, the British sea captain William Bligh became governor. His reforms triggered conflict with the corps. On Jan. 26, 1808, the commander of the New South Wales Corps, George Johnston, arrested Bligh and took control of the colony. In 1809, the government of the United Kingdom appointed Lachlan Macquarie governor. Macquarie brought his own troops to replace the New South Wales Corps. He arrested Johnston and regained control of the colony.

Macquarie's administration. Macquarie had a liberal, tolerant policy toward convicts and *emancipists* (pardoned convicts). These policies angered wealthy free settlers, who thought they were superior to the emancipists. In 1819, British officials appointed John Thomas Bigge to lead an investigation of the colony. Bigge's report was critical of Macquarie's policies. Bigge recom-

mended the extension of *assignment,* the practice of assigning convicts to free settlers who put them to work. He also concluded that transportation did not discourage crime and should be made more severe. Because of Bigge's report, the British recalled Macquarie to England and increased the severity of the convict system. After the 1820's, life for convicts became much stricter.

End of transportation. Free immigrants had been arriving in Australia since 1788, attracted by free land grants and cheap convict labor. By 1828, those born in the colony already made up almost one-fourth of the population, and free people outnumbered convicts.

Opposition to convict transportation became widespread during the 1830's. In the United Kingdom, many reformers questioned the effectiveness of transportation as a way to stop crime. In Australia, free immigrants objected to living in a prison colony. Cheap convict labor kept wages low, and restrictions on civil liberties were greater than those in the United Kingdom.

In 1838, a committee led by the British colonial official Sir William Molesworth examined transportation and the convict system. The committee, known as the Molesworth Committee, recommended that the government end transportation to New South Wales and Van Diemen's Land and abolish assignment. The British government followed the recommendations and stopped transportation to New South Wales in 1840, suspended it in Van Diemen's Land in 1846, and officially abolished it there in 1852. In Western Australia, convict transportation started in 1850 and was not abolished until 1868. There, convicts, or *exiles,* as they were called, provided labor that the struggling colony desperately needed. Altogether, more than 160,000 convicts were sent to Australia from 1788 to 1868.

The Molesworth Report was a victory for the anti-transportation movements in Australia. But it also had a harmful impact because it portrayed the colonies as deeply tainted and corrupted by convicts. This inaccurate picture of Australia disappointed and shocked the colonists. This portrayal had a lasting impact on Australian society into the 1900's. It made many Australians ashamed and sensitive about their convict origins.

Mapping the continent. Two British navigators, Matthew Flinders and George Bass, completed the exploration of Australia's coastlines in the late 1700's and early 1800's. Flinders was the first European to sail completely around the continent. He suggested the name *Australia,* and Governor Macquarie adopted it.

The settlers in New South Wales explored the area around Sydney during the early 1800's. In 1824, the Australian explorer Hamilton Hume and a British-born sea captain named William Hovell opened up an overland route from Sydney to the future site of Melbourne. In 1829 and 1830, the British explorer Charles Sturt sailed down the Murray River into the sea, near what is now Adelaide. His exploration opened the way for the establishment of the colony of South Australia in 1836. In 1829, the British sea captain Charles Fremantle landed on Australia's southwest coast and claimed the entire western part of the continent for the United Kingdom.

In 1860 and 1861, Robert O'Hara Burke, an Irish-born explorer, and William John Wills, a British-born explorer, became the first white people to cross the continent from south to north. They died on the return trip south. John McDouall Stuart, a Scottish-born explorer, made the first round trip between the south and north coasts in 1861 and 1862.

Aboriginal people were great explorers and vital guides during this period. They guided the European parties, found food and water, and acted as peacemakers when they communicated with other, hostile Aboriginal groups. The Europeans rarely acknowledged these individuals and their contributions, however.

Expansion. In 1831, the British introduced *assisted migration* to the colonies. Under this system, officials raised money to help run the colonies and to assist migration to Australia. Only land within the colonies' settled areas could be sold. Between 1831 and 1840, more than 40,000 assisted immigrants arrived in Australia. By 1850, their total number was more than 110,000.

As the wool industry flourished, some *sheep graziers* (farmers who graze sheep) moved out into new country and settled illegally on land beyond the legal limits of settlement. They were soon called *squatters.* By 1840, they had occupied most of Victoria and eastern New South Wales and had reached the Darling Downs in present-day Queensland. By the early 1850's, the colonies of Tasmania, Western Australia, South Australia, and Victoria had been established.

Aboriginal peoples. British officials ordered the early governors to protect and establish friendly relations with the Aboriginal peoples. Eventually, colonial authorities created land reserves and encouraged missionary activity for the Aboriginal and Torres Strait Islander peoples. However, these policies were often ineffective.

In 1789, smallpox brought to north Australia by fishing crews from Makassar spread across the continent. In some groups, such as the Cadigal people near Sydney, all but a few people died. Diseases new to Australia also arrived with the Europeans. Disease and violent conflicts with settlers devastated the Aboriginal population.

When the Europeans first arrived, the Aboriginal peoples usually tried to draw them into their own familial and legal systems. As it became clear that the Europeans would not respect the Aboriginal society, Aboriginal communities resisted colonization. This resistance was strong but usually short-lived. Although the Aboriginal warriors were frightening and powerful, and their spears and other weapons were deadly, they could not defeat troops on horseback armed with guns.

Most Europeans did not understand or value Aboriginal ways, and they assumed the land belonged to no one. Squatters claimed the right to take Aboriginal land without compensation. When Aboriginal peoples resisted the invasion of their land and attacked settlers, officials ordered deadly raids. *Dispossession* (the taking of land) meant the loss of Aboriginal food sources and ways of life. Aboriginal societies began to crumble.

Some Aboriginal people survived these crises, and many of them stayed with their land for as long as they could. A small number managed to get some of their land back through land grants and reserves.

The discovery of gold in April 1851, near Bathurst, New South Wales, and soon after in Victoria, changed Australia's economy and society. Gold stimulated the production and distribution of goods. It attracted a large, new population that supported the manufacturing industry. Miners poured into Australia. By early 1852, the first miners and their families arrived from overseas. The number of Australian colonists soared from about 400,000 in 1850 to more than 1,100,000 in 1860.

Political changes. By 1856, the United Kingdom had granted self-government to all the colonies except Western Australia. Because of convict labor in that colony, steps to self-government were postponed there until the late 1800's.

Squatters settled in New South Wales north and west of Brisbane. In 1859, the United Kingdom created the colony of Queensland out of this area, with Brisbane as its capital. Western Australia received representative government in 1870 and a parliament in 1890.

Land reform. By 1860, thousands of disappointed gold miners wanted to buy plots of land and take up farming. But squatters held most of the best farmland. During the early 1860's, the colonial legislatures passed

Australian prime ministers

Name	Dates served	Party	Name	Dates served	Party
Edmund Barton	1901-1903	Protectionist	Francis M. Forde	1945	Labor
Alfred Deakin	1903-1904	Protectionist	Ben Chifley	1945-1949	Labor
Chris Watson	1904	Labor	Robert G. Menzies	1949-1966	Liberal
George H. Reid	1904-1905	Free Trade	Harold E. Holt	1966-1967	Liberal
Alfred Deakin	1905-1908	Protectionist	John McEwen	1967-1968	Country
Andrew Fisher	1908-1909	Labor	John G. Gorton	1968-1971	Liberal
Alfred Deakin	1909-1910	Fusion	William McMahon	1971-1972	Liberal
Andrew Fisher	1910-1913	Labor	Gough Whitlam	1972-1975	Labor
Joseph Cook	1913-1914	Liberal	Malcolm Fraser	1975-1983	Liberal
Andrew Fisher	1914-1915	Labor	Robert Hawke	1983-1991	Labor
William M. Hughes	1915-1917	Labor	Paul Keating	1991-1996	Labor
William M. Hughes	1917-1923	Nationalist	John Winston Howard	1996-2007	Liberal
Stanley M. Bruce	1923-1929	Nationalist	Kevin Michael Rudd	2007-2010	Labor
James Scullin	1929-1932	Labor	Julia Gillard	2010-2013	Labor
Joseph A. Lyons	1932-1939	United	Kevin Michael Rudd	2013	Labor
Earle Page	1939	Country	Tony Abbott	2013-2015	Liberal
Robert G. Menzies	1939-1941	United	Malcolm Turnbull	2015-2018	Liberal
Arthur Fadden	1941	Country	Scott Morrison	2018-	Liberal
John Curtin	1941-1945	Labor			

laws to redistribute the squatters' land. These *selection acts* allowed individuals to select a small block of land. Selectors had to live on their land, cultivate and fence it, and pay for it. Selection was less successful than its supporters expected. Many farms were too small, and the environment was often unsuitable for agricultural use. Many people who took up the land knew nothing about farming. Squatters often used illegal means to keep their farms intact. However, selection succeeded where the land was suitable for crop growing and dairy farms, and in places that also had ready access to markets. In some parts of Victoria, New South Wales, and Queensland, selection boosted the agriculture industry.

By the 1880's, colonial governments had begun to set aside the drier regions for grazing use. They introduced new settlement plans in the 1890's to further divide the large landholdings into small family farms.

Economic changes. Historians have called the period from 1860 to 1890 *the long boom.* The discovery of gold during the 1850's and 1860's boosted the Australian economy. Agriculture and manufacturing industries grew. Railroad construction increased greatly. The railroads opened up new areas for settlement, lowered transport costs, and carried such bulky goods as wheat.

Despite the boom, life was hard for the working classes. Wages were low, working hours were long, and many workplaces were dangerous. Unemployment was common. Without a social security system, unemployed people relied on aid from charities. These difficult conditions contributed to a rise in the reform and labor union movements. In the late 1800's, the colonial governments passed several factory acts regulating workplace safety and hours and wages of workers.

By the late 1880's, the economic boom had begun to falter. Public and private debt rose greatly during the 1880's. Unemployment soared, reaching crisis proportions in 1893 and 1894. In 1893, the Australian banking system suffered a near collapse. Victoria was the hardest hit. Recovery from the depression was slow. Only Western Australia escaped the depression because the discovery of gold created a boom economy.

The struggle for women's rights. Even though women played an essential role in building the new nation, they were treated as second-class citizens in the early and middle 1800's. In most places, they could not vote and were excluded from most employment. Deserted or widowed women were often left in poverty. Wives married to abusive husbands had little prospect of escape because divorce and property laws favored men. In 1870, the average number of children in a family was seven. Many women died in childbirth, so having large families was a danger for them. The 1880's were a turning point for Australian women. Colonial governments amended divorce laws to be fairer to women. Female education levels rose. Women won the right to vote in South Australia in 1895 and in Western Australia in 1899.

Federation. The 1890's saw the first steps toward the federation of the six Australian colonies. A growing number of Australians believed the colonies would be better off as a single nation with a unified government. A new sense of Australian identity favored a united, white Australia. The writings of Mary Gilmore, Henry Lawson, Banjo Paterson, and Steele Rudd illustrated this view.

In 1897 and 1898, a federal convention drew up a constitution for Australia. The people approved it in balloting during 1898 and 1899, and Australian leaders submitted it to the British Parliament in 1900. The United Kingdom approved it, and the Commonwealth of Australia came into being on Jan. 1, 1901. However, Australians were still British citizens, and the United Kingdom continued to control Australia's foreign policy.

Building a nation. The federal Parliament met in Melbourne until a site for a national capital could be selected. At first, Australia had three political parties—the Protectionists, the Labor Party, and the conservative Free Traders. The Protectionists wanted high *tariffs* (taxes on imports) to protect Australian industries from foreign competition. The Free Traders wanted low tariffs or none. The Labor Party represented the labor unions. Protectionist leader Edmund Barton became Australia's first prime minister. No single group held a majority in the House of Representatives between 1901 and 1910.

By 1909, Parliament agreed to adopt a national tariff. With this solution, the major issue separating the Free Traders and Protectionists had gone. The two groups joined together as the Fusion Party in 1909. The name was changed to the Liberal Party shortly afterward.

Prosperity returned to Australia during the early

1900's. Australia's *gross domestic product*—that is, the value of all goods and services produced by the country—soared. Production of wool, wheat, and other agricultural products rose. New railroads were built.

Social policies. White women won the right to vote in federal elections in 1902. States that had not yet given women the vote were forced to grant it. At the same time, the federal government took the right to vote away from Indigenous people not already registered to vote. White Australians did not consider them citizens of the new nation and did not count them in the census.

Most white Australians had British ancestry and believed that non-Europeans were inferior to them. They passed the Immigration Restriction Act of 1901, which prevented non-European immigration to Australia. This act was the basis of the White Australia policy, an anti-immigration policy that lasted for more than 60 years.

Numerous women's groups campaigned for social reform, and Australia became known for its groundbreaking social welfare policies. In 1910, the government introduced pensions for the elderly and for sick people. Some state governments introduced workers' compensation. In 1912, women's lobbying achieved the establishment of a maternity allowance for white mothers.

The Stolen Generations. The new Constitution prohibited the federal government from making laws and policies for Indigenous peoples. Over the first half of the 1900's, most Australians expected Australia's Indigenous peoples to die out. The governments of the states and territories increased policies of segregation and control. By 1912, all of the state governments except Tasmania passed legislation that allowed authorities to take Aboriginal and Torres Strait Islander children from their families and place them in institutions and foster homes. The children who were taken from their homes are often called the *Stolen Generations.*

World War I (1914-1918). When the United Kingdom declared war on Germany on Aug. 4, 1914, Australia was automatically at war. The government formed the Australian Imperial Force (AIF). By the end of 1914, more than 50,000 men had enlisted. They were sent with troops from New Zealand to train in Egypt, where the term *ANZAC (Australian and New Zealand Army Corps)* was coined to describe them. Australian troops played important roles at battles on the Gallipoli Peninsula in present-day Turkey and on the Western front in Europe.

More than 58,000 Australian soldiers died and over 152,000 were wounded, the highest casualty rate in proportion to total number of troops among the Allies.

Between the wars. Two new political parties were founded in Australia after World War I. The conservative Australian Country Party (now the National Party) was formed at the national level in 1920. The Communist Party of Australia formed in 1920. The capital was transferred from Melbourne to Canberra in 1927.

The period between the two world wars was initially prosperous for Australia. After 1929, however, the country fell into the grip of the Great Depression, the worldwide economic slump of the 1930's. In the worst of the Depression, nearly a third of the country's workers had no job. The Depression lasted until 1936, when a general world recovery took effect.

The period between the wars was significant for Aboriginal peoples. In New South Wales, the government took back nearly 13,000 acres (5,260 hectares) of land given to Aboriginal peoples through official reserves and individual grants, often giving it to white farmers and returning white soldiers. This process started a move of Aboriginal people to the cities. It led Aboriginal peoples and non-Aboriginal supporters to form the first activist groups promoting Aboriginal rights.

World War II (1939-1945). Australia entered World War II on the side of the United Kingdom on Sept. 3, 1939. The government announced the formation of the Second AIF, but enlistment was slow. The Second AIF fought in battles in Crete, Greece, and northern Africa.

On Feb. 19, 1942, the Japanese launched the first of more than 60 air raids against Darwin. In May 1942, three Japanese submarines entered Sydney Harbour. The United States Navy, with the Royal Australian Navy, defeated the Japanese in the Battle of the Coral Sea in May 1942. From then until the end of the war, Australia was the base for the Allied offensive against Japan.

Women played a significant role in the war effort. Many joined the services. Others were drafted into factory jobs, in such areas as weapons production. They also took jobs left by the men, often in areas where women had previously been excluded. These women for the first time received the same wages as men.

Postwar Australia. The war boosted Australia's manufacturing industry. The status of women increased, particularly in the work force. The country's ethnic compo-

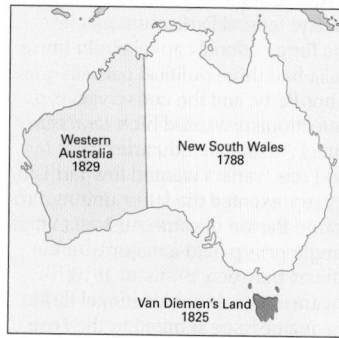

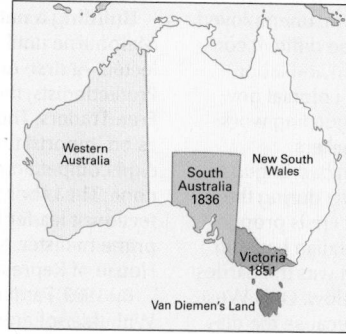

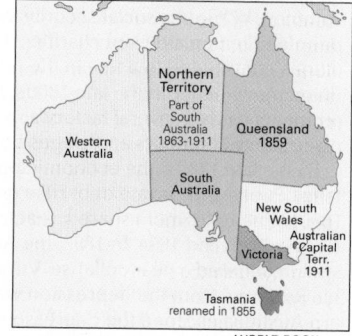

WORLD BOOK maps

In 1829, Western Australia became the third British colony in Australia. The British had established New South Wales in 1788 and Van Diemen's Land in 1825.

In 1836 and 1851, the United Kingdom founded two more colonies—South Australia and Victoria. The land for the colonies was taken from New South Wales.

By 1911, the map of Australia looked much as it looks today. Queensland and the mainland territories were set up. Van Diemen's Land was renamed Tasmania.

sition changed with postwar immigration. In all, 853,953 assisted immigrants arrived between 1947 and 1960.

The Labor Party governed from 1941 to 1949, when it was defeated in parliamentary elections. The Liberals then formed a government with the Country Party. Liberal and Country Party coalitions held power until 1972.

The 1950's and the 1960's were years of peace, prosperity, and political stability for many Australians. A mineral boom aided economic growth. Marriage and childbirth rates rose, along with home ownership levels. A generation of Australians emerged from depression and war into lives of well-being and security.

The women's movement reemerged in a new and more radical form in the late 1960's. One of its major international leaders was the Australian writer Germaine Greer. The feminists of the 1960's and 1970's believed that women should be equal in every sphere of life, and all jobs and public positions should be open to them.

The campaign for Indigenous rights forced its way into Australian public awareness in the 1960's. Indigenous people held strikes to demand better working conditions, equal pay, and the right to own their ancestral lands. In 1962, Aboriginal and Torres Strait Islander people received the right to vote in national elections. A constitutional referendum in 1967 allowed the federal government to legislate on their behalf. The first Indigenous land claims were made in the late 1960's, and groups petitioned the United Nations for compensation for the injustices done to them. In 1971, for the first time, Indigenous people were included in the national census.

The Vietnam War led many people to question both the war and their society in general. The war was fought between the Communist-led nationalists of North Vietnam and anti-Communists in South Vietnam supported by the United States. In 1965, the first Australian troops went to South Vietnam. Opposition to the war began in Australia almost immediately. By the late 1960's, opposition was widespread. Mass antiwar demonstrations took place in 1970 and 1971. When the soldiers returned home in 1973, few public welcomes greeted them.

Political upheavals. In 1972, the Labor Party won a majority in the House of Representatives. Labor leader Gough Whitlam became prime minister. No elections were held for the Senate, which remained under the control of a Liberal-Country coalition. The Whitlam government passed important reforms but was plagued by problems, including an economic recession. In 1975, a coalition of the Liberal and National parties blocked the approval of funds needed to run the government. A constitutional crisis followed, and Governor General John Kerr removed Whitlam from office. Kerr named Malcolm Fraser, head of the Liberal Party, to serve as prime minister until new elections could be held.

The Liberal-National coalition won elections in late 1975 and in 1977 and 1980. Fraser remained prime minister. In 1977, Don Chipp, a former Liberal minister, formed a party called the Australian Democrats, which held the balance of power in the Senate after 1980. The Labor Party, led by Bob Hawke, regained power in 1983 and won elections in 1984, 1987, and 1990. In 1991, the Labor Party elected Paul Keating as party leader. He replaced Hawke as prime minister. The Labor Party won elections in 1993, and Keating remained prime minister.

A coalition of the National and Liberal parties won general elections in 1996, 1998, 2001, and 2004. John Howard, the Liberal leader, served as prime minister.

Indigenous land decisions. The struggle for land rights won a victory in 1992. That year, the High Court ruled in the case of *Mabo v. Queensland* that Aboriginal and Torres Strait Islander peoples had legal title to their land before European settlers took it. The *Mabo decision,* as it is often called, recognized that native title still existed where the people had remained on their land. *Native title* refers to the rights of native peoples under their traditional laws and customs.

In 1993, the federal government passed the Native Title Act. This law recognized and protected ownership rights to the ancestral lands of Aboriginal and Torres Strait Islander peoples. A 1996 High Court ruling called the *Wik decision* was equally important. The Wik people of the Cape York peninsula succeeded in their challenge to have native title recognized in areas where graziers had leases. The court ruled that graziers' leases had not replaced native title, but that the two had coexisted.

Iraq War. The Howard government supported the U.S.-led "war on terror," a response to the Sept. 11, 2001, terrorist attacks against the United States. It also supported the U.S.-led war against Iraq, which began in 2003. That year, Howard's government sent troops to serve in Iraq. The allied forces quickly gained control of Iraq and ended the rule of dictator Saddam Hussein. Some Australian troops stayed in Iraq after the fall of Hussein's government to take part in peacekeeping operations. Australia's participation in the Iraq War was unpopular with many Australians. In 2009, Australian military forces were formally withdrawn from Iraq. See **Iraq War.**

Refugees. In the early 2000's, thousands of people attempted to sail to Australia from Indonesia in search of political *asylum* (shelter and protection). The Royal Australian Navy diverted many of them to Christmas Island, an Australian territory in the Indian Ocean. The refugees were held there until the government could process their asylum claims. Under the Howard government, many of the refugees were sent to the Pacific Islands nations of Nauru and Papua New Guinea for processing.

The Labor Party regained power in 2007 elections. Kevin Rudd became prime minister. In 2008, Rudd's government closed the Pacific Islands detention centers. Also that year, Rudd issued a formal apology for grief, suffering, and loss caused among Australia's Indigenous peoples by the policies of previous governments.

In 2010, Rudd's deputy, Julia Gillard, successfully challenged him for leadership of the Labor Party. She became Australia's first female prime minister. In 2012, the government reopened the facilities in Nauru and Papua New Guinea and began transporting asylum-seekers from Christmas Island to those two countries.

Recent developments. Kevin Rudd challenged Gillard for Labor leadership and again became prime minister in June 2013. In September, the Liberal-National coalition regained power in a general election. Liberal leader Tony Abbott became prime minister. In 2015, Malcolm Turnbull challenged Abbott for leadership of the Liberal Party and became prime minister. The coalition remained in power after parliamentary elections in 2016. In 2017, the Australian government closed the detention center in Papua New Guinea. Some asylum-seekers who had been held there and in Nauru were sent to the United States for resettlement.

Scott Morrison replaced Turnbull as leader of the Liberal Party in 2018 and became prime minister. In 2019, Morrison led the coalition to victory in federal elections and remained in office as prime minister.

From late 2019 to early 2020, bushfires burned millions of acres of land in Australia, especially impacting heavily populated areas of eastern Australia. In 2020 and 2021, Australians also faced the health crisis and financial challenges of the COVID-19 pandemic. Federal, state, and territorial governments implemented measures to stop the spread of the disease. Australia's vaccination program to fight the disease began in February 2021, but some policies to limit new outbreaks continued. See **COVID-19.**

David Carter, Grace Karskens, Clement Macintyre, and Adrian Mitchell

Related articles in *World Book* include:

Biographies

Anderson, Judith
Assange, Julian
Bruce, Sir David
Burnet, Sir Macfarlane
Florey, Lord
Gibson, Mel
Gillard, Julia
Grainger, Percy
Greer, Germaine
Howard, John W.
Jackman, Hugh

Kelly, Ned
Keneally, Thomas
Kenny, Elizabeth
Macquarie, Lachlan
McCullough, Colleen
Melba, Dame Nellie
Menzies, Sir Robert Gordon
Morrison, Scott

Murdoch, Rupert
Parkes, Sir Henry
Rudd, Kevin
Michael
Simpson and his donkey
Sutherland, Joan
Torres, Luis Vaez de
Travers, P. L.
White, Patrick
Wilkins, Sir Hubert

Characteristic animal life

Bandicoot
Bearded dragon
Bogong moth
Bowerbird
Cane toad
Cassowary
Cockatoo
Cuscus

Dingo
Dugong
Echidna
Emu
Glider
Honeyeater
Kangaroo
Koala
Kookaburra
Lyrebird

Marsupial
Marsupial mouse
Mound bird
Numbat
Parakeet
Parrot
Platypus
Possum
Quoll

Tasmanian devil
Tasmanian tiger
Tiger snake
Wallaby
Wallaroo
Weaver
Wombat

Characteristic plant life

Acacia
Beefwood

Bottle tree
Eucalyptus

Kava
Silky oak

Cities

Adelaide
Brisbane
Canberra
Darwin

Hobart
Melbourne
Newcastle

Perth
Sydney
Wollongong

Natural features

Australian Desert
Barossa Valley
Botany Bay
Coral Sea
Daintree rain forest
Great Barrier Reef

Great Victoria Desert
Indian Ocean
Lake Eyre
Lake Macquarie
Lake Torrens
Mount Kosciuszko

Murray River
Pacific Ocean
Tasman Sea
Torrens River
Torres Strait Islands
Uluru

States and territories

Australian Capital Territory
New South Wales
Norfolk Island

Northern Territory
Queensland
South Australia

Tasmania
Victoria
Western Australia

Other related articles

Aboriginal peoples of Australia
Anzac Day

Bank (Australia and New Zealand)
Boomerang

Colombo Plan
Conservation (Australia)
Cook, James
Dreamtime
Exploration (Exploring the Pacific; Exploring Australia's interior)
Great Depression (Effects in Australia)
Immigration

Motion picture (Films in postwar Australia)
National park (Australia)
Outback
Political party (In Canada and Australia)
Stolen Generations
Television (In Australia and New Zealand)
Transportation of convicts
Woman suffrage (Australia)

Outline

I. Government
   A. The federal government
   B. State government
   C. Local government
   D. Political parties
   E. The armed forces

II. People
   A. Population and ancestry
   B. Language
   C. The Indigenous peoples of Australia

III. Ways of life
   A. City life
   B. Country life
   C. Food and drink
   D. Recreation
   E. Education
   F. Religion

IV. The arts
   A. Literature
   B. Painting
   C. Music and dance
   D. Theater and motion pictures
   E. Architecture

V. The land
   A. Land regions
   B. Mountains
   C. Deserts
   D. Rivers
   E. Lakes
   F. Underground water
   G. The Great Barrier Reef

VI. Climate

VII. Animals and plants
   A. Native animals
   B. Native plants
   C. Introduced species

VIII. Economy
   A. Service industries
   B. Manufacturing
   C. Mining
   D. Agriculture
   E. Forestry and fishing
   F. Tourism
   G. International trade
   H. Transportation
   I. Communication

IX. History

Australian Aborigines. See Aboriginal peoples of Australia.

Australian Capital Territory (ACT) is the site of Canberra, Australia's capital. The ACT covers 910 square miles (2,358 square kilometers). It includes the urban area of Canberra as well as a national park, recreation areas, and historic and scenic sites. The 2016 Australian census reported that the ACT had 397,397 people.

The average rainfall in Canberra is about 36 inches (91 centimeters) a year. The average temperature is 69 °F (21 °C) in January and 42 °F (6 °C) in July.

Aboriginal peoples, the earliest inhabitants of Australia, lived in the region at least 21,000 years ago. In 1820, British explorers became the first white people to reach the area. In 1900, the British Parliament approved the Commonwealth of Australia Constitution Act. This act established the Commonwealth of Australia and provided for a federal government area with its own territory.

In 1909, Charles R. Scrivener, a New South Wales district surveyor, recommended the present site of Canberra. The ACT was established on Jan. 1, 1911. In 1915, the Jervis Bay Territory was created on the New South Wales coast and added to the ACT as a port. In 1989, the ACT gained powers of self-government like those in the Australian states. Afterward, the Jervis Bay Territory ceased to be governed as part of the ACT. Voters elect a parliament, the Legislative Assembly.   Jack Waterford

See also **Canberra.**

Australian cattle dog is a breed of dog that originated in Australia during the 1800's. It was developed from several breeds of farm dogs, including collies and kelpies. Farmers and ranchers use Australian cattle dogs to herd cattle. These dogs nip at the heels of the cattle to keep them from straying. The dogs also make excellent watchdogs and affectionate pets. They stand from 17 to 20 inches (43 to 51 centimeters) high and weigh 35 to 45 pounds (16 to 20 kilograms). They have short, thick coats and bushy tails. Many of the dogs are blue and may have black, blue, or tan markings on the head, and tan markings on the chest and legs. Others are red. Many have red speckles all over the body. Puppies are born with white coats. Their color and markings appear in a few months. The Australian cattle dog has been known by several other names, including the *Australian heeler,* the *Queensland heeler,* the *Queensland blue heeler,* and the *blue heeler.*   Critically reviewed by the American Kennel Club

See also **Dog** (picture: Herding dogs).

Australian Desert refers to three deserts that cover most of western and central Australia—the Great Sandy Desert, the Gibson Desert, and the Great Victoria Desert. These deserts are not as dry as most deserts and have a thin cover of vegetation. The Great Sandy Desert stretches south to the Gibson Desert. It covers about 110,000 square miles (285,000 square kilometers). Peter Egerton Warburton first walked over it in 1873. That same year, Ernest Giles became the first European to reach the 60,000-square-mile (156,000-square-kilometer) Gibson Desert. The Great Victoria Desert runs south from the Gibson to the Nullarbor Plain (see **Australia** [physical map]). See also **Great Victoria Desert.**   D. N. Jeans

Australian pine. See Beefwood.

Australian shepherd is a medium-sized dog originally bred for herding livestock. The breed was developed in the United States. It got its name because many sheepherders who came from Australia in the late 1800's used similar dogs to herd their flocks. Australian shepherds are often called "Aussies." The Aussie stands 18 to 23 inches (46 to 58 centimeters) tall at the shoulders and weighs about 45 to 65 pounds (20 to 29 kilograms). It has a straight to wavy coat that may be blue or red *merle* (dark blotches on a lighter background), black, or red, often with white or tan markings. Aussies are intelligent and protective, and they make good pets.

Critically reviewed by the United States Australian Shepherd Association

© Shutterstock

The Australian shepherd has strong herding instincts.

Australian terrier is a small dog once used to guard mines and tend sheep in Australia. People now keep these terriers chiefly as pets. Australian terriers have harsh, straight coats, with a soft-haired topknot on their heads. The coats may be blue- or silver-black, with tan markings on the head and legs. The Australian terrier weighs about 12 to 14 pounds (5.4 to 6.4 kilograms). The breed originated in Australia about 1885.

Critically reviewed by the American Kennel Club

See also **Dog** (picture: Terriers).

Australopithecus, *AW struh loh PIHTH uh kuhs,* is a group of early humanlike creatures. These creatures lived in Africa from about 4 million to 1 million years ago. Members of the *genus* (group of species) *Australopithecus* are called *australopithecines.* Their remains are among the oldest known *hominin* fossils. In scientific classification, hominins make up the group that includes human beings and prehistoric humanlike species.

Australopithecines stood upright and walked on two legs. They grew about 3 ½ to 5 feet (110 to 150 centimeters) tall and had large projecting faces with large molar teeth. The size of their brains was about one-third the size of a modern human brain. The male australopithecines were larger than the females.

Most anthropologists recognize at least seven species of *Australopithecus.* They are, from oldest to most recent, *A. anamensis, A. afarensis, A. africanus, A. aethiopicus, A. garhi, A. boisei,* and *A. robustus.* Although all the australopithecines had large faces and molars, *A. aethiopicus, A. robustus,* and *A. boisei* had much larger jaws and teeth than the other species. These three species are often called the *robust australopithecines.* The other species are called *gracile* (slender) *australopithecines.* Some anthropologists put the robust species in a separate genus, called *Paranthropus.*

Scientists think that humans developed from a species of australopithecine. However, they are not sure which species is ancestral to the first humans. The first humans appeared about 2 million years ago.

Australopithecine fossils were first recognized in 1924 when the South African anthropologist Raymond Dart identified a child's skull that had been found at Taung, near Vryburg, South Africa. Dart named the creature *Australopithecus africanus.* He believed it was a human ancestor, but most scientists thought it was an extinct ape. Additional fossils found over the next 35 years convinced scientists that *Australopithecus* was a hominin.

In 1974, researchers discovered a partial skeleton of a female australopithecine at Hadar, Ethiopia. The fossil is about 3.2 million years old. Nicknamed "Lucy," she walked upright but had arms that, in proportion to her body, were longer than those of modern people. In 1978, researchers at Laetoli, Tanzania, found fossil footprints together with fossilized bones of a hominin that lived 3.6 million years ago. Anthropologists have classified "Lucy" and the Laetoli fossils as *Australopithecus afarensis.* In 2010, anthropologists announced the discovery of a new gracile species called *Australopithecus sediba* at a site called Malapa in South Africa. It is about 2 million years old. Features of the skeleton show that *A. sediba* could walk upright and possibly make and use stone tools, as could the earliest humans.   Alan E. Mann

See also **Laetoli fossil site; Prehistoric people** (Prehuman ancestors).

Austria is known for its picturesque mountain scenery. The Alps and their foothills dominate Austria's landscape. Heiligenblut village, *shown here,* lies in a Central Alpine valley in the Carinthia region of southern Austria. Thick forests also cover much of the land.

© Johanna Huber, SIME/4Corners Images

Austria

Austria is a small country in central Europe famous for its beautiful mountain scenery. The towering Alps and their foothills stretch across the western, southern, and central parts of the country. In many areas, broad, green valleys separate the mountains. Austria has many lovely, mirrorlike lakes. Thick forests cover much of the land.

Austria has no coastline. It shares boundaries with the countries of Switzerland and Liechtenstein to the west, Germany and the Czech Republic to the north, Slovakia and Hungary to the east, and Slovenia and Italy to the south.

Vienna is Austria's capital and largest city. It lies on the Danube River in the northeastern part of the country. Most of Austria's people live in cities and towns.

Austrians take great pride in the fact that their country has long been a leading cultural center of Europe. The cultural institutions and scenic beauty of Austria attract tens of millions of tourists each year.

Austria was once the core of one of the great powers of Europe. Austria began as a military border territory of the Holy Roman Empire in the late 900's and became a *duchy* (territory ruled by a duke) of the empire in 1156. In the late 1200's, the Habsburg (also spelled *Hapsburg)* family gained control of Austria and became identified with Austria. The House of Habsburg, also known as the House of Austria, developed into the most powerful

dynasty in the empire. From 1438 to 1806, except from 1740 to 1745, the Habsburgs ruled the empire. The Holy Roman Empire ended in 1806, and the Austrian Empire, founded in 1804, replaced it. The Austrian Empire became the Dual Monarchy of Austria-Hungary in 1867. This kingdom split into several states at the end of World War I in 1918. The territories of present-day Austria formed the Austrian republic. The republic endured two decades of economic difficulty and political unrest.

From 1938 to 1945, Austria was part of the German *Third Reich* (Third Empire), the Nazi term for the empire in which they hoped to unite all Germanic peoples. After Germany's defeat in World War II (1939-1945), the Allies

Facts in brief

Capital: Vienna.
Official language: German.
Official name: Republik Österreich (Republic of Austria).
Area: 32,387 mi² (83,882 km²). *Greatest distances*—east-west, 355 mi (571 km); north-south, 180 mi (290 km).
Elevation: *Highest*—Grossglockner, 12,461 ft (3,798 m) above sea level. *Lowest*—Neusiedler Lake, 377 ft (115 m) above sea level.
Population: *Estimated 2022 population*—8,963,000; density, 277 per mi² (107 per km²); distribution, 59 percent urban, 41 percent rural. *2020 official government estimate*—8,901,064.
Chief products: *Agriculture*—apples, beef and dairy cattle, corn, grapes, hogs, potatoes, poultry, sugar beets, wheat. *Manufacturing*—chemical products, electronic equipment, glass, iron and steel, machines and tools, motor vehicles, paper and pulp, processed foods and beverages, textiles and clothing, wood products. *Mining*—gypsum, iron ore, magnesite, natural gas, petroleum, salt, stone, tungsten.
National anthem: "Land der Berge, Land am Strome" ("Land of Mountains, Land at the River").
Money: *Basic unit*—euro. One hundred cents equal one euro. The schilling was taken out of circulation in 2002.

Steven Beller, the contributor of this article, is the author of A Concise History of Austria *and other books on Austrian history and culture.*

© f1 online/Alamy Images

The Federal Assembly building in Vienna is the meeting place of both houses of the Austrian legislature. The building, designed in the Greek Classical style, dates from the late 1800's.

occupied Austria until 1955. Since then, Austria has been a neutral country. It has benefited from both economic and political stability and has become a prosperous nation. In 1995, Austria joined the European Union (EU), an organization of European nations that works for economic and political cooperation among its members.

Government

Austria is a federal republic made up of nine provinces: Burgenland, Carinthia, Lower Austria, Salzburg, Styria, Tyrol (or Tirol), Upper Austria, the city of Vienna, and Vorarlberg. Austria's Constitution was adopted in 1920. All Austrian citizens who are 16 years and older may vote.

The president is Austria's head of state. The people elect the president to a six-year term. The president may serve any number of terms but no more than two in a row. The president's duties include appointing ambassadors, signing treaties, and swearing in certain officeholders. The president also acts as commander in chief of the armed forces. The president does not have the power to declare war or to *veto* (reject) bills passed by Austria's parliament, the Federal Assembly.

The chancellor and Council of Ministers run the Austrian government. The *chancellor* (prime minister) serves as head of government. Generally, the president appoints as chancellor the leader of the political party with the most seats in the Nationalrat. The Nationalrat is the more important of the two houses of the Federal Assembly. On the chancellor's advice, the president also appoints members of the Council of Ministers to head the government departments. The chancellor and Council of Ministers set government policies and are responsible to the Nationalrat. The Nationalrat may force the chancellor and Council of Ministers to resign by rejecting their policies in a *vote of no confidence.*

The Federal Assembly consists of two houses, the Nationalrat (National Council) and the Bundesrat (Federal Council). Members of the Nationalrat are elected by the people to five-year terms. But new elections may take place sooner if the Nationalrat dissolves itself, or if the president dissolves it on the chancellor's advice. The

© Loveshop/Shutterstock

Austria's civil flag has three stripes of red, white, and red. The state flag includes the coat of arms in the center.

The coat of arms was adopted in its present form in 1945. Use of an eagle to symbolize Austria dates from the 1200's.

WORLD BOOK map

Austria is a landlocked country in central Europe. Eight other European countries surround Austria.

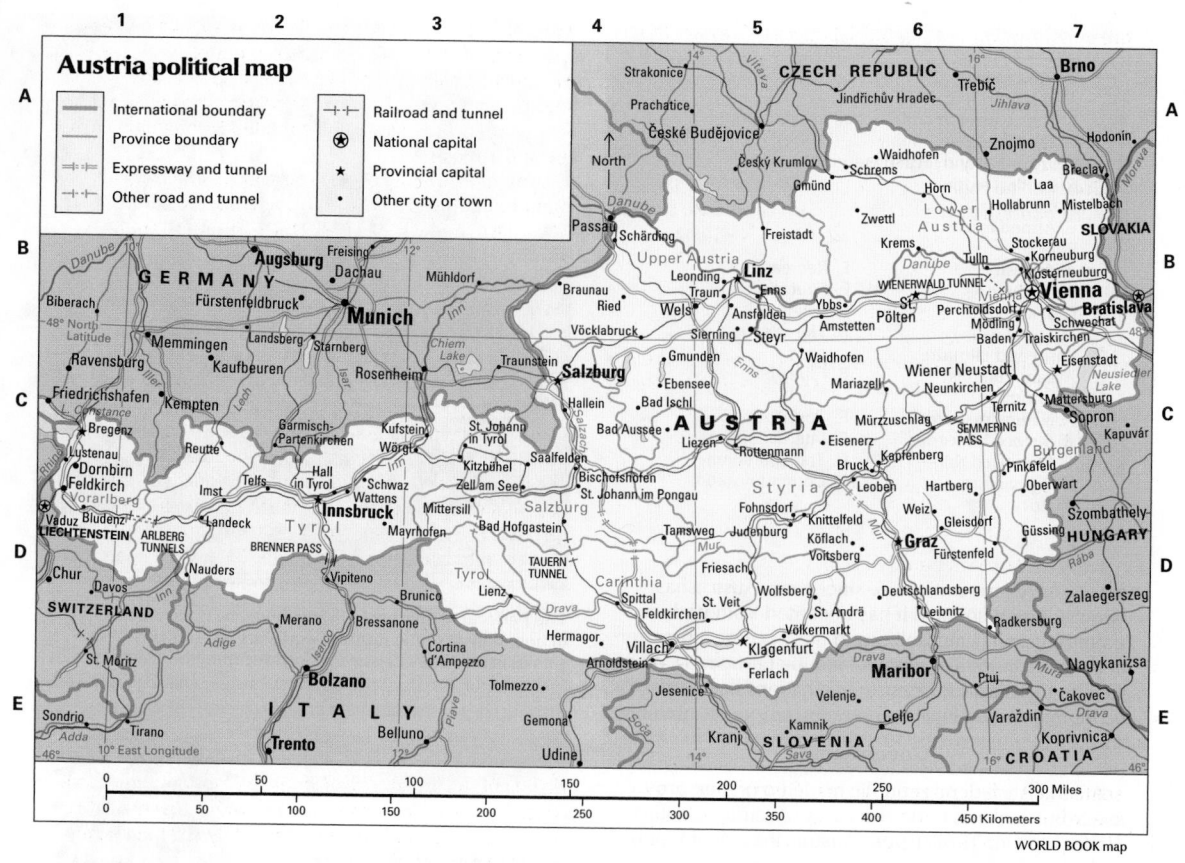

Austria political map

▬ International boundary	┼┼ Railroad and tunnel
▬ Province boundary	⊛ National capital
╪╪ Expressway and tunnel	★ Provincial capital
┼┼ Other road and tunnel	• Other city or town

WORLD BOOK map

Austria map index

Bundesrat's members are elected by the country's nine *Landtags* (provincial legislatures). Members of the Bundesrat serve as long as the Landtag that chose them stays in power. The number of members a province has in the Bundesrat varies according to population.

Provincial and local government. The people in each province elect Landtag members to terms of up to five or six years, depending on the province. Each Land-

tag chooses the governor of the province. The provinces are subdivided into more than 2,000 *municipalities* (units of local government). Voters in each municipality elect a governing council, which selects one of its number to serve as mayor. Vienna is both a province and a municipality. Its municipal council serves as the provincial legislature, and its mayor serves as governor.

Political parties. Two political parties control the

great majority of seats in the Nationalrat. They are the center-left Social Democratic Party of Austria and the conservative Austrian People's Party. Other parties include the environmentalist Greens and two parties on the far right—the Alliance for the Future of Austria and the Freedom Party of Austria.

Courts. The Supreme Court of Justice is Austria's highest court of appeal in civil and criminal cases. The Supreme Constitutional Court determines whether laws are constitutional, and the Supreme Administrative Court is the highest court for cases that challenge the activities of government agencies. Four provincial courts hear appeals of decisions made by lower courts. Various special courts handle juvenile matters and labor disputes.

Armed forces. Austria's armed forces consist of an army with an air wing but no navy. Austrian men must serve at least six months in the army, usually with additional periods of follow-up training later. Women serve in the armed forces on a voluntary basis.

People

Most of Austria's people live in the lowland areas of the country—in the east and just south of the Danube River. About a fifth of the people live in Vienna, the country's capital and largest city.

Ancestry. Many different groups of people have settled in Austria. Each group mixed with other people and so helped shape the ancestry of present-day Austrians. In ancient times, the people of Austria included Celts and Romans. Later, various Germanic and Slavic groups settled in Austria. After the 1300's, Austria attracted people from many parts of central Europe and parts of the Habsburg empire, such as Italy and Spain. Many immigrants came to Austria during the Cold War, the rivalry between Communist and non-Communist nations that lasted from the late 1940's to the early 1990's. Large numbers of people fleeing from Communism in Czechoslovakia and Hungary settled in Austria. In the 1990's, the tensions surrounding the breakup of Yugoslavia led some people from that region to immigrate to Austria.

Language. Almost all Austrians speak German, the country's official language. In different parts of the country, the people speak *dialects* (local forms) of German.

A number of Austrians speak another language as their first language. In the province of Burgenland, for example, there are communities of people who speak Croatian. Carinthia has a number of people who speak Slovenian. Small groups of people in Vienna speak either Czech or Slovak. Other languages spoken as a first language include Magyar (also called Hungarian), Serbian, and Turkish.

Way of life. Most city dwellers in Austria live in apartment buildings. Others live in single-family homes. Many farm and village families live in single-family homes. Housing styles vary from region to region. In Burgenland, many homes are simple in design and covered with a kind of plaster called *stucco*. The provinces of Tyrol and Vorarlberg have many wooden houses called *chalets* similar to those of Switzerland. Most chalets have a steep, pointed roof with wide, overhanging eaves.

Austrians wear clothing much like that worn in other European countries and in North America. On special occasions, many Austrians wear traditional national or regional costumes. Men may wear a green-trimmed, gray wool suit consisting of a coat and *knickers*—short, loose-fitting trousers gathered just below the knee. Women may wear a peasant costume called a *dirndl*, which has a full skirt, an apron, and a close-fitting top that is worn over a blouse and laced up the front.

Many Austrian dishes have been influenced by Czech, German, or Hungarian cooking. Popular meats in Austria include beef, chicken, pork, sausage, and veal. An Austrian dish called *Wiener schnitzel* (breaded veal cutlet) has become a favorite in many countries. Popular side dishes in Austria include dumplings, noodles, and potatoes. Austrians drink beer or wine with many meals. The delicious cakes and pastries created by Austrian bakers have become world famous.

Festivals and holidays play an important part in Austrian life. Some festivals date from pre-Christian times. One such festival held in parts of the Tyrol has become part of the late winter merrymaking that precedes the solemn religious season of Lent. Some people pretend to chase away the "evil spirits" of winter. Wearing special costumes and masks, they march through the streets and wave large sticks in the air.

Social welfare. The Austrian government provides comprehensive welfare services. Under the national social insurance program, workers may receive disability,

Salzburg, one of Austria's major cities, attracts visitors from all over the world. The people shown here are gathered at one of the city's many outdoor cafes. Hohensalzburg Fortress, the city's chief landmark, stands in the background.

maternity, old-age, sickness, survivors', or unemployment benefits. Austria also has a national health insurance program for all citizens. The costs of both programs are shared by insured people; employers; and the federal, provincial, and local governments.

Since 1919, Austrian law has limited the workday to eight hours and has guaranteed employed people annual holidays. Today, most employed people who have been on the job for one year or longer receive at least a 25-day vacation with pay each year. In 1975, the workweek became limited to 40 hours.

Recreation. Austrians love the outdoors, and their country's many forests, lakes, and mountains offer opportunities for a variety of outdoor sports. In winter, the people especially enjoy ice skating, skiing, and tobogganing. Other popular winter sports include bobsledding, ice hockey, and ski jumping. Favorite summer sports include boating, fishing, hiking, mountain climbing, swimming, and water skiing. The people also enjoy bicycling, camping, picnicking, and playing soccer.

Austrians love the arts as well as sports. Ballets, concerts, motion pictures, operas and operettas, and plays are all popular.

Education. Almost all adult Austrians can read and write. Austrian children between the ages of 6 and 15 are required to attend school. Most students attend free public schools. The rest attend private schools, which may charge a tuition fee.

Austria has several universities, technical colleges, and fine arts colleges. The University of Vienna is the country's largest university.

Religion. About 65 percent of the people in Austria are Roman Catholics. Muslims and Protestants each account for about 5 percent of the population. Austria has a small Jewish population, mostly in Vienna. The Austrian government gives financial support to many religious institutions, including the private schools of the Roman Catholic Church and several other recognized religions.

The arts. Austria has been a leading cultural center in Europe. The country has made outstanding contributions in architecture, literature, painting, and theater. However, Austria's most important cultural achievements have been in music.

Music. Austria has produced many great composers. During the late 1700's and early 1800's, Joseph Haydn helped make the symphony one of the most important forms of musical composition. Haydn and Wolfgang Amadeus Mozart became the leading composers of the Classical period of music. Mozart wrote masterpieces in a wide range of musical forms. Many people consider his *Don Giovanni* (1787) the world's greatest opera.

The German composer Ludwig van Beethoven spent most of his life in Austria. Most of his nine symphonies and his opera, *Fidelio* (three versions: 1805, 1806, 1814), were composed and first performed in or near Vienna. In the early 1800's, Franz Schubert of Vienna created chamber music, symphonies, and over 600 *lieder* (German-language art songs). Hugo Wolf continued the lieder tradition in the late 1800's. Gustav Mahler and Anton Bruckner wrote many symphonies, which are considered some of the finest Austrian contributions to music during the Romantic era. Johannes Brahms, a German composer who combined the Romantic and Classical traditions, also lived in Vienna. Johann Strauss and his son, Johann Strauss, Jr., composed their famous waltzes and operettas in Vienna.

Arnold Schoenberg became one of the most revolutionary composers of the 1900's. He developed a new system of composition called the *twelve-tone technique.* Schoenberg influenced many composers, including his fellow Austrians Alban Berg and Anton Webern.

Austria continues to make important musical contributions today. The Vienna Boys' Choir, Vienna Philharmonic, Vienna State Opera, and Vienna Symphony have achieved international fame. The Salzburg Festival is one of the great annual musical events. Students from all over the world study at Austria's fine music schools.

Architecture. Austria has some of Europe's best examples of Baroque architecture. Beginning in the 1600's, buildings in the Baroque style featured elaborate decorations and an abundance of paintings and sculptures. The architects intended these buildings to express the power and glory of the Roman Catholic Church, the Austrian aristocracy, and the Habsburg dynasty. The finest examples of Austrian Baroque architecture include the *Karlskirche* (Church of St. Charles, named for St. Charles Borromeo) in Vienna and the Church of the Holy Trinity in Salzburg. Johann Bernhard Fischer von Erlach designed both churches. Other examples include the Belvedere Palace in Vienna, designed by Johann Lucas von Hildebrandt, and the Benedictine monastery in Melk, designed by Jakob Prandtauer.

Austria also has many churches, palaces, and other buildings designed in the Rococo style of the 1700's. Rococo architecture is even more decorated than Baroque, but lighter.

© INTERFOTO/Alamy Images

Scenic resort towns lie along many lakes in the Salzkammergut area of central Austria. In St. Gilgen, *shown here,* a waterfront scene shows boats and visitors on Lake Wolfgang. Mountains of the Alps rise in the background.

The Vienna Boys' Choir performs a holiday concert at the Vienna Konzerthaus. With performances around the world, the choir has achieved international fame.

During the late 1800's and early 1900's, Otto Wagner developed a simplified, *functionalist* style of architecture, based on the belief that a building's function should determine its style. Adolf Loos further developed this architectural functionalism. Wagner and Loos are regarded as two of the founding figures of the Modern Movement in architecture.

Literature. People in Austria love the theater, and many of the country's most important writers have been playwrights. Franz Grillparzer wrote plays in the early to middle 1800's that drew on classical German drama as well as Austrian folk plays. Ferdinand Raimund wrote plays in the folk tradition with elements of fairy tales, while Johann Nestroy wrote political satires often disguised as fantasies.

During the late 1800's and early 1900's, such writers as Arthur Schnitzler and Hugo von Hofmannsthal created a Viennese literary tradition famous for its artistic style and psychological depth. Such authors as Robert Musil, Franz Werfel, and Stefan Zweig further developed this tradition of psychological fiction. These authors of such fiction were inspired partly by the theories of Sigmund Freud, the Austrian physician who developed psychoanalysis as a method of treating mental illness. Karl Kraus became one of the greatest satirists of the early 1900's. In 2004, Elfriede Jelinek became the first Austrian writer to receive the Nobel Prize in literature.

Painting. Gustav Klimt, who worked in the late 1800's and early 1900's, was one of Austria's first modern painters of international importance. He is known for his flat, two-dimensional, decorative portraits. Two of Klimt's followers—Egon Schiele and Oskar Kokoschka—became the leading artists of Austrian Expressionism, a movement that emphasized strong emotional content.

Land and climate

Mountains cover about three-fourths of Austria. The Alps stretch across the western, southern, and central parts of the country. A separate mountainous area, the Granite Plateau, lies in the north. The country's highest point, the mountain Grossglockner, rises 12,461 feet (3,798 meters) above sea level in central Austria.

The Danube, the country's longest river, flows 217 miles (350 kilometers) from west to east through northern Austria. Almost all Austrian rivers flow into the Danube. Austria's largest lake is Neusiedler Lake. Part of this lake lies in Hungary. The Austrian part covers 52 square miles (135 square kilometers).

Land regions. Austria has six main land regions. They are (1) the Granite Plateau; (2) the Eastern Forelands; (3) the Alpine Forelands; (4) the Northern Limestone Alps; (5) the Central Alps; and (6) the Southern Limestone Alps.

The Granite Plateau forms Austria's northernmost region. It consists of hills and mountains that are made up mostly of granite and partly covered by thick forests.

The Eastern Forelands lie southeast of the Granite Plateau. The northern part is a lowland called the Vienna Basin. Its fertile soil helps make it Austria's chief agricul-

The interior of Innsbruck Cathedral, a Roman Catholic church, has tall columns and a richly decorated ceiling in the Baroque style. Catholics are a majority of Austria's population.

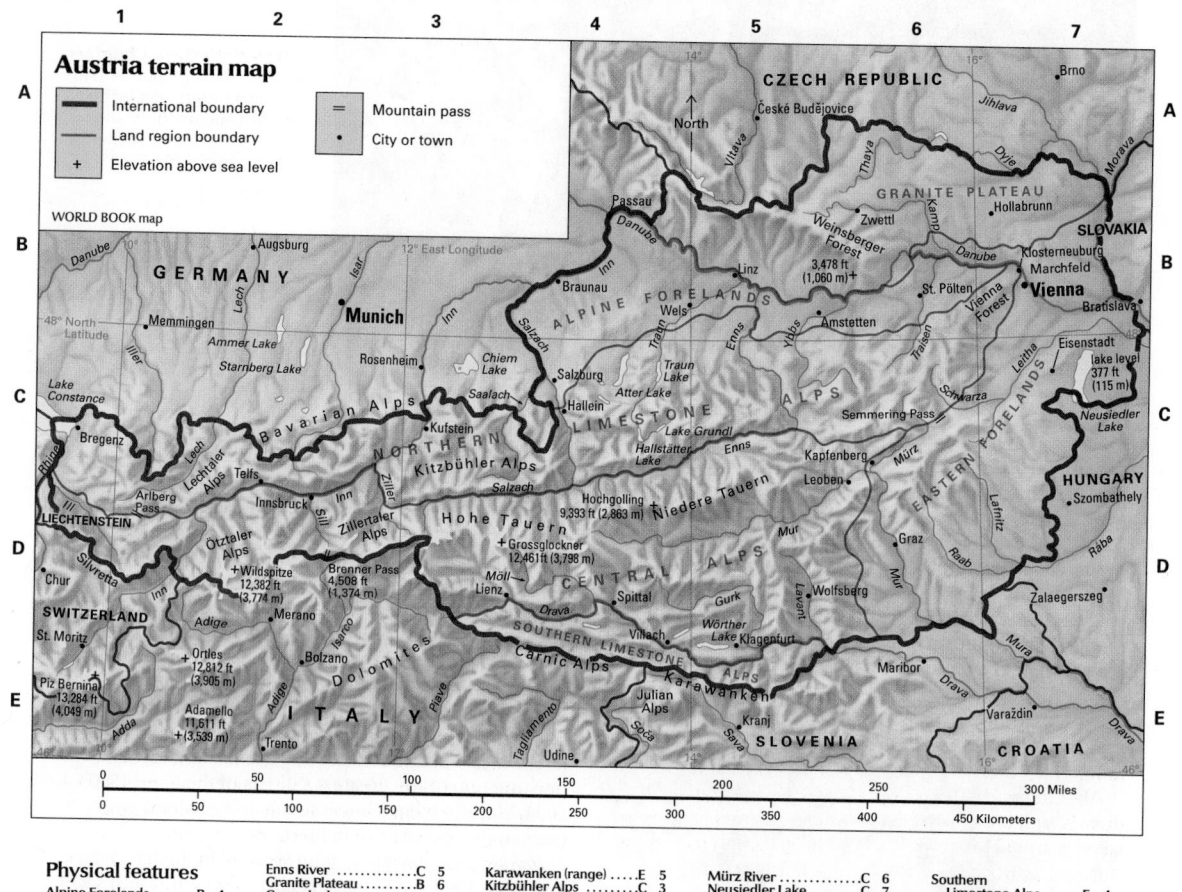

Austria terrain map

International boundary	Mountain pass
Land region boundary	City or town
+ Elevation above sea level	

WORLD BOOK map

Physical features

Alpine Forelands	B 4	Enns River	C 5	Karawanken (range)	E 5	Mürz River ....C 6
Arlberg Pass	D 1	Granite Plateau	B 6	Kitzbühler Alps	C 3	Neusiedler Lake ......C 7
Atter Lake	C 4	Grossglockner		Lafnitz River	D 6	Niedere Tauern ......D 5
Brenner Pass	D 2	(mountain)	D 3	Lake Constance	C 1	Northern
Central Alps	D 4	Gurk River	D 5	Lake Grundl	C 4	Limestone Alps ....C 4
Danube River	B 4	Hallstätter Lake	C 4	Lavant River	D 5	Ötztaler Alps ....D 2
Drava River	D 4	Hochgolling (mountain)	D 4	Lech River	C 2	Raab River ....D 6
Eastern Forelands	C 6	Hohe Tauern	D 3	Leitha River	C 7	Rhine River ....C 1
		Ill River	D 1	Möll River	D 4	Salzach River ....C 4
		Inn River	D 2	Mur River	D 5	Semmering Pass ....C 6

Southern	
Limestone Alps	E 4
Traisen River	C 6
Traun Lake	C 4
Vienna Forest	B 6
Weinsberger Forest	B 5
Wildspitze (mountain)	D 2
Wörther Lake	E 5
Ybbs River	B 5
Zillertaler Alps	D 3

tural area. The southern part consists of rolling hills and broad valleys, with the land becoming flatter in the east.

The Alpine Forelands lie south of the Granite Plateau and west of the Eastern Forelands. The region is made up of hills and low mountains.

The Northern Limestone Alps rise south and southwest of the Alpine Forelands. The mountains in this region consist of limestone. The region is marked by high plateaus; steep, forested slopes; and jagged peaks. Several large lakes formed by ancient glaciers dot this mountainous region.

The Central Alps are separated from the Northern Limestone Alps to the north by a series of valleys. Unlike the Northern Limestone Alps, the Central Alps do not consist of limestone but of such rocks as granite and gneiss. The Central Alps have Austria's highest mountains. Glaciers cover many parts of the mountains.

The Southern Limestone Alps lie south of the Central Alps. A series of valleys separates the two regions. The physical features of the Southern Limestone Alps resemble those of the Northern Limestone Alps.

Climate. Austria has four sharply defined seasons. The country's climate is influenced by both west and east winds. Warm, moist winds blowing eastward from the Atlantic Ocean affect the climate of western and central Austria. These winds bring rain, snow, and other forms of precipitation and help produce moderate temperatures throughout the year. Dry winds blowing westward from the Asian plains are hot in summer and cold in winter. Partly as a result of these winds, eastern Austria has less precipitation and more extreme temperatures than western and central Austria.

Within the western, central, and eastern areas, Austria's climate varies from place to place, partly because of differences in altitude. Local winds also influence the climate. For example, warm, dry winds called *foehns* cause sudden rises in temperature in some mountain valleys in winter. Because they may rapidly melt mountain snow, foehns sometimes cause destructive avalanches (see **Foehn**).

January temperatures in Austria average about 27 °F (−3 °C). July temperatures average about 67 °F (19 °C). The country receives an average of about 25 inches (64 centimeters) of precipitation yearly.

Economy

Austria's economy is based mostly on private ownership of businesses. The country's economy was severely

The Danube, the longest river in Austria, flows from west to east through the northern part of the country. It runs through the city of Krems, *shown here,* in the northeast.

© Giovanni Simeone, SIME/4Corners Images

damaged by the breakup of the Habsburg dynasty in 1918. Wartime destruction and defeat in World War II (1939-1945) brought further economic distress to Austria. However, postwar financial aid from the United States helped boost Austria's economy.

In the late 1940's, the Austrian government *nationalized* (transferred from private to state ownership) most of the companies in several chief industries, including coal and metal mining; electric power production; iron and steel production; and oil drilling and refining. Since the 1980's, the government has *privatized* many of these industries, returning them to private ownership.

After the early 1950's, Austria rapidly became an industrialized nation. Today, service industries have overtaken manufacturing as the country's leading industry. Austria has become a prosperous country with little poverty or unemployment.

Natural resources. During the Middle Ages, from about the 400's to the 1400's, Austria was famous for its minerals, especially iron from the Erzberg (Iron Ore Mountain) in the Styria province and silver from the Tyrol province. Today, mineral deposits either have become depleted or are too low in quality to meet the country's needs. The Erzberg still has much iron ore, but Austria must import higher-grade ores. Most of Austria's petroleum and natural gas reserves are in the Lower Austria province, but these reserves are insufficient for the country's demands. As a result, Austria depends upon large imports of petroleum and gas.

Austria is one of the world's leading producers of magnesite, which is used to make such products as heat-resistant bricks and artificial stone. The country also mines gypsum, salt, stone, and tungsten.

Austria's rich forests, which cover about 45 percent of the country, provide plentiful lumber, paper, and other products. Spruce and fir are commercially important trees. Strict conservation laws and extensive replanting programs ensure the preservation of forests.

Austria's swift-flowing rivers are another important natural resource. They provide energy for many hydroelectric power stations, which produce more than half of the nation's electric power.

Service industries, taken together, account for about 70 percent of both Austria's employment and its *gross domestic product* (GDP)—the total value of goods and services produced within a country in a year. The community, government, and personal services group employs more people than any other economic activity. The privatization of businesses has reduced the government's influence in the economy, but the state still has total or partial control over several of Austria's major companies. The finance, insurance, real estate, and business services group contributes more to Austria's GDP than any other industry group. Many foreign investors own shares in Austria's banks, and many Austrians have invested in banks in central and eastern Europe. Hotels, restaurants, and shops in Austria benefit from tourism.

Manufacturing. The production of metal, especially iron and steel, and the manufacture of metal products—including automobiles, locomotives, machines, and tools—once dominated Austrian manufacturing. Today, however, manufacturing has become more varied. Austria's factories now also produce chemical products, clothing and textiles, electronic equipment, glass and porcelain products, paper, processed foods and beverages, and wood products.

Factories are scattered throughout Austria, but the heaviest concentration is in the Vienna area. There is a strong emphasis in Austrian manufacturing on high quality rather than mass production. Many factories are small or medium-sized. Austria is known for its craftworkers, who produce excellent glassware, jewelry, needlework, porcelain objects, woodcarvings, and other handicrafts. One of the country's best-known products is Swarovski crystal.

Agriculture. Austria is so mountainous that only about 20 percent of the land can be used for growing crops. But the country's farmers use modern machinery and scientific farming methods. As a result, they can supply most of the food needed by the people. All Austrian farms are privately owned. Since the late 1940's, there has been a trend toward larger farms. But most farms in Austria are still small.

Dairy farming and livestock production are the main sources of farm income. Austria's farmers produce all the meat and milk needed by the people. The country's farmers raise beef and dairy cattle, chickens, hogs, and turkeys. Many of these farm animals are raised in the northern section of Austria.

The best croplands are in the Vienna Basin. But farm plots can be found in every province. Austria's leading crops include apples, barley, corn, grapes, pears, pota-

Austria's gross domestic product

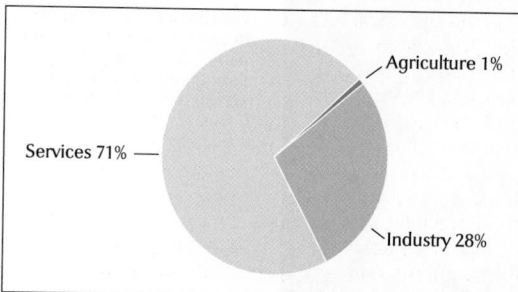

- Agriculture 1%
- Services 71%
- Industry 28%

Austria's gross domestic product was $386,587,000,000 in 2016. The gross domestic product is the total value of goods and services produced within a country in a year. *Services* include community, government, and personal services; finance, insurance, real estate, and business services; trade, restaurants, and hotels; and transportation and communication. *Industry* includes construction, manufacturing and mining, and utilities. *Agriculture* includes agriculture, forestry, and fishing.

Production and workers by economic activities

Economic activities	Percent of GDP produced	Employed workers	
		Number of people	Percent of total
Finance, insurance, real estate, & business services	24	547,100	13
Community, government, & personal services	20	1,204,300	29
Manufacturing & mining	19	681,200	16
Trade, restaurants, & hotels	18	866,400	21
Transportation & communication	9	340,300	8
Construction	6	350,100	8
Utilities	3	47,500	1
Agriculture, forestry, & fishing	1	183,500	4
Total	100	4,220,400	100

Figures are for 2016.
Source: Statistics Austria; International Monetary Fund.

toes, sugar beets, vegetables, and wheat. Winemaking is an important industry in Austria.

Tourism. Austria is one of Europe's most popular vacation spots. Tens of millions of tourists visit the country every year. About half of Austria's tourists come from Germany. Many others come from Italy, the Netherlands, and Switzerland. Innsbruck, Kitzbühel, and other sports centers in the Alps attract many winter vacationers, especially skiers. In summer, the lakes of Carinthia and of the Salzkammergut area in central Austria are popular recreation spots. Vienna's art galleries, concert halls, and museums also attract many tourists, as do the summer music festivals held throughout the country.

International trade. Austria depends heavily on trade, especially trade of manufactured goods with other European nations. Austria imports some types of machinery and vehicles and exports other types. Other imports include chemicals, foods, and petroleum. Other exports include forest products, especially paper and pulp, and iron and steel.

Austria's chief trading partner is Germany. Both countries are members of the European Union (EU). EU members have removed almost all tariffs and other restrictions on imports of manufactured goods from one another. In addition, Austria trades with China, the Czech Republic, France, Italy, Switzerland, the United Kingdom, and the United States.

Transportation. Austria has an excellent road network. Almost all Austrian families own an automobile. Railroads link almost all cities and towns. The federal government owns most of the nation's railroad tracks. Both buses and trains provide fast and frequent passenger service. Many mountain areas have cable railways.

Austria's national airline, Austrian Airlines, operates international and domestic flights. Vienna has Austria's chief international airport. Graz, Innsbruck, Klagenfurt, Linz, and Salzburg also have important international airports. The Danube River is a major shipping route for trade between Austria and nearby countries. Passenger vessels also travel on the Danube.

Communication. Austria has many regional and national newspapers. The country's leading daily newspapers include *Kleine Zeitung, Kurier, Neue Kronen Zeitung,* and *Österreich. Wiener Zeitung,* founded in 1703, is one of the world's oldest daily newspapers. The federal and provincial governments own the nation's main radio and television stations. Private radio and television stations are also available. People who own a radio or television set pay a license fee. Austria has a high rate of cell phone and Internet usage.

History

Early years. People have lived in what is now Austria for thousands of years, but historians know little about the earliest inhabitants. They do know that after about 800 B.C., the people mined and traded iron ore and salt. These people were part of a cultural group known as the Celts, which eventually spread through much of central and eastern Europe. Archaeologists have found the earliest evidence of Celtic culture at the village of Hallstatt, near Salzburg.

By 15 B.C., the Romans had made Austria south of the Danube River part of their empire. In the late A.D. 100's, mainly Germanic tribes from the north began to invade Roman Austria, weakening Roman control. The Roman Empire split into two parts in the late 300's, and the western part collapsed in 476. Various groups—including Avars, Slavs, and a Germanic people who became the Bavarians—invaded and settled in Austria.

In the late 700's, Austria came under the rule of Charlemagne, king of a Germanic people called the Franks. After Charlemagne's death in 814, the Frankish empire gradually broke up. In the 900's, Magyars, the national ethnic group of Hungary, overran Austria. But the king of Germany, Otto I, defeated them in 955. Austria then came under his rule. In 962, the pope crowned Otto emperor of what later became known as the Holy Roman Empire. The Holy Roman Empire lasted until 1806. Austria became the empire's most important state.

In 976, Holy Roman Emperor Otto II had given control of northeastern Austria to Leopold I of the Babenberg family. In 1156, Holy Roman Emperor Frederick I increased the importance of this area by declaring it a duchy. In 1192, the Duchy of Styria, south of the Duchy of Austria, also came under Babenberg rule. In 1238, the

Skiers glide downhill at a mountain resort in the Tyrol region of western Austria. Ski resorts in Austria's Alps attract numerous tourists and vacationers each year. The country is widely known for its outdoor sports.

© HP Huber, SIME/4Corners Images

© IML Image Group/Alamy Images

Austrian bakeries are known for their delicious cakes and pastries. The chefs shown here are working in the kitchen of a bakery in Vienna. Other foods popular in Austria include dumplings, noodles, and *Wiener schnitzel* (breaded veal cutlet).

Duchy of Austria was divided into two administrative parts, Upper and Lower Austria.

The Habsburgs. The last Babenberg duke died without an heir in 1246. King Ottokar (also spelled Otakar) II of Bohemia then gained control of the Babenberg duchies of Austria and Styria, plus some lands to the south. In 1273, the princes of Germany elected Rudolf I, a member of the Habsburg family of Switzerland, as Holy Roman emperor. Rudolf defeated Ottokar in battle

in 1278 and began to acquire for his family the lands that the king had taken.

In the early 1300's, the Habsburgs lost control of the Holy Roman crown. The empire was a patchwork of territories ruled by various families, including the Habsburgs. In 1359, the great-grandson of Rudolf I, Rudolf IV, made a claim, based on forged documents, to the title of archduke of Austria. Other European rulers did not recognize this claim until 1453. In the next few centuries, the Habsburgs acquired many new territories, including most of the regions that make up present-day Austria.

In 1438, a Habsburg had again been elected Holy Roman emperor. From then on, the Habsburgs held the title almost continuously. The House of Habsburg, also called the House of Austria, became the chief dynastic power of the Holy Roman Empire. One of the greatest Habsburgs was Maximilian I. In 1496, he arranged for his son, Philip, to marry the daughter of the king and queen of Spain. Philip's son became King Charles I of Spain in 1516 and Holy Roman Emperor Charles V in 1519. In 1556, Charles gave up the two thrones. Spain went to his son, and Austria and the title Holy Roman emperor went to his brother, Ferdinand I. The Habsburgs thus became divided into Spanish and Austrian branches.

Ferdinand I had become king of Bohemia and claimed Hungary in 1526. Some Hungarian nobles supported him, and others tried to make a Hungarian nobleman their king. Meanwhile, the Ottoman Empire conquered most of Hungary. Ottoman forces besieged Vienna in 1529 and again in 1683. Both sieges failed. The Habsburgs gained control of almost all of Hungary soon after the 1683 siege.

In 1618, Protestants in Bohemia revolted against their Habsburg ruler, Ferdinand II. Ferdinand was a strong supporter of the Counter Reformation, a movement that led to renewal within the Catholic Church. The Protestants in Bohemia were defeated in 1620. But their revolt led to the start of the Thirty Years' War (1618-1648), a series of political and religious wars that involved most European nations. The Peace of Westphalia, which ended the war, weakened Habsburg authority in the Holy Roman Empire but strengthened the family's control over their lands in Austria. The peace treaty declared that the ruler of each state within the empire could determine the religion of that territory. The Habsburgs forced Catholicism on Austria's large Protestant population.

Wars in the 1700's and 1800's. The last Habsburg king of Spain died in 1700. Both Austria and France

The Habsburg lands

In 1282, almost all of what is now Austria, outlined in red, formed part of the Holy Roman Empire. The Habsburg family controlled the areas shown in yellow. In 1526, the Habsburg lands included Bohemia, part of Hungary, and other areas.

————— Boundary of present-day Austria

0   300 Miles
0   300 Kilometers

Important dates in Austria

15 B.C. Romans controlled Austria south of the Danube River.
A.D. 100's Germanic tribes from the north began to invade Roman Austria, and Roman control started to weaken.
476   The Roman Empire collapsed in Western Europe.
976   The Holy Roman emperor put Leopold I of the Babenberg family in control of northeastern Austria.
1278   Holy Roman Emperor Rudolf I began to acquire the duchies of Austria and Styria for the Habsburgs.
1438-1806 Austria's House of Habsburg was the most important dynastic power in the Holy Roman Empire.
1804-1806 The Austrian Empire was established, and the Holy Roman Empire dissolved.
1867   Austria-Hungary was established.
1914   Austria-Hungary's declaration of war on Serbia began World War I.
1918   Austria-Hungary was defeated in World War I. The Habsburgs were overthrown, and Austria became a republic.
1938   Adolf Hitler made Austria part of Germany.
1939-1945 The Allies defeated Germany in World War II.
1945-1955 The Allies occupied Austria.
1955   The Austrian State Treaty guaranteed Austrian independence.
1995   Austria joined the European Union, an economic and political organization of European nations.

claimed the throne. The War of the Spanish Succession (1701-1714) followed. Austria won Belgium and Spain's Italian lands. A French prince became king of Spain.

Charles VI, the Habsburg heir, became Holy Roman Emperor in 1711. In 1713, Charles publicly announced a decree based on a secret family succession agreement that was made in 1703. Charles added a provision to the ordinance stating that the Habsburg lands should remain united. He also included that, in the event of not having a direct male heir, his daughters' succession claims should take priority over those of the daughters of his older brother and predecessor, Joseph I. Joseph's daughters normally would have come before Charles's daughters in the line of succession. This decree served to strengthen the succession claim of Charles's prospective children over those of Joseph. Known as the Prag-

Emperor Francis I and Empress Maria Theresa at Schönbrunn Castle, surrounded by their 12 children (1756), oil on canvas painting by Martin van Meytens; Chateaux de Versailles et de Trianon, Versailles, France (Daniel Arnaudet, Art Resource)

Maria Theresa became ruler of Austria, Bohemia, and Hungary in 1740. This painting shows Maria Theresa, *seated at right,* with her husband, Francis I, *seated at left,* and 12 of their children.

matic Sanction, this law became especially significant when it became clear that Charles indeed would have no direct male heir. Charles sought and obtained the acceptance of this document, first from the nobles of all of the Habsburg-ruled lands by 1724, and then from the rulers of the principal European states. By doing so, Charles secured the succession of his oldest daughter, Maria Theresa, as the Habsburg heir.

After Charles VI died in 1740, several states challenged Maria Theresa's right to rule. In the War of the Austrian Succession (1740-1748), Maria Theresa established her rights as ruler of Austria, Bohemia, and Hungary. But she lost nearly all of Silesia to Prussia. In the Seven Years' War (1756-1763), she tried to regain Silesia but failed.

Austria suffered many defeats in the Napoleonic Wars of the late 1700's and early 1800's. In these wars, Napoleon I of France fought successfully for many years against an alliance of major European powers, including Austria. Napoleon conquered large parts of the Holy Roman Empire, and in 1806 Emperor Francis II dissolved the empire. Francis had declared himself emperor of Austria in 1804 to ensure that he would still have imperial standing. After 1806, he reigned as Emperor Francis I of Austria. Napoleon was finally defeated in 1815.

Metternich and revolution. The major political figure in Austria from 1809 to 1848 was Prince Klemens von Metternich, who served as minister of foreign affairs. Metternich played a leading role at the Congress of Vienna. The congress was a series of meetings of European political leaders that arranged the peace settlement following the Napoleonic Wars. The congress returned to Austria most of the land it had lost. Austria exchanged Belgium for Venetia, an area in northeast Italy. The congress also set up the German Confederation, a loose union of independent states. Austria and Prussia began a struggle to lead the confederation.

During the 1800's, early liberalistic and nationalistic ideas swept across Europe. These ideas, particularly the belief that people had a right to govern themselves, triggered revolutions in many areas of Europe. Because Metternich feared revolution, he tried to put down all nationalist movements in the Austrian Empire. But in 1848, revolution began in France and spread to Austria, Bohemia, the German states, and Hungary. In Vienna, revolutionaries demanded that Metternich resign and that a constitutional government be set up. Metternich fled to England. Revolts also broke out in the Austrian-controlled states in Italy. But by late 1849, the Austrian army had put down all revolts.

At this time, Italy and Germany were not unified countries but were each divided into numerous small states. During the 1860's and 1870's, unification movements in Italy and Germany weakened the Austrian Empire. In Italy, the kingdom of Sardinia, which included the island of Sardinia and the Piedmont region of Italy, led the unification movement. Austria declared war on Sardinia in 1859, but Italian and French forces defeated the Austrians. As a result, Austria lost the Lombardy region of northern Italy and could not prevent Italian unification. In 1866, Prussia used a minor dispute to spark the Seven Weeks' War, in which Italy and Prussia quickly defeated Austria. Austria had to give Venetia to the new Kingdom of Italy, and the German Confederation was dissolved.

Austria-Hungary in 1914

The Austrian Emperor Franz Joseph set up the Dual Monarchy of Austria-Hungary in 1867. It consisted of the Austrian Empire and the Kingdom of Hungary. Austria-Hungary reached its greatest size in 1914, the year World War I began. The country broke up in 1918, at the end of the war.

☐ Austrian Empire

☐ Kingdom of Hungary

—— Boundary of present-day Austria

WORLD BOOK map

Prussia formed a new German empire without Austria.

Austria-Hungary. In 1867, Emperor Franz Joseph agreed to Hungarian demands for greater *autonomy* (self-rule) and status. In the resulting Dual Monarchy of Austria-Hungary, both the Austrian Empire and the Kingdom of Hungary were ruled by the Habsburg monarch. The two countries were united in their conduct of foreign, military, and joint financial affairs. But each country had its own government to handle all other matters.

In the late 1800's and early 1900's, Slavs and other minority groups in Austria-Hungary also demanded the right to govern themselves. Serbia led a movement to unite the region's Slavs. In 1908, Austria-Hungary added the territory of Bosnia-Herzegovina in southeast Europe to its empire. Serbia wanted control of this area because many Serbs lived there. In 1914, Gavrilo Princip, a Serb from Bosnia-Herzegovina, assassinated Archduke Franz Ferdinand, heir to the Austro-Hungarian throne. Austria-Hungary then declared war on Serbia, starting World War I (1914-1918). In this war, the Central Powers—Austria-Hungary, Germany, and other nations—fought the Allies—France, Russia, the United Kingdom, and later the United States. The Allies won the war.

After World War I. A defeated Austria-Hungary signed an armistice on Nov. 3, 1918. On November 12, the last Habsburg emperor was overthrown, and Austria became a republic. Many Austrians wanted to make Austria part of Germany. However, the Treaty of St.-Germain, signed by Austria and the Allies in 1919, forbade such a union. In addition, the treaty established Austria's present boundaries. In 1920, Austria adopted a democratic constitution.

Austria had many political problems after the war. The two major parties—the conservative Christian Social Party and the socialist Social Democratic Workers' Party—often clashed with each other. The Austrian Nazi Party also became an increasing menace. In March 1933, Chancellor Engelbert Dollfuss of the Christian Social Party adjourned the Federal Assembly. In February 1934, he outlawed the Social Democratic Party. Dollfuss then ruled Austria as a dictator. But Austrian Nazis assassinated him in July 1934 because of his strong opposition to Adolf Hitler, the Nazi dictator of Germany. Dollfuss was

succeeded by Kurt von Schuschnigg, who struggled to maintain Austrian independence against Nazi pressure.

In March 1938, German troops marched into Austria and seized the country unopposed. Hitler then announced the *Anschluss* (union) of Austria and Germany. Austria became part of Nazi Germany, whose quest for power led to World War II (1939-1945). Hitler's forces conquered most of continental Europe and, in the "Final Solution" of the Holocaust, killed about 6 million Jews. Austrians took full part in both the military campaigns and the Holocaust. The Allies, including France, the Soviet Union, the United Kingdom, and the United States, defeated Germany in 1945.

After World War II, Austria was divided into American, British, French, and Soviet zones of occupation. But

Wide World

The German dictator Adolf Hitler, *front left,* visited Vienna in April 1938. His troops had seized Austria the month before. Hitler had then announced the union of Austria and Germany, which lasted until Germany's defeat in World War II in 1945.

the four powers allowed Austria to set up a single *provisional* (temporary) government based on the 1920 Constitution. After elections in November 1945, a national government was formed. It included leaders of the People's Party (formerly the Christian Social Party) and the Socialist Party (formerly the Social Democratic Party). This *coalition* government—that is, a government including two or more parties—helped stabilize Austria. In 1955, the Allies ended their occupation of the country. The Austrian State Treaty of 1955, between the Allies and Austria, guaranteed Austrian independence. To obtain independence, Austria agreed to be permanently *neutral*—that is, completely uninvolved in international military affairs. Later in 1955, Austria joined the United Nations (UN).

As a neutral nation, Austria became a channel for the exchange of ideas between the non-Communist countries of Western Europe and the Communist countries of Eastern Europe. Vienna hosted nuclear arms talks and became the home of a number of UN agencies.

Austria had coalition governments until 1966, when the People's Party, led by Chancellor Josef Klaus, won a majority of seats in the Nationalrat. After the 1970 elections, the Socialist Party formed a coalition government, with Bruno Kreisky as chancellor. The Socialists gained a majority in the Nationalrat in 1971 and kept it until 1983.

Following losses in the 1983 elections, the Socialists formed a coalition with the Freedom Party to keep control of the government. Kreisky resigned as chancellor, and Fred Sinowatz of the Socialist Party succeeded him.

Kurt Waldheim, a former UN secretary-general, was elected president of Austria in 1986. During the election campaign, records surfaced indicating Waldheim might have been involved in Nazi war crimes during World War II. He denied taking part in war crimes, and an investigation found no evidence that he had done so. But he had lied about his wartime record, which led to both domestic and international outrage. After Waldheim's election, Sinowatz resigned as chancellor and was succeeded by another Socialist, Franz Vranitzky.

Elections in 1986 brought an increase in support for the Freedom Party, which had moved to the far right under its leader Jörg Haider. Vranitzky refused to enter a coalition with Haider and instead formed a new coalition with the People's Party in 1987. Vranitzky began a policy of facing up to Austria's past. He became the first Austrian chancellor publicly to accept Austria's responsibility for war crimes committed when Austria was part of Nazi Germany, from 1938 to 1945. The coalition of the Socialist and People's parties kept its majority in elections in 1990, 1994, and 1995. In 1991, the Socialist Party changed its name to the Social Democratic Party. Chancellor Vranitzky retired in 1997. Viktor Klima, also of the Social Democratic Party, then became chancellor.

Recent developments. Elections in 1999 gave Haider's right-wing Freedom Party the second largest number of seats in the Nationalrat. In 2000, the conservative People's Party formed a coalition with Haider's group. In 2006, Nationalrat elections led to a coalition between the Social Democratic Party, led by Alfred Gusenbauer, and the People's Party. Gusenbauer then became chancellor. In 2008, Werner Faymann succeeded Gusenbauer as Social Democratic Party leader and as chancellor at the head of a new coalition government.

In 2015, Austria began accepting large numbers of refugees fleeing war and terrorism in the Middle East and northern Africa. In national elections in 2016, anti-immigrant sentiment resulted in advances for the far-right Freedom Party. In May, Faymann resigned as chancellor and as Social Democratic Party leader. Railway executive and businessman Christian Kern was named chancellor and leader of the Social Democrats.

After 2017 elections, the People's Party formed a coalition with the Freedom Party, and People's Party leader Sebastian Kurz became chancellor. Kurz resigned in May 2019 following a scandal involving leaders of the Freedom Party, his coalition partner. Brigitte Bierlein, the president of the Constitutional Court, became acting chancellor. In early 2020, months after the 2019 elections, the People's Party formed a coalition with the Green Party, and Kurz returned as chancellor.

In 2020 and 2021, the COVID-19 pandemic caused major social and economic disruptions in Austria. In March 2020, authorities closed many businesses and gathering places to limit the spread of the disease. Vaccines became available to most Austrians in 2021, leading to a decline in infections. See **COVID-19.**   Steven Beller

Related articles in *World Book* include:

Biographies

For biographies of Austrian composers, see the list of *Related articles* at the end of the **Classical music** article. See also:

Adler, Alfred	Maria Theresa
Charles I	Maximilian I
Charles V (Holy Roman emperor)	Meitner, Lise
	Mendel, Gregor J.
Charles VII (Holy Roman emperor)	Mesmer, Franz A.
	Metternich
Ferdinand II	Otto I, the Great
Ferdinand III	Otto II (Holy Roman emperor)
Francis II	Pauli, Wolfgang
Franz Ferdinand	Schiele, Egon
Franz Joseph	Schnitzler, Arthur
Freud, Anna	Schrödinger, Erwin
Freud, Sigmund	Steiner, Rudolf
Hofmannsthal, Hugo von	Straus, Oscar
Klimt, Gustav	Waldheim, Kurt
Kokoschka, Oskar	Wiesenthal, Simon
Landsteiner, Karl	Zweig, Stefan
Mach, Ernst	

Cities

Graz	Innsbruck	Salzburg	Vienna

History

Austerlitz, Battle of	Pragmatic Sanction
Austria-Hungary	Revolution of 1848
Czech Republic (History)	Saint-Germain, Treaty of
Europe, Council of	Seven Weeks' War
Germany (History)	Seven Years' War
Habsburg, House of	Succession wars
Holy Roman Empire	Thirty Years' War
Hungary (History)	Vienna, Congress of
Italy (History)	World War I
Nazism	World War II

Other related articles

Alps	Danube River
Brenner Pass	German language

Austria-Hungary, also called the Austro-Hungarian Monarchy and the Dual Monarchy, was a country in central Europe from 1867 until 1918. It was formed from the Austrian Empire, which included the Kingdom of Hungary. Austria had gained control of Hungary in the late 1600's. But in the mid-1800's, several military defeats weakened Austria's power. Hungary's demand for equal status with Austria led to the formation of Austria-Hungary. The Habsburg (also spelled *Hapsburg)* family, an influential line of rulers who held thrones in Europe as early as 1273, governed the country. Austria-Hungary gained control of the neighboring province of Bosnia-Herzegovina in 1878 and annexed it in 1908.

The monarchy covered about 260,000 square miles (673,000 square kilometers). About 51 million people lived in Austria-Hungary, including 24 million Slavs, 12 million Germans, 10 million Magyars, and many smaller groups. Each group kept its own customs and language.

The cultural life of Austria-Hungary was outstanding. Influential thinkers, such as the physician Sigmund Freud, lived and worked in the capital city of Vienna. Composers Gustav Mahler and Arnold Schoenberg also contributed to the country's artistic achievements.

The people of Austria-Hungary lived mostly in peace and prosperity. Its two governments—one in Vienna for Austria and the other in Budapest for Hungary—provided efficient public services and improved the welfare of the people. But neither government was able to control the growing desire for self-determination among many of Austria-Hungary's ethnic groups.

In 1914, Gavrilo Princip, a Serbian from Bosnia-Herzegovina, killed Archduke Franz Ferdinand, the heir to the throne of Austria-Hungary. Franz Ferdinand was seen as a threat to the union of South Slavic people. The act also was a protest of Austria-Hungary's control of Bosnia-Herzegovina. Most Serbs believed Serbia, which lay south of Austria-Hungary, had a right to the province.

The assassination caused Austria-Hungary to declare war on Serbia. Russia promised to support Serbia. Then Germany, Austria-Hungary's ally, declared war against Russia and Russia's ally, France. Germany invaded Belgium to attack France, and the United Kingdom joined the fight in support of Belgium. World War I had begun.

During the war, Austria-Hungary sent troops to Italy and many other locations on the Eastern Front. The army performed well under difficult conditions, but morale became low as the war dragged on. By late 1917, thousands of soldiers had deserted. Some Czech troops joined the Allied forces.

After the war ended in 1918, the new states of Austria, Hungary, and Czechoslovakia were formed entirely from Austria-Hungary's territory. Other land went to Italy, Poland, Romania, and the Kingdom of the Serbs, Croats, and Slovenes (later called Yugoslavia). The breakup of Austria-Hungary marked the end of the empire of the Habsburg family.　　　　John W. Boyer

See also Austria; Franz Ferdinand; Hungary.

Austrian Succession, War of the. See Succession wars (The War of the Austrian Succession).

Austro-Prussian War. See Seven Weeks' War.

Author. See the various literature articles, such as American literature; Russian literature. See also the *Arts* section of the various country articles, such as Brazil (The arts). See also Literature; Writing.

Authoritarianism, *uh* THAWR *uh* TAIR *ee uh* NIHZ *uhm,* is any form of government in which relatively few people run the country, and the rest of the population takes little part in decision making. Authoritarian states may prohibit, severely restrict, or manipulate elections to suit their own purposes. They may limit the powers of

legislatures that represent the people, such as a parliament or congress, and restrict individual freedom. Authoritarianism includes such types of government as absolute monarchy, dictatorship, and totalitarianism.

The goals and methods of authoritarian governments vary. In a totalitarian state, for example, the leaders try to change society according to a set of doctrines. In an absolute monarchy or a dictatorship, the ruler may be interested only in gaining personal wealth and power. Some authoritarian states exercise cruel and unjust use of power, but others may not. Democratic states occasionally may adopt authoritarian methods of rule during a war or other emergency.　　　Alexander J. Groth

Related articles in *World Book* include:

Absolutism	Dictatorship	Totalitarianism
Despotism	Fascism	Tyranny

Authority. See Power (Forms of power).

Autism, *AW tihz uhm,* is a serious medical disorder that appears in young children and persists throughout life. It is characterized by limited ability to communicate and interact with other people. Some symptoms may be present in infancy, but the condition becomes more noticeable as affected children reach the age when their peers are beginning to speak in phrases and participate in social play. The United States Centers for Disease Control and Prevention (CDC) estimates that autism and related disorders, *Asperger syndrome* and *pervasive developmental disorder,* occur in about 1 out of every 59 children. Health experts refer to these similar disorders collectively as *autism spectrum disorders.* Boys are more commonly affected than girls.

The American psychiatrist Leo Kanner first described the symptoms in the 1940's. He chose the name *autism,* from the Greek word for *self,* referring to the children's apparent lack of interest in other people.

Symptoms. Autism is diagnosed by a variety of symptoms that can occur in different combinations and range from mild to severe. But diagnosis requires that all cases have symptoms from each of these categories: (1) abnormal social interaction, (2) abnormal communication, and (3) restricted and repetitive interests and behaviors.

Abnormal social interaction in individuals with autism is reflected in such behaviors as failure to seek comfort from a parent and lack of eye contact. Children with autism may not respond when their name is called or play with other children. They do not understand the social behaviors necessary to make friends or work with teachers. This lack of social contact isolates people with the disorder from many experiences by which most people come to understand the world.

Abnormal communication. Most children with autism do not develop language as early as others, and some never develop language. Problems with communication extend to gestures and facial expression, as well as language. Affected children with fluent speech may talk endlessly about a single subject or use words in a way that is abnormally precise and literal. Others exhibit a speech pattern called *echolalia,* where they repeat what is said to them instead of giving their own response.

Restricted and repetitive interests and behaviors. Some children with autism appear to have only one interest, such as clocks, airplanes, or calendars, and spend their time pursuing that interest, excluding all others. Repetitive movements, such as hand flapping, rocking, or head banging, are common. Children may exhibit repetitive behaviors in other ways, such as placing toys in a line rather than playing with them. Children with autism often insist on sameness and become distressed by changes in their environment or routine.

Causes. Scientists know that autism is caused by an abnormality in brain development. This abnormality may begin before birth. However, the nature of the abnormality has been difficult to describe. The symptoms are so complex that no single area of the brain can account for all of them. Even so, there is one consistent finding in the brains of people with autism. People with autism have a lower number of *Purkinje cells (pur KIHN jee)* compared with other people. These cells are important in coordination of movement and may also play a role in higher brain functions, such as planning and language. Scientists do not know, however, what part the reduction of Purkinje cells plays in symptoms of autism.

Scientists have also identified a combination of certain factors that may indicate that an infant is at risk for developing autism. They found that infants with a small head size at birth who then experience a sudden and excessive growth in head size in the first year of life have an increased risk of developing autism.

Scientists know that susceptibility to autism is inherited. They have observed in families that parents, siblings, and other relatives of a child with autism often have some symptoms of the disorder. In addition, the diagnosis is more common in relatives than would be expected by chance. Children fathered by older men have a higher chance of developing autism than do those with younger fathers. About 1 percent of people with autism have duplicated or missing genes on one of the pair of chromosomes designated *chromosome 16.* Researchers believe that autism likely results from the interaction of several genes that may be on different chromosomes.

Scientists also know that environmental factors play a role in autism and related disorders. Women exposed to *rubella,* also called *German measles,* or certain drugs during early pregnancy have an increased risk of having a child with autism. Some people with autism have intellectual disability, but autism occurs among people of all levels of intelligence. The brains of children with autism tend to be somewhat larger than normal, while children with intellectual disability, alone, tend to have small brains. This suggests the causes of the two conditions are different, even though they may occur together.

Treatment. There is no cure for autism, but early detection and treatment can improve the lives of children with the disorder. *Behavioral intervention,* where the child is rewarded for progress toward more typical behavior, is often helpful. Many children respond with improvements on tests of language and intelligence. Drug therapy can reduce repetitive behavior in some patients. With treatment, some children with autism are able to take part in regular school classes. For others, the same treatments seem to have little effect. Scientists hope new treatments will become available as they learn more about the biology of autism.   Patricia M. Rodier

Autobiography is a type of biography in which the author tells the story of his or her own life. Autobiographies give readers an inside view of the lives of interesting people. They also may provide eyewitness descriptions of historical events or accounts by people who helped shape such events. Some people use autobiographies to explain or justify actions in their lives. Some autobiographies are inspired by feelings of nostalgia for the author's past. Still others are written by celebrities who feel they can earn money from the public's curiosity about their lives.

The first genuine autobiography is generally considered to be the *Confessions* (about A.D. 400) by the early Christian leader Saint Augustine. It tells of his spiritual struggles and triumphs. *The Autobiography of Benjamin Franklin* (1789) is perhaps the most famous American autobiography. Many authors have written novels that are largely autobiographical. For example, the Irish novelist James Joyce's *Portrait of the Artist as a Young Man* (1916) closely resembles his early life. Some authors have written novels in the form of autobiographies. For example, the English author Jonathan Swift wrote *Gulliver's Travels* (1726) as a ship's surgeon's autobiographical account of experiences in strange lands. Some authors have written autobiographical poems. Examples include works by two British poets, William Wordsworth's *The Prelude* (1850) and John Betjeman's *Summoned by Bells* (1960).

H. George Hahn

See also **Literature for children** (Books to read [Biographies and autobiographies]).

Autocracy, *aw TAHK ruh see,* is a form of government in which one person holds supreme power. This person cannot be restricted, according to law, by any institution or group of citizens from doing whatever he or she wishes. However, some autocratic leaders have used the appearance of *public accountability* (being answerable to the people) and elections to conceal their autocracies. The Russian government under the czars from the mid-1500's to the early 1900's was an autocracy. Dictator Adolf Hitler's government in Germany from 1933 to 1945 was also a form of autocracy. Many countries have been controlled by autocrats since World War II ended in 1945. These autocrats included Idi Amin Dada of Uganda and Mu'ammar Muhammad al-Qadhāfī of Libya. See also **Dictatorship; Government.**

Thomas S. Vontz

Autogiro, *AW tuh JY roh,* is a type of heavier-than-air craft that is supported in the air by a rotor instead of by fixed wings, as an airplane is. Most autogiros have short, stubby wings for balance. An autogiro's rotor spins by itself as it passes through the air. The craft differs from a

NYT Pictures

Autogiros have a helicopterlike rotor to keep them aloft and a nose propeller to pull them forward. These aircraft were flown mainly during the 1920's and 1930's. This photograph, taken in 1930, shows autogiros flying over New York City.

helicopter, whose rotor is always powered by an engine. The chief purpose of an autogiro's engine is to provide thrust to pull the vehicle through the air.

The rotor is set in motion through the use of gears and a clutch connected to the engine. These gears are disconnected in flight, but the rotor blades continue to revolve. A hinge at each blade's hub makes the rotor somewhat flexible. When the airflow strikes each rotating blade, *lift* (upward pull) occurs. In addition, autogiros are designed in such a way that when airflow strikes the blades, it also causes them to be pulled forward around their hubs. This forward pull causes the blades to *autorotate* (rotate by themselves) and hold the craft aloft.

An autogiro can fly from 20 to 140 miles (32 to 225 kilometers) per hour. It cannot *hover* (stay motionless in the air) like a helicopter. But an autogiro requires an extremely short take-off run and can descend almost vertically to land in a small space.

Juan de la Cierva, a Spanish inventor, flew the first successful autogiro in 1923. Autogiros were later produced in Europe, the United States, and Japan. They were eventually replaced by helicopters, which are quicker and more maneuverable. Roger E. Bilstein

Autograph is anything handwritten. It often refers to a person's signature. But it also may be a lengthy example of writing, such as letters, documents, and manuscripts. The term *autograph* comes from the Greek words *autos,* meaning *self,* and *graphein,* meaning *to write.*

Collecting autographs. The hobby of collecting autographs is called *philography,* from a Greek word meaning *love of writing.* People collect many kinds of autographs. Some collect signatures or other handwritten materials of authors, composers, movie stars, or sports heroes. Others focus on certain events, such as the signing of the Declaration of Independence, a presidential election, or the space program. Some try to acquire a complete set of autographs of the presidents of the United States, the justices of the U.S. Supreme Court, Nobel Prize laureates, or Academy Award winners.

Collectors use a number of terms to identify different types of autographs. A letter completely handwritten and signed is called an *autographed letter signed* (A.L.S.). A letter either typed or handwritten by another person but actually signed by the subject is known as a *letter signed* (L.S.). The terms *autographed document signed* (A.D.S.) and *document signed* (D.S.) usually refer to legal items, such as bank checks or receipts.

Collectors may request autographs from celebrities either in person or by letter. They may also buy autographs at auctions or from dealers who guarantee the authenticity of the autographs they sell. Most beginning autograph collectors do not have the knowledge to determine whether an autograph is genuine. Many years of study are required to learn to verify handwriting and to become familiar with different types of paper and ink.

Inexperienced collectors also may mistake other kinds of signatures for genuine handwritten signatures. For example, some people have secretaries who sign their mail. Some individuals send out mass-produced letters or signed photographs to collectors who request their autographs. These *facsimile autographs* can be identified because they are not addressed to a specific person. Many famous people use a mechanical device called an *Autopen* to sign autographs. The machine can

sign 3,000 signatures in eight hours. The only way to recognize an Autopen autograph is to compare two of them. All Autopen autographs are identical, but no two handwritten autographs are exactly alike.

The value of autographs varies widely. Some signatures sell for less than $5, while some handwritten letters sell for thousands of dollars. The value of many autographs depends on supply and demand. William Henry Harrison served as president of the United States for only one month in 1841 before he died. Therefore, the supply of his autograph as president is quite small. On the other hand, a number of well-known figures, such as Daniel Webster and Henry Wadsworth Longfellow, wrote many letters during their lifetime, and so their autographs are relatively inexpensive.

In all cases, the content of an autograph helps determine its value. For example, a letter written by astronaut Neil A. Armstrong that describes his walk on the moon is extremely valuable. A brief typed "thank you" letter signed by the astronaut would be relatively inexpensive.

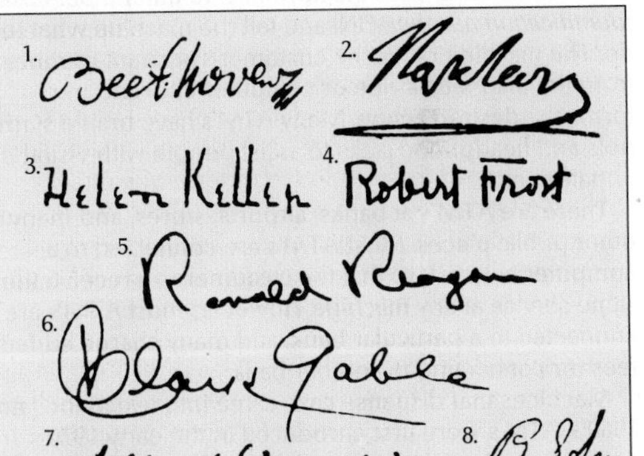

Universal Autograph Collectors Club

Autographs of famous people. (1) Ludwig van Beethoven; (2) Napoleon Bonaparte; (3) Helen Keller; (4) Robert Frost; (5) Ronald Reagan; (6) Clark Gable; (7) Albert Einstein; (8) Robert E. Lee; (9) Mark Twain; (10) Douglas MacArthur; (11) George Washington Carver; (12) Abraham Lincoln; (13) Geronimo, who signed his name vertically, as shown above; (14) Sigmund Freud; (15) Alexander Graham Bell; (16) Winston Churchill; (17) Babe Ruth.

Preserving autographs. A collector may mount autographs in albums or put them between sheets of acid-free paper to help prevent them from turning yellow with age. Some collectors place autographs in transparent envelopes in a loose-leaf binder. These envelopes protect autographs from dirt and rough handling. Libraries usually place valuable autographs in manila folders. Herman Darvick

For examples of autographs, see **Declaration of Independence; Emancipation Proclamation.**

Automated teller machine (ATM) is a computer terminal that functions as a miniature financial institution. ATM's enable people to make a variety of banking transactions at any time. For example, a customer can use an ATM to make a bank deposit, withdraw cash, get account information, transfer funds between accounts, or get a cash advance on a credit card.

To use an ATM, a customer must have a special plastic card with a magnetic stripe across the back or an embedded computer chip. The customer inserts the card into the ATM and uses the keyboard to enter a *personal identification number* (PIN) and tell the machine what to do. The machine reads the customer's account number from the magnetic stripe or computer chip and performs the desired action. Many ATM's have braille symbols and headphone jacks to assist people with visual impairment.

There are ATM's at banks, airports, stores, and many other public places. Most ATM's are connected to a computer network so that the customer can receive the same service at any machine. However, most ATM's are connected to a particular bank, and many charge added fees for connecting to another bank.

Machines that dispense cash came into use in the late 1960's. ATM's were first introduced in the early 1970's and became popular in the 1980's. William T. Verts

See also **Bank** (picture); **Smart card.**

Automatic flight control system (AFCS), sometimes called an *automatic pilot* or *autopilot,* is a device that automatically steers aircraft. The device controls a craft using information provided by sensors along with a detailed set of computerized instructions. An AFCS reduces the amount of work a pilot must do, makes navigation easier, and improves fuel economy and flight safety. In addition, an AFCS can take over control of particularly difficult flight operations from a pilot. It can thus aid a pilot faced with such situations as landing in poor visibility or flying low to avoid radar detection.

How an AFCS works. An AFCS is part of the *avionics* (flight electronics) of an aircraft. The heart of a modern AFCS system is a computer with many high-speed digital processors. The processors communicate with other airplane systems and equipment, including *gyroscopes, accelerometers,* a *compass,* and an *air-data system.* The gyroscopes, accelerometers, and other equipment provide information about the vehicle's *attitude* (orientation in relation to the horizon), altitude, and velocity. A special compass provides information on the craft's *heading* (direction) relative to magnetic north. The air-data system provides data associated with the movement of the aircraft through the atmosphere.

The AFCS processors perform complex calculations using a set of *control modes.* Typical modes include those that maintain an aircraft's altitude, airspeed, head-

ing, and designated flight path. The processors then issue control signals to various *servo* (or *servomechanism) units.* These units have motors and hydraulic devices that move the throttle and the craft's control surfaces—the ailerons, elevator, and rudder.

In a *fly-by-wire system,* a computer combines instructions from the pilot with those of an AFCS to improve flight safety. Such a system can, for example, prevent a pilot from endangering the aircraft by exceeding a certain airspeed or angle of descent or ascent.

Many airplanes include a device called a Global Positioning System (GPS) receiver that can contribute data to the AFCS. A GPS receiver can determine a plane's position in space by calculating its distance from 3 or more satellites in the GPS network. Each of the 24 satellites in this network continually broadcast their positions.

History. In 1912, Lawrence Sperry invented and flight-tested an automatic gyroscopic stabilizing device for airplanes using four gyroscopes. In 1932, the Sperry Gyroscope Company, founded by Lawrence's father, Elmer A. Sperry, developed an automatic pilot. This device enabled American aviator Wiley Post to make the first solo flight around the world in 1933 (see **Post, Wiley**).

In 1998, the Insitu Group, a developer of long-range unpiloted aircraft, together with the University of Washington, flew a pilotless plane across the Atlantic Ocean for the first time. The aircraft was directed by an AFCS using a GPS receiver for navigation. It took off from Newfoundland and landed in Scotland, crossing 2,030 miles (3,270 kilometers). Brian Nicklas

See also **Global Positioning System; Gyroscope; Servomechanism; Sperry, Elmer Ambrose.**

Automatic pilot. See Automatic flight control system.

Automatic transmission. See Transmission.

Automation is the use of machines to perform tasks that require decision making. Automation is used for a wide variety of jobs that are too complex or dangerous for people to do, for repetitive tasks that many people would find boring, and for work that would be extremely costly if done by people.

Uses of automation. Automated systems can make decisions that are beyond the capacity of people to make. For example, many cities use automated systems to coordinate their traffic lights to smooth the flow of traffic. Sensors in the pavement determine the number and speed of vehicles on the street and send the data to a computer. The computer decides how to time each traffic light in the area and sends signals to the lights.

Automated systems can also make decisions more quickly than people can. For example, high-speed military aircraft sometimes fly at low altitudes to avoid detection by enemy radar. To avoid hitting obstacles, these aircraft use automated guidance systems that can react much faster than a pilot can.

Repetitive, simple jobs can be boring for people to do for long periods. Automated machinery is well suited to these routine tasks, such as assembling, inspecting, and packaging manufactured products.

Automated machinery can operate in places unsafe for people. Automated systems are used for repairing underwater pipelines at high pressures. Robots paint automobiles using spray paint that would harm people.

Automated systems can do some jobs more quickly

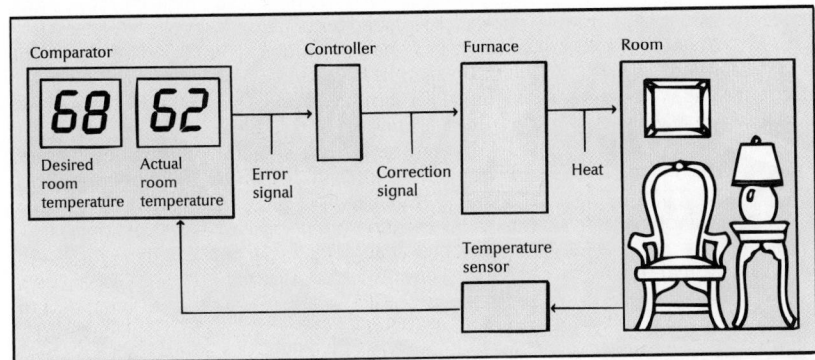

Automated temperature control relies on *feedback*. The actual room temperature is measured by a sensor and *fed back* to a comparator that compares it with the desired temperature. Any difference between the two temperatures causes an error signal to be sent to a controller, which sends a correction signal to the furnace to adjust the heat flowing to the room.

WORLD BOOK illustration by Bill and Judie Anderson

and cheaply than people can. In many stores, checkout clerks use an *optical scanner* to read bar codes printed on product packaging. The scanner sends signals to the store's computer, which relays price and product information to the cash register. The computer records the sale, keeping a tally of how much of each item remains in stock. It can even place orders to restock items. The use of automation also allows companies to save money they otherwise would have to spend to make hazardous work areas safe for human workers. In addition, a manufacturing robot may be able to perform different tasks by having its program changed, allowing one robot to do the work of several single-task machines.

How automation works. An automated system has devices called *sensors* that pick up information about the results of the machine's operation. Sensors may also sense certain environmental conditions that affect the machine's performance. Information "read" by the sensors is fed directly back to the system, enabling the machine to adjust its operation as needed. Such a system of self-regulation is called *feedback*.

Feedback is what makes automation different from *mechanization* (the use of machinery to replace human workers or work animals). A mechanized industrial robot, for example, does not use feedback and therefore cannot adapt its operation to changing conditions.

The basic elements of feedback can be illustrated by an automated home heating system, which maintains a certain room temperature using *input* and *output*. The input is the thermostat setting—that is, the desired room temperature. The output is the actual temperature. The input tells the system what the output should be. An automated system needs sensors to measure output. The heating system's sensor is a thermometer that measures room temperature. Sensors in other systems measure such variables as pressure, size, and weight.

Automated systems compare the actual output with the desired output through devices called *comparators*. In a heating system, the thermostat acts as the comparator. It compares the thermometer reading with the temperature for which the thermostat has been set. If the actual output of the system differs from the desired output, the comparator sends an error signal to a *controller*. The controller decides how to correct the error in output. The thermostat in a heating system functions as a controller as well as a comparator. In some feedback systems, the controller may be a computer.

The part of any automated system that is controlled by feedback and changes the output is called the *process*. The controller directs the process to correct the output. In a home heating system, the process is the furnace. The thermostat turns the furnace on to raise the room temperature or shuts the furnace off to lower the room temperature.

History of automation. The first industrial application of automation was a *flyball governor*, a device that regulated the speed of a steam engine. James Watt, a Scottish engineer, constructed this device in 1787.

In the 1900's, automated controls were applied to many processes. Automated steering systems controlled by gyroscopes were first used in ships in the 1920's and came into regular use in airplanes in the 1930's (see **Automatic flight control system**).

Additionally at this time, the quality of telephone signals was improved by using amplifiers controlled by feedback. Automated controls used in chemical production and petroleum refining date from the early 1900's. World War II (1939-1945) further stimulated the development of automation. Automatically aimed antiaircraft guns, using radar and electronics equipment, were introduced in 1944.

The first industrial robot was used in 1961. It was controlled by a computer and worked in an automobile assembly plant. Many robots are now used in the electronics industry and in the production of automobiles, airplanes, and heavy construction machinery. Since the late 1970's, the use of computers to run machines has greatly stimulated development.

Automation and jobs. A large number of people expect an increase in automation to cause unemployment as workers are replaced by machines. However, while the use of automation eliminates low-skill jobs, it increases the demand for highly skilled workers. A large number of skilled people are needed to design, build, and maintain automated systems. In addition, automation may enable manufacturers to lower prices and increase sales. As sales increase, employment may rise.

Amy Sue Bix

Related articles in *World Book* include:
Artificial intelligence
Computer
Cybernetics
Labor movement (The challenge of automation)
Robot
Servomechanism
Technology
Unemployment (Types of unemployment)

Automobiles have shaped modern society perhaps more than any other technology. The development of automobiles led to the construction of vast highway systems. Many cities have complex systems of overpasses, underpasses, ramps, and interchanges, such as the one shown here.

Automobile

Automobile is a wheeled machine that serves as the most important form of transportation in the world. People drive about 800 million passenger cars along the world's roads and highways—about 1 car for every 9 people. Trucks transport huge amounts of food, clothing, and other products across vast distances. Since their invention in the late 1800's, automobiles have shaped the way people do business and live their lives. Few technologies have changed the world as much as the automobile has.

A car moves by producing power and channeling it to the wheels, spinning them. Like the human body, a car includes a number of systems that work closely together. Each system is itself a complex machine. Most systems in an automobile have many moving and computerized parts. Some systems work to produce power or transfer it to the wheels. Others work to support the car or provide information to the driver.

All cars use energy to power their motion. Most cars have *internal-combustion engines*. Such engines use energy stored in gasoline or diesel fuel by burning it. Other cars have an *electric motor*. The motor uses energy stored in a rechargeable battery. *Hybrid cars* combine an internal-combustion engine with an electric motor.

Manufacturing a car requires years of planning. Engineers use computer programs to model how the car will look and perform. They build sample cars and test how well the samples work in a variety of conditions. All the parts of the car must be made from scratch or bought. Then, automakers bring the parts together on an *assembly line*. An automobile assembly line is a row of workers. Each worker performs an assigned task, such as inserting a part. The car then passes along to the next worker until it is finished.

Auto manufacturers and related industries employ millions of people throughout the world. This fact causes the health of the auto industry to be closely tied to the health of the world economy. The popularity of automobiles has given rise to vast networks of highways. Gas stations, motels, and fast-food restaurants owe their existence to the popularity of the automobile.

Automobiles also have their disadvantages. Millions of people have died in car accidents. The construction of car-friendly roads and cities has destroyed or displaced many natural habitats. Cars also cause pollution.

The history of automobiles was shaped by many inventors, engineers, and businesspeople. Cars were once too expensive for most people. But they became cheaper and more plentiful after the introduction of *mass production*. Mass production involves the use of interchangeable parts, machines, and moving assembly lines to produce large quantities of nearly identical goods. By the late 1920's, a few large companies came to dominate the car market.

In the early 2000's, relatively new markets for cars—such as China and India—were growing fast. But the automobile industry, shaken by a global recession, struggled to adapt to demands for greater fuel efficiency and less pollution. Changing consumer preferences, safety concerns, and government regulation reshaped automobile designs and reduced the dominance of the big car companies.

Automobile systems

When a driver steps on an automobile's gas pedal, the car accelerates. This action and reaction may seem simple. However, a number of complex systems—each consisting of many moving parts—must work together to make it happen. The car's power system, connected to the gas pedal, generates motion within the vehicle. The *power train*—which includes the transmission and the drive system—channels this motion from the car's power system to spin its wheels. Meanwhile, the car's support system holds the car's frame up from the wheels. Steering and brake systems enable the driver to control the moving car. The electrical system connects most of the other systems together.

All of a car's systems use a number of technologies and scientific principles to work. Physical laws govern the spinning, pushing, and pulling motions of a car's engine, axles, wheels, and other internal parts. *Hydraulics*—a branch of physics involving pressure from fluids—plays a major role in steering and brake systems. Most

modern cars rely on electronics and advanced computer technology to coordinate their systems.

Power systems. A car's power system consists of one or more *power plants*. A power plant is a machine that generates power. Power plants generate electric power for a car's lights and computerized parts. But their main purpose is to generate power for spinning

Interesting facts about automobiles

The word *automobile* was first applied to the horseless carriage in France about 1890. It comes from the Greek word *autos,* meaning *self,* and the French word *mobile,* meaning *moving.*

A nation on wheels. The United States has about 12 percent of the world's passenger cars. Americans drive about 3 trillion miles (5 trillion kilometers) a year.

Car owners. About 88 percent of all U.S. households own a car, and about 35 percent own two or more.

Vacation travel. People in the United States use their automobiles for about 80 percent of all vacation trips.

Fuel consumption by motor vehicles in the United States totals about 170 billion gallons (645 billion liters) a year—an average of about 656 gallons (2,480 liters) for each motor vehicle.

Hybrid cars. The number of hybrid cars sold in the United States annually has increased significantly, from about 2,300 in 2000 to about 385,000 in 2015.

Insurance premiums paid on car policies of all types in the United States total about $210 billion a year.

Sources: U.S. Department of Commerce; U.S. Department of Energy; *Ward's Motor Vehicle Facts & Figures,* Ward's Communications, Inc.

© Tesla Motors, Inc.

An electric car, such as the Tesla Roadster shown here, does not use gasoline, unlike most cars. Instead, a rechargeable battery powers an electric motor that moves the car.

The major systems of an automobile

This diagram illustrates the major systems of a car with a front-mounted gasoline engine, an automatic transmission, and front-wheel drive. The power system produces the force that moves the car. The power train transfers power from the engine to the driving wheels. The steering and brake systems help the driver control the vehicle. The suspension system supports the car, and the electrical system produces and distributes the electric power that ignites the fuel and runs the lights, windshield wipers, and many options.

WORLD BOOK diagram by Paul Perreault

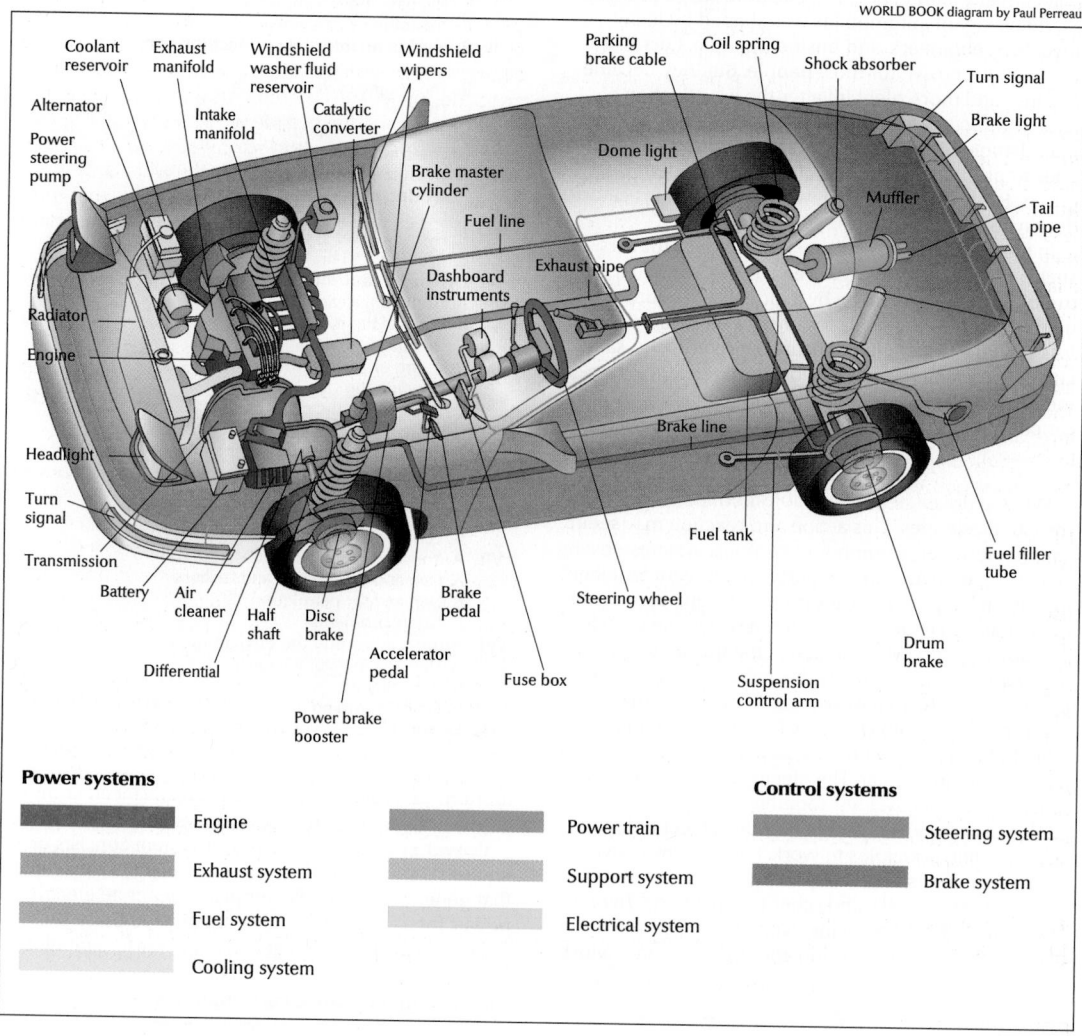

Power systems

Engine

Exhaust system

Fuel system

Cooling system

Power train

Support system

Electrical system

Control systems

Steering system

Brake system

the wheels. There are two main kinds of power plants in modern automobiles: (1) internal-combustion engines and (2) electric motors.

Internal-combustion engines generate power from the energy stored in fuel. Gasoline and diesel are the most common engine fuels. They are made from petroleum. Petroleum is called a *fossil fuel* because it comes from the fossilized remains of long-dead plants. Some engines can use *biofuels.* Biofuels are made from plant crops. Other engines use propane, natural gas, or hydrogen as fuel.

Electric motors generate power from large batteries. Several forms of batteries are available in modern cars. They include lead-acid, nickel, and lithium batteries.

Both fuel and batteries are extremely dense energy sources. They can provide enough power for long

drives without taking up much space or weighing down the car. For more details on how a car's power system works, see the sections *Powering an internal-combustion car* and *Powering electric and hybrid cars* below.

From power plant to wheels. The power train, also called the *drive train,* connects a car's power plant to the wheels. It channels the motion generated by the power system through a series of connected moving parts. Eventually, the motion reaches the wheels and spins them to make the car move. The power train consists of two main systems, the transmission and drive system.

The transmission regulates the spinning motion generated by the power system before it reaches the wheels. The transmission gets power from the spinning motion of the *flywheel,* a heavy disc connected to the car's engine or motor.

In physics, spinning objects—such as flywheels—have two related characteristics: *speed* and *torque*. Speed is simply the rate at which the wheel rotates. Torque refers to the strength of twisting force. Within the car, torque tends to drop as speed increases, and vice versa. The transmission varies the amounts of torque and speed from the flywheel using devices called *gears*.

One way to think about the relation between speed and torque is to consider wrenches. A person might use two different wrenches to loosen a nut by rotating it. To start, the person uses a long-handled wrench. It is easier to turn a tight nut with a long-handled wrench, because such a wrench provides more twisting force or torque. But once the nut loosens and becomes easier to spin, less torque is required to rotate it. The person would then switch to a short-handled wrench to spin the nut at a faster rate. The short handle can spin faster because it has to rotate a shorter distance than the long handle.

The transmission's gears work much like wrenches with different-sized handles. A stopped car, like a tight nut, requires a large amount of torque to begin moving. The *first gear,* also called *low gear,* provides the greatest torque and so is used to start moving a car. But like a long-handled wrench, the first gear sacrifices speed for its high torque. As the car moves faster, less torque is needed. Thus, the transmission switches to higher gears. Like the short-handled wrench, higher gears spin faster with less torque.

Switching from lower to higher gears enables a car to use power more efficiently. Most cars have one reverse gear and from three to five gears for moving forward. A car with an *automatic transmission* switches gears automatically. Such cars use a computer system to sense the ideal gear for the car's motion.

In a car with a *manual transmission,* the driver has to switch between gears. To do so, the driver presses down a pedal called the *clutch.* The clutch disengages the transmission from the car's power plant. The driver then moves a leverlike device called the *gearshift* to change between gears.

The drive system carries power from the transmission to the set of wheels that moves the car. Depending on the automobile, these may be the front wheels only, the back wheels only, or all four wheels.

With *front-wheel drive,* the front wheels not only steer the car but also drive it. Such cars combine the engine, transmission, and *differential* under the hood. The differential is a set of gears connected to the transmission. In a turn, it enables an outside wheel to rotate faster than an inside wheel. The differential is necessary because through a corner, the outside wheel must travel farther than the inside one. A short bar called a *half shaft* transfers power from the differential to the wheels.

Automobiles with *rear-wheel drive* have a long *drive shaft* that transfers power to the back wheels. The differential is in the back of the car. Rear-wheel drive cars have better weight distribution, which can improve the car's handling.

Four-wheel drive vehicles deliver power to all four wheels. A device called a *transfer case* distributes the power between the front and rear wheels. Driving with all four wheels provides good traction on rough or slippery terrain.

Front-wheel drive cars can be cheaper and more compact than other types. They also require less power. Most passenger cars and vans have front-wheel drive. Pickup trucks, commercial vans, and sports cars typically use rear-wheel drive. Vehicles with four-wheel drive include some sport utility vehicles (SUV's) and light trucks.

Controlling the car. Two main control systems enable a car's driver to navigate the road. They are the steering system and the brake system.

The steering system controls the front wheels. The driver operates the system with the steering wheel. The steering wheel connects to the car's front wheels through the *steering shaft.* Turning the steering wheel causes gears at the bottom of the shaft to turn. The gears, in turn, connect to the car's wheels.

Most cars have *power steering,* which enables drivers to more easily turn the vehicle's wheels. Power steering

Transferring power to the wheels   The drive train carries power from the engine to the wheels. A key part of the drive train in a front-wheel drive car is the transaxle, which consists of the transmission and the differential. The transmission has gears that vary the speed and *torque* (twisting force) of the engine power. The differential enables the outside front wheel to rotate faster when the car turns a corner.

WORLD BOOK diagram by Graham Studios

Engine

Power from engine

Wheels are turned

Transaxle housing

Location of transmission

Power to wheel

Half shaft

Half shaft

Location of differential

Power to wheel

Steering the car The steering system guides the front wheels. The steering wheel sits atop the steering shaft. When the driver turns the steering wheel, the steering shaft twists. The twisting operates the steering gears. The gears push and pull on the tie rods, causing the wheels to turn in the desired direction. With power steering, an engine-powered *hydraulic* (fluid) system helps operate steering gears.

WORLD BOOK diagrams by Graham Studios

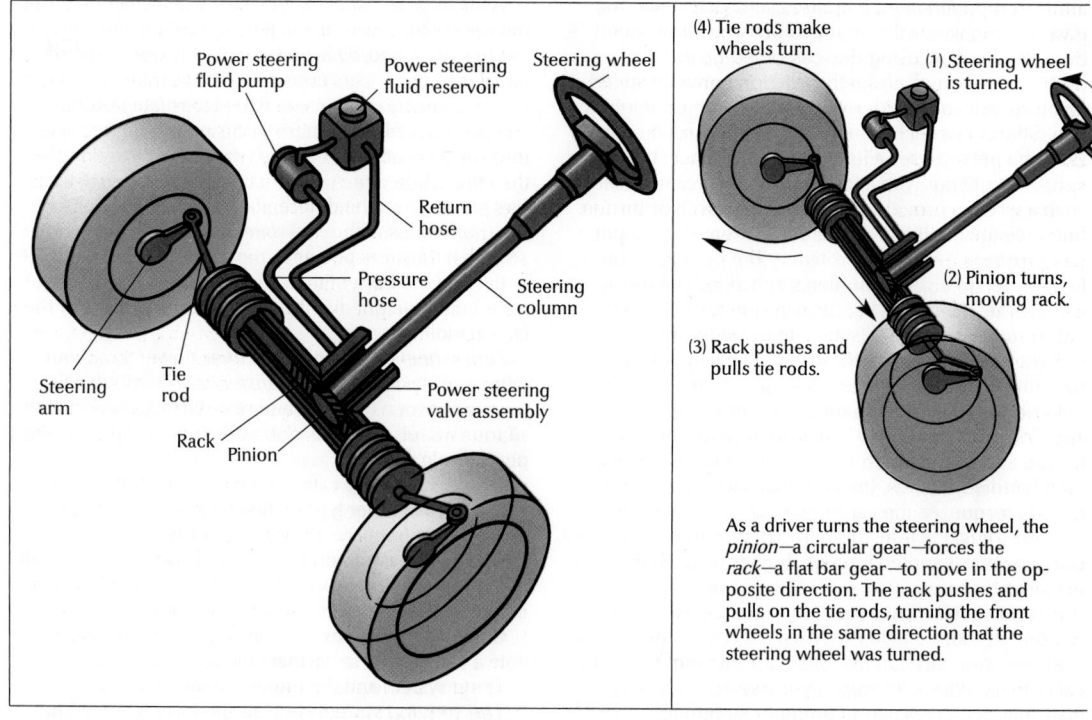

As a driver turns the steering wheel, the *pinion*—a circular gear—forces the *rack*—a flat bar gear—to move in the opposite direction. The rack pushes and pulls on the tie rods, turning the front wheels in the same direction that the steering wheel was turned.

uses a hydraulic system, which produces pressure from a fluid, to help move the wheels.

The brake system slows or stops an automobile. Cars have brakes on all four wheels. The brake system relies on hydraulic pressure. When a driver steps on the brake pedal, fluid goes through lines connected to each wheel. In *disc brakes,* pressure from this fluid forces a pad to rub against a disc attached to the moving wheels. The resulting friction slows or stops the wheels. All cars have disc brakes on their front wheels. Some cars have another kind of brake, called *drum brakes,* on their back wheels. The parts that rub against each other are shaped differently in drum brakes.

Power brakes make it easier to force fluid through the brake system. Power brakes use the difference in pressure between the air in the engine and the air outside to squeeze the brake fluid faster. They make it easier to push down the brake pedal. But they do not stop a car any faster than regular brakes.

Many cars have an *antilock-braking system.* Such a system prevents the wheels from locking up entirely during braking, helping to prevent skidding. It is especially useful on wet roads. A computer varies pressure on the brakes, preventing lockup.

Supporting the car involves tires, wheels, axles, and the *suspension system.* In the past, a rectangular steel frame on the bottom of the car supported the rest of the car's weight, much as a skeleton supports the weight of a body. Today, few cars have a separate body and frame. Instead, their entire structures are welded together.

The suspension system helps smooth the ride of passengers and cargo over twists and bumps in the road, somewhat as shoes protect a person's feet. The system keeps the wheels in contact with the road. But it allows them to move up and down with holes or bumps in the road surface without shaking the entire car.

Most suspension systems consist of springs and mechanical devices known as *shock absorbers,* also called *shocks.* As a tire hits a bump, the wheel is forced upward, and the spring and shock compress. As the road levels out again, the spring and shock rebound, forcing the wheel back down.

The passenger compartment, sometimes called the cabin or cab, is the area of a car or truck in which people sit. It contains seating and the pedals and steering wheel that the driver uses to control the car. It also has a number of other systems that provide comfort, convenience, or information to the people in the car.

The *dashboard,* a panel under the windshield, houses important displays and controls. Instrument readouts above the steering wheel typically display information about the car's performance. For example, the *speedometer* displays a car's speed. The *odometer* records the total distance a car has been driven. A fuel gauge tells how much gas remains in the tank. Many cars also display information about oil pressure, battery voltage, and engine temperature. Dashboards may also house warning lights that alert drivers to problems with the car's parts or systems.

Virtually all cars have a heater. It blows air warmed by

engine heat into the interior of the vehicle. Most cars also have an air conditioner, which draws on engine power to circulate cool air.

Other devices accessible on the dashboard include audio equipment and computerized displays that help give directions. Controls for power door locks, windows, and mirrors are typically on the inside of the doors. Levers near the steering wheel control the car's turn signals, windshield wipers, and headlights. Many cars also have a computerized mechanism called *cruise control.* Cruise control keeps the car moving at a set speed without the driver having to step on the gas.

Almost all automobiles are equipped with safety features, notably seat belts and airbags. Seat belts restrain passengers if a car crashes. An airbag is a bag that rapidly fills with gas in a collision, acting to cushion the passengers. Without such safety features, passengers in a collision would be thrown from their seats and smash into the windshield, dashboard, steering wheel, or seat backs, causing injuries or deaths.

Providing electric power. A automobile's electrical system ties many of its other systems together. The electrical system typically controls the starting and ignition systems, the lights, and the devices and displays inside the passenger compartment.

A 12-volt battery stores energy to start the car. This action cranks the engine to life. The engine, in turn, powers an alternating-current generator. The generator produces power for the electrical system and recharges the battery.

Hybrid vehicles have an additional battery pack, typically above 100 volts. The battery pack provides electric power that turns an electric motor that moves the car. If the battery pack's charge gets low, the 12-volt battery restarts the internal-combustion engine so the automobile can continue to move. For more information about how hybrid cars work, see the section on *Powering electric and hybrid cars.*

Powering an internal-combustion car

The power system lies at the heart of an automobile. In most cars, it includes an internal-combustion engine. In addition, it includes several subsystems that feed into the engine and help maintain it.

Most automobiles have an engine under their front hood. The engine typically works by burning a mixture of gasoline and air. The explosive force from burning this mixture creates motion in the engine's parts. This motion makes its way through the power train to spin the car's wheels. Some internal-combustion engines use diesel fuel or a biofuel instead of gasoline. The term *internal-combustion engine* refers to the fact that fuel is *combusted* (burned) inside the engine.

Both gasoline and diesel engines are housed in structures called *engine blocks.* Both types operate with similar *engine cycles.* The cycle starts when a person turns the car's ignition key. Electric current from the car's 12-volt battery powers the *ignition system,* which causes a starting motor to crank the engine. Both gasoline and diesel engines also have the same support systems, including (1) the fuel system, (2) the exhaust system, (3) the cooling system, and (4) the lubrication system.

The engine block, also called the *cylinder block,* houses the engine's internal parts. In particular, it contains a number of hollow cylinders. Inside the cylinders, solid metal *pistons* move up and down. The motion of the pistons is driven by the explosive force of burning fuel. The pistons, in turn, drive a spinning *crankshaft* connected to the car's transmission.

The number and arrangement of cylinder cavities varies from car to car. Smaller cars typically have from 2 to 5 cylinders. Larger cars can have anywhere from 6 to 12 cylinders. Engines with more cylinders are generally more powerful.

In most cases, the cylinders are arranged either in a straight line or in a V-shaped formation. Engines are

Stopping the car   The brake system slows or stops the car. Most cars have disc brakes on their front wheels and drum brakes on their rear wheels. Hydraulic pressure operates both types. Pressing the brake pedal forces fluid from the master cylinder through the brake lines to the brakes. The pressure of the fluid forces a friction material to rub against the discs or drums on the wheels.

WORLD BOOK diagram by Graham Studios

Drum brake
Parking brake cables
Mechanical parking brake handle
Brake line
Brake line
Power brake booster
Brake pedal
Brake line
Brake shoe
Master cylinder
Caliper
Disc
Brake drum
Disc brake
Disc brake
Drum brake

Powering an internal-combustion car

The typical internal-combustion engine burns a mixture of gasoline and air inside closed cylinders. As the fuel burns, it produces expanding gases that force each piston down inside its cylinder. This downstroke provides the power that ultimately moves the car. Connecting rods transmit this power to the crankshaft, which converts the pistons' up-and-down movement into rotary movement.

WORLD BOOK diagrams by Paul Perreault

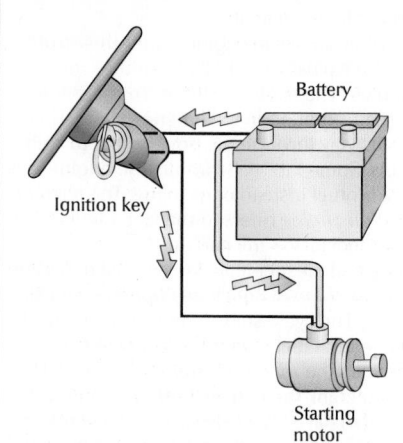

Ignition begins when the key turns the starting switch. Electric power flows from the battery to the starting motor, which cranks the engine.

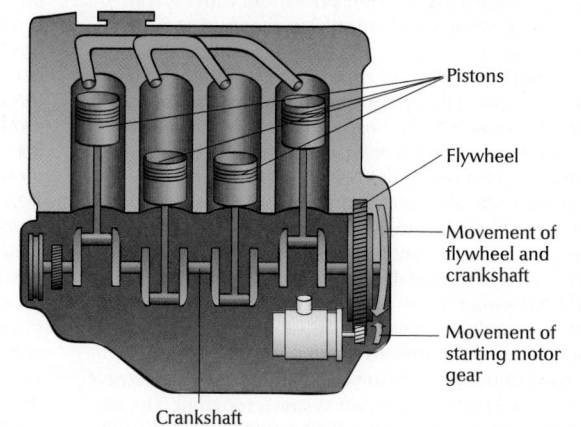

Cranking takes place as the starting motor spins the flywheel. The flywheel turns the crankshaft, which starts the pistons moving up and down in the cylinders and activates the fuel pump.

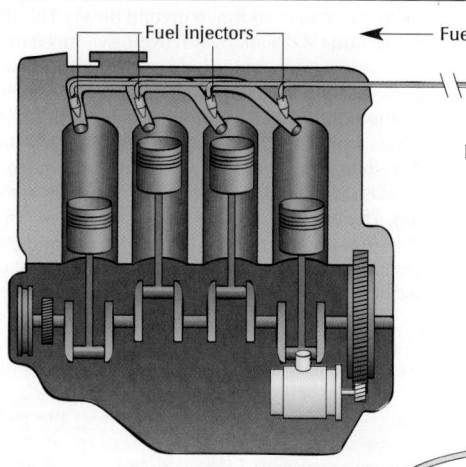

Pressing the accelerator opens the throttle, letting the pistons draw the fuel mixture into the cylinders. The fuel pump supplies gasoline under high pressure to the fuel injectors, which deliver it to the cylinders.

The engine runs as the battery feeds electric power through the coils. A computer in the engine signals each coil to fire each of its two spark plugs at the right time. Sparks from the plugs ignite the fuel, and the pistons go into a rapid, pumplike action. As the pistons move up and down, connecting rods turn the crankshaft. The rods transfer energy from the power stroke to the crankshaft and flywheel, which transmit energy to the car's transmission. The engine is now providing the power to move the car.

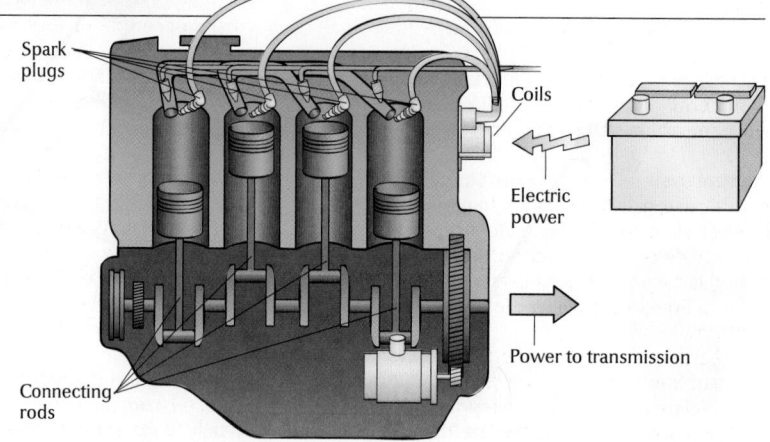

named for the number of cylinders and their arrangement. For example, a *straight-4* engine has four cylinders in a straight line. A *V-8* engine has eight cylinders arranged in a V-shape.

The engine cycle. In most cars, the engine operates in a *four-stroke cycle*. The four strokes, or stages, of the cycle are (1) intake, (2) compression, (3) power, and (4) exhaust.

During the first stage—the intake stroke—the piston moves down in its cylinder. At the same time, air is drawn into the empty cylinder cavity. The air enters from an *intake valve* that opens. In some engines, fuel is also pumped in from the car's fuel system.

The second stage, compression, begins when the cylinder is full of air. The intake valve closes and the piston moves up the cylinder, *compressing* (squeezing) the air. Squeezing the air has an effect similar to squeezing a balloon, making it more likely to explode. Fuel may be compressed along with the air, or it may be pumped in separately. In a diesel engine, the mixture explodes on its own. In gasoline engines, electric sparks from *spark plugs* set the mixture on fire.

The force of the explosion starts the third stage, the power stroke. The explosion pushes the piston back down. The burned gases remain in the cylinder.

The fourth stage, exhaust, allows those burned gases to escape through an *exhaust valve*. The valve opens as the piston moves back up, pushing the burned gases out. The exhaust valve connects to the exhaust system, which cleans the burned gases before releasing them into the open air. With the exhaust stroke complete, the exhaust valve closes, and the cycle starts again from the beginning. The entire four-stroke cycle can take less than a second.

The pistons are connected to the crankshaft. As the piston moves down, it causes the crankshaft to spin— much as the pushing of a foot pedals a bicycle. The spinning crankshaft, in turn, connects to the car's transmission and causes the flywheel to rotate, along with all the other systems and parts connected to the flywheel. Thus, the up-and-down motion of the pistons creates the motion that eventually spins the car's wheels.

Computers regulate the cycles of modern engines. A control unit gathers data about the engine's speed, air pressure, temperature, and other factors. It uses this information to control the timing of the spark plugs and the fuel flow. It makes adjustments hundreds of times a minute.

For more information, see the article **Gasoline engine**. To learn about other types of engines used in some cars, see the articles **Diesel engine; Rotary engine; Turbine**.

The fuel system stores fuel in a car's gas tank, prepares it for use, and transports it to the engine. Most fuel tanks hold from 12 to 20 gallons (45 to 76 liters). They are made of steel or plastic. Before the fuel can be burned in the engine, the fuel system must first transform it into fine droplets, and then into a gas that can mix with air.

Older cars used a device called a *carburetor* to create a mixture of fuel and air in the cylinders. But carburetors were inefficient and caused much pollution.

Most cars produced since the late 1980's use a different system called *fuel injection*. The system times and delivers a precise amount of fuel to the engine's cylinders. A pump—either in the fuel tank or on the engine— forces pressurized fuel through *fuel lines*. The fuel lines connect to needlelike injectors in the engine. A *single-point* system injects fuel from a single injector into a pipe that branches and feeds into the cylinders. But most cars today use *multiport* or *direct injected* systems. Such systems have separate injectors for each cylinder. An electric current opens the needlelike valve in the injectors, allowing pressurized fuel to spray out.

The exhaust system channels, cleans, and cools the burned waste gases from the engine cycle. It then releases them into the air. In the fourth stage of the engine cycle—the exhaust stroke—these gases are squeezed out of the cylinder through the exhaust valve. The valve leads to a structure called the *exhaust manifold*. In some cars, the manifold is a single pipe. In others, it is a set of pipes.

The exhaust manifold channels the gases into a cleansing device called a *catalytic converter*. The inside of a catalytic converter is somewhat like the inside of a honeycomb. It is divided into many cells. The cells are coated with certain rare metals, including platinum, palladium, and rhodium. As the waste gases flow over the metals, chemical processes break the pollutants down into safer substances.

The gases that leave the catalytic converter, though cleaned, are still much hotter than the outside air. If released into the air, the hot gases would expand rapidly and create loud noise. A final device in the exhaust system, the *muffler*, cools the gases before releasing them. The muffler consists of a series of tubes pierced with holes. It slows down the gases, cooling them, before letting them out of the car.

The cooling system keeps the engine from overheating. The engine cycle involves repeated explosions in the cylinders. It results in high temperatures that, without cooling, could damage the engine. The cooling system works by channeling the engine heat elsewhere.

The cooling system pumps a *coolant*—a mixture of about half water and half antifreeze—around the cylinders. The areas around the cylinders that hold coolant are called *water jackets*. The coolant absorbs heat from the cylinders as it flows through the water jackets.

The hot coolant then passes through copper or aluminum tubes in the *radiator*. Fins on the radiator—also made of copper or aluminum—absorb heat from the coolant. The coolant, having given its heat to the fins, returns to the engine, where the process starts over.

The now-hot fins, in turn, are cooled by air that flows around them. The air is drawn by the motion of the car and, at slower speeds, the motion of a fan. The heated air can be used to heat the car's interior in cold weather. Otherwise, it is pumped out of the car.

The lubrication system keeps the parts of the engine moving smoothly. It delivers oil that coats the moving parts of the engine with a thin film. The film helps the parts slide over each other. It reduces friction, which can slow or damage the engine. The oil also helps cool the engine.

Oil is stored in a pan under the engine. A pump circulates oil from the pan, through a filter, through lines, and finally to the engine. The filter removes impurities from the oil, protecting the engine.

Powering electric and hybrid cars

Electric cars use an electric motor powered by a rechargeable battery to turn the wheels. Hybrid vehicles have both an electric motor and an internal-combustion engine. They can run either device or both at the same time. In hybrid and electric cars, the battery can be recharged when the car brakes. Hybrid vehicles thus use much less fuel than cars with only an internal-combustion engine. Electric cars use no fuel at all in their power system.

Electric automobiles have existed since the late 1800's. But early electric cars were slower than cars with internal-combustion engines. In addition, the cars could at first only be used in the few large cities that had access to electric power. Electric cars thus fell out of favor.

Today, improvements in battery technology and wide access to electric power make electric cars more practical. Hybrid cars, which combine an electric motor and an internal-combustion engine, offer consumers the strengths of both types of vehicles.

Electric motors are devices that convert electric power to mechanical motion. This conversion is possible because electricity and magnetism, in physics, are closely related. When an electric current flows through a metal conductor, it creates a magnetic field around that conductor. Like a bar magnet, this field has a north and a south pole. When a magnet's north pole is brought near another magnet's south pole, they attract each other. But when two north poles or two south poles are brought close together, they *repel* (push away) each other.

In a car's electric motor, the conductor sits inside a second magnetized device, called the *stator.* The conductor can turn, but the stator is fixed in place. When current flows through the conductor and magnetizes it, the stator's magnet attracts and repels the conductor. These interactions cause the conductor to spin around.

The spinning conductor is connected to a shaft called the *rotor.* The rotor, in turn, connects to the car's transmission. The transmission transfers the rotor's spinning motion to the wheels.

Hybrid power systems come in two main types, *series* and *parallel.* In a series hybrid vehicle, the electric motor is the only device that is connected to the transmission. Its internal-combustion engine powers a second electric motor. This second motor, in turn, acts as a generator. It is used only to recharge the first motor's battery pack. Energy flows from the engine to the secondary motor, to the battery, to the primary motor, and finally to the car's transmission.

In a parallel design, both the internal-combustion engine and the electric motor are connected to the car's transmission. Through the use of a computer and gear clutches, the car can use either the engine or the motor—or both in combination—to move the wheels.

Batteries and braking. In electric and hybrid cars, current runs from the battery to the electric motor to power the car. However, the nature of electric motors allows current to run in the opposite direction as well, recharging the battery. Electric and hybrid cars take advantage of this fact in a process called *regenerative braking.* The brakes in most cars slow a spinning wheel by applying friction. The friction converts much of the wheel's energy into heat, slowing its spin. In regenerative braking, the wheel's spin is channeled backward through the car's drive system and transmission and into the electric motor. There, the kinetic energy spins the magnetized conductor around. This motion generates an electric current that flows back into the battery, recharging it.

Regenerative braking can greatly increase the distance an electric car can travel before being plugged into a power source to recharge. In hybrid cars, it increases the distance the car can travel before refueling. However, hybrid and electric vehicles still use standard brakes to stop quickly at higher speeds.

Driving an automobile

To drive an automobile, a person must understand how the machine works and how to control it. A person must also know and obey the rules of the road. Most countries require drivers to earn licenses. To earn a license, a person must pass a series of tests. Careless or unlawful drivers may lose their licenses.

In addition, many states and countries require drivers to purchase car insurance. The insurance covers potential damage to a driver's car, as well as potential damage to other vehicles, property, and people. Drivers who are young or have records of accidents or traffic violations usually must pay more for car insurance.

Operating a car normally requires the use of both hands and at least one foot. Most cars are started by turning a key, which cranks the engine to life. Some hybrid and electric vehicles are started by pushing a power button instead of turning a key.

Once the car is started, the driver presses down the brake pedal and shifts the transmission from park to either *reverse* or *drive* to move the car. Most cars, once in reverse or drive, will begin moving as soon as the driver stops pressing the brake—without having to press the gas pedal. The gas pedal is used to accelerate the car.

Levers near the steering wheel enable drivers to control various features on their cars. One lever operates the car's *turn signals,* blinking lights on the car's exterior. Drivers use turn signals to let other drivers know when they intend to turn left or right. They also use them to

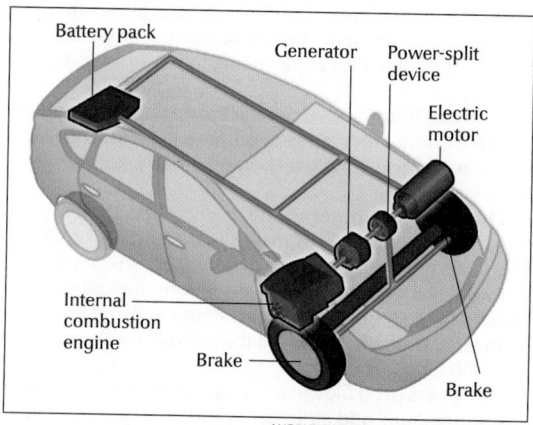

WORLD BOOK illustration by Matt Carrington

A hybrid car is powered by an internal combustion engine and a battery-driven electric motor. Braking spins a generator connected to the battery pack, recharging the battery.

Do's of safe driving

Fasten your safety belt snugly before starting the engine.
Drive defensively—always think ahead.
Obey all traffic regulations.
Drive at a safe speed.
Reduce speed at night, in bad weather, and in heavy traffic.
Yield the road to emergency vehicles that flash a light or sound a siren. Pull far to the right and stop.
Drive in the passing lane only when passing.
Allow vehicles behind you to pass when drivers indicate they want to do so and passing conditions are favorable.
Signal by hand or light your intention to turn, pass, or change lanes.
At intersections, yield the right of way:
1. To pedestrians.
2. To drivers ahead of you.
3. To a driver on the right, if you both arrive at an intersection at the same time.
4. To through traffic, if you are turning left.

Don'ts of safe driving

Never pass a car unless you have plenty of open road ahead. Come back into line only after the car you have passed is visible in your rear-view mirror.
Never pass a stopped bus without taking precautions. A passenger may step into your path from in front of the bus.
Never park with any part of your car in a driving lane.
Never coast with gears in neutral.
Never weave from lane to lane in traffic.
Never cut across a curve.
Never drive past a STOP sign without stopping, even though there is no traffic, and even though the car ahead of you has halted and moved on.
Never pull into traffic until your car's engine is running smoothly.
Never park a car facing traffic. It confuses other drivers, especially at night, and is illegal in most places.
Never drive with your bright lights on when other cars are approaching, or when following another car.

signal when changing lanes. Other levers control windshield wipers, headlights, and cruise control.

Drivers use mirrors to see behind and to the sides of their cars. The *rearview mirror* above the windshield provides a view through the car's back window. Using the rearview and side mirrors, drivers can get a good view around their vehicles. But all vehicles have *blind spots*—that is, places to the side and rear of the vehicle that are not visible in any of the mirrors. Some types of automobiles, such as trucks, have trailers or other objects blocking the view out their back windows. They

thus have no rearview mirrors. Drivers of such vehicles must use only their side mirrors to navigate and so have a much larger blind spot. It is important to note the blind spots of other drivers on the road to avoid surprising them and, possibly, colliding with them.

Rules of the road help to coordinate traffic and prevent accidents. Many rules are enforced by law. Signs and traffic lights tell drivers when to stop the car or yield to cross traffic or pedestrians.

Signs also show speed limits. Police officers use radar guns to measure the speeds of vehicles. The officers can

Standard traffic signs

The main aids to safe driving are the traffic signs seen on all American highways. These signs (1) regulate traffic, (2) warn of dangerous road conditions, or (3) give vital information.

Octagon		Always requires a complete stop—not merely a slowdown.
Round		Always means there is a railroad crossing just ahead.
Diamond		Always warns of a certain danger, such as a sharp curve.
Triangle		Always means yield the right of way by slowing or stopping.
Rectangle		Always gives important instructions or directions.

Safe following distances

A driver can determine the safe following distance by using the *two-second rule*. The driver selects a fixed object in the road ahead. When the vehicle ahead passes the object, the driver counts "one-thousand-one, one-thousand-two." If the driver's vehicle reaches the object before the count is completed, he or she is following too closely. If road or weather conditions are not good, the driver should increase the count to four or five seconds. This graph shows some safe following distances based on the two-second rule.

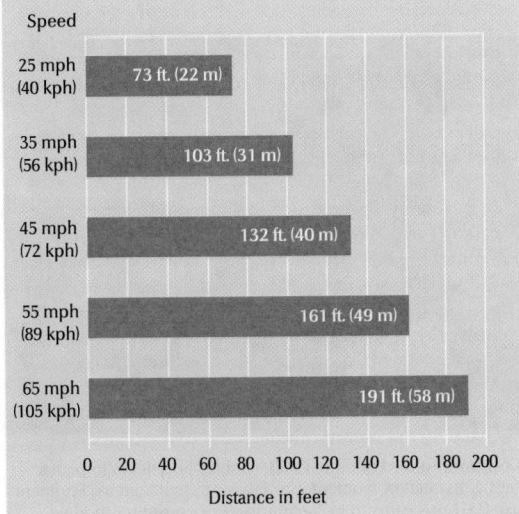

Speed

25 mph (40 kph) — 73 ft. (22 m)
35 mph (56 kph) — 103 ft. (31 m)
45 mph (72 kph) — 132 ft. (40 m)
55 mph (89 kph) — 161 ft. (49 m)
65 mph (105 kph) — 191 ft. (58 m)

0 20 40 60 80 100 120 140 160 180 200

Distance in feet

pull over drivers who exceed the speed limit.

In addition to following signs and traffic rules, drivers have other responsibilities. Drivers must remain alert to avoid accidents—especially while turning, speeding up, changing lanes, or performing other maneuvers. It is illegal to drive under the influence of alcohol or other drugs. Such substances slow or change a person's reactions, which can lead to deadly accidents. Some cities limit or ban such dangerous distractions as cell phone use and text-messaging while driving. In some places, it is illegal to ride in a car without a seat belt. Drivers also must see that their cars are properly maintained. Poorly functioning cars can be dangerous on the road.

Defensive driving means anticipating danger to avoid accidents. A defensive driver stays alert to all possibilities, such as other vehicles slowing down, entering the roadway, or stopping suddenly. A defensive driver adjusts the car's speed and position to suit visibility, the road, and traffic conditions. He or she slows down before entering a curve and yields the right of way. A defensive driver also signals well in advance before turning or changing lanes.

Building an automobile

To maintain interest and sales, most automakers bring out new car models every year. But most new models are updates on existing models. New model designs may correct problems in earlier models, add new features, or give the car a fresh look to attract new buyers. High costs prevent automakers from making major changes or introducing entirely new cars every year.

Developing a new vehicle, or even merely updating one, is a complex task. It requires many people, technologies, and parts. The whole process, from idea to finished car, may take from two to four years. Automakers therefore try to predict several years in advance what kind of cars buyers will want.

Planning the car. The first step in developing a new car is typically market research. Manufacturers survey car owners and people in the age or income groups they would like to target as potential buyers. Car designers plan an entire car's design based on such people's likes and dislikes, from the interior fabrics to the exterior

colors. They use *computer-aided design* (CAD) to create hundreds of drawings and models. They can then quickly test, modify, and re-create the models.

Traditionally, modelers used clay to turn the computer drawings into a *concept car*—a full-sized model that resembled a real car. Other specialists created interior models of the car's seats and instrument panel. Next, workers built a fiberglass body based on the clay concept car and interior models. The fiberglass model was given real tires, glass windows, doors, and interior and exterior decorations to look as much like the final product as possible. After further reviews, development on the new car began in full force.

Today, the auto industry uses fewer models because computers can accurately simulate many of a car's physical properties. For example, car models were once exposed to a wind tunnel to study how air flowed around the vehicle. Computer simulations today can provide the same information quicker and more cheaply.

Engineering the parts. After the car design is settled, a team of engineers plans every part of the car. Some parts, such as the engine and transmission, may be reused from previous models. But many other parts are newly created.

Engineers rely on computer programs to design parts and combine them into the working systems that make up the car. Computer programs also help make *dies*—the precision tools that shape metals and other materials into parts.

Testing the car. As the car's parts are engineered, manufacturers assemble *prototypes* (working samples) of the vehicle to test how it performs. The prototypes are often run for 24 hours a day, covering 100,000 miles (160,000 kilometers) or more, to test their endurance and *emission levels*. Emission levels are the amounts of pollutants, such as carbon monoxide and hydrocarbons, released in the car's exhaust. Carmakers also crash prototypes into walls to test their safety. Computers can model how well a car will protect its occupants in a collision. But government safety standards require actual crash tests.

Prototypes are typically much more expensive to produce than finished cars, costing hundreds of thousands

© age fotostock/SuperStock

Computer-aided design (CAD) enables engineers to plan a car's construction, from interior fabrics to paint colors. Engineers use CAD programs to make hundreds of computer models.

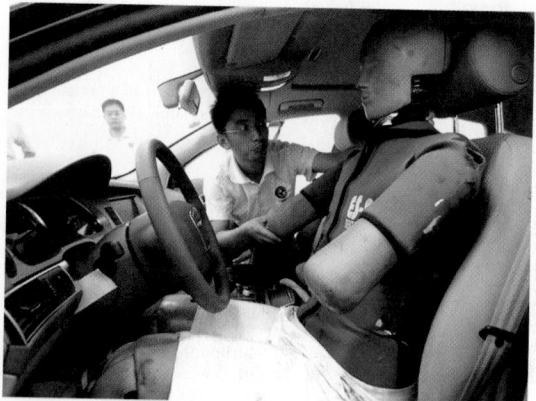

© Xinhua/Landov

A crash test dummy is used in the design of car safety systems, including airbags. Many automakers test cars by deliberately crashing them to determine how well they protect passengers.

**Assembling
an automobile**

These drawings show some of the chief steps involved in assembling an automobile using *unitized body construction.* In this method of assembly, manufacturers build the car body and attach the engine and other chassis parts to it along a main assembly line. Assembly and testing include hundreds of separate operations and take about two days from start to finish.

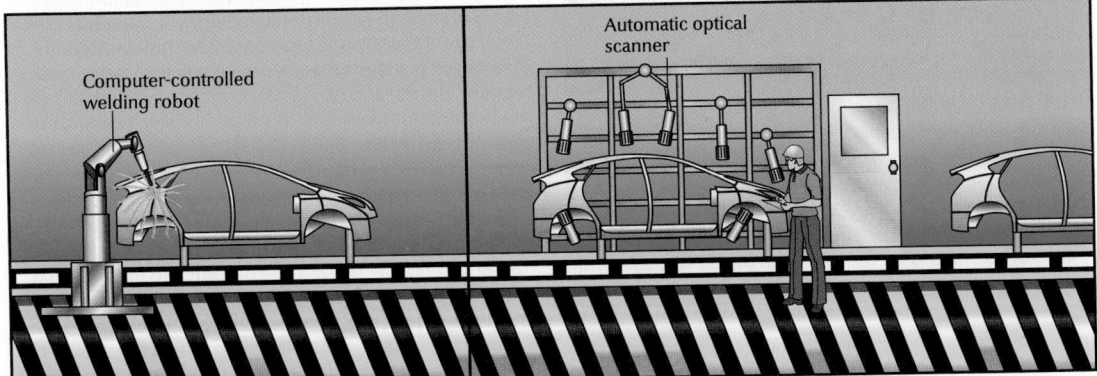

Assembling the body. After the main body parts are brought together for assembly, computer-controlled welding robots automatically weld the parts together, *above left.* Then, devices called *automatic optical scanners* use laser beams and electronic cameras to check the body, *above right.* They measure the parts to make sure they fit together accurately.

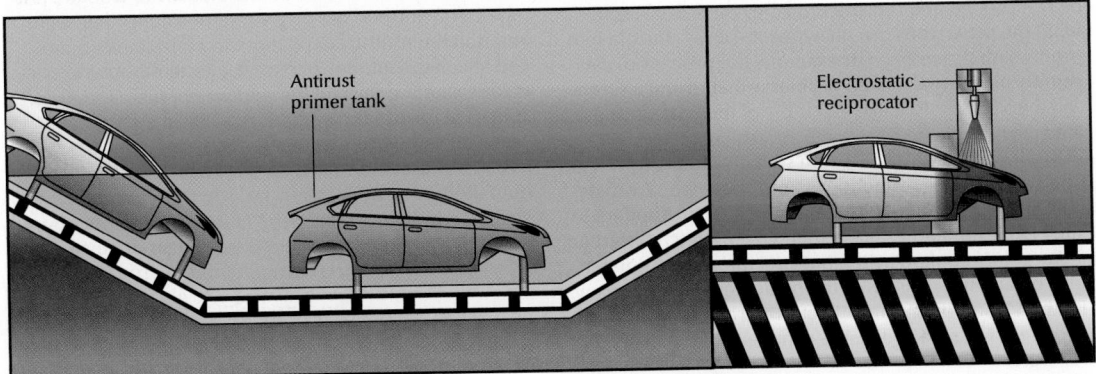

Painting the body. The body is dipped in a tank of *primer*—a paint that helps protect the body from rust. Automatic devices called *electrostatic reciprocators* spray on the final coats of paint. The fine droplets of paint are electrically charged so that they are attracted to the surface of the automobile body, which has an opposite charge. In this way, little paint is wasted.

WORLD BOOK illustrations by Jay Bensen

Chassis assembly and quality assurance. After the body has been painted, the chassis—including the engine, axles, and wheels—is attached to it. The windows, seats, and trim are also added. The car is tested at several points during assembly. At the quality assurance station at the end of the assembly line, technicians make a final check of the car's interior and exterior.

© Bloomberg/Getty Images

A wind tunnel can be used by automotive engineers to test the effects of airflow on a new car prototype. The tunnel blows a stream of air at the car at a uniform speed.

of dollars each. They are built without the cost savings that come from manufacturing many cars at once on an assembly line. If the prototypes fail the tests, they must be redesigned and remade until they pass. But assembling the prototypes can give manufacturers insight into production processes. For example, the process of assembly may reveal design problems that manufacturers can then correct to make assembly of the final car more efficient.

Buying materials. Based on specifications developed by engineers, automakers purchase the raw materials and parts to make the finished car. The suppliers of such parts sometimes make them from scratch based on a blueprint supplied by the manufacturer. The supplier may be another division of the manufacturer's company. But much automotive manufacturing relies on outside suppliers. Outside and inside suppliers *bid* (compete) for work.

Manufacturing includes the final steps of building a car. It involves making the car's parts and, finally, assembling them. Gathering all of the parts that make up a finished car together in one place poses its own challenge.

Companies use planning programs to schedule parts deliveries to their plants for use in production.

Computers also control many of the power-driven tools called *machine tools* that create a car's parts. In a process called *metal stamping,* pressing machines shape metal into forms determined by engineering dies. Small presses stamp out such parts as brackets and handles. Huge presses create a car's trunk lids, floor, roof, fenders, doors, and hood. Many parts of car bodies are made from lightweight fiberglass, plastics, or *composite materials* instead of metal. Composite materials consist of two or more substances. Most such parts are molded instead of stamped.

Another process, *casting,* involves pouring molten metal into a mold. The metal solidifies in the shape of the required part. The engine block is the main car part made by casting. Blocks are cast from iron, *iron alloys* (mixtures of iron and other metals), or aluminum.

Forging shapes steel or iron into the desired form by hammering. Crankshafts and certain pieces of the suspension system are forged. *Machining* involves using various tools to cut, grind, and shape precision parts, such as those used in engines and transmissions. Other processes are used to shape a car's plastic equipment.

After the parts have been manufactured, workers put together a finished car on an assembly line. They weld and bolt the exterior parts together, install the engine, and attach the interior parts. Final assembly also includes painting the car and adding *options.* Options are special features—for example, back-seat DVD players or seat warmers—that can vary among cars in the same model. An assembly line may turn out up to 75 cars per hour. Robots perform many tasks on an assembly line, such as welding and painting. Quality inspectors examine the work with cameras and lasers that precisely measure how the parts fit together.

The auto industry

Automobiles cost a great deal to produce, and most manufacturers operate out of wealthy countries. In many countries, automobiles make a major contribution to the economy. The auto industry is closely tied to a number of other important industries that together provide tens of millions of jobs worldwide.

© Norm Betts, Landovs

An assembly line enables the quick and efficient manufacture of automobiles. Robots on an assembly line perform many tasks, such as welding parts together.

Automobile features
worldbook.com/ca-15

Where cars are made. The top four countries for automobile production are China, Germany, Japan, and the United States. Other major producers include Brazil, Canada, the Czech Republic, France, India, Mexico, Russia, South Korea, Spain, and the United Kingdom. Some large corporations own or control several automobile companies, often in more than one country. Many developing nations assemble cars and trucks for automakers based in other countries. Many other countries make the parts that are used in automobiles.

Each country's auto industry developed around the unique conditions of its local economy, society, and market. For example, Japan's auto producers have tended to make small cars designed for fuel efficiency rather than power. Such cars appeal to consumers in Japan, where fuel is expensive and many streets are too narrow or crowded for big cars.

A number of German companies have targeted the luxury and sports car market. Other German companies offer low-cost passenger cars. German companies also produce about half of the diesel automobiles in the European Union. Most diesel passenger cars in the United States are imported from Germany.

Canada, Japan, the United States, and the countries of western Europe long had most of the world's automobiles. But in the early 2000's, the automobile markets in China and India grew rapidly. In 2009, for the first time, more cars were sold in China than in the United States. China was also the fastest-growing auto manufacturer in the world. The country has limited roads and depends on imported oil. Thus, Chinese manufacturers produce many smaller, fuel-efficient vehicles. China's industry also emphasizes hybrid and electric vehicles to take advantage of the electric power produced by the country's large coal supply.

Economic impact. Automobile manufacture depends on many other industries for various parts. These industries include the computer, glass, electronics, petroleum, plastics, rubber, steel, and textile industries. Furthermore, many people have jobs in car salesrooms, repair shops, and finance offices. Other people work in advertising developing car commercials. Small companies that make car parts employ hundreds of thousands of workers. In the United States, for example, about 2.5 million people are employed in jobs tied to the automobile industry.

For much of society, the widespread influence of the auto industry has transformed the nature of work. During the 1900's, millions of people left farms to live in cities and work in factories tied to carmaking. In the United States, such factories provided jobs to minority groups and recent immigrants. Work on assembly lines and other factory jobs required few specialized skills. Thus, the work of skilled artisans and craftspeople gave way to mechanized, unskilled labor. The industry also needed a large number of new managers and engineers to design and oversee car production and make business decisions.

Before the automobile became part of life in industrialized countries, average people owned few possessions and had little money. Many of them were enriched by the jobs provided by the auto industry and by the facilities and services that support car owners. Wages in the auto industry tended to be higher than hourly pay in

service industries. Higher incomes helped create a *consumer culture* (way of life that revolves largely around the purchase of goods). Advertising grew in importance as people had more money to spend and cars enabled them to drive to a wider variety of stores.

The health of the auto industry is closely tied with the overall economic health of many countries and that of the entire world. In 2007, a global *recession* (economic slump) began. In 2008, the auto industry suffered a severe downturn. At the same time, unemployment surged in many countries, deepening the recession.

The U.S. auto industry once consisted of three large corporations known as the "Big Three"—Chrysler Group LLC, General Motors (GM), and Ford Motor Company. But in 2009, two of the companies—Chrysler and GM—went bankrupt during the recession. The two companies reorganized with government assistance. All three companies produce a variety of cars and light trucks under a number of trade names. They have thousands of suppliers, including such large corporations as United States Steel Corporation, General Electric Company, and TRW Automotive.

Automobiles and society

Perhaps no technology has shaped modern society as much as the automobile has. A vast system of roads now connects distant places, communities, and economic markets. The automobile industry generates a huge amount of economic activity around the world. For some people, cars offer a sense of identity and social status. Automobiles have also introduced new dangers from collisions and reckless driving.

Demand for services and facilities. As automobiles became more popular, their use required the creation of new *infrastructure* (essential services and facilities) to support them. Such infrastructure includes paved roads, gas stations, repair shops, and everything else that enables cars to function smoothly.

Roads. Before the automobile, most roads were little more than dirt paths. They were dusty in dry weather and rutted and muddy in winter. Rivers and coastal waters served as the main routes for the flow of people and goods. Today in developed countries, cars and trucks carry most people and goods along highway systems that crisscross the land.

Beginning in the 1920's, national governments became involved in building better roads to connect major cities. Funding for such roads originally came from taxes on gasoline. Some of the earliest roads for automobiles were undivided highways that could be dangerous. After about 1950, more effort went into constructing divided highways to increase safety. Such highways have a strip of land called a *median strip* to separate lanes of traffic going in opposite directions. Highway designers also built many freeways and expressways. These roads achieved a safer, smoother traffic flow by limiting where vehicles can enter and leave.

Some highways became national landmarks. In the United States, Route 66—also known as the "Mother Road"—connects the Midwest to southern California. Other famous highway systems include Italy's Autostrade and Germany's Autobahnen. In India and China, new roads support the explosive growth of automobile ownership.

Automobile production in selected countries since 1960

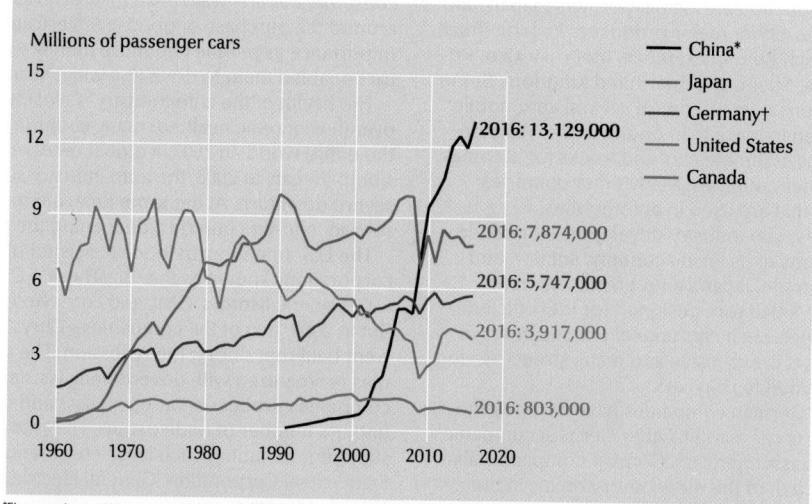

Millions of passenger cars

— China*
— Japan
— Germany†
— United States
— Canada

2016: 13,129,000
2016: 7,874,000
2016: 5,747,000
2016: 3,917,000
2016: 803,000

*Figures prior to 1991 are unavailable for China.   †Figures prior to 1990, the year of Germany's reunification, are for West Germany only.
Source: *Ward's Motor Vehicle Facts & Figures*, Ward's Communications, Inc.

Leading automobile-manufacturing countries

Number of passenger cars produced in 2016

China	13,129,000
Japan	7,874,000
Germany	5,747,000
United States	3,917,000
India	2,621,000
Spain	2,354,000
South Korea	2,092,000
Mexico	1,993,000
Brazil	1,781,000
United Kingdom	1,670,000

Source: *Ward's Motor Vehicle Facts & Figures*, Ward's Communications, Inc.

Leading automobile-manufacturing states and provinces

Number of passenger cars produced in 2016

Ontario	803,000
Michigan	725,000
Ohio	649,000
Kentucky	533,000
Alabama	415,000
Tennessee	404,000
Indiana	373,000
Mississippi	283,000
Kansas	279,000
Georgia	112,000

Source: *Ward's Motor Vehicle Facts & Figures*, Ward's Communications, Inc.

Fast highways offer convenience for traveling citizens. They also serve as critical routes for national defense and evacuation planning.

In the United States especially, expressways link cities and the suburbs around them. But some such links have contributed to the decline of inner cities by allowing people and businesses to move to the suburbs. Some critics claim that city-based expressways are unsightly. In Europe, many highways stop short of entering cities.

Other infrastructure. Alongside the world's highways lie gas stations, truck stops, restaurants, repair shops, camps, and motels. Such establishments sprang up to service the growing numbers of drivers and cars.

Gasoline was only available to drivers at general stores at first. But starting in 1905, gas stations became a roadside fixture. The architecture of gas stations evolved over the 1900's. Early gas stations looked like small homes. Modern gas stations feature wide canopies, self-service pumps, and convenience stores.

Early drivers traveling long distances were forced to camp on the side of the road and bring their own food.

As automobile touring became more popular, the demand grew for places to sleep along the road. Such places included tourist cabins and, later, motels.

Restaurants also developed along the highways, including early "greasy spoon" diners. In the 1940's, roadside chain restaurants, such as Howard Johnson's, became popular. These, in turn, lost customers to fast-food restaurants, such as McDonald's. Many such restaurants are designed around the automobile, offering drive-through food services.

A type of infrastructure called the *power grid* channels electric power from power plants to homes and other buildings. Electric cars, in particular, rely on the power grid to recharge after use. Power plants for cities typically produce extra electric power that is not used—power that electric cars can store in their batteries. Electric cars may become even more convenient to use when widespread improvements to power grids offer drivers more places to "plug in" their cars.

Demand for petroleum. The rise and dominance of the petroleum industry is closely linked to automobiles.

Automobile registrations in the United States and Canada since 1900

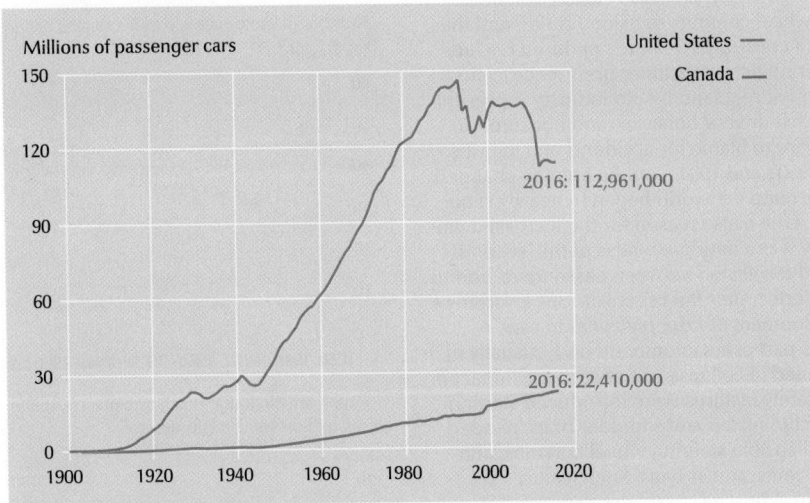

Millions of passenger cars

United States —
Canada —

2016: 112,961,000

2016: 22,410,000

Figures are for passenger cars only. Registrations for trucks, vans, and sport utility vehicles are not included.
Sources: Federal Highway Administration; Statistics Canada.

Leading countries in automobile registrations

Total number of registered passenger cars in 2013

United States	●●●●●●●●●●●●	120,214,000
Japan	●●●●●●	60,035,000
China	●●●●●◖	55,930,000
Germany	●●●●◖	43,851,000
Russia	●●●●	39,320,000
Italy	●●●◖	36,963,000
United Kingdom	●●●◖	31,918,000
France	●●●◖	31,650,000
Brazil	●●●◖	31,339,000
Mexico	●●◖	24,286,000

Source: *Ward's Motor Vehicle Facts & Figures,* Ward's Communications, Inc.

Leading states and provinces in automobile registrations

Total number of registered passenger cars in 2016

California	●●●●●●●●●●●●	14,768,000
Texas	●●●●●●◖	8,287,000
Ontario	●●●●●●◖	8,037,000
Florida	●●●●●●◖	7,855,000
Quebec	●●●●◖	5,187,000
New York	●●●●	4,891,000
Ohio	●●●◖	4,694,000
Pennsylvania	●●●●	4,640,000
Illinois	●●●◖	4,525,000
North Carolina	●●●	3,546,000

Sources: U.S. Department of Transportation; Statistics Canada.

Petroleum was once used mainly as kerosene to light lamps. But as gasoline derived from petroleum became critical to the use of automobiles, petroleum suppliers became big international businesses.

Earth has only a limited supply of petroleum and other fossil fuels. As more and more is used, what remains will become increasingly expensive. Petroleum prices rise and fall according to demand for petroleum and the supply available to meet that demand. In general, an increase in demand causes prices to rise. An increase in supply can cause prices to fall. In the 1920's and the 1970's, "scares" about running out of petroleum drove up the price of gasoline. In the long term, as consumers continue to use up the world's fossil fuels, lower supplies will lead to even higher gas prices. High gas prices can deeply affect the design of cars, driving behavior, and car purchasing decisions.

The countries that drive the most cars and so consume the most petroleum are among the world's wealthiest. Petroleum-producing nations tend to be, in contrast, poorer. This inequality can create resentment

and mistrust between petroleum-consuming and petroleum-producing nations.

As with any valuable resource, petroleum can also create political conflict. Countries that depend on imported oil have struggled to control petroleum-producing areas. Some historians have argued that the desire for petroleum contributed to the outbreak of many modern wars. Many people also worry that the need to secure a steady supply of petroleum too strongly influences the foreign policy of car-owning, petroleum-consuming countries.

Safety problems. Every year, about 1 ¼ million people die in car accidents around the world. In the United States, accidents occur almost daily in every area of the country. The scene of such an accident is generally cleaned up and has disappeared within hours. Occasionally, crosses or flowers mark the site of a fatal crash.

Despite the many deaths from automobile accidents, consumers and the industry paid little attention to automobile safety until the 1950's. Before that time, the typical American car had dashboards with numerous hard knobs, brakes and tires of poor quality, and windshield glass that shattered easily. Cars also lacked seat belts. Their steering wheel columns remained rigid—and thus, dangerous—in a crash. Such features endured because of manufacturer neglect, consumer preferences, and a lack of government regulation. Auto industry representatives claimed that drivers' behavior, and not automobile designs, were to blame for accidents and injuries.

During the 1950's and 1960's, public opinion changed. Governments around the world began to heavily regulate auto safety. One major reason for the increased emphasis on safety was a new awareness of the "second crash"—that is, the collision between passengers' bodies and the car's interior, after the car crash. This awareness led to the development of *crumple zones* in cars. A crumple zone is part of an automobile body, usually in the front, designed to collapse and absorb the impact of a crash. Other safety features were introduced starting in the 1960's, including lap and shoulder belts, padded dashboards, collapsible steering wheel columns, antilock braking systems, and airbags. Such features are now standard on almost all passenger cars.

Despite improvements, safety problems remain. Engineers design most cars to have a low *center of gravity*—that is, to keep most of the car's weight low. A low center of gravity makes a vehicle hug the road and handle better. Sport utility vehicles, however, have high centers of gravity because of their greater height, boxy design, and high ground clearance. A high center of gravity makes them vulnerable to rolling over in a crash.

In addition, reckless driving remains a constant source of danger. Drivers under the influence of alcohol or other drugs cause accidents that injure or kill hun-

Motor vehicle traffic deaths in the United States

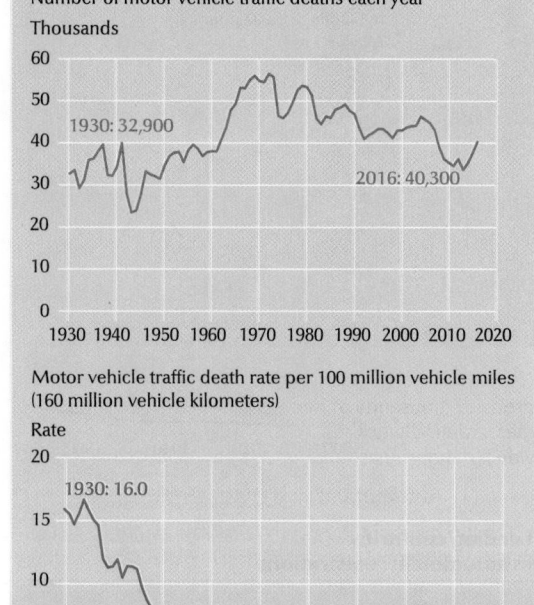

Number of motor vehicle traffic deaths each year
Thousands

1930: 32,900

2016: 40,300

1930 1940 1950 1960 1970 1980 1990 2000 2010 2020

Motor vehicle traffic death rate per 100 million vehicle miles (160 million vehicle kilometers)
Rate

1930: 16.0

2016: 1.18

1930 1940 1950 1960 1970 1980 1990 2000 2010 2020

Source: National Safety Council.

Highlights in the history of the automobile

Nicolas-Joseph Cugnot of France built two steam-powered road vehicles.

Jean Joseph Étienne Lenoir of France patented an internal combustion engine.

◯ 1769-1770   ◯ 1801-1803   ◯ 1860   ◯ 1865

Richard Trevithick of England developed a four-wheeled steam carriage for transporting passengers.

England passed the "Red Flag Law," which ended development of automobiles there for about 30 years.

WORLD BOOK illustration by Oxford Illustrators Limited

The Cugnot steam tractor was one of two steam-powered road vehicles built by French military engineer Nicolas-Joseph Cugnot in 1769 and 1770. These were the first self-propelled road vehicles.

Six-wheeled steam carriages provided regular passenger service in England in the mid-1800's. By the late 1800's, opposition by railroad and stagecoach companies had effectively ended the use of such steam carriages in England.

© Qilai Shen, Bloomberg/Getty Images

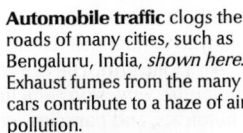

Automobile traffic clogs the roads of many cities, such as Bengaluru, India, *shown here.* Exhaust fumes from the many cars contribute to a haze of air pollution.

On the road
worldbook.com/cb-15

dreds of thousands of people each year. New technologies, especially text messaging on mobile phones, provide a dangerous source of distraction for many drivers.

Automobiles and the environment

During the early 1900's, a number of experts warned that the widespread use of internal-combustion engines could damage the environment and deplete the world's limited supply of fossil fuels. But cars with internal-combustion engines soon became overwhelmingly popular, and most people ignored such concerns. As a result, much of the modern world's economy and infrastructure has come to depend on automobiles powered by fossil fuels. Thus, reducing the environmental impact of cars and their use of fossil fuels requires reshaping

and rethinking important and established parts of our society—a serious challenge.

Damage to natural habitats. Roadways and other automobile infrastructure have altered the landscape in many places. Roads and highways cut through forests and other natural habitats. Wherever there are roads, fast-moving cars endanger deer and other animals that try to cross the road. Runoff from paved highways and parking lots may contain oil and other dangerous chemicals from cars. These pollutants may seep into the ground or enter rivers and streams, harming plants and animals.

Many car parts, such as tires, batteries, and used motor oil, are not *biodegradable*—that is, they are not broken down by nature after they are thrown away. Noise

American inventor Sylvester H. Roper built a steam-powered vehicle that received much attention.

William Morrison of Des Moines, Iowa, built a six-passenger car that ran on electric power.

| 1860's | 1885 | c. 1891 | 1891 |

Gottlieb Daimler and Karl Benz of Germany developed forerunners of the gasoline engines used today.

The French company Panhard et Levassor designed a front-engine, rear-wheel drive auto.

Mercedes-Benz

The Benz carriage was one of the first vehicles powered by a four-stroke gasoline engine. Karl Benz and Gottlieb Daimler developed the engine separately in 1885.

State Historical Society of Iowa

An electric car built by William Morrison in the early 1890's became the first successful vehicle of its kind produced in the United States.

Free Library of Philadelphia

The Panhard et Levassor was the first gasoline-powered car with a front-mounted engine and rear-wheel drive.

and light from cars can also disrupt the natural cycles of many living things.

Air pollution. The burning of gasoline and diesel fuel generates *emissions*—including exhaust gases, other chemicals, and particles—that pollute the air. Many automobile emissions, such as carbon monoxide and sulfur dioxide, are poisonous to plants, animals, and people. Nitrogen oxide, another pollutant in automobile exhaust, reacts with chemicals called *hydrocarbons* and sunlight to form a substance called *ozone.* Near Earth's surface, ozone helps create a thick yellow haze called *smog.*

Automobile emissions first received significant attention in Los Angeles during the 1950's. The number of cars in the region had more than doubled in a little over a decade, greatly increasing the amount of car exhaust. Much of Los Angeles lies in the San Fernando Valley, a natural basin that traps exhaust fumes. The increased emissions, combined with the unique landscape, produced smog that often blanketed the city. Eye irritation and damage to vegetation were commonplace.

Automobile manufacturers did little to reduce emissions until the 1960's, when the federal government intervened. Car manufacturers gradually added equipment that cleaned car emissions, such as catalytic converters. California, in particular, set strict standards for vehicle emissions. In 1989, the state adopted a long-term plan to combat air pollution in Los Angeles and the surrounding area. Los Angeles still ranks among the U.S. cities with the worst air pollution, but its air quality has begun to improve.

Global warming. Many scientists consider automobile use to be a major factor in global climate change.

Earth's average surface temperature has risen since the mid-1800's in a trend called *global warming.* Global warming results chiefly from an increase in *greenhouse gases* in the atmosphere. These gases trap heat from the sun, acting much like the glass roof and walls of a greenhouse. Carbon dioxide, one of the main greenhouse gases, makes up the largest portion of the waste gases produced by automobiles. Scientists believe global warming, if unchecked, will greatly harm both the natural environment and human society.

History

The origin of the automobile can be traced to Europe. But it first became a major form of transportation in the United States. Most European cars were built by hand. They were expensive, and few people could afford them. In the early 1900's, Ransom E. Olds, Henry Ford, and other American auto pioneers began mass-producing cars. The demand for affordable cars grew rapidly. Automobiles saw action near the battlefields of two world wars. The auto industry soon spread around the world. As automobiles became a vital part of human society, automakers developed new cars to suit changing consumer tastes and the demands of government regulation.

Early automobiles. Automobiles first emerged during a period of great social and technological change called the Industrial Revolution, which began in the late 1700's. Throughout Europe at this time, new machines and factories transformed the way many people worked and lived. Inventors in Europe dreamed of a "horseless carriage." Steam, used to power many machines at the

Charles E. and J. Frank Duryea demonstrated the first successful American gasoline-powered car.	Pioneer automobile manufacturer Henry Ford built his first successful gasoline-powered car.	Ransom E. Olds built 425 autos to begin the mass production of cars in the United States.
○ 1893-1894 ○ 1895	○ 1896	○ 1901
	The Michelin company of France introduced the first tires with compressed air for use on cars.	The Spindletop gusher marks the discovery of huge oil fields in eastern Texas.

WORLD BOOK illustration by
Oxford Illustrators Limited

The Duryea, the first successful U.S. gasoline car, was built by brothers Charles and Frank Duryea in the 1890's.

Smithsonian Institution

The Stanley steamer was one of the most famous steam-powered cars. Francis and Freelan Stanley, identical twin brothers, built the first one in 1897.

Culver

The discovery of huge oil deposits in eastern Texas in 1901 aided the growth of the auto industry by making gasoline more plentiful and cheaper.

time, seemed the obvious power source.

The steam car. In 1769 and 1770, Nicolas-Joseph Cugnot, a French military engineer, built the first self-propelled road vehicles. One of them carried passengers. The other was a three-wheeled steam tractor for hauling heavy guns. In 1801 and 1803, Richard Trevithick of the United Kingdom demonstrated four-wheeled passenger vehicles powered by steam. But he lacked the money to continue his work.

During the 1820's and 1830's, the United Kingdom made many attempts to promote and develop steam cars. But such efforts failed in the face of competition from railroad and stagecoach companies. Furthermore, early steam cars were noisy contraptions that damaged roads, filled the air with smoke, and frightened horses. Sometimes, they blew up.

In 1865, the Red Flag Law greatly limited the use of automobiles in the United Kingdom. Under the law, a steam car could go no faster than 4 miles (6 kilometers) per hour in the country and 2 miles (3 kilometers) per hour in town. To warn of its approach, a signalman had to walk ahead of the vehicle, swinging a red flag by day and a red lantern by night. These restrictive measures effectively ended automobile development in the United Kingdom for about 30 years.

In the United States, an inventor named Oliver Evans demonstrated a steam-operated dredge mounted on a boat in 1805. Evans put wheels on the boat and drove the gigantic machine—which weighed about 20 tons (18 metric tons)—through the streets, to the harbor, and into the water. During the 1860's, another American inventor, Sylvester H. Roper, developed a much smaller steam vehicle that looked more like a present-day automobile. Many other Americans experimented with steam cars during the late 1800's. The number of U.S. companies that made steam cars grew rapidly. One of the most successful firms was founded by twin brothers, Francis E. and Freelan O. Stanley. They built the famous "Stanley steamer" car.

Steam cars had big disadvantages. At first, it took a long time for the fire to heat the boiler. Inventors eventually solved that problem, but the cars remained heavy and expensive. Over time, manufacturers gradually stopped making steam-powered cars. In 1924, the Stanley brothers' company—one of the last steam car manufacturers—went bankrupt.

The electric car. About 1891, William Morrison, an American inventor, built a successful electric car. Electric cars quickly became popular because they were quiet, easy to operate, emission-free, and reliable. In 1900, they accounted for 38 percent of all U.S. car sales.

However, most electric cars could travel no faster than 20 miles (32 kilometers) per hour. The batteries had to be recharged at least every 50 miles (80 kilometers). In addition, they could not be used in rural areas that did not have electric power. By 1905, only a few of the cars sold were electrics.

The gasoline car. Early automobiles owed their designs to the development of other technologies, such as the bicycle. But perhaps the most critical technology was the internal-combustion engine. Étienne Lenoir, a Belgian living in France, is usually credited with inventing the internal-combustion engine. In 1860, he patented a two-stroke engine that used gas obtained from heating

Henry Ford founded the Ford Motor Company.

Ford introduced the Model T. William C. Durant set up General Motors.

General Motors introduced the electric self-starter, invented by Charles F. Kettering the year before.

1903   1904   1908   1912   1913

Henry M. Leland of the Cadillac Automobile Company began building cars using interchangeable parts.

Ford installed a moving assembly line in his auto factory, dramatically cutting production time and costs.

General Motors Corporation

The curved-dash Oldsmobile, the first mass-produced car, was driven up the steps of the Michigan Capitol in a publicity stunt.

AP/Wide World

Assembly-line methods were improved by Henry Ford. Ford used the moving assembly line to produce the Model T, the most popular U.S. car of the early 1900's.

Motor Vehicle Manufacturers Association

Road building boomed with the increased popularity of the automobile. In 1916, workers began building a nationwide U.S. highway system.

coal. A spark generated from a battery and coil ignited the gas. Lenoir's engine was noisy and inefficient, and it tended to overheat. About 250 of his engines were sold and used to power pumps and machines.

In 1876, Nikolaus August Otto, a German inventor, developed a four-cycle engine. Like modern automobiles, his engine had steps for intake, compression, power, and exhaust. Two German engineers who had once worked for Otto—Gottlieb Daimler and Wilhelm Maybach—designed a "high-speed engine" in 1885. Their engine could rotate 600 times per minute. They built several experimental vehicles between 1885 and 1889. Maybach also designed a carburetor for mixing air and gasoline in 1893.

Karl Benz, a German engineer, was the first to link the internal-combustion engine with a wheeled vehicle. In 1885 and 1886, he built a tricycle powered by the engine. In 1889, he exhibited the design at the Exposition Universelle, a world's fair in Paris. By 1893, he had created an improved four-wheel car with a powerful engine. The vehicle proved reliable, and Benz sold more than 100 of his cars by 1898.

Benz's invention was soon improved on by Émile Constant Levassor, a French inventor. Levassor took Daimler's engine and attached it to the front of a vehicle. This car proved itself fast and well designed in the 1895 Paris-Bordeaux-Paris race.

The birth of the automobile industry. Until 1900, Europe led the world in automobile development and production. Peugeot, a French firm, started making automobiles in 1890. Another French company, Renault, began producing cars in 1898. Fiat of Italy began operation in 1899. France and Germany became the first large automobile production centers.

The first successful gasoline car in the United States was manufactured by the Duryea Brothers. Charles E. and J. Frank Duryea completed their car in 1893. Some American bicycle and carriage manufacturers began producing automobiles around the same time. Many quickly failed. But eventually, after 1900, the center of the auto industry shifted from Europe to the United States. Production of American cars increased from fewer than 5,000 in 1900 to more than 1 ½ million in 1916.

Mass production. Many historians credit the 1901 Oldsmobile as the first mass-produced car. More than any car before, this automobile was built of parts made by outside suppliers and shipped to the assembly plant. In 1904, Henry M. Leland further developed mass production when he took charge of the Cadillac Automobile Company. Leland began building cars using interchangeable parts. Such parts could be used to assemble or repair any car of the same model. Previously, most parts were made to fit only one particular car.

Henry Ford, an American industrialist, perfected the mass production of cars. Ford believed that there existed a huge market for cheap, reliable automobiles. He understood mass production as a way to achieve both reliability and low cost. In 1908, Ford started production of the Model T. In 1913, he installed a moving assembly line in his car factory. A chain pulled the car's frame through the plant. Workers on each side assembled the car by adding parts brought to them on conveyor belts. This process resulted in huge savings in production time and costs.

U.S. auto production fell for the first time, as a result of World War I (1914-1918).

The Big Three—Ford, GM, and Chrysler—accounted for most U.S. car production.

○ 1918   ○ 1921   ○ 1920's   ○ 1922

Walter P. Chrysler became president of the company that later became the Chrysler Corporation.

Low-pressure, or balloon, tires were introduced, giving a more comfortable ride.

Motor Vehicle Manufacturers Association

Motor vehicles played a major role during World War I (1914-1918). Trucks moved soldiers and supplies from place to place.

Culver

A 1920's boom in the auto industry put more cars on the road in the United States. Traffic clogged 42nd Street in New York City in this 1922 photograph.

General Motors Corporation

GM's Chevrolet became the top-selling U.S. car in the late 1920's, a distinction it held almost every year until the late 1980's. A 1927 Chevy is shown here.

Classic and collector cars

A number of historic automobiles are prized by collectors for their distinctive designs. Classic cars of the 1920's and 1930's were luxury cars with custom-built bodies. During the 1950's and 1960's, automakers designed sleek sports cars, such as the Corvette; luxury cars, such as the Cadillac; and fast "muscle cars," such as the Firebird Trans Am.

Richard A. Brown from *Car Collector*

1928 Cadillac 341 Sport Phaeton

Dennis Adler from *Car Collector*

1935 Mercedes-Benz 500K Special Roadster

Dennis Adler from *Car Collector*

1942 Lincoln Continental Coupe

© Mark Williamson, Alamy Images

1957 Cadillac Series 62 Coupe

© culture-images/Alamy Images

1966 Chevrolet Corvette Sting Ray

© Performance Image/Alamy Images

1969 Pontiac Firebird Trans Am

Alfred P. Sloan became president of GM. He introduced new car models every year.

Production slumped to 1,300,000 vehicles, the lowest number since 1918.

The United Automobile Workers (UAW) union was founded in Detroit.

○ 1923   ○ 1930   ○ 1932   ○ 1935   ○ 1939

United States motor vehicle production fell 36 percent due to the Great Depression.

Fully automatic transmission and air conditioning were introduced.

Motor Vehicle Manufacturers Association

The 1932 Ford was one of the first cars with a V-8 engine. In spite of its new model, Ford, like most other auto firms, suffered hard times in the 1930's.

Dorothea Lange

Rickety cars carried many farm families to new homes in California during the mid-1930's, after drought in the Great Plains.

AP/Wide World

Strikes by auto workers led to improved wages and working conditions. In 1936, these workers held a strike at a Flint, Michigan, GM plant.

Technological advances. As the auto industry expanded, various advances made vehicles safer, more comfortable, and easier to operate. One major development was the introduction of the electric self-starter. Charles F. Kettering, an American engineer, invented it in 1911. General Motors installed the first electric starters on its 1912 Cadillacs.

Before the self-starter, people had to insert a crank into the front of the engine and turn it by hand until the engine started. Hand-cranking was difficult and sometimes dangerous. As soon as the engine started, the crank would begin to spin fast and powerfully. As a result, people suffered broken thumbs, broken wrists, and other injuries from hand cranks. The self-starter helped lead to an increasing number of women drivers.

War and depression. Great changes occurred in the auto industry between the start of World War I (1914-1918) and the end of World War II (1939-1945). There were far fewer manufacturers, but they could produce far more cars. Competition changed from simple mass production to broad marketing programs. The marketing campaigns involved market research, product development, distribution, advertising, and publicity. Most of the pioneers who helped found the auto industry retired or died. Corporations, rather than individuals, began to run most automobile companies.

World War I was the first conflict that showcased the military value of automobiles. In September 1914, German forces advanced on Paris. The French used Paris taxicabs to rush soldiers to the battlefront. In 1916, the Allies saved Verdun, France, from German capture by carrying fresh troops and supplies to the battle in trucks.

Carmakers produced many war goods, including military trucks, tanks, and airplane engines.

During the war, people in the United States continued to purchase cars for personal use. But automobile production fell for the first time in 1918, largely as a result of a shortage of materials. After the war, the industry expanded again.

The rise of the Big Three. An economic slump struck the United States in 1920 and 1921. The sagging economy badly hurt the U.S. auto industry. In response, large auto companies shifted their leadership. In 1923, Alfred P. Sloan became president of General Motors. He developed several ideas that the entire industry came to adopt. Sloan encouraged car sales by changing model styling each year. This tactic is often described as *planned obsolescence*—that is, the intentional design of products to become outdated soon after purchase.

Sloan also set up a system of group management for GM. Each of the company's car divisions became independent and responsible for its own operations—though the head of the company maintained tight control. This organizational structure proved effective for managing the huge companies that the major automakers eventually became.

GM and other companies built cars that offered comfort, style, and speed at reasonable prices. Such cars proved tough competition for Ford's Model T, which ended production in 1927. Ford introduced a new car, the Model A, in the same year. The Model A became the top-selling car in 1928, but it held that distinction for only a short time.

Throughout the 1920's, the large automakers lowered

Automakers turned to manufacturing military equipment during World War II.

Hudson and Nash-Kelvinator combined to form American Motors Corporation (AMC).

| Early 1940's | 1948 | 1954 | 1956 |

Tubeless tires were introduced. Their casing was made airtight by an inner liner.

The Highway Act called for building a system of interstate highways.

Motor Vehicle Manufacturers Association

Army tanks were produced by the automobile industry during World War II (1939-1945).

Motor Vehicle Manufacturers Association

The Studebaker represented the "new look" in automobiles after the end of World War II. Cars became longer, wider, and lower, like the 1947 model shown here.

Motor Vehicle Manufacturers Association

Freeway construction began full force with passage of the Highway Act of 1956. The act called for building 41,000 miles (66,000 kilometers) of interstate highways.

Special-performance automobiles

Mercedes-Benz USA

A Mercedes-Benz is a German car known for its quality engineering. The model shown here is an S-Class luxury coupe.

Audi of America, Inc.

An Audi sports car is a German automobile with a powerful engine and stylish design. The model shown here is the R8.

Fiat Chrysler Automobiles

A crossover sport-utility vehicle (SUV), like this Jeep Grand Cherokee, combines features of an SUV and a station wagon.

© Ford Motor Company

A Ford pickup truck has an open compartment for cargo. The F-150, *shown here,* is one of the top-selling automobiles ever.

American cars became larger, heavier, and more loaded with options, such as automatic transmission.

Ford introduced the Mustang, the first compact car to feature sporty styling.

Late 1950's   1959   1964

Imported cars gained 10 percent of the U.S. auto market. U.S. automakers began introducing compact cars.

© ClassicStock/Alamy Images

Large motor hotels sprang up along interstate highways during the 1950's. These conveniently located hotels catered to Americans on the go.

UPI/Bettmann

The West German Volkswagen Beetle arrived in great numbers in the United States beginning in the 1950's. It was a big hit with American consumers.

Motor Vehicle Manufacturers Association

The Ford Mustang, introduced in 1964, quickly became a favorite with car buyers. The Mustang was smaller and sportier than most other compacts.

prices, cutting profits to increase sales. Eventually, only companies that could manufacture and sell large numbers of cars quickly and cheaply could stay in business. The number of U.S. automakers dropped sharply—from 108 in 1923 to only 44 by 1927.

The Great Depression was a worldwide economic slump that began in October 1929. It hit the automobile industry hard. In the United States, production of all vehicles fell 36 percent in 1930, and an additional 29 percent in 1931. By 1932, output had plunged another 44 percent, reaching the lowest volume since the war year of 1918.

Ford and Chrysler lost money during the Great Depression. However, GM made a profit throughout the 1930's. By the end of the decade, the Big Three controlled over 85 percent of the car market. Many firms had gone bankrupt. Others had survived by shifting to truck production.

World War II. Automobile manufacture in Europe was halted in 1939 by the outbreak of World War II. In the United States, the automakers converted their production facilities to making war equipment, becoming the "Arsenal of Democracy." They made not only military trucks, jeeps, and personnel carriers, but also tanks, aircraft and aircraft engines, ammunition, artillery, and marine engines.

The postwar years. After the war, the auto industry resumed civilian production. The return of former servicemen and women, the enormous growth of the suburbs, and the unsatisfied demand for cars during the war all created a huge market for automobiles. By 1960, 77 percent of all U.S. families owned a car, and 15 percent owned two or more. Roads and highways began to look the same everywhere, bordered by motels, fast-food restaurants, filling stations, and shopping centers. More than ever, the United States was a nation on wheels.

During the 1950's, performance and styling became

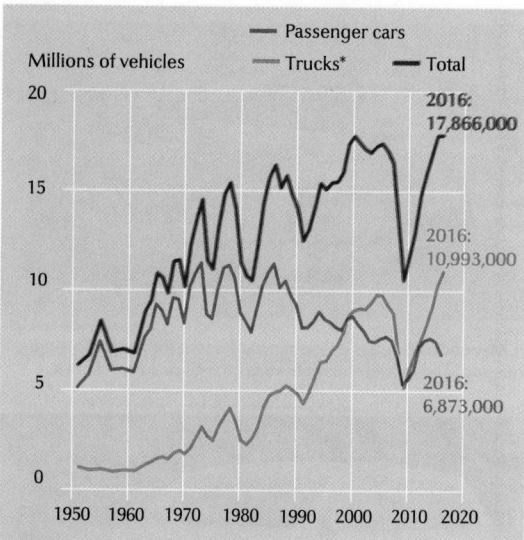

Car and truck sales in the United States since 1950

Millions of vehicles

— Passenger cars
— Trucks*
— Total

2016: 17,866,000

2016: 10,993,000

2016: 6,873,000

1950 1960 1970 1980 1990 2000 2010 2020

*Includes sport utility vehicles and minivans.
Source: *Ward's Motor Vehicle Facts & Figures*, Ward's Communications, Inc.

Ralph Nader wrote *Unsafe at Any Speed,* which led to new safety regulations.

A worldwide petroleum shortage helped make fuel-efficient cars popular.

1965   1968   1970's   1974

Devices that reduce exhaust fumes became standard equipment on U.S. cars.

A nationwide speed limit of 55 mph (89 kph) was established in the United States.

AP/Wide World

AP/Wide World

UPI/Bettmann

Front-seat shoulder belts became required equipment in automobiles in 1968. During the 1960's, car buyers began calling for such safety measures.

Imports from Japan gained a significant share of the U.S. auto market during the 1970's. Thousands of Japanese cars awaited delivery in Boston, *shown here.*

Long lines at filling stations were the result of a worldwide oil shortage in the 1970's. In Los Angeles, cars waited for a turn at the gas pump, *shown here.*

A sport utility vehicle (SUV), such as this GMC Yukon Denali, is a rugged vehicle originally designed for rough terrain but used by many people for everyday driving. SUV's first became popular in the 1990's.

keys to selling. American cars grew longer, wider, and lower. Automatic transmissions became available in low-priced cars. Engine power and electric motors operated air conditioning, brakes, seats, steering, and the tops of convertibles.

By the late 1950's, imports—especially the West German Volkswagen Beetle—began to take a growing share of the U.S. market. Imports reached 10 percent in 1959. They then temporarily declined until the late 1960's.

In 1964, Ford introduced the Mustang, which was smaller and sportier than most American cars. Car buyers loved the Mustang at first sight. The same year, Pontiac came out with the GTO, marking the era of the "muscle car" in the United States. Muscle cars were midsize cars with big, powerful engines, usually V-8's. They were fast, but many were also unsafe due to inadequate brakes. The popularity of muscle cars faded by the 1970's.

The growth of government regulation. In 1965, an American lawyer named Ralph Nader wrote *Unsafe at Any Speed.* The book attacked Chevrolet's Corvair in particular and the auto industry in general for emphasizing profits and style over safety. Corvair sales plunged, and Chevrolet stopped producing the car in 1969.

Until then, the U.S. auto industry had operated largely free of government regulation. The situation changed in the 1960's, partly because criticism of the automobile had increased, especially after Nader's book appeared. The 1966 National Traffic and Motor Vehicle Safety Act ordered certain changes to promote automobile safety.

Japan first surpassed the United States as the world's leading manufacturer of cars.

The speed limit on rural U.S. interstates was allowed to rise to 65 mph (105 kph).

| 1980 | 1980's | 1987 | 1995 |

Japanese automakers built seven assembly plants in the United States.

The 65 mph speed limit on rural U.S. interstates was abolished, allowing each state to set its own limit.

The minivan became popular during the 1980's. Its success provided a financial boost to Chrysler, which introduced the vehicle in 1984.

Japanese auto plants in the United States, such as this Nissan plant in Smyrna, Tennessee, first appeared in the 1980's.

Aerodynamic designs, like this Miata by Mazda, presented one of the "hottest" new looks for automobiles in the early 1990's.

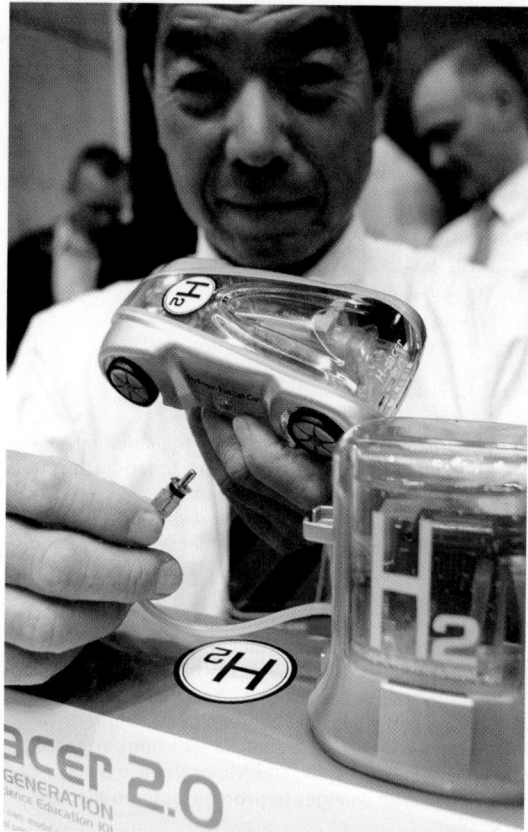

© Kim Kyung-Hoon, Reuters/Landov

A fuel cell converts chemical energy to electric energy, which can be used to power automobiles. This model car is powered by a fuel cell that combines oxygen from the air with hydrogen.

The rise of international automaking. During the 1960's, the auto industries of France, Italy, Spain, Sweden, and West Germany prospered. The Soviet Union and Italy agreed to produce Italian Fiat cars in the Union of Soviet Socialist Republics. The Australian auto industry thrived, and Argentina and Brazil expanded production. Japan, however, made the most dramatic progress. Japanese production skyrocketed from about 50,000 cars in 1958 to more than 2 million by 1968.

A worldwide petroleum shortage during the 1970's resulted in high gasoline prices and long lines at filling stations. Many families with large automobiles switched to smaller, lightweight cars that were more fuel efficient. In the United States, imported cars became popular because of their fuel efficiency. By 1980, imports had captured more than 25 percent of the U.S. market, and Japanese cars accounted for more than 80 percent of those sales.

Challenges to the Big Three. The oil shortage led the U.S. Congress to pass a law in 1975 requiring manufacturers to make cars more fuel efficient. The 1974 cars averaged 14 miles per gallon (6 kilometers per liter) of gasoline. Under the new law, the 1985 models had to average 27 ½ miles per gallon (11.7 kilometers per liter). The Big Three met the requirements by building lighter cars with smaller engines and by making mechanical im-

provements. However, they could not match the Japanese automakers in quality. Congress later demanded even greater fuel efficiency in the 1990's.

The shift in consumer preference from large cars to small ones helped Japan surpass the United States as the world's largest automaker for the first time in 1980. The shiploads of imported cars pouring into the United States stunned the Big Three. The price of a new car rose sharply during the early 1980's. As a result, people kept their old cars longer before buying a new one.

Chrysler, in deep financial trouble, needed $1 ½ billion in government-guaranteed private loans to survive. Lee Iacocca, head of Chrysler, turned the company around for a time. Chrysler received the loans in 1980 and repaid them within three years. In 1984, Chrysler introduced a line of small passenger vans called *minivans* that achieved huge success in the marketplace. In 1987, the company bought American Motors Corporation, which the French automaker Renault had largely controlled since 1977.

In 1981, the United States and Japanese governments placed voluntary restrictions on the export of Japanese cars to the United States. The restrictions encouraged Japanese car manufacturers to produce vehicles in the United States themselves. By the late 1990's, several Japanese manufacturers had assembly plants in the United States.

The 2000's. Light trucks and sturdy SUV's became increasingly popular in the United States. In the 1990's, production of such vehicles surpassed that of passenger cars in the United States. This shift toward big, fuel-hungry vehicles eventually created problems for United States automakers after a global recession began in 2007. As the economic downturn took hold, demand for vehicles dropped. American automakers struggled to survive. Chrysler and GM received billions of dollars in loans from the U.S. federal government. Despite these loans, both Chrysler and GM filed for bankruptcy in 2009. GM quickly emerged from bankruptcy, but Chrysler did not.

Gasoline prices soared in 2008, soon after the recession had begun. As a result, more consumers purchased fuel-efficient vehicles, including hybrids and electric

© Dominic Lipinski, PA Photos/Landov

A charging station provides electric power to recharge the batteries of electric cars. A network of convenient charging stations could make electric cars more practical for drivers.

Toyota Motor Company

A hybrid automobile, such as this Toyota Prius, combines a battery-driven electric motor with another power source—in this case, a gasoline engine.

cars. For example, the number of hybrid cars sold in the United States increased from about 8,000 in 2000 to about 290,000 in 2009. Manufacturers who made fuel-efficient cars also benefited from a United States government program called the Car Allowance Rebate System. The program, popularly known as "Cash for Clunkers," gave car owners up to $4,500 for trading in older cars with poor gas mileage for newer, more fuel-efficient vehicles.

Rising gas prices also led to other efforts to reduce consumption. For example, engineers and scientists worked to power cars with *fuel cells.* Fuel cells convert chemical energy to electric energy, rather than burning gasoline. Some automobiles were manufactured to run on biofuels, including ethanol, a type of alcohol made from crops such as corn and sugar cane.

Despite technological advances, the auto industry faces many challenges. The industry still manufactures many large, inefficient vehicles, but rising fuel costs have made them less popular with consumers. Safety concerns have also caused problems. In 2010, the Japanese automaker Toyota Motor Company had to recall millions of vehicles because their gas pedals could become stuck, causing the cars to accelerate out of control.

Christopher Depcik and John A. Heitmann

Related articles in *World Book* include:

Biographies

Bendix, Vincent
Benz, Karl
Buick, David Dunbar
Chevrolet, Louis
Chrysler, Walter Percy
Daimler, Gottlieb
Dodge brothers
Durant, William Crapo
Duryea brothers
Evans, Oliver
Ford, Henry
Ford, Henry, II
Haynes, Elwood
Iacocca, Lee
Kaiser, Henry John
Kettering, Charles Franklin
Maybach, Wilhelm
Nash, Charles William
Olds, Ransom Eli

Stanley brothers
Studebaker, John Mohler
Willys, John North

Automobile industry

Daimler AG
Ford Motor Company
General Motors Company
Porsche AG
Toyota Motor Corporation
United Automobile Workers
Volkswagen AG

Automobile parts and devices

Airbag	Ignition
Battery	Induction coil
Bearing	Muffler
Brake	Radiator
Carburetor	Rotary engine
Catalytic converter	Shock absorber
Diesel engine	Speedometer
Electric generator	Starter
Electric motor	Thermostat (Uses)
Flywheel	Tire
Fuel injection	Torsion bar suspension
Gasoline engine	Transmission
Gear	Turbine
Governor	

Kinds of motor vehicles

All-terrain vehicle
Ambulance
Bus
Electric car
Hot rod
Hybrid car
Jeep
Motorcycle
Recreational vehicle
Sport utility vehicle
Sports car
Truck

Other related articles

Air pollution
Antifreeze
Assembly line
Automobile, Model
Automobile racing
Driving while intoxicated
Gasoline
Horsepower
Hydraulics
Insurance (Automobile insurance)
Interstate Highway System
Mass production
Motel
National Safety Council
No-fault insurance
Road
Steam engine
Streamlining
Traffic
Trailer
Transportation

Automobile models
worldbook.com/cc-15

Additional resources

Level I

Graham, Ian. *Cars.* Raintree Steck-Vaughn, 1999. Discusses automobile design.
Graham, Ian, and Salariya, David. *Cars.* Watts, 2000.
Petty, William. *Some Cars Can Swim.* Copper Beech, 1999.

Level II

Brazendale, Kevin, ed. *The Encyclopedia of Classic Cars.* Rev. ed. Thunder Bay Pr., 1999.

Georgano, Nick, ed. *The Beaulieu Encyclopedia of the Automobile.* 2 vols. Fitzroy Dearborn, 2000.

Kollins, Michael J. *Pioneers of the U.S. Automobile Industry.* 4 vols. Soc. of Automotive Engineers, 2002.

Lewis, Lucinda. *Roadside America: The Automobile and the American Dream.* Abrams, 2000.

Toboldt, William K., and others, eds. *Automotive Encyclopedia.* Rev. ed. Goodheart-Willcox, 2000.

Automobile, Model, is a small-scale copy of a car. Many people enjoy making and collecting model cars as a hobby. Some hobbyists collect many different types of model cars. Others collect only cars from a certain period or specialize in models of racing cars, antique cars, or cars of historic value.

Some models are unique, handcrafted cars made of clay, wood, plastic, or plaster of Paris. But the most popular type of model is made of molded plastic and is sold as a kit. Because of modern advances in plastics molding, manufacturers can produce kits of very detailed

Roy Ritola, Inc.

A model automobile may be a copy of a historic, modern, or imaginary car. This model is of a Mercedes-Benz 540, a version of the German car that was popular during the 1930's.

models at a low cost. Many types of vehicles, including sports cars, trucks, racing cars, and unusual show cars,are available in model kits. The kits include step-by-step instructions on how to assemble the models and require such tools as pliers, a sharp knife, and a small drill. Popular kits include replicas of the stock cars used in such races as the Daytona 500. People can also collect die-cast metal models or plastic promotional models of current cars that can be obtained from car dealers.

Some hobbyists have favorite models they build as *stock.* A stock car looks like the real car as it was produced at the factory. Others prefer to *customize* their cars. This means that they give them special touches or features, such as elaborate paint jobs, unusual decorations, or molded plastic wheels.

Some people enjoy the excitement of radio control (R/C) car racing. In the early years of radio control racing, the model cars used fuel-powered model airplane engines. Now most radio control cars are powered by a battery-operated electric motor. The motor drives the wheels through a set of gears. A carefully tuned transmitter controls the car's speed and steering. The transmitter sends radio signals to a receiver built into the car.

In racing, each participant has an assigned channel or frequency that prevents cars from receiving conflicting signals from other competitors' transmitters. Most R/C car races last 8 or 10 minutes. The car that finishes the most laps on a track during the time limit wins the race.

Some model car hobbyists enter the Pinewood Derby. Pinewood Derby cars are wooden blocks that can be shaped to look like racing or passenger cars. The races are held on downhill ramps. Winners in a series of races compete with other winners until the car that finishes first in the final race is named champion. Participants in the derby can also win prizes for the best-designed car, for superior workmanship, or for the most original car.

Critically reviewed by the Model Car Collectors Association

Automobile insurance. See Insurance (Automobile insurance).

Radlauer Productions

Radlauer Productions

Radio control model cars are operated by radio signals transmitted to long, thin antennas attached to the car's hood, *left.* At the start of a road race, *right,* operators prepare to guide their cars with radio signals they send from handheld transmitters.

© Jonathan Ferrey, Getty Images

Stock cars whip around a turn during the annual Daytona 500 race in Daytona Beach, Florida.
Stock car racing is the most popular kind of automobile racing in the United States.

Automobile racing

Automobile racing is a thrilling sport that tests the speed and performance of automobiles and the skill and daring of drivers. Each year, millions of spectators around the world attend a wide variety of automobile races. One of the most famous is the Indianapolis 500, which attracts hundreds of thousands of people yearly.

Much of automobile racing's popularity lies in the great variety of racing cars and racing events. The vehicles range in size from small, open karts (formerly called *go-karts)* to large sedans. However, all racing cars can be divided into two major groups: (1) production cars and (2) cars built specifically for racing. Production cars are factory-made passenger cars converted into racing cars. Most cars built only for racing are not designed to carry passengers. Automobile races range from 1,000-foot (0.3-kilometer) *drag races* that last only seconds to *rallies* that may cover great distances and last weeks.

There are two major types of racing tracks, *oval tracks* and *road-racing courses.* Oval tracks vary from less than ⅕ mile (0.3 kilometer) to more than 2 ⅗ miles (4.2 kilometers) long. They have straightaways and banked turns. Most oval tracks have an asphalt or concrete surface, but some have a dirt surface.

Road-racing courses resemble country roads. They have straightaways, hills, and a variety of turns. Many turns are described by their names, such as *hairpin, dogleg,* and *ess.* Some courses include sections of pub-

lic roads or are combined with oval tracks. Races are faster on big oval tracks than on road courses because cars can maintain higher speeds on banked turns than on sharp, irregularly shaped turns. Road courses in the United States range from less than 2 miles (3.2 kilometers) to more than 5 miles (8 kilometers) long.

Events called *street races* have become increasingly popular in automobile racing. Such a race is run on a temporary course on city streets. The most famous street race is the one held annually in Monaco. Street races have also been held in such North American cities as Detroit, Michigan; Long Beach, California; and Toronto, Canada.

Alongside both oval tracks and road-racing courses are special areas called *pits,* where drivers make servicing stops and refueling stops during a race. In the pits, a skilled crew changes tires, refuels, and may make minor adjustments and repairs. The pit stops often take only seconds to complete. A delay in the pits can lose the race for a driver. Pit crews are part of large professional racing teams. Such teams also include car designers and builders, engineers, computer technicians, mechanics, and a promotional staff.

Safety measures

Automobile racing is a highly dangerous sport, but many steps have been taken over the years to make it as safe as possible for both spectators and drivers. Strong guardrails and heavy fencing protect spectators from cars that have gone out of control. On many oval tracks, SAFER (Steel And Foam Energy Reduction) barriers are attached to concrete walls to absorb the energy of a crash and protect the driver. SAFER barriers consist of special foam pads behind structures of steel tubing.

A driver's most important piece of safety gear is a rac-

Sylvia Wilkinson, the contributor of this article, is the author of many books on automobile racing, including the series World of Racing *and a history of stock car racing,* Dirt Tracks to Glory.

Kinds of automobile racing courses and tracks

Most races are held on *oval tracks* or *road-racing courses*. Oval tracks have fast-banked turns. Road-racing courses have some sharp turns. On a combined road course and oval track, races may be run on the combined course or only the oval track. *Drag strips* are straight.

WORLD BOOK diagram by Linda Kinnaman and Isaiah Sheppard

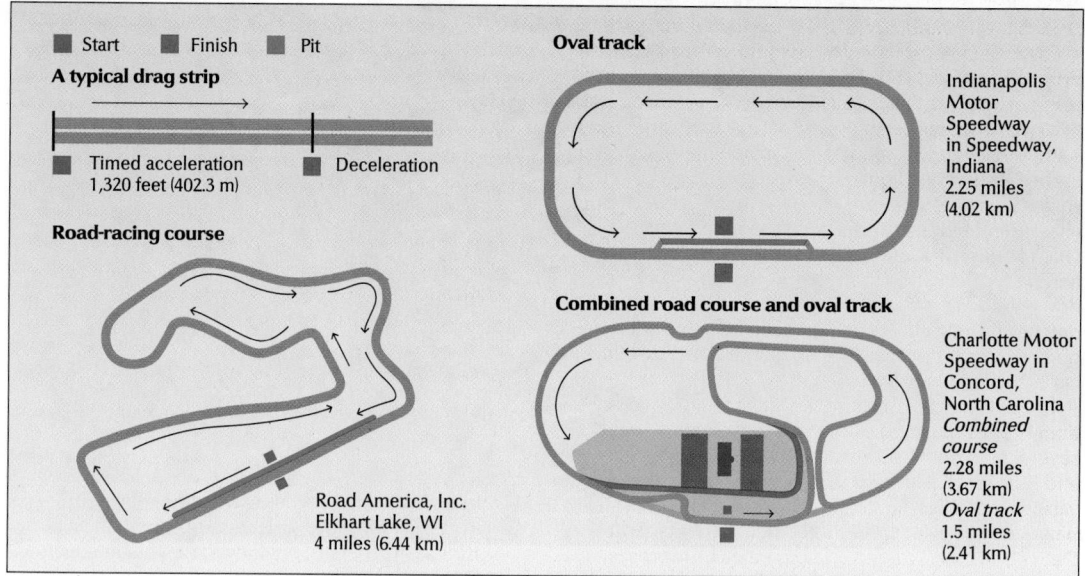

■ Start　■ Finish　■ Pit

A typical drag strip

■ Timed acceleration 1,320 feet (402.3 m)　■ Deceleration

Road-racing course

Road America, Inc.
Elkhart Lake, WI
4 miles (6.44 km)

Oval track

Indianapolis Motor Speedway in Speedway, Indiana
2.25 miles (4.02 km)

Combined road course and oval track

Charlotte Motor Speedway in Concord, North Carolina
Combined course
2.28 miles (3.67 km)
Oval track
1.5 miles (2.41 km)

ing helmet. Such a helmet has a hard outer shell made of fiberglass or carbon fiber and a foam-cushioned, flame-resistant lining. Drivers also wear flame-resistant clothing from head to toe. Under their helmet, some drivers wear a flame-retardant head covering that resembles a ski mask called a *balaclava.*

Lap and shoulder belts are standard safety equipment on racing cars. A device known as the HANS *(head and neck support)* reduces the chance of serious injury caused by the violent movement of a driver's unrestrained head and helmet. Every car also has a built-in structure to help protect a driver's upper body if the car rolls over. A racing car with an *open cockpit—*that is, without a roof—has a *roll bar,* a dome-shaped metal bar that arches over the driver's head. A car with a roof has a *roll cage,* a structure of steel tubes that prevents the roof of an overturning car from collapsing.

A racing car carries fuel in a leak-resistant *fuel cell* within a metal or plastic fuel tank. A fuel cell consists of a strong, rubberlike bladder usually filled with a spongy material or foam that absorbs the fuel and helps keep it from spraying in case of a crash. The fuel cell foam also prevents fuel from sloshing around in the tank during a race, which makes a car harder to control.

Many race sites have medical facilities to provide emergency treatment to injured drivers in the event of a crash. In some cases, helicopters are available to rush injured drivers to nearby hospitals.

Sponsorship

The cost of building or buying a racing car and keeping it in top condition makes automobile racing one of the most expensive sports. For this reason, most professional racing teams have sponsors. A sponsor may be a wealthy person or a manufacturing company, such as an automobile maker or a household products company.

In return for their financial support, manufacturers advertise their products on the racing cars and on the uniforms of the drivers and crews. Television coverage of races also gives sponsors exposure.

Racing organizations

The Fédération Internationale de l'Automobile (FIA) regulates organized automobile racing in about 145 countries throughout the world. The Automobile Competition Committee for the United States (ACCUS) governs U.S. racing as part of FIA. Six racing organizations are members of ACCUS. They are the National Association for Stock Car Auto Racing (NASCAR), the Sports Car Club of America (SCCA), the National Hot Rod Association (NHRA), the United States Auto Club (USAC), IndyCar, and the International Motor Sports Association (IMSA). Canada is represented in the FIA by ASN (National Sporting Authority) Canada FIA. Each group establishes *classes* (divisions) of races for the type of racing it governs and specifies the cars in a class.

Kinds of automobile racing

There are six major kinds of auto racing: (1) Formula One racing, (2) sports car racing, (3) Indy racing, (4) stock car racing, (5) drag racing, and (6) sprint and midget racing.

Formula One racing features the most technologically advanced cars. Each Formula One car is designed and manufactured individually. The cars have a single seat, an open cockpit, and *open wheels* (no fenders). They are built according to a *formula* (set of specifications) drawn up by the FIA. The formula dictates tire *configuration* (design) and *chassis* and engine limits as well as the car's weight and aerodynamic limits. A car's chassis is its base frame, wheels, and other parts necessary for operation of the car. *Aerodynamics* refers to the design of the car's body so that it can move through the air as quickly and efficiently as possible. Formula One cars are also called *Grand Prix* (pronounced *grahn PREE)* cars. The races in which the cars compete include the French term *Grand Prix* (Great Prize) in their names.

Formula One cars are designed on some of the same principles as airplanes. Like the *fuselage* (body) of an airplane, a Formula One car uses *monocoque* construction. In this type of construction, the car's central structure is a single-piece, tube-shaped shell made of carbon fiber and other durable, lightweight materials. This structure, sometimes called the *tub,* serves as both the body and chassis and bears the mechanical stresses. A Formula One car has front and rear wings. The flow of air over and under the wings and other devices produces a downward force that presses the car to the ground. This *downforce* holds the car to the road, which enables it to go faster through turns. The engine of a Formula One car is behind the driver.

Grand Prix races make up the most famous international series of racing events on road courses, with several held on the streets of such cities as Monaco and Singapore. The series consists of about 20 races in various countries, including Brazil, Canada, China, Japan, Russia, Spain, the United Kingdom, and the United States. The races are governed by the FIA representative in each country.

Grand Prix races are held on exceptionally challenging courses. The races range from about 160 to 190 miles (260 to 305 kilometers) in length. Cars reach speeds of more than 238 miles (381 kilometers) per hour on straightaways and may go as slow as 30 miles (48 kilometers) per hour around sharp turns. The first driver to finish the required number of laps around the course wins. The top 10 drivers receive points. The driver who earns the most points in Grand Prix races in a year wins the World Drivers' Championship. There is also a Constructors' Championship for manufacturers based on the same point system.

Sports car racing consists of events for production cars, modified production cars, and specially built *sports-racing* and formula cars. Most sports car races are held on road courses or on combined road courses and oval tracks. The SCCA oversees many sports car races across the United States, including a National Championship event each year for numerous car classes.

Endurance races are among the most popular sports car events. Such races last from less than 6 hours to 24 hours. The winner is the driver who completes the most laps within the specified time or becomes the first to cover the required distance. During an endurance race, cars make regular pit stops to refuel, change tires, and alternate drivers. Two or more drivers usually take turns driving the car during the race. The most famous sports car endurance race is the 24 Hours of Le Mans, held each year in Le Mans, France. Other famous endurance races include a 24-hour race in Daytona Beach, Florida, and a 12-hour race in Sebring, Florida.

Some endurance cars have *turbocharged* engines. Turbocharging increases the power of a small engine by using the energy from the engine's exhaust gases to spin a windmill-like pump. The pump forces a large volume of a fuel-and-air mixture into the engine's *combustion chamber,* where the mixture is burned. The greater

Thomas Zimmermann, FPG

Formula One racing features cars with one seat, a rear engine, and front and rear wings. They have no roof or fenders. The wings produce a *downforce* that presses the cars to the ground.

the volume of the fuel-and-air mixture in the engine's combustion chamber, the more power is released and the more energy is converted into the car's speed.

Indy racing. In 2008, the Indy Racing League (IRL) and Champ Car merged into one organization, adopting the name and rules of the Indy Racing League. The racing organization is now called IndyCar. The cars are high-powered open-wheel vehicles that resemble Formula One cars. They have one seat, an open cockpit, and monocoque construction. To provide downforce, the cars have front and rear wings plus a *ground-effects underbody.* This underbody is created by two structures called the *side pods,* one on each side of the cockpit. Each side pod has a curved *ground-effects panel* on its underside. These panels direct the flow of air moving under the car so that a low-pressure area, or partial vacuum, is created beneath the car. The resulting suction helps hold the car to the track. The side pods also create an area to hold radiators and other car parts, and they help protect the driver from side impacts.

Indy cars have turbocharged engines that are fueled by a form of alcohol called *ethanol.* Ethanol allows engines to remain cooler at higher power settings than gasoline. It also ignites less easily than gasoline, reducing the risk of fire in case of a crash.

Races range from 150 to 500 miles (240 to 805 kilometers) long. Indy cars can average more than 200 miles (320 kilometers) per hour on oval tracks, with top speeds up to 240 miles (386 kilometers) on straightaways. At first, Indy car races ran only on oval tracks. Today they often race on road and street courses.

Indy cars are named after the Indianapolis 500, the premier annual event for IndyCar. This race takes place on the 2 ½ mile (4.02-kilometer) Indianapolis Motor Speedway in Speedway, Indiana. There are 33 starting positions. Drivers with the highest average speeds in four qualifying laps earn the chance to race. The first driver to complete the 200 laps around the track—a distance of 500 miles (805 kilometers)—wins the race. All the drivers share in the largest *purse* (amount of prize money) in automobile racing, which has exceeded $10 million. First prize has reached more than $2 million.

© Mark Weber

Sports-car racing is popular in the United States and Canada. The cars are built especially for automobile racing. They race on road courses or on combined road courses and oval tracks.

Stock car racing, which originated in the South, is the most popular kind of automobile racing in the United States. Stock cars are based on passenger cars sold by U.S. manufacturers. The biggest stock car races are restricted to late-model sedans. The cars are specially built for racing, but from a distance they look like ordinary passenger cars. They have an engine mounted in the front, fenders, doors, and a windshield. Drivers sit in the usual upright position.

Stock cars have steel bodies and are therefore much heavier than other kinds of racing cars. Stock cars that are raced in the Monster Energy NASCAR Cup (formerly the Sprint Cup) series have a minimum weight of 3,400 pounds (1,540 kilograms), compared with about 1,500 pounds (680 kilograms) for an Indy car. However, a stock car's large, powerful engine enables it to reach speeds of 200 miles (320 kilometers) per hour.

Most major stock car races are held on oval asphalt tracks. The distance around the tracks ranges from about ⅝ mile (0.8 kilometer) to 2 ⅗ miles (4.2 kilometers) for *superspeedways,* such as the one in Talladega, Alabama. A superspeedway has wide, high-banked turns that enable cars to make the turns at speeds up to 200 miles (320 kilometers) per hour.

Nearly all stock car races are held in the United States. NASCAR governs U.S. competition, including the Monster Energy NASCAR Cup Series championship. Cup races range from about 215 to 600 miles (345 to 965 kilometers). Highlights of this series of about 40 races include the Daytona 500 in Daytona Beach; the Allstate 400 at the Brickyard at Indianapolis Motor Speedway; the Sharpie 500 in Bristol, Tennessee; and the UAW-Ford 500 in Talladega. NASCAR also governs a series for racing vehicles that have the body of a pickup truck mounted on the chassis.

Drag racing. A drag race is a high-speed race on a straight paved track called a *drag strip.* Drag races are traditionally ¼-mile (0.4-kilometer) long, and some cars cross the finish line in less than four seconds. The fastest cars reach speeds of more than 300 miles (480 kilometers) per hour. Such cars use a parachute at the rear to slow them down to a stop.

Drag-racing cars range from mass-produced passen-

ger cars to unusual-looking models built only for racing. The three main types of professional drag-racing cars are (1) Pro Stock, (2) Top Fuel, and (3) Funny Cars. All of these cars burn high-octane racing gasoline.

Pro Stock cars are especially built for racing but must resemble commercially made cars. However, the car body and engine may be from different manufacturers.

Top Fuel cars, also called *dragsters,* are named for the high-energy fuel they burn. The car bodies are not required to resemble production cars. Top Fuel cars have an engine in the rear, one seat, and a long, slender frame. They have huge rear tires that increase speed by applying more than 7,000 horsepower to the road. The front wheels on Top Fuel cars are narrow, like bicycle wheels, to reduce drag.

Funny Cars must have a body that resembles a particular model of passenger car. However, the *wheelbase* (distance between front and rear axles) must be shorter than that of standard passenger cars. Their strange appearance led to the class being named Funny Cars.

Hundreds of cars may race in a *drag meet.* The cars race two at a time, accelerating from a standing start. The losing car is eliminated, and the winner advances in the competition to race against another car. The elimination continues until only two cars are left. The winner of the last round is the meet champion.

The NHRA supervises the major drag races in the United States and Canada. Each year, it conducts more than 20 events in which drivers earn points toward the Mello Yello Drag Racing Championship. Important events in the series include the Winternationals in Pomona, California; the Gatornationals in Gainesville, Florida; and the U.S. Nationals in Indianapolis.

Other kinds of racing. *Sprint cars* are open cockpit cars that race mainly on dirt oval tracks. The cars have powerful front engines and open wheels. They often have large wings mounted on the roll cage for better downforce.

Midgets are smaller than sprint cars. They have highly modified small engines in the front that produce more than 300 horsepower. Midget tracks are usually ⅙ mile (0.3 kilometer) to ½ mile (0.8 kilometer) in length. Most races last 30 laps.

The *quarter midget* is a popular small racing car. It has an open cockpit and open wheel with the engine in the rear. Many successful drivers raced quarter midgets while still in elementary school.

A *kart* is the smallest racing vehicle. Many race drivers begin their careers in karting. Children as young as 8 years old, as well as adults, compete in kart races, which are generally held on miniature road racing tracks. See **Kart racing.**

A *Formula Atlantic* looks like a small Formula One or Indy car. The car has front and rear wings and a Toyota engine. Formula Atlantics race on oval asphalt tracks and on road-racing courses. They can go as fast as 160 miles (260 kilometers) per hour. Formula Atlantic racing is popular in the United States for young drivers who hope to move up to Formula One or Indy car racing.

Two rugged forms of racing are *off-road races* and *rallies.* Popular vehicles for off-road races include small trucks produced by such manufacturers as Nissan, Toyota, and Mazda. Most off-road races are long-distance events run on rough desert terrain.

National Hot Rod Association

In a drag race, two cars at a time compete against each other, accelerating from a standing start. The fastest drag cars can travel more than 300 miles (480 kilometers) per hour.

Most rally cars are production models, some of which have four-wheel drive. The chief kinds of rallies are *amateur rallies* and *pro-rallies*. Road rallies are held on public roads and feature some of the longest automobile events. Pro-rallies are held on rugged back roads. The SCCA governs the major U.S. rallies.

Vintage racing has become extremely popular. Such racing involves competition between historic cars that range in age from the late 1800's to just a few years old. Events differ in size, with some drawing as many as 600 entrants. The cars include sports cars, open-wheel cars, stock cars, and sedans. A broad variety of competitions are sanctioned by numerous vintage racing clubs.

The world's fastest cars are jet-powered vehicles. These cars do not race against other cars but against the clock to break the world land speed record. Most speed trials consist of two runs, each of which includes several miles to build speed, a 1-mile (1.6-kilometer) timed segment, and several miles to slow down.

History

The sport of automobile racing began in the 1890's. The first races were run on the open public roads between towns. Many of the courses were hilly, sharply winding dirt roads. Drivers often lost control of their cars and crashed, sometimes injuring spectators standing along the road.

Growth of organized automobile racing. The world's first automobile-racing organization, the Automobile Club de France, was established in 1895. Later that year, it supervised the first actual automobile race—a 732-mile (1,178-kilometer) round trip between Paris and Bordeaux, France. The winners averaged 15 miles (24 kilometers) per hour. That same year in the United States, J. Frank Duryea, a pioneer automobile maker, beat five other drivers in a race from downtown Chicago to the suburb of Evanston and back.

The most famous open-road races in the United States, the Vanderbilt Cup races, began on Long Island in New York in 1904. But the crowds along the road were difficult to control, and so the races were held in several other places around the country after 1910, such as Savannah, Georgia. In 1916, the races were discontinued. In time, more and more races in Europe and the United States were run on tracks designed specifically

Start   Finish

Stop in pit and consult an official   Reduce speed

Stop racing   About to be overtaken

WORLD BOOK illustrations

Automobile-racing flags signal the start and finish of a race. During a race, other flags tell drivers to consult an official, to reduce speed, to stop racing, or that they are about to be overtaken by another car.

for automobile racing.

The first Grand Prix race took place on a large course near Le Mans, France, in 1906. It was supervised by the Fédération Internationale de l'Automobile (FIA), which was established in 1904 to govern international automobile racing. The Indianapolis Motor Speedway opened in 1909, and the first Indianapolis 500 was run in 1911. The Grand Prix series began in 1920. The first 24-hour endurance race for sports cars was held in Le Mans in 1923. Organized stock car racing began in 1936 in Daytona Beach. The first Grand National (now Monster Energy NASCAR Cup) race for stock cars took place in Charlotte, North Carolina, in 1949. In 1950, the FIA established the World Drivers' Championship for Grand Prix drivers.

Development of racing cars. The earliest racing cars were simply the first automobiles. These heavy, open vehicles had poor brakes and were hard to steer. Racing cars thus became trimmer and faster in the 1920's and 1930's. Competition among carmakers also hastened the development of racing cars.

The major automobile races were canceled during World War II (1939-1945). The development of the rear-engined racing car in the mid-1950's revolutionized the sport. It enabled drivers to lean back and so conform to a car's streamlined body. By the early 1960's, rear-engined vehicles had almost completely replaced front-engined race cars. In 1962, Colin Chapman, an English racing car designer, introduced monocoque construction to Formula One cars with the Lotus 25. Wings appeared on racing cars in the mid-1960's. In 1978, Chapman introduced the Lotus 79 ground-effects car.

Automobile racing today. Racing car designers are always seeking ways to make cars run faster. But some racing organizations are changing their rules for safety reasons. In the early 1980's, for example, Grand Prix teams began trying to control corner speeds with more restrictive rules that governed aerodynamic technology.

Earlier racing cars used electronics only in the ignition system. Today, electronic technology is used in the engine, suspension, transmission, brakes, and other major components of many racing cars. Media technology can provide viewers of televised races with much technical information about the performance of the cars and drivers.

Top drivers of the 1990's and early 2000's included Helio Castroneves and Ayrton Senna of Brazil; Paul Tracy and Jacques Villeneuve of Canada; Juan Pablo Montoya of Colombia; Mika Hakkinen of Finland; Sébastien Bourdais of France; Michael Schumacher of Germany;

Formula One World Drivers' Championship

Year	Driver	Country	Year	Driver	Country	Year	Driver	Country
1950	Giuseppe Farina	Italy	1974	Emerson Fittipaldi	Brazil	1998	Mika Hakkinen	Finland
1951	Juan M. Fangio	Argentina	1975	Niki Lauda	Austria	1999	Mika Hakkinen	Finland
1952	Alberto Ascari	Italy	1976	James Hunt	United Kingdom	2000	Michael Schumacher	Germany
1953	Alberto Ascari	Italy	1977	Niki Lauda	Austria	2001	Michael Schumacher	Germany
1954	Juan M. Fangio	Argentina	1978	Mario Andretti	United States	2002	Michael Schumacher	Germany
1955	Juan M. Fangio	Argentina	1979	Jody Scheckter	South Africa	2003	Michael Schumacher	Germany
1956	Juan M. Fangio	Argentina	1980	Alan Jones	Australia	2004	Michael Schumacher	Germany
1957	Juan M. Fangio	Argentina	1981	Nelson Piquet	Brazil	2005	Fernando Alonso	Spain
1958	Mike Hawthorn	United Kingdom	1982	Keke Rosberg	Finland	2006	Fernando Alonso	Spain
1959	Jack Brabham	Australia	1983	Nelson Piquet	Brazil	2007	Kimi Räikkönen	Finland
1960	Jack Brabham	Australia	1984	Niki Lauda	Austria	2008	Lewis Hamilton	United Kingdom
1961	Phil Hill	United States	1985	Alain Prost	France	2009	Jenson Button	United Kingdom
1962	Graham Hill	United Kingdom	1986	Alain Prost	France	2010	Sebastian Vettel	Germany
1963	Jim Clark	United Kingdom	1987	Nelson Piquet	Brazil	2011	Sebastian Vettel	Germany
1964	John Surtees	United Kingdom	1988	Ayrton Senna	Brazil	2012	Sebastian Vettel	Germany
1965	Jim Clark	United Kingdom	1989	Alain Prost	France	2013	Sebastian Vettel	Germany
1966	Jack Brabham	Australia	1990	Ayrton Senna	Brazil	2014	Lewis Hamilton	United Kingdom
1967	Denis Hulme	New Zealand	1991	Ayrton Senna	Brazil	2015	Lewis Hamilton	United Kingdom
1968	Graham Hill	United Kingdom	1992	Nigel Mansell	United Kingdom	2016	Nico Rosberg	Germany
1969	Jackie Stewart	United Kingdom	1993	Alain Prost	France	2017	Lewis Hamilton	United Kingdom
1970	Jochen Rindt	Austria	1994	Michael Schumacher	Germany	2018	Lewis Hamilton	United Kingdom
1971	Jackie Stewart	United Kingdom	1995	Michael Schumacher	Germany	2019	Lewis Hamilton	United Kingdom
1972	Emerson Fittipaldi	Brazil	1996	Damon Hill	United Kingdom	2020	Lewis Hamilton	United Kingdom
1973	Jackie Stewart	United Kingdom	1997	Jacques Villeneuve	Canada			

Indianapolis 500 winners

Year	Driver	Mph	Kph	Year	Driver	Mph	Kph	Year	Driver	Mph	Kph
1911	Ray Harroun	74.59	120.04	1951	Lee Wallard	126.24	203.16	1987	Al Unser, Sr.	162.18	261.00
1912	Joe Dawson	78.72	126.69	1952	Troy Ruttman	128.92	207.48	1988	Rick Mears	144.81	233.05
1913	Jules Goux	75.93	122.20	1953	Bill Vukovich	128.74	207.19	1989	Emerson Fittipaldi	167.58	269.69
1914	René Thomas	82.47	132.72	1954	Bill Vukovich	130.84	210.57	1990	Arie Luyendyk	185.98	299.31
1915	Ralph De Palma	89.84	144.58	1955	Bob Sweikert	128.21	206.33	1991	Rick Mears	176.46	283.98
1916	Dario Resta	84.00	135.18	1956	Pat Flaherty	128.49	206.78	1992	Al Unser, Jr.	134.48	216.42
1919	Howdy Wilcox	88.05	141.70	1957	Sam Hanks	135.60	218.23	1993	Emerson Fittipaldi	157.20	252.99
1920	Gaston Chevrolet	88.62	142.62	1958	Jimmy Bryan	133.79	215.31	1994	Al Unser, Jr.	160.87	258.90
1921	Tommy Milton	89.62	144.23	1959	Rodger Ward	135.86	218.65	1995	Jacques Villeneuve	153.62	247.23
1922	Jimmy Murphy	94.48	152.05	1960	Jim Rathmann	138.77	223.33	1996	Buddy Lazier	147.96	238.12
1923	Tommy Milton	90.95	146.37	1961	A. J. Foyt	139.13	223.91	1997	Arie Luyendyk	145.83	234.69
1924	L. L. Corum and			1962	Rodger Ward	140.29	225.77	1998	Eddie Cheever	145.16	233.61
	Joe Boyer	98.23	158.09	1963	Parnelli Jones	143.14	230.36	1999	Kenny Brack	153.18	246.52
1925	Peter De Paolo	101.13	162.75	1964	A. J. Foyt	147.35	237.14	2000	Juan Pablo Montoya	167.50	269.57
1926	Frank Lockhart	95.90	154.34	1965	Jim Clark	150.69	242.51	2001	Helio Castroneves	153.60	247.20
1927	George Souders	97.55	156.99	1966	Graham Hill	144.32	232.26	2002	Helio Castroneves	166.50	267.96
1928	Louis Meyer	99.48	160.10	1967	A. J. Foyt	151.21	243.35	2003	Gil de Ferran	156.29	251.52
1929	Ray Keech	97.59	157.06	1968	Bobby Unser	152.88	246.04	2004	Buddy Rice	138.52	222.93
1930	Billy Arnold	100.45	161.66	1969	Mario Andretti	156.87	252.46	2005	Dan Wheldon	157.60	253.63
1931	Louis Schneider	96.63	155.51	1970	Al Unser, Sr.	155.75	250.66	2006	Sam Hornish, Jr.	157.08	252.80
1932	Frederick Frame	104.14	167.60	1971	Al Unser, Sr.	157.74	253.86	2007	Dario Franchitti	151.77	244.25
1933	Louis Meyer	104.16	167.63	1972	Mark Donohue	162.96	262.26	2008	Scott Dixon	143.57	231.05
1934	Bill Cummings	104.86	168.76	1973	Gordon Johncock	159.04	255.95	2009	Helio Castroneves	150.32	241.92
1935	Kelly Petillo	106.24	170.98	1974	Johnny Rutherford	158.59	255.22	2010	Dario Franchitti	161.62	260.10
1936	Louis Meyer	109.07	175.53	1975	Bobby Unser	149.21	240.13	2011	Dan Wheldon	170.27	274.02
1937	Wilbur Shaw	113.58	182.79	1976	Johnny Rutherford	148.73	239.36	2012	Dario Franchitti	167.73	269.94
1938	Floyd Roberts	117.20	188.62	1977	A. J. Foyt	161.33	259.64	2013	Tony Kanaan	187.43	301.64
1939	Wilbur Shaw	115.04	185.14	1978	Al Unser, Sr.	161.36	259.68	2014	Ryan Hunter-Reay	186.56	300.24
1940	Wilbur Shaw	114.28	183.92	1979	Rick Mears	158.90	255.72	2015	Juan Pablo Montoya	161.34	259.65
1941	Mauri Rose and			1980	Johnny Rutherford	142.86	229.87	2016	Alexander Rossi	166.63	268.17
	Floyd Davis	115.12	185.27	1981	Bobby Unser	139.08	223.83	2017	Takuma Sato	155.40	250.10
1946	George Robson	114.82	184.78	1982	Gordon Johncock	162.03	260.76	2018	Will Power	166.94	268.66
1947	Mauri Rose	116.34	187.23	1983	Tom Sneva	162.12	260.91	2019	Simon Pagenaud	175.79	282.91
1948	Mauri Rose	119.81	192.82	1984	Rick Mears	163.61	263.30	2020	Takuma Sato	157.82	253.99
1949	William Holland	121.33	195.26	1985	Danny Sullivan	152.98	246.20	2021	Helio Castroneves	190.69	306.89
1950	Johnny Parsons	124.00	199.56	1986	Bobby Rahal	170.72	274.75				

Monster Energy NASCAR Cup Series champions*

Year	Driver	Year	Driver
1949	Red Byron	1985	Darrell Waltrip
1950	Bill Rexford	1986	Dale Earnhardt
1951	Herb Thomas	1987	Dale Earnhardt
1952	Tim Flock	1988	Bill Elliott
1953	Herb Thomas	1989	Rusty Wallace
1954	Lee Petty	1990	Dale Earnhardt
1955	Tim Flock	1991	Dale Earnhardt
1956	Buck Baker	1992	Alan Kulwicki
1957	Buck Baker	1993	Dale Earnhardt
1958	Lee Petty	1994	Dale Earnhardt
1959	Lee Petty	1995	Jeff Gordon
1960	Rex White	1996	Terry Labonte
1961	Ned Jarrett	1997	Jeff Gordon
1962	Joe Weatherly	1998	Jeff Gordon
1963	Joe Weatherly	1999	Dale Jarrett
1964	Richard Petty	2000	Bobby Labonte
1965	Ned Jarrett	2001	Jeff Gordon
1966	David Pearson	2002	Tony Stewart
1967	Richard Petty	2003	Matt Kenseth
1968	David Pearson	2004	Kurt Busch
1969	David Pearson	2005	Tony Stewart
1970	Bobby Isaac	2006	Jimmie Johnson
1971	Richard Petty	2007	Jimmie Johnson
1972	Richard Petty	2008	Jimmie Johnson
1973	Benny Parsons	2009	Jimmie Johnson
1974	Richard Petty	2010	Jimmie Johnson
1975	Richard Petty	2011	Tony Stewart
1976	Cale Yarborough	2012	Brad Keselowski
1977	Cale Yarborough	2013	Jimmie Johnson
1978	Cale Yarborough	2014	Kevin Harvick
1979	Richard Petty	2015	Kyle Busch
1980	Dale Earnhardt	2016	Jimmie Johnson
1981	Darrell Waltrip	2017	Martin Truex, Jr.
1982	Darrell Waltrip	2018	Joey Logano
1983	Bobby Allison	2019	Kyle Busch
1984	Terry Labonte	2020	Chase Elliott

*The Monster Energy NASCAR Cup Series was called the Grand National Championship from 1949 to 1971, the Winston Cup Championship from 1972 to 2003, the Nextel Cup Championship from 2004 to 2007, and the Sprint Cup Championship from 2008 to 2016.

Arie Luyendyk of the Netherlands; Fernando Alonso of Spain; Dario Franchitti and Lewis Hamilton of the United Kingdom; and several drivers from the United States, including Michael Andretti, Dale Earnhardt, Sr., Jeff Gordon, Jimmie Johnson, Tony Stewart, and Al Unser, Jr. Star drivers who emerged later in the 2000's include Will Power of Australia; Sebastian Vettel of Germany; Max Verstappen of the Netherlands; Scott Dixon of New Zealand; and Kyle Busch, Joey Logano, Alexander Rossi, and Martin Truex, Jr., of the United States.

Several women have achieved success in automobile racing. In 1977, Janet Guthrie of the United States became the first woman to race in the Indianapolis 500. In 2009, Danica Patrick finished third, the highest finish by any woman in the history of the race. In 2008, Patrick had become the first woman to win an Indy car race when she won the Indy Japan 300. Shirley Muldowney, an American drag racer, won the Top Fuel Winston World Championship in 1977, 1980, and 1982. Sylvia Wilkinson

Related articles in *World Book* include:

Andretti, Mario	Hill, Graham	Patrick, Danica
Breedlove, Craig	Hot rod	Petty, Richard
Chevrolet, Louis	Indiana (pictures)	Rickenbacker,
Earnhardt, Dale	Kart racing	Eddie
Earnhardt, Dale, Jr.	Le Mans	Soap Box Derby
Foyt, A. J.	NASCAR	Sports car
Gordon, Jeff	Oldfield, Barney	Unser, Al, Sr.

Autopsy, *AW tahp see,* is an external and internal examination of the dead. It is also called *necropsy* and *post mortem examination.* The law requires that a physician or a coroner's jury verify every cause of death. If the physician knows that death is from natural causes, he or she signs the death certificate and no autopsy need be performed. If uncertain of the conditions leading to the cause, however, the physician may ask for an autopsy for scientific reasons. A medical examiner or coroner may legally insist on an autopsy when death results from suicide, homicide, or unknown causes. See also **Forensic pathology; Medical examiner.** John I. Thornton

Autry, Gene (1907-1998), became famous for his roles as a singing cowboy in Western films from the 1930's through the early 1950's.

Orvon Gene Autry was born on Sept. 29, 1907, in Tioga, Texas, near Pilot Point. He began recording cowboy songs in 1929 and made his first hit record, "That Silver-Haired Daddy of Mine," in 1931. Autry wrote more than 250 songs, including such hits as "Tears on My Pillow" (1941) and "Here Comes Santa Claus" (1947). He also made popular recordings of "Back in the Saddle Again" (1939), "Rudolph the Red-Nosed Reindeer" (1949), "Frosty the Snowman" (1950), and "Peter Cottontail" (1950).

In 1934, Autry moved to Hollywood, California, to appear in motion pictures, and he made his first film that same year. He acted in more than 100 Western movies and also continued to perform as a singer. During the 1950's, Autry began a successful business career. In 1960, he became an owner of the Los Angeles Angels baseball team, which played its first season in 1961. He was elected to the Country Music Hall of Fame in 1969. Autry died on Oct. 2, 1998. Lee Rector

Autumn is the season after summer and before winter. In the Northern Hemisphere, autumn weather extends from late September through November. In the Southern Hemisphere, autumn weather begins in March and continues through May. People living in the tropics rarely consider autumn a distinct season because the temperatures there change little from month to month. Many Atlantic Ocean hurricanes occur during autumn.

During autumn, many kinds of trees shed their leaves, which then fall to the ground. For this reason, many people call autumn *fall.* Autumn also serves as harvesttime for many crops. Many autumn holidays and festivals began as harvest celebrations.

In the middle latitudes, early autumn days generally feel warm, and nights are cool. As autumn progresses, the air becomes chillier, and the number of daylight hours decreases, particularly in the polar regions. Birds migrate toward the equator. Frost often forms at night, and the first light snows fall. Jon E. Ahlquist

See also **Equinox; Indian summer; Season.**

Autumnal equinox. See Equinox.

Auxin, *AWK sihn,* is the name of a group of hormones that help control plant growth. Plant embryos, young leaves, and the tips of stems and roots produce auxins that influence the growth of different parts of plants. Auxins play an important role in plant *tropisms* (bending movements). For example, the stems or leaves of many plants bend toward light. Such movement, called *positive phototropism,* occurs because auxins accumulate on the dark side of the stem or leaf stalk, causing the cells on that side to lengthen. This elongation gradually bends the stem or leaf toward the light.

Artificially produced auxins are widely used in weedkillers. They are also used to promote root formation on plant cuttings, to stimulate the growth of seedless fruits,

and to prevent sprouting in stored potatoes and onions.
Joseph E. Armstrong

See also **Hormone** (Plant hormones); **Tropism**.

Avalanche is a mass of snow that slides down a mountain slope. Most avalanches result from weather conditions that cause snow on a slope to become unstable. Such disturbances as heavy winds, earth tremors, and explosions can send the snow sliding down the mountain. Skiers have started many avalanches.

There are three chief kinds of avalanches. A *dry snow avalanche* consists of powdery snow and air that may move faster than 100 miles (160 kilometers) per hour. A *wet snow avalanche* is a mass of wet, dense snow that typically moves slower than a dry snow avalanche. In a *slab avalanche,* a solid portion of snow breaks loose as a slab and splits into pieces as it slides.

Experts can often recognize the conditions that lead to avalanches by studying the terrain, snow, and weather in an area. To help control avalanches, they use explosives to reduce snow build-up. They also replant trees on slopes, and erect barriers.   Sidney R. Nagel

Avant-garde, *AH vahn GAHRD,* is a term used to describe people in any field who break with tradition and conventional standards in their work. But the term is especially used to describe movements in the arts. Avant-garde artists emphasize experimental and original methods. They sometimes attack past and present attitudes about art in the interest of creating a better future.

Avant-garde was a French military term, meaning an advance guard ahead of the main army. It was first used in its current meaning by the French socialist leader Henri de Saint-Simon in 1825. In the 1800's, most avant-garde art promoted social reform. But in the late 1800's, a doctrine of "art for art's sake" developed. It emphasized the form of art itself, regardless of its effect on society.

Events of World War I (1914-1918) led to the return of reform-based avant-garde art. These works criticized European culture and contributed to political and social reform movements after the war. But some artists in the early 1900's wanted to restore to art its primary creative function. For example, the German artist Kurt Schwitters created collages from fragments of newsprint and discarded items, including buttons, cloth, stamps, and wood. He also wanted to weaken the authority of conventional art forms. Avant-garde ideals became especially important in the mid-1900's, when artists tended to combine art forms, such as architecture, films, music, painting, sculpture, and theater.   Stephen C. Foster

See also **Cage, John; Dadaism; Duchamp, Marcel; Performance art; Schwitters, Kurt; Surrealism.**

Average is a number that is typical of a group of numbers. It provides one measure of the center of the numbers. People often think of an average as a *mean,* or *arithmetic average.* A mean is the sum of a group of numbers divided by the number of numbers in the group. For example, the average, or mean, of 4, 5, 5, 7, and 14 is 7—that is, 35 (the sum of the five numbers) divided by 5 (the number of numbers).

Other numbers are also typical of a group of numbers, including the *median* and the *mode.* A median is the middle number of a series of numbers arranged in numerical order, but only if there is an odd number of numbers. If the number of numbers is even, the median is the mean of the middle two numbers. The *mode* is the number that occurs most often in a group. In the example, the median and mode are both 5.   Michael D. Larsen

See also **Mean; Median; Mode; Statistics** (Probability).

Avi, *AH vee* (1937-   ), is the pen name of Edward Irving Wortis, a popular American author of children's literature. Avi is best known for his historical fiction. He won the 2003 Newbery Medal for *Crispin: The Cross of Lead* (2002). The novel is set in England during the 1300's. The suspenseful story describes the adventures of a 13-year-old peasant boy falsely accused of a crime.

Avi's other novels include *Captain Grey* (1977); *Night Journeys* (1979) and its sequel, *Encounter at Easton* (1980); *The Fighting Ground* (1984); *S.O.R. Losers* (1984) and its sequel, *Romeo and Juliet—Together (and Alive!) at Last* (1987); *Wolf Rider* (1988); *The True Confessions of Charlotte Doyle* (1990); *Nothing But the Truth* (1991); *Don't You Know There's a War On* (2001); *Iron Thunder* (2007); *City of Orphans* (2011); *Sophia's War* (2012); *Old Wolf* (2015); and *The Unexpected Life of Oliver Cromwell Pitts* (2017) and its sequel, *The End of the World and Beyond* (2019). Avi wrote a fictionalized story called *The Man Who Was Poe* (1989). *The Traitors' Gate* (2007) is based on the life of Charles Dickens. *Strange Happenings* (2006) and *The Most Important Thing: Stories About Sons, Fathers, and Grandfathers* (2016) are short-story collections. *Poppy* (1995) is the first book in Avi's "Tales from Dimwood Forest" series for younger readers. The series is illustrated by the American artist Brian Floca.

Wortis was born on Dec. 23, 1937, in New York City. His sister nicknamed him "Avi," which he adopted as his pen name. Avi received degrees in history and the theater from the University of Wisconsin in 1959 and 1962. He earned a master's degree in library science from Columbia University in 1964. His first book was a collection of stories for beginning readers called *Things That Sometimes Happen* (1970).   Ann D. Carlson

Avian influenza, also called *bird flu,* is an infectious disease of birds that is occasionally transmitted to human beings. The disease is caused by the type A influenza virus. Waterfowl, including wild ducks, sea birds, and shore birds, naturally carry this virus but generally do not develop the disease itself. But infected domestic birds, such as chickens, ducks, and turkeys, are likely to develop a rapidly fatal form of the disease. A number of human beings have also died from avian influenza.

After avian influenza is introduced into a flock, it can spread quickly. It spreads through waste matter from infected birds and through contaminated water, feed, and equipment, such as cages and the trucks used to transport birds. There is no treatment for avian influenza. Vaccination helps reduce the symptoms in birds but does little to prevent avian influenza from spreading. Infected flocks are usually killed to prevent spread of the disease.

The first known human outbreak of avian influenza occurred in Hong Kong in 1997. Several more outbreaks have occurred, mostly in China, Thailand, and Vietnam, and they have resulted in the slaughter of millions of domestic birds. Most human cases of avian influenza have come from contact with infected birds or contaminated surfaces. Health officials are concerned about a possible *pandemic* (worldwide occurrence) of the disease. They closely monitor outbreaks of avian influenza to watch for any transmission to human beings.   Daniel R. Perez

See also **Influenza.**

The Boeing Company

Modern airplane factories are a vital part of the aviation industry, which also includes airline and airport operations. This Boeing Company plant near Everett, Washington, produces Boeing 747, 767, and 777 jumbo jets, some of which are lined up awaiting delivery to major passenger airlines.

Aviation

Aviation is a term that includes all the activities involved in building and flying aircraft, especially airplanes. The first successful airplane flights did not take place until 1903. Yet today, airplanes affect the lives of people almost everywhere. Giant airliners carry passengers and cargo between the world's major cities in a matter of hours. Planes and helicopters rush medicine and other supplies to the farthest islands and deepest jungles. Farmers use airplanes to seed fields, count livestock, and spray crops. Aviation has also changed the way nations make war. Modern warfare depends on the instant striking power of jet fighters and bombers and the rapid supply capabilities of jet transports. Helicop-

ters and other special aircraft are also important in military aviation.

Hundreds of thousands of airplanes are used throughout the world. They range from small planes with room for only a pilot to enormous jumbo jets, which can carry hundreds of passengers. To produce and operate all these airplanes requires the skills of millions of workers in many countries—from the engineers who design the planes to the mechanics and pilots who service and fly them. Many government agencies also work to make flying safer and more dependable. All these activities together make up the *aviation industry.* The industry's two major activities are (1) the manufacture of aircraft and aircraft components, such as engines, and (2) the operation of airlines. The manufacture of aircraft, together with the manufacture of spacecraft, missiles, and related electronic equipment, is often called the *aerospace industry.*

The aviation industry began on Dec. 17, 1903, near Kit-

Roger E. Bilstein, the contributor of this article, is Professor of History Emeritus at the University of Houston-Clear Lake, and the author of several books on aviation, including Flight in America: From the Wrights to the Astronauts.

ty Hawk, North Carolina. That day, Orville and Wilbur Wright—two brothers who operated a bicycle-manufacturing shop in Dayton, Ohio—made the world's first successful piloted airplane flights. They had built their airplane after studying the writings of other aviation pioneers and after experimenting with gliders, kites, and wind tunnels.

Within a few years, several small factories in Europe and the United States were producing airplanes. Daredevil fliers bought many of these planes and used them to put on thrilling air shows. The governments of various countries also began to buy airplanes to build small air forces. The daring feats of the early fliers and the development of military airplanes greatly encouraged the growth of the aviation industry.

By the late 1930's, airplanes had become an important means of transportation. Then, in the 1950's, engineers developed jet airliners—and air travel grew at an even faster rate. In 1960, the world's airlines carried about 100 million passengers. By the late 2010's, they carried more than 4 billion passengers annually.

Almost from the beginning of the aviation industry, the governments of most nations have been deeply involved in its activities. Airplanes have such great importance as weapons of war that many countries have encouraged and financed improvements in airplane design for military reasons. Most nations have also supported the development of *civil aviation* (the operation of nonmilitary aircraft).

Although aviation includes all types of heavier-than-air craft, this article deals chiefly with airplanes. To learn about the two other main types of heavier-than-air craft, see **Glider** and **Helicopter**. The **Airplane** article traces the history of human efforts to fly and the development of the airplane. It also describes how a plane flies, how pilots navigate, and how planes are built. For a discussion of space flight, see **Space exploration**.

The aviation industry

The aviation industry can be divided into five branches: (1) aircraft manufacturing, (2) general aviation activities, (3) airline operations, (4) airport operations, and (5) aviation support industries.

Aircraft manufacturing. Aircraft companies produce chiefly airplanes, but many also manufacture gliders, helicopters, and parts for spacecraft. Some parts factories and assembly plants are owned by *conglomerates,* enormous corporations that control a number of firms in largely unrelated fields. Most aircraft used around the world are manufactured in the United States.

The Russian aerospace industry produces aircraft and equipment for use throughout the former Eastern bloc—that is, the former Soviet Union and its Eastern European allies. Russia also exports military aircraft to many other countries. BAE Systems, based in the United Kingdom, and the European Aeronautic Defence and Space Company (EADS), based in the Netherlands, are major European manufacturers of aircraft and other aerospace products. Other countries with important aerospace industries include Brazil, Canada, China, India, Israel, Japan, and South Africa. Many other nations have facilities for aircraft repair and maintenance.

Manufacturers produce three main types of airplanes: (1) general aviation planes, (2) commercial transport planes, and (3) military planes. General aviation activities range from business and personal flying to rescue services. Most general aviation planes are small propeller-driven airplanes with one or two engines. Many businesses use jets. Commercial transport planes are large airplanes used to carry both passengers and cargo or cargo only. Airlines operate these planes. The smallest commercial transports carry from 20 to 100 passengers, and the largest, called *jumbo jets* or *airbuses,* carry several hundred. Most commercial transports are jet planes with two, three, or four engines. Military planes include bombers, fighters, and military transports owned by the governments of various countries and operated by their armed forces. See **Airplane** (Types of airplanes).

In some countries, the government wholly or partly owns some or all aircraft companies. All aircraft companies in the United States and some other countries are privately owned. But many depend heavily on government orders for military planes, engines, missiles, or spacecraft. Many U.S. manufacturers—such as the Boeing Company, General Electric Company, and the Lockheed Martin, Northrop Grumman, and United Technologies corporations—receive large government contracts.

A modern jet airliner costs millions of dollars to build. A small company cannot afford to build such a plane, and even large companies often have trouble acquiring the necessary funds. Many companies have *merged* (combined) to cut costs. These mergers have produced some of the world's largest aerospace companies, including BAE Systems, Boeing, and EADS.

A number of European nations have cooperated in special aircraft-manufacturing projects. For example, the British and French governments formed a partnership called a *consortium* to share the cost of building a supersonic transport (SST), the Concorde. An SST was designed to carry passengers at speeds faster than that of sound (see **Airplane** [Supersonic airplanes]).

General aviation activities include pleasure flying, land surveying, giving flying instructions, inspecting telephone lines, scattering seed, and spraying crops. Another important general aviation activity is using light planes to provide transportation. Most *air taxi services,* also called *commuter airlines,* use compact, twin-engine planes to carry passengers—usually fewer than 20—on short flights. Air taxi services serve small communities and provide connecting flights to large airports. Some air taxi services have planes large enough to carry more than 20 passengers. Some large airlines also provide air taxi service.

Many businesses have their own aircraft that are used to fly officials and salespeople to out-of-town assignments. General aviation planes also carry cargo and passengers in areas of the world that do not have highways or railroads.

In Australia, a specialized aviation service called the Royal Flying Doctor Service supplies medical treatment to people living in remote areas. People who are ill or require medical advice use radio to contact a doctor at the nearest base. The doctor may advise the patient by radio or may arrange for a light plane to pick up the patient. Air ambulances in other parts of the world provide specially equipped airplanes to fly patients to hospitals.

Airline operations. Almost every country has at least one airline. In some countries, the government wholly

Cameramann International, Ltd. from Marilyn Gartman Agency

Airline operations involve carrying cargo as well as passengers. Most commercial transport planes carry both passengers and cargo. Other transports haul cargo only.

© Thinkstock

Airport operations focus on providing runways and navigation aids as well as facilities to load, refuel, and repair planes. This aerial photo shows San Francisco International Airport.

or partly owns one or more airlines. For example, Singapore Airlines, the national airline of Singapore, is partly state-owned. During the 1990's, many governments encouraged privatization of airlines to curb costs and increase efficiency.

There are two main types of airline service—*scheduled flights* and *nonscheduled flights.* Scheduled flights are made over certain routes according to a timetable. Nonscheduled flights are mainly *charter* flights for customers who want to hire a plane to fly to a particular place at a particular time.

In the United States, airlines must receive permission from the federal government to use commercial transport planes for scheduled flights. The airlines that the government approves for such flights are called *certificated airlines.* The term *scheduled airlines* is often used in the United States for the certificated airlines, though these lines may also make some nonscheduled flights. To receive government certification, an airline's planes and pilots must meet government standards.

A majority of airlines carry both passengers and cargo. Airliners usually carry a certain amount of freight on

passenger flights. In addition, a large number of passenger airlines operate transport planes that carry only cargo. A few certificated airlines in the United States specialize in carrying cargo and make no passenger flights.

Sometimes, airlines have financial problems due to low passenger traffic, debts from purchasing new aircraft, and increasing costs, such as the rising cost of jet fuel. In the 1970's, many airlines cut their airfares and developed various bargain ticket plans to attract passengers. These steps led to huge increases in passenger traffic. High operating costs led many small airlines to merge with larger airlines. By the late 1990's, many airlines had also formed alliances for ticketing and for scheduling certain routes.

In most European countries, the government has combined two or more airlines to form a large national airline. Various European airlines have also formed consortiums to help cut expenses. The members of an airline consortium cooperate in such matters as purchasing aircraft and training pilots.

Airport operations. Airports provide the fuel and the runways, navigation aids, and other ground facilities needed for air travel. Generally, only a few of a country's airports have the facilities to handle large passenger planes. Additional small airfields serve light planes or specialized aircraft, such as helicopters or seaplanes. Cities or public corporations own most large airports. Most small airports are private airfields owned by organizations or individuals. See **Airport.**

Aviation support industries provide a wide variety of supplies and services to airlines, airports, pilots, and passengers. Some companies furnish repair services or fuel for airplanes. *Freight forwarders* make arrangements for shipping air cargo. Various food services prepare meals to be served on passenger flights. Some insurance brokers specialize in flight insurance, and some lawyers specialize in air law. Private weather bureaus supply pilots with specialized information not provided by government weather services.

Aviation agencies and organizations

Aviation agencies. A majority of countries have government agencies that enforce air safety regulations and handle related economic matters. In the United States, the Federal Aviation Administration (FAA) establishes

© Thinkstock

General aviation activities include the operation of *air taxi services,* which fly small numbers of passengers over relatively short distances in small planes.

the rules that all planes must follow when flying in the United States. One of the agency's most important jobs is to operate a network of *air route traffic control centers* throughout the United States and its territories. Each control center uses Automatic Dependent Surveillance-Broadcast (ADS-B) technology, which uses the Global Positioning System (GPS). GPS technology makes use of a network of navigation satellites to enable pilots anywhere on Earth to determine their location. A control

Aircraft nationality marks

Most civil aircraft carry one or two letters or a number and a letter to identify their nationality. This *nationality mark* is painted on both sides of the fuselage or tail. It also is displayed on the underside of the wing. Numbers or letters following the nationality mark on a plane are the *registration mark* issued to that particular plane in its own country. Each country that belongs to the International Civil Aviation Organization (ICAO) reports its nationality mark to the organization. This table lists the nationality marks of selected ICAO members.

Afghanistan	**YA**	Kuwait	**9K**
Algeria	**7T**	Latvia	**YL**
Argentina	**LQ, LV**	Liberia	**A8**
Armenia	**EK**	Lithuania	**LY**
Australia	**VH**	Luxembourg	**LX**
Austria	**OE**	Malaysia	**9M**
Azerbaijan	**4K**	Mexico	**XA, XB, XC plus**
Bangladesh	**S2**		**national emblem**
Belgium	**OO**	Morocco	**CN**
Bolivia	**CP**	Myanmar	**XY, XZ**
Brazil	**PP, PR, PS, PT, PU**	Nepal	**9N**
Bulgaria	**LZ**	Netherlands	**PH**
Cambodia	**XU**	New Zealand	**ZK, ZL, ZM**
Cameroon	**TJ**	Nicaragua	**YN**
Canada	**C, CF**	Nigeria	**5N**
Chile	**CC**	Norway	**LN**
China	**B**	Pakistan	**AP**
Colombia	**HJ, HK**	Panama	**HP**
Congo, Democratic		Paraguay	**ZP**
Republic of the	**9Q**	Peru	**OB**
Costa Rica	**TI**	Philippines	**RP**
Côte d'Ivoire	**TU**	Poland	**SP**
Cuba	**CU**	Portugal	**CR, CS**
Czech Republic	**OK**	Romania	**YR**
Denmark	**OY**	Russia	**RA**
Ecuador	**HC**	Saudi Arabia	**HZ**
Egypt	**SU**	Singapore	**9V**
Estonia	**ES**	Slovakia	**OM**
Ethiopia	**ET**	South Africa	**ZS, ZT, ZU**
Finland	**OH**	Spain	**EC**
France	**F**	Sri Lanka	**4R**
Germany	**D**	Sudan	**ST**
Ghana	**9G, 9GR**	Sweden	**SE**
Greece	**SX**	Switzerland	**HB plus**
Guatemala	**TG**		**national emblem**
Honduras	**HR**	Syria	**YK**
Hungary	**HA**	Tanzania	**5H**
Iceland	**TF**	Thailand	**HS**
India	**VT**	Tunisia	**TS**
Indonesia	**PK**	Turkey	**TC**
Iran	**EP**	Uganda	**5X**
Iraq	**YI**	Ukraine	**UR**
Ireland	**EI, EJ**	United Arab Emirates	**A6**
Israel	**4X**	United Kingdom	**G**
Italy	**I**	United States	**N**
Japan	**JA**	Uruguay	**CX**
Jordan	**JY**	Uzbekistan	**UK**
Kazakhstan	**UP**	Venezuela	**YV**
Kenya	**5Y**	Vietnam	**XV**
Korea (North)	**P**	Yemen	**7O**
Korea (South)	**HL**	Zimbabwe	**Z**

center helps planes in its vicinity follow the *airways,* also called *air routes,* to which they are assigned (see **Airplane** [Air navigation]). The FAA also issues licenses to pilots. In addition, every newly manufactured airplane must be issued an FAA certificate of *airworthiness* before it may be flown. This certificate states that the airplane has been inspected and is in good flying condition. See **Federal Aviation Administration.**

Almost every U.S. state has an agency to regulate and improve aviation within its borders. These agencies handle airport construction, registration of airplanes and pilots, and similar matters. Many local governments also have aviation agencies. These agencies deal mainly with the operation and maintenance of local airports.

In Canada, the federal government regulates civil aviation. Transport Canada, a government department, deals mainly with such matters as registration of aircraft, licensing of pilots, and establishment of air navigation facilities. The Canadian Transportation Agency handles the economic regulation of Canadian airlines.

Similar regulatory activities are carried out by national agencies in other countries. Such agencies include the United Kingdom's Civil Aviation Authority (CAA). These agencies are involved in such issues as air-traffic control and registration of airplanes and pilots.

The International Civil Aviation Organization (ICAO) is an agency of the United Nations (UN). Almost every country belongs to the ICAO. The organization sets up common air safety standards among member countries and tries to increase cooperation in other matters concerning international aviation. See **International Civil Aviation Organization.**

Other aviation organizations include various groups formed to further their own special interests. The groups include airline operators, airplane manufacturers, and pilots. For example, U.S. and Canadian airline operators belong to the Air Transport Association of America. Operators of international airlines in countries throughout the world belong to the International Air Transport Association. See **Air Transport Association of America; International Air Transport Association.**

History of the aviation industry

Beginnings. The successful piloted flights of a powered airplane by Orville and Wilbur Wright in 1903 marked the beginning of the practical aviation industry. After these flights, the Wright brothers tried to sell the design for their plane to the United States and various European governments. But many people at the time remained skeptical that flying machines could even work.

Meanwhile, a few European inventors also had built airplanes. In the 1890's, the German glider pioneer Otto Lilienthal had manufactured a limited production series of special gliders for experimental use. In 1905, French brothers Charles and Gabriel Voisin started the world's first airplane-manufacturing company. The Voisins began making a few made-to-order planes at a small factory outside Paris. Within a few years, other European fliers also started manufacturing companies. They included Louis Blériot and the brothers Henri and Maurice Farman in France; and Frederick Handley Page, A. V. Roe, and T. O. M. Sopwith in the United Kingdom.

In 1907, Glenn H. Curtiss, an American flier and airplane designer, started the first airplane company in the

United States, in Hammondsport, New York. Curtiss sold his first plane to the newly organized Aeronautic Society of New York for $5,000. This was the first sale of a commercial airplane in the United States.

By 1908, the Wright brothers had made several public flights and dazzled audiences with their airplane's flying ability. That same year, the U.S. Army Signal Corps ordered a specially built Wright plane, for which the government paid $30,000. This was the world's first military plane. In November 1909, wealthy German backers helped the Wright brothers form the German-Wright Company. Later that year, the Wrights established the Wright Company in New York City, with a factory in Dayton, Ohio. In the autumn of 1909, a young automobile mechanic and salesman named Glenn L. Martin began to manufacture airplanes in an abandoned church in Santa Ana, California. Within a few years, his company became a leading U.S. producer of military planes.

The world's first great aviation meeting was held in 1909 near Reims, France. Manufacturers displayed 38 airplanes. Several of the planes on show were offered for sale to the public—a sign of growing confidence in the airplane.

The first flying regulations. In 1905, a group of French flying enthusiasts established the Fédération Aéronautique Internationale (FAI) in Paris. One of the FAI's main duties was to regulate the sport of flying. It also ruled on world speed, altitude, and other flying records. The FAI still has this function. The Aero Club of America was also founded in 1905. It regulated flying in the United States, sponsored exhibitions and races, and issued licenses to U.S. pilots.

In 1908, Kissimmee, Florida, passed the world's first law regulating airplanes. The law required the registration of local aircraft and regulated their speed and altitude when flying over the town. In 1911, Connecticut passed the first state law regulating aviation. The law required anyone who owned or operated an airplane within the state to register the plane and obtain a pilot's license.

World War I (1914-1918). When World War I began in Europe, even the largest airplane factories turned out only a few planes a year. The factories quickly increased production to meet the demands of the warring nations. Airplane builders used newly designed engines to put fighters and bombers into the skies. Such well-known manufacturers as Farman, Handley Page, and Voisin built many of these planes. Other European manufacturers also became famous for their warplanes. They included Morane-Saulnier and Nieuport in France; Fokker and Junkers in Germany; and Bristol, de Havilland, Hawker, Short, and Vickers in the United Kingdom. By the war's end, designers had created such aircraft as the British Vickers Vimy bomber and the American Curtiss NC-4, which both flew across the Atlantic Ocean in 1919.

The United States entered the war in 1917 with about 110 military planes. The government immediately set a production goal of 29,000 airplanes a year. But the airplane companies had little or no experience with mass-production methods. The nation's automobile manufacturers, on the other hand, had developed assembly lines before the war and used them to turn out thousands of cars yearly. Various automakers helped set up assembly lines in the airplane factories.

The United States had no designs of its own for bombers or fighters. But American engineers designed a powerful airplane engine called the Liberty. Several U.S. companies began to mass-produce the United Kingdom's de Havilland D.H. 4 bombers and equip them with Liberty engines. The principal producer was the Dayton Wright Aeroplane Company, which was organized in 1917. Wilbur Wright had died of typhoid fever in 1912, and Orville sold his interest in the Wright Company to a group of investors in 1915. Although Orville had no financial interest in the Dayton Wright Company, he allowed the firm to use the Wright name in its title. The companies founded by Curtiss and Martin also became major producers of military planes during the war. Although U.S. factories did not meet their production goal of 29,000 planes a year, they had built almost 15,000 military planes by the end of the war.

In 1916, two airplane companies were established on

National Air and Space Museum, Smithsonian Institution

Early airplane factories, such as this French plant of 1908, produced only a few planes at a time—and almost entirely by hand. Mass production began with the manufacture of warplanes during World War I (1914-1918). Before the war, airplanes were used mainly for sport.

National Air and Space Museum, Smithsonian Institution

Airplanes raced against automobiles in the early days of aviation. This 1914 race at Columbus, Ohio, was between the famous auto racer Barney Oldfield and the daredevil pilot Lincoln Beachey. The finish was so close that no one knows who won.

the West Coast of the United States. They were the Boeing Company, which was founded in Seattle by William E. Boeing, and the Lockheed Corporation (now Lockheed Martin Corporation), which was founded in Santa Barbara, California, by the brothers Allan and Malcolm Loughead. The Boeing and Lockheed companies were too small to make many planes during the war. But in time, they became two of the nation's leading aircraft manufacturers.

The first airlines. The Wright brothers and other early fliers occasionally took passengers for short plane rides. In 1910, a Wright airplane flew 70 pounds (32 kilograms) of silk from Dayton to Columbus, Ohio—perhaps the first air freight shipment in history. The world's first regular airplane passenger service began in the United States in 1914, but it lasted only a few months. A pilot named Tony Jannus used a small seaplane to fly passengers across Tampa Bay, between St. Petersburg and Tampa, Florida. On May 15, 1918, the U.S. government started the world's first permanent airmail service. Army pilots flew the mail between New York City, Philadelphia, and Washington, D.C.

After World War I, thousands of military planes became available for civilian use. In 1919, bombers were used to start nearly 20 small passenger airlines in France, Germany, the United Kingdom, and several other European countries. One of these airlines, founded by Henri and Maurice Farman, began the world's first regular international airline service. The company used old Farman bombers to make weekly passenger flights between Paris and Brussels, Belgium.

By 1924, passenger airlines were operating in 17 European countries as well as in Africa, Australia, and South America. Several of these airlines are still active. They include KLM Royal Dutch Airlines (now part of Air France-KLM) of the Netherlands, Germany's Lufthansa, and Australia's Queensland and Northern Territory Aerial Services (QANTAS). Beginning in the mid-1920's, the

governments of many countries started to combine two or more private airlines to form a large national airline. In 1924, the United Kingdom became the first major power to form a national, government-owned airline, Imperial Airways.

Aviation progress. Many small passenger airlines were formed during the early 1920's. But most lasted only a few months because they could not attract enough customers. Most people considered flying a dangerous sport rather than a safe means of transportation.

In the United States, the federal government's main interest in aviation was to improve airmail service. In 1920, airmail routes extended from New York City to San Francisco. Mail planes operated only during the day, however. To help the mail pilots fly their open-cockpit planes at night, the government installed beacon lights at airports along the transcontinental route. Each light could be seen as far as 50 miles (80 kilometers) away. By 1924, night-flying techniques enabled planes to get mail from New York City to San Francisco in 24 hours.

In 1925, the U.S. Congress passed the Kelly Air Mail Act, which gave private airlines the job of flying the mail. The government then signed contracts with 11 companies formed to carry the mail. Henry Ford, the famous automobile maker, owned one of these airlines. In 1926, Ford's airline became the first airline to carry U.S. mail. Within a few months, all 11 companies were flying mail between major U.S. cities. Some of the airlines also began carrying passengers. In 1926, airlines in the United States carried only about 6,000 passengers. In 1930, they carried more than 400,000.

Several U.S. aircraft companies were also started during the 1920's. In 1920, an engineer named Donald Douglas helped organize an aircraft company in Santa Monica, California. It became the Douglas Company the following year, later part of McDonnell Douglas Corporation, and later still part of the Boeing Company. In 1923, the Consolidated Aircraft Corporation was founded in East Greenwich, Rhode Island. It took over the air-

National Air and Space Museum, Smithsonian Institution

Post-office planes began flying U.S. mail in 1918. This plane is being loaded with mail for a transcontinental flight in 1923. Private airlines began flying the mail in 1926.

United Airlines

Early airliners, such as this Ford Tri-Motor, carried about 10 passengers, who bundled up in coats to keep warm. This Tri-Motor was flown by National Air Transport (NAT), one of the first successful U.S. airlines. NAT began carrying mail in 1926 and passengers in 1927. It became part of United Airlines in 1931.

plane designs of the Dayton Wright Company. The Pratt and Whitney Company began making aircraft engines in Hartford, Connecticut, in 1925. In 1929, the Curtiss and Wright companies merged to form the Curtiss-Wright Corporation. Grumman Aircraft (now part of Northrop Grumman Corporation) also started business in 1929 on Long Island, New York.

The rapid increase in aviation activity led Congress to pass the Air Commerce Act in 1926. This act was the first federal law to regulate aviation in the United States. It provided for a system of airways and navigation aids across the country. The act also called for rules governing the manufacture of airplanes and the licensing of airplanes and pilots. A Bureau of Air Commerce was set up

to carry out these measures.

The industry comes of age. Air transport continued to grow during the early 1930's. By 1935, the United States had four major domestic airlines—American, Eastern, Transcontinental and Western Air (later called Trans World Airlines), and United. Smaller regional airlines included Braniff, Delta, and Northwest. The country also had a major international airline—Pan American World Airways (Pan Am)—which flew to Latin America. Many European governments continued to form large national airlines, such as Air France (now part of Air France-KLM).

To meet the growing demand for faster, larger airliners, manufacturers began to produce twin-engine planes, such as the Boeing 247 and the Douglas DC-3. The DC-3 appeared in 1935 and soon became the world's most popular transport plane. A number of companies, including Martin (now Lockheed Martin Corporation) in the United States and Short in the United Kingdom, started to make large, four-engine seaplanes called *flying boats.* In the 1930's, flying boats made the first passenger flights across oceans. New firms were also started in the 1930's, such as North American Aviation and United Aircraft (now United Technologies), which took over production of Pratt and Whitney engines.

By the late 1930's, flying was an important means of travel in most of the world. In 1938, the world's airlines carried nearly 3 ½ million passengers.

The rapid growth of civil aviation created a need for more effective government regulation. In 1938, the U.S. Congress established the Civil Aeronautics Authority to deal with every aspect of civil aviation. The authority included a five-member board, which, in 1940, became the Civil Aeronautics Board. It also included an administrative office, which became the Civil Aeronautics Administration (CAA) in 1940.

World War II (1939-1945). The peace treaty that ended World War I prohibited the manufacture of military aircraft in Germany. Nevertheless, several German aircraft firms were founded during the 1920's. They included the famous Heinkel and Messerschmitt companies. In the mid-1930's, Heinkel, Messerschmitt, and other German firms, such as Dornier and Junkers, secretly

Boeing Co.

Huge flying boats began carrying passengers on ocean flights during the 1930's. In 1939, Pan American World Airways used this Boeing 314 Clipper to start regular transatlantic service.

made hundreds of bombers and fighters for the German air force. On Sept. 1, 1939, German dive bombers attacked Poland, and World War II began. One European country after another fell to the Germans. Finally, the United Kingdom was left nearly alone to fight off the German air force. British aircraft companies, such as Avro, de Havilland, Handley Page, Hawker, and Supermarine, quickly increased their production of warplanes.

The United States produced about 2,100 military planes in 1939. Both Germany and Japan had larger air forces. The huge Mitsubishi corporation produced many of Japan's warplanes, including the famous Zero fighter. After the United States entered the war in December 1941, U.S. airplane production increased tremendously. More than 40 companies took part in a gigantic effort to supply the United States and its allies with military planes. Many companies enlarged their factories and hired additional workers. Assembly lines began working round the clock. By 1944, production had reached nearly 100,000 transport planes, bombers, and fighters a year.

By the end of the war, U.S. factories had built more than 300,000 aircraft. Germany, Japan, the Soviet Union, and the United Kingdom had also produced many thousands of planes. During the war, aircraft production had become the world's leading manufacturing industry.

A new age of flight. In 1937, British inventor Frank Whittle built the first successful jet engine. The first jet airplanes were developed for military use. Germany flew the first jet aircraft in 1939. By 1942, both the United Kingdom and the United States had developed experimental jet planes for military use.

After World War II, aircraft manufacturers began the development of jet airliners. In 1952, British Overseas Airways Corporation (BOAC), now British Airways, started jet passenger flights with de Havilland Comets. But the flights were stopped after several Comets exploded in the air. Investigators discovered serious flaws in the plane's structure. De Havilland engineers then designed an improved Comet. In 1958, BOAC used the new Comets to begin jet passenger service across the Atlantic Ocean. American companies also built successful jet transports in the late 1950's, and these aircraft quickly dominated international air transportation. In 1959,

Aviation speed records*

Speed In mph	In kph	Date	Aircraft	Aviator	Place
38.0	61.2	Oct. 5, 1905	Wright Flyer III	Wilbur Wright (United States)	Dayton, OH
108.18	174.1	Sept. 9, 1912	Deperdussin Racer	Jules Védrines (France)	Chicago
222.97	358.84	Oct. 18, 1922	Curtiss R-6	William Mitchell (United States)	Mount Clemens, MI
294.38	473.76	Sept. 3, 1932	Granville Gee Bee R-1	James H. Doolittle (United States)	Cleveland
304.98	490.82	Sept. 4, 1933	Wedell-Williams "44"	James Wedell (United States)	Chicago
469.22	755.14	April 26, 1939	Messerschmitt Me 209 V1	Fritz Wendel (Germany)	Augsburg, Germany
606.25	975.66	Nov. 7, 1945	Gloster Meteor F Mk 4	Hugh J. Wilson (United Kingdom)	Herne Bay, United Kingdom
670.98	1,079.84	Sept. 15, 1948	North American F-86A-1 Sabre	Richard L. Johnson (United States)	Muroc, CA
698.5	1,024.13	Nov. 19, 1952	North American F-86D Sabre	J. Slade Nash (United States)	Salton Sea, CA
755.14	1,215.28	Oct. 29, 1953	North American YF-100A Super Sabre	F. K. Everest, Jr. (United States)	Salton Sea, CA
822.26	1,323.3	Aug. 20, 1955	North American F-100C Super Sabre	Horace A. Hanes (United States)	Edwards Air Force Base, CA
1,132.13	1,821.99	March 10, 1956	Fairey Delta 2	L. Peter Twiss (United Kingdom)	Ford/Chichester, United Kingdom
1,207.6	1,943.44	Dec. 12, 1957	McDonnell F-101A Voodoo	Adrian E. Drew (United States)	Edwards Air Force Base, CA
1,404.09	2,259.66	May 16, 1958	Lockheed YF-104A Starfighter	Walter W. Irwin (United States)	Edwards Air Force Base, CA
1,483.85	2,388.03	Oct. 31, 1959	Mikoyan E-66	Georgi Mossolov (Soviet Union)	Jukowski-Petrowskol, U.S.S.R.
1,525.96	2,455.79	Dec. 15, 1959	Convair F-106A Delta Dart	Joseph W. Rogers (United States)	Edwards Air Force Base, CA
1,606.32	2,585.12	Nov. 22, 1961	McDonnell F4H-1F Phantom II	Robert B. Robinson (United States)	Edwards Air Force Base, CA
1,665.89	2,680.99	July 7, 1962	Mikoyan E-166	Georgi Mossolov (Soviet Union)	Podmoskownoe, U.S.S.R.
2,070.1	3,331.5	May 1, 1965	Lockheed YF-12A	Robert L. (Fox) Stephens and Daniel Andre (United States)	Edwards Air Force Base, CA
2,193.16	3,529.56	July 28, 1976	Lockheed SR-71A	Eldon W. Joersz (United States)	Edwards Air Force Base, CA

*This table shows aviation speed records set over a straight course.

American Airlines used the first of these—the Boeing 707—to start transcontinental jet service from New York City to Los Angeles.

The beginning of jet airline service created new challenges. Large jetliners carried nearly 200 passengers, and the crash of one of these planes could cause heavy loss of life. New hazards were also created along the world's air routes as airplanes flew faster and in greater numbers than ever before. In 1958, the U.S. government combined the CAA and several other agencies to form the Federal Aviation Agency. The agency was given the job of establishing and enforcing air safety regulations and air traffic procedures in the United States. It was renamed the Federal Aviation Administration in 1967.

By 1970, jet transports had replaced propeller-driven planes on most major airlines. In 1970, Pan Am became the first airline to offer jumbo jet service, using Boeing 747's. France and the United Kingdom began passenger service with their SST, the Concorde, in 1976.

Industry mergers. Beginning in the 1950's, several large aerospace companies were formed by mergers. In 1954, the General Dynamics Corporation took control of Consolidated Vultee (Convair). In 1967, McDonnell Aircraft merged with Douglas Aircraft to form the McDon-

nell Douglas Corporation, and North American Aviation and Rockwell-Standard merged, forming the North American Rockwell Corporation. In 1973, this firm merged with Rockwell Manufacturing Company to become Rockwell International Corporation.

Internationalization became an important trend in the aviation industry beginning in the 1960's. The term refers to cooperative manufacturing programs in which firms from different nations share research, development, and production costs. The consortium formed by the British and French to build the Concorde SST was an early program of this type. Another successful program has been Airbus. This consortium, which manufactures commercial transport aircraft, has involved most countries in western Europe.

United States aviation firms moved slowly into internationalization in the 1970's. Manufacturers in Canada, Italy, Japan, and the United Kingdom produced major parts of the McDonnell Douglas DC-10 transport, which began commercial service in 1971. Some U.S. firms have formed partnerships with foreign companies to manufacture European-designed aircraft in the United States. For example, during the 1980's, McDonnell Douglas produced the British-designed Harrier—a V/STOL (Vertical/Short Take-Off and Landing plane)—in partnership with British Aerospace (see **V/STOL**).

Airline safety concerns. Beginning in the 1960's, airliner hijacking, also called air piracy, became a serious problem. In 1970, hijackers throughout the world seized 49 airliners and forced the pilots to fly to destinations off their routes, often to other countries. In the 1980's, terrorist sabotage became a serious risk as several airliners were blown up in flight.

In response to the hijackings, aviation authorities tightened airport security regulations. These regulations include the inspection of aircraft, passengers, and baggage for hidden guns, bombs, or other weapons. Most countries have laws against hijacking and terrorism. But laws differ from country to country. The ICAO develops procedures to help member countries establish consistent methods to prevent and investigate hijackings. See **Airport** (Airport security); **Hijacking; Terrorism.**

Deregulation and mergers. In the late 1970's, the Civil Aeronautics Board began to ease its controls over airline fares and routes in the United States to encourage greater competition and better service. In 1978, Congress passed the Airline Deregulation Act. This law provided for the gradual removal of economic controls of the airline industry. The Civil Aeronautics Board was dissolved in 1984. New airlines soon began to form, and existing ones rapidly expanded their services.

Deregulation in the United States allowed domestic airlines to compete in many international markets. Many U.S. airlines formed alliances with overseas carriers to simplify ticketing. Many U.S. airlines also developed *hub and spoke* systems. In such a system, many flights connect at a central airport. In manufacturing, several mergers in the 1990's led to the disappearance of historic U.S. airplane builders, such as McDonnell Douglas, which merged into Boeing. International partnerships became increasingly significant, with Airbus capturing one-third of the world market in jet airliner sales in the 1990's.

Recent developments. On Sept. 11, 2001, terrorists hijacked four commercial airplanes, crashing two into

Important dates in aviation history

1903	Orville and Wilbur Wright of the United States made the world's first successful airplane flights.
1905	Charles and Gabriel Voisin of France started the first airplane-manufacturing company.
1907	Glenn H. Curtiss started the first airplane-manufacturing company in the United States.
1914	The world's first scheduled airline began service across Tampa Bay between St. Petersburg and Tampa, Florida. But the airline lasted only a few months.
1918	The U.S. government used Army pilots to start the world's first permanent airmail service.
1919	The first successful scheduled airlines began to operate in Europe. They used converted World War I bombers.
1925	Private airlines began carrying U.S. airmail.
1926	The first successful scheduled airlines in the United States began operations.
1926	The U.S. Congress passed the Air Commerce Act, the first federal law to regulate aviation in the United States.
1952	British Overseas Airways Corporation (now British Airways) started jet passenger service with de Havilland Comets.
1958	The U.S. Congress established the Federal Aviation Agency (FAA) to deal with air safety and air traffic control. The agency became the Federal Aviation Administration in 1967.
1959	American Airlines started jet service across the United States with Boeing 707's.
1970	Pan American World Airways (Pan Am) began jumbo jet service with Boeing 747's.
1970	A group of European countries founded Airbus to compete with U.S. production of jet airliners.
1976	Air France and British Airways began passenger service with supersonic transport planes.
1984	The Civil Aeronautics Board was dissolved as part of the U.S. government plan to deregulate the airline industry.
2001	In response to terrorist attacks in New York City and Washington, D.C., on September 11, the U.S. Congress created the Transportation Security Administration to take over air safety functions from the FAA.
2003	Air France and British Airways discontinued all supersonic transport plane flights.
2010	A volcanic eruption in Iceland caused most of Europe's major airports to close for several days.

the towers of the World Trade Center in New York City and one into the Pentagon Building outside Washington, D.C. The fourth hijacked plane crashed in Somerset County, Pennsylvania. After the hijackings, U.S. airports and airlines sought new ways to protect against terrorist attacks. Congress passed legislation requiring federal employees to handle all passenger and baggage inspection in U.S. airports by the end of 2002. A newly created agency, the Transportation Security Administration, took over air safety functions from the FAA.

Fears of terrorism and a sluggish world economy contributed to a decline in air travel in the early 2000's. In 2003, British Airways and Air France discontinued all Concorde flights because the flights were no longer profitable. In 2008, Delta Air Lines, Inc., merged with Northwest Airlines to form one of the world's largest commercial airlines. The 2010 merger of United Airlines and Continental Airlines created another huge carrier. In 2011, British Airways merged with Iberia, but both airlines continued to operate under their own names.

Unmanned aerial vehicles (UAV's), also called *drones*, became increasingly important during the 2000's for military operations. Such planes have no pilot and are controlled remotely to gather intelligence or attack enemies.

In 2010, a volcanic eruption in Iceland closed most of Europe's major airports for several days. Aviation authorities grounded planes to avoid ash and particles in the air that could damage engines and endanger flights.

Careers in aviation

The aviation industry employs many kinds of skilled workers. They include aeronautical engineers, computer specialists, electricians, flight attendants, flight engineers, flying instructors, mechanics, pilots, radar specialists, and radio operators. In the United States, many jobs in the aviation industry require FAA certification. For example, air traffic controllers, aviation mechanics, flight engineers, and pilots must have FAA certificates.

Some schools offer courses in preparation for such careers as aviation mechanic, computer specialist, and radio operator. Aeronautical engineering and some other highly skilled professions require a college education. Most pilots obtain their training at flying schools or in military service. Some high schools and colleges also offer courses in flying. See **Airplane** (Learning to fly).

Jobs in general aviation. Many pilots work for air taxi services, business firms, and other organizations that use light planes. In many countries, flying light planes for commercial purposes requires a *commercial pilot license.* In the United States, the FAA issues these licenses to pilots 18 years old or older who have at least 250 hours of flying experience and who pass the physical, written, and flight examinations.

Jobs with airlines and airports. In most countries, airline pilots and copilots must obtain a special license. They must pass a thorough physical examination, as well as written and flight examinations. In the United States, airline pilots and copilots must have an FAA *airline transport pilot license.* To obtain this license, they must be at least 23 years old and have a commercial pilot license and 1,500 hours of flight time.

Some airlines use flight engineers. On long flights, the engineers watch the many instruments in the cockpit that tell how the engines are operating. Most airlines require their flight engineers to have a commercial pilot license. Airlines prefer to hire flight attendants who have some college, business, or nursing training. Skilled mechanics are needed for airliner maintenance.

Jobs in the aircraft industry. Aircraft manufacturers hire electricians, machine tool operators, mechanics, and other skilled workers to make and assemble airplanes. The industry also employs engineers to design aircraft and experienced pilots to test-fly planes.

Jobs with government agencies. Government agencies in many countries hire radar and radio operators to work at air traffic control centers. They also hire mechanics and pilots as safety agents. Many local aviation agencies also need engineers, mechanics, and pilots. Some large cities hire pilots as flying police officers or to perform rescue services.   Roger E. Bilstein

Related articles. See **Airplane** with its list of *Related articles* and the *Transportation* section of the various state, province, country, and continent articles. See also the following articles:

Biographies

Blériot, Louis	De Seversky, Alexander Procofieff	Hughes, Howard R.
Boeing, William E.		Link, Edwin A.
Curtiss, Glenn H.	Fokker, Anthony H. G.	Sikorsky, Igor I.
		Wright brothers

Other related articles

Air force	Jet stream
Air Force, United States	Manufacturing
Airmail	National Aeronautic
Airport	Association
Careers (Transportation and material moving)	National Air and Space Museum
Federal Aviation Administration	Radar
Great-circle route	Test pilot
Jet propulsion	Transportation
	Tuskegee Airmen

Outline

I. **The aviation industry**
  A. Aircraft manufacturing
  B. General aviation activities
  C. Airline operations
  D. Airport operations
  E. Aviation support industries

II. **Aviation agencies and organizations**
  A. Aviation agencies
  B. The International Civil Aviation Organization
  C. Other aviation organizations

III. **History of the aviation industry**

IV. **Careers in aviation**
  A. Jobs in general aviation
  B. Jobs with airlines and airports
  C. Jobs in the aircraft industry
  D. Jobs with government agencies

Aviation medicine. See **Aerospace medicine.**

Avicenna, *AV ih SEHN uh* (980-1037), also known as Ibn-Sina, *IHB uhn SEE nah,* was a Muslim physician, philosopher, astronomer, and poet. He wrote *Canon of Medicine* (about 1025), used as a medical text for over 600 years. It is still occasionally used in Asia. Avicenna's major philosophical work, *The Cure* (1027), presented his interpretation of the philosophy of Aristotle. Of all his books, it had the greatest effect on Western thought.

Avicenna was born near Bokhara (now Buxoro in Uzbekistan), then a part of Persia ruled by the Samanid dynasty. He began to practice medicine at 16. When only 20, he was known as the most learned person of his time.   Matthew Ramsey

Avignon, *ah vee NYAWN* (pop. 92,378; met. area pop. 529,190), is an agricultural center and a historic city in

The Papal Palace in Avignon was the home of the popes of the Roman Catholic Church from 1309 to 1377. The building at the far left, topped by a statue of the Virgin Mary, is the cathedral. The other buildings are part of the palace complex.

© Tomsickova Tatyana, Shutterstock

southeastern France. It lies along the Rhône River in one of France's richest agricultural regions. For location, see **France** (political map). Avignon is a trading center for wine, fruits, vegetables, and other goods produced in its area. Other economic activities include shipping, food processing, and the manufacture of chemicals, leather, machine tools, soap, and textiles. A major theater festival is held there each summer. The city is the capital of the Vaucluse *department* (administrative district).

Roman soldiers established a colony on the site of what is now Avignon in the 100's B.C. From 1309 to 1377, Avignon served as the home of the popes and, as such, the center of Christianity (see **Pope** [The troubles of the papacy]). The Papal Palace, where the popes lived, is an architectural masterpiece and a major tourist attraction. Walls that were built around the city to protect the popes still stand.   Mark Kesselman

Ávila Camacho, *AH vee LAH kah MAH choh,* **Manuel,** *mah NWEHL* (1897-1955), a Mexican political leader, served as president of Mexico from 1940 to 1946. As president, he promoted closer relations with the United States and encouraged U.S. investment in Mexico. During World War II (1939-1945), he allied Mexico with the United States against the Axis Powers and initiated the *bracero* (day laborer) program. This program sent Mexican agricultural workers to the United States. See **Mexico** (During and after World War II).

Ávila Camacho was born on April 24, 1897, in Teziutlán, Puebla, Mexico. When he was 17, Ávila Camacho joined the uprising led by Venustiano Carranza against President Victoriano Huerta (see **Carranza, Venustiano**). Ávila Camacho later fought with Lázaro Cárdenas and Plutarco Elías Calles against the rebellion of Adolfo de la Huerta in 1923. In the late 1930's, during the presidency of Cárdenas, Ávila Camacho served as secretary of national defense. He died on Oct. 13, 1955.   W. Dirk Raat

Avocado is a fruit that grows in tropical and subtropical climates. The fruit may be round, oval, or pear-shaped. Its skin color ranges from green to dark purple, depending on the variety. Avocados have a yellow-green pulp and contain one large seed.

Avocados are highly nutritious. They are rich in vitamins, minerals, and oil. People eat avocados fresh in dips, salads, and desserts. Guacamole, a popular Mexican dish, is made with mashed avocados, onions, tomatoes, cilantro, garlic, and salt. Avocados are also used to make milk shakes and ice cream.

Avocados are native to Mexico, Guatemala, Jamaica, and Cuba, but they now grow in many parts of the world. Mexico is the leading avocado-producing country. Other leading producers include Chile, Indonesia, and the United States. California and Florida produce most of the U.S. avocado crop.

Avocado trees grow up to 30 to 60 feet (9 to 18 meters) tall. They have spreading branches with dark green leaves and small, greenish-white flowers. In some varieties, it is estimated that only one fruit is harvested for every 5,000 flowers. To help guarantee fruit development and uniformity, the stems of avocado seedlings are grafted to the stems of selected varieties.

The many varieties of avocados are divided into three main groups—(1) Mexican, (2) Guatemalan, and (3) West Indian. Mexican avocados have smooth, thin skins. The fruits are small, and few weigh more than ½ pound (0.2 kilogram). Guatemalan avocados have thick, rough skins and may weigh over 3 pounds (1.4 kilograms). West Indian avocados are about the same size as the Guatemalan fruits, but they have leathery skins.   Jaime E. Lazarte

Scientific classification. The avocado's scientific name is *Persea americana.*

WORLD BOOK illustration by Kate Lloyd-Jones, Linden Artists Ltd.

Avocados have a yellow-green pulp that surrounds one large seed. Avocado trees bear broad leaves and small flowers.

Avocet, *AV uh seht,* is a type of long-legged wading bird. The *American avocet* is most common west of the Mississippi River, from Canada to the Mexican border. It is about 17 inches (43 centimeters) long and has a white body and black wings. The head and neck are streaked with brown during the breeding season. The long, flat bill curves upward. Another avocet species, the *pied avocet,* lives throughout much of Africa, Asia, and Europe. Pied avocets resemble American avocets, except they have both black and white plumage on the head.

The avocet feeds by scraping its bill along the bottom

WORLD BOOK illustration by John Rignall, Linden Artists Ltd.
The American avocet is a wading bird whose long legs and long, curved bill help it feed in shallow-water areas.

of shallow pools to collect small water animals, which it eats. It also eats other food that floats on or in the water. Harmful insects form part of its diet. Fritz L. Knopf

Scientific classification. Avocets make up the genus *Recurvirostra*. The American avocet's scientific name is *Recurvirostra americana*. The pied avocet is *R. avosetta*.

Avogadro, *AH vuh GAH droh*, **Amedeo,** *AH mah DEE oh* (1776-1856), an Italian physicist, proposed in 1811 his famous hypothesis, known as *Avogadro's law*. The law states that equal volumes of all gases at the same temperature and pressure contain the same number of chemical units. Avogadro distinguished between gases composed of complex units (molecules) and gases made up of simple units (atoms). He could calculate from gas densities the amount of matter in atoms and molecules. The leading scientists of Avogadro's time rejected his hypothesis until 1858, when the Italian chemist Stanislao Cannizzaro reintroduced it and developed it further.

Avogadro also introduced a basic unit of quantity in chemistry called a *mole* (see Mole). Still widely used, a mole contains 6.022137×10^{23} atoms or molecules of a single substance. This quantity is referred to as *Avogadro's number*. Avogadro was born on Aug. 9, 1776, in Turin. He died on July 9, 1856. See also **Chemistry** (Development of physical chemistry). Melvyn C. Usselman

Avoirdupois, *AV uhr duh POYZ*, is a system of weights used for common commodities such as coal, grain, and foodstuffs. It is used primarily in the United States. The word *avoirdupois* comes from French words meaning *goods of weight*. The basis of the system is the pound, which equals 0.454 kilogram. An avoirdupois pound contains 16 ounces or 7,000 grains. Each ounce contains 16 drams, so 1 dram equals 27.344 grains. One grain equals 64.799 milligrams. Two other systems of weight, the *Troy* and *apothecaries'* systems, also have grains that equal 64.799 milligrams. The Troy and apothecaries' pounds, however, equal 5,760 grains. Richard S. Davis

See also **Ounce; Pound; Ton; Troy weight; Weights and measures.**

Avon, Earl of. See Eden, Sir Anthony.

Avon, *AY vuhn,* **River,** is the name of nine rivers in the United Kingdom. Four are in England, three in Scotland, and two in Wales. Three of the English rivers are open to public navigation. They are described below. The name Avon is from the Welsh word for river, *afon.*

The Upper Avon, often called the Warwickshire Avon, rises near Naseby, in Northamptonshire. It flows about 95 miles (150 kilometers) through Warwickshire, Worcestershire, and Gloucestershire. For location, see **England** (terrain map). The Upper Avon joins the River Severn at Tewkesbury. Towns on the river include Rugby, Warwick, and Stratford-upon-Avon, birthplace of the playwright William Shakespeare.

The Lower Avon, also called the Bristol Avon, rises near Chipping Sodbury in Gloucestershire. It flows about 60 miles (100 kilometers) through the picturesque countryside of Wiltshire and Somerset to the Bristol Channel. It passes through Bath and Bristol.

The East Avon, or Hampshire Avon, rises near Devizes, in Wiltshire, and flows about 70 miles (110 kilometers) south through Hampshire and Dorset. It empties into the English Channel at Christchurch. Salisbury stands on its banks. Molly Warrington

AWOL. See Desertion.

Ax, also spelled *axe*, is a chopping tool. It has a single-edged or double-bladed head attached to a handle. Ancient axes had heads of stone, copper, bronze, or iron. Modern axeheads are made of steel or steel alloy. Ax handles, called *hafts*, were traditionally hardwood. Modern hafts are also made from plastic or fiberglass.

People have long used chopping and throwing axes as weapons. In the Middle Ages (about the A.D. 400's through the 1400's), warriors wielded battle-axes and long poleaxes. Today, loggers use various types of axes to cut down and split trees. Firefighters' axes help them break into burning buildings. Amy Sue Bix

See also **Tomahawk; Weapon.**

Axiom, *AK see uhm,* is a mathematical statement that is assumed to be true. An example of an axiom is the *parallel postulate* of geometry. The parallel axiom states that "through a point not on a given line, one, and only one, line may be drawn that is parallel to the given line." The ancient Greeks distinguished between axioms and *postulates*. They considered axioms to be universal, self-evident truths that could not be proved. Postulates, on the other hand, were assumed to be true as the basis for a specific field of study, such as geometry. Today, most mathematicians no longer make this distinction. See also **Geometry** (Axiomatic system). Eli Maor

Axis refers to alliances formed among Germany, Italy, and Japan before and during World War II (1939-1945). In 1936, Italy and Germany joined in an alliance called the Rome-Berlin Axis. The term Axis was used to suggest that all Europe rotated about a line between these two capitals. Japan joined the alliance in 1940, and it became the Rome-Berlin-Tokyo Axis. Bulgaria, Hungary, Romania, and the German-created states of Croatia and Slovakia became Axis satellites. Donald M. McKale

See also **World War II** (table; maps).

Axle. See Wheel and axle.

Axum. See Aksum.

Ayckbourn, *AYK bawrn,* **Alan** (1939-   ), is a British playwright known for dark, thought-provoking comedies about middle-class life. The audience laughs at his characters but often realizes that they lead sad, empty lives. For example, in *Woman in Mind* (1985), a neglected homemaker invents an imaginary family who become more real to her than her own family. Ayckbourn is noted for his intricate plot structures and clever use of stage space. *The Norman Conquests* (1973) is really three plays, each about events set in different parts of a country home at the same time. In *Taking Steps* (1979), one set represents three places. The plays *House* and *Garden* (both 2000) are performed in two separate theaters by the same cast at the same time.

© David Levenson, Getty Images
Alan Ayckbourn

Ayckbourn first gained international notice with *How the Other Half Loves* (1969). His other plays include *Absurd Person Singular* (1972), *Absent Friends* (1974), *Bedroom Farce* (1975), *Sisterly Feelings* (1979), *A Small Family Business* (1987), *Man of the Moment* (1988), *The Revengers' Comedies* (1989), *Communicating Doors* (1994), *Things We Do for Love* (1997), *Comic Potential* (1999), and *Private Fears in Public Places* (2005).

From 1972 to 2009, Ayckbourn served as the artistic director of the Stephen Joseph Theatre in Scarborough, where most of his comedies have premiered. He was born on April 12, 1939, in London. Ayckbourn was knighted in 1997. His book *The Crafty Art of Playmaking* appeared in 2003.   Thomas P. Adler

Aycock, Charles Brantley (1859-1912), was a leader in developing public education in the United States South. As the Democratic governor of North Carolina from 1901 to 1905, Aycock argued for the creation of new schools, including the first rural high schools, and new teacher-training facilities. Later educational reformers used his legislation as a model in much of the South.

Aycock was born on Nov. 1, 1859, in Wayne County, North Carolina. He received a law degree from the University of North Carolina in 1880. Aycock died on April 4, 1912, while campaigning for a seat in the U.S. Senate. A statue of Aycock represents North Carolina in the U.S. Capitol.   Luther Spoehr

Aye-aye, *EYE eye,* is a rare tree-dwelling mammal of Madagascar with woolly, brownish fur and a long, bushy tail. It is closely related to a monkeylike animal called the lemur. The aye-aye weighs 5 to 7 pounds (2 to 3 kilograms) and measures about 3 feet (1 meter) long from head to tail. It has large eyes like a lemur but features unusually large ears.

The aye-aye becomes most active at night, when it hunts for food. The animal bores into trees with its large, rodentlike front teeth. It then uses its long, clawed third finger to probe inside and extract insects and their *larvae* (young) to eat. During the day, aye-ayes hide in the forks of trees, among vines, and in nests made of twigs. They mostly live and feed alone, coming together only to breed. Young aye-ayes stay with their mothers until they can survive on their own.

The government of Madagascar protects aye-ayes

© Javarman/Shutterstock

The aye-aye lives in the forests of Madagascar. Its large eyes and ears help it move around easily at night.

with laws that forbid hunting them. However, habitat destruction and *poaching* (illegal hunting) endanger the animal's survival. Small populations live throughout Madagascar, but the precise number of aye-ayes in the wild remains unknown.   Randall L. Susman

Scientific classification. The aye-aye's scientific name is *Daubentonia madagascariensis.*

See also Lemur.

Ayers Rock. See Uluru.

Ayllón, *eyel YAWN,* **Lucas Vásquez de** (1480?-1526), a Spanish colonizer, founded the first European settlement in what is now the United States. The settlement, on what is now the nation's southeast coast, survived for only a few months.

Ayllón was born in Toledo, Spain. In 1504, he arrived in the Americas and served as a judge for the Spanish government on the island of Hispaniola. Ayllón became wealthy, partly by trading in Indian slaves. He also sponsored voyages to the coast of what may have been present-day South Carolina or Georgia. The first voyage, in 1521, was led by the Spanish explorer Francisco Gordillo. Ayllón heard reports that the land Gordillo saw, which became known as Chicora, was rich in natural resources and resembled southern Spain. In 1526, Ayllón led an expedition of about 600 people to colonize Chicora. The colony Ayllón founded, called San Miguel de Gualdape, was probably on Sapelo Sound in what is now Georgia. The colonists soon suffered from starvation and disease. Many, including Ayllón, died there. The survivors returned to Hispaniola.   Helen Delpar

Azalea, *uh ZAYL yuh,* is the name of a group of flowering shrubs. Azaleas grow mostly in North America and eastern Asia. Most North American azaleas are *deciduous*—that is, they lose their leaves every autumn. Asian *species* (kinds) usually are evergreen and remain green all year. Azaleas can be grown in gardens. These plants also occur wild in woodlands, often in swamp areas.

Azalea blossoms range in color through all shades of pink, red, white, yellow, and purple. Their long, conspicuous *stamens* (stalks that contain pollen) extend beyond the petals. A long, slender capsule covered with hairlike parts holds the seeds.

Numerous species of azaleas grow in North America. These shallow-rooted plants live best in well-drained acid soil. They especially thrive in partial shade with filtered sunlight. Azalea plants bloom during the months of May and June in the Northern Hemisphere.

Fred T. Davies, Jr.

Scientific classification. Azaleas are in the genus *Rhododendron*. A common North American azalea is *R. canescens*.

See also **Bonsai** (picture); **Flower** (Garden perennials [picture]); **Heath**.

Azerbaijan, *AH zuhr by JAHN,* is a country in the Caucasus Mountain region on the western shore of the Caspian Sea. It lies mostly in southwestern Asia, but part of northern Azerbaijan is in Europe. An area of Azerbaijan called the Naxçivan Autonomous Republic lies west of the rest of the country, separated by Armenian territory.

The country's full name in Azerbaijani, the official language, is Azərbaycan Respublikasi (Republic of Azerbaijan). Baku is its capital and largest city. Azerbaijan became independent in 1991, after nearly 70 years as a part of the Soviet Union.

Government. Under Azerbaijan's Constitution, which became effective in 1995, the president is the country's most powerful government official. The people elect the president to a seven-year term. A Cabinet of Ministers, headed by a prime minister, helps carry out the operations of government. The president appoints the Cabinet members. A 125-member parliament called the Milli Mejlis (National Assembly) makes the country's laws. Voters elect the assembly members to five-year terms. All citizens 18 years old or older may vote. The main units of local government include the Naxçivan Autonomous Republic and districts, cities, and villages. Azerbaijan has a Supreme Court and regional courts.

Azerbaijan's armed forces include a land force, an air force, and a navy. Men are required to serve in the armed forces.

Nagorno-Karabakh, a territory in southwestern Azerbaijan, is populated mainly by Armenians and controlled by ethnic Armenian military forces. The region has its own elected government. However, no country recognizes Nagorno-Karabakh as an independent nation.

People. Most of Azerbaijan's people are ethnic Azerbaijanis. Armenians, Lezgins, and Russians make up the largest minority groups.

In Azerbaijan's cities, most people live in multistory apartment buildings. In rural areas, most of the people live in one- or two-story houses.

Most Azerbaijanis are Shī`ite Muslims. Many Armenians are Christians who belong to the Armenian Church. It resembles the Eastern Orthodox Churches in its beliefs. Many Russians are Russian Orthodox Christians.

Most people in Azerbaijan wear clothing similar to that worn by North Americans and Europeans. On holidays, some men wear a traditional costume consisting of pants, a long shirt, boots, and a long jacket. Some rural women wear wide skirts and blouses with long, wide sleeves. Muslim women in rural areas often wear a black shawl that covers the head and shoulders and may be drawn over the face.

The Azerbaijani language developed from the languages of Persians and Turkic people who once inhabited the region. Azerbaijani closely resembles Turkish.

Azerbaijanis enjoy *pilaf* (a rice dish) and a variety of grilled and boiled meats, including beef, goat, and lamb. Traditional dishes include *bozartma* (mutton stew) and *dovga* (soup made of yogurt, meat, and herbs). Tea and wine are popular drinks.

Facts in brief

Capital: Baku.
Official language: Azerbaijani.
Area: 33,436 mi² (86,600 km²). *Greatest distances*—north-south, 240 mi (385 km); east-west, 295 mi (475 km).
Elevation: *Highest*—Bazardyuzyu, 14,652 ft (4,466 m) above sea level. *Lowest*—Caspian Sea coast, 92 ft (28 m) below sea level.
Population: *Estimated 2022 population*—10,280,000; density, 307 per mi² (119 per km²); distribution, 56 percent urban, 44 percent rural. *2020 official government estimate*—10,067,100.
Chief products: *Agriculture*—apples, barley, cattle, cotton, grapes, potatoes, sheep, tomatoes, wheat. *Manufacturing*—chemicals, oil field equipment, refined petroleum, steel. *Mining*—aluminum, copper, iron, natural gas, petroleum, salt.
Flag: The flag's three horizontal stripes are light blue, red, and green. In the flag's center is a white crescent and star.
Money: *Basic unit*—Azerbaijani manat.

Soccer is a popular sport in Azerbaijan. Many people walk or swim for recreation. Men spend much of their leisure time talking with one another in teahouses.

Azerbaijanis are known for their handwoven rugs. Also, their brightly patterned shawls are highly admired.

Nearly all adults in Azerbaijan can read and write. The government requires children to attend school from the ages of 6 to 15. The country has several universities.

Land and climate. The Caucasus Mountains rise in northern Azerbaijan, and the Little Caucasus Mountains stretch across western Azerbaijan. The area north of the mountains is considered part of Europe. The area south

Azerbaijan

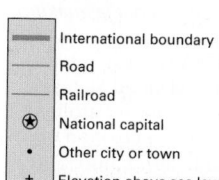

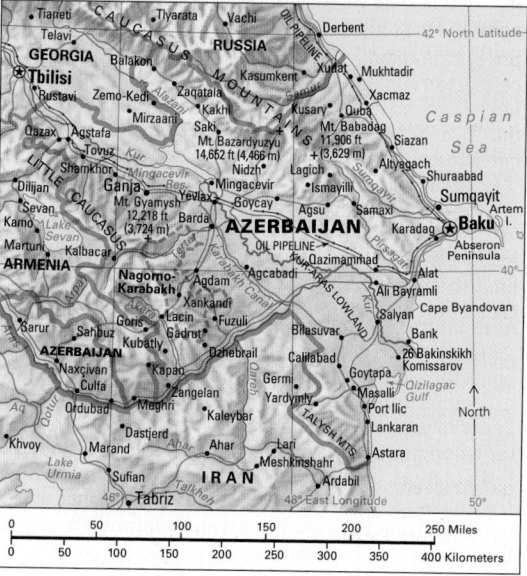

WORLD BOOK maps

© Serguei Fedorov, Woodfin Camp, Inc.

Baku, Azerbaijan's capital, lies on the Caspian Sea. It serves as the country's chief port. Refineries in Baku process petroleum, Azerbaijan's chief source of income.

of the range is considered part of Asia. Azerbaijan's highest mountain, Bazardyuzyu, rises 14,652 feet (4,466 meters) above sea level in the Caucasus Mountains.

The rugged Armenian Plateau, a land broken by deep gorges, covers part of southwestern Azerbaijan. The Kur, the country's main river, flows through the central valley between the mountain ranges and across a broad, dry plain called the Kur-Aras Lowland. From the lowland, the Kur drains into the salty Caspian Sea. The Kur's main tributary, the Aras, flows along part of Azerbaijan's southern border. Other important rivers in Azerbaijan include the Terter and the Akera. The rivers serve as a source of irrigation water and energy. The Mingacevir dam on the Kur River provides hydroelectric power for Baku and the Ganja industrial region.

Summers in the lowlands are long and hot. Winters are cool. The lowlands have an average temperature of 79 °F (26 °C) in August and 39 °F (4 °C) in January. Parts of the Caucasus Mountains have average temperatures of 56 °F (13 °C) in August and 21 °F (6 °C) in January. Annual precipitation ranges from about 5 to 15 inches (13 to 38 centimeters) in most of the country's lowland areas. The highlands and a region in southeastern Azerbaijan on the Caspian Sea receive about 40 to 55 inches (100 to 140 centimeters) of precipitation every year.

Economy. Industry accounts for about half of the value of Azerbaijan's economic production. The country's industrial activities include building oil field equipment, mining, processing chemicals, producing steel, and refining petroleum. The chief industrial cities are Baku, Ganja, and Sumqayit.

Petroleum ranks as the country's most important mined product by far. The largest producing oil fields lie in the Baku region, in the Caspian Sea, and on the sea's western shore. Oil pipelines link Baku with ports on the Mediterranean Sea and Black Sea. Azerbaijan's other mined products include aluminum, copper, iron, natural gas, and salt.

Agriculture employs about two-thirds of all Azerbaijani workers. Farmers in the lowlands grow such crops as apples, barley, cotton, grapes, potatoes, tomatoes, and wheat. Some farmers raise silkworms for the raw

silk industry. Herders raise cattle, goats, and sheep on mountain slopes. The Caspian Sea is a source of fish.

Azerbaijan's main export is crude petroleum. It also exports cotton and food. The country imports food, machinery, metals, and vehicles. Azerbaijan's trading partners include Indonesia, Italy, Russia, Turkey, and the United Kingdom.

Internet and cell-phone usage has increased rapidly since the early 2000's. A port at Baku handles most of the country's trade on the Caspian Sea. The main international airport is at Baku.

History. People have lived in what is now Azerbaijan since prehistoric times. Medes invaded the region in the 700's B.C. Later invaders were Persians of the Achaemenid Empire in the 500's B.C. and the Macedonian general Alexander the Great in the 300's B.C. Persians of the Sasanian dynasty controlled much of the region from the A.D. 200's until the 600's, when the Arabs conquered the area. The Arabs introduced the religion of Islam.

From the 1000's to the 1200's, Turkic tribes migrated into the region in large numbers and mixed with the Persians who lived there. These people became the ancestors of the Azerbaijanis. In the early 1500's, Azerbaijan fell to the Safavid Empire, which ruled Iran. The Ottoman Empire took control from the Safavids in the late 1500's but lost it to them again in the early 1600's.

In the early 1800's, Russia gained control of what is now Azerbaijan. Under Russia, industry, especially petroleum production, developed in Azerbaijan. By the late 1800's, Baku had become the world's leading producer of refined petroleum.

In 1917, revolutionaries known as Bolsheviks (later called Communists) seized control of the Russian government. In 1918, Azerbaijani nationalists set up an independent state in western Azerbaijan. But the Russians regained the area in 1920.

Soviet rule. In early 1922, Azerbaijan, Georgia, and Armenia combined to form the Transcaucasian Republic under Russia's leadership. Later that year, the Transcaucasian Republic joined Byelorussia (now Belarus), Russia, and Ukraine to form the Soviet Union. In 1936, the three parts of the Transcaucasian Republic became separate republics of the Soviet Union. Azerbaijan was called the Azerbaijan Soviet Socialist Republic.

The Soviet Union established a powerful central government and took control of Azerbaijan's industry and land. The Soviet Union *collectivized* agriculture in Azerbaijan—that is, it severely restricted private farming and transferred control of farms to the government. The Soviet rulers destroyed many Azerbaijani traditions, and they tried to reduce the influence of Islam. They closed down almost all mosques and religious schools in Azerbaijan. But the Soviets also built roads, schools, modern housing, hospitals, and communication systems.

Independence. The Soviet government maintained strict control until the late 1980's. In 1989, Azerbaijan declared that its own laws overruled the laws of the Soviet Union. In August 1991, conservative Communist officials failed in an attempt to overthrow the Soviet president, Mikhail S. Gorbachev. During the upheaval that followed, Azerbaijan and several other republics of the Soviet Union declared their independence. In December, Azerbaijan joined other republics in a loose association called the Commonwealth of Independent States. The

Soviet Union was formally dissolved on December 25.

In 1992, the Azerbaijani government slowly began to pass laws that encouraged a market economy. However, most of the economy continued under government control. Most of the people remained poor. Abulfaz Elchibey was elected president in 1992. In 1993, a rebel uprising forced Elchibey to flee the capital, Baku. Heydar Aliyev was appointed acting president and then was elected president. He was reelected in 1998.

Dispute over Nagorno-Karabakh. An area known as Nagorno-Karabakh in southern Azerbaijan has been a source of dispute between Azerbaijan and neighboring Armenia. Most of its people are Armenians, and Armenia claims the area. In early 1988, Nagorno-Karabakh petitioned to become part of Armenia. This action triggered fighting between Azerbaijanis and Armenians for control of Nagorno-Karabakh. About 200,000 Azerbaijanis—almost all those who lived in Armenia—fled to Azerbaijan. About 250,000 Armenians fled Azerbaijan for Armenia. In 1994, the two countries declared a cease-fire, but fighting continued from time to time. Ethnic Armenian forces controlled Nagorno-Karabakh and some of the surrounding Azerbaijani territory. Nagorno-Karabakh established its own elected government.

Recent developments. In the 1990's, Azerbaijan made progress in selling government-owned farmland and businesses to private owners. It signed agreements with foreign oil companies for supplies of oil from the Caspian Sea. The deals proved profitable for Azerbaijan.

In 2003, Heydar Aliyev did not run for reelection as president. Voters elected his son Ilham to succeed him and reelected Ilham in 2008. In 2009, voters approved amending the Constitution to allow the president to run for an unlimited number of terms. Ilham Aliyev was reelected in 2013 and 2018. In 2020, fighting flared between Azerbaijan and Armenia. Azerbaijan gained some lands in and near Nagorno-Karabakh. A truce arranged by Russia allowed Azerbaijan to keep these lands and some other nearby areas.   Nancy Lubin

See also **Baku; Caspian Sea; Caucasus; Caucasus Mountains.**

Azimuth, *AZ uh muhth,* is a measure along the horizon of the angle between an object and a reference point. The reference point is usually due north, and the angle is measured in a clockwise direction. An object that lies due east would have an azimuth of 90°. A wind of direction 270° is blowing from the west. Azimuth may also be measured counterclockwise from due south. In this case, an object of azimuth 135° would lie to the northwest. The reference point can be made even clearer by giving the direction as S 135° W.

The azimuth of an object above or below the horizon is found using an imaginary circle called a *great circle.* One such circle passes through the object from a point directly above the observer. The azimuth is measured from the point where this circle intersects the horizon. To locate the object, its altitude must also be known.

Surveyors use azimuth to help determine boundary points. Soldiers use it to direct artillery fire. Astronomers and navigators use it to locate objects in the sky.

Glenn Schneider

Azores, *AY zohrz* or *uh ZOHRZ,* are a group of nine islands that belong to Portugal. They are in the North Atlantic Ocean, about 800 miles (1,300 kilometers) west of

The Azores are a group of islands in the North Atlantic Ocean. The islands, which belong to Portugal, lie about 800 miles (1,300 kilometers) west of the Portuguese mainland.

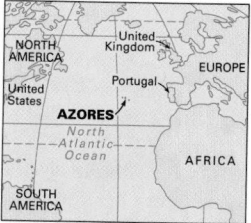

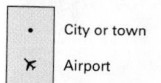

•   City or town

✕   Airport

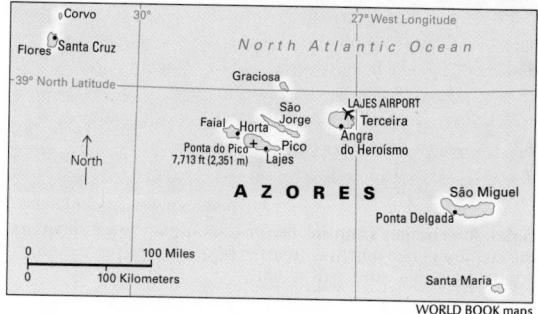

WORLD BOOK maps

Portugal. The Azores lie in the path of air and cable lines that link Europe and North America. The islands cover 897 square miles (2,322 square kilometers) and have a 320-mile (515-kilometer) coastline.

About 245,000 people live in the Azores. Through the years, many Azoreans have immigrated to the United States. More people of Azorean descent live in the United States than live in the Azores. The most important city in the Azores is Ponta Delgada, on São Miguel Island.

The Azores form the peaks of an underwater volcanic mountain chain that extends through the mid-Atlantic Ocean from Iceland nearly to Antarctica. Earthquakes are fairly common in the Azores. Much of the land is hilly and wooded, but it yields corn, grapes, and citrus fruits.

The navigator Gonzalo Cabral claimed the Azores for Portugal in 1431. No one lived there at the time Cabral arrived. But the Portuguese soon colonized the islands. The British used the Azores as a naval base in the warfare against Nazi submarines in World War II (1939-1945). Portugal, though neutral, honored an ancient treaty that allowed the British to use the islands in time of war. The United States has military installations in the Azores. In the mid-1970's, many Azoreans objected to Portugal's tight rule over the islands. Under the 1976 Portuguese Constitution and its later revisions, the Azores became an *autonomous* (self-governing) region of Portugal. But some Azoreans continued to call for complete independence.   Douglas L. Wheeler

See also **Flores Island.**

Azov, *AZ awf* or *uh ZAWF,* **Sea of,** is a large, shallow inland sea bounded by Ukraine and Russia. It is connected with the Black Sea by the Kerch Strait (see **Black Sea** [map]). The Sea of Azov covers about 14,500 square miles (37,600 square kilometers). It is only about 46 feet (14 meters) deep. Its western end is called the Sivash, or Putrid Lake, because of the many foul-smelling marshes and lagoons there. The lagoons yield important chemicals for industry. The Don River flows into the Gulf of Taganrog, which lies at the northeastern end of the sea. Ice and storms make shipping on the Sea of Azov dangerous in winter.   Leslie Dienes

The Pyramid of the Sun
rises above the Valley of Mexico in the ancient city of Teotihuacán, near present-day Mexico City. The city was an important religious center for the Aztec, though it was built centuries before by a culture unknown to them. The Aztec believed that Teotihuacán had been built by an ancient race of giants. Later, the gods met there and created the world in which the Aztec lived.

Human sacrifice
worldbook.com/az-15

© Free Agents Limited/Corbis

Aztec

Aztec were an American Indian people who ruled a mighty empire in Mexico during the 1400's and early 1500's. The Aztec had one of the most advanced civilizations in the Americas. They built cities as large and complex as any in Europe at that time. They also practiced a remarkable religion that affected every part of their lives. To worship their gods, the Aztec developed a sophisticated ritual system, built towering temples, and created huge sculptures. They held impressive religious ceremonies featuring dancing, musical performances, and the bloody sacrifices of animals and human beings.

The name *Aztec* is also commonly applied to the people who founded the city of Tenochtitlan (pronounced *tay nohch TEE tlahn).* It stood on the site of present-day Mexico City and, according to legend, was established in 1325. Its people referred to themselves by the names *Colhua-Mexica, Mexica,* and *Tenochca.* In the 1400's, the city and its allies conquered many groups in central and southern Mexico, forming the Aztec Empire. Tenochtitlan became the capital. The empire was destroyed by the Spaniards, who conquered Tenochtitlan in 1521. But the Aztec left a lasting mark on Mexican culture. *Aztec* also refers to this larger group of Indians who made up the empire. This article uses *Aztec* in that sense.

The Aztec Empire

The center of Aztec civilization was the Valley of Mexico, a huge, oval basin about 7,500 feet (2,300 meters) above sea level. Although the valley was in the tropics, its high altitude gave it a mild climate. The surrounding lowlands had a hotter, wetter climate.

The Aztec Empire included as many as 20 million people in about 400 cities and towns. Most were concentrated in the Valley of Mexico, but the empire extended well beyond that. The largest city was the capital, Tenochtitlan, which occupied an island in Lake Texcoco. *Causeways* (raised earthen roads) linked the city to the mainland. On a nearby island to the north stood the city of Tlatelolco, a commercial center. Both Tenochtitlan and Tlatelolco lay within the borders of what is now Mexico City. Present-day Mexico City covers much of the bed of Lake Texcoco, which was drained during the 1600's. In 1473, warriors of Tenochtitlan conquered Tlatelolco and united the two cities. When the Spaniards arrived in the 1500's, Tenochtitlan may have had a population of about 200,000. The Spaniards were astonished by its complexity and richness when they first saw it. No Spanish city had so many people. They compared it to Constantinople (now Istanbul, Turkey), the capital of the Ottoman Empire, and to other great European cities.

The emperor of the Aztec was called the *huey tlatoani* (great speaker). A council of high-ranking nobles chose him from the members of the royal family. The emperor, who was considered to have both human and supernatural abilities, had immense political power. However, he had to consult the council of nobles when making important decisions. Military units were stationed in key locations throughout the empire to keep it secure. Most of these units were commanded by a great noble, who often also served as governor of the territory. An elaborate system of government offices administered the affairs of the empire. Many of the top positions were hereditary, but service to the emperor was another way for a person to obtain high office.

Aztec society had four main classes: (1) nobles, (2) commoners, (3) serfs, and (4) slaves. Among nobles and commoners, closely related families belonged to groups called *calpollis.* The members of a calpolli owned an area of land in common, and each family was allowed to farm a plot large enough for its needs. In addition to their calpolli land, most nobles had their own private land or received government land for use during their term in public office. Commoners made up the

David Carrasco, the contributor of this article, is Neil L. Ruden-stine Professor of the Study of Latin America at Harvard Divinity School and the coauthor of Moctezuma's Mexico: Visions of the Aztec World.

The Aztec empire had its capital at Tenochtitlan, which stood on the site of present-day Mexico City. The empire was established during the 1400's, when the Aztec and their allies conquered much of central and southern Mexico.

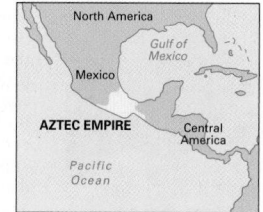

WORLD BOOK maps

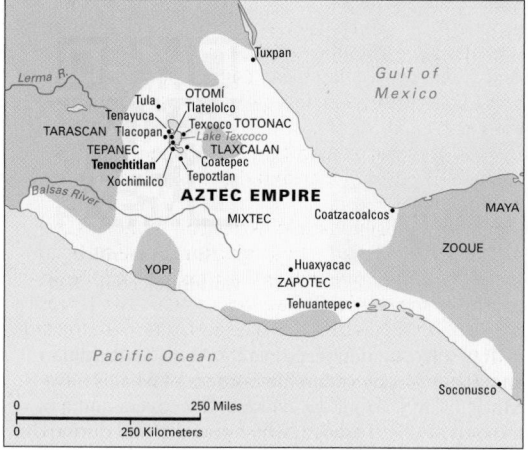

majority of the population, and many made a living by farming their calpolli plots. Serfs worked the land held by nobles and remained on the land when a new noble acquired it. Slaves were considered property, but their children were born free. Many slaves had been captured in war, and the Aztec also purchased slaves from other groups. Other slaves were criminals or people who could not pay their debts.

Way of life

Religion was extremely important in Aztec life. The people devoted much of their time to religious practices, such as praying, singing, dancing, pilgrimages, and offerings. They even waged war largely to obtain prisoners to sacrifice to their gods.

The Aztec worshiped many gods and goddesses, each of whom ruled one or more human activities or aspects of nature. The Aztec economy was based largely on farming, and so the people had many agricultural divinities. They included Centéotl, a corn god; Tláloc, a rain and fertility god; and Xipe Totec, associated with springtime and regrowth. Other major gods included Tezcatlipoca, an all-powerful divinity; Tonatiuh, the sun god; Mictlantecuhtli, ruler of the dead; and Xiuhtecuhtli, the fire god. Huitzilopochtli, a war god, was the special guardian of the people of Tenochtitlan. Xochiquetzal was a goddess of fertility, weaving and other women's crafts, flowers, and beauty. The god Quetzalcoatl was associated with civilization and learning. However, he sometimes took the form of Ehécatl, god of the wind.

The Aztec held many religious ceremonies. The most important observed planting, harvesting, and other events in the agricultural year. The purpose of many ceremonies was to motivate people to work together to ensure good crops by winning the favor of the gods.

Human and animal sacrifice played a vital role in the ceremonies. The Aztec regarded the human body and all living things as gifts from the gods. They believed that a divine power resided in three parts of the body—the head, the heart, and the liver. The Aztec thought that the gods required a ritual payment in the form of human hearts and blood to remain strong. Human sacrifices were elaborate, dramatic ceremonies designed to magically transform the human victims into living representatives of the gods before they were sacrificed. Often, priests slashed open the chest of a living victim and tore out the heart. Worshippers sometimes ate portions of a victim's body. They may have thought that the dead person's strength and bravery passed to anyone who ate a portion of the flesh. Most victims were male prisoners of war or slaves. The Aztec also sacrificed women and occasionally, to the god Tláloc, children.

Most religious activities took place inside walled ceremonial centers. The chief structures within the centers were *teocallis*. A typical teocalli consisted of a wide, solid base, upon which rose steep stairsteps. Priests climbed the stairs to reach a temple dedicated to a divinity at the top. The ceremonial centers also included royal palaces, gardens, living quarters for priests, sacred pools for ritual cleansing, and racks holding the skulls of sacrificial victims. In addition, many centers had a *tlatchli* (playing court) for a game called *ullamaliztli* that resembled a mixture of soccer and basketball. The players tried to hit a rubber ball through a ring with their hips and knees. They could not use their hands or feet.

The Aztec had a 260-day religious calendar. Priests used the calendar to determine lucky days for such activities as sowing crops, building houses, and going to war. The Aztec also had a 365-day solar calendar. It consisted of 18 months of 20 days each plus 5 extra days.

Drawing from the *Codex Florentino* (mid-1500's); © American Museum of Natural History, New York City

Human sacrifice played a major role in Aztec religion. This drawing by an Aztec artist shows priests cutting out a victim's heart. Clay flutes broken during the ceremony lie nearby.

© Free Agents Limited/Corbis

Xiuhtecuhtli was the Aztec god of fire. This statue shows Xiuhtecuhtli *(shee oo tay KOO tlee)* seated with his arms folded to receive sacrifices. The Aztec worshiped many gods, each of whom ruled one or more human activities or aspects of nature.

Every 52 years, the Aztec held a great celebration called the Binding of the Years or the New Fire Ceremony. Before the celebration, people throughout the empire let their hearth fires go out and destroyed some of their kitchenware. At the start of the new 52-year cycle, the priests lit a fire on the chest of a sacrificial victim. People pricked themselves to add their blood to the sacrifice. Fire bearers delivered the sacrificial fire to towns and cities throughout the empire. Then the people relit their hearth fires from the new fire and feasted.

Family life. The typical Aztec household consisted of a husband and wife, their unmarried children, and a number of the husband's relatives. All members of this extended family, including the children, helped with the work. The husband's chief responsibility was to support the family, usually by farming or craftwork. The wife's duties included weaving the family's clothing, raising girls in the home, and cooking the family's food.

Boys were educated by their father until about the age of 10. They then attended a school run by their calpolli or—especially if they belonged to the nobility—a school connected with a temple. Calpolli schools provided general education and military training. Temple schools offered a religious education, which prepared boys to become priests or other leaders. Some girls also attended the temple schools, but the majority learned household skills at home. The Aztec married at an early age, women at about 16 and men at about 20.

Food. Many types of corn and squash were staples of the Aztec diet. The principal food was a thin corn-meal pancake called a *tlaxcalli*. In Spanish, it is called a *tortilla*. The Aztec used tlaxcallis to scoop up other foods or wrapped them around bits of meat and vegetables to form tacos. Aztec cooking was rich and spicy. Many dishes had sauces flavored with chili peppers.

Hunting and, to a lesser extent, fishing provided animal protein for the Aztec diet. Game animals included deer, rabbits, and such birds as ducks and geese. The only animals raised for meat were dogs and turkeys.

The Aztec used the juice of maguey plants to make an alcoholic beverage called *octli*. Chocolate drink was also a favorite beverage, but only the wealthy could afford to have it often.

Clothing. Aztec women wore a loose, sleeveless blouse and a wraparound skirt. Men wore a cloth around their hips and a cloak knotted over one shoulder. The poorer people used cloth made from maguey fibers, but richer people had cotton clothing. The amount of decoration on a garment further indicated the wealth and social rank of the wearer. When the Spaniards first arrived in Tenochtitlan, they were amazed by the elaborate and rich clothing of the Aztec nobles.

Shelter. Most houses for Aztec commoners were simple and designed for usefulness rather than beauty. In the highlands, the houses were made of adobe. In the lowlands, they had thatched roofs, and the walls were made of branches or reeds plastered with clay. In addition to the main dwelling, most families had several other buildings, including a storehouse and a small sweat house, where the family took steam baths. Wealthy Aztec families had large adobe or stone houses finely decorated and built around a patio.

Arts and crafts. Aztec sculptures, which decorated temples and other buildings, were among the most elaborate in the Americas. The most famous surviving Aztec sculpture is the large, circular Calendar Stone, which represents the Aztec universe. The stone measures about 12 feet (3.7 meters) in diameter. In its center is the face of the sun god Tonatiuh. Other carvings

12 ft. (3.7 m) in diameter; Instituto Nacional de Antropología e Historia, Mexico City

The Aztec Calendar Stone was used in ceremonies honoring the sun god Tonatiuh. His face is in the center of the stone. Other carvings represent the Aztec universe.

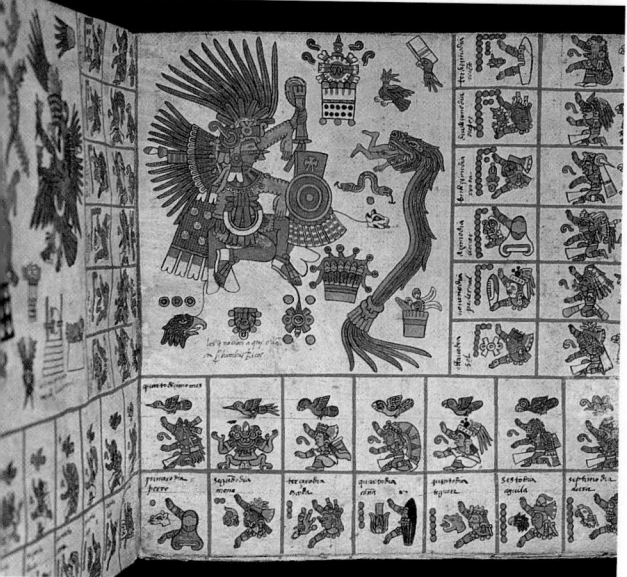

Codex Borbonicus (early 1500's); Bibliothèque du Palais Bourbon, Paris (Giraudon/Art Resource)

Aztec writing consisted of small pictures called *pictographs.* This page from an Aztec book shows Xipe Totec, *left,* the god of spring, and the god Quetzalcoatl, who appears as a snake, *right.*

represent the days of the Aztec month and religious symbols related to the sun god. Many archaeologists believe that Aztec priests placed the hearts of human sacrifices on the stone.

The Aztec produced various forms of oral literature, including poetry and traditional accounts of their history. When Spanish priests studied this oral tradition, they were deeply impressed by the elaborate metaphors and prose used by the Aztec speakers.

Music played a major part in religious services. The chief instruments were drums, flutes, and rattles.

Aztec craftworkers used feathers to make cloaks, headdresses, and other garments. Other crafts included metalworking, pottery, weaving, and woodcarving.

Language. The Aztec spoke a language called Nahuatl. It belongs to a large group of Indian languages known as the Aztec-Tanoan or Uto-Aztecan family. This language family also includes the languages spoken by the Comanche, Pima, Shoshone, and other tribes of western North America.

The Aztec used a form of writing called *pictographic writing,* which consisted mostly of images, pictures, and scenes. Some pictures symbolized ideas. Others stood for the sounds of syllables. For example, the Aztec town of Coatepec was represented by a snake and a hill. The Nahuatl words for *snake* and *hill* were *coatl* and *tepetl,* which together sounded like Coatepec. This system of writing was not developed enough to provide full expression of ideas, and so the Aztec combined pictorial images with oral explanation or interpretation. They used the pictorial system alone for business records, censuses, and tax lists.

Warfare was considered a religious duty by the Aztec. They fought not only to enlarge their empire but also to take prisoners to sacrifice to the gods. The high-est goal for a young man was to be a successful warrior. Men who took many captives in battle were rewarded with land, high social rank, and important government offices. Warriors wore costumes that symbolized their accomplishments and rank.

Aztec methods of combat were designed primarily to capture prisoners rather than to kill. The chief weapon was a wooden club edged with sharp pieces of the volcanic glass obsidian. This weapon, called a *macuahuitl,* was effective for disabling an opponent without killing him. The Aztec also used bows and arrows and spears. A spear-throwing device called an *atlatl* increased the range and force of their spears. For protection, warriors carried shields and wore armor of tightly quilted cotton.

Economy

Agriculture formed the basis of the Aztec economy. Corn was the most important crop. Farmers also grew avocados, beans, squashes, sweet potatoes, tomatoes, and many other crops. The lowlands provided such tropical products as cotton, papayas, rubber, and cacao beans, from which chocolate is made.

The basic agricultural tool was a pointed stick for digging. In the densely forested lowlands, farmers practiced *slash-and-burn agriculture.* They chopped down and burned a section of forest, then planted crops in the clearing. The ashes fertilized the soil. In the highlands, the Aztec cut terraces into the hillsides to increase the amount of level farmland. They also dug irrigation systems to water their crops. In addition, farmers turned areas of shallow lakes into cropland by scooping up mud from the lake bottoms to form islands. These islands were called *chinampas.* The farmers regularly added fresh mud, which was extremely fertile. As a result, the chinampas yielded huge crops. Lake Xochimilco in Mexico City still has many chinampas. Although they do not float, they are often called *floating gardens.*

Trade and transportation. The marketplace was a major center of Aztec life. The market at Tlatelolco was the largest in the Americas. It displayed nearly every kind of merchandise available in the Aztec world. The Spanish explorer Hernán Cortés reported that more than 60,000 people visited it daily. There were also many smaller markets throughout the empire. Government officials supervised the trading.

Merchants called *pochteca* traveled throughout the empire on trading expeditions and also served as spies. The merchants employed many bearers, who marched in long caravans with heavy loads on their backs. People of the lowlands traded such goods as cacao beans, cotton, jaguar pelts, rubber, and tropical bird feathers. In return, they received goods from the highlands. These goods included obsidian—which was used for knives and weapons—and a variety of manufactured products.

The Aztec had no system of money as we know it. They usually traded goods and services for other goods and services. But the Aztec used cacao beans and other widely acceptable goods somewhat as we use money.

The Aztec used the wheel only in toys, and they had no beasts of burden. As a result, the people themselves carried all their goods on land. Dugout canoes were an important means of transportation in the Valley of Mexico, which had many lakes, canals, and other waterways.

History

The Aztec migration. According to legend, the ancestors of the Aztec came to the Valley of Mexico from a place in the north called *Aztlan* or *Chicomoztoc* (Place of Seven Caves). Their supreme deity inspired them to leave their homeland and travel until they found a new home, which would be marked by an eagle eating a serpent on a blooming cactus. The name *Aztec* comes from *Aztlan.* The Aztec wandered for many years before settling in the valley in the 1200's. At first, they were subjects of people who lived in the area. But in 1325, the legend says, they founded their own city, Tenochtitlan.

Middle American growth of the Aztec empire. By the early 1400's, Tenochtitlan had become a powerful city that controlled the region around it, forming a city-state. Tenochtitlan joined with Texcoco and Tlacopan, two other city-states in the Valley of Mexico, to form an alliance. Tenochtitlan became the most powerful member of the alliance and began to build the Aztec empire. Under Montezuma I, who ruled from 1440 to 1469, the alliance conquered large areas to the east and south. Montezuma's name is also spelled *Moctezuma* or *Motecuhzoma.* His successors expanded the empire until it extended between what are now Guatemala and the Mexican state of San Luis Potosi. Hundreds of conquered towns paid heavy taxes in goods to the empire. When Montezuma II became emperor in 1502, the Aztec empire was at the height of its power.

The Spanish conquest. In 1519, the Spanish explorer Hernán Cortés landed on the east coast of Mexico. After several skirmishes and setbacks, he began a march inland to the Aztec capital. He and his troops were eventually joined by many Indians who had been conquered by the Aztec and resented their heavy taxes and brutality. For reasons that are still mysterious, Montezuma II did not oppose the advancing Spaniards with military force. Instead, he tried to use religious magic to discourage them from coming to the capital. Some scholars think he believed Cortés represented the creator god, Quetzalcoatl, and his Toltec incarnation, *Topiltzin Quetzalcoatl,* who had ruled centuries before. An Aztec legend said that Quetzalcoatl had sailed away to the east, the direction from which the Spaniards came. Cortés eventually entered Tenochtitlan and made Montezuma a prisoner in his own palace.

In 1520, the Spaniards massacred Aztec dancers, priests, and musicians at a sacred ceremony. The Aztec rebelled and drove the invaders from their city. Montezuma died that year, probably from wounds received early in the rebellion. Cortés and the Spaniards retreated, but soon reorganized their army and attacked Tenochtitlan in May 1521. Montezuma's successor, Cuauhtemoc, surrendered in August of the same year.

The Aztec heritage. Little Aztec architecture remains. The Spaniards considered it their duty as Christians to wipe out the temples, idols, sacrifices, and all other traces of the Aztec religion. They destroyed Tenochtitlan and built Mexico City on the ruins. However, archaeologists have excavated the site of the Great Temple in downtown Mexico City. They have uncovered all four sides of the building and recovered thousands of objects, including jewelry, pottery, statues, wall carvings, and remains of animal and human sacrifices. Archaeologists have restored some other Aztec buildings, including temples at Tenayuca and Tepoztlan near Mexico City. The National Museum of Anthropology in Mexico City has a large collection of Aztec art.

Drawing by an unknown Aztec artist from *History of the Indies of New Spain* (late 1500's) by Diego Durán; Biblioteca Nacional, Madrid, Spain (Ampliaciones y Reproducciones MAS)

The Spanish conquest in 1521 destroyed the Aztec empire. This drawing shows Aztec warriors, *right,* fighting to recapture a palace from the Spaniards, *left.* One Aztec wears an eagle costume, and one a jaguar suit. Warriors earned the right to wear such costumes by taking many prisoners.

The marketplace was a center of Aztec life. It displayed nearly every kind of merchandise available in the Aztec world. Merchants employed many bearers, who marched in long caravans with heavy loads on their backs. This painting from the mid-1900's depicts the market at Tlatelolco in the Aztec capital. The Spanish explorer Hernán Cortés reported that more than 60,000 people visited it daily. There were also many smaller markets throughout the Aztec Empire.

Detail of *Great City of Tenochtitlan* (1929-1945), a fresco mural by Diego Rivera; National Palace, Mexico City (Granger Collection)

Thousands of people in Mexico have Aztec ancestors, and many speak a modern form of Nahuatl. Many Mexican place names, including Acapulco and Mexico itself, come from Nahuatl, as do the English words *avocado, chocolate,* and *tomato.* Such Mexican painters as José Orozco, Diego Rivera, and David Siqueiros have used Aztec themes in their work. Foods of Aztec origin, including chili, chocolate, and tacos, have become popular in many countries. Descendants of the Aztec also live in the United States, especially in California and Texas. Many Mexican Americans take pride in the creative aspects of Aztec culture.   David Carrasco

Related articles in *World Book* include:

Chocolate (History)
Cortés, Hernán
Cuauhtemoc
Hispanic Americans (In Mexico)
Indian, American (pictures: Aztec Indians; Aztec merchants; The city of Tenochtitlan)
Latin America (The conquest of the American Indians)
Manuscript (picture: Aztec manuscript)
Mexico (The Toltec and the Aztec; The Spanish conquest)
Mexico City (City of the Aztec)
Montezuma II
Mythology (Aztec mythology)
Tarascan Indians
Tenochtitlan
Toltec Indians

Questions

Why did Montezuma II fail to oppose Cortés?
How many days are in a month in the Aztec solar calendar?
Why did the Aztec want prisoners of war?
When was the Aztec Empire at its height?
What were *chinampas?*
How did the Aztec move their goods on land?
Why did the Aztec perform human sacrifices?
What are two popular foods of Aztec origin?
Where was the Aztec capital of Tenochtitlan?
Why are so few Aztec buildings left?

Additional resources

Apte, Sunita. *The Aztec Empire.* Children's Pr., 2010. Younger readers.
Bodden, Valerie. *Aztec Empire.* Creative Education, 2014. Younger readers.
Brumfiel, Elizabeth M., and Feinman, G. M., eds. *The Aztec World.* Abrams, 2008.
Carrasco, Davíd, and Sessions, Scott. *Daily Life of the Aztecs.* 2nd ed. Greenwood, 2011.
Smith, Michael E. *The Aztecs.* 3rd ed. Wiley-Blackwell, 2011.
Villela, Khristaan D., and Miller, M. E. *The Aztec Calendar Stone.* Getty Research Inst., 2010.

Aztec Ruins National Monument lies in northwestern New Mexico. It contains ruins of a Pueblo Indian town of the 1100's, including a 500-room dwelling place. The ruins were misnamed Aztec by American settlers of the 1800's. The monument was established in 1923. For its area, see **National Park System** (table: National monuments).   Critically reviewed by the National Park Service

Azurite, *AZH uh ryt,* is a blue mineral that contains copper. Azurite is mined as a copper ore, but most azurite is used for ornamentation. Small stones are polished and mounted in jewelry. Slabs are shaped into decorative objects such as bowls. Artists once used ground azurite as a pigment for paint. Azurite's chemical formula is $Cu_3(CO_3)_2(OH)_2$. Its crystal structure is *monoclinic* (see **Crystal** [Classifying crystals]). Azurite is found throughout the world, usually in the same location as *malachite,* a similar mineral that is green. But the best crystals come from Chessy, near Lyon, France. Fine azurite also occurs in Australia, Greece, Mexico, Namibia, Romania, Russia, and the United States.   Kenneth J. De Nault

See also **Mineral** (picture: Azurite).